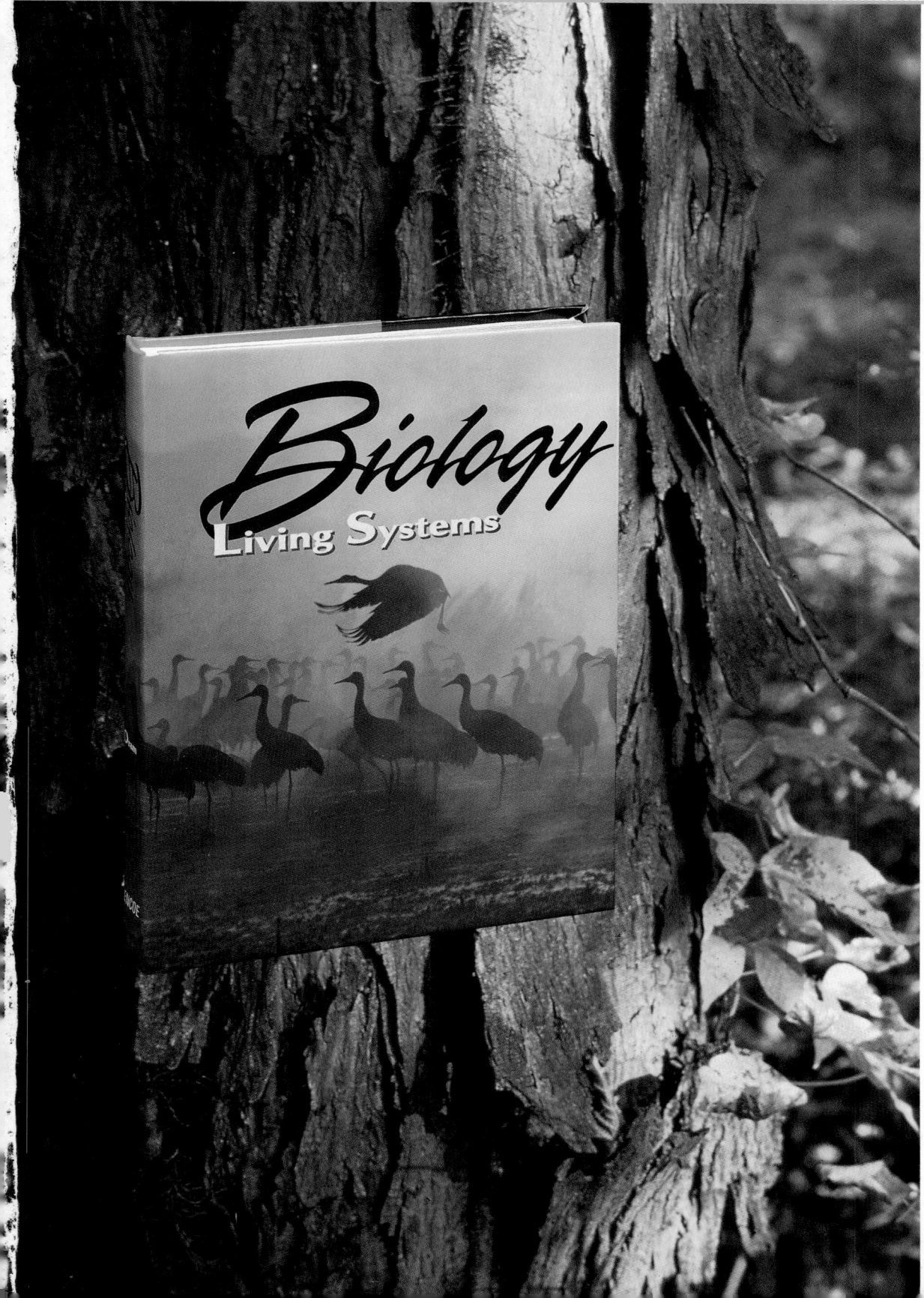

Sometimes students can't see the forest for the trees.

Now, Glencoe brings the forest into focus with the NEW Biology: Living Systems.

GLENCOE

Now, your students will focus more on the forest and less on the trees.

"I can't see the forest for the trees." We've all heard that old phrase thousands of times. But it takes on a special meaning when it's applied to many of today's biology programs. Too often, these programs fail to tie all the facts together effectively. They get caught up in minor details. And they don't encourage students to make the kind of meaningful connections that could help them understand biology's big ideas.

The answer? Taking a major step in a different direction. Focusing more on the forest and less on the trees, so students can see the big picture for the first time. That's what Glencoe's *Biology: Living Systems* has to offer.

Our unique systems approach structures the book's presentation around six basic biology themes: Evolution, Unity Within Diversity, Use of Energy, Patterns of Change, Systems and Interactions, and the Nature of Scientific Inquiry. Through this approach, you can encourage students to recognize similarities rather than differences, so concepts are more cohesive.

This program offers unequaled support materials and a comprehensive **Teacher Wraparound Edition**, to give you more opportunities to extend lessons, assess your students' progress, and challenge them to achieve even more.

Linking ideas
Recurrent themes make the big picture easier to see.

Biology: Living Systems has always been innovative. But our new edition goes even further to help students understand the fundamental interactions and connections that exist between living things and their environment.

The six basic themes, which are continually reinforced and reapplied throughout the text, give students a solid structure to build their understanding around. At the same time, fundamental concepts, such as photosynthesis, are continually reintroduced in different contexts, so students' understanding can progress far beyond basic facts and terms.

Engaging students
Once they get their hands on biology, they'll never let go.

With *Biology: Living Systems*, your students can do it all. They can conduct, design, and evaluate their own experiments through **Investigation**, a one-of-a-kind inquiry lab found in each chapter. They can discover a new twist on classroom activities with **Minilabs**, which require just a little time and little or no equipment. They can develop their critical thinking and problem solving skills with **Thinking Labs**. Quite simply, they can get their hands on what they're learning and discover the biologist in themselves.

Applying biology
Students see how biology lessons come to life in everyday things.

Biology: Living Systems was designed to motivate students by continually showing them how biology issues enter their lives in countless ways every day. Through the narrative and specially designed features in every chapter, students can discover the biology connection with art, literature, current issues, technology, and careers.

We link ideas to bring students closer to the big ideas.

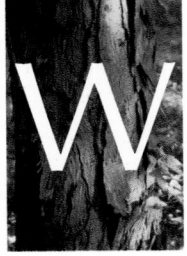

We start simple, and work from there. But, unlike most biology texts, which don't effectively connect ideas together, *Biology: Living Systems* focuses on concept reinforcement, from the very first page. Material is constantly reintroduced throughout the text to help students grasp the fascinating processes of biology while they gain a thorough understanding of each element in the process.

As they re-examine each basic idea in new contexts and learn to apply concepts, students will begin to see the big picture more clearly.

Food and Energy Needs in a Community

Zebra mussels also threaten clam populations, another valuable fishing resource. Clams, though larger than the new invaders, are also mussels. This means that they also have two shells hinged together. Zebra mussels attach to clam shells. The sheer weight of piled-on zebra mussels prevents clams from opening their shells, thus restricting their food intake.

Food as an Energy Source The connection between food and life is obvious, as well as common to all life forms. Just what is it about food that makes it so important? In a word, the answer is energy.

Energy is the ability to do work. Work is anything that causes motion. When you read about the four common characteristics of life in the first section, you learned that all organisms carry on certain kinds of biological work—reproducing, growing, developing, and maintaining homeostasis. Organisms must have energy to keep this work going. Without energy, a zebra mussel could not expel eggs and sperm for reproduction, or close its shell to preserve moisture and maintain homeostasis. Nor could you perspire or shiver to maintain homeostasis in your own body. The zebra mussel, you, and every other organism gets energy for biological work from food. Energy fuels the work of life just as surely as gasoline fuels an automobile engine and keeps its parts functioning. Every organism uses the energy from some of the materials in food as fuel for the functions needed to keep it alive.

Producing Food Maintaining an adequate food supply is critical in any community. Each community has an orderly system through which organisms obtain food from other organisms. Certain members of a community are food **producers.** That is, they make food. In some communities, plants—such as trees, grasses, and shrubs—and certain bacteria are the producers. In the communities invaded by zebra mussels, algae are the producers.

Among most producers, the ingredients in the food-making recipe are carbon dioxide and water. **Chlorophyll,** a green substance in the producers, traps light from the sun. Sunlight provides the energy for the work of combining carbon dioxide and water. Simple sugars are the finished product. Oxygen, given off while the manufacture is taking place, is the by-product. The whole process is called **photosynthesis.**

The light energy of the sun is converted during photosynthesis to chemical energy in the form of simple sugars. Thus, these sugars are good sources of energy and hence food for the producer itself. But producers do not use all the simple

Figure 1-8 Zebra mussels belong to a group of mollusks that have two shells. The shells offer protection and help maintain homeostasis.

Figure 1-9 During photosynthesis, carbon dioxide and water (raw materials) react to form sugars (end products) and oxygen (a by-product). Without the photosynthetic process, life on Earth would not exist.

Energy from sunlight

Carbon dioxide from air and water from soil⟶ Simple sugars and oxygen

Chlorophyll in leaves

CO₂

Water

SCIENCE OF LIFE

FOR EXAMPLE:

In the first chapter, students are introduced to the fundamental concept of photosynthesis.

Objectives

Describe the interaction of white light with objects including chlorophyll molecules.

Relate the events of the light reactions to those of the Calvin cycle in photosynthesis.

Analyze the relationship between photosynthesis and cellular respiration.

6.2 Photosynthesis

The energy you need to run, think, and grow is released in the process of cellular respiration. The key ingredient in this process, of course, is the energy-rich molecule glucose. But where does glucose come from? How is it produced? What makes it energy-rich? As you know, algae, some bacteria, and plants are producers in almost every ecosystem on Earth. These producers absorb energy from sunlight and convert it to chemical energy stored in organic molecules including glucose. To understand how this process occurs, you must first learn a little about the properties of light itself.

Light

Light is a form of radiant energy. Besides light, radiant energy includes radio waves, microwaves, X rays, and gamma rays. All radiant energy travels in waves. The distance between one wave crest and the next is called the **wavelength** of the waves, as shown in Figure 6-8. The human eye is sensitive to radiant energy with wavelengths of about 400 to 700 nm. The abbreviation *nm* stands for *nanometer,* which is one billionth of a meter. This mixture of wavelengths of radiant energy that is visible to humans is called white light.

The Visible Spectrum When white light passes through a prism, the prism separates it into a range of colors. This range of colors that make up white light is known as the **visible spectrum.** The colors of the spectrum are usually given as red, orange, yellow, green, blue, and violet. Red light has the longest wavelength of the visible spectrum, and violet light has the shortest wavelength. Ultraviolet and infrared wavelengths, on either end of the visible spectrum, are invisible to humans.

white light passing broken into a shorter wavelengths ore by the prism ngths (red). distance from he next. Where are d infrared light ctrum?

Crest

Trough

FLOW OF ENERGY

In Chapter 6, while students begin to learn about the flow of energy, photosynthesis is covered again in detail, to help build the connection and deeper understanding.

The interactions between a community of organisms and the environment are give-and-take relationships. Organisms take from their environment materials and energy needed for life, and, as they are used, they are transferred back to the environment. Because there is a tight relationship between a community of organisms and the environment, there is a delicate balance among the many forms of life in a healthy ecosystem.

How do organisms interact with each other? Perhaps the most obvious way in which different populations of organisms interact is by feeding upon one another. Because food is a source of energy, availability of food is a limiting factor for many animal populations. You are well aware by now that all organisms require energy in order to carry out their many functions. In almost all ecosystems, the original source of that energy is sunlight. The light can be used directly only by autotrophs such as grasses, trees, or algae. In photosynthesis, autotrophic organisms trap light energy and change it to chemical energy stored in the form of sugars and other organic compounds.

Because only photosynthetic autotrophs can trap and change light energy to chemical energy, all other organisms depend on them for their energy sources. Energy stored in energy-rich organic molecules is transferred from one organism to another as organisms feed upon each other within an ecosystem. In this way, each organism represents a feeding step, or **trophic level,** in the passage of energy and materials.

All organisms within an ecosystem have functions in that ecosystem. An organism's **niche** describes how an organism fits into an ecosystem. Where an organism lives, what it eats and what eats it, and how it interacts with all the biotic and abiotic parts of the ecosystem describe its niche. Since each organism plays a unique role, no two organisms can occupy the same niche in an ecosystem.

28.1 INTERACTIONS AMONG ORGANISMS ❧ **787**

In Chapter 28, on ecosystems, photosynthesis is again introduced so students can see how it plays a role in the way organisms interact.

Hands-on experience designed to challenge and motivate.

These short **Minilabs**, which can be set up and completed in much less than a class period, help provide immediate concept reinforcement as students move from topic to topic. Many of them can be used as demos or take-home activities.

Minilab 1

Is blubber an adaptation?

Spoon 40 g of shortening into a plastic sandwich bag. Place a test tube filled with room-temperature water and a thermometer into this bag. Then place another test tube with room-temperature water and a thermometer into another plastic bag with no shortening. Fasten the bags close to the top of the test tubes with rubber bands. Working on the outside of the bag, gently spread the shortening evenly over the surface of the test tube. Place these two bagged test tubes and another unbagged test tube with the same contents into a beaker of ice water. Record the temperature of each tube as you begin, then every minute for 30 minutes.

Analysis *Compare the time needed for each tube of water to cool to the temperature of the ice water. What is the purpose of the tube with no insulation? The tube with only the plastic bag?*

*B*iology: Living Systems offers an unprecedented number of opportunities for students to gain valuable hands-on experience, with a wide variety of labs in the student text and in supplemental lab manuals.

Most labs can get your students to go through the motions. But these labs can get them to go the extra distance, by putting them in charge of the learning process.

Our Investigation Labs are nothing like the cookbook-style labs you've seen so many times before. These unique open-ended labs, which are ideal for cooperative group work, encourage students to design their own labs, ask their own questions, and evaluate their own progress. Because we develop them slowly, with less-complicated problems and plenty of guiding questions, students never feel overwhelmed. But they always feel challenged to find out more.

INVESTIGATION

Optimum Temperature

Humans are most comfortable with a surrounding temperature around 23°C. When it is too hot, we feel uncomfortable and start to sweat. When it is too cold, we begin to shiver and are equally uncomfortable. Thus, humans have an optimum temperature, a temperature at which they are most comfortable. Do all living things share the same optimum temperature for life activities? No. The optimum temperature for a deep-sea fish is quite different from that of a desert coyote.

Yeast cells also have an optimum temperature for life processes. In this investigation, you will design and then carry out an experiment to determine the temperature at which yeast best carries out fermentation. Carbon dioxide is given off during the process of alcoholic fermentation. Therefore, it can be used as a means for judging the rate at which yeast cells carry out this process. To help you get started, look at the diagram at the right. It shows how you could measure carbon dioxide gas given off by yeast cells during fermentation.

Problem
What is the optimum temperature for yeast cell fermentation?

Safety Precautions
Wear safety goggles when pouring and mixing liquids. Use caution with hot plates and hot liquids. Use mitts or hot pads when handling hot beakers.

Hypothesis
Have your group agree on a hypothesis to be tested. Record your hypothesis.

Experimental Plan
1. Review the discussions of aerobic respiration and fermentation in this chapter. Note particularly the reactants involved.
2. Examine the materials provided by your teacher. Then, as a group, make a list of the possible ways you might test your hypothesis using the materials available.
3. Agree on one way that your group could investigate your hypothesis.
4. Design an experiment that will (a) use a control, (b) test only one variable at a time, and (c) allow for the collection of quantitative data.
5. Prepare a list of numbered directions. Include a list of materials and the quantities you will need.

Checking the Plan
Discuss the following points with other group members to decide the final procedures for your experiment. Make any needed changes in your plan.
1. What materials will you use to grow your yeast?
2. What will you measure to determine the rate of fermentation?
3. What factor will you vary in your experiment?
4. What factors will you control in your experiment?
5. To what range of temperatures will you expose the yeast? Why?
6. What food will you use?
7. How will you determine appropriate amounts of yeast and food to use?
8. How long will you carry out the experiment?
9. How many tubes of yeast will you expose to each temperature?
10. Have you designed and made a table for collecting data?

Make sure your teacher has approved your experimental plan before you proceed.

Data and Observations
Carry out your experiment, make any needed measurements, and complete your data table. Design and complete a graph of your results.

Analysis and Conclusions
1. What conditions did you keep constant in the experimental group? What one condition varied?
2. What differences did you observe between experimental groups? Were these differences due to temperature differences? Explain how you know.
3. Explain how you were able to determine the optimum temperature for fermentation in yeast.
4. Was your hypothesis supported by your data? If not, suggest a new hypothesis that is supported by your data.
5. List several ways that your methods may have affected the outcome of the experiment. Suggest ways that you might improve your methods.
6. Write a brief conclusion to your experiment.

Going Further
Based on this lab experience, design another experiment that would help to answer any questions that arose from your work. What factors might you allow to vary if you kept temperature constant? Assume that you will not be doing this lab in class.

— Test tube
— Water
— Plastic pipet
— Metal washers or other weight
— Yeast and food

This is where lessons and life come together.

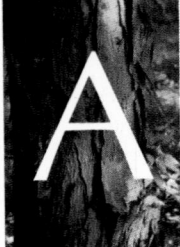

As they walk to school, cut the grass, or even sit down for lunch, your students come face-to-face with the big ideas in biology. But they won't realize it unless they learn to make connections between the expected and the unexpected.

With the help of these **Connections** features, which explore areas ranging from history to leisure, students will discover that biology lessons aren't always found between the covers of a book. They can be found in every facet of everyday life.

Connections features help students explore the often unexpected ways biology crosses over into other disciplines . . . and daily living.

CHEMISTRY CONNECTION

Spider Silk

The U.S. Army is definitely interested. So is the Navy. Medical equipment makers, their own experiments, and even the world of high fashion is keeping a close watch on new developments.

What is at the center of all this interest? Some new synthetic wonder fabric, the product of advanced chemical research? No, the fabric is spider silk, and scientists are trying to unravel its chemical and genetic properties so that it can be commercially produced. **Wonder Thread** The reason for

unique characteristics. Ounce for ounce, spider silk is five times stronger than steel. Furthermore, it's incredibly elastic; spider silk can be stretched up to 130 percent of its original length before it snaps. Spider silk is waterproof, and it's nonallergenic, too.

Commercially produced spider silk would have hundreds of uses. But before it can be produced in a laboratory, scientists first must discover how it is produced by spiders.

Internal Chemistry Spiders produce a variety of silks—dragline silk for dropping out of sight when threatened, capture silk for weaving

GLOBAL CONNECTION

Cultural Evolution

Whether the ability to communicate with language first evolved among the Cro-Magnons or earlier, there is certainly no doubt about its impact on the lives of humans. Speech was made possible by evolution of a large and complex brain.

The development of language coincided with accumulation of knowledge. Older people could teach younger ones about all they had discovered, thus avoiding the need for people to learn everything on their own.

Using Tools At first, improved patterns of speech may have led to ideas for making better tools. With new tools came an increase in the

ability to hunt larger animals and to make clothing, shelters, and new inventions such as boats. With each of these advances, humans had a better chance of surviving. Notice, however, that the changes in humans were not changes that

affected their gene pools, but were because of changes in human cultures. Instead of being molded by changes in their environment, humans began to alter or avoid the effects of that environment. Unlike all other organisms, learning and intuition began to surpass mutations and recombination as causes of change in the human species.

Learning to Farm Early hominids were hunters and gatherers. They hunted large mammals and gathered grains, nuts, berries, and other fruits. From about

Biology, Technology, and Society

This exclusive feature includes in-depth segments on **Considering the Environment, Issues,** and **Biotechnology,** to help students explore the impact of biology on important issues that affect them and society.

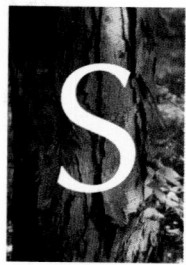

kills reinforcement is included in each chapter with the **Section Review**, which features questions, critical thinking exercises, and a **Skill Review**, to help students develop their abilities in a variety of skill areas.

At the end of the text, the **Skill Handbook** gives students a handy reference and introduction to each skill that is reinforced and applied throughout the text.

SKILL HANDBOOK

Organizing Information

Classifying

You may not realize it, but you impose order on the world around you. If your shirts hang in the closet together, your socks take up a corner of a dresser drawer, or your favorite CDs are stacked in groups according to recording artist, you have used the skill of classifying.

Classifying is grouping objects or events into groups based on common features. When classifying, you first make careful observations of the group of items to be classified. Select one feature that is shared

by some items in the group but not others. Place the items that share this feature in a subgroup. Place the remaining items in a second subgroup. Ideally, the items in the second subgroup will have some feature in common with one another. After you decide on the first feature that divides the items into subgroups, examine the items for other features and further divide each subgroup into smaller and smaller groups until the items have no features in common.

How would you classify a collection of CDs? Classify the CDs based on observable features. You

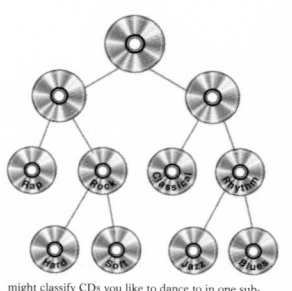

might classify CDs you like to dance to in one subgroup and CDs you like to listen to in another. The CDs you like to dance to could be subdivided into a rap subgroup and a rock subgroup. Note that for each feature selected, each CD only fits into one subgroup. For example, you wouldn't place a CD into both rap and rock categories. Keep selecting features until all the CDs are classified. The chart shows one method of classification.

Remember, when you classify, you are grouping objects or events for a purpose.

Sequencing

A sequence is an arrangement of things or events in a particular order. A common sequence with which you are familiar is students sitting in alphabetical order. Think also about baking chocolate chip cookies. Certain steps have to be followed in order for the cookies to taste good.

When you are asked to sequence things or events,

876 ꬵ SKILL HANDBOOK

The Skill Review, which is found at the end of each lesson, directs students to apply an important thinking process using information from the preceding lesson. Students are referred to the **Skill Handbook** if they need help.

Section Review

Understanding Concepts

1. You are examining a unicellular organism with an electron microscope. What clues would enable you to determine whether the organism is a bacterium?
2. Some bacteria can break down cellulose in plants. How might this be beneficial to humans?

3. Is endospore formation a form of reproduction among bacteria? Explain.
4. **Skill Review—Classifying:** Set up a classification of bacteria based on their structural features and means of obtaining energy. For more help, refer to Organizing Information in the **Skill Handbook**.

5. **Thinking Critically:** A bacterium is discovered that does not obtain energy from organic molecules and does not undergo photosynthesis. How does it obtain its needed energy?

Thinking Lab

INTERPRET THE DATA

How can you determine chromosome numbers in plants?

Background

In the plant kingdom, a pattern of reproduction occurs that is called alternation of generations. Each generation looks different and serves different functions. *Sporophyte* generations form *spores* by meiosis while *gametophyte* generations form *gametes* by mitosis. Spores form directly into gametophytes. Gametophytes always form sporo-

phytes after gametes fuse at fertilization. Sporophyte generations are always diploid while gametophyte generations are always haploid.

You Try It

Examine the table shown here. Information is provided for four plants, A to D. **Interpret the data** and fill in any of the missing chromosome numbers.

Chromosome numbers

	Sporophyte	Gametophyte	Spore	Gamete
A	20			
B			12	
C				8
D		34		

You can use **Thinking Labs** in class to reinforce lessons and encourage critical thinking. Or you can use them as homework assignments, since they don't require equipment to complete. With several categories of *Thinking Labs*, which give students all the background information they need, problem solving in a simulated lab context can become a part of every lesson.

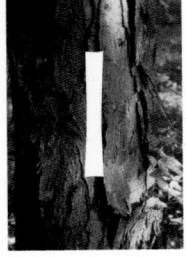

Teach with it once. And you'll never want to teach without it.

It's all right here, right where you need it. Background information, teaching strategies, planning guides . . . everything you need to make lesson enrichment less time consuming.

With our **Teacher Wraparound Edition**, you can access lab materials, alternate assessment strategies, hands-on learning options, and strategies to help you address any ability level or learning style. With this new edition, you can even see where to integrate program resources and explore bioethical and societal issues.

Biology: Living Systems puts it all right here, at the point of instruction. Because the more we do with each page, the more you can do in each class.

SECTION 7.2

Prepare

Key Concepts
The events of meiosis are presented in detail. Differences between meiosis in males and in females are explained. The importance of meiosis in adaptation, variation, and evolution is discussed.

Key Terms
diploid, homologue, zygote, gamete, fertilization, haploid, sexual reproduction, meiosis, spore, genetic recombination

Materials
• Gather materials for Minilab 2.

1 Focus

Objectives
The objectives are listed on the student page. Remind students to preview these objectives as a guide to this numbered section.

Brainstorming
Have students make a list of reasons why the cells of most organisms contain two identical sets of chromosomes. Students will likely list several possible reasons. When they have exhausted their possibilities, add the word *variation* to the list if it isn't already present. Explain that variation is important to the maintenance of a species. Meiosis provides a mechanism for variation. Point out that the importance of the process will be discussed later in the chapter, but students first need to understand the process. **L1** **COOP LEARN**

Objectives

Sequence the series of events by which reproductive cells are produced in complex plants and in animals.

Analyze the significance of meiosis with respect to adaptation and evolution.

Figure 7-11 **Human cells contain 23 pairs of chromosomes, or 46 chromosomes. Here, enlarged photographs of stained chromosomes have been cut up and arranged by pairs.**

182 ❧ CELLULAR REPRODUCTION

7.2 ## Production of Reproductive Cells

How many chromosomes does it take to make a cell? Would you guess that it depends on the kind of organism? If that's your guess, your thoughts are headed in the right direction. The number of chromosomes per cell does vary from one kind of organism to another.

Your cells have, and always have had, 46 chromosomes. The cells of fruit flies have eight. Does this mean, then, that every cell cycle in mature humans passes along 46 chromosomes to daughter cells? Or that every cell cycle in mature fruit flies passes along eight? The answer would be yes, in every cycle except among one class of cells—namely the cells that form reproductive cells. The job of reproductive cells is to produce offspring like the parent organism. The way chromosomes are distributed to reproductive cells differs from mitosis. And it's largely a matter of numbers.

Chromosome Numbers and Characteristics

Think for a moment about what happens when a male and female butterfly mate. Their reproductive cells unite to form a single cell that is the beginning of a new butterfly. What would happen if each of those reproductive cells contained the same number of chromosomes as all other cells in the butterfly? The offspring's cells would have twice the number of chromosomes as its parents' cells. In reality, however, the number of chromosomes does not double. Instead, it remains constant from one generation to the next. Understanding how this happens begins with a close-up look at cells and chromosomes.

Diploid Cells Chromosomes vary in a number of ways, including size and shape. All body cells of a given kind of organism normally have the same kinds and numbers of chromosomes. In the diagrams in Figure 7-8, you saw the stages of mitosis in a cell having four chromosomes. Did you notice that among those four, there were two large and two small chromosomes? In the cells of animals, chromosomes usually come in pairs, as shown by the two shades of the same color in Figure 7-8. Cells of many simple plants such as mosses, and cells of other simple organisms such as fungi, do not have such paired chromosomes. More complex plants, such as carrots and cabbages and oak trees, have paired chromosomes as animal cells do. Human cells have 23 pairs of chromosomes, as shown in Figure 7-11; fruit fly cells have four pairs. Cells having two of each chromosome are said to be **diploid.** The diploid number of chromosomes is represented by $2n$, where n = the number of different pairs. Humans have 23 different pairs, so $2n = 46$.

MULTICULTURAL CONNECTION

Chromosome Numbers: In 1887, Edouard-Joseph-Louis-Marie van Beneden, a Belgian scientist, discovered that each species has a fixed number of chromosomes. He also observed the formation of haploid cells.

In 1954, J. Hin Tijo and Albert Levan showed that each human cell has 46 chromosomes.

PROGRAM RESOURCES

Teacher Classroom Resources
Study Guide, pp. 40-42 **L1**
Critical Thinking/Problem Solving, p. 7 **L2**
Color Transparency #10 **L1** **LEP**
Investigating Living Systems, Lab 19, p. 77 **L2**

182

Alternate Labs, located at the bottom of the *Teacher Wraparound Edition*, provide supplemental text-driven laboratory activities, perfect for concept reinforcement or extra practice.

---

standing of that process. During cellular respiration, some of the energy released by breaking the bonds of food molecules such as glucose is used to make ATP from ADP. These ATP molecules are then used as needed. Processes that require oxygen are called *aerobic processes*. Respiration in most cells makes use of oxygen and is called **aerobic respiration.**

Aerobic Respiration Aerobic respiration involves many reactions that follow one another in a particular sequence. The first several steps take place in the cell's cytoplasm. The products of the last of these early reactions move into the mitochondria, where the process called the citric acid cycle takes place. The process as a whole is exergonic. It can be summarized in the following equation.

$$C_6H_{12}O_6 + 6O_2 + 38ADP + 38 P_i \xrightarrow{\text{enzymes}} 6CO_2 + 6H_2O + 38ATP$$

glucose oxygen   carbon water
                                  dioxide

This equation shows that aerobic respiration in some cells can release enough energy from a molecule of glucose to produce 38 ATP. Not all the steps of the process are exergonic, however. Early steps in the breakdown of glucose use the energy of two ATP. So, the maximum net ATP that can be produced is 36 molecules. ATP production from the breakdown of glucose is not always that efficient, however. Note that aerobic respiration does not produce 38 ATP in every cell. In general, about 39 percent of the energy available in glucose is transferred to molecules of ATP. The rest escapes as heat. More important than the exact number of ATP molecules produced, though, is this basic point: During cellular respiration, the energy of one glucose molecule is released bit by bit and transferred to many molecules of ATP.

Figure 6-5 summarizes the interrelationships among aerobic respiration, ATP, ADP, and the work of the cell. This series of chemical events is sometimes referred to as the ATP-ADP cycle. The diagram shows that during aerobic respiration, the energy of glucose is transferred to ADP and inorganic phosphate, forming ATP, which can then be used as a free energy source for cellular work.

High

Potential energy

Energy

$C_6H_{12}O_6 + 6O_2$

ATP

Maximum of 38 ATP per glucose molecule

Cell activities

Energy

Low

$6CO_2 + 6H_2O$

ADP + P_i

6.1 ENERGY FOR CELLS ● **147**

Minilab 1

Can you detect energy released by a biological reaction?

Half fill a test tube with a 3 percent solution of hydrogen peroxide. **CAUTION:** *Wear goggles. Wash away any spills immediately with water.* Use a thermometer to take the temperature of the liquid in the tube. Add one or two small chunks of fresh liver to the tube. Observe what happens. After one minute, take the temperature again.
Analysis *What evidence of a reaction did you observe? Was the reaction endergonic or exergonic? What is your evidence? Considering that the reaction was carried out by living tissue, what do you think was responsible for the breakdown of hydrogen peroxide? Do you think this reaction could be used by cells to do biological work? Why or why not?*

Figure 6-5 When sugar burns in air, it releases CO_2, H_2O, and a lot of energy at once. In respiration, the same process occurs, but step by step, releasing a little energy at a time and storing it in ATP.

SECTION 6.1

Minilab 1

Purpose
Students observe a temperature rise as evidence of energy released by an enzyme reaction.

Skills
observe and infer, recognize cause and effect

Teaching Strategies
- **Safety Precautions:** Students should wear goggles and aprons. You should perform the activity before class in order to see what is likely to happen.
- **Troubleshooting:** Sometimes the reaction mixture foams over the top of the test tube, so students should use test-tube racks and work over newspaper.
- Ask students if they have ever applied hydrogen peroxide to a cut or sore. Ask them to relate what happened to what they observe in this activity.
- Consider performing the glowing splint test to show that oxygen is produced by the reaction.

Expected Results
Students should observe a rise of a few degrees in the reaction mixture. If reactions are too slow to give a rise in temperature, try again using liver that has been more finely diced.

Answers
A new substance (oxygen gas) was formed. The reaction was exergonic because heat was released. An enzyme (catalase) present in liver carried out the reaction. The reaction probably could not do useful work because all the energy was released in the form of heat.

✔ Assessment
Performance: Have students carry out tests with other materials including diced raw potatoes, ground beef, radishes, diced leaves, and so on. Ask students to draw conclusions regarding the prevalence of this enzyme in living things.

Other features of our Teacher Wraparound Edition:

4-Step Lesson Plan, which includes the highly effective Focus, Teach, Assess, and Close cycle, helps you make every lesson as thorough–and effective–as possible.

Program Resource Boxes show you the most effective way to correlate resources into your daily lessons, so you can spend less time planning.

Projects provide a number of interesting opportunities to reinforce concepts through cooperative learning activities.

Portfolio provides a variety of portfolio-building suggestions, which help you to assess student performance over time.

Performance Tasks are a valuable tool to help you gauge how well your students can analyze, formulate, and solve problems in authentic assessment situations.

PORTFOLIO

Have students write one or two paragraphs interpreting the diagram in Figure 6-5 on page 147. Ask them to include a sentence or two discussing the contrast between the photo and the diagram. ■

MEETING INDIVIDUAL NEEDS

For those students working below grade level, ask the following questions about the diagram in Figure 6-5. Where did the oxygen at the top of the arrow come from? Where did the ADP at the bottom of the cycle come from? Where did the glucose at the top of the arrow come from? What happens to the CO_2 and H_2O formed? What happens to the ATP formed? **LEP**

147

The most comprehensive and innovative package of support materials available.

Assessment. Enrichment. Labs. Technology. Here is everything you need to make every lesson more powerful, and every hour more productive.

Reinforcement and Enrichment

Study Guide Masters provide students with section-by-section activities to guide their reading, while the **Teacher Edition** gives you tips on how to use this resource most effectively.

Concept Mapping Masters for each chapter help students draw relationships between concepts as they complete each map.

Critical Thinking/Problem Solving Masters encourage students to develop and use higher-level thinking skills to examine and solve problems in new ways.

Hands-on Learning

Two **Lab Manuals,** containing more than 160 classroom-tested activities and experiments, helps you build the ideal lab program for your biology course.

• **Investigating Living Systems** features structured experiments that require very simple equipment and supplies, and even includes instructions to help you construct inexpensive equipment of your own.

• **Probing Levels of Life,** designed for the better equipped lab, uses more living materials and requires students to create their own lab reports.

Assessment

Chapter Assessment uses short answer and open-ended questions to help you assess student understanding, chapter by chapter, so you can determine any trouble spots as they arise.

Computer Test Bank Package, available in Apple, IBM, and Macintosh versions, gives you the flexibility to add your own problems and edit existing questions to make creating your own chapter tests more convenient.

Instructional Aids

Transparency Package includes *over 59* new transparencies, many with overlays, to help you add color and emphasis to key concepts. Packaged in a 3 ring binder for ease of storage and protection. Also included:

- **Transparency Workbook** features blackline versions of the full color transparencies and supplemental worksheets for added review and reinforcement of important concepts.

Spanish Resources provides Spanish translations of chapter and lesson objectives, main ideas, glossary terms, and definitions. Ideal for bilingual classrooms.

Lesson Plan Booklet, which includes correlations for lessons, objectives, features, and program resources, is your complete planning resource.

Technology

Videodisc Correlations for Optical Data and Videodiscovery biology laserdisc programs allow you to use these resources with *Biology: Living Systems* with the sweep of a light pen.

Science and Technology Videodisc Series which features 7 discs containing over 280 videoreports produced and narrated by TV's "Mister Wizard," lets students catch a glimpse of real scientists exploring current problems and technological developments, so they can discover biology's influence in day-to-day living.

Science and Technology Videodisc Teacher Guides help you integrate the exciting videoreports in the Science and Technology Videodisc Series with lessons from *Biology: Living*

Systems. Each Videodisc **Teacher Guide** includes a bar code directory plus teaching strategies, research updates, and complete narration for each videoreport.

Infinite Voyage Video Series (20 VHS Videotapes) brings the amazing live action and animated sequences of this award-winning PBS series to your biology classroom, for added enrichment . . . and enjoyment. Includes a **Teacher Guide**.

Lab Partner Software is a spreadsheet and graphing program that allows you and your students to record, collect, and graph data from laboratory activities simply and effectively. A **User Guide** is also available to assist students through the programs.

Glencoe Science Professional Development Series

Exploring Environmental Issues incorporates open-ended projects to help students investigate many of the environmental issues found in today's headlines, so they understand how these issues can affect their lives.

Cooperative Learning Resource Guide helps you turn almost any classroom situation into an opportunity to put the effectiveness of group learning to work.

Performance Assessment in the Biology Classroom uses a variety of performance-based tasks and skills assessments to help you assess student mastery of important thinking processes and skills.

Alternate Assessment in the Science Classroom explains nontraditional methods of assessment such as performance assessments and portfolios. In addition to strategies, this component also provides samples of questions, report forms, and scoring rubrics.

To get the big picture, the choice is perfectly clear.

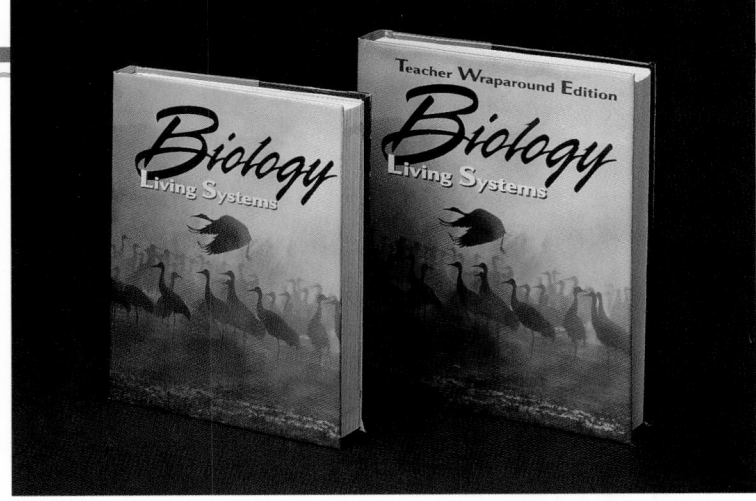

You have to get Biology: Living Systems.

Student Edition	0-02-800672-0
Teacher Wraparound Edition	0-02-826294-8
Teacher Classroom Resources	0-02-826295-6
Study Guide	0-02-826296-4
Study Guide, Teacher Edition	0-02-826308-1
Critical Thinking/Problem Solving Booklet	0-02-826313-8
Concept Mapping	0-02-826321-9
Investigating Living Systems Lab Manual	0-02-826297-2
Investigating Living Systems Lab Manual, Teacher Edition	0-02-826298-0
Probing Levels of Life Lab Manual	0-02-826299-9
Probing Levels of Life Lab Manual, Teacher Edition	0-02-826300-6
Spanish Resources	0-02-826310-3
Transparency Package	0-02-826306-5
Videodisc Correlations	0-02-826304-9
Science and Technology Videodisc Series	0-02-826149-6
Biology: Living Systems Science and Technology Videodisc Teacher Guide	0-02-826305-7
Infinite Voyage Video Series Package, 20 VHS videos *(individual videos also available)*	0-02-826510-6
Lab Partner Software	
Demonstration Package (IBM 3.5" & 5.25" disks)	0-02-826470-3
Apple (3.5" & 5.25" disks)	0-675-02487-0
IBM (3.5" & 5.25" disks)	0-675-17271-3
Chapter Assessment	0-02-826301-4
Computer Test Bank Package	
Apple (3.5" & 5.25" disks)	0-02-826302-2
IBM (3.5" & 5.25" disks)	0-02-826303-0
Macintosh (3.5" disks)	0-02-826309-X
Glencoe Science Professional Development Series	
Performance Assessment in Biology	0-02-826322-7
Alternate Assessment in the Science Classroom	0-02-826429-0
Cooperative Learning Resource Guide	0-02-826430-4
Exploring Environmental Issues	0-02-826312-X
Lesson Plan Booklet	0-02-826311-1

GLENCOE
Macmillan/McGraw-Hill

5/93
SC90799-3

For more information contact your nearest regional office or call 1-800-334-7344.

1. Northeast Region
GLENCOE
17 Riverside Drive
Nashua, NH 03062
603-880-4701
800-424-3451

2. Mid-Atlantic Region
GLENCOE
5 Terri Lane, Suite 5
Burlington, NJ 08016
609-386-7353
800-553-7515

3. Atlantic-Southeast Region
GLENCOE
Brookside Park
One Harbison Way, Suite 101
Columbia, SC 29212
803-732-2365

4. Southeast Region
GLENCOE
6510 Jimmy Carter Boulevard
Norcross, GA 30071
404-446-7493
800-982-3992

5. Mid-America Region
GLENCOE
4635 Hilton Corporate Drive
Columbus, OH 43232
614-759-6600
800-848-1567

6. Mid-Continent Region
GLENCOE
846 East Algonquin Road
Schaumburg, IL 60173
708-397-8448
800-762-4876

7. Southwest Region
GLENCOE
320 Westway Place
Suite 550
Arlington, TX 76018
817-784-2100
800-828-5096

8. Texas Region
GLENCOE
320 Westway Place
Suite 550
Arlington, TX 76018
817-784-2100
800-828-5096

9. Western Region
GLENCOE
610 East 42nd Street, #102
Boise, ID 83714
208-378-4002
800-452-6126
Includes Alaska

10. California Region
GLENCOE
15319 Chatsworth Street
P. O. Box 9609
Mission Hills, CA 91346
818-898-1391
800-423-9534

Glencoe Catholic School Region
GLENCOE
25 Crescent Street
1st Floor
Stamford, CT 06906
203-964-9109
800-551-8766

Canada
Maxwell Macmillan Canada
1200 Eglinton Avenue, East
Suite 200
Don Mills, Ontario M3C 3N1
Telephone: 416-449-6030
Telex: 069.59372
Telefax: 416-449-0068

Overseas and Hawaii
Macmillan/McGraw-Hill
International
10 Union Square East
New York, NY 10003
Telephone: 212-353-5700
Telefax: 212-353-5894

Printed on recycled paper.

Teacher Wraparound Edition

Biology
Living Systems

GLENCOE
Macmillan/McGraw-Hill

New York, New York   Columbus, Ohio   Mission Hills, California   Peoria, Illinois

A
GLENCOE
PROGRAM

Biology

Living Systems

Student Edition
Teacher Wraparound Edition
Study Guide, SE and TE
Investigating Living Systems, SE and TAE
Probing Levels of Life, SE and TAE
Assessment
Videodisc Correlations
Science and Technology Videodisc Series Teacher Guide
Transparency Package
Concept Mapping
Exploring Environmental Issues
Critical Thinking/Problem Solving
Spanish Resources
Lesson Plans
Computer Test Bank

Contributing Authors

Alton Biggs
Allen High School
Allen, TX

Linda Lundgren
Bear Creek High School
Lakewood, CO

Albert Kaskel
Evanston Township High School
Evanston, IL

Devi Mathieu
Sebastopol, CA

Send all inquiries to:

GLENCOE DIVISION
Macmillan/McGraw-Hill
936 Eastwind Drive
Westerville, OH 43081

ISBN 0-02-826294-8

Printed in the United States of America

1 2 3 4 5 6 7 8 9 - RRD-W - 00 99 98 97 96 95 94 93

TABLE OF CONTENTS

Teacher Guide

Student Edition

Philosophy and Themes

Since its inception in 1973, **Biology: Living Systems** has led the way in providing a fresh and innovative approach to biology education that appeals to students and teachers alike. By its very organization, the "systems approach" focuses on the important concepts and ideas of biology, leading students to understand and appreciate the world of life not in terms of the many differences among organisms, but rather in terms of their common characteristics.

This new edition of **Biology: Living Systems** continues that successful approach with an up-to-date and streamlined text that places even greater emphasis on conceptual understanding, the development of important ideas of biology, and the relationship between biology and the everyday lives of students through connections to biotechnology, the arts, literature, history, and ethics. Exploration of ideas is favored over excessive terminology, understanding and application of concepts over memorization of facts, the big picture over endless, encyclopedic detail.

How can students be helped to see the big picture? The text's organization enables them to do so. In **Biology: Living Systems,** topics are presented from the simplest to

the most complex levels of organization, and the text continually and logically builds upon and reinforces previously learned material. Students reexamine basic ideas in different contexts, and, as they do so, begin to make meaningful connections. For example, the importance of photosynthesis becomes increasingly appreciated as it is studied at levels ranging from the details of its chemistry to its significance in the biosphere.

The sequence of topics is complemented by emphasis on six themes. These themes are not an end, but rather a means to an end. Emphasis on themes contributes to the big picture by focusing learning on connections among major ideas and concepts. The thematic approach contributes to students' comprehension of fundamental life processes, understanding of interactions among organisms, and appreciation of how biologists have come to know what they know. **Biology: Living Systems** emphasizes the following themes:

Evolution
All organisms are related in that they are descendants of the first forms of life on Earth. Evolution is the process by which organisms are adapted to changing environments and by which one species may give rise to another. Evolutionary relationships identify closely related organisms and explain both similarities and differences among them. The diversity of life on Earth is a product of evolutionary change. This theme is developed not only where the process of evolution is discussed, but also, for example, in chapters dealing with classification and the five kingdoms of life and in comparisons of adaptations for maintenance and reproduction.

Unity Within Diversity
Though life on Earth today is represented by millions of species, those species face similar problems. Moreover, they solve them in similar ways. In order to survive, all organisms must carry out the same basic functions. General patterns of carrying out life functions are easily recognized, and these patterns form a common bond that unites the many different organisms alive today. The theme is evident in discussion of topics ranging from cell structure and function to the genetic code to patterns of digestion.

Use of Energy
In order to carry out basic functions, organisms require a continual source of energy and a means of extracting and utilizing that energy. Energy flow pervades every level of biological organization from cell to biosphere. This theme is explored in numerous contexts: photosynthesis and respiration, need for enzymes, ATP and its uses, the link between exergonic and endergonic reactions, and energy flow through ecosystems.

Patterns of Change

Organisms are constantly exposed to and influenced by changes of different types. Some are cyclical; others are less regular. This theme becomes apparent in the exploration of such topics as animal and plant life cycles, recycling of nutrients, patterns of population growth, and ecological succession.

Systems and Interactions

No single part at any level of organization operates independently. Proper functioning depends on coordinated relationships. Parts of organisms interact with one another, and organisms, in turn, are interdependent as well. This theme is stressed in the study of the interaction of organelles within cells, cells within tissues, organs within systems, and systems within organisms. It is also apparent in such topics as feeding relationships, symbiotic associations, and recycling of materials. Organisms also interact with physical aspects of their environment, each affecting the other.

The Nature of Scientific Inquiry

Science is not a "subject to be learned." It is an activity, a process by which we learn about the physical world. Students learn about the fundamental methods common to scientific inquiry and see evidence of those methods as classic experiments leading to the development of major principles are discussed and analyzed. More significantly, students are afforded the opportunity to do science themselves throughout the course. Each chapter includes **Minilabs** that stimulate interest and a **Thinking Lab** that fosters analytical thinking. The **Investigation** in each chapter provides students with an opportunity to act like real scientists. Far from the "cookbook" labs that require students to confirm what they have already learned, many of the **Investigations** require students to formulate hypotheses and then design controlled experiments to test them.

Biology: Living Systems makes sense for teachers, too. It is replete with features that will help you stimulate the interest of, provoke curiosity among, and motivate your students. Within each chapter are thought-provoking, relevant, and contemporary discussions that extend or build upon topics treated in the core text—subjects that involve students in decision making; enable them to perceive connections to mathematics, other sciences, and nonscience disciplines; and promote critical thinking. **Section Review** and **Chapter Review** questions reflect the text's philosophy in that they focus on understanding of themes and principles, relationships among ideas, and application of knowledge to new situations, both hypothetical and real.

In addition, the *Teacher Wraparound Edition* contains a wealth of material that will save you time and help you achieve your teaching goals. Among its many features are suggested teaching strategies; information related to each lab exercise; demonstrations; discussion of relevant issues of science, technology, and society; and answers to all questions.

Biology: Living Systems provides your students with a program that promotes true learning about the science of biology. Reflecting current thought about the goals of secondary science education and how those goals can best be met, it actively engages students in the processes of science and directs them to a meaningful understanding of biology, the study of life.

Biology: Living Systems —
Connects Students to the Big Ideas in Biology

Finally, students can understand the ideas that, when woven together, form a big picture of what biology is all about. Relationships among major concepts are established through a thematic approach that links together ideas from one chapter to the next. Learning by doing further increases student comprehension as students design their own lab investigations and discover the biologist in themselves. Discovery continues as students read about and make connections between biology and other disciplines. A whole new world awaits your students in *Biology: Living Systems,* a program that focuses on relevance and understanding the big picture.

The Big Picture

When was the last time you asked a student to make a connection between two major concepts, and he or she was at a loss for words? If that has ever happened in your classroom, *Biology: Living Systems* is the program for you. *Biology: Living Systems* offers students the chance to see the forest as well as the trees by making connections between major ideas in biology. Biology is more than just a list of vocabulary terms to memorize—it's an exciting world of discovery that sometimes eludes students. But, in *Biology: Living Systems* the big picture of what biology is all about becomes crystal clear because major ideas are woven together in a thematic context. From chapter to chapter, the relationships among concepts are reintroduced and reinforced—not introduced and forgotten. Vocabulary terms are kept to a minimum, allowing students to focus on what's important— the big ideas of biology. Students see how all the parts of biology fit together, all the while seeing how biology relates to their lives. All of these benefits are wrapped up in a visually exciting book that invites students to explore the wonders of biology.

Making Connections

Biology comes alive through connections and applications that emphasize the relationships between biology and other disciplines. Students see that many different kinds of "trees" grow in the biology "forest," and that all of these trees together make biology a richly rewarding course of study. **Connections** to art, literature, leisure, history, health, psychology, math, and other sciences make for a more stimulated and well-rounded student. **Global Connections** highlight the contributions of individuals and societies of diverse cultures. **Issues** provide opportunities to develop viewpoints on topics of controversy. **Considering the Environment** features enlighten students about ever-growing environmental concerns. **Biotechnology** and **Career Connections** round out the selection of features that show students how biology relates to them and how colorful and exciting that relationship can be.

Skill Development

Ample support for skill development is provided through **Skill Review** questions, a complete **Skill Handbook, Thinking Labs,** and **Lab Interpretation** questions in the **Chapter Review. Skill Review** questions appear at the end of each numbered section. They are supported by a comprehensive **Skill Handbook,** which is located in the student textbook and so is easily accessible to students. Students receive help developing critical thinking skills, scientific method skills, and organizing skills. **Thinking Labs** provide opportunities to manipulate data and practice critical thinking skills without the fuss. No lab materials are required, so you save time on setups. **Lab Interpretation** questions at the end of each chapter reinforce and extend the content in the labs, while enabling students to further hone their skills.

Self-Discovery

What makes biology exciting to students is working in the lab, observing living things, and tackling concrete problems that challenge them to find their own answers. *Biology: Living Systems* is the first textbook to provide more than the same, tired "cookbook" labs you've seen hundreds of times before. Students work cooperatively to develop their own experimental designs in the **Investigations.** They discover firsthand that developing procedures for studying a problem is not as hard as they thought it might be. Watch your students grow in confidence and ability as they progress through the self-directed **Investigations.** In addition to the **Investigations,** *Biology: Living Systems* offers **Minilabs. Minilabs** are short activities that require simple materials and minimal guidance from the teacher. **Minilabs** can be student-directed, or you may wish to do some of them as classroom demonstrations.

Preparing Students for Open-ended Lab Experiences

To prepare students for **Investigations,** you should follow the guidelines in the ***Teacher Wraparound Edition,*** especially in the sections titled **Possible Procedures** and **Teaching Strategies.** In these sections, you will be given information about what demonstrations to do and what questions to ask students so that they will be able to design their experiment. Your introduction to an **Investigation** will be very different from traditional lab introductions in that it will be designed to focus students on the problem and stimulate their thinking without giving them directions for how to set up their experiment. Different groups of students will develop alternative hypotheses and alternative procedures. Check their procedures before they begin. In contrast to some "cookbook" labs, there will not be just one "right" answer. Finally, students should be encouraged to use questions that come up during the **Investigation** in designing a new experiment.

If you feel that your students are not prepared to begin designing experiments, you may want to practice some paper and pencil lab designs using the following format: Select a simple biological scenario and ask students to design an experiment that will test a hypothesis they make about the problem presented in the reading. Give them a set of questions that will lead them to an appropriate experimental design. An example follows:

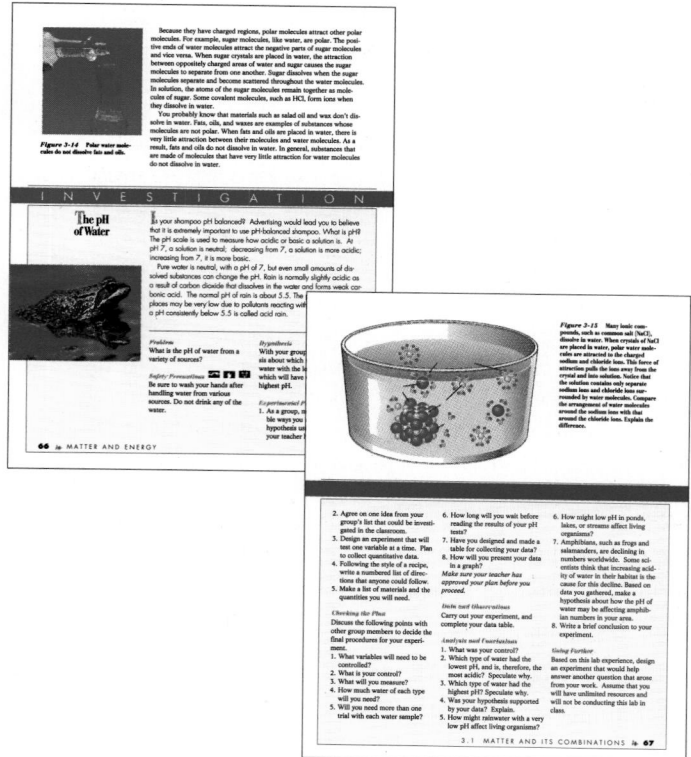

Background

Stingrays, both male and female, are equipped with organs that detect the minute electrical fields given off by living organisms. Scientists speculate that during mating season, male stingrays find female stingrays by locating the electrical fields given off by the females.

Experimental Plan

1. State the problem posed by the reading.
2. To what other factors (excluding electricity) might male stingrays be responding in their search for females?
3. State a hypothesis about how male stingrays find female stingrays.
4. In a cooperative group, brainstorm a list of ways to test the stated hypothesis.
5. What variables are important?
6. From the list generated in Step 4, design an experiment to test one variable. List materials needed and a step-by-step procedure in a numbered list similar to a recipe.
7. What variables will be measured?
8. How many stingrays will be tested?
9. How many trials will be run?
10. How will controls be incorporated?
11. How can the results be graphed?

Possible Experimental Designs

1. Prepare two models of female stingrays. Incorporate electricity into one and not the other. Introduce both of them into the environment of a male stingray. Measure the amount of time he spends with each model.
2. Cover the electrical organs of female stingrays to prevent electrical fields from escaping. Compare the amount of time males spend with normal females to ones that have their electrical organs covered.

If students need further help, you may wish to guide them step by step through the **Investigations** in Chapters 1 and 2. These **Investigations** are designed to be more structured than **Investigations** in other chapters by offering students additional help in designing and setting up experimental procedures. For students who are still uncomfortable with developing their own experiments, ***Biology: Living Systems*** also offers traditional labs in several forms. **Alternate Labs** in the ***Teacher Wraparound Edition*** give specific procedures for students to follow. Two lab manuals, ***Investigating Living Systems*** and ***Probing Levels of Life,*** provide more than 160 lab experiences that address the ability levels of all students.

Supplementary Materials

The *Teacher Classroom Resources* is designed to enhance the *Biology: Living Systems* program by assisting the teacher in all areas of biology instruction. Use the components of the *Teacher Classroom Resources* as time-saving teaching aids in the planning, instruction, evaluation, and enrichment of your biology classes. Each component of the *Teacher Classroom Resources* is described below.

Reinforcement and Enrichment

The *Study Guide* contains masters that help students read and understand the major concepts of each numbered section. An added bonus is a vocabulary review page for each chapter. The *Study Guide* is also available in a consumable student edition.

Exploring Environmental Issues in the Biology Classroom provides opportunities for students to explore a variety of environmental topics. Activities are open-ended and encourage students to make decisions about current environmental issues.

Reinforce connections within and among concepts and processes by using the *Concept Mapping* book. Each master challenges students to construct visual representations of relationships among particular chapter concepts.

The *Critical Thinking/ Problem Solving* book provides masters that require students to apply knowledge and higher-level thinking skills to analyze new situations and solve problems.

Laboratory Manuals

A well-rounded laboratory program is an integral part of the high school biology curriculum. Glencoe offers two lab manuals that provide students with a variety of laboratory experiences and reinforce biology principles encountered in *Biology: Living Systems. Investigating Living Systems* provides structured laboratory experiences for students who still need guidance in the lab. Less-structured lab explorations are provided in a second lab manual, *Probing Levels of Life.* Each lab manual provides opportunities for the manipulation of apparatus, observation, data gathering and processing, and interpretation to form conclusions. Together, *Investigating Living Systems* and *Probing Levels of Life* provide the perfect complement to the open-ended **Investigations** in the *Student Edition.*

SUPPLEMENTS

Instructional Aids

The ***Transparency Package*** lets you conduct a review or test in living color. The package includes 59 full-color transparencies, many with a label overlay. Included in the ***Transparency Package*** are student worksheets and accompanying instruction strategies for use with each transparency.

The ***Lesson Plans*** book provides a complete teaching plan for each numbered section of the textbook. Each plan is geared to the teaching cycle employed in the ***Teacher Wraparound Edition*** and contains a complete list of all the resources available for that section.

Help your Spanish-speaking students get more out of your science lessons by reproducing pages from the ***Spanish Resources*** book. In addition to a complete English-Spanish glossary, the book contains translations of all objectives, key terms and definitions, and summary statements for each chapter of the student text.

Part of the Glencoe Science Professional Development Series, the ***Cooperative Learning Resource Guide*** provides strategies for implementing cooperative learning techniques in your classroom.

Assessment

The ***Chapter Assessment*** book includes short-answer and open-ended questions to let you assess students' understanding of important ideas in each chapter.

The ***Performance Assessment*** book enables you to assess students' mastery of important skills and processes in biology through a variety of performance-based tasks.

Computer Test Banks, available in IBM, Macintosh, and Apple versions, provide the ultimate flexibility in designing and creating your own test instruments. Program features include selection of sections to be tested, number of questions for each section, objectives to be tested, total number of questions on a test, inclusion or exclusion of specific questions, and multiple test forms. Teachers may also add their own questions or modify existing questions.

Another offering from the Glencoe Science Professional Development Series is ***Alternate Assessment in the Science Classroom,*** which provides practical strategies for using alternate forms of assessment.

Technology

Using the barcode directory in the ***Videodisc Correlations*** book, you can access all the images in Videodiscovery's and Optical Data's life science videodiscs that correlate to ***Biology: Living Systems.***

The ***Science and Technology Videodisc Series Teacher Guide*** shows teachers how to use the high-interest videoreports in the laserdisc series to enhance their biology lessons.

The award-winning PBS series "Infinite Voyage" provides some of the best live-action and animation sequences available to enrich your biology program.

Together, the components of the ***Teacher Classroom Resources*** give you a complete program that is flexible enough to meet all your teaching needs.

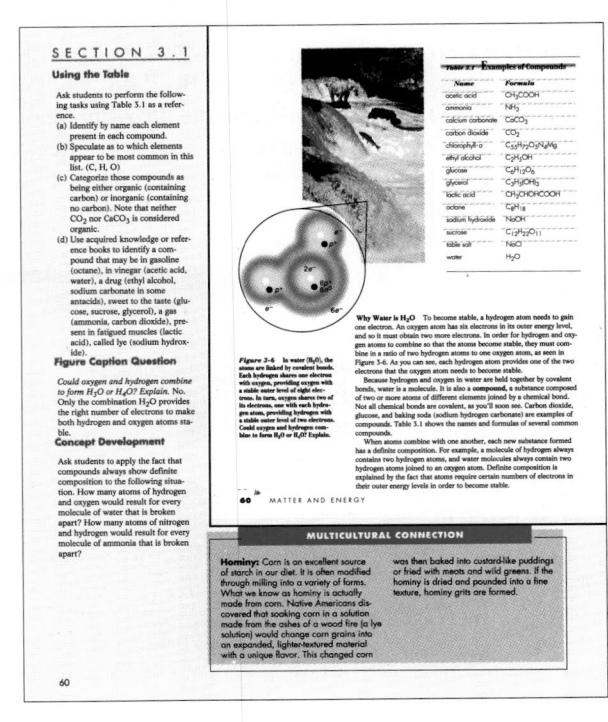

Using Your *Biology: Living Systems Teacher Wraparound Edition*

The ***Teacher Wraparound Edition*** is designed to make teaching ***Biology: Living Systems*** as easy as possible. Nearly all relevant teacher information is presented in wraparound margins. In addition, two pages of planning guides precede every chapter as interleaves.

Interleaves

The two interleaf pages that precede each chapter contain complete planning information for that chapter. The **Chapter Organizer** lists the objectives, text features, and laboratory activities for each numbered section. Also correlated to each section are all the components of the ***Teacher Classroom Resources***, including worksheets and color transparencies.

To aid the teacher with laboratory planning, a chart of lab materials needed for the **Investigations, Minilabs,** and **Alternate Labs** is provided. Finally, the **Key to Teaching Strategies** provides information on how the teaching strategies have been coded for varying ability levels.

Wraparound Margins

The bulk of the teacher information is conveniently placed in the margin next to the student page. Each unit opener has a **Unit Overview** that gives a broad picture of unit coverage. **Theme Development** gives a general overview of the themes developed. **Advance Planning** includes lists of materials to be ordered in advance of teaching the unit. The relationship of the photos to the content of the unit is discussed in **Using the Photo. Previewing the Chapter** discusses how the chapters fit together and overarching content ideas.

At the beginning of each chapter, the **Chapter Overview** previews the main ideas presented in the chapter. A list of the **Key Terms** presented in the chapter is provided. **Introducing the Chapter** assists the teacher by providing information about the visual link between biology concepts and real-world situations. A **Theme Development** section describes how the themes of the text are incorporated into the chapter. **Tying to Previous Knowledge** presents strategies to help the student see the connection between the current chapter and earlier lessons. A comprehensive **Assessment Planner** provides suggestions for evaluating your students' progress.

Teaching Cycle

Each numbered section starts with **Prepare,** which contains **Key Concepts** and **Key Terms.** In most sections, a **Materials** list assists the teacher in advance preparation of laboratory or demonstration materials. The **Prepare** section is followed by a comprehensive, four-part teaching cycle designed to help students learn biology concepts most efficiently.

1 Focus

The first step in teaching any set of concepts or skills is to focus the students' attention. After objectives are previewed with students, a focus idea is provided for each section. This idea may include a demonstration, analogy, activity, or discussion idea that helps to motivate and focus the class so the lesson can begin.

2 Teach

The primary aim of the ***Biology: Living Systems Teacher Wraparound Edition*** is to give you the tools to accomplish the task of getting biology concepts and problem-solving skills across to your students. Most of these tools are presented under **Teach.** Many teaching suggestions are provided under a series of clearly defined headings, such as **Background, Using the Illustration, Enrichment, Misconception,** and others. Also under **Teach** can be found **Connections** to other disciplines; **Different Viewpoints in Biology; Science, Technology, and Society;** and **Bioethics.** You are also provided with information needed to teach each of the special features of the ***Student Edition*** such as: **Investigations, Thinking Labs, Minilabs, Global Connections, Issues, Considering the Environment, Biotechnology, Career Connections,** and **Connections.**

3 Assess

To assist you in monitoring students' progress and adjusting your teaching accordingly, a **Check for Understanding** idea is provided for you in each section. For students who are having trouble, a suggestion immediately follows the **Check for Understanding** hint. The **Reteaching** tip suggests a way to teach the same concepts or facts differently to adjust to students' individual learning styles. For those students in the class who do not need additional help understanding the lesson, **Extension** ideas are provided immediately following the **Reteaching** tips. These enrichments allow students to go on while others are reviewing the section.

4 Close

Closing the lesson is the last but also one of the most important steps in teaching the section because it helps students bring things together in their minds to make sense of what went on in the section. The *Biology: Living Systems Teacher Wraparound Edition* gives you a variety of ways to provide effective closure to a section. The **Close** options are activities, discussions, demonstrations, or analogies that summarize the section, bridge to the next section, or provide an application of the section.

And There's More

At the bottom of many pages in the *Biology: Living Systems Teacher Wraparound Edition* is a **Student Journal** or a **Portfolio** suggestion. Ample suggestions are also provided for **Meeting Individual Needs** of students with diverse learning styles and abilities. **Multicultural Connections** in each chapter look at the contributions of other cultures to biology as well as the impact of biology on those cultures. Answers to all **Section Review** and **Chapter Review** questions are presented in the margin for quick and convenient reference. There are **Program Resources** boxes throughout each section to assist you in planning which of the many resources available are appropriate for your students.

As you review the *Biology: Living Systems Teacher Wraparound Edition,* you will discover that you and your students are considered very important. With the enormous number of teaching strategies provided by the *Teacher Wraparound Edition,* you should be able to accomplish the goals of your curriculum. The materials allow and encourage adaptability and flexibility so that both student needs and curricular needs can be met.

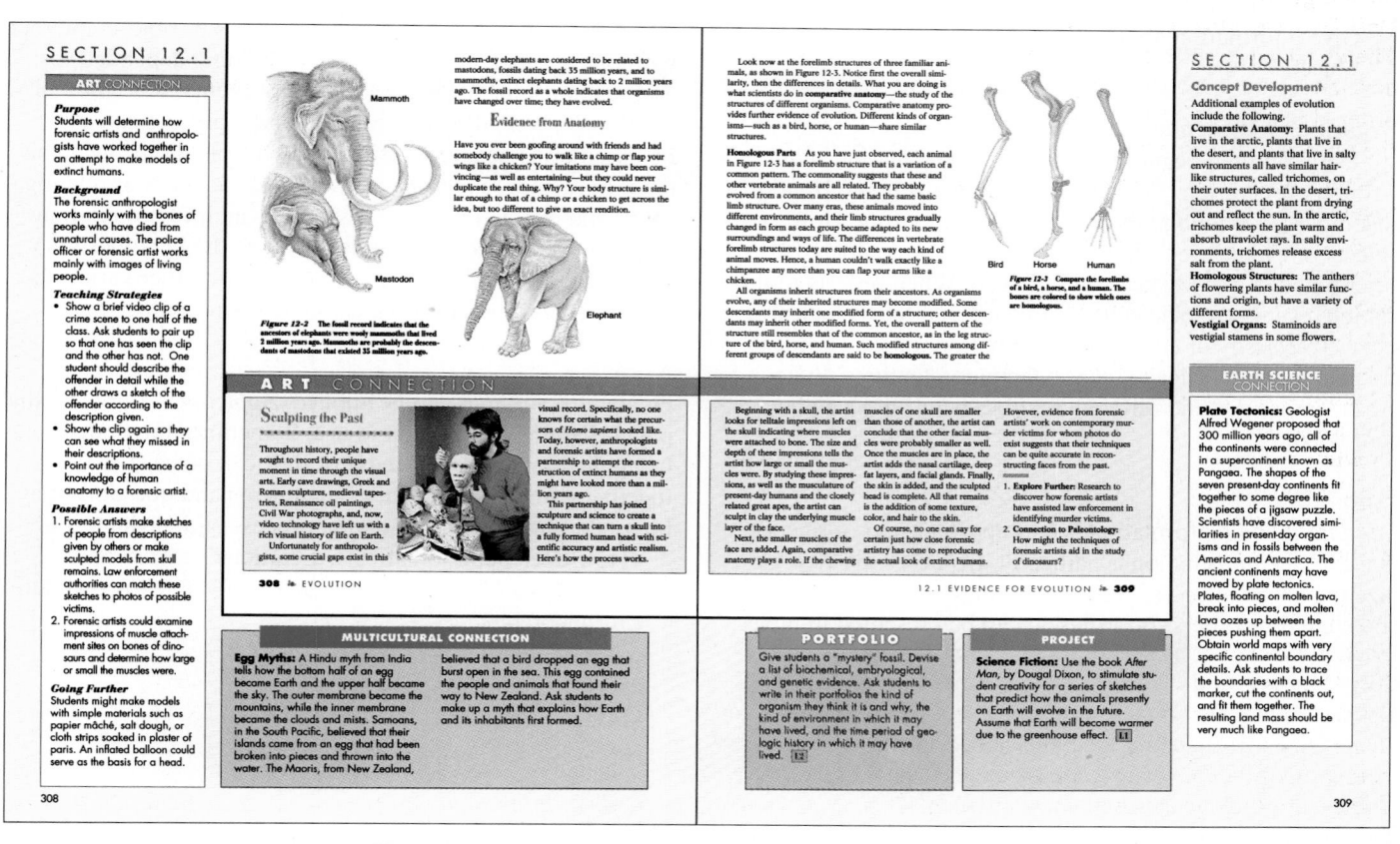

Developing and Applying Thinking Skills

Science is not just a collection of facts for students to memorize. Rather, it is a process of applying those observations and intuitions to situations and problems, formulating hypotheses, and drawing conclusions. This interaction of the thinking process with the content of science is the core of science and should be the focus of science study. Students, much like scientists, will plan and conduct research or experiments based on observations, evaluate their findings, and draw conclusions to explain their results. This process then begins again, using the new information for further investigation.

Thinking Skills

Observing

What are the thinking processes? The most basic process is *observing*. Through observation—seeing, hearing, touching, smelling, tasting—the student begins to acquire information about an object or event. Observation allows a student to gather information regarding size, shape, texture, or quantity of an object or event. The following statements and questions might be posed to students to focus their observations:

"Describe what the objects feel like."
"List the shapes that you see."
"What characteristics can you observe?"
"Give information about the size and quantity of the objects."

Organizing Information

Students can then begin to organize the information acquired through observation. This process of organizing information encompasses *ordering, organizing,* and *comparing.* How the objects or events are ordered, categorized, or compared is determined by the purpose for doing so. When ordering information, events are placed in a sequence that tells a logical story. To *classify* or *categorize* information, objects or ideas are compared in order to identify common features. By looking at similarities and differences, objects or ideas can be compared.

Communicating

Communicating information is an important part of science. Once all the information is gathered, it is necessary to organize the observations so that the findings can be considered and shared by others. Information can be presented in tables, charts, a variety of graphs, or models that make it easier to consider the facts. The following statements and questions may assist students in organizing the information so that it may be communicated to others.

"Compare these objects on the basis of color and shape."
"What information would you use to classify these objects?"
"Order your data according to weight."
"Present your facts on a bar graph."

Inferring

Inferences are logical conclusions based on observations and are made after careful evaluation of all the available facts or data. Inferences are a means to explain or interpret observations. They are a prediction or hypothesis that can be tested and evaluated. The teacher may pose the following questions to focus students on the process of inferring:

"What predictions can you make based on the outcome of this experiment?"
"What can you infer from the classification of these data?"
"Discuss the data that support your prediction."

Relating

Another process to be discussed here is *relating* cause and effect. This process focuses on how events or objects interact with one another. It also involves examining dependencies and relationships between objects and events. Since not all relationships are directly observable, the process can also be based on logical conclusions drawn from all the available data. In science, experiments involve the process of relating cause and effect. The hypothesis states an inferred relationship between objects or events. Then, as the hypothesis is tested, each variable that may interact with other variables to affect the results must be carefully controlled.

Applying

Finally, the findings can be applied. *Applying* is a process that puts scientific information to use. Sometimes the findings can be applied in a practical sense or they can be used to tie together complex data. These statements and questions may be used to focus students on the process of applying:

"How does pollution affect vegetation?"
"What does the phenotype of an organism tell you about its genotype?"

Interaction of Content and Process

Biology: Living Systems encourages the interaction between science content and thinking processes. We've known for a long time that hands-on activities are a way of providing a bridge between science content and student comprehension. ***Biology: Living Systems*** encourages the interaction between content and thinking processes by offering literally hundreds of hands-on activities that are easy to set up and do. In the ***Student Edition,*** the **Thinking Labs** and **Minilabs** require students to make observations, and collect and record a variety of data. **Investigations** require students to design, conduct, and evaluate their own experiments. **Skill Review** questions at the end of each section provide students with another opportunity to practice the thinking processes relevant to the material they are studying. The **Skill Handbook** provides examples of the processes that students may refer to as they do the **Skill Review** exercises.

At the end of each chapter, students use the thinking processes as they complete **Understanding Concepts, Applying Concepts, Lab Interpretation,** and **Connecting Ideas** questions. **Biology, Technology, and Society** and **Connections** connect the science content to other disciplines. In each case, students apply thinking processes as they answer the questions at the end of the feature.

Thinking Processes in the *Teacher Wraparound Edition*

Thinking processes are also featured throughout the ***Teacher Wraparound Edition.*** In the margins are suggestions for students to write in a **Student Journal.** Keeping a journal encourages students to communicate their ideas, a key process in science. The journal may be used to record findings, explore a related topic, or make inferences based on an activity they have just completed. **Project** ideas require the use of thinking process skills as students research and complete each activity.

Concept Mapping

Concept mapping helps the student make abstract information more concrete and useful by visually representing relationships among concepts. A concept map can show the interaction of a series of events, describe the stages of a process, or present a hierarchy of procedures. Further information on concept mapping and a concept map for each chapter can be found in the ***Concept Mapping*** booklet of the ***Teacher Classroom Resources.***

Skills Map

On page 14T, you will find the **Skills Map,** which indicates how frequently thinking process skills are encouraged and developed in ***Biology: Living Systems.***

Minilab 2

What do flower parts really look like?

Use a flower to observe and record the following in a table: number of sepals, number of petals, number of stamens, pistil. Use a scalpel to make a cross-section cut through the ovary. CAUTION: *Be careful when using a scalpel.* Record numbers and arrangement of young seeds. Prepare a wet mount of the anther and record the shapes of pollen grains as seen under low power. **Analysis** *What are the functions for all the parts in your table? How did the numbers of sepals, petals, and stamens compare? How many compartments could you see in your cross section of the ovary? What was the shape of the pollen grains?*

Section Review

4. ***Skill Review—Making Tables:*** Make a table comparing carbohydrates, lipids, and proteins. Compare them in terms of the elements they contain, the building blocks of which they are composed, and their functions in living organisms. For more help, see Organizing Information in the **Skill Handbook.**

Thinking Lab

INTERPRET THE DATA

What may cause "fish kills" in the summer?

Background
In late summer, fish may die off in small lakes as water temperatures rise. Are the fish boiling? This is not likely, as the water doesn't get that hot. What else could be affecting them?

You Try It
Examine the data in the table. It shows the amount of dissolved oxygen available at different water temperatures. The amount of oxygen available to fish is in units marked ppm or "parts per million." A reading of 8 ppm means 8 parts oxygen for 1 million parts of water. The higher the ppm reading, the more oxygen there is. Prepare a graph and then **interpret the data.**

Water temperature	Amount of dissolved oxygen
30°C	7.8 ppm
20°C	9.0 ppm
10°C	10.5 ppm
0°C	14.1 ppm

Why do fish require oxygen? What happens to dissolved oxygen as water temperatures rise? When they fall? Explain why fish may die off when water temperatures rise.

SKILL HANDBOOK

Making and Using Tables

Browse through your textbook, and you will notice many tables both in the text and in the labs. The tables in the text arrange information in such a way that it is easier for you to understand. Also, many labs in your text have tables to complete as you do the lab. Lab tables will help you organize the data you collect during the lab so that it can be interpreted more easily.

Most tables have a title telling you what is being presented. The table itself is divided into columns and rows. The column titles list items to be compared. The row headings list the specific characteristics being compared among those items. Within the grid of the table, the collected data are recorded. Look at the following table and then study the questions that follow it.

Effect of Exercise on Heartbeat Rate

Pulse taken	Heartbeat rate	
	individual	class average
at rest	73	72
after exercise	110	112
1 minute after exercise	94	90
5 minutes after exercise	76	75

What is the title of this table? The title is "Effect of Exercise on Heartbeat Rate." What items are being compared? The heartbeat rate for an individual and the class average are being compared at rest and for several durations after exercise.

What is the average heartbeat rate of the class 1 minute after exercise? To find the answer, you must locate the column labeled "class average" and the row "1 minute after exercise." The data contained in the box where the column and row intersect is the answer. Whose heartbeat rate was 110 after exercise? If you answered the individual's, you have an understanding of how to use a table.

Making and Using Graphs

After scientists organize data in tables, they often display the data in graphs. A graph is a diagram that shows a comparison between variables. Since graphs show a picture of collected data, they make interpretation and analysis of the data easier. The three basic types of graphs used in science are the line graph, bar graph, and pie graph.

A line graph is used to show the relationship between two variables. The variables being compared go on two axes of the graph. The independent variable always goes on the horizontal axis, called the *x*-axis. The independent variable is the condition that is manipulated. The dependent variable always goes on the vertical axis or *y*-axis. The dependent variable is any change that results from manipulating the independent variable.

SKILL HANDBOOK 879

SKILLS MAP

Chapters

SKILL	1	2	3	4	5	6	7	8	9	10	11	12	13	14	15	16	17	18	19	20	21	22	23	24	25	26	27	28	29	30
ORGANIZING INFORMATION																														
Classifying	SR		SR ML	ML TL	I SR						ML	I	SR	SR ML I,TL	SR ML	SR	SR			ML SR			ML SR						ML	
Sequencing			SR	TL		SR ML	SR ML		I SR	I SR		ML SR		I TL			SR	TL SR	ML SR	SR	ML SR	SR	ML SR	TL SR	SR				SR ML	SR
Concept Mapping																	TL	TL												
Making and Using Tables	SR ML I		SR	SR		ML	ML			ML	SR		SR	TL	SR ML	SR ML		I,TL ML SR	I SR	SR	SR							SR	SR	SR
Making and Using Graphs								SR																		SR				
THINKING CRITICALLY																														
Observing and Inferring	SR ML	ML I TL	ML I	ML I	ML SR	ML TL		SR	ML	SR ML	I	TL I		ML I	SR ML I	I TL	ML	ML	ML	I ML TL	ML	ML	ML	ML	TL ML	ML I	I ML	ML	I	I
Comparing and Contrasting	ML I	ML	ML I	ML I	I ML	ML SR	ML			ML			ML	ML	I ML	TL ML	ML I	I ML	ML	ML			ML SR	ML	ML SR	ML SR I	ML SR	ML	ML TL	ML
Recognizing Cause and Effect	ML I TL	I TL				ML SR	TL		TL	TL ML			I ML		SR ML		I TL		TL		SR ML I,TL	ML TL	ML TL		ML SR	ML	TL	ML SR		
Measuring in SI	ML SR		ML		I			SR					I								ML	ML			TL				ML	TL
Interpreting Scientific Illustrations										TL I	ML			TL					TL				TL		TL				ML TL	TL
PRACTICING SCIENTIFIC METHODS																														
Observing	I				I	ML	ML	TL	I	ML	ML		SR		ML		ML	SR	ML				ML	ML	I	I	I	ML	ML	I
Forming a Hypothesis	I	ML I	TL	I		I TL	I TL	I	TL	I	TL I	I	I TL	I	SR	I	I ML			I		I		I	I	I	I	I	ML	I
Designing an Experiment to Test a Hypothesis	ML I TL	I SR	TL	SR	ML	I SR	I		TL		TL I	I SR			I		I I							SR		SR TL		ML I	ML	SR
Separating and Controlling Variables		ML SR		I	ML	I ML	I		ML	ML	TL I		ML			TL	I TL		ML TL		ML				TL					
Interpreting Data	I TL	ML I TL	ML TL	ML TL	ML	TL	I TL	I	ML	TL ML	TL ML	TL ML	I TL	I	TL	TL	I TL	TL I	ML TL	ML TL	I TL	ML I TL		I TL	ML TL I	ML TL ML	I TL ML	TL I	I ML	I ML

Key: TL = Thinking Lab, ML = Minilab, I = Investigation, SR = Skill Review

14T

Assessment

What criteria do you use to assess your students as they progress through a course? Do you rely on formal tests and quizzes? To assess students' achievement in science, you need to measure not only their knowledge of the subject matter, but also their ability to handle apparatus; to organize, predict, record, and interpret data; to design experiments; and to communicate orally and in writing. *Biology: Living Systems* has been designed to provide you with a variety of assessment tools, both formal and informal, to help you develop a clearer picture of your students' progress.

Performance Assessment

Performance assessments are becoming more common in today's schools. Science curriculums are being revised to prepare students to cope with change and with futures that will depend on their ability to think, learn, and solve problems. Although learning fundamental concepts will always be important in the science curriculum, the concepts alone are no longer sufficient in a student's scientific education. Performance assessments differ in formality and complexity, but in most cases, the teacher observes a pupil or group of pupils involved in an activity and rates the performance and/or the products that result from the activity. Background information and specific examples of performance assessment are included in Glencoe's *Alternate Assessment in the Science Classroom. Biology: Living Systems* provides numerous opportunities to observe student behavior both in informal and formal settings. The laboratory activities present many instances where you can informally observe students and evaluate their understanding of both concepts and process skills. Each **Investigation, Thinking Lab,** and **Minilab** contains suggestions that will enable you to assess students' understanding of how the lab relates to the concepts presented in the text.

Another approach for assessing student mastery of concepts and skills in the laboratory is provided in Glencoe's *Performance Assessment in the Biology Classroom.* It features 30 laboratory exercises that enable you to evaluate students' skills in handling laboratory equipment and students' knowledge of laboratory processes.

Group Performance Assessment

Recent research has shown that cooperative learning structures produce improved student learning outcomes for students of all ability levels. *Biology: Living Systems* provides many opportunities for cooperative learning and, as a result, many opportunities to observe group work processes and products. Glencoe's *Cooperative Learning Resource Guide* provides strategies and resources for implementing and evaluating group activities. In cooperative group assessment, all members of the group contribute to the work process and the products it produces. For example, if a mixed ability, four-member laboratory work group conducts an activity, you can use a rating scale or checklist to assess the quality of both group interaction and work skills. An example, along with information about evaluating cooperative work, is provided in the booklet *Alternate Assessment in the Science Classroom.* All four members of the group are expected to review and agree on the data sheet produced by the group. You can require each member to certify the group's results by signing the data sheet or lab report. In this approach, all members of the group receive the same grade on the work product. Research shows that cooperative group assessment is as valid as individual assessment. Additionally, it reduces the marking and grading work load of the teacher.

Portfolios: Putting It All Together

The purpose of a student or cooperative group portfolio is to present examples of the individual's or group's work in a "non-testing" environment. A portfolio is simply a method for assembling and presenting selected examples of work products. The process of assembling the portfolio should be both integrative (of process and content) and reflective. The performance portfolio is *not* a complete collection of all worksheets and other assignments for a grading period. At its best, the portfolio should include integrated performance products that show growth in concept attainment and skill development. You can structure the portfolio development process by establishing categories and other limiting specifications. An essential component in portfolio development is the composition of a submission letter or reflective paper that lists the contents of the portfolio and discusses growth in knowledge, attitudes, and skills.

Biology: Living Systems presents a wealth of opportunities for performance portfolio development. Each chapter contains projects, enrichment activities, investigations, skill reviews, library research opportunities, and connections with life, society, and literature. Each of these student activities results in a product. A mixture of these products can be used to document student growth during the grading period.

Finally, *Biology: Living Systems* strongly suggests the use of student journals. Students are encouraged to write observations, descriptions, and reflections in their journals. They are also encouraged to include diagrams and drawings. Excerpts from the student journal can be included in the individual or group portfolio. Additionally, as many writers have discovered, the journal will be an excellent resource for developing the reflective submission letter or paper.

PORTFOLIO

Give students a "mystery" fossil. Devise a list of biochemical, embryological, and genetic evidence. Ask students to write in their portfolios the kind of organism they think it is and why, the kind of environment in which it may have lived, and the time period of geologic history in which it may have lived. **L2**

Content Assessment

While new and exciting performance skill assessments are emerging, paper-and-pencil tests are still a mainstay of student evaluation. Students must learn to conceptualize, process, and prepare for traditional content assessments. Presently and in the foreseeable future, students will be required to pass pencil-and-paper tests to exit high school, and to enter college, trade schools, and other training programs.

Traditional content assessment forms such as matching, multiple choice, and short essay items are effective in sampling content and can be quickly marked and scored. *Biology: Living Systems* contains numerous strategies and formative checkpoints for evaluating student progress toward mastery of science concepts. Throughout the chapters in the *Student Edition,* **Section Review** questions and application tasks are presented. This spaced review process helps build learning bridges that allow all students to confidently progress from one lesson to the next.

After instruction for the chapter is completed, a summation of the major concepts is presented. Small groups of students can research the major concepts in the chapter and present restatements of their meaning in writing and as oral reports to the class.

After the main idea presentations, the formal review process for the written content assessment can begin. *Biology: Living Systems* presents a two-page **Chapter Review** at the end of each chapter. Individual students or cooperative groups of three to five students can respond to these items to check their understanding of science terms, concepts, critical thinking skills, and problem solving techniques. By evaluating the student responses to this extensive review, you can determine if any substantial reteaching is needed.

For the formal content assessment, a three-page test is provided in the *Biology: Living Systems Chapter Assessment* booklet for each chapter in the student text. The first page of the test includes objective-type questions (multiple choice, true-false, fill-in) that test knowledge. Pages two and three include numerous short-answer and essay items that require students to apply and relate concepts. If your individual assessment plan requires a test that differs from the **Chapter Test** in the resource package, customized tests can be easily produced using the *Computer Test Bank.*

PLANNING GUIDE

Planning Your Course

Biology: Living Systems provides flexibility in the selection of topics and content that allows teachers to adapt the text to the needs of individual students and classes. In this regard, the teacher is in the best position to decide what topics are to be presented, the pace at which the content is covered, and what material should be given the most emphasis. To assist the teacher in planning the course, a planning guide has been provided.

Biology: Living Systems may be used in a full-year course of two semesters covering the text activities and chapter-end materials. It is assumed that a year-long course in life science will have 180 periods of approximately 45 minutes each. The sections of each chapter are classified as core or enrichment. A basic biology program would include core sections. These sections are essential for a minimum program in biology. After presenting the essential sections in each chapter, you may have the time to select from the additional, enrichment topics.

Please remember that the planning guide is provided as an aid in planning the best course for your students. You should use the planning guide in relation to your curriculum and the ability levels of the classes you teach, the materials available for activities, and the time allotted for teaching. You may decide to extend the scope and time devoted to certain topics through the use of enrichment activities and **Teacher Classroom Resources** presented in the teacher margins and on the interleaf pages preceding each chapter. The planning guide will assist you in developing and following a schedule that will enable you to complete your goals for the school year or semester.

Planning Guide for Biology: Living Systems

Unit	Chapter	Class Sessions	Core	Enrichment
1	1	6	1.1, 1.2, 1.3	
	2	4	2.1, 2.2	
2	3	8	3.1 (except Acids and Bases), 3.2 (except Reactions of Biological Compounds), 3.3 (except Coenzymes)	Acids and Bases, Reactions of Biological Compounds, Coenzymes
	4	5	4.1, 4.2	
	5	6	5.1, 5.2 (except Evolution of Eukaryotes)	Evolution of Eukaryotes
	6	6	6.1, 6.2	
3	7	6	7.1 (except Control of the Cell Cycle), 7.2	Control of the Cell Cycle
	8	7	8.1, 8.2, 8.3 (except Many Genes—One Effect, Expression of Genes)	Many Genes—One Effect, Expression of Genes
	9	6	9.1, 9.2	
	10	6	10.1 (except Composition of Eukaryotic Chromosomes), 10.2 (except Other Causes of Genetic Variation)	Composition of Eukaryotic Chromosomes, Other Causes of Genetic Variation
	11	6	11.1 (except Analysis of Genetic Disorders, 11.2	Analysis of Genetic Disorders
4	12	6	12.1, 12.2, 12.3	

Unit	Chapter	Class Sessions	Core	Enrichment
	13	6	13.1, 13.2 (except Other Patterns of Evolution, The Tempo of Speciation)	Other Patterns of Evolution, The Tempo of Speciation, 13:3
	14	3	14.1, 14.2	
	15	7	15.1, 15.2 (except Nutrition in Ancient Bacteria), 15.3 (except Fungus-like Protists), 15.4	Nutrition in Ancient Bacteria, Fungus-like Protists
	16	5	16.1, 16.2	
	17	9	17.1, 17.2, 17.3	
5	18	8	18.1, 18.2, 18.3	
	19	5	19.1 (except Control of Differentiation, Embryonic Induction); 19.2	Control of Differentiation, Embryonic Induction
	20	7	20.1, 20.2, 20.3	
	21	7	21.1, 21.2 (except Exchange of Materials), 21.3	Exchange of Materials
	22	5	22.1 (except Control of Breathing), 22.2 (except Control of Osmotic Balance)	Control of Breathing, Control of Osmotic Balance
	23	6	23.1 (except The Evolution of Disease), 23.2, 23.3	The Evolution of Disease
6	24	5	24.1, 24.2 (except Hormone Action)	Hormone Action
	25	6	25.1, 25.2 (except The Senses)	The Senses
	26	5	26.1, 26.2 (except Energy for Skeletal Muscle Contraction, Ciliary and Flagellar Motion)	Energy for Skeletal Muscle Contraction, Ciliary and Flagellar Motion
7	27	6	27.1, 27.2 (except Interspecific Competition, Intraspecific Competition)	Interspecific Competition, Intraspecific Competition
	28	6	28.1 (except Pyramids of Numbers and Biomass), 28.2	Pyramids of Numbers and Biomass
	29	6	29.1 (except From Pond to Forest), 29.2 (except Unique Ocean Communities)	From Pond to Forest, Unique Ocean Communities
	30	6	30.1, 30.2, 30.3	

Alternate Approaches

You may choose to teach the chapters in an order other than as presented in the Planning Guide. The guides on this page show how chapters can be rearranged if you choose to teach the course with an ecological or human biology approach. Each of these guides shows use of all chapters in the text; however, if you are interested in teaching a minicourse or one-term course, only the chapters marked with asterisks are needed. Each guide also shows the main emphasis of the topics presented in each of the alternate approaches. These guides, like the original planning guide, should be used as frameworks for your planning and not as rigid plans.

Ecological Approach

Chapters	Emphasis
1-2*	Contemporary problems in ecology Introduction to communities Common characteristics of life Methods of science
14-17*	Bases for classification Survey of organisms—their adaptations to various environments
27-30*	Population dynamics Flow of energy and materials Interaction and interdependence of organisms and their environment Protection of the environment Conservation of resources
3-13	Basic chemistry Cell structure and function Cellular basis of reproduction, principles of genetics, DNA function, heredity and environment Evolution—adaptations to changing environments
18-26	Life functions

*Include these chapters in a one-term ecology course.

Human Biology Approach

Chapters	Emphasis
1-6*	Humans have the same needs and perform the same basic life functions as other organisms Methods of science Chemistry as a basis for understanding physiology Cell physiology
12-13*	Human evolution
18-26*	Human body systems
27*	Human population growth
30*	Impact of human activities on the environment
7-10*	Genetics, role of DNA
11*	Human genetics
14-17	Classification and survey of organisms
28-29	Effect of humans on ecosystem structure and function, ecological succession, and world biomes

*Include needed portions of these chapters in a one-term human biology course.

Cooperative Learning in the Biology Classroom

What Is Cooperative Learning?

In cooperative learning, students work together in small groups to learn academic material and interpersonal skills. Group members learn to "sink or swim together" in that they are responsible for the group accomplishing an assigned task as well as for learning the material themselves. When compared to competitive or individual accountability, in which students work against each other or alone, cooperative learning fosters academic, personal, and social success for all of your students.

Recent research supports the benefits of cooperative learning. It shows that cooperative learning results in

- development of positive attitudes toward science.
- choosing to take more science courses as electives.
- positive attitudes toward science carrying over to positive attitudes toward school.
- lower drop-out rates for at-risk students.
- building respect for others regardless of race, ethnic origin, or sex.
- increased awareness of diverse perspectives.
- increased capability for problem solving in sciences.
- increased realization of potential for all students in science classes.
- development of kindness, sensitivity, and tolerance.

Establishing a Cooperative Classroom

Cooperative groups in high school usually contain from two to five students. If students are not experienced in working in groups, you may consider grouping students in pairs and then joining the pairs later to form groups of four or five.

Generally, it is best to assign students to heterogeneous groups that contain a mixture of abilities, genders, and ethnicities. The use of heterogeneous groups exposes students to ideas different from their own and helps them to learn to work with persons different from themselves.

Students may also be randomly assigned to groups, or they can be allowed to select their own groups. Consider using random grouping to let students get acquainted at the beginning of the year or for students to learn to work with all students in the class. As a general rule, it is not good to allow students to choose groups until students have experience with cooperative learning. Have student-selected groups work together when students have interests in common.

Initially, cooperative learning groups should work together for only a day or two. After the students are more experienced, they can do group work for longer periods of time. Some teachers change groups every week, while others keep groups together during the study of a chapter or unit.

Regardless of the duration you choose, it is important to keep groups together long enough for each group to experience success and to change groups often enough that students have the opportunity to work with others.

Preparing for Cooperative Learning

It is necessary to prepare the students for working in cooperative groups. When first starting out, it is important that students understand that they are responsible for themselves as well as other group members learning the material. Before beginning, specify what interpersonal behaviors are necessary for people to work together. Discuss the basic rules for effective cooperative learning: (1) listen while others are speaking, (2) respect other people and their ideas, (3) stay on task, and (4) be responsible for your own actions. Students can learn and practice other interpersonal skills such as speaking quietly, encouraging other group members to participate, checking for understanding, disagreeing constructively, reaching a group consensus, and criticizing ideas rather than people.

You can structure the learning task to promote the participation of each group member by the arrangement of your classroom and the provision of materials. Limiting the materials available to accomplish the assigned task forces students to share them. Also, consider assigning students roles that contribute to accomplishing the group task.

Before teaching the lesson, you must decide on the academic task and the interpersonal skills students will learn or practice in groups. Prepare the students for the academic task by teaching any material they might need to know and by giving specific instructions for the task.

Explain your criteria for evaluating group and individual learning. Specify the interpersonal skills they will be working on and how these skills will be evaluated. Explain the sharing of materials and assuming of roles.

The **_Teacher Wraparound Edition_** codes the activities and teaching suggestions for which cooperative learning strategies are appropriate. The code COOP LEARN appears at the end of such suggestions. For additional help as you prepare to teach the lessons cooperatively, refer again to these pages of background information on cooperative learning.

Using Cooperative Learning Strategies

The **_Cooperative Learning Resource Guide_** of the **_Teacher Classroom Resource Package_** provides valuable background and much practical help for selecting cooperative learning strategies. The booklet suggests methods for teachers to use to facilitate the cooperative groups as well as methods for trouble shooting and evaluation.

During a cooperative learning activity, spend most of your time monitoring the functioning of groups. Praise group cooperation and good use of interpersonal skills. When students are having trouble with the task, answer questions, clarify the assignment, reteach, or provide background as needed. When answering questions, make certain that no students in the group can answer the question before *you* reply.

Evaluating Cooperative Learning

At the close of the lesson, reinforce student learning by having groups share their products or summarize the assignment. Answer any questions about the lesson. Use the criteria discussed at the beginning of the lesson to evaluate and give feedback on how well the academic task was mastered by the groups. Since students are responsible for themselves and other group members learning the material, you can evaluate group performance during a lesson by frequently asking questions of group members picked at random. Other forms of group evaluation include having each group take a quiz together or having all students write and choosing one student's paper at random to grade. Assess individual learning by your traditional method.

To assess the learning of interpersonal skills, have students evaluate how well they used interpersonal skills. Groups can list what they did well and what they could do to improve. Have groups share their analysis with the class and summarize the analysis of the whole class.

Meeting Individual Needs

Each student brings his or her own unique set of abilities, perceptions, and needs into the classroom. It is important that the teacher try to make the classroom environment as receptive to these differences as possible and to ensure a good learning environment for all students.

It is important to recognize that individual learning styles are different and that learning style does not reflect a student's ability level. While some students learn primarily through visual or auditory senses, others are kinesthetic learners and do best if they have hands-on exploratory interaction with materials. Some students work best alone and others learn best in a group environment. While some students seek to understand the "big picture" in order to deal with specifics, others need to understand the details first, in order to put the whole concept together.

In an effort to provide all students with a positive science experience, this text offers a variety of ways for students to interact with materials so that they can utilize their preferred method of learning the concepts. The variety of approaches allows students to become familiar with other learning approaches as well.

Ability Levels

The activities are broken down into three levels to accommodate all student ability levels. ***Biology: Living Systems Teacher Wraparound Edition*** designates the activities as follows:

L1 activities are basic activities designed to be within the ability range of all students. These activities reinforce the concepts presented.

L2 activities are application activities designed for students who have mastered the concepts presented. These activities give students an opportunity for practical application of the concepts presented.

L3 activities are challenging activities designed for the students who are able to go beyond the basic concepts presented. These activities allow students to expand their perspectives on the basic concepts presented.

Limited English Proficiency

In providing for the student with limited English proficiency, the focus needs to be on overcoming a language barrier. Once again, it is important not to confuse ability in speaking/reading English with academic ability or "intelligence." The following ideas may help you to structure learning for the LEP student:

1. Visual and experimental teaching is important. Use demonstrations to clarify ideas. For example, in discussing the "domino effect," do a demonstration using dominoes.
2. Make use of "independent" (especially small group) activities. Small group work allows for more participation and discussion by LEP students.
3. Concepts need to be presented and worked out in a variety of ways. Try to relate the concepts to situations of relevance to the student. Provide examples, use nonverbal strategies, and model the concept whenever possible.
4. Check for understanding frequently. Provide opportunities for students to do sample evaluation items similar to those on tests.

In general, the best method for dealing with LEP students, as well as variations in learning styles and ability levels, is to provide all students with a variety of ways to learn, apply, and be assessed on the concepts. Look for the symbol **LEP** in the teacher margin for specific strategies for students with limited English proficiency.

The chart on pages 22T-23T gives additional tips you may find useful in structuring the learning environment in your classroom to meet students' special needs. In the extended margins of the ***Teacher Wraparound Edition*** there is one or more **Meeting Individual Needs** strategies for each section.

MEETING INDIVIDUAL NEEDS

	DESCRIPTION	SOURCES OF HELP/INFORMATION
Learning Disabled	All learning disabled students have an academic problem in one or more areas, such as academic learning, language, perception, social-emotional adjustment, memory, or attention.	*Journal of Learning Disabilities* *Learning Disability Quarterly*
Behaviorally Disordered	Children with behavior disorders deviate from standards or expectations of behavior and impair the functioning of others and themselves. These children may also be gifted or learning disabled.	*Exceptional Children* *Journal of Special Education*
Physically Challenged	Children who are physically disabled fall into two categories—those with orthopedic impairments and those with other health impairments. Orthopedically impaired children have the use of one or more limbs severely restricted, so the use of wheelchairs, crutches, or braces may be necessary. Children with other health impairments may require the use of respirators or other medical equipment.	Batshaw, M.L. and M.Y. Perset. *Children with Handicaps: A Medical Primer.* Baltimore: Paul H. Brooks, 1981. Hale, G. (Ed.). *The Source Book for the Disabled.* New York: Holt, Rinehart & Winston, 1982. *Teaching Exceptional Children*
Visually Impaired	Children who are visually disabled have partial or total loss of sight. Individuals with visual impairments are not significantly different from their sighted peers in ability range or personality. However, blindness may affect cognitive, motor, and social development, especially if early intervention is lacking.	*Journal of Visual Impairment and Blindness* *Education of Visually Handicapped* American Foundation for the Blind
Hearing Impaired	Children who are hearing impaired have partial or total loss of hearing. Individuals with hearing impairments are not significantly different from their hearing peers in ability range or personality. However, the chronic condition of deafness may affect cognitive, motor, and social development if early intervention is lacking. Speech development also is often affected.	*American Annals of the Deaf* *Journal of Speech and Hearing Research* *Sign Language Studies*
Limited English Proficiency	Multicultural and/or bilingual children often speak English as a second language or not at all. The customs and behavior of people in the majority culture may be confusing for some of these students. Cultural values may inhibit some of these students from full participation.	*Teaching English as a Second Language Reporter* R.L. Jones (Ed.). *Mainstreaming and the Minority Child.* Reston, VA: Council for Exceptional Children, 1976.
Gifted	Although no formal definition exists, these students can be described as having above-average ability, task commitment, and creativity. Gifted students rank in the top 5% of their class. They usually finish work more quickly than other students, and are capable of divergent thinking.	*Journal for the Education of the Gifted* *Gifted Child Quarterly* *Gifted Creative/Talented*

MEETING INDIVIDUAL NEEDS

With careful planning, the needs of all students can be met in the science classroom.

TIPS FOR INSTRUCTION

1. Provide support and structure; clearly specify rules, assignments, and duties.
2. Establish situations that lead to success.
3. Practice skills frequently. Use games and drills to help maintain student interest.
4. Allow students to record answers on tape and allow extra time to complete tests and assignments.
5. Provide outlines or tape lecture material.
6. Pair students with peer helpers, and provide class time for pair interaction.

---

1. Provide a clearly structured environment with regard to scheduling, rules, room arrangement, and safety.
2. Clearly outline objectives and how you will help students obtain objectives. Seek input from them about their strengths, weaknesses, and goals.
3. Reinforce appropriate behavior and model it for students.
4. Do not expect immediate success. Instead, work for long-term improvement.
5. Balance individual needs with group requirements.

---

1. Openly discuss with the student any uncertainties you have about when to offer aid.
2. Ask parents or therapists and students what special devices or procedures are needed, and if any special safety precautions need to be taken.
3. Allow physically disabled students to do everything their peers do, including participating in field trips, special events, and projects.
4. Help non-disabled students and adults understand physically disabled students.

---

1. As with all students, help the student become independent. Some assignments may need to be modified.
2. Teach classmates how to serve as guides.
3. Limit unnecessary noise in the classroom.
4. Encourage students to use their sense of touch. Provide tactile models whenever possible.
5. Describe people and events as they occur in the classroom.
6. Provide taped lectures and reading assignments.
7. Team the student with a sighted peer for laboratory work.

---

1. Seat students where they can see your lip movements easily, and avoid visual distractions.
2. Avoid standing with your back to the window or light source.
3. Using an overhead projector allows you to maintain eye contact while writing.
4. Seat students where they can see speakers.
5. Write all assignments on the board, or hand out written instructions.
6. If the student has a manual interpreter, allow both student and interpreter to select the most favorable seating arrangements.

---

1. Remember, students' ability to speak English does not reflect their academic ability.
2. Try to incorporate the student's cultural experience into your instruction. The help of a bilingual aide may be effective.
3. Include information about different cultures in your curriculum to help build students' self-image. Avoid cultural stereotypes.
4. Encourage students to share their cultures in the classroom.

---

1. Make arrangements for students to take selected subjects early and to work on independent projects.
2. Let students express themselves in art forms such as drawing, creative writing, or acting.
3. Make public services available through a catalog of resources, such as agencies providing free and inexpensive materials, community services and programs, and people in the community with specific expertise.
4. Ask "what if" questions to develop high-level thinking skills. Establish an environment safe for risk taking.
5. Emphasize concepts, theories, ideas, relationships, and generalizations.

Multicultural Awareness

"Multicultural education is an idea stating that all students, regardless of the groups to which they belong, such as those related to gender, ethnicity, race, culture, social class, religion, or exceptionality, should experience education equality in the schools."—James Banks

American classrooms reflect the rich and diverse cultural heritages of the American people. Students come from different ethnic backgrounds and different cultural experiences into a common classroom that must assist all of them to learn. The diversity itself is an important focus of learning experience.

Diversity can be repressed, creating a hostile environment; ignored, creating an indifferent environment; or appreciated, creating a receptive and productive environment. Responding to diversity and approaching it as a part of every curriculum is challenging to a teacher, experienced or not. The goal of science is understanding. The goal of multicultural education is to promote an understanding of how people from different cultures approach and solve the basic problems all humans have in living and learning. ***Biology: Living Systems*** addresses this issue. In the **Global Connections** features of the ***Student Edition,*** information is provided about people and groups who have traditionally been misrepresented or omitted. The intent is to build awareness and appreciation for the global community in which we all live.

The ***Biology: Living Systems Teacher Wraparound Edition*** also includes **Multicultural Connections** that offer additional opportunities to integrate multicultural materials into the curriculum. By providing these opportunities, ***Biology: Living Systems*** is helping to meet the five major goals of multicultural education:

1. promoting the strength and value of cultural diversity
2. promoting the human rights of and respect for those who are different from oneself
3. promoting alternative life choices for people
4. promoting social justice and equal opportunity for all people
5. promoting equity in the distribution of power among groups

Two books that provide additional information on multicultural education are:

Banks, James A. (with Cherry A. McGee Banks). ***Multicultural Education: Issues and Perspectives.*** Boston: Allyn and Bacon, 1989.

Banks, James A. (with others). ***Curriculum Guidelines for Multiethnic Education.*** Washington, DC: National Council for the Social Studies, 1977.

Managing Activities in the Biology Classroom

Laboratory Safety

The activities in **Biology: Living Systems** are designed to minimize dangers in the laboratory. Even so, there are no guarantees against accidents. However, careful planning and preparation as well as being aware of hazards can keep accidents to a minimum. Numerous books and pamphlets are available on laboratory safety with detailed instructions on preventing accidents. However, much of what they present can be summarized in the phrase: *Be prepared!* Know the rules and what common violations occur. Know the Safety Symbols used in this book (see p. 26T). Know where emergency equipment is stored and how to use it. Practice good laboratory housekeeping and management by observing these guidelines:

CLASSROOM/LABORATORY

1. Store chemicals properly. (For details see p. 28T.)
2. Store equipment properly.
   a. Clean and dry all equipment before storing.
   b. Protect electronic equipment and microscopes from dust, humidity, and extreme temperatures.
   c. Label and organize equipment so that it is accessible.
3. Provide adequate work space.
4. Provide adequate room ventilation.
5. Post safety and evacuation guidelines.
6. Be sure safety equipment is accessible and works.
7. Provide containers for disposing of chemicals, waste products, and biological specimens. Disposal methods must meet local guidelines.
8. Use hot plates whenever possible as a heat source. If burners are used, a central shutoff valve for the gas supply should be available to the teacher. Never use open flames when a flammable solvent is in the same room.

FIRST DAY OF CLASS/LABS (with students)

1. Distribute and discuss safety rules, safety symbols, and first aid guidelines. Have students refer to Appendix I on pages 930-931 to review safety symbols and guidelines.
2. Review safe use of equipment and chemicals.
3. Review use and location of safety equipment.
4. Discuss safe disposal of materials and laboratory cleanup policy.
5. Discuss proper laboratory attitude and conduct.
6. Document students' understanding of the above points. Have students sign a safety contract and return it.

BEFORE EACH INVESTIGATION

1. Perform each investigation yourself before assigning it.
2. Arrange the lab in such a way that equipment and supplies are clearly labeled and easily accessible.
3. Have available only equipment and supplies needed to complete the assigned investigation.
4. Review the procedure with students, emphasizing any caution statements or safety symbols that appear.
5. Be sure all students know the proper procedures to follow if an accident should occur.

DURING THE INVESTIGATION

1. Make sure the lab is clean and free of clutter.
2. Insist that students wear goggles and aprons.
3. Never allow a student to work alone in the lab.
4. Never allow students to use a cutting device with more than one edge.
5. Students should not point the open end of a heated test tube toward anyone.
6. Remove broken glassware or frayed cords from use. Also clean up any spills immediately. Dilute solutions with water before removing.
7. Be sure all glassware that is to be heated is of a heat-treated type that will not shatter.
8. Remind students that hot glassware looks cool.
9. Prohibit eating and drinking in the lab.

AFTER THE INVESTIGATION

1. Be sure that the lab is clean.
2. Be certain that students have returned all equipment and disposed of broken glassware and chemicals properly.
3. Be sure that all hot plates and electrical connections are off.
4. Insist that each student wash his or her hands when lab work is completed.

SAFETY SYMBOLS

The **Biology: Living Systems** program uses safety symbols to alert you and your students to possible laboratory dangers. These symbols are explained below. Be sure your students understand each symbol before they begin an investigation or skill.

DISPOSAL ALERT
This symbol appears when care must be taken to dispose of materials properly.

ANIMAL SAFETY
This symbol appears whenever live animals are studied and the safety of the animals and the students must be ensured.

BIOLOGICAL HAZARD
This symbol appears when there is danger involving bacteria, fungi, or protists.

RADIOACTIVE SAFETY
This symbol appears when radioactive materials are used.

OPEN FLAME ALERT
This symbol appears when use of an open flame could cause a fire or an explosion.

CLOTHING PROTECTION SAFETY
This symbol appears when substances used could stain or burn clothing.

THERMAL SAFETY
This symbol appears as a reminder to use caution when handling hot objects.

FIRE SAFETY
This symbol appears when care should be taken around open flames.

SHARP OBJECT SAFETY
This symbol appears when a danger of cuts or punctures caused by the use of sharp objects exists.

EXPLOSION SAFETY
This symbol appears when the misuse of chemicals could cause an explosion.

FUME SAFETY
This symbol appears when chemicals or chemical reactions could cause dangerous fumes.

EYE SAFETY
This symbol appears when a danger to the eyes exists. Safety goggles should be worn when this symbol appears.

ELECTRICAL SAFETY
This symbol appears when care should be taken when using electrical equipment.

POISON SAFETY
This symbol appears when poisonous substances are used.

PLANT SAFETY
This symbol appears when poisonous plants or plants with thorns are handled.

CHEMICAL SAFETY
This symbol appears when chemicals used can cause burns or are poisonous if absorbed through the skin.

SOLUTION PREPARATION

Preparation of Solutions

It is most important to use safe laboratory techniques when handling all chemicals. Many substances may appear harmless but are, in fact, toxic, corrosive, or very reactive. Always check with the manufacturer or with Flinn Scientific, Inc., (312) 879-6900. Chemicals should never be ingested. Be sure to use proper techniques to smell solutions or other agents. Always wear safety goggles and an apron. The following general cautions should be used.

1. Poisonous/corrosive liquid and/or vapor. Use in the fume hood. Examples: *acetic acid, hydrochloric acid, ammonia hydroxide, nitric acid.*
2. Poisonous and corrosive to eyes, lungs, and skin. Examples: *acids, limewater, iron(III) chloride, bases, silver nitrate, iodine, potassium permanganate.*
3. Poisonous if swallowed, inhaled, or absorbed through the skin. Examples: *glacial acetic acid, copper compounds, barium chloride, lead compounds, chromium compounds, lithium compounds, cobalt (II) chloride, silver compounds.*
4. Always add acids to water, never the reverse.
5. When sulfuric acid and sodium hydroxide are added to water, a large amount of thermal energy is released. Sodium metal reacts violently with water. Use extra care if handling any of these substances.

Aceto-orcein stain (7): To make a 9:1 solution of 2% aceto-orcein stain, add 9 mL of 2% aceto-orcein stain to 1 mL of 1N HCl.

Alpha amylase enzyme solution (20): To prepare a 1% solution, dissolve 1 g of enzyme in 99 mL of distilled water.

Benedict's solution (10, 20): Dissolve 173 g sodium citrate and 100 g sodium carbonate in 700 mL water over a hot plate. Filter. Dissolve 17.3 g copper sulfate in 100 mL water. Slowly add to the first solution. Add water to a total volume of 1 L.

Bromthymol blue (1, 22): Add 0.1 g bromthymol blue powder to 2000 mL water. Solution should be bright blue. If not, add one drop of HCl at a time, swirling to mix. Check color.

Bromthymol yellow (6): Dissolve 0.1 g of bromthymol blue in 2 L of water. Add vinegar drop by drop, stirring constantly until the solution turns yellow and remains yellow after standing for 10 minutes.

Charate (29): Burn birch or balsa wooden dowels. Do not burn them to ash. Grind the charred dowels to a fine powder. Alternately, soak the charred dowels in water for 2 days and use the water to treat seeds.

Congo red (5, 15, 20): Add 3 g Congo red dye to 100 mL distilled water. Dilute to the desired strength.

Fertilizer solution (27): To make a 1% fertilizer solution, mix 1 g 5-10-5 fertilizer with 99 mL water. For a 0.1% serial dilution, mix 1 mL 1% solution with 9 mL water. For a 0.01% serial dilution, mix 1 mL 0.1% solution with 9 mL water.

Gibberellin solution (24): Prepare a 500-ppm solution by dissolving 1 g gibberellin in 2 L of water.

Glucose solution (3): For 10% glucose solution, dissolve 10 g of glucose in 90 mL water.

Hay infusion (15, 27, 29): Add a few wheat seeds and a pinch of hay to 500 mL of water in a 1-L jar.

Hydrochloric acid (17): For a 0.0001M solution of HCl, dilute 8.3 mL of stock 12M concentrated HC1 to 1 L with distilled water. To make a 0.0001M HCl solution, remove 1 mL solution and dilute it to 1.0 L with distilled water.

Iodine solution (Lugol's) (5): Dissolve 1.5 g potassium iodide in 25 mL water. Add 1 g iodine crystals. (10): Dissolve 1 g iodine crystals and 2 g potassium iodide in 100 mL water. (18, 20):Dissolve 5 g of potassium iodide in 50 mL of water. Add 1.5 g of iodine crystals. Dilute to 500 mL for use.

Lactose solution (20): For a 10% lactose solution, dissolve 10 g of lactose in 90 mL water.

Maltose solution (20): For a 10% maltose solution, dissolve 10 g of maltose in 90 mL water.

Methyl green (5): Dissolve 1 g methyl green in 1 mL glacial acetic acid. Dilute with distilled water to 100 mL.

Methylene blue stain (5, 7, 11, 15): Dissolve 1.5 g methylene blue in 100 mL ethyl alcohol. Dilute by adding 10 mL of solution to 90 mL water. (4): For a 0.02M solution of methylene blue, dissolve 0.6 g methylene blue in 100 mL water.

Pesticide solution (30): To prepare 1%, 5%, 10%, and 20% solutions of pesticide, mix: 1 g pesticide with 99 mL water; 5 g pesticide with 95 mL water; 10 g pesticide with 90 mL water; 20 g pesticide with 80 mL water.

Phenol red (4): Mix 0.4 g phenol red in 100 mL water to make stock solution. Transfer 1 mL stock solution to 100 mL water for use.

Potassium dichromate (4): For a 0.02M potassium dichromate solution, dissolve 0.6 g $K_2Cr_2O_7$ in 100 mL water.

Potassium permanganate (4): For a 0.02M solution of potassium permanganate, dissolve 0.3 g $KMnO_4$ in 100 mL water.

Salmon testes solution (9): Add 0.5 mL sodium acetate to 0.5 mL salmon testes solution.

Salt solution (4): For a 30% salt solution, dissolve 30 g salt in 70 mL water. For a 6% solution, dissolve 6 g salt in 94 mL water. For a 20% solution, dissolve 20 g salt in 80 mL water. (27): For a 1% solution, dissolve 1 g salt in 99 mL water. Follow procedures under fertilizer solution for making 0.1% and 0.01% serial dilutions.

Sodium hydroxide (17): For a 0.00001M solution of NaOH, first prepare a 0.1M solution by dissolving 4.0 g NaOH in 1 L water. Remove 10 mL and dilute to 1 L with distilled water. Remove 10 mL of this second solution and dilute to 1 L with distilled water. (23): For a 0.01M solution of NaOH, first prepare a 0.1M solution by dissolving 4.0 g NaOH in 1 L water. Remove 100 mL of solution and dilute to 1.0 L with distilled water.

Starch solution (10): Soak a handful of oat cereal (regular, not instant) in 250 mL water. Mash oats with a spoon. Allow to settle for 10-15 minutes. If supernatant liquid is not milky, repeat mashing. Drain off supernatant and use. (20): Make a liter of 1% starch solution by stirring a slurry of cornstarch and cold water into boiling water. Cool thoroughly before using.

Sucrose solution (6): For a 20% sucrose solution, dissolve 20 g sucrose in 80 mL water. (20): For a 10% sucrose solution, dissolve 10 g of sucrose in 90 mL water.

Yeast culture (5): Add 1/4 package dry baker's yeast to 225 mL distilled water, 25 mL molasses, and 10 dry beans. (6): Add one package yeast to 40 mL water. (18): Add 1/2 package activated yeast to 400 mL water and three teaspoons table sugar. Keep solution in an incubator at 38°C overnight. For solution 2, add 1/2 package activated yeast to 400 mL water.

Chemical Storage and Disposal

General Guidelines

Be sure to store all chemicals properly. The following are guidelines commonly used. Your school, city, county, or state may have additional requirements for handling chemicals. It is the responsibility of each teacher to become informed as to what rules or guidelines are in effect in his or her area.

1. Separate chemicals by reaction type. Strong acids should be stored together. Likewise, strong bases should be stored together and should be separated from acids. Oxidants should be stored away from easily oxidized materials, and so on.
2. Be sure all chemicals are stored in labeled containers indicating contents, concentration, source, date purchased (or prepared), any precautions for handling and storage, and expiration date.
3. Dispose of any outdated or waste chemicals properly according to accepted disposal procedures.
4. Do not store chemicals above eye level.
5. Wood shelving is preferable to metal. All shelving should be firmly attached to the wall and should have anti-roll edges.
6. Store only those chemicals that you plan to use.
7. Hazardous chemicals require special storage containers and conditions. Be sure to know what those chemicals are and the accepted practices for your area. Some substances must even be stored outside the building.
8. When working with chemicals or preparing solutions, observe the same general safety precautions that you would expect from students. These include wearing an apron and goggles. Wear gloves and use the fume hood when necessary. Students will want to do as you do whether they admit it or not.
9. If you are a new teacher in a particular laboratory, it is your responsibility to survey the chemicals stored there and to be sure they are stored properly or disposed of. Consult the rules and laws in your area concerning what chemicals can be kept in your classroom. For disposal, consult up-to-date disposal information from the state and federal governments.

Disposal of Chemicals

Local, state, and federal laws regulate the proper disposal of chemicals. These laws should be consulted before chemical disposal is attempted. Although most substances encountered in high school biology can be flushed down the drain with plenty of water, it is not safe to assume that is always true. It is recommended that teachers who use chemicals consult the following books from the National Research Council:

Prudent Practices for Handling Hazardous Chemicals in Laboratories. Washington, DC: National Academy Press, 1981.

Prudent Practices for Disposal of Chemicals from Laboratories. Washington, DC: National Academy Press, 1983.

These books are useful and still in print, although they are several years old. Current laws in your area would, of course, supersede the information in these books.

DISCLAIMER

Glencoe Publishing Company makes no claims to the completeness of this discussion of laboratory safety and chemical storage. The material presented is not all-inclusive, nor does it address all of the hazards associated with handling, storage, and disposal of chemicals, or with laboratory management.

EQUIPMENT LIST

NONCONSUMABLE ITEM	INVESTIGATION	MINILABS	ALTERNATE LAB
acetate	424		
aluminum foil	424, 676, 764, 818	678	
animal shells	310		
animals, pictures			458
apron		65, 71, 147, 155	
aquaria	36	11	
aquarium with pump	764		
aquarium lids with 15- & 75- watt fluorescent bulbs	36		
atlas of U.S.		830	
baby food jars	66		318
backpack	378	592	
bag		340	
bags, plastic sandwich	452, 856	100, 340, 414	346
balance	104, 742	65, 855	318, 428
basin			620
beakers	66, 104, 148, 552, 658, 764	16, 100, 269, 340, 564, 615, 642	154, 428, 762, 816, 848
bird bones	742		
bookbag		592	
books	338		
bottles		862	
Bunsen burner	658		
calculator		47, 327, 622	
calendars, blank		327	
chalk		71	
clock with second hand	424	340	
colored pencils			154
cork		367	
coverslips	120,178	122, 130, 285, 307, 367, 405, 433, 485, 492	44, 106, 126, 176, 398, 816
crayons	120, 178		
culture dish	452	11	126
cups		615, 774	208
depression glass slide			398
dimmer switch	36		
dish, shallow		855	154
dissecting tray			14
dissection pins		367	
dropper	178, 406, 552, 716, 764	269, 367, 405, 485, 554	44, 73, 106, 266, 546, 704, 816, 848
dropper bottle	22, 66		
duct tape			704
EKGs: normal and abnormal		598	
envelopes		367	
exoskeletons	742	732	
feathers		855	
field guide		471	458, 800
fish net		615	
flag marker tape, plastic			346
flashlight			704
flasks, 250- or 500-mL	616		
food containers, small plastic	310		
forceps	658	340	44, 106, 126, 154, 176
funnel	552	862	42, 546
glass rod		485	
glass tube	798		
glass tubing, bent	616		
gloves	378		848
goggles	310, 798	65, 71, 147, 155	848
graduated cylinder	104, 310, 424, 616, 676, 742, 798	269	73, 266, 428, 546

EQUIPMENT LIST

NONCONSUMABLE ITEM	INVESTIGATION	MINILABS	ALTERNATE LAB
grease pencil	66		
grip tester	294		
hair dryer	424		
hole stoppers	616, 798		
hot plate	148, 552, 658	269	154
incubator			526
karyotype, normal			284
karyotypes, with disorders			284
lamp, portable	452		
lens, hand		71	488, 704
library sources on blood cells			646
light bank	856		
light meter			800
light source	746, 818	774	
limestone		71	
magic markers	258		
magnifiers			848
magnifying glass	294		
marble		71	
marking pens	178, 204, 520, 658	564	620, 704
masking tape	66, 230, 520, 658, 818	646 706	428
measuring cup			620
meterstick		47, 719	318, 346
metric ruler	120, 294, 452 520, 658	804	232, 318
microscope	120, 178, 338, 406, 716	91, 122, 130, 181, 282, 285, 307, 377, 405, 433, 441, 485, 492, 515, 683, 732	44, 106, 126, 176, 284, 398, 488, 598, 646, 688, 816 318, 458
microscope, binocular	452, 764	11	
microwave oven	520	263	
milk cartons	204, 856	263	
modeling clay	310, 856	186, 678, 800	
mortar and pestle		546	
nickel		598	
oven mitts	148, 552		
overhead projector	378		
pan, shallow	798		
paper clips		367	
paper punch	258, 658	348	
pennies	742		
petri dish	204, 406, 490, 520 658, 716, 818	519, 615	526
pH paper color chart		862	
photographs, insects & cats		455	
photos from remote-sensing satellites		763	
pine cones, male		492	
pipettes	120, 148, 452	122, 130	
plastic tygon	798		
Potential Vegetation Map		830	
pots	204		176
probe			14
razor blade	120, 178	91	
refrigerator			526
rubber bands	452	155, 340	
rubber tubing	798		
ruler	258, 676, 764, 856	763, 744	266, 704
sand	204, 856	91	
saxophone reed		91	
scalpel		441	14, 176

EQUIPMENT LIST

NONCONSUMABLE ITEM	INVESTIGATION	MINILABS	ALTERNATE LAB
scissors	104, 204, 230, 310 424, 520, 676, 818	678, 804	44, 526, 598
sea urchin spine		732	
shoebox, plastic			730
shoes	378		
slides	120, 178, 338	11, 91, 122, 130, 285, 307, 367, 433, 441, 485, 492, 554	106, 126, 176, 398
soda bottle, 2-L			620
soda pop can pull tab		367	
sphygmomanometer	596		
spoon			428
spoons, plastic		340	208
spray bottle		414	
stethoscope	596		
stirring rod	66	239	
string	258	186, 367	
test tubes	22, 66, 148, 178, 452, 552, 798, 856	71, 147, 155, 239, 269, 340, 564, 800	73, 266, 546
test-tube holder	22, 178, 552		
test-tube rack	552, 798, 856	147	73, 266, 704
thermal mitts		269, 815	
thermometer tubes with caps, plastic			704
thermometers	36, 148, 452, 764	147, 340, 615	526, 800
thread, colored	104		44, 232
thread, nylon		91	
tongs	552		
transparency sheets	378		
turtle skeleton		732	
tweezers		33, 492, 804	
twine			800
twist ties		367	
washers, steel	148		
watch glass		11	176
watch with second hand	36	592, 615, 622	346
water bottle		263	
wood stakes			800
wood sticks		263	
yardstick		47	
yarn	258, 424		
yogurt containers		424	

CONSUMABLE ITEM	INVESTIGATION	MINILABS	ALTERNATE LAB
antacid tablets		71	
barley seeds			546
bean seeds		519	208
beans, navy			762
beans, pinto			762
birdseed		471	
bones, chicken or beef	310, 742	732	
bread, day-old	490	414	
broad beans (Vica faba)			176
caffeine solution	716		
candy pieces		367	
cartilage	742		
cheesecloth			546
cologne	406		
construction paper, 6 colors	230, 258, 452		704

EQUIPMENT LIST

CONSUMABLE ITEM	INVESTIGATION	MINILABS	ALTERNATE LAB
cotton balls	596		
cotton swabs	490, 676		
cough syrup		100	
dialysis tubing	104, 552		
diatomaceous earth		307	
distilled water	22, 66	862	266, 730
egg white	452		
eggshells		71	
filter paper		815	428
food coloring		100	
fruit samples: apple, kiwi, orange, pineapple		564	
gelatin capsule			232
gelatin solution		564	
graph paper, metric	452		
grass seed	818		
hamburger, uncooked	120		
hand lotion	406		
ice	452	340, 615	
labels	204, 676, 856	71, 263, 269, 485, 642, 800, 804, 862	208, 266, 526, 598
lens paper		441, 485, 493, 804	
lettuce	120	91, 227	
lima beans			398
litmus paper			800
liver, raw	452	147	
macaroni, elbow			346
matches		367	
meat chunks	742		
moss capsule		433, 492	
mouthwash		100, 646	
newspapers	310	147	
notebook	378		
oil	856	855	
onion	178, 490	122	
onion bulbs	120, 178	122, 227	266
owl pellets		33	
paper cups	204, 310, 676	227	
paper towels	104, 204, 424, 520, 742, 818, 856	33, 239, 519, 678, 855	106, 176, 526
peat moss	798		
peat pots	856	263	
petroleum jelly	310, 676		398
pH paper	66	862	
pipe cleaners		186	
plaster of paris	310		
plastic wrap		155	
poster board	258		
potato	120		
potting soil		774	208
radish seeds		678, 774	
rain samples		862	
Readi-Earth	204		
salmon testes solution		239	
salt dough		186	
seeds, radish or bean	520	263, 367	
shortening		340	
soda, diet		65	
soda, regular		65	
soil	204, 490	263, 804, 815	428, 816
soil samples		815	
straws, flexible	22		620
sunscreen	406		

CONSUMABLE ITEM	INVESTIGATION	MINILABS	ALTERNATE LAB
talcum powder		91	
tally cards		348	
tape, clear	258, 338, 424, 742	678	526
TesTape		554	73
tobacco seeds	204		
toothpicks	120, 658, 676	16, 285, 519, 544, 646, 706	398
vermiculite	204, 856	263	176
wax paper	310, 424		154
wheat grains	406		
yeast	120, 148	485	
yogurt culture			398

LIVING ORGANISM	INVESTIGATION	MINILABS	ALTERNATE LAB
algae	120		
animals, live			458
bean plants	676, 856	800	
coleus		227	
crayfish			730
Daphnia	716		704, 848
duckweed	764		
E. coli culture	658		
Elodea	22, 36, 126	155	106, 126
fern sorus		433	
fern frond with sporangia		492	
flower petals		91	
flowers		441	
geranium		227	
goldfish		615	
grasshoppers			318
hay			816
insect larvae			526
leaves	310, 338		816
lichen		377	
liverwort		377	
mussels	22	11, 16	
Planaria	452		704
plant material	658		
pond scum		91	
protozoans	406		
puffball		732	
snails		11	
Sphagnum moss			428
spider plant		227	
Ulva		377	
vinegar eels (*Turbatrix aceti*)			704
Wandering Jew		227	

CHEMICALS	INVESTIGATION	MINILABS	ALTERNATE LAB
aceto-orcein stain			176
agar		646	
alginate	310		
alpha amylase enzyme solution	552	269	
ammonia	66		
beet juice, canned		100	

CHEMICALS	INVESTIGATION	MINILABS	ALTERNATE LAB
Benedict's solution	552	269	
bleach		285	
bromthymol blue	22, 616	155, 800	
carmine powder		16	
charate	818		
detergent	856		266
disaccharides		554	
ethanol		239	154
fertilizer solution	764, 818, 856		
gibberellin solution	676		
glucose		554	
glucose solution			73
HCl			176
hydrogen peroxide	798	147	
insecticides	856		
iodine	552	100	154, 546
isopropyl alcohol		239	
LactAid		554	
Lugol's solution	120	130	
methyl cellulose	406		
methylene blue stain	120, 178	122, 130, 285	
molar HCl	452		
molar NaOH	452		
nail polish, clear	338		
NaOH solution		642	
nitric acid solution	764		
pesticides (rotene, pyrethrum)			848
phenolphthalein		642	
rubbing alcohol	596		266
salt	104		
salt solution	452, 764		106
sodium acetate		239	
starch solution	552	269	546
sucrose	148		
sugar		485	
vinegar	66	71, 155	
window cleaner			266

PRESERVED SPECIMENS	INVESTIGATION	MINILABS	ALTERNATE LAB
animals			458
diatom slides		732	
embryos of whitefish, sea urchin, roundworm (*Ascaris*)		181	
fertilized egg, prepared slide		515	
human red blood cells, prepared slide	282	598	
human sickled red blood cells, prepared slide		282	
Hydra slides			488
mammalian adrenal gland slide			688
Obelia		377	
pancreas tissue, prepared slide		683	
Paramecium slides	120		488
prepared slides of thyroid gland, testes, ovaries			688
preserved animal specimens		455	
sand dollar		732	
specimens of freshwater mussels or clams			14
Spirogyra slides			488
unfertilized egg, prepared slide		515	

SUPPLIER ADDRESSES

Equipment Suppliers

Carolina Biological Supply Co.
2700 York Road
Burlington, NC 27215

Central Scientific Company
11222 Melrose Avenue
Franklin Park, IL 60131

Edmund Scientific Company
103 Gloucester Pike
Barrington, NJ 08007

Fisher Scientific Company
4901 W. LeMoyne Avenue
Chicago, IL 60615

Nasco
901 Janesville Avenue
Fort Arkinson, WI 53538

Sargent-Welch Scientific Co.
7300 N. Linder Avenue
Skokie, IL 60077

Sargent-Welch Scientific of
Canada, Ltd.
285 Garyray Drive
Weston, Ontario
Canada M9L 1P3

Turtox/Cambosco
8200 S. Hoyne Avenue
Chicago, IL 60620

Ward's Natural Science
Establishment, Inc.
5100 W. Henrietta Road
Rochester, NY 14692

Audiovisual Distributors

Access Network
295 Midpark Way SE
Calgary, Alberta,
Canada T2X 2A8

Benchmark Films, Inc.
145 Scarborough Road
Briarcliff Manor, NY 10510

BFA Educational Media
468 Park Avenue S.
New York, NY 10016

Clearvue, Inc.
6365 N. Avondale Ave.
Chicago, IL 60631-1996

Coronet/MTI Film and Video
Distributors of LCA
108 Wilmot Road
Deerfield, IL 60015

Educational Media International
Box 1288
175 Margaret Place
Elmhurst, IL 60126

Encyclopaedia Britannica
Educational Corp. (EBEC)
310 S. Michigan Avenue
Chicago, IL 60604

Films, Inc.
5547 N. Ravenswood Avenue
Chicago, IL 60640

Films for the Humanities and Sciences, Inc.
743 Alexander Rd.
Princeton, NJ 08540

Image Entertainment
9333 Oso Avenue
Chatsworth, CA 91311

Insight Media, Inc.
121 W. 85th St.
New York, NY 10024

International Film Bureau, Inc. (IFB)
332 S. Michigan Avenue
Chicago, IL 60604

National Geographic Society
Educational Services
17th and "M" Streets, NW
Washington, DC 20036

Optical Data Corporation
P.O. Box 4919
30 Technology Drive
Warren, NJ 07059

Pyramid Film and Video
Box 1048
Santa Monica, CA 90406

SRA
Macmillan/McGraw-Hill
Blacklick, OH 43004-0543

Sunburst Communications
39 Washington Avenue
Pleasantville, NY 10570

SysCon Corporation
2686 Dean Drive
Virginia Beach, VA 23452

Time-Life Videos
Time and Life Building
1271 Avenue of the Americas
New York, NY 10020

VideoDiscovery
1515 Dexter Avenue N.
Suite 400
Seattle, WA 98109

Software Distributors

Academic Hallmarks
P.O. Box 998
Durango, CO 81302

Career Aids, Inc.
20417 Nordhoff
Chatsworth, CA 91311

CompuWare Corporation
1008 Abington Road
Cherry Hill, NJ 08034

CONDUIT
The University of Iowa
Oakdale Campus
Iowa City, IA 52242

Cygnus Software
8002 E. Culver
Mesa, AZ 85207

Diversified Educational Enterprises, Inc.
725 Main Street
Lafayette, IN 47901

Educational Activities, Inc.
P.O. Box 392
Freeport, NY 11520

Educational Materials and
Equipment Company (EME)
P.O. Box 2805
Danbury, CT 06813-2805

Focus Media, Inc.
839 Stewart Avenue
P.O. Box 865
Garden City, NY 11530

Gemstar (Classroom Consortia
Media, Inc.)
P.O. Box 050228
Staten Island, NY 10305

IBM Educational Systems
Department PC
4111 Northside Parkway
Atlanta, GA 30327

Intellectual Software
562 Boston Avenue
Bridgeport, CT 06610

Micro-ED, Inc.
P.O. Box 24750
Edina, MN 55424

Queue, Inc.
562 Boston Avenue
Bridgeport, CT 06610

Scholastics Software
730 Broadway
New York, NY 10003

BIBLIOGRAPHY

Student Readings

Alexander, R. McNeill, ed., *The Encyclopedia of Animal Biology,* New York, Facts on File, 1987.

Baskin, Yvonne, "DNA Unlimited." *Discover,* July, 1990.

Batra, Suzanne W.T., "Deceit and Corruption in the Blueberry Patch." *Natural History,* August, 1987.

Berreby, David, "Artificial Blood." *Discover,* April, 1991.

Caldwell, Mark, "How Does a Single Cell Become a Whole Body?" *Discover,* November, 1992.

Cochran, M. Ford, "Back from the Brink—Chestnuts." *National Geographic,* February, 1990.

Cohen, Joel E., "How Many People Can Earth Hold?" *Discover,* November, 1992.

Dussourd, David E., "The Vein Drain: Or How Insects Outsmart Plants." *Natural History,* February, 1990.

Freedman, David H., "The Aggressive Egg." *Discover,* June, 1992.

Hanson, Betsy, "Message in a Barrel." *Discover,* June, 1992.

John, B., and K.R. Lewis, "The Meiotic Mechanism." *Carolina Biology Reader.* Burlington, NC.: Carolina Biological Supply Co., 1984.

Kiester, Edwin, Jr., "A Bug in the System." *Discover,* February, 1991.

Martin, Glen. "Spring Fever." *Discover,* October, 1992.

Miller, John A., and Irwin L. Slesnick. "Difficult Decisions: Acid Rain." *The Science Teacher,* March, 1989.

Miller, Kenneth R., *Energy and Life.* Carolina Biology Reader, Burlington, NC: Carolina Biological Suppy Co., 1988.

Noonan, David. "Genes of War." *Discover,* October, 1990.

Ravven, Wallace, "In the Beginning." *Discover,* October, 1992.

Sapolsky, Robert M., "Junk Food Monkeys." *Discover,* September, 1989.

Trefil, James, "Seeing Atoms." *Discover,* June, 1990.

Walker, Tim, "Butterflies and Bad Taste." *Science News,* June 1, 1991.

Wilson, Edward O., "The Diversity of Life." *Discover,* September, 1992.

Teacher Readings

Allard, David W., and Royce L. Granberry, "Osmosis Revisited." *The American Biology Teacher,* November/December, 1992.

Beardsley, Tim. "Teaching Real Science." *Scientific American,* October, 1992.

Brouse, Deborah E., "Population Education." *The Science Teacher,* December, 1990.

Byrne, Kevin B., ed., *Responsible Science: The Impact of Technology on Society.* New York, Harper and Row, 1986.

Chiras, Daniel D., "Teaching Critical Skills in the Biology and Environmental Science Classrooms." *The American Biology Teacher,* November/December, 1992.

Diamond, Jared, "Double Trouble." *Discover,* August, 1988.

DiSpezio, Michael A., "Retroviruses—Gaining an Understanding." *The Science Teacher,* October, 1990.

Foote, MaryAnne, "The Birds and the Bees . . . and the Bats." *The Science Teacher,* April, 1990.

Keown, Duane, "Teaching Evolution—Improved Approaches for Unprepared Students." *The American Biology Teacher,* October, 1988.

Levinton, Jeffrey S., "The Big Bang of Animal Evolution." *Scientific American,* November, 1992.

Margulis, L., and K.V. Schwartz, *Five Kingdoms: an Illustrated Guide to the Phyla of Life on Earth.* New York, W.H. Freeman and Co., 1988.

Meadows, Jack, *The Great Scientists,* London, Oxford University Press, 1987.

Miller, John A., and Irwin L. Slesnick, "Difficult Decisions: Acid Rain." *The Science Teacher,* March, 1989.

Offner, Susan, "A Plain English Map of the Human Chromosomes." *The American Biology Teacher,* Febuary, 1992.

Okebukola, Peter A., "Concept Mapping with a Cooperative Learning Flavor." *The American Biology Teacher,* April, 1992.

Rubin, Amran, and Pinchas Tamir, "Meaningful Learning in the School Laboratory," *The American Biology Teacher,* November/December, 1988.

Storey, Richard D., and Jack Carter, "Why THE Scientific Method?" *The Science Teacher,* December, 1992.

Wilson, Edward O., "Threats to Biodiversity." *Scientific American,* September, 1989.

Yager, Robert E., "Assess All Five Domains of Science." *The Science Teacher,* October, 1987.

Biology
Living Systems

GLENCOE

Macmillan/McGraw-Hill

New York, New York   Columbus, Ohio   Mission Hills, California   Peoria, Illinois

Biology
Living Systems

Student Edition
Teacher Wraparound Edition
Study Guide, SE and TE
Investigating Living Systems, SE and TAE
Probing Levels of Life, SE and TAE
Assessment
Videodisc Correlations
Science and Technology Videodisc Series Teacher Guide
Transparency Package
Concept Mapping
Exploring Environmental Issues
Critical Thinking/Problem Solving
Spanish Resources
Lesson Plans
Computer Test Bank

Send all inquiries to:

GLENCOE DIVISION
Macmillan/McGraw-Hill
936 Eastwind Drive
Westerville, OH 43081

ISBN 0-02-800672-0

Printed in the United States of America

1 2 3 4 5 6 7 8 9 - RRD - W - 00 99 98 97 96 95 94 93

Raymond F. Oram

is a teacher/administrator at the Peddie School, Hightstown, New Jersey, with more than 30 years of teaching experience. Mr. Oram chairs the Science Department, as well as teaching classes in introductory biology, honors biology, and advanced placement biology. Mr. Oram received his A.B. degree from Princeton University and his M.S.T. from Union College, Schenectady, New York. He is a member of several professional organizations, including NABT, NSTA, and AAAS. In 1976, Mr. Oram was recognized with the Princeton Prize for Distinguished Secondary School Teaching in the State of New Jersey. He also has been named Master Teacher, has received the Outstanding Classroom Teacher Award, and is holder of the Casperson Chair in Science, all at the Peddie School.

Paul J. Hummer, Jr.

taught seventh grade life science and high school biology from 1958 to 1986 in Frederick County, Maryland, public schools. He is currently Assistant Professor of Education at Hood College in Frederick, Maryland. Mr. Hummer received a B.S. in Education from Lock Haven State University, Pennsylvania, and an M.S. degree from Union College. He was the 1972 Maryland recipient of the Outstanding Biology Teacher Award, NSTA STAR Award recipient in 1972, and the 1984 Maryland recipient of the Presidential Award for Excellence in Teaching Science and Mathematics.

CONTRIBUTING AUTHORS

Albert Kaskel
Evanston Township High School
Evanston, IL

Linda Lundgren
Bear Creek High School
Lakewood, CO

CONTENT CONSULTANTS

Jerry Downhower, Ph.D.
Department of Zoology
The Ohio State University
Columbus, OH

Donald G. Kaufman, Ph.D.
Department of Zoology
Miami University
Oxford, OH

Melissa S. Stanley, Ph.D.
Department of Biology
George Mason University
Fairfax, VA

David G. Futch, Ph.D.
Department of Biology
San Diego State University
San Diego, CA

Peter N. Petersen, Ph.D.
Science Department
Wilcox High School
Santa Clara, CA

Richard Storey, Ph.D.
Department of Biology
Colorado College
Colorado Springs, CO

James A. Gavan, Ph.D.
Department of Anthropology
University of Missouri
Columbia, MO

Fred David Sack, Ph.D.
Department of Plant Biology
The Ohio State University
Columbus, OH

E. Peter Volpe, Ph.D.
School of Medicine
Mercer University
Macon, GA

READING CONSULTANT

Barbara S. Pettegrew, Ph.D.
Department of Education
Otterbein College
Westerville, OH

REVIEWERS

David G. Cowles
Victor Central High School
Victor, NY

Kathy Hoppin
Wheatland High School
Wheatland, CA

Mary E. Schwartz
Hamilton Heights High School
Arcadia, IN

John E. DeMary
Loudoun Valley High School
Purcellville, VA

Susan Hutchinson
Benicia High School
Benicia, CA

Demby Sejd
McLean High School
McLean, VA

John W. Fedors
Greenwich High School
Greenwich, CT

Priscilla Jane Lee
Venice High School
Los Angeles, CA

Thomas Phil Talbot
Skyline High School
Salt Lake City, UT

Lois Mayo
Pius X Central High School
Lincoln, NE

UNIT ONE

The Nature of Biology 2

TABLE OF CONTENTS

TABLE OF CONTENTS

UNIT THREE

The Continuation of Life 166

UNIT FOUR

Evolutionary Relationships   302

UNIT
FIVE

Life Functions of Organisms   480

UNIT SIX

Controlling Living Systems 668

UNIT SEVEN

Interactions in the Environment 756

INVESTIGATIONS

Here's your chance to explore your creativity. INVESTIGATIONS give you an opportunity to act like a biologist and develop your own plans for studying a question or problem. You'll find that there's more than one way to explore biology!

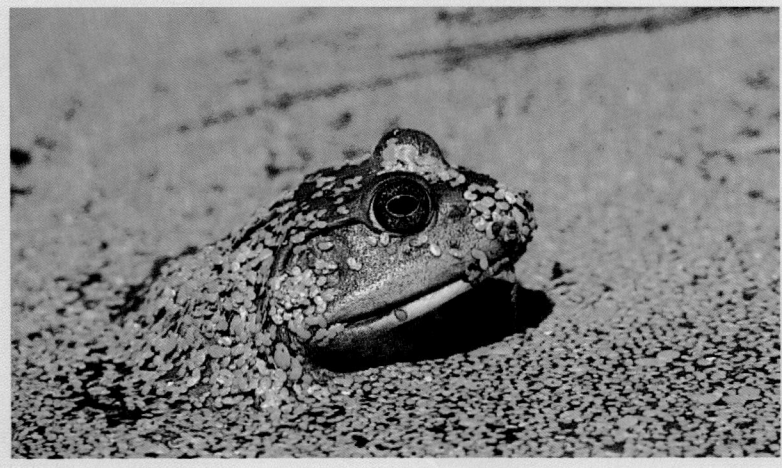

MINILABS

Want to see it for yourself? Then try it! Discover for yourself how something works. Just as a picture is worth a thousand words, a MINILAB may be worth hours of reading.

MINILABS

THINKING LABS

Sharpen up your pencil and your wit because you'll need them. THINKING LABS offer a unique opportunity to evaluate someone else's experiments and data without the mess.

——

ISSUES

What are some aspects of biology that have an impact on society? Develop your own viewpoint on the ISSUES that might be controversial. Learn how to live with biology and use it to enrich your life.

CONSIDERING THE ENVIRONMENT

Do you take for granted that when you flip the switch, the light will come on? Developing alternate ways to provide energy without damaging the environment is one problem that challenges scientists and people like you. Find out how people can make a difference.

GLOBAL CONNECTIONS

How are people in Mexico adapted to a high-altitude lifestyle? How do Native Americans view animals? These and other intriguing questions are answered as you explore these GLOBAL CONNECTIONS.

INTERDISCIPLINARY CONNECTIONS

It may not have occurred to you that biology is an integral part of all your courses. Learn in these features how biology is connected to art, literature, and other subjects that interest you.

Health

Science and Math

INTERDISCIPLINARY CONNECTIONS

Art

Literature

History and Economics

BIOTECHNOLOGY

What new advances have been developed in the last decade from applying biological principles? Explore these new developments and find out how they improve the quality of life.

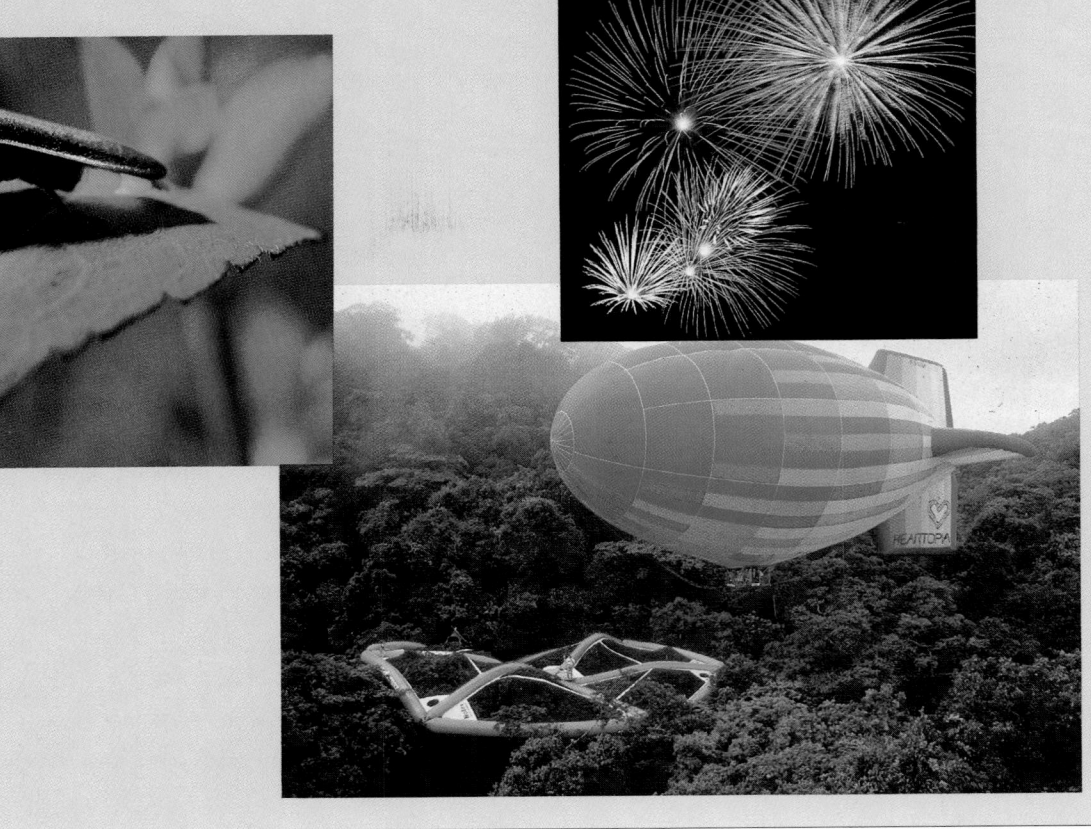

CAREER CONNECTIONS

How can you use biology to develop a career? Find an idea from the CAREER features presented in your textbook. Then plan for an exciting future of discovery.

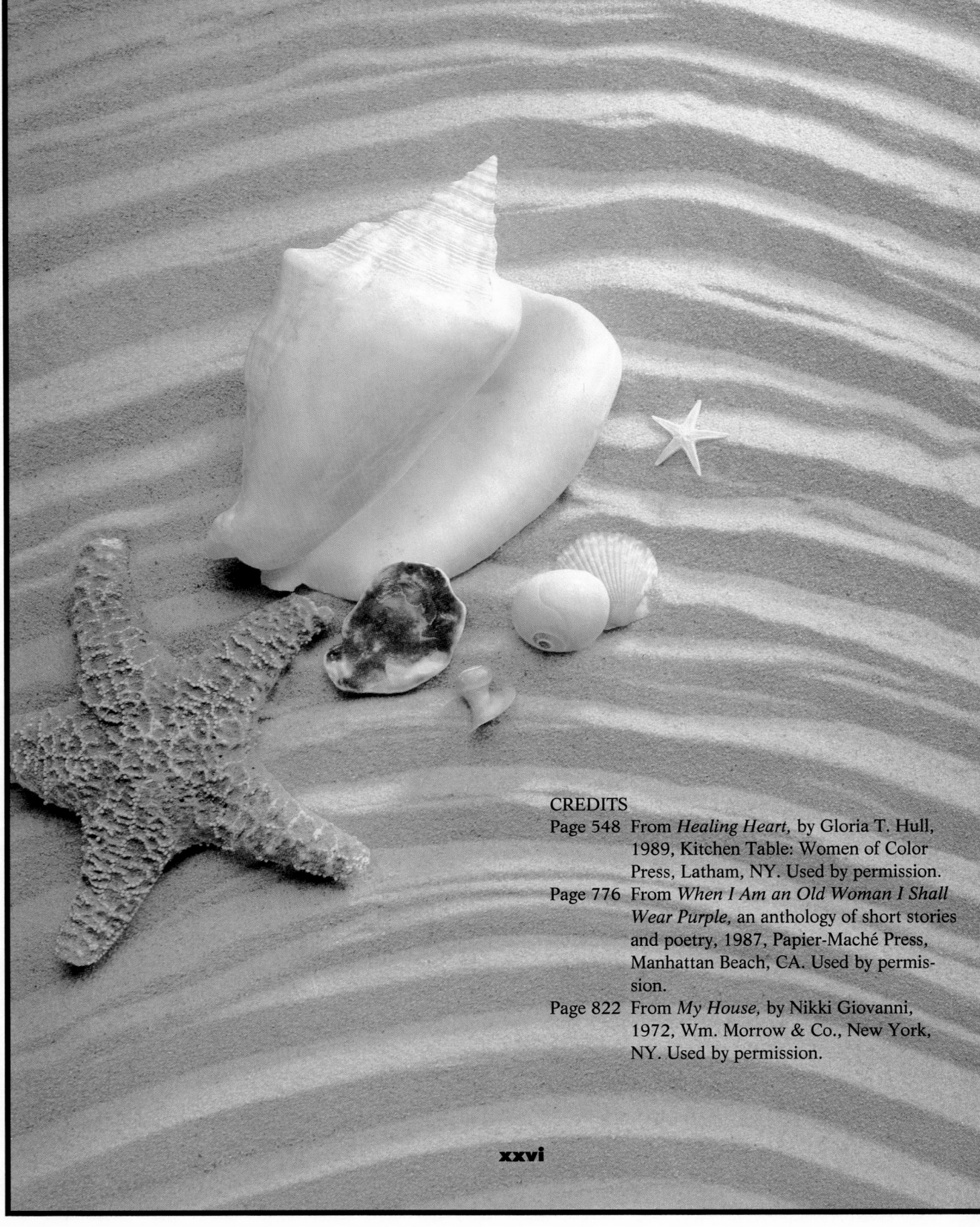

CREDITS

Page 548 From *Healing Heart,* by Gloria T. Hull, 1989, Kitchen Table: Women of Color Press, Latham, NY. Used by permission.

Page 776 From *When I Am an Old Woman I Shall Wear Purple,* an anthology of short stories and poetry, 1987, Papier-Maché Press, Manhattan Beach, CA. Used by permission.

Page 822 From *My House,* by Nikki Giovanni, 1972, Wm. Morrow & Co., New York, NY. Used by permission.

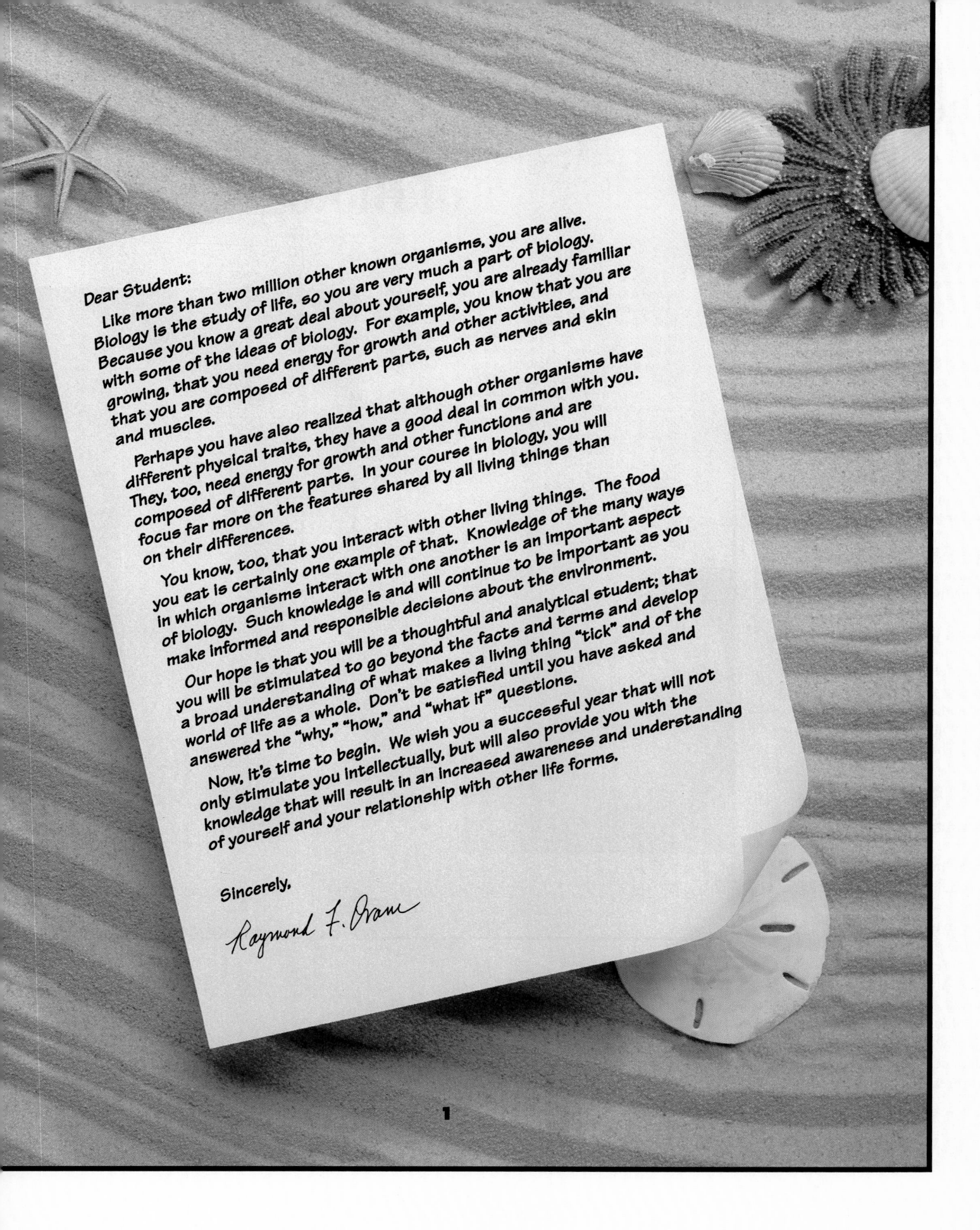

Dear Student:

Like more than two million other known organisms, you are alive. Biology is the study of life, so you are very much a part of biology. Because you know a great deal about yourself, you are already familiar with some of the ideas of biology. For example, you know that you are growing, that you need energy for growth and other activities, and that you are composed of different parts, such as nerves and skin and muscles.

Perhaps you have also realized that although other organisms have different physical traits, they have a good deal in common with you. They, too, need energy for growth and other functions and are composed of different parts. In your course in biology, you will focus far more on the features shared by all living things than on their differences.

You know, too, that you interact with other living things. The food you eat is certainly one example of that. Knowledge of the many ways in which organisms interact with one another is and will continue to be important as you make informed and responsible decisions about the environment. Such knowledge is and will continue to be important as you make informed and responsible decisions about the environment.

Our hope is that you will be a thoughtful and analytical student; that you will be stimulated to go beyond the facts and terms and develop a broad understanding of what makes a living thing "tick" and of the world of life as a whole. Don't be satisfied until you have asked and answered the "why," "how," and "what if" questions.

Now, it's time to begin. We wish you a successful year that will not only stimulate you intellectually, but will also provide you with the knowledge that will result in an increased awareness and understanding of yourself and your relationship with other life forms.

Sincerely,

Raymond F. Oram

1

The Nature of Biology

Unit Overview

This introductory unit consists of only two chapters, which are designed to stimulate student interest both in biology and in the way science attempts to answer questions and solve problems concerning the world of life. Interest is generated and curiosity immediately sparked in Chapter 1 as students examine a contemporary ecological dilemma and the difficulties in solving the many problems associated with it. In Chapter 2, students become active participants as they explore the methods of science.

Theme Development

The themes that students will encounter throughout the course are introduced in this unit. As they learn about the problems caused by the invasion of North America by zebra mussels in Chapter 1, they are exposed to the themes of energy, systems and interactions, patterns of change, evolution, and unity within diversity. They also begin to get a feel for methods of inquiry, a theme more fully developed in Chapter 2.

Advance Planning

Chapter 1
- Prepare bromthymol blue solution and order live mussels and *Elodea* for the Investigation.
- Order live mussels, snails, and carmine powder for the Minilabs.
- Order preserved mussels or clams for the Alternate Lab.

Chapter 2
- Order *Elodea* for the Investigation.
- Order owl pellets for Minilab 1.
- Order slides of the letter *e* and colored threads for the Alternate Lab.

The Nature of Biology

Optical telescopes like this one "see" images from space by collecting light energy and focusing it onto sensors. Unlike the facets of an insect's eye, the mirrors of some optical telescopes can be moved as Earth moves. This enables optical telescopes to have a much wider field of view.

Insects with compound eyes, such as this dragonfly, see individual pictures through many facets. Each of the dragonfly's 28 000 facets perceives a slightly different picture than any other, but when merged, the pictures give the insect a much larger field of view. Compound eyes are just one type of vision found in insects.

2

If you could look through a dragonfly's eyes, what would you see? Dragonflies, like many insects, have compound eyes made of many facets. Light rays from a small area fall on a single facet and are concentrated on light-sensitive cells below. Information from each facet is collected and interpreted as a mosaic of the insect's field of view.

In what ways do people collect information about their world? Scientists collect information about the planets and other objects in space with optical tele-scopes such as the Keck Telescope on Mauna Kea, Hawaii. The Keck Telescope has 36 hexagonal mirrors, each 1.8 meters wide, that reflect light energy from space. The light energy is focused onto sensors and collected. Gathering and interpreting information about the world around us is one important part of science inquiry. In this unit, you will learn how inquiry and other scientific methods help you explore the nature of biology.

aspects common to most scientific research. Through their participation in the Investigation, they come to understand the logic of and need for controlled experimentation. The chapter concludes with an examination of microscopes and their uses and a discussion of SI measurements.

Introducing the Unit

Using the Photos

Just as a powerful telescope can provide data about distant stars or planets, an insect's eye receives visual information about its immediate environment. Telescopes are human-engineered devices that function similarly to a biological "invention"—the eye. Gathering information about the physical world is a necessity for organisms and a hallmark of scientific inquiry. Instruments such as telescopes enable scientists to extend the range of their senses as they attempt to learn more about the physical world.

Previewing the Chapters

Unit 1 provides students with an exciting glimpse of modern biology as a dynamic science, how that science is done, and how the knowledge gained is applied.

Chapter 1 centers around a study of very real and immediate problems that have resulted from an invasion of North American waters by European zebra mussels. The chapter weaves together the consequences of the invasion and the biology of zebra mussels, and, in so doing, introduces students to basic ideas of biology. Students explore the importance of interactions among organisms in communities and the relationship between organisms and their physical surroundings. They learn of the universal need for energy and, in a special feature, the major ways in which energy is used by organisms. In another feature, they are briefly introduced to the concept of biological evolution and how evolution explains both the diversity of life on Earth and the unity that exists within that diversity.

In Chapter 2, students find that science is a process—a way of learning. They are introduced to a discussion of how scientists do their work—not by *the scientific method,* but rather the *methods* of science. Students come to see that there is no single formula for learning about the world in which we live, but they also come to realize that there are several

ORGANIZER
C H A P T E R 1

SECTION	OBJECTIVES	TEXT LABS/FEATURES
1.1 Rowdy Newcomers in the Great Lakes (2 days)	**Relate** various characteristics of zebra mussels to the problems they cause. **Characterize** living things based on four broad life functions.	**Characterizing Life:** What distinguishes living things? p. 8 **Minilab 1:** How do a snail and mussel compare? p. 11
1.2 Community Misfits (2 days)	**Discuss** how energy is made available to all members of a community. **Distinguish** between producers and consumers and between photosynthesis and cellular respiration. **Relate** the zebra mussels' food and energy needs to the biological problems it causes.	**Minilab 2:** How do mussels get food? p. 16
1.3 Now That They're Here (2 days)	**Discuss** how organisms are influenced by nonliving factors of their environment. **Explain** how the process of evolution has resulted in a great diversity of life forms and why there is unity within the diversity. **Apply** knowledge of the biology of zebra mussels to possible methods of controlling them.	**Unity Within Diversity:** Alike but Different, p. 20 **Investigation:** Mussels and Their Environment, p. 22 **Thinking Lab:** How do physical factors affect zebra mussels? p. 24
BIOLOGY, TECHNOLOGY, AND SOCIETY		**Biotechnology:** Watching the Brain at Work, p. 26 **Career Connection:** Radiology technician, p. 26 **Issues:** Rare Animals as Pets, p. 27

LAB MATERIALS

INVESTIGATION	MINILAB	ALTERNATE LAB
page 22 bromthymol blue solution distilled water dropper bottle *Elodea* stems mussels paper, white straw test tubes test-tube holder	**page 11** aquarium binocular microscope culture dish glass slide mussels snails watch glass **page 16** beaker carmine powder mussels toothpicks	**page 14** dissecting trays preserved specimens of freshwater mussels or clams probe scalpel

TEACHER CLASSROOM RESOURCES	OTHER RESOURCES
Study Guide, p. 1 ***PLL:** *Life: Common Characteristics,* p. 1 **Exploring Environmental Issues:** *Water, Water Everywhere,* p. 1	***STVS:** *Lizard Invasion,* Ecology (Disc 6, Side 1) **Color Transparency 27:** *Mollusk Body Systems*
Study Guide, pp. 2-3 **Concept Mapping,** p. 1 ***PLL:** *Life in a Square Meter Community,* p. 3 ****ILS:** *Biological Communities,* p. 1	
Study Guide, pp. 4-6 **Critical Thinking/Problem Solving:** *Controlling Zebra Mussel Populations,* p. 1	***STVS:** *Hydrilla Killer,* Ecology (Disc 6, Side 1)
Assessment Materials **Chapter Assessment,** pp. 1-4 **Performance Assessment in Biology,** p. 2 **Alternate Assessment in the Science Classroom** **Computer Test Bank**	**Spanish Resources** **Cooperative Learning Resource Guide** **Videodisc Correlations** (to Optical Data's and Videodiscovery's videodiscs)

* Probing Levels of Life
** Investigating Living Systems

* Science Technology Videodisc Series

Key to Teaching Strategies

The following designations will help you decide which activities in the teacher margin are appropriate for your students.

L1 Level 1 activities should be within the ability range of all students.

L2 Level 2 activities should be within the ability range of the average to above-average student.

L3 Level 3 activities are designed for the ability range of above-average students.

LEP LEP activities are appropriate for Limited English Proficiency students.

COOP LEARN Cooperative Learning activities are designed for small group work.

ADDITIONAL RESOURCES

Infinite Voyage *Life in the Balance*
From mass extinctions in the past to rain forest destruction today, this video details some of the effects of humans on the biosphere and suggests ways for humans to interact more equitably.

Audiovisual
Coping with Change, video, Films for the Humanities and Sciences.
Energy, video, Benchmark Films, Inc.

Software
Diversity of Life, J and S, Apple.

BIOLOGY—THE SCIENCE OF LIFE

Chapter Overview

Students jump right into the study of biology as they examine the complex and contemporary ecological problems resulting from the invasion of North American waters by zebra mussels. As they examine the story, students relate the mussels' characteristics to the problems they are causing. They also become familiar with the features common to all organisms and come to understand that a knowledge of biology is important in helping to solve the problems caused by the mussels.

Continuing with the zebra mussel story, students next explore basic concepts of community life and begin to appreciate the idea that organisms interact and are interdependent. They come to see the importance of food as an energy source and learn that energy is needed for all biological work. A study of the flow of energy and materials through a community reinforces their understanding of the interaction among organisms and develops the idea that energy, unlike materials, cannot be recycled.

Students complete the chapter by examining the importance of physical factors of the environment, again relating that idea to the zebra mussel story. They then analyze possible solutions to the problems, and see that many approaches, both physical and biological, may be needed. They also learn how changes in the environment, both physical and biological, may lead to evolution, and that evolution explains both the diversity of life and the unity that exists within that diversity.

BIOLOGY—THE SCIENCE OF LIFE

A FISH TANK may be a small world but it is by no means a simple one. It teems with life and life's diversity. Start with the obvious—the fish. They're all swimming around in the same water, but do you see any two that are exactly alike? How many are the same size, the same color, or have identical tails and fins? Those filmy green plants you see floating near the top of fish tanks are alive too. And what's going on under the rocks at the bottom? There may be life there too, unseen, but just as much a part of the scene as the fish and plants. How much attention do these living things seem to pay to one another? It may seem as if they pay no attention to their fellow occupants, but don't be fooled. Each one does matter to the others.

There would be no mistaking the little snail in the photo for a fish. It may live in a fish tank, but it doesn't look or behave anything like a fish. Who says life has to be all the same anyway? Did you ever think about what might happen if no one had any other forms of life to relate to? Would we even be here? In the exciting journey you are about to undertake, you will find that living things do indeed differ in many ways. That much you can tell just by looking around you. But, living things also are alike in some very fundamental ways that may not be readily apparent. Add to that an understanding of the interdependence that they share and you have the basis for deep appreciation for the science of living things—biology.

4

KEY TERMS

adaptation	decomposer	homeostasis
biology	development	organism
cellular respiration	energy	organization
chlorophyll	evolution	photosynthesis
community	food chain	producer
consumer	growth	reproduction

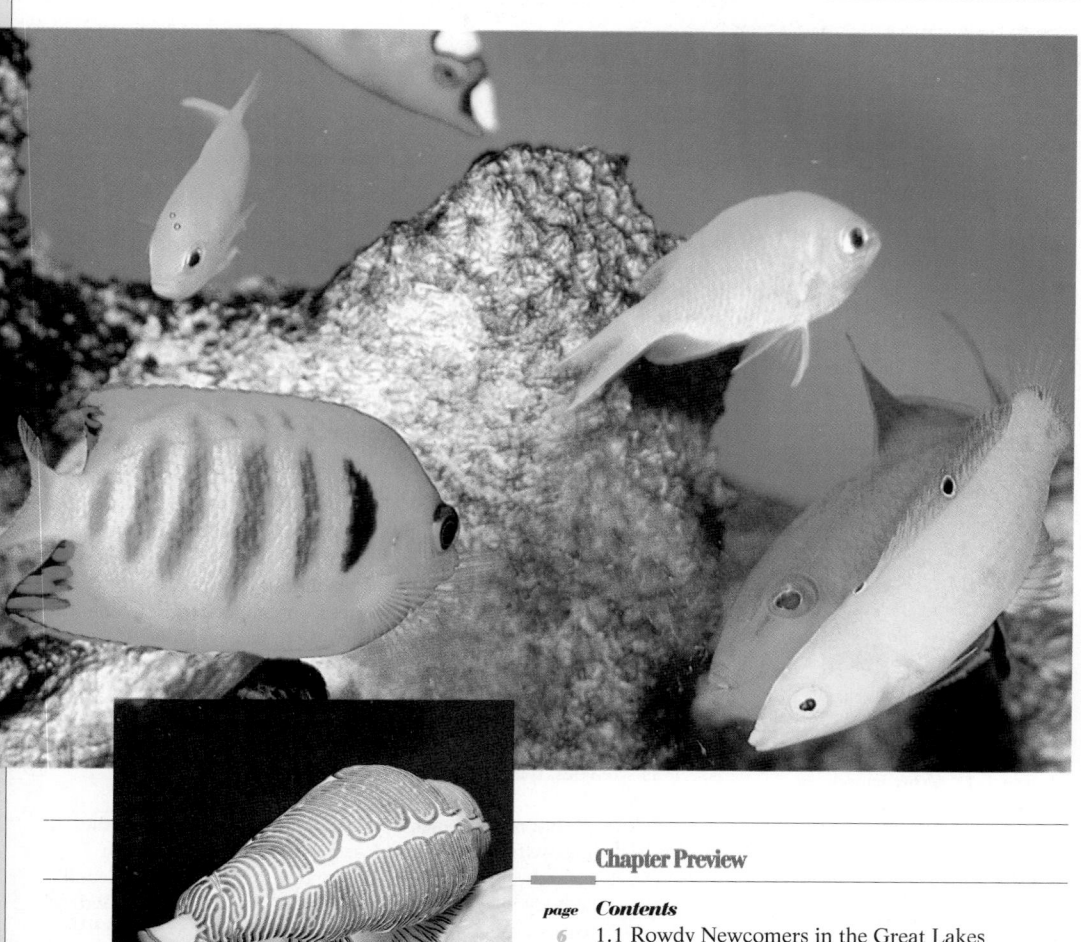

The fish, the snail, and the plants in a fish tank depend on one another—for food, oxygen, protection, support. Can you think how? Now imagine yourself sitting under the green boughs of a tall tree. The tree gives you shade on a hot, sunny day. Now, what might you be doing to return that favor?

Chapter Preview

Introducing the Chapter

A discussion of the aquarium photo on pages 4 and 5 can lead, in a general way, to most of the themes and concepts introduced in this chapter. Begin by having students identify the different kinds of organisms in the aquarium. Push them to name unseen organisms, too. As they name organisms, make lists on the board, each list representing a different kingdom. Make the point, at the end, that the world of life is diverse. Now, ask students to suggest ways that the organisms, despite the differences in their physical appearances, are similar. Lead them by suggesting they think about the functions the organisms carry out. Such a discussion can make clear the idea that there is unity within diversity.

Theme Development

As they study Chapter 1, students will be introduced to important themes that will be emphasized throughout the entire course: evolution, energy, patterns of change, systems and interactions, unity within diversity, and the nature of scientific inquiry. Make certain that you identify each theme and inform students that they will continue to study examples of each as they proceed with their study of biology.

Tying to Previous Knowledge

Ideas introduced in this chapter can be related to students' previous knowledge in many ways. Students are probably familiar with other contemporary ecological issues, and you may wish to have them identify some current problems such as ozone depletion, destruction of tropical rain forests, or oil spills at sea. Each issue has an impact on communities of organisms and affects interactions among them. Relate other concepts by asking basic questions related to students' lives. Why must you eat? Why do you have to breathe? How do you depend on plants? What's so important about bacteria?

ASSESSMENT PLANNER

Choose assessment strategies from the following pages to evaluate the progress of your students.

Prepare

Key Concepts

Students learn the characteristics common to all organisms and discover some of the problems that can result when an organism is introduced into a new area.

Key Terms

reproduction, growth, development, homeostasis, organization, biology, organism

Materials

- Gather mussels, snails, glass slides, watch glasses, and culture dishes for Minilab 1.
- Gather prepared slides of embryological development in a bivalve, sea urchin, frog, and cat for the Microscope Activity.

1 Focus

Objectives

The objectives are listed on the student page. Remind students to preview these objectives as a guide to this numbered section.

Using an Analogy

Ask students to think of examples illustrating how "too much" of something that is ordinarily benign or beneficial can become a problem. Humans need to grow, but cancer is a condition of too much growth. Automobiles are very useful, but too many can result in traffic tie-ups. Burning fuels for heat and energy is necessary, but too much combustion causes air pollution. Point out that the environment is healthiest when the living and nonliving things in it are in balance. When the balance is disrupted, problems occur. **LEP**

Objectives

Relate various characteristics of zebra mussels to the problems they cause.

Characterize living things based on four broad life functions.

1.1 Rowdy Newcomers in the Great Lakes

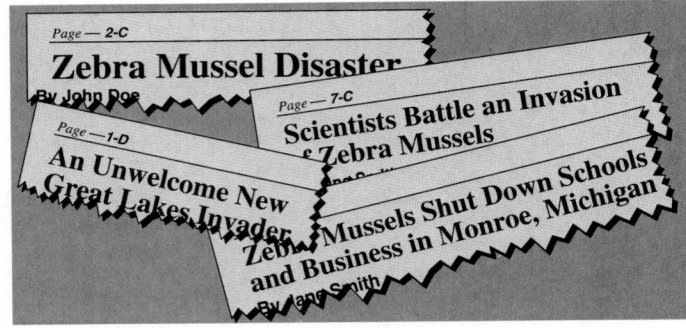

Troublemakers often make headlines. The zebra mussel crowd, which arrived in the Great Lakes in the mid-1980s, falls into the troublemaking category. It has been grabbing national headlines ever since.

Considering the zebra mussel's bad press, you might expect to confront some monstrous demon if you came face to face with one. If you live along the shore of Lake Erie or one of the other Great Lakes, you may actually have done just that. You can easily hold one of the little creatures in the palm of your hand. Even a full-grown and hefty one is petite enough to nestle in the bowl of a soup spoon with room to spare. As far as size goes, the zebra mussel seems innocent enough, even insignificant.

How does a zebra mussel stack up when it comes to looks? On the outside, which consists of a cream-colored shell striped with brown lines—much as a zebra is striped in black and white—it looks not at all unpleasant. The body inside the shell is headless, armless, legless, and boneless. It's hairless too—unless you think that tuft of 200 or so little threads sticking out near its foot looks something like hair. Yes, it has a blob of a foot—just one—but no toes. Put this way, the picture may not sound very flattering, at least to a human being. But among other zebra mussels, it's just the usual shape and order of existence.

Figure 1-1 Zebra mussels get their name from the alternating bands of brown and cream that color their shells. These small mollusks are spreading rapidly throughout freshwater lakes and streams in the United States, where they are causing a multitude of problems.

Enter and Multiply

It's that part about "other zebra mussels" that stirs up trouble. There are so *many* of them! There may have been only a few when they first arrived, probably as stowaways. Zebra mussels have lived in the freshwater lakes and rivers of Europe for several centuries. But they are not native to the Americas. As far as anybody knows, a party or several parties of zebra mussels still in their infancy rode along in the freshwater ballasts of European cargo ships crossing the Atlantic Ocean. Ballast is water

PROGRAM RESOURCES

Teacher Classroom Resources

Study Guide, p. 1 **L1**
Probing Levels of Life, Lab 1, p. 1 **L2**
Exploring Environmental Issues, p. 1 **L3**
Color Transparency #27 **L1** **LEP**

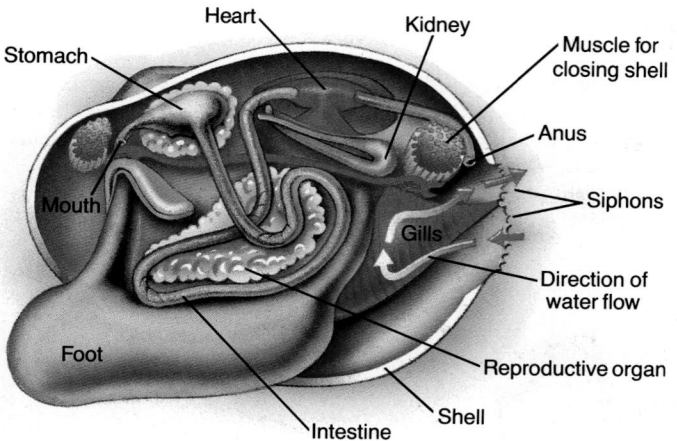

Figure 1-2 A zebra mussel has two shells for protection and a foot for burrowing into the mud or sand. Water containing food and oxygen is taken in by way of one siphon. Wastes are expelled by another siphon.

pumped into the hold of a ship to add weight and help steady the seagoing vessel. When the ships—probably in late 1985 or early 1986—emptied their holds into Lake St. Clair to take on fresh ballast, they spilled their young passengers into American waters. Nobody knew or noticed; the passengers would have been too small to attract attention even if anyone had been looking.

The transported youngsters grew up. By the time they were two years old, they were sexually mature. They became parents, grandparents, great grandparents, and so on. Keep in mind that we're talking big families here. Each female zebra mussel produces about 400 live young each year. And this is only a fraction of the eggs she produces. If all her eggs survived, she would produce an unimaginable 40 000 offspring each year. But 400 offspring a year is quite enough to swell the entire population of zebra mussels into a menace—a menace that has already spread into all the Great Lakes, most of New York's inland waterways, and the Mississippi, Ohio, and Illinois rivers.

A researcher digging for clams in Lake St. Clair was the first to identify the newcomers in 1988. By then, the first arrivals would have been full grown and recognizable. By the time another year went by, the zebra mussels were numerous enough to assume troublemaking status—in a number of ways and in a number of places.

Figure 1-3 Native to the Caspian Sea, zebra mussels are thought to have crossed the Atlantic Ocean in the ballast of cargo ships. They probably first entered the Great Lakes system from Lake St. Clair.

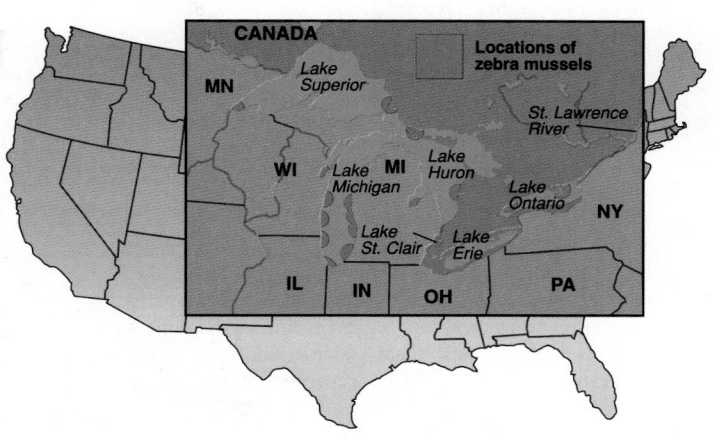

2 Teach

GEOGRAPHY CONNECTION

World Traveler: Zebra mussels are native to the Caspian Sea. On a world map, show students how zebra mussel larvae could have spread from one European port to another via interconnecting rivers and lakes. Remind students that the mussel invaded the waterways of Europe long ago, but didn't make its way across the Atlantic until the 1980s.

Using the Illustration

You may wish to point out that zebra mussels are bivalves, mollusks having two, hinged shells. The illustration shows the anatomy of a typical bivalve mollusk. Other bivalves include clams, scallops, and oysters.

STUDENT JOURNAL

Have students select a plant or animal that lives near home or school. Ask them to write an article that describes the organism's appearance and proves it is a form of life. Challenge students to explain at least one way the organism maintains homeostasis and to give at least four examples of structural or operational organization. For example, a dandelion can maintain homeostasis by maturing quickly and producing seeds that withstand drought and freezing. The plant is made up of cells, which are in turn organized into stems, leaves, roots, and flowers. The plant provides shelter or food for other organisms in the community. L1

CHARACTERIZING LIFE

Traits of Living Things:
Teaching strategies on pages 8 and 9 relate to the material under Characterizing Life. This material represents core concepts that form the basis for understanding the story of the zebra mussel. Use the teaching strategies on these two pages to teach students about the characteristics of living things.

Microscope Activity

Have students examine prepared slides of fertilization and development in several different organisms, such as a bivalve, sea urchin, frog, and cat. Point out that all organisms begin life as a fertilized egg, also called a zygote. During development, cells grow and differentiate based on instructions in the master code contained in the sperm and egg. **L1**

Demonstration

Demonstrate the organization of living organisms by showing students models or illustrations of the cell and its components, an organ system such as the human digestive system, and a community such as a pond or forest. Point out that the division of labor in beehives is one level of organization. The fact that bees pollinate flowers, which develop into fruit that feeds birds and other animals, is another level of organization. **LEP**

Attack

In a lake or river untouched by human settlement, nearly grown zebra mussels usually head for rocks either lying at the bottom of the water or wedged into shorelines under the surface of the water. There, those hairy little threads, which in reality are more like tiny strands of tape with incredible sticking power, grab hold on a rock. Thus attached, each young zebra mussel becomes anchored to the spot where it will spend the rest of its life.

CHARACTERIZING LIFE

What distinguishes living things?

If you expect to get a good grade in biology this year, you know you will have to perform certain actions—like studying for tests and paying

attention in class. Such functions help characterize good students in any subject. Biologists, too, refer to certain functions when they describe and define life. Broadly speaking, all organisms carry out four functions that distinguish them as living creatures.

Reproduction The production of offspring is **reproduction,** probably the most obvious of all the characteristics of life. Living things reproduce. Nonliving things do not.

Among many kinds of organisms, including the zebra mussel, each new life begins with a fertilized egg. At appropriate times, male zebra mussels release sperm into their watery environment. Shortly thereafter, female zebra mussels expel eggs into the same waters. When a sperm and egg connect, fertilization is accomplished.

A fertilized egg contains the raw materials for life and certain chemicals. One of those chemicals holds a master code, which determines how the raw materials within the egg combine. Following the instructions of the master code, the egg will eventually turn into a new organism that will take the form of a zebra mussel—or a giraffe, whale, horse, or whatever kind of organism the parents are. Each time reproduction occurs among parents in a particular group of organisms, the same set of coded instructions is passed on from one generation to the next.

Growth and Development Young organisms get bigger. As they do, they take on the special traits that identify them as members of a particular group of organisms. Such are the processes of growth and development. **Growth** is an increase in the amount of living material in an organism. **Development** is the series of changes an organism undergoes in reaching its final, adult form.

Fertilized eggs of the zebra mussel begin to grow at once. During their early stages of growth, the young zebra mussels, called larvae, float around freely in surface waters and currents. The zebra mussel larvae do not yet resemble adult zebra mussels. That comes later.

After about three weeks, the young zebra mussels attach to a surface. At this point, their bodies begin to develop into new, adult forms. They develop gills for obtaining oxygen, siphons for taking in food, and body parts necessary for reproduction. Two shells, hinged together so that they can open to draw in water or snap shut to protect the soft, defenseless body, also develop. At the same time, the zebra mussels continue to

MEETING INDIVIDUAL NEEDS

Help students with limited English proficiency (LEP) develop vocabulary and oral skills by teaming them up with native English speakers. Have the students work together to learn the definitions of the terms introduced in this section and study the events that have resulted from the introduction of zebra mussels into the Great Lakes. Have LEP students practice oral skills by explaining to their partners the meaning of each term studied and describing how zebra mussels have affected the Great Lakes. **LEP**

COOP LEARN

Zebra mussels aren't fussy about having "all-natural" addresses. Any solid surface will do. Human-produced junk or debris that people have tossed into the water suits them just fine. So do the hard surfaces of submerged pipes and channels that humans have built for taking in or discharging water. And in the Great Lakes region, people have built many such structures along the shores. They use them to get water for drinking, running air conditioners, cooling the machinery that operates factories and electric power plants, or doing any other work that requires large quantities of water.

increase in size. The largest get to be about 4 centimeters across before they stop growing.

Homeostasis   Outward growth and development end when an organism reaches adulthood, but other life functions continue. One of them is concerned with maintaining proper conditions for the internal workings of the organism regardless of what happens in the external environment. If a zebra mussel's body is to carry on life processes, it needs to be surrounded by water. What happens if the organism is removed from its watery environment? It will conserve moisture by closing its shells. Thus encased, a zebra mussel can continue to carry on normal life processes in dry surroundings for several days. It survives because it has managed to maintain **homeostasis,** the steady state of the internal operation of an organism regardless of external changes.

Your own body offers more familiar examples of homeostasis. The temperature at which your body works with maximum efficiency is 37°C. What happens when hot weather or some other source of heat raises your body temperature?

The free-floating larval stage of a zebra mussel bears little resemblance to the adult.

Your body gets rid of excess heat by perspiring. When you're outside in cold weather, your body temperature begins to fall. Your muscles may start to contract rapidly and you begin to shiver. The internal muscle action generates heat and raises your body temperature to the proper level.

Organisms face constant changes in their environments. If they are to survive these changes, their bodies must be able to respond in ways that maintain homeostasis.

Organization   Each function or life process that an organism performs is vital to its existence. But none is isolated from the others. All come together and interact with

one another to create a single, orderly living system. Such precise **organization** is characteristic of all life forms. When a zebra mussel opens its shells, for example, it is coordinating its activities with its feeding needs. When it closes its shells, the organism can no longer take in food but it will have protection from danger, a more immediate need than food intake in given circumstances.

Organization shows itself in the way an organism is put together as well as in the ways the organism operates. For every body function, there is a body part—a basic body structure—to perform it. Those body structures take different forms, but they, too, are linked together in the single living system. The zebra mussel has a structure called a siphon for taking food into its body. From the siphon, the food passes to other body structures.

Cells–the basic unit of life–are also organized. Different kinds of cells grouped together make up complex structures. Altogether, these structures are organized into an even more complex system of interacting structures and functions involved in the business of life.

Misconception

Students may be under the impression that insects are the only animals that undergo metamorphosis (a distinct change in form during development) as they grow and develop. Metamorphosis is also characteristic of the growth and development of mollusks (including zebra mussels, clams, snails), crustaceans (crabs, shrimp), echinoderms (sea urchins, sea stars), and other animals.

Brainstorming

Have students select a few familiar organisms (such as apple trees, frogs, birds, humans) and discuss ways in which each one maintains homeostasis. Begin by asking students to identify environmental factors that change, such as temperature, light, water availability, and food supply. Then ask for ways each organism deals with these changes. *In cold temperatures, apple trees become dormant, losing leaves and storing sap in roots; birds fluff their feathers; humans shiver.* Ask students to identify some of the limits past which an organism cannot maintain homeostasis. *Fish out of water, plants without light.*   COOP LEARN

Using the Illustration

Other bivalves, such as the marine mussel, *Mytilus edulis,* also have sticky byssal threads with which they adhere to the substrate. This adaptation makes it possible for the organisms to remain attached, even with fast-moving water currents.

The Invasion Continues

Within the first year after their presence became known, zebra mussels colonized the water intake pipes of facilities all around Lake Erie on both the U.S. and Canadian sides. In the city of Monroe, Michigan, young zebra mussels about one centimeter across were attached to electric power plant intake surfaces in the summer of 1988. Only about 200 mussels clung to each square meter of surface area. A year later, an average of 700 000 clung to each square meter of surface. Zebra mussels attach to one another's shells as easily as to any other hard surface. So with this many mussels piled up on one another, the power plant's intake tubes and other surfaces were covered with a layer of zebra mussels some four centimeters thick. Water lines became clogged and flows were reduced. In some places, heated water from power-plant equipment killed and dislodged the animals, but their shells remained and accumulated. At the same time, the dead bodies emitted a foul odor.

Similar colonies built up in pipes of the drinking-water treatment facilities in Monroe. By December of that year, the pipes and other equipment were so clogged that city water intake was severely reduced. Schools and businesses had to close down for two days due to water shortages.

The zebra mussel has earned a bad name in other places, too. Swimmers and sunbathers walking along many beaches are now careful to wear sandals. They have to protect their bare feet from knicks and scrapes inflicted by sharp edges of the now-too-familiar striped shells that wash ashore. The putrid odor of decaying mussel bodies has ruined some beaches.

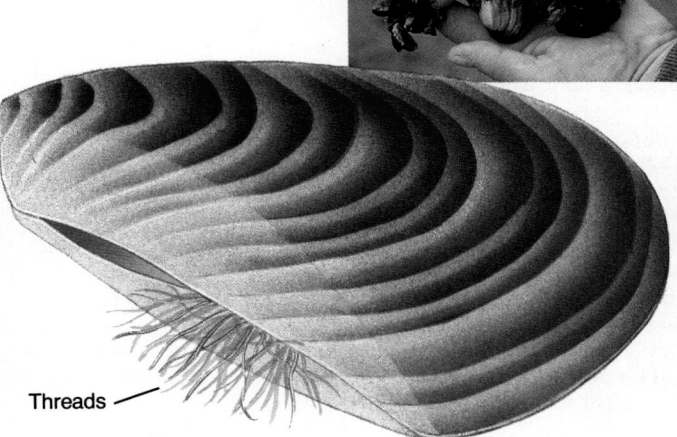

Figure 1-4 Zebra mussels attach to rocks or other surfaces by means of sticky threads. The mussels are capable of sticking to anything, including each other, and can quickly clog pipes and encrust any available surface.

Threads

Boaters find colonies growing on and weighing down hulls. Detached, dead animals wash into marine engines, where they damage parts and give off bad odors. Zebra mussel colonies stick to the underwater portions of floating channel markers placed in river or lake channels to guide boaters away from unseen dangers. The added weight of the mussel colonies sinks many channel markers and so deprives boaters of essential safeguards.

A Scientific Approach

What is to be done about the striped invaders in the Great Lakes? Probably, the first impulse is to scrape the zebra mussels away from their moorings. And that's exactly what has been done in many places under attack. In fact, scraping has been about the only workable method so far. But it's no firm solution to the problem. The zebra mussels are right back within a year. Workers who do the scraping often have to enter dangerous underwater passageways. The continual expense of scraping adds millions of dollars to the operating costs of power plants and water-treatment facilities.

Clearly, some heavy input of knowledge and investigation is needed if the zebra mussel problem is to be brought to a successful conclusion. In this case, such input can come from science. And since the zebra mussel is a living creature, that science will be biology. *Bios* is the Greek word for *life* or *way of life*. **Biology,** then, is the study of life. Its subjects are all the components of the biosphere, that thin envelope of space surrounding and projecting a short distance below Earth's surface in which all forms of life reside. The work of the biologist is to investigate and enlarge our understanding of the biosphere.

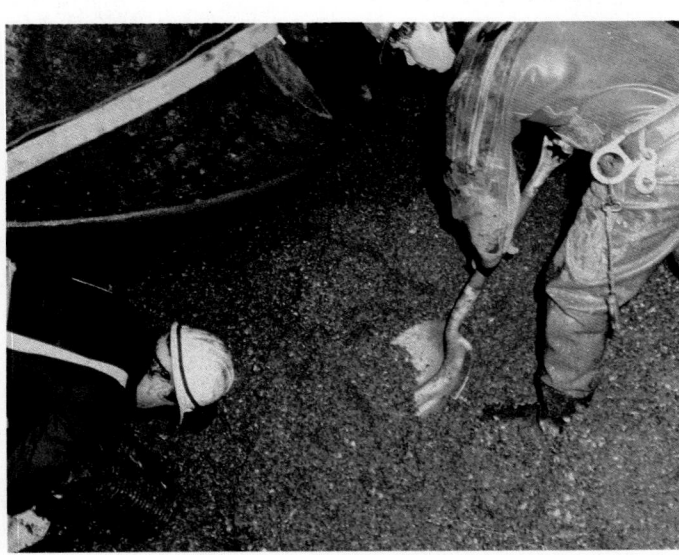

Figure 1-5 **Zebra mussels are removed by the truckload from some underground water pipelines. In many areas, daily removal is necessary just to keep pipelines clear.**

☰ Minilab 1

How do a snail and mussel compare?

Before removing them from the aquarium, observe the movements and locations of the mussels and snails in the aquarium. Remove a snail and place it on a glass slide until it becomes attached. **CAUTION:** *Use care when handling live animals.* Invert the slide over a watch glass, and observe with a binocular microscope the structure and functioning of the snail's foot. Remove a mussel from the aquarium and place it in a culture dish with aquarium water to cover the shells. Note what happened to the shells as you made the transfer. Note any changes after the mussel has been in the culture dish for 10 minutes. Make a chart of similarities and differences between the snail and the mussel.

Analysis   *What do the locations of the snail and the mussel in the aquarium tell you about where these animals might live in a lake? How do the snail and mussel move?*

PORTFOLIO

Invite students to make drawings of their observations of the snail and the mussel during the Minilab. Have them label important structures—such as the foot, shell, and mantle—of each organism, and use arrows or sequential diagrams to indicate motion, where applicable. Ask students to write a brief paragraph comparing the similarities and differences of these two mollusks. **L1**

SECTION 1.1

Minilab 1

Purpose
Students will compare and contrast a freshwater snail and a freshwater mussel.

Skills
compare and contrast, make and use tables, observe and infer

Teaching Strategies
- **Safety Precautions:** Caution students to handle live animals with care.
- Live freshwater mussels and snails may be purchased from biological supply houses. Set them up in a large aquarium with a deep layer of gravel into which the mussels can burrow. Make sure students use dechlorinated water or water from the aquarium.

Expected Results
Similarities: both covered with shells, move very slowly, and live in the water. Differences: snails have a single shell and glide on a muscular foot; mussels use their foot to burrow; snails have a head with a pair of tentacles, while mussels do not; mussels can open and close their shells.

Answers
1. The snail will most likely be attached to the side of the aquarium, on vegetation, or on the filter apparatus, while the mussel will be partly buried in the gravel, indicating that the mussel lives on the bottom while the snail lives on surfaces of rocks or vegetation.
2. The snail puts down a slime trail and glides along on its foot. The mussel uses its foot to burrow.

✔ Assessment
Performance: Examine a live land snail and explain how it is similar to and how it is different from the pond snail. The land snail moves faster than the pond snail and has similar features: head with tentacles, muscular foot that produces a slime trail, and a single shell. It lives exclusively on land in damp places.

Figure Caption Question

How do these organisms differ? How are they alike? Both are flowering plants and show the characteristics of living things. Bird of paradise plants undergo photosynthesis. Pitcher plants also are consumers, digesting insects trapped inside the pitcher.

3 Assess

Check for Understanding

List the terms introduced in this section on one side of a work sheet. List their definitions on the other side in a different order. Have students match terms with definitions. **L1**

Reteach

Have pairs of students explain to each other how the mussels reproduce, grow, and maintain homeostasis.

Extension

Have students list all the levels of organization they can think of that are associated with an ant. The interiors of its cells are organized; it has systems for digestion, reproduction, and locomotion; individuals are organized into colonies; colonies build nests in the soil and depend on their surroundings for food, water, and air. **L2**

✔ Assessment

Knowledge: Have students list, define, and give examples of the four characteristics that distinguish living organisms from nonliving things. **L1**

4 Close

Activity

Have students play a game in which one team names a common or familiar organism and one of the four characteristics of life. The other team must explain how the organism meets the criterion for that characteristic. For example, the answer to "birds and organization" could be "they build nests" or "they have digestive systems." **L1** **COOP LEARN**

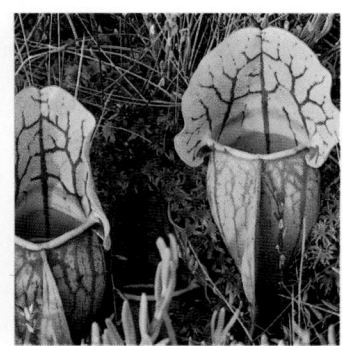

Diversity

Figure 1-6 Enormous diversity exists among the two million types of living things that inhabit Earth. Shown here are a bird of paradise flower and a pitcher plant. How do these organisms differ? How are they alike?

A biologist could give us some basic information about the zebra mussel without ever seeing one. First of all, the zebra mussel carries on life processes. One of these processes is reproduction. Given their growing numbers in the Great Lakes, who could doubt the zebra mussels' capacity to reproduce? In addition to reproducing, each zebra mussel will also grow and develop. Finally, a zebra mussel must maintain the internal processes that go on in its body, and be able to keep the different parts of its body working together as a unit. How can a biologist be sure of these things? He or she knows them because the core of scientific knowledge already amassed shows that these four functions are common to all organisms. *(See Characterizing Life, page 8.)* An **organism** is anything capable of carrying on life processes.

Nobody knows exactly how many different kinds of organisms inhabit our planet. So far, scientists have identified more than 2 million. How many of them can you list if you take a minute to think about it? Don't forget human beings, like yourself. Remember, too, things like oak trees and rosebushes as well as dogs, cats, and zebra mussels. How would you describe and compare the differences among the various organisms on your list? Just thinking about that question gets a little overwhelming. For now, leave the answers up to more experienced biologists. It is enough for you to remember that all organisms are alike in that they share similar life processes and requirements for life. Biologists, too, keep this in mind as they search for ways people can deal with the recently arrived organisms now troubling American waterways.

Section Review

Understanding Concepts

1. Explain why zebra mussel populations in North America exploded so quickly.
2. How is the lifestyle of adult zebra mussels related to the problems they cause in water intake pipes?
3. In what ways are you like a zebra mussel?

4. **Skill Review—Observing and Inferring:** You collect organisms from a nearby pond and transfer them to an aquarium. Among the organisms is an animal that you think is a fish. Over time, though, the animal begins to form legs, and its tail seems to be disappearing. What life function(s) are you observing? For more help, see Thinking Critically in the **Skill Handbook**.
5. **Thinking Critically:** Explain the following statement about organisms: Like produces like.

Answers to Section Review

1. Adult female zebra mussels produce 400 surviving young each year.
2. The intake pipes provide suitable points of attachment and zebra mussels may settle upon other zebra mussels, thus clogging the pipes.
3. Humans, zebra mussels, and all other organisms carry out similar life functions and have similar requirements for life.

4. **Skill Review—Observing and Inferring:** Growth and development are being observed.
5. **Thinking Critically:** When organisms reproduce, they produce offspring of the same kind.

1.2 Community Misfits

"Their presence could be catastrophic." That is how one Canadian scientist summed up his view of zebra mussels in the Great Lakes. His concern rests on the biological knowledge that, like any other organism, zebra mussels don't live alone.

Life and the Community

Each time zebra mussels settle down in a new American lake or river, they join a community of many other kinds of organisms. A **community** is an assortment of life forms within a given place where all the organisms interact and depend upon one another in various ways. You observe organisms interacting in a community when you see robins unearthing worms, squirrels using trees as nesting sites, or bees tracking pollen from one flower to another. Animal parents caring for their young are also interacting within a community.

The aquatic communities that zebra mussels invade teem with bacteria—the simplest and tiniest forms of life. The bacteria either lodge in bottom mud or are suspended in the water. Floating above in the surface water are tiny algae and different kinds of microscopic animal life. Of course, there are also many larger and more obvious animals—fish, waterfowl, worms, frogs, and native mussels such as clams.

Right from the start, biologists have worried about the many ways in which zebra mussels could and probably have already begun to disrupt Great Lakes communities. For example, the shallow, rocky edges of shorelines are favored anchoring spots for zebra mussel colonies. Some fish, such as walleye and lake trout, reproduce only in these waters. Large zebra mussel colonies could interfere with the reproduction of these kinds of fish and so reduce their numbers. Walleye and trout are important to Great Lakes fishing industries. Reduction in their numbers would hurt both fishers and people who like to eat the fishers' catches.

Objectives

Discuss how energy is made available to all members of a community.

Distinguish between producers and consumers and between photosynthesis and cellular respiration.

Relate the zebra mussel's food and energy needs to the biological problems it causes.

Figure 1-7 Zebra mussel colonies are typically found along rocky shorelines of freshwater lakes, such as the Great Lakes. Other organisms that inhabit Great Lakes communities include the walleye. What other types of communities can you name?

1.2 COMMUNITY MISFITS 🐟 **13**

Key Concepts
Students develop an understanding of how energy moves through living communities.

Key Terms
community, energy, producer, chlorophyll, photosynthesis, consumer, cellular respiration, food chain, decomposer

Materials
- Gather live mussels, beakers, dechlorinated water, carmine powder, and toothpicks for Minilab 2.
- Gather preserved mussels and dissection equipment for the Alternate Lab.

1 Focus

Objectives
The objectives are listed on the student page. Remind students to preview these objectives as a guide to this numbered section.

Using an Analogy
Compare zebra mussels "hitchhiking" across oceans in ship ballast with fruit flies or other insects "hitchhiking" across state or national borders in automobiles. Ask students if they have ever encountered an agricultural checkpoint when crossing a state line. Were they asked to give up plants or produce they had with them? Point out that these precautions help keep hitchhiking pests out of important agricultural areas.

Figure Caption Question
What other types of communities can you name? Freshwater pond or stream, meadow, city park and woodland are some examples.

2 Teach

Misconception

Students may not realize that many familiar plants are not native to North America, but were imported from other regions. Many have become successfully established here, sometimes at the expense of native plants. For example, oats and rye imported into California from Europe have taken over large areas of land once covered by native bunch grasses. Have students look up information on familiar plants and find out whether or not they are native to their area.

Microscope Activity

Have students examine wet mounts of *Elodea* leaves. Point out the green, chlorophyll-containing structures and tell them these are the sites of photosynthesis. You do not need to introduce the term *chloroplast* at this time.

Figure 1-8 Zebra mussels belong to a group of mollusks that have two shells. The shells offer protection and help maintain homeostasis.

Figure 1-9 During photosynthesis, carbon dioxide and water (raw materials) react to form sugars (end products) and oxygen (a by-product). Without the photosynthetic process, life on Earth would not exist.

Energy from sunlight

Chlorophyll in leaves

Carbon dioxide from air and water from soil⟶
Simple sugars and oxygen

CO_2

Water

14 BIOLOGY—THE SCIENCE OF LIFE

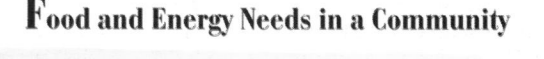

Food and Energy Needs in a Community

Zebra mussels also threaten clam populations, another valuable fishing resource. Clams, though larger than the new invaders, are also mussels. This means that they also have two shells hinged together. Zebra mussels attach to clam shells. The sheer weight of piled-on zebra mussels prevents clams from opening their shells, thus restricting their food intake.

Food as an Energy Source   The connection between food and life is obvious, as well as common to all life forms. Just what is it about food that makes it so important? In a word, the answer is energy.

Energy is the ability to do work. Work is anything that causes motion. When you read about the four common characteristics of life in the first section, you learned that all organisms carry on certain kinds of biological work—reproducing, growing, developing, and maintaining homeostasis. Organisms must have energy to keep this work going. Without energy, a zebra mussel could not expel eggs and sperm for reproduction, or close its shell to preserve moisture and maintain homeostasis. Nor could you perspire or shiver to maintain homeostasis in your own body. The zebra mussel, you, and every other organism gets energy for biological work from food. Energy fuels the work of life just as surely as gasoline fuels an automobile engine and keeps its parts functioning. Every organism uses the energy from some of the materials in food as fuel for the functions needed to keep it alive.

Producing Food   Maintaining an adequate food supply is critical in any community. Each community has an orderly system through which organisms obtain food from other organisms. Certain members of a community are food **producers.** That is, they make food. In some communities, plants—such as trees, grasses, and shrubs—and certain bacteria are the producers. In the communities invaded by zebra mussels, algae are the producers.

Among most producers, the ingredients in the food-making recipe are carbon dioxide and water. **Chlorophyll,** a green substance in the producers, traps light from the sun. Sunlight provides the energy for the work of combining carbon dioxide and water. Simple sugars are the finished product. Oxygen, given off while the manufacture is taking place, is the by-product. The whole process is called **photosynthesis.**

The light energy of the sun is converted during photosynthesis to chemical energy in the form of simple sugars. Thus, these sugars are good sources of energy and hence food for the producer itself. But producers do not use all the simple

---

ALTERNATE LAB: Mussel Anatomy

Purpose
Students examine the external morphology and internal anatomy of a freshwater mussel.

Materials
dissecting trays, scalpels, probes, preserved specimens of freshwater mussels or clams
Safety Precautions: Caution students to use great care with scalpels. Tell them never to cut toward the free hand. Also

caution students to use care with probes.

Procedure
Give the following directions to students.
1. Examine the outer shell of the mussel. Locate the hinge and the valves (the two halves of the shell).
2. Run a scalpel between the valves to sever the adductor muscles that hold them together. Pull away the upper valve.

3. Locate the mantle, which is the sheet of tissue lining the inner surface of the shell.
4. Pull away any mantle tissue covering the soft body parts of the mussel. Locate and identify as many internal parts as possible. *Students should be able to discern gills, a foot, byssal threads, flaplike palps, and perhaps the gonads and digestive gland.*

sugars they make for food. They convert some of the sugars into other, more complex substances that are rich in energy and can be stored for later use. The producer also uses some of the other complex substances to build new cells and body structures.

Consuming Food   Not only do producers make food for themselves, they also serve as food sources for other members of the community—those that are unable to produce their own. Organisms that cannot make their own food are **consumers.**

Some consumers, like leaf-grazing deer, feed directly on producers. When a consumer feeds on a producer, it converts some of the producer's complex substances into another sugar, known as glucose. Although glucose is not the *only* energy-rich food consumers use, it is the most important one. Producers and consumers convert the energy in glucose and other sugars to a usable form of energy through a process called **cellular respiration.** Energy converted during cellular respiration drives the biological work of life.

Zebra mussels are consumers that feed directly on producers—the microscopic algae in the water. As a zebra mussel draws water into its body, it filters algae out of the water through its siphon structures. Much of the algae is used as food as it passes through the digestive system of the zebra mussel. Some, however, is of no use to the zebra mussel and is expelled.

Small, shrimplike animals occupying surface waters also feed on algae. These small animals are food for small fish, which in turn are food for large fish—like walleye, trout, and bass. In this way, food is passed from producers through a series of consumers. Such a passage of food and the energy it contains is called a **food chain.** Different sets of organisms create different food chains. Each organism in the chain helps distribute energy that originates with the sun throughout the community.

One zebra mussel may not eat much, but thousands of zebra mussels together represent one hearty appetite. This many zebra mussels can eat a lot of algae. Thus, the feeding activities of zebra mussels could disrupt

Figure 1-10 **Producers convert light energy to chemical energy, which they may use or which may end up as an energy source for consumers (left). Two-shelled mollusks have two siphons, one for drawing in water, and one for expelling water (right). As water is drawn into the body, microscopic food particles contained in it are extracted by the gills and then passed along to the mouth. Using this siphoning action, zebra mussels are capable of filtering great volumes of water.**

1.2 COMMUNITY MISFITS **15**

Display

Have students work in groups to create bulletin board or poster displays that illustrate how energy moves from sunlight to producers and consumers. Assign a different community to each group. Possibilities include forest, grassland, lake, ocean, and freshwater stream. L1   LEP   COOP LEARN

MATH CONNECTION

Cleanup Crew: The zebra mussel has provided at least one benefit in some waters. Since each mussel can filter as much as a liter of water every day, these organisms are being used to clear up heavy growth of microscopic algae in some European lakes. Have students calculate how much water a clump of 200 mussels can filter in an hour, then calculate how much water a clump of 700 000 mussels can filter in an hour. $1 L/24 h = 0.04 L/h$; $0.04 L \times 200 = 8 L/h$; $0.04 L \times 700 000 = 28 000 L/h$ L1

Analysis
Have students draw the structures they observe and describe the function of each. The shell protects the mussel's body; the mantle secretes the shell; gills absorb oxygen and direct food toward the mouth; the foot is used for burrowing; byssal threads are used for attachment; labial palps form the entrance to the digestive system.

✔ Assessment
Skill: Have students compare the functions of the external and internal structures of the mussel with structures found in other organisms, including humans. For example, the shell is analogous to the bony skeleton of vertebrates. Gills correspond to lungs, the foot to limbs or muscles, and palps to the mouth. Reproductive and digestive structures are functionally similar to those of other organisms. L1

Minilab 2

Purpose
Students will observe the filtering action of mussels.

Skills
observe and infer, recognize cause and effect

Teaching Strategies
- **Safety Precautions:** Warn students that carmine powder is a dye that will stain clothes and skin. Caution students to handle mussels with care and return them to the aquarium when finished.
- Freshwater mussels may be purchased from biological supply houses.
- Introduce the activity by asking students how animals that have no ability to move get their food. Ask students to examine their mussel and think of other ways in which it is suited for its habitat.

Expected Results
The mussels will set up a water current, taking in the carmine powder within minutes. What this says about the mussel is that it does not discriminate as to what it takes into its body, so it could be easily poisoned if a chemical could be found that would kill only mussels and no other life forms.

Answers
1. Answers will vary. In general, the mussel will filter the carmine powder in minutes.
2. The filtering power of large numbers of mussels in a small space would be very great.

✔ Assessment
Skill: You are a scientist of the future who has been given the responsibility of designing a new mussel to breed with the existing problem mussels. Your new mussel will have characteristics that will benefit rather than harm the environment. In your journal, draw a diagram of your mussel of the future and explain how it benefits the environment.

Minilab 2

How do mussels get food?

Mussels take in water through one siphon, filter out food particles, and let the water out of another siphon. Place a mussel in a beaker of dechlorinated water. **CAUTION:** *Use care when handling live animals. Do not disturb it for 10 minutes. Carefully add an amount of carmine powder that will fit on the end of a flat toothpick. Draw a diagram of the path taken by the carmine powder through the water, into the mussel, and out of the mussel.*

Analysis *How long did it take for the carmine powder to enter the mussel? What does this tell you about the filtering power of mussels?*

Figure 1-11 **Even the simplest food chain includes producers, consumers, and decomposers. Note that decomposers act on the wastes of all organisms in the chain, not just the last consumer.**

entire food chains. With fewer algae to go around, there would be fewer small, shrimplike animals, fewer small fish, and finally fewer walleye and other larger fish. In addition, the food materials that zebra mussels do not use settle to the bottom. There they add to the food supply of bottom-dwelling animals. These bottom dwellers could thus become more numerous and further disrupt the community.

Consumers categorized as **decomposers** complete every food chain. Decomposers feed on the dead remains and waste products of living organisms. Mushrooms on a rotting log, for example, are decomposers. As with all decomposers, their feeding causes decay.

Flow of Food in a Community

Planet Earth holds only a given supply of water, carbon dioxide, and other materials that living things need to carry out life processes. Even so, life goes on. There are always enough of these materials for generation after generation of producers and consumers. How can that be? Why doesn't the supply run out? It's because the same materials are used over and over again. Materials used for making food flow in a continuous cycle through the food chains of communities.

Cycling Food Materials All the links in a food chain—producers, consumers, and decomposers—constantly undergo cellular respiration. They give off the waste products of cellular respiration—water and carbon dioxide—as they use the energy in sugars and other fuels. The water and carbon dioxide are released into the environment. Water and carbon dioxide, of course, are the substances needed for photosynthesis. The food chain's producers take in water and carbon dioxide from the environment and use it to carry on photosynthesis. In the process, they make sugars

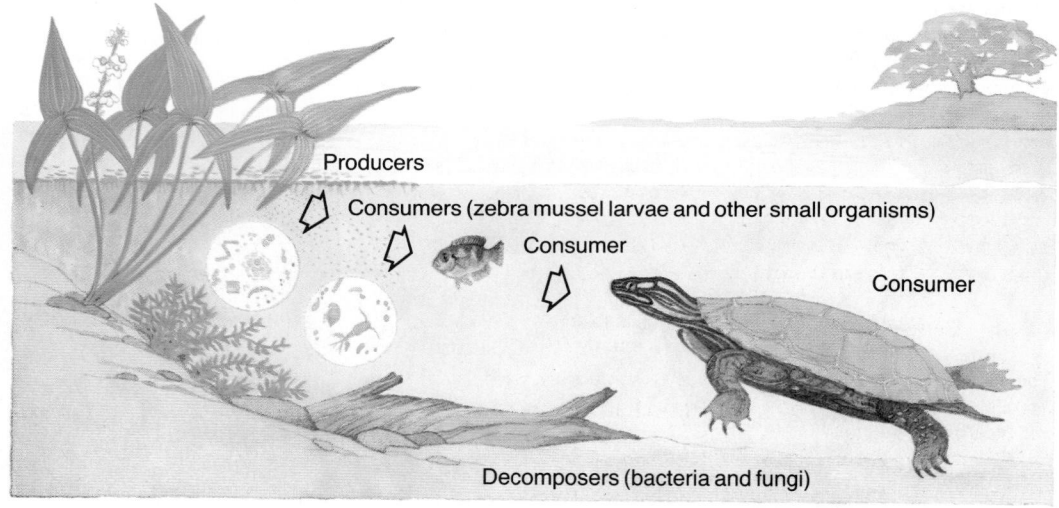

Producers
Consumers (zebra mussel larvae and other small organisms)
Consumer
Consumer
Decomposers (bacteria and fungi)

STUDENT JOURNAL

Have students choose an organism from the Great Lakes community and describe, from the perspective of that organism, the flow of energy through the community before and after the invasion of the zebra mussels. Possibilities include trout, bass, walleye, native clams, and small crustaceans such as *Daphnia*. From the trout's perspective, for example, energy comes from arthropod larvae that constitute the fish's primary food supply. Before zebra mussels arrive, there is plenty of food, and the fish use that energy to grow and reproduce. After zebra mussels arrive, their exploding population consumes so much microscopic algae that little energy is available to the arthropods, so even less energy reaches the trout. L1 and other energy fuels, and release oxygen into the environment. Oxygen, as you have read, is needed by most organisms, including producers, for cellular respiration. Thus, the processes of photosynthesis and cellular respiration constantly interact. Producers and consumers constantly exchange the materials needed for life processes.

Unlocking Resources in Wastes At the same time a food chain's organisms are obtaining food and using its energy for carrying on life processes, they are also producing wastes. Eventually, organisms die. Organisms' wastes and dead remains contain certain materials needed for carrying on life processes. If these materials were allowed to stay and accumulate in wastes and dead remains, there eventually would not be enough materials available to living organisms in a community. But decomposers, such as fungi and some kinds of bacteria, prevent this from happening.

Many decomposers are able to use the fuels still left in the wastes and remains of other organisms for cellular respiration. As with all organisms, the cellular respiration of decomposers releases carbon dioxide and water that can be cycled back to producers. But decomposers also carry on other processes. These processes break down and release nitrogen, sulfur, and phosphorus into the environment. All three of these substances are taken up by producers, which need them to make the more complex materials that also cycle through food chains.

In lake communities beset by zebra mussels, bacteria decompose wastes and dead organisms that settle to the bottom. If organisms deprived of food by zebra mussels begin to die in great numbers, the number of bacteria and volume of bottom decomposition will increase. That decomposition would consume great amounts of oxygen during the cellular respiration of the bacteria. Significant decreases in oxygen supplies could in turn lead to an even greater number of deaths in the community and higher volumes of decomposition on the bottom. The end result, biologists fear, would be that materials would not be cycled efficiently enough to sustain life in the community.

Flow of Energy in a Community

The path that energy takes as it passes through a community is more like a straight line than a circle. Instead of going from producer to consumer and back again, it changes form after it has been used to do work. Try this bit of work: Vigorously rub your hands together. Did you feel heat? The energy it took to rub your hands was changed to heat as you did the work

Figure 1-12 The products of photosynthesis are involved in respiration, while the products of respiration are involved in photosynthesis. Thus, materials are continuously cycled between the two processes.

Demonstration
Demonstrate the flow of energy and materials through a community by having students sow seeds of garden cress, leaf lettuce, radishes, or other quick-growing salad plants in pots on a sunny windowsill. Explain to students as they watch the seedlings grow that they are witnessing the cycling of food materials: water and nutrients from the soil and carbon from the carbon dioxide in the classroom air (possibly exhaled by students) are transformed, using the energy from sunlight, into plant tissue. Let students continue the cycle by eating the plants when the plants are large enough to harvest.

Outdoor Activity
Pair students up and take them outdoors to a park, lawn, or vacant lot. Assign each pair a plot of land and ask them to find producers, consumers, and decomposers, or evidence of each. For example, if they cannot see any decomposers, they might be able to find a decaying leaf or other evidence of decomposition.
L1   LEP

PROJECT

Problem Species: Have students work in small groups to report on organisms that have been introduced into North America. Examples are the sea lamprey, water milfoil, the Japanese beetle, and Dutch elm disease. Ask students to find out how these pests were transported, what kinds of problems they cause, and methods used to control them. COOP LEARN

PORTFOLIO

Assign individuals or pairs of students a plot of land in a lawn, park, flower bed, or weed lot. Have students draw and label examples of producers, consumers, and decomposers (or evidence of them) from that area. If possible, have students identify some of the organisms they've drawn. L1

3 Assess

Check for Understanding

Describe to students some of the organisms in a simple community they have not yet studied, such as a sandy beach. Have students describe how energy flows from sunlight into and through the organisms in that community. **L1**

Reteach

Have students close their eyes and listen as you describe what happens to the energy of sunlight as it enters a chloroplast and is used to make chemical energy in the form of simple sugars; the simple sugars are converted to more complex substances; the complex substances are used by the plant for growth or eaten by a consumer; and so on through a food chain.

Extension

Have students write a short paper describing the flow of energy from sunlight into their own bodies during the past 24 hours. How did they use that energy? **L3**

✔ Assessment

Portfolio: Ask students to describe and illustrate the difference between the cycling of materials in a community and the flow of energy through that community. *Materials are recycled; energy is not recycled.* **L1**

4 Close

Brainstorm

Have students brainstorm an imagined scenario about what might happen if Earth stopped receiving energy from sunlight. Temperatures would decrease, and photosynthesis would stop. At first, there would be fuel to burn for heat and food stores to eat, but these eventually would be consumed. Although Earth would still have plenty of carbon, oxygen, and other raw materials, life could not continue without the constant energy input needed to move these materials through the system. **L1** **COOP LEARN**

18

of moving them. That energy still exists—in the form of heat released into the environment. You cannot reuse that energy to do additional work. You will have to take more energy from the fuel substances in food you eat.

In a food chain, energy sources are passed from one organism to another, first from producer to consumer and then from consumer to consumer. Once an organism uses a unit of energy for any kind of work, be it rubbing hands together or doing any other biological work, the energy cannot be reused. Thus—unlike such materials as water and sugars, oxygen and carbon dioxide, nitrogen and sulfur—energy is not cycled. Instead, it changes into heat, one of several forms that energy takes.

As you know, energy drives the processes, functions, and activities of life. Energy must always be available in the form of fuels made by producers. To make the fuels, producers must have a constant source of energy for photosynthesis. That energy comes from the sun in the form of light. Most communities, including those under attack by zebra mussels, could not survive without the sun and its energizing light.

Figure 1-13 As energy is transferred from one organism to another in a food chain, it is used by the organisms for work and lost as heat. Therefore, there must be a constant supply of energy from the sun for living systems to function.

Section Review

Understanding Concepts

1. How is a candy bar you eat related to moving your muscles?
2. A catfish feeds on algae in an aquarium. Which of these organisms is a producer? A consumer? Which undergoes photosynthesis? Cellular respiration?
3. A forest community consists of trees, birds, insects, deer, bacteria, worms, ferns, mosses, squirrels, toadstools, spiders, snakes, and mice. List, in order, the organisms that might form a food chain composed of four links. Which of the organisms would act as decomposers?
4. **Skill Review—Making Tables:** Using the organisms listed in question 3, make a table that divides them into producers and consumers. For more help, see Organizing Information in the **Skill Handbook**.
5. **Thinking Critically:** If it were possible to decrease the size of algae populations, would such a decrease affect the size of zebra mussel populations? Explain.

Answers to Section Review

1. By the process of cellular respiration, energy from the sugars in the candy bar is converted to energy the body can use for muscle contraction.
2. The algae are producers and undergo photosynthesis. The catfish is a consumer. Both organisms undergo cellular respiration.
3. Tree→ insect→ bird→ snake. Decomposers include toadstools and bacteria.
4. **Skill Review—Making Tables:** Producers: trees, ferns, mosses. Consumers: birds, insects, deer, bacteria, worms, squirrels, toadstools, spiders, snakes, mice.
5. **Thinking Critically:** Because algae are the food source for zebra mussels, a decrease in the algae population would lead to a decrease in the zebra mussel population.

1.3 Now That They're Here

According to one U.S. scientist, "There won't be one answer to the zebra mussel problem. We are going to need a bag of tricks." Indeed, science and industry are attacking the dilemma from a number of different standpoints. Their approaches take into account not only the biological communities invaded by the zebra mussels but also the physical environment.

Interactions in the Physical Environment

In any community, organisms respond to and interact with other living things. At the same time, they also respond to and interact with the physical environment. For example, a whole colony of zebra mussels can filter a great deal of water as each organism siphons out algae for food. A colony can filter so much water, in fact, that the water around the site becomes very clear. From the human point of view, this interaction with the physical environment could be a possible benefit.

From the zebra mussel point of view, physical factors of the North American environment help explain why the organisms have succeeded in multiplying so fast. For one thing, the zebra mussel finds North American water temperatures to its liking. The mussels can survive and reproduce at temperatures between 7°C and 32°C. Water currents in North American lakes and streams have also proved beneficial. The currents flow gently enough to allow young zebra mussels to attach easily, and evenly enough to deliver a steady food source. The waters also contain calcium, an important substance in the makeup of zebra mussel shells. In their search for ways to combat the zebra mussel, science and industry are looking at ways to change the physical environment so that it is less favorable for the zebra mussel.

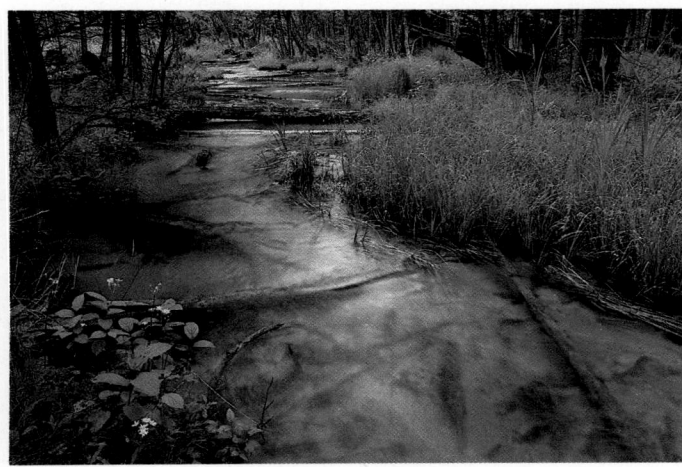

Figure 1-14 The filtering action of zebra mussels can cause the water in which they live to become as crystal clear as this stream.

Objectives

Discuss how organisms are influenced by nonliving factors of their environment.

Explain how the process of evolution has resulted in a great diversity of life forms and why there is unity within the diversity.

Apply knowledge of the biology of zebra mussels to possible methods of controlling them.

Prepare

Key Concepts
Students discover that the environment has influenced the evolution of organisms, that there is unity within the diversity of Earth's organisms, and that environmental changes can influence population size.

Key Terms
evolution, adaptation

Materials
- Gather live mussels, aquarium plants, test tubes, soda straws, and bromthymol blue solution for the Investigation.

1 Focus

Objectives
The objectives are listed on the student page. Remind students to preview these objectives as a guide to this numbered section.

Audiovisual
Show five to six color slides that show environments in which organisms live (wet, dry, hot, cold, windy). Ask students to identify what effects the environment can have on the organisms not seen in the pictures.
[LEP]

PROGRAM RESOURCES

Teacher Classroom Resources
Study Guide, pp. 4-6 [L1]
Critical Thinking/Problem Solving, p. 1 [L2]

2 Teach

PHYSICS CONNECTION

Conservation of Energy:
The Law of Conservation of Energy, formulated in 1845 by H. Helmholtz and J.R. Mayer, states that "energy can neither be created nor destroyed." The law applies to both living and nonliving systems, and has contributed to our understanding of the importance of interrelationships in nature.

Bioethics

Helpful Zebra Mussels:
Zebra mussels aren't all bad. Dutch biologists have introduced them into lakes to clear up water that is overgrown with microscopic algae. These introduced mussel populations are kept in check by predators—diving ducks and fish species that aren't found in the Great Lakes. In Germany and the Netherlands, scientists have tried using zebra mussels to filter pollutants from the effluent of chemical plants. Have students debate the pros and cons of introducing a foreign organism, such as the zebra mussel, into an area to help solve an environmental problem. Who would be responsible if the introduction caused unforeseen problems? Who should have the authority to make such decisions? **COOP LEARN**

Figure 1-15 Keeping pipes and waterways clear of zebra mussel buildup is an ongoing battle. One method of cleaning off the tiny invaders is to spray them with water heated to between 45°C and 55°C.

Some Answers for Industry

Shippers and lakeshore industries and drinking-water plants are still using scraping procedures to clear surfaces of zebra mussel clogging. They have also developed some improved screening devices that keep small larvae as well as larger forms of zebra mussels out of some water intake entrances. But these answers do not take care of all the problem areas.

Another possible control is to deprive the zebra mussels of oxygen, which you may recall they need for cellular respiration. Adding chemicals that contain sodium and chlorine removes oxygen from water that is sealed off in a given area. Lack of oxygen will kill zebra mussel larvae quickly, but adult zebra mussels can survive for several days without fresh oxygen. That often means that a plant using this method to clear clogged pipes will have to close down for several days while the affected areas are out of operation. Many factories and plants that provide drinking water to large cities cannot afford such lengthy shutdowns.

Increasing the speed of the current, if methods become available, might also prove worthwhile. A faster flow of water would prevent maturing forms of the organisms from settling and attaching. Electric currents sent

UNITY WITHIN DIVERSITY

Alike but Different

Basic life functions combined with the need for energy unite all of Earth's different kinds of organisms in a common bond that defines life. The statement you just read hints at one of the wonders of life. Life is amazingly diverse; although scientists have counted 2 million different forms, there may be another 4 million yet to be identified. All those life forms exhibit the same life functions and the same need for energy. How did such unity within such diversity come about?

Evolution Clues to life's riddle of unity within diversity lie in the environment and how organisms interact with and respond to it. Adding change and time factors to the clues brings us right up to the answer, which in a word is *evolution*. Change in organisms over time is the meaning of **evolution**.

Environments Differ Environments differ from place to place on Earth today, and they differ from environments of the past. In any environment, organisms have traits suited to that environment. These traits, which develop according to an organism's coded instructions, are known as **adaptations**.

Algae, for example, have the traits needed to produce chlorophyll for photosynthesis. Zebra mussels are adapted to draw in water, filtering out the algae and digesting substances from the algae they take in. Deer, which live in an entirely different environment from that of zebra mussels or algae, are adapted to browse on leaves for nourishment.

Environments Change Changes to environments occur slowly, very slowly over the space of countless centuries. Populations of organisms living and interacting within that environment also change, slowly and over a long period of time. If enough changes occur, or if

20 🐚 BIOLOGY—THE SCIENCE OF LIFE

PORTFOLIO

Have students imagine that they are managers of a power company that is experiencing zebra mussel problems. What actions would they take to solve the problem? Remind them that if they close the plant for any length of time, people will be without power. **L1**

MULTICULTURAL CONNECTION

Insect Adaptations: One way biologists study diversity is by investigating animal behavior. Dr. Charles Henry Turner, an African-American scientist, was a pioneer in the field of insect behavior. His experiments showed that bees recognize colors and patterns, moths hear, and ants use light as well as chemical trails to find their way home.

through water have also been found to interfere with attachment. As a last resort, new pipes could be built and buried beneath the sand. Europeans, long experienced with zebra mussel harassment, put in such underground structures as long as a century ago. At that time, the Europeans were just beginning to build their first power plants. Americans expect to spend at least 4 billion dollars in the 1990s just to get rid of mussels already in intake pipes. New construction projects to install underground pipes would cost even more.

In those pipes that are exposed to zebra mussel intrusion, Europeans sometimes flush the pipes with water heated to between 45° and 55°C. At these temperatures, both adult and immature zebra mussels die; they can survive at temperatures no higher than 32°C. The flushing must be done at least three times a year. It usually requires some scraping as well, because some of the organisms remain attached. In the United States, widespread use of this method could increase water temperatures in lakes and rivers. The impact could be harmful to other communities.

Some Biological Possibilities

In the long run, probably the best solution to America's zebra mussel dilemma is to control the growth of the population rather than try to kill off and remove colonies as they arise. One of the reasons zebra mussel populations have soared so quickly in the United States is that no native consumers feed on zebra mussels.

changes are dramatic, a new type of organism may arise.

Therein lies the secret of the diversity of life forms on Earth. Earth's first life forms appeared some 3 billion years ago and have been evolving ever since. The first forms of life gradually gave rise to other, new forms, which in turn evolved into still other kinds of organisms.

The great diversity among the many kinds of organisms challenges scientists in a number of ways. First, there is the challenge of discovering and counting all the different life forms. Then there is the challenge of making sense of their differences and similarities. Take the zebra mussel. There are thousands of other animals whose bodies are boneless, like the zebra mussel's. There are also thousands of animals that have shells, some of which—like those of clams and oysters—open and close the way the zebra mussel's do. Although they do not have shells, slugs, squids, and octopuses also have many traits similar to those of the zebra mussel. Intriguing likenesses and differences exist throughout all 2 million of today's known life forms.

Kingdoms of Living Things
Biologists bring order to life's diversity by dividing and classifying organisms into a series of groups and subgroups. The first grouping is that of kingdom. A kingdom is the broadest division in the classification of organisms. There are five kingdoms, each with its own name and each encompassing organisms with certain traits. You will study the organization of and representatives belonging to these five kingdoms—Monerans, Protists, Fungi, Plants, and Animals—when you read Chapters 15, 16, and 17.

UNITY WITHIN DIVERSITY

Alike but Different
Teaching strategies on page 21 relate to the material under Unity Within Diversity. This material represents core concepts that form the basis for understanding how the environment affects organisms such as the zebra mussel. Use the teaching strategies on this page to teach students about adaptations in organisms, what adaptations have to do with an organism's environment, and how organisms in different environments show different adaptations.

Display
Using models, illustrations, or live or preserved specimens, show students examples of organisms from each of the five kingdoms of living things. Introduce the idea that, in general, organisms have become increasingly complex over the course of evolution.
LEP

Different Viewpoints in Biology

Six Kingdoms
Biologists are proposing a sixth kingdom, the archaebacteria. The archaebacteria have cell structures composed of chemicals different from those found in other monerans. The archaebacteria include three groups of organisms that live in extreme environments that can't be tolerated by most other organisms: very salty, hot acid sulfur springs, and other anaerobic conditions.

MEETING INDIVIDUAL NEEDS

Show slides of organisms with various adaptations. Have students try to name one or two adaptations of each organism that haven't been discussed. Encourage them to think of internal adaptations as well as morphological ones. LEP

STUDENT JOURNAL

Have students write about organisms that are introduced into farms, gardens, or greenhouses to control pests. These organisms include ladybugs, lacewings, praying mantis, and *Bacillus thuringensis*. Information on many of these organisms can be found in *Common Sense Pest Control* by Olkowski, Daar, and Olkowski, Taunton Press, 1991. L1

Mussels and Their Environment

Time Allotment
1-1/2 class periods

Objectives
Upon completing this investigation, students will be able to:
- analyze the effect of mussels on their environment.
- summarize how mussels and other organisms in a lake depend on each other.

Skills
observe, form a hypothesis, design an experiment, separate and control variables, interpret data, recognize cause and effect, compare and contrast, make and use tables

Materials
2 mussels, 2 *Elodea* stems, 4 test tubes, test-tube holder, clean straw, bromthymol blue solution in a dropper bottle, sheet of white paper, distilled water

Safety Precautions: Caution students to handle live mussels with care. Have students wear aprons to protect clothing from bromthymol blue solution. Caution students not to inhale bromthymol blue.

Preparation
- Freshwater mussels may be ordered from a biological supply house. You might want to ask for small ones of uniform size.
- See page 27T for preparation of bromthymol blue.

Possible Procedures
Allow variations of the following setups. Set up test tubes with:
1. bromthymol blue solution
2. solution with mussel only
3. solution with mussel and plant
4. solution with plant only
Keep in a warm, lighted area overnight and observe results during the next class period.

Control Through Predation Introducing zebra mussel predators, organisms that kill and eat zebra mussels for food, might be one form of control. One such group of predators, in fact, may have already arrived—again from Europe and probably in the same way that the zebra mussels arrived. The predators are goby fish, and they seem to have an appetite for zebra mussels, shells and all. But biologists are not celebrating. The goby fish also eat the same kinds of small animals that walleye and lake trout eat. There is a danger that the goby will rob these valuable fish of their food supply and thus reduce their numbers.

Interfering with Reproduction Another, and perhaps the most promising, biological approach focuses on tampering with the zebra mussels' reproductive pattern. If successful, both the size of zebra mussel populations and their spread to new waterways could eventually be decreased. Furthermore, no other organisms in the community would be adversely affected.

INVESTIGATION

Mussels and Their Environment

Why do you breathe? You breathe in oxygen, which is needed by your body for breaking down food and converting the energy it contains to a form your body can use. What do you breathe out? Carbon dioxide. This gas is a waste product from the breakdown of food. Does a mussel "breathe"? Like you, a mussel needs oxygen for the conversion of energy into usable forms through cellular respiration. Mussels, of course, get oxygen from the water that surrounds them. Does a mussel breathe out? If a mussel takes in oxygen and gives off carbon dioxide, how will this gas exchange affect the ecosystem in which it lives? Consider other organisms that live in the water with the mussel. They, too, exchange gases with their watery environment. What one organism gives off, another may use. In this way, organisms in a food chain make materials available to each other. In this lab, you will see how the mussel affects its environment and how other organisms might be dependent on the mussel.

Problem
How do mussels affect their environment?

Safety Precautions
Bromthymol blue will stain clothing and skin. Do not drink bromthymol blue. Wash your hands at the end of the lab.

Experimental Plan
1. Fill a test tube with distilled water. Add a drop or two of bromthymol blue until you have a very light blue color. Check the color by holding it against a piece of white paper.
2. Place a clean straw into the test tube and blow into the bromthymol blue solution. Do

Teaching Strategies
- Advise students to wash their hands at the end of the lab.
- To prevent reuse, students should dispose of their used straws in a trash can you have designated.
- Make sure that students understand that carbon dioxide makes the bromthymol blue turn yellow.
- When checking their plans, make sure students are using mussels, plants, and bromthymol blue solution. Even if their plan is not quite right, the group should be

allowed to proceed. They will learn to make a better plan the next time if they see for themselves by comparison with other groups where they went wrong.
- **Troubleshooting:** Very small mussels may take two days to give off enough carbon dioxide to turn the solution yellow.
- Tell students that their bromthymol blue solution should be a very light blue. If it is too dark, the mussel may die.

Zebra mussels begin reproducing when they detect an explosive growth in the algae on which they feed. Reproducing at that time ensures a plentiful supply of food for the young. If the adult zebra mussels could be tricked into reproducing at a time when algae are less plentiful, far fewer mussel offspring would survive. Biologists might accomplish such trickery if they find substances that would cause males to release sperm and females to release eggs at the wrong times in the algae life cycle.

Another possibility would be to trick males and females into releasing sperm and eggs at widely spread time intervals. Because sperm and eggs live only a short time, fertilization would not occur. Yet another approach arises from the fact that adult zebra mussels stuff themselves with food just prior to reproducing. They need extra food to get the extra energy they need for producing sperm and eggs. Biologists are searching for a substance that would cause the mussels to close their shells, and thus prevent food intake. Such a substance, though, would have to be one that doesn't interfere with the feeding routines of similar animals, like clams.

Figure 1-16 The goby is a natural predator of the zebra mussel. However, it also eats the same foods that walleye and lake trout eat. What are the possible effects of an increasing goby population?

- Encourage students to develop a long list of possibilities for ways that the mussel might affect its environment.

Data and Observations
Student data tables will have columns headed: bromthymol blue, mussel, mussel and plant, plant. Rows may be headed: color at start, color at end.

Data Analysis
1. Carbon dioxide produced by the mussel caused the bromthymol blue to change to yellow. The aquarium plant didn't produce carbon dioxide, so the bromthymol blue stayed blue. In the test tube with the plant and mussel, the mussel produced carbon dioxide, some of which was used by the plant. The solution, therefore, turned yellowish/blue.
2. Outcomes will depend on methods used. Some students may omit certain parts of the setup. Some may use more bromthymol blue. Results should be similar, but not necessarily identical.
3. Students may suggest including more experimental groups than they did the first time, or testing with different chemicals, such as chemicals that detect oxygen.
4. Mussels produce carbon dioxide, which plants use.
5. A huge number of mussels may produce so much carbon dioxide that organisms will be deprived of needed oxygen.

✔ **Assessment**
Portfolio: Have students write a lab report to place in their portfolios.

Extensions
Ask students to think about what nutrients mussels need to survive, what organisms eat mussels, what temperature mussels need, how much oxygen they use, what the effect of acid rain might be on mussel survival, or what effect the death of many mussels might have on a lake system.

---

not get any of the solution in your mouth. Continue to blow into the solution until you notice a color change.
3. In your group, decide what may have caused the color change.
4. Do you think the color of bromthymol blue solution would change if a water plant were placed in the test tube overnight in bright light? Why or why not? What about a mussel? What about a mussel and a plant?
5. In your group, make a list of possible ways the mussel might affect its environment.
6. From the list you have made, select an effect you could test with bromthymol blue solution, a mussel, and a water plant.
7. Make a prediction about what you think will happen during your investigation.
8. You will be provided with several test tubes, one of which

should contain only bromthymol blue solution so you will have a basis for comparison at the end of your investigation.
9. Following the style of a recipe, write a numbered list of directions that anyone could follow.
10. Make a list of the materials you will need.
11. Make a table in which to record what happens. In your table, you may want to include the type(s) of organism(s) you tested and the colors observed in the bromthymol blue.

Make sure your teacher has approved your plan before you proceed further.

Data and Observations
Carry out your investigation and record what happens in your table.

Analysis and Conclusions
1. What happened to the bromthymol blue in which you put a

mussel? An aquarium plant? An aquarium plant and a mussel? Explain.
2. Compare your outcome with those of other groups. How do the outcomes compare? Explain.
3. If you were going to do this same investigation again, what would you do differently? Why?
4. Explain how mussels and plants in a pond are dependent on each other.
5. How might the balance of living things in the pond be upset if the mussels increased in huge numbers?

Going Further
Based on this lab experience, plan another investigation that helps to determine more about the relationship between mussels and their environment. Assume that you will have unlimited resources and will not be conducting this lab in class.

Figure Caption Question

Refer to Figure 1-16 on page 23.
What are the possible effects of an increasing goby population?
Increasing numbers of gobies may result in a decreased food supply for other fish. Without enough food, these fish may not be able to survive.

3 Assess

Check for Understanding

Ask students to answer the following questions. Describe at least three types of trouble the mussels have caused, and why these problems did not occur in the mussel's native environment. Describe some of the solutions that have been proposed, and explain any drawbacks to those solutions. **L1**

Reteach

Have pairs of students play "hangman" using the terms introduced in this chapter. **COOP LEARN**

Extension

Have students write about what they think must have happened to the Great Lakes community as the number of humans living along its shores increased over the past 200 years. **L3**

Change and the Environment

All of the solutions biologists are exploring involve human-made changes in the environment. Scientists want to restrict these changes to ones that conflict with the adaptations of zebra mussels only. Nature also makes changes in the environment. Natural disasters such as floods, fires, or volcanic eruptions can arise suddenly and have drastic effects on entire biological communities.

For the most part, natural disasters occur infrequently. More gentle and more predictable changes, however, go on constantly in both physical and biological environments. Responding to change in various ways is part of everyday living for organisms. As you have just read, for example, zebra mussel reproduction takes place in response to changes in algae growth. Many organisms, especially those that live on land, face seasonal changes every year. Many kinds of plants respond to cooler temperatures

Thinking Lab

INTERPRET THE DATA

How do physical factors affect zebra mussels?

Background
What do you think would happen to living things in a lake if the oxygen dissolved in the water disappeared? What would happen to the same living things if the temperature of the water were raised 10°C? Most likely, these changes in the physical factors of the lake would have an adverse effect on life in the lake. In Europe, zebra mussels building up in water pipelines have been controlled to some degree by periodic flushing of water pipes with hot water. Oxygen can be eliminated from a sealed water system by adding specific chemicals. Zebra mussels can live for a few days without oxygen, but eventually they die.

You Try It
Interpret the data in the table below and answer the following questions.

1. In which water temperatures do zebra mussels die more quickly?
2. What is the relationship between water temperature, dissolved oxygen, and death of zebra mussels?
3. If you were the manager of a water system contaminated with zebra mussels, which method of mussel control would you use? Speculate about the advantages and disadvantages of each method.

Table 1.1 **Zebra Mussel Death Rates**

Water Temp (°C)	Day 0	Day 1	Day 2	Day 3	Day 4	Day 5	Day 6	Factors Studied
17-18	7.5	—	0.7	0.03	—	0	0	dissolved oxygen mg/L
	0	—	0	0	—	90	100	% dead mussels
20-21	9.6	0.08	0	—	0	—	—	dissolved oxygen mg/L
	0	0	10	—	100	—	—	% dead mussels
23-24	7.1	0.33	0	0	—	—	—	dissolved oxygen mg/L
	0	0	48	100	—	—	—	% dead mussels

Thinking Lab

INTERPRET THE DATA

Purpose
Students will interpret the effect of water temperature on dissolved oxygen.

Skills
interpret data, recognize cause and effect

Teaching Strategies
• Temperatures on p. 19 assume the availability of oxygen. To separate the effects of temperature and oxygen, researchers who collected the data used sublethal temperatures.

Answers
1. 23°C—24°C
2. Warmest water had least oxygen to begin with; mussels in this water died first. Remaining mussels died as oxygen was used up.
3. Water—pros: immediate death; cons: death of other organisms. Oxygen—pros: other organisms can escape; cons: takes longer; pipeline shutdown.

✔ **Assessment**
Portfolio: Have students describe controls for an explosively breeding fish species with no natural predators.

of autumn by losing their leaves. For many consumers, this means a reduction in food supply. Some consumers might respond by migrating to areas where food is abundant. Others might hibernate, thus reducing their need for food during the long winter of barren plants.

Patterns of change are part of the natural world and influence the lives of all organisms. Humans are the only organisms who can make choices and decisions about how to respond to changes in the natural world. They can also make decisions about how or how not to introduce changes themselves. As you have seen, biologists apply caution as they consider changes aimed at combating zebra mussels. But one change they have persuaded government leaders to make relates to the dumping of ships' ballast. Ships' crews are now required to release ballast offshore, in saltwater ocean areas, instead of waiting until they put in at freshwater ports. In this way, they should eliminate the future risk of changing communities by introducing unwelcome misfits like zebra mussels.

Figure 1-17 Natural disasters lead to changes in living systems. Most change, however, is regular and does not disrupt the system.

LOOKING AHEAD

In THIS CHAPTER, you looked over the shoulders of biologists as they predicted outcomes of the zebra mussel presence. By now, you probably appreciate how important it is that scientists find a way to prevent those outcomes from disrupting life in our lakes and rivers. In the next chapter, you will get an idea of how biologists go about finding solutions. You will see that scientists follow similar steps and procedures as they attack any scientific problem. Altogether, these steps and procedures make up a kind of formula for research and investigation—the never-ending story of science.

Section Review

Understanding Concepts

1. What physical factors promote growth of zebra mussel colonies in intake pipes?
2. Octopuses and zebra mussels are two types of mollusks. Each animal has unique characteristics. The octopus has no shell, and the zebra mussel has two shells. How did those different characteristics originate? How are the two mollusks the same?
3. Is it likely that zebra mussels could establish colonies in swiftly moving streams? Explain.
4. **Skill Review—Classifying:** You observe that spider monkeys and rhesus monkeys have many features in common. How can you explain their similarities? For more help, see Thinking Critically in the **Skill Handbook**.
5. **Thinking Critically:** You discover an organism that seems to be rooted in the soil. How could you decide whether that organism is a fungus or a plant?

Answers to Section Review

1. Water temperatures are suitable, and currents are gentle enough to permit young mussels to attach. Slower water currents also permit transport of food particles.
2. The different characteristics are adaptations to different ways of life. Adaptations arise through evolution. The basic body structure of the two mollusks is similar.
3. The current in such streams would prevent attachment of the mussels or could possibly dislodge those that managed to attach.
4. **Skill Review—Classifying:** Both monkeys have evolved adaptations for life in a particular kind of environment—trees.
5. **Thinking Critically:** A plant is a producer and would show green color due to the presence of chlorophyll. A fungus is a consumer, lacking chlorophyll.

✔ Assessment
Performance: Use the school yard, a fence row, or a wooded area for a field trip. Have students record the physical factors that affect the organisms they see. Choose two or three factors and have the students orally explain how these factors affect the organism's survival. **L1**

4 Close

Brainstorm

Have students brainstorm a series of approaches to dealing with the zebra mussel population. Ask students if there are any approaches discussed in the text that they would like to experiment with or elaborate on. Invite students to propose and discuss new ideas of their own. Have students explain how they could test their idea to see if it works. **L1**

CHAPTER 1

BIOLOGY, TECHNOLOGY, AND SOCIETY

Biotechnology

Purpose
Students discover that advances in technology offer increasingly revealing looks into the workings of the human organism.

Teaching Strategies
- Show students a diagram of the areas of the human cerebral cortex that are associated with speech and language, motion, taste, smell, and sight.

Possible Answers
1. Modern radiological devices use minimum amounts of radiation and can be used to discover cancerous tissue early so it can be removed before spreading to the rest of the body.
2. Possible answers include nuclear power plant operators, astronauts, and long-distance truck and bus drivers.

Going Further
Have students investigate and discuss other high-technology medical devices, such as MRI (Magnetic Resonance Imaging), or the use of lasers and fiber-optic probes in surgical procedures. L2

BIOLOGY, TECHNOLOGY, AND SOCIETY

Biotechnology
Watching the Brain at Work

For centuries, people have puzzled over this question: What does a thought look like?

PET Medical equipment that has already been in use for several years provides clues to the answer. A PET (positron emission tomography) machine can give doctors a peek inside the brain. Here's how it works.

Energy comes in many different forms. In this chapter, you've read that sunlight is a form of energy and food contains chemical energy. Certain elements also emit energy. These radioactive elements, as they are called, have proven to be indispensable medical tools. PET is just one technique that uses radioactive elements to produce images of the inside of the body. Before the PET machine can do its job, a patient is given a simple sugar (glucose) solution tagged with a radioactive element. After this solution moves into the brain, the radioactive tracer gives off particles like X rays, thus allowing a computer to trace its location. The PET machine shows the location on a color computer monitor. The more active the brain is, the more it uses the sugar solution. And the greater the use of sugar by the brain, the brighter the spot on the monitor.

During the PET scan, the doctor may vary the patient's exposure to sound or sight in order to watch for changes in the brain's image. By comparing images of a patient's brain during different activities, researchers have identified specific areas of the brain used for seeing, hearing, speaking, and thinking.

MANSCAN A device newer than PET is the mental activity network scanner, or MANSCAN for short. This device, which fits over a patient's head like a soft helmet, takes a picture of brain activity every 4 milliseconds. (A millisecond is one-thousandth of a second.)

One application of MANSCAN is to study short-term memory. This component of thought, which involves remembering and using something that has just been learned, is often disturbed by serious head injuries or Alzheimer's disease. MANSCAN can record brain-wave patterns to predict whether a person is about to perform a memory task correctly. This application of MANSCAN may be useful in diagnosing brain diseases and in testing the effectiveness of drugs or methods of rehabilitation.

Another potential use of MANSCAN could be in a kind of brain monitor for people in jobs involving extremely critical decisions, such as airline pilots or brain surgeons. By putting on the MANSCAN helmet for a quick "checkup," these people could predict the onset of mental fatigue before their job performance began to decline.

Researchers expect that an even more detailed picture of the working brain may result when PET and MANSCAN, plus yet-to-be-developed technologies, are teamed up.

1. **Issue:** Exposure to radioactive elements has been linked to diseases such as cancer. How can the use of radioactive elements be justified?
2. **Connection to Social Studies:** What are some other careers or jobs in which you think a MANSCAN "checkup" would be useful? Why?

CAREER CONNECTION

Radiology technicians need specialized training to work with new technology such as PET and MANSCAN machines. People working in these careers in hospitals and medical schools must have an interest in and aptitude for science and mathematics as well as people skills.

CAREER CONNECTION

Have students interview a radiology technician at a local hospital or medical office to find out about the educational background and physical and social skills required for the job.

Rare Animals as Pets

How would you like to have a herd of Indian elephants in your backyard? Does a basement full of rare Rothschild's myna birds sound appealing? Or how about a snow leopard basking in the sunshine on your patio? In about 850 American homes, exotic pets like these are cared for through the Fish and Wildlife Service's Captive-Bred Wildlife Registration program.

Animal Adoption   Lovers of exotic animals have to meet some strict requirements before they can keep rare animals as pets. (Obviously, even a small herd of elephants would need more roaming room than the average suburban backyard has to offer.) However, the people who can take on such a project do it for reasons besides personal enjoyment. They are concerned about the dwindling number of animals in the wild and want to give them a safe place to grow up and reproduce. Loss of animals or plants, or any other type of organism from the wild, reduces diversity.

Problem Pet Owners   You probably know people who enjoy the attention they get from wearing unusual clothing and owning out-of-the-ordinary things. This personality trait can be fun, but when it extends to possessing rare animals, the results can be rather cruel. Take, for example, a black bear. When it is a cub, it looks like an overgrown teddy bear. People who think the bear would make a cuddly pet may be in for a surprise in a few months because a bear is and always will be a wild animal. Even

if its claws and some of its sharpest teeth are removed, a bear is still capable of behaving as it would in the wild and may act aggressively toward its owners.

By the time wild animal owners realize they have a problem, they find that it is nearly impossible to give a bear, tiger, or wolf to a zoo. The animal may have developed undesirable behaviors or habits and be unfit for life in a zoo. The pet these owners once loved could end up on a kind of ranch where hunters pay a fee to shoot animals. Birds, which are easier to place in new homes, present a different kind of problem. Birds often outlive their owners. Parrots, for example, can live to be 90 years old.

Illegal Entry   With wild pets not as potentially dangerous as bears, lions, or snakes, there are other factors to consider. A wild bird is probably a safe enough animal in a home, but people planning to buy one should consider where it has come from. Up to 20 million birds are taken from the wild each year—a number that could push many species near extinction. Half a million of these birds end up legally in the United States each year, while another 100 000 are smuggled in. As many as 60 percent of captured birds are thought to die in transit to the United States. Why so many? Consider parrots. Parrots

are sometimes taken across the Mexican-U.S. border in the hubcaps of cars. It isn't surprising that they can't survive the trip.

Many animal collectors justify keeping exotic pets by claiming that they are saving them from death as natural habitats are reduced or destroyed. Would these animals be better off if their habitats were preserved?

Understanding the Issue
1. Would you like to participate in the Wildlife Registration program? Why or why not?
2. Why do you think that preserving a wild animal's natural habitat is often difficult?

Readings
- Luoma, J.R. "Born to Be Wild." *Audubon,* Jan.-Feb., 1992, pp. 50-58.
- Yerton, Stewart. "Rare Species and Red Tape." *New York Times,* June 25, 1992, pp. C-1.

Issues

Purpose
Students gain a deeper understanding of the survival requirements of wild animals.

Teaching Strategies
- Point out that humans do act as caretakers of wild or rare animals, not in the home but in zoological parks and wildlife refuges. Also, zoologists sometimes breed endangered animals, such as the California Condor, in captivity, then release the young to the wild to continue a natural life cycle.

Possible Answers
1. Some students may feel that the responsibility would be too great, or they may realize that they don't have the space or financial resources to successfully meet the needs of a wild or rare animal. Others might enjoy the challenge of meeting the animal's needs.
2. Preservation of wildlife habitats often competes with the needs or desires of humans, such as dirt bike trails that can destroy plant cover and cause damaging erosion, or the need to build homes, schools, and offices in areas populated by rare or endangered species.

Going Further
Have students investigate the steps and requirements involved in getting a permit to keep a rare animal of their choosing. Or have them look into local wild animal rescue or captive breeding programs. **L1**

CHAPTER REVIEW

Summary

Summary statements can be used by students to review the major concepts of the chapter.

Language of Biology

Answers should go beyond defining the terms. Accept any reasonable answer that uses the term correctly and in the proper context.

Understanding Concepts

1. All of the organisms release carbon dioxide in the process of cellular respiration. The carbon dioxide is taken up by the plants and used in photosynthesis. The sugars and oxygen produced are used in cellular respiration, again releasing carbon dioxide.
2. Decomposers must be present to recycle the materials contained in dead organisms and wastes.
3. Light is necessary for photosynthesis. Without light, life in the aquarium would soon cease to exist.
4. A flow of water is needed to bring the mussels both food and oxygen.
5. growth and development; energy
6. These changes bring more sugars and oxygen to cells, materials necessary for cellular respiration. Thus, more energy can be made available during exercise. These changes illustrate homeostasis.
7. Organization disappears as decomposition occurs. When an organism is alive, energy is available to maintain organization.
8. The larvae float freely and can spread far and wide before settling down.
9. In everyday conversation, the word *adapt* means to adjust to a new situation, and individuals adapt within a short period of time. Populations of organisms become adapted to changing environments over a long period of time by the process of evolution.

Summary

The more than 2 million different kinds of organisms are distinguished on the basis of physical characteristics. The focus of a modern course in biology, however, is not on differences among various forms of life, but rather the common features shared by all.

Living things do not live alone, but exist together in communities. They do so because they are interdependent. A fundamental way in which organisms depend upon one another is for food.

Through photosynthesis, most producers use the energy of sunlight to make substances that become food for other organisms. That food, and the energy it contains, is made available to all members of a community through food chains. Through cellular respiration, both producers and consumers release the energy of substances in food to perform biological work.

In any community, materials are cycled but energy is not. To exist, almost all communities must have a continual input of energy in the form of sunlight.

Energy released during cellular respiration is used for a variety of functions: reproduction, growth and development, homeostasis, and organization. These functions are common to all organisms.

In addition to their need for energy to carry out functions, all organisms share other common features. They interact with one another and with the physical aspects of their environment, and they respond to patterns of change. Although evolution has resulted in the great diversity of living things on Earth, the common features of organisms have been retained over time. Though diverse, the many forms of life can be classified into five kingdoms.

Language of Biology

Write a sentence that shows your understanding of each of the following terms.

adaptation	evolution
biology	food chain
cellular respiration	growth
chlorophyll	homeostasis
community	organism
consumer	organization
decomposer	photosynthesis
development	producer
energy	reproduction

Understanding Concepts

1. An aquarium consists of several plants, a variety of fish, and snails. How does each type of organism contribute to cycling of materials in the aquarium?
2. What other kinds of organisms must be present in the aquarium in order for cycling of materials to continue over time? Explain.
3. Could life in the aquarium continue to exist if the aquarium were placed in the dark? Explain.
4. Could zebra mussels colonize intake pipes if there were no continuous flow of water into those pipes? Explain.
5. Before it is a butterfly, an insect is a fertilized egg and then a caterpillar. What common features of life do these facts illustrate? What is needed for those features to occur?
6. Your heart beats more quickly and you breathe more rapidly when you exercise. How are such changes beneficial? Of what common feature of life are those changes an example?
7. What happens to the organization of an organism when it dies? What is the cause? Why does it not happen when the organism is alive?
8. How are the stages of development of zebra mussels an adaptation for spreading to new areas?

Applying Concepts

10. The predator might also prey upon other species, reducing their numbers and possibly disrupting food chains.
11. Oxygen is needed for cellular respiration.
12. Examples are forests, grasslands, deserts, streams, or lakes. They differ in terms of the organisms present, but are similar in that they all require energy, must recycle materials, and show complex interactions.
13. Most organisms have adaptations for a particular set of environmental conditions.
14. Producer→ decomposer. The two types of organisms can effectively recycle needed materials.
15. No. The piece of potato has not increased in terms of amount of living material.
16. Availability of water would determine the extent of plant life and thus the amount of energy trapped during photosynthesis. Food production affects all members of the community. Amount of sunlight affects the kinds of plant life, as does content of soil. Amount of light may also affect the kinds of organisms in the other four kingdoms.

9. When you begin a new course in school, you usually adapt to the way your teacher wants you to do your homework. How is the meaning of the word "adapt" in everyday conversation different from the biological meaning of the word?

Applying Concepts

10. Suppose a predator of zebra mussels is found. The advantage of introducing such a predator into waters where the mussels are found is clear. What disadvantages might follow introduction of the predator?
11. One suggested method of dealing with the problem of intake pipes clogged with zebra mussels is to block the intake of oxygen. Why would this be an effective method?
12. Identify several different types of natural communities. What do they have in common? How do they differ?
13. Why can most organisms live only in a certain type of community?
14. What would be the simplest possible food chain in a community? Explain.
15. A piece of potato immersed in water absorbs some of the water and swells. Has the piece of potato grown? Explain.
16. How would each of the following physical factors be important in a forest community: availability of water; direct sunlight versus shade; type of soil?
17. Why are there no algae at the bottom of a deep lake or ocean?
18. **Biotechnology:** How is MANSCAN used to monitor brain activity?
19. **Issues:** Explain the types of problems that arise as a result of keeping wild animals as pets.

Lab Interpretation

20. **Investigation:** If you had a chemical solution that was red in the absence of oxygen and green in the presence of oxygen, what color would the following solutions be after exposure to bright light for 24 hours? Explain.

a. Solution with mussel
b. Solution with water plant
c. Solution with mussel and water plant
d. Solution alone

21. **Minilab 1:** You are walking along an ocean beach when a very unusual specimen rolls up to your feet in the waves. It looks somewhat like a rock and somewhat like a shell. It is crusted over with a hard buildup of a substance that you cannot scrape off, so you cannot see it well. What could you do to tell if it is a relative of a snail or mussel?
22. **Thinking Lab:** Various types of mussels were tested for their tolerance to heated water. Results are illustrated in the graph below. Which species might live in the tropics, which in temperate climates, and which in the far north? Explain.

Connecting Ideas

23. How is the adaptation of filtering food related to other adaptations characteristic of adult zebra mussels?
24. What is the common requirement necessary for all the following activities? A firefly lights up. A muscle in your arm contracts. A leaf produces simple sugars. A zebra mussel closes its shells.

17. Light does not penetrate to those depths.
18. By taking a picture of brain activity every 4 milliseconds, MANSCAN can be used to study various brain activities.
19. Some animals can be dangerous. Some birds outlive their owners.

Lab Interpretation

20. a. Red, mussel uses oxygen
    b. Green, plant gives off oxygen
    c. Slightly reddish, mussel uses some of the oxygen given off by the plant
    d. Slightly reddish, water has some dissolved oxygen in it
21. Students may suggest looking for snaillike movement, a head, and tentacles, or allowing it to remain undisturbed in a container of sea water to see if there are two shells that will open.
22. Tropics-A, north-B, temperate-C; tropical fish should survive longer in warmer water.

Connecting Ideas

23. **Evolution:** Filter feeding is an adaptation that enables immobile zebra mussels to trap food.
24. **Energy:** Each activity listed is an example of biological work. Each requires energy.

ORGANIZER
CHAPTER 2

SECTION	OBJECTIVES	TEXT LABS/FEATURES
2.1 Methods of Science (2 days)	**Relate** the various methods used by scientists to learn about the natural world. **Apply** your understanding of a controlled experiment to the testing of a hypothesis.	**Minilab 1:** How do observations help you make an educated guess? p. 33 **Investigation:** Light and the Rate of Photosynthesis, p. 36 **Thinking Lab:** How can you test dog food commercial claims? p. 39 **Global Connection:** The Iceman Unfreezes History, p. 40 **Career Connection:** Anthropologist, p. 41
2.2 Tools of the Trade (2 days)	**Compare and contrast** the compound light microscope, the transmission electron microscope, and the scanning electron microscope. **Measure** objects using the International System of Measurement.	**Minilab 2:** What is the area of your classroom? p. 47
BIOLOGY, TECHNOLOGY, AND SOCIETY		**Physics Connection:** An Unusual Idea for Testing Global Warming, p. 49

LAB MATERIALS

INVESTIGATION	MINILAB	ALTERNATE LAB
page 36 aquaria aquarium lids with 15 and 75-watt fluorescent bulbs dimmer switch *Elodea* plants thermometer watch	**page 33** owl pellets paper towels tweezers **page 47** calculator meterstick yardstick	**page 44** coverslips eyedropper forceps microscope scissors slide of letter "e" threads, colored

TEACHER CLASSROOM RESOURCES	OTHER RESOURCES
Study Guide, pp. 7-9 **Concept Mapping,** p. 2 **Critical Thinking/Problem Solving:** *Identifying Scientific Methods,* p. 2 ****ILS:** *Solving a Problem with a Scientific Method,* p. 13 **Exploring Environmental Issues:** *Sources of Water Pollution,* p. 3	***STVS:** *Research in the Pinelands,* Ecology (Disc 6, Side 1)
Study Guide, pp. 10-12 ***PLL:** *The Compound Microscope—A Biological Tool,* p. 6 ***PLL:** *Microscopic Measurement,* p. 11 ****ILS:** *Use of the Light Microscope,* p. 5 ****ILS:** *Techniques for Better Microscope Use,* p. 9 ****ILS:** *Using SI Units,* p. 17	***STVS:** *Using Bacteria to Detect Carcinogens,* Plants and Simple Organisms (Disc 4, Side 1) **Color Transparency 1:** *A Compound Microscope*
Assessment Materials **Chapter Assessment,** pp. 5-8 **Performance Assessment in Biology,** p. 4 **Alternate Assessment in the Science Classroom** **Computer Test Bank**	**Spanish Resources** **Cooperative Learning Resource Guide** **Videodisc Correlations** (to Optical Data's and Videodiscovery's videodiscs)

* **Probing Levels of Life**
** **Investigating Living Systems**

* **Science Technology Videodisc Series**

Key to Teaching Strategies

The following designations will help you decide which activities in the teacher margin are appropriate for your students.

L1 Level 1 activities should be within the ability range of all students.

L2 Level 2 activities should be within the ability range of the average to above-average student.

L3 Level 3 activities are designed for the ability range of above-average students.

LEP LEP activities are appropriate for Limited English Proficiency students.

COOP LEARN Cooperative Learning activities are designed for small group work.

ADDITIONAL RESOURCES

Infinite Voyage *Unseen Worlds*
From Egyptian mummies to human hearts and brains, new tools enable biologists and other scientists to see images that were previously unknown.

Audiovisual
Inquiring into Life, video, Coronet/MTI.
Scientific Methods: An Introduction and Problems, two sound filmstrips, SRA.

Software
Biological Principles, Apple/IBM, Queue.
Characteristics of a Scientist, Apple II, Learning Arts.

C H A P T E R
2
BIOLOGY AS A SCIENCE

Chapter Overview

Students first learn that science is a process that produces knowledge about nature and that scientists attempt to explain the causes of the effects they observe. They find out that there is no fixed way to do this, but that there are several elements common to most scientific investigations. Students are led to understand these elements as they explore the roles of observation and data collection, interpretation of data, and formation of explanations of data. They then learn that an explanation must be tested by experimentation and that an experiment must be designed to reduce doubt about the cause of an effect. They are introduced to the concept of a controlled experiment as they carry out the Investigation. They also learn the value of graphing data, where applicable. They find out that not all research lends itself to experimentation, and examine the importance of integrity in and the limits of science.

Next, students compare and contrast compound light microscopes, transmission electron microscopes, and scanning electron microscopes in terms of their magnification and resolving power. They complete the chapter by studying basic ideas of SI measurement and its usefulness.

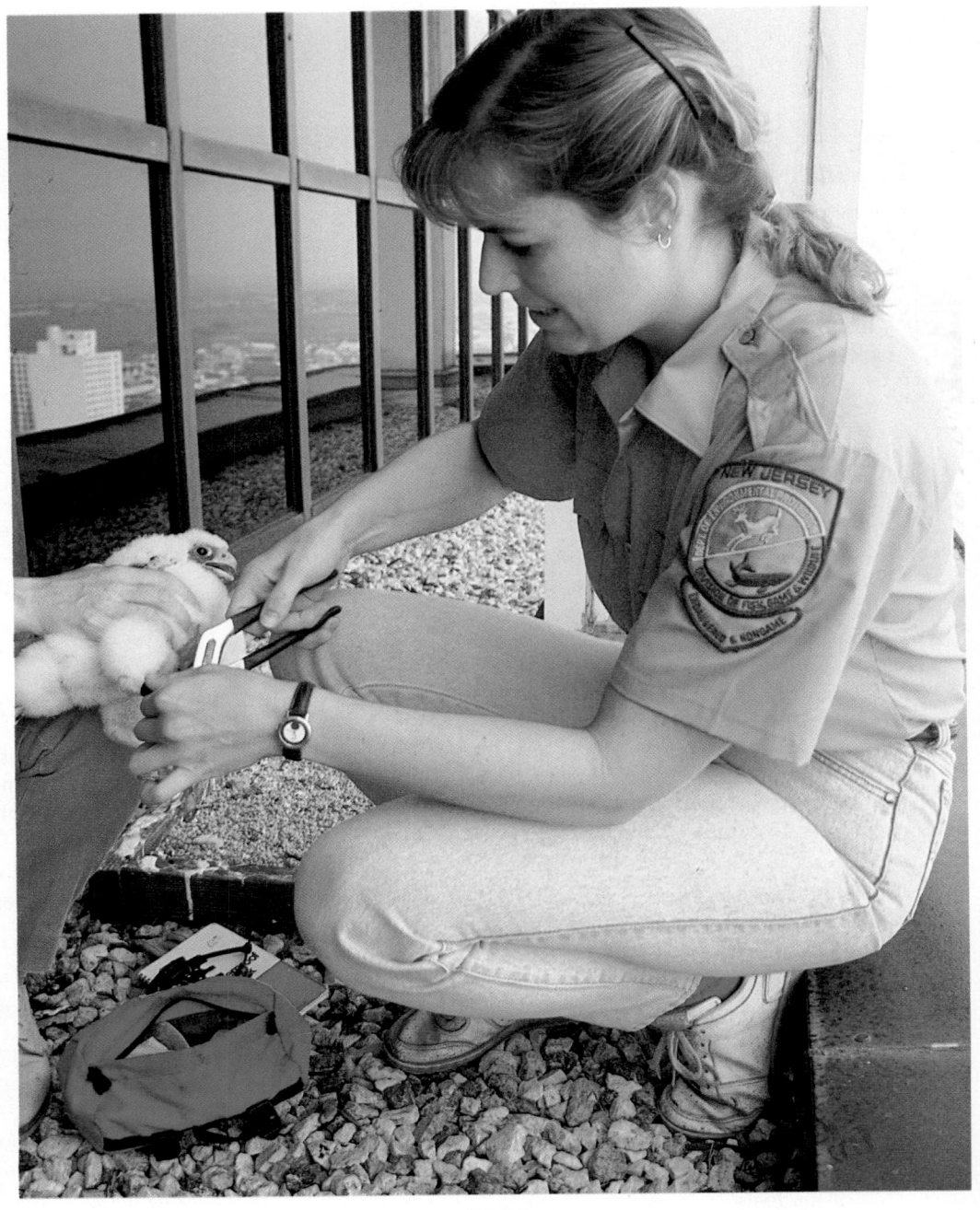

30

KEY TERMS

control group
controlled experiment
data
dependent variable
experiment
experimental group
hypothesis
independent variable

International System of
  Measurement (SI)
law
resolving power
scanning
  electron microscope (SEM)
science
technology

theory
transmission electron microscope (TEM)

2

BIOLOGY AS A SCIENCE

HAVE YOU EVER watched a nature program on television and wished you could have the opportunity to travel to strange places and study exotic animals? What may have looked like a wonderful vacation and adventure to you is serious business for the scientists who spend weeks, months, and even years out in the field gathering information about the world of biology. These scientists study and collect information about organisms, such as physical characteristics, what they eat, how they reproduce, and how they interact with other living things and their environment.

The naturalist in the photograph is trying to learn more about a population of falcons that inhabits a specific area of the eastern United States. Part of the investigation includes capturing and banding individual birds. If this bird is recaptured in some other place, information recorded on the band will be collected and added to a body of knowledge that scientists throughout the world have collected on peregrine falcons. How do scientists from one country follow and understand the work of scientists who live in another country? In this chapter, you will learn about the methods most scientists follow as they conduct their investigations. You will become familiar with some of the tools that biologists use. You also will learn about the universal system of measurement that enables scientists from all over the world to communicate the results of their investigations.

Suppose you found an animal that had been banded or tagged. What information might you learn about that animal from the band?

Chapter Preview

Contents

C H A P T E R

2

Introducing the Chapter

Begin the chapter by discussing the photograph on page 30. Most students envision scientists dressed in white coats, hunched over a microscope or peering at a bubbling liquid and surrounded by fancy equipment in an indoor laboratory. Point out that much of science occurs in the field as shown in the photograph. Lead students to the idea that science is a learning process, and ask them to identify some of the methods that both the field scientist and laboratory researcher carry out. As a means of emphasizing that the methods of science set it apart from other disciplines, ask students how the work of a scientist differs from that of a poet or historian. Students should be familiar with activities such as data collection, hypothesis formation, and experimentation.

Theme Development

This chapter introduces the final theme that will be woven throughout the text: methods of inquiry. Students focus on the methods common to most scientific inquiry and have an immediate opportunity to put that knowledge to use in the Minilabs, Thinking Lab, and Investigation.

Tying to Previous Knowledge

The discussion of the methods of science, including the Investigation in this chapter, makes use of students' understanding of the process of photosynthesis. Emphasize to students how previous knowledge can be put to use in forming explanations and designing experiments.

ASSESSMENT PLANNER

Choose assessment strategies from the following pages to evaluate the progress of your students.

Prepare

Key Concepts
The methods of science and the limits of science are defined. Students apply the methods of science to solve a problem.

Key Terms
science, technology, data, hypothesis, experiment, controlled experiment, independent variable, experimental group, control group, dependent variable, theory, law

Materials
- Gather owl pellets, paper towels, and tweezers for the Minilab.
- Gather aquaria, *Elodea* plants, aquaria lids with 15-watt and 75-watt bulbs, dimmer switch, water, watch, and thermometer for the Investigation.

1 Focus

Objectives
The objectives are listed on the student page. Remind students to preview these objectives as a guide to this numbered section.

Discussion
Allow students to discuss historical developments of science that led to new discoveries. Be prepared to provide some time references. As an example, some students will likely think that certain discoveries like nuclei in cells (Robert Brown, 1820s) or how blood circulates (William Harvey, 1620s) are much older than they are. As the class discussion continues, you might illustrate the events with a time line on the bulletin board.

Objectives

Relate the various methods used by scientists to learn about the natural world.

Apply your understanding of a controlled experiment to the testing of a hypothesis.

2.1 Methods of Science

Have you ever tried to figure out what an object in a closed box might be? Perhaps you shook the box or tilted it back and forth. You listened to the sound of the object as it moved within the box. You tried to determine its size, shape, weight, and perhaps the material it was made of. As you manipulated the box, you were making observations about it, and, based on your previous knowledge and experience, were ruling out certain conclusions and leaving open other possibilities. Finally, you narrowed your choices further and made a decision about what the object was. In trying to solve the puzzle of what was in the box, you were following the kinds of procedures that scientists use to learn about the natural world. Before continuing with this chapter, do the Minilab on page 33. Find out how sharp your powers of observation really are.

Development of Science

Think about the times when you tried to figure out what was inside a box. Perhaps you were curious because the object inside was a present for your birthday. Humans have always been curious about the natural world. They see effects and try to determine the causes of those effects. Why, for example, does the sun always disappear from the western sky and reappear in the east? Why do birds migrate when the seasons change, and how do they know where to go?

People long ago attempted to explain nature and make use of what they learned. Explanations based on reason were assumed correct and passed on from one generation to the next. In the 1500s people began to question the explanations of earlier generations. They developed new explanations based on the information they discovered. Much of the new information concerned earth, physical, and biological sciences. Galileo and Copernicus revolutionized the study of the planets, while Newton's laws of gravity and motion led to a new field of physics. In biology, the English scientist, Robert Hooke, used an early microscope to discover that cork is made of many boxlike structures he called cells.

Figure 2-1 **Migrating geese often fly in a V-shaped formation. Can you explain why?**

Modern biology began in the 1800s. By then scientists observed that all organisms are made up of cells, and that all life comes from preexisting life. The theory of evolution was proposed, as were the principles of heredity. Such findings were important for two reasons. They applied to all organisms, and they provided a basis for later discoveries.

What brought about these discoveries? It was a new way of learning about nature. One of the most important factors in good science is asking the right questions. Many discoveries made in the last 100 years are still valid because the scientists who made them were good detectives.

Allow students to research a scientist who made an important contribution. Have students include in their journals an epitaph they might have written for the scientist. [L2]

Teacher Classroom Resources
Study Guide, pp. 7-9 [L1]
Concept Mapping, p. 2 [L1] [LEP]
Critical Thinking/Problem Solving, p. 2 [L2]
Investigating Living Systems, Lab 4, p. 13 [L2]
Exploring Environmental Issues, p. 3 [L3]

What Is Science?

What does the word *science* mean to you?

Science as a Process   You may think of science as a list of terms to be memorized or facts to be learned, but that is not what science is. **Science** is a *process* that produces a body of knowledge about nature. As you read this book, you will learn a great deal of information about what is currently known about living things. You will also learn about the research leading to some of this information. You will work like a scientist and get a feel for how science is carried out.

Applied Science   You know that science is carried out because people are curious. They want to learn more about nature. Some people enjoy gaining knowledge for its own sake. Others want to apply the knowledge for a useful purpose. Applying knowledge to real problems is **technology,** or applied science. For example, some scientists wanted to know how traits are transmitted to offspring. Their curiosity led to the field of genetics. The scientific knowledge of genetics has been used to produce plants that grow faster and bacteria that produce drugs.

Remember that scientists note effects and attempt to explain the causes of those effects. There is no fixed way to do this; scientists arrive at explanations in many ways. Each situation is different. Several factors play a role in learning about nature. Among them are careful and thorough observations, interpretation of what is observed, explaining what is observed, and testing to see if those explanations are "on the right track." These steps do not always follow a precise order, and a scientist may go back and forth many times between many steps to solve a puzzle.

Observation

Observations about the natural world are the heart of science. A scientist may notice something that sparks his or her curiosity and then decide to observe it very carefully over a period of time. Often, this may lead to reading what is already known about the subject or related subjects. Sometimes an observation may seem unimportant at first. However, it may lead to something very important. The discovery of the role of DNA came about in such a way.

Collecting Data   Observations lead to collecting bits of information about the natural world. Information can come from observations in the field, such as the average measurements of sunflowers growing in slightly different habitats. Some information can be gathered from observations made during experiments. For example, an experiment might include monitoring the development of tadpoles into frogs when they have been exposed to different chemicals. All of the information gathered from observations is called **data**. Data need not be numerical. For example, data about the shapes or colors of butterfly wings are in the form of words.

Figure 2-2   **Observation includes collecting data on living things and making observations. How do you know these organisms become frogs?**

SECTION 2.1

Misconception
Almost all students will consider technology to be the answer to every difficult problem facing society. Point out that technology solves some problems, but creates others. Technology that produces greater amounts of food, for example, leads to increased population.

Audiovisual
The film *Technological Failures*, available from Screenscope, compares past and present technologies.

Figure Caption Question
How would you record data about the objects shown in this photograph? by listing characteristics of organisms such as size, shape, color, hardness, and body parts

Brainstorming
Ask students to think of everyday problems they could solve by using scientific methods. List the problems on the blackboard. If students are hesitant about offering examples, you may make a suggestion or two such as which toothpaste to use or which dress would be a better buy. Make the point that almost all problems students have can be solved using scientific methods. **COOP LEARN**

Reinforcement
Ask students if they have ever made a hypothesis or drawn a conclusion that was incorrect. Emphasize that in science there must be the possibility of making a wrong hypothesis. Explain that scientists make more incorrect hypotheses than correct ones. This is one of the reasons science is said to be self-correcting.

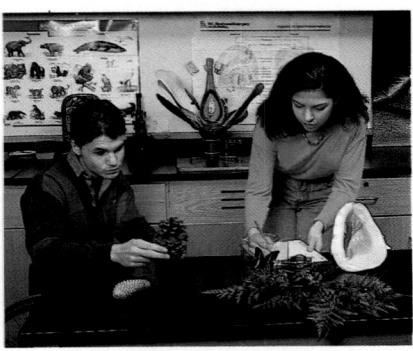

Figure 2-3 **How would you record data about the objects shown in this photograph?**

Making Observations   Suppose you are walking around your school, a park, or the area near where you live and you notice a particular flowering plant. As you walk along admiring the flowers, you notice that some plants are taller than others. You continue your walk, forgetting the flowers as something else catches your attention.

Later, you remember something about the different sizes of the plants, and you go back for another look. Upon closer observation, you see that there are indeed marked differences in the sizes of the plants. The taller ones are the ones exposed to more direct sunlight. The plants in the shade seem, on average, to be quite a bit shorter. Returning with a tape measure, you record data—the heights of plants in sun and in shade.

Interpretation and Explanation

What do you do with data you have recorded? If you are thinking like a scientist, you would be curious about the size differences of the plants you saw on your walk and begin thinking about what might cause those differences. One possibility is that some of the plants are younger than others, but you know they were all planted a few years ago at about the same time. You also discount the idea that the plants in the sun are growing in better soil than those in the shade, because you know that the soil is the same for both groups of plants.

Using Reason   What you have been doing is trying to reason things out. You have been attempting to interpret what you observed and have been doing so on the basis of previous observation and knowledge. You are being logical as you sort through possible causes of the difference in the height of these plants.

You know that plants carry out photosynthesis and that they require light in order to do so. The explanation seems clearer to you now. You assume that the plants exposed to more light over a long period of time grow taller because they produce more sugars by photosynthesis than the plants in the shade. If they produce more sugars, you reason, they can also produce more materials needed for growth. This leads you to a broader point. Light probably influences the rate of photosynthesis in all plants, not just the plants you observed.

Making a Conclusion   You have reached a conclusion by analyzing your observations and by sorting through possible causes of the effect you noted. Your explanation accounts for the data originally gathered through your observations. Your explanation could be stated: "Plants exposed to brighter light over a long period of time grow taller because they undergo photosynthesis more quickly." A statement that explains and relates data is called a **hypothesis.** Scientists do not always state formal hypotheses as they carry out their work. However, they do continually develop ideas that explain their observations and guide them in their further research. Can you think of any other statement to explain why some plants are shorter than the others? Could you collect data to support your explanation?

34 🔖 BIOLOGY AS A SCIENCE

PROJECT

Making Observations: Ask students to make observations about living things around their homes, school grounds, or local park. They are to observe for a week, one hour a day, and record their observations on a poster to display in the classroom. Suggest that they choose one organism or group of organisms to observe. Examples might include watching birds around a bird feeder, a pet cat exploring the yard, or movements of tulips as the sun travels across the sky. They may want to observe at different times of day during the week to identify different types of activity.

Testing the Explanation

You have explained the difference in height of plants satisfactorily to yourself, but forming an explanation does not in itself solve the problem. Many earlier "scientists" stopped at the point of coming up with an explanation. They made the explanation the conclusion of their work. An explanation, whether a formal hypothesis or not, must be tested. Only if there is a test can a scientist be certain whether or not an explanation is realistic. A hypothesis is only a tool for further study of a problem.

A good explanation not only explains the data, but also predicts new data. Scientists ask themselves, "If sunlight causes plants to grow taller, will a lack of sunlight result in shorter plants?" Asking such questions, in other words, making predictions, is a major step in doing science. By asking questions, scientists find ways to test their explanations. Explanations are most often, but not always, tested by **experiments**.

Designing the Experiment

Let's return to your explanation. How can you test whether your idea that brighter light leads to an increase in rate of photosynthesis is correct? Think about the idea of *rate* of photosynthesis. Rate means how much photosynthesis occurs per unit of time. How can you detect rate? You know that sugars are produced during photosynthesis. Can you somehow measure how much sugar is produced in a given amount of time? That seems unlikely, because sugar is produced within the leaves of the plant. You are stumped until you remember that photosynthesis also results in the production of oxygen. Oxygen is released from a plant during photosynthesis, so, you reason, if you could somehow measure how much oxygen is given off, you would have an indirect way of measuring the rate of photosynthesis.

Figure 2-4 Some cacti in the desert grow very tall, yet other desert plants stay short. How would you explain this difference?

The Need to Reduce Doubt

Remember, you are trying to determine the cause of a particular effect. In this case, the effect is a greater rate of photosynthesis and the cause, you believe, is brighter light. In carrying out your experiment, you must eliminate all doubt about cause and effect. You have to make sure, if you can, that any differences in rate of photosynthesis you might observe are due to differences in brightness of light and no other factor. Now try the following investigation. See if you can devise and conduct an experiment that will confirm or disprove the hypothesis.

Chalkboard Example

Before students come to class, place about 400 mL of water with a few drops of food coloring in a one-liter beaker. Slowly pour about 400 mL of cooking oil on top of the water. When students come into the room, have them examine the beaker without touching it. Once class has started, have students list their observations on the chalkboard, make hypotheses, and then list other methods of science they would use to answer their hypotheses. LEP

Figure Caption Question

Some cacti in the desert grow very tall, yet other desert plants stay short. How would you explain this difference? Students may hypothesize that cacti are more efficient in producing food or in retaining water to use for growth. Any explanation will show them how experimentation begins.

Concept Development

Explain the importance of a control in an experiment. Use the terms *independent variable, dependent variable, control group* and *experimental group* as you explain how to conduct an experiment.

Display

Make a bulletin board display that shows how scientific problems are solved. LEP

Teacher FYI

Although their findings were often inaccurate because they did not perform controlled experiments, the natural philosophers had a rational approach that has had a tremendous impact on science. The natural philosophers proposed that there is a natural cause for every natural process. Scientists today agree that this statement is one of the natural philosophers' most important contributions to science.

MEETING INDIVIDUAL NEEDS

It will be extremely important that students be able to design and conduct investigations as they use this text. Provide considerable background and practice in the methods of science for students working below grade level. Before going on to the next chapter, be certain that all students understand the concepts associated with experimental design.

INVESTIGATION

Light and the Rate of Photosynthesis

Time Allotment

1 class period

Objectives

Upon completing this Investigation, students will be able to:

- understand the significance of and have the opportunity to design a controlled experiment.
- describe how the amount of light influences the rate of photosynthesis.

Skills

observe and infer, recognize cause and effect, form a hypothesis, design an experiment, interpret data

Materials

two small aquaria, *Elodea* plants, aquarium lid with 15-watt fluorescent bulb, aquarium lid with 75-watt fluorescent bulb, dimmer switch, water, watch, thermometer

Preparation

Instead of dimmer switches, bulbs of different wattages, such as 25, 40, 60, and 75, can be used. At least one member of each group should have a watch if a wall clock clearly visible to all is not available.

Possible Hypotheses

The hypothesis is given to students in this investigation.

Possible Procedures

- Sufficient gravel should be placed in each aquarium to allow *Elodea* sprigs to be securely anchored.
- The amount and temperature of the water and number of *Elodea* sprigs in each aquarium should be identical, and the size of the sprigs should be as close as possible.
- One aquarium will be the control, containing *Elodea* sprigs exposed to the 15-watt light source. The *Elodea* sprigs in the other aquarium, which will be exposed to varying brightness of light, will be the experimental group.

INVESTIGATION

Light and the Rate of Photosynthesis

How can you measure the amount of oxygen given off by a plant? After all, you can't see oxygen coming from a plant. Or can you? You have an aquarium that contains plants, and you have noticed bubbles appearing around those plants. You never paid much attention to those bubbles before, but now you realize that those bubbles are bubbles of oxygen. The design for carrying out your experiment now becomes clear. You can estimate the rate of photosynthesis by counting the number of bubbles coming from aquatic plants in a given period of time, such as 20 minutes.

Problem

You begin by stating the problem you are trying to solve. In this case, you want to know if brighter light increases the rate of photosynthesis, so your problem statement might be: Does brighter light increase the rate of photosynthesis?

Hypothesis

Now you must prepare a hypothesis that might explain your observations. A hypothesis is usually written using an if/then format. Your hypothesis might be stated as: If the level of light influences the rate of photosynthesis, then increasing the amount (brightness) of light should increase the rate of photosynthesis.

Safety Precautions

Be careful when working with plant materials. Make sure that electrical wires do not touch the water unless they are intended for use in aquaria.

Experimental Plan

1. Now you are ready to write your experimental plan. An experimental plan details the steps you must take to collect data to test your hypothesis. Begin by listing what materials you will need. In this experiment, you will need to collect the following materials from your teacher: 2 small aquaria, 2 *Elodea* plants, an aquarium lid with a 15-watt fluorescent bulb, an aquarium lid with a 75-watt fluorescent bulb attached to a dimmer switch, water, a watch, and a thermometer.
2. Working in a group enables each group member to participate in the experiment. Scientists often work cooperatively. In this experiment, plan to work with several classmates. Each classmate may be assigned a different job, such as collecting materials, making observations, or recording data.
3. Use the materials to design an experiment. The experiment must be a controlled experiment. A **controlled experiment** is one in which all variables are the same except the one being tested (the one factor presumed to be the cause of the effect). The variable being tested is the **independent**

- In preparation for data collection, the dimmer switch (or bulb) in the experimental group would be set to provide light brighter than 15 watts.
- Students should experiment with the dimmer switch and decide on settings to be used during the experiment before beginning.
- The bulbs for each aquarium should be switched on simultaneously.
- Students should count and record the number of bubbles given off by the *Elodea* in each aquarium during two-minute intervals

up to 20 minutes. In order to have more than one trial for each setting, however, it may be necessary to count bubbles for periods of less than 20 minutes.

- At the end of 20 minutes, the dimmer switch should be set to provide greater brightness (or the bulb changed) and the above procedure repeated.
- Students should continue the procedure until the 75-watt level of brightness is tested. If separate bulbs are used, students should allow the bulbs to cool each time.

variable. In a controlled experiment, only this independent variable changes. All the other variables must be kept constant so that you are sure the results you observe are due to changes in the variable being tested. To have a controlled experiment, two groups must be tested. The group in which the independent variable is changed, or manipulated, is known as the **experimental group;** the group in which all the variables remain constant, including the independent variable, is known as the **control group.**

4. Make sure that your experiment tests only one variable at a time. All factors, in both control and experimental groups, must be treated exactly alike except for the independent variable. In this experiment, the independent variable will be the amount of light. The amount of water, number of plants, temperature, and location of aquaria will remain constant.

5. Allow for the collection of quantitative data (data that use numbers in reporting results). For example, you may need to count bubbles given off by a plant in a given period of time. In this experiment, the number of bubbles given off is the dependent variable. The **dependent variable** is any change that results from the manipulation of the independent varible. You could count the bubbles given off every two minutes, for example. Create a table for recording data. A data table in your experiment might

list the numbers of bubbles given off by plants in each aquaria every two minutes.

6. Discuss the following points with your group. If necessary, change your experiment to meet these criteria.
   (a) What is your control group?
   (b) Which independent variable will you manipulate?
   (c) What variables need to be controlled?
   (d) What data will you collect and how will you measure them?
   (e) How will you record your data?
   (f) How many trials will you carry out? Why?

7. Write specific numbered directions for your experiment.

8. Conduct your experiment.

Data and Observations

During the experiment, observe what happens as a result of changes you made in the independent variable. Write down in the data table what you have observed. As you complete each trial of the experiment, record the data. In this experiment, you might record the number of bubbles produced by a plant in the aquaria every two minutes up to 20 minutes.

Analysis and Conclusions

At the end of the experiment, study the data collected

in the data table for analysis and make some conclusions based on your results. The analysis may include answering questions such as these:

1. How did you determine your control group?
2. How did you determine your experimental group?
3. What variable did you test?
4. What variables did you keep the same in all groups?
5. Do your data support or reject your hypothesis? How?
6. Do your experimental results verify the hypothesis? Why?

Going Further

After you have analyzed your data and reached some conclusions, you may want to design another experiment that would answer another problem. Or you may want to revise your hypothesis or change the variable being tested to make sure that you have reached the correct conclusion.

Teaching Strategies
- Ask each group to let you know when they have completed their experimental design and are ready to begin. Check the design and make suggestions, if necessary.
- Make certain that the number and size of *Elodea* sprigs is the same in each aquarium.
- Check to see whether students have set up an appropriate table for collecting data.
- Caution students who will be counting bubbles to pay close attention during each trial.
- Because this is the first opportunity for students to set up an experiment on their own, you might want to ask them to explain their reasoning and to identify their control and experimental groups and the independent and dependent variables.

Data and Observations
The only data to be collected are the number of bubbles given off during each time interval. These data are to be recorded in appropriate tables. If several trials are used for each level of brightness, data for the trials should be averaged and recorded in the data table.

Data Analysis
Students should have observed an increase in the number of bubbles given off with each increase in brightness. The data support the hypothesis that an increase in the brightness of light causes an increase in the rate of photosynthesis.

✔ Assessment
Skill: Have students write a discussion of controlled experimentation and the need for it. Then have them apply their understanding by explaining how they would set up a controlled experiment to test a hypothesis of their own choosing. This work should be included in their portfolios.

Extensions
Have students design and/or carry out an experiment to test the influence of another factor on the rate of photosynthesis such as temperature or amount of carbon dioxide available.

SECTION 2.1

Audiovisual

Interpreting Data: Testing a Hypothesis, a film available from Journal Films, demonstrates how to make observations, collect and interpret data, and make graphs.

Using the Illustration

Emphasize that each kind of graph illustrates data in a particular way. Some graphs are more useful for illustrating data than others. Have students discuss the differences between the kinds of graphs. LEP

Reinforcement

Prepare three sets of data. Each set of data should best be used with one of the types of graph discussed. Have students construct graphs using the data. You may wish to have students work alone or in small groups for guided practice. L1 COOP LEARN

Enrichment

Have students bring in graphs that they have cut from newspapers or magazines. Have them analyze why the particular kinds of graphs were chosen over other types. Then have them analyze the information on the graphs. L1

Concept Development

Point out to students that the results of an experiment often lead to more questions. Such questions lead to further observations, hypotheses, and experiments. Emphasize that unlike most other fields, the work of science is never completely finished.

After the Experiment

Now that you have completed the experiment, it's time to study your data. Having conducted several trials for each group, you decide to average the data for each group. You can then analyze your data and determine what they tell you.

Analyzing Your Data   In your experiment, you might find that the plants exposed constantly to a 15-watt bulb give off almost the same number of bubbles during each two-minute interval. However, the plants exposed to brighter and brighter light give off differing amounts of bubbles during each two-minute interval as the brightness is increased. The data seem to show a relationship between the brightness of light and the rate of oxygen produced. To be sure, you want to make a visual picture of the data. How can you produce this picture?

Scientists use several ways to show data, including line graphs, bar graphs, and pie charts. Line graphs plot data on an *x*-axis and a *y*-axis and show the relationship between independent and dependent variables. In this experiment, what is the independent variable? What is the dependent variable? In a line graph, the data for the independent variables are always plotted on the horizontal or *x*-axis. Data for the dependent variables are plotted on the *y*-axis. Data points show where information about the two variables meet. Bar graphs use bars instead of data points to plot the data and are a good way to show comparisons among groups when data are not dependent on one another. Pie charts or pie graphs show what percentage, out of 100 percent, a specific piece of information represents. Look at the graphs in Figure 2-5. Which one tells you what percent of Earth's water supply is found in glaciers? Which one tells you that males and females differ in the amount of calories used while engaged in the same activities. Samples of line, bar, and pie graphs are shown in Figure 2-5. For more information on graphs, turn to the **Skill Handbook.**

Figure 2-5   **Different kinds of data can be shown graphically in line graphs, bar graphs, and pie graphs.**

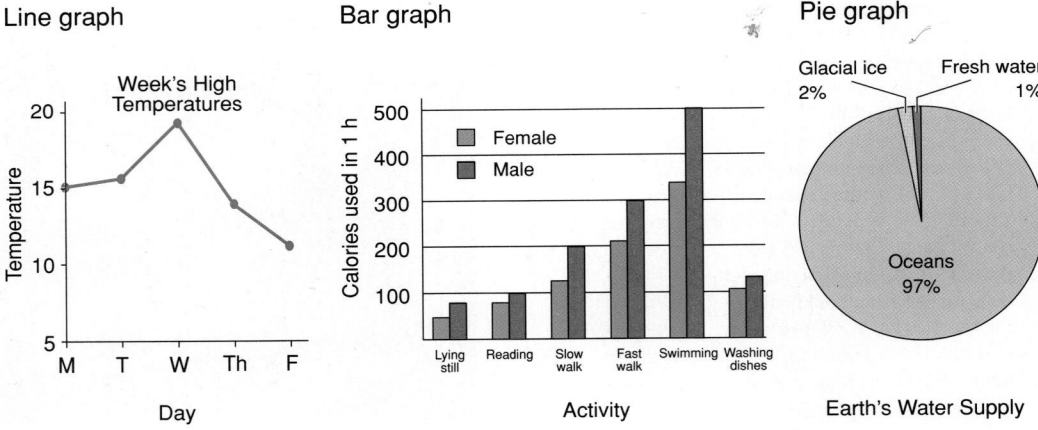

Line graph

Bar graph

Pie graph

PORTFOLIO

Ask students to bring an article from a magazine or newspaper that contains a graph and reports some scientific findings. Have them identify the type of graph used and state why this graph is best to explain the findings reported. They should include the article, graph, and their analyses in their portfolios. L1

You decide that a line graph is the best way to show your data. Your line graph shows the average total number of bubbles given off during the entire 20-minute period for each brightness setting. The data, it seems, support your explanation.

Interpreting a Graph   Figure 2-6 shows a line graph representing data gathered from an experiment similar to yours. Notice what happens to the rate of oxygen production in the experimental group. As you follow the lines you should notice that the number of bubbles given off is greater at the higher brightness settings. This starts you thinking about other matters. Is there a maximum brightness of light above which no further increase in rate of photosynthesis occurs? Maybe other variables interact with light to influence rate of photosynthesis. Could temperature play a role? How about amount of carbon dioxide available to plants? These kinds of questions could lead you to search for new observations, new explanations, and new experiments to test those explanations. These are the kinds of activities that scientists do all the time. Rarely does a single experiment satisfy their curiosity.

Sometimes, even though an explanation seems logical and reasonable, an experiment yields data that show the explanation to be incorrect. In such a case, the explanation must be revised and sometimes even discarded entirely. If the explanation is changed or a new one proposed, a new experiment must, of course, be carried out to test it.

Figure 2-6   This graph shows the number of bubbles given off over a 10-minute period. Compare this graph to the graph made at the end of the Investigation. Are they similar? Can you explain why?

Different Viewpoints in Biology

Interpreting Data
Biologists often disagree about how to interpret data. Usually the differences are the result of whether the biologists accept data as the result of causes and effects. As an example, statistics show that crimes increase during the time of a full moon. Some scientists consider this evidence that the full moon causes people to become more violent and commit more crimes. Other scientists see no cause-and-effect relationship and suggest that the additional moonlight may just make it easier for criminals to see and get around at night.

Figure Caption Question
This graph shows the number of bubbles given off over a 10-minute period. Compare this graph to the graph made at the end of the Investigation. Are they similar? Can you explain why? Both graphs show that more bubbles are given off as light intensity increases.

Thinking Lab
ANALYZE THE PROCEDURE

How can you test dog food commercial claims?

Background
You are going to test dog food commercial claims with a litter of three male and two female puppies. Five weeks after they are weaned, you start your test.

You Try It
Puppies are fed only "Puppy Chow Wow" for the next four weeks. The table shows your collected data. You conclude the following after four weeks: "Puppy Chow Wow" gives your puppies shiny coats, good health,

and good mass gain. The commercial's claims are correct. **Analyze the procedure** and describe any errors that you believe were made. How might the procedure be changed in the future if redoing this experiment?

Week	Average Mass Gain	General Appearance
1	25 g	frisky
2	38 g	healthy
3	49 g	shiny coats
4	52 g	very frisky

Thinking Lab
INTERPRET THE DATA

Purpose
Students are exposed to an experimental setup in which no control is used.

Skills
observe and infer, recognize cause and effect, interpret data

Teaching Strategies
• It should be emphasized that the experiment, whether it relies on quantitative

or qualitative data, is lacking in the ability to compare the puppy chow to a control group.

Answers
Students' answers will vary. Most students will recognize the lack of a control group for comparison. Students may suggest establishing specific criteria for judging dog appearance as well as the need for a

control group of dogs being fed some other food brand.

✔ **Assessment**
Performance: Have one group of students write a script for a short play that shows the results of this lab. Have a different group of students perform the play. By their actions, others should be able to identify researchers, dogs, and pet food company executives.

Reinforcement

Have students imagine that they are professional scientists in the fields of their choice. Ask them to write a one-page paper that explains whether they use controlled experimentation or comparisons in their research, or both. Their papers should give some indication of the kinds of work they do. **L1**

Enrichment

Have a behavioral scientist from a university visit your class to discuss how he or she uses both categories of research.

Figure 2-7 Scientists often use collections such as this to help them identify organisms found in the field.

Research Without Experimentation

Performing an experiment to test an explanation is one type of research, but not all research lends itself to controlled experimentation. Often, scientists carry out their work by making comparisons. For example, a scientist who finds a bone of an extinct animal may make certain conclusions about that animal by comparing its bone to bones of animals that are currently alive. Many important conclusions about evolution are made on the basis of this type of research rather than controlled experiments in a laboratory. Naturalists are biologists who conduct research by making observations in nature. Naturalists often collect data "in the field"—that is, they collect organisms, observe behavior, and identify organisms as part of their research. Field work, such as collecting and identifying insects, is another type of research that does not involve experimentation. Such research, though, does involve other important elements of the process of science, including careful observation and sound reasoning.

GLOBAL CONNECTION

Purpose
In this essay about the 1991 discovery of a human frozen for more than 5000 years, students glimpse how anthropologists piece together clues to understand the past. The explanation ties in to the discussion of research without experimentation on this page.

Teaching Strategies
Have students describe what they think it would have been like to live 5000 years ago. Ask how they came to have these beliefs. Point out that this essay explains how scientists research the past.

Possible Answers
1. The age was determined by radioactive carbon dating.
2. To identify the closest living descendants, scientists would complete DNA sequencing studies on the mummy and living humans.

Going Further
Students may find out more information about this topic by researching news magazines such as *National Geographic* and *Natural History*.

GLOBAL CONNECTION

The Iceman Unfreezes History

Do you think scientists and anthropologists have learned everything there is to know about the past? It's easy to feel that way because there is so much information. But every so often, something happens to remind us that the past is still a mystery.

Discovery of the Iceman In September 1991, a hiker in the Alps along the border between Austria and Italy found the body of a man who had been frozen in a glacier for 5300 years. That discovery is changing some ideas about the Stone Age. The Iceman, as he is called, is the oldest human found with his brain and organs still inside. Scientists think that his body was frozen by wind and cold and then enclosed in ice, which preserved him for 53 centuries. Although some of his clothing and tools were lost or damaged as he was cut from the glacier, enough remained to give anthropologists some new ideas about how humans lived in the late Stone Age.

Ideas About Stone Age Changed Stone Age people had been thought to wear crude skin clothing, but the Iceman was dressed in leather shoes and a robe made of pieces of different animal skins sewn together in a mosaic-like pattern. The skill required to make such a robe has led anthropologists to think that the Iceman did not make the robe himself, but rather that he may have been part of a community in which people did different kinds of work.

Other things about the Iceman have also changed ideas about the Stone Age. Although no hair remained on his skull, hairs about 9 cm long found on his clothes indicate that humans were cutting their hair as early as 5300 years ago. The Iceman had tattoos on his lower spine, behind a knee, and on an ankle. Tattoos had been thought to originate about 2500 years after the Iceman lived. He also carried, strung on a leather cord, two mushrooms that are known to help fight infections. Anthropologists think they may be part of the oldest known first-aid kit.

Anthropologists are also fascinated by a fur quiver that held arrows, two of which had flint points and feathers attached by a resin-like glue. The feathers are set

40 🐾 BIOLOGY AS A SCIENCE

MEETING INDIVIDUAL NEEDS

Visually Impaired: To help students who are visually impaired understand how they could become scientists, bring in recordings of bird songs that are used to identify species. Have all the students close their eyes to listen, then ask if they are able to distinguish between several related species by hearing alone. Visually impaired students may find that they are more attuned to noticing slight differences in sounds and thus have a greater facility for identifying birds by song.

Reporting on Research

Scientists publish the results of their work in scientific journals to be shared with other scientists around the world. Most of what is published does not include final answers to a question. Numerous articles, for example, have come out about various aspects of research centering on AIDS. To be acceptable and useful to other scientists, a description of an experiment and its results must be reproducible; that is, the same experiment should always yield the same results, wherever and whenever it is conducted. Scientists must be able to rely upon the work of other scientists in their field. They learn from others' work as they carry out their own research. Thus, integrity is of the utmost importance to the scientific community. Scientists must make every effort to carry out their work thoroughly and carefully and to report their results accurately and honestly.

Reporting on research often leads to a flurry of related research. An example was the discovery of penicillin. Penicillin is a chemical produced naturally by a mold. Other scientists, upon learning of the discovery of penicillin, began a search for other molds that produce similar drugs. Scientific knowledge builds upon the foundations of previous findings. An important discovery provides a basis for and stimulates further work.

at an angle that would help keep the arrow on a straight course. Anthropologists now suspect that Stone Age hunters knew quite a bit about the principles of flight. In addition to the quiver, which anthropologists had not known to exist this early, the Iceman carried a rucksack with a U-shaped wooden frame, not unlike a backpack, and a leather pouch that resembles the "fanny packs" worn today.

As scientists and anthropologists study the Iceman's internal organs and analyze his DNA, they hope to learn more about his diet and his immune system. They are also trying to piece together the story of how he died. The discovery of the 5300-year-old Iceman may be rewriting prehistory.

1. **Explore Further:** How were scientists able to determine the Iceman's age?
2. **Connection to Genetics:** Scientists think they may be able to identify the closest living descendants of the Iceman. How might this be possible?

How Laws are Made:
Have students discuss the differences between how a law is arrived at in society and in science. Ask students if it is easier to break a societal law or a scientific law. Have them give their reasons.

Figure Caption Question

What is the difference between a theory and a law? A law is a statement of events that always occur in nature; a theory is an explanation of the law.

3 Assess

Check for Understanding

Have students outline the section and give a brief summary of the major headings in the outline. Make sure they have included information on the scientific method.

Reteach

Have students cut articles reporting science findings from newspapers or magazines and bring them to class. Working in pairs, have students analyze the articles for scientific methods. If necessary, provide a list of the methods on the chalkboard.

COOP LEARN

Laws and Theories

It is not at all unusual for scientists in different labs to be working on the same basic research. It is important for you to realize they often interpret data and test explanations in different ways, and it is not unusual for them to come up with different explanations for those data. Explanations and hypotheses are not carved in stone and are always subject to further revision. It is always possible, and, in fact, often the case, that new data or novel ways of interpreting data will cause revision of an existing explanation. No explanation in science is final. Rather, you should think of science as an ongoing process in which knowledge of the world is constantly refined and improved. For these reasons, scientists shy away from using the word *proof,* which suggests something final or without other possible explanation. You may use the word *proof* in mathematics, but it really has no place in science.

Development of Theories Many hypotheses, although subject to revision, have held up well over long periods of time. Such hypotheses, usually major ones, that have stood the test of time are known as **theories.** Major theories are ones that are the guiding principles of science. In biology, for example, Charles Darwin's explanation of how evolution occurs through natural selection is known as a theory because it guides scientists in their understanding of how change in organisms occurs. Common usage of the word *theory* suggests a guess or an uncertainty, such as, "This is only a theory, but..." The opposite meaning is true in science. A theory is as close to a complete explanation as science can offer. However, like a hypothesis, a theory is always subject to revision.

Figure 2-8 Charles Darwin, left, developed the theory of natural selection to explain how evolution occurred. Sir Isaac Newton, right, discovered the law of universal gravitation. What is the difference between a theory and a law?

Charles Darwin

Theory of Evolution

Sir Isaac Newton

Law of Gravity

Statements of Natural Events Hypotheses and theories are explanations of observations. On the other hand, **laws** are statements about events that always occur in nature. You know, for example, that gravity will always cause an object that rolls off a window ledge to fall to the ground below. This observation and others like it about falling objects can be stated as the law of gravitation. The statement or law does not explain *why* the object falls to the ground below. It merely says that it does. Scientists use theories to explain the law.

PORTFOLIO

Sailors of the 14th century believed that Earth was flat. Portuguese navigators, however, believed it to be round. Ask students to imagine they are sailors on a ship with a Portuguese navigator. Have them write in their portfolios imaginary diary entries including an explanation for their belief that Earth is flat. Now have them write an explanation for the navigator's belief that Earth is round. Ask them if these explanations are theories or laws. They are theories. Now ask them to write in their diaries how they would test each explanation. Ask students how we know which theory comes closest to reality.

What Science Cannot Do

A hallmark of the process of science is developing ideas that can be tested. The test results may show that the explanation is partly or totally incorrect.

Limits to Science   An explanation that is not testable poses a limit on science, at least until a means of testing becomes possible. Sometimes testing requires the development of new equipment or procedures. For example, relatively little was known about the structure and functions of cells until the electron microscope was invented and better means of chemically analyzing cell parts were discovered.

Science and Morality   Some ideas are not scientifically testable at all. The process of science cannot test and determine, for example, what is morally or socially correct or incorrect. Morality and human behavior are important issues, but decisions about those issues cannot be made by science. For example, science has produced a great understanding of how the genetic code works, and it is now possible to introduce new bits of genetic information into an organism. However, science cannot determine whether that knowledge should be used to create races of "superhumans." Similarly, science can gather information about and predict consequences of destroying a rain forest, but it cannot make the decision whether or not to do so. Science can provide information to people about the natural world. It is up to the people to decide how to make use of that information.

Figure 2-9   **Observations by scientists show that clear-cutting tropical rain forests leads to soil erosion. What people choose to do with this information may be a political or moral issue, not a scientific one.**

Section Review

Understanding Concepts

1. Why is the word *process* used in defining science?
2. You notice moths resting on dark tree trunks. There seem to be more dark-colored moths than light-colored ones. You also notice that birds sweep down and feed on the moths. Suggest an explanation for the observation that there are more dark-colored than light-colored moths.

3. Can you think of another equally possible explanation for the observations described in question 2?
4. ***Skill Review—Designing an Experiment:*** How might you design an experiment to test the hypothesis that young seedlings need light in order to develop normally? Assume you have whatever equipment you think you need. For more help, see Practicing Scientific Methods in the **Skill Handbook**.

5. ***Thinking Critically:*** You observe that bees seem to visit only bright-colored flowers in a garden, ignoring white ones. What might be the cause of the bees' behavior pattern?

Extension

Ask students to propose a problem for a science fair project. Have them prepare a time line that will allow them to include scientific methods, including reporting their findings. The time line should end in time to enter the proposal in the local science fair.

✔ Assessment

Skill: Assess the observational skills of students by providing each with a different common object such as a tube of toothpaste, a twig, or a flower and having them write 20 observations about the object and five hypotheses that could be investigated using scientific methods. L1

4 Close

Analogy

Working in groups of three or four, have students think of an analogy for scientific methods. They could use any decision-making process for this analogy, such as choosing among several options when buying a car. The group should use butcher paper and markers to illustrate the analogy and present it to the class. Students should report how the analogy is similar and how it is different from the methods used by scientists.
COOP LEARN

Answers to Section Review

1. Science is a procedure, a way of doing things, that leads to knowledge about nature.
2. The dark-colored moths might be better camouflaged against the tree trunks.
3. The light-colored moths may taste better to the birds.
4. **Skill Review—Designing an Experiment:** A controlled experiment can be set up in which all factors are the same except for amount of light. The control group consists of seeds that will be planted in soil, watered, and placed in sunlight. Seeds in the experimental group will be planted and watered, but will not be exposed to light.
5. **Thinking Critically:** It can be assumed that the bees are attracted by the bright colors.

Prepare

Key Concepts

Types of microscopes are compared and contrasted in this section. Students practice using the International System of Measurement.

Key Terms

resolving power, transmission electron microscope (TEM), scanning electron microscope (SEM), International System of Measurement (SI)

Materials

- Gather metersticks, yardsticks, and calculators for students to use in the Minilab.

1 Focus

Objectives

The objectives are listed on the student page. Remind students to preview these objectives as a guide to this numbered section.

Activity

Before students arrive in the classroom, put five small dots close together on the chalkboard. The dots should be so close together that from the back of the classroom they appear to be a single, small dot. Once students are seated, ask them how many dots are on the chalkboard. Have them get closer until they can resolve the separate dots. Point out that resolution is more important to scientists than magnification. **L1**

Objectives

Compare and contrast the compound light microscope, the transmission electron microscope, and the scanning electron microscope.

Measure objects using the International System of Measurement.

Figure 2-10 The compound light microscope allows light to pass through an object and through two or more lenses that enlarge the image.

Eyepiece

Objectives

Stage

Light source

Base

2.2 Tools of the Trade

Observation, as you have learned, is a key element in the methods of science. Many observations can be made directly as a scientist uses his or her senses of sight, smell, taste, touch, and hearing. Modern scientists often extend the limits of their own senses by using equipment such as telescopes to view the sky or tracking and recording instruments that detect sounds of animals. Because biology often calls for a study of extremely small objects, such as a tiny organism or certain parts of a cell, observations often require the use of microscopes.

Functions of a Microscope

One reason biologists use a microscope is to magnify a very small object that cannot be readily studied using the naked eye. Only by using a microscope, for example, can the thousands of cells that compose even a thin leaf be seen.

Resolving Power   Suppose you were examining a leaf using a microscope and you focused on an individual cell. Within that cell are many smaller parts. Many of those parts are very close to one another. Depending on the distance between the parts and the type of microscope you are using, you may or may not be able to distinguish among the parts. They might look like one object. Have you ever walked along abandoned railroad tracks? As you look off into the distance, you can distinguish the two rails of the tracks as being separate. Your eyes can distinguish them as being distinct objects. Looking as far as you can see, though, you may no longer be able to tell the two tracks apart. In the distance, they appear as one. Just as you have the ability to distinguish two objects as being separate, the microscope can also distinguish between two objects. The ability of a microscope to distinguish two objects as being separate is known as its **resolving power.**

The Compound Light Microscope   In your biology course, you will use a compound light microscope. Such a microscope uses glass lenses that focus light passing through an object. These microscopes can magnify up to about 2000 times and have a resolving power of about 500 nanometers (nm). A nanometer is a unit of measure that will be discussed shortly. Two objects closer together than 500 nm will be seen as one object when viewed with a light microscope.

ALTERNATE LAB: Using the Light Microscope

Purpose

Students will become familiar with the parts of the compound light microscope, learn how to prepare a wet mount, and observe how the image is reversed.

Materials

microscope, colored threads, scissors, forceps, eyedropper, water, coverslips

Procedure

Give the following directions to students.
1. Uncover your microscopes. Watch as your teacher points to and names each part of the microscope and goes over rules for using the microscope.
2. Collect the materials you and a partner will need for preparing a wet mount. Prepare a wet mount of a thread by cutting a small piece of colored thread,

placing it in one drop of water, and covering with a coverslip. Observe the wet mount using first low and then high power.
3. Move the slide back and forth and right and left to observe how the image in a microscope moves.
4. Make a second wet mount by placing three different colors of thread over one another. Observe under low and

Electron Microscopes

For greater magnification and resolving power biologists rely on electron microscopes. Such microscopes typically magnify hundreds of thousands of times and have a resolving power as great as 0.2 nm. Thus, they provide much greater detail and enable biologists to study inner and outer structures of even the smallest cells. As the name suggests, an electron microscope utilizes a beam of electrons, rather than light, to illuminate the object being viewed.

The Transmission Electron Microscope In order to view parts of very small structures, biologists use the **transmission electron microscope (TEM).** The sample to be studied is frozen or embedded in plastic and then sliced into very thin sections. Thus, living specimens cannot be viewed. The electrons are focused by magnets instead of glass lenses. The electrons form an image that can be photographed or seen on a screen. The TEM has played an important role in the study of cell parts. It reveals details that aid in understanding how those parts function.

The Scanning Electron Microscope Another kind of electron microscope permits a view of surfaces not possible with the TEM. This microscope, called a **scanning electron microscope (SEM),** has a lower magnification but produces a three-dimensional image. This is possible because the beam of electrons does not pass through the object. Rather, it sweeps across it and bounces off. As it does so, it causes electrons to be knocked loose from the object. These electrons produce patterns seen as an image on a television-like screen. Knowledge of the surfaces of cells, for example, is important in studying cancer. Interactions of cells with one another and with chemicals can also be studied using the SEM.

Figure 2-11 **Can you tell which photograph came from a TEM and which came from an SEM? The same organism, *Amyloodinium*, is shown as photographed by a TEM (a) and by an SEM (b). Magnifications: 3900× (a); 4200× (b)**

a

b

2 Teach

Display

Make a bulletin board display using photomicrographs from magazines, newspapers, and other sources. Identify the type of microscope responsible for each image. **LEP**

Misconception

Students will probably think that magnification is more important than resolution for a microscope. Point out that microscopists are interested in the details of the object being viewed. Magnification does not increase the detail; resolution does.

Chalkboard Example

Use the chalkboard to make diagrams of the different kinds of microscopes. Label the glass lenses of compound light microscopes and magnetic lenses of electron microscopes. **LEP**

Concept Development

Scanning electron microscopes can make three-dimensional images of living material. However, the electron bombardment does kill the cells or organisms if not done quickly.

Audiovisual

Show *The Microscope, An Indispensable Instrument,* a film available from Chevron Corporation. The film shows sophisticated microscopes at work, including electron microscopes and X-ray microscopes. **LEP**

---

high power. Use the fine focus knob to focus on each thread.

5. Replace the cover and clean microscope lenses using tissue paper or lens paper.

Analysis

Ask students to answer the following questions.

1. How do you prepare a wet mount? *By placing a specimen in a drop of water on a microscope slide and*

covering with a coverslip.

2. Why could you not keep all three threads in clear focus at the same time on high power? *The plane of focus is too shallow.*

3. Draw the slide as it appeared in the microscope.

4. Draw and label the parts of the microscope you used.

✔ **Assessment**

Skill: Place a prepared slide of the letter "e" on the stage of a microscope. Have the student focus first on low power and then on high power using correct procedures. Repeat this procedure for every student. Students who fail to master this skill should receive additional attention. **L1**

Size of Electrons Compared to Light: Resolution of a microscope is dependent upon the wavelength that is able to go between two objects. As the wavelength of light is much larger than the wavelength of an electron, transmission electron microscopes have a greater resolution.

Science, Technology, and Society

Microscope Detects Atoms: A new kind of microscope, the scanning tunneling electron microscope or STEM, has a resolution so small that it can detect individual atoms in a molecule.

Using the Table

Use Table 2.1 to give students practice with using the prefixes with liters, grams, and seconds. **LEP**

Audiovisual

A Metric America from Media Incorporated has an emphasis on prefixes. To illustrate reasons for switching to the metric system, you might also show the film *Metres, Litres, and Grams* from General Motors Corporation. **LEP**

Demonstration

You can demonstrate the use of SI by measuring different amounts of materials for students to see. As an example, cut a millimeter piece of ribbon and a meter piece of ribbon. Then set up graduated cylinders with a milliliter of colored water, or a beaker with a liter of colored water. Make a gram pile of salt and a kilogram pile. **LEP**

The International System of Measurement

You just learned that resolving power of microscopes is measured in terms of units called nanometers. You've probably never heard of such a unit. What does it represent and where does it come from?

Recall that scientists publish articles in journals to report on their research. Imagine the difficulty they would have interpreting the data if several different systems of measurement were used. For example, suppose a scientist in New York reported using 25 ounces of a chemical to do an experiment. A scientist in Germany would have to accurately convert the number of ounces to grams before being able to repeat the experiment. Errors could easily be made. To prevent errors and confusion, scientists worldwide use a universal language of measurements and its symbols. Those measurements and symbols are known as the **International System of Measurement,** or **SI** (from the French title, Système Internationale d'Unités). SI is a modern form of the older metric system and is now used in most countries. One major advantage of SI is that it is a decimal system. It is based on tens, multiples of tens, and fractions of tens. Because it is a decimal system, it is much easier (and more logical) to use than the English system. Although the names of the units used to measure length, mass, volume, and time differ, the decimal system applies to all of them.

Use of Prefixes

In the SI, fractions and multiples of tens are expressed by the use of prefixes. Consider, for example, measurements of length.

Measuring Length   The unit of length with which you may be familiar is the meter (m). One meter is slightly longer than a yard. In any fraction or multiple of the meter, the name of the unit—meter—remains. Consider fractions of meters. One meter is equal to ten *deci*meters, or, to put it another way, there are ten decimeters in a meter. A hundredth of a meter is a *centi*meter (cm), and a thousandth of a meter is a *milli*meter (mm). Length of cells or parts of cells are much smaller than any of these units.

Table 2.1   **P**refixes in SI

kilo	thousand	kilometer
deka	ten	dekameter
deci	tenth	decimeter
centi	hundredth	centimeter
milli	thousandth	millimeter
micro	millionth	micrometer
nano	billionth	nanometer

Have students create a book for children that shows uses for SI, illustrates the prefixes, and tells about the different units of length, mass, and volume. **L1**

Teacher Classroom Resources
Study Guide, pp. 10-12 **L1**
Probing Levels of Life, Labs 3, 4, pp. 6, 11 **L2**
Investigating Living Systems, Labs 2, 3, 5, pp. 5, 9, 17 **L2**
Color Transparency #1 **L1** **LEP**

Such objects are often measured in *micro*meters (µm) or *nano*meters (nm). One meter contains a million micrometers and a billion nanometers. Prefixes are also used to express multiples of meters. A *deka*meter is equal to ten meters, and a *kilo*meter equals a thousand meters. You can see these prefixes and their meanings in Table 2.1. Information about SI can be found in Appendix G.

Measuring Mass, Volume, and Time These same prefixes are used in measurements of mass, liquid volume, and time. For example, in SI, mass is measured in units called grams (g). Mass is the amount of material of which something is composed. For example, a nickel has a mass of about 5 grams. One milligram (mg) represents 0.001 grams, just as one millimeter equals 0.001 meters. The unit of measurement for liquid volume, for example the amount of cola in a clear plastic bottle, is measured in a unit called the liter (L). Many soft drinks are sold in two-liter bottles. What part of a liter is a centiliter? Time is measured in seconds. What does a nanosecond mean?

Because of the decimal basis of the metric system, the same value can be expressed in different units. One centimeter could also be written as one-hundredth of a meter (0.01 m), ten millimeters (10 mm), or even one-hundred-thousandth of a kilometer (0.000 01 km).

Figure 2-12 Using this photograph, figure out the volume of the object by water displacement. Use milliliters in your answer. Would it be easier, harder, or the same to figure out the volume using a cylinder marked in ounces?

Measuring Area Areas and solid volumes can be calculated using SI measurements. To find the area of a rectangle measuring 5 cm by 3 cm, you multiply its length times its width. This rectangle has an area of 15 cm^2. To find solid volume, you multiply length times width times height. Thus, a bricklike cell measuring 100 micrometers long by 40 micrometers wide by 10 micrometers thick has a volume of 40 000 µm^3.

2.2 TOOLS OF THE TRADE 🐾 **47**

Figure Caption Question

What is the solid volume of this cheese brick in centimeters? In millimeters? Volume is height × width × length, so volume of the cheese brick is 10 cm × 15 cm × 40 cm = 6000 cm^3. In millimeters, it is 100 mm × 150 mm × 400 mm = 6 000 000 mm^3.

3 Assess

Check for Understanding

Conduct a lab practical to see if students understand SI, how to measure, and the use of the prefixes. You can set up stations at which students must perform some measurement using the gram, liter, or meter units. **L1**

Reteach

If you find that students are unable to make the measurements necessary in the lab practical, the concepts may be retaught using peer tutoring. Pair a student who understands the concepts with one who does not. Have pairs complete the lab practical together after reteaching. **COOP LEARN**

Extension

Have students create a poster that summarizes their understandings of the SI measurement system. **L2**

✔ Assessment

Skill: Have students measure the volume of the room in cubic meters and then figure out how many liters of water the room could hold if it were a swimming pool. **L1**

4 Close

Activity

Remove photomicrographs from the bulletin board display suggested on page 45. Pass the photomicrographs to pairs of students. Ask the students to analyze the photomicrographs and discuss the kind of microscopes used, the magnification, and the resolution of each one. **L1** **COOP LEARN**

Figure 2-13 What is the solid volume of this cheese brick in centimeters? In millimeters?

Working with SI A little common sense will go a long way toward making you feel more confident in working with SI. Use logic to check your work. For example, suppose you were asked to convert 5.2 kilometers to meters. Do you divide or multiply? You know that a kilometer is 1000 times the length of a meter, and that a meter is only one-thousandth of a kilometer. If you are converting 5.2 kilometers to meters, it is reasonable that the answer should be a number larger than five because there are many meters in one kilometer. By simple math, you multiply 5.2 times 1000 and reach your answer: 5.2 kilometers equal 5200 meters. Now try another problem. Convert 5200 meters to millimeters. What is your answer? (Multiply 5200 by 1000 = 5 200 000 mm.) You will have opportunities to make use of and improve your skills in SI measurements as you conduct lab work throughout this course. With a little practice, you will find SI an easier system to work with than the English system.

LOOKING AHEAD

SCIENTISTS THROUGHOUT the world use the same methods, tools, and system of measurement to find answers for their questions. As you complete this course, you will use some of the same tools, follow similar methods, and use the same system of measurement to further your own understanding of biology. You will also come to the realization that biology, indeed all fields of science, cannot be studied in isolation. What is learned in one particular field of science is usually related to other areas of science as well. In the next chapter, you will study some basic principles of chemistry. Knowledge of those principles will also add to your understanding of organisms.

Section Review

Understanding Concepts

1. In a book, you see two photographs of the same kind of cell as viewed through two different microscopes. What looks like one solid mass in one photograph is seen as a cluster of dots in the other. Explain the difference.
2. As viewed with an electron microscope, a pollen grain is seen to have a bumpy surface. What kind of electron microscope is probably being used? Explain.
3. The dots seen in one of the photographs mentioned in question 1 are known to measure 2 micrometers across. Express that measurement in terms of nanometers.
4. **Skill Review—Measuring in SI:** Find the sum, in grams, of the following: 816 milligrams + 527 centigrams + 5.1 kilograms. For more help, see Thinking Critically in the **Skill Handbook**.
5. **Thinking Critically:** One mL of water has a mass of 1 g. Suppose a student has a cylinder marked off with mL lines. How can the student determine the mass of an object using such a cylinder?

Answers to Section Review

1. The microscope that enables dots to be seen has greater resolving power.
2. An SEM is being used. Such an electron microscope provides a three-dimensional view of surfaces.
3. 2000 nanometers
4. **Skill Review—Measuring in SI:** 816 mg = 0.816 g; 527 cg = 5.27 g; 5.1 kg = 5100 g. Total = 5106.086 g.
5. **Thinking Critically:** After noting the volume of the water, the student can carefully lower the object into the cylinder. The volume of the water in the cylinder can then be noted. The difference between final volume and initial volume can be calculated in mL. That number equals the mass of the object in grams. The object has displaced that volume of water.

Physics Connection

An Unusual Idea for Testing Global Warming

A greenhouse is a glass building in which plants are grown. The glass lets in sunlight to warm the building and then keeps in the heat, so that the greenhouse stays warmer than the temperature outside. On Earth, sunlight that reaches Earth's surface is radiated back as heat. Some of this heat is absorbed by water and carbon dioxide and trapped in the upper air, where it keeps our atmosphere warm.

A Rise in Temperature Scientists think that more carbon dioxide is being released into the air than can be stored in the oceans and used by plants. As excess carbon dioxide in the air increases, more heat is trapped inside Earth's atmosphere. Some scientists speculate that the result may be a slow rise in the temperature of Earth's surface.

The idea that the temperatures of Earth's air and water are rising is a hypothesis, an idea that some scientists think to be true. In order to test their hypothesis, they have to conduct experiments. Direct measurement of surface warming of Earth is difficult, however, and it could take centuries to detect a valid trend. Recently, an international team of scientists, led by Walter Munk of the United States and Andrew Forbes of Australia, has proposed a

way to measure global warming by sending sound waves through the ocean. Their unusual plan is called the Heard Island Experiment.

The Heard Island Experiment
The speed at which sound travels through water is determined mostly by the temperature of the water; the warmer the water, the faster sound travels. By transmitting sound from one point to another, you can get a measure of the average temperature of the water along the path of the sound. Global ocean warming of only 0.005 degrees Celsius a year would reduce by several tenths of a second the time it takes a sound wave to travel. Munk and Forbes think that monitoring water temperatures of ten paths for about ten years will reveal whether there is a warming trend in the oceans.

The first phase of their experiment took place in January 1991. Munk and Forbes lowered three loudspeakers into the ocean around Heard Island, 1200 kilometers north of the coast of Antarctica. They sent a series of sound transmissions to 19 receiving stations in the Atlantic, Pacific, and Indian Oceans. The purpose of the January 1991 test was to determine whether the signal could be heard by the receivers. Once they determine the

exact signal needed in order to make sensitive temperature measurements, the scientists hope to begin a long-term experiment.

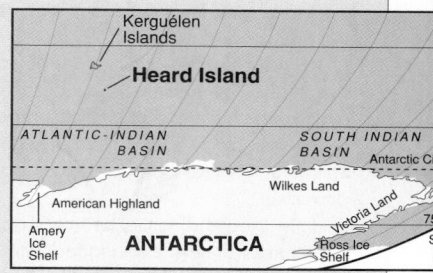

Verifying Global Warming Not all scientists think the experiment will demonstrate global warming. They say that it takes ten years for ocean water to warm to the temperature of the air. Global warming may be verified first by less costly experiments, such as measuring air temperature. They also question the accuracy of the test.

1. **Explore Further:** A buildup of carbon dioxide (CO_2) and other gases in the upper atmosphere may lead to global warming. What are the causes of increased CO_2?
2. **Writing About Biology:** Why do scientists worry about global warming?

CHAPTER 2
BIOLOGY, TECHNOLOGY, AND SOCIETY

Physics Connection

Purpose
Students will learn that scientists are trying to use a technology that allows accurate measurement of the speed of sound in water to determine if global warming is occurring. The measurement system used is SI.

Teaching Strategies
- Ask students why scientists would want to know if Earth is getting warmer. *Even a small increase or decrease in global temperature could cause devastating climatic changes.*
- Ask students why scientists don't directly measure warming of Earth's surface. *It would be difficult and take a very long time to develop a trend.*

Possible Answers
1. Increased carbon dioxide is caused chiefly by burning fossil fuels, a human activity.
2. Scientists worry about global warming because it could have disastrous consequences on farming, climate, and coastal cities, which could be flooded as sea levels rise.

Going Further
Have students brainstorm other indirect ways to measure increasing global temperatures. Increase or decrease in sea levels, increase or decrease in glacial melt, and similar measurements have all been suggested as being as accurate and less costly than measuring the speed of sound in oceans.

CHAPTER 2
CHAPTER REVIEW

Summary

Summary statements can be used by students to review the major concepts of the chapter.

Language of Biology

Answers should go beyond defining the terms. Accept any reasonable answer that uses the term correctly and in the proper context.

Understanding Concepts

1. That information has been learned as a result of science. Science is a process by which knowledge about nature is obtained.
2. The early "scientists" provided an explanation, but did not test that explanation through controlled experimentation. People know today that life comes from life.
3. Fleming might have stated: A chemical produced by *Penicillium* spread to the bacteria and killed them.
4. His hypothesis offered the prediction that the chemical produced by *Penicillium* could, by itself, kill the bacteria, and that the mold did not have to be present.
5. The mold could be grown in a liquid into which it would secrete the presumed chemical. The liquid could then be added to the bacteria, which, if the hypothesis is correct, should die. As a control, some of the same liquid, in which no mold had grown, should be added to some bacteria.
6. Such a hypothesis would be useless because it cannot be tested.
7. What is learned in the course of pure research can often be applied in a practical way. Fleming's discovery led to use of penicillin and spurred searches for other antibiotic drugs.
8. Fleming's explanation is not considered a law. It relates an effect to its cause, whereas laws simply state effects. In addition, the explanation applied to a very specific observation.

Summary

Science is an ongoing process that produces a body of knowledge about the natural world. It is a unique field of study because of the methods by which that knowledge is gained.

The methods used by scientists vary, depending upon the questions they are attempting to answer. However, scientific research centers on careful and thorough observations, reasoning and insight, explanations of observations, and, usually, a means of testing those explanations. There is no specific order in which these activities are carried out. Rather, scientists most often go back and forth among the activities, refining their thinking and conclusions as they do so.

Where possible, scientists test their explanations, or hypotheses, by means of controlled experiments. Such experiments make use of a control group and an experimental group and should have only one variable factor. This experimental design reduces doubt about cause and effect.

If the results of an experiment do not confirm the hypothesis, a new explanation can be devised and tested. Most often, the results of one experiment lead a scientist to other, related experiments.

Results of scientists' research are published in journals where they can help other scientists and spur further work. The integrity of scientists is, therefore, of the utmost importance.

Microscopes are important to the work of many biologists, extending the limits of the observations they may make. Microscopes vary in terms of both magnification and resolving power. Use of SI to express numerical data provides a universal language of numbers and measurements understandable by scientists around the world.

Language of Biology

Write a sentence that shows your understanding of each of the following terms.

control group	law
controlled experiment	resolving power
data	scanning electron
dependent variable	microscope (SEM)
experiment	science
experimental group	technology
hypothesis	theory
independent variable	transmission electron
International System	microscope (TEM)
of Measurement (SI)	

Understanding Concepts

1. One of the things you will learn this year is how blood circulates through your body. Is such information "science"? Explain.
2. Some early "scientists" concluded that eels arise from mud at the bottom of the ocean. They came to that conclusion because, like the ocean bottom, eels are slimy. That conclusion was accepted as a true explanation of the production of eels. What methods of science were missing in reaching that conclusion? What knowledge do you possess today that would lead you to reject such a conclusion?
3. Alexander Fleming's discovery of penicillin came from an unexpected observation. He noted that bacteria growing in lab glassware died when that glassware was contaminated by a mold called *Penicillium*. He reasoned that a chemical produced by the mold spread out and destroyed the bacteria. Fleming then reasoned that the chemical alone, without the mold being present, should also kill the bacteria. He assumed he could obtain the chemical by growing the mold in a liquid medium. What formal hypothesis might Fleming have stated?

9. In science, experiments must be reproducible. If a scientist is not careful, the results will not be reproducible.
10. Use of a TEM necessitates killing of cells being observed.

4. What prediction did Fleming offer based on his hypothesis?
5. Based on the information given in question 3 above, how would you test Fleming's hypothesis? What would your control be?
6. Suppose Fleming had explained his observations by stating that the mold sent out evil spirits that caused the death of bacteria. Why would such an explanation be useless?
7. Fleming did not set out to find substances that kill bacteria, but his experiments showed that such substances exist. How do his findings show the relationship between science and technology?
8. Was Fleming's explanation a law? Explain.
9. Suppose a scientist hurried through his research and was not careful in reporting and analyzing his data and conclusions in a paper. Why would that be a problem?
10. Why can't scientists use a TEM to study the details of how cells reproduce?

Applying Concepts

11. A student wishes to test the hypothesis that plants grow fuller if a certain mineral is added to their soil. The student uses two groups of plants, cacti and geraniums. The cacti, since they are desert plants, are given little water and are grown in a hot environment. The geraniums are given more water and are grown in a cooler environment. The mineral is added only to the soil in which the geraniums are growing. Is the student conducting this experiment properly? Explain.
12. How would you conduct the experiment in question 11 above?
13. You look through a light microscope and observe some microorganisms. The diameter of your field of vision is 1500 μm and you estimate that 50 of the organisms could fit across that diameter. How big is a single organism?
14. Express your answer to question 13 in terms of nanometers.
15. A student records the following data for the height, in centimeters, of certain kinds of plants growing in a field: 42.6, 39.4, 37.9, 44.0, 35.6, 41.7, and 40.1. What is the average height of these plants expressed in meters?

16. Convert the following: (a) 818 grams to kilograms; (b) 6.26 liters to centiliters; (c) 121 640 millimeters to meters; (d) 316 seconds to milliseconds.
17. **Global Connection:** Why do anthropologists want to know what kind of community the Iceman lived in? How do his robe, quiver, and tattoos give cultural anthropologists ideas about the social development of his community?
18. **Physics Connection:** Why do the researchers in the Heard Island Experiment need to record data on water temperature for 10 years?

Lab Interpretation

19. **Investigation:** Suppose your experiment with the rate of photosynthesis shows no difference in number of bubbles when plants are exposed to different amounts of light. Would you throw your data out and try the experiment again, or would you revise your hypothesis and test it through experimentation? Explain your answer.
20. **Thinking Lab:** Explain why it might have been better to use either male or female puppies in your study of puppy food.
21. **Minilab 1:** Suppose you were given an animal such as a turtle to observe as the "object." What observations could you make about the turtle, besides describing its outside appearance, if you didn't want to dissect it?

Connecting Ideas

22. Suppose an experiment was designed that interfered with the ability of a certain part of an organism to carry out cellular respiration. Results of the experiment show that the part can no longer carry out its normal function. Why?
23. How might you carry out an experiment to test the idea that the presence of large numbers of zebra mussels might lead to a decrease in the number of other consumers in the kinds of communities in which zebra mussels live?

23. **Systems and Interactions:** A body of water recently invaded by zebra mussels could be chosen as a site for study. Sampling could be done to ascertain the numbers of other consumers in the area. As time goes on and the size of the mussel population increases, the water could be sampled again and the numbers of other consumers determined.

PROGRAM RESOURCES

Teacher Classroom Resources
Chapter Assessment, pp. 5-8 L1
Performance Assessment in Biology, p. 4 L2
Alternate Assessment in the Science Classroom
Computer Test Bank L1

CHAPTER 2

Applying Concepts

11. The test is not a controlled experiment. It consists of numerous variables.
12. Students' answers should reflect their comprehension of controlled experimentation. The experiment should consist of a control group and an experimental group in which all factors are identical except for the one being tested, the independent variable. In this case, that factor is the mineral.
13. Each organism is 30 μm long.
14. 30 000 nm
15. 40.2 cm = 0.402 m
16. (a) 0.818 kg; (b) 626 cL; (c) 121.64 m; (d) 316 000 msec
17. Answers to such questions provide new information about life during the Stone Age. These discoveries suggest that Stone Age people were much more advanced than previously thought.
18. It will take that long to determine whether temperature differences, if they occur, really signify global warming.

Lab Interpretation

19. Students may throw out the data, redo the experiment, or revise their hypotheses. Accept any answer that shows understanding of the scientific method.
20. Using both male and female puppies introduces a variable that is not being controlled. Male and female puppies may grow at different rates regardless of the type of food they eat.
21. Students may describe its color, texture, method of walking, size, weight, behavior, and other observations such as presence of legs, eyes, tail, head, claws, toes, and so on.

Connecting Ideas

22. **Energy:** Cellular respiration is necessary to release energy for biological work. Without a means of releasing energy, the part cannot function.

Energy and the Cell

Unit Overview

Unit 2 introduces students to cell structure and function, tying in the acquisition and utilization of energy by cells. As a prelude to these topics, students first explore basic chemistry in Chapter 3, being presented with just enough background information necessary for an understanding of the chapters that follow. Chapter 4 relates membrane structure to function, and Chapter 5 examines structure and function of organelles and other cell parts. Building upon both Chapter 1 and previous chapters in this unit, students then study details of energy flow in respiration and photosynthesis in Chapter 6.

Theme Development

The theme of energy is developed in Chapter 3, applied in the study of cell structure and function in Chapters 4 and 5, and emphasized in Chapter 6 as students examine, compare, and contrast the processes of respiration and photosynthesis. Systems and interactions is a theme stressed in both Chapters 4 and 5 as students come to appreciate the concept that the many parts of a cell work together in making the cell the basic unit of structure and function. The theme is also evident in the discussion of respiration and photosynthesis as interdependent processes.

Advance Planning

Chapter 3
- Order pH paper for the Investigation.
- Procure marble or limestone and seashells for Minilab 2.
- Prepare glucose solution and order grease pencils and TesTape for the Alternate Lab.

Energy and the Cell

Fireflies and hatchet fish produce light by bioluminescence. In fireflies, light helps in mate recognition. Hatchet fish, which live deep in the ocean, produce light in organs under their eyes. This light may help attract prey or aid vision.

Neon lights contain gases under low pressure inside glass tubes. Each gas gives off light of a certain color when electricity is passed through the tube. For example, neon glows orange-red, and mercury vapor glows bright blue.

52

Chapter 4
- Order dialysis tubing for the Investigation.
- Prepare iodine solution for Minilab 2.
- Order *Elodea* and prepare salt solution for the Alternate Lab.

Chapter 5
- Order algae, protozoan, and yeast cultures, *Elodea,* and *Paramecium* slides; prepare Lugol's solution and methylene blue stain for the Investigation.
- Order *Paramecium* cultures and prepare methylene blue stain and Lugol's solution for the Minilabs.

- Order *Elodea* for the Alternate Lab.

Chapter 6
- Prepare bromthymol blue and order *Elodea* for Minilab 2.
- Prepare iodine solution for the Alternate Lab.

You see them everywhere, those signs on storefronts that glow in the dark. Red, yellow, green, or blue lights like these are called neon lights, but, really, they may contain any one of several types of gases including neon, argon, mercury vapor, or helium. These gases are trapped inside a transparent tube of glass under low pressure. When an electric current is passed through the tube, the gas inside is energized and begins to glow. Neon lights thus work by converting electrical energy to light energy.

Many other organisms use light to send messages. Have you ever stayed up late on a summer night to catch fireflies? By alternating flashes of light, fireflies communicate to other members of their species.

The emission of light by an organism is called bioluminescence. Bioluminescence results from a chemical reaction in which chemical energy is converted directly to light energy. How energy is used in cells, and how it is converted from one form to another, is the focus of this unit.

Introducing the Unit

Using the Photos

Both bioluminescence and the flashing of a neon sign depend upon energy transformation. Transformation of energy is crucial to living systems. Most life forms depend, directly or indirectly, on transformation of light energy to chemical energy by photosynthetic producers. Chemical energy in molecules of sugars and other organic compounds is released and transferred to ATP molecules during fermentation or cellular respiration. Energy in ATP, in turn, is used for endergonic reactions in living things. Once used, that energy escapes as heat. Thus, a constant source of energy—light—is needed to sustain most life on Earth.

Previewing the Chapters

Chapter 3 begins with a discussion of basic atomic structure, followed by an explanation of covalent and ionic bonding. Students come to distinguish among elements, compounds, and solutions, and between acids and bases. Building on this knowledge, students then compare the structures and functions of biologically important molecules—carbohydrates, lipids, and proteins—and learn how they are built up or broken down by condensation and hydrolysis reactions. Students then focus upon energy, distinguishing between potential and kinetic energy and coming to understand the concept of energy transformation. Finally, they examine the concept of activation energy and learn how enzymes lower activation energy during cellular reactions.

Having examined the means by which materials enter and leave cells in Chapter 4, students then relate that information to organelle structure and function in Chapter 5. In studying cell parts, they learn where materials go after entering the cell and how they are used. Students also learn the source of useful products and wastes that exit the cell. Interaction of cell parts is emphasized throughout the chapter. As a result, students come to understand the cell as a dynamic unit of life.

Chapter 6 begins with the idea that exergonic and endergonic reactions are linked. After learning that ATP is a universal source of chemical energy for endergonic reactions, students study production of ATP and aerobic respiration and fermentation. How "fuel" molecules of respiration are produced follows logically as students study the light reactions and Calvin cycle. They complete the chapter by examining the interdependence of respiration and photosynthesis and refining their understanding that materials are recycled but energy is not.

Knowledge of material learned in Chapter 3 provides a sound basis for student understanding of the fluid mosaic model in Chapter 4. After studying the development of the cell theory, students learn the properties of the plasma membrane and then come to see how the fluid mosaic model explains those properties.

ORGANIZER
CHAPTER 3

SECTION	OBJECTIVES	TEXT LABS/FEATURES
3.1 Matter and Its Combinations (3 days)	**Model** the structure of an atom in both words and diagrams. **Compare** the formation of covalent and ionic bonds. **Explain** how substances dissolve in water and how some substances form acidic or basic solutions.	**Minilab 1:** How much sugar is in a can of soda pop? p. 65 **Investigation:** The pH of Water, p. 66
3.2 Biological Chemistry (3 days)	**Relate** the structure of a carbon atom to the complexity of carbon compounds. **Compare** the structures and functions of carbohydrates, lipids, and proteins. **Distinguish** between condensation and hydrolysis reactions.	**Minilab 2:** What materials contain CO_2 in the form of carbonates? p. 71 **Thinking Lab:** Why do monarch butterflies contain two different chemicals for defense? p. 72
3.3 Energy and Reactions (2 days)	**Distinguish** between potential energy and kinetic energy by using an example. **Discuss** the relationship between a reaction and activation energy. **Describe** the means by which an enzyme carries out a cellular reaction.	**Health Connection:** Proteins in Vegetarian Diets, p. 80
BIOLOGY, TECHNOLOGY, AND SOCIETY		**Considering the Environment:** Recycling Batteries, p. 84 **Chemistry Connection:** There's More than Food in Your Food, p. 85 **Career Connection:** Food technologist, p. 85

LAB MATERIALS

INVESTIGATION	MINILAB	ALTERNATE LAB
page 66 ammonia baby food jars, or beakers, 50-mL distilled water droppers grease pencil masking tape pH paper stirring rods test tubes vinegar, white water samples	**page 65** apron balance goggles soda, diet in aluminum can soda, regular in aluminum can **page 71** antacid tablets lens, hand apron marble or lime- chalk stone eggshells seashells goggles test tubes labels vinegar	**page 74** glucose solution graduated cylinder grease pencil medicine dropper TesTape test tubes test-tube rack

TEACHER CLASSROOM RESOURCES	OTHER RESOURCES
Study Guide, pp. 13-14	***STVS:** *Images of Atoms,* Chemistry (Disc 2, Side 1) ***STVS:** *Treating Acid Lakes,* Chemistry (Disc 2, Side 2) **Color Transparency 2:** *Ionic and Covalent Bonding*
Study Guide, pp. 15-16 **Concept Mapping,** p. 3 **Critical Thinking/Problem Solving:** *Sugars and Isomers,* p. 3 ***PLL:** *Detecting Compounds Made by Living Things,* p. 15 ***PLL:** *Molecules of Biological Importance,* p. 18 ***PLL:** *Amino Acid Chromatography,* p. 20 ****ILS:** *Carbohydrates: Chemistry and Identification,* p. 21 ****ILS:** *Proteins: Chemistry and Identification,* p. 27 ****ILS:** *Fats: Chemistry and Identification,* p. 31	
Study Guide, pp. 17-18 **Exploring Environmental Issues,** *Energy: Renewable and Nonrenewable,* pp. 17-18; *What's Your Energy Quotient?* pp. 19-22 ***PLL:** *Extracellular Enzymes,* p.23 ****ILS:** *Proof of Enzyme Action,* p.35	
Assessment Materials **Chapter Assessment,** pp. 9-12 **Performance Assessment in Biology,** p. 6 **Alternate Assessment in the Science Classroom** **Computer Test Bank**	**Spanish Resources** **Cooperative Learning Resource Guide** **Videodisc Correlations** (to Optical Data's and Videodiscovery's videodiscs)

* Probing Levels of Life
** Investigating Living Systems

* Science Technology Videodisc Series

Key to Teaching Strategies

The following designations will help you decide which activities in the teacher margin are appropriate for your students.

L1 Level 1 activities should be within the ability range of all students.

L2 Level 2 activities should be within the ability range of the average to above-average student.

L3 Level 3 activities are designed for the ability range of above-average students.

LEP LEP activities are appropriate for Limited English Proficiency students.

COOP LEARN Cooperative Learning activities are designed for small group work.

ADDITIONAL RESOURCES

Infinite Voyage *Miracles by Design*
New materials created by chemistry are changing biology. Artificial skin and stainless steel hips are just two of the new materials now in use.

Audiovisual
Atoms and Molecules, video, Frey Scientific.
Enzymes: Regulators of Body Chemistry, video, Insight Media.

Software
Chemicals of Life I and II: The Structure of Matter, IBM, Gemstar.
Enzyme Investigations, Apple/64K, Queue.

3

MATTER AND ENERGY

Chapter Overview

Students begin the chapter by learning about the structure of atoms and how they combine to form compounds by forming covalent and ionic bonds. They learn to write and interpret chemical formulas and equations. Then, students examine the solution process and learn to distinguish between acids and bases.

Based on this information, students will then study the structure of organic substances as well as the structures and functions of carbohydrates, lipids, and proteins. They will also find out how these molecules are formed and broken down by condensation and hydrolysis reactions.

Finally, students will explore the role of energy in chemical reactions. They will come to understand how enzymes serve to lower activation energy so that reactions can occur at cellular temperatures.

KEY TERMS

acid	enzyme
activation	ion
energy	ionic bond
amino acid	isomer
base	kinetic energy
carbohydrate	lipid
chemical	molecule
formula	nucleic acid
coenzyme	polypeptide
compound	polysaccharide
covalent bond	potential
electron cloud	energy
element	protein
energy level	solution

MATTER AND ENERGY

HUMMINGBIRDS—the animal world's equivalent to today's modern helicopter. If you've ever been lucky enough to spot one of these tiny creatures, you may have marvelled at the way it can dart backward and forward and then hover over a flower. Appearing more like insects than birds, hummingbirds have the most rapid wing beats of all birds—up to 100 wing beats per second! Like the huge motors in modern helicopters, hummingbirds accomplish their unique method of flight by expending large amounts of energy. In fact, hummingbirds have the highest energy output for their size of all warm-blooded animals.

You know that nonliving things such as helicopters and cars need energy to move and function. In the same way, living things need energy to carry out life processes. You need energy to think, digest food, grow, and move in gym class, just as hummingbirds need energy for their brand of aerial acrobatics. For a long time, scientists have known that the ability to carry out life processes distinguishes living things from nonliving things. However, all life processes involve changes in matter and energy. Therefore, scientists know that in order to understand life processes, they must first understand the properties of matter and how energy interacts with matter when changes take place. In this chapter, you'll explore the structure, properties, and changes of matter, including the matter involved in life processes.

54

CHAPTER

3

Introducing the Chapter

Have students examine the photographs of the hummingbirds on pages 54 and 55. Ask them to contrast the flight of a hummingbird with that of a helicopter. What parts make a helicopter fly? A hummingbird? Is the basic matter of which both are composed the same? Draw students into a discussion of the need for energy for flight and have them compare the "fuels" used by birds and helicopters. **LEP**

Theme Development

This chapter introduces students to the theme of energy, specifically with respect to chemical change. Transformation and conservation of energy are stressed, as is the concept of activation energy and the role of enzymes. The importance of carbohydrates and fats as energy sources is also emphasized.

Tying to Previous Knowledge

Photosynthesis and cellular respiration are processes crucial to most life forms. These processes can be referred to and better understood by applying knowledge of chemical reactions, chemical formulas and equations, structure of simple sugars, potential and kinetic energy, transformation of energy, and the function of enzymes.

Imagine being as active as a hummingbird. How much food do you suppose you'd have to eat if you used energy at the same rate that a hummingbird does?

Chapter Preview

page	Contents
56	3.1 Matter and Its Combinations
65	Minilab 1
66	Investigation *The pH of Water*
70	3.2 Biological Chemistry
71	Minilab 2
72	Thinking Lab *Make a Hypothesis*
78	3.3 Energy and Reactions
80	Health Connection *Proteins in Vegetarian Diets*
	BIOLOGY, TECHNOLOGY, AND SOCIETY
84	Considering the Environment *Recycling Batteries*
85	Career Connection *Food Technologist*
85	Chemistry Connection *There's More Than Food in Your Food*

55

ASSESSMENT PLANNER

Choose assessment strategies from the following pages to evaluate the progress of your students.

Assess, pp. 68-69, 76-77, 82-83
Portfolio, pp. 61, 65, 67, 75, 76, 77, 82
Alternate Lab, pp. 74-75
Thinking Lab, p. 72

Minilab 1, p. 65
Minilab 2, p. 71
Investigation, pp. 66-67
Chapter Review, pp. 86-87

Prepare

Key Concepts

Students will be introduced to the structure of matter and the changes that matter undergoes. Near the end of the section, special emphasis is placed on the properties of water, dissolving, solutions, and pH in order to provide a background for understanding biological processes taking place in the water solution.

Key Terms

electron cloud, energy level, element, covalent bond, molecule, compound, ion, ionic bond, chemical formula, solution, acid, base

Materials

- Purchase cans of diet and regular soda of the same brand for Minilab 1. Also gather balances and aquaria or large beakers to hold the cans.
- Gather samples of rain, pond, lake, and distilled water for the Investigation. Purchase pH paper.

1 Focus

Objectives

The objectives are listed on the student page. Remind students to preview these objectives as a guide to this numbered section.

PROGRAM RESOURCES

Teacher Classroom Resources

Study Guide, pp. 13-14 **L1**
Color Transparency #2 **L1**
LEP

Objectives

Model the structure of an atom in both words and diagrams.

Compare the formation of covalent and ionic bonds.

Explain how substances dissolve in water and how some substances form acidic or basic solutions.

Figure 3-1 **The left photo shows atoms of carbon and oxygen as seen by a scanning tunneling microscope. (Magnification: 14 000 000×) As you see, scientists are now able to arrange atoms into shapes. The right diagram is a model of an atom. Notice the small nucleus made up of protons and neutrons and the much larger cloud of electrons in three energy levels. The darkest regions in the cloud represent places where electrons are most likely to be found.**

3.1 Matter and Its Combinations

You live in a world of both living and nonliving things. In Chapter 1, you learned about the important features of organisms, and from your everyday experience you know the difference between what is alive and what is not. Although very different, both living and nonliving things are made of matter, and all matter is composed of the same building blocks—atoms.

Atoms

Helicopters and hummingbirds, stereos and spiders, textbooks and trees—these things have very different visible characteristics. All of them, though, are composed of matter. Matter is anything that has mass and occupies space. All matter, in turn, is composed of small particles called atoms. Atoms are basic building blocks that you cannot see. They are so small that even the most powerful microscopes cannot photograph their details, as Figure 3-1 shows. Most atoms measure between 0.1 and 0.5 nm in diameter. The unit nm (nanometer) is one billionth of a meter.

Atomic Structure   To understand why atoms behave as they do, let's look first at their structure. Though tiny, atoms are composed of still smaller particles, the major ones being protons, neutrons, and electrons. Protons and neutrons are packed tightly in the nucleus of an atom. Protons are positively charged and are represented by the symbol p^+. Neutrons have no charge and are represented by the symbol n^0. Moving rapidly outside the nucleus are the electrons, which are represented by the symbol e^-. Electrons are negatively charged. In an uncombined atom, the number of protons equals the number of electrons. Therefore, the atom as a whole is neutral because it has no electric charge.

Electron energy levels

Nucleus containing protons and neutrons

To illustrate the fact that an atom is neutral, assign a positive charge (proton) to five students and a negative charge (electron) to five other students. Ask these "charges" to stand in front of the classroom. Advise students that a negative and positive cancel one another out and result in a neutral condition. Ask students to form pairs of opposite charges. Ask those seated what the resulting charge would

be on each group. All groups should be neutral. To demonstrate unbalanced charges on ions, ask groups of unequal numbers of positive and negative charges to form. Point out that if more electrons are present than protons, then the overall charge will be negative, but if more protons are present than electrons, then the overall charge will be positive. **LEP**
COOP LEARN

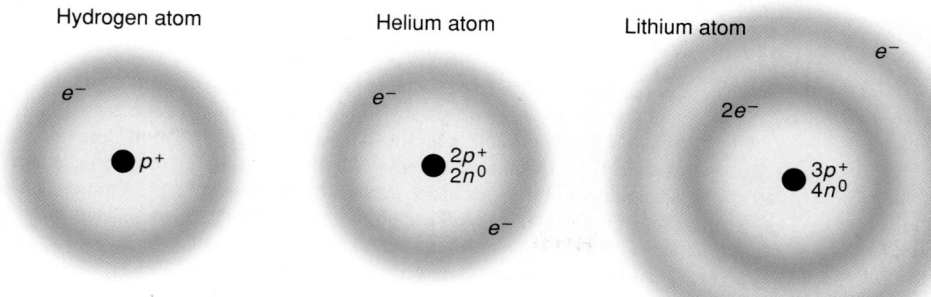

Hydrogen atom Helium atom Lithium atom

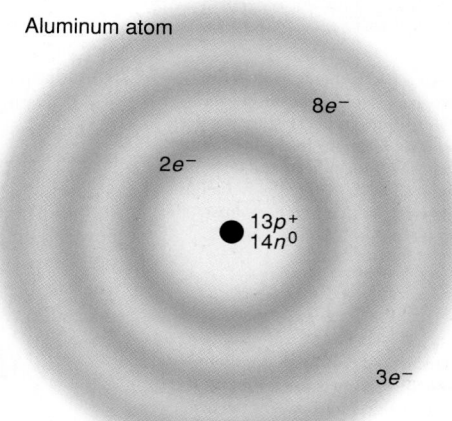

Aluminum atom

A scientist's idea or picture of how something works is called a model. Models help to picture atomic structure, as seen in Figure 3-1. As you can see from this diagram, the nucleus is at the center and the electrons are moving in a region around it. Electrons do not travel in fixed paths. Rather, they move anywhere within a probable region around the nucleus. The region or space that electrons occupy while moving around the nucleus is known as the **electron cloud.**

To give you an idea of what typical atoms are like, let's look at models of some simple atoms. Hydrogen atoms are the most abundant atoms in the universe and are also the simplest because they consist of only one proton and one electron. Helium is the gas used to fill balloons that float in air. A helium atom contains two protons and two neutrons in its nucleus and two electrons in the electron cloud. Lithium is a soft, silvery metal. A typical lithium atom has three protons and four neutrons in its nucleus and three electrons in the electron cloud.

Electron Energy Levels If you saw models of many atoms, you would note that there are several different regions in which electrons travel about the nucleus. These regions are called **energy levels**. As electrons increase in energy, they occupy energy levels farther from the nucleus. Each energy level is a region of space in which it is highly probable that an electron of a certain energy will be located. The first energy level can hold a maximum of only two electrons. Look at Figure 3-2. Note that in a helium atom, the first energy level has two electrons and, therefore, is full.

If an atom contains more than two electrons, those additional electrons must occupy higher energy levels farther from the nucleus. Look at the model of a lithium atom in Figure 3-2. Two electrons fill the first energy level, but the third is in the second energy level, a region farther away from the nucleus. The second energy level can hold eight electrons. Higher levels can hold even greater numbers of electrons. The third level holds a maximum of 18 electrons. Thus, an atom of aluminum, which has 13 electrons, has two in the first energy level, eight in the second, and the remaining three in the third level.

Figure 3-2 **Shown here are models of hydrogen, helium, lithium, and aluminum atoms. Notice that the first energy level can hold only two electrons. It is full in a helium atom. The third electron in a lithium atom must occupy the second energy level. In the aluminum atom, you can see that the second energy level is full with eight electrons. The three remaining electrons must occupy a third level. Note that in every atom the number of protons ($p+$) is the same as the number of electrons ($e-$).**

Demonstration
Place a thermometer into a large test tube half full of 3% hydrogen peroxide solution (available in drugstores). Ask a student to read the temperature of the liquid and to describe the liquid. Add a piece of raw liver the size of a pencil eraser to the liquid. Observe the reaction and then read the temperature again. Ask students to describe what happened and to discuss the kinds of changes that occurred. Ask them to suggest the source of the heat that raised the temperature.

2 Teach

Reinforcement
Prepare a chart that lists the following information along the top: location, charge, symbol. List the following along the side: electron, neutron, proton. Have students complete the chart. L1

Building a Model
Have students use mini-marshmallows, toothpicks, and different colored gumdrops to build models of some of the simpler elements studied. Marshmallows may represent neutrons while specific colored gumdrops may represent electrons and protons. L1 LEP

Brainstorming
Ask students to use Figure 3-2 as a guide while they complete diagrams for the elements beryllium, carbon, fluorine, neon, and sodium. Supply students with numbers of the protons and neutrons for these elements. They must predict the electron arrangements on their own. L2 COOP LEARN

STUDENT JOURNAL
Ask students to pretend that they are atoms. Ask them to write a paragraph describing what they look like and what everything around them looks like. Students should be encouraged to use their imaginations. However, they must still describe the basic structure of an atom and should describe other atoms around them. L1 LEP

MEETING INDIVIDUAL NEEDS
Visually Impaired: Have students who are visually impaired arrange fellow classmates to represent an atom. Assign roles to classmates to represent protons, neutrons, and electrons. Protons and neutrons will remain stationary, forming the nucleus of the atom. Electrons will move slowly around the nucleus representing the electron cloud. LEP COOP LEARN

SECTION 3.1

Periodic Table: Introduce students to the periodic table. A wall chart or transparency will enhance the discussion. Show the correlation between atomic number and proton/electron number moving horizontally across the table rows. Introduce some of the more common biological elements and their symbols.

Using Science Terms

Correlate the term *neutr*on with its *neutr*al charge. Ask students to explain how the term *neutral* is used in a nonscientific context. Also, correlate *electr*on with *electr*icity and *proton* with its charge of *positive*.

Science, Technology, and Society

Detecting Damaged Heart Muscle: An isotope called thallium-201 is used to detect damaged heart muscle after a heart attack. This isotope will accumulate only in normal, undamaged heart muscle. Thus, it is a useful tool to determine where and to what extent a heart has been damaged. Contact a local hospital and determine the cost, risk to patient, advantages, and disadvantages of using this isotope.

Figure 3-3 Some radioactive isotopes are useful in diagnosing and treating illnesses because they collect in certain locations in the body. This image of a human head and neck was produced by detecting the radiation from isotopes that had been injected into the person's body.

Figure 3-4 A hydrogen atom is not stable by itself because its energy level has only one electron. Two electrons make the atom stable. As a result, two hydrogen atoms share electrons and bond with each other, forming a molecule written as H_2. Then the atoms are stable because, by sharing, each has two electrons—at least part of the time.

Elements

So far, you've considered separate atoms of hydrogen, helium, lithium, and aluminum. What about a group of all one kind of atom, such as a sheet of aluminum foil or all the helium gas inside a balloon? Substances such as these, composed of only one type of atom, are known as **elements.** The number of protons in the nucleus determines the type of atom (or element). For example, every atom of aluminum has 13 protons, and every atom of helium gas inside a balloon has two protons.

Although the number of protons in a given element is always constant, atoms of the same element can differ in the number of neutrons. Such atoms are called isotopes of that element. For example, the most abundant isotope of hydrogen contains no neutrons, but other hydrogen isotopes containing one and two neutrons also exist in nature. Some isotopes are unstable and can break down, giving off radiation in the process. These radioactive isotopes are important in biological research because they can be substituted for non-radioactive atoms in molecules. However, the radiation can be dangerous to organisms.

For example, suppose a scientist wants to find out what happens to a certain weed killer when it is sprayed on plants. A sample of the weed killer can be made using atoms of the radioactive isotope, carbon-14, which has eight neutrons in the nucleus. The more abundant isotope of carbon, carbon-12, has only six neutrons in the nucleus. The weed killer is now said to be "tagged" or "labeled" because it can be detected by its radioactivity. Now, the weed killer can be traced as it enters the plant. The scientist can find out whether the chemical stays in the plant, enters the soil, travels to other plants, or is broken down into other chemicals.

Molecules

You are no doubt familiar with many other elements—gold, lead, oxygen, and copper, to name a few. In all, there are more than 100 elements. But you know from your own experience that there are many more than 100 different substances in the world. These other substances are formed when atoms combine with one another.

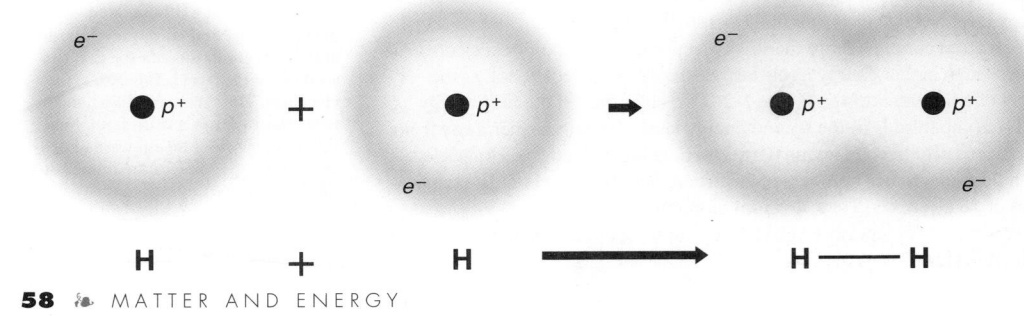

Lead Poisoning: Have students research the topic of lead poisoning. They may wish to report their findings in an oral report to the class, or you may ask them to submit a written report. Their project may focus on one aspect of lead poisoning such as cause, symptoms, prevention, prevalence of the problem locally and/or nationally, or treatment for those individuals afflicted. Some students may wish to research the levels of lead that are considered toxic in the environment. Visiting county or city government labs may also be a means to determine how tests for the presence of lead in drinking water or paint are conducted. The problem of mercury poisoning may be an alternate topic. L2

Why Atoms Form Bonds   When atoms combine, their outer energy levels become stable. They are then more resistant to change. Except for atoms of hydrogen and helium, atoms have electrons in two or more energy levels. An outer energy level becomes stable when it contains a total of eight electrons. Nitrogen, for example, has five electrons in its outer energy level. When a nitrogen atom combines with other atoms, its outer energy level must acquire three more electrons to become stable. An atom such as hydrogen, however, with only one energy level, becomes stable when that level holds its maximum of two electrons. Thus, hydrogen must acquire only one electron to become stable.

One way in which atoms combine is by sharing electrons, as in Figure 3-4. Hydrogen atoms do this when they combine with each other. The electrons travel in the space between and around the two nuclei.

Combined atoms are held together by forces called chemical bonds. When atoms combine by sharing electrons, a **covalent bond** results. A covalent bond can be represented by a line drawn between the atoms, as in Figure 3-4. A combination of two or more atoms joined by a covalent bond is called a **molecule.**

Compounds

In nature, hydrogen gas exists in the form of hydrogen molecules, composed of two covalently bonded hydrogen atoms. Oxygen gas also exists as molecules, each consisting of two atoms of oxygen covalently bonded. Figure 3-5 shows molecules of oxygen and hydrogen in motion. If these molecules collide at normal room temperature, nothing will change. However, if heat is added, the molecules will react to form molecules of water. The additional energy—heat—caused the molecules to speed up and collide with more force. As a result, the covalent bonds in the hydrogen and oxygen molecules were broken and the atoms of hydrogen and oxygen recombined in a new way to form molecules of water.

Figure 3-5   In the reaction shown here, nothing happens until enough heat is added to make a few hydrogen and oxygen molecules collide with sufficient force to break bonds. Water is the product of the reaction. After the reaction starts, the energy released causes the remaining molecules to react. The equation for this reaction is written

$$2H_2 + O_2 \rightarrow 2H_2O$$

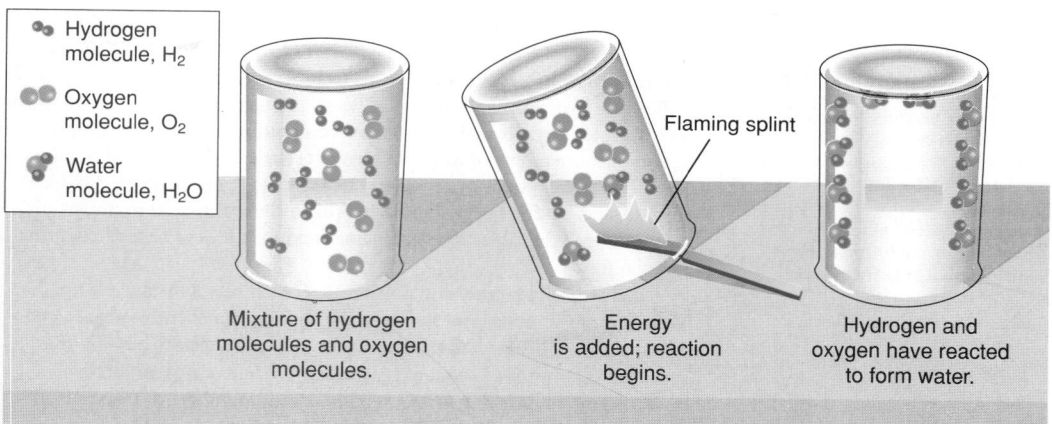

- ⚬⚬ Hydrogen molecule, H_2
- ⬤⬤ Oxygen molecule, O_2
- ⬤ Water molecule, H_2O

Mixture of hydrogen molecules and oxygen molecules.

Energy is added; reaction begins.

Flaming splint

Hydrogen and oxygen have reacted to form water.

Concept Development

Point out that only the electrons of an atom's outermost energy level are involved in bonding, whether covalent or ionic. Ask students to diagram molecules of the compounds CH_4, CO_2, and NH_3. Remind students that the use of a line connecting atoms of elements is a way of indicating a covalent bond. Ask why a molecule of oxygen gas is written as O=O with two lines. **L1** **LEP**

Demonstration

Illustrate the fact that energy is needed to initiate the combining of elements into compounds. Use a strike-anywhere kitchen match for this demonstration. Without an energy input, the match does not ignite. With added energy, it does ignite and change chemically. The initiating energy comes from the heat generated by friction as the match head is rubbed across a rough surface.

Bioethics

Isotope Risk: All isotopes used in medical procedures carry some risk to the patient because they emit radiation. Students should discuss the question of whether the benefit of using these radioactive isotopes outweighs their possible side effects and/or risk to the patient. Have students find out what the risks and benefits are from the use of such isotopes as iodine-131, technetium-99, cobalt-60, and iron-59. Have students form their own opinions based on their own research of this topic. A larger list of medically useful isotopes and their applications can be found in the Miscellaneous Tables section of The Merck Index. **L2** **COOP LEARN**

MEETING INDIVIDUAL NEEDS

To better illustrate compound formation, exhibit a clean copper penny (pre-1984), sulfur powder, an empty stoppered test tube labeled "Oxygen," and a small jar containing some crystals of copper sulfate. Allow students to observe and then record descriptions of copper, sulfur, oxygen, and copper sulfate. Explain that the compound called copper sulfate contains all these elements in a chemically com- bined form. Write the formula for this compound on the chalkboard ($CuSO_4$). Have students compare the lists and emphasize the differences in properties between the uncombined elements on one hand and the compound on the other. **LEP** **COOP LEARN**

Using the Table

Ask students to perform the following tasks using Table 3.1 as a reference.

(a) Identify by name each element present in each compound.

(b) Speculate as to which elements appear to be most common in this list. (C, H, O)

(c) Categorize those compounds as being either organic (containing carbon) or inorganic (containing no carbon). Note that neither CO_2 nor $CaCO_3$ is considered organic.

(d) Use acquired knowledge or reference books to identify a compound that may be in gasoline (octane), in vinegar (acetic acid, water), a drug (ethyl alcohol, sodium carbonate in some antacids), sweet to the taste (glucose, sucrose, glycerol), a gas (ammonia, carbon dioxide), present in fatigued muscles (lactic acid), called lye (sodium hydroxide).

Figure Caption Question

Could oxygen and hydrogen combine to form H_3O or H_4O? Explain. No. Only the combination H_2O provides the right number of electrons to make both hydrogen and oxygen atoms stable.

Concept Development

Ask students to apply the fact that compounds always show definite composition to the following situation. How many atoms of hydrogen and oxygen would result for every molecule of water that is broken apart? How many atoms of nitrogen and hydrogen would result for every molecule of ammonia that is broken apart?

Figure 3-6 In water (H_2O), the atoms are linked by covalent bonds. Each hydrogen shares one electron with oxygen, providing oxygen with a stable outer level of eight electrons. In turn, oxygen shares two of its electrons, one with each hydrogen atom, providing hydrogen with a stable outer level of two electrons. Could oxygen and hydrogen combine to form H_3O or H_4O? Explain.

Table 3.1 Examples of Compounds

Name	Formula
acetic acid	CH_3COOH
ammonia	NH_3
calcium carbonate	$CaCO_3$
carbon dioxide	CO_2
chlorophyll-a	$C_{55}H_{72}O_5N_4Mg$
ethyl alcohol	C_2H_5OH
glucose	$C_6H_{12}O_6$
glycerol	$C_3H_5(OH)_3$
lactic acid	$CH_3CHOHCOOH$
octane	C_8H_{18}
sodium hydroxide	$NaOH$
sucrose	$C_{12}H_{22}O_{11}$
table salt	$NaCl$
water	H_2O

Why Water is H_2O To become stable, a hydrogen atom needs to gain one electron. An oxygen atom has six electrons in its outer energy level, and so it must obtain two more electrons. In order for hydrogen and oxygen atoms to combine so that the atoms become stable, they must combine in a ratio of two hydrogen atoms to one oxygen atom, as seen in Figure 3-6. As you can see, each hydrogen atom provides one of the two electrons that the oxygen atom needs to become stable.

Because hydrogen and oxygen in water are held together by covalent bonds, water is a molecule. It is also a **compound,** a substance composed of two or more atoms of different elements joined by a chemical bond. Not all chemical bonds are covalent, as you'll soon see. Carbon dioxide, glucose, and baking soda (sodium hydrogen carbonate) are examples of compounds. Table 3.1 shows the names and formulas of several common compounds.

When atoms combine with one another, each new substance formed has a definite composition. For example, a molecule of hydrogen always contains two hydrogen atoms, and water molecules always contain two hydrogen atoms joined to an oxygen atom. Definite composition is explained by the fact that atoms require certain numbers of electrons in their outer energy levels in order to become stable.

60 ● MATTER AND ENERGY

MULTICULTURAL CONNECTION

Hominy: Corn is an excellent source of starch in our diet. It is often modified through milling into a variety of forms. What we know as hominy is actually made from corn. Native Americans discovered that soaking corn in a solution made from the ashes of a wood fire (a lye solution) would change corn grains into an expanded, lighter-textured material with a unique flavor. This changed corn was then baked into custard-like puddings or fried with meats and wild greens. If the hominy is dried and pounded into a fine texture, hominy grits are formed.

Ions

Not all chemical compounds result from the sharing of electrons. Another kind of bond is possible. Some atoms attract electrons much more strongly than other atoms. When these two types of atoms combine to form compounds, they do not share electrons. Instead, electrons are transferred from one atom to another as the atoms acquire stable outer energy levels. Figure 3-8 shows how sodium and chlorine atoms combine to form the compound sodium chloride, better known as table salt. The sodium atom, by losing one electron, attains a stable outer level of eight electrons. The chlorine atom obtains the electron lost from sodium, so it, too, has a stable outer level of eight electrons.

Charges on Ions After an atom loses or gains electrons, it has an unbalanced electric charge. After losing an electron, a sodium atom has 11 positive charges (protons) but only ten negative charges (electrons). It is positive by one charge, 1+. Similarly, the chlorine atom, after gaining one electron, is negative by one charge, 1−. Such charged atoms (or sometimes groups of atoms) are called **ions.** In this case, a sodium atom has become a sodium ion, and a chlorine atom has become a chloride ion. Note that negatively charged ions formed from single elements have names ending in -*ide.* The names are slightly different from the names of the elements.

Because sodium and chloride ions are oppositely charged, they attract each other. This force of attraction between ions is called an **ionic bond.** The number and kind of charge on each ion determine the composition of a compound. In an ionic compound, the positive and negative charges must balance each other so the net charge is zero. In sodium chloride, only one of each kind of ion is needed, because the 1+ charge of a sodium ion balances the 1− charge of a chloride ion.

Comparing Covalent and Ionic Bonding Let's compare ionic and covalent substances. You have learned that covalent substances consist of

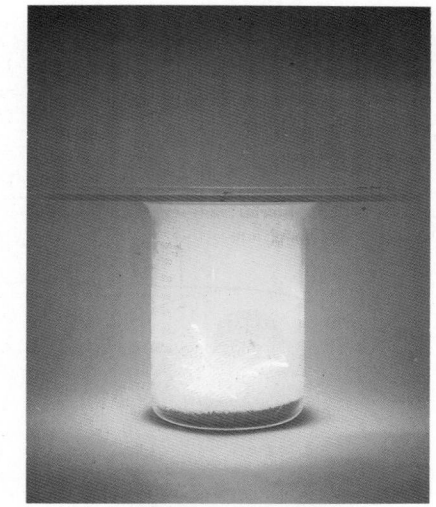

Figure 3-7 **This photo shows sodium reacting with chlorine, forming common salt. The violent reaction produces both light and heat.**

Figure 3-8 **When sodium and chlorine react, they form sodium chloride, an ionic compound. After the reaction, each sodium ion has a positive charge, and each chloride ion has a negative charge. As a result, there is a force of attraction between the two ions of opposite charge. This force is an ionic bond.**

Ionic bond

| Sodium atom | + | Chlorine atom | ➡ | Sodium + ion | + | Chloride − ion |
| Na | + | Cl | ➡ | NaCl | | |

3.1 MATTER AND ITS COMBINATIONS **61**

PORTFOLIO

Have students make atomic diagrams of elements not illustrated in the text, such as magnesium and silicon. Supply the students with the number of protons but not the number of electrons. Magnesium has 12 protons; silicon has 14 protons.

Have students diagram a model of the formation of an unfamiliar ionic compound such as magnesium chloride, $MgCl_2$; calcium oxide, CaO; or sodium

sulfide, Na_2S. Advise them that these compounds have ionic bonds. Students should pattern their diagrams on Figure 3-8. **L3**

Using an Analogy

Ask students to describe and/or give an example of a code or symbol system that they are familiar with. Relate this example to the system of using symbols for elements. Possible symbols that might be suggested by students are the symbols for male and female, universal traffic sign symbols, sign symbols for washrooms, and symbols used for various controls in a car. Code examples may include the three letters used to designate airports. **L1** **LEP**

Brainstorming

Provide the symbols for some of the more common elements to your students. Ask them to name the element that they believe corresponds to the symbol. Provide the names of other common elements and ask students to predict the symbol that corresponds to these elements.
COOP LEARN

Teacher FYI

Baking soda, $NaHCO_3$, is commonly called sodium bicarbonate. The correct chemical name is, however, sodium hydrogen carbonate.

Discussion

Ask students to once again use Table 3.1 to determine the number of atoms present in $3NH_3$, $5C_2H_5OH$, $4CaCO_3$, and $3C_3H_5(OH)_3$.

Figure 3-9 Crystals of common salt are cube-shaped. If you could magnify one corner of a salt crystal several million times, you would see the cubic arrangement of positive sodium ions and negative chloride ions shown below. Notice that there are no molecules of sodium chloride, only separate sodium and chloride ions.

Sodium ion
(Na$^+$)

Chloride ion
(Cl$^-$)

individual particles called molecules. For example, a glass of water consists of more than one septillion individual water molecules, each distinct from the others. On the other hand, ionic compounds do not consist of separate molecules. A crystal of table salt, as seen in Figure 3-9, is made up of a continuous network of alternating sodium and chloride ions held tightly by their electric attraction for one another. There are no separate and distinct units of sodium chloride, just sodium ions and chloride ions in a one-to-one ratio.

Symbols and Formulas

Though scientists around the world use different languages, they have a standard way of referring to the elements. Each element is represented by a symbol. Some symbols consist of one letter. For example, symbols of the four elements most abundant in living systems are C (carbon), H (hydrogen), O (oxygen), and N (nitrogen). Other symbols contain two letters—Ca for calcium, Zn for zinc, and Mg for magnesium. Notice that when a symbol consists of two letters, the second letter is not capitalized.

Chemical Formulas A group of symbols called a **chemical formula** shows the number and kind of each atom in a compound. The chemical formula for water is H_2O. Subscripts in a formula represent the number of atoms of an element. For example, in the chemical formula for water, there are two hydrogen atoms for every oxygen atom. When a symbol is not followed by a subscript, it is understood to represent one atom or ion. For example, the formula CO_2 for carbon dioxide indicates one atom of carbon and two atoms of oxygen.

Numbers in front of a formula apply to the entire formula. For example, $5H_2O$ means that there are five molecules of water. How many atoms are there in $5H_2O$? There are three atoms in each water molecule—two hydrogen and one oxygen. Therefore, in five molecules, there would be five times three atoms—15 atoms altogether.

62 🌶 MATTER AND ENERGY

Properties of Matter

Properties are the characteristics that scientists use to describe matter. For example, a piece of iron might have a certain color, hardness, and texture. It might have a mass of 1.5 kg, a volume of 190 cm³, and be molded in the shape of a gear. Such features that describe a piece of matter are called physical properties. Another characteristic of iron is that it will combine chemically with oxygen in the air to form rust. Iron will also be eaten away chemically by acids spilled on it. Characteristics such as these describe how iron behaves in contact with other elements or compounds. These characteristics are called chemical properties.

Chemical Change

Think back to the formation of water from atoms of hydrogen and oxygen. Isn't water very different from the hydrogen and oxygen gases from which it was formed? Think, too, about wood burning in a fireplace. Burning occurs as molecules in the wood combine with oxygen molecules. Invisible gases, including carbon dioxide and water vapor, are formed. Aren't these substances quite different from wood and oxygen? What has happened? In both examples, a chemical change has occurred. A chemical change involves the breaking of bonds and the formation of new ones. Chemical changes are also called chemical reactions.

Characteristics of Chemical Changes   In a chemical change, new combinations of atoms are produced, forming new substances with new properties. For example, when wood burns, large molecules that make up the solid wood break apart, combine with oxygen, and rearrange to form small molecules of gaseous carbon dioxide and water.

Chemical changes occur constantly within organisms and are essential for maintaining life. For example, digestion of a spaghetti lunch involves chemical changes. In these changes, large starch molecules that the body can't absorb are broken into small sugar molecules that the body can absorb. Then, in cellular respiration, chemical reactions break the bonds of sugar molecules, release energy, and form CO_2 and H_2O. You'll learn more about the processes of respiration and digestion later in your biology course.

Figure 3-10   In this photo, you can see several physical properties of iron. You can also see the result of one of iron's chemical properties—the fact that it combines with oxygen in the air to form rust.

Figure 3-11   Just as the rusting of iron is a chemical change, so is the digestion of starch in spaghetti. In your body, digestion chemically changes the starch to smaller sugar molecules, which can be absorbed and transported to cells. In cells, further chemical changes may break the sugar down into CO_2 and H_2O, giving off energy in the process.

63

Chemical Equations

How can you describe the chemical change that we commonly call the rusting of iron? One way is to say that a gray piece of iron became brown and flaky on the surface exposed to air. Unfortunately, this description uses a lot of words and doesn't provide much information about what reacted and what new substance formed. Instead, scientists describe chemical reactions (changes) by using a system of chemical shorthand. For example, when iron rusts, it reacts chemically with oxygen, forming iron oxide. This reaction is represented as follows.

$$Fe + O_2 \rightarrow Fe_2O_3$$

Such a representation of a chemical reaction is called a chemical equation. Iron and oxygen are called reactants, and iron oxide, Fe_2O_3, is called the product. This equation is read, "Iron plus oxygen yields iron oxide."

Why Chemical Equations Must Be Balanced Chemical equations are like algebraic equations in that both sides must represent the same quantity. In other words, the number of atoms of each element on each side of the arrow must be equal. Why is this so? Have you ever heard of the Law of Conservation of Mass? This law states that during a chemical reaction, mass is neither created nor destroyed. Therefore, the above equation must be written as follows:

$$4Fe + 3O_2 \rightarrow 2Fe_2O_3$$

Such an equation is said to be *balanced*, because the number of atoms of each element on each side is the same.

When you burn natural gas to cook food or heat your home, methane molecules (CH_4) combine with oxygen molecules (O_2) in the air. The products are CO_2 and H_2O. Study Figure 3-12, and note how the written equation represents the way the molecules change. Count the number of each type of atom in the reactants and in the products. Are the numbers equal? If so, the equation is balanced.

Figure 3-12 This diagram shows what happens as methane burns. Compare the models to the written equation. You should realize that scientists do not balance equations to make life difficult for students. They do it because, as you see here, only a *balanced* equation really represents the actual numbers of atoms, ions, and molecules involved in a chemical reaction.

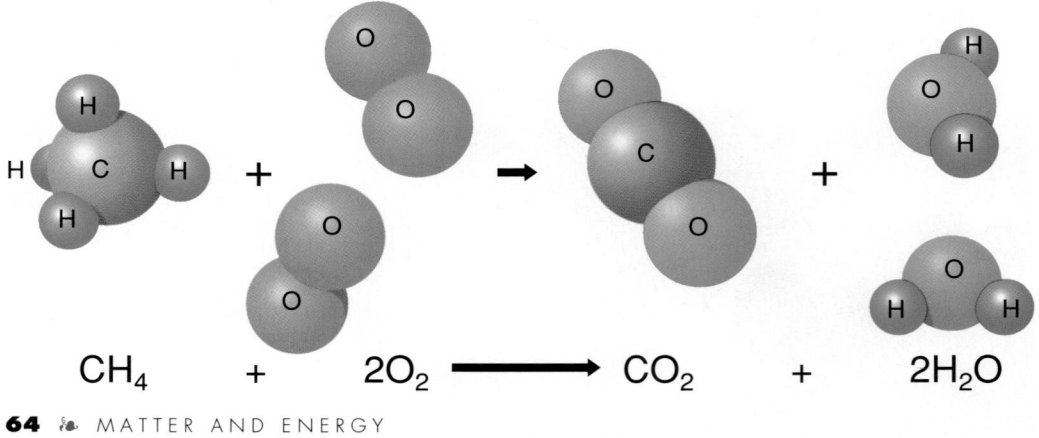

$$CH_4 + 2O_2 \longrightarrow CO_2 + 2H_2O$$

64 MATTER AND ENERGY

Solutions

Have you ever made a fruit-flavored drink by stirring a powdered drink mix in a glass of cold water? If so, you've mixed different substances without starting a chemical reaction. No bonds were broken and no bonds were formed. After thorough stirring, you formed a mixture that was the same throughout; that is, every part of the mixture is the same.

Now, suppose you dissolved 1 g of table salt, NaCl, a compound, in 100 mL of water. You have made salt water. If you stir 2 g of the same salt in another beaker containing 100 mL of water, you would again have salt water. Each beaker containing salt water would be the same throughout, but the two mixtures would differ in composition. The second beaker would contain a greater amount of salt in the same amount of water.

Both the fruit drink and the salt water are examples of solutions. **Solutions** are mixtures that are the same throughout but have variable compositions, depending on how much of one substance is dissolved in the other.

How Substances Dissolve   Why do some substances dissolve in water and others do not? The answer depends not only on the nature of the substance, but also on the nature of water. Look at Figure 3-13. In a water molecule, the nucleus of the oxygen atom attracts electrons more strongly than do the hydrogen nuclei. Thus, at any given time, there are more electrons near the oxygen nucleus, and electrons are pulled away from the hydrogen nuclei. As a result, the oxygen part of the water molecule has a slight negative charge, while the hydrogen part of the molecule has a slight positive charge. Molecules that have oppositely charged regions are called polar molecules.

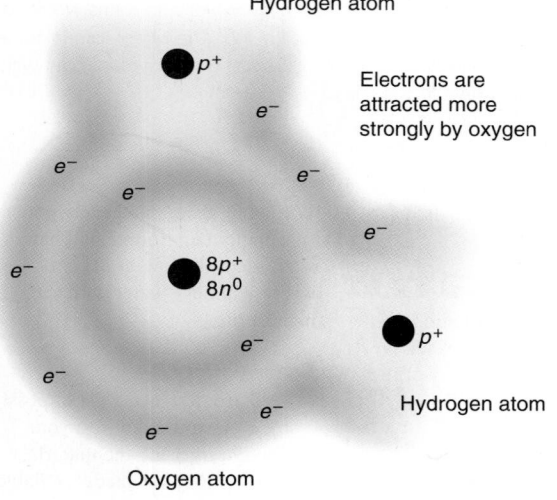

Hydrogen atom

Electrons are attracted more strongly by oxygen

$8p^+$
$8n^0$

p^+

Hydrogen atom

Oxygen atom

Minilab 1

How much sugar is in a can of soda pop?

Place a can of diet soda and a can of the same brand of regular soda (with sugar) in a filled aquarium. Be sure both cans are made of aluminum, not steel, and are exactly the same in construction. What do you observe? Assume both cans contain the same volume of liquid. Predict which type of soda has more mass. On what do you base your prediction? Mass each can on a balance. Which has more mass? Determine the difference in mass between the two cans. What accounts for this difference?

Analysis   How much sugar is there in a can of the regular soda pop you tested? What happens when sugar is dissolved in soda pop? Is this process a chemical change? How can you tell?

Figure 3-13   In reality, hydrogen and oxygen do not share electrons equally in covalent bonds. Oxygen "hogs" the electrons because it attracts them more strongly than hydrogen. This condition causes water molecules to be polar. Do you think that water molecules would attract each other? Why?

Negatively charged end

− + Positively charged end

Polar water molecules

Minilab 1

Purpose
Students discover that two solutions can look identical but have different densities as a result of the substances dissolved in them.

Skills
observe and infer, measure in SI

Teaching Strategies
- **Safety Precautions:** Have students wear aprons and goggles.
- Pour out samples of each type of soda in clear, labeled containers to show students that the two appear identical.
- **Troubleshooting:** You should try cans of several brands to be sure they give the desired result. Test cans with a magnet to be sure they are not steel. Note that most drinks are actually sweetened with high-fructose corn syrup or similar material. However, it is equivalent to dissolved sugar.

Expected Results
The can containing diet soda will float and the one with dissolved sugar will sink because although the volumes of liquid in the cans are the same, one is heavier because it contains dissolved sugar.

Answers
Differences may be in the range of 15 g to 25 g. When sugar dissolves, polar water molecules attract polar parts of the sugar molecules and pull them into solution. It is a physical change because no new substances were formed.

✔ Assessment
Portfolio: Have students write an evaluation of the lab for placement in their portfolios.

Figure Caption Question
Do you think water molecules would attract each other? Why? Yes. Water molecules are polar and, thus, the positive side of one molecule attracts the negative side of another.

MEETING INDIVIDUAL NEEDS

Visually Impaired: Have students make solutions consisting of powdered fruit drink mix and water. Balances will be needed along with graduated cylinders, water, and beakers. Have students prepare 1%, 5%, and 10% solutions. Students should judge the strength of the solutions by their colors. Students should explain why this series of beakers illustrates the concept of mixtures as well as solutions. Visually impaired students might be teamed up with students who are not impaired when preparing the series of solutions. Caution students not to taste or drink the solutions.   **COOP LEARN**

The pH of Water

Time Allotment
1 class period if water samples are available in class

Objectives
Upon completing this investigation, students will be able to:
- State typical pH values for water sources in the local community.
- Demonstrate the correct technique for using test papers.

Skills
interpret data, observe and infer

Materials
wide-range pH paper; droppers or stirring rods; 2 test tubes or other small glass containers for water samples; 5 beakers, 50 mL, or 2 baby food jars; masking tape or grease pencil for labeling

Safety Precautions: Caution students not to taste or drink any of the water samples, however innocuous they may seem.

Preparation
Obtain water samples from a variety of sources including lakes, ponds, streams, tap water from wells and treated municipal water supplies, bottled mineral water, ocean, and fresh rainwater. Have distilled water, white vinegar, and weak ammonia solution available as controls.

Possible Hypotheses
Because students have heard of acid rain, they may suggest that rainwater has the lowest pH. This is not likely to be supported by results in most locations.

Possible Procedures
- Demonstrate the technique for using test papers. Students should not dip paper into sample supply, but instead should apply a drop of the sample with a clean dropper or a stirring rod. They should never touch the test portion of the paper.
- Have students take some of each water sample in a separate clean, numbered test tube. They should immediately record the identity of each water sample in a data table.

Figure 3-14 Polar water molecules do not dissolve fats and oils.

Because they have charged regions, polar molecules attract other polar molecules. For example, sugar molecules, like water, are polar. The positive ends of water molecules attract the negative parts of sugar molecules and vice versa. When sugar crystals are placed in water, the attraction between oppositely charged areas of water and sugar causes the sugar molecules to separate from one another. Sugar dissolves when the sugar molecules separate and become scattered throughout the water molecules. In solution, the atoms of the sugar molecules remain together as molecules of sugar. Some covalent molecules, such as HCl, form ions when they dissolve in water.

You probably know that materials such as salad oil and wax don't dissolve in water. Fats, oils, and waxes are examples of substances whose molecules are not polar. When fats and oils are placed in water, there is very little attraction between their molecules and water molecules. As a result, fats and oils do not dissolve in water. In general, substances that are made of molecules that have very little attraction for water molecules do not dissolve in water.

INVESTIGATION

The pH of Water

Is your shampoo pH balanced? Advertising would lead you to believe that it is extremely important to use pH-balanced shampoo. What is pH? The pH scale is used to measure how acidic or basic a solution is. At pH 7, a solution is neutral; decreasing from 7, a solution is more acidic; increasing from 7, it is more basic.

Pure water is neutral, with a pH of 7, but even small amounts of dissolved substances can change the pH. Rain is normally slightly acidic as a result of carbon dioxide that dissolves in the water and forms weak carbonic acid. The normal pH of rain is about 5.5. The pH of rain in some places may be very low due to pollutants reacting with water. Rain with a pH consistently below 5.5 is called acid rain.

Problem
What is the pH of water from a variety of sources?

Safety Precautions
Be sure to wash your hands after handling water from various sources. Do not drink any of the water.

Hypothesis
With your group, make a hypothesis about which source will have water with the lowest pH and which will have water with the highest pH.

Experimental Plan
1. As a group, make a list of possible ways you might test your hypothesis using the materials your teacher has made available.

Teaching Strategies
- If this is the first time your students have designed an experiment, refer them to the Investigations in Chapters 1 and 2.
- Have students make a bar graph of their data. The pH scale should run from 1 to 14 vertically, and the horizontal axis should list the source of the samples. Have them include the acidic, basic, and neutral controls, too.

Data and Observations
Natural water samples are likely to be on the acidic side with pHs in the range of 5.0 to 6.5.

If, however, you have hard water from wells or other sources, it may have been in contact with limestone and may have pHs of 8 or 9.

Data Analysis
1. distilled water
2. Answers will vary. Water is often acidic, though, because of dissolved CO_2. Also, ponds that contain large amounts of decaying plant matter often have acidic pHs.
3. Seawater, well water, and some mineral water are the most likely candidates to be basic.

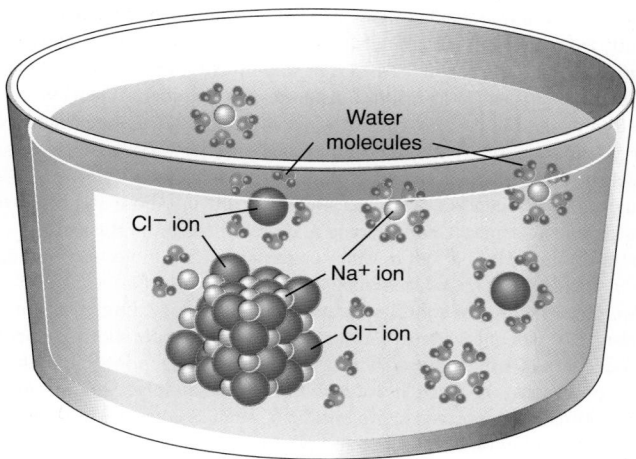

Figure 3-15 Many ionic compounds, such as common salt (NaCl), dissolve in water. When crystals of NaCl are placed in water, polar water molecules are attracted to the charged sodium and chloride ions. This force of attraction pulls the ions away from the crystal and into solution. Notice that the solution contains only separate sodium ions and chloride ions surrounded by water molecules. Compare the arrangement of water molecules around the sodium ions with that around the chloride ions. Explain the difference.

4. Answers will vary from group to group. Students should provide plausible explanations.
5. Students should realize that much depends on what happens to the acid rain when it falls. It may do harm by acidifying ponds, lakes, and streams. It also may harm plants. However, in some areas, soil can neutralize most of the acidity, at least for a time.
6. It will kill or weaken many organisms and favor others.
7. Many normal water sources are slightly acidic. Acidity only becomes a problem if it drops consistently below 5.5 or so. Values lower than this might have a detrimental effect on amphibians.
8. Student conclusions should not go beyond what they can objectively state from what they have observed.

✔ **Assessment**

Portfolio: Have students write a report on the investigation, including observations, graphs, and conclusions, in their journals. Each student should write a paragraph telling whether he or she believes an acid water sample could have originated as acid rain. If possible, provide students with a map showing acid rain patterns. Have students include their journal entries in their portfolios.

Extensions

Ask students to consider what they would do if they found a pond in the area that had a pH of about 4. How would they experiment to try to pin down the source of the acidity?

---

2. Agree on one idea from your group's list that could be investigated in the classroom.
3. Design an experiment that will test one variable at a time. Plan to collect quantitative data.
4. Following the style of a recipe, write a numbered list of directions that anyone could follow.
5. Make a list of materials and the quantities you will need.

Checking the Plan

Discuss the following points with other group members to decide the final procedures for your experiment.
1. What variables will need to be controlled?
2. What is your control?
3. What will you measure?
4. How much water of each type will you need?
5. Will you need more than one trial with each water sample?

6. How long will you wait before reading the results of your pH tests?
7. Have you designed and made a table for collecting your data?
8. How will you present your data in a graph?
Make sure your teacher has approved your plan before you proceed.

Data and Observations

Carry out your experiment, and complete your data table.

Analysis and Conclusions

1. What was your control?
2. Which type of water had the lowest pH, and is, therefore, the most acidic? Speculate why.
3. Which type of water had the highest pH? Speculate why.
4. Was your hypothesis supported by your data? Explain.
5. How might rainwater with a very low pH affect living organisms?

6. How might low pH in ponds, lakes, or streams affect living organisms?
7. Amphibians, such as frogs and salamanders, are declining in numbers worldwide. Some scientists think that increasing acidity of water in their habitat is the cause for this decline. Based on data you gathered, make a hypothesis about how the pH of water may be affecting amphibian numbers in your area.
8. Write a brief conclusion to your experiment.

Going Further

Based on this lab experience, design an experiment that would help answer another question that arose from your work. Assume that you will have unlimited resources and will not be conducting this lab in class.

Figure Caption Question

Compare the arrangement of water molecules around the sodium ions with that around the chloride ions. Explain the difference. The positive ends of water molecules are attracted to negative chloride ions, whereas the negative ends are attracted to positive sodium ions.

Building a Model

Suggest that students use a model such as four stacks of three pennies each arranged in a tight cluster to represent sugar molecules in a crystal. Then ask them to rearrange the pennies to represent sugar molecules in solution. They should separate all 12 pennies wide apart on a tabletop to represent the dissolved molecules.

Using the Illustration

Have students use Figure 3-15 on page 67 as a model for the following task. Predict the appearance of a similar diagram showing a salt such as magnesium bromide, $MgBr_2$, after dissolving in water. **L1** **LEP**

Reinforcement

Have students explain why (a) one end of the water molecule is positive and the other is negative, (b) the sodium ion is positive, (c) the chloride ion is negative, (d) the positive end of a water molecule is attracted to a negative ion, (e) the negative end of a water molecule is attracted to a positive ion.

Figure Caption Question

Which has the higher concentration of OH⁻ ions, ammonia solution or blood? Ammonia solution because it has a higher pH.

3 Assess

Check for Understanding

Provide a list of names of several common elements. Ask students to (a) give the correct chemical symbol for each element, (b) diagram the element's nucleus using symbols to show numbers of protons and neutrons, (c) use symbols to indicate electron numbers and locations within energy levels.

How Ionic Compounds Dissolve   In water, ionic compounds behave differently from covalent compounds. Consider table salt (sodium chloride) as an example. Earlier, you learned that sodium chloride is not composed of molecules. Instead, it is made of separate, charged ions. When salt is added to water, the positive ends of water molecules attract the negatively charged chloride ions, and the negative ends of other water molecules attract the positively charged sodium ions. This attraction is strong enough to break the ionic bond, causing the positive sodium and negative chloride ions to separate and become scattered throughout the water. Thus, a solution of table salt in water consists of water molecules, sodium ions, and chloride ions, as seen in Figure 3-15.

An understanding of solutions is important in biology. Organisms may consist of 70 percent water or more, and many substances, both covalent and ionic, are dissolved in that water. The chemical reactions that make up life processes take place in water solution. Ions dissolved in the water of organisms are important to life functions, such as conduction of nerve impulses, contraction of muscles, and photosynthesis.

Acids and Bases

You might think that pure water would consist of only H_2O molecules. However, in about two molecules per billion, one proton of a hydrogen atom breaks away from a water molecule. This process forms a positively charged hydrogen ion (H^+) and a negatively charged hydroxide ion (OH^-). See Figure 3-16. The numbers of hydrogen and hydroxide ions that exist are equal, because one ion of each kind is produced from the breakup of every water molecule. Any solution in which the concentration of hydrogen and hydroxide ions is equal is called a neutral solution.

What happens if you dissolve in water some substance that changes the balance between the concentration of hydrogen and hydroxide ions? When hydrogen chloride gas dissolves in water, the molecules of HCl separate into hydrogen and chloride ions. The solution now has a greater concentration of hydrogen ions than hydroxide ions. Such a solution is called an **acid,** in this case, hydrochloric acid. Similarly, if the ionic substance sodium hydroxide is dissolved in water, the solution will contain a greater concentration of hydroxide ions than hydrogen ions. Such a solution is called a **base.** Solutions of acids typically have a sour taste. Lemons

Figure 3-16   A tiny fraction of water molecules breaks apart and forms ions. Each molecule that ionizes forms one hydrogen ion and one hydroxide ion. Therefore, in pure water, the numbers of hydrogen ions and hydroxide ions will be equal. It's important to note that a hydrogen ion is just a bare proton. In water, it is always surrounded by water molecules attracted to it because of its positive charge.

$$H_2O \longrightarrow H^+ + OH^-$$

68 ❧ MATTER AND ENERGY

pH Values of Common Foods: Have students test a variety of familiar foods and juices with pH paper. Ask them to record their data in a self-designed chart. If possible, have them test some of the items named in Figure 3-17 to verify their pH values. Ask them to group the liquids and items tested into three categories: acid, base, and neutral (between pH 6 and 8). Have students report their findings to the class or have them write a formal lab report of their project. **L1**

and grapefruit are sour because they contain citric acid. Solutions of bases, like soapy water, have a sharp, bitter taste, and they feel slippery.

The pH Scale   The concentration of hydrogen ions in solutions is indicated by a set of numbers called the pH scale, which runs from 0 to 14. See Figure 3-17. Pure water, having an equal concentration of hydrogen and hydroxide ions, has a pH of 7. A pH of 7 represents a neutral solution. Numbers below 7 represent acids. The lower the number, the greater the concentration of hydrogen ions and the more acidic the solution. Numbers above 7 represent bases. The higher the number, the lower the concentration of hydrogen ions and the more basic the solution.

The pH of solutions is important to living systems. The pH of water and soil, for example, is one of the factors that determines the kinds of organisms that can live there. Also, pH can influence the chemical reactions that can occur in an organism. For example, in order for digestion to occur properly in the human stomach, the pH there must be about 2. Human blood must be maintained at a pH slightly above 7.

Figure 3-17   Shown here are the pH values of some common materials. Which has the higher concentration of OH⁻ ions, ammonia solution or blood?

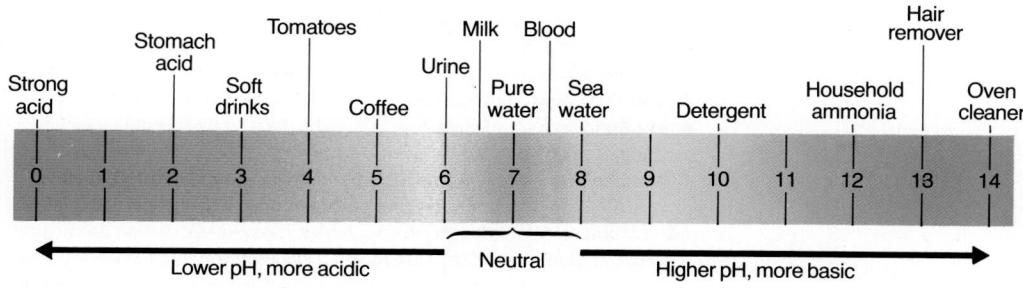

Section Review

Understanding Concepts

1. Carbon is a key element in living things. A typical carbon atom has 6 protons and 6 neutrons in the nucleus. Describe the electron arrangement of a carbon atom. How many covalent bonds would a carbon atom usually form? Explain your reasoning.

2. When an aluminum atom forms an ionic bond, will it gain or lose electrons? How many electrons does an aluminum ion have? What is its charge?

3. Calcium chloride, $CaCl_2$, is an ionic compound composed of calcium and chloride ions. If you could see the particles in a solution of calcium chloride dissolved in water, what would you see? Explain.

4. **Skill Review—Classifying:** Atoms having the same number of electrons in their outermost energy levels have similar properties. The following is a list of atoms and their total number of electrons. Divide the atoms into two groups, each having similar properties: lithium—3;

magnesium—12; sodium—11; potassium—19; beryllium—4. For more help, refer to Organizing Information in the **Skill Handbook.**

5. **Thinking Critically:** Neon has a total of ten electrons. Why does neon not react with other atoms?

SECTION 3.1

Reteach

Supply the following pairs of terms or phrases to students. Have them explain how each set of terms is related and how they differ and/or are alike. (1) compound, element (2) ionic bond, covalent bond (3) atom, ion (4) electron number and charge, proton (5) bond, outer-level electrons (6) number and charge (7) acid, base

Extension

Provide students with a small amount of sulfur in a sealed container. Ask them to describe the physical characteristics of this element and diagram an atom of the element. Ask them to diagram a sulfide ion.

✔ Assessment

Oral: Ask students to describe how electrons and protons are related to the charge of an ion and to provide an example and explain the difference between products and reactants in a chemical reaction.

4 Close

Demonstration

Have students build a model of an element such as oxygen using classmates to represent protons, neutrons, and electrons. Extend the model to show ion formation. LEP

Answers to Section Review

1. There are two electrons in the first energy level and four in the second. A carbon atom usually forms four covalent bonds because it must share four electrons to attain a total of eight electrons.

2. An aluminum atom will lose three electrons, resulting in an aluminum ion having ten electrons and a charge of 3+.

3. Calcium ions, chloride ions, and water molecules would be seen. The calcium and chloride ions separate from one another because of the polar nature of the water molecules. There would be twice as many chloride ions as calcium ions.

4. **Skill Review—Classifying:** Group 1 would contain lithium, sodium, and potassium because each has one electron in its outer energy level. Group 2 would contain magnesium and beryllium because

each has two electrons in its outer energy level.

5. **Thinking Critically:** A neon atom has eight electrons in its outer energy level. Therefore, it is stable in an uncombined form.

Prepare

Key Concepts

Students will look at the four main classes of organic compounds present within all living matter. The chemical makeup and properties of carbohydrates, lipids, proteins, and nucleic acids will be studied.

Key Terms

isomer, carbohydrate, polysaccharide, lipid, protein, amino acid, polypeptide, nucleic acid

Materials

- Purchase antacid tablets and gather materials that contain calcium carbonate such as eggshells, seashells, chalk, limestone, and/or marble chips.

1 Focus

Objectives

The objectives are listed on the student page. Remind students to preview these objectives as a guide to this numbered section.

Discussion

Ask students if they would sweeten their food with sugar or starch. All will respond that they would use sugar. Advise them that starch is actually a compound formed from many sugar molecules joined together. **L1**

2 Teach

Discussion

Ask students to draw a model of the element carbon. Verify that the placement of electrons is correct—two in the inner level, four in the outer level. Ask them to predict how many electrons are needed to make the atom stable. Ask how carbon may accomplish this task. Why does carbon bond to four hydrogen atoms to make methane? How are hydrogen atoms becoming stable by bonding with carbon? **L1**

Objectives

Relate the structure of a carbon atom to the complexity of carbon compounds.

Compare the structures and functions of carbohydrates, lipids, and proteins.

Distinguish between condensation and hydrolysis reactions.

3.2 Biological Chemistry

What's your favorite food? Do you like pizza? Frozen yogurt? Spaghetti? A juicy steak? As you know, these foods contain parts and products of living things, which are composed of a variety of compounds. Biological compounds are much more complex than any we have looked at so far. Many of them contain thousands of atoms or more. Though they are more complex, the properties and behavior of these substances are explained by the same principles of chemistry that apply to substances in the nonliving world.

Carbon Compounds

Originally, because most carbon compounds were known to be associated only with organisms, scientists called them organic compounds. Later, chemists analyzed them and learned to make organic compounds in the laboratory. Today, organic compounds are defined as those compounds that contain carbon. All substances not classified as organic are called inorganic substances. A few carbon compounds, such as carbon dioxide, CO_2, are not classified as organic.

Carbon atoms have six electrons, two in the first level and four in the second. In order to have a stable outer level of eight electrons, carbon must obtain four more electrons. It usually does so by sharing electrons, forming covalent bonds.

Not only can carbon atoms form bonds with atoms of different elements, they can also bond to other carbon atoms. This property explains why carbon compounds can be so complex. Sometimes carbon atoms join together, making long chains that form a skeleton to which other kinds of atoms are joined. In other organic molecules, carbon atoms are bonded to form ringlike structures, and these rings may be bonded to one another.

Figure 3-18 The simplest organic substance is methane, shown here in four different ways. Notice that carbon atoms form four covalent bonds in a pyramid shape called a tetrahedron. The diagram on the right shows how a methane molecule would look if you could see it. The two formulas on the left represent two convenient ways of writing formulas for methane.

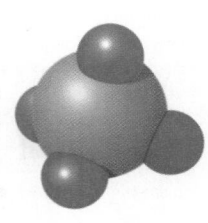

MEETING INDIVIDUAL NEEDS

Visually Impaired: Building models of a methane molecule can be accomplished with visually impaired students by using Styrofoam balls of different sizes and taffy apple sticks to hold the model parts together. **L1** **LEP**

PROGRAM RESOURCES

Teacher Classroom Resources
Study Guide, pp. 15-16 **L1**
Concept Mapping, p. 3 **L1** **LEP**
Probing Levels of Life, Labs 5, 6, 7, pp. 15, 18, 20 **L2**

Structural Formulas   Recall that chemical formulas show the kinds and numbers of atoms in a molecule. Such formulas can also be written for organic molecules. More often, though, structural formulas are used to better represent organic molecules. Structural formulas show not only the kinds and numbers of atoms in a molecule, but also their arrangement. Methane, the major component of natural gas, is the simplest organic compound. Methane has the chemical formula CH_4, as shown in Figure 3-18. Its structural formula shows that each of the four hydrogen atoms is bonded to the central carbon atom. If the formula were shown in three dimensions, it would resemble a pyramid, the true shape of the molecule. Each line drawn between atoms represents a covalent bond, the sharing of one pair of electrons.

Some covalent bonds involve sharing of more than one pair of electrons between atoms. A structural formula with two lines between atoms, such as C=C or C=O, indicates a double covalent bond, the sharing of two pairs of electrons.

Isomers   To see why it is important to use structural formulas to represent organic compounds, examine Figure 3-19. Count the number of each kind of atom in each structural formula and determine the chemical formula of each. As you can see from the diagram, some organic molecules may have the same chemical formula, but different structural formulas. Such molecules are called **isomers.** Isomers have different physical and chemical properties that are important to organisms. By showing structural formulas, one isomer can be easily distinguished from another.

2-methylpropane
C_4H_{10}

Butane C_4H_{10}

Figure 3-19   Here you can see the advantage of writing structural formulas to represent organic compounds. Both of these compounds have exactly the same chemical formula, C_4H_{10}. However, they are two different compounds because they have different structures. One is called butane, and the other is 2-methylpropane.

Although CO_2 is a gas, much of it in nature is combined in inorganic carbonate compounds, usually calcium carbonate. Obtain several carbonate-containing materials, such as dry eggshell, a piece of seashell, a bit of chalk, a piece of antacid tablet, and a chip of marble or limestone. Place each sample in a separate labeled test tube. Pour enough vinegar (weak acetic acid solution) into each container to cover each sample about 1 cm deep. Use a hand lens to observe what happens to each sample. If bubbles form, carbon dioxide is being produced in the reaction.

Analysis   *How do you know that what you observed is a chemical change? Which of your samples come from living things? Consider that CO_2 gas is a major contributor to the greenhouse effect in Earth's atmosphere. What do you think would happen if organisms that manufacture carbonate compounds were to die off?*

Minilab 2

Purpose
To demonstrate the existence of inorganic carbon compounds produced by living things.

Skills
classify, observe and infer

Teaching Strategies
• **Safety Precautions:** Have students wear aprons and goggles.
• Don't use an effervescent antacid. Check the label to see that the antacid contains carbonates.
• It may be possible to get natural chalk, crushed shells, and similar materials from pet supply stores or stores that sell animal feed. Use 5% vinegar instead of 4%.
• **Troubleshooting:** If materials are slow to react, have students warm the tubes or you could demonstrate the reactions in large test tubes using dilute hydrochloric acid instead of vinegar.

Expected Results
All materials contain carbonates and should produce bubbles of CO_2.

Answers
A new substance (CO_2) with different properties (a gas) is produced. All samples, perhaps even the $CaCO_3$ in the antacid tablet, come ultimately from living things. If students doubt this, have them research the origins of chalk, limestone, and marble. The amount of CO_2 in the atmosphere would increase, thus increasing the greenhouse effect and increasing temperatures.

✔ **Assessment**
Skill: Ask students to use their observations from this activity to devise a method for testing rock samples in the field to determine which rocks contain carbonates. They should specify materials and write out a stepwise procedure.

STUDENT JOURNAL

Ask students to explain and summarize in paragraph form why structural formulas are more informative than chemical formulas. Some students could create an analogy for the comparison. One example is attempting to describe a house by giving the number of boards and nails and other materials used in its construction. They should also include the concept of differentiating among isomers within their paragraphs. Diagrams may be used when needed to enhance the explanation. **L1**

SECTION 3.2

Reinforcement

If possible, exhibit or have students construct a model of the methane molecule. Students often cannot see the tetrahedral shape as represented on flat paper. **L1** **LEP**

Building a Model

Have students use toothpick sections and colored gumdrops to build models of ethane (C_2H_6) and propane (C_3H_8). Ask students if they can construct isomers of these structures of ethane. They cannot. Now have them build a model of butane (C_4H_{10}). Ask students if they can now construct an isomer. They should be able to construct one isomer. **L1** **LEP**

Brainstorming

The formula for sucrose is $C_{12}H_{22}O_{11}$. Ask students to account for the difference between the number of each kind of atom in two molecules of glucose compared to one molecule of sucrose. The difference is H_2O, or one molecule of water.

Figure 3-20 Look at the structural formulas for glucose and fructose. If you count the atoms of carbon, hydrogen, and oxygen, you'll discover that both sugars have the same chemical formula. Glucose is abundant in corn syrup; honey contains fructose. Simple sugars such as these are examples of carbohydrates.

Glucose

Fructose

Carbohydrates

Are you hungry? Picture a thick cheeseburger on a bun and a side order of fries. When you eat a meal like this, you're really enjoying several biologically important groups of organic compounds. One of these groups is carbohydrates. **Carbohydrates** are organic compounds composed of carbon, hydrogen, and oxygen with a ratio of two hydrogen atoms to each oxygen atom. Sugars and starches, such as those found in the hamburger bun and fries, are typical examples of carbohydrates. In living things, many carbohydrates serve as energy sources for life processes. In fact, the sugar glucose is a "fuel of life" for many different organisms.

Simple Sugars Glucose, $C_6H_{12}O_6$, is an example of the simplest type of carbohydrate, a monosaccharide, or simple sugar. Fructose, the sugar contained in many fruits, is also a monosaccharide. It has the same chemical formula as glucose, $C_6H_{12}O_6$, but differs in structure. Another isomer of glucose is galactose, a monosaccharide in milk.

Two simple sugars can bond together to form organic compounds called double sugars, or disaccharides. Table sugar, sucrose, is a double sugar composed of one molecule of glucose and one of fructose. Lactose, milk sugar, is composed of one molecule of glucose bonded to one of galactose. Maltose consists of two glucose molecules bonded together. Sucrose, lactose, and maltose are isomers of one another. They all have the formula $C_{12}H_{22}O_{11}$.

Thinking Lab

MAKE A HYPOTHESIS

Why do monarch butterflies contain two different chemicals for defense?

Background
The monarch butterfly has two chemical defense systems. As a caterpillar, the monarch eats milkweed leaves. These leaves contain a bitter-tasting toxic substance, which the butterfly stores in its body. As a butterfly, the monarch migrates to southern regions where

there are few milkweeds. There, it takes in different toxic chemicals from the nectar of certain flowers.
You Try It
Make a hypothesis to explain how toxic chemicals work as a defense system for monarchs. Keep in mind that some major predators for monarchs are birds

and reptiles. However, they are usually only made ill by the toxic substances. Describe an experiment that would test your hypothesis. What additional information would you need? Why would the presence of these chemicals benefit the species as a whole but not necessarily the individual?

72 ꙮ MATTER AND ENERGY

Thinking Lab

MAKE A HYPOTHESIS

Purpose
Students observe that organisms consume organic chemicals for defense.

Skills
design an experiment, form a hypothesis

Teaching Strategies
• Many reference books have photos showing a bird being made ill after the consumption of a monarch.

Answers
Students should describe experiments in which the behavior of predators toward the monarch is observed both before and after the predator has attempted to consume a monarch. Some individuals must be killed and consumed in order to "teach" the predator to avoid monarchs.

✔ Assessment
Skill: Ask students what types of predators would be deterred by this defense strategy. Students should conclude that this strategy requires an organism capable of being made ill by the poison but not killed and which is capable of learning new behavior from one or two encounters with monarchs.

Figure 3-21 Materials such as cotton, wood, and paper consist mainly of cellulose, a polysaccharide. Grains and potatoes contain starch, another polysaccharide. Both cellulose and starch are carbohydrates made of chains of glucose units, but the units are linked differently. Starch molecules are long spiral chains of glucose units.

Starch—a polysaccharide

Polysaccharides   Long chains of monosaccharides joined together form the most complex carbohydrates, **polysaccharides.** Hamburger buns and fries contain a polysaccharide known as starch. Starch is provided by plants. During the growing season, many plants produce more simple sugars than they use for energy. This excess sugar is converted to starch for storage. During critical periods, plants can change starch back to simple sugars, which can be used by the plant as its energy source in cellular respiration. When you digest the starch contained in the bun and fries, you convert it to glucose, which you then use as an energy source. Humans store excess glucose in the liver and muscles in the form of a starchlike compound called glycogen. Like starch in plants, glycogen can also be converted to glucose and used as an energy source when the need arises. However, not all carbohydrates are used as energy sources. For example, another plant polysaccharide, cellulose, is used for structural purposes in the cell walls of plants. Cellulose, glycogen, and starch are all made of chains of glucose molecules. They differ in the patterns by which the molecules are linked.

Lipids

Besides carbohydrates, a tasty cheeseburger meal contains another group of organic compounds, fats. The cheese in cheeseburgers and the burger itself contain fats. French fries are usually cooked in oil. Fats and oils, along with waxes, belong to a class of organic compounds called lipids. Like carbohydrates, **lipids** are also composed of carbon, hydrogen, and oxygen, but unlike carbohydrates, the number of hydrogen atoms per molecule is much greater than the number of oxygen atoms. For example, one common lipid has the formula $C_{57}H_{110}O_6$. Lipids produced by animals are usually solid fats, but those produced by plants are usually liquid oils. Waxes are produced by both plants and animals.

Figure 3-22   This photo shows some sources of lipids in our diets. In general, butter and the fat in meat contain more saturated fatty acids than do oils from plants, which contain more unsaturated fatty acids. Which examples have more double bonds?

SECTION 3.2

Discussion

Use Figure 3-20 as a guide to asking the following questions. (a) Are the total numbers of atoms in glucose and fructose the same or different? (b) Are the total numbers of C, H, and O atoms the same or different? (c) In view of the fact that the numbers of atoms are the same, exactly how does glucose differ from fructose? (d) Might this difference between these two molecules be obvious if structural formulas were not available?
LEP

Using Science Terms

Ask students to define *mono-*, *di-*, and *poly-* prefixes as they apply to the three different sugars. Ask students to correlate the three prefixes with the terms *simple sugar, double sugar,* and *complex sugar.* LEP

Demonstration

Have students taste a disaccharide such as sucrose. Then ask them to taste starch, a complex polysaccharide. How do their tastes differ? Ask them to describe the appearance of both carbohydrates. A hand lens may be helpful. Ask students to speculate why the two substances taste different even though both are composed of linked monosaccharides.
CAUTION: *Do not allow students who are diabetic to taste these substances.*

Teacher FYI

The lipid with the formula $C_{57}H_{110}O_6$, referred to in the text, is the fat *tristearin* and is abundant in beef fat and cocoa butter.

Figure Caption Question

Which examples have more double bonds? peanut butter, vegetable oils

---

PROGRAM RESOURCES

Teacher Classroom Resources

Critical Thinking/Problem Solving, p. 3
L2

Investigating Living Systems, Labs 6, 7, 8, pp. 21, 27, 31 L2

Display

Bring in samples of animal and plant fats for students to observe. Animal fats may consist of the fat trimmed from bacon, steaks, or chops. Plant fats include peanut, corn, olive, canola, and cottonseed oils. Ask students to feel both types. Ask them to describe and record any similarities and/or differences between the two fat types that they observe. Be sure students wash hands thoroughly after touching fats. **L1** **LEP**

Brainstorming

Ask students to list several ways in which the chemical compositions and structural formulas of carbohydrates and lipids are similar and different.
COOP LEARN

Teacher FYI

The terms *saturated* and *unsaturated* were originally used before chemists understood organic structure. Compounds were considered unsaturated if they "took up" (reacted with) bromine or chlorine. Compounds that took up no halogen to begin with were said to be saturated. Today, chemists know that the halogens were reacting with double bonds present in the compounds. Thus, double bonds mean that the compound is unsaturated.

Figure 3-23 Typical fats contain three fatty acids bonded to a glycerol molecule. The structure of a fat (top) shows how the fatty acids are linked to glycerol. It also demonstrates the structural differences between saturated and unsaturated fatty acids.

In animals, excess fats in the diet, along with excess sugars that have been converted to fats, are stored and used as energy reserves. The storage of fats is an adaptation that guards against critical times when food is scarce. Lipids also form part of the structure of cell membranes (Chapter 4). In some animals, lipids protect parts of nerve cells, speed the transmission of nerve impulses, and provide insulation from the cold.

The Structure of Fats Fat molecules are built from two types of simpler molecules—fatty acids and glycerol. There are many different types of fatty acid molecules, but all have one part in common, a group of atoms called a carboxyl group (—COOH). In the structural formula of a fatty acid, shown in Figure 3-23, the letter *R* represents a long chain of carbon and hydrogen atoms to which the carboxyl group is attached. The exact number of these atoms varies among fatty acids; thus, for simplification, the chain is written as *R*.

The kinds of bonds between carbon atoms in fat molecules also vary. Fatty acids in which carbon atoms are linked by single covalent bonds are said to be saturated, while those having one or more double covalent bonds are said to be unsaturated. As Figure 3-23 shows, saturated fatty acids are filled, or saturated, with more hydrogen atoms than unsaturated molecules. This difference is important to your health. Scientists generally agree that substituting vegetable oils that have a high proportion of unsaturated fatty acids for animal fats in the human diet lowers the risk of heart and circulatory diseases.

Cholesterol is another lipid you have probably heard of. The molecular structure of cholesterol is quite different from that of other lipids. However, cholesterol is classified as a lipid because, like other lipids, it is insoluble in water. In many organisms, especially animals, cholesterol is produced in the body. It is used in the formation of cell membranes and the manufacture of many hormones. Later, you'll learn how an excess of cholesterol in the human body can cause health problems.

74 MATTER AND ENERGY

ALTERNATE LAB: How Sensitive is TesTape?

Purpose
Students will determine the percentage at which glucose can no longer be detected by TesTape.

Materials
TesTape, test tubes, test tube rack, medicine dropper, graduated cylinder, grease pencil, 10% glucose solution (See page 27T.)

Procedure
Give the following directions to students.
1. Place 9 mL of water in each of six test tubes. Mark the tubes 1 through 6 and arrange them in a test tube rack.
2. Use a medicine dropper to add 20 drops of 10% glucose solution to tube 1 and mix the tube by shaking.
3. Use a clean dropper to add 20 drops of liquid from tube 1 to tube 2 and mix tube 2 by shaking.
4. Repeat the previous steps of dilution using clean droppers for all six tubes. The dilutions of the tubes will be: tube 1 = 1% glucose, tube 2 = 0.1% glucose, tube 3 = 0.01% glucose, and so on.
5. Touch a drop of the liquid from each test tube to a small piece of TesTape.
6. Note and record the color of the tape for each tube in a self-designed data table.

Proteins

In hamburger as well as other meats and seafood, the largest group of organic molecules belongs to another class of compounds, the **proteins.** Unlike carbohydrates and lipids, proteins are not normally used as energy sources by organisms. Some are used in the building of living material, such as the muscle from which burgers are made. Others have functional roles, such as carrying out chemical reactions, fighting disease, or transporting particles into or out of cells. These functions are very specific, and each requires a protein with different structural characteristics.

The Structure of Proteins   Like carbohydrates and lipids, protein molecules are composed of carbon, hydrogen, and oxygen atoms. In addition, they contain nitrogen and sulfur. A single protein molecule may be built from chains of hundreds or even thousands of simpler compounds called **amino acids**. Most of the 20 different amino acids that make up most proteins have a central carbon atom to which is bonded a carboxyl group, a hydrogen atom, and an amino group ($-NH_2$). Also attached to the carbon atom is the rest of the molecule, the part that makes each amino acid different. It is represented by the letter R, as seen in Figure 3-25.

When amino acids bond to one another, they are known as peptides. Two amino acids linked together form a dipeptide. Many bonded together are a **polypeptide.** Polypeptides differ from one another by the kind, number, and sequence of amino acids. To see why there are so many different proteins possible, try this exercise. How many other words can you make from the letters in the word STOP? In the same way that the 26 letters of the alphabet form many words with special meanings, the 20 amino acids in proteins can form an almost endless variety of polypeptides having different properties.

Figure 3-24   Feathers, spider webs, wool, and silk are made up of proteins. In fact, feathers consist mostly of the same protein, keratin, that makes up human nails and hair.

Figure 3-25   Proteins are made of long chains of amino acid units. The left photo is a computer image of a molecule of immunoglobin. In the right diagram, the shaded area shows the structure that is present in almost every amino acid. Structures of two of the simpler amino acids are shown also. The R group in more complex amino acids can include longer chains, sometimes with ring structures and atoms of sulfur.

General structure of an amino acid

Alanine

Valine

3.2 BIOLOGICAL CHEMISTRY 🐚 **75**

Chalkboard Example

Write the formula for glucose as $C_6H_{12}O_6$ on the board. Write another glucose formula directly below, and have students add the total carbons, hydrogens, and oxygens. Their totals will be 12, 24, and 12, respectively. Write the formula for sucrose on the board. Show them that the loss of H_2O from the two glucose molecules will account for the formula for sucrose, $C_{12}H_{22}O_{11}$.

Demonstration

Ask students to taste and observe the physical characteristics of glucose. Glucose tablets are available in drugstores. Crush them before showing students. Have them record their observations. Ask them to taste and observe the physical characteristics of maltose, which is available as malt tablets in specialty food stores or drugstores. Have students record their observations. Students may be surprised at the difference in taste, considering that maltose is a disaccharide made from two glucose units. **CAUTION:** *Do not allow students who are diabetic to taste the sugars.*

Using an Analogy

Obtain some Lego blocks. Ask your students to model the formation and breakdown of polysaccharides and polypeptides by hydrolysis and condensation reactions. If blocks are not available, use paper clips. LEP

COOP LEARN

3 Assess

Check for Understanding

Students should be able to name the types of molecules used to form disaccharides and polysaccharides, lipids, and proteins. They should also be able to correctly use the terms *hydrolysis* and *condensation* in sentences describing how small molecules are assembled or how large molecules are broken apart.

Protein structure is very complex. A protein molecule may consist of just one polypeptide or two or more polypeptides bonded together. In addition, each protein has a distinct, three-dimensional shape that is crucial to the protein's function. For example, the proteins that form fingernails and hair are long and fiberlike. Some other proteins, such as hemoglobin in your blood, have a globular shape. That is, they are like a sphere with a lumpy surface.

Nucleic Acids

Every organism contains molecules that form a code that controls the organism's basic appearance and behavior. These molecules belong to a fourth class of biological compounds called **nucleic acids**. Nucleic acids include DNA and RNA and are the most complex of all biological molecules. Deoxyribonucleic acid (DNA) and ribonucleic acid (RNA) control the cell's activities. DNA usually forms the genetic code of organisms, and RNA works to carry out the instructions of that code. You'll learn more about the structure and function of nucleic acids in Chapters 9 and 10.

Reactions of Biological Compounds

As you recall, the disaccharides sucrose, maltose, and lactose all have the formula $C_{12}H_{22}O_{11}$. Does this formula surprise you? Do you think it should be $C_{12}H_{24}O_{12}$ because these molecules consist of two monosaccharides each having the formula $C_6H_{12}O_6$? If you think that two hydrogen atoms and an oxygen atom are missing, you're thinking clearly.

Condensation Reactions Remember that in order for a chemical reaction to occur, bonds must be broken and new bonds must be formed. Figure 3-26 shows the formation of maltose from two molecules of glucose. In one glucose molecule, a bond to one hydrogen atom is broken. In the other, the bond to an —OH group is broken. During the reaction, these three atoms bond with one another to form a molecule of water. This water molecule accounts for the two hydrogen atoms and one oxygen atom that seemed to be missing. At the same time, the glucose molecules form new bonds with each other. The new disaccharide molecule is made by removing water from the original molecules. This chemical process is called *condensation*

Figure 3-26 **Large molecules in living things often consist of smaller molecules bonded to each other by condensation reactions. This diagram shows how the disaccharide, maltose, is built by the condensation of two glucose molecules. The —H and —OH that are removed form a molecule of water.**

Glucose   Glucose   Maltose

Dipeptide + Water ⟶ Amino acid + Amino acid
                                    Glycine   Alanine

and is a common reaction in organisms whenever larger molecules are made from smaller units. For example, amino acids from the foods you eat are linked by condensation reactions to form the larger proteins needed by your cells for growth and maintenance.

Hydrolysis   Large molecules are converted to smaller ones by a process that is the reverse of condensation. Because this process involves the addition of water, it is called *hydrolysis*. Hydrolysis reactions are important to living things because complex molecules must be broken down into simpler ones before they can be used by cells. Digestion, for example, involves the breakdown of proteins in food into amino acids. Figure 3-27 shows such a reaction in which a dipeptide is converted to two amino acids. Notice that the reaction breaks the bond that links the amino acids together. During the hydrolysis, a nitrogen atom from one amino acid bonds to a hydrogen atom, and a carbon atom from the other amino acid bonds to an —OH group. Both the —H and —OH groups come from a water molecule. These processes of hydrolysis and condensation illustrate the importance of water to living things.

Figure 3-27   Some biological processes, such as digestion, require that large molecules be broken down into smaller units, usually by hydrolysis reactions. Shown here is the hydrolysis of a dipeptide into two amino acids. Compare this diagram with Figure 3-26. Can you see that the two processes are the reverse of each other?

Section Review

Understanding Concepts

1. Why are organic compounds usually more complex than inorganic compounds?
2. Why do you think the variety of proteins is so much greater than that of carbohydrates or lipids?
3. Suppose 100 amino acids are linked together in a cell, one at a time, to form a polypeptide chain. How many molecules of water will be removed in this synthesis?

4. **Skill Review—Making Tables:** Make a table comparing carbohydrates, lipids, and proteins. Compare them in terms of the elements they contain, the building blocks of which they are composed, and their functions in living organisms. For more help, see Organizing Information in the **Skill Handbook.**

5. **Thinking Critically:** One gram of fat releases 2.5 times as much energy as an equal amount of glucose. Why does the body normally use glucose for energy and store fat instead of using fat and storing glucose?

Reteach
Ask students to model the formation of a polysaccharide, lipid, and protein through the use of models made from paper clips or stacking blocks.

Extension
Have students make a physical model of the hydrolysis reaction shown in Figure 3-27 using model kits or Tinkertoy parts with pasted-on labels. Ask them to exhibit the model to the class and demonstrate both hydrolysis and condensation showing the addition and elimination of a water molecule, respectively. **L3**

✔ Assessment
Portfolio: Ask students to construct a concept map that covers the main ideas and relationships of this section. **L1**

4 Close

Activity
Pass out enlarged photocopies of a food label to all students. Ask them to read the nutritional information. Then have them describe in as much detail as possible the chemical composition of the carbohydrates, fats, and proteins listed on the label. Have them speculate from this information on how our bodies obtain needed fats, proteins, and carbohydrates. Also ask them to predict where within our bodies each of these three chemical groups may end up. **L1**

Answers to Section Review

1. Carbon atoms form four covalent bonds including bonds with other carbon atoms. Thus, carbon compounds may consist of long chains or rings of carbon atoms.
2. Unlike carbohydrates and lipids, which are composed of just a few kinds of building block molecules, proteins are built of 20 different kinds of amino acids. The number and sequence of amino acids in a protein makes each one unique.

3. 99 water molecules will be removed.
4. **Skill Review—Making Tables:**
   Elements contained—carbohydrates: carbon, hydrogen, and oxygen; lipids: carbon, hydrogen, and oxygen; proteins: carbon, hydrogen, oxygen, nitrogen, and sulfur. Building blocks—carbohydrates: monosaccharides; lipids (fats): fatty acids and glycerol; proteins: amino acids. Functions—carbohydrates: energy

source, energy reserve, plant cell walls; fats: energy reserves, cell membranes, insulation, nerve transmission; proteins: structural material, enzymes, transport of particles in and out of cells.
5. **Thinking Critically:** Glucose is readily available from stored glycogen. Fat must go through a more complex series of enzyme reactions in order to yield molecules that can enter cell respiration.

Prepare

Key Concepts

Students learn to distinguish between potential and kinetic energy. They will study how enzymes lower activation energy, thus allowing cells to carry out chemical reactions at low temperatures.

Key Terms

potential energy, kinetic energy, activation energy, enzyme, coenzyme

Materials

- Purchase Alka Seltzer tablets for the demonstration of activation energy.

1 Focus

Objectives

The objectives are listed on the student page. Remind students to preview these objectives as a guide to this numbered section.

Demonstration

Ask students to stand up at their desks and feel the temperature of the desk seat. Ask them to explain why the seat temperature is warmer than the surrounding air. Have them try to explain what it is they sense as heat and where this heat is coming from.

`L1`

2 Teach

Chalkboard Example

Diagram a structural formula of glucose on the board. Ask students to count the number of bonds present. Ask students if the bond lines represent potential or kinetic energy. Ask how it will be possible to convert from one energy form to another.

Objectives

Distinguish between potential energy and kinetic energy by using an example.

Discuss the relationship between a reaction and activation energy.

Describe the means by which an enzyme carries out a cellular reaction.

3.3 Energy and Reactions

You have probably heard that you need lots of energy for both running and thinking. What is energy? The best way to define energy is to describe what it does. Moving a car requires energy. So does melting ice. Both of these events involve motion. In a car, it's the motion of pistons and gears. With the melting ice, it's the motion of water molecules. Whenever anything moves, work is done. Therefore, energy is the ability to do work—in other words, to cause motion.

Energy is most evident to you when it is changing from one form to another. Electrical energy flowing through a light bulb changes to light, enabling you to read. Electrical energy is changed to energy of motion in the motor of a fan. The motion of the fan blades moves air, creating a breeze that cools you. In a gas oven, chemical energy changes to heat, which cooks your food. Energy changes aren't limited to the nonliving world, however. All life processes involve energy, too. Therefore, energy changes are necessary for organisms to carry out these processes.

Transformation of Energy

Does a ball have energy? Imagine carrying a ball to the top of a flight of stairs. How would you get the ball back down to the bottom of the stairs? You could push the ball over the edge of the top step so that it bounced step by step down the stairs. Or, you could drop it directly over the railing to fall quickly to the floor below. In both cases, when the ball moves downward it does work, perhaps by knocking over a lamp.

Now think about a log in a fireplace. As the wood burns, energy in the form of heat and light is released. This energy can then warm a room or pop popcorn.

Figure 3-28 You can easily see energy doing work in this antique locomotive. The energy released by the burning of wood or coal is converted to the energy of motion of the locomotive's pistons and wheels.

MEETING INDIVIDUAL NEEDS

To help students who may have difficulty with the analysis of a ball doing work as a result of falling, remind them that when the ball hits an object, the object moves. Work is done whenever anything is moved. Compare the action to a bowling ball doing work by knocking down pins. Ask students to trace the path of the energy used to do the work of knocking down pins. `LEP`

a

b

Types of Energy Both the ball at the top of the stairs and the wood in the fireplace have a type of energy called potential energy. **Potential energy** is the energy of position, and is sometimes called stored energy. What is the source of the potential energy in the ball and the wood? Energy was used to carry the ball to the top of the stairs where it could fall and do work. The potential energy of molecules in wood is chemical energy—energy that is stored in the bonds of the molecules in wood cells during photosynthesis. As a ball bounces down stairs, potential energy is converted to **kinetic energy,** the energy of motion. When the ball comes to rest at the bottom of the stairs, it has lower potential energy. Similarly, the products formed from the burning of wood have a lower potential energy than the original wood molecules had.

Survival of organisms depends upon the chemical energy stored in energy-rich molecules like those in wood. When a reaction occurs, the bonds break, energy is released, and the potential energy is converted to kinetic energy that can be used by cells for biological work. For example, through a series of chemical reactions, chemical energy is transformed to electric energy in the bodies of electric eels or to light energy in fireflies.

Conservation of Energy When energy is transformed in living organisms, is there any loss of energy? Suppose you earn $10 performing an after-school job. That $10 was paid to you by your employer, who got it from another source. You use the $10 to buy a snack that costs $1.25, receiving $8.75 in change. Of this, $5 goes into your savings account, and you gradually spend the rest. What has happened to that original $10? Has it disappeared? No. It still exists, but in different forms and belonging to different people.

Figure 3-29 This skier (a) increased his potential energy by riding to the top of the hill on a lift. Now, his increased potential energy is changing to kinetic energy as he skis downhill. In a similar way, the potential energy gained by this cheetah (b) from its last meal is stored in molecules in its cells. Now, the cheetah is converting some of that potential energy to kinetic energy by chasing another meal.

SECTION 3.3

Teacher FYI

The role of bioluminescence is rather diverse. Deep-sea fish release light to attract a mate or to attract prey. For example, the dogfish shark *Spinax niger* will startle its prey with light emitted from a series of ventrally located body organs. Certain stinkhorn fungi such as "foxfire" emit a yellow-green glow that attracts insects that aid in distribution of its spores. Squid emit light that enables them to locate and therefore remain in a school with related species. Both male and female fireflies emit light to attract one another for mating.

Demonstration

To illustrate the role of temperature as a means for speeding up a chemical reaction, perform the following demonstration. Obtain three 250-mL beakers. Place 150 mL of ice water in the first. Label it "cold." Place 150 mL of room-temperature water in the second and label it "room." Place 150 mL of hot water from the tap in the third. Label it "hot." Show Alka Seltzer tablets that you intend to add to each beaker at the same time. Ask students to speculate in which beaker the reaction will occur fastest. Perform the demonstration. Discuss the fact that the tablet is undergoing a chemical reaction that results in the release of carbon dioxide gas. Have students relate the speed of the reaction to the temperature of the water in which it occurs and suggest reasons for the differences.

Concept Development

Ask students to develop a numbered list of the characteristics of enzymes that appear on pages 81 and 82. Their lists may include such information as proteins, globular, not used up in a reaction, lower activation energy, are specific, not permanently changed, etc. **L1** **COOP LEARN**

Using Science Terms

Have students look up and record the meaning of the term *catalyst.* Ask them to relate the meaning of this word to enzymes. **L2**

Enrichment

Have students check the labels on several different brands of laundry detergents. Ask them to record the brand names for those that contain or list an enzyme in their chemical composition. Have students speculate as to the role of this enzyme in laundry detergents. **L3**

Brainstorming

Have students attempt to visualize and then explain the problem of carrying out chemical reactions within an organism if enzymes were not present. They should conclude that high temperatures would be necessary and that the organism would have to operate on heat much as a car's engine does.

The same idea is true of energy transformations. When energy is transformed, it does not disappear. It is conserved, and the total amount of energy in a system remains constant. When wood burns, for example, energy is released as light and heat. In addition, some of the energy that was stored in the wood still exists as chemical energy in the bonds of the products formed, carbon dioxide and water. But all of the original energy is accounted for. The total amount of energy released plus the energy remaining in the bonds of the products is equal to the amount of energy originally in the wood and the oxygen molecules with which it reacted. This idea can be stated as the Law of Conservation of Energy. This law states that in chemical reactions, energy is neither created nor destroyed.

Activation Energy

Although a ball will fall down a flight of stairs, it needs a push to get started. The same is true of chemical reactions. You learned earlier that hydrogen gas and oxygen gas will not react to form water without an input of energy, usually as heat. The added energy causes some of the molecules to move faster and collide with more force. When the hydrogen and oxygen molecules hit each other hard enough, bonds break, and the reaction starts. The minimum amount of energy required to start a chemical reaction is called **activation energy.** Some reactions do not require very high temperatures and will begin at room temperature or below. In self-sustaining chemical reactions, such as burning, the activation energy needed to keep the reaction going comes from the energy given off by the molecules that have already reacted.

HEALTH CONNECTION

Proteins in Vegetarian Diets

Have you ever seen a house with walls built of bricks that were salvaged from an old building that had been torn down? The new house may look nothing like the old building, yet it is built of the same units. This process is similar to what takes place when you eat protein in your diet.

As you know, proteins are composed of long chains of basic building blocks, amino acids. In order to build the kinds of proteins that humans need, you eat proteins from a variety of sources.

Digestion breaks up the chains of amino acids in the dietary protein. The free amino acids are then used in your own cells to build new proteins for body structures or to act as enzymes. Without proteins, humans cannot survive for long. In fact, lack of protein causes a disease called kwashiorkor, which you may have seen on TV or in photographs from areas where there is famine.

Meat and fish are major sources of protein in the diet. In fact, many people in the United States consider these foods to be essential to a healthy life. Although meat and fish are good sources of protein, they're not the only ones. Plants also contain proteins. The big difference between animal proteins and plant proteins is that they contain different combinations of amino acids. Because humans are animals, animal protein has an advantage in that it contains the amino acids we need in the proportions we need them. Of the 20 common amino

STUDENT JOURNAL

Students are to assume that they are energy trapped within a candle made from beef tallow. They are to report in a written paragraph as to where they are located and if they are in a kinetic or potential form. They are to also speculate as to how their energy came to be in the tallow of the candle. Their paragraph should continue to describe where their energy goes as the candle burns. As a conclusion to their paragraph, they must address the issue of conservation of energy. Are they now in a new form and what might become of them, or how might they now be used in this new form? **L1**

Enzymes

Think again about wood in a fireplace. Although oxygen molecules are in constant motion and bouncing off the wood molecules, the wood does not burst into flame. A very high temperature, such as that of a burning match, is needed to provide enough activation energy to start the reaction. The reactions of living organisms cannot depend on heat as a source of activation energy. First, the high temperature needed would destroy cells. Second, heat would be far too random a source of activation energy. Like a flame in a fireworks factory, it could trigger many different reactions at once. To function properly, cells must carry out specific reactions at definite times.

How, then, do reactions get started in cells? Cells contain **enzymes,** proteins that lower the activation energy required and allow reactions to occur at the normal temperatures of cells. Each enzyme is specific; it guides only one type of cell reaction. In addition, enzymes are not permanently changed or used up during a reaction, so a given enzyme can be used over and over again. Most enzymes are globular proteins with particular three-dimensional shapes. The shape of an enzyme is crucial to the reaction it controls.

Reactants in cellular reactions are called substrates. Most enzymes are named by adding the suffix *-ase* to part of the name of the substrate in the

Figure 3-30 The basketball player has to shoot with more energy when the basket is higher. When the basket is lower, the player can accomplish the same task using less energy. You can compare this situation to the action of an enzyme. An enzyme lowers the amount of energy needed to begin a chemical change.

---

acids, humans can manufacture 12 from smaller molecules. The other eight must be obtained from proteins in the diet. The problem with plant protein is that no one plant protein provides all the needed amino acids.

However, a carefully planned vegetarian diet can supply the proper protein balance. By combining a cereal grain (such as rice, wheat, or corn) with a legume (such as peas, beans, or peanuts), the necessary combination of amino acids is supplied. The old favorite of rice and beans from the southern

United States is a good example of such a dish, as is a corn tortilla with frijoles (beans). This method of combining foods is called protein complementarity and is the manner by which millions of people maintain a diet balanced in amino acids. For this effort they get a bonus— plant proteins don't come bundled with animal fat that might cause additional health problems.

1. **Explore Further:** Plan a meatless meal that is balanced in amino acids. Use a vegetarian cookbook to find recipes that your family would enjoy. Which parts of the recipe supply the needed amino acids?

2. **Solve the Problem:** Imagine that you are in charge of feeding a poor country that is largely desert and has no access to the sea. What could you do to help your people eat a healthy diet?

HEALTH CONNECTION

Purpose
Students learn that vegetarian diets must contain a balance of amino acids.

Background
The essential amino acids are isoleucine, leucine, lysine, methionine, phenylalanine, threonine, tryptophan, and valine.

Teaching Strategies
- Assign students to cooperative learning groups of four or five to gather answers for the questions that follow this feature. L1 COOP LEARN

Possible Answers
1. Student meals will vary. However, the recipes should include grains such as corn, rice, or wheat, along with legumes such as peas, beans, or peanuts. Grains supply tryptophan and methionine, which are lacking in legumes. Legumes supply isoleucine and lysine, which are lacking in grains.
2. The most reliable sources of essential amino acids in the diet are meat and animal products such as eggs and cheese. However, desert areas can support only limited grazing herds. If crops can be grown, then it is essential that they not be limited to a single crop but must be balanced between grains and legumes.

Going Further
Have students do research on the disease "kwashiorkor" and its symptoms. It often occurs when a child is weaned and is placed on a diet of plant starch. L3

SECTION 3.3

Using an Analogy

Have students diagram a "see-through" version of a lock and its corresponding key not yet inserted into the lock. Ask several students to diagram their models on the chalkboard. Have students explain the following from their diagrams. Which part of the diagram corresponds to (a) the substrate, (b) the enzyme, and (c) the active site? `L1` `LEP`

`COOP LEARN`

Brainstorming

Using any lock-and-key model from the Analogy activity just described, ask students to explain how the model supports the idea that (a) enzymes are specific for their substrates, (b) enzymes are not used up, (c) enzymes are not permanently changed in a reaction, and (d) enzymes may be used over and over in a reaction. `L1`

Concept Development

Ask students to list characteristics of coenzymes. Their lists should include such items as: nonprotein, helper molecules to enzymes, made of vitamins, reusable, needed in small amounts, etc. `L1`

3 Assess

Check for Understanding

Provide students with a diagram of an enzyme with a novel shape for its active site. Have students draw a corresponding substrate shape that would fit with this enzyme. `L1`

`LEP`

---

reaction the enzyme controls. For example, the enzyme that guides the conversion of maltose to glucose is called maltase. Some enzymes, such as pepsin, which works in your stomach, were assigned names before the present naming system was adopted.

A Model of Enzyme Function

For many years, scientists worked to determine how enzymes and substrates interacted to carry out reactions. As a result of this research, scientists developed a model of how enzymes work. Enzymes were pictured as fitting together with their substrate molecules like a key fits a lock. You know that every lock has a specific key that opens it. The surfaces of the lock and key fit together. Similarly, part of an enzyme's surface, called its active site, fits together with the substrate molecule(s). This description of enzyme function is called the lock-and-key model.

Induced Fit Model   More recently, scientists have modified the lock-and-key model. Research shows that the shape of the enzyme's active site and the shape of the substrate need not match exactly. When the enzyme and substrate join, the shape of the enzyme changes slightly, making the fit between enzyme and substrate more exact. In other words, the enzyme is a flexible key. This modern model is called the *induced fit model.* Modification of the lock-and-key model shows how explanations in science change when scientists make new discoveries.

   Let's look at a common biological reaction—the formation of a larger protein molecule from single amino acid molecules. The reaction is shown in Figure 3-31. Suppose a cell has two amino acids that are to be joined to form a dipeptide. There is an enzyme for this type of reaction. How does it react with just the right amino acids among the many other molecules moving around in the cell? As you know, enzymes function on the basis of matching surfaces. In this case, the active site of the enzyme fits together only with the two amino acid substrates. The joining of substrates and enzymes lowers activation energy by placing the reactants in a position favorable for bonding. As the reaction continues, bonds in each amino acid are broken, a molecule of water is removed, and the two amino acids bond to one another, forming a dipeptide.

Figure 3-31   **This diagram shows the induced-fit model of an enzyme reaction. Notice how the shape of the enzyme changes and conforms to the shape of the substrates. Even so, a particular enzyme fits with only certain substrates. Thus, the induced-fit model is just a slight modification of the older lock-and-key model.**

Amino acid — Amino acid — Substrates

Active site — Enzyme (cutaway view) — Enzyme-substrate complex

Induced fit

Unchanged enzyme — + — + H_2O — Dipeptide

PORTFOLIO

Students should design and then diagram a series of steps that would illustrate the lock-and-key model for enzyme action. Provide them with an original substrate shape and the shapes of the new molecules that result from the substrate's undergoing a hydrolysis reaction. Have them label active site, substrate, enzyme, and products. They are then to redraw and label their models to depict a more current model of enzyme action using the induced-fit model. A short paragraph should be included to explain how the two models differ from one another and how the two models are alike. A second paragraph should be included to describe the characteristics of all enzymes and explain why they are needed in living organisms. `L1`

Using computers, scientists are identifying the structure of the active sites of some enzymes, as well as the part of the substrates that match those active sites. Such computer analyses not only verify the induced fit model, but also provide detailed information about how a particular reaction occurs.

Coenzymes

Just as people sometimes require helpers to carry out a job, enzymes sometimes require helpers in order to carry out reactions. These non-protein helper molecules are called **coenzymes.** Many coenzymes are made from vitamin molecules or fragments of vitamin molecules. Like enzymes, they are reusable and are needed in only small amounts.

Some coenzymes join temporarily with enzymes, changing the enzyme's active site and enabling it to fit with the substrate. Other coenzymes act as transfer agents, shuttling atoms, parts of atoms, or entire groups of atoms from one substrate to another.

LOOKING AHEAD

LIFE PROCESSES carried out by organisms involve chemical reactions and energy. Enzymes control these reactions, allowing them to occur at temperatures suitable to living systems. Most of the chemical reactions of organisms occur within cells. In the next two chapters, you will apply your knowledge of matter and energy as you explore the structure of cells and how the various parts of cells interact to carry out life processes upon which the cell and the entire organism depend. ✿

Section Review

Understanding Concepts

1. You turn on a tape deck and the reels in the cassette begin to rotate. How does this example illustrate energy transformation?

2. Suppose you start a fire by using a magnifying glass to focus the sun's image on some paper. What is the source of activation energy for this reaction? What is the source of activation energy after the fire has started and the magnifier is taken away?

3. Explain how the enzyme maltase can control a reaction involving maltose, but not one involving sucrose.

4. **Skill Review—Sequencing:** Using Figure 3-31 as a reference, outline the sequence of events that occurs in an enzyme-controlled reaction. For more information, see Organizing Information in the **Skill Handbook.**

5. **Thinking Critically:** To function properly, cells must carry out thousands of reactions and do so at the appropriate times. How might the organization of cells be different if enzymes were not required for each of these many reactions?

3.3 ENERGY AND REACTIONS ✿ **83**

Answers to Section Review

1. If batteries powered the recorder, chemical energy was first converted to electrical energy and then to mechanical energy.

2. The concentrated sunlight was absorbed by the paper and changed to heat. This heat provided the activation energy. Because the burning of paper is exothermic, some of the energy released provides activation energy for continued burning.

3. Maltose consists of two bonded glucose units, whereas sucrose consists of a glucose bonded to a fructose. If the active site of the enzyme maltase fits with maltose, it will not fit with sucrose.

4. **Skill Review—Sequencing:** When a substrate collides with the active site, it fits and attaches, causing the enzyme to change shape somewhat. By holding the substrate in a certain position, the enzyme lowers the activation energy for the reaction. The reaction occurs. The product is released from the enzyme.

5. **Thinking Critically:** Without enzymes, reactions would occur randomly. Cells would have to be organized to take in materials and eliminate wastes at much greater rates because reactions would continue to occur but products would not always be needed by the cell.

SECTION 3.3

Reteach
Ask students to write sentences making a link between the words or phrases in the following pairs.
(a) kinetic energy/potential energy
(b) energy in wood/energy released as wood burns (c) chemical reaction/conservation of energy
(d) enzyme/substrate (e) lock-and-key model/induced-fit model (f) enzyme/coenzyme

Extension
Using the dipeptide formed in Figure 3-31, have students design an enzyme that would allow for a hydrolysis reaction of the dipeptide into two amino acids. Ask them to diagram the enzyme and reaction. **L3**

✔ Assessment
Skill: Use this question to assess student ability to sequence information. List the steps that occur in the induced-fit model of enzyme action. **L1**

4 Close

Activity
Have a student take his or her temperature using the "underarm" technique. Have the class explain where the energy absorbed by the thermometer came from. Ask whether this energy was potential or kinetic and in what form this energy was released in the body. The energy (heat) is kinetic because it involves the motion of molecules. It was transformed from chemical (potential) energy. **L1**

Considering the Environment

Purpose
Students will be introduced to the possibility of recycling batteries to avoid pollution.

Teaching Strategies
- Have students work in cooperative learning groups. Provide them with needed reference materials, and ask them to research answers to the questions at the end of this feature. Written answers may be included in each student's portfolio. **L1** **COOP LEARN**

Possible Answers
1. A chemical compound containing mercury was used in the shaping and finishing of hats. Somehow, this compound was ingested or inhaled by hat workers and caused mercury poisoning. One symptom is mental confusion.
2. Students may identify the problems of battery-powered vehicles as being related to the production and disposal of the batteries being used in the vehicles. Others may address the problem of low speeds and limited ranges associated with the battery-powered vehicle. However, more important is the pollution resulting from the burning of fossil fuels to generate the electricity needed to recharge the batteries.

Going Further
Ask students to contact auto supply stores and electronics stores to see if they know of recyclers that take discarded batteries. If these recyclers are local, a team of students could visit them with a camera and videotape interviews and possibly some of the processes involved in the recycling process. **L3** **COOP LEARN**

BIOLOGY, **T**ECHNOLOGY, AND **S**OCIETY

Considering the Environment
Recycling Batteries

Batteries are wonderful! They provide us with a source of electrical energy that does not depend on a cord connected to a wall outlet. They make possible flashlights, cordless phones, boom boxes, digital watches, portable computers, hearing aids, smoke detectors, heart pacemakers, remote controls, and electric cars.

However, there is a dark side to batteries—some contain very toxic substances. Lead, mercury, and acids are just three of the most common. If these substances are ingested by humans, they can cause injury or even death.

Mercury, for example, can cause birth defects and brain and kidney damage. It doesn't take much mercury to be dangerous. The mercury in just one button battery from a wristwatch in six tons of garbage is enough to exceed government safety standards. What can be done?

One answer to this problem is recycling. When batteries are recycled, the environment is protected and, at the same time, scarce resources are conserved. Suppose you discard a car battery, which contains several lead plates and terminals. To build a new battery to replace the old one, new lead must be mined and then refined using great amounts of energy and causing considerable pollution at the mine and refinery. Even after all this, not all of the lead in the ore is recovered. However, reclaiming the lead from a recycled battery takes much less energy and causes less pollution. Moreover, the lead that would have been mined is still there for future generations.

Most stores that sell car batteries will offer a few dollars trade-in value for a battery that can be recycled. Many jewelry, camera, and department stores will recycle button batteries when they sell you new ones. At present, fewer than half of the states require stores to accept batteries for recycling. Most merchants are responsible and are proud to tell you of their efforts. Those who don't recycle may be encouraged to do so if their customers think it is important.

Another solution in some cases is to use rechargeable batteries. These batteries are usually made from nickel and cadmium. These elements are also toxic, and the battery costs more than a regular battery. However, a rechargeable battery will last up to 40 times longer. Thus, even when it is worn out, there is only about 1/40 of the waste.

1. **Connection to Literature:** The Mad Hatter in Lewis Carroll's *Alice in Wonderland* was not an entirely fictional character. People who made hats sometimes suffered from a disease that causes "madness." Research how hats were made at the time of the story and find out what caused the Hatter's madness.
2. **Explore Further:** The cause of much of the air pollution today in the United States is the internal combustion engine in automobiles. One proposed solution to this problem is electric cars powered by large, rechargeable batteries. What are some of the problems with battery-powered vehicles? Electric cars are sometimes referred to as nonpolluting. Do you think this is true?

CAREER CONNECTION

For more information on Food Technologists, have students contact local universities to determine the requirements for admission to a food technology program. Looking through the articles and ads in a trade journal in food technology is a quick way of learning what food technologists do.

Chemistry Connection

There's More Than Food in Your Food

Pick up any box of crackers and look at the ingredients label. Sometimes it looks as if the entire chemical industry was involved in making that cracker. Actually, there is a plan behind that list of ingredients, but it's not evil. One of the reasons for the list is that there is a problem with food—it spoils. This is not a worry if you live where you can grow food all year. You'll always have fresh food. However, if you live where there are seasons, you can eat fresh food in summer and fall, but you'll have to depend on preserved food the rest of the year. Food preserved in September will probably have to last until the following June or July.

The earliest food additives were preservatives. Natural materials, such as salt, were added to meat and fish to keep them from spoiling. Salt is still used today along with hundreds of other additives. As a result, a cracker made in October is still fresh in April. Additives combined with packaging methods, such as canning, allow us to enjoy foods like pineapple from Hawaii at reasonable prices in and out of season.

Some food additives are vitamins and minerals added to foods that do not naturally contain them. Before food additives, diseases such as rickets and scurvy were common, especially among children. Rickets

is a disease in which bones do not develop naturally and become soft. It is caused by a lack of vitamin D. Enriching milk, bread, and other foods with vitamin D has nearly wiped out rickets.

Iodine is needed for proper thyroid function. Lack of iodine causes a disease called goiter. Seafood contains iodine, so coast dwellers don't usually get the disease. People who don't have regular access to seafood can avoid goiter by eating foods that contain an iodine additive. The most common iodized food is salt.

But not all additives are safe for everyone. For example, monosodium glutamate, called MSG, is sometimes added to make foods taste better. However, a small percentage of the population is allergic to MSG. Another example is sulfites, additives used to keep green vegetables green and crisp. Sulfite-treated food can cause a serious allergic reaction in some people.

Food processing companies are regulated by a federal agency called the Food and Drug Administration (FDA). The FDA requires extensive testing of additives before they are allowed to be used. Even so, an additive may be approved, but later be found to be unsafe. In that case, the FDA can order that substance banned and all foods containing it destroyed.

1. **Explore Further:** The FDA has a special responsibility to ban food additives that might cause cancer. Find out about an additive called red dye number 2. What was it used for? What research led to its being banned?

2. **Connection to History:** In the days of sailing ships and the far-flung European colonial empires, naval vessels were at sea for many months at a time. During these voyages, many sailors used to come down with a disease called scurvy. Research the symptoms, cause, and cure of this disease.

CAREER CONNECTION

Food technologists research the chemical, physical, and biological properties of food. They do this to learn how to properly process, preserve, package, distribute, and store food. Some food technologists develop new products, while others concentrate on ensuring quality and safety standards.

CHAPTER 3 MATTER AND ENERGY 85

Point out to students that the British and Dutch navies took limes on board their ships to provide vitamin C. On German ships, sauerkraut was used for the same purpose.

Going Further
Have students determine why salt and sugar can be used as preservatives and how canning preserves food. Some students could find out how treating food with radiation prevents spoilage and how the public is reacting to this new form of preservation. **L2**

CHAPTER 3

Chemistry Connection

Purpose
Students are introduced to some of the chemical additives that are included in our food. Their helpful (and sometimes harmful) effects are explored.

Background
Most food additives are used to preserve food. Some retard or prevent the growth of bacteria and/or fungi within the food. Others retard oxidation to prevent rancidity and staleness in foods that contain fats or oils.

Teaching Strategies
- Assign students to work in cooperative groups. Provide them with photocopies of at least 10 different food labels. The specific food from which the label is being used should also be included. Ask them to identify the additives that are being used to preserve or enhance flavor in these foods. Have them compile a list of the different foods and the additives or preservatives that were added to them. Some labels include the purpose for each additive. Try to find one or two examples of this type of label to provide students. **COOP LEARN**

Possible Answers
1. Red dye number 2 (also called amaranth) was used to color foods, drugs, and cosmetics. Russian researchers, in experiments on rats, found that it could cause cancer, prevent pregnancy, and cause stillbirths. The dye's use in food, drugs, and cosmetics was banned in the United States in 1976.
2. Scurvy is a vitamin deficiency disease caused by a lack of vitamin C in the diet. It results in the development of fragile capillaries, causing them to hemorrhage at various sites. Specific symptoms include swollen and bleeding gums, anemia, shortness of breath, lack of appetite, hemorrhaging in skin and under nails, and eventual cardiac failure. The cure is to provide ascorbic acid by increasing fresh fruits and vegetables in the diet.

CHAPTER 3

CHAPTER REVIEW

Summary

The summary can be used by students to review the major concepts of the chapter.

Language of Biology

Answers should go beyond defining the terms. Accept any reasonable answer that uses the term correctly and in the proper context.

Understanding Concepts

1. The number of atoms or ions in a molecule or ionic compound is determined by the number of electrons each atom must have to attain a stable outer energy level.
2. There are four different kinds of atoms in $NaHCO_3$. There are 12 atoms in $4PbI_2$, four lead atoms and eight iodine atoms.
3. A chemical equation must be balanced because the law of conservation of mass always holds true in chemical reactions. The balanced equation accounts for all the matter present before and after a reaction. The equation is balanced.
4. The positive ends of water molecules will attract the negative iodide ions, and the negative ends of water molecules will attract the positive potassium ions. The attraction of the ions will break ionic bonds, causing the potassium and iodide ions to separate. The polar nature of water molecules will cause individual sugar molecules to separate from one another, but the covalent bonds of the sugar molecules will not be broken.
5. in the solution whose pH is 10
6. Melting of ice and snapping a twig in two are not chemical changes. No bonds are broken and no new substances are formed.
7. (a) hydrolysis; (b) condensation; (c) condensation
8. covalent bonds

Summary

Atoms are the basic building blocks of all matter, both living and nonliving. Atoms combine with one another, producing more complex arrangements of matter, such as molecules and ionic compounds, which have definite compositions. As a chemical reaction occurs, bonds are broken, new bonds are formed, and new substances having different properties are produced.

Substances dissolve in water to form solutions, which are mixtures that are the same throughout. Solutions may be acidic, basic, or neutral depending on the relative concentrations of hydrogen and hydroxide ions.

Biologically important organic compounds are covalently bonded and include carbohydrates, lipids, proteins, and nucleic acids. These molecules are formed from and can be converted to simpler molecules by condensation and hydrolysis reactions.

There are two types of energy—potential and kinetic. Energy is never lost during energy transformations.

Every chemical reaction requires a certain amount of activation energy to begin. In cells, enzymes lower the activation energy to a point at which reactions can occur at lower temperatures. Coenzymes often work along with enzymes in biological reactions.

Language of Biology

Write a sentence that shows your understanding of each of the following terms.

acid	ion
activation energy	ionic bond
amino acid	isomer
base	kinetic energy
carbohydrate	lipid
chemical formula	molecule
coenzyme	nucleic acid
compound	polypeptide
covalent bond	polysaccharide
electron cloud	potential energy
element	protein
energy level	solution
enzyme	

Understanding Concepts

1. Explain why molecules and ionic compounds have definite composition.
2. How many different kinds of atoms are there in $NaHCO_3$? How many atoms are in $4PbI_2$?
3. Why must a chemical equation be balanced? Is the following a balanced equation?

$$N_2 + 3H_2 \rightarrow 2NH_3$$

4. Potassium iodide, KI, is an ionic compound. Suppose you add some KI crystals to a beaker of water. Describe and explain what happens as the crystals dissolve. Will sugar crystals dissolve the same way? Explain.
5. A chemist tests two solutions. One has a pH of 6, the other a pH of 10. In which solution is the concentration of hydrogen ions less than the concentration of hydroxide ions?
6. Which of the following are not examples of chemical changes? Explain your reasoning.
   (a) A piece of paper burns. (b) Ice melts. (c) A twig is snapped in two. (d) A cell converts sucrose to glucose and fructose.
7. Classify each reaction below as either hydrolysis or condensation.
   (a) conversion of starch to glucose
   (b) synthesis of a polypeptide from amino acids
   (c) production of a fat from fatty acids and glycerol
8. Ethane, C_2H_6, is a gas composed of molecules. What kind of bonds are present in ethane?
9. Using diagrams, show how an enzyme would carry out the hydrolysis of maltose.
10. How does an enzyme lower the amount of activation energy needed to begin a reaction?

9. The diagrams should show matching shapes between the substrate maltose and the active site of the enzyme and should follow the sequence shown in Figure 3-31. Water should be shown as a reactant and two molecules of glucose as products.
10. An enzyme holds the substrates in a position that favors bonds breaking and new bonds forming.

PROGRAM RESOURCES

Teacher Classroom Resources
Chapter Assessment, pp. 9-12 `L1`
Performance Assessment in Biology, p. 6 `L2`
Alternate Assessment in the Science Classroom
Computer Test Bank `L1`

Applying Concepts

11. Ion X has a charge of 3+. Ion Y has a charge of 1–. In what ratio would the two ions combine to form a compound? Write its formula.
12. What atomic particles are most important in determining chemical reactions? Explain.
13. Pentane, C_5H_{12}, is an organic compound containing single covalent bonds. Draw structural formulas for two isomers of pentane.
14. What is incorrect in this structural formula?

$$H - \underset{\underset{H}{|}}{\overset{\overset{H}{|}}{C}} = \underset{\underset{H}{|}}{C} - \underset{\underset{H}{|}}{\overset{\overset{H}{|}}{C}} - H$$

15. Each enzyme operates most efficiently at a particular pH. For example, pepsin breaks down proteins in the stomach, where the pH is about 2. However, pepsin could not break down protein in the intestine, where the pH is about 8. Can you suggest an explanation of how pH might affect enzymes?
16. **Chemistry Connection:** Look up information about the sweetener aspartame. Is it chemically related to proteins, carbohydrates, or fats? Aspartame is not used in foods to be cooked because it breaks down when the food is heated. What sort of reaction do you think would cause it to break down?
17. **Health Connection:** It is generally advisable for vegetarians to eat combinations of foods that provide a complete set of amino acids at a single meal instead of eating one food in the morning and another in the evening. Why do you think this advice is valid?

Lab Interpretation

18. **Investigation:** You have tested the pH of the water of six ponds in your locality. The results you obtained are shown in the following graph. You know that a farmer in your area has been applying lime (a base) to the soil. In another location, an abandoned coal mine is producing some acid runoff. According to your results, which ponds are most likely to have been affected by the lime and the mine runoff? Explain.

19. **Minilab 1:** You are trying to figure out whether unlabeled cans of soda pop are diet pop or regular pop. What could you do to figure it out without opening the cans?
20. **Minilab 2:** A contractor has promised to install marble tile in your kitchen. Upon examining the tile, you believe that the tile is really plastic. Describe a chemical test you could carry out to determine whether the tile might be marble. Would a positive test prove that the tile is really marble? Explain.
21. **Thinking Lab:** A certain fly makes one toxic chemical during its larval stage and another during its adult stage. What would you predict about the predators of each stage of the life cycle of this fly? Why?

Connecting Ideas

22. In Chapter 1, you encountered the word *photosynthesis*. What sort of energy transformation takes place during photosynthesis?
23. You will learn later how DNA forms a code for the manufacture of proteins. Suppose a change in an organism's DNA causes a change in the amino acid sequence of a certain enzyme. The resulting enzyme has unusual properties. How might such a change be important to a group of organisms?

19. You could measure the mass of both cans. The can with the greater mass is probably the regular pop.
20. Place a few drops of dilute acid such as vinegar in an inconspicuous spot. If the tile is marble, bubbles of CO_2 gas will be produced as the $CaCO_3$ of marble reacts with the acid. The test proves only that the tile contains a carbonate.
21. The fly may have one predator at the larval stage and a different predator at the adult stage. The first is susceptible to the toxin produced by the larva. The second is susceptible to the adult's toxin.

Connecting Ideas

22. **Energy:** Light energy is transformed to chemical energy.
23. **Evolution:** The novel enzyme might allow the organism to utilize different molecules as energy sources. Such a change might enhance the survival of the organism. Many other answers are possible. Accept any logical answer.

Applying Concepts

11. The ions will combine in a ratio of 1X : 3Y. Its formula is XY_3.
12. The electrons are most important. They determine the bonding among atoms.
13. The following structures show the possible answers.

$$H - \overset{\overset{H}{|}}{\underset{\underset{H}{|}}{C}} - \overset{\overset{H}{|}}{\underset{\underset{H}{|}}{C}} - \overset{\overset{H}{|}}{\underset{\underset{H}{|}}{C}} - \overset{\overset{H}{|}}{\underset{\underset{H}{|}}{C}} - \overset{\overset{H}{|}}{\underset{\underset{H}{|}}{C}} - H$$

14. The first carbon atom on the left has five covalent bonds, rather than four. One less hydrogen should be attached to that carbon.
15. The pH may alter the shape of an enzyme. If an enzyme's active site is altered, it will not be able to match its substrate.
16. Aspartame is a dipeptide, composed of aspartic acid and phenylalanine. It would be broken down by a hydrolysis reaction.
17. Neither food alone provides all essential amino acids. For protein to be synthesized, all amino acids must be present at the same time.

Lab Interpretation

18. Pond B appears to have been affected by the lime. Ponds D and F may have been affected by acid runoff. The pH of pond B is much higher than normal, whereas ponds D and F have acidic pHs.

ORGANIZER
C H A P T E R
4

SECTION	OBJECTIVES	TEXT LABS/FEATURES
4.1 Membrane Structure (2 days)	**Describe** the discovery of cells and the development of the cell theory. **Relate** the properties of the cell membrane to its structure.	**Minilab 1:** Which items show evidence of cell organization? p. 91 **History Connection:** Ernest Everett Just, p. 95
4.2 Membrane Function (3 days)	**Demonstrate** the various ways by which substances enter and leave cells. **Compare and contrast** the processes of passive transport and active transport.	**Global Connection:** Fish Out of Water, p. 98 **Career Connection:** Fish farmer, p. 99 **Minilab 2:** Are plastic bags permeable to certain molecules? p. 100 **Thinking Lab:** Can pore size be used to determine molecule size? p. 102 **Investigation:** Osmosis in a Model Cell, p. 104
BIOLOGY, TECHNOLOGY, AND SOCIETY		**Biotechnology:** Cold Storage, p. 111 **Health Connection:** Fiber to the Rescue? p. 112

LAB MATERIALS

INVESTIGATION	MINILAB	ALTERNATE LAB
page 104 balance beakers, 2-3 small dialysis tubing graduated cylinder paper towels salt scissors thread	**page 91** flower petals lettuce microscope pond scum razor blade, single-edge sand saxophone reed slides talcum powder thread, nylon **page 100** beakers (or cups) beet juice, canned cough syrup food coloring iodine mouthwash plastic bags	**page 106** coverslips dropper *Elodea* sprigs forceps microscope paper towels salt solution, 6% slides

TEACHER CLASSROOM RESOURCES	OTHER RESOURCES
Study Guide, pp. 19-20 ****ILS:** *The Basic Unit of Life,* p. 39	***STVS:** *Diagnosing Disease with Glowing Cells,* Human Biology (Disc 7, Side 1) **Color Transparency 3:** *The Plasma Membrane*
Study Guide, pp. 21-24 **Concept Mapping,** p. 4 **Critical Thinking/Problem Solving:** *Separating Sea Urchin Cells,* p. 4 ***PLL:** *Qualitative and Quantitative Plasmolysis,* p. 25 ****ILS:** *Cell Membranes and Permeability,* p. 47	***STVS:** *Natural Time-Release Capsules,* Human Biology (Disc 7, Side 1) ***STVS:** *White Cells in Action,* Human Biology (Disc 7, Side 1) **Color Transparency 4:** *Osmosis*
Assessment Materials **Chapter Assessment,** pp. 13-16 **Performance Assessment in Biology,** p. 8 **Alternate Assessment in the Science Classroom** **Computer Test Bank**	**Spanish Resources** **Cooperative Learning Resource Guide** **Videodisc Correlations** (to Optical Data's and Videodiscovery's videodiscs)

* Probing Levels of Life
** Investigating Living Systems

* Science Technology Videodisc Series

Key to Teaching Strategies

The following designations will help you decide which activities in the teacher margin are appropriate for your students.

- **L1** Level 1 activities should be within the ability range of all students.
- **L2** Level 2 activities should be within the ability range of the average to above-average student.
- **L3** Level 3 activities are designed for the ability range of above-average students.
- **LEP** LEP activities are appropriate for Limited English Proficiency students.
- **COOP LEARN** Cooperative Learning activities are designed for small group work.

ADDITIONAL RESOURCES

Infinite Voyage *A Taste of Health*
Diet and health are intimately related, as students will see in this video. Eating a balanced diet will result in better health.

Audiovisual
Diffusion, video, Frey Scientific.
The Plasma Membrane, video, Coronet/MTI.

Software
Osmosis and Diffusion, Apple/IBM, EME.

4

THE CELL AND ITS ENVIRONMENT

Chapter Overview

The chapter begins with an account of the development of the cell theory. Students will learn that all cells are surrounded by a liquid environment that is a source of needed materials and a site for waste removal. Students will understand that materials entering and leaving cells must do so by passing across the plasma membrane.

Next, students will study the fluid mosaic model of plasma membrane structure and the means by which it was developed. They will examine the molecular composition of membranes and the roles of each type of molecule.

Having examined the processes of diffusion and osmosis, facilitated diffusion, and active transport, students will develop an understanding of how the fluid mosaic model explains the properties of cell membranes. They will also explore the processes of endocytosis and exocytosis, and study the function of plant cell walls.

THE CELL AND ITS ENVIRONMENT

SOME HOMES are surrounded by fences—tall or short, wooden or metal or brick, plain or fancy. Fences can have several functions. They can be decorative. They can define property boundaries. They can enclose and protect the home and family within. Although fences may differ in form and function, they have one thing in common—gates. A gate is a passage through which people and materials enter and leave the home. Without a gate, people within the home could not survive, because food and other supplies could not be brought in and waste materials could not leave.

Cells, too, are enclosed by "fences." Every cell is surrounded by a membrane, such as the one shown in the electron micrograph opposite. A cell's membrane func-

tions to protect and enclose the cell structures within. It has gates—some permanent, some temporary—that allow materials into and out of the cell. But not all kinds of particles can enter the cell, and not all kinds can exit. The membrane is selective. It controls the traffic of substances passing in and out of the cell. Water and dissolved substances necessary for maintaining the life of the cell enter through the membrane, and poisonous wastes exit. If needed molecules cannot pass through the membrane on their own, a cell can help get those particles through. How? In this chapter, you will read about the structure and function of the cell membrane and how this structure is vital to the survival of all organisms.

88

KEY TERMS

active transport
cell theory
cell wall
diffusion
dynamic equilibrium
endocytosis
exocytosis
facilitated diffusion
fluid mosaic model
middle lamella

osmosis
passive transport
phagocytosis
pinocytosis
plasma membrane
selectively permeable membrane
transport protein
vesicle

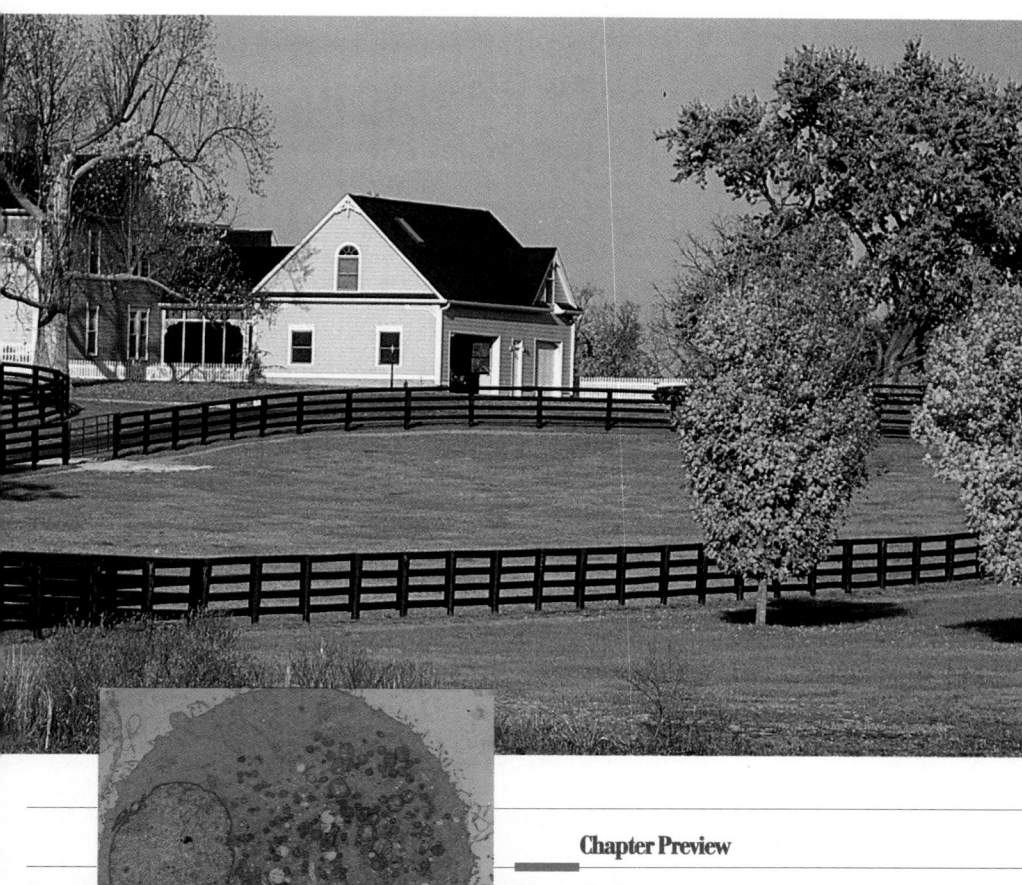

When you sweat, your body loses water and dissolved substances. Sport drinks can replenish the body's supply. Where do these substances go when you drink them? How do they get through the barriers surrounding your cells?
Magnification: 8000×

Chapter Preview

ASSESSMENT PLANNER

Choose assessment strategies from the following pages to evaluate the progress of your students.

Assess, pp. 95-96, 109-110
Portfolio, pp. 91, 93, 98, 102, 103, 110
Alternate Lab, pp. 106-108
Thinking Lab, p. 102

Minilab 1, p. 91
Minilab 2, p. 100
Investigation, pp. 104-105
Chapter Review, pp. 114-115

Introducing the Chapter

Have students look at the photograph of fences on pages 88-89. Lead them in a discussion of a fence's roles in protection and as a boundary, and ask them if fences are designed such that what is inside remains inside and what is outside cannot enter. Compare people entering or leaving a property through a gate in the fence with the kinds of particles that enter or leave a cell through its plasma membrane. Contrast a fence, which is not selective, with the selectively permeable plasma membrane. Although people pass through a gate in a fence by only one means, there are several different ways by which particles may enter or leave a cell. **L1**

Theme Development

One theme stressed in this chapter is unity within diversity. Though the plasma membranes of cells may vary in terms of their permeability characteristics, those membranes, as well as the membranes of organelles, have the same basic fluid mosaic structure. In addition, all cells must take in and rid themselves of certain basic kinds of materials. Also addressed in the chapter is the theme of methods of inquiry, as applied to development of the cell theory and of the fluid mosaic model.

Tying to Previous Knowledge

The structure and function of the plasma membrane can be related to concepts of matter and energy learned in the previous chapter. Students will come to see that knowledge of such topics as polar molecules, lipid and protein structure, and energy are important in explaining the structures of organisms and the functions those structures perform.

Prepare

Key Concepts

Students will be introduced to the cell theory, properties of the plasma membrane, and the roles of the membrane components.

Key Terms

cell theory, plasma membrane, selectively permeable membrane, fluid mosaic model

Materials

- Gather saxophone reed, talcum powder, flower petals, lettuce leaves, sand, pond scum, and nylon thread for Minilab 1.

1 Focus

Objectives

The objectives are listed on the student page. Remind students to preview these objectives as a guide to this numbered section.

Activity

Ask students to brainstorm a list of functions they think a cell would have to carry out. After completing their lists, students should make a diagram of an imaginary cell with imaginary parts that carry out each function on their lists. For example, if taking in food is on the list, they might make a large mouth in the outer covering of the cell. Encourage students to be creative. **L1** **LEP** **COOP LEARN**

Objectives

Describe the discovery of cells and the development of the cell theory.

Relate the properties of the cell membrane to its structure.

Figure 4-1 Robert Hooke designed this microscope (left) to observe cork cells (right). The microscope has three lenses and is beautifully finished in gold-embossed leather. Magnification (right): 250×

4.1 Membrane Structure

In earlier chapters, you learned about the great diversity of organisms on Earth today. You had a glimpse of the variety of organisms in each of the five kingdoms. But remember that all the different life forms have much in common. The obvious external differences among such organisms as alligators, toadstools, and rosebushes might not suggest that different kinds of organisms share many features, but internally they share a very basic characteristic. All are composed of the same fundamental units of life—cells. As brick buildings can look very different, so, too, can organisms. The buildings are all built of bricks; the organisms are all built of cells. Bricks are lifeless clay, but cells are alive with activity. The eyes reading this page are made up of living cells. What do you suppose is going on in those cells right now?

The Cell Theory

You have probably known about cells for many years and take for granted the idea that they are fundamental parts of organisms. However, this idea took nearly 200 years to develop. The first discovery of cells was recorded in 1665. Robert Hooke, an English scientist, used a primitive microscope to examine razor-thin slices of cork, part of the bark of an oak tree. He saw, as in Figure 4-1, that cork is composed of many similar compartments, empty cubicles that he named cells. They were so tiny that he estimated there to be more than a billion cells per cubic inch of cork.

The cork cells that Hooke observed were dead. He actually saw only their stiff outer borders, which he named walls. Hooke's discovery spurred further research by others. Limited by poor microscopes, however, these researchers made slow progress. Gradually, discoveries by a number of scientists led to a more accurate picture of living cells. It was

MULTICULTURAL CONNECTION

Ancient Medicine: Ancient Egyptians have contributed to medicine by giving the world its first doctors. These physicians had an excellent knowledge of herbal and food remedies. Even though they did not know of vitamin C, they prescribed meals with onions, known to have large amounts of vitamin C, as a treatment of scurvy, a disease caused by a lack of vitamin C.

MEETING INDIVIDUAL NEEDS

Visually Impaired: For Minilab 1, pair students who are visually impaired with sighted students who can explain what is seen under the microscope. **COOP LEARN**

learned, for example, that cells are filled with a jellylike fluid and that most cells house a round, central structure that stands out from the rest of the cell. Although these individual discoveries were important, the idea of cells being the basic structural units of all organisms was a long time coming. In 1838, Matthias Schleiden, after completing a lengthy study of plant structure, concluded that all plants are composed of cells and that cells are the basis of a plant's functions. A year later, Theodor Schwann concluded the same things about animals. Then, in 1858, another important generalization was made. Rudolf Virchow stated that all cells come from other living cells.

The discoveries of other scientists and the generalizations made by Schleiden, Schwann, and Virchow came to form the basis of one of biology's most important concepts, the **cell theory.** The cell theory states that:

1. All organisms are composed of one or more cells or cell fragments.
2. The cell is the basic unit of structure and function in organisms.
3. All cells are produced from other cells.

You learned that a theory is a major hypothesis that has stood the test of time. Because it applies to all organisms, the cell theory is a cornerstone of modern biology. It is important in another way, too. The cell theory fits the theory of evolution: All organisms are descendants of an original organism, which was a single cell. As organisms evolved, they retained and shared the cell as the basic unit of structure and function.

Properties of the Plasma Membrane

Each cell, whether an entire organism or a small part of an organism, lives in a fluid environment. Amoebas are surrounded by the water of a lake or pond. Most cells of land plants are bathed by water that enters the plant from the soil. Your cells are in contact with fluids as well. Blood and tissue fluids bathe each of the cells in your body. Cells must obtain materials from and release substances into their moist environment.

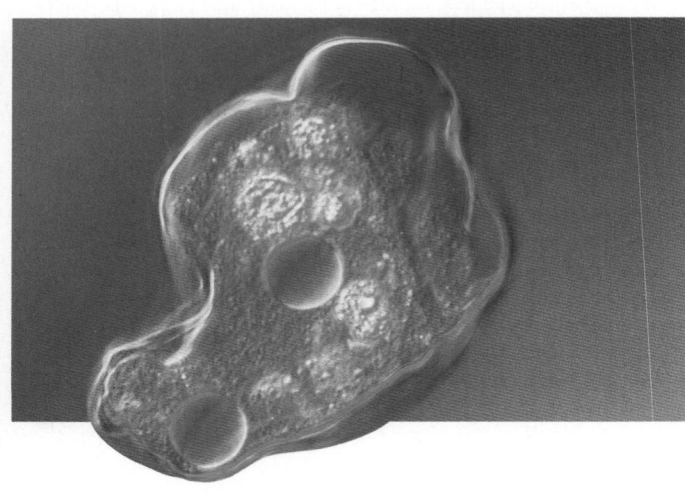

Figure 4-2 **All cells are surrounded by a membrane, which separates the cell contents from the outside environment. This amoeba is a single-celled organism. Magnification: 160×**

91

Teacher FYI

Brain cells need a constant supply of glucose, which is water soluble, making it easily passed through the brain cell membranes. If deprived of glucose even for a few seconds, the brain will lapse into unconsciousness.

Science, Technology, and Society

Brain Drugs: The pharmaceutical industry is developing new ways to get drugs into brain cells. Because nerve cell membranes are not permeable to many particles that permeate most cells, many drugs cannot enter the brain. If the drug can be linked to a carrier "taxi" of fat, it can sometimes be moved across the barrier. This action is similar to a soap bubble merging into another after contact. After entering the brain, the drug is released from its carrier by an enzyme.

Using an Analogy

- Explain to students that the lining up of the nonpolar fatty acid tails and the polar phosphate heads of the membrane could be compared to the action of magnets repelling each other. LEP

- Another useful analogy about the action of a cell membrane is that of a ball pool. Students may have played in ball pools in kiddie play areas at shopping malls. Ask them to remember how the balls acted to stay in even layers as children moved in and out of the pool. The balls separated easily as children moved through, and immediately moved back into open places as the children's feet passed through. The balls represent the phospholipids and the children represent substances moving in and out of the membrane. LEP

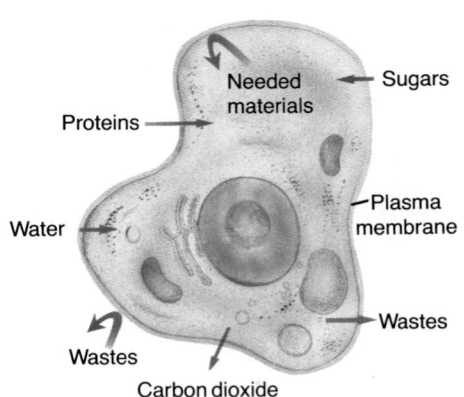

Figure 4-3 A cell must remove wastes and keep other wastes from entering. Likewise, it must take in and keep needed materials while maintaining a balance with its surroundings.

The Plasma Membrane If each cell is a separate unit of life, it must have a boundary separating it from other cells and from its environment. The outer boundary of a cell, the **plasma membrane**, encloses the cell's contents. The membrane is also the cell's gatekeeper. It regulates which particles can enter and leave the cell. Proper cell functioning depends on passage of materials across the plasma membrane. For example, amino acid and glucose molecules move from an animal cell's environment, across the membrane, and into the cell's interior. Once inside, the amino acids can be linked to form polypeptides, and the glucose can be used in cellular respiration. Carbon dioxide produced during respiration passes from inside the cell, across the membrane, and out into the environment. These functions of the plasma membrane are directly related to its structure.

Selective Permeability Long before much was known about the structure of the plasma membrane, biologists had learned a great deal about its properties. They knew that only certain molecules were able to pass through, or permeate, the membrane. Such a structure was called a **selectively permeable membrane**. A tea bag also is a selectively permeable membrane. It is permeable to water molecules but not to tea leaves. This property is important, because only those particles that are used by the cell or that must be expelled should cross the membrane. If all particles could pass in or out freely, the cell could not maintain its organization. The chaos would be like a parking lot without the white lines and painted arrows, with cars driving in and out anywhere and parking any which way.

Cells differ in terms of the particles they use and those that must be expelled. Thus, different types of cells are permeable to different particles. In addition, the permeability of a membrane to a certain particle may change from time to time.

Certain particles can cross the plasma membrane more freely than others. Small particles can pass through more easily than large ones. Lipids and particles that are soluble in lipids can cross the membrane more readily than particles that are insoluble in lipids. In general, small ions do not cross the membrane as easily as uncharged particles of about the same size, and some ions can permeate the membrane more readily than others.

A Model of the Plasma Membrane

You learned from your study of enzymes that scientists often propose models to explain known properties. Biologists have offered several models of plasma membrane structure over the last 50 years. The models have been revised as new ways of investigating the plasma membrane have been developed. Since the 1950s, electron microscopes and improved techniques for biochemical analysis have been especially important in studying the plasma membrane.

92 ⋅ THE CELL AND ITS ENVIRONMENT

Figure 4-4   The two cells shown here side by side illustrate clearly that each is bounded by a plasma membrane made of two layers. Magnification: 200 000×

The Lipid Bilayer   When viewed through an electron microscope, the plasma membrane appears as two thin lines, as in Figure 4-4. Chemical analysis has shown that the membrane consists of a lipid bilayer, made up of two layers of molecules called phospholipids. The phospholipids composing each of the two layers are different. Look back at Figure 3-23. The diagram represents a molecule of a lipid, made up of one molecule of glycerol joined to three fatty acid molecules.

Now look at Figure 4-5b. One of the fatty acid molecules has been replaced by a group of atoms called a phosphate group. This group is attached to the part of the glycerol molecule away from the fatty acids. Fatty acids are nonpolar molecules and do not dissolve in water. The phosphate group, however, is polar and easily dissolves in water. These properties determine the way the two layers of phospholipids are arranged. Because they are soluble in water, the polar phosphate heads of the phospholipids point toward the outside and inside of the cell, where water is plentiful. The nonpolar fatty acid tails of the phospholipids point away from water, toward the middle of the membrane. As a result, the two layers of phospholipids face one another, as Figure 4-5a shows. This arrangement of phospholipids into two layers is a result of their physical and chemical properties when in a watery environment. The layers form spontaneously. Once formed, the bilayer in membranes can be maintained without expenditure of energy by cells.

Figure 4-5   Two layers of phospholipids form the structure of a membrane (a). Each phospholipid has a polar head and two nonpolar tails (b). Which end of the molecule will dissolve in water?

a

b

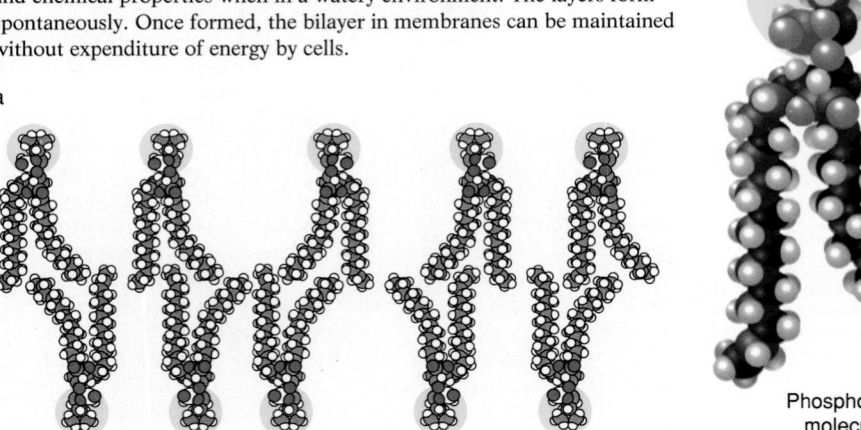

Polar head

Phosphate group

Fatty acids

Phospholipid molecule

4.1 MEMBRANE STRUCTURE   **93**

Figure Caption Question
Which end of the molecule will dissolve in water? The polar head dissolves in water.

Different Viewpoints in Biology

Why do cells age?
One leading theory of aging states that the body deteriorates because it produces destructive free radicals. These agents impair the functioning of cell membrane components. An alternative hypothesis holds that genes control aging. Other studies indicate that interactions between the nervous and endocrine systems are involved in aging. In terms of evolution, perhaps animals have not evolved maintenance systems that prevent aging because the energy required for that process is more effective for survival of the species if it is put into reproduction. You might ask your students to discuss the pros and cons of development of techniques that would delay aging.

Using the Illustration
Students can make a model of a triglyceride using gumdrops, or marshmallows, and toothpicks. By replacing one fatty acid with a phosphate group, students will be able to visualize the structure of a phospholipid, as shown in Figure 4-5b.

Using an Analogy

In discussing the flexibility of a cell membrane, you may want to compare the cell membrane to a balloon that expands as it is blown full of air and then contracts as air is released.

LEP

Building a Model

Ask students to make a salt dough model of a cell membrane. They could do this in their groups with each group member taking a part in explaining to you how its model works. The recipe for salt dough is: 2 parts salt to 1 part flour; add water and mix with hands until the dough has the consistency of bread dough and does not stick to your hands. L1

LEP   COOP LEARN

PHYSICS CONNECTION

Lasers: Lasers are devices that amplify light waves and concentrate them in a penetrating beam that a surgeon can use as a scalpel. Photons of light in a laser pass back and forth between mirrors, causing more and more photons to be emitted from atoms. You could compare this reaction to a chain reaction in a nuclear reactor. Lasers have been used by surgeons to unclog obstructed arteries, break up kidney stones, and clear cataracts. Surgical lasers are highly selective, penetrating and leaving the exterior intact while destroying interior tissue. Laser surgery can be so specific that it targets just one cell. A highly focused laser can create a small temporary hole in a membrane so that DNA can be inserted for genetic engineering procedures.

Using the Illustration

Ask students why it might be beneficial for a cell if its plasma membrane contains cholesterol.

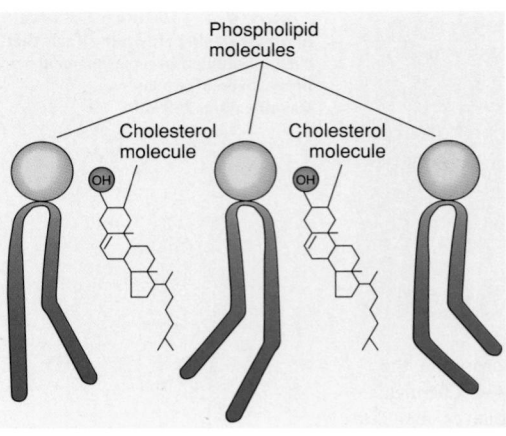

Figure 4-6 Cholesterol molecules embedded in the bilayer stabilize the plasma membranes of some eukaryotic cells and make them more rigid. Cholesterol also helps to keep the fatty acid tails apart.

This lack of energy use by the cell does not mean that the membrane is inactive. If you could see the individual molecules of the membrane, you might be surprised to see that the membrane is a dynamic structure. Within each layer, the fatty acid tails can wag back and forth, and entire phospholipids can glide sideways through their layer. These properties make the bilayer act like a very fine film of oil. Rigid molecules of cholesterol are embedded in the bilayer of many cells, where they bind to and restrict movement of the phospholipids (Figure 4-6). This binding makes the plasma membrane strong, as well as flexible.

Membrane Proteins   Scientists have long known that the plasma membrane contains proteins in addition to phospholipids. Until the 1970s, it was thought that the two lines seen with an electron microscope represented protein coats on either side of the bilayer, and that the membrane was like a lipid sandwich between two "slices" of protein. A new technique showed this to be an incorrect interpretation. Plasma membranes were separated from the rest of cells and then frozen. The frozen membranes were then fractured to expose the area between the two lines. Examination of the fractured membranes revealed many bumps in the phospholipid bilayer, as seen in Figure 4-7. These bumps are proteins.

Results of the freeze-fracture technique have shown that proteins are scattered throughout the bilayer, like raisins in a slice of raisin bread. Some proteins are partly or totally embedded in the bilayer. Others lie on the surface of either the outer or inner phospholipid layer. Like phospholipids,

Figure 4-7 The interior surface of a red blood cell membrane can be seen using an electron microscope, after the membrane has been prepared by the freeze-fracturing technique. The bumps are proteins embedded in the membrane. Magnification: 100 000×

94 ✿ THE CELL AND ITS ENVIRONMENT

PROGRAM RESOURCES

Teacher Classroom Resources
Study Guide, pp. 19-20 L1
Color Transparency #3 L1 LEP
Investigating Living Systems, Lab 10, p. 39 L2

proteins have polar and nonpolar areas that determine their position in the bilayer. Proteins, too, can migrate sideways within the bilayer, but not as rapidly as the phospholipids. Because components of the membrane are constantly moving, like a fluid, and because the membrane has a pattern of proteins embedded in it, this current model of membrane structure is called the **fluid mosaic model.** This structure, shown in Figure 4-8, is closely related to the membrane's function.

Figure 4-8   The fluid mosaic model is the current model of membrane structure.

HISTORY CONNECTION

Purpose
Students will study the work of Ernest Everett Just, an African American cell biologist.

Teaching Strategies
• Ask students what they think it might have been like for a black scientist with an idea different from the accepted view in the early 1900s.

Possible Answers
1. Most biologists of the time thought that the cytoplasm was under the control of the nucleus and did not serve any function in that it was not a living part of the cell. Today scientists know that both the cytoplasm and cell membrane are essential parts of the cell.
2. The plasma membrane was considered to be a passive structure because scientists had no way to know about the complex chemical reactions going on in this structure. Scientists of the time were focusing on the nucleus as the important part of the cell and ignoring the plasma membrane.

Going Further
Have students report on the work of other biologists who were producing important research at the same time as Just.

HISTORY CONNECTION

Ernest Everett Just

As a teenager, Ernest Just (1883-1941) left South Carolina with few academic skills other than reading. He completed high school and college in New Hampshire, graduating with honors in 1907, and joined the teaching staff of Howard University.

Just devoted his life to research in cell biology and embryology. He studied fertilization in marine organisms and the importance of the cell surface in the development of these organisms. While conducting this research, he began to realize that all parts of a cell were important to the cell's activity. Just came to believe that the plasma membrane was an active part of the cell, not just a passive covering. He also believed that the cytoplasm was as important as the nucleus in determining a cell's activities. These ideas were controversial at that time. (Remember that much of the information we have today about cells was not known at that time.)

Because of his unpopular views, Just and his work were not fully appreciated in his lifetime, even though he was later shown to be correct. He did, however, publish numerous articles and authored two books, including *The Biology of the Cell Surface.* In 1915, he was the first person to receive the Spingarn Medal, awarded annually to an African-American who has had outstanding achievement in his or her field.

1. **Explore Further:** Just's belief that all parts of a cell influence the cell's activities was considered controversial when it was first proposed. Find out what the popular scientific belief of the time was. Compare this belief with what scientists currently believe.
2. **Writing About Biology:** Write a short paragraph explaining why you think the plasma membrane was once considered to be a passive structure.

STUDENT JOURNAL
Students may not know what a mosaic is. Bring an example of this type of art or use a photograph in an art book to help students understand the concept of the fluid mosaic model. Have students write a paragraph in their journals explaining the concept of a mosaic. LEP

3 Assess

Check for Understanding
Make several diagrams of cell membrane structure on the chalkboard or on a transparency. Ask students to pick the one that is correct and write a paragraph defending their choice, explaining why the others are incorrect. You might want to put labels on your diagrams and tell students that they must use those words as part of their explanation. L1

Reteach

Tell students that they are cell membrane doctors. They must decide what part of the cell membrane is missing or what is wrong in each of the following descriptions.

1. The bumps in the phospholipid bilayer are missing.
2. The phospholipid bilayer is unrestricted in its movement.
3. The plasma membrane is weak.
4. Polypeptides are not formed inside the cell.
5. Cell respiration stops.
6. There is no polar part to the membrane.
7. Specific chemicals can no longer recognize the cell membrane.

Answers: 1. Proteins are missing. 2. Cholesterol is missing. 3. Cholesterol is missing. 4. Amino acids are not transported into the cell. 5. Glucose is not transported into the cell. 6. Phosphate groups are missing. 7. Proteins are missing.

Extension

Ask students to look up information about the key experiment by Gorter and Grendel that demonstrated that the cell membrane is a bilayer. Have them report on the procedures the scientists used, their final conclusions, and also the serious mistakes they made during the course of their investigation. **L3**

✔ Assessment

Knowledge: Give students a diagram of the cell membrane that is missing parts. Ask them to draw in the needed parts. Also ask them specifically how the membrane without the parts they have added would be different in its function. **L1** **LEP**

4 Close

Activity

Tell students that they are going to be tour guides of a cell membrane display at a museum. They should prepare a script to use as they point out various parts of the cell membrane. **L1**

Inner membrane

Outer membrane

Figure 4-9 **The membranes of internal cell parts, such as this mitochondrion, also have a fluid mosaic structure. The photomicrograph shows the internal structure of the mitochondrion, magnified about 81 000 times.**

Roles of the Membrane Components The phospholipid bilayer serves mainly a structural role in the plasma membrane and forms most of the cell's outer boundary. Its chemical properties allow it to act as a barrier across which most particles cannot pass. The membrane proteins play more functional roles. Many of the proteins regulate which particles can pass across the membrane. Other proteins serve as enzymes and take part in chemical reactions. Still others act as markers that are recognized by chemicals from both inside and outside the cell. Some of these markers are involved in fighting disease. Other markers are important in recognition of other cells. Thus, in many respects, the plasma membrane can be thought of as a communication center.

Most cells have internal structures that are themselves enclosed by membranes. These internal membranes also have a fluid mosaic structure. The kinds and arrangements of the phospholipids and proteins vary from one such membrane to another. Thus, each membrane has its own distinct permeability characteristics. These differences are important because, as you will learn in Chapter 5, each cellular part carries out its own set of chemical reactions. The membrane of each cell part lets in and out those particles used or produced by that part's particular functions.

Section Review

Understanding Concepts
1. Explain how the plasma membrane is like a liquid.
2. Could different cells in your body perform different functions if their membranes were all permeable to exactly the same materials? Explain.
3. Why did it take almost 200 years after Robert Hooke's discovery for scientists to develop the cell theory?

4. ***Skill Review—Making Tables:*** Construct a table comparing how easily the following particles pass across membranes: lipids vs. nonlipids; small particles vs. large particles; neutral particles vs. ions; particles soluble in lipids vs. particles not soluble in lipids. For more help, refer to Organizing Information in the **Skill Handbook**.

5. ***Thinking Critically:*** Suppose you added some phospholipids to water. If you could see individual molecules, how would the phospholipids be arranged? Explain.

Answers to Section Review

1. Most of the plasma membrane is composed of a phospholipid bilayer in which individual phospholipids can move. Proteins embedded in the membrane can also move. Such movement makes the membrane like a fluid.
2. Different functions require particular sets of particles from the environment and result in production of different wastes or products. Each type of cell must be permeable to the particles it needs and those it must expel.

3. Scientists were limited by poor microscopes.
4. **Skill Review—Making Tables:** Those particles that pass through more readily: lipids, small particles, neutral particles, lipid-soluble particles.
5. **Thinking Critically:** The phospholipids would be arranged in a circle consisting of two layers. The charged heads would be facing the water, and the fatty acid tails would face one another.

4.2 Membrane Function

Now that you have a picture of the plasma membrane and its structure, think again about its role as a gatekeeper. Keep in mind that the membrane is selectively permeable. You can make use of what you've learned about the membrane's structure to understand how particles enter and leave cells and why all membranes are not permeable to the same substances.

Diffusion

Suppose you had a collection of 500 marbles, which you kept neatly in an open box on a table. That is a very organized, or nonrandom, arrangement. Marbles do not place themselves neatly in a box. They are there because of the energy you used to put them there. Now, suppose the box is knocked over and falls to the floor. Out come the marbles, bouncing off one another, the floor, the furniture, and the walls. Eventually, the marbles stop moving. Their arrangement now is anything but organized. In fact, it is quite random. In nature, there is a tendency toward randomness. Energy is required for nonrandomness. Think about the organization of your room or locker. Is it random or nonrandom? Do your socks place themselves neatly in a drawer? Do your books line themselves up on a shelf? What must you do to achieve greater organization of your socks and books?

Random Movement   The example of the marbles illustrates an important physical process. Placing some blue crystals of copper sulfate, an ionic compound, into a beaker of water shows the same process, Figure 4-10. At first, the crystals settle to the bottom, and the water is colorless. After a time, the water near the crystals appears blue, and gradually the blue color spreads throughout the water.

Figure 4-10   Copper sulfate, a blue crystalline compound, diffuses through water, distributing copper and sulfate ions evenly throughout. The solution turns bluer as diffusion proceeds.

Objectives

Demonstrate the various ways by which substances enter and leave cells.

Compare and contrast the processes of passive transport and active transport.

Prepare

Key Concepts
Students will compare diffusion and osmosis, and learn how facilitated diffusion, active transport, endocytosis, and exocytosis allow materials to enter and leave the cell.

Key Terms
diffusion, dynamic equilibrium, osmosis, passive transport, transport protein, facilitated diffusion, active transport, endocytosis, vesicle, phagocytosis, pinocytosis, exocytosis, cell wall, middle lamella

Materials
- Gather food coloring, beet juice, iodine, mouthwash, and cough syrup for Minilab 2.
- Gather dialysis tubing for the Investigation.
- Gather *Elodea* for the Alternate Lab.

1 Focus

Objectives
The objectives are listed on the student page. Remind students to preview these objectives as a guide to this numbered section.

Demonstration
As class begins, ask a student to wrap two pieces of hard candy in wax paper. Grape or cherry sour balls work well. Ask another student to hit the candy with a hammer so that one piece breaks into several large pieces, and the other is pulverized. Into one small beaker of water, place one whole candy; into another, place the large pieces of candy; into a third, the smashed candy. During the class, ask students to observe what is happening in the beakers. Which candy dissolved first? Which candy had the most surface area? How do you think the amount of surface area affects the rate at which the candy dissolves? Compared to the volume, which has a larger surface area—a large cell or a small cell? Which cell would take in materials faster—a large cell or a small cell? L1 LEP

PROGRAM RESOURCES

Teacher Classroom Resources
Study Guide, pp. 21-24 L1
Concept Mapping, p. 4 L1 LEP
Probing Levels of Life, Lab 9, p. 25 L2

2 Teach

Purpose
Students will compare and contrast ways that fish historically have been preserved.

Teaching Strategies
- Ask students what causes spoilage. Ask them what might happen if they were to eat spoiled food.
- A week before class, put a dried apple slice, a fresh apple slice, and some applesauce in containers in the classroom. Ask students to observe what has happened to the three types of apple and explain these results.

Possible Answers
1. Drying would be healthier because a high salt diet makes people prone to high blood pressure.
2. Fish will lose flavor more quickly than meat because the chemical processes will continue and waste products will collect.
3. Smoldering hardwood is the source of smoke used for smoking food. Researchers recommend that smoked food in the diet be limited because chemicals in the smoke are toxic.

Going Further
Ask students to bring in samples of food items that have been preserved in various ways. Enclose the samples in plastic bags and observe to see which remain spoilage free the longest at room temperature.

CAREER CONNECTION

For more information, contact a government fish hatchery or a fish farm.

Material moving into cell = Material moving out of cell

Figure 4-11 In dynamic equilibrium, there is motion but no net change.

When copper sulfate is first added to water, the copper ions and sulfate ions are all concentrated in one area—in the crystals. The position of the ions in the water is nonrandom. With time, though, the ions begin to separate. They move about randomly, colliding with one another, with the water molecules, and with the sides and bottom of the beaker. At each collision, ions bounce off and move in new directions. Random movement of the ions results finally in their uniform distribution throughout the water. Unlike the marbles, which stop moving because of friction, the ions continue to move about. The water becomes and stays blue because equal numbers of copper ions are entering and leaving any given region of water at any given time. The position of the ions in the water has become more random.

Diffusion of Particles Random movement of ions and other particles is called **diffusion.** Diffusion results in the net movement of particles from a region of greater concentration to a region of lesser concentration. With time, the particles become evenly distributed throughout the container. After this point, particles continue to move randomly and collide with one another, but the numbers of particles entering and leaving an area are equal. This condition, in which there is continuous movement but no overall change, is called **dynamic equilibrium,** Figure 4-11.

Particles may diffuse through the air, through water and other liquids, and across membranes. For example, the molecules that give toast its aroma

---

GLOBAL CONNECTION

Fish Out of Water

Freshly caught fish is a real treat to eat. The fresher it is, the better it tastes. It doesn't take long, however, before unpreserved fish starts to smell bad and taste worse. Most spoilage is caused by the growth of bacteria and other microorganisms. In the days before refrigeration, fish-eating people around the world came up with other ways to preserve seafood. The most common were drying and salting. These methods are still used today.

Drying Water is vital to most biological processes. If you remove most of the water from in and around fish cells, microorganisms can't grow—at least not well. The seafaring people of Northern Scandinavia are old masters of the art of drying fish. So are the Eskimos. But perhaps the most dramatic example of preservation by drying comes from the Native Americans of pre-Columbian Peru.

Living high in the Andes Mountains, they would freeze fish in the frigid night air and dry it in the hot daytime sun. In the daytime heat, the low atmospheric pressure of the high mountains allowed much of the fish meat's water, frozen during the night, to turn directly from ice to vapor. This was freeze-drying, a technique we consider very modern.

Salting Salting is related to drying in that it works by affecting water in cells. In the salting process, however, the water under attack is in the microorganism. When salt is added to meat, the watery environment of the cells is loaded with a high concentration of ions. The water inside the microbes' cells contains a lesser concentration of ions. Water flows out of the microbes' cells into the surrounding environment, restoring osmotic

---

PORTFOLIO

Ask students to work in pairs to make a list of substances having an odor that would permit detection of diffusion of those molecules through the air. Students should design an experiment in which they determine which solutions diffuse fastest. They should write a lab report for inclusion in their portfolios. **L1** **COOP LEARN**

STUDENT JOURNAL

Ask students to examine the effects of high and low temperature on diffusion. They could simply add food coloring to water of different temperatures and time how long it takes for the molecules to become evenly distributed. Students should make graphs of their data in their journals and speculate how differences in temperatures would affect diffusion into and out of cells. **L1** waft by diffusion from near the toaster, where they are more concentrated, through the air to your nose at the breakfast table, where they are less concentrated. The bumping and colliding of the air and molecules from the toast move the particles outward from their source. Eventually, dynamic equilibrium is reached and the smell of toast fills the entire kitchen.

Diffusion Through Membranes   Diffusion is a physical process that explains how some particles permeate a membrane. Particles that can diffuse across cell membranes include lipids and those particles that dissolve in lipids, such as oxygen and carbon dioxide. As an example, consider a plasma membrane surrounded by and permeable to small lipid molecules. Assume more lipid molecules are outside than inside the cell. Because they are in random motion, the molecules bump into one another and into the membrane. So many of the molecules strike the membrane that most pass through it. A greater concentration of the lipid molecules on the outside means a greater chance of their hitting and passing across the membrane from the outside than hitting and crossing the membrane from the inside. As the number of lipid molecules inside the cell increases, the chance of lipid molecules leaving the cell increases. Eventually, dynamic equilibrium occurs. The molecules continue to move, but the numbers entering and leaving the cell are equal. A net movement from a region of greater concentration outside the cell, to a region of lesser concentration inside the cell, has occurred.

---

balance. The microbes dry up and die.

Europeans and Americans first used salting in the late 1600s to preserve red meat during shipping. This method was later used for preserving fish. Unfortunately, salting wasn't as well suited to preserving fish as it was to preserving red meat. Most of the fish shipped came from salt waters. The microbes that attack saltwater fish are quite at home in a salty environment. So, while a 2 percent salt solution would easily preserve red meat, fish required a 12 percent salt solution.

Brine   If salt and vinegar are combined to make a strong brine, however, a much more effective fish

preservative is produced. Most microbes that attack fish can't survive in such an acidic environment. Brine solutions have long been used in Eastern Europe and Scandinavia. The pickled herring you find in the supermarket is preserved in brine.

1. **Connection to Health:** If you had to preserve food without refrigeration, do you think that drying or salting would be healthier? Why?
2. **Explore Further:** The enzymes in fish cells remain active at normal room temperatures, unlike the enzymes in meat from mammals. How does this fact influence the keeping quality of fresh fish?

3. **Writing About Biology:** Another method of preserving food is by smoking. Learn more about this method of food preservation and write a short paper about the subject.

CAREER CONNECTION

Fish farmers raise fish as crops, just as other farmers might grow corn or a rancher might raise cattle. Fish farmers make sure that plenty of eggs are fertilized and safely hatched, and that fish are properly fed and raised for the table.

Bioethics

Fetal Cell Research: Tissue from aborted human fetuses has been used to treat a variety of human ailments from Alzheimer's disease to Parkinson's disease. Nerve cells from aborted fetuses have been used to repair damaged spinal cords. Have a class discussion about the ethics of using fetal tissue for medical research. Make sure both sides of the issue are discussed.

Using an Analogy

Give students this analogy. A playground is surrounded by a fence with gates. Children are kept in and criminals kept out. The gates have locks and only certain people have keys to get in. Security guards patrol the gates and fences. Small children are carried through the gate while others can go through if they have an ID card. Trash is taken out by a truck through a different gate. Ask students to compare the parts of this analogy to what they know about the functioning of cell membranes. LEP

ART CONNECTION

SEM Art: David Scharf has brought the world of the scanning electron microscope into the realm of art. His amazing pictures of cells, pollen grains, tiny insects, and plant parts have been used by magazines and are in museums and galleries. While most scientists use the electron microscope to observe and study the structure of organisms, Scharf has opened this microscopic world so we may look at these structures and specimens as art. Ask students to look in the text at some of the photos taken with the aid of an electron microscope and note the captions indicating size. Compare these sizes to familiar objects.

MEETING INDIVIDUAL NEEDS

Ask a group of gifted students to contact and interview a cell biologist at a nearby college, university, or biology research facility to determine trends and conclusions of research on cell membranes. Students could take slides of the facility they visit and present them to the class. L3

PROGRAM RESOURCES

Teacher Classroom Resources
Color Transparency #4 L1 LEP
Investigating Living Systems, Lab 11, p. 47 L2
Critical Thinking/Problem Solving, p. 4 L2

Minilab 2

Purpose
Students will determine whether various colored substances will diffuse through a membrane.

Skills
classify, observe and infer, compare and contrast, interpret data

Teaching Strategies
- **Safety Precautions:** Iodine is poisonous. Students should avoid spilling on skin or inhaling vapors.
- Clear plastic cups can substitute for the five small beakers.
- Tea, coffee, or phenol red may also be tested. See page 27T.
- Place beaker with bag containing iodine overnight in the dark.
- Phenol red will diffuse through plastic after 24 to 48 hours.
- Review the meaning of the terms *permeable, impermeable,* and *selectively permeable.*
- Ask students to review direction of water flow with different concentrations of molecules inside and outside the bag, and have them predict the movement of molecules, assuming the membranes are permeable to all molecules being tested.
- Make the iodine solution by dissolving 1 g iodine crystals (I_2) and 2 g potassium iodide (KI) in 100 mL water.

Expected Results
Discuss how students will be able to evaluate if molecules diffuse across the membrane.

Answers
Typical results, using Glad pleated sandwich bags, will show no diffusion except for iodine solution. Student data will vary, depending on brand of plastic bag used and length of time that bag remains in water. Plastic bags and plasma membranes are both selectively permeable.

✔ Assessment
Oral: Ask students to make comparisons between cell membranes and the plastic-bag model being used.

Minilab 2

Are plastic bags permeable to certain molecules?

Place the following into separate plastic bags: food coloring in water, canned beet juice in water, iodine in water, mouthwash, and cough syrup. Seal the bags. Place each bag in a separate small beaker of water. Observe the color of the beaker water 24 hours later.

Analysis *What conclusion can you make regarding permeability of plastic bags to those molecules tested? How is a plastic bag similar to a plasma membrane?*

Osmosis

The diffusion of water into and out of cells across a selectively permeable membrane is so common that it is given a special name, **osmosis.** For any cell to survive, it must be in osmotic balance with its watery environment. Osmotic balance occurs when the movement of water into and out of a cell is equal, that is, when dynamic equilibrium occurs.

Osmotic Balance in the Blood Consider a red blood cell, which is in osmotic balance with its surrounding liquid, blood plasma. The cell and the plasma both contain water and dissolved substances. Although not necessarily the same, the substances are in equal concentrations in the plasma and in the cell. Thus, the concentration of water is the same in the plasma and in the cell. If the blood cell is removed from the plasma and placed in pure water, however, it is no longer in osmotic balance. The pure water contains no dissolved particles, so the concentration of water outside the cell is greater than inside. A net movement of water molecules into the cell begins. So much water enters so quickly that the blood cell swells and bursts, Figure 4-12b. This is why IVs given to patients are usually solutions of sugar and salts rather than pure water.

Osmotic Balance in Freshwater Plants Red blood cells are not normally surrounded by pure water. They have no adaptations that enable them to adjust to the difference in concentration of water, and so they burst. Many cells, however, do normally live in a freshwater environment, and they have evolved ways of maintaining osmotic balance. For example, *Elodea* is a freshwater plant often seen in home aquariums. Like the red blood cell in pure water, cells of *Elodea* contain water with dissolved particles, and so water tends to move into the cells. However, the cells do not burst. The net movement of water inward is slight but does not continue, because the cell's tough outer wall balances the pressure of the small amount of water that enters. By pressing inward to counterbalance the outward pressure of the water, the cell wall prevents additional water from entering the cell. This adaptation—the cell wall—enables the cells to survive. Cells of land plants maintain osmotic balance in the same way.

What would happen if an *Elodea* plant were placed in salt water? The concentration of water molecules would be greater inside the cells than outside. As a result, there would be a net movement of water outward. Such loss of water causes the cell contents to shrink, Figure 4-12c. Continued water loss may lead to the death of cells and of an entire plant.

Diffusion and Osmosis as Passive Transport Osmosis and diffusion are processes by which water, lipids, and lipid-soluble particles permeate membranes. These substances either are able to dissolve in the lipid bilayer or are small enough to squeeze between the phospholipids in the membrane. Their passage across membranes is due to their net random motion from a region of greater concentration to a region of lesser concentration. The cell plays no active role and does no work in moving the particles. This type of movement of particles across membranes is called **passive transport,** because the cell uses no energy to move the particles.

100 🖎 THE CELL AND ITS ENVIRONMENT

STUDENT JOURNAL

Ask students to answer the following question in their journals: Why are there no unicellular animals 30 mm in diameter? Tell them that they must explain their answer in terms of diffusion and osmosis. **L1**

PROJECT

Dry Cells: Have students do library research to get background for the following project. Design a cell membrane that would function well under conditions of extreme drought. Students should make a diagram of their cell membrane and write a description of how it functions. **L3**

EFFECTS OF WATER CONCENTRATION ON CELLS

Water Concentrations	Red Blood Cell	*Elodea*

a   Equal water concentrations

Cell unchanged

Cell unchanged

H_2O

H_2O

b   Greater water concentration outside cell — pure water

Cell bursts

Cell swells

H_2O

H_2O

c   Greater water concentration inside cell — salt water

Cell shrinks

Cell contents shrink

H_2O

H_2O

Water molecules

Dissolved substances

Figure 4-12   As a result of osmosis, cells respond differently when the water concentration inside the cell is equal to, greater than, or less than the water concentration in the environment.

4.2 MEMBRANE FUNCTION   **101**

Enrichment

The cell membrane is like a switchboard that can merge a variety of signals or send the signals down different paths, depending on what the cell needs. The molecules that coordinate the cell's responses to outside signals are called G proteins, referring to the guanine nucleotides to which they bind. G proteins play an important role in most cell activities. **L3**

Demonstration

- Set up two or more thistle tubes covered with selectively permeable membranes. Compare rates of osmosis in varying concentrations of colored sugar or salt solutions by filling each tube with solution and placing the base in a beaker of distilled water. **L1**
- Illustrate osmosis by watering a small plant with salt water at the beginning of class. By the end of class, the plant will have wilted. Ask students what would happen to crops in dry climates when salts accumulate in soil. **L1**

Using the Illustration

Make flash cards by pasting a copy of one of the cells in Figure 4-12 on each of six cards. Have students identify the concentration of the solution in which the cell has been placed. **L1**

Discussion

Ask students what would happen to freshwater protozoans if they were suddenly released into salt water. What would happen to a patient's blood cells if pure water were substituted for physiological saline in an IV bottle? **L1**   **COOP LEARN**

MEETING INDIVIDUAL NEEDS

Visually Impaired: For students who are visually impaired, ask a group to make a diagram of the cell membrane and also to illustrate the basic concepts of Figure 4-12 with string and lines of glue that are raised when dry. **LEP**   **COOP LEARN**

STUDENT JOURNAL

Show students some Gary Larson cartoons about cells. Each of his books has at least one cartoon about cells. Tell students to make, as a group, their own cartoon about cells. It must illustrate a concept about cell membranes. Ask students to sketch the cartoon with its caption into their journals. **L1**   **COOP LEARN**

SECTION 4.2

Enrichment

The Nobel Prize in Physiology was awarded in 1991 to German scientists Erwin Neher and Bert Sakmann for proving that certain membrane proteins dot the outer membranes of cells and permit the cell to take in and let out charged atoms. They found that specific cell membrane channels accept only certain size ions and ions with specific charges. They developed a technique called patch clamping that allowed them to isolate and study a single channel.

Demonstration

Add a bit of phenolphthalein as you prepare a gelatin block. Put the block into dialysis tubing. Suspend the gelatin in the tubing over a solution of ammonium hydroxide. Ask students to account for the color change that occurs. During the discussion, make sure that the idea of diffusion is brought out. Ask students what might happen if the block were larger or smaller. `L1`

Figure 4-13 **Channel proteins provide water-filled passages through which small dissolved particles, such as ions, can diffuse.**

Channel protein

Facilitated Diffusion

Most particles needed by cells—such as certain ions, sugars, and amino acids—may be in greater concentration outside the plasma membrane than inside. However, they cannot dissolve in the lipid bilayer and are too large to squeeze through. How can such particles, so important to cells, permeate the membrane? You read earlier that many membrane proteins play a role in the passage of particles. Such proteins are known as **transport proteins.** Use of transport proteins to aid, or facilitate, the passage of particles across the plasma membrane is called **facilitated diffusion.** Because the particles move from a region of greater concentration to one of lesser concentration, facilitated diffusion is a form of passive transport.

In facilitated diffusion, each transport protein is highly selective and aids the passage of only certain particles. Transport proteins are so selective because each one has a distinctive shape and charge that allows passage of only one kind of particle. There are several types of transport proteins.

Channel Proteins Among the simplest types of transport proteins are protein channels, also called pores. These channels, shown in Figure 4-13, extend through the bilayer and form water-filled tunnels that allow certain ions to pass through. Different ions pass through different pores. Which ion passes through a given pore depends on the size and charge of the ion and the inside diameter of the channel. The polar (charged) regions of the channel protein itself are also important. You know that like charges (++ or – –) repel each other; opposite charges (+– or –+) attract each other.

Thinking Lab

INTERPRET THE DATA

Can pore size be used to determine molecule size?

Background
Particle movement across living cell membranes may be influenced by conditions such as pore size, particle size, or particle charge. The following table shows the results of an experiment in which four molecules (W-Z) were passed through three different membranes (A-C) with varying pore sizes.

You Try It
Interpret the data to predict the size of the molecules based on their movement through the membranes. Assume that

pore size is the only condition influencing molecule movement. Note: One nanometer (nm) = 1/1 000 000 mm.

Membrane	Pore Size	Can Molecule Pass Through Pore?			
		W	X	Y	Z
A	1 nm	no	yes	no	no
B	2 nm	no	yes	no	yes
C	3 nm	yes	yes	no	yes

Completing the following statements may help with interpreting the data.

Molecule W is larger than _____ nm but smaller than _____ nm.

Molecule X is smaller than _____ nm.

Molecule Y is larger than _____ nm.

Molecule Z is larger than _____ nm but smaller than _____ nm.

How could you determine the exact size of molecule Z if membranes with different known pore sizes were available?

Thinking Lab

INTERPRET THE DATA

Purpose
Students will evaluate how particle size influences passage of a particle through a membrane.

Skills
classify, interpret data, sequence

Teaching Strategies
• Have students make a chart to help them visualize the sizes of W - Z.

Answers
W = 2-3 nm; X < 1 nm; Y > 3 nm; Z = 1-2 nm

Obtain a membrane with a pore size larger than 1 nm but smaller than 1.9 nm. If a molecule passes through, it is between 1 and 1.9 nm in diameter. If a molecule does not pass through, it is larger than 1.9 nm. Continue the process

using membranes whose pore sizes are progressively smaller than 1.9 nm but larger than 1 nm.

✔ Assessment
Portfolio: Have students write an evaluation of the Thinking Lab for their portfolios.

Even if an ion is small enough to pass through a pore, the charge of the ion and of part of the channel protein may prevent it from doing so. For example, because particles of the same charge repel one another, a positively charged ion may be repelled by the positively charged part of a channel protein.

Carrier Proteins   Other transport proteins, called carrier proteins, work in a more complex way. It is thought that for carrier proteins, a particle on one side of the membrane fits into a part of the protein, like two pieces of a puzzle. Once the particle has joined the carrier protein, the shape of the protein changes so that the particle is released on the other side of the membrane. Having released the particle, the protein's original shape is restored, and it is free to combine with another of the same kind of particle. This series of events is shown in Figure 4-14.

Some carrier proteins act as gates. Figure 4-15 shows that when a certain particle combines with the carrier protein, the shape of the carrier changes so that the gate opens, allowing a different kind of particle to pass through. Many ions enter cells through gates. A gate opens when a hormone attaches to it, and the ions then pass through.

Whether passive transport occurs by osmosis, diffusion, or facilitated diffusion, it always involves a net movement of particles from a region of greater concentration to a region of lesser concentration. The particles pass across the membrane without any energy input from the cell.

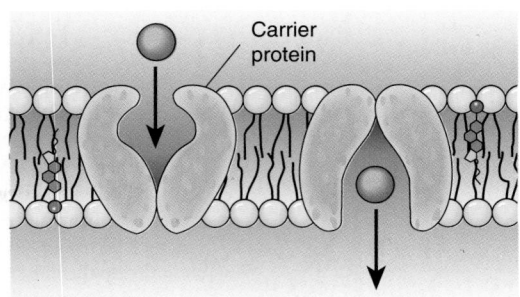

Figure 4-14   **Carrier proteins change shape to allow certain molecules to cross the plasma membrane.**

Figure 4-15   **Gate proteins open to allow passage of particles, when a "signal" molecule combines with the gate. When the signal molecule is released, the gate closes.**

Gate protein

4.2 MEMBRANE FUNCTION **103**

INVESTIGATION

Osmosis in a Model Cell

Time Allotment
Students may wish to collect data after 30 or 45 minutes and then 24 hours later. Long waiting time will result in more dramatic changes in mass or volume.

Objectives
Upon completing this investigation, students will be able to:
- determine the direction of water flow based on salt concentration on both sides of a membrane.
- form a hypothesis on how osmosis affects movement of water.

Skills
separate and control variables, observe and infer, compare and contrast, form a hypothesis

Materials
2-3 small beakers, 2-3 strips of dialysis tubing (each 15 cm long), thread, scissors, salt, water, balance, graduated cylinder, paper towels

Preparation
- To open dialysis tubing, soak in water for 5 minutes and rub between thumb and first finger, causing tubing to separate into a tube.
- You may wish to prepare salt solution in advance. Prepare a 30% salt solution by adding 30 g sodium chloride to 70 mL water.

Possible Hypotheses
1. If salt solution surrounds a dialysis bag filled with water, the bag will gain in mass as water moves into bag through osmosis (or liquid volume in beaker will decrease as water moves into bag).
2. If salt solution surrounds a dialysis bag filled with water, the bag will lose mass as water moves out of bag through osmosis (or liquid volume in beaker will increase as water moves out of bag).

Possible Procedures
- Control may consist of a dialysis bag filled with water and placed into a beaker filled with water, or a bag filled with salt solution and surrounded by salt solution.

Active Transport
Passive transport is like the events that occur when the bell rings to end class. Students who were sitting in a nonrandom way before the bell rang now begin to move around randomly. They may even bump into one another as they move about. Eventually, they move toward and through the door, and scatter in many directions through the hallways. They have moved from an organized state (a region of greater concentration inside the classroom) to a less organized state (a region of lesser concentration outside the classroom). Like putting the marbles in a box, energy will be necessary to get the students back in the classroom—to move them from a region of lesser concentration to one of greater concentration.

INVESTIGATION

Osmosis in a Model Cell

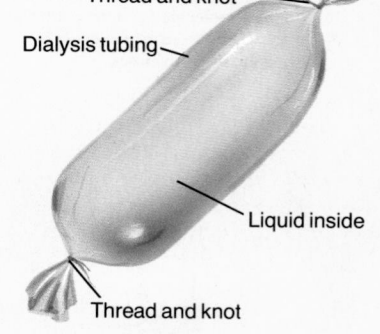

Twisted end
Thread and knot
Dialysis tubing
Liquid inside
Thread and knot

It is very difficult to measure or see osmosis actually occurring in cells because of the small size of most cells. However, if an artificial membrane that acts in some ways like a real plasma membrane could be found, then a study of osmosis using a model would be possible.

Dialysis tubing is such a membrane. It is a sausage casing-like material and is permeable to water molecules. Thus, it is possible to study osmosis using a cell model with a dialysis membrane. A dialysis bag filled with liquid appears at the left.

In this lab, you will design and then carry out an experiment to determine if certain molecules that surround a model cell result in net movement of water by osmosis. Work in a group of three or four classmates.

Problem
Will certain liquids surrounding a model cell filled with tap water result in the net movement of water by osmosis?

Safety Precautions
Wear safety goggles and an apron when mixing and pouring all liquids.

Hypothesis
Have your group agree on a hypothesis to be tested. Record your hypothesis.

Experimental Plan
1. Examine the materials provided by your teacher. Then, as a group, make a list of the possible ways you might test your hypothesis using the materials available.
2. Agree on one way that your group could investigate your hypothesis.

- Variable to be tested is the difference in solution surrounding the bag compared to liquid inside bag.
- If students prepare their own salt solutions, the concentration used may vary from one group to another.

Teaching Strategies
- If this is the first time your students have designed an experiment, refer them to the Investigations in Chapters 1 and 2.
- Encourage students to run several trials if time permits and then average their data.

- Advise students to double membrane over on ends and tie thread tightly to prevent leakage.

Data and Observations
Data collection may consist of:
(a) mass changes in bags. Use a balance to measure.
(b) liquid volume changes in beakers. Use a graduated cylinder to measure.
(c) changes in bag plumpness. Use diagrams of before and after to illustrate changes.

Pumps Can a cell ever move particles from a region of lesser concentration to a region of greater concentration? Yes, but to do so the cell must expend energy to counteract the random motion of the particles. Energy from the cell causes the movement of the particles to become less random. Because the cell's energy is required to move the particles, this type of movement is called **active transport.** Transport proteins known as pumps are used in active transport. They are embedded in the plasma membrane. Each pump can bind to a particular particle whose shape fits it. Chemical energy is then used to alter the shape of the pump so that the particle to be moved is released on the other side of the membrane. Once the particle is released, the pump's original shape is restored.

(d) changes in bag diameters. Measure diameter of bags before and after by circling bags with a string and then measuring length of string.
Sample data charts:

Bag	Original Mass	Final Mass
in water	32 g	32 g
in salt	34 g	21 g

OR

Bag	Original beaker volume	Final beaker volume
in water	200 mL	200 mL
in salt	200 mL	218 mL

Data Analysis

1. Student answers will vary. They may say the bag in salt water decreased in volume or mass, or the liquid in the beaker increased. Or, students may say the bag in water did not change in mass or volume. The bag placed in salt water did show a change, or bag in water showed no change.
2. Student answers will vary. Osmosis occurred in the bag surrounded by salt water, resulting in a mass change compared to the control bag.
3. Water was able to pass through the bag into the beaker of salt water, resulting in a mass decrease of the bag (or an increase in the volume of surrounding liquid).
4. The bag filled with water and placed in a beaker of water was a control. It serves as a basis for comparison between itself and a bag differing only by the liquid that surrounds it.
5. Student answers may vary depending on their original hypothesis. A new hypothesis may be stated that suggests that bags filled with water and surrounded by salt will lose mass.
6. Student answers may include not drying bags before massing them (double-check that bags are dry), leakage of liquid from bags (repeat several trials or reprepare bags), errors in massing (remass all bags several times before and after).
7. Answers may include allowing all bags to remain in beakers for same length of time and using same volume of liquid inside and outside of bags.

3. The variables in this experiment might be the salt concentration outside of the bags, the length of time allowed for water movement to occur, and the amount of liquid inside and outside the bags. Design an experiment that will (a) use a control, (b) test only one variable at a time, and (c) allow for the collection of quantitative data.
4. Prepare a list of numbered directions. Include a list of materials and the quantities you will need.

Checking the Plan

Discuss the following points with other group members to decide the final procedures for your experiment. Make any needed changes in your plan.
1. What will be your control?
2. What one variable are you going to test?
3. What data are you going to collect and how are you going to measure it?
4. How long will you carry out the experiment?

5. What variables, if any, will need to be controlled?
6. How many trials will you carry out?
7. What will be the role of each classmate in your group?
8. Have you designed and made a table for collecting data?

Make sure your teacher has approved your experimental plan before you proceed further.

Data and Observations

Carry out your experiment, make any needed measurements, and complete your data table. Design and then complete a graph or visual representation of your results.

Analysis and Conclusions

1. What changes did you observe among the bags or the liquids in which the bags had been placed? How did these changes relate to the salt concentrations of the liquids in which the bags were placed?
2. What evidence do you have that net intake or loss of water due to osmosis did or did not occur?

3. What evidence do you have that dialysis tubing is permeable to water?
4. What was your control and how is it used to explain your results?
5. Was your hypothesis supported by your data? If not, suggest a new hypothesis that is supported by your data.
6. List several sources of experimental errors that may have influenced your data, and suggest ways in which each error source might be corrected.
7. What were several variables that had to be controlled? How were they controlled?
8. Write a brief conclusion to your experiment.

Going Further

Based on this lab experience, design an experiment that would help to answer a question that arose from your work. Assume that you will not be doing this lab in class. Record this information as part of your conclusion.

4.2 MEMBRANE FUNCTION **105**

8. The important points should state that, experimentally, it was found that a bag filled with water and placed into a beaker of salt water will lose liquid to the beaker. The process responsible was osmosis. Osmosis had occurred and was supported by data.

✔ Assessment

Knowledge: Have students write a summary of what they learned from this Investigation. They can write an evaluation in their journals.

Extensions

Ask students the following questions. What effect will different salt concentrations have on the rate of osmosis? What effect will waiting 48 hours have on the results? What effect will different solutions (sugar, maple syrup, fruit juice, coffee) have on osmosis? Have students think about additional experiments that could be done to answer these questions.

Figure Caption Question

Why is ATP needed to move these particles through the membrane? ATP, or energy, is needed to counter-act the random motion of particles.

Building a Model

Students could build a plasma membrane using foam balls as the polar heads, yarn as saturated fats, and pipe cleaners as unsaturated fats. Plastic netting could hold the parts together. Various channels and other cell membrane features should be shown. Students should use creativity and ingenuity in putting their cell membranes together. **L1** **LEP** **COOP LEARN**

Using an Analogy

Membrane fluidity is the result of saturated and unsaturated fatty acids in the tails of phospholipid molecules. Saturated fats can be compared to books stacked tightly on a shelf. They are rigid and highly organized. Unsaturated fats can be compared to warped books that cannot be tightly packed. You can get your hand between the books more easily and move them. **LEP**

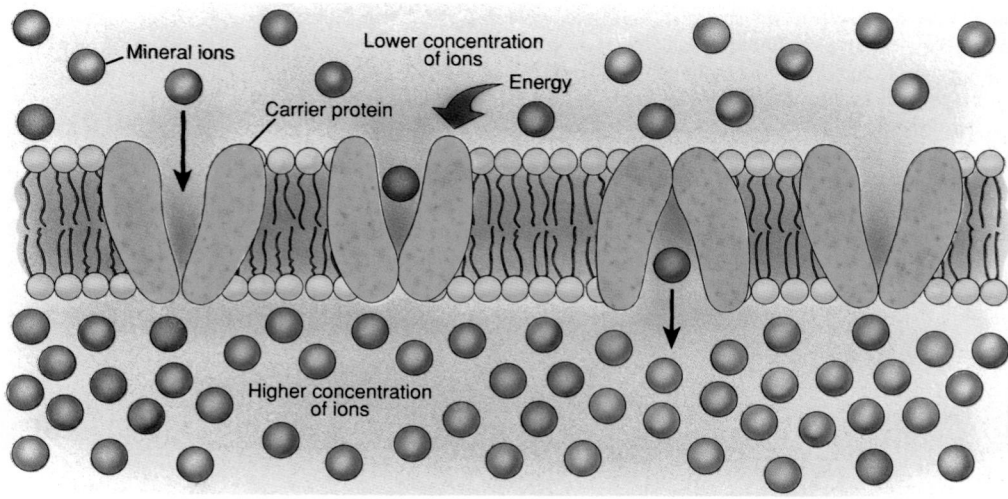

Figure 4-16 In active transport, energy from ATP is used to modify the shape of a carrier protein. This change allows the movement of an ion or molecule through the membrane from a region of lower concentration to one of higher concentration. Why is ATP needed to move these particles through the membrane?

Active transport through a membrane may occur in either direction. Cells in the gills of a marine fish actively pump out salts even though the concentration of salts in the sea water is greater than that in the fish's fluids. Such outward movement of salts maintains the osmotic balance between the fish's cells and body fluids. In other cases, active transport is used to bring particles into a cell even when their concentration in the cell is already greater than that outside. Root cells of plants often take in large quantities of needed ions from soil by active transport.

Transport and the Fluid Mosaic Model   Now that you've studied the structure of membranes and the passage of particles across them, think again about the fluid mosaic model. The model certainly explains the properties of the membrane. Lipids and lipid-soluble particles permeate easily by diffusion because they dissolve in the lipid bilayer. Smaller particles pass across readily because they can fit between the phospholipid molecules. Larger particles or those insoluble in lipids may pass across with the aid of transport proteins, either channels or carriers. Small neutral particles cross more freely than ions because they are neither attracted to nor repelled by charged parts of the molecules in the membrane. Membranes made up of different lipids and transport proteins are permeable to different particles, and permeability of a given membrane may change, depending on the position of its lipids and proteins.

Endocytosis and Exocytosis

Not all materials that enter a cell do so by passing through the membrane. Some materials can be surrounded by a portion of the plasma membrane, which then encloses the material, pinches off from the rest of the membrane, and releases the material on the other side. **Endocytosis** is the

106 ▲ THE CELL AND ITS ENVIRONMENT

ALTERNATE LAB: Plasmolysis in *Elodea*

Purpose
Students will compare *Elodea* cells before and after adding salt solution.

Materials
Elodea sprigs, slides, coverslips, microscopes, paper towels, 6% salt solution (See page 27T.), dropper, forceps

Procedure
Give the following directions to students.

1. Put two drops of distilled water on a slide.
2. Add an *Elodea* leaf. Leaves from the tip of the plant work best.
3. Cover the leaf with a coverslip and observe under the microscope on low and high power. Note the location of the chloroplasts in relation to the cell wall.
4. Add a drop of 6% salt solution next to the coverslip. Place a piece of paper

towel next to the cover slip on the opposite side from the salt solution. The paper towel will draw the distilled water out from under the coverslip, and the salt solution will replace it. Watch under the microscope as this is happening.
5. Plasmolysis occurs as the cell contents shrink and the water flows out of the cell. Note the location of the chloroplasts relative to the cell wall.

process by which the plasma membrane engulfs and then takes in substances from a cell's environment.

Phagocytosis Endocytosis is common in unicellular organisms, such as amoebas, which depend on smaller organisms for food. Figure 4-17 shows that after food is detected, the amoeba's plasma membrane engulfs the food organism by flowing over and enclosing it. That portion of the membrane then forms the border of a small sac, called a **vesicle,** which breaks away and moves to the cell's interior. The food in the vesicle will be digested later. Endocytosis is also used by some cells of multicellular organisms. For example, some kinds of white blood cells protect you against disease by engulfing and then digesting bacteria and other foreign particles that enter your body. The form of endocytosis in which solid chunks of material are taken in is called **phagocytosis.**

Pinocytosis Endocytosis may also involve taking in liquid droplets. The process is the same as in phagocytosis, but drops of liquid rather than solid particles are engulfed. This form of endocytosis, in which liquid droplets are taken in, is called **pinocytosis.**

Receptor-aided Endocytosis Sometimes, specific molecules are brought into the cell by a third form of endocytosis, called receptor-aided endocytosis. Molecules of a substance outside the cell first link up with proteins called receptors in the plasma membrane. The receptors, with their bound molecules, move to one area of the membrane. An indentation, or pit, in the membrane then forms, eventually breaking away to form a vesicle. The vesicle, containing both the entering substance and the receptors, is brought into the cell. The molecules separate from the receptors and are released into the cell's interior. The vesicle, still containing the receptors, then returns to the outer part of the cell where it and its receptors become part of the plasma membrane once again. Cholesterol, necessary for the manufacture of new membranes in many cells, enters a cell this way.

Figure 4-17 **Endocytosis can involve either phagocytosis or pinocytosis, depending upon whether the material to be brought into the cell is a solid chunk or a liquid.**

SECTION 4.2

Using Science Terms
Have students use a dictionary to learn the meanings of the prefixes *endo-, exo-, pino-,* and *phago-.*

Misconception
It is easy for students to confuse phagocytosis and pinocytosis. Make sure they understand that phagocytosis involves solids and pinocytosis involves liquids. Also make sure that they understand that endocytosis takes several different forms and is not a specific method of entry, but a more generic term that includes phagocytosis, pinocytosis, and receptor-aided endocytosis.

Phagocytosis

Pinocytosis

4.2 MEMBRANE FUNCTION **107**

---

6. Make a diagram of the *Elodea* cell before and after plasmolysis. Label the cell wall, chloroplasts, and cell membrane.
7. Draw a drop of distilled water under the coverslip, as in step 4. The salt water will be replaced by distilled water.

Analysis
Ask students to answer the following questions.

1. Is plasmolysis reversible? Explain. *Yes, the cells recovered when the salt water was removed.*
2. Describe the location of chloroplasts before and after adding salt solution. *Before adding salt solution, the chloroplasts were distributed throughout the cell. After adding salt water, the chloroplasts were clumped together.*
3. Explain what happened to the cell when

it was plasmolyzed and why it happened. *Water flowed out of the cell because the water was in higher concentration inside.*
4. Which way did the water move across the cell membrane? Why? *Water flowed out of the cell because the water was in higher concentration inside.*
5. Did the cell wall change shape during plasmolysis? Why or why not? *The cell*

Using the Illustration

Go over the steps of receptor-aided endocytosis in Figure 4-18 to make sure students understand the process.

Enrichment

Have interested students do a written library research report on the membranes in the cells of caribou legs. During the long arctic winter, keeping caribou legs and feet warm would waste too much energy. The lower parts of caribou legs maintain a temperature near freezing. Of course, cell membranes would have to be different from the cell membranes of other animals if they are to survive this temperature. **L3**

Chalkboard Example

Draw on the chalkboard examples of the following cells: very thin flat cells, cells with invaginations to increase the surface area, and cells with extensions of the plasma membrane. Ask students to explain how each of these cells has overcome surface-to-volume problems. **L1**

Misconception

Many students think that plant cells do not have cell membranes, only cell walls. Explain to students that the cell wall does not play a role in determining permeability characteristics of the cell.

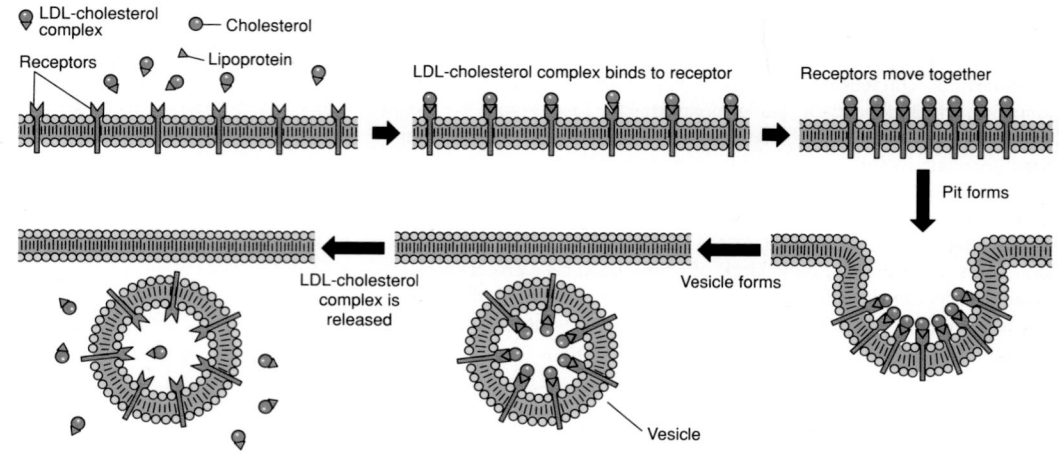

Figure 4-18 When a cell needs cholesterol, it synthesizes receptors for low-density lipoproteins and incorporates them into the plasma membrane. Each receptor binds to an LDL-cholesterol complex, which is then brought into the cell by endocytosis.

Cholesterol molecules destined for use by body cells are found in the blood in the form of low-density lipoproteins, LDLs. Because it is insoluble in water, cholesterol cannot dissolve in the liquid part of blood. Therefore, the body wraps cholesterol molecules in water-soluble protein envelopes, forming lipoprotein molecules that can dissolve in blood. It is the LDLs that combine with receptors on cell membranes. These events are summarized in Figure 4-18.

Exocytosis A reverse process of endocytosis is used to rid some cells of wastes, such as undigestible particles, or to secrete substances, such as hormones, needed elsewhere. The substances are first enclosed in a vesicle that has a membrane with fluid mosaic structure. The vesicle moves toward the plasma membrane, breaks open, and fuses with part of the plasma membrane. As this occurs, the contents of the vesicle are expelled. This process, known as **exocytosis,** is diagrammed in Figure 4-19.

Figure 4-19 Cell products or wastes, enclosed in vesicles, are released to the surroundings by exocytosis.

108 THE CELL AND ITS ENVIRONMENT

A L T E R N A T E   L A B :   Plasmolysis in *Elodea,* continued

wall bulged out slightly. Because it is rigid, it did not change shape greatly.

6. Define plasmolysis. *Plasmolysis is the movement of water out of a cell from a region of higher concentration to one of lower concentration.*

7. Did the salt move across the cell membrane? Why or why not? *The salt did not move across the membrane because the membrane is impermeable to salt.*

8. Think of a situation in everyday life in which osmosis is important. *Crispness in fresh vegetables and fruits.*

✔ Assessment

Performance: Tell students that you will provide them with two uncooked eggs that have had their shells removed by being soaked for 24 hours in white vinegar. These eggs must be handled very carefully.

They are still covered with their protective membrane. Have students design and conduct an experiment in which they determine if osmosis will occur through this membrane. Provide distilled water, 20% salt solution, and beakers. Make sure students gather quantitative data, and illustrate it in graphic form. Have students write lab reports and put them in their portfolios. **L1**

Figure 4-20 Plant cell walls are composed of cellulose. The cellulose molecules form interconnecting fibers that are interwoven in a strong network. The network protects a plant cell and gives the plant support. Magnification: 20×

Cell Walls

In many organisms, the plasma membrane is not the outermost cellular boundary. Plants, most algae, fungi, and bacteria have a **cell wall** that lies outside the plasma membrane. Remember that cell walls were the only parts of cork cells that Robert Hooke observed in 1665. Cell walls of plants and algae are composed largely of the polysaccharide cellulose. Wood products, paper, cotton, and rayon are made from the cellulose cell walls of plants. Fungal and bacterial cell walls are each composed of different materials.

Cellulose is arranged in rows of fibers stacked in layers, as Figure 4-20 shows. Spaces between the fibers allow water, ions, and other particles to pass through. Thus, the wall does not play a role in determining a cell's permeability characteristics. However, the cell wall is important in other ways. It provides protection and, in land plants, also provides support. The wood supporting a giant redwood tree consists of the cell walls of hollow, dead cells.

Figure 4-21 These giant redwood trees could not grow so large if their cells did not have tough cellulose walls.

4.2 MEMBRANE FUNCTION **109**

3 Assess

Check for Understanding

Use a three-dimensional model or a large, unlabeled diagram to quiz students orally. Ask questions such as: Explain, using this model, how the cell membrane works. Where are the protein molecules and what is their function? How would this cell react if it were put in a 20% salt solution? Why? What is the importance of the bilayer structure of the cell membrane?

Reteach

Remove a central cylinder of a raw white potato, leaving about 7 mm of potato tissue at the bottom. Fill the hole with concentrated sucrose solution. Put a one-hole stopper with a glass tube into the hole. Seal the edges of the stopper with melted paraffin to prevent leakage around the stopper. Place the potato in a beaker of water. Use a ring stand with a clamp to support the glass tube. Students will observe osmosis occurring.

Extension

Scientists have proposed many models for the structure of the cell membrane. Ask a group of students to prepare a report about how the concept of the structure of the cell membrane has changed over the years. They should include the work of Gorter and Grendel, Danielli and Davson, and Singer and Nicholson. They should make sketches of the different models and show how new research contributed to changes in the old models. **L3** **COOP LEARN**

MULTICULTURAL CONNECTION

Exploring Biology: Wilfred Denetclaw learned to love nature and the living world as he grew up in New Mexico on a Navajo reservation. In Navaho Community College at Shiprock, he learned about the world of biology research. Upon transferring to Fort Lewis College, he earned his B.S. in biology in 1983. That same year, he was accepted to U.C. Berkeley. His research involved experimenting with how cells communicate and transport materials through cell membranes. He currently works on a team with other scientists studying the Ca^{2+} leak channels in muscle cells of patients with Duchenne muscular dystrophy. When asked how he likes being a cell biologist, Wilfred says it is "fun and exciting," and he feels "like an explorer."

Performance: Provide student groups with a plate of plain agar with three equidistant holes in the agar. Tell them to put three drops of 0.02M potassium dichromate in one hole, three drops of 0.02M potassium permanganate in another, and three drops of 0.02M methylene blue in the third hole. (See page 27T.) At the end of the class period, they should make observations and explain them in their portfolios. Give students metric rulers so they can gather quantitative data. Their discussions should include explanations of diffusion of a liquid in a solid. Methylene blue diffuses the slowest, while potassium permanganate diffuses the fastest. Some students may come to the conclusion that the different rates of diffusion are the result of the different molecular weights of the molecules, methylene blue being heaviest. **L1**

COOP LEARN

4 Close

Analogy

Ask students in their groups to make a list of the analogies in the section. They should describe how each analogy fits the cell membrane, then make their own analogy of the cell membrane comparing it to a communication or transportation system.

L1   **COOP LEARN**

After plant cells divide, a new cell wall forms as cellulose is deposited outside the plasma membrane. This cell wall is known as the primary cell wall. Formation of the primary cell wall continues as long as the cell continues to grow. Between the two primary cell walls of adjacent cells lies an area called the **middle lamella.** It is composed of pectin, a cellular cement that binds adjacent cells together. If the pectin breaks down, the cells become less tightly bound, a process that occurs as fruit ripens. After completing their growth, many plant cells, such as those from a redwood, deposit more cellulose, thus forming a secondary cell wall. This secondary wall, which lies inside the primary wall, makes the cell wall even stronger and provides the degree of support a large plant requires.

LOOKING AHEAD

YOU HAVE READ how the structure of the plasma membrane is related to the ways particles pass across it. The foods you eat cannot nourish your body unless the nutrients they contain enter your cells. As you study the next two chapters, you will see that whether the nutrient particles enter by passive transport or active transport, once inside a cell they are used by cellular structures in processes that maintain your body and keep it alive. Cellular wastes that could build up and kill the cell pass across the membrane and out into the surrounding fluid. In a multicellular organism, many such individual cells group together to form different tissues that work together as a team to form your body parts.

Section Review

Understanding Concepts

1. You forget to water your garden and notice that the plants have become wilted and limp. Explain what has happened to the plant cells. What will happen to the plant cells if you now water the plants?
2. Cells produce carbon dioxide during cellular respiration. Explain how carbon dioxide leaves cells.

3. A unicellular organism that normally lives in salt water is transferred to a beaker of fresh water. What will happen to the cell? Why?
4. ***Skill Review—Designing an Experiment:*** How could you design an experiment that would allow you to see the effect of salt water on an *Elodea* plant? For more help, refer to Practicing Scientific Methods in the **Skill Handbook.**

5. ***Thinking Critically:*** How are active transport and facilitated diffusion similar? How are they different?

Answers to Section Review

1. The plant cells, which had a greater concentration of water than the soil, lost water by osmosis. If water were added to the soil, it would move into the plant cells by osmosis.
2. There is a greater concentration of carbon dioxide molecules in the cell than in the surrounding liquid. Carbon dioxide molecules will move from the cell into the surrounding liquid.

3. In fresh water, there is a greater concentration of water outside the cell than inside, so there will be a net movement of water by osmosis into the cell, which may burst.
4. **Skill Review—Designing an Experiment:** Wet mounts of an *Elodea* leaf could be made using fresh water and salt water. The two slides could be observed and compared.

5. **Thinking Critically:** Both processes require transport proteins to permeate the membrane. Facilitated diffusion is a form of passive transport. The particles move from a region of greater concentration to one of lesser concentration, and the cell expends no energy. In active transport, the cell must expend energy to move particles from a region of lesser concentration to one of greater concentration.

BIOLOGY, TECHNOLOGY, AND SOCIETY

Biotechnology
....
Cold Storage

Now here's a chilling thought! Freeze the body of someone who has just died of a disease, then wait until medical science has progressed enough to revive and cure the patient.

When Does Death Occur? The use of this technique is attractive to many people. After all, they point out, a person was once considered dead when his or her heart stopped. Now physicians can restart a heart, and death is considered to occur when brain activity stops. But even in a person whose brain activity has ceased, the individual brain cells and body cells remain alive for a short time. So perhaps the patient may still be curable by the standards of future medicine. And, supporters continue, we've long been able to freeze and revive individual cells and even small embryos. Why not whole bodies?

The Controversy It's easy enough to freeze and preserve whole bodies, but so far, there's no safe way to defrost them. And some scientists doubt that the damage done to cells will ever allow the process to be worthwhile. Those who believe in the procedure, which is known as cryonic suspension, are betting that future medical technology *will*

be able to repair or rebuild bodies right down to the cellular level.

The Freezing Process In order for cryonic suspension to work, the body must be frozen to a temperature of –130°C or lower. The freezing process puts enormous stress on the cells.

As the body temperature drops, water between cells turns to ice. All the salts, sugars, and other solids dissolved in the water become concentrated in the still-liquid water, a much higher concentration than exists inside the cell. Water flows out of the cell, keeping the concentration of salts and sugars inside and outside of the cell in equilibrium. A cell losing water is similar

to a balloon losing air—it shrinks.

Meanwhile, water between the cells continues to freeze, the concentration of solids outside the cell continues to rise, and water continues to flow from the inside to the outside of the cell. In time, the cell becomes little more than a tiny mass of membrane and extremely concentrated solids embedded in ice.

Damaged Cells The stress this process puts on the cell can damage the cell's membrane structure and distort essential cell proteins. If such a damaged cell is defrosted, it will no longer work properly.

Today's cryonic techniques use protective agents to shield the cell from damage. But some of the

---

BIOLOGY, TECHNOLOGY, AND SOCIETY

Biotechnology

Purpose
Students will recognize the benefits and limitations of cryonic preservation of the human body. Damage to cell membranes and intercellular connections are pointed out. Students will find this intriguing because they might be faced with having to decide one day if the expense of having their bodies frozen is worth it for the benefits promised.

Teaching Strategies
- Begin by asking students if they would consider having their bodies frozen when they die in the hopes that medical science would be able to unfreeze them and cure their ailments in the future. Ask students to make a list of the pros and cons of cryonic preservation before reading the article, and then add to their lists after reading the article.

Possible Answers
1. Inheritance laws would have to be reconsidered as unfrozen people would need access to their money and property. Laws regarding property rights would have to be reconsidered. Could a frozen body own property?
2. No, because she paid a great deal of money and signed a contract, which stated that her body could only be removed from cryonic suspension to be cured.

Going Further
Contact your nearest cryonic preservation facility to arrange for a group of students to interview the director.
L2

Health Connection

Purpose

Students will be able to distinguish the differences in the actions of the two types of fiber in foods and become more aware of their own food selections. They also will be alerted to examining health claims of food very carefully.

Background

After all the national publicity about cholesterol and fat, many well-meaning parents put their babies on skim milk and low-fat diets. For the first time in our country's history, pediatricians began to see failure to grow and nutritional deficiencies in babies from homes where income was not a problem. Parents need to know that infants and young children need a diet higher in fat than people who have stopped growing. Infants, toddlers, and young children need whole milk in order to accommodate growth of many new cell membranes.

Teaching Strategies

- Prior to reading the article, ask students if they know the difference between water-soluble and water-insoluble fiber. Ask them why they need fiber in their diets.

protective agents themselves are toxic and damage the cells.

Even more damage occurs between cells. Because cells are organized in groups, the spacing between them is important. The space between cells is usually no more than about 5 micrometers. (A micrometer is one-millionth of a meter.) The ice crystals formed in cryonic preservation, however, are generally about 30 micrometers in diameter. So as the intercellular water freezes, it pushes the cells apart. Many vital cell-to-cell junctions are invariably torn.

Ice crystals cause similar damage to the capillaries, which provide blood flow to the cells. The average capillary is only 8 micrometers in diameter and can only stretch so much before bursting.

To date, no whole organ, let alone an entire body, has ever been fully restored after being frozen to the temperatures long-term storage requires. Yet, animal brains have survived extremely low temperatures without apparent damage.

For so cold a topic, cryonics continues to light bright fires in many imaginations.

1. **Connection to Law:** Suppose many of those people declared dead and preserved in cryonic suspension prove to be curable in the future. How might some laws have to be changed?
2. **Issue:** There is a case of a woman who was declared dead and placed in cryonic suspension. The coroner suspected that her death might have been due to foul play. He wanted her body removed from cryonic suspension for autopsy. How would you have ruled if you were the judge?

Health Connection

Fiber to the Rescue?

A few years ago, an unlikely hero began grabbing headlines around the world for supposedly saving lives and offering people the promise of a healthier future. This overnight media sensation was a long-time staple of winter breakfast tables—oatmeal, or more specifically, oat bran. According to scientific studies, oat bran seemed to possess the ability to lower levels of cholesterol in the bloodstream.

Cholesterol, a lipid component of membranes, long had been associated with clogged arteries and an increased risk of heart attack. Some nutritionists suggested that cholesterol might be brought under control with a daily dose of oats. Soon, oat bran began appearing on grocer's shelves in a variety of foods: oat-bran cookies, oat-bran muffins—even oat-bran tortilla chips!

The oat-bran frenzy began to fizzle when new studies failed to duplicate earlier promising results. Nevertheless, scientists were intrigued and began studying the nutritional role of dietary fiber more closely.

Indigestible and Indispensable
The indigestible cell walls of plant cells, found in fruits, vegetables, and whole grains, are called fiber. Fiber, an essential part of everyone's diet, comes in two forms—water-soluble and water-insoluble.

Water-soluble fiber, found in such foods as apples, carrots, and oats, appears to lower blood cholesterol. Water-insoluble fiber, such as that present in brown rice, lentils, and wheat bran cereals, provides

Panel 1: OK, HOBBES, I NEED YOU TO HELP ME MEMORIZE MY LINE FOR THE PLAY. / SURE.

Panel 2: I'M THE ONION, AND I SAY, "IN ADDITION TO SUPPLYING VITAL NUTRIENTS, MANY VEGETABLES ARE A SOURCE OF DIETARY FIBER."

Panel 3: OK, READY? / READY. GO AHEAD. "IN ADDITION...." / WAIT. HOLD IT. I'M NOT IN CHARACTER YET. WHAT MOTIVATES AN ONION?

Panel 4: FAME, I SUPPOSE. THIS COULD BE A BIG BREAK.

the roughage that stimulates the muscles of the digestive tract and prevents constipation.

Different Fibers, Different Functions   Scientists still don't understand fully how fiber affects cholesterol. Recent studies, however, provide some interesting clues.

Cholesterol is broken down in the liver to form bile acids. These bile acids help to break down fats in the stomach and small intestine.

After the bile acids have done their work, the small intestine absorbs them for reuse later.

Carrot pectin, a water-soluble fiber, acts like a sponge, absorbing bile acids and preventing the small intestine from reabsorbing them. Thus, the liver must break down additional cholesterol to make more bile acids. The result is lower cholesterol levels in the blood-stream.

Scientists still have not pin-pointed all of the exact mecha-

nisms that enable dietary fiber to do its work. One thing is clear, however. Fiber is now recognized as an essential component in a bal-anced, nutritious diet.

1. **Explore Further:** Which foods provide the greatest amount of fiber? Which provide the least amount?
2. **Writing About Biology:** Explain why vegetarian diets are likely to be higher in fiber than nonvege-tarian diets.

These scanning electron micrographs show a healthy, unclogged artery (left) and an artery clogged with cholesterol (right). What will happen if the artery becomes completely blocked? Magnification: left, 3×; right, 4×

Possible Answers

1. Greatest: fruits, vegetables, and whole grains. Least: meat, fish, dairy products, refined grains.
2. Vegetarians exclusively eat plant materials in the form of vegeta-bles, fruits, and grains. Even though some vegetarians eat fish and dairy products, most of their diet consists of plant material.

Figure Caption Question

What will happen if the artery becomes completely blocked? If an artery becomes completely blocked, a heart attack or stroke can occur, or tissue may die because cells do not receive oxygen.

Going Further

Ask students to go to the market, examine the ingredients labels of cold cereal boxes, and make a list of how much fiber there is in various types of cereal. Nutritionists recommend that your morning cereal have at least 4 grams of fiber per serving. Ask stu-dents to put stars by the cereals they eat, and circle the ones that have an appropriate amount of fiber. L1

113

CHAPTER REVIEW

Summary

Summary statements can be used by students to review the major concepts of the chapter.

Language of Biology

Answers should go beyond defining the terms. Accept any reasonable answer that uses the term correctly and in the proper context.

Understanding Concepts

1. The cell theory applies to all organisms and complements the theory of evolution as well.
2. A human cell is surrounded by blood or other fluids composed of water plus dissolved substances. A plant cell is surrounded by water containing fewer dissolved substances. A human cell in such an environment would take in water by osmosis and burst.
3. Membranes of different cells have different transport proteins.
4. Most particles are neither lipids nor lipid soluble.
5. At the spill, the molecules are in a region of greater concentration. As they randomly bounce off one another and off molecules in the air, they undergo a net movement from a region of greater concentration to one of lesser concentration; a person across the room will begin to smell them.
6. Energy is needed for nonrandomness. Lack of energy results in randomness.
7. Some ions may enter by means of channel proteins. Other ions may enter when one chemical combines with a gate, changing the gate's shape.
8. Passive transport does not require an expenditure of energy by the cell and is like a sled moving down a hill. Active transport requires energy, just as energy is needed to pull the sled back to the top of the hill.
9. Channel proteins are not openings in the membrane. They are open-

ings bounded by proteins embedded in the membrane.
10. Endocytosis does not involve passage across the membrane. Instead, the membrane engulfs a particle, and the membrane and the enclosed particle move into the cell.

Applying Concepts

11. An amoeba's plasma membrane probably lacks cholesterol. Presence of cholesterol would make the membrane less flexible.
12. The alga must be using active transport to

Summary

Cells were first discovered by Robert Hooke. Over a period of almost 200 years, study of a variety of cells resulted in the establishment of the cell theory.

Cells are surrounded by a liquid environment from which they obtain needed materials and in which they dump their products and wastes. Each cell is bordered by a plasma membrane, which regulates the passage of these substances.

According to the fluid mosaic model, the plasma membrane, as well as the membranes of internal parts of cells, consists of a phospholipid bilayer that provides strength and flexibility. Embedded in the bilayer are proteins. Many proteins determine to which particles a given membrane is permeable.

In passive transport, the cell uses no energy. Movement of particles across the membrane is due to the energy of the moving particles themselves and results in net movement from a region of greater concentration to one of lesser concentration. Diffusion, osmosis, and facilitated diffusion are forms of passive transport.

In active transport, the cell uses energy to move particles from a region of lesser concentration to a region of greater concentration. Some substances do not pass across membranes, but enter or leave cells by endocytosis and exocytosis.

Language of Biology

Write a sentence that shows your understanding of each of the following terms.

active transport	osmosis
cell theory	passive transport
cell wall	phagocytosis
diffusion	pinocytosis
dynamic equilibrium	plasma membrane
endocytosis	selectively permeable
exocytosis	membrane
facilitated diffusion	transport protein
fluid mosaic model	vesicle
middle lamella	

Understanding Concepts

1. Why is the cell theory so important to the science of biology?
2. How is the environment of your cells different from that of a plant cell? Could one of your cells exist in the environment of a plant cell?
3. Use the fluid mosaic model to explain how different cells are permeable to different particles.
4. Why is it not possible for most particles to pass across a membrane by diffusion?
5. A student on the other side of the lab accidentally spills some alcohol. Explain, in terms of molecules, why you can smell it.
6. How is energy related to random and nonrandom states of matter?
7. Identify and compare two ways that ions may enter cells by passive transport.

8. Why is passive transport often referred to as a downhill process and active transport as an uphill process?
9. Pores are often thought of as definite openings in a membrane. Does this definition fit the channel proteins of a plasma membrane? Explain.
10. How does the process of endocytosis differ from diffusion, facilitated diffusion, and active transport?

Applying Concepts

11. Do you think that the membrane of an amoeba has much, if any, cholesterol in it? Explain your reasoning. Hint: Think about how an amoeba takes in food.

---

take in iodide ions, because the ions are moving from a region of lesser concentration to one of greater concentration.
13. The cell lacking the membrane proteins will likely die, for it will be unable to take in needed particles or rid itself of wastes without the help of the missing proteins.
14. The process occurring is endocytosis; specifically, phagocytosis. She would next see the membrane totally enclose the material. Then the membrane, with its enclosed material, would break away and move inside the cell.

12. A single-celled alga living in the ocean is found to contain ten times as many iodide ions as are present in an equal volume of sea water. The cell continues to take in even more iodide. What process must the cell be using to take in these ions? Explain the process.

13. Suppose a cell has just reproduced. One of the new cells cannot make several transport proteins that cells of this type usually have. Will the cell be able to survive?

14. A cell biologist has taken a photograph of a plasma membrane as viewed through an electron microscope. She notices that part of the membrane was closing around a bit of solid material outside the cell. What process is occurring? What would happen next if the cell were still alive?

15. You are observing a freshwater cell in pure water. You slowly add small amounts of salt to the water. Considering that the cell's membrane is permeable to water but not to salt, how will the size of the cell change as the salt is added? Why?

16. Certain cells of a snake produce venom, a large molecule. How will the venom leave the cells in which it is produced?

17. Would phospholipids move more rapidly or less rapidly if a membrane contained no cholesterol? Why?

18. **Global Connection:** Some people sprinkle salt on weeds to kill them. Why would salt have this effect?

19. **Health Connection:** What substance in cereals makes them such good sources of dietary fiber? Why do you think this substance serves as roughage in the digestive tract?

Lab Interpretation

20. **Investigation:** An experiment was done using three dialysis bags, labeled A, B, and C. Before the experiment began, all of the bags appeared like the unlabeled bag shown in the next column. Bags A, B, and C were filled with a 20 percent sugar solution and were placed into different liquids in separate beakers. Predict the nature of the liquids in which each bag was placed, compared with the liquid inside the bag. (Assume each bag is impermeable to sugar.) Explain your answers.

21. **Investigation:** Assume that the dialysis tubing in question 20 is impermeable to sugar but not to water. Diagram a model of the dialysis tubing showing its pore size in relation to the sizes of water and sugar molecules.

22. **Minilab 2:** If you were to repeat the experiment in Minilab 2, but place the test liquids in the beakers and the water in the bags, what would be the outcome? Explain your results.

Connecting Ideas

23. Your blood contains more oxygen than your body cells, so oxygen diffuses from the blood into the cells. However, dynamic equilibrium is not reached. Why?

24. A single-celled organism makes a transport protein that no other cell of that type has made before. How might that transport protein be important in the future of this population of organisms?

Connecting Ideas

23. **Use of Energy:** The oxygen that enters cells is continually used in the process of cellular respiration.

24. **Evolution:** The new transport protein may enable the organism to take in a molecule that increases its chances of survival.

PROGRAM RESOURCES

Teacher Classroom Resources

Chapter Assessment, pp. 13-16 L1

Performance Assessment in Biology, p. 8 L2

Alternate Assessment in the Science Classroom

Computer Test Bank L1

15. As salt is added, the concentration of water inside the cell becomes greater than that of the surrounding water. Thus, the cell will shrink as a result of a net movement of water outward.

16. The venom will most likely leave by means of exocytosis.

17. They would move more rapidly without cholesterol to bind them.

18. Addition of salt will result in a net movement of water out of the plant cells. The cells will become dehydrated and may die.

19. Plant cell walls are a source of dietary fiber in cereals. The fiber in cereals is water-insoluble.

Lab Interpretation

20. Bag C was placed into a liquid that was 20% sugar and 80% water. Bag A was placed into a liquid that contained more than 80% water and less than 20% sugar. Water moved into the bag from high to low concentration of water. Bag B was placed into a liquid that contained less than 80% water and more than 20% sugar. Water moved out of the bag.

21.

22. The plastic membrane is still permeable and impermeable to the same specific molecules tested. Therefore, if it was permeable to iodine before, the molecules of iodine will diffuse from high concentration outside the bag to low concentration inside the bag. Those molecules to which the bag is impermeable will not move into the bag.

SECTION	OBJECTIVES	TEXT LABS/FEATURES
5.1 Structure of Cells (2 days)	**Recognize** general differences between the cells of unicellular and multicellular organisms. **Describe** how cells are arranged into increasingly complex levels of organization. **Discuss** how cell organelles contribute to the efficiency of cellular functions.	**Investigation:** Sizes of Cells, p. 120 **Minilab 1:** What are the differences between onion root and onion bulb cells? p. 122
5.2 Functions and Interactions of Cell Parts (4 days)	**Compare** the structure and function of cell organelles, including the nucleus, mitochondrion, chloroplast, lysosome, endoplasmic reticulum, Golgi body, vesicle, and vacuole. **Discuss** how the functions of ribosomes, endoplasmic reticulum, and Golgi bodies are interrelated. **Describe** the structure and function of other eukaryotic cell parts.	**Chemistry Connection:** Spider Silk, p. 128 **Minilab 2:** Why are stains used when observing cells? p. 130 **Thinking Lab:** What organelle directs cell activity? p. 130
BIOLOGY, TECHNOLOGY, AND SOCIETY		**Biotechnology:** Culturing Artificial Skin, p. 138 **Issues:** Don't Let the Sun Catch You Fryin', p. 139 **Career Connection:** Cytologist, p. 139

LAB MATERIALS

INVESTIGATION	MINILAB	ALTERNATE LAB
page 120 algae coverslips *Elodea* hamburger, uncooked lettuce Lugol's solution methylene blue stain metric ruler microscope onion bulb *Paramecium* slide pipette potato protozoans razor blade slides toothpicks yeast culture	**page 122** coverslips methylene blue stain microscope onion bulb ring tissue onion root pipette slides **page 130** coverslips Lugol's solution methylene blue stain microscope *Paramecium* culture pipette slides	**page 126** coverslips culture dish *Elodea* plants forceps microscope slides

TEACHER CLASSROOM RESOURCES	OTHER RESOURCES
Study Guide, pp. 25-26 **Exploring Environmental Issues:** *Save Our Skins,* pp. 9-10 ***PLL:** *Basic Cell Structure,* p. 27	***STVS:** *Salt-Resistant Crops,* Plants and Simple Organisms (Disc 4, Side 2)
Study Guide, pp. 27-30 **Concept Mapping,** p. 5 **Critical Thinking/Problem Solving:** *Cell Organelles and Their Functions,* p. 5 ****ILS:** *Normal and Plasmolyzed Cells,* p. 51	***STVS:** *Bacterial Control of Mosquitoes,* Plants and Simple Organisms (Disc 4, Side 1) **Color Transparency 5:** *The Cell*
Assessment Materials **Chapter Assessment,** pp. 17-20 **Performance Assessment in Biology,** p. 10 **Alternate Assessment in the Science Classroom** **Computer Test Bank**	**Spanish Resources** **Cooperative Learning Resource Guide** **Videodisc Correlations** (to Optical Data's and Videodiscovery's videodiscs)

* **Probing Levels of Life**
** **Investigating Living Systems**

* **Science Technology Videodisc Series**

Key to Teaching Strategies

The following designations will help you decide which activities in the teacher margin are appropriate for your students.

L1 Level 1 activities should be within the ability range of all students.

L2 Level 2 activities should be within the ability range of the average to above-average student.

L3 Level 3 activities are designed for the ability range of above-average students.

LEP LEP activities are appropriate for Limited English Proficiency students.

COOP LEARN Cooperative Learning activities are designed for small group work.

ADDITIONAL RESOURCES

Infinite Voyage *Crisis in the Atmosphere*
Our atmosphere protects Earth from harmful rays of the sun, but air pollution is destroying it. Students will learn what the problems are and how they can help to reduce air pollution.

Audiovisual
Living Cells, video, Insight Media.
Structure of the Cell Video, video, Frey Scientific.

Software
Cells, Apple II/IBM, Queue.

INSIDE THE CELL

Chapter Overview

After learning about sizes and shapes of cells, students learn that unicellular organisms are versatile, whereas cells of multicellular organisms have evolved specialized adaptations. They become familiar with biological levels of organization from cell to organism and appreciate that interdependence is a characteristic of each level.

Students become familiar with the idea of division of labor as it applies to individual cells. As students study the organelles and parts of eukaryotic cells, they learn not only about the specific functions carried out, but also how the various cell parts are interdependent.

Finally, students learn about the endosymbiosis model of the evolution of eukaryotes from prokaryotes and the evidence supporting that model.

INSIDE THE CELL

A TWO-TON ELEPHANT is made of the same tiny units of life as an ant crawling on the ground at its feet. Elephants and ants, whales and shrimp, horses and humming-birds—all organisms, large and small, are made up of cells. Although cells exist in different shapes and sizes, most cells are so small they can be seen only with the aid of a microscope. Microscopic organisms, such as bacteria and *Amoeba,* consist of single cells. Larger forms of life, like ants and elephants, are composed of thousands, millions, or even trillions of cells. The size of an organism depends on the number of cells that compose it, rather than the size of those cells.

The activities that take place within cells constitute the processes of life. What are those processes? What lies inside the plasma membrane, and what happens there? In this chapter, you will take a look inside a typical cell and learn about the forms and functions of the parts within it. You will learn how the cells of single-celled organisms differ from the cells that make up many-celled organisms such as plants and animals. You also will find out how the cells of multicellular organisms are organized, and how they evolved from simpler forms.

KEY TERMS

centriole	microfilament
chloroplast	microtubule
chromatin	mitochondria
chromosome	nucleoli
cilia	nucleus
cytoplasm	organ
endoplasmic	prokaryote
reticulum	ribosome
eukaryote	symbiosis
flagella	system
Golgi body	tissue
lysosome	vacuole
metabolism	

Introducing the Chapter

Ask students to think about the photographs of the elephant and the diatom on pages 116 and 117. Remind them of the cell theory as you lead them to the point that both these organisms (and all others) are composed of the same microscopic units of life—cells. Ask them if they remember that the cell is the basic unit of function as well as structure, and lead them in a discussion of the kinds of functions that cells must carry out. Close examination of different visible parts of the two organisms as well as mention of internal parts can lead to a discussion of levels of biological organization. **L1**

Theme Development

Unity within diversity is one important theme of this chapter. Students will observe that all cells have certain basic parts and functions. The theme of systems and interactions is also stressed as the idea of interaction among organelles is developed.

Tying to Previous Knowledge

Cells can carry out their functions only if the raw materials they need can pass through their membranes. Similarly, both wastes and some needed products made within cells must be able to leave cells. The various parts of cells and their functions can be related to the different means by which materials involved in those functions enter and leave cells.

What one thing does the organism in the photograph (magnification: 725×) have in common with green beans, mushrooms, and you? Can you think of any other trait that these organisms share?

Chapter Preview

ASSESSMENT PLANNER

Choose assessment strategies from the following pages to evaluate the progress of your students.

Assess, pp. 124, 137
Portfolio, pp. 122, 124, 130, 132
Alternate Lab, pp. 126-127
Thinking Lab, p. 130

Minilab 1, p. 122
Minilab 2, p. 130
Investigation, pp. 120-121
Chapter Review, pp. 140-141

Prepare

Key Concepts

Students will differentiate between the function of cells in unicellular and multicellular organisms and identify the stages in the division of labor from cells to organisms.

Key Terms

tissue, organ, system, cytoplasm, metabolism

Materials

- Gather transparent rulers, Lugol's solution or methylene blue stain, and the variety of plant and animal cells for the Investigation.
- Gather two onions, razor blades, slides, coverslips, and methylene blue stain for the Minilab.

1 Focus

Objectives

The objectives are listed on the student page. Remind students to preview these objectives as a guide to this numbered section.

Discussion

Place the following words on the chalkboard: *fuel cell, prison cell, battery cell, weather cell.* Ask students to discuss what they think the meaning of each word is, then direct them to discuss what each name has in common with the others (cell). Point out that each of the cells mentioned is made of a single unit of an object and contains some type of matter. Tell them that these cells are made of nonliving matter and that they are going to focus on living cells that are units of living things. L1 LEP

Objectives

Recognize general differences between the cells of unicellular and multicellular organisms.

Describe how cells are arranged into increasingly complex levels of organization.

Discuss how cell organelles contribute to the efficiency of cellular functions.

5.1 Structure of Cells

You have seen photographs and drawings of cells. Perhaps you've also looked at cells that have been frozen, stained, or prepared in some other way for viewing under a microscope. These images can make cells seem dull and inactive, because they show you only a single instant in the life of a cell. Instead, imagine you have a microscope that allows you to watch what's actually happening inside a living cell—perhaps one of the cells of your own body.

An amazing number of activities are taking place inside a living cell. Molecules are passing into and out of the cell through the plasma membrane. Inside the cell, there is constant motion. Molecules are constantly being transported from one area to another. Some molecules are being joined to create new substances, while others are being broken down into smaller parts. You've entered a dynamic factory of life, where large numbers of very complex manufacturing processes are going on.

Characteristics of Cells

When you look at a photograph, you see a flat, two-dimensional representation of something you know is actually three-dimensional. Pictures of cells can make them seem like circles, squares, or rectangles. Cells, however, are actually spheres, cubes, or bricks. Many cells can change their shapes, and some also have spikes, bulges, or other strange extensions. Cells vary in size as well as shape. Bacteria are among the smallest cells; some are less than half a micrometer (written as the Greek symbol μm) across. One micrometer is equal to one thousandth of a millimeter (1μm = 1/1000 mm). Twenty thousand bacterial cells, side by side, would measure about one centimeter. A human egg cell is large by comparison, measuring nearly a millimeter in diameter. It would only take about 10 egg cells, side by side, to measure one centimeter.

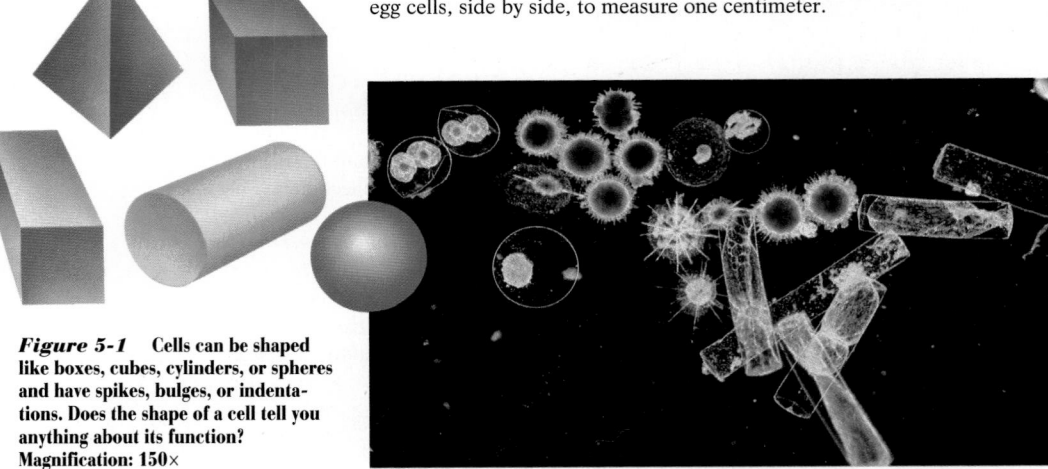

Figure 5-1 **Cells can be shaped like boxes, cubes, cylinders, or spheres and have spikes, bulges, or indentations. Does the shape of a cell tell you anything about its function? Magnification: 150×**

118 INSIDE THE CELL

MEETING INDIVIDUAL NEEDS

Have students who are having problems with vocabulary write a list of words in their journals that they do not understand. Direct them to use the text and a dictionary to write a short phrase that describes each word. When doing independent practice with the students who need more help, have students explain to you what each word means. Help students relate two or more words or concepts, for example, *unicellular* organisms perform all functions within one cell, while *multicellular* organisms have many cells and each group of cells performs a specific function. LEP

a

b

c

Unicellular Organisms   Bacteria, *Amoeba,* certain algae, and yeasts are examples of single-celled, also called unicellular, organisms. Because these organisms are made up of only a single cell, that one cell has to be able to perform all the functions necessary for life. Some of these cells, like *Amoeba,* must be able to obtain food and oxygen from the environment and, by cellular respiration, release the energy in food molecules. That energy is required for functions such as reproduction, production of enzymes, elimination of waste products, and motion. Unicellular algae must take in carbon dioxide and water and convert them to sugars in the process of photosynthesis. Then, through cellular respiration, they, too, obtain the energy needed for their functions. All unicellular organisms must be versatile, because they must do everything for themselves.

Multicellular Organisms   Many-celled, also called multicellular, organisms evolved from unicellular life forms. Almost all cells of multicellular organisms have retained the ability to carry out very basic functions, like enzyme production, that first evolved among their unicellular ancestors. However, some of the cells of multicellular organisms are adapted for performing specific tasks. For example, not all of the cells of a tree are capable of photosynthesis. Only cells that contain chlorophyll can perform this function. The food produced by these chlorophyll-containing cells is transported to other parts of the tree. Most of your cells cannot transmit messages from one part of your body to another; only your nerve cells can. Cells that are adapted for specific functions are said to be specialized.

Figure 5-2   Examples of unicellular organisms include ***Gloeocapsa*** (a), ***Oscillatoria*** (b), and ***Euglena*** (c). Some unicellular organisms are found in colonies or attached to one another to form long chains. However, the cells remain independent.
Magnifications: 400× (a), 100× (b), 180× (c).

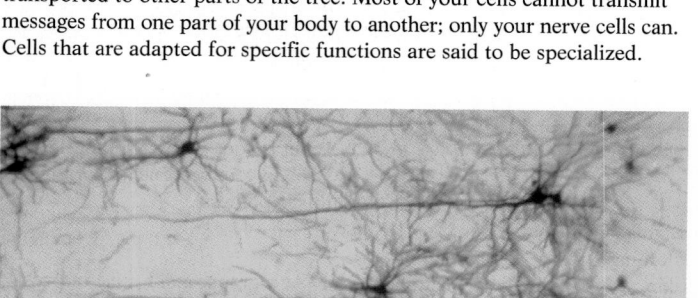

Figure 5-3   Some cells are specialized to carry out specific functions in multicellular organisms. What functions do these human nerve cells carry out? Magnification: 300×

2 Teach

Reinforcement

To reinforce the idea of how small bacteria are, tell students that 1000 bacteria 0.5 micrometers wide would fit side by side across the period at the end of any sentence on this page.

Using the Photo

- Ask students to look at Figure 5-1 on page 118 and compare the geometric shapes with the shapes of the cells and tell which cells are similar to any of the geometric shapes. **L1** **LEP**
- In Figure 5-2, students will notice that single-celled *Oscillatoria* do not occur as single cells but are connected to one another to form a filament. Filaments of *Oscillatoria* are not multicellular because each cell remains independent of the others. **L1** **LEP**
- Have students relate how the nerve cell in Figure 5-3 is similar in shape to an electrical or telephone wire. Reinforce the idea that shape and structure of a cell are important to the function it serves. **LEP**

Figure Caption Question

- *Does the shape of a cell tell you anything about its function?* Students should be able to guess that shape does play a role in the function of a cell.
- *What functions do these human nerve cells carry out?* Nerve cells carry messages between the brain and other body cells.

Concept Development

Emphasize that cells with and without chloroplasts release energy for the work of the cell through respiration.

STUDENT JOURNAL

Direct students to read the first paragraph at the top of page 120. Give them the following information and questions to write in their journals.

Red blood cells carry oxygen to other cells and are shaped like donuts or a sphere in most animals. Assuming that cells would change to these shapes—cone, cube, ballpoint pen—ask the following questions:

1. Would the cell still be able to carry oxygen?
2. What problems would the red blood cells have moving through the blood vessels?
3. Write a statement that explains why cells that perform a certain function must have a specific shape to carry out their functions. **L1**

SECTION 5.1

INVESTIGATION

Sizes of Cells

Time Allotment
1 1/2 class periods

Objectives
Upon completing this investigation, students will be able to:
* use the microscope as a measuring device.
* compare and contrast sizes of plant and animal cells.

Skills
compare and contrast, measure in SI, observe, classify

Materials
microscope, slides and coverslips, prepared *Paramecium* slide, dropping pipette, transparent mm ruler, razor blade, toothpicks, methylene blue, Lugol's solution, a variety of live cells: *Elodea,* various protozoans, lettuce, potato, onion bulb, yeast culture, uncooked hamburger, algae
Safety Precautions: Remind students that stains may be permanent on clothing and long-lived on skin. If stains are spilled on skin, they should rinse immediately. They should wash their hands at the end of the lab. If they obtain cheek cells with toothpicks, they should dispose of the toothpicks properly.

Preparation
Protozoans and algae can be purchased from biological supply houses or collected from local sources; yeast culture can be prepared one day before needed by adding 1/4 package of dry baker's yeast to 225 mL distilled water, 25 mL molasses, and 10 dry beans. Transparent rulers can be made by making a transparency of rulers from a photocopy and cutting them with scissors from the transparency. Preparation time: about one hour. Refer to page 27T for additional solution preparation directions.

Possible Hypotheses
Some students may hypothesize that plant cells will be larger; others may suggest animal cells will be larger.

Cells average about 200 microns in size. Students' estimates will vary

Although multicellular organisms must be able to perform all the functions necessary for life, each cell need not be equipped to do everything. Instead, the many different kinds of specialized cells interact to keep the organism alive. Specialized cells are dependent on one another. For example, many animals depend on their blood cells to transport the oxygen all the other cells need. If the blood cells fail to function properly, the animal may not be able to survive. Specialized cells often have shapes or sizes that enable each type of cell to perform its function more efficiently. Nerve cells carry messages from one part of your body to another. What shape would you expect nerve cells to be?

Levels of Organization in the Living World

Think for a moment about what it's like to be part of a team. You may be a member of a softball, soccer, or football team. Perhaps you've joined a choir, band, or drama troupe. Your coach or director organizes the mem-

I N V E S T I G A T I O N

Sizes of Cells

How big is a cell? The first thought that comes to mind is "very small." However, nerve cells in your body can be 1.5 m long! An ostrich egg cell is about 100 mm in diameter. This egg cell is able to grow larger than other cells because its food, the yolk, is inside the cell. Other cells must take in materials for survival through their surfaces. As a cell gets larger, its need for materials may exceed the ability of the surface to let materials in. As a cell increases in size, it has proportionately less surface area to volume.

In this lab, you will determine the size of plant and animal cells. Your teacher will supply a small, transparent millimeter ruler and a variety of plant and animal cells. If you have trouble seeing the cells, you might use Lugol's solution or methylene blue stain. You can measure the diameter of the field of view under low power with your millimeter ruler. There are 1000 micrometers (µm) in 1 mm. It might be easier to make your cell measurements in micrometers because cells are very small.

Problem
How big are cells?

Safety Precautions
Stains may be permanent on clothing and last a long time on skin. Rinse immediately if spilled on skin. Wash your hands at the end of the lab.

Hypothesis
What is your group hypothesis? Explain your reasons for forming this hypothesis.

Experimental Plan
1. As a group, make a list of possible ways you might test your hypothesis using the materials your teacher has made available.

120 🐚 INSIDE THE CELL

and their reasons will be based on the *Paramecium* or other cells they remember seeing magnified.

Possible Procedures
* Ask students if they have ever had to estimate a measurement. An example might be estimates of distance made while driving a car. Ask what strategies they use to make estimates. Bring out the idea of making comparisons.
* Ask students to read the introductory materials and ask them to measure the

low-power field of view with their transparent millimeter ruler.
* Ask them how many microns there are in a millimeter.
* Ask them how many microns there are in the diameter of their field of view.
* Ask them to focus their prepared slide of *Paramecium* under low power and estimate its size in microns.
* As students discuss their strategies, ask groups how they are making their estimates.
* Make sure they have a strategy for estimating before they begin with live cells.

bers of your group in a way that takes advantage of each individual's talents and abilities. You do your part, and you depend on the other team members to do theirs. You work together. Similarly, the specialized cells of multicellular organisms work together to accomplish a task.

Tissue A group of cells that have the same basic structure and function is called a **tissue.** For example, the cells that make up the muscle tissue in your legs work together to enable you to walk. Nerve cells are grouped into tissues that extend throughout your body to carry messages to and from your brain. Epithelial tissue forms the protective outer layer of your skin and the lining of your internal cavities. Plant tissues include protective tissues, such as bark, and conductive tissues that transport water, minerals, and organic molecules from one part of the plant to another.

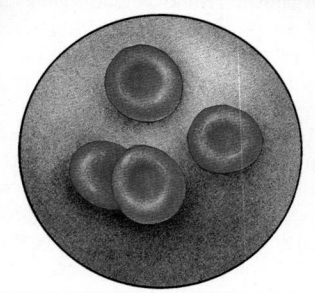

2. Agree on one idea from your group's list that could be investigated in the classroom.
3. Design an experiment in which you collect quantitative data.
4. Following the style of a recipe, write a numbered list of directions for your experiment that anyone could follow.
5. Make a list of materials and the quantities you will need.

Checking the Plan

Discuss the following points with other group members to decide the final procedures for your experiment.
1. How many cell types will you use?
2. Is it important to use both plant and animal specimens?
3. How many cells of each type will you measure?
4. Under what circumstances will you need to use stain?
5. In what way will estimation be used in your calculations?

6. If you measure the field of view with the millimeter ruler, how can this information be useful in determining the sizes of cells?
7. Have you designed and made a table for collecting data?

Make sure your teacher has approved your experimental plan before you proceed further.

Data and Observations

Carry out your experiment; make your measurements; and complete your data table. Make a graph of your results.

Analysis and Conclusions

1. What was the average size of the cells you measured?
2. Which are larger, plant or animal cells? Speculate why.
3. Which cell type was smallest? Speculate about why it is an advantage for that species of cell to be so small.
4. Which cell type was largest? Speculate about why it is an advantage for the cell of that species to be larger.
5. Why do you think cells are different sizes?

Going Further

Based on this lab experience, design an experiment that would help to answer another question that arose from your work. Assume that you will have unlimited resources and will not be conducting this lab in class.

4. The largest cell would most likely be a protozoan. A protozoan must carry on all the life functions of an organism and therefore needs space inside for a variety of organelles.
5. Cells are different sizes because they carry on different functions.

Teaching Strategies

If this is the first time your students have designed an experiment, refer them to the Investigations in Chapters 1 and 2.
- You may wish to review proper microscope handling and technique before doing this inquiry.
- Explain to students that they need to develop a method to make accurate estimates of cell sizes. Do not give them this method, but lead them with questioning to develop the strategy if they have trouble.
- Use of low power is recommended.
- Explain that cheek cells may be obtained by gently scraping inside the cheek with the flat end of a toothpick.

Data and Observations

Cells will vary in size from 25 to 300 microns (length). Under low power (eyepiece 10×, objective 10×), the field of view is 1.5 mm or 1500 microns. If six *Elodea* cells fit across one diameter of the field of view, then each cell is 1/6 the field of view or 1/6 of 1500 microns, 250 microns in length. If a single cheek cell takes up 1/8 of the diameter of the field of view, then the cell is about 1/8 of 1500 microns or about 200 microns in length.

Data Analysis

1. Answers will vary from 50 microns to 150 microns.
2. Plant cells are generally larger. Plant cells must make their own food and contain chloroplasts, an organelle not needed by animal cells. Perhaps plant cells that contain chloroplasts are larger for this reason.
3. The smallest cell type will depend on what cells students observed. Blood cells would probably be smallest. The smaller the cell, the greater the ratio of surface area to volume. This permits the cell to take in and give off materials quickly. This ability would be important to a red blood cell that carries oxygen.

✔ Assessment

Skill: Give each group a prepared slide of a cell they have not seen and ask them to measure it using the microscope.

Extensions

Give students prepared slides of various types of tissue such as connective, blood, muscle, nerve, and others you might have available. Ask them to measure the sizes of cells in these tissues, determine which tissues have the largest cells and which have the smallest cells, and speculate why.

Minilab 1

Purpose
Students will observe and compare the differences between different cell types from the same organism.

Skills
observe and infer, compare and contrast

Teaching Strategies
- It takes about a week to grow onion roots from a bulblet with its base immersed in water. Scrape the base of the bulblet gently with a knife before setting it in the top of a test tube of water.
- Use "onion sets" from a nursery or biological supply house. Onions from the grocery store may have been treated with chemicals.
- **Safety Precautions:** Advise students to use extreme care when handling a razor blade.

Expected Results
Bulb cells will be larger and have thicker cell walls than root cells. Bulb cells may be larger because they serve as storage for food, while root cells can take in water quickly if they are smaller.

Answers
Differences in the two types of cells: Onion bulb cells are larger, have a rectangular appearance, thicker cell walls, and easily distinguished nucleus and granules in the cytoplasm. Root cells are smaller, or may vary in size, nucleus not distinct in all of the cells, and have thinner cell walls. They are alike in that they are arranged in a regular sequence and they both have cell walls. They are different because the roots absorb water and the bulb stores materials.

✔ Assessment
Performance: Give students prepared slides of other cells from different tissue types from the same species. Ask them to observe and record the differences in the cells and speculate about why these cells are different.

Minilab 1

What are the differences between onion root and onion bulb cells?

Remove a small section of the inner transparent membrane of a raw onion ring cut from a bulb. **CAUTION:** *Be careful when using a razor blade.* Make a wet-mount slide of this tissue with a drop of methylene blue. With a razor, cut a paper-thin cross section of onion root from a bulb that has sprouted roots. Make a wet-mount slide of this tissue with a drop of methylene blue. Observe both of these preparations under the microscope.

Analysis *How are the two cell types alike? How are they different? Speculate about why these differences occur.*

Organ   Just as the cells of a tissue work together like team members to accomplish a task, tissues also join forces to perform more complex functions. The tissues within a leaf work together to carry out the complicated process of photosynthesis. Chlorophyll-containing tissue absorbs sunlight, while other tissues obtain the carbon dioxide, water, and minerals needed to trap the energy of sunlight in the chemical bonds of simple sugars and other carbohydrates. Still other tissues move the sugars out of the leaf to other parts of the plant. All of the tissues in the leaf work together to provide food and other nutrients for the plant. A leaf is an organ of the plant. An **organ** is a structure composed of many different tissues that work together to perform a particular function. Your stomach is another organ.

System   Your stomach stores food and begins the digestion of proteins. It cannot completely digest an entire meal, however. Other organs, including the liver and the large and small intestines, are needed to complete the process. A group of organs working together is known as a **system.** Your stomach is part of your digestive system. Other human organ systems include the respiratory, circulatory, and reproductive systems.

Organism   Multicellular organisms are composed of a group of organ systems working together. You might think that an organism represents the highest level of organization in the living world, but it doesn't. Think about your neighborhood. It's a community made up of many people, plants, and animals. As you know, organisms live together in communities. A forest community, for example, consists of trees, bushes, flowers, birds, mammals, and other forms of life. There are even higher levels of organization in the living world. You will learn more about them later in this course.

As you can see, each level of organization—cell, tissue, organ, system, organism, and community—involves interdependence. Cells that are dependent on each other form tissues. Tissues that work together form organs. Organs depend on other organs to function as a system. Systems work together to form an organism, and organisms cooperate in forming communities.

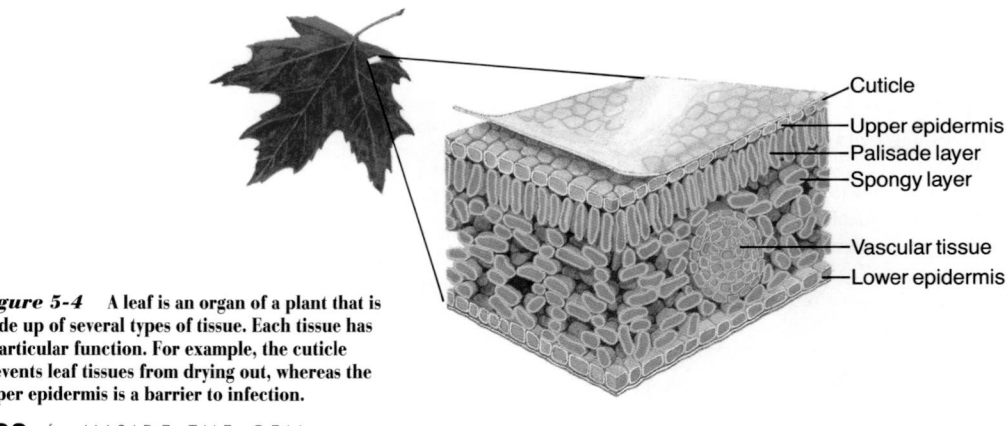

Figure 5-4   A leaf is an organ of a plant that is made up of several types of tissue. Each tissue has a particular function. For example, the cuticle prevents leaf tissues from drying out, whereas the upper epidermis is a barrier to infection.

122 🦠 INSIDE THE CELL

PORTFOLIO

Direct students to refer to the section on systems. Tell students there are four systems in a home: electrical, plumbing, heating, and structural. Tell them to list the component parts that would be analogous to organs in a living thing that make up the specific system in a home. The answers you can expect are: electrical: wires, bulbs, sockets, meter, appliances, switch and socket plates, circuit breaker; plumbing: pipes, drains, toilets, sinks, tubs; heating: furnace, air conditioner, heat pump, wires, fireplace, chimney, ducts; structural: lumber, shingles, cement blocks, bricks, siding.

Have students write a paragraph about how the "organs" of one system work together. Relate this to how organs work together in an organism. **L1**

Figure 5-5 A coral reef is one type of community in which organisms cooperate. The place you live is another type of community. How do organisms in your community cooperate?

Cytoplasm

When Hooke made the first observations of cells, he saw only dead, empty cells. The fact that living cells contain a substance called **cytoplasm** was not recognized until the 1830s. Analysis of cytoplasm shows that it consists of about 70 percent water and about 30 percent proteins, fats, carbohydrates, nucleic acids, and ions. Its consistency is like a gelatin dessert that has not completely solidified. The exact composition of cytoplasm varies from cell to cell and is always changing because the substances it is made of are constantly involved in chemical reactions. So much chemical change takes place within a cell that 100 000 proteins can be made in a cell each second!

Cellular reactions both build up and tear down complex molecules. The sum of all chemical changes in cells is called **metabolism.** Some chemical reactions, such as condensation or hydrolysis, occur in one or just a few steps. Often, though, a complex set of related reactions is involved, as in the processes of photosynthesis and cellular respiration.

Figure 5-6 Cytoplasm contains a complex mix of enzymes, sugars, and amino acids. Cells are filled with cytoplasm, as you can see in this color-enhanced photograph. Magnification: 15 000×

5.1 STRUCTURE OF CELLS **123**

Reinforcement

Have students differentiate a cell from a tissue and explain the relationship between the two.

Figure Caption Question

How do organisms in your community cooperate? Students may answer that mice eat grass seed, cats eat mice, cats are pets; other students may describe garbage collectors, bus drivers, and postal carriers—people whose jobs help others in the community.

Demonstration

Use the directions on a pack of gelatin to make enough liquid gelatin to give each student 10 mL in a small cup. Have students stir the liquid gelatin with a plastic spoon and describe the consistency of the gelatin. Tell students that the thickness of liquid gelatin is similar to cytoplasm, and some cytoplasm is thicker than what they see in their cups. Point out that the gelatin they use today is about 3 to 5 percent solids and 95 to 97 percent water. Ask them how this is similar to or different from cytoplasm. **L1**

CHEMISTRY CONNECTION

The Chemical Basis of Life: Cells are the smallest parts of an organism that are considered to be alive. Cells are living things, but they are made up of nonliving things—molecules—and molecules are made up of atoms connected by chemical bonds. Molecules interact with other molecules through chemical reactions. Life has a chemical basis because cells are made up of chemicals. Have students look at numerous nonliving materials like rocks, glass slides, and sand, and have them write several sentences explaining how these materials are similar to living things.

PROGRAM RESOURCES

Teacher Classroom Resources
Study Guide, pp. 25-26 **L1**
Exploring Environmental Issues, pp. 9-10 **L3**

3 Assess

Check for Understanding

Have students write a short paragraph listing in order the levels of organization in multicellular organisms and write a sentence describing each level of organization and how it relates to the one before it. **L1**

Reteach

Develop an analogy using the school and students to help students understand the levels of organization in living things. Relate a student in the biology class to a cell, the entire class to a tissue, all students in the 10th grade to an organ, all students in the school as a system, and the school building with all of the people as an organism.

Extension

Ask students to do library work to find out how unicellular organisms are being used to benefit humans. Have them concentrate on how they are used to make new products and medicines. **L3**

✔ Assessment

Portfolio: Have students develop a concept map for this section using the following concepts: cell, tissue, organ, system, organism, unicellular, multicellular, and cytoplasm. Make sure they connect lines to show relationships among the concepts.

4 Close

Discussion

Assign two students to put their concept maps on a transparency. Have each student explain the major concepts of the section using their concept maps on the overhead projector. As they are presenting their concept maps, you may call on other students to ask them to explain why certain concepts are connected with lines. **L1** **COOP LEARN**

Organization Within Cells

Figure 5-7 Various functions of the cell are performed in cell organelles. Magnification: 400×

Imagine that you and some friends are planning a costume party. How would you get ready for the big night? One or two of you might gather recordings of your favorite dance music, while another group arranges for the food, and another takes charge of all the decorations. You would divide up the labor.

Division of labor is evident at all levels of biological organization. You've already seen how tissues, organs, systems, organisms, and communities illustrate this idea. Division of labor is also an important factor in the lives of individual cells. Some cellular reactions occur in the cytoplasm. Thousands and thousands of reactions take place in a cell at the same time. Would it be efficient to have all these reactions going on in the cytoplasm? Just as you would use different pans when baking a cake and cooking soup, the cell includes many structures that carry on different chemical reactions. These specialized structures found in the cytoplasm are called organelles.

The various functions performed by different organelles are interdependent and contribute to the survival of the entire cell. Recall that many internal cell parts are enclosed by membranes that have a fluid mosaic structure, and those membranes vary in terms of the particles to which they are permeable. These membranes allow organelles to be separated from one another and from the cytoplasm. The membranes maintain separate environments where particular sets of reactions can occur.

Section Review

Understanding Concepts
1. Compare current knowledge of the basic structure of cells with what Hooke knew.
2. *Paramecium* is a unicellular consumer. What functions must it carry out that most cells of a multicellular organism would not carry out?
3. Would you expect a nerve cell and a muscle cell to have the same size and shape? Explain.

4. **Skill Review—Observing and Inferring:** You observe two photographs of cells as viewed by an electron microscope. You find many structures common to both cells, but one cell contains many additional structures. Which is probably a unicellular organism? For additional help, see Observing and Inferring in the **Skill Handbook**.

5. **Thinking Critically:** All cells of a multicellular organism carry out cellular respiration. Why don't multicellular organisms have specialized cells for this function?

Answers to Section Review

1. Hooke saw only dead cells bordered by the cell wall. He had no idea of the presence of cytoplasm or organelles, much less their functions or how they interact.
2. *Paramecium* must carry out functions such as food-getting and digestion, obtaining oxygen from the external environment, and expelling carbon dioxide and wastes into the external environment.
3. These are specialized cells and have different shapes. Many nerve cells, which conduct impulses, are long and thin like a wire. Muscle cells have a shape suited to their role in contracting and relaxing.
4. **Skill Review—Observing and Inferring:** The unicellular organism is the one with additional structures.
5. **Thinking Critically:** Cellular respiration releases the energy needed by every cell for its functions.

5.2 Functions and Interactions of Cell Parts

You learned in Chapter 4 the various ways in which materials enter cells. Some of these materials are used to assemble new molecules that contribute to cell growth. Others are used to make molecules that regulate the cell's functions or the functions of other cells. Still others are sources of energy that fuel these activities. It is during these metabolic processes that by-products are formed. You have also learned how by-products leave the cell. Now you are ready to study how each of the organelles and other cell parts function, and how they work together to make cells the basic units of life.

Cell Types

Almost all cells found in the living world contain organelles that are surrounded by a membrane. Cells that possess a membrane-bound organelle called a nucleus are known as **eukaryotes,** meaning cells that contain a nucleus. Plant, animal, protist, and fungi cells are examples of eukaryotic cells. Cells that do not have a membrane-bound nucleus are called **prokaryotes,** meaning before a nucleus. Bacteria are prokaryotes because they lack a nucleus and other membrane-bound organelles. Prokaryotes contain one type of organelle that synthesizes proteins, but most metabolic functions take place in the cytoplasm. The vast majority of cells in the living world are eukaryotic.

Figure 5-8 **Trees, ferns, fungi, birds, flowers, insects and worms are all composed of eukaryotic cells. Eukaryotic cells are found in most multicellular organisms.**

Objectives

Compare the structure and function of cell organelles, including the nucleus, mitochondrion, chloroplast, lysosome, endoplasmic reticulum, Golgi body, vesicle, and vacuole.

Discuss how the functions of ribosomes, endoplasmic reticulum, and Golgi bodies are interrelated.

Describe the structure and function of other eukaryotic cell parts.

SECTION 5.2

Prepare

Key Concepts
Students will distinguish between the various cell organelles and relate the function of each organelle to its structure.

Key Terms
eukaryote, prokaryote, ribosome, endoplasmic reticulum, Golgi body, mitochondria, nucleus, chromatin, chromosome, nucleoli, chloroplast, lysosome, vacuole, microfilament, microtubule, centriole, cilia, flagella, symbiosis

Materials
• Gather slides, coverslips, filter paper, methylene blue stain, Lugol's solution, and *Paramecium* for the Minilab.

1 Focus

Objectives
The objectives are listed on the student page. Remind students to preview these objectives as a guide to this numbered section.

Discussion
Make a transparency for the overhead projector from the owner's manual showing the "exploded" parts of a lawn mower. Ask the students what would happen if one of the parts of the lawn mower was missing. Ask them what they think would happen if one of the parts of their cells were missing.

2 Teach

Using Science Terms
Write the words *prokaryote* and *eukaryote* on the chalkboard and underline *pro, eu,* and *karyo*. Write the word *before* under *pro, true* under *eu,* and *nucleus* under *karyo*. Have students figure out what *prokaryote* means (a cell "before the nucleus" or "without a nucleus") and what *eukaryote* means (a cell with a "true nucleus"). **L1** **LEP**

MEETING INDIVIDUAL NEEDS

Physically Challenged: Have students who are having trouble understanding this chapter use their journals to outline the cell parts and their functions. Make sure they organize this material so it can be used for reinforcement as they look over their notes in the journal. When doing independent practice with students who need more help, have students explain to you what each word means.

Help them put an outline together that covers only the major concepts. Physically challenged students may need to use the computer to add to their journals. **LEP**

Misconception

Make sure that students understand the similarity in functions of cell organelles and organs of multicellular organisms. They may think that organelles are the same in structural complexity as an organ. Point out that both are made of molecules, but only organs are made of layers of cells called tissues.

Using an Analogy

Compare the ribosomes that are attached to the rough endoplasmic reticulum to small beads that are glued to the outside of a flexible soda straw. Point out that the endoplasmic reticulum snakes its way through the cytoplasm of the cell. **LEP**

Using Science Terms

Write the words *endoplasmic reticulum* on the chalkboard and underline *endo, plasmic,* and *reticulum*. Write the word *inside* under *endo, molded* under *plasmic,* and *network* under *reticulum*. Have students figure out what the term *endoplasmic reticulum* means (a molded network inside a cell). Ask the students if the diagram of endoplasmic reticulum in Figure 5-9 fits the definition using the translation of the root words. **L1** **LEP**

Reinforcement

Explain that the manufacture of proteins by the ribosomes is a condensation reaction in which smaller molecules, amino acids, are made into larger molecules, proteins.

Eukaryotic Cell Organelles

Just as a newborn baby's major task is to transform food and oxygen for its own growth and development, a newly produced cell must make the proteins it needs to carry out its specialized tasks. These proteins might be used, for example, as enzymes.

Ribosomes and Endoplasmic Reticulum Proteins are made from amino acids at organelles called **ribosomes,** tiny particles that are composed of RNA and protein. The electron microscope shows that some ribosomes float freely in the cytoplasm. Proteins synthesized at free ribosomes are used in chemical reactions that occur in the cytoplasm. Free ribosomes are found in the cytoplasm of both prokaryotic and eukaryotic cells. Ribosomes are the most common organelle in any cell. A single prokaryotic cell may have as many as 15 000 ribosomes; a eukaryotic cell contains many more. In eukaryotic cells, other ribosomes are attached to the membranes of the **endoplasmic reticulum,** or ER. The ER is a network of interconnected, flattened, or tubelike structures that end in blind alleys, as Figure 5-9 shows. The ER on which ribosomes are located has a bumpy appearance and is known as rough ER. Proteins made on ribosomes of rough ER enter channels in the ER membrane and are transported to other parts of the cell. Do you see how the tubular structure of the ER is suited to its function of transport?

Endoplasmic reticulum that lacks ribosomes is known as smooth ER. In human liver cells, enzymes located in membranes of smooth ER break down harmful substances, such as alcohol. Other proteins in the smooth ER membrane serve as enzymes to produce phospholipids. Rough and smooth ER are sometimes connected. In these cases, the smooth ER may help in the transport of proteins coming from the rough ER.

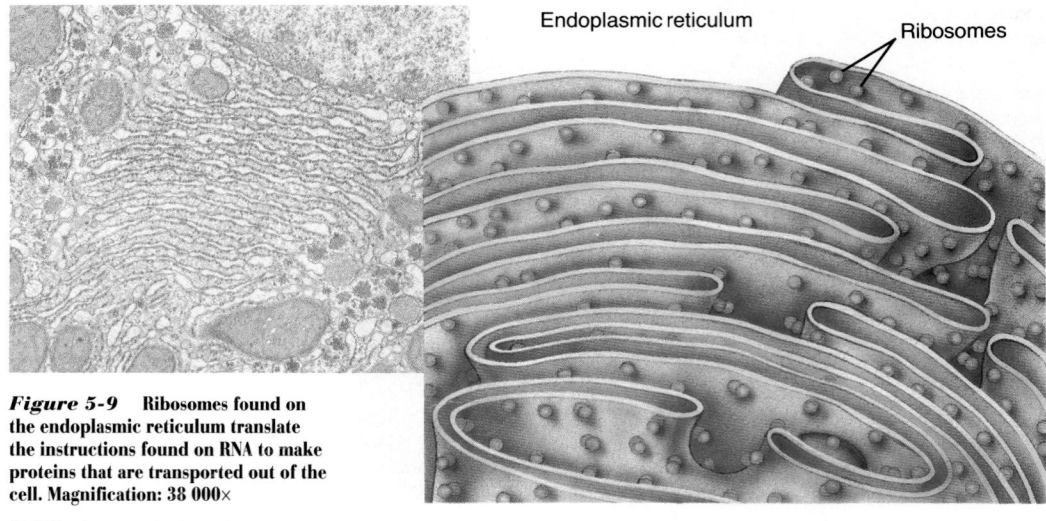

Endoplasmic reticulum

Ribosomes

Figure 5-9 **Ribosomes found on the endoplasmic reticulum translate the instructions found on RNA to make proteins that are transported out of the cell. Magnification: 38 000×**

126 INSIDE THE CELL

ALTERNATE LAB: Does cytoplasm move in plant cells?

Purpose
Students will observe movement of cytoplasm (cyclosis) of cells in *Elodea* leaves.

Materials
Elodea plants in culture dish with water, light microscope, slide, coverslip, forceps

Procedure
Give the following directions to students.
1. Add a drop of water to a clean microscope slide.
2. Use forceps to remove a leaf from the bright green growing tip of an *Elodea* plant.
3. Place the leaf in the drop of water and add a coverslip.
4. Locate the leaf on low power, then switch to high power for observations.
5. Look at the cells near the edge of the leaf that have numerous oval, green chloroplasts until you find cells going through cyclosis.
6. Determine whether the cytoplasm is moving in the same direction in all of the cells.
7. Make drawings of your observations in your journal.

Analysis
Ask students to answer the following questions.

Golgi bodies

Sacs of protein moving out

Figure 5-10 At the edges of the Golgi bodies, vesicles containing proteins pinch off and move to other locations in the cell. Golgi bodies are the delivery system in a eukaryotic cell. Magnification: 48 000×

Golgi Bodies   Lying close to the ER are sets of flattened, slightly curved sacs, as shown in Figure 5-10. Although they seem to resemble ER, they are more disklike than ER and much smaller. These groups of saclike structures are known as the **Golgi bodies.**

When proteins reach the end of rough ER, they are surrounded by a small sac called a vesicle formed from the ER membrane, which then breaks away from the ER. This vesicle moves toward the membrane of the nearest sac of a Golgi body, fuses with it, and empties its protein molecules into it. The proteins pass from one sac to another in vesicles formed from the Golgi membrane. These are the vesicles visible near the Golgi bodies in Figure 5-10. Like pieces of mail coming into a post office, the various proteins traveling through the Golgi body are sorted and eventually sent to their proper destination inside or outside of the cell. While the proteins are in each sac, they are modified chemically. This modification is part of the process by which proteins are properly identified and sorted. The sorted proteins are packaged in a vesicle formed from the final Golgi sac. Each vesicle contains proteins needed for a particular function. For example, some vesicles contain enzymes that will remain in the cell. Other vesicles contain hormones that will be transported to other cells in the same organism. Some may contain chemicals, such as poisons, that will eventually be used to affect other organisms. Vesicles that contain materials intended for use outside the cell fuse with the plasma membrane and release the materials through exocytosis.

Interaction among ribosomes, ER, and Golgi bodies illustrates how various parts of a cell work together. It also shows that the many membranes present in cells are interchangeable. For example, vesicles formed from ER and Golgi membranes can fuse with the cell membrane. They can be recycled from one part of a cell to another. This shuttling of membranes is possible because they all have the same basic fluid mosaic structure.

5.2 FUNCTIONS AND INTERACTIONS OF CELL PARTS ❧ **127**

Discussion Questions

Dragonflies have been clocked at speeds of 64 to 96 kilometers per hour as they fly across a pond. Ask students which muscle tissues of the dragonfly have the most mitochondria—leg or wing muscles?

CHEMISTRY CONNECTION

Purpose
This feature can be used to reinforce the concept of interaction among the various organelles in the cells of the spider's abdomen in the production of silk. Because they understand that many different kinds of silk are made, students should understand that each is probably made of different proteins.

Teaching Strategies
Tell students to read the assignment prior to coming to class to discuss the topic of spider silk. Some questions to use during the discussion are:
1. How do you suppose scientists found out that spider silk is stronger than steel, and is also elastic, waterproof, and nonallergenic?
2. What other properties do you think spider silk has?
3. Why does the spider have to produce many types of silk?

Possible Answers
1. To stop the bleeding of a deep wound; the spider silk gave the clotting agents in the blood a surface on which to clot. It could serve as a medium for tissue culture for skin grafts.
2. It would take a great number of spiders to produce enough silk threads to make enough material to make a shirt or dress.

Going Further
Find out what materials bulletproof vests are made of and whether spider silk could be used as a material for this item.

`L2` `COOP LEARN`

Mitochondria   The alarm clock rings, but you turn it off for another 40 winks. When you finally wake up, you have 15 minutes to get ready and out the door, so you skip breakfast. Two hours later, you find yourself nodding off in math class, or unable to keep up with your partner in science. What's wrong? You didn't give your body the energy it needs to perform to the best of its ability.

The cell needs energy to perform to the best of its ability, too. An organelle in eukaryotic cells provides the energy "breakfast" that cells need. **Mitochondria,** found in all eukaryotic cells, are the powerhouses of cells. Organic molecules are broken down in mitochondria to release energy. This energy is then used to produce other molecules that release energy needed for cell reactions. The more energy a particular cell needs, the more mitochondria it is likely to have. Mitochondria are often found in groups in portions of the cell that use a lot of energy. Although they are among the largest organelles in the cell, mitochondria vary in size and shape. Mitochondria may look like spheres, cylinders, or peanuts. They may be large in cells that use a lot of energy, such as heart muscle cells. A slice through a mitochondrion, as seen in Figure 5-11, reveals that it has a double membrane. The final reactions in cellular respiration take place on the inner membrane. The inner membrane is highly folded within the fluid-filled central cavity. The membrane's many folds increase the surface area for these final steps. With more surface area, more reactions can occur, and more energy can be released.

CHEMISTRY CONNECTION

Spider Silk

The U.S. Army is definitely interested. So is the Navy. Medical equipment manufacturers are conducting their own experiments, and even the world of high fashion is keeping a close watch on new developments.

What is at the center of all this interest? Some new synthetic wonder fabric, the product of advanced chemical research? No, the fabric is spider silk, and scientists are trying to unravel its chemical and genetic properties so that it can be commercially produced.

Wonder Thread   The reason for all the interest in spider silk is its unique characteristics. Ounce for ounce, spider silk is five times stronger than steel. Furthermore, it's incredibly elastic; spider silk can be stretched up to 130 percent of its original length before it snaps. Spider silk is waterproof, and it's nonallergenic, too.

Commercially produced spider silk would have hundreds of uses. But before it can be produced in a laboratory, scientists first must discover how it is produced by spiders.

Internal Chemistry   Spiders produce a variety of silks—dragline silk for dropping out of sight when threatened, capture silk for weaving webs to snare prey, cocoon silk for

Outer membrane

Inner membrane

Mitochondrion

Figure 5-11 The final chemical reactions of cellular respiration take place on the inner membranes of mitochondria. The energy molecules produced diffuse across the membranes of the mitochondria into the cytoplasm. Magnification: 90 000×

MATH CONNECTION

Organelle Size: To reinforce how small organelles are, tell students that some cells have mitochondria that are between 2 to 8 micrometers long. Draw a circle on the chalkboard and tell students that this circle is the size of the period at the end of a sentence in their textbook. The period is approximately 500 micrometers in diameter. Ask the students how many small and large mitochondria could fit across the diameter of the period.

500/2 = 250
500/8 = 62.5

Remind students that they are not able to see these small structures with the unaided eye because they are beyond the resolving power of the human eye. Resolving power is the ability of a lens to distinguish between two objects. L1

protection and insulation, and more. Although types of silk vary, production methods are similar.

Within a spider's abdomen are several silk glands. Each gland is filled with soluble proteins made of chains of amino acids. Cells in the glands that produce these proteins use a lot of energy. High energy use in a cell means there are lots of mitochondria in the cell. These cells produce large amounts of protein, too, so they also have numerous ribosomes.

The proteins produced in one silk gland pass through a narrow tube on their way to the spinnerets, spigot-like structures on the spider from which the silk is extruded. As the soluble proteins pass through the narrow tube, the proteins' molecules are forced to align in the same direction, forming a solid thread up to 34 amino-acids long. The proteins that make up the extruded silk have stiff, rodlike regions that give the silk its strength, and curved, springy regions that give it elasticity.

In order to manufacture large quantities of spider silk, scientists will first have to engineer the genes responsible for producing silk proteins. These genes will then be implanted in cooperative organisms, such as lab bacteria or yeast. Scientists hope that these genetically altered hosts will become miniature silk factories, making commercially produced silk a reality.

─────

1. **Explore Further:** How has spider silk been used by healers throughout history? What medical applications does it have for the future?
2. **Writing About Biology:** Explain why scientists can't use spiders themselves to produce commercial quantities of silk.

PROGRAM RESOURCES

Teacher Classroom Resources

Study Guide, pp. 27-30 L1

Critical Thinking/Problem Solving, p. 5 L2

Probing Levels of Life, Lab 10, p. 27 L2

Color Transparency #5 L1 LEP

Investigating Living Systems, Lab 12, p. 51 L2

Concept Mapping, p. 5 L1 LEP

Science, Technology, and Society

Chemotherapy: One protein in cancer cells may induce the cells to resist a number of other chemicals, allowing the cancer cells to grow. Scientists have found a protein in the plasma membrane of cancer cells that pumps lethal chemicals from the cells. This protein attracts toxic molecules and carries them out of the cell through the membrane. Normal cells also have this protein, but it does not perform the same way in normal cells as it does in cancer cells. In yeast cells, this same protein was found to secrete a hormone that triggers sexual reproduction. Does this protein secrete a useful chemical? Scientists hope to find out how the cancer cells use this protein to negate the benefits of chemotherapy.

Minilab 2

Purpose
Students will practice the technique of staining and make observations of the effects of staining cells.

Skills
observe and infer, interpret data

Teaching Strategies
- Protozoans and other cells are stained to demonstrate specific details of the cell. Vital stains, such as methylene blue, do not kill the cell immediately, but allow it to carry on life functions as the stain is absorbed slowly.
- Methylene blue is absorbed by the nucleus and granules in the cytoplasm. It is usually used in concentrations of 0.1 to 0.01 percent. In a 0.5 percent solution, it may be used to trigger discharge trichocysts in *Paramecium.*
- Lugol's solution stains cilia and flagella a reddish-brown. Glycogen absorbs this stain. Lugol's is made by using 1.5 g potassium iodide in 25 mL of water, then adding 1 g of iodine.
- **Safety Precautions:** Students should be cautioned that the stain will color their clothing permanently and skin temporarily. If it is spilled on skin, they should rinse well immediately.
- Refer to page 27T for solution preparation directions.

Expected Results
Lugol's solution stains the cilia.

Answers
1. Granules might be food particles ingested by the *Paramecium.* They might indicate areas of other membrane-bound organelles.
2. Lugol's stain is absorbed by cilia.

✔ Assessment
Performance: Ask students to use two other stains such as methyl green and Congo red on live *Paramecium* cultures. Ask them to note what parts of the cell are stained by these dyes. (Methyl green: trichocyst; Congo red: food vacuoles in which digestion is complete.)

130

Minilab 2

Why are stains used when observing cells?

Prepare a slide of *Paramecium* and observe it under the microscope. Add a drop of dilute methylene blue to the edge of the coverslip. Place filter paper at the opposite edge of the coverslip to draw out the fluid. Notice that the nucleus and granules in the cytoplasm absorb the stain. Prepare another slide of *Paramecium*. Add a drop of Lugol's solution in the same way as described above.

Analysis   *What do you think the granules in the cytoplasm are? What organelles absorb the Lugol's stain?*

Nucleus   As in any organization, the cell must have an area of central control to coordinate the many activities that take place within it. In eukaryotic cells, that control area is the **nucleus,** which is separated from the rest of the cell by a double membrane. Inside the nucleus is a dense mass of material called **chromatin,** which looks something like a tangled mass of string. Chromatin is composed of individual chromosomes. **Chromosomes** are composed of proteins and DNA, the genetic code. The DNA contained in the nucleus ultimately controls all the activity that takes place in the cell. It does so by making RNA. The DNA remains in the nucleus, but the RNA can move from the nucleus into the cytoplasm. Some RNA acts as a messenger, carrying out the instructions of the genetic code by directing the synthesis of proteins at the ribosomes.

Before a cell reproduces, its chromosomes are copied. Then, when the cell begins to reproduce, the chromosomes that make up the tangled mass of chromatin become separate and distinct. During reproduction, one set of chromosomes goes to the nucleus of each new cell. Thus, each offspring cell contains the genetic information required to control its activities.

Although the nucleus is enclosed in its own membrane, it must communicate with the rest of the cell. Definite openings called pores in the nuclear membrane allow some large molecules, such as RNA, to pass between the nucleus and the cytoplasm. Other materials move within portions of ER that are joined to the nuclear membrane.

Parts of some chromosomes consist of multiple copies of DNA that make the RNA present in ribosomes. The RNA molecules produced in the nucleus stand out as prominent bodies known as **nucleoli.**

Thinking Lab
INTERPRET THE DATA

What organelle directs cell activity?

Background
Acetabularia, a type of marine algae, grow as single, huge cells 2-5 cm in height. The nuclei of these cells are in the "feet." Different species of these algae have different kinds of caps, some petal-like and others like umbrellas. If a cap is removed, it quickly regenerates. If both cap and foot are removed from the cell of one species of algae and a foot from another species is attached, a new cap will grow. This new cap will have a structure with characteristics of both species. Then, if this new cap is removed, the next cap that grows will be like the cell that donated the nucleus.

The scientist who discovered these properties was Joachim Hämmerling. He wondered why the first cap that grew had characteristics of both species, yet the second cap was clearly like that of the cell that donated the nucleus.

You Try It
Look at the diagrams below and **interpret the data** to explain the results. Why is the final cap like the one from which the nucleus was taken?

Nucleus

Nucleus

Thinking Lab
INTERPRET THE DATA

Purpose
Students will describe the function of the nucleus in the cell.

Teaching Strategies
- Before students read the lab, ask them to speculate about what might happen to a protozoan that had its nucleus removed.

Answers
The nucleus directs cap production. The first cap was an intermediate type because the cytoplasm still contained cap-producing substances from the original nucleus. The second cap grew after the original cap-producing substances were used up.

✔ Assessment
Portfolio: Ask students to make diagrams in their portfolios of their speculations about interchanging nuclei between various cells.

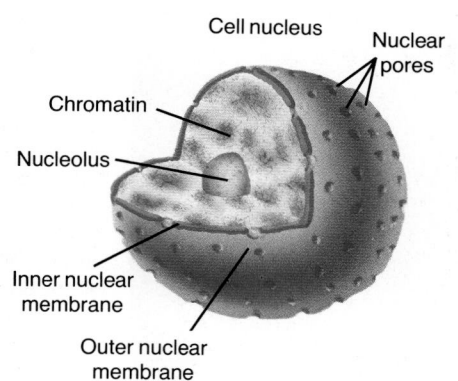

SECTION 5.2

Using Science Terms

Write the word *chromatin* on the chalkboard and ask the students if they know what the word means. Tell them that *chromatin* means color. Biologists didn't know what chromatin's function was, so they called it chromatin because it was a cell part that stained a dark color. **LEP**

Other Eukaryotic Cell Structures

In addition to the organelles discussed above, some eukaryotic cells contain additional organelles, such as plastids and lysosomes. The use of new, high-voltage electron microscopes has increased our understanding of other cell structures and led to the discovery of some new ones, including parts that help cells move.

Plastids While all eukaryotic cells have mitochondria, a nucleus, ribosomes, ER, and Golgi bodies, only certain cells of some plants and algae contain organelles called plastids. Some plastids are used to store lipids and starches, whereas others contain pigments. The most common pigment-containing plastids are **chloroplasts.** Chloroplasts contain chlorophyll and other pigments required for photosynthesis. Remember, only those plant cells that actually carry out photosynthesis contain chloroplasts. A chloroplast consists of a double membrane surrounding an interior filled with liquid and numerous internal membranes. During photosynthesis, the internal membranes trap light energy, which is used to produce simple sugars or other organic molecules.

Figure 5-12 The nucleus contains chromatin and a nucleolus. It communicates with the rest of the cell through pores in the outer membrane. Magnification: 1750×

Figure 5-13 A chloroplast is a double-walled organelle found in plants and some algae. The internal membranes of a chloroplast trap sunlight used in photosynthesis. Magnification: 40 000×

Concept Development

Explain to the students that prior to the development of the electron microscope in the 1930s, the structures of most of the cell parts were not clearly visible. The biologists referred to the objects they saw in the cells that they could not distinguish clearly as "inclusion bodies" because they were cell parts that were included inside the cell.

Teacher FYI

Chloroplasts, like prokaryotic cells, contain a single circular chromosome of DNA. Chloroplasts and mitochondria can grow, duplicate their DNA, and reproduce. Also, chloroplasts cannot be manufactured by the cell. These facts help to support the endosymbiotic hypothesis.

PROJECT

Cell Model: Give students directions for building a three-dimensional model of a cell. This project should be started after completion of Section 5.2. Direct students to use household materials that do not easily rot or break down. Some items to use are soda straws, thread, beads, and polystyrene. The cell model should have a cell wall and/or membrane and nucleus as well as any other five parts the students choose. The organelles should be made as close to scale as possible. Students can use their text to get an idea of the relative sizes of cell parts. A key should be placed on the model and list (a) which materials represent which organelles, (b) the amount of time spent on the model, and (c) student name. **L1** **COOP LEARN**

SECTION 5.2

Using Science Terms

Write the word *lysosome* on the chalkboard and underline the words *lyso* and *some*. Write the word *loosening* under *lyso* and *body* under *some*. Explain that the two parts of the word describe the chemical property of the lysosome. Have students figure out what the word *lysosome* means (a body that dissolves). Ask the students what they think the lysosome dissolves and how it fits the definition using the translation of the root words. **L1** | **LEP**

Figure 5-14 An *Amoeba* traps food and takes it in by phagocytosis. Phagocytosis continues as lysosomes fuse with vesicles containing food and release digestive enzymes to break food down. Magnification: 80×

Lysosomes   Remember the process of phagocytosis described in Chapter 4? Phagocytosis is the means by which cells like *Amoeba* trap and take in food. That food must be digested before the cell can make use of the glucose, amino acids, and other substances the food contains. Organelles called **lysosomes** are vesicles formed from the Golgi bodies. Lysosomes contain digestive enzymes that break down food. For example, as *Amoeba* takes in food by phagocytosis, the food is enclosed in a vesicle (sometimes called a food vacuole). A lysosome fuses with the vesicle and releases digestive enzymes into it. The enzymes break the food down into smaller molecules, such as amino acids and glucose, which can diffuse across the vacuole's membrane and out into the cytoplasm. What do you think happens to the amino acids? How are they used? What about the glucose? Lysosomes are also used to digest worn out cell parts. Their components may be recycled or digested to provide energy. Lysosomes are found mostly in animal or animal-like cells.

The segregation of digestive enzymes within lysosomes is an example of the importance of enclosing certain chemicals and reactions within membranes. If lysosomes were to break open, the enzymes released could destroy the entire cell. The cell is protected from the digestive enzymes by the lysosome's membrane.

Vacuoles   Cells often produce substances that are stored for later use. **Vacuoles** are fluid-filled, membrane-bound structures that store these substances. Many vacuoles act as cellular reservoirs for food, water, and minerals. In plant cells, small vacuoles merge to form a single, large vacuole, which nearly fills the mature cell. Many unicellular freshwater protists have unique contractile vacuoles, so named because as they contract they act as pumps for removing excess water. A contractile vacuole is an example of an adaptation for maintaining osmotic balance in a freshwater environment.

Figure 5-15 In plant cells, vacuoles merge to form a single, large vacuole that contains digestive enzymes, amino acids, carbohydrates, and cellular waste products. Magnification: 7800×

132 INSIDE THE CELL

Cytoskeleton   Proteins in a cell are also used in the manufacture of long, thin structures that give shape and support to the cell. These structures are referred to as the cytoskeleton. The cytoskeleton provides a framework for the cell, much as your bony skeleton provides the framework for your body.

One structure of the cytoskeleton, called a **microfilament,** is composed of the proteins actin and myosin. Microfilaments are found in many types of eukaryotic cells. In addition to providing structural support, microfilaments assist in cell movement. For example, they make it possible for you to use your muscles. When you stretch an arm or bend a knee, your muscles contract. Your muscles depend on microfilaments to make those contractions. Microfilaments are also involved in changing the shapes of cells and in the movement of some unicellular organisms, such as *Amoeba.*

Another structure of the cytoskeleton is called a **microtubule,** which is usually longer and thicker than a microfilament. Some microtubules extend all the way from the center of the cell, near the nucleus, to the area just inside the cell membrane. These microtubules help certain organelles to move from place to place within the cell. Vesicles and mitochondria, for example, travel along microtubule "tracks" rather than just drift through the cytoplasm.

Figure 5-16   The cytoskeleton of eukaryotic cells is not stable, but is always being assembled and disassembled. The cytoskeleton of a cell can be seen in this specially treated photograph. Magnification: 1100×

Centrioles

Chromosomes

Figure 5-17   In cells of animals and some algae and fungi, two pairs of centrioles play a role in cell division.

Centrioles   Microtubules also serve as components of some organelles. For example, cells of animals and some algae and fungi contain two pairs of **centrioles,** which play an important role in cell reproduction. Each centriole is composed of sets of microtubules arranged to form a cylinder. Figure 5-17 shows how centrioles function in cell division.

Cilia and Flagella   Microtubules play yet another role in the cell. They are an important component of two cell parts that are involved in motion of the cell. **Cilia** and **flagella** are flexible projections that extend outward from the cell, though they are still surrounded by the cell membrane. Flagella are longer than cilia and fewer in number. The arrangements of microtubules in cilia, flagella, and centrioles are very similar.

5.2 FUNCTIONS AND INTERACTIONS OF CELL PARTS **133**

Misconception

Students may have difficulty distinguishing between the microfilaments and microtubules. Explain that microfilaments are solid and thread-like while microtubules are hollow and tube-shaped.

Using an Analogy

To help students better understand the role of the cytoskeleton, ask them if they have ever seen the scaffolding used inside a building that is being remodeled. Tell them that sometimes the scaffolding is held in place by thick wires, ropes, or small boards attached to the main scaffolding. Explain that the scaffolding is similar in structure and function to the microtubules in the cell; the wires, ropes, or small boards attached to the scaffolding are similar to the structure and function of the microfilaments in a cell. Have students compare the microfilaments and microtubules in Figure 5-16 with a scaffold on a building being remodeled. Ask them which parts appear to be thicker and why. (Microtubules are, because they control the shape of the cell.) [LEP]

Using Science Terms

Write the word *centriole* on the chalkboard and ask the students what word in the English language sounds similar to *centriole* (*center*). Tell them that the root word means "center." Biologists had observed centrioles adjacent to the nucleus, which was usually in the center of the cell, hence the name centrioles. [L1] [LEP]

New Microscope Developed in Japan: The acoustic microscope was developed by Japanese scientists to inspect minute electronic parts on the assembly line. It is a light microscope with an ultrasound probe. It is better than a conventional light microscope in that the cells and tissues do not have to be stained; staining kills cells and stops all metabolic activity. This microscope emits sound waves through the cells and changes the returning sound waves into a visual picture of the cell. This new microscope will be useful in testing the reaction of cells to drugs or examining tissue without doing a biopsy or surgery. Ask students to find out more about how ultrasound works.

SECTION 5.2

Using an Analogy

Explain to students that the flagella on unicellular organisms cause movement through a fluid, similar to the way an airplane propeller moves an airplane forward in air. **LEP**

Using Science Terms

Have students find out what language the words *cilium* and *flagellum* are derived from (Latin). Have them use the meanings of the words to describe the properties of cilium (eyelash) and flagellum (whip). **L1**

Figure Caption Question

What are cilia made of? Cilia are made of microtubules.

Different Viewpoints in Biology

New Cell Organelle or a Protein?

Biologists Leonard Rowe and Nancy Kedersha may be responsible for adding a new cell organelle to Table 5.1 in the future. Researchers who reported on an eight-sided, barrel-shaped object seen in cells believed the object to be a protein. However, Rowe and Kedersha are convinced that this object is a cell organelle, rather than a protein. Rowe and Kedersha developed a technique to make the barrel-shaped object more visible for microscopic observation. They knew about eight-sided holes in the nuclear membrane through which molecules travel, so they reasoned that these eight-sided barrels could possibly carry materials such as RNA from the nucleus to the ribosomes. Until these objects are isolated from cells and studied, no one knows if they are new organelles or proteins floating in the cytoplasm of eukaryotic cells.

Figure 5-18 This *Paramecium* moves by the whiplike motion of its cilia. What are cilia made of? Magnification: 1500×

The whiplike motions of cilia or flagella enable unicellular organisms to move around in their environment. Cilia and flagella are also found in some cells of multicellular organisms. For example, portions of the cells that line your windpipe have numerous cilia. These cells do not move, but the motion of the cilia moves mucus up and out of your lungs. A sperm cell moves by means of a single flagellum.

Figure 5-19 illustrates generalized animal and plant cells. The drawings are based on observations made using an electron microscope. While such drawings are good for review of cell parts, keep in mind that they do not represent any particular cell. Cells vary in shape and size as well as the kind and number of organelles they contain. Table 5.1 lists the structures of eukaryotic cells and their functions.

Table 5.1 Eukaryotic Cell Structures

Structure	Found in Cells of	Functions
Cell wall	Plants; algae; fungi	Support; protection
Centrioles	Animals; some algae and fungi	Cell reproduction
Chloroplasts	Plants; algae	Photosynthesis
Cytoplasm	All eukaryotes	Metabolism
Endoplasmic reticulum	All eukaryotes	Intracellular transport of proteins (rough and smooth); smooth ER enzymes break down substances
Golgi bodies	All eukaryotes	Modification and packaging of some proteins; in plants, secretion and processing of carbohydrates
Lysosomes	Mainly animals or animal-like cells	Digestion within cells
Microfilaments	All eukaryotes	Movement; support
Microtubules	All eukaryotes	Movement; support
Mitochondria	All eukaryotes	Break down organic molecules to release energy for cell reactions
Nucleolus	All eukaryotes	Production of ribosomes
Nucleus	All eukaryotes	Control of cellular activities and reproduction
Plasma membrane	All eukaryotes	Boundary; regulates passage of materials into and out of cells
Ribosomes	All eukaryotes	Protein synthesis
Vacuoles	Most prominent in plants and algae	Storage, digestion, maintenance of osmotic balance

134 INSIDE THE CELL

STUDENT JOURNAL

Have students make a list of the cell parts in decreasing size starting with the largest and proceeding to the smallest. Tell them to use Figure 5-19 and other references to find answers. Have them list the number of each part they think is present in a cell. Have them explain why some cell parts are more numerous than others. **L1**

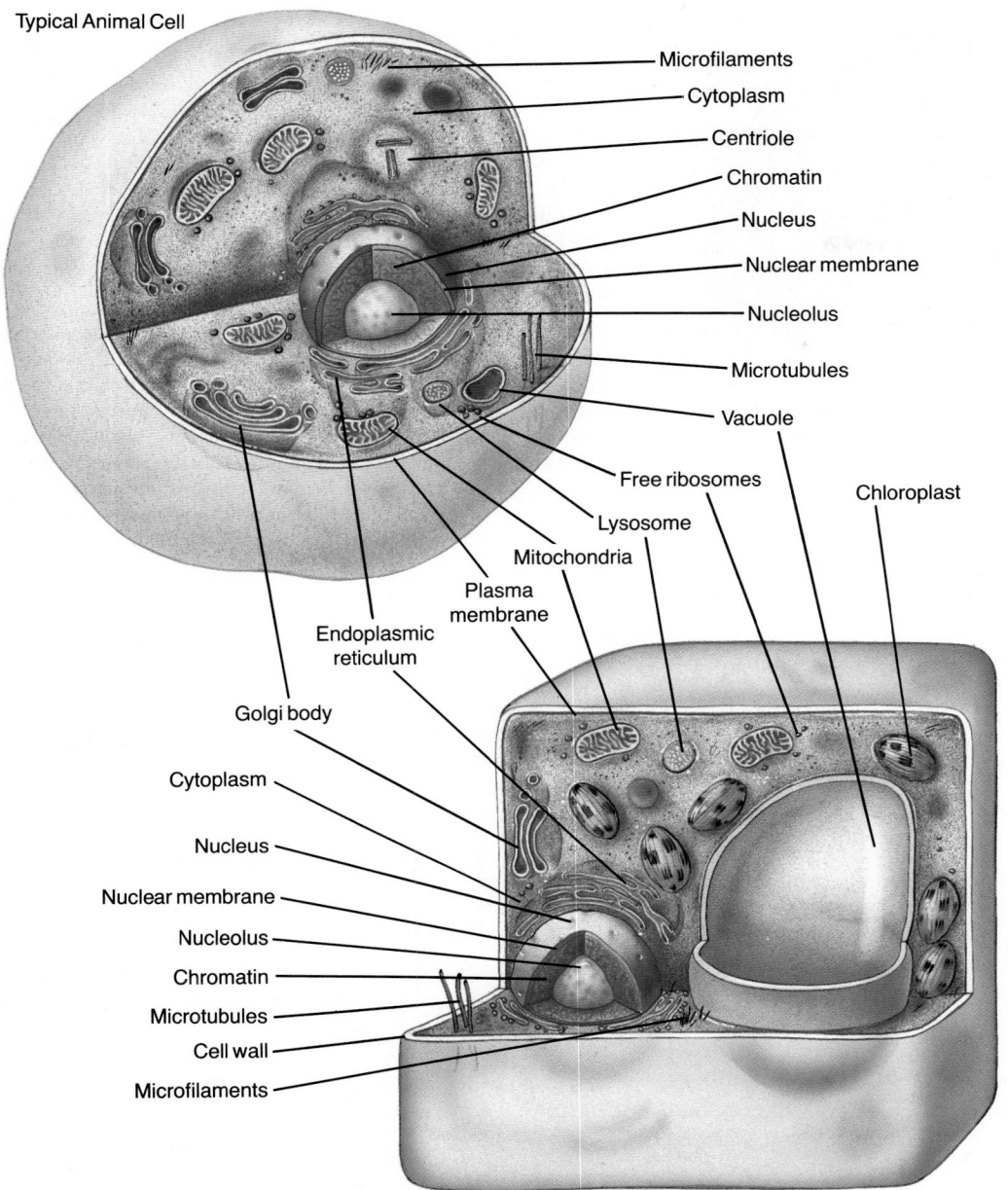

Typical Animal Cell

- Microfilaments
- Cytoplasm
- Centriole
- Chromatin
- Nucleus
- Nuclear membrane
- Nucleolus
- Microtubules
- Vacuole
- Free ribosomes
- Lysosome
- Mitochondria
- Plasma membrane
- Endoplasmic reticulum
- Golgi body
- Cytoplasm
- Nucleus
- Nuclear membrane
- Nucleolus
- Chromatin
- Microtubules
- Cell wall
- Microfilaments
- Chloroplast

Typical Plant Cell

Figure 5-19 **The structures of typical plant and animal cells show their similarities and differences.**

5.2 FUNCTIONS AND INTERACTIONS OF CELL PARTS ● **135**

Using the Illustration

Use Table 5.1 and Figure 5-19 to review the parts of the cell and their functions, and to describe their parts. Call on a student to name the cell part, describe its physical properties, location within the cell, and its function. Have students relate how the structure or other features of the organelle are important in carrying out its functions. **L1** **LEP**

Display

If you have commercial models of plant and animal cells, have students use the models to reinforce their understanding of the location of the cell parts. **LEP**

Bioethics

Selling Your Cells: A doctor removed a man's enlarged spleen. In culturing the cells of the spleen, he found that they produced a large amount of a protein that stimulates the growth of blood cells. After several years of research, a drug made from this protein was tested and found to bring the blood count to normal in several AIDS patients. The man who unknowingly donated the spleen to research now states that the doctor owes him money for his cells because the doctor signed a paper that stated the diseased spleen would be destroyed. The drug company that developed the new drug from the man's spleen would not have this drug if it were not for his spleen. Divide the class into two teams to debate whether patients should receive money for cells removed from their bodies that are used in research. Should the researchers be required to ask patients for permission to use their cells? **COOP LEARN**

STUDENT JOURNAL

Have students make their own sketch of the cell using Figure 5-19, other references, and cell models you may have in the classroom. Direct students to label organelles they put in their sketches. **L1** **LEP**

Figure 5-20 A lichen is an example of symbiosis between fungi cells and the cells of monerans or protists. Magnification: 67×

Evolution of Eukaryotes

Prokaryotes such as bacteria were the first organisms to evolve. As you have learned, these simple cells had no nucleus. They did have DNA, but it was in the form of a single, double-stranded, circular chromosome. Prokaryotes then and now are essentially the same. Today's bacteria lack a nucleus, but do have a single chromosome. These prokaryotes also lack organelles such as ER, Golgi bodies, and most of the other cell parts you have studied. Ribosomes, although present, are smaller than those of eukaryotic cells. Table 5.2 compares some of the features of prokaryotes and eukaryotes.

Symbiosis Scientists have combined logic and indirect evidence to piece together the puzzle of how eukaryotes might have evolved from prokaryotes. The most widely held model is called the symbiotic theory. It is based on the idea of **symbiosis,** a relationship in which two organisms live in close association. For example, certain bacteria living in a cow's intestine produce an enzyme that digests cellulose. Without the bacteria, the cow wouldn't be able to digest grass. Without the cow's intestine as a place to live, and cellulose and other foods provided by the cow, bacteria would die. Both the cow and the bacteria benefit from this symbiotic relationship.

Evidence for Symbiotic Theory The symbiotic theory states that sometime during evolution, prokaryotic cells were engulfed by other cells to become the ancestors of eukaryotes. That is, prokaryotic cells became the symbiotic partners of other cells, giving rise to the eukaryotic cells. Evidence for the symbiotic theory comes from the study of mitochondria and chloroplasts. Both these organelles contain their own DNA, RNA, and ribosomes. These structures seem to duplicate what is already present

Table 5.2 **Comparison of Prokaryotes and Eukaryotes**

Prokaryotes	Eukaryotes
no true nucleus or nuclear membrane	true nucleus and nuclear membrane
single circular chromosome of double-stranded DNA	several linear chromosomes of DNA and protein
no mitochondria, ER, Golgi bodies, lysosomes	mitochondria, ER, Golgi bodies, lysosomes
photosynthetic membrane, if present, not enclosed in organelle	photosynthetic membrane, if present, in chloroplasts
cell wall, if present, containing murein or other substances	cell wall, if present, containing cellulose or other substances
no microtubules in flagella	microtubules in flagella and cilia
smaller ribosomes	larger ribosomes

elsewhere in the cell. Why do mitochondria and chloroplasts have their own versions of these structures? It is thought that modern mitochondria and chloroplasts are what remains of what were once free-living prokaryotes. These prokaryotes were engulfed by and remained within other prokaryotes, forming a symbiotic relationship. If mitochondria and chloroplasts were once free-living, it makes sense that they would have equipment for synthesizing proteins and regulating their reproduction. Also, like the DNA of prokaryotes, the DNA of mitochondria and chloroplasts is circular, and their ribosomes are smaller. Furthermore, their enzymes for making nucleic acids and proteins are similar to those found in prokaryotes.

This model of the origin of eukaryotes is logical and appealing, but incomplete. How, for example, did the nuclear membrane, the various membrane-bound organelles, and all the other eukaryotic cell structures evolve? These questions have not yet been answered.

Figure 5-21 Prokaryotic cells do not have a nucleus, but they do have double-stranded DNA. The DNA of prokaryotes is found in a circle within the cell. Magnification: 6000×

LOOKING AHEAD

DIVISION OF LABOR is a characteristic of cells. Organelles and other cell parts carry out particular functions efficiently. Together, all the parts contribute to the survival of the cell, the basic unit of living systems. So far, the functions of the organelles have been identified, but not studied in detail. In the next chapter, you will explore two of those functions—cellular respiration and photosynthesis—in greater depth. You will learn how both processes are essential to an organism's ability to meet its energy requirements, and how the two processes are related.

Section Review

Understanding Concepts

1. A unicellular organism is discovered. It has DNA and ribosomes, but neither mitochondria nor ER. Is the cell a prokaryote or eukaryote? Explain.
2. Observing a photograph made using an electron microscope, a biologist sees what appears to be a small, saclike structure between the ER and a nearby Golgi body. What is the structure and what does it contain?
3. Why must digestion that occurs within a cell occur inside the food vacuole instead of in the cytoplasm?
4. *Skill Review—Classifying:* Divide cell parts into two categories—those found in all eukaryotic cells and those present in only some eukaryotic cells. List the function(s) of each part. For more help, see Organizing Information in the **Skill Handbook**.
5. *Thinking Critically:* Based on your answer to question 4, explain why eukaryotes have the parts in common that they do.

5.2 FUNCTIONS AND INTERACTIONS OF CELL PARTS **137**

Answers to Section Review

1. The cell is a prokaryote because it lacks membrane-bound organelles.
2. The sac, a vesicle, contains proteins being transported from the ER and Golgi body.
3. The membrane prevents the enzymes used in digestion from digesting molecules of the cell itself.
4. **Skill Review—Classifying:** Parts in all eukaryotic cells: plasma membrane, nucleus, ribosomes, ER, cytoplasm, Golgi bodies, microfilaments, microtubules, mitochondria. Parts in some eukaryotic cells: cell wall, chloroplasts, centrioles, lysosomes, vacuoles.
5. **Thinking Critically:** The parts in common are those necessary for essential functions.

SECTION 5.2

3 Assess

Check for Understanding
Have students use their journal entries about cell parts. Ask students specific questions that lead to matching cell organelles with their functions, sizes, and shapes. If done orally, you could place students in small cooperative groups so they have access to information in two to three journals. **L1** **COOP LEARN**

Reteach
Students who are still confused about the function of cell parts and the relationship to size and shape can be asked to review cell parts in small groups by using Table 5.1, Figure 5-19, and models of cells you have in the classroom. **LEP** **COOP LEARN**

Extension
Provide students with an opportunity to design their own cell with the same organelles as those listed in this section. Tell them they may use any shape, size, and number of parts they wish. Have each student write a page describing his or her new cell. **L3**

✔ Assessment
Skill: Have students develop a concept map for this section using all of the cell parts. Tell them to use their journals, portfolios, and texts for this information. Make sure they connect lines to show relationships between the different cell parts. You can give students a grade based on how well they tied the concepts together. **L1**

4 Close

Discussion
Tell the students to close their texts and open their minds for a review of the cell parts. Give them the name of a cell part or function and ask them to give you the response requested in return. Also ask them why biologists are reluctant to call the cytoplasm a cell organelle.

BIOLOGY, TECHNOLOGY, AND SOCIETY

Biotechnology

Purpose

This feature can be used to reinforce the concept of tissues and organs because skin is the largest organ in the body.

Background

Students should understand that researchers have developed a procedure to grow large sheets of skin from small amounts of skin from a burn patient. Skin from a close relative or another person was used to replace burned skin in the past, but skin grafts of this type did not always grow because the body of the person who received the transplant usually rejected it. Students should understand that the knowledge gained in the research lab today often results in useful products in the future.

Teaching Strategies

Tell students to read the assignment prior to coming to class and prepare answers to these questions.

1. Why is skin considered an organ?
2. How many layers of skin are there?
3. What other kinds of tissue are found in the epidermis? Dermis?
4. What is the function of each layer of skin?
5. Infer why the upper epidermis is dead skin.
6. Infer why the lower epidermis is considered to be alive.
7. Why was the artificial skin placed in a medium of proteins and nutrients similar to blood?

Possible Answers

1. To replace scars from moles or other growths that have been removed as well as from operations or accidents.
2. Research with animals closely related to humans has provided the medical community with useful technology that has saved lives or corrected defects in humans.

BIOLOGY, TECHNOLOGY, AND SOCIETY

Biotechnology

Culturing Artificial Skin

On a warm July day in 1983, life changed suddenly for two brothers, Jamie and Glen Selby, ages five and six. The boys were using a solvent to remove paint from their bodies when the solvent ignited. By the time the flames were extinguished, Jamie and Glen had suffered third-degree burns over nearly 90 percent of their bodies.

The prognosis for the two Wyoming boys was grim. Skin is the body's first defense against injury and infection. When both the outer and inner layers of the skin are burned away, as they are in third-degree burns, bacteria and other harmful organisms have access to the body's systems. Doctors expected Jamie and Glen to develop massive infections, go into shock, and die.

That's not what happened, however. The brothers were airlifted to the Shriners Burn Institute in Boston, Massachusetts, where nickel-sized pieces of their unburned skin were cultured into thin sheets of epithelial cells. This artificial skin was grafted onto the boys' burned bodies where it grew and formed new, permanent skin.

The Structure of Skin   How is artificial skin produced? Skin has two layers of cells: the dermis, which is the thick, inner layer; and the epidermis, the thin, outer layer. The dermis is made up of connective tissue. Within the dermis are oil and sweat glands, hair follicles, blood vessels, and nerves.

The epidermis consists of 20 layers of scalelike epithelial cells. These cells, called keratinocytes, are produced in the basal area of the epidermis. As new keratinocytes are produced by mitosis, the older cells begin dehydrating and dying as they are pushed upward toward the skin's surface. Finally, these cells are shed.

Growing Epidermis   The process of culturing artificial skin begins with some type of culture medium on which the skin cells can grow. Keratinocytes are placed onto the medium and washed with a liquid mixture of proteins and nutrients similar to those found in the blood vessels of the dermis.

The keratinocytes divide and multiply. Eventually, a thin layer of epidermis is formed, and the sheet of artificial skin is ready for use.

Problems Yet to Be Overcome

There remain hurdles to be overcome before the use of artificial skin as a replacement for burned skin is perfected. For example, artificial skin is quite fragile—bacteria can attack and dissolve artificial epidermis.

Artificial skin can set off the body's immune response. If the skin has been cultured from cells from another donor, chances are the body will reject the new skin.

Nevertheless, the promise of artificial skin is quite real. Jamie and Glen Selby, and thousands of burn victims like them, are proof that tissue culturing has become much more than just an experimental procedure. It's a lifesaver.

1. **Explore Further:** What other applications exist for commercially produced artificial skin?
2. **Issue:** Should animals be used to test the effectiveness of artificial skin as a treatment for severe burns?

Going Further

Find out how pig skin was used to help burn patients recuperate before the development of artificial skin.   **L2**

Don't Let the Sun Catch You Fryin'

During the Victorian era in the late 19th and early 20th centuries, no woman of manners and social standing ever would have exposed her skin to the sun's rays. Wide-brimmed hats and parasols were considered essential accessories for a woman on any sunny day.

By the middle of the 20th century, however, sunbathing had gained popularity as a favorite leisure pastime. A well-bronzed complexion was considered a sure sign of health and vitality among whites, and hats and parasols were exchanged for sunglasses and sun-tan oils.

Today, however, the "cult of the sun" finally may be coming to an end. The incidence of malignant melanoma, a virulent and often fatal skin cancer, continues to rise dramatically. In the United States today, 32 000 people are diagnosed with melanoma, and 6000 people die from it, each year. By the year 2000, some researchers estimate that one in 90 Americans will develop this disease. A major culprit, scientists agree, is ultraviolet radiation from the sun.

Two different wavelengths of light cause damage to the skin. Ultraviolet A (UVA) is long-wavelength solar radiation that penetrates the epidermis and travels down to the dermis. There, UVA attacks two proteins, collagen and elastin, which give skin a smooth, supple look. UVA destroys these proteins, and the result is wrinkled, sagging skin.

Ultraviolet B (UVB) is shorter-wavelength solar radiation that does its damage in the epidermis. UVB rays destroy certain DNA bonds in the nuclei of cells called keratinocytes. Although these cells have the ability to repair their destroyed DNA, sometimes a cell rearranges the repaired genetic material incorrectly. The result is a damaged cell that may begin multiplying uncontrollably, leading to skin cancer.

Although scientists agree that solar radiation is the cause of most skin cancers, there is some disagreement about why skin cancer, particularly malignant melanoma, has suddenly become so prevalent.

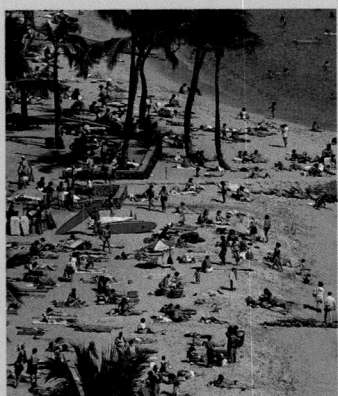

Many scientists blame the ozone layer, which blocks much harmful solar radiation. As polluting gaseous chemicals, such as chlorofluorocarbons, rise up into the atmosphere, they destroy part of the ozone layer, allowing greater amounts of solar radiation to strike Earth.

Other scientists are skeptical of this hypothesis, claiming instead that the rise in skin cancers can be tied to lifestyle changes. More people are spending more time outdoors, often wearing less clothing than they did in the past. The result is increased exposure to UV radiation.

Despite some differences of opinion, scientists do agree on ways to prevent skin cancers. You can reduce your exposure to the sun, and use specially formulated sunscreens with sun protection factor (SPF) numbers of 30 or above. Protecting yourself *from* the sun, it seems, is the only sure way to prevent damage—potentially fatal damage—*by* the sun.

Understanding the Issue
1. Many people still consider a tan both healthy and glamorous. What are some ways these perceptions might be changed?
2. Do you think it's okay to sunbathe as long as you use sunscreens? Explain your reasoning.

Readings
- Saltus, Richard. "Genetic Damage and Skin Cancer." *Technology Review*, February-March 1992, pp. 11-12.
- Fischman, Ben. "Sun: Let the Fryer Beware." *Science World*, May 1991, pp. 4-6.

CAREER CONNECTION

If you enjoy solving mysteries, a career in cytology may be right for you. A **cytologist** discovers and analyzes previously unknown cell structures. Cytologists specialize in the study of plant cells and animal tissue to increase their understanding of the basic unit of all life—the cell.

CAREER CONNECTION

Contact a cytologist at the laboratory of a local hospital, university, or biological research laboratory. He or she can connect you to a network that will give you career information. Some laboratories provide on-the-job training for entry-level medical technician aides.

Going Further
1. Find out why sunscreen has different numbers and the relationship of the numbers to the skin tone and length of exposure. **L1**
2. Find out how sunscreen can work if it appears transparent when rubbed on the skin. **L2**

CHAPTER 5

Issues

Purpose
This feature can be used to reinforce how the environment can cause damage to an important organ—the skin. The new knowledge the students learned about culturing artificial skin allows them to apply their knowledge of the living layer of the epidermis, the keratinocytes. They will see that even scientists disagree about the cause of the increase in skin cancer. This reinforces the idea that disagreement among scientists leads to more experimentation.

Teaching Strategies
Tell students to read the assignment prior to coming to class and prepare answers to these questions.
1. What part of a cell is changed by UV light to cause skin cancer?
2. Why is there disagreement among scientists as to the cause of skin cancer?
3. How could scientists find out which of the two hypotheses is correct?
4. Find a source of statistics that shows the rate of skin cancer among lighter- and darker-skinned people. State which shows a higher incidence and find out why this is true.
5. How does the answer to the above question show what some scientists believe or do not believe about skin cancer?

Possible Answers
1. If there is an increase in skin cancer among people who spend their time in the sun with unprotected skin, people may change their attitude about the relationship of excessive exposure of the skin to sunlight and skin cancer.
2. You may not reduce the possibility of getting skin cancer but you may reduce the probability of getting skin cancer.

CHAPTER REVIEW

Summary

Summary statements can be used by students to review the major concepts of the chapter.

Language of Biology

Answers should go beyond defining the terms. Accept any reasonable answer that uses the term correctly and in the proper context.

Understanding Concepts

1. Muscles must receive a "signal" from a nerve in order to contract.
2. The part is an organ because it is composed of several different types of tissues.
3. A root cell has no chloroplasts. Chloroplasts are found in photosynthetic cells only.
4. Ribosomes would be abundant at the site of the synthesis of the proteins. ER, Golgi bodies, and vesicles would also be numerous.
5. Protein synthesis begins on free ribosomes and is completed on ribosomes of rough ER. The protein enters the rough ER and is passed to a Golgi body in a vesicle. As the protein passes from one Golgi sac to another, it is chemically altered for packaging in a final vesicle. The vesicle moves to the plasma membrane, where it is expelled by exocytosis.
6. Mitochondria would be required because energy is needed for the beating of the flagella.
7. microfilaments
8. Ribosomes are essential for synthesis of proteins, which are needed by all cells.

Applying Concepts

9. The bacterium is brought into the white blood cell by phagocytosis and digested within a food vacuole. The enzymes needed for digestion were made on ribosomes, passed through the ER and a Golgi body, and packaged in a lysosome. Undigestible parts are expelled by exocytosis.

Summary

Multicellular organisms evolved from versatile unicellular ancestors. As they did so, their cells became specialized and interdependent.

Cells of multicellular organisms work together in increasingly complex levels of organization. Thus, the entire organism, as well as each of its many cells, benefits from division of labor.

Division of labor in eukaryotes is made possible by the many organelles and cell parts of the cytoplasm. These parts provide for separate environments within the cell, each performing its own particular function, but working together to maintain the life of the cell.

Prokaryotes, the first cells to evolve, are very simple in structure, lacking the complexity of their eukaryotic descendants. The symbiotic model suggests how evolution of eukaryotes from prokaryotes might have occurred.

Language of Biology

Write a sentence that shows your understanding of each of the following terms.

centriole	microfilament
chloroplast	microtubule
chromatin	mitochondria
chromosome	nucleoli
cilia	nucleus
cytoplasm	organ
endoplasmic reticulum	prokaryote
eukaryote	ribosome
flagella	symbiosis
Golgi body	system
lysosome	tissue
metabolism	vacuole

Understanding Concepts

1. Nerves and muscles are two kinds of specialized cells in animals. How do muscles depend upon nerves?
2. You dissect a part of an animal and find it contains nerves, muscles, and epithelium. What is the level of organization of the part?
3. In answer to a quiz question, a student identifies the parts of a root cell: cell wall, cytoplasm, chloroplast, and nucleus. What is incorrect in that answer? Explain.
4. What organelles would be especially numerous in a cell specialized for secreting a protein hormone?
5. Based on your answer to question 4, outline the steps that would occur to produce and secrete that hormone.
6. Sperm cells must swim to an egg. What kind of internal organelle would sperm cells require in large numbers? Why?
7. When an animal cell reproduces, the parent cell membrane pinches in, and eventually the cell breaks in two. What cell structure might play a role in this pinching-in process?
8. Explain why bacteria can survive without membrane-bound organelles, but not without ribosomes.

Applying Concepts

9. A white blood cell in your body engulfs a bacterium and digests it. By what process is the bacterium brought into the cell? Where and how is it digested? Where were the enzymes needed for digestion produced and packaged? How would the undigestible parts of the bacterium be expelled from the white blood cell?
10. Can you suggest a reason why large pores are present in the nuclear membrane but absent in the plasma membrane?

---

10. Large pores are necessary for passage of complex molecules, such as RNA, from the nucleus to the cytoplasm.
11. Consumers must digest food. They cannot make it as producers can.
12. cellular respiration
13. Bursting of lysosomes would release enzymes that might digest and destroy cells of which they are a part.
14. Most reactions occur in the cytoplasm. Because they lack organelles and division of labor, prokaryotes are less efficient.
15. Such grafts would not be rejected. If too much time were required, it would probably be worth the risk to use artificial skin from cells cultured from another donor in order to try to prevent infection. Perhaps time could be bought until artificial skin made from the person's own cells could be produced.
16. The friend may be healthy now, but his or her tan indicates exposure to sunlight, a known cause of skin cancer.

11. Why are lysosomes found mainly in cells of consumers?

12. Other than protein synthesis and reproduction, what other single basic function must all prokaryotes be able to perform?

13. Can you explain how lysosomes might be related to the aging process? (Hint: What might go wrong?)

14. Given that prokaryotes have no membrane-bound organelles, where do you suppose most of their chemical reactions are carried out? Compare their efficiency to that of eukaryotes.

15. **Biotechnology:** Why would it be an advantage for burn victims to receive skin grafts of artificial skin grown from their own skin cells? Would your answer be different if it took a long time to grow enough new skin to cover the burned areas?

16. **Issues:** Your best friend jogs, drinks a lot of water, eats a balanced vegetarian diet, gets enough sleep, doesn't smoke, and has a nice tan. Is your friend healthy? Why?

Lab Interpretation

17. **Investigation:** The following are microscopic fields of view. Estimate the sizes of the objects in these diagrams. Explain how you got your answers.

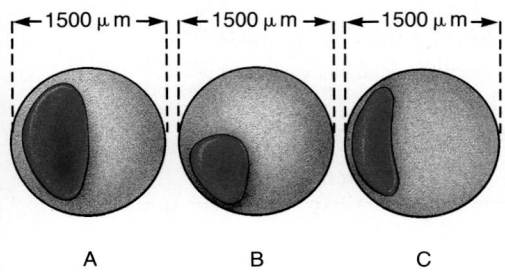

A   B   C

18. **Thinking Lab:** Examine the diagrams of the cells below. Predict what might happen if the cells are recombined as indicated. Draw diagrams of what the resulting cells might look like.

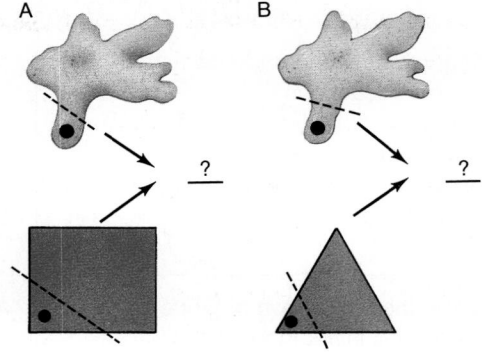

19. **Minilab 1:** You are trying to classify some protozoans and need to know whether they have cilia or flagella. They move very fast, and even slowing them with methyl cellulose does not allow you to make this determination. What could you do to determine if they have cilia?

Connecting Ideas

20. *Paramecium* is a unicellular, freshwater protist. What osmotic problem does it face? What organelle would you expect it has to solve that problem?

21. Some biologists think that the membranes inside eukaryotic cells might have evolved from parts of the cell membrane that broke off and moved inside the cell. What evidence would support that hypothesis?

Lab Interpretation

17. A. 750 micrometers; B. 575 micrometers; C. 500 micrometers. Estimate what portion of the diameter of the field of view the object covers; then calculate the estimate by multiplying this fraction by the diameter of the field of view.

18. Answers will vary, but in general the cell should look like a combination of the two cells.

19. You could use the stain, Lugol's solution, as it stains cilia.

Connecting Ideas

20. **Uses of Energy:** *Paramecium* faces the problem of taking in water by osmosis. Using energy, its contractile vacuole can pump out the water that enters.

21. **Unity Within Diversity:** All membranes of a cell have the same basic fluid mosaic structure. Study of cells shows that a membrane of one organelle may become part of another, such as a vesicle from ER joining with the membrane of a Golgi body or a lysosome's membrane becoming part of the plasma membrane as exocytosis occurs.

PROGRAM RESOURCES

Teacher Classroom Resources
Chapter Assessment, pp. 17-20 **L1**
Performance Assessment in Biology, p. 10 **L2**
Alternate Assessment in the Science Classroom
Computer Test Bank **L1**

SECTION	OBJECTIVES	TEXT LABS/FEATURES
6.1 Energy for Cells (3 days)	**Distinguish** between endergonic and exergonic reactions. **Explain** how ATP is used in linking exergonic and endergonic reactions in cells. **Compare** the processes of aerobic respiration and fermentation.	**Minilab 1:** Can you detect energy released by a biological reaction? p. 147 **Investigation:** Optimum Temperature, p. 148 **Leisure Connection:** Hitting the Wall, p. 150
6.2 Photosynthesis (3 days)	**Describe** the interaction of white light with objects including chlorophyll molecules. **Relate** the events of the light reactions to those of the Calvin cycle in photosynthesis. **Analyze** the relationship between photosynthesis and cellular respiration.	**Minilab 2:** Under what conditions do plants take up CO_2? p. 155 **Thinking Lab:** Does light color influence the rate of photosynthesis? p. 156 **Economics Connection:** Yeasts: Raising Economic Dough, p. 158
BIOLOGY, TECHNOLOGY, AND SOCIETY		**Biotechnology:** Enlightened Product Testing Using Bioluminescence, p. 162 **Considering the Environment:** Alternative Sources of Energy, p. 162 **Career Connection:** Biochemist, p. 163

LAB MATERIALS

INVESTIGATION	MINILAB	ALTERNATE LAB
page 148 beaker hot plate oven mitts pipettes sucrose test tubes thermometer washers, steel yeast	**page 147** apron goggles hydrogen peroxide liver, fresh newspapers test tubes test-tube rack thermometer **page 155** apron bromthymol blue *Elodea* sprig goggles plastic wrap rubber bands test tubes vinegar	**page 154** beakers, 400-mL *Coleus* plant colored pencils dish, shallow ethanol forceps hot plate iodine solution waxed paper

TEACHER CLASSROOM RESOURCES	OTHER RESOURCES
Study Guide, pp. 31-32 **Exploring Environmental Issues:** *Water, Water Everywhere?* pp. 1-2; *Is It Getting Hot in Here?* pp. 7-8 ***PLL:** *Measurement of Chemical Energy in Food,* p. 30 ***PLL:** *Yeast Fermentation,* p. 32 ****ILS:** *Cell Energy,* p. 53 ****ILS:** *Factors Influencing the Rate of Yeast Respiration,* p. 57	***STVS:** *Farming Indoors,* Plants and Simple Organisms (Disc 4, Side 2) **Color Transparency 6:** *Glycolysis and Fermentation* **Color Transparency 7:** *Aerobic Respiration*
Study Guide, pp. 33-36 **Concept Mapping,** p. 6 **Critical Thinking/Problem Solving:** *Two Factors Affecting Photosynthesis,* p. 6 ***PLL:** *Analysis of Plant Pigments,* p. 35 ***PLL:** *Some Aspects of Photosynthesis,* p. 37 ****ILS:** *Influencing the Rate of Photosynthesis,* p. 61 ****ILS:** *Chloroplast Pigment Analysis,* p. 65	***STVS:** *Detecting Climate Changes in Tree Rings,* Plants and Simple Organisms (Disc 4, Side 2) **Color Transparency 8:** *Photosynthesis and Aerobic Respiration*
Assessment Materials **Chapter Assessment,** pp. 21-24 **Performance Assessment in Biology,** p. 12 **Alternate Assessment in the Science Classroom** **Computer Test Bank**	**Spanish Resources** **Cooperative Learning Resource Guide** **Videodisc Correlations** (to Optical Data's and Videodiscovery's videodiscs)

* **Probing Levels of Life**
** **Investigating Living Systems**

* **Science Technology Videodisc Series**

Key to Teaching Strategies

The following designations will help you decide which activities in the teacher margin are appropriate for your students.

L1 Level 1 activities should be within the ability range of all students.

L2 Level 2 activities should be within the ability range of the average to above-average student.

L3 Level 3 activities are designed for the ability range of above-average students.

LEP LEP activities are appropriate for Limited English Proficiency students.

COOP LEARN Cooperative Learning activities are designed for small group work.

ADDITIONAL RESOURCES

Infinite Voyage *The Champion Within*
Why do some people stay fit as they age whereas others don't? Students will learn about energy and the human body in this video.

Audiovisual
Photosynthesis and Respiration, video, Frey Scientific.
The Isolation and Metabolism of Mitochondria, video, Films for the Humanities and Sciences.

Software
Photosynthesis: Unlocking the Power of the Sun, Apple II/IBM, Thoroughbred.
Respiration, Apple II/TRS-80 Model III, J and S.

6

THE FLOW OF ENERGY

Chapter Overview

As the chapter begins, students study the concept of free energy and learn to distinguish between endergonic and exergonic reactions. They find out that the free energy required for endergonic reactions in cells comes from exergonic reactions involving ATP.

Students then learn how ATP is replenished by the processes of aerobic respiration and fermentation and come to understand why more energy is released by the former than the latter.

Students next study light and find that we see colored objects because of reflected wavelengths while absorbed wavelengths are transformed to other forms of energy. This knowledge is applied to the role of chlorophyll and carotenoids in photosynthesis. Students will come to understand how the light reactions of photosynthesis prepare for the Calvin cycle and how photosynthesis and respiration are related.

THE FLOW OF ENERGY

PICTURE YOURSELF in a lush, wet, tropical rain forest like the one shown here. The hot sun is shining brightly on thick stands of tall trees. Small birds and mammals feed noisily in the canopy high above the jungle floor, and swarms of insects fill the air with an endless buzzing sound. The jungle is full of life! But tropical rain forests are not just things of beauty. And, to the billions of organisms living in rain forests, the huge, broad-leaved plants and trees provide more than a well-protected habitat. They also convert the sun's energy to energy that can be used by living things for movement, growth, and reproduction. In fact, plants in tropical rain forests convert a large portion of all the sun's energy converted by living organisms.

From the dry, hot deserts of Northern Africa to the dense pine forests of North America, all life depends on organisms that carry out photosynthesis. Through the process of photosynthesis, producers convert the energy of sunlight to chemical energy carried in organic molecules. Thus, this stored energy is passed through the food chains to all living organisms. The energy used by organisms to carry out their life processes can ultimately be traced to the biological work of producers. But how do organisms get this energy? In this chapter, you will investigate how organisms use the energy made available by photosynthesis to fuel their own processes and explore the vital process, photosynthesis, itself.

KEY TERMS

absorption spectrum	exergonic
aerobic respiration	free energy
	grana
alcoholic fermentation	lactic acid fermentation
anaerobic	light reactions
ATP	stroma
Calvin cycle	visible spectrum
carotenoid	wavelength
endergonic	

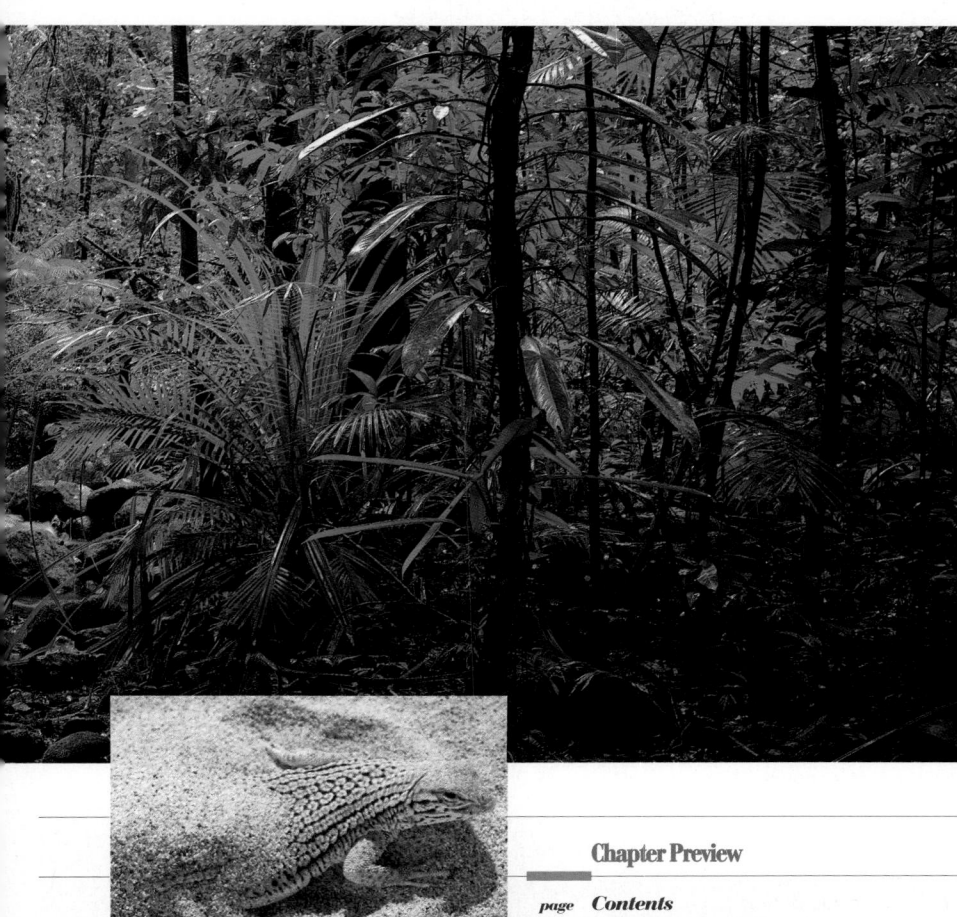

Introducing the Chapter

Have students study the photographs on pages 142 and 143. Ask them to list organisms that they would expect to find in a rain forest and a desert. Have them classify these organisms as producers or consumers. What is the source of energy for producers? For consumers? Ask students to predict a possible food chain in a rain forest and in a desert. Review the fundamental ways energy is used by all living systems in a community. **L1**

Theme Development

As the chapter title clearly implies, the major theme of the chapter is energy. Producers use light energy for photosynthesis. This energy is converted to chemical energy in the bonds of simple sugars and other molecules. Organisms release energy in those molecules and use it for life functions. The theme of unity within diversity is also exemplified. For example, nearly all organisms, both producers and consumers, use ATP as a source of energy for endergonic reactions.

Tying to Previous Knowledge

This chapter concludes the opening unit. Students will draw upon and expand their understanding of such concepts as photosynthesis, cellular respiration, food chains, the fact that matter is recycled and energy is not, basic chemistry, energy transformations, and the structure and functions of mitochondria and chloroplasts.

Compared to a rain forest, a desert has a very sparse supply of living things. However, just as in a rain forest, all organisms, including this desert lizard, rely on the work of photosynthesis to supply energy for life.

Chapter Preview

143

ASSESSMENT PLANNER

Choose assessment strategies from the following pages to evaluate the progress of your students.

Assess, pp. 151, 160-161
Portfolio, pp. 147, 149, 151, 160, 161
Alternate Lab, pp. 154-155
Thinking Lab, p. 156

Minilab 1, p. 147
Minilab 2, p. 155
Investigation, pp. 148-149
Chapter Review, pp. 164-165

Prepare

Key Concepts

Students will be introduced to exergonic and endergonic reactions, which will later be related to the ATP-ADP cycle. The processes of aerobic respiration and fermentation replenishing ATP will then be introduced.

Key Terms

free energy, endergonic, exergonic, ATP, aerobic respiration, anaerobic, lactic acid fermentation, alcoholic fermentation

Materials

- Purchase 3% hydrogen peroxide and a small piece of fresh liver for Minilab 1.
- Purchase yeast from your local supermarket.

1 Focus

Objectives

The objectives are listed on the student page. Remind students to preview these objectives as a guide to this numbered section.

Discussion

Ask students to respond to and discuss the following questions. Explain why most living things, including humans, need oxygen. What happens to the oxygen once it is in our lungs? Where does the CO_2 that we exhale come from and how is it produced? Students may not have ready answers for these questions. Use them to lead into the section.

Objectives

Distinguish between endergonic and exergonic reactions.

Explain how ATP is used in linking exergonic and endergonic reactions in cells.

Compare the processes of aerobic respiration and fermentation.

Figure 6-1 An exergonic process releases free energy. This energy is transformed to light by the caterpillar on the left in a process called bioluminescence. The skunk cabbage on the right carries out the endergonic process of photosynthesis. It also generates heat in an exergonic process. This heat melts the snow surrounding the plant.

6.1 Energy for Cells

Have you ever heard the loud booming of exploding fireworks on the Fourth of July or the crackling of a bolt of lightning in a thunderstorm? What do these events have in common? As you may have guessed, events such as these release enormous amounts of energy. What about playing a tape on your stereo, running a fan, or making toast in a toaster? These activities require energy. In the everyday world, activities that require energy get that energy from some energy-releasing event. For example, the energy that heats the coils in your toaster may have started out as the energy of water rushing through the turbine of an electric generator. Now let's see how energy-releasing and energy-absorbing events are linked in living things.

ATP

As you know, living organisms also require energy to function. You need energy to think just as a plant needs energy to grow, and as a dog needs energy to run. But where do living organisms get their energy? What are the energy-releasing events in the living world?

Free Energy As you learned in previous chapters, in order for organisms to carry out life processes, their cells must have energy available to do biological work. This energy available to do work is called **free energy.** For example, free energy is needed for the contraction of a muscle cell, the active transport of ions and molecules across a cell membrane, and the synthesis of proteins from single amino acids. Chemical reactions, such as these, that require free energy are called **endergonic** reactions.

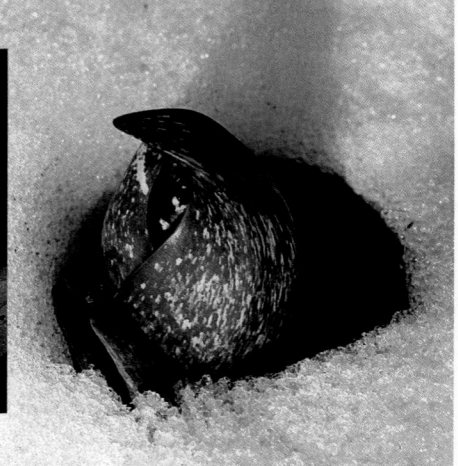

144 THE FLOW OF ENERGY

In Chapter 3, you learned that cellular reactions require enzymes to lower the activation energy needed to cause the reaction. However, endergonic reactions in organisms need more than just enzymes and activation energy. They also require an input of free energy because products of endergonic reactions have higher potential energy than the reactants.

Sources of Free Energy The free energy required for endergonic reactions must come from energy released by other chemical reactions in the cell. These energy-releasing reactions are called **exergonic** reactions. Because free energy cannot just "wait around" until it is needed, both exergonic and endergonic reactions must be linked together for a cell to carry out biological work.

In cells, most of the free energy to drive endergonic reactions comes from an exergonic reaction involving a molecule known as adenosine triphosphate, commonly called **ATP**. The structure of ATP is shown in Figure 6-2. ATP can be represented as A–P–P–P, where the A stands for the adenosine part of the molecule and –P–P–P represents three bonded phosphate groups.

Releasing Free Energy from ATP When the bond between two phosphate groups of ATP is broken, free energy is released. One type of exergonic (energy-releasing) reaction involving ATP is a hydrolysis reaction in which ATP reacts with water, the last phosphate group is broken off, and energy is released. The products of the reaction are adenosine diphosphate, ADP, which has only two phosphate groups, and free inorganic phosphate, P_i.

$$ATP + H_2O \rightarrow ADP + P_i + energy$$

The energy released in this reaction is used to produce heat in warm-blooded animals and to drive some processes, such as active transport. In another type of reaction, the phosphate group removed from ATP is attached to another molecule, raising the potential energy of that molecule.

Figure 6-2 **Hydrolyzing ATP to ADP and inorganic phosphate releases free energy. The reverse process stores free energy given off by other processes. This method of storing and releasing energy is called the ATP-ADP cycle. Why do you think that all successful life forms have both long-term and short-term mechanisms for storing energy?**

Adenine

Three phosphates
Ribose
Adenosine triphosphate (ATP)

Exergonic
Free energy released
+ H₂O
Endergonic
Free energy absorbed

Adenine

Two phosphates
Ribose
+ HO–P–OH
Inorganic phosphate
Adenosine diphosphate (ADP)

2 Teach

Brainstorming
Ask students to name chemical reactions that occur within the human body that require free energy. They can use the concepts and/or information described earlier in Chapter 3. Any reaction involving condensation is correct. Therefore, all reactions that form complex carbohydrates, proteins, or fats would be good examples. **L1** **COOP LEARN**

Using Science Terms
- Ask students to review or look up the meaning of the prefixes *end-* and *ex-*. *End-* is related to *endon*, meaning "inside," while *ex-* is related to *exo* meaning "outside." The root *ergon* is the Greek word meaning "work" or "energy." Have students explain in their own words how the words *endergonic* and *exergonic* reflect the meaning of their parts. **L1** **LEP**
- Ask students to correlate the meanings of the prefixes *di-* and *tri-* with the structural formulas for ATP and ADP. **L1** **LEP**

Figure Caption Question
Why do you think that all successful life forms have both long-term and short-term mechanisms for storing energy? Short-term storage (ATP) is needed to provide ready energy for biological processes. Long-term storage provides a reserve for times when food for respiration is not immediately available.

MEETING INDIVIDUAL NEEDS

Visually Impaired: Prepare cutout models of the component parts of ATP—one adenosine molecule and three phosphate groups. Use a jigsaw puzzle format so that parts can be interlocked. Have each part correctly labeled. Ask students to construct ATP and then convert it to ADP while describing the energy change taking place. **LEP**

STUDENT JOURNAL

Ask students to write a journal entry that reflects the changes that occur in an ATP molecule as it is converted to ADP. Emphasis should be on (a) how the potential energy changes when changing from ATP to ADP and back, (b) how the molecules are able to change back and forth, and (c) what function they have in the life of a cell. **L1**

Reinforcement

Use equation 1 on page 146 to illustrate the point that energy is released as ATP is changed to ADP. Use equation 2 to illustrate the point that energy is absorbed as glucose and fructose combine to form sucrose.

Brainstorming

Using the equation on page 147, ask students to answer the following questions.

(a) Which are the reactants?
(b) Which are the products?
(c) Why must there be 6 CO_2 and 6 H_2O molecules?
(d) What happens to the $38P_i$ molecules to the left of the arrow?
(e) Why does the equation represent an aerobic reaction?
(f) Where did the atoms of carbon present in carbon dioxide come from originally?
(g) Where do the molecules of CO_2 end up when this reaction occurs in your body? [L1] [COOP LEARN]

Figure 6-3 When plants make sucrose (table sugar) from glucose and fructose, an input of energy is required. That energy comes from the breakdown of ATP to ADP and inorganic phosphate.

Figure 6-4 All organisms require food molecules that can be broken down to release energy. In a bear, much of that energy is used to make fat molecules, which can be broken down to release heat and energy for body functions as the bear hibernates in winter.

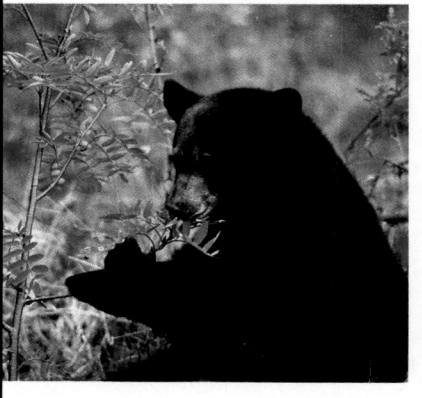

Linking Energy Release and Energy Use As an example of how ATP is used to link exergonic and endergonic reactions, consider a reaction in which glucose and fructose are combined to make the disaccharide sucrose. The making of sucrose is endergonic, because the product, sucrose, has more potential energy than the reactants, glucose and fructose. The reaction can be summarized in two main steps.

(1) ATP + glucose $\xrightarrow{\text{enzyme}}$ ADP + glucose – P

(2) glucose – P + fructose $\xrightarrow{\text{enzymes}}$ sucrose + P_i

Net: ATP + glucose + fructose $\xrightarrow{\text{enzymes}}$ sucrose + ADP + P_i

Do you see how one reaction is linked to the other? First, the attachment of phosphate to glucose transfers some of the potential energy of ATP to glucose. Next, the glucose phosphate combines with fructose to form sucrose and a free phosphate group. Thus, the energy from the conversion of ATP to ADP (an exergonic reaction) is used to form the chemical bond between glucose and fructose (an endergonic reaction). ATP seems to have evolved as a main energy link between exergonic and endergonic reactions, because the amount of free energy it transfers is suitable for most cellular reactions.

Respiration with Oxygen

As you just learned, after a molecule of ATP is used and energy is released, a molecule of ADP and inorganic phosphate remain. How do cells replenish the supply of ATP? Cells can maintain their supply of ATP by rejoining ADP and phosphate. But, a source of free energy is needed to bond the free phosphate to ADP and form a molecule of ATP. As you know, free energy must come from exergonic reactions. What are those reactions?

How ATP Is Replenished All organisms require food for energy. In animals, glucose is a food molecule commonly available as an energy source, although other molecules such as fatty acids can also be used. You have learned that the process by which the energy is made available for work is cellular respiration, an exergonic process. Now, let's refine our understanding of that process. During cellular respiration, some of the energy released by breaking the bonds of food molecules such as glucose is used to make ATP from ADP. These ATP molecules are then used as needed. Processes that require oxygen are called *aerobic processes.* Respiration in most cells makes use of oxygen and is called **aerobic respiration.**

Aerobic Respiration Aerobic respiration involves many reactions that follow one another in a particular sequence. The first several steps take place in the cell's cytoplasm. The products of the last of these early reactions move into the mitochondria, where the process called the citric acid cycle takes place. The process as a whole is exergonic. It can be summarized in the following equation.

$$C_6H_{12}O_6 + 6O_2 + 38ADP + 38\ P_i \xrightarrow{enzymes} 6CO_2 + 6H_2O + 38ATP$$
glucose oxygen   carbon water
           dioxide

This equation shows that aerobic respiration in some cells can release enough energy from a molecule of glucose to produce 38 ATP. Not all the steps of the process are exergonic, however. Early steps in the breakdown of glucose use the energy of two ATP. So, the maximum net ATP that can be produced is 36 molecules. ATP production from the breakdown of glucose is not always that efficient, however. Note that aerobic respiration does not produce 38 ATP in every cell. In general, about 39 percent of the energy available in glucose is transferred to molecules of ATP. The rest escapes as heat. More important than the exact number of ATP molecules produced, though, is this basic point: During cellular respiration, the energy of one glucose molecule is released bit by bit and transferred to many molecules of ATP.

Figure 6-5 summarizes the interrelationships among aerobic respiration, ATP, ADP, and the work of the cell. This series of chemical events is sometimes referred to as the ATP-ADP cycle. The diagram shows that during aerobic respiration, the energy of glucose is transferred to ADP and inorganic phosphate, forming ATP, which can then be used as a free energy source for cellular work.

Minilab 1

Can you detect energy released by a biological reaction?

Half fill a test tube with a 3 percent solution of hydrogen peroxide. **CAUTION:** *Wear goggles. Wash away any spills immediately with water.* Use a thermometer to take the temperature of the liquid in the tube. Add one or two small chunks of fresh liver to the tube. Observe what happens. After one minute, take the temperature again.

Analysis *What evidence of a reaction did you observe? Was the reaction endergonic or exergonic? What is your evidence? Considering that the reaction was carried out by living tissue, what do you think was responsible for the breakdown of hydrogen peroxide? Do you think this reaction could be used by cells to do biological work? Why or why not?*

Figure 6-5 **When sugar burns in air, it releases CO_2, H_2O, and a lot of energy at once. In respiration, the same process occurs, but step by step, releasing a little energy at a time and storing it in ATP.**

$C_6H_{12}O_6 + 6O_2$

High

Potential energy

Energy

ATP

Maximum of 38 ATP per glucose molecule

Energy

Cell activities

Low
$6CO_2 + 6H_2O$

ADP + P_i

Minilab 1

Purpose
Students observe a temperature rise as evidence of energy released by an enzyme reaction.

Skills
observe and infer, recognize cause and effect

Teaching Strategies
- **Safety Precautions:** Students should wear goggles and aprons. You should perform the activity before class in order to see what is likely to happen.
- **Troubleshooting:** Sometimes the reaction mixture foams over the top of the test tube, so students should use test-tube racks and work over newspaper.
- Ask students if they have ever applied hydrogen peroxide to a cut or sore. Ask them to relate what happened to what they observe in this activity.
- Consider performing the glowing splint test to show that oxygen is produced by the reaction.

Expected Results
Students should observe a rise of a few degrees in the reaction mixture. If reactions are too slow to give a rise in temperature, try again using liver that has been more finely diced.

Answers
A new substance (oxygen gas) was formed. The reaction was exergonic because heat was released. An enzyme (catalase) present in liver carried out the reaction. The reaction probably could not do useful work because all the energy was released in the form of heat.

✔ **Assessment**
Performance: Have students carry out tests with other materials including diced raw potatoes, ground beef, radishes, diced leaves, and so on. Ask students to draw conclusions regarding the prevalence of this enzyme in living things.

PORTFOLIO

Have students write one or two paragraphs interpreting the diagram in Figure 6-5 on page 147. Ask them to include a sentence or two discussing the contrast between the photo and the diagram. **L2**

MEETING INDIVIDUAL NEEDS

For those students working below grade level, ask the following questions about the diagram in Figure 6-5. Where did the oxygen at the top of the arrow come from? Where did the ADP at the bottom of the cycle come from? Where did the glucose at the top of the arrow come from? What happens to the CO_2 and H_2O formed? What happens to the ATP formed? **LEP**

INVESTIGATION

Optimum Temperature

Time Allotment
1 class period to assemble equipment and complete the experiment; one-half period to analyze data and answer questions

Objectives
Upon completing this investigation, students will be able to:
- Relate rate of fermentation to temperature.
- Suggest ways to design experiments so that they yield comparable data across multiple trials.

Skills
design an experiment, separate and control variables

Materials
Per group of four students: 5 large test tubes, 5 disposable plastic pipets, thermometer, yeast, sucrose (table sugar), beaker, hot plate, mitts for handling hot glassware, 10 steel washers that fit inside test tubes

Preparation
Prepare a 20% sucrose solution by dissolving 20 g of sucrose in 80 mL of water. Prepare the yeast suspension by adding a packet of yeast to 40 mL of water.

Possible Hypotheses
Students will probably suggest that the reaction will become faster as temperature increases.

Possible Procedures
- Have students set up test tubes according to the illustration. Lumps of modeling clay formed around the neck of the pipet can be used instead of steel washers.
- Students must control the temperature in each tube by immersing it in a water bath held at a constant temperature. Students should use individual thermometers to determine the temperature inside each test tube. They should not start to count bubbles until the tube temperature reaches the temperature of the bath.

ATP as the Cell's Energy Currency   Consider this comparison. Suppose you work for another person, and that person pays you with a $100 bill. It's not very convenient to buy lunch with a $100 bill, and you certainly wouldn't want to stuff one in the slot of a soft drink machine. Smaller bills and coins are much more convenient for daily expenses. In the same way, all the energy from the breakdown of a glucose molecule is a very inconvenient amount for a cell. Instead, respiration "makes change," storing small amounts of energy in each ATP. The energy stored in a molecule of ATP is a convenient amount for most cell reactions. That's why scientists often speak of ATP as a cell's energy currency.

INVESTIGATION

Optimum Temperature

Humans are most comfortable with a surrounding temperature around 23°C. When it is too hot, we feel uncomfortable and start to sweat. When it is too cold, we begin to shiver and are equally uncomfortable. Thus, humans have an optimum temperature, a temperature at which they are most comfortable. Do all living things share the same optimum temperature for life activities? No. The optimum temperature for a deep-sea fish is quite different from that of a desert coyote.

Yeast cells also have an optimum temperature for life processes. In this investigation, you will design and then carry out an experiment to determine the temperature at which yeast best carries out fermentation. Carbon dioxide is given off during the process of alcoholic fermentation. Therefore, it can be used as a means for judging the rate at which yeast cells carry out this process. To help you get started, look at the diagram at the right. It shows how you could measure carbon dioxide gas given off by yeast cells during fermentation.

Problem
What is the optimum temperature for yeast cell fermentation?

Safety Precautions
Wear safety goggles when pouring and mixing liquids. Use caution with hot plates and hot liquids. Use mitts or hot pads when handling hot beakers.

Hypothesis
Have your group agree on a hypothesis to be tested. Record your hypothesis.

Experimental Plan
1. Review the discussions of aerobic respiration and fermentation in this chapter. Note particularly the reactants involved.
2. Examine the materials provided by your teacher. Then, as a group, make a list of the possible ways you might test your hypothesis using the materials available.
3. Agree on one way that your group could investigate your hypothesis.
4. Design an experiment that will (a) use a control, (b) test only

148 THE FLOW OF ENERGY

- Guide students to a cooperative arrangement in which each group maintains a water bath at a different temperature. Then each group can run a tube in each bath. Baths should range from 0°C to about 90°C. Try to have more skilled students maintain the high-temperature baths.
- Counting bubbles for ten minutes should be sufficient, although students should decide how long to count.
- Student controls may vary, but an appropriate control would be a tube containing a mixture of yeast with plain water.

Teaching Strategies
If this is the first time your students have designed an experiment, refer them to the Investigations in Chapters 1 and 2.
- Guide students to realize that they do not have to take readings at just certain temperatures. Otherwise, they may waste time trying to adjust temperatures of water baths.
- **Troubleshooting:** When students take readings at temperatures significantly below room temperature, have them cool the test tube and the pipet with its mixture separately before putting the pipet into the tube.

Anaerobic Processes

Have you ever lifted a heavy object and held it until you felt your muscles starting to give out? When your muscles become fatigued like this, it is because your muscle cells are not receiving enough oxygen to carry out aerobic respiration. Instead, muscle cells are undergoing anaerobic processes to release needed energy. **Anaerobic** processes take place in the absence of oxygen. Some bacteria carry out the entire process of respiration without using oxygen. More familiar, though, are two anaerobic processes called lactic acid fermentation and alcoholic fermentation.

one variable at a time, and (c) allow for the collection of quantitative data.

5. Prepare a list of numbered directions. Include a list of materials and the quantities you will need.

Checking the Plan

Discuss the following points with other group members to decide the final procedures for your experiment. Make any needed changes in your plan.

1. What materials will you use to grow your yeast?
2. What will you measure to determine the rate of fermentation?
3. What factor will you vary in your experiment?
4. What factors will you control in your experiment?
5. To what range of temperatures will you expose the yeast? Why?
6. What food will you use?
7. How will you determine appropriate amounts of yeast and food to use?
8. How long will you carry out the experiment?
9. How many tubes of yeast will you expose to each temperature?

10. Have you designed and made a table for collecting data?

Make sure your teacher has approved your experimental plan before you proceed.

Data and Observations

Carry out your experiment, make any needed measurements, and complete your data table. Design and complete a graph of your results.

Analysis and Conclusions

1. What conditions did you keep constant in the experimental group? What one condition varied?
2. What differences did you observe between experimental groups? Were these differences due to temperature differences? Explain how you know.
3. Explain how you were able to determine the optimum temperature for fermentation in yeast.
4. Was your hypothesis supported by your data? If not, suggest a new hypothesis that is supported by your data.
5. List several ways that your methods may have affected the outcome of the experiment. Suggest

ways that you might improve your methods.

6. Write a brief conclusion to your experiment.

Going Further

Based on this lab experience, design another experiment that would help to answer any questions that arose from your work. What factors might you allow to vary if you kept temperature constant? Assume that you will not be doing this lab in class.

— Test tube

— Water

— Plastic pipet

— Metal washers or other weight

— Yeast and food

6.1 ENERGY FOR CELLS **149**

Extensions

Have students devise methods for determining the effects of (1) yeast quantity or (2) sucrose concentration on the rate of reaction at optimum temperature. If time permits, students should try these experiments. **L2**

Ask students to draw a general conclusion about enzyme activity over a range of temperatures. They should realize that too high a temperature also decreases enzyme activity (because it destroys the enzyme). **L1**

Data and Observations

Students should prepare data tables having water temperature in the left column and number of bubbles per X minutes in the right column. A third column could include average bubbles per minute. If students' data can be made comparable, plot the data of all groups on the same graph, thus making the trend more visible to students.

Data Analysis

1. Time and amounts of sucrose and yeast are held constant. Temperature varied.
2. The difference should be the rate at which CO_2 bubbles were given off. Yes, because temperature was the only variable condition.
3. The temperature at which CO_2 bubbles were given off at the greatest rate is the optimum temperature.
4. Student answers will vary. They may suggest hypotheses with different optimum temperatures.
5. Possibilities include miscounting bubbles in tubes reacting at faster rates, not counting bubbles for the same length of time in each tube, and failing to maintain the temperature in a tube at a constant level. Students should suggest ways to ensure consistent data in future experiments.
6. Students should make a concise conclusion that takes into account only the data and observations they collected and how those data correspond to the conditions of the experiment. Students should find optimum temperatures from 40°C to 60°C.

This will eliminate the possibility of water being drawn into the pipet because of uneven cooling.
• Demonstrate how to fill a pipet and point out that pipets should be only three-quarters full.
• You may want to mix the entire quantity of sucrose and yeast just as students are ready to fill pipets. You should try to keep this mixture cold so that the reaction will be fresh each time.

Figure Caption Question

- *Why does the oxygen supply to cells become limited during exercise?* Even with lungs and heart working at a high rate, the O_2 need becomes greater than the blood can supply.

- *What do you think causes fermentation to stop?* Ethanol builds up in the mixture and has a toxic effect on yeast. Even though yeast may not be killed, fermentation stops.

LEISURE CONNECTION

Purpose
Students will realize that energy sources other than glucose are available to the body.

Teaching Strategies
Make an analogy between glycogen storage and a bank account. Once all the money is used up from the account (glycogen), one must dip into long-term savings (fat) for cash.

Possible Answers
1. More body fat is a large source of available energy but increases body mass and detracts from performance.
2. Sprinters do not use up stored glycogen as do long-distance runners.
3. A possible answer is yes. With only 4 km to go, fat reserves may be enough.

Going Further
Have students determine which source, "energy bars" or a pasta meal, would supply the body with more glycogen reserves before a race. **L2**

Figure 6-6 With strenuous exercise, lactic acid fermentation begins because oxygen cannot reach the cells fast enough to meet energy demands. Why does the oxygen supply to cells become limited during exercise? Read more about this subject in the Leisure Connection below.

Lactic Acid Fermentation Ordinarily, muscles would carry out aerobic respiration, using oxygen to break down glucose and transfer energy to ATP. If not enough oxygen is available, the early steps of glucose breakdown continue to occur because they do not require oxygen. However, without oxygen, the later steps, which produce carbon dioxide and water, cannot continue. Instead, muscles carry out a process called lactic acid fermentation. **Lactic acid fermentation** is an anaerobic process in which enzymes break down a glucose molecule into two lactic acid molecules, transferring energy to ATP in the process. The following equation summarizes lactic acid fermentation.

$$C_6H_{12}O_6 + 4ADP + 4P_i \xrightarrow{enzymes} 2CH_3CHOHCOOH + 4ATP$$
glucose   lactic acid

Compare this equation with the previous equation for aerobic respiration. Lactic acid fermentation produces many fewer ATP molecules than would be produced in aerobic respiration. However, it does provide a mechanism by which muscles can keep on working when oxygen can't reach them fast enough. It is the accumulation of lactic acid in muscles that causes the pain of muscle fatigue. Besides animal cells, some microorganisms also carry out lactic acid fermentation. Examples include the bacteria used to produce sauerkraut and buttermilk.

LEISURE CONNECTION

Hitting the Wall

Perhaps you have seen marathon runners strain toward the finish line, cheeks hollow and eyes glazed. Some cross the finish line and collapse, gasping, on the ground. Others cannot even finish.

These runners have "hit the wall." The wall refers to a point in a run at which a drop in energy production causes a sudden decrease in performance. With some runners, this drop can occur within a single mile, while other runners can run for more than 40 miles without hitting the wall. Beyond the wall, the runner's legs often feel heavy and leaden. Moving the body takes so much effort that some people compare it to trying to run while carrying a bear.

You can understand what happens when runners hit the wall if you remember that ATP supplies energy to the muscles, and is produced by the cellular respiration of glucose. Most of the glucose used during long-distance running comes from glycogen stored in muscle tissue and the liver. Because the body can store only limited amounts of glycogen, long-distance runners often exhaust their stores before the end of a run.

At this point, the body begins to metabolize fat for energy. However, metabolizing fat is a more complex process than simply oxidizing sugar obtained from glycogen. Meanwhile, the runner attempts to use energy faster than the body can produce it by this slower process. At this point, the runner "hits the wall."

1. **Explore Further:** Explain how additional body fat would help or hinder a runner trying to extend the collapse point.
2. **Explore Further:** Why is hitting the wall more likely to be a problem for a long-distance runner than for a sprinter?
3. **Solve the Problem:** Suppose a runner in a marathon hits the wall at 38 km. Should that runner try to finish the race? Why or why not?

MULTICULTURAL CONNECTION

Preserving Food by Fermentation: Certain bacteria found naturally in a variety of foods use the food as an energy source and carry out lactic acid fermentation. The process is responsible for the formation of a number of specific cultural foods. Hawaiians make poi by fermenting taro root, Japanese make soy sauce by fermenting soybeans, and Koreans make a spicy dish called kimchee by fermenting bok choy (Chinese cabbage). The familiar German dish, sauerkraut, also results from the fermentation of cabbage. Some cultures in southwestern Asia and northern Africa have traditionally preserved milk by fermenting it to form yogurt or similar products. The acid formed by fermentation allows the yogurt to be kept unrefrigerated for a time.

Alcoholic Fermentation   Many plant cells and microorganisms can carry out another type of fermentation called alcoholic fermentation. **Alcoholic fermentation** is an anaerobic process in which enzymes break down a glucose molecule into two molecules of ethanol and two molecules of carbon dioxide, transferring energy to ATP. The following equation summarizes alcoholic fermentation.

$$\underset{\text{glucose}}{C_6H_{12}O_6} + 4ADP + 4P_i \xrightarrow{\text{enzymes}} \underset{\text{ethanol}}{2C_2H_5OH} + \underset{\substack{\text{carbon} \\ \text{dioxide}}}{2CO_2} + 4ATP$$

In industry, yeast is used to ferment sugars from grain, fruit, or other sources in order to produce ethanol. Ethanol is the alcohol found in beer, wine, and other alcoholic beverages. It is also useful as a gasoline additive. Alcoholic fermentation is important in baking as well. Yeast added to dough carries out fermentation, breaking down carbohydrates in the flour. Bubbles of the carbon dioxide produced are trapped in the dough, causing it to rise. When the dough is baked, the alcohol produced by fermentation evaporates, raising the dough even more.

Energy Yield from Fermentation   The early steps of both types of fermentation are the same as those of aerobic respiration, requiring two ATP molecules to provide energy. So, even though fermentation produces four ATP molecules, the net ATP produced is only two molecules. This amount is only about 5 percent of the maximum ATP available from aerobic respiration. Still, by using up glucose at a rapid rate, some cells can produce ATP by fermentation almost as fast as by aerobic respiration, at least for a short time.

Some cells, such as certain bacteria, rely entirely on fermentation or other anaerobic processes for energy. Other cells, like yeast and muscle cells, switch between aerobic respiration and fermentation, depending on the amount of oxygen present.

Figure 6-7   **Fermentation by yeasts generates carbon dioxide, which makes the dough rise. The alcohol produced in the same process evaporates during baking. When yeast is used to ferment a solution containing a lot of sugar, fermentation eventually stops although sugar and yeast are still present. What do you think causes fermentation to stop?**

Section Review

Understanding Concepts

1. A friend tells you that the burning of a campfire must be an endergonic process because starting the fire required the heat from a match. Would you agree? Explain your answer.

2. Suppose a cell combines molecules A and B to produce molecule C in an endergonic reaction. Explain how ATP may be used in this type of reaction. Include the idea of free energy in your answer.

3. Suppose two cells are producing energy at the same rate by breaking down glucose—one by aerobic respiration and one by alcoholic fermentation. What conclusion can you draw about the rates at which waste would have to be removed from the two cells? Explain your reasoning.

4. *Skill Review—Designing an Experiment:* How would you design an experiment to determine whether the rate of alcoholic fermentation in yeast cells differs when cells use fructose instead of glucose? For more help, see Practicing Scientific Methods in the **Skill Handbook.**

5. *Thinking Critically:* The lactic acid produced during lactic acid fermentation is transported to the liver and converted to glucose. Do you think that reaction would require ATP? Explain.

Prepare

Key Concepts

Students study the nature of light and its interaction with chlorophyll. Photosynthesis is analyzed with special attention to both light reactions and the Calvin cycle. Respiration and photosynthesis are related to one another, and the energy flow for these two processes is correlated.

Key Terms

wavelength, visible spectrum, absorption spectrum, carotenoids, light reactions, grana, stroma, Calvin cycle

Materials

- For Minilab 2, purchase sprigs of Elodea plants from a local pet store. Purchase bromothymol yellow indicator from a supply house.

1 Focus

Objectives

The objectives are listed on the student page. Remind students to preview these objectives as a guide to this numbered section.

Discussion

Exhibit a plant to the class. Ask students how the plant differs from animals with respect to energy. Ask specifically if the plant carries on respiration, how it obtains energy, and what its source of food is. **L1**

Objectives

Describe the interaction of white light with objects including chlorophyll molecules.

Relate the events of the light reactions to those of the Calvin cycle in photosynthesis.

Analyze the relationship between photosynthesis and cellular respiration.

Figure 6-8 **White light passing through a prism is broken into a spectrum because shorter wavelengths (violet) are bent more by the prism than longer wavelengths (red). Wavelength is the distance from one wave crest to the next. Where are ultraviolet light and infrared light located on the spectrum?**

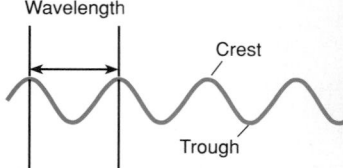

Wavelength

Crest

Trough

6.2 Photosynthesis

The energy you need to run, think, and grow is released in the process of cellular respiration. The key ingredient in this process, of course, is the energy-rich molecule glucose. But where does glucose come from? How is it produced? What makes it energy-rich? As you know, algae, some bacteria, and plants are producers in almost every ecosystem on Earth. These producers absorb energy from sunlight and convert it to chemical energy stored in organic molecules including glucose. To understand how this process occurs, you must first learn a little about the properties of light itself.

Light

Light is a form of radiant energy. Besides light, radiant energy includes radio waves, microwaves, X rays, and gamma rays. All radiant energy travels in waves. The distance between one wave crest and the next is called the **wavelength** of the waves, as shown in Figure 6-8. The human eye is sensitive to radiant energy with wavelengths of about 400 to 700 nm. The abbreviation *nm* stands for *nanometer,* which is one billionth of a meter. This mixture of wavelengths of radiant energy that is visible to humans is called white light.

The Visible Spectrum When white light passes through a prism, the prism separates it into a range of colors. This range of colors that make up white light is known as the **visible spectrum.** The colors of the spectrum are usually given as red, orange, yellow, green, blue, and violet. Red light has the longest wavelength of the visible spectrum, and violet light has the shortest wavelength. Ultraviolet and infrared wavelengths, on either end of the visible spectrum, are invisible to humans.

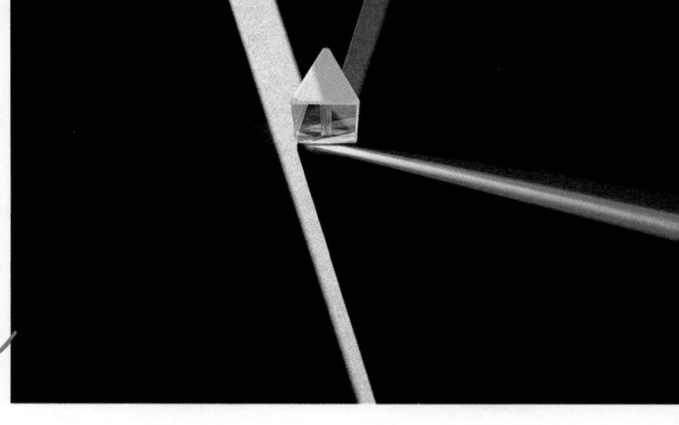

Why Objects Appear Colored Molecules in colored objects absorb some wavelengths of light and reflect others. The color of an object depends on which wavelengths it reflects. For example, a red car looks red because it reflects more red light than other colors of light. A white shirt looks white because it reflects all colors. Likewise, a dark blue sweater looks blue because it reflects some light in the blue part of the spectrum and absorbs most other wavelengths of light.

If you've ever worn a dark-colored sweater outdoors on a sunny day, you probably remember feeling warm. The darker the material, the greater the amount of light that is absorbed. The light energy that is absorbed changes to heat. As you'll see, light energy can sometimes be changed to forms other than heat.

Chlorophyll and Other Pigments

Light energy can be changed to chemical energy. Photosynthesis is the process by which producers store energy from sunlight as chemical energy in organic molecules, mainly in molecules of carbohydrates. Organisms that carry out photosynthesis contain colored pigments that absorb light energy and convert it to chemical energy. Among these pigments, the green pigment known as chlorophyll is the most important in photosynthesis. There are several types of chlorophyll, but in plants, chlorophyll *a* is the most important. In eukaryotes, such as plants and algae, chlorophyll is found in chloroplasts. However, prokaryotes, such as photosynthetic bacteria, have no chloroplasts. Chlorophyll of photosynthetic bacteria is most often attached to membranes in the cytoplasm.

How Chlorophyll Interacts with Light Producers usually appear green because of the presence of chlorophyll. Chlorophyll is green because it reflects light in the green and yellow parts of the visible spectrum. Chlorophyll absorbs most other wavelengths of visible light. This pattern of absorption and reflection can be demonstrated by passing white light through a solution of chlorophyll *a* and then through a prism.

Figure 6-9 **The color of an object depends on which colors of the spectrum it reflects. Some animals have distinct colors as camouflage or to distract and confuse predators. The bright colors of many other animals tell potential predators to beware because they are poisonous.**

Figure 6-10 **In blue-green bacteria such as the *Anabena* (left), chlorophyll is found on membranes within the cytoplasm. (Magnification: 400×) In plants and algae, such as the *Spirogyra* (right), chlorophyll is contained within chloroplasts. (Magnification: 100×)**

153

SECTION 6.2

2 Teach

Building a Model

Two empty coffee cans of the same size with thermometers placed through their plastic caps can be used to measure the difference in light absorption. Thermometers should fit tightly through the lids so that their bulbs are suspended midway in the can. Cover one can with white paper and the other with black paper. Allow sunlight to strike both cans. Compare the changes in their temperatures. LEP

Figure Caption Question

Where are ultraviolet light and infrared light located on the spectrum? Ultraviolet has shorter wavelengths than visible violet light and is located above the violet in the photo. Infrared has longer wavelengths than visible red and is located below red.

CHEMISTRY CONNECTION

Separating Leaf Pigments: It is possible to remove the pigments from a leaf and separate them by paper chromatography. Less soluble compounds remain near the bottom of the paper and more soluble compounds are carried higher.

Soak ground leaves in warm alcohol and apply the extract to a 12-cm strip of filter paper in a narrow band about 2 cm from the bottom of the strip. Place the filter paper into a test tube containing a small amount of acetone (available as clear fingernail polish remover—check the label). The test tube should be tightly sealed after placing the paper in it. Just the bottom edge of the paper should dip into the solvent. Pigments will separate as the solvent moves up the paper. L2

PROJECT

Growing Plants Under Lights: The use of special growing lights has become a popular way to aid the growth of plants indoors. Have your students correspond with a manufacturer, distributor, or retailer of these light bulbs and request information on the light spectrum provided by these specialized lamps. In some cases, information is printed on the carton in which the lamps are packaged. Have students grow plants under traditional light bulbs, grow lights, and sunlight to determine the differences in plant growth that result.

SECTION 6.2

Microscope Activity

Have students prepare wet mounts of tomato cells from within the juicy part of the fruit. Note the cells and the red colored plastids (chromoplasts) that are present. These plastids contain carotene and xanthophyll pigments. Wet mounts of flower petals may also be used to observe the variety of pigments present in their cells' plastids. **L1**

Using Science Terms

Have students correlate the term *carotenoid* with the orange color of the carrot root. **L1** **LEP**

Discussion Questions

Ask students to answer the following questions using the equation on page 155. What was the original source of carbon atoms in the simple sugar? What was the original source of hydrogen atoms in the simple sugar? Why are six molecules of carbon dioxide and water needed? Why can the formula for this simple sugar represent either fructose or glucose?

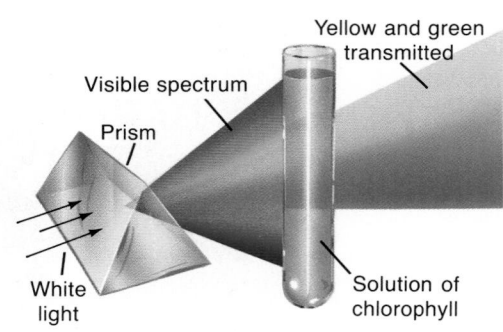

Figure 6-11 **When white light strikes chlorophyll, it absorbs colors in the red, blue, and violet parts of the spectrum. Thus, chlorophyll appears yellow-green. The graph on the right shows the absorption spectrum of chlorophyll.**

Because some wavelengths are absorbed by the chlorophyll, the spectrum produced is called an **absorption spectrum,** as shown in Figure 6-11. Violet and red wavelengths are greatly absorbed, as well as some blue wavelengths. During photosynthesis, these absorbed wavelengths are transformed from light energy to chemical energy.

Other Colored Pigments Besides chlorophyll *a* and *b,* chloroplasts also contain yellow, orange, and red pigments called **carotenoids.** Carotenoids absorb mainly blue and green wavelengths of light, and pass this energy to chlorophyll *a.* Thus, other wavelengths are also important in photosynthesis. Chlorophylls and carotenoids interact to absorb the light energy necessary for photosynthesis.

Carotenoids and other pigments are also present in other parts of a plant. These yellow, orange, and red colors are most often seen in the flowers and fruits of plants. A different assortment of carotenoids is present in leaves but is often masked by the green color of chlorophyll. In northern latitudes, the manufacture of chlorophyll usually stops in autumn. With less chlorophyll present, the carotenoids and other pigments become visible, so leaves turn from green to yellow, orange, and red.

Figure 6-12 **When leaves lose chlorophyll in the fall, the colors of other pigments become visible. These colors were previously masked by the green color of chlorophyll.**

154 🍂 THE FLOW OF ENERGY

ALTERNATE LAB: Is Chlorophyll Needed for Photosynthesis?

Purpose
Students learn that starch is present only in regions of a leaf that have chlorophyll.

Materials
Coleus plant, hot plate, colored pencils, two 400-mL beakers, 85% ethanol, forceps, shallow dish, wax paper, iodine solution
CAUTION: Students must wear aprons and goggles and use oven mitts when removing hot beakers from hot plate. Do

not boil alcohol. Do not use a burner or a hot plate with exposed coils.

Procedure
Give the following directions to students.
1. Remove one leaf from a *Coleus* plant and draw it using colored pencils.
2. Prepare a water bath using a hot plate, 400-mL beaker, and 200 mL of water. When the water is boiling, add the leaf and boil it for 2 minutes.

3. Turn hot plate to low. Use forceps to remove the leaf and place it aside.
4. Pour 50 mL of alcohol into a second 400-mL beaker and place it on the hot plate set to low. The alcohol should be warm but should not boil.
5. Place the leaf into the warm alcohol until it has lost all of its green color.
6. Turn off hot plate. Remove the leaf using forceps and place it into a

Overview of Photosynthesis

Photosynthesis occurs only in producers—some bacteria, algae, and plants. In photosynthetic bacteria and most algae, photosynthesis occurs in all cells. With evolution of green plants, however, certain cells became specialized for this process. As you study photosynthesis, think about a familiar plant, such as a tree. As you will learn in Chapter 21, chloroplasts, the organelles of photosynthesis, are located in just some, not all, of the cells of a tree.

Like cellular respiration, photosynthesis is a set of many separate, related reactions. Taken as a whole, these reactions are endergonic, and the ultimate source of energy needed for the reactions to occur is external—light. The many reactions of photosynthesis can be summarized by the following equation.

$$6CO_2 + 6H_2O \xrightarrow[\text{light energy}]{\text{enzymes, chlorophyll}} C_6H_{12}O_6 + 6O_2$$

carbon dioxide · water · simple sugar · oxygen gas

This equation tells us that molecules of carbon dioxide and water are combined into simple sugars by enzymes, and oxygen is given off as a by-product. Energy for the process of photosynthesis comes from light energy absorbed by chlorophyll. Simple sugars are represented in the equation by the formula $C_6H_{12}O_6$, which can represent fructose, glucose, or other six-carbon sugars.

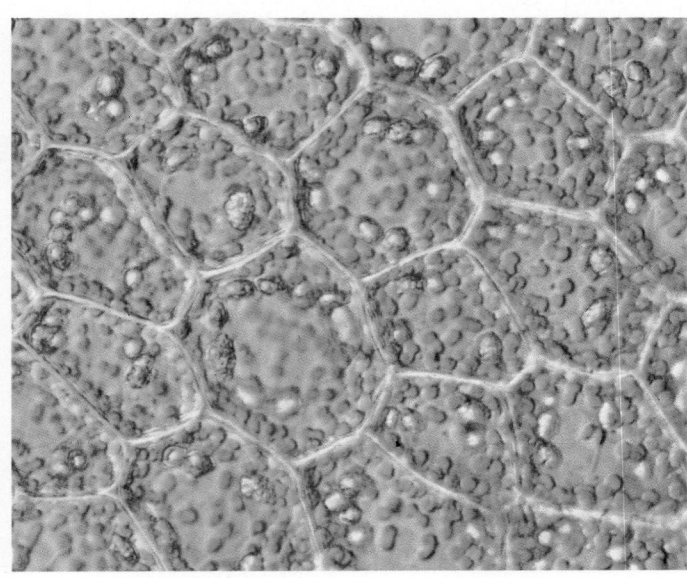

Figure 6-13 In plants and algae, photosynthesis takes place in chloroplasts. The green objects inside these leaf cells are chloroplasts. Magnification: 100×

Under what conditions do plants take up CO₂?

Place one sprig of Elodea, a common aquarium plant, into each of two test tubes. Fill each tube almost to the top with bromothymol yellow solution. Cover each tube with a small piece of clear plastic wrap and secure it with a rubber band. Place one tube in bright light (not direct sunlight), and place the other tube in a dark place. Compare the colors of both tubes over a 24-hour period. The yellow color of bromothymol yellow indicates that carbon dioxide is present. The color changes to a green/blue color as carbon dioxide is removed.

Analysis Which plant removed carbon dioxide? What evidence do you have? What happened to the carbon dioxide that was removed? Why did one plant remove carbon dioxide but not the other?

Minilab 2

Purpose
Students see that more CO_2 is taken up by plants in the light.

Skills
observe and infer, separate and control variables

Teaching Strategies
- **Safety Precautions:** Have students wear apron and goggles.
- To prepare bromothymol yellow solution, dissolve 0.1 g of bromothymol blue in 2 L of water. Add vinegar drop by drop, stirring constantly until the solution turns yellow and remains yellow after standing for 10 minutes.
- **Troubleshooting:** Do not put tubes in direct sunlight because the Elodea will be damaged.

Expected Results
The tube exposed to light turns blue, whereas the other tube either remains yellow or turns blue much later.

Answers
The plant in the light used up carbon dioxide. The evidence is that the solution turns blue. The CO_2 was used to make simple sugars. Only one plant had light energy available to drive photosynthesis.

✔ Assessment
Knowledge: Ask students what they think the results would have been if the indicator tested for oxygen release. L2

---

7. Pour off the water and add iodine solution. Allow the leaf to remain in the iodine for several minutes.
8. Remove the leaf with forceps and rinse it quickly in water. Smooth it out on a piece of wax paper and study the areas of dark and light brown.
9. Draw the leaf again, shading in the areas of dark and light brown.

shallow dish of water. *Gently* unfold until it is flat.

Analysis
Ask students the following questions.
1. Explain how the areas of starch compare to the color pattern on the original leaf. *The starch was located where the leaf was green or dark red.*
2. Explain the connection between photosynthesis and the location of the starch. *Photosynthesis requires chlorophyll and occurred only where the starch was located.*

3. Explain why it was necessary to remove the chlorophyll from the leaf. *The chlorophyll would have masked the results of the iodine test.*

✔ Assessment
Skill: Using the same technique, have students design an experiment that would determine how fast a leaf will deplete its starch reserves when placed in the dark.

Figure Caption Question
What would be an adaptive advantage of having chlorophyll-containing membranes in stacks? Stacks make light absorption more efficient. Light that gets past the first layer may be absorbed by the second, third, and so on.

Reinforcement
Ask students to make a diagram of a typical chloroplast like the one shown in Figure 6-14. Have them label thylakoids, grana, and stroma. Students should add clusters of chlorophyll molecules to the thylakoid membrane. Now, ask students to add the following labels to their diagram: (a) site of the light reactions and (b) site of light absorption. Note that both labels should be pointing to the thylakoid membrane. Have students add more labels to this diagram as they study the Calvin cycle to show the pathways of raw materials and products. **L1** | **LEP**

Microscope Activity
Students can examine chloroplasts under the microscope by using either living or preserved materials. Elodea chloroplasts will be visible when a single leaf is removed and prepared as a wet mount. Elodea cells will also show cyclosis or movement of the chloroplasts within the cells' cytoplasm. Increasing the amount of light on the wet mount tends to stimulate cyclosis. Living or preserved moss "leaves" may also be used to examine chloroplasts. Other material useful for observing chloroplasts would be spirogyra (either fresh or preserved) and lettuce leaves. **L1** | **COOP LEARN**

Chloroplast · Thylakoid membrane · Stroma · Grana

Figure 6-14 Inside a chloroplast, chlorophyll molecules are located on the thylakoid membranes, which are arranged in stacks called grana. The fluid around the thylakoids is called stroma. Sugars are synthesized in the stroma. A chloroplast has a second outer membrane not shown here. What would be an adaptive advantage of having chlorophyll-containing membranes in stacks?

The Light Reactions

The whole process of photosynthesis is divided into two main sets of reactions. The first set is known as the light reactions. The **light reactions** are so named because they involve a series of changes that convert light energy into chemical energy.

Trapping Energy from Light When you studied cell structure in Chapter 5, you learned that a chloroplast contains internal membranes. These membranes are called thylakoid membranes. They have a fluid mosaic structure and have chlorophyll and carotenoid molecules embedded along with the proteins in their bilayers. Part of these thylakoid membranes are arranged in stacks called **grana,** seen in Figure 6-14. It is on these internal membranes that the light reactions occur.

Thinking Lab
INTERPRET THE DATA

Does light color influence the rate of photosynthesis?

Background
A student took four similar plants and exposed each plant to a different colored light for 24 hours. She then measured the amount of starch present within each plant's leaves. She chose to measure starch because starch is a major product formed from the sugars produced by photosynthesis.

You Try It
In her experiment, the student obtained the data shown in the following table.

Plant	Color of Light	Starch Present (in milligrams)
A	red	72 mg
B	yellow	10 mg
C	green	13 mg
D	blue	68 mg

Interpret the data given in the table. State a conclusion that you would draw from the data given in the table. Be sure to limit your conclusion to the conditions of the experiment. Based on the data given, what colored light bulbs would be best for growing plants indoors? What colors would be the poorest? What sort of results do you think the student would obtain if she had grown one plant under white light? List two things the student might do to improve her experiment.

Thinking Lab
INTERPRET THE DATA

Purpose
Students will correlate light color with the efficiency of photosynthesis.

Skills
observe and infer, interpret data

Teaching Strategies
• Ask students what they suppose the student actually did to conduct her experiment. Why didn't she measure glucose?

How did she obtain different colors of light?

Answers
Red or blue lights seem to give the best results. Green and yellow are poorest. Students may suggest that the plant under white light would produce more starch than a plant grown under either red or blue light alone. The student should make

sure that lights were of equal intensity and that the leaf samples were of equal mass.

✔ **Assessment**
Knowledge: Have students write a paragraph correlating the experimental results to the absorption spectrum of chlorophyll and explaining why these results would be expected.

During these reactions, light is absorbed by chlorophyll and carotenoids. When these molecules absorb light, their energy increases and that energy is passed along to electrons in a specific chlorophyll molecule. When electrons absorb energy, they move to higher energy levels and are said to be excited. Next, the excited electron in this chlorophyll molecule leaves the molecule. Then, by a series of steps, the energy of the excited electron is used to bond a molecule of inorganic phosphate to ADP to form an ATP molecule. Thus, energy that originally came from sunlight becomes stored as chemical energy in the bonds of ATP molecules. Energy from light is now available to do biological work.

Splitting of Water Another part of the light reactions involves the water used in photosynthesis. As light is transformed to chemical energy and stored in the bonds of ATP, water molecules are split into hydrogen ions, electrons, and oxygen. The electrons replace those lost by chlorophyll, and the oxygen is given off as a by-product. The hydrogen ions become attached to organic carrier coenzymes called NADP and are used in later steps of photosynthesis.

Note that the light reactions of photosynthesis do not involve carbon dioxide, and no sugars are produced. In summary, the light reactions involve three main events.

1. Light energy is absorbed and converted to chemical energy in the bonds of ATP.
2. Water is split into hydrogen ions, oxygen, and electrons.
3. Hydrogen ions from water are attached to carrier coenzymes for use in later steps of photosynthesis.

Figure 6-15 In the light reactions, there are really two events involving chlorophyll. In one event, energy from the sun boosts electrons from chlorophyll to a higher energy level. As these electrons lose energy, that energy is used to form ATP molecules. Electrons lost from chlorophyll are replaced by electrons from water. This action breaks water into hydrogen ions and oxygen gas. In the second event, the energy of other electrons is raised again by light. This time, the electrons' energy is used to attach hydrogen ions (H⁺) to carrier coenzymes called NADP to form NADPH. The ATP and NADPH generated in the light reactions are used in the Calvin cycle, the part of photosynthesis that makes sugars.

Brainstorming
When looking at a balanced equation for photosynthesis, such as the one on page 155, students will note that both products formed contain oxygen atoms. Students should try to determine the source of each oxygen atom on the right side of the equation. Remind them to read the section marked "Splitting of Water" carefully, and to study Figure 6-15. **L1**
COOP LEARN

Concept Development
Review the changes that occur to a water molecule when it is split into hydrogen ions, electrons, and oxygen atoms. Use a model or chalkboard diagram of a water molecule showing all electrons. You may have made one in Chapter 3. Remove hydrogen protons (H⁺ ions). Then separate a neutral oxygen atom (nucleus plus eight electrons). Have students note what remains (two electrons). Ask them to relate this to the water-splitting reaction shown in Figure 6-15.

Discussion Questions
Ask students to trace energy changes that occur as light energy strikes a chlorophyll molecule. Ask them to correlate the changes during the light reaction to any similar changes that took place during respiration (generating ATP).

HISTORY CONNECTION

The Importance of Sugar: Have students research the history of sugar production and its social and economic importance. Sugar cane originated in India and was brought from Europe to the West Indies on Columbus's second voyage in 1493. Sugar became a major export from the New World. Because many people were needed to work in the cane fields, sugar production was also a major reason for the importation of slaves from Africa. Have students find out what happened to the original inhabitants of the islands. **L2**

PROJECT

Starch Depletion in the Dark: Use the technique of the Alternate Lab on pages 154-155 to determine how much time is needed for a plant to deplete its starch reserves when placed in the dark. A plant with many leaves, such as a geranium, must be used so that students can remove a different leaf each day to test for the presence of starch. Another technique is to mask the top half of a leaf with aluminum foil each day for 10-15 days and then pick and process them all at once. With this technique, students will have to devise a way to label each leaf.

Purpose
Students will correlate a biological process with the economic value of the process.

Teaching Strategies
You may wish to review the equation for this process. It appears on page 151. Emphasize the facts that yeast cells, like all living things, need food; that yeast uses glucose or other sugars as food and, in the process, converts it to alcohol and carbon dioxide; and that the reaction does not require oxygen.

Possible Answers
1. It should speed up the process because the yeast would not have to break down starch to obtain sugar.
2. An argument for baking is that most bread products depend on yeast, and the quantity of baked bread is huge. An argument for brewing is that the raw materials are relatively cheap and the products relatively expensive. Nutrition is probably not a good choice because of low volume and lack of acceptance.
3. Yeast could be mixed with a culture's traditional foods to provide extra nutrition. Extra yeast could be added to foods already made with yeast. Other arguments are possible.

Going Further
Have students prepare wet mounts of yeast and observe under high power. Bake bread in the classroom. Prepare two types, one with and one without yeast. Compare the two baked samples and explain how and why they differ. **L1**

The Calvin Cycle

Thylakoid membranes, the site of the light reactions, are surrounded by a fluid that contains many enzymes and other molecules. This fluid part of a chloroplast is called the **stroma,** and the molecules within it are used in the manufacture of sugars. This process of synthesizing sugars is known as the **Calvin cycle.** In a sense, the Calvin cycle is the "synthesis" part of photosynthesis.

Events of the Calvin Cycle Consider what must happen in the Calvin cycle. Sugars are composed of carbon, hydrogen, and oxygen atoms, so these atoms must be present in the reactants. Also, because sugars have more potential energy than the reactants from which they are made, a source of free energy is needed. If you study Figure 6-16 carefully, you can understand how the light reactions and the Calvin cycle are related. As you recall, the light reactions provide hydrogen ions as well as a source of energy, ATP. Along with these hydrogen ions and ATP, the plant uses carbon dioxide it has obtained from the environment. The carbon dioxide is a source of carbon and oxygen atoms. The reactions of the Calvin cycle convert that carbon dioxide to sugars. Appendix C provides more details about the Calvin cycle.

Products of the Calvin Cycle The molecules produced in the Calvin cycle are not glucose, but rather molecules of three-carbon sugars. Some of these three-carbon sugars are used directly as energy sources, while others are converted to other molecules, such as lipids, amino acids, and parts of nucleic acids. Two of the three-carbon molecules can be combined to form

Yeasts: Raising Economic Dough

You have probably smelled bread baking at home or near a bakery. Does it seem possible that the tantalizing aroma could result from fungi in the dough? Yeasts are indeed types of fungi. Yeasts obtain their energy by fermenting sugars.

No record exists of the first use of yeast in baking. It is thought that, originally, flour and water were left standing until naturally occurring yeasts multiplied and fermented the carbohydrates in the dough. Thereafter, the baker saved a small amount of dough to use for "starter" in the subsequent batch of bread. Because varying amounts and types of yeast along with bacteria can develop, this method is unpredictable. Some bread is still fermented by using starter dough. It is called sourdough because its high acidity gives it a sour taste. The acidity results from acetic and lactic acids produced by some types of yeast and bacteria.

For most types of bread, modern bakers use pure cultures of selected strains of yeast grown in sterile, formulated liquid media. *Saccharomyces cerevisiae* are the fungi in bakers' yeast.

Yeasts leaven (raise) dough by fermenting carbohydrates such as glucose, fructose, maltose, and sucrose. One product of fermentation is carbon dioxide, which creates most of the leavening effect as it is released and forms bubbles in the elastic dough.

Alcohol is another product of fermentation. When dough is baked, the alcohol evaporates and raises the dough a little more.

The production of alcohol by fermentation is economically important,

MEETING INDIVIDUAL NEEDS

Have students working at or below grade level explain the: (a) source and function for carbon dioxide in the Calvin cycle, (b) source and function for hydrogen in the Calvin cycle, (c) source and function for ATP in the Calvin cycle, (d) requirement for two 3-carbon sugars to form one glucose molecule.

PROJECT

Starch Shapes: There are many different types of starch grains. Each type will have a distinct shape when observed under the microscope. Have students prepare wet mounts of starch scraped from corn, rice, peas, chestnut (if available), water chestnut, sweet potato, bean, acorn, oat, and ginger. A very light iodine stain will aid in seeing the grains under the microscope. **L1**

Sunlight

H_2O

O_2

Light reactions (on thylakoids)

ATP

NADPH (carrier of H$^+$)

CO_2

Enzymes of Calvin cycle (in stroma)

$C_6H_{12}O_6$ (simple sugars)

Chloroplast

six-carbon sugars such as glucose and fructose. However, most plants contain very little free glucose. Why? The glucose often combines with fructose to form sucrose, which is transported to other parts of the plant. Other glucose molecules are joined to form starch, which can be stored in stems, roots, or seeds. The starch molecules can later be reconverted to glucose, which can yield energy in cellular respiration. Still other glucose molecules are used to form cellulose to build new cell walls. Thus, even though photosynthesis produces three-carbon sugars, the equation is usually written to indicate $C_6H_{12}O_6$ as one of the products. A principal reason for writing the equation this way is that sucrose, starch, and cellulose are all made of six-carbon sugar units.

Figure 6-16 The Calvin cycle takes place in the stroma. Enzymes combine CO_2 from air or water with hydrogen from NADPH and energy from ATP to form 3-carbon simple sugars. Many of these sugars are used to form 6-carbon sugars, which make up sucrose, starch, and cellulose.

too. For example, fortunes have been made by the manufacture and sale of beer, another product made possible by yeast-caused fermentation. Beer brewers use yeast to ferment a malted grain, such as barley, with hops and water. Malting involves allowing the grain to begin to germinate. In this process, an enzyme converts starch stored as a food reserve in the grain to simpler sugars, mainly maltose, a disaccharide made of two glucose units. Thus, sugar becomes available as an energy supply to the germinating seedling. In brewing, the germination process is stopped by heating

as soon as most of the starch is converted. The alcohol and carbon dioxide in beer are products of fermentation.

A by-product of beer brewing is the nutrient-rich yeast that settles out during the aging and filtering process. This yeast is such a concentrated source of nutrients that some nutritionists have proposed it as a partial solution to world hunger.

Unfortunately, most people don't like the taste of nutritional yeast. Brewers' yeast has a bitter flavor. Some other types of yeast, such as torula yeast, are milder in flavor and richer in nutrients.

1. **Explore Further:** How would adding simple sugars affect the leavening action of the yeast in bread dough?

2. **Explore Further:** Which use of yeast would you judge to be more profitable: baking, brewing, or nutrition? Argue in support of your opinion.

3. **Solve the Problem:** Propose some strategies for using nutritional yeast to alleviate famine and malnutrition, in spite of people's preference for other foods.

Misconception

Students often believe that plants obtain all their food from the soil. Typically, they have heard of "plant food" or fertilizers and know that they are added to soil. Plants not only make their own carbohydrates during photosynthesis, they also make vitamins, fats, and amino acids using the products of photosynthesis. The soil provides a source of water and nitrogen, potassium, phosphorus, sulfur, and other elements that are needed to form proteins, coenzymes, and molecules such as chlorophyll. You may wish to have students grow plant cuttings in pure water. They may continue to grow for weeks with no additional minerals being added to the water, but they will not flourish as will plants grown in soil.

Different Viewpoints in Biology

Dark Reactions
The Calvin cycle is often referred to as the "dark reactions." Most biologists now prefer to avoid the term *dark reactions* because these reactions must have the products of the light reactions to operate. The Calvin cycle is also sometimes called the Calvin-Benson cycle.

Brainstorming

Have students cite evidence that plants store starch in roots and other parts. Ask them to name the type of chemical reaction involved with the formation of starch from glucose molecules. Students may cite items they know to be starchy foods. If students wish to confirm their suggestions, have them perform iodine-starch tests on the plant parts they name. **L1**

PROGRAM RESOURCES

Teacher Classroom Resources
Study Guide, pp. 33-36 **L1**
Concept Mapping, p. 6 **L1** **LEP**
Probing Levels of Life, Labs 13, 14, pp. 35, 37 **L2**

Critical Thinking/Problem Solving, p. 6 **L2**
Color Transparency #8 **L1** **LEP**
Investigating Living Systems, Labs 15, 16, pp. 61, 65 **L2**

Bioethics

Desertification: Carbon dioxide for photosynthesis is always available in the atmosphere. Water is also needed for photosynthesis but is not always available, especially in deserts. In Africa, the fringe of the Sahara Desert moves southward by 6 km each year. This advancing of desert is known as desertification.

What is causing this continuing change? One factor is the lack of rain in that area of the world since 1968. Little can be done to correct the lack of rain. But, what humans have done to contribute to this problem can be corrected. Semi-arid regions at the edge of desert are in a delicate balance. Many of these areas have been cleared and converted to the growing of crops. When the poor soil fails to produce crops, the land is often converted to grazing, thus destroying natural vegetation at the desert's edge. It is this vegetation that stabilizes the soil and "holds back" the desert. Eventually the desert claims the land. However, changes in human farming and grazing practices can reduce the rate of desertification.

3 Assess

Check for Understanding

Have students explain the literal meaning of *photosynthesis*. Ask them to relate this meaning to what takes place in the light reactions (photo-) and the Calvin cycle (-synthesis). **L1**

Energy Relationships

Figure 6-17 Here you see the interrelationship between chloroplasts and mitochondria. The chloroplast uses light energy to synthesize high-energy molecules (sugars) from CO_2 and H_2O, giving off O_2 gas in the process. The mitochondrion uses O_2 to break down sugars, releasing the stored energy to make ATP from ADP, giving off CO_2 and H_2O. Note that the chloroplasts and mitochondria might be in the same cell or in different cells of the same organism. In many cases, the chloroplasts are in one organism (a producer), and the mitochondria are in another (a consumer).

As you finish studying this chapter, it is important for you to think about cellular respiration and photosynthesis together, not as separate processes.

Relating Photosynthesis and Respiration In some ways, photosynthesis is the opposite of respiration. For example, respiration is exergonic while photosynthesis is endergonic. More significant, though, is that photosynthesis and cellular respiration are interdependent processes. One could not occur without the other, because the reactants (raw materials) of one reaction are the products of the other, and vice versa.

During photosynthesis, low-energy molecules of carbon dioxide and water are converted to high-energy molecules of sugar. Sunlight provides the energy to build these sugar molecules. Once formed, sugars are a rich source of energy for all organisms. Producer organisms themselves obtain energy from the breakdown of sugars. Sugars or products made from them are also passed along to consumers.

Photosynthesis
$6CO_2 + 6H_2O + \text{light energy} \rightarrow$
$C_6H_{12}O_6 + 6O_2$

Cellular respiration
$C_6H_{12}O_6 + 6O_2 \rightarrow$
$6CO_2 + 6H_2O + \text{energy}$

Ask your students to prepare a chart that compares the processes of photosynthesis and respiration. Some of the comparisons to be made should include: organisms that carry out each process, organelles where reactions occur, names of pathways or cycles used, whether energy is released or absorbed, raw materials and products formed.

Students should describe the journey of an atom of carbon in a carbon dioxide molecule entering a plant. Assume that this molecule was just released from an animal as a product of respiration. The journey should continue until the carbon atom passes through the plant, becomes a part of starch or cellulose, and ends up again as waste from respiration. **L1**

Why Continuous Energy Input Is Needed Whether in the cells of producers or consumers, sugars are broken down by cellular respiration. As respiration occurs, what was originally light energy is transferred to ATP, which is then used for biological work. But energy of ATP, once used, cannot be recycled. The reason is that whenever energy is used to drive endergonic reactions in cells, some of that energy escapes as heat. This is why living systems require a continuous input of energy.

When you work or play hard, much of the energy used to contract muscle cells is transformed to heat. Also, warm-blooded animals usually require more food than cold-blooded animals of the same size because much of the energy from the food is transformed to heat to maintain body temperature.

But the low-energy carbon dioxide and water molecules produced by respiration are recycled through the environment; producers use them to make new sugars by photosynthesis. Thus, more energy-rich molecules are made available. This is why sugars are referred to as the "crossroads" of energy in living systems.

LOOKING AHEAD

YOU HAVE NOW TRACED the flow of energy from sunlight to chemical energy in energy-rich molecules of simple sugars. Energy from the breakdown of energy-rich molecules is used to make ATP molecules, which provide energy in convenient amounts to do the biological work of cells. One very important way in which cells use energy is in the production of new cells. In the next chapter, you will find out why cells reproduce, how they do so, and how that reproduction is controlled.

Section Review

Understanding Concepts

1. You are looking at a blue mailbox outdoors in the sun. Describe what happens when the sunlight strikes the box that enables you to see it and distinguish its color.
2. Suppose you have an orange-colored substance. What colors of light would that substance absorb? Reflect? What happens to the light energy the object absorbs?
3. Describe photosynthesis in terms of energy transformations and relative potential energy of the reactants and products involved.
4. **Skill Review—Recognizing Cause and Effect:** How would photosynthesis be affected if:
   (a) a plant were placed in air having a higher concentration of CO_2?
   (b) a plant could not make enough NADP?
   (c) a chloroplast were missing carotenoid molecules?
   (d) a plant failed to absorb enough phosphate ions?
   (e) water were in short supply? Explain your reasoning for each answer. For more help, see Thinking Critically in the **Skill Handbook.**
5. **Thinking Critically:** Not all cells of a leaf carry out photosynthesis. Picture a leaf as being composed of several layers of cells. In which layer(s) do you think the photosynthetic cells would be located? Explain your reasoning.

SECTION 6.2

Reteach
Have students explain with respect to photosynthesis the relationships that exist between the following pairs: (a) light reactions and Calvin cycle, (b) stroma and Calvin cycle, (c) respiration and photosynthesis.

Extension
There are certain plants such as Indian pipe *(Monotropa uniflora)* and dodder *(Cuscuta sp.)* that lack chlorophyll. Have students look up these plants and tell how they are able to survive. **L2**

✔ Assessment
Portfolio: Have students link the major concepts of this section by using a concept map. Include information such as the reactants and products of photosynthesis, the fate of each reactant, sites of chemical changes within the chloroplast, pathways of energy, origin of atoms in products formed, and intermediate products such as ATP and NADPH.
L1 **LEP**

4 Close

Activity
Ask students to list all foods they consumed on the previous day. Then, ask them to divide the list into two groups: (a) those foods formed directly by photosynthesis and (b) those foods not directly formed by photosynthesis. Help students realize that the energy available in all food can be traced to photosynthesis.
L1

Answers to Section Review

1. You see the box because it reflects light. More blue wavelengths are reflected and others are absorbed. Therefore, the box appears blue.
2. The substance would absorb green, blue, violet, some yellow, and some red. It would reflect light in the orange region of the spectrum. The light energy that is absorbed is transformed mostly to heat.
3. During photosynthesis, light energy is transformed first to chemical energy of ATP and then to chemical energy of simple sugars or other organic molecules. The potential energy of the products is greater than that of the reactants.
4. **Skill Review—Recognizing Cause and Effect:** (a) The rate would increase because carbon dioxide is a reactant. (b) The rate would decrease because NADP is needed to transfer hydrogen ions to the Calvin cycle. (c) The rate would decrease because carotenoids trap wavelengths that chlorophyll *a* cannot trap. (d) The rate would decrease because phosphate ions are necessary for formation of both ATP and NADP. (e) The rate would decrease because water is a reactant in the process.
5. **Thinking Critically:** They would be close to the upper surface of the leaf where light absorption is most efficient.

CHAPTER 6

BIOLOGY, TECHNOLOGY, AND SOCIETY

Biotechnology

Purpose
Students will learn that there are alternate techniques available for the routine testing of chemicals, drugs, and foods to prove that they are not harmful to humans.

Background
The entire reaction for bioluminescence is as follows:

$$\text{reduced luciferin} + ATP + O_2$$

$$\xrightarrow{\text{luciferase}} \text{oxidized luciferin} +$$

$$P_i\!-\!P_i + H_2O + AMP + \text{light}$$

Teaching Strategies
- Bioluminescent bacteria, such as *Vibrio fischeri,* are available from biological supply houses. Demonstrate the bioluminescent properties of these organisms. Ask students to propose experiments to determine if specific chemicals are harmful to these bacteria as judged by changes in their bioluminescent activity. **L2**

Possible Answers
1. Bacteria are life forms that lack a nervous system. There is not the stigma associated with experimentation on life forms that experience pain.
2. Bioluminescence test results are reliable enough to inform researchers that no further testing is needed.

Going Further
Students can work with firefly bioluminescence by using a kit available from supply houses. The kit contains all needed chemicals and firefly abdomens. **L3**

BIOLOGY, TECHNOLOGY, AND SOCIETY

Biotechnology

Enlightened Product Testing Using Bioluminescence

No one likes to test consumer products on animals, but the public and the government demand that products be proven safe and free of harmful substances. As a result, scientists are looking for alternative methods of testing product toxicity.

One such method involves the use of bioluminescent bacteria. It is more sensitive than animal testing.

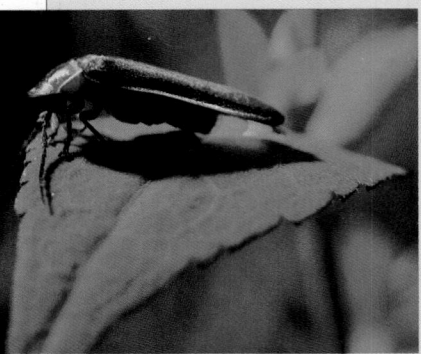

If a chemical kills or damages bioluminescent bacteria, the bacteria lose their ability to produce light. This result suggests to the researcher that the tested material could be toxic or irritating to humans.

A familiar example of bioluminescence is the emission of light by fireflies and many other organisms. Light is emitted by an organism when oxygen combines with a substance called luciferin in the presence of the enzyme luciferase and energy in the form of adenosine triphosphate (ATP). Therefore, changes in the levels of ATP can be detected by monitoring changes in the degree of bioluminescence.

Such tests, called bioluminescence assays, are used for many different purposes. For example, they were used at a medical school in Israel to detect the presence of the HIV virus, and in Sweden to detect the presence of bacteria in urine. A researcher at the University of Miami School of Medicine uses bioluminescence to monitor the effect of chemical or radiation treatment on uterine cancer cells.

Because federal laws require testing of some products on animals and humans, bioluminescence assays cannot entirely replace animal testing. However, when used as preliminary screening tests, they can avoid subjecting animal or human subjects to unnecessary risk.

1. **Issue:** Why might researchers be less concerned about harming bacteria than about harming mammals by toxicity testing?
2. **Explore Further:** Why don't researchers test substances on animals if bioluminescence assays strongly suggest that a substance is harmful?

Considering the Environment

Alternative Sources of Energy

You may have heard that air pollution regulations are getting tougher, but they are lenient compared to a law passed in the 1300s. Edward I, an English king, forbade the burning of coal because of its terrible smell. The penalty for burning it was death. Because there were few other energy alternatives in England at the time, the law was eventually repealed.

Today, emissions from burning fossil fuels—coal, petroleum, natural gas—are still a problem. These emissions can impair health, damage forests and wildlife, and even corrode marble statues. For this reason, and because fossil fuel supplies are limited, humans are seeking new energy sources.

Solar Energy As you know, the sun is the ultimate source of energy for all life forms. It is also the source of the energy in fossil fuels, which are the remains of living things. However, the use of sunlight directly, solar energy, is considered a modern idea even though it has been used directly for thousands of years.

Unfortunately, unless additional equipment is used, sunlight isn't sufficiently concentrated to produce the high temperatures needed for generating electricity and powering machinery. Also, the sun isn't a reliable energy source in places where it is cloudy or where days are short.

To achieve the high temperatures needed to generate electricity, large areas covered with flat or curved reflectors concentrate sunlight by focusing it onto a small area, usually tubes of water, which then boils to produce steam. The steam spins the blades of a turbine connected to an electrical generator.

Hydropower People don't usually think of hydropower, or energy from moving water, as derived from the sun. Yet the sun's energy evaporates water, which then falls to Earth as rain and runs from high ground to low. For centuries, humans have used the kinetic energy of moving water to turn waterwheels, which power small mills, grindstones, saws, and even looms for weaving cloth.

Today, hydroelectric power plants harness moving water to generate electricity. Usually, the plant has a dam that raises the level of the water behind it much higher than the power plant at the bottom

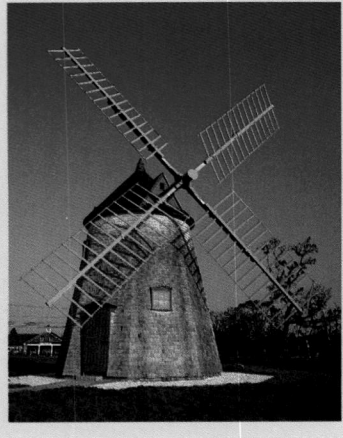

of the dam, which increases the gravitational potential energy of the water. As electricity is needed, water is released with tremendous force. The rushing water turns the blades of a turbine, which in turn spins generators.

Wind Power By heating Earth's surface unevenly, the sun creates wind. For example, when air over a warm region is heated, its density decreases and it rises. Cooler air from other regions rushes in, creating wind.

The energy of wind was among the first forms of energy harnessed by humans. Sailors used it to move ships; people built windmills to pump water and grind grain. Thousands of wind machines are now in use. Usually, wind farms, with many wind-powered electric generators connected together, supply electrical energy for communities. Like direct sun, the use of wind power is limited to areas where wind is relatively strong and steady. In the United States, California has the most wind farms.

Fossil fuel gradually replaced wind and water power because

fossil fuel was convenient, reliable, cheap, easily transported, and supplied energy on demand. Inventions such as the steam engine, the internal combustion engine, and the technology to generate electricity escalated demand for fossil fuels.

As oil sources became unreliable, and people began to be more concerned about environmental quality, interest in ancient energy sources such as sunlight, wind, and water revived. Engineers reached back into the distant past for "new" sources of energy to move civilization forward.

1. **Solve the Problem:** Study a map of the world. Select some areas where you think solar energy would be a useful source. Select others that you believe have potential for hydropower and still others where wind power could be developed. On what factors did you base your choice?

2. **Explore Further:** Why does burning fossil fuels release carbon dioxide?

3. **Explore Further:** What are some possible adverse environmental effects of hydropower?

CAREER CONNECTION

As a **biochemist**, you would study the chemical composition and processes of living organisms, and the effects of substances on them. You might work in the research laboratory of a pharmaceutical company trying to determine how molecules of varying structures might affect a certain enzyme reaction. In a government laboratory, you might try to find out how toxins from disease organisms affect an important food crop such as corn.

---

2. Fossil fuels are composed of carbon or carbon compounds. Their oxidation results in CO_2 production.

3. Most hydropower requires damming rivers. This action floods valleys, drowns forest, and destroys existing wildlife habitat.

Going Further

Students may wish to build small model wind towers. The possibility of constructing a solar collector from aluminum foil is possible. The rise in temperature at the center of the collector can be demonstrated with the use of a thermometer. **L1**

CAREER CONNECTION

A career as a biochemist will require a college degree, usually a masters or a doctorate. A biochemistry major has requirements similar to a chemistry major but with additional courses in biological sciences. Courses in physics and mathematics are also recommended. To learn more about a career as a biochemist, contact the American Chemical Society or a university.

Purpose

Students are introduced to alternative energy sources, but they discover that all these sources depend on the sun's energy.

Background

It is estimated that by the year 2000, the United States will obtain 25% of its energy needs from renewable sources (hydropower, solar, wind, geothermal, and burning of biomass) and 75% from nonrenewable sources (nuclear, natural gas, oil, and coal).

Teaching Strategies

- Have students work in small groups to arrive at a consensus to the following questions: (a) What is meant by renewable and nonrenewable energy resources? (b) Why are solar, wind, and hydropower considered to be renewable energy alternatives? (c) What is the renewable component to these three energy forms? (d) Why are fossil fuels such as coal and oil nonrenewable? (e) Why should research in alternative energy sources concentrate more on renewable rather than on nonrenewable sources? **L1**

Possible Answers

1. Any country or region of a country that receives sun during a large portion of the day would be a good choice for solar energy—deserts and surrounding regions plus regions close to the equator. Hydropower depends on large quantities of moving water. Therefore, any region that has mountainous areas with steadily flowing rivers should have potential for hydropower. Also, methods are being developed to obtain energy from ocean waves and tidal flow. Countries located in regions where the prevailing winds are constant or in areas that contain windy mountain passes are suitable for wind power. Certain areas along coastlines can take advantage of strong onshore and offshore winds.

CHAPTER 6

CHAPTER REVIEW

Summary

Summary statements can be used by students to review the major concepts of the chapter.

Language of Biology

Answers should go beyond defining the terms. Accept any reasonable answer that uses the term correctly and in the proper context.

Understanding Concepts

1. Once activated, an exergonic reaction releases energy. In an endergonic reaction, more than activation energy is required. A source of free energy is required as well.
2. endergonic—reactants lower than products; exergonic—reactants higher than products
3. The first step must be endergonic because energy is released. Glucose phosphate has higher potential energy.
4. ATP provides a suitable source and amount of free energy to carry out most endergonic biological reactions.
5. As ATP is converted to ADP and inorganic phosphate, energy is released. Because ADP and inorganic phosphate have less potential energy than ATP, energy is needed to make more ATP. That energy comes from glucose or other energy-rich molecules in an exergonic process.
6. The reaction in cells is a series of many steps, allowing the energy released little by little to be trapped and used to make ATP.
7. Carbon comes from carbon dioxide, hydrogen from water, and oxygen from carbon dioxide. The oxygen released is from water.
8. Photosynthesis will not occur. The chloroplast's membranes, pigments, and enzymes must be present.
9. Carotenoids absorb certain wavelengths that chlorophyll *a* cannot and pass that energy along to the chlorophyll *a*.

10. Both producers and consumers require oxygen for aerobic respiration.
11. protection, controlling evaporation, transport of water to the leaf, transport of sugars away from the leaf, and allowing carbon dioxide into the leaf

Summary

Many cell processes involve endergonic reactions. Such reactions require free energy, which is released in an exergonic reaction that is linked to the endergonic reaction. Free energy needed to drive endergonic reactions in cells is transferred from the conversion of ATP to ADP molecules.

Energy required to form ATP from ADP and phosphate is transferred from the breakdown of energy-rich molecules such as glucose during aerobic respiration or fermentation. Aerobic respiration releases much more energy per glucose molecule than does fermentation. Thus, many more ATP molecules can be produced from a single glucose molecule by aerobic respiration.

In photosynthesis, light energy absorbed by chlorophyll is used to build three-carbon simple sugar molecules from the raw materials carbon dioxide and water. Oxygen is a by-product of the process. These simple sugars can be used directly as energy sources, or used to make more complex molecules, such as fats and amino acids. They can also be used to form glucose, most of which is changed to disaccharides, starch, or cellulose.

The sugars produced by the Calvin cycle of photosynthesis have higher potential energy than the raw materials. This added energy was converted from sunlight during the light reactions.

Cellular respiration and photosynthesis are interdependent processes, because the products of one process are recycled and used as the raw materials of the other. Once the energy-rich molecules that are the products of photosynthesis have been broken down to release energy for biological work, some energy is lost as heat. Thus, a continuous input of energy in the form of sunlight is necessary for life on Earth.

Language of Biology

Write a sentence that shows your understanding of each of the following terms.

absorption spectrum	exergonic
aerobic respiration	free energy
alcoholic fermentation	grana
anaerobic	lactic acid fermentation
ATP	light reactions
Calvin cycle	stroma
carotenoid	visible spectrum
endergonic	wavelength

Understanding Concepts

1. Explain why biological reactions that are exergonic require an enzyme only, but endergonic reactions require an enzyme and ATP.
2. Compare the relative potential energies of reactants and products in endergonic reactions with those in exergonic reactions.
3. An ATP molecule is used in the first step of cellular respiration, producing a molecule of glucose phosphate and a molecule of ADP. Is this process exergonic or endergonic? How do you know? Which has higher potential energy, glucose or glucose phosphate?
4. Why do you think that ATP is referred to as the "energy currency" of living organisms?
5. Tell what happens in the ATP-ADP cycle.
6. When sugar burns in air, it reacts quickly, giving off heat and light as water and carbon dioxide are formed. Aerobic respiration of sugar in cells involves the same overall reaction. How does the reaction in cells differ from the reaction in air?
7. Examine the equation summarizing photosynthesis on page 155. What is the source of each of the atoms in the molecules of sugar produced? What is the source of the oxygen given off?
8. Suppose you have a test tube containing chlorophyll and water. If you bubble carbon dioxide into the tube and shine light on it, will photosynthesis occur? Explain.

PROGRAM RESOURCES

Teacher Classroom Resources
Chapter Assessment, pp. 21-24 L1
Performance Assessment in Biology, p. 12 L2
Alternate Assessment in the Science Classroom
Computer Test Bank L1

9. An experiment can be done showing that wavelengths of light, other than blue and red, the wavelengths absorbed by chlorophyll *a*, are necessary for photosynthesis. How can this observation be explained?

10. How is the oxygen produced during photosynthesis important to both producers and consumers?

11. The leaf is the organ of photosynthesis in most plants, but only some of its cells carry out photosynthesis. Other leaf parts perform functions needed for photosynthesis to take place. What are some of those functions?

Applying Concepts

12. The title of this chapter is "The Flow of Energy." Summarize the flow of energy in most living systems beginning with light energy.

13. An important scientific law states that the total amount of free energy in the universe is declining. How does the process of cellular respiration illustrate that law? Hint: Remember the definition of free energy.

14. Imagine a sealed container that light can enter. It contains producers, but the only consumers are those that carry out lactic acid fermentation. Could the life in that container continue to exist? Explain.

15. Would the survival period of the organisms in the container in the previous question be longer if consumers that undergo aerobic respiration were present? Explain.

16. **Economics Connection:** What simple clue, requiring no special equipment, would indicate that yeast in a sugar solution are undergoing fermentation rather than aerobic respiration?

17. **Considering the Environment:** Large arrays of photovoltaic cells can convert sunlight into electric energy to power homes. What provison would be necessary in such a system to be able to have power on cloudy days?

Lab Interpretation

18. **Investigation:** Suppose you want to determine the optimum pH for fermentation of glucose by yeast cells. State a hypothesis and describe an experiment that you could do to test it. What factors would you keep constant?

19. **Minilab 1:** A student carries out an experiment similar to the one described in Minilab 1. The student uses two test tubes, records the temperature in each tube every 30 seconds, and prepares the following graph from the data. Use the graph to answer the following questions. (a) Which tube probably contained liver chunks? How do you know? (b) According to the graph, when were the liver chunks added? How do you know? (c) Which tube was the experimental control? How would the student's conclusion have differed if there had been no control? Why? (d) Predict the temperatures of tubes A and B if they were allowed to stand for 20 minutes more. Explain your reasoning.

20. **Minilab 2:** Suppose you prepare two test tubes with Elodea sprigs and bromothymol blue solution. The blue color indicates that there is almost no CO_2 present. Then, instead of placing the tubes in the light, you place both in the dark for 24 hours. Predict what you would see after 24 hours. Explain your observations. Hint: Review Section 6.1 of your text.

Connecting Ideas

21. Active transport requires ATP. What role does ATP play in this process?

22. During aerobic respiration, a molecule binds to the product of one reaction, pulls it through the membrane of a mitochondrion, and transfers it to another molecule. What kind of molecule does this? How do you think the molecule passes through the membrane?

Applying Concepts

12. During photosynthesis, light is transformed to chemical energy of ATP and then to chemical energy in the bonds of sugars or other energy-rich molecules. In both aerobic respiration and fermentation, energy in the bonds of sugars or other molecules is released and used to form ATP. The energy of ATP is used for endergonic reactions, after which it is transformed to heat.

13. The energy released during cellular respiration is used to carry out life functions and is then transformed to heat, which is not available to do more biological work.

14. The producers could not survive because lactic acid fermentation releases no CO_2, which the producers need for photosynthesis.

15. Yes, because aerobic respiration produces CO_2, and the producers produce sugars and oxygen needed for aerobic respiration.

16. The smell of alcohol is the clue that fermentation is occurring.

17. A mechanism such as an array of batteries is necessary to store the electric energy.

Lab Interpretation

18. Here is a sample hypothesis. If the optimum pH for yeast fermentation is 7, then the rate at which bubbles of CO_2 are released should be greatest at this pH. Use the same setup as in the Investigation. Add acid or base to samples of sugar solution to obtain a range of pH values. Allow each tube to ferment at the optimum temperature and count the number of bubbles released per 10 min. Constants would be amount of sugar solution, amount of yeast suspension, and temperature.

19. (a) Tube B contained liver chunks because it had a rise in temperature indicating that energy was given off by a reaction. (b) It isn't possible to tell for sure. A good assumption would be that the chunks were added at 2 min. because the temperature rise began at 2.5 min.

(c) Tube A was the control. No temperature rise was observed; therefore, Tube A probably contained only hydrogen peroxide solution. (d) The temperature of tube B was already declining at 5.5 min. Therefore, it is likely that the reaction had nearly stopped. After 20 min., it is likely that tube B would have cooled to the same temperature as tube A.

20. The tubes would be yellow after 24 hours because cellular respiration would continue, releasing CO_2 as a product.

Connecting Ideas

21. **Energy:** ATP provides the energy to change the shape of a pump so that particles can be moved from a region of lesser to greater concentration.

22. **Systems and Interactions:** The molecule passes across the mitochondrial membrane by means of a transport protein.

The Continuation of Life

Unit Overview

Unit 3 treats the fundamental process of reproduction from cellular and biochemical points of view. Chapter 7 focuses on mitosis and meiosis as students learn how both body cells and reproductive cells are produced and how meiosis, in combination with fertilization, results in variation among offspring. In Chapter 8, students study Mendel's experiments and apply his laws and the ideas of probability to the solution of genetics problems. Chapter 9 presents the experimental evidence that led to the discovery of DNA as the genetic material and discusses its structure, its role in coding for synthesis of polypeptides, and the nature of the code. Then, in Chapter 10, students learn how the DNA code is actually deciphered in polypeptide synthesis. Students conclude their study of the unit with Chapter 11, in which they learn about examples of human genetic disorders, their symptoms, and possible treatments and cures.

Theme Development

Students will recognize the theme of energy as it applies to mitosis, meiosis, DNA replication, and polypeptide synthesis. Unity within diversity is appreciated as students recognize that mitosis and meiosis are functions common to all eukaryotes, and that DNA function is a characteristic of all organisms. Patterns of change is evident in the discussion of variation resulting from meiosis and fertilization, mutations, and gene duplications. Systems and interactions is stressed in the study of the processes mentioned above. Finally, methods of inquiry is evident in the discussion of spontaneous generation, Mendel's experiments, discovery of DNA, and human genetics.

The Continuation of Life

The Rosetta Stone, shown below, provided an important clue to the deciphering of Egyptian hieroglyphic writing because it had three translations of the same text side by side. Other codes have been broken when scientists called cryptologists learned to recognize patterns of letters or proper names, such as the name and title of a king.

The model of DNA is based on the work of many people. The clues used to decipher this code were discovered over a period of 30 years, and were contributed by scientists from many disciplines. How do scientific methods enable scientists to decipher a code such as this one?

166

Advance Planning

Chapter 7
- Prepare methylene blue stain and order prepared slides of onion root tips for the Investigation.
- Order prepared slides of onion root tips and animal mitosis (whitefish, sea urchin, or roundworm) for Minilab 1.
- Prepare aceto-orcein stain and order hydrochloric acid for the Alternate Lab.

Chapter 8
- Order tobacco seeds for the Investigation.

Chapter 9
- Prepare salmon testes solution for Minilab 2.
- Procure empty gelatin capsules for the Alternate Lab.

Chapter 10
- Order alpha-amylase enzyme and prepare Benedict's and starch solutions for Minilab 2.

Chapter 11
- Procure a grip tester for the Investigation.
- Order prepared slides of human red blood cells, both normal and sickled, and prepare methylene blue stain for the Minilabs.
- Order karyotypes for the Alternate Lab.

The discovery of the Rosetta Stone was a dramatic breakthrough for linguists, scientists who study and translate languages. Linguists recognized one of the languages on the stone as Greek, and the other two as forms of ancient Egyptian. At that time, linguists were not able to translate either of the Egyptian languages. The Greek text stated that the same information was written on the tablet in all three languages. Working with this valuable clue, linguists over the next 30 years were able to decipher the hieroglyphic writing that appeared on many of the ancient Egyptian monuments.

Just as translating hieroglyphic writing depended upon breaking a code, identifying and translating the code of life depended upon many different lines of investigation over a long period of time. Learning how the code of life was deciphered, and understanding how the code is translated, is the focus of Unit Three, The Continuation of Life.

Introducing the Unit

Using the Photos

Like the linguists who used the Rosetta Stone to decipher hieroglyphics, scientists used a variety of clues, based upon many experiments and techniques, to reveal the mystery of the genetic code. Breaking the DNA code led not only to a basic scientific understanding of how that complex molecule functions in polypeptide synthesis, but also to a broader understanding of genetics and to technological advances such as recombinant DNA and gene therapy. Discovery of DNA and the means by which it encodes information is a prime example of how science continually builds upon previous knowledge.

Previewing the Chapters

Chapter 7 builds a strong foundation for this unit, focusing on the downfall of spontaneous generation, the cell cycle, and mitosis and meiosis. Students learn that both processes contribute to genetic continuity and that meiosis is an important source of variation.

With this background, students then explore genetics in Chapter 8. Mendel's experiments and laws, as well as non-Mendelian patterns of heredity, are studied, and the principles of probability are used in solving genetics problems. Students associate meiosis with genetics as they study the chromosome theory of heredity.

In Chapter 9, students learn first of the discovery of DNA as the genetic material and then of the double helix model. They study DNA replication and learn that DNA codes for polypeptides. They complete the chapter by examining the nature of that code.

Chapter 10 continues the story of DNA, focusing first on transcription and then on translation. Students then relate phenotypes to DNA and polypeptide synthesis. They study eukaryotic chromosomes, learning that those chromosomes contain multiple copies of some genes and much DNA that is nonfunctional. Students

examine sources of variation and recombinant DNA techniques.

All previous material in this unit is put to use as students study human genetic disorders in Chapter 11. They come to understand how those disorders result from chromosomal or gene abnormalities and are able to correlate the causes and symptoms of genetic disorders with DNA and polypeptide synthesis. They conclude the chapter by examining possible treatments and cures.

ORGANIZER
C H A P T E R
7

SECTION	OBJECTIVES	TEXT LABS/FEATURES
7.1 Life from Life—Cells from Cells (3 days)	**Describe** the debate surrounding spontaneous generation and how Redi's and Pasteur's experiments ended that debate. **Sequence** the events of the cell cycle in which new body cells are produced. **Analyze** the ways in which events of the cell cycle are controlled.	**Math Connection:** Why Cells Divide, p. 174 **Investigation:** Growth of Onion Root Tips, p. 178 **Thinking Lab:** Where is the nuclear membrane during mitosis? p. 180 **Minilab 1:** How is animal mitosis different from plant mitosis? p. 181
7.2 Production of Reproductive Cells (3 days)	**Sequence** the series of events by which reproductive cells are produced in complex plants and in animals. **Analyze** the significance of meiosis with respect to adaptation and evolution.	**Minilab 2:** How can you make a model of meiosis? p. 186
BIOLOGY, TECHNOLOGY, AND SOCIETY		**Biotechnology:** Aging: Can We Stop the Clock? p. 191 **Medicine Connection:** Hope for Spinal Cord Injury Patients, p. 193 **Career Connection:** Occupational therapist, p. 193

LAB MATERIALS

INVESTIGATION	MINILAB	ALTERNATE LAB
page 178 coverslip dropper marking pen, extra fine tip methylene blue stain microscope onion bulblet prepared slide of onion root tip razor blade, single-edge slide test tube test-tube holder	**page 181** microscope prepared slides of: onion root tips; embryos of white fish, sea urchins, or roundworm *Ascaris* **page 186** pipe cleaners string yarn, or modeling clay, or salt-dough	**page 176** aceto-orcein stain broad beans (*Vica faba*) coverslip forceps HCl microscope paper towels pot scalpel slide vermiculite watch glass, covered

TEACHER CLASSROOM RESOURCES	OTHER RESOURCES
Study Guide, pp. 37-39 **Concept Mapping,** p. 7 ***PLL:** *Spontaneous Generation,* p. 40 ***PLL:** *Significance of Time and Mitosis,* p. 42 ****ILS:** *Mitosis,* p. 69 ****ILS:** *Time for Mitosis,* p. 73	***STVS:** *Plant Clones,* Plants and Simple Organisms (Disc 4, Side 2) ***STVS:** *Nerve Regeneration in Garfish,* Animals (Disc 5, Side 2) **Color Transparency 9:** *Mitosis*
Study Guide, pp. 40-42 **Critical Thinking/Problem Solving:** *Meiosis in Males and Females,* p. 7 ****ILS:** *Comparing Mitosis and Meiosis,* p. 77	**Color Transparency 10:** *Meiosis*
Assessment Materials **Chapter Assessment,** pp. 25-28 **Performance Assessment in Biology,** p. 14 **Alternate Assessment in the Science Classroom** **Computer Test Bank**	**Spanish Resources** **Cooperative Learning Resource Guide** **Videodisc Correlations** (to Optical Data's and Videodiscovery's videodiscs)

* Probing Levels of Life
** Investigating Living Systems

* Science Technology Videodisc Series

ADDITIONAL RESOURCES

Infinite Voyage *The Living Clock*
How does time affect living things? From aging to timing of flowering, nature is full of cycles. Students will see how timing is important in natural cycles.

Audiovisual
Meiosis: The Key to Diversity, video, Insight Media.
Mitosis Video, video, Frey Scientific.

Software
Meiosis, Apple 128K/MAC/IBM, EME.
Mitosis, Apple II, Learning Arts.

CELLULAR REPRODUCTION

Chapter Overview

Students begin the chapter by analyzing the experiments of Redi and Pasteur, which led to the downfall of spontaneous generation and the acceptance of the theory of biogenesis. They come to understand how that theory and the cell theory, developed about the same time, complement one another.

Reminded of the fact that all cells come from other cells, students then explore the reasons why most cells must reproduce. They study the cell cycle of eukaryotes and then the stages of mitosis. Next, students learn of factors that control the cell cycle, and then compare binary fission in prokaryotes to mitosis in eukaryotes.

After distinguishing between diploid and haploid cells, students see the logic behind the process of meiosis. They then study and compare the stages of meiosis in male and female animals. Finally, they come to realize that meiosis not only results in genetic continuity, but also, along with fertilization, leads to genetic recombination, which is important for evolution.

CELLULAR REPRODUCTION

ALL ORGANISMS, great and small, start with a single cell. Then they begin to grow. Young animals, such as bear cubs and human teenagers, seem to spend much of their time eating and growing. Their growth is especially apparent as they increase in body size and weight. Less obvious is the growth that occurs in adults. They may not be growing larger or heavier, but their cells are continuously being renewed and replaced. Cuts are healed, the lining of the intestine is regrown, and worn blood cells are replaced.

Growth is the result of a cell's ability to reproduce itself. New body cells are produced from other, already existing cells when one cell becomes two. Whether growth occurs in young animals or in adults, new cells are produced that contain the same genetic information as the cells from which they came. But when a new individual, such as you or a bear cub, is first produced, specialized reproductive cells come together. This joining of reproductive cells, one from each parent, produces an individual with a unique combination of genetic material. In this chapter, you will study the process that produces and replaces body cells and the process that produces reproductive cells needed for the formation of new individuals. You will see that, although the two processes differ, they both ensure *continuance*. The first process of cell reproduction results in continuance of an individual's growth and life. The second—the formation of reproductive cells—assures continuance of the species to which that individual belongs.

KEY TERMS

anaphase
binary fission
cell cycle
cell plate
centromere
chromatid
diploid
fertilization

gamete
genetic recombination
haploid
homologue
interphase
meiosis
metaphase
mitosis

prophase
sexual reproduction
spindle
spontaneous generation
spore
telophase
zygote

Is this a cell of a cub or kitten, starfish or guppy, worm or butterfly? Whatever the identity of the organism, we know that it's growing because cell reproduction is underway. Magnification: 315×

Chapter Preview

Contents

Introducing the Chapter

The photograph on these two pages can serve as a focal point to get this chapter going. Those bear cubs will grow into some very large animals. Remind students that all organisms are composed of cells, and lead them to the conclusion that an increase in number of cells must be associated with growth. Building on what they have previously learned about the nuclei of eukaryotic cells, ask them what parts of the nucleus are most crucial in terms of cell reproduction and why. Once they recall that the chromosomes are in the nucleus and that they contain DNA, students should be able to reason out the general idea that chromosomes must be replicated and that each new cell must have the same set of chromosomes as the parent cell. Calling attention to the photo of the cell on this page, point out that cell reproduction is carried out in a very precise way.

Theme Development
The theme of unity within diversity should become apparent as students begin to appreciate the idea that all cells must replicate and pass on their genetic message to daughter cells; however, different processes have evolved to carry out that function. Patterns of change is a theme that can be related to the discussion of how meiosis and fertilization lead to variation among organisms and serve as raw materials for evolution.

Tying to Previous Knowledge
Students will build upon their knowledge of cell structure and function as they examine the various cell parts that play a role in the processes of mitosis and meiosis.

ASSESSMENT PLANNER

Choose assessment strategies from the following pages to evaluate the progress of your students.

Prepare

Key Concepts

A historical development of the theory of biogenesis is briefly presented, and the process of mitosis is described in detail.

Key Terms

spontaneous generation, interphase, mitosis, cell cycle, prophase, spindle, chromatid, centromere, metaphase, anaphase, telophase, cell plate, binary fission

Materials

- Gather broad beans, aceto-orcein stain, vermiculite, and HCl for the Alternate Lab.
- Collect onion bulblets, methylene blue, and mitosis slides for the Investigation.
- Order prepared slides of mitosis in onion root tip cells and animal cells for Minilab 1.

1 Focus

Objectives

The objectives are listed on the student page. Remind students to preview these objectives as a guide to this numbered section.

Demonstration

Demonstrate Redi's experiment disproving spontaneous generation. Place *Drosophila* food in two culture vials attached to a population growth chamber. Cover one of the vials with netting so that the flies cannot reach the food. After the *Drosophila* have been in the chamber for approximately one week, larvae and pupae can be observed along the sides of the uncovered vial, but not in the covered vial. This is analogous to Redi's experiment with meat and houseflies.

Objectives

Describe the debate surrounding spontaneous generation and how Redi's and Pasteur's experiments ended that debate.

Sequence the events of the cell cycle in which new body cells are produced.

Analyze the ways in which events of the cell cycle are controlled.

7.1 Life from Life—Cells from Cells

Suppose you were to plant a partly eaten apple, or perhaps just drop it on the ground. Under the right conditions, a seedling sprouts and eventually grows into a mature apple tree. Each new growing season, pollen from blossoms on the tree reaches the eggs of other blossoms and more seeds are formed. Thus, the potential for more apple trees continues.

Continuity exists among all life forms. Butterflies mate, the female deposits her fertilized eggs on a leaf, and those eggs hatch into caterpillars that change form and eventually become mature butterflies. These examples, though different in their details, illustrate a major idea: Living things are produced from other living things of the same kind.

Debating Spontaneous Generation

In the past, people were not all so certain that like produces like. Many myths prevailed to explain the origin of some organisms. According to some myths, eels came from the slime at the bottom of rivers and oceans, and maggots arose from decaying meat.

Testing the Myths A number of scientists in the past accepted the myths because the scientists were not applying some very basic methods of science. Often, the myths themselves were the result of insufficient observations and data. In modern terms, the myths were hypotheses; and hypotheses, however logical they may be, are only explanations of what a scientist has observed. As you know, the validity of a hypothesis must be determined by controlled experiments. Some early scientists did perform experiments, but they did not use proper controls. The results of such faulty experiments convinced those scientists that some nonliving things could give rise spontaneously to living things, an idea that is known as **spontaneous generation**.

In 1668, Francesco Redi performed a simple, but well-thought-out, controlled experiment to test the commonly held belief that maggots were spontaneously generated from decaying meat. Redi had observed that maggots became flies and that flies were always found near decaying meat. He suspected that the maggots in meat actually arose from the eggs of flies that landed on the meat, rather than from the meat itself. To test his suspicion,

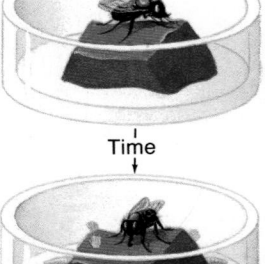

Figure 7-1 **Redi's experiment showed that maggots do not spontaneously generate from decaying meat.**

Air circulates through cloth.

Time

Eggs and maggots do not appear.

Time

Eggs and maggots appear on meat.

170 CELLULAR REPRODUCTION

Redi placed a piece of meat in each of two jars and tightly covered one jar with a piece of cloth so that air, but not flies, could reach the meat. The other jar was left open. In a few days, Redi observed that maggots were crawling on the meat that was exposed to flies. In the sealed jar, maggots never developed. The experiment showed that maggots are the offspring of houseflies, that they develop into flies just like the parents that produced them, reproduce, and, in turn, produce more maggots.

Two More Centuries Over the next few years, the conflict about how maggots and other familiar organisms come into existence gradually subsided. Then, in 1675, the world of microorganisms was discovered. A major event in itself, this discovery reopened the split between scientists who believed in spontaneous generation and those who did not. Those who believed quickly assumed that these never-before-seen organisms were spontaneously generated. The debate, which was to last for almost another 200 years, raged again.

Disproving Spontaneous Generation

Finally in 1864, Louis Pasteur, a great French scientist, devised an elegant experiment that ended the debate. Pasteur's findings from earlier research had revealed the existence of reproductive cells called spores. Pasteur hypothesized that these spores were carried on dust particles in the air, where they were inactive, but that they developed into active microorganisms when nutrients were available.

At the time, air was believed to be an essential ingredient necessary for spontaneous generation; it was supposed to contain a vital force necessary to generate life. Pasteur realized that to disprove spontaneous generation, he would have to conduct an experiment in which spores were kept from entering the nutrient-rich solutions, called infusions, in which microorganisms grow, but air was allowed to enter. To conduct such an experiment, he designed a novel flask that had a long, S-shaped neck, as seen in Figure 7-3. He prepared infusions and boiled them thoroughly, allowing steam to flow throughout the flask. The heat killed any organisms that were present in the infusion, and steam killed any spores clinging to the glass. Pasteur predicted that air entering the neck of the flask would contain dust and spores, but that they would be trapped in the curve of the neck and never reach the infusion. The infusion would remain clear and free of microorganisms.

Pasteur's prediction proved to be correct. His experiment showed that microorganisms, like other, more familiar organisms, are not spontaneously generated, even in the presence of air.

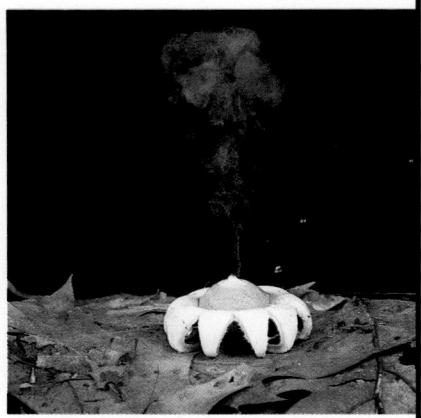

Figure 7-2 Fungi, such as this Earth star, shoot millions of tiny spores into the air. If a spore lands where nutrients are available, it starts to grow. Why might this occurrence have seemed to be spontaneous generation to early scientists?

Figure 7-3 Pasteur's experiment is diagrammed here. His flasks are on display at the Pasteur Institute in Paris. They are still free from growth of microorganisms after almost 150 years!

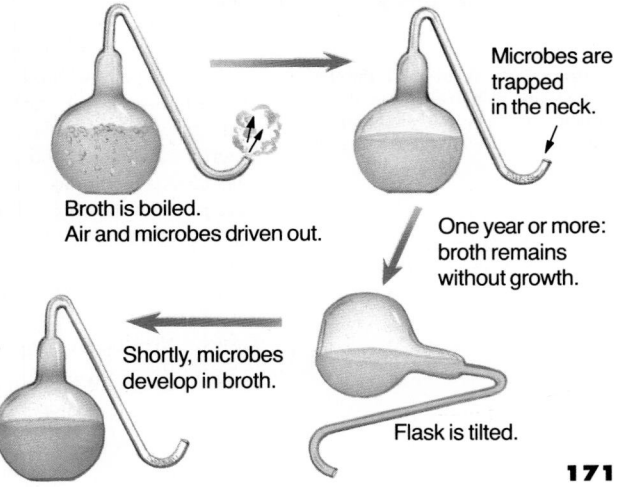

Broth is boiled. Air and microbes driven out.

Microbes are trapped in the neck.

One year or more: broth remains without growth.

Flask is tilted.

Shortly, microbes develop in broth.

171

2 Teach

Concept Development
Reinforce the fact that science is tentative and self-correcting. Redi's experiment showed that familiar organisms that could easily be seen come only from preexisting organisms. Many people still believed that microscopic organisms arose spontaneously, and the debate continued until Pasteur settled it. Although it is not likely to happen, science will be ready to alter its concept of spontaneous generation of any organism if it is ever demonstrated by repeatable experiments.

Science, Technology, and Society

Pasteurization: Pasteur's demonstration that bacteria do not grow spontaneously in broth has been put to widespread use in our society. Technology today allows processing and pasteurization of food with supervision of only a few workers. Without the process of pasteurization, milk, canned foods, beer, and hundreds of other food items would spoil quickly. This would result in a tremendous increase in cost to consumers.

Using the Illustration
After discussing the unique design of Pasteur's flasks using Figure 7-3, have students write a summary of Pasteur's experiment. **L1**

Figure Caption Question
Why might spore germination have seemed to be spontaneous generation to early scientists? Spores could not be seen with the naked eye, so fungal growth seemed to have arisen spontaneously.

SECTION 7.1

Using Science Terms

Point out that the prefix *bio* in the word *biogenesis* is from the Greek *bios,* meaning "life." The suffix *genesis,* from the Latin, means "origin." Ask students to explain why the word *biogenesis* is used in the theory name. *The theory explains that life originates from life.* Have them list other words that contain this prefix or suffix. *Biology, bioengineering, organogenesis* **L1** **LEP**

Demonstration

You can demonstrate that diffusion rate limits cell size by preparing unflavored gelatin in pH indicator solution. (Dissolve a packet of unflavored gelatin according to package directions, using dilute phenolphthalein solution in place of water.) **CAUTION:** If the indicator solution contains alcohol, do not heat over an open flame. Once the gelatin has hardened, you can cut it up into blocks that are one, two, and three centimeters on a side. Place all three blocks into a dilute solution of sodium hydroxide for five minutes, making sure that they are not touching each other. Remove the blocks and rinse them with water. Cut the blocks down the middle and measure the volume of each block that remains uncolored. Students will see that the sodium hydroxide has penetrated each block equally, but the volume of penetration is different. This demonstration illustrates one reason why cells remain small. **LEP**

Audiovisual

- Show the 28-minute film *Cell Reproduction,* McGraw-Hill Films.
- Many good audiovisual materials are available from your local chapter of the American Cancer Society.

Pasteur's work led to a major biological theory: At the present time and under present conditions on Earth, all organisms are produced from other organisms. That statement, known as the theory of biogenesis, tied in nicely with the cell theory, formulated at about the same time. The cell theory states that cells are the basic units of life, and that all cells are reproduced from other cells. Thus, by the late 19th century, scientists were working with two theories indicating that all life must come from life.

Reproduction of Body Cells

Think back to the apple tree or the butterfly discussed earlier in the chapter. The lives of the two organisms, like those of every other kind of organism, involve a cycle. Offspring are produced. They grow and take on their familiar traits as they mature, and at some point they reproduce, giving rise to descendants that repeat the pattern.

The cells that make up organisms go through a similar cycle. Cell reproduction occurs when parent cells divide. Two new daughter cells arise from each parent cell. Ongoing production of new cells serves several vital functions. Early in the development of a multicellular organism, an increasing number of cells contributes to overall growth and to the production of the many different cell types that will make up the mature organism. After reaching full development, the organism needs new cells to repair damaged tissue, replace cells that are lost from outer surfaces, and resist disease.

Small Is Better Cells come in different sizes, but almost all are microscopic, as you know. Why must cells be so small? Why doesn't each parent cell just keep growing, instead of dividing over and over again into small daughter cells?

Picture a balloon as you begin to inflate it. At first, the surface area of the balloon is large compared to the volume of air inside. But what happens as more air enters? The volume of air gets larger and larger and increases faster than the surface area of the balloon.

The same relationship between surface area and volume exists in a cell. As a cell grows larger, the volume of its cytoplasm increases more quickly than the surface area of its plasma membrane. Now recall that needed materials must enter, and cell products and wastes must leave, through a cell's plasma membrane. As the volume of cytoplasm increases, more and more particles must pass through the membrane to keep the cell functioning. If a cell continued to grow unchecked, it would eventually reach a point where the surface area of its plasma membrane would not be great enough to meet the cell's needs. The cell either would starve because of a lack of nutrients or would become poisoned because of a buildup of wastes. Cells stop growing or they reproduce before that point is reached.

The Cell Cycle When you view cells through a microscope, you will most often see them in a non-reproducing state. The nuclear membrane is

Figure 7-4 **A coconut is the seed of a coconut palm tree. The seed sprouts and begins to grow. Eventually, a mature multicellular tree is formed.**

clearly visible, and inside the nucleus, one or more nucleoli can be readily seen. If proper stains have been used, the chromatin, a mass of long, thin intertwined chromosomes, will stand out. This non-reproducing stage, in which a cell spends most of its life, is called **interphase.**

Interphase begins when cell reproduction is completed. Early in interphase, the newly produced cells are using energy to carry out the basic cell functions you have studied. In addition, new cell parts such as ribosomes and mitochondria are produced. New centrioles are made in animal cells, and chloroplasts are made in certain plant or algal cells.

In eukaryotes, the DNA of chromosomes is wound like a thread around spools of proteins, as seen in Figure 7-5. These wound spools, in turn, are highly coiled and arranged to form thick strands. It is these strands that make up the chromatin present in an interphase nucleus. Later, these strands will condense (shorten and thicken) and will become visible as distinct chromosomes.

Remember that the genetic information in DNA is used by the cell to make proteins. Some of these proteins function in cell parts, and others function as enzymes needed for cellular reactions. To survive, each daughter cell must have the same DNA instructions as its parent cell. Because DNA resides in the chromosomes, each daughter cell must have the same number of chromosomes as its parent cell. How can that happen?

About midway through interphase, each chromosome and the DNA it contains replicates. To replicate is to make an exact copy. Chromosome replication cannot be seen directly, but chemical tests show that it occurs. This replication provides a second set of chromosomes. Following chromosome replication, the final events of interphase occur. Then, two identical sets of chromosomes will be equally distributed to daughter nuclei during another part of the cell cycle called **mitosis.** Mitosis is usually, but not always, accompanied by division of the rest of the cell to produce two daughter cells. After mitosis and cell division are completed, the new daughter cells enter interphase. Together, interphase and mitosis make up the **cell cycle.**

Figure 7-5 **The DNA in eukaryotic chromosomes is wrapped around spools of proteins and is highly coiled.**

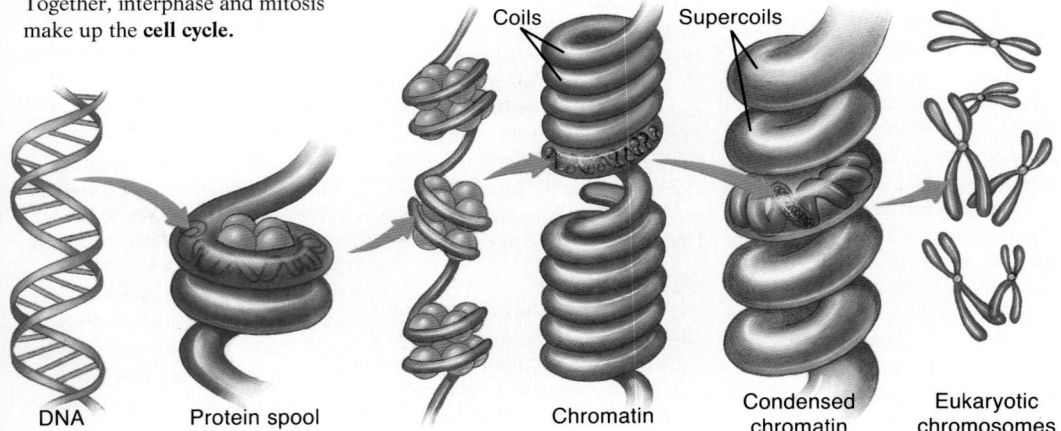

Coils   Supercoils

DNA   Protein spool   Chromatin   Condensed chromatin   Eukaryotic chromosomes

CHEMISTRY CONNECTION

Replication of DNA: The chemical tests that show that replication is occurring measure the amount of nitrogen bases inside the nucleus. Between the beginning of interphase and the end of interphase, the amount of nitrogen bases doubles. Assays of the relative amounts of each base in the chromosomes prove that the chromosomes replicate.

Microscope Activity

Students can make smears of their cheek cells and stain them with methylene blue to see cells in interphase. (See page 27T.) **CAUTION:** Methylene blue will permanently stain clothing. **L1**

Concept Development

Mention that many of the vocabulary terms in this section and the next will use the suffix *phase,* which means stage. The stages are arbitrary, and the end of one phase blends into the next without stopping. The edges of the phases are often difficult to distinguish.

Using an Analogy

A cut rubber band wound tightly around a pencil can be used to represent the coiling of DNA around a protein. Have students point out the similarities and differences between the rubber band and pencil and the DNA and its associated protein. Similarities are that both coil tightly, that the rubber band and DNA are linear, and that the pencil and protein represent points for the coiling. Differences include that one is microscopic and the other is macroscopic; DNA is made of nitrogen bases, phosphate groups, and deoxyribose and pencils are composed of carbon and cellulose. **LEP**

MEETING INDIVIDUAL NEEDS

To demonstrate chromosome thickening to students who are learning disabled, remove a telephone cord from a phone. Have students stretch out the cord. Discuss how it is long and thin. Allow the cord to return to its usual position. Make sure they understand that the cord shortens and thickens when it goes back into position. Explain that this is comparable to what happens to chromosomes during prophase of mitosis when the chromatin condenses. **LEP**

Misconception

Students often think that cells in all tissues continue to divide throughout life. Point out that there are tissues in which the cell cycle stops after a certain period. If nerve cells in humans are killed, they will not be replaced by mitosis and cell division of living nerve cells. In plants, mitosis occurs only in meristems. All growth in plants results from simple enlargement of cells derived from meristems.

MATH CONNECTION

Purpose
This feature gives a mathematical explanation for why cells must be small. The surface-to-volume ratio of a cube is used as an analogy for a cell.

Teaching Strategies
Ask students if they have ever seen or heard about monster movies with titles like "The Blob." Most students will be familiar with such movies. Then ask them if such giant, single-celled monsters are possible. Most students will answer in the negative. Tell them that the reason such monsters cannot exist is mathematical. Then, have them read the feature and answer the questions at the end.

Possible Answers
1. 24 cm^2:8 cm^3 or 3:1
2. Well-chewed food has a greater surface-to-volume ratio than less-well-chewed food.
3. Large cells may have several nuclei scattered throughout the cytoplasm.

Going Further
Have a class discussion of the processes that require large surface-to-volume ratios. Include digestion, excretion, and transport in the discussion. L1

COOP LEARN

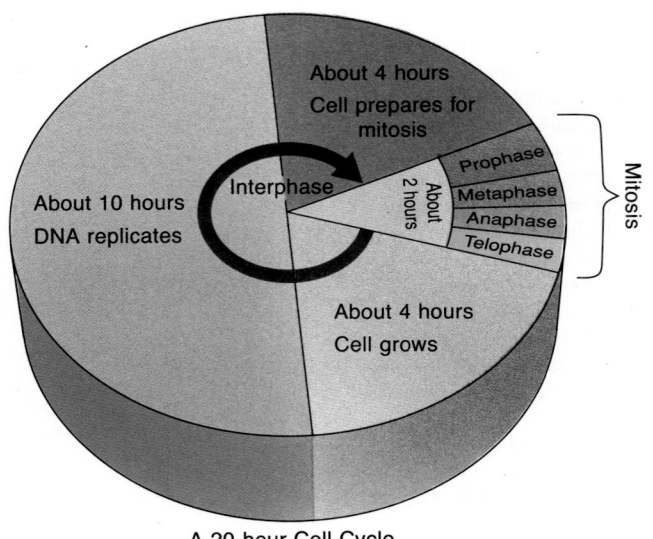

A 20-hour Cell Cycle

Figure 7-6 This cell cycle is typical for some actively dividing cells of mammals. Note that the largest portion of time is spent in interphase.

Mitosis

Suppose, during an investigation with your microscope, you were to catch a living cell in the mitosis portion of its cell cycle. You might think of yourself as having a seat for a four-act drama. Each act, however, follows the previous one without a pause or curtain close. Your program tells you that the drama you are witnessing occurs in most of the cells of eukaryotes. The program also reminds you that the main characters, the chromosomes, prepared for the drama during interphase when they replicated. You are already familiar enough with the plot to know that the drama will end when the chromosomes have distributed the replicas equally among new nuclei of new cells. So turn down the lights and watch the players in action.

M A T H   C O N N E C T I O N

Why Cells Divide
. . . .

One hundred trillion cells—that's approximately how many make up your body. As you can imagine, each cell is very small. If you could line up 1000 of those cells, they would total less than 2 centimeters in length—only about the width of your thumbnail.

How does cell size in other living things compare? You might expect the cells of a mouse to be tiny and those of an elephant to be gigantic. Surprisingly, these animals have something in common with each other and with you. The cells in mice, elephants, and humans are all about the same size.

Why Small? Whatever the size of the whole organism, the cells remain small. That's because it is advantageous for cells to have as much surface area as possible. Through this all-important surface area, cells absorb oxygen and nutrients and give off carbon dioxide and wastes. A larger surface area allows more of this interchange to go on. In addition, the smaller cell size means that the incoming nutrients have to travel a shorter distance to reach the center of the cell.

Surface-to-Volume The diagram on the next page shows how surface area is related to volume. The first cube, which is 1 centimeter on each side, has a volume of 1 cubic centimeter (height × width × depth).

Its surface area is 6 square centimeters (height × width × 6 sides of the cube). Comparing the surface area to the volume produces a ratio of 6/1, or 6.

Using the same math on the second cube, which is 4 centimeters on each side, yields a surface area of 4 × 4 × 6, or 96, and a volume of 4 × 4 × 4, or 64. Thus, this cube has a smaller surface-to-volume ratio—96/64, or 1.5. Even though it is larger, the second cube has a relatively smaller surface area than the first cube.

Now look what happens when the larger cube is divided into 64 small cubes. The large cube still has the same volume, 64, but it now has a total surface area of 384 (1 × 1 × 6 × 64 cubes), and its surface-

174 🐾 CELLULAR REPRODUCTION

MEETING INDIVIDUAL NEEDS

Visually Impaired: If you have students make models of chromosomes that demonstrate the events of mitosis, it will be necessary to modify the models for students who are visually impaired. One way to do this is with tactile modifications. For instance, if you are making the chromosomes from tubing, you can roughen the surface of one part of the tube so that students can distinguish it from a different tube. Also, you can use tubes of different lengths to show differences in chromosomes.

Act One—Prophase The first act among the four stages of mitosis—**prophase**—opens with disintegrating nucleoli. The thick strands of chromatin are forming loops and condensing, growing thicker and shorter in the process. Separate chromosomes cannot yet be seen clearly.

A little later, the nucleoli have disappeared completely. Chromosomes become clearly visible, and the nuclear membrane is beginning to break down. In animal cells, the two pairs of centrioles begin to separate and migrate toward opposite poles of the cell. Microtubules form between the two pairs of centrioles and become assembled into tiny fibers. These fibers, located between the centrioles, form a football-shaped structure called the **spindle**. Some fibers are quite short, extending just a short distance from the centrioles. Many of the longer fibers overlap one another at the equator (center) of the spindle. Although most non-animal eukaryotic cells lack centrioles, they do have spindles.

Still later in prophase, the nuclear membrane has completely disappeared. Chromosomes appear even more distinct. The fact that replication has occurred is noticeable because the chromosomes are double-stranded structures. Each strand is a replica of the other and is called a **chromatid**. The two chromatids of a chromosome, called sister chromatids, are joined at a region of attachment, the **centromere**. The centromere region of the chromosome serves not only to attach the two chromatids to each other but also to attach the chromosome to the microtubules of the spindle.

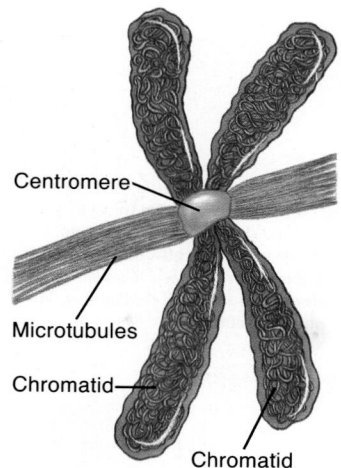

Centromere

Microtubules

Chromatid

Chromatid

Figure 7-7 This metaphase chromosome has two sister chromatids held together at the centromere and attached to spindle microtubules.

to-volume ratio increases from 1.5 to 6. The divided cube has a much greater surface area.

To get an idea of relative surface area, pretend that the large cube and the individual parts of the divided cube are gift boxes. Suppose that you are wrapping each gift box in fancy paper. You'd need a lot more paper to wrap all of the small boxes than to wrap the one large box. However, you could store either the one large box or all of the small boxes in the same space because their volumes are equal.

1. **Solve the Problem:** Figure out the surface-to-volume ratio of a cube that is 2 centimeters on each side.

2. **Connection to Health:** Keeping in mind surface-to-volume ratio, why do you think it would take less time to digest food that is well chewed?

3. **Solve the Problem:** A nucleus can exert control over only a limited volume of cell contents. What adaptation might a large cell have to overcome this problem?

	Volume	Surface Area	Surface-to-Volume Ratio
	1	6	6
	64	96	1.5
	64	384	6

PORTFOLIO

Have students draw and caption a six-block cartoon strip. The first block should show interphase, and the remaining blocks should depict the stages of mitosis and cell division. Student drawings should include the important structures and indicate proper movements of the structures, but may have a humorous twist. **L1**

SECTION 7.1

Teacher FYI

A fast-moving subfield of cytology is the study of the structure and function of chromosomes. The concept that chromosomes are ordered in the interphase nucleus has been around for 100 years, but evidence for the hypothesis didn't appear until 1981.

The lily, *Ornithogalum virens*, has only three pairs of chromosomes. Geneticist Terry Ashley discovered that the three chromosomes are joined to each other in a specific order at their tips. The tips of the chromosomes also attach at specific points to the inner membrane of the nucleus. This internal order may determine cell polarity and the order of the chromosomes during mitosis.

Concept Development

The spindle, centrioles, and asters together are known as the mitotic apparatus. Explain to students that it is the mitotic apparatus that moves the chromosomes during mitosis.

Demonstration

Use two pieces of tubing stuck together by putty to demonstrate sister chromatids, the structures produced by the replication of a chromosome. Show students how the sister chromatids separate in anaphase, producing two single-stranded chromosomes. Explain that the cell usually divides in telophase or shortly after, and the cell cycle begins again. **LEP**

EARTH SCIENCE CONNECTION

Why do spindles have equators? In geology, the study of Earth, the equator is an imaginary line around the middle of Earth halfway between the North Pole and the South Pole. Ask students why biologists refer to a spindle as having an equator. *The equator of the spindle is an imaginary line around the middle of the spindle halfway between its poles where the centrioles migrate.*

How do chromosomes move?

The exact mechanism of how spindle fiber microtubules cause the separation of sister chromatids is not understood. Many biologists believe that the microtubules are disassembled by depolymerization at the centromere end and that the chromatids "crawl" up the shortening fibers. Other scientists believe that the microtubules depolymerize at the pole ends, and the chromatids are pulled to the poles.

Figure Caption Question

What two differences do you notice?
Animal cells have centrioles; plant cells do not. Plant cells divide in two by the formation of a cell plate; animal cells divide in two by a pinching in of the plasma membrane.

Reinforcement

- Give students additional practice relating the sequence of the cell cycle. Call out a stage of the cell cycle. Have students write the stages immediately preceding and following the stage you call out. **L1**

- Provide students with photomicrographs of cells in mitosis. Have students sketch the photomicrographs on their own paper and label as many structures as they are able to observe. **L1**

Figure 7-8 Identify the characteristics of each stage in the cell cycle, and note the differences between mitosis in animal cells (diagrams) and in plant cells (photos). What two differences do you notice? Magnification (photos): 1000×

INTERPHASE

Nucleus

Chromatin

Centrioles

Act Two—Metaphase The players proceed immediately with the short second act, **metaphase.** The chromosomes become attached to the spindle when the microtubules of the spindle "capture" the chromosomes by their centromeres. Interaction of the spindle fibers causes the chromosomes to move agitatedly, as if they were dancing. Eventually, the chromosomes move to the equator of the spindle and become aligned. The dangling chromatids may face in any direction. Once the chromosomes are thus aligned on the spindle's equator, the next act proceeds directly.

Act Three—Anaphase The centromeres split at the beginning of **anaphase,** the third stage of mitosis. The two sister chromatids of each chromosome begin to separate from one another and move apart. Each one heads toward a pole of the spindle. Although the details are not fully understood, action of microtubules facilitates the movement of the chromatids. The microtubules slide past each other, causing the spindle as a whole to become flattened and elongated. The poles move farther apart and the sister chromatids are pulled to opposite poles. Each sister chromatid now behaves as a separate chromosome. As anaphase ends, there is one set of single-stranded chromosomes at each end of the cell.

Act Four—Telophase The final stage of mitosis, **telophase,** opens as two cells begin to form from one. The plasma membrane of animal cells begins to pinch together at the cell's center, as a ring of microfilaments attached to the membrane contracts. Rigid cell walls, however, prevent plant cells from pinching in. In most plants, a **cell plate** begins to appear, growing outward from the middle of the cell. The cell plate may form from membranes of Golgi bodies or from endoplasmic reticulum (ER). From the cell plate will come the plasma membranes of the two new plant cells. Later, cell walls form between the membranes.

PROPHASE

Spindle fibers

Doubled chromosome

Disappearing nuclear membrane

176 ⬩ CELLULAR REPRODUCTION

ALTERNATE LAB: The Cell Cycle of Broad Beans

Purpose

Students will observe and diagram the cell cycle in plants.

Materials

broad beans (*Vica faba*), scalpel, 2% aceto-orcein stain (See page 27T.), covered watch glass, vermiculite, pot, glass slide, coverslip, forceps, 1*N* HCl, paper towels, microscope

Procedure

Soak two beans in water overnight. Plant the beans in a pot of moist vermiculite. After about five days, the root will have grown to 3 cm in length. Cut off the end 3 mm with a sharp scalpel and return the seeds to the pot. In one week, 15 to 20 secondary roots will have grown laterally from the primary root. Ten to 20 minutes before class, cut off the end 3 mm of each lateral root, and place these tips in about

2 mL of a 9:1 solution of 2% aceto-orcein stain and 1*N* hydrochloric acid in a watch glass. You can obtain these solutions from a biological supply house or purchase concentrated solutions and dilute them yourself. Students will use these stained root tips. Give the following directions to students.

1. Using forceps to hold the root tip, remove it from the stain. **CAUTION:** The staining solution will permanently stain clothing and burn the skin. If any

Telophase ends with events in reverse order from those with which mitosis began. The nucleoli reappear, and a nuclear membrane encloses each set of chromosomes. The nuclear membrane forms from ER. Meanwhile, chromosomes lose their distinct outlines and once again appear as a mass of chromatin.

In animal cells, when cell division is completed, the cell membrane pinches together so that the single parent cell is separated into two daughter cells. In plants, the cell plate is completed to form the daughter cells. Thus, mitosis accomplishes its mission. New cells are produced, each of which contains the same set of genetic information as the parent cell.

Control of the Cell Cycle

Most of the cells in your body are in one or another stage of the cell cycle at this very moment. At least some of your skin cells, stomach-lining cells, and countless other cell types are probably producing daughter cells. It has been estimated that 25 million cell divisions occur every second in the adult human body.

Rate of Cell Division   Different types of cells divide at different rates. Some types of cells, such as those in bone marrow that form red blood cells, reproduce rapidly to keep up with the need for new blood cells. In these cells, the cycle lasts less than an hour. At the other extreme, certain nerve and muscle cells never reproduce once they mature. They remain in interphase as long as they live. Human liver cells divide only when new cells are needed to repair a wound. It is important in a multicellular organism that a balance be maintained among the many kinds of cells in the body. If one kind of cell begins to reproduce too rapidly, the normal organization of the organism will be disrupted. This kind of disruption occurs in cancer, when the rapid, uncontrolled division of one kind of cell invades and disrupts cells in other tissues.

METAPHASE

Chromosomes line up at equator

Centromere

Sister chromatids

ANAPHASE

Nuclear membrane reforms

TELOPHASE

Chromatids pull apart at centromere

7.1 LIFE FROM LIFE—CELLS FROM CELLS ❧ **177**

MATH CONNECTION

Many from Few: Have students calculate the number of cells produced by mitosis from a single cell after 10 cell cycles. Then have them make a graph showing their results. The graph will show doubling at each cell cycle, ending with 1024 cells. Point out that this kind of doubling is called logarithmic or exponential growth in mathematics. **L1**

Activity

Have students germinate corn seeds. Once the root is about 1 cm in length, cut 10 mm from the tip. After five days, have students observe the root again and note any changes. Measure the distance between the new roots and the end of the primary root. Where are the roots farthest apart? *The roots get farther apart near the seed.* Ask students to tell where most of the cells undergoing mitosis are located. *the tip of the root* **L1**

Using the Illustrations

Have students compare the photo and the diagram for each stage of mitosis to determine similarities and differences between mitosis in plant and in animal cells. It may be helpful if students first draw diagrams of the stages of mitosis in a plant cell, based on the photos, before they make their comparisons.

stain is splashed out of the watch glass, immediately wash the affected area.
2. Cut off the first 1 or 2 mm of the root tip and place it on a clean slide.
3. Using the edge of a paper towel, blot around the root to remove excess staining solution, and add one drop of water. Add a coverslip.
4. Place the slide, coverslip up, between two layers of paper towels on the table.

Using a pencil eraser or thumb, apply pressure to the coverslip area in order to squash and spread the root tip.
5. Using the microscope on low power, locate the meristematic region of the root tip. Once you have located this more darkly stained area, examine it under high power.

Analysis
Ask students to answer these questions.

1. Compare the stages of mitosis in the broad bean squash with photographs in the textbook.
2. Using your own bean tip squash, draw and label each stage of the cell cycle.

✔ **Assessment**
Knowledge: Have students relate the events of mitosis to its importance in body cells.

Growth of Onion Root Tips

Time Allotment

1 class period, then 10 minutes a day for 1 week

Objectives

Upon completing this investigation, students will be able to:
- analyze root tips to determine the regions of rapid growth.
- demonstrate understanding of mitosis.

Skills

observe and infer, form a hypothesis, design an experiment, interpret data

Materials

onion roots from bulblet growing in water in test tube, test-tube holder, single-edge razor blade, extra-fine-tip permanent marking pen, methylene blue (See page 27T.), droppers, slide and coverslip, microscope, prepared slide of onion root tip

Preparation

One month and again one week before conducting this lab, "plant" an onion bulblet in the top of a test tube filled with water. Gently scrape the base of each bulblet with a knife before "planting." Be sure that the base of the bulblet is always in water. Make sure light is adequate when leaves begin to form. Use onion bulblets from a biological supply company or onion sets from a local nursery, as onions from a grocer may have been treated with chemicals to prevent sprouting.

Possible Hypotheses

1. Roots are growing more rapidly near the tip of the root.
2. Roots are growing more rapidly near the bulb.

Possible Procedures

- Students might make thin-section slides and compare numbers of cells in mitosis in younger roots and in older roots. Or, they might make marks with a permanent marker at specific intervals on a root and measure the change in

Regulation of the Cell Cycle How is the cell cycle regulated? Scientists are just now beginning to understand some of the many mechanisms that seem to be involved. One factor that influences cell division is cell-to-cell contact, Figure 7-9. Most normal cells will divide repeatedly until they come in contact with another cell. Then cell division stops. If cells are isolated from one another and grown in a nutrient medium, they will reproduce until the spaces between them are filled with cells. As soon as a continuous layer of cells is formed, they stop dividing.

When cells stop dividing, they always seem to stop at the same point in the cell cycle—just before DNA replication begins in interphase. Once a cell passes this point, it is committed to completing the cell cycle. Scientists are trying to identify the control mechanisms that operate at this point in interphase. Because many factors that affect the cell cycle have already been identified as being chemical in nature, scientists are concentrating their search on chemical controls. Several different proteins have been discovered and identified. In frog eggs, a protein was discovered that controls the onset of mitosis. This control protein is present during interphase but not during mitosis. Later studies showed that the

I N V E S T I G A T I O N

Growth of Onion Root Tips

When you were born, you probably weighed about 7 pounds. If you gained 2 pounds in the first month, you increased your weight by 29 percent. If you weigh 125 pounds now and gain 2 pounds in a month, you are increasing your weight by 1.6 percent. Clearly, at the beginning stages of life, growth is very rapid. Certain parts of organisms also tend to grow more rapidly than others. In this lab, you will examine growing onion roots and determine what part of the root is growing most rapidly. You will observe the root with a microscope, as well as observe growth of particular sections of the root over a number of days. Your teacher will supply methylene blue for staining any microscope slides you may wish to prepare.

Cells in this cross section of onion root tissue are in various stages in the cell cycle. Magnification: 1000×

Problem

What part of an onion root grows most rapidly?

Safety Precautions

Use care when handling a razor blade. Methylene blue stains clothing permanently and skin temporarily. Wash your hands at the end of the lab.

Hypothesis

What is your group's hypothesis? Explain your reasons for making this hypothesis.

Experimental Plan

1. As a group, make a list of possible ways you might test your hypothesis using the materials your teacher has made available.

178 🔬 CELLULAR REPRODUCTION

the intervals each day for a week.
- Methylene blue is chosen as the stain for this lab although it is not the traditional one. More complex preparation with potentially toxic chemicals is traditional when preparing onion root tip slides. For use by students, methylene blue will serve the purpose of finding cells in mitosis. They will be stained darker than nuclei not in mitosis. Methylene blue is not an appropriate stain for identifying stages of mitosis.
- If onion bulblets (onion sets) are not available, garlic bulbs can be substituted, or cut-

tings of the houseplant *Zebrina pendula*, commonly known as wandering Jew, could be placed in dechlorinated tap water one week prior to the lab. The adventitious roots formed could be used in the same way as onion roots.

Teaching Strategies

If this is the first time your students have designed an experiment, refer them to the Investigations in Chapters 1 and 2.
- Ask students if they grew faster when they were babies or when they were in their early teens. Hold up the onion bulblet

a
Culture dish
containing nutrients

Cells

b

d

c

Figure 7-9 When cells are grown in a culture dish, they will divide only until they come into contact with other cells (a). If some of the cells are removed (b), the cells at the edge of the gap begin to divide again (c). Cell division stops when the dish is covered by a single layer of cells (d).

"planted" for a week and ask how long they think it took for it to grow as much as it has. Does all growth occur at the same rate? What causes growth and what determines how fast a part of an organism grows? Hold up the onion bulblet "planted" for a month and ask how long they think it has been growing. Ask students to observe a prepared slide of an onion root tip under a microscope. Explain that they will be able to see cells in various stages of mitosis. Ask them which part of the onion root they think is growing fastest. Tell students that they can plan an experiment in which they use the microscope to answer this question, or they can develop a method of observing growth of onion roots over a number of days.

Data and Observations
If students examine onion root tip slides, they should make a bar graph showing the number of cells in mitosis in one field of view for each part of the root examined. If students measure lengths of root tip, they should plot days (x axis) vs. length of root (y axis) for various root parts.

Data Analysis
1. Onion roots grow fastest at their tips.
2. Direct measurement or number of cells undergoing mitosis should be cited as evidence.
3. Answers will vary.
4. Incorrect measurements or poor staining techniques will cause errors.
5. Answers will vary.
6. Onion roots grow fastest in meristem regions.
7. Research on rapidly growing cells can be used in studies of cancer because cells grow rapidly and uncontrollably in this disease.
8. Answers will vary but most students will conclude that roots grow from the region near the tip.

2. Agree on one idea from your group's list that could be investigated in the classroom.
3. Design an experiment that will test one variable at a time. Plan to collect quantitative data.
4. Following the style of a recipe, write a numbered list of directions that anyone could follow.
5. Make a list of materials and the quantities you will need.

Checking the Plan
Discuss the following points with other group members to decide the final procedures for your experiment.
1. What variables will need to be controlled?
2. What is your control?
3. What will you measure or count? How will you determine which part of the root tip is growing fastest?
4. How many cells or roots will you count, measure, or examine?

5. Have you designed and made a table for collecting data?

Make sure your teacher has approved your experimental plan before you proceed further.

Data and Observations
Carry out your experiment, make your measurements, and complete your data table. Make a graph of your results.

Analysis and Conclusions
1. According to your results, which part of the onion root is growing fastest?
2. What is the experimental evidence for this conclusion?
3. Was your hypothesis supported by your data? Explain.
4. If your hypothesis was not supported, what types of experimental error could be responsible?
5. Consult with other groups that

used different procedures to examine this problem. Were their conclusions the same as yours? Why or why not?
6. Speculate about why onion roots grow rapidly in some regions and not in others.
7. Some scientists have a keen interest in finding out why certain cells undergo rapid division and others do not. Speculate about why research on rapidly growing cells is important.
8. Write a brief conclusion to your experiment.

Going Further
Based on this lab experience, design an experiment that would help to answer a question that arose from your work. Assume that you will have unlimited resources and will not be conducting this experiment in class.

✔ Assessment
Portfolio: Have students write up summaries of the Investigation and include them in their portfolios. Summaries should include graphs.

Extensions
Students can investigate roots of other species or grow roots under other environmental conditions to see if they get the same results.

Minilab 1

Purpose
Students will compare mitosis in plant and animal cells.

Skills
make and use tables, compare and contrast, observe

Teaching Strategies
- **Safety Precautions:** Have students use microscopes with care.
- Prepared slides can be purchased from a biological supply house.

Expected Results
Students will notice similarities and differences in several stages.

Answers
Late prophase, metaphase, and anaphase are similar in plants and animals. Early prophase is different because plants do not have centrioles and asters from which spindle fibers radiate. Telophase is different. In plant cells, the formation of a cell plate divides the cell. Animal cells divide by pinching in two.

✔ Assessment
Skill: Students should make diagrams showing and comparing the stages of mitosis in plants and animals. When they are completed, they should be exchanged and critiqued.

Concept Development
Reinforce the concept of molecular control of mitosis by reviewing the structure and function of relevant biomolecules. Include a review of amino acids, ATP, and proteins.

control protein must be activated by still other proteins during interphase before it can do its job. Once the control protein is activated, it can begin the events of mitosis by acting as an enzyme that transfers a phosphate group from ATP to another molecule. The added phosphate group activates this molecule which, in turn, can begin a series of events that activates other molecules. It is this complex chain of activations that sets in motion the events of mitosis, such as breakdown of the nuclear membrane and formation of the spindle.

Several genes that appear to be required for cell division have been discovered and identified in both yeasts and humans. Researchers are trying to determine what role these genes play and how they exert control over the cell cycle.

In most cells, the events of the cell cycle will not begin until various checkpoints have been properly completed. For example, mitosis will not begin unless DNA has been replicated and, where necessary, repaired.

Figure 7-10 Prokaryotes reproduce by binary fission. Each new cell receives a copy of the single chromosome.

Chromosome (DNA)

DNA replication

Thinking Lab
MAKE A HYPOTHESIS

Where is the nuclear membrane during mitosis?

Background
During prophase of mitosis, the nuclear membrane disappears. It reappears at the end of telophase. Where is the nuclear membrane during mitosis? Electron microscope studies show that during prophase, small saclike vesicles appear in the cytoplasm. In late anaphase, these vesicles disappear.

You Try It
Make a hypothesis to explain what might be happening to the nuclear membrane during mitosis. Draw a diagram to show these events, making sure that your diagram fits both the electron microscope data and your hypothesis. Then, describe an experiment that would test your hypothesis. What results would you expect if your hypothesis were correct?

Thinking Lab
MAKE A HYPOTHESIS

Purpose
Students will explain what happens to the nuclear membrane during mitosis.

Skills
recognize cause and effect, form a hypothesis, design an experiment

Teaching Strategies
- Review endocytosis and exocytosis in Chapter 4 and the function of vesicles

in Chapter 5 to refresh students' memories about the role of vesicles in cells.

Answers
A variety of hypotheses might be acceptable. One might be that the nuclear membrane takes on another form during prophase and is packaged in the vesicles that appear at that time. Students might design an experiment that determines the

chemical makeup of the nuclear membrane, then determines the chemical makeup of the vesicles. Similarities would suggest that the nuclear membrane was packaged in the vesicles.

✔ Assessment
Portfolio: Have students add their lab write-ups, including diagrams and designed experiments, to their portfolios.

Similarly, separation of chromatids will not take place until all chromosomes are properly attached to spindle fibers. And, the formation of two daughter cells will not occur until the chromosomes have arrived at opposite poles of the cell.

New knowledge about control of the cell cycle comes from basic research carried out in many labs by many different scientists. As more and more is learned about this subject, that knowledge may be used to replace cells damaged by injury or disease, to allow organisms to live longer lives, or to control the spread of cancers.

Cell Reproduction in Prokaryotes

Prokaryotes have but a single chromosome. Unlike eukaryotic chromosomes, that single chromosome is circular rather than linear. Prokaryotic chromosomes have little or none of the proteins associated with the DNA of eukaryotic chromosomes, so there are no protein spools either.

Prokaryotes cannot be said to have a cell cycle. In fact, their simple structure does not include the cell parts necessary for mitosis to occur. However, like all cells, they must replicate their DNA and distribute the two copies equally to daughter cells. Prokaryotes do so by a process called **binary fission**, shown in Figure 7-10.

As binary fission begins, the single chromosome is attached to the inside of the cell membrane. There a duplicate chromosome is formed. The new chromosome also attaches to the cell membrane, at a point near the first chromosome. While this attachment occurs, growth of new cell membrane and cell wall material between the attachment sites separates the two copies of the chromosome and elongates the cell. At the midpoint in the length of the cell, which is now about twice its original size, more new membrane and wall form and begin to push inward. As this inward growth continues, the two chromosomes become separated. Two separate daughter cells are produced, each with the same genetic material.

Minilab 1

How is animal mitosis different from plant mitosis?

Rapidly growing tissues will have more cells undergoing mitosis than tissues that are not growing rapidly. Root tips of plants and developing embryos of animals are rapid growers. Examine prepared slides of the cells of onion root tips and the developing embryos of whitefish, sea urchins, or the roundworm, *Ascaris*. Observe differences between mitosis in plant cells and in animal cells. Make diagrams of your observations in a chart to compare each stage of the cell cycle in plant cells and animal cells.

Analysis   *Which stages are alike in plant and animal cells? Explain. In which stages are there differences? Explain.*

Section Review

Understanding Concepts

1. You prepare a nutrient infusion, which you pour into two flasks of the same size. You boil both infusions for the same amount of time. You seal one flask tightly with plastic wrap and place a wad of cotton loosely in the neck of the other. What hypothesis are you testing, and what results do you expect? Why do you expect these results?

2. A parent cell has a total of 12 chromosomes. How many chromosomes will each of its daughter cells contain? Why must they contain that number?

3. You are observing a prepared slide of many cells of one type of animal tissue. You notice that the cells are in various stages of the cell cycle. In what stage will most of the cells be? Why?

4. ***Skill Review—Sequencing:*** Sequence the activities of chromosomes during the cell cycle. For more help, refer to Organizing Information in the **Skill Handbook.**

5. ***Thinking Critically:*** Review Pasteur's experiment. What kind of control might he have carried out? Explain the reasoning behind that control.

3 Assess

Check for Understanding

Draw a cell in interphase on the board. Have students supply the labels for the drawing. Then proceed with each stage of mitosis. At each step, students should provide the labels for the drawings. L1

Reteach

If students fail to comprehend the importance of mitosis or to be able to relate the phases, divide the class into groups. Provide each group with a worksheet that shows drawings of mitosis. Have the groups label the drawings and discuss the reasons cells may undergo mitosis. L1

Extension

Tell students to imagine that they are a cell in interphase. Have them explain orally what kind of cell they are and what their journey through the cell cycle would be like. L2

✔ Assessment

Performance: Draw several stages of mitosis on the board. Include errors in your drawings such as drawing centrioles in a plant cell or drawing sister chromatids moving to the same pole. Have students find the errors. L1 COOP LEARN

4 Close

Discussion

Have students discuss the similarities and differences between mitosis in eukaryotes and binary fission in bacteria.

Answers to Section Review

1. The experiment tests the hypothesis that air must be present for spontaneous generation to occur. The flask sealed with plastic wrap would later show no signs of life. However, microorganisms probably would appear in the flask that was plugged with cotton. The experiment would seem to verify the hypothesis, but spontaneous generation did not occur. Rather, spores entered the second flask.

2. Each daughter cell will also contain 12 chromosomes. Each cell must have a complete set of genetic information.

3. Most cells would be in interphase, the longest stage of the cell cycle.

4. **Skill Review—Sequencing:** Chromosomes are replicated during interphase. In prophase, they condense and become visible. During metaphase, each chromosome becomes attached by its centromere to a spindle fiber. Centromeres split during anaphase, and one chromatid of each chromosome is pulled to each pole. During telophase, the chromosomes become indistinct once again.

5. **Thinking Critically:** Pasteur could have constructed other flasks with straight necks through which spores could enter.

Prepare

Key Concepts

The events of meiosis are presented in detail. Differences between meiosis in males and in females are explained. The importance of meiosis in adaptation, variation, and evolution is discussed.

Key Terms

diploid, homologue, zygote, gamete, fertilization, haploid, sexual reproduction, meiosis, spore, genetic recombination

Materials

• Gather materials for Minilab 2.

1 Focus

Objectives

The objectives are listed on the student page. Remind students to preview these objectives as a guide to this numbered section.

Brainstorming

Have students make a list of reasons why the cells of most organisms contain two identical sets of chromosomes. Students will likely list several possible reasons. When they have exhausted their possibilities, add the word *variation* to the list if it isn't already present. Explain that variation is important to the maintenance of a species. Meiosis provides a mechanism for variation. Point out that the importance of the process will be discussed later in the chapter, but students first need to understand the process. `L1` `COOP LEARN`

Objectives

Sequence the series of events by which reproductive cells are produced in complex plants and in animals.

Analyze the significance of meiosis with respect to adaptation and evolution.

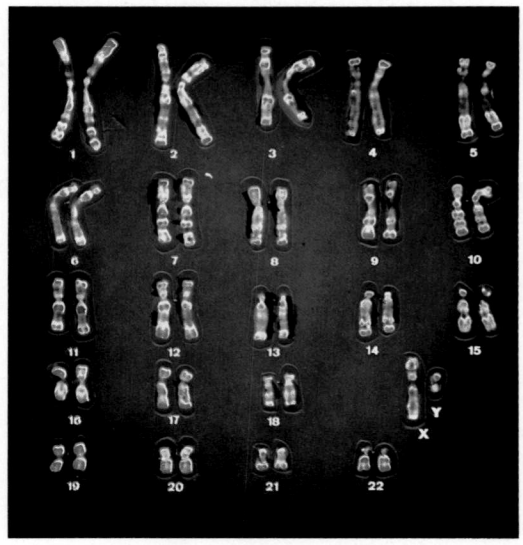

Figure 7-11 Human cells contain 23 pairs of chromosomes, or 46 chromosomes. Here, enlarged photographs of stained chromosomes have been cut up and arranged by pairs.

7.2 Production of Reproductive Cells

How many chromosomes does it take to make a cell? Would you guess that it depends on the kind of organism? If that's your guess, your thoughts are headed in the right direction. The number of chromosomes per cell does vary from one kind of organism to another.

Your cells have, and always have had, 46 chromosomes. The cells of fruit flies have eight. Does this mean, then, that every cell cycle in mature humans passes along 46 chromosomes to daughter cells? Or that every cell cycle in mature fruit flies passes along eight? The answer would be yes, in every cycle except among one class of cells—namely the cells that form reproductive cells. The job of reproductive cells is to produce offspring like the parent organism. The way chromosomes are distributed to reproductive cells differs from mitosis. And it's largely a matter of numbers.

Chromosome Numbers and Characteristics

Think for a moment about what happens when a male and female butterfly mate. Their reproductive cells unite to form a single cell that is the beginning of a new butterfly. What would happen if each of those reproductive cells contained the same number of chromosomes as all other cells in the butterfly? The offspring's cells would have twice the number of chromosomes as its parents' cells. In reality, however, the number of chromosomes does not double. Instead, it remains constant from one generation to the next. Understanding how this happens begins with a close-up look at cells and chromosomes.

Diploid Cells Chromosomes vary in a number of ways, including size and shape. All body cells of a given kind of organism normally have the same kinds and numbers of chromosomes. In the diagrams in Figure 7-8, you saw the stages of mitosis in a cell having four chromosomes. Did you notice that among those four, there were two large and two small chromosomes? In the cells of animals, chromosomes usually come in pairs, as shown by the two shades of the same color in Figure 7-8. Cells of many simple plants such as mosses, and cells of other simple organisms such as fungi, do not have such paired chromosomes. More complex plants, such as carrots and cabbages and oak trees, have paired chromosomes as animal cells do. Human cells have 23 pairs of chromosomes, as shown in Figure 7-11; fruit fly cells have four pairs. Cells having two of each chromosome are said to be **diploid**. The diploid number of chromosomes is represented by $2n$, where n = the number of different pairs. Humans have 23 different pairs, so $2n = 46$.

Homologues In diploid cells, each chromosome of a pair has the same basic structure. The two members of each pair are called homologous chromosomes, or simply **homologues.** The DNA of each homologue carries information for the same traits as its partner, although the specific information may differ. For example, each homologue may carry the instructions for eye color. The instructions on one homologue may be for brown eyes; the instructions on the other homologue may be for blue eyes. The combination of the two instructions determines the eye color of the individual. That same homologous pair of chromosomes carries information for perhaps thousands of other inherited traits as well.

Meiosis Rather than Mitosis

Where do diploid plant and animal cells get their two homologues of each chromosome pair, and why does it matter? The answer to both questions goes back to the beginning—when two parent organisms mate to produce a single cell. That single cell is a fertilized egg called a **zygote.**

Haploid Sex Cells A zygote results from the union of two different kinds of **gametes,** which are the sex cells. One gamete is a sperm from the male parent. The other is an egg from the female parent. The fusion of egg and sperm to form a zygote is called **fertilization.** All your body cells originated from a single zygote and were produced as a result of mitosis and cell division. Your body cells each contain 46 chromosomes. Cells of your parents also contain 46 chromosomes, and cells of their parents, too.

Sex cells of complex plants and animals, which must unite to form a zygote, differ from body cells in an important way—they do not have the diploid number of chromosomes. Sex cells contain only *one* chromosome from each homologous pair. Cells such as eggs and sperm that contain one chromosome of each homologous pair are said to be **haploid.** The haploid number is represented by n. In human gametes, $n = 23$.

Reproduction that involves the production and subsequent fusion of sex cells is called **sexual reproduction.** Fusion of haploid gametes to form a diploid zygote, which then develops to produce a mature multicellular adult, is the key feature of sexual reproduction. If you think about it, you will realize that fertilization restores the diploid number of chromosomes.

Haploid from Diploid Haploid cells cannot be produced by mitosis. Instead, they are produced by **meiosis,** the process by which haploid

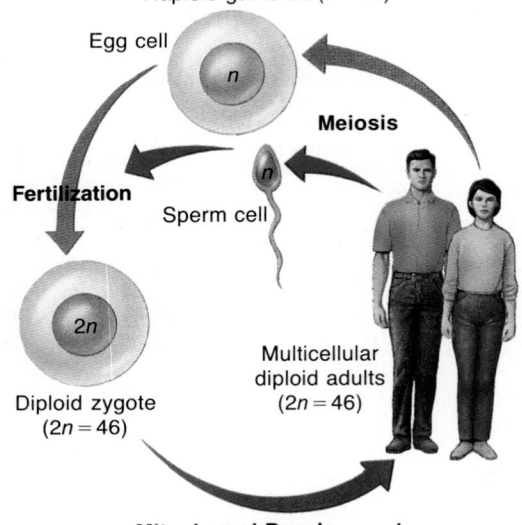

Haploid gametes ($n = 23$)
Egg cell
Meiosis
Fertilization
Sperm cell
n
$2n$
Multicellular diploid adults ($2n = 46$)
Diploid zygote ($2n = 46$)
Mitosis and Development

Figure 7-12 In a sexual life cycle, the doubling of the chromosome number that results from fertilization is balanced by the halving of chromosome number that results from meiosis.

---

2 Teach

Bioethics

***In-vitro* Fertilization:** *In-vitro* fertilization is a procedure that joins sperm and eggs outside the body. It is performed in cases where a woman cannot become pregnant without medical help. The sperm may be from the husband or from a donor. Eggs may be from the wife or from a donor. Fertilized eggs (actually two-day-old embryos) are then implanted into the wife or into a surrogate. Ask students to consider the ethics of this procedure. If the procedure is ethical, who should pay for it—insurance companies or the individuals receiving the embryo? Accept the reasoning of students who consider the procedure positive as well as those who do not. Use the discussion to alert students that they are using their decision-making skills to clarify their own values. **L2**
COOP LEARN

Teacher FYI

Evidence indicates that in diploid cells, the chromosomes remain segregated as haploid sets, making homologous pairing during meiosis a relatively simple matter. If the haploid chromosome sets are ordered identically, they may face each other across the nucleus.

Reinforcement

Have students explain the difference between the results of mitosis and those of meiosis. They should include that mitosis results in two cells with the same number of chromosomes as the parent cell, whereas meiosis results in four cells with the haploid number of chromosomes. The results of mitosis are body cells; the results of meiosis are sex cells in animals and spores in plants.

MULTICULTURAL CONNECTION

Similarities: Societies throughout the world have similarities in many genetically controlled features including hair types, skin color, height, and facial shape. Ask students why people of Asian, European, or African descent vary in such features. *Features controlled by genetics are found on the chromosomes. Because cultures of people were unable to travel great distances for thousands of years,* *they associated mainly among themselves. Thus, genetic instructions that control such features remained within given groups.*

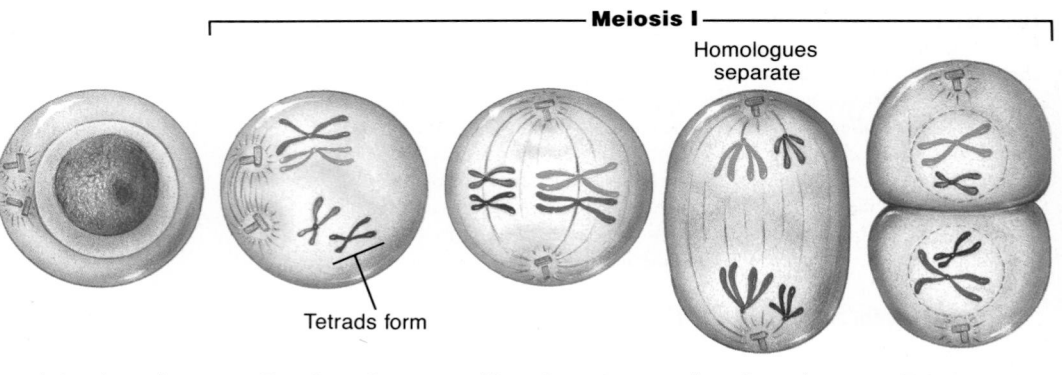

Homologues
separate

Tetrads form

| Interphase I | Prophase I | Metaphase I | Anaphase I | Telophase I |

Audiovisual

Meiosis: Sex Cell Formation is an excellent 16-minute film available from the Encyclopedia Britannica Educational Corporation.

Using Science Terms

The Greek word *meiosis* means "lessening." Ask students to explain why the term given to this process is applicable. *Meiosis is the reduction, or lessening, of the number of chromosomes by one half.* [LEP]

Using the Illustration

Use Figure 7-13 to emphasize the point that each of the four haploid cells resulting from meiosis has one half the number of chromosomes as the original diploid cell. [LEP]

Chalkboard Example

Draw and label the events of meiosis on the chalkboard. Make nonhomologous chromosomes different colors and shapes for easier recognition. Point out that one of the most important events of meiosis, the reduction of the chromosome number by one half, occurs in meiosis I. [LEP]

Figure Caption Question

Is this an animal or a plant cell? How do you know? This is an animal cell; it has centrioles. Plant cells do not contain centrioles. Also, the cell in the figure divides in two by the pinching in of the cell membrane, not by forming a cell plate.

Challenge

Challenge students to invent a mechanism for demonstrating how the plasma membrane of an animal cell pinches together in anaphase and telophase. Allow students to use any common objects as models, such as balloons, string, wire, etc. [L2]
[COOP LEARN]

Figure 7-13 **These diagrams show meiosis for a cell with a diploid number of 4. Is this an animal or a plant cell? How do you know? Compare the diagrams of meiosis with those of mitosis on pages 176 and 177.**

nuclei are formed from diploid nuclei. Meiosis usually is accompanied by cell division. In animals, meiosis results in production of haploid gametes, sperm and egg.

Meiosis is not limited to animal cells. It also occurs in the life cycles of plants, multicellular algae, fungi, and in some unicellular organisms. In plants and some algae and fungi, meiosis results in the production of haploid spores, not gametes. A **spore** is a small reproductive cell that can develop into a new haploid organism. Unlike a gamete, a spore may give rise to a multicellular individual without first fusing with another cell. In unicellular organisms, meiosis often produces haploid nuclei instead of spores or gametes. In any case, meiosis always involves two successive divisions—meiosis I and meiosis II. The controls operating when meiosis occurs are much the same as those operating when mitosis occurs.

Unlike mitosis, which occurs in most kinds of body tissues, meiosis occurs only in certain reproductive tissues. Correct meiosis ensures that gametes will have the right *number* and *kinds* of chromosomes. As a result, the zygote formed from the union of two gametes will also contain the proper number and kinds of chromosomes.

Meiosis in Male Animals

The main events of meiosis are diagrammed in Figure 7-13 on these two pages. As in the case of mitosis, you can think of meiosis as a series of acts in a drama that progresses without a pause from beginning to end. You will recognize the players and many of the scenes, but the plot takes some extra twists and ends differently.

Meiosis I Early in meiosis I, chromosomes do not appear to be double stranded. However, studies show that the chromosomes have replicated during interphase, as they do before mitosis. A bit later in prophase I, a crucial event occurs—the homologous chromosomes move close together. Each pair of homologues comes together so that matching sections along the length of their chromatids lie side by side. During this time, the non-

184 CELLULAR REPRODUCTION

─────── Meiosis II ───────

Prophase II   **Metaphase II**   **Anaphase II**   **Telophase II**

Sister chromatids separate

sister chromatids of two homologues may be wound around one another, Figure 7-14. Soon, the double-stranded condition of the chromosomes, indicating that replication has occurred, becomes clear. Because two homologous chromosomes pair, and because each chromosome of a homologous pair is double stranded, a quadruple chromatid structure called a tetrad is formed.

While the chromosomes are coming together, some events similar to mitosis occur in the cell. The nucleoli and nuclear membrane disappear, the centrioles move apart, and the spindle forms. The major difference between this prophase and prophase of mitosis is that the homologous chromosomes are paired in prophase I of meiosis.

At metaphase I of meiosis, tetrads consisting of homologous pairs of chromosomes line up at the equator of the spindle. This is a second differ- ence between mitosis and meiosis because, as you read, homologous chro- mosomes do not pair during metaphase in mitosis.

A third important difference between mitosis and meiosis occurs at the beginning of anaphase I and involves the centromeres. Remember that anaphase in mitosis begins by a splitting of the centromeres, so that the sister chromatids can be separated and pulled to opposite poles. At anaphase I of meiosis, the centromeres do not divide, and sister chro- matids do not separate. Instead, one homologous chromosome of each pair goes to each pole, and the sister chromatids stay attached to each other. Thus, meiosis I separates the homologues of a homologous pair of chromosomes, not the sister chromatids of individual chromosomes.

With the tetrads thus separated, the cell membrane begins to pinch inward. In telophase I, the original cell divides to form two cells, each of which contains one member of every homologous pair (*n*). However, each chromosome is still double stranded and consists of two chromatids that are still joined together.

Meiosis II   After a short interphase, during which no replication of DNA or chromosomes occurs, meiosis II begins. Meiosis II is much like mitosis. Each of the two cells may skip early events, and the chromosomes move

Figure 7-14   **Late in prophase I, homologous chromosomes come together to form a tetrad. Arms of non-sister chromatids may wind around each other.**

Non-sister chromatids

Homologues

Do chromosomes communicate?

If chromosomes are attached to one another in some specific order, as has been suggested, it is possible that they may affect each other's activity. Gabriel Dover, of Cambridge University, says, "There are so many surprises... in the eukaryotic genome these days, so the idea might well turn out to be true." Since there is no direct evidence for this, most scientists disagree with the possibility of such communication. Instead, they accept the current view that the ordered events of meiosis have a genetic basis for what appears to be a very orderly process.

Concept Development

Point out the major differences between mitotic prophase and prophase I of meiosis. In prophase of mitosis, the chromosomes condense and begin to line up randomly along the equator of the spindle. In prophase I of meiosis, homologous chromosomes, each with two chromatids, condense and begin to line up side by side, forming tetrads along the equator of the spindle. Then contrast anaphase of mitosis with anaphase I of meiosis. In anaphase of mitosis, the chromatids of the diploid set of chromosomes separate. In anaphase I of meiosis, one of each homologous chromosome pair separates to produce the haploid number of chromosomes in each resulting cell.

SECTION 7.2

Minilab 2

Purpose
Students will make models of the stages of meiosis to help them understand how the chromosome number is halved.

Skills
sequence, observe, compare and contrast, recognize cause and effect

Teaching Strategies
- Salt dough can be prepared by adding water to one part flour and one part salt until bread dough consistency results. The dough should not be sticky. If it is, add more flour. Five cups of salt and five cups of flour will make enough for a class of 30 working in groups of three or four.

Expected Results
Students will better understand the process of meiosis after making models.

Answers
Meiosis causes an exact halving of the chromosome number when the centromeres fail to divide during anaphase I. One homologue of each homologous pair moves to each pole, thus halving the chromosome number. This separation is able to occur because homologous chromosomes pair up during prophase I.

✔ Assessment
Knowledge: Have student groups examine each other's models of each stage of meiosis for errors.

`COOP LEARN`

Using the Photos
Ask students to examine Figure 7-15 and suggest how the shape of the sperm cell might relate to its function. Guide students to see that the tail gives the sperm mobility. Contrast this to the shape of the egg. Make sure that students understand that even though the egg is much larger than the sperm (note the magnifications), both contain the same number of chromosomes.

Minilab 2

How can you make a model of meiosis?

On your lab table, assemble string, yarn, and two colors of pipe cleaners. The string can represent the cell membrane and nuclear membrane; yarn can be uncoiled, unreplicated chromosomes; pipe cleaners can be replicated chromosomes. Move the cell parts into positions that represent the process of meiosis. As an alternative, use a baseball-size piece of salt dough or modeling clay to represent the stages. As the model moves from one stage to the next, take the pieces from the previous stage and form them into the next stage.

Analysis How does meiosis cause an exact halving of the genetic material of a cell? Can you identify the crucial event in meiosis that causes the chromosome number to be halved?

directly to the equator. The centromere of each chromosome splits, and sister chromatids are pulled toward opposite poles. Thus, separation of the chromatids occurs in the second meiotic division. By the time meiosis II is completed, each new nucleus contains single-stranded chromosomes, as seen in Figure 7-13, telophase.

The overall outcome of meiosis in male animals is the formation of four haploid cells, immature sperm, from one diploid cell, Figure 7-16. Each of the four haploid cells has half as many chromosomes as the original parent cell. A flagellum then forms from one of the centrioles of each cell as it matures. The flagellum helps the mature sperm to swim toward an egg, thus aiding fertilization.

Meiosis in Female Animals

Production of eggs by meiosis in a female animal follows the same general pattern as sperm production in males. But there are some interesting differences. Meiosis I in human females begins before birth, as early as the twelfth week of fetal development. Meiosis then stops until sexual maturity is reached many years later. At that point, several cells continue meiosis I on a cyclic basis. Usually, however, only one cell survives per cycle. The surviving cell divides during meiosis I to produce two cells of unequal size. The larger cell enters meiosis II. The smaller cell may do so as well, but if it does, the cells produced from it die. During meiosis II, the larger cell divides unequally once again. The smaller cell dies, but the larger one matures into an egg. Figure 7-16 compares the major events of meiosis in male and female animals.

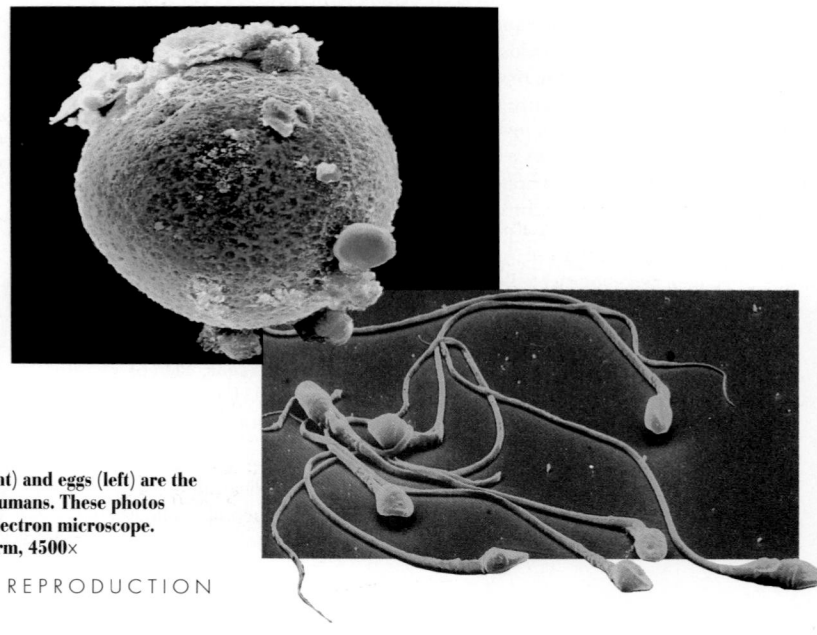

Figure 7-15 Sperm (right) and eggs (left) are the final products of meiosis in humans. These photos were taken with a scanning electron microscope. Magnification: egg, 470×; sperm, 4500×

186 CELLULAR REPRODUCTION

PROJECT

Meiosis Model: Have students design and build a model, or set of models, that can be used to demonstrate the process of meiosis. Students might make chromosome models from colored 1/4-inch tubing to demonstrate meiotic events. Models may be built of any materials the students provide, including clay, wood, Styrofoam, or even cakes. Each model should be clearly labeled to show what stage of meiosis the cell is in. Alternatively, students might build a model to demonstrate male or female gametogenesis that occurs after meiosis.
`L1` `LEP`

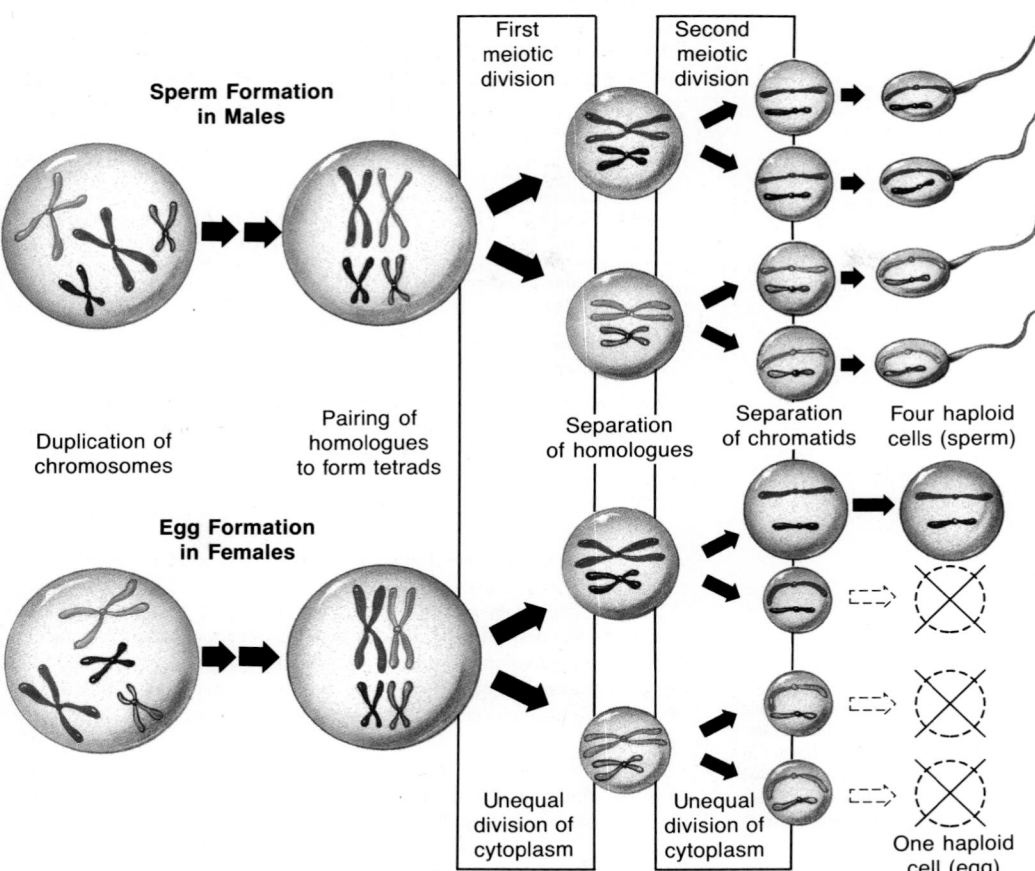

Sperm Formation in Males

Duplication of chromosomes

Pairing of homologues to form tetrads

First meiotic division

Separation of homologues

Second meiotic division

Separation of chromatids

Four haploid cells (sperm)

Egg Formation in Females

Unequal division of cytoplasm

Unequal division of cytoplasm

One haploid cell (egg)

Figure 7-16 **Compare the products of meiosis in male and in female animals.**

Although a sperm must be in final form before fertilization can occur, an egg may be fertilized before it is fully mature. In some animals, fertilization triggers the second meiotic division in a female. In a male, four sperm develop from each cell that undergoes meiosis, but in a female, only one egg develops from each cell that undergoes meiosis. In what way might unequal cell division resulting in production of one large egg be adaptive?

Importance of Meiosis

Meiosis may produce sperm or eggs in animals, or spores in plants, algae, and fungi. No matter which type of organism it is, each of these reproductive cells contains the haploid number of chromosomes. Thus, each carries genetic information in a form that can be passed to the next generation. If meiosis did not occur, the life cycle could not continue.

7.2 PRODUCTION OF REPRODUCTIVE CELLS 🐾 **187**

Reinforcement

Give students additional practice discriminating between meiosis in males and in females. List facts about each process and have students tell if the fact is a part of meiosis in males, females, or both. Examples might include: produces eggs (female); equal cytoplasm division between the cells produced (male); half the number of chromosomes as in the parent diploid cell (both).

Using the Illustration

If students have trouble listing facts outlined in the Reinforcement, use Figure 7-16 to reteach these concepts.
LEP

Science, Technology, and Society

Fertility Drugs: Drugs are available that cause females to produce large numbers of eggs. These drugs are called fertility drugs because they increase fertility. Human females who have had difficulty becoming pregnant often take these drugs. Many times, a resulting pregnancy will produce multiple births.

Demonstration

You can demonstrate the unequal distribution of cytoplasm in meiosis in females by using a ball of clay. First, divide the clay into two unequal pieces. State that each piece represents one cell with a nucleus having half the original number of chromosomes, but with each chromosome being made up of two chromatids as it was in mitosis. Explain that the smaller cell doesn't have enough food stored in the cytoplasm, so it dies. Then divide the remaining large piece of clay unequally again. This time, tell students that each piece of clay represents a cell with half the original number of chromosomes, but with each chromosome being made up of a single chromatid. The smaller cell dies, leaving one viable egg. **LEP**

Misconception

Since human females usually produce a single egg each month, some students may think that males produce sperm at only one time of the month. A similar misconception may be held that since males produce sperm constantly, so do females produce eggs constantly. Clarify the timing and production of each sex cell.

Display

Make a bulletin board display of photographs of various plants and animals. Challenge students to research the diploid and haploid numbers of chromosomes in each organism. Extend the display by discussing whether there are any trends in chromosome numbers. Students should see that two species of organisms may have the same chromosome number, but that complexity of the organism and chromosome number have little correlation. L1 COOP LEARN

Brainstorming

Inform students that many organisms reproduce both asexually and sexually. Have students offer suggestions for the advantages and disadvantages of each form of reproduction. Student responses should indicate that asexual reproduction is faster and more efficient than sexual reproduction, but that variations do not occur with asexual reproduction. Sexual reproduction is slower, requires more energy, and is less efficient than asexual reproduction but allows for variations and evolution. L1 COOP LEARN

Using the Table

Use Table 7.1 to further reinforce the differences and similarities between mitosis and meiosis. L1 LEP

Enrichment

Point out that homologous pairs of chromosomes may cross over in prophase I of meiosis. If this occurs, the genes on these chromosomes will be rearranged. This provides additional variation and explains why sometimes traits that are known to be inherited together get separated. L2

Table 7.1 **Comparison of Mitosis and Meiosis**

	Mitosis	*Meiosis*
Occurs in	all body cells	certain cells of reproductive organs
Number of cells produced per parent cell	two	four (three may die)
Chromosome number of parent cell	diploid (2n) or haploid (n)	diploid (2n)
Chromosome number of daughter cells	same as parent cell	haploid (n)
Kind of cell produced	various cells, such as skin and bone	animal gametes or certain spores
Function	genetic continuity from cell to cell	genetic continuity between generations; promotes variation

Figure 7-17 **Traits such as height and skin color can be reshuffled by genetic recombination. If changes in the environment occur, an individual with a different combination of traits may have a better chance of survival.**

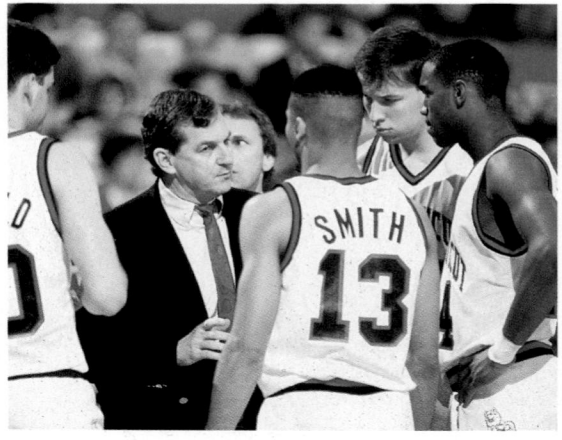

The Variation Advantage Meiosis provides for more than the transfer of genetic information. Combined with fertilization, which is needed for sexual reproduction, meiosis also provides the means for variation among offspring. Reproduction by mitosis alone produces little or no variety in offspring.

The variety arising from meiosis and fertilization is a little like a game of cards. The deck is shuffled before it is dealt. Shuffling rearranges the cards so that you play each hand with a different set of cards.

Meiosis is a process that reshuffles chromosomes—and the genetic information they carry. In this case, the hands played contain the genetic information that will be passed to offspring. In any population, there are variations among organisms. Such differences arise from various combinations of chromosomes.

How is this variation important to a species? Variation provides a better chance for survival of some organisms if changes in the environment should occur over time. By ensuring that individuals will have slightly different traits, nature keeps many hands in the game. Thus, the chance of producing too many individuals with undesirable combinations of genes is decreased. Adaptations of organisms result from genetic variations that enable them to survive in a particular environment.

188 CELLULAR REPRODUCTION

PORTFOLIO

Have students create a poster, using photographs or words cut from magazines, that demonstrates the similarities and differences between the processes of mitosis and meiosis. L1

Chromosome Combination Possibilities How does meiosis increase variety? Consider an animal whose diploid number is four—two pairs. Such an animal will produce gametes having two chromosomes, one of each pair. How many possible combinations of chromosomes may appear among the gametes? Look at Figure 7-18. The parent cell, shown in metaphase I, has two pairs of homologous chromosomes—*A* and *a*; *B* and *b*.

When the cell at the left completes meiosis, the gametes produced from it contain two possible chromosome combinations—*A* with *B* or *a* with *b*. The cell at the right produces gametes with different combinations—*a* with *B* or *A* with *b*. (Notice that there is always one member of each homologous pair in each gamete.) The particular combination of chromosomes in a gamete depends on how the chromosomes lined up at the equator during meiosis I. In this example, four combinations of chromosomes are possible among the gametes.

Now consider the possible combinations of chromosomes in zygotes produced by the union of these gametes. Figure 7-19 on page 190 shows that 16 different combinations of chromosomes may be produced. You have read that homologous chromosomes carry information for the same traits, but that the information may be in a different form. For example, one homologue may carry information for brown eyes; the other may carry information for blue eyes. Also, a single chromosome may carry information for thousands of traits. Thus, combinations of chromosomes resulting in many different features are possible among offspring. Some combinations may be more useful to an organism's survival than others. This reshuffling of chromosomes and the genetic information they carry is one of the mechanisms for what is called **genetic recombination**. Genetic recombination is a source of important raw material in the process of evolution—inheritable variation.

Figure 7-18 **How chromosomes are combined in gametes depends on how homologues line up during metaphase I of meiosis, an event that is a matter of chance.**

Using the Illustration
Use Figure 7-18 to visually demonstrate how variation occurs. First explain the variation to students visually and then give them a mathematical explanation.

3 Assess

Check for Understanding
Make up packs of cards using postcard stock or heavier paper. Place the name or a drawing of a phase of meiosis or a description of an important event of meiosis on each card. Arrange students in groups of four, and give each group one pack of cards. Have students shuffle the deck and pass out all of the cards. Students then identify their cards to the other students in their group. If the card contains a term or drawing, the student identifies it. If the card contains an event, the student adds additional information about when the event occurs and why the event is important. **L1** | **LEP** | **COOP LEARN**

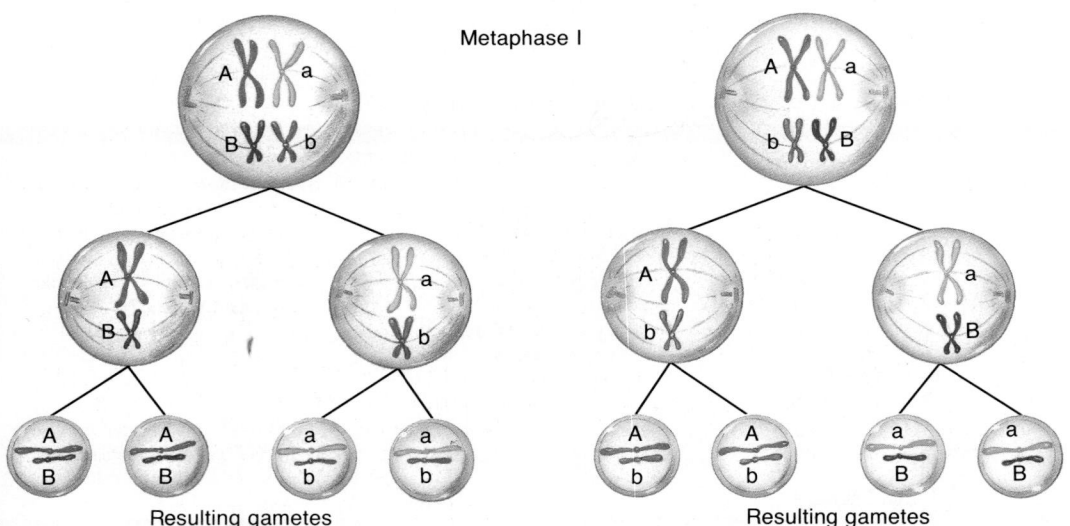

Metaphase I

Resulting gametes   Resulting gametes

STUDENT JOURNAL

Have students create an original cartoon that demonstrates meiosis in not less than an eight-block cartoon strip. The events shown may be represented by a likeness of a cell, or by an imaginary representation. Thorough captions should accompany each cartoon block. Each stage of meiosis should be represented. Because meiosis is cyclic, students may begin with any stage. Grade the project as follows:

- Give ten points for a cartoon strip containing eight blocks that demonstrate the correct sequence of meiotic events.
- Add ten points for originality.
- Add ten points for artistic representation.
- Subtract five points for each block out of sequence.
- Subtract five points for each incomplete or incorrect caption. **L1**

Reteach

Ask students why the second meiotic division is necessary if the chromosome number is halved during meiosis I. They should recognize that although the numbers are halved at the end of meiosis I, the chromosomes are still double stranded. Meiosis II is necessary to restore single-stranded chromosomes in the cell. **L1**

Extension

Ask interested students to calculate how many chromosomes would be in the body cells of a human after four generations if gametes were formed by mitosis rather than by meiosis. *Cells would contain 736 chromosomes instead of 46.* **L3**

✔ Assessment

Skill: Call on students randomly to draw the stages of meiosis on the chalkboard. Have other students label each stage. **L1**

4 Close

Discussion

Show students a diagram of a stage of mitosis or meiosis. Have them identify the process and the stage. Ask what clues helped them identify the process.

Figure 7-19 When gametes contain different combinations of chromosomes, fertilization leads to genetic recombination and increased variety among offspring.

Possible arrangement of chromosomes in sperm

Possible arrangement of chromosomes in eggs

Possible combinations of chromosomes in zygotes (in boxes)

LOOKING AHEAD

IF MEIOSIS IS the *process* of ensuring that genetic information is passed from one generation to the next, then what is the *content* of that information? You will find answers to this question in the next chapter. You will discover how traits are passed on from parents to offspring, and why offspring have combinations of characteristics different from their parents. Then you will solve problems in order to predict or explain results of matings between different parents.

Section Review

Understanding Concepts

1. Most cells of a certain animal contain 20 chromosomes. Some of its cells, though, are found to contain 10 chromosomes. What kinds of cells contain 10 chromosomes and by what process were they produced? Compare the 10 chromosomes in those cells to the 20 chromosomes in the other cells.
2. A certain cell has two pairs of chromosomes—*C* and *c*; *D* and *d*.

Gametes produced from this cell are found to have the following chromosome combinations: *C* and *D*, *C* and *d*; *c* and *D*, *c* and *d*. How can these different combinations be explained?

3. Most members of a population of animals have dark fur. Some offspring are produced, though, with light fur. Under what conditions might this difference be important to these animals in the future?

4. **Skill Review—Sequencing:** Sequence the activities of chromosomes during meiosis I. For more help, refer to Organizing Information in the **Skill Handbook**.

5. **Thinking Critically:** What events of meiosis I are critical if each cell produced by the end of meiosis is to have the haploid number of chromosomes? In what way are these events important in the production of genetic recombination?

Answers to Section Review

1. Reproductive cells, formed by meiosis, would contain 10 chromosomes. The 10 chromosomes in the reproductive cells would consist of one member of each homologous pair of chromosomes present in nonreproductive cells.
2. These combinations are a function of how homologous pairs of chromosomes line up during metaphase I.
3. The light fur might camouflage those

animals from predators if the environment became colder with more snow cover.

4. **Skill Review—Sequencing:** Homologous pairs of replicated chromosomes move together during prophase I, forming tetrads. During metaphase I, the tetrads attach to the spindle. In anaphase I, one homologue of each pair is pulled toward each pole; the

centromeres do not split. Each chromosome in telophase I is double stranded.

5. **Thinking Critically:** Moving together of homologues during prophase I, followed by separation of homologues rather than chromatids during anaphase I, are crucial events. The various ways in which homologous pairs line up during metaphase I make possible different combinations of chromosomes.

BIOLOGY, TECHNOLOGY, AND SOCIETY

Biotechnology

Aging: Can We Stop The Clock?

How old do you think "old" is? Thirty? Forty? Seventy? Your answer might be similar to that of Bernard Baruch, an advisor to several U.S. presidents. Baruch said, "I will never be an old man. To me, old age is always 15 years older than I am." Baruch died at 95, possibly with the same attitude about age.

However you define old age, the reality is that you, just like everyone else, are on your way toward it. In fact, aging has already begun to dull your senses of taste and hearing. You no longer have taste buds on the roof of your mouth, as a baby has. Nor can you hear as well as a baby, who is able to hear the "silent" noise of a high-pitched dog whistle.

Of course, the signs of aging are much easier to spot in people of your grandparents' generation. Graying hair, stronger glasses, and weaker muscles are just some of those signs.

As more people live longer, they want to understand the changes they face as they grow older. They also want to know why aging occurs and whether or not it is inevitable. Scientists are providing some answers as they study the aging process.

The Wear-and-tear Model   One of the older models of aging could be called the "wear-and-tear" model. This model compares the human body to a machine, such as an automobile. You expect a car to last a certain length of time before its parts break down or wear out. Like a machine, the human body can be overworked and its "repairs" neglected. Under the wear-and-tear model, it seems logical that too much work and stress could shorten a person's life span.

The Ticking-clock Model
Other researchers claim that aging seems to be programmed into the genes of a human body. Scientist Leonard Hayflick tried to demonstrate this idea by growing fibroblasts, a type of skin cell, under accelerated conditions in his laboratory. He discovered that cells taken from fetuses divided about 50 times, then slowed their rate of division, stopped, and died. Fibroblasts from adults divided fewer times before dying. Repeating the experiment with other types of body cells yielded about the same number of divisions. Under normal conditions within the human body,

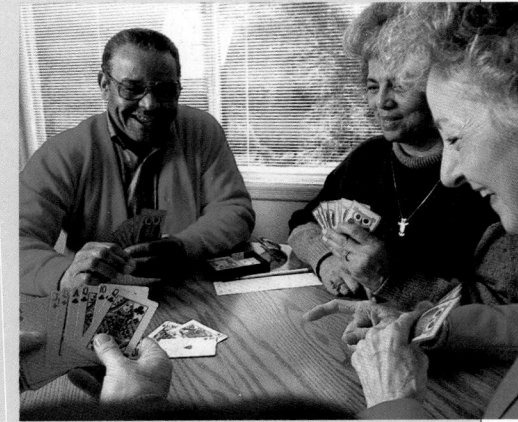

these 50 divisions would take place over 100 to 115 years, which Hayflick decided is probably the upper limit of a life span. Hayflick hypothesized that the entire human body may be tuned to a biological time clock that ticks off the years of life. He left for other scientists the question of whether or not this clock could be reset.

The Malfunctioning-body Model
Another factor that probably contributes to aging is the increasing chance that an older body's immune system will malfunction. As the defenders of the body age,

---

Biotechnology

Purpose
Students will compare several biological models for the aging process. They will be able to connect the processes of cell division and mitosis with aging.

Background
New evidence for the ticking-clock model suggests that the ends of DNA molecules are protected by a section of DNA much like the plastic tip on a shoelace. Some of this tip wears away with each cell division. When the tip is gone, the DNA becomes damaged, and the cell dies.

Teaching Strategies
- Ask students what Baruch meant by his statement as quoted in the feature.
- Discuss each of the models as students read them. Have students relate reasons they agree or disagree with each model.   **COOP LEARN**
- Have students do independent research for an extension if they show particular interest in the aging process.   **L3**

Possible Answers
1. Life expectancy for all males in the United States is approximately 74; it is approximately 78 for all females. In Southeast Asia, the life expectancy is 59. In Africa, the life expectancy is 51. Factors accounting for the differences are cultural stresses, diet, and genetic factors.
2. 1 048 576; approximately 1 followed by 15 zeros
3. Student answers will vary. Some students will agree that the statement is true because thinking about the past makes one old. Others will disagree, stating that simply counting the years doesn't increase age in and of itself.

4. Student answers will vary. Some students will say biotechnology should be used, while others will disagree. Positive results might include longer lives for them, their family, or friends. Negative results might include an increased population size resulting in less energy and other resources available for individuals. An aging human population would also create health care problems and would result in difficulties in supporting large numbers of older people.

Going Further

Allow students to choose the one model they think is most promising. Have them work in groups to design an experiment that would test the hypothesis of the model. Designs may be as complex or simple as students choose, but should clearly indicate scientific methods including controls, methods, and materials. **COOP LEARN**

---

they become less efficient in recognizing and responding to invasions of organisms that can harm the body. These aging defenders can confuse disease-causing invaders with the body's own cells and mistakenly attack the "good guys."

Other mistakes could involve the molecules that carry the genetic instructions for making proteins in the cell. If these molecules malfunction, the wrong directions would be used as the cell builds its proteins. To understand this breakdown in communications, imagine a contractor who plans to use 16-penny nails in building a house. If the message were garbled on the way to the carpenter and became "Use 16 nails," the house certainly wouldn't be sturdy. With incorrect instructions for its building activities, a body cell wouldn't be sturdy, either.

The Waste-buildup Model

Another factor interfering with cell construction could be the cellular wastes that build up inside a cell. With wastes lying around, it becomes more difficult for a cell to carry out its functions, just as it is hard to prepare dinner in a kitchen cluttered with unwashed dishes from lunch. If there is too much of this unneeded cellular material clogging a cell, the cell could "choke" on its own waste and die.

The Free-radical Model

One of the newest models of aging involves free radicals. Not a political group, as the name might suggest, these substances are unstable particles that are formed in the cell during normal metabolism, especially

when oxygen combines with unsaturated fats. Free radicals are fast moving and have one free, unpaired electron. Because of this unpaired electron, a free radical is attracted to and can steal an electron from other molecules. The resulting union of molecule and free radical can cross-link the molecules of a cell. Cross-links may prevent DNA from passing on its information and result in cancer, or they may cause breakdowns in the normal functioning of the body. If a free radical steals an electron from the protein, collagen, in connective tissue of skin or joints, this cross-linking can show up as wrinkled skin or stiff joints. And if an electron is stolen from a phospholipid molecule in a cell membrane, a hole could be punctured in the membrane. This would kill the cell.

Because the number of free radicals increases with exposure to sunlight, air pollution, tobacco smoke, and the normal breakdown of fat within the cell, damage can be extensive. Scientists are studying the action of some compounds, such as vitamins A, C, and E. These vitamins seem to work by scavenging unpaired electrons from free radicals before they cause damage.

As scientists continue to study cells looking for additional clues to the aging process, they have encountered a contrast that might someday be put to use. While most human cells run out of dividing time on the biological clock, cancerous cells may keep on dividing indefinitely. This contrast poses a challenge for biologists: Can they find a way to exchange some properties of normal and cancerous cells? If such a trade is possible, aging cells might be given a new lease on life. They may continue to divide, while the dangerous, uncontrolled division of cancerous cells is brought to a halt.

---

1. **Explore Further:** What is the average life expectancy of males and females born today in the United States? In some Asian countries? In some African countries? What factors might account for the differences among countries?

2. **Connection to Math:** When cells divide, one cell becomes two, and two become four. Calculate how many cells there would be after 20 divisions. If you can, continue to 50 divisions.

3. **Connection to Social Studies:** The Hopi Indians of the American Southwest have this saying: "It is well not to count the years. That makes one old." Do you agree with this saying? Why or why not?

4. **Issue:** Should biotechnology intervene to lengthen the average life span? What positive and negative effects might result?

192 CHAPTER 7 CELLULAR REPRODUCTION

Medicine Connection

Hope for Spinal Cord Injury Patients

It was a hot day, and the lake looked so cool and inviting. Fourteen-year-old Dan dived into what appeared to be eight feet of water. It was only three. Dan became one of the estimated 10 000 people in the United States who suffer spinal cord injuries every year.

Spinal Cord Injury The future for people like Dan could be a lifetime of paralysis. Some of the paralysis associated with spinal cord injury seems to be caused by the body's own responses to the trauma. When the spinal cord is injured, the body responds in a series of events. First, free radicals released from injured cells attack the membranes of surrounding cells. Then, endorphins, the body's natural painkillers, cause a sharp drop in the amount of blood flowing to the damaged area. A reduced flow of blood means that nerve cells in the spinal cord are deprived of crucial nutrients and oxygen. Finally, the molecules that transmit nerve impulses pour out of injured cells and bind to surrounding cells, causing cellular swelling and damage.

Drug Treatment Some drugs are able to counteract each of these bodily responses. If the drugs are administered quickly enough, within a few hours of injury, they could mean a difference between total paralysis below the site of injury and being able to move.

These drug treatments were developed in accord with the long-held belief that nerve cells cannot replace themselves. Unlike skin and stomach-lining cells, nerve cells were thought never to divide after a person is born. Scientists believed that once the nerve pathways were injured, they would never heal. Recently, researchers discovered that this belief is not always true. Under some conditions, nerve cells *can* divide and grow.

Because of this discovery, a new drug seems to hold promise for spinal cord injury patients. This newcomer, presently called GM-1, is a chemical extracted from the brains of cows. In laboratory tests on animals, GM-1 has been shown to protect nerve cells after damage to the spinal cord. Even more encouraging, GM-1 showed in similar tests that it could actually stimulate regeneration of injured nerve cells and cause new nerve cells to grow. Researchers are especially excited because the drug seems to restore the function of paralyzed muscles.

Much research and testing remains to be done, but doctors say they are hopeful that soon they can begin to consider spinal cord injury as treatable rather than incurable.

1. **Connection to Health:** Why is an injury to the spinal cord so serious?
2. **Connection to Genetics:** How might new drugs like GM-1 help people born with spinal cord defects?

CAREER CONNECTION

Occupational therapists help people with serious injuries to regain independence in their daily lives. For example, these professionals may teach a paralyzed patient how to turn the pages of a book by using a motor that is activated by breathing into a tube.

Medicine Connection

Purpose
This feature ties research aimed at better treatment techniques of spinal cord injury with drugs that may alter the ability of nerve cells to undergo mitosis.

Teaching Strategies
- Ask students why a broken arm of a starfish can regenerate into a new animal, but humans cannot even replace a finger. *Regeneration requires mitosis, a process that is stopped in many organs after their formation.* Relate the regenerative ability of starfish to mitosis and the inability of a finger to regenerate to the inability of nerve cells to undergo mitosis in the body.

Possible Answers
1. Nerve tissue does not usually regenerate by mitosis, so an injury to the spinal cord cannot be repaired.
2. GM-1 might make the nerve cells of the spinal cord divide, repairing the spinal cord defects.

Going Further
Allow students to create a bulletin board for current events relating to reports of other medical research from newspaper and magazine clippings. **COOP LEARN**

CAREER CONNECTION

Students may find out more about occupational therapists by checking with the therapy department in the nearest medium- or large-size hospital. They may also write to The American Institute of Biological Sciences, 730 11th Street, NW, Washington, DC 20001-4584.

CHAPTER 7

CHAPTER REVIEW

Summary

Summary statements can be used by students to review the major concepts of the chapter.

Language of Biology

Answers should go beyond defining the terms. Accept any reasonable answer that uses the term correctly and in the proper context.

Understanding Concepts

1. The microorganisms developed from bacteria and spores that entered the pot of soup.
2. Students should use the information in the text to make their drawings. Each daughter nucleus should contain six chromosomes, three homologous pairs.
3. Pasteur believed that microorganisms present in infusions develop from spores. He had to allow air in to satisfy those who believed air was needed for spontaneous generation to occur.
4. The cell cycle would stop at that point. Until DNA has been replicated, the events of mitosis will not begin.
5. The volume grows more rapidly than does the surface area. If the volume becomes too large, materials cannot be exchanged rapidly enough across the membrane to meet the cell's needs.
6. Students should use the information in the text to make their drawings. Each daughter nucleus, at the end of meiosis II, should contain three single-stranded chromosomes, one of each homologous pair.
7. No, the replicated chromosomes would probably not be divided equally between the two daughter cells.
8. The two parents are carrying genetic instructions for short wings, even though they have long wings. Short wings are possible among some offspring because offspring can have combinations of chromosomes different from those of their parents.

9. Meiosis I—haploid cells are produced from diploid cells.
10. Mitosis ensures that each daughter cell will have the exact same genetic information as the parent cell.

Applying Concepts

11. Such a cell might arise if, during mitosis, one pair of chromatids failed to separate during anaphase. It could also arise if one gamete missing a chromosome fused with a normal gamete. The abnormal gamete could be produced if both members of a homologous pair of chromosomes were pulled to the same pole. (This would also result in another gamete having an extra chromosome.)
12. The results suggest that a signal is needed to initiate DNA replication. The nerve cell must lack that signal, probably a chemical in the cytoplasm.
13. The offspring would be produced by mitosis and cell division. All such offspring would be genetically identical to one another and to the parent, unlike organisms produced by sexual reproduction, which exhibit variations.

Summary

Pasteur's experiment leading to the downfall of spontaneous generation also led to the theory of biogenesis, a theory that ties in nicely with the idea that all cells come from other cells.

New eukaryotic cells arise during cell cycles that are regulated by interaction of many proteins and external agents. When a cell cycle includes mitosis, as in the reproduction of most body cells, the chromosomes are first replicated and then distributed equally to daughter cells. Each daughter cell receives the same set of genetic instructions originally present in the parent cell. Prokaryotic cells distribute their replicated chromosomes to daughter cells by binary fission.

A cell cycle involving meiosis also requires chromosome replication, but results in the formation of specialized reproductive cells that contain only half the number of chromosomes as their parent cells. This reduction in the number of chromosomes ensures that the chromosome number will remain constant from generation to generation. Meiosis and fertilization result in genetic recombination, important in the variation of organisms, and therefore important in evolution.

Language of Biology

Write a sentence that shows your understanding of each of the following terms.

anaphase	interphase
binary fission	meiosis
cell cycle	metaphase
cell plate	mitosis
centromere	prophase
chromatid	sexual reproduction
diploid	spindle
fertilization	spontaneous generation
gamete	spore
genetic recombination	telophase
haploid	zygote
homologue	

Understanding Concepts

1. A pot of leftover soup is not refrigerated and sits out overnight. A student takes some of the soup into his science class and examines a drop under the microscope. He discovers microorganisms in the soup and concludes that they formed from the soup itself. What could you teach him about his conclusion?
2. Make a series of labeled diagrams illustrating mitosis in an animal cell in which $2n = 6$.
3. Why did Pasteur believe that in order to disprove the idea of spontaneous generation, he had to design a flask that allowed air to enter but kept spores out?
4. How would the cell cycle be affected if DNA were prevented from replicating? Why?
5. What is the relationship between a cell's surface area and its volume as the cell grows? How does this limit cell size?
6. Make a series of labeled diagrams illustrating meiosis in an animal cell in which $2n = 6$.
7. Would binary fission be an efficient means of cell reproduction if prokaryotes had several chromosomes instead of just one?
8. Explain how two fruit flies having long wings can produce some offspring having short wings.
9. Which part of meiosis—meiosis I or meiosis II—is sometimes called the reduction division? Why?
10. What is accomplished by mitosis in terms of the genetic information of a cell?

194 CHAPTER 7 CELLULAR REPRODUCTION

Applying Concepts

11. How might you explain the production of a human cell that had only 45 chromosomes?

12. If a nucleus from a nondividing type of cell, such as a nerve cell, is transplanted into a skin cell whose nucleus is undergoing DNA replication, within minutes DNA replication begins in the chromosomes of the transplanted nerve cell nucleus. What do the results of this experiment suggest about control of the cell cycle?

13. Some organisms reproduce in such a way that their offspring arise from just a single cell of the parent. Which method of cell reproduction would such reproduction involve? Compare the variety among offspring produced in this way with the variety among offspring resulting from fertilization of an egg by a sperm.

14. Suppose a cell had four homologous chromosomes of each type instead of two. How many homologous chromosomes of each type would be in the daughter cells produced by mitosis? By meiosis?

15. In what ways does cell reproduction in prokaryotes and eukaryotes differ? Could mitosis or meiosis occur in prokaryotes? Why or why not?

16. Colchicine is a chemical that prevents the formation of microtubules. What would be the effect of adding colchicine to cells just before mitosis were to begin?

17. At one time, interphase was referred to as the "resting phase" of mitosis. Why do you think this description is no longer used?

18. Damage to nerves is often permanent. Why is it sometimes not possible to recover from such damage?

19. In some organisms, mitosis is not followed by cell division. Describe what the cellular structure of these organisms might look like.

20. **Math Connection:** Why is it important for incoming nutrients to reach the interior of a cell quickly?

21. **Medicine Connection:** Why do you think it is important to administer drugs quickly after spinal cord injury?

Lab Interpretation

22. **Investigation:** Bean roots were marked into three equal sections (A, B, and C), with A being closest to the root tip and C being farthest from the root tip. The length of each section was measured each day for five days. Total growth in each section is indicated in the graph below. In which section of the root is growth fastest? Explain.

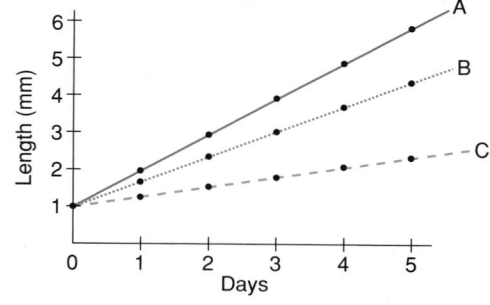

23. **Thinking Lab:** A scientist studying certain cells finds that Golgi bodies disappear at the same time that there is an increase in the numbers of vacuoles. Hypothesize what might be happening in this cell.

24. **Minilab 1:** A cell undergoes a problem during mitosis in that spindle fibers form in only one half of the cell. The spindle fibers that do form are associated with centrioles at only one pole of the cell. If this cell continues in mitosis, predict what might happen. Is this a plant cell or an animal cell? How do you know?

25. **Minilab 2:** When a large-scale model is made of something that occurs on a small scale, it is often easier to understand. Why? Explain the parts of meiosis that were easier to understand after making a model.

Connecting Ideas

26. How do certain events in the control of the cell cycle illustrate that energy is needed for the biological work of cell reproduction?

27. You learned in Chapter 5 how various parts of cells interact. What parts interact during mitosis?

Connecting Ideas

26. **Energy:** Energy is necessary for such functions as DNA replication, building the spindle, movement of spindle fibers and their attached chromosomes, and for initiating the events of mitosis.

27. **Systems and Interactions:** Some examples of interaction include attachment of chromosomes to spindle fibers, action of microfilaments to pinch in the cell membrane in animal cells, and formation of the cell plate in plant cells from ER or Golgi bodies.

14. The daughter cells produced by mitosis would contain four of each type. The cells produced by meiosis would have two of each type.

15. Prokaryotes have a much simpler means of cell reproduction (binary fission) than do eukaryotic cells, whose reproduction involves mitosis. Neither mitosis nor meiosis could occur in prokaryotes. They lack the structures necessary for those processes to be carried out.

16. Addition of colchicine would stop mitosis in prophase because spindle fibers could not be formed. The cell, which would remain in that stage, would be $4n$.

17. During interphase, the cell is actively producing new organelles, synthesizing proteins, and carrying out basic life functions.

18. The remaining undamaged nerves cannot reproduce. Thus, no new nerves are produced to replace the damaged ones.

19. The cell would consist of many distinct nuclei. Each nucleus would have the same number of chromosomes.

20. Cells use nutrients continuously. If it took too long for some of those nutrients to reach the cell's interior, the cell might not be able to survive.

21. Administration of the drugs very soon after the injury can counteract the body's responses to the injury, thus decreasing the chances of total paralysis below the point of the injury.

Lab Interpretation

22. The root grew fastest in section A, closest to the tip. This is where the meristem is located.

23. The Golgi bodies may be producing materials that are incorporated into vacuoles. The Golgi bodies disappear after their work is done.

24. Chromosomes might not separate after metaphase or they might all move to the side of the cell with the spindle. This would be an animal cell because it has centrioles.

25. Answers will vary.

ORGANIZER
CHAPTER 8

SECTION	OBJECTIVES	TEXT LABS/FEATURES
8.1 Principles of Genetics (3 days)	**Discuss** Mendel's experiments and his results. **Explain** the three principles of genetics Mendel obtained through his experiments. **Solve** genetics problems using Punnett squares.	**Minilab 1:** How does sample size affect results? p. 199 **Investigation:** Predicting Plant Genotypes, p. 204
8.2 Solving Genetics Problems (2 days)	**Apply** the rules of probability to solve genetics problems. **Demonstrate** the inheritance of traits resulting from incomplete dominance, codominance, and multiple alleles.	
8.3 The Chromosome Theory of Heredity (2 days)	**Discuss** the development of the chromosome theory of heredity. **Apply** the laws of probability to solve genetics problems involving sex-linked traits. **Explain** how the expression of a pair of genes may be influenced by other genes as well as by the environment.	**Math Connection:** Crossing Over as a Tool to Determine Gene Location on Chromosomes, p. 216 **Career Connection:** Genetic counselor, p. 217 **Minilab 2:** What are some human variations? p. 218 **Thinking Lab:** What pattern of inheritance allows for the prediction of a genotype when phenotypes are known? p. 218
BIOLOGY, TECHNOLOGY, AND SOCIETY		**History Connection:** What if Mendel had picked different traits? p. 220 **Issues:** Inbreeding: Helpful or Harmful? p. 221

LAB MATERIALS

INVESTIGATION	MINILAB	ALTERNATE LAB
page 204 labels marking pens milk cartons paper cups paper towels petri dishes pots Readi-Earth (optional) sand scissors soil tobacco seeds vermiculite	**page 199** No special materials are needed for this lab. **page 218** No special materials are needed for this lab.	**page 208** bean seeds cups labels potting soil spoons, plastic

TEACHER CLASSROOM RESOURCES	OTHER RESOURCES
Study Guide, pp. 43-44 **Concept Mapping,** p. 8 ***PLL:** *Probability and Mendelian Genetics,* p. 44 ***PLL:** *Drosophila Genetics,* p. 49 ****ILS:** *Finding Phenotypes and Genotypes for One Trait,* p. 81 ****ILS:** *Finding Phenotypes and Genotypes for Two Traits,* p. 85	***STVS:** *Obesity and Heredity,* Human Biology (Disc 7, Side 2) ***STVS:** *Selective Breeding in Cows,* Plants and Simple Organisms (Disc 4, Side 1)
Study Guide, p. 45 **Critical Thinking/Problem Solving:** *Evolution of a Leopard Population,* p. 8	***STVS:** *Selective Breeding in Micro-Pigs,* Plants and Simple Organisms (Disc 4, Side 1) **Color Transparency 11:** *Punnett Squares* **Color Transparency 12:** *A Dihybrid Cross*
Study Guide: pp. 46-48 ****ILS:** *Heredity or Environment?* p. 89	***STVS:** *Breeding Fruit Flies,* Plants and Simple Organisms (Disc 4, Side 1)
Assessment Materials **Chapter Assessment,** pp. 29-32 **Performance Assessment in Biology,** p. 16 **Alternate Assessment in the Science Classroom** **Computer Test Bank**	**Spanish Resources** **Cooperative Learning Resource Guide** **Videodisc Correlations** (to Optical Data's and Videodiscovery's videodiscs)

* Probing Levels of Life
** Investigating Living Systems

* Science Technology Videodisc Series

Key to Teaching Strategies

The following designations will help you decide which activities in the teacher margin are appropriate for your students.

L1 Level 1 activities should be within the ability range of all students.

L2 Level 2 activities should be within the ability range of the average to above-average student.

L3 Level 3 activities are designed for the ability range of above-average students.

LEP LEP activities are appropriate for Limited English Proficiency students.

COOP LEARN Cooperative Learning activities are designed for small group work.

ADDITIONAL RESOURCES

Infinite Voyage *The Geometry of Life*
The discovery of the structure and function of DNA has changed how scientists view heredity. Students will learn how understanding DNA gives humans the opportunity to look for cures for inherited diseases.

Audiovisual
Basic Genetics, video, Frey Scientific.
Factoring in Mendel, video, Films for the Humanities and Sciences.

Software
Genetics Problem Shop, Apple II, EME.
Mendelbugs, Apple, Focus.

HEREDITY

Chapter Overview

Students will first learn about Mendel's experiments, his interpretation of his data, and the tests that confirmed his hypothesis. They will come to understand the principles of dominance, segregation, and independent assortment and be introduced to modern terminology of genetics.

Next, students will apply Mendel's ideas and the concept of probability to solve genetics problems involving complete dominance, incomplete dominance, and multiple alleles.

Students will then study the development of the chromosome theory of heredity and learn how to solve genetics problems involving sex-linked traits. Finally, they will find that expression of a given pair of genes depends upon all other genes as well as the environment.

HEREDITY

HAVE YOU EVER stopped to admire a butterfly flitting from flower to flower? Butterflies belong to a group of insects called Lepidoptera, from the Greek words *lepis,* which means "scale," and *pteron,* which means "wing." The scales on a butterfly's wing form the beautifully colored, sometimes iridescent pattern you see. The different kinds of butterflies can be identified by the particular patterns on their wings. Monarch butterflies, for example, have an orange and black pattern, while tiger swallowtails are yellow, edged with black, blue, and orange.

What causes a monarch butterfly's wings to be orange and black? The same thing that causes a zebra to be striped and causes you to have blue, brown, or green eyes. Heredity. The pattern of scales on a butterfly's wing is inherited; it is passed from parent to offspring. While many traits are shared by all organisms of the same kind, the *forms* of traits may vary among offspring. All traits are transmitted from one generation to the next by microscopic bits of matter on the chromosomes of gametes. The same bits of matter that control the butterfly's intricate and brilliantly colored pattern of scales also help determine the color of your eyes, the texture of your hair, and your sex. And what sex you are, male or female, may, in turn, affect which other traits you inherit. What may seem most surprising about heredity is that the occurrence of many traits is largely determined by probability—the "roll of the dice."

196

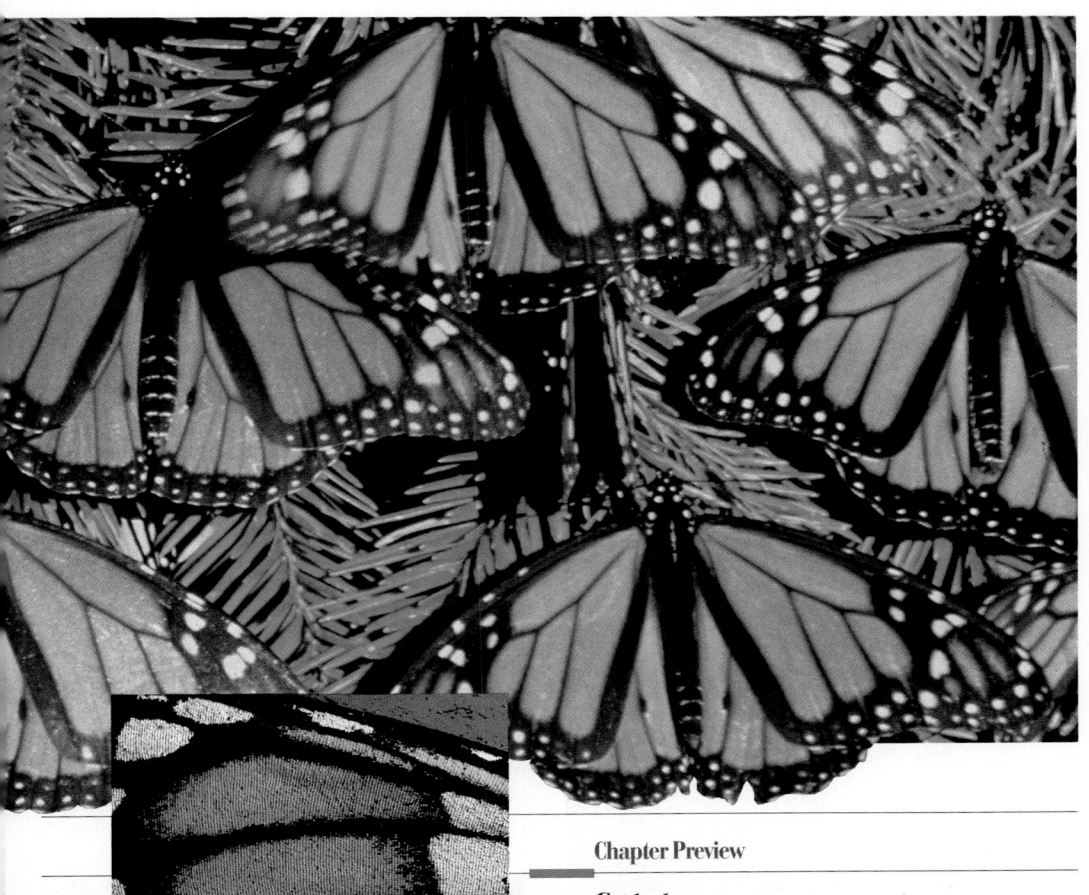

What would monarch butterflies look like if the pattern of scales on their wings changed with each generation? What problems might this cause for these butterflies?

Chapter Preview

197

Introducing the Chapter

Beginning with a discussion of the photographs on pages 196 and 197, lead students in a discussion of visible traits of a variety of familiar organisms, including themselves. Have them come to the conclusion that such traits are passed from parents to offspring. Ask the following questions, having them concentrate on human traits as they think about the answers. What determines an organism's traits? Do all offspring in a family have the same traits? Do they have some traits of each parent or a blend of traits? How are traits passed from parents to offspring? Can the traits an organism will have be predicted? **L1**

Theme Development

A theme that is stressed in this chapter is patterns of change. This becomes apparent in solving genetics problems. Also emphasized is the theme methods of inquiry, which pervades the discussion of the work of Mendel, Sutton, and Morgan as each contributed to our understanding of genetics.

Tying to Previous Knowledge

Sexual reproduction results in offspring having sets of characteristics different from one another and from their parents. The traits an organism has are largely a matter of chance, depending upon the particular combination of genes an offspring inherits. Genes are located on chromosomes, and the possible combinations of chromosomes are understood in terms of the events of meiosis and fertilization studied in Chapter 7.

ASSESSMENT PLANNER

Choose assessment strategies from the following pages to evaluate the progress of your students.

Assess, pp. 206, 211, 219
Portfolio, pp. 202, 205, 206, 213, 218
Alternate Lab, pp. 208-209

Thinking Lab, p. 218
Minilab 1, p. 199
Minilab 2, p. 218
Investigation, pp. 204-205
Chapter Review, pp. 222-223

Prepare

Key Concepts

Students will distinguish between dominant and recessive traits, homozygous and heterozygous genotypes, and be able to summarize the experiments and results of Gregor Mendel.

Key Terms

heredity, genetics, dominant, recessive, gene, allele, genotype, phenotype, homozygous, heterozygous

Materials

- Gather tobacco seeds, soil, and planting trays for the Investigation.

1 Focus

Objectives

The objectives are listed on the student page. Remind students to preview these objectives as a guide to this numbered section.

Activity

Set up 5 to 6 small plastic containers each containing a different fish (goldfish, guppy, bluegill, etc). Have students observe the fish and list the similar features that they all share (eyes, scales, fins). Have them list differences among the fish (size and color of scales, size, shape and number of fins). After the activity, have the students discuss their observations. Explain that they have described some inherited traits found in fish. Point out that some of the traits are similar in all fish because they are defining characteristics of all fish. Tell students they will learn more about how living things inherit their traits in this chapter. L1

Objectives

Discuss Mendel's experiments and his results.

Explain the three principles of genetics Mendel obtained through his experiments.

Solve genetics problems using Punnett squares.

8.1 Principles of Genetics

You know that like produces like. Cats produce cats, fruit flies produce fruit flies, and maple trees produce maple trees. Offspring are like their parents in that you can easily recognize them as the same kind of organism. But are offspring and parents exactly alike? Certainly the colors of kittens in a litter are not identical. Some kittens may have a color very much like one of the parents, but others may have a color not seen in either parent. Whenever offspring are produced by sexual reproduction, they vary from one another and from each of their parents.

Why is the last statement true? Recall from Chapter 7 that each parent contributes a set of DNA instructions, located on chromosomes, to its offspring. These two sets of chromosomes can combine in many ways, depending upon how they line up at the equator during meiosis I. The particular combination of the two sets of parental chromosomes in the zygote determines the traits the offspring will develop. This passing of traits from parent to offspring is called **heredity.** Can we predict what traits the offspring are likely to have if we know the traits of their parents? Are we able to determine what kinds of genetic information parents must have by analyzing the traits of their offspring? Answers to these questions can be formulated through genetics experiments. **Genetics** is the science of heredity.

Origin of Genetics

The basis for what we know about genetics came from the work of Gregor Mendel (1822-1884). Mendel was a monk in a monastery in Czechoslovakia. He went to Vienna to study science and mathematics

Figure 8-1 Kittens from the same litter can have similar or very different colors. The chromosomes each kitten inherited from its parents determine its unique color pattern.

Figure 8-2 Through experiments with common pea plants, Mendel discovered basic laws of inheritance.

198 HEREDITY

MEETING INDIVIDUAL NEEDS

Visually Impaired, Physically Challenged: For the visually impaired and physically challenged students, make a large Punnett square by dividing a sheet of paper into four equal-size squares with a marking pen. The symbols for various traits can be put on 2″ × 2″ cards and placed on the sides of the Punnett square to show the gene contents of the sperm and eggs. Make other 2″ × 2″ cards

showing the genes in possible offspring. Students will be able to place the genes inside the Punnett square and read the genotype and determine the phenotype. L1 LEP COOP LEARN to become a teacher. After two years, Mendel returned to the monastery, where he tended the monastery garden and experimented with plants. He also taught at a local school. In 1866, Mendel published the results of eight years of experiments and analysis. His work was ignored until 1900, when it was finally recognized as a major new development in biology. As you read about Mendel, keep in mind the methods of good science. All of them are shown in Mendel's creative work.

Mendel's Experiments

Mendel worked with the common pea plant. Pea plants are grown easily and produce large numbers of offspring in a short time. Certain varieties of pea plants have sets of clearly different characteristics that remain unchanged from one generation to the next. Mendel found that these traits or characteristics are hereditary—they are passed from generation to generation. For example, pea flowers are either purple or white. The stems of pea plants are either short or tall. Mendel's work was to determine how these traits were transmitted from parent to offspring.

Mendel planned his experiments very carefully. He chose traits of pea plants that had clear-cut differences to test. He studied the offspring of many generations, not only the first, and he worked with a large number of plants, realizing that this would increase the chances that his results would be meaningful. He counted the offspring and analyzed the numbers mathematically. This quantitative data helped him support his findings. Mendel was looking for general trends to form a basic set of rules about the transmission of traits.

Mendel chose a total of seven traits to work with in his first experiments on pea plants. Those traits are shown in Figure 8-3.

Figure 8-3 **Mendel chose seven traits of peas with clearly different forms for his experiments.**

	Seed shape	Seed color	Flower color	Flower position	Pod color	Pod shape	Plant height
Dominant trait	round	yellow	purple	axial (side)	green	inflated	long
Recessive trait	wrinkled	green	white	terminal (tips)	yellow	constricted	short

---

Minilab 1

How does sample size affect results?

The ratio of males to females born in a population should be 50/50. Your class should show this balance, but does it? Count the number of males and females in your class. What is the ratio? The ratio may not be 50/50. One reason is that your class is a very small sample size. Now count the brothers and sisters of your classmates and total the number of males and females. How do these totals compare to the expected 50/50 ratio? How does this sample size compare to just your class? Redo the count and this time include all brothers, sisters, and first cousins of the members of your class. How do these totals compare to the 50/50 ratio? How does this sample size compare to your original sample size?

Analysis *How does sample size affect results?*

STUDENT JOURNAL

Have the students write their understanding of Mendel's principle of segregation in their journals. Tell them to include the concepts of dominant, recessive, homozygous, heterozygous, allele, genotype, and phenotype. As they write their analysis, tell them to write it as though they were explaining it to a friend who has no idea what Mendel's principle is or what any of the terms mean. Have them use construction paper strips 4" × 1$\frac{3}{4}$" of different colors to represent the chromosomes that separate from each other. Have them include the parental, F_1, and the F_2 generations in their models. L1 LEP

---

2 Teach

Using the Table

Have students study each pair of traits in Figure 8-3. Be sure students are able to distinguish the differences. Ask students to think of any problems Mendel may have had in distinguishing between these traits in his experiments.

Minilab 1

Purpose

For students to discover how sample size affects results.

Skills

interpret data, make and use tables

Teaching Strategies

- Begin this Minilab by reviewing the 50:50 chance for male and female children being born.

Expected Results

Students should find that as the sample size increases, the ratio of males to females becomes closer to 50:50.

To determine just how close the 50:50 ratio is, use this formula:

$$\frac{\text{Total males in survey}}{\text{Total students in survey}} \times 100 = \% \text{ males}$$

Use the same formula to determine female percentages. Example:

$$\frac{\text{Total females in survey}}{\text{Total students in survey}} \times 100 = \% \text{ females},$$

$91/173 \times 100 = 53.7\%$ females

Answers

As sample size increases, observed data will come closer to the expected 50:50 ratio.

✔ **Assessment**

Performance: Use a coin to represent males (heads) and females (tails). Perform a brief activity that will reflect the fact that a small sample size will not yield a 50:50 ratio of males to females when a coin is flipped but a large sample size will approach this expected ratio. Prepare a brief report and include your data.

Discussion Question

Mendel knew that pea plants were self-pollinating plants. Suppose the pea plants that Mendel worked with had cross-pollinated easily. How could this have caused him problems developing his principles of heredity? *If pollen from a plant with one kind of genes had cross-pollinated with a plant having another set of genes, the offspring would not have shown the expected traits.*

Brainstorming

Ask students why Mendel used pollen from a purple-flowering plant to pollinate a white-flowering plant and also used pollen from a white-flowering plant to pollinate a purple-flowering plant. You can develop the concept of reciprocal crosses after the students have given their answers.

 L1   COOP LEARN

Figure 8-4   In his experiments, Mendel carefully opened and removed the male structures from the flowers he did not want to self-fertilize. He then transferred male gametes (pollen) from another plant to fertilize the flower.

Pea Flower Structures

Male structures

Female structures

Pollen Transfer

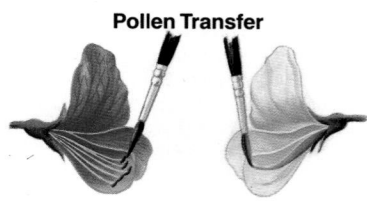

Figure 8-5   Mendel's cross of pure purple-flowered plants with pure white-flowered plants resulted in an F₁ generation of all purple-flowered plants.

Mendel's Results

Pea plants reproduce sexually. Both male and female sex organs are in the same flower. Normally, male gametes fertilize eggs of the same flower. After many generations, offspring still have the same features as the parents. Such plants are said to be pure. In his experiments, Mendel crossed a plant having a certain trait with a plant having the opposite trait. For example, he crossed pea plants that produced purple flowers with plants that produced white flowers. He transferred the pollen of one plant to another plant as shown in Figure 8-4.

In some cases, the pollen was obtained from purple-flowered plants and transferred to plants with white flowers. The opposite combination was also done. Mendel found that in every case, the offspring of this cross yielded offspring that all had purple flowers. The offspring of a parental cross are called the first filial, or F_1 generation.

Mendel was impressed that there were no plants that produced white flowers in the F_1 generation. He allowed members of the F_1 generation to reproduce in the usual fashion.

The offspring of the second cross are called the second filial, or F_2 generation. Mendel's results for this cross were very revealing. Of the 929 offspring produced, 705 plants produced purple flowers and 224 plants produced white flowers. These numbers give a ratio very close to three purple-flowered plants to one white-flowered plant.

Mendel noted that for each trait there is one form that dominates the other. Based on the results for the F_1 generation, the trait for purple flowers is the **dominant** trait. The other trait, in this case white flowers, disappears in the F_1 generation and is called a **recessive** trait. Mendel conducted this experiment using several other traits of pea plants. In each case, he obtained the same results. From his experiments, he concluded that one form of a hereditary trait, the dominant trait, dominates or prevents the expression of the recessive trait. This is now known as the principle of dominance.

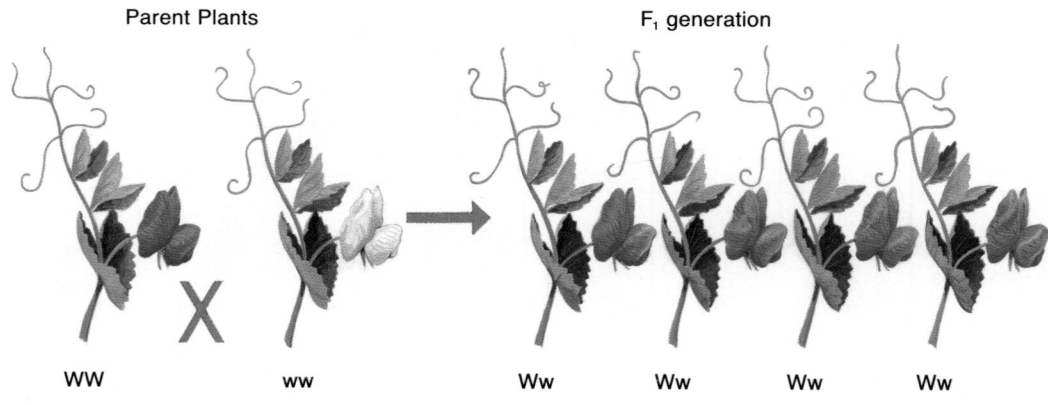

Parent Plants   F₁ generation

WW   ww   Ww   Ww   Ww   Ww

200 🖙 HEREDITY

PROGRAM RESOURCES

Teacher Classroom Resources

Study Guide, pp. 43-44 L1
Concept Mapping, p. 8 L1 LEP
Probing Levels of Life, Labs 17, 18;
   pp. 44, 49 L2
Investigating Living Systems, Labs 20, 21;
   pp. 81, 85 L2

Mendel's Hypothesis

In Mendel's crosses, the recessive trait disappeared in the F_1 generation but reappeared in the F_2 generation. To explain this result, Mendel made certain assumptions. Each pea plant is produced as a result of the union of a sperm and an egg. He reasoned that for every trait, there must be a pair of factors. One must come from the sperm and one must come from the egg. He called the factors *characters,* but we now call them **genes.** Mendel represented the genes by symbols. A dominant gene is represented by a capital letter. A recessive gene is represented by the same letter but in lowercase. For example, if the gene for purple flowers (dominant) were W, then the gene for white flowers (recessive) would be w. The two genes combine in the fertilized egg so that each new pea plant contains two genes for each trait.

Gene Segregation   In Mendel's experiments, the pure parental plants each had two identical genes for a trait. Purple-flowered plants (dominant) were WW. White-flowered plants (recessive) were ww. Mendel reasoned that the two genes segregate (separate) during gamete formation. Sperm and eggs would have just one gene for each trait. Therefore, the gametes of purple-flowered parents should have the W gene, and gametes of white-flowered parents should have the w gene. As a result, all F_1 plants should be Ww, the only possible combination. Because the W gene is dominant to the w gene, all F_1 plants would have purple flowers.

If Mendel's assumptions were correct, all F_1 plants *(Ww)* should produce half their gametes with the W gene and half with the w gene. There would be three possible combinations in the F_2 generation—*WW, Ww,* and *ww*. The chance of W and w gametes combining would be twice as great as other possible combinations. These possibilities can be expressed as a ratio—1 *WW*:2 *Ww*:1 *ww*. Both *WW* and *Ww* plants will produce purple flowers, while *ww* plants will produce white flowers. This result represents a ratio of 3 purple-flowered plants:1 white-flowered plant. This is, in fact, what Mendel observed.

Figure 8-6   **The cross of individuals from the F_1 generation resulted in approximately one white-flowered pea plant for every three purple-flowered plants.**

F$_1$ generation

F$_2$ generation

Ww   Ww   Ww   Ww   Ww   ww

8.1 PRINCIPLES OF GENETICS **201**

SECTION 8.1

Reinforcement
Assign students who have difficulty focusing on a complex concept, such as gene segregation, to rewrite Mendel's hypothesis in a step-by-step format in their own words. They should use the key concepts from the text. This work can be put in their journals and used for review. **L1**
COOP LEARN

Concept Development
- Tell students that Mendel had no information about meiosis or cell division, and had no idea that chromosomes had any relationship to how traits are inherited. Mendel's success in explaining his experimental results was due, in most part, to his understanding and use of mathematics, especially statistics, as he analyzed, verified, and explained his data.
- Remind students that Mendel worked with six other traits besides flower color. Direct them to work with data that Mendel obtained from his experiments (below) to see how he arrived at his conclusions about segregation. In each case, Mendel allowed the heterozygous F_1 to self-pollinate. Tell students to make Punnett squares and use calculators. Have students write a paragraph stating how they think Mendel arrived at his conclusions. **L1**

Number of offspring in F$_2$

Trait	Dominant	Recessive
stem length	787	277
pod color	428	152
pod shape	882	299
seed shape	5474	1850
seed color	6022	2001
flower color	705	224
flower position	651	207

PROJECT

Specimen Collection: Have the students make a collection of photos or specimens of closely related living things such as leaves, seashells, skulls from a taxidermist, or preserved specimens. Leaves that have fallen on the ground in the autumn may be collected, dried, and pressed in a catalog. Have them organize and bring the collection into class to display to the rest of the students. Direct them to make a list of traits that all of the closely related specimens share as well as a list of the traits that are different in each specimen. Tell them to use the physical properties of the specimens as traits. **L1** **LEP**

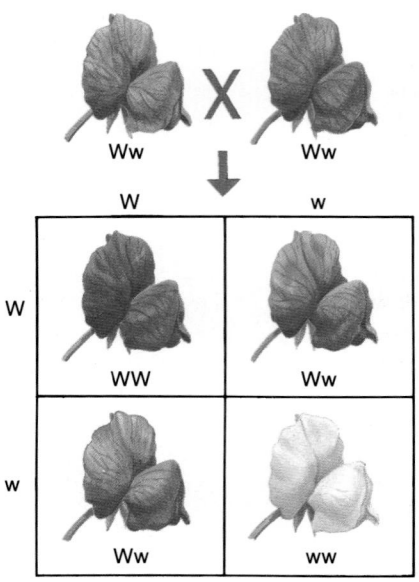

Figure 8-7 The results of Mendel's F₁ cross are shown in this Punnett square. Here there are three possible gene combinations: *WW, Ww,* and *ww.*

Punnett Squares Results of crosses can be predicted with Punnett squares (Figure 8-7). A Punnett square is a chart used to determine the possible combinations of genes among offspring. Across the top of the square are written the gametes produced by one parent. The gametes produced by the other parent are listed along the left side of the square. The square is then filled in by listing all the possible combinations of gametes. Each square in the chart represents a possible zygote.

The Test of Segregation

Mendel was able to explain what he observed in his experiments. His conclusions about dominant and recessive traits and his hypothesis that genes segregate when gametes are formed grew from his experiments. His first experiments alone did not mean that his explanation was correct; another test was needed to confirm his hypothesis. Mendel did this test after predicting the outcome of yet another cross.

Mendel predicted that if F₁ generation purple-flowered plants were crossed with white-flowered plants, he would get ratios different from any of his previously obtained ratios. According to his hypothesis, F₁ purple-flowered plants are *Ww* and white-flowered plants are *ww*. Purple-flowered plants produce both *W* and *w* gametes, while white-flowered plants produce only *w* gametes. Mendel predicted that the possible combinations in offspring resulting from a cross between *Ww* and *ww* parents would be *Ww* (purple) and *ww* (white). He predicted also that the numbers of each would be about the same. When Mendel performed the experiment, he obtained about half (50%) purple-flowered and half (50%) white-flowered plants. The same ratio was observed when he did the same experiment using plants having other traits.

Figure 8-8 A cross between a purple-flowered plant with the genes *Ww* and a white-flowered plant with the genes *ww* results in 50% purple-flowered plants and 50% white-flowered plants. What are the genotypes of the offspring?

202 ❦ HEREDITY

As a result of his experiments, Mendel assumed his hypothesis was correct. His hypothesis and data led him to form the principle of segregation—during gamete formation the pair of genes responsible for each trait separates so that each gamete receives only one gene for each trait. The gametes unite to produce predictable ratios of traits among the offspring.

Terminology

Many inherited traits, like the color of pea plant flowers or the length of a fruit fly's wings, take different forms. For many traits, such as those of the pea plants in Mendel's experiments, there are two forms. Each alternative form of a gene for a certain trait is called an **allele.** For example, the trait expressed as seed shape is determined by the alleles R and r. The trait of flower color in the previous examples was determined by the alleles W and w.

The combination of alleles for a given trait is referred to as the **genotype.** For example, RR, Rr, and rr are possible genotypes controlling seed shape in pea plants; the two seed shapes possible are round or wrinkled, with round being dominant to wrinkled. The appearance of a trait as determined by a given genotype is called the **phenotype.** Round and wrinkled are possible phenotypes of seed shape. In this example, the genotype RR would produce a round seed. The genotype Rr would also produce a round seed. The genotype rr would produce wrinkled seeds.

Did you notice that different genotypes in the example above may result in the same phenotype? Some phenotypes, such as the shape of pea seeds, are visible. However, many, such as human blood type, are not.

When each cell of an organism contains two of the same alleles for a given trait, the organism is **homozygous** for that trait. RR and rr are homozygous genotypes. To avoid confusion, the terms *homozygous dominant* and *homozygous recessive* are used. When each cell of an organism contains two different alleles for a trait, such as Rr, that organism is **heterozygous** for the trait.

Genotype	Phenotype	Homologous chromosomes	
RR		R allele	R allele
Rr		R allele	r allele
rr		r allele	r allele

Figure 8-9 **The combination of alleles in the chromosomes of an individual, its genotype, produces its physical appearance, its phenotype.**

8.1 PRINCIPLES OF GENETICS **203**

Demonstration

Cut four 5" circles from a piece of posterboard. Use a marker to write RY on one circle, Ry on the second, rY on the third, and ry on the fourth. Draw 4 lines on the chalkboard to represent two separate pairs of chromosomes. Write the gene symbols R, r, Y, and y, one on each chromosome.

Using the circle, demonstrate how gametes can be determined when two traits are involved. Place masking tape hinges on the unmarked sides of each circle. Tape the circle with RY on the board beneath the chromosomes labeled $RrYy$. Show how the chromosome with R and the chromosome with Y separate independently and show up in a gamete. Repeat with the other three gametes.

EARTH SCIENCE CONNECTION

Fossils and Genetic Traits: Rock layers containing fossils are helpful in comparing the genetic traits of organisms that lived in the past. Paleontologists compare the phenotypic variations of closely related specimens over geological time and determine what changes have occurred. Sometimes a new ridge on a seashell or a change in the shape of the exoskeleton of a trilobite shows a change that can be attributed to a genetic trait. Have students look at a group of closely related fossils and let them compare the parts of the shell with recent specimens and list similarities and differences. They can report their findings in their journals and use their observations during a class discussion.

INVESTIGATION

Predicting Plant Genotypes

Time Allotment
Initial day of preparation = 1 class period, 5 minutes each consecutive day, final day = 1 class period.

Objectives
Upon completing this investigation, students will be able to:
- Observe and record colors of offspring from three different parental genotypes.
- Determine parental genotypes based on ratios of observed phenotypes.

Skills
form a hypothesis, design an experiment, separate and control variables, interpret data

Materials
For growing the seeds, petri dishes (plastic), small pots or empty milk cartons, small paper cups, soil, sand, vermiculite or Readi-Earth, labels, marking pens, paper towels, scissors

Preparation
Tobacco seeds need to be purchased in advance from a biological supply house. Seeds are available from Carolina Biological Supply Co. Order:
(a) 17-8400 green : albino tobacco seeds, 3:1 ratio
(b) 17-8410 green : yellow green : yellow seeds, 1:2:1 ratio
(c) 15-9080 green

Possible Hypotheses
If a genotype for a batch of seeds cannot be determined until the seeds mature, then growing the seeds and seeing the phenotype should help in predicting genotype.

Possible Procedures
- Students' procedures should include counting the number of each phenotype appearing for the three tobacco seed batches. Experiments should last one to two weeks. 50 seeds per batch is recommended. Students' investigations should include controlling the amount of

Two Traits

After Mendel's first set of experiments, he studied the inheritance of two traits at once. For example, what types of plants would develop from a cross between a parent plant that produced peas that were round and yellow *(RRYY)* and a parent plant that produced peas that were wrinkled and green *(rryy)*. Remember that the law of segregation states that each gamete must contain one allele for each trait. Therefore, the gametes of the yellow, round parent should have the alleles *Y* and *R* and the wrinkled, green parent would produce gametes with *y* and *r* alleles. If they do, F_1 plants would all have the genotype *RrYy* and the phenotype round and yellow. Mendel found these results.

I N V E S T I G A T I O N

Predicting Plant Genotypes

It may be difficult to predict traits for tobacco plants if provided with only their seeds. But, if these seeds were planted and allowed to grow, certain traits would appear. You might even be able to predict the genotypes and phenotypes of the parents based on the appearance of traits in the offspring.

In this lab, you will design and then carry out an experiment to determine the genotypes of three tobacco seed batches. It should be pointed out in advance that the two seed batches to be used will yield plants that appear either all green in color or some green and some albino (white). Use these genotypes for help: *CC* = green, *Cc* = green, and *cc* = albino (white). Another batch will yield some green, some yellow-green, and some yellow. Use these genotypes: *GG* = green, *GY* = yellow-green, and *YY* = yellow.

Work in a group of three or four students.

Problem
Predict the genotype for each tobacco seed batch based on the appearance of color in the mature plants.

Hypothesis
Have your group agree on a hypothesis to be tested. Record your hypothesis.

Experimental Plan
1. Examine the materials provided by your teacher. Then, as a group, make a list of the possible ways you might test your hypothesis using the materials available.
2. Agree on one way that your group could investigate your hypothesis.
3. Design an experiment that will allow for the collection of quantitative data.
4. Prepare a list of numbered directions. Include a list of materials and the quantities you will need.

light and water each pot gets each day. Each should also contain the same number of seeds.

Teaching Strategies
- Students are *not to be told* which batch of seeds they are receiving. Batches should be identified simply as A, B, and C. However, they must keep the batches separate and plant them in different containers or petri dishes. You may wish to provide all student groups with the same batch designations, that is, batch A may by 3:1 green to albino,

batch B may be 1:2:1 green to yellow green to yellow, and batch C may be the all green seeds.
- Allow about 6 to 8 days for seed germination. If using conventional pots or paper cups, have students place seeds only 2 to 3 mm below surface of soil. Distribute about 50 seeds per batch.

Data and Observations
The sample data chart at right gives representative data. Student charts and data will vary.

The Principle of Independent Assortment The F_1 cross presented another problem to Mendel. The F_1 plants had the genotype *RrYy*. He knew that gametes produced by these plants must contain one of each kind of allele. But, do the alleles segregate independently of each other during gamete formation? Or do they stay in the same combination, *RY* or *ry*? Mendel hypothesized that they segregate independently and that the possible gametes would be *RY, Ry, Yr,* and *ry*. Given these possible gametes, the F_2 generation would show a phenotypic ratio of 9:3:3:1, or 9 round and yellow:3 round and green:3 wrinkled and yellow:1 wrinkled and green. These results are shown in the Punnett square in Figure 8-10. Again, Mendel's experiments verified his prediction. From his results, he formulated the principle of independent assortment. It states that genes for different traits segregate independently during gamete formation.

Checking the Plan

Discuss the following points with other group members to decide the final procedure for your experiment. Make any needed changes in your plan.
1. What data are you going to collect?
2. How long will you carry out the experiment?
3. How many seeds of each batch will you use?
4. What variables, if any, will have to be controlled? (Hint: Think about the amount of light, water, and temperature.)
5. What will be the role of each classmate in your group?
6. Have you designed and made a table for collecting data?

Be sure your teacher has approved your experimental plan before you proceed.

Data and Observations

Carry out your experiment, make any needed observations, and complete your data table. Design and then complete a graph or visual representation of your results.

Analysis and Conclusions

1. Why was it necessary to grow the seeds into plants in order to "read" the seeds' phenotypes?
2. Using the information provided in the introduction regarding genotype and phenotypes, describe the difference between the inheritance pattern of the green gene C and the green gene G.
3. What were some of the variables that you had to consider in this experiment? Explain how they could have influenced your data if not taken into account.
4. For the batch of seeds that provided all green plants, are you able to predict exactly the genotypes of (a) the parents that formed these seeds? Explain. (b) Each plant observed? Explain.
5. For the batch of seeds that provided some green and some albino plants, are you able to predict exactly the genotypes of (a) the parents that formed these seeds? Explain. (b) Of each plant observed? Explain.

6. For the batch of seeds that provided some green, yellow-green, and yellow plants, are you able to predict exactly the genotypes of (a) the parents that formed these seeds? Explain. (b) Each plant observed? Explain.

Going Further

Based on this lab experience, design an experiment that would help to answer another question that arose from your work. Assume that you will be doing this lab in class. Record this information as part of your conclusion.

Data Analysis

1. Seeds contain the genetic instructions for traits in an adult plant. Growing the seeds allows these gene traits to be expressed.
2. The gene *C* is inherited as a completely dominant trait. The gene *GG* is inherited with a pattern of incomplete dominance.
3. All plants had to receive the same amount of water. All plants should be placed in the same type of soil. Nutrients in one soil type could influence or retard the growth of one batch.
4. (a) No—parent plants may have been *CC* and *CC* or *CC* and *Cc*. (b) No—plants may be green with a *Cc* or *CC* genotype.
5. (a) Yes—the parents must have been *Cc* and *Cc*. These are the only possible parental genotypes that will yield a 3:1 green to albino ratio of offspring. (b) No for the green plants. They may have been *CC* or *Cc*. Yes for the albino plants. They are all *cc*.
6. (a) Yes—parents both had to be *GY*. This is the only genotype combination that will yield offspring with a 1:2:1 green to yellow green to yellow ratio of offspring. (b) Yes—with incomplete dominance, each genotype has a corresponding phenotype.

✔ Assessment

Portfolio: Prepare a report of this investigation for your portfolio. In addition, calculate the expected ratios for the three different seed types. Compare the expected ratios of phenotypes to the corresponding ratios of observed phenotypes. Explain why observed and expected ratios are very similar for each seed batch but not necessarily exactly alike.

Extensions

Students may suggest that amount of light being given to plants may alter expression of genotypes. Students may suggest that fertilizers be provided to the pots to see if this will alter expression of genotypes. Will similar results be obtained from other seed species if one knows the genotypes of the parents?

Data Table

Seed Batch	Observed Phenotypes	Number of Each Phenotype Observed	Possible Parent Genotypes
A	green albino	40 10	Cc and Cc
B	green yellow green yellow	12 28 10	GY and GY
C	green	50	CC and CC or CC and Cc

Figure Caption Question
How many different phenotypes and genotypes result from this cross? nine genotypes and four phenotypes

3 Assess

Check for Understanding
Give the students several monohybrid genetics problems, one at a time, and have them solve them using Punnett squares. Give a blank overhead transparency to several students and have each of them complete a specific problem on the transparency. **L1**

Reteach
Give students a dihybrid problem to see if they are able to determine the gametes, set up a Punnett square, and determine the phenotypes of the offspring. Use the cross *PPTt ✕ PpTT*, where *P* = purple, *p* = white, *T* = tall, and *t* = short. Ask them to explain why they did not get a 9:3:3:1 ratio of offspring. Students can put results in their journals.

Extension
For students who have mastered the dihybrid problem, give them a problem that involves three pairs of genes. Let them set up a Punnett square and solve the problem. **L3**

✔ Assessment
Portfolio: Have students develop a concept map for this section using the following terms: *allele, dominant, gene, genotype, heredity, heterozygous, phenotype,* and *recessive.* **L1**

4 Close

Discussion
Have students make concept maps using the terms in this section. Ask volunteers to put their maps on the board and explain them to the class. As they are presenting their concept maps, you may call on other students to ask them to explain why certain concepts are connected together. This is an opportunity for a final review for all of the students. **L1** **COOP LEARN**

F₁ cross
RrYy ✕ RrYy

- round yellow
- round green
- wrinkled yellow
- wrinkled green

Figure 8-10 The F₂ generation of a two-trait cross clearly shows that alleles segregate independently of one another. How many different phenotypes and genotypes result from this cross?

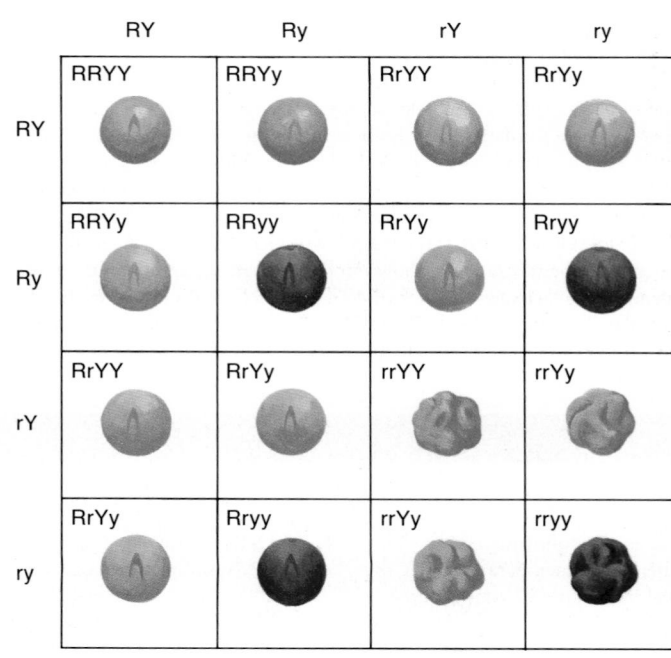

A Two-Trait Problem Try another problem involving two traits. In guinea pigs, the gene for rough coat (*R*) is dominant over the gene for smooth coat (*r*). The gene for black color (*B*) is dominant over the gene for albino (*b*). A heterozygous black, smooth-coated male is bred to a heterozygous black, rough-coated female. Use a Punnett square to solve this problem. What genotypic and phenotypic ratios could you expect among their offspring?

Section Review

Understanding Concepts
1. Explain how two black mice, when mated, can produce some offspring that are white.
2. Apply the law of segregation to explain the kinds of gametes produced by an animal that has the genotype *Aa*.
3. One parent is homozygous for a certain trait, and the other is heterozygous. What fraction of their offspring would you expect to be heterozygous?
4. **Skill Review—Observing and Inferring:** The offspring of a cross between two red-flowered plants show a ratio of three red-flowered plants to one white-flowered plant. Which trait is dominant? What must the genotypes of the parents be? For more help, see Observing and Inferring in the **Skill Handbook.**
5. **Thinking Critically:** In pea plants, tall is dominant over short. Suppose you have a tall plant but don't know whether it is homozygous or heterozygous. How could you find out?

206 🐾 HEREDITY

Answers to Section Review

1. Each parent mouse carries an allele for white. If gametes each containing an allele for white unite, a white offspring will be produced.
2. The law states that each gamete contains one gene for each trait. Because the parent has both *A* and *a* alleles, gametes containing each of those alleles will be produced.
3. Half the offspring are expected to be heterozygous.
4. **Skill Review—Observing and Inferring:** The trait for red flowers is dominant. Each parent must be heterozygous.
5. **Thinking Critically:** The plant should be crossed with a short plant, whose genotype is known (two recessive alleles). If any offspring are short, then the tall parent plant is heterozygous.

8.2 Solving Genetics Problems

When you toss a coin, the chances of getting a head and the chances of getting a tail are equal, or about 50-50. Stated another way, there is an equal probability of tossing a head and tossing a tail. This probability can also be written as a ratio—1 head:1 tail or 1/2 heads:1/2 tails. These ratios are what you expect, but the results do not always come out that way. The probability of getting a 1:1 ratio of heads to tails increases with the number of tosses. You will probably come closer to the expected ratio if you toss the coin ten times rather than twice. And you will do even better if you toss the coin 100 times. You can use these principles of probability to solve genetics problems.

Probability and Genetics

What ratio of head and tail combinations might you expect if you toss two coins together? For each toss, the chance of getting a head or the chance of getting a tail is 1/2. The tossing of the two coins must be considered independent events. The probability that both coins will land heads is the product of each independent event or $1/2 \times 1/2 = 1/4$.

Figure 8-11 shows the possible combinations of heads and tails when you toss two coins together. You can see that the chance of a heads-tails combination is twice as great as the chance of either a heads-heads or a tails-tails combination. Thus, the expected ratio is 1/4 heads-heads:1/2 heads-tails:1/4 tails-tails. Looking at this mathematically, you can see that the chances of heads and tails of one coin toss have been multiplied by the chances of the second coin toss.

Multiplying the chances of independent events occurring to determine the chance of those occurring together is a basic law of probability. It is also the basis for solving problems in genetics.

> (1/2 heads + 1/2 tails) × (1/2 heads + 1/2 tails) =
> 1/4 heads-heads + 1/4 heads-tails +
> 1/4 heads-tails + 1/4 tails-tails =
> 1/4 heads-heads + 1/2 heads-tails + 1/4 tails-tails

Objectives

Apply the rules of probability to solve genetics problems.

Demonstrate the inheritance of traits resulting from incomplete dominance, codominance, and multiple alleles.

| 1/2 chance heads | 1/2 chance tails | 1/2 chance heads | 1/2 chance tails |
| 1/4 chance 2 heads | 1/2 chance heads tails | | 1/4 chance 2 tails |

Figure 8-11 Each toss of a coin has a probability of being a head or a tail. To find the probability of combinations of tosses in a row, multiply the individual probabilities, as shown above.

8.2 SOLVING GENETICS PROBLEMS 🔊 **207**

Prepare

Key Concepts
Students will relate how probability is used to solve genetics problems, and compare patterns of inheritance in multiple alleles and incomplete dominance with the patterns of inheritance set forth by Mendel.

Key Terms
incomplete dominance, multiple alleles, codominance

Materials
* Get pinto and kidney beans and bags for the Focus activity.

1 Focus

Objectives
The objectives are listed on the student page. Remind students to preview these objectives as a guide to this numbered section.

Activity
Place students in groups of two. Give each team a paper bag and have them add to it 50 pinto and 50 kidney beans. Ask them to predict how many pinto and kidney beans they will get if they pull 10 beans from the bag. *5/10 for each* Have them select a bean and record its type. They should return the bean before they select the next one. Have students record data on the chalkboard. Add each column and discuss the class data. Ask students to calculate the chance of selecting two kidney beans in a row. *1/2 × 1/2 = 1/4* What other combinations could occur? *pinto, kidney; kidney, pinto; pinto, pinto* Have students select two beans in a row and record their data. Students should repeat this 19 times and determine if their observed results were close to the expected results. Collect class data and discuss results based on probability. **L1** **COOP LEARN**

2 Teach

Overhead Example

Draw a Punnett square on a transparency with a permanent marker. Write the genetic cross *Ss* × *Ss* at the top using one color for one parent and a second color for the other parent so students are able to determine the source of the gametes. Use washable pens to write the alleles. Show students how to solve the problem by using the five steps listed. Have the students follow as you present the lesson. You may want to have a student come to the projector and fill in one of the four squares as you are presenting the lesson. Point out that the heterozygous genes appear in two of four squares, and this explains why 2/4 of the offspring are heterozygous. Relate the results to probability. **L1**

LEP

Concept Development

Tell students that the Punnett square was developed by an English geneticist, R.C. Punnett. His technique gave geneticists a visual way of interpreting a genetic cross—especially dihybrid crosses. He also developed several hypotheses about genetic systems with collaborators.

In the last section, you used Punnett squares to predict the results of crosses. This chart helps determine the possible combinations of genes among offspring. In effect, the Punnett square helps you multiply the chances of different alleles combining. The following example will show you how probability works in solving genetics problems.

In fruit flies, the gene for straight wings *(S)* is dominant over the gene for curled wings *(s)*. Two heterozygous straight-winged flies are mated. What ratios of genotypes can you expect from this cross? Below are the steps to follow in solving this kind of problem.

1. Write the genotype of each parent.
   male heterozygous straight = *Ss*
   female heterozygous straight = *Ss*
2. Use the law of segregation to list the different alleles that may be carried by the gametes of each parent.
   male *Ss* = *S* and *s*
   female *Ss* = *S* and *s*
3. Write the different alleles from the male parent along the top of the Punnett square. Write the alleles from the female parent down the side.
4. Fill in the boxes with the possible combinations of alleles in the offspring.
5. Determine the ratio of genotypes. The denominator of your fraction should be the total number of boxes in your square. Make sure to group similar genotypes. In this case, the genotypic ratio is 1/4 *SS*:1/2 *Ss*:1/4 *ss*.

What are the ratios of phenotypes in the offspring? To determine the phenotypic ratio, interpret the genotypic ratio:

1/4 *SS* = straight winged
1/2 *Ss* = straight winged
1/4 *ss* = curled winged

Therefore, the phenotypic ratio is 3/4 straight winged:1/4 curled winged.

Figure 8-12 **Combinations of characters among offspring can be determined by using Punnett squares. Sperm and egg possibilities are listed along the top and the left side of the square. Possible offspring are shown inside the Punnett square.**

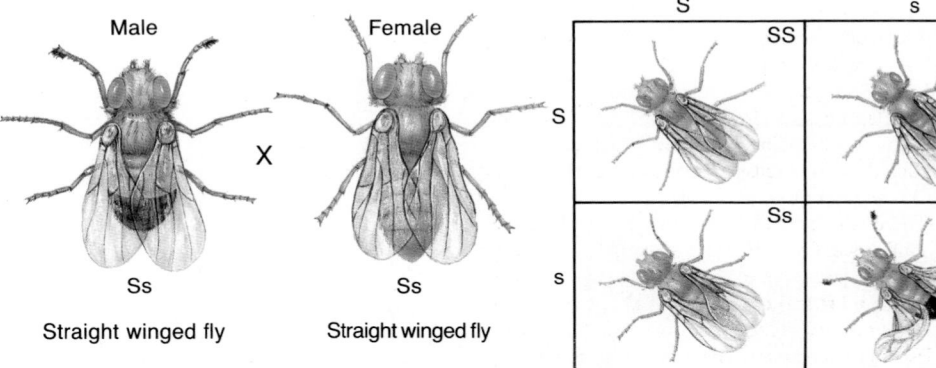

Male
Ss
Straight winged fly

X

Female
Ss
Straight winged fly

208 HEREDITY

Purpose
Students will determine the similarities and differences in traits of different bean seeds and make predictions about what the plants will look like when the seeds are planted.

Materials
5 different kinds of bean seeds from the grocery store placed in cups for groups of 3–4 students, potting soil, cups, plastic spoons, labels

Procedure
Give the following directions to students:
1. Set up a data table.
2. Sort the seeds in the cup into like groups.
3. Make observations as to the color, size, shape, texture, and markings on the seeds.
4. Record observations on data charts.
5. Discuss and report on observations such as similar and different traits.
6. Make a hypothesis as to what the plants will look like if the seeds are planted. Focus on any similarities and differences, such as will the larger seeds produce larger plants? Will the larger or smaller plants sprout first? Will the plant parts from each type of bean be similar or different?

Solving genetics problems with Punnett squares applies the laws of probability. When you write the alleles for each parent, you are actually representing probabilities. For the problem above, you write *S* and *s* along the top and side because it is probable that half of all gametes that go into producing the next generation will contain the *S* allele and half will contain the *s* allele. Whether a gamete with an *S* allele combines with a gamete containing an *S* allele or one containing an *s* allele is also a matter of chance. When you fill in the boxes of the Punnett square, you are really multiplying independent chance events to determine the chances of their occurring together. The results are genotypic and phenotypic ratios.

Remember that these are *expected* genotypic and phenotypic ratios. For the problem above, those ratios tell you that out of every four offspring produced, three are expected to have straight wings and one is expected to have curled wings. But, as with tossing a coin, expected results and actual results do not always agree. It is possible—but less probable—that two heterozygous straight-winged flies could produce four offspring with straight wings. It is even less probable—but still possible—that the offspring all would have curled wings. The larger the number of offspring produced, the more likely it is that the actual ratios will be close to the expected results.

Incomplete Dominance

In Mendel's original experiments, he studied seven different pairs of traits in garden pea plants. In every case, one form of the trait always completely dominated the other. Dominant and recessive traits are not always as clearly defined as the seven pea plant traits Mendel studied.

For example, plants called four o'clocks have alleles for red flowers and white flowers, but neither of these colors is dominant. In these plants, heterozygous genotypes result in pink flowers. This pattern of inheritance is known as **incomplete dominance.** It appears that the parental genes blended together to form an intermediate color. Actually, incomplete dominance of two alleles results in the possibility of three different phenotypes because neither allele is dominant over the other. The third phenotype, which results when the two alleles combine in an offspring, is an intermediate form of the other two phenotypes, not a blending of the two. If heterozygous pink flowers are allowed to self-pollinate, the colors red and white return in the offspring.

Punnett squares can be used to solve problems involving incomplete dominance. For example, try to solve this problem: What genotypic and phenotypic ratios could you expect from a cross between a red four o'clock and a pink four o'clock? The two alleles for flower color are represented as *R* (red) and *R'* (white). Use a Punnett square to solve the problem.

Figure 8-13 In incomplete dominance, neither allele is dominant to the other. Three completely different phenotypes are possible. The third phenotype is intermediate between the other two.

8.2 SOLVING GENETICS PROBLEMS **209**

Misconception

Most students assume that all traits are inherited in a Mendelian pattern controlled by a dominant or recessive gene. Students have difficulty explaining traits for eye color, hair color, height, skin color, or any traits involving more than two phenotypes in an offspring. As you present this section, make sure they understand that Mendel's principles represent one pattern of inheritance or genetic system. You can refer to incomplete dominance and multiple alleles as examples of two more genetic systems. Point out that the pattern of inheritance is different in each known genetic system.

---

7. Plant the seeds.
8. Observe, record, and water the seeds daily for at least two weeks.

Analysis
Ask students to answer these questions.
1. List the traits that all bean seeds share. *Shape*
2. List the traits that are different in the bean seeds. *Color, size, pattern of color on the seed coat, weight*

3. What similarities did the seeds have as they were sprouting? *They all came up through the soil in the same way with the seed coat protruding on the end of the growing plant.*
4. Were the leaves and stems alike or different in their traits as the plants grew? *They were basically the same shape but slightly different in color and some of the leaves were smaller.*

5. How would you be able to tell which seed grew into what plant if the labels on the cups were lost? *Wait until the plant produces fruit and look at the color of the seeds.*

✔ Assessment
Knowledge: Ask the students to write how the growing plants were similar or different from what they expected based on their observations. L1

Chalkboard Example

Draw two lines on the chalkboard to represent two chromosomes. Place the three gene symbols on each chromosome. Point out that any one of the three genes can be found at the loci on the two chromosomes. Tell them these are called multiple alleles because more than two alleles control the trait. Have them look at the genotypes in Table 8.1 to see how many different combinations the three genes can form.

Figure Caption Question

If all these children had blood type O, what are the probable genotypes of the parents? Both parents, probably have type O blood. It is possible that both could have either $I^A i$ or $I^B i$, but not probable.

Concept Development

Point out that the ABO blood group was introduced in paternity suits nearly 60 years ago. It was used primarily to prove who was not the father of the child. The test could not prove who the father was because there are too many persons that have the same blood type. If the person who claimed he was not the father of the child had the same blood type as the child, tests using other blood groups could be done for confirmation.

Multiple Alleles

You have learned that two alleles act together to produce a phenotype. Although each *organism* normally has just two alleles for a trait, more than two alleles may be possible for that trait in the *population*. In the human population, for example, three alleles govern blood type: I^A, I^B, and i. Human blood types are therefore determined by **multiple alleles,** a set of three or more different alleles controlling a trait. In humans, both I^A and I^B are dominant over i. But I^A and I^B are codominant. Like incomplete dominance, **codominance** results when one allele is not dominant over the other. Unlike incomplete dominance, in which the presence of both alleles results in an intermediate third phenotype, codominance results in both alleles being expressed equally.

From Table 8.1 you can see that six genotypes and four phenotypes are possible for human blood types. The four blood phenotypes are *A*, *B*, *AB*, and *O*.

Table 8.1 Blood Groups in Humans

Phenotypes (Blood Types)	Genotypes
A	$I^A I^A$ or $I^A i$
B	$I^B I^B$ or $I^B i$
AB	$I^A I^B$
O	ii

Figure 8-14 The three alleles in humans that govern blood type are a familiar example of multiple alleles. If all these children had blood type O, what are the probable genotypes of the parents?

Using the information above, try to solve this problem: A woman having type *O* blood marries a man having type *AB* blood. What are the expected genotypic and phenotypic ratios among their children? Use a Punnett square to determine your ratios.

You can also use Mendel's laws to determine information about parents based on knowledge of the offspring they have produced. Consider this problem, for example: A woman who has type *B* blood marries a man who has type *A* blood. They have five children, all with type *AB* blood. What are the most *probable* parental genotypes?

To solve this problem, first think about the children. Each child has type *AB* blood. Therefore, each genotype must be $I^A I^B$. What is the source of each allele in each child? One allele came from its mother, and the other from its father. Now consider the parental possibilities.

MULTICULTURAL CONNECTION

American Indians and Animals: Animals were important in the culture of the American Indians. They were used for food and clothing, and the hides were used for shelter. The traits of animals have been an important part of the folklore and culture. Some of their tales describe how they got their phenotypic traits. For instance, one tale tells that the owl got its large eyes and short neck because it was always stretching its neck to see what was going on around its roost and got its big eyes so it could see at night. The names of tribal members were basically animal names that described the phenotypic traits that the person "acquired" from the animal. For instance, the name Silent Eagle was given to a person who was swift and who hunted quietly and with great accuracy.

The mother could be either $I^B I^B$ or $I^B i$. The father could be $I^A I^A$ or $I^A i$. But if all five children are $I^A I^B$, both parents are most probably homozygous. Each child's I^A gene came from the father, while the I^B gene came from the mother. If either of the parents were heterozygous, some other blood types would probably occur among the children. Using this reasoning, the mother's genotype is probably $I^B I^B$, and the father's is probably $I^A I^A$.

Coat color in rabbits is a visible trait that is governed by multiple alleles. Different combinations of these four alleles produce four different coat colors as seen in Figure 8-15. In this case, the alleles involved have a dominance relationship with each other.

Figure 8-15 Different combinations of four alleles produce different coat colors in rabbits: the wild type or agouti rabbit (CC, Cc^ch Cc^h, or Cc) (a); light grey rabbit (c^ch c^ch, c^ch c^h or c^ch c) (b); an albino with black points (c^h c^h or c^h c) (c); and an albino rabbit (cc) (d).

b

c

d

a

Section Review

Understanding Concepts

1. What are the chances of tossing four pennies at the same time and having them all come up tails?
2. What genotypic ratio could you expect from a cross between an organism having the genotype *Dd* and an organism with the genotype *DD*?
3. Watermelons with a round shape are crossed with those having a flat-

ter shape. Some offspring have an oval shape. Explain.

4. *Skill Review—Making and Using Graphs:* In guinea pigs, rough coat (*R*) is dominant over smooth coat (*r*), and black (*B*) is dominant over albino (*b*). Make a pie graph showing the ratio of different genotypes expected when a guinea pig having the genotype *BbRr* is crossed with one having the

genotype *bbRr*. For more help, see Organizing Information in the **Skill Handbook.**

5. *Thinking Critically:* A man with blood type *B* marries a woman with blood type *A*. Their first child has blood type *O*. Explain. What other blood types are possible for their future children?

Answers to Section Review

1. 1/16
2. 1/2 *DD* + 1/2 *Dd*
3. The trait for shape illustrates incomplete dominance.
4. **Skill Review—Making and Using Graphs:** The graph should show 12.5% each of the genotypes *BbRR*, *Bbrr*, *bbRR*, and *bbrr* and 25% each of the genotypes *BbRr* and *bbRr*.

5. **Thinking Critically:** Each parent must be heterozygous. Other possible blood types are A, B, and AB.

SECTION 8.2

Teacher FYI

The symbol for an albino rabbit with black points is c^h. The "h" stands for Himalayan, which is a breed of rabbit with black points—face, ears, feet, and tail. Himalayan is also a breed of cat that is a Persian crossed with a Siamese. These cats also have black points.

3 Assess

Check for Understanding

Give students the ratios of some offspring in a cross involving the concept of incomplete dominance and have them work back to determine the genotype of the parents. **L1**

Reteach

For students who are still having difficulty understanding how to solve genetics problems, work with small groups of students at the chalkboard so they can see how the gametes are placed at the side of the Punnett square and how the genotype is formed.

Extension

For students who have mastered the problems of this section, have them find out what other living things inherit traits by multiple alleles and report their findings to the class. **L3**

✔ Assessment

Oral: Have students explain the difference between codominance and incomplete dominance, citing examples of each and how these words relate to each other. **L1**

4 Close

Analogy

Ask the students what would happen if they mixed the same amount of red paint and white paint together. Ask them to tell you what the resulting color would be. When they say pink, tell them that this is similar to what happens in traits that show incomplete dominance. **LEP**

Prepare

Key Concepts

Students will describe the chromosome theory of heredity and relate how it helped biologists develop an understanding of sex determination in animals. They will compare and contrast inheritance patterns in sex-linked genes, multiple genes, and modifier genes with patterns of inheritance according to Gregor Mendel.

Key Terms

sex chromosomes, autosome, sex-linked traits, continuous variation, multiple genes, modifier gene

Materials

1 Focus

Objectives

The objectives are listed on the student page. Remind students to preview these objectives as a guide to this numbered section.

Discussion

Ask students to discuss why they think it took 35 years for scientists to rediscover Mendel's patterns of inheritance. Have students present a quick review of Mendel's principles and use this information to bridge into what chromosomes have to do with inherited traits. Use the Teacher FYI to give some background for the discussion. L1

Objectives

Discuss the development of the chromosome theory of heredity.

Apply the laws of probability to solve genetics problems involving sex-linked traits.

Explain how the expression of a pair of genes may be influenced by other genes as well as by the environment.

Figure 8-16 Grasshopper chromosomes are shown during a mitotic cell division. Homologous pairs of chromosomes can be found.

8.3 The Chromosome Theory of Heredity

Gregor Mendel explained simple patterns of inheritance without knowing of the existence of chromosomes or of how they are packaged in gametes by means of meiosis. Not until the early 1900s did scientists begin to connect cellular processes and genetic principles to understand how genetic information is transmitted. New knowledge not only helped us understand how traits are physically passed from one generation to the next, but also enabled us to explain different patterns of inheritance that do not follow Mendelian principles.

Mendel had concluded that there are two characters, which we now call genes, for each trait, both of which were transmitted to offspring. He had also concluded that these characters segregate during gamete formation—each gamete has just one character per trait. Later, when new staining techniques allowed scientists to observe chromosomes in cells, it was revealed that each diploid cell has one homologous pair of chromosomes of each type and that a zygote inherits both homologues. Furthermore, homologous chromosomes segregate during meiosis—each gamete has only one homologue of a pair.

In the early 1900s, a young scientist named Walter Sutton took these new observations and the results of Gregor Mendel and began making his own observations. His work ultimately resulted in a new theory.

Mendel's Work Rediscovered

Walter Sutton, while a student at Columbia University, proposed that Mendel's hereditary factors (genes) are carried on chromosomes. Sutton made this proposal after observing meiosis in grasshoppers. Sutton saw that during meiosis the chromosomes in each grasshopper cell lined up in pairs and that each pair of chromosomes was the same size and shape.

Sutton next observed that the homologous pairs of chromosomes segregate during meiosis so that each gamete receives one chromosome from each pair. He then reasoned that when fertilization occurs, the resulting zygote has a full set of homologous chromosomes.

produces gamete with · w allele

produces gamete with · W allele

W · w

Homologous chromosomes

Figure 8-17 Each new organism receives one allele for a gene from each parent. The phenotype of an organism results from the combination of alleles it receives.

212 🐾 HEREDITY

From his observations, Sutton found that chromosomes do indeed behave like Mendel's factors. During meiosis, chromosomes follow each of Mendel's principles of heredity. This led Sutton to propose the chromosome theory of heredity—Mendel's hereditary factors (genes) are carried on chromosomes.

Scientists soon realized that organisms have many more hereditary characteristics than they have chromosomes. For example, humans have 46 chromosomes, but we certainly have more than 46 inherited characteristics. Because of this, Sutton reasoned that each chromosome must carry hundreds of genes.

Although Sutton's observations give good evidence that genes are located on chromosomes, many scientists were not convinced. The work of Thomas Hunt Morgan, a biologist from the United States, supported Sutton's work and ultimately confirmed the chromosome theory of heredity.

Figure 8-18 Fruit flies (*Drosophila melanogaster*) have four pairs of chromosomes. Three pairs are autosomes and the other two chromosomes are sex chromosomes.

Sex Determination

Drosophila, commonly known as fruit flies, are small (about 2 mm in length), easily handled, and produce many offspring in about two weeks. For these reasons, *Drosophila* have played an important role in the study of genetics.

Thomas Hunt Morgan (1866-1945) helped pioneer the use of fruit flies to study genetics. Early in Morgan's research, he discovered that chromosomes of male and female *Drosophila* cells are slightly different, as seen in Figure 8-18.

Because the *X* and *Y* chromosomes differ between the sexes, they are called **sex chromosomes.** Other chromosomes are called **autosomes.** Thus, both female and male *Drosophila* have three pairs of autosomes and one pair of sex chromosomes. A female normally has three pairs of autosomes and two *X* chromosomes. A male normally has three pairs of autosomes, an *X* chromosome, and a *Y* chromosome.

All the gametes produced by a female fruit fly will contain an *X* chromosome. The male fruit fly's *X* and *Y* chromosomes are not homologous, but they behave as a homologous pair during meiosis. They separate from each other during gamete formation. Thus, half the male's gametes will contain the *X* chromosome, and half will contain the *Y* chromosome. The possible combinations of *X* and *Y* chromosomes among offspring can be determined as with other traits, as seen in Figure 8-19. Using probability methods, you can determine that half the offspring would have the genotype *XX* (female). The other half would have *XY* (male).

Such a pattern of sex determination is evident in many organisms, including humans. However, the pattern is different in some organisms. In grasshoppers, for example, males have only one *X* chromosome but no *Y* chromosome, while females have two *Y* chromosomes.

Figure 8-19 This Punnett square shows that half the possible offspring in fruit flies are female and half are male.

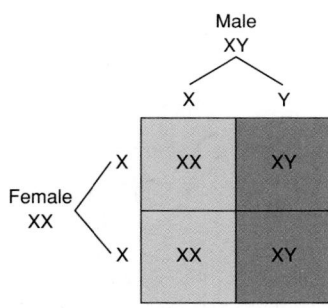

Genotypic ratio = 1/2 XX : 1/2 XY
Phenotypic ratio = 1/2 female : 1/2 male

Bioethics

Sex Determination: A scientist named David Page was investigating why some males are born with two *X* chromosomes and some females are born with an *X* and a *Y* chromosome. Using DNA analysis of the *X* and *Y* chromosomes, he found a section on the *Y* chromosome that is not similar to the *X* chromosome. He called this the Testis Determining Factor gene (TDF) because he hypothesized that this gene codes for formation of testis in males. He found the TDF gene absent on the *Y* chromosome of an *XY* female. Without this gene, no testis could be produced by this female.

What were the results with males having two *X* chromosomes? Neither of the *X* chromosomes should carry the TDF gene, but he found the TDF gene on the second *X* of the male. The *XX* male should have developed as a female, but the presence of the TDF gene caused a male to develop instead of a female.

There is technology under development, that might eventually be used to change the sex of an individual by inserting the TDF gene into the developing embryo before the sex glands begin to form. This could give livestock breeders the desired sex in the offspring. Suppose humans decided that they wanted all boys or all girls. Should geneticists be allowed to insert this gene in a newly forming embryo? Should a couple be able to decide what sex their child will be? What do you think are some other possible uses or misuses of this new information?

Different Viewpoints in Biology

Sex Check: Chromosome testing of female athletes was first used in the 1968 Olympics. It was done to find males who were competing as female athletes. Since this testing began, not one male has been found competing as a female. A chromosome test, using cheek cells, shows how many X chromosomes a person has. The results are based on the theory that males have a single X and females have two X chromosomes. This test should be foolproof, but some females fail this test because they have a Y chromosome in place of or in addition to the second X. Some males show up as females in the test because they can have two X chromosomes in addition to a Y. A female with the Y chromosome has the reproductive organs of a female, and a male with two X chromosomes has the reproductive organs of a male. For this reason, some doctors and human geneticists oppose this test because they conclude that the presence of the reproductive organs shows the sex of the individual, not what sex chromosomes he or she has. The Olympic Committee disagrees with these doctors and geneticists and uses the chromosome test. For additional information, see Grady, Denise. "Sex Test of Champions." *Discover,* June 1992, pp. 78-82.

Figure 8-20 **In fruit flies, red eyes (right) are dominant to white eyes (left). The allele for eye color is carried on the X chromosome.**

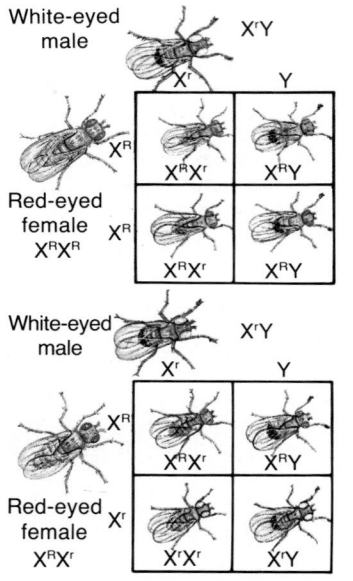

Figure 8-21 **Assuming eye color is sex-linked, results predicted with Punnett squares agree with Morgan's experimental results. The parental and F$_1$ crosses he did are shown here.**

White-eyed male — X^rY

Red-eyed female X^RX^R

	X^r	Y
X^R	X^RX^r	X^RY
X^R	X^RX^r	X^RY

White-eyed male — X^rY

Red-eyed female X^RX^r

	X^r	Y
X^R	X^RX^r	X^RY
X^r	X^rX^r	X^rY

Sex-linked Inheritance

In 1910, Morgan made an unexpected discovery about how the sex of an organism can be related to inheritance of a trait. He made this discovery studying eye color in fruit flies. He found a male fly with white eyes. This fly was produced from a pure line having only red eyes.

Morgan decided to cross this white-eyed male with red-eyed females. Assuming that red eye color (*R*) was dominant over white eye color (*r*), Morgan expected to find all red-eyed offspring in the F$_1$ generation. He also expected the F$_1$ flies, when interbred, to produce a ratio of three red-eyed flies to one white-eyed fly. He did, in fact, get these results.

However, there was something unusual about the F$_2$ generation. Morgan noted that the white-eyed flies in this generation were all males. There were no white-eyed females. Because white eye color seemed to be linked with sex, it was called a **sex-linked trait.**

Morgan's Explanation Morgan knew of the hypothesis that genes are located on chromosomes and used that idea to form a hypothesis of his own. Morgan's hypothesis was that the alleles for eye color are carried only on the X chromosome, and that there are no alleles for eye color on the Y chromosome. If this were true, then the parental cross had been between red-eyed females (X^RX^R) and white-eyed males (X^rY), as illustrated in Figure 8-21. The results of the cross—the F$_1$ generation—had been red-eyed males (X^RY) and red-eyed females (X^RX^r). And the F$_2$ generation had been red-eyed females (X^RX^R or X^RX^r), red-eyed males (X^RY), and white-eyed males (X^rY). Morgan's hypothesis explained his previous data by showing how all white-eyed flies in the F$_2$ generation had to be males.

However, a hypothesis should also predict new facts. Morgan predicted that he could produce white-eyed females by breeding an F$_1$ red-eyed female (X^RX^r) with a white-eyed male (X^rY). When such a cross was done, Morgan's prediction was confirmed. There were white-eyed females among the offspring. This confirming evidence also helped support the hypothesis that genes are carried on chromosomes, because Morgan's explanation was based on that concept.

Sex-linked Traits and Punnett Squares Morgan's discovery of sex-linked traits and his explanation of how they are inherited show that problems involving such traits can also be solved using Punnett squares. If information given in a problem tells you that a trait is sex-linked, you assume that the trait is carried on the X chromosome because it carries more information than the smaller Y chromosome. In humans, very few genes are located on the nonhomologous portion of the Y chromosome, and therefore few traits are sex-linked this way. A few genes in humans are Y-linked. These traits are only expressed in males and are transmitted from father to son. Consider the sex chromosomes and the genes they carry together as a unit (for example, X^R) when determining the kinds of gametes produced by each parent. When you determine phenotypic ratios, do so by including the sex as well as the trait of the offspring.

Try solving the following problem: In a certain imaginary animal, the gene for black coat color (*B*) is dominant over the gene for orange coat color (*b*), and the trait is sex-linked. Determine the expected genotypic and phenotypic ratios among the offspring produced by the mating of a heterozygous female and a black male.

Many Genes—One Effect

Inheritance involving incomplete dominance, codominance, multiple alleles, and sex-linkage does not follow the patterns first discovered by Mendel. However, in each case, the phenotype is determined by a single pair of interacting alleles. Some other patterns of heredity are not controlled that way. Traits in humans, such as height, hair, eye and skin color, are all controlled by more than one pair of alleles. Many traits in other organisms are also controlled this way.

For example, consider the length of ears of corn. If ear length in corn were governed by a simple case of complete dominance, only two lengths would be found: long and short. If ear length were controlled by a single pair of genes showing incomplete dominance, three phenotypes could be expected: long, medium, and short. However, ears of corn are not just long or short, or even long, medium, or short. Instead, a whole range of phenotypes exists, from long to short. The presence of many phenotypes, from one extreme to another, is an example of **continuous variation**.

The graph in Figure 8-22 relates ears of corn and their lengths. How could you explain these data? Assume that, in this case, ear length is controlled by two pairs of genes (*A* and *a; B* and *b*) located on different pairs of homologous chromosomes. Both pairs of genes contribute to ear length in an additive fashion. Suppose that *AABB* represents the longest ears, and *aabb* produces the shortest ears. A cross between *AABB* and *aabb* parents would result in F₁ offspring that are *AaBb* with medium-length ears.

F₁ CROSS

Genotypic ratio = 1/16 AABB : 1/8 AABb : 1/8 AaBB :
    1 1/4 AaBb : 1/16 AAbb : 1/6 aaBB :
    1/8 Aabb : 1/8 aaBb : 1/16 aabb
Phenotypic ratio = 1/16 longest : 1/4 long : 3/8 medium :
    1/4 short : 1/16 shortest

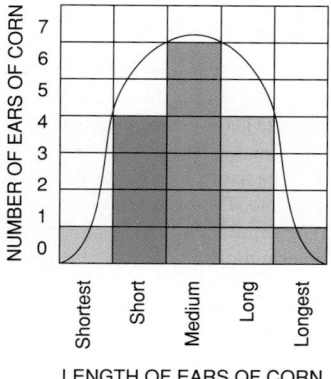

Figure 8-22 **When two pairs of genes determine a trait, many different phenotypes (continuous variation) are possible in the F₂ generation (left). A graph of the distribution of ear lengths in corn (right) is bell-shaped. Medium-length ears occur most often.**

8.3 THE CHROMOSOME THEORY OF HEREDITY ❧ **215**

Concept Development

- Use the data from Morgan's explanation and develop Punnett squares for the P, F₁, and F₂ generations to show how Morgan developed his hypothesis and arrived at his conclusions.
- Tell students that this pattern of inheritance is also called polygenic inheritance. This type of inheritance comes from two or more pairs of genes on two or more pairs of chromosomes. Explain the difference between this pattern of inheritance and multiple alleles by stating that any one of several genes is found at a given locus on a single pair of chromosomes in multiple allele inheritance.

Misconception

Students think that the *X* and *Y* chromosomes are so named because of their shapes, but the *X* chromosome was given the name *X* merely to identify it. When a second sex chromosome was discovered, it was named *Y* after the next letter of the alphabet.

Problem Solving

A wildflower commonly found in the eastern United States has been recorded to have seven different and distinct flower colors when it blooms. Each plant has numerous flowers, and the flowers on the same plant are always the same color. Have students use their knowledge of genetics to explain how the plant inherits these traits. Devise a genetic system to explain your ideas. **L2**

Purpose

This feature introduces the concept of chromosome mapping. It allows students to use their knowledge of meiosis as it applies to crossing over.

Teaching Strategies

- Have students bring calculators to class. Students should first determine which genes are farthest apart. Now that they know the position of bar eye and cut wing, they can subtract or add values to the locus for each gene.

Possible Answers

1. 12.5 ruby eye
   25 cut wing
   41 mini wing
   62 bar eye
2. You may wish to use construction paper strips and have students glue these on large posterboard.
3. Use an analogy for crossovers by holding a chain labeled a through g in front of the students and asking them where it will break. Their response will usually be, "Anywhere there is a weak link." Ask them if there is a greater chance that the chain will break between a and b or a and g. Develop the idea that the closer the links, the less chance there is of breaking.

Going Further

Have students find out why the earliest completed chromosome maps were with fruit flies and corn and why it has taken so long to find the loci of a few genes on human chromosomes. Students could report on the work of A.H. Sturdivant and his model for mapping chromosomes. **L2**

If you cross these F_1 corn plants, the F_2 offspring exhibit a broad range of genotypes and phenotypes, as Figure 8-22 shows. Relate the phenotypic ratios to the graph in the figure. The genotype *AaBb*, medium-length ears of corn, is the one most often expected. *AABB* (longest) and *aabb* (shortest) are seldom expected. The rest of the expected genotypes correspond to various intermediate lengths. Some ears would be longer than medium; some would be shorter. When these crosses are actually made, the results largely agree with those predicted by the Punnett square.

Geneticists explain continuous variation in terms of **multiple genes,** a pattern of inheritance in which many genes affect a single trait. Human skin color shows continuous variation and is also thought to be determined by multiple genes.

M A T H C O N N E C T I O N

Crossing Over as a Tool to Determine Gene Location on Chromosomes

You are asked to find the location for cities B, C, and D on a map. Try it. The solution is not difficult but requires a little logic. You are told the following:

> **Distance Between Cities**
> A and C is 50 km
> D and C is 25 km
> D and B is 100 km
> B and A is 175 km

This same type of application can be used to determine the location of specific genes on a chromosome if you assume that genes are like cities and the map corresponds to a chromosome. The problem with mapping genes on a chromosome is determining how you can measure distance between genes. The size of chromosomes is very small and the distance between genes is, there-

fore, almost impossible to measure by direct observation. Luckily for scientists, an event that occurs between chromosomes called crossing over allows them to make these types of measurements indirectly. Thus, they are able to prepare chromosome maps showing positions and distances between genes.

What is crossing over, and how does it allow for mapping of genes on chromosomes? Remember that during early events of meiosis, the four chromatids from each homologous pair of chromosomes line up

Homologous chromosomes   Gametes

Non-sister chromatids

Gametes

216 HEREDITY

For more information, have students contact a local hospital or university and ask about careers in genetic counseling.

Expression of Genes

Genes can interact with one another to control various other patterns of inheritance. Actually, most characteristics that make up an individual's phenotype are not inherited in Mendel's simple patterns. For example, consider the color of your eyes. Brown color in human eyes (*B*) is due to the presence of a pigment called melanin. People with blue eyes (*b*) have no melanin in their eyes. You know, however, that many other eye colors—such as gray, hazel, and green—exist. Those other colors are due to the presence of other genes inherited along with the *B* and *b* alleles. These other **modifier genes** affect eye color by influencing the amount, intensity, and distribution of melanin in cells of the eye.

with corresponding genes appearing side by side. To help simplify this idea, only one set of homologous chromosomes is shown. As meiosis continues, the homologous pairs are pulled apart and the resulting four gamete cells with their chromosome and gene combinations are shown. However, the arms of non-sister chromatids may overlap as shown on page 216. Overlapping may lead to an actual breaking off and exchange of chromosome ends during this early phase of meiosis. This overlapping and exchange of chromosome parts, along with their genes, is called crossing over. Note that the gametes have a different arrangement of genes on their chromosomes as a result of crossing over. The percent of these crossed-over traits appearing in offspring is then used as a means for determining gene location on a chromosome. This is true because the frequency or amount of cross-over that occurs corresponds to the location of genes on a chromosome. Genes that cross over more often with one another are far-ther apart on the chromosome than are genes that cross over less often.

On a chromosome map, the distance between genes is stated in map units. Thus, the distance between map units is an indication of the amount of or percentage of crossing over occurring between genes.

1. **Solve the Problem:** If one map unit = 1% crossing over, determine the location of the following genes on the chromosome map:

Percent of Cross Over
Cut wing and bar eye = 37
Cut wing and ruby eye = 12.5
Mini wing and cut wing = 16
Mini wing and ruby eye = 28.5
Ruby eye and bar eye = 49.5

Draw a diagram of this fruit fly chromosome and locate its genes with their correct distances in map units on your diagram. Note that the location of the ruby eye gene is already positioned for you in map units.

2. **Explore Further:** Build a model using tape and wool strands to show homologous chromosomes and their four chromatids. Add labels to indicate which are non-sister chromatids. (a) Show how these chromatids appear during prophase 1 of meiosis if no crossing over were to take place. (b) Show how these chromatids appear during early phases of meiosis if crossing over does occur.

3. **Writing About Biology:** Offer a possible explanation as to why genes located on the same chromosome will have higher percentages of cross-over when farther apart than if they are closer together. Use your model in question 2 to help illustrate and support your explanation.

CAREER CONNECTION

Genetic counselors are individuals who are trained in the field of genetics. Their training allows them to test, advise, and counsel people on the possibility of genetic diseases appearing in their families.

Science, Technology, and Society

The Human Genome Project: The project of mapping all of the genes of the human chromosomes, the human genome, has become quite controversial due to the amount of money and time devoted to the project. Several scientists think it will take decades to accomplish this. Some are concerned that too much money will be spent on this project while other projects do not get funded. David Cohen thinks that it can be done faster and claims that he has already mapped 67% of the human genome; by 1993, he expects to finish the job. Cohen, with money from the French muscular dystrophy association, began his search for the gene that causes muscular dystrophy. They gave him the money because he said he was going to use robots to process the DNA and this would take less time to accomplish. While searching for this gene, he has mapped a large chunk of the human genome. Cohen hopes to focus on treatment of muscular dystrophy after he locates the gene causing the defect. The defective gene can then be replaced by gene therapy. Since there are more than 3500 human genetic disorders, who will pay for the research and treatment to treat each one when the gene that causes it is identified?

Minilab 2

Purpose
To observe some genetic variations in humans.

Skills
observe and infer, interpret data

Teaching Strategies
- Review the traits being used with your students.

Expected Results
There are many possible combinations of traits. Have students give both phenotypes and genotypes. Classroom tallys will vary but will illustrate the fact that few students show the exact same combination of traits.

Answers
Everyone, except identical twins, has a unique combination of genes that result in a unique phenotype. Although people can look similar, gene combinations make it impossible to look exactly like someone else.

✔ Assessment
Performance: Provide students with the following genotypes and have them convert them to phenotypes:
(a) *OOwwTt*
(b) *ooWwtt*
(c) *oowwTT*
Provide students with the following phenotypes and have them convert them to *all possible* genotypes:
(a) Oriental eye, no widow's peak, no tongue roller
(b) Non-oriental eye, widow's peak, no tongue roller

Minilab 2

What are some human variations?

Read this list of human traits and their alleles:
- Oriental eye shape = *O*
- Non-oriental eye shape = *o*
- Widow's peak = *W*
- No widow's peak = *w*
- Tongue roller = *T*
- No tongue rolling = *t*

Record a list of all the possible combinations of these three traits in one person. Then, tally the number of students in your class fitting each category. Predict the possible genotypes for each category.

Analysis *Explain why it is almost impossible for two people, except for identical twins, to look exactly alike.*

It is the rule, not the exception, that many genes interact to control a phenotype. Because most traits are controlled by several genes working together, an individual may have alleles for a particular trait but not show that trait. For example, a person may have the genotype *Bb* but have blue eyes if a modifier gene prevents melanin from being produced.

Another factor that determines the expression of genes is the environment in which an organism develops. In fruit flies, for example, the gene for vestigial wings is expressed differently at different temperatures. Flies with small, vestigial wings bred at 29°C will have offspring with larger wings. But vestigial-winged flies bred at temperatures below 29°C will have offspring with small wings. The difference probably results from how enzymes operate at different temperatures. A higher temperature may deactivate an enzyme, preventing a reaction from occurring and thereby changing a phenotype.

In general, the development of any organism is affected by the environment. At low altitudes, trees may grow to be several hundred feet tall. At high altitudes, with fewer nutrients and harsher conditions, the same trees will only reach a height of several feet. Less dramatic conditions can also affect an organism's development. A corn plant may have the genotype for long ears of corn. But the soil in which the corn is planted may be poor, or a drought may occur during the growing season. Each of these events can affect the phenotype, with the result that the corn produces short ears or even no ears.

Thinking Lab

INTERPRET THE DATA

What pattern of inheritance allows for the prediction of a genotype when phenotypes are known?

A	B	C
HH	HT	TT

Background
An inherited blood disease called thalassemia affects red blood cells. A person with thalassemia minor has normal cells and abnormal cells. The abnormal cells lack hemoglobin. Thalassemia major results in all abnormal cells.

You Try It
The following diagrams show the blood cells and genotypes of three people. **Interpret the following data:** If HH = normal red cells, HT = thalassemia minor, and TT = thalassemia major, predict the (a) phenotypes of persons A, B, and C; (b) possible genotypes of

A, B, and C's parents; and (c) phenotypes of children born to parents when both have thalassemia minor, and when one is normal and one has thalassemia major. Which pattern of inheritance tells you genotypes when phenotypes are known? Why?

Thinking Lab

INTERPRET THE DATA

Purpose
Genotypes can be determined in some cases from phenotypes.

Teaching Strategies
- Review the role of hemoglobin and red blood cells in the human body.

Skills
interpret data, observe

Answers
(a) normal, thalassemia minor, thalassemia major, respectively
(b) A's parents = *HH* and *HH, HH* and *HT, HT* and *HT*
B's parents = *HH* and *HT, HT* and *HT, HT* and *TT*
C's parents = *HT* and *HT, HT* and *TT, TT* and *TT*

(c) normal or thalassemia minor or thalassemia major—all children will have thalassemia minor.
(d) Incomplete dominance. There is no dominant or recessive gene so there is no hybrid or heterozygous state.

✔ Assessment
Portfolio: Have students write a short summary of this Thinking Lab in their portfolios.

Figure 8-23 Eye color is determined by the interaction of many genes.

In summary, phenotypes—the expression of traits—are more complicated than early biologists thought. Whether a certain trait is expressed depends upon the particular alleles for that trait, all other alleles carried by the organism, and the environment in which the organism develops.

LOOKING AHEAD

THE LAWS of probability can be used to predict the likely results among all the offspring of a genetic cross. The genes themselves carry the code that determines which traits an individual offspring inherits. Just what is the structure of a gene? And what is the nature of the genetic code it helps carry? You'll discover the answers to these questions in the next chapter.

Section Review

Understanding Concepts

1. Colors of wheat kernels range from white to dark red, with various shades of pink in between. By what pattern of inheritance is this trait controlled? Sketch a graph that would represent this distribution of colors.

2. In fruit flies, the gene for red eyes (R) is dominant over the gene for white eyes (r) and is sex-linked. If an offspring is a white-eyed female, and her female parent has red eyes, what must the genotype of her male parent be?

3. Explain how the environment can affect the expression of various traits in an organism.

4. **Skill Review—Observing and Inferring**: Sutton proposed his chromosome theory of heredity after observing meiosis in grasshopper cells. Explain what Sutton observed and what inferences he made on which he based his theory. For more help, see Practicing Scientific Methods in the **Skill Handbook**.

5. **Thinking Critically:** Certain rabbits are white except for black fur on their feet, tail, ears, and nose. If a patch of fur is removed from a rabbit's back, and that area is covered by an ice pack, the fur that grows back will be black. How can you explain this fact?

Answers to Section Review

1. The data suggest inheritance due to multiple genes. The graph would be bell shaped with most offspring being a medium-red color.
2. The male parent must be X^rY.
3. Temperature can affect gene expression as can soil conditions, water, and altitude.
4. **Skill Review—Observing and Inferring:** Sutton came to the conclusion that genes are located on chromosomes. More specifically, he reasoned that the two alleles controlling a particular trait are located on a pair of homologues.
5. **Thinking Critically:** This fact shows the influence of environment on the expression of genes. The cold temperature probably favors activity of the enzyme that produces black pigment.

SECTION 8.3

3 Assess

Check for Understanding

Give students a set of problems in which they try their skills at solving problems related to sex-linked traits and many genes-one effect. **L1**

Reteaching

For students who are still having difficulty understanding how the X and Y chromosomes are different, make a drawing of these chromosomes on the board and explain that the reason they are called nonhomologous is that some parts of the X chromosome are not found on the Y chromosome. **LEP**

Extension

For students who have mastered the problems of this section, have them find out whether all animals have XX and XY chromosomes as sex chromosomes. Have them report their findings to the class. **L3**

✔ Assessment

Performance: Give the students scissors, construction paper, and glue and tell them to develop a model that shows the differences between the patterns of inheritance in many genes-one effect and multiple alleles. Tell them to label all parts of their model and write a brief description explaining the differences in the genetic systems. **L1**

4 Close

Using an Analogy

Assign three cooperative learning groups to make a presentation on one of the following genetic systems: sex linkage, many genes-one effect, and modifier genes. Tell them to discuss the pattern of inheritance by showing a Punnett square on the chalkboard or overhead projector. After each team presents their discussion have them compare and contrast their genetic system with the other two.

History Connection

Purpose
Students are going beyond the concepts in the chapter to gain an understanding of gene linkage.

Background
Students will find out how Mendel benefited by picking the seven genes he did. Mendel's traits were found on seven different chromosomes. Had he picked an eighth trait, he would not have obtained the ratios that helped him explain his principles of heredity. Some historians think Mendel did work with an eighth pair of genes but did not get the ratios he saw in the other crosses, and thus, abandoned the eighth trait.

Teaching Strategies
- Make a drawing on the chalkboard that shows two homologous chromosomes with two different genes on the same chromosome. Go through the steps of forming gametes during meiosis and ask students how the number of gametes is different from independent assortment. Tell them if the genes were not linked, they would get four different gametes. Explain that linked genes cannot separate independently during meiosis.

Possible Answers
1. No, because he would not get the 9:3:3:1 phenotypic ratios he obtained from non-linked genes.
2. If the genes were linked, you would get 3 black, short: 1 white, long; and if not linked you would get 9 black, short: 3 black, long: 3 white, long: 1 white, short.
3. The phenotype does not tell you whether the genes are linked or not. You would have to plant the seeds to observe the phenotypes of the offspring.

Going Further
Have students find out how scientists found the gene for Alzheimer's disease. **L3**

220

BIOLOGY,
TECHNOLOGY, AND
SOCIETY

History Connection
What if Mendel had picked different traits?

Mendel provided us with our basic understanding of genetics and established several laws, which you have studied in this chapter. Mendel also was very lucky or very smart with the choice of traits that he used in his studies. Why was he lucky?

Assume that yellow pea seed color = *Y* and green color = *y*, round pea seed shape = *R* and wrinkled = *r*. What Mendel may have observed in offspring after making a cross of *YyRr* × *YyRr* parents is shown in Table A.

Table A

Offspring phenotypes	Number observed	Ratio
Yellow, round	1841	9
Yellow, wrinkled	611	3
Green, round	618	3
Green, wrinkled	202	1

His data were the foundation for the formation of his law of independent assortment. This law states that genes for different traits segregate independently during gamete formation. This law is the basis for predicting the gene combinations in gametes. For example, when both parents are heterozygous for two traits, the following gene combinations are possible in gamete cells:

YR, Yr, yR, and *yr*. The observed appearance of these two traits in the offspring and the ratio of phenotypes supports the law established by Mendel. A phenotypic ratio of 9:3:3:1 when both parents are heterozygous for both traits being studied is what Mendel predicted and observed. Mendel was lucky because he picked genes located on different pairs of chromosomes.

But how lucky was Mendel? What if the two gene traits that Mendel worked with, pea seed color and seed shape, were both located on the same chromosome? Would he have observed the same ratios in the offspring? Would he have been able to demonstrate his law of independent assortment?

Genes for different traits located on the same chromosome are called

linked genes. This refers to the fact that the genes are found on the same chromosome. How would this have altered Mendel's observations, data, and formation of the law itself? Let's see. The diagram shows a pair of homologous chromosomes with the two traits used before. This time, however, they are linked. The parent genes are still heterozygous for both traits. The difference will be in the distribution of genes into gamete cells and the resulting combinations in the offspring. This is where gametes containing linked genes differ from gametes in which genes are not linked. The diagram shows the gametes formed when the genes are linked. Table B shows the data that one might observe for these two linked traits.

Replication prior to meiosis   Gametes possible

Table B

Offspring phenotypes	Number observed	Ratio
Yellow, round	1361	3
Green, wrinkled	452	1

Compare these data to those in Table A. Note that the ratios and phenotypic results are different with genes that are linked versus those that are not linked. Mendel was lucky because the traits he used were not linked. How might he have explained his data if the genes were linked?

1. **Solve the Problem:** Could Mendel have used data from linked genes to help formulate the law of independent assortment? Explain.
2. **Explore Further:** Describe the experimental procedure that you would use to determine whether or not the following genes are linked: *B* = black fur in guinea pigs, *b* = white fur, *S* = short fur length in guinea pigs, *s* = long fur. Describe the phenotypic ratios that would result in each situation, and explain how you would interpret your data.
3. **Writing About Biology:** Why is it impossible to tell, looking at a parent plant, if the genes for two heterozygous traits are linked or not?

Issues

Inbreeding: Helpful or Harmful?

There are laws in many states that forbid the marriage of first cousins. These laws are intended to prevent inbreeding. Inbreeding is the mating of individuals who are closely related. Why should such a law exist? What are the effects of inbreeding?

Inbreeding has led to offspring that show many harmful traits. This can be explained genetically. Certain recessive traits are prevented from showing because an organism may be heterozygous for these traits. It can be assumed that close relatives will also be heterozygous for these same traits. Mating two individuals who are both heterozygous for the same traits will increase the chance of both recessive genes appearing in the offspring. Thus, a higher number of recessive harmful traits may show up in the offspring.

Inbreeding is frequently used by animal and plant breeders. It is not uncommon for a male dog to be mated with his female offspring during breeding programs. The chance for harmful recessive traits in the offspring is increased.

Examples of inbreeding are plentiful in domesticated animals and especially dogs. Miniature poodles are good examples of problems associated with inbreeding. Have you ever noticed the dark brown stains appearing in the corners of a white poodle's eyes? These stains are the result of plugged tear ducts. Tears usually flow naturally from eye to tear duct to inside the nose. It's the same in humans. That's why you have to blow your nose after crying. Tear stains are certainly not harmful to the life of a poodle, but other inbred problems such as dislocated shoulders, epilepsy, diabetes, and collapse of the windpipe often are.

The healthiest dogs are usually those with the least inbreeding. Mutts rarely show the problems seen in bred varieties. Humans breed dogs and other animals for the traits they wish to have in their pets or in their farm animals or crops. However, these traits bring with them the many problems associated with inbreeding.

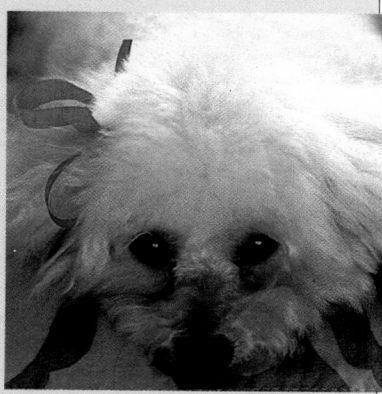

1. **Solve the Problem:** Several dogs in a new litter show genetic problems at birth. What steps should the breeder take to prevent these same problems from appearing in future litters?
2. **Writing About Biology:** Wolves, foxes, and coyotes rarely show any genetic problems that are typical of inbreeding. Write a paragraph explaining why this is true. How is this fact a benefit to a population?

Issues

Purpose
To show students how genetics is applied in plant and animal breeding.

Background
Students should understand that inbreeding increases the chance for homozygous recessive traits that are harmful to show up in a population with a higher-than-normal frequency. Many of the small animals used in medical research are from lines that have been inbred through numerous generations.

Teaching Strategies
- Inform students that inbreeding is found in plants as well as animals. Mendel used inbred lines of peas. Inbreeding in plants helped develop strains with desired phenotypes for agricultural use. Point out that even though these plants had desired phenotypes, some were not as disease resistant as the plants that were not inbred. Now, geneticists are crossing two different inbred lines of the same plant to try to make the plants more disease resistant. Gene therapy may even be used on plants to mask undesirable genes.

Possible Answers
1. The breeder should try to find out if the dogs are from an inbred line and only mate pairs that they suspect will not produce offspring with the harmful traits. If they have one or several dogs in a litter with genetic problems, they should not use any of the individuals from that litter for breeding stock.
2. The young of wolves, foxes, and coyotes that have genetic abnormalities do not survive in the wild and therefore do not pass on any of the harmful genes in the population.

Going Further
Have students find out more about the inbred animals used in medical research and whether any problems occur through inbreeding. **L2**

CHAPTER REVIEW

Summary

Summary statements can be used by students to review the major concepts of the chapter.

Language of Biology

Answers should go beyond defining the terms. Accept any reasonable answer that uses the term correctly and in the proper context.

Understanding Concepts

1. Each parent must be heterozygous since they produce some recessive (yellow) offspring. The yellow offspring are Pp and the purple offspring are PP or Pp, the latter being more probable.
2. Long wing is dominant based on the 3:1 ratio among the offspring. The parents were both heterozygous. Two-thirds of the long-winged offspring would be expected to be heterozygous.
3. The approximate 9:3:3:1 ratio among the offspring suggests that each parent was heterozygous for both traits.
4. The results are unexpected. By probability, it would be expected that 1/4 of the offspring would have blue eyes. However, actual results do not always correspond to predicted results.
5. 1/64
6. Assume female is homozygous for red eyes. Female parent = $ttXRXR$. Male parent = $TtXrY$.

$$TtX^rY \times ttX^RX^R$$

	tX^R
TX^r	TtX^RY^r
tX^r	ttX^RY^r
TY	TtX^RY
tY	ttX^RY

7. On the basis of his initial experiment, Morgan saw that only male flies had white eyes. He associated the inheritance of that trait with the fact that males have a unique chromosome, the Y, and assumed that the Y chromosome lacked a gene for eye color.
8. The Y chromosome is smaller and carries fewer genes. A Y-linked gene is always passed from father to son. Punnett square should show all males inheriting Y-linked trait.

Summary

Mendel's laws of dominance, segregation, and independent assortment can be applied to analyze many patterns of inheritance. Punnett squares, based on the laws of probability, can be used to solve a variety of genetics problems dealing with both Mendelian and other patterns of inheritance.

Observations that tied together Mendel's laws and the activities of chromosomes during meiosis led to the hypothesis that genes are on chromosomes. Discovery of how sex is determined and of sex-linked traits strengthened that hypothesis.

Expression of genes as a particular phenotype depends not only upon the alleles governing that phenotype, but also upon all the other genes of the organism and the environment in which the organism develops.

Language of Biology

Write a sentence that shows your understanding of each of the following terms.

allele	homozygous
autosome	incomplete dominance
codominance	modifier gene
continuous variation	multiple alleles
dominant	multiple genes
gene	phenotype
genetics	recessive
genotype	sex chromosome
heredity	sex-linked trait
heterozygous	

Understanding Concepts

1. Suppose that in outer space there exist creatures whose traits are inherited by Mendel's laws. Purple eyes (P) are dominant over yellow eyes (p). Two purple-eyed creatures mate and produce six offspring. Four of them have purple eyes, and two have yellow eyes. What are the genotypes of the parents and the offspring?
2. Two long-winged fruit flies produced 49 short-winged and 148 long-winged offspring. Which trait do you assume is dominant? Why? What were the probable genotypes of the parents? About how many of the long-winged offspring would you expect to be heterozygous?
3. You inspect an ear of corn and find the following number of kernels: 461 purple and starchy, 142 purple and sweet, 156 yellow and starchy, 53 yellow and sweet. What genotypes did the parent corn plants probably have? Support your answer by working out the cross.
4. In humans, brown eyes (B) are dominant over blue eyes (b). Two heterozygous brown-eyed parents produce eight children, all brown eyed. Do these results surprise you? What idea about genetics do the results illustrate?
5. The probability of any one child being a boy is 1/2. What is the probability that six children in a family will all be boys?
6. In fruit flies, the gene for tan body color (T) is dominant over the gene for ebony color (t). The gene for red eyes (R) is dominant over the gene for white eyes (r). The latter trait is sex-linked. Calculate the expected genotypic and phenotypic ratios resulting from a cross between a homozygous ebony female with red eyes and a heterozygous tan male with white eyes.
7. Explain why Morgan reasoned that the gene for eye color in fruit flies is carried on the X chromosome but not the Y chromosome.
8. Why are few sex-linked traits in humans located on the Y chromosome? How are Y-linked traits transmitted? Draw a Punnett square showing the transmission of a Y-linked trait.

Applying Concepts

9. This trait is an example of codominance. Two roans would be expected to produce 1/4 red, 1/2 roan, and 1/4 white. If the genes controlling coat color were completely dominant, then a horse would have hairs all of one color.
10. The narrow-eyed fly could be crossed with a round-eyed female and then with a female offspring produced by that cross. If narrow eyes are found only among male offspring, then the trait is probably sex linked.

Applying Concepts

9. A cross between a homozygous red horse and a homozygous white horse produces an offspring with a coat coloring called roan. Examination of the roan's coat reveals the presence of both red and white hairs. How is this pattern of inheritance explained? What results would you expect if two roan horses were crossed? How do you know that the genes controlling coat color are not completely dominant over each other?

10. Doing experiments with fruit flies, you unexpectedly find a male fly having narrow eyes. Normal flies have round eyes. How could you determine whether the gene for narrow eyes is autosomal or sex-linked?

11. In chickens, the gene for a rose comb (*R*) is dominant over the gene for a single comb (*r*). The gene for a pea comb (*P*) is dominant over the gene *p*, which also produces a single comb. When *R* and *P* are both present, they combine to produce what is called a walnut comb. Calculate the phenotypic ratio expected from a cross between two chickens with the genotypes *RrPp*.

12. **History Connection:** Describe the experimental procedure you would use to determine whether or not the following genes are linked: *B* = black fur in guinea pigs; *b* = white fur; *S* = short fur; *s* = long fur. Describe the phenotypic ratios that would result in each situation and explain how you would interpret your data.

13. **Issues:** Suggest a way a breeder of a particular show dog could obtain the traits he wanted in the dogs without inbreeding.

Lab Interpretation

14. **Minilab 1:** Your high school is co-ed with 82 females and 67 males in the sophomore class. The entire school has 322 females and 317 males. Explain why the numbers for sophomores and the entire school may or may not be close to 50:50 for males and females.

15. **Minilab 2:** List your phenotypes for the three traits described in the Minilab. Predict the possible genotypes that you might have for these three traits. Explain why you cannot be certain about having a homozygous dominant condition for any of the three traits.

16. **Thinking Lab:** The roots of radish plants are either long, round, or oval. (a) What type of gene inheritance pattern might this suggest? (b) Assign genotypes to the traits if an oval radish parent crossed with an oval yields 121 long, 246 oval, and 117 round. (c) How could you grow only oval radish plants?

17. **Investigation:** How many generations of tobacco plants would you have to observe to determine the actual genotype of a parent plant?

Connecting Ideas

18. Relate the law of segregation to the events of meiosis.

19. Explain the scientific methodology Mendel used in his experiments. Why is it important to have carefully thought out procedures when conducting experiments?

Single combs

Rose comb

Pea comb

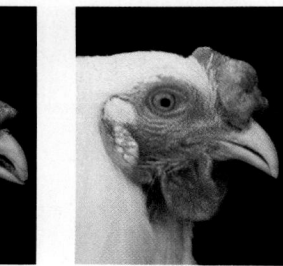

Walnut comb

CHAPTER 8 HEREDITY **223**

Connecting Ideas

18. **Patterns of Change:** The pair of genes controlling a particular trait is located one each on a pair of homologous chromosomes. The pair of homologues separate during meiosis and recombine to produce new traits among offspring.

19. **Methods of Inquiry:** Mendel chose clearcut hereditary differences; he worked with a large number of individuals to get statistically significant data; and he analyzed his data quantitatively.

11.

RrPp	×	RrPp	

	RP	Rp	rP	rp
RP	RRPP	RRPp	RrPP	RrPp
Pp	RRPp	RRpp	RrPp	Rrpp
rP	RrPP	RrPp	rrPP	rrPp
rp	RrPp	Rrpp	rrPp	rrpp

12. Cross a homozygous black, short with a white, long and then interbreed the offspring. If the genes are not linked, then the expected phenotypic ratio is 9 black, short: 3 black, long: 3 white, short: 1 white, long. If the genes are linked, the expected phenotypic ratio is 3/4 black, short: 1/4 white, long.

13. The breeder could breed dogs of the same kind, but not of the same "family."

Lab Interpretation

14. Sample size may be influencing the data.

15. Homozygous dominant traits are difficult to predict because it cannot be determined from a dominant phenotype if the organism is homozygous dominant or heterozygous. Both genotypes show the same phenotype. Only recessive traits that appear can be predicted with 100% accuracy.

16. (a) Lack of or incomplete dominance (b) Answers may vary but should be similar to this pattern: Long = *LL*, Oval = *LO*, Round = *OO*. (c) Begin with one parent radish plant that must be long, the other must be round. *LL* and *OO* will yield only *LO* or oval.

17. One generation (the one observed by students) for the 3 green: 1 albino and the 1 green: 2 yellow green: 1 yellow. The all green plants may require two generations to show if the parents were *GG* × *GG* or *GG* × *Gg*.

SECTION	OBJECTIVES	TEXT LABS/FEATURES
9.1 Structure of DNA (3 days)	**Sequence** the experimental evidence that led to the conclusion that DNA is the chemical of which genes are composed. **Diagram** the double helix model of DNA. **Demonstrate** the replication of DNA.	**Minilab 1:** How is a clone made? p. 227 **Investigation:** A Classroom Model of DNA, p. 230 **Art Connection:** Craig Schaffer—Sculptor, p. 232
9.2 The Role of DNA (3 days)	**Discuss** the evidence for the fact that DNA codes for proteins. **Demonstrate** an understanding of the DNA code.	**Thinking Lab:** How can crop plants be genetically engineered to produce higher yields? p. 238 **Minilab 2:** What does DNA look like? p. 239 **History Connection:** Har Gobind Khorana, p. 240
BIOLOGY, TECHNOLOGY, AND SOCIETY		**Biotechnology:** Transgenic Organisms—What Are They and Who Owns Them? p. 243 **Issues:** Genetic Profiles and Denying Health Care and Employment, p. 244 **Career Connection:** Lab technician, p. 245

LAB MATERIALS

INVESTIGATION	MINILAB		ALTERNATE LAB
page 230 construction paper, 10 pieces each of 6 different colors per group masking tape scissors	**page 227** garden plants, such as: lettuce onion houseplants, such as: *Coleus* geranium spider plant Wandering Jew small containers (paper cups)	**page 239** ethanol (or Everclear) isopropyl alcohol paper towels salmon testes solution sodium acetate stirring rod (or coffee stirrers or pipettes) test tubes	**page 234** gelatin capsule (empty) metric ruler thread, 10 m

TEACHER CLASSROOM RESOURCES	OTHER RESOURCES
Study Guide, pp. 49-51 **Critical Thinking/Problem Solving:** *DNA Replication,* p. 9 ***PLL:** *DNA Models,* p. 53	***STVS:** *Bacteriophage,* Plants and Simple Organisms (Disc 4, Side 1) **Color Transparency 13:** *DNA Replication*
Study Guide: pp. 52-54 **Concept Mapping:** p. 9 ****ILS:** *DNA and RNA,* p. 91	***STVS:** *New Grains,* Plants and Simple Organisms (Disc 4, Side 2) ***STVS:** *Genetic Engineering in Barley,* Plants and Simple Organisms (Disc 4, Side 1)
Assessment Materials **Chapter Assessment,** pp. 33-36 **Performance Assessment in Biology,** p. 18 **Alternate Assessment in the Science Classroom** **Computer Test Bank**	**Spanish Resources** **Cooperative Learning Resource Guide** **Videodisc Correlations** (to Optical Data's and Videodiscovery's videodiscs)

* Probing Levels of Life
** Investigating Living Systems

* Science Technology Videodisc Series

Key to Teaching Strategies

The following designations will help you decide which activities in the teacher margin are appropriate for your students.

L1 Level 1 activities should be within the ability range of all students.

L2 Level 2 activities should be within the ability range of the average to above-average student.

L3 Level 3 activities are designed for the ability range of above-average students.

LEP LEP activities are appropriate for Limited English Proficiency students.

COOP LEARN Cooperative Learning activities are designed for small group work.

ADDITIONAL RESOURCES

Infinite Voyage *The Future of the Past*
Do art and science work together? Art restoration is one area where they do. Students will see how chemistry is used to restore art masterpieces in this video.

Audiovisual
DNA and Genes, video, Frey Scientific.
DNA: The Molecule of Heredity, video, Films for the Humanities and Sciences.

Software
DNA: The Master Molecule (Part I), Apple 128K/MAC/IBM 256K, EME.

9

CHEMISTRY OF THE GENE

Chapter Overview

Students will study two classic experiments that led to the conclusion that DNA is the chemical genes are composed of. They will learn about DNA structure and the means by which this structure was discovered by Watson and Crick.

Students will learn how Watson and Crick's model offered a clue as to how DNA replicates, and they will study the means by which such replication occurs.

Students then learn how, based on both logic and experiments, scientists determined that genes, segments of DNA molecules, code for the synthesis of polypeptides. Finally, they find that each codon in a gene represents a particular amino acid and that the code is a universal one.

CHEMISTRY OF THE GENE

TAP A KEY on a computer keyboard, and a symbol appears on the screen. Tap another key, and a different symbol appears. With more than 100 keys on an expanded computer keyboard, almost anything the human mind can think of can be created—in words or in pictures. The trick, however, is to tap the keys in the correct sequence.

All organisms are created using the same chemicals. Almost any trait you can think of— color, size, temperament—can be coded for by these chemicals. The trick is to get these chemicals arranged in a particular order.

All the people in this photograph are made up of the same parts—arms, legs, eyes, hearts, and so on. Each of those parts is made up of tissues. Each of those tissues is made up of cells. Each of those cells is made up of chemicals. All people are made up of the same chemicals. It's the way these chemicals are put together that makes us different. Just as combinations of the 26 letters of our alphabet can make up many thousands of words, combinations of chemicals are used to produce the many thousands of characteristics that make us human. We are alike in many ways because we are made of the same chemicals. We look different because we are made up of different combinations of those chemicals.

As letters can be combined to form sentences, so chemicals can be combined to form molecules of DNA. What is DNA? It's what makes you, you.

224

KEY TERMS

adenine	guanine
bacteriophage	nucleotide
codon	thymine
cytosine	

Introducing the Chapter

Discuss the photograph on pages 224 and 225 with your students. Have them identify differences in the traits of people pictured. Remind them of what they have just learned about genes and the inheritance of traits. Review the idea that phenotypes, the traits they have identified in the photo, are the expression of genotypes. Now have them examine the DNA model pictured on page 225. Explain that the model is of DNA, a chemical, and that each gene is part of a DNA molecule. Point out that DNA must carry the code that results in the expression of genotypes. Lead them to the conclusion that DNA must be replicated and why.

Theme Development

Unity within diversity is one of the themes stressed in this chapter as students learn that genes of all organisms are composed of DNA and that the DNA code is a universal one. Methods of inquiry is a second important theme, one that is emphasized by an account of the numerous scientists whose research led to the discovery of DNA as the genetic material and to the current model of DNA structure.

Tying to Previous Knowledge

Students have previously learned about the cell cycle during which DNA of chromosomes is replicated. DNA is then divided between daughter nuclei during mitosis or meiosis. They have also studied several patterns by which traits may be inherited. Now students will begin to understand more clearly what DNA is, how it is replicated during interphase, and that it determines phenotypes by coding for particular polypeptides.

This model of DNA was generated by a computer. How does your body generate actual DNA?

Chapter Preview

page   *Contents*

225

ASSESSMENT PLANNER

Choose assessment strategies from the following pages to evaluate the progress of your students.

Assess, pp. 235-236, 242
Portfolio, pp. 227, 231, 235, 239, 240, 245
Alternate Lab, pp. 234-235
Thinking Lab, p. 238

Minilab 1, p. 227
Minilab 2, p. 239
Investigation, pp. 230-231
Chapter Review, pp. 246-247

Prepare

Key Concepts

Students are introduced to the history of the discovery that DNA is the chemical genes are composed of. The chemical structure of the DNA molecule is then described in detail.

Key Terms

bacteriophage, adenine, guanine, thymine, cytosine, nucleotide

Materials

- Purchase plants such as begonias, coleus, or geraniums. These plants are to be used for cloning in Minilab 1.
- Gather colored construction paper and scissors for the models of DNA in the Investigation.

1 Focus

Objectives

The objectives are listed on the student page. Remind students to preview these objectives as a guide to this numbered section.

Discussion

Ask students what they have in common with bacteria, molds, plants, and all other organisms. Direct their attention to the chemical similarity of chromosomes. Alert them to the fact that all life forms do share a common chemical that makes up the chromosomal material of all cells.

2 Teach

Using Science Terms

Have students define the term *transforming* in their own words. Ask them to use the word in a sentence and then have them apply or use the word as Griffith might have. **L1**

Objectives

Sequence the experimental evidence that led to the conclusion that DNA is the chemical of which genes are composed.

Diagram the double helix model of DNA.

Demonstrate the replication of DNA.

9.1 Structure of DNA

A new house is about to be built. The house will consist of many rooms. Those rooms will be similar in many ways, but will vary according to the activities that will take place within them—cooking, sleeping, or relaxing. Before building can begin, a set of plans called blueprints must be created. The blueprints provide the instructions for building the entire house and each of its parts. Building a house requires the coordinated efforts of many workers. Each worker needs a set of plans to build a particular part of the house, so the blueprints must be duplicated and given to each worker before work can begin.

Like the blueprints needed to build a house, the plans for making a new organism must be copied from the parent organisms and passed on to newly produced cells. Each cell of an organism then has instructions for its development in the form of a genetic blueprint. The cells of an organism are, like the rooms of a house, the same in many basic ways. However, just as a kitchen is specialized for cooking, cells are also specialized to perform certain functions.

What are the genetic blueprints made of? Although you know that genes direct the expression of traits that an organism will develop, what are genes, exactly? What chemicals are they made of? How can a chemical be copied? We'll explore the answers to these questions, and how the answers were discovered, in this chapter.

Heredity and Chemistry

In 1928, researcher Fred Griffith was studying the disease pneumonia, caused by a bacterium called *Streptococcus pneumoniae*. One strain of these bacteria consists of cells enclosed within a jellylike outer capsule and is referred to as smooth. Another strain has cells that are not enclosed by a capsule. Cells without a capsule are called rough. Smooth cells cause pneumonia, but rough cells do not.

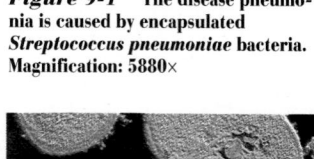
Figure 9-1 The disease pneumonia is caused by encapsulated *Streptococcus pneumoniae* bacteria. Magnification: 5880×

Griffith injected a mixture of dead smooth cells, killed by heat, and living rough cells into mice. He expected the mice to remain healthy, because rough cells do not cause pneumonia and because the smooth cells were dead. However, some of the mice died of pneumonia. On examining the blood of the dead mice, Griffith made an unexpected observation—living smooth *Streptococcus pneumoniae* cells were present. He concluded that somehow the dead smooth cells influenced the rough cells to become smooth. An inherited trait of rough cells must have changed in the presence of dead smooth cells. This kind of change in a bacterial trait is called a bacterial transformation.

226 CHEMISTRY OF THE GENE

PROGRAM RESOURCES

Teacher Classroom Resources

Study Guide, pp. 49-51 **L1**
Probing Levels of Life, Lab 19, p. 53 **L2**
Color Transparency #13 **L1** **LEP**
Critical Thinking/Problem Solving, p. 9 **L2**

PROJECT

Avery's Experiments: Have students research the following: (a) what were the steps that Avery took to determine that DNA was the transforming principle; (b) the type of protein found associated with chromosomes; (c) how DNA from one bacterium can actually enter the cells of another bacterium to bring about DNA transformation. **L2**

Changes in Traits How could a trait change as it had done in these experiments? Scientists suspected that a chemical in the dead smooth cells caused the change. To test this hypothesis, colonies of smooth cells were ground up to release their chemicals. The chemicals were removed from the cells in a solution called an extract. It was thought that a chemical in the extract would cause transformation.

The extract from the smooth bacteria was added to a new set of culture dishes containing only rough cells. After many colonies had formed, examination of the dishes showed that many of these colonies now contained both rough and smooth cells. The new smooth cells caused pneumonia when they were injected into healthy mice. The extract had changed the inherited traits of the rough cells, just as the hypothesis had predicted. A chemical in the extract changed the form of one strain of bacteria, and this change in traits was passed on to the offspring. This chemical was thus called the transforming principle.

Identifying the Transforming Principle The work of many scientists helped to identify the transforming principle. Earlier chemical analyses of cells showed that the chromosomes of eukaryotic cells contain about equal amounts of proteins and a chemical, deoxyribonucleic acid (DNA). Most scientists believed hereditary information in a cell was contained in the proteins, because they are more complex than the chemical components of DNA. In 1943, O.T. Avery demonstrated that DNA was the transforming principle in bacterial cells, but this information did not convince scientists that DNA is the primary hereditary mechanism in *all* cells.

Figure 9-2 A mixture of heat–killed smooth cells and living rough cells caused mice to die of pneumonia (a). Rough cells growing in a culture with an extract of living smooth cells were changed to smooth cells, an example of bacterial transformation (b).

Minilab 1

How is a clone made?

How would you like to have a clone of yourself? Clones are organisms that have the same genetic makeup as the parent organism and are produced by asexual reproduction. Clones of some orders of animals can be made from body cells of a parent by fission or budding. Clones of some plants can be made by cutting off a leaf and placing the cut end of the leaf in water. After a few days, roots will form and the plant can be potted. Try to clone a variety of plants by this method. Investigate garden plants and houseplants.
Analysis *Which plants made clones quickly? What is the adaptive value of the ability of a plant to make a clone?*

Minilab 1

Purpose
Students will describe and make a clone of a plant and determine common plants that can be cloned.

Skills
observe and infer, interpret data

Teaching Strategies
- Many students will have the misconception that a clone is a copy of an organism as described in science fiction books and films. Show students common houseplants such as coleus, wandering jew, geraniums, and spider plants. Ask them how they could quickly get a new plant of each of the ones you display.
- Clones of common houseplants such as coleus, wandering jew, geraniums, and spider plants can be made easily in one week.

Expected Results
Many plants cannot be cloned from a leaf, including many garden plants such as lettuce and onions.

Answers
1. Student answers will vary.
2. Plants can reproduce quickly from parts that might be broken off. Plants living in areas where storms are common would be at an advantage to reestablish if they could form clones.

✔ Assessment
Portfolio: Ask students to write in their portfolios predictions of which of the following plant parts could be most easily cloned into new plants and speculate why: needles from a pine tree, tulip flower on a stem, or a thick-stemmed houseplant leaf.

STUDENT JOURNAL

Have students pretend to be O.T. Avery. Upon their discovery that DNA is the transforming principle, have students write letters to their nonscience friends explaining what they have discovered and the possible significance of those discoveries for the future. Remind students that this discovery was made in 1943. **L1**

PORTFOLIO

Ask students to prepare a "time line" of the historical events leading up to the Watson and Crick model of DNA. Students should include dates that are listed on pages 226, 227, 228, and 230. Have students design and select the format themselves. Dates, scientists' name(s), and their contributions should be included. **L1**

Using Science Terms

Ask students to look up the meaning of the term *bacteriophage.* Ask them why this term is appropriate in describing how a virus reacts to its host cell. `L1` `LEP`

Chalkboard Example

Diagram a large outline of a bacteriophage on the board. Use two different colored chalks to indicate locations of sulfur and phosphorus. Prepare a second outline diagram of the bacteriophage attached to a bacterial host. Diagram the location of the colored sulfur and phosphorus after the injection of viral DNA into the host cell. Ask students this key question: What evidence shows that it is indeed the injected viral DNA that controls the events within the host cell? What type of control might Hershey and Chase have used with their experimentation using bacteriophages?

Different Viewpoints in Biology

Support for DNA as Genetic Material

Biologists look for additional information to support a finding or theory. This was the case with the role of DNA as the genetic material. One bit of added evidence was the fact that prior to mitosis, cells double their amount of DNA. During mitosis, this DNA is equally distributed into the two newly formed cells. If DNA is not the genetic material, then why is there a need for distributing DNA to all new daughter cells equally? It appeared that DNA indeed was important in carrying the genetic material for all future cell generations, thus the need to first double the amount in a reproducing cell and then the need to distribute exactly half to all future cells.

Figure 9-3 Bacteriophages are viruses that attack bacteria. They consist of a hexagonal head and a complex tail. Magnification: 60 000×

Evidence for DNA   Scientists studying heredity began to focus on DNA as the genetic material as a result of many experiments. One of the most important experiments was performed by Alfred Hershey and Martha Chase in 1952. Hershey and Chase experimented with viruses. Viruses can reproduce only by invading specific cells. Viruses that attack bacteria, known as **bacteriophages,** or phages, consist of an outer coat of protein and an inner core of DNA. That simple structure, seen in Figure 9-3, seemed ideal for resolving the debate about whether protein, DNA, or a combination of the two controlled heredity.

Bacteriophages attach to cells, and within an hour the cells contain hundreds of new viruses. The cells soon burst, releasing the viruses, which can then attack other cells. Hershey and Chase knew that the protein coat of a bacteriophage contains sulfur but not phosphorus, and that a phage's DNA contains phosphorus but not sulfur. Using this information, these researchers infected bacterial cells with bacteriophages. After infection had begun, they shook the infected cells in a blender, then spun them in a centrifuge to separate the cells from materials remaining outside the cells. What did they discover? Sulfur from the bacteriophages remained outside the bacterial cells, but phosphorus was found *inside* the bacterial cells. In other words, the protein coats of the bacteriophages remained outside the cells, but the phage's DNA had moved into the bacterial cells. It was the phage's DNA that entered cells and directed them to create new bacteriophages. This experiment clearly demonstrated that DNA, not protein, carries the information needed for reproduction and that DNA is the chemical genes are made of.

A Model of DNA

Although DNA was first discovered in a laboratory in 1869, its chemical components were not known until the 1920s. P.A. Levine, a biochemist, showed that DNA can be broken down into a sugar (deoxyribose), a phosphate group, and four nitrogen-containing bases. These bases are **adenine** (A), **guanine** (G), **thymine** (T), and **cytosine** (C). In Figure 9-4,

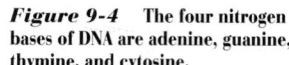

Figure 9-4 The four nitrogen bases of DNA are adenine, guanine, thymine, and cytosine.

Adenine (A)

Guanine (G)

Thymine (T)

Cytosine (C)

228 ◈ CHEMISTRY OF THE GENE

Have students working at or above grade level: (a) write the problem that Hershey and Chase might have stated at the start of their experiment; (b) write a hypothesis that Hershey and Chase might have used with their experiment; (c) explain how Hershey and Chase might have interpreted their data if sulfur were found to enter the bacterial cell while phosphorus remained on the outside; (d) explain how they might have interpreted their data if both sulfur and phosphorus entered the cell. `L2`

One DNA Nucleotide

Phosphate

Deoxyribose

Hydrogen bond

Adenine (A)

Thymine (T)

Guanine (G)

Cytosine (C)

Figure 9-5 **A nucleotide consists of a phosphate group, a sugar molecule, and one of four nitrogen bases. The shaded area shows an adenine molecule.**

the chemical structure of each base is shown. Notice the colored shapes. Each shape refers to that specific base in the figures that follow. It will be easy to tell what chemicals are shown in the drawings if you keep in mind what the shapes represent as you examine the other figures in this chapter.

Levine deduced that each base was attached to a molecule of sugar, and each sugar was then attached to a phosphate group to form a single molecule called a **nucleotide.** Each nucleotide is named for the base it contains. For example, an adenine nucleotide contains adenine. Figure 9-5 shows the arrangement of the three parts of a nucleotide. Many nucleotides are linked together to form a long chain of DNA.

Bases Appear in Matching Quantities Other scientists studying the chemical structure of DNA made some important discoveries. Erwin Chargaff analyzed the content of many different kinds of DNA. He found that the nitrogen bases do not occur in equal proportions. In the DNA of any given species, the amounts of adenine and thymine are always the same, and the amounts of guanine and cytosine are always the same. This piece of information helped solve the problem of how DNA could be complex enough to be the chemical controlling heredity.

A Classroom Model of DNA

Time Allotment
1 class period

Objectives
Upon completing this investigation, students will be able to:
- Design and construct a model for DNA replication.
- Demonstrate, with a model, DNA replication.

Skills
sequence, observe

Materials
construction paper, 8 1/2 × 11, six colors, 10 pieces of each color per group; scissors, 2 per group; masking tape

Safety Precautions: Remind students to be careful when using scissors.

Preparation
Obtain construction paper in six different colors. Obtain a three-dimensional model of DNA from a biological supply house or pictures showing the coiled helix of DNA.

Possible Procedures
- Suggest to students that they choose to make the sugar a yellow, 5-sided shape; phosphate, a purple round shape; thymine, a red lock shape; adenine, a green key shape to match; guanine, an orange rectangle with inverted side; cytosine, a blue rectangle with protruding side to match. The students' nucleotide would consist of a person representing a phosphate linked to a person who is a sugar by placing an arm over a shoulder to form an L shape. A person representing a base would link to the sugar by placing an arm over the shoulder at a 45-degree angle.
- The placard may be attached to shirt fronts with masking tape.
- Other models might also be acceptable provided they follow the basics of DNA replication. Be sure to check the group's model idea before students demonstrate.

Describing DNA How is genetic information carried in DNA? To answer this question, James Watson, a biologist, and Francis Crick, a physicist, compiled all the information available about DNA. They knew that DNA is a large molecule composed of sugars, phosphate groups, and four bases. They knew that the amounts of adenine and thymine are always equal, as are the amounts of guanine and cytosine. But how are these components arranged?

Two other discoveries helped complete the picture. Linus Pauling, in 1950, showed that a protein's chains of amino acids are often arranged in the shape of a helix. He speculated that DNA might have a similar shape. Maurice Wilkins and Rosalind Franklin were experts in a technique that bombards molecules with X rays, allowing the molecules to be photographed and visualized. Some of their photographs of DNA showed patterns that looked like turns of a giant helix. Crick and Watson, using all available information as well as their knowledge of chemistry, set about building a model of DNA that fit all the known facts. They first concluded that the DNA molecule must be in the form of a helix, or spiral, composed

---

INVESTIGATION

A Classroom Model of DNA

Have you ever been in a restaurant with your friends and suddenly had a thought you didn't want to forget? To keep from forgetting, you probably wrote your thought on a paper napkin. In the early 1950s, Rosalind Franklin provided, in her X-ray pattern studies of DNA, the clues James Watson and Francis Crick needed to construct a three-dimensional model of DNA. Where and how did they think about the possibilities for the structure of DNA? They brainstormed with pencils on paper napkins in restaurants. They tinkered in their lab with bits of wire, plastic, and string. In this lab, you will use colored construction paper and your fellow students in the class to make a working model of DNA replication.

Problem
How can a model of DNA replication be made?

Safety Precautions
Use care with scissors.

Experimental Plan
1. As a group, you will receive ten pieces of each of six colors of construction paper.
2. The six colors will correspond to the six different molecules that make up the DNA molecule.
3. Decide what shapes you will use to represent each of the six molecules.
4. Using paper and pencil, brainstorm, in your group, a list of possible ways various shaped placards could be held by students in the class as they move through a representation of the process of DNA replication.
5. Select the best idea and, following the style of a recipe, write a numbered list of directions that anyone could follow.

230 CHEMISTRY OF THE GENE

Teaching Strategies
- Tell students that they may need to cut some of their paper in half to have enough of one color, but that they should make their molecules large enough to be seen as a classroom demonstration.
- Explain that students in the class will be holding the placards they make, and that they need to be visible to those watching.
- A group that needs a simpler form of this activity may choose to demonstrate only the bonding of bases, splitting of these bonds,

and formation of new bonds with the parent bases.
- Students may choose to have hand holding or hands on shoulders to indicate bonding, but they need to show respect for those who do not wish to be touched in this way.
- You may wish to have students demonstrate only the model you decide has the best potential for success. After the demonstration, ask the class to give feedback about positive aspects of the model as well as negative aspects.

of a single chain of nucleotides. Each nucleotide must be joined to the next by the sugar-phosphate backbone.

One Chain or Two However, Watson and Crick calculated that a single chain of DNA would have only half the density known for DNA. They realized that a molecule of DNA must be composed of two chains of nucleotides. But how are the two chains joined? The fact that, in any DNA molecule, the numbers of adenine and thymine nucleotides are always equal, and the numbers of guanine and cytosine nucleotides are always equal, gave them the answer.

Watson and Crick built a model of DNA in which the two chains of nucleotides are joined. Using wire and tin, they constructed a ladder-like model in which the uprights of the ladder are composed of the sugar and phosphate parts of the nucleotides. The rungs are composed of the nitrogen bases of the nucleotides. Each rung contains two nitrogen bases held together by what are called hydrogen bonds. Only two bonding arrangements are possible: adenine with thymine, and guanine with cytosine.

---

6. Cut out the number of hand-held, large placards you will need to model DNA replication by students in your class. Label each placard with the name of the molecule it represents.
7. Decide how you will identify the bonds that hold your molecule together.
8. Decide how you will demonstrate your model. Decide what each group member will contribute during the demonstration.

Checking the Plan

Discuss the following points with other group members to decide the final procedures for your model.
1. Have you incorporated all the parts of the DNA molecule into your model and most, if not all, of the students in class?
2. Does your model come apart, just as DNA "unzips" during replication?

3. Does your model include the idea of new molecules being added on to each half of the DNA molecule once it is unzipped?
4. Do you have two molecules identical to the original when you have completed your modeling of DNA replication?

Make sure your teacher has approved your model before you proceed further.

Observations

Use the time given to you by your teacher to demonstrate your model. Be effective and efficient in your distribution of shapes and your directions for movement of students.

Analysis and Conclusions

1. What did you learn about DNA by making a model of its replication?
2. Did you use the "ladder" comparison to make your model? If so, what kind of molecules made

up the sides of the ladder? What molecules made the rungs?
3. Explain how, during replication, DNA is able to make an exact copy of itself.
4. What was the easiest part of making your model?
5. What was the most difficult part of making your model?
6. Write a brief summary of how DNA replicates.

Going Further

Based on this lab experience and Table 9.1 on page 241, prepare a model of a DNA strand that codes for the following molecules: phenylalanine, tryptophan, and argenine in that order. You may use the same materials for this model or expand on an idea that you think might work better. Assume that you will have unlimited resources and will not be conducting this lab in class.

---

together, and the bases cytosine and guanine bond together. The chains of nucleotides are twisted around each other to form a double helix or spiral.

When replication takes place, the bases come apart at the center of the "rung," and new nucleotides are added to the parent DNA strands. Each new DNA molecule is an exact replicate of the parent strand.

✔ **Assessment**

Portfolio: Sketch on the chalkboard a set of shapes that represent nucleotide parts. A

square might represent a base; a triangle, sugar; a rectangle, phosphate. Ask students to make a diagram in their portfolios of DNA replication by using these shapes to represent nucleotides.

Extensions

Ask students to expand, on paper, ideas for their current model to include codons for specific amino acids.

- Ask students to speculate about the mechanism at work during replication to ensure an exact copy of the original. If they have no ideas, ask them what should be done to ensure an exact copy if they decided they wanted to build a new house or building exactly like the one they are living in. Lead them to discuss how blueprints are used.

Data and Observations

Students' models will vary. Be sure that they represent adenine bonded with thymine and guanine with cytosine. The bonds will be represented by holding hands or linking arms to shoulders. Nucleotides will be L-shaped with phosphates bonded to sugars, and the base at a 45-degree angle with the sugar. When the DNA unzips, the bases come apart by dropping hand connections, and new nucleotides come in to take their places by joining hands in the appropriate order. The end result should be two new DNA strands.

Data Analysis

1. Students should have a clearer picture of DNA structure as a result of making a model.
2. The sugar and phosphate groups are the ladder sides, whereas the bases are the rungs.
3. After the parent nucleotides "unzip," new nucleotides are added in a specific order due to the fact that adenine joins only with thymine and cytosine only with guanine. As a result, each new DNA molecule is an exact copy of the parent DNA.
4. Answers will vary.
5. Answers will vary.
6. DNA is made of units called nucleotides. Each nucleotide consists of a phosphate, base, and sugar (deoxyribose) molecule. Many nucleotides joined together form a DNA molecule. DNA structure is often compared to a ladder in which the sides are made of alternating sugar and phosphate molecules and the rungs of two bases joined together. The bases adenine and thymine bond

Purpose

A parallel is made between the approach that an artist uses when attempting a new piece of art and the methods that scientists use when solving problems.

Teaching Strategies

Assign students to work in cooperative groups. Ask them to: (1) define the terms *chaotic* and *retrospective;* and (2) list the steps that scientists use as they attempt to solve a problem. Have each group decide on an imaginary art project to be undertaken. The group should write out the steps that an artist would undertake in this project to parallel the steps listed for the scientist.

Possible Answers

1. Student answers will vary. Those who agree may point out the similarity between undertaking an experiment with unknown results and undertaking a work of art with unknown results. Those who disagree may feel that art has no parallel to science because art deals with one's imagination while science deals with the interpretation of data.
2. Frank Lloyd Wright used a lot of wood and stone in the exteriors, interiors, and furniture of his buildings. He is most famous for his ability to design buildings that fit their location.

Going Further

Ask students to choose six works of art that depict some aspect of nature. Have them note and record the artists' names as well as the titles of the art pieces. Ask them to explain the correlation between what the artist has depicted and nature itself. L1

Adenine and guanine belong to a group of nitrogen bases called purines. Thymine and cytosine belong to a different group of nitrogen bases known as pyrimidines. Bonding in the DNA molecule only occurs between a purine and a pyrimidine because of their chemical structures. In fact, the chemical structure of adenine enables it to bond *only* with thymine.

ART CONNECTION

Craig Schaffer— Sculptor

Take a double helix, add two parallel lines, and mix. What do you get? If you are sculptor Craig Schaffer, you get six-sided stars that double as candlesticks. By looking at the double helix of DNA in a different way, Schaffer interpreted the structure of life itself into art with a religious context for a Jewish house of worship. Interpreting the structure of DNA as art is only one of the ways in which Schaffer has been inspired by natural forms. He

uses stone, wood, metal, and even plastic to explore the artistic possibilities of the natural world.

"People think that art and science are at opposite ends of the poles," says Schaffer, "but really they are very similar." The sculptor believes that artists and scientists share several traits—both are very curious about the world around them, and both perform experiments to test their ideas. Like a scientist, an artist often begins with a question, or hypothesis. How does shape influence function? Are there repeating patterns in seemingly chaotic structures? These are some of the questions artists may ask as they begin to explore new possibilities. Artists follow the scientific method, Schaffer explains, because they begin each new work with a different question. They try something new, then learn from the results. As in scientific inquiry, the results of an experiment are not always what you expect. Often an artist may move along a different path as a result of one experiment, just as a scientist's experiments often lead to a new hypothesis.

As a sculptor, Craig Schaffer tries to explore the artistic possibilities of both science and mathematics. He has created sculpture for clients such as Princeton University and the Mathematical Association of America, and has had various

other commissions around the country. Schaffer is especially interested in combining various disciplines in his work. One of his double helix designs graces the Congregation Beth Tikvah in Columbus, Ohio. The double helix structure of DNA offered the sculptor an opportunity to combine a natural form with religious interests to create a six-sided star shape, which is a Jewish symbol.

Schaffer feels that you can learn how an artist evolves by viewing work from various times in the artist's life. At a retrospective show, you can see how an artist's perspective has changed over time. Why, for example, would an artist paint the same mountain over and over again throughout his or her life? Schaffer explains that, each time, the artist wanted to know what would happen if one variable was altered. Scientists operate in exactly the same way.

1. **Writing About Biology:** Schaffer believes that art and science share common traits. Do you agree with him? Explain why.
2. **Explore Further:** Many artists are interested in natural forms. Find out what made the work of Frank Lloyd Wright so original, and how natural forms influenced his work.

MEETING INDIVIDUAL NEEDS

Have students working at grade level or below perform the following tasks: (a) Assign a letter A, T, C, or G to each student. Have them write a large assigned letter on a sheet of paper. Ask about six students to line themselves up at the chalkboard with the letters that you have already written there. Have them explain why they lined up as they did. (b) Have the remaining students line themselves up in front of the classroom to illustrate DNA replication. Ask them to explain why they lined up as they did. LEP

The same is true for guanine and cytosine. Do you see why the amounts of adenine and thymine in a DNA molecule are always the same?

Either base of a pair may be on either nucleotide chain, and the sequence of base pairs may vary along the entire length of the DNA molecule. The two chains of nucleotides run in opposite directions and are twisted around one another to form a double helix. The twisting results in indentations along the molecule, known as major grooves and minor grooves. These grooves play a role in the activation of genes. Figure 9-6 shows the double helix model constructed by Watson and Crick.

Study the model of DNA shown in Figure 9-6. Notice the base pairing in the structure of DNA. The order of these bases makes up the genetic code. Differences in the order of bases are what make one species different from another. Make certain you understand DNA structure. As you look at the drawing of a DNA molecule, think again about the role of DNA. How does a chicken egg become a chicken? Remember that DNA is the chemical that genes are made of. A gene is one sequence of nucleotides along a DNA molecule. One DNA molecule, therefore, contains many genes. The simplest known virus has 5000 paired bases in its DNA. A single human cell contains about 6.6 billion base pairs in its nuclear DNA. The amount of DNA in a single human cell carries as much information as 600 000 printed pages of 500 words each. If all this DNA were stretched out in a line, it would measure almost two meters. Not all of the DNA in a cell carries genetic information. The portion that does contains about 50 000 to 100 000 genes.

Figure 9-6 The double helix structure of DNA results from pairing of the four bases and the angles of their chemical bonds.

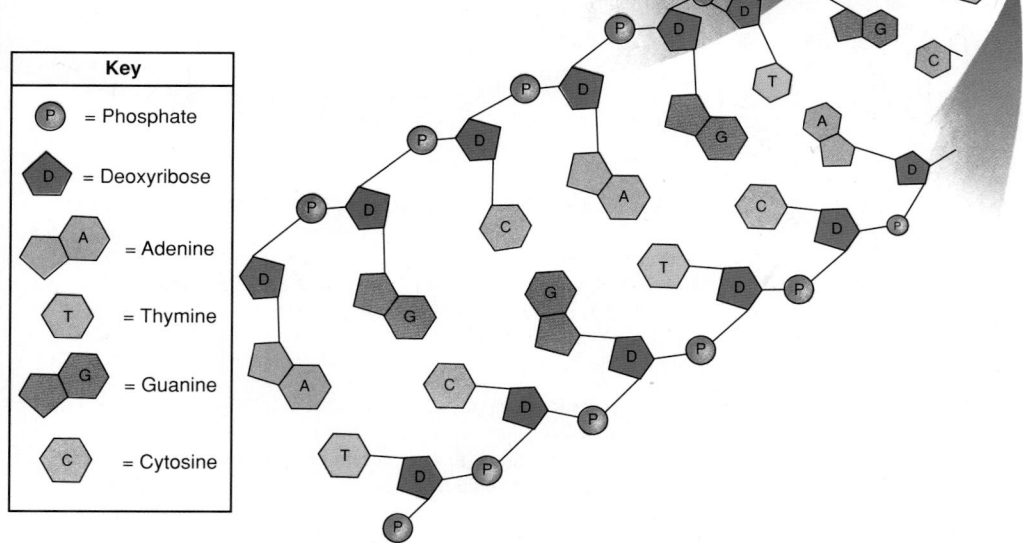

Key

P	= Phosphate
D	= Deoxyribose
A	= Adenine
T	= Thymine
G	= Guanine
C	= Cytosine

9.1 STRUCTURE OF DNA **233**

SECTION 9.1

Reinforcement

Ask students the following questions: (a) a cell has been chemically analyzed and shows 0.0047 g of cytosine. Predict the amount of guanine present; (b) explain why the amount of cytosine present will not help in determining the amount of thymine. **L1**

Using the Illustration

Have students refer to Figure 9-6 as they answer the following questions: (a) what do the two almost ribbon-like bands toward the top of the diagram represent chemically; (b) is the rule regarding one purine and one pyrimidine illustrated correctly; (c) is the rule of only an A and T or C and G pairing together illustrated correctly; (d) how many different nucleotide types are illustrated; (e) what specific molecules (not including the opposite base) does each nitrogen base attach to; and (f) how does the illustration convey the idea that DNA is a helix? **L1**
COOP LEARN

Concept Development

Ask students to define a gene. Is the number of nucleotides specific for a gene according to the information given here? Explore regulating or controlling traits and see if students can come up with a hypothesis that might account for different genes on a DNA strand when the only differences along its length are four nitrogen bases.

MULTICULTURAL CONNECTION

Phenylketonuria: A disease called phenylketonuria (PKU) is caused by a mutation in a gene that controls the enzyme phenylalanine hydroxylase. Children born with PKU cannot break down phenylalanine, so it accumulates in the blood, leading to mental retardation. PKU is most common among Israeli Jews who emigrated from Yemen. Studies have found that Yemenite Jews from 22 families all are missing the same piece from the phenylalanine hydroxylase gene.

Although these families came from 25 different towns in Yemen, all are descended from people who lived in San'a, the capital of Yemen, in the 17th century. Scientists now believe they will be able to find one ancestor who had the original mutation.

SECTION 9.1

Using Science Terms

Make sure that students are familiar with the terms *eukaryotic, prokaryotic, mitosis,* and *binary fission.* Ask students to look up the meaning of the term *replication* using a dictionary. Have them explain how this term is applicable to the process that DNA undertakes. **L1**

Misconception

Most students believe that DNA is somehow replicated within the cell as a process having no connection to chromosomal events previously studied. Remind students that chromosomes are composed of DNA, and the cell's chromosomes replicate or duplicate just prior to mitosis and meiosis.

Demonstration

A zipper could be used to represent a model of DNA prior to replication. Purchase a zipper and hold it up for the class to examine. Ask students: (a) what does each side of the zipper represent, (b) what process regarding nitrogen base bonds is being represented as the two sides are unzipped, (c) what is actually needed now in the model to fit along each open side of the zipper and what would these correspond to in the molecules that form DNA, and (d) how many zippers would be needed to illustrate replication? **LEP**

Figure 9-7 DNA replication results in exact copies of genetic information that can be passed on to offspring. Replication is possible because of base pairing.

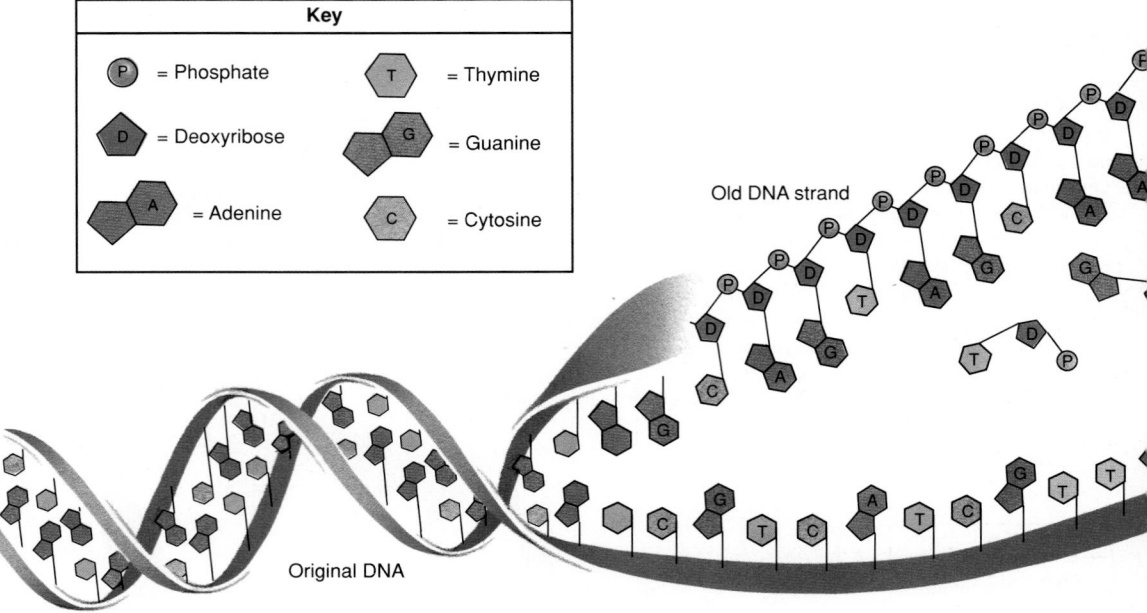

Replication of DNA

How are genes passed on to offspring when a cell reproduces? Recall from Chapter 7 that in a eukaryote, many chromosomes are duplicated during mitosis. A prokaryote does not undergo mitosis. Instead, its single chromosome is duplicated in the cytoplasm as binary fission occurs. In spite of these differences, replication of the DNA of both eukaryotic and prokaryotic chromosomes is basically the same. It is also the same in mitochondria and chloroplasts.

Watson and Crick's model suggested how DNA replication might occur. They hypothesized that each original chain of nucleotides in DNA acts as a template, or mold, for making a new chain. Because of base-pairing rules, A with T and G with C, new nucleotides would be put in place according to the sequence of bases in each parent chain. Watson and Crick's hypothesis was tested experimentally by other researchers, and found to be correct.

How DNA Is Replicated One requirement for genetic material is the ability to provide exact copies of itself. How can DNA accomplish this? Replication of DNA begins as a protein binds to a section of DNA called the origin. Once that binding occurs, an enzyme begins breaking the hydrogen bonds between nitrogen bases that hold the two chains of nucleotides together, and the double helix begins to unzip. These actions

---

A L T E R N A T E   L A B :   Modeling and Measuring the Size of a DNA Molecule

Purpose
In this activity students will measure a model of a bacterial chromosome.

Materials
empty gelatin capsule (from druggist), metric ruler, 10-meter-long piece of thread

Procedure
Give the following directions to students.
1. Set up a data table similar to the one shown.

2. Measure the length of a gelatin capsule in millimeters. Record the capsule length in the data chart.
3. The length of the capsule is about 10 000 times the length of an actual *E. coli* bacterial cell. Its shape is very similar to that of the capsule. Record the *actual* length of a bacterial cell in the data chart.

4. To determine the length of an *E. coli* chromosome, measure the length of a strand of thread in millimeters. Record this length in the data table.
5. The thread strand is 10 000 times the actual length of a bacterial chromosome. Calculate and record the actual length of a bacterial chromosome in the chart.

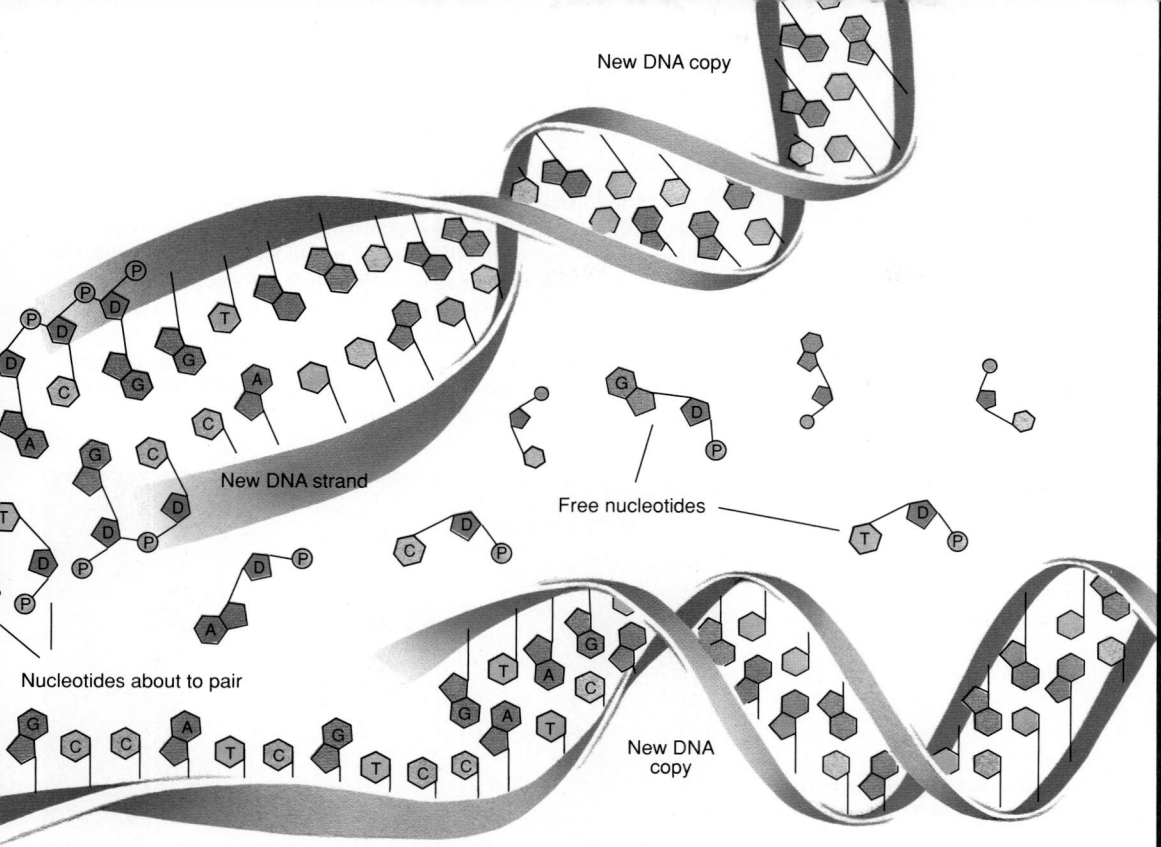

New DNA copy

New DNA strand

Free nucleotides

Nucleotides about to pair

New DNA copy

begin at several places along the DNA molecule; as sections unzip in both directions, the unzipped sections eventually merge and the result is an entirely unzipped molecule. As the chains of nucleotides separate, a complex enzyme (DNA polymerase) binds to each of the separated parent chains. The enzyme sweeps along, bonding new nucleotides to the nucleotides of the parent chain. Addition of nucleotides occurs in opposite directions on the two chains—from top to bottom on one chain, from bottom to top on the other. The nucleotides are matched by base pairing in the same order as one of the parent chains. That is, if one nucleotide on the parent chain has adenine as a base, the new nucleotide added will have the base thymine. As a result, each new chain is a complement of one of the two parent chains.

The replication of the DNA in a human cell takes about four hours. An enzyme then bonds the nucleotides together in the new replicated chain. ATP energy is needed for many of these steps, such as breaking the bonds between nucleotides and adding new nucleotides to the growing chains. Each new DNA molecule consists of one parent chain and one new chain and is a replica of the parent molecule. Recently, a protein that inhibits

SECTION 9.1

3 Assess

Check for Understanding
Have students explain the following word relationships:
(a) bacteriophage and bacteria;
(b) nitrogen bases and adenine, thymine, guanine, and cytosine;
(c) nucleotides and nitrogen base, sugar and phosphoric acid molecules;
(d) nitrogen bases and base pairing;
(e) DNA and a double helix. **L1**

Using the Illustration
Have students use Figure 9-7 to answer the following questions: (a) what is meant by the label "original DNA"; (b) what is meant by the label "new DNA strand"; (c) in what organelle of the cell is this process of replication occurring; (d) what part of the illustration represents the unzipped portion of DNA; (e) what molecules alternate to form the ribbon-like parts; (f) explain how the models of molecules enable you to see the difference between purines and pyrimidines and provide examples of each. **L1** **LEP** **COOP LEARN**

---

6. Calculate how many times longer the bacterial chromosome length is when compared to the length of the bacterial cell. Record this data in the chart.
7. Pull the capsule apart. Attempt to fit the thread chromosome into the capsule cell. Close the capsule.

Data Table

Capsule length	= 20 mm
Actual bacterial cell length	= 0.002 mm

Model chromosome length	= 10 000 mm
Actual chromosome length	= 1 mm

Analysis
Ask students to answer the following questions.
1. Compare the length of a bacterial chromosome to the length of a bacterial cell. *Chromosome length is much greater (500×) than cell length.*

2. Explain how it might be possible for a bacterial chromosome to fit easily into the actual cell. *DNA is highly coiled and thin.*

✔ **Assessment**
Portfolio: Have students explain in a short paragraph the value of using a model in science. This paragraph may be placed in their portfolios.

Reteach

Have students diagram a railroad track with exactly 20 ties. Ask them to redraw the tracks and ties, only this time the track is twisted and overlaps at every 10 ties. Ask them to label the molecules that would correspond to DNA at the correct positions on the railroad track diagram.

Extension

Have students research the significance and meaning of the statement that the two sides of DNA are anti-parallel to one another. **L3**

✔ Assessment

Performance: Prepare 2 sets of 3 × 5 cards with the words: bacterial transformation; Avery; Griffith; DNA transforming principle in bacterial cells; bacteriophages; Hersey and Chase; Levine; chemical structure of DNA; Chargaff; adenine matches thymine; Watson and Crick; double helix. Divide class into two groups. Give each group a set of cards. Then give them five minutes to match names with discoveries. Have the winning group explain their matches.

4 Close

Analogy

Provide students with a piece of Velcro. Ask them to assume that the Velcro is a section of DNA. Students are to name the various molecules that form DNA and locate these same molecule positions on the Velcro model. **L1**

replication has been discovered. It attaches to the origin and prevents the breaking of bonds between nucleotide chains. This protein, along with the one that starts replication, plays an important role in regulating the replication part of the cell cycle.

Replication Mistakes During DNA replication, some mistakes may occur. Although rare, such copying mistakes may be serious because each cell must have exact copies of DNA to function properly. The number of mistakes that are actually passed on, though, is extremely small because a cell can repair its DNA. Special repair enzymes "proofread" the newly made DNA for errors. They remove any incorrect nucleotides. Other enzymes then insert the correct ones. DNA repair reduces the chance of errors to about one in every billion nucleotides. Mistakes that are not corrected result in variations in genetic material.

Figure 9-8 A variation in chickens called the frizzle trait results in weak, stringy feathers. Caused by a single mistake in DNA, this trait also results in chickens with enlarged hearts and spleens, changes in kidneys, and decreased egg-laying abilities.

Section Review

Understanding Concepts

1. How did the results of Hershey and Chase's experiment finally change the notion that genes were made of proteins?
2. Would Watson and Crick's first idea that DNA is a single chain of nucleotides offer an explanation of how DNA replicates? Explain.

3. One chain of a DNA molecule has the nucleotide sequence C, C, G, C, T. What is the sequence of nucleotides on its partner chain?
4. **Skill Review—Sequencing:** Sequence the steps that occur in the replication of a DNA molecule. For more help, see Organizing Information in the **Skill Handbook**.

5. **Thinking Critically:** Why is it important that a signal for stopping DNA replication be part of the cell cycle?

Answers to Section Review

1. Hershey and Chase used bacteriophages, whose only components are proteins and DNA. Their experiments showed that DNA controls reproduction.
2. If DNA were a single chain of nucleotides, the replication process would not occur. A complementary chain of nucleotides could be made from an original chain, but it would have a different sequence of nucleotides. The two chains would not be replicas.

3. G, G, C, G, A.
4. **Skill Review—Sequencing:** After a protein binds to the origin, an enzyme breaks the hydrogen bonds between the nitrogen bases of the two chains. The double helix begins to unzip. This unzipping occurs at several places and proceeds in both directions. DNA polymerase binds to each of the separated parent chains and moves along, adding

complementary nucleotides to each chain. Another enzyme bonds the nucleotides of the newly formed chains to one another. Mistakes are rare, but most are repaired by enzymes that "proofread" the newly made DNA.
5. **Thinking Critically:** Lack of such a signal would result in production of excess copies of DNA molecules. Each cell must have the proper number of DNA molecules.

9.2 The Role of DNA

Blueprints are drawings that show the dimensions of each room of a house, how one room is joined to another, and the locations of plumbing and electrical wires. DNA, like a blueprint, contains information for cells to function and for the organism made up of those cells to develop as a whole. That information is in the form of a code. Before you can decipher the code, you need to know exactly what kind of information the code carries. What instructions does DNA give to a cell? The answer to that question involves proteins.

Genes and Proteins

Proteins are molecules made up of 20 kinds of amino acids. In cells, hundreds of amino acids may be linked to form long chains called polypeptide molecules. Two or more polypeptides may be joined to make a particular protein. The kind and sequence of amino acids make the shape of one polypeptide different from another. Shapes of proteins are related to their particular functions. Recall from Chapter 4, for example, the importance of the shape of enzymes, which govern every cellular reaction.

All organisms make proteins. Consider two simple organisms, *Amoeba* and *Paramecium*. Both of these unicellular forms take in basically the same raw materials. What makes one cell different from the other? The answer is the kinds of enzymes and other proteins each contains. Because cells have different sets of enzymes, they use their raw materials in different ways. Their chemical reactions vary; as a result, they have unique features.

Multicellular organisms differ as well, and for the same reason. Individual organisms of the same species have many of the same proteins. Your hemoglobin is the same as the hemoglobin of any other human being; your pet dog's hemoglobin, however, is different. Similarity of proteins is one way scientists identify the species of newly discovered organisms. However, even among species there can be variations in proteins. Some human beings, for example, have sickle cell anemia. Their hemoglobin differs from normal hemoglobin, but it is still human hemoglobin and not like that of any other species.

Figure 9-9 This polypeptide was formed by six amino acids. The shaded areas show where amino acids are bonded chemically to form the polypeptide.

Objectives

Discuss the evidence for the fact that DNA codes for proteins.

Demonstrate an understanding of the DNA code.

Prepare

Key Concepts
The relationship between DNA as a code and protein formation is established. Genes are defined and their roles in protein synthesis and the genetic code are described.

Key Terms
codon

Materials
- Gather supplies needed for Minilab 2. Obtain test tubes and ethanol. Purchase testes material. See page 239 for sources of salmon testes.

1 Focus

Objectives
The objectives are listed on the student page. Remind students to preview these objectives as a guide to this numbered section.

Analogy
Write out a sentence that uses only three-letter words and one that uses only four-letter words. Students are to pick the four letters they wish to use. Is this a difficult task? Explain to students that their cells are busy doing almost the same thing. L1 LEP

2 Teach

Using Science Terms
Review the meaning of the terms *protein, amino acid, polypeptide,* and *enzyme.* Ask students to correctly use each word in a sentence. Have them explain how all four terms are related to one another. LEP

PROGRAM RESOURCES

Teacher Classroom Resources
Study Guide, pp. 52-54 L1
Concept Mapping, p. 9 L1 LEP
Investigating Living Systems, Lab 23, p. 91 L2

MEETING INDIVIDUAL NEEDS

Challenge students working at or above grade level to record the sequence of amino acids present in normal human hemoglobin. Ask them to identify the one amino acid in the sequence that differs in a person with sickle-cell anemia. Have them also determine the limitations that are imposed on a person with sickle-cell anemia. L2

Genetics and PKU: The proposal that genes carry the information that codes for proteins was made by English doctor Archibald Garrod. He studied the disorder phenylketonuria and hypothesized that the disease was caused by a lack of enzymes that should have been made if the proper genes were present. He was correct in his hypothesis. Today we know that the disorder is due to the lack of the enzyme phenylalanine hydroxylase, which converts phenylalanine to tyrosine. It is a recessive genetic disorder. About two percent of the U.S. population carries the recessive gene in its heterozygous state. Phenylalanine, when not converted to tyrosine, is converted by another enzyme to a toxic substance and results in mental retardation to the individual if no medical or dietary treatment is provided.

Chalkboard Example

To convey the "one-gene one-enzyme" concept, use the following example on the board: (a) Draw the conversion of phenylalanine to tyrosine as a chemical reaction. Above the arrow, include the word *enzyme*. (b) Draw the same reaction but leave off the word *enzyme*. Ask students whether the reaction will or will not occur. (It will not.) Ask them to explain their answers.

Relationship Between Proteins and Genes Proteins are unique. Genes are unique. Could there be a relationship between genes and proteins? Perhaps the role of genes is to carry information for the synthesis of proteins. That idea was first proposed early in this century, when a physician noted that several inherited diseases result from the absence of a necessary enzyme or the presence of a defective enzyme (remember, enzymes are proteins). Normal individuals who have at least one dominant gene make normal enzymes and do not have the disease. Individuals who have two recessive genes do not produce the normal enzyme and have the disease. Thus, there was evidence, based on analysis of family histories, that genes are associated with synthesis of proteins.

Genes Direct Protein Synthesis In 1941, researchers learned that each gene contains information for the synthesis of a particular enzyme. Since that time, it has been learned that genes contain information for making not only enzymes, but also all other kinds of proteins. Because many proteins are made of two or more different polypeptides, each gene must control the synthesis of a particular polypeptide. Hemoglobin, the protein that carries oxygen in your blood, is a protein composed of four polypeptide chains—two of one kind and two of another. Two genes are involved, each coding for the synthesis of one kind of polypeptide. After the polypeptides are synthesized, they join to form hemoglobin.

Thinking Lab

DESIGN AN EXPERIMENT

How can crop plants be genetically engineered to produce higher yields?

Background
Scientists can remove DNA from bacteria that kill insect pests and inject it into plant cells. They coat microscopic metal particles with bacterial DNA and shoot them into plant cells with a tiny gun. As these cells reproduce, this bacterial DNA is incorporated into the new plant cells. The bacterial DNA codes for a substance that kills only the insects that are plant pests, such as moth larvae. When moth larvae feed on plant tissue that includes cells with bacterial DNA, they die. Other insects, however, are not affected. By incorporating bacterial DNA into plant cells, scientists can give plants traits that they do not ordinarily have in order to protect them from pest organisms.

You Try It
Weeds can reduce crop yields by 70 percent. **Design an experiment** similar to the one described to produce crop plants resistant to herbicides, chemicals that kill plants. Farmers would benefit from these plants because they could selectively kill weeds without harming crop plants. Fewer chemicals would result in less harm to the environment. Think about how cells take in materials, how cells reproduce, and how DNA replicates to guide your design. What would be the advantages of crops that are resistant to herbicides? What would be the disadvantages of such plants? Think about how they would affect other organisms in the environment.

238 ‎ CHEMISTRY OF THE GENE

Thinking Lab

DESIGN AN EXPERIMENT

Purpose
Students will explain the process by which crop plants can be genetically engineered.

Skills
design an experiment, form a hypothesis

Teaching Strategies
• Before they have read this lab, ask students to imagine that they are farmers who grow tomatoes. Ask them what would be ideal characteristics of the plant for the most profit from the crop. Explain that biotechnology has created plants that have some of these traits.

Answers
Advantages: Plants that are free of diseases, pests, and have other ideal characteristics will be easier and less costly to care for. Disadvantages: The public will have to be reassured that genetically engineered plants are safe.

✔ **Assessment**
Knowledge: Ask students to summarize what they have learned about the techniques of genetic engineering and the issues involved in this lab.

The DNA Code

Now you know that genes code for polypeptides. But what exactly are genes? At this point, let's define a gene as a segment of a DNA molecule that carries the code for the synthesis of a particular polypeptide. Polypeptides are composed of amino acids. The sequence and kinds of amino acids make one polypeptide different from another. Therefore, a gene must carry a code for putting particular amino acids together in a certain order. What part of DNA might carry the code? Only the sequence of base pairs along a DNA molecule varies. Experiments have shown that it is this sequence of bases along one of the two chains of a DNA molecule that carries the code.

Coding for Proteins   There are 20 amino acids, but DNA contains only four kinds of bases. Thus, a single base cannot represent an amino acid. Likewise, a sequence of two bases in a row such as AA, CG, TA, or GT cannot represent an amino acid. The four bases taken two at a time yield only 16 possible sequences. Considering three bases at a time, however, gives more than the 20 combinations needed. In fact, it provides 64 possible combinations of bases. Think of the 26 letters in the English alphabet. They can be combined in various ways to make thousands of words. Experiments have shown that three bases in a row do act as the code for amino acids. Each set of three bases representing an amino acid is known as a **codon**. Because there are 64 possible codons and only 20 amino acids, some amino acids have more than one codon. The cell "reads" these codons, and links together certain amino acids to form a particular polypeptide. DNA language in the nucleus is converted to protein language in the cytoplasm.

Minilab 2

What does DNA look like?

DNA is pictured as a coiled helix in most diagrams. What does it look like in a test tube? Extract DNA from salmon testes using the following procedure:

1. Add 1 mL of cold ethanol to the cold test tube of salmon testes preparation given to you by your teacher. Add the ethanol by letting it run slowly down the inside of the test tube. A layer of ethanol should float on the salmon testes preparation.
2. Use a stirring rod to stir at the point where the two liquids come together. The DNA will cling to the stirring rod.

Analysis   What does DNA look like? DNA can be extracted more easily from rapidly dividing cells. What does this tell you about salmon testes cells?

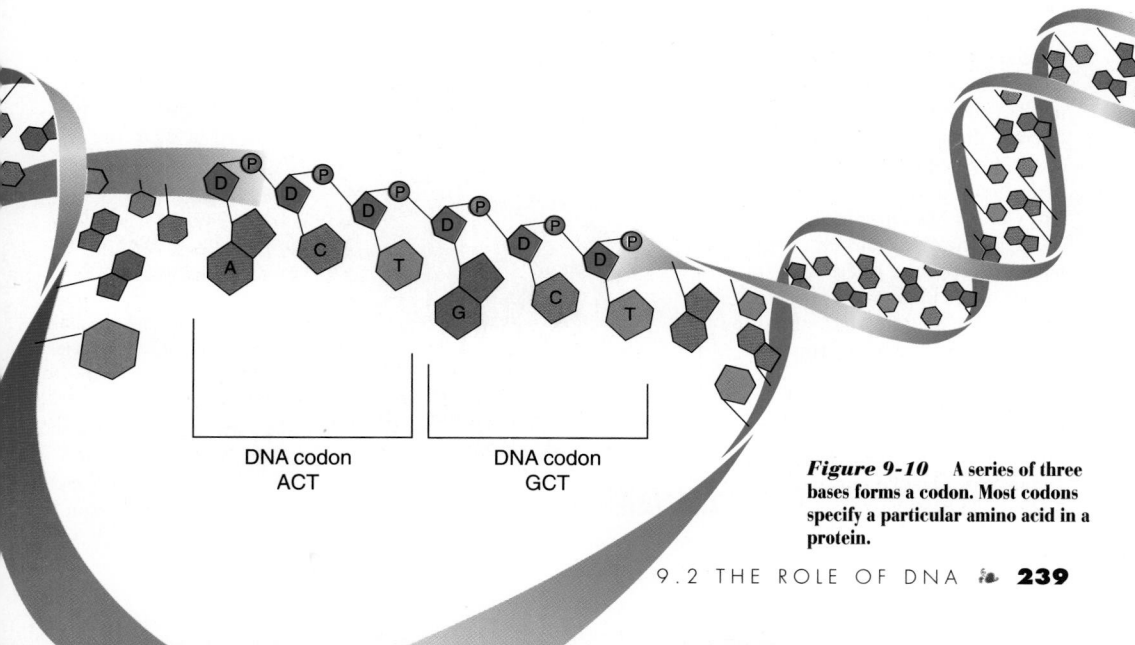

Figure 9-10   A series of three bases forms a codon. Most codons specify a particular amino acid in a protein.

Minilab 2

Purpose
Students will see DNA and spool it in their test tubes.

Skills
observe and infer, interpret data

Teaching Strategies
- Salmon testes prepared for spooling may be purchased from biological supply companies.
- Prepare solutions by slowly adding 0.5 mL (10 drops) sodium acetate to 0.5 mL salmon testes solution. Mix gently.
- Because the amounts of solution are small, 15-mL test tubes work best.
- Keep all solutions in refrigerator or on ice until they are ready to be used.
- 95% ethanol, Everclear, or isopropyl alcohol can be used.
- The precipitated DNA can be removed from the rod, blotted on paper towels, and dried.
- Coffee stirrers or pipettes may be used instead of glass rods.

Expected Results
DNA will form a thin, white thread of gelatin-like substance on the stirring rod.

Answers
1. thin white thread of gelatin-like substance
2. They are rapidly dividing.

✔ Assessment
Portfolio: This extraction of DNA is called "spooling." Ask students to write in their journals why this is an appropriate term for this lab. They should include this entry in their portfolios. The DNA extracted is like a thread. The stirring tool used is like a spool on which the thread is wound.

PROJECT

Amino Acid Diagrams: Use references to determine the names and structural formulas for the 20 different important amino acids. Make a set of poster-sized diagrams. Have students do the research, others do the printing, and others be responsible for the hanging or mounting of the diagrams.

COOP LEARN

STUDENT JOURNAL

The following two statements are no longer scientifically accurate but are commonly heard among nonscientists. Research these two statements and explain why they are indeed "out of date." (1) Science is now beginning to crack the genetic code. (2) Everyone has his or her own unique genetic code. **L1**

Purpose

The feature emphasizes the fact that the DNA code uses a three-letter system. Three nitrogen bases are required to code for one amino acid. Initial research work to break this code is described.

Teaching Strategies

- Have students use the table that appears on page 241 to interpret Khorana's work by asking them to name the specific amino acids coded for by AGA and GAG.
- Have students determine what amino acids are coded for by AG and GA. What might be the significance of this finding?

Possible Answers

1. Possible answers may suggest that each scientist attempts to answer a hypothesis that may be similar to hypotheses of other scientists. Also, scientists must be able to verify and reproduce the same findings and data as those reported. The more confirmation from different scientists, the more confidence one can place in the hypothesis and its data.
2. Marshall Nirenberg worked with the RNA sequence UUU-UUUUUU and discovered that the amino acid phenylalanine was coded at ribosomes. Severo Ochoa was able to synthesize the formation of RNA with the use of an enzyme called polynucleotide phosphorylase.

Going Further

Allow students to practice using the DNA code by providing them with other triplet series of nitrogen base codons and having them convert these codons to amino acids. **L1**

The Genetic Code Table 9.1 shows the various codons and the amino acids they represent. All but two amino acids are represented by two or more codons. In codons that are synonyms, the first two nucleotides are usually the same. Valine, for example, is coded for by four different codons, but all begin with the two nucleotides cytosine and adenine. Notice that three of the 64 codons do not represent amino acids. These are the codons at the end of a gene. They act as stop signals, like periods at the end of sentences, that signify the end of the code for a particular polypeptide. It is important to understand that the codons are read in only one direction. Reading the codon in reverse does not result in the same amino acid. In Table 9.1, the codon for serine is AGC, whereas the codon for alanine is CGA. The nucleotides are arranged in a specific order and read in one direction only.

The DNA code is a universal one. That is, with rare exceptions, a codon representing a given amino acid in one organism represents the same amino acid in another organism. This tells us that the DNA code must have arisen very early in the evolution of life and then been passed down unaltered to all later life forms. How was DNA passed down to later life forms? Replication of DNA ensured that exact copies of DNA were made. These copies were passed on to offspring unaltered.

HISTORY CONNECTION

Har Gobind Khorana

Cracking any code can be a monumental task or a simple one, depending on how complex the initial code happens to be or what equipment is available for decoding. For scientists who were trying to crack the genetic code, the task was indeed monumental. In the early 1960s, a biochemist named Har Gobind Khorana synthesized small nucleic acid molecules in the laboratory. Nucleic acids were known at the time to carry genetic information, and the exact structure of some nucleic acid molecules was already determined. Khorana was able to produce an artificial molecule in which two or three nucleotides were repeated over and over in a known sequence. For example, one sequence was AGAGAGAGAGAG. When Khorana combined his synthetic nucleic acids with the proper materials, these acids caused proteins to be synthesized just as proteins are

made in the cell. By comparing the proteins made with the known structure of these synthetic acids, Khorana was able to determine which portions of the nucleic acid were the codes for each protein. For example, the molecule in which A and G were repeated over and over resulted in the production of two amino acids made by the codons AGA and GAG. For this work on the genetic code, Har Gobind Khorana shared a Nobel Prize for Medicine in 1968 with two other researchers.

1. **Writing About Biology:** Explain why many scientific discoveries are made by several people working together.
2. **Explore Further:** Find out who shared the Nobel Prize with Khorana, and what each person contributed to the final result.

240 CHEMISTRY OF THE GENE

PORTFOLIO

Ask students to make a large diagram of a typical animal cell. Most of the detail should be left out except for the nucleus, cytoplasm, and cell membrane. Include labels for these three parts. Have them add the following statements to their diagrams: (a) site of DNA; (b) site of free nucleotide codons; (c) site of new protein formation under direction of DNA; (d) site of DNA replication. Each statement should have clearly marked locations within the cell. **L1**

Table 9.1 The DNA Code

First Base in Codon	Second Base in Codon				Third Base in Codon
	A	G	T	C	
A	phenylalanine	serine	tyrosine	cysteine	A
	phenylalanine	serine	tyrosine	cysteine	G
	leucine	serine	stop	stop	T
	leucine	serine	stop	tryptophan	C
G	leucine	proline	histidine	arginine	A
	leucine	proline	histidine	arginine	G
	leucine	proline	glutamine	arginine	T
	leucine	proline	glutamine	arginine	C
T	isoleucine	threonine	asparagine	serine	A
	isoleucine	threonine	asparagine	serine	G
	isoleucine	threonine	lysine	arginine	T
	methionine	threonine	lysine	arginine	C
C	valine	alanine	aspartate	glycine	A
	valine	alanine	aspartate	glycine	G
	valine	alanine	glutamate	glycine	T
	valine	alanine	glutamate	glycine	C

Figure 9-11 What do you and this leaf insect have in common? Both the insect and you have DNA that codes for the same amino acids.

Science, Technology, and Society

Telomeres: Telomeres were hypothesized to exist as long ago as the early 1940s. They were discovered in the early 1980s to actually exist in many different species, but only recently have telomeres been found on human chromosomes. What are telomeres, where are they found, and what do they do? Telomeres are the tip ends of all chromosomes. They consist of the nucleotide sequence TTA GGG. This sequence of bases does not carry any genes. Instead, it is a region on the chromosome that directs the cell not to continue to add bases when DNA replicates. The discovery that more than 100 different species of organisms all show telomere caps of exactly the same base sequences of TTA GGG is additional evidence that DNA has been around for as long as life itself.

Bioethics

Data Must Be Reproducible: David Baltimore was appointed president of Rockefeller University in 1990. He resigned this position in 1991. Baltimore is a noted molecular biologist who was awarded the Nobel Prize at the age of 37. Why his quick departure from the university? Much of the problem centered around a paper that he published in 1986 with several other scientists. Other labs were unable to produce the same data as were reported by Baltimore and his group. Scientific findings must be reproducible; otherwise the results can be questioned. This pressure over "faulty" reporting caused his resignation. He has since returned to working in a laboratory and is now focusing on HIV research.

MEETING INDIVIDUAL NEEDS

Ask those students working below grade level to do the following task: (a) name the amino acids that are coded for by the following sequence of bases—TAC, CGG, GAG, AAT, TAG; (b) name all possible nitrogen base sequences in DNA if a polypeptide had the following sequence of amino acids—valine, proline, glutamine, tryptophan, methionine.

Figure Caption Question

Why is this ability important to the preservation of species? DNA is unique to each species and is passed from parent to offspring, a way to maintain the integrity of a species.

3 Assess

Check for Understanding

Ask students to explain how the following are related:
(a) amino acids, polypeptides, and proteins;
(b) genes, enzymes, and proteins; and
(c) DNA bases, codon, and proteins.

Reteach

Ask students to prepare an outline of the ideas found in Section 9.2. They are to use all main headings and subheadings.

Extension

Have students determine through the use of Table 9.1 on page 241 which codons are synonyms. Have them list the synonym codons with the amino acids they code for.

✔ Assessment

Skill: Provide students with the opportunity to decode a series of nine nitrogen bases into their proper amino acids. Ask students to form these amino acids into a polypeptide. They are to label the following: nitrogen base, codon, amino acid, polypeptide. L1

4 Close

Analogy

Provide students with the Morse code. Have them write out a code sentence using only letters coded for by three symbols (dots and/or dashes) and then translate the sentence into actual letters. Have students make parallels between the Morse code and what they have learned about DNA and its coding pattern. L1

Figure 9-12   These fossil organisms passed on their DNA code to their offspring. Why is this ability important to the preservation of species?

LOOKING AHEAD

DISCOVERING THE STRUCTURE of DNA and the nature of genetic information is only one step in understanding how cells produce proteins. Although you know that genes code for the assembly of polypeptides, and that polypeptides make up proteins, how does this information get from the DNA in a cell's nucleus to the cytoplasm or the organelles where proteins are synthesized? In the next chapter, you will study the means by which cells decipher the code to make polypeptides and where this synthesis takes place. You will also see how subtle changes in DNA can lead to variation among organisms.

Section Review

Understanding Concepts
1. Identical twins have exactly the same sets of DNA. How does that fact support the idea that genes code for synthesis of proteins?
2. Several human diseases are associated with production of hemoglobin. How would you expect the hemoglobin of diseased people to compare with that of normal people?

3. What would be the minimal number of different genes between normal people and those having a disease associated with hemoglobin? Explain.
4. **Skill Review—Sequencing:** Use Table 9.1 to sequence the amino acids coded for by the following sequence of codons: GAG CTC AAC. For more help, see

Organizing Information in the **Skill Handbook.**
5. **Thinking Critically:** How can you explain that two genes can vary in terms of one nucleotide pair yet code for exactly the same polypeptide?

Answers to Section Review

1. Identical twins have the same phenotypes. Phenotypes result from proteins and genes code for proteins. Therefore, they have the same genes, which are composed of DNA, and DNA must code for synthesis of proteins.
2. The amino acid sequence of one or both of the polypeptide chains of hemoglobin would be different.
3. Only one gene need be different. One different gene would result in one of the two hemoglobin chains being different, affecting the hemoglobin molecule as a whole.
4. **Skill Review—Sequencing:** The sequence is leucine—glutamate—leucine.
5. **Thinking Critically:** The two different nucleotides may act as codons for the same amino acid.

BIOLOGY, TECHNOLOGY, AND SOCIETY

Biotechnology

Transgenic Organisms—What Are They and Who Owns Them?

Suppose you were given an assignment to redesign any type of living thing. What would you redesign? Would you design a human who is resistant to all disease, or a tomato the size of a basketball? What other possibilities can you think of? Is this something that will never be possible? What do you think? The possibility of redesigning living things may sound like science fiction, but the opportunity for accomplishing this is here today, thanks to genetic engineering. Scientists already have the ability to redesign living things. They can remove genes from one organism and insert them into another. This provides them with an opportunity to place desirable gene traits from one living thing into another living thing that is missing those traits. Organisms that have genes derived from other organisms are called transgenic organisms.

What are some examples of this type of technology? Scientists have perfected transgenic tobacco and tomato plants that are resistant to virus attack. A virus infection could reduce crop yield or destroy an entire crop. Resistance to a disease-causing virus, therefore, increases the harvest of a particular crop. Potato, cotton, and corn plants are now designed with built-in insect resistance. Moth and butterfly larvae and adult beetles that once fed upon these plants no longer do so. Tomatoes also are now available with genes inserted that slow down the process of spoilage. This makes storage, shipping, and stocking of tomatoes in supermarkets less of a problem. The chances of seeing a rotten tomato may be reduced in just a year or two. Are scientists using this new technology with animals, too? Animals such as goats, sheep, and cows are being used to produce milk that contains high levels of chemicals that can be used against hemophilia, cancer, and emphysema. These transgenic animals may even be used to form a protein that helps to break up blood clots.

An interesting question arises from the formation of all transgenic organisms. Who owns them? Do scientists or the companies that have done the research on producing them own the organisms that they have created? The Supreme Court of the United States was asked this very question. According to the court's decision, the ownership or patent for these organisms does indeed belong to the company or scientist who designed them through research. The court stated that a "patent can be granted on anything under the sun which can be made by man." This decision is one reason that companies today are investing millions of dollars in research to produce transgenic organisms. It is hoped that the tools of biotechnology will help scientists produce new drugs or improve food production and quality for all of us.

CHAPTER 9 CHEMISTRY OF THE GENE ❦ **243**

---

2. Many students may feel that this is too much tampering with life when and if new organisms are created. Others may be fearful of creating organisms that could prove harmful to other life forms including humans. Those in favor of this research may feel that new life forms may provide new products that can be used by humans.

3. Student answers may vary. Selective breeding is typically conducted among members of the same species. Transgenic organisms are not limited to similar species but involve the transferring of genes from one species to another.

4. Students' answers are limited only by their imaginations. Examples might include: Tomatoes Forever, or Cornacopia.

Going Further

Have students correspond with some of the genetic engineering companies and ask for information regarding the type of transgenic organisms they are researching and what they hope to accomplish with their research. **L2**

Biotechnology

Purpose
The concept of altering the genetic makeup of an organism is introduced. The feature expands on the idea that all life forms contain the same genetic codes, and therefore the ability to move genes from one organism to another is not without a scientific basis. Once new genes are introduced into different life forms by scientists, who owns them? This question is answered in this feature.

Background
A specific example of work on transgenic plants may be used to demonstrate the nature of this type of research. An herbicide called "Roundup" contains a chemical called glyphosate. It is used by farmers to kill off unwanted weeds. Unfortunately, it also kills off many commercial plants. However, researchers have found a line of hybrid petunia plants that are resistant to the herbicide. Their task is to introduce the gene properties for this resistance into commercial crops.

Teaching Strategies
- Have the class work in groups. Assign them the task of redesigning several different life forms in any manner that they wish. However, they must defend or explain their reasoning.
- Ask class members to prepare a debate as to who should own transgenic organisms. Limit the debate teams to three students per side.

Possible Answers
1. Student answers may vary. Transgenic may be the combination of two words, *trans* for transfer and *genic* for gene. Transgenic organisms have had the genes from some other life form transferred into their gene makeup.

CHAPTER 9

Issues

Purpose

Students will have an opportunity to evaluate the information gained by mapping the human genetic code. Will this new information be helpful or possibly harmful for each individual?

Background

It will take 15 years to map out the entire 100 000 genes found on the 46 human chromosomes. The information gained will identify genes that contribute to the development of many illnesses and will result in better preventive and therapeutic measures.

Teaching Strategies

- Have students work in cooperative groups to research the following:
  (1) define the terms *genome, genetic disease, lethal;*
  (2) provide examples of genetic diseases;
  (3) construct a large diagram depicting one human chromosome and add to it any of the gene locations already known and established. Each group can be assigned a different chromosome number, and this will provide a large display that could be exhibited along the classroom walls.
  References may have to be provided.
- Prepare a debate between student groups—those in favor of releasing information about a person's genome and those opposed to releasing this type of information.
- Have interested students correspond with a variety of insurance companies to determine their policies regarding insured people who find out that they have a genetic disorder.

1. **Writing About Biology:** Why is the term "transgenic" very appropriate for genetically engineered organisms?
2. **Issue:** Should scientists use biotechnology to develop new organisms?
3. **Explore Further:** Scientists have been selectively breeding new plants and animals for centuries. Is the formation of transgenic organisms different or similar? Explain.
4. **Solve the Problem:** Design product names for the following genetically engineered organisms: tomatoes that do not rot, oranges with more juice, corn cobs with more kernels.

Issues

Genetic Profiles and Denying Health Care and Employment

You are ready to try out for the football team. You have been working out over the summer and have gained enough weight not to make a fool of yourself on the football field. You go to the doctor for a physical exam, and you are ready to start practice on the first day of school. But wait. The doctor ran a test from a sample of your blood and found out that you carry a gene for bone cancer. The school, after receiving this report, is not willing to insure you against injury. No insurance means that you cannot play football.

The situation just described is fictional, but it may become a possibility in the future. How? Scientists will soon be able to read the genes on all 46 human chromosomes. This will enable them to analyze each person's genome (all their genes) for genetic diseases.

Is this new knowledge about your genetic makeup good news or bad news? Let's look at the good news first. If you find out at an early age that you are at high risk genetically for a particular disease, you may be inclined to have checkups more often. You might even wish to have a specific organ removed before it becomes a problem. This will work, of course, only if the organ is not vital for life. You may wish to change or alter your diet or begin certain therapy programs that may help reduce the effects of a certain disease. The possibility of passing this genetic disease on to your offspring is also an important piece of information to help you decide whether to have children. Doesn't it seem that knowing in advance about the possibility of having a certain genetic disease is a good thing?

Unfortunately, such information may not be all to your benefit. Once your genetic makeup becomes known, it could be used against you. For example, say you apply for life or health insurance. The insurance company may decide not to insure you because you have a gene that results in a disease called Huntington's chorea. This disease usually does not show up until a person is about 40 years old. But in the meantime, you may break your arm in a fall, or come down with a viral disease, and have no insurance to pay for your medical bills. What if you are denied insurance coverage because you may come down with a genetic disease in your forties, but meanwhile you contract cancer in your twenties? What if a future employer obtains your genetic profile and finds out about genetic diseases in your genome? Will this employer hire you, or hire someone who is less at risk of contracting a genetic disease? Often, the cost of health insurance is the responsibility of the employer. It eventually may cost employers more if they hire employees with higher risks of becoming ill than those who have lower risks. Employers could discriminate against people because of their genetic makeup.

Should a person be informed about his or her own genome? How will a person react to knowing that he or she carries the gene for some lethal genetic disease? Is your genome your own private business or are others entitled to know all about your genome, like they know your social security number?

Some researchers believe that information about genomes should only be available to individuals who are at risk of passing a genetic

disease on to a future child. These people may have a parent or relative with a certain disease, and wish to know what their chances are of carrying a defective gene. Genetic counselors work with families to help them make decisions about whether to have children or not. However, many people may carry a defective gene without being aware of it. Researchers don't believe a person should be forced to find out information about his or her genome if such information is not wanted.

Understanding the Issue

1. Should a person's genome be protected by law as something private? Explain your answer.
2. Huntington's chorea, a genetic disease, causes early death. By the time a person finds out that he or she has the disease, the gene that causes the disease may have already been passed on to his or her children. (a) Would

you want to know if you have the gene for Huntington's chorea? Explain your answer. (b) Would you want to know if your children have received this lethal gene from you? Explain your answer. (c) As a child from a parent with this disease, would you want to know if you are or are not carrying the gene? Explain your answer.
3. If you are told that you have the gene for Huntington's chorea, would you want your health insurance company or your employer to know this? Explain why.

Readings

- Brownlee, Shannon. "The Assurances of Genes: Is Disease Prediction a Boon or a Nightmare?" *U.S. News and World Report,* July 23, 1990, p. 57.
- Zoler, Mitchel L. "Genetic Tests: Can We Afford the Answers?" *Medical World News,* Jan. 1991, p. 32.

CHAPTER 9 CHEMISTRY OF THE GENE 245

CHAPTER 9

Possible Answers

1. Students may have opposite views. Some may feel a person's genome should remain private just as personal information may only be released at a person's discretion. Others may feel that this information should be available to doctors so that they can anticipate and prepare for future medical problems.
2. (a) Yes—so that I can gain proper medical attention for myself. No—I wouldn't want to know. (b) Yes—so that they can also benefit from any advances made in the treatment of the disease. No—the guilt associated with knowing that I transmitted the disease to them is too great a burden to live with. (c) Yes—so that I in turn do not have children who may receive the defective gene. No—I would be willing to take my chances and want children of my own regardless.
3. Yes, if the employer and/or insurance company already has a known policy when dealing with such cases. No, especially if not sure how they might react to this information.

Going Further

Have students read the articles mentioned at the end of this feature and have them write a report, which may be placed in their portfolios. Students may be interested in finding out about the problems that faced Woody Guthrie during his battle with Huntington's chorea. **L2**

CHAPTER REVIEW

Summary

Summary statements can be used by students to review the major concepts of the chapter.

Language of Biology

Answers should go beyond defining the terms. Accept any reasonable answer that uses the term correctly and in the proper context.

Understanding Concepts

1. The DNA of the heat-killed smooth cells was not altered by the heat. That DNA entered some of the rough cells. Some of the DNA carried a code for production of a capsule, which some rough cells began producing.
2. The DNA of the phages had already been injected into the bacteria.
3. If the two chains of the double helix were unwound, the molecule would have the shape of a ladder.
4. The original molecule should first be shown. The other chain would have the nucleotide sequence ATC CTC TGA. The parent molecule should then be shown unzipping, and complementary nucleotides should then be shown being added. A final drawing should show two complete, double-stranded DNA replicas.
5. Brother and sister would have more similar proteins because they have more genes in common than do two cousins.
6. Some proteins consist of more than one polypeptide. Thus, several genes may be responsible for the production of one protein.
7. Only the sequence of base pairs along a DNA molecule varies. The sugars and phosphates are identical along the entire molecule.
8. A codon is three nucleotides in a row that represents one particular amino acid. A polypeptide is a sequence of many amino acids. The sequence is determined by the sequence of codons in DNA.

9. A DNA molecule consists of many genes, each coding for a particular polypeptide. The stop codon is a signal indicating where the code for a particular polypeptide ends.

Applying Concepts

10. Adding a nucleotide would change the sequence of codons from the point of addition to the rest of the gene. From that point on, the polypeptide would consist of the wrong sequence of amino acids.

11. The gene consists of 100 codons; 300 nucleotides (excluding the stop signal).
12. People who are homozygous recessive cannot make a needed protein.
13. DNA from bacteria that can synthesize the needed amino acid can be extracted. That DNA could be added to a culture containing the necessary raw materials for making the amino acid. Bacteria that cannot make the amino acid can be added to the culture. If some of the bacteria survive, it is because they have been transformed.

Summary

Griffith's discovery of bacterial transformation led to later experiments showing that DNA seemed to be the chemical of which genes are composed. Hershey and Chase's experiments made use of the reproduction of phages to show finally that genes are indeed made of DNA, not protein.

Watson and Crick's model shows DNA to be a double helix composed of two chains of nucleotides joined together by hydrogen bonds between nitrogen bases. Adenine can bond only to thymine, and cytosine can bond only to guanine. During replication of DNA, the two chains separate, and each chain acts as a template, guiding the formation of a new partner chain. Because of base-pairing requirements, two replica DNA molecules are produced from the parent molecule.

Evidence based first on logic and later on experimentation revealed that genes, segments along a DNA molecule, carry a code for the synthesis of a polypeptide. Each codon represents one amino acid in the polypeptide chain.

Language of Biology

Write a sentence that shows your understanding of each of the following terms.

adenine	guanine
bacteriophage	nucleotide
codon	thymine
cytosine	

Understanding Concepts

1. In terms of DNA, explain what happened to living rough cells when they were mixed with heat-killed smooth cells. (Hint: DNA is stable under high temperatures, whereas other organic molecules are not.)
2. Explain why the phages that were dislodged from bacterial cells in a blender consisted of just their outer coats.
3. How is the idea of DNA as a ladder related to the double helix model?
4. Use a series of drawings to illustrate the events of replication of a DNA molecule, assuming one chain of the parent molecule has the nucleotide sequence TAG GAG ACT.
5. Which two people, brother and sister or two cousins, would be more similar in terms of proteins? Why?
6. Explain why it is more precise to say that a gene carries a code for the synthesis of a polypeptide than for a protein.

7. Why is it logical to assume that the sequence of base pairs of DNA, rather than the sugars and/or phosphates, carries the code for synthesizing polypeptides?
8. Explain the relationship among codons, amino acids, and a polypeptide.
9. Why must stop codons be present along a DNA molecule?

Applying Concepts

10. Suppose an error occurred in replication of a gene so that one nucleotide was added. How would that error affect the polypeptide coded for by that gene?
11. A gene carries the code for a polypeptide consisting of 100 amino acids. How many codons are in the gene? How many nucleotides?
12. PKU is a genetic disease resulting in a form of mental retardation. It occurs in people having two recessive genes. Normal people are either homozygous dominant or heterozygous. What is the likely cause of the disease?

13. Most bacteria of a certain type can synthesize an amino acid they need from raw materials that enter their cells. Some forms of these bacteria cannot. Assuming you had the equipment necessary to extract DNA from bacteria, how could you demonstrate the idea of bacterial transformation?

14. Bacteria are growing and reproducing on culture dishes in a lab. Colonies of the bacteria are clearly visible on the medium in the dishes. A biologist discovers one morning that the bacteria in many dishes have disappeared and that no other organisms are visible on the medium. What is a likely reason for the disappearance of the bacteria?

15. Suppose a molecule of DNA has replicated but one error occurred and was not corrected or repaired. What will the DNA molecules produced after the next replication and in future replications be like? What might the result of this error be?

16. **History Connection:** Why is an understanding of chemistry often important in biology? Use the information in the History Connection to explain your answer.

17. **Art Connection:** Sculpture is one art form in which the shapes of natural forms such as chemicals can be expressed. Name an art form in which the following could be expressed: colors, light, language, relationships.

Lab Interpretation

18. **Investigation:** Based on your paper model of DNA, design on paper another model of DNA. Use toothpicks for chemical bonds and various kinds of candy or dry cereal for the molecules. Give a brief set of directions for putting together your DNA molecule. Trade your directions with another group. See if they can visualize and draw the DNA molecule you designed.

19. **Thinking Lab:** Corn plants are killed by a specific bacterial disease. A scientist discovers a weed that is resistant to this bacterial disease. Using genetics, what could the scientist do to make corn plants have the same resistance to the disease as the weeds?

20. **Minilab 1:** You are starting your own business, a greenhouse nursery, in which you will grow and sell houseplants. You have very little money to invest in this business. How could the principle of cloning help you save money?

21. **Minilab 2:** DNA can be more easily extracted from rapidly dividing cells. If you were going to extract DNA from cells other than the ones used in this Minilab, what other cells might you try?

Connecting Ideas

22. Transformation is an accident in which a bacterium receives a new gene. Because bacteria are haploid, all offspring of the transformed cell will have the trait coded for by the new gene. How might transformation be important to a population of bacteria?

23. Is replication of DNA an endergonic reaction? How do you know?

14. It is possible that the bacteria were destroyed by bacteriophages.

15. The DNA molecules produced thereafter will all contain the same error. The error could result in an inability to produce a protein, which might be harmful or cause death.

16. Khorana could not have deciphered the genetic code if he did not have a knowledge of chemistry.

17. Possible answers: colors—paintings; light—photography; language—poetry; relationships—a play or novel.

Lab Interpretation

18. Answers will vary. Students may make their model directions with items such as toothpicks pushed into miniature marshmallows, jelly beans, puffed rice, and other soft snack items.

19. Remove the DNA segment that confers resistance to the disease from the weed. Bombard corn plants with microscopic metal particles coated with the DNA removed from the weed. The corn plants will use the weed DNA as they form new cells with resistance to the bacterial disease.

20. You could buy 25 plants of several varieties and use cuttings of stems of these plants to start new plants rather than purchasing 100 of several varieties of plants.

21. onion root tips, testes from other animals, embryonic cells, fertilized eggs

Connecting Ideas

22. **Evolution:** The transformed bacteria might gain a trait that enables them to adapt more easily to their environment, thus improving their chances for survival.

23. **Uses of Energy:** DNA replication is endergonic. It requires both enzymes and ATP.

ORGANIZER

CHAPTER 10

SECTION	OBJECTIVES	TEXT LABS/FEATURES
10.1 Polypeptide Synthesis (3 days)	**Analyze** the process of transcription in prokaryotes and eukaryotes. **Sequence** the events that occur during translation. **Relate** genes and polypeptide synthesis to the expression of phenotypes.	**Thinking Lab:** Which parent provides the genes in organelle DNA? p. 256 **Investigation:** Modeling Cell Processes, p. 258
10.2 Sources of Variation (3 days)	**Infer** several ways in which genetic variation may arise. **Sequence** the events in a cell that lead to cancer. **Relate** techniques used in recombinant DNA technology and the uses of that technology.	**Minilab 1:** Can mutations be observed? p. 263 **History Connection:** Jumping Genes, p. 264 **Health Connection:** Dr. Jane C. Wright, p. 267 **Minilab 2:** Do biotechnology products help us? p. 269
BIOLOGY, TECHNOLOGY, AND SOCIETY		**Biotechnology:** DNA Fingerprinting—A New Weapon Against Crime, p. 271 **Career Connection:** Crime laboratory technician, p. 272 **Issues:** Dying with Dignity: Who Decides? p. 272

LAB MATERIALS

INVESTIGATION	MINILAB		ALTERNATE LAB
page 258 crayons construction paper magic markers paper punch poster board ruler string tape yarn	**page 263** labels microwave oven milk cartons peat pots (optional) plastic cups (optional) seeds, 2 different groups from same plant species soil vermiculite (optional) water bottle wood sticks	**page 269** alpha-amylase enzyme beaker Benedict's solution dropper graduated cylinder lab burner or hot plate labels starch solution test tubes thermal mitts	**page 266** chemicals, household, such as: detergent rubbing alcohol window cleaner distilled water dropper graduated cylinder labels onion bulbs, small ruler test tubes, 18 x 150 mm test-tube rack

TEACHER CLASSROOM RESOURCES	OTHER RESOURCES
Study Guide, pp. 55-56 **Concept Mapping,** p. 10 ***PLL:** *Modeling Protein Synthesis,* p. 55 ****ILS:** *tRNA and Protein Building,* p. 95	**Color Transparency 14:** *Transcription: DNA to RNA* **Color Transparency 15:** *Translation: RNA to Protein*
Study Guide, pp. 57-60 **Critical Thinking/Problem Solving:** *Mutations,* p. 10	***STVS:** *Viruses and Plant Diseases,* Plants and Simple Organisms (Disc 4, Side 1) ***STVS:** *Microinjecting Polygenes,* Plants and Simple Organisms (Disc 4, Side 1)
Assessment Materials **Chapter Assessment,** pp. 37-40 **Performance Assessment in Biology,** p. 20 **Alternate Assessment in the Science Classroom** **Computer Test Bank**	**Spanish Resources** **Cooperative Learning Resource Guide** **Videodisc Correlations** (to Optical Data's and Videodiscovery's videodiscs)

* Probing Levels of Life
** Investigating Living Systems

* Science Technology Videodisc Series

Key to Teaching Strategies

The following designations will help you decide which activities in the teacher margin are appropriate for your students.

L1 Level 1 activities should be within the ability range of all students.

L2 Level 2 activities should be within the ability range of the average to above-average student.

L3 Level 3 activities are designed for the ability range of above-average students.

LEP LEP activities are appropriate for Limited English Proficiency students.

COOP LEARN Cooperative Learning activities are designed for small group work.

ADDITIONAL RESOURCES

Infinite Voyage *Insects: The Ruling Class*
There are more insects than any other animal group. In this video, students can see the wide variety of insects and their roles in their environments.

Audiovisual
DNA Techniques, video, Films for the Humanities and Sciences.
Translating the Code, video, Frey Scientific.

Software
DNA: The Master Molecule (Part II), Apple 128K/MAC/IBM 256K, EME.
Gene Machine, Apple 64K, Queue.

FROM GENES TO PROTEINS

Chapter Overview

Students will continue their study of DNA, learning about the process of transcription as it occurs in both prokaryotes and eukaryotes. They will then find out how messenger RNA and transfer RNA work together during translation to synthesize the polypeptide coded for by the gene.

Next, students will come to understand the relationship between genotypes and phenotypes in terms of DNA and protein synthesis. They will find that the eukaryotic chromosome consists of multiple copies of some genes and that the majority of DNA is nonfunctional.

Sources of variation will be explored as students learn about mutations of genes and chromosomes, and gene duplications. They will study the genetic basis of cancer and will learn about recombinant DNA techniques.

KEY TERMS

anticodon	plasmid
carcinogen	point
clone	mutation
deletion	recombinant
exon	DNA
insertion	ribosomal
intron	RNA (rRNA)
messenger	transcription
RNA	transfer RNA
(mRNA)	(tRNA)
mutagen	translation
mutation	uracil
oncogene	

248

FROM GENES TO PROTEINS

ALBINO ORGANISMS, such as the rabbits shown in the large photo, have no color. Their tissues do not contain the pigments needed for normal coloration. Complete albinos have white or very pale fur, feathers, or hair. Their skin and eyes look pink, because there is no pigment to mask the red color of the blood vessels in the iris of the eye and the top layers of skin. You may be more familiar with partial albinos, such as domesticated ducks and geese, which have white feathers and pale skin but show some color in their eyes, beaks, or legs. Although albinism is unusual, it does occur in many organisms, including flowering plants, insects, rabbits, koalas, and humans.

The genes of albino organisms do not code for a normal enzyme that makes pigment. Since albinism is a recessive trait, an organism that shows normal coloration could have a gene for albinism, and that gene could be passed to the organism's offspring. Offspring that inherit a gene for albinism from each parent will express an albino phenotype.

How did genes for unusual traits like albinism develop? How do the cells of an organism follow the instructions contained in its DNA to manufacture proteins such as the enzyme that makes a pigment? In this chapter, you will find out how DNA is involved in protein synthesis. You will learn how genetic material can be altered, and what can happen as a result. You will also find out how geneticists have learned to alter DNA to develop organisms that have specific traits.

248

If a normal brown rabbit, like the one above, and an albino rabbit were side by side in a field, which would be more likely to escape the eye of a hungry hawk? Why do you think albinism is extremely rare in the wild?

Chapter Preview

249

Introducing the Chapter

Students have previously learned that many traits exist in one of two forms. Emphasize this point by calling their attention to the photographs on pages 248 and 249. Students know, too, that the traits brown and albino in rabbits are controlled by genes, and that genes are composed of DNA. Lead them into the chapter by posing questions such as the following: Assuming the gene for brown is dominant to the gene for albino, what are the possible genotypes of the brown rabbit? the albino? How, in terms of DNA, do the two alleles controlling color differ? How do alleles originate? Are the two phenotypes the result of different proteins? How do the genetic codes of the two alleles actually result in production of proteins, and how are proteins related to the phenotypes? **L1** **COOP LEARN**

Theme Development

The theme of unity within a diversity is exemplified as students come to see that the essential features of transcription and translation are common to all cells. The systems and interactions theme becomes apparent in the study of how the various cell structures and chemicals interact to produce the polypeptide coded for by a gene.

Tying to Previous Knowledge

This chapter is a logical extension of many aspects of genetics previously learned in this unit. Many ideas can now be more fully understood. Among them are how the genetic code is deciphered to produce a polypeptide, how new alleles and new genes arise, the chemical difference between alleles, and how particular combinations of alleles (genotypes) actually result in phenotypes.

ASSESSMENT PLANNER

Choose assessment strategies from the following pages to evaluate the progress of your students.

Assess, pp. 259-260, 270
Portfolio, pp. 255, 259, 260, 262, 263, 273
Alternate Lab, pp. 266-267
Thinking Lab, p. 256
Minilab 1, p. 263

Minilab 2, p. 269
Investigation, pp. 258-259
Chapter Review, pp. 274-275

Prepare

Key Concepts

Students will study how the genetic information in DNA is used to synthesize polypeptides and how DNA is related to the expression of genetic phenotypes. Transcription and translation will be studied in detail.

Key Terms

uracil, transcription, messenger RNA (mRNA), ribosomal RNA (rRNA), intron, exon, translation, transfer RNA (tRNA), anticodon

Materials

- Gather poster board and yarn for the Investigation.

1 Focus

Objectives

The objectives are listed on the student page. Remind students to preview these objectives as a guide to this numbered section.

Chalkboard Example

Draw a large cell outline on the chalkboard. Include two chromosomes in the nucleus and add two human gene traits (such as blood type and ear lobe shape) to the chromosomes. Ask students to (a) explain why the diagram oversimplifies gene and chromosome numbers in human cells; (b) speculate on how gene messages located in the nucleus are able to influence the appearance of these traits in the cell itself and in the proper tissues of a human. **L1**

Objectives

Analyze the process of transcription in prokaryotes and eukaryotes.

Sequence the events that occur during translation.

Relate genes and polypeptide synthesis to the expression of phenotypes.

10.1 Polypeptide Synthesis

As you grow, the cells that make up your body increase in number. When each cell reproduces, the genes it contains are replicated and passed to its daughter cells. You have learned that genes carry the instructions needed by each new cell to make its polypeptides. Each gene is a segment of a DNA molecule and consists of a chain of nucleotides. The information for making a polypeptide lies in the sequence of those nucleotides. You also know that the DNA needed for making most of a cell's proteins is located in the nucleus, but that proteins are synthesized outside the nucleus, at the ribosomes. Once scientists understood this much about the role of DNA in heredity, they began looking for the answers to two basic questions. First, how does the information in DNA get from the nucleus to the ribosomes? And once the information arrives, how is it used by the ribosomes to make the polypeptide it represents?

Transcription

Geneticists began to understand how the information in DNA moves into the cytoplasm when they discovered that another kind of nucleic acid, ribonucleic acid (RNA), is found not only in the nucleus, but also in the cytoplasm. They also learned that RNA forms part of the ribosomes and that cells actively making polypeptides contain more RNA than cells less active in polypeptide synthesis. These facts suggested that RNA, as well as DNA, is involved in the manufacture of proteins.

Structure of RNA Like DNA, RNA is a nucleic acid made up of a sugar, a phosphate, and four bases. Although there are several forms of RNA, each form shares three basic characteristics that distinguish it from DNA. First, RNA is usually composed of a single chain of nucleotides, rather than the double chain characteristic of DNA. Second, RNA contains the sugar ribose, rather than deoxyribose. Third, instead of the base thymine, RNA contains **uracil.**

Figure 10-1 The difference between thymine and uracil and between ribose and deoxyribose involves only a few atoms. Uracil and ribose in RNA take the places of thymine and deoxyribose in DNA.

Thymine   Uracil

Deoxyribose   Ribose

Formation of RNA Cells synthesize proteins as they are needed. When it is time to build a protein, the gene for each polypeptide in that protein is activated. Near each gene is a region of DNA that acts as a start signal for the synthesis of the needed polypeptide. A complex enzyme, like the one that unzips DNA during replication, binds to this region of DNA. Once the enzyme is attached, a series of events much like those of DNA replication begins. The two chains of the DNA begin to "unzip" at the start signal. Notice in Figure 10-2 that only one chain of the DNA molecule acts as a template for RNA. RNA nucleotides match up with the DNA template until a stop signal is reached. The RNA nucleotides bond together to form a single-stranded molecule of RNA, which breaks away from the DNA chain. The two DNA chains then rejoin.

250 🔬 FROM GENES TO PROTEINS

MEETING INDIVIDUAL NEEDS

For students who need help in correlating similarities and differences between DNA and RNA, ask them to build models of these molecules using colored gum drops and small pieces of toothpicks. For components that are similar in both molecules, such as phosphoric acid, adenine, cytosine, and guanine, have students use the same color gum drop. For components that differ between DNA and RNA, such as thymine, uracil, ribose, and deoxyribose, use different colored gum drops. Students should make a color key so that other students can verify if the correct component choices were used. **LEP**

COOP LEARN

Key

P = Phosphate
D = Deoxyribose
R = Ribose
A = Adenine
T = Thymine
G = Guanine
C = Cytosine
U = Uracil
= DNA backbone
= RNA backbone

DNA double helix

DNA strand

DNA strand

RNA strand

RNA strand

Figure 10-2 In order to make RNA, the DNA chains must be opened and copied. The accuracy of the RNA is assured by base pairing. The photograph shows many RNA molecules being produced from the same section of DNA. Magnification: 6700×

10.1 POLYPEPTIDE SYNTHESIS 🔹 **251**

2 Teach

Using Science Terms

Students should review, define, and provide an example, where appropriate, for the following terms: base, nucleotide, polypeptide, ribosome, nucleic acid. Without a clear understanding of these terms, much of the subsequent information will not be understood or mastered. **LEP**

Using the Illustration

While using Figure 10-2, students are to make the following observations and comparisons: (a) how does DNA differ from RNA in terms of nitrogen bases, sugar molecules, and number of strands; (b) how are DNA and RNA similar in terms of their overall appearance or construction; (c) compare the original and eventual location of DNA and RNA molecules within the cell after the process of transcription has taken place. **L1** **LEP**

CHEMISTRY CONNECTION

Structural Formulas:
Students should be able to use the structural diagrams from Chapter 9 as well as those from Figure 10-1 to calculate the molecular formulas for ribose and deoxyribose. Have students decide if these sugar molecules "fit the pattern" of the typical six-carbon carbohydrate molecules studied in previous chapters. Have students categorize the molecule uracil as being either a purine or a pyrimidine, and have them explain how they were able to make their decision. It may be necessary to review the purine/pyrimidine anatomy from Chapter 9. **L2**

STUDENT JOURNAL

Using Figure 10-2 as a guide, have students write a brief report explaining the occurring events. The report is to be written through the eyes of an RNA nucleotide that is present. Suggestions for students may be: Explain where they are located, what is surrounding them, what is happening around them, and what the future may hold for them. **L1**

PROJECT

Onion Root Tips: Have students grow onion root tips. Removing the tips and staining them with Feulgen stain (available from biological supply houses) will allow students to observe the chromosomal (DNA) material within cells. Some supply houses will furnish all reagents and directions for proper use in a kit form. **L2**

Using Science Terms

Have students look up the meaning of the terms *transcription* and *transcribe* in a dictionary. Have them record the definitions of these two terms as they relate to non-biological processes or use. Then, ask them to explain how the definitions and word usage of the non-biological definitions relate or correlate to the biological use of the term *transcription*. `L1` `LEP`

Enrichment

RNA is transcribed from only one side or strand of the DNA double helix molecule. This side is referred to as the "sense side." The side or strand not used is called the "antisense side." The side that serves as the sense side for one gene may be the antisense side for another gene.

Chalkboard Example

Take a moment to review with simple line diagrams on the board how the two cell types, prokaryotic and eukaryotic, differ from one another in their anatomy and organelles. `LEP`

Figure Caption Question

What characteristic of prokaryotes makes simultaneous transcription and translation possible? Prokaryotes have no nucleus; their DNA is located in the cytoplasm.

The sequence of bases composing the new RNA molecule is complementary to the base sequence of the DNA template on which it was made. For example, a DNA chain with the sequence AGC TTA TCC AGG will code for RNA with the sequence UCG AAU AGG UCC. (Notice that in RNA, U takes the place of T.) The process of making RNA from DNA is called **transcription.** RNA transcribed from DNA that codes for a polypeptide is called **messenger RNA (mRNA).** Not all DNA, however, codes for polypeptides. For example, some DNA codes for the RNA that makes up the ribosomes. This type of RNA is called **ribosomal RNA (rRNA).** Both mRNA and rRNA are transcribed from DNA.

Transcription in Prokaryotes   In prokaryotes, transcription is a relatively simple process. Prokaryotes have no nucleus, and the ribosomes lie close to the DNA in the cytoplasm. As a result, the first part of the mRNA molecule attaches directly to the ribosomes even as the rest of the molecule is still being transcribed (Figure 10-3). Assembly of amino acids into proteins begins right away.

Transcription in Eukaryotes   In eukaryotes, the transcription process is more complex. You learned in Chapter 7 that the DNA of eukaryotic chromosomes is wound around protein spools. The DNA must be unwound from the spools before transcription can begin. Otherwise, the enzyme that begins the process could not attach to the start signal region.

It took the careful work of many scientists to figure out the details of polypeptide synthesis. As this work was going on, one researcher made an unexpected discovery. In eukaryotes, after a new mRNA molecule is transcribed from its DNA template, the mRNA breaks up into pieces. When these pieces reassemble to form the finished mRNA molecule, portions of the original are left out, making the finished strand shorter than the original. Why does the original mRNA molecule break up into pieces? What is discarded when the pieces are spliced back together?

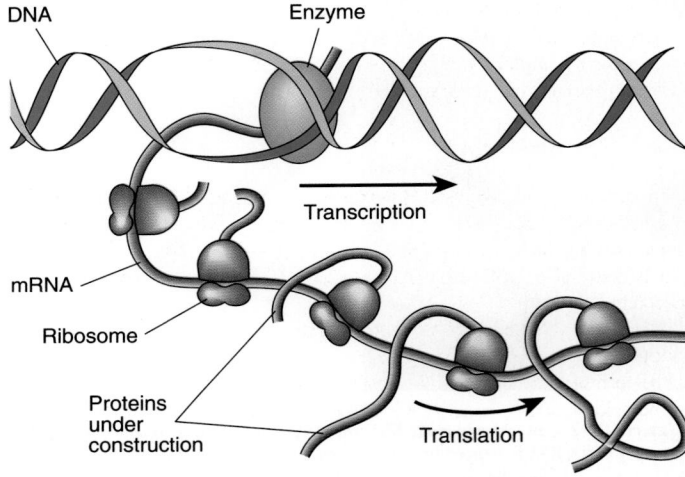

Figure 10-3   **In prokaryotes, as the genetic message is transcribed from DNA to mRNA, ribosomes attach to the forming mRNA, and translation begins simultaneously. What characteristic of prokaryotes makes simultaneous transcription and translation possible?**

- **Visually Impaired:** Visually impaired students may be helped in learning transcription and translation if you prepare large colored cardboard models of DNA and RNA nucleotides held onto a large fabric backdrop with Velcro. You can move the models as needed to properly position them in the formation of DNA or RNA.

- For students reading below grade level, give added practice in transcribing the genetic code from DNA to RNA language. Provide them with a DNA code such as TTC CAA GAC TCC GAG CTA and have them rewrite it in RNA language. Also, provide students with a segment of RNA such as UAC GCC UCC AGC CGU AUU and have them convert back to DNA language. `LEP`

Exons

Gene (DNA)

Introns

Transcription

mRNA formed

Finished mRNA

mRNA processing

Nuclear pore

To the ribosomes

Nucleus

Cytoplasm

Further research revealed that the original mRNA molecule produced by transcription contains many sets of nucleotides that do not code for amino acids. These *inter*vening sets of nucleotides are called **introns.** The sets of nucleotides that do code for amino acids are called **exons,** because they are *ex*pressed. After a new mRNA molecule is transcribed, and before it can function in protein synthesis, the introns must be removed and the exons spliced together. The removing of introns from mRNA is known as mRNA processing and is diagrammed in Figure 10-4. When processing is complete, the finished mRNA molecule moves through pores in the nuclear membrane and travels to the ribosomes.

Figure 10-4 During mRNA processing, introns are cut out and exons are spliced together. These events occur in the nucleus of the cell. What happens to the mRNA molecule after processing is completed?

Translation

In eukaryotes, processed mRNA attaches to a free ribosome in the cytoplasm and polypeptide synthesis begins. In many cases, synthesis is completed on free ribosomes. In other cases, the free ribosome and its attached strand of mRNA bind to rough ER, where protein synthesis is completed.

Messenger RNA carries the genetic information—a sequence of RNA codons—that represents a particular order of amino acids. Making the proper protein requires deciphering the information and assembling the amino acids it calls for. Synthesis of a polypeptide from the information carried by an mRNA molecule is called **translation.** How is mRNA "language" translated into protein "language"?

10.1 POLYPEPTIDE SYNTHESIS ◆ **253**

Using Science Terms

Have students look up the meaning of the term *translation* in a dictionary. Have them record definitions of this term as they relate to non-biological processes or use. Then, ask them to explain how the non-biological definitions and usage of the term relate or correlate to the biological use of the term *translation.* **L1** **LEP**

Figure Caption Question

What happens to the mRNA molecule after processing is completed? It moves through the pores in the nuclear membrane to the ribosomes in the cytoplasm.

Reinforcement

Ask students to write a sentence that contains a number of extra letters in many of the words. Have them pass their sentence to other students to correct or process. Their classmates are to identify the letters removed as introns and those retained as exons. **COOP LEARN**

MEETING INDIVIDUAL NEEDS

Provide students who are working below grade level with the following diagram of a DNA sequence. Each letter from A to G identifies a specific DNA portion or sequence.

A   B   C   D   E   F   G
intron intron exon intron exon exon intron

Ask students to predict and then correctly write down the sequences that will be discarded during processing (A B D G). Have them explain why these sequences are discarded. Have them predict and then correctly write down what the sequence will be for a processed RNA molecule using the correct letters A - G. (C E F) Have them explain why these sequences remain. **LEP**

Reinforcement

Have students make the following connections or correlations: (a) similarity of codon and anticodon regions in terms of length; (b) differences as to where the codon and anticodon regions are located; (c) what is attached to codon or anticodon regions; (d) location of tRNA in cell before being brought to ribosomes; (e) difference in appearance of tRNA and mRNA. **L1**

Enrichment

Students will need to refer back to Table 9.1 on page 241 for completion of this exercise. Their task is to work backwards in translation and transcription to determine the anticodon sequence of tRNA bases, codon sequence of mRNA, and DNA sequence of bases for specific amino acids. For example, predict the above information starting with the amino acid histidine. Two correct answers are possible: GUA-CAU-GTA or GUG-CAC-GTG. You may provide students with as many or as few original amino acids as you feel are needed to reinforce and enrich the individual members of your class. **L2**

Using the Illustration

Have students examine Figure 10-5. Ask them to answer the following questions after studying the figure. (a) What small units are used to form a polypeptide molecule? (b) How exactly does the cell know what the correct sequence of amino acids must be as the polypeptide is formed? **L1**
LEP

Concept Development

The nucleus has been the site of the majority of processes that have been described in this chapter. Ask students to list the events covered in Chapters 9 and 10 that occur within the nucleus. Student lists may include such events as transcription, processing, removal of introns, replication of DNA, unzipping of DNA prior to RNA formation, rejoining of DNA after transcription. **L1** **COOP LEARN**

Figure 10-5 A polypeptide is made when the mRNA code is translated. Each mRNA codon pairs with the anticodon of tRNA carrying an amino acid. When the first two amino acids bond together, the tRNA attached to the first amino acid is released. The ribosome then moves along the mRNA strand to the next codon, continuing the process of translation.

The Role of Transfer RNA Picture an mRNA molecule attached to a ribosome. In the surrounding cytoplasm are molecules of all 20 amino acids. If a polypeptide is to be made, the amino acids must be carried to the ribosomes. This job of bringing amino acids to the ribosomes is performed by yet another type of RNA, **transfer RNA (tRNA)**. Like other types of RNA, transfer RNA molecules are transcribed from certain regions of DNA in the nucleus. A tRNA molecule is a single chain of nucleotides folded into a cloverleaf shape and then bent over on itself. Each tRNA combines with and carries only one type of amino acid. Enzymes and ATP are used to join an amino acid to one end of the tRNA molecule. At the other side of the tRNA molecule is a set of three bases that is specific to the type of amino acid the tRNA carries. This set of bases is called an **anticodon**. Each type of tRNA has a different anticodon, which can bind only to the complementary mRNA codon for that amino acid.

The Joining of Codons and Anticodons Correct translation depends upon proper joining of mRNA codons and tRNA anticodons. Follow Figure 10-5 as you read how translation occurs.

As translation begins, a ribosome attaches to the first codon of the mRNA strand. At the same time, a tRNA molecule approaches, carrying its amino acid. If the tRNA anticodon recognizes the mRNA codon, the

STUDENT JOURNAL

Ask students to use Table 9.1 on page 241 to complete this project. Have students design an 18-base sequence for a section of DNA. It should start with the codon TAC and end with a proper stop codon. Have them record and label the mRNA sequence that would form during transcription, the tRNA anticodons that would match during translation, and the proper amino acid that would be carried to the ribosome via tRNA. Students are to also describe or name the location within a cell where the events recorded take place. **L1**

Messenger RNA chain

two molecules join. For example, the first codon, which acts as a start signal, is usually AUG. AUG codes for the amino acid methionine, so a tRNA molecule that carries this amino acid will have the anticodon UAC. The UAC anticodon and the AUG codon match up and join together. The tRNA with its attached amino acid remains joined to the first mRNA codon as the ribosome moves along the mRNA strand, exposing the next mRNA codon. Again, the proper tRNA with its amino acid joins the mRNA strand.

Formation of a Polypeptide   Once the first and second amino acids are in place, they bond together. The first tRNA is then released, making it available to bring another molecule of its amino acid to a ribosome. The process continues as the ribosome moves along the mRNA strand; thus, a polypeptide chain grows. Amino acids are added to a chain at the rate of about 15 per second. At the end of the mRNA strand is one of three codons—UAG, UAA, or UGA—that stops the translation process. There are no tRNA molecules with anticodons to match these codons. When the ribosome reaches one of these codons, translation stops and the completed polypeptide chain breaks away from its assembly line. The new polypeptide molecule may be ready to function in cellular processes, or it may join with other polypeptides to form a more complex protein molecule.

10.1 POLYPEPTIDE SYNTHESIS   **255**

Teacher FYI

The genetic code is said to be universal. However, it may not be when it comes to mitochondrial DNA and RNA. The mRNA codons of AGA and AGC usually code for the amino acid arginine. Instead, they are read as stop codons in mitochondrial DNA. An AUA codon codes for methionine in mitochondria rather than the usual isoleucine. Differences in the code of mitochondria add additional support to the theory that mitochondria were at one time free-living organisms that evolved separately, then became incorporated into primitive eukaryotic cells.

MATH CONNECTION

Mitochondrial DNA:
Mitochondria have their own DNA. Human mitochondrial DNA has been measured at 15 570 bases in length. Have students calculate the number of: (a) mRNA bases that would be needed during transcription (15 570); (b) tRNA bases involved with translation (15 570); (c) amino acids that are carried by tRNA (15 570 divided by 3, or 5190). **L1**

The translation process is basically the same for both prokaryotes and eukaryotes. Recall, however, that in prokaryotes translation may begin even before transcription is completed. Also, prokaryotes have no ER. All translation takes place on free ribosomes.

You may remember that the DNA and ribosomes found in mitochondria and chloroplasts are very similar to those of prokaryotes. Mitochondria and chloroplasts synthesize some of the polypeptides needed for their own functioning by carrying out the processes of transcription and translation in the same way prokaryotes do. However, most of the proteins needed by these organelles are coded for by nuclear genes. The proteins are synthesized on ribosomes in the cytoplasm and then move into the organelles.

Summary The path from genes to proteins can be summarized briefly.

1. DNA stores instructions for polypeptide synthesis.
2. The DNA instructions are transcribed into mRNA, which carries the information from the nucleus into the cytoplasm.
3. Ribosomes and tRNA interact with mRNA to translate the information and build polypeptides.

Each cell of an organism has the same set of genes as every other cell in that organism. A cell doesn't make every protein for which it has instructions, however. Proteins are made to order—they are synthesized only when they are needed and in the quantity needed. This means that only certain genes are expressed at any one time. The kinds of proteins synthesized by a cell differentiate it from other kinds of cells in an organism. For example, many of the proteins made by a muscle cell are different from those made by a nerve cell.

Thinking Lab

INTERPRET THE DATA

Which parent provides the genes in organelle DNA?

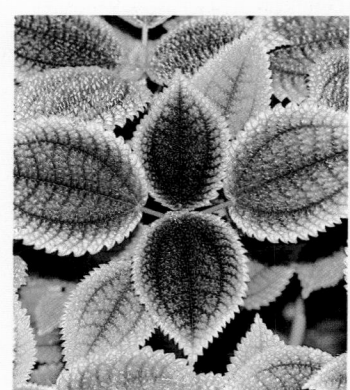

Background
DNA has been found in mitochondria and chloroplasts. The DNA in chloroplasts controls traits such as the appearance of white patches in a leaf caused by a lack of chlorophyll. This trait is known as a variegated leaf.

You Try It
The following genetic crosses were performed many times, with the same results each time.

1. A variegated female plant crossed with a variegated male plant produces all variegated offspring.
2. A variegated female plant crossed with a non-variegated male plant

produces all variegated offspring.

3. A non-variegated female plant crossed with a variegated male plant produces all non-variegated offspring.
4. A non-variegated female plant crossed with a non-variegated male plant produces all non-variegated offspring.

Interpret the data to determine which parent is responsible for giving the variegated trait to its offspring. Explain how the data support your answer. Draw a diagram tracing the inheritance of this trait through cell division.

256 FROM GENES TO PROTEINS

Thinking Lab

INTERPRET THE DATA

Purpose
Students will interpret data to discover that the female plant is responsible for the transmission of an organelle DNA trait.

Skills
interpret data, recognize cause and effect

Teaching Strategies
• Bring a variegated spider plant, Coleus, or ivy plant into the classroom.

• Discuss organelle DNA as an exception to Mendelian genetics patterns. Ask if a plant might be able to form chloroplasts if the fertilized egg cell contained no chloroplasts. The answer is no.

Answers
The female parent is responsible for giving the variegated trait to offspring. The offspring will always appear identical to the

female parent regardless of the trait present in the male parent.

✔ **Assessment**
Knowledge: Ask students how it might be possible to locate where in a plant the production of eggs and the production of sperm take place. Ask them to speculate on the process that is responsible for egg and sperm cell formation in plants.

Transcribed strand

DNA

Transcription

mRNA

Start codon — Termination codon

tRNA

Translation

Anticodon

PROTEIN — Met — Lys — Phe — Gly

Amino acid

Figure 10-6 When the genetic message in one of the two DNA strands is transcribed into mRNA, the resulting mRNA has codons that are complementary to those in the DNA strand. The tRNA anticodon, then, has the same base sequence as the original DNA codon, except for having uracil instead of thymine.

DNA and Phenotypes

What you have learned about DNA and protein synthesis can explain some concepts of genetics. Consider coat color in guinea pigs. Black fur (*B*) is dominant to albino (*b*). Guinea pigs having the genotype *BB* or *Bb* will be black. Guinea pigs with the genotype *bb* will be albino. Can these patterns of inheritance be explained at a chemical level?

Genes consist of DNA that codes for specific proteins. Suppose the *B* allele carries a code that directs the synthesis of a particular enzyme, an enzyme being a protein. That enzyme aids in the conversion of a substance in the cells of the guinea pig to melanin, a black pigment. Thus, a guinea pig that is *BB* or *Bb* will be able to make melanin and will be black. The *b* allele is a mutant form of the *B* allele. Its nucleotide sequence, and so its code, is slightly different. Because of the difference, the enzyme needed to make melanin is defective and cannot function properly. Therefore, a *bb* guinea pig cannot make melanin. Its phenotype will be albino.

You have seen how genetic information is expressed by transcription and translation into specific proteins, which in turn bring about an organism's phenotype. The phenotype of an individual is the result of the particular proteins that are produced as the individual's genes are expressed. Thus, all phenotypes have a chemical basis.

Figure 10-7 Phenotypes result from the combination of proteins produced by a given set of alleles. The black guinea pig has a black coat because its DNA codes for the enzymes that make the pigment melanin. The white guinea pig cannot make melanin because its DNA contains a defective gene. What are the possible genotypes of these two guinea pigs?

SECTION 10.1

Figure Caption Question

What are the possible genotypes of these two guinea pigs? The black guinea pig can be either *BB* or *Bb*. The white guinea pig must be *bb*.

Using the Illustration

Students are to use Figure 10-6 as a guide as they complete the following task. Provide students with this sequence of bases on DNA: AAT-CGT-GCA-ATG-CTG. Advise them that this is the side of DNA that is not transcribed. They are to: (a) complete the side of DNA that is transcribed, (b) transcribe this side into mRNA codons, (c) determine the mRNA anticodons that correspond to the mRNA codons. [L1] [LEP]

Brainstorming

Using the example of guinea pig coat color, have students do the following: (a) create their own model of the DNA (make it at least 9 bases long) that could represent the nucleotide sequence for a guinea pig having black fur; (b) create their own model of the DNA that could represent the nucleotide sequence for a guinea pig having white fur. Remember, its nucleotide sequence should only be slightly different from the sequence for black fur; (c) explain how the codes for black and white fur are interpreted differently by the cells of these two guinea pigs. [L1] [COOP LEARN]

Using Science Terms

Have students redefine the terms *genotype* and *phenotype*. Have them include an example of each term taken directly from the guinea pig story on this page. [L1] [LEP]

MEETING INDIVIDUAL NEEDS

For students who are working above grade level, have them explain the correlation between sickle cell anemia and the particular protein that is produced by these individuals, as compared to normal hemoglobin and the particular protein produced by those individuals. Why and how do the proteins of these individuals differ? Ask students to research the advantage of the sickle cell trait (a mild form of sickle cell anemia) shown by those individuals against malaria. [L3]

Using an Analogy

Ask students to explain the meaning of the terms *nonfunctional DNA* and *functional DNA*. Have them compare functional and nonfunctional information on a videotape to these same two terms in DNA. Ask how disturbing it would be to play and view this type of tape and why. **L1** **LEP**

INVESTIGATION

Modeling Cell Processes

Time Allotment
one class period

Objectives
Upon completing this investigation, students will be able to:
- Make models of the processes of transcription, translation, and protein formation.
- Understand how transcription and translation function in protein synthesis.

Skills
sequence, compare and contrast, interpret scientific illustrations

Materials
paper, construction paper or poster board, paper punch, string, tape, magic markers or crayons, rulers, yarn

Preparation
Gather materials for the lab.

Possible Procedures
The actual models may vary from group to group. However, the following is one possible student interpretation of how each model might appear and function.
- DNA molecule: Students will have paper signs supported by string around their necks. The signs may be marked A, G, T, or

---

Composition of Eukaryotic Chromosomes

Using a variety of new techniques to analyze chromosomes, geneticists have continued to discover surprising facts about these structures. One unexpected finding is that the vast majority of the DNA in a eukaryotic chromosome does not code for polypeptides. Some of this DNA codes for other kinds of molecules, such as ribosomal RNAs and transfer RNAs. But much of the DNA doesn't code for any functional RNA.

Nonfunctional DNA   As you have seen, some DNA codes for introns that are removed from mRNA before it leaves the nucleus. Other DNA serves as start and stop signals for transcription. Still other types of noncoding DNA have base sequences similar to, but not exactly like, genes

---

INVESTIGATION

Modeling Cell Processes

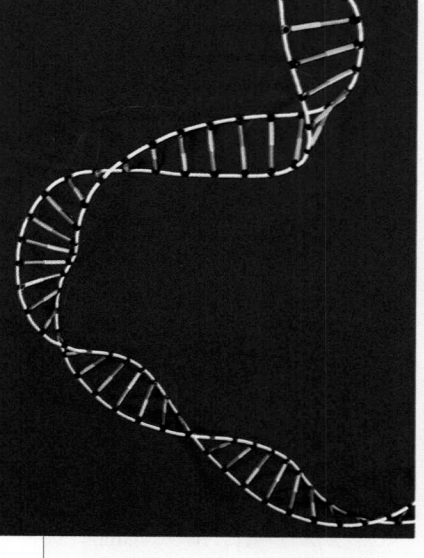

Scientists often use models to explain complex processes or to aid in better understanding of an event. The events of transcription, translation, and protein formation within a cell are difficult to see. The understanding of how and when they occur is critical to the understanding of normal and even abnormal cell functioning. Models will be designed to better illustrate these complex cellular processes.

Problem
How can models using your classmates be designed to illustrate the processes of transcription, translation, and protein formation as they occur within a eukaryotic cell?

Experimental Plan
1. As a group, make a list of possible ways you might design your models using the materials your teacher has made available. Remember, classmates are to be used as an actual part of the modeling process. HINT: A student with a paper sign hung over his or her neck can easily represent a DNA or RNA nitrogen base. Holding hands can represent molecular bonds.
2. Agree on one idea from your group's list that would be a correct model showing each process listed in the Problem section.
3. Write a numbered list of directions that could be followed to build and execute your models. You may also want to diagram the models to be used with each directional step.
4. Make a list of materials and the quantities you will need.

C. A line of students will stand in front of the class. They will be held together in line with lengths of yarn attached with tape from student to student at their shoulders. Opposite them will be another line of students with signs marked in a similar way. However, those students directly opposite one another must be matched, with either an A to a T or a C to a G. The matched pairs of A/T and C/G can hold hands to signify base pair bonds. Length of the model will be determined by the number of classmates and the plans of each group.

- Transcription: The DNA model should open along the length of held hands. Other students with different signs around their necks will now represent mRNA. Color choice of paper for mRNA should be different from color choice for DNA to reflect the difference between the sugar of DNA (deoxyribose) and the sugar of RNA (ribose). Their signs must also reflect the fact that no T is present but is replaced with U. A single line of students again held together with taped yarn should line up opposite one side of the opened DNA.

that code for polypeptides. These DNA regions are called pseudogenes (false genes) and do not code for functional polypeptides. And some DNA has no known function.

Repeating DNA Sequences   The picture becomes even more puzzling when we learn that each cell has multiple copies of many DNA sequences. Some of these repetitious regions consist of pairs of bases that are repeated over and over again, thousands and even millions of times. Other repetitious regions appear to be multiple copies of genes.

In some cases, the presence of repetitive DNA is an advantage to a cell. For example, there are many copies of the genes that code for tRNAs and rRNAs. Having multiple sets of these genes allows the cell to make these RNAs quickly and in great quantities, an advantage when a busy cell must synthesize proteins rapidly.

Check for Understanding

Ask students to explain the following relationships:
(a) DNA—genetic code
(b) DNA—mRNA
(c) mRNA—tRNA
(d) transcription—translation
(e) codon—anticodon
(f) tRNA—amino acid
(g) amino acid—polypeptide   `L1`

Checking the Plan

Discuss the following points with other group members to decide the final procedures for your model building.
1. How many students will actually be needed in your model?
2. Can the same student assume a second or third role in the model-building process at a later time to conserve on the number of students needed?
3. Your model may have to use all the students in your class. Make sure that the model or plan designed by your group will provide specific enough directions so that other students not in your group will be able to execute your plan with little confusion.
4. Who will be in charge of actually directing the student models?
5. Who will be in charge of explaining the events that are occurring to either the students participating or to any students observing the modeling?

6. Who will be in charge of designing and drawing any needed signs?

Make sure your teacher has approved your experimental plan before you proceed further.

Data and Observations

Carry out the model building one group at a time. For example, if there are five class groups, each group will be allowed to build and demonstrate the workings of its model. Again, realize that each group may wish to use the entire class as part of its model.

Analysis and Conclusions

1. How did your group represent DNA and how many base pairs were used? How did your group model differ from other models at this step?
2. How did your group represent mRNA and transcription? How did your group model differ from other group models at this step?

3. How did your group represent tRNA, translation, and protein or polypeptide formation? How did your group model differ from other group models at this step?
4. How did your group determine the specific amino acid to use with a particular mRNA codon? How did your group model differ from other group models at this step?
5. Based on all group presentations, explain any errors that were made and how these errors should be corrected. List suggestions that could improve your model or other groups' models.
6. Explain the role of models in science.

Going Further

Based on this activity, design other models that would illustrate (a) transcription and translation in prokaryotic cells, (b) how a mutation might alter the formation of a polypeptide, and (c) the possible sites where mutations might occur.

10.1 POLYPEPTIDE SYNTHESIS ❧ **259**

Which side they line up on is optional. However, again their bases must fit the DNA sequence. That is, A of DNA can match only with U of mRNA. T of DNA can match only with A of mRNA. C of DNA can match only with G of mRNA. G of DNA can match only with C of mRNA. Hands may be held temporarily between the DNA and RNA.

- Translation: mRNA moves away from DNA but stays together as a single line of molecules. Other students will represent tRNA molecules. These molecules will consist of groups of three students. Their signs again should match the color for mRNA. Behind each group of three should be a student representing an amino acid. This student should indicate that he or she is amino acid X, Y, or Z. The amino acid should be attached to the tRNA molecule by holding onto the back of the three bases of tRNA, or through the use of yarn. tRNA molecules now must match with the mRNA bases. That is, the sequence of the three bases in each tRNA must fit the sequence of three bases in mRNA.
- Protein formation: Amino acids brought by tRNA molecules will now join together by holding hands. This will signify the formation of a protein or polypeptide.

Teaching Strategies
- Models may have to be broken down to provide enough students for building the next model.

Data Analysis
1-5. Answers will vary depending on student models.
6. Models are often used to explain complex scientific processes or to aid in better understanding of an event.

✔ Assessment
Portfolio: Have students write an evaluation

of the lab for their portfolios. They should describe in their own words how the modeling of these complex cell processes helped them to better understand how proteins are formed. Students should summarize what they learned and how models are useful as a teaching tool.

Extensions
Students can design models to help them understand gene and chromosome mutation, concepts that will be studied later in this chapter. `LEP`   `COOP LEARN`

Reteach

Provide a series of DNA bases (at least 6). Have students trace the events that occur: (a) within the nucleus; (b) from nucleus to ribosomes; (c) at ribosomes. L1

COOP LEARN

Extension

Ask students to diagram a DNA molecule consisting of the proper number of bases per turn of the helix. (Most DNA has 10.) Their model should be no more than two turns in length. Included in their model should be labels indicating sense and antisense sides, nitrogen base names, nucleotide group (purine or pyrimidine), sugar, and phosphate. L2

✔ Assessment

Portfolio: Have students summarize the major concepts of this section by creating a flow chart describing the steps from DNA code to polypeptide in order of occurrence within a cell. L1

4 Close

Discussion

Have students describe events during the life of a cell when rapid protein synthesis is needed. If help is needed, ask students to think in terms of mitosis/meiosis or when a cell is busy forming proteins for export (pancreas cells, thyroid gland cells, stomach lining cells).

Figure 10-8 Only a very small percentage of the DNA in a eukaryotic chromosome actually codes for polypeptides. The rest of the DNA has other functions, or no known function at all. In contrast, about 90 percent of a prokaryotic cell's DNA codes for polypeptides.

Key
■ = Pseudogene
■ = Gene that codes for rRNA
□ = Gene that codes for tRNA
■ = Gene that codes for polypeptide
□ = Intron
■ = Start and stop signals

Repetitive DNA segments represent about 30 percent of a chromosome's total DNA, while the other 70 percent consists of single copies of genes. However, most of these single copies are pseudogenes that are never transcribed. It has been estimated that only about one percent of the total DNA in a eukaryotic cell actually codes for polypeptides.

Clearly, these recent findings indicate that some of our initial ideas about heredity were far too simple. For example, we now know that there may be hundreds or thousands of alleles of some genes in a single cell, not just the two proposed by Mendel. These findings also show that much remains to be explained about the DNA of eukaryotes. Why is so much of the DNA nonfunctional? How did it arise? Why does it exist if it is not needed? Possible answers to some of these puzzling questions will be proposed in the next section of this chapter.

Section Review

Understanding Concepts

1. Why are transfer RNAs necessary for translation? What critical role do they play?
2. Suppose a chain of DNA has the base sequence GCC TAT ACA CCT. Describe transcription of that chain and list the sequence of nucleotides in the mRNA chain produced.
3. A fertilized frog egg produces an mRNA molecule consisting of 2000 nucleotides. That same mRNA mole- cule, when it reaches the ribosomes, has only 951 nucleotides. Explain the difference in the size of the two mRNA molecules.
4. **Skill Review—Observing and Inferring:** You are examin- ing two different types of cells. One type of cell is part of a gland spe- cialized for producing an enzyme needed for digestion. The other is part of a tissue specialized for trans- mitting nerve impulses, a process that does not involve proteins. In which type of cell would you expect to find more RNA? Why? For more help, see Thinking Critically in the Skill Handbook.
5. **Thinking Critically:** Suppose that, in a certain plant, the gene for green seeds, *G*, is dominant to the gene for colorless seeds, *g*. In terms of DNA function, explain why the genotype *GG* or *Gg* results in green seeds, while the genotype *gg* results in colorless seeds.

Answers to Section Review

1. Because each tRNA has an anticodon that matches the complementary mRNA codon for the amino acid it carries, the proper amino acid will be placed in the proper position in the growing polypeptide chain.
2. An enzyme binds to the start signal near each gene and the DNA unzips. RNA nucleotides are put in position and bonded together, forming an mRNA molecule that breaks away from the DNA. The DNA strands then rejoin. The mRNA molecule would have the sequence CGG AUA UGU GGA.
3. The mRNA molecule originally con- tained both introns and exons. The introns were removed and the exons spliced together.
4. **Skill Review—Observing and Inferring:** The gland cell would con- tain more RNA, used for synthesizing the enzymes that the cell produces.
5. **Thinking Critically:** A plant having at least one *G* allele has the code for synthesizing an enzyme that results in production of a green pigment. The homozygous recessive plant lacks a *G* allele and cannot produce the func- tional enzyme.

10.2 Sources of Variation

You probably copy homework assignments off the board each day in school. Have you ever copied one incorrectly? Perhaps instead of copying an assignment that called for answering questions 1-15, you misread the 5 and wrote a 3 instead. When you did your homework, you answered questions 1 through 13, leaving out two of the assigned questions. DNA is usually replicated correctly, but mistakes do occur. Some mistakes arise during the copying process, while others result from external factors. Such mistakes can have important consequences for organisms and their offspring.

Mutation

The mechanisms that control transfer of hereditary traits from a cell to its daughter cells usually produce accurate results. However, when mistakes in the replication of genetic material occur, a daughter cell will contain genetic material different from that of its parent cell. Such mistakes are called **mutations,** and can arise from changes to individual genes or changes in the arrangement of genes on a chromosome.

Gene Mutations   Many gene mutations arise spontaneously as DNA is replicated. Although most replication errors are corrected, some escape detection. In one type of gene mutation, called a **deletion,** a nucleotide is left out. As Figure 10-10 shows, leaving out a nucleotide shifts the reading of the DNA message over by one nucleotide, resulting in synthesis of a polypeptide with an altered amino acid sequence. The same result can occur with an **insertion,** a type of mutation in which an extra nucleotide is added to a chain during replication. Deletion and insertion mutations

Objectives

Infer several ways in which genetic variation may arise.

Sequence the events in a cell that lead to cancer.

Relate techniques used in recombinant DNA technology and the uses of that technology.

Figure 10-9   Mutations occur in all organisms. Curly wings in *Drosophila,* the short legs of a bassett hound, seedless fruit such as oranges and grapes, and a protruding "Hapsburg" lip in humans each arose as the result of a mutation.

10.2 SOURCES OF VARIATION ▲ **261**

SECTION 10.2

Prepare

Key Concepts

Various types of mutations and their effects on polypeptide formation are described in detail. Causes and consequences of mutations are discussed and the concept of recombinant DNA is introduced.

Key Terms

mutation, deletion, insertion, point mutation, mutagen, carcinogen, oncogene, recombinant DNA, plasmid, clone

Materials

- Order irradiated seeds for Minilab 1. Begin to gather empty student milk cartons to be used as plant growth chambers.
- Order alpha-amylase from a supply house for use in Minilab 2.
- Buy onion bulbs for the Alternate Lab.

1 Focus

Objectives

The objectives are listed on the student page. Remind students to preview these objectives as a guide to this numbered section.

Discussion

Ask students to describe what they believe is the meaning of the term *mutant.* Ask for examples of mutations and elicit from students what they believe are the major causes for mutations appearing in organisms.
L1   COOP LEARN

MEETING INDIVIDUAL NEEDS

This exercise may be helpful for students working below grade level. The following sentence represents a set of bases in DNA. Each letter represents a nucleotide.
YOU CAN SEE THE CAT EAT THE RAT.

Illustrate the effect of a deletion by dropping out the C in cat. The sentence now is shifted as follows: YOU CAN SEE THE ATE ATT HER AT. Ask students if the sentence still makes sense.

Illustrate the effect of an insertion by using the same correct sentence but adding a letter such as an extra S at the word *see.* The sentence now would read: YOU CAN SSE ETH ECA TEA TTH ERA T. Ask students if the sentence still makes sense. Ask them to design their own three-letter-word sentence and illustrate its changes with a letter insertion and a deletion.   LEP

2 Teach

Misconception

Students believe that most mutations are harmful and result in the formation of hideous or bizarre appearances, such as a two-headed horse. The majority of mutations may be neither helpful nor harmful. Most go unnoticed due to their often subtle changes in the nature of a protein.

Using Science Terms

Have students explain the meaning of the expression *a polypeptide is usually not functional.* **L1** **LEP**

Reinforcement

Ask students to provide a series of at least nine DNA bases. Ask them to determine and record the amino acids that are coded by their sequence. This will require that students refer to Table 9.1 on page 241 of the text. Then students should alter the sequence by only one base by leaving it out to simulate a deletion (the deleted base should be the first in sequence of any triplet). Rewrite the changed amino acid sequence to illustrate the effect of a deletion. Have students repeat the exercise twice more to illustrate an insertion and a point mutation. Have them explain why a mutation will: (a) not influence future generations if occurring in a body cell; (b) influence future generations if occurring in a gamete. **L1**

Figure Caption Question

If three nucleotides are inserted or deleted, the protein will probably be functional. Why? An entire codon is added or deleted, which will add or delete a single amino acid to the polypeptide. This change most likely will produce a functional polypeptide.

Figure 10-10 The protein formed as a result of a point mutation may be able to function because only one amino acid is affected. Deletions and insertions, however, affect all amino acids that are coded beyond the point of the mutation. The effect on the protein is usually disastrous. If three nucleotides are inserted or deleted, the protein will probably be functional. Why?

result in amino acid sequences that are very different from those coded for by normal genes because all the amino acids in the polypeptide beyond the point at which the mutation occurred will be affected. The polypeptide produced by the mutated gene, if one can be produced at all, is usually not functional.

In a **point mutation,** a base substitution occurs, and one nucleotide is substituted for another. This type of gene mutation affects only one amino acid in the polypeptide. With such a small change in its structure, the polypeptide may be able to function normally or nearly normally.

Deletions, insertions, and point mutations all result spontaneously from errors in copying. Gene mutations may also result from exposure to environmental factors, such as radiation, high temperature, and a variety of chemicals. External agents that cause mutations are called **mutagens.** Many mutagens exert their effect by breaking the chemical bonds of DNA molecules or by causing unusual bonds to form. Some of these mutagens are known to play a role in the development of many forms of cancer.

Once a gene mutation has taken place, regardless of its cause, the altered gene is copied as if it were correct. After all, DNA replication is a predetermined series of chemical events. A cell has no way of knowing that it is copying a mistake. Mutations that occur in a body cell of an organism may damage the organism or perhaps even cause its death, but they are not important to the organism's descendants. However, mutations that occur in the sex cells may affect an entire population of organisms, because the information can be passed from one generation to the next.

262 FROM GENES TO PROTEINS

MEETING INDIVIDUAL NEEDS

An exercise similar to that on page 261 can be used to illustrate a point mutation. Use the same sentence, and substitute a T for the H in *the.* Can the sentence still be read and understood, as is the case with point mutations? Have students explain how the polypeptide formed from the mutated sentence might differ from the original polypeptide. **LEP**

PORTFOLIO

Have students summarize in their own words how insertions, deletions, and point mutations affect protein synthesis. Diagrams can accompany the summary.

New Alleles It may have occurred to you that gene mutations result in new forms of genes, or, in other words, new alleles. Polypeptides produced from the transcription and translation of new alleles are often so different that they are useless or even harmful to the cell. Rarely is a new allele immediately beneficial to an organism, and most new alleles have little effect at the time they occur. They are also usually, but not always, recessive to the original allele, especially if they produce a useless product or none at all. The normal allele can produce enough useful product to mask the presence of the useless product. Because most organisms are diploid, even harmful or lethal recessive alleles may be passed to offspring and gradually spread through a population. This can happen because the effect of the recessive allele is masked by the dominant allele. Over time, many new alleles can spread through a population, adding to a storehouse of variety that may eventually become important to the species.

Chromosome Mutations Changes may occur in chromosomes as well as in genes. Chromosome mutations occur in several different ways. For example, parts of chromosomes can be broken off or lost during mitosis or meiosis. Sometimes, these broken parts rejoin the chromosome from which they came, but they may attach backwards or at the wrong end of the chromosome. Also, they may reattach to a different chromosome. Any of these changes can result in abnormal information in the cell's genetic material. Because each chromosome consists of many genes, chromosome mutations can have serious effects on the distribution of genes to gametes during meiosis. Gametes that should have complete haploid sets of genes may end up with double doses of some genes and a complete lack of others. Most chromosome mutations are not passed on, either because the zygote fails to develop, or, if it does, the mature organism is incapable of producing offspring.

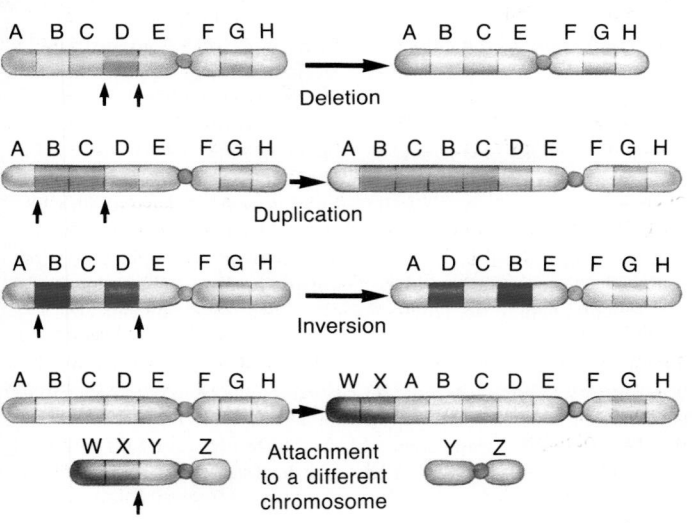

Deletion

Duplication

Inversion

Attachment to a different chromosome

Figure 10-11 **Chromosomal mutations occur in many different ways. A deletion removes a segment of a chromosome, a duplication repeats a segment, and an inversion is caused by breakage followed by attachment backwards. Breakage and attachment of the fragment to another chromosome can also occur.**

10.2 SOURCES OF VARIATION ❧ **263**

PROJECT

Growing Cells: It is possible to have students prepare cell smears from vertebrate blood samples. These smears will provide white blood cells that are undergoing mitosis and will yield visible chromosomes under the microscope. Students will gain experience in growing cells using tissue culture techniques and will also learn how to halt mitosis chemically, as well as how to properly stain cells for viewing of chromosomal material. Kits are available from biological supply houses. **L3**

Chalkboard Example

Demonstrate the events that occur during nondisjunction of chromosomes (failure of homologous chromosomes to separate during meiosis). Show the step-by-step changes responsible for the formation of a gamete that contains an extra chromosome and a gamete containing no copy of the chromosome. Show students that when nondisjunction occurs, two different abnormal sex cells can result, one with too many chromosomes and one with too few chromosomes. Have students predict the chromosome number at fertilization of these two cell types if fused with a normal human gamete. **LEP**

Brainstorming

- Have students predict the actual events that cause a failure of homologous chromosomes to separate during meiosis. **L3** **COOP LEARN**

- Ask students to explain how it was possible for the genes Barbara McClintock had studied to move from one chromosome to a different chromosome, or to move to a new area on the same chromosome. It may be necessary to explain to students that many of the concepts or ideas regarding chromosome and gene mutations during her time of research were not as yet known or well understood. **L2** **COOP LEARN**

A
B
A
B

Reattachment

A
B
A
B

C
D
E

C
D
E

Sister chromatids

Figure 10-12 **When a piece of a chromatid breaks off and attaches to its sister chromatid, duplication of genes occurs.**

Other Causes of Genetic Variation

You have learned that a cell has multiple copies of many DNA sequences and that some of these sequences are duplicate genes. New genes can arise when these duplicate genes undergo slight changes in their nucleotide sequence. Because the new gene is quite similar to the original, it is likely to code for a polypeptide that may be able to function in a new way.

Types of Gene Duplication Gene duplication may occur in different ways. During meiosis, homologous chromosomes may fail to segregate properly, causing both homologues to move to the same pole. This failure to separate can lead to production of an offspring having an entire extra chromosome. That offspring would have duplicates of all the genes on that chromosome. Another type of duplication occurs when a piece of a chromatid breaks off and attaches to its sister chromatid, as Figure 10-12 shows. One chromatid would have several duplicate genes. If this duplication occurred during meiosis, one of the offspring would inherit those extra copies.

You have doubtless pictured genes as fixed sections of DNA, located at particular points along a chromosome. That is usually true, but as Barbara McClintock discovered four decades ago, some genes can actually move from one area of a chromosome to another or from one chromosome to another. Such genes, called jumping genes, often leave a copy of them-

HISTORY CONNECTION

Jumping Genes

It was not until almost 40 years after Barbara McClintock first discovered what she called the jumping gene that the scientific community recognized its importance to genetic theory. McClintock began her research in the 1940s by studying the effects of crossing corn plants that had different kernel colors and textures. She observed kernel color patterns that could only be explained if genes moved around on chromosomes. This was a star-

tling interpretation. At the time, genes were thought to be fixed at a specific place on a specific chromosome. The results of McClintock's experiments led her to conclude that some genes, instead of being fixed, move around on a chromosome, affect each other's functionings, and cause massive mutations.

Dr. McClintock presented her experimental data to her fellow scientists. They initially did not accept her conclusion because it was contrary to how they thought genes should behave. Then, in the late 1960s, jumping genes were discovered in fruit flies, yeast, and

bacteria. Scientists are just now beginning to realize how important her work was and how jumping genes bring diversity to a species. Jumping genes have actually led to the further study and suspicion that some movable genes may be the descendants of viruses. Jumping genes may even be responsible for producing specific tumor cells that result in certain cancers.

Because of the importance of her work, Barbara McClintock was awarded the Nobel Prize for Physiology and Medicine in 1983. She continued her work with corn until her death in 1992 at the age of 90.

264 FROM GENES TO PROTEINS

PROJECT

Genetic Disorders: A number of human disorders result from chromosomal abnormalities. Have students use references to determine the names of some of these disorders, the problems they cause, and the chromosomal mutations responsible. They may research Edwards Syndrome, Patau Syndrome, Turner Syndrome, Klinefelter Syndrome, and Cri-Du-Chat Syndrome. **L2**

PROGRAM RESOURCES

Teacher Classroom Resources
Study Guide, pp. 57-60 **L1**
Critical Thinking/Problem Solving, p. 10 **L2**

selves before jumping to another position. Thus, the cell would have two or more copies of the same gene. Some of those copies could later undergo slight change, resulting in new functional genes.

Importance of Gene Duplication   The importance of gene duplication as a source of new genetic variation has yet to be determined. There is evidence, though, that it does occur. For example, the form of hemoglobin produced by a human fetus is different from that produced by the adult. The genes that code for the two forms of hemoglobin are located close to one another on the same chromosome, and are only slightly different from one another. One may have arisen by duplication from the other, and changed slightly over time so that it now codes for a slightly different polypeptide chain.

Creation of new genes as a result of duplication would explain some of the puzzling features of the DNA of eukaryotic chromosomes. It would certainly explain the many copies of certain genes, such as those that code for rRNA. It may also explain the presence of pseudogenes. It is likely that pseudogenes are duplicate genes that have been slightly modified so that they no longer code for functional polypeptides.

A slightly different result of duplication may be another source of new genes. It is the exons of a gene that code for amino acids. Each exon can be thought of as a set of nucleotides that codes for a series of amino acids. It is possible that several exons from different genes along a chromosome could be duplicated, then move to and become inserted into another chromosome. Putting exons together in new combinations would form new sequences of nucleotides resulting in codes for new polypeptides.

1. **Explore Further:** Find out what a virus is and how its genetic material differs from that of living things.
2. **Writing About Biology:** Find out how tumor cells that are not cancerous differ from those that are. Write a short report.
3. **Explore Further:** What evidence led Dr. McClintock to conclude that genes could jump from one chromosome to another?

10.2 SOURCES OF VARIATION **265**

HISTORY CONNECTION

Purpose
Students will note that McClintock's discoveries were the first evidence that genes move about. The discoveries also show how science constantly evolves as new evidence is presented to change or alter old ideas or theories.

Background
The terms *transposon* and *transposable controlling elements* are sometimes used to describe the genes that move between chromosomes and upon the same chromosome.

Teaching Strategies
* Ears of corn are available from biological supply houses. You may wish to demonstrate the appearance of jumping gene traits on these ears. Purchase ears that show a typical 3:1 or 9:3:3:1 ratio of traits.

Possible Answers
1. Viruses are considered to be nonliving chromosomal matter that shows some living traits. They contain genetic material in the form of DNA or RNA.
2. Tumor cells that do not cause cancer remain in one place within the body of the organism in which they are growing. Malignant tumor cells can spread to other sites within the body.
3. Her work involved the appearance or disappearance of purple color in the aleurone covering of corn seeds, as well as the appearance of colored swirls on certain seeds of Indian corn.

Going Further
Allow students to study the ears of corn that were used as a demonstration. Have them predict the genotypes of parents that could contribute to the phenotype ratios observed. L1
LEP

MEETING INDIVIDUAL NEEDS

Use the sentence in the exercise on page 261 to illustrate the effect of pseudogenes by adding the words PIG DOG to the sentence. The sentence now reads:

YOU CAN SEE THE CAT EAT THE PIG DOG RAT.

Ask students if the sentence still makes sense. Ask them to identify the pseudogenes. Ask them to design their own three-letter-word sentence and illustrate the effect of pseudogenes.

Carry the example one step further by having students design a sentence with exons that are duplicated and are then moved into another sentence, where they form a new combination of words. LEP

Figure 10-13 Duplication of a gene followed by random mutations and natural selection can lead to two genes with different functions. In the absence of gene duplication, the mutation on the left would be lethal if it produces a nonfunctional protein. With a duplicated gene, the same mutation that would otherwise be lethal is not disadvantageous, because the original gene continues to produce the normal protein. With time, several mutations can accumulate in the duplicated gene.

Normal gene → Mutation only → Mutated gene → Abnormal protein (nonfunctional) → Selection against defective gene

Normal gene → Gene duplication and mutation → Normal gene / Mutated gene → Normal protein / Abnormal protein (nonfunctional) → Additional mutations and selection → Two genes with different functions

You read in Chapter 8 that meiosis and fertilization are processes that reshuffle alleles, leading to genetic variation. You now know that new alleles may be produced by mutation and new genes by duplication of previously existing genes and parts of genes. Over time, the new genes and alleles may spread through a population. The continual production of new alleles and their reshuffling during meiosis and fertilization provide for genetic variation among the individual organisms in a population. The production of new functional genes provides for the evolution of greater complexity.

Cancer

Earlier you studied the cell cycle and learned of the events that control cell growth and reproduction. Although the cell cycle usually results in production of normal cells having the proper genetic information, sometimes the cycle is altered and abnormal cells are produced. These abnormal cells differ in shape from normal cells and have unique proteins in their membranes. Some of these cells have unusual numbers of chromosomes, and many have abnormal chromosomes that have been produced through chromosome mutations. The abnormal cells reproduce, forming more cells like themselves. Unlike other mature cells, many can migrate around the body and take hold in other organs. Such cells are said to be malignant, or cancerous. They reproduce in an uncontrolled way, eventually crowding out normal cells and destroying the tissues and organs to which they have spread. Because almost any body cell can become malignant, cancer is not a single disease. Rather, there are many forms of cancer, depending on which type of body cell has become malignant.

Figure 10-14 Melanoma is a deadly type of skin cancer that is caused by excessive exposure to sunlight.

266 FROM GENES TO PROTEINS

ALTERNATE LAB: A Screening Test for Possible Carcinogens

Purpose
Students will grow onion bulbs in a variety of chemical solutions to screen for possible carcinogens.

Materials
18 × 150 mm test tubes, test-tube rack, labels, dropper, distilled water, small onion bulbs, ruler, graduated cylinder, household chemicals (minimum of four)

Procedure
Give the following directions to students.
1. Obtain five onion bulbs and locate the root end. It will contain small dried remains of roots.
2. Fill a test tube to the very top with distilled water. Label it "control."
3. Place one onion bulb onto the mouth of the test tube so that the bulb rests on the tube lip. The root end must be in the water.
4. Prepare four tubes as in step 3, but replace the water with 4 test solutions. Chemicals such as window cleaner, rubbing alcohol, and detergent may be used. Label each tube.
5. Prepare a data table and record the total combined length of all roots present on each bulb in each tube.
6. Wait 4 - 5 days. Then measure the total

Causes of Cancer: Mutation What causes normal cells to be transformed to malignant ones? It is now known that genetic changes are ultimately to blame. Genes that control the normal events of the cell cycle mutate. When such mutations occur, normal cell cycle controls no longer operate. The mutations may be inherited, or they may be triggered by a **carcinogen,** a cancer-causing agent in the environment. Tobacco smoke, X rays and other forms of radiation, and a variety of chemicals are known carcinogens. No matter how the mutation occurs, the genes that mutate are ones that code for proteins involved in controlling normal cell growth and reproduction. When such a gene mutates, it becomes a cancer-causing gene, called an **oncogene.** Because mutations are passed on, descendant cells inherit the oncogene, and a tumor, a large mass of cancer cells, forms. Several genetic changes must occur to transform a healthy cell to a cancerous one, and some of the steps involve oncogenes. Each change probably affects the cell cycle in a different way.

Causes of Cancer: Viruses Some viruses are known to cause cancer in animals. These viruses may cause cancer simply because their presence in the animal cell disrupts the function of normal genes. Viruses can also cause cancer if they carry an oncogene into an animal cell when they infect the cell. The oncogene becomes part of the animal cell's chromosome, where it disrupts the normal events of the cell cycle, causing cancer.

HEALTH CONNECTION

Dr. Jane C. Wright

You could say that practicing medicine was in her genes, but after reading this chapter and the next, you'll know that isn't true. But it was a very distinguished and powerful heritage that pulled Jane Wright (1919–) into medicine. Her father, an eminent surgeon, was one of the first African-American graduates of Harvard Medical School, and her grandfather was an early graduate of Meharry Medical College, a school for former slaves.

After practicing for several years as a family doctor, Dr. Wright was offered the opportunity to do cancer research and began the work that has brought her national and international fame. Her research into chemotherapy, the use of chemicals to treat cancer, has made her an international authority on the subject.

Chemotherapy is often the last resort in the treatment of cancer, after surgery and radiation therapy fail. In chemotherapy, various drugs are used, either alone or in combination, to try to kill or stop the spread of cancer cells. Every year, new chemotherapy drugs are developed. Dr. Wright tests these drugs on cancer cells in test tubes and in animals to see if the drugs are effective in killing the cancer cells. If a drug shows promise, it is tested in humans and eventually made available to doctors for use in treating cancer.

Dr. Wright has published more than 100 articles on cancer chemotherapy. She believes chemotherapy treatments are becoming more effective with the development of new and more powerful drugs. But she thinks new drugs still need to be discovered, and perhaps she will be the researcher to do it.

1. **Explore Further:** Find out how surgery and radiation therapy are used in the treatment of cancer.
2. **Solve the Problem:** Why are increasingly more powerful drugs dangerous to use in chemotherapy?

HEALTH CONNECTION

Purpose
Students will be exposed to the variety of methods that exist today in the treatment of cancer.

Teaching Strategies
• Assign students to cooperative learning groups. Ask each group to review and define the meaning of the following terms: cancer, malignant tumor, radiation therapy, chemotherapy. Have them also ask the school nurse to provide them with a list of cancer warning signs. **LEP** **COOP LEARN**

Possible Answers
1. Surgery is used to remove a malignant tumor. Radiation therapy attacks the cancer cells by slowing down or stopping their reproduction.
2. A drug used to stop the growth of cancer cells may interfere with the growth of normal cells as well.

Going Further
Have students do some library research to determine which organs and tissues in the human body seem to be most prone to cancer. Have them prepare a list of possible carcinogens that they may be exposed to every day. **L3**

combined length of all roots that now appear in each tube. Record your data.

Analysis
Ask students to answer the following questions.
1. Explain how you were able to assess that a specific chemical was a possible carcinogen. *lack of root growth compared to control tube*
2. You may not have evidence that the chemicals tested were actually carcinogens.
(a) How could you verify that these chemicals are carcinogens? *examine the cells microscopically*
(b) What might you have been observing in the experiment if these chemicals reduced root growth? *inhibitors of mitosis*
3. What was the value of doing this experiment if one cannot prove that a chemical is a carcinogen? *It is a screening technique.*

✔ **Assessment**
Skill: Draw the following in your journal: (a) a normal onion root cell and its 16 chromosomes as seen in prophase of mitosis; (b) onion root cells and their chromosomes if the cells are cancerous. Label both diagrams. **L1** **LEP**

SECTION 10.2

Figure Caption Question

How are recombinant plasmids produced? Plasmids and the foreign genes are cut at specific points, using an enzyme. The foreign gene inserts itself in the open plasmid and, because the ends match, the plasmid is spliced together.

Bioethics

Ethical Decisions: How can one make a decision as to the ethics of a new technology, such as recombinant DNA, being right or wrong? Ethicists have to be guided in their decisions and use three general principles when making a decision. (1) Beneficence: This principle asks the question "Will a decision result in a greater balance of good over harm?" It can be applied to whole groups of people as well as to only one individual. (2) Respect for autonomy: All individuals have self worth and dignity, which should be respected by others, even if their values differ from yours. (3) Justice: Every person has a right to basic needs such as food, shelter, and education. Therefore, all individuals must be treated equally regardless of their position, merit, or status in the community. Use of these guidelines will avoid the "free for all" type of debate or discussion that might result when discussing bioethics in class.

Cancer researchers have begun to identify different oncogenes, and they are attempting to determine the proteins for which the oncogenes code. When these proteins are discovered, their effects on the cell cycle will be analyzed. Knowing the effects of these abnormal proteins will also further understanding of proteins that control the cell cycle in a normal way. All this knowledge will perhaps lead to more effective treatment and cure of cancers.

Variation Through Technology—Recombinant DNA

In Chapter 9, you learned that discovery of DNA as the genetic material of all organisms came from a series of experiments in which genetic transformation took place. Transformation is one of the ways genetic variation arises in bacteria. It occurs when a bacterial cell absorbs a gene from another cell. The cell that gains the gene exhibits the phenotype of the cell that donated the DNA.

Scientists have made practical use of their knowledge of transformation by learning how to transfer a gene artificially from a donor organism to a bacterium. The DNA of the bacterium that has been altered by insertion of a foreign gene is called **recombinant DNA.** The bacterium transcribes and translates the foreign gene to produce the protein for which the foreign gene codes.

Plasmids   How is this genetic engineering accomplished? The cytoplasm of a bacterium contains, in addition to its main chromosome, small circular pieces of DNA called **plasmids.** Plasmids are the structures with which the foreign DNA is recombined. The technique involves making many recombined plasmids and putting them together with bacteria that will

Figure 10-15   **Using recombinant DNA techniques, *E. coli* bacteria can be engineered to produce a desired protein such as human insulin. How are recombinant plasmids produced?**

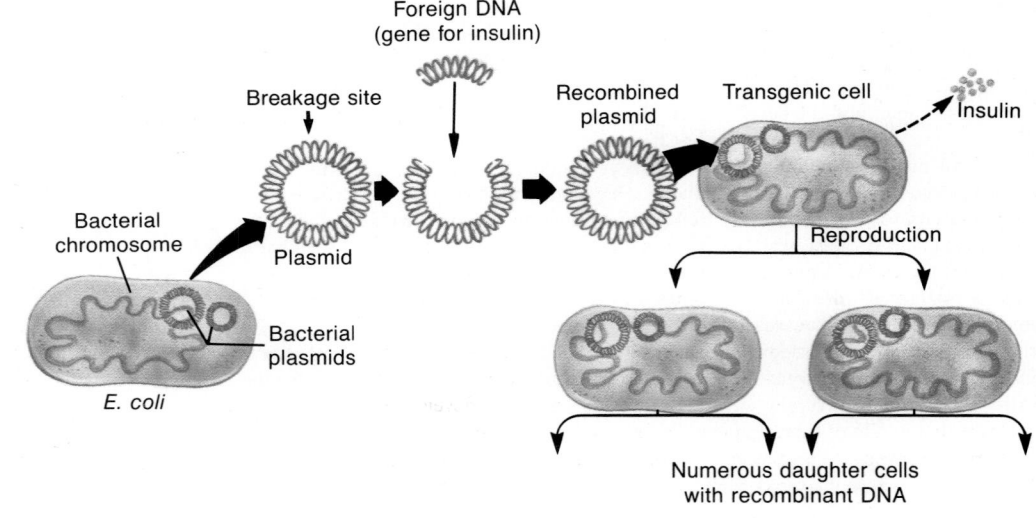

268 ▲ FROM GENES TO PROTEINS

MULTICULTURAL CONNECTION

Cancer Incidence: The incidence and distribution of cancer varies by country and race. Ask students to discuss possible causes for the data. Suggest genetic or environmental causes.

Type of Cancer	Highest Occurrence	Lowest Occurrence
Skin	Queensland, Australia	Bombay, India
Esophagus	N.E. Iran	Nigeria

Type of Cancer	Highest Occurrence	Lowest Occurrence
Lung	England	Nigeria
Stomach	Japan	Uganda
Liver	Mozambique	Norway
Prostate	U.S.	Japan
Colon	Connecticut, U.S.	Nigeria
Mouth	India	Denmark
Rectum	Denmark	Nigeria
Bladder	Connecticut, U.S.	Japan
Cervix	Colombia	Israel
Breast	Connecticut, U.S.	Uganda

absorb them. The bacteria that take up the recombined plasmids will begin to produce large quantities of the protein for which the foreign gene codes.

For example, insulin, a hormone important in the treatment of a form of diabetes, is produced commercially this way. Recombinant DNA techniques have enabled researchers to produce this protein in purer form and in much larger quantities than was formerly possible.

Obtaining the Foreign Gene   How is the foreign gene obtained? There are several approaches, but one of the most reliable is to synthesize it. First, a cell that specializes in producing the desired protein must be found, because such a cell will contain many mRNA molecules that carry the genetic code for the protein. These mRNA molecules are identified and isolated. With the help of an enzyme obtained from a virus, a single-stranded DNA molecule is produced from the mRNA molecule by a process that is the reverse of transcription. The single-stranded DNA is converted to double-stranded form, using an enzyme normally used by cells for DNA replication. This double-stranded DNA is the desired gene. Next, thousands of copies of the gene must be made. Making many copies of a gene by these methods is known as gene cloning. **Clones** are genetically identical copies. You will learn more about clones when you study reproduction.

Inserting the Foreign DNA   Before the foreign DNA can be inserted into the plasmid, the plasmid must first be broken open at a specific point and changed from circular to linear form. The circle must be broken at that point where the nucleotides of the plasmid's DNA will match the nucleotides of the foreign DNA. This is accomplished using enzymes that are known to break DNA only at specific points. These enzymes are used on both the plasmid and the foreign DNA. The two segments of DNA with matching ends then join, and the plasmid regains its circular shape. The recombinant plasmids are then placed into a liquid medium containing billions of bacterial cells and chemicals that favor the cells' absorption of the plasmids. A few bacteria take up the plasmids and, if the recombinant DNA has located properly, begin to produce the desired protein, which they secrete into the medium. The protein is extracted from the medium, purified, and put to use.

Applying Recombinant DNA Techniques   Although early work in recombinant DNA was limited to bacterial cells, recent advances have enabled geneticists to develop modified techniques that can be applied to eukaryotic cells as well. In some cases, foreign genes are inserted into whole organisms. In other cases, the genes are inserted into isolated cells grown in a culture medium. For example, scientists recently inserted into fertilized goat eggs a human gene for a protein that dissolves blood clots. The recombined fertilized eggs were then implanted into female goats for development. Two of the eggs picked up the foreign gene and developed into baby goats, one male and one female. These animals are called transgenic organisms because they contain genetic material from two species. The transgenic female goat secretes the clot-dissolving protein in her milk.

Minilab 2

Do biotechnology products help us?

The enzyme alpha-amylase can be recovered efficiently through means of biotechnology from a fungus. This enzyme is used to speed up the chemical change of starch to glucose. Test a starch solution for the presence of glucose using Benedict's solution. Combine starch with alpha-amylase, wait 15 minutes, and test again for glucose. Test a sample of the enzyme alone for glucose. Explain your results. Offer a possible commercial use for this enzyme, knowing that starch is not sweet while glucose is.

Analysis   *How might the recovery of an enzyme from a microorganism illustrate biotechnology?*

Figure 10-16   **This bacterial DNA plasmid contains genes that make bacteria resistant to certain antibiotics. Magnification: 50 000 ×**

Minilab 2

Purpose
Students will treat starch with alpha-amylase to observe the enzymatic reaction. Students will suggest some commercial uses for this enzyme, and infer how the enzyme can be produced in large quantities.

Skills
observe and infer, compare and contrast, separate and control variables, interpret data

Teaching Strategies
- **Safety Precautions:** Advise students to use thermal mitts and handle hot objects with care.
- For preparation of solutions, see page 27T.
- Enzyme is available in liquid form from a biological supply house.
- Set up a boiling water bath by heating a beaker of water on a hot plate or lab burner.
- Add 5 mL of starch and 5 drops of enzyme. Mix and wait 15 minutes before testing for glucose.

Expected Results
Starch or amylase alone will give a negative test for glucose. Starch plus alpha-amylase will test positive for glucose because the enzyme catalyzes the conversion of starch to simple sugars.

Answers
Starch or amylase alone does not contain glucose. Amylase speeded up the change from starch to glucose.

Glucose may be used as a sweetener in foods and beverages. Starch is available in cereals and potatoes.

Bacteria may not normally produce this enzyme. Through biotechnology, bacteria have been modified so that they can make amylase, thus providing a previously unavailable source of this chemical.

✔ Assessment
Oral: Have students outline the lab on the chalkboard, explaining the procedure for the tests and why the results were achieved. They should demonstrate an understanding of what happened in each test tube.

MULTICULTURAL CONNECTION

Oil Cleanup: Ananda M. Chakrabarty used recombinant DNA techniques to develop an "oil-eating" bacterium that would be of great assistance as a means for helping with ecological cleanup after oil spills. His contribution was not only important to science but he also was awarded the first patent for a genetically engineered organism.

STUDENT JOURNAL

Have students write a short paper discussing the possible role of recombinant DNA techniques in the future. Ask students to consider both the pros and cons of genetic engineering.

3 Assess

Check for Understanding

Have students explain the relationships between the following word groups:
(a) insertion—deletion
(b) recombinant DNA—variation
(c) carcinogen—oncogene
(d) mutagens—cancer L1   LEP

Reteach

Divide the class into groups. Have each group prepare a concept map of the major topics and concepts in this section. Have a presenter from each group share the group's map with the rest of the class. COOP LEARN

Extension

Have student groups prepare a bulletin board that shows the steps used in recombinant DNA technology. Have them use a specific example in their presentation. L2   COOP LEARN

✔ Assessment

Oral: Students should be able to describe at least four different mechanisms by which genes and chromosomes contribute to the observation of variation among organisms. They should also be able to describe three causes of cancer and be able to explain the role of recombinant DNA in helping society. L1

4 Close

Discussion

Have students explain why the DNA of a foreign organism that has been transferred to a bacterium will work normally to form proteins in this new environment. Make sure students understand the universality of the genetic code. COOP LEARN

Scientists have produced transgenic plants that resist disease and spoilage. Special recombinant DNA techniques have been needed for use with plants because the tough cell walls of plant cells make it difficult for the foreign genes to be inserted. Foreign genes can be inserted into these cells by one of several methods. In one method, the foreign genes are inserted into a bacterium or a virus, which infects the plant cells and transfers the gene to the plant's genetic material. In a second method, "bullets" of metal particles coated with foreign DNA are shot into the plant cells using a device known as a "gene gun." Other methods punch temporary holes in the cell wall or dissolve the cell wall altogether. In any of these ways, the cells that successfully pick up the foreign gene may reproduce and develop into mature plants. Newly developed techniques such as these hold promise for the production of transgenic crops that are both hardier and more nutritious than conventional crops. The techniques will also enable people to produce more food at less expense.

Transgenic organisms are used not only to produce a wide variety of desired proteins, but also as a basic research tool to study genes and their control mechanisms. Recombinant DNA techniques will doubtless continue to yield benefits that will improve health, alter food crops, and benefit the economy.

LOOKING AHEAD

YOU HAVE now explored how the genetic information in DNA is used to synthesize polypeptides and how DNA is related to expression of phenotypes. In the next chapter, you will relate this information to human genetics and the causes and symptoms of hereditary disorders. Geneticists are using knowledge of DNA and protein synthesis in their efforts to diagnose, treat, and cure those disorders.

Section Review

Understanding Concepts

1. Explain how a gene mutation can be lethal, yet be passed on from one generation to another. How can such mutations prove lethal to a later generation?

2. Which would likely be more of a problem—an insertion mutation that occurs near the beginning of a gene or toward the end of a gene? Why?

3. Many fertilized eggs begin, but never complete, development. These eggs usually contain abnormal genetic material. Which is more likely to be responsible, a gene mutation or a chromosome mutation? Explain.

4. **Skill Review—Sequencing:** Sequence the steps used in recombinant DNA work with bacteria. For more help, see Organizing Information in the **Skill Handbook**.

5. **Thinking Critically:** Why would a new polypeptide produced as a result of the rearrangement of exons be more likely to be functional than a polypeptide produced by a random gene mutation?

Answers to Section Review

1. The mutant allele can be masked by a dominant allele. If two heterozygotes mate, 1/4 of their offspring may be homozygous recessive, a lethal combination.

2. An insertion near the beginning of a gene would be more of a problem because all of the codons after the point of the insertion (and the amino acids for which they code) would be affected.

3. A chromosome mutation is more likely to be responsible because many more genes would be involved. This type of mutation is more likely to be lethal.

4. **Skill Review—Sequencing:** See page 269 of the text for a discussion of the steps of recombinant DNA work.

5. **Thinking Critically:** The exons code for segments of proteins that function. New combinations of such segments might also function, but in a slightly different way.

BIOLOGY, TECHNOLOGY, AND SOCIETY

Biotechnology

DNA Fingerprinting—A New Weapon Against Crime

In violent crimes such as murder and rape, physical evidence is often left at the scene of the crime. Blood, skin, hair, or sperm cells may be the only evidence that the police have. A suspect can be arrested and found guilty long after a crime has been committed. How do police use the cells they have found to prove that a suspect is guilty? They are able to identify the DNA in the cells as having come from the suspect, using a technology known as DNA fingerprinting. How does DNA fingerprinting work and how is it used?

Why DNA Fingerprinting Works
Genetically, we are what we are because of our DNA. We are all human because we all have 46 chromosomes made up of sequences of DNA. Half of these sequences come from our mother and half from our father. Every one of us is distinct because each new combination of egg and sperm is different. Thus, except for identical twins, every human has DNA that is different and unique. But because the original sequences come from our parents, our DNA will show similarities to our parents' DNA.

DNA fingerprinting takes advantage of the differences in base sequences in individuals. There are about 3 billion base pairs that make up the DNA of a human. Most of the DNA, such as the genes that control cellular respiration and other life processes, are common to all humans. However, some areas of DNA, the repetitive noncoding sequences found between genes, are highly variable. It is this variability that makes the DNA of each person unique.

The Technique DNA, both from the cell sample found at the crime scene and from a suspect's blood cells, is first isolated and purified. The DNA is then treated with enzymes that chop it up at specific places in the molecule. This produces about one million DNA fragments of differing lengths. The fragments are separated according to size by electrophoresis, a technique that uses an electric field to separate molecules or charged particles embedded in a jellylike material.

After separation, the fragments can be identified by treating them with various radioactive probes. These probes are pieces of radioactively labeled, single-stranded DNA with base sequences that may be complementary to those in the repeating sequences of the samples. If a probe matches the repeating sequences in the DNA being tested, the two pieces of DNA bind together. The location of the DNA fragments that have bound to the probe can be detected because they are radioactive. A pattern of bands is produced that resembles the bar codes you see every day on groceries and other products. It is this bar code pattern that is the DNA fingerprint.

Analysis The bar code produced by the DNA found at the scene of the crime is compared with that of the DNA from the suspect's blood cells. If the patterns match, the two samples of DNA most likely came from the same individual. The probability of two individuals having matching DNA fingerprints has been calculated to be about one chance in 9.34 billion—about double the present population of the world. Therefore, it is almost a certain conclusion that the suspect is guilty.

CHAPTER 10 FROM GENES TO PROTEINS ꆧ **271**

Biotechnology

Purpose
Students are introduced to the technique of DNA fingerprinting and learn how this technique can be used in a variety of different situations. They will be able to see that this test relies on the uniqueness of each person's DNA and may be used as a specific means for identifying a person's cells or tracing his or her heritage.

Background
The enzymes used to chop up the DNA as part of the process are called restriction enzymes. This step and electrophoresis separation are necessary because of the large size of human DNA. Without these steps, all that would result would be a smear of human chromosomal material that could not be analyzed.

Teaching Strategies
• Collect and copy 8 bar codes, labeled A-H, from food packages. Try to use bar codes that are equal in size and that initially appear similar in their patterns. These eight codes will represent the DNA from possible criminal suspects. Then supply students with a bar code taken from a suspected criminal's skin cells discovered at the scene of a crime (use a copy of one of the eight codes). Have students match the skin cell DNA with the suspects' DNA (bar codes A-H) and identify the criminal by letter.

Possible Answers
1. Student answers will vary. Some may state that the evidence is quite convincing if it is almost impossible for two individuals on Earth to have the same DNA. Others may feel that laboratory techniques may not be refined enough to use this type of technology to convict a criminal, regardless of the nature and/or severity of the crime.

2. Cell surface proteins are inherited traits that are controlled by DNA. Donors can be screened to see if their DNA (gene traits) closely matches that needed by the organ recipient.

3. As is the case with any evidence at the scene of a crime, the criminal does not leave it there intentionally. Therefore the case may be made that this is not evidence that should be discounted because it constitutes a person testifying against him or herself.

Going Further

Kits (Edvotek and Carolina Biological Supply) are available that will allow students to perform some of the same techniques described in this feature. Teachers will need to have electrophoresis equipment available for use with these kits. **L3**

How Is DNA Fingerprinting Used?
You have just read how DNA fingerprinting can be used to prove that a particular suspect is guilty of a crime. The technique can also be used to prove that a suspect is innocent. If the suspect's DNA fingerprint does *not* match that of the evidence, he or she is almost assuredly innocent.

DNA fingerprinting has several other uses. It has been used to determine paternity by comparing the DNA of a child, its mother, and two or more possible biological fathers. It also can be used to establish family relationships between individuals living in different countries. These family relationships are important in solving immigration disputes. And finally, DNA fingerprinting has been used in studying animal populations to determine the amount of genetic diversity in the population. These data should be useful in studying ecology and evolution of animal populations.

1. **Issue:** Discuss what you think the proper role for DNA fingerprinting should be in court cases. Should it be the deciding evidence in cases that involve the death penalty? What about cases of assault or rape? What about cases that establish paternity?

2. **Connection to Health:** To treat certain diseases, some patients require transplants of organs or bone marrow. One problem with transplants is that the body will reject those whose cell surface proteins do not closely match the recipient's. Hypothesize about how DNA fingerprinting might be used to treat these patients.

3. **Connection to Government:** The Fifth Amendment to the Constitution of the United States prohibits forcing people to testify against themselves. Discuss whether using a person's blood or other body part that was obtained involuntarily as evidence constitutes a person testifying against him or herself.

Issues

Dying with Dignity: Who Decides?

The 85-year-old woman was rushed to the hospital on New Year's Day. She could not breathe, so doctors placed her on a respirator. After five months of trying to wean her from the machine that was helping her breathe, her doctors transferred her to a chronic care facility. In only a few weeks, however, the woman was taken back to the hospital when her heart stopped. Doctors managed to restart her heart, but the patient had lapsed into a coma that doctors believed was permanent.

The woman was connected to many machines that breathed for her, fed her, and kept her organs functioning. She lay in her hospital bed with tubes and wires attached to her body. After several weeks, doctors became convinced that her treatment was doing no good and that she would never recover. Yet, her family refused to allow doctors to remove the machines.

After many months, the hospital went to court, asking for an independent opinion on whether treatment should be continued. A hearing was held, and the court decided that the husband should make medical decisions for his incapacitated wife. The machines remained, and the woman finally died 18 months after her illness began.

Medical Futility This case illustrates the concept of medical futility. Are doctors morally obligated to administer treatment that they believe will not benefit the patient? For example, if a patient suffering from untreatable lung cancer needs a kidney transplant because of kidney failure, must a doctor perform one? Or would a transplant be futile? Some people might argue that a transplant would prolong life. Others might say that, in the end, the patient would still die of cancer. In our society, doctors are not obliged to do what will be futile, but legal decisions have shown that futility is difficult to define.

Who Decides? If the woman in the above case had been conscious, she could have communicated her wishes about whether life-sustaining treatment should be used to prolong her life. It is when a patient is no longer mentally competent to make such decisions that problems arise. In December, 1991, the first United States law to address this issue went into effect. This law, the Patient Self-Determination Act, requires all hospitals and other medical care facilities to inform patients of the laws of that state regarding the making of advance health care decisions before patients are no longer capable of making the decisions themselves.

There are two ways a person can plan in advance in case such medical decision-making becomes necessary. First, a person can write a living will, in which he or she makes a statement outlining preferences for treatment or nontreatment under different conditions. Second, a person can sign a power of attorney for health care, in which the decisions are entrusted to someone who knows the person well and knows the person's feelings.

Assisted Death Some terminally ill patients feel that they should have control over the conditions of their death. They feel that prolonging their life by technological means is inhumane and robs them of their right to die with dignity. Many of these patients have asked their doctors to assist them in dying.

Assisted death, called euthanasia, can be either passive or active. Passive euthanasia is the withholding of life-prolonging treatment. If a doctor does not attempt to resuscitate a terminally ill patient whose heart has stopped beating, the doctor is practicing passive euthanasia. On the other hand, if the doctor administers a lethal dose of a drug to end a patient's painful life at the patient's request, that is active euthanasia. Many people concerned with the right to die feel that, if a doctor knows the patient's feelings well and knows that the patient is competent to make this decision, active euthanasia should be allowed. Other people believe that active euthanasia is "killing," whereas passive euthanasia is "letting die." At the present time, active euthanasia is illegal in the United States.

Active euthanasia has been performed in The Netherlands since the 1980s. Although it is illegal, the practice has been tolerated as long as doctors follow strict guidelines. A British medical institute recently published a report in which it appeared to endorse active, as well as passive, euthanasia. In the United States and elsewhere in the

Western world, passive euthanasia is widely accepted. However, active euthanasia is a morally, politically, and legally debated issue. As the right-to-die movement becomes more widespread, laws no doubt will change.

1. **Understanding the Issue:** Should a person have the right to decide when to die? Explain. Some state laws dictate what must be done for terminally ill patients who cannot make decisions for themselves. Discuss why such laws are or are not desirable.
2. **Writing About Biology:** Research the idea of a living will. What is its purpose? Write a living will for yourself that clearly states what you would like done without unnecessarily restricting a doctor or relative from using his or her judgment in an uncertain situation.

Readings
- Gustaitis, R. and E.W.D. Young. *A Time to be Born, a Time to Die.* Reading, MA: Addison-Wesley, 1986.
- Orentlicher, David. "The Right to Die After Cruzan." *The Journal of the American Medical Association,* Nov. 14, 1990, p. 2444.

sions. Note that if I am in a coma or vegetative state for more than two weeks, then all treatment aimed at keeping me alive shall cease.

Going Further
Have students read the article and/or book listed at the bottom of page 273. Have them write a report on their readings and include it in their portfolio. L2

Issues

Purpose
Students will be presented with an aspect of life that they normally do not associate with genes—the aging and death of a person.

Teaching Strategies
- Have students work in two groups to prepare a debate on the issue of euthanasia. You will assign group positions for and against. Groups will have to do some research before their presentations are made. If class members are already involved with the debate team, appoint them as leaders within each group. COOP LEARN
- Ask students to research the pros and cons of euthanasia. Ask for specific students to present their findings to the class.
- Present the following word list to student groups and have them determine definitions for: *chronic, coma, futility, competent.*

Possible Answers
1. This question may be answered either way. Requesting death if ill could prevent the person from receiving a new cure that could help prolong his or her life. However, people should be given control over their own bodies to decide if they wish to continue living or not. The state laws controlling whether a person does or does not receive treatment can be argued with the same two points as expressed above.
2. A living will specifies the medical treatment to be administered or appoints an agent to act on the behalf of a person who might be unable to make a decision regarding his or her own medical treatment if incapacitated. The agent has the authority to make all decisions regarding the treatment of the person who established the living will. Example: If I am in a situation where I am no longer able to make any decisions regarding my medical care and/or treatment, I am appointing my friend, Jack Nymark, as the person who shall be in charge of making these deci-

CHAPTER 10

CHAPTER REVIEW

Summary

Summary statements can be used by students to review the major concepts of the chapter.

Language of Biology

Answers should go beyond defining the terms. Accept any reasonable answer that uses the term correctly and in the proper context.

Understanding Concepts

1. The processed mRNA attaches to a ribosome. A tRNA molecule with an anticodon complementary to the first mRNA codon carries an amino acid coded for by that first codon. It moves to the ribosome, where its anticodon and the first mRNA codon join. The ribosome then moves to the second mRNA codon. The process is repeated. The two amino acids form a bond, and the first tRNA molecule leaves the ribosome. This process continues until the ribosome moves to the stop codon. At this point, the polypeptide breaks away.

2. Each allele codes for a different functional protein. When both proteins are made, the organism has an intermediate phenotype.

3. GGA.

4. The cell will not be able to make a sufficient number of ribosomes and will be unable to synthesize proteins quickly enough. The cell could not survive.

5. This fact reveals an exception to the one gene-one polypeptide hypothesis. In effect, some genes can code for several different polypeptides, depending on how mRNA is processed.

6. The mutation in a diploid organism will most often result in a recessive allele, whose effect will be masked by the normal, dominant allele. Haploid organisms have just one allele for each trait. Assuming the haploid organism survives with the mutant gene, it will have a new trait, which will be inherited by all its offspring.

Summary

Messenger RNA carries information from the DNA in the genes to the sites of protein synthesis in the cytoplasm. The DNA information carried by each gene on the many chromosomes of a eukaryotic cell, or on the single chromosome of a prokaryote, is first transcribed into mRNA. Transfer RNA then acts as an interpreter to translate the nucleic acid language into the protein language, and a polypeptide is synthesized at the ribosomes.

Polypeptides are synthesized by a cell only when they are needed and only in the quantity needed. The phenotype of an organism is determined by the polypeptides produced by its cells, which in turn is determined by its DNA. Only a tiny fraction of the DNA of eukaryotes carries information for polypeptides.

Mutations can occur in single genes or in chromosomes and may occur spontaneously or as a result of external agents. In addition to random mutations, which produce new alleles, entirely new genes may arise from duplication and modification of pre-existing genes or by rearrangement of gene parts. Production of new alleles and genes adds to the variations present within a population.

Cancer is a disease that is caused by mutations in the genes that control the cell cycle. Viruses play a role in causing some kinds of cancer.

A variety of recombinant DNA techniques can be used to mass-produce quantities of useful proteins. These techniques are also important tools used to study cell mechanisms.

Language of Biology

Write a sentence that shows your understanding of each of the following terms.

anticodon	mutation
carcinogen	oncogene
clone	plasmid
deletion	point mutation
exon	recombinant DNA
insertion	ribosomal RNA (rRNA)
intron	transcription
messenger RNA (mRNA)	transfer RNA (tRNA)
	translation
mutagen	uracil

Understanding Concepts

1. A short chain of processed mRNA has the nucleotide sequence AUA CCG GAC UCA. The last codon is a stop signal. Explain the series of events by which a polypeptide is synthesized from this mRNA sequence.

2. Based on your knowledge of DNA and polypeptide synthesis, how might you explain incomplete dominance?

3. A tRNA molecule has the anticodon GGA. What DNA base sequence was used to produce the codon that will bind to this anticodon?

4. A new cell is produced that has just a few copies of each of the genes needed for making rRNA. What cell function would be affected? Could the cell survive?

5. Sometimes the exons of a newly synthesized mRNA molecule can be spliced together in several different ways. Each processed mRNA molecule then codes for a different polypeptide. How does this fact fit in with the one gene-one polypeptide hypothesis?

6. Why would a mutation in a haploid organism have a much more immediate effect on the entire population than a mutation in a diploid organism?

7. How might a pseudogene be important in the future of a population?

8. How could you determine whether a single chain of nucleotides is RNA or DNA?

7. A pseudogene could undergo modification, resulting in a new functional gene that might promote survival.

8. Chemical analysis of the chain would provide the answer. RNA contains ribose and uracil. DNA contains deoxyribose and thymine.

Applying Concepts

9. The two alleles differ in only one nucleotide.

10. It was probably a point mutation, because only one amino acid is different.

11. The DNA could be neither replicated nor transcribed properly.

12. The creeper allele is lethal.

13. The fact that light is given off by the plant into which the foreign gene was inserted provides an indirect way of knowing that the desired foreign gene has been taken up by the plant.

14. The genes probably arose as a result of duplication followed by modification of the duplicated gene.

15. The sequence of bases along DNA molecules is important. Attaching some DNA

Applying Concepts

9. The difference between a normal hemoglobin molecule, coded for by a dominant allele, and the abnormal hemoglobin molecule that causes the disorder sickle-cell anemia, coded by a recessive allele, is only one amino acid in one of the hemoglobin polypeptide chains. In terms of DNA, how do the two alleles differ?

10. Assume the abnormal allele for sickle-cell anemia was produced by a random mutation. What kind of mutation was it? How do you know?

11. Ultraviolet light causes two successive thymine nucleotides along a chain of DNA to bond with one another instead of to the adenine nucleotides of the complementary chain. What effects would result from this mistake?

12. An allele in chickens, when present with the normal allele, results in the phenotype called creeper, in which the chicken has short legs and walks improperly. Two heterozygotes are crossed, but 1/4 of the eggs fail to develop. What does that tell you about the creeper allele?

13. Sometimes foreign genes are inserted into plants along with another gene that produces light (as in a firefly). How might the gene for light production be useful in recombinant DNA work?

14. Many digestive enzymes have been found to have very similar nucleotide sequences. How might the genes that code for these enzymes have originated?

15. You might think that a piece of a chromosome that breaks off but attaches backwards to its original chromosome would not cause a problem because all the genes are still present. Suggest reasons why such a chromosome mutation could, in fact, cause a problem.

16. What is cancer? How do cancer cells differ from normal cells?

17. **Issues:** The deaths of many terminal cancer patients occur when vital organs stop functioning. These organs may be located far from the original site of the cancer. How can cancer spread to distant organs?

18. **Biotechnology:** Forensic lab technicians compare the blood of a rape suspect with sperm recovered at the crime scene. What concept forms the basis of this method of identifying crime suspects?

Lab Interpretation

19. **Investigate:** The following diagrams are "birds-eye" views of student models. Describe the errors that you are able to detect.
    (a) Model of DNA

Tape

A-T-T-C-G-G-A-C-U   = row of students facing below

‖ ‖ ‖ ‖ ‖ ‖ ‖ ‖ ‖ } Hands

T-A-A-G-G-C-T-G-T   = row of students facing above

(b) Model of mRNA undergoing transcription, using the bottom row from above as a template

A-T-T-C-C-G-U-C-U

(c) Model of tRNA for amino acid X

20. **Minilab 1:** Suggest two ways in which a gene mutation might slow or prevent the process of germination from occurring in a seed.

21. **Minilab 2:** Explain why, in this experiment, it was necessary to test the enzyme itself for the presence of glucose.

22. **Thinking Lab:** Explain why traits determined by organelle DNA are inherited in the pattern observed in this experiment.

Connecting Ideas

23. Suppose a cell synthesizes a protein that will leave the cell and be used by other cells. How does the protein travel from the ribosomes where it is made, through the cell, and out?

24. Different blood types are due to the presence of different proteins on the surfaces of red blood cells. Red cells of people with type O blood have no proteins of this type. In terms of DNA function, explain (a) why the genotype $I^B i$ results in type B blood and (b) why the genotype $I^A I^B$ results in type AB blood.

backwards could place start and stop signals in the wrong place. It could also reverse the base sequences of genes.

16. Cancer is a general term for a variety of diseases characterized by production of cells having abnormal shapes and membrane proteins and often unusual numbers of chromosomes.

17. Unlike other cells, cancer cells can migrate throughout the body. As they invade new areas, they grow uncontrollably, crowding out healthy cells and destroying tissues and organs.

18. All cells of an individual contain the same DNA sequences. If repeating sections of the two DNA samples match, even though the two samples are from different types of cells, the suspect is almost certainly guilty.

Lab Interpretation

19. a. There should be no U in DNA; T would not pair with U; G never pairs with G.
    b. There should be no T in mRNA. It should read as follows: A-U-U-C-C-G-A-C-A
    c. There should be no T in tRNA. An anticodon has only 3 bases.

20. The mutation may cause a change in the seed coat, making it impermeable to water. The mutation may alter the embryo within the seed, preventing its normal pattern of development. The mutation may result in death of the seed.

21. If the enzyme contains glucose, then the source of glucose was not from the reaction between starch and the enzyme.

22. The egg contributes all the cytoplasm, including the organelles, to the zygote. The sperm is too small to contain much cytoplasm.

Connecting Ideas

23. **Systems and Interactions:** The protein enters the rough ER and is passed, in a vesicle derived from the ER membrane, to a nearby Golgi body. The protein passes from one Golgi compartment to

the next in a vesicle. The protein leaves the Golgi body in a vesicle, and is expelled by exocytosis.

24. **Systems and Interactions:** (a) The I^B allele codes for B proteins while the i allele codes for no protein. Thus the person has type B blood. (b) The I^A allele codes for A proteins and the I^B allele codes for B proteins. Because both proteins are synthesized, the person has type AB blood, an example of codominance.

SECTION	OBJECTIVES	TEXT LABS/FEATURES
11.1 Human Genetic Disorders (3 days)	**Explain** the symptoms of cystic fibrosis. **Demonstrate** how modern knowledge and techniques have led to understanding the cause of genetic disorders. **Discuss** examples of other inherited disorders, their symptoms, and their causes.	**Thinking Lab:** Is snoring inherited? p. 281 **Minilab 1:** How do normal red blood cells compare to red blood cells of patients with sickle-cell anemia? p. 282 **Minilab 2:** Can sex differences be observed in human body cells? p. 285 **History Connection:** Heredity and the Amish, p. 286
11.2 Prevention and a Possible Means of Cure (3 days)	**Demonstrate** how genetic counseling can be used to provide parents with information about the possibility of having a child with a genetic disorder. **Describe** techniques that permit diagnosis of a genetic disorder in the unborn. **Discuss** gene therapy and how it might be used to cure genetic disorders.	**Global Connection:** Tracking Deadly Medicine, p. 292 **Investigation:** Variation in Human Hands, p. 294
BIOLOGY, TECHNOLOGY, AND SOCIETY		**Issues:** Gender on Demand, p. 297 **Biotechnology:** In Utero Treatments for Genetic Disorders, p. 299 **Career Connection:** Neonatologist, p. 299

LAB MATERIALS

INVESTIGATION	MINILAB	ALTERNATE LAB
page 294 grip tester magnifying glass metric ruler	**page 282** microscope prepared slides: human red blood cells human sickled red blood cells **page 285** bleach coverslips methylene blue stain microscope slides toothpicks	**page 284** karyotype, normal karyotype, disorders: Down syndrome Edwards syndrome Klinefelter syndrome Pateau syndrome tetraploidy triploidy XXX syndrome XYY syndrome microscope

TEACHER CLASSROOM RESOURCES	OTHER RESOURCES
Study Guide, pp. 61-63 **Concept Mapping,** p. 11 **Critical Thinking/Problem Solving:** *Genetic Disorders: Causes and Symptoms,* p. 11 ***PLL:** *Human Chromosome Karyotyping,* p. 59 ***PLL:** *Human Pedigree Genetics,* p. 61 ****ILS:** *Pedigree Studies,* p. 99 ****ILS:** *A Chromosome Study,* p. 103	***STVS:** *Detecting Cystic Fibrosis,* Human Biology (Disc 7, Side 2)
Study Guide, pp. 64-66 ****ILS:** *Sex-Linked or Not Sex-Linked?* p. 105	
Assessment Materials **Chapter Assessment,** pp. 41-44 **Performance Assessment in Biology,** p. 22 **Alternate Assessment in the Science Classroom** **Computer Test Bank**	**Spanish Resources** **Cooperative Learning Resource Guide** **Videodisc Correlations** (to Optical Data's and Videodiscovery's videodiscs)

* Probing Levels of Life
** Investigating Living Systems

* Science Technology Videodisc Series

Key to Teaching Strategies

The following designations will help you decide which activities in the teacher margin are appropriate for your students.

L1 Level 1 activities should be within the ability range of all students.

L2 Level 2 activities should be within the ability range of the average to above-average student.

L3 Level 3 activities are designed for the ability range of above-average students.

LEP LEP activities are appropriate for Limited English Proficiency students.

COOP LEARN Cooperative Learning activities are designed for small group work.

ADDITIONAL RESOURCES

Infinite Voyage *The Search for Ancient Americans*
Are all native Americans related? Scientists agree that humans migrated to North America over a land bridge connecting Siberia and Alaska.

Audiovisual
Genetic Testing, video, Films for the Humanities and Sciences.
The Human Genome, video, Films for the Humanities and Sciences.

Software
Human Genetic Disorders, Apple 64K, Queue.

11

HUMAN GENETICS

Chapter Overview

Students begin this chapter by studying the causes of several human genetic diseases. They not only learn about the symptoms of the diseases, but also about the causes of those symptoms. They also find out that some diseases are the result of more than a single pair of alleles and explore the idea of heterozygote superiority. They investigate sex-linked diseases and learn about Down syndrome, a disorder due to a chromosome abnormality.

Students then learn about genetic counseling, techniques that can be used to diagnose genetic disorders in fetuses, and the promise of gene therapy as a means of curing certain genetic diseases.

276

KEY TERMS

amniocentesis
chorionic
  villus biopsy
fetoscopy
gene therapy

genetic
  counseling
karyotype
trisomy
ultra-
  sonography

11

HUMAN GENETICS

GROWING WITHIN its mother's uterus, this developing human appears to have the potential for living a long and healthy life. Even now, eye and hair color have already been determined by its genes. This individual's genes may also have determined that it will develop a disorder that makes breathing difficult, weakens the lungs, and shortens a person's normal life expectancy. How can a parent, who has a history of this disorder in the family, be assured that this new individual is healthy? A test can be done using the white blood cells of the developing human. The cells are studied for signs of the abnormal gene that causes the disease. Results showing that this individual has normal genes bring welcome relief to the parents.

You and each one of your friends are the expression of many thousands of genes. If two children received their genes from the same parents, why does one child inherit a fatal genetic disorder while the other does not? What is the probability that a new baby sister will suffer from the same disorder? How soon after conception can the parents find out about the health of the child and what, if anything, can be done to correct an abnormality? In this chapter, you will read about the symptoms of some inherited disorders and how some genetic disorders are passed on. You will learn why some disorders affect mostly males. You will also learn how doctors discover if an individual has a genetic disorder even before its birth.

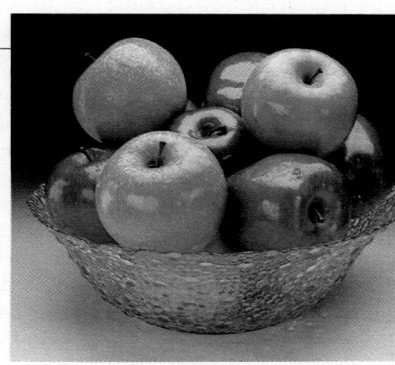

Color blindness is a gentic disorder that affects a person's ability to distinguish the colors red and green. How might these apples look to someone who is colorblind? What problems might a person with this disorder encounter every day?

Chapter Preview

277

CHAPTER 11

Introducing the Chapter

Begin this chapter by initiating a discussion of the photograph on page 276. The fetus is developing according to the set of genes it received from its parents. Suppose each parent was normal. Will the fetus develop into a normal, healthy child as well? Ask your students how it is possible for two healthy parents to produce a child who is born with a genetic disease. Is it possible to predict the chances of having a healthy child? Point out that some genetic diseases or developmental abnormalities can now be diagnosed and corrected even before the child is born. **LEP**

Theme Development

The major theme running throughout the chapter is methods of inquiry. Students will investigate how modern techniques, including technological applications based on our modern understanding of DNA, come into play in furthering understanding of the cause of symptoms of genetic diseases and in diagnosing and developing possible courses of treatment as well as cures.

Tying to Previous Knowledge

All the principles of genetics studied by students so far come to bear on the study of human genetics. Students will see that both Mendelian and non-Mendelian patterns of inheritance apply to humans. They will see how genetic counseling depends upon knowledge of patterns of genetics, too. Knowledge of DNA will help students to develop a more thorough understanding of the causes of the symptoms of genetic diseases and will enable them to understand the idea of gene therapy and its uses.

ASSESSMENT PLANNER

Choose assessment strategies from the following pages to evaluate the progress of your students.

Prepare

Key Concepts

Students will distinguish the nature of inheritance patterns of the most common genetic disorders known to be caused by single genes, sex-linked genes, and chromosome abnormalities.

Key Terms

trisomy, karyotype

Materials

- For Minilab 1, obtain prepared slides of sickled red blood cells and normal red blood cells. Have microscopes available.
- For Minilab 2, gather slides, coverslips, toothpicks, methylene blue, and microscopes.

1 Focus

Objectives

The objectives are listed on the student page. Remind students to preview these objectives as a guide to this numbered section.

Discussion

Ask students to give examples of human behavior patterns that seem to be due almost entirely to heredity. Reflexes such as blinking your eyes when an object comes suddenly toward your face or pulling your hand away from something hot are examples. You might have an interesting discussion about behaviors such as aggression, speech, and sexual behavior. How much of these behaviors is learned and how much is hereditary? **L1**

Objectives

Explain the symptoms of cystic fibrosis.

Demonstrate how modern knowledge and techniques have led to understanding the cause of genetic disorders.

Discuss examples of other inherited disorders, their symptoms, and their causes.

Figure 11-1 **Cystic fibrosis results from inheriting a recessive allele for the disorder from each parent. The inheritance pattern for two heterozygous parents is shown here.**

11.1 Human Genetic Disorders

Like other organisms, you inherited genes that have determined your individual traits—your blood type, your skin color, whether your earlobes are attached or free, and the enzymes your body uses for cellular respiration. Inheritance of human traits can be explained by the same principles used to explain hereditary patterns in other organisms. So, too, can the inheritance of many human disorders. Scientists have known for many years that disorders, like other human phenotypes, are associated with production of abnormal proteins. Now, knowledge of DNA and the use of modern research techniques are permitting scientists to begin analyzing disorder-causing genes and pinpoint how the abnormal proteins actually cause the disorders.

Cystic Fibrosis

How often have you read a book and found a misspelled word among the hundreds or thousands of words used? Even with careful proofreading, a mistake will sometimes occur. A similar situation may occur with human genes. Unfortunately, those mistakes may result in a person who suffers from an inherited disorder. Cystic fibrosis (CF) is the most commonly inherited genetic disorder among white people. It is estimated that one white person in 20 carries the recessive allele that causes this disorder. As a result, one in 2000 babies is born with CF. This statistic translates into four or five babies being born with this fatal disorder in the United States every day.

Symptoms of CF Several body systems are affected by CF. Normally, a thin, free-flowing fluid is secreted that lubricates the passageways of the lungs and intestinal tract. CF represents a malfunctioning of the mucus-secreting glands of the body. Thick mucous secretions build up in the air passages and lungs. The mucus blocks the passage of air into and out of the lungs, causing lung damage. Almost all affected individuals have a history of wheezing and coughing. Recurrent infections weaken the lungs even more. In most CF patients, thick mucous secretions damage the pancreas and prevent or reduce the flow of digestive enzymes to the intestines. These enzymes are essential for the breakdown and absorption of food.

Scientists know that CF affects the transport of ions such as sodium and chloride across the cell membrane. This affects the movement of salt and water in and out of cells that line the lungs and digestive system. As a result, the usually thin mucus that coats these surfaces dehydrates, becomes thick and sticky, and accumulates.

The Cause of CF The discovery that CF patients have defective mechanisms for transporting chloride ions across the cell membrane led to the idea that the recessive CF allele might code for an abnormal cell membrane protein. This abnormal protein might be part of a membrane protein, or another protein that is needed for passage of chloride ions out of the cell. Eventually, the existence of such a membrane protein was established, and it was found that it doesn't operate properly in CF patients. In 1989, the gene that codes for this protein was found.

A person without CF has an allele that codes for a normal cell membrane protein. In a person with CF, the recessive allele codes for an abnormal protein. Actually, there are several different CF alleles. Depending on which two recessive alleles they may have, CF patients suffer from different symptoms, some more severe than others.

Recent Developments in CF In recent years, increased knowledge of CF and advances in medicine have improved the quality of life for people with the disorder. Physical therapy, breathing exercises, modern antibiotics, and special diets allow many patients to live longer and lead more normal lives. However, even with these recent advances, the disorder continues to be fatal. Identification of the CF alleles, along with analysis of the defects in the proteins for which they code, offers possibilities for better means of prevention and treatment. Perhaps even a cure may be found in the future. We will return to these exciting possibilities later in the chapter.

Figure 11-2   Normal cell membranes have membrane proteins that allow cells to maintain normal levels of chloride. CF-affected cell membranes have membrane proteins that do not function properly and prevent the movement of chloride ions across the membrane. People affected with CF need daily therapy to loosen mucus buildup in the lungs.

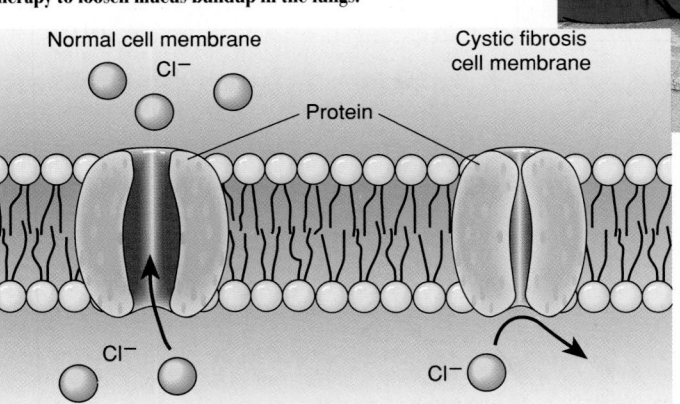

Normal cell membrane

Cystic fibrosis cell membrane

Protein

Cl⁻

Cl⁻

Cl⁻

2 Teach

Science, Technology, and Society

Gene Therapy for Cystic Fibrosis: Scientists have developed a method of administering gene therapy to patients with CF. A genetically engineered cold virus carrying a working gene will replace the defective gene that causes CF problems in the lungs. The viruses will be sprayed into the nose and lungs of a select group of patients. It is hoped that these viruses will invade the lung tissue, spread the corrected DNA into the affected cells, and reduce the production of the thick mucus that clogs the lungs. This strategy has worked well in laboratory tissue cultures. Cultures of CF cells, when exposed to the genetically engineered virus, took in the corrected genetic information and began to get rid of salt rather than trapping it inside. This therapy does not offer a long-term cure. Because cold viruses will not insert their genes permanently, the viruses will need to be readministered after three months.

STUDENT JOURNAL

Select a tabloid news article about a genetic disorder. Discuss the sensational and insensitive manner of presentation in the article. Ask students to rewrite the article in a way that shows knowledge of the genetic disorder and sensitivity toward people with this problem. Ask them to dispel any myths associated with the disorder and alleviate fears and prejudices. **L2**

Activity

Have students taste PTC paper available for genetic studies from biological supply houses. Explain that the ability to taste PTC is inherited as a dominant single-gene trait. Students could take pieces of paper home to test family members and then prepare a pedigree of the inheritance of this trait. In a pedigree, squares are males, circles are females, and shading indicates that the trait is in the individual's phenotype. Have students use Figure 11-3 as an example of a pedigree. Theirs will probably be much simpler. **L1** **LEP**

Bioethics

The Right to Know—And Not to Know: A test is currently available for people who are at risk for Huntington's disease. This test is 95%–98% accurate. Psychiatric studies of people who have been tested show that people who are tested and find out that they have the gene and will get the disease do not become significantly depressed when they get this news. In fact, they are less depressed than those who have not been tested or whose test results are inconclusive. Why do think people might feel this way? Would you want to know if you were going to get this disease or if your children were going to get the disease? Should people be required to know even if they don't want to know? Why or why not? If an insurance company pays for a genetic screening test, should it have the right to know the results of the test? Should health or life insurance companies require genetic testing as a prerequisite for buying insurance? Should employers have the right to know about an employee's genetic screening tests? Why or why not?

Huntington's Disease

Cystic fibrosis is caused by a recessive gene. In fact, most human genetic disorders result from a homozygous recessive genotype. Huntington's disease, however, is caused by a dominant gene. Thus, a person heterozygous for Huntington's disease will have this fatal disease. Symptoms of Huntington's disease usually appear by the time a person is about 40 years old. Deteriorating brain cells may cause the person to become clumsy, irritable, depressed, and suffer memory loss. As the disease progresses, these symptoms become more severe, resulting in the uncontrollable jerking of arms and legs. Further loss of muscle coordination, memory, and the ability to speak are symptoms of advanced stages of the disease. Death usually occurs within 20 years after the onset of the first symptoms.

Finding the Huntington's Gene The year 1983 provided an important milestone in the search for the cause of Huntington's disease. Until then, scientists could only reason that this disease was caused by a dominant gene by using the laws of probability when applied to genetics. Remember that offspring of a parent having a trait expressed by a dominant gene have a 50 percent chance of also having that trait. Experience showed that children of a person with Huntington's disease had a 50 percent chance of getting the disease. In 1983, a geneticist was finally able to show where the Huntington's gene is located. Scientists hoped that discovery of the exact location of the gene on the chromosome would quickly follow. A special foundation consisting of workers in six different laboratories was formed specifically to achieve this goal. In early 1993, the exact location of the gene that causes Huntington's disease was found.

Figure 11-3 **A pedigree of five generations of a family with Huntington's disease shows family relationships, the sex of each individual, and whether or not an individual is affected with Huntington's.**

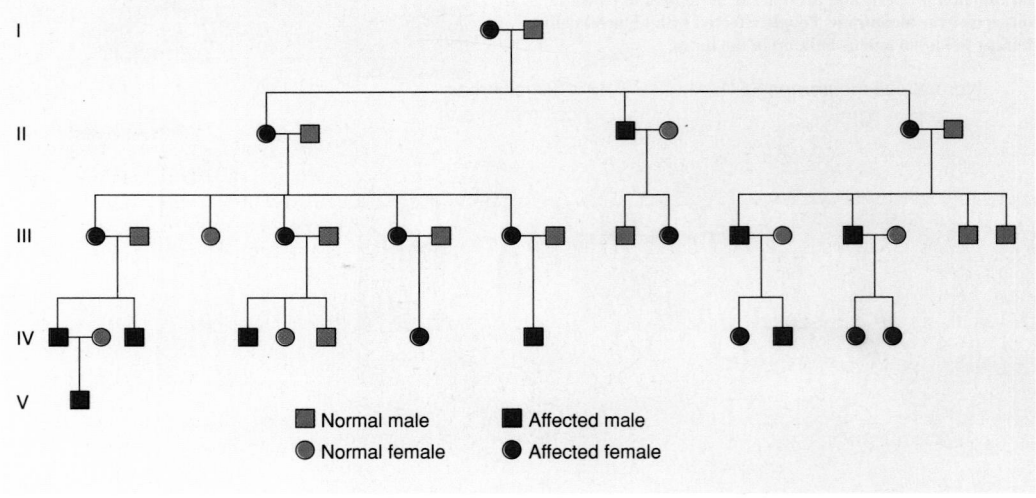

■ Normal male   ■ Affected male
● Normal female   ● Affected female

280 HUMAN GENETICS

MULTICULTURAL CONNECTION

A Huntington's Case History: In 1979, geneticist Nancy Wexler led a research team to conduct investigations of a community in Venezuela that had the largest concentration of Huntington's victims in the world. One hundred suffered the disease and 1100 were at risk. In 1981, she collected skin and blood samples for DNA testing from hundreds of Venezuelans and began developing pedigrees. The family trees included more than 3000 related people. Even though the largely uneducated population was initially afraid of what the researchers wanted to do, Wexler and her team and Huntington's victims the world over will always appreciate the cooperation of this large family, as so much was learned from this pedigree about the inheritance and manifestation of the disease.

The discovery is credited to the foundation of scientists in the United States, England, and Wales who were working toward this goal—the Huntington's Disease Collaborative Research Group. For the estimated 25 000 Americans who currently have the disease, the discovery of this gene's exact location is an important one.

Now that the location of the Huntington's gene is firmly established, scientists can begin analyzing its nucleotide sequence. They can also compare the dominant allele to the recessive allele, and then, perhaps, the proteins coded by each allele can be analyzed and compared. The crucial variations in the proteins that lead to destruction of the brain cells can be identified.

Knowing the Future   Have you ever waited for the results of a major exam knowing that your participation in a special activity depended on the results? Notification of a passing grade brings happiness and relief. Failure brings disappointment. Imagine how you might feel if the exam you needed to pass was whether or not you carried the allele for Huntington's disease. Today, persons with a family history of the disease can be tested to see if they have the allele. Finding out that they don't have the allele provides relief from the fear of developing the disease and passing it along to children. On the other hand, learning that they have the allele and will face a slow death can be devastating. Many people prefer to live with uncertainty rather than experience the fear created by knowing the disease will eventually strike. These people decide against being tested. Woody Guthrie, one of America's most beloved folk singers and songwriters, died of Huntington's disease. His son , Arlo Guthrie, and his daughters have elected not to be tested for the disease that claimed their father.

Figure 11-4 **Woody Guthrie (1912-1967) died of Huntington's disease.**

Thinking Lab

DESIGN AN EXPERIMENT

Is snoring inherited?

Background
Have you ever been kept awake at night because someone near you was snoring? For many years, evidence has pointed to the fact that snoring was associated with weight gain, alcohol consumption, a disorder in which people pause in breathing during sleep, and other unknown causes. Extra fat in the walls of air passages makes them "rattle" when people assume certain positions during sleep. Alcohol's effect on the muscles of the tongue, other respiratory structures,

and the brain can also produce snoring. More recent evidence is also pointing to genetic causes of snoring. Researchers report that relatives of people who snore are twice as likely to snore as relatives of people who do not snore.

You Try It
Make a hypothesis and design an experiment that would investigate the idea that snoring has some genetic basis. Think about parts of the mouth and throat that you could investigate that might be involved in snoring.

Activity
Tell students that they are geneticists of the future opening a clinic that will do genetic screening for CF, Huntington's disease, sickle-cell anemia, diabetes mellitus, heart disease, personality disorders, and other disorders with a genetic basis. Ask them to develop a one-minute public service announcement for TV that will advertise their services. If you wish, you can videotape the presentations and show them all at once. L1
COOP LEARN

Enrichment
Suppressor genes that are associated with the development of cancer have recently been discovered. When they are functioning properly, these genes do not allow abnormal growth; however, when they malfunction or disappear, cells grow out of control and become cancerous. Researchers found that the p53 suppressor gene stopped cancer cells from growing in laboratory cultures. Scientists are working on a drug to replace the function of the damaged p53 gene.

Thinking Lab

DESIGN AN EXPERIMENT

Purpose
Students will examine the idea that snoring has a genetic basis.

Skills
design an experiment, separate and control variables

Teaching Strategies
• Variations in mouthparts such as tongue length, soft palate, length of lower jaw bone, and others that can be measured contribute to snoring.

Answers
Students should select two groups of families, ones that snore and ones that do not and compare the two groups. Students may select a variety of mouthpart measurements to investigate; or they may choose a different experimental design.

✔ **Assessment**
Portfolio: Some people may have features that make them especially suited for a particular sport. Have students pick three sports and describe three specific behaviors with the accompanying ideal body characteristics that make them especially suited to this sport. Tell whether the ideal features are acquired or genetic.

Minilab 1

Purpose
Students will compare and contrast under the microscope normal and sickled red blood cells.

Skills
observe, interpret scientific illustrations

Teaching Strategies
- Prepared slides of blood cell types can be obtained from a biological supply house.
- Explain to students that there are two forms of the disorder, one in which half of the red cells are spherical and another in which all the red blood cells are sickled. When all the cells are sickled, very little oxygen can reach body cells. When half the cells are sickled, more oxygen can reach the body.

Expected Results
Students should be able to see apparent differences in normal red blood cells and sickled red blood cells.

Answers
1. Mutated hemoglobin cannot carry enough oxygen to body cells.
2. Students' diagrams should show normal, easy movement of normal red blood cells through capillaries. The sickled-cell diagram should show cells getting stuck, building up, and eventually clogging the capillary.

✔ Assessment
Portfolio: Ask students to make Punnett squares to analyze and answer the following question. If both parents carry the gene for sickle-cell anemia, what are the chances that their children will have sickle-cell anemia?

Minilab 1

How do normal red blood cells compare to red blood cells of patients with sickle-cell anemia?

Sickle-cell anemia is a genetic disorder in which the gene for one chain of hemoglobin, the molecule in red blood cells responsible for carrying oxygen, is mutated. Normal red blood cells have a spherical disc shape. Examine, under low and high power, prepared slides of normal red blood cells and sickled red blood cells. Draw diagrams of both types of cells.

Analysis *Explain what problems are caused by mutated hemoglobin. Make two simple diagrams—one showing how normal red blood cells would pass through capillaries and another showing what happens when sickled cells pass through capillaries.*

Sickle-Cell Anemia

Just as the recessive CF allele causes a fatal disorder most often in white people, another recessive allele causes the disorder sickle-cell anemia most often in blacks. About one of every 500 Americans of African descent has the disorder. Sickle-cell anemia results when the structure of hemoglobin is genetically changed. Hemoglobin, a protein found in red blood cells, is made of four polypeptide chains—two alpha chains and two beta chains. Hemoglobin combines with oxygen in the lungs and transports the oxygen to body cells for use in cellular respiration. While most of us take for granted that our cells will receive the amounts of oxygen they need, people suffering from sickle-cell anemia are not so fortunate.

Sickle-cell anemia is the result of a mutation in the gene that codes for one of the polypeptide chains of hemoglobin. The mutant hemoglobin allele differs from the normal allele in the sixth codon. Just one nucleotide of that codon is different, but that difference results in one amino acid difference in the beta polypeptide chains coded for by the two alleles. The slight difference in the structure of abnormal hemoglobin molecules makes them less soluble and causes them to form crystals within the red blood cells. These crystals distort the red cells, changing their shape from the normal disc shape to sickled, as seen in Figure 11-6.

The formation of crystals of abnormal hemoglobin prevents hemoglobin from carrying enough oxygen to cells. In addition, the sickled red cells are rigid and cannot pass through capillaries as easily as normal red cells. As a result, those capillaries can be blocked. Severe pain, fever, and weakness are some of the symptoms caused by the blocked capillaries. Strokes that result in paralysis may also occur in young children.

alpha chain

O₂ binding sites

beta chain

alpha chain

beta chain

a

b

Figure 11-5 Normal hemoglobin molecules (a) are composed of four protein chains and four iron-containing chemical groups, each of which can hold one oxygen molecule. Sickle-cell hemoglobin (b) is slightly different in structure from normal hemoglobin. This difference prevents these cells from carrying as much oxygen and results in their sickled shape.

PROJECT

Hemophilia: Learn more about the history of hemophilia. Write about its role in the downfall of the Russian monarchy. Write about the current treatment. Is there a difference in the treatment of males and females? **L2**

PORTFOLIO

Do library research on the current status of the human genome project. Look into why there was opposition to beginning this project. What are the benefits to be gained by mapping the human genome? **L2**

While many affected with sickle-cell anemia die while still young, some sickle-cell patients now live past age 40. Treatment for sickle-cell anemia involves a variety of approaches, including transfusions, antibiotics to treat infections, and drugs that increase the oxygen-carrying capacity of the red cells. Recently, scientists have been using mice to help study sickle-cell anemia. Fertilized mouse eggs are injected with DNA containing the normal allele for one of the hemoglobin chains together with the allele that codes for the other abnormal chain. The mice produce human sickle hemoglobin. Scientists hope that studies using these mice will provide useful information about sickle-cell anemia. Future experiments should provide new information that produces better means of dealing with the disorder.

Figure 11-6 Scanning electron micrographs of normal red blood cells (left) and sickled cells (right) shows the difference in their appearances. Magnification: 11 550×

Analysis of Genetic Disorders

Finding the cause of genetic disorders might be compared to successfully putting together the pieces of a puzzle. Disorders such as CF, Huntington's, and sickle-cell anemia are the result of mutant alleles. Locating the defective allele for each disorder might be compared to completing a very simple jigsaw puzzle. However, not all genetic disorders are explained in terms of a single pair of alleles. Many, such as diabetes mellitus, heart disease, and certain personality disorders, are believed to be the result of multiple genes. Complicating the problem of multiple genes is the fact that expression of genes is influenced by all the other genes an organism possesses. Successfully analyzing these disorders might be compared to completing a three-dimensional jigsaw puzzle with 100 interlocking pieces.

There are more harmful or lethal alleles in the human population than you may think. Just as every book may have a few misspelled words, it is estimated that every person carries five to eight harmful genes. Given that fact, why aren't more people born with hereditary diseases? One answer is that most of the harmful alleles are recessive; in other words, their effects are hidden by the presence of the normal allele. Another possibility is that although many zygotes carry harmful alleles, most of these zygotes never complete development.

11.1 HUMAN GENETIC DISORDERS **283**

Bioethics

Perceived Perfection: Have students in groups make a list of what they consider to be the most desirable human characteristics. Next, have them make another list of important people or heros in their own lives. Ask them if these people have all the characteristics on their first list. Now explain to students that in Nazi Germany the leadership used what was called eugenics, the philosophy of improving the intellectual, economic, and social levels of humans by allowing reproduction only in people determined to be superior. The Nazis misused concepts of genetics to justify hatred and extermination of entire groups of people. Ask students how we can ensure the improvement of the human condition using progress being made and new strategies being developed in the field of genetics, and at the same time prevent prejudice and hatred from developing as we decide on "desirable human characteristics."

MULTICULTURAL CONNECTION

Flo Hyman: Flo Hyman, black olympian, was the star of the U.S. women's volleyball team in the 1984 Olympic games, helping them to win a silver medal. During a game in Japan in 1986, she collapsed and died due to a ruptured aorta caused by Marfan's syndrome. This disorder is inherited as an autosomal dominant gene, but is difficult to detect.

HISTORY CONNECTION

Early Genetics: Questions of heredity and evolution of humans were very important to ancient Greek philosophy. The Greeks were interested in explaining the origin and organization of the universe, living systems, and human life. They theorized that semen is formed in small particles throughout the body, then transferred to the blood, transported to the testicles, and transferred during intercourse. They also thought that females formed, in a similar fashion, semen that combined with the male semen. They agreed that semen was involved in inherited traits, but disagreed about which parent contributed more to the appearance of the offspring. Most Greeks also believed that traits acquired by parents could be passed on to children.

Figure Caption Question

What are the phenotypic and genotypic ratios of this cross?
Genotypic ratios— $1/4 X^H X^H$: $1/4 X^H X^h$: $1/4 X^H Y$: $1/4 X^h Y$
Phenotypic ratios— 1 normal daughter: 1 carrier daughter: 1 normal son: 1 hemopheliac son

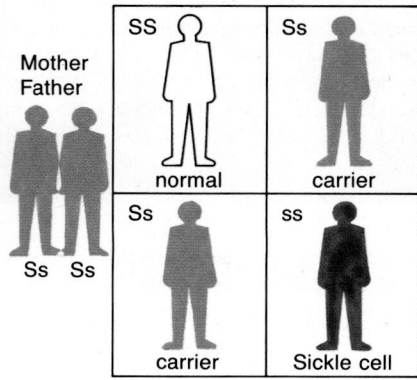

Figure 11-7 **The mosquito in the photograph, the female *Anopheles,* is responsible for the spread of malaria. The Punnett square shows the inheritance of the sickle-cell trait. The offspring that are homozygous recessive or heterozygous for the sickle-cell trait are more resistant to malaria.**

Heterozygote Superiority In some cases, although a certain allele is harmful in the homozygous state, that same allele actually presents an advantage to a heterozygous individual. Let's take another look at sickle-cell anemia. In the United States, one in ten African Americans carries the abnormal allele. However, depending on the area of Africa in which they live, as many as four out of ten Africans carry the allele for sickle-cell anemia. How can the difference be explained?

Malaria is a debilitating disease prevalent in parts of Africa, but uncommon in the United States today. Malaria is caused by a unicellular organism that invades red blood cells. Here the parasites multiply and soon rupture the blood cells. The newly released parasites invade other red blood cells and repeat the cycle. Periodic destruction of blood cells produces chills and fever and chronic illness. Some types of malaria can be fatal if untreated. People homozygous for normal hemoglobin are susceptible to malaria. Those who are heterozygous or homozygous for the sickle-cell hemoglobin resist malaria because the parasite does not thrive in cells with sickle hemoglobin. Therefore, in parts of Africa where malaria is prevalent, heterozygotes tend to live longer than people having the other genotypes. Unfortunately, those homozygous for sickle-cell usually die quite young. The likelihood of two heterozygotes producing children is great, and genetics tells us that every two out of four of those children will be heterozygotes, like the parents. Thus, the incidence of the recessive allele in African black populations remains high even though such a high incidence also results in many offspring having sickle-cell anemia. Because malaria is uncommon in the United States, heterozygotes have no such advantage, and over the years, the frequency of the recessive allele has declined due to natural selection.

284 HUMAN GENETICS

ALTERNATE LAB: Karyotyping

Purpose
Students will observe human karyotypes and determine which ones are not normal. Then they will match the karyotype with the genetic disorder from a list provided.

Materials
Gather copies of a normal karyotype, and ones with the following disorders: triploidy, tetraploidy, Pateau syndrome, Edwards syndrome, Down syndrome,

Turner syndrome, Klinefelter syndrome, XYY syndrome, and XXX syndrome. Actual karyotypes may be available through a nearby genetics screening unit. You can also find them in human genetics books such as *Human Heredity, Principles and Issues* by Michael R. Cummings. Give students an information sheet with descriptions of each of the disorders. Include characteristics and prognosis, also chromosome abnormality.

Procedure
Give the following directions to students.
1. Examine the karyotypes for the above nine genetic disorders.
2. Compare the normal karyotype with the abnormal ones. Write in a table what is wrong with each one.

Analysis
Ask students to answer the following questions.

The condition in which heterozygotes have an advantage over both homozygous genotypes, as in the case of sickle-cell anemia in Africa, is known as heterozygote superiority. This phenomenon may apply to other human genetic disorders as well.

The Results of a Higher Survival Rate Another reason that the frequency of some harmful alleles remains high has developed in recent years. In those countries with modern health care, people having some genetic disorders are living long enough to reproduce. Their genes, therefore, are passed on. For example, earlier in this century there was no treatment for people with a severe form of diabetes mellitus. Then, in 1922, insulin injections to control diabetes became available. Instead of dying young, diabetics began to lead more normal lives, to live longer, to marry, and to pass their genes to their descendants.

Sex-linked Disorders

You know that genes for many sex-linked traits are carried on the X chromosome, and fewer are carried on the Y. Some of those genes are the cause of disorders or abnormalities in humans.

Hemophilia How often have you gotten a small cut and noticed that very little blood was lost because a clot formed quickly? Clotting of the blood that leaks from a scratch or cut is familiar to almost everyone. In persons with hemophilia, however, a protein necessary for clotting is absent. Consequently, the smallest injury can lead to a life-threatening loss of blood. Hemophilia is due to a recessive allele on the X chromosome. If a boy's mother is heterozygous, he has a 50 percent chance of inheriting the X chromosome with the hemophilia allele from his mother. If a male inherits an X chromosome with the hemophilia allele, he will be a "bleeder." The Y chromosome does not carry the normal allele to provide the clotting factor.

Figure 11-8 A cross of parents with normal blood clotting shows the probability of hemophiliac offspring if the mother carries the hemophilia gene. A female hemophiliac is rare because she must receive a gene for hemophilia from each parent. What are the phenotypic and genotypic ratios of this cross?

Minilab 2

Can sex differences be observed in human body cells?

Barr bodies are structures in cells that stain dark in human females. Normally, in human females, only one X chromosome is active. The other X chromosome becomes inactive during the development of the embryo and results in a Barr body. Prepare a microscope slide of your cheek cells and examine it for Barr bodies. Your teacher will give you information on slide preparation. Observe under low power and switch to high power. Barr bodies will appear as darkly stained spots inside the nuclear membrane. Observe a slide of a student of the opposite sex. Females will have Barr bodies in many cells and males will not have any.

Analysis How are male and female cheek cells alike? How are they different? If a doctor found Barr bodies in cells being studied during amniocentesis, what could be concluded?

SECTION 11.1

Minilab 2

Purpose
Students will observe their own cheek cells. They will be able to describe how sex can be determined by observing Barr bodies cheek cells.

Skills
observe, classify

Teaching Strategies
- Students should use methylene blue to stain their cheek cells. Too much will cause the cells to be hard to see.
- Methylene blue will stain.
- Used slides and coverslips should be placed in containers of 10% household bleach.

Expected Results
Students will be able to see the differences between male and female cells.

Answers
1. The cells are alike in shape and size and contain the same organelles. Females have Barr bodies; males do not.
2. The child is a female.

✔ Assessment
Performance: Give students prepared slides of cheek cells or slides you have prepared from your cheek cells. Ask them to tell if the individual is male or female and explain why.

---

1. How did you determine what was wrong with the karyotypes? *comparison to normal and finding differences in number of chromosomes*
2. How did you match the physical descriptions of disorders with the karyotypes? *severe disorders had greater chromosome abnormality*
3. What are some ways of controlling these disorders in a population? *prenatal testing, good prenatal care, not using alcohol or drugs of any kind during pregnancy, eliminating air pollution and other environmental hazards, limiting intake of chemicals in foods, and proper nutrition during pregnancy*

✔ Assessment
Oral: In 1980, a California couple thought they were at risk for Tay-Sachs disease because they were descended from Eastern European Jews. They underwent tests and were informed that they were not at risk. Their child developed Tay-Sachs disease soon after being born; the parents sued the laboratory that did the testing. The suit charged that the child's life was a "wrongful life." If you were the judge, would you award damages to the child and parents? Why or why not? (In the actual case, the court found that the child and parents were entitled to damages.) **L1**

Purpose

Students will study the founder effect and genetic drift and learn how these phenomena have affected Amish communities.

Background

The 15 000 Amish of Lancaster County Pennsylvania are all descended from 200 Swiss Anabaptist farmers. They are commonly called "Pennsylvania Dutch," an anglicized misnomer of "deutsche," the dialect the Amish speak.

Teaching Strategies

• Ask students to think about what life might be like without TV, computers, electric lights, or any electrical appliances in the home. Bring out the advantages of living a simpler life so that students will gain respect and appreciation for a group of people who may be very different from them.

Possible Answers

1. The Amish would be easier to study because they have large families, do not marry outside their culture, get good medical care, and do not use alcohol, drugs, or tobacco, factors which can mask or confuse certain disorders.

2. The Amish have high incidences of the disorders manic-depression, a psychiatric problem; glutaric aciduria, a metabolic deficiency in which the protein glutaric acid builds up and damages muscles, liver, and nerves.

Going Further

Have students research more about the history and traditions of the Amish.

As with other diseases, modern technology has helped lengthen the life span and improve the quality of life for hemophiliacs. One treatment consists of blood transfusions to restore lost blood. Another involves giving the patient the missing clotting factor. Research based on recombinant DNA techniques is being done to try to make the clotting factor available in greater quantities and at a practical price.

Color Blindness   Imagine looking at a bowl of shiny red and green apples and not being able to distinguish which was which. Some people don't have to imagine such a situation because they aren't able to see the colors red or green. For them, anything that is red or green appears brown. These people have red-green color blindness, another sex-linked

H I S T O R Y   C O N N E C T I O N

Heredity and the Amish

The Amish of Lancaster County, Pennsylvania are part of a remarkable group of people. The Amish were founded in the 1690s as an offshoot of the Swiss Mennonite Church. The group now living in Lancaster County is descended

from a handful of Swiss Amish who came to America in the 1720s. Like most other Amish communities in the United States, they have maintained a way of life that has changed

little in 300 years. Unlike other Amish communities, they also have the misfortune to maintain an unusually high rate of Ellis-van Creveld syndrome in their population.

Ellis-van Creveld syndrome is an autosomal recessive genetic disorder. People born with this disorder have short arms and legs. They may also have extra fingers or toes. What is it about the Lancaster Amish population that makes them more susceptible to this syndrome? The answer may lie in Amish culture and history, and in two genetic principles known as the founder effect and genetic drift.

The Amish form a relatively closed community. They live a very simple life. They wear the same style of plain, homemade clothing that their ancestors wore three centuries ago. Such things as buttons are rejected as too fancy. Amish clothes are fastened with hooks and eyes or straight pins.

The Amish live a life close to the earth and the basic needs of daily life. They don't use electricity in their homes. You won't find any computer programmers or electrical engineers in Amish communities. Even though they are famous as fine farmers and craftsmen, tractors and power tools are usually forbidden. Hand tools are used for woodworking and horses for farming. While some Amish men will drive cars or trucks as part of their work for non-Amish employers, they do their own traveling in horse-drawn carriages.

This way of life keeps the Amish outside the mainstream of American society. They take care of each other so well that poverty is almost unknown. In most cases, they don't socialize or marry outside of the

286 HUMAN GENETICS

PROGRAM RESOURCES

Teacher Classroom Resources
Study Guide, pp. 61-63 `L1`
Concept Mapping, p. 11 `L1` `LEP`
Probing Levels of Life, Labs 21, 22, pp. 59, 61 `L2`

Critical Thinking/Problem Solving, p. 11 `L2`

Investigating Living Systems, Labs 25, 26, pp. 99, 103 `L2`

trait. Red-green color blindness is caused by a defect in either of two alleles located on the X chromosome. Dominant forms of these alleles code for red and green receptor molecules that are present in light-capturing cells of the eye. These molecules absorb red or green wavelengths of light and transform their energy into nerve impulses to the brain. In a male, if either recessive allele is present on the X chromosome, abnormal receptors are made. Red and green will not be properly distinguished. In females, both X chromosomes must have at least one of the two recessive alleles for her to be color-blind. In some cases, either the red or green receptor allele is actually missing entirely.

SECTION 11.1

Analogy

To dramatize independent assortment, ask students to pair off and line up in pairs. Students should then intermingle as if they were at a party. Next ask a few of the pairs to switch partners to form new pairs. Explain to students that the pairs that did not switch represent genes that are linked together on the same chromosome, while those that did switch represent genes that were located on different chromosomes and were able to independently assort themselves. Those linked on the same chromosome were unable to assort independently. **L1**

LEP **COOP LEARN**

Amish community. This type of closed community does not allow for much genetic variability. The same genes are continually passed along in the population.

The vast majority of the Lancaster County Amish are descended from about 200 common ancestors who came to the U.S. in the late 1720s. Two hundred people is not a lot to start a community. At least one of those 200 was almost certainly a carrier of Ellis-van Creveld syndrome.

Imagine how such a gene would act in a small, closed community. If only one of the original 200 carried the gene, he or she made up just 1/2 of 1 percent of the population. But if that person passed the gene along to half of his or her children, and those children passed the gene along as well, it wouldn't be long before a large number carried the gene. After several generations, carriers would inevitably marry each other, and 1/4 of their children would be born with the syndrome. This phenomenon is called the founder effect.

Imagine now what would happen if the gene-carrying founder had many children. The percentage of carriers would probably rise, increasing the number who would eventually be born with the disorder. On the other hand, what if the gene-carrying founder had few chil-

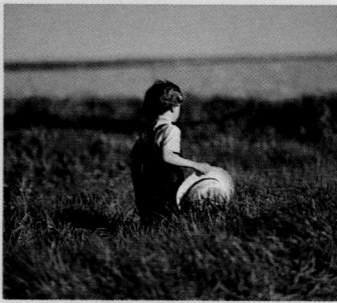

dren? The percentage of carriers would probably drop. If it dropped to zero, the gene would be lost from the population. Such change in the gene pool, resulting from chance, is known as genetic drift. Amish families are usually large, so chance favors having genes—such as the one causing Ellis-van Creveld syndrome—passed along from gen-

eration to generation in fairly high numbers.

Fortunately for geneticists, family history is very important to the Amish, so they keep good records of their ancestry. They also seek good medical care for themselves and each other. By allowing geneticists to study their medical records and family trees, the Amish have contributed a great deal to the understanding of Ellis-van Creveld syndrome and how genetic disorders affect populations through the founder effect and genetic drift.

1. **Writing About Biology:** Suppose you were studying a genetic disorder and found two excellent examples of populations with a history of that disorder. One was in an Amish community and the other in your town. Both had good family records. Would one be easier to study than the other? Why?
2. **Explore Further:** Find another example of the founder effect and genetic drift in the Amish or any other population.

CHEMISTRY CONNECTION

Liposomes: A liposome is a hollow, spherical structure consisting of phospholipids, the same molecules that form the cell membrane. They can envelop materials including drugs, cosmetics, and genetic materials. Liposomes can transport genetic materials by endocytosis through the cell membrane. There are a variety of problems associated with getting genetic materials into cells. A liposome can "deceive" the cell by hiding the DNA inside until it arrives in the cytoplasm.

PORTFOLIO

Ask students to collect articles about human genetics from the local newspapers for two to three weeks. They should mount them on paper, summarize the important points, and list the bioethical issues that might be raised by the articles. After the list, they should write about their opinions on these issues. **L1** **LEP**

Enrichment

Women scientists have often found themselves marginalized in a world of mostly male scientists. Very few sources indicate that Nettie Stevens, a graduate of Bryn Mawr College, was the first scientist to observe that sex, in humans, is determined by the X and Y chromosomes.

3 Assess

Check for Understanding

Ask students to pair up and conduct interviews. One student should assume the role of a person with a particular genetic disorder. The other should interview him or her with the following questions: What causes your disorder? What are its symptoms? In what way does your disorder limit your lifestyle? What research is being done to help with a cure or treatment? What treatment do you get? **L1** **COOP LEARN**

Chromosome Abnormalities

Some inherited defects are due to abnormalities in the structure or number of chromosomes rather than particular alleles. For example, the most common cause of Down syndrome is nondisjunction. Nondisjunction is the failure of paired chromosomes to separate during meiosis. This results in one gamete having too many chromosomes and the other too few. The presence of three of one kind of chromosome is known as **trisomy**. This cause of Down syndrome is known as trisomy 21.

Karyotyping Certain chromosomal abnormalities can be detected by looking at a picture of human chromosomes called a **karyotype.** Karyotypes are made by taking a blood sample and separating out the white cells. A chemical is added that stops the white cells in metaphase of mitosis. Water is added to the cells to cause them to swell and burst, releasing chromosomes. The chromosomes are then stained and photographed. The photograph is enlarged and each individual chromosome is cut out and matched with its homologue. The chromosomes are arranged by size and numbered. Visible chromosomal abnormalities can be easily identified by looking at the chromosomes. Geneticists can see large chromosome abnormalities such as extra chromosomes or added or deleted pieces of chromosomes. Additional chromosomes often cause multiple abnormalities. In a deletion, a portion of a chromosome is missing. Sometimes, a deleted portion of a chromosome attaches to another chromosome. This is called a translocation. The karyotype in Figure 11-9 shows the karyotype of an individual with Down syndrome.

Figure 11-9 **The photograph shows human chromosomes in metaphase of mitosis. The karyotype shows an extra 21st chromosome. This indicates an individual with Down syndrome.**

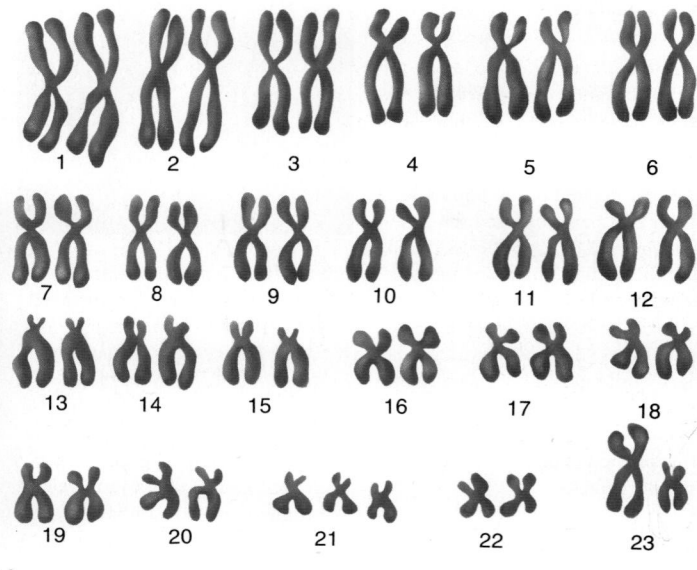

288 HUMAN GENETICS

Characteristics of Down Syndrome

People with Down syndrome have varying degrees of mental retardation, from mild to severe. They are usually shorter than normal. Many are born with heart, intestinal, or vision problems. They are susceptible to infection and have an increased risk of developing a form of blood cell cancer known as leukemia. Sixty years ago, most people with Down syndrome died before the age of ten. Now, with better care, the average life span has increased to 30 years. About 25 percent of people with Down syndrome now live to be 50.

Some cases of Down syndrome are due not to nondisjunction, but to a different chromosome abnormality. This abnormality is caused when most of the 21st chromosome breaks off and fuses to another chromosome, usually chromosome number 14. This is a translocation. When a gamete containing this part of chromosome 21 and another normal gamete combine, the zygote has three copies of chromosome 21. This event is the cause of about four percent of Down syndrome cases. This cause of Down syndrome is most likely to occur in infants born to mothers over the age of 40. The exact reason for this is not yet known.

Geneticists are currently studying the DNA of chromosome 21 in an effort to answer many questions about Down syndrome. They need to identify which of the estimated 1500 genes on that chromosome are the cause of Down syndrome. They want to know the proteins coded for by those genes in an effort to understand why the various symptoms occur. They also want to determine why the presence of three of each gene, rather than the usual two, is so harmful.

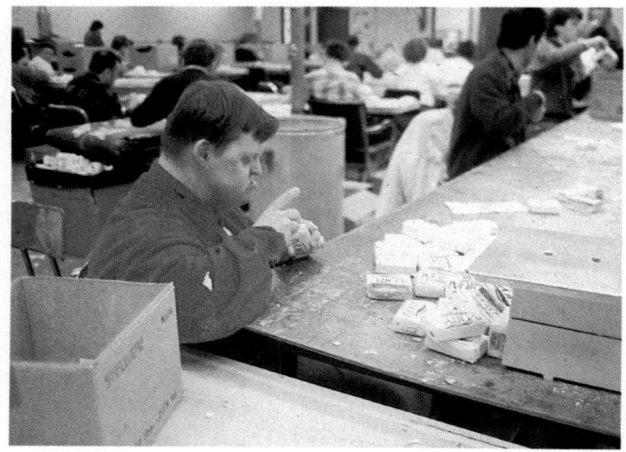

Figure 11-10 **Many individuals with Down syndrome live very productive lives.**

Section Review

Understanding Concepts

1. Explain how the defect in the membrane protein responsible for the transport of chloride ions is related to symptoms of CF.
2. How are the cause and onset of symptoms in Huntington's disease different from those of CF and sickle-cell anemia?
3. Relate the structure of abnormal hemoglobin to the symptoms of sickle-cell anemia.
4. **Skill Review—Making Tables:** Make a table that compares the following genetic disorders in terms of their causes and symptoms: CF, Huntington's disease, sickle-cell anemia, hemophilia, red-green color blindness, and Down syndrome. For more help, see Organizing Information in the **Skill Handbook.**
5. **Thinking Critically:** The organism that causes malaria requires oxygen carried by red blood cells. Why might heterozygotes for sickle-cell anemia be resistant to malaria?

Reteach

Tell students to make a chart of each of the disorders mentioned in the chapter. They should have columns for cause, symptoms, current research, and treatment. LEP

Extension

Ask students to find karyotypes of males and females of different species and compare them to human karyotypes. L3

✔ Assessment

Portfolio: Ask students in groups to prepare a proposal for funding for research on a specific genetic disease. Tell them that they are a team of scientists who would like to continue some important research but have run out of funds. They are applying to the National Science Foundation. They should explain the disorder they have chosen, what research has accomplished to date, why the course they are choosing to take is important, and how they expect to proceed. L1 COOP LEARN

4 Close

Demonstration

Prepare large transparent chromosomes with labels for use on the overhead projector. Ask students to explain problems they see such as deletions, inversions, duplications, and translocations. Show, with large transparent chromosomes, other specific problems that can be demonstrated in the karyotypes of various genetic disorders. LEP

Answers to Section Review

1. The normal membrane protein moves chloride ions across membranes of cells lining the lungs and certain digestive organs. This prevents mucus in the air passages and lungs from becoming too thick. The defective membrane protein cannot move chloride ions properly, the mucus becomes too thick, and the passageways become blocked.
2. Huntington's disease is caused by a dominant allele. Symptoms do not appear until around age 40.
3. The abnormal hemoglobin cannot carry sufficient oxygen and also causes the red cells to become sickle shaped. The tissues deprived of oxygen, the distorted cells block capillaries, resulting in pain, fever, weakness, and strokes.
4. **Skill Review—Making Tables:** One column identifying the genetic disorders, one describing their symptoms, and one identifying causes
5. **Thinking Critically:** The red cells of heterozygotes do not carry as much oxygen as those of people who are homozygous dominant because one of their two alleles codes for abnormal hemoglobin. Thus, there is not enough oxygen present in their blood for the malaria-causing organism's needs.

Prepare

Key Concepts

Students will study genetic counseling and various types of diagnosis in the uterus: amniocentesis, chorionic villus biopsy, ultrasonography, and fetoscopy. Gene therapy will also be considered.

Key Terms

genetic counseling, amniocentesis, chorionic villus biopsy, ultrasonography, fetoscopy, gene therapy

Materials

• For the Investigation, gather millimeter rulers and magnifying glasses.

1 Focus

Objectives

The objectives are listed on the student page. Remind students to preview these objectives as a guide to this numbered section.

Discussion

Ask students why they think harmful genes stay in the population.

Objectives

Demonstrate how genetic counseling can be used to provide parents with information about the possibility of having a child with a genetic disorder.

Describe techniques that permit diagnosis of a genetic disorder in the unborn.

Discuss gene therapy and how it might be used to cure genetic disorders.

Figure 11-11 With today's diagnostic techniques and genetic counseling, parents can have information about the health of their child long before it is born.

11.2 Prevention and a Possible Means of Cure

Research is providing knowledge of the causes of many genetic disorders. Researchers are identifying and analyzing the genes that cause genetic disorders and defects in the proteins they encode. But being able to relate genes and proteins to the symptoms of a genetic disorder is just a beginning. In the United States alone, more than 200 000 babies each year are born with genetic disorders or congenital disabilities—disabilities that are acquired during development and not through heredity. Although many of these disorders are minor, others cause severe health problems, and some are eventually fatal. The knowledge gained through basic research must be applied to improve and extend the lives of people afflicted with these disorders and, perhaps in the not-too-distant future, to prevent or cure them.

Genetic Counseling

When a couple is expecting a baby, a question they hear often is, "What do you want, a boy or a girl?" Most prospective parents answer, "I don't care as long as it's healthy." It used to be that the parents had to wait until the baby was born to find out the answers to both of these questions. Today there are techniques available to give parents not only information about the sex of their baby but also information about the health of their unborn child.

A person trained in genetics can give parents information about the chances of their child having a genetic disorder. This process is called **genetic counseling.** This type of counseling is very valuable to couples with a history of hereditary disorders in their families. The counselor studies the family histories of the couple, and uses knowledge of basic patterns of heredity and newly developed diagnostic techniques to inform the parents of possible disorders that may be passed on.

Suppose, for example, that a couple is concerned about the possibility of having a child with Tay-Sachs. Tay-Sachs is an autosomal recessive disorder that is not apparent at birth. Babies homozygous for Tay-Sachs appear normal for the first few months. By eight to nine months of age, however, the first symptoms appear. This disorder results in the degeneration of the nervous system. Neither parent knows if he or she is heterozygous, or a carrier of the recessive allele for the disorder. A blood test has been developed that will tell parents whether they carry the recessive allele. Individuals who are heterozygous have half the normal level of the enzyme missing in children with Tay-Sachs.

290 ❧ HUMAN GENETICS

The counselor would provide the couple with information based on this test. If neither parent is a carrier, or if only one is, they would be told that there is no chance for them to have a child with Tay-Sachs. However, if both parents carry that allele, the counselor would explain to them that there is a one in four chance of their having a child with the disorder. With genetic counseling, parents would know the possibility of having a child with a genetic disorder.

While genetic counseling can provide important information about the probability of a child being born with a genetic disorder, it can't tell if a specific individual will be afflicted. Parents must turn to other methods for that answer.

Diagnosis in the Uterus

Down syndrome is a genetic disorder that is known to occur significantly more often in children born to mothers over the age of 35. Is there any way for parents to know whether their child will have Down syndrome?

Amniocentesis   When Down syndrome is a result of trisomy 21, examining the chromosomes of a developing fetus could determine whether the fetus is normal or not. Techniques are available for doing just that. The most frequently used technique is called **amniocentesis.** This is a process in which a sample of the fluid surrounding the fetus is withdrawn through a long, thin needle. The fluid contains fetal cells that are then grown in the correct conditions in a lab. A karyotype of the chromosomes is then made to determine whether the child has three, or the normal two, number 21 chromosomes. While amniocentesis can confirm the presence of Down syndrome, it can't determine the severity of the disease. However, the parents at least know if the fetus is affected.

Figure 11-12   **In amniocentesis, amniotic fluid is withdrawn, and the fetal cells contained in it are studied. Ultrasonography (shown in the photograph) determines the position of the fetus before amniocentesis. This is a 25-week fetus.**

Amniotic fluid

Fetus

11.2 PREVENTION AND A POSSIBLE MEANS OF CURE ❧ **291**

GLOBAL CONNECTION

Purpose

Students will study how Tay-Sachs disease affects patients and why Ashkenazic Jews tend to show more of this disease than other groups.

Teaching Strategies

• Before they read the feature, ask students if they have ever known anyone with this genetic disorder. Promote the idea that there are many people with genetic disorders. Genetic disorders are not contagious illnesses. Many individuals with genetic disorders can live full and productive lives. However, many genetic disorders do have more serious effects.

Possible Answers

1. Tay-Sachs has been reported among the Amish, Italian Catholics, and a group of non-Jewish Canadians.

2. A diet low in amino acid phenylalanine minimizes symptoms. Newborns are screened for PKU to prevent possible effects. Carriers are identified by measuring the hex-A level in their blood. If these results are inconclusive, then white blood cells or tears can be tested to confirm the diagnosis.

Going Further

Ask students to do library research about genetic diseases and disorders that seem to be more common in certain groups of people than in others.

Amniocentesis can also be used to diagnose several other disorders, such as sickle cell anemia and hemophilia, caused by defective alleles rather than chromosomes. For these diseases, a karyotype is not useful. Instead, the fluid is analyzed for the presence or absence of certain molecules that indirectly indicate presence of the disease.

Results of tests done after amniocentesis may not be available for ten days in cases where a karyotype is required. That amount of time is needed to grow enough cells for microscopic examination. A new variation of the test is being tried that will yield results in as little as two days. Artificial chromosomes known as probes are inserted into the nuclei of the cells extracted from the fluid. The probes, which contain a substance that glows under fluorescent light, attach themselves to the fetal chromo-

GLOBAL CONNECTION

Tracking Deadly Medicine

A bottle of medicine can be a priceless cure—or a deadly poison. Which it will be is a question of dosage. Digitalis, for example, is a

medicine that has given additional years of life to people with weak hearts. Yet an overdose will end a life quickly.

Sometimes a population will develop a natural defense against a disease. And sometimes individuals can overdose on that natural

defense. In this chapter, you've already seen one classic example in sickle-cell trait and sickle-cell anemia. Being heterozygous for the trait protects against malaria while being homozygous recessive for the anemia—an "overdose" of the protection—can kill. Less well understood is Tay-Sachs, which wasn't recognized as probably being the deadly form of a natural defense until the early 1970s.

Just as sickle-cell anemia is most common among people descended from Central Africans, Tay-Sachs is most likely to haunt those of Eastern European Jewish ancestry, known as Ashkenazic Jews. It was by studying this population that medical detectives tracked down clues to much of Tay-Sach's nature.

Babies born with Tay-Sachs have a genetic defect that prevents their bodies from making a vital enzyme called hexosaminidase A. In some forms of the disease, the enzyme is

made but isn't active. Hexosaminidase A breaks down a fatty substance, called G_{M2} ganglioside, produced in your nerve cells.

Without the hexosaminidase A, G_{M2} ganglioside builds up in the nerve cells until it reaches toxic levels. Tay-Sachs babies seem normal at birth, but over a period of several months, they become listless, suffer convulsions, and lose whatever control of their bodies they may have learned. They go blind and lose touch with the world around them. It's rare for a Tay-Sachs baby to survive to its fourth birthday.

You have two copies of the gene that creates hexosaminidase A, one inherited from each of your parents. You only need one to code for the enzyme to prevent Tay-Sachs. A Tay-Sachs baby must inherit two recessive hexosaminidase A-producing genes—one from each parent.

Worldwide, about one baby in every 400 000 is born with Tay-Sachs. But among Eastern European Jews and their descendants, the disorder historically affected about one birth out of every 3600. Why should this population be 100 times more

PORTFOLIO

Radiation, infectious agents, and drugs and chemicals are groups of agents that can cause gene mutations. Have students do library research to find out the details of problems caused by specific agents in each group and in their portfolios make a summary and explain what could be done both by individuals and by legislators to prevent or correct these problems. **L3** somes. Fetal cells are then examined under a microscope using fluorescent light. The number of visible probes and the chromosomes to which they attach can be used to determine whether a fetus has a chromosomal defect. As more and more individual disease-causing genes are located on chromosomes, probes may be used to spot them as well.

Chorionic Villus Biopsy   Because of possible injury to the fetus, the earliest amniocentesis can be conducted is the 14th week of pregnancy. Another method, called **chorionic villus biopsy,** can be performed as early as the ninth week. Cells from a tissue called the chorion, which is part of the structure by which the fetus is linked to its mother in the uterus, can be removed. These cells have the same chromosomes as the fetus and can be karyotyped and analyzed as in amniocentesis.

prone to the disorder than the rest of the world?

Medical science got its first peek at a possible answer to that question in a 1972 study of how grandparents of Ashkenazic Tay-Sachs babies died. Since the babies had Tay-Sachs, they must have inherited one defective hexosaminidase A gene from each parent. All the parents had to be heterozygous for Tay-Sachs. That, in turn, meant that each parent had at least one parent who was also heterozygous. At least 50 percent of the babies' grandparents had to have a single defective gene.

The study showed that only one of the 306 grandparents in the study had died of one of the most common killers of their day: tuberculosis (TB). This was at a time when as much as 20 percent of the deaths in Eastern European cities were caused by TB. Was it possible that being heterozygous for Tay-Sachs gave some protection against tuberculosis?

More evidence appeared in 1983 when studies showed that the Ashkenazic population with the highest concentration of Tay-Sachs heterozygotes was also the population with the highest rate of TB. At first glance, that might make it seem as though being heterozygous for Tay-Sachs offers no protection against TB at all. But remember— it's the population with the greatest frequency of TB that would be most likely to evolve a defense. After all, sickle-cell trait evolved in Central Africa, where malaria caused the greatest number of deaths. It didn't in Norway, where malaria isn't a problem.

Still, that evidence doesn't answer the question of why a defense against TB would arise among Eastern European Jews but not among the general population. To solve that mystery, we have to look at history.

For nearly 2000 years, the Jews of Europe made their living in various businesses in an urban setting. Large numbers of them were crowded into ghettos, separated from the rest of the city.

The Jews, confined to their ghettos, remained genetically distinct. When a defense arose, it was passed along within this stable population, spreading throughout the generations.

So far, nobody knows how carrying one defective hexosaminidase A gene helps defend against TB. In fact, the suspicion that the defect is such a defense has yet to be proven. There is, however, still more evidence that being heterozygous for Tay-Sachs provides some advantage.

Despite the fact that Tay-Sachs is incurable, it no longer strikes as many Ashkenazic families as it once did. That's because it's now possible to screen for the defective gene. As a result, carriers have been able to avoid having babies. Today, thanks to the routine testing of high-risk couples, Tay-Sachs disease is no longer more likely to strike an American Ashkenazic family than it is to appear in any other.

1. **Find Out:** What populations other than those of Ashkenazic descent are prone to Tay-Sachs?
2. **Connection to Medicine:** PKU is another disorder caused by an autosomal recessive allele. What treatment is available for this disorder?

MEETING INDIVIDUAL NEEDS

Have students research the latest genetic breakthroughs, such as finding the gene for Huntington's disease. Have students report on their findings to the class. Be sure they have a handout and involve the class in their presentations.

L3

Enrichment

Fragile X syndrome, the most common inherited form of mental retardation, is an X linked trait with an abnormal occurrence pattern. Twenty percent of male carriers of the mutation transmit the disorder to their children without developing the disorder themselves. The gene which causes this disorder has been discovered and named FMR-1. In people with fragile X syndrome, the base sequence of nucleotides CGG has been altered. Carriers of fragile X have twice as many copies; and people severely affected have thousands of extra copies. The base sequence is thought to replicate many times from one generation to the next, causing symptoms to worsen.

Different Viewpoints in Biology

The Study of Alzheimer's Disease

In 1991, three different genetically engineered mice with lesions like those of Alzheimer's disease were used by neuroscientists researching treatment for the disease. One scientist claimed that the mice produced beta-amyloid plaques and tangles of protein indicative of Alzheimer's disease. However, other researchers could not duplicate this data and accused the original researcher of tampering with the data. They say that diseased human brain tissue was adjacent to mouse tissue on the original slides prepared of the mouse brains. Fortunately, many other genetically engineered mice are being developed for continued study of Alzheimer's disease.

INVESTIGATION

Variations in Human Hands

Time Allotment

1 class period to design experiment, 10 minutes each day for a week for training and observations, 1 class period for data analysis.

Objectives

Upon completing this investigation, students will be able to:

- Distinguish between inherited and environmentally produced features of human hands.
- Describe genetic variation of human hands.

Skills

observe and infer, form a hypothesis, design an experiment, separate and control variables, and interpret data

Materials

metric ruler, one per group; magnifying glass, one per group; grip tester, several for the class (Grip testers measure hand grip quantitatively. They are available from biological supply companies and some shops where athletic equipment is sold. You might be able to borrow some from the P.E. department in your school.)

Safety Precautions: Caution students not to force bending hands or fingers beyond what is comfortable.

Preparation

Assemble materials for student groups.

Possible Hypotheses

There are no right or wrong hypotheses.

- Flexibility is inherited while writing ability is produced by the environment.
- Strength of the hand is produced by the environment while mid digit hair is inherited.

Possible Procedures

- Students may decide to try to have a group practice and train for a week to develop a hitchhiker's thumb or double jointedness, and train to write with the non-preferred hand for a week.

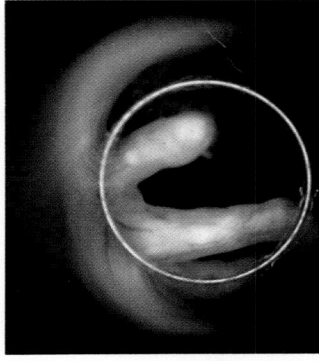

Another kind of test is being developed that can be performed even earlier. During gestation, a few fetal blood cells enter the mother's bloodstream. The fetal and maternal blood cells can be distinguished from each other and the fetal blood cells examined for chromosome abnormalities.

Ultrasonography So far, all of the techniques discussed depend on analysis of cells or fluid to determine fetal abnormalities. Two other techniques can be used to observe the fetus for abnormalities. One technique called **ultrasonography** is often used to determine the position and anatomy of a fetus. During the process, an ultrasound probe is passed back and forth over the mother's abdomen. The probe emits high-frequency sound waves that "echo" from the tissues of the fetus. Different tissues have different densities. These differences in density cause the sound waves to echo back at different wavelengths that, when put together by a computer, form an image on a screen. These images, called echograms, allow physicians to spot abnormalities, such as certain forms of heart disease. Ultrasound is also used prior to amniocentesis to determine fetal position. This reduces the risk of injuring the fetus when the needle is inserted into the mother's abdomen.

Figure 11-13 An 18-week fetus viewed through an endoscope.

INVESTIGATION

Variations in Human Hands

Do you have a "hitchhiker's thumb"? Can you bend just the first knuckle of your fingers without bending others? Do you have hair on the middle section of your fingers? How large is your hand span? Can you easily push your thumb down to touch the side of your wrist? These traits as well as all other features of your body are determined in part by genes. Almost all human traits are determined by multiple gene pairs rather than by one pair of genes. In addition, some traits may be influenced by the environment. For these reasons, it is difficult to determine which traits are dominant and which are recessive. In this investigation, you will compare features of classmates' hands and hypothesize which features of the hand are inherited and which may be produced by the environment.

Problem

Which features of the hand are probably inherited and which may be produced by environment?

Safety Precautions

Do not force bending your hands and fingers beyond what is comfortable.

Hypothesis

What is your group's hypothesis? Explain your reasons for making this hypothesis.

Experimental Plan

1. As a group, make a list of possible ways you might test your hypothesis using the materials your teacher has made available.

294 ● HUMAN GENETICS

- Students might compare the grip strength of the preferred hand to the non-preferred hand of a group of classmates and ask students to compare mid digit hair on their hands to that of other family members.

Teaching Strategies

- Differences between the preferred and the non-preferred hand may indicate environmental influence. The preferred hand may be stronger as measured by a grip tester, and slightly larger.
- Environmentally produced features might be fingernail length, color, and shape; cal-

luses; fingerprints worn down on preferred hand; hangnails; scars; visible injuries; roughness or smoothness of skin; tan; and freckles.

- Inherited traits would be length of fingers; "hitchhiker's thumb"; flexible or "double joints"; mid digit hair; skin color unless altered by sun or chemicals; number of fingers, unless altered by accident.
- Some features might be a combination of heredity and environment: number of moles; ability to play piano or other musical instrument; manual dexterity; strength; size

Fetoscopy Direct observation of the fetus and surrounding tissues is also possible. After determining the position of the fetus by means of ultrasonography, a technique called **fetoscopy** can be used. The technique makes use of a device called an endoscope. The endoscope can be inserted through a small incision in the mother's abdomen. The fetus is viewed directly through the endoscope tube. At the same time, an image of the fetus is seen on a screen. Using instruments inserted into the endoscope, small samples of skin or blood may be withdrawn for study as in amniocentesis. Fetoscopy has been used to give a transfusion to a fetus. It also has been used to remove excess fluid around the brain of a fetus.

Gene Therapy

The amount of information geneticists have discovered in the last 20 years is staggering. It was only in 1973 that the first recombinant DNA methods were successfully used. Since then, recombinant DNA technology has led to the development of techniques that allow geneticists to locate the positions of some genes that cause genetic disorders. Nucleotide sequences of normal alleles and the harmful counterparts can be compared, as can

2. Agree on one idea from your group's list that could be investigated in the classroom.
3. Design an experiment that will test one variable at a time. Plan to collect quantitative data as well as make other observations.
4. Following the style of a recipe, write a numbered list of directions that anyone could follow.
5. Make a list of materials and the quantities you will need.

Checking the Plan

Discuss the following points with other group members to decide the final procedures for your experiment.
1. What are the variables in your experiment?
2. How have you set up a control?
3. How many traits will you count?
4. What traits will you measure or count?

5. How many students' hands will you measure, observe, or examine?
6. Have you designed and made a table for collecting data?

Make sure your teacher has approved your experimental plan before you proceed further.

Data and Observations

Carry out your experiment; make your measurements and observations; and complete your data table. Make a graph of your results.

Analysis and Conclusions

1. Was your hypothesis supported by your data? Explain.
2. According to your results, which traits are most likely inherited and which are most likely produced by environment?
3. What is your experimental evidence for your conclusion in question 2?

4. Consult with another group that used a different procedure to examine this problem. Were their conclusions the same as yours?
5. Do you know of other human traits scientists are studying to determine which is more important, heredity or environment, in influencing their development?
6. Write a brief conclusion to your experiment.

Going Further

Based on this lab experience, design an experiment that would help to answer another question that arose from your work. Assume that you will have unlimited resources and will not be conducting this lab in class.

of hands; lines on palms; and dryness of skin.
- Demonstrate, or ask a student to demonstrate, what it means to have "double-jointed" fingers. (The fingers can be bent so only the first joint bends without bending the others.) Ask students to demonstrate a "hitchhiker's thumb." Ask them to look at their hands to see if they have hair on the mid digit. Ask students to examine their hands for calluses. Ask them how many are right-handed and how many are left-handed and how many play the piano. Ask them to predict whether their right or their left hand has a stronger grip. Finally, ask them, but do not answer the question, which of these traits they think are inherited and which are produced by the environment.

Data and Observations
1. The data should indicate that training to develop a hitchhiker's thumb does not help.
2. The data should indicate that mid-digit hair may be inherited.

Data Analysis
1-4. and 6. Answers will vary depending on experimental procedures and results.
5. Cancer, diseases, learning.

✔ Assessment
Portfolio: Have students write an evaluation of this lab for placement in their portfolios. Have students suggest at the conclusion of their evaluation other human features that could be studied to see if they were inherited or environmentally produced. Weight might be one example.

Extensions
When a scientist completes an experiment, another experiment often comes to mind when making observations and analyzing data. This experimental plan is part of the lab and not an option. Students might decide to investigate additional hand features or feet or other body characteristics in a similar way.

3 Assess

Check for Understanding

Ask students to describe several techniques that are used to detect genetic diseases. L1

Reteach

Tell students that they are the directors of a museum that is designing an exhibit about prevention and possible cures for genetic diseases. Ask them to brainstorm a list of possible exhibits and ways to present information to the general public.

Extension

Ask students to present updated information about the human genome project. L3

✔ Assessment

Performance Assessment: Make a transparency of a karyotype of a genetic disorder such as Down syndrome. Tell students that they are genetics counselors and must tell parents that because there is a history of this condition in their families, their future children may be at risk. Students should use the transparency as if they were explaining Down syndrome to the parents, then tell them about various testing procedures that could be done during a pregnancy, and end with some discussion of what gene therapy can do now and the potential for the future. All of this should be in written form in the portfolio.

4 Close

Discussion

Ask students to collect data regarding book-carrying behavior of males and females in the school. They should come to class with this data. Have a discussion about whether the results are genetic or influenced by the environment. L1

the amino acid sequences of the proteins for which they code. Such analysis enables scientists to understand the basic causes of the symptoms of a genetic disease, as in the case of CF.

Suppose a person suffering from CF could receive the normal allele for the protein that is not functioning correctly. The patient's cells could then begin making the proper protein, chloride ions could be pumped normally, and the thick mucus associated with the disease would no longer be present.

Although all of this sounds like a plot from a science fiction novel, it isn't. The treatment of genetic diseases by introducing normal genes into body cells is called **gene therapy.** Gene therapy has already been successfully done in a few cases. More tests have been approved and are planned for the near future.

LOOKING AHEAD

You NOW KNOW how abnormalities of genes and chromosomes can cause genetic disorders in humans. Such abnormalities and the disorders they cause can be considered variations within the human population that tragically affect the health of specific individuals. While you may focus on the situation of a specific individual, variations are also important to the long-term health of an entire population. The information being discovered by scientists may someday lead to methods that eliminate inherited disorders. Such discoveries may also lead to a human population that is generally more healthy. In the next chapter, you will explore how changes in a population's genes can be important to the evolution of that population over long periods of time.

Section Review

Understanding Concepts
1. PKU is a disease caused by the failure of an enzyme to break down the amino acid phenylalanine. This can result in mental retardation. It is caused by a recessive allele on an autosome. What information would a genetic counselor provide to the two parents, each of whom was found to carry that allele?

2. Explain why ultrasonography is used before amniocentesis is done.
3. Could chorionic villus biopsy be used to determine the existence of a disease caused by defective alleles? Explain.
4. **Skill Review—Forming a Hypothesis:** Scientists have developed several methods for introducing genes into body cells. White blood cells and viruses are two

methods already being used. Form your own hypothesis about how scientists use one of these two methods. For more help, see Practicing Scientific Methods in the **Skill Handbook.**
5. **Thinking Critically:** Could the technique of gene therapy described in this section be useful in the case of Huntington's disease? Explain.

Answers to Section Review

1. The chances of PKU are one in four.
2. Ultrasonography locates the position of the fetus to prevent injury.
3. Chorionic villus biopsy can only detect possible chromosomal defects. Only fetal cells are examined, not chemicals.
4. **Skill Review—Forming a Hypothesis:** Scientists could insert new genes into a harmless virus's chromosome and introduce the virus into the human body. Hopefully the

virus when invading human cells would insert new genes into the human's DNA.
5. **Thinking Critically:** The idea of gene therapy is to introduce a missing dominant gene, which will produce the protein missing when a person is homozygous recessive. Huntington's disease is caused by a dominant gene, so the technique described could not be used.

BIOLOGY, TECHNOLOGY, AND SOCIETY

Issues

Gender on Demand

People like to have some choice about the important things in their lives. What kind of work they do, who they marry, and whether or not they'll have children are all good examples. But when it comes time to have a child, the decision of whether to have a son or a daughter has always been out of our control.

Over the centuries, people have come up with all sorts of methods for influencing the sex of their offspring. Techniques have involved such things as getting pregnant when a north wind is blowing, eating a raw egg, and trying to conceive while wearing boots. You've probably already figured out the trouble with these methods—they don't work.

In most cases, there's no reason for couples to choose a sex for their baby except that they'd prefer a son or a daughter. But the ability to select a child's gender could be a great blessing to couples at risk of passing along a sex-linked disorder, such as hemophilia. Usually only males suffer from the disorder, but females carry it. A woman carrying the hemophilia gene has a very good reason to want daughters instead of sons.

There's still no way to guarantee either a daughter or a son, but modern medicine has found ways of improving the odds. The most successful methods involve ways of separating sperm carrying the X chromosome from those carrying the Y chromosome. The Y-carrying sperm tend to swim faster than X carriers, so one method involves separating the faster sperm from the slower ones. Another method uses a centrifuge and differences in the sperms' masses to separate them.

Both these techniques boast a success rate of 70 to 85 percent, but both are far from being a sure thing. They also have the disadvantage of requiring the sperm to be artificially placed in a woman's reproductive tract.

Another recently popular method doesn't require so much outside help, but is far more controversial. It's based on the theory that chemical changes inside a woman's reproductive system favor the success of either the X- or Y-carrying sperm at different times. Supposedly, the X sperm have an advantage from two to 24 hours before ovulation and Y-carrying sperm are more likely to fertilize the egg 36 hours after ovulation.

This theory led to a home kit intended to help prospective parents with their timing. It was sold in many drug stores, with the manufacturer professing a 77 to 98 percent success rate. The Food and Drug Administration disagreed, however, saying that there was no evidence to back up such a claim.

CHAPTER 11 HUMAN GENETICS **297**

Issues

Purpose

Students will analyze the pros and cons of parents being able to select the sex of their children and learn why this selection might be possible in the future.

Teaching Strategies

- Before students have read the selection, ask them which they think that they would want first, a son or a daughter, if they decide to have children in the future. Have a discussion about their reasons.
- Review exactly how the SRY gene functions. Use a diagram on the chalkboard, as students may be confused without a visual illustration.
- After they have read the selection, ask them if they still feel the same way.
- Ask them to discuss with adults they know whether they had a preference for sons or daughters and why. Ask them to report this information back to the class.

Possible Answers

1. Some students might say that it should be covered by insurance because it is just another part of medical care. Others will say that it should not be covered because it is an optional choice, just as having a face lift is an option that is not covered by many insurance plans. However, some will say that if the choice is based on a possible medical problem such as hemophilia, then insurance should pay.

2. There will be more men than women. Fewer men will be able to marry and there will be fewer children, resulting in population decline. Women might lose rights in a male-dominated population. The population might become more aggressive, with more war and fighting. Men would have to do many of the jobs traditionally done by women.

3. They might begin to favor daughters because there would be so many eligible men to choose from to marry, and they might realize that the population will continue to decline if there are more and more men. On the other hand, laws might be changed to make polygamy acceptable.

Going Further

Ask students to tally in their class the total number of boys and girls in their families. Ask them why, if male and female offspring occur at a ratio of approximately 50:50, some families have only boys or only girls.

The manufacturer withdrew the product after being investigated for misleading consumers.

Something more definite may someday come from a discovery announced in mid-1990. A team of genetic researchers found a tiny string of DNA on the Y chromosome that they believe to be the gene that determines whether an embryo will become a male or a female. The gene, known as SRY, functions much like a switch. If it's present, it "turns on" a long sequence of reactions that determines the development of sex

organs. The hormones produced by the sex organs trigger the rest of the process: hormones from ovaries result in a female body while those from testes cause a male body to develop.

The researchers who discovered SRY think that they might be able to use the gene to influence the sex of mice and cattle. They are opposed, however, to using it on humans. Besides a host of technical problems, they believe the procedure would be unethical.

They aren't alone. Many people are uncomfortable with the idea of being able to select a baby's gender as easily as choosing his or her first pair of shoes. One great concern deals with the problem of sexual equality.

Many Eastern cultures value sons more than daughters. Some people worry that, once gender selection becomes simple, people from those cultures will choose to have far more boys than girls. That could cause social problems when those many boys and few girls reach marrying age. They also note that women tend to have fewer rights in many of these countries. Any movement towards women's rights could be seriously endangered if men make up the majority of the population.

Others argue that the problems could be easily avoided with regulation. Simply allow every couple to select a son once and a daughter once. After that, they must take the luck of the draw. That would keep the sexes from ever becoming far out of balance.

But that, according to some, might only lead to more subtle problems. The threat of men numerically overrunning women isn't a real concern in the United States. Here families tend to want balance—both sons and daughters. Still, some studies have indicated that, if they had their choice, more American families would choose to have a son first and daughter second than the other way around. Other research has suggested that the order of birth has some effect on personality traits, with firstborns

tending to be more assertive and achievement-oriented than later children. Therefore, the argument goes, there's a risk that the overall male population would grow increasingly more aggressive than the overall female population.

Proponents of gender choice consider that risk small compared to the benefit of being able to help control the birth rate in many poor and overpopulated countries. A family with three daughters wouldn't have to keep trying to have a son. A family with four sons wouldn't have to keep trying to get a daughter. Everyone could have both a son and a daughter in just two childbirths.

Yet, while the controversy has already begun, so far it's all largely theoretical. The reality of guaranteed gender selection is some time away. For now, everyone is still assured of getting either their first or second choice.

Understanding the Issue

1. Treatment to increase the chance of having either a boy or girl is expensive. Do you think this cost should be covered by medical insurance? Why or why not? What if the purpose is to avoid having a son with a sex-linked genetic disorder?

2. What problems do you see developing in a country that values sons over daughters 20-25 years after gender selection becomes available?

3. Suppose a country that now values sons over daughters developed a population with three times as many men as women. How do you think that would affect the way parents selected their children's genders?

Biotechnology

In Utero Treatments for Genetic Disorders

The defeat of many diseases has long depended upon early diagnosis and treatment. For families prone to severe genetic disorders, however, early diagnosis just meant early heartbreak and little chance for hope. Take the recessive disorder known as Hurler's syndrome, for example. Symptoms appear within two years of birth, but nothing can be done about them. Death before age 10 is almost certain.

When medical science devised ways to test embryos for Hurler's syndrome, parents carrying the genetic defect that causes the disease gained the option of aborting a pregnancy. But there was still no treatment in sight.

Today, it's possible that Hurler's syndrome and many similar genetic disorders can actually be cured. The key, as in other types of disorders, lies in early diagnosis and treatment. But "early" means earlier than ever before—not just before symptoms appear, but about 22 weeks before the child is even born.

Hurler's syndrome is caused by a defective gene unable to make an enzyme called alpha-iduronidase. Body cells need this enzyme to break down a group of complex carbohydrates known as muco-polysaccharides. Without the enzyme, these carbohydrates accumulate to toxic levels, creating the lethal symptoms of Hurler's syndrome.

Alpha-iduronidase is one of several vital enzymes produced in the body's stem cells. These are the cells that manufacture blood cells. In adults, they're located in the bone marrow. But they first develop in a fetus's liver. They start migrating to the bone marrow when the fetus is about 14-16 weeks old.

There's no way known to repair defective alpha-iduronidase genes—or any other genes—at any age. If a fetus has Hurler's syndrome, its stem cells will never produce the needed enzyme. But a technique called stem-cell transplantation may make up for the defect. The idea is to give the fetus cells that will make substances its flawed genes keep it from making for itself.

When healthy stem cells are transplanted into the fetus's liver in time, the healthy cells migrate to the bone marrow along with the rest of the cells. If they take, they may produce enough healthy blood cells to prevent the disorder from appearing.

Stem-cell transplants hold great hope for curing a wide variety of genetic disorders. Enzyme deficiencies, such as Hurler's Syndrome, are prime candidates for the treatment. Almost any disease caused by defective stem cells could be targeted, as long as the disease can be diagnosed within 14 weeks of conception.

However, stem-cell transplants are still both experimental and controversial. The greatest controversy is based on the problem of finding healthy cells to transplant. The best source of these cells is tissues from miscarried fetuses. Many people are opposed to using the tissues of these fetuses for experimental procedures.

1. **Issues:** Why might some people be opposed to using tissues from miscarried fetuses for research? How might society benefit from research using these tissues?
2. **Find Out:** Find other diseases or disorders that are candidates for treatment with stem-cell transplants.

299

in its genetic makeup, with many inactive genes.

2. Bone marrow transplants are given to people with cancers of the blood such as leukemia. Patients who have damage to bone from disease or injury can be given special stem cell preparations that will allow bone replacement. Fetal tissue has also been successfully transplanted into people with Parkinson's disease.

Biotechnology

Purpose

Students will study a procedure for curing Hurler's syndrome. In this procedure, healthy stem cells are transplanted into the liver of a fetus that has a defective gene preventing the formation of the enzyme alpha-iduronidase.

Background

The development of radioactive probes for detection of abnormal alleles has revolutionized diagnosis of genetic disorders of the fetus. Synthetic nucleotide sequences probe to find a complementary sequence among restriction fragments that code for portions that would be missing if the child has the specific disorder being screened. If the probe cannot make a match, the child is diagnosed with the disorder. Such probes are currently available for disorders such as hemophilia, sickle-cell anemia, and Duchenne muscular dystrophy. With the lifting of the ban on fetal tissue research in early 1993, perhaps more progress will be made in learning about transplanting stem cells to eliminate the disorders that can be detected now with such precision.

Teaching Strategies

- Before students read this selection, ask them if they know anyone who has had a bone marrow transplant. Ask them what the transplant accomplished.
- Ask them how they feel about using tissue from aborted fetuses for transplant into patients who would surely die without it. Explain to students that fetal tissue contains cells with genes that are turned on that adult tissue may have already turned off.

Possible Answers

1. Opposition may result from lack of knowledge about how important the research is for curing certain diseases. Some people think that abortion is morally wrong and, therefore, that using aborted fetal tissue is also morally wrong. Some may not understand that adult tissue may be very different

CHAPTER 11
CHAPTER REVIEW

Summary

Summary statements can be used by students to review the major concepts of the chapter.

Language of Biology

Answers should go beyond defining the terms. Accept any reasonable answer that uses the term correctly and in the proper context.

Understanding Concepts

1. Such knowledge is useful in order to determine the causes of disease symptoms and may also lead to a means of treatment.
2. The disease is sex linked.
3. Multiple genes might be responsible for the disease. It is also possible that development of the disease depends in part on the presence of other genes.
4. Heterozygotes may carry a disease-causing recessive allele, but that allele may confer an advantage that neither homozygous genotype provides. Thus, the frequency of the recessive allele remains high in the population even though the homozygous recessive genotype results in the disease.
5. This form of color blindness is due to an autosomal gene, whereas red-green color blindness is sex linked.
6. The chromosome abnormality results from nondisjunction of the sex chromosomes.
7. It would reveal the sex.
8. Chorionic villus biopsy can be performed earlier in pregnancy.
9. The defective membrane protein does not pump chloride ions across the membrane. As a result, water and sodium ions fail to pass across the membrane, and the mucus is thick. The mucus clogs the passageways that are lined by cells having the defective membrane protein.

Summary

Using modern techniques, the locations of many genetic disorder-causing genes have been determined. In some cases, the nucleotide sequences of the genes have been worked out and compared to those of normal alleles, and the proteins coded for by the two alleles have been compared. Such work provides information that explains the symptoms of the disorder.

Many human genetic disorders are caused by defective alleles, both autosomal and on sex chromosomes. Although these alleles cause disorders in certain combinations, they may also benefit a population when in other combinations.

Genetic counseling can help prospective parents determine the chances of having children with an inherited disorder. A variety of techniques can determine whether a fetus will have a disorder or not. Gene therapy offers the promise of replacing defective genes with normal ones.

Language of Biology

Write a sentence that shows your understanding of each of the following terms.

amniocentesis
chorionic villus biopsy
fetoscopy
gene therapy

genetic counseling
karyotype
trisomy
ultrasonography

Understanding Concepts

1. Why is it important to know the nucleotide sequences of harmful genes and the abnormalities in the proteins for which they code?
2. Muscular dystrophy is an inherited disorder in which the muscle tissue gradually breaks down. It almost always occurs in males. What does that suggest about its genetic basis? Explain.
3. How might you explain the genetic basis of a disorder that occurs with equal frequency among both sexes and that does not follow basic patterns of Mendelian inheritance?
4. Explain the idea of heterozygote superiority with respect to human genetic disorders.
5. In a rare form of color blindness, a person cannot distinguish the color blue. This abnormality, when it does occur, affects both males and females and in equal numbers. Explain this pattern of inheritance and compare it to that involved in red-green color blindness.

6. Males having Klinefelter syndrome are found to have two X chromosomes and one Y. What is the genetic basis of that chromosome abnormality?
7. Besides the presence of chromosome abnormalities, what else could amniocentesis reveal about chromosomes of a fetus that parents might be eager to know?
8. What advantage does chorionic villus biopsy have over amniocentesis?
9. How does the defective cell membrane protein in CF patients affect transport of materials across the cell membrane? What is the result?
10. How can a pedigree help a geneticist get information about a certain genetic disorder?

10. The pedigree can reveal the pattern of inheritance and can also provide information about genotypes of individuals.

Applying Concepts

11. Ultrasonography can be used to determine the condition of organs such as the liver, pancreas, and ovaries. Doctors can determine the size of these organs and if there are any abnormalities.
12. The alleles causing those diseases arose in certain groups of people by mutation.

Because people tend to reproduce among members of their own group, the disease tends to be most prevalent in the group in which it first arose.

13. Amniocentesis is performed later, CVS earlier. In amniocentesis, fetal cells in amniotic fluid are analyzed, providing information about both chromosome and gene defects. In chorionic villus biopsy, cells from the chorion are analized.
14. The transfusions will contain normal red blood cells, thus relieving the symptoms of sickle-cell.

Applying Concepts

11. A very common use of ultrasonography is to determine the size and position of a developing fetus. What other organs do you think could be examined using ultrasonography? What could it show?

12. Can you suggest a reason why certain human genetic diseases, such as CF and sickle-cell anemia, occur more frequently among one group of people than another?

13. Compare amniocentesis with chorionic villus biopsy.

14. Why are transfusions useful in treating people with sickle-cell anemia?

15. Human eggs fertilized outside the body will develop normally for a time. If separated at the eight-cell stage, each cell can still develop properly when placed in the mother's womb. Do these facts suggest a means for early detection of genetic abnormalities? Explain what might be done.

16. What is the likelihood that a female would inherit hemophilia? Draw a Punnett square to support your answer.

17. **History Connection:** Explain how the founder effect works in the transmission of a trait in a small, closed population.

18. **Global Connection:** What evidence is there that being heterozygous for Tay-Sachs is a protection against TB?

Lab Interpretation

19. **Investigation:** You hypothesize that having the second toe longer than the big toe is an inherited trait. What experimental procedure would you follow to test your hypothesis? What else would you need to do before you could say your hypothesis was confirmed?

20. **Minilab 1:** Examine diagrams of microscopic views of human red blood cells. Tell which has sickle-cell anemia, which has sickle-cell trait, and which one is normal. Explain how you know.

21. **Minilab 2:** Examine the microscopic views of diagrams of human cheek cells. Which one is male and which one is female? How do you know?

A   B

22. **Thinking Lab:** A scientist would like to test the hypothesis that grinding teeth during sleep has a genetic basis. Current research suggests that it is due to an improper bite. How might the scientist begin the investigation? What might be involved?

Connecting Ideas

23. Healthy people have cell membrane proteins that do not function properly in CF patients. ATP is necessary for these membrane proteins to function. By what process are the ions moved across the membrane?

24. Explain the relationships between DNA, genes, alleles, and chromosomes. How does specific information about chromosomes and their parts help in perhaps one day finding a cure for a specific genetic disorder?

15. Eggs could be fertilized outside the body when parents are both heterozygous. The eggs could be examined for genetic diseases.

16. The zygote must contain two X chromosomes, each bearing a recessive allele. The mother would have to be heterozygous and the father a hemophiliac.

17. Even though an allele is originally present in only one or a few individuals, it may increase in frequency if it is passed on to those individuals' offspring. Because the offspring reproduce only with others in the same small population, more and more individuals will carry the allele. With time, the number of heterozygotes increases, as does the likelihood of two heterozygotes reproducing.

18. Heterozygotes are less likely to contract TB, and heterozygotes are most numerous in populations where TB is common.

Lab Interpretation

19. You would have to measure toe length in children in families in which only one parent had longer second toes and in families whose big toes were longer. To conclude that your hypothesis is correct, you would sample a large number of individuals and have the majority show a longer second toe.

20. Normal red blood cells have a distinct disc shape. Sickled cells are half-moon shaped.

21. A. Female: has Barr bodies.
    B. Male: no Barr bodies.

22. The scientist would begin his investigation by studying the bites of people who do not grind their teeth. He might then take mouth and tooth measurements and correlate them to families in which both parents and children grind their teeth at night. Some variables would be the type of improper bite, an overbite or underbite; the age of the individuals; and their habits—stress.

Connecting Ideas

23. **Uses of Energy:** The process is active transport. Energy of ATP is

---

used to change the shape of the pump that moves chloride ions across the membrane.

24. **Methods of Inquiry:** Genes are made of DNA and are located on chromosomes. Alleles differ in the sequence of their nucleotides. By comparing proteins coded for by different alleles and learning about the functions of all the genes on a given chromosome, it may be possible for researchers to develop treatments or even cures for diseases caused by both gene and chromosomal abnormalities.

Evolutionary Relationships

Unit Overview

This unit begins by presenting various lines of evidence for evolution and the central concept of natural selection. Evolution of adaptations and of entirely new groups of organisms, including humans, is then explained. Following this, students will apply their understanding of evolution as they examine the modern basis of classification. The unit concludes with an evolutionary overview of viruses and the five kingdoms of life.

Theme Development

Two major themes are addressed in this unit—evolution and unity within diversity. Students are introduced to the former in Chapters 12 and 13 as they study the fact that evolution occurs and the means by which it occurs. In Chapters 14 through 17, students come to appreciate that evolution explains the great diversity of life on Earth, past and present, and explore evolutionary innovations as they survey examples of life, forms of the major phyla within each kingdom. They will also understand that, though diverse, organisms have many characteristics in common.

Advance Planning

You may wish to consider a trip to a zoo, aquarium, botanical garden, or museum. Such a trip will not only afford students an opportunity to observe a variety of life forms, but will also provide direct evidence that will stimulate discussion of adaptations, speciation and evolutionary relationships, and taxonomy.

Chapter 12
• Order alginate and plaster of paris and procure animal shells for the Investigation.
• Order diatomaceous Earth for Minilab 1.
• Order live grasshoppers for the Alternate Lab.

Evolutionary Relationships

Chickens have been artificially selected for different traits for many years. This Rhode Island Red is bred for its good taste and good egg-laying ability. Other breeds of chicken may produce more eggs or more meat. Why isn't the Rhode Island Red a different species than the White Leghorn?

What kind of food do you think this finch eats? This is only one of the 14 species of finches that Darwin identified on the Galapagos Islands. Each species has a different type of beak that is related to the type of food it eats. Think of a woodpecker and a sparrow. Can you tell from their beaks that they eat different kinds of foods?

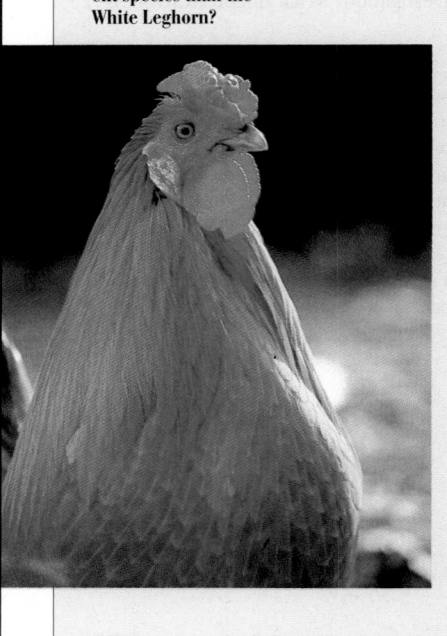

302

Chapter 13
• Procure flag marker tape (surveyor's tape) for the Alternate Lab.

Chapter 14
• Order live and preserved specimens for Minilab 2: lichen, liverwort, *Obelia,* and *Ulva.*

Chapter 15
• Order methyl cellulose and protozoan culture for the Investigation.
• Order or prepare active yogurt culture for the Alternate Lab.

Chapter 16
• Order or procure fern sori and moss capsules for Minilab 1.
• Order or procure *Sphagnum* moss for the Alternate Lab.

Chapter 17
• Order hydrochloric acid, sodium hydroxide, and *Planaria* cultures for the Investigation.
• Order preserved animal specimens for Minilab 1.
• Order preserved animal specimens for the Alternate Lab.

The Galapagos Islands are home to many unusual organisms, such as giant tortoises, flightless cormorants, and marine iguanas. But to Charles Darwin, the most interesting organisms were the many species of finches. How could so many species of finches exist in such a small area? Darwin's thoughts about these finches and other organisms he saw on his voyage in the 1830s led to his ideas on natural selection.

Variations among organisms have enabled humans to produce desirable organisms that would not occur in nature. Artificial selection for desirable traits has resulted in cows that produce more milk, disease-resistant corn, and seedless grapes.

Selection, either artificial or natural, only works because of the great genetic diversity that exists among species. In this unit, you will learn how variations among organisms enable evolution to occur, and how relationships among organisms of the present can be determined by exploring the evolutionary relationships of the past.

Knowing this, students will then study in Chapters 15, 16, and 17 viruses and representative organisms from major phyla of each kingdom. As they do so, they will begin to appreciate both the unity and diversity of life and how both are explained in terms of evolutionary change.

Introducing the Unit

Using the Photos
Ask students to compare the two kinds of animals shown here. Ask if the two are related in any way. Students might say that chickens and finches are not related but then point out that they are both birds and therefore more closely related than a chicken and a tree. Birds make up a class of the animal kingdom and show enormous variety. Ask students to list and describe other birds. Invite them to think of other flightless birds. Show them a picture of a dodo, a flightless bird that became extinct around 1680. The dodo is illustrated in Lewis Carroll's *Alice in Wonderland.* Sailors on ships that visited the island of Mauritius killed the fearless birds for food and released pigs and monkeys that ate the dodo's eggs. This example of extinction can lead you into a discussion of the importance of conserving gene pools of rare species.

Previewing the Chapters
As students examine different lines of evidence that evolution occurs in Chapter 12, they will come to see that those lines of evidence support one another, leading to the inescapable conclusion that evolution is a fact. They will then learn about Darwin's work and the clues that led him (and Wallace) to the concept of natural selection, the concept that explains how most evolutionary change takes place.

In Chapter 13, students will examine how Darwin's ideas can be applied to explain the origin of adaptations and of new species. They will also study how speciation may result from polyploidy or chance events and genetic drift. They will learn about evolutionary patterns including convergence and adaptive radiation and will explore both the biological and cultural evolution of humans.

With basic principles of evolution behind them, students will see in Chapter 14 that evolutionary relationships form the basis of modern taxonomy and that an organism's classification represents its phylogeny.

SECTION	OBJECTIVES	TEXT LABS/FEATURES
12.1 Evidence for Evolution (2 days)	**Recognize** how various lines of evidence suggest that evolution occurs. **Apply** your knowledge of evolution to explain resistance of bacteria to penicillin.	**Minilab 1:** What are microfossils? p. 307 **Thinking Lab:** Do rock layers provide clues for judging their age? p. 307 **Art Connection:** Sculpting the Past, p. 308 **Investigation:** Forming Your Own Fossil, p. 310
12.2 Darwin's Explanation (2 days)	**Analyze** how Darwin's observations led him to conclude that life forms change over time. **Explain** the process of natural selection. **Apply** modern knowledge of genetics to the theory of natural selection.	**Global Connection:** The Question of Color, p. 320
12.3 Origin of Life (2 days)	**Sequence** the events that might have led to the evolution of complex organic molecules and the first prokaryotes. **Discuss** the events leading to evolution of autotrophs and the consequences of that evolution.	**Minilab 2:** Can a calendar represent geologic time? p. 327
BIOLOGY, TECHNOLOGY, AND SOCIETY		**Issues:** Biodiversity: Which Species Should Be Saved? p. 330 **Biotechnology:** Dating Fossils, p. 331 **Career Connection:** Archaeologist, p. 331

LAB MATERIALS

INVESTIGATION	MINILAB	ALTERNATE LAB
page 310 alginate animal shells bones, chicken or beef clay food containers, small plastic goggles graduated cylinder leaves newspapers paper cups petroleum jelly plaster of paris scissors waxed paper	**page 307** coverslips diatomaceous earth microscope slides **page 327** blank calendars calculator	**page 318** balance grasshoppers jars, baby food size with lids magnifying glass, or microscope, binocular meterstick metric ruler

TEACHER CLASSROOM RESOURCES	OTHER RESOURCES
Study Guide, pp. 67-68 **Concept Mapping,** p. 12 ****ILS:** *Biochemical Evidence for Evolution,* p. 109	***STVS:** *Fossil CAT Scan,* Earth and Space (Disc 3, Side 2) ***STVS:** *Carbon-14 Dating,* Chemistry (Disc 2, Side 2) **Color Transparency 16:** *The Geologic Time Scale*
Study Guide: pp. 69-70 **Critical Thinking/Problem Solving:** *Darwinian Theory: A Genetic Interpretation,* p. 12 ***PLL:** *Natural Selection in Populations,* p. 64	***STVS:** *Resistance to Pesticides in Cockroaches,* Ecology (Disc 6, Side 2) **Color Transparency 17:** *Natural Selection*
Study Guide: pp. 71-72 **Exploring Environmental Issues:** *The Rain Forest,* pp. 39-40 ***PLL:** *Coacervates—A Model of Life's Origins,* p. 68	
Assessment Materials **Chapter Assessment,** pp. 45-48 **Performance Assessment in Biology,** p. 24 **Alternate Assessment in the Science Classroom** **Computer Test Bank**	**Spanish Resources** **Cooperative Learning Resource Guide** **Videodisc Correlations** (to Optical Data's and Videodiscovery's videodiscs)

* Probing Levels of Life
** Investigating Living Systems

* Science Technology Videodisc Series

Key to Teaching Strategies

The following designations will help you decide which activities in the teacher margin are appropriate for your students.

L1 Level 1 activities should be within the ability range of all students.

L2 Level 2 activities should be within the ability range of the average to above-average student.

L3 Level 3 activities are designed for the ability range of above-average students.

LEP LEP activities are appropriate for Limited English Proficiency students.

COOP LEARN Cooperative Learning activities are designed for small group work.

ADDITIONAL RESOURCES

Infinite Voyage *Living with Disaster*
Nature is always unpredictable, yet living things manage to survive and prosper in spite of natural disasters. Students will explore the responses of living things to natural disasters in this video.

Audiovisual
The Human Influence, video, Films for the Humanities and Sciences.
The Record of the Rocks, video, Films for the Humanities and Sciences.

Software
Natural Selection, Apple 128K, EME.
Origin of Life, Apple II, EME.

EVOLUTION

Chapter Overview

Students begin their study of evolution by examining the evidence for the process, which includes the fossil record, comparative studies, genetics, and direct observation.

Next, students learn about the evidence that provided Darwin with clues that helped him form his theory of natural selection. They will find that Wallace had come to the same conclusions as Darwin. Using Darwin's ideas as well as the modern concept of population genetics, students will be able to explain evolutionary changes.

Finally, students will examine the heterotroph hypothesis of the origin of life and the evidence that supports that hypothesis.

EVOLUTION

WHAT YOU SEE here is like a photograph of a photograph. Someone took a picture of the fossil embedded in the rock, developed the film, and made a print on paper—all within a matter of days or possibly even hours. The image in the rock is actually the preserved form of the bones from an ancient organism's body, one that lived on Earth perhaps millions of years ago. The process of fossilization may have taken thousands of years for the surrounding sediments to become rock-hard. Does it remind you of any living organisms you have seen?

The canyon walls shown in the small photo could be called a big-screen image of the past. Like ribbons of time, layers of different rock formations run across the cliff faces. Each layer records an episode in Earth's geologic history. A few organisms that lived out their lives during various geologic episodes may have become encased in the layers. The fossilized organisms are entries in the record of life. As you will see in this chapter, such traces of past organisms give us clues about how and when life evolved. They help us understand how organisms are related to one another and how the present is tied to the past.

KEY TERMS

autotroph
chemosynthesis
comparative anatomy
comparative biochemistry
comparative embryology
embryo
fossil
gene pool
heterotroph
homologous
natural selection
ozone layer
population
selective breeding
theory of natural selection
vestigial

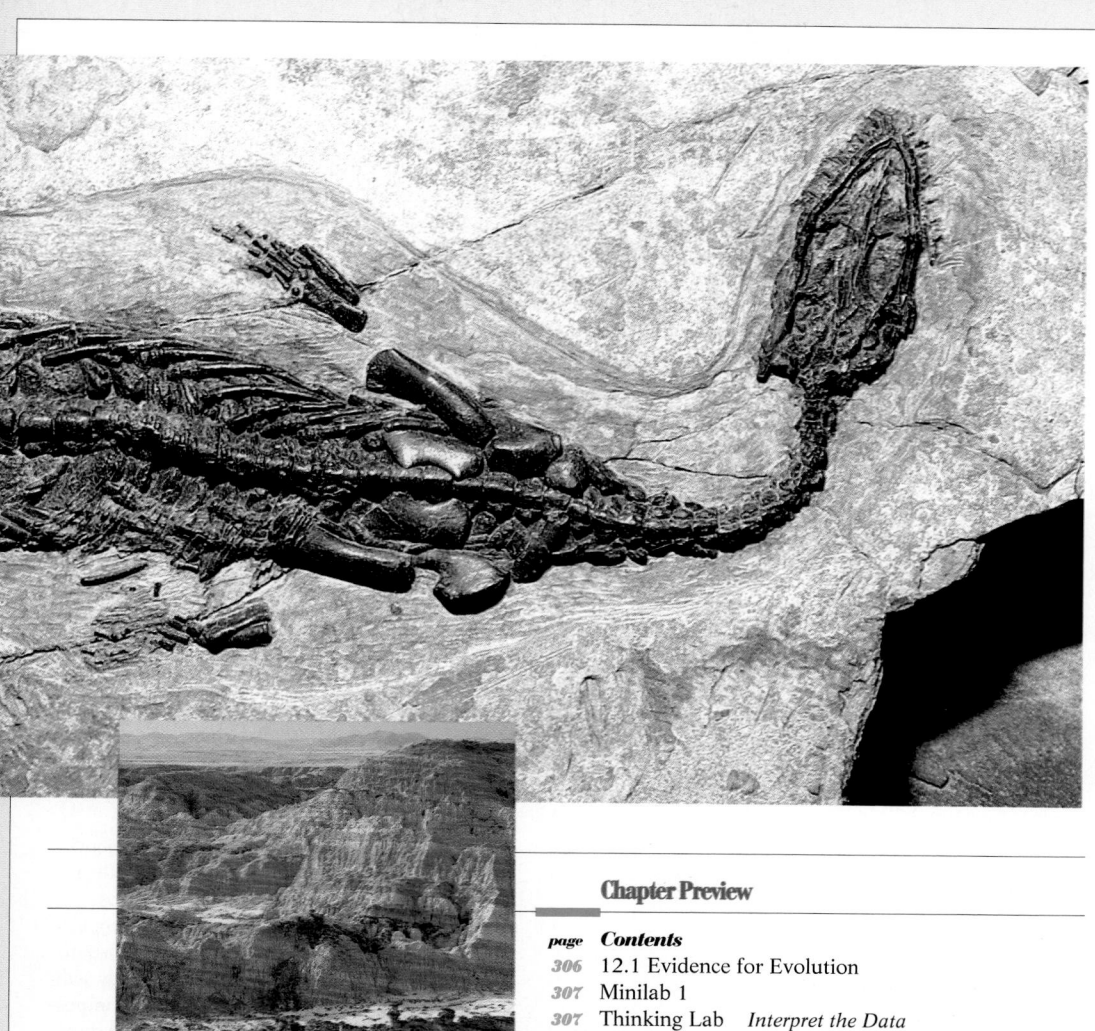

What are the records of your past life? How will your great-great-grandchildren know what you looked like and what your life was like?

Chapter Preview

305

Introducing the Chapter

Have students examine the photograph on page 304 and begin a general discussion of fossils. The fossil record provides a history of life on Earth. Ask students to identify extinct organisms that they know about such as dinosaurs, giant ferns, or trilobites. Ask them if there are present-day life forms that resemble extinct forms of life. What does the answer to that question suggest about life on Earth? How can the idea of evolution be explained?

Theme Development

Evolution is the prominent theme addressed in this chapter as students examine the means by which evolution occurs. Students will see that methods of inquiry in science do not always involve experimentation. However, experimentation does play a role in the study of some aspects of evolution, such as for DNA analyses, meticulous field work, careful analysis of fossil discoveries, and logical comparisons.

Tying to Previous Knowledge

In the broad sense, everything that students have learned about biology so far can be related to evolution. In teaching this chapter, you can refer back to many topics in terms of evolution and natural selection. For example, have students realize that processes they have studied, such as cellular respiration and mitosis, are adaptations. So, too, is a cell a highly adapted structure, as are the many organelles that interact to keep it alive. Remind them of the symbiosis model of eukaryotic evolution. Stress that current knowledge of genetics provides a broad base for our understanding of variations among organisms.

ASSESSMENT PLANNER

Choose assessment strategies from the following pages to evaluate the progress of your students.

Assess, pp. 315, 323, 328-329
Portfolio, pp. 307, 309, 311, 312, 320, 325
Alternate Lab, pp. 318-319
Thinking Lab, p. 307

Minilab 1, p. 307
Minilab 2, p. 327
Investigation, pp. 310-311
Chapter Review, pp. 332-333

Prepare

Key Concepts

Evidence for evolution is presented. Students will examine evidence from the fossil record, anatomy, embryology, biochemistry, genetics, and direct observation.

Key Terms

fossil, comparative anatomy, homologous, vestigial, embryo, comparative embryology, comparative biochemistry, population, selective breeding

Materials

- For Minilab 1, obtain diatomaceous earth.
- For the Investigation, obtain plaster of paris, alginate from your dentist, petroleum jelly, wax paper, clay, plastic food containers, newspapers, animal shells, plant parts, and small, clean chicken bones.

1 Focus

Objectives

The objectives are listed on the student page. Remind students to preview these objectives as a guide to this numbered section.

Demonstration

Obtain a roll of toilet tissue with 1000 sheets. Tell students that the roll of paper represents all time since life evolved. Walk around the room unrolling about 845 sheets. Tell students that the 845 sheets represent the time it took for the first invertebrates to evolve. Unroll 43 sheets, the time it took for the first jawed fishes to evolve. Unroll another 57 sheets, the time it took for the first dinosaurs to appear. Then unroll 13 sheets, the time for mammals to appear; then 29 sheets, the time for the first placental mammals to evolve. The remaining 12 sheets represent the time it took for the first humans to evolve. Each sheet represents about 3.5 million years; therefore, the last sheet is the approximate time that humans have been on Earth. LEP

306

Objectives

Recognize how various lines of evidence suggest that evolution occurs.

Apply your knowledge of evolution to explain resistance of bacteria to penicillin.

12.1 Evidence for Evolution

You didn't have to sign up for a biology course to discover that a great many different life forms inhabit Earth. You had already experienced them all around you—in trees and smaller plants, in birds and insects, in animals and humans. You may even have puzzled over the existence of such great diversity. How did elephants and elm trees, or mushrooms and mice end up on the same planet? On the other hand, you may have wondered how horses and zebras could be so different from each other and yet so much alike. Perhaps you wondered about chimps and humans in the same way.

Fossil Evidence

So far, you have learned that there are millions of different kinds of life forms on Earth. They all evolved. Remember from Chapter 1 that evolution means change over time. During the course of evolution, some life forms retained closer relationships with one another than others. But how do we know that evolution continues to occur? How does evolution account for the relationships that we observe among existing organisms?

A Fossil Is Formed Most organisms depart this world without a trace. They die; their remains decay; nothing is left to show that they ever lived. But there are exceptions. Occasionally, one or more actual parts, such as bones, of an organism or even a whole organism is preserved or petrified. Sometimes, a mold or cast of an organism is left in a rock. Any such trace of an organism that lived long ago is a **fossil.**

Some organisms were fossilized when they became trapped and quickly frozen in ice or enclosed in amber, which is resin from ancient coniferous trees. Such fossils can be very clear and revealing. They also are very rare. Most commonly, sand or clay surrounds a tooth, a bone, or other hard part of an organism soon after the organism dies. The sand or clay sediments prevent the body part from decomposing. In time, the sediments around the dead organism turn to rock. Sometimes a shell or skeleton may be preserved with very little change to its chemical makeup. Sometimes, minerals filter into the body of the preserved organism's part or parts and the organism also turns to rock. The organism has become petrified.

Figure 12-1 Fossils in the lower layers of sedimentary rock are older than those found in upper layers. Often, the layers of rock can be dated by types of fossils they contain.

306 EVOLUTION

The Fossil Record   Fossils give us information about kinds of organisms that have existed on Earth. Thanks to the layering in sedimentary rock, fossils also give us clues as to when the organisms may have lived. Think of it this way: You stack up newspapers by adding each day's edition to the top. As long as the stack remains undisturbed, the oldest paper is on the bottom and the newest is on the top. In much the same way, particles of weathered rocks settle in layers like the layers in a cake and form sedimentary rocks. Fossils found in the undisturbed lower layers of sedimentary rocks are usually older than those found in undisturbed upper layers. Scientists have determined the relative times of appearance and disappearance of many kinds of organisms from the locations of their fossils in sedimentary rock layers.

Often many fossils are found together at the same location, probably because all the organisms died together in a flood, volcanic eruption, or some other disaster. One site discovered in China consists of sediments from an ancient seafloor dating back 570 million years. More than 70 previously unknown fossil animals were discovered at that site.

Fossil studies often show that the majority of organisms from older layers are generally simpler in body structures than ones from younger layers. The types of fossil organisms change from one layer to the next. Thus, we can conclude that life forms became more complex over time. However, many of the simple life forms found as fossils still exist. Many others have become extinct.

Important as it is, the fossil record remains incomplete. Because fossil formation has occurred so rarely, the record may never be complete enough to show every step in the evolution of Earth's life forms. Because soft tissues are rarely preserved, it is certain that not every kind of organism that ever lived has left a record. Nevertheless, many fossils that show strong similarities to existing organisms have been found. For example,

Minilab 1

What are microfossils?

Certain fossils are so small that they can only be observed with a microscope. They are called microfossils. Prepare a wet mount of fossil "powder" taken from sedimentary rock. Examine the sample under low and high power. Make diagrams of what resembles shells of organisms. Using Appendix A, attempt to identify these organisms. You have three clues for help: size, where it lived, and the structure being viewed.
Analysis   *How do you know that fossils once lived in water? Explain why these fossils may not have been destroyed over time.*

Thinking Lab

INTERPRET THE DATA

Do rock layers provide clues for judging their age?

Background
The law of superposition states that most sedimentary rocks are laid down in horizontal layers. The fossils in these layers increase in age from top to bottom as long as the layers have not been disturbed. The two formations shown here are formed from sedimentary rocks and have not been disturbed in position. Rock layers of like colors are the same age.

You Try It
Use the law of superposition to answer the following questions. **Compare** rock formations 1 and 2.
1. Which layer in each formation is the oldest? Explain how the fossil records in these two layers compare.
2. Which layer is the youngest? Explain how their fossil records will compare.
3. Which layers are the same age? Compare their fossil records.

---

2 Teach

Concept Development
Explain that amber is fossilized resin extruded in Tertiary times from coniferous trees. Insects were occasionally trapped in the honey-colored amber. One specimen of a spider included traces of its thread, indicating the immediate nature of the preservation.

Minilab 1

Purpose
Students will observe diatoms.

Skills
make a wet mount, use a microscope, compare and contrast, classify

Teaching Strategies
• The fossil powder is diatomaceous earth, available from any biological supply house. The powder consists of millions of fossil skeletons of marine diatoms.
• Direct students to Appendix A for identification of simple organisms.
• **Safety Precautions:** Caution students to use care when handling the microscope and making wet mounts.

Answers
Sedimentary rock results from the deposition of sediment in water. Diatoms live in water. The shell of this organism is hard and therefore can withstand damage by pressure.

✔ **Assessment**
Oral: Students should explain how a rock that is above sea level could contain fossil shells of marine organisms.

Thinking Lab

INTERPRET THE DATA

Purpose
Students will learn to identify relative age of rocks by their fossils.

Skills
observe and infer, interpet the data

Teaching Strategies
• A model of superposition can be constructed with layers of clay.

Further Background
Explain that the top layers of formation 2 may be missing due to erosion.

Answers
1. E is oldest in 1, C′ is oldest in 2. Fossil records will be alike if sediments are the same age. (Note: both layers being the oldest does not make them equal in age.)

2. A is youngest in 1, A′ is youngest in 2. Fossil records will be alike.
3. B, C, and D in 1 are equal in age to A′, B′, and C′ in 2. Fossil records will be alike if sediments are the same age.

✔ **Assessment**
Portfolio: Ask students to research the meaning and use of index fossils.

ART CONNECTION

Purpose

Students will determine how forensic artists and anthropologists have worked together in an attempt to make models of extinct humans.

Background

The forensic anthropologist works mainly with the bones of people who have died from unnatural causes. The police officer or forensic artist works mainly with images of living people.

Teaching Strategies

* Show a brief video clip of a crime scene to one half of the class. Ask students to pair up so that one has seen the clip and the other has not. One student should describe the offender in detail while the other draws a sketch of the offender according to the description given.
* Show the clip again so they can see what they missed in their descriptions.
* Point out the importance of a knowledge of human anatomy to a forensic artist.

Possible Answers

1. Forensic artists make sketches of people from descriptions given by others or make sculpted models from skull remains. Law enforcement authorities can match these sketches to photos of possible victims.

2. Forensic artists could examine impressions of muscle attachment sites on bones of dinosaurs and determine how large or small the muscles were.

Going Further

Students might make models with simple materials such as papier mâché, salt dough, or cloth strips soaked in plaster of paris. An inflated balloon could serve as the basis for a head.

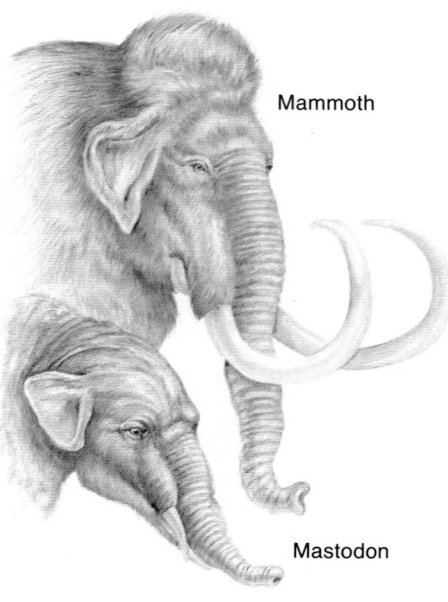

Mammoth

Mastodon

Figure 12-2 The fossil record indicates that the ancestors of elephants were wooly mammoths that lived 2 million years ago. Mammoths are probably the descendants of mastodons that existed 35 million years ago.

modern-day elephants are considered to be related to mastodons, fossils dating back 35 million years, and to mammoths, extinct elephants dating back to 2 million years ago. The fossil record as a whole indicates that organisms have changed over time; they have evolved.

Evidence from Anatomy

Have you ever been goofing around with friends and had somebody challenge you to walk like a chimp or flap your wings like a chicken? Your imitations may have been convincing—as well as entertaining—but they could never duplicate the real thing. Why? Your body structure is similar enough to that of a chimp or a chicken to get across the idea, but too different to give an exact rendition.

Elephant

ART CONNECTION

Sculpting the Past

Throughout history, people have sought to record their unique moment in time through the visual arts. Early cave drawings, Greek and Roman sculptures, medieval tapestries, Renaissance oil paintings, Civil War photographs, and, now, video technology have left us with a rich visual history of life on Earth.

Unfortunately for anthropologists, some crucial gaps exist in this visual record. Specifically, no one knows for certain what the precursors of *Homo sapiens* looked like. Today, however, anthropologists and forensic artists have formed a partnership to attempt the reconstruction of extinct humans as they might have looked more than a million years ago.

This partnership has joined sculpture and science to create a technique that can turn a skull into a fully formed human head with scientific accuracy and artistic realism. Here's how the process works.

MULTICULTURAL CONNECTION

Egg Myths: A Hindu myth from India tells how the bottom half of an egg became Earth and the upper half became the sky. The outer membrane became the mountains, while the inner membrane became the clouds and mists. Samoans, in the South Pacific, believed that their islands came from an egg that had been broken into pieces and thrown into the water. The Maoris, from New Zealand, believed that a bird dropped an egg that burst open in the sea. This egg contained the people and animals that found their way to New Zealand. Ask students to make up a myth that explains how Earth and its inhabitants first formed.

Look now at the forelimb structures of three familiar animals, as shown in Figure 12-3. Notice first the overall similarity, then the differences in details. What you are doing is what scientists do in **comparative anatomy**—the study of the structures of different organisms. Comparative anatomy provides further evidence of evolution. Different kinds of organisms—such as a bird, horse, or human—share similar structures.

Homologous Parts As you have just observed, each animal in Figure 12-3 has a forelimb structure that is a variation of a common pattern. The commonality suggests that these and other vertebrate animals are all related. They probably evolved from a common ancestor that had the same basic limb structure. Over many eras, these animals moved into different environments, and their limb structures gradually changed in form as each group became adapted to its new surroundings and ways of life. The differences in vertebrate forelimb structures today are suited to the way each kind of animal moves. Hence, a human couldn't walk exactly like a chimpanzee any more than you can flap your arms like a chicken.

All organisms inherit structures from their ancestors. As organisms evolve, any of their inherited structures may become modified. Some descendants may inherit one modified form of a structure; other descendants may inherit other modified forms. Yet, the overall pattern of the structure still resembles that of the common ancestor, as in the leg structure of the bird, horse, and human. Such modified structures among different groups of descendants are said to be **homologous**. The greater the

Bird   Horse   Human

Figure 12-3 **Compare the forelimbs of a bird, a horse, and a human. The bones are colored to show which ones are homologous.**

Beginning with a skull, the artist looks for telltale impressions left on the skull indicating where muscles were attached to bone. The size and depth of these impressions tells the artist how large or small the muscles were. By studying these impressions, as well as the musculature of present-day humans and the closely related great apes, the artist can sculpt in clay the underlying muscle layer of the face.

Next, the smaller muscles of the face are added. Again, comparative anatomy plays a role. If the chewing muscles of one skull are smaller than those of another, the artist can conclude that the other facial muscles were probably smaller as well. Once the muscles are in place, the artist adds the nasal cartilage, deep fat layers, and facial glands. Finally, the skin is added, and the sculpted head is complete. All that remains is the addition of some texture, color, and hair to the skin.

Of course, no one can say for certain just how close forensic artistry has come to reproducing the actual look of extinct humans.

However, evidence from forensic artists' work on contemporary murder victims for whom photos do exist suggests that their techniques can be quite accurate in reconstructing faces from the past.

1. **Explore Further:** Research to discover how forensic artists have assisted law enforcement in identifying murder victims.
2. **Connection to Paleontology:** How might the techniques of forensic artists aid in the study of dinosaurs?

PORTFOLIO

Give students a "mystery" fossil. Devise a list of biochemical, embryological, and genetic evidence. Ask students to write in their portfolios the kind of organism they think it is and why, the kind of environment in which it may have lived, and the time period of geologic history in which it may have lived. [L2]

PROJECT

Science Fiction: Use the book *After Man*, by Dougal Dixon, to stimulate student creativity for a series of sketches that predict how the animals presently on Earth will evolve in the future. Assume that Earth will become warmer due to the greenhouse effect. [L1]

Concept Development
Additional examples of evolution include the following.
Comparative Anatomy: Plants that live in the arctic, plants that live in the desert, and plants that live in salty environments all have similar hairlike structures, called trichomes, on their outer surfaces. In the desert, trichomes protect the plant from drying out and reflect the sun. In the arctic, trichomes keep the plant warm and absorb ultraviolet rays. In salty environments, trichomes release excess salt from the plant.
Homologous Structures: The anthers of flowering plants have similar functions and origin, but have a variety of different forms.
Vestigial Organs: Staminoids are vestigial stamens in some flowers.

EARTH SCIENCE
CONNECTION

Plate Tectonics: Geologist Alfred Wegener proposed that 300 million years ago, all of the continents were connected in a supercontinent known as Pangaea. The shapes of the seven present-day continents fit together to some degree like the pieces of a jigsaw puzzle. Scientists have discovered similarities in present-day organisms and in fossils between the Americas and Antarctica. The ancient continents may have moved by plate tectonics. Plates, floating on molten lava, break into pieces, and molten lava oozes up between the pieces pushing them apart. Obtain world maps with very specific continental boundary details. Ask students to trace the boundaries with a black marker, cut the continents out, and fit them together. The resulting land mass should be very much like Pangaea.

INVESTIGATION

Forming Your Own Fossil

Time Allotment
1 or 2 class periods

Objectives
Upon completing this investigation, students will be able to:
- Recognize how a fossil is formed in nature.
- Solve problems by trial and error.
- Identify different kinds of fossils.

Skills
measure in SI, design an experiment, make a model, work cooperatively in groups, observe and infer, classify

Materials
- plaster of paris, alginate, petroleum jelly, wax paper, scissors, clay, plastic food containers, paper cups, graduated cylinders, newspapers for covering lab desk surfaces, safety goggles, animal shells such as snail or oyster, small clean chicken or beef bones, small leaves or plants
- **Safety Precautions:** Have students wear safety goggles and aprons while handling modeling materials.

Preparation
Obtain plaster of paris from a hardware store. Mix powder and water slowly to form a thin paste for pouring. Obtain alginate from your dentist or dental supply company. Follow the directions on the container for proper mixing with water. Alginate sets and hardens up very quickly within minutes. Plaster of paris takes hours to harden and is less expensive than alginate. Obtain other materials required as listed below. Students may wish to use their own objects for fossil formation.

Possible Procedures
- All groups may not be successful in their first attempt at forming a fossil. Problems may arise in terms of incorrect mixtures or improper sequence of procedural steps.
- Procedures that students follow will vary depending on the type of fossil being formed. Imprints of

number of homologous structures that different kinds of organisms share, the closer the relationship among them. Which do you think is a closer evolutionary relative of a cat, a dog or a lizard? Why?

Homologous parts among descendants of a common ancestor are often similar in structure, in function, or in both structure and function. However, similarities in function alone do not indicate common ancestry. For example, you know that the wings of both birds and insects have the same function in flight, but it is also clear from comparative anatomy that they are not homologous. The wings of birds and insects developed from entirely different structures in two completely unrelated groups of ancestors, as supported by fossil evidence.

Vestigial Organs   Examine the drawing of the vestigial structures in Figure 12-4. Notice the difference in the sizes of the caecum in a horse

INVESTIGATION

Forming Your Own Fossil

Trace Fossil

Fossils form when an organism part or an entire organism is preserved in sediments before it has a chance to decay. One common type of fossil is formed from petrified bones or shells. Body parts such as bones or shells often become harder with chemical changes to the structure's minerals. Trace fossils are simply tracks or impressions of plants or animals left in soft sediment that eventually hardens. A soft body part of an organism may become buried in sediment that hardens with time. If the organism then dissolves and decays, a mold remains in the hard sediments. A mold can sometimes become filled with minerals that harden into a cast or copy of the original organism. Fossils, regardless of the type and how formed, provide a chance to look back in time. They serve as a source of evidence for evolution.

Problem
How is a fossil formed?

Safety Precautions
Handle all materials safely. Wear an apron when measuring, mixing, and pouring all powders.

Experimental Plan
1. As a group, make a list of possible ways you might design your procedure using the materials your teacher has made available.

Your teacher will provide your group with any needed information concerning correct handling of materials.
2. Agree on one method from your group's list that could be tried in the classroom.
3. Following the style of a recipe, write a numbered list of directions that anyone could follow.
4. Make a list of the materials and the quantities you will need.

310   EVOLUTION

leaves, shells, or bones pressed directly onto the surface of freshly prepared alginate or plaster of paris would be the simplest approach. Both materials may be poured into plastic containers or paper cups.
- Molds will consist of the entire object being buried within the alginate or plaster. The object should be covered with petroleum jelly first to aid in its removal. These objects will not actually decay as in nature but will have to be freed from the plaster or alginate by cracking or chipping away of the surrounding materials. Two different layers of alginate or plaster may be used to bury the fossil. The layers can be separated with wax paper with the fossil between the layers.
- Casts can be made by forming a clay model of the object to be fossilized. This model may then be buried in plaster of paris or alginate.

and in a human. Structures that have no function in the living organism, but may have been used in the ancestors, are said to be **vestigial.** Vestigial structures may be homologous with still-used structures in other related organisms. For example, the human appendix, a small wormlike tube connected to the large intestine, is vestigial in humans. However, in other animals that graze on plants, a similar but much larger structure, the caecum, is used for digesting this tough, fibrous plant material.

How do vestigial organs come about? At one time in the past, a vestigial structure was useful for the organism's way of life. As time passed, the organism changed in form and behavior as it became adapted to a new lifestyle. The structure, although reduced in size and function, continues to be inherited as part of the organism's body plan.

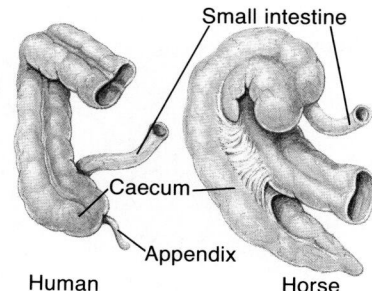

Figure 12-4 When compared with the caecum of a horse, the caecum and appendix of humans is thought to be vestigial.

Checking the Plan

Discuss the following points with other group members to decide the final procedures for your simulation.

1. What will be used as the original object to be fossilized?
2. Will the original object be destroyed in the procedure or will it be recovered? This is an important consideration if the object you choose to fossilize is a personal possession of one member of your group.
3. Will your fossil be a petrified original, a trace, a mold, or a cast?
4. How much time will be needed to prepare your fossil?
5. Assign specific roles and jobs for each member of your group.
6. If unsuccessful in forming a fossil the first time, be prepared to record and correct any errors that were made. Make modifications in your original procedure, and repeat the experiment if time permits.

Cast Fossil

Make sure your teacher has approved your experimental plan before you proceed further.

Data and Observations

Carry out your experiment. Diagram and label the original object used for the fossil as well as the final fossil produced.

Analysis and Conclusions

1. Based on this activity, record your own definition of a fossil.

2. Determine why the fossil you formed fits the category of petrified fossil, trace, mold, or cast.
3. Describe how the fossil that you formed is both alike and different from the original object used to form your fossil.
4. Suggest how the procedure that you used to form your fossil may have differed from the procedure that takes place in nature.
5. Assume that your fossil is real and had formed millions of years ago. What data could be taken from your fossil that might help scientists in their studies of evolution?
6. If your fossil-forming technique was not successful, explain why and describe the procedure changes you would make in a second trial.

Going Further

Based on this lab experience, design another procedure that would allow you to form another fossil type. Record this information as part of your conclusion.

differs from that which takes place in nature during fossil formation.

Extensions

Kits for embedding of specimens in plastic are available from Carolina Biological Supply. These kits will enable students to prepare professional quality mounts of almost any type of organism.

Teaching Strategies

- When students appear to use incorrect amounts of modeling materials, try to suggest further experimentation without giving them the answers.
- Allow students to carry out their own designs as long as no safety hazard presents itself.
- When students remove the plaster or alginate from their fossils, make sure that safety goggles are worn by all group members.

Data and Observations

Examine students' diagrams to ensure accurate identification of their fossils.

Data Analysis

1. Answers will vary but should convey the fact that a fossil is evidence of a once-living organism.
2. Answers will vary but should include the definition for the type of fossil they formed. A comparison should then be made regarding their fossil and how it fits the accepted definition.
3. Answers will vary. For example, a student's fossil and original object may be identical in size and shape but differ in terms of chemical makeup.
4. Answers will vary. Students may discuss the time needed to form a fossil in nature. They may discuss the actual deposition of sediments in nature versus the adding of plaster or alginate. They may discuss the difference between the object used in class and the natural object.
5. Answers will vary. Students may describe specific physical characteristics of their fossil or discuss the nature of surrounding fossils.
6. Answers will vary. Students may describe errors made in preparing the plaster or alginate, not waiting long enough for the materials to harden, or waiting too long before pouring them.

✔ Assessment

Knowledge: Have students write an evaluation of the lab for placement in their portfolios. They should include an explanation of how their procedure

Activity

Provide students with mounted skeletons of representative groups of animals: a chicken, turtle, fish, cat,
human, and others that may be available. Ask them to identify homologous bones and compare their functions. Ask them how the shapes and
sizes of the homologous bones reflect
their similar functions. **L1** **LEP**
COOP LEARN

Display

Ask students to make a display of
local fossils. What do they reveal
about the past history of the area?
Have them find out if your state has a
declared state fossil. If not, have them
decide, after their research and collection, what fossil would best represent the state. You may want to have
them write a letter to state officials
proposing a state fossil. **L1**
COOP LEARN

Field Trip

Take a trip to a nearby site where fossils or exposed rock layers may be
observed. Ask students to make
sketches of their observations.

Human — Gill slits, Limb bud, Head, Heart, Tail, Umbilical cord, Gill slits, Vertebrae

Pig — Tail, Limb bud

Embryo at 4th week   Fetus at 12th week   At birth

Figure 12-5   Although at the fourth week of development it is difficult to tell which embryo is a pig or a human, by the 12th week the two fetuses are easily distinguished.

Evidence from Embryology and Biochemistry

Anatomy of mature organisms isn't the only area where comparisons
point to evidence of evolution. Scientists also compare and contrast
embryos, which are the early stages of developing plants or animals. The
study of developing organisms, known as **comparative embryology,** shows
a number of relationships not obvious in the fully grown organism.

If you viewed an early human embryo and an early pig embryo side by
side under a microscope, you'd have a hard time telling them apart. The
more alike the development of two organisms is, the more closely related
they are thought to be. Thus, the pig and the human must be closely
related. They probably inherited the same basic body plan from a common ancestor. As the pig and human embryos progress in their development, their patterns become more and more different. In their later stages
before birth, they attain their distinct and more familiar forms.

Studies of organisms on a biochemical level, which constitute **comparative biochemistry,** also provide evidence of evolution. Biochemical
comparisons show, for instance, that the structure of hemoglobin in a
chimpanzee strongly resembles the structure of human hemoglobin. That
is, the sequence of amino acids in chimpanzee and human hemoglobin is
almost the same. The amino acid sequence of human hemoglobin and dog

312 🐾 EVOLUTION

PORTFOLIO

Give students about 50 "fossil" Styrofoam
packing pellets that are different shapes,
sizes, and colors. Ask them to group the
closely related ones together by using
observations of their "anatomy" (structure), "biochemistry" (color), and "embryology" (similarities between ones that are
smaller and ones that are bigger). Ask
them to give names based on structural
features to their fossil groups and justify
their placement into particular groups.
Have them put all their findings in writing
in their portfolios. Popcorn varieties may
be used if you cannot find enough variety
in Styrofoam pellets. **L1** **LEP**

hemoglobin shows less similarity. It appears then that humans and chimpanzees have a more recent common ancestor than do humans and dogs. Much research today focuses on comparing sequences of amino acids in organisms to reveal relationships. Some scientists say that these studies provide the most fundamental evidence for evolution.

Genetic Evidence

Our understanding of evolution deepens with the expanding fossil record, with new studies in amino acid sequencing, and with all the other lines of evidence you have just read about. The fact that so many different lines of evidence exist strengthens the conclusion that evolution occurs. We have seen that change in life forms occurs over time, but how are these changes brought about?

A Basis for Change Each generation of a given kind of organism is linked to the next by genes (DNA). But genes and the chromosomes that carry them can both mutate. Mutations, as explained in Chapter 10, are mistakes that occur in the genetic material. The mutation and duplication of existing alleles can give rise to new alleles or genes, and, thus, to new proteins. In addition, meiosis and fertilization reshuffle alleles. In other words, within any breeding group, or **population,** of organisms, there is constant change over time. Production of new alleles and genetic recombination could be called the raw materials of the process of evolution.

Humans unknowingly used the potential for change in organisms thousands of years ago when they first domesticated plants and animals. Working with wild plants in their environment, humans developed crops such as barley, wheat, and corn. They also learned to tame wild animals such as cattle and dogs for food and protection. In each case, people selected only individuals with the most desirable traits and bred them so the traits would be passed on to the offspring. They repeated the steps generation after generation. Without realizing the effects of their breeding practices, humans were directing the evolution of many kinds of plants and animals. Today we call such practices **selective breeding.** Farmers, horticulturists, pet breeders, and scientists still use selective breeding to improve domestic plant and animal varieties.

Figure 12-6 **Beef cattle are a product of selective breeding. There are six major breeds in the United States. They are the Aberdeen Angus (shown here), Brahman, Charolais, Hereford, Polled Hereford, and Sinmental.**

12.1 EVIDENCE FOR EVOLUTION **313**

SECTION 12.1

Guest Speaker
Ask a researcher to visit your class and exhibit some gel electrophoresis patterns that show actual "runs." Ask them to interpret the differences and similarities in the proteins from different sources.

Reinforcement
Ask students what types of conditions favor fossil formation and what types of conditions were unfavorable for fossil formation.

Concept Development
When comparing the biochemistry of organisms to determine evolutionary relationships, it would be ideal if their DNA could be compared directly. A comparison of proteins is easier. Ask students to use their knowledge of protein synthesis to show that comparing proteins ultimately reveals information about DNA.

Brainstorming
Give students the following instructions. Your group is in the business of breeding race horses. Scientists have told you that the latest studies show that performance is 35 percent heritable and 65 percent training and nutrition. The body features that are most important in a winning horse are the ability to clear lactic acid quickly from the muscles and the ability to circulate blood to bring oxygen quickly to the muscles. In your group, brainstorm a list of features you would select for winning horses. After you have made your list, put stars beside the six or seven features that you think will be most important and justify your choices.
L1 COOP LEARN

STUDENT JOURNAL

Tell students to assume that they are in the business of developing better breeds of their choice of domestic animal such as chickens, beef cattle, dairy cows, or others of special interest. They must decide what characteristics they will be selecting for and why. For example, if they decide they want to produce chickens that lay larger eggs, they will have to decide what features of the chicken will need to be changed and justify the importance of larger eggs. In order to do this assignment effectively, students will need to do library research as well as use imagination and creativity. L1

SECTION 12.1

HEALTH CONNECTION

Cockroach Control: The German cockroach is the major indoor roach in North America. Cockroaches are notoriously filthy and carry the *Salmonella* bacteria that cause food poisoning and possibly the virus that causes Hepatitis A. A single, fertilized roach can be the cause of a colony of up to a million offspring each year. Control of these pests has been by baiting, trapping, spraying, and squashing. Cockroaches have shown an intense power of resistance to many common insecticides. Some strains in Florida seem to be impossible to kill.

An insecticide called hydramethylnon affects a cell's ability to release energy. The cockroach eventually runs out of energy, falls asleep, and never wakes up. Hydroprene, another insecticide, causes sterility in cockroaches, but this process takes about seven months to have any impact. A more natural approach to population control of the cockroach was discovered by a cockroach breeding facility in California when 3 million of their roaches were killed by a yeast infection. The yeast used all the energy provided by the insect's metabolism and the cockroaches starved to death.

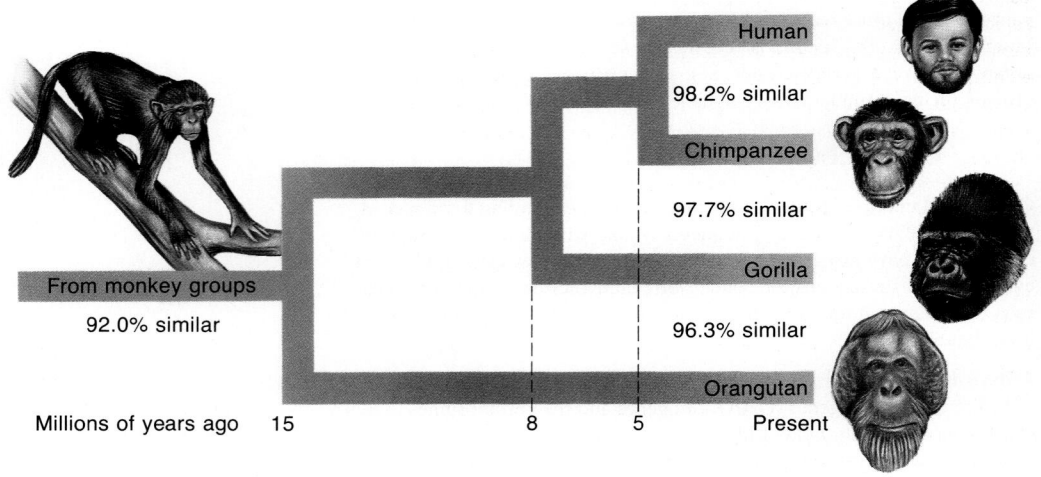

Figure 12-7 Comparisons of DNA nitrogen based sequences show that chimpanzees are more closely related to humans than to gorillas or other apes.

A Basis for Relationships Knowledge of genetics can help us understand more than how changes in genotypes and phenotypes come about. Genetics can also tell us how different groups of organisms are related back through time. Biologists first analyze the base sequences of DNA in the genes of one kind of organism. Then they examine genes controlling the same or similar traits among different kinds of organisms. As in other comparative studies, the greater the similarity, the closer the relationship. The DNA of humans and chimpanzees, for example, is 99 percent identical. Between humans and other mammals, 80 percent of the DNA is identical. Again, the evidence points to a close relationship between humans and chimpanzees.

Biologists have developed a timetable that they believe reflects the rate at which mutations occur over given time spans. Using these mutation rates, scientists have estimated the time when certain descendants began to go their separate genetic ways from a common ancestor. Mutation rates, like other lines of evidence, show that chimpanzees and humans branched off from a common ancestor at a comparatively recent point in evolution.

Direct Observation

Do you now find it easier to picture evolution? You won't be alone if you answer that the evidence that organisms have changed over time described so far seems somewhat indirect. If so, it's because the changes you were reading about took place so slowly over such a long time that no one could possibly have observed them directly. (Regardless of the fact that humans were not yet around for most of the changes!) There is, however, other evidence for evolution that can be observed directly. The evidence comes from evolutionary changes that occur rapidly and on a regular basis.

314 EVOLUTION

MULTICULTURAL CONNECTION

South American Agriculture: Six thousand years ago, pre-Incan Indians in South America were cultivating the common white potato. When they cultivated this plant, they practiced selective breeding to improve the quality of the potato from one generation to the next.

PROJECT

Fossil Fuels: Write about the formation of coal and oil. Make a map of areas where coal and oil are found in the U.S. and the world. L2

Rapid Evolution   The reaction of bacteria to penicillin often results in rapid evolutionary change. Penicillin, the chemical from the *Penicillium* mold, kills many kinds of bacteria. When penicillin is added to bacteria in a culture dish, a clear zone forms indicating death of the bacteria in that zone. Sometimes, however, a few bacteria may survive and reproduce to form visible, living colonies. Each colony will consist of millions of cells that are resistant to penicillin.

When penicillin is added to a culture dish, it changes the environment of the bacteria. Resistance to penicillin becomes vital for the survival of a bacterium. All the bacteria that have no resistance will die. As in any other group of organisms, there are variations in the genetic material among bacteria. Those few individuals with a gene for penicillin resistance will survive and go on to reproduce. Thus, this group of bacteria has evolved, or changed over time. The organisms that continue to live and reproduce after the change in the environment are adapted to the new environment.

Evolution Causes Health Problems   As you may have already guessed, penicillin-resistant bacteria create a serious health problem. Bacteria cause many diseases in humans and animals. You probably have taken penicillin or other antibacterial drugs, commonly called antibiotics, to combat an illness. On average, each bacterium in a colony will divide every 20 minutes. It is easy to see why evolution in bacteria can be rapid. When resistant forms of bacteria evolve, existing drugs will no longer kill them. For this reason, scientists need to search continually for new antibiotics to treat bacterial diseases.

Rapid evolution has also occurred among pest organisms such as weeds and insects exposed to pesticides. As these organisms have evolved a resistance to these chemicals, stronger chemicals have been used and are often applied in greater amounts. But, pesticide use endangers non pest organisms too. For example, DDT interferes with reproduction in large birds, such as falcons and pelicans. Some of these powerful chemicals have also caused health problems among the workers who apply them.

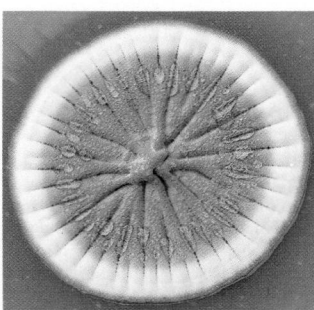

Figure 12-8   **The discovery that bacteria could be killed (the clear areas in the culture in the top photo) by a chemical released by the penicillin fungus (bottom) was made by Sir Alexander Fleming in 1928. The bacteria not killed by this or other antibiotics are resistant strains.**

Section Review

Understanding Concepts
1. Which organism would you expect to have evolved first, a spider or a lizard? Why?
2. Why should you complete a prescribed course of antibiotics to treat a bronchial infection?
3. Would vestigial structures make any sense if organisms did not evolve? Explain.

4. *Skill Review—Predicting:* You are part of a team collecting fossils at a new site. The fossils are embedded in sedimentary rock. You discover a fossil of an animal in a low layer of rock that looks something like a modern insect. Knowing about the fossil record, what would you expect to see in similar fossils found in upper layers of rock? For more

help, see Representing and Applying Data in the **Skill Handbook.**
5. *Thinking Critically:* Why is it logical to say that if two animals have similar proteins, they are probably closely related genetically?

3 Assess

Check for Understanding
Tell students that they are archaeologists working on evidence gained by studying a fossil. Put the following clues on cards. 1 Paleozoic era. 2 No bones. 3 No cell walls. 4 Shell-like imprint. They are trying to determine the type of organism the fossil once was. Give the group clue card 1. Ask them to brainstorm a list of possible organisms based on this clue. Give students clue card 2. From their brainstormed list in 1, they should select a set of possibilities. Follow with cards 3 and 4 in the same manner. For student reference, put up a transparency of the geologic time scale with listings of organisms. **L1**
COOP LEARN

Reteach
Ask students to write a note to a friend. Their note should explain what they understand about evolution and what they still find difficult to understand. They should fold the note and exchange notes with another student in the class. The other student should answer the note with an explanation in his or her own words.

Extension
Students could describe famous fossil hoaxes, such as the Piltdown man described in England in 1912. **L2**

✔ Assessment
Performance: Provide student groups with an assortment of laboratory glassware. Ask them to classify it based on some perceived evolutionary trend. Students should propose a chart showing the lines of descent. **L1** **LEP**

4 Close

Discussion
Show slides or a filmstrip of a trip through the Grand Canyon. Ask students how a trip through the Grand Canyon reinforces their understanding of evolution. **LEP**

Answers to Section Review

1. Because a lizard is more complex, it probably evolved later than a spider.
2. If a course of antibiotics is not completed, the bacteria with a higher resistance to the drug will still remain and the infection will therefore increase. It will then require a new and probably stronger dose of another antibiotic to cure the infection.
3. By definition, vestigial structures have no function. Therefore, their presence can only

be logically explained in terms of evolution. Such structures were functional among the ancestors of the organisms that possess the structures today.
4. **Skill Review—Predicting:** The student would expect to see other fossils more closely resembling a modern insect.
5. **Thinking Critically:** Proteins are coded for by DNA. Similarity in proteins, therefore, indicates similarity in DNA.

Prepare

Key Concepts

Students will study Darwin's observations during his famous voyage and his development of the theory of natural selection, and learn about population genetics.

Key Terms

natural selection, theory of natural selection, gene pool

Materials

1 Focus

Objectives

The objectives are listed on the student page. Remind students to preview these objectives as a guide to this numbered section.

Discussion

Obtain a large picture of a polar bear to show to students. Ask students why polar bears have white fur. Have students imagine that polar bears had a variety of fur colors in the past. Ask them to explain why polar bears are only white in color. At the end of the discussion, explain to them that polar bears actually have black skin and that the hairs are colorless. Ask them how these characteristics aid in polar bear survival. **L1**

Objectives

Analyze how Darwin's observations led him to conclude that life forms change over time.

Explain the process of natural selection.

Apply modern knowledge of genetics to the theory of natural selection.

Figure 12-9 Darwin's voyage in *HMS Beagle* (left) took him south from England, around Cape Horn, and north to the Galapagos Islands; a journey (right) that led to the conclusion that evolution occurs.

12.2 Darwin's Explanation

What will you be doing six or seven years from now? Perhaps you will be working at a new job, or maybe still going to school. A little less than 200 years ago, a young Englishman named Charles Darwin (1809-1882) was still trying to decide his future. By the time he was in his 20s, he had tried both medical school and law school, and liked neither. Long nature walks interested him more.

Darwin: Gathering Data

While attending Cambridge University, Darwin became friends with a professor of natural history. The professor encouraged the young student to apply for a job aboard *HMS Beagle,* a British survey ship used for making voyages of scientific discovery. Darwin's knowledge of biology and geology impressed the captain of the *Beagle.* Darwin got the job of ship's naturalist. At the age of 22, he began the first and only sea voyage of his life. No one, including Darwin, guessed what that voyage would one day mean to science.

Observing Biodiversity The *Beagle* left England for a five-year, around-the-world voyage in December of 1831. As ship's naturalist, Darwin began immediately to collect, study, and store specimens of the ocean's marine life. After crossing the Atlantic Ocean, the *Beagle* made many stops along the east and west coasts of South America. Darwin went ashore to study the land environment and to collect fossils.

Based on studies of fossils and observations in comparative anatomy, some people of Darwin's time had already guessed at the idea of evolution. Few scientists of the day, however, accepted evolution as fact. They did not have the body of evidence that scientists have now. In fact, Darwin avoided using the term *evolution* because it was used at that time to describe the theory that embryos contained fully formed but miniature versions of the adult. As you can guess, the light microscope was not sufficiently high-powered to test this hypothesis.

During his voyage, Darwin read a book by a contemporary scientist, Charles Lyell. Lyell discussed how changes occur over time in geology. Lyell's ideas, together with Darwin's own observations of both geology and living organisms studied during his voyage, caused Darwin to think and ask questions. With the knowledge that environmental features of Earth change, it was clear to Darwin that organisms adapted to their environments must also change to remain adapted. If populations of organisms do change, he considered, how does the change occur?

In the Galapagos For Darwin, the answers to his questions pointed to evolution, or, as he described it, descent with modification. In other words, structural or functional changes occur from one group of descendants to the next, and so on. Studies into comparative anatomy that Darwin made during his voyage seemed to confirm his guess. Organisms he studied on the Galapagos Islands, about 600 miles west of South America, offered especially convincing evidence. Forms of life, such as giant tortoises and marine swimming lizards (iguanas), not found anywhere else on Earth, lived on the Galapagos. These animals were at once unique and yet similar to other forms of the same animals common in other parts of the world. The similarities between Galapagos plants, birds, amphibians, and reptiles and those of distant lands persuaded Darwin that despite their uniqueness, the Galapagos organisms were all related to the more common forms. By the end of the trip, Darwin was convinced that evolution occurs—that life forms can and do change. But as yet, he still needed to test these ideas before he could or would attempt to explain how or why such changes happen.

Figure 12-10 **The Galapagos Islands are renowned for their unusual animal and plant life. The giant tortoises (left) are the largest on Earth. The marine iguanas (right) have become adapted to feeding on algae underwater.**

SECTION 12.2

2 Teach

Concept Development
Develop interest in Darwin's theory by bringing a copy of *Origin of Species* to class. Read selected chapter titles and sections of the text. Point out that there were no illustrations in the original edition.

Activity
- Tell half of your student groups that they are personnel managers on board Darwin's ship, *HMS Beagle*. They must design a position description for a group of assistants for Darwin and his research. The other half of the groups should write resumes, one per group, of their qualifications for the job. Ask students to choose one person to be the interviewer and another to be the job applicant. Have the interviews conducted while other group members watch. L1 COOP LEARN

- Ask students to develop a brief MTV video segment illustrating Darwin's voyage and discoveries. They should be creative and use props and music. You might videotape their presentations and later show them all at once to the class. L1 LEP COOP LEARN

MULTICULTURAL CONNECTION

From a Woman's Viewpoint:
Scientist Adrienne Zihlman proposes that women have been left out of the story of human evolution because male scientists have led the field in the study of human evolution. For example, she says that the idea that bipedalism developed because men had to have their arms free for hunting is not the complete answer. Women also had to have their arms free for their job of gathering food. Her opinions are not supported by a large part of the anthropological community, still mostly male.

PROGRAM RESOURCES

Teacher Classroom Resources
Study Guide, pp. 69-70 L1
Probing Levels of Life, Lab 23, p. 64 L2
Color Transparency #17 L1 LEP
Critical Thinking/Problem Solving, p. 12 L2

SECTION 12.2

Misconception

Students often believe that characteristics acquired during an organism's lifetime can be passed on to its offspring.

Activity

Use the cooperative learning strategy, expert groups. Divide up this section of the chapter into four parts. Assign responsibility for different parts to students in their home groups. Ask students who are assigned the same part to get together, read their pages, and design ways of presenting the material to their home group. When students move back to their home groups, they should take turns presenting their material. **L1**

COOP LEARN

Discussion Question

A colorless, blind millipede lives in caves. In response to light, it demonstrates avoidance behavior and curls up. Ask students, what is the adaptive value of this behavior? *The curling of the millipede may expose less of its body to UV light to which it has no protection. The light may represent the intrusion of a predator through a crack in the cave ceiling. In this case, curling may make the millipede appear smaller and pebble-like, thereby being unsuited as food.*

Darwin's Explanation: Natural Selection

Charles Darwin spent the next 20 years after his voyage studying his collections as well as living organisms to help him explain to the world how evolution occurs. His methods of inquiry followed sound principles of scientific investigation. He collected still more organic specimens, he studied breeds of different animals, and he made countless additional observations in his greenhouse. After many years of evaluating his data, two facts led Darwin to hypothesize that change occurred resulting in descent with modification.

A Struggle for Existence The idea for the first fact Darwin investigated came originally from an essay about population growth by Thomas Malthus. Malthus proposed that the human population was growing faster than the food supply needed to feed it. Darwin applied Malthus's idea not to humans, but to other forms of life. He knew that in nature there is commonly an overproduction of offspring. In other words, many of the offspring produced by organisms die before reaching maturity. For example, a mouse will give birth to six young. Imagine how many mice there would be in the world if every litter of six young mice survived, and every female mouse gave birth to 150 young and none died! Earth would be a large, mouse-infested planet within a short time. Darwin realized that there must be a struggle for existence among individuals. Darwin envisioned many kinds of struggles—competition for food and space, escape from predators, and ability to find shelter. Only some of the individuals in any population survive the struggle long enough to produce offspring of their own. But which ones?

Figure 12-11 **Two factors lead to gradual changes in new generations of species. (a) Traits in individuals that can compete successfully and reproduce will be passed on. (b) Traits in individuals that have been artificially selected will be passed on to new generations.**

a

b

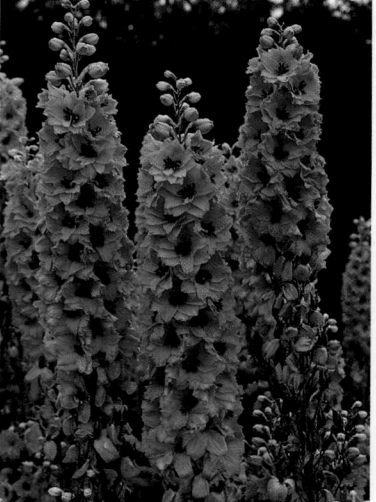

ALTERNATE LAB: Which Grasshoppers Jump Farthest?

Purpose
Students will analyze adaptations that make grasshoppers suited for jumping.

Materials
grasshoppers, metric rulers, meter sticks, balance, magnifying glass or binocular microscope, baby food jars with holes in lids

Procedure
Give the following directions to students.

1. Observe three grasshoppers of different sizes in three separate baby food jars.
2. Hypothesize which grasshopper will jump farthest. Explain your reasoning.
3. Take the mass of each grasshopper, measure the length of different segments of their hind legs, and count or measure other features and write this information in a table.
4. Place the grasshoppers, one at a time, on a pencil line drawn on the floor as the starting position. Measure the length of the first jump made from that line. Do not make noises or touch the grasshopper to make it jump. Record all results in a table.
5. Take turns with the grasshoppers, allowing them a rest in their jars between jumps.
6. Carry out 10 trials with each grasshopper, take an average of the results, and make a graph of your data.

Artificial Selection   The second fact that Darwin examined came from his inquiries into selective breeding. Darwin knew that plant and animal breeders generated new varieties of desirable plants and animals by selecting parents with desired traits. He observed that in any population, individuals have different variations of traits that can be inherited. For example, plants vary in color, height, mass, and number of seeds produced. Among animals, cows vary in amount of milk produced, sheep vary in the thickness of their wool, and chickens vary in the numbers of eggs they produce. Plant and animal breeders select parents having desired characteristics and breed them to produce preferred offspring. Darwin observed that breeders do not use individuals as parents if they have less desirable traits. He wondered if there were some force in nature similar to this *artificial selection* practiced by breeders.

Evolution Explained   The two facts, a struggle for existence and artificial selection, gave Darwin the information he needed to explain descent with modification. He observed that variations exist among all groups of organisms. Those individuals with the traits that aid them in coping with their environment have a better chance of surviving and, thus, leave more offspring. The offspring, in turn, tend to have the same traits and so are adapted to the environment.

As an example of this evolution, imagine that long ago among a population of spadefoot toads, a few had a louder mating croak and longer toes on the back feet. The population lived in a desert where rain comes only a few times each year. As you know, the young of toads can survive only in water. Two things are vital to a present-day desert spadefoot toad. First, it must be able to bury itself in the ground when there is no available water for breeding. The toad uses its back feet to dig itself down into the soil. The toads can survive buried in the caked mud for many months. Second, when rain falls, the toads must be fast to emerge and mate before the water is evaporated by the hot daytime sun of the desert. You may now begin to understand why the toads with the louder mating croak and longer back toes were the ones best suited to the environment in which they lived. Any toads with less-adapted traits would have left fewer offspring. The water would be gone before the tadpoles were fully mature and able to bury themselves. Darwin noted that individuals with traits not suited to their environment leave fewer, if any, offspring. In time, those individuals lose in the struggle for existence.

Figure 12-12   **The spadefoot toad is just one animal that has successfully evolved to survive in desert conditions.**

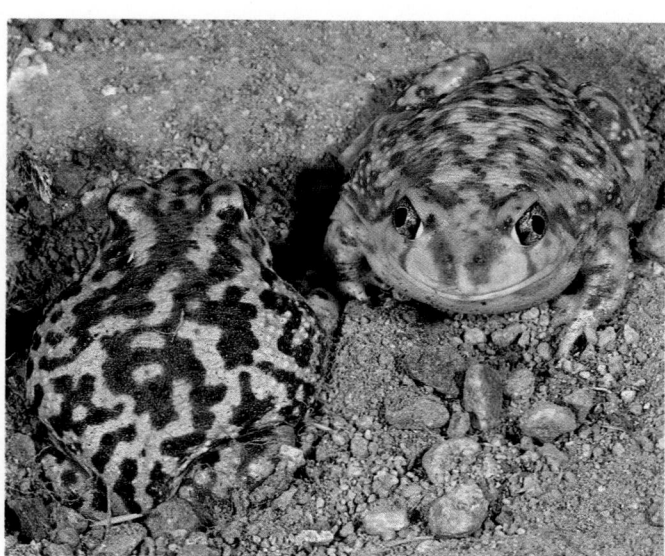

12.2 DARWIN'S EXPLANATION **319**

SECTION 12.2

Different Viewpoints in Biology

The Gaia Hypothesis
James Lovelock, a British biochemist, hypothesized that Earth has evolved into a superorganism. He calls this idea the Gaia hypothesis, in which Earth's physical features are likened to a skeleton; the oceans, lakes, and rivers to blood; and the atmosphere to breath. Plants and animals interact with Earth to keep it alive. According to Lovelock, the environmental conditions of Earth are actively made fit and altered by life itself. The Gaia hypothesis is controversial but can help us look at the physical evolution of Earth, and the evolution of life not as two separate events but as a closely integrated process.

Misconception

Students often think that evolution occurs with some purpose. They say that animals or plants developed certain features "in order to" adapt to a change in the environment. Point out that variations exist in populations. Certain variations become beneficial when new conditions develop. The organisms with the best-suited variations survive and produce offspring, and the others die before they can reproduce. In this way, a group of organisms becomes adapted to its environment.

Analysis
Ask students to answer the following questions.
1. Which grasshopper had the longest jumping distance? Which had the shortest jump? *Answers will vary. Larger grasshoppers generally jump farther.*
2. How might a grasshopper protect itself against predators? *By jumping away when a predator approaches, and by* blending in with the surroundings.
3. What might happen to grasshoppers that are not able to jump as far? *They might be eaten by predators.*
4. Speculate about how grasshoppers might evolve if their predators were eliminated. *Answers will vary. The removal of a selection pressure may not result in any change, or it may result in a broader variation in jumping distance with more grasshoppers capable of a* shorter jumping distance. Removal of predators could also result in a wider variety of body colors—camouflage would be less important.

✔ **Assessment**
Performance: Ask students to design a similar experiment with a frog. **L1**

Discussion

Ask students to give examples of natural situations in the wild or experimental situations in labs in which evolution can be seen occurring. L1

Figure Caption Question

What are some animals that produce offspring in these enormous numbers? Students may list fishes, amphibians, echinoderms, mollusks, worms, or any other group of invertebrate animal.

Enrichment

A bacterium, *Bacillus thuringienis* (Bt), was developed for use as an effective biological control in the 1950s. Some insects developed resistance to Bt. From 1986 to 1989, the number of insects with resistance doubled. How could this means of control be used so that insects would not develop resistance? *Use Bt sparingly every few years and use other insecticides in alternate years.*

Critical Thinking

Certain salamanders lay eggs of slightly different sizes. Several summers pass with drier conditions than usual. The larger eggs survive the drought conditions more often than the smaller eggs. What will happen to the egg size of this salamander if these conditions continue?

Library Research

Ask students to discover the current biological ideas available to Darwin at the time he formulated his theory of evolution. L2

Figure 12-13 **Many plants, such as these in the squash family, overproduce seeds. There is a greater chance that some seeds will survive to produce their own offspring. What are some animals that produce offspring in these enormous numbers?**

Since the struggle for existence goes on unaided in nature, Darwin realized that any selection that occurs in a population is natural. The organisms that survive the day-to-day struggle are best fitted or adapted. Darwin related changes in organisms to a natural force or selection pressure that his lifetime work had set out to discover. In the course of **natural selection,** the best adapted individuals in a population survive and produce offspring that are likewise well adapted. The least adapted individuals produce fewer offspring, which, along with their parents, may die young and leave still fewer offspring.

According to Darwin's model, natural selection is an interaction of organisms and environment. Evolution, then, does not occur according to a plan or goal, as in artificial selection. It is rather a matter of variations and chance. Variations that arise either do or do not fit the environment. Suitable variations are passed on from one generation to the next; other variations are eventually lost to the population. The following sequence summarizes Darwin's explanation of how organisms evolve. They make up what we now call Darwin's **theory of natural selection.**

(1) In nature there is a tendency toward overproduction.
   For example, mice, watermelons, ants, fish, dandelions, and mosquitoes are well-known overproducers.

GLOBAL CONNECTION

The Question of Color

Take a walk down a busy boulevard in any major city in the United States and look closely at the people around you. You'll notice a rainbow of skin colors, from the palest white to the darkest black-brown. Why do humans, who all belong to the species *Homo sapiens,* have such a broad variation in skin color? The reason can be traced to a combination of events in history and human cellular biology. However, to fully understand this interaction, you will need to know the importance of skin color to human health.

When human skin cells are exposed to ultraviolet (UV) radiation, lipids in the cells are converted to vitamin D. Vitamin D is essential to human health because it aids the body in absorbing calcium from foods. Too little vitamin D can lead to rickets, a bone disease from calcium deficiency that results in brittle, misshapen, and easily broken bones. Too much vitamin D can result in excess calcium in the blood plasma, causing kidney stones and extra bone formation in the tendons.

How does your body regulate the production of vitamin D from sunlight? The key is melanin, the pigments in skin cells that help turn the skin dark as it is exposed to rays of the sun. Melanin absorbs UV radiation. The more melanin pigments in the skin, the less UV radiation is absorbed by lipids for the production of vitamin D.

How, then, can we account for differences in human skin colors? We know that people who live within equatorial latitudes have dark skin due to the large amounts of melanin pigments in their skin cells. Thus, despite constant exposure to intense UV radiation, these people do not manufacture too much vitamin D because their melanin pigments absorb much of the sunlight.

People who live in the northern latitudes have fewer melanin pigments and are exposed to much less sunlight. The lower levels of UV are absorbed by lipids and, therefore, sufficient vitamin D is produced.

All the available anthropological evidence suggests that the species *Homo sapiens* originated as dark-skinned people in the tropical regions of Africa. So, how did blond-haired, blue-eyed Scandinavians evolve? If humans were all originally dark-skinned, why didn't everyone remain dark?

PORTFOLIO

Ask students to collect pine cones, milkweed pods, or dandelion or sunflower heads gone to seed. Have them count the number of seeds in each and make graphs of the average number for each plant. Ask them to write about the advantage of high seed production, why the variation in number of seeds is important, and what the chances are for survival of each seed. L1

(2) Not all offspring that are produced survive.
   For example, many bacteria treated with antibiotics will die. Not all seeds from a watermelon will grow and thrive.
(3) Variations exist in any population.
   For example, some spadefoot toads mature faster than others.
(4) Variations are inherited.
   For example, the long fur of a cat will be passed on to the cat's offspring. The color patterns of many insects are the same from generation to generation.
(5) Those individuals with variations that are suitable for their environment will live longer and leave more offspring on average than will individuals not having the variations. Thus, suitable variations will tend to be passed on and unsuitable ones lost.
   For example, penicillin-resistant bacteria will survive and reproduce after treatment with this antibiotic.
(6) The resulting population as a whole will change as it becomes better adapted to its environment.
   For example, an entire population of mosquitoes evolves a resistance to an insecticide.

When people with dark skin from the lower latitudes first began migrating north, they probably didn't fare well because of limited levels of sunlight. Their melanin pigments would have absorbed too much sunlight, and their bodies may have produced too little vitamin D. Diseases like rickets have commonly been found in northern human fossils.

Lighter-skinned people, however, would have been at an advantage. Natural selection clearly would favor these paler humans. With fewer melanin pigments to absorb UV radiation, their bodies were able to continue manufacturing enough vitamin D to prevent disease. In short, lighter-skinned people were adapted to this new environment; darker-skinned people were not. As natural selection continued to operate over tens of thousands of years, the number of people with lighter skin grew in the northern latitudes. Today, the availability of improved medical care has allowed for people of all skin colors to reside safely together in any region of Earth.

1. **Explore Further:** Find out how vitamin D deficiency in humans is avoided in areas of low sunlight. How do light-skinned people protect themselves from high levels of UV radiation?

2. **Issue:** Throughout history, skin color has been used as a justification for hatred, prejudice, and discrimination. Write a brief essay explaining how your own attitudes about skin color have been affected by your knowledge of evolution.

12.2 DARWIN'S EXPLANATION **321**

PROJECT

Adapting to Survive: Ask one half of your students to write an essay from the perspective of a plant or animal from 350 million years ago. They should discuss their adaptations to the environment of the time. Ask them to give their essay to a student who has not written yet. This student should write from the perspective of the same or a similar plant or animal today. They should write about how they have changed over the course of geologic history, or why they died out. The focus in both essays should be on adaptations.

`L2` `COOP LEARN`

GLOBAL CONNECTION

Purpose
Students will be able to interpret the evolution of different skin colors based on the amount of exposure to UV light.

Teaching Strategies
• Ask students how many of them wear sunscreen when they are outdoors.
• Ask them if they know what happens to skin that has a great deal of sun exposure. (Skin becomes at high risk for skin cancer and wrinkles.)
• Explain that most wrinkling of skin is the result of sun exposure, not age or genetics as previously believed.
• Point out that in the last few years, skin cancer cases are increasing in teenagers because of their desire to be tan.
• Explain that melanin is formed from the amino acid tyrosine.

Possible Answers
1. Vitamin D is added to milk and other foods. Light-skinned people protect themselves from UV radiation by wearing sunscreen, clothing with long sleeves, long skirts or pants, hats with large brims, and sunglasses with UV protection, and by staying indoors during the midday and early afternoon sun.
2. Students should explain that variation in skin color resulted from natural selection and should not affect our perception of people any more than variations of other bodily characteristics. Prejudice and discrimination based on skin color are learned behaviors with no genetic or biological basis.

Going Further
Ask students to design an experiment that would determine the effectiveness of various brands of sunscreen with the same SPF numbers.

Demonstration

Cut holes larger than marbles on the ends of three shoeboxes. Place 15 red and 15 white marbles in each box. Explain to students that the white marbles represent genes for poor eyesight and the red marbles represent genes for good eyesight in the shoebox populations. Shake the boxes until 10 marbles fall out of each. Ask students what this action represents. Count the number of red and white marbles that remain in each box. Ask students what will happen to populations with more white marbles if no new genes are introduced. **LEP**

Figure Caption Question

What are the gene frequencies of the tenth generation? 60 percent *A* and 40 percent *a*

Wallace's Same Conclusion   Darwin was not alone in his investigation into evolution. A fellow scientist, Alfred Wallace, had made his own observations on journeys to other remote parts of the world. While resting from malarial fever in the West Indies, Wallace happened to read Malthus's essay on population. Within two days, he arrived at the same basic explanation as Darwin.

Wallace did not know that Darwin had also been developing a theory of the process behind evolution. He wrote to share his views with Darwin and to seek Darwin's opinions. Wallace's letter arrived shortly before Darwin planned to publish *On the Origin of Species, by Means of Natural Selection,* a book describing his years of observations and the supporting evidence that led to his explanation of evolution.

Lyell and other scientists suggested that Darwin and Wallace both present short summaries of their ideas at a joint meeting of scientists, which they did. After that, Darwin went on to publish his book in 1859. Darwin is the scientist most often remembered as the pioneer in evolution. But the idea of natural selection should properly be credited to both Wallace and Darwin.

Darwin himself could not explain the cause of variations or how they are passed on. He knew nothing about genes, much less about mutations and duplications, and nothing about meiosis and recombination. This lack of knowledge, however, did not detract from his lifelong work of explaining descent with modification. What we know about genetics today, in fact, supports Darwin's theory of natural selection.

Population Genetics

Have you ever wondered if individuals could evolve? By now you have probably recognized, as Darwin did, that it is a group of related individuals—a population, not an individual organism—that evolves. The genotype or genetic material of an individual remains constant. But, over time, the genes within a population may change. New alleles arise and are recombined, thus producing novel phenotypes.

Geneticists picture the entire collection of genes among a population as its **gene pool.** Each new offspring in the population draws its genes from this collection. It is the gene pool that evolves. The study of gene pools and the changes they undergo is called population genetics.

322 🦎 EVOLUTION

Give students culture dishes of mixtures of cornstarch and water mixed in the proportions of two parts cornstarch to one part water. This is a non-newtonian fluid that will shatter and break when hit, yet ooze and pour when moved slowly. Do not give students this information, but ask them to stir, squeeze, and tap this substance with their fingers to determine the properties themselves. After they have observed what this substance is like, tell them that next week Earth's entire surface will become coated 30 cm deep with this substance. Ask them to design an animal that will be adapted to this substance. They should draw this animal in their journals and make a written explanation of how it is adapted. **L1** **LEP**

Observing Gene Pool Changes Imagine a population of insects in which alleles *A* and *a* exist. The number of times you can expect to see any allele in a population is often described as its frequency. In our imaginary population, the frequency of allele *A* is 80 percent and the frequency of allele *a* is 20 percent. When the population's mature individuals reproduce, they will produce countless numbers of gametes—80 percent carrying the *A* allele and 20 percent the *a* allele. Those gametes represent the gene pool—for *A* or *a* alleles—from which the genotypes of the next generation will be drawn. Because the individuals reproduce sexually by meiosis, some genotypes will be *AA*, some *Aa*, and others *aa*.

Suppose that after ten generations, the frequency of the two alleles changes; now only 60 percent of the alleles are *A* while 40 percent are *a*. The change in percentages indicates that the gene pool has evolved.

Natural Selection in Gene Pools How do gene pools evolve? Gene pools evolve in a number of ways. One important way is by the process of natural selection. The genotypes—*AA, Aa,* or *aa*—dictate certain phenotypes. Phenotypes are the expression of the alleles that exist in populations. Suppose, for example, that the alleles *A* and *a* control the color of an insect. Insects with the *A* allele are greenish brown; insects with the *a* allele are dark brown. Because the *A* allele is dominant, most of the insects will be greenish brown. Some phenotypes are better suited to the environment than others. Suppose the phenotypes resulting from the genotypes *AA* and *Aa* are not as adapted to the environment as the ones resulting from *aa*. If, for example, the greenish-brown insects are more easily seen than the dark brown insects, they will be reduced in numbers much faster by hungry birds. Individuals having the *AA* or *Aa* phenotypes will not live as long or leave as many offspring as organisms that are *aa*. In this case, the number of *A* alleles or greenish-brown insects in the population will decline, and the number of dark brown insects with *a* alleles will increase. By analyzing gene frequencies, biologists can determine if a species is near extinction.

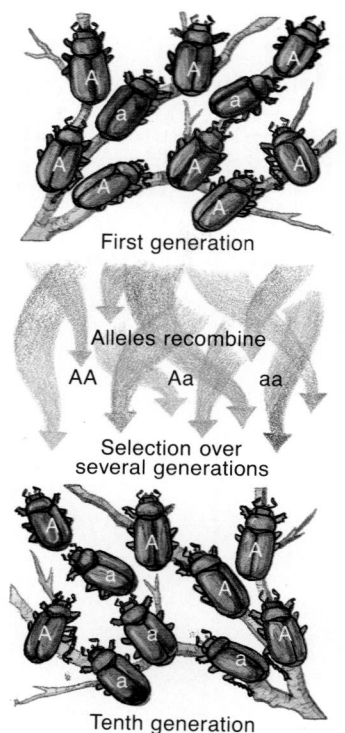

First generation

Alleles recombine

AA   Aa   aa

Selection over several generations

Tenth generation

Figure 12-14 The evolution of a population can be determined by comparing the gene pools of different generations. The gene frequencies in the first generation are 80 percent *A* and 20 percent *a*. What are the gene frequencies of the tenth generation?

Section Review

Understanding Concepts

1. Darwin discovered flightless cormorants on the Galapagos Islands. How might the discovery of this unusual bird have influenced his thinking about evolution?
2. Suppose snakes evolved from reptile ancestors that had legs. Explain how that evolution might have occurred.

3. How does evolution of resistance to a pesticide illustrate natural selection?
4. **Skill Review—Designing an Experiment:** How would you conduct an experiment to test the hypothesis that insects resistant to a low dose of insecticide may also become resistant to higher doses? For more help, see Practicing Scientific Methods in the **Skill Handbook**.

5. **Thinking Critically:** Cauliflower, brussels sprouts, and cabbage are closely related garden vegetables. They are all descendants of one type of wild plant. How might these plants have evolved?

3 Assess

Check for Understanding
Make a poster that illustrates a population of a species. Remove a couple of the pictures. Ask students how these organisms might have been removed. Ask them to predict what happens to populations when some members are removed. Ask them to compare how the loss of population members might affect a large population as compared with the effect on a small population. **L1**   **LEP**

Reteach
Ask students to make a list of the main points of the theory of evolution by natural selection. Ask them to explain why evolution is a property of populations, not individuals.

Extension
Ask students to write a report on the historical development of evolutionary ideas. They should include the work of Buffon, Lamarck, Lyell, Malthus, and Wallace. **L3**

✔ Assessment
Performance: Ask students to dramatize the life, voyage, findings, and discoveries of Darwin. They should be creative and use their imaginations while presenting accurate science. **L1**

4 Close

Discussion
Ask students to list ways that the topic of evolution is relevant to their lives today and how it might be relevant in the future.

Answers to Section Review

1. Darwin might have concluded that flightless cormorants were similar to flying cormorants he had observed elsewhere. Perhaps flightless forms evolved over time in this new, predator-free habitat.
2. Those reptile ancestors that had a variation for shorter legs were somehow more suited to a change in their environment. Thus, they may have lived longer and produced more offspring than their longer-legged counterparts. In succeeding generations, natural selection again may have favored the reptiles with shorter legs. Eventually, the entire population would lack legs.
3. Some insects exposed to a pesticide happen to have a variation that enables them to resist the pesticide. Those insects will tend to live longer and leave more offspring; that is, they will be naturally selected.
4. **Skill Review—Designing an Experiment:** The insects could be sprayed with a higher dose of the insecticide. A few may resist the higher dose, survive, and produce offspring. Over time, more and more of the population will resist the higher dose.
5. **Thinking Critically:** They are products of selective breeding.

Prepare

Key Concepts

Students will study how the formation of organic compounds led to the evolution of prokaryotes, autotrophs, and finally the higher forms of life.

Key Terms

heterotroph, autotroph, chemosynthesis, ozone layer

Materials

- For the Minilab 2, gather paper, pencils, and calculators.

1 Focus

Objectives

The objectives are listed on the student page. Remind students to preview these objectives as a guide to this numbered section.

Discussion

Ask students what Earth might be like today if life had never begun on this planet. Lead them to ideas about atmospheric oxygen and ultraviolet protection from the ozone layer.

Objectives

Sequence the events that might have led to the evolution of complex organic molecules and the first prokaryotes.

Discuss the events leading to evolution of autotrophs and the consequences of that evolution.

12.3 Origin of Life

Whose imagination hasn't been kicked into overdrive by video Earthlings making space visits to imaginary planets, where they mingle with incredible creatures in strange environments? Rev up your fantasies now and climb into an imaginary time machine. You are going to visit a planet every bit as strange—and hostile—as any you have seen on a video screen. The planet is Earth. You won't recognize it, though, because it is still at the beginning of its time.

Formation of Organic Compounds

Your time of arrival is about 4.6 billion years ago, which is when scientists believe Earth first came into being. Advisedly, you put on your protective clothing and respirating equipment. You could not survive a second without them. The overall scene is one of violence. Prolonged lightning and erupting volcanoes surround you. Meteorites and ultraviolet radiation (UV) make surface heat fearsome. There are no signs of life anywhere. You decide to leave and come back later—a long time later, perhaps after life has come to the planet. You wonder how that life will evolve, but you don't care to stick around in these unfriendly conditions long enough to find out.

Simple Molecules from the Atmosphere All the many forms of life on Earth today are descended from a common ancestor, found in a population of primitive unicellular organisms. What were those first cells like? How do we know? What events led up to their formation? No traces of those events remain, and scientists can't travel backward in time to witness what happened. Instead, they turn to scientific methods of observing data, forming hypotheses, making predictions, and constructing experiments to test their predictions.

Formation of complex organic molecules

Inorganic to organic molecules

Nucleic acids

Hydrothermal vents

4.5 billion years ago

Primordial Conditions: Alexander Oparin's ideas about the origins of life assume that constant sunlight and a large supply of organic compounds in ancient seas allowed the formation of a high degree of structural and functional organization resulting in life forms. This last idea was contrary to those previously held stating that life began as basic molecules. Oparin's ideas stimulated Stanley Miller to attempt to reproduce primordial conditions in the laboratory.

324

Earth's primitive atmosphere was far different from today's. In 1936, Alexander Oparin, a Russian biochemist, proposed that the primitive atmosphere consisted of the gases methane (CH_4), ammonia (NH_3), hydrogen (H_2), and water vapor (H_2O). Other scientists have since suggested that the atmosphere consisted mainly of water vapor and small amounts of nitrogen gas (N_2). Did you miss oxygen gas, so important to life as we know it today? Most of Earth's oxygen 4.6 billion years ago was probably in the form of metal oxides or water vapor. Oxygen was, therefore, not available as a gas.

Whatever the exact makeup of the primitive atmosphere might have been, the four elements most common in today's organic compounds—carbon, hydrogen, oxygen, and nitrogen—are thought to have been part of it. With time, Earth's crust gradually cooled. Runoff from torrential rains gathered to form oceans. Meanwhile, ultraviolet radiation and lightning continued to bombard the atmosphere. Scientists assume that these energy sources broke the bonds in the gas molecules, thereby releasing atoms to form simple organic compounds.

If scientists are correct in their assumption, then it should be possible to predict that organic compounds will form if primitive gases are exposed to high energy sources. Stanley Miller, a graduate student at the University of Chicago, tested that hypothesis in 1953 when he simulated conditions of the early atmosphere. In a setup like the one shown in Figure 12-15, Miller circulated steam through ammonia, methane, and hydrogen and subjected the mixture to electricity. At the end of one week, he found amino acids and a variety of other simple organic molecules in the

Electrodes

Methane, ammonia, water vapor, and hydrogen

Condenser cools

Stopcocks to obtain samples

Water

Organic compounds

Figure 12-15 At about the same time that Miller discovered that the red goo at the bottom of his flask was rich in amino acids, it was also learned that DNA carries the code for amino acids.

Primitive pre cells

Prokaryotes

3.5 billion years ago

Figure 12-16 In one billion years from the beginning of time on Earth, prokaryotes such as present-day photosynthetic bacteria had emerged.

12.3 ORIGIN OF LIFE 🐾 **325**

2 Teach

Bioethics

Dinosaurs from Flies:
Jurassic Park, by Michael Crichton, is a fiction book about bringing genetically engineered dinosaurs back to life. Copies of dinosaur DNA were made using a laboratory technique called the polymerase chain reaction. Using this technique, nucleotides could be connected in the order they appeared in the original organism. This DNA was injected into unfertilized reptile eggs, which then developed into dinosaurs. Even though dinosaur DNA currently is not available, some scientists think that it may be found in the future in flies, preserved in amber, that may have bitten dinosaurs in the ancient past. If ancient life could be genetically engineered today, what new regulations would be needed to ensure that ancient life forms would not become a problem for present-day living organisms? What should be done with life forms that might be made with this technique? Should they be used for research, put in zoos, or introduced into selected wild habitats?

PORTFOLIO

Geologic Time Table: Assign one group of students to each of the geologic time eras. The groups should prepare a report on the climate, geological events, and dominant life forms of each era. This report should include diagrams and sketches as well as written descriptions, all to be included in student portfolios. L1 COOP LEARN

PROGRAM RESOURCES

Teacher Classroom Resources
Study Guide, pp. 71-72 L1
Exploring Environmental Issues, pp. 39-40 L3
Probing Levels of Life, Lab 24, p.68 L2

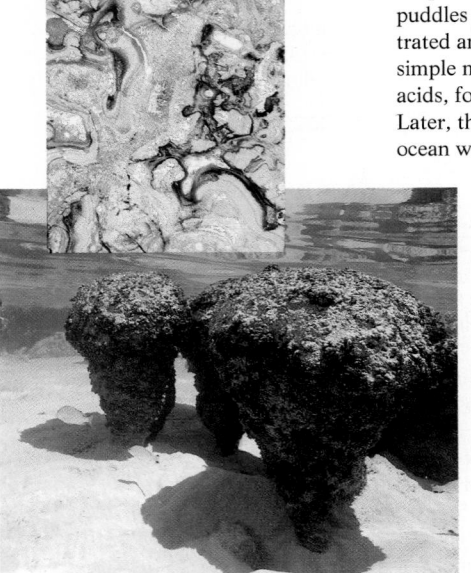

Figure 12-17 The species of photosynthetic bacteria that cover these mounds on the west coast of Australia have existed for over three and a half billion years. The mounds are made up of the fossils (inset) of these ancient prokaryotes.

condensed water vapor at the bottom of the chamber. The assumption that organic compounds were produced in the early atmosphere, then, seems to be a valid one. It is the one most widely held among researchers in the field today.

Complex Molecules from Simple Molecules? Simple organic molecules are necessary for life, but so are more complex molecules. How did complex molecules form? One assumption holds that the heavy rains washed simple organic molecules into the early oceans. In some places, say in puddles of water along a shoreline, the simple molecules became concentrated and were exposed to surface warmth. Under these conditions, the simple molecules may have reacted to form larger molecules. Amino acids, for example, might have joined to form short polypeptide chains. Later, the molecules could have been washed farther out into deeper ocean waters.

The First Organisms: Heterotrophs

The ocean was probably the cradle of life. That is, Earth's first organisms are believed to have evolved in the ocean. Modern scientists use knowledge of biochemistry to help them see through the window of this watery nursery.

Primitive Pre-cells Picture a situation, as modeled in Figure 12-16, in which complex organic molecules, polypeptides, nucleotides, and simple and complex carbohydrates are floating in the water. Various inorganic ions complete the mixture and form a chemical soup. If some sort of membrane were to form around groups of these molecules and ions, a kind of pre-cell condition would result. Models explaining how this could happen have been designed and tested.

The primitive cell could not truly be alive, however, without a means of obtaining energy for its functions. And once life processes started, the cell would need a means of reproduction to keep the processes going. Scientists have hypothesized about early energy sources and reproduction.

Anaerobic respiration Oparin and later scientists have suggested that simple organic molecules in the ocean, such as sugars, may have crossed the membranes and entered the pre-cells. At first, some inorganic molecules may have acted as enzymes that break the bonds in the sugars and release energy. A compound similar in function to ATP could have trapped that energy to fuel activities within the pre-cell. Later, polypeptide chains that formed in the soup may have taken over the role of enzymes. Because oxygen gas was not yet available, respiration in these early stages of cellular evolution must have been anaerobic.

DNA and Reproduction All cells, as scientists observe them today, depend upon DNA to code for their enzymes and other proteins. How and when DNA first evolved and became linked to protein synthesis is not known. But some of the very earliest cells must have been the scene of DNA activity, because all of their descendants inherited a universal genetic code. The first cells able to obtain energy and reproduce under the guidance of DNA were prokaryotes. According to Oparin, these early prokaryotes were **heterotrophs,** which means that they required a supply of organic material from the environment. These early heterotrophs were like some present-day bacteria. They obtained their energy from simple chemical reactions.

Later Organisms: Autotrophs

As the supply of simple molecules for heterotrophs was used up, life forms that used the available supplies more efficiently were at an advantage. This competition for food may have led to the evolution of cells that had the ability to make their own food. Organisms that make their own food are **autotrophs.** Autotrophs produce their own food—through photosynthesis or chemosynthesis. You learned in Chapter 6 that photosynthesis is a process that uses carbon dioxide, water, and energy from the sun to make food. **Chemosynthesis** is a process in which an organism uses the energy from chemical reactions to produce food. For example, chemosynthesis occurs in present-day bacteria that live in places where no sunlight can reach but also where there is no oxygen. It is, therefore, possible that life forms in the early anaerobic conditions on Earth used chemosynthesis to obtain energy. The oldest fossils found, dated at 3.5 billion years, are similar to today's bacteria that live in extreme habitats such as deep ocean vents, highly salty coasts, or hot sulfur pools.

Early prokaryotes that became adapted to living in light would have had an advantage as the supplies of organic molecules were used up. They must have eventually evolved a process of making their own complex molecules. Any genetic variations enabling certain cells to use light energy to make food would have been naturally selected. The first photosynthetic autotrophs evolved.

Photosynthesis and the Oxygen Revolution You will recall that the process of photosynthesis results in the production and release of oxygen. After photosynthesis evolved to the state in which we know it today, oxygen (O_2) would have become available.

It's too bad no one was around to applaud. The increase of oxygen in the drama of evolution changed the course of life forever. The change was so drastic that scientists call it the oxygen revolution. Once oxygen became abundant, aerobic respiration could evolve. As a result,

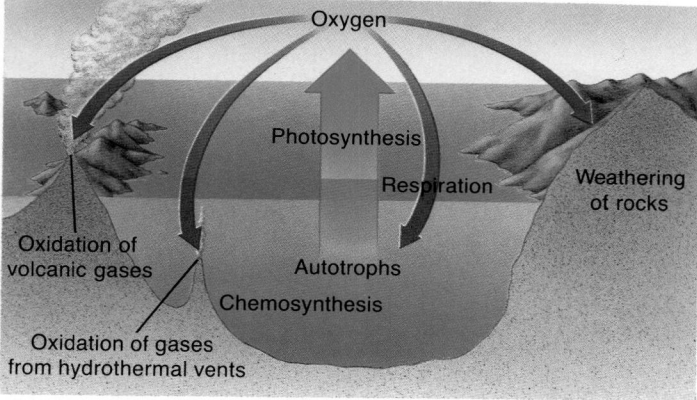

Figure 12-18 Early oxygen buildup resulted from photosynthesis by early autotrophs. The oxygen was then available for respiration, the oxidation of volcanic gases, and the weathering of rocks.

12.3 ORIGIN OF LIFE **327**

Minilab 2

Can a calendar represent geologic time?

Draw an outline of a calendar for the entire year. Calculate how one day corresponds to the total time scale being used in Figure 12-19. For example, if the first event occurred 550 000 000 years ago, one day on the calendar equals about 1 500 000 years (365 divided into 550 000 000).

Analysis How many years are represented by one day? How does your calendar help you to judge the rate of evolutionary change in different groups of organisms?

Minilab 2

Purpose
Students will construct a time line and use it to illustrate evolutionary events. **COOP LEARN**

Skills
sequence, make a model, interpret data, calculate

Teaching Strategies
- This activity will make an excellent cooperative group project.
- Have students indicate with colors and labels the times of each epoch and period.
- You may wish to photocopy calendar outlines in advance for your students. The blocks designated for each day should be large enough so that events can be recorded within the space provided.
- If students show difficulty visualizing what they are to do, explain that they are condensing the events of millions of years into a time sequence that they can relate to—one calendar year.

Answers
1. Student calculations should show one day corresponding to about 12 330 000 years.
2. The calendar will become very crowded in December with a number of events occurring toward the very end of the month. Thus, the pace of evolutionary change initially was very slow.

✔ Assessment
Performance: Have students prepare a similar time line, only this time all events must be placed onto a single month of 30 days in length. They should use the same events as they did for the preparation of the year calendar.

Figure Caption Question

In what era did humans first appear?
Cenozoic

Science, Technology, and Society

Searching for Extraterrestrial Life: Ask students how many think that life may have evolved on other planets or in other galaxies. On October 12, 1992, astronomers began a new search for intelligent life beyond the solar system. Scientists hope to hear messages from other forms of life that may exist in the Milky Way, 80 light-years from Earth. The receiving system consists of radio receivers coupled to state-of-the-art pattern recognition systems and signal processing equipment. The new system can gather the same amount of data in five minutes that previously had taken 32 years. If alien messages are heard, it could give biologists more information about the origins of life.

3 Assess

Check for Understanding

Ask students to make a list of steps of the origin of life beginning with simple molecules and ending with complex life forms. **L1**

Reteach

Tell groups of four students to debate some of the ideas about the origin of life. **COOP LEARN**

Figure 12-19 This representation of the Geologic Time Scale makes clear that the enormous diversity of ancient and present-day life evolved over a comparatively short duration. In which era did humans first appear?

more energy could be extracted from food molecules. With increased energy, greater organization and complexity among primitive cells could evolve. Still later, eukaryotes, with their complex organelle system and DNA enclosed in a nucleus, made an entrance that led to the enormous diversity of multicellular organisms today.

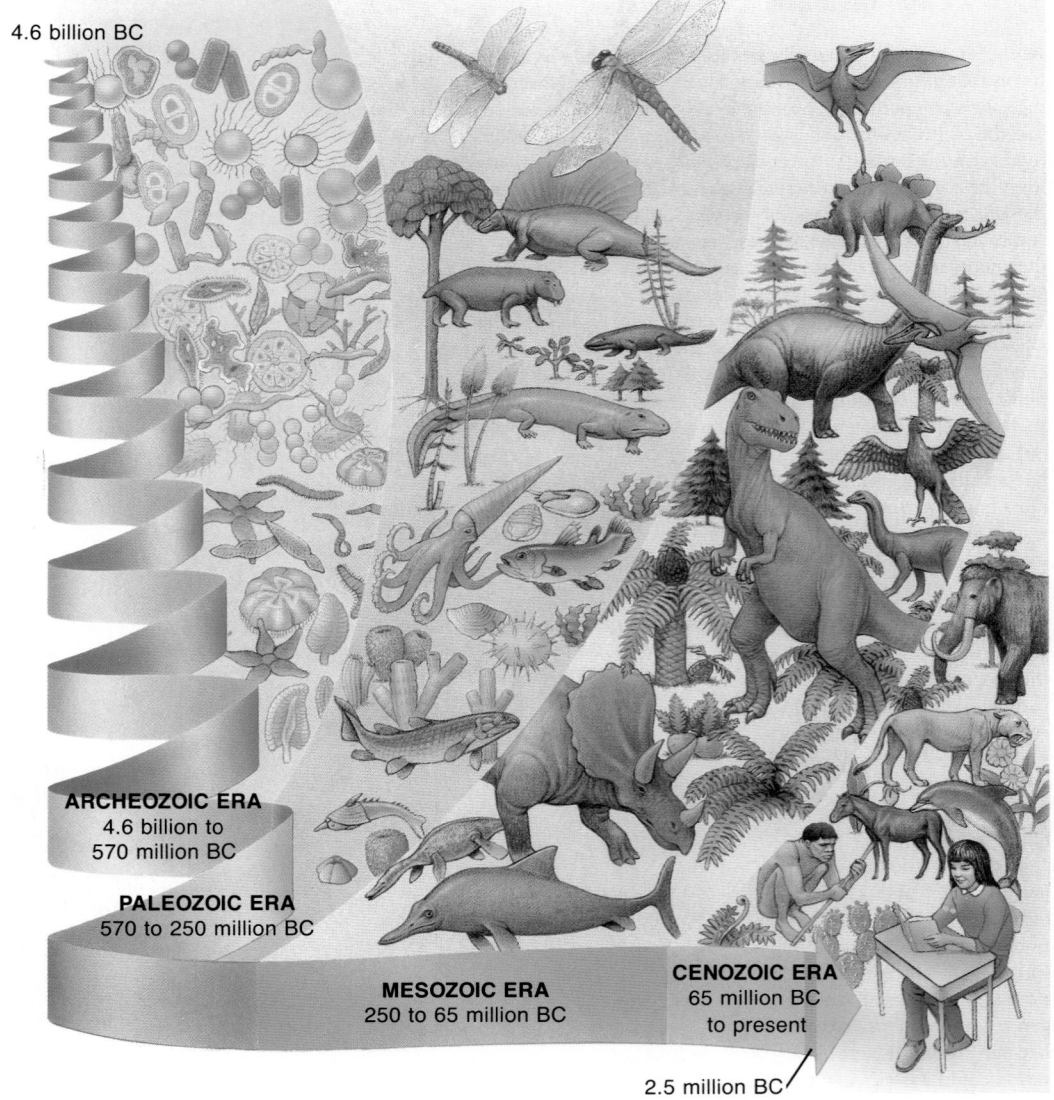

4.6 billion BC

ARCHEOZOIC ERA
4.6 billion to 570 million BC

PALEOZOIC ERA
570 to 250 million BC

MESOZOIC ERA
250 to 65 million BC

CENOZOIC ERA
65 million BC to present

2.5 million BC

328 EVOLUTION

MEETING INDIVIDUAL NEEDS

Some students may have problems with sequencing. Provide a variety of materials to deal with the sequences in this chapter. They could write lists of the sequential events, read their lists into tape recorders, and play them back. Make flash cards with sketches of the sequences and encourage these students to work with the cards. **LEP**

PROJECT

What starts an ice age?: Ask students to read the *Science News* article "Devil's Hole Heats up Debate Over Ice Ages," October 10, 1992, pages 142-143. This article reviews ideas about how the ice ages began. Ask students to explain the most recent evidence and compare it with older theories. **L3**

An Explosion of Life Over time, oxygen would have been present in large amounts in the atmosphere. Lightning converted much of the atmospheric oxygen to ozone molecules (O_3). The molecules collected in an **ozone layer** ten to 15 miles above the surface of Earth. The ozone layer blocked most UV radiation, and so prevented any further synthesis of organic molecules in the atmosphere. At the same time, it shielded emerging life forms from UV's harmful effects and thus allowed an explosive evolution of new organisms.

More than 500 million years ago, the early eukaryotes in the sea already included red, green, and brown algae, and a host of invertebrates from sponges to crabs. Later, by 300 million years ago, fishes, amphibians, and reptiles, and massive treelike ferns and large forests of coniferous trees had evolved.

Examine Figure 12-19 to compare the fossil record of life forms found from different periods in geologic history. Note that organisms during the Archeozoic Era, which represents nearly 90 percent of Earth's history, were very simple in form. The explosion of diverse life forms that occurred in the Paleozoic Era probably reflects the oxygen revolution. Notice how the fossil record provides evidence for evolution.

LOOKING AHEAD

THE THEORY of natural selection is central to any understanding of evolution. As you dig deeper into your studies of evolution, you will see how natural selection can result in new adaptations within a given population of organisms. New evidence for relationships among organisms is continually being presented in the areas of molecular biology, population studies, and genetics. You will trace the origin of completely new populations and species with the help of these modern studies. The most fascinating story of the history of a species is probably that proposed for humans to be described in Chapter 13.

Section Review

Understanding Concepts

1. Why are techniques such as examination of the fossil record and comparative studies of structures or genes not useful in learning about the origin of life?

2. Why could organisms today not exist in conditions like those thought to be present on early Earth?

3. Why would chemosynthesis have been an advantage for early prokaryotes?

4. **Skill Review—Sequencing:** Sequence the major events leading to the evolution of the first cells. For more help, see Organizing Information in the **Skill Handbook**.

5. **Thinking Critically:** How could the evolution of aerobic respiration have permitted evolution of more complex organisms?

Extension

The end of the Permian is characterized by mass extinction. A variety of explanations have been proposed. New evidence has been found in the Siberian Traps, an expanse of volcanic rock. Ask students to look up this new evidence and the ideas proposed that are coming out of this discovery about the mass extinction at the end of the Permian. **L3**

✔ Assessment

Knowledge: Give students mixed sequences of the origins of organic compounds, development of prokaryotes, and development of complex organisms. Ask them to put the sequence in correct order and justify their choices. **L1**

4 Close

Show the film *Origins of Life* by McGraw-Hill. This film shows that of billions of possible organic molecules, only 50 are functional in life processes.

Answers to Section Review

1. Neither technique can be applied to steps leading to the first organisms. There are no fossils or structures to analyze.

2. Organisms today could not exist in the atmosphere thought to be present on early Earth and would also be damaged by UV energy.

3. Chemosynthesis would have provided a means of obtaining energy as the supply of organic nutrients dwindled.

4. **Skill Review—Sequencing:** (1) formation of organic molecules in the atmosphere; (2) formation of more complex organic molecules; (3) accumulation of complex organic molecules in the ocean; (4) formation of a membrane around organic molecules and ions; (5) evolution of anaerobic respiration; (6) reproduction under control of DNA.

5. **Thinking Critically:** Aerobic respiration supplies a great deal more energy than anaerobic processes. Energy is needed to maintain organization. With a greater supply of energy, early cells could have become more highly organized and complex. Some energy could also be used for movement.

Issues

Purpose

Students are encouraged to examine the problem of extinction by examining the idea that genetic diversity in a species may need to be considered before deciding which species to save.

Teaching Strategies

- Before students read this selection, ask them to decide in their groups which of a list of ten endangered plants and animals they would save from extinction if they could only pick one. Ask them to justify their choice. You can get current lists of endangered species from your state Division of Wildlife or from the U.S. Fish and Wildlife Service.
- After they finish reading the selection, ask them to reevaluate their list and their justification.
- Make sure students understand what "close genetic cousins" are.
- Discuss with students why it is important to keep a gene pool as large as possible. Ask them what might happen to a species that lost diversity in its genes. Ask them to apply these same ideas to closely related species.

Possible Answers

1. Discuss biodiversity in general and explain that for our planet to remain in balance, it will be important to preserve as much variety as possible. Plants give off oxygen and keep the supply of oxygen in our atmosphere at a level that can support all life.
2. Tropical rain forests have more biodiversity than any other regions on Earth. By destroying tropical rain forests, we are limiting biodiversity more than destruction of any other areas on Earth.

Going Further

Ask students to do library research to determine which species of animals, because of their small numbers, lack

---

BIOLOGY, TECHNOLOGY, AND SOCIETY

Issues

Biodiversity: Which Species Should Be Saved?

They stare out at you from emotion-charged public service advertisements. They star in wildlife documentaries chronicling the disappearance of many forms of life on Earth. "They" are the endangered plant and animal species of Earth.

For decades, biologists have endeavored to identify plant and animal species headed toward extinction and to devise ways of saving them. Lately, however, dissenting voices have asked, where will conservationists find the time, the money, and the technology to save all the threatened species on Earth? And, even if this rescue effort were possible, the voices add, is it necessary?

Consider the Facts: The total number of species on Earth is still unknown. Millions of species have yet even to be identified. Furthermore, many species share such a similar evolutionary history that their genetic differences are slight. Perhaps it is time, some scientists are saying, to adopt a new goal: the preservation of biodiversity, which describes the broad variety of living things on Earth.

Earth is home to many different species. Preserving this biodiversity doesn't mean preserving all species; rather, it means protecting species

that and represent a broad spectrum of variation.

For example, suppose scientists have identified ten species of falcons. Five of these species are endangered and face extinction. Three of the five endangered falcon species are close genetic cousins of a falcon that is not endangered. Which of the endangered falcon species should we protect?

Not too long ago, the answer might have been "all of them." Today, however, some scientists would suggest that the two genetically distinct falcons should be saved. If the close cousins become extinct, much of their genetic heritage will be preserved in the group of nonendangered species.

Investing in the Future: Some conservationists reject this approach. They argue that even the subtle differences between close genetic cousins are important and worth

preserving. The loss of any species through human neglect is, they say, a potential biological tragedy. A plant species allowed to disappear may be the one that contained the chemistry to cure disease, and an animal species may have secreted a substance for some other technological breakthrough.

Although the issue is likely to be debated for decades to come, the process of evolution may have already shown us the way. Throughout Earth's history, species have continuously appeared and disappeared. Nature, it seems, has been preserving biodiversity for as long as species have existed.

Understanding the Issue

1. How would you respond to someone who suggested that saving plant species wasn't as important as saving animal species?
2. Today, vast areas of tropical rain forests are being destroyed. How will this affect biodiversity?

Readings

- "So Much to Save." *The Economist*, June 13, 1992, p. 94.
- Mlot, Christine. "The Science of Saving Endangered Species." *Bioscience*, Feb. 1989, pp. 68-70.

---

of genetic variability, and resulting inbreeding, are having serious genetic problems. **L2**

Biotechnology

Dating Fossils

If you think you have problems finding dates, imagine the problems of the paleontologist who's just unearthed a fossil skull. The skull appears to be quite old, but the question is, "exactly how old?" The answer can come from a variety of dating techniques that scientists use to date fossils precisely.

Radioisotope Dating: In the past, paleontologists have dated bones and fossils by two standard methods—radiocarbon dating and potassium-argon dating. Radiocarbon is an unstable form of carbon, carbon-14, that changes or decays into nitrogen-14 atoms at a known rate. When an organism dies, the levels of radiocarbon continue to decrease within the bones. The age of a fossil can, therefore, be estimated from its present-day levels of carbon-14. Radiocarbon dating is useful for fossils less than 40 000 years old.

Other isotopes are necessary to date older fossils. Potassium-argon dating depends on the decay of potassium-40 to argon-40 and calcium-40. Half of the original atoms of potassium in a rock sample will decay to argon-40 in 1.3 billion years. The age of the rocks can, therefore, be estimated from present-day levels of potassium-40. The decay of potassium-40 is so slow that this dating method is useful only for fossils in surrounding rocks more than 500 000 years old.

Comparing Amino Acids: There remains a 460 000-year gap for which other dating techniques are needed. At one time, amino acid racemization (AAR) gained some popularity. Amino acids manufactured during an organism's life do not disappear when the organism dies. Instead, they slowly change from one isomeric form to another (a process called racemization). By measuring the ratio of the levels of the two isomeric forms, scientists can estimate the age of the organism.

Measuring Trapped Electrons:

Two other techniques that developed from research in chemistry and physics are becoming more popular in the dating of fossils up to two million years old. Luminescence dating and electron spin resonance (ESR) are both based on the measurement of buildup of the trapped electrons caused by radiation. The difference in the two techniques is that luminescence dating can only be used to date flint tools or pottery—items that have been subjected to high temperatures at the time of their formation; ESR can be used to date bones, coral, shells, or tooth enamel. The development of these two methods could probably lead to the unravelling of the mystery of the evolutionary history of humans.

1. **Issue:** One group of anthropologists says that humans evolved 200 000 years ago in Africa. Another group says that humans evolved later in Asia. Why is it important for scientists to use more than one method of dating fossils?

2. **Explore Further:** Use the library to find out how mitochondrial DNA has been used in determining the place of human origins.

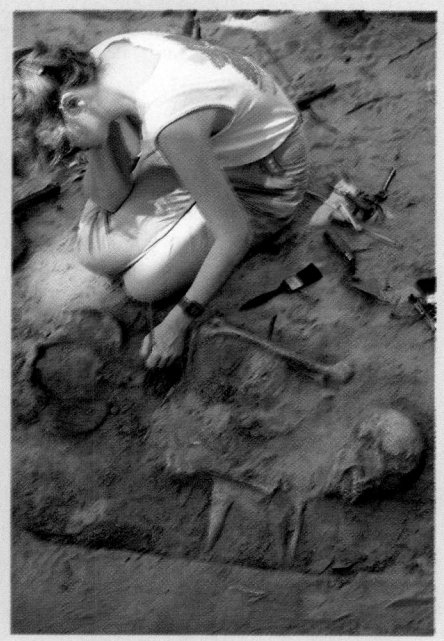

Going Further

Ask students to read "End of the Proterozoic Eon" in *Scientific American,* October 1991, pages 64-73. They should write about the dating technique used to help determine that oxygen levels increased in the atmosphere of early Earth, thereby making conditions suitable for more complex organisms. **L3**

Purpose

Students will learn about the benefits and disadvantages of a variety of methods of dating fossils.

Teaching Strategies

- Use bottle caps from soft drinks to illustrate radioactive decay. Put 50 bottle caps in a cardboard box. Shake the box. Open the box and take out all the bottle caps that are face down. Repeat this procedure for several trials. Explain to students that this is a model that illustrates how radioactive decay works.

- Ask students to make a summary table of fossil-dating methods.

- Ask students which method of fossil dating would be best for fossils known to be:
  (1) more than 600 000 years old.
  (2) less than 30 000 years old.
  (3) about 250 000 years old.
  (4) human fossils.

Possible Answers

1. **Issue:** All the measurements of fossil ages made using various dating techniques are only estimates. Using a variety of methods to date fossils will help to pinpoint an age more precisely. Also, if an approximate geologic time period cannot be determined by examining the fossil, the scientist would use a variety of methods because the techniques available are useful only within certain time periods of Earth's history.

2. **Explore Further:** Because DNA in mitochondria is transmitted only from the egg and not the sperm, lineages based on this DNA do not follow Mendelian genetics. It is possible to trace human origins back from mother to grandmother to great-grandmother. When this type of study is done, some scientists have concluded that modern humans share mitochondrial DNA from a single female ancestor from Central Africa who lived about 200 000 years ago.

CHAPTER 12

CHAPTER REVIEW

Summary

Summary statements can be used by students to review the major concepts of the chapter.

Language of Biology

Answers should go beyond defining the terms. Accept any reasonable answer that uses the term correctly and in the proper context.

Understanding Concepts

1. The ancestors of the fish used their eyes. As their descendants moved into a new environment in which there was no light, some variations occurred that may have coincided with loss of vision. The fish with these variations were selected.
2. An animal breeder who understands that variations are inherited will be able to produce organisms with all the desired traits.
3. Darwin might have concluded that the two populations are evolving different variations in slightly different environments.
4. Malthus reasoned that availability of food could limit human population growth. The earliest heterotrophs faced a food supply problem.
5. Individual organisms do not change during their lifetime. Over time, however, the gene pool of a population changes, giving rise to organisms having traits different from those of their ancestors.
6. Artificial selection is a process by which humans choose as parents organisms having traits important to humans. In natural selection, organisms having traits best suited to the environment more often become parents.
7. Plants evolved during the Paleozoic era. Animals evolved in the Archeozoic era.
8. The oxygen revolution began when photosynthesis evolved. Free oxygen permitted the evolution of aerobic respiration among early organisms, leading to greater

Summary

Study of the fossil record and comparisons of anatomy, embryology, chemistry, and genes of organisms provide a wealth of evidence that evolution occurs. Results of selective breeding and direct observations of changes in populations strengthen that assumption.

Darwin and Wallace recognized the importance of variations among organisms and that variations can be inherited. The two scientists independently formed the theory of natural selection to explain how evolution occurs. Modern understanding of genetics confirms and expands that theory.

Although direct evidence to explain the origin of life is not available, scientists have proposed models and tested hypotheses about how the first cells and organisms evolved. One hypothesis proposes that the first cells were heterotrophic prokaryotes and that autotrophs evolved later.

Language of Biology

Write a sentence that shows your understanding of each of the following terms.

autotroph	gene pool
chemosynthesis	heterotroph
comparative anatomy	homologous
comparative biochemistry	natural selection
	ozone layer
comparative embryology	population
	selective breeding
embryo	theory of natural selection
fossil	vestigial

Understanding Concepts

1. Blind cave fish have eyes but do not use them to find their prey. Explain why they have these apparently useless structures.
2. How might an understanding of genetics be useful to an animal breeder?
3. Two populations of wildflowers are found in nearby meadows. There are slight differences among members of each population, such as flower color and leaf shape. How might Darwin have interpreted these facts?
4. Relate the situation faced by the first heterotrophs to the idea proposed by Malthus.
5. Why is it more correct to speak of the evolution of populations rather than of individual organisms?
6. Compare the terms *artificial selection* and *natural selection*.

7. Using Figure 12-19 as a reference, determine when plants began to evolve on land? Animals?
8. Explain the cause and consequences of the oxygen revolution.

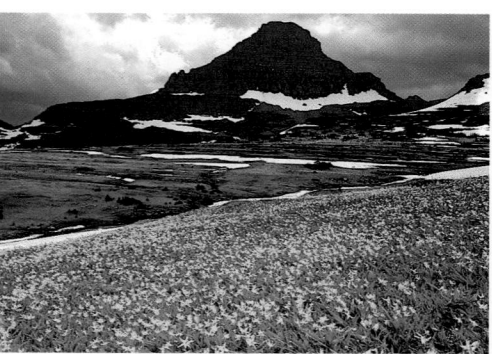

complexity. Some oxygen was converted to ozone, which would have been harmful to emerging land organisms.

Applying Concepts

9. Originally, tan-colored insects were camouflaged from predators. As green plants began to invade the area, green-colored insects had an advantage. Over time, the population evolved such that there were more green insects than tan ones.

10. In the original gene pool, the frequency of the allele for tan was much greater than the frequency of the allele for green. The gene pool evolved as the frequency of the allele for tan declined and the frequency of the allele for green increased.
11. Though the first living things arose from nonliving materials, they did so over a billion years' time and were simple cells.
12. The theory accounts for the evolution of the first living things.

Applying Concepts

9. Suppose a population of tan-colored insects inhabits a sandy area. Over time, the area becomes grown over by a population of green plants. Use Darwin's ideas to explain how and why the insect population might evolve to be green in color.

10. Explain the same evolution of insects asked about in the question above, but this time in terms of population genetics.

11. Is the evolution of the first living thing an example of spontaneous generation as described in Chapter 7? Defend your answer.

12. The theory of biogenesis, as you read in Chapter 7, states that all organisms are produced from other organisms. Why does it also state that biogenesis only refers to organisms at the present time and under present conditions on Earth?

13. Some biologists have proposed that organic molecules or even simple life forms reached Earth by hitching rides on meteorites. Even if that were true, why is that suggestion not very useful in the study of the origin of life?

14. How might mutations and immigration of the same kind of organism from another population affect a population's gene pool?

15. Darwin recognized the existence of variations and the fact that they are inherited. However, he knew nothing about genetics. How do (a) events of mitosis, meiosis, and fertilization, (b) mutation and crossing over, and (c) the role of DNA support his theory?

16. Explain why further synthesis of simple organic compounds in the atmosphere is not possible.

17. The DNA code is basically the same in all organisms. For example, a bacterium is able to use the information from human genes to make proteins when the human genes are inserted into it using genetic engineering techniques. What does this fact suggest about evolution?

18. In a population, flower color is represented by two alleles. The population consists of 10 *BB* flowers and 10 *bb* flowers. What are the allele frequencies?

19. If a population of palm trees were planted on a mountain in the Rockies, would you expect them to evolve into a new species? Explain.

20. **Global Connection:** How do humans avoid the effects of natural selection in adverse environmental conditions?

21. **Issues:** You know that diversity means a condition of being different or having various forms or qualities. In your own words, explain what biodiversity is and why maintaining it is important.

Lab Interpretation

22. **Minilab 1:** A layer of microfossils is found in nature. Directly above it is a layer of sedimentary rock with no microfossils. How might you explain this difference?

23. **Thinking Lab:** A young rock layer is found exposed at Earth's surface with a much older layer exposed nearby. What might explain why younger layers are missing from the top of the older layer?

24. **Investigation:** Amber is a hardened, resinlike material that sometimes may hold trapped insects. Describe a simple way of making an amber-trapped fossil without using amber.

Connecting Ideas

25. Explain the frequencies of the alleles for sickle-cell anemia in populations of African Americans and native black Africans in terms of population genetics.

26. Relate the model of the origin of life presented in this chapter to the model of evolution of eukaryotes by symbiosis as described in Chapter 5.

CHAPTER 12 EVOLUTION **333**

---

26. **Evolution:** The heterotroph hypothesis explains the evolution of the first prokaryotes, both heterotrophic and autotrophic, and anaerobic and aerobic. According to the symbiosis model, some aerobic prokaryotes invaded anaerobic ones, evolving into mitochondria. Similarly, some early autotrophic prokaryotes took up residence in other prokaryotes, giving rise to chloroplasts.

---

13. That explanation would not explain how the life forms evolved in the first place.

14. Both mutations and immigration would alter gene frequencies.

15. (a) Events of mitosis, meiosis, and fertilization explain how traits are passed to offspring as well as variation. (b) Mutation and crossing over are causes of variation. (c) The role of DNA explains variations on a biochemical level.

16. The components of the atmosphere are different.

17. The DNA code arose early in the evolution of life.

18. 50% B : 50% b

19. It is doubtful that palm trees would have the variations that would enable them to survive in such a different environment.

20. Humans alter or protect themselves from adverse conditions.

21. Biodiversity refers to the many different organisms present in a community. Maintaining biodiversity is important so as not to disrupt interactions within a community and to preserve species that may have practical value.

Lab Interpretation

22. The layer above may have been deposited from sediments formed in a body of water not suitable for the existence of this specific fossil organism.

23. Erosion via water or wind may have removed the younger layers.

24. Students may suggest using an ice cube or gelatin to trap a "fossil" within it.

Connecting Ideas

25. **Evolution:** In Africa, heterozygotes are naturally selected because that genotype confers resistance to malaria. Thus, the frequency of the recessive allele remains high even though homozygotes die from malaria or sickle-cell anemia. In the U.S., heterozygotes have no advantage. People with sickle-cell anemia have been selected against and the frequency of the recessive allele has declined.

333

SECTION	OBJECTIVES	TEXT LABS/FEATURES
13.1 Adaptation (2 days)	**Sequence** the steps in the evolution of new adaptations. **Compare** three different types of adaptations.	**Investigation:** Variation in Numbers of Stomata, p. 338 **Minilab 1:** Is blubber an adaptation? p. 340
13.2 Origins of Species (2 days)	**Contrast** various ways in which speciation may occur. **Compare** gradualism and punctuated equilibrium. **Determine** the survival value of mimicry and camouflage.	**Thinking Lab:** Why are finches that survive drought larger with bigger beaks? p. 345 **Minilab 2:** How do adaptations aid survival? p. 348 **Literature Connection:** How the Crow Came to Be Black, p. 350
13.3 Human Evolution (2 days)	**Describe** the characteristics of primates. **Sequence** the major trends in human evolution.	**Global Connection:** Cultural Evolution, p. 356
BIOLOGY, TECHNOLOGY, AND SOCIETY		**Physics Connection:** Honeybee Heating and Cooling, p. 360 **Issues:** Interbreeding to Save a Species, p. 361 **Career Connection:** Naturalist, p. 361

LAB MATERIALS

INVESTIGATION	MINILAB	ALTERNATE LAB
page 338 book, large heavy leaves microscope nail polish, clear slides tape, clear	**page 340** bags, plastic beaker ice rubber bands shortening spoon, plastic test tubes thermometers watch or clock with a second hand **page 348** bag forceps hole punch paper, black paper, white tally cards	**page 346** bag, plastic flag marker tape, plastic macaroni, elbow meterstick watch with a second hand

TEACHER CLASSROOM RESOURCES	OTHER RESOURCES
Study Guide, p. 73 **Exploring Environmental Issues:** *Going, Going, Gone,* pp. 31-32 ***PLL:** *Adaptation,* p. 70 ****ILS:** *A Human Variation with Possible Adaptive Value,* p. 113 ****ILS:** *Animal Adaptations,* p. 117 ****ILS:** *Seed Adaptations,* p. 119	***STVS:** *Temperature Regulation in Dogs,* Animals (Disc 5, Side 2) ***STVS:** *March of the Spiny Lobster,* Animals (Disc 5, Side 1)
Study Guide, pp. 74-75 **Concept Mapping,** p. 13 **Critical Thinking/Problem Solving:** *Selection Pressures,* p. 13 ***PLL:** *Variation Within a Species and Between Species,* p. 73	***STVS:** *Horseshoe Crab,* Ecology (Disc 6, Side 1) ***STVS:** *Aphid Mimics,* Ecology (Disc 6, Side 1)
Study Guide, pp. 76-77 ***PLL:** *Evolutionary Changes in Primates,* p. 75 ****ILS:** *Evolutionary Changes in Primates,* p. 123	
Assessment Materials **Chapter Assessment,** pp. 49-52 **Performance Assessment in Biology,** p. 26 **Alternate Assessment in the Science Classroom** **Computer Test Bank**	**Spanish Resources** **Cooperative Learning Resource Guide** **Videodisc Correlations** (to Optical Data's and Videodiscovery's videodiscs)

* Probing Levels of Life
** Investigating Living Systems

* Science Technology Videodisc Series

Key to Teaching Strategies

The following designations will help you decide which activities in the teacher margin are appropriate for your students.

L1 Level 1 activities should be within the ability range of all students.

L2 Level 2 activities should be within the ability range of the average to above-average student.

L3 Level 3 activities are designed for the ability range of above-average students.

LEP LEP activities are appropriate for Limited English Proficiency students.

COOP LEARN Cooperative Learning activities are designed for small group work.

ADDITIONAL RESOURCES

Infinite Voyage *The Great Dinosaur Hunt*
Traditional views of dinosaurs are changing due to the work of many field scientists. Students will learn how some dinosaurs cared for hatchlings and lived in herds in this new look at dinosaurs.

Audiovisual

Selection and Adaptation, video, Films for the Humanities and Sciences.
The Evolution of Man, video, Films for the Humanities and Sciences.

Software

Evolution, Apple II, Conduit.
Survival of the Fittest, Apple II, EME.

13

ADAPTATION AND SPECIATION

Chapter Overview

In this chapter, students will apply their understanding of natural selection to several topics in evolution. First, they will examine the origin of adaptations and the concept of descent with modification. They will be able to distinguish among and give examples of structural, physiological, and behavioral adaptations.

Next, students will learn about the species concept and examine factors leading to speciation: geographic isolation, genetic drift, and polyploidy. They will explore the trends of adaptive radiation and convergence, and analyze and compare the ideas of gradualism and punctuated equilibrium.

Students conclude the chapter by studying the origin of humans. They will begin to form a picture of human evolution as they examine trends revealed by a study of fossils of australopithecines and other hominid ancestors.

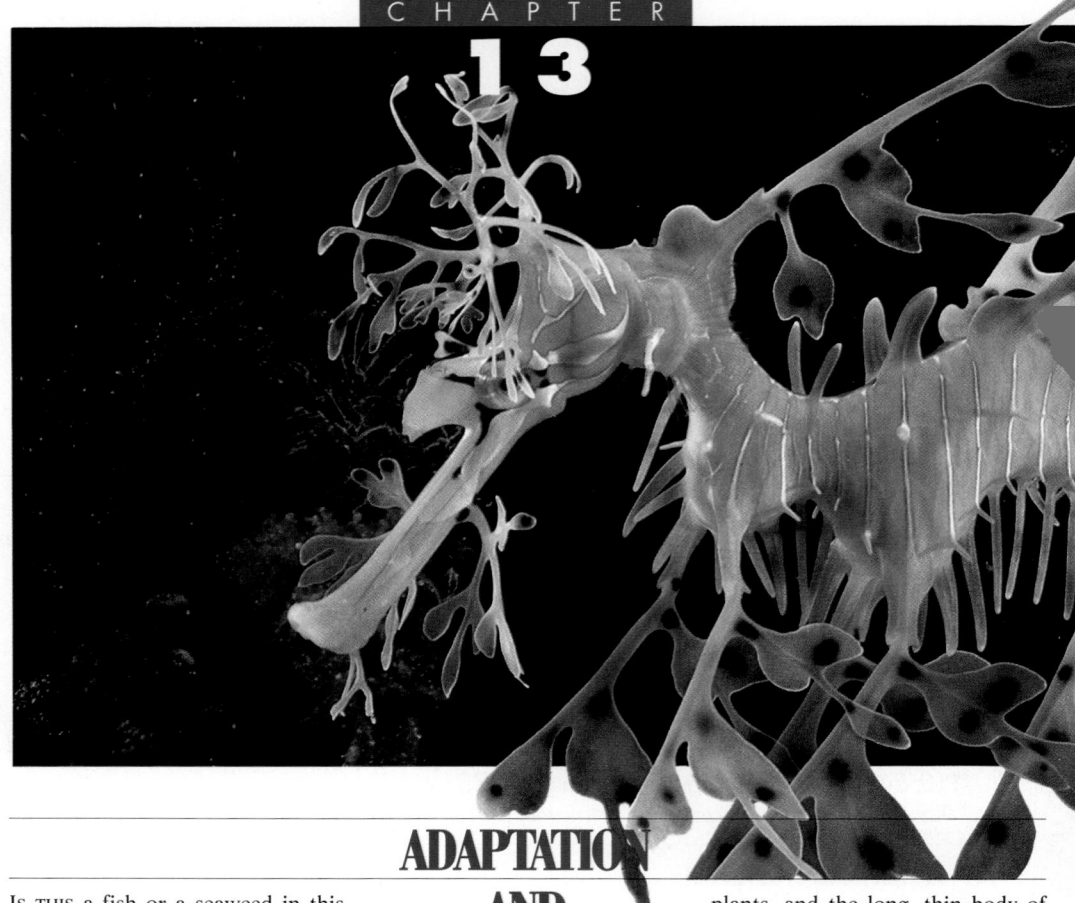

CHAPTER

13

ADAPTATION AND SPECIATION

IS THIS a fish or a seaweed in this photograph? Perhaps you weren't fooled, but a predator, such as a larger fish, might have missed this tasty morsel. The fish you see hiding among the plants is called a leafy sea dragon. The sea dragon possesses large, fanlike fins that resemble the leaves of kelp seaweed, in which it generally hides. In addition, the sea dragon can hold itself upright to further camouflage itself from predators. These fish use the underwater kelp as a home base for feeding and reproduction. The sea dragon's close relatives, sea horses and pipefishes, also have the ability to swim vertically among the seaweed in order to hide from predators. Sea horses have a grasping tail, which they use to hold firmly onto underwater plants, and the long, thin body of the pipefish very much resembles the grasses it calls home. Can you see how these features enable sea dragons and their relatives to survive in this watery environment?

All organisms possess features that enable them to survive and eventually reproduce in a particular environment. Trees possess leaves that capture the sun's energy so they can produce food and survive. Mammals have fur or hair that insulates them from the cool temperatures of the environment. In Chapter 12, you learned how the process of natural selection causes the enormous variety of life forms on Earth. In this chapter, you'll consider how adaptations evolve and how they eventually can lead to the evolution of species.

334

When you're in a crowd, do you feel hidden? When you wear brightly colored clothes, do you expect to frighten people away? Do you have predators to run from?

CHAPTER
13

Introducing the Chapter

Discussion of the photograph on pages 334-335 should provoke a lively discussion of adaptations. Begin by challenging your students to name as many structural adaptations of the leafy sea dragon as they can. Have them analyze how each structure they name is adaptive. Then ask them to think about ways in which the animal's behavior complements its structure. Ask them if they can think of some physiological adaptations as well, and stress the idea that the sea dragon, like all organisms, is a complex set of adaptations. As time permits, follow the same exercise by analyzing adaptations of familiar organisms including the students themselves.

Theme Development

The themes of evolution and methods of inquiry are intertwined throughout the chapter. Change in organisms with time is seen with respect to both evolution of adaptations and of entirely new groups of organisms. The differing viewpoints concerning the tempo of evolution and the kinds of evidence used to determine the events of human evolution illustrate that science cannot always offer absolute answers and that alternative hypotheses not only exist, but are healthy in science.

Tying to Previous Knowledge

The chapter builds primarily upon and calls for application of the theory of natural selection. Students will make use of that principle in being able to analyze and explain how new adaptations as well as new species evolve. It will be useful, also, to remind students of how their knowledge of genetics can be applied to the topics in this chapter.

Chapter Preview

335

ASSESSMENT PLANNER

Choose assessment strategies from the following pages to evaluate the progress of your students.

Assess, pp. 341, 351, 358
Portfolio, pp. 339, 340, 341, 347, 348, 351, 353, 358
Alternate Lab, pp. 346-347
Thinking Lab, p. 345

Minilab 1, p. 340
Minilab 2, p. 348
Investigation, pp. 338-339
Chapter Review, pp. 362-363

Prepare

Key Concepts

Students will distinguish between variation and adaptation and the various types of adaptation: structural, physiological, and behavioral. They will study the evolution of complex adaptations and the interactions of adaptations.

Key Terms

structural adaptation, physiological adaptation, behavioral adaptation

Materials

- For the Investigation, gather slides, microscopes, and one geranium plant covered by a large plastic bag. Students can provide clear nail polish, clear tape, large books for pressing leaves, and leaves with smooth, not fuzzy, surfaces.
- For Minilab 1, gather shortening, test tubes, sandwich bags, thermometers, rubber bands, ice cubes, and beakers.

1 Focus

Objectives

The objectives are listed on the student page. Remind students to preview these objectives as a guide to this numbered section.

Demonstration

Place an onion bulb on the desk of each group of students. Ask them to make a list of features that make the onion plant suited to its environment. Compile their lists of features on the chalkboard. Then ask them to explain the function of an onion bulb. Cut an onion in half. Ask them to hypothesize how the onion's aroma helps it survive. Explain that the chemicals responsible for making a person cry also prevent bacteria and fungi from growing on and in onion bulbs. Lead up to the fact that the traits of onions that enable them to survive and reproduce are called adaptations.
L1

Objectives

Sequence the steps in the evolution of new adaptations.

Compare three different types of adaptations.

13.1 Adaptation

Have you ever wondered why some trees have pointed needles while others have broad, flat leaves? Why do dogs and cats have sharp, needlelike teeth while humans have rather flat teeth? As you learned in the last chapter, the answers to these questions can be explained by Darwin's theory of natural selection. In this section, you will apply Darwin's theory to explain the differences among different kinds of organisms.

Origin of Adaptations

The pointed needles of trees such as pines, firs, and spruces and the flat leaves of trees such as maples and magnolias are features that enable them to survive in different environmental conditions. A broad-leaved tree would not survive very well in a hot, dry desert or in a cold, dry region of the far north. Too much water would be lost faster than it could be replaced. The sharp teeth of dogs and cats are also traits that are important to survival. You have read that any trait that aids the chances of survival and reproduction of organisms is called an adaptation. Because sharp teeth in dogs and cats and needle-shaped leaves in pine trees enable these organisms to survive, adaptations can also be thought of as traits that increase an organism's fitness to the environment or that increase the probability of an organism passing its genes on to the next generation. How do adaptations arise?

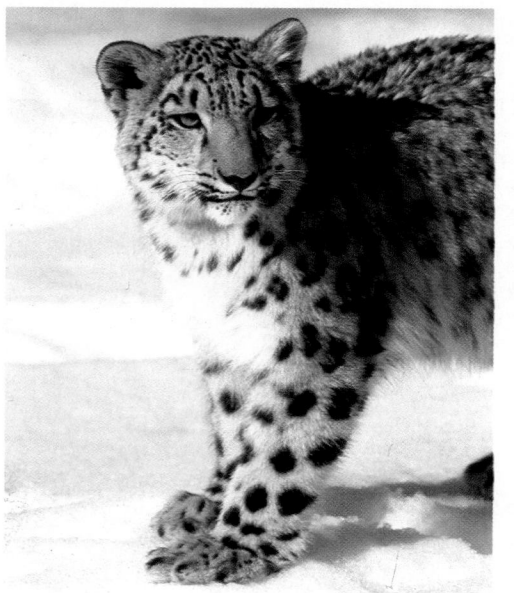

Figure 13-1 The beautiful snow leopard has deadly teeth and claws. What other adaptations for survival does it have?

Distinguishing Variations and Adaptations
Adaptations may evolve as certain variations increase in frequency within a population of organisms. But note that the words *variation* and *adaptation* do not mean the same thing. A variation may improve fitness, but it may also reduce it. For example, the sharpness and length of claws in a population of leopards is an adaptation that allows them to capture the foods they need to survive. Occasionally, some of these cats may have very long, needlelike claws, or some cats may have shorter and less sharp claws. If a leopard develops claws that are too short, this cat may not be able to catch its prey. The fitness of this animal has been reduced. Only variations that aid survival up to and including the reproductive stage will be preserved by natural selection. Over time, all members of a population will have inherited that variation, at which point the original variation becomes an adaptation. That adaptation will be a general characteristic of the entire population, like needles on pine trees or eyespots on fish. Adaptations, then, are products of evolution by natural selection. Variations are the raw materials upon which natural selection acts.

336 ADAPTATION AND SPECIATION

MEETING INDIVIDUAL NEEDS

Students with learning disabilities will benefit from using visualization techniques. Make a large set of cards with a printed word and visual example of the concepts from this section. Tell the students to look closely at a card for 10 seconds, then close their eyes and imagine that card being placed on a bulletin board. With eyes closed, they should focus on their bulletin board card for about 10 seconds.

Do the same for each card. The next day, put the key terms, one at a time, on the chalkboard. Ask students to close their eyes and look at their imaginary bulletin boards and explain what they see. Reassure them that they may not remember all of the concepts the first time. Show pictures again if necessary. L1 LEP

The Evolution of Complex Adaptations One of the more common misconceptions about evolution by natural selection is that adaptations arise all at once, as a result of some giant mutation or massive mistake in the genetic message. Some of you may have considered it difficult to comprehend, for example, how a complex structure such as the eye could possibly be the product of a mistake. Your confusion would be understandable. However, complex adaptations do not evolve instantly by giant mutations.

Adaptations do not arise overnight. Keep in mind that evolutionary changes occur over many, many generations of a species. Adaptations evolve slowly as a result of a series of small adaptive changes or modifications, each change representing a slight variation from the traits of the previous generation. Remember from Chapter 12 that Darwin referred to this idea as "descent with modification." But, it is important to recognize that natural selection does not invent. It only acts to modify in each successive descendant what already exists. Adaptations in organisms you see today are the result of chance variations that arose at a particular time in the evolutionary history of that type of organism. For example, if the variations for piercing mouthparts in mosquitoes had not arisen, mosquitoes probably would not be as successful as they are today.

When we marvel at a structure as complex as an eye, we are looking at a product of the ongoing process of evolution. You can better understand how an eye might have evolved if you picture a series of changes during the evolution of the eye. Each step along the way provided organisms with slightly better vision (Figure 13-2).

a

b

c

d

Figure 13-2 Simple animals such as flatworms (a) have groups of light-sensitive cells to detect direction of light. More complex animals have visual systems that form images. In mollusks (b) the images are blurry. The images are focused for a turtle (c) and are enhanced by color in the eagle (d) and many other vertebrates.

2 Teach

Figure Caption Question
What other adaptations for survival does it have? a thick fur coat that protects against freezing temperatures

Concept Development
Explain that there are traits on which the environment does not act. Therefore, these traits do not evolve as rapidly because selection pressures are lower.

CHEMISTRY CONNECTION

Chemical Evolution:
Evolution also occurs at the macromolecular level. Through selection, amplification, and mutation, large populations of related biological molecules can be directed to evolve toward a particular goal. For example, a chemist interested in producing a new drug might want to produce a molecule that will bind to a specific toxin. First, a variety of molecules are introduced to the toxin. The ones that bind are saved; the ones that do not are discarded. In another example, molecules that inhibit the clot-forming protein, thrombin, are evolving in researchers' labs. Scientists began with billions of different single-stranded, genetically engineered DNA molecules. Some bound strongly to thrombin, some bound a little, and some did not bind. Through repeated rounds of amplification, and washing away of unwanted DNA, the best DNA evolved. This type of manufactured evolution may eventually lead to industrial applications and new, helpful drugs.

PROGRAM RESOURCES

Teacher Classroom Resources
Study Guide, p. 73 L1
Exploring Environmental Issues, pp. 31-32 L3
Probing Levels of Life, Lab 25, p. 70 L2
Investigating Living Systems, Labs 29-31, pp. 113-119 L2

INVESTIGATION

Variation in Numbers of Stomata

Time Allotment
2 class periods separated by 1 week

Objectives
Upon completing this investigation, students will be able to:
- Analyze the variation in numbers of stomata on leaves of local trees.
- Identify factors that may determine variation in numbers of stomata on leaves of the same species.

Skills
form a hypothesis, design an experiment, measure in SI, recognize cause and effect, interpret data, make graphs, work cooperatively in groups

Materials
- For each group, provide one slide and a microscope. Students can provide leaves, clear nail polish, clear tape, and a large book for pressing leaves. Provide a prepared slide of stomata.
- **Safety Precautions:** Make sure students can identify poisonous plants in your area.

Preparation
For your introductory demonstration, prepare a slide of leaf stomata in the following manner: Apply a band of clear nail polish to cover about 1/8 of the lower surface of a leaf of a common local tree. Choose a plant with smooth, not hairy or velvety, leaves. Apply the polish at the collection site. When the polish is dry, place the leaf in a phone book for a few days. Place a strip of transparent tape over the polish and lift off gently. Affix the tape to a microscope slide. A coverslip is not necessary.

Possible Hypotheses
Variation in numbers of stomata on leaves is determined by genetics, rainfall of a region, habitat type, and position on the plant. Alternative hypotheses might include: (a) Leaves of sugar maple trees on stream banks will have more stomata than maple trees in meadows. (b) Leaves of young red oaks have more stomata

By studying simple through complex organisms, biologists know that the eye began only as a group of light-sensitive cells. The ability to distinguish between light and dark was an advantage because it enabled organisms to avoid danger and exploit new food resources more efficiently than organisms without this adaptation. Later, over time, new variations arose that resulted in the formation of a simple lens providing a blurry image. Seeing even a blurred image is an advantage over seeing no image at all. Later changes led to a sharpening of focus, and, probably at the same time, still other changes permitted color vision. Can you see how each step along the way was due purely to chance appearances of variations? The structure becomes more adaptive and improves an animal's chances of survival and, therefore, the passing of its genes to offspring. The same process was involved in the evolution of each and every complex structure of plants and animals.

INVESTIGATION

Variation in Numbers of Stomata

Have you ever been outside early in the morning and found the grass wet with dew? Where does this water come from? You know it didn't rain the night before, yet the grass is wet as if it did. Some of this water condensed from the air as it touched cool surfaces. Some of the water came from inside the plant. Plants give off water through stomata, which are tiny openings in their leaves. In many plants, the majority of stomata are on the lower surface of the leaves. Each stoma is surrounded by two guard cells. When the plant has access to plenty of water, the guard cells are plump and swollen with water. In this condition, the stomata are open and water can escape from the plant. When the plant does not have enough water, the guard cells become limp and the stomata close. In this lab, you will try to determine how numbers of stomata vary within the same species of plant.

Problem
How do the numbers of stomata on leaves of plants of the same species vary?

Safety Precautions
Make sure you can identify and avoid poisonous plants in your area such as poison ivy and poison oak.

Hypothesis
After observing the prepared slide of stomata provided by your teacher, hypothesize how much variation you might expect in numbers of stomata on leaves of one kind of local tree or shrub. What might produce this variation?

Experimental Plan
1. As a group, make a list of possible ways you might test your hypothesis using the materials your teacher has made available.
2. Decide on a common local species of tree or shrub from

than leaves on old red oaks.

Possible Procedures
- Make sure that students in one group have collected leaves from the same species.
- Caution students to wait until their leaves dry before putting them in the book.
- Explain how to prepare slides of leaf stomata.
- Have students compare their data with those of other groups that used the same and different species and with those groups that used different criteria for collection.
- Student collections will reflect their hypotheses. There will be variations in the species

of leaves collected, the numbers collected, and how counts are made microscopically.

Teaching Strategies
- Explain how to count and average numbers of stomata in different fields of view. They should first locate stomata under low power, change to high power, and count all the stomata in their field of view. They will then move the slide to show a different portion of the leaf and count the stomata in this new field of view. Explain that an average can be taken of several fields of view of one leaf and another average of fields of

Types of Adaptations

If you think about it, any organism, as it presently exists, can be thought of as a bundle of adaptations. For example, the shape of a bear's teeth and face, the length of its fur, and the way it behaves are adaptations that interact to promote its fitness in the environment in which it lives. Although the many adaptations of an organism may work together, we can examine them individually and classify them by type.

Structural Adaptations   The most obvious adaptations are those involving structure or anatomy. Traits such as the structure of a bird's beak, the hoof of a horse, or the shape of a tooth are called **structural adaptations.** Many obvious structural adaptations in animals are for obtaining food. A woodpecker's tongue, for example, is narrow and very long. It can probe

view from several leaves of the same plant.

- **Enrichment:** Ask each group to observe prepared slides of stomata. Explain how guard cells function.
- **Discussion Question:** Ask students why variations exist in all species.

Data and Observations

Average number of stomata in different leaves

There are more stomata on leaves of maple trees near water than in a field.

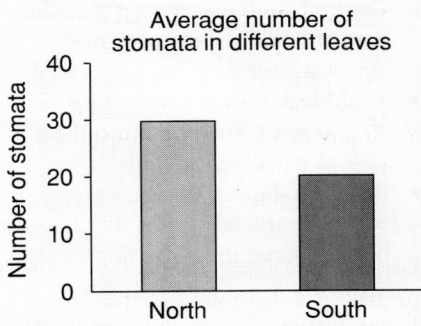

Average number of stomata in different leaves

There are more stomata on the north side of beech trees than on the south side of the trees.

Extensions

Ask students to suggest ways of expanding their work to investigate the effects of other habitat factors.

Data Analysis

1. Hypotheses may or may not have been supported depending on the climate, genetics, and habitat of the plants.
2. Conclusions will vary depending on the experimental design. Plants in wet climates and wet habitats will generally have more stomata than plants in dry climates and dry habitats.
3. Fewer stomata may be reflected by dry climates or dry habitats.

---

which to collect leaves. It should have leaves with smooth rather than fuzzy surfaces.
3. Make sure your collection procedures will provide uniform samples. To assure this, remember that a tree might have different numbers of stomata at different ages, in different habitats, at different heights, on different sides of the tree, and on different positions on the twig.
4. Agree on one idea from your group's list that could be investigated in the classroom.
5. Following the style of a recipe, write a numbered list of directions that anyone could follow.
6. Make a list of materials and the quantities you will need.

Checking the Plan

Discuss the following points with other group members to decide the final procedures for your experiment.
1. What variables will need to be controlled?
2. What is your control?

3. What will you count or measure?
4. How many leaves from how many trees will you examine?
5. Have you designed and made a table for collecting data?

Make sure your teacher has approved your experimental plan before you proceed further.

Data and Observations

Carry out your experiment, make your counts, and complete your data table. Make a graph of your results.

Analysis and Conclusions

1. Was your hypothesis supported by your data? Explain.
2. Write a brief conclusion for your experiment.
3. What is your experimental evidence for your conclusion in question 2?
4. What types of experimental error could have affected your results?
5. Compare your results with those of another group. Write a brief summary of this comparison.

6. What factors might affect the numbers of stomata on leaves of the plant species you studied?
7. If the climate in your area gradually became drier over the next ten years, how might the number of stomata on leaves be affected? Explain in terms of adaptation.

Going Further

Based on this lab experience, design an experiment that would help determine variation in numbers of stomata in houseplants. Assume that you will have unlimited resources and will not be conducting this lab in class.

Clear tape

Nail polish

13.1 ADAPTATION **339**

---

4. Plants may not have been the same age. Some leaves may have been collected from different heights, different habitats, or different positions on the stems.
5. Results will be different if different groups examined different species of plants, examined plants in different habitats, or examined plants of different ages.
6. climate, age of plant, genetics, collection height on the plant, direction leaf was facing, or different positions on the stem
7. Fewer stomata; plants with more stomata might lose too much water and die.

✔ **Assessment**

Skill: Ask students to design an experiment that will determine the effect of pollution on the functioning of stomata. Provide materials for them to conduct the experiment and have them write up and place their conclusions in their portfolios.

Minilab 1

Purpose
Students will determine the effect of solid shortening as insulation.

Skills
separate and control variables, make a model, compare and contrast, recognize cause and effect

Materials
Each group will need 3 test tubes, a plastic spoon, 40 g of shortening, 3 thermometers, 3 plastic bags, 1 large beaker, 3 rubber bands, ice, and a watch with a second hand.

Teaching Strategies
- Ask students what kinds of animals have blubber. Ask them in what way blubber is an adaptation to the animal's environment.
- Ask students to make a hypothesis and give reasons for their setup before they begin.
- Caution students to keep their fingers off the shortening to make cleanup easier.
- **Troubleshooting:** Shortening should not be emptied into the sink as it will clog drains.
- Provide a bucket of hot, soapy water for the test tubes that have been covered in shortening.

Expected Results
The uninsulated tube will cool to ice-water temperature in about five minutes; the one with a plastic bag will cool in about ten minutes; and the one with shortening in about 30 minutes—about six times as long.

Answers
The tube with no bag is the control; the tube with only the plastic bag is to test if the plastic bag alone offers insulation. The insulating effect is due to air trapped in the bag.

✔ Assessment
Portfolio: Ask students to design an experiment to determine how thick solid shortening on test tubes should be to achieve maximum insulation against ice water. Have students conduct this experiment and write their conclusions in their portfolios.

Minilab 1

Is blubber an adaptation?

Spoon 40 g of shortening into a plastic sandwich bag. Place a test tube filled with room-temperature water and a thermometer into this bag. Then place another test tube with room-temperature water and a thermometer into another plastic bag with no shortening. Fasten the bags close to the top of the test tubes with rubber bands. Working on the outside of the bag, gently spread the shortening evenly over the surface of the test tube. Place these two bagged test tubes and another unbagged test tube with the same contents into a beaker of ice water. Record the temperature of each tube as you begin, then every minute for 30 minutes.

Analysis *Compare the time needed for each tube of water to cool to the temperature of the ice water. What is the purpose of the tube with no insulation? The tube with only the plastic bag?*

---

small openings in trees that have been pecked away by the bird's sharp beak. Insect larvae living beneath the bark are picked out by the tongue and eaten by the woodpecker. An anteater's sticky tongue inserted into an anthill attracts ants as it moves. If the ants touch the tongue, they stick to it. When the anteater pulls its tongue in, the ants are easily trapped.

Structural adaptations for obtaining food do not always involve parts of the mouth. The adaptations of the angler fish provide a good example of this. Protruding from the top of the angler fish's skull is a long filament that is broad and flat at its tip. It hangs in front of the fish's mouth and attracts prey, much like a fishing lure. When the prey bites at the lure, the angler fish sucks the prey into its mouth. Some deepwater angler fish of the North Atlantic also have fins that are modified to glow in the dark waters. Prey are attracted by the glowing fins and so are easily trapped.

Of course, not all structural adaptations involve food-getting, and many are internal rather than external. For example, the strong muscular walls of your heart are an adaptation that enables it to pump blood throughout the body. Some single, microscopically thin nerve cells extending from your spinal cord to your leg are adapted to carry rapid nerve impulses.

Physiological and Behavioral Adaptations Other adaptations are associated with functions in organisms. The enzymes needed for digestion, clotting of blood, or muscular contractions in animals fall into this category, known as **physiological adaptations.** Such adaptations have a chemical basis. Other examples include the poison venom of a snake, the proteins used in a spider's web, and the ink of an octopus.

Organisms are also adapted in their responses to the environment. Birds migrate in search of food, squirrels hunt and store nuts, wolves track their prey, and plant stems grow toward the light. Such responses are examples of **behavioral adaptations.**

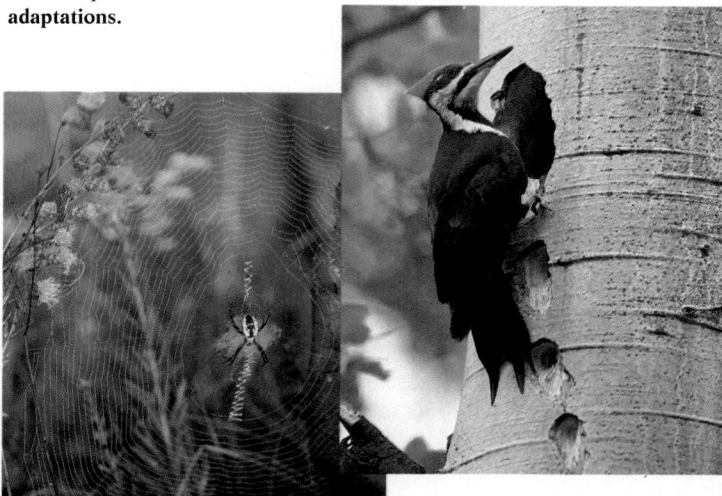

Figure 13-3 The spider's web (left) is the result of a physiological adaptation and enables the spider to catch its prey. The woodpecker's long tongue (right) is a structural adaptation for obtaining food.

340 ADAPTATION AND SPECIATION

STUDENT JOURNAL

Ask students what might happen if all the insects in the world were suddenly destroyed. Have them explain what might happen over the course of hundreds of years to the other organisms in your area if this were to happen. They should give explanations in terms of evolution of adaptations. L1

PORTFOLIO

Have students design a magazine cover for a special issue on adaptation and variation. The cover should illustrate all the concepts from this section of the chapter. L1

Figure 13-4 Many kinds of animals migrate. Some animals, including fish and birds such as these red-winged blackbirds, migrate to find food and a less severe climate. Some animals migrate to breed. The longest journey by any migratory animal is traveled by the Arctic tern, which flies more than 35 000 miles each year.

Interactions of Adaptations Isolating and classifying adaptations is really an artificial process, because in nature, adaptations often depend upon each other. For example, the migration of birds can be classified as a behavioral adaptation. These regular, seasonal, and mass movements of birds could not occur without a set of structural adaptations such as feathers, lightweight bones, and strong flight muscles. The migration also requires the interplay of many physiological adaptations—nerves that signal the muscles, the ability of the muscles to contract, and cellular respiration to provide the ATP energy needed. Before the actual migration even begins, other physiological adaptations, such as the release of chemicals from sex glands before a spring migration, must signal the birds that the time for migration is approaching.

Section Review

Understanding Concepts

1. The thorns on a rosebush protect the plant from animals that might eat it. What type of adaptation are thorns?
2. Name two human adaptations not described in this section. Describe how each is adaptive for humans.
3. In a population of brown-colored insects, an occasional variation of body color is yellow. List the stages in the evolution of a population of yellow-colored insects following a change in the environment to more desertlike conditions.
4. *Skill Review—Classifying:* Classify each of the following adaptations as either behavioral, structural, or physiological: (a) bees build a hive; (b) a young duckling follows its mother; (c) a wood-pecker's beak is pointed and sharp; (d) use of ATP; (e) photosynthesis; (f) the flat shape of a leaf. For more help, see Organizing Information in the **Skill Handbook**.
5. *Thinking Critically:* What might happen to plants that are pollinated by flies if insecticides are constantly used in their community?

13.1 ADAPTATION 🐾 **341**

Answers to Section Review

1. structural
2. Answers can include externally visible structural adaptations, internal structures, and physiological adaptations.
3. Originally, yellow insects were less likely to survive; brown insects were naturally selected because they were hidden against their background. As the environment began to change, yellow insects had an advantage. They tended to live longer and leave more offspring than the brown insects. Over time, the population came to consist of more yellow insects.
4. **Skill Review—Classifying:** (a) behavioral; (b) behavioral; (c) structural; (d) physiological; (e) physiological; (f) structural
5. **Thinking Critically:** A decrease in the population size of the flies would probably lead to a decrease in the plant population because fertilization would be reduced.

3 Assess

Check for Understanding

Tell students that DDT is an insecticide first introduced in the early 1940s. In ten years, resistant strains of insects were reported everywhere in the world. It was banned in the United States in 1973. Ask students to explain, in terms of adaptation and evolution, how resistance to an insecticide might develop. L1

Reteach

Give each student group a culture dish of wild birdseed mixed with sunflower seeds and cornmeal. Give each student a different kitchen utensil or tool, for example tweezers, a tea strainer with large holes, tongs, or a teaspoon to represent a bird's beak. Tell students to take turns "eating" seeds with their "beaks." Ask students to explain in terms of adaptation how their "beaks" are adapted to "eating" certain foods. LEP
COOP LEARN

Extension

Give students a number of different mammal skulls or skeletons. Ask them to distinguish the adaptations they find and infer what each animal's lifestyle might have been. L3
COOP LEARN

✔ Assessment

Portfolio: Ask students to study the variation of a local species. They might examine cone size of a species of gymnosperm, length of dandelion stems, or mass of seed pods. Students should make graphs of their data and explain the importance of the variations they find. L1

4 Close

Demonstration

Bring in a large number of broad leaves from one species of tree and needles from another species. Ask students to use the leaves to demonstrate their understanding of variation and adaptation. L1 LEP

SECTION 13.2

Prepare

Key Concepts

Students will study how species originate and evolve. They will distinguish between geographic isolation, reproductive isolation, genetic drift, polyploidy, and adaptive radiation and how each contributes to evolution. Other evolutionary trends brought about by convergence, hiding from predators, and close association will also be considered.

Key Terms

species, geographic isolation, speciation, divergent evolution, reproductive isolation, genetic drift, adaptive radiation, convergent evolution, gradualism, punctuated equilibrium

Materials

For Minilab 2, use a hole puncher to make 100 white and 100 black dots for each group.

1 Focus

Objectives

The objectives are listed on the student page. Remind students to preview these objectives as a guide to this numbered section.

Activity

Give each group two different species of tropical fish in a small bowl. Make sure they are very different from each other in a variety of ways. Ask students to make a list of the differences between the two fish. Ask them how these differences might reflect differences in the lifestyles of these fish.

 L1 **LEP**

Objectives

Contrast various ways in which speciation may occur.

Compare gradualism and punctuated equilibrium.

Determine the survival value of mimicry and camouflage.

Figure 13-5 The spotted horsemint is just one species of plant in the mint family. It is, clearly, a distinct organism from a turtle. But, can you be sure that the four turtles shown here are separate species? They are all classified in the same genus.

Spotted horsemint

13.2 Origins of Species

If the flowers in a population of horsemints become more brightly colored over time, are the plants still the same kind of plant? If the necks in a population of turtles get longer over time, are the animals still the same species? You have seen that new adaptations arise as a result of the process of natural selection. A species can include a broad range of variations. But how do plants, animals, or any other species evolve in the first place? How do new forms of life evolve? Can the evolution of new species be explained by natural selection?

Defining a Species

Horsemints are one kind of organism. Turtles are another. It's easy to distinguish between these two organisms because of some very obvious physical differences. However, if you compared a wood turtle, a spotted turtle, a bog turtle, and a western pond turtle, the differences are not so obvious. Each of these kinds of turtle is a separate species. It is easy to say that a plant and an animal are not the same species. It is easy to distinguish a cat from a turtle. But, when you study the four turtles shown in Figure 13-5, the differences are not as striking as the similarities. Now consider a golden retriever and an Irish setter. You will recognize these dogs as different, but would you call them separate species? Actually, both dogs are in the same species. But why are they considered the same species when they have such obvious differences?

Biological Species Early biologists working on the classification of organisms faced a similar dilemma. Organisms could be assigned to different species on the basis of physical features alone. Organisms are today more often classified according to a biological species concept. According to this concept, a **species** is a group of organisms that can interbreed and produce fertile offspring in nature. A species is the expression of all the genes in every population of that species. There is a gene pool for each species. Because mating between different species is rare, genes seldom pass from one gene pool to another.

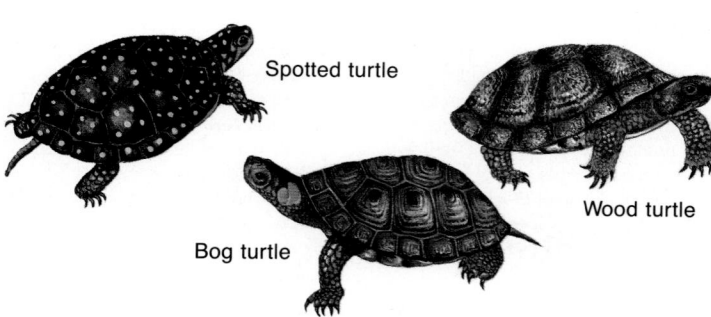

Spotted turtle

Wood turtle

Bog turtle

Western pond turtle

342 ADAPTATION AND SPECIATION

Some species have been seen to interbreed, but they rarely produce fertile offspring. A well-known example is in the breeding of a female horse and a male donkey to produce a mule. Horses and donkeys are separate species, but mules are sterile, and therefore unable to mate with other mules to produce more mules. Therefore, according to our biological species definition, horses and donkeys are distinct species. Another exception to the biological species concept is when a lion and a tiger are brought together in captivity to produce a liger (or tiglon). From the many similarities shared by lions and tigers, it is clear that they are related. However, in the wild, lions and tigers do not live together and are separated by thousands of miles. As you know, tiglons are not found in the wild, and lions and tigers are recognized as separate species.

When Darwin visited the Galapagos islands, he discovered a group of birds that have since come to be known as Darwin's finches. Darwin recognized 14 species divided among four genera of finches on the islands. The Galapagos finches differ mainly in their feeding behaviors, beak structures, and body sizes. Biologists have shown that the beaks are structural adaptations for the different foods they eat. For example, the three species of ground-living, seed-eating finches all have rather short and strong beaks useful in breaking the hard shells of seeds. On the other hand, the insect-eating finches have pointed beaks used for probing into holes in trees or flowers. There is also a very unusual finch with a stout beak that is used to grasp twigs or cactus thorns for use as a tool to probe into the insect's burrow until it emerges.

Because the different species of Galapagos finches share so many features, Darwin concluded that they must have had a common ancestor. Since the birds had many similarities with a species of finch commonly found on the South American mainland, he argued that the ancestor of the island finches came from the mainland group.

Figure 13-6 The beaks of Darwin's finches can be compared to different types of tools. Each tool, or beak, is adapted to dealing with a different job.

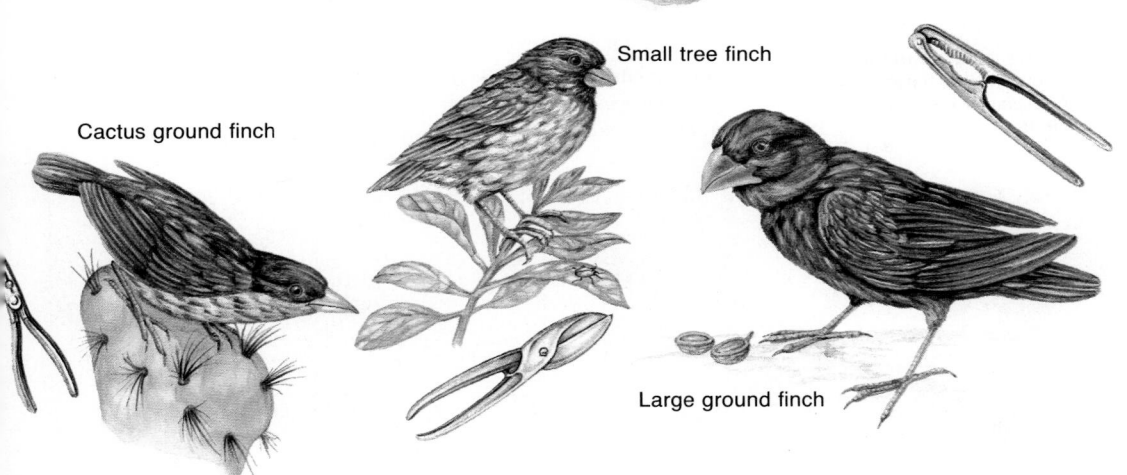

Woodpecker finch

Small tree finch

Cactus ground finch

Large ground finch

13.2 ORIGINS OF SPECIES **343**

MEETING INDIVIDUAL NEEDS

Ask gifted students to evaluate data using correlations, Chi-square, or other statistical procedures. L3

SECTION 13.2

2 Teach

LITERATURE CONNECTION

A Bee Metaphor: Use the cooperative learning strategy *acknowledging contributions* to carry out the following activity. Ask students to read the poem *The Bee* by Emily Dickinson. You can find it in an anthology of poetry in the school library. You will need to tell students that a chrysoprase is a light green gemstone. Ask them to write a list of all the things the bee is compared to in the poem. Have them make another list of the bee's body part to which the comparison applies. Finally, they should explain in a third list how the comparison reflects the lifestyle of the bee. L1 COOP LEARN

Concept Development

Darwin's finches belong to three groups distinguished by the ways they feed and types of food they eat. The ground finches feed on seeds of various sizes. The tree finches are insect and fruit eaters. The warbler finch makes up the third group. It has a slender beak suited to searching over leaves and branches for insects. Because the warbler finch is so different from other Galapagos finches, scientists have questioned whether it is related to the others. Some scientists think that its ancestor is related to a bird common to Latin America and South America.

Enrichment

Have students examine the variation in the number of spurs on grasshopper legs. Ask them to hypothesize how the spurs function. Ask them to design an experiment that would test their hypothesis. If they think that the spurs assist their jumping, they might test that by having them jump on a smooth, oiled surface and also on one not oiled. L1 COOP LEARN

SECTION 13.2

Concept Development

You may wish to introduce the term *ecological niche* at this time. As individual organisms arrived at the sterile conditions of a newly formed volcanic island, such as the Galapagos Islands, there must have been available many empty niches to which they could become adapted with very little competition.

Different Viewpoints in Biology

Are tropical species old or new?

Traditional views propose that the huge diversity in the tropics is the result of organisms originating in this warm climate. This is the evolutionary cradle hypothesis. Another view recently considered is that species evolved elsewhere and later moved to the tropics. This is the evolutionary museum hypothesis. In a new study, scientists found that of the 26 orders known by well-preserved fossils, the number originating in the tropics is about equal to the number originating elsewhere. This would indicate that the tropics may not be different from other regions in species' origins. However, because the collection of fossils, in the past, has been mainly from temperate regions, it is possible that the tropical species have been underestimated. There is obviously more room for further research before the cradle of evolution is determined.

Figure 13-7 **The Abert squirrel (top), of the southern rim of the Grand Canyon, and the Kaibab squirrel (bottom), of the northern rim, are two distinct species that probably evolved from a common ancestor as a result of geographic isolation.**

Figure 13-8 **Speciation of the Galapagos island finches occurred by geographic isolation and natural selection.**

Evolution of Species

What starts the evolution of an ancestral species into new species? Often, the evolution begins with a geological change that isolates one part of a population from another.

Geographic Isolation When a river, canyon, or mountain is formed, the populations of plants and animals in the region can often be split apart. This type of separation results in what is known as **geographic isolation.** Because the gene pools of the newly separated groups are isolated, individual organisms of the two groups cannot interbreed. If the new environments have differing conditions, different variations may become naturally selected, and the gene pools of the two new populations gradually become distinct. Mutations arise randomly in each population, genes are recombined in different ways, and as time passes, each isolated group will evolve different traits in response to its own environment. The evolution of the lion and the tiger may have occurred in this way. If the groups remain isolated, they might eventually reach a point where they can no longer interbreed, even when the geographic barrier is removed. They are now separate species only because their gene pools are isolated. Evolution of a new species is called **speciation.**

This sequence of events has been applied to the explanation of the evolution of the Galapagos finches. Somehow, possibly by being blown off course during a tropical storm, some ancestral finches got to the islands. Unable to return because of great isolation from the mainland, the finches became permanently separated from others of their own species. Because the two environments were different, the island birds evolved differently from their mainland relatives. Geographic isolation also exists between each island and between birds on different parts of each island. As a result, many gene pools evolved independently of one another, producing the 14 species of finches existing today in addition to the more common mainland finch. When one species evolves into two or more species with different characteristics, this process is called **divergent evolution.**

Reproductive Isolation Perhaps the greatest factor in the evolution of the Galapagos finches was that the gene pools of the 14 groups were geographically isolated, preventing interbreeding. As the gene pools became

344 ADAPTATION AND SPECIATION

PROGRAM RESOURCES

Teacher Classroom Resources
Study Guide, pp. 74-75 `L1`
Concept Mapping, p. 13 `L1` `LEP`
Probing Levels of Life, Lab 26, p. 73 `L2`
Critical Thinking/Problem Solving, p. 13 `L2`

more and more different by chance mutations, a number of other factors prevented interbreeding among the finches. The present 14 species of finches have different mating habits, and mating occurs at different times of the year.

When there is no interbreeding, and gene exchange among species is prevented, a condition known as **reproductive isolation** exists. In some cases, sperm of one species cannot fertilize eggs of another species. Even if eggs are fertilized, gene and chromosome differences between the species are so great that they almost always prevent normal development of an embryo. Those offspring that do develop, however, are often sterile.

Genetic Drift Another driving force in speciation can arise following geographic isolation. Imagine a large population of leafhoppers that lives throughout a forest on a remote island somewhere in the Pacific Ocean. One day, a local volcano erupts and hot lava covers all but small and remote portions of forest where some leafhoppers survive. The genetic variation in the individual leafhoppers' gene pools, and therefore the range of variations, will have been drastically reduced. In small populations, the chances are high that some alleles will be lost. For example, there is a greater chance that predators will completely remove one kind of phenotype from the population if it has only a few individuals. It is a matter of chance which alleles are lost to the population. They may not have any adaptive value. However, if the alleles control variations that are adaptive, the species may become endangered, Figure 13-9.

Rapid changes in the numbers and kinds of genes in a small, isolated population are known as **genetic drift.** Such random changes in gene pools may lead to the evolution of new species—populations of distinct organisms that are reproductively, isolated.

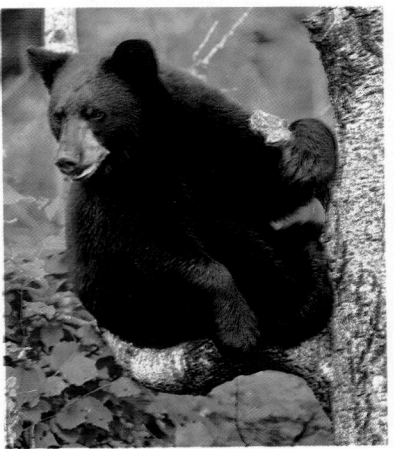

Figure 13-9 The range of *Ursus americanus*, the American black bear, once spanned across the whole of the United States. It is now listed as threatened or endangered in the few states where it can still be found.

Thinking Lab
MAKE A HYPOTHESIS

Why are finches that survive drought larger with bigger beaks?

Background
One of the Galapagos islands is inhabited by a ground finch that eats seeds. Normally, ground finches feed on a variety of grass and herb seeds that are small. Sometimes, as the supply of grass seeds is used up, the finches will feed on larger seeds of larger plants. Occasionally, drought hits the island and grasses and herbs disappear. The ground finches that survive are larger and have bigger beaks than the ones that do not survive.

You Try It
Make a hypothesis about why surviving ground finches are larger and have bigger beaks than the ones that die during years of drought. Make a complete title and caption for the graph shown here. Explain, based on the graph, what is happening to beak size of ground finches. Why?

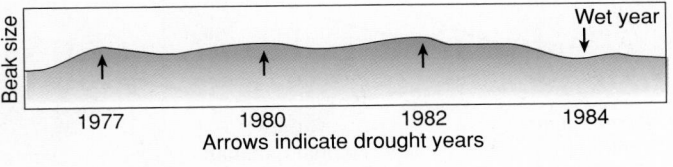

Beak size

Wet year

1977 1980 1982 1984
Arrows indicate drought years

13.2 ORIGINS OF SPECIES **345**

Thinking Lab
MAKE A HYPOTHESIS

Purpose
Students will hypothesize why the frequency of a trait would increase.

Skills
form a hypothesis, interpret data

Teaching Strategies
• Be sure students understand that the variation of larger beak size already exists in the population.

Further Background
Rapid evolution can also be seen in an increase in tolerance of some species of grasses to high concentrations of lead.

Answers
One hypothesis might be that only birds with larger beaks could eat large seeds. Possible title: Beak Size of Galapagos Finches in Response to Drought Years.

Caption: Following a drought, beak size of surviving Galapagos finches is larger than average. Explanation: The selective pressure of drought allows only the birds with larger beaks to survive.

✔ Assessment
Oral: Ask students to make a hypothesis about what might be causing an increase in tuberculosis.

Bioethics

Loss of Biodiversity: Ask students what part of the world first comes to mind when loss of biological diversity is considered. Most likely they will say "tropical rain forests." Many programs to save the rain forest have had much publicity; however, marine systems are in similar, if not worse, trouble. Biological diversity of the oceans is declining. Technology such as satellite imaging and computer modeling is currently available and can be used for studying biodiversity of the oceans.

Concept Development
Discuss the idea that our view of the world is like a snapshot of one moment in time. Earth has changed in the past and will continue to change in the future. Changes will result in new life forms and more extinctions. An animal such as a cheetah that is well adapted today is not assured that it will exist in the future, as we have learned from the example of the dinosaurs.

SECTION 13.2

Concept Development

An autopolyploid occurs when a single species doubles its chromosome number. These tetraploids fertilize themselves or can be fertilized by other tetraploids within the population. These mutants cannot mate with the regular, diploid members of the population and are separated from them by reproductive isolation, forming the start of a new species. Allopolyploids occur when two different species combine their chromosomes. An example is a cross between radish and cabbage. These hybrids are usually sterile but often more hardy than either parent and may reproduce asexually to form a new species. Sometimes these allopolyploids double up their chromosomes by autopolyploidy, and then a few seeds could be formed. These unusual hybrids are often giant sized and completely fertile. It is clear that speciation by polyploidy has been important in plant evolution from the fact that 25 to 50 percent of all plants are polyploids.

Although geographic isolation plays an important role in most cases of speciation, it is not the only factor that leads to the origin of a new species. A new species may evolve in the same geographic area as the ancestral species as a result of changes in chromosome number. This kind of speciation is far more common in plants than in animals.

Speciation by Polyploidy How can changes in chromosome number lead to the evolution of new species? As you learned in Chapter 8, a set sequence of events must occur during meiosis for organisms to reproduce successfully. What would happen in a diploid (2n) plant if, during meiosis, the pairs of homologous chromosomes did not separate at the first division? The gametes produced would each have two sets of chromosomes. The gametes would not be haploid (n), but diploid (2n).

As you may have guessed, if two diploid (2n) gametes were to fuse in fertilization, the offspring would then have four of each kind of chromosome. In other words, they would not be the usual diploid (2n) plants. They would be tetraploid (4n). These offspring, if they survived, would be able to undergo a normal meiosis because each pair of homologous chromosomes would line up as usual on a spindle fiber. One chromosome of each pair would be pulled to each pole in the first division, as shown in Figure 13-10. The second division would proceed normally, and gametes produced would be diploid (2n). At fertilization, the diploid gametes would unite to produce tetraploid (4n) offspring.

When organisms contain some multiple of the normal number of chromosomes, they are called polyploid organisms. Tetraploid (4n) plants are often bigger and produce larger flowers and fruits than their diploid (2n) ancestors. Suppose that a tetraploid plant was fertilized by one of its diploid parent plants. Not all chromosomes would have a partner when gametes are formed by meiosis in this hybrid offspring plant. There is, therefore, reproductive isolation between the two kinds of plants. They behave as separate species. Many important crops, such as wheat, cotton, and apples, and beautiful garden flowers, such as chrysanthemums and daylilies, have been developed by breeders who can engineer the doubling up of chromosomes and hybridize the resulting polyploids.

Figure 13-10 **Follow the stages of speciation by polyploidy. Many cultivated garden flowers, such as the chrysanthemum (inset), have been developed by selecting and hybridizing polyploid individuals.**

ALTERNATE LAB: Winter Survival

Purpose
Students will discover the kinds of adaptations useful for a small herbivore.

Materials
elbow macaroni, plastic flag-marker tape, a meter stick, one sandwich bag per pair, a watch with a second hand

Procedure
Give the following directions to students.

1. Work in pairs. Each pair will count out 100 pieces of macaroni into a plastic bag.
2. In an outside grassy area, mark off an area 3 m × 3 m.
3. One partner will scatter 100 pieces of macaroni over the marked-off area.
4. The other partner will be a mouse foraging for food in the winter. The only food available is in the marked area.

5. Find five pieces of macaroni while your partner times you. This time will be equal to one winter day. Five pieces of food is the amount needed for survival for one day.
6. Time how long it takes the mouse to find food for each of 12 days, meaning 12 trials. Do not let the mouse take more than five pieces in one day.
7. Record the data in a table and note the

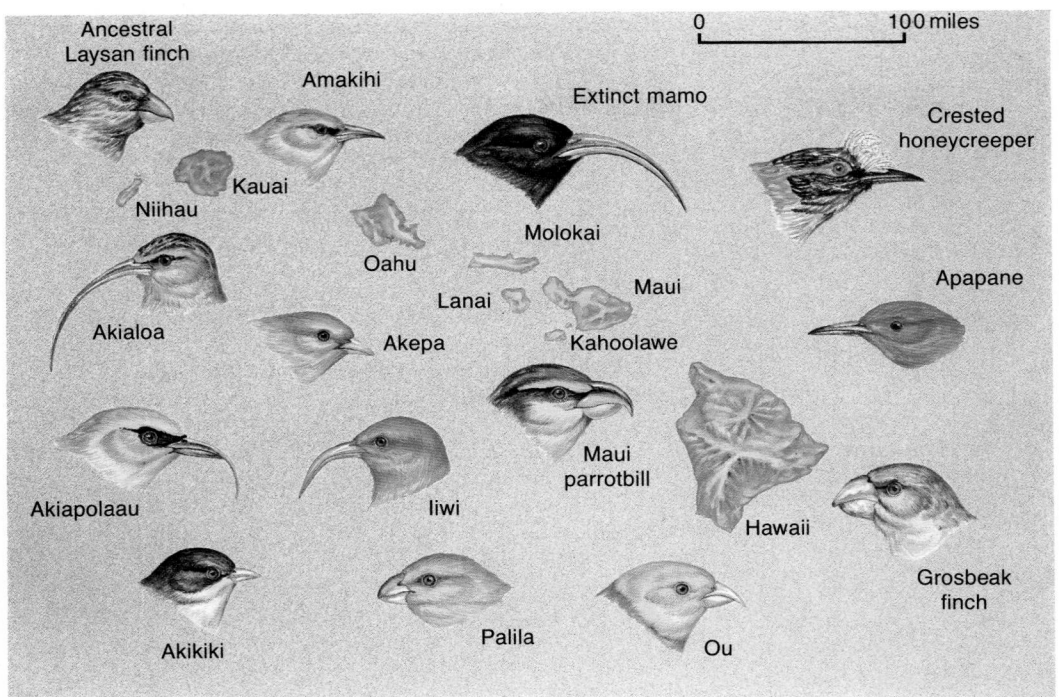

Concept Development

Just as Darwin's finches evolved into many new species, the fruit fly, *Drosophila*, on the Hawaiian Islands has evolved into a huge number of species. There are more than 1250 species of *Drosophila* found in the world, over 400 of them found only on the Hawaiian Islands, with more species still being discovered. The opportunities for the ancestral *Drosophila* must have been similar to the opportunities found by the finches: many empty niches. Today, Hawaiian *Drosophila* species are highly adapted to host plants for larval development and food.

Figure Caption Question

For what kinds of foods do you think each beak is adapted? Large, strong beaks are adapted for breaking open large, woody seeds; long, pointed beaks are adapted for reaching into crevices of bark for insects; short beaks are adapted for small seeds and flying insects.

Adaptive Radiation   As you learned earlier, Darwin's finches evolved into many new species within different environments of the Galapagos islands from one kind of ancestor. This pattern of divergent evolution is common among populations on isolated islands, such as the Galapagos and Hawaiian islands. How did the ancestors of all island species get there in the first place? Biologists have suggested that a small population of birds, seeds, or other organisms may have been blown off course onto isolated islands or other remote places during heavy storms. If the new environment were not too different from that of the original habitat, and the competition for food and space from other island populations were not too severe, the organisms would have had a high chance of survival.

The Hawaiian islands, like the Galapagos, have an extraordinary wealth of rare species of plants and animals not found anywhere else on Earth. Similar to the broad array of species of Darwin's finches, there have existed in Hawaii 22 species of Hawaiian honeycreepers—beautiful birds that feed on nectar, seeds, and insects. Nine of the 22 species have become extinct over the last 200 years. The plumage of the Hawaiian honeycreepers displays colors of plain greens and greys to bright reds, yellows, and black, Figure 13-11. The ancestor of all the honeycreepers in Hawaii probably crossed the 2000 miles of Pacific ocean from the American mainland some 5 million years ago.

Figure 13-11   **If Darwin had landed on the Hawaiian islands, he would have observed a similar, though more dramatic, example of adaptive radiation in the honeycreepers as the example he found in his finches. For what kinds of foods do you think each beak is adapted?**

---

day that the mouse died. This will be the day that it does not get all five pieces of food in one day.
8. Compare data from other class partners.

Analysis

Ask students to answer the following questions.
1. When did most of the mice die? Explain. *Most mice died near the end of the winter when food was scarce.*

2. What adaptations did the mice have that gathered the most food in the least time? *They might have had more physical strength, been larger, faster, or smarter.*
3. How do you think your results would compare with results of real mice in the wild? *Answers will vary. Mice in the field would have to compete with each other and with other animals for available food.*

✔ **Assessment**

Performance: Have students design another similar experiment in which the animal surviving the winter is a predator, such as a weasel, and the prey, which are mice, try to escape the predator. Run the experiment. Ask students to gather data, make graphs, and write their conclusions in their portfolios. **L1**

Minilab 2

Purpose
Students will examine the effects of protective coloration on survival of a population.

Skills
make a model, interpret data, recognize cause and effect

Materials
black and white paper, forceps, paper lunch bags, tally cards

Teaching Strategies
- Spread 100 white dots and 100 black dots of punched paper over a sheet of black paper.
- Tell students that the time it takes to place the paper insect in the bag and mark the tally card is the simulated eating time. Remind students that they cannot pick up more than one paper insect at a time. You may wish to have a group of students pool their results, or have the class put results on the chalkboard before answering questions. Ask students what might happen if the environment changed color.

Answers
Predators eat insects that are a different color from the color of the background. The ones that were the same color as the background were camouflaged. The camouflaged insects would survive and reproduce more of their own kind. The insects with colors that stand out the most would be eaten and not reproduce.

✔ Assessment
Skill: Ask students to design an experiment in which they determine the effect of protective coloration on a population of worms. Provide them with yarn pieces of a variety of colors. Tell them that the pieces of yarn represent the worm population.

Figure Caption Question
Which of these two animals needs air to breathe? dolphins

Minilab 2

How do adaptations aid survival?

Some insects are better adapted than others for survival. Imagine you are a bird predator of insects. Your insects are colored either white or black. Use a paper hole punch to punch 100 dots from a sheet of white paper. Repeat with a sheet of black paper. These dots will represent white and black insects. Place both white and black insects on a black sheet of paper. Work in pairs and see how many insects of each color your partner can collect in two minutes.

Analysis *How does color affect the survival rate of an insect? What might happen over time to a similar insect population in the wild?*

The islands of Hawaii, the Galapagos, and many other island groups around the world provide large numbers of distinct and separate habitats. When a population of immigrants increased, split up, and radiated out into separate habitats, new species evolved. Each species became adapted to a particular role in the new habitat. Similar to Darwin's finches, the Hawaiian honeycreepers have many roles. They display a broad variation in bill shape, feeding behavior, and body size. For example, one species has a straight bill like that of a woodpecker. There are no woodpeckers in the Hawaiian islands. The role of a woodpecker has been filled by this species of honeycreeper.

The divergent evolution and adaptation of species to different roles in new habitats is called **adaptive radiation**. For adaptive radiation to occur, three conditions must be met.
(1) The ancestral form must reach the new environment.
(2) The ancestral form must have some basic adaptations suited to the new habitat.
(3) The new environment must be free from competition with similar, better, or equally adapted species.

Darwin's finches, Hawaiian honeycreepers, and a vast array of other island plants and animals have met these conditions and have successfully evolved by adaptive radiation.

Other Patterns of Evolution

Most often, evolution results in new species that are different from one another as described in divergent evolution. Sometimes, though, convergent evolution occurs. **Convergent evolution** is a process in which species that are not closely related evolve similar traits. Convergent evolution usually occurs in unrelated species that have similar roles and live in similar environments.

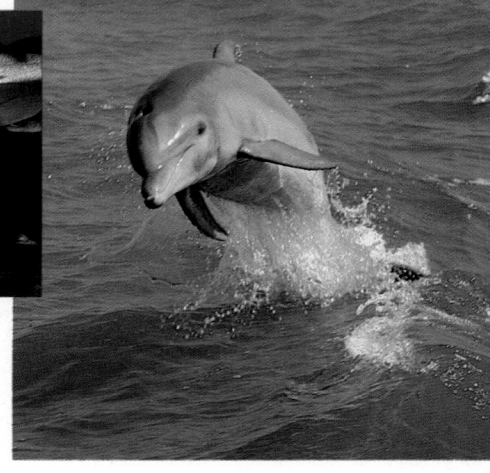

Figure 13-12 Although dolphins (right) have the same streamlined body shape as many kinds of fishes (left), their body structures are homologous with those of other mammals, not with fishes. Which of these two animals needs air to breathe?

348 🐾 ADAPTATION AND SPECIATION

PORTFOLIO

To one group of students, give a variety of seeds from one family of plants such as the mustard family (Brassicaceae). To another group, give a variety of seeds from the cereal plants (family Poaceae); to another, give seeds from another family such as the legumes (family Fabaceae). Ask students to put them in petri dishes with wet paper towel circles cut to fit the bottom of the dish. Over the course of a week, ask students to note germination times, appearance, shape, and size of the first leaves in each plant family. Develop the idea that these plants share a gene pool from a common ancestor in each family group. Students should write data in tables and compare and explain class data in their portfolios. **L2** **COOP LEARN**

Similar But Not Related Examples of convergent evolution are easy to spot. Think about fish and dolphins. The ancestor of all fish was a simple marine organism. Dolphins, though, are descendants of land mammals. Fish and dolphins, then, are not at all closely related. How are fish and dolphins similar? Both have a streamlined shape for swimming. Fish have fins, but the finlike structures of dolphins are not homologous; they are really modified limbs. The similarities between fish and dolphins can be explained in terms of their environment. Both organisms evolved in water. In the two groups, natural selection favored variations suited for an aquatic environment. But the two groups did not undergo convergent evolution in all their traits. For example, fish have gills, but dolphins have lungs. Each type of animal can live in water with these organs, but dolphins must come to the surface for oxygen. Can you think of other differences between these sea animals?

Figure 13-13 The honeybee is a valuable insect pollinator. Many popular fruits, such as apples and oranges, would not develop without them. What kinds of flowers might be pollinated by butterflies?

Hiding from Predators As you know, in the world of nature, the rule is survival. If one animal is a tasty meal for another larger and stronger animal, then the only way it will survive is if it can hide. The ability to hide from predators is a well-known adaptation observed among animals. One seemingly clever strategy in animals is to deceive.

The process of natural selection has provided many animals with structural or behavioral adaptations that copy or mimic their surroundings to avoid detection. Look back at the chapter opener. The fish disguised by nature rests among the seaweed, unnoticed by hungry predators that pass by. The insect that looks like a leaf will have a good chance of surviving when a passing bird stops to rest for a midday meal. The animal that looks like its surroundings or like something a predator would avoid is preserved by natural selection.

Evolving Together Populations of organisms do not evolve isolated from one another. Rather, as you know, different organisms live together within communities and interact in many ways. Often, these interactions involve complex relationships and affect the evolutionary history of the organisms. Are you familiar with flowering plants that are pollinated by insects, bats, or birds? Plants benefit by having pollen transferred from one flower to another, thus increasing the chances for successful reproduction. The pollinators benefit by obtaining nectar or pollen for food. Over time, this interaction has led to some interesting, mutual adaptations in many plant and animal species.

13.2 ORIGINS OF SPECIES 🐝 **349**

Figure Caption Question
What kinds of flowers might be pollinated by butterflies? flowers with long, tubular petals such as daisies, catchflies, phlox, and milkweeds

Misconception
Stress that the environment doesn't cause changes in the traits of species. Variations exist within a species. When the environment changes, certain variations may be better suited to the new conditions. These types will survive and reproduce while others die out.

Science, Technology, and Society

Antifreeze Proteins: When the Antarctic ocean turned cold and icy, all but one group of fishes died out. The survivors, a group of perchlike teleosts, had evolved an adaptation to the extremely cold water temperatures. These fish have the ability to produce proteins with the properties of antifreeze—compounds that depress the freezing point of body fluids. However, these antifreeze compounds have little effect on the melting point of frozen blood. Antifreeze compounds commonly used in technology are ethylene glycol, sodium chloride, and other salts, which equally depress both freezing and melting points. Scientists are studying these naturally occurring antifreeze proteins to help them understand the way in which ice crystals grow. If we could prevent formation of ice crystals, maybe we could control ice formation in the atmosphere or in biological fluids held in long-term storage. The formation of ice crystals in fluids such as blood is biologically destructive.

Purpose
Students will discover the importance of myths in a culture.

Teaching Strategies
- Before students read the selection, ask them to recall the traditional childhood stories that were told to them by their families. Ask them why these tales continue to be told to one generation after another and if there are morals to any of these stories. Encourage students of different cultural backgrounds to share stories from their family traditions.
- Have students read myths about how the world and organisms came to be from a variety of cultures.

Possible Answers
1. Answers may include the following. The snowshoe hare is white in winter and brown in summer, allowing it to blend into its surroundings. The female mallard duck is a brownish color, as are the grasses in which she builds her nest.
2. A myth is a traditional story that explains a part of the world view of a group of people. A legend is a story that is passed down from one generation to another but is not verifiable. A fable is a fictitious narrative of supernatural happenings that often include animals that speak as humans. A parable is a fictitious narrative with a moral or religious statement. An allegory expresses truths about human conduct or experience using symbolic fictional figures, while a tale is an imaginative narrative.

The Tempo of Speciation

Up to this point, you have seen that sometimes speciation can occur rapidly over a few generations. But how long did it take for the enormous variety of organisms, from *amoeba* to human, or from alga to oak tree, to evolve? Biologists have proposed that the evolution of all existing species occurred over very long periods of time—millions of years—during which time small adaptive changes slowly built up in populations. That idea of slow and steady change in species is known as **gradualism**.

Other biologists have described evidence suggesting that some speciation occurs much more suddenly. They explain that species probably remain constant for long periods of time. However, a sudden change in environmental conditions—such as warmer temperatures or drought—will interrupt, or punctuate, the steady rate of evolution. New species become established and remain constant for millions of years or until new changes in the environment occur. This idea of slow evolution punctuated by short events of rapid evolution was given the name **punctuated equilibrium**. It is important to note that the term *rapid* must be thought of in terms of geological time—maybe as long as 100 000 years.

How the Crow Came to Be Black

According to Good White Buffalo of the Brule Sioux nation, crows were once white. They were also friends of the buffalo, and warned them when Native American hunters approached the herd, much to the resentment of plains Indians who depended on buffalo for food.

A young brave captured the leader of the crows and hurled him into the fire. The crow escaped, promising never to warn the buffalo again. He was singed black, and ever since, all crows have been black.

Folklore includes a variety of stories passed orally from person to person and generation to generation within a given culture. Many prescientific explanations for the origins and conditions of the world appear in folklore as myths.

The myths of a given culture center on what that culture considers important. "How the Crow Came to Be Black" illustrates the importance of buffalo to the plains tribes.

Biologists today know color has evolved through natural selection and species adaptation. In many species, color serves important survival functions. For example, Arctic foxes turn white in winter and can hide from predators against the snow.

Although evolution may provide us with many a tale of origins of weird and wonderful life forms, probably none would be as simple, or simplistic, as the myths and legends passed on from generation to generation in folk tales.

1. **Explore Further:** Give examples of species in which color aids an animal's survival.
2. **Connection to English:** Use your dictionary to distinguish among the meanings for myth, legend, fable, parable, allegory, and tale. Use your library to discover the Greek fables by Aesop that explain how other animals came to be.

350

Adapted Seeds: Tell students that they should design the ideal seed for a plant that lives in a very dry, windy place with a short growing season and a variety of animals that are seed eaters. First, they will have to do some library research to find out the kinds of seeds found in plants that live under these conditions. **L2**

Evidence of gradualism has been pointed out in the fossil record. For example, as you have read in Chapter 12, modern-day elephants can be traced back through mammoths to mastodons that lived more than 30 million years ago. This evidence clearly shows how some species have gradually changed over a long period of time. Other fossil evidence indicates that some species have

remained the same over long periods of time and then, quite suddenly in geological terms, they became extinct and new species appeared. Punctuated equilibrium would explain these patterns in the fossil record. For example, the fossil record indicates that about 570 million years ago, there was a sudden appearance of enormous numbers of multicellular invertebrates. Cambrian fossils seem to indicate that, before that time, only monerans and protists existed.

Discussions over the rate at which evolution occurs are ongoing among biologists. The major problem with interpreting the fossil record is that only hard parts of organisms are preserved. There may have been changes in the soft tissues of evolving species that obviously cannot be studied. The most likely explanation may be that some species have evolved gradually, while others evolved rapidly. It should not surprise you that scientists offer alternate hypotheses to explain observations. As you know, hypotheses are subject to change in light of new evidence and as biological research continues.

Figure 13-14 There are many more kinds of organisms now than there were 300 million years ago. Many of those ancient forms, such as the extinct arthropods called trilobites (left), show strong similarities to present-day forms, which, in this case, are the horseshoe crabs (right).

Section Review

Understanding Concepts
1. Why is geographic isolation necessary for most cases of speciation?
2. Does the idea of punctuated equilibrium mean that the theory of natural selection is incorrect? Explain.
3. Explain why it was not possible for Darwin to find animals such as wolves or cats on the Galapagos islands.

4. **Skill Review—Observing:** You discover two groups of butterflies living in fields not too far from one another. The butterflies are similar in appearance, but their markings are not identical. What clue would you need to determine whether they are members of the same or different species? For more help, see Practicing Scientific Methods in the **Skill Handbook**.

5. **Thinking Critically:** A population of spiders is divided by a river, and the two gene pools begin evolving differently over time so that each group of spiders has some unique adaptations. A drought causes the river to dry up before the two groups have become distinct species. Explain what may happen to the two groups.

Answers to Section Review

1. Geographic isolation prevents interbreeding among members of what was originally a single population. Thus, changes in the two gene pools are not shared. The two populations diverge and may eventually be recognized as distinct species.
2. According to the idea of punctuated equilibrium, speciation may occur rapidly as a result of a sudden change. Speciation can also occur gradually by natural selection.
3. Ancestors of such animals would not have had a natural means of reaching the islands.
4. **Skill Review—Observing:** If butterflies of the two populations interbreed and produce fertile offspring in nature, then they are members of the same species.
5. **Thinking Critically:** The two populations will doubtless interbreed and produce fertile offspring. The changes in their gene pools will gradually disappear.

3 Assess

Check for Understanding
Show students a picture of a white Himalayan rabbit with a black pigmented nose, paws, and tail. Explain to them that if you shave a patch of fur on its back and place an ice pack over the shaved fur spot on its back, the fur will grow in as black. Ask students how this example shows the interaction of genes and the environment. *The color of the fur is affected by temperature.* L1

Reteach
Ask students to examine a variety of seashells. Ask them to explain the difference between variation and adaptation for these shells. L1

Extension
Ask students to capture moths at night by attracting them with light. After putting the moths in the refrigerator to immobilize them, tell students to use a toothpick to uncoil the proboscis of a variety of moths. Caution students to handle the moths with care so they may later be released. They should examine variation of this trait. L3

✔ Assessment
Portfolio: Tell students that individuals of a species of a freshwater snail live longer and grow bigger when the population is hunted by crayfish. Snails preyed on by crayfish grew to 7 mm and lived for about three to five months. Snails living in streams with no crayfish grew to 4 mm and lived for 11 to 14 months. Ask students to explain why a population of snails being preyed upon by crayfish has larger snails. L1

4 Close

Demonstration
Provide students with toy models of animals. Ask students to describe the adaptations they see in their animals and how they may have evolved. L1

LEP   COOP LEARN

Prepare

Key Concepts

In this section, students will study primate adaptations, human origins, and the African origins of humans.

Materials

1 Focus

Objectives

The objectives are listed on the student page. Remind students to preview these objectives as a guide to this numbered section.

Demonstration

Cut open a pomegranate. For students who have not eaten this fruit, show them the individual compartments and the seeds enclosed in each one. Explain that having fingers and an opposable thumb is very useful for eating such a fruit. This demonstration could lead to the making of a list on the chalkboard of unique primate characteristics as students suggest them. L1

2 Teach

Writing About Biology

Ask students to go back in time to Africa and write, from the point of view of an ancient ancestor, about the events of his or her day. L1

Objectives

Describe the characteristics of primates.

Sequence the major trends in human evolution.

13.3 Human Evolution

Everyone's familiar with the behavior of humans. Humans plant crops and gather food. Humans breed animals to use for work, food, and protection, and humans play video games, work on computers, and build cities. Like all other forms of life, humans are products of evolution by natural selection. What evidence is there for the evolution of humans, and what adaptations have led us to the unique place we have on Earth today?

Primate Adaptations

To begin to answer the question of what makes humans unique, we must step back in time. Humans, like any other organism, can be grouped to show relationships. Humans are members of a group of mammals known as primates—animals that include lemurs, monkeys, chimpanzees, and gorillas. Humans and other primates share several traits.

One such trait is a relatively high level of problem-solving ability. Relative to body weight, primates have the largest brains of any mammals. This adaptation for large brain size has allowed primates to survive and compete in a variety of environments, such as tropical rain forests, dry savannahs, and cool, northern forests. All primates have flexible shoulders and forelimbs that can be rotated. These adaptations allow them to swing from branch to branch among the trees.

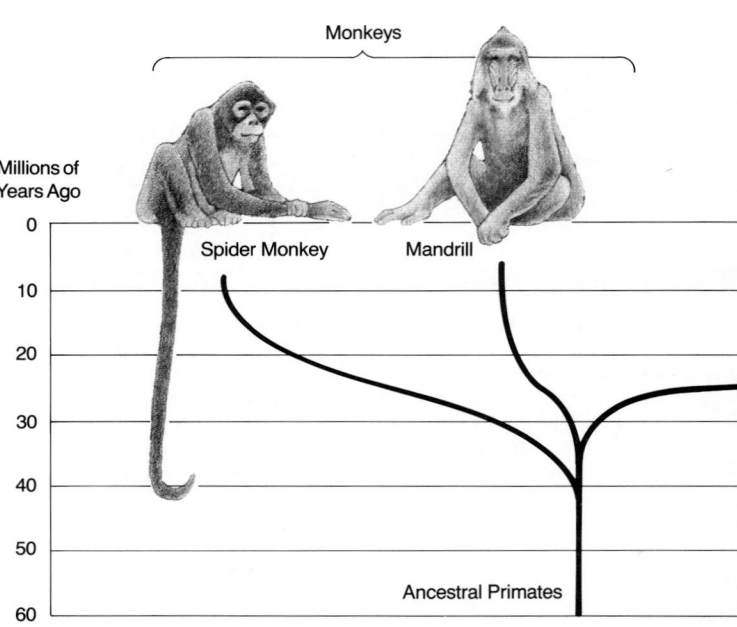

Figure 13-15 The ancestors of present-day primates probably evolved from primates such as the lemur (left photo). Primates share traits such as fingernails, four pairs of incisors (biting teeth), and opposable thumbs.

352 ⚜ ADAPTATION AND SPECIATION

STUDENT JOURNAL

Ask students to travel 2000 years into the future in a time machine. They should write in their journals a description of what humans look like. They should base this on the environmental changes that may occur in the future and also on the fact that natural selection will have limited humans to those adapted to the environment at that time. L1

MEETING INDIVIDUAL NEEDS

Visually Impaired: For students who are visually impaired, lab materials may be labeled with sandpaper lettering for ease in identification. Discussion during lab could be tape recorded so that the student could listen to it again at a later date. Ask other students in the group to read instructions aloud. LEP
COOP LEARN

Another unique adaptation among primates is the structure of the hand. Unlike non-primate mammals, which have paws with claws, primates have extremely flexible hands consisting of five independent digits with fingernails and toenails. Primate hands have an opposable thumb—one that touches the fingers of the same hand and can grasp objects. The overall flexibility of the primate hand allows it to be used as a structure of locomotion and to manipulate objects.

Large brains, opposable thumbs, and rotating forelimbs are just some of the adaptations common to all primates. Because these traits are shared by all primates, biologists agree that the traits were probably present in the earliest primate ancestors. As monkeys and then apes evolved, there were further modifications that added to the success of these primates in a variety of environments. Apes include gibbons, orangutans, gorillas, and chimpanzees. There are more characteristics shared among humans, chimpanzees, and gorillas than among any other primates (Figure 13-15).

African Origins

The story of human evolution begins approximately 8 million years ago in Africa. During this time, scientists propose, a population of ancestral apes diverged into two groups. One group would eventually evolve into the African apes—chimpanzees and gorillas. The other group, a population of small-bodied apes, would lead to modern humans. This group gained the ability to walk upright on two legs.

Gorilla

Human

Figure 13-16 **The ability to grasp objects between a thumb and the other digits is a characteristic common to all primates, and not unique to humans.**

SECTION 13.3

Misconception
- Many students think that hominids and dinosaurs existed at the same time.
- Some students will have the mistaken belief that all primates other than humans are more related to each other than to humans. Recent genetic studies have indicated that the chimpanzee and gorilla are more related to humans than to orangutans or other primates.

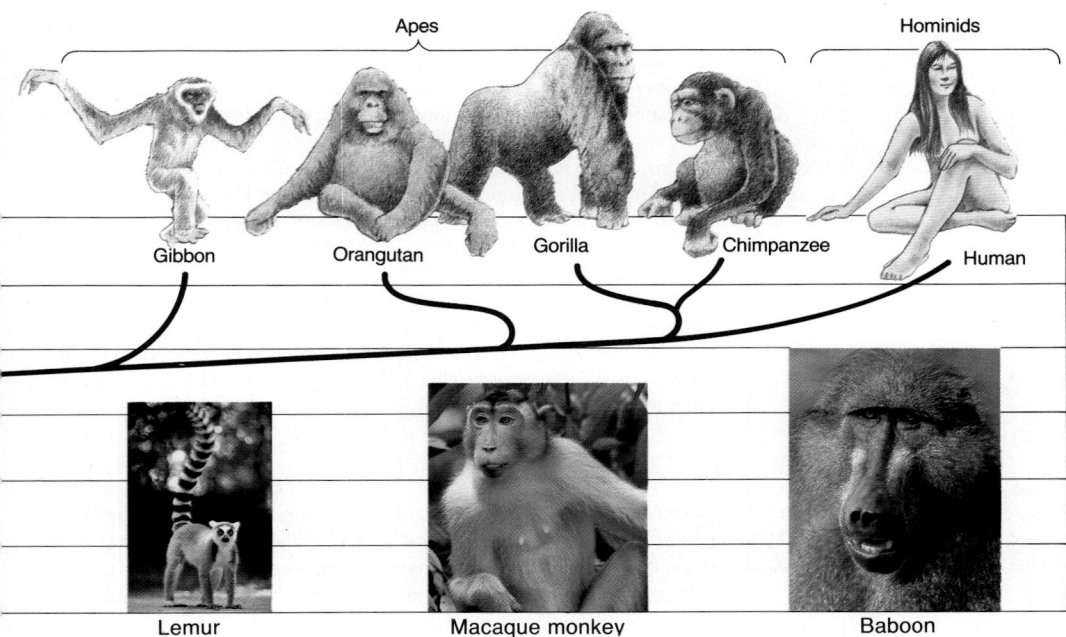

Apes — Hominids
Gibbon — Orangutan — Gorilla — Chimpanzee — Human
Lemur — Macaque monkey — Baboon

13.3 HUMAN EVOLUTION **353**

PROGRAM RESOURCES

Teacher Classroom Resources
Study Guide, pp. 76-77 L1
Probing Levels of Life, Lab 27, p. 75 L2
Investigating Living Systems, Lab 32, p. 123 L2

PORTFOLIO

Ask students to examine diagrams of skeletons of primates and humans. Ask them to make a table in their portfolios listing the parts of the skeleton that make them uniquely primate and the functions of those parts. They should include the foramen magnum, pelvis for upright walking, rotating shoulders, opposable thumbs, and others. L1

Misconception

- Evolution is often portrayed as a tree. The "primitive" organisms are placed at the base of the trunk. The "advanced" organisms are placed at the top of the tree. In fact, a more realistic view of relationships of organisms is like a view of the crown of a tree. All the present-day species can be seen on one level together. Extinct species are further down the tree.

- Students often think that human evolution means that humans evolved from chimpanzees. Tell students that evolutionary theory does not suggest that humans have evolved from any modern primate. Explain that evolutionary theory suggests that humans and apes evolved from a common ancestor in the geologic past. The common ancestor was probably apelike.

Human Ancestors Thus far, there is no complete fossil record for the time period when humans first began to diverge from apes. However, there is now a large collection of fossils for the humanlike apes that lived in Africa from about 5 million years ago. Most often, only small fragments of bone and teeth are discovered. However, anthropologists can tell a great deal from these meager findings. In attempting to trace the course of human evolution, the fossils are analyzed and a variety of structural adaptations are compared. Among them are skull traits including brain capacity, relative sizes of bones, and joint structure. Based on evidence such as this, anthropologists classify each and every fossil of human bone. As you might imagine, classifying extinct humans on the basis of a few bones or teeth is difficult at best, and interpretations often differ among groups of anthropologists.

Southern Ape The oldest fossils of human ancestors were discovered in several areas of Africa. These fossils were named australopithecines because *austral* means southern and *pithekos* is Greek for ape. Several species of southern ape have been discovered. *Australopithecus afarensis* was first discovered in East Africa and has been dated at 3.5 million years old. This ancient primate was called Lucy by her discoverer, who was a fan of the pop group The Beatles. He was playing their hit song that included this name at the time of his find. Studies of Lucy and other fossils of this species indicate they had an average brain capacity approximately the size of chimpanzee brains. Lucy was three feet tall, and it was determined that she must have had a mass of 66 pounds, about the same as you weighed when you were in fourth grade. Since Lucy, other specimens of the southern ape have been found, and they date back to 5 million years ago. These early human ancestors, although they walked on two legs, were probably clumsy by modern standards. Their arms were longer in relation to body size than those of modern humans, and their legs were quite short. From the study of these limb proportions and joint structures, scientists agree that this species may have spent a great deal of time in the trees. They probably returned there for safety and feeding.

In addition to Lucy, anthropologists have recognized three more species of australopithecines. The evidence suggests that there was adaptive radiation among these southern apes in Africa. They all evolved and lived in Africa from 5 million to 1.5 million years ago. The skulls of southern apes had a smaller brain capacity than skulls of modern humans. Although the face and teeth were similar to those of modern humans, if the australopithecines were alive today, scientists would not consider them to be human.

Figure 13-17 The oldest fossils of *Australopithecus* make up the skeleton of a young female. Using this 3 million-year-old skeleton, an artist provides us with an impression of these human-like apes.

Rocking the anthropological world, a second "Lucy" is discovered in southern Uganda.

The Origin of Humans

Modern humans, meaning you and all the people on this planet, are classified as *Homo sapiens*. During the last half million years of the time of the australopithecines, the first human ancestor arose. Fossils recognized as belonging to the same group as modern humans are called hominids. Hominids include handy man, upright man, and modern man.

354 ADAPTATION AND SPECIATION

Fossil Footprints: The eruption of a volcano 3.6 million years ago in the Rift Valley of what is now Tanzania created a layer of ash through which 20 different kinds of animals ran for cover. Their tracks were found only recently by scientists. More fossil animal tracks have been found here at Laetoli than anywhere else in the world. Included with the other animals are the tracks of three hominids.

One sequence of about 25 meters shows a very small hominid walking beside a much larger one. Behind, another followed, stepping in the footprints made by the largest of the three. Anthropologists ask, was the smallest holding the hand of the largest? It is remarkable to think about a family in Tanzania 3.6 million years ago being related in some way to us.

Figure 13-18 Early hominids first learned how to make and use tools from rocks (a). Upright man, *Homo erectus*, learned how to use fire (b). Neanderthals, an early form of modern humans, used ceremonies to bury their dead, as evidenced by these remains (c).

a

b

c

Handy Man   After southern apes, the next oldest known hominid is dated at more than 1.8 million years old. The brain capacity was larger than that of any earlier southern ape. Stone tools were found with these fossils, indicating that these hominids were handy at making and using tools for their everyday lives. These hominids were named *Homo habilis,* meaning handy man.

There is evidence that handy man collected stones from many miles away from where they lived. They used other stones to reshape them into tools for chopping, scraping, cutting, and hammering. They probably used the tools to make weapons for hunting purposes and for butchering the meat once caught and killed. Toolmaking is an important human behavioral trait rarely seen in other animals. The ability to make and use tools is a strong indicator of the handy man's learning abilities.

Upright Man   Anthropologists have suggested that *Homo habilis* gave rise to a new species that appeared more than 1 million years ago. More recent than handy man, this species is called *Homo erectus,* meaning upright man. This hominid had a rather humanlike face, flat, but with very large brow ridges and a lower jaw that sloped back with no chin. The skulls have a larger brain capacity than those of handy man.

What makes upright man different from handy man? They had learned to make and use fire! The first evidence that people had discovered the importance of fire is found with remains of the *Homo erectus* people. There is ample fossil evidence that the upright man was an excellent hunter, and discovery of hearths in caves indicates that these people used fire and lived together in groups. There is fossil evidence that these ancestors of modern humans began to migrate about 1 million years ago, and they spread throughout Africa, Asia, and possibly into Europe. Upright man became extinct about 300 000 years ago.

13.3 HUMAN EVOLUTION   **355**

Purpose
Students will examine how the development of culture has enabled humans to avoid natural selection.

Teaching Strategies
- Ask for volunteers to make posters of the steps in development of human culture.
- Ask other students to construct a concept map that represents the sequence of human cultural evolution.
- Ask students to distinguish between cultural evolution and evolution by natural selection.

Possible Answers
1. Answers will vary. Tangelos are a cross between an orange and a tangerine. Broccoflower is a cross between cauliflower and broccoli. Native Americans are known to have developed corn, squash, and pumpkins as sources of food.
2. One possible topic might be leafcutter ants. Leafcutter ants live in colonies of several million. They grow and tend crops of fungi below the ground. Workers cut leaves into small pieces and carry them back to the colony. Smaller workers chew the leaf pieces into a mulch, which they spread in underground chambers. Even smaller workers "plant" fungal hyphae in the mats of leaf pieces. After the fungi are growing, nurse ants carry larvae to feed on areas of the best fungal growth.

Going Further
Ask students to select an invention of the industrial revolution and explain how it changed people's lifestyles. L1

Modern Man The emergence of modern humans, *Homo sapiens*, remains a tricky puzzle today due to scanty fossil evidence and controversial dating. Yet there is ample evidence to sketch out a basic picture for the origin of our species. It is known that by about 100 000 years ago, populations of *Homo sapiens* appeared in Europe, Africa, and Asia. These first people of our species lived between 100 000 and 40 000 years ago and possessed features typical of both *H. erectus* and of ourselves.

Best known among the first *Homo sapiens* are the Neanderthals, so named because the original fossils were discovered in the Neander Valley in Germany. Neanderthal fossils have been found in Europe and Southwest Asia. Neanderthals were a short, powerfully built group. Their thick skulls were somewhat flat with heavy brow ridges, and like *H. erectus,* they lacked a chin. Neanderthals and modern man show similar brain capacities, and they both developed ceremonies for the burial of the dead. The view that Neanderthals were simply brutish cavemen is incorrect. Rather, there is excellent evidence which suggests that Neanderthals were efficient hunters and creative artists.

What happened to the Neanderthals, and how did modern humans emerge? Until recently, many scientists believed that populations of Neanderthals in Europe and Asia evolved directly into the different groups of modern *Homo sapiens*. However, recent archaeological and

GLOBAL CONNECTION

Cultural Evolution

Whether the ability to communicate with language first evolved among the Cro-Magnons or earlier, there is certainly no doubt about its impact on the lives of humans. Speech was made possible by evolution of a large and complex brain.

The development of language coincided with accumulation of knowledge. Older people could teach younger ones about all they had discovered, thus avoiding the need for people to learn everything on their own.

Using Tools At first, improved patterns of speech may have led to ideas for making better tools. With new tools came an increase in the ability to hunt larger animals and to make clothing, shelters, and new inventions such as boats. With each of these advances, humans had a better chance of surviving. Notice, however, that the changes in humans were not changes that affected their gene pools, but were because of changes in human cultures. Instead of being molded by changes in their environment, humans began to alter or avoid the effects of that environment. Unlike all other organisms, learning and intuition began to surpass mutations and recombination as causes of change in the human species.

Learning to Farm Early hominids were hunters and gatherers. They hunted large mammals and gathered grains, nuts, berries, and other fruits. From about

PROJECT

Early Use of Tools: Ask students to report on the first use of tools by *Homo habilis*. First, they should describe the differences between *Homo habilis* and species of Australopithecus from which they were derived. L1

Figure 13-19 The skull of *Australopithecus afarensis* (left) has a cranial capacity of 400 cm³. In *Homo erectus* (center) it is 850 cm³, and in modern *Homo sapiens* (right) the average volume is 1360 cm³. The evolution of the human brain spans 3 million years. By how much has brain size increased during this time?

SECTION 13.3

Figure Caption Question
By how much has brain size increased during this time? by 960 cm³ or 70 percent

Discussion Question
Ask students to imagine that the world's population of nearly 5 billion people is reduced to a village of 100 people with the same proportions of ethnic groups as there are in the world today. Ask them to estimate how many would be Asians (58), how many would be Africans (12), how many Western Europeans (10), how many Latin Americans (8), Eastern Europeans (6), North Americans (5), and Australian/New Zealanders (1). **L1**

10 000 years ago, our ancestors began to sow seeds, tend crops, and protect livestock. This change to an agricultural lifestyle led to permanent settlements and different cultural practices. Growing of crops reduced competition for food; thus, population size increased and permanent homes could be established.

Intellectual Explosion
Cultural evolution also led to a much more recent development in the history of humans, the Industrial Revolution. In the early 19th century, many societies became more technological than agricultural. Factories produced new products, new methods of transporta-

tion were invented, sanitation was improved, and electricity changed the lives of humans in countless ways. The products of modern technology have become important parts of our daily lives. They include not only CD players and air conditioners, but more importantly, drugs and medical equipment that save and prolong lives. But cultural evolution and an increased human population has its downside, too. As you are aware, the ways humans interact with one another and with the environment are often destructive.

Will our future cultural advances keep our planet and its species safe from extinctions?

1. **Connection to Genetics:** What new species of plant foods have humans produced within the last few centuries?
2. **Writing About Biology:** Describe social organizations in a group of animals other than humans.

13.3 HUMAN EVOLUTION **357**

Different Viewpoints in Biology

Human Origins
Scientists continue to debate how, when, and where modern humans originated. One opinion suggests that modern humans have no one single home. Humans, according to this group, originated in Africa and then slowly developed modern forms in all parts of the world. On the other side of the debate, scientists claim that Africa alone gave rise to all modern humans. Even though mitochondrial DNA studies demonstrate evidence that favors the single-origin or "Eve" theory, fossil evidence favors the multi-regional theory of human origins.

MATH CONNECTION

Evolutionary Time Line:

Have students prepare a time line that shows when the following major events occurred: invasion of the land by plants, extinction of the dinosaurs, diversification of primates, and evolution of humans. Ask, in relation to the entire history of Earth, what percent of time have humans been around? *Less than 1 percent.* **L1**

3 Assess

Check for Understanding

Write lists of human ancestors and their characteristics on the chalkboard. Ask students to match the characteristics with the ancestor. **L1**

Reteach

Have each group of students prepare a list of 10 questions from this section. Ask groups to exchange and answer the questions. **COOP LEARN**

Extension

Ask students to prepare an illustrated report on the methods artists use to reconstruct fossil humans. **L2**

✔ Assessment

Skill: Provide students with a hypothetical example of a fossil suspected of belonging to a human ancestor. Include information gained from the example such as particular age, sex, jaw shape, and so on. Ask students to determine where and if the example fits into the evolutionary scheme of humans. **L1**

Figure 13-20 Artistic creation is an anthropologist's clue to ancient hominid levels of abstract thought. This beautiful carving of mammoth ivory depicting two reindeer is about 15 000 years old. What can you deduce from such an artifact? Magnification: 0.5×

genetic evidence suggests that this may not be true. The new evidence supports an origin of modern humans, *Homo sapiens*, in Africa perhaps as early as 200 000 years ago. Scientists now believe that this population of modern humans quickly spread throughout Europe, Africa, and Asia. By 30 000 years ago, Neanderthals were extinct and modern man had spread throughout most parts of the world. The most famous among the early modern peoples are the Cro-Magnons. Discovered in France, they were fully modern in height, skull structure, skeleton, teeth, and brain size. Not only were they advanced toolmakers, they were also talented artists. It is fairly certain that these people also used language.

The evolution of complex language and the use of symbols must have led to an increased ability to communicate ideas and to make plans with others. These capabilities might have made the difference between success and extinction as the groups competed with one another for survival.

In 30 000 years, modern humans have adaptively diverged into a wide range of groups differing physically and culturally. Probably the most obvious differences to have evolved among peoples of the world include more than a thousand languages and hundreds of cultural and ethnic social practices. These differences, however, reflect only minute cultural differences. With widespread global travel among all groups of humans, speciation by geographic isolation has not occurred. The species *Homo sapiens* has remained as one.

Figure 13-21 This is just one phylogenetic tree that suggests the ancestry of *Homo sapiens*. How many years ago did modern humans first arise?

PORTFOLIO

Ask students to write about their own cultural or ethnic heritage in their portfolios. Ask them to bring something to class that is indicative of their heritage and tell about its importance. **L1**

PROJECT

The Geography of Blood: Have students look up the distribution of blood groups and speculate about human migration based on the distribution of blood groups. **L3**

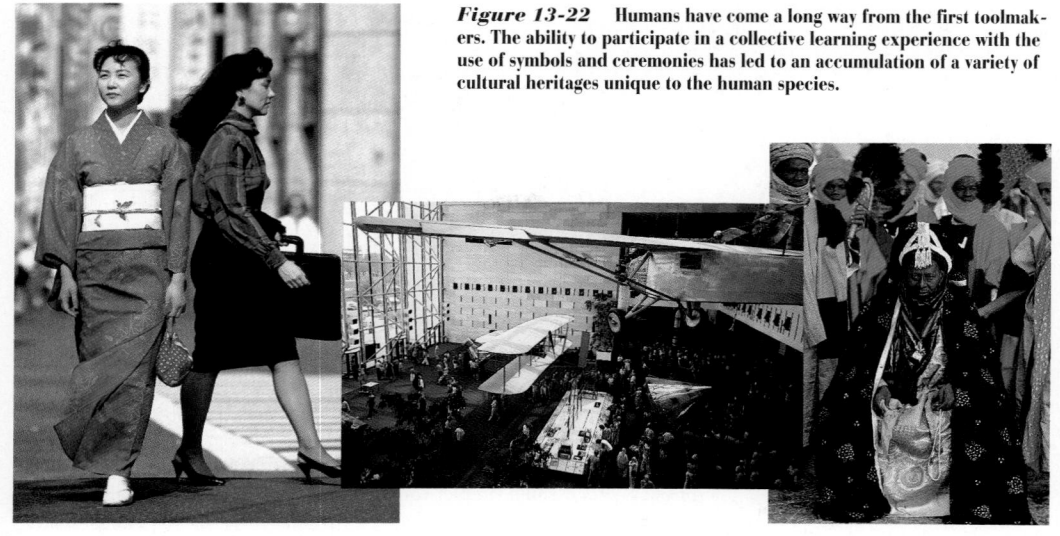

Figure 13-22 Humans have come a long way from the first toolmakers. The ability to participate in a collective learning experience with the use of symbols and ceremonies has led to an accumulation of a variety of cultural heritages unique to the human species.

SECTION 13.3

4 Close

Demonstration

Ask students to work in pairs. One partner should use masking tape and tape the thumbs of the partner so that thumbs are immobilized by the sides of their hands. The partner should give the subject a peanut and tell him or her to remove the shell. Have the partners trade positions. Ask students to describe the difficulty of not having an opposable thumb. **L1** **LEP** **COOP LEARN**

LOOKING AHEAD

Sᴘᴇᴄɪᴇs ʙᴇᴄᴏᴍᴇ adapted to their environments. As the environment changes, variations better suited to these new conditions are naturally selected and the population as a whole evolves. Information from evolution also helps to show relationships among species, which can then be used to classify organisms. You will find out that classification of species is a way of presenting their evolutionary history.

Section Review

Understanding Concepts

1. Why is it not biologically accurate to say that fossil humans are the missing link between apes and modern humans?
2. What evidence would scientists use to determine the diet of fossil humans? Explain your answer.
3. How can we determine relationships of modern humans to australopithecines, *Homo habilis*, and Neanderthals?
4. **Skill Review—Making Tables:** Make a table that compares australopithecines, upright man, Neanderthals, and Cro-Magnons in terms of where and when they lived, their brain size, and their general appearance. For more help, see Organizing Information in the **Skill Handbook.**
5. **Thinking Critically:** The average height of humans in the United States has increased by several inches during this century. Explain how that change in height might have evolved.

Answers to Section Review

1. The idea of a missing link suggests that fossil humans evolved from apes.
2. Tooth and jaw structure can be studied to determine whether the early humans ate meat, plants, or both.
3. Relationships are determined by study including brain capacity, sizes of bones, number and structure of teeth, skull shape, and dating of fossils. Structural features are studied and compared.

4. **Skill Review—Making Tables:** Students should construct a table with four rows, one for each primate, and four columns, one for each characteristic. The table should contain the following information. Australopithecines lived in Africa, 1.5 to 5 million years ago, 400 cm³ brain size, humanlike teeth; Upright man lived in Africa, Asia, and Europe, 300 000 to 1 million years ago, 850 cm³ brain size,

large brow ridges; Neanderthals lived in Europe and Asia, 30 000 to 100 000 years ago, 1360 cm³ brain size, heavy brow ridges; Cro-Magnons lived in Europe, 30 000 years ago, 1360 cm³ brain size, modern human features.

5. **Thinking Critically:** Better diet and health care may be responsible for the change.

Physics Connection

Purpose

Students will compare refrigeration and air conditioning to methods honeybees use to cool their hives. They will also learn how honeybees keep warm in winter.

Teaching Strategies

- Before they read the article, ask students what they could do to cool off on a hot summer day. Ask them what they could do to stay warm on a cold winter day.

- Ask them if they know how patients who have high fevers can be cooled. Point out that by putting water on the skin and allowing it to evaporate, the body is cooled.

- Ask, what is recommended treatment for people who are suffering from hypothermia, the cooling of the body due to exposure to extreme cold? *Warm them with your own body heat, preferably within the warmth of a sleeping bag.*

Possible Answers

1. Freon is a chlorofluorocarbon chemical used in air conditioners. Chlorofluorocarbons released into the atmosphere destroy the high atmospheric ozone layer that protects Earth from dangerous ultraviolet rays. To reduce this problem, other methods have been developed for air conditioners.

2. Honeybees have fuzzy bodies that trap pollen while they seek nectar from flowers. When a bee flies to another flower, some of the pollen may rub off onto the stigma as the bee searches for nectar.

BIOLOGY,

TECHNOLOGY, AND

SOCIETY

Physics Connection
Honeybee Heating and Cooling

Would it surprise you to learn that honeybees have cooling systems similar to air conditioning and refrigeration? Humans have used water for cooling for millennia, and so have honeybees.

Water helps cool for several reasons. It draws thermal energy from its surroundings to change its physical state from solid to liquid or from liquid to vapor. Therefore, evaporating water or melting ice draws heat from the air around it. Water is a better conductor of heat than air, so water will conduct heat away from a body or hot object faster than any surrounding air.

Humans use these physical principles in refrigeration and air conditioning systems, which draw heat from the surroundings to evaporate liquid. Honeybees use the same physical process in a simpler form. In hot weather, honeybees spread water over their honeycomb, then use their wings to fan it.

Honeybees also use strategies for staying warm in cold weather. Unlike other social insects, they remain active throughout winter in the hive, actively metabolizing. To maintain body temperature, they huddle together. As external temperatures drop, the bees conserve

thermal energy by clustering more tightly. The cluster of bees moves and feeds as a unit over the honeycomb.

1. **Issue:** Why is air conditioning harmful to the environment, and how can we reduce the problems?

2. **Explore Further:** How are honeybees adapted to pollinating flowers?

360 CHAPTER 13 ADAPTATION AND SPECIATION

Going Further

Ask students to test what type of sock is best for holding in heat. Have them put thermometers into beakers of water at body temperature and place these beakers inside a variety of socks made of different materials such as cotton, wool, acrylic, nylon, silk, or polyester. They should see which temperature drops most after 20 minutes. They could try the same experiment with wet socks. **L1** **LEP**

Issues

Interbreeding to Save a Species

The Florida panther and the gray wolf are registered as endangered species. Once a species has been recognized as endangered, its members receive protection under the law. They may not be killed, and in many cases their habitats are protected from development. However, the protection of the Florida panther may be questioned based on claims that it is no longer a pure species. Although only 50 panthers remain in the Everglades habitat, genetic analysis has indicated that some panthers have interbred with South American cougars that were released into the wild.

The gray wolf's endangered status was challenged by state farm bureaus in Indiana, Montana, and Wyoming because some had interbred with coyotes. Therefore, the petitions charged, the gray wolf species was not pure, but contained many hybrids.

What Is a Species? If you have heard *species* defined as a group of organisms that will not interbreed with another group, you might wonder how a species can be impure. If breeding between species is possible, what, then, is a species? The answer depends upon the definition of species.

Most taxonomists use outward appearances for their classifications. Field biologists who want to classify an organism cannot immediately identify the other organisms with which it can breed. It is much easier to classify by structure. Only with extensive breeding programs can a research scientist discover the

limits of the breeding group. When offspring are neither healthy nor able to reproduce, the species limits may have been identified.

Too Pure to Save? Without complete knowledge of what constitutes a species, you can probably appreciate the challenge facing those who are responsible for registering a species as endangered.

Another problem facing those in charge of protecting endangered species is that sometimes the efforts to keep these species genetically pure may work against the goal of preserving the species. For example, in the case of a group of organisms

with a very small population, breeding among individuals only within that population can result in genetic weaknesses that threaten the group's survival. Most Florida panthers have few offspring and many display abnormalities. In such a case, interbreeding with the cougars may produce offspring that are healthier and more resistant to disease.

Understanding the Issue

1. If you were in charge of protecting the small, inbred population of an endangered subspecies, would you try to keep the population pure, or interbreed if necessary to ensure the survival of its members' descendants? Explain your reasons.
2. How might protecting a species be a threat to local economics?

Readings

- Mlot, Christine. "The Science of Saving Endangered Species." *Bioscience* 2, 1989, p. 68.
- Radetsky, Peter. "Cat Fight." *Discover,* July 1992, pp. 56-63.

CAREER CONNECTION

As a **naturalist,** you might monitor species in the wild, study an ecosystem, or work to save an endangered species. You might also monitor pollution levels and their effects on organisms in the wild. You probably would work for a government agency such as a park or forestry service, a university, or a museum of natural history.

CAREER CONNECTION

For more information about the career of naturalist, students can contact the National Park Service, the State Park System, or a nearby natural history museum.

Issues

Purpose
Students will examine the problems scientists face in defining a species. The students will analyze the problems of endangered species.

Teaching Strategies
- Make a display of endangered animals and discuss with students the reasons for their being endangered.
- Contact the U.S. Fish and Wildlife Service to get more information on the Florida panther and the gray wolf. Also find out which wildlife refuges provide habitats for these species and have students write to them to find out about the latest information regarding the status of these animals. **L2**
- Invite a guest speaker from the U.S. Fish and Wildlife Service to talk to your class about law enforcement in their endangered species programs.

Possible Answers
1. Students' answers will vary depending on their views. Interbreeding would probably be more desirable than letting a species die out just because it was not pure. In nature, the less variation a population has, the more susceptible it will be to environmental pressure. Therefore, in terms of survival of life in general, preserving more varieties of genes, even in mixed species, may help in sustaining life on Earth in the long term.
2. Student answers might include that local economies could suffer in areas where a species of plant or animal has always been used for food or some other useful product. Examples of this have occurred with certain seals, whales, and the forests of the northwest.

Going Further
Ask students to contact a nearby zoo and ask about their breeding programs to save endangered species. **L1**

CHAPTER REVIEW

Summary

Summary statements can be used by students to review the major concepts of the chapter.

Language of Biology

Answers should go beyond defining the terms. Accept any reasonable answer that uses the term correctly and in the proper context.

Understanding Concepts

1. Most human behavior is not an adaptation. It was not naturally selected and is not genetically controlled.
2. Many structures having similar functions are the product of convergence and do not indicate a close relationship.
3. Because geographic isolation would have been necessary for the evolution of the many species, they could not have evolved in the same forest. They must have invaded the forest after they evolved, and they remain as separate species because they are now reproductively isolated.
4. Evolution of land vertebrates is an example of adaptive radiation. Their common ancestor must have had a means of reaching the new environment, must have had basic adaptations for that environment, and must not have had competition from similar or better-adapted species.
5. Neanderthals and Cro-Magnons could have interbred because they were members of the same species. *Homo erectus* and *H. habilis,* however, were members of different species and therefore could not have interbred.
6. The various hominids were geographically isolated from one another. As new alleles and genes arose in their gene pools, natural selection resulted in the evolution of different adaptations. Over time, the various groups diverged from one another and evolved into

---

Summary

Adaptations, which promote fitness, evolve slowly as previously existing adaptations are modified through changes in the environment and chance events.

Most instances of speciation result after geographic barriers split an original species into two or more isolated groups. Some cases of speciation occur without isolation as a result of chromosome mistakes.

Adaptive radiation is movement of individuals into new environments where they become separate species. In convergence, organisms that are not related evolve similar traits due to living in similar environments.

Fossil evidence of hominids reveals much about the evolution of humans in Africa and their migration to all parts of the world. As time passed, evolution of language enabled humans to become adapted culturally.

Language of Biology

Write a sentence that shows your understanding of each of the following terms.

adaptive radiation
behavioral adaptation
convergent evolution
divergent evolution
genetic drift
geographic isolation
gradualism
physiological adaptation
punctuated equilibrium
reproductive isolation
speciation
species
structural adaptation

Understanding Concepts

1. Is most human behavior an adaptation in the same sense as migration of birds? Explain.
2. Do structures having similar functions necessarily indicate close evolutionary relationships? Explain.
3. Many species of millipedes are found to inhabit the same forest. Could they all have evolved there? Explain.
4. The thousands of land vertebrates (amphibians, reptiles, birds, and mammals) are descended from a type of fish. What pattern of evolution does this example illustrate? What conditions had to be met in order for the land vertebrates to evolve?
5. Based on their classification, is it possible that Neanderthals and Cro-Magnons could have interbred? Explain. Could *Homo erectus* and *H. habilis* have interbred? Explain.

6. Explain how the evolution of various hominids illustrates the way in which speciation most often occurs.
7. Suppose a small part of an original population is isolated after a disaster and is in an environment quite different from that before the disaster. Why might it very rapidly evolve into a new species?
8. Trace the evolutionary steps from the beginnings of increased brain size in southern apes to the development of complex language in Cro-Magnons.
9. The digestive tracts of cows contain bacteria that can digest the cellulose in the grass the cows eat. Cows lack an enzyme that would help digest cellulose. Can you explain how the cow/bacteria relationship might have originated?

---

distinct species.

7. In a small, isolated population, rapid changes in gene frequencies may occur as a result of genetic drift, and the environment in which the survivors find themselves may be different. Drift and selection may alter the gene pool to such an extent that the isolated population may quickly evolve into a new species.
8. Brain size more than tripled as humans evolved. With greater brain size came greater intelligence. Humans began to learn more about their environment and to find

ways to avoid its effects. Development of language enabled humans to pass on that knowledge to others. Thus, humans could profit from what others before them had learned.

9. The bacteria probably gained adaptations that permitted them to live within the cows' digestive tracts, thus gaining access to food. The cows probably evolved adaptations that facilitated entry of the bacteria and made the digestive tract a suitable habitat for the bacteria.

Applying Concepts

10. Consider the various geographic groups of humans such as Pygmies, Inuits, Polynesians, and Hottentots. What factors may have led to their evolution? Will these geographic groups someday evolve into separate species? Discuss.

11. Colchicine is a chemical that can be used to induce polyploidy. How might such a chemical be used to benefit society?

12. Suppose another ice age develops in the distant future. How would the response to such a change differ between humans and other organisms if both are to survive?

13. Organisms that have variations that can be used in new ways in new environments are said to be preadapted. How was preadaptation important to Hawaiian honeycreepers?

14. Many animals have adaptations known as courtship behavior. This kind of behavior enables males and females of the same species to recognize one another and stimulates them to mate. Besides the fact that courtship behavior promotes reproduction of a species, how else is it important?

15. **Global Connection:** Why does cultural evolution result in more rapid changes in humans than does biological evolution?

16. **Issues:** If a nearly extinct species is released into a new habitat with an unlimited food supply and no competition, what might happen to the species?

Lab Interpretation

17. **Thinking Lab:** Flies are sprayed with a new chemical pesticide on Monday for five weeks. The flies that remain alive are counted each Monday. Based on the graph below, predict how many flies will be left in week five. Explain these results.

Number of flies surviving after pesticide application

18. **Minilab 2:** A marshland in New Jersey has plants with bright green vegetation, dark brown stems, and bright red berries. Describe how a frog that lives in this marsh and is difficult to spot might look.

19. **Investigation:** Analyze the following data of numbers of stomata on leaves of one tree species. What might the data tell you about the rainfall in the areas where the data were collected?

Average number of stomata at low power in ten leaves of ten trees of one species

Connecting Ideas

20. Give reasons why a mule would be sterile.
21. How might viruses and the host cells they invade have evolved?

Connecting Ideas

20. **Evolution:** Because the mule was produced from a cross between two distinct species, it does not have homologous pairs of chromosomes.

21. **Evolution:** The host cells evolved adaptations that prevented viruses from invading them while the viruses evolved adaptations that allowed them to do so.

CHAPTER 13

Applying Concepts

10. The various human groups, due to both biological and cultural evolution, have many differences. However, because the groups are not now geographically isolated, they will not evolve into distinct species. Over time, with more interbreeding between groups, they may become more similar.

11. Use of colchicine could lead to artificial evolution of new plants.

12. Humans would use technology to avoid the effects of the cold. Other organisms would depend on the chance occurrence of genetic changes that would enable them to withstand the cold.

13. The ancestors of the honeycreepers were probably adapted to the climate of Hawaii and to make use of various food sources available in that new environment.

14. Courtship behavior maintains reproductive isolation among species. Mating between members of different species results in abnormal development or sterility of offspring.

15. Biological evolution depends upon chance genetic changes acted upon by natural selection over a long period of time. Advances resulting from cultural evolution, such as the invention of a machine, may benefit an entire population very quickly.

16. The size of the population will increase. It is also possible, if the organisms are geographically isolated, that the population could diverge, leading to a new species.

Lab Interpretation

17. 400 flies—The flies are developing resistance to the chemical pesticide spray. Only the ones with resistance can survive.

18. Answers will vary; but, in general, the frog would be mainly bright green with some dark brown streaks and perhaps red spots.

19. Texas and Colorado have drier climates than Nebraska and Kansas.

SECTION	OBJECTIVES	TEXT LABS/FEATURES
14.1 The Concept of Classification (2 days)	**Explain** the concept of binomial nomenclature. **Discuss** how various lines of evidence are used to classify organisms. **Develop** the concept of a phylogenetic diagram.	**Minilab 1:** Can you classify nonliving things? p. 367 **Art Connection:** John James Audubon, p. 368 **History Connection:** William Montague Cobb, p. 372
14.2 A System of Classification (1 day)	**Demonstrate** how each successive taxon is more specific than the previous taxon. **Discuss** why the number of kingdoms of organisms has changed over time.	**Minilab 2:** What traits are used to classify an unknown organism? p. 377 **Investigation:** Making a Key, p. 378 **Thinking Lab:** What traits are used to classify organisms into kingdoms? p. 380
BIOLOGY, TECHNOLOGY, AND SOCIETY		**Biotechnology:** Modern Tools for Classification, p. 383 **Issues:** In Competition: Fish or Dam? p. 384 **Career Connection:** Taxonomist, p. 385

LAB MATERIALS

INVESTIGATION	MINILAB	ALTERNATE LAB
page 378 10-20 miscellaneous items per group: backpacks, gloves, laboratory equipment, notebooks, pens, shoes; overhead projector; transparency sheets (clear acetate)	**page 367** envelopes; miscellaneous items, such as: candy pieces, cork, coverslip, dissection pin, glass slide, match, medicine dropper bulb, paper clip, seeds, soda pop can pull tab, string, twist tie; overhead projector **page 377** microscope; organisms, such as: lichen, liverwort, *Obelia*, *Ulva* (sea lettuce)	**page 370** art of organisms

TEACHER CLASSROOM RESOURCES	OTHER RESOURCES
Study Guide, pp. 79-80 **Critical Thinking/Problem Solving:** *Evaluating Methods of Classification,* p. 14 ***PLL:** *Binomial Nomenclature,* p. 82 ****ILS:** *Classification,* p. 129	***STVS:** *Naming Fish,* Animals (Disc 5, Side 2) ***STVS:** *Insect Museum,* Animals (Disc 5, Side 1)
Study Guide, pp. 81-84 **Concept Mapping,** p. 14 **Exploring Environmental Issues:** *Going, Going, Gone,* pp. 31-32 ***PLL:** *Construction and Use of a Dichotomous Key,* p. 80 ****ILS:** *Using and Making a Biological Key,* p. 133	***STVS:** *Fungal Collection for Research,* Plants and Simple Organisms (Disc 4, Side 1)
Assessment Materials **Chapter Assessment,** pp. 53-56 **Performance Assessment in Biology,** p. 28 **Alternate Assessment in the Science Classroom** **Computer Test Bank**	**Spanish Resources** **Cooperative Learning Resource Guide** **Videodisc Correlations** (to Optical Data's and Videodiscovery's videodiscs)

* Probing Levels of Life
** Investigating Living Systems

* Science Technology Videodisc Series

Key to Teaching Strategies

The following designations will help you decide which activities in the teacher margin are appropriate for your students.

L1 Level 1 activities should be within the ability range of all students.

L2 Level 2 activities should be within the ability range of the average to above-average student.

L3 Level 3 activities are designed for the ability range of above-average students.

LEP LEP activities are appropriate for Limited English Proficiency students.

COOP LEARN Cooperative Learning activities are designed for small group work.

ADDITIONAL RESOURCES

Infinite Voyage *To the Edge of the Earth*
Organisms have adapted to living conditions in many extreme environments, from the Tibetan plateau to underwater caves. New organisms are still being discovered in some of these areas.

Audiovisual
Classification: Order Out of Chaos, two sound filmstrips, SRA.
Classifying Living Things, video, Insight Media.

Software
Classification, Apple/IBM/Commodore 64, Diversified Educational Enterprises.
Classification, Apple 64K, J and S.

CLASSIFICATION

Chapter Overview

Students begin the chapter by analyzing the need for classification as a means of bringing order to a group of related objects. They will learn about Linnaeus's system of binomial nomenclature as well as modern bases of establishing evolutionary relationships. They will learn that classification is an indication of an organism's phylogeny and gain an understanding of a phylogenetic diagram.

Students will study the various taxonomic categories and compare the classifications of several familiar animals. Finally, they will understand why a five-kingdom classification system is used by many biologists today.

CLASSIFICATION

IMAGINE IT'S the beginning of a new semester, and your science teacher has given you a research assignment. You ride your bicycle to the public library to look for a book on your topic. In the library, row after row of shelves stand before you. Thousands of books line the shelves. How do you find a book on your specific topic? You might begin with the card catalog or the computerized catalog system. You look for your research subject and find a book that looks interesting. The Dewey decimal number tells where a book is located. When you go to the shelf to find your specific book, you will also find other books on the same topic. That's because similar books are classified together.

The same kind of situation faces biologists. Biologists deal with millions—not just thousands—of organisms. How do they locate information about a certain organism? How do they communicate with one another about their findings? Scientists have devised a classification system for all organisms, just as a classification system was created for all books. Instead of a number, the biological classification system assigns each organism a two-part name. Similar names are assigned to related organisms. Of course, the organisms aren't neatly arranged on a shelf for the biologist to study, but information about the organisms can be. That is the true benefit of classification—it enables us to organize information about the world.

364

KEY TERMS

binomial	order
nomenclature	phylogeny
class	phylum
family	taxa
genus	taxonomy
kingdom	

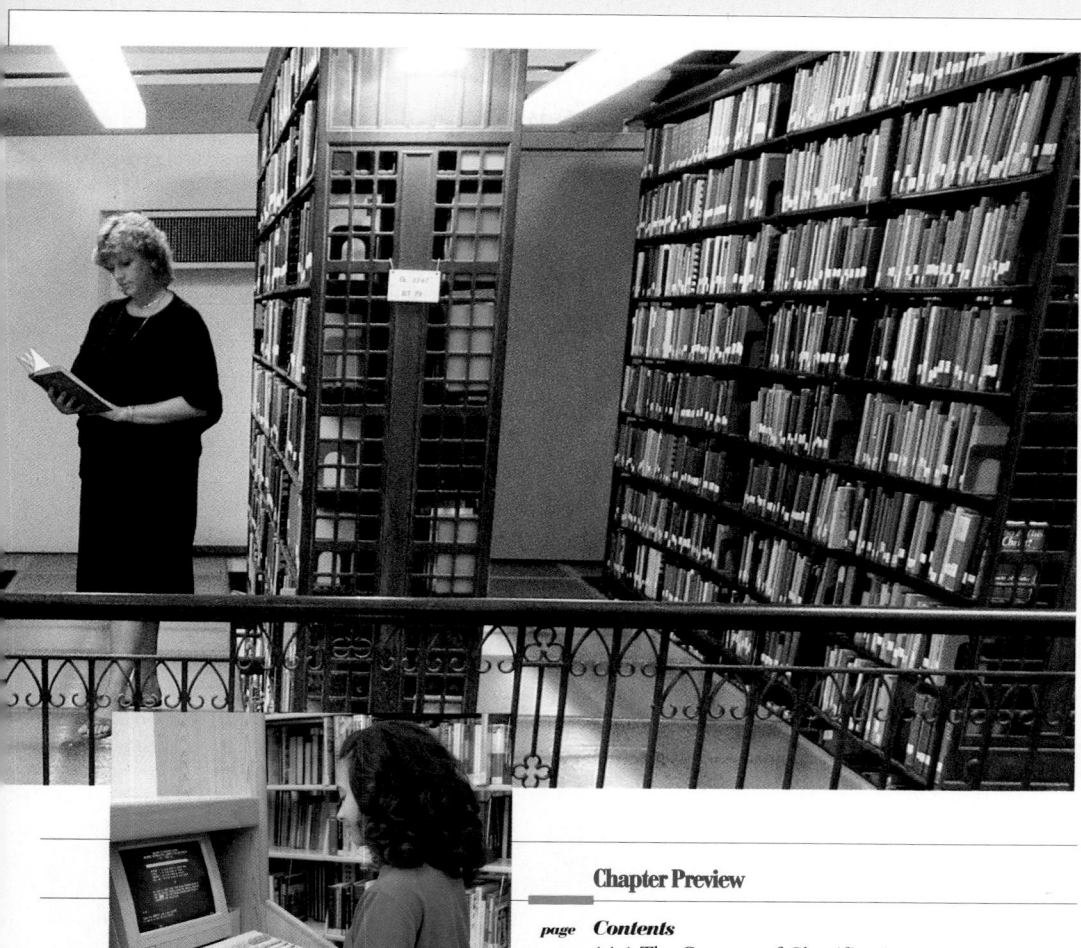

How could you find a book about biology among the thousands of books in the library if there were no classification system?

Introducing the Chapter

A discussion of the photograph on pages 364 and 365 will serve as a familiar example of the importance of classification. Books are classified into various broad categories—reference materials, fiction, and nonfiction, for example. Based on these broad classifications, books in certain categories are then further arranged by subject area; nonfiction books may be subdivided into groups such as history, geography, and science. Science books are more specifically arranged by topic—biology, chemistry, geology, and physics. Finally, each book is given a specific catalog number. Similarly, organisms are classified in categories from broadest to most specific. Both systems provide an orderly means of studying, whether it be books or organisms.

Theme Development

The chapter stresses the themes of evolution and methods of inquiry. Organisms are classified on the basis of evolutionary relationships. Various methods of science are employed to determine those relationships.

Tying to Previous Knowledge

Students have just completed a study of evolution. What they have learned will contribute to their understanding of taxonomy. Principles such as divergence and adaptive radiation explain the origin of new species from common ancestors and also provide insight into why some organisms are more closely related than others. The idea of convergence, conversely, should remind students that functional similarities among organisms are not evidence for common ancestry and therefore do not indicate close relationships.

Chapter Preview

Contents

ASSESSMENT PLANNER

Choose assessment strategies from the following pages to evaluate the progress of your students.

Assess, pp. 374-375, 382
Portfolio, pp. 367, 373, 374, 375, 381
Alternate Lab, pp. 370-371
Thinking Lab, p. 380

Minilab 1, p. 367
Minilab 2, p. 377
Investigation, pp. 378-379
Chapter Review, pp. 386-387

Prepare

Key Concepts

Students will be introduced to the need for classifying organisms and the system of using binomial nomenclature. They will also learn what tools are used currently for investigating and determining relationships for classification.

Key Terms

taxa, taxonomy, binomial nomenclature, genus, phylogeny

Materials

- Gather items to be placed within envelopes for Minilab 1. Items are typically inexpensive pieces of lab equipment available in the classroom.

1 Focus

Objectives

The objectives are listed on the student page. Remind students to preview these objectives as a guide to this numbered section.

Demonstration

Hold up a starfish (sea star) skeleton and a preserved fish for the class (or use photos of these two animals). Ask students to list as many similar traits for the two animals as they can. The list will be rather short. Ask if the two animals are both fish. Their list of similarities is very short because the animals are not as related as the similarity of their common names might suggest. A need for a system of classification to group those living things that are closely related can now be introduced. **L1**

Objectives

Explain the concept of binomial nomenclature.

Discuss how various lines of evidence are used to classify organisms.

Develop the concept of a phylogenetic diagram.

14.1 The Concept of Classification

Have you ever played in a school band or listened to one perform? The various musical instruments in a band are placed into several groups—brass, percussion, or woodwind. Or think about the last motor vehicle you rode in. Was it a car, a truck, a bus, or a van? Each of these broad groups can be subdivided into several more specific groups. For example, woodwind instruments include clarinets, saxophones, and oboes. Cars may be sedans, coupes, or convertibles. As a new musical instrument is developed, it can be placed in the proper category in the classification system. The same is true of a new motor vehicle. A classification system brings order and logic to instruments, vehicles, or any group of related objects.

The Need for Classifying Organisms

Just as musical instruments or motor vehicles can be classified, so, too, can organisms. Biologists classify organisms in categories called **taxa,** (*sing.,* taxon). The science of classification is, therefore, called **taxonomy.** Just as a classification system for instruments brings order to a band, a classification system for organisms brings order to the great diversity of life forms. It also serves as a basis for identifying unfamiliar organisms. New organisms are being discovered continually. Such organisms may be placed in existing taxa, or, if they are unique, a new taxon may be formed. For example, recent exploration of marine caves has led to the discovery of more than 20 new kinds of crustaceans, the taxon of organisms that includes shrimp, lobsters, and crabs.

Figure 14-1 **New taxa may be created in order to classify newly-discovered organisms, such as these marine tube worms.**

366 CLASSIFICATION

Have students needing more help in understanding the need for classification analyze a page of the classified ads from your local newspaper. Ask them (a) why the page is called the classified ads; (b) how difficult it would be to locate an ad if the page were not organized or grouped into categories; (c) what is the advantage of classifying ads; (d) to design some other way of classifying the ads that appear on the page; (e) if there is only one correct way to classify or might it be possible to classify in several different ways; (f) what is one way in which the information in an entire newspaper is not classified; and (g) to provide other examples from their daily lives that illustrate systems of classification. **LEP**

Classifying organisms not only results in order, but also provides a logical means of naming organisms. Common names are inadequate for biologists' purposes. The word *frog*, for example, probably conjures up a certain mental image for you, but it is inaccurate as a scientific label. A biologist would need to know what *kind* of frog it is. Is it a grass frog, a tree frog, or a bullfrog? Consider also the common word *worm*. You probably think of a long, slimy animal that lives in soil, but biologists know of various kinds of worms, including roundworms, flatworms, and segmented worms. Also, organisms such as ringworms, mealworms, and acorn worms are not worms at all. A ringworm is a fungus, a mealworm is an insect in the larval stage, and an acorn worm is a simple relative of vertebrates.

In addition, common names vary from country to country and from language to language. They may even vary among people who speak the same language. For example, a puma, a cougar, and a mountain lion are all the same organism. The need for one scientifically accepted name for each kind of organism is clear. Scientific names can be used to identify a particular organism even when the scientists studying that organism do not speak a common language. All scientific names given to organisms are in Latin, or in a Latin style, as Latin is no longer used in everyday conversation.

Binomial Nomenclature

Many early biologists devised classification schemes. Aristotle divided organisms into two groups—plants and animals. In Aristotle's system, plants were classified on the basis of structure and size—herbs, shrubs, and trees. Animals were subdivided on the basis of where they lived—air, land, or sea. Yet a classification system should have the same basis for all groupings. In the 18th century, Carolus Linnaeus developed a classification system based on just one characteristic—structural features.

Minilab 1

Can you classify nonliving things?

Your teacher has provided you with an envelope containing a variety of items. Your task is to group these items into a self-designed classification system. Assume these objects all belong to the same large group, such as plants or clothing fasteners. Your classification scheme should first divide the objects into several smaller groups, then divide each of these into even smaller groups. Record the traits used for each category of your classification scheme. **Analysis** What trait was used to first divide your objects? Was this same trait used by all classmates? Why must only one scheme be used to classify living things?

Figure 14-2 The word *frog* can be applied to a tree frog (a), a grass frog (b), or a bullfrog (c), even though they are quite different organisms.

a

b

c
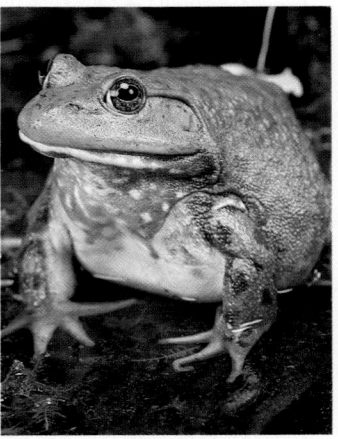

14.1 THE CONCEPT OF CLASSIFICATION 367

2 Teach

Minilab 1

Purpose
The purpose of the activity is to help students visualize how classification schemes are organized and to give them the opportunity to create their own classification schemes.

Skills
classify, sequence, observe and infer

Teaching Strategies
- Suggestions for items within the envelope to be classified could include: coverslip (plastic), glass slide, dissection pin, piece of candy, soda pop can pull tab, paper clip, small cork, plant seed, match, bulb from medicine dropper, twist tie, piece of string. You may wish to use any item that is available in class or from home.

Expected Results
Student classification schemes will vary. Make sure that the traits being used to separate groups are logical. As a means for demonstrating different students' schemes, have one student at a time position his or her objects onto an overhead projector plate according to the classification sequence. Then allow the class to determine the rationale used for the scheme. If a student has prepared a correct and logical classification of the objects, the rationale should be obvious to his or her classmates.

Answers
Answers will vary; no; scientists have agreed on which traits should be used to group all living things into the five kingdoms. Without agreement no uniform system for classification would exist.

✔ Assessment
Portfolio: Have students write an evaluation of the lab for their portfolios, summarizing what was observed.

MULTICULTURAL CONNECTION

Plant Names Commonly Used:
Various plants throughout the world have different names. They are, however, the same plant. For example, in the Caribbean Islands a pod is called St. John's bread, but in the U.S. it is called carob. In India, a certain seed is called plantago but here it is called psyllium. In Central America it is pepo, but in the U.S. it is pumpkin seed. People in the West

Indies call it myristica but we call this spice derived from a seed nutmeg. In Italy the plant is called belladonna, but in the U.S. it is called deadly nightshade. The problems and possible confusion that arise when common names are used is prevented when scientific names are used.

ART CONNECTION

Purpose
Students will be introduced to the artist and will learn that not only did Audubon draw birds in a unique manner, but he also was a taxonomist in the sense that he studied a variety of traits of birds.

Teaching Strategies
- Attempt to locate books that use drawings of Audubon's work. Display them for the class to examine.
- Have students list some of the traits or characteristics other than physical appearance that Audubon studied.
- Have students look up the meaning of such terms as *pictorial, prey, ornithological, frank, meticulously, extinct,* and *threatened.* Ask them to write out these definitions and to explain how they relate to the feature.

Possible Answers
1. Student answers will vary. Possible answers include habitat reduction through human development, contribution of pollutants such as oil spills and use of insecticides/pesticides that may also harm birds, capture of birds for use as pets, destruction of birds during hunting, and use for human food.
2. 1760 yards = 1 mile, 1760 yards × 1760 = 3 097 600 square yards per mile, 2 birds per square yard = 6 195 200 birds per square mile, three square miles = 18 585 600 birds.

Going Further
Have students research the names of those 33 species that have become extinct and the 150 that are threatened in North America. Have them include the scientific names and common names. **L2**

According to Linnaeus, each type of organism was a distinct species. If two organisms had the same set of features, they belonged to the same species. Different species having similar features were classified together in broader groups. Although Linnaeus thought that species were unchangeable—that they did not evolve—his decision to group organisms on the basis of structure was significant. In fact, many of his groupings are still used today.

Linnaeus made a second contribution to the study of life. He introduced a two-part system called **binomial nomenclature** for naming and classifying organisms. In this system, each organism is given a two-word Latin name. The first word, a noun, is the **genus** (*pl.,* genera) to which an organism belongs. The second word, an adjective, is the specific name. Genus and specific name together constitute the species name of an organism.

Genus and species are different taxa. A genus is a broader category than a species. Thus, a single genus may contain many different species. For example, cats belong to the genus *Felis,* but there are many species of

ART CONNECTION

John James Audubon

John James Audubon (1785-1851) could hardly have been happier. The Pennsylvania woods teemed with birds. Nearly every day in 1803, Audubon went into the woods with his gun. However, unlike other hunters, he didn't put the contents of his game bag into the stew pot. Instead, he arranged his birds in front of his drawing board and carefully sketched their features.

Audubon's lifestyle was not acceptable to his French father, who had sent his son to America with instructions to manage a mine on family property. The older man could see little future in drawing birds. Next, he tried to make a businessman of Audubon, setting him up as a partner in a general store in Kentucky. Predictably, the venture failed because Audubon found new birds to study closer to the frontier territory.

Audubon was dissatisfied with the way other artists depicted birds. They usually stuffed a dead bird and used it as a model. Audubon thought that the resulting paintings looked stiff and unnatural, so he tried something different. He built a wooden frame and stretched wire screen across it. Arranging a dead bird in a lifelike position, he wired it to the screen. He then made his initial drawing on paper lined with squares the same size as those in the screen. This method allowed him to draw the bird life-size, with each part in exact scale. He found a way to make his paintings look even more lifelike by attaching string to the bird's wings and tail so he could

change their positions. Audubon also included pictorial information about the birds by painting them in their natural settings, often showing their prey and nests.

368 CLASSIFICATION

PROGRAM RESOURCES

Teacher Classroom Resources
Study Guide, pp. 79-80 **L1**
Probing Levels of Life, Lab 29, p. 82 **L2**
Investigating Living Systems, Lab 33, p. 129 **L2**
Critical Thinking/Problem Solving, p. 14 **L2**

PROJECT

Scientific Dinner: Have students obtain a menu from a good restaurant. Ask them to list 10 main dishes, 5 appetizers, 2 soups, and 2 salads. Then have students find out the scientific names for the foods listed. Ask them to prepare a menu of a complete dinner with only scientific names. See if their classmates can figure out the items being served. **L2**

cats. A wildcat is *Felis sylvestris,* an ocelot is *Felis pardalis,* a cougar is *Felis concolor,* and a house cat is *Felis catus.* The same is true of plant genera. Oak trees belong to the genus *Quercus.* A red oak is *Quercus rubra;* a white oak is *Quercus alba.* Note that in writing a scientific name, the first letter of the genus is capitalized, but the first letter of the species is not. Genus and species names are always underlined or italicized. If you are discussing a particular genus, the genus name may be abbreviated by using only the first letter. When discussing cats, for example, *Felis sylvestris* may be written as *F. sylvestris.* Botanists discussing oak trees would discuss *Q. rubra* and *Q. alba.*

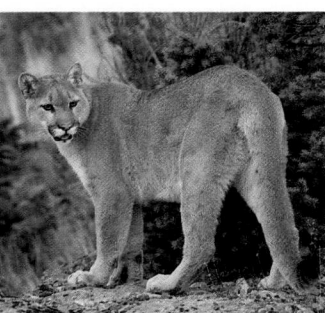

Figure 14-3   The wildcat *Felis sylvestris* (left) shares a genus with the cougar *Felis concolor* (right).

In 1820, Audubon began an 1800-mile journey by flatboat down the Ohio and Mississippi rivers, along what was then the western boundary of the United States. His plan was to study and paint the birds he found between Cincinnati and New Orleans, and eventually to document all the different kinds of birds found in the country.

Audubon wrote a book, *The Birds of America.* Unable to find a publisher in the United States, Audubon went to England to have the book published. It immediately became popular in the United States and Audubon was a celebrity, even being entertained by President Andrew Jackson.

To accompany his book of bird paintings, Audubon wrote an ornithological biography. He included his frank opinion of the bald eagle, the species chosen as the national bird. Audubon wrote that he agreed with Benjamin Franklin, who accused the bird of "bad moral character" because of its habit of stealing fish caught by the hawk. (Franklin suggested that the wild turkey would make a better symbol for the nation.)

In another part of the biography, Audubon described watching migrating passenger pigeons in 1813. He said, "The air was literally filled with pigeons; the light of noon-day was obscured as by an eclipse." Enthusiastic hunters, in search of both food and sport, lowered the pigeon population drastically, although Audubon was confident that the numbers would remain high. A century later, the world's last surviving passenger pigeon died in a Cincinnati zoo.

The passenger pigeon, the nearly extinct whooping crane, and more fortunate species that continue to survive are all meticulously pictured in Audubon's works. Thanks to Audubon, the world has a record of the vanished American wilderness. His drawings have also been the basis for countless guidebooks that allow today's birdwatchers to identify what they see nesting in trees and on the wing.

1. **Issues:** In Audubon's time, there were about 700 species of birds on the North American continent. Today, 33 are extinct and 150 others are threatened. What do you think are some reasons for the decline?

2. **Mathematics Connection:** Audubon made a rough calculation of how many passenger pigeons there were in a flock. He figured that the birds flew 60 miles per hour in a column about one mile wide. If a flock took three hours to pass overhead, and two birds occupied one square yard of space, how many birds would that flock contain?

Using Science Terms

Have students look up the meaning of the terms *binomial* and *nomenclature.* Have them explain why the use of these two terms is appropriate for how the system of naming organisms is designed and used. **L1** **LEP**

Different Viewpoints in Biology

Lumpers and Splitters

Taxonomists do not always agree as to the scheme to be used for classification. There are two groups, the lumpers and the splitters. Taxonomists who see many differences among related organisms and therefore place them into many taxonomic groups are called *splitters.* Those who see only a few important differences and classify into fewer groups are called *lumpers.* Have your students provide an example of what might be the classification of breakfast cereals as seen by lumpers and splitters. For example, lumpers may group cereals into two categories: hot and cold. Splitters may group on the basis of what plant provided the basic cereal source such as oat, wheat, corn, or rice cereal.

A second problem among taxonomists is that of deciding what trait to use in the classifying scheme or deciding if all traits are to be given equal importance. For example, if protein sequencing is most important, then humans and chimpanzees are most closely related. However, if sexual structure and behavior is considered, then orangutans and humans are most closely related.

STUDENT JOURNAL

Ask students to record the rules for naming organisms in the binomial nomenclature system. Have them include those ideas found on pages 368 and 369. Have them provide an example for each rule. Encourage students to use examples not already used in the text. Refer them to Appendix A for examples of other organism names. **L1**

MEETING INDIVIDUAL NEEDS

Binomial nomenclature sometimes can be better understood when familiar names that are similar to or derived from the Latin name are used as examples. Provide students with these scientific names and ask them to name the organism: *Hippopotamus amphibius, Mus musculus, Crocodylus americanus, Citrus aurantium.* **LEP**

Software
The Taxonomy Game, Queue

Audiovisual
Show the filmstrip *Five Kingdoms of Life—Introduction,* Carolina Biological Supply Company.

Teacher FYI
Horses, tapirs, and rhinoceroses, along with zebras and asses, belong to a group of ancient mammals called Perissodactyls. These are hoofed animals with an odd number of toes; the axis of the foot passes through the middle toe. Typically, they will have three toes. Teeth also show a specific characteristic where the premolar teeth are completely molarized. This increases the efficiency of the animals' ability to grind and crush hard plant material. The first known fossils of the perissodactyls appear in the early Eocene age. By the middle of Tertiary times, these animals were the dominant ungulates in most of the world.

Using Science Terms
Have students use a dictionary to determine the literal meaning for the word *homologous.* Ask them to explain why this definition is appropriate when used with classification.

Determining Relationships

The science of taxonomy became more exact when evolution and the theory of natural selection were explained. Since that time, classification has been based upon ancestry of organisms. Organisms that have a common ancestor are considered related and are grouped together. For example, the various species of cats are all classified in the same genus because they have evolved from a common ancestor. Dogs are in a different genus, *Canis,* because they are descended from a different ancestor. The closer the evolutionary relationships of organisms, the more similar their classification.

Classifying Based on Structure Once evolution was recognized, taxonomists began to use two main lines of evidence for classification: the fossil record and homologous structures. Fossils often provide clues that help scientists determine relationships among organisms. The fossil record shows clearly the evolution of the horse, for example. Scientists also have ample fossil evidence to show that horses, tapirs, and rhinoceroses evolved from a common ancestor. However, the fossil record is rarely this complete, so other lines of evidence are needed for classifying most organisms. Figure 14-5 shows how homologous structures were used to determine that walruses, seals, and sea lions belong to the same group. The reason so much of Linnaeus's classification system still remains valid is that he used the idea of homologous structures without realizing it. By using structure as his basis, Linnaeus was grouping organisms on the basis of evolutionary relationships.

However, fossils and homologous structures can sometimes provide information that is misleading or inconclusive. Also, the presence of structures similar in function that have resulted from convergence can and do mislead taxonomists. As time went on, other lines of evidence came into use.

Classifying Using Biochemistry and Development As new scientific tools such as microscopes became more precise, taxonomists began to use

Figure 14-4 Relationships among organisms are easy to see when the fossil record is complete, as in the evolution of the horse.

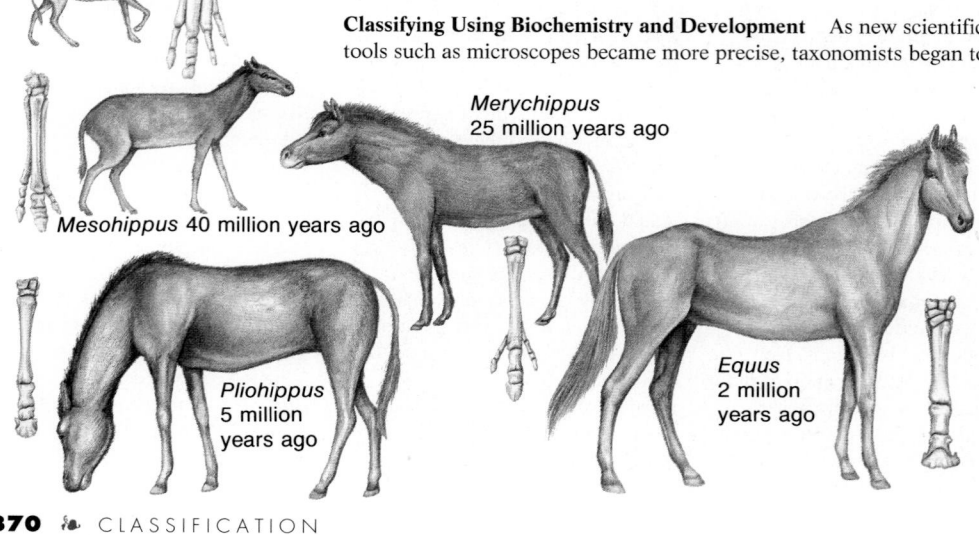

Eohippus
55 million
years ago

Mesohippus 40 million years ago

Merychippus
25 million years ago

Pliohippus
5 million
years ago

Equus
2 million
years ago

370 ❧ CLASSIFICATION

ALTERNATE LAB: Classifying Organisms

Purpose
Students will have an opportunity to decide on a specific trait that is to be used in assigning organisms to a particular taxon.

Materials
art of organisms A through F

Procedure
Give the following directions to students.

1. Obtain a copy of organisms from your teacher.
2. Classify the organisms into different taxa. Traits to be used have already been decided upon. Use this table as a guide for your classification.
3. Prepare a table that will allow you to record your data. Note that each organism has been assigned a letter for identification. List these letters across the

top of your table and the taxon names along the side.

Taxon	Characteristic to be used
Kingdom	producer or consumer
Phylum	real or false organism
Class	habitat where it lives
Order	type of appendages
Family	number of appendages
Genus	body covering
Species	head adornment

Walrus

Flipper bones

Front

Rear

Sea lion

Seal

new information to identify relationships among organisms. For example, comparative embryology has revealed that the major group to which vertebrates—including humans—belong is most closely related to the group that includes the starfish and its relatives. Such a conclusion would be difficult to reach on the basis of adult structure alone. Comparative biochemistry finally established the ancestry of the horseshoe crab, seen in Figure 14-6. As the name suggests, this animal was thought to be a true crab. Yet blood studies showed differently. It is now classified as a relative of spiders.

Figure 14-5 The similarity of bone structure in the flippers of the walrus, sea lion, and seal provides evidence of common ancestry.

Figure 14-6 Biochemical studies show that the horseshoe crab is related to spiders, not crabs.

14.1 THE CONCEPT OF CLASSIFICATION 🐚 **371**

Analysis
Ask students to answer the following questions.
1. (a) How many similar taxa were shared by organisms A and C? *Four*
(b) What does this tell you about their similarities? Why? *Their appearances are more similar when they share more taxa.*

2. (a) How many similar taxa were shared by organisms D and F? *Two*
(b) What does this tell you about their similarities? Why? *Their characteristics and appearances are not similar, so they share few taxa.*
3. (a) What taxons are used when assigning a scientific name? *Genus and species*

371

Purpose

Students will become aware of the fact that a person trained in anatomy will sometimes have to research fine details such as the measurements of heel bones to show similarity between individuals. A trait as minor as heel bone length can yield quantitative data in support of a hypothesis.

Teaching Strategies

- Have students verify the meaning of the following words: *anatomist, cadaver, ethnicity, comparative anatomy.*
- Provide students with X rays obtained from a hospital of the heel area of adults. Have students measure and then prepare a histogram of their measurements. The class can work in cooperative groups.
  COOP LEARN

Possible Answers

1. Answers may vary. Religious belief may prevent people from donating their bodies or organs.
2. Hitler claimed that only Germans were a superior race and therefore it should have been impossible for someone who was not a pure Aryan to win an Olympic event.

Going Further

Have students research and report on the Olympic records established by Jessie Owens.
L1

Brainstorming

Ask students to explain the relationship between relatedness and similar DNA. They should be able to correlate relatedness and similar DNA with the fact that DNA is inherited, but, more importantly, is passed from one generation of organisms to another.

Figure 14-7 Guinea pigs may resemble rodents, but they have been reclassified based on DNA studies.

Classifying on a Molecular Basis Today, studies at the molecular level play a major role in determining evolutionary relationships. Analyses of proteins and/or DNA can often reveal relationships that could not be determined in any other way. The idea is quite simple: Organisms having many proteins or genes in common are closely related.

For example, guinea pigs, shown in Figure 14-7, were classified for many years with mice and squirrels as rodents. However, when scientists compared the guinea pig's proteins with those of other rodents and those of other types of mammals, they found significant differences in the sequences of amino acids. Taxonomists concluded that the guinea pig does not share a common ancestry with rodents, and it is now classified in a new group of its own.

In one method of comparing DNA, the DNA from each of two organisms is separated into single strands. The DNA of one of the organisms is made radioactive, and the DNA of both organisms is then mixed. Base pairing causes the single strands to bond with each other, forming double-stranded molecules. Bonding will occur only where the genes, or sequences of bases, are complementary. The bonding is detected because one set of DNA is radioactive. The greater the amount of bonding, the more closely related the two organisms. Using this method, scientists have been able to match the DNA of humans with other primates. For example, 93 percent of the base pairs of human and macaque DNA match up, showing a close evolutionary relationship between these species.

Not only can DNA reveal close evolutionary relationships, it can also be used to determine *when* two organisms began to diverge from their

HISTORY CONNECTION

William Montague Cobb

Six hundred human skeletons may sound like something from a horror movie, but the collection was instead an important teaching tool for Dr. William Montague Cobb (1904-1990). He used the skeletons to help train more than 6000 physicians while he worked for more than 40 years as an anatomist at the Howard University Medical School in Washington, D.C. Each of the skeletons, which came from cadavers used in the school's dissecting lab, is documented by race, ethnicity, and place of birth. This careful documentation makes the collection invaluable in the study of comparative anatomy. Dr. Cobb became especially well-known for his research on the physical growth and development of African Americans.

Dr. Cobb's expertise in comparative anatomy put his name in the headlines on sports pages in the 1930s. At the time, Jesse Owens, an African American track star, was breaking world records at college athletic meets. He excelled in the 100- and 200-meter dash as well as the broad jump and other events. Two of the records he set stood for more than 20 years.

Some jealous people contended that Owens had an unfair advantage because of what they called the natural athletic ability of blacks. A specific contention was that blacks had a longer heel bone, which gave them greater leverage. After making extensive measurements, Dr. Cobb was able to conclude that hard work and courage, not physical characteristics, were at the heart of Owens's remarkable accomplishments.

372 🐾 CLASSIFICATION

Have students write a paragraph that describes the following: (a) how you as a blood-eating insect can get dinosaur DNA into your gut, (b) how by chance you end up fossilized in amber, (c) what scientists might learn from the analysis of dinosaur DNA, (d) how scientists will reconstruct the proteins that were made by dinosaur DNA. **L2** common ancestor. Mitochondrial DNA is used in this type of study. Because scientists theorize that mitochondrial DNA mutates at predictable rates, it may provide a molecular clock for dating evolutionary events.

Mitochondrial DNA from different species can be analyzed and compared. The number of differences in base sequences is a function of how long the organisms have been evolving. By comparing the differences in the base sequences of the DNA and using predicted rates of mutation, scientists can establish how long the two organisms have been diverging. Using this approach, along with evidence from the fossil record and other biochemical evidence, scientists have determined that chimpanzees and humans began to evolve from a common ancestor only 5 million years ago.

It may surprise you to learn that DNA of ancient organisms can also be analyzed, if scientists are lucky enough to find it. Usually, DNA is destroyed as a dead organism decomposes, but some bits of it may survive under certain conditions. Many researchers hope to be able to analyze DNA from dinosaurs. They expect to get samples of dinosaur blood from biting insects preserved in amber. Some unusually well-preserved leaves of a magnolia tree that lived 20 million years ago provided an opportunity for DNA analysis. Scientists used a new technique that produces many copies of DNA in a short period of time, providing enough DNA to be studied. One particular gene coding for an enzyme in photosynthesis was analyzed and compared with the same gene in a modern magnolia. What was discovered? Out of a total of 820 base pairs, 803 remained the same. Such studies help determine evolutionary relationships.

Figure 14-8 **Humans and chimpanzees evolved from a common ancestor. Various lines of evidence show that gibbons, orangutans, and gorillas also evolved from the same common ancestor.**

Science, Technology, and Society

Cytochrome C: A technique that relies on protein comparison between organisms is used to supply information on relatedness. Similar sequences of amino acids are evidence of common ancestry. One technique compares a protein called cytochrome c that is present in mitochondria of almost all organisms. The amino acid sequences of this protein in humans and chimpanzees are identical for all 104 positions. The sequence in the rhesus monkey differs by only one position from the sequence in humans and chimps. Human cytochrome c differs from that of dogs by 13 amino acid sequences. This number jumps to 31 when humans are compared to tuna.

MATH CONNECTION

Comparing Hemoglobin: Provide students with the following sequences of amino acids (in abbreviated form) from a portion of hemoglobin in humans, horses, and gorillas: Human = leu-gly-asp-val-leu-val-cys-val-leu-ala-his-his-phe-gly-lys. Gorilla = leu-gly-asp-val-leu-val-cys-val-leu-ala-his-his-phe-gly-lys. Horse = leu-gly-asp-val-leu-val-leu-val-val-ala-arg-his-phe-gly-lys. Ask students to: (a) calculate the number of differences in amino acids between human, gorilla, and horse, and (b) calculate the percent difference between the three organisms. Answers: (a) no difference between humans and gorillas, but horse hemoglobin differs by three amino acids; (b) horses differ from humans and gorillas by 20 percent. L1   COOP LEARN

In the 1960s, Dr. Cobb became troubled that African Americans did not have equal access to the hospitals in Washington, D.C., and that the city's medical society was also segregated. He organized and led the negotiating team that corrected both of these injustices. As president of the National Association for the Advancement of Colored People from 1976 to 1982, Dr. Cobb continued to champion civil rights in the medical profession and beyond.

1. **Issue:** Medical schools need human bodies to teach medical students about anatomy. What do you think are the pros and cons of donating one's organs or body after death to a medical school?
2. **Explore Further:** Why do you think it was so personally embarrassing to Adolf Hitler, dictator of Germany from 1933 to 1945, to see Jesse Owens excel in the Olympics held in Berlin?

14.1 THE CONCEPT OF CLASSIFICATION **373**

PORTFOLIO

Have students use Table 14.1 on page 377 and Table 14.2 on page 387 to record: (a) where one could find grasshoppers and fossils of mastodons; (b) the reason for the species name of dogs; and (c) the reason for the cartoon character Felix the Cat's name. Students may include these in their portfolios. L1

Enrichment

Provide students with the following information regarding the Suborder and Family, respectively, to which each animal belongs: giant panda = Caniformia, Ailuropodidae; red panda = Caniformia, Procyonidae; bear = Caniformia, Ursidae. Ask what can be told regarding characteristics of these three animals based on their classifications. **L1** **COOP LEARN**

Software

Classification, Queue

Audiovisual

Show the laserdisc *The Biology Encyclopedia,* Carolina Biological Supply Company.

Different Viewpoints in Biology

Panda Classification Still in Doubt?

Not all scientists agree with the current classification scheme for the giant panda. Drs. D.D. Davis and V. Sarich have classified the giant panda with bears. Drs. H. Heine and I. Pogloyen-Neuwall classify both the red and the giant panda in the family Ailuropodidae.

---

3 Assess

Check for Understanding

Have students explain the relationship that exists between the following word groups:

(a) taxa—classification
(b) common names—binomial nomenclature
(c) genus and species—scientific name
(d) structure—homologous
(e) function—analogous **L1**

Phylogeny

When taxonomists classify an organism, they are really providing the evolutionary history, or **phylogeny,** of the organism. Each taxon can be thought of as representing a different step in an organism's phylogeny.

For more than 100 years, the phylogeny of the giant panda has been in doubt. First studied in 1869 in western Asia, the giant panda was classified as a bear on the basis of its physical appearance or structure. Later, it was thought to behave more like the red panda and was classified with raccoons. As the debate continued, some scientists argued for the bear classification; others for the raccoon. Structure and behavior suggested to some taxonomists that the panda be placed in a group of its own. To confuse the issue further, the giant panda has a thumb, a structure found only in primates. In pandas, however, that thumb is not a true opposable thumb, but a sixth digit that evolved from a wrist bone. The panda's thumb and primates' thumbs are the result of convergence, so the presence of a thumb cannot be used to establish common ancestry.

Recent work shows just how important the use of several lines of evidence can be in classification. Using the technique of studying radioactive DNA strands described previously, scientists learned that the giant panda

Figure 14-9 Red pandas have long been classified with raccoons. When the giant panda was classified with red pandas, it became a "relative" of raccoons, too. The actual relationships among the raccoon (a), red panda (b), giant panda (c), and black bear (d) were determined using several lines of evidence.

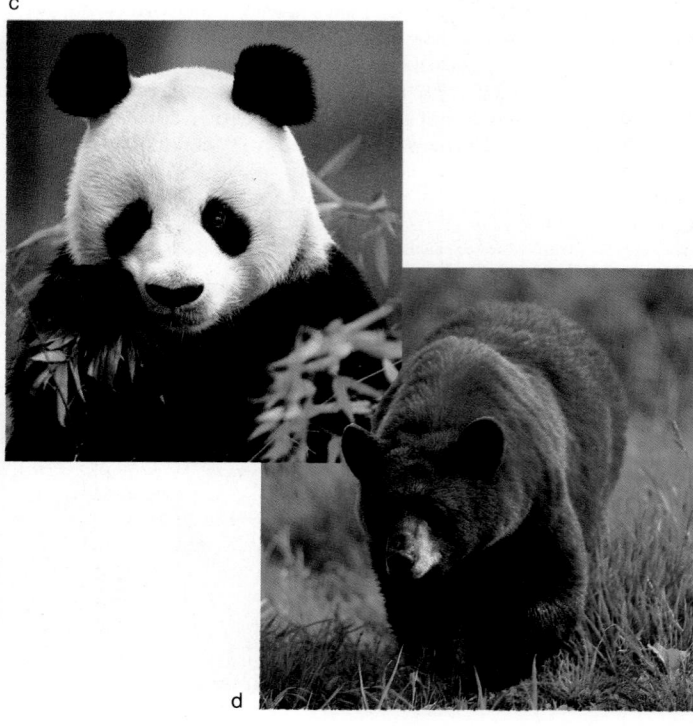

374 CLASSIFICATION

PORTFOLIO

Ask students to spend some time examining the photos on this page. Have them prepare a list that provides as many similarities as they can see among all the animals. A chart may be helpful in grouping and/or analyzing their observations. Have students prepare a second chart that lists as many differences among the four animals as they can see. Using only their observations, ask students to predict how these four animals are related and how they should be classified. Ask students to explain why the use of only physical characteristics makes it difficult to show phylogeny and accurate classifications among animals. **L1**

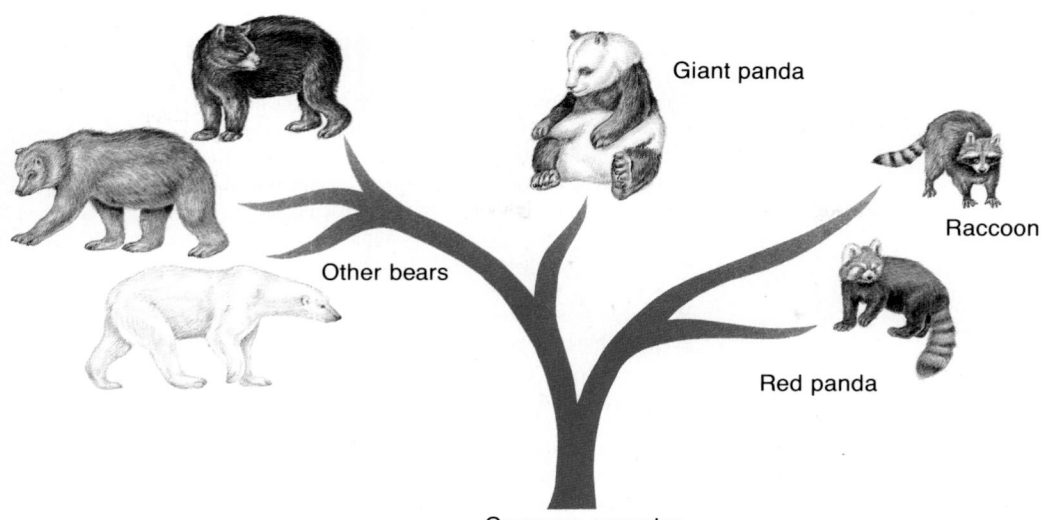

Giant panda

Other bears

Raccoon

Red panda

Common ancestor

is more closely related to bears than to raccoons. Biochemical comparisons of enzymes and other proteins led to the same conclusion. With these techniques, along with fossil evidence, the evolutionary histories of the giant panda, the bear, and the raccoon have now been more clearly established.

Figure 14-10 represents those histories in the form of what is called an evolutionary or a phylogenetic diagram. You can see that both bears and raccoons descended from a common ancestor. You can also see that the giant panda is a bear and the red panda is a raccoon. Each fork in the branches of an evolutionary diagram represents a point at which offspring of a common ancestor gave rise to different descendant groups. You can also see from this story how misleading common names can be.

Figure 14-10 The phylogenetic diagram of giant pandas shows that pandas are more closely related to bears than raccoons.

Section Review

Understanding Concepts
1. Consider a horse, a cow, and a wolf. Which two of them would have the more similar classifications? Why?
2. Give several reasons to explain why binomial nomenclature is useful.
3. Cite one example of how different lines of evidence can be used to establish evolutionary relationships.

4. *Skill Review—Classifying:* Based on your own knowledge, set up a scheme to place the following organisms in groups and subgroups: apple tree, baboon, butterfly, eagle, earthworm, fern, frog, human, jelly-fish, moss, oak, toad, tulip, wasp. For more help, see Organizing Information in the **Skill Handbook**.

5. *Thinking Critically:* Suppose the molecular clock technique indicates that an organism began evolving from its ancestor a certain number of years ago. What other line of evidence should yield the same basic data?

SECTION 14.1

Reteach
- Ask students to describe as much information as they can about the use of, advantages of, and rules for using scientific names.
- Have students briefly describe the methods used today by scientists that allow for determining relationships among organisms.

Extension
Have students determine those characteristics used in comparative embryology that established that the starfish and its relatives are more closely related to vertebrates than other invertebrate groups. **L3**

✔ Assessment
Portfolio: Have students summarize the major concepts of this section by designing a concept map that includes the use of binomial nomenclature and the techniques used to establish relationships. **L1** **LEP**

4 Close

Discussion
Have students explain why: (a) the wings of birds and bats are homologous and analogous, (b) the wings of birds and moths are analogous but not homologous, (c) taxonomy relies on homologous rather than analogous structures. **L1**

Answers to Section Review

1. Based on physical characteristics, the cow and the horse would have the more similar classifications. For example, both are plant eaters; the wolf eats meat.
2. Binomial nomenclature provides an accurate name for each organism that is recognized by scientists worldwide. It also is specific; for example, each type of cat or oak tree has a different name.
3. Because they share many homologous structures, it can be concluded that a human and a macaque are closely related. This conclusion is supported by comparing the two organisms' DNA, which is 93 percent alike.

4. **Skill Review—Classifying:** The organisms should first be grouped as plant or animal (or, producer or consumer). Within the plant group, moss and fern could be placed in separate sub-groups. The apple tree, oak, and tulip would make up another subgroup. Among the animals, earthworm and jelly-fish would be grouped separately. Butterfly and wasp would be classified together. Frog, toad, eagle, baboon, and human would make up a large subgroup, which could be subdivided.

5. **Thinking Critically:** The fossil evidence should support this conclusion.

Prepare

Key Concepts

The categories or taxons used in the classification scheme are looked at briefly. Organization and the problems that result from an imperfect system of five kingdoms are described.

Key Terms

kingdom, phylum, class, order, family

Materials

- Gather the "unknown" organisms suggested for Minilab 2. This would include slides of *Obelia* or *Ulva,* lichens, or liverworts.
- Materials needed for the Investigation should be located or remind students to bring specific items such as notebooks, pens, or backpacks to class.

1 Focus

Objectives

The objectives are listed on the student page. Remind students to review these objectives as a guide to this numbered section.

Activity

Have students place the following organisms into two groups: oak tree, dog, human, moss, bat, horse, mouse, cockroach, rose bush, corn, squirrel, geranium. Ask them to explain the trait or traits used to form the two groups. Would there be any problems with these two category groups if 100 organisms were used? Have students explain why. **L1**

Microscope Activity

Use prepared slides to study the appearance of *Euglena.* Slides are available from biological supply houses, or if available, these protists may be located in pond water. Have students diagram what they see and ask them to list those characteristics that tend to make *Euglena* plant-like and animal-like. **L1** **LEP**

Objectives

Demonstrate how each successive taxon is more specific than the previous taxon.

Discuss why the number of kingdoms of organisms has changed over time.

14.2 A System of Classification

Think again about classifying everyday objects like motor vehicles. In any system, you usually first assign the objects to very broad categories. Motor vehicles might be one broad group of objects used for travel. Other such groups might be wind-powered vehicles and animal-drawn devices. Beyond the broad group, you can then assign each object to increasingly more specific groups. You've seen, for example, that cars comprise subgroups such as sedans and convertibles. You could classify sedans as two-door or four-door models. You could further group each of these by type of engine. With each subdivision, the object is classified into a more specific category. Within each subdivision, the members are more like each other.

Taxa

When an organism is assigned to a species, it has been classified as specifically as possible. The genus to which that species belongs is a slightly more general taxon because several species may be members of that genus. The complete classification system includes five more taxa, for a total of seven.

The seven taxa form a series. The broadest taxon is the **kingdom.** Kingdoms are divided into increasingly more specific taxa. These are, in order, **phylum, class, order,** and **family.** Genus and species are last. Each taxon narrows the number of organisms of the previous group. Therefore, the number of organisms included in each taxon becomes smaller and smaller. Each species is one certain type of organism.

That sequence is classification in its simplest form. But classification is often more complex because each of these major groups may be further subdivided. For example, each phylum may be divided into several subphyla. The phylum that vertebrates belong to contains three subphyla, of which one is Vertebrata. A single species may be made up of several subspecies. Subspecies are sometimes called breeds, varieties, or races. The various breeds of domestic dogs, for example, are all subspecies.

Figure 14-11 **The seven taxa used to classify organisms include the division, a taxon at the phylum level. Organisms in the Plant and Fungi Kingdoms are classified in divisions rather than phyla.**

376 CLASSIFICATION

PROGRAM RESOURCES

Teacher Classroom Resources
Study Guide, pp. 81-84 **L1**
Concept Mapping, p. 14 **L1** **LEP**
Exploring Environmental Issues, pp. 31-32 **L3**
Probing Levels of Life, Lab 28, p. 80 **L2**
Investigating Living Systems, Lab 34, p. 133 **L2**

MEETING INDIVIDUAL NEEDS

Ask students who are having trouble seeing that taxa become more specific to try classifying different types of candy. Using the Candy Kingdom, they should try to classify chocolate versus non-chocolate candy (phylum), milk chocolate versus non-milk chocolate (class), plain milk chocolate versus milk chocolate with nuts, raisins or peanut butter (order), and so on.

Some Examples of Classification

What would the complete classification of a common house cat (*Felis catus*) be? First, a cat is classified as an animal based on the very broad characteristics of all animals. Like all other animals, for example, a cat doesn't make its own food, but eats other organisms. Cats are also multi-cellular organisms. Using these and other characteristics, the cat is placed in Kingdom Animalia.

A cat is then put into the Phylum Chordata and, because it has a back-bone, into the subphylum Vertebrata. This subphylum includes the seven classes of fish, amphibians, reptiles, birds, and mammals. You can see the rest of the classification of a common house cat in Table 14.1. Each group represents more specific characteristics than the previous group.

Now compare the classification of a cat with that of a dog. Because cats and dogs share the same broad characteristics, they are in the same kingdom, phylum, subphylum, class, and order. But at the family level, the classification diverges. The different families represent different branches of animal evolution. Each of the remaining groups is, of course, also different from the others.

Minilab 2

What traits are used to classify an unknown organism?

Your teacher will provide you with an organism you've never seen before. Your task is to classify it by kingdom. Observe and record as many traits as you can see with the naked eye, then observe under the microscope. Record additional traits. Review your list. Use your list to determine the kingdom to which you believe this organism belongs.

Analysis *What kingdom does this organism belong to? What traits helped you decide which kingdom to place the organism in? Explain why.*

Table 14.1 **Classification of Some Animals**

Taxon	House Cat	Dog	Human	Grasshopper
Kingdom	Animalia	Animalia	Animalia	Animalia
Phylum	Chordata	Chordata	Chordata	Arthropoda
Subphylum	Vertebrata	Vertebrata	Vertebrata	
Class	Mammalia	Mammalia	Mammalia	Insecta
Order	Carnivora	Carnivora	Primates	Orthoptera
Family	Felidae	Canidae	Hominidae	Locustidae
Genus	Felis	Canis	Homo	Schistocerca
Species	Felis catus	Canis familiaris	Homo sapiens	Schistocerca americana

---

SECTION 14.2

2 Teach

Minilab 2

Purpose
Students will have an opportunity to use scientific methods to classify unknown living things.

Skills
classify, compare and contrast, sequence, observe and infer

Teaching Strategies
- Suggestions for unknown organisms may be *Ulva* (sea lettuce), any lichen, a liverwort with reproductive bodies, or *Obelia*.
- It may be of interest to have certain students share their observations and decision-making process with the class. You may also wish to refer students to Appendix A, which describes traits and provides examples of the five kingdoms.
- Students may work in groups of two or three to reduce the number of samples needed.

Expected Results
The objective with this Minilab is not to determine exactly what kingdom the organism belongs to, but to allow students to observe and then use traits as a basis for classification. Therefore, determining the correct kingdom is not important. Typically, if the organism is green and macroscopic, students will place the organism in the Plant Kingdom. If green and microscopic, it will be placed in the Protist Kingdom. *Obelia* will most likely be placed in the Protist Kingdom.

Answers
There are no correct answers to the questions. However, the choice of those traits used should justify or support the kingdom choice.

✔ Assessment
Skill: Your teacher has provided you with a piece of coral. Use your powers of observation to support the idea that coral is not a plant but is indeed the remains of an animal.

STUDENT JOURNAL

Have students look up the classification of domesticated animals such as horses, cows, pigs, or chickens. Ask them to compare these organisms to those listed in Table 14.1. In their journals, ask students to prepare a table similar to Table 14.1 listing the classifications of the organisms they have looked up. Ask them to identify which organisms in their tables are most closely related to the organisms in Table 14.1.

INVESTIGATION

Making a Key

Time Allotment

1 class period

Objectives

Upon completing this investigation, students will be able to:

- Identify the pattern used in the construction of a biological key.
- Construct a key.
- Understand how a key may be used to identify objects.

Skills

classify, sequence, observe and infer, interpret data

Materials

between 10 and 20 items belonging to students, such as shoes, backpacks, pens, notebooks, gloves; or laboratory equipment; or other items found in classrooms

Preparation

An ideal number of objects per group would be between 10 and 20. The advantages of using shoes are that (1) a class of 20 students can provide 4 groups of 10 shoes each; (2) the same objects will be keyed in different ways in different groups; (3) students will bring them to class on their feet and will not have to be reminded of bringing a specific item to class on a specific day; (4) you will not have to secure the items for keying in advance of class; (5) each shoe can be identified with a student. To determine if the group keys are designed properly, any shoe picked at random from a group can be keyed out and returned to its rightful owner.

One disadvantage to using shoes is that the economic levels of various students may relate to the shoes they wear. Be aware that this activity may prove embarrassing for certain students. Students from certain cultural backgrounds may be uncomfortable showing their feet to others as well.

Possible Hypotheses

If a key is properly designed, it can be used to identify whose shoes belong to whom. If a key is developed correctly, it will be organized in a way similar to the key shown with jays.

Now compare the cat and dog with humans. How closely do humans seem to be related to dogs and cats? How many levels of classification do humans have in common with dogs and cats? At what level do the classifications differ?

Finally, compare these three animals with the grasshopper. The only common taxon among the grasshopper, cat, dog, and human is kingdom—all these organisms are classified as animals. Because the grasshopper's characteristics are different from those of the other animals, so, too, is its classification.

The grasshopper is classified in the Phylum Arthropoda. What major difference among organisms would cause a taxonomist to place a newly-discovered animal into the Phylum Chordata rather than the Phylum Arthropoda? How are you different from a grasshopper?

INVESTIGATION

Making a Key

You wish to identify a friend in a crowd. You do it by looking for certain key traits that you associate with your friend. If your friend has red hair or is very tall, you might first use hair color or height to screen the crowd and narrow down your search. It's usually an easy task if the crowd is not too large. However, what if you were asked to pick out a person from a crowd but had never seen this person before? That complicates things a bit. How would you do it? You would need a list of that person's traits in order to help identify him or her. How do scientists identify an organism that they are not familiar with? They use almost the same technique as you would use to pick out a person you have never met before. The scientist uses a tool called a biological key. These types of keys list traits of living things, which allows you to identify the organism in question down to its scientific name. Below is an example of what a key might look like if you were attempting to identify jaybirds.

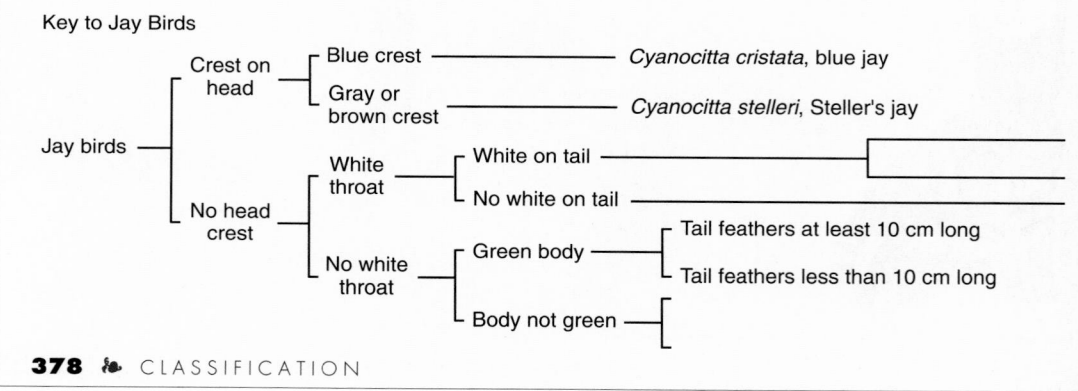

Key to Jay Birds

Possible Procedures

- Advise students in advance to bring in the objects they will be classifying.
- If using shoes, the shoe may be identified by owner's name.
- If using laboratory equipment, students should be told the name for specific items that they may not be familiar with such as Florence or Erlenmeyer flasks, etc.
- If they look at the jaybird key example, students will note that once a bird is keyed out or identified, it is no longer used in the key. A well-designed key will show a pattern at

The Kingdom Problem

You know from Chapter 2 that most biologists today use a five-kingdom system of classification. These kingdoms include the monerans, protists, fungi, plants, and animals. Examples of organisms in each kingdom are shown in Figure 14-12 on page 381. All organisms once were classified as either plants or animals. This two-kingdom scheme was reasonable for most familiar, multicellular organisms. After all, it is not difficult to distinguish a plant like a cactus from an animal like a coyote.

However, the discovery of microscopic organisms posed a problem. Some unicellular forms could easily be classified into one kingdom or the other, but many did not fit neatly into either group. For example, an organism called *Euglena* has characteristics common to both kingdoms.

Problem

How can you design a key?

Hypothesis

What is your group's hypothesis? Explain your reasons for forming this hypothesis.

Experimental Plan

1. As a group, make a list of possible ways you might construct a key to identify by name the objects given to you by your teacher.
2. Agree on one idea from your group's list.
3. Assign responsibilities within your group for the various tasks to be done.

Checking the Plan

1. Your key must identify all objects given to your group.
2. All objects must be identified by name (or at least by the owner's name).
3. The key ends for a specific item when its name is given.

4. Note that each set of traits at each fork in the key tend to be opposites of one another. For example, the first fork in the example key compares a crest on the head to its opposite (no crest).
5. A person not familiar with the objects used by your group should be able to use your key and correctly key out any object from your group.

Data and Observations

Carry out your design by writing a key that identifies the objects given to your group.

Analysis and Conclusions

1. What is actually used as the basis for designing each different subcategory or fork on your key?
2. Try your key out with other groups. If it works, what does this tell you about your key design? If it does not work, what does this tell you about your key design?

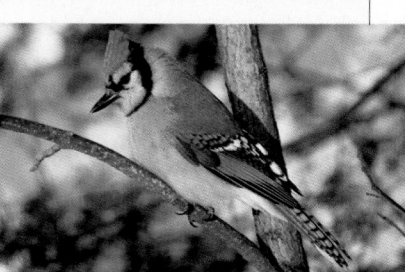

3. Assume that all groups in the class began with the exact same objects. Might all keys be exactly alike? Explain. Is it proper to say that only one key is correct? Explain.
4. Explain the value of a biological key.
5. List several examples of when keys may be useful tools.

Going Further

Based on this activity, design another key that would also work for the identification of the objects provided you. Record this key as part of your experimental report.

✔ Assessment

Skills: Ask students to prepare a key that identifies six individuals. Two of the six must include you (the teacher) and one school administrator. The other four are to be classmates in this classroom.

Extensions

Locate examples of biological keys. Have students examine them and, if possible, use them in the identification of a set of organisms.

SECTION 14.2

each fork of contrasting traits. Look for this in the keys that each group produces. The test as to whether or not a group's key is correct comes when a person totally unfamiliar with the key is able to identify any object correctly by using the key.

Teaching Strategies

• Have one member of each group write the key onto a sheet of clear acetate. This will allow each group to display its key on an overhead projector and thus allows other classmates to use the displayed key to identify the objects. This technique will also quickly point out any errors that have been made in a group's organization of its key.

Data and Observations

Allow students to share keys and objects from other groups. This technique will also quickly allow students to identify any errors that have been made in an original group's organization of its key if unfamiliar students cannot use the key correctly.

Data Analysis

1. Specific traits or characteristics are being used in the construction of a key.
2. (a) If the key works correctly, it has been properly designed. (b) If the key does not work correctly, it is improperly designed.
3. (a) No—each group may have used different traits in their key design. (b) No—no one design is correct. If the key works, it is designed properly.
4. Keys enable scientists or nonscientists to identify organisms that are unfamiliar to them.
5. Answers will vary. Students may cite key use in identifying birds, insects, grass types, flowers, plant diseases, bacteria, minerals, rocks, and poisonous snakes.

Bioethics

Animal Experimentation: Should experimentation on animals be allowed and/or continued? In favor of continuing this type of research, supporters state that (a) the life expectancy of humans has increased by almost 25 years this century as a direct result of animal research, (b) computer modeling cannot replace actual testing on living things, (c) humans have always used animals for food, fiber, and transportation, and this is merely an extension of that use, (d) animals are not poorly treated or neglected during any phase of research. Those opposed to animal research state that (a) modeling with computers can provide enough data to replace animal research, (b) poor treatment of and cruelty to experimental animals does occur. Some individuals feel that experimentation should be allowed only for essential research and should be discontinued for the development of products such as cosmetics.

Euglena is mobile, like an animal, yet autotrophic, like a plant. To confuse the matter further, at certain times *Euglena* may lose its chlorophyll and become heterotrophic.

Other problems arise with a two-kingdom system. For example, how should fungi such as mushrooms and molds be classified? They are like plants in that they do not move, but they are heterotrophic like animals. What about slime molds? They are heterotropic and move like *Amoeba*, but they produce spores like fungi. Sponges, sea anemones, and coral all are animals, but they resemble plants.

Based on current knowledge of evolutionary relationships among organisms, the five-kingdom system has solved some of these problems. Identifying cells as prokaryotes or eukaryotes helped classify many microscopic organisms. Remember from Chapter 5 that prokaryotic cells have no nucleus. All monerans are prokaryotes. However, other classification systems have been proposed. That's not surprising because biologists often interpret data in different ways. One proposed system is based on six kingdoms. The sixth kingdom consists of a group of extremely ancient bacteria that are different in certain respects from other bacteria. Some taxonomists, therefore, argue that these bacteria represent a different major branch of evolution. You'll learn about these bacteria in the next chapter. However, this book will use the five-kingdom system, as presented in Appendix A. Use it as a reference when needed.

Thinking Lab
INTERPRET THE DATA

What traits are used to classify organisms into kingdoms?

Background
Today's classification scheme uses a five-kingdom system. The separation of all life forms into these five main groups is based on shared characteristics.

You Try It
Copy the outline provided. Complete it by writing the listed terms in the correct bracket spaces. When complete, the outline should provide a logical and

correct guide to the traits of the five kingdoms. Terms: usually unicellular, autotrophic, prokaryotic, eukaryotic, multicellular, heterotrophic, ingest food, absorb food.

All organisms
[ ] ———————————————————— Monerans
[ ] [ ] ———————————————————— Protists
[ ] [ ] ———————————————— Plants
[ ] [ ] [ ] — Fungi
[ ] — Animals

Thinking Lab
INTERPRET THE DATA

Purpose
Students will complete a classification scheme.

Skills
classify, sequence, make and use tables

Teaching Strategies
• This lab may be completed as homework and included in the students' portfolios.

Answers
See completed outline.

✔ Assessment
Knowledge: Have students explain the difference between word pairs in the outline.

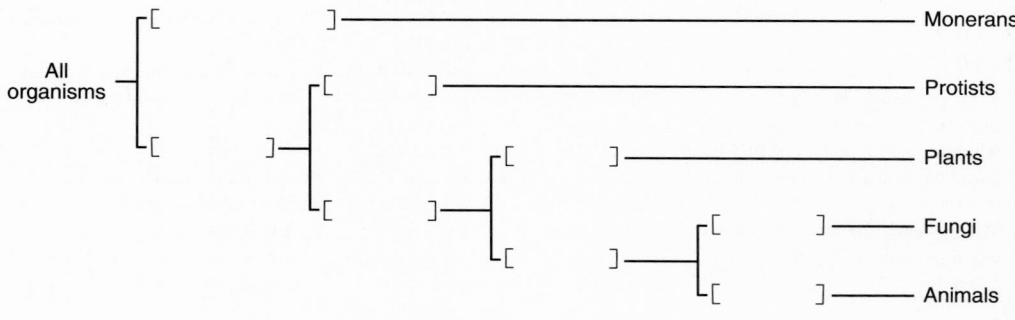

All organisms
— prokaryotic ———————————————— Monerans
— eukaryotic
— usually unicellular ———————————— Protists
— multicellular
— autotrophic ———————————— Plants
— heterotrophic
— absorbs food — Fungi
— ingests food — Animals

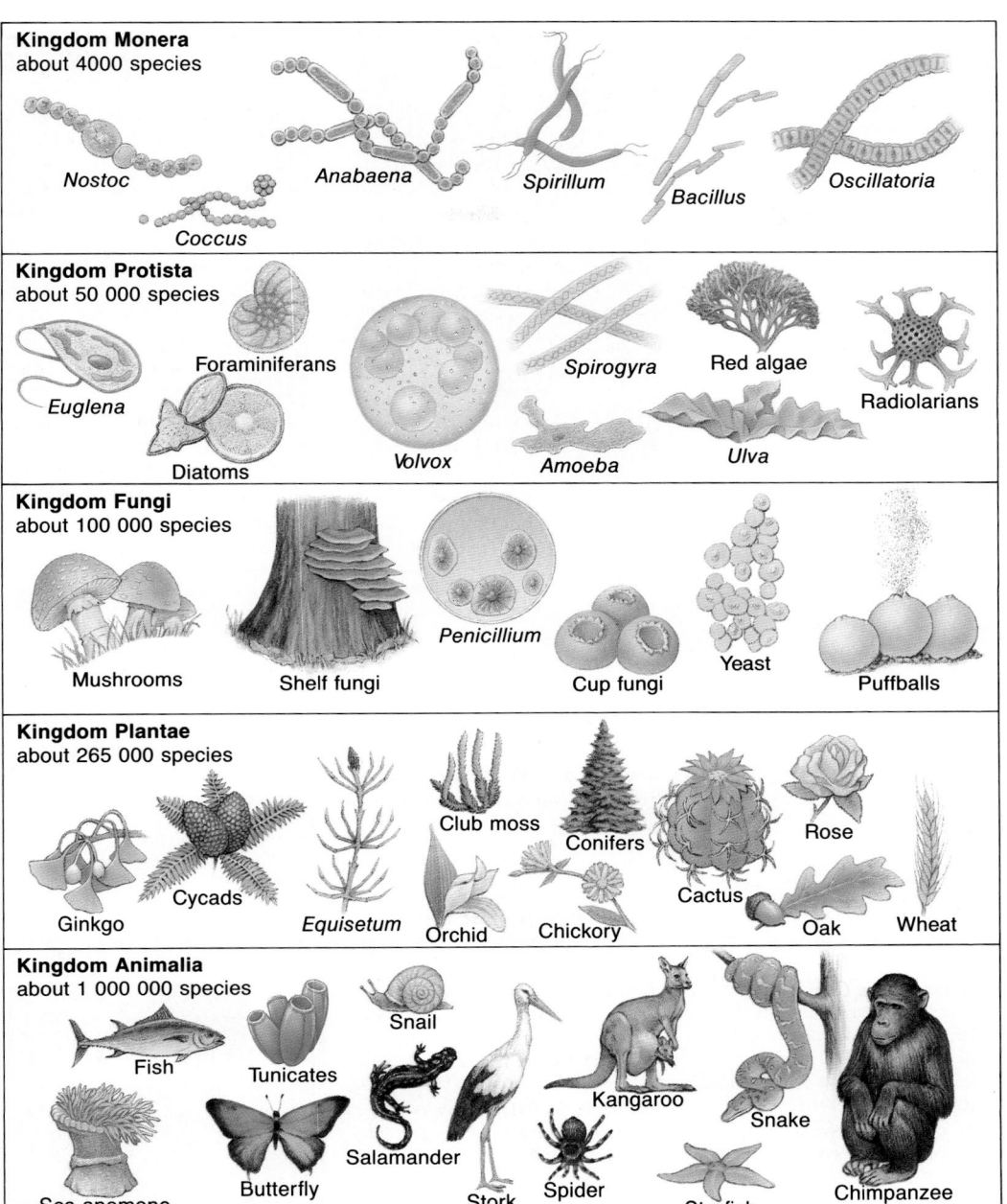

Kingdom Monera
about 4000 species

Nostoc Anabaena Spirillum Bacillus Oscillatoria
Coccus

Kingdom Protista
about 50 000 species

Foraminiferans Spirogyra Red algae Radiolarians
Euglena Diatoms Volvox Amoeba Ulva

Kingdom Fungi
about 100 000 species

Mushrooms Shelf fungi Penicillium Cup fungi Yeast Puffballs

Kingdom Plantae
about 265 000 species

Cycads Club moss Conifers Rose Cactus
Ginkgo Equisetum Orchid Chickory Oak Wheat

Kingdom Animalia
about 1 000 000 species

Snail Kangaroo Snake
Fish Tunicates Salamander Spider Chimpanzee
Sea anemone Butterfly Stork Starfish

Figure 14-12 The five kingdoms of life include the Monera, Protista, Fungi, Plant and Animal Kingdoms.

SECTION 14.2

Reinforcement

Review the terms *autotrophic, heterotrophic, unicellular, eukaryotes,* and *prokaryotes.* Ask students to provide not only definitions of each term but also an example of each. L1 LEP

Using the Illustration

Have students examine Figure 14-12. Then ask them to explain or answer the following questions: (a) What trait or traits are shared by all kingdoms? (b) How do the Monerans differ from all other kingdoms? (c) How are certain Monerans plant-like and animal-like? (d) How do the Protists differ from the Fungi, Plants, and Animals? (e) What traits do Protists share with some Plants and Animals? (f) How do the Fungi differ from other kingdoms and what traits do they share? (g) How does the Plant Kingdom differ from other kingdoms and what traits do they share? (h) How does the Animal Kingdom differ from other kingdoms and what traits do they share? L1 LEP
COOP LEARN

Misconception

Present students with a piece of coral and a sea fan. Ask them to indicate the kingdom to which these organisms belong. Almost without exception, students will place these organisms into the Plant Kingdom. Ask them the basis for their decision. If plants, why are they not green? What further information would be needed to correctly classify these two organisms?

CHEMISTRY CONNECTION

Chemistry Dependent:
Living things depend on chemistry. DNA is made up of sugars, phosphate groups, and nitrogen bases. All living things are thus composed of the same chemicals. Genes that are inherited determine the sequence of amino acids produced in cells, which in turn determine the proteins produced by organisms. Thus, chemistry is the basis of life on Earth.

PROJECT

Using Five Kingdoms: Ask students to check around their homes or apartments and bring in a list of examples of how members of the five kingdoms are used in art, room decorations, room furniture, or in the actual construction of the room itself. Their lists should include the item as well as the kingdom to which it belonged. This list may be added to their portfolios. L1

PORTFOLIO

Have students prepare a key that could be used to identify the five kingdoms. Have them verify that their key works by allowing other classmates to try it. Have students review the proper organization and construction of a biological key before undertaking this assignment. L1 COOP LEARN

3 Assess

Check for Understanding

Have students explain the relationships that exist between the following:
(a) taxon order from kingdom to species and specificity;
(b) subspecies and breeds or varieties;
(c) Animal Kingdom and not being able to make food; and
(d) two-kingdom system and problems associated with the discovery of microscopic life forms. **L1**

Reteach

- Have students list the taxon names from most specific category to least specific category.
- Use the classification scheme for the African elephant on page 387 to illustrate that taxa become more selective moving from kingdom to species.
- Describe some of the problems associated with a two-kingdom system for classification and how the five-kingdom system has solved some of these problems.

Extension

Prepare a classification scheme for poodles, Great Danes, collies, and greyhounds. Include a highly specific taxon level not typically used within the chapter. Explain why and when this level would be needed. **L2**

✔ Assessment

Performance: Have students prepare a key of the five kingdoms. Give each student five organisms or photographs of organisms. Have them classify the organisms into kingdoms. Have them explain why they placed organisms into particular kingdoms.

4 Close

Activity

Have students design a sentence whose words begin with the first letters of the taxon category names. The letters to be used are K-P-C-O-F-G-S. For example: Kind people can...etc.

a

b

Figure 14-13 Which of these is a plant and which is an animal? Structure alone is not enough to classify an animal like the sponge (a) and a loofah (b), the dried fruit of a plant in the gourd genus *Luffa.*

LOOKING AHEAD

VARIOUS LINES of evidence—structural, biochemical, molecular—are used to establish evolutionary relationships. From this evidence, a five-kingdom system for classifying organisms has been developed. In Chapter 15, you will learn about the diversity of and evolutionary relationships among organisms of three kingdoms—monerans, protists, and fungi. You'll also study the unique viruses, which are not classified in any kingdom.

Section Review

Understanding Concepts

1. Explain why two organisms classified in the same family must also be in the same order.
2. Based on Table 14.1, which taxa would a gorilla and a human have in common? Defend your answer.
3. Relate the classification of an organism to its phylogeny.

4. *Skill Review—Classifying:* Use Appendix A to classify a bee down to order. For more help, see Organizing Information in the **Skill Handbook.**
5. *Thinking Critically:* What structural features put humans, cats, and dogs in the same taxa through the class level? What characteristics place humans in a different order from cats and dogs?

Answers to Section Review

1. Family is a more specific taxon than order.
2. kingdom, phylum, subphylum, class, and order
3. The classification of an organism is based on evolutionary relationships. Each taxon can be thought of as a point at which a particular organism diverged from organisms not sharing that taxon.

4. **Skill Review—Classifying:** Kingdom Animalia, Phylum Arthropoda, Class Insecta, Order Hymenoptera.
5. **Thinking Critically:** All three belong to Class Mammalia on the basis of features such as presence of mammary glands, hair or fur, and bearing their young alive. Unlike cats and dogs, humans have features such as upright posture, a larger brain, and hands with fingers rather than paws.

BIOLOGY, TECHNOLOGY, AND SOCIETY

Biotechnology

Modern Tools for Classification

For years, biologists working in the rain forests gazed longingly upward at the rain forest canopy looming 30 m above their heads. High up in what one naturalist called "an undiscovered continent" live up to 40 percent of the world's species of plants and animals. Previously, except for a few daredevils using ropes to climb to the top, scientists could only crane their necks to peer through binoculars at a world that was tantalizingly out of touch.

Parts of that world can now be explored at arm's length from a 42-meter tower on Barro Colorado Island, near the Panama Canal. Allowing even greater access is a construction crane set up near Panama City. A gondola on the end of the crane's 36-meter arm can be maneuvered to any height up to 30 meters and to any position on a circular area more than 60 meters in diameter.

A team of French biologists took a more lofty approach to reaching the rain forest canopy in French Guiana. Deciding to reverse previous methods and work from top to bottom, scientists rigged up an inflatable raft to sit atop the towering trees. They used a hot-air dirigible to carry aloft a set of rubber pontoons interlaced with fiber netting and balance it on the canopy.

The resulting 600 m² of work space is shared by teams of scientists from eight countries. It takes some daring to make the 15- to 30-minute ascension via ropes and harnesses, but once they have arrived at the "treehouse," scientists can move about in the canopy with relative safety.

Back on the ground with their samples from the canopy, biologists can use a new computer database to identify and classify the species they have collected. Appropriately called "Linnaeus," the system uses distinguishing features of taxonomic groups to guide identification. It directs a user to make a series of binary choices, such as:

1a. Animal with a carapace
1b. Animal without a carapace

Each succeeding choice narrows the possibilities until the species is finally identified.

Another useful tool in classification is the scanning electron microscope, which allows study of a living thing's DNA. This genetic material is unique for each species.

1. **Connection to Music:** In writing out DNA sequences, scientists use the letters A, T, G, and C to refer to molecules' chemical sub-units. Looking at a DNA sequence, a biochemist who is an amateur musician decided to change Ts to Es and tried playing the resulting "notes" on a music synthesizer. Try playing or singing a random series of the notes A, E, G, and C to see how DNA "sounds."

2. **Writing About Biology:** Some scientists call taxonomy "a window backwards into evolution." What do you think this description means?

3. **Issue:** Most scientific studies carry some risk of harming the subject of the study. What risks do you think could be associated with studying the rain forest canopy?

Going Further

Extend the answer to question 1 above by asking students how different the "sound" of RNA would be. Have students demonstrate their answers. Ask students to report on or discuss what the immediate or future value of research such as that being undertaken in rain forests is to society.

CHAPTER 14

BIOLOGY, TECHNOLOGY, AND SOCIETY

Biotechnology

Purpose

Students will be introduced to an unusual taxonomic study of an ecologic zone that previously resisted study. The need for a taxonomic system becomes apparent when attempting to determine if new species are being observed.

Teaching Strategies

- Have students work in cooperative groups to locate the specific areas and countries where this research is being conducted.
- Ask students to determine with meter sticks what exactly corresponds to: (a) a circle with a diameter of 60 m, (b) an area of 600 m². Use the school gym or an outdoor area to make these measurements.
- Measure off a 60-meter diameter circle on school grounds. Have students canvass this area and record the names of all known species of living things observed. Tally the number of unknown species also found.
- You may wish to ask students with musical ability to demonstrate the "answer" to question 1 for the entire class. Use of voice, guitar, or even harmonica would be ideal for the classroom demonstration.

Possible Answers

1. The rhythm of the four notes will vary but not the notes themselves.
2. This idea may be related to the ability of the taxonomist to predict when a specific group of organisms may have split off or evolved from its ancestors.
3. Destruction of, or injury to, organisms that are collected for study in the canopy may result. Further disruption may occur to certain organisms dependent in some way on those collected for study. Disruption of the normal habitat where these organisms live is occurring.

383

CHAPTER 14

Issues

Purpose

Students are exposed to several environmental issues that have and have not been resolved in favor of environments or the species that occupy these environments. They will also be made aware of how the government and outside pressure groups (both for and against saving the environment) may influence legislation related to environmental issues.

Background

In 1981, snail darter populations were found in a number of tributaries of the Little Tennessee River. By 1983, the status of the snail darter was changed from endangered to threatened by the U.S. Fish and Wildlife Service.

Teaching Strategies

Allow students to work in cooperative groups as they:

- answer the questions at the conclusion of this feature.
- design new questions or issues raised by the feature.
- do library research to determine how the Endangered Species Act of 1973 can be interpreted and to determine how often the law is enforced. Students should also research the penalties imposed on those who break this law.
- determine the distinction between endangered and threatened species. They should provide examples of each category and provide examples of organisms that have been moved off the lists due to conservation efforts.

In Competition: Fish or Dam?

In the mid-1970s, the construction of a $120 million dam on the Tennessee River was halted due to a fish only 8 cm long. This fish, called the snail darter, was not much to look at. In fact, it had been completely overlooked for centuries. Yet this unremarkable little fish kicked off a campaign that threatened to cancel a dam construction project that would provide hydroelectric power for a large area of Tennessee, create a lake, and increase recreational opportunities for state residents and visitors.

"Fish or Dam?" shouted headlines across the United States. Environmentalists and developers took their corners in one of the first tests of the Endangered Species Act passed by Congress in 1973. The act seemed to cover all bases, making it illegal for an endangered species to be "killed, hunted, collected, harassed, harmed, pursued, shot, trapped, wounded, or captured." In addition, it provided for the protection of such a species'

critical habitat, the living area a species needs in order to survive.

Soon after the Endangered Species Act went into effect, scientists discovered that the snail darter only existed in a portion of the Tennessee River scheduled to be flooded by dam construction. Efforts by conservationists succeeded in getting the snail darter declared an endangered species. In spite of protests, the United States Supreme Court halted construction of the dam—but only for a while.

The Dam is Built Proponents of the dam convinced their congressional representatives to pass a special bill to exempt this particular dam from compliance with the act. The dam was built, and some snail darters were transported to another river. Humans and their needs for electrical power, a larger water supply, recreation, and jobs had prevailed over the needs of a tiny fish.

Owls Versus Loggers In 1987, another small animal gained prominence in the news. The northern spotted owl was threatened by the loss of its habitat in the old-growth forests of the Pacific northwest. Timber companies wanted to continue logging these forests. Loggers feared they would lose their jobs if the northern spotted owl was given legal preference over their needs for jobs and income. Environmentalists tried to generate support for the owl by selling stuffed toy replicas of the bird, emphasizing its big, dark eyes. Loggers reacted by donning T-shirts that claimed, "I love spotted owls—on a sandwich" and "Save a logger. Eat an owl." Jobs

were at stake, and loggers were infuriated that "outsiders" would threaten their way of life and their livelihoods.

Seeking to capitalize on the feelings of loggers and their families, President Bush campaigned hard in the area in 1992. He threatened to refuse to sign a renewal of the Endangered Species Act. Like many people in the northwestern United States, the President believed that it was time to make people more important than animals, even endangered ones. Some people felt that it was time to rewrite the act to allow economic considerations to override the preservation of species.

The Earth Summit Similar sentiments came up at the first Earth Summit, held in 1992 and attended by representatives from all over the world. Efforts by developed countries such as the United States to dictate conservation practices met with disdain from developing countries. After all, they reasoned, the United States had prospered by cutting down its own forests and exploiting its other natural resources. To them, it seemed hypocritical of the U.S. to deny other countries the same route to industrialization and prosperity.

Protection and Economics Environmental scientists have been trying to show people that preserving the environment also benefits people in monetary terms. A researcher from the Massachusetts Institute of Technology recently finished a study that weakens the jobs-versus-environment argument. Professor Stephen Meyer looked at the relationship between jobs and environmental regulation in each state between 1982 and 1989. Although he expected to find a negative relationship, the results were quite the opposite: Environmental protection and economic development were mutually supportive.

Some American companies are also discovering on their own that they can save money by protecting the environment. For example, one huge corporation started pollution-prevention measures in 1970. Those measures translated into big savings—$670 million over 20 years.

Protecting Tropical Forests
Today, the public's attention is focused on the rain forests of South America and Asia. These rain forests cover only seven percent of Earth's surface but contain at least half of all plant and animal species. Unfortunately, rain forests are disappearing at the rate of about 70 000 square kilometers each year. They are cleared for subsistence farming and pasture for cattle. Ironically, the land these farmers clear remains useful for grazing or farming for only a few short years because most of the nutrients in rain forests are in the abundant plants, not in the soil. When the plants are cleared or burned, the soil that is left is deficient in essential nutrients such as minerals. After two or three years of planting crops, the few nutrients in the soil are used up. The soil will no longer support crops. So farmers are forced to clear more land, and the cycle of destruction continues.

The best hope for the conservation of rain forests is to find ways

for people to use them productively without destroying them. Some efforts, such as collecting certain nuts from rain forest trees, are under way right now. The race is also on to collect and test rain forest plants for medicinal uses. At least 1400 tropical plants may contain substances active against cancer. In addition to medicines, the rain forests may also contain new types of foods that could help to feed a hungry world. Scientists believe that rain forests contain more than 4000 species of edible fruits and vegetables. Only a tiny fraction of these foods are cultivated today.

Many scientists have read in the fossil record a tragic future for Earth's plant and animal species if the loss of endangered organisms accelerates. They believe that mass extinction is possible.

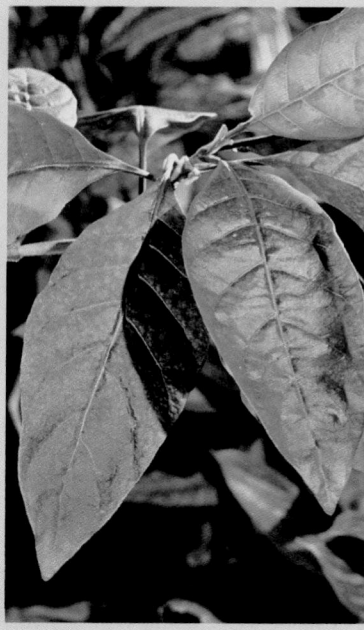

CAREER CONNECTION

Taxonomists study and classify organisms. They work in museums, research laboratories, universities, and scientific societies. Taxonomists often travel to all parts of the world to study endangered organisms. Taxonomists have a broad-based education, including biology, chemistry, anatomy, physiology, evolution, biochemistry, ecology, and genetics.

---

1. **Understanding the Issue:** What response could you make to Brazilians who insist that their country has a right to use its resources in any way it wants?

2. **Solve the Problem:** Imagine you were a congressional representative from a northwestern state in which loggers would lose their jobs if the spotted owl were protected to the full extent of the law. How could you save the owl and jobs for the loggers?

Readings
- Korn, Peter. "The Case for Preservation." *The Nation*, March 30, 1992, pp. 414-417.
- Adams, Robert. "Can We Find a Way to Balance the Survival of Endangered Species with the Livelihoods of People?" *The Smithsonian*, March 1992, p. 8.

- Order or collect owl pellets. Allow students to dissect these pellets. Relate student findings to food chains and control of rodent populations. Have students calculate the number of prey consumed by one owl per year based on the average number of skeletons found per pellet. Assume that an owl throws up one pellet every 24 hours. **L2** **COOP LEARN**

Possible Answers
1. Student answers will vary. However, one approach is to say that Brazil today is not isolated from all other countries. Ecological changes within one country can disrupt the ecology worldwide.
2. Student answers may vary. One approach would be to reach a compromise to limit the amount of logging in an area where spotted owls live. Another approach would be to relocate the owls to a different geographic area much as was done with the snail darters.

Going Further
Ask students to read the articles listed at the bottom of this feature. Have them either: (a) make reports to the class, (b) write reports and submit them as part of homework assignments, or (c) write reports and place them in their portfolios. **L2**

CAREER CONNECTION

Most universities and colleges do not offer a formal degree in taxonomy. Have students write or call your local museum to determine the type of training or formal education required and what the future job opportunities are for a taxonomist.

CHAPTER REVIEW

Summary

Summary statements can be used by students to review the major concepts of the chapter.

Language of Biology

Answers should go beyond defining the terms. Accept any reasonable answer that uses the term correctly and in the proper context.

Understanding Concepts

1. Many different species have the same common name; e.g., fish, frog. Also, some common names are misleading, such as cuttlefish, which is not a fish at all.
2. The genus name is a noun. The species name is an adjective describing that noun. For example, *Quercus alba* = white oak.
3. Such knowledge provided a logical basis for classification. Organisms having common ancestry are grouped together. The closer the evolutionary relationships, the more similar the classification.
4. By comparing DNA, scientists can determine relationships at the genetic level. The greater the amount of common DNA shared by organisms, the closer their relationship.
5. The date could be established by analyzing the mitochondrial DNA of the two organisms. This DNA is predicted to mutate at a certain rate. The number of base sequence differences between the two organisms indicates how long ago they began to diverge from a common ancestor.
6. DNA analysis, comparison of proteins, and fossil evidence together indicated that the panda is more closely related to bears than to raccoons.
7. There are many subspecies of house cats; e.g., Siamese, Persian, and Manx.
8. Although it is an animal, the grasshopper's more specific traits

---

Summary

Classification of organisms brings order to the great diversity of life. Each organism is assigned a two-part name—genus and species—recognized by scientists everywhere.

Taxonomy today classifies organisms on the basis of their evolutionary relationships. Using evidence based on fossils, homologous structures, and comparative studies of chemistry, embryos, proteins, and DNA, scientists can determine an organism's phylogeny.

Organisms are classified in a series of taxa, each of which represents a set of more specific characteristics. The broadest taxon is the kingdom; the most specific, the species. Most classification systems today are based on five kingdoms.

Language of Biology

Write a sentence that shows your understanding of each of the following terms.

binomial nomenclature	order
class	phylogeny
family	phylum
genus	taxa
kingdom	taxonomy

Understanding Concepts

1. Explain why common names of organisms are not scientifically acceptable.
2. How are the genus and species names of organisms related?
3. How did knowledge of evolution and natural selection improve the science of taxonomy?
4. How does knowledge of DNA make for more accurate classification of organisms?
5. Two organisms were found to have begun evolving from a common ancestor 15 million years ago. Other than fossil evidence, explain how that fact could be determined.
6. How were various lines of evidence combined to establish the giant panda's phylogeny?
7. Do you think various subspecies exist within *Felis catus*? Explain.
8. Why do you think a grasshopper is classified in a different phylum from the other animals classified in Table 14.1?

Applying Concepts

9. Certain lemurs and raccoons have similar patterns of coat coloration. Why would that similarity *not* be useful in determining the closeness of their evolutionary relationship?
10. All the following organisms are animals. Based on your everyday knowledge of these animals, place them into three different phyla. No technical terms are expected: ant, clam, crow, lobster, octopus, pig, shark, snail, spider, turtle.
11. *Amoeba* has many characteristics in common with the animals listed in question 10 above. Why is it not classified in the same kingdom? Refer to Chapter 2 or Appendix A for help.
12. Guess the common name of each of the following organisms: *Rattus norvegicus; Equus zebra; Elephus maximus; Pinus ponderosa; Camelus bactrianus.*
13. Several species of plants are known to have evolved from a common ancestor beginning 26 million years ago. Suppose the groups of plants are known by colors. One group includes species

---

are far different from those of the chordates. For example, it has an external skeleton and jointed legs and antennae.

Applying Concepts

9. The color patterns are a product of convergence. They do not indicate common ancestry.
10. Phylum 1: ant, lobster, spider. Phylum 2: clam, octopus, snail. Phylum 3: crow, pig, shark, turtle.

11. Although *Amoeba* is animal-like in that it is heterotrophic and can move, it is not multicellular; nor does it have nerves, which are animal characteristics.
12. rat; zebra; elephant; pine; camel

REVIEW

known as yellow, golden, and red. Fossil evidence and molecular clock techniques indicate that yellow evolved 8 million years ago, golden evolved 12 million years ago, and red evolved 17 million years ago. Another group includes green, which evolved 14 million years ago, and blue, which evolved 22 million years ago. Construct an evolutionary diagram for these species.

14. Sharks, skates, and rays have internal skeletons made of cartilage. How does this fact help taxonomists place these organisms into the correct taxa? Without any other information, to what taxa can you identify these organisms in the classification scheme?

15. **Biotechnology:** Study Table 14.2, then answer the following questions: What can you infer about the relationships of these organisms? From their family names? From their order names? If a mastodon were alive today, could it mate with an African elephant to produce fertile offspring? Explain your answers.

16. **Issues:** The California condor is an endangered bird species, once limited to only 39 individuals. At enormous expense, the last few surviving condors were captured and have been bred successfully in captivity. Should money be spent to save species on the verge of extinction? Why?

Lab Interpretation

17. **Investigation:** Complete the following incomplete key for classifying writing instruments. Key out the following: ballpoint pen, pencil, felt-tip marker.

Writing tools ⟶ Uses ink ⟶ .... / ....
⟶ ....

18. **Thinking Lab:** What traits are shared by the Animal and Fungi Kingdoms? How are you able to separate organisms into their correct kingdoms?

19. **Minilab 2:** An organism is found to be a consumer and can move about. Will these traits be enough to classify it into its proper kingdom? Why?

Connecting Ideas

20. Could members of different genera mate and produce fertile offspring? Could members of different subspecies? Explain.

21. How can the similar characteristics of two different species, such as tiger and cheetah, be explained?

Table 14.2 **Elephants and Their Relatives**

	African elephant	Asian elephant	Woolly mammoth	American mastodon
Kingdom	Animalia	Animalia	Animalia	Animalia
Phylum	Chordata	Chordata	Chordata	Chordata
Subphylum	Vertebrata	Vertebrata	Vertebrata	Vertebrata
Class	Mammalia	Mammalia	Mammalia	Mammalia
Order	Proboscidea	Proboscidea	Proboscidea	Proboscidea
Family	Elephantidae	Elephantidae	Elephantidae	Mastodontidae
Genus	Loxodonta	Elephas	Mammuthus	Mastodon
Species	Loxodonta africana	Elephas maximus	Mammuthus primigenius	Mastodon americanus

CHAPTER 14 CLASSIFICATION ⚜ **387**

Connecting Ideas

20. **Evolution:** Members of different genera could not produce fertile offspring. Because they diverged from a common ancestor, their gene pools evolved and have become quite different. Members of different subspecies, however, all belong to the same species and could interbreed.

21. **Evolution:** The two species have diverged from a common ancestor relatively recently. Thus, their similar genes control development of many similar traits.

13.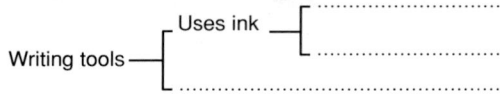
yellow / golden / red / green / blue

14. Internal skeletons are characteristics of vertebrates. Thus, the three organisms are in Kingdom Animalia, Phylum Chordata, and Subphylum Vertebrata.

15. The organisms are closely related based on the fact of their common classification through the order taxon. They have a common ancestor. They are all elephants or elephant-like. A mastodon, if alive today, could not breed with an African elephant (or Asian elephant either). Only members of the same species can interbreed.

16. Some students may argue that it is worth spending money to save an endangered species because an organism, once extinct, is gone forever. Others might argue that the money could be better spent solving problems faced by humans.

Lab Interpretation

17. Key should show writing tools as original term, diverging to uses ink and does not use ink; does not use ink flows to pencil; uses ink flows to felt tip and marker or tip, not felt and ball-point pen.

18. Both kingdoms share being multicellular and consumers. Animals move about and digest food that is first taken in. Fungi absorb digested food and do not move about.

19. No, you must know if it is unicellular or multicellular. Unicellular may place it in the Protist Kingdom, and multicellular may place it in the Animal Kingdom.

SECTION	OBJECTIVES	TEXT LABS/FEATURES
15.1 Viruses (1 day)	**Infer** how the structure of a virus is related to its function. **Compare** the reproductive cycles of viruses.	**Global Connection:** Who were the real conquerors? p. 392
15.2 Kingdom Monera (2 days)	**Describe** the basic characteristics of bacteria. **Compare** the various means of nutrition found among bacteria. **Demonstrate** knowledge of how bacteria are beneficial in nature and useful to humans.	
15.3 Kingdom Protista (2 days)	**Compare** the features of the various phyla of algae. **Distinguish** among the protozoan phyla. **Relate** the characteristics of slime molds to their life cycle.	**Minilab 1:** Is there life in a drop of pond water? p. 405 **Investigation:** The Effect of Chemicals on Protozoans, p. 406 **History Connection:** Protists Change a Country, p. 408
15.4 Kingdom Fungi (2 days)	**Compare** the characteristics of the different phyla of fungi. **Explain** how the organisms of which a lichen is composed benefit one another.	**Thinking Lab:** Why would farmers put noodles on their crops? p. 411 **Art Connection:** *Three Mushrooms* by Roberto Juarez, p. 412 **Minilab 2:** What do fungi need to grow? p. 414
BIOLOGY, TECHNOLOGY, AND SOCIETY		**Considering the Environment:** Fighting Pollution with Bacteria, p. 416 **Medicine Connection:** A Lucky Accident, p. 417 **Career Connection:** Microbiologist, p. 417

LAB MATERIALS

INVESTIGATION	MINILAB	ALTERNATE LAB
page 406 cosmetics (such as hand lotion, cologne, sunscreen, etc.) dropper methylcellulose microscope petri dishes, sterile pond water protozoans wheat grains, boiled	**page 405** coverslips dropper pond water microscope **page 414** bread, day-old bakery plastic bags, self-sealing spray bottle	**page 398** coverslips depression glass slide lima beans, soaked microscope petroleum jelly slides toothpicks yogurt culture

TEACHER CLASSROOM RESOURCES	OTHER RESOURCES
Study Guide, p. 85 **Exploring Environmental Issues:** *Why Are Wetlands Important?* pp. 41-42	***STVS:** *Mapping a Virus,* Plants and Simple Organisms (Disc 4, Side 1) **Color Transparency 18:** *Viral Replication*
Study Guide, p. 86 ***PLL:** *Morphology and Staining of Bacteria,* p. 84	***STVS:** *Bacterial Miners,* Plants and Simple Organisms (Disc 4, Side 1) ***STVS:** *Energy-Integrated Farm,* Ecology (Disc 6, Side 2)
Study Guide, pp. 87-88 **Concept Mapping,** p. 15 ***PLL:** *Morphology of Green Algae,* p. 87 ***PLL:** *Size and Structure of Protozoa,* p. 89 ****ILS:** *A Comparison of Some Monerans and Protists,* p. 137 ****ILS:** *Algal Plants,* p. 143	**Color Transparency 19:** Structures of *Paramecium* and *Euglena*
Study Guide, pp. 89-90 **Critical Thinking/Problem Solving:** *Fields of Fungi,* p. 15 ***PLL:** *Morphology and Growth of Fungi,* p. 91 ***PLL:** *Morphology of Lichens,* p. 93 ****ILS:** *Lichens,* p. 141	***STVS:** *Soil Crusts in the Desert,* Plants and Simple Organisms (Disc 4, Side 1) **Color Transparency 20:** *Life Cycle of Bread Mold* **Color Transparency 21:** *Life Cycle of a Mushroom*
Assessment Materials **Chapter Assessment,** pp. 57-60 **Performance Assessment in Biology,** p. 30 **Alternate Assessment in the Science Classroom** **Computer Test Bank**	**Spanish Resources** **Cooperative Learning Resource Guide** **Videodisc Correlations** (to Optical Data's and Videodiscovery's videodiscs)

* Probing Levels of Life ** Investigating Living Systems

* Science Technology Videodisc Series

Key to Teaching Strategies

The following designations will help you decide which activities in the teacher margin are appropriate for your students.

L1 Level 1 activities should be within the ability range of all students.

L2 Level 2 activities should be within the ability range of the average to above-average student.

L3 Level 3 activities are designed for the ability range of above-average students.

LEP LEP activities are appropriate for Limited English Proficiency students.

COOP LEARN Cooperative Learning activities are designed for small group work.

ADDITIONAL RESOURCES

Infinite Voyage *Secrets from a Frozen World*
Students will see that Antarctica is a living laboratory that can serve as an early warning system for global change.

Audiovisual
Fungi, video, SRA.
The Protozoa; Bacteria, video, Insight Media.

Software
Protozoa, Apple/IBM/MAC, Cambridge Development Laboratory.

CHAPTER
15

VIRUSES AND MICROORGANISMS

Chapter Overview

Students begin the chapter learning that viruses are not organisms, but rather are particles capable of reproduction at the expense of specific host cells. Students then explore the various reproductive strategies of both DNA and RNA viruses.

Students then study the structure of bacteria, their reproduction, and various modes of nutrition. They distinguish between true and ancient bacteria and come to appreciate the many ways bacteria are important, both ecologically and economically.

Next, students come to understand the logic behind biologists' adding the protist kingdom, and study and compare the three main groups of protists—algae, protozoans, and slime molds. As they learn about these groups, they grasp the concept that these organisms do not fit neatly into plant or animal kingdoms.

Students conclude the study of simple organisms as they learn about the basic structure and means of reproduction of the major groups of fungi and of lichens and their roles in nature and/or industry.

388

KEY TERMS

ascus	mutualism
asexual repro-	mycelium
duction	parasite
basidium	plasmodium
endospore	provirus
hypha	pseudopodium
lysogenic	retrovirus
cycle	rhizoid
lytic cycle	saprophyte

CHAPTER 15

VIRUSES AND MICROORGANISMS

THESE MUSHROOMS are members of the Kingdom Fungi. Like all fungi, they have no chlorophyll, so they cannot perform photosynthesis. Instead, they obtain energy by digesting organic material from the forest floor. The cap of a mushroom is only a small part of the organism. Most of a fungus consists of masses of tiny hairlike filaments that live within soil and decaying matter. The small photo shows some of these filaments.

In the early 1990s, an enormous fungus was discovered in the state of Washington. It covers an area of 2.5 square miles, the equivalent of more than a thousand football fields! Most fungi, of course, are not nearly as large.

Mushrooms exist in many different shapes, sizes, and colors. The fungus kingdom also contains organisms other than mushrooms. The mold that grows on stale bread is a fungus. So is the yeast that makes bread dough rise. In this chapter, you will learn the characteristics all fungi have in common, and find out what kinds of organisms belong to the Kingdoms Monera and Protista. You will discover that organisms from these two kingdoms and from Kingdom Fungi have similarities as well as differences. In addition, this chapter will describe viruses and give you a chance to think about whether or not viruses should be considered members of the living world.

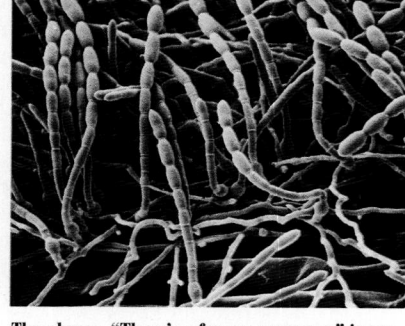

The phrase, "There's a fungus among us" is certainly true when you realize that soil contains billions of these fungal filaments.
Magnification: 1500×

Chapter Preview

ASSESSMENT PLANNER

Choose assessment strategies from the following pages to evaluate the progress of your students.
Assess, pp. 394, 399-400, 409, 415
Portfolio, pp. 393, 396, 401, 405, 407, 409, 413, 416
Alternate Lab, pp. 398-399
Thinking Lab, p. 411

Minilab 1, p. 405
Minilab 2, p. 414
Investigation, pp. 406-407
Chapter Review, pp. 418-419

Introducing the Chapter

Begin the chapter by focusing discussion on the photograph on page 388. Ask students if they think mushrooms are simple organisms. You might lead them by asking them to think about the complexity of organization in a mushroom as compared to that in a grasshopper, pine tree, or themselves. Have students identify other organisms they consider simple. As they do so, list the organisms in separate columns on the board and then ask students why you've created those separate columns. They may recall that the columns represent three kingdoms—monerans, protists, and fungi. Students may not think about viruses in the context of your discussion, but you can easily lead them to the topic by asking them to identify the cause of diseases such as chicken pox or AIDS. **COOP LEARN**

Theme Development

Students will recognize the theme of unity within diversity as they begin to understand that, though diverse, members of the same phylum share basic features as do all members of a given kingdom. Evolution is stressed in several ways. For example, students will learn of the various adaptations present among these organisms and viruses, and explore possible explanations of the origins of the different groups.

Tying to Previous Knowledge

Students have learned that evolution explains the diversity of life on Earth, past and present. In studying this chapter, they can see the "products" of evolution: adaptations of individual organisms and the divergence that led to the phyla in the three kingdoms of simple organisms. Remind them that classification is based on evolutionary relationships, and stress the traits that have led biologists to classify simple organisms in three kingdoms and in different phyla within each of those kingdoms.

Prepare

Key Concepts

The basic structure of viruses is described. Their varying methods of reproduction within host cells are examined, and the issue of whether or not viruses are alive is discussed.

Key Terms

lytic cycle, provirus, lysogenic cycle, retrovirus

Materials

1 Focus

Objectives

The objectives are listed on the student page. Remind students to preview these objectives as a guide to this numbered section.

Discussion

Poll the class. How many have ever had a fever blister or cold sore? Ask if these problems eventually go away, if they are capable of being passed on to someone else, if they are caused by a "germ" or seem to just happen, and what a germ is. **L1** **COOP LEARN**

2 Teach

MATH CONNECTION

TMV: Draw a line 132 mm in length. This represents a tobacco mosaic virus magnified 450 000 times. Have students calculate this virus's actual length in millimeters, micrometers, and nanometers.
Note: 1000 μm = 1 mm
1 000 000 nm = 1 mm
School microscopes may be capable of showing objects that are larger than 0.0002 mm. Ask students if they will be able to observe this virus with their class microscope.

Objectives

Infer how the structure of a virus is related to its function.

Compare the reproductive cycles of viruses.

15.1 Viruses

When's the last time you had a cold or the flu? Do you remember being vaccinated against polio or measles when you were younger? Those diseases—as well as AIDS, mumps, and chicken pox—are caused by viruses. Viruses are extremely tiny particles that reproduce themselves but are not cells. Therefore, viruses cannot truly be called organisms and are not classified in any kingdom. Yet, viruses play a significant role in the lives of humans and all other organisms.

Structure of Viruses

More than a century ago, scientists discovered that many bacteria can cause disease. These scientists developed ways to isolate and identify disease-causing bacteria. They learned how to filter bacteria from liquids, grow them in the laboratory, and observe them under the microscope. The causes of some diseases, though, could not be isolated by these procedures. These mysterious disease-causing agents passed through the filters that would trap bacteria. They could not be grown in the laboratory, and they were invisible even with the aid of a microscope. These undiscovered causes of disease were named *viruses,* from the Latin word for poison. By 1935, laboratory methods and equipment had become more sophisticated, and the first virus was isolated from diseased tobacco plants. Since then, hundreds of viruses have been isolated and identified.

Chemical analysis shows that all viruses are composed of an outer protein coat that encloses a nucleic acid. Some viruses contain DNA; others contain RNA. Viruses are so small they cannot be seen with a light microscope. However, the first electron microscopes were developed about the same time viruses were discovered. These new instruments enabled biologists to see viruses for the first time. The shapes of viruses vary widely and include spherical, rodlike, cubical, and many-sided forms, Figure 15-1.

Unlike all true organisms, even the most simple bacteria, viruses have no cellular structure. They have no cytoplasm, organelles, or membrane to isolate them from their environment. Viruses do not carry out respiration or other common life processes, except that they do reproduce themselves. For this function, they require the chemicals and ribosomes of the healthy cells they invade.

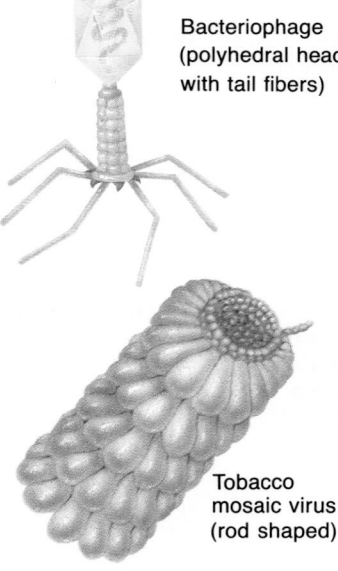

Figure 15-1 **Virus particles have a variety of shapes.**

Bacteriophage (polyhedral head with tail fibers)

Tobacco mosaic virus (rod shaped)

AIDS virus (spherical)

Polio virus (polyhedral)

 390 VIRUSES AND MICROORGANISMS

PROGRAM RESOURCES

Teacher Classroom Resources
Study Guide, p. 85 **L1**
Exploring Environmental Issues, pp. 41-42 **L3**
Color Transparency #18 **L1** **LEP**

STUDENT JOURNAL

Direct students to enter the following in their journals. Assume that you are a virus that has just invaded a host cell. You can speak to the cell and it can answer you back. What would you tell your host cell if asked why you are there and what you want? What would you tell your host cell as to its fate? What might your host cell answer for each question? **L1**

LYTIC CYCLE

① **Attachment** — Bacteriophage
— Nucleic acid core
— Bacterial host cell
— Bacterial host DNA

② **Entry**

Nucleic acid injected into cell

③ **Replication**

Host DNA destroyed; new viral nucleic acids and proteins made

④ **Formation**

New virus particles assembled

⑤ **Lysis and Release**

Host cell breaks open; new virus particles released

Figure 15-2 During the lytic cycle, a virus takes over the total metabolic activities of its host cell, makes many copies of itself, and destroys the cell.

Viral Cycles

When a virus invades a cell, new viruses are produced. The invaded cell, called a host cell because it provides materials to the virus, usually is destroyed. Let's examine this reproductive process in greater detail, using a virus containing DNA as an example.

Lytic Cycle A virus can identify and infect a potential host cell only if part of the viral coat can match a specific receptor site on the membrane surface of the host cell, much like jigsaw puzzle pieces must match in order to fit together. For example, the virus that causes AIDS can attack only certain white blood cells, tobacco mosaic virus can invade only the leaf cells of the tobacco plant, and bacteriophages can infect only certain bacterial cells. Once the virus recognizes its host, it is able to attach itself to the host cell membrane. After attachment, the viral DNA is usually injected into the host cell. In some cases, rather than injecting its DNA into the host, the entire virus enters the cell. The DNA is then released from the protein coat. In either case, once the viral DNA is inside, it takes over the workings of the cell using the host cell's ribosomes, amino acids, enzymes, and ATP to make more viruses. Even the host cell's DNA is broken down to provide raw material for making new viruses. The viral DNA is replicated to provide genetic material for new viruses. Viral DNA is also transcribed to make mRNA, which codes for viral coat proteins and several enzymes. Some of these enzymes are used to assemble new viruses from the new coats and DNA copies. Others are used to lyse, or break open, the host cell after the new viruses have been assembled. After lysis, which can occur as quickly as 20 minutes after attachment, the newly made viruses are released to attack other host cells. This process is called the **lytic cycle** and is diagrammed in Figure 15-2.

Reinforcement

Have students list traits that describe viruses, and compare these traits to eukaryotic organism traits or eukaryotic cells already studied. **L1**

Bioethics

AIDS: AIDS is a viral disease that can be transmitted from one person to another in a variety of ways. One way in which the disease can be transmitted is when a person comes in contact with the blood from a person with AIDS. What might be the chance of a person who has AIDS, such as a dentist, passing the virus to a patient during a routine extraction or filling? Ask students if health care workers who carry the AIDS virus should be allowed to treat patients.

Using an Analogy

Compare the injection of viral DNA into a host cell to a syringe, needle, and a person's arm. Expand the analogy by having students explain which part of the virus corresponds to the contents of the syringe, the plastic portion of the syringe, and the arm of the person. Continue to expand the analogy by referring to those viruses that inject their entire coat and contents into a host cell. What part of the syringe now corresponds to the virus parts? **LEP**

Using the Illustration

While looking at Figure 15-2, have students answer the following questions. What is a chemical name for the injected nucleic acid core? What serves as the raw material for new viral nucleic acids and proteins? **L1** **LEP**

Concept Development

When comparing viral reproduction to cell reproduction, ask how they are alike and how they are different. Of what genetic significance would it be to the virus if its protein coat is or is not injected into the host cell? Explain why.

Hosts: Specific viruses will infect only specific host cells. For example, the HIV virus only attacks T4 white blood cells. Have students compile a list of at least 5 viral diseases and the specific type of host cell invaded by the virus. Library research will be needed to complete the project. Have students determine a possible explanation for the specificity among host cells. **L2**

Have students working at grade level or below prepare either a concept map or a flowchart that describes the series of steps and expected changes that take place during a lytic virus cycle. **L1** **LEP**

Concept Development
Have students compare lytic and lysogenic cycles (a) in terms of time needed for completion, (b) as to how they both begin, (c) in terms of incorporation into the host cells' chromosomes, (d) in terms of a need for triggering viral reproduction in the host cell, and (d) in terms of how they both end for the host cell. **L1**

COOP LEARN

LYSOGENIC CYCLE

① **Attachment and Entry**   ② **Provirus Formation**

Bacterial host chromosome   Provirus

③ **Cell divides**

Provirus is inactive but is replicated with the host cell chromosome

Lysogenic virus injects its nucleic acid into a bacterium

Viral nucleic acid becomes part of the host chromosome as a provirus

Figure 15-3 **Lysogenic viruses don't destroy their host. The viral nucleic acid becomes a part of the host cell chromosome and is called a provirus.**

Lysogenic Cycle A different kind of viral reproductive cycle was discovered in 1953, when scientists noticed that certain bacteria unexpectedly lysed after being exposed to external factors such as UV light or X rays. This event led researchers to discover that viral DNA may sometimes become integrated into the host cell's chromosome. When this occurs, the viral DNA is known as a **provirus.**

Cells containing proviruses, rather than immediately being taken over and destroyed, continue to carry on their normal functions for a time. As a host cell reproduces, the provirus it contains is replicated along with the host's DNA. A provirus may cause some phenotypic changes in its host because the viral DNA is transcribed and translated to make proteins along with the host's genes. The provirus also prevents other viruses from entering and destroying the host. When a cell that contains a provirus is

Who were the real conquerors?

For centuries, history books have described how the Americas were invaded by European explorers. Columbus arrived in 1492, and others soon followed. The powerful Aztec empire, whose largest city had about 100 000 inhabitants, was conquered by only 1000 soldiers under Cortes in 1519-21. Twelve years later, Pizarro and an even smaller army conquered the Incan empire in Peru. The native people they met had never seen horses or guns before, but they were good warriors. And they far outnumbered the Europeans. How were the Spanish able to conquer them?

The Real Conquerors Some historians believe that disease played a more important role than horses and guns. In the 50 years after Columbus landed, smallpox reduced the native population by half—some say by as much as 90 percent. Between a third and half of the Aztecs died of smallpox when the Spanish first invaded their empire. Only about 1000 Native Americans survived in Cuba and the Antilles after an epidemic in 1518. And smallpox wiped out thousands of Incas in the 1530s.

Selective Killers Why did smallpox kill only the Native Americans? Smallpox had been common in Europe, killing many children. Those who lived to be adults had developed an immunity to the disease. But, they carried the virus that causes smallpox in their bodies.

Epstein-Barr: In the United States, exposure to the Epstein-Barr virus will result in infectious mononucleosis. It is not a fatal disease and seems to be most common among teenagers. However, if you lived in certain parts of Africa or New Guinea, you might end up with a quite different disease. You could develop massive cancerous tumors in the jaw and neck and could die within days. The disease is then called Burkitt's lymphoma. Why should the same virus bring about two different sets of symptoms depending on where one lives? Scientists are puzzled as to why the sharp differences exist but have suggested genetic differences, malnutrition of those living in Africa and New Guinea, or the possibility of other diseases such as malaria affecting the viruses' behavior.

exposed to environmental factors like X rays, UV light, or certain chemicals, the provirus is triggered to become active. The viral DNA takes over the machinery of the cell. New viruses are manufactured, the host cell lyses, and the new viruses are released to invade other cells. It was this series of events that scientists observed in 1953 when they exposed bacteria to radiation. Cells containing proviruses are said to be lysogenic, in other words, subject to lysing. This pattern of viral reproduction is called the **lysogenic cycle,** Figure 15-3.

RNA Viruses

Viruses containing RNA go through the same lytic and lysogenic cycles as DNA viruses. In most RNA viruses, the viral RNA both replicates to make new viral RNA and serves directly as mRNA to form new viral proteins by translation. When new viruses have been assembled, the host cell lyses.

RNA viruses that enter the lysogenic cycle are very unusual. They contain RNA, but their host cells' genetic material is DNA. How, then, can the viral RNA attach to the host's DNA to become a provirus? These viruses contain a unique enzyme, reverse transcriptase, which reverses the normal transcription process. Instead of transcribing DNA into RNA, reverse transcriptase transcribes RNA into DNA. Once the DNA has been transcribed, it can become double stranded by replication and join the

RNA LYTIC CYCLE

Figure 15-4 The RNA in RNA viruses replicates itself to make more viral RNA and serves as mRNA to make viral proteins by translation. Note that production of this type of RNA virus does not involve the host nucleus. What types of viral proteins are made by translation?

There had been no epidemics of smallpox in the Americas before 1492. Native Americans are thought to have come to North America by migrating across the Bering Strait from Siberia to Alaska. They lived for long periods in the freezing Arctic region before moving south. Any viruses and bacteria they brought with them would have been killed by the cold while being transmitted from host to host. Thus, the Native Americans had no immunity to smallpox and the other diseases that existed in Europe.

When the Europeans landed, the smallpox viruses they carried swept through the native cities and villages like fire through a dry forest. They killed children and adults alike. Sick and dying, the people could not defend themselves.

There were other epidemics as well. Cholera, plague, diphtheria, and other diseases caused by bacteria also killed many Native Americans. Like the smallpox virus, these bacteria were new to the Americas. Some historians think that after the Pilgrims landed in

Plymouth in 1620, 90 percent of the Native Americans died from diseases brought by the English colonists.

1. **Connection to Medicine:** Why are there no smallpox epidemics in the world today?
2. **Issue:** Germ warfare is the use of harmful microorganisms as weapons in war. Why is germ warfare so dangerous? What do you think should be done to prevent its use?

STUDENT JOURNAL

Have students explain through the use of an outline, flowchart, or concept map how the two kinds of RNA viruses complete their life cycles once they enter a host cell. Then, have them explain how these series of events differ from those of a DNA virus that has invaded a host cell. L1 LEP

PORTFOLIO

Direct students in the following activity. Assume that you are to enter a debate regarding the issue of whether or not viruses are alive. You do not know to which side of the debate you will be assigned. Prepare and list materials or ideas that support viruses as being living things, and also those that support viruses as being nonliving. L1

Figure Caption Question
What types of viral proteins are made by translation? Viral proteins include coat proteins and enzymes needed for making viral components and assembling new viruses.

GLOBAL CONNECTION

Purpose
Students will be introduced to a viral disease called smallpox. They will learn that exposure to a disease-causing agent can result in immunity against that disease. If one has no immunity toward a disease, contraction of that disease may be fatal.

Teaching Strategies
• Cooperative groups allow students to work together in researching and answering questions. Have students determine what a vaccine is, how the injection of a vaccine can provide immunity to a disease such as smallpox, and why the subjecting of humans to the pustules of cowpox could provide immunity to smallpox. L2 COOP LEARN

Possible Answers
1. Smallpox was officially announced to be eradicated from the world in May of 1980. A very strong program of vaccination worldwide has accounted for the lack of such an epidemic.
2. Germ warfare is not selective. That is, it may be intended to destroy enemy soldiers but it may also destroy innocent populations not involved in a war. World agreement among all countries should prohibit its use as a possible weapon during war time.

Going Further
Ask students to find out how soon after birth the smallpox vaccine should be given. What form does the smallpox vaccine take and how is it made? L1

3 Assess

Check for Understanding

Verify that students can explain the following relationships.
(a) protein, nucleic acid, virus structure
(b) virus structure differs from cell structure
(c) lytic cycle, lysogenic cycle
(d) RNA, reverse transcriptase, retroviruses L1

Reteach

Have students prepare a diagram of a bacteriophage with all parts labeled and its true size indicated. Have them make a series of diagrams to illustrate how the lytic cycle allows for reproduction of the virus. LEP

Extension

Have students research the growth curves of bacterial cells (references for this will be found later in this chapter). Have them compare the growth curve of bacteria to that of a typical lytic virus. A graph would be helpful in comparing the two curves. L3

✔ Assessment

Oral: Students should be able to describe what traits viruses share with cells, what processes viruses share with living organisms, what traits are different for viruses when compared to cells, and what processes are different when viruses are compared to living organisms. L1 LEP

4 Close

Discussion

Have students name some viral diseases that they have contracted. Have them explain the mode of transmission for each disease (how they think they caught it). Ask them the type of medication that is useful in treating viral infections. Do these drugs cure the disease or merely treat the symptoms? Why does it take a week to cure a cold but if medicine is taken, it will take 7 days? L1

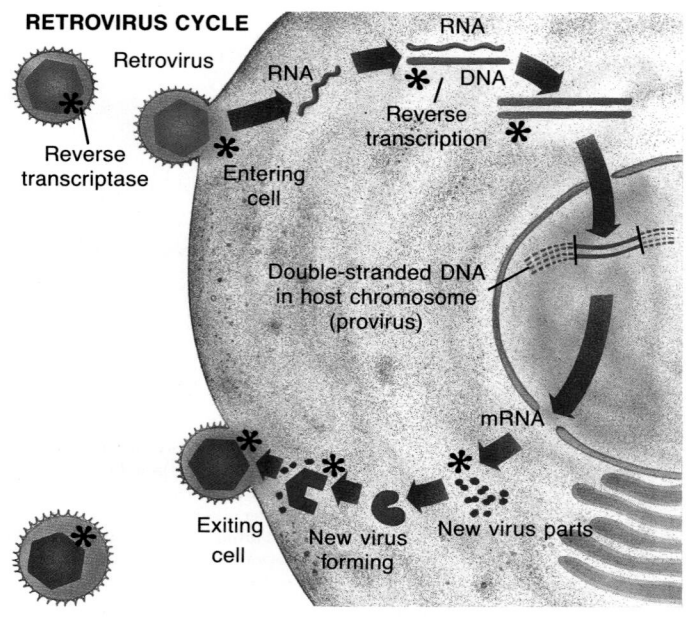

RETROVIRUS CYCLE

Retrovirus
Reverse transcriptase
Entering cell
RNA
RNA
* DNA
Reverse transcription
Double-stranded DNA in host chromosome (provirus)
mRNA
Exiting cell
New virus forming
New virus parts

Figure 15-5 **A retrovirus enters a host cell and its RNA undergoes reverse transcription. Eventually, a double-stranded molecule of DNA is produced and becomes a provirus, remaining in the host cell's nucleus.**

host's chromosome. The viral DNA may remain dormant as a provirus for a long period of time, or it may start directing the production of new viruses very soon. Because they perform transcription backwards, these viruses are called **retroviruses** (*retro* means backward). The virus that causes AIDS is an example of a retrovirus.

Some Questions

Is a virus alive? The answer is debatable. Because viruses don't have most of the basic features associated with living systems, you could conclude that a virus does not qualify as a living organism. However, viruses can perform the most universal function of life. They can reproduce.

A question that may be more important is, how did viruses evolve? It might seem reasonable to think that viruses, because of their simple structure, resemble the very first forms of life that appeared on Earth. But that explanation doesn't seem likely when you consider that viruses require true cells in order to reproduce. According to one hypothesis, viruses may be descendants of a more complex living system that lost certain features as it became highly specialized for one function only—reproduction. Another hypothesis states that viruses may have arisen after DNA escaped from a cellular organism. In either case, viruses now consist mainly of the bare chemical necessities for reproduction, nucleic acids.

Section Review

Understanding Concepts

1. Why must viruses take over host cells in order to reproduce?
2. Explain how viral nucleic acid can enter a host cell and not destroy it.
3. Why can't a bacteriophage infect human cells?
4. *Skill Review—Observing and Inferring:* A microbiologist added some viruses to a bacterial culture. At that time and every hour for 8 hours, he removed a sample of liquid from the culture and determined the number of viruses present in the sample. The number of viruses in each sample was 15, 17, 49, 128, 385, 386, 386, and 387. Explain what was happening in the bacterial culture. For more help, refer to Thinking Critically in the **Skill Handbook**.
5. *Thinking Critically:* What kinds of human cells must be hosts for the viruses that cause colds?

Answers to Section Review

1. Viruses have the genetic instructions for producing more viruses, but they lack the "equipment" needed to carry out the instructions: raw materials, enzymes, ATP, and ribosomes.
2. The viral nucleic acid may become integrated with the host cell's DNA, forming a provirus.
3. Each virus recognizes receptors in the membranes of specific host cells.

4. **Skill Review—Observing and Inferring:** The number of viruses increased rapidly initially as they reproduced within bacterial cells. However, that viral reproduction caused the death of the bacteria. As bacterial hosts died, viral reproduction slowed and the number of viruses remained essentially constant.
5. **Thinking Critically:** Cells of the upper respiratory tract are hosts to cold viruses.

15.2 Kingdom Monera

We know that living forms have dwelt on Earth for at least 3.5 billion years, because that is the age of the oldest fossils discovered. Those fossils are monerans. All monerans are bacteria. Although bacteria are simple in structure, they carry out the familiar functions of life and so are included in the classification of living organisms. Monerans are classified in a kingdom of their own because they are prokaryotes. All other organisms are eukaryotes. Two main groups of monerans, the ancient bacteria and the true bacteria, exist on Earth today. Some monerans have probably evolved very little over billions of years. The ancient bacteria give us some ideas about what the very first living organisms may have been like and what conditions were like on primitive Earth.

Characteristics of Bacteria

There are bacteria everywhere you look—in air, soil, water, on the surface of your desk, on your skin, even inside your body. A single bacterium is too small to be seen without the aid of a microscope. Bacteria often grow in colonies, which can become visible if they grow large enough, Figure 15-6. Let's find out what a typical bacterium looks like.

Structure   You have already learned that, as prokaryotes, monerans have no true nucleus and no membrane-bound organelles. Monerans have cell walls that protect the bacterium and help to maintain osmotic balance between the bacterium and its environment. Many bacterial cell walls are made of a substance found only in monerans. The antibiotic penicillin destroys these bacteria because it hinders the production of this substance. The bacterium cannot reproduce because it can no longer make new cell walls.

Often, the cell wall is surrounded by another structure, an outer capsule that offers the bacterium additional protection. This capsule may make it possible for bacteria to infect humans, that is, to escape destruction by the body's defenses. For example, cells of *Pneumococcus,* a pneumonia bacterium, can cause the disease only if they have capsules. *Pneumococcus* cells lacking capsules are not infectious.

Figure 15-6   **Each bacterial colony on this streak plate arose from a single cell, which underwent many generations of cell division. There are millions of cells in a bacterial colony.**

Objectives

Describe the basic characteristics of bacteria.

Compare the various means of nutrition found among bacteria.

Demonstrate knowledge of how bacteria are beneficial in nature and useful to humans.

Prepare

Key Concepts
The major traits of bacteria, including structural, reproductive, and physiological, are examined. The various groups of bacteria and their nutritive strategies are covered, as well as the economic importance to humans and all of nature.

Key Terms
endospore, asexual reproduction, parasite, saprophyte

Materials
• Make bean water for the Alternate Lab.

1 Focus

Objectives
The objectives are listed on the student page. Remind students to preview these objectives as a guide to this numbered section.

Activity
Ask students to prepare a wet mount of a sentence period taken from a magazine page. Have them estimate the period size while under the microscope. Tell them that the average low-power field diameter is 1.4 mm. Ask them to "guesstimate" the number of bacteria that could fit in a row across the period (about 175 if average bacterial size is 0.002 mm and period size is 0.35 mm). Caution students to use care when handling the microscope and making wet mounts. **L1**

2 Teach

Concept Development
Ask student groups to make a list of the major differences between prokaryotic and eukaryotic cells. It may be necessary to have them review some of these differences from Chapter 5. **L1** **COOP LEARN**

Brainstorming

Have students explain the consequences to future generations of bacteria if endospores were to contain only cytoplasm and no DNA. Ask how an endospore might differ from a cell wall or capsule that surrounds most bacterial cells. L1

COOP LEARN

Teacher FYI

Examples of endospore-forming bacterial species and the diseases they cause include *Bacillus anthrax* (anthrax in domesticated animals such as cattle), *Clostridium tetani* (tetanus), *Clostridium botulinum* (food poisoning), and *Clostridium perfringens* (gas gangrene).

Using an Analogy

Asexual reproduction capacity is best illustrated as follows. Ask students if they would rather have $10 every 20 minutes for 13 hours or one penny doubled every 20 minutes for 13 hours. Point out that the growth rate of bacteria as they undergo asexual reproduction is like the second example ($400 by arithmetic growth or more than $5 million by exponential growth). LEP

Using the Illustration

Ask students to trace the diagram appearing as Figure 15-8. Have them use the labels provided to identify its parts and add a brief function next to each cell part. Suggest that students place their completed diagrams in their portfolios. L1 LEP

Figure 15-7 The rod-shaped bacillus, round coccus, and spiral-shaped spirillum are common shapes of bacteria. Magnification: 3500×, 26 000×, 19 000×, respectively

Some bacteria possess flagella and are able to move around. Bacterial flagella are simpler in structure than are eukaryotic flagella and are made of different materials.

Most bacterial cells have one of three shapes. They may be spherical, rod-shaped, or spiral-shaped. Many bacteria, especially the rod-shaped ones, are adapted for withstanding harsh conditions. When living conditions become unfavorable for one of these bacteria, a tough, protective wall forms around its DNA and a small bit of its cytoplasm, producing a highly resistant, dormant structure called an **endospore.** The rest of the cell may then die. However, the endospore can resist long periods of boiling, or years of freezing or drought. When conditions once again become favorable, the endospore develops into an active cell.

Reproduction A bacterium reproduces by simply dividing into two cells. This method of reproduction, called binary fission, is a form of **asexual reproduction.** Asexual reproduction is the production of one or more genetically identical offspring from a single parent. In many types of bacteria, the new cells separate from one another. However, in some species, the new cells remain attached to form pairs, chains, or clusters. Even though these cells are grouped together, each one acts as an independent organism.

Figure 15-8 Bacteria are prokaryotes with a cell wall and a single chromosome. Cells of some species are surrounded by a protective capsule. Some may have one or more flagella.

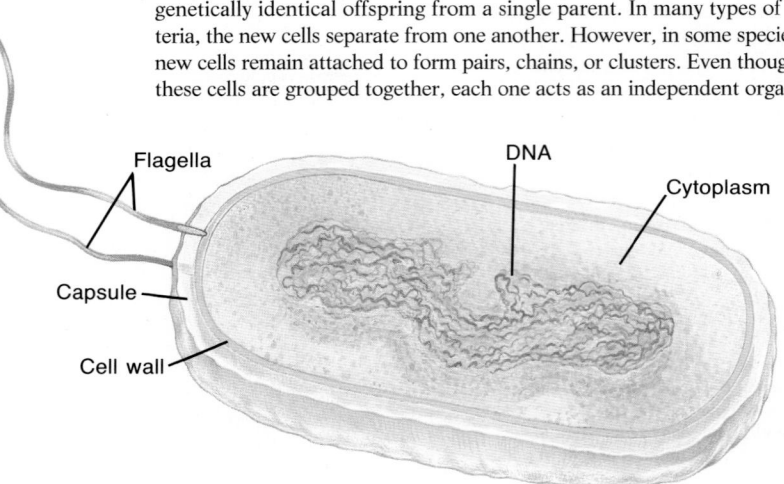

Flagella

DNA

Cytoplasm

Capsule

Cell wall

396 VIRUSES AND MICROORGANISMS

Nutrition in True Bacteria

Bacteria are successful not only because of their ability to withstand harsh conditions, but also because they have evolved a wonderful variety of ways to obtain energy. It seems that every potential food source can be used by some kind of bacteria. Though most true bacteria are heterotrophs and obtain energy from the organic molecules they take in, many are autotrophs. True bacteria have also developed different methods of respiration to break down stored food and release energy. Some respire aerobically and can grow only in the presence of air. Others release energy anaerobically and cannot grow when air is present. Still others can release energy either way. If oxygen is available, they respire aerobically. If not, they become anaerobes, organisms that release energy in the absence of air.

Heterotrophs   Heterotrophic bacteria are found everywhere. Because they require complex organic molecules as their energy source and are not adapted for trapping the food that contains these molecules, these bacteria must absorb nourishment from their surroundings. Many heterotrophs are **parasites,** organisms that live in or on other organisms. The organisms that are invaded, and on which parasites live, are called hosts. Parasites always cause harm to their hosts in some way. Other heterotrophic bacteria are **saprophytes,** organisms that feed on dead organisms or other organic wastes. These bacteria are extremely important in nature because they help recycle the nutrients contained in decomposing organisms and waste materials. Were it not for saprophytes, dead matter would soon envelop Earth's surface. Eventually, life would stop as carbon and other elements became unavailable for new growth.

Photosynthetic Autotrophs   Several types of true bacteria are autotrophic; they use inorganic molecules or light to obtain energy. One type, the blue-green bacteria, traps the energy in sunlight by photosynthesis. During photosynthesis, they convert carbon dioxide and water to organic material and release oxygen. This group of monerans was probably very important in generating oxygen early in life's history. The blue-green bacteria do not always look blue-green in color. In addition to chlorophyll *a*, they usually contain a blue pigment, though some may contain red or yellow pigments as well. So, depending on the combination of pigments present in a particular species, it may be blue-green, black, yellow, green, or red. The Red Sea was named for the large masses of red-pigmented bacteria that grow on its surface. Because they are prokaryotes, the blue-green bacteria have no chloroplasts. Their chlorophyll and other pigments are located on simple, flattened membranes within the cytoplasm.

Figure 15-9   **Bacterial cells reproduce by binary fission, producing two cells of equal size. Why can't bacteria undergo mitosis? Magnification: 26 000×**

15.2 KINGDOM MONERA 🐚 **397**

Misconception

Step on a rusty nail, get a puncture wound, and you may get lockjaw, or tetanus. Ask students what the cause of tetanus is and most will tell you it is either the rust on the nail or bacteria living on the nail. Those that answer bacteria living on the nail are partially correct. The nail provides the puncture wound, but the ground where the nail was found contains bacteria that normally live in the soil. They are responsible for causing tetanus. Also, the tetanus-causing bacteria are anaerobes and will grow rapidly in the oxygen-free environment provided by a deep puncture wound. A small sample of soil added to a petri dish of agar and incubated in the absence of air will yield bacterial colonies in 24 hours. A nail placed on a petri dish of agar under the same conditions will yield no bacteria or very few colonies of bacteria in 24 hours.

Microscope Activity

Provide students with prepared slides of heterotrophic and autotrophic bacteria. Certain supply houses can supply the three heterotrophic shapes on one slide. Have students make colored diagrams of what they see under high-power magnification. Ask them to indicate the approximate size of the cells by using the diameter of their high-power field (typically 0.35 mm) as a guide. Have students briefly state the similarities and differences seen in the two cell types.
L1   LEP

Figure Caption Question

Why can't bacteria undergo mitosis? Mitosis is division of the nucleus. Bacteria have no nucleus.

PROJECT

Anaerobes: A number of harmful bacteria are anaerobes. Have students use references to determine the names of these bacterial species and the diseases they cause. Students should also determine how the method of treatment for diseases caused by anaerobes may differ from those caused by aerobic bacteria. L1

MEETING INDIVIDUAL NEEDS

For students working below grade level, verify that the following terms are understood: *heterotroph, organic molecules, autotroph, aerobic respiration, anaerobic fermentation, photosynthetic, inorganic molecules, prokaryotes.* Have them use each term correctly in a sentence or have them group opposites such as aerobic-anaerobic, autotroph-heterotroph. LEP

Reinforcement

Have students refer to Appendix A on classification. Ask them to note the pattern used in the overview of each kingdom, which presents one way that a kingdom may be classified using a series of traits and branching lines. Have students prepare a similar scheme that uses the different categories of bacteria as the main traits on the branching lines. Information will be needed from pages 397, 398, and 399. Ask students to carry the branching as far as possible with the information provided. L1 LEP

CHEMISTRY CONNECTION

Methane: Have students diagram the structural formula for methane. Advise them that its molecular formula is CH_4. Ask them to write a balanced equation that shows the combination of carbon dioxide and hydrogen gas to form methane and water ($CO_2 + 4H_2 \rightarrow CH_4 + 2H_2O$). To illustrate the properties of methane, simply light a lab burner as a demonstration. The gas being burned is mostly methane. It is normally an odorless gas, but chemicals are added to it to give it an odor so that gas leaks can be detected. Based on the demonstration, have students propose a possible economic or commercial role for the bacteria that are methane producers.

L2

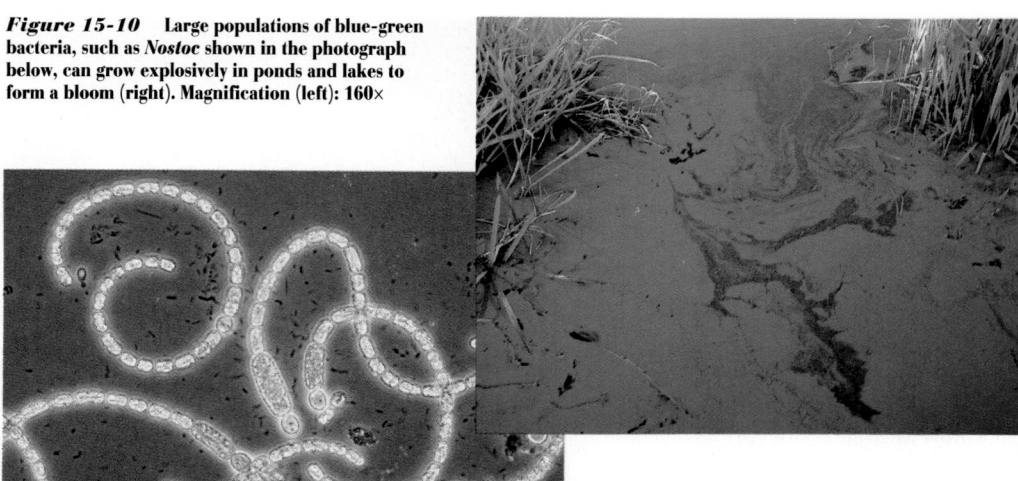

Figure 15-10 Large populations of blue-green bacteria, such as *Nostoc* shown in the photograph below, can grow explosively in ponds and lakes to form a bloom (right). Magnification (left): 160×

Blue-green bacteria are common in ponds, lakes, puddles, streams, and even moist places on land. They are important producers in aquatic communities, and many species are important in converting atmospheric nitrogen into a form that plants can use.

Chemosynthetic Autotrophs   Some true bacteria are autotrophic but not photosynthetic. They do not derive energy from sunlight. Instead, they use a process called chemosynthesis to trap energy released from the breakdown of inorganic materials such as sulfur and nitrogen compounds. Some chemosynthetic bacteria are important in converting nitrogen and sulfur compounds in the environment to forms that can be used readily by plants.

Nutrition in Ancient Bacteria

The ancient bacteria live under conditions that may be very similar to those found when life was first evolving on Earth. All of the known ancient bacteria live without oxygen and are autotrophs. Some live in places where no other organisms can exist today.

Methane-Producing Bacteria   Members of one group of ancient bacteria inhabit swamps, marshes, and other environments where there is a great deal of decaying plant matter. Bacteria from this group also inhabit the digestive tracts of humans and other mammals, particularly grazing mammals such as cattle, horses, and deer. Some of these bacteria are found in sewage treatment plants. These bacteria obtain energy by chemosynthesis. They convert carbon dioxide and hydrogen to methane, which is sometimes called marsh gas. For this reason, they are known as methane-producing bacteria. Since methane can be used as a fuel, it is possible that these bacteria could be put to practical use. They would not only aid in the decomposition of dead organisms and organic waste, but also convert those substances into a usable product.

398 ᴥ VIRUSES AND MICROORGANISMS

ALTERNATE LAB: Demonstrating Bacterial Motility

Purpose
Students will learn how to prepare a hanging drop slide and will verify that some species of bacteria show the ability to move.

Materials
Sample A—yogurt with active cultures diluted with water; Sample B—bean water (a handful of dried lima beans added to 200 mL of water 5 days before the lab); Sample C—toothpick scrapings of gums

and teeth, mixed with a drop of water; glass coverslip; petroleum jelly; microscope; depression glass slide; toothpicks

Procedure
Give the following directions to students.
1. Place petroleum jelly on your fingertip and rub all 4 borders on one side of the coverslip to make a ring.
2. Use a toothpick to add a drop of sample A to the center of the coverslip on

the side *with* the petroleum jelly.
3. Invert a depression glass slide and position the depression directly over the drop on the coverslip. Press lightly together to form a seal between the coverslip and slide.
4. Invert the slide quickly. The bacterial sample should hang as a drop from the coverslip.
5. Examine the slide under high power of your microscope. Reduce the amount of

Salt-Loving Bacteria   Other groups of ancient bacteria inhabit even harsher habitats. Members of one group, the salt-loving bacteria, live in salt lakes. They are the only prokaryotic organisms that inhabit the Great Salt Lake and the Dead Sea.

Heat- and Acid-Loving Bacteria   Another group of ancient bacteria occupies very hot and acidic areas. They are known as heat- and acid-loving bacteria. Some members of this group are producers that live deep in the ocean near underwater volcanoes and thermal vents. Others live in hot sulfur springs, such as those in Yellowstone National Park, which have temperatures near 80°C and a pH as low as 2, Figure 15-11.

Comparing Ancient Bacteria and True Bacteria   The ancient bacteria differ from the true bacteria in several ways. Their cell walls and the lipids in their plasma membranes have a different structure. The sequences of bases in the tRNAs and rRNAs of ancient bacteria are quite different from those of true bacteria. Ancient bacteria also react differently to antibiotics. You can see why ancient bacteria are classified separately from the true bacteria. Some biologists feel the ancient bacteria should be classified in a separate kingdom. Perhaps the ancient bacteria, the true bacteria, and the eukaryotes share a common ancestor that was a very early form of life on Earth.

The Importance of Bacteria

What would life on Earth be like if there were no decomposers to break down dead plant material, the bodies of dead animals, and the waste products generated by all living things? Eventually, all the nutrients needed for life would be bound up in this dead matter and waste. The raw materials needed to support new life would no longer be available.

Figure 15-11   Ancient bacteria are the only organisms that can inhabit hot sulfur springs, such as this one in Yellowstone National Park.

Different Viewpoints in Biology

Are they really ancient?
Eocytes is the name given to those organisms that live near thermal vents in the ocean floor. They are considered to be ancient bacteria and are therefore grouped with the archaebacteria. Recently, a group of scientists from the University of California sequenced a protein that is involved with protein synthesis. To their surprise, the sequence of amino acids that make up this protein is identical in all eocytes and in all eukaryotic cells that they studied. So, where should the archaebacteria be classified now—or is more biochemical evidence needed for molecular taxonomy?

3 Assess

Check for Understanding
Have students explain the following word relationships.
(a) bacteria—Kingdom Monera—prokaryotes
(b) cell wall—capsule—round—rod—spiral
(c) binary fission—asexual reproduction
(d) oxygen—aerobes—no oxygen—anaerobes
(e) parasite—saprophyte
(f) autotroph—heterotroph
(g) decomposers—recyclers L1
LEP

---

light. Motility is observed if motion of bacteria is in one direction. NOTE: The shimmering effect that you might see from some of the bacteria is not motility.
6. Make a table and record observations.
7. Repeat steps 1-6 for samples B and C.

Analysis
Ask students to answer these questions.
1. Which bacterial samples show motility? What is your evidence? *Typically, bean*

broth will show good motility. Bacteria can be seen moving across field of view.
2. Were you able to see flagella on any of the bacteria that were motile? Offer a possible reason for your answer. *No, too small, in constant motion.*
3. Explain why it was necessary to use a hanging drop technique rather than simply placing bacteria on the slide and adding a coverslip. *A hanging drop pro-*

vides a 3-D environment that does not impede motility.

✔ Assessment
Performance: Have students make diagrams of what the bacteria observed in the three samples might actually look like if greatly enlarged. Be sure they include important cellular parts that might be present. Students should show flagella for only those that were motile. L1   COOP LEARN

Reteach

Ask students to prepare an outline of this section. There should be as many subsections as possible in covering the major chapter concepts.

Extension

Have students research how antiseptics, disinfectants, sterilizing, canning, freezing, salting, smoking, and cooling are used as techniques aimed at reducing bacterial growth. How does each process or technique work? **L2**

✔ Assessment

Knowledge: Have students explain the following major ideas or concepts, using either a written or verbal format. What is the structural basis for the Kingdom Monera? How do bacterial cells differ from eukaryotes in terms of structure and reproduction? How do bacteria vary in their nutritive needs? Why are they important to the world and to humans? **L1**

4 Close

Demonstration

Project 35-mm colored slides on the classroom screen. The slides should be of all three shapes of bacterial heterotrophs, as well as examples of autotrophic bacteria. Ask students to describe as many things as possible about each organism being viewed.
L1 **LEP** **COOP LEARN**

Figure 15-12 The holes in Swiss cheese are caused by bubbles of carbon dioxide produced by the bacteria that give the cheese its flavor. Cheese is made in large vats such as this one.

Bacteria play an important role in nature. Most of Earth's decomposers are bacteria that break down organic matter into basic components that can be reused by other organisms. Without bacteria, this recycling of life-sustaining materials could not take place.

Bacteria are also very important to human economy because they are needed for a variety of industrial processes. For example, the dairy industry makes yogurt and buttermilk by adding certain bacteria to milk. As the bacteria multiply, they secrete substances that flavor the milk. Production of cheese depends on bacteria that cause milk products to turn to solids. Bacteria are indirectly involved in milk production. Certain bacteria that live in the stomachs of cows aid in the digestion of plant materials. Without this help, cows would not be able to obtain the nutrients they need to produce milk. Bacteria break down the material that holds together flax and hemp fibers, freeing the fibers for use in making linen or rope. Animal skins are tanned into leather with the help of bacteria. Many of today's antibiotics are produced by bacteria.

While many bacteria are very helpful, others can be harmful and dangerous. The role of bacteria in disease is discussed in Chapter 23.

Section Review

Understanding Concepts

1. You are examining a unicellular organism with an electron microscope. What clues would enable you to determine whether the organism is a bacterium?
2. Some bacteria can break down cellulose in plants. How might this be beneficial to humans?
3. Is endospore formation a form of reproduction among bacteria? Explain.
4. **Skill Review—Classifying:** Set up a classification of bacteria based on their structural features and means of obtaining energy. For more help, refer to Organizing Information in the **Skill Handbook**.
5. **Thinking Critically:** A bacterium is discovered that does not obtain energy from organic molecules and does not undergo photosynthesis. How does it obtain its needed energy?

Answers to Section Review

1. If the cell lacks a nucleus and membrane-bound organelles, it is a bacterium.
2. Cellulose consists of many glucose molecules linked together. Humans cannot utilize cellulose as an energy source, but they can utilize glucose.
3. Endospore formation is not a means of reproduction. Part of one cell becomes an endospore which, under favorable conditions, will become one active cell.

4. **Skill Review—Classifying:**
   1A usual tRNA and mRNA base sequences............go to 2
   1B unusual tRNA and mRNA base sequences............go to 3
   2A parasitic or saprophytic.................heterotrophic true bacteria
   2B photosynthetic or chemosynthetic.............autotrophic true bacteria

3A produce methane...methane-producing ancient bacteria
3B live in salt water ....salt-loving ancient bacteria
3C live in hot springs...heat-and-acid-loving ancient bacteria

5. **Thinking Critically:** The bacterium is chemosynthetic. It obtains energy from the breakdown of inorganic molecules.

15.3 Kingdom Protista

By now, you understand that classification of Earth's living organisms requires more than two kingdoms. When biologists realized that some organisms were neither plants nor animals, the first new kingdom they added to their classification system was the Kingdom Protista. Protists are a diverse group of organisms. They may appear to have little in common, and they are difficult to classify. However, protists do share several features.

Protists are all eukaryotes, and they probably arose from prokaryotes. Most are unicellular, but some have a simple multicellular structure. Some are heterotrophic, others autotrophic, and some may switch from one form of nutrition to the other. The Kingdom Protista is made up of three groups of organisms: plantlike protists, which are called algae; animal-like protists, known as protozoans; and funguslike protists.

Plantlike Protists: The Algae

You may have seen seaweeds washed up on a beach, or the greenish film that often forms in still ponds or on the sides of a home aquarium. These are just a few examples of algae. Algae range in size from microscopic, single-celled forms to multicellular seaweeds that may reach 100 meters in length. Algae first appeared on Earth about 550 million years ago. The vast majority are autotrophs and are important sources of food for both freshwater and marine animals. Algae are classified on the basis of their color and structure.

Euglenoids   Euglenoids are unicellular algae that have characteristics associated with both plants and animals. Like animals, they lack cell walls and move by means of a flagellum. Like plants, they are photosynthetic. One species, *Euglena,* provides a good example of why protists are difficult to classify. This organism, pictured in Figure 15-13, is usually autotrophic. However, if exposed to a period of darkness, it will lose its chloroplasts

Objectives

Compare the features of the various phyla of algae.

Distinguish among the protozoan phyla.

Relate the characteristics of slime molds to their life cycle.

Figure 15-13   **Euglenoids contain many specialized structures, including contractile vacuoles that pump excess water out of the cell and an orange-red eyespot that detects light. Magnification (photo): 450×**

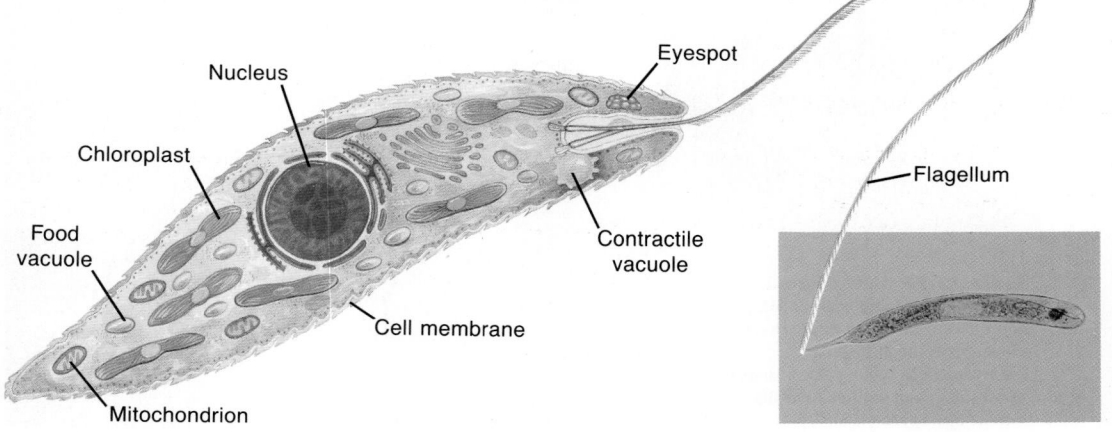

Nucleus

Eyespot

Chloroplast

Food vacuole

Flagellum

Contractile vacuole

Cell membrane

Mitochondrion

15.3 KINGDOM PROTISTA ✿ **401**

SECTION 15.3

Prepare

Key Concepts
Characteristics of the Kingdom Protista will be presented with emphasis on similarities and differences among members of this kingdom's three groups. Protist relationships to other organisms such as humans will also be described.

Key Terms
pseudopodium, mutualism, plasmodium

Materials
- Gather pond water or puddle samples for Minilab 1.
- Purchase living cultures from a biological supply house for the Investigation. Gather chemicals to be tested on the protists.

1 Focus

Objectives
The objectives are listed on the student page. Remind students to preview these objectives as a guide to this numbered section.

Discussion
Ask students what malaria, ice cream, and toothpaste all share in common. Give students an opportunity to think about the answer before you explain that members of the Kingdom Protista are involved with products used in the making of toothpaste and ice cream and are responsible for malaria. [L1]

PORTFOLIO

Ask students to copy the diagram of *Euglena,* labeling the structures and adding the following statements: regulates water concentration within cell, controls cell, contains DNA, traps energy, sensitive to light, allows for movement, releases energy, photosynthetic organelles, responsible for food production, replaces cell wall. [L1] [LEP]

STUDENT JOURNAL

Have students prepare a chart that summarizes the similarities and differences studied so far between *Euglena* as a typical plantlike protist, *Pneumococcus* as a typical heterotrophic moneran, and *Nostoc* as a typical autotrophic moneran. They should include information regarding size, color, cell organization and contents, habitat, classification, etc. [L1] [LEP]

2 Teach

Different Viewpoints in Biology

Old is Older

Han and Runnegar have discovered algal fossils in the iron-rich rock layers of Michigan. What was discovered are remains of the extinct eukaryote *Grypania spiralis.* Upon dating these rocks, it was found that their age was 2.1 billion years old. Previously, the oldest eukaryotic fossils had been dated at 1.7 to 1.8 billion years of age. This pushes back the time most scientists believe that eukaryotes evolved on Earth.

Microscope Activity

- Obtain prepared slides or living specimens of *Euglena, Volvox, Chlamydomonas,* and *Spirogyra.* Have students observe these specimens under both low- and high-power magnification. Ask them to prepare a chart that lists similarities and differences for these four algae. **L1** **LEP**

- Obtain a sample of diatomaceous earth from your earth science teacher. Have students prepare a wet mount of this material. Ask them to diagram any evidence that can be seen which supports the fact that this material had a living origin. Have them prepare a wet mount of aquarium side wall scrapings and compare what they see to the wet mount of diatomaceous earth. Caution students to use care in making wet mounts and handling the microscope. **L1**

Figure 15-14 The glassy cell walls of diatoms are covered with many beautiful markings. Magnification: 300×

and become heterotrophic. You have learned that unicellular organisms must be very versatile, because they must carry out all life functions in a single cell. Note the many specialized structures in the diagram of *Euglena.*

Golden Algae Most members of this phylum are unicellular. Their colors range from yellow-green to golden-brown, depending on the pigments they contain. Most common and best known among them are the diatoms, pictured in Figure 15-14. Diatoms inhabit both fresh and salt water and are the most numerous of the many microscopic producers that float near the ocean surface. Their many shapes and colors make diatoms some of nature's most beautiful organisms. Each diatom is composed of a two-part outer shell, one part of which overlaps the other like the lid of a box. The shell consists of a cell wall impregnated with a glasslike material. When diatoms die, their glass shells do not decay. They drift to the ocean bottom, where large masses of them collect into deposits called diatomaceous earth. Diatomaceous earth can be mined and has many uses. It serves as an abrasive ingredient in scouring powders, cosmetics, and toothpaste. It can also be used to filter small particles from juices and other liquids.

Green Algae The green algae belong to a very diverse phylum that includes both unicellular and multicellular species. Most are found in freshwater habitats, though many live in moist areas on land. Some live in salt water, and some even inhabit other organisms. The green algae are thought to be the ancestors of the plant kingdom, partly because the cells of green algae and plants contain the same kinds of chlorophyll and other pigments. Note the great diversity of forms within this phylum, as shown in Figure 15-15. Some, like *Spirogyra,* are filaments. Others, such as *Volvox,* are globe-shaped groups of cells called colonies. Species like *Ulva*

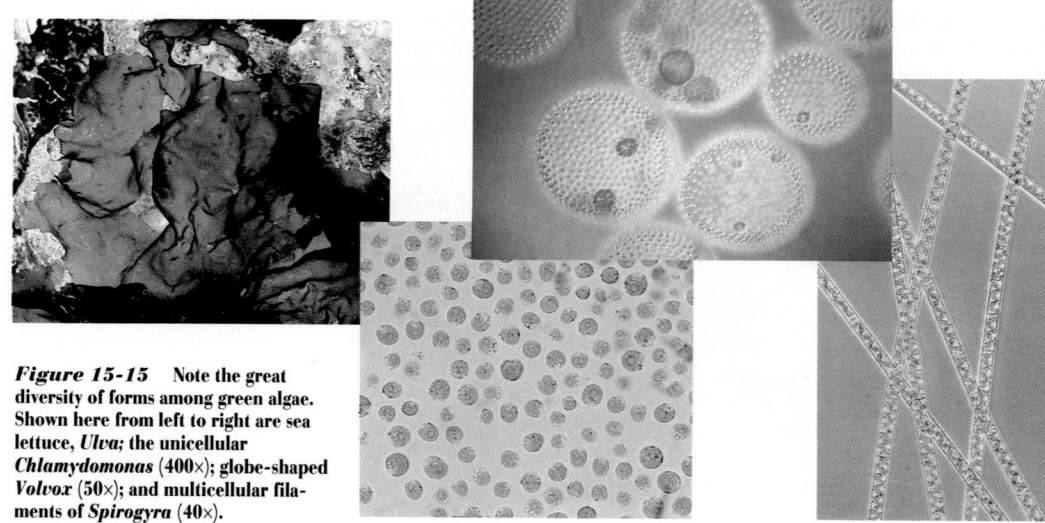

Figure 15-15 Note the great diversity of forms among green algae. Shown here from left to right are sea lettuce, *Ulva;* the unicellular *Chlamydomonas* (400×); globe-shaped *Volvox* (50×); and multicellular filaments of *Spirogyra* (40×).

402 VIRUSES AND MICROORGANISMS

PROJECT

Food for Growth: Have students design and conduct an experiment that determines if growth and reproduction of *Euglena* will increase with the addition of nutrients to the growth medium. If supplied with nutrients, the organism is capable of rapid reproduction. Evidence of its reproductive capabilities is seen as an increasingly green coloration in the container in which the organism is living. Typically, spring water should be used and a 0.1% fertilizer solution (5-10-5) can be prepared. (See page 27T.) Students should use controls and also be aware of the need for light by these algae. Results will be observed within 7 to 10 days. Kits and supplies such as the spring water, *Euglena,* and fertilizers are available from biological supply houses. **L1** **COOP LEARN**

Figure 15-16 These photos of kelp, a brown alga, show the structures that resemble roots, stems, and leaves. The round structures are filled with air and help the alga float on the water's surface, where it can photosynthesize.

resemble a lettuce leaf. The bodies of some larger species have parts that resemble the stems, leaves, or roots of true plants. However, algae do not have tissues or organs as plants do, though some division of labor among cells may occur. For example, most or all of the cells in a multicellular alga may contain photosynthetic pigments and perform photosynthesis. Some of those same cells may also participate in reproduction, while others do not. As the green algae evolved, they became increasingly complex, as division of labor among groups of cells increased. While asexual reproduction still occurs, most species are also capable of reproducing sexually, and many have evolved life cycles similar to those of plants.

Brown Algae   Also known as seaweeds, brown algae are complex multicellular organisms that live mainly in salt water. In addition to chlorophyll, they contain a pigment that gives them their brown color. Some species are among the largest of all algae. Many brown algae have a thick body with specialized parts. *Laminaria,* for example, has a rootlike structure, a stemlike portion, and leaflike parts, Figure 15-16. Many species grow in cool water along rocky coasts. They are anchored to the rocks by their rootlike parts. Some, like *Sargassum,* float unattached at the surface of warmer waters. *Sargassum* grows so densely that it covers much of the surface of the Atlantic Ocean near Bermuda, forming an area of millions of square kilometers known as the Sargasso Sea.

Brown algae are an important commercial source of iodine. Some brown algae, called kelp, can be used as fertilizer or as food for humans. Other species are a source of algin, which is used to thicken ice cream and other foods.

Red Algae   This phylum contains multicellular forms that are more complex in structure than the other phyla of algae. Most live in salt water, but a few occupy freshwater or land environments. Their bright red color, which is due to a red pigment, and their feathery shapes make many species beautiful.

15.3 KINGDOM PROTISTA 🐟 **403**

SECTION 15.3

Using Science Terms

- Ask students to define in their own words the meaning of *multicellular, asexual reproduction,* and *sexual reproduction.* Then, have them check for a formal definition of these terms and compare their definitions to a more accurate or correct one. **L1** **LEP**

- The term *seaweed* is used to describe certain algae. Ask students to explain why this term, and especially the ending *weed,* might be an appropriate term to use in describing them. **LEP**

Using an Analogy

Ask students how their school's building or organization shows specialization. Ask students if the entire school, however, serves one main function in spite of its separate parts, areas, or departments. What is that one main function? Introduce the term *division of labor.* How does the school's organization demonstrate a division of labor? Compare it to the division of labor seen in algae. Ask how an alga benefits from division of labor. **LEP**

Demonstration

Alginate or algin is available in many supermarkets on the shelf next to instant puddings and gelatin products. If not available, ask the manager of your local McDonald's for a sample. Have your students taste it and describe its taste, texture, and other properties. Discuss why alginate is used with foods and what properties make it an excellent medium for growing bacteria.

MULTICULTURAL CONNECTION

Eating Algae: Although they are not a popular food in the United States, various red algae are used by the Japanese in soup and as a part of sushi (raw fish dishes). The Japanese cultivate beds of these algae along their shores for ease in harvesting. NOTE: Dried algae may be purchased from an oriental food store so students can taste it.

MEETING INDIVIDUAL NEEDS

Ask students working below grade level to prepare a chart that summarizes the similarities and differences studied so far between a typical unicellular plant-like protist, a typical brown alga, and a typical red alga. Include information regarding size, color, cell organization, habitat, and classification. Have students refer to Appendix A for information on classification names. **LEP**

PHYSICS CONNECTION

Light Absorption: Why is it that blue light can penetrate to depths of 270 meters? The colors in the visible spectrum range from violet to blue to green to red. Correspondingly, the wavelengths for these colors become longer. Therefore, the wavelengths of the violets, blues, and greens are shorter than those of the yellows and reds. In the ocean, the absorption of visible light is greater for the long-wavelength colors; thus, the short wavelengths are transmitted to greater depths. Ask students who are SCUBA divers how colors change as one descends into ocean depths. Most natural colors can only be seen in the first 15 to 20 meters of water. As one descends, colors become more monochromatic in the blue-green family.

Brainstorming

Algae need mineral nutrients as well as light in order to survive and grow. These nutrients are comparable to fertilizers added to soil to enhance plant growth. Ask students if the nutrients available in the ocean would be more abundant near shore or further out away from shore. Ask them where these nutrients come from. See if students can correlate nutrient availability with where the majority of algal growth occurs. (near the shore) **COOP LEARN**

Microscope Activity

Order a living culture of *Amoeba* from a biological supply house. Allow students to prepare wet mounts of these protists. Use a depression slide, or add toothbrush bristles to the slide to avoid crushing the organisms when a coverslip is added. Most amoebas will be found at the bottom of the container in which they are shipped. Caution students to make wet mounts and use the microscopes with care.

L1 **LEP**

Figure 15-17 **The branched filaments of this red alga are hooked, enabling it to cling to other algae and to rocks and mud.**

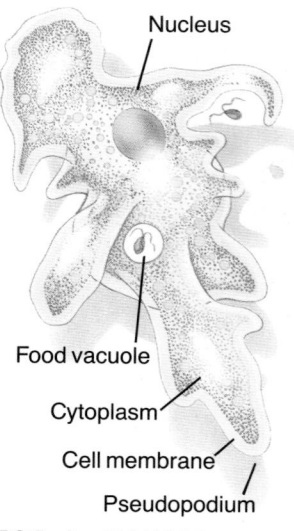

Figure 15-18 **The shape of an amoeba changes constantly as pseudopodia form. Note the small protist about to be captured, and the protist in the food vacuole that is ready to be digested. Magnification (photo): 100×**

Nucleus

Nucleus

Food vacuole

Cytoplasm

Cell membrane

Pseudopodium

404 VIRUSES AND MICROORGANISMS

The pigments present in red algae enable them to live and photosynthesize at greater ocean depths than any other group of algae. Most wavelengths of light, such as the red and violet wavelengths that are absorbed by chlorophyll, do not penetrate ocean water very deeply. This is why organisms that have chlorophyll cannot live deep in the ocean. However, some of the pigments in red algae are able to trap blue light, the wavelengths that penetrate the water most deeply. That light energy can then be used in photosynthesis. A species of red algae discovered in the Bahamas grows at a depth of nearly 270 meters. Not all red algae live at such great depths. Many live anchored in mud along the shore.

Red algae are used in a variety of ways. Some species are used as food by humans. Agar is a substance made from red algae and used to make culture media for growing bacteria in the laboratory. Other substances obtained from red algae are used in making ice cream, puddings, and cake icing.

Animal-like Protists: The Protozoans

The second major group of protists is made up of unicellular, animal-like organisms known as protozoans. Most protozoans can move, and their classification is based on their method of locomotion. Protozoans are heterotrophs and have evolved a variety of adaptations for obtaining food. Some actively trap food, while others are parasites and live at the expense of a host.

Rhizopods   One of the simplest and most often studied of the protozoans is *Amoeba*, a member of the phylum known as rhizopods. Members of this phylum move by means of extensions of the plasma membrane called **pseudopodia,** which means "false feet." Formation of pseudopodia is made possible by a flexible plasma membrane and the constant movement of cytoplasm. Pseudopodia are used not only for locomotion, but also for engulfing food. By means of phagocytosis, food is surrounded by pseudopodia and brought into the cell for digestion.

PROJECT

Observing Protists: Paramecia can be observed feeding if they are provided with a small amount of yeast boiled in an 0.5% solution of Congo red dye. (See page 27T.) Have students make a wet mount using a drop of paramecium culture and a drop of yeast suspension. The red yeast will be seen being swept into the oral groove and being funneled into newly forming food vacuoles. Order

Paramecium multimicronucleatum for this study. It is also possible to observe the contractile vacuoles by adding a small amount of Chinese ink (available in stick form from art supply stores) to a wet mount of paramecia. The ink tends to concentrate in the vacuoles, making them more visible. **L1**

Two groups of rhizopods that inhabit the ocean are interesting because they have mineral skeletons. Members of one group, the forams, have chalklike outer skeletons. Those in the other group, the radiolarians, have internal, glasslike skeletons. Skeletons of forams make up much of the limestone and chalk on Earth, including the white cliffs of Dover, England.

Ciliates   Members of another phylum of protozoans, the ciliates, move by the beating of the many cilia that project from their surfaces. The cilia also play a role in food-getting by sweeping food into the cell. This phylum includes the familiar *Paramecium.* Examine Figure 15-19. You can see that a paramecium has many specialized parts. It is, in fact, one of the most complex of all unicellular organisms, containing specialized organelles for taking in and digesting food, eliminating undigestible materials, and pumping out excess water to maintain osmotic balance. Ciliates are so complex that they have two types of nuclei. A large macronucleus controls the cell's metabolism. A smaller micronucleus is involved in reproduction. Some ciliates have many micronuclei.

Flagellates   Members of another phylum of protozoans, the flagellates, move by means of flagella. Some flagellates are free-living and inhabit either fresh or salt water. Many species, though, live within other organisms. One such flagellate, a member of genus *Trypanosoma,* is transmitted to humans by the tsetse fly. This protist lives in the blood of humans and releases a poisonous substance that attacks the nervous system, causing weakness and then death. This disease is called African sleeping sickness. Another flagellate inhabits the digestive tract of termites, where it secretes enzymes that digest the wood the termites eat. This relationship, which benefits both organisms, is known as **mutualism.** The termite benefits by having its food digested, and the flagellate benefits by receiving shelter and a constant supply of wood.

Minilab 1

Is there life in a drop of pond water?

Use a dropper to collect a sample of water from a pond or puddle of muddy water. Place a drop on a microscope slide and cover it with a coverslip. Examine the slide first on low power of your microscope, then on high power. Draw what you see.
Analysis   *Can you identify by kingdom any organisms you find? If you see any protists, can you identify the group they belong to? What characteristics did you use to make your identifications?*

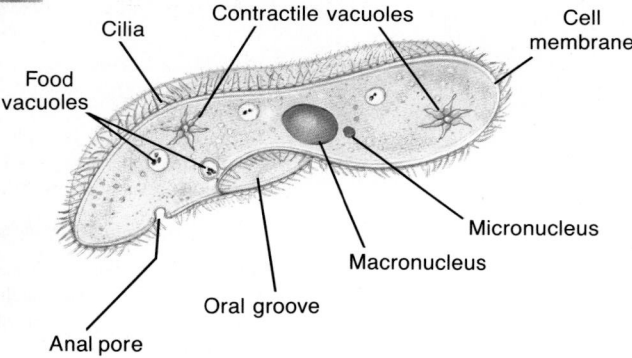

Figure 15-19   **Trypanosoma** (left) is a parasitic flagellate. **Paramecium** (right) contains many specialized structures. Note the two nuclei. The oral groove is lined with cilia that sweep tiny organisms into the cell, where they are digested. Undigested wastes leave through the anal pore. Contractile vacuoles pump water out of the cell. Magnification (photo): 1000×

Cilia

Contractile vacuoles

Cell membrane

Food vacuoles

Micronucleus

Macronucleus

Oral groove

Anal pore

15.3 KINGDOM PROTISTA   **405**

INVESTIGATION

The Effect of Chemicals on Protozoans

Time Allotment

1 class period to design and set up experiment and 10 minutes daily for 1 to 2 weeks

Objectives

Upon completing this Investigation, students will be able to:

- Measure the life span of protozoans to determine how sensitive they are to chemicals.
- Describe the importance to humans of research on protozoans' sensitivity to chemicals.

Skills

observe and infer, form a hypothesis, design an experiment

Materials

- sterile petri dishes, pond water, boiled wheat grains, cosmetics, microscopes, methyl cellulose, droppers
- **Safety Precautions:** Ask students to wash their hands at the end of the lab.

Preparation

- Obtain methyl cellulose and cultures of protozoans from a biological supply house.
- Boil the pond water for 20 minutes, and autoclave or boil petri dishes to ensure that there will be no contamination of the cultures.
- Boil the wheat grains and add one to each petri dish of pond water.

Possible Hypotheses

1. The control protozoans will live as long as the ones exposed to 1%, 0.1%, and 0.01% solutions of hand lotion.
2. The control protozoans will live longer than the ones exposed to 1%, 0.1%, and 0.01% solutions of hand lotion.

Possible Procedures

- A possible procedure involves making dilutions of cologne so pond water will be 1%, 0.1%, and 0.01% cologne. One dish will have no cologne. Add 10 drops of

Sporozoans Some protozoans, the sporozoan phylum, reproduce by tiny, sporelike structures. Remember that spores are small reproductive cells that can develop into new organisms.

Sporozoans have no cilia or flagella. Because they have no means of movement, they cannot actively trap food. Therefore, they live as parasites and obtain their food from the host's tissues. The sporelike reproductive structures are specialized for penetrating host cells and tissues. In this way, sporozoans obtain food.

Some sporozoans cause diseases in humans and animals. Most dreaded of all the sporozoans are members of the genus *Plasmodium*. These sporozoans are transmitted by certain mosquitoes and are responsible for causing malaria, a disease that has caused millions of human deaths. Every year, more that 200 million people are infected with malaria, mostly in tropical climates. In Africa alone, at least a million people die of malaria each year.

INVESTIGATION

The Effect of Chemicals on Protozoans

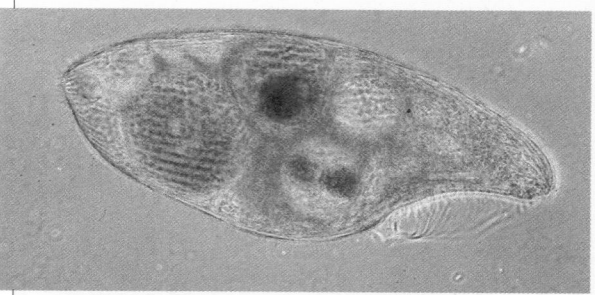

Magnification: 300×

How many different kinds of cologne, eyeshadow, and mascara are on the market? All cosmetics, fragrances, sunscreens, hair sprays, and similar products must be thoroughly tested to be sure they are safe for human use. A variety of animal experiments are conducted as a part of the testing process. Rabbits were commonly used to test new eye products. Because of questions raised about the use of animals in these tests, laboratories are developing different methods of testing cosmetics. Some researchers believe that all cells behave in similar ways. If a new cosmetic causes problems for protozoan cells, it may cause problems for cells in the human body also. In this lab, you will test the effects of chemicals on the life span of protozoan cultures.

Problem

How do chemicals affect the life span of protozoan cultures?

Safety Precautions

When handling chemicals, use guidelines given by your teacher. Wash your hands at the end of each lab period.

Hypothesis

Make a hypothesis about how a specific chemical, either a specific cosmetic or a pure compound or element, would affect the life span of a protozoan culture. Explain your reasons for making this hypothesis.

406 VIRUSES AND MICROORGANISMS

---

original protozoan culture to each dish. Allow to sit for 5 minutes. Make a slide of one drop of the culture in a drop of methyl cellulose. Count a portion of the low-power field of view. Each day, make a new slide in the same way and count the same portion of the field of view. Variations in procedures would include dilutions, types of cosmetics, types of protozoans, and counting procedures.

- Protozoans commonly used in the classroom include *Paramecium, Amoeba, Stentor, Vorticella, Spirostomum,*

Didinium, and *Blepharisma. Blepharisma,* because of its large size and pink color, is easy to see. All are relatively easy to maintain in sterile pond water with a wheat grain nutrient supply. Because of their fast movement, you will need to supply methyl cellulose and advise students to add one drop to each slide they prepare in order to slow movement.

- Review with students how to make serial dilutions.
- Ask students to label their droppers and not mix them from one culture to another.

Funguslike Protists

While algae clearly resemble plants, and protozoans are very much like animals, the third group of protists is similar in many respects to fungi. Funguslike protists are all heterotrophs.

Slime Molds   One phylum, the slime molds, has a fascinating and unique life cycle with features not only of fungi, but also of protozoans. At some stages of life, a slime mold is unicellular, while at other times it is multicellular.

Some species of slime molds begin their life cycle as a colorful, slimy mass containing many nuclei. This mass, called a **plasmodium,** slowly oozes along the forest floor over rotting logs and other decaying matter. Like a giant amoeba, the plasmodium engulfs bacteria and small particles of organic matter by phagocytosis. Thus, slime molds are decomposers.

Experimental Plan

1. As a group, make a list of possible ways you might test your hypothesis using the materials your teacher has made available.
2. Agree on one idea from your group's list that could be investigated in the classroom.
3. Design an experiment that will test one variable at a time. Plan to collect quantitative data.
4. Following the style of a recipe, write a numbered list of directions that anyone could follow.
5. Make a list of materials and the quantities you will need.

Checking the Plan

Discuss the following points with other group members to decide the final procedures for your experiment.

1. What variables will need to be controlled?
2. What is your control?
3. What dilutions of your chemical will you use?

4. What will you measure or count?
5. What portion of a field of view will you count?
6. How many fields of view will you count each time?
7. For how many days will you conduct your experiment?
8. Have you designed and made a table for collecting data?

Make sure your teacher has approved your experimental plan before you proceed further.

Data and Observations

Carry out your experiment, make your measurements, and complete your data table. Make a graph of your results.

Analysis and Conclusions

1. According to your results, was your protozoan sensitive to the chemical you tested?
2. What is your experimental evidence for your conclusion in question 1?

3. Was your hypothesis supported by your data?
4. If your hypothesis was not supported, what types of experimental error could be responsible?
5. Consult with another group that used a different chemical. Were their conclusions the same as yours? Why or why not?
6. Do you think a larger or smaller amount of your chemical might produce different results? Why or why not?
7. How did your chemical affect the life span of your protozoan culture?
8. Write a brief conclusion to your experiment.

Going Further

Based on this lab experience, design an experiment that would help to answer a question that arose from your work. Assume that you will have unlimited resources and will not be conducting this lab in class.

Teaching Strategies

- Choose a variety of cosmetics: hand lotions, cologne, and sunscreens make good choices. You may also want to supply items such as tooth-filling material (from dentist) and other elements and compounds such as lead, copper, brass, plastic, stainless steel, iron filings, nickel, and aluminum.
- If cultures are too thick to count entire fields of view, students may count portions of fields of view, as long as they count the same portion, such as 1/4, each time.

Data and Observations

The graph below indicates that paramecia were not affected by cologne.

The graph below indicates that paramecia exposed to 1% cologne died in 5 days, while the others survived. The keys for the two graphs are the same.

Data Analysis

1-8. Answers will vary.

✔ Assessment

Portfolio: Have students add their lab write-ups, including graphs, to their portfolios.

Extensions

Students might decide to investigate other protozoans, other cosmetics, or other dilutions.

Purpose
Students will learn that protists have a huge impact on farming losses and on food spoilage.

Teaching Strategies
- Ask students to determine the name of the organism responsible for the potato blight epidemic in Ireland.
- Ask them to determine if Ireland is still a large producer of potatoes and where within the United States they are grown.
- Consult with farmers or the Department of Agriculture to determine the methods used to rid or control fungus pests amongst crops. How do they prevent fungus growth?

Possible Answers
1. *Plasmopara viticola* is the organism that was responsible for causing downy mildew on grapes. The protist was naturally found in the U.S. and was brought by accident to France, where it attacked their grapevines. Pasteur discovered the cause of this disease.
2. Water molds and true fungi are similar in that their lifestyles are both parasitic or saprophytic. Their reproduction is by spores. Both release enzymes into their hosts' tissues and absorb the digested foods. Water molds have cell walls of cellulose while true fungi have walls of chitin.

Going Further
A funguslike protist called *Saprolegnia* can be easily grown and observed. Place a chunk of beef into the classroom aquarium or allow a dead goldfish to remain in the tank. In several days, it will be covered with white fuzz. Have students make wet mounts of this fuzz and observe under low and high power. **L1**

Figure 15-20 Slime molds produce an amoeba-like feeding stage called a plasmodium (left). When food becomes scarce, reproductive structures, called fruiting bodies, form (right). Magnification: (right) 10×

When food or moisture becomes scarce, the plasmodium may slow down and undergo an amazing change. It develops many reproductive structures that produce spores by meiosis. The spores are released and spread by wind and rain. When food and moisture become available, the spores germinate and develop into flagellated swarm cells. These cells are attracted to each other by a chemical they secrete. Two flagellated swarm cells fuse to form a zygote that loses its flagella and begins to move like an amoeba. The production of a new plasmodium involves division of the nucleus by mitosis, and growth without cell division. Thus, many nuclei are formed within the plasmodium. Sometimes several plasmodia fuse to form a larger plasmodium.

HISTORY CONNECTION

Protists Change a Country

In the 1800s, most people in Ireland were farmers. Potatoes were the most important crop and were the main part of the Irish diet. In the fall of 1845, a large part of the potato crop molded. The following year, the entire potato crop was wiped out in one week. The potatoes had been infected with potato blight.

Potato blight is caused by a water mold, a funguslike protist. The spores of this protist multiply most rapidly in cool, damp weather.

It rained constantly in Ireland from May 1845 until March 1846. The rainy weather continued during the summer and fall of 1846. Conditions were perfect for the protist to grow rapidly.

The potato blight changed the course of Ireland's history. There were more outbreaks of potato blight in Ireland until 1860, and a quarter of a million people starved to death or died of typhoid fever in the epidemics that followed. Ireland's population dropped by one-third. With fewer people to farm, Ireland's economy suffered.

The disease changed America's history, as well. A million and a half Irish farmers fled to the United States to begin new lives. These people and their descendants have enriched American life in many fields, including industry, politics, and entertainment.

1. **Writing About Biology:** Another water mold damaged and almost destroyed the French wine industry in the 1870s. Find out more about this disease and write a short report. What famous scientist played a part in discovering the cause of this disease?
2. **Explore Further:** Find out how the water molds are similar to true fungi and how they differ.

PROGRAM RESOURCES

Teacher Classroom Resources
Study Guide, pp. 87-88 **L1**
Concept Mapping, p. 15 **L1** **LEP**
Probing Levels of Life, Labs 31, 32, pp. 87, 89 **L2**
Investigating Living Systems, Labs 35, 37, pp. 137, 143 **L2**
Color Transparency #19 **L1** **LEP**

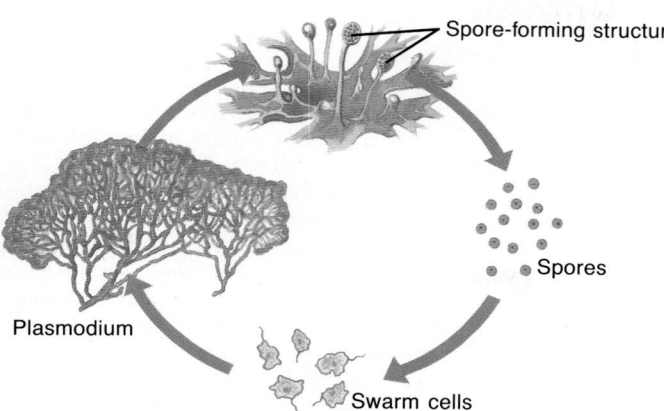

Spore-forming structures

Figure 15-21 The life cycle of a slime mold has several stages.

 Spores

Plasmodium

Swarm cells

The Interest in Slime Molds The slime molds are interesting to biologists because their life cycles involve many changes in form. These different forms resemble other forms of life. Spore production resembles reproduction in fungi. The individual, flagellated swarm cells and the plasmodium are like protozoans. Biologists study slime mold development to try to better understand the development of more complex organisms.

Evolution of Other Kingdoms Based on structural similarities, many taxonomists argue that certain organisms in each of the three groups of protists gave rise to the other kingdoms. According to this hypothesis, algae evolved into plants, protozoans into animals, and funguslike protists into fungi. Chemical analysis, however, suggests other possibilities. Perhaps a common ancestor gave rise to protists as well as to the fungi, plant, and animal kingdoms. Because the fossil evidence is so sparse, it is difficult to know the exact origins and relationships of the various kingdoms.

Section Review

Understanding Concepts

1. Euglenoids and flagellates have much in common. Explain why both are considered protists but also why they are classified in different groups.

2. In what ways are brown algae more complex than most other phyla of algae?

3. What would be the first clue you might look for to determine whether a newly discovered unicellular protist is an alga or a protozoan?

4. **Skill Review—Recognizing Cause and Effect:** If a photosynthetic protist lost its chloroplasts, under what conditions would it be able to survive? For more help, refer to Thinking Critically in the **Skill Handbook**.

5. **Thinking Critically:** Based on information presented in this section, what biological method might be devised to rid a house of termites?

Answers to Section Review

1. Both are considered protists on the basis of their simple structure. Both are unicellular eukaryotes. Although both groups are motile by means of flagella, euglenoids are usually photosynthetic whereas flagellates are always heterotrophic.

2. Not only are brown algae generally larger than algae in other phyla, they also have a greater degree of specialization; for example, parts resembling roots, stems, and leaves.

3. The presence of chloroplasts would indicate that the protist is an alga.

4. **Skill Review—Recognizing Cause and Effect:** Such a protist could survive only if a suitable food source were available and it had a means of taking in that food.

5. **Thinking Critically:** If termites could somehow be prevented from harboring the flagellates that digest the cellulose in the wood, then the termites could not survive.

SECTION 15.3

3 Assess

Check for Understanding

Have students explain the following:
(a) traits of protists.
(b) examples of how euglenoids, golden algae, green algae, brown algae, and red algae are alike and how they differ.
(c) examples of how rhizopods, ciliates, flagellates, and sporozoans are alike and how they differ.
(d) traits of slime molds. **L1**

Reteach

Provide students with the names of all groups studied in this section. Ask them to describe as many characteristics as possible for each group.

Extension

Have students investigate how the flagella and cilia of protists differ from the flagella seen in bacteria. **L2**

✔ Assessment

Portfolio: Students are to prepare a classification outline similar to the type used with the overview introduction in Appendix A. However, their outline is to be based initially on methods of locomotion. The first branch, therefore, must divide protists into as many groups as needed based on how or if they move about. **L1** **LEP**

4 Close

Activity

Have students work in groups of two. Each group is to diagram a protist assigned by you. Diagrams are to be placed on 5 × 8 file cards. You are to hold the diagrams up for the class to see one at a time. Class members are to describe as many facts as they can regarding each example. **L1** **LEP** **COOP LEARN**

Prepare

Key Concepts

Students will be introduced to the Kingdom Fungi. The major traits of the three phyla forming this kingdom will be examined.

Key Terms

hypha, mycelium, rhizoid, basidium, ascus

Materials

• Purchase the bread and plastic bags needed for Minilab 2.

1 Focus

Objectives

The objectives are listed on the student page. Remind students to preview these objectives as a guide to this numbered section.

Demonstration

Hold up a package of store-bought yeast, a moldy orange, and a store-bought mushroom. Elicit answers from students as to whether or not all samples are alive. Then try to determine what, if anything, all have in common. Provide some closure to the discussion by pointing out that these samples are living things and that all belong to the Kingdom Fungi. L1

2 Teach

Concept Development

Ask students to explain how the two terms *saprophyte* and *parasite* differ. Ask them to categorize each of the following as being either parasitic or saprophytic examples and explain their answers: athlete's foot, bread mold, bracket fungus on dead tree, bracket fungus on living tree, mold on orange, mold on jelly. L1

Discussion Questions

Ask students to explain the relationship between hyphae and mycelium, hyphae and asexual spores, and spore formation and classification. L1

COOP LEARN

410

Objectives

Compare the characteristics of the different phyla of fungi.

Explain how the organisms of which a lichen is composed benefit one another.

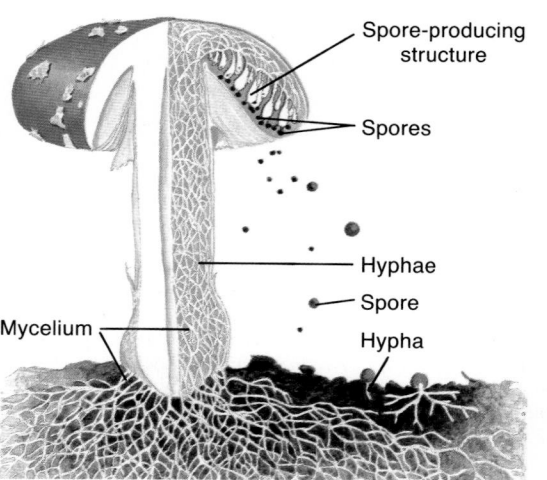

Figure 15-22 Hyphae form the basic structure of fungi. The reproductive part of the organism, known as a mushroom, is composed of densely packed hyphae. Spores are produced in the mushroom.

Spore-producing structure

Spores

Hyphae

Spore

Hypha

Mycelium

15.4 Kingdom Fungi

You are probably familiar with many types of fungi. Some you eat, such as mushrooms; others, like molds on bread or oranges, eat the food you want to eat. You may also have seen fungi growing from the trunk of a tree or a fallen log. In these examples, the fungi are obtaining food from other organisms or parts of organisms. In nature, many fungi play important roles in decomposing dead organisms and wastes. By breaking down dead material and waste products, fungi release nutrients needed for the growth of plants. However, fungi also can cause severe economic damage when they feed upon valuable crops. Although fossils of fungi are scarce, evidence suggests that they probably first appeared about 500 million years ago and that they evolved later than the algae. Fungi are plantlike in that they are stationary, and animal-like in that they are heterotrophic. Because most fungi cannot move to trap their food, they are either parasites or saprophytes; that is, they absorb their food from the living or dead tissues of other organisms.

Structure of Fungi

Most true fungi are made up of very thin filaments called **hyphae**. In some fungi, each hypha is a tube-shaped mass of cytoplasm containing many nuclei. No crosswise cell walls divide the hypha into separate cells. In other fungi, cross walls divide the hyphae into distinct cells.

Hyphae grow and branch out to form a mat of filaments called a **mycelium.** The visible part of a fungus is only a small part of the mycelium. Most of the mycelium is embedded in the soil or in the tissues of the host organism and cannot be seen.

Most fungi reproduce by forming thick-walled spores both by mitosis and by meiosis. Thick cell walls of both hyphae and spores are adaptations that prevent drying. This adaptation permits fungi to live and reproduce on land. Most fungi produce asexual spores by mitosis in structures located at the tips of specialized hyphae. These hyphae extend outward from the food source and give a fungus its fuzzy appearance.

Fungi are classified according to the way they produce spores during sexual reproduction. Each group is named for the sexual structures it forms.

Zygote Fungi

The common bread mold, *Rhizopus,* is a member of the phylum known as zygote fungi, as shown in Figure 15-23. Zygote fungi are so named because specialized hyphae from two different organisms

---

can meet and fuse to form a zygote. This zygote becomes a thick-walled spore, called a zygospore, that is resistant to harsh conditions. Other hyphae, called stolons, spread along the surface of the organism's food supply or substrate. Still other hyphae, **rhizoids,** anchor the fungus to the food source. Thus, rhizoids resemble roots in function. Enzymes secreted by the rhizoids break food molecules into simpler molecules, which are absorbed by the rhizoids and diffused throughout the mold.

Most relatives of bread mold are saprophytes. As a result of their activities, valuable materials are returned to the soil and atmosphere. However, some species are parasites and cause diseases by feeding on plants such as potatoes and cereal grains. These species produce rhizoids that penetrate the tissues of the host plant, thus robbing it of nutrients.

Club Fungi

This phylum includes mushrooms, shelf fungi, rusts, smuts, and puffballs. Members of this phylum are called club fungi because they possess club-shaped structures, called **basidia,** in which the sexual spores are formed.

When you eat a mushroom, you are actually consuming only the reproductive part of the organism. In the soil beneath the mushroom is a branching network of hyphae, the mycelium, that obtains nourishment in much the same way as bread mold. The cap portion of the mushroom begins as a small outgrowth of the mycelium in the soil. As the hyphae push through the soil, they develop a stalklike section and an umbrella-shaped cap that are composed of tightly packed masses of hyphae, as seen in Figure 15-22. On the underside of the cap, arranged like spokes of a wheel, are gills on which basidia are located. Each basidium produces four spores. When the spores mature, they are released from the basidium and dispersed by the wind.

Figure 15-23   *Rhizopus* forms asexual spores by mitosis in black spore cases called sporangia, located at the tips of upright hyphae. These hyphae and sporangia give the fungus a fuzzy appearance. *Rhizopus* also produces sexual spores. By what process are sexual spores produced? Magnification: 5×

Thinking Lab

DESIGN AN EXPERIMENT

Why would farmers put noodles on their crops?

Background
Why does William Connick make pasta with fungi? Connick is a researcher who was working on a project to develop a natural weed killer that would kill a weed called hemp sesbania. This weed can take over fields of cotton, soybeans, and rice. Connick knew that a particular fungus kills this weed. However, it would be difficult to spread the spores of the fungus on fields because spores are very

light in weight and would blow away. The fungus would have to be packaged, without using killing chemicals or high temperatures, into a stable material with a long shelf life. An effective number of fungal spores would have to be used, and they would need a food source to get them to start growing.

You Try It
Speculate about the characteristics of pasta that inspired Connick to make it

into what he called "pesta." **Design an experiment** that Connick might have done to determine how many fungal spores should be put into pesta to make it an effective weed killer. Think about at what stage in the growth of the crop the pesta should be applied for maximum effectiveness. What characteristics of pasta make it a suitable substance for packaging fungi for use as a weed killer?

Concept Development
Ask students to describe the names of structures formed and the various roles of hyphae as they relate to reproduction, securing food, and spreading across a surface.

Microscope Activity
- *Rhizopus* can be easily grown about four to five days before use by rubbing several moistened pieces of bread across any outdoor soil. Place bread in a plastic sandwich bag and observe daily for signs of growth. Once mold growth appears, allow students to observe using stereoscopes if available. Keep mold covered while observing or the structures will dry out. This can best be done by placing small sections of the bread and mold into closed petri dishes. L1
  LEP
- Have students remove one gill from the underside of a store-bought mushroom. Place it between two glass slides and press down hard on the top glass with thumbs. Removing the top slide, add water and a coverslip and observe under high power for spores. Prepared commercial slides may also be purchased and used. L1 LEP

Enrichment
Mushroom farm kits are available from biological supply houses and make an interesting long-term classroom project. L1 COOP LEARN

Figure Caption Question
By what process are sexual spores produced? Sexual spores are produced by meiosis.

Thinking Lab

DESIGN AN EXPERIMENT

Purpose
Students will determine why fungal spores are added to pasta.

Skills
design an experiment, separate and control variables

Teaching Strategies
- Ask students to list the characteristics of pasta that are important to fungi.

Answers
Students may design an experiment that makes pesta with equal amounts of flour and water and increasing numbers of fungal spores. They will probably say that the pesta should be applied to the field with the crop seeds. Characteristics of pasta that make it a suitable substance for packaging fungus include long shelf life, does

not use killing chemicals or high temperature in preparation, flour would provide food for fungus, spores would stay in place on the soil, does not harm crop plants.

✔ Assessment
Performance: Have students write a journal entry describing Connick's reasoning for making pasta with fungi. Entries should be written as if Connick were writing.

SECTION 15.4

Misconception

Place a cooked mushroom into a silver spoon or on a silver coin. If it blackens the silver, it is unfit to eat and is poisonous. True or false? Most students have heard that this tale is true. However, it has no scientific merit. Silver tarnishing or blackening can result from a variety of chemical reactions, none of which are related to the chemicals present in mushrooms.

Teacher FYI

The most notorious of all poisonous mushrooms are those from the genus *Amanita. Amanita phalloides, A. brunnescens, A. tenuifolia, A. verna,* and *A. bisporigera* are examples. Most poisons are complex cyclic proteins composed of either seven or eight amino acids. Their effects on the human body may differ. Typically, they fall into three categories. (1) Proteins that disrupt cell membranes. Cellular lysosomes, endoplasmic reticuli, and the plasma membrane itself are damaged with the various chemical compounds present within or on these organelles being released. (2) Disruption of the cell's nucleolus and its ability to store and metabolize RNA. (3) Disruption of kidney tubules' normal functioning. The poisons normally filtered from the body via kidney tubules are unable to be eliminated and are returned to the bloodstream.

Figure 15-24 The poisonous mushroom on the left and the edible mushroom on the right look similar. Wild mushrooms should never be eaten unless they have been identified by an expert.

While many mushrooms are edible, many more are not. Poisonous mushrooms are commonly called toadstools. Toadstools can cause illness, and some can cause death, if eaten. Many poisonous mushrooms closely resemble edible species, as shown in Figure 15-24. It takes a great deal of study and training to learn how to tell the difference between edible and poisonous species. An untrained person should never eat unidentified mushrooms found growing wild.

Whereas mushrooms are valuable to humans, many other club fungi are harmful. Mycelia of rusts, for example, invade the internal parts of wheat, oats, rye, and other plants, and can destroy entire crops. Geneticists have developed some strains of plants that are resistant to these parasites.

ART CONNECTION

Three Mushrooms by Roberto Juarez

Fungi come in many shapes and colors. Some are round or circular, resembling cups or plates. Bird's nest fungi look just like a nest with small white eggs inside. Fungi come in many colors, too: white, pink, yellow, orange, green, blue, even black. It is no wonder, then, that the shapes and colors of fungi have inspired artists in their work.
The Artist One such artist is

Roberto Juarez. His father is Mexican American, his mother Puerto Rican. From the time he was small, he drew what he saw around him. It wasn't until college, however, that he realized he could become an artist. Since 1979, Juarez has exhibited his drawings and paintings in galleries across the United States and in Europe.
The Painting In several of his paintings, Juarez uses mushrooms as his main subject. In one, called *Three Mushrooms* (1986), the mushrooms float or fly above a sea of fungi. The mushrooms are dark,

perhaps menacing. Their gills can be seen through the cap. Light seems to shine on the shapes behind, but not on the mushrooms. The background looks a little like a slide under a microscope. The colors are the colors of fungi. Juarez painted the picture on a piece of burlap, which gives the shapes a rough surface.

Many of Juarez's paintings have an ironic quality. There is often a background like the one in this painting that forms a pattern of shapes and colors. Hanging above this pattern is something that goes with it, and also does not. In *Three*

412 🍄 VIRUSES AND MICROORGANISMS

PROJECT

Fungus Fun: Hold a class contest to see who can grow the biggest, ugliest, most colorful fungus in class within one week's time. Students can bring in their starter mold by collecting samples such as moldy oranges or bread. One or two students could supply enough starter mold for the entire class. Allow students to determine how to use the starter mold, as well as where within the classroom to store the mold. Light, dark, warm, or cool areas may be selected by students. Fungi should be grown in closed containers to prevent spore contamination of the classroom. Appoint a student committee for the final judging. The prize for the winners—a gift-wrapped chunk of blue cheese. **Caution:** *Students who are allergic to molds should not participate in the contest. They can act as judges.* **L1** **COOP LEARN**

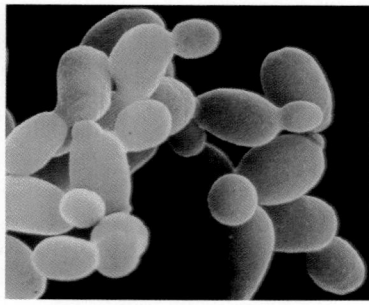

Sac Fungi

Yeasts, cup fungi, and powdery mildews are all members of the phylum known as the sac fungi. Each of these organisms possesses a saclike structure called an **ascus.** Sexual spores are produced by meiosis in the ascus.

Yeasts are unusual fungi in that they are unicellular and lack hyphae. They are important in both the brewing and baking industries. They are also very important in scientific research, because they are simple eukaryotes and can be studied easily. Yeasts have proven to be of value in research on recombinant DNA and in the study of diseases such as cancer and AIDS. Cellular processes such as respiration also have been studied by using yeasts as research organisms.

Figure 15-25 Cup fungi (left) and yeasts (right) are both sac fungi. Yeasts are unusual fungi in that they only have one cell. Magnification (right): 18 000×

Mushrooms, the mushrooms go with the background shapes because they are all circular. Yet, the mushrooms are separated from the background by their dark color. They seem to hang in the air with no connection to anything around them.

1. **Writing About Biology:** What do the shapes and colors in Juarez's picture mean to you?
2. **Connection to Agriculture:** Many kinds of mushrooms are grown for food. What are some of the different kinds of mushrooms you can eat?

ART CONNECTION

Purpose
Students should come to realize that nature supplies the subject matter for many paintings and art forms. Even fungi, not the most prominent of living things, can be used as an art subject.

Teaching Strategies
* Provide students with needed references. Then, having them work in cooperative groups, ask students to: identify the technical parts or names of the structures that are shown; determine if all three mushrooms are possibly of the same genus or species and provide evidence for their answer; and describe the type of fungi other than mushrooms that might lend themselves to a painting such as the one seen here. **COOP LEARN**

Possible Answers
1. Students may or may not like the color selection used by the artist. Shapes and colors may present a soothing or comforting feeling. Some students may feel that the background detracts from the painting.
2. The most common store species available are *Agaricus bisporus* or *A. campestris.* Morels and shiitake mushrooms are also most prized edible forms.

Going Further
Have interested students prepare mushroom spore prints. Place a mushroom cap, with stipe removed, gill side down onto a piece of white paper, and allow to remain undisturbed for 24 to 48 hours. Spores will fall from the gills and form a distinct pattern resulting in an interesting art form. Have students brainstorm and then experiment with ways to preserve the spore prints.
L1 **LEP** **COOP LEARN**

PORTFOLIO
Allow students to examine and then report on the appearance of yeast. Students can easily get yeast cells to reproduce asexually by budding. The results of the process can be seen microscopically with ease. Have students design an experiment to determine the type of sugar that best stimulates budding. This experiment can be added to their portfolios. **L2**

MULTICULTURAL CONNECTION
Matzo: Bread that has been made with yeast or baking powder is called leavened bread. The term *leavened* refers to the rising action of carbon dioxide on the dough, giving it a fluffier texture. Some ethnic groups use unleavened bread in their diet. Matzo is used by Jews during the Passover holiday. Matzo is a very dry and flat dough lacking the soft texture of leavened breads.

Minilab 2

Purpose
Students will determine what factors are required for fungal growth.

Skills
observe and infer, compare and contrast, recognize cause and effect, interpret data

Teaching Strategies
- Bread should be sprinkled lightly with water. Water can be placed in a plastic spray bottle and sprayed on the bread.
- Bakery bread, rather than grocery bread, should be used in this experiment because it does not contain preservatives. Day-old bread should be used.

Expected Results
Students should see mold growth on the moist bread within a week. There should be no growth on the dry bread.

Answers
Students should observe mold on the moist bread. Fungi need food, water, and a warm, dark place in which to grow.

✔ Assessment
Knowledge: Have students make a list of factors required for growth of fungi.

Minilab 2

What do fungi need to grow?

Sprinkle a slice of bread lightly with water. Place it in a self-sealing plastic sandwich bag. Place a dry slice of bread in a second plastic bag. Seal both bags and put them in a warm, dark place for a week.
Analysis *What do you observe? What do fungi need for growth?*

Other types of fungi are also important in industry and medicine. One species of *Penicillium* mold is used in the production of penicillin. Other species of *Penicillium* are used in making cheeses such as Roquefort and Camembert. Enzymes produced by these molds give the cheeses their distinctive flavors.

Lichens

Most noticeable in desolate regions, but found throughout the world, are organisms called lichens. A lichen is a "dual organism" consisting of a fungus and a green organism, either a blue-green bacterium or a green alga. The mycelium of the fungus surrounds the cells of the green organism. Lichens grow on soil, rocks, and trees. Some grow flat and close to the surface, Figure 15-26, while others grow upward and may appear shrublike.

The Living Arrangement of Lichens Lichens can live in barren places such as on bare rock or on Arctic ice. Neither the fungus nor the green organism could survive alone in such harsh environments. What kind of living arrangement do the two organisms have? The green organism is autotrophic; it provides food for itself and the fungus by means of photosynthesis. Exactly how the fungus aids the green organism is not clear.

Table 15.1 **Summary of Major Characteristics of Monerans, Protists, and Fungi**

Kingdom	Common Name	Structure	Nutrition	Importance
Monera	true bacteria	prokaryotic mainly unicellular	heterotrophic; autotrophic (photosynthetic, chemosynthetic)	producers; disease; industry; decomposers
	ancient bacteria		chemosynthetic	producers
Protista	euglenoids golden algae	unicellular	autotrophic (photosynthetic)	producers in aquatic habitats; industry
	green algae brown algae red algae	mostly multicellular		
	rhizopods ciliates flagellates sporozoans	unicellular	heterotrophic	consumers; parasites; disease
	slime molds	unicellular and multicellular stages	heterotrophic	decomposers
Fungi	zygote fungi club fungi sac fungi	multicellular; hyphae	heterotrophic	decomposers; disease; medicine

414 ❧ VIRUSES AND MICROORGANISMS

PROGRAM RESOURCES

Teacher Classroom Resources
Critical Thinking/Problem Solving, p. 15 [L2]
Color Transparency #20 [L1] [LEP] , #21 [L2] [LEP]
Investigating Living Systems, Lab 36, p. 141 [L2]

PROJECT

Lichens: Have students place a thin slice of washed lichen in a petri dish with moistened paper towels on the bottom. Cover the petri dish and place it under lights. Examine the lichen every day for a week for evidence of algal growth. Add water if the lichen appears to be drying out. Students may wish to make diagrams to show the changes that occur to the lichen. [L1]

MEETING INDIVIDUAL NEEDS

Refer students working at grade level or above to Appendix A. Have them record the phylum names for all protists. After listing examples of organisms in each phylum, have them use references to determine the literal meaning of the phylum names. Have students correlate the meaning of the phylum name with the corresponding phylum trait already studied. [L2]

Perhaps the fungus provides it with protection and moisture, because the lichen can survive drying, whereas the green organism by itself cannot. The fungus also may be a source of inorganic materials. A lichen is an example of a living arrangement based on mutualism.

The Role of Lichens Lichens sometimes serve as food for animals. An example is reindeer moss, an Arctic species that is eaten by reindeer and caribou. Lichens serve yet another important ecological function. They can actually help create soil in rocky or barren regions. The fungus portion of the lichen secretes acids that begin the breakdown of rock into particles of soil. When lichens die, they decompose, thus enriching the soil they helped produce. Eventually, the soil becomes rich enough to support the growth of more complex, true plants.

Summary Many of the phyla contained in the Kingdoms Monera, Protista, and Fungi have been described in this chapter, but there are many more. It would take several chapters to describe them all. Table 15.1 summarizes the major characteristics of the phyla that have been included here. The common names of the phyla have been used rather than the technical names. You can see how diverse these three kingdoms are. For more information on these groups, see Appendix A.

Figure 15-26 Some lichens are leaflike, others are shrublike, and still others, such as the lichens shown here, form crustlike growths on rocks.

LOOKING AHEAD

YOU HAVE explored important features of the viruses and of the organisms that make up the Kingdoms Monera, Protista, and Fungi. Certain of these simple organisms are thought to be the ancestors of more complex and familiar living things. In the next chapter, you will study the major groups of another kingdom, the plants. You will learn about the evolution of adaptations that have made different groups of plants suited to life in particular habitats.

Section Review

Understanding Concepts

1. Explain why fungi must be either parasites or saprophytes.
2. Why do you think fungi were previously classified as plants?
3. How can you explain the fact that mushrooms just seem to pop up out of the ground and do so in about the same place each year?
4. **Skill Review—Forming a Hypothesis:** Why can't the separate organisms of which a lichen is composed live in places where the lichen can live? For more help, refer to Practicing Scientific Methods in the **Skill Handbook**.
5. **Thinking Critically:** How could you determine whether a newly discovered fungus is a relative of *Rhizopus* or of a mushroom?

Answers to Section Review

1. Fungi, although heterotrophic, are sessile and lack adaptations for trapping food. They must absorb organic matter from other organisms or from wastes or dead organisms.
2. Fungi are stationary like plants, and some have plantlike adaptations such as being "rooted" in soil.
3. The mycelium of a fungus is present in the soil year round. It is part of that mycelium that develops aboveground.
4. **Skill Review—Forming a Hypothesis:** Neither the fungus nor the photosynthetic organism can exist in harsh conditions. The fungus would have no food source and the photosynthetic organism would dry out.
5. **Thinking Critically:** In a relative of *Rhizopus*, sexual spores would be produced from zygotes. A relative of a mushroom would produce sexual spores in basidia.

3 Assess

Check for Understanding

Have students explain the following word connections or relationships.
(a) economic importance to humans—fungal growth
(b) ecological importance to all living things—fungal growth
(c) spores, gills, basidia
(d) sac, ascus, reproduction
(e) mutualism, lichens, algae, fungi L1

Reteach

There are five main sections within the Kingdom Fungi heading. Ask students to prepare a concept map of the main ideas found in these five sections. LEP

Extension

Students are to pick one fungus responsible for crop losses and follow its life cycle. Specific examples might be rusts (*Puccinia graminis*) or smuts (*Ustilago zeae*). Another topic might be the formation of LSD from the ergot fungus *Claviceps purpurea*. L3

✔ **Assessment**

Performance: Have students prepare wet mounts of *Peziza*, a cup fungus available preserved from biological supply houses. A small amount of the cup region prepared using a squash technique will yield sacs containing ascospores. Have students observe their squashes under low and high power and identify the structures seen. Have them name the group (sac fungi) to which this specimen belongs. L1

4 Close

Discussion

The following anecdote can be presented to the class for analysis.

Growing mushrooms commercially is accomplished in caves. The only major expense is bringing in enough light so that photosynthesis can occur. Is this a correct interpretation or not? L1

Considering the Environment

Purpose
Students will gain an understanding of how monerans can be put to use to clean up the environment.

Background
Bacteria are normally present in soil. The species that are most commonly present are *Arthrobacter,* followed by *Pseudomonas, Clostridium,* and *Bacillus.*

Teaching Strategies
- Have students work in groups to learn the amount of oil spilled by the *Exxon Valdez* and if or how Exxon made restitution to those whose jobs and businesses were lost as a consequence of the disaster. They might also research the bioremediation process that was used, the organism used, and write a follow-up of the disaster and cleanup. COOP LEARN
- You might want to assign this reading as homework and have students place their answers to the questions in their portfolios.

Possible Answers
1. The bacteria that were encouraged to reproduce rapidly could themselves have adverse effects on other life forms. Using a fertilizer to increase bacterial growth could result in the rapid reproduction of harmful bacteria also present on the beaches.
2. Plants typically remove minerals from the soil via their root systems. Therefore, it is a natural extension to develop plants that can selectively remove certain metals from the soil. In New Jersey, ragweed is being used to remove lead from the ground around a former factory site. Plants are being used in Russia to remove radioactive waste from the site of the nuclear power plant disaster.

Considering the Environment
Fighting Pollution with Bacteria

You may have thought all bacteria were harmful. Think again. Some bacteria are working to clean up the damage we have done to our environment.

Oil Spills In 1989, the ship *Exxon Valdez* was carrying crude oil south from the Alaska pipeline. When the ship hit ground, a hole was ripped

in its hull and millions of gallons of oil spread along the Alaskan coast. In some places, the oil soaked two feet deep into the beaches. There seemed no way to clean up the spill. Then scientists decided to enlist the help of bacteria that live on the beaches.

Scientists knew that some bacteria naturally break down hydrocarbons, the main type of molecule found in oil, and that these bacteria lived on the Alaskan beaches. The problem was that there were not enough of these bacteria to handle the huge load of oil. To make the bacteria multiply faster, the scientists sprayed a fertilizer along 70 miles of coastline. Within 15 days, the number of bacteria had tripled. The beaches that had been treated were much cleaner than those that had not. The bacteria continued to work for five months. Without this bacterial "scouring," Alaska's beaches might still be covered with oil.

What makes bacteria such good cleaning agents? They break down toxic chemicals, such as the hydrocarbons in oil, into simple harmless substances like carbon dioxide and water. The bacteria that do this dirty cleanup work are found in soil and water—anywhere we have left our pollution. With the right fertilizer, bacteria grow quickly. And when

they have done their work, they die.

Bioremediation This process of using living things to get rid of toxic materials is called bioremediation. It is being used to clean up gasoline that leaks into the soil under gas stations. At plants that process wood pulp, scientists are using microorganisms that break down phenols, a poisonous by-product of the process. The bacteria reproduce quickly and convert the phenols into harmless salts. Recently, scientists have found bacteria that break down polychlorinated biphenyls (PCBs), the deadly toxins that can get into our water supplies as waste products of certain industries. Other scientists are experimenting with bacteria that break down explosives, such as TNT, and with bacteria that can clean up the acid drainage that seeps out of abandoned coal mines.

Given that Americans make more than 600 million tons of toxic waste a year, bioremediation may soon become a big business. Microbiologists are studying ways to speed up the work of bacteria. The most common method of bioremediation is to increase the growth rate of bacteria found naturally at the pollution site, as the scientists did in Alaska. If the right bacteria are not present, scientists can grow

Going Further
Students might want to test the idea that bacteria are present in the soil, in ocean water, or on beaches. Sterile petri dishes with sterile nutrient agar can be used to investigate this idea.
L2

them in a laboratory and then add them to the soil.

Other Uses of Bioremediation The soil is not the only place bioremediation is being tried. Bacteria are used in sewage treatment plants to clean water and are even going to work against acid rain. When coal containing sulfur burns, the sulfur is released into the air, where it forms acid rain. Bacteria that "eat" sulfur are being used to treat the coal before it is burned and change it into a cleaner-burning fuel.

If scientists can identify microorganisms that attack all the kinds of waste we produce, expensive treatment plants and dangerous toxic dumps might be put out of business.

1. **Solve the Problem:** What new problems might result from using bacteria to fight pollution?
2. **Explore Further:** Scientists are also experimenting with common plants, such as ragweed, to take lead and other metals out of soil. This is called green remediation. How does green remediation work and where is it being tried?

Medicine Connection

A Lucky Accident

In 1928, Alexander Fleming, an English bacteriologist, was studying the bacteria that cause infections on the skin and in the throat. Fleming put some bacterial cells in a petri dish and put the dish aside. When he examined the bacterial growth, he saw that a fungus had appeared as a contaminant in the culture, and the bacteria surrounding the fungus had died. Where there was no fungus, the bacteria were growing. Fleming studied the fungus and discovered that it produced a substance that was toxic to bacteria. Because the fungus belonged to the genus *Penicillium,* Fleming named the substance penicillin. Growth of the fungus was an accident, but Fleming's curiosity and careful investigation took advantage of that accident.

Penicillin as a Medicine Ten years passed before anyone thought of using penicillin for medicine. Howard Florey, another English scientist, knew that penicillin killed bacteria without harming humans or animals. At the time, England was at war with Germany and many soldiers were dying from gangrene

infections in wounds. Florey thought that penicillin might kill the bacteria that cause gangrene. Because England's factories were busy producing weapons and supplies for the war, they were not able to mass-produce penicillin. In 1941, Florey came to the United States, where he convinced American drug companies to make penicillin for use on the battlefield.

Production Begins Production of penicillin was one of the fastest successes in medical history. Most of the drug companies in the United States worked together to produce and test the new antibiotic. By 1943, they were able to produce penicillin in large enough quantities to help the English and American soldiers.

The First Uses Florey went to North Africa to oversee the first uses of penicillin on the battlefield. Penicillin was combined with sulfa drugs and put directly in the wound. Then the wound was closed. The penicillin and sulfa drugs worked together to kill the bacteria, and the wound healed. Because of Fleming's accidental discovery, thousands of soldiers' lives were saved during World War II.

1. **Explore Further:** What diseases are treated with penicillin today?
2. **Solve the Problem:** How does penicillin kill bacteria? Why isn't it harmful to human cells?

CAREER CONNECTION

Microbiologists study bacteria, viruses, fungi, and protists to learn how they work. These scientists may study ways to prevent diseases, study how microbes affect the way plants grow, and look for ways to use microbes to clean up the environment.

CAREER CONNECTION

For more information, have students contact a local hospital or your state university and ask about careers in microbiology. Microbiologists typically will have a degree in virology, bacteriology, or mycology (study of fungi).

Medicine Connection

Purpose
Students will be able to better understand the importance of good observing skills in science as well as learn more about the role of fungi in producing antibiotics.

Background
Various antibiotics destroy or inhibit microbes by disrupting cell wall synthesis, cell membrane synthesis, protein synthesis, nucleic acid formation, or specific metabolic pathways.

Teaching Strategies
- Have students work in groups to: determine the meaning of the terms *bacteriologist, contaminant, toxic, gangrene infection,* and *serendipity* (ask how it applies to the discovery of penicillin); learn the literal meaning of the term *antibiotic;* research the name of the organism responsible for gangrene and whether it is an aerobe or an anaerobe; learn if current antibiotics are still made directly from fungi or if antibiotics are made commercially now on a chemical rather than a natural basis; and answer the questions at the end of this feature. **COOP LEARN**

Possible Answers
1. *Streptococcus* infections such as pneumonia, scarlet fever, and sore throat; food poisoning from *Salmonella;* gonorrhea; syphilis.
2. Penicillin interferes with the ability of bacteria to form peptidoglycans, chemicals found in their cell walls. Human cells do not have cell walls and therefore are not affected by the antibiotic's action.

Going Further
Kits are available from biological supply houses (Carolina Biological Supply) that will allow interested students to test different antibiotics on the growth of selected bacterial species. **L3**

CHAPTER REVIEW

Summary

Summary statements can be used by students to review the major concepts of the chapter.

Language of Biology

Answers should go beyond defining the terms. Accept any reasonable answer that uses the term correctly and in the proper context.

Understanding Concepts

1. A retrovirus contains reverse transcriptase, which transcribes viral RNA to DNA. This enters the host cell's nucleus and becomes a provirus. The other type of RNA virus undergoes a lytic cycle. Its RNA is used as a template for making more viral RNA and also serves as mRNA for synthesizing viral proteins.
2. Some symptoms, such as irritation to the nasal passages, are caused by viruses destroying cells in that area as they carry out the lytic cycle.
3. Chemosynthesis may have evolved first. It is a less complex process, requires no sunlight, and makes use of a variety of inorganic chemicals that might have been present on early Earth.
4. Many of the organisms in these three phyla have a more complex structure than that of other algae.
5. Fungal spores are specialized reproductive cells. Endospores are an adaptation to withstand harsh conditions. They are not reproductive cells.
6. Euglenoids are motile, a characteristic associated with animals. However, like plants, they are photosynthetic. Moreover, some may become heterotrophic and others are always heterotrophic.
7. A colonial alga may represent a transitional stage of evolution in which very similar cells became grouped together to form a single unit. Some of those cells evolved specialized roles, a characteristic

Summary

Viruses are particles of protein and nucleic acid that resemble living things only in their ability to reproduce. To do so, however, they must invade and take over the materials and energy sources of specific host cells. As the viruses reproduce, the host cells are sometimes destroyed.

Monerans are mostly unicellular, prokaryotic organisms known as bacteria. Included in this kingdom are the older, ancient bacteria and the true bacteria. A major reason for the success of bacteria is the diversity of ways they have evolved for obtaining energy.

The most diverse kingdom of organisms is the protists. Included in this eukaryotic kingdom are algae, protozoans, and funguslike species. These groups may have given rise to plants, animals, and fungi, respectively.

Kingdom Fungi includes multicellular heterotrophs that absorb nutrients from living organisms, from the wastes produced by other organisms, or from dead organisms. While many parasitic fungi cause harm, other fungi are very important in the recycling of nutrients. Many fungi are useful to humans.

Language of Biology

Write a sentence that shows your understanding of each of the following terms.

ascus	parasite
asexual reproduction	plasmodium
basidium	provirus
endospore	pseudopodium
hypha	retrovirus
lysogenic cycle	rhizoid
lytic cycle	saprophyte
mutualism	
mycelium	

Understanding Concepts

1. Compare how a retrovirus and the other type of RNA virus invade and replicate within their host cells.
2. How can the symptoms of viral diseases such as the flu be related to the reproductive cycles of the viruses that cause the diseases?
3. Which do you think might have evolved first, chemosynthesis or photosynthesis? Explain your answer.
4. In some classification systems used today, green, brown, and red algae are classified as plants rather than algae. Can you suggest a reason for that classification?
5. How are bacterial endospores different from fungus spores?
6. How do characteristics of euglenoids illustrate some of the problems of classifying organisms?
7. Some green algae are colonial forms that are made up of many individual cells connected together. The cells have developed specialized functions, but still remain independent. Explain how colonial algae may represent a step in the evolution of multicellular algae.
8. In what ways do *Euglena* and *Paramecium* show that division of labor is important in unicellular organisms?
9. How do slime molds resemble other protists as well as fungi?
10. Why do you think fungi are now classified in a kingdom of their own?

of multicellular organisms.
8. Both have unique organelles that enable them to carry out all life functions.
9. Like fungi, slime molds are heterotrophic and reproduce by means of spores. The plasmodium and swarm cells resemble protozoans.
10. Fungi lack the features by which plants and animals are classified. It is more logical to assume that fungi represent a line of evolution distinct from that of either plants or animals.

Applying Concepts

11. Without a cell wall, mycoplasmas could not maintain osmotic balance in fresh water without bursting. Body fluids of their hosts are similar to their cell contents.
12. Drugs might be developed that prevent the retrovirus from recognizing or entering its host cell, or that would interfere with reverse transcription of the viral RNA.
13. Detection of light would not be important in the life of a heterotrophic euglenoid.

Applying Concepts

11. Mycoplasmas are bacteria that lack cell walls. How might that feature be related to the fact that all mycoplasmas are parasites within other organisms?

12. How might you develop drugs that prevent the reproduction of a retrovirus, using knowledge of its reproductive cycle?

13. Some species of euglenoids are always heterotrophic. Do you think such species have a light-sensing eyespot? Explain.

14. How do you think protozoans were classified in a two-kingdom system? Explain.

15. How could you easily distinguish between a unicellular alga and a blue-green bacterium?

16. Fungi may be harmful to crops. In what way are they helpful?

17. Is a virus a parasite? Explain.

18. Can penicillin be used to treat a viral infection? Why or why not?

19. Sometimes, during a lytic cycle, a small part of a host bacterium's DNA may be enclosed in a new phage. If this phage then attacks another bacterium, it will carry a portion of the first host's DNA into the second host. How is this process a possible source of variation among bacteria?

20. **Considering the Environment:** Why might it be better to clean up a site by using bacteria that naturally grow there rather than by bringing new bacteria to the site?

21. **Medicine Connection:** Today, the United States government must approve the use of all drugs. Sometimes it takes years before a drug is proved to be effective and safe for use. Is this time lag justified, or should new drugs be used, as penicillin was, as soon as they are developed?

This British soldier lichen forms shrublike growths. Each "soldier" is 1 to 2 cm tall.

Lab Interpretation

22. **Investigation:** What would the following graph indicate about a new sunscreen being tested for safety?

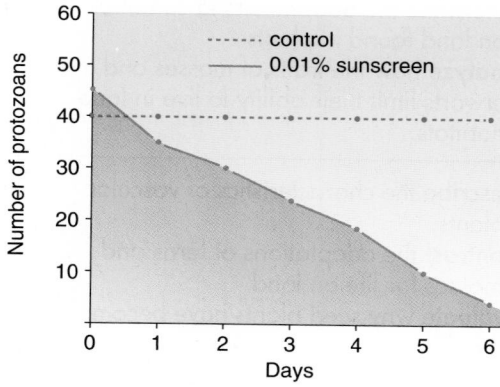

Protozoan numbers in 0.01% sunscreen vs. control

23. **Thinking Lab:** How can a fungus be used as an effective weed killer?

24. **Thinking Lab:** Why might using a fungus to control weeds be more desirable than using chemical controls?

25. **Minilab 2:** Why did you place the plastic bags containing slices of bread in a warm, dark place? Would you have gotten similar results if you had placed the bags in the refrigerator? Why or why not?

Connecting Ideas

26. Thinking back to conditions that were believed to have existed on primitive Earth, why is it reasonable to assume that ancient bacteria may have been the first organisms to evolve?

27. Lichens are sometimes called pioneer organisms because they are among the first organisms to move into a barren area. Why are lichens well suited for this role?

14. Protozoans were classified as animals because most are motile and all are heterotrophic.

15. The alga is a eukaryote. Its chlorophyll is located in chloroplasts, and it contains a nucleus.

16. Fungi recycle nutrients required by the crop plants.

17. A virus is a parasite in the sense that it cannot reproduce unless it makes use of its host cell's raw materials, energy sources, enzymes, and ribosomes.

18. Penicillin has no effect on viruses. Viruses are not cells.

19. The DNA from the first bacterium may code for a protein not coded for by the second bacterium's DNA. Receiving that DNA may aid the survival of the second bacterium.

20. The imported bacteria might not thrive in a new environment. They might also disrupt the ecological balance at the site.

21. Student opinions will vary. Some might argue "better safe than sorry." Others might believe that the benefit of a new drug outweighs its possible risks.

Lab Interpretation

22. The sunscreen kills protozoans. Further testing needs to be done to determine its safety on other living cells.

23. Fungus spores of a species that kills a specific weed can be made into a stable form such as a pesta and sprinkled onto crop fields.

24. A fungus is more specific than chemical control, is less toxic to other living things, and is not polluting to the environment.

25. Fungi need warmth and darkness for optimal growth. They may grow eventually in the refrigerator, but will do so very slowly.

Connecting Ideas

26. **Evolution:** Conditions in the early ocean may have been similar to those in which these bacteria thrive today.

27. **Systems and Interactions:** The two organisms of which lichens are composed interact to form a unit that can survive. Even in barren areas, the autotrophic organism can produce food for both itself and the fungus because the fungus protects and holds moisture for the autotroph.

ORGANIZER

C H A P T E R

16

SECTION	OBJECTIVES	TEXT LABS/FEATURES
16.1 From Water to Land (2 days)	**Determine** the adaptations to conditions on land found in plants. **Analyze** how the traits of mosses and liverworts limit their ability to live in land habitats.	**Investigation:** Leaf-Cuticle Models, p. 424 **Thinking Lab:** What adaptations were necessary for plants to move onto land? p. 427
16.2 Vascular Plants (3 days)	**Describe** the characteristics of vascular plants. **Contrast** the adaptations of ferns and mosses for life on land. **Evaluate** why seed plants have become the dominant plants on Earth.	**Minilab 1:** How do mosses and ferns compare? p. 433 **Global Connection:** Corn: The Native American Grain, p. 438 **Art Connection:** *Affection* by Patricia Gonzalez, p. 440 **Minilab 2:** What do flower parts really look like? p. 441
BIOLOGY, TECHNOLOGY, AND SOCIETY		**Biotechnology:** Plants: Earth's Major Energy Trappers, p. 443 **Issues:** How shall our forests be harvested? p. 444 **Career Connection:** Forestry technician, p. 444 **Considering the Environment:** Controlling Pests, p. 445

LAB MATERIALS

INVESTIGATION	MINILAB	ALTERNATE LAB
page 424 acetate graduated cylinder hair dryer paper towels scissors tape aluminum foil watch or clock waxed paper yarn yogurt containers, empty	**page 433** coverslips fern sorus microscope moss capsule slides **page 441** flower lens paper microscope scalpel slides	**page 428** balance, pan beaker, 50-mL filter paper funnel graduated cylinder, 100-mL masking tape soil/sand mixture *Sphagnum* moss spoon

TEACHER CLASSROOM RESOURCES	OTHER RESOURCES
Study Guide, pp. 91-92 ***PLL:** *Mosses, Club Mosses, and Horsetails,* p. 95 ****ILS:** *Liverworts, Mosses, and Ferns,* p. 147 **Exploring Environmental Issues,** *Hold onto That Soil,* p. 15; *Thank a Tree,* p. 37	***STVS:** *Water Hyacinth,* Plants and Simple Organisms (Disc 4, Side 2) **Color Transparency 24:** *Alternation of Generations* **Color Transparency 29:** *Life Cycle of a Moss*
Study Guide, pp. 93-96 **Concept Mapping,** p. 16 **Critical Thinking/Problem Solving:** *Using a Key to Identify Trees,* p. 16 ***PLL:** *Ferns, Gymnosperms, and Angiosperms,* p. 98 ***PLL:** *Classification of Fruits,* p. 101 ****ILS:** *Liverworts, Mosses, and Ferns,* p. 147	***STVS:** *City Trees,* Plants and Simple Organisms (Disc 4, Side 2) ***STVS:** *Insecticides from Desert Plants,* Plants and Simple Organisms (Disc 4, Side 2) **Color Transparency 30:** *Life Cycle of a Fern* **Color Transparency 32:** *Flower Structures*
Assessment Materials **Chapter Assessment,** pp. 61-64 **Performance Assessment in Biology,** p. 32 **Alternate Assessment in the Science Classroom** **Computer Test Bank**	**Spanish Resources** **Cooperative Learning Resource Guide** **Videodisc Correlations** (to Optical Data's and Videodiscovery's videodiscs)

* Probing Levels of Life
** Investigating Living Systems

* Science Technology Videodisc Series

Key to Teaching Strategies

The following designations will help you decide which activities in the teacher margin are appropriate for your students.

L1 Level 1 activities should be within the ability range of all students.

L2 Level 2 activities should be within the ability range of the average to above-average student.

L3 Level 3 activities are designed for the ability range of above-average students.

LEP LEP activities are appropriate for Limited English Proficiency students.

COOP LEARN Cooperative Learning activities are designed for small group work.

ADDITIONAL RESOURCES

Infinite Voyage *Life in the Balance*
From mass extinctions in the past to rain forest destruction today, this video details some of the effects of humans on the biosphere and suggests ways to mitigate some of those effects.

Audiovisual
Patterns in Green, video, Coronet/MTI.
The Life Cycle of Plants, video, Films for the Humanities and Sciences.
The Kingdom of Plants, video, Insight Media.

Software
Plants, Apple, J and S.

16

PLANT ADAPTATIONS

Chapter Overview

Students begin the chapter by examining the evidence that plants evolved from green algae and by gaining an understanding of the adaptations necessary for plants to live on land. They study general solutions to the problems of life on land—retaining water, gas exchange, reproduction, and transport in a dry environment—and then examine how nonvascular plants are adapted to solving those problems. Students then explore the concept of the plant life cycle and alternation of generations, applying that concept to the life cycle of a moss.

Next, students study the evolution of major groups of vascular plants: club mosses, horsetails, ferns, and seed plants. As they learn about each group, they compare their adaptations for land life and will come to realize why certain groups are more successful than others.

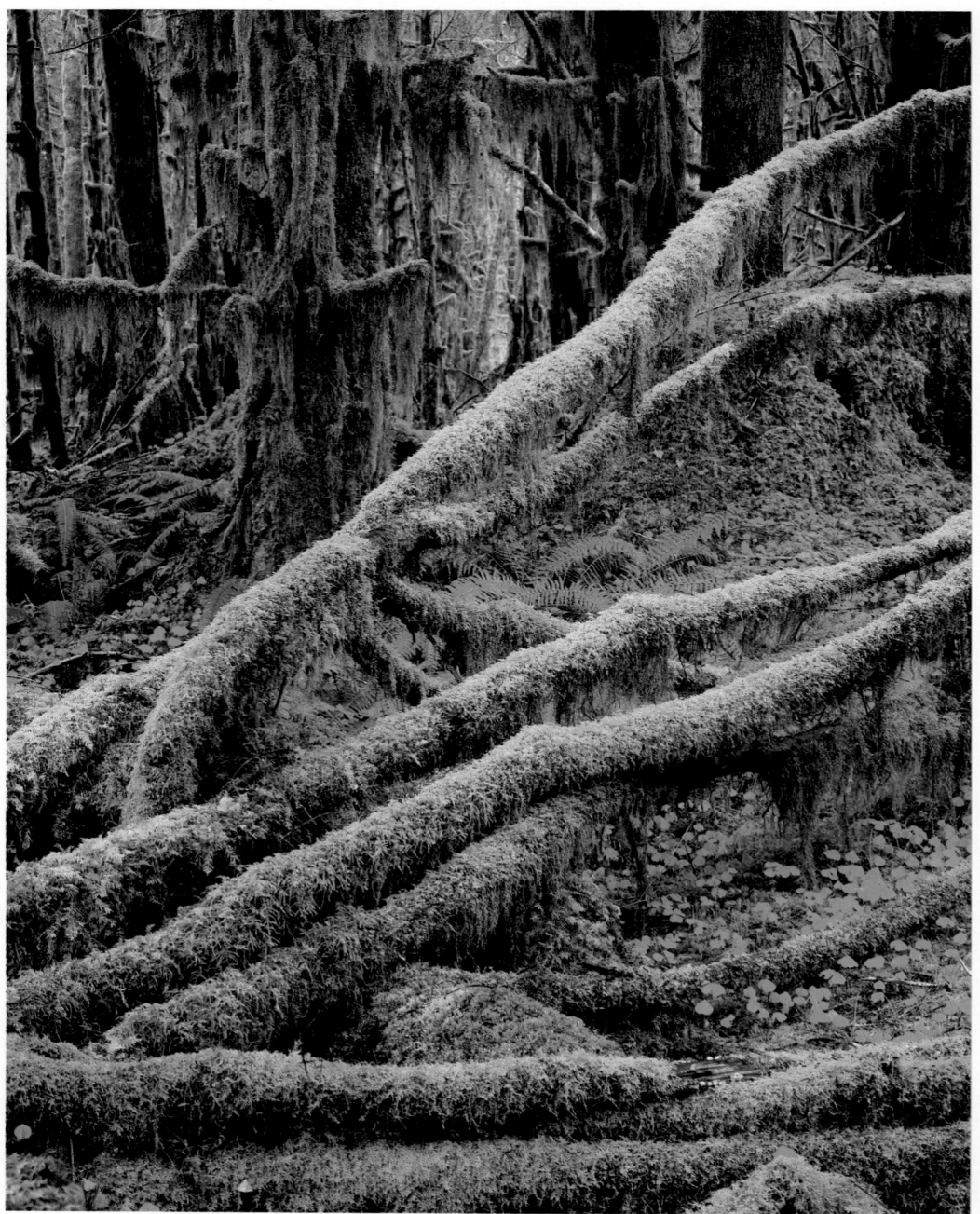

420

KEY TERMS

16

PLANT ADAPTATIONS

MOSSES LIVE IN damp, shady places. Individual moss plants are very small and easy to overlook, but they often grow together in dense mats covering soil, bark, or gaps between stones. Mosses are probably very similar to some of the first plants that appeared on Earth, and may have evolved from green algae that lived in ancient swamps, lakes, and oceans. Mosses, unlike their ancestors, can live on land. But they cannot survive or reproduce unless they are surrounded by at least a thin film of moisture.

Many other plants, including trees, are also thought to have descended over millions of years from ancient green algae. However, trees have evolved a number of adaptations that enable them to survive under conditions unsuitable for mosses. For example, some trees can grow and reproduce in hot, dry climates. Trees also have adaptations that enable them to grow much larger than any moss. What are these adaptations, and how did they arise? In this chapter, you will learn about the differences between mosses, ferns, coniferous trees, and flowering plants. You will find out that the plant kingdom contains a huge variety of organisms adapted for life in all kinds of environments, from sandy deserts and coastlines to snowy mountains, fertile valleys, vast flatlands, and even lakes.

Imagine you are planting a garden. What kinds of plants would grow best in the shade? Where would you plant a magnolia tree? What survival needs do the tree and shade plants have in common? How do their needs differ?

Chapter Preview

ASSESSMENT PLANNER

Choose assessment strategies from the following pages to evaluate the progress of your students.
Assess, pp. 430, 442
Portfolio, pp. 426, 430, 433, 436, 442
Alternate Lab, pp. 428-429
Thinking Lab, p. 427

Minilab 1, p. 433
Minilab 2, p. 441
Investigation, pp. 424-425
Chapter Review, pp. 446-447

Introducing the Chapter

The photographs on pages 420 and 421 can be used to initiate a discussion of the diversity of plant life with which students are familiar. The photos depict mosses, nonvascular plants; and magnolia blossoms, parts of an angiosperm, a group of more complex plants. Have students identify plants they know and categorize them by groups. They will probably name ferns and several examples of conifers as well as a wide variety of angiosperms. Ask students where each type of plant lives, leading them to the idea that some, like mosses, are limited in habitat, whereas others, conifers and flowering plants, occupy a wider range of environments. Follow up on this by asking students why different plants live in different habitats. This discussion will provide a logical introduction to the approach of the chapter.

Theme Development

Evolution is a theme quite obviously woven throughout this chapter. It is apparent in the discussion of green algae as the ancestor of plants, and in terms of the adaptations for land life that have arisen among the descendants of those algae and the relationships among various plant groups. Unity within diversity is exemplified by the idea that all plants must be adapted to the same problems of life on land, but the adaptations vary greatly among the different groups.

Tying to Previous Knowledge

Students will make use of their understanding of evolution as they study adaptations of plants. As you teach the material presented, incorporate ideas where applicable such as speciation, descent with modification, adaptive radiation, and convergence.

Prepare

Key Concepts

Students will study the origins of plants from algae and movement to the land with associated problems and adaptations. Algae, mosses, and liverworts will be considered.

Key Terms

cuticle, vascular tissue, thallus, gametophyte generation, sporophyte generation, alternation of generations

Materials

- For the Investigation, gather empty yogurt containers, tin foil, paper towels, yarn, scissors, graduated cylinders, wax paper, tape, hair dryer, and acetate.
- Purchase or obtain algae, mosses, liverworts, and duckweed for the Microscope Activities.

1 Focus

Objectives

The objectives are listed on the student page. Remind students to preview these objectives as a guide to this numbered section.

Activity

Give each group live samples, mounts, or prepared slides of algae, mosses, and liverworts. If you cannot collect them from your local area, they may be ordered from biological supply companies. Ask students to observe the specimens at low power; then ask them to make diagrams and tell how they are alike and how they are different in appearance. **L1**

Objectives

Determine the adaptations to conditions on land found in plants.

Analyze how the traits of mosses and liverworts limit their ability to live in land habitats.

Figure 16-1 **The storage of sugars in plants and green algae takes the form of polysaccharides that make up starch, whereas storage of sugars in bacteria, fungi, and animals takes the form of glycogen. The scanning electron micrograph (left) shows starch grains in a potato cell. (Magnification: 100×) The transmission electron micrograph on the right shows the starch grain in *Chlamydamonas*, a unicellular green alga. (Magnification: 6000×)**

16.1 From Water to Land

Where do plants live? Have you seen lily pads floating on a pond, vines clinging to the side of a building, trees towering hundreds of feet from the forest floor, or ferns growing along a stream bank? These are just a few examples of the many environments plants can occupy. Plants are an important part of any community of living organisms. They are the producers that use the energy of sunlight to turn water and soil nutrients into food needed by themselves and their consumers. They provide shelter for caterpillars, owls, pythons, koalas, and a multitude of other organisms. Plants are also indispensable to human economy. We build homes from wood, weave cloth from cotton or other plant fibers, and make medicines from a variety of roots, leaves, and flowers. Plants were used to make the paper this book is printed on, and perhaps the desk or chair you're sitting on, and probably some of the clothes you are wearing.

Origin of Plants

All the plants on Earth today are probably descendants of green algae that dwelt in ancient oceans. This conclusion is based on three pieces of evidence. First, both green algae and plants have cell walls containing cellulose. Second, their cells contain the same kinds of chlorophyll and carotenoid pigments. Third, the product of photosynthesis in both green algae and plants is starch, which is stored in plastids in the cytoplasm.

Starch

422 ❧ PLANT ADAPTATIONS

Life in the Water   As you read in Chapter 15, green algae are protists that live in water or very moist places. Water generally provides a very stable environment; temperatures remain fairly even, dissolved nutrients are plentiful and easily absorbed into cells, and, of course, there is never a shortage of water. As a result of this stability, green algae, which first appeared on Earth about a billion years ago, have survived as fairly simple organisms. They don't need to transport water or nutrients from one part of the organism to another because algal cells can obtain these materials directly from the surrounding water or from other cells that are in direct contact with the water. Similarly, each algal cell is either capable of photosynthesis or located near a cell that can carry out photosynthesis. Gametes or developing embryos don't need to be protected from drying out. They are simply released into the water, where fertilization and development occur. Some green algae have soft tissues that allow these protists to float, but none that provide structural support. Their support is the watery environment. They are perfectly adapted to their environment.

Life on Land   Life on land is more demanding than life in the water. On land, there are wide variations in temperature and in the amount of water and nutrients available. What are some of the problems that plants overcame as they became adapted to life on land?

(1) They needed protection from drying out.
(2) They needed to exchange gases with the surrounding air.
(3) They needed a transport system to provide all the cells in a multicellular body with nutrients.
(4) They needed support to grow upright on land.

Figure 16-2   The cells of a green alga, such as the filamentous *Chara*, can obtain nutrients directly from their watery environment (left). The gametes of *Chara* need no protection from drying out (right). Magnification: 20×

2 Teach

Microscope Activity
Ask students to observe duckweed that has been collected locally or purchased from a biological supply house. Tell students that it is not an alga in spite of the fact that it lives on water. Ask them to examine it under low power and explain why it is not an alga. Students should be able to see that a single duckweed plant consists of a leaf with vascular tissue and a root. **L1**

Enrichment
In addition to structural features that made life possible on land, plants developed symbiotic relationships with mycorrhizae—fungi in the soil that aid the plant in taking up phosphorus and other ions. The fungus uses sugars from the plant roots. In some relationships, the mycorrhizae live within the root cells and are called endomycorrhizae. Endomycorrhizae are characteristic of about 80 percent of all vascular plants and have also been found in the fossil forms of early plants.

MULTICULTURAL CONNECTION

Plant Chemistry: Eloy Rodriguez, a Mexican American, grew up in south Texas where his aunts cultivated medicinal gardens in their backyards. His interest in their gardens and how they treated various ailments and infections with teas and ointments made from plants grew into a lifetime interest. Rodriguez is now a plant chemist making a career of examining and testing the chemical relationships between plants and animals. For example, scientists studying chimpanzees noticed that when chimps ate *Aspilia* leaves, they did not seem to enjoy them. When chemists extracted chemicals from the leaf, they found that they killed disease-causing bacteria, fungi, and parasitic worms.

INVESTIGATION

Leaf Cuticle Models

Time Allotment
2 class periods

Objectives
Upon completing this investigation, students will be able to:
- Discover the value of using models to help solve a problem.
- Evaluate data and draw conclusions.

Skills
make a model, work cooperatively in groups, separate and control variables, recognize cause and effect, observe and infer

Materials
empty yogurt containers, paper towels, yarn, scissors, graduated cylinders, water, wax paper, tape, watch or classroom clock, hair dryer, acetate, tin foil

Possible Procedures
- Model design will vary from group to group. One possible design might be two yogurt cups with water and a tin foil cover. Yarn could be threaded through two holes in the foil and into the water. A paper towel would be laid over the moist yarn, which acts as a wick to keep the towel moist. This would be the control, representing a leaf with no cuticle. The experimental model would be set up in the same way but with a plastic or wax-paper covering of the paper towel to represent a leaf with a cuticle. Another design might be like the one shown on the student page.
- Students could measure the amount of water loss over a period of time such as 24 hours. Students should be encouraged to make a data table.
- With the design shown on the page, students could measure the amount of time needed to dry out the paper toweling. Use of the hair dryer is optional.

Through natural selection, plants have evolved a variety of adaptations for coping with the harshness of land conditions. These adaptations involve the evolution of different tissues that perform tasks for survival on land. A variety of plant adaptations have evolved that protect the plant body, gametes, and embryos from drying out during fertilization and development. Some tissues absorb water and dissolved nutrients from the soil, and exchange gases with the air. Some are adapted for photosynthesis, and others distribute water, nutrients, and the food produced by photosynthesis to all parts of the plant. Cells with rigid cell walls provide structural support, which enables the plant to grow upright.

INVESTIGATION

Leaf-Cuticle Models

For water-dwelling plants to evolve into land dwellers, many problems had to be overcome. For example, how might land plants prevent their drying out when once out of a water environment? A waterproof covering over their leaf surfaces might have been an adaptation that would certainly help. Land plants do have such an adaptation, called a cuticle. A cuticle forms a thin surface coating on most land-dwelling plants. Its waterproof quality is provided by a waxy secretion of cutin from the outer cells of a plant. The cuticle acts as a barrier to water evaporation, much as a covering of plastic wrap keeps your food from drying out when placed in the refrigerator.

A waxy cuticle, magnification: 286×

Problem
How can a model be built to show that a plant's cuticle reduces water evaporation?

Experimental Plan
1. As a group, make a list of possible ways that you might design a model to test the idea that a cuticle does reduce evaporation. Keep in mind the materials that your teacher has made available.
2. Agree on one model from your group's list that could be built in the classroom.
3. Refine your model to:
   (a) Construct a control model without a cuticle and an experimental model with a cuticle.
   (b) Make sure that your models and the actual conducting of the experiment will test only one variable.
   (c) Plan to collect quantitative data from your models for comparison.
   (d) Design a table that will compare the data of the control model with the experimental model.
4. Following the style of a recipe, write a numbered list of directions that anyone could follow in building and using your models. Include diagrams of the two models that you plan to build.
5. Make a list of materials and the quantities you will need.

Teaching Strategies
- The control model should have no "cuticle" such as a wax or plastic cover, whereas the experimental model should have a coating representing a cuticle.
- Experimental and control models must be placed in exactly the same conditions. If using a moistened paper towel, both towels must receive the same amount of water and heat from the hair dryers.

Data and Observations
Student answers will vary depending on model design and execution of the experiment. Data tables will vary with the type of model designed.

Data Analysis
1. plastic cups = soil water, string = roots or root hairs, paper towel = leaf surface, wax paper = cuticle

Preventing Water Loss Water that moves into a plant cell by osmosis will also move out of the cell. It is important that land plants have mechanisms for retaining water in their cells. Most plants have a waxy layer, called the **cuticle,** that covers the outer surface of the plant body. The waxy substance is secreted by the epidermal cells. The cuticle helps prevent water loss by forming a watertight seal to the outer cell walls.

Exchanging Gases with the Air All plants take in carbon dioxide and release oxygen during photosynthesis. While the waxy cuticle covers most of a plant's surface, there are small openings, or pores, through which these gases can pass. Before carbon dioxide, or any other gas, can diffuse

Checking the Plan

Discuss the following points with the other group members to decide the final procedures for building and using your models.
1. Which will be your control model? How will it differ from the experimental model?
2. What steps in the design and procedure must be taken to make sure that only one variable is being used?
3. How will you measure the evaporation of your model?
4. How many trials will you carry out?
5. Have you designed and made a table for collecting data?
6. What specific role will each member of your group perform?
7. Make any needed changes in your list of directions or model diagrams.

Make sure your teacher has approved your models and experimental plan before you proceed further.

Data and Observations

1. Build your models.
2. Use your models to collect data and complete your data table.
3. Make a graph of your data or

present your data using some other visual format.

Analysis and Conclusions

1. What model parts correspond to actual plant parts?
2. Explain how the function of model parts did or did not differ from the functions of their corresponding actual plant parts.
3. (a) What were you measuring in the models?
   (b) How does this compare to what actually occurs in a plant?
4. (a) Describe and explain how data from your control model and experimental model differed.
   (b) What were some of the variables that had to be held constant during the experiment? Explain.
5. Does your model data help support the conclusion that a cuticle reduces water evaporation from a plant? Explain how.
6. Use your group's data and models while consulting with other groups to answer the following:
   (a) How did other group models differ from yours?
   (b) How did other group data compare with yours?

(c) What conclusions might be made if other group models and data show similar or different trends from yours?
7. Write a brief conclusion about the value of models in science.

Experimental model

Tape   Wet paper   Wax
        towel   paper
Control
model

Going Further

Based on this lab experience, design another experiment or model that would help to compare a different plant adaptation to life on land. Assume that you will have unlimited resources and will not be building the model in class.

2. Yarn and roots both absorb water; however, roots are composed of living cells. Leaves are photosynthetic and alive, whereas toweling is not. Both wax paper and a cuticle are nonliving, and both are a waxy material.
3. (a) rate at which water evaporates from the control versus the experimental model.
   (b) similar—evaporation rates may vary with the type of leaf or whether it does or does not contain a cuticle.
4. (a) The control model should show faster water loss.
   (b) amount of water added to paper towels; placement of models in same environmental conditions
5. The model should confirm the role of a cuticle in reducing water loss.
6. (a) Answers will vary.
   (b) Answers will vary.
   (c) models may not really be testing for water loss through evaporation; improper collection of data; lack of control over variables; testing for a different hypothesis
7. Models allow scientists to conduct experiments and gather data that might otherwise be difficult or impossible to gather.

✔ Assessment

Performance: Have students prepare a line graph to represent their data. There should be three lines: one representing their control, one their experimental model, and one the expected results.

Extensions

Some possible questions that arose during the experiment may have been: What is the effect of larger leaf surface on evaporation rate? What is the influence of wind on evaporation rate? Have students design experiments to test these factors.

PROGRAM RESOURCES

Teacher Classroom Resources
Study Guide, pp. 91-92 **L1**
Probing Levels of Life, Lab 35, p. 95 **L2**
Color Transparency #24, 29 **L1** **LEP**
Investigating Living Systems, Lab 38, p. 147 **L2**

SECTION 16.1

HISTORY CONNECTION

The Father of Botany:

Theophrastus (372–287 B.C.) was a philosopher of ancient Greece who is known as the father of botany. He wrote more than 200 books and is best known for his botany books in which he covered such topics as plant distribution, propagation, germination, and cultivation. He gave detailed descriptions of more than 500 kinds of plants from as far away as India. Theophrastus obtained information from his pupils who came from far away and from people who had been in military campaigns away from Greece and had knowledge of plants from other parts of the world. He classified plants into trees, shrubs, undershrubs, and herbs. He distinguished between dicotyledons and monocotyledons, and between angiosperms and gymnosperms. Theophrastus was careful to substantiate his statements with observed facts, thereby also establishing a method of scientific investigation that is still used today.

Figure Caption Question

Why are vascular tissues essential for one organism but not the other? The palm tree lives on land and grows many meters tall far from the water supply essential for life. The alga lives in the water and doesn't need special tissues to transport water around the body.

---

through a cell membrane and into a cell, it must be dissolved in water. This necessity poses no problem for algae, since they are not coated with a cuticle and they take in carbon dioxide that is already dissolved in the water surrounding them. But plants must obtain carbon dioxide from the air. All plants have evolved in such a way that their internal cells are surrounded by a film of water. As a gas passes through this film, it is dissolved in the water and can then be absorbed by the cell.

Transport of Nutrients Think for a moment about the difference between a cell belonging to a thin filament of a green alga floating in a pond and a cell located deep inside the stem of a palm tree (Figure 16-3). The algal cell absorbs water, nutrients, and carbon dioxide directly from the water. It contains chloroplasts and produces its own food. But what about the tree cell? It contains no chloroplasts, nor is it exposed to sunlight, so it cannot produce its own food. It is nowhere near the soil, so it can't absorb water and nutrients. To survive, this cell needs a way to get food, water, and other nutrients from the leaves and roots of the tree.

Tissues that transport materials from one part of a plant to another are called **vascular tissues.** Plants that possess vascular tissues are called vascular plants, and those that do not are called nonvascular plants. These are the two major groups that make up the plant kingdom. Vascular plants are far more numerous than nonvascular plants. The trees, shrubs, flowers, and ferns you are familiar with are vascular plants. Nonvascular plants are much less well known.

Nonvascular Plants

In the plant kingdom, the term *division* is usually used in the classification of major groups. You will remember that in the animal kingdom, the major groups are phyla. There are several divisions of vascular plants, but only one division of nonvascular plants. Most nonvascular plants can be grouped into one of two classes—the mosses or the liverworts.

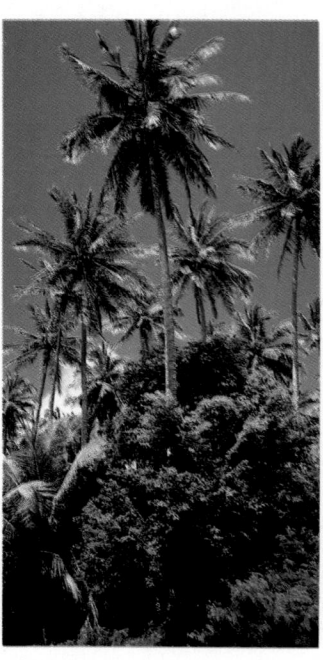

Figure 16-3 Compare the cellular organization in a palm tree and a filamentous green alga. Why are vascular tissues essential for one organism but not the other?

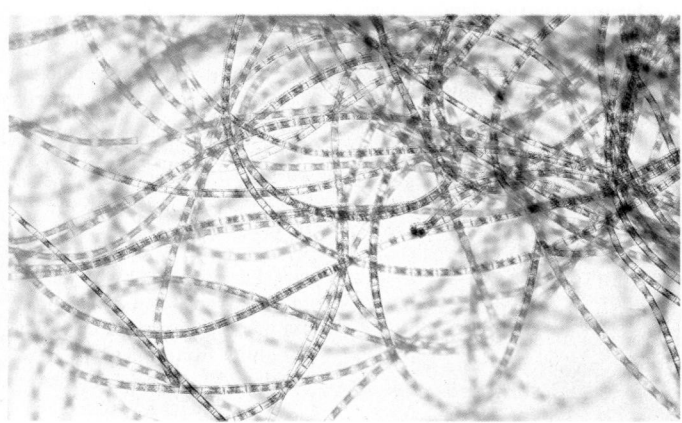

426 🌿 PLANT ADAPTATIONS

PORTFOLIO

Ask students to plan a presentation in which they use transparencies they have designed, posters, and live specimens to explain to a group of fifth graders the evolution of plants from water to land. They should write the details of their plan in their portfolios and, if possible, actually do the demonstration. **L2**

STUDENT JOURNAL

Ask students to take photographs or cut out pictures from seed catalogs of common local wild plants. Some should be water plants, others land plants. In their journals, they should prepare a photo essay about the adaptations of these plants to water and land. **L1**

Identifying Nonvascular Plants   Mosses and liverworts are quite similar. They contain chlorophyll and, therefore, are green in color. Individual plants are almost always very small, often no more than two or three inches high, and are usually found growing in clumps or dense carpets. They grow on soil, rocks, or rotting wood, and a few are adapted to life in water. Mosses are feathery or velvety in texture, and have thin, leaflike structures attached to a tiny upright or creeping stalk, as shown in Figure 16-4. Some liverworts are creeping plants that look like mosses, but most liverworts are flat and leathery in appearance, also shown in Figure 16-4. The flat, liverlike body of a liverwort is called a **thallus.**

Most species of mosses and liverworts inhabit shady, damp areas. Moisture retained by a covering of mosses or liverworts helps promote the decay of rotting wood or other organic matter. In this way, mosses and liverworts help build soil. They also help stabilize soil and prevent erosion by wind and water.

Figure 16-4   Mosses (top) and liverworts (bottom) are land plants that have a low resistance to drying out. They are most often found in the damp regions of the world such as the bogs of temperate regions and rain forests of the tropics.

Thinking Lab

INTERPRET THE DATA

What adaptations were necessary for plants to move onto land?

Background
Most biologists would agree with the theory that the green algae are the ancestors of plants. Most present-day green algae spend all of their life cycle in water. The following traits show how they are well adapted to this environment.

(a) Water helps to support the algal plant body.
(b) All algal cells have access to carbon dioxide and water.
(c) Algal cells cannot dry out.

(d) Most photosynthesis occurs along the top surface of a multicellular alga because only these cells receive direct light.

You Try It
Describe the traits that evolved in land plants which helped overcome the problem of moving to life on land. Use the features of algae described above for comparison. **Explain** how each trait may have led to adaptations in land plants.

Thinking Lab

INTERPRET THE DATA

Purpose
To determine adaptations for life on land.

Skills
interpret data, recognize cause and effect, compare and contrast, observe and infer

Teaching Strategies
• Explain that although algae are not adapted to life on land, they should not be thought of as primitive organisms.

Answers
Land plants were able to adapt to a land environment by evolving: (a) vascular and supportive tissue in the root, stem, and leaves to allow the plant to remain upright; (b) roots or rhizoids and leaves with stomata for gas exchange; (c) a cuticle; and (d) broad, flat leaves arranged on the stem in a manner that allows for maximum light

exposure.

✔ **Assessment**
Knowledge: There are a number of marine algae that have air bladders on their fronds. Have students explain how this type of adaptation might be of value to these algae.

Microscope Activity
Ask students to examine the rhizoids of a moss under low and then high power. They should make drawings and describe how this structure is related to its function. **L1**

Concept Development
Tell students to use an eraser to break open the spore capsules of a variety of mosses. They should prepare wet mount slides of the spores and diagram their shapes. Ask them to compare the external appearances of spores from the different species. **L1**

Teacher FYI
Like lichens, mosses are very sensitive to air pollution and are reduced in numbers near cities or other areas with high levels of pollution.

SECTION 16.1

Activity

Have students crush a dry sporangium of a moss such as *Funaria*, *Bryum*, *Sphagnum*, or *Polytrichum* over liquid media or agar prepared for moss culture from a biological supply house. Spores will germinate in about two weeks, and branched protonemata will form in four weeks. Several cultures should be prepared as some may become contaminated.

Enrichment

Mosses, numbering up to 10 000 species, are found almost everywhere on Earth. In the arctic and the antarctic, they are the most common species of plant. Although not found in deserts, they are able to withstand long periods of dryness. They are not able to absorb water from the air and must have free water to reproduce, as well as for growth and development.

Misconception

Many plants look like mosses that are only superficially similar. For example, "Spanish moss" is actually a flowering plant, a relative of the pineapple (Bromeliaceae).

Transporting Water and Nutrients   Mosses and liverworts do not have tissues that make up the roots, stems, or leaves like those of vascular plants. The leafy structures of mosses and leafy liverworts are generally made up of several layers of tissues only one or two cells thick. The thallus of a liverwort is, likewise, just a few cells thick. Instead of roots, mosses and liverworts have rootlike structures called rhizoids that anchor them to the soil, wood, or water where they live. Like roots, the rhizoids absorb water by osmosis and also take in dissolved nutrients.

Once water and nutrients have been absorbed into the cells of the rhizoids, these molecules move by osmosis and diffusion directly into the cells of the moss stalks or cells of the liverwort body. Sugars produced during photosynthesis in the leafy structures of the moss or thallus of the liverwort also move through the plant by diffusion. This type of transport does not move molecules very far or very quickly. However, transport by diffusion is adequate for nonvascular plants because they are small and the distances molecules must be transported are not great. For the same reason, nonvascular plants can grow only very close to or directly upon a source of nutrients, such as soil on the ground or on the branches of a tree in a wet, tropical forest.

Like all plants, mosses and liverworts have pores through which air enters the plant body. The cells lining these pores are covered with a thin film of water. Carbon dioxide from the air dissolves in the water, then diffuses through the cell membranes. Oxygen is released from the plant by the same process operating in reverse.

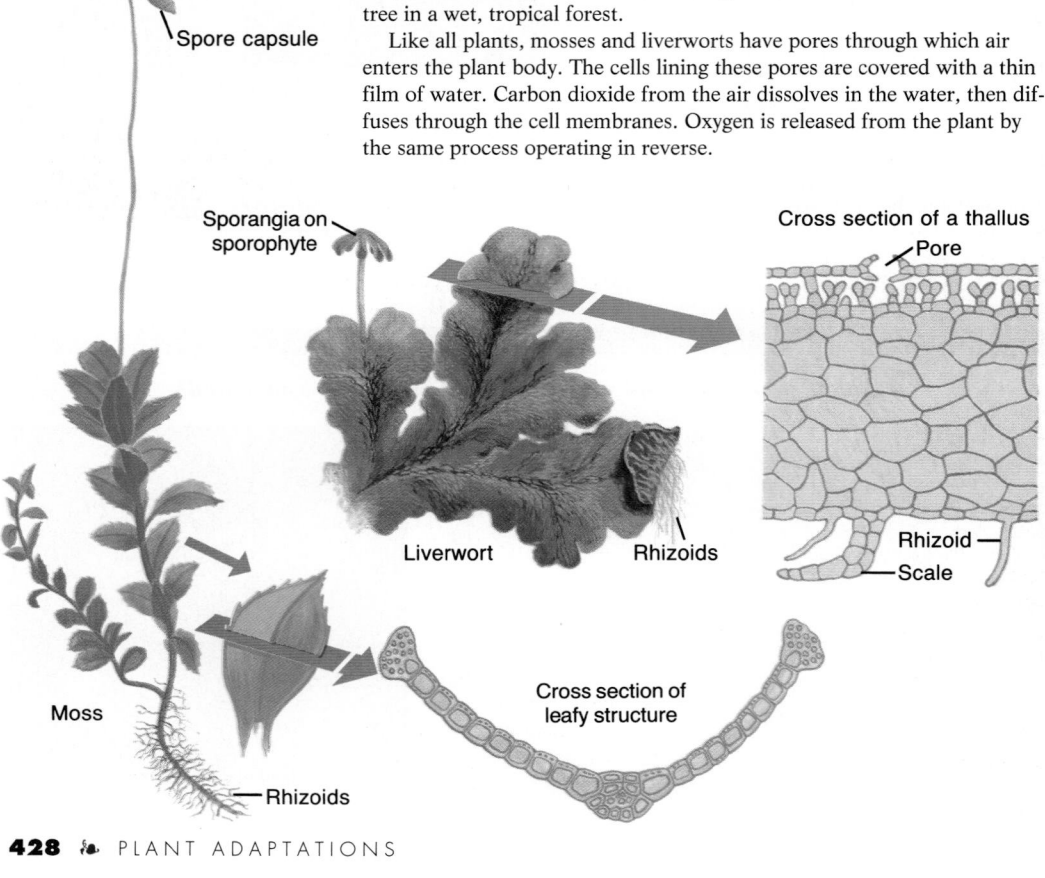

Figure 16-5   Sections through the leaflike structure of a moss (left) and the thallus of a liverwort (right) reveal the simple organization of cells and lack of vascular tissues for transport of water and nutrients.

Spore capsule

Sporangia on sporophyte

Liverwort

Rhizoids

Cross section of a thallus

Pore

Rhizoid

Scale

Cross section of leafy structure

Moss

Rhizoids

428 PLANT ADAPTATIONS

ALTERNATE LAB: How does *Sphagnum* moss help the soil?

Purpose
Students will determine how the addition of *Sphagnum* moss to soil improves its water-holding capacity.

Materials
soil and sand mixture, *Sphagnum* moss, 250-mL beakers (2), pan balance, 100-mL graduated cylinder, masking tape, spoon, funnel, filter paper

Procedure
Give the following directions to students.
1. Mass 10 g of soil/sand mixture and place it in a beaker. Label the beaker "soil."
2. Mass 10 g of soil/sand mixture and place it in a second beaker. Weigh 10 g of *Sphagnum* moss and add it to the soil. Mix thoroughly with a spoon. Label the beaker "soil-moss."

3. Measure 100 mL of water in a graduated cylinder. Pour the water into the first beaker. Measure and pour 100 mL of water into the second beaker. Wait five minutes.
4. Write a hypothesis to describe the amount of water that will be absorbed by the soil in each beaker.
5. Insert a funnel lined with filter paper into the graduated cylinder.

Spores
Germinating spore
Young leafy gametophyte
Sperm
Male reproductive structure
Egg
Female reproductive structure
Fertilization
HAPLOID *n*
Meiosis
DIPLOID 2*n*
Capsule
Young sporophyte develops from zygote
Zygote

The Plant Life Cycle

The lives of all plants including liverworts and mosses consist of two alternating stages, or generations. The **gametophyte generation** in plants is the stage responsible for the development of gametes. All the cells of the gametophyte are haploid (*n*). The second stage is called the **sporophyte generation,** which is responsible for the production of spores. The sporophyte generation is made up of diploid (2*n*) cells. A typical plant life cycle that is made up of this **alternation of generations** is shown in Figure 16-6.

In a moss, the gametophyte generation makes the green, leafy carpets with which you are probably most familiar. The sporophyte generation of a moss makes up the stalks and the capsules where spores are produced by meiosis. Plants of the moss gametophyte generation are haploid and have male and female reproductive organs. Sperm produced in the male organ of a moss swim, by means of flagella, through surface rain or dew to a female organ, which contains the egg. The moisture required by mosses and liverworts for sexual reproduction explains why these nonvascular plants still live in wet habitats. The female reproductive structure provides a moist, protected environment in which fertilization can take place and the embryo can develop.

The embryo develops into a diploid stalk, which is the beginning of the sporophyte generation. A capsule forms at the tip of the stalk and cells inside undergo meiosis to form spores. Spores are adapted to life on land. They have walls that are tough and resist evaporation. When moss spores settle on moist land, they may develop into new haploid plants, thus continuing the plant life cycle.

Figure 16-6 The typical alternation of gametophyte and sporophyte generations in a plant is illustrated here by a moss. What are the products of meiosis in a plant?

16.1 FROM WATER TO LAND ⁂ **429**

Figure Caption Question

How are these characteristics useful as indicators of relationships? The similar traits of unrelated species indicate similar origins. Traces of vascular tissues may indicate relationships to vascular plants but may not be evidence that mosses gave rise to vascular plants. The direction of evolution may have been to reduction of vascular tissues in mosses.

3 Assess

Check for Understanding

Enlarge and photocopy key illustrations from the chapter. Make them into transparencies, and ask students to explain each one. **L1** **LEP**

Reteach

Photocopy diagrams from the chapter, cut them out without captions, and place them on cards. Give each group a set of five cards and ask them to write appropriate captions for each card. **COOP LEARN**

Extension

Ask students to examine soil that is growing under mosses and compare it with soil that is growing under grasses in a lawn. They might examine the soil microscopically and do chemical analysis or test the pH. **L2** **COOP LEARN**

✔ Assessment

Portfolio: Show students a club moss. Ask students what they could do to determine if the plant really is a moss. Ask them to write in their portfolios about how they would study and test this plant to determine if it is a true moss. **L1**

4 Close

Filmstrip

Show a film or filmstrip about mosses and liverworts. Show part of it without sound and ask students to make up narration for that section.

Figure 16-7 The young gametophyte of a moss (top) shows close similarity to a filamentous green alga. A few mosses, such as *Funaria* (left), show traces of vascular tissues in their leaves and stems (right). How are these characteristics useful as indicators of relationships?

Although adapted for life on land, nonvascular plants are not as common or widespread as vascular plants. They need a more moist environment in which to carry on reproduction, photosynthesis, and other life functions. Because adequate water is not available everywhere, nonvascular plants are limited to moist habitats. Their size is also limited because they lack vascular tissues or thick-walled cells for transport or structural support. Because they cannot grow very tall, neighboring plants can easily overgrow them, cutting them off from sunlight and gases.

As you can see, nonvascular plants have more similarities with algae than with vascular plants. For this reason, many biologists consider nonvascular plants the most ancient plants alive today. The close resemblance of the newly developing gametophyte generation to filamentous green algae helps support the theory that nonvascular plants evolved originally from ancient green algae. But there is also another theory that could explain the origin of nonvascular plants. Biologists have observed that some nonvascular plants have traces of vascular tissue. The presence of this tissue could indicate that nonvascular plants are just another relative of vascular plants.

Section Review

Understanding Concepts

1. List the reasons why land is a more demanding environment than water.
2. You collect several plants growing near the edge of a pond. How can you tell which are mosses?
3. How are rhizoids similar to and different from roots?
4. **Skill Review—Making Tables:** Construct a table listing how mosses are adapted for life on land. For more help, refer to Organizing Information in the Skill Handbook.
5. **Thinking Critically:** How are tropical or temperate rain forests perfect habitats for mosses?

Answers to Section Review

1. Land is a much less stable environment than water. Wide temperature variations exist and amounts of water and minerals may also vary. There are problems of drying out, gas exchange in a dry environment, transport, and support.
2. Mosses lack true roots, stems, and leaves and produce spores in capsules.
3. Rhizoids, like roots, absorb water and minerals from the soil. However, they are only one or a few cells.
4. **Skill Review—Making Tables:** Protection from evaporation—cuticle, spores. Sexual reproduction—live in moist habitat. Transport—osmosis and diffusion. Exchanging gases—pores.
5. **Thinking Critically:** Both habitats receive a constant supply of water and therefore provide the perfect environment that meets the needs of mosses.

16.2 Vascular Plants

According to the fossil record, the earliest vascular plants appeared on Earth about 400 million years ago. Since then, land conditions have changed, new habitats have appeared, and plants adapted for survival in those new habitats have gradually evolved. As a result, the number and diversity of plant species has increased vastly. One of the adaptations that enabled plants to survive in new environments was the evolution of vascular tissues. Vascular plants have roots, stems, and leaves that are supplied by vascular tissues.

Possession of vascular tissue is the major difference between vascular and nonvascular plants. But, there is also another important difference—in vascular plants, the diploid, sporophyte generation is larger and more conspicuous than the haploid, gametophyte generation. As vascular plants have evolved, the gametophyte generation has become so much smaller than the sporophyte that most vascular plants no longer have an independent gametophyte generation. The gametophyte remains only as a few cells dependent on the body of the sporophyte. The sporophyte is the stage that contains vascular tissues.

Simple Vascular Plants

Imagine traveling back almost 400 million years in time to observe Earth's ancient vascular plants. As you look around the damp, swampy forest, you see huge flying insects, but no birds, no mammals—not even any dinosaurs. These animals don't appear until much later in Earth's history. You also notice that there are no flowers—just leafy plants and many extremely tall but unfamiliar-looking trees (Figure 16-9). These plants, after they die, will gradually be transformed into the vast deposits of coal that will provide humans with fuel hundreds of millions of years later.

Club Mosses There are plants today that strongly resemble fossils of vascular plants that formed ancient forests. Among these plants are the club mosses, which first appeared about 390 million years ago. Some grew as tall as 100 feet and had rootlike stems at the base of the trunk. Most species died out about 280 million years ago, when Earth's climate became drier and cooler.

Objectives

Describe the characteristics of vascular plants.

Contrast the adaptations of ferns and mosses for life on land.

Evaluate why seed plants have become the dominant plants on Earth.

Figure 16-8 The gametophyte and sporophyte plant structures of a simple vascular plant such as a club moss are distinct and separated by the processes of fertilization and meiosis.

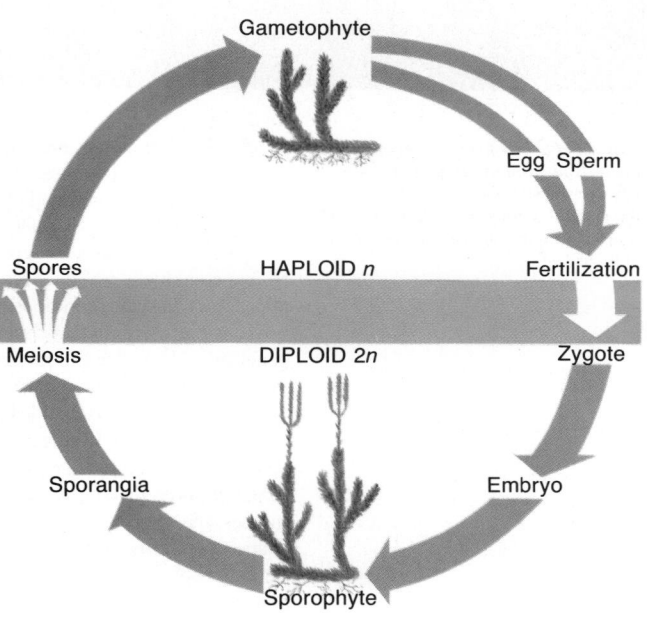

Gametophyte

Egg Sperm

Spores HAPLOID *n* Fertilization

Meiosis DIPLOID 2*n* Zygote

Sporangia Embryo

Sporophyte

16.2 VASCULAR PLANTS **431**

PROGRAM RESOURCES

Teacher Classroom Resources
Study Guide, pp. 93-96 L1
Concept Mapping, p. 16 L1 LEP
Probing Levels of Life, Labs 35, 36, 37, pp. 95-101 L2

Key Concepts

Students will compare and contrast groups of vascular plants, from simple to complex in their organization. The study of the evolution of horsetails, club mosses, ferns, gymnosperms, and angiosperms will allow students to recognize and distinguish among a variety of plant adaptations.

Key Terms

sporangia, rhizome, seed, gymnosperm, conifer, pollen, angiosperm, fruit, sepal, petal, stamen, anther, pistil, ovary, style, stigma

Materials

- Obtain fresh or preserved samples of mosses and ferns with capsules and sori for Minilab 1.
- Obtain fresh or preserved flowers for Minilab 2.

1 Focus

Objectives

The objectives are listed on the student page. Remind students to preview these objectives as a guide to this numbered section.

Activity

Make a display of a variety of prepared foods such as boxes of cereal, pasta, rice, and potato chips; cans of beans, olives, and chili peppers; jars of pickles and mustard; and bottles of cranberry juice and molasses. Also have a variety of fresh foods such as carrots, celery, and peanuts. Ask students to make a list describing each plant and the part of the plant from which the food is derived. Students will most likely not recognize all the plants or plant parts. However, this activity is intended to raise their awareness about sources of foods. L1 LEP

2 Teach

Teacher FYI

The club moss *Lycopodium* is used in holiday decorations such as wreaths. Spores of some species of *Lycopodium* are highly flammable and have been used in the manufacture of fireworks and by early flash photographers as flash powder to provide light to take photographs.

Enrichment

Spike mosses are similar to club mosses. One species of spike moss (*Selaginella*), the resurrection plant, is adapted to desert conditions. These plants are sometimes available in plant nurseries. When water is not available, the plant curls up and looks dead. But when it rains, the resurrection plant unfurls its green leaves and begins making food again. The plant can go through this process many times.

Demonstration

If specimens of club mosses and horsetails are available, show students the cones that hold spores. Show how horsetails come apart at the nodes and show the hollow stems. The leaves are reduced to a ring of scales around each node. Demonstrate the silica content of their stems. **LEP**

Figure 16-9 **Ancient and extinct plants from around 320 million years ago were mostly relatives of present-day simple vascular plants and were the source of Earth's nonrenewable supply of fossil fuels.**

Modern club mosses are much smaller than their ancestors. They grow close to the ground and are found mostly in damp forests, though some live in desert or mountain climates. One species found in forests in the northern United States is called the ground pine because of the plant's evergreen and pine-treelike growth habit. The name *club moss* comes from a combination of their resemblance to true mosses and the clublike appearance of their reproductive structures. The plant shown in Figure 16-10 is the sporophyte generation of the club moss. The gametophyte generation is smaller and much less conspicuous, and sometimes remains buried in the soil. Like other vascular plants, the sporophyte of a club moss has roots, stems, and leaves.

A major advance in this group of vascular plants was the evolution of leaves that are adapted for reproduction and hold structures called sporangia. **Sporangia** are reproductive structures that produce spores. In club mosses, the sporangia-bearing leaves cluster together to form a clublike shape. As in mosses, the spores grow into new gametophyte plants. For new sporophytes to be produced, sperm must swim through a film of water to the eggs.

432 🌿 PLANT ADAPTATIONS

Horsetails The horsetails represent another group of simple vascular plants. Like the early club mosses, early horsetails were tree-sized members of the ancient forest community. Today's horsetails are much smaller and are usually found growing in damp soil. As in club mosses, the sporophyte generation is the most conspicuous, with small, triangular-shaped and paper-thin leaves that circle each joint of the slender, hollow stem. The name *horsetail* refers to the bushy appearance of the plant. Sporangia-bearing leaves form a conelike structure at the tips of some stems. Some horsetails are called scouring rushes because they are impregnated with silica, an abrasive substance, and have been used to scour cooking utensils.

Ferns

Appearing in the fossil record at about the same time as club mosses and horsetails, the ferns evolved into more species than any of these other groups of vascular plants. The ferns were especially prominent members of Earth's ancient plant population, their tall treelike forms creating vast fern forests. Some tree-sized ferns still exist today, primarily in the tropics. Although ferns are still abundant, most modern species are much smaller than their ancestors. You may have seen shrub-sized ferns on the damp forest floor or along stream banks. Some species float in water or are rooted in mud, whereas others live in dry areas. Some even cling to the sides of rocky cliffs. Ferns that inhabit dry regions become dormant when moisture is scarce, but resume growth and reproduction when water is available.

Figure 16-10 **The spores in club mosses (left) and horsetails (right) are formed in sporangia on the upper surfaces of small leaves, which are clustered together in conelike structures at the tips of sporophyte stems.**

Minilab 1

How do mosses and ferns compare?

Make a table to compare the following observations for a moss and a fern: overall size, structures for obtaining water, structures for plant support, and structures for making food. Make wet mounts of the food-making structures. Observe under low and high power. Describe evidence for photosynthetic ability. Prepare wet mounts of the contents of a moss capsule and a fern sorus. Compare these structures.

Analysis *How do the functions of the structures compare? What evolutionary advances do ferns show over mosses?*

Minilab 1

Purpose
Students will compare the structures of mosses and ferns.

Skills
make and use tables, use a microscope, make a wet mount, compare and contrast

Teaching Strategies
- **Safety Precautions:** Caution students to use care when handling the microscope.
- **Troubleshooting:** Students may confuse the fern's underground stem (rhizome) for roots.
- Moss spores can be observed by crushing a capsule. The spores of ferns can be observed within sporangia that are clustered within each sorus.
- Wet mounts of mosses will easily show chloroplasts within cells because of their thin nature. Fern fronds will not show individual cells as easily. Encourage students to make a jagged tear of the fern frond and concentrate on observing the torn edge, thus allowing them to see individual cells.

Expected Results
Tables may compare plant size, structures for water absorption, structures for support, structures for photosynthesis, and reproductive structures.

Answers
Spores are used for reproduction in both mosses and ferns. Ferns are larger in size and contain vascular tissue within their roots, stems, and leaves. These structures are lacking in a moss. Both plants are land adapted, having structures for obtaining water from the soil, tissues for photosynthesis, chloroplasts within leaf cells, and spores for reproduction.

✔ Assessment
Knowledge: A friend tells you that his or her house fern is diseased and has spots that suddenly appeared on the underside of all the fronds. Offer an explanation for what this "disease" might be.

Misconception

Students may think that the sori on the underside of fern fronds are insects or a fungal disease. Explain to them that these are clusters of sporangia that in some species are covered by an indusium and in other species are fully exposed.

Brainstorming

Explain to students in detail how coal was formed: In the Paleozoic, the land was covered by forests of giant tree ferns, horsetails, and club mosses. As the climate became colder in the Mesozoic, the giants became extinct, leaving behind the smaller species that exist today. The gigantic plants were pressed into the mud, causing a buildup of peat on the forest floor. As more plant material accumulated, it became compacted and there was a buildup of pressure and heat that caused the eventual transformation to lignite coal. Further compaction produced bituminous coal, and finally anthracite. Ask students why they think the ancient plants became extinct, and if coal beds could form today. *As the climate became cooler and drier, it was harder for plants with swimming sperm to compete with seed-bearing plants. Coal probably could not form today because the conditions for coal formation are not right. Modern-day decomposers prevent the necessary buildup of large amounts of plant material.* **COOP LEARN**

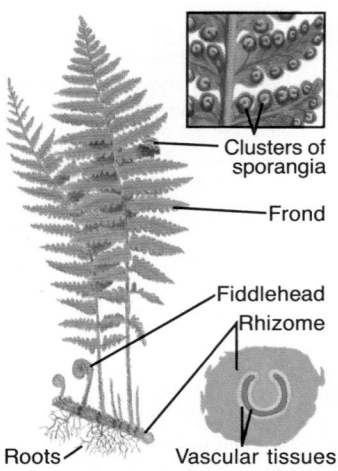

Figure 16-11 ***Dryopteris* (top) is a fern common throughout the temperate regions of the world. It has the typical fern structures of fronds with sporangia, rhizomes, and fiddlehead shoots. The ostrich fern (left) is unusual in having sporangia only on distinct fertile fronds. The trunk of a tree fern (right) is formed by upright growth of the rhizome.**

Clusters of sporangia

Frond

Fiddlehead

Rhizome

Roots

Vascular tissues

Like the club mosses and horsetails, it is the sporophyte generation of the fern that has roots, stems, and leaves with vascular tissues and is the plant commonly recognized as a fern. In most ferns, the main stem forms an underground clump under the soil surface. This thick, underground stem is called a **rhizome**. Rhizomes are underground food storage organs in which many of the cells are filled with starch. The apparently upright stems of tree ferns that extend aboveground are in reality formed by the masses of leaf bases that grow from the rhizome underground. Roots descend from the rhizome into the soil. The fern's leaves, usually called fronds, are often highly subdivided and sometimes have a lacy appearance, as shown in Figure 16-11.

Life Cycle   The sporophyte generation of a fern is the stage that is most familiar. Spores are produced inside sporangia, which are usually located in clusters on the undersides of the fronds, but sometimes are formed on separate stalks (Figure 16-11). As in the club mosses, haploid fern spores are produced by meiosis and released into the air. If a spore comes to rest in favorable conditions, it develops into a tiny, nonvascular gametophyte in which the gametes are formed. As in club mosses and nonvascular plants, the sperm must swim through water for fertilization to take place. The zygote develops into the new, diploid sporophyte fern plant.

Adaptations for Life on Land   The sporophyte generation of a fern is not limited in size because it has vascular tissues that provide both transport and structural support. As with nonvascular and vascular plants alike, water loss is reduced in ferns by the presence of a waxy cuticle covering the stems and fronds. Ferns have an additional adaptation that helps prevent water loss. They have cells that can control the size of the pores on the plant's surface. When water is scarce, the pores decrease in size.

434 PLANT ADAPTATIONS

Ferns, club mosses, and horsetails are like nonvascular plants in that they must live in a moist environment where there is enough water to allow sperm to swim to the egg during sexual reproduction. Because the gametophyte generation of these plants is nonvascular, water must be readily available for absorption and transport by osmosis. These spore-bearing plants are not completely adapted to a life on dry land.

The Seed-bearing Plants

Although spore-producing vascular plants dominated the ancient forests 300 million years ago, they were not the only plants present. Early seed-bearing plants, though fewer in number, also had begun to emerge. About 280 million years ago, when club mosses, ferns, and other spore producers had reached their greatest numbers and diversity, Earth's climate changed. There began long periods of drought and freezing weather, and glaciers began to form. Many spore-producing plants became extinct during these times of unsettled conditions. But, a few seed-bearing plants had adaptations that enabled them to survive and reproduce even in areas where there was little water. As the numbers of spore producers decreased, the seed-bearing plants began to take over. As Earth's climate continued to change, these ancient plants underwent adaptive radiation and evolved into many new and different species.

What is a seed-bearing plant? It is one that bears a structure called a seed, which protects the young plant embryo. A **seed** consists of an embryo with a food supply enclosed in a tough, protective coat. It is one of the adaptations that has enabled seed-bearing plants to be so successful in the many environmental conditions now found on Earth. The embryo is protected during harsh conditions, and when those conditions improve, the embryo can continue its development. The seed-bearing plants are far more diverse and numerous than any other plants living today. They can be classified into two major groups: those that produce seeds enclosed in a fruit, and those with seeds that are not enclosed.

Figure 16-12 **The gametophyte of a fern is heart-shaped. The gametes are formed in organs within or near the notch of the heart. In what kind of habitat would you expect to find a fern gametophyte? Magnification: 6×**

Figure 16-13 **The major distinction between an angiosperm (left) and a gymnosperm (right) can be made by examining their seeds. In the mountain ash (left), the seeds are enclosed within berries. In the cycad (right), the seeds are completely exposed. Why are both of these plant species so successful?**

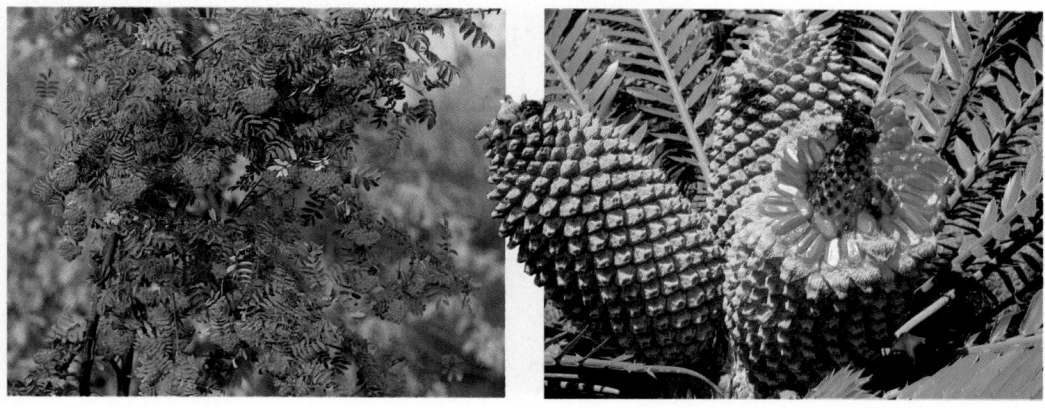

Science, Technology, and Society

Musical Reeds: Over the years, most woodwind players buy reeds by the hundreds, shape them with knives, test them, and may find only two goods ones out of 100. Then, after all that, the reed often lasts only four weeks. As a result, several botanist/musicians are testing ways to preserve the life of a reed. Another idea is that synthetic materials could be developed that would produce the quality sound made by natural reeds. All agree the American cane *Arundinaria donata*, a giant reed related to bamboo, makes the best sound. Studies show that the crystalline structure of the tissues in this plant enable it to diffuse vibrations effectively. Gummy lignins and moisture-holding pectins make the reed flexible. Other studies show that saliva may leach pectins out of the reed, thereby preventing it from holding moisture. Bacteria and leaching may cause the eventual breakdown of reed quality. Scientists are currently using chemical analysis, X-ray diffraction, and infrared spectroscopy in their research to develop a better woodwind reed.

Figure Caption Question

- *In what kind of habitat would you expect to find a fern gametophyte?* a moist or wet habitat
- *Why are both of these plant species so successful?* They are both well adapted to their environments. They both produce abundant offspring.

MULTICULTURAL CONNECTION

Small-farm Common Sense: Dr. Booker T. Whatley, an African American and retired professor of horticulture at the Tuskegee Institute in Alabama, says that his interest in agriculture began as he grew up on his parents' small farm. Dr. Whatley developed the "Foxy Lottie" grape and the Carver sweet potato by artificial selection. He also is known for his book on farming methods that have led to the success of many small farmers, important in this day when most farming is done as huge agribusinesses. His ideas combine science with common sense. For example, he suggests that farmers keep guinea fowl, voracious insect eaters. To keep deer and rabbits away, he discovered that stringing bags of human hair around the plot was effective. When the animals smell the hair, they stay away.

Demonstration

Demonstrate how to use field guides to recognize important characteristics of leaf arrangement and shape for the identification of different conifers in your area. `LEP`

Enrichment

Gnetophytes have some characteristics in common with flowering plants, indicating that flowering plants may have descended from them. For example, the xylem of flowering plants and gnetophytes both have vessel cells, whereas all other gymnosperms have tracheids—xylem cells with closed ends.

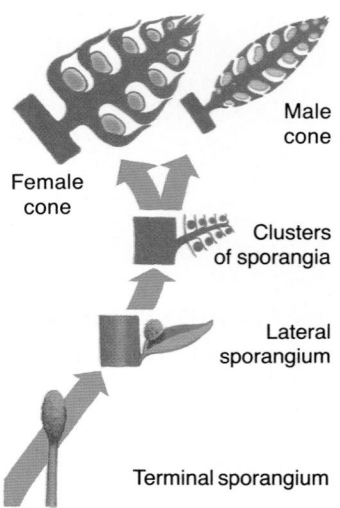

Figure 16-14 The evolution of the male and female cones of gymnosperms probably began with a terminal sporangium. The sporangia then developed in the angles of leaves. The stems became condensed, and the sporangia and leaves formed a woody cone.

Gymnosperms According to the fossil record, the first seed-bearing plants to appear were those that produce seeds with no enclosing tissue. This group is commonly called the **gymnosperms,** a name that means "naked seeds." One group of gymnosperms are the cycads—true relics of the past. Two hundred million years ago, cycads were widespread and existed with the dinosaurs. Now, only nine genera survive in remote places around the world, and they are often grown as curiosities in botanic gardens.

Conifers The most familiar and numerous of the gymnosperms are the **conifers,** so named because their seeds develop on the woody scales of reproductive structures that form cones. Modern conifers include pine, fir, juniper, spruce, and giant redwood trees. It is hypothesized that cones evolved from spore-bearing leaves or branches of ancestral gymnosperms. Each scale on the cone is actually a small leaf or tiny, reduced branch, and along with their attached reproductive structures, they have become woody and clustered together to form a male or female cone.

Conifers are distributed over most of Earth. They were widespread 150 million years ago. Huge petrified trunks of conifers from that time can be seen today at the Petrified Forest National Park in Arizona. Huge coniferous forests were once widespread in all temperate regions. The greatest coniferous forest once ranged from Alaska along the Pacific coast, and south to northern California. Ninety percent of this forest in the United States has been felled. What remains is the Pacific Northwest coniferous forest, which is the habitat of the largest and oldest trees on Earth. Today, coniferous forests are found mainly in northern latitudes of North America, Scandinavia, and Russia, where they provide much of the lumber used in human commerce.

Figure 16-15 The petrified trunks of trees that are scattered throughout the Petrified Forest National Park in Arizona are the fossils of ancient and now extinct gymnosperms that lived 200 million years ago. When the trees were buried by volcanic ash and mud, the original wood tissues were slowly replaced with silica deposits.

436 PLANT ADAPTATIONS

The Protection of Sperm In all gymnosperms, the sporophyte generation is dominant, and cells of the gametophyte develop within the tissues of the sporophyte. This characteristic has proved to be a vital adaptation to the development of plants capable of surviving in harsh, dry climates. You know that in the plants so far studied, moisture is essential for sperm to reach an egg. Conifers and all other seed-bearing plants have a mechanism that accomplishes fertilization without the need for a watery environment. The sperm of all seed plants is enclosed in protective structures called **pollen.**

In conifers, the many grains of pollen develop from the male gametophytes inside the male sporangium of a male cone. A pollen grain is composed of the male gametophyte with four haploid cells housed inside a tough outer wall, which resists evaporation and provides protection for the sperm that will later develop within. Pollen grains released from the male cone are scattered by wind or air currents. Two of the haploid nuclei disintegrate. The pollen grains that land inside a female cone continue their development, first by producing two sperm nuclei and then by fertilizing the egg inside each female sporangium. After fertilization, the embryo remains attached to the female cone, where it develops into a seed. When mature, most gymnosperm seeds are released into the wind. Both the pollen grains and the seeds of a pine have wings that help them stay aloft when they are carried by the wind away from the parent plant (Figure 16-16). The pollen grain and the seed are two more adaptations of plants for life on land.

Other Gymnosperm Adaptations How are gymnosperms able to grow so tall? Vascular tissue that transports water to all parts of a plant is made of cells with very hard cell walls. In trees, these cells are surrounded by thick-walled fibers that help in providing support to woody plants. This woody tissue of trees, especially of coniferous trees, makes up the wood that we burn as fuel and make into houses, furniture, and paper. The support

Figure 16-16 The Scotch pine, *Pinus sylvestris* (right), originated in Scotland but has been planted throughout Europe, Asia, and the United States. The production of pollen and seeds in the Scotch pine (left) is typical of all conifers.

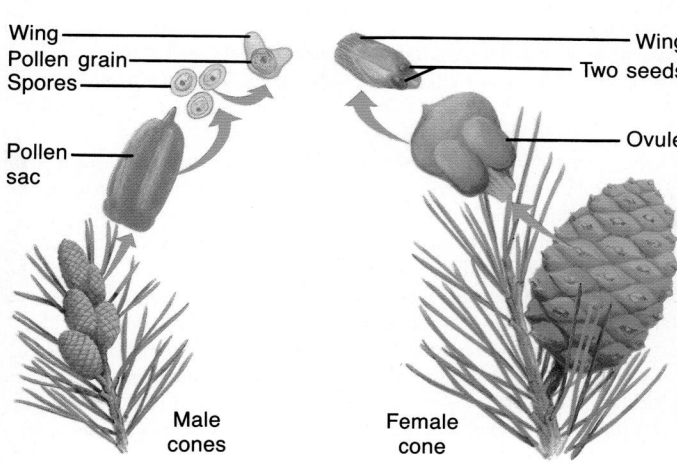

Wing
Pollen grain
Spores

Wing
Two seeds

Pollen sac

Ovule

Male cones

Female cone

Chalkboard Example

Display male and female pine cones from the same tree. Draw a diagram on the chalkboard illustrating cross pollination, fertilization, and development of the gymnosperm seed. **LEP**

CHEMISTRY CONNECTION

Chemical Protection:

Conifers have a variety of chemicals with which they protect themselves. The resins of conifers, the sticky material that is often seen extruding from the tree bark, contain terpenoids. Terpenoids are used to make the paint thinner turpentine, but the tree uses terpenoids as an insect repellent. Terpenoid resins also help to protect the tree from infection of fungi and viruses by sealing the cuts in the plant. Animals, such as deer, that browse on vegetation are repelled by the strong smell of terpenoids.

Activity

Ask students to examine vegetation maps of the world, and, on their own blank map of the U.S., shade in areas where conifers are common. Ask them to describe these environments and speculate why these areas are most suitable for the growth of conifers. **L1**

PROJECT

Gymnosperms from the Air: Ask students to look at a series of aerial photos or satellite images of your area as far back as you have history of the area. You might find this information from the local planning office or from government offices in your area involved in environmental protection. Landsat satellite remote sensing photos are available from Landsat Data Users Notes, 4300 Forbes Blvd., Lanham, MD 20706. Ask students to determine what is happening to areas that have gymnosperms. If you do not have gymnosperms in your area, you may want to request maps with data from another part of the country. **L3**

SECTION 16.2

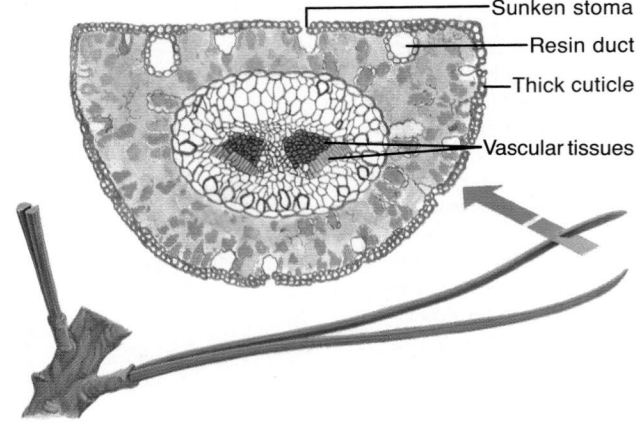

Sunken stoma
Resin duct
Thick cuticle
Vascular tissues

Figure 16-17 The leaves of pines are always in groups of two, three, or five needles. Because of the needlelike leaf's small surface area, water loss is reduced.

provided by woody tissue enables giant redwoods, for example, to grow to heights of more than 100 meters. Tall, upright growth offers several advantages to a plant. For example, a plant that grows taller than its neighbors does not have to compete with other plants for access to sunlight. Tall, upright growth can also help in the broad dispersal of pollen and mature seeds.

Adaptations for reducing water loss include the development of bark, a feature that is shared by all seed-bearing trees. Bark serves as a protective covering that helps prevent water loss through the stem. The needle-shaped leaves characteristic of conifers also have adaptations for preventing water loss. They are shaped somewhat like rolled-in leaves, and pore openings are sunken beneath a thick layer of cuticle, as shown in Figure 16-17. Conifer needles are covered with a thick, waterproof cuticle, and their long, thin shape reduces the surface area from which water can evaporate.

GLOBAL CONNECTION

Corn: The Native American Grain

Before humans learned to save seeds from year to year to grow annual crops, they lived as hunter-gatherers. Living in this way meant constant traveling in search of animal herds and wild fruits, vegetables, and grains. Often, when food was scarce, people starved. In time, people discovered that seeds could be saved and planted each year to provide a regular supply of food. Corn was one of the earliest crops to be domesticated.

The development of corn as a major human food source began with the Toltecs and Aztecs in Mexico. About 7000 years ago, a

wild corn that produced edible kernels was discovered. Over many generations, the Aztecs and others selected and traded corn. Corn is wind-pollinated, so the crop required little care other than weeding and watering. *Tripsacum*, a wild grass, also produced large edible grains, and it was planted along with corn.

When the wind stirred the corn tassels, cross-pollination between the two grain crops occurred. The result was the establishment of a new plant called *Teosinte*, a cross between a wild corn and *Tripsacum*. When *Teosinte* was planted with true corn, another new and stronger plant was produced.

Corn was so important to these early farmers that their culture was built around it, and they worshiped

a god of corn. Largely as a result of their development of corn and other agricultural practices, the Aztecs developed a great empire.

By the time Columbus came to America in 1492, Native Americans of both North and South America were growing many kinds of corn. Flint corn, which has a very hard, smooth kernel, was the kind most widely grown. Flour corn was grown by the Aztecs and Incas. Its soft kernels made it easy to grind into flour, the main ingredient in tortillas, a major part of the regional diet today.

Because corn was an easy crop to grow and it was plentiful, it had a symbolic place in the culture of many Native American tribes. In the Tewa Tribe of New Mexico, for instance, summer is the time of the

438 PLANT ADAPTATIONS

Angiosperms

About 200 million years ago, yet another group of plants began to emerge. Within the next 80 million years, the flowering plants became the most prominent plant group in the fossil record. The flowering plants are commonly called **angiosperms**, a term that means "seeds in a vessel." The vessel that contains the seeds of angiosperms is what you know to be a **fruit.** There are more than 250 000 species of angiosperms.

Most of the plants you are familiar with are probably angiosperms, partly because this plant group provides most of the plant food that humans eat. Angiosperms include wild and cultivated flowers such as dandelions, poppies, and chrysanthemums; they produce grains such as oats, wheat, rye, and rice; they form fruits such as strawberries, tomatoes, peaches, and cucumbers; and they provide us with vegetables such as spinach, broccoli, onions, and carrots. Angiosperms are also important to the survival of many other animals besides humans. Without flowering plants, biodiversity on Earth would disintegrate.

Figure 16-18 **Flower form is used for classifying plants into families. Can you point out the flowers here that belong to the daisy family?**

Blue Corn Chief, while winter is the time of the White Corn Chief. When a child is named, its mother offers two perfect ears of corn, one white and one blue, to the six sacred directions, and prayers are said for good fortune.

Many Native American tribes consider corn a sacred plant. Much rain is needed for corn to grow well. Before the Hopi and Zuni tribes developed the practice of irrigation, corn dances were part of a ritual to bring rain, and other dances were performed to thank the gods for a bountiful harvest.

The early English colonists were taught to plant corn by Native Americans who lived in northeastern North America. The colonists and the Spanish explorers not only used it as a food source, they exported it to Europe and beyond. From these beginnings sprang a plant that is now grown all over the world and is a major food source for both humans and their livestock.

1. **Connection to History:** Another plant from South America that influenced world history has the scientific name *Solanum tuberosum.* Research and report on how this plant influenced the history of Europe and North America in the mid-1800s.
2. **Connection to Genetics:** One of the most influential scientists working with corn in the 20th century was Barbara McClintock. Find out the variety of corn she worked with and what she discovered.

LITERATURE CONNECTION

Native American Poetry: Give each group an anthology of Native American poetry. Ask them to find poems that refer to plants. Ask students to make a list of the plants to which the poems refer. Ask them to explain how or why the poet used that specific plant in the poem.

Figure Caption Question

Can you point out the flowers here that belong to the daisy family? Students may recognize that three of the flowers share characteristics that will make them members of Asteraceae, the daisy family.

MULTICULTURAL CONNECTION

The Beginning of Agriculture: Scientists have discovered carbonized seeds that were most likely cultivated 8000 years ago. This archaeological site in the African savanna may challenge the current assumption that African agriculture began in Egypt about 6400 years ago. Other investigators think that plant cultivation began in southwest Asia around 12 000 years ago.

Purpose
Students will observe and analyze a metaphor of a flowering vine in a painting by Patricia Gonzalez.

Teaching Strategies
- Ask students why artists may be inspired to paint plants. Ask students how an understanding of botany might help an artist.

Possible Answers
1. Some climbing and creeping vines attach themselves with structures called tendrils. Tendrils are modified leaves or parts of leaves such as leaflets, stipules, or petioles. Rambling types of shrubs, such as roses, rest on other plants and fasten themselves with thorns or prickles. English ivy has adventitious roots that grow from the climbing stem, whereas plants such as morning glory climb by coiling their stem around a support.
2. Most pigments used in paintings are inorganic. They include ocher and burnt sienna from soils; and cadmium yellow, viridian green, and zinc white from minerals. Some pigments are from plants such as black walnut, black-eyed Susan, buttercups, and dandelion. Cochineal is a red dye made from the dried female bodies of a scale insect that lives on cactus plants. Orchil, used to make purple, comes from several different varieties of lichen. Many of these natural pigments are now made synthetically.
3. Van Gogh painted irises, chestnut trees, cypresses, and many orchard trees in bloom, but he seemed to prefer sunflowers as the subject of many of his works.

Flower Structure Angiosperms have many traits in common with the gymnosperms, including vascular tissues and pollen. However, the reproductive structures of angiosperms and gymnosperms differ. Angiosperms have reproductive organs in flowers rather than in cones.

Like the scales of a cone, a flower consists of several rows of structures on a short stem that are homologous with leaves and which function as reproductive organs. Use Figure 16-19 to follow the description of a typical flower. The outer row of leaves that make up a flower are called **sepals;** they enclose and protect a flower in its bud stage. When the flower bud opens, the sepals may fall off. Sometimes, though, you can still see them surrounding the base of the open flower. You are probably familiar with the colorful petals of garden flowers. **Petals** make up the next inner row or rows of leaflike structures of the flower. Petals have many functions important to the reproductive success of a flowering plant. Often, they are brightly colored, highly perfumed, provide a convenient landing platform for insects, and dispense nectar, a sugary solution that provides many insects and birds with a high-energy food supply. Some flowers do not have showy petals. For example, grass plants, maple trees, and corn have small, inconspicuous flowers.

Affection
by Patricia Gonzalez

This oil-on-canvas painting hangs in a private collection in New York. To understand this picture, imagine what the scene would be without the flowering vine. The stark, forbidding view is transformed into a lush garden covered with brilliant blooms. The title, *Affection,* seems to suggest a metaphor of a clinging vine and the closeness of friendship. Perhaps the artist used the vine to express close family ties that are a major part of the Hispanic culture. Love and affection can make lives very beautiful, just as the flowering vine has enriched the painted landscape. Utilizing the colors and forms of Earth, the artist has produced a striking portrayal of the strength that exists within the family and within the Hispanic culture.

Educated in England and Colombia, Gonzalez now lives and paints in Houston, Texas. Most of the images she creates come from fantasy rather than living models.

1. **Explore Further:** There are many different flowering vines. Research to find out how these plants hold onto their supports.
2. **Chemistry Connection:** What are some sources of pigments used in paintings?
3. **History Connection:** Find out which plants Vincent Van Gogh preferred to paint.

440 PLANT ADAPTATIONS

Grain for Bread: Ask students to bring in bread recipes from other cultures that use a variety of grains. Tell students about amaranth, once the Aztecs' most widely cultivated crop. It produces huge numbers of seeds that are high in the amino acid lysine. It grows well in hot climates where other grains are hard to grow. When Cortez arrived in Mexico in 1519, he banned the growing of amaranth because the Aztecs also used the red dye of the flowers for religious ceremonies. In the 1970s, scientists began experimental cultivation again. Buy amaranth flour or baking mix and ask students to use it to bake pancakes. L1

At the center of the rows of petals are male and female reproductive organs that also are homologous with leaves. Many plants have both male and female structures. Sometimes only **stamens,** the male reproductive organs of a flower, are present. Many trees, such as oaks and willows, have male flowers consisting only of sepals and stamens (Figure 16-19). A stamen produces the male gametes and pollen inside the **anther,** which sits at the top of a short stalk called the filament. Sometimes only a **pistil,** the female reproductive organ, sits in the center of a flower. Within the swollen base of a pistil is the **ovary,** where the female gametes are produced. The neck of the ovary is called the **style** and at the tip of the style is a rough or sticky surface called the **stigma.** Usually, however, all four kinds of flower structures—sepals, petals, stamens, and pistils—are present. You will learn how all these structures are important to the reproduction of flowering plants in Chapter 18.

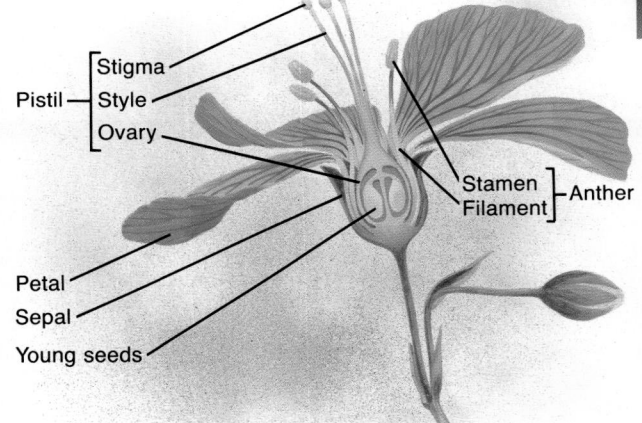

Minilab 2

What do flower parts really look like?

Use a flower to observe and record the following in a table: number of sepals, number of petals, number of stamens, pistil. Use a scalpel to make a cross-section cut through the ovary. **CAUTION:** *Be careful when using a scalpel.* Record numbers and arrangement of young seeds. Prepare a wet mount of the anther and record the shapes of pollen grains as seen under low power. **Analysis** *What are the functions for all the parts in your table? How did the numbers of sepals, petals, and stamens compare? How many compartments could you see in your cross section of the ovary? What was the shape of the pollen grains?*

Figure 16-19 **Flowers are the organs of reproduction in angiosperms. The diversity of flower structures indicates their enormous success. From the male and female catkins of a walnut (left) to the spiny cluster of small tubular flowers of the thistle (center) to the showy floating heads of a water lily (right), flowering plants have evolved many ways to ensure the continuation of the species.**

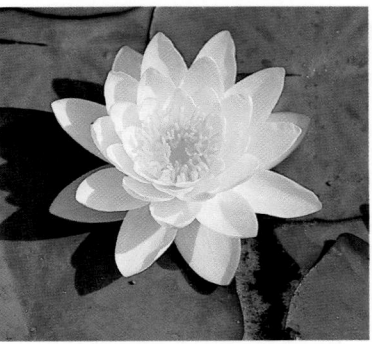

Minilab 2

Purpose
Students will identify the structures of a flower.

Skills
compare and contrast, use a microscope, make a cross section, make and use tables

Materials
microscope, glass slide, lens paper, scalpel, flower

Teaching Strategies
- **Safety Precautions:** Caution students to take care when using a scalpel and when using a microscope.
- Obtain fresh flowers from a garden or a florist shop. Preserved flowers are available from biological supply houses.
- Irises and gladiolus are not recommended for dissection because the sepals and petals are both colorful and fused together. Also avoid using any composites such as chrysanthemums or daisies.

Expected Results
Student tables may vary depending on the flowers being used.

Answers
Sepals and petals protect internal flower parts. Petals also attract animals. Stamens produce pollen in anthers. Pistils trap pollen and produce ovules. The ovules contain eggs and form future seeds after fertilization. The pollen contains sperm.

The numbers of petals, sepals, and stamens will be multiples of three, four, or five and be similar within each flower.

The number of compartments of the ovary will be one, two, three, or five. The shape of the pollen grain will be oval or round with different wall patterns.

✔ Assessment
Performance: Have students tape representative flower parts to a sheet of paper. Have them label each part and indicate if the part is male, female, or neither.

MULTICULTURAL CONNECTION

Biocontrol Beginnings in China:
Mandarin oranges are severely attacked by black ants, caterpillars, and other pests. The Chinese have controlled insect pests by biological means for 1700 years, a method introduced to the West only in this century. The Chinese use of yellow, citrus-killer ants to protect mandarin trees is still in use today. Bridges of bamboo are stretched between trees to allow the ants to move easily from tree to tree. The ants hunt and eat the pests that would consume the oranges. This method of protection continues successfully in China today.

3 Assess

Check for Understanding

Ask students to write lists of adaptations of club mosses, horsetails, ferns, gymnosperms, and angiosperms. **L1**

Reteach

Give each group a live example or a picture of a club moss, horsetail, fern, gymnosperm, and angiosperm. Ask them to point out features that make each group unique.

Extension

Ask a group of students to visit a local nursery and ask what kinds of evergreens are most suited for your local area. Have them find out where these evergreens are native and what makes them suited for your climate. **L2**

✔ Assessment

Portfolio: Tell students that they are to design the ultimate weed. Each student should make a diagram and write a description of this weed and how it lives. They will need to demonstrate their knowledge of plant adaptations and their importance to plant survival. **L1**

4 Close

Activity

Plan a field trip to a botanical garden, arboretum, or greenhouse. Ask students to make a list of the plant adaptations they discover. **L1**

Figure 16-20 **Butterflies and moths visit flowers for their nectar, which is often produced at the bottom of long tubular flowers.**

Other Angiosperm Adaptations   The angiosperms are the most successful plants on Earth. Most of that success is due to adaptations that have made reproduction possible under a variety of conditions. For example, the dispersal of pollen by wind is a fairly random method. There is little control over whether a pollen grain lands on any female reproductive structure, much less on one belonging to the same species. Therefore, a flower that depends on wind produces a great deal of pollen. Many flowering plants, as you read in Chapter 13, depend on insects to transport pollen from one flower to another flower of the same species. Less pollen is wasted, and less is needed.

Another adaptation in flowering plants that provides success in a variety of conditions is the protection and dispersal of seeds inside a fruit. You will read in Chapter 18 how fruits are formed following fertilization and how important fruits are to the survival of the individual species.

As you finish this chapter, think about the major features of each group of plants you've studied. What kinds of environments does each group inhabit? What is their typical size, now and in the past? How have their reproductive structures changed over time? Can you recognize members of each group growing near your home or school? Use Appendix A to help you distinguish the divisions and classes of the plant kingdom.

LOOKING AHEAD

YOU HAVE learned how plants descended from aquatic algae and evolved adaptations that enabled them to occupy a broad range of habitats on land. Did these same trends occur in animals? Features that enable animals to exploit both land and water environments will be described in the next chapter. You will also see that animals had to overcome some of the same problems as plants as they began to fill more habitats on land. 🦋

Section Review

Understanding Concepts

1. How are the cones of club mosses and horsetails similar to those of conifers?
2. In what ways are ferns better adapted for life on land than are nonvascular plants?
3. How has the evolution of pollen been important to the survival of land plants? What other traits of plants are important to their survival on land?
4. **Skill Review—Classifying:** Set up a system to classify the divisions of vascular plants on the basis of their adaptations for survival on land. For more help, see Organizing Information in the **Skill Handbook**.
5. **Thinking Critically:** Why does it seem probable that angiosperms evolved from primitive gymnosperms?

Answers to Section Review

1. The cones of each of these plants consist of structures that have evolved from modified leaves to which are attached the spores.
2. Ferns have vascular tissues, which not only transport materials but also provide support, thus permitting larger size and the ability to grow further from water.
3. Seeds protect the embryo and help disperse the offspring. Evolution of pollen removed the restriction of a moist habitat for sexual reproduction. Sperm within pollen grains are protected from dehydration. Woody tissues provide support for photosynthetic tissues, which allows them to compete better for available light.
4. **Skill Review—Classifying:** Though answers may vary, the classification scheme should begin by distinguishing vascular plants on the basis of no seeds versus seeds. The eight divisions of vascular plants can be studied in Appendix A.
5. **Thinking Critically:** Angiosperms, like gymnosperms, have vascular tissue and pollen. Gymnosperms are found to appear in the fossil record a long time before angiosperms.

BIOLOGY, TECHNOLOGY, AND SOCIETY

Biotechnology

Plants: Earth's Major Energy Trappers

Almost all of the energy used here on Earth comes from the sun. Very small amounts come from nuclear reactions and geothermal sources such as volcanoes, hot springs, and natural steam vents. However, approximately 90 percent of our energy needs today are met with solar energy that was captured by ancient and now extinct plants and stored within their cells millions of years ago. These ancient plant remains are called fossil fuels and are found buried deep in Earth. One fossil fuel that affects almost everyone's life today is petroleum. But, there's a problem—we're using petroleum faster than it can be formed.

A Finite Supply   The total world petroleum consumption since we first began to use it has been about 550 billion barrels. Known reserves of oil and gas have dropped rapidly since 1970. Today's reserves are estimated at about 990 billion barrels. It is also estimated that undiscovered, recoverable quantities of oil may total about 500 billion barrels. In other words, at the present rate of usage, the supply of fossil fuels may cease to be a dependable source of energy not long after the year 2000. This fuel shortage is critical because fossil fuels are used for

more than heating buildings and moving vehicles down the road.

Our Energy-dependent Society
Fossil fuels are the raw materials from which plastics, fabrics, some medicines, and other products are made. When fossil fuels are burned,

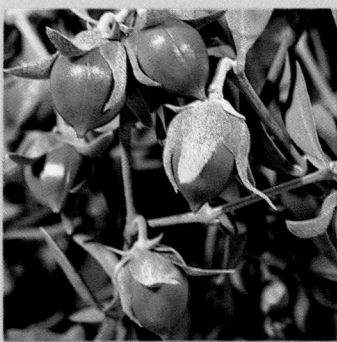

their stored energy is no longer available for use in other products. The modern world is dependent on easy access to energy. Computers, for example, are totally dependent on energy, and most industrial processes are very energy-intensive. Without abundant energy, today's society could not function. What can be done?

Solutions   One answer to the fuel shortage could be to use an energy resource that can be constantly

renewed. For example, you may have seen service stations advertising gasohol as a fuel for automobiles. This is a mixture of 10 percent ethanol and 90 percent gasoline. Ethanol is a resource that can be replenished yearly. It is a by-product from the processing of foods such as potatoes, sugar beets, sugar cane, grain, or corn. Presently, the United States grows a surplus of these crops. By blending alcohol into a fuel, gasoline can be conserved. For example, 10 gallons of a 10 percent gasohol blend contains one gallon of ethanol and nine gallons of gasoline. Thus, the gasoline supply could be stretched by approximately 10 percent if everyone used gasohol.

New Energy Supplies   Another future option might be provided by a desert plant called jojoba (ho HO bah). The jojoba produces peanut-sized seeds that are almost 50 percent oil. This oil is very versatile and could possibly be used as a substitute for fuel and other products that are made from petroleum today. Currently, it is used to make products as diverse as lubricating oil, face creams, and low-cholesterol salad dressing.

At present, jojoba oil is very expensive because it is extracted

put that effort into production of alternative sources. Recycle all products that are nonrenewable.

2. The solar cell has two layers of silicon wafers that produce their own electrical field. The energy of photons frees an electron in the silicon to move around in the crystal and also creates a "hole" or positive charge that balances the free electron. Positive charges move to one layer of the wafer and negative charges to the other layer. The difference in electrical potential allows electrical current to flow.

Going Further
Tell students that they are going to measure the amount of biomass in a square meter of weeds. Ask them to collect weeds, both above and below ground parts, from one square meter of a local area thick with weeds. They should wash off the soil, dry the plants until crisp, and then take their total masses. Ask students if they think that there might be enough weeds in the area to use for biomass fuel. L1

BIOLOGY, TECHNOLOGY, AND SOCIETY

Biotechnology

Purpose
Students will study the problem of diminishing supplies of fossil fuels and gain perspectives on alternative fuel sources.

Background
In a one- to two-week period, the sun transmits more energy to Earth's surface than the amount combined in all of the reserves of stored energy of all the fossil fuels. The sun's energy is inexhaustible, clean, and free. However, it is not uniform in amount each day, is not available at night, is difficult to capture and store economically, and is expensive to convert to electricity. Even though people of ancient times may not have understood the science behind the power of the sun, they recognized its importance. Egyptians believed that the sky was a falcon with one eye forming the sun, and the other, the moon. The Incas of ancient Peru thought that at night the sun swam under the Earth until morning when it rose. They believed that the sun was a god as did the Aztecs of ancient Mexico. A new form of energy under investigation is biomass. This includes all types of plant matter and organic solid waste. Plants are a form of stored solar energy that is released as gas when plants are burned or when they decompose.

Teaching Strategies
- Ask students to make lists of times they may have been aware of the power of the sun. Lists may include getting a sunburn, walking through a greenhouse, drying clothes on the line, or observing signs of spring.

Possible Answers
1. Guidelines might include some of the following: Allocate a limited amount of use or mining of a particular fuel each year. Reduce or stop all mining or production and

BIOLOGY, TECHNOLOGY, AND SOCIETY

Issues

Purpose
Students will compare and contrast two methods of cutting the forest: clear-cutting and sustained yield.

Background
To the environmentalist, sustained yield would also include increasing paper recycling to reduce the demand for pulpwood, growing timber on rotations of 100 to 200 years, taking precautions to protect topsoil, minimization of road building and logging that compacts soil and causes erosion, clear-cutting in small patches of less than 15 acres, leaving some dead trees to provide wildlife cover, and using natural predators to control severe pest outbreaks.

Teaching Strategies
- Ask students what they personally can do to cut down on the use of wood and paper products. Ask them if they think that more wilderness areas should be preserved in the United States.
- Have students investigate how much recycling of paper is going on in the community and in the school. Ask them to find out if the paper products bought by the school and the local government contain recycled fibers.

Possible Answers
1. Clear-cutting—For: Economical, easy, replantings of one species make later harvesting easier, can reharvest in 30 to 40 years. Against: Does not supply ideal habitat for wildlife, allows soil erosion, environmentally destructive. Sustained Yield—For: Provides continued good habitat for wildlife, erosion of soil less likely, environmental protection and protection of a variety of species. Against: Costs more to harvest timber, get less timber, need more miles of road built.

---

from beans that usually are hand gathered from scattered wild plants in the desert. It has only recently been grown efficiently as a crop.

1. **Issue:** In about 100 years, humans have consumed approximately 25 percent of the recoverable petroleum that took millions of years to form. Propose and defend some guidelines that could govern the use of nonrenewable resources such as petroleum, iron, gold, copper, zinc, and lead.

2. **Connection to Physics:** Plants aren't the only things that can convert and store solar energy. Find out and describe how a silicon solar cell works.

Issues

How shall our forests be harvested?

When Europeans first arrived in the Americas, millions of acres of forest greeted them. Most were full-grown stands containing millions of mature trees. While Native Americans used few trees in their lives, the Europeans viewed them as a commercial resource to be exploited. In addition, the colonists used large amounts of wood for housing and fuel. At first, this wasn't a problem because there were so few colonists and so many trees. But the population grew, cities made of wood sprang up, and mechanical methods of harvesting trees were developed.

Clear-cutting Today, our ability to harvest trees exceeds the ability of the forests to regenerate. Additionally, the economics of mechanical harvesting makes it cheaper and more efficient to cut down every tree in an area and then replant, rather than select out a few fully mature trees at a time. The replantings are usually of one species and spaced to facilitate later mechanical harvesting. Thirty to 40 years later, the area can easily be harvested again. This method of forestry is called clear-cutting.

Sustained Yield At one time, forests were managed for sustained yield, where only the mature trees were cut on a regular schedule. This allowed the forest to yield smaller amounts of wood at each cutting, but it did so steadily every few years. In addition, sustained-yield harvesting allowed for a diverse forest in which many species could flourish, including animals and birds that require forests to survive.

Which Method to Choose? Recently, there has been much controversy over what philosophy should govern how our forests are managed. This is important because much of the land being logged is public land, and some of the organisms that live there are rare or endangered. Some large companies claim that they cannot compete in the lumber business if forced to selectively cut trees. They claim that it is too expensive and inefficient.

Opposing groups take the position that forests are a resource we hold in trust for future generations to use and enjoy and that they should be preserved. They claim that a variety of species is important to the survival of a community.

Understanding the Issue
1. Write down the main points for and against clear-cutting and sustained-yield forestry. Prepare a balanced presentation.

---

2. Long-term effects: Soil erosion, destruction of wildlife habitat, and reduced biological diversity. Alternatives: Develop "agroforestry," a practice that involves growing the natural forest and food crops side by side. Governments could pass laws that prevent any future destruction of rain forest land.

Going Further
Ask students to help restore a degraded area of forest or grassland in the local area. **L1**

2. Many large groups of poor people are homesteading in the forests of South America. They clear-cut and then burn a region of forest land on which they grow crops until the soil is depleted of nutrients. They then move on to another forest region. What is the long-term effect of this practice? What are some alternatives you can suggest?

Readings
- Sanoff, A.P. "The Greening of America's Past." *U.S. News &* *World Report,* October 19, 1992.
- Wilson, E.O. "Rain Forest Canopy: The High Frontier." *National Geographic,* December, 1991.

Considering the Environment
Controlling Pests

All life competes for survival. Food, water, space, sunlight—they're all objects of competition by organisms struggling to live and reproduce. Some of the best at this competition are insect pests.

Problems with Control Some of the earliest methods of insect pest control were mechanical. Farmers simply picked harmful bugs off their plants. However, this method only works over small areas. One of the early and most effective methods, still in use today, was to kill pests with chemical poisons. This method had several drawbacks.

First, some of the chemicals used, such as arsenic for killing aphids, were as dangerous to the farmers as they were to the pests. Second, some of the chemicals did not break down in the soil and were transferred to other untargeted species, such as bees and birds, that are helpful to humans. Third, as the pests were affected by the chemicals, the less resistant ones died. The survivors reproduced and passed their resistance on to their offspring. Thus, the pests adapted and the chemicals had less and less effect.

Biological Control Recently, biologists have been studying biological control of insect pests. Biological control is the use of one organism to control the population of another. A common example of this method of biologically controlling pests is the use of ladybird beetles to eat aphids that destroy crops and flowers.

The Neem Tree Another example of biological control is using the leaves and seeds of the neem tree from India and Burma. The leaves are placed in grain bins to repel insects. The seeds, when ground up and dissolved in water, are sprayed on plants as an insect repellent. Japanese beetles, a major plant pest, will starve to death rather than eat a neem-protected plant.

The insect-repellant chemical compounds produced by the neem tree are called limonoids. There are about 20 limonoids . One closely resembles a hormone that causes caterpillars to shed their skin during metamorphosis. When this limonoid is eaten, the caterpillar does not make enough of its own hormone, fails to mature, and dies.

The chances of any pest adapting to all 20 limonoids is very remote. Scientists hope to produce an insecticide that targets the pests but does not harm useful organisms, and that breaks down into harmless compounds in the soil.

1. **Explore Further:** The bacterium *Bacillus thuringiensis* has been used for years to control garden pests. Find out how this organism controls pests and what the pros and cons of its use are.
2. **Issue:** One source of new chemicals is the tropical rain forests. Right now, these forests are rapidly being destroyed. Discuss the long-term effects of this behavior.
3. **Literature Connection:** Read Rachel Carson's *Silent Spring.* Find out what problems she identified and what pesticides were the cause of the problems.

Going Further
Ask students to debate the following issue: Should farmers be given economic incentives to use biological controls? **L1**   **COOP LEARN**

Considering the Environment

Purpose
Students will examine the problems associated with pest control.

Background
A variety of natural predators, parasites, and disease-causing bacteria and viruses can be used for pest control. Males of some species of insect pests can be raised and sterilized, then released in large numbers. Pheromones, extracted from an insect pest, can be used to lure pests into traps. Insect hormones can be extracted from insects and applied at certain stages of the life cycle to prevent appropriate development.

Teaching Strategies
- Ask students how insects are controlled in their homes. Ask them if they think it is appropriate to spray for mosquitoes in their town, and for roaches or termites in their homes. Ask them to explain their answers.

Possible Answers
1. It causes a lethal disease in many caterpillars, which prey on vegetables. Pros: Chemicals not introduced into environment, specific to target organism. Cons: Insects could develop resistance.
2. Biological diversity will diminish; undiscovered species will disappear even before they are described; potential medicines, pesticides, and other important chemicals will go undiscovered.
3. Rachel Carson found that a variety of harmful pesticides and herbicides were being passed along in food chains and concentrated at each step. She discussed many of the chemicals in terms of their cancer-causing potential and harm being done to nontarget species such as beneficial insects, birds, domestic animals, and humans. Her main targets were the chlorinated hydrocarbons such as DDT and chlordane, the organophosphorus insecticides such as parathion, and a variety of weed killers.

CHAPTER 16

Chapter Review

Summary

Summary statements can be used by students to review the major concepts of the chapter.

Language of Biology

Answers should go beyond defining the terms. Accept any reasonable answer that uses the term correctly and in the proper context.

Understanding Concepts

1. The cell walls are composed of cellulose. Cells contain the same kinds of chlorophyll and carotenoids. Both store starch in plastids.
2. Vascular tissue increased the efficiency of transport and permitted larger size. All have evolved modified leaves bearing sporangia.
3. The gametophyte is dominant in mosses and liverworts, but the sporophyte predominates among vascular plants, most of which have small gametophytes lacking vascular tissues.
4. Ferns are smaller and possess a rhizome. Fronds are broader as opposed to the narrow needles of gymnosperms. Sporangia are found on fern fronds; gymnosperm spores are produced in cones.
5. Both are modified leaf structures.
6. Modification of leaves led eventually to highly complex structures such as cones and flowers, which produce sperm protected within pollen grains and, after fertilization, embryos are contained within seeds. The seeds, in turn, are partially or completely protected.
7. Both have vascular tissue that aids in support. Cells of vascular tissues in conifers are surrounded by thick-walled fibers that increase the degree of support possible. Ferns are limited to a moist habitat because sperm are not protected and must be able to swim to eggs. In conifers, sperm are protected from drying out by the thick wall that forms the pollen grain, which

Summary

Plants are thought to have evolved from green algae. As they did so, they became adapted to life on land, a much harsher environment than water.

Nonvascular plants include mosses and liverworts. Though not complex, these plants have adaptations that provide the ability to survive on land. In many ways, though, they are like algae in that they are restricted to a moist habitat and are limited in size.

Evolution of vascular tissue enabled later plants to transport materials more efficiently and grow larger in size. Club mosses, horsetails, and ferns have adaptations more suited to life on land than do the nonvascular plants, but must live in moist areas because of their mode of sexual reproduction.

The evolution of pollen, seeds, and woody tissues has enabled the seed plants to live in drier areas. Because of their efficient means of pollen and seed dispersal, flowering plants have become the most successful group of plants today.

Language of Biology

Write a sentence that shows your understanding of each of the following terms.

alternation of generations	pollen
angiosperm	rhizome
anther	seed
conifer	sepal
cuticle	sporangium
fruit	sporophyte generation
gametophyte generation	stamen
gymnosperm	stigma
ovary	style
petal	thallus
pistil	vascular tissue

Understanding Concepts

1. Explain why algae are thought to be the ancestors of mosses and liverworts.
2. Identify and explain the importance of new structures that evolved among club mosses, horsetails, and ferns.
3. Compare the dominant stages of the life cycle in nonvascular and vascular plants.
4. Based on external structure, how could you distinguish between a fern and a gymnosperm?
5. How are the scales of a cone and the petals of a flower homologous structures?
6. How was the modification of leaves for reproduction important in the evolution of plants?
7. Compare the adaptations for support and reproduction in conifers and ferns.

8. Why was the evolution of seeds so important?
9. Give two reasons why angiosperms are more successful than gymnosperms.

446 CHAPTER 16 PLANT ADAPTATIONS

is transported by wind from male to female cones.
8. Seeds provide a means for surviving unfavorable conditions and contain a source of nourishment for early development.
9. Pollination in angiosperms is dependent on intricate associations with insects, birds, or mammals as well as on wind, thus increasing the chances for fertilization. Seeds are completely protected within fruits, which also aid in the seeds' dispersal.

Applying Concepts

10. Dispersal of seeds avoids competition with parent plants.
11. The tree should show green algae as the common ancestor, with the two main branches indicating nonvascular and vascular plants. The nonvascular branch should be divided into mosses and liverworts. Smaller branches of the vascular branch should indicate ferns, club mosses, horsetails, gymnosperms, and angiosperms. Each group should be named at the "tip" of each branch.

Applying Concepts

10. Why is it beneficial to have seeds dispersed away from parent plants?

11. Construct a phylogenetic tree that shows the evolution of plants from their common ancestor. Hint: The tree should have two major branches. What are they?

12. Coniferous forests are the major kinds of communities in Canada. Why do you think conifers are so abundant in that country?

13. How might flowers with pollen dispersed by wind differ from flowers with pollen transported by insects?

14. What might happen to nonvascular plants and plants like club mosses and ferns if exposed to long periods of drought?

15. How might the distribution of plants on Earth be affected by a significant increase in worldwide temperature?

16. **Biotechnology:** What might be the effect on agriculture of using large amounts of corn to produce fuel? How might it affect price and availability of corn as a food?

17. **Issue:** Forests all over the world take in carbon dioxide and give off oxygen. What could be some possible effects on other life forms if the forests are destroyed by forestry practices?

Lab Interpretation

18. **Minilab 1:** What evolutionary similarities do mosses and ferns share?

19. **Minilab 2:** Guard cells and stomata should have been seen when observing the wet mounts of the plant's food-making structures. Which plant showed these structures?

20. **Investigation:** Some plants, such as water lilies, have a cuticle only on their top leaf surface. A student applied petroleum jelly to the underside of such a plant and used a second plant as a control. Use the following graph to predict answers to these questions.

(a) Which plant may have had petroleum jelly applied to its underside? How do you know?

(b) Which plant was the control? Explain.

Connecting Ideas

21. How would you explain the origin of a plant with no chlorophyll, such as the Indian pipe found in northern forests?

22. Two new plants are discovered in a tropical rain forest. They are similar in many respects. How could you determine if they are descendants of a common ancestor?

CHAPTER 16 PLANT ADAPTATIONS **447**

Connecting Ideas

21. **Evolution:** Indian pipe probably descended from a photosynthetic ancestor. It lost chlorophyll as it became adapted to a saprophytic lifestyle.

22. **Evolution:** The plants could be studied in terms of anatomy and genetics. Presence of many homologous structures would possibly indicate common ancestry. Analysis of their breeding patterns and DNA would reveal how closely the plants are related.

12. Conifers are well adapted to withstand harsh conditions common in Canada. Especially important adaptations are production of pollen and seeds. Needle-shaped leaves reduce surface area and have pores sunken beneath the cuticle.

13. Flowers pollinated by wind are less conspicuous. They often lack large, brightly colored petals.

14. Each of these kinds of plants requires at least a thin film of moisture through which sperm swim to eggs. Drought would thus prevent sexual reproduction, interrupting the life cycle. The thin, leafy structures would eventually dry out and die.

15. Increase in temperature could decrease the range of plants requiring water for sexual reproduction. The range of gymnosperms in the northern latitudes might be limited by the warmer temperatures. Present-day tropical plants might spread to today's temperate areas.

16. If fossil fuel supplies decline rapidly in the future, more corn would have to be grown to provide ethanol. If that happened, there might not be an ample supply of corn for use as food, and the price would increase.

17. Almost all organisms require oxygen for cellular respiration. Destruction of forests could cause a decline in oxygen that would threaten human health as well as almost all other life forms.

Lab Interpretation

18. Mosses and ferns both produce sperm with flagella on small gametophytes that depend on moisture for fertilization. Both produce spores in sporangia.

19. Stomata are present in ferns.

20. (a) Plant A had petroleum jelly applied to its underside. The amount of water lost was lower than plant B. (b) Plant B was the control and showed greater water loss than plant A.

ORGANIZER
CHAPTER 17

SECTION	OBJECTIVES	TEXT LABS/FEATURES
17.1 Invertebrates (3 days)	**Compare** the features of sponges and cnidarians. **Explain** how flatworms are more complex than sponges and cnidarians. **Diagram** the symmetry of an organism.	**Investigation:** Responses of Planarians to Environmental Stimuli, p. 452 **Minilab 1:** What are the characteristics of animals? p. 455
17.2 Divergence of Animal Phyla (3 days)	**Describe** the features of roundworms, segmented worms, mollusks, and arthropods. **Discuss** how evolution of many features has contributed to the success of arthropods.	**Global Connection:** Fellow Beings on the Land—The Native American View of Animals, p. 460
17.3 Echinoderms and Chordates (3 days)	**Compare** the features that evolved in echinoderms and chordates. **Describe** the characteristics of vertebrates. **Analyze** why certain adaptations were necessary before vertebrates could live on land.	**Thinking Lab:** What is the function of ringed seal whiskers? p. 466 **Minilab 2:** What types of food do different birds prefer? p. 471 **Literature Connection:** Gorillas in the Mist, p. 472
BIOLOGY, TECHNOLOGY, AND SOCIETY		**Considering the Environment:** White Death in the Coral Reefs, p. 475 **Career Connection:** Oceanographer, p. 475 **Issues:** Drawing the Line on Animal Pain, p. 476

LAB MATERIALS

INVESTIGATION	MINILAB	ALTERNATE LAB
page 452 bags, plastic sandwich; construction paper, black; culture dish; egg white; graph paper, metric; ice; lamp, portable; liver, raw; metric ruler; microscope, binocular; molar HCl; molar NaOH; pipettes; *Planaria*; pond water; rubber bands; salt solution; test tubes; thermometers	**page 455** photographs, insects and cats preserved animal specimens **page 471** bird seed field guide	**page 458** animals (either live, pictures, or preserved specimens) binocular microscope field guide

TEACHER CLASSROOM RESOURCES	OTHER RESOURCES
Study Guide, p. 97 ***PLL:** *Diversity of Lower Invertebrates,* p. 103 ***PLL:** *Constructing a Key to the Lower Invertebrates,* p. 105 ****ILS:** *A Survey of Some Animal Phyla,* p. 151	***STVS:** *Jellyfish,* Animals (Disc 5, Side 1) **Color Transparency 26:** *Body Structures of Sponges and Cnidarians*
Study Guide, pp. 98-99 ***PLL:** *Identification of Aquatic Insect Larvae and Juveniles,* p. 106 ****ILS:** *Earthworm Anatomy,* p. 155 ****ILS:** *Arthropods,* p. 161 **Exploring Environmental Issues,** *Sharing the World with Wildlife,* p. 33	***STVS:** *Nematodes,* Animals (Disc 5, Side 1) **Color Transparency 25:** *Body Development* **Color Transparency 27:** *Mollusk Body Systems* **Color Transparency 28:** *Earthworm Body Systems*
Study Guide, pp. 100-102 **Concept Mapping,** p. 17 **Critical Thinking/Problem Solving:** *Is Migration Learned or Inherited?,* p. 17 ***PLL:** *Diversity of Vertebrates,* p. 108 ****ILS:** *Starfish,* p. 165	***STVS:** *Sea Urchins and Power Plants,* Animals (Disc 5, Side 1) ***STVS:** *Animal Models of Human Physiology,* Human Biology (Disc 7, Side 2)
Assessment Materials **Chapter Assessment,** pp. 65-68 **Performance Assessment in Biology,** p. 34 **Alternate Assessment in the Science Classroom** **Computer Test Bank**	**Spanish Resources** **Cooperative Learning Resource Guide** **Videodisc Correlations** (to Optical Data's and Videodiscovery's videodiscs)

* Probing Levels of Life
** Investigating Living Systems

* Science Technology Videodisc Series

Key to Teaching Strategies

The following designations will help you decide which activities in the teacher margin are appropriate for your students.

L1 Level 1 activities should be within the ability range of all students.

L2 Level 2 activities should be within the ability range of the average to above-average student.

L3 Level 3 activities are designed for the ability range of above-average students.

LEP LEP activities are appropriate for Limited English Proficiency students.

COOP LEARN Cooperative Learning activities are designed for small group work.

ADDITIONAL RESOURCES

Infinite Voyage *The Search for Ancient Americans*
Native Americans migrated across the Bering Strait from Siberia. New tools are helping scientists study ancient cultures to learn more about their lives.

Audiovisual
Animal Life Cycles and Activities, three sound filmstrips, SRA.
Introduction to Invertebrates, video, Insight Media.

Software
Animals, Apple, J and S.
Vertebrates, Apple, J and S.

17

ANIMAL ADAPTATIONS

Chapter Overview

Students begin the chapter by surveying simple invertebrates—sponges, cnidarians, and flatworms. As they study the basic features of these animals, they come to see the increasingly complex adaptations that have evolved among each phylum.

Next, students examine characteristics of more complex invertebrate phyla from roundworms through arthropods. Not only do they come to appreciate the distinctive traits of each phylum, but they also learn of their evolutionary relationships. They find out, too, why these animals are grouped together as one major branch on the tree of animal evolution.

Students complete their study of animal phyla by examining features of and learning about evolutionary relationships among animals that have followed a different evolutionary path—the echinoderms, hemichordates, and chordates. They learn about vertebrate characteristics and compare the adaptations of each class within that subphylum.

ANIMAL ADAPTATIONS

EARTH IS HOME to an unbelievable number of different types of animals. Some are as familiar as your pet dog or a robin. Others are unfamiliar. Who would think that this coral reef is a marine mountain made of living animals? Unlike mountains that rise from the ground when forces within Earth uplift layers of rock, this reef is built by individual coral animals that live on the skeletal remains of earlier coral generations. The reef itself is shelter for many other amazing animals. Sea anemones, clown fish, sponges, crabs, and moray eels are at home on the reef. As you study each of these animal species, you will find a great diversity in body forms, body functions, and behavior. The crab shown on the next page has a very different form than any of the other reef animals. Its body functions and behaviors are also different. Yet, in spite of the differences, this crab and the other animals have many similarities. They all reproduce, respond to stimuli, grow, and depend on other organisms for their source of energy.

Looking at all of the different animals may cause you to wonder how this great diversity came about. In this chapter, you will learn why certain animals are considered to be more advanced than others. You will trace the evolution of different forms, functions, and behaviors from the simplest animals to the most complex. You will discover how the adaptations allow each kind of animal to be successful within its own environment.

448

KEY TERMS

anterior	endotherm
appendage	exoskeleton
bilateral	invertebrate
symmetry	mesoderm
coelom	posterior
dorsal	radial
ectoderm	symmetry
ectotherm	ventral
endoderm	vertebra
endoskeleton	vertebrate

Suppose you awoke one morning and found yourself transformed into an organism such as the crab pictured here. What changes would you have to make to adjust to this organism's lifestyle?

Chapter Preview

449

Introducing the Chapter

The photograph of the coral reef on page 448 could be used to initiate a discussion of the diversity of animal life. You might consider asking students to cite examples of relatives of the animals seen in the photo. List these animals on the board in groups of related organisms. Ask students to identify the common characteristics of each group. Then ask students to name other groups of animals not shown in the photograph, and have them discuss some of their characteristics. After discussing different types of animals with different features, conclude the discussion by having students identify the features that all groups have in common. This type of discussion would serve to remind students about basic ideas of taxonomy and evolution that they have previously studied.

Theme Development

This chapter focuses on the themes of evolution and unity within diversity. Throughout the chapter, evolutionary relationships among animal phyla are stressed, as are the adaptations that have evolved among those phyla. Students will come to appreciate the theme of unity within diversity as they recognize common features found among all members of a given phylum.

Tying to Previous Knowledge

Students will make use of their understanding of evolution and of principles of taxonomy in this chapter. As you teach the material, it will be useful to remind them about ideas such as divergence and speciation, descent with modification, and the origin of adaptations. Have them recall, too, the various taxa and apply that information as appropriate—for example, as you go over subphylum vertebrata and the various classes within the subphylum.

ASSESSMENT PLANNER

Choose assessment strategies from the following pages to evaluate the progress of your students.

Prepare

Key Concepts

Students will distinguish the major similarities and differences between sponges, cnidarians, and flatworms.

Key Terms

vertebrate, invertebrate, ectoderm, endoderm, radial symmetry, bilateral symmetry, anterior, posterior, dorsal, ventral, mesoderm

Materials

- For the Investigation, gather culture dishes, dechlorinated water, metric rulers, portable lamp, black construction paper, test tubes, hot plates, thermometers, ice or plastic ice cubes, plastic sandwich bags, rubber bands, 1% salt solution, small pieces of raw liver, small pieces of raw egg white, 0.0001 molar HCl and 0.00001 molar NaOH that have a pH of 4 and 9, respectively, pipettes, graph paper, binocular microscopes, pond water for *Planaria*, and *Planaria*.

1 Focus

Objectives

The objectives are listed on the student page. Remind students to preview these objectives as a guide to this numbered section.

Activity

Ask students to observe with a binocular microscope live *Hydra*, a freshwater sponge, and *Planaria*. Ask them to write a list of characteristics they observe in these animals. Ask them how they are alike and how they are different. If you do not have access to live specimens, use prepared slides. L1 LEP

Objectives

Compare the features of sponges and cnidarians.

Explain how flatworms are more complex than sponges and cnidarians.

Diagram the symmetry of an organism.

17.1 Invertebrates

Suppose a visitor from another solar system happens to land in your neighborhood. This visitor wants to study the various life forms on Earth. You suggest that the local zoo and aquarium are great places to find out about animals. So the visitor spends a day with gorillas, snow leopards, macaws, cobras, killer whales, dolphins, sharks, and sea lions. At the end of the day, the visitor journeys back to its home planet thinking it has learned all about Earth's animals. Actually, the visitor has learned very little, because most of the animals in zoos and aquariums belong to a group of animals that represent only five percent of the entire animal kingdom.

You know that organisms are classified according to their body structures. An informal way of classifying animals is based on whether or not they have a backbone. Most of the animals with which you are familiar have a backbone, yet about 95 percent of all animals have no backbone. Animals with backbones are called **vertebrates** and are grouped into one subphylum within the classification system. Animals without backbones are called **invertebrates** and are grouped into about 30 different phyla.

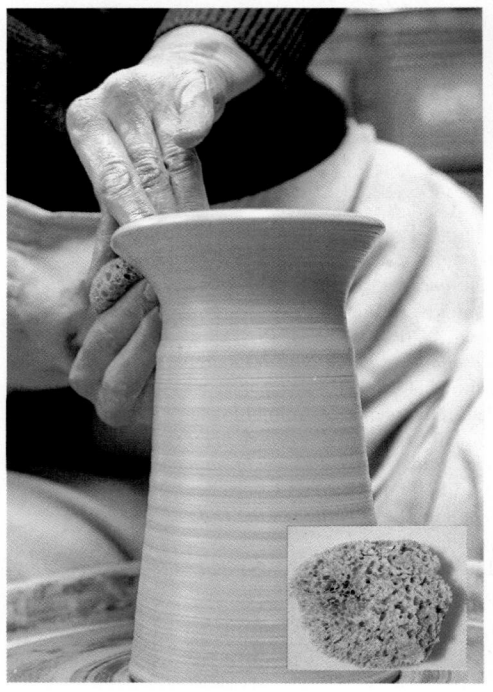

Figure 17-1 The natural sponge used by a potter is the "skeleton" of a once-living animal.

Sponges

Have you ever watched a vase being shaped on a potter's wheel? As the wheel spins and the vase rises out of the clay, the potter uses a natural sponge to keep the clay moist. It's difficult to believe that the natural sponge was once a living animal. Sponges are the least complex invertebrate. Most of the 8000 species live in saltwater environments, although a few do inhabit fresh water. The various species exhibit a variety of sizes, shapes, and bright colors such as yellow, red, and orange.

Body Structure   A sponge is made of two layers of cells and a central cavity. While a sponge doesn't have tissues, organs, or systems, it does have specialized cells that carry out specific functions. The outer layer of the sponge is composed of flat cells that provide protection for the animal. The inner layer has cells with flagella that constantly move back and forth, creating water currents in the sponge. The water currents help to draw food and oxygen into the sponge and carry wastes out of the sponge. Water enters through the hundreds of pores that penetrate the sponge's body. It exits from one or more larger pores, usually located near the top of the sponge. This method of obtaining nutrients in sponges is adaptive because sponges are sessile animals. Sessile animals are attached to some object, such as a rock or shell, on the ocean bottom. Adult sponges are not able

---

MEETING INDIVIDUAL NEEDS

Visually Impaired: Provide students who are visually impaired with a variety of dried specimens of sponges and other invertebrates from this chapter. Some organisms may not be appropriate for this activity but many are. Students who are visually impaired could use their tactile sense to observe shapes and textures of these organisms. LEP

PROJECT

Commercial Fishing: Ask a group of students to report about commercial sponge fishing. L2

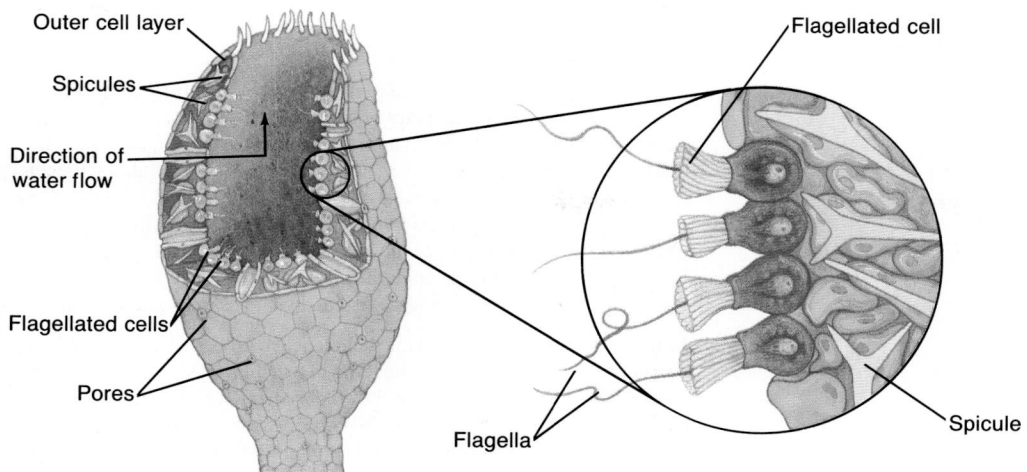

Outer cell layer
Spicules
Direction of water flow
Flagellated cells
Pores
Flagella
Flagellated cell
Spicule

to move about looking for food or shelter. Would a sessile animal need a means of support? Think again about the potter's sponge. What the potter uses to shape the clay is actually the remains of the sponge's support framework. This elastic substance appears as a meshlike network when viewed very closely. Not all sponges, however, have this meshlike elastic network. In fact, sponges are classified according to the mineral content and shape of their support structures called spicules. Some sponges have glasslike structures that form a lattice. Other sponges have massive support structures made of calcium, the same mineral found in bone.

Reproduction   Because sponges are sessile, they need a way of reproducing that doesn't require movement of individuals. To solve this problem, sponges reproduce both sexually and asexually. Asexual reproduction occurs when small fragments of the parent sponge break off, float away, settle to the ocean floor, and grow into a new sponge. While this type of reproduction results in a new sponge, it doesn't allow for any genetic variability. Because the parent sponge and the new sponge have exactly the same genes, the new sponge is an identical copy of the parent. In asexually reproducing sponges, only mutations provide for variability.

Many sponges are hermaphrodites. A hermaphroditic animal produces both sperm and eggs. However, hermaphroditic sponges do not fertilize their own eggs. The sperm are released into the water and fertilize eggs that are retained between the two cell layers of other sponges. After a period of development within the sponge, embryos are released and swim about until they attach themselves to a rock or shell. The advantage of sexual reproduction lies in the recombination of genetic material, which results in genetic variability. An additional advantage to being hermaphroditic is that an individual animal can mate with any other individual of its own species because it can produce both types of gametes.

Figure 17-2   **Although sponges do not have true tissues, they are composed of several different types of cells. The flagella of the flagellated cells help water move through the sponge. Food particles are pulled from the water by these flagella for use by the sponge. Sponges also have an inner support system of spicules. Why do you think this support system is beneficial?**

2 Teach

Activity
Ask students to examine a variety of species of dried marine sponges. Have them cut off a small section of each sponge, and find the mass of the dry sponge and then the mass after being soaked in water for 20 minutes. Have them do the same with a variety of commercial sponges. Ask them which type of sponge holds the most water and why. **L1** **LEP**

Figure Caption Question
Why do you think this support system is beneficial? The spicules allow the sponge to be upright in the water column. This allows them to obtain food more easily.

Field Trip
Take a field trip to a tide pool or visit a marine aquarium in a zoo or pet shop. Ask students to make comparative observations and diagrams of sponges, corals, and sea anemones. Ask them to hypothesize how these animals feed, move, and protect themselves.

Microscope Activity
Have students observe and make diagrams of prepared slides of sponges, sponge larvae, and spicules. Have them observe with a hand lens or binocular microscope and draw diagrams of the freshwater sponge, *Spongilla*, which can be purchased from biological supply houses. **L1**

Misconception
Many people know that natural sponges were once alive, but some think that they are plants rather than animals.

PROGRAM RESOURCES
Teacher Classroom Resources
Study Guide, p. 97 **L1**
Probing Levels of Life, Labs 38, 39, pp. 103, 105 **L2**
Investigating Living Systems, Lab 39, p. 151 **L2**
Color Transparency #26 **L1** **LEP**

INVESTIGATION

Responses of Planarians to Environmental Stimuli

Time Allotment
1 class period

Objectives
Upon completing this investigation, students will be able to:
- test responses of planarians to an environmental stimulus.
- interpret planarian responses in terms of adaptive value to their lifestyle.

Skills
form a hypothesis, design an experiment, separate and control variables, interpret data

Materials
Planaria, at least 2 per group; culture dish with pond water; metric ruler; portable lamp; black construction paper; test tubes; boiling water bath; thermometers; ice or plastic ice cubes; plastic sandwich bags; rubber bands; 1% salt solution; small pieces of raw liver; small pieces of egg white; solutions of 0.0001 molar HCl and 0.00001 molar NaOH that have a pH of 4 and 9, respectively; dropping pipettes; metric graph paper; binocular microscopes; container of pond water for used *Planaria*. See page 27T for solution preparation.

Safety Precautions: Caution students to use care with electrical cords. They should not get them wet. Students using acids and bases should wear goggles. Rinse immediately if acid or base gets on skin. Have students wash hands thoroughly after the lab.

Preparation
Prepare 1% salt solution by placing 1 g salt in 99 mL water. *Planaria* can be found under rocks in streams that are relatively pollution free and where aeration is supplying oxygen or they may be ordered from biological supply houses. As an alternative, you can modify this experiment using pond or land snails, brine shrimp, or *Daphnia*.

Cnidarians

The rhythm of a jellyfish's undulating body has a hypnotic effect as you watch it move through the water of an aquarium exhibit. The delicate tentacles and transparent body invite the curious observer to reach out and touch the strange body. However, such an act can be painful, for the tentacles are long, armlike structures containing stinging cells that shoot out poisonous filaments. These stinging cells are called cnidocytes, hence the phylum name *cnidaria*. While the sting of small jellyfish is painful and irritating, the sting of large cnidarians, such as the Portuguese man-of-war, is strong enough to kill large fish and seriously harm humans.

Body Structure The cnidarians include jellyfish, corals, *Hydra*, and sea anemones. Most live in salt water. The two cell layers of the sponges have evolved into two tissue layers in the cnidarians. Recall that tissues are organized groups of cells carrying out specific jobs. This organization into tissues is a major evolutionary trend leading to the development of more

INVESTIGATION

Responses of Planarians to Environmental Stimuli

When the mail carrier comes into your yard, your dog barks. When you use your can opener, your cat comes running. When you see an advertisement for a pizza bubbling with cheese, your mouth waters. All animals react to stimuli in their environments. Planarians are freshwater flatworms that live on organic debris. They glide over rocks or gravel in the water on a slippery trail of mucus that they make. In this lab, you will determine how planarians respond to a variety of stimuli.

Problem
How do planarians respond to environmental stimuli?

Safety Precautions
Make sure you do not let electrical cords get wet. Wear goggles when working with acids or bases. Immediately rinse spills on skin.

Wash your hands at the end of the lab.

Hypothesis
Make a hypothesis about how planarians would react to a specific environmental stimulus. Explain your reasons for making this hypothesis.

Possible Hypotheses
- Planarians swim away from light and toward the dark.
- Planarians prefer cooler over warmer temperatures.
- Planarians prefer liver over egg white.

Possible Procedures
- Put small bits of liver and egg white (same size pieces) on opposite sides of the culture dish. Place worm equidistant from each food source. Measure distance traveled and time. Calculate rate of movement. Conduct 10 trials.

- Place a drop of pH 4 and a drop of pH 8 solution at opposite sides under water at the bottom of the culture dish. Insert both drops at the same time. Place the worm in the middle at the same time also. Observe and record as above. Conduct the same experiment with plain water.

Teaching Strategies
- Keep *Planaria* in pond water or dechlorinated tap water. Dechlorinate by letting it stand for two days.
- To feed *Planaria*, place them in another container with bits of liver and cooked egg

Figure 17-3   Some jellyfish, such as this giant pelagic jellyfish, can be extremely large. This jellyfish can have tentacles up to 15 feet long. Some tiny fish and crabs, impervious to the stinging cells of the jellyfish, hide among its tentacles.

white. Allow them to feed for two hours once a week. Be sure that the water you keep them in is changed every few days and has no traces of food materials as bacterial growth will begin.

- Rate of movement of the worm can be calculated by dividing the distance traveled in cm by the time it takes to travel that distance in seconds.
- Students testing the effect of light should make sure the temperature is controlled.
- Metric graph paper may be placed under the culture dish and squares counted to determine distance moved.

Data and Observations

Number of Squares Worm Crosses in One Minute in pH 4, 7, and 9: Average of 10 trials.

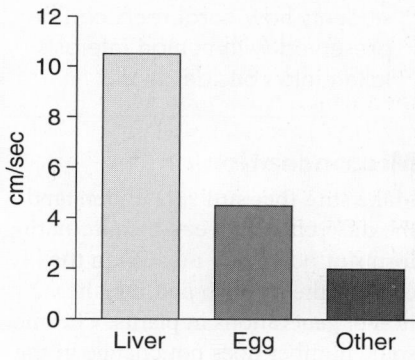

Rate of Movement of Worm Toward Liver, Egg, and Other Parts of Dish: Average of 10 Trials.

Experimental Plan

1. As a group, make a list of possible ways you might test your hypothesis using the materials your teacher has made available.
2. Agree on one idea from your group's list that could be investigated in the classroom.
3. Design an experiment that will test one variable at a time. Plan to collect quantitative data.
4. Following the style of a recipe, write a numbered list of directions that anyone could follow.
5. Make a list of materials and the quantities you will need.

Checking the Plan

Discuss the following points with other group members to decide the final procedures for your experiment.

1. What variables will need to be controlled?
2. What is your control?

3. What will you measure or count?
4. How many worms will you test?
5. How many trials will you run?
6. Have you designed and made a table for collecting data?

Make sure your teacher has approved your experimental plan before you proceed further.

Data and Observations

Carry out your experiment; make your measurements; and complete your data table. Make a graph of your results.

Analysis and Conclusions

1. According to your results, how do planarians respond to the stimulus you selected?
2. What is your experimental evidence for your conclusion in question 1?
3. Was your hypothesis supported by your data? Explain.

4. If your hypothesis was not supported, what types of variation in your method could be responsible?
5. Consult with other groups that tested different environmental stimuli. What were their conclusions?
6. In what way is the response of the planarians you tested an adaptation to their lifestyle?
7. Explain the planarian responses tested by other groups in terms of adaptive value to the animal.

Going Further

Based on this lab experience, design an experiment that would help to answer another question that arose from your work. Assume that you will have unlimited resources and will not be conducting this lab in class.

17.1 INVERTEBRATES   **453**

Data Analysis

1-7. Answers will vary according to student investigations.

✔ Assessment

Portfolio: Have students write an evaluation of the lab for placement in their portfolios. They should be sure to evaluate their procedures in the evaluation.

Extensions

When a scientist completes an experiment, another experiment often comes to mind when making observations and analyzing data. This experiment is an integral part of the lab and not an option. Students might choose to test other invertebrates with similar tests, or test other variables. They could test the effects of crowding on the same responses, raise or lower the water temperature, or try other foods.

Misconception

Make sure that students understand the difference between the alternating forms of polyp and medusa in the life cycle of the jellyfish and the alternation of generations in plants. Chromosome number does not change in the jellyfish as it does in plants that undergo alternation of generations.

3 Assess

Check for Understanding

Give students a variety of prepared slides of jellyfish, hydra, sea anemones, coral, sponges, and flatworms, all with their labels covered. Ask them to identify what they see.

 L1

Reteach

Ask students to divide up into groups of four with a large piece of butcher paper for each group. As a group, they should draw the basic body plan of a sponge, cnidarian, and flatworm.

454

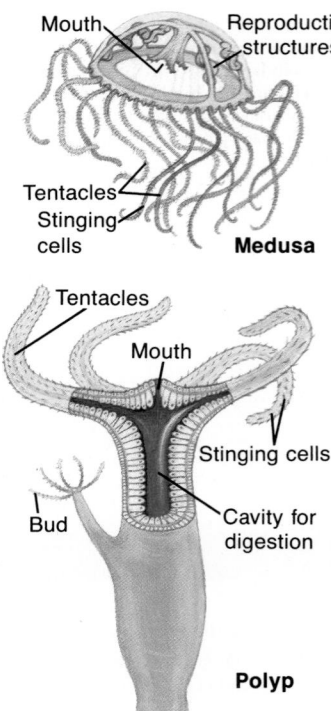

Figure 17-4 Cnidarians come in one of two body shapes. The motile medusa (top) is umbrella- or bell-shaped. The sessile polyp (bottom) is vase-shaped. Each form has the phylum-distinguishing stinging cells located in the tentacles.

Figure 17-5 A radially symmetrical animal can be cut lengthwise through the center in any direction and result in two equal halves. A bilaterally symmetrical organism shows mirror symmetry; the right and left sides are nearly identical. Organisms such as amoebas and sponges show no symmetry.

454 ANIMAL ADAPTATIONS

complex animals. The outer layer of cells is called the **ectoderm,** and the inner cell layer is called the **endoderm.** In cnidarians, a jellylike layer separates the ectoderm and endoderm. True nerve cells are arranged within the bodies of cnidarians and serve to coordinate the activities of the animal.

Cnidarians have a hollow body that is either vase-shaped as in a polyp, or umbrella-shaped as in a medusa. A single body opening called the mouth passes food into the hollow body and ejects wastes. Surrounding the mouth are numerous tentacles, the cnidarian's means of capturing prey and defending itself. Each tentacle has a number of stinging cells, which are used to poison or entangle prey. When prey brush against the tentacles, the stinging cells discharge and immobilize the prey. The tentacles then surround the food and transfer it to the mouth. Digestion occurs within the hollow body.

Reproduction Cnidarians reproduce both sexually and asexually. Many polyps reproduce asexually by producing buds, which are small outgrowths that eventually grow into new polyps. Sexual reproduction is accomplished by the production of gametes. All medusa-shaped cnidarians reproduce sexually. Like sponges, cnidarians are hermaphroditic. Each individual is capable of producing both eggs and sperm. Eggs and sperm are released into the water, where they fuse and develop into a new individual.

Body Symmetry

Animals exhibit one of two types of body symmetry. Some animals, such as sponges, have no definite body shape. Animals without a specific body shape are called asymmetrical. Cnidarians have a body plan called radial symmetry. Picture a bicycle wheel with the spokes arranged around a central point. No matter where the wheel is divided through the central point, a mirror image is produced. In **radial symmetry,** body structures of the animal are arranged equally around its center like a bicycle wheel.

Most animals have bilateral symmetry. In **bilateral symmetry,** the body is divided through the midline, from head to tail, to produce roughly identical left and right halves. Other cuts would not produce identical halves, as they would in a radially symmetrical animal. Bilateral symmetry is an adaptation for movement. Thus, animals with bilateral symmetry have definite areas named in relation to the direction of movement. Generally the front end, or **anterior,** has a head while the back end, or **posterior,** has a tail. There is also a definite top or back called the **dorsal** side, and a bottom or belly called the **ventral** side.

Radial symmetry   Bilateral symmetry   Asymmetry

Flatworms

Have you ever taken your cat or dog to the veterinarian because it had a tapeworm? Those parasitic worms belong to a phylum of flat, elongated animals known as flatworms. Flatworms are the simplest animals with bilateral symmetry. They have an advantage over sponges and cnidarians in being able to move forward in a certain direction. Flatworms are also the simplest animals with organs and organ systems. These systems are described below.

Body Structure   In addition to the inner and outer tissue layers that cnidarians have, flatworms have a middle, or third, tissue layer called the **mesoderm.** The evolution of mesoderm allowed for increasing complexity in organisms. The anterior end of a planarian has a primitive brain and sensory organs that allow it to sense danger and food more easily. Two nerve cords run the length of the body, in addition to a primitive digestive system. Like cnidarians, flatworms have a single opening, the mouth, through which food enters the body and undigested materials are removed. The planarian uses muscles and cilia located on its ventral surface to move toward food or away from danger. Muscles allow for controlled movement, even though movement is slow. Balance of internal fluids is maintained by a network of cells that draw excess fluids out of the tissues. However, systems for gas exchange, waste removal, and transport have not evolved in this phylum.

In addition to free-living forms such as planarians, this phylum also includes many parasitic animals. Flukes and tapeworms, for example, have complex life cycles during which they invade several different hosts, including humans.

Reproduction   Flatworms reproduce both sexually and asexually. Some members can reproduce asexually by breaking apart, with each part growing missing body parts to become a complete animal. Each part will grow, or regenerate, into an identical animal. Flatworms are also hermaphroditic. Two individuals will join together and exchange sperm to cross-fertilize the eggs. Genetic variability is insured by this exchange of genetic material.

Minilab 1

What are the characteristics of animals?

Observe carefully the group of animals given to you by your teacher. What are some of the characteristics of these organisms? Describe characteristics of their bodies, senses, movement, and behaviors. Think of these same characteristics of your own body.

Analysis   *List the ways that you and these organisms are the same and ways that you differ. What characteristics do you and these organisms share? Does each of the organisms have distinct head and tail regions? Does each have a method of locomotion? Do all the organisms have the same number of appendages?*

Section Review

Understanding Concepts
1. Compare the food-getting adaptations of sponges and cnidarians.
2. In what ways are cnidarians more complex than sponges?
3. What kind of symmetry do you have? Explain.

4. **Skill Review—Classifying:** Set up a classification key that would enable you to identify animals as sponges, cnidarians, or flatworms. For more help, see Organizing Information in the **Skill Handbook.**

5. **Thinking Critically:** Some species of sponges, as adults, become attached to the backs of crabs. How might that attachment benefit the sponge?

Answers to Section Review

1. Sponges are filter feeders. Cnidarians catch prey with stinging cells.
2. Cnidarians have true tissues, which form the ectoderm and endoderm layers. Cnidarians also have nerve cells; sponges don't. While sponges are sessile, some cnidarians can move and all are adapted for capturing prey.
3. Humans have bilateral symmetry, a body plan composed of roughly identical left and right halves.
4. **Skill Review—Classifying:**
   1A no tissues..............sponges
   1B tissues.................go to 2
   2A two tissue layers.......cnidarians
   2B three tissue layers.....flatworms
5. **Thinking Critically:** The sponge might have an advantage in obtaining food as the crab moves from one area to another.

Minilab 1

Purpose
Students will make observations of several groups of animals in the animal kingdom and describe characteristics that they have in common.

Skills
observe and infer, compare and contrast

Teaching Strategies
Give students sets of preserved specimens and photographs of a variety of insects and a variety of cats.

Expected Results
Students should find that all the organisms need to obtain food, breathe, have a method of defense, get rid of waste, and reproduce.

Answers
Humans and cats both have systems for digestion, respiration, and circulation. They both also have appendages and developed sense organs.

✔**Assessment**
Portfolio: Have students write a short paragraph in their portfolios describing the general characteristics of animals.

Extension

Ask students to read the Greek myth about *Hydra*, the water monster with nine heads. Ask them if this mythical animal has any characteristics of a real *Hydra*. **L2**

✔**Assessment**
Portfolio: Ask students to prepare a want ad for a newspaper advertising a home and homesite for each of the animals mentioned in the chapter. Tell them the homes should be described in detail with nearby adequate food sources. **L1**

4 Close

Audiovisual

Show films, slides, or filmstrips about animals presented in this section.

Prepare

Key Concepts
Students will study the increasingly complex bodies and lifestyles of roundworms, segmented worms, mollusks, and arthropods.

Key Terms
coelom, exoskeleton, appendage

Materials
None

1 Focus

Objectives
The objectives are listed on the student page. Remind students to preview these objectives as a guide to this numbered section.

Activity
Bring in a fresh shovel full of garden, lawn, meadow, or forest soil. Have students examine it for nematodes with hand lenses or binocular microscopes. Explain to students that thousands of species of roundworms are found in soil. Most of them are free-living species that help cycle soil nutrients. Some species are plant parasites that jab a sharp, arrow-like structure into plant root cells. Enzymes are injected, which digest cell contents subsequently sucked into the body of the worm. `L1`

2 Teach

Using the Diagram
Use the cross sections in Figure 17-7 to discuss coeloms, muscle layers, or lack of them.

Objectives

Describe the features of roundworms, segmented worms, mollusks, and arthropods.

Discuss how evolution of many features has contributed to the success of arthropods.

Figure 17-6 Roundworms were among the first organisms to have two body openings.

Figure 17-7 The basic body plans of the animal phyla are (1) no body cavity, (2) a false body cavity, and (3) a true body cavity. In organisms with a true coelom, the digestive tube is suspended in the body cavity.

17.2 Divergence of Animal Phyla

So far, you have followed the evolution of increasingly complex body plans beginning with sponges and moving to the cnidarians and the flatworms. The phyla discussed in this section show continued advances in the complexity of body structure.

Roundworms

Roundworms are one of the most numerous types of animal. They live in both salt and fresh water, in the soil, and even as parasites within other animals. These cylindrical animals are tapered at each end and have two distinct body openings—a mouth and an anus. The presence of a mouth, gut, and anus represent a much more efficient adaptation than the one-opening, mouth-only body plan of the cnidarians and flatworms. The passage of food in one direction through the worms allows for regional specialization. Specific areas of food intake, digestion, absorption, and excretion are developed in the digestive system. In roundworms, there are separate male and female sexes, and reproduction is always sexual. What can you say about the genetic variability possible in these animals?

Patterns of Development

Cnidarians, as you will recall, have only two tissue layers—endoderm and ectoderm. There is no body cavity between these layers. Flatworms also lack a body cavity, but do have a third layer, the mesoderm, in which primitive organ systems are located. Roundworms show further advancement in the body plan. The roundworm body plan has sometimes been referred to as a tube within a tube. These animals are the first to have a body cavity, which develops between the endoderm and mesoderm. This fluid-filled cavity gives the animal a firmness similar to a long, water-filled balloon. The body cavity is only partially lined with mesoderm, and organs are suspended within the cavity. The fluid provides some protection and support for the organs. It also provides resistance for the muscles, which run only along the length of the body, to work against.

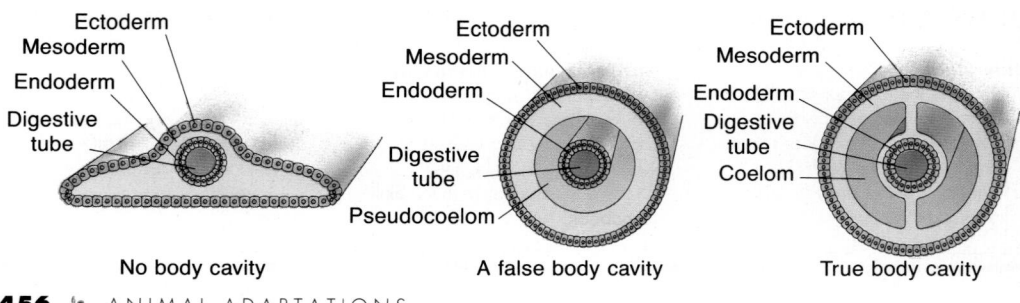

No body cavity | A false body cavity | True body cavity

PROGRAM RESOURCES

Teacher Classroom Resources
Study Guide, pp. 98-99 `L1`
Probing Levels of Life, Lab 40, p. 106 `L2`
Investigating Living Systems, Labs 40, 41, p. 155, 161 `L2`
Color Transparency #25, 27, 28 `L1` `LEP`
Exploring Environmental Issues, p. 33 `L3`

PROJECT

Pet Parasites: Ask a group of students to visit a veterinary clinic to see how microscopic analysis and diagnosis is done for parasitic worms in domestic animals. They should take photos of the lab and the procedure and show their slides or display their photo essay to the class. `L3`

The rest of the phyla in the animal kingdom have a true body cavity called a coelom. The **coelom** is a body cavity that forms within the mesoderm. As it develops, the coelom becomes completely lined with mesoderm. Notice the differences between the cross sections shown in Figure 17-7. In animals with coeloms, some organs develop from the mesoderm, becoming surrounded by a thin layer of this tissue in the process. This arrangement supports and protects the organs. More complex organ systems are therefore possible. The fluid within the coelom keeps the organs moist and may also provide some support for the body.

Segmented Worms

You've seen that major differences exist among animal groups, particularly in body plan. Other differences in developmental patterns also can be observed among groups. Animals with coeloms—segmented worms, mollusks, arthropods, echinoderms, and chordates—can be divided again into two major evolutionary groups based on differences in early development. Segmented worms, mollusks, and arthropods represent one group. Echinoderms and chordates represent the other.

Did you ever see an earthworm crawling across a parking lot or sidewalk after a rainstorm? If you look carefully at the worm, you will see individual segments on its body. Most of these segments contain the same internal structures. A common earthworm can have about 100 segments and be several centimeters long.

Earthworms and other segmented worms have several advantages over the flatworms and roundworms. Their body cavity is a true coelom. They also have several organ systems for controlling body functions. Their complex digestive system includes an esophagus, an intestine, and an anus. The circulatory system has two main blood vessels that transport materials to and away from body cells. Most segments contain a pair of excretory organs that remove body wastes. While earthworms exchange gases through their skin, aquatic members of this group have gills in paddlelike structures that stick out from each segment. The nervous system includes a primitive brain and nerve cord. The muscular system is composed of outer circular muscles and inner longitudinal muscles. Some species of segmented worms have separate sexes although the earthworms are hermaphroditic.

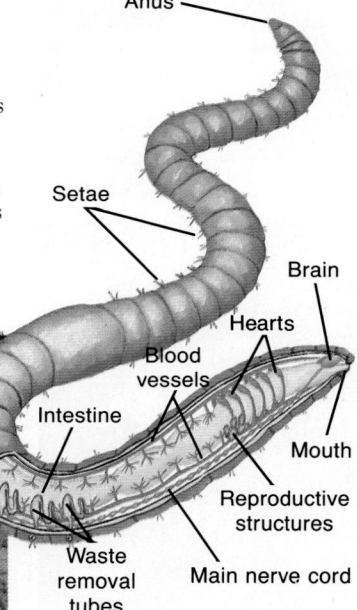

Figure 17-8 **The segmentation of an earthworm is internal as well as external. Many structures repeat in each segment. The external bristles, setae, help the earthworm move.**

Anus

Setae

Brain

Hearts

Blood vessels

Intestine

Mouth

Reproductive structures

Waste removal tubes

Main nerve cord

SECTION 17.2

Science, Technology, and Society

Medical Uses for Leeches: Leeches are popular in the field of medicine again, but not for blood letting. The saliva in the European leech, *Hirudo medicinalis*, has a blood thinner known as hirudin. This substance could prove useful for people who get blood clots that cause heart attacks. When tested on pigs, which have cardiovascular systems similar to humans, hirudin was 10 times as effective as heparin, the current drug in use for thinning the blood.

Concept Development

Animals without a cavity between the gut and the outer wall are called the acoelomates. Examples of these animals are sponges, cnidarians, and flatworms. Rotifers and roundworms are pseudocoelomates—animals that have body cavities not completely lined with mesoderm.

Mollusk Poetry: Ask students to read the poem "The Shell" by James Stephens, found in many anthologies of British poetry. Ask what caused the person in the poem to imagine the scene presented. This poem was written in the early 1900s. Ask students what parts of the poem could be true in today's world. Speculate about why the shell sparked the imagination of the listener. **L1**

Bioethics

Living Jewelry? The Humane Society says that hermit crabs should not be worn as jewelry. This fad began at a gift shop selling hermit crabs. The owner put a chain through a hole in the crab's shell so the hermit crab could be worn as a necklace. Hermit crabs spend their time on shore living in the shells of dead mollusks. Owners of hermit crab jewelry say that they give the crab food and water and follow all the care directions that come with the jewelry. Others say that the hermit crab needs to be on solid ground. Ask your students if they think that wearing hermit crabs is cruelty to animals. Ask them if they would buy hermit crab jewelry for themselves or for a gift.

Mollusks

Have you ever walked along the seashore collecting shells that have washed up on the beach? Or, have you read a restaurant's menu that offered steamed clams, fried squid, and escargots (snails) in garlic and butter? If so, then you are familiar with some of the diverse group of animals called mollusks—organisms with a soft body enclosed by a shell or shells. Although many different kinds of mollusks exist, they all have certain features in common. They are bilateral, have three tissue layers and a coelom, and also have both a mouth and an anus.

Most mollusks, except for the group that includes clams and oysters, have a well-developed head. Sensory organs such as eyes and tentacles are located on the head, along with a tongue-like organ—the radula—that has hard teeth used for scraping algae off rocks. A muscular organ called the foot moves mollusks across the bottom of their ocean or freshwater habitats or even over dry land. The single foot has been modified into tentacles or arms in the squid and octopus and is used for food-getting and movement. A mass of organs for digestion, reproduction, excretion, and circulation is located above the foot. This is known as the visceral mass. A unique folded tissue called the mantle hangs down over the visceral mass and creates a cavity where the gills are located. Calcium carbonate, which is used to form the shell, is secreted from the mantle. On the basis of both internal and external features, it would seem that mollusks and segmented worms are not at all closely related. However, comparison of embryos indicates that they probably evolved from a common ancestor.

Scientists have found that the shell-less mollusks, the squid and octopus, are both exceptionally intelligent animals. They are capable of learning behavior and adapting their actions to locate and capture prey. Their behavior is more like the behavior of vertebrates than invertebrates.

Figure 17-9 Mollusks are a group of animals that are very diverse in size and shape. However, all mollusks have the same basic body plan. The body plan of a mollusk is shown below. A bay scallop (top left), day octopus (bottom left), banded snail (right).

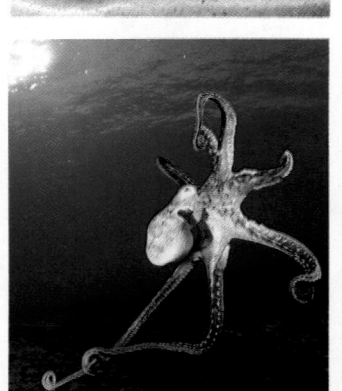

Labels: Heart, Shell, Gills, Stomach, Anus, Siphon, Mantle, Mouth, Foot, Brain, Radula

ALTERNATE LAB: Making a Classification Key

Purpose
Students will make careful observations of the characteristics of a variety of animals. They will write a classification key identifying each organism based on physical characteristics.

Materials
A variety of animals—pictures, preserved specimens, or live animals may be used. Try to include specimens from several phyla. Binocular microscopes may be needed depending on specimens. Field guides, textbook

Procedures
Give the following directions to students.
1. Make careful observations of each of the animals. Record your observations on a data sheet.
2. Write a dichotomous key to identify each of the animals you have been given. Be sure to use sets of opposite traits in your keys. For example,
1a. has wings; 1b. does not have wings.
If you need more help, refer to Organizing Information in the Skill Handbook.
3. Using the classification appendix in this book, field guides, and other resources, check to see if your key is accurate.

Arthropods

You watch as the heroine walks slowly down a dark staircase in an old castle. The only light comes from a smoky torch she holds in one hand. A sudden noise causes her to swing around. As she turns, something brushes across the side of her face. A sigh of relief escapes her when she realizes that the large spider hanging from its silky thread is only interested in finding a juicy insect and not in harming her. This scene is *not* typical of how Hollywood has presented spiders, bees, shrimp, lobsters, and other arthropods as major villains in science fiction and horror movies. Hollywood's arthropods usually lose the battle, while in real life, they are one of nature's most successful groups. About a million species of these animals have been found. They live in more habitats than any other group of animals. Indeed, if numbers of species or diversity indicate success, then the arthropods win hands down.

A Link Between Two Groups   Arthropods have several features in common with the segmented worms, the most prominent being body segments. Scientists have also found an animal that seems to be a link between the segmented worms and arthropods. Figure 17-10 shows *Peripatus*. This animal is segmented and has a soft outer skin like the segmented worms, but it also has stumpy legs with claws and a transport system like that of some arthropods. The phylum to which *Peripatus* belongs may have branched off from the evolutionary line leading to arthropods.

Novel Adaptations   Several important adaptations have led to the amazing success of arthropods. A hard outer covering, or **exoskeleton,** protects the animal from predators, prevents loss of water from the body through evaporation, and provides support for tissues and organs. The exoskeleton also provides a point of attachment for muscles. The ends of the muscles are attached to different segments, thus enabling movement.

Arthropods have pairs of jointed appendages. An **appendage** is a structure—such as an arm, leg, or antenna—that grows out of the body. In arthropods, the jointed appendages have evolved into a variety of sizes and shapes based on their functions. Some are used for walking, swimming, feeding, spinning webs, or gathering sensory information. Because of the exoskeleton, muscles, and jointed appendages, arthropods have evolved a variety of movements much more complex than those of any animal discussed so far. Consider the speed, height, and suddenness of a grasshopper's jump, or the graceful flutter of a butterfly's wings during flight.

Figure 17-10   *Peripatus*, the most likely link between segmented worms and arthropods, can be found in the rain forests of South America.

Figure 17-11   All arthropods have pairs of jointed appendages. This moth is an arthropod. What pairs of appendages do you observe?

Figure Caption Question
What pairs of appendages do you observe? Students should list wings, legs, and antennae.

17.2 DIVERGENCE OF ANIMAL PHYLA **459**

Analysis

Ask students to answer the following questions.

1. Were there any animals that had no distinctive characteristics?
2. Arrange your specimens in order from least complex to most complex. What features did you use to arrange your organisms? *Answers will vary depending on specimens.*

3. Use your classification appendix to determine if your arrangement of organisms was correct. What changes did you have to make? *Answers will vary.*

✔ **Assessment**

Portfolio: Have students write a summary of what they have learned from this activity for their portfolios. In their summaries,

ask students to reflect on the importance of making careful observations. They should also include their data sheet and their keys in their portfolios.

Purpose

Students will study the Native American view of the unity of the natural world and relationship between people and animals in this world: Humans share the world with animals and do not control it.

Teaching Strategies

Ask students if they know people who are very much in touch with the natural world and the animals in it. Ask them to think about what might have happened in the lives of these people or what cultural factors might have given them this view. Point out that people who live close to the land might think about nature in a different way than people who have grown up and lived in cities all their lives.

Possible Answers

1. A Norse myth explains creation in the following way: In the North there was a cold realm of death and the South was the land of fire. In between, there was a chasm of nothing. Twelve rivers poured freezing ice into the chasm, and from the South fiery clouds turned the ice to mist. From the drops of water in the mist came frost maiden gods and the first giant. A god killed the giant and made the Earth and sky from him—the sea from his blood, the Earth from his body, and a walled-in protected space from his eyebrows. In this space, the first man and woman were created by the gods from trees—the man from an ash tree and the woman from an elm. They were the parents of all humans. In this myth, the daily life of the Norse people in an icy climate with long dark winters can be

Arthropods differ from segmented worms because their segments are fused together into distinct body regions or compartments. Evolution of such regions is associated with greater specialization, with particular functions being carried out in specific sections. This is an advance over duplicating a function in each individual segment, as in the excretory organs of annelids.

A variety of well-developed sensory organs confers another evolutionary advantage to the arthropods. The complex nervous system receives information from these sensory organs. Antennae provide information about sounds, odors, tastes, and touch sensations.

GLOBAL CONNECTION

Fellow Beings on the Land—The Native American View of Animals

There is no one people called "Native Americans" or "American Indians." There are hundreds of different Native American peoples, all with differing beliefs and cultures. So there is no single Native American way of considering animals. There are, however, some broad, underlying ideas that various Native Americans hold in common, though they may express them differently.

Native American beliefs generally include a strong tie between people and the land. They stress the unity of the entire natural world, including both animate and inanimate objects and such phenomena as the wind and the rain.

In such a world view, it's only natural that animals have an important place. Rather than seeing animals as lower creatures fit only for work or food, Native American traditions often portray animals as beings as important as or even more important than humans. Many cultures stress the importance of giving great respect even—or especially—to animals hunted as food.

Some Northwestern Native American peoples, for example, considered salmon, a major food source, to be higher beings who took the form of fish for the purpose of feeding people. If such beings weren't treated respectfully, they might become angry and never return as salmon again.

Often, animals were depicted as the descendants of great animal spirits responsible for the creation of the world or for the origination of social customs. The roles they play in Native American myths and legends not only illustrate how certain natural things came to be, but also communicate cultural values.

An Iroquois legend, for example, tells about how the owl made the Creator angry by greedily demanding too much and arrogantly sticking his beak in where it didn't belong. Rather than giving the owl what he asked for, the Creator gave him a short neck so he wouldn't be able to crane his neck to look where he shouldn't and big ears so that he could better hear what he was told.

A Papago myth tells of the Creator being saddened by the thought that the beautiful children,

MULTICULTURAL CONNECTION

Chinese Fable: A Chinese fable tells the tale of Mussel and Bird: Mussel lived in the cliffs on the edge of the ocean where it was drowsily opening its shell to the warmth of the sunshine. Bird swooped down from the sky to snatch a meal from the shell. Mussel quickly snapped shut and closed tightly on Bird's bill. Mussel told Bird that if it didn't take its beak out of the shell, Bird would die in three days.

Bird told Mussel that if it didn't open its shell, it would die in three days. Neither would listen to the other. A child came by and picked up Bird and Mussel locked together and took them home where they were put into the family stew pot. Ask students what the moral of this story is. Ask them if this Chinese fable would apply to cultures in many parts of the world. Have them explain their answers.

Visual images are gathered by sets of simple eyes and a unique pair of compound eyes. The multiple lenses or facets allow an arthropod to view images from all around it at the same time. This is one reason why it is so difficult to successfully swat at and hit a fly.

Reproduction in arthropods is mainly sexual, many species with internal fertilization. Males form sperm that are deposited into the female's body. This process provides a greater chance of success because the sperm are deposited in the same area where the eggs are released. Animals that have internal fertilization are no longer dependent on a water environment to carry the sperm to the eggs.

the lovely leaves, and the colorful flowers would all grow old and die. To preserve some of the beauty, he took the beautiful sights and sounds around him and created butterflies, only to be reproached by the birds. The birds were upset that the Creator had given butterflies the melodious songs that belonged to them. Realizing that it wasn't right to take from the birds what was meant to be unique to them, the Creator let the butterflies keep their colors but took back their songs.

In the preceding legends, there is a creator distinct from the animals. But often it's an animal, or an animal spirit, who is responsible for some or all of creation.

Much Northwestern Native American lore deals with Coyote— an anthropomorphic hero and ancestor of the animal that shares his name. One story from the Nez Perce´ tells how Coyote tricked and killed a monster who was eating all his fellow animals. To celebrate his victory, Coyote created a new animal from the monster's remains. He cut up the monster's body, throwing the pieces in all directions.

Wherever a piece landed, a tribe of Native Americans came into being.

Note that this myth doesn't show humans being created as a dominant species, but simply as a new animal. They are to share the world, not control it. And while other Native American tribes had different myths, this one depicts an attitude shared by virtually all.

1. **Writing About Biology:** Compare the story of Coyote creating people to the creation story of some other culture. What similarities and differences are there in the way the two tales portray the relationship of humans and animals to nature and each other?
2. **Issues:** Even today, animals play a large part in Native American religious practices. The American Indian Religious Freedom Act, signed into federal law in 1978, was supposed to assure Native Americans' rights to exercise their religions. Even

so, some Native Americans have been prosecuted for using eagle feathers in their ceremonies. Eagles are also protected by federal law as an endangered species. What do you think should take precedence: Native Americans' rights to religious freedom or maximum protection of an endangered species?

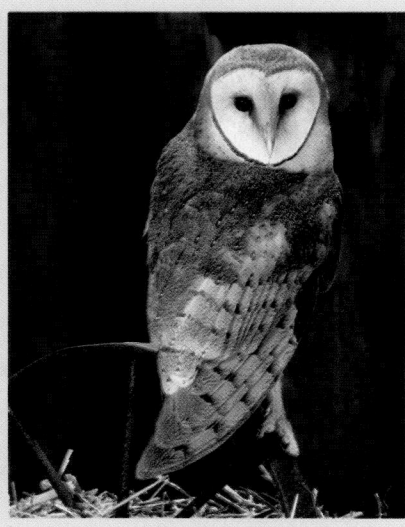

17.2 DIVERGENCE OF ANIMAL PHYLA ❧ **461**

SECTION 17.2

GLOBAL CONNECTION

seen. Animals do not play a part, perhaps because the ice was the most important challenge they faced daily. It was natural for them to look at creation of people from trees because they could see trees alive and surviving even through the icy winters, surviving as they wanted to themselves.
2. Student views will vary on this issue and all should be respected. Those who do not have strong religious and spiritual beliefs or those who have an intense dedication to preservation of the natural world might say that it is wrong to have eagle feathers in possession. Those with strong religious and spiritual ties may feel that the exercise of religious freedom of humans should take precedence over protection of endangered species.

Going Further
Read about and report on how the buffalo was important, both in a religious sense and to the daily life of the Native Americans of the plains. **L2**

3 Assess

Check for Understanding
Put the following list on the chalkboard: nervous system, digestive system, excretory system, circulatory system, respiratory system, and skeletal system. Ask students to tell which phylum of invertebrates was first in the course of evolution to have that system. **L1**

Reteach
Ask students to make a concept map using the information in Table 17.1. Students should refer to Concept Mapping in the Skill Handbook for more information.

MEETING INDIVIDUAL NEEDS

Visually Impaired: Provide students who are visually impaired with a variety of arthropod skeletons. Some of these would include a crab shell, a lobster shell, and a dried grasshopper, beetle, and butterfly. Have students observe each skeleton tactilely and tape record their observations.

PORTFOLIO

Many young children and some adults are afraid of spiders. Ask students to make a plan in their portfolios and later present their plans to a nearby elementary school class to help them overcome their fear of spiders and to realize how they are important to the natural world as well as being beneficial to humans. Included should be a presentation of local spiders—both poisonous and nonpoisonous. **L1**

Extension

Annual slug races are held in several towns in the Pacific northwest. The track consists of a large table with six straight, narrow lanes with an infield of artificial turf. Ask students to plan a "snail race" with either land snails or pond snails. They should decide on what surface would work best and make sure conditions are the same for all snails. **L2**

✔ Assessment

Performance: Set up a lab practical with preserved animals, live animals, and prepared slides of animals studied in this chapter. Ask students to identify the phylum to which each animal belongs as well as describing the features that make it characteristic of that group and also describing important adaptations the animal has to its environment. **L1**

4 Close

Activity

Give groups of students a live crayfish. Ask them to observe its actions in a culture dish of shallow pond water. They may try to feed it and stimulate it in a variety of ways that will not harm it, such as exposing it to light and dark or touching various parts gently with a cotton swab. Have them write a list of structural and behavioral adaptations the crayfish has to its environment. **COOP LEARN**

Table 17.1 Summary of Major Characteristics of Invertebrates

Phylum	Sponges	Cnidarians	Flatworms	Roundworms	Segmented Worms	Mollusks	Arthropods
Locomotion	none	sessile; free-swimming	muscles; cilia	muscles	muscles	muscles	muscles, skeleton
Symmetry	none	radial	bilateral	bilateral	bilateral	bilateral	bilateral
Number of body openings	pores	one	one	two	two	two	two
Number of tissue layers	none	two	three	three	three	three	three
Nervous system	none	nerve net	present	present	present	present	present
Digestive system	none	none	present	present	present	present	present
Excretory system	none	none	none	present	present	present	present
Circulatory system	none	none	none	none	present	present	present
Respiratory system	none	none	none	none	present	present	present
Skeletal system	none	none	none	none	none	none	exoskeleton

Sponge   Sea anemone   Leech   Mussel   Crayfish

Section Review

Understanding Concepts

1. What features seen in roundworms are not present in less complex invertebrates?
2. Why is a true body cavity an important evolutionary development?
3. What evidence links the segmented worms, mollusks, and arthropods as closely related phyla?

4. **Skill Review—Sequencing:** Develop a sequence for the new features found among the roundworms, segmented worms, and arthropods. For more help, see Organizing Information in the **Skill Handbook.**

5. **Thinking Critically:** You have only microscopic slides of cross sections of two animals to study. What clues would help you decide which is a flatworm and which is a roundworm?

462 ❧ ANIMAL ADAPTATIONS

Answers to Section Review

1. Roundworms have separate sexes, two body openings, and a primitive body cavity in which internal organs are suspended and which aids in movement.
2. Evolution of a true body cavity, the coelom, supports and protects internal organs, allowing for greater complexity. The fluid within the coelom provides support.
3. Presence of a coelom as well as a similar pattern of early development link these three phyla.

4. **Skill Review—Sequencing:** Roundworms: primitive coelom, separate sexes, two body openings. Segmented worms: segmentation, circulatory system, excretory organs, gills in some forms, more controlled movement. Arthropods: exoskeleton, jointed appendages, distinct body regions,

well-developed sensory organs, more complex nervous system, internal fertilization in some forms.

5. **Thinking Critically:** Unlike the flatworm, the roundworm has a digestive tube and a body cavity.

17.3 Echinoderms and Chordates

Segmented worms, mollusks, and arthropods represent one major path of evolutionary development. The next organisms you will learn about are those animals scientists think have followed another path of evolutionary development.

Echinoderms

Its seems unlikely, from just looking at them, that the feather star, sea cucumber, and starfish all belong to the same animal phylum. Yet they are all members of the group of marine animals called echinoderms, or spiny-skinned animals. It also seems unlikely that echinoderms are considered the most advanced group of invertebrates. After all, these animals exhibit radial symmetry, a characteristic not seen since the very simple invertebrates. Scientists know, however, that echinoderms have bilateral symmetry in their larval stage. Echinoderms also have several well-developed organ systems. One exception to these well-developed systems is their nervous system, which is not centralized. A nerve ring is usually located around the mouth with nerves radiating to other parts of the animal's body. This decentralization works well in animals with radial symmetry because it allows them to respond to stimuli coming from any direction.

As mentioned, the name of this phylum means "spiny skinned." The name is appropriate because spines project through the skin of these animals. The spines are made of calcium carbonate plates that link together to form an **endoskeleton,** which is an internal framework or support system. Reproduction in echinoderms is usually sexual. Gametes are released into the water, and fertilization occurs externally. Echinoderms have an amazing ability to regenerate parts. Some reproduce asexually this way by breaking apart, with each part then regenerating the missing body parts.

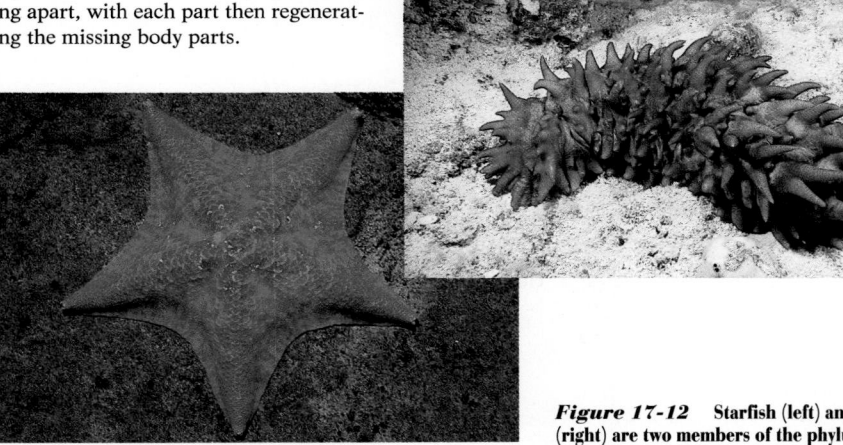

Figure 17-12 **Starfish (left) and sea cucumbers (right) are two members of the phylum Echinodermata.**

Objectives

Compare the features that evolved in echinoderms and chordates.

Describe the characteristics of vertebrates.

Analyze why certain adaptations were necessary before vertebrates could live on land.

---

2 Teach

Demonstration

Use a live or preserved starfish or sea urchin to demonstrate the physical characteristics of the echinoderms.

`LEP`

Misconception

Starfish is a commonly used name, but many scientists call these organisms sea stars. Students may think that the name "starfish" means that these animals are closely related to or are fish.

Microscope Activity

Ask students to observe and sketch the stages of sea urchin development in prepared slides. Have them compare the symmetry of adult sea urchins with larval sea urchins. `L1`

Concept Development

Phylum Hemichordata, the "half-chordate" phylum, consists of about 90 species of acorn worms, soft-bodied animals that live in burrows in the sand and mud of the seashore. Another small phylum, Chaetognatha, the arrow worms, consists of about 70 species that also share characteristics with echinoderms and chordates. Arrow worms, ranging in size from 0.6 cm to 7 cm long, are the most common predator in the marine plankton of shallow seas all over the world.

Figure 17-13 This acorn worm (*Saccoglossus kowalewskii*) belongs to the phylum Hemichordata. This species is common to the Atlantic coast of North America.

Echinoderms have a unique water-pumping system that includes a series of internal canals connected to external body parts called tube feet. Echinoderms utilize this system to catch food, move, and for gas exchange. While the movements caused by this system of locomotion are not very fast, animals such as the starfish prey on clams and oysters. Speed isn't necessary to locate these stationary prey. However, this system does allow the starfish to exert a constant, pulling force to open the shells of its prey. You will learn more about the water-pumping system of echinoderms in Chapter 26.

Hemichordates

Once classified in the chordate phylum, these animals are now classified in a phylum of their own. In fact, hemichordates are so named because of the characteristics they share with chordates. These characteristics include a nerve cord running along the dorsal side of the animal and gill slits (discussed later). However, the nerve cords of hemichordates and chordates are not homologous structures, thus indicating that they do belong in separate phyla.

Hemichordates also share certain characteristics with echinoderms. Most notably, the larval stage shows bilateral symmetry. The similarities among the three groups lead biologists to believe that echinoderms, hemichordates, and chordates evolved from a common ancestor.

Chordates

Remember when the alien visitor went to the zoo and aquarium to learn about animals? Most of the animals the alien was able to study in these places belong to a phylum known as the chordates. In fact, it's likely that most of the animals with which you are familiar belong to this group. You, too, are a member of the chordate phylum.

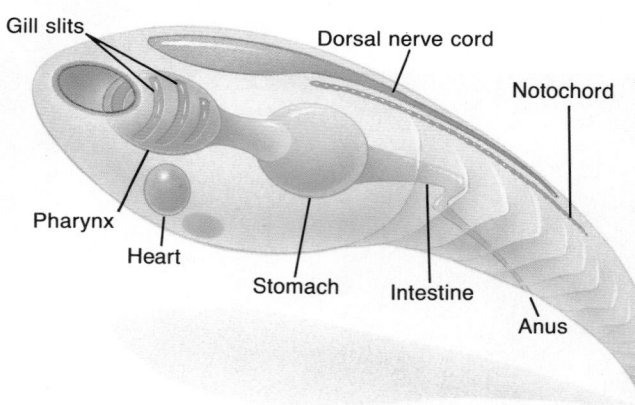

Figure 17-14 This generalized chordate shows all the chordate characteristics: a dorsal nerve cord, notochord, and gill slits.

464 ANIMAL ADAPTATIONS

All chordates have three common characteristics: a notochord, a dorsal nerve cord, and gill slits or gill pouches. Each characteristic is present at some time during the life cycle of a chordate. However, in some animals the characteristic might appear only during the embryonic stage.

The first characteristic, the notochord, is a dorsal rod made of cartilage. This rod is flexible, yet firm enough to provide support for the animal's body. The dorsal nerve cord is a group of nerves that form a hollow tube. It is located above the notochord. The gill slits or pouches are perforations in the pharynx or throat. In some animals, these slits develop into gills that are used for gas exchange. Other chordates have gill slits only in the larval stage. Which of these three characteristics do you still have?

Chordate Subphyla   The chordate phylum is divided into three subphyla. Two subphyla include animals that do not have backbones. One of these two subphyla includes marine organisms known as tunicates. Tunicates are sessile animals that grow singly or in colonies attached to rocks. They have a tough outer covering, called a tunic, and two body openings. When disturbed, contractions of the body force water out of the openings, thus earning these animals the common name of sea squirt.

The second subphylum of chordates without backbones includes the lancelets. These marine animals have streamlined bodies that are pointed at each end. In fact, they bear some resemblance to a small fish. Although lancelets can swim, they usually live partly buried in sand. There, they feed on microscopic organisms that are drawn into the mouth by the beating of cilia that line the oral cavity.

Figure 17-16   Unlike tunicates, lancelets retain all chordate characteristics throughout their lives.

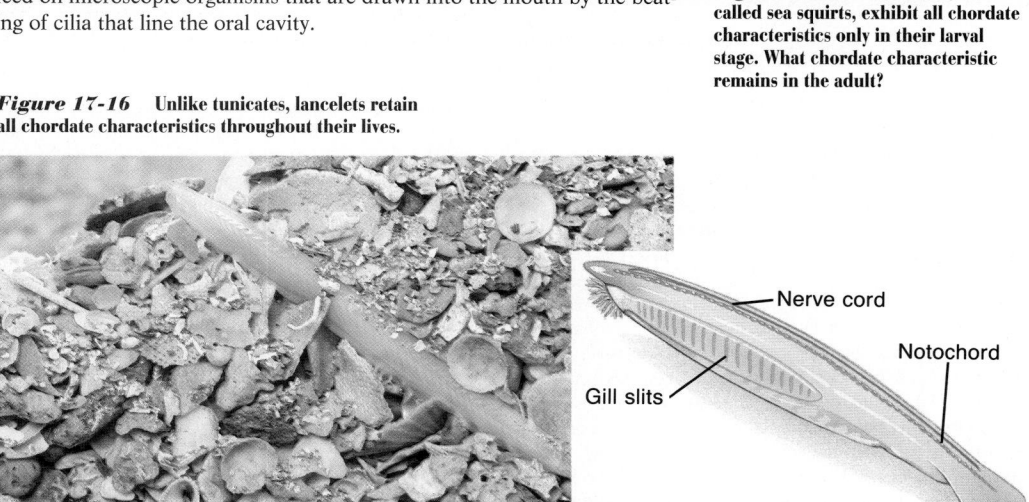

— Incurrent siphon
— Excurrent siphon
— Gill slits
— Intestine
— Tunic
— Heart
— Stomach

Figure 17-15   Tunicates, also called sea squirts, exhibit all chordate characteristics only in their larval stage. What chordate characteristic remains in the adult?

Nerve cord
Notochord
Gill slits

Concept Development

Tunicates belong to the subphylum Urochordata. Most of these small tubular animals live attached to objects on the seafloor. They take in water through one tube and force it out another in a process known as filter feeding. Lancelets belong to the subphylum Cephalochordata. At one time, biologists thought that lancelets were degenerate fish whose structures had been reduced during the course of evolution. Recently discovered fossil forms, 550 million years old (before the appearance of fish), show that they evolved as a group separate from fish.

Figure Caption Question

What chordate characteristic remains in the adult? the gill slits

Activity

Ask students to compare and contrast preserved or mounted specimens of tunicates and lancelets. Examination with a binocular microscope could also be done. Ask them to make diagrams of the animals and describe their lifestyles. **L1** **LEP**

17.3 ECHINODERMS AND CHORDATES **465**

MULTICULTURAL CONNECTION

Island Biology: Dr. Alexander Cruz remembers growing up in the Puerto Rican neighborhoods of New York City. He was fascinated by the wildlife in vacant lots and filled his room with collections of the animals he found. After completing his studies in biology, he became interested in island ecology. He studied and compared birds and other animals and plants of islands adjacent to mainlands. Currently, he does field work on the islands of Trinidad, Hispaniola, and Puerto Rico, and the mainland tropical rain forests of Venezuela and Mexico. He is concerned about the disappearance of the world's rain forests to lumbering and agriculture.

Concept Development

The first known vertebrates were small jawless fish called ostracoderms that appeared on Earth more than 500 million years ago. Scientists hypothesize that all other vertebrates can be traced back to the ostracoderms. The first modern fish appeared about 225 million years ago during the Triassic period.

Demonstration

When describing the difference between cartilage and bone, you might have students feel the flexibility of the cartilage in their ears.

LEP

Vertebrate Characteristics The third and largest of the chordate subphyla are the vertebrates. Vertebrates have a backbone, made of bony segments or cartilage, that develops around the notochord or replaces it. The bony or cartilaginous segments making up the backbone are called **vertebrae.** Vertebrae provide protection for the animal's spinal cord. They also fit together in a way that allows great flexibility of movement. It is from these structures that the group receives its name. In addition, the backbone is the major support structure of the endoskeleton. Unlike the endoskeleton of echinoderms, the endoskeleton of vertebrates is made of living cells and tissue. This adaptation allows the support structure to grow with the animal—which means that vertebrates can grow to enormous sizes. Whales, elephants, and the extinct dinosaurs are proof of the success of this adaptation.

The nervous system of vertebrates has evolved into a highly efficient system with a complex brain that is separated into different regions, each with different functions. The regionalization allows for more specialization. Greater sensitivity to sounds, odors, images, and vibrations, as well as increased intelligence, resulted in vertebrates having much more complex behaviors than the invertebrates. As in arthropods, the nervous system also interacts more with other systems of the body. For example, it interacts with the muscles that are attached to the endoskeleton. The interaction of the muscular, skeletal, and nervous systems means vertebrates have greater speed and agility than most other animals.

Thinking Lab

INTERPRET THE DATA

What is the function of ringed seal whiskers?

Background
You have seen cats carefully washing their faces and whiskers. Many mammals have whiskers. Ringed seals that live in the cloudy water of Lake Saimaa in Finland may use their whiskers for finding the six pounds of fish they need to eat each day. With only six feet of visibility in the water, seals must use some other means besides sight to find fish. Biologists think that the seals may be using echolocation, emitting sounds and detecting the echoes, with their whiskers. The seal makes vocal clicking sounds that may be picked up by whiskers as the sound bounces back off a nearby object or fish. Biologists know that the whiskers of most mam-

mals have about 150 nerve fibers attached to them, while ringed seals' whiskers have 1200 nerve fibers attached. Biologists hypothesize that the extra nerve fibers may be involved in echolocation.

To test their hypothesis, a team of biologists placed several ringed seals in an indoor pool. The pool had reduced visibility similar to that of their natural habitat. One hundred fish were added to the pool. The biologists noted that each seal caught six fish. Next, the biologists blocked the seals' whiskers with a cover and conducted the same experiment. Here, each seal caught an average of two fish. The biologists concluded that their hypothesis was correct.

You Try It
Interpret the biologists' results. Were they correct in their conclusions? What was missing? Suggest other methods biologists might use to determine the purpose of the extra nerve fibers.

Thinking Lab

INTERPRET THE DATA

Purpose
Students will interpret the data to determine the function of ringed seals' whiskers.

Skills
design an experiment, interpret the data, separate and control variables

Teaching Strategies
• Ask students if they know how a cat

uses its whiskers.

Further Background
Seals belong to the order Pinnipedia. Others in the order include sea lions and walruses. They are all aquatic carnivores and swim using flippers.

Answers
Yes, they were correct. Whiskers seem to be important in the ability of the seal to

find fish. They need to do the experiment again and cover the eyes, then the ears, to determine whether vision or hearing is involved in finding fish.

✔ Assessment

Knowledge: Ask students to design an experiment to determine the function of whiskers in another animal.

Another important adaptation is the evolution of jaws. As jaws evolved, new and more efficient ways of eating were developed. Rather than depending on sucking, rasping, or filter feeding as most invertebrate groups do, animals with jaws and teeth can grasp and hold on to prey. They have a distinct advantage in the competition for food.

Evolution of Vertebrate Classes

Vertebrates are subdivided into two major groups, the fish and the tetrapods—vertebrates with legs. Fish are streamlined, aquatic organisms that breathe by means of gills and move about by means of fins. There are three living fish classes, one of which lacks jaws.

Jawless Fish   Jawless fish include the lampreys, a familiar animal to people who live along the Great Lakes. These parasites have been responsible for great losses to the sport and commercial fishing industries. Lampreys have a sucker-shaped mouth that is lined with sharp teeth. They use their mouth to pierce the flesh of trout or other fish, and then feed on the blood and tissue of the host.

Cartilagenous Fish   The two remaining fish classes have jaws. One, in fact, was immortalized for this distinctive characteristic in a movie by the same name. We are talking, of course, about sharks, skates, and rays—the cartilagenous fish. These fish have skeletons composed entirely of cartilage and skin that is covered with toothlike scales. Although they breathe by means of gills, the gill openings are not covered. The evolution of hinged jaws in this group is associated with a more predatory way of life. Cartilagenous fish probably evolved from a group of armored fish that lived more than 400 million years ago.

Figure 17-17   The round, jawless mouth of a lamprey is lined with sharp, toothlike structures.

Figure 17-18   The many sharp teeth, great size, and quickness of sharks make them fierce predators.

17.3 ECHINODERMS AND CHORDATES   **467**

SECTION 17.3

Guest Speaker

Ask an expert on fly fishing to demonstrate fly fishing to your class. Ask the expert to demonstrate fly tying and explain how knowledge of fish behavior and entomology are important for successful fly fishing.

Different Viewpoints in Biology

Amphibian Population Decline

Biologists disagree about why the populations of amphibians are dwindling worldwide. Some think that stocking lakes and streams with fish causes a large number of tadpoles and eggs to be eaten by the stocked fish. Others think that because amphibian skin readily absorbs toxic chemicals, the pollution in water is killing them directly. In specific areas where amphibians are collected for sale, numbers are declining. Others think that global environmental problems are causing the decline: increased CO_2, worldwide warming, and increased ultraviolet light.

Demonstration

Play a recording of frog calls. They are available through biological supply companies and some public libraries. Ask students to speculate about why frogs call. *mating calls, territorial calls, distress calls*

Activity

Ask each group of students to observe and describe behaviors of a live frog. They should describe how these behaviors may have evolved: *swimming, jumping, feeding, breathing*

Bony Fish   Bony fish probably arose from the same armored ancestor that gave rise to the cartilagenous fish. As their name implies, these animals have skeletons of bone. The flattened, bony scales along with the slimy covering of mucus on the body protect and streamline the animal. Instead of the exposed gills that cartilagenous fish have, these fish have gill coverings composed of hard plates.

Figure 17-19   Although bony fish come in a wide variety of sizes and shapes, they all have the same basic structures, as shown in this French Angel fish.

Amphibians   Four other classes of vertebrates are grouped together based on the presence of legs, as opposed to fins. Most primitive among these classes are the amphibians—frogs, salamanders, toads, and newts.

The ancestor of today's amphibians was the lobe-finned fish that lived about 350 million years ago. The lobe-finned fish had two characteristics that favored their ability to survive on land, at least for short periods of time. The lobed fins enabled movement on dry surfaces. Primitive lungs supplemented the gills in delivering oxygen to the body. Scientists speculate that millions of years ago, there was a drought that caused shallow lakes and stream beds to dry up. Lobed-finned fish would have been able to survive the drought and reproduce by seeking out new, deeper sources of water. Natural selection would favor the survival of these animals, and their traits for surviving on land would be passed to their offspring.

Fishing Reels: The fishing reel was invented by the Chinese by the third century. A painting by a Chinese artist from 1129 A.D. is the oldest picture of a fishing reel. No representation of fishing reels is known from the West before 1651. The fishing reel was devised from an idea first used in warfare, a piece of artillery that could fire javelins attached to cords so they could be retrieved for reuse.

Over the course of millions of years, genetic mutations and natural selection would lead to further modifications in traits, and animals with primitive legs would appear. The evolution of primitive legs set the stage for the adaptive divergence of land vertebrates. That divergence led not only to the evolution of amphibians, but also to reptiles, birds, and mammals.

Most modern amphibians, like their early ancestors, are still chained to the water for reproduction. Water provides a protective, moist environment for developing embryos. And, because fertilization is external in most water-dwelling vertebrates, the water provides a medium for sperm to reach the eggs. Most amphibians have gills in the larval stage and lungs as adults. Thus, they spend part of their life cycle in the water and part of it on land.

Reptiles   If vertebrates were to move completely away from water, adaptations for different modes of reproduction and development, as well as for preventing dehydration, were necessary. In vertebrates, such adaptations first appeared among the reptiles. Reptiles evolved from an amphibian ancestor nearly 300 million years ago. These animals, which include lizards, snakes, turtles, and alligators, don't require water for reproduction or development. Major advancements that allowed for the separation from water were internal fertilization of the eggs and protection of the eggs by an outer covering—the shell. A reptilian egg can be compared to a hen's egg. Each has a yolk—the food supply for the developing embryo—and a water supply. As adults, reptiles have well-developed lungs for gas exchange. Their dry, scaly skin prevents evaporation of body fluids. Most reptiles have legs that are positioned under the body, an adaptation that allows quicker movement on land.

Figure 17-20   This Tiger salamander (*Ambystoma maculatum*) can be found across most of North America from the plains to high-elevation forests. Although it has a wide range, it must have water for reproduction.

Figure 17-21   The English viper of Costa Rica (**right**) **and an American alligator** (**left**) **are representatives of the reptile class.**

17.3 ECHINODERMS AND CHORDATES ❧ **469**

PHYSICS CONNECTION

Dinosaur Locomotion:
Scientists are using techniques from physics and engineering to determine whether dinosaurs moved slowly or ran with speed. Scientists and engineers have developed mathematical relationships that have made it possible to calculate the speeds of moving dinosaurs. As an animal increases in size, the leg strength is proportional to the cross section of the limb. The formula v/gl, where v is running speed, g is the acceleration of gravity (9.8 m/sec), and l is the leg length, helps, along with stride lengths, make it possible to calculate the running speed of dinosaurs. The faster an animal runs, the longer its stride, as long as the animal is larger than a house cat. In addition, the faster an animal runs, the greater the forces are on its feet. For example, when a person sprints, the force on the foot is 3.5 times the body weight. Fast running requires strong bones. Scientists used force plates, (pressure-sensitive panels in the floor) to measure the forces on the feet of a variety of modern animals as they walked and ran. Then, stresses on leg bones could be measured. Scientists concluded that dinosaurs could have run as fast as any modern mammal with similar strength leg bones. The huge plant-eating sauropods may have been able to run as fast as an elephant, about 5 m/sec, and *Triceratops* about the speed of a white rhinoceros, 7 m/sec, about the speed of a fast human run.

SECTION 17.3

Concept Development

Birds preen their feathers to clean them and remove parasites such as mites and lice. Preening also "zips together" feather barbs that have separated. Open spots along the feather allow air to rush through and prevent flight. Many birds secrete oil from a gland at the base of the tail. During preening they spread oil through their feathers to keep them waterproof.

Microscope Activity

Provide students with microscope slides of quill, contour, and down feathers. Have students draw diagrams of the feathers and label barbs, barbules, vanes, and shafts. **L1**

Activity

Ask students to take the masses of bones of approximately the same size in birds and mammals. You might ask students to bring in cooked bones from poultry and meat, or use bones from purchased skeletons. They will find that bird bones have less mass than others.

Birds Birds are believed to have evolved from a small, two-legged dinosaur more than 150 million years ago. Today's birds have several features in common with reptiles. Protective scales cover their legs, and they have a tough beak that is similar to that of some reptiles. Like reptiles, birds also have shelled eggs.

Birds have one feature that no other group of animals possesses—feathers. Feathers, which are modified scales, are associated with the ability of birds to fly. Flight is a major innovation among the vertebrates. Other vertebrates, such as flying fish or squirrels, can glide for short distances. However, only birds and bats (mammals) are capable of sustained flight. Birds are by far the strongest fliers, some species migrating for thousands of miles from breeding grounds to wintering grounds. Large, strong muscles in the breast and lightweight, hollow bones also allow for flight.

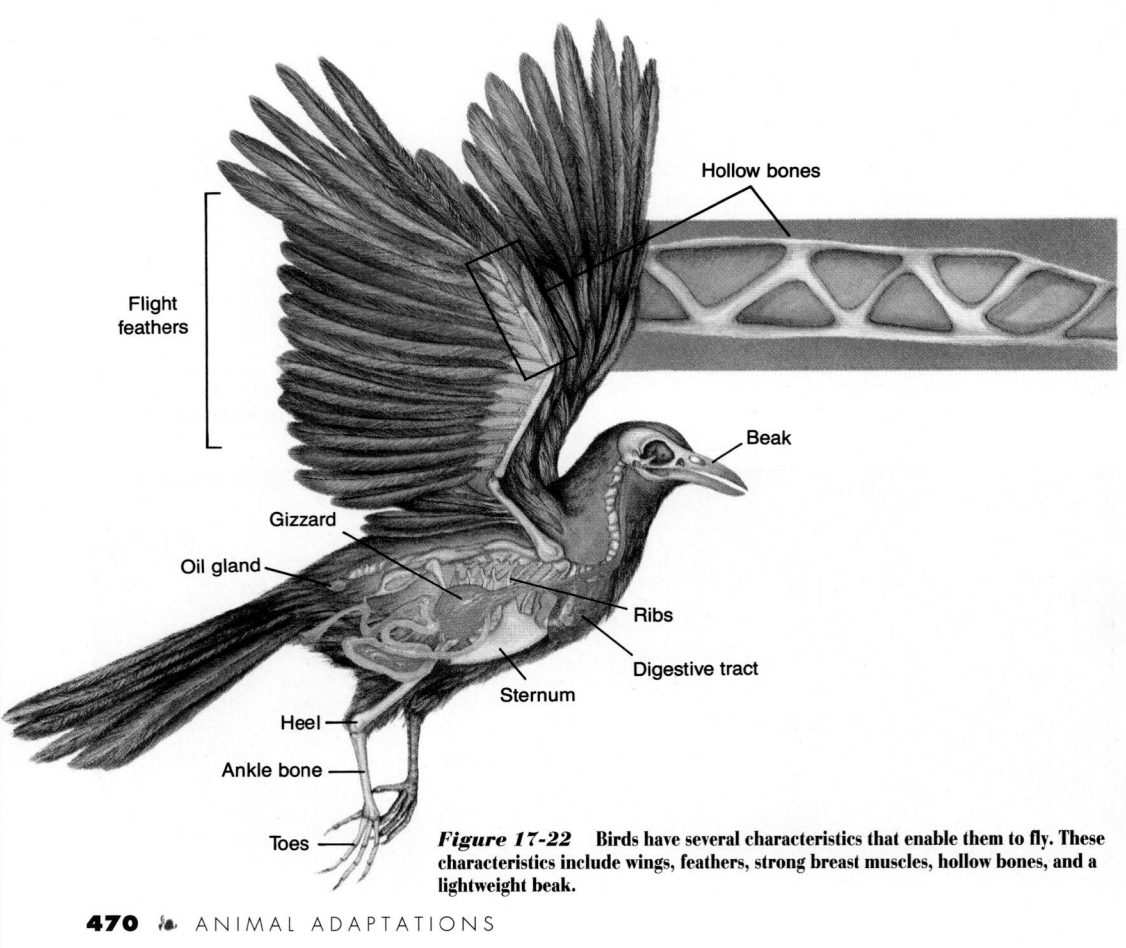

Figure 17-22 **Birds have several characteristics that enable them to fly. These characteristics include wings, feathers, strong breast muscles, hollow bones, and a lightweight beak.**

470   ANIMAL ADAPTATIONS

Birds in Art: Birds were important in the arts and crafts of the Incas of Peru in the 11th century. The Inca bird was different from the birds used in arts and crafts of Native Americans. The Zuni, one of the Pueblo tribes of Native Americans, used a geometrically shaped "rain bird" on their pottery. The Hopi also used geometric shapes in creating the birds on their pottery. Ask students to find examples of these birds in pictures of pottery, and point out the differences in the styles of making the bird shapes.

Quite possibly one of the most important adaptations that enabled birds to conquer the air is one that can't be observed directly. This adaptation involves the method by which birds regulate their internal body temperature. Birds have high energy requirements due to their aerial lifestyle. Maintenance of a constant body temperature is necessary for the internal chemical processes that are required to sustain high levels of activity. Animals that maintain a constant body temperature through internal metabolic actions are called **endotherms.** Regardless of the external temperature, an endothermic animal is able to remain active. For example, an owl is able to hunt even in much cooler nighttime temperatures, but a snake must seek shelter once the sun sets.

Endothermy is in direct contrast to temperature regulation in fish, amphibians, and reptiles, which are ectotherms. **Ectotherms** are animals whose body temperature can change with the temperature of the environment. Unlike endotherms, ectotherms generally have low metabolisms and are less active. To help regulate internal body temperature, ectotherms rely on a variety of behaviors. You may have seen a turtle sunning itself on a log in the cool morning, or retreating to the shady undergrowth of the shore during the hot afternoon. Both actions help the turtle to regulate its body temperature. Sunning itself increases its internal temperature, while retreating to the shade lowers its temperature.

Why is temperature regulation so important in the first place? The enzymes necessary for metabolism function best at temperatures near 40°C. Vertebrates must keep their internal temperature close to 40°C for optimum enzyme functioning.

Figure 17-23 **Birds that winter in cold climates, such as this cardinal, must have a constant abundant food supply to maintain their body temperatures. Ectotherms such as this collared lizard need to sun themselves to raise their body temperatures. Why do they need to raise their temperatures?**

Minilab 2

What types of food do different birds prefer?

Observe birds in your backyard, schoolyard, or nearby park for several days. Obtain a field guide and identify several of the most common species you see. Obtain several different sizes and types of birdseed. Place the seed out for the birds and record the type of food each species of bird prefers.

Analysis *Which types of seed did the birds prefer? Relate the bird's size, beak shape, and any other physical characteristics to the food type each preferred. Based on your observations, make a hypothesis about a bird's physical characteristics and the type of food it prefers.*

Minilab 2

Purpose
Students will learn how to make observations. They will also see that different birds prefer different foods based on size and beak shape.

Skills
observe, form a hypothesis

Teaching Strategies
You may wish to point out which species of birds are most likely to be found in your area. This activity will probably work the best in the winter months when food is not as abundant.

Expected Results
Depending on the species of birds in your area, students should see that birds with larger beaks will prefer larger seeds such as sunflower seeds. Smaller birds will prefer small seeds.

Answers
Students should answer that size and beak shape determine a bird's food preference. Accept all logical hypotheses.

✔ Assessment
Portfolio: Have students keep an observation log during this activity. They should record date, weather conditions, and any other anecdotal information along with their bird observations. This log as well as the results of their activity should be part of their portfolios.

Figure Caption Question
Why do they need to raise their temperatures? Lizards need to warm up for metabolic activity to work at an optimum level, for movement, digestion, etc.

STUDENT JOURNAL

Have students write a short story describing a day in the life of an endotherm or ectotherm. Students should develop characters and a plot. The stories should provide information about the lifestyle of the organism.

LITERATURE CONNECTION

Purpose

Students will get an overview and be inspired to read the book or see the movie version of Dian Fossey's *Gorillas in the Mist.*

Teaching Strategies

Ask students if they are familiar with another primate researcher, Jane Goodall, and her work with the wild chimpanzee. Goodall, like Fossey, has spent years living in the African wilds observing and recording the behaviors of chimpanzees.

Possible Answers

1. Answers will vary, but some students may notice that the book focuses and presents a great deal more information about the lives of the gorillas, while the movie version may seem to emphasize the human aspects of the endeavor as well as the political and social aspects of the country and its people.
2. The extreme conservationist would allow no human action or interaction in natural areas. The extreme opposing view would use all natural areas and organisms strictly for the benefit of humans. A middle ground might be the following. Replace what you take. If a forest is cut, trees should be replanted. Learn about the environment. Think about the consequences of your lifestyle and live a more environmentally aware life.

Going Further

Have students research the work of Jane Goodall and compare her work and Dian Fossey's work.

Mammals Mammals are thought to have evolved from a group of endothermic, mammal-like reptiles. Exactly when the first true mammals appeared is difficult to tell, but about 70 million years ago there was a sudden, dramatic increase in the number of mammal species. This increase in mammal diversity followed the extinction of the dinosaurs, leading scientists to believe that the two events were directly related. Since then, mammals have come to occupy every conceivable habitat—on land, in water, and even in the air.

LITERATURE CONNECTION

Gorillas in the Mist

In the 18 years she lived among them, Dian Fossey came to know mountain gorillas better than any other human being. Her book, *Gorillas in the Mist,* tells how she transformed herself from an occupational therapist in America to a field zoologist in the wilds of Rwanda, as well as one of the foremost authorities on mountain gorilla behavior. In the process, she survived violent weather, life on dangerous mountain slopes, dealings with witch doctors (friendly and unfriendly), and political upheaval.

The book is not only Fossey's story. It's also the tale of four gorilla families. The reader gets to know the gorillas as Fossey did, each as an individual with its own personality.

Blended in with Fossey's exploits as a zoological researcher, the adventures of daily gorilla life, and scientific information on gorilla behavior is the story of the fight for the gorillas' very existence. Fossey tells of her struggle to protect the mountain gorillas from illegal hunting and the destruction of their habitat. Her efforts included hiring private anti-poacher patrols to remove traps and make poaching as difficult as possible in and around her research area.

Dian Fossey was found murdered in her Rwanda camp in 1985—two years after the publication of her book. Many believe that she was killed by poachers angered by her forceful attempts to protect the gorillas.

Gorillas in the Mist is a stirring legacy left by a dedicated researcher whose work led her down many unexpected paths. Fossey's life and work stand as an example and inspiration to biologists, naturalists, and lovers of animals.

1. **Explore Further:** Obtain from your local library copies of the book and movie versions of *Gorillas in the Mist.* First read the book, then view the movie. How do the two differ? Which did you prefer?
2. **Writing About Biology:** Many people view conservation versus development to be an all-or-none issue. Write a paragraph describing a middle ground on this type of issue.

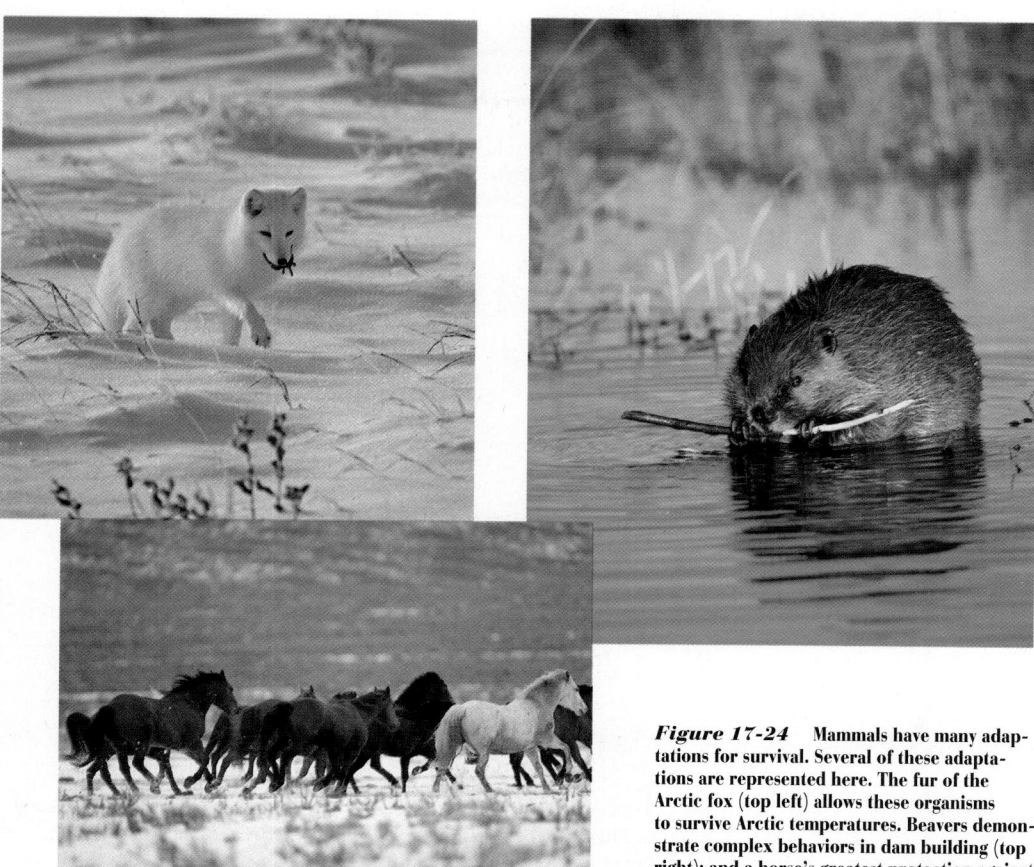

Figure 17-24 Mammals have many adaptations for survival. Several of these adaptations are represented here. The fur of the Arctic fox (top left) allows these organisms to survive Arctic temperatures. Beavers demonstrate complex behaviors in dam building (top right); and a horse's greatest protection against predators is its speed.

There are several reasons for their success. First, mammals feed their young with milk from mammary glands. This adaptation helps to ensure survival of the offspring by providing them with a readily available, nutrient-rich food source. A second adaptation that aids offspring survival is internal development of the young. This protection during development gives mammals the best chance of having a fertilized egg mature into an adult. Third, mammals have hair for insulation. This adaptation, in addition to endothermy, helps them to maintain a constant body temperature. Fourth, mammals are extremely agile. The legs are positioned under the body, allowing for greater speed. Finally, mammals have complex nervous systems, thus allowing for complex behaviors and increased intelligence.

Table 17.2 summarizes the characteristics of vertebrates. As you review this table, make sure that you can explain how the evolution of new features allowed each class to be successful.

17.3 ECHINODERMS AND CHORDATES **473**

SECTION 17.3

Demonstration
Bring in a small mammal such as a mouse, rat, gerbil, or hamster. Offer it appropriate food and ask students to observe it for a few minutes. Ask them to make a list of adaptations the animal has to its natural environment.

Brainstorming
Ask students why mammals live everywhere—below the surface of the Earth, in lakes, oceans, in deserts, and on frozen ice caps. *They have a variety of adaptations, such as endothermy, hair, high rate of metabolism, internal fertilization and development, care of young, variations in teeth types, large brain size, and methods of food getting, that make them suited to a wide variety of environments.* **COOP LEARN**

Misconceptions
Raccoons do not wash their food before eating it. Racoons have poor eyesight and therefore obtain a lot of information from the sense of touch. Racoons handle their food before eating it. It is this behavior that perhaps gave rise to the notion that raccoons wash their food before eating it. Camels do not store water in their humps; the hump is made of fat, which is stored food. These food stores allow the camel to survive long periods in the desert without food. They also allow the rest of the body to lose heat more rapidly than if fat covered the body in a continuous subcutaneous layer.

3 Assess

Check for Understanding
Give students a copy of a chart similar to the one in Table 17.2 in which you have left blank spaces for them to fill in.

Reteach
Ask students to make a concept map using the ideas in Table 17.2. Students should use Concept Mapping in the Skill Handbook for more information.

473

Extension

Ask students in groups of seven to role play a town meeting about what to do about the overpopulation of deer in the local area. One student should portray a hunter, another an animal rights activist, another a wildlife biologist, another a manager of a new development, another a farmer, another a state game manager. Prepare role cards for students and tell them they must stick to the position assigned to them, even if they disagree. **L2** **COOP LEARN**

✔ **Assessment**

Portfolio: Tell students that they are genetic engineers of the year 3000. They have been given the responsibility of developing a new animal, for use as meat for humans, from the genes of ones that currently exist. The world has become too warm to successfully raise cattle and the meat will replace today's hamburger. Tell students to describe their animal, justify its use as a meat source to replace cattle, and make a diagram of it in their portfolios. **L1**

4 Close

Field Trip

Take students to a nearby zoo or animal park. Ask them to make a list of the animals they observe and describe their adaptations, behavior, and where they live in the wild. **LEP**

Table 17.2 **Summary of Characteristics of Vertebrates**

Class	Examples	Outer Covering	Body Temperature	Limb Structure	Gas Exchange	Fertilization
Jawless fish	lamprey, hagfish	slimy skin	ectotherm	unpaired fins	gills	external
Cartilagenous fish	shark, skate, ray	scales	ectotherm	2 pairs of fins	gills	internal
Bony fish	perch, bass, trout	scales and slimy skin	ectotherm	2 pairs of fins	gills	external
Amphibians	frog, toad, salamander	slimy skin in most forms	ectotherm	2 pairs of legs; no claws	gills; lungs	external
Reptiles	turtle, lizard, snake, alligator	dry, scaly	ectotherm	2 pairs of legs; claws	lungs	internal
Birds	robin, eagle, pelican	feathers; scales on legs	endotherm	1 pair of wings; 1 pair of legs with claws	lungs	internal
Mammals	bear, whale, kangaroo	hair/fur	endotherm	2 pairs of legs; claws in most forms	lungs	internal

LOOKING AHEAD

THE NEARLY 2 million different species making up all of the five kingdoms illustrate the great diversity of life on Earth. Remember, though, that there is unity within that diversity. The many forms of life carry out the same basic life processes. One of the most fundamental of these processes is reproduction. In Chapter 18, you will learn about the basic patterns of reproduction that occur and study specific examples of how each pattern is carried out.

Section Review

Understanding Concepts

1. In which way are echinoderms and chordates similar?
2. What characteristics of vertebrates allow them to be such a successful group?
3. What advantages do endotherms have over ectotherms?
4. **Skill Review—Classifying:** Construct a classification key that could be used to identify the various classes of vertebrates. For more help, see Organizing Information in the **Skill Handbook**.
5. **Thinking Critically:** Based on features discussed in this section, explain why reptiles do not have to eat as much or as often as birds.

474 ANIMAL ADAPTATIONS

Answers to Section Review

1. Like chordates, larval echinoderms are bilaterally symmetrical.
2. Vertebrates have a complex brain and nervous system that interacts with the muscular system, allowing for speed and agility. They have jaws, which enable them to grasp and hold prey.
3. Endotherms maintain a constant body temperature most favorable for metabolism. Endotherms are not so restricted in habitat or activities as are ectotherms.
4. **Skill Review—Classifying:** Students may construct a key similar to this one. Accept all reasonable answers.
   1A no jaws.....................jawless fish
   1B jaws........................go to 2
   2A skeleton of cartilage........cartilagenous fish
   2B skeleton of bone.............go to 3
   3A fins........................bony fish
   3B legs........................go to 4
   4A external fertilization.......amphibians
   4B internal fertilization.......go to 5
   5A ectotherms...................reptiles
   5B endotherms...................go to 6
   6A feathers....................birds
   6B fur.........................mammals
5. **Thinking Critically:** Reptiles do not have the high energy demands of birds.

BIOLOGY, TECHNOLOGY, AND SOCIETY

Considering the Environment

White Death in the Coral Reefs

Around the world, oceanographers and other environmental scientists are becoming alarmed as a record number of coral reefs turn white and sometimes die. The delicate color we think of as coral doesn't belong to the coral itself. Individual coral animals, known as polyps, have a clear body over a limestone skeleton. Polyps live in tight colonies and, as each dies, it leaves its skeleton behind for another polyp to grow on. Where, then, does the coral color come from?

The Color of Coral The algae, zooxanthella and their chloroplasts give coral polyps their green, yellow and brown colors. This algae lives symbiotically with the coral. During the day, the algae produce oxygen and simple sugars through photosynthesis. These products become available to the coral polyps for food. In return, the algae get carbon dioxide and nitrogen produced by the polyps as waste. The cooperation works beautifully for both organisms, creating—over millions of years—the coral reefs of today. But the system is delicate and easily disrupted.

If the polyps' environment becomes poor and they become stressed, they will eject their algae. The coral then turns white because the limestone skeletons become

visible through the polyps' clear body tissue. Because it looks as if the coral reef has been bleached, the effect is known as coral bleaching.

Causes of Bleaching A lot of things can cause the stresses that lead to coral bleaching; pollutants and poisons in the water, damage from hurricanes, changes in water salinity, and natural diseases are among them. But a major cause is overly warm water.

Coral can survive only in a relatively narrow range of temperatures. A difference of only one degree above normal annual high temperatures for only a few weeks can cause coral reefs to bleach. A jump of only four degrees above normal highs can cause bleaching in a few days.

Worse, if a reef is already stressed by something, a small additional stress from another source can cause coral bleaching. For example, a slight warming that would otherwise pose no danger can start bleaching if the coral is already stressed from a recent hurricane.

Many oceanographers and environmental scientists consider the increased incidence of coral bleaching a possible early indicator of global warming. But, because there aren't yet any long-term data on coral, it will be some time before definite conclusions are possible.

CAREER CONNECTION

Oceanographer is the general name for scientists who study the sea. They may study the composition or movements of the water itself, the plant or animal life that lives there, or underwater geology. Many have recently developed specialties in such topics as ocean conservation, public policy, and archaeology. Virtually any study having to do with the sea is fair game for an oceanographer.

CHAPTER 17 ANIMAL ADAPTATIONS **475**

CAREER CONNECTION

For more information, have students contact a local college or university for information about careers in oceanography. If you live near the shore, you may ask them to get in touch with marine institutes, marine parks, or marine conservation agencies.

escape from the atmosphere around Earth. This cooling might shorten growing seasons, reduce plant growth, increase the size of the polar ice caps, or begin a new ice age. Reduced growth of marine algae might reduce the amount of oxygen in the atmosphere.

Going Further

Ask students to look up information about other symbiotic relationships between organisms. How does environmental stress affect these symbiotic relationships? **L2**

Considering the Environment

Purpose

Students will study the symbiotic relationship between the coral polyp and the algae that live inside their bodies. They will learn how this symbiotic relationship is disrupted by environmental stress to produce "bleaching" and eventually death of the reef.

Background

Coral reefs flourish at water temperatures between 25°C and 29°C. In Bali, reefs have been badly damaged by coral miners smashing the reef for its raw materials. In Sri Lanka, an extensive government coastal management program is compensating more than 10 000 people for loss of employment as a result of prohibition of reef mining. The Caribbean island of Bonaire established Bonaire Marine Park where the effects of tourism and research on the reef can be closely monitored, controlled, and eliminated in areas of the reef that become threatened.

Teaching Strategies

If anyone has done any snorkeling in areas where there are coral reefs, have them describe their experience to the class. Show slides, films, or videos of coral reefs. Show students pieces of coral skeleton.

Possible Answers

1. Algae, fish, mollusks, and a huge variety of other vertebrates and invertebrates
2. Plants might not photosynthesize as quickly due to lower amounts of CO_2 available to them, and as a result, grow more slowly and not complete formation of reproductive structures at the end of the growing season. As a result, there might be fewer plants. Lower amounts of CO_2 might lead to general cooling due to a less thick blanket of CO_2 allowing heat to

Issues

Purpose

Students will examine both sides of the issue of using animals for testing cures for diseases, cosmetics, and military weapons.

Background

In the early 1920s when cosmetic companies did not test their products, *The Journal of the American Medical Association* published the results of a study of use of mascara containing a synthetic aniline dye. Users were reported to have complications ranging from eye irritation to disfigurement, blindness, and death. A particular hair dye was found to cause swelling of the face, eyelids, larynx, inflammation of the skin with cracking, blistered scalp, impaired eyesight, spreading of infection leading to long-term hospitalization, and permanent blindness. The toxins arsenic, quinine, resorcin, and mercury were common ingredients in cosmetics and personal care products. The development of the Draize test for ocular irritation was heralded by the medical community as a way to prevent senseless blinding and death.

Teaching Strategies

- Prior to having students read the article, ask if they can list diseases that can be cured or treated as a result of animal testing. Possibilities include: polio, diabetes, rubella, arthritis, cerebral palsy, coronary heart disease, and kidney disease.
- Ask them to discuss the problem of comparing the techniques of older science with modern science.
- Tell students that many of the animal rights groups are nonprofit agencies and some are businesses that make a profit.
- If they support animal rights, ask them which groups they would rather support, the nonprofit or the for-profit businesses and why.

There have been many other factors in recent years that may have greatly contributed to the frequent bleachings, including epidemics of coral diseases, large numbers of strong hurricanes, and surges in the populations of animals that prey on coral.

Fortunately, coral reefs can survive short periods of bleach-ing. If the stress on a reef ceases, polyps will regain their algae and color in a matter of weeks. Frequent or long-lasting bleach-ings, however, have already killed several reefs.

1. **Find Out:** Name three other marine plants or animals that are endangered when a coral reef dies.

2. **Writing About Biology:** Some scientists think it is possible that loss of the coral reefs may result in a noticeable drop in the amount of carbon dioxide being made in the world. What effects on global ecology might such a drop have?

Issues

Drawing the Line on Animal Pain

There are few issues in the world of science as emotionally charged as the issue of experimentation on animals. Each side has horror stories to back up its point of view.

The literature of those who fight for animal rights is filled with tales of cruelty to animals. There are accounts of animals blowtorched in burn studies, deafened or addicted to drugs in studies of social behavior, systematically and painfully poisoned to determine levels of tox-icity, and much more—all without anesthetics.

Scientists who work with animals have their own tales to tell. They often hear stories of children dying from diseases that can't be cured today, but which may someday be eliminated through animal research. They also tell stories of people who are alive today because of treatments developed through animal research.

Cystic fibrosis (CF) is a case in point. Cystic fibrosis is a hereditary disease caused by a defective gene. Until recently, most people born with CF suffered painful death in childhood. By the mid-1980s, treatment had progressed enough to allow more than half of the victims to survive into their twenties. The treatment, say experimenters, could not have been developed without animal research. As this book is being written, there's finally hope that the disease can be cured. The cure is being tested on monkeys.

Most advanced surgical techniques have been developed with animal tests. Coronary bypass operations and organ transplants are examples. Animal experiments led to the eradication of smallpox, a dreaded killer that became the first disease to be entirely wiped out by modern medicine. It's impossible to know how many lives have been saved by penicillin and the polio vaccine we've come to take for granted—both of which were tested and proven on animals. Thousands of people with diabetes are alive today because of the animal research that led to our understanding of insulin.

Most animal rights proponents are willing to allow research necessary to save lives, provided that the animals are treated as humanely as possible. But many question whether much of the research is truly necessary. They claim that a great deal of the work could be done with computer simulations, and they suspect that animals are only used because it's less expensive than developing alternate methods.

Experimenters counter that computer simulations are only useful in studying a system that's fully understood. Medical research, they say, deals with so many unknown factors that no accurate simulation is possible.

But there's more to animal testing than the medical research that might one day save your life. There's cosmetic research as well. One of the most notorious tests involves putting cosmetic ingredients directly onto the eyeballs of live rabbits to see just how irritating they are. Rabbits are used because their eyes don't make tears to wash the irritating substances away. Public opposition to such practices has lead several cosmetic companies to abandon animal tests. There are now stores devoted entirely to selling cosmetics and other products developed without research on animals.

A highly controversial area is military research that tests weapons on animals. Many animal rights activists are appalled by the idea of killing and mutilating animals for the sole purpose of testing the ability to destroy. On the other side is the view that military actions are an unavoidable evil in our world. Should war develop, having adequate knowledge of the destructive power of our weapons could save the lives of countless soldiers and civilians. Should our country be in danger, the knowledge might be critical in making decisions that could mean the difference between victory and defeat.

The questions don't stop at the treatment of animals in the laboratory. Even when animals are treated humanely, as most are, there's the problem of what to do with test subjects once research is finished. Many are routinely killed. Some can theoretically be released into the wild, but preparing them to survive on their own can be an extremely

expensive process lasting years. Others will never be able to live alone in the wild and are unfit to be pets. Caring for them can be costly. Furthermore, many animal rights activists maintain that dooming animals to a life in captivity is in itself cruel.

There are two extreme positions—one that any activity that causes animals to suffer is wrong, the other that any animal suffering leading to improved conditions for humans is justified. In between there are no easy answers.

Understanding the Issues

1. Under what conditions, if any, do you think experimentation on

animals is justified? Defend your view.

2. Suppose you discovered that your favorite shampoo was tested on animals in painful experiments to determine how irritating its ingredients might be. Would you change brands? Think of whatever it is you're most looking forward to buying right now. Suppose it was developed with animal tests. Would you change your mind about buying it?

3. Should the criteria for animal testing be the same for all types of animals? Is experimentation on a rat more justifiable than experimentation on a chimpanzee?

Readings

- Ritvo, Harriet. "Toward a More Peaceable Kingdom." *Technology Preview,* February/March, 1992, p. 54.
- Karpati, Ron. "A Scientist: 'I Am the Enemy.'" *Newsweek,* December 18, 1989, p. 12.

Possible Answers

1. Some students may say that it is morally wrong to experiment on animals for any reason. Others may say animal experimentation is permissible, provided that human lives are being saved. Others may say that any kind of animal research is acceptable because researchers care for and treat animals in a humane way.

2. Some students will not want to purchase a shampoo developed with animal testing because they do not believe humans should consider their needs to be more important than those of animals. Others will say they want to keep their scalps and vision intact and would not feel safe using a shampoo that had not been tested on animals.

3. Some students will say that the criteria should be the same for all animals because they all have the same rights. Others will say that more advanced forms of animal life have more rights to protection than animals not as closely related to humans.

Going Further

Have students go to drugstores and cosmetic counters and find products labeled "No animal testing." Are these products becoming more prevalent?

CHAPTER REVIEW

Summary

The summary can be used by students to review the major concepts of the chapter.

Language of Biology

Answers should go beyond defining the terms. Accept any answer that uses the term correctly and in the proper context.

Understanding Concepts

1. Sexual reproduction can occur within a single organism. However, when that happens, there is less variety among offspring than when two parents are involved.
2. Tissues are composed of various kinds of cells that function together. Evolution of different kinds of tissues provided an opportunity for higher levels of organization and more specialization of parts.
3. A segmented worm has a true coelom, body segments, excretory organs, gills (some forms), and more controlled movement.
4. Being radially symmetrical allows an animal such as a cnidarian to obtain food coming from any direction.
5. If the endotherm were to survive in a warmer climate, adaptations promoting cooling would have to evolve; e.g., loss of fur and/or insulation or behaviors that would generate less heat.
6. Both groups of animals evolved a means of internal fertilization and a shelled egg for development of young.
7. Reptiles have dry, scaly skin, while amphibians generally have a moist, slimy skin. Reptiles have internal fertilization, but amphibians have external fertilization. Jawless fish have slimy skin and unpaired fins, whereas bony fish have scales and slimy skin and two pairs of fins.
8. Vertebrae protect the spinal cord, provide support, and permit flexibility of movement. The endo-

Summary

About 95 percent of all animals are invertebrates, animals with no backbone. Sponges are the least complex of the invertebrates. They are made of two layers of cells and lack tissues, organs, and systems. Sponges are sessile heterotrophs.

The cnidarians have two tissue layers with a jellylike substance between them. They have a primitive nerve network, a single body opening, and some type of locomotion. Cnidarians are radially symmetrical—all their body parts are arranged equally around a center point.

The flatworms have bilateral symmetry and distinct head and tail regions. They have three tissue layers and distinct organs. Their nerves are arranged into a ladderlike system and they have a primitive digestive system.

Based on their pattern of early development, one group of animals, the segmented worms, mollusks, and arthropods, are thought to have diverged from a common ancestor. New adaptations that evolved in these organisms include a coelom, separate sexes, two body openings, true systems, segmentation, body sections, and features that permitted life on land.

The other main group of animals includes echinoderms, hemichordates, and chordates. The chordates include the subphylum of vertebrates, which have evolved a variety of adaptations for life in water and on land.

Language of Biology

Write a sentence that shows your understanding of each of the following terms.

anterior	endotherm
appendage	exoskeleton
bilateral symmetry	invertebrate
coelom	mesoderm
dorsal	posterior
ectoderm	radial symmetry
ectotherm	ventral
endoderm	vertebra
endoskeleton	vertebrate

Understanding Concepts

1. How is being a hermaphrodite both a benefit and a disadvantage to an organism?
2. How did evolution of tissues allow for more complexity in an organism?
3. Other than segmentation, what other features would allow you to distinguish between a roundworm and a segmented worm?
4. How is being radially symmetrical a benefit to a sessile organism?
5. What adaptations would an endotherm from a cold environment have to make if it were relocated to a tropical climate?
6. Broadly speaking, what adaptations evolved in both insects and reptiles that allowed them to be successful away from water?
7. Based on information in Table 17.2, explain how you could distinguish between reptiles and amphibians. How could you distinguish between the jawless fish and bony fish?
8. Identify the features that evolved among vertebrates and explain the importance of each.
9. Explain the adaptations that led to the evolution of land vertebrates.
10. Compare and contrast the body plans of segmented worms and arthropods.

skeleton grows with the animal, allowing some vertebrates to grow quite large. The complex nervous, muscular, and skeletal systems have resulted in complex behaviors and greater speed and agility.
9. Lobed fins and primitive lungs of lobe-finned fish were adaptations that enabled those animals to survive a drought and find a source of water in which to reproduce. As fins were modified into legs and lungs became more efficient, amphibians gradually evolved.
10. Both segmented worms and arthropods are segmented, but in arthropods, the segments

are fused into distinct regions or sections.

Applying Concepts

11. The sponge is sessile and the clam moves very slowly. Both extract food from their watery environment by means of filter feeding.
12. The exoskeleton protects against predators and loss of water, provides support, and aids in locomotion. Jointed appendages have evolved to function in various ways—locomotion, feeding, and sensory perception.

Applying Concepts

11. In what ways are mollusks with two shells, such as clams, similar to sponges?
12. Why are arthropods such a successful group?
13. How are a starfish and a hydra similar? How are they different?
14. Arthropods and mollusks are very successful groups of animals. In what ways are they similar?
15. Why do many ectotherms migrate or hibernate? Do endotherms do so for the same reason?
16. What hypothesis could you make to explain the advantages of sessile animals and parasites having both male and female sex organs even though their free-living relatives have separate sexes?
17. **Considering the Environment:** Why do many oceanographers and environmental scientists consider an increase in coral bleaching to be a possible early indicator of ocean pollution?
18. **Global Connection:** Why do you think animals became so important in Native American culture?

Lab Interpretation

19. **Investigation:** You would like to know if a particular species of hydra is temperature sensitive. The graph below shows numbers of these organisms active in samples observed under a microscope at various temperatures. From the data on the graph, determine the optimum temperature range for this hydra. What experimental procedure would you follow to check if the data shown on this graph are accurate?

Activity of Hydra at various temperatures

20. **Thinking Lab:** Assume that an animal's ability to use its whiskers for echolocation would require that more nerve fibers be attached to the whiskers. A scientist finds that animal A has 200 nerve fibers attached to each whisker; animal B, 150 nerve fibers; animal C, 900 nerve fibers; and animal D, 1000 nerve fibers. Which animals, would you hypothesize, might use their whiskers for echolocation? Why do you think that?
21. **Minilab 2:** Observe the teeth of the animals pictured below. From your observations, what types of food do you think each eats? Explain your answer.

Connecting Ideas

22. In what ways are animals similar to protozoa? How are they different?
23. In what ways was the evolution of insects and reptiles similar to that of plants?

13. Both have radial symmetry and lack a centralized nervous system. Both are chunk feeders; the starfish has two body openings while the hydra has one. The starfish has true organs and systems. The starfish can move; the hydra is sessile.
14. Both have complex sensory adaptations and nervous systems. Both have skeletons that work along with muscles and limbs or appendages for locomotion.
15. As a means of adjusting to external temperatures and food
16. Both sessile animals and parasites are less likely to find a mate than are free-living forms. Having both male and female sex organs, they are able to reproduce sexually without a mate.
17. Pollutants accumulate in the water, stressing the coral. Increased cases of coral bleaching may be associated with increased pollution of ocean waters.
18. Native Americans lived very close to the land. Animals were a means of food and transportation and a source of danger.

Lab Interpretation

19. The graph shows that this species of hydra is most active at 25°C, and somewhat active between 20°C and 30°C. To check the data, an experiment could be set up to observe hydra at various temperatures and record activity.
20. Animals C and D, because they have more nerve fibers attached to their whiskers
21. The dog has sharp ripping teeth most useful for eating meat. The mouse has teeth most useful for eating seeds and gnawing. The rabbit and horse have long, flat incisors and large chewing teeth best suited for eating grasses.

Connecting Ideas

22. **Unity Within Diversity:** Both groups are heterotrophic and must obtain food as predators or parasites. However, protozoa are unicellular, and, therefore, by

---

definition, cannot be nearly so complex as animals.
23. **Evolution:** Both insects and reptiles evolved adaptations that enabled them to live on land—a means of internal fertilization and a shelled egg that protects the embryo. Mosses and ferns require water for sexual reproduction, but their embryos are protected by the female reproductive structure.

Life Functions of Organisms

Unit Overview

Unit 5 covers functions common to all or almost all organisms and is organized in such a way that students continually build upon previous knowledge. Reflecting the systems approach, the chapters in this unit draw examples from all five kingdoms of life with special emphasis on human anatomy and physiology. Chapter 18 focuses on reproduction, both asexual and sexual. Chapter 19 presents a discussion of development. In Chapter 20, students learn how nutrients are processed by heterotrophs. After studying transport in Chapter 21, students explore the relationship of transport to gas exchange, excretion, and maintenance of osmotic balance in Chapter 22. A study of infectious diseases and the immune system in Chapter 23 concludes the unit.

Theme Development

Systems and interactions is made evident as the various structures that contribute to each life function are examined. Students also strengthen their understanding of unity within diversity as they realize that a great variety of organisms must carry out the same basic functions, but are adapted to do so in a variety of ways. Evolution is evident in the study of adaptations that allow organisms to carry out life functions.

Advance Planning

Chapter 18
- Procure or order fern fronds, moss, and male pine cones for Minilab 2.
- Order *Hydra, Paramecium,* and *Spirogyra* slides.

Chapter 19
- Order prepared slides of fertilized eggs, unfertilized eggs, and developmental stages for Minilab 1.
- Order insect larvae for the Alternate Lab.

Life Functions of Organisms

This close-up view of the hooks and eyes of de Mestral's locking tape shows how the two strips connect. The Swiss mountaineer hoped that his invention would replace metal zippers as a clothing fastener. Why do you think this has not happened?

Cocklebur seeds have hooks that enable them to cling to animal fur and other types of materials. Other plants have seeds that float in the wind or on water.

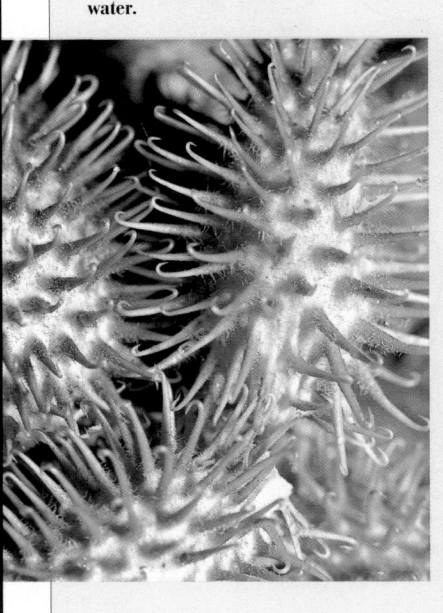

480

Chapter 20
- Prepare alpha amylase enzyme solution, Benedict's solution, iodine solution, and starch solution for the Investigation. Order dialysis tubing.
- Order TesTape and prepare solutions of lactose, maltose, sucrose, and glucose for Minilab 1.
- Prepare iodine and starch solutions for the Alternate Lab.

Chapter 21
- Procure a sphygmomanometer and a stethoscope for the Investigation.

- Procure normal and abnormal EKGs for Minilab 2.
- Order prepared slides of human blood for the Alternate Lab.

Chapter 22
- Prepare bromthymol blue solution for the Investigation.

Chapter 23
- Order *E. coli* culture for the Investigation.
- Order or prepare sodium hydroxide, phenolphthalein, and agar for the Minilabs.
- Order prepared slides of human blood.

W hy do seeds like the cocklebur have hooks, spines, barbs, or bristles? The seeds of flowering plants are dispersed by wind, water, or as hitchhikers on organisms that move from place to place. The dispersal of seeds far away from the parent plant reduces competition with the parent for sunlight and water.

In 1948, a Swiss mountaineer named George de Mestral discovered that cockleburs attached to fibers by way of tiny hooks and wondered if this same technique could be used to fasten clothing. Working with a weaver, de Mestral developed two strips of cloth, one with tiny hooks and the other with smaller eyes. Today, de Mestral's locking tape is used to secure items in space, seal the chambers of artificial hearts, and, of course, to fasten clothing from diapers to tennis shoes. The reproductive strategies of a plant led to an invention that has changed how people do things. Reproduction is just one of the life functions that you will examine in this unit.

In Chapter 23, students learn about causes and transmission of infectious diseases and how the immune system functions in protecting against them. Students compare nonspecific and specific means of defense, the principles of immunity, and means of prevention and treatment of diseases.

Using the Photos

De Mestral's fasteners imitate the hooks of cockleburs. Many advances in health care have been made possible by the design of equipment that mimics normal body functions. For example, a heart-lung machine duplicates the functions of the organs for which it is named in the same way that a dialysis machine takes on the role that cannot be properly performed by diseased kidneys. Similarly, plastic devices can replace diseased valves in the heart, and artificial pacemakers can take over control of the heartbeat.

Previewing the Chapters

Chapter 18 begins with a look at various modes of asexual reproduction. Students then study conjugation in simple organisms, followed by the angiosperm life cycle. Next, students compare solutions to common problems of fertilization in several animal groups. The chapter ends with a study of human reproduction.

Following logically from Chapter 18, Chapter 19 is a study of development in plants and animals: first early stages and then later events. Students come to see the different solutions to problems of development that have evolved among animals and also examine factors that control differentiation.

In Chapter 20, students compare nutrient requirements of autotrophs and heterotrophs, and compare patterns of food getting and digestion in a variety of organisms.

In Chapter 21, students explore the similarities and differences between plant and animal transport systems. The human circulatory system is emphasized, as are the structure and functions of blood.

Chapter 22 analyzes gas exchange, excretion, and maintenance of osmotic balance. Students come to realize the important role the circulatory system plays in those functions in animals.

SECTION	OBJECTIVES	TEXT LABS/FEATURES
18.1 Asexual Reproduction (2 days)	**Compare** and **give examples** of different forms of asexual reproduction. **Hypothesize** how asexual reproduction is an adaptation in plants and animals.	**Minilab 1:** What conditions favor budding in yeast? p. 485
18.2 Sexual Reproduction (3 days)	**Compare** conjugation in different organisms. **Explain** the generalized life cycle of plants. **Relate** the idea of alternation of generations to the life cycle of a typical flowering plant.	**Investigation:** Growing Bread Mold, p. 490 **Minilab 2:** How do spores and pollen compare? p. 492 **Thinking Lab:** How can you determine chromosome numbers in plants? p. 494
18.3 Sexual Reproduction in Animals (3 days)	**Distinguish** between external and internal fertilization in animals. **Relate** human reproductive structures to functions in females and males. **Compare** estrus in mammals with the menstrual cycle in humans.	**Health Connection:** Fetal Alcohol Syndrome, p. 498 **Career Connection:** Midwife, p. 499 **Literature Connection:** Native American Names, p. 502 **Art Connection:** Family Group, p. 504
BIOLOGY, TECHNOLOGY, AND SOCIETY		**Issues:** And Baby Makes Three? p. 506 **Biotechnology:** Cloning Humans: Is It Possible? p. 507

LAB MATERIALS

INVESTIGATION	MINILAB		ALTERNATE LAB

page 490
bread
cotton swab
onion (optional)
petri dish
soil
	page 485
	coverslips
	glass rod
	labels
	lens paper
	medicine
	  dropper
	microscope
	slides
	sugar
	yeast
		page 492
		coverslips
		fern frond with
		  sporangia
		lens paper
		microscope
		moss with capsules
		pine cones, male
		slides
		tweezers
			page 488
			hand lens
			Hydra slides
			microscope
			Paramecium slides
			Spirogyra slides

TEACHER CLASSROOM RESOURCES	OTHER RESOURCES
Study Guide, p. 103 **Concept Mapping,** p. 18 ***PLL:** *Reproduction in Yeasts,* p. 110 ***PLL:** *Vegetative Reproduction in Duckweed,* p. 112 ***PLL:** *Regeneration in Planarians,* p. 115 ****ILS:** *How Common Are Bacteria and How Quickly Do They Reproduce?* p. 169 ****ILS:** *Reproduction in Fungi,* p. 171 ****ILS:** *Regeneration: A Form of Asexual Reproduction,* p. 175	***STVS:** *Super Trees,* Plants and Simple Organisms (Disc 4, Side 2) **Color Transparency 20:** *Life Cycle of Bread Mold* **Color Transparency 21:** *Life Cycle of a Mushroom*
Study Guide, pp. 104-105 **Critical Thinking/Problem Solving:** *Reproduction in Flowering Plants,* p. 18 ****ILS:** *Flower Anatomy,* p. 181 ****ILS:** *Moss Plants and Alternation of Generations,* p. 177	***STVS:** *Bats as Pollinators,* Plants and Simple Organisms (Disc 4, Side 2) **Color Transparency 33:** *Life Cycle of a Flowering Plant*
Study Guide, pp. 106-108 **Exploring Environmental Issues:** *Organically Grown,* p. 13	***STVS:** *Alligator Courtship,* Animals (Disc 5, Side 2) **Color Transparency 34:** *The Human Reproductive System* **Color Transparency 50:** *Frog Body Systems*
Assessment Materials **Chapter Assessment,** pp. 69-72 **Performance Assessment in Biology,** p. 36 **Alternate Assessment in the Science Classroom** **Computer Test Bank**	**Spanish Resources** **Cooperative Learning Resource Guide** **Videodisc Correlations** (to Optical Data's and Videodiscovery's videodiscs)

* **Probing Levels of Life**
** **Investigating Living Systems**

* **Science Technology Videodisc Series**

Key to Teaching Strategies

The following designations will help you decide which activities in the teacher margin are appropriate for your students.

L1 Level 1 activities should be within the ability range of all students.

L2 Level 2 activities should be within the ability range of the average to above-average student.

L3 Level 3 activities are designed for the ability range of above-average students.

LEP LEP activities are appropriate for Limited English Proficiency students.

COOP LEARN Cooperative Learning activities are designed for small group work.

ADDITIONAL RESOURCES

Infinite Voyage *The Living Clock*
How does time affect living things? From aging to the timing of flowering, natural cycles affect all living things.

Audiovisual
Courting, video, Frey Scientific.
Reproduction and Gender, video, Films for the Humanities and Sciences.

Software
Animal Reproduction, Apple II/TRS-80/Model III, J and S.
Plant Reproduction, Apple II/TRS-80/Model III, J and S.

18

REPRODUCTION

Chapter Overview

As they study this chapter, students discover that various patterns of reproduction are shared by a wide variety of organisms. They will first learn about asexual reproduction, studying examples of organisms that undergo fission, budding, fragmentation, and spore formation.

Next, students will compare sexual and asexual reproduction and discover the advantages to a population of sexual reproduction. They will examine conjugation in a variety of simple life forms, identify the stages of a plant life cycle, and examine the life cycle of angiosperms.

Students complete the chapter by focusing on sexual reproduction among animals. They will come to understand the problems associated with fertilization and how those problems are solved by animals with external and internal fertilization. Students will complete their study of reproduction as they learn the basic anatomy and physiology of human reproduction.

KEY TERMS

budding	oviduct
conjugation	ovulation
endosperm	ovule
estrus	pollination
follicle	regeneration
fragmentation	scrotum
hermaphro-	semen
dite	testes
hormone	uterus
menstrual	vagina
cycle	vegetative
menstruation	reproduction

REPRODUCTION

ONE MOMENT, a large, milky white seed pod hangs from the stem of a milkweed plant. The next moment—poof! The pod suddenly bursts open, and feathery white seeds are cast to the breeze. Hundreds of such seeds may be scattered by the wind—some perhaps to favorable spots on the ground where they germinate and grow into new milkweed plants. In fact, the enormous number of seeds that a single milkweed plant produces increases the chances that the plant will successfully reproduce.

Many plants overproduce seeds; this helps ensure continuation of the species. After all, the chances that a single milkweed seed or tomato seed or watermelon seed will take root may be limited by many environmental factors. The chances that at least one out of hundreds will survive and grow is much better. Likewise, many animals overproduce offspring. A

toad, for example, may produce as many as 10 000 tadpoles in one clutch. Some large spiders produce more than 2000 offspring at a time. In contrast, some organisms—including humans—normally produce just one offspring at a time.

Regardless of the numbers, the result of reproduction is new members of the species. Reproduction involves the transfer of genetic information from parent to offspring—information that tells how the new species member will be structured and how it will function. In some organisms, the genetic information in the offspring is exactly the same as in the parent; in others, the information is a combination of information from two parents. In this chapter, you'll explore the different ways in which organisms from each of the five kingdoms reproduce.

If your school grounds had ten milkweed plants, and every plant produced 500 seeds each year, and every seed grew to be an adult plant, how long would it be before you would have to move to another school?

Chapter Preview

Contents

ASSESSMENT PLANNER

Choose assessment strategies from the following pages to evaluate the progress of your students.

Assess, pp. 486-487, 495-496, 505
Portfolio, pp. 486, 491, 492, 496, 497, 500
Alternate Lab, pp. 488-489
Thinking Lab, p. 494

Minilab 1, p. 485
Minilab 2, p. 492
Investigation, pp. 490-491
Chapter Review, pp. 508-509

Introducing the Chapter

Use the photographs on pages 482 and 483 to introduce the concept of an organism's life cycle. Ask students to identify, in general, the stages leading from one generation to the next. Remind them that reproduction is a means of passing on the genetic code of DNA. Then have them focus on organisms with which they are familiar—for example, a plant such as milkweed, an animal such as a cat, or themselves. Discuss with students the roles of spores, pollen, seeds, sperm, and eggs. Have them calculate the problem posed on the photograph of the milkweed flowers. In three years, there would be more than 1 billion milkweed plants! Point out that the basic elements of life cycles are quite similar even though organisms can be quite different. **L1**

Theme Development

Although the chapter draws upon all the themes, systems and interactions and unity within diversity are most evident. Systems and interactions is illustrated in the interaction of the parts involved in the reproductive process. The idea of unity will be appreciated when students realize that, although different, organisms face the same problems in reproducing, that there are only several main patterns of reproduction, and that a wide variety of organisms share each of those patterns.

Tying to Previous Knowledge

This chapter builds upon students' knowledge of genetics and of evolution. Students will make use of their understanding of genetics at the cellular and biochemical level—mitosis, meiosis, and DNA function—as they explore reproduction at the level of the organism. They will also have a sound basis for an understanding of the adaptive significance of the various reproductive structures.

Prepare

Key Concepts

Students are introduced to the process of asexual reproduction and are provided with specific examples of this process occurring in different kingdoms.

Key Terms

budding, vegetative reproduction, fragmentation, regeneration

Materials

- Purchase yeast in your local supermarket for Minilab 1.
- Prepare the following solution 24 hours in advance of Minilab 1: Add 1/2 package of activated yeast to 400 mL water and three teaspoons of table sugar. If possible, keep this solution in an incubator at 38°C overnight. Prepare a second solution with the remaining yeast and 400 mL water on the morning of the activity.

1 Focus

Objectives

The objectives are listed on the student page. Remind students to preview these objectives as a guide to this numbered section.

Demonstration

Show your students a potato tuber and an onion bulb. Ask them how they think these parts are useful to the plant. Bring the ideas around to the function of reproduction.

2 Teach

Using Science Terms

Have students look up the literal meaning of *binary* and *fission*. Have them explain why these terms are appropriate for what they define in asexual reproduction. **L1**

Objectives

Compare and **give examples** of different forms of asexual reproduction.

Hypothesize how asexual reproduction is an adaptation in plants and animals.

18.1 Asexual Reproduction

Did you ever see a tulip begin to emerge from beneath the soil in early spring? Have you ever noticed new grass growing in what had been almost bare ground? Did you ever see a green shoot start to develop from the eye of an old potato? If you answered yes to any of these questions, you've seen evidence of asexual reproduction. In each case, a new organism was produced from a single parent, with no new combination of genetic material. The tulip, the grass plants, and the sprouting potato are all genetically identical to the individual parents that produced them.

You'll find organisms that reproduce asexually in each of the five kingdoms. In fact, in monerans, asexual reproduction is the only method by which offspring are produced. Many other organisms can undergo either asexual or sexual reproduction, which involves the combining of two sets of genetic information. As you have seen in Chapter 16, plants have a life cycle in which there is an alternation of haploid and diploid generations. One generation reproduces by mitosis; the next generation reproduces by meiosis.

Reproduction by Splitting

There are several kinds of asexual reproduction. In one kind, the parent organism divides into two new offspring by splitting into two. Monerans normally reproduce by binary fission. In binary fission, the DNA in the parent cell duplicates, then the cell divides into two identical cells. Under ideal conditions, some monerans can divide into two new organisms every ten to 20 minutes. In unicellular protists such as *Amoeba* and *Euglena,* the process of asexual reproduction occurs by mitosis and cell division and takes several hours. First, the DNA in the nucleus duplicates, then the nuclear membrane breaks down, and eventually the cell divides into two.

Figure 18-1 Asexual reproduction by binary fission in prokaryotes (left, magnification: 30 000×) and by mitosis and cell division in unicellular eukaryotes such as *Paramecium* (right) results in offspring and parents with identical genetic information.

MEETING INDIVIDUAL NEEDS

Ask students to prepare a list that includes as many characteristics or traits associated with asexual reproduction as possible. Advise them to include any information that is also described in this section. **LEP**

STUDENT JOURNAL

Have students pretend they are a bacterium that is ready to start reproduction. They should describe their process of binary fission. Have them now pretend they are a *Euglena* and describe their asexual reproduction by mitosis and cell division. **LEP**

Cell division in the protist *Paramecium* is more complex because, as described in Chapter 15, it has two kinds of nuclei. The smaller micronucleus controls reproduction, while the large macronucleus controls other cellular processes.

Reproduction by Budding

A second method of asexual reproduction involves the growth and separation of a small part of a parent organism to form a new organism. In some organisms, a miniature and complete version of the parent grows out from the parent body, breaks off, and develops into an adult. In animals, such as *Hydra* and sea anemones, and in fungi, such as yeast, this process is called **budding.** In plants, this kind of asexual reproduction is called **vegetative reproduction.** For example, in strawberry plants, spider plants, and many kinds of grasses the new plants form at the end of thin, creeping stems that grow out from the parent plant. When the young plants become rooted to the ground, the stem that joins them to their parent eventually rots away. The new plants will then grow to be independent adult plants.

There are other forms of vegetative reproduction. Have you ever planted tulip bulbs, gladiolus corms, or potato tubers? Bulbs, corms, and tubers are food storage organs that allow a plant to survive over winter or during a drought. When the temperature and water supplies are good for growth, the organs begin to produce leaves. The food that is stored in the organs is used as an energy source for development of new parts such as stems and leaves. Food made during the growing season is stored in new underground storage organs at the end of the season. Many new bulbs, corms, or tubers are produced each year. If you have ever dug up bulbs, corms, or tubers, you may have noticed that you had more at the end of the season than what you planted in the spring. Your plants have reproduced by vegetative reproduction.

Figure 18-2 Miniature *Hydra* buds grow out from one parent (left). In a similar way, tiny *Gladiolus* corms form from a single parent during its growing season (right).

Minilab 1

What conditions favor budding in yeast?

Make two wet mounts, one from yeast in water and the other from yeast in water plus sugar. Note, only a very small drop of each is needed. Label the two slides accordingly. Examine each mount under the microscope. Using high power, look for signs of budding in the two mounts. Make diagrams of several cells from each slide. Label each diagram as with or without sugar.
Analysis   *What is budding? Which yeast cells have more buds? Explain why.*

Minilab 1

Purpose
Students will observe yeast cells and compare nutrient requirements for asexual reproduction.

Materials
Provide two yeast solutions for the class. For each group, provide a compound microscope, glass slides, coverslips, labels, lens paper, water, and medicine droppers.

Skills
use a microscope, make a wet mount, compare and contrast, observe and infer

Teaching Strategies
- **Safety Precautions:** Caution students to use care when handling the microscope and making wet mounts.
- Remind students to use very little of each solution in preparing their wet mounts and to stir the solution prior to drawing off a sample.
- **Troubleshooting:** If students have difficulty seeing individual cells under high power, their solutions are probably too dense with yeast cells. They should add a drop of water to further dilute and blot excess water with a paper towel.
- Review with students what a budding yeast cell may look like prior to their observations.

Expected Results
Students should see cells that are undergoing budding in the sugar solution but not in the plain water.

Answers
Budding is a process of asexual reproduction. New cells form from a parent cell, increase in size, and then break free. The slide with added sugar shows more budding. The sugar provides energy for reproduction.

✔ Assessment
Knowledge: Ask students to record their answers and diagrams in their journals.

PROGRAM RESOURCES

Teacher Classroom Resources
Study Guide, p. 103 `L1`
Concept Mapping, p. 18 `L1` `LEP`
Probing Levels of Life, Labs 42, 43, 44, pp. 110, 112, 115 `L2`
Color Transparency #20 `L1` `LEP`
    #21 `L2`
Investigating Living Systems, Labs 43, 44, 45, pp. 169, 171, 175 `L2`

MEETING INDIVIDUAL NEEDS

Have students design a table with three columns. Across the top are to be written *Type, Definition,* and *Example.* Under *Type,* they should write *budding* and *vegetative reproduction.* Ask for three examples of budding and three of vegetative reproduction. Definitions should be based on the information presented on this page. `L1` `LEP`

Demonstration

Use an iodine/potassium iodide solution to demonstrate the appearance and storage of starch in potato tubers. Add a few drops of I•KI solution to the exposed surface of the tuber. A blue-black color indicates a positive test for starch. This amyloid reaction may also be demonstrated on other storage organs such as bulbs and corms.

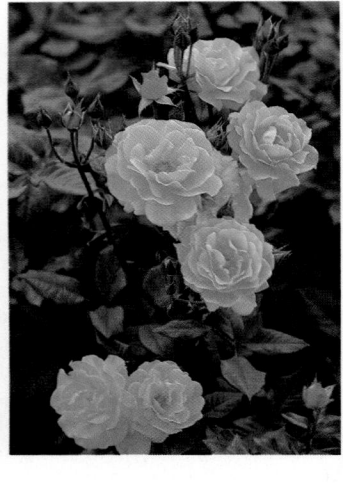

Figure 18-3 **Repair of damaged tissue is common to most organisms. In starfish (left), whole new arms can be regenerated. Regeneration of tissue helps a gardener to graft beautiful rose plants to the stems of disease-resistant rose plants (right).**

Reproduction by Fragmenting

A third kind of asexual reproduction is actually a form of repair to damaged or broken parts of organisms. Sometimes a small part of an organism breaks off, and the piece grows by mitosis to replace all the missing, major body tissues. In this process, called **fragmentation,** each small, broken piece of organism develops into a whole, new adult, exactly like its parent. For example, a sponge, planarian, or starfish can grow from a small fragment of a parent. The replacement or regrowth of missing parts is called **regeneration.** Planarians and starfishes show remarkable powers of regeneration as you can see in Figure 18-3. If a starfish is damaged by predators or harsh weather conditions, many of the broken pieces will often regenerate all the missing parts and eventually form a small population of starfishes, all exactly alike. When fragmentation occurs in a filamentous prokaryote, such as the cyanobacterium *Nostoc,* regeneration occurs by binary fission.

Gardeners often use the natural process of regeneration to form new plants artificially from small pieces of selected plants. One way to do this involves taking cuttings from a plant stem of the kind of plant you want to reproduce. If you place a stem cutting in moist sand, the piece of stem develops roots, which anchor the cutting and begin absorbing water and minerals. Other plant parts then develop by regeneration. In the same way, you can use roots, such as those of chrysanthemums, and leaves, such as those of begonias, for cuttings.

Many garden shrubs and fruit trees are artificially produced. For example, a cutting of a good fruit-producing tree is bound into a cut on the branch of a young branch or trunk of another tree that may be more resistant to disease. If this grafting process, in which the tissues of two stems of different but related plants regenerate and grow together, is successful, a shoot of the cutting will eventually produce healthy fruits. Apples, cherries, roses, and peaches are often reproduced in this artificial way.

3 Assess

Check for Understanding

Ask students to explain the correlation between these word pairs:
(a) asexual reproduction—mitosis
(b) splitting—binary fission
(c) budding—vegetative reproduction
(d) fragmentation—regeneration
(e) parthenogenesis—asexual reproduction L1 LEP

PROJECT

Regeneration: Have students cut a planarian into pieces to simulate fragmentation. Have them observe regeneration. Allow students to discover the problems encountered with attempting to grow the regenerated parts. L1

COOP LEARN

PORTFOLIO

Have students design a procedure to grow plants asexually from leaves or stem cuttings. Allow students to decide on the medium (water, soil, sand) in which to place the plant part. Have them use plant containers from discarded food products. Have them record data, write up their project, and place in their portfolios. L1

COOP LEARN

Spores and Parthenogenesis

The fourth method of asexual reproduction involves the production of spores. Spores are produced by a variety of organisms—algae, some protozoans, many fungi, and plants. Some spores are produced by mitosis; others by meiosis. Some are diploid (2n), whereas others are haploid (n). All spores have features in common. Each spore contains DNA and a small mass of cytoplasm surrounded by a tough outer wall. This wall protects the spore until it encounters conditions that are favorable for growth. It also prevents the contents within from drying out, an important adaptation for organisms that live on land. Some organisms produce and release large numbers of spores, which are carried far and wide by water currents or wind. Production of many spores and their dispersal further increases the chances that some spores will find suitable places for growth.

You've examined asexual reproduction in some simpler animals, plants, and monerans. More complex animals can undergo asexual reproduction too. For example, some insects, such as aphids and honeybees, may sometimes reproduce by means of parthenogenesis. During this process an unfertilized egg develops into an adult. For example, the queen honeybee lays both fertilized and unfertilized eggs. The fertilized eggs develop into females, mostly workers. The unfertilized haploid eggs become males called drones. The only function of drones appears to be that they mate with the queen.

Moss spores

Figure 18-4 **A queen bee (left) lays fertilized eggs that develop into workers (right), and unfertilized eggs that develop into drones (center) by parthenogenesis. Mosses are one kind of plant that reproduces by spores (above).**

Section Review

Understanding Concepts
1. Compare asexual reproduction in a bacterium and a unicellular alga.
2. How are fragmentation and budding similar? How are these two methods different?
3. Explain how the term *budding* could be applied to asexual reproduction of a flowering plant.

4. ***Skill Review—Forming a Hypothesis:*** You discover an enormous population of clover in your lawn and observe that the plants are all identical. You know that just two weeks ago there were only one or two clover plants. How could you explain the rapid increase in the production of clover? For

more help, see Practicing Scientific Methods in the **Skill Handbook.**
5. ***Thinking Critically:*** What trait of spores makes them more efficient than any other means of asexual reproduction?

Reteach
Ask each student to design a series of four questions from every major heading in this section. Have students exchange questions. They should answer the questions given to them and return the answers to the original question designer for grading. Discuss any questions that may have been answered incorrectly. **L1**

Extension
Have students determine the meaning of the word *clone*. Ask them how a clone fits the category of asexual reproduction and have them research how the technique is used. **L2**

✔ Assessment
Performance: Have students design an experimental procedure that will explain and illustrate the ability of some plants to produce new plants asexually from stem and leaf parts. **L1** **COOP LEARN**

4 Close

Discussion
Relate the story to your students of the fish farmers who were finding starfish in their oyster beds. Starfish feed on oysters. To destroy the starfish, the fish farmers would cut them up and throw them back into the ocean. Over time, the number of starfish exploded rather than diminished. Have students explain why and how they might have reduced the starfish population. **L1**

Answers to Section Review

1. In bacteria, prokaryotes, the process is binary fission. In an alga, asexual reproduction involves mitosis and cell division.
2. Fragmentation and budding are both means of asexual reproduction. In the former, a part of a parent organism breaks off and then the parent regenerates its missing part. In budding, a new organism develops from its parent and then breaks off as a complete organism.

3. Vegetative reproduction in a flowering plant is similar to budding in an animal. For example, plants such as strawberries and grasses develop as outgrowths from stems of the parent plant. They eventually become complete and separate plants as the stems that join them to the parent rot away.

4. **Skill Review—Forming a Hypothesis:** Because the plants are all identical, and two weeks seems too short a time for plants to grow from seeds, it can be assumed that they were produced asexually by vegetative reproduction.
5. **Thinking Critically:** Spores are produced in great numbers, are adapted to withstand harsh conditions, and are lightweight for easy dispersal.

Prepare

Key Concepts
The process of sexual reproduction is introduced. Examples of sexual reproduction are examined in monerans, protists, and fungi. Reproduction and the alternation of generations in plants is looked at in detail.

Key Terms
conjugation, ovules, pollination, endosperm

Materials
- Gather suitable materials to use as a food source for mold growth in the Investigation.
- Obtain male pine cones and either fern fronds with sori or moss with capsules for Minilab 2.
- Obtain slides of reproductive stages of *Paramecium*, *Spirogyra*, and *Hydra* for the Alternate Lab.

1 Focus

Objectives
The objectives are listed on the student page. Remind students to preview these objectives as a guide to this numbered section.

Discussion
Ask students if only animals form egg and sperm cells. Most will say that this is true. Point out that all organisms produce gametes. When one gamete fertilizes another that is much larger, they are distinguished by the terms *sperm* and *egg*.

Objectives

Compare conjugation in different organisms.

Explain the generalized life cycle of plants.

Relate the idea of alternation of generations to the life cycle of a typical flowering plant.

Figure 18-5 *Chlamydamonas* is a unicellular green alga with one cup-shaped chloroplast (left, magnification: 500×). Sexual reproduction is by conjugation (right).

18.2 Sexual Reproduction

In the previous section, you studied different means of asexual reproduction. You saw how to get new potatoes from an old potato and how two starfishes develop from one. You know that new plants can develop from shoots of mature plants, and that spores help many organisms reproduce asexually. While all these organisms may undergo asexual reproduction, they are also capable of reproducing sexually.

Conjugation

Whereas asexual reproduction is a splitting process that always involves one parent, sexual reproduction is the fusion of two different sets of DNA. Over evolutionary time, sexual reproduction has become the major form of reproduction among organisms. Although there are differing views on how it first evolved, the reason that sexual reproduction has become more common is generally agreed upon. When two different sets of DNA fuse, genetic recombination occurs, resulting in variety among offspring. As you learned in Chapter 12, variations are the raw materials for adaptation and evolution. With the exception of monerans, almost all forms of life are capable of some means of sexual reproduction.

Conjugation in Algae   Most kinds of organisms reproduce by fusion of two kinds of gametes, eggs and sperm. During the process of fertilization, a zygote is formed. Eggs are often much larger in size than sperm. In most algae, sexual reproduction is by the fusion of two gametes that are similar in size. However, in a few algae, there are different mating strains that come together and form connecting tubes through which genetic material is transferred. The sexual process by which genetic material is transferred from one cell to another by cell-to-cell contact is called **conjugation**. During conjugation, the DNA of the two strains of an alga is combined.

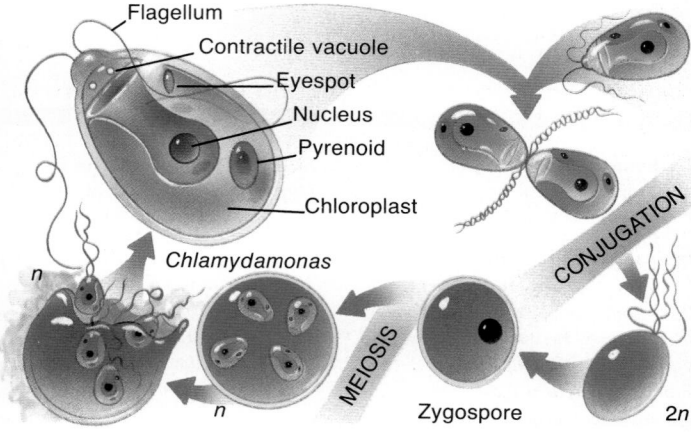

ALTERNATE LAB: Reproduction

Purpose
Students will compare the reproductive methods used by a variety of organisms.

Materials
microscope, hand lens, prepared slides of *Paramecium* undergoing (a) fission and (b) conjugation, prepared slides of *Spirogyra* undergoing conjugation, prepared slides of *Hydra* with (a) buds and (b) either spermaries or ovaries

Procedure
Give the following directions to students.
1. Observe different slides of *Paramecium* that show either no reproduction, fission, or conjugation.
2. Diagram all three stages. Construct a data table to record data.
3. Observe different slides of *Spirogyra* that show no reproduction or conjugation.
4. Diagram the two examples.
5. Observe slides of *Hydra* with a hand lens. One shows no reproduction occurring, another shows budding, the third shows either spermaries or ovaries.
6. Diagram the three examples.

Analysis
Ask students to answer the following.
1. Explain how, during reproduction,

Figure 18-6 The bread mold *Rhizopus* is a mass of fine hyphae that can reproduce asexually by spores or sexually by conjugation.

Sporangia / Spores / ASEXUAL REPRODUCTION / + mating type (n) / Hypha / Hypha / mating type (n) / SEXUAL REPRODUCTION / CONJUGATION / Zygospore (2n) / MEIOSIS

Conjugation in Fungi Conjugation can also be seen in fungi, such as the *Rhizopus* shown in Figure 18-6. Conjugation in this bread mold occurs between different types of hyphae, often labeled *plus* and *minus*. The many nuclei in fungal hyphae are all haploid (*n*). The plus and minus hyphae don't look different, but chemicals produced by each type of hypha cause them to be attracted to each other. Many nuclei acting as gametes move into the tip of each branch. Then, a cell wall forms behind the nuclei. The walls between the tips of the branches join and break down, allowing pairs of gametes to come together and fuse. The result is numerous diploid (2*n*) zygotes. A tough outer wall then develops around all the zygotes and forms a single zygospore.

Zygospores are adapted to extreme temperatures or dry conditions. After a period of dormancy, however, all but one of the zygotes breaks down. The remaining zygote undergoes meiosis, producing four haploid (*n*) spores. In turn, three of these spores die. The surviving spore develops a new hypha with a terminal sporangium and many asexual spores, which eventually produce new plus or minus strains of *Rhizopus*.

Conjugation in Bacteria Although bacteria have not been observed to reproduce sexually, a few bacteria are known to transfer genetic material from one cell to another in conjugation. As in bread mold, there are two different mating types that can be called plus and minus.

Only plus and minus bacteria can conjugate. During conjugation, a bridge of cytoplasm forms between the two bacteria. A plasmid moves from the plus cell through the bridge and into the minus cell. Therefore, the minus cell has received genes it did not have before, and it now becomes a plus cell. Genetic recombination has occurred, but not reproduction because there has been no increase in the number of cells. However, bacteria receiving genes from other bacteria can pass those genes on to offspring via binary fission.

Figure 18-7 Bacteria exchange genetic material by forming connecting bridges of cytoplasm.

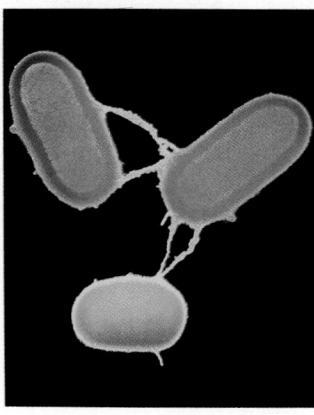

2 Teach

Using Science Terms
Have students look up the Latin meaning of the term *conjugate*. Ask them to relate it to the way the term is used with algae. **L1**

Reinforcement
Review the meaning of the terms *haploid* and *diploid*. Ask how these terms relate to chromosomes within a cell. Also review the significance of the use of *n* and 2*n*. Ask the following questions to test their understanding. A cell has a 2*n* number of 40. What is its haploid number? *20* A cell has an *n* number of 14. What does this mean if you could count its chromosomes? *Haploid cells would have 14 chromosomes.* What would be the diploid number for this cell? *28* **L1**

Using the Illustration
Refer students to Figure 18-6 and have them answer the following questions: (a) Are the spores formed from the zygospore and the sporangia *n* or 2*n*? *They are both* n. (b) What cell process preceded the forming of these spores? *meiosis* (c) If the zygospore is diploid, what must this tell you about the chromosome number of both mating types? *Both are haploid.* (d) Why are four spores produced by a zygote? *Four cells result from meiosis.* **L1** **LEP**

Brainstorming
Ask students to compare the functions of zygospores and bacterial endospores. **L1**

Paramecium cells differ in appearance from cells not undergoing reproduction. *Two cells are seen attached end to end with splitting; two cells appear side by side in conjugation.*

2. Explain how *Spirogyra* appear during conjugation. *Two strands lie side by side and join up.*

3. Explain the appearance of *Hydra* undergoing budding and forming either spermaries

or ovaries. *A bud appears as a small animal attached to the parent, whereas a spermary or ovary appears as a small bump on the side of the parent.*

✔ Assessment
What evidence do you have that asexual reproduction occurs in different kingdoms? What evidence do you have that sexual reproduction is not limited to one kingdom?

SECTION 18.2

INVESTIGATION

Growing Bread Mold

Time Allotment
1 class period

Objectives
Upon completing this investigation, students will be able to:
- identify mold growth.
- identify those conditions that promote spore growth of mold.
- compare data between groups and offer explanations for any difference in forming conclusions.

Skills
design an experiment, separate and control variables, make and use tables, compare and contrast, measure in SI, recognize cause and effect, work cooperatively in groups

Materials
mold source; water; cotton swabs; petri dishes; plastic bags with seals; commercial mildew inhibitor sprays; hand lens; bread with preservatives; bread without preservatives; alternate food sources for mold such as raw slices of potatoes, cooked rice, and oatmeal; plastic grids; marking pencils; graduated cylinder; incubator; refrigerator

Preparation
Bread mold is easily grown in preparation for this lab as follows: At least a week prior to the start of this lab, place a slice of any type of bread into a petri dish. Rub a moist cotton swab along the soil outdoors. Moisten the bread with water. Then, rub the cotton swab along the bread's surface. Cover the dish and store at room temperature. Mold growth should appear within two or three days. Alternate mold source—rub a moist cotton swab along the base of an onion that shows black spots near roots. Spots (spores) may be inside the first layer of onion skin.

Possible Hypotheses
1. A refrigerator should reduce or prevent growth of spores.
2. Food sources with added water will show more growth of mold.

Plant Life Cycles

You've learned that plants reproduce asexually in a number of ways. Perhaps you already know that plants can also reproduce sexually with male and female gametes. You may recall from Chapter 16 that plants have a life cycle in which a gametophyte stage and a sporophyte stage alternate. The two stages make up two generations of plants. One generation is haploid (n) and produces gametes and the other generation is diploid ($2n$) and produces spores.

How exactly does the alternation of generations occur? Figure 18-8 shows the life cycle in a flowering plant. You will remember from Chapter 16 that during the gametophyte stage of the cycle, the plant is haploid. Its cells have one of each pair of chromosomes. Through mitosis, it produces eggs and sperm that also have half the normal number. Two gametes, produced from one or two parent plants, fuse to form a zygote, which develops into the next, or sporophyte, stage of the plant life cycle.

The sporophyte stage is diploid because its cells have two of each kind of chromosomes. Through meiosis, the sporophyte produces spores, each with half the number of chromosomes. The spores develop into new gametophyte plants and the plant life cycle continues.

INVESTIGATION

Growing Bread Mold

Magnification: 12×

Spores are reproductive cells that germinate under proper conditions to form new offspring. Spores are a common means of reproduction in fungi, protists, and some kinds of plants, such as mosses. The air is full of spores. Many are so small, they may seem like nothing more than dust particles. Not all spores find suitable conditions to grow, which probably accounts for the fact that the world is not covered in mold!

Mold spores are easily grown from the bread mold fungus *Rhizopus nigricans*. The spores give the mold its characteristic black color. Spores may be collected from a parent fungus with a damp cotton-tipped swab.

Problem
What conditions are best for the germination and growth of mold spores?

Safety Precautions
Wash your hands after handling fungi. Dispose of mold growths according to your teacher's directions.

Hypothesis
Working in groups, develop a hypothesis that could be tested to demonstrate the most suitable conditions for spore growth in bread mold.

Experimental Plan
1. Agree upon a way to test your two variables. Keep in mind the available materials.

Possible Procedures
- Different conditions in which to test mold growth could be dry versus moist, warm versus cold, light versus dark, food substrate with mold retardants versus food substrate with no retardants, different kinds of foods, or use of commercial mold or mildew inhibitor versus no commercial inhibitor.

Teaching Strategies
- To make a grid for measuring mold growth area, prepare a pencil diagram of a grid using lines spaced 2.5 mm apart. Make copies as if for a transparency.

Data and Observations
Examine student data tables for recordings of observations that compare mold growth in contrasting conditions.

Data Analysis
1. Student answers will vary. An example might be that if warm temperatures speed up mold germination and growth, then spores kept in a warm environment will show more growth than those kept in a cool

Mature sporophyte

Embryo

Flower

Zygote

Diploid generation (2n)

MEIOSIS

FERTILIZATION

Haploid generation (n)

Megaspore

Egg — Female gametophyte

Sperm — Male gametophyte

Microspore

Figure 18-8 The alternation of sporophyte and gametophyte generations is typical for all plants. What two cell processes separate the two generations?

Figure Caption Question
What two cell processes separate the two generations? meiosis and mitosis

environment. A student might test this by using two dishes containing the same food and moisture. Spores are added to both dishes. One dish is kept at room temperature while the other is placed in a refrigerator.

2. Student answers will vary. An example might be that the amount of food and type of food should be the same, amount of water added to each dish and amount of mold spores should be the same in both dishes. If one is placed in a refrigerator, then the other dish should be placed in the dark at room temperature because it is dark inside a refrigerator. Student answers may vary. For example, two dishes receiving no mold spores but receiving the same food and moisture as the others should be placed one in the refrigerator and one at room temperature.

3. An example could be no growth in a control dish at room temperature after eight days, and 80 cm^2 of growth in the experiment at room temperature.

4. Student answers will vary. For example, warm temperature tends to speed up germination and growth of *Rhizopus nigricans*.

5. Student answers will vary. For example, another group may have placed one dish in an incubator at 38°C. The growth in the dish at 38°C may be more rapid than in the dish at room temperature. A group's conclusions may agree with another group's; however, more extensive mold growth may be due to the other group following a different procedure.

6. Answers will be similar to the examples given for 1 through 5.

2. Determine how many spore samples you will need.
3. Remember to test only one variable at a time and use suitable controls for each condition.
4. List the conditions for possible mold growth.
5. Choose the conditions you wish to use to test mold growth.
6. Record your procedure and list materials that you will need.

Checking the Plan

1. Be aware of other possible variables that will have to be controlled.
2. What will be your control?
3. What quantitative data will you collect and how will you record these data?
4. How long will you allow the experiment to run?

5. How many trials will be used to test each variable?
6. Assign roles for your plan.

Make sure your teacher has approved your experimental plan before you proceed further.

Data and Observations

Carry out your experiment and develop a table to record your data.

Analysis and Conclusions

1. State your hypothesis. Describe the way in which your first variable was tested.
2. Which variables had to be controlled? What was your control?
3. Use quantitative data to compare the control group and the experimental group.
4. Based on your answer from

question 3, draw a conclusion for how the condition being tested influenced mold growth of *Rhizopus nigricans*.
5. Locate another group in your class that tested the same condition. How did their procedure differ from your group's? How did their data differ and how did their conclusions differ? Explain a possible reason for any differences.
6. Repeat questions 1-5 for your second variable being tested.

Going Further

Based on this lab experience, design an experiment that would determine the conditions of growth for yeast cells. Assume that you will have limited resources and will be conducting the lab in class.

Extensions

Students could use a different mold such as *Penicillium* from an orange. They might wish to treat the food source with different acids or bases to determine the effect of pH on germination and growth of mold spores. Some students could experiment with spores from ferns or moss plants.

✔ Assessment

Portfolio: Ask students to write a summary of their findings for their portfolios. Ask them to offer suggestions for making various food products less susceptible to spoilage from mold growth.

Minilab 2

Purpose
Students will compare the structure and function of spores and pollen.

Skills
use a microscope, make a wet mount, make and use tables, compare and contrast, observe and infer

Materials
male pine cone—fresh or preserved, fern frond with mature sori—fresh or preserved, moss with sporophyte capsule, microscope, glass slides, coverslips, tweezers, lens paper

Teaching Strategies
- **Safety Precautions:** Caution students to use care when handling the microscope and making wet mounts.
- Wet mounts of pine pollen are easily prepared by pulling off one small microsporophyll with tweezers and mashing the contents of the sac (microsporangium) under a coverslip and slide.
- Fern sori can be picked off and mashed under a coverslip.

Expected Results
Pine pollen—large reproductive cell with wings or air bladders, will form sperm nuclei; Fern spore—reproductive cell, smaller than pine pollen, rough coat, will form fern prothallus; Moss spore—reproductive cell, smaller than fern spore, rough coat, will form a moss protonema.

Answers
All cells are formed by meiosis, are haploid in chromosome number, and each is part of the gametophyte generation.

✔ Assessment
Skill: Provide students with anthers from a flower. Have students identify the type of cell present within the anther. They will have to prepare wet mounts of the tissue, squash it, and observe under the microscope. Although the cells they observe may be young microspores, students will probably identify them as pollen grains.

Minilab 2

How do spores and pollen compare?

Obtain a male pine cone, and a fern frond with sporangia, or a moss with capsules. Prepare wet mounts of pine pollen and fern or moss spores. Observe each cell type under a microscope and make diagrams of each. Prepare a data table that compares structure and function for pollen and spores. Use your text to include the following information.

Analysis *By what process is each cell formed? Is each cell type haploid or diploid? Is each cell a part of a sporophyte or gametophyte generation?*

The relative importance of gametophyte and sporophyte generations varies from one type of plant to another. For example, mosses spend more time in the haploid gametophyte stage; following fertilization, the diploid sporophyte grows out from the body tissues of the gametophyte parent and lives for just a short time. As vascular plants evolved more complex tissues and systems, the diploid sporophyte became predominant and the haploid gametophyte became short lived, nonvascular, and quite small. In seed plants, which you'll examine shortly, the gametophyte is short lived and consists of only a few cells embedded within the sporophyte.

What advantage is there to a life cycle spent mostly in the diploid sporophyte stage? Remember that haploid organisms have just one allele for each trait, but diploid organisms have two. The presence of two alleles has several advantages. First, the effect of a harmful or lethal allele can be masked if it is recessive. Second, a greater variety of phenotypes can be expressed with two alleles for each trait as, for example, in incomplete dominance, codominance, and multiple genes. Having a greater number of phenotypes provides greater opportunities for differences upon which natural selection can act.

Life Cycle of a Flowering Plant

When you look at a flowering plant, you are observing a sporophyte. All of its many parts—roots, stem, leaves, and flowers—are composed of diploid cells. Recall from Chapter 16 that the flower is the organ of reproduction in these plants.

Figure 18-9 The female gametophyte in a flowering plant develops from the single-celled megaspore. The gametes form in each ovule of a flower.

Gametes in a Flower   Keep in mind that all the parts of a flower are composed of diploid cells. Cell divisions in the anthers and ovaries of a flower lead to the production of spores. Look at Figures 18-9 and 18-10 as you read how eggs and sperm of flowering plants are produced.

Meiotic cell divisions occur within the ovary. You have read in Chapter 16 that the ovary is the structure in the pistil where the seeds are eventually formed. Within the ovary are one or more **ovules** that will one day become seeds if fertilization occurs. A diploid cell in the ovule divides by meiosis to produce four haploid spores. However, only one large spore—a megaspore—survives. Within this megaspore, the nucleus then divides by mitosis to form two haploid nuclei. Mitosis continues until a total of eight haploid nuclei are produced. These nuclei and the cytoplasm around them form the embryo sac or female gametophyte. Eventually, one of the nuclei becomes an egg cell. Two others move to the center of the embryo sac, and a membrane forms around them.

Within each anther, diploid cells also divide by meiosis to produce four small haploid cells known as microspores. Within each microspore, the nucleus then divides by mitosis to form two haploid nuclei; one becomes the nucleus that will help the growth of a pollen tube into the stigma, and the other divides to form two sperm. The three cells of the microspore make up the male gametophyte. When the outer wall of the microspore hardens, the structure becomes a pollen grain. The walls of pollen grains have beautifully intricate patterns that can be used to identify individual species of plants.

Flower

Anther

Diploid cell

Meiosis

Microspores (*n*)

Mitosis

Mitosis of one nucleus

Two haploid nuclei

Pollen grains released

Haploid tube cell

Hard coat

Haploid sperm cells

Pollen grain

Figure 18-10   The male gametophyte of a flowering plant develops from a single microspore in the anthers of stamens. One pollen grain (right) develops from each male gametophyte.

18.2 SEXUAL REPRODUCTION **493**

Concept Development
Review the following important ideas with your students.
(a) Why is the sporophyte generation so named or what type of reproductive cells does it form? *It produces spores.*
(b) Why is the gametophyte generation so named or what type of reproductive cells does it form? *It produces gametes.*
(c) Meiosis usually results directly in the formation of sex cells in animals. Is this also the case for plants? *No, meiosis in plants results first in spores.*
(d) In animals, the diploid organism produces sperm and egg via meiosis. In plants, the diploid generation produces what type of cell and by what process? *The diploid generation produces spores by meiosis.* **L1**

Microscope Activity
Prepared slides of cross sections of flowers showing megaspore and embryo sac development are available. Slides of pollen development are also available. **L1**

Reinforcement
Mitosis occurs within the embryo sac to form a total of eight nuclei. Have students determine the number of divisions that must take place to form these cells from the original one cell. **L1**

MEETING INDIVIDUAL NEEDS

- Have students diagram a vertical cross section of a flower. The diagram should indicate all major flower parts and should also show cutaway sections through the anther and ovary. The anther should indicate pollen cells and the ovary should indicate ovules. Have students label all parts. **L2**
- Have students working at average or below grade level prepare an outline that indicates the steps that take place within an ovule as it becomes an embryo sac. Have them also prepare an outline of the steps that take place within the anther as pollen grains are formed. **L1**

Misconception

Hay fever sounds as if it is a disease caused by hay. Ask students who suffer from the disorder the real meaning of hay fever. They should be able to tell the rest of the class that it is an allergic reaction to pollen. Typically, it is pollen from ragweed or other weeds rather than from hay itself that the student is allergic to. Ask students when the "hay fever season" occurs. It correlates with the time of the year when plants are reproducing and shedding their pollen into the air. Typically, this occurs in early fall, also the time of harvesting. To help resolve the misconception, ask students to prepare wet mounts of the anthers of almost any flower. Their field of view will be loaded with microscopic pollen cells, the culprits in hay fever.

PHYSICS CONNECTION

Ultraviolet Light: Bees can see ultraviolet light and therefore can detect markings on flowers that humans are unable to see. Review the electromagnetic spectrum with students. The range of visible light extends from wavelengths of 0.4 to 0.7 millimicrons. UV radiation is between 0.2 and 0.4. Have students correlate UV with being on either the "short" or the "long" end of the spectrum. L2

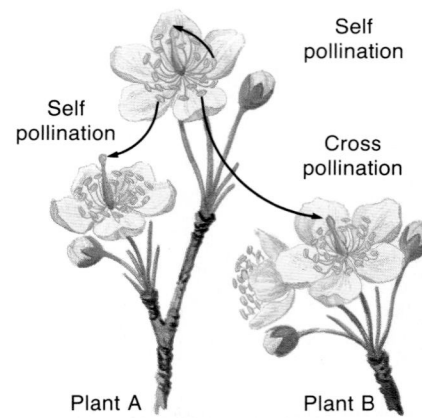

Figure 18-11   When pollen is transferred from one plant to another in cross-pollination, genetic material is exchanged. Self-pollination involves the genetic material of one parent.

The three nuclei of the ovule and the two sperm nuclei of the pollen all contribute to the fertilization of a flowering plant, as you will read about next.

Pollination   In order for plants to reproduce sexually, the gametes in a pollen grain and an ovule must meet and fuse. The pollen grain must first be transferred from an anther of a stamen to the stigma of a pistil. This transfer is called **pollination.**

It is possible that a plant that has flowers with both male and female sex organs can be pollinated by its own pollen. This self-pollination can occur in a single flower or between two flowers on the same plant, as shown in Figure 18-11. On the other hand, cross-pollination occurs when the pollen from one plant is transferred to the stigma of another plant. Both self- and cross-pollination involve genetic recombination; however, cross-pollination results in more variety in the offspring because the two gametes come from different parents.

How is pollen transferred? In some cases, insects are the pollinators. The rugged walls of pollen grains and the hairy bodies of insects will often easily stick together. Pollen grains on the body of an insect that visits a new flower may then be transferred to the sticky or rough stigma as the insect passes over. In flowers that are pollinated by insects, the petals are often large, attractively colored, or scented. The flowers that are not showy are usually pollinated by wind or flies. In wind-pollinated flowers, there is often an abundant production of pollen. In fly-pollinated flowers, the flowers often have the smell of rotting meat. Other flowers are pollinated by birds, bats, and even mice.

Once pollination occurs and one or more pollen grains land and stick on a stigma, each grain begins to grow. The tube nucleus leads the growth of a pollen tube from one end of the pollen grain. The tube grows through the tissue of the style and heads toward an ovule within the ovary. The

Thinking Lab

INTERPRET THE DATA

How can you determine chromosome numbers in plants?

Background
In the plant kingdom, a pattern of reproduction occurs that is called alternation of generations. Each generation looks different and serves different functions. *Sporophyte* generations form *spores* by meiosis while *gametophyte* generations form *gametes* by mitosis. Spores form directly into gametophytes. Gametophytes always form sporo-

phytes after gametes fuse at fertilization. Sporophyte generations are always diploid while gametophyte generations are always haploid.

You Try It
Examine the table shown here. Information is provided for four plants, A to D. **Interpret the data** and fill in any of the missing chromosome numbers.

	Chromosome numbers			
	Sporophyte	Gametophyte	Spore	Gamete
A	20	■	■	■
B	■	■	12	■
C	■	■	■	8
D	■	34	■	■

Thinking Lab

INTERPRET THE DATA

Purpose
Students will correlate the processes of mitosis and meiosis with the events occurring in plant life cycles.

Skills
make and use tables, calculate, sequence, concept mapping, recognize cause and effect

Teaching Strategies
• Review the typical life cycle of an animal

first, with emphasis on the diploid generation forming gametes directly via meiosis. In plants, however, an extra event or stage occurs that requires the gametophyte generation to form gametes via mitosis.

✔ **Assessment**
Knowledge: Have students make a concept map of a typical life cycle for a plant.

Answers

Chromosome Numbers			
Sporo-phyte	Gameto-phyte	Spore	Gamete
A	20	10	10	10
B	24	12	12	12
C	16	8	8	8
D	68	34	34	34

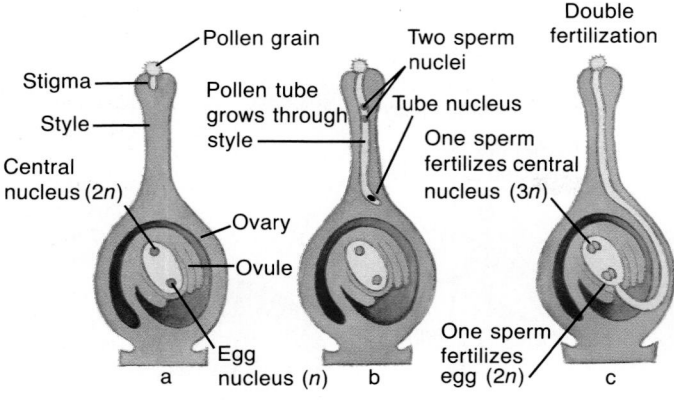

Stigma —
Style —
Central nucleus (2n) —
— Pollen grain
— Ovary
— Ovule
— Egg nucleus (n)

Pollen tube grows through style
Two sperm nuclei
— Tube nucleus

Double fertilization
One sperm fertilizes central nucleus (3n)
One sperm fertilizes egg (2n)

a   b   c

two sperm nuclei follow the tube nucleus down the pollen tube and through a small opening into the ovule.

Double Fertilization   Within an ovule, one of the sperm nuclei fuses with the two nuclei in the center of the ovule, forming a triploid (3n) nucleus that eventually develops into a food supply for the new plant. The other sperm nucleus fertilizes the egg to form a zygote. This double fertilization is typical for all flowering plants. Zygote formation marks the beginning of a new diploid sporophyte generation.

The triploid nucleus divides many times to form a mass of tissue called the **endosperm**. Endosperm is the food source that provides energy for the new plant's early development. The outer covering of the ovule hardens into a protective coat. At this point, the ovule has become a young seed. The seed contains an embryo sporophyte plant and the food source needed for its early growth.

Fruits: Nature's Way of Dispersal

Soon after fertilization, most of the flower parts of the parent plant begin to die. However, the ovary, in which the developing seeds are located, enlarges rapidly. The enlarged ovary becomes the fruit. You're certainly familiar with fleshy sweet fruits, such as oranges, apples, grapes, and peaches. Many of the plant foods you call vegetables are actually fruits, too—tomatoes, green beans, corn, and cucumbers. You will realize from this list that sometimes fruits are not all fleshy, and that some have only one seed. Besides corn, other grains such as wheat, rice, and oats are single-seeded, dry fruits. Flowering plants can be identified just by examining the forms of their fruits.

Figure 18-12   **Each seed in a flowering plant results from double fertilization within the female gametophyte (left). Without insects, the majority of flowering plants would not be pollinated (right).**

Figure 18-13   **Many fruits, such as cereal grains, and a variety of nuts have a dry, not fleshy, wall and hold only one seed.**

18.2 SEXUAL REPRODUCTION **495**

Discussion
Discuss the following ideas with your students.
1. Go over the use of the term *double fertilization.* Point out that the same egg cell is not fertilized twice.
2. What is the function of an endosperm? *a food supply for the plant embryo*
3. What will develop from a fertilized ovule? *a seed*
4. What will develop from a newly formed seed? *a new plant* L1

Brainstorming
Small white seeds are often found in a watermelon. They contrast sharply with the large black seeds that are often so numerous. Ask students to infer what the white seeds are. *unfertilized ovules* Ask students, what general statement can be made about the number of pollen cells needed on the stigma of the watermelon flower in relation to the number of black seeds within the watermelon fruit? *A large number, equal to the number of seeds, would be necessary.* L1

3 Assess

Check for Understanding
Ask students to explain: (a) the role of sexual reproduction in organisms and how it differs from asexual reproduction. *Sexual reproduction provides for genetic variation from two parents, whereas asexual reproduction requires only one parent and therefore does not result in genetic variation.* (b) what type of cell was responsible for forming sporophyte generations and what type of cell they will in turn form. *A zygote forms a sporophyte, which in turn forms haploid spores.* (c) what type of cell was responsible for forming gametophyte generations and what type of cell they will in turn form. *A spore forms a gametophyte, which in turn forms haploid gametes.* L1

Reteach

Have students create questions that are related to the section. Give each student a chance to answer at least one question. LEP   COOP LEARN

Extension

Have students trace the gradual changes in size of gametophyte and sporophyte generations that occur as one moves through the plant kingdom from mosses to ferns to flowering plants. L1

✔ Assessment

Portfolio: Have students create two concept maps that describe the events associated with megaspore and microspore formation. L1

4 Close

Demonstration

Bring several fruits into class. Examples might be avocados, watermelons, plums, squash, string beans, tomatoes, and peanuts within their shells. Ask students to classify them as either fruits or vegetables or neither. Once their categories have been determined, cut each one open to reveal the seeds protected within the fruit wall. Ask students to reclassify them again into the original categories. L1   COOP LEARN

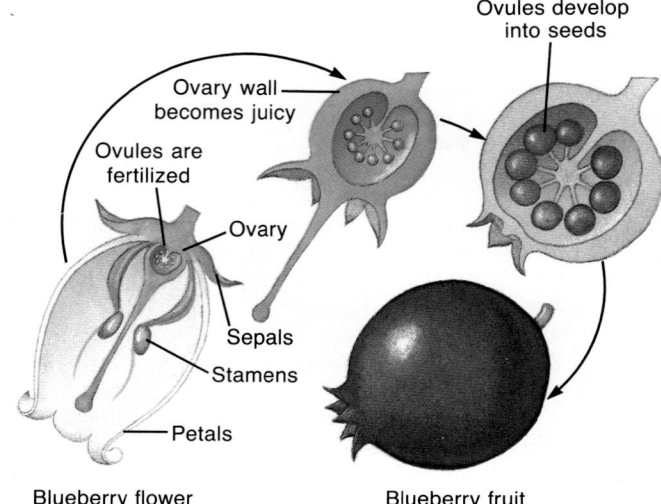

Figure 18-14 The fleshy tissue of a fruit usually develops from the wall of the ovary as shown here in a blueberry. The seeds develop from each fertilized ovule.

Ovules develop into seeds

Ovary wall becomes juicy

Ovules are fertilized

Ovary

Sepals

Stamens

Petals

Blueberry flower

Blueberry fruit

Fruits initially protect the seeds, but they are also important in dispersing seeds. Many fruits are eaten by animals. The hard seeds pass unharmed through the digestive systems and are deposited in the animal's wastes away from the parent plant. Animals that gather nuts may drop and lose many of these dry fruits. The nuts, such as acorns, will then grow away from the parent plant. Some fruits have their own dispersal mechanisms. For example, when seeds of the squirting cucumber are ripe, the pressure inside the cylindrical fruit builds up until the end wall explodes. The seeds are shot out over great distances. The winged fruits of maples, dandelions, and elms are carried by wind. Other fruits, such as water lily nuts, float away from the parent plant. Still others with hooks will stick to clothes of humans or the fur of passing animals. Dispersal of seeds is important. If seeds began to germinate in the shadow of the parent plants, they would need to compete with the parents for sunlight, oxygen, carbon dioxide, and water. Dispersal of fruits and seeds reduces this competition.

Section Review

Understanding Concepts

1. In what ways are conjugation in bacteria and bread mold similar? How are they different?
2. How is the life cycle of a moss different from that of a dandelion?

3. Explain why the gametophyte generation of a flowering plant cannot become an independent plant.
4. **Skill Review—Sequencing:** Sequence the series of events from pollination through seed formation.

For more help, see Organizing Information in the **Skill Handbook.**
5. **Thinking Critically:** Why are seeds good food sources for humans and other animals?

496 🐾 REPRODUCTION

Answers to Section Review

1. In both cases, genetic recombination occurs between two organisms. Conjugation in bacteria does not result in reproduction because no new bacteria are reproduced. In a bread mold, offspring are produced.
2. In moss, the gametophyte is predominant, the sporophyte produces spores and then dies. In a dandelion, the sporophyte is predominant. The gametophyte never

develops into an independent plant.
3. The gametophyte is modified such that certain nuclei or cells become gametes.
4. **Skill Review—Sequencing:** (1) pollen grain lands on stigma; (2) pollen tube grows; (3) sperm nuclei move down pollen tube toward ovule; (4) sperm nuclei enter ovule; (5) one sperm nucleus fertilizes the egg, forming a diploid zygote; (6) other sperm nucleus fuses

with other two nuclei in ovule, forming a triploid cell; (7) zygote develops into embryo of new sporophyte; (8) triploid cell develops into endosperm; (9) wall of ovule forms seed coat.
5. **Thinking Critically:** The endosperm, which is an energy source needed for early development of the sporophyte, is also a suitable energy source for consumers.

18.3 Sexual Reproduction in Animals

You've learned about the intriguing life cycle of plants in which diploid and haploid stages alternate. Is the same true of the bird outside the window, your family's pet dog, and other members of the animal kingdom? The answer is no. Life cycles of animals differ in several ways from those of plants. Unlike plants, animals have a life cycle in which there is no alternation of haploid and diploid generations. For almost all animals, the organism is always diploid. Only an animal's gametes are haploid. As you've already learned, simpler animals such as sponges may reproduce either asexually or sexually. In more complex forms, though, sexual reproduction is predominant.

Fertilization

In animals, as in plants, gametes are produced in sex organs. Sperm are produced from cells of **testes,** and, just as in plants, eggs are produced from cells within ovaries. Among many simpler animals, both kinds of sex organs develop in the same individual. These animals are called **hermaphrodites.** However, as animals became more complex over time, separate sexes—males and females—became more usual. Why would separate sexes be an adaptation? For the same reason you learned cross-pollination in plants was adaptively beneficial, the fusion of DNA from two separate parents leads to more variation among the offspring. As you know from Chapter 12, variation is necessary for adaptation and evolution to occur. For the most part, in hermaphrodites, such as earthworms and clams, two different parents exchange gametes.

Figure 18-15 **This young elephant developed within the body of its mother after the fusion of male and female gametes from separate parents.**

Objectives

Distinguish between external and internal fertilization in animals.

Relate human reproductive structures to functions in females and males.

Compare estrus in mammals with the menstrual cycle in humans.

Concept Development

Ask students if they can explain why frogs "croak." Most will not be aware of the connection between reproduction and vocalizations in animals. The male frog croaks to attract a female. Have students think of other kinds of mating calls. **L1**

PHYSICS CONNECTION

Lake Temperatures: Temperatures of bodies of water vary depending on their geographic location, depth of the water, turnover of the water, and season of the year. The Great Lakes can be used as an example. In the summer, water surface temperatures may reach 22°C, forming a narrow band at the surface called the epilimnion. This upper band lies above a second layer of rapidly changing temperatures called the thermocline. Temperatures drop from 21°C to 8°C in just a few meters. Below the thermocline, temperatures may level off at about 7°C in the widest band, called the hypolimnion. By contrast, in winter, the temperature of the Great Lakes' water may vary from 0°C at the surface (below the ice cover) to only 4°C at the lake bottom.

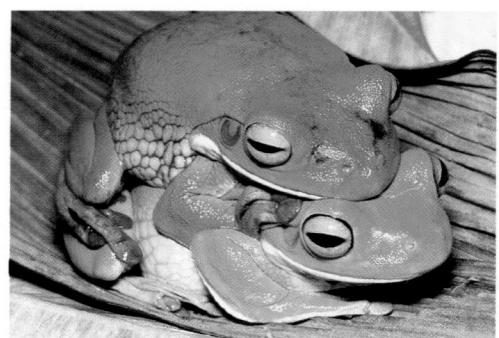

Figure 18-16 Mating behaviors in animals can ensure the fertilization of eggs even though this occurs outside the parent's body.

Successful sexual reproduction in animals first depends on fertilization of the egg by a sperm. In animals such as sponges, cnidarians, most worms, and many fishes and amphibians, fertilization occurs outside the female. But in insects, reptiles, birds, mammals, and some fishes and amphibians, fertilization occurs within the female. Do you remember from Chapter 17 that the evolution of internal fertilization was an adaptation that may have helped animals to survive on land?

Whether external or internal, fertilization is no sure thing. Because gametes are delicate, they must be protected. The life span of gametes is short; therefore, the timing of their release must be matched so that both sperm and eggs are present together. Also, because sperm and eggs would dehydrate in a dry environment, they must remain in a moist environment. A liquid medium is also important for another reason—for sperm to be able to swim to an egg. Animals have a variety of adaptations that ensure fertilization.

External Fertilization   In general, animals with external fertilization meet the need for moisture by reproducing in water. But an ocean, a lake, or even a pond is a vast amount of water and is full of risk and danger. The chances of sperm finding eggs are decreased in so large a volume of water. In addition, exposed eggs may be eaten by other animals. Unfavorable physical factors such as lack of oxygen, extreme temperatures, and pollutants may destroy the gametes. How, then, do these animals survive? Animals with external fertilization release huge numbers of

---

HEALTH CONNECTION

Fetal Alcohol Syndrome

Seven-year-old Jason has lots of friends. He is outgoing, loving, and very energetic. Unfortunately, he is off to a poor start at school because he has trouble remembering his numbers and letters and he can't pay attention to his work for as long as most children his age. Jason's problems are not really his fault; they're his mother's.

Jason's mother loves him very much. She was thrilled when she found out she was going to have a baby. Her pregnancy was a time of celebration, including parties with beer, wine, and other alcoholic drinks. Although she never drank enough to get drunk, she unknowingly did damage to Jason. She didn't realize that alcohol crossed over into her developing baby's blood.

Fortunately for Jason, his symptoms of FAE (Fetal Alcohol Effect) are not as severe as they might be. Some children whose mothers drink heavily during pregnancy are born mentally retarded and physically malformed. They may have a whole range of physical problems, including a deformed skull, heart defects, poor eyesight and hearing, bad teeth, and stunted growth. Most of these problems, called FAS (Fetal Alcohol Syndrome) will last a lifetime.

Each year, more than 50 000 babies with alcohol-related defects are born in the United States. One-fourth of these babies have damage severe enough to be termed FAS. Some researchers think that FAS is

498 REPRODUCTION

PROJECT

***Obelia* Life Cycle:** *Obelia* is a marine animal found in the Phylum Cnidaria. It carries out a life cycle that alternates between an asexual and a sexual generation. However, unlike these stages in plants, both stages are diploid. Ask students to use references that explain this complex life cycle. Allow students to study prepared slides of the organism. **L2**

STUDENT JOURNAL

Ask students to prepare a table for their journals listing all the animal phyla. Refer them to Appendix A for guidance in the headings and numbers of phyla. Using references, ask them to determine and indicate in the table which phyla carry out internal or external fertilization or both methods of reproduction. **L1** gametes at one time. A female salmon, for example, lays from 2000 to 10 000 eggs during spawning. There is safety in numbers in that at least some of the eggs are fertilized and have a greater chance of survival.

Other adaptations help ensure fertilization. The eggs of some animals such as frogs are enclosed in a jellylike layer that protects and insulates them. Also, many animals follow patterns of courtship behavior that lead to the release of sperm and eggs at precisely the same time. In frogs, for example, the male clasps tightly to the back of a female and stimulates the release of both their gametes.

Internal Fertilization Internal fertilization removes the dangers of predators and harsh environmental conditions for the gametes. Inside the female parent's body, eggs are retained in reproductive organs. When sperm enter the female's body, they move in a direct path toward the eggs. The reproductive organs provide a moist and protective environment for sperm and eggs. The only time sperm are exposed is when they leave the male body and before fertilization. During these times, they are protected from drying out by a fluid in which they are able to swim to the egg. When the chances of fertilization are high, fewer eggs are produced.

Figure 18-17 **When a male insect deposits sperm into the body of a female, fertilization is internal and loss of eggs to predators is reduced.**

the cause of 20 percent of all cases of mental retardation in the U.S.

Michael Dorris learned this statistic in a heartbreaking way. Half Native American himself, Dorris adopted a three-year-old boy whose Sioux parents had died from alcohol abuse. The boy, now grown up, is still undersized, a slow learner, and unlikely to lead a truly independent life. Dorris, who tried everything to help his son, says sadly, "If you wouldn't give your kid a bottle of gin the day after birth, why give it one the day before?"

Perhaps the most tragic fact about FAS is that it is entirely preventable. Even an alcoholic woman can have a baby free of FAS—if she stops drinking before she becomes pregnant.

1. **Issue:** Some people think that mothers who refuse to stop drinking should be jailed to control their access to alcohol. What arguments for and against this proposal can you provide?
2. **Writing About Biology:** What advice would you give a friend

who says, "I'm worried about FAS, so I'll stop drinking as soon as I find out I'm pregnant"?

CAREER CONNECTION

A **midwife** helps a pregnant woman during labor and birth of her baby. Around the world, nearly 800 000 midwives help in the birth of three-fourths of the babies born each year. In the United States, many universities now train registered nurses to become midwives.

MEETING INDIVIDUAL NEEDS

Ask students to prepare a table that lists these two categories across the top: "Features of External Fertilization" and "Features of Internal Fertilization." Have them list as many features for these categories as possible. Information may be obtained from pages 498 to 500. LEP

CAREER CONNECTION

For more information, contact your local hospital or a nursing college.

HEALTH CONNECTION

Purpose
This feature illustrates the effects that a pregnant mother's behavior has on fetal development.

Background
Alcohol has been shown to act as a teratogen, a chemical responsible for causing birth defects.

Teaching Strategies
• Bring in labels from alcoholic beverages. Use this as a means for discussing the impact of such labeling on levels of alcohol consumption by pregnant women.
• Provide these facts—one to two ounces of alcohol per day during pregnancy leads to a ten percent risk of FAS. Two to three ounces brings about a 19 percent risk.

Possible Answers
1. For: the cost of caring for the FAS child will eventually need to be covered by tax dollars. Against: the personal rights of the mother would not be considered.
2. Answers will vary. It will be useful to point out here that often pregnancy is not realized until several weeks have passed. By that time, sufficient alcohol may have been consumed to have already damaged the fetus.

Going Further
Have students research the meaning of the term *teratogen*. *Greek, meaning "monster causing"*

SECTION 18.3

Brainstorming

Ask students to speculate on the frequency with which the estrous cycle occurs in mice and dogs. Based on their own experiences with these pets, students will explain that the estrous cycle must be very frequent for mice but infrequent for dogs. The rate of reproduction in mice is much greater than that in dogs. Estrus for mice is every four days and every six months for dogs.

Using the Illustration

Ask students to study Figure 18-18. Have them identify only those organs that form part of the reproductive system and to speculate as to the nature of the tissue forming the uterus. Is it muscle, connective tissue, or cartilage? Ask them to defend their decision. **L1**

Figure Caption Question

What is the name of the opening to the uterus? cervix

Although sperm may be deposited within the female's body, there is no guarantee that her eggs are ready to be fertilized. Adaptations for proper timing are still important. Earthworms and many female insects have storage organs where sperm can be kept alive for months or even years. As the female's eggs mature, they can be fertilized with immediately available sperm. In birds, proper timing is ensured by elaborate courtship behaviors.

The Estrous Cycle

In many mammals, including dogs, rats, and whales, the female is receptive to mating at only a few times each year. These receptive times are known as periods of **estrus** or heat. What controls this cycle of events in mammals? The production and release of eggs and sperm would never happen without chemicals called hormones released by the body. A **hormone** is a chemical that is produced in one part of an organism and then is transported to another part, where it causes a response. During estrus, sex hormones control the release of eggs and the receptive behavior of the female. At the peak of the estrous cycle, when the female is in estrus, changes in her behavior are perceived by the male. He senses these changes as her readiness for mating. It is at that point in the cycle that her eggs are released by the ovary and can be fertilized.

Human Reproduction

Humans, like other mammals, have internal fertilization. Figure 18-18 shows the human female reproductive system. On each side of a female's abdominal cavity is an ovary. Within the ovary are groups of cells called **follicles,** where eggs develop from cells that divide by meiosis.

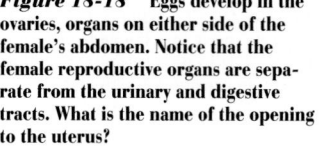

Figure 18-18 Eggs develop in the ovaries, organs on either side of the female's abdomen. Notice that the female reproductive organs are separate from the urinary and digestive tracts. What is the name of the opening to the uterus?

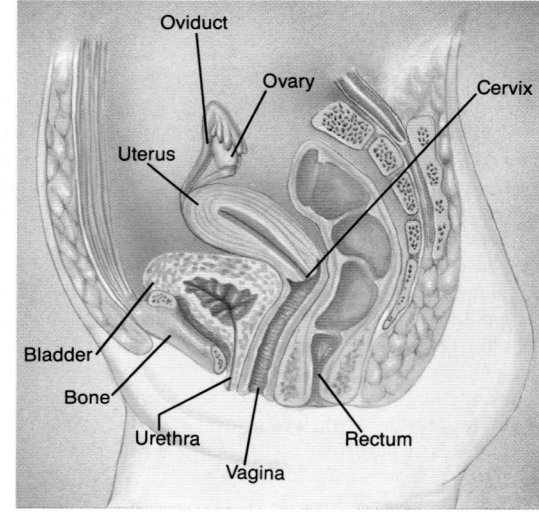

500 🐾 REPRODUCTION

PORTFOLIO

Have students imagine that they are an egg within a follicle. Ask them to describe their surroundings, who their friends are, how they spend their time, and what their future may hold. Then, using Figure 18-18 as a guide, have them explain where a possible trip may take them. **LEP**

Ovulation   Very close, but not attached, to each ovary is an opening to a tube called an **oviduct.** When an immature egg is released from a follicle, a process called **ovulation,** it is usually pulled into the oviduct by tiny cilia that line the opening of this tube. The left and right oviducts join to form a thick-walled, muscular organ called the **uterus.** Within the hollow uterus, a fertilized egg will develop. The uterus narrows to a small neck called the cervix, which becomes plugged during the development of a fetus. Usually, the cervix opens to the **vagina,** which leads to the outside of the female's body and is the passageway along which sperm pass on their way to the uterus.

Sperm Formation   Figure 18-20 shows the human male reproductive system. The testes of the male are two oval structures within an external sac called the **scrotum.** In many animals, the testes are within the abdomen. But in humans and some other mammals, sperm require a temperature slightly lower than that of the body. The position of the testes away from the body in an external structure is therefore adaptive.

Sperm are produced from cells of the testes and then transferred along a series of highly coiled tubes. As sperm leave these tubes, they pass several structures that add fluids. Each sperm has a flagellum that helps it swim in these fluids. The combination of sperm and the fluids is called **semen.** Semen leaves the male's body through the penis.

Conception   During sexual intercourse, semen is ejected by a series of muscular contractions from the male's urethra into the female's vagina. Although millions of sperm may enter the vagina, only a few thousand of them will pass through the cervix into the uterus. Many of these enter the oviduct, where fertilization usually occurs if an egg is present. However, only one sperm fertilizes the egg. As soon as one sperm penetrates the

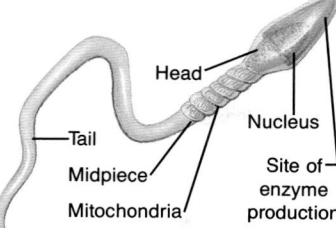

Figure 18-19   A mature sperm has a head containing the nucleus and a tail with mitochondria, which is shed after the sperm head penetrates the egg.

Figure 18-20   Sperm develop in the testes, organs within sacs outside the male's abdomen. Notice that the urinary and reproductive tracts have one shared passage. Why do sperm need to be stored outside the body cavity?

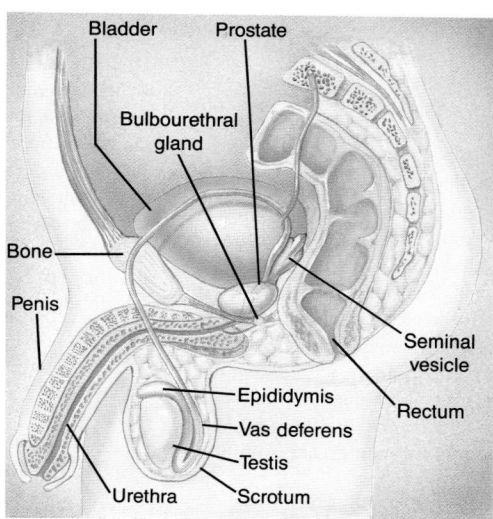

18.3 SEXUAL REPRODUCTION IN ANIMALS **501**

Different Viewpoints in Biology

The Aggressive Egg

Typically, it is the sperm that is described as the aggressor in fertilization. Sperm search out the egg and then push through the material that encloses it to bring about conception. This view is changing as greater importance is being assigned to the egg. It is now thought that the egg may act as the aggressor. Molecules on the egg's surface hook together with counterparts on the sperm's surface, fastening the sperm to the egg until the egg can absorb the sperm's head. Sperm are no longer described as active burrowers. If they were, they would burrow into any surface they encounter. They constantly bump into the walls of the uterus and oviduct.

Using the Illustration

Have students examine Figure 18-20. Ask them to name only those organs that form part of the reproductive system. Have them speculate as to the nature of the tissue forming the vas deferens and urethra. Is it muscle, connective tissue, or cartilage? Can they name the glands that may contribute to the supply of semen? **L1**

Figure Caption Question

Why do sperm need to be stored outside the body cavity? Body temperature is too high for normal sperm development.

MEETING INDIVIDUAL NEEDS

Ask students to perform the following tasks. Have them trace Figure 18-20 using only the side view diagram. Then have them use arrows on their diagram to trace the path of sperm from testes through the entire reproductive system to the urethra. Have them label their diagram to indicate the function of the various organs. **L1** **LEP**

Teacher FYI

A human female contains 2 million primary oocytes six months prior to birth. The number then continues to decline. At birth, the number is 1 million, and at puberty the number has dropped to 400 000. At birth, all oocytes are held at prophase I of meiosis. After puberty, meiosis I is completed in one oocyte per month, but again, they are held at metaphase II until just before release into the fallopian tubes. Less than 500 oocytes are ever released from the ovaries from the time of puberty to menopause.

LITERATURE CONNECTION

Purpose
To introduce the importance of providing a native American offspring with a name.

Teaching Strategies
- Have students read the feature as homework. Answers to the questions may be placed in their portfolios.
- Assign groups within the class and undertake the survey described in question 1.

Possible Answers
1. Names today will vary from those most commonly used 20 or 30 years ago.
2. Answers will vary. Typically, nicknames will describe some event in which the person excels, such as "Speedy," or may even point out some physical attribute possessed by the person, such as "Curly."

Going Further
Ask students to write about naming traditions from other cultures.

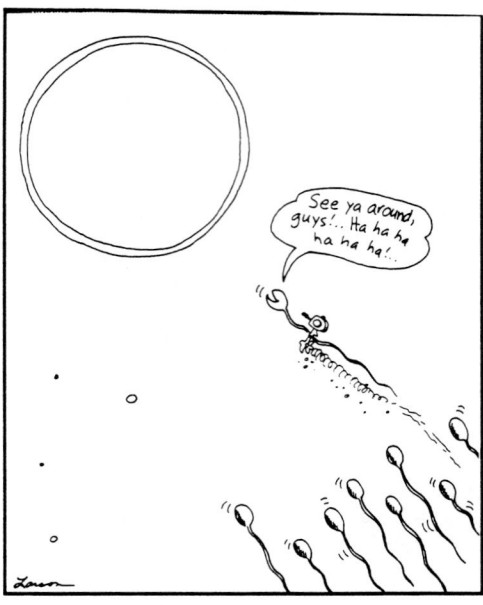

egg, the cell membrane of the egg becomes unresponsive to the attempts of other sperm to break the egg's outer barrier. Penetration of the egg by the sperm triggers the almost-mature egg to complete meiosis. Then the haploid nuclei of sperm and egg combine to form the diploid zygote.

If a zygote is formed, it moves along the oviduct toward the uterus, where development will occur. A pregnancy begins when the embryo becomes embedded in the uterine wall, which has thickened and become enriched with blood vessels since just prior to the time of ovulation. Ovulation occurs in the average, sexually mature female on a near-monthly basis as a result of the female's menstrual cycle.

The Menstrual Cycle

Beginning on average around age 12, and continuing until about age 50, human females undergo a series of changes similar to those of the estrous cycle. These hormonally controlled changes result in the **menstrual cycle**. During this cycle, an egg matures and is released

LITERATURE CONNECTION

Native American Names

Columbus started the confusion. Thinking he had discovered a new trade route to India, he called the people living in the Americas "Indians." More confusion arose when the European settlers tried to learn the personal names of the Native Americans they encountered. The Europeans discovered that the original inhabitants of the land often changed their names as they grew older. A childhood name might be exchanged for a new one at adolescence, or after a first battle or an important dream. Another cultural mystery to Europeans was that some Native Americans considered their names so personal and sacred that only a bad-mannered person would address them directly by those names.

Naming the Baby The Native American tradition of naming babies is a practice that survives today among many tribes. A baby might be called simply "boy" or "girl" until he or she is several months old. By that time, the baby has developed some personality. A tribe elder observing the baby will then know enough about his or her personal traits to suggest a name that seems to fit. That name might be one given to honor a dead ancestor, or it might come from a dream of the baby's mother or father. You can read an account of how the famous Shawnee chief, Tecumseh, received his name in the book *Panther in the Sky,* by James Alexander Thom. Thom writes that Tecumseh's father saw a birth sign, a yellow-green shooting star, and that sign determined the child's name, Panther in the Sky or Tecumseh.

Respect for a Name Even after a Native American child grows up, his or her name can change. In some tribes, names are considered a personal possession that can be loaned, pawned, given away, or even thrown away. Following the death of a family member, all the surviving members of the family

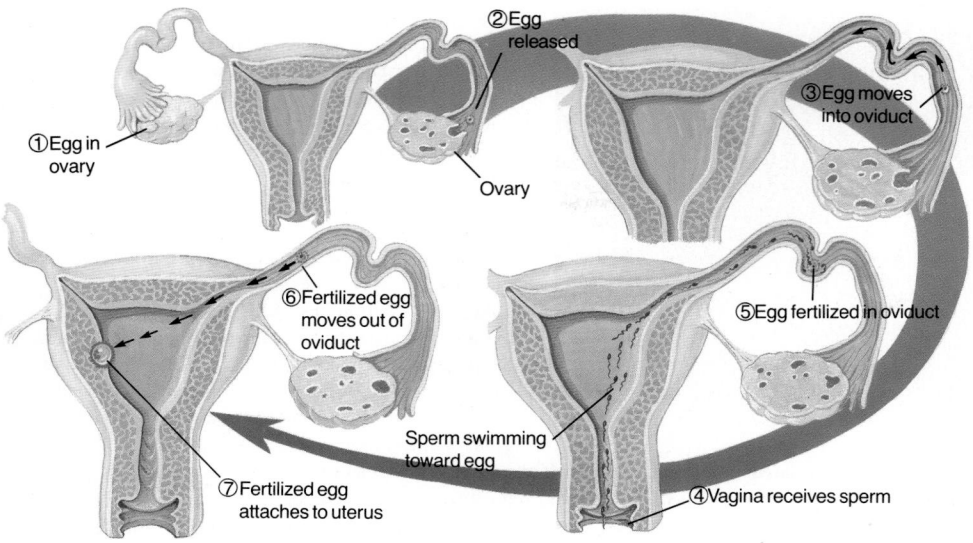

Figure 18-21 Follow the steps in the movement of an egg from the ovary to when it becomes embedded in the wall of the uterus following fertilization.

① Egg in ovary
② Egg released
③ Egg moves into oviduct
Ovary
④ Vagina receives sperm
⑤ Egg fertilized in oviduct
⑥ Fertilized egg moves out of oviduct
⑦ Fertilized egg attaches to uterus
Sperm swimming toward egg

may take new names and avoid saying any word that suggests the name of the deceased for many years to come.

Because of misunderstandings, many Native American names have been made fun of. For instance, the name "Stinking Blanket" may have caused snickers among Europeans. However, attitudes about that name changed significantly after hearing an explanation of its source: An Indian brave fought so long and hard against his enemies that he never had time to stop and change his horse's saddle blanket. Similarly, the name "Crazy Horse" sounds different when the word "crazy" is correctly translated as "recklessly brave."

Today, many Native Americans have two personal names. One name might be an ordinary one used for convenience. The other and more important name is the tribal name, which establishes membership in the tribe.

1. **Explore Further:** Do a survey in your school to learn the most common first names for boys and girls. Ask older family members about popular first names when they were young.
2. **Connection to Social Studies:** Nicknames often reveal more about a person than his or her real

name does. What are some nicknames among your friends or among sports stars? Why do you think these nicknames were given?

18.3 SEXUAL REPRODUCTION IN ANIMALS **503**

MEETING INDIVIDUAL NEEDS

Ask students to prepare a time line that plots the events described in Figure 18-21. A second time line is to plot the events of the menstrual cycle. Have students also indicate on the time line when fertilization is most likely to occur and the time span during which fertilization can occur if sperm are introduced.

Bioethics

Birth Control or Abortion?: A drug called RU-486 is commonly used in France to induce an abortion within hours of a known conception. The drug interferes with the production of progesterone. The uterus lining does not continue to develop, and a fertilized egg will not become implanted. Menstruation will occur as if fertilization had not happened. Of more than 50 000 French women who have used it, few are recorded as having any side effects, and most consider it preferable to traditional and often later abortion methods. It is considered by some to be a means of birth control. Myron Allukian, past president of the American Public Health Association, says that the drug should be made available in the United States. The National Right to Life Committee opposes the introduction of what they consider to be an abortion pill. The drug, recently released in England, is not yet available in the United States.

Science, Technology, and Society

STDs: The incidence of gonorrhea and syphilis has been dropping in Europe, Australia, and Japan. However, these sexually transmitted diseases (STDs) are rising sharply in the United States. Ask students to research the cause, symptoms, and current treatment for each of the two STDs mentioned as an increasing problem in this country. Ask them to speculate as to why there is a rise in this country and not in other modern civilizations.

Using Science Terms

Ask students to look up the Latin meaning for the term *menstruate*. Ask them how this term correlates to the Latin definitions. *Menstruous means "monthly" in Latin.* L1

ART CONNECTION

Purpose
To show the importance and responsibility of a family to its children.

Teaching Strategies
• Ask students to research the topic of life expectancy. How does this relate to the role of grandparents in the family unit?
• Ask students to discuss how the longer life spans have added to the responsibilities of parents who must provide for both their children and parents at the same time.

Possible Answers
1. A typical family today may not consist of two parents. It may consist of one parent and grandparents or no grandparents. Children may be cared for by professionals in day care facilities.
2. Single parents often have difficulty finding work that allows for time off to care for a sick child. One income is often inadequate to support an average lifestyle for a family with one parent. The children often lack the role model of the male or female parent who is not present.
3. Have students share their reports on adults' views of an ideal family.

Going Further
Have students research which cultures traditionally take responsibility for the care of grandparents within their own household. Which do not?

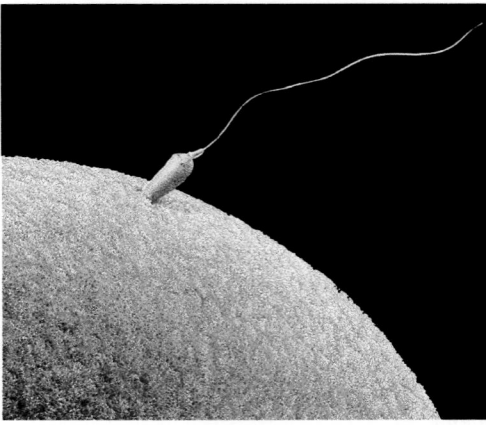

Figure 18-22 This false-colored illustration of a human egg and sperm shows their relative sizes. Magnification: 1500×

by an ovary at ovulation, and the uterus is prepared for a possible pregnancy. However, unlike estrus in other mammals, the human female's readiness for mating is not limited to this or any one particular time.

Each menstrual cycle lasts for about 28 days and consists of four different phases: thickening of the uterine tissue, ovulation, passage of the egg into the uterus, and loss of egg and uterine tissue via the vagina. This last phase, called **menstruation,** marks the onset of a new cycle and lasts about five days. Once menstruation has ended, a new egg begins to mature, and the uterine tissue once again is prepared for pregnancy. Ovulation usually occurs about midway through the cycle. It is at this time and for perhaps a day or two more that if sperm are already present in or are introduced into the vagina, fertilization can occur. If an egg is fertilized and the embryo becomes embedded in the uterine wall, pregnancy begins. The menstrual cycle ceases throughout pregnancy. You'll discover how hormones interact to control the events of the menstrual cycle and pregnancy in Chapter 24.

ART CONNECTION

Family Group

For all of history, the survival of our species has depended on our ability to reproduce. However, we have learned that just producing offspring is not enough. Without constant care and attention, even well-fed babies will not develop well, nor will they gain weight.

Early representations of females in art stressed fertility by portraying pregnancy because of the importance of continuation of the family line by reproduction. Some more recent artists have gone beyond just showing fertility. Henry Moore, a 20th century English sculptor, is one such artist. In 1949, he developed a bronze sculpture called

"Family Group," which shows a nurturing family spirit. The parents are providing protection and care for the child. Henry Moore was influenced early in his career by Mexican and African art. His works in stone, wood, and bronze have simple lines, and many look weathered. Several of his sculptures depict families or mothers with their children.

1. **Writing About Biology:** How does Moore's sculpture relate to what you know about today's families?
2. **Issue:** The number of single-parent families has increased greatly over the past few decades. What are some of the problems these parents encounter as their children grow up?

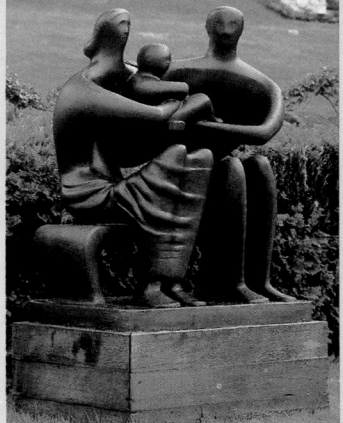

3. **Connection to Social Studies:** Talk to an adult about his or her view of the ideal family. Write a brief report on your impressions.

504 🔬 REPRODUCTION

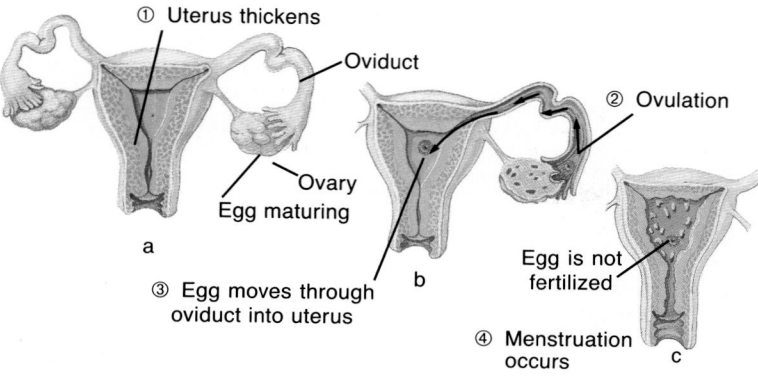

① Uterus thickens
Oviduct
Ovary
Egg maturing
a

② Ovulation
③ Egg moves through oviduct into uterus
b
Egg is not fertilized
④ Menstruation occurs
c

Figure 18-23   The wall of the uterus thickens and becomes engorged with blood in preparation for pregnancy. The wall lining falls away during menstruation if fertilization does not occur.

LOOKING AHEAD

THERE ARE various patterns of reproduction among different kinds of organisms. Obviously, there is a good deal of diversity. However, it's also important to focus on what the many different kinds of organisms have in common. How does reproduction in different kinds of organisms compare? Whether reproduction is asexual or sexual, the result is newly produced offspring. These offspring must then undergo a period of development. You'll discover that development in plants and animals follows similar patterns, and you'll also explore how genetics controls that development.

Section Review

Understanding Concepts

1. Compare the numbers of eggs produced at one time by a cat and a fish. Explain the reason for the difference.
2. How are humans adapted for solving the problems of fertilization?
3. Explain why it is important for animals with internal fertilization to have precise timing for the release of their gametes.
4. *Skill Review—Making Tables:* Make a table listing how animals with external and internal fertilization are adapted to the conditions required for fertilization. For more help, see Organizing Information in the **Skill Handbook**.
5. *Thinking Critically:* A species of frogs in Puerto Rico lives in trees, where they reproduce by external fertilization. What conditions must be present in those trees that enable these frogs to reproduce?

Issues

Purpose

The feature illustrates how technology has come to the aid of couples who are unable to have children naturally, and it also addresses the ethical and legal problems that can result when modern methods are used to aid in pregnancy.

Background

The cost for in-vitro fertilization (IVF) may run between $3000 and $10 000 and it has a success rate of between 10 and 15 percent. Artificial insemination, where sperm are introduced into the vagina of the mother in a laboratory setting, is a technique that has been used for years and is common in the dairy industry today.

Teaching Strategies

- Ask groups of students to define *in vitro* and *surrogate*.
- Have students examine and discuss some of the questions associated with IVF such as:
  (a) For how long should embryos be frozen?
  (b) Will wealthy parents hire poor surrogate mothers to bear their children? Is this wrong if the surrogate is paid for her nine-month job?
  (c) What should be done to extra fetuses if the mother can only maintain two in her uterus but actually has six that are frozen?

Possible Answers

1. Answers may vary. Doctors could disclose the cost and complications that are possible, explain laws that prohibit selling of eggs or fetuses, and provide counseling before a program in IVF is commenced.
2. Answers may vary. Early detection of a disease in the zygote will reduce the need for therapeutic

---

Issues

And Baby Makes Three?

How many people does it take to conceive a baby? The question may seem silly, but sometimes the answer isn't two. The couple must turn to a third person—a doctor—to help them conceive. Between eight and 15 percent of couples cannot conceive a child despite years of trying. The man's sperm count may be low. The woman may not ovulate, her oviducts may be blocked, or the fertilized egg may not implant in her uterus. In all of these cases, pregnancy seems impossible. Or it did, that is, before in vitro fertilization, a procedure during which sperm and egg are brought together outside the body and then returned to the uterus.

A Miracle Baby When a couple decides to try in vitro fertilization, the woman is given fertility drugs so that more than one egg will ripen during ovulation. Using modern techniques, a doctor can remove the ripe eggs from the ovaries and fertilize them in a glass laboratory dish. Placing sperm and egg in direct contact increases the chances of fertilization. One or more fertilized eggs, called zygotes, are then placed in the uterus and the rest are usually frozen. If a zygote implants in the wall of the uterus, an embryo will develop. If it does not, the pro-

cedure can be repeated using the remaining fertilized eggs.

What if the woman no longer has a uterus or is unable to produce eggs? In the first case, the zygote may be placed in the uterus of another woman, called a surrogate, who agrees to carry the fetus to birth and then return the fully developed baby to the couple. If the woman is unable to produce eggs, an egg from another female, called a donor, can be fertilized with the man's sperm and then placed in the woman's uterus. In both cases, two parents have now become three.

For the couple who has been unable to conceive a baby, in vitro

fertilization may seem like a miracle worth any price. They have the baby they always wanted. But is it all that simple? Some couples find there are unforeseen complications.

Risky Business To increase the chances of pregnancy, more than one fertilized egg is generally introduced into the uterus. One woman who received four eggs found herself pregnant with quadruplets.

Sometimes, couples freeze fertilized eggs for later use. One couple who did this divorced shortly afterwards. The woman asked the court to give her custody of the frozen zygotes. The husband objected, however, saying he, too, should have a say in what happens to the zygotes fertilized by his sperm.

When a couple receives eggs from a donor or pays a surrogate mother to carry the fetus, the question of who is the real mother may come up as a legal issue. Several couples have found themselves in court fighting for custody of the baby they thought was theirs.

While there are more than 200 centers in the United States and Canada that offer in vitro fertilization, and they have given thousands of couples their only hope of having a child, there are many legal and ethical questions yet to be resolved.

---

abortions later, and parents may wish to have a child in spite of knowing that they have a genetic disease. If there are defects, a prepared couple will be able to provide the proper care immediately.
3. Yes, federal funds will allow people with less money to use IVF techniques, or federal funds can improve research in this area. No, money can be better spent on research for cancer or heart disease, or the use of IVF might violate religious principles.

Going Further

Have students debate the issue of whether or not they would inform their child if it were conceived through IVF or via a surrogate mother.

Biotechnology

Purpose

This feature points out the status of research in the field of cloning. It also illustrates how cloning may be considered as another reproductive strategy for future humans.

Understanding the Issue

1. What, if any, regulations on in vitro fertilization do you think are necessary?
2. Doctors can now test zygotes for genetic defects. Explain why you think this is good or bad.
3. Should the current ban on use of federal funds for in vitro fertilization be lifted? Why or why not?

Readings

- "Mixed Blessings." *Health*, Vol. 22, Nov. 1990, pp. 64-67.
- "And Donor Makes Three." *Newsweek*, Sept. 30, 1991, pp. 60-61.
- "The Rights of Frozen Embryos." *Time*, July 24, 1989, p. 63.

Biotechnology

Cloning Humans: Is It Possible?

It is the twenty-first century. A young women walks out of a medical clinic with a new liver, one her body will not try to reject because it came from her clone. Several years before, the woman had been cloned, or genetically duplicated. The fetus developed in a test tube womb, and once the clone grew, it was frozen in liquid nitrogen. When the woman developed liver cancer, the liver was removed from her clone and put into her body. If the cancer spreads to other organs, if her heart or lungs become diseased, or if she loses an arm or leg in an accident, these body parts can also be replaced from her clone. "This way I will always be young," she thinks.

This scene may not be as impossible as it sounds today. The concept fascinates the human mind, and many science fiction writers have explored the idea since.

Starting with Frogs Cloning is the making of an exact copy of an organism; thus the genes—and all the parts—of the clone are identical to those of the original organism. Scientists have been working on reproducing exact genetic copies of

animals since the 1950s. By pulling the nucleus out of the cell of a frog embryo and injecting it into an egg cell from which the chromosomes had been removed, scientists were first able to grow a tadpole. Since then, they have successfully cloned sheep, rabbits, and cows in the same way. By cloning cows that give the best milk, for example, the quality of the herd can be kept genetically consistent.

So far, scientists have been able to clone animals using only cells from embryos. Scientists understand that all of the genes present in the cell of an embryo are still present in the cells of the different tissues, but they are not all turned on for action. When they discover how the genes are switched on and off, they may be closer to understanding how to clone humans.

Stay Forever Young Some biologists are already working on ways to make adult body cells of vertebrates revert back to their original embryonic stage, when all the genes were active. One biologist has successfully placed the nucleus of a red blood cell from a frog into a frog's egg cell that isn't quite mature. She

found that the metabolic process that occurs in the egg helped to activate the genes in the introduced adult nucleus. The biologist has so far been successful in cloning a tadpole from a blood cell until it reached the stage of forming limb buds.

Cloning began with frogs. This latest research on frogs could mean that the power to clone human adult cells is not far away.

1. **Issue:** Not everyone thinks that biologists should try to clone humans. What are some of the arguments against cloning?
2. **Connection to Genetics:** In 1990, the United States organized the Human Genome Project. A genome is all the genes in one cell. What is the goal of this project?

Background

During frog cloning, the egg cell that receives the new nucleus has had its original nucleus destroyed. In effect, the receiving cell is a surrogate that provides only cytoplasm to the frog about to be formed.

Teaching Strategies

- Have students read the feature as homework and ask them to place their answers to the questions in their portfolios.
- Have students design a flowchart or outline for the procedure to be used in cloning a frog. This procedure is briefly mentioned in the feature.

Possible Answers

1. Student answers may vary. Cloning may lead to eugenics, the ability to create a race with certain physical features. Cloning violates the rights of the fetus, especially if it is to be used only for spare parts. Who will make the decision about which human will be cloned and why?
2. The goal is to understand the genetic makeup of humans. By mapping the human genome, scientists hope to discover the location of all genes and be able to identify the location for those associated with specific disorders.

Going Further

Ask students to describe the advantages of cloning plant material. Are the advantages of cloning animals the same? Why or why not?

Summary

Summary statements can be used by students to review the major concepts of the chapter.

Language of Biology

Answers should go beyond defining the terms. Accept any reasonable answer that uses the term correctly and in the proper context.

Understanding Concepts

1. Sexual reproduction produces variety among offspring. Such variety is important in terms of evolution.
2. All these structures are protective adaptations. The seed coat protects the embryo within. The outer wall of a pollen grain protects and prevents dehydration of the haploid male nuclei inside. The wall of a spore protects the young haploid gametophyte.
3. The ovary from which such a fruit developed contained many ovules. Each ovule developed into a seed.
4. Animals having external fertilization produce large numbers of gametes. Production of many gametes is common when the chances of successful fertilization are not great. At least some gametes will enter into fertilization. The idea is the same for fungal spores. At least some spores will encounter conditions suitable for germination.
5. Most amphibians and mosses require some moisture in which sperm can swim to eggs. Thus, both are restricted to a moist habitat.
6. In all these organisms, fertilization occurs internally. Internal fertilization is necessary if these organisms are to be able to live in dry areas on land.
7. Exchange of gametes between hermaphrodites results in a greater degree of variation among offspring because of the exchange of genetic material.

Summary

Asexual reproduction occurs among members of all kingdoms and, in general, is the only means available to monerans. It may occur by binary fission, budding or vegetative reproduction, fragmentation, or spore formation. Each of these processes results in offspring that are genetically identical to the parent and to one another.

Sexual reproduction involves gametes that combine DNA and produce offspring different from one another and from the parents. Conjugation is a form of sexual reproduction carried out by bacteria, some algae, and fungi. More complex organisms, though, produce male and female gametes.

Plants have a life cycle in which the sporophyte and gametophyte generations alternate with one another. The diploid sporophyte generation is the major stage in angiosperms.

Animals do not undergo alternation of diploid and haploid generations, and only their gametes are haploid. Eggs of animals are fertilized either internally or externally, and animals have many adaptations that ensure fertilization.

Language of Biology

Write a sentence that shows your understanding of each of the following terms.

budding	ovulation
conjugation	ovule
endosperm	pollination
estrus	regeneration
follicle	scrotum
fragmentation	semen
hermaphrodite	testes
hormone	uterus
menstrual cycle	vagina
menstruation	vegetative reproduction
oviduct	

Understanding Concepts

1. What is the adaptive advantage of sexual reproduction?
2. How are a seed coat, a pollen grain, and a spore wall adaptive structures?
3. How can you explain the fact that many fruits have more than one seed?
4. Fungi release spores in great numbers. What kinds of animals produce gametes in great numbers? What are the advantages of high production of spores or gametes?
5. What do most amphibians and mosses have in common in terms of reproduction? How does that similarity affect both kinds of organisms in terms of their habitats?

6. How is sexual reproduction in a flowering plant similar to that in a reptile, bird, or mammal? Why?
7. What is the adaptive advantage for hermaphrodites to exchange sperm and eggs with other individuals?

---

8. Mammals have a constant body temperature that is too high for the production of healthy sperm. The temperature in the scrotum is lower. Amphibians and reptiles are ectotherms whose body temperature is not too high for sperm production.
9. Both cycles involve hormonal changes. Estrus also involves changes that lead the female to mate only when her eggs are mature. Mating (intercourse) in the human female is not linked to the time when her egg is mature.

10. The spores contain eight chromosomes. The gametes contain eight chromosomes. The zygote contains 16 chromosomes.

Applying Concepts

11. Although cnidarians may have a life cycle in which the two body forms alternate with each other, both stages are diploid. Only the gametes are haploid. Thus, this is not an example of alternation of generations.

8. Why is sperm production in animals such as amphibians or reptiles located internally, whereas in mammals sperm is produced in an external structure?

9. Compare estrus in a cat with the menstrual cycle of a human.

10. A sporophyte plant has cells containing 16 chromosomes. How many chromosomes are in the spores of this plant? The gametes? The zygote?

Applying Concepts

11. Recall that many cnidarians have a life cycle in which polyp and medusa stages alternate. Is this an example of alternation of generations? Explain why or why not.

12. How may vegetative reproduction be an advantage to plants invading a new habitat?

13. How are reproductive hormones important to the survival of a species?

14. A gametophyte plant dies because it has inherited a lethal allele. The sporophyte plant that produced it had the allele but did not die. Why?

15. Grasshoppers mate in spring, and eggs are fertilized in the summer. What adaptation for proper timing of release of gametes must grasshoppers have?

16. Bacteria normally produce substances essential for their growth. Two cultures of mutant bacteria are discovered that cannot grow without the addition of these substances. The two cultures require two different substances. If the two cultures are mixed and then placed on a solid medium without the added substances, a few bacteria begin to grow. Explain how this could happen.

17. Parasites are often hermaphrodites. How is that trait an advantage?

18. How are the conditions for fertilization in animals also met by flowering plants?

19. Does fragmentation and regeneration always involve reproduction of an organism? Explain.

20. **Issues:** What are some reasons why women may not be able to conceive?

21. **Biotechnology:** As you know, your skin can regenerate after it has been damaged. How is this characteristic important to doctors who attend severely burned patients?

Lab Interpretation

22. **Minilab 1:** How is budding in yeast similar to the formation of potatoes?

23. **Minilab 2:** Describe how each type of cell, spore or pollen, would have eventually developed if you could continue to observe it.

24. **Investigation:** Offer a possible reason why: (a) dry crackers do not mold when lying out of their wrapper for months, (b) moist dog food is sealed in individual meal packets.

Connecting Ideas

25. When self-pollination occurs, the two sets of DNA that fuse come from the same plant. How will this fertilization result in variety among the offspring?

26. Why was the requirement for moisture not a problem in the process of fertilization for early life forms?

12. Vegetative reproduction can occur more rapidly. Thus, the plant can colonize the new habitat in a short time.

13. Reproductive hormones guide development of sexual structures, gametes, and mating behaviors.

14. The gametophyte has only one allele for each trait. The lethal allele was masked by a dominant allele in the sporophyte.

15. The female grasshopper can store sperm until her eggs are mature.

16. Some of the bacteria must have undergone conjugation. The mutant receiving the normal gene could survive and pass on both normal genes to its offspring.

17. The parasite can reproduce whether or not other parasites of the same species are present.

18. Pollen delivers sperm to eggs without the need for water. The sperm are protected within the pollen grain and the female's reproductive structures, and the egg is protected within the ovule.

19. No. For example, a lizard might replace part of its tail and a starfish can regenerate part of an arm.

20. A man's sperm count may be too low. A woman's oviducts may be blocked, her hormones may not be released, or the zygote does not become implanted.

21. It is possible to remove healthy skin from an undamaged area and transplant it to the burned area. The skin removed will be replaced by regeneration.

22. Budding in yeast is the asexual production of new yeast cells. Potatoes are also formed asexually from a single parent.

23. Pollen would have formed two sperm nuclei and a pollen tube nucleus. Spores would have formed the young gametophyte.

24. (a) Mold spores require water in order to germinate.
    (b) Sealed packets prevent spores from getting into the package.

PROGRAM RESOURCES

Teacher Classroom Resources
Chapter Assessment, pp. 69-72 **L1**
Performance Assessment in Biology, p. 36 **L2**
Alternate Assessment in the Science Classroom
Computer Test Bank **L1**

Connecting Ideas

25. **Patterns of Change:** The particular combination of genes in sperm and egg will be different because meiosis results in many possible combinations of chromosomes among gametes.

26. **Evolution:** Early life forms evolved in the ocean. Thus, their gametes could be shed into the external environment without danger of desiccation.

SECTION	OBJECTIVES	TEXT LABS/FEATURES
19.1 Early Stages of Development (2 days)	**Sequence** the early stages of animal development. **Explain** embryo formation and germination in angiosperms. **Describe** how differentiation is controlled.	**Minilab 1:** What does sea urchin development look like? p. 515 **Minilab 2:** Will seeds grow without stored food? p. 519 **Investigation:** The Effect of Microwave Radiation on Seed Germination, p. 520 **Thinking Lab:** What factors are important in sea urchin development? p. 523
19.2 Patterns of Animal Development (3 days)	**Relate** the events of metamorphosis and development within an amniotic egg to the needs of animal embryos. **Describe** the formation and functions of the placenta.	**Art Connection:** Storytellers: The Birth and Development of an Art Form, p. 532 **Psychology Connection:** Infant Learning, p. 534 **Career Connection:** Psychologist, p. 535
BIOLOGY, TECHNOLOGY, AND SOCIETY		**Considering the Environment:** Seed Banks, p. 538 **Biotechnology:** Fetal Surgery—An "Out-of-Body" Experience, p. 539

LAB MATERIALS

INVESTIGATION	MINILAB	ALTERNATE LAB
page 520 marking pens masking tape metric rulers microwave oven paper towels petri dish scissors seeds (radish or bean)	**page 515** microscope prepared slides: fertilized egg unfertilized egg stages of development **page 519** bean seeds paper towels petri dish toothpicks	**page 526** incubator insect larvae labels paper towels petri dish refrigerator scissors tape thermometer

TEACHER CLASSROOM RESOURCES	OTHER RESOURCES
Study Guide, pp. 109-110 **Critical Thinking/Problem Solving:** *Frog Development: The Early Stages,* p. 19 ***PLL:** *Development of Seeds into New Plants,* p. 117 ****ILS:** *Fruits and Seeds,* p. 185 ****ILS:** *Chick Development,* p. 189	***STVS:** *Brain Development,* Human Biology (Disc 7, Side 1) ***STVS:** *Seed Banks,* Plants and Simple Organisms (Disc 4, Side 2)
Study Guide, pp. 111-114 **Concept Mapping,** p. 19 **Exploring Environmental Issues:** *Organically Grown,* pp. 13-14 ***PLL:** *Effects of Salt Concentration on Development of Brine Shrimp,* p. 119 ***PLL:** *Development of a Chicken Embryo,* p. 121 ****ILS:** *Fruit Fly Development,* p. 193 ****ILS:** *Insect Metamorphosis,* p. 195	***STVS:** *Reptilian Sex Change,* Animals (Disc 5, Side 2) ***STVS:** *Development of Walking in Chicks,* Animals (Disc 5, Side 2) **Color Transparency 35:** *Insect Metamorphosis* **Color Transparency 36:** *Amniotic Egg* **Color Transparency 37:** *Fertilization and Fetal Development*
Assessment Materials **Chapter Assessment,** pp. 73-76 **Performance Assessment in Biology,** p. 38 **Alternate Assessment in the Science Classroom** **Computer Test Bank**	**Spanish Resources** **Cooperative Learning Resource Guide** **Videodisc Correlations** (to Optical Data's and Videodiscovery's videodiscs)

* **Probing Levels of Life**
** **Investigating Living Systems**

* **Science Technology Videodisc Series**

Key to Teaching Strategies

The following designations will help you decide which activities in the teacher margin are appropriate for your students.

L1 Level 1 activities should be within the ability range of all students.

L2 Level 2 activities should be within the ability range of the average to above-average student.

L3 Level 3 activities are designed for the ability range of above-average students.

LEP LEP activities are appropriate for Limited English Proficiency students.

COOP LEARN Cooperative Learning activities are designed for small group work.

ADDITIONAL RESOURCES

Infinite Voyage *Fires of the Mind*
The brain is the least understood organ in the human body. This video explores the brain at work, offers new insight into learning, and looks at how memories are made.

Audiovisual
A New Life, video, Films for the Humanities and Sciences.
Development of the Amphibian Embryo, video, Frey Scientific.

Software
Plant: A Plant Growth Simulator, Apple/IBM/Commodore 64, DEE.

19

DEVELOPMENT

Chapter Overview

Students begin the chapter by examining and comparing early development in starfish, frog, and chick. Students learn that although differences exist among the animals, they share a basic pattern of development consisting of cleavage, gastrulation, and, among vertebrates, neurulation stages. In addition, students come to see that cell division and morphogenesis are the main events of early development.

Next, students study embryonic structure, early development, and germination in a flowering plant and examine both similarities to and differences between such plants and animals. They then learn that differentiation is a consequence of different sets of genes being active in different cells of the embryo.

Students conclude their study of development as they learn about patterns of later development in animals—metamorphosis, amniotic egg, and placental development. They come to realize that these vastly different patterns are different solutions to solving fundamental problems faced by any developing animal: need for food, a means of gas exchange, excretion, and protection.

KEY TERMS

allantois	hypocotyl
amnion	larva
blastocoel	meristem
blastula	meta-
chorion	morphosis
cleavage	morpho-
cotyledon	genesis
differentiation	neural tube
embryonic	nymph
induction	placenta
epicotyl	pupa
gastrula	radicle
germination	umbilical cord

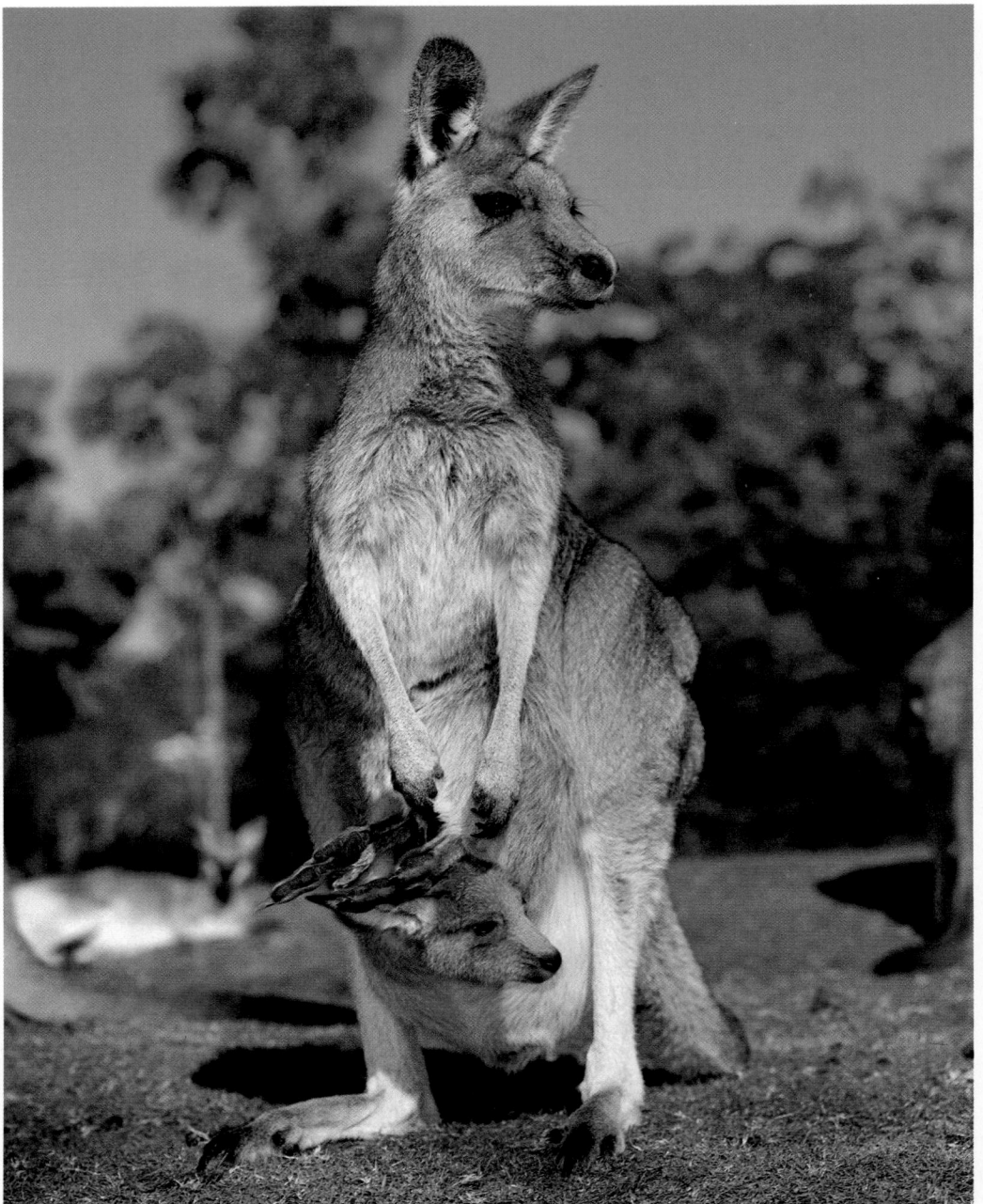

510

19

DEVELOPMENT

PERHAPS THE most unusual animals are the diverse group of mammals that live mainly in Australia—the marsupials. Most remarkable about marsupials, such as the kangaroo pictured opposite, is the presence of a skin pouch that is used to protect and nurture the new offspring. Marsupial offspring are born very tiny and physically immature. In some kangaroo species, they spend only 30 days inside the mother's uterus. Once born, kangaroo babies crawl into their mother's pouch and attach themselves to a nipple inside. There they remain—feeding, growing, and developing—for

five to eleven months until fully developed, preparing for life in the outside world.

The evolutionary success of a species depends, in large part, on adaptations related to development from a fertilized egg to a mature organism. Animals and plants have a variety of adaptations to ensure the survival of offspring to maturity. In this chapter, you will learn how the offspring of some animals and plants grow and develop. You will find out how their adaptations work to bring offspring to maturity and prepare them for the outside environment.

Baby kangaroos are only about the size of honey-bees when they are born and crawl into their mother's pouch. Can you imagine what your development would have been like if your mother had a pouch?

Chapter Preview

ASSESSMENT PLANNER

Choose assessment strategies from the following pages to evaluate the progress of your students.

Assess, pp. 523-524, 536-537
Portfolio, pp. 512, 515, 523, 529, 530, 531, 535, 536, 538
Alternate Lab, pp. 526-527
Thinking Lab, p. 523

Minilab 1, p. 515
Minilab 2, p. 519
Investigation, pp. 520-521
Chapter Review, pp. 540-541

19

Introducing the Chapter

Examination of the photograph on page 510 should serve to spark a lively discussion of development. Have your students identify ways in which development of a kangaroo within its mother's pouch is adaptive. Ask them to identify other methods of animal development and examples of organisms that develop by those methods. Are some methods more efficient than others? If so, why? Does germination of seeds have anything in common with development in animals? Your goal here is to lead them to see that, though details of development vary, the basic events of development are the same for all organisms. **COOP LEARN**

Theme Development

Unity within diversity is a major theme addressed as students learn that basic events of early development are common to both plants and animals, that all animal embryos have fundamental needs, and that they develop according to one of a few basic patterns, each of which meets those needs in different ways. The theme of patterns of change is emphasized as students explore the sequence of events during development in animals and flowering plants.

Tying to Previous Knowledge

This chapter is a logical follow-up to the previous chapter on reproduction. Reminding students of what they've just learned about reproduction in animals and flowering plants as you teach development in those organisms will enable them to fill in the gaps and thus improve their understanding of the complete life cycle. Students can also draw upon their understanding of evolution as they analyze patterns of development from the point of view of adaptations to common problems. Their knowledge of DNA function will be put to use as they explore the idea that selective gene activity is the key to differentiation.

Prepare

Key Concepts

Developmental changes occurring in animals and plants following fertilization are studied. The mechanisms behind these changes are examined.

Key Terms

cleavage, blastula, blastocoel, morphogenesis, gastrula, neural tube, differentiation, cotyledon, hypocotyl, epicotyl, radicle, meristem, germination, embryonic induction

Materials

- Purchase prepared slides of sea urchin development from a biological supply house for use in Minilab 1.
- Bean seeds for Minilab 2 may be purchased at a supermarket.
- Seeds for the Investigation may be purchased from your local supermarket. A variety of seeds should be made available for students. Arrange with your home economics department for use of microwave ovens.

1 Focus

Objectives

The objectives are listed on the student page. Remind students to preview these objectives as a guide to this numbered section.

Demonstration

Pass a plastic-embedded or preserved specimen of a caterpillar for all students to see and study briefly. Ask them the type of animal they have observed. Most will be able to call it by its common name (caterpillar), but few will realize that it is an intermediate stage in the development of a moth or butterfly. Elaborate on this idea if you wish. **L1** **COOP LEARN**

Objectives

Sequence the early stages of animal development.

Explain embryo formation and germination in angiosperms.

Describe how differentiation is controlled.

19.1 Early Stages of Development

You have probably seen buds forming on trees, leaves or flowers opening, and fruits enlarging and ripening. These events signal the development of new plant parts. And as you've probably observed, these events occur gradually and in many separate stages. From a single cell—the zygote—a new organism is produced. At first, repeated cell divisions produce a mass of similar looking cells. Later, the embryo starts to take on a definite shape, and specialized parts begin to form—tissues, organs, and systems. Similar changes occur as the body plan of a newly produced animal unfolds. What series of events results in the production of a new organism, and how are those events guided and coordinated?

Animal Development—Cleavage

As you know, development is a series of changes leading to formation of a mature organism. Scientists first studied animal development using animals that develop in water. Animals such as frogs, starfish, and sea urchins were studied because they were easy to raise and observe. With new technological advances, it became possible to study development in birds, reptiles, and mammals as well. Perhaps the most important finding of these early studies was that, although there are differences in the early stages of development among different types of animals, there is a general scheme that applies to all of them.

Figure 19-1 Frog eggs have a darker, pigmented animal pole and a lighter colored vegetal pole. The eggs are surrounded by a jelly coat that swells when they are deposited in water. This swollen jelly protects the eggs.

512 DEVELOPMENT

PORTFOLIO

Ask students to design an experimental procedure that will allow one to measure the ratio of yolk to albumen in a chicken egg. Have students speculate on how this ratio would compare in a starfish egg, frog egg, and chicken egg. The design should be written up as a formal experimental procedure and placed in the students' portfolios. **L2**

PROGRAM RESOURCES

Teacher Classroom Resources
Study Guide, pp. 109-110 **L1**
Probing Levels of Life, Lab 45, p. 117 **L2**
Critical Thinking/Problem Solving, p. 19 **L2**
Investigating Living Systems, Labs 48, 49, pp. 185, 189 **L2**

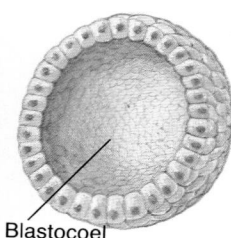

Blastocoel

Cleavage

In sexually reproducing animals, immediately after the fertilization of an egg by a sperm cell, development begins with a rapid series of cell divisions. Because the original zygote is split up, or cleaved, into many smaller cells during initial development, this process is known as **cleavage**. The group of cells produced as a result of cleavage is called a **blastula**. As you will learn, the pattern of cleavage varies among animals and is related to the amount and distribution of yolk in the zygote. Yolk is a thick protein and lipid substance that serves as a food source for the developing embryo. Cell division occurs more slowly in areas of the embryo where there is a lot of yolk because the thick yolk interferes with cleavage.

Cleavage in a Starfish Figure 19-2 shows cleavage in a starfish. The small amount of yolk in the zygote is evenly distributed. As cell division occurs without growth, the newly produced cells become smaller and smaller. The original zygote finally becomes a ball of cells, like a mass of soap bubbles, surrounding a hollow area called the **blastocoel**.

Cleavage in a Frog Now examine Figure 19-3, which shows cleavage in a frog. The frog zygote has a darker, pigmented animal pole and a lighter-colored vegetal pole. Most of the light-colored yolk is in the vegetal pole, and its presence has an effect on the pattern of cleavage. Early cleavage results in production of cells of about equal size, but as cleavage progresses, cells in the animal pole divide more rapidly than those in the vegetal pole. As a result, the cells in the animal pole are smaller and more numerous than those of the vegetal pole. Unlike the starfish, the frog blastula at this point resembles a more solid ball of cells, but it, too, contains a blastocoel filled with fluid (Figure 19-3, upper right).

Figure 19-2 Cleavage in a starfish results in a blastula (far right) that resembles a hollow ball of soap bubbles. The cells in the blastula are all about the same size. Magnification (photos): 400×

Figure 19-3 The first two cell divisions in the frog embryo are from pole to pole. The third division is perpendicular to the polar axis and results in the formation of four smaller cells at the animal pole and four larger cells at the vegetal pole. Magnification (photos): 20×

Blastocoel

19.1 EARLY STAGES OF DEVELOPMENT 🐾 **513**

SECTION 19.1

2 Teach

Brainstorming
Ask students to identify the cell process responsible for the rapid series of cell divisions that follows fertilization. **L1** **COOP LEARN**

Concept Development
Ask students to sequence the following terms or events in the order in which they occur during development: fertilization, sperm, egg, blastula, cleavage, zygote.

Using Science Terms
Have students check on the derivation of the word part *coel*. Have them explain how the term *blastocoel* relates to the derived meaning. **L1** **LEP**

Building a Model
Supply students with a predetermined amount of modeling clay shaped into a ball about the size of a plum. Advise them that this clay ball represents a starfish zygote. Ask them to illustrate the series of changes that occur to the zygote as it goes through cleavage and becomes a blastula with a blastocoel. **L1** **LEP** **COOP LEARN**

Using the Photos
Have students examine Figures 19-2 and 19-3. Ask them to prepare a table that is divided into two columns marked *similarities* and *differences*. Have them list as many similarities and differences as they can observe between these two sets of photos. **L1** **LEP**

PROJECT

Frog Eggs: Preserved frog eggs in various stages of development are available from biological supply houses. Have students examine these stages with a stereoscopic microscope or hand lens. Student diagrams may be made, and labels can be added showing the stage name as well as a brief description of the events that are occurring. **L1**

MEETING INDIVIDUAL NEEDS

Ask students working below grade level to prepare a flowchart of the events that occur within a frog egg as it goes from fertilization through blastula with blastocoel. The format to be used should appear as follows:
ZYGOTE → RAPID CELL → ETC. DIVISIONS

 LEP

Reinforcement

Have students summarize the differences in cleavage seen among starfish, frogs, and chickens. Ask them to also indicate any similarities that are seen among all three animals.

Building a Model

- Surface-to-volume ratio may be illustrated through the use of sugar cubes. Provide students with 27 cubes and ask them to stack the cubes into a large cube with three small cubes on each side. Have them consider this large cube of 27 smaller cubes as a single large cube. Have them calculate and record the surface area and volume for this large cube. Now ask them to determine the total surface area and total volume for all 27 individual cubes. Which value changes as one calculates surface area to volume for one large cube versus surface area to volume for 27 small cubes? Have students relate their findings to the events occurring during cleavage. **L1** **LEP**

- Provide students with an uninflated, round balloon. Have them blow up the balloon to about the size of a grapefruit to represent a starfish blastula. Then ask them to model indentation and subsequent formation of the archenteron (this can be done by having them push their fingers into the side of the balloon), and formation of a blastopore. Have them identify the following structures on their balloon model: ectoderm, archenteron, blastopore, endoderm, disappearing blastocoel. **L1** **LEP**

Using Science Terms

Have students relate the term *genesis* as it is used in the Bible to how it is used in the term *morphogenesis*. **L1** **LEP**

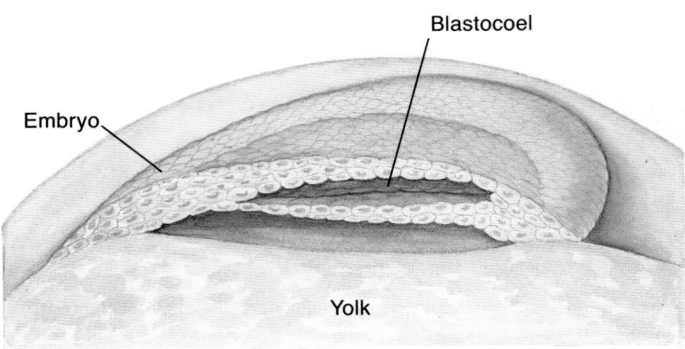

Figure 19-4 Cleavage in a chick embryo is limited to a small area at the top of the yolk. There is so much yolk that it is not cleaved through, and only a small disk of cells is produced.

Cleavage in a Chick   Figure 19-4 shows cleavage in a chick embryo. As you might expect, this cleavage pattern is quite different from those of both starfish and frogs because the chick egg contains a large amount of yolk. The embryo is a small area on top of the yolk. Because cleavage cannot cut through the yolk easily, a disk of cells, and not a ball, forms on top of the yolk like a cap, as the embryo undergoes cell division.

In all these examples, cleavage produces a mass of many cells from one original cell. Cell division occurs so quickly that there is little or no growth of the embryo at first. Why does cleavage occur first, and why is it necessary? One reason is that cleavage produces the raw materials—many cells—needed for production of a new multicellular animal. Division of the zygote into many smaller cells increases the surface-to-volume ratio of each cell in preparation for the rapid uptake of oxygen and nutrients that will be needed during the explosive growth of the embryo. Formation of the blastocoel is another reason why cleavage is important. The blastocoel is necessary to provide a space for movement of cells in the next stage of development.

Animal Development—Morphogenesis

If you think about it, you will realize that an embryo cannot just acquire more and more cells. It also begins to take on a form characteristic of its species. The term *morphogenesis* comes from two Greek words meaning "beginning structure." **Morphogenesis,** then, literally means the beginning of form or structure. That form begins to take shape during the next stage of animal development and occurs as blastula cells begin moving from one place to another.

Starfish Morphogenesis   In a starfish blastula, for example, morphogenesis begins when the outer layer of cells surrounding the blastocoel, called the ectoderm, begins to push inward at one end. This inward movement produces a small indentation. As cell division continues and more and

Suggest to students that they prepare a series of diagrams that would accurately reflect the changes that are described for a chick from zygote to blastula. The presence of yolk in the chicken egg can be ignored for the diagrams. They should label the various stages. A brief description below each diagram should explain the events that are taking place. **L1**

Visually Impaired: Students who are visually impaired may benefit from the following model. A single large ball of clay may represent a blastula. The formation of the small indentation that represents the inward movement of cells can be accomplished by having students push in one side of the clay. This will allow them to feel the ectoderm, endoderm formation, blastopore, and archenteron.

more cells move inward, the blastocoel begins to disappear, and a new cavity forms in its place. This cavity, the archenteron, will later develop into the digestive tract. The archenteron opens to the outside through an opening called the blastopore. Later, the blastopore will become the anus, and the mouth will form from a second opening that develops at the opposite end of the archenteron. Thus, with this early movement of cells comes the first evidence of body systems seen in mature organisms. Although the shape of the embryo has changed, it is no larger than the zygote was. Real growth still has not occurred.

Notice from Figure 19-5 (center) that instead of one layer of cells, the blastula now has two layers. The ectoderm cells that migrated inward have created a second layer, called the endoderm, that lies up against the inside of the ectoderm. You can picture how this happens if you think about collapsing an uninflated basketball so that the wall on one side of the ball is pushed in against the inside of the wall on the opposite side. Part of the outer wall of the basketball will form a second layer as you push it inwards, and the original interior of the basketball will disappear as a new hollow area is created.

Later, a third layer, the mesoderm, will form between the ectoderm and endoderm, further adding complexity to the developing embryo. This rearrangement of cells changes the blastula to a cup-shaped form called a **gastrula.** The entire process of cell movement, and the formation of a triple-layered embryo, is called gastrulation.

Frog Morphogenesis   Gastrulation doesn't occur in exactly the same way in a frog, because a frog blastula is a different shape and contains a greater amount of yolk concentrated in the vegetal pole. Instead of ectoderm cells pushing in, some animal pole cells first move inward through a slitlike blastopore that forms midway between the animal and vegetal

Figure 19-5   Gastrulation in the starfish occurs when the outer layer of cells begins to form an indentation (left). As the cells push inward, the blastocoel becomes smaller and the archenteron forms in its place (center). A third layer of cells, the mesoderm, forms between the ectoderm and the endoderm (right).

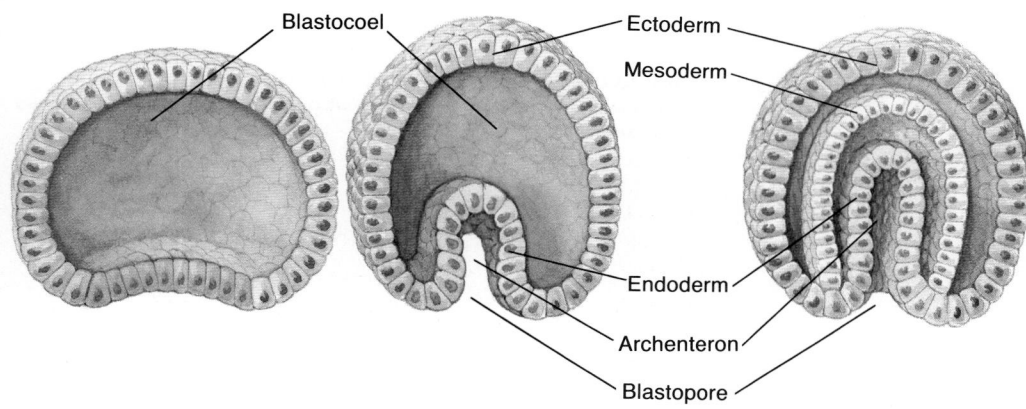

Blastocoel

Ectoderm

Mesoderm

Endoderm

Archenteron

Blastopore

19.1 EARLY STAGES OF DEVELOPMENT   **515**

▤ Minilab 1

What does sea urchin development look like?

Using low power of your microscope, examine prepared slides of the stages of sea urchin development. You should examine slides of an unfertilized egg, a fertilized egg, and stages of development up to the gastrula. Draw and label diagrams of the stages as you examine them.

Analysis   *What happens to the size of the cells as development progresses? Speculate about a major difference between development of a sea urchin and that of a human. What are some similarities?*

Minilab 1

Purpose
Students will examine prepared slides of sea urchin embryos to study the stages of development.

Skills
sequence, observe, compare and contrast

Teaching Strategies
- **Safety Precautions:** Urge students to use care when handling the microscopes.
- Sea urchin *(Arbacia)* or starfish development slides can be purchased from biological supply houses. The stages of development will be in random order on the slide.
- If your slides show a morula stage, tell students that the morula is a solid ball of cells. It becomes a blastula when the blastocoel forms.
- The fertilized egg will be surrounded by a fertilization membrane, and the nucleolus will not be visible. The unfertilized egg does not have a fertilization membrane, and the nucleolus is visible. The morula is a uniformly colored solid ball of small cells. The blastula appears as a similar ball, but the cells on the outside are lighter in color because the ball is hollow.

Expected Results
Students will note that cells become smaller and more numerous as development proceeds.

Answers
Cells get smaller. Major difference: human development is internal, sea urchin development is external. Similarity: early stages (up to blastula stage) will be very much alike.

✔ Assessment
Skill: Have students make drawings of sea urchin development in correct sequence and add their drawings to their portfolios.

MEETING INDIVIDUAL NEEDS

Have students working at grade level or below explain the fate of: the blastocoel as the ectoderm pushes in, the archenteron, and the blastopore. Ask them to name the layer or part that forms as: the ectoderm pushes inside the blastula, the ectoderm and endoderm are formed, and the blastula forms a cup-shaped structure.   **LEP**

STUDENT JOURNAL

You are a single cell that is part of a starfish blastula. Describe what things look like around you before morphogenesis begins. Describe some of the events that begin to unfold around you as you observe morphogenesis.   **L1**

Teacher FYI

Development is best understood in a roundworm called *Caenorhabditis elegans.* Cell death plays an important role in development. As a fertilized egg, many cell divisions occur and then all but six cells die. These remaining cells reproduce to form exactly 558 cells, which will form intestines, muscles, nerve cells, and an outer body wall. After three days, the worm has exactly 959 cells. Then, exactly 113 cells die. Why is this animal so good as a research tool for development? It is transparent and its few cells can easily be studied under a microscope. With so few cells, the fate of each cell can be traced. Each cell at a very early age already is programmed as to what its future fate will be. Also, every worm undergoes the same number of cell divisions at the same time and in the same place. Its growth and developmental schedule never changes.

Using the Table

Have students examine Table 19.1. Ask them to use a dictionary to determine the meaning of the prefixes *ecto, endo,* and *meso.* Have them explain why these three layers are so named, based on the prefix meanings. Ask students to note any correlation between the general location of the organs in the human body for each tissue layer and the location of the three tissue layers themselves. `L1`

`LEP`

Using Science Terms

Ask students to use a dictionary to locate at least five words that begin with the prefix *ecto.* They should record these words along with a definition and correlate the meaning or relationship of these words with the term *ectoderm.* Have them repeat the same tasks for the prefixes *endo* and *meso.* `L1`

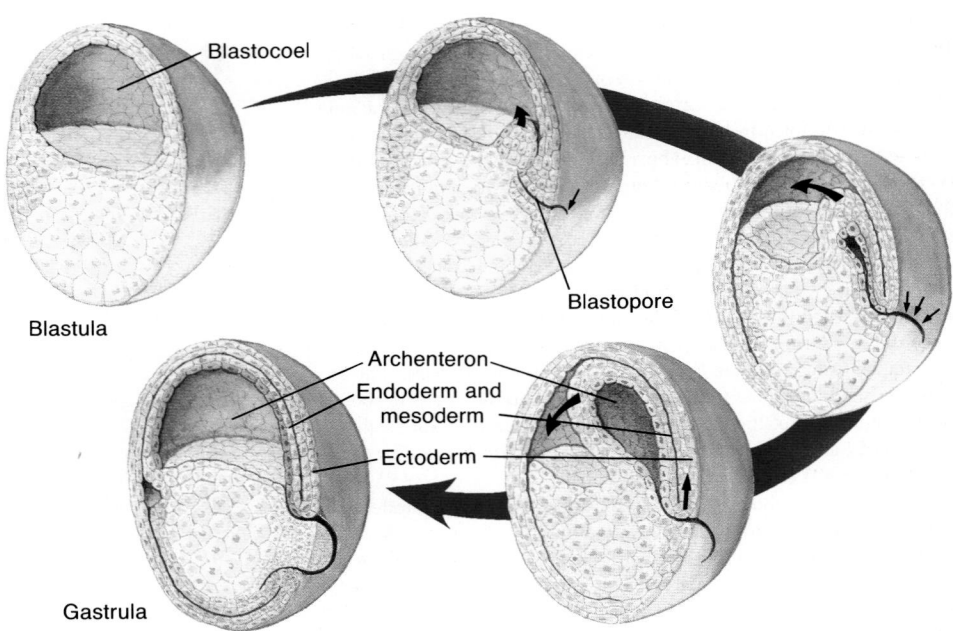

Figure 19-6 Gastrulation in the frog embryo involves movement of cells through the slit-like blastopore into the blastocoel. Note the formation of the archenteron.

poles, Figure 19-6. Later, cells on the surface of the embryo move to the blastopore until, eventually, the entire sheet of ectoderm cells that forms the surface of the embryo streams inward, as if being pulled in by an unseen pulley. As with gastrulation in the starfish, the blastocoel is replaced by the archenteron, and three tissue layers are eventually formed. If a frog gastrula is viewed from the outside, the entire embryo is dark-colored as a result of dark-pigmented ectoderm cells moving down from the animal pole and then back up and over the light-colored cells of the vegetal pole to the blastopore.

Table 19.1 Structures Produced by Tissue Layers

Ectoderm	Mesoderm	Endoderm
brain	skeleton	pancreas
spinal cord	muscles	liver
nerves	gonads	lungs
skin (outer layer)	excretory system	lining of digestive system
eye cup and lens	skin (inner layer)	
nose and ears		

MEETING INDIVIDUAL NEEDS

Provide students working at or below grade level with three photocopied diagrams of the human body showing bone, muscle, spinal cord, brain, kidneys, liver, lungs, and pancreas. Have students use a colored pencil to shade in and label those body parts formed from ectoderm. Have students use the other two diagrams and different colors to shade in and label those body parts formed from endoderm and from mesoderm. Table 19.1 is to be used as a guide. `L1` `LEP`

The cell movements and changes that occur in gastrulation mark the beginning of a definite shape for the embryo. At this point of development in the frog and starfish, there is no visible evidence of any differences in the cells of the embryo, other than size and yolk content. The cells are merely arranged into three tissue layers. However, those three tissue layers are crucial for giving rise to specialized parts later in development. Table 19.1 lists some structures that develop from each of the layers in a vertebrate.

Animal Development—Neurulation

After the completion of gastrulation in a frog (and other vertebrates), further changes can be seen along the back, or dorsal, surface of the embryo. Morphogenesis continues as ectoderm cells along the dorsal side of the embryo divide rapidly and elongate to form a flat plate. Then the sides of this plate rise up, buckling into two folds along the entire length of the embryo. These folds meet and fuse together to form a hollow structure called the **neural tube,** which pinches off from the rest of the ectoderm. These events mark the beginning of the nervous system in the developing embryo. The brain and spinal cord soon form from the neural tube. Figure 19-7 shows the development of the neural tube, called neurulation, in the embryo.

Formation of the brain and spinal cord is an example of **differentiation,** changes that result in the formation of specialized parts. During further development, all the various parts of the embryo develop. Cell division, morphogenesis, and differentiation will continue until development is completed. Because the supply of food and raw materials available to the early embryo is limited, the embryo changes shape but little real growth occurs. When differentiation is completed and the young organism can feed, a period of rapid growth begins.

Figure 19-7 As the sides of the neural plate fold upward and inward, a hollow tube is formed. This tube later becomes the spinal cord and brain. Magnification (photo): 250×

Neural plate

Ectoderm

Neural tube

19.1 EARLY STAGES OF DEVELOPMENT ✦ **517**

Figure Caption Question

Why are identical twins identical in appearance? Because they were formed from a single fertilized egg, they have the same DNA, which codes for identical traits.

Concept Development

Have students make comparisons between identical and fraternal twins in terms of number of eggs needed for each, number of sperm needed for each, which are most common, their DNA, and their appearance. Twins occur about once in every 80 to 90 pregnancies. About two-thirds of all twins are fraternal. L1

Brainstorming

Advise students that the technical term for identical twins is *mono-zygotic*, while the term that describes fraternal twins is *dizygotic*. Ask them to analyze the meaning of the two terms and explain why they appropriately describe each type of twinning. L2 COOP LEARN

Chalkboard Example

Illustrate the formation of identical and fraternal twins, drawing the correct number of eggs and sperm for each. Use a flowchart format in your illustration. Then, ask students to explain and diagram on the board how the following formations might be possible: identical triplets, triplets with two identical twins and one fraternal, and fraternal triplets. LEP

Demonstration

Check with students and teachers to identify sets of identical and fraternal twins in your school. Invite them to class and have your students ask questions of them, if the twins are willing to be interviewed by their peers. Have students attempt to keep some type of tally regarding the questions and twin responses in an attempt to determine whether identical twins show more similar personality traits than do fraternal twins.

Identical Twins

One sperm · One egg

Early embryo splits in two

Fraternal Twins

Two sperm · Two eggs

Uterus

Figure 19-8 Identical twins form from a single fertilized egg that divides into two cell masses. Fraternal twins develop from two fertilized eggs. Why are identical twins identical in appearance?

Twinning

Occasionally, as an early embryo begins to develop, the cells of the embryo separate into two cell masses, rather than remaining as one embryo. Each of these cell masses, however, still undergoes the processes of gastrulation and differentiation to develop into a new and complete animal. Thus, two animals are produced instead of one. Because they came from the same fertilized egg, the animals have the same sets of DNA and, therefore, are physically identical. These two animals are identical twins.

The more common fraternal twins are not alike, because they develop when each of two different eggs is fertilized by a different sperm. Fertilization occurs at about the same time, and development of the embryos takes place simultaneously. Each zygote begins life with a different set of DNA instructions. Therefore, fraternal twins are no more alike than any other brothers or sisters. Fraternal twins are not as common in humans as are single births because females normally produce only one egg each menstrual cycle. Must fraternal twins be the same sex? Must identical twins be the same sex? Why?

Development in Flowering Plants

As you have learned, seeds from angiosperm plants are structures containing an embryo that has developed from a zygote. Events leading to production of a plant embryo are somewhat different from the early stages of animal development.

518 ❧ DEVELOPMENT

MEETING INDIVIDUAL NEEDS

- Have students working below grade level prepare a concept map that deals only with the topic of identical and fraternal twinning. They may work in cooperative groups or individually. If done in a cooperative setting, collect some representative maps, make transparencies, and place them on the overhead projector. LEP COOP LEARN

- **Visually Impaired:** Provide students who are visually impaired with a small ball of clay to represent a developing embryo. Ask them to model the specific event that must take place in order to form identical twins. Have them explain the action they took with the clay. Then ask them what they would need and how their models might differ if they were to represent fraternal twins.

Cleavage and Morphogenesis After the zygote is formed, it divides by mitosis, producing two cells of different sizes. One of these cells, through continued cell division, gives rise to the embryo. The second cell gives rise to an elongated structure that will function in transport of nutrients from the parent plant to the forming embryo. The embryo continues to undergo cell division and growth, forming three kinds of tissues that will later develop further. Unlike cleavage in an animal embryo, early cell division and growth in the embryo of a flowering plant occur at the same time. Nor does morphogenesis occur as a result of cell movement as it does in animals. Instead, morphogenesis comes about as a result of different rates and patterns of cell division in the different parts of the embryo. To understand development in plants, you need to think about the structures seen in mature plants. Embryos of vascular plants contain structures that will eventually develop into roots, stems, and leaves. Like animal embryos, the embryos in seeds of flowering plants also contain a food source that provides the energy needed for early growth and cell division. Remember from Chapter 18 that the food source of a flowering plant embryo is the endosperm. As the food supply in the endosperm is used up, the cotyledons become the major food storage organs of the seed. A **cotyledon** is a leaflike storage organ that develops from the upper part of the embryo and to which the embryo is attached. The embryos of some flowering plants have one cotyledon; most have two.

Embryo Structure Figure 19-9 shows the fully developed embryo of a bean seed. It consists of three regions. The **hypocotyl** is the stalklike part of the embryo attached just below the cotyledons. The hypocotyl will eventually form the stem and part of the root. At the upper end of the hypocotyl, attached above the cotyledons, is the **epicotyl**. The epicotyl will form a pair of small leaves, which open early in development. At the lower end of the hypocotyl is the **radicle**, which forms the root. The epicotyl and radicle develop from regions of cell division known as **meristems**. Meristems are found in many places of growth in mature plants, as well as in the embryo. They produce cells that develop into new parts each growing season. Thus, unlike animals, many plants continue to develop new structures throughout their lifetimes.

Seed Germination Once the embryo has been formed, a seed enters a period of inactivity or dormancy that may last for long periods of time, even years in some cases. Only when a seed is placed in a suitable environment will the dormancy be broken. **Germination,** the development of a seed into a new plant, occurs if conditions such as the amounts of oxygen and moisture and a suitable temperature are favorable for growth.

Will seeds grow without stored food?

Soak six bean seeds in water overnight. The following day, carefully remove the seed coat from five of the seeds. Separate the two halves of the seeds. Using a toothpick, very gently remove the embryo from each of the five seeds. Place the embryos on a moist paper towel in a petri dish. As a control, place the sixth seed, which has not been disturbed, on the moist paper towel. Cover the petri dish. Store the petri dish in a warm place and examine it every day for several days.
Analysis What did you observe? Can a plant embryo grow without food? What is the food source for a bean embryo?

Figure 19-9 The large fleshy cotyledons of bean seeds store food that was absorbed from the endosperm when the seed developed. Note that the plant embryo inside the seed is not yet green. Why is that so?

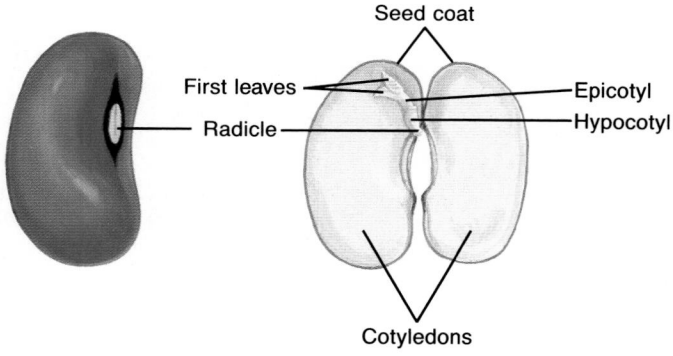

Seed coat
First leaves
Radicle
Epicotyl
Hypocotyl
Cotyledons

Minilab 2

Purpose
Students will determine whether a plant embryo can grow without a food source.

Skills
observe and infer, compare and contrast, interpret data

Teaching Strategies
- Soak the bean seeds overnight to soften them.
- The process of removing the entire embryo from the seed will result in some embryos being broken or mutilated. Discard these damaged embryos.
- Keep the paper towel in the petri dish moist.
- **Troubleshooting:** Students should exercise great care in removing embryos.

Expected Results
Isolated embryos may begin to grow if part of the cotyledon is left attached, but they will not develop properly or completely.

Answers
The isolated embryos did not grow to become plants. The food source for a bean embryo is the cotyledons.

✔ **Assessment**
Performance: Have students write evaluations of the lab in their journals.

Figure Caption Question
Why is a plant embryo inside the seed not yet green? It has no chlorophyll and cannot photosynthesize because it is inside the seed, not exposed to sunlight. Its food source is the cotyledons.

Discussion Questions
Relate the following questions to the events associated with seed germination. Why is oxygen needed by a seed? How does soil contribute oxygen to plants? Why do seeds typically germinate in the spring and not in the late fall or winter? **L1** **COOP LEARN**

PROJECT

Plant Growth: Have students plant soaked bean seeds in small, *clear* plastic cups filled with sand. Seeds are to be positioned along the outside edge of the cup so that their growth can be viewed through the cup. Students should determine the growth rate of the radicle, hypocotyl, lower part of stem, and epicotyl. Data should be recorded in a data table. **L2**

MEETING INDIVIDUAL NEEDS

Ask students working below grade level to prepare a concept map that deals only with the structures present in a bean seed. The following terms must be included in the map: *cotyledon, hypocotyl, epicotyl, radicle,* and *meristem.* Allow students to work either independently or in cooperative groups.
LEP **COOP LEARN**

The Effect of Microwave Radiation on Seed Germination

Time Allotment
1 class period, then 5 days of 10-minute observations

Objectives
Upon completing this investigation, students will be able to:
- Measure the results of microwave radiation on the germination of seeds.
- Describe the importance of the results of this experiment.

Skills
make and use tables, observe and infer, form a hypothesis, design an experiment

Materials
petri dishes (4), paper towels, seeds such as radish or beans with rapid germination time, metric rulers, masking tape, scissors, permanent marking pens, microwave oven
Safety Precautions: Be sure students follow instructions when using the microwave oven.

Preparation
A few days before the start of the lab, place 20 radish seeds on two wet paper towel circles in a petri dish sealed with masking tape. Keep the paper towels moist.

Possible Hypotheses
1. Microwaving for 15 seconds, 30 seconds, and 45 seconds on low power causes the same reduction in percent germination of seeds.
2. Microwaving for less than 30 seconds does not change germination in seeds; more than 30 seconds reduces percent germination.

Possible Procedures
- A possible procedure might be to place 20 radish seeds in each of four petri dishes. Microwave three dishes on medium setting for 10, 20, and 30 seconds, respectively. The fourth dish is the control. Add two circles of wet paper towels to each dish under the seeds. Count

The radicle is the first part of the embryo to emerge from the seed. It becomes the primary root of the plant. The area behind the radicle, the hypocotyl, lengthens, forming an arch that pushes the bean cotyledons above the soil. The part of the hypocotyl that remains in the soil becomes the upper part of the primary root. The aboveground portion becomes the lower part of the stem. The two cotyledons separate and the epicotyl emerges, forming part of the stem and the first leaves. While these events take place, the cotyledons shrink in size as the food they contain is absorbed and used by the developing plant.

INVESTIGATION

The Effect of Microwave Radiation on Seed Germination

Did you ever grow plants from seeds? The backs of the seed packages said that germination would take five days for some kinds of seeds, seven days for some seeds, two weeks for others, and three weeks for still others. Farmers select crops based on how long it takes for seeds to germinate and plants to grow. The length of time that growing conditions in the area are suitable for a particular crop is also important. If these conditions could be altered in specific ways, farmers would be able to alter planting schedules and types of crops to make their harvests larger and more profitable. In this lab, you will try to alter the germination time of seeds by treating them with microwave radiation.

Problem
What is the effect of microwave radiation on the germination of seeds?

Safety Precautions
Follow instructions for using the microwave oven.

Hypothesis
Make a hypothesis about the effect of varying doses of microwave radiation on seed germination. Explain your reasons for making this hypothesis.

Experimental Plan
1. As a group, make a list of possible ways you might test your hypothesis, using the materials your teacher has made available.
2. Agree on one idea from your group's list that could be investigated in the classroom.
3. Design an experiment that will test one variable at a time. Plan to collect quantitative data.
4. Following the style of a recipe, write a numbered list of directions that anyone could follow.
5. Make a list of materials and the quantities you will need.

520 ⬩ DEVELOPMENT

germinated seeds each day for five days.
- Alternatively, place 25 bean seeds on two circles of wet paper towel in each of four petri dishes. On the following day, expose the seeds in three dishes to 20, 40, and 60 seconds, respectively, of low-level microwaves. Do not microwave one group of seeds. Count germination for five days.

Teaching Strategies
- Pass around the seeds germinating in a petri dish. Ask students if they have ever planted seeds. Ask them if they remember how long it took for seeds to germinate. What conditions are necessary for germination of most seeds? Write the list they generate on the board: Warmth and moisture are needed, soil and light are not. Ask students how various environmental factors might alter germination rate. Discuss pollution, acid rain, and ionizing radiation.
- Make sure all seeds are treated in the same oven, as power levels vary from one oven to another.

Plant Development You have learned that plant development doesn't involve movement of cells, as occurs during animal development. Rather, plants develop as cell division and growth occur, and more and more layers of cells build up. As an example of further plant development, consider a developing plant root. At the tip of the root is a root cap that protects the delicate root as it pushes downward through the soil. Just behind this cap is a meristem region that continually produces new cells. Cells forming near the root tip replace root cap cells as they are worn away. At the same time, cells on the opposite side of the meristem expand

Germination of a Bean Seed

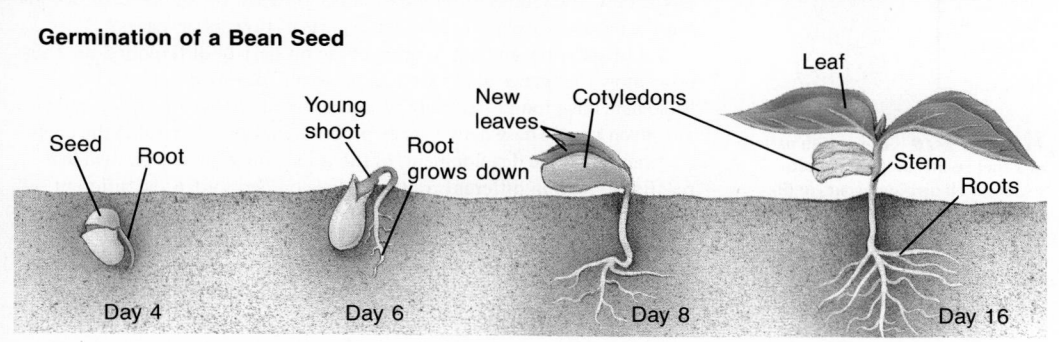

Seed · Root · Young shoot · Root grows down · New leaves · Cotyledons · Leaf · Stem · Roots · Day 4 · Day 6 · Day 8 · Day 16

Checking the Plan

Discuss the following points with other group members to decide on the final procedures for your experiment.

1. What variables will need to be controlled?
2. What is your control?
3. What will you measure or count?
4. What power levels will you use in the microwave?
5. How many seconds will you use at each power level?
6. How many groups of seeds will you use?
7. How many seeds will you use in each group?
8. Have you designed and made a table for collecting data?

Make sure your teacher has approved your experimental plan before you proceed further.

Data and Observations

Carry out your experiment, make your measurements, calculate percentages of germination, and complete your data table. Make a graph of your results.

Analysis and Conclusions

1. Was your hypothesis supported by your data? Explain.
2. What is the effect of microwave radiation on seed germination?
3. Consult with other groups and compare your results with theirs. How do you account for the similarities? The differences?

4. Speculate about why your results turned out as they did.
5. How might the size of your seeds determine the outcome of your experiment?
6. In what way might farmers benefit from the kind of lab results you obtained in this experiment?
7. Write a brief conclusion based on the results of your class or several classes.

Going Further

Based on this lab experience, design an experiment that would help to answer a question that arose from your work. Assume that you will have unlimited resources and will not be conducting this lab in class.

19.1 EARLY STAGES OF DEVELOPMENT **521**

- Make sure students use one power setting and vary the time, or one time and vary the power setting. They should not vary both in a single experiment.
- Remind students to keep their paper toweling moist during the course of their experiment.
- Tell students that germination has occurred as soon as the seed coat is broken.

Data and Observations

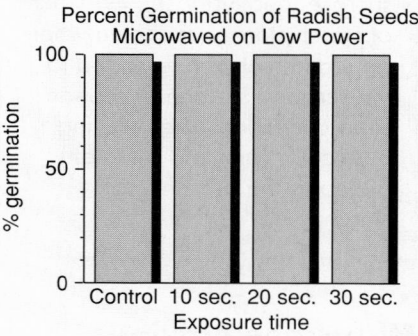

Percent Germination of Radish Seeds Microwaved on Low Power

These results show that low-power microwave radiation of 30 seconds or less does not affect germination of radish seeds.

Percent Germination of Bean Seeds Microwaved for 10 Seconds

Results indicate that 10 seconds of microwave radiation at low and medium powers does not alter germination of bean seeds, but the same time at high power decreases germination of bean seeds.

Data Analysis

1-4. Answers will vary. Students may notice that low levels or small amounts of microwave time speed germination. This may be due to the fact that water in the embryo is heated, causing faster germination.

5. Because larger seeds have more water, it takes more radiation to produce the same amount of heat in the seed.
6. If the growing season is short in an area, increased speed of germination might allow a farmer to plant crops not normally suited to that area.
7. Answers will vary.

✔ Assessment

Skill: Have students summarize the lab and write evaluations in their journals.

Extensions

Students may decide to experiment with different amounts of time and levels of microwaves, use different seeds, or use plants at various stages after germination. **L1**

Starch: Starch is the form in which plants typically store their carbohydrates. Photosynthesis produces simple sugar molecules, which are then converted into long chains of starch by condensation. Starch is technically called amylose. Typically, students will recall that almost all sugars they have studied end in the letters *ose* (glucose, sucrose, deoxyribose). Evidence of starch storage is shown when an iodine solution is added to the scraped surface of a bean seed cotyledon. The resulting blue color (amyloid reaction) indicates the presence of starch.

Microscope Activity

Obtain prepared slides of onion *(Allium)* root tips. Have students observe these slides under low and then high power. They should be able to locate the root cap with ease. It is located at the end of the root and contains cells that are not in mitosis (therefore showing no mitotic figures). The meristem area is directly behind the root cap and can be distinguished by the large number of mitotic figures. Behind the meristem region is the zone of elongation, which can be distinguished by elongating cells. Have students make diagrams of the root tip, indicate in a general way with labels and brackets where the different areas are located, and write a brief statement as to the function of each area. **L1**

Region of maturation

Root hair

Region of elongation

Meristem region

Root cap

Figure 19-10 The growth pattern of a root results in three definite regions. Cell division occurs in the meristem region. Lengthening of the root occurs in the region of elongation. Cell specialization occurs in the region of maturation.

Figure 19-11 Shown here is part of the experiment described on this page. Nuclei from blastula and gastrula cells were also transplanted into frog eggs, with similar results.

in length, adding to the total length of the root and aiding the root in pushing more deeply into the soil. Next to this lengthening region are older, more mature cells. It is here that differentiation of plant tissues begins. Tissues for uptake of water and minerals; transport of water, minerals and food; food storage; and protection all form here. In some angiosperms, another kind of meristem forms, producing cells that will develop into more transport tissue as the plant ages. The addition of such transport tissue causes the root to grow in diameter as well as in length.

Control of Differentiation

A zygote or, in the case of asexual reproduction, a single cell, contains a set of DNA that guides its development. All the many cells of the developing organism inherit that same set of DNA. If all cells contain the same DNA, how, then, does differentiation occur? How do animal cells become muscle or skin, or plant cells become parts of flowers or leaves?

Scientists are beginning to unravel the mystery of differentiation. They now know that genes are "switched on or off" during development. Biologists have found that only certain genes are active in a given cell at any given time. These active genes produce enzymes that guide the chemistry, and thus the development, of the cells. Different sets of chemical reactions result in different traits. As development proceeds, different sets of genes become activated, and cells become more and more specialized.

Actually, biologists have suspected for many years that genes may be switched on and off. Experiments conducted with frogs supported this idea. In one experiment, nuclei from blastula cells, gastrula cells, and intestinal cells of a tadpole were transplanted into unfertilized eggs from which the nuclei were destroyed by ultraviolet radiation. Many of these eggs developed into normal frogs. These offspring were clones because they were genetically identical to their parents. This experiment showed that the nuclei of cells in various stages of development still have the full set of DNA instructions. The same DNA was present in the nuclei when

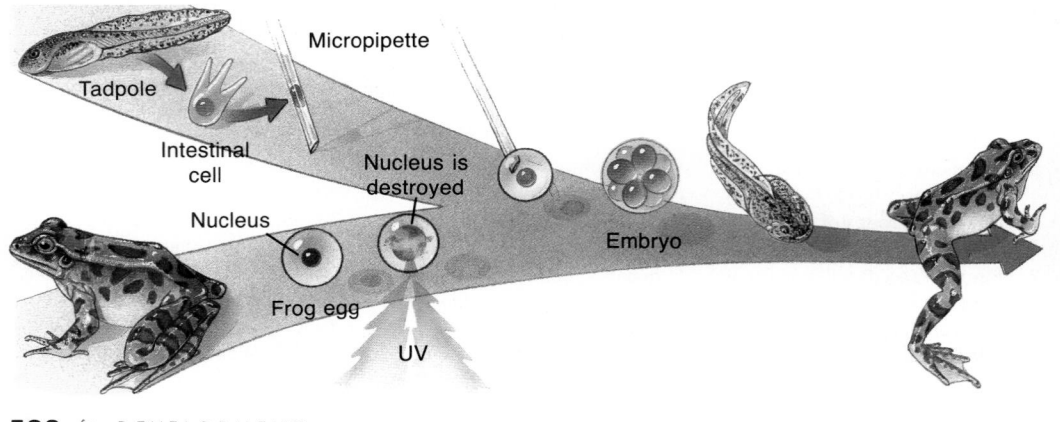

Tadpole

Micropipette

Intestinal cell

Nucleus is destroyed

Nucleus

Frog egg

UV

Embryo

Growing Seeds: Seeds are classified as either monocot or dicot depending on the number of cotyledons present. Ask students to hypothesize whether a seed with two cotyledons will germinate faster and produce a longer root within five days than a seed with one cotyledon. Have students design an experiment to test their hypotheses. Allow them to execute their plans. Remind them that the masses of the seeds should be as similar as possible.

Alternately, have students hypothesize and test whether a large seed will germinate faster and form a longer root in three days than a smaller seed. Provide students with bean and radish seeds as two good extremes in seed size. **L2** they were parts of blastula, gastrula, or intestinal cells, so some of the DNA must not have been operating. But, when the nuclei were placed in the egg cells, the DNA was switched on again. Something in the cytoplasm must have interacted with the DNA to switch it on.

Today, scientists are working to understand what causes genes to be switched on and off. Such gene regulation is probably involved in many developmental processes. How is a salamander limb regenerated? How do cells become changed in cancer? These processes are thought to be the result of different genes being switched on and off. Thus, these problems are important challenges of modern biological research.

Embryonic Induction

Using evidence gathered from studies in the 1920s, scientists know that if genes are to be switched on and off during development, some kind of chemical signal is needed. Genes respond to the signal by becoming either activated or inactivated. Scientists have learned that the relative position of embryo parts is an important factor in gene regulation.

Thinking Lab
INTERPRET THE DATA

What factors are important in sea urchin development?

Background
At one time, you were a single fertilized egg cell. How did the complexity of your body with millions of cells develop from such a simple beginning? The information coded in the genes of this single cell directs descendant cells to change in form and function in countless ways.

Fertilized sea urchin eggs contain stored food in the lower half of the

egg, called the vegetal pole, and specific mRNA and protein molecules in the upper, or animal, pole of the egg. The first two cell divisions occur from pole to pole. The third division occurs at right angles to the polar axis. When an eight-cell sea urchin embryo is divided into two sections, the resulting embryos are different, depending on how the division is made.

You Try It
The following diagram illustrates the results of an experiment in which eight-cell sea urchin embryos are divided in two ways. **Interpret the data,** in terms of the importance of the nucleus and cytoplasm, in development of sea urchins. What do you think the animal and vegetal poles contribute to the developing embryo?

Animal pole

Vegetal pole

Animal pole

Vegetal pole

19.1 EARLY STAGES OF DEVELOPMENT **523**

Thinking Lab
INTERPRET THE DATA

Purpose
Students will interpret the data of a classic experiment in differentiation.

Skills
interpret scientific illustrations, interpret data, recognize cause and effect

Teaching Strategies
• Tell students that the larvae formed

from a horizontal division of the embryo are both abnormal. The larva formed from the four cells of the animal pole has cilia but is permanently arrested at the blastula stage. The larva produced from vegetal cells looks relatively normal but lacks a mouth, cilia, and spicules. Larvae produced from longitudinally divided embryos are normal.

Answers
Elements in both poles are necessary for development of normal larvae. The vegetal pole contributes stored food; the animal pole contributes mRNA and proteins.

✔ **Assessment**
Portfolio: Have students write a summary of the lab for their portfolios.

Different Viewpoints in Biology

Is sex of an organism genetic or environmental?
Most would agree that the basis for determining the sex of an animal is genetic. However, the Atlantic silversides fish proves that both factors may be operating. When temperatures in the water are low at the start of a season, the fish being born are females. Then, as the water warms during the season, the fish born are males. The advantage of more females being born in the early part of a season allows for longer growth and greater size. Greater size also means more egg production. Thus, forming females in cold water may actually be an adaptation for survival.

3 Assess

Check for Understanding
Have students explain the relationship between each word group.
(a) mitosis—cleavage
(b) blastula—ball
(c) blastocoel—hollow center
(d) morphogenesis—movement of cells
(e) ectoderm—endoderm
(f) ectoderm—endoderm—mesoderm
(g) triple layers—gastrulation
(h) neural tube—brain—spinal cord
(i) bean embryo—epicotyl—hypocotyl—radicle **L1** **LEP**

Reteach

Take each word pair or group from the Check for Understanding on page 523 and have students write a short paragraph that explains the events being described without actually using the key words themselves. Share these paragraphs with the class and have them determine the word pairs being described. **L1** **COOP LEARN**

Extension

Have students make an analogy comparing seed dormancy and germination with an animal's hibernation and normal activities. Ask them to compare what happens to the needs for oxygen and food during hibernation and seed dormancy, and these same needs when normal animal activity and germination occur. **L2**

✔ Assessment

Skill: Students are to prepare a flowchart of the changes that occur from fertilization through development of the neural tube in a frog. **L1**

4 Close

Activity

Ask students to design a simple series of questions that shows the next step or structure that follows or appears in sequence. For example, "A radicle will form a ___." Have students exchange these questions with a classmate who is to complete them and return them to the original designer for correction. **L1**
COOP LEARN

Figure 19-12 The development of many structures is induced by other tissues lying near the structures. Formation of the frog tympanic membrane, the external hearing organ, is induced by the cartilage beneath it.

Inducers The results of these early studies led to the development of the concept of embryonic induction. **Embryonic induction** occurs when one part of an embryo somehow influences, or induces, the development of another part of the embryo. During induction, one tissue releases a chemical that passes to another tissue. That chemical, called the inducer, acts as the signal for differentiation. In the development of nervous tissue, for example, the mesoderm cells release an inducer that activates a gene (or genes) in the ectoderm. Ectoderm cells then develop into nervous tissue.

Although the specific chemical involved in nervous system development has not been identified, other inducers are known. Perhaps the best known inducers are hormones. For example, in humans, differentiation of testes or ovaries depends upon the presence of male sex hormones. The hormones induce the tissue to become testes. If the male hormones are absent, the tissue becomes ovaries.

The Role of Cytoplasm Factors other than induction also play a role in guiding differentiation of an embryo. During cleavage, division of cells can occur in such a way that the chemical composition of cytoplasm begins to vary from cell to cell. For example, some cells may contain more yolk than others. Also, different areas of the embryo become surrounded by slightly different chemical and physical environments. Such differences may act as signals that regulate genes. A domino effect can occur, where signals received by some cells result in production of chemicals that act as signals for other cells. As more and more signals are received, cells may become increasingly committed to a specialized structure and function. Most likely, these signals act by switching on genes in a specific order at specific times. Those genes, in turn, guide the overall unfolding of the animal's body plan.

Section Review

Understanding Concepts
1. How does the cleavage stage in animal development prepare for gastrulation?
2. How is neurulation an example of morphogenesis?

3. In what ways does early development in a plant differ from that in animals?
4. *Skill Review—Sequencing:* Sequence the steps in germination of a bean seed. For more help, refer

to Organizing Information in the **Skill Handbook.**
5. *Thinking Critically:* Suggest a reason why morphogenesis in plants cannot occur by the movement of cells, as it does in animals.

524 🐾 DEVELOPMENT

Answers to Section Review

1. Cleavage produces a ball of many cells, some of which will move inward during gastrulation. The hollow interior of the blastula provides a space into which those cells will migrate.
2. Neurulation creates a form or shape, a hollow tubelike area, from which the brain and spinal cord will later form.
3. In plants, reproduction and growth of cells occur at the same time.

Morphogenesis occurs as a result of different rates and patterns of cell reproduction, as opposed to the movement of cells that occurs in animals.
4. **Skill Review—Sequencing:** (1) Dormancy is broken. (2) The radicle emerges, developing into the primary root. (3) The hypocotyl appears, arching upward above the soil and forming the upper part of the root and lower part of

the stem. (4) The cotyledons separate, and the epicotyl, which gives rise to part of the stem and first leaves, emerges. (5) The cotyledons shrink as the food within them is used up during the events of germination.
5. **Thinking Critically:** Plant cells are surrounded by a rigid cell wall. Thus, movement of cells is impossible.

19.2 Patterns of Animal Development

Although animal embryos at the gastrula stage have a long way to go before they develop into mature organisms, they are still living organisms. As living organisms, they must be adapted for obtaining food, exchanging gases, and excreting wastes. As delicate organisms, they also require a means of protection and must be kept moist. Though the pattern of development up through gastrulation is basically the same in all animals, the patterns of later development vary among different groups of animals.

Metamorphosis

Most animals that develop outside the female go through a series of remarkable changes as they reach adult form. Animals such as frogs, toads, insects, crabs, clams, and starfish all share this pattern of development, called **metamorphosis**, in which they go through a series of changes in body structure. The changes that occur during metamorphosis aid developing organisms in meeting their life needs.

Metamorphosis in Frogs   Shortly after the gastrula stage, frogs, many insects, and many marine animals quickly develop into a **larva**, an immature stage that can live on its own. Larvae usually bear no resemblance to the final, mature form, but will change into that final form with time.

Fertilized frog eggs develop for one or two weeks within their jellylike blanket, obtaining energy from the yolk, and exchanging gases and getting rid of wastes by diffusion. The color pattern of their eggs, dark on top and light on the bottom, provides protection by camouflaging them from predators. To predators swimming above the eggs, the dark color they see blends with the bottom of the stream or pond. Predators swimming below the egg mass see the light color that blends with the sky.

Objectives

Relate the events of metamorphosis and development within an amniotic egg to the needs of animal embryos.

Describe the formation and functions of the placenta.

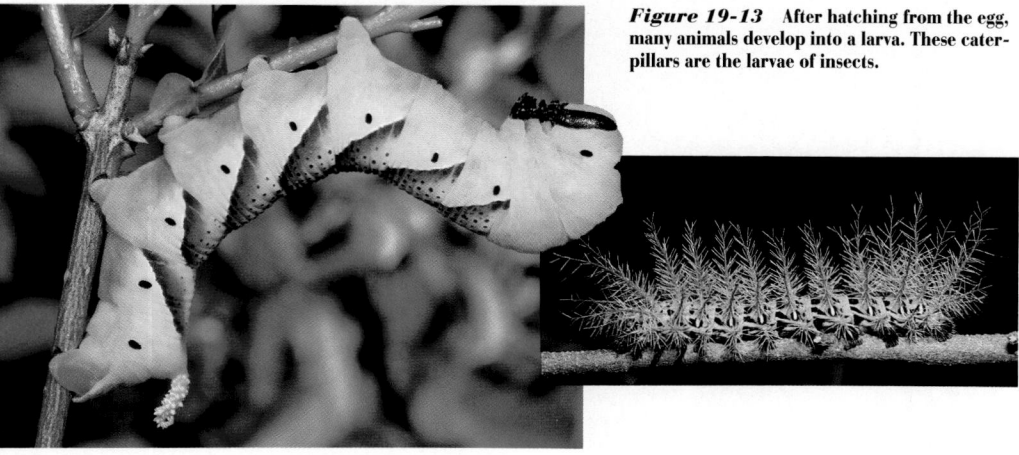

Figure 19-13   **After hatching from the egg, many animals develop into a larva. These caterpillars are the larvae of insects.**

19.2 PATTERNS OF ANIMAL DEVELOPMENT ❧ **525**

PROJECT

Tadpoles: Living tadpoles are available from biological supply houses. Encourage interested students to research the effect of adding iodine to the water of tadpoles that are undergoing metamorphosis, or the effect of water temperature on the rate of metamorphosis. **L2**

Prepare

Key Concepts
Events occurring during frog and insect metamorphosis are discussed. The contributions of an amniotic egg and internal development aiding in the success of land animals are studied and emphasized.

Key Terms
metamorphosis, larva, pupa, nymph, amnion, allantois, chorion, placenta, umbilical cord

Materials
• Order insect larvae for the Alternate Lab.

1 Focus

Objectives
The objectives are listed on the student page. Remind students to preview these objectives as a guide to this numbered section.

Discussion
Ask students if they can offer any evidence that they were totally dependent on their biological mother during development for all life needs. Discuss the significance of and technical name for the belly button (umbilicus). Ask why the structure name does *not* justify its previous function. Ask why certain fruits are called navel oranges. **L1**
COOP LEARN

2 Teach

Using Science Terms
Ask students to look up the derivation of the term *metamorphosis.* Ask them to explain why the term is appropriate when used to explain changes in development. Have them use the term in a sentence that does *not* have a scientific theme. **LEP**

SECTION 19.2

Using the Illustration

Ask students to examine Figure 19-14. Which figures in the illustration depict larval stages? Which figures depict tadpoles? Which figures depict adults or near adults? Compare the color of the adult to that of the larva, and explain why this coloration is well suited for the environment in which it lives. Explain how the tadpole and adult differ in their means of obtaining oxygen and in the type of food they eat. **L1** **LEP**

PHYSICS CONNECTION

Dissolved Gases: Oxygen comprises about 20% of the gases in air. Air dissolves in water. The result is a gas-liquid solution. The gas or air may not be visible but it is present. Ask students if they can see the dissolved carbon dioxide gas in soft drinks when the bottle is closed. They will agree that the gas is easily seen when the cap is removed and the pressure within the bottle is reduced.

Display

Purchase the various stages of frog metamorphosis from a biological supply house. They typically are available as mounted specimens within plastic. This makes them well suited for display purposes and for student examination. **L1** **LEP**

The larval form of the frog—the tadpole—is an animal that is probably familiar to you. Very young tadpoles are inactive, but changes soon begin to occur. A long, tapering tail and three pairs of external gills develop. Because the embryo is now too large to exchange gases and excrete wastes by diffusion, this exchange takes place in the gills. Gills pick up oxygen that is dissolved in the water and release carbon dioxide into the water. Until the larval structures are fully formed, the embryo must rely on its attached yolk, originally stored in the egg, as a source of both raw materials and energy. The fully formed larva has no yolk remaining as a food source, but it can now feed, using its small teeth to scrape algae and plant matter from rocks in the water. Tadpoles are protected from predators by their coloration, which enables them to hide, and by their ability to swim rapidly.

As tadpoles grow and mature, further changes occur. First, the hind legs, then the front legs, begin to appear, and the tail begins to disappear. Internally, a pair of lungs develop, and the circulatory system becomes coordinated with the lungs and skin. Eventually, the lungs and skin will be able to obtain oxygen directly from the air and get rid of carbon dioxide. There are also changes in the digestive system as the tadpole's diet switches from plants to insects. As development proceeds, new structures are formed to replace old structures, which are broken down. For example, the tadpole's tail is broken down and its components are taken into the body. Many of the materials from which these old structures were composed are used as an additional energy source for the developing frog. The many steps in metamorphosis take about three months in the common leopard frog, Figure 19-14, but the exact length of time depends on the temperature of the water.

Figure 19-14 **Metamorphosis in the frog involves an aquatic tadpole stage and a terrestrial adult stage. Note the formation of gills and eyes in the tadpole.**

External gills

Eye

526 DEVELOPMENT

ALTERNATE LAB: Insect Metamorphosis

Purpose

Students will determine whether different temperatures can alter the rate at which insect larvae become pupae.

Materials

petri dishes (3), insect larvae *, paper towels, labels, scissors, thermometer, water, tape, incubator, refrigerator

* Order *Drosophila,* housefly, or *Sarcophaga* larvae from a biological supply house.

Procedure

Give the following directions to students.
1. Cut out four circles of paper towel to fit the bottom of each of three petri dishes. Stack the circles in the bottom of the dishes.
2. Moisten the circles with water.
3. Add 10 insect larvae to each dish.
4. Cover each dish, tape it closed, and label it with your name, date, and either *room, cold,* or *warm.*

5. Place one dish in each of three environments: the classroom, an incubator set at 30°C, and a refrigerator set at 5°C.
6. Make a data table and record the temperatures of each environment.
7. Examine the dishes each day for five days. Record the numbers of larvae that have become pupae at each temperature.
8. Check and add more water to each dish as needed to keep the toweling moist.

Using the Illustration

Have students examine Figure 19-15. Ask them to explain, interpret, or answer the following. What structures are being shown on the underside of the leaf? What is the purpose of the large, balloon-like diagram in the upper left corner? Describe the appearance of the larva. Describe two adaptive values or reasons for having the female deposit her eggs on leaves. Describe the appearance of the pupa. Is the pupa also a free-living stage that feeds independently? Describe how the adult differs from both larval and pupal stages. **L1** **LEP**

Brainstorming

Ask students how they would modify Figure 19-15 to illustrate that metamorphosis is a life cycle pattern that occurs over and over again. **COOP LEARN**

Enrichment

Have students determine the usage of or difference between a chrysalis and a cocoon. Have them research the life cycle of *Bombyx mori* (silkworm) and report the economic importance of this insect. To add a challenge to this enrichment, do not tell them that the organism they are checking on is the silkworm. Allow them to determine this on their own. **L2**

Figure 19-15 Complete metamorphosis in insects is shown in the development of a butterfly. The egg undergoes changes, becoming a larva and then a pupa. The adult emerges from the pupa.

Complete Metamorphosis in Insects   After internal fertilization, the eggs of insects are deposited by the female in places such as water, soil, plants, or other animals, where they develop and grow to maturity. If you've ever looked at the undersides of leaves, you may have seen such eggs. The young embryos enclosed in the eggs obtain food from the yolk. They exchange gases and release wastes by diffusion through a porous shell, which also protects the embryo. Eventually the embryo hatches, begins to feed, and undergoes metamorphosis.

Most insects undergo complete metamorphosis, which occurs in four stages—egg, larva, pupa, and adult. In complete metamorphosis, a fertilized egg first develops into a wormlike larva such as a fly maggot or the caterpillar of a butterfly or moth. Protected by its exoskeleton and camouflage coloration, an insect larva is free-living and secures its own food. This food is, of course, needed as an energy source for the larva, but it is also important for the changes that follow.

After a period of rapid growth, the larva becomes inactive and develops into a **pupa**, a stage in which tremendous change occurs. Because it is inactive, the pupa is usually enclosed within some type of protective case. During the pupal stage, the tissues of the animal are completely reorganized. The source of energy needed for this change is the food eaten during the larval stage. After a period of time, a fully formed adult emerges from the pupa.

19.2 PATTERNS OF ANIMAL DEVELOPMENT **527**

Using Science Terms

Have students use a dictionary to check the Latin meaning of the word *nymph.* Have them explain how this meaning applies to the way in which we use the word. **L1**

Misconception

Students believe that chickens will only lay eggs if a rooster is present. Typically, no roosters are present nor are they needed during egg production by hens. A hen will produce eggs just as a human female will produce eggs without the presence of males. In both cases, the role of the male is to fertilize eggs but not to control the production of them.

Brainstorming

Ask students how it is possible for bird or reptilian eggs to be fertilized when the egg is surrounded by a shell. Students may offer a variety of solutions to the problem. The female stores sperm in the oviduct of her reproductive tract. As eggs without a shell pass this area, sperm fertilize the egg. A shell then forms around the egg. **COOP LEARN**

Enrichment

Have students carefully open a fresh chicken egg and pour the contents into a shallow dish. Have them note the thin membrane that surrounds the yolk and keeps it intact. Have them locate the small white disk that appears on the yolk surface. Ask them what this might be. Advise them that this is actually the egg, or blastoderm. This is the site of fertilization if the egg were fertilized. **L1**
COOP LEARN

Figure 19-16 Grasshoppers are insects that exhibit incomplete metamorphosis. A female deposits fertilized eggs in the ground. A nymph hatches from the egg and grows in size. Eventually, the nymph will develop wings and a reproductive system, and become an adult.

Incomplete Metamorphosis   Some insects, such as grasshoppers, undergo a gradual or incomplete metamorphosis, as seen in Figure 19-16. Their life cycle includes only three stages—egg, nymph, and adult. The female grasshopper digs a hole in the ground and deposits her fertilized eggs in the hole. A fertilized grasshopper egg hatches into a **nymph,** an immature stage that closely resembles the adult but is smaller and wingless. Note in Figure 19-16 that the nymph also has a large head, compared to the adult insect. As a nymph develops into an adult, it grows in size and usually forms wings. Internally, a reproductive system also develops.

The Amniotic Egg

If you've ever seen a mass of frog eggs in the water, you've probably noticed that there are hundreds, perhaps thousands, of such eggs. The laying of such large numbers of eggs is an adaptive strategy of some animals to ensure survival of offspring. Because the eggs and the developing larvae of these animals are eaten by so many predators, many eggs must be produced to ensure survival of a few. And because the eggs are fertilized externally, they must be laid in water. Water keeps the eggs moist and serves as a medium for transporting sperm.

Survival on Land   An important adaptation that allowed reptiles and birds to survive on land was internal fertilization. After fertilization occurs within the female, the zygote travels down the oviduct as a shell develops around it. In reptiles, the shell is tough and leathery; in birds, it is brittle and porous.

Membranes   In addition to the shell, four membranes later develop around the embryo. The innermost of these, the **amnion,** is a fluid-filled sac in which the embryo floats. The amniotic fluid keeps the embryo moist, and the waterproof shell offers protection and prevents evaporation. Because of the presence of the amnion, eggs of birds and reptiles are known as amniotic eggs. Evolution of the amnion, along with that of the shell and internal fertilization, allowed development to occur on land.

Connected to the digestive region of the embryo is a membrane sac called the **allantois.** Because the developing embryo is a living organism, it produces waste products, and these are excreted into and collected in the allantois. When a reptile or bird hatches, it leaves behind the allantois and its collected wastes. Thus, the allantois can be thought of as an embryonic garbage bag.

528 🦗 DEVELOPMENT

PROGRAM RESOURCES

Teacher Classroom Resources
Study Guide, pp. 111-114 **L1**
Concept Mapping, p. 19 **L1**   **LEP**
Exploring Environmental Issues, pp. 13-14
   L3
Probing Levels of Life, Labs 46, 47,
   pp. 119, 121 **L2**

Color Transparency #35, 36, 37 **L1**
   LEP
Investigating Living Systems, Labs 50, 51,
   pp. 193, 195 **L2**

Also attached to the developing digestive system of the embryo is the yolk sac, a membrane that encloses the yolk. The fatty yolk, along with the protein-rich white of the egg, is a food source for the developing embryo. The yolk sac contains blood vessels through which the food passes to the embryo's cells.

Beneath the porous shell lies a very thin membrane, the **chorion,** which encloses the other three membranes. Part of the chorion lies close to the allantois. Together, these two membranes function in gas exchange. Oxygen passes across the porous shell and through the membranes of the chorion and the allantois. The oxygen diffuses into blood moving through the vessels of the allantois and is carried back to the embryo. Carbon dioxide leaves the embryo, traveling in the opposite direction.

You may have noticed a small pocket of air trapped near the blunt end of an egg. It is especially noticeable when you remove the shell from a hard-boiled egg. Near the end of its development period, a bird obtains additional oxygen by poking its beak through the membrane into this air pocket. Using this air, the bird's lungs start working. The bird then begins to break open its shell and breathes air from outside.

Figure 19-17 Some reptiles lay amniotic eggs, an adaptation for life on land. These Eastern hognose snakes are just hatching. Note the leathery shell of reptile eggs.

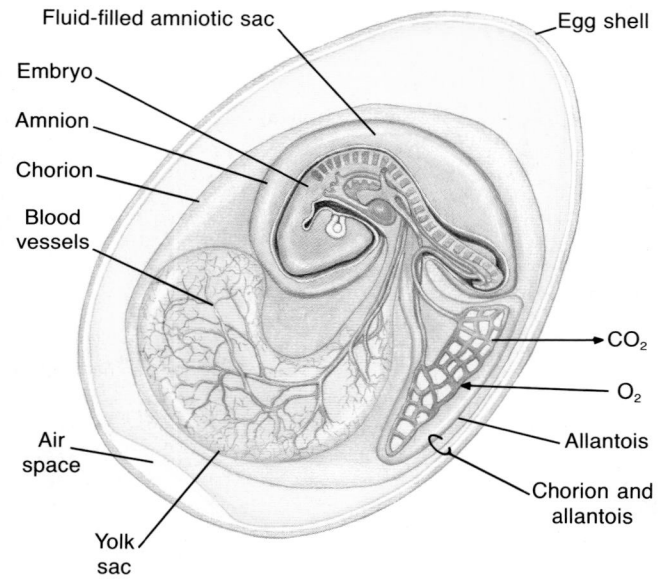

Fluid-filled amniotic sac
Egg shell
Embryo
Amnion
Chorion
Blood vessels
CO₂
O₂
Allantois
Air space
Chorion and allantois
Yolk sac

Figure 19-18 An amniotic egg provides protection, a food source, and a means of gas exchange and waste removal. What is the food source?

19.2 PATTERNS OF ANIMAL DEVELOPMENT **529**

SECTION 19.2

Figure Caption Question
What is the food source in an amniotic egg? the yolk

Using the Illustration
Have students examine Figure 19-18. Ask them to answer the following questions. What might be the role of the blood vessels that cover the yolk? How might food stored in the egg white, or albumen, eventually reach the developing embryo? What structure in the developing egg might be analogous to our lungs?

Brainstorming
Ask students to explain how and why each of the following may or may not interfere with normal development of an egg: a non-permeable material such as wax covering the eggshell, removal of the shell without damaging any structures beneath it, having no yolk or albumen, having no chorion and allantois, and having no air space at the egg's end. **COOP LEARN**

Demonstration
Bring a hard-boiled egg to class. Have students carefully remove the shell from the rounder (blunt) end. Ask them to locate the air space that appears at this end. Have them open the other end for comparison. Point out the membranes that are located directly beneath the shell. They are the inner and outer shell membranes, not the chorion or allantois. **L1**
COOP LEARN

MEETING INDIVIDUAL NEEDS
Have students working at or below grade level trace Figure 19-18 onto a sheet of paper. Ask them to label all structures. Then, in addition to the labels, have students describe briefly the function of the labeled parts, placing this information next to the appropriate label. You may wish to have them place their completed diagrams into their portfolios. **LEP**

PORTFOLIO
Ask students to draw a developing chick in an egg. Have students draw arrows of four colors to show the direction of food as it moves from its source to the embryo, the direction of oxygen from outside the egg to the embryo, the direction of carbon dioxide from the embryo to outside the egg, and the direction of wastes from the embryo to the storage site. **L1**

Fetal Development: Have students prepare a graph that illustrates the change in size of a developing human fetus from day 24 to day 266. Provide students with the following data.

Day	Length
24	3.0 mm
28	5.0 mm
35	1.3 cm
56	2.5 cm
84	10.0 cm
112	20.0 cm
126	30.5 cm
266	53.0 cm

Have students decide on the proper spacing of units for time and length. The completed graphs may be placed in their portfolios. **L1**

Enrichment

Have students use Appendix A to name the technical categories used in the classification of placental and marsupial mammals. Have them evaluate the closeness of these two animal types based on where their classification categories differ. **L3**

Using the Illustration

Have students examine Figure 19-20. Ask them the following. Explain how the large circled diagrams of fertilization and blastula differ. Explain the events that have brought about the change from a single-celled egg to the many cells in the blastula. Where does the event of fertilization actually occur along the pathway of female organs? Define what the term *implantation* refers to. What structure already is forming in the large circular diagram marked *implantation* that anchors the embryo to the uterus? How would all events in the diagram differ if no sperm had been present? **L1**

Figure 19-19 **Placental mammals feed their young milk that is produced in mammary glands.**

Figure 19-20 **The eggs of placental mammals are fertilized in the oviduct. The zygote then begins development before implantation in the uterus.**

Internal Development

In the chapter opener, you learned that the offspring of the pouched group of mammals, the marsupials, develop inside the female's uterus for only a short period of time. Because marsupials have no means of providing the embryo with food and oxygen, and removing carbon dioxide and wastes, for a longer period of time, the offspring develop in the uterus only briefly and are born very tiny and physically immature. In most mammal groups, however, more complete development of the embryo occurs within the mother. If complete internal development is to occur, there must be methods for a continuous food supply, gas exchange, and waste removal. These methods are found in another group of mammals—the placentals. In these mammals, tissue called the **placenta** is formed from both the mother's uterus and the embryo itself. Exchange of gases between the embryo and the mother occurs in the placenta. Also, the placenta is the site where nutrients are obtained and wastes are removed. Humans, dogs, rats, horses, and deer are examples of placental mammals.

Development of the Placenta   Prior to fertilization in placental mammals, the uterus becomes thickened, and its blood supply increases. After an egg is fertilized in the oviduct, the newly formed zygote divides to form a blastula that travels down the oviduct to the uterus. During this time, the embryo obtains nutrients from a small amount of yolk. On the sixth or seventh day after fertilization, the blastula attaches to the spongy wall of the uterus. Cells of the blastula produce enzymes that digest away some of the thick uterine lining, and the embryo becomes embedded in the uterine wall. The attaching and embedding of the embryo within the uterus is called implantation. This event marks the start of pregnancy.

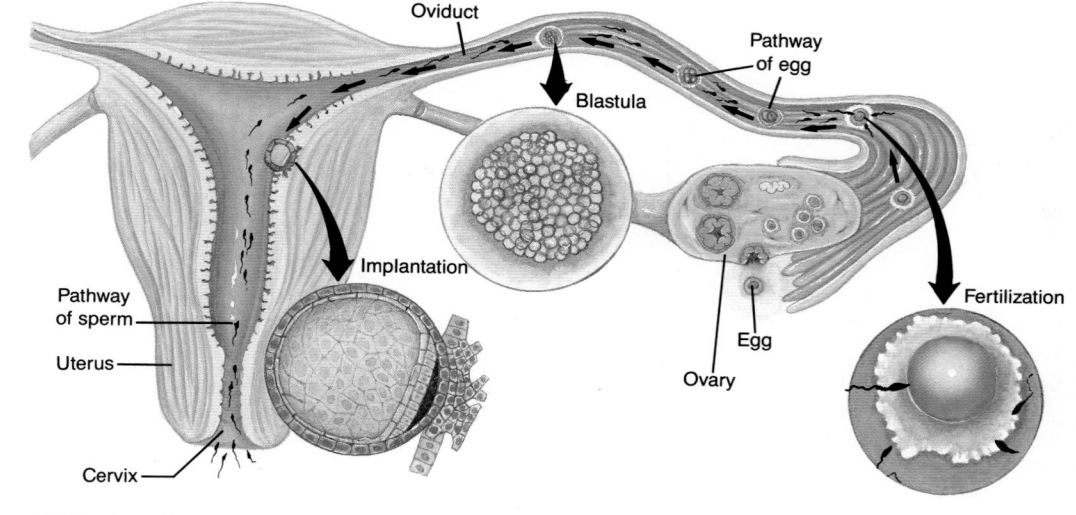

530 🐾 DEVELOPMENT

Menstrual Myths: The menstrual period has always been surrounded by myth. The word *taboo* may come from the Polynesian word for menstruation. Not all the myths are negative, however. A girl's first period is greeted with celebration in some areas, for it means that she can now have children. Canada's Naskapi, for example, create elaborate caribou veils for women during their first menses.

Apache girls kneel on a sacred deerskin during a four-day celebration of their first menstrual period.

Figure 19-21 Protective membranes surround the developing embryo in the uterus. The placenta serves as a site for the exchange of gases, nutrients, and wastes between the mother and the fetus. Materials are transported to and from the fetus through blood vessels in the umbilical cord. There is no direct connection between the circulation system of the fetus and that of its mother.

As implantation occurs, an amnion, similar to the amnion of bird and reptile eggs, begins to form around the embryo. In addition to the amnion, the other membranes found in the amniotic egg develop. In placental mammals, however, these membranes are modified for different functions and some become part of the placenta. For example, as the placenta develops, fingerlike projections of the chorion begin to grow into the uterine wall. In these projections, small blood vessels—capillaries—develop from the allantois and become part of the placenta. The rest of the placenta is made of uterine tissue. The capillaries in the placenta are part of the embryo's circulatory system. As these capillaries form, the embryo's heart and circulatory system are also developing. In humans, these changes occur during the fourth week of development.

Functions of the Placenta The embryo is connected to the placenta by the **umbilical cord,** which contains large blood vessels that transport blood between the embryo and the placenta. These blood vessels are formed from the allantois. There is a separate placenta and umbilical cord for each developing embryo, except for most identical twins, who share a common placenta.

Concept Development

- Events in the formation of the placenta require four weeks. At that time, the embryo begins to receive nourishment from the mother. What did the embryo depend on for nourishment until this time?
- Have students record the following terms: *blastula, chorion, amnion, allantois,* and state what each of these parts becomes in a placental mammal. As a special challenge, ask them to take these same four structures and explain what each becomes in the chicken egg during development. L2

Using an Analogy

Ask students to explain the function and structure of the "umbilical cord" that connects an astronaut to the space capsule during a space walk. Why is the cord called by this name? Is it an appropriate name? Why? LEP

Brainstorming

In a technique called chorionic villus sampling, a tube or catheter is passed through the vagina and uterus, and a small sample of chorionic villi (the fetal portion of the placenta) is removed from the developing embryo for analysis. Have students explain how this technique can be used to determine genetic and chromosomal information about the embryo before it is born. Also, have students explain how the possibility of sampling the mother's cellular material by mistake could happen. Why would this technique not work before the mother is at least four weeks pregnant? L1 COOP LEARN

PORTFOLIO

Have students design and then draw a time line that illustrates the following human events: egg released from ovary, egg fertilized, zygote becomes a blastula as it travels down oviduct, implantation into uterus lining, continued growth and development for next 258 days. If providing the events to students, provide them in a scrambled order. L1

MEETING INDIVIDUAL NEEDS

Ask those students who are working below grade level to prepare a flowchart sequencing the changes that are described in the text subsection, Development of the Placenta. Only those events of major importance are to be included. This is not to be a concept map, but those students who can visualize the assignment better as a concept map may use this format. LEP

Brainstorming

Certain chemicals and cells can move across the placenta from mother to embryo. Ask students to consider each of the following short scenarios. (1) Children born to mothers with HIV are also HIV positive. How does this happen? Is this a case of movement across the placenta? (2) A mother's blood type is AB but her child's blood type is O. Can blood cells move across the placenta? (3) A mother has syphilis and her child is born with congenital syphilis. What organism is responsible? Is this a case of movement across the placenta? (4) Babies are born with antibodies against the common cold. Chemically, what are antibodies? Is this an example of movement of materials across the placenta? **L3** **COOP LEARN**

Blood pumped by the embryo's heart enters arteries of the umbilical cord and circulates through the capillaries of the placenta. The blood comes into close contact with the blood in the mother's uterine wall. The two blood supplies normally do not mix together, but they are close enough so that certain materials diffuse between them. The mother's blood carries nutrients digested by her system and oxygen taken in by her lungs. Some of these molecules diffuse from her blood to the embryo's blood in the capillaries of the placenta. Water and vitamins also pass from mother to embryo. The blood then travels to the embryo through a vein in the umbilical cord and circulates through the embryo's blood vessels. The oxygen and nutrients diffuse from the blood into the embryo's body cells. At the same time, carbon dioxide leaves the embryo's cells and enters its blood. At the placenta, the carbon dioxide diffuses into the mother's blood and is later exhaled by her lungs. Excretory products are also transferred to the mother at the placenta to be excreted later by her. The amniotic fluid cushions the embryo and keeps it moist. Thus, placental development provides an embryo with a favorable environment until it is

ART CONNECTION

Storytellers: The Birth and Development of an Art Form

"They aren't just pretty things I make for money," says Pueblo artist Helen Cordero of her storyteller figures, adding that her work comes

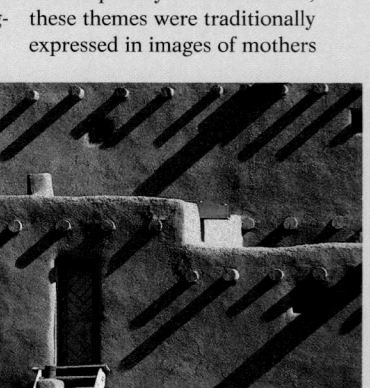

from her heart. In making her first clay figure of a storyteller, Cordero created a new form to express two common themes in art: the interaction between humans and their descendants, and the systems by which culture is passed on. In the Pueblo pottery of New Mexico, these themes were traditionally expressed in images of mothers

singing to their children. Although most Pueblo pottery has taken the form of functional pots and vessels decorated with geometric designs, clay figures have flourished in the last century, especially at Cochiti Pueblo.

Late in life, Cordero, who lives at Cochiti Pueblo, began to make clay figures. At one of her first exhibits, her figures attracted the attention of a collector, who bought all of her work. He later ordered a number of commissioned pieces, including a singing mother with her children.

Shaping the singing mother reminded Cordero of her grandfather, a famous Pueblo storyteller. She formed a clay image of him telling stories to his five grandchildren. Because Cordero herself was one of the grandchildren, the piece was a self-portrait as well as a portrait of her grandfather. The figure of her grandfather was the first of many storyteller figures by Cordero.

532 DEVELOPMENT

PROJECT

Fetal Pathways: Provide students with a large copy of this diagram and five different colored pencils.

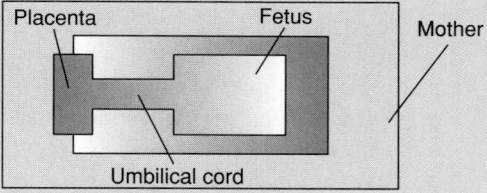

Have students use a series of short, colored arrows to follow the pathways that food molecules, oxygen, carbon dioxide, vitamins and water, and excretory products will take between mother and fetus. Have students use a different colored pencil for each pathway and provide a key to identify each pathway. **L1**

ready to exist independently. All the needs of the developing embryo are provided for within the mother's body. Because placental development meets an embryo's needs so well, the embryo's chances of survival are very good. Fewer eggs need to be produced to ensure continuity of the species.

Birth

As development proceeds, the embryo grows and causes the uterus to expand. After about eight weeks, the embryo is called a fetus. The developing fetus is nourished by the placenta for the entire gestation period, the period of internal development. In humans, the gestation period lasts about 266 days, about nine months. This time span is divided into three trimesters, each equal to three months. During the first trimester, all the body systems of the embryo begin to form. During the second trimester, growth and maturation of fetal tissues continue. The fetus triples its mass during the third trimester. Figure 19-22 on page 536 shows human development.

19.2 PATTERNS OF ANIMAL DEVELOPMENT **533**

SECTION 19.2

Teacher FYI

The hormone oxytocin produced by the pituitary gland is responsible for the ensuing three stages of labor. Stage 1 is a dilation stage whereby the amnion and chorion are forced into the cervical canal by contractions of the uterus. The cervix slowly dilates, and the amniotic and chorionic sacs rupture, causing fluid to escape via the vagina. Stage 2, called the expulsion stage, occurs as contractions of the uterus become stronger and are aided by the voluntary contraction of abdominal muscles. The fetus is forced through the cervical canal and vagina. In stage 3, the membranes along with the placenta are expelled. On occasion, the fetus cannot be pushed from the uterus and a surgical procedure called a cesarean section is performed. A vaginal birth may be impossible due to the position of the fetus (breech position) or the mother's pelvic opening being too small. About one in five births today are cesarean. The term originated from the fact that Julius Caesar was delivered in this manner.

534

At the end of the gestation period, hormones secreted by the mother interact to start labor, a series of contractions of the uterine muscles. The amniotic sac bursts, and the cervix and the opening of the vagina dilate. As contractions become more frequent and intense, the fetus is pushed downward in the uterus. Usually the fetus is in a head-down, face-down position. Further contractions push the fetus headfirst out of the mother's body through the vagina. This expulsion of a fetus from the uterus is called birth, and is followed by a final series of contractions that expels

PSYCHOLOGY CONNECTION

Infant Learning

"The assumption used to be that there was practically nothing going on in the heads of these infants," says UCLA psychologist Randy Gallistel. "Now we can see that many of the foundations of adult thinking are present at a very early age." The findings of numerous studies support his statement.

In fact, research conducted at Johns Hopkins University indicates that human babies are born capable of making logical inferences and perceiving simple cause-and-effect relationships. When babies a few hours old were repeatedly given sugar from the left side after their foreheads were stroked by researchers, the babies began to turn to the left whenever their foreheads were stroked. If no sugar was provided, they cried.

Cognition
Cognition is the process by which humans gain meaning from what the senses perceive. The senses provide the brain with raw information. During infancy, humans develop the ability to learn about, draw meaning from, and act upon this sensory information. They learn to relate events, experiences, and sensory perceptions.

Sense Perception at Birth The ability to see, hear, smell, taste, and touch all develop in the fetus before birth. Although infants are born with all five senses, perception and discrimination are not well developed. Even so, babies can recognize mothers by voice or scent within their first month of life.

Newborns seem to seek information about their environment, and they prefer certain kinds of sensory stimuli. For example, they prefer vivid colors, sweet tastes, language sounds, and certain odors. Babies examine patterns methodically, as though trying to learn about them.

Sense Perception in the First Six Months By the time infants are three or four months old, they begin to understand that objects have constant shapes and sizes. They can tell objects apart by their size, shape, and color. They also discriminate between complex sounds.

Before six months of age, infants can tell whether or not a person's lip movements match the speech sounds they hear. They also know that objects continue to exist even when hidden from view, and that two objects cannot occupy the same space.

534 DEVELOPMENT

the placenta, a stage called afterbirth. In humans, the umbilical cord is tied and cut immediately after birth. The remainder of the cord dries up and falls off the baby after several days. The navel is the place where the umbilical cord was attached to the baby's body.

In reptiles, birds, and mammals, most differentiation is completed before the young animal is hatched or born. After that, mostly growth occurs. The period of growth varies from animal to animal. In humans, it lasts for about 18 to 21 years.

In 1992, a study at the University of Arizona suggested that infants as young as five months of age can count and perform simple addition and subtraction. For example, if an infant watched a researcher place first one, then another doll behind a screen, the infant expected to see two dolls when the screen was removed.

You might wonder how a researcher determines what infants know, believe, or expect, given that they cannot speak. When infants see something different from what they expect, they stare at it longer than when they see something they predicted. Researchers use this tendency to evaluate infants' predictions. For example, in the study just mentioned, an infant watched a researcher place two dolls behind the screen. If the researcher then removed the screen, revealing only one doll, the baby registered surprise by staring longer than when it saw the two dolls it expected to see.

Informally and in research settings, infants reveal the connections they make in various ways as they interact with their environment. You may have watched babies smile, laugh, cry, and explore objects as they made connections. Perhaps researchers who establish that infants are capable of complex cognitive processes are only proving what mothers have always known.

1. **Connection to Neonatology:** The experiment at Johns Hopkins University suggests that infants made incorrect cause-and-effect connections and incorrect inferences. How, then, does the research support the statement that babies have the ability to extract cause and effect and make logical inferences?
2. **Solve the Problem:** How could the methods used at the University of Arizona be used to demonstrate that babies know objects continue to exist even when hidden from view?
3. **Solve the Problem:** If an infant did not understand that objects exist even when hidden from view, how would this affect his or her performance on the test for mathematical ability at the University of Arizona?
4. **Connection to Health:** Based on the information in this feature, what could a parent do to provide sensory stimulation and information for a young infant? How can their interaction with families help babies learn about their environment?
5. **Explore Further:** What role does sensory stimulation play in infant development? What effect does sensory deprivation have on young humans and animals?

Bioethics

Fetal Tissue Implants: A number of human diseases have the potential for being treated through fetal tissue implants. Cells from an aborted fetus may be implanted into a Parkinson's disease, juvenile diabetes, or muscular dystrophy patient. Fetal tissue is not rejected by the recipient's immune system, so these transplanted cells grow and take over the function of the diseased tissue. Research in the field of fetal tissue implantation was halted in the United States from 1988 until 1993 because of a government ban. Those who think the ban should be reinstated believe that this type of research creates a market for fetal tissue and, thus, increases the number of abortions. Those opposed to the ban claim that the issue should not be linked to the possible increase in abortions. Should the government be involved with setting this type of policy? Should researchers be looking for non-human fetal tissues with which to experiment? Should this research be allowed?

3 Assess

Check for Understanding

Ask students to compare and contrast the following.
(a) incomplete versus complete metamorphosis
(b) method of obtaining oxygen in a frog larva versus in an adult frog
(c) amniotic egg structure versus frog egg structure
(d) food, oxygen, waste removal in a developing amniotic egg versus in a developing placental mammal
(e) protective structures in an amniotic egg versus in a developing placental mammal **L1**

Figure 19-22 These photos show selected stages of the 9-month development that produces a human baby. A six-week human embryo (a) shows paddles for hands and feet on limb buds, and a large head with forming eyes and ears. (Magnification: 10×) At eight weeks (b), facial features become more obvious and hands and feet more developed. (Magnification: 7×) At eleven weeks (c), fingers and toes are clearly visible, and the rib cage can be seen just beneath the elbow. At 22 weeks (d), a human fetus is well-developed and grows rapidly. If born prematurely at this time, however, it can survive only with special care. After nine months (e), a baby is born.

536 DEVELOPMENT

PORTFOLIO

Have students prepare a graph that plots age (x axis) against mass, using the following data. Ask them how many weeks mark each trimester and what percent of the total mass the fetus has gained in each. Does mass gain appear to be about equal throughout the developmental time? They should use specific percentages to support their answers. **L2**

Age of Fetus (weeks)	Mass (grams)
4	0.5
8	1.0
12	15.0
16	100.0
20	300.0
24	650.0
28	1100.0
32	1700.0
36	2400.0
38	3300.0

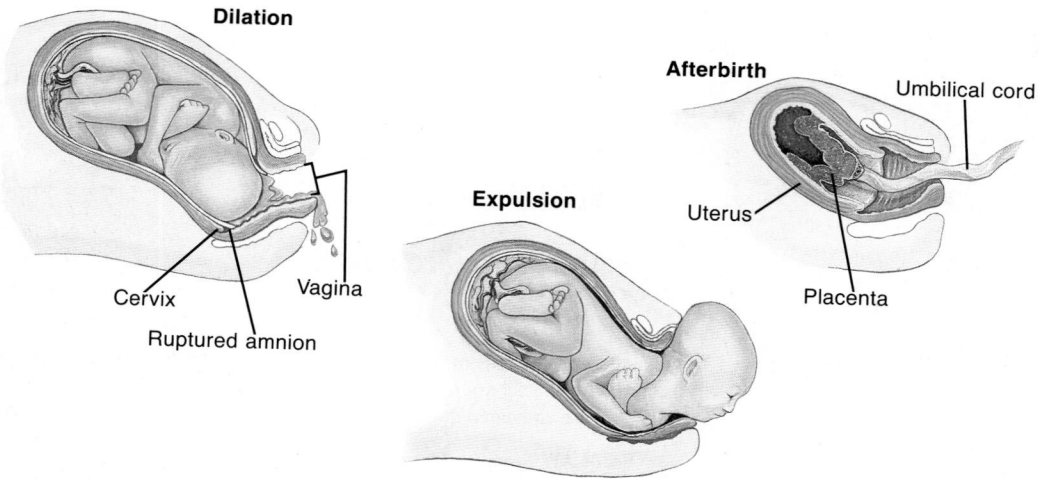

Dilation

Afterbirth
Umbilical cord

Expulsion

Uterus

Cervix

Vagina

Placenta

Ruptured amnion

Figure 19-23   The stages of birth are dilation, expulsion, and afterbirth.

LOOKING AHEAD

IN THIS CHAPTER and the last, you have studied two related processes—reproduction and development. In the next chapter, you will learn how organisms obtain the materials they need for growth and for energy, and what happens to those materials once they enter the organism. You will compare the needs of autotrophs and heterotrophs, and examine why heterotrophs must have specialized means of processing the materials they obtain from the environment. Finally, you will examine different ways in which heterotrophs are adapted to carry out that processing.

Section Review

Understanding Concepts

1. Why must the embryo of a frog quickly become a larva?
2. Both insects and birds develop within shelled eggs. Do they have the same pattern of development? Explain.

3. Explain why frogs, reptiles, and placental mammals, in that order, produce decreasing numbers of eggs at one time.
4. *Skill Review—Making Tables:* Make a table listing the adaptations that butterfly, bird, and human embryos have for obtaining food,

exchanging gases, excreting wastes, protection, and keeping moist. For more help, refer to Organizing Information in the **Skill Handbook.**
5. *Thinking Critically:* Why do you think fertilized insect eggs are often deposited in soil or water?

Reteach

Each of the points listed in Check for Understanding on page 536 is to serve as the basis for a review. Divide the class into five groups. Assign one question to each group. Have them prepare a complete answer to their question. Ask them to present their answer to their classmates.
`COOP LEARN`

Extension

Ask students to compare the role of the membranes that surround an amniotic egg and the role of these membranes in a placental mammal. What are the similarities and differences in terms of structures formed from these membranes during development? `L3`

✔ **Assessment**

Knowledge: Have students prepare a time line that compares events in a frog undergoing metamorphosis, a chicken egg in development, and development in a placental mammal such as a human.

4 Close

Activity

Students are to assume that they are a molecule of oxygen. Have them trace their path from the air through those structures of an amniotic egg to the embryo. `L1`

Answers to Section Review

1. The early embryo quickly consumes its limited supply of yolk and gets too big to exchange gases or excrete wastes by means of diffusion.
2. Insects undergo metamorphosis during which they change from larva or nymph to adult. Birds undergo their entire development within the shelled egg. All needs are met by both patterns.
3. The chances for successful completion of

development are successively greater in each of these animals. Thus, fewer eggs must be produced at one time.
4. **Skill Review—Making Tables:** Obtaining food: butterfly—yolk, then larva feeds; bird—yolk; human—via placenta. Exchanging gases: butterfly—diffusion, then as a larva; bird—via allantois and chorion, then from air space; human—via placenta. Excretion: butterfly—diffu-

sion, then as a larva; bird—stored in allantois; human—via placenta. Protection: butterfly—first shell, then exoskeleton; bird—shell and parent; human—mother. Keeping moist: butterfly—first shell, then exoskeleton; bird—amnion; human—amnion.
5. **Thinking Critically:** Soil and water provide moisture for early insect embryos.

CHAPTER 19

BIOLOGY, TECHNOLOGY, AND SOCIETY

Considering the Environment

Purpose
Students will learn that the link that connects one plant generation to the next is the seed. Human efforts to prevent plant extinction center around the preservation of this link by the formation of seed banks.

Teaching Strategies
- Have students review the meaning of the following terms: *ecosystem, extinct, habitats, endangered, crossbreed, germ plasm.*
- Students may work in cooperative groups to answer the questions at the conclusion of this feature.
- Alternatively, ask students to read the feature independently and place answers to the questions in their portfolios.
- Have students correspond with the United States National Seed Storage Laboratory in Fort Collins, Colorado, asking for more information on their program and the process used to preserve and store seeds.

Possible Answers
1. An ecosystem must have the same nutrients, daily temperature, moisture, amount of sunlight, and seasonal variation as did the original environment from which the extinct plant came.
2. Introduce students to the use of the *Readers' Guide to Periodical Literature* for researching their topic or for gaining information on which species are endangered.

BIOLOGY, TECHNOLOGY, AND SOCIETY

Considering the Environment

Seed Banks

There are banks to hold your money, sperm banks, and even banks for blood and body organs. Scientists also have formed seed banks. The deposits made in these banks are exactly what you would expect from its name—seeds. Seeds from all over the world are frozen and stored in vats of liquid nitrogen. Someday, they will be removed from the vats and germinated.

Why do seeds need to be stored?
Seeds are the link from one generation of plants to the next. One in ten plant species is in danger of becoming extinct, due to agricultural practices, development by humans, and changes in climate and ecosystems. As Earth changes over time, species that cannot adapt to the changes become extinct, and new species evolve. If a plant species becomes extinct, there is no way to get it back. Extinction is forever.

Groups and individuals are making efforts to save the habitats of endangered species, with varying degrees of success. Fortunately, plant species themselves are much easier to preserve than are entire ecosystems. A seed bank is a means of saving plants that are in danger of becoming extinct. To ensure the survival of existing plant species, many groups have established seed banks to store seeds from plant species, with special attention to those that are endangered.

How Seeds Are Stored More than 3 million seed samples are frozen and stored worldwide in about 100 seed banks. Seed storage has become a global enterprise, with groups collaborating on storage facilities for seeds from many nations. Should plant species become extinct in the future, stored seeds may be used to reintroduce the species in suitable habitats. Scientists of the future could also crossbreed plants that have desirable traits with plants from the past. This technique could be used to produce new species of crop plants that grow faster or contain more nutrients, in case of escalating demand for food in the future.

Unfortunately, many seed storage projects are beset by problems. For example, the temperatures at which seeds are stored in some seed banks are too high to protect them from spoilage. In some banks, plant samples are lost, and so is identifying information.

A Global Initiative To solve these problems, an international group of researchers, environmentalists, and agricultural industry representatives met in 1991. They issued a global initiative calling for establishment of a nonprofit organization that will fund and support research for preserving plant germ plasm to safeguard future generations of existing plant life. Without plants for food, most living things cannot survive. The "interest" that seed banks pay on seed deposits is that all living things benefit. Seed banks will help make the best seeds available for growing food for the future. Scientists will also be able to place extinct plant species back into the wild when a new and suitable environment is found.

1. **Connection to Ecology:** Before an extinct plant species could be introduced into a new environment, what conditions would need to be present?
2. **Explore Further:** Research a plant species that is classified as endangered. Write a paragraph or two about the reasons for its endangerment and the existing efforts to save it from extinction.

Going Further
Have interested students read the following articles and report back to the class or place a written report in their portfolios.
Gibbons, Ann. "Saving Seeds for Future Generations." *Science,* Nov. 8, 1991, p. 804.
Shell, Ellen Ruppel. "Seeds in the Bank Could Stave Off Disaster on the Farm." *Smithsonian,* Jan. 1990, pp. 94-105. L2

Biotechnology

Fetal Surgery—An "Out-of-Body" Experience

Imagine that you (or your spouse) are just 18 weeks pregnant when your doctor informs you that the fetus has an obstruction in its urinary tract. The obstruction is causing a backup of urine into the kidneys. If the obstruction is not cleared, it could lead to the deterioration of the fetus's kidneys, a fatal condition known as hydronephrosis. Normally, babies with this condition are operated on soon after birth to clear the blockage. But what if the blockage is so severe that normal fetal development is

being threatened and the life of the fetus is in danger? The only possible solution to the problem is to operate on the fetus before it is born. But there are risks for both mother and fetus if this is done. What would you do? In 1986, a couple named Williams had to make such an impossible choice.

The Williams's fetus was diagnosed as having hydronephrosis. Blockage was so severe that the fetus would almost certainly die before it could be born. Even though they knew that there was

some risk involved, the Williamses believed that the blockage had to be removed if there was even a small chance of saving their baby. The Williamses were good candidates for a new type of treatment — surgery on a fetus while it is still in its mother's uterus. Called fetal surgery, this new technique is helping to save fetuses with congenital defects by operating on them before they are born.

What is involved in fetal surgery? In the Williams's case, doctors made incisions in the mother's abdomen and uterus, siphoned out the amniotic fluid, then lifted the tiny fetus halfway out of the mother's uterus. Making an incision in the fetus's lower abdomen, doctors created an external opening between the bladder and the abdomen so that the urine could drain out of the fetus's body and into the amniotic fluid. Then they placed the fetus back into the uterus, replaced the amniotic fluid, and sewed the mother's uterus and abdomen closed. A few months later, the Williamses welcomed a normally developed baby girl into their family. Later, surgery permanently repaired the blockage.

There are several types of congenital defects that can be corrected through fetal surgery. Hydrocephalus, a condition in which excess fluid builds up in the brain, can lead to brain damage unless the fluid is drained as the fetus grows. Fetal surgery allows doctors to place a drainage shunt in the brain of such a fetus to prevent such damage. Congenital diaphragmatic

hernia (CDH) is a condition in which there is a hole in the diaphragm, the muscle that helps the lungs inflate. In severe cases of CDH, other organs move through the hole into the chest area, and the lungs have no room to develop properly. Babies born with CDH are routinely operated on at birth, but if the condition is severe, they invariably die for lack of well-developed lungs. Fetal surgery allows doctors to repair the hole in the diaphragm before lung development is affected.

Are there any adverse effects of fetal surgery? The surgery itself may lead to premature birth, and the newborn dies of complications unrelated to the fetal surgery. But for parents of fetuses with life-threatening congenital defects, the reward is worth the risks.

1. **Issue:** Some medical researchers are opposed to the use of fetal surgery. They feel that the mother will lose her right to make decisions about her own body if the rights of the fetus are considered to be more important than those of the mother. Should parents have the right to decide whether or not to proceed with fetal surgery if it is an option?

2. **Explore Further:** Some congenital disorders can be corrected during pregnancy by treating the mother. Find out about fetal cardiac dysrhythmia, in which there are irregularities or disturbances in the fetal heartbeat. Why can this disorder be treated with medication given to the mother?

Biotechnology

Purpose
The discussion of fetal surgery in this feature illustrates the fact that abnormalities can occur in development of a fetus. Modern techniques are now available for detecting and correcting some of these problems before birth.

Teaching Strategies
- Make sure that students know the meaning of the following terms: *urinary tract, congenital defects, adverse effects, premature birth.* Have them work in cooperative groups to define these terms.
- Ask students to determine the derivation of the terms *hydronephrosis* and *hydrocephalus.*
- Ask students to explain why doctors had to replace the amniotic fluid when placing the Williams's fetus back into the mother's uterus.
- Have students determine which organs push into the chest cavity if a fetus has CDH and why this is a problem.

Possible Answers
1. Some students may feel that the parents are the only ones who should be allowed to decide the fate of their future child. Others may feel that the safety and life of the fetus should be given preference over the decisions made by the parents.
2. Cardiac dysrhythmia results from errors in the conduction network of nerve cells that control the heartbeat cycle. Drugs given to the mother will pass into her bloodstream, through the placenta, and into the body of the fetus, thus alleviating or controlling any cardiac problems of the fetus.

Going Further
Have interested students find out why hydrocephalus can lead to brain damage. Where does the fluid come from and where does it go? L2

CHAPTER REVIEW

Summary

Summary statements can be used by students to review the major concepts of the chapter.

Language of Biology

Answers should go beyond defining the terms. Accept any reasonable answer that uses the term correctly and in the proper context.

Understanding Concepts

1. The plant embryo is protected by the seed coat and the fruit, and the bird embryo by its shell. Endosperm is food for the plant embryo, yolk is the food for the bird.
2. Differences among the cells signal different sets of genes to be switched on or off. Once that happens, the cells no longer have the capacity to give rise to an entire organism.
3. In a starfish, there is little yolk, which is evenly distributed, and cleavage produces a ball of uniformly sized cells. Gastrulation occurs as cells push in on one side of the blastula. In a frog, there is more yolk in the vegetal pole, inhibiting cleavage there. The blastula, therefore, consists of more and smaller cells in the animal pole and fewer, larger cells in the vegetal pole. Gastrulation occurs as cells from the animal pole migrate inward through a slitlike indentation.
4. A fully differentiated cell still retains all the genetic information for a complete carrot plant. Only some of those genes must have been active in the root cell.
5. Certain drugs can pass across the placenta and alter the chemical environment of embryonic cells.
6. The area will probably develop into skin because its genes for eye development have not yet been switched on.
7. The area will develop into part of the eye because its genes for eye development have been switched on.

8. No. The lines farther from the meristem would be farther apart because cells in those areas would have undergone the most elongation.
9. The yolk sac functions as a food source. The allantois is a repository for waste and, along with the chorion, functions in gas exchange. The amnion protects and provides moisture for the embryo.
10. Not only are all the needs of the developing embryo provided during development, but the protection afforded by the mother is far

---

Summary

Early development in animals begins with cleavage. Morphogenesis occurs during gastrulation, producing in most animals an embryo consisting of three tissue layers. The pattern of cleavage and gastrulation is influenced by the amount and distribution of yolk present in the zygote.

Development of plant embryos is characterized by cell division and growth that occur at the same time. Morphogenesis in plants comes about by differences in the rates and patterns of cell division, rather than by the movement of cells. Earlier events set the stage for differentiation, most of which comes later in development.

Development is guided by genes. Cells in different parts of embryos receive chemical signals that switch some genes on or off. The particular set of active genes in a cell guides its chemistry and thus its characteristics.

All animal embryos require food, a means of gas exchange and excretion, protection, and moisture. Different patterns of development—metamorphosis, the amniotic egg, and internal development—have evolved to meet these requirements.

Language of Biology

Write a sentence that shows your understanding of each of the following terms.

allantois	hypocotyl
amnion	larva
blastocoel	meristem
blastula	metamorphosis
chorion	morphogenesis
cleavage	neural tube
cotyledon	nymph
differentiation	placenta
embryonic induction	pupa
epicotyl	radicle
gastrula	umbilical cord
germination	

Understanding Concepts

1. With respect to protection and food during development, what do flowering plant and bird embryos have in common?
2. In some animals, early embryos consisting of as many as eight cells can be separated into two groups, and each will develop into a normal organism. If cells are separated later, though, normal development of two animals will not occur. Why?
3. Compare cleavage and gastrulation in a starfish and a frog. Explain the reasons for the differences.
4. A single cell from the root of a carrot is placed on a culture medium. The cell begins dividing, producing an unorganized mass of cells at first. Later, though, an entire carrot plant develops. What do these results indicate about how development is controlled?

5. Why do you think that certain drugs can result in birth defects?
6. Suppose an area of an embryo that normally develops into part of the eye is transplanted next to the area that develops into skin, before the eye area begins differentiating. What will probably happen to it? Why?
7. Suppose the area that normally develops into part of the eye is transplanted after it has begun differentiating. What will probably happen to it? Why?
8. Suppose you marked evenly spaced lines on a very young developing plant root. Would the lines still be evenly spaced after the root has grown? Explain.
9. Describe the function of each of the four membranes in an amniotic egg.

superior to protective adaptations present among other animal groups.

Applying Concepts

11. The root absorbs water and minerals the young plant needs during germination.
12. By the time the cotyledons have shriveled and fallen away, the young plant is capable of photosynthesis.
13. Many desert seeds have high concentrations of inhibitors. Germination begins only

10. Why is development more efficient in placental mammals than in any other group?

Applying Concepts

11. Why does the primary root of a flowering plant develop first?
12. How can a young angiosperm continue to develop after its cotyledons shrivel and fall away?
13. Hormones that inhibit germination are diluted by water moving into the seeds. As the hormones are diluted, their effect decreases. Do you think desert seeds would have high or low concentrations of such hormones? Explain.
14. What kind of twins might be produced if gastrulation occurred at two places in the same embryo? Explain.

15. Explain how a baby can be born addicted to drugs if its mother were a drug abuser during pregnancy.
16. How might a double-yolked hen's egg be produced?
17. What might be an adaptive advantage to the dormancy period of seeds before germination?
18. **Considering the Environment:** Why are seeds easier to preserve than whole plants?
19. **Psychology Connection:** What assumptions was the University of Arizona researcher making in analyzing the behavior of the infants she tested for understanding of addition? What could she verify for certain by observation?

Lab Interpretation

20. **Investigation:** A scientist hypothesizes that ionizing radiation at low levels will not affect seed germination. The results of the experiment are illustrated in the graph below. Do the results support the hypothesis? Why or why not? Interpret the results of the experiment.

Percent germination of bean seeds after exposure for one minute to ionizing radiation of different levels

21. **Thinking Lab:** Identical twins are formed when the fertilized egg divides into two separate cells. If the early stages of human development are similar to those of sea urchin development, what must happen during this cell division to ensure that each twin is an exact copy of the other?
22. **Minilab 2:** Why was the sixth seed needed in this experiment? What was its purpose?

Connecting Ideas

23. In what way do larvae serve a function similar to that of seeds?
24. Relate the events of fertilization and development in a human, paying attention to adaptations for each.

cord forms. As blood passes through the capillaries in the placenta, wastes and carbon dioxide diffuse from embryo to mother, who expels them. At the same time, food and oxygen pass from the mother's blood to the embryo's and are taken back to the embryo and circulated.

when sufficient water to see the plant through its development dilutes the inhibitors.
14. What is known as Siamese twins might be produced. They would be joined where the "double" gastrulation occurred.
15. The drugs would pass across the placenta, exerting the same addictive effect on the fetus as on the mother.
16. Two eggs become enclosed within the same shell as they travel along the oviduct.
17. Dormancy ensures that the embryo will not continue developing until conditions suitable for germination have been met.
18. Seeds are smaller and remain dormant for long periods of time.
19. The researcher assumed that the infant had made a prediction based on addition and the prediction was at variance with its observation. She could verify only that infants stared longer at wrong numbers of objects than at right numbers of objects.

Lab Interpretation

20. The results do not support the hypothesis. The seeds at low radiation levels have low levels of germination compared to the control. Seeds at high radiation levels do not germinate at all.
21. Nucleus and cytoplasm must have elements equally divided.
22. The sixth seed showed that intact embryos grow and develop normally, using food in the cotyledons.

Connecting Ideas

23. **Unity Within Diversity:** Both larvae and seeds can be dispersed, thus reducing competition between parents and offspring.
24. **Systems and Interactions:** The egg is fertilized within the oviduct and begins development as it travels toward the uterus. After implantation has taken place, an amnion forms around the embryo. Chorionic projections invade the uterine wall, and capillaries form within them. Later, the umbilical

SECTION	OBJECTIVES	TEXT LABS/FEATURES
20.1 Patterns of Nutrition and Digestion (2 days)	**Distinguish** between the nutrient requirements of autotrophs and heterotrophs. **Compare** intracellular and extracellular digestion. **Explain** the need for digestion.	**Literature Connection:** Akasha (Gloria) Hull, p. 548
20.2 Digestion in Animals (2 days)	**Compare** patterns of digestion in animals having one body opening with those having two body openings. **Describe** the process of filter feeding in several different animals. **Relate** the processes of physical digestion and chemical digestion.	**Investigation:** Modeling Digestion, p. 552 **Minilab 1:** Are enzymes specific for their substrates? p. 554
20.3 Nutrition and Digestion in Humans (3 days)	**Explain** the importance of a balanced diet. **Identify** physical and chemical aspects of digestion in each part of the human digestive system. **Compare** the absorption and transport of sugars and amino acids with that of fatty acids and glycerol.	**Global Connection:** Salt of the Earth, p. 560 **Minilab 2:** Which fruits keep gelatin from jelling? p. 564 **Thinking Lab:** Why are Michael's data different? p. 564 **History Connection:** Lillie Rosa Minoka-Hill, p. 568
BIOLOGY, TECHNOLOGY, AND SOCIETY		**Health Connection:** Does cholesterol count? p. 571 **Issues:** Are liquid diets a losing proposition? p. 572 **Career Connection:** Dietitian, p. 572

LAB MATERIALS

INVESTIGATION	MINILAB		ALTERNATE LAB
page 552 alpha amylase enzyme solution beakers, 400-mL and 250-mL Benedict's solution dialysis tubing dropper funnel hot plate iodine solution oven mitts starch solution test tubes test-tube holder test-tube rack tongs	**page 554** disaccharides: lactose maltose sucrose dropper glucose LactAid marking pencils slides TesTape toothpicks	**page 564** beakers fruit samples, mashed: apple kiwi orange pineapple gelatin solution markers test tubes	**page 546** barley seeds cheesecloth dropper funnel graduated cylinder iodine solution mortar and pestle starch solution test tubes

TEACHER CLASSROOM RESOURCES	OTHER RESOURCES
Study Guide, p. 115 ***PLL:** *Ingestion and Digestion in Protists,* p. 125 ****ILS:** *Fungal Nutrition,* p. 199	
Study Guide, pp. 116-117 **Critical Thinking/Problem Solving:** *Feeding and Digestion:* *Earthworms vs. Sponges,* p. 20 ***PLL:** *Ingestion and Digestion in Hydra and Planaria,* p. 127	***STVS:** *Mosquito Feeding,* Animals (Disc 5, Side 1) **Color Transparency 27:** *Mollusk Body Systems* **Color Transparency 28:** *Earthworm Body Systems* **Color Transparency 47:** *Crustacean Body Systems* **Color Transparency 48:** *Starfish Body Systems* **Color Transparency 49:** *Fish Body Systems* **Color Transparency 50:** *Frog Body Systems* **Color Transparency 51:** *Bird Body Systems*
Study Guide, pp. 118-120 **Concept Mapping,** p. 20 ***PLL:** *Digestion of Starches, Proteins, and Fats in Humans,* p. 129 ****ILS:** *Protein Digestion,* p. 201 ****ILS:** *A Nutrition Study,* p. 203 ****ILS:** *Digestive System of Frog and Human,* p. 205	***STVS:** *Measuring Body Fat,* Human Biology (Disc 7, Side 2) **Color Transparency 38:** *The Digestive System* **Color Transparency 52:** *Human Body Systems*
Assessment Materials **Chapter Assessment,** pp. 77-80 **Performance Assessment in Biology,** p. 40 **Alternate Assessment in the Science Classroom** **Computer Test Bank**	**Spanish Resources** **Cooperative Learning Resource Guide** **Videodisc Correlations** (to Optical Data's and Videodiscovery's videodiscs)

* Probing Levels of Life
** Investigating Living Systems

* Science Technology Videodisc Series

Key to Teaching Strategies

The following designations will help you decide which activities in the teacher margin are appropriate for your students.

L1 Level 1 activities should be within the ability range of all students.

L2 Level 2 activities should be within the ability range of the average to above-average student.

L3 Level 3 activities are designed for the ability range of above-average students.

LEP LEP activities are appropriate for Limited English Proficiency students.

COOP LEARN Cooperative Learning activities are designed for small group work.

ADDITIONAL RESOURCES

Infinite Voyage *A Taste of Health*
Diet and health are intimately related, as students will see in this video. Eating a balanced diet will lead to better health.

Audiovisual
Digestion, video, Frey Scientific.
Eat Smart, video, PBS Video.

Software
Digestion, Apple II/TRS-80/Model III, J and S.
Digestion Simulator, Apple 48K, Focus.

C H A P T E R

20

NUTRITION AND DIGESTION

Chapter Overview

Students first distinguish between the nutrient requirements of autotrophs and heterotrophs. They come to understand that because heterotrophs must take in complex organic molecules, these must be digested into molecules small enough to permeate membranes. Students then compare patterns of intracellular and extracellular digestion, examining examples of each.

Students next explore patterns of digestion in animals. As they do so, they see why a digestive system with one-way traffic of food is more efficient than a system with two-way traffic. Students also contrast filter feeding and chunk feeding and come to see how each is related to the animals' ways of life.

Students complete the chapter by studying nutrition and digestion in humans. In so doing, they learn how both physical and chemical events contribute to thorough digestion, and they examine adaptations that promote efficient absorption and transport of nutrients.

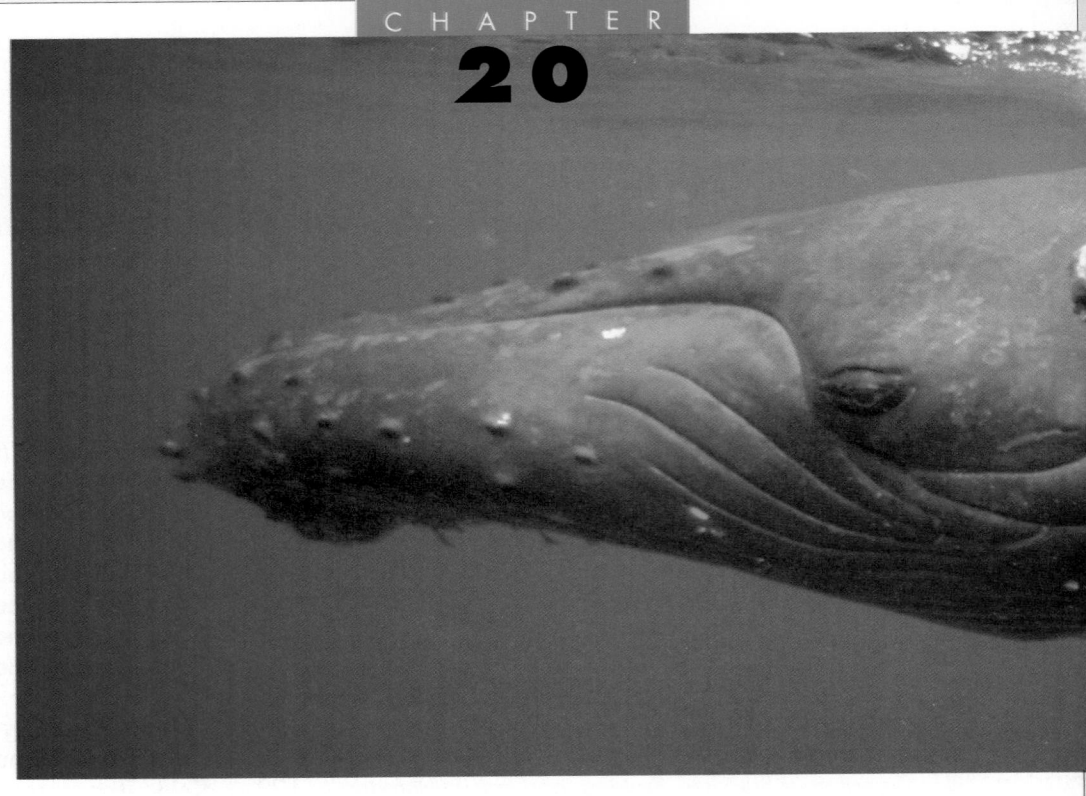

C H A P T E R

20

NUTRITION AND DIGESTION

THE HUMPBACK WHALE you see above can grow to a length of 15 meters, literally as long as some houses. Its mass is thousands of kilograms. How is this enormous animal able to nourish its massive bulk? Believe it or not, humpback whales are filter feeders. As they suck in water, they use their baleen to filter small invertebrates from the water. Baleen, shown in the smaller photo of a gray whale, are comblike structures that trap small crustaceans and other plankton. The whale then licks the baleen and swallows its meal.

Every organism requires nutrients to survive. How does a tree obtain food? How are cheetahs and clams alike in getting food? Do sponges and whales have anything in common? In this chapter, you will read about nutrition in organisms that make their own food and in organisms that must take in food. You'll learn how some consumers simply absorb nutrients and how others, like the blue whale, filter food from their watery environment. You'll see how still other consumers, such as the *Hydra* and the human, obtain food in chunks and must break it apart to digest it. Finally, you'll discover that although heterotrophs get food in different ways, they all need to break down the complex molecules of food into smaller molecules that can enter cells.

KEY TERMS

anus	intracellular
bile	digestion
colon	large intestine
crop	nutrient
digestion	pancreas
esophagus	peristalsis
extracellular	pharynx
digestion	salivary gland
gallbladder	small intestine
gastrovascular	stomach
cavity	villi
gizzard	

Imagine having combs in your mouth and having to make a meal out of whatever became stuck in them. It's a system that works well for whales because of the environment they live in.

Introducing the Chapter

Start the chapter by asking students why they must eat, leading them to the idea of the components of food and how those components are used. Then, refer them to the photograph of the blue whale on page 542. Lead them to understand that the whale requires the same types of food materials as they do, and extend that idea to other heterotrophs as well. Next, have students contrast the filter-feeding method of food-getting in animals like the whale with chunk feeding in humans and many other animals. Remind students of the structure of the plasma membrane, and lead students to infer the need for digestion. **LEP**

Theme Development

Systems and interactions is a theme that pervades the chapter as students learn how the parts of digestive systems work with one another to accomplish the function of digestion. The theme is evident in another context as well—the interaction of digestive and circulatory systems in more complex animals. Students will also perceive the theme of unity and diversity as they recognize the commonality among digestive systems as well as the different ways in which the fundamental tasks of obtaining, digesting, absorbing, and transporting food are carried out.

Tying to Previous Knowledge

Many previously learned concepts are reinforced in this chapter. For example, students will see evidence of different levels of biological organization as they compare digestion in different organisms. They will also recognize the importance of the idea of division of labor with respect to digestive functions, whether it be in a paramecium or a human. Their knowledge of biologically important molecules and their smaller building blocks, along with hydrolysis, pH, and chemical change, will also be applied, as will their understanding of cell membrane structure and function.

Chapter Preview

Contents

543

ASSESSMENT PLANNER

Choose assessment strategies from the following pages to evaluate the progress of your students.
Assess, pp. 549, 555-556, 569-570
Portfolio, pp. 544, 549, 553, 554, 556, 558, 560, 564
Alternate Lab, pp. 546-547
Thinking Lab, p. 564
Minilab 1, p. 554

Minilab 2, p. 564
Investigation, pp. 552-553
Chapter Review, pp. 574-575

Prepare

Key Concepts

Autotrophs and heterotrophs require the same organic substances for life processes. They differ, however, in that autotrophs make their own substances, whereas heterotrophs must obtain them from outside sources. Digestion of nutrients may occur within cells or may occur outside of cells.

Key Terms

nutrient, digestion, intracellular digestion, extracellular digestion

Materials

- Obtain barley that may be germinated for the Alternate Lab. Germination requires about two days.

1 Focus

Objectives

The objectives are listed on the student page. Remind students to preview these objectives as a guide to this numbered section.

Activity

Ask students to list foods that they have eaten in the past few days. Place this list on the chalkboard. Then, ask students to determine if each food came primarily from an autotroph or a heterotroph. Assign the letter A or H next to each food. Then, ask what the heterotrophs used for food. Place the appropriate letter after each heterotroph. Students will quickly realize that all foods can be traced back to autotrophs. **L1**

2 Teach

Brainstorming

Plants require vitamins. Ask students to discuss where autotrophs are able to obtain these organic substances. Make sure that they understand that plants make their vitamins from simple compounds formed originally by photosynthesis. **COOP LEARN**

Objectives

Distinguish between the nutrient requirements of autotrophs and heterotrophs.

Compare intracellular and extracellular digestion.

Explain the need for digestion.

20.1 Patterns of Nutrition and Digestion

A giraffe browses on the leaves of a tree and a horse grazes on grass. A hawk captures and feeds on a snake, and a tapeworm absorbs some of the food that moves through a cow's intestines. A mushroom soaks up organic matter from the soil, an amoeba traps a smaller protozoan, and you munch a pizza. You know that you and all other heterotrophic organisms must take in food. The trees and grass that giraffes and horses eat are autotrophs, which make their own food. The need for food is a universal characteristic of life.

Nutrient Requirements

Everything that lives needs food. If the cells of living organisms are to grow and divide, carry on respiration, synthesize proteins, and perform all other life functions, they need a constant source of energy and raw materials. Food contains complex organic molecules that can supply both energy and raw materials. These complex molecules and the simpler substances that are used in life processes are called **nutrients.**

Nutrition in Autotrophs Autotrophs need the same kinds of organic substances that heterotrophs obtain by eating food. But autotrophs don't eat. Instead, they build the needed organic substances by using water, carbon dioxide, and minerals absorbed from their surroundings. For example, in the case of an apple tree, water and minerals present in the soil easily pass through plasma membranes and into cells of the plant's roots and are transported to the leaves. Carbon dioxide enters the plant through openings in the leaves, where photosynthesis converts water and carbon

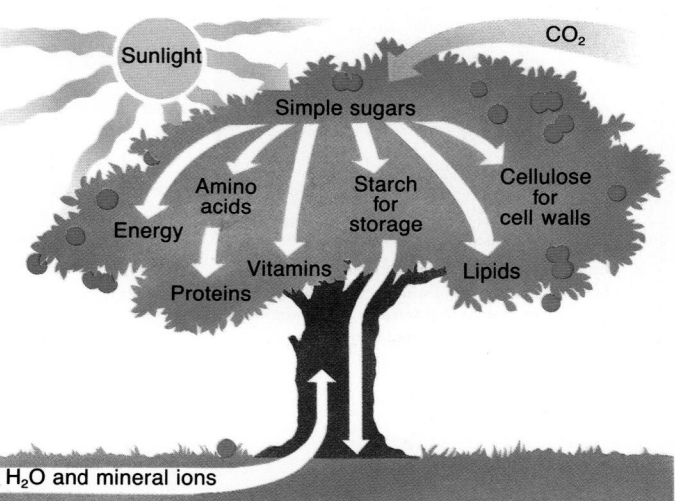

Figure 20-1 Autotrophs produce simple sugars by photosynthesis. These sugars are the raw materials for building nearly all other substances the plant needs. The word *autotroph* literally means "self feeder." Explain how the drawing illustrates the meaning of *autotroph.*

544 NUTRITION AND DIGESTION

---

dioxide into simple sugars. Some of these simple sugars are used as a source of energy for the plant cells. However, most of them are used to build more complex molecules, such as starch and cellulose, or combined with minerals to form lipids and amino acids which are needed for growth and other life functions.

Nutrition in Heterotrophs   Heterotrophs obtain their nutrients by eating autotrophs and/or other heterotrophs. Many heterotrophs, including humans, hawks, and sea anemones, consume fairly large chunks of food. To make use of the nutrients in the food, each chunk must be broken down into smaller and smaller particles until it is in the form of molecules small enough to pass through a plasma membrane. The process of converting complex organic molecules to simpler ones that can pass through a cell membrane is called **digestion**. Digestion is a chemical process involving enzymes that carry out a series of hydrolysis reactions. Review hydrolysis on page 77 in Chapter 3. Large, complex food molecules, such as fats, carbohydrates, and proteins, must be converted by hydrolysis to smaller molecules of fatty acids, glycerol, monosaccharides, and amino acids. These products of digestion are molecules that are small enough to pass through plasma membranes.

Not all nutrients required by heterotrophs are in the form of large, complex molecules. They also include simpler molecules, such as water, minerals, and vitamins, that readily pass across cell membranes with little or no need for digestion.

Figure 20-2   In contrast to autotrophs, heterotrophs must take in food, most of which is in the form of complex molecules. These molecules are broken down by digestion to yield simple molecules which are used as building blocks to form materials that the heterotroph needs.

20.1 PATTERNS OF NUTRITION AND DIGESTION   **545**

Using Science Terms

Have students review the actual meaning for prefixes *hetero-* (other) and *auto-* (self). Ask them to determine the actual meaning for the root *trophic* (nourishing). Ask them to explain why the words *autotrophic* and *heterotrophic* are useful for describing plants and animals.   L1

LEP

Figure Caption Question

Explain how the drawing illustrates the meaning of autotroph. The tree takes in H_2O, CO_2, and minerals and "feeds itself" by making food.

Discussion Questions

Have students answer the following questions.

(a) What smaller molecules are formed during hydrolysis of fats?
(b) What smaller molecules are formed during hydrolysis of carbohydrates?
(c) What smaller molecules are formed during hydrolysis of protein?
(d) What type of substance carries out each of the reactions just described?   L1   COOP LEARN

Enrichment

• Humans chew food to reduce the size of the food chunks and increase surface area. Ask students to research the function of each type of human tooth. Have them correlate the tooth type with an example of food used in our diet. Ask students to make a statement saying why good dental health is important to good nutrition.   L2

• Ask students to look up the meaning of the terms *herbivore, carnivore,* and *omnivore*. Have them provide examples of animals that fit each definition and list foods that are eaten by each animal.   L1

MEETING INDIVIDUAL NEEDS

• Ask students working at or below grade level to place the following terms under the headings "Must be digested" and "No need for digestion": *vitamins, proteins, fats, water, minerals, carbohydrates.*   LEP

• Diagram a cell membrane on the chalkboard. Include a variety of pore sizes on the membrane. Ask students working at or below grade level to predict and diagram sizes of molecules that can and cannot pass through the variety of pore sizes. Ask them how this exercise relates to digestion.   L1

LEP

Using Science Terms

- Have students look up the derivation of the term *phagocytosis*. Ask them to explain why the term is well suited in describing the method by which an amoeba feeds. **L1**
- Ask students to list four words that begin with the prefix *intra-*. Ask them to explain how the prefix suggests where digestion is occurring when describing the pattern seen in *Paramecium* or *Amoeba*. **L1** **LEP**

Microscope Activity

Students can easily prepare a wet mount in order to observe feeding by *Paramecium*. Prepare food for paramecia by boiling yeast suspended in a 1% solution of congo red. Allow the yeast to cool, and add a very small amount to a wet mount of paramecia. Students should be able to observe cilia sweeping the dyed yeast into the organism's oral groove and the formation of a food vacuole. High power is recommended. The addition of a small amount of methyl cellulose solution will help to slow the organisms, making student viewing easier. **L1**

Digestion in Heterotrophs

Because heterotrophs obtain food by eating other organisms, they have a variety of adaptations that enable them to get and digest food. These adaptations include specialized structures along with physical and chemical processes.

Intracellular Digestion A variety of specialized structures for the crucial functions of food-getting and digestion have evolved in heterotrophs. Even organisms as simple as water-dwelling protozoans are well adapted for taking in and digesting food efficiently.

Amoeba and *Paramecium* both feed on microorganisms, which are digested inside a food vacuole. In *Amoeba*, the food vacuole is formed as food is being captured. This process, called phagocytosis, is shown in Figure 20-3. In *Paramecium*, the action of cilia creates a current that draws food into the organism's oral groove. The food is swept to the bottom of the groove, where a food vacuole forms around it. In both of these protozoans, digestion begins when a lysosome fuses with the food vacuole. Enzymes from the lysosome convert large, complex food molecules into smaller molecules that can pass through the membrane of the vacuole and enter the cytoplasm of the cell. These molecules are then available for use in cell metabolism. In *Paramecium*, the food vacuole slowly moves through the cytoplasm as digestion proceeds. Such movement ensures that nutrients are distributed to all parts of this unusually large and complex protozoan. Digestion that takes place inside a cell is called **intracellular digestion**.

Figure 20-3 The photo on the left shows an amoeba trapping prey. (Magnification: 100×) The prey will be taken in by the process of phagocytosis, as shown below. Enzymes digest the food inside a food vacuole, and the nutrients are absorbed into the cytoplasm.

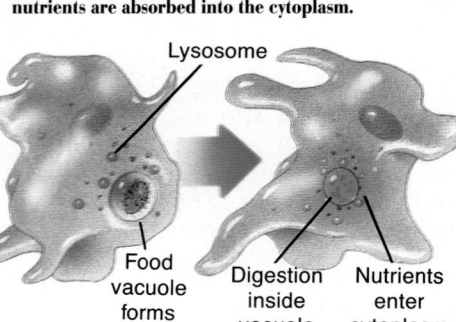

Amoeba — Prey organism — Lysosome — Food vacuole forms — Digestion inside vacuole — Nutrients enter cytoplasm

546 NUTRITION AND DIGESTION

ALTERNATE LAB: Digestion

Purpose
Students extract an enzyme from germinating seeds and observe its action.

Materials
barley seeds, 7 test tubes, funnel, droppers, cheesecloth, mortar and pestle, iodine solution, starch solution, graduated cylinder. To germinate barley, soak in water overnight, wrap in wet towels, and seal in a plastic bag for another 24 hours.

Procedure
Give the following directions to students.
1. Place 2 tsp. of germinating barley seeds into a mortar. Add 20 mL of cold water. Crush the seeds completely with the pestle and allow to sit for 10 minutes.
2. Filter the mixture through a funnel lined with cheesecloth. The filtrate contains the enzyme diastase.
3. Add 5 mL of starch solution to each of six test tubes. Number the tubes from 1 to 6. Use a medicine dropper to add 2 drops of iodine solution to each tube.
4. Add materials to the test tubes one at a time as instructed in step 5. After preparing each tube, mix it by swirling and then observe its color after 2 minutes. Record your observations in a data table. Use a scale from 0 to 10 to indicate the degree of blue color. Let 10 equal darkest blue and 0 equal no color.

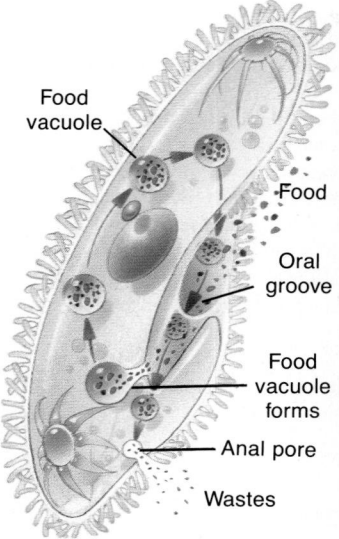

Food vacuole

Food

Oral groove

Food vacuole forms

Anal pore

Wastes

Figure 20-4 In *Paramecium*, a food vacuole forms at the bottom of the oral groove. The vacuole moves throughout the cytoplasm as its contents are digested. This mechanism helps distribute nutrients evenly throughout the cell. Solid wastes are expelled through the anal pore. The photo shows a paramecium that has been fed dyed yeast cells so that its food vacuoles can be seen more easily. **Magnification: 250×**

Not all material consumed by heterotrophs is digestible, so adaptations for eliminating undigestible material are important. In *Amoeba*, elimination takes place by exocytosis, a process opposite to phagocytosis. In elimination by exocytosis, the food vacuole moves to the plasma membrane and merges with it. Then, the indigestible particles that remain in the food vacuole are ejected from the cell. In *Paramecium*, a vacuole containing indigestible food fuses with an opening in the cell membrane called the anal pore. The food waste is ejected from the cell through this pore.

Although autotrophs obtain organic nutrients primarily by building them from simpler materials, they sometimes need to digest complex molecules. For example, many of the sugars produced by an apple tree during spring and summer is not needed for that year's growth. It is transported to the tree's roots as sucrose, where it is converted to starch and stored in plastids within the root cells. During the following spring, those starch molecules are digested. The resulting sucrose molecules are then transported to the upper parts of the tree, where they supply energy for growth and development of new leaves and flowers.

Extracellular Digestion Intracellular digestion is an efficient means of breaking down starch molecules in root cells as well as the tiny microorganisms consumed by an amoeba. But the diets of humans, birds, earthworms, clams, and other multicellular heterotrophs consist of much larger pieces of food that are too large to be taken into cells for digestion. Instead, large pieces of food are completely or partly digested outside the organism's cells. This process is called **extracellular digestion** and may take place within a cavity inside an organism, or it may take place completely outside the organism.

20.1 PATTERNS OF NUTRITION AND DIGESTION **547**

Brainstorming

Gathering sap from sugar maple trees to make maple syrup is an event that occurs each year in late winter or early spring in some regions. Ask students to explain where the sugar was stored and in what chemical form it was stored. Ask them to suggest reasons why maple trees can be tapped only during this certain time of year.

COOP LEARN

LITERATURE CONNECTION

Purpose
The feature illustrates that food is important for reasons other than nutrition.

Teaching Strategies
- Obtain cookbooks or recipes that feature foods of the rural South. Discuss the recipes with your students. Ask how many students in class have tried some of the foods mentioned.
- Have students describe some dishes that are typical of their ethnic or cultural background.

Possible Answers
1. Changes may take place because certain foods are no longer available or are not available in areas where they now live. Diet may also change because of health reasons.
2. Answers may include special dishes prepared in celebration of specific holidays, traditional dishes prepared by grandparents or other older relatives, and dishes that are typical of countries from which parents or grandparents came.
3. room surroundings, type of dishes being used, music in background, good conversation

Some heterotrophs, such as protozoans and animals, have the mobility needed to find, take in, and digest food. Fungi, although they are also heterotrophs, are generally not mobile and cannot capture food. Instead, fungi obtain food in other ways.

Have you ever seen a piece of bread covered by a blanket of black fuzz? The fuzz is a mold, usually *Rhizopus,* which obtains nutrients from the starch and other materials in the bread. The short, rootlike rhizoids of the mold penetrate the bread where they can absorb food. But starch molecules are too large to pass through the cell's plasma membrane. The rhizoids release enzymes into the bread that convert the starch into glucose. The rhizoids absorb the glucose and pass it to the rest of the mold, as shown in Figure 20-5. Other saprophytic fungi, such as mushrooms and cup fungi, digest and absorb organic matter from the soil in much the same way. Many bacteria also secrete digestive enzymes into their surroundings. These bacteria and fungi decompose dead materials and recycle the nutrients those materials contain.

LITERATURE CONNECTION

Akasha (Gloria) Hull

Make no mistake about it:
Mother love has taste.

That's what
seasons the beans
and salts the roast
and makes the cabbage taste
good
(even when they're just
cooked in bacon grease).

These lines are from "The Taste of Mother Love," a poem written in the early 1970s by Akasha Hull (1944-   ). As she wrote it, she was remembering the days she spent in her mother's sunny yellow kitchen in Shreveport, Louisiana. That kitchen, with its shabby, broken-back chairs but an abundance of affection, was the center of family life in Hull's Louisiana home. Hull recalls, "Meals were never anything fancy, but my father always made

sure we had enough to eat. Whatever there was, my mother always managed to make it taste special, to feed both our bodies and our spirits."

As she grew up, Hull faithfully followed her mother's recipes, but the resulting dishes never tasted quite the same. They were missing that one special ingredient: her mother's love.

Nearly a quarter century later, Hull shudders a little at the mention of roast and bacon grease. Although she is now a strict vegetarian, she says, "I still have that Black Southern good cooking in my palate. It's a challenge to make vegetarian fare satisfy me in the same way." A lot of garlic, tamari, and cayenne pepper, plus a generous portion of mother love for her own family, meets that challenge. Hull emphasizes that she is maintaining the connection to her mother's cooking while growing in her own way.

Hull is now a Professor of Women's Studies and Literature at the University of California, Santa Cruz. She is an inspiring symbol of African American womanhood to her students. She advises students who share her heritage to "honor our culture, and nurture both the body and the spirit because they make one."

Explore Further
1. Ask older family members if their diets have changed over the years. If there have been changes, find out the reasons.
2. Think ahead to the time when you will be grown and living on your own. What food do you think you will most want to eat when you visit your old home?
3. **Connection to Psychology:** What elements besides flavor contribute to a person's enjoyment of a meal?

STUDENT JOURNAL

Have each student write a journal entry that describes what an amoeba must do in order to gather food, what happens once it has captured the food, and what events occur within the food vacuole. L1

Mold

Bread

Rhizoids of mold penetrating bread

Digested food　Enzymes

Some plants are not only capable of photosynthesis, but are also capable of digesting insects. These insectivorous plants are often found in soils that are low in nitrogen and other important nutrients. Insects provide a needed supply of these nutrients. Venus's-flytrap, pitcher plant, and sundew are plants that have unique adaptations for the trapping and extracellular digestion of insects.

In a Venus's-flytrap, each leaf is bordered by spines and is hinged along its middle. When sensory hairs on the leaf are stimulated by the touch of an insect, the leaf quickly closes. The crossed spines trap the insect inside. Digestive enzymes are then secreted into the hollow formed by the folded leaf, where digestion occurs. Small molecules such as amino acids are absorbed by the leaf cells and transported throughout the plant. In the sundew and the pitcher plant, as in Venus's-flytrap, natural selection has resulted in the modification of leaves to form insect traps.

Figure 20-5 A Venus's-flytrap secretes enzymes onto trapped insects and absorbs the resulting nutrients. Bread mold carries out extracellular digestion by releasing enzymes from rhizoids into the bread.

Section Review

Understanding Concepts
1. Why do autotrophs get most of their nutrients in the form of simple molecules rather than complex organic molecules?
2. Why do heterotrophs have specialized structures for digestion whereas autotrophs usually do not?
3. How is digestion in fungi and insectivorous plants similar?

4. **Skill Review—Making Tables:** Construct a table that compares the digestion of starch by a plant, a bread mold, and *Amoeba*. For each organism, indicate where the digestion occurs, the kind of molecule produced by digestion, and whether the digestion is intracellular or extracellular. For more help, refer to Organizing Information in the **Skill Handbook**.

5. **Thinking Critically:** A starfish can pry open the shells of a clam. It then pushes its stomach through its mouth into the clam. The stomach secretes enzymes that begin digesting the clam. What type of digestion is this and why is it necessary?

3 Assess

Check for Understanding
Ask students to explain the relationship between the words or phrases in the following pairs.
(a) autotroph—heterotroph
(b) carbon dioxide—simple sugar
(c) lysosome—digestion
(d) phagocytosis—exocytosis

Reteach
Have students write a sentence using each word or phrase in the section "Check for Understanding." Ask them to use these sentences to help make the comparisons.

Extension
Many animals that are carnivores are able to eat one meal every few days and survive. Animals that are herbivores appear to eat almost constantly in order to survive. Offer an explanation for why this difference relates to the type of food being eaten. L2

✔ Assessment
Portfolio: Ask students to prepare a flowchart that summarizes the events that take place in a paramecium from capturing food to elimination of undigestible material. L1

4 Close

Discussion
Ask students to examine the animal phyla listed in Appendix A and describe any adaptations or specialized structures that animals in each phylum use to obtain food.

Answers to Section Review

1. Autotrophs, unlike heterotrophs, are able to convert the simple nutrients they take in, by photosynthesis and subsequent reactions, into the complex organic nutrients they require.
2. Food of heterotrophs contains complex organic molecules too large to permeate cell membranes. These must be converted to molecules small enough to do so. Plants usually do not take in such complex molecules.
3. Both fungi and insectivorous plants employ extracellular digestion. In fungi, it occurs completely outside the organism. Within the insectivorous plants, it occurs within a specialized cavity.
4. **Skill Review—Making Tables:** Location: plant—within individual cells; bread mold—outside the mold; *Amoeba*—in a food vacuole. Product

of digestion in all three: glucose. Type of digestion: plant—intracellular; bread mold—extracellular; *Amoeba*—intracellular.
5. **Thinking Critically:** This is extracellular digestion. It is necessary because the starfish lacks adaptations for taking in large bits of food.

Prepare

Key Concepts
Animals with a single opening to the digestive system have two-way traffic for food and wastes, and distribution of nutrients is by diffusion. Animals with two openings have one-way traffic through a continuous tube, and distribution of nutrients is usually by a transport system.

Key Terms
gastrovascular cavity, anus, pharynx, esophagus, crop, gizzard

Materials
- Obtain dialysis tubing, Benedict's solution, and cornstarch for the Investigation.
- For Minilab 1, obtain LactAid liquid enzyme and TesTape from a drugstore.

1 Focus

Objectives
The objectives are listed on the student page. Remind students to preview these objectives as a guide to this numbered section.

Demonstration
Place two small beakers onto the overhead projector and add a 1% starch solution until each is 1/3 full. Add 3 to 4 drops of iodine solution to each. Add 10 to 15 mL of your saliva to one beaker, mix, and note time and color of both beakers. Ask students to continue to note the color of each beaker. After 5 minutes, ask them to offer a possible explanation for why the beaker with your saliva became lighter in color compared to the other beaker.

Objectives

Compare patterns of digestion in animals having one body opening with those having two body openings.

Describe the process of filter feeding in several different animals.

Relate the processes of physical digestion and chemical digestion.

20.2 Digestion in Animals

From high atop a tree, an owl spots a field mouse. With precision, it swoops down and takes the mouse in its talons. How does the owl digest its meal? Once digested, how does the food reach all of its body cells? Because animals are complex organisms, elaborate adaptations have evolved for taking in and digesting food and then distributing nutrients to cells. You'll see, though, that there are only a few general patterns of digestion.

Two-way Traffic

You learned in Chapter 17 that cnidarians and flatworms have only one body opening, the mouth. That single opening is used both for taking in food and eliminating material that isn't digested. As a result, there is two-way traffic within the animal. While cnidarians lack organs specialized for digestion, they do have a variety of cells with different functions for trapping and digesting food.

Hydra, as shown in Figure 20-6, is a typical cnidarian. When mature, *Hydra* is sessile, so it can't chase after prey. Like other cnidarians, though, *Hydra* has tentacles to trap prey organisms that pass close by. *Hydra* does not have organs of vision, so it must employ other senses to locate prey. It has sensory cells that are sensitive to touch and can detect chemicals given off by potential prey organisms moving through the water.

To catch prey, *Hydra* extends its tentacles, which are covered with stinging cells. The filaments of the stinging cells are forcefully ejected toward the prey. Some filaments wrap around the prey, trapping it. Filaments of stinging cells also have tips that look like barbed harpoons,

Figure 20-6 Like humans, *Hydra* is a chunk feeder and carries out extracellular digestion. Unlike humans, *Hydra* has only one body opening which both takes in food and eliminates wastes. Magnification: 25×

Tentacles
Mouth
Food
Gastrovascular cavity
Enzymes begin digestion
Small bits are taken into cells where digestion is completed

550 NUTRITION AND DIGESTION

PROGRAM RESOURCES

Teacher Classroom Resources
Study Guide, pp. 116-117 **L1**
Critical Thinking/Problem Solving, p. 20 **L2**
Color Transparency #27, 28, 47-51 **L1** **LEP**
Probing Levels of Life, Lab 49, p. 127 **L2**

PROJECT

Studying Stinging Cells: Cnidarians use stinging cells to stun their prey. Ask students to use the library to determine the nature of the poison in the stinging cells, whether the poison is lethal to humans, what triggers the stinging cells to explode, the mechanism that fires the stinging cells, and which cnidarians form the most toxic poison. **L2**

which pierce the prey and discharge a poison that paralyzes or kills it. Once the prey is captured, the *Hydra* uses its tentacles to draw the prey to its mouth and push the prey through.

Digestion in *Hydra* begins in the hollow, water-filled **gastrovascular cavity,** which extends into the tentacles. Lining the cavity are numerous gland cells that secrete digestive enzymes. In the cavity, the enzymes begin breaking food into smaller bits. This process is an example of extracellular digestion. Animals, like *Hydra,* that take in relatively large pieces of food are known as chunk feeders. Because *Hydra's* prey is generally larger than any one of its cells, you can see how extracellular digestion is important for chunk feeders.

The *Hydra's* digestive process does not end in the body cavity. Some of the cells lining the cavity take in smaller bits of food by phagocytosis. Food vacuoles are formed, intracellular digestion takes place, and nutrients diffuse into the cytoplasm. Because *Hydra* consists of only two layers of cells, digested food can diffuse readily to all of the animal's other body cells. No cell is far from a source of nutrients.

One-way Traffic

Think about an automobile assembly line. As a partially built car moves along the line, workers attach parts in a logical order. An assembly line is organized and efficient because the process moves in one direction, and specialized tasks can be performed at each stop.

The digestive systems of most animals function something like automobile assembly lines, but in reverse. In fact, they might better be called "disassembly lines." The digestive pathway through which the food moves is essentially a hollow tube known as the digestive tract. Food enters through the mouth and travels along the digestive tract, where it is broken down physically and chemically into smaller and smaller pieces. Undigested material does not travel back to the mouth, but is eliminated through a second body opening, the **anus.** The anal opening, which first evolved among wormlike animals such as roundworms, makes it possible for food to travel through the animal in one direction only. One-way traffic also allows for a long digestive tract providing thorough, efficient digestion. As a result, the digestive process could be divided into a series of stages. At each stage, food particles are broken down until they are the right size for the next stage, continuing through a series of steps until the particles are small molecules. Then, digestion is complete.

Figure 20-7 Shown here is a diagram of a digestive tract with two openings. This type of digestive system exists in animals from roundworms to humans. Note, however, that not every animal has all of these regions. Also, functions are not always as clearly separated as in this diagram. Why does a digestive system with two openings generally work more efficiently than a system with only one opening?

Mouth, where food is evaluated and moistened

Region for physical breakdown of food

Region for additional digestion and nutrient absorption

Region for waste storage

Region for food storage (in some animals)

Region for chemical digestion

Anus, where waste is expelled

20.2 DIGESTION IN ANIMALS **551**

2 Teach

Using Science Terms
Ask students to check the actual meaning of the term *gastrovascular.* Have them explain how a hydra's cavity serves both a gastric and vascular function. **L1** **LEP**

Microscope Activity
Obtain prepared slides of *Hydra.* Have students use a hand lens or the low-power lens of a microscope to observe and diagram the animal. Ask them to label gastrovascular cavity, mouth, body, and tentacles. Students can add the labeled diagram to their portfolios. **L1**

Using an Analogy
Have students diagram a part of a city showing one-way and two-way streets. Traffic can be represented by arrows. Ask them to relate the digestive pathways in *Hydra* and in a roundworm to one of the types of streets and explain their conclusions. **L1** **LEP**

Figure Caption Question
- *Why does a digestive system with two openings generally work more efficiently than a system with only one opening?* With two openings, food can move continuously through the system, and different parts of the system can have specialized functions.
- **Page 553:** *Why do you suppose the intestine is so long compared to the rest of the digestive tract?* The long intestine represents adaptation to provide the largest practical surface area and the longest time of passage for maximum absorption.

MEETING INDIVIDUAL NEEDS

- Ask students working at or below grade level to make a diagram of a hydra and label the body, gastrovascular cavity, and mouth. Using a series of arrows and labels, have students trace the path of food into the gastrovascular cavity. Using arrows and labels of another color, have students trace the path of undigested food out of the gastrovascular cavity. **LEP**

- Have students working at or below grade level list the nine major animal phyla. Tell them to use Appendix A as a reference if necessary. Have them list after each phylum name whether the animals within the phylum typically have one or two openings to the digestive system. Students may omit sponges to simplify the task of assigning numbers. **LEP**

Modeling Digestion

Time Allotment

1 1/2 class periods

Objectives

Upon completion of this investigation, students will be able to:

- describe some advantages and limitations of using models.
- describe chemical digestion of a complex organic molecule.

Skills

separate and control variables, observe and infer

Materials

1-inch dialysis tubing, 400-mL beakers, 250-mL beakers, droppers, funnels, test tubes, test-tube holder, test-tube rack, hot plate, tongs, oven mitts, starch solution, Benedict's solution, iodine solution, alpha amylase enzyme solution

Safety Precautions: Do not use hot plates with exposed coils. Remind students to use mitts and spring-type test-tube holders to handle hot beakers and test tubes. Benedict's and iodine solutions are toxic.

Preparation

- Cut dialysis tubing into 20-cm lengths and soak in water 5 min or until soft and pliable. Prepare iodine solution by dissolving 5 g of KI in 50 mL of water and then dissolving 1.5 g of iodine crystals in this solution. Dilute to 500 mL for use. Make 1% starch solution by stirring a slurry of 10 g of cornstarch into 1 L of boiling water. Continue to boil until clear. Cool thoroughly before using. It is suggested that you purchase prepared Benedict's solution and fungal amylase from a supply house. Prepare a 1% solution by dissolving 1 g of enzyme in 99 mL of distilled water.

Possible Hypotheses

Students will probably suggest that maltose will be found outside the tubing after digestion. Students may diverge on whether starch and/or maltose will remain inside the tubing.

One-way Traffic in an Earthworm An earthworm is an example of an animal that has two body openings. Use Figure 20-8 to identify the parts of the digestive system of an earthworm. The earthworm's mouth moistens the food, which is then sucked in by muscle contractions of the **pharynx.** From the pharynx, the food moves through the **esophagus,** where continued muscle contractions push the food into a stretchable organ, the **crop,** where the food can be stored. From the crop, the food passes into the thick-walled **gizzard.** With the aid of coarse soil particles taken in with the food, the muscular contractions of the gizzard grind the food into smaller particles.

I N V E S T I G A T I O N

Modeling Digestion

The lining of the intestine is a selectively permeable barrier. It allows the passage of nutrients from digested foods through its cells and into the bloodstream or lymph, but molecules of undigested foods cannot pass across this barrier. Dialysis tubing may be used as a model for the intestinal lining. You will use starch as food and amylase as a digestive enzyme. You can then determine if the products of starch digestion indeed pass through the membrane.

Starch, in the presence of amylase enzyme, changes chemically to maltose, a disaccharide. Benedict's solution reacts with maltose. To carry out this test, mix equal amounts of the solution in question with Benedict's solution in a test tube and heat the tube in a hot water bath for 5 minutes. A color change from the original blue to either green, yellow, red, or rust indicates that maltose is present. The presence of starch can be detected by the blue color produced when iodine is added.

Problem

Is dialysis tubing (a model for human intestines) permeable to the products of starch digestion?

Safety Precautions

Wear goggles and an apron. Benedict's and iodine solutions are toxic. Avoid contact with skin and eyes. Wash away spills immediately.

Hypothesis

With your group, make a hypothesis regarding what substances you will find inside and outside the dialysis tubing after starch digestion has taken place.

Experimental Plan

1. Work with a group assigned by your teacher. Form a hypothesis that could be tested using starch, dialysis tubing, Benedict's solution, iodine solution, beakers, and the enzyme amylase.

2. Decide on a way to test your group's hypothesis. Keep the available materials in mind as you plan your procedure. Note that dialysis tubing can be soaked in water until soft and then opened into a tube. To fill the tubing, tie it in a tight knot at one end, then use a dropper or small funnel to add liquid.

Possible Procedures

- Each group should prepare three bags. The first will contain only starch solution; the second will contain a 1:1 mixture of starch and enzyme solutions; the third will contain enzyme solution only. Bags should be prepared one at a time and placed into marked beakers of water.
- On the first day, have students carry out tests on the water in each beaker after the bags have sat in it for a few minutes. After 24 hours, students should repeat these tests and test the contents of the bags as well.

Hold bags over clean beakers and pierce them, allowing contents to fall into beakers.

Teaching Strategies

- Demonstrate the technique for carrying out Benedict's test and the safe use of a hot-water bath. Beakers for water baths should be less than half full.
- Demonstrate how to tie and fill a dialysis bag. Bags should be rinsed off in clean water after filling and before placing in beakers. To confirm that bags are sealed, have students wipe them dry with tissue, wait a minute, and then wipe again with dry tissue.

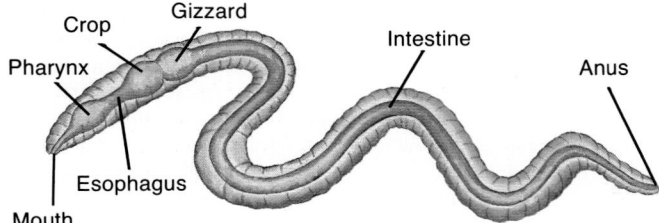

Crop Gizzard
Pharynx
Intestine
Anus
Esophagus
Mouth

Figure 20-8 The digestive system of the earthworm provides one-way traffic during digestion. Why do you suppose the intestine is so long compared to the rest of the digestive tract?

• If enough time is available, encourage students to be rigorous in their experimental design by running Benedict's and iodine tests on the solutions to be used before they are placed in the bags.

• Note that Benedict's solution tests for any reducing sugar including glucose and is not specific for maltose.

Data and Observations

On the first day, students should find no evidence of either maltose or starch in the water in the beaker. After 24 hours, only the beaker with the enzyme-starch mixture should show a positive Benedict's test. The bag with only starch should give a positive starch test and a negative Benedict's test. The bag with only enzyme should give negative tests. The bag with the starch-enzyme mixture should give a positive Benedict's test and may give a positive starch test.

Data Analysis

1. See Data and Observations.
2. Students should conclude that starch was broken down to maltose by amylase and that maltose was small enough to pass through the dialysis membrane. Students should cite evidence from chemical tests.
3. Students' answers should be based entirely on experimental observations. If original hypotheses were acceptable, students should look for sources of error (primarily mixups and leaks).
4. Starch is being broken down into sugars small enough to pass through membranes by an enzyme similar to the one used in this experiment.
5. to break down starch molecules into sugars small enough to pass through dialysis tubing
6. Because enzymes are specific for their substrates, no reaction would have occurred in either case and solutions in the beaker would never test positive for sugar.
7. No. The conclusions of an experiment are always limited to the factors studied. You would have to test other foods and enzymes.

Finally, tie the open end tightly. Work over a pan or several layers of newspaper to catch spills. The filled tubing should look like a small sausage. You'll need about 15 cm of tubing, and the filled part should be about 10 cm long. Remember that you can test for maltose with Benedict's solution and for starch with iodine solution.

3. Remember to test only one variable at a time and use suitable controls.
4. Record your procedure and list the materials that you will need.

Checking the Plan

1. What controls will be used and what factors will have to be controlled?
2. How will you be certain that no maltose is present in any of the solutions before the experiment begins? How will you determine that maltose diffused through the dialysis tubing and that the tubing did not just leak some of its contents into the surrounding water?
3. What data will you collect and how will it be recorded?
4. How long will your experiment

run and how many trials will be needed?
5. Assign roles for this investigation.

Make sure your teacher has approved your experimental plan before you proceed further.

Data and Observations

Carry out your experiment. Prepare a data table to record your findings.

Analysis and Conclusions

1. After digestion had taken place, what substances were in the water surrounding the dialysis tube? What substances remained inside the dialysis tube? What is your evidence?
2. Write a conclusion to your experiment stating what your data showed about the permeability of the dialysis tubing. Explain how your observations support your conclusions. Base your conclusions entirely on your observations.
3. Did your data support your original hypothesis? Explain. If the data did not support your hypothesis, write a revised hypothesis that takes into account what you observed.

4. Assume that the tubing is a reasonably accurate model of the human intestine. Make a statement about what must be taking place during starch digestion in the intestine.
5. Explain the role of the enzyme in this investigation.
6. How might your data have been different if protein had been used instead of starch but the same enzyme had been used? Explain. How might your data have been different if a different enzyme had been mixed with the starch? Explain.
7. Does your experiment offer evidence that all foods must be digested in order to pass across dialysis tubing? Explain.
8. Considering your answer to question 7, explain the value of using models in science.

Going Further

Based on the results of this experiment, design an experiment that would help to answer another question that arose from your work. Assume that you will have limited resources and will be conducting the lab in class.

20.2 DIGESTION IN ANIMALS **553**

---

8. Models are useful when it is difficult to work with materials such as living intestine. However, models are useful only when they provide the same results as the system in question would provide.

✔ Assessment

Portfolio: Have students report on this Investigation by creating a flowchart. Have them write their hypothesis at the top and then describe each step in a box with arrows pointing to the next steps. When tests were done, the question being answered by the test should be in the box followed by arrows labeled "yes"

or "no." Students should state their conclusions at the end, explaining how those conclusions are supported by what the flowchart shows.

Extensions

Have students devise procedures to test the effects of other factors on the breakdown of starch by amylase. Factors could include temperature, pH, enzyme concentration, and so on.

Minilab 1

Purpose

Students will observe the specificity of an enzyme that breaks the disaccharide lactose into simple sugars.

Skills

compare and contrast, interpret data

Teaching Strategies

- Obtain LactAid in liquid form and TesTape from a drugstore. Prepare 10% solutions of the disaccharides sucrose, maltose, and lactose. Provide water and a 10% glucose solution as controls. For solution preparations, see page 27T.
- Provide students with droppers, toothpicks, marking pencils, and glass slides. If you have plastic plates with wells for microscale experiments, here is an ideal place to use them.
- Advise students on the use of TesTape. Have them use 2-cm strips. Caution them not to touch the end to be used for testing. Have each group observe the change in TesTape from yellow to green by using glucose solution.
- To be rigorous, it is advisable for students to test all solutions with TesTape before mixing them on slides. Guide students to make this conclusion.

Expected Results

Only lactose will yield a positive test for glucose after being mixed with the lactase enzyme. All other disaccharides will remain negative.

Answers

The activity suggests that they are very specific. However, only one enzyme was tested with three possible substrates. If the enzyme had contained glucose, all mixtures would have given positive tests. Also, students may have tested the enzyme separately.

✔ Assessment

Oral: Refer students to the discussion of active sites, substrates, and enzyme specificity in Chapter 3, and ask teams to provide illustrated explanations of what occurred in this activity.

Minilab 1

Are enzymes specific for their substrates?

Disaccharides are chemically changed to simple sugar molecules by enzymes. In this lab, you will determine whether a certain enzyme is specific for only one disaccharide. Add two drops of a solution of each common disaccharide onto different marked glass slides. Test for glucose using TesTape. Record your data in a data table. Wipe off your slides. Again add two drops of each disaccharide solution to the slides. This time, add one drop of enzyme solution to each sugar solution. Mix each solution with a different toothpick. Wait five minutes and then test for glucose. Record your data.

Analysis *Does this activity show that enzymes are very specific for their substrates? How do you know that the enzyme did not contain glucose?*

Physical processes such as chewing or grinding are important first steps in the digestive processes of many animals including humans. These actions break chunks of food into many smaller particles. Breaking up food in this way increases the total surface area of the food many times. For instance, breaking a chunk of food into 1000 smaller chunks increases the surface area about ten times. The increased surface area allows more enzyme molecules to come into contact with the food, thus breaking it down more efficiently.

Chemical Digestion In the earthworm, the ground food passes from the gizzard into the intestine. The intestine is the longest portion of the digestive tract, and carries out the final stages of digestion. In the intestine, enzymes break the food particles into simple nutrient molecules that can pass into cells through a plasma membrane. In addition, some water and dissolved minerals are absorbed in the intestine. Undigested material is passed out of the earthworm through the anus.

Absorption and Distribution Once the food has been digested, it must be absorbed and transported to all of the earthworm's body cells. Initially, the nutrient molecules pass across the membranes of cells lining the intestine. It is important that the earthworm absorb as many of the nutrient molecules as possible from the intestine. Nutrients that are not absorbed before they reach the anus will be passed out of the body and lost to the worm that expended the energy to digest them.

What does the inside of an earthworm's intestine look like? If you were to slice through a tube and look at the cut end, you would see a cross section of the tube's interior, which forms a circle. Now picture the same circle but with a fold that extends downward from the top into its interior, as shown in Figure 20-9. Which circle would have the greater interior surface area for absorbing food? If you said the circle with the fold, you would be right. An earthworm has a fold of tissue extending along its entire length, increasing the inner surface area of the intestine. This increased surface greatly increases the absorption of digested food.

Figure 20-9 **Compare the drawings of an intestine with and without an infolding of tissue. Can you see how this adaptation increases the surface area available for absorbing nutrients? The photo on the right shows a cross section through the intestine of an earthworm. Magnification: 10×**

Circle with fold

Circular cross section

554 NUTRITION AND DIGESTION

PORTFOLIO

Have students make a stylized diagram of an earthworm's digestive system. Essentially, it should look like a long tube with some expanded areas representing the pharynx, crop, gizzard, and intestine. Label the areas responsible for physical changes and those responsible for chemical changes. Label those areas responsible for enzyme production, absorption of digested food, and elimination of undigested food. Use a series of short arrows to show the pathway of food through the digestive system. Label the arrows at both ends "one-way traffic." Have students suggest which organ in the earthworm's digestive system is most important and have them explain why. **L1**

Once nutrients have been absorbed by the cells of the intestine, they cannot be distributed to other cells by simple diffusion, as in *Hydra*. The body of an earthworm is much thicker than the body of a *Hydra*, and most of an earthworm's cells are too far from the intestine to receive nutrients directly by diffusion. Instead, nutrients from the cells of the intestine pass into the bloodstream by means of small blood vessels in the tissues of the intestine. As the blood flows through the rest of the earthworm's body, nutrients pass from it and into the body cells.

Filter Feeding

The animals you are most familiar with are probably chunk feeders. Most birds, fish, mammals, reptiles, and amphibians consume fairly large pieces of food that are digested as they move through the digestive tract. But there are a number of aquatic animals that feed on tiny organisms or microscopic bits of organic matter suspended in water. These animals obtain their food by passing water through a part of their body that strains out the food. They are known as filter feeders.

What kinds of animals are adapted for filter feeding? This method of obtaining food makes sense for sessile or slow-moving species that are not adapted for chasing prey or taking in large bits of food. Sponges and certain mollusks fit this category.

Digestion in Sponges   Sponges are sessile and do not have a mouth opening or digestive tract for taking in and breaking down large food particles. They have cells with flagella that draw water into the sponge through its many pores. As the water passes through the sponge, microorganisms and other food particles are filtered out, captured, and ingested by individual cells. The food is digested inside these cells, and the nutrients pass on to other cells by diffusion.

Figure 20-10   Sponges can be very large, as shown in the photo below. Even so, all sponges obtain food in the same way. The arrows in the diagram show how water flows through the sponge. Food particles become trapped in the mucus of the collar cells, are taken in by phagocytosis, and digested in food vacuoles. Sometimes, entire food vacuoles are transferred to amoebocytes which travel throughout the sponge.

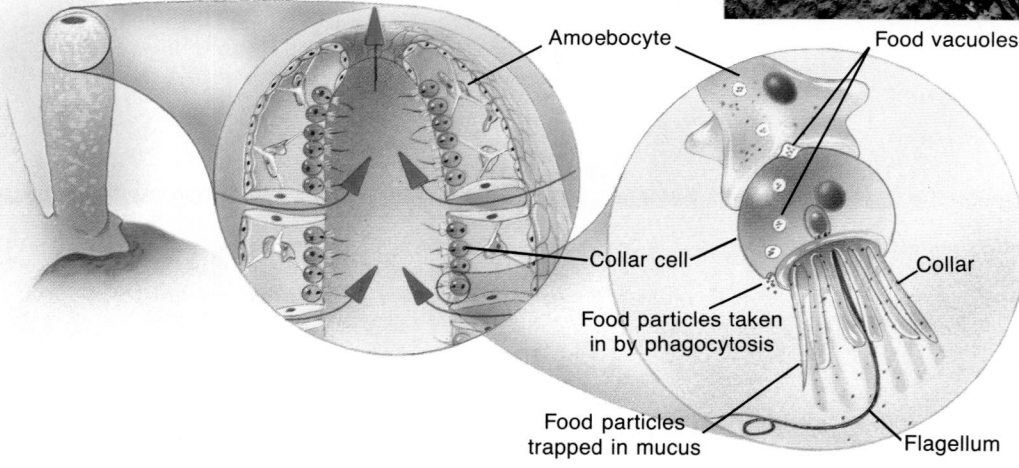

Amoebocyte

Food vacuoles

Collar cell

Collar

Food particles taken in by phagocytosis

Food particles trapped in mucus

Flagellum

20.2 DIGESTION IN ANIMALS   **555**

Reteach

Ask students to take each group of words in the Check for Understanding section and explain how they relate to nutrition and digestion. Also ask for an example of an organism that illustrates groups a, b, d, and f.

Extension

Many mollusks, such as clams and oysters, are sessile organisms that filter feed. Have students use Appendix A to name the different classes in this phylum. Ask them to determine which classes exhibit filter feeding. Have them describe the types of feeders found in each class. **L2**

✔ Assessment

Portfolio: Have students compare the events of digestion in animals that have one-way traffic to those that have two-way traffic. A labeled diagram of a representative example of each should be provided. **L1**

4 Close

Discussion

Provide the following animal examples to your class: baleen whale, hydra, earthworm, clam, human, sponge. Ask them to determine if each animal (a) shows one-way or two-way traffic, (b) is sessile or motile, (c) has only one digestive opening, (d) has a separate mouth and anus, (e) is a chunk or filter feeder, and (f) has a bloodstream for distribution of nutrients.

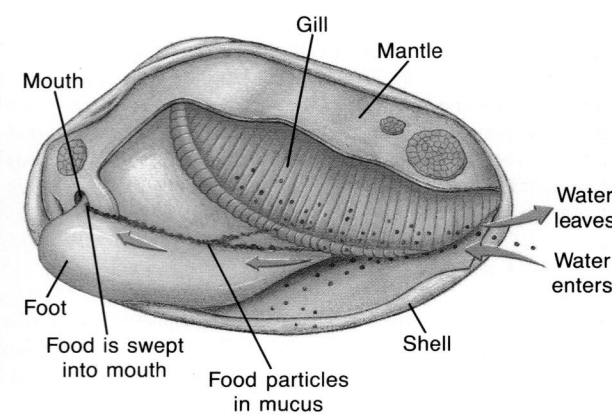

Figure 20-11 Like sponges and some whales, clams are also filter feeders. The diagram shows a clam with part of the upper mantle cut away. You can see how a clam collects food particles on its gills and passes them to the mouth. Its digestive system consists of a stomach and intestine, which are located beneath the structures you see in the diagram. Why do you think that filter feeding is such a successful adaptation for many animals in an aquatic environment?

Other Filter Feeders Filter-feeding mollusks such as clams, oysters, and mussels are much more complex than sponges and have true digestive systems. They have sieve-like gill structures that strain out food particles from the water that passes through them. These particles become embedded in a layer of mucus, which is continuously swept by cilia into the mouth. From there, food passes through the esophagus, stomach, and intestine. Digestion in the stomach and intestine is both extracellular and intracellular.

Filter feeding has evolved as an efficient feeding strategy for larger animals that live on tiny organisms scattered through a large volume of water. You have read in the opening to this chapter that baleen whales are adapted for filter feeding. It may surprise you to learn that many other vertebrates are filter feeders. Ducks and flamingoes use their bills to strain food from the water. Tadpoles and some types of fish remain stationary while sucking in water and filtering tiny food particles from it. The evolution of different structures that perform similar functions—sieve-like gills of mollusks and the baleen of whales, for example—illustrates convergent evolution.

Section Review

Understanding Concepts
1. What is the adaptive advantage of a digestive system with two openings?
2. How are the length and inner surface area of the intestine important in digestion?

3. A barnacle is a sessile crustacean. How do you think it obtains food?
4. **Skill Review—Sequencing:** List the series of structures through which food passes in an earthworm, and describe the function of each of those structures. For more help,

refer to Organizing Information in the **Skill Handbook**.
5. **Thinking Critically:** Do you think the mouth and throat structures of chunk feeders are very similar to those of closely related species that filter feed? Explain.

Answers to Section Review

1. Food travels in one direction. Different regions of the digestive tube can be specialized for specific aspects of digestion. Therefore, the process is more efficient.
2. The length allows for thorough digestion of the food. A large surface area is an adaptation for maximum absorption of the digested food.

3. It is sessile and aquatic; therefore it is likely that the barnacle obtains food by filter feeding.
4. **Skill Review—Sequencing:** Mouth takes in food. Pharynx and esophagus transfer food to crop, where it is stored. The gizzard grinds the food into smaller pieces, thus increasing its surface area. The food then passes to the

intestine, in which chemical digestion and absorption occur. Undigested food is expelled from the anus.
5. **Thinking Critically:** The filter feeders have adaptations that enable them to separate food from the water they take in. Chunk feeders have adaptations for admitting and then breaking apart and swallowing larger bits of food.

20.3 Nutrition and Digestion in Humans

Do you eat the same foods every day? Maintaining the health of your body requires many different nutrients, and varying your diet is the best way to get them. Your digestive system is adapted for the thorough digestion and absorption of many types of food.

Human Nutrition

Humans are heterotrophs, so our food includes complex molecules that must be digested and simple substances that don't require digestion. The complex nutrients are carbohydrates, fats, and proteins. The simple nutrients are vitamins, minerals, and water. It is important not only to consume foods containing all these nutrients, but also to consume them in the right proportions. In other words, we all need to eat a balanced diet.

A Balanced Diet   Nutrition is the study of nutrients and how they are used by the body. For many years, nutritionists recommended that a balanced diet include several portions of food from each of four basic food groups—breads and cereals, fruits and vegetables, eggs and dairy products, and meats. More recent guidelines refer to five basic food groups and include suggestions for the number of servings from each group that a healthy individual should consume every day. These new guidelines are represented by the food pyramid shown in Figure 20-12.

Objectives

Explain the importance of a balanced diet.

Identify physical and chemical aspects of digestion in each part of the human digestive system.

Compare the absorption and transport of sugars and amino acids with that of fatty acids and glycerol.

**Fats, oils, and sweets
USE SPARINGLY**

**Milk, yogurt, and cheese group
2-3 SERVINGS**

**Meat, poultry, fish, dry beans, eggs, and nuts group
2-3 SERVINGS**

**Vegetable group
3-5 SERVINGS**

**Fruit group
2-4 SERVINGS**

**Bread, cereal, rice, and pasta group
6-11 SERVINGS**

Figure 20-12   You can see from this food pyramid that it's easy to maintain a balanced diet and still eat a great variety of tasty, attractive foods. The diagram shows the number of recommended servings per day of each food group.

SECTION 20.3

Prepare

Key Concepts
Students will determine that a balanced diet requires the proper intake of nutrients, regardless of source. The breakdown of complex food molecules in the digestive tract is accomplished by many different organs as well as the enzymes that are produced by these organs.

Key Terms
salivary gland, peristalsis, stomach, small intestine, gallbladder, bile, pancreas, villi, large intestine, colon

Materials
- Purchase unflavored gelatin from a supermarket for Minilab 2. Also purchase fresh pineapple, apple, kiwi, and oranges.

1 Focus

Objectives
The objectives are listed on the student page. Remind students to preview these objectives as a guide to this numbered section.

MULTICULTURAL CONNECTION

Flemmie Kittrell: Flemmie Pansy Kittrell was born in Henderson, North Carolina. She attended Cornell University where she received a Ph.D. in nutrition. Kittrell was the first African American woman to receive a doctorate in nutrition. She served as the head nutritionist at Howard University from 1944 to 1973. Her field of interest was related to the feeding of infants in African American communities of North Carolina. Until her death in 1980, she served as Emeritus Professor of Nutrition at Howard University.

Activity

Draw lines of the following length below one another on the chalkboard, and indicate each line's length: 1 m, 3 m, 5 m, 7 m, 9 m, 12 m. Fold lines when you run out of width. Ask students which line best represents the length of the human adult digestive tract. Place the number of votes after each line. Advise them that the length is about 9 meters. Have them explain how such a long length of "guts" can fit into their body size and why such a long length might be needed. **L1**

2 Teach

Misconception

Ask students if the following are true or false. (a) Vitamins from foods are superior to those taken in tablet form. (b) Vitamins provide energy. The chemical composition of a vitamin is the same, whether received naturally from foods or in a tablet. Vitamins supply no energy to the body. Carbohydrates, fats, and proteins are the only energy sources.

Using the Table

Have students reorganize Table 20.1 as follows. Prepare two columns marked "Food" and "Mineral." Prepare three rows marked "Milk," "Meats," and "Vegetables." Have students complete their tables. Ask them which foods supply the greatest variety of minerals.

MATH CONNECTION

Cost of Food Processing:
How does the cost of prepared foods compare to their raw or natural equivalents? Determine the cost and mass of a potato. Calculate the cost per gram. Determine the cost and mass of a bag of frozen french fries. Calculate the cost per gram for this prepared food. Ask students to perform this same type of calculation for tomatoes (in season) versus tomato juice or canned tomatoes.

Eating a balanced diet provides your body with a daily supply of all the essential nutrients. If one or more nutrients are missing from the diet for a period of time, malnutrition can result. For example, inadequate protein in the diets of growing children can lead to weight loss, liver damage, and anemia. Table 20.1 lists some of the minerals that are important to health. Table 20.2 lists symptoms of some vitamin deficiencies.

Table 20.1 **Some Important Minerals**

Mineral	Sources	Function
Calcium	Milk, cheese, meats, vegetables, whole-grain cereals	Blood clotting, muscle contraction, bone and tooth formation
Iron	Liver, leafy vegetables, meats, raisins	Production of hemoglobin, part of molecules used in respiration
Iodine	Seafood, iodized table salt	Part of hormone that controls rate of metabolism
Magnesium	Leafy vegetables, meats, potatoes	Proper functioning of some enzymes
Phosphorus	Milk, meats, eggs, vegetables	Bone and tooth formation, part of ATP and nucleic acids
Potassium	Vegetables, bananas	Conduction of nerve impulses
Sodium	Table salt, vegetables	Conduction of nerve impulses, maintaining osmotic balance

Table 20.2 **Some Important Vitamins**

Vitamin	Sources	Deficiency Symptoms
A	Green and yellow vegetables, eggs, fruits, liver	Night blindness, dry skin
B-1	Whole-grain cereals, liver, other meats, nuts, most vegetables	Weak muscles, paralysis (beriberi)
B-2	Milk, cheese, eggs, liver, whole-grain cereals	Poor vision, sores in and around mouth
B-12	Liver, other meats, eggs, milk products	Anemia
C	Citrus fruits, tomatoes, some vegetables	Loose teeth, bleeding gums, swollen joints, poor muscle development (scurvy)
D	Milk, egg yolk, fish liver oil, also made in skin	Soft bones, deformed skeleton (rickets)
K	Green vegetables, liver, also made by intestinal bacteria	Slow blood clotting

558 🦴 NUTRITION AND DIGESTION

PORTFOLIO

Students should prepare a written report that attempts to answer the following questions.
1. Explain how plants are able to obtain minerals if they are autotrophic.
2. Explain how plants are able to obtain vitamins if they are autotrophic.
3. Explain how both carnivorous and herbivorous animals are able to obtain minerals.
4. Explain how both carnivorous and herbivorous animals are able to obtain vitamins.

Figure 20-13 You might enjoy eating a meal like this one. The problem, though, is that you would be eating large quantities of fats and sugar and relatively small quantities of proteins, vitamins, and minerals. In other words, the meal is high in Calories, but low in nutrition.

Figure 20-14 Vegetarians can obtain all essential amino acids by eating certain combinations of foods such as corn (used to make tortillas) and beans (in the filling of refried beans).

Diet and Obesity Are you fond of potato chips, candy bars, cookies, and soda? These foods fall into the fats, oils, and sweets portion of the food pyramid. They aren't harmful if eaten in moderation, but including too many of them in your diet can contribute to health problems. Often called junk foods, they contain large proportions of sugar and/or fat, but very little protein and few vitamins and minerals. It's true that sugar and especially fat are good energy sources for the body. However, when we try to make a meal of junk foods, we take in much more sugar and fat than we would in a balanced diet. A diet containing a lot of junk food can lead not only to vitamin deficiencies and malnutrition, but also to obesity. Obesity is a condition of being overweight. It results when the body takes in more food than it needs. The extra food that isn't broken down to release energy is stored in the body as fat. Obesity usually can be avoided by eating a balanced diet with moderate portions and getting plenty of exercise.

Vegetarian Diet Your cells must have all 20 amino acids available if they are to make the many proteins needed to build enzymes, muscles, connective tissue, skin, and other tissues. Human cells can manufacture 12 of the 20 amino acids from other nutrients. But the remaining eight amino acids cannot be manufactured in the body. Thus, they are often called the essential amino acids and must be supplied in food. Meat and dairy products supply our major sources of protein and all of the essential amino acids.

For a variety of reasons, many people decide to become vegetarians—they choose not to eat meat. Some vegetarians further limit their diet by eating only plant foods and avoiding seafood, eggs, and dairy products as well as meat. But, while many vegetables, nuts, and grains are sources of protein, they are not as protein-rich as animal products. How, then, do vegetarians maintain a balanced diet?

Individual vegetables and grains supply different combinations of essential amino acids, but none contains all of them. Therefore, a person on a vegetarian diet must include a variety of cereals, grains, peas, beans, and nuts that, taken together, contain proteins having the eight essential amino acids.

20.3 NUTRITION AND DIGESTION IN HUMANS **559**

CHEMISTRY CONNECTION

Essential Amino Acids: Eight essential amino acids cannot be synthesized by humans. They include lysine, leucine, isoleucine, methionine, phenylalanine, threonine, tryptophan, and valine. Other amino acids can be synthesized by body cells through a process known as transamination. This process transfers an amino group from an amino acid to a substance such as an intermediate in respiration.

Enrichment

Gather food labels from junk foods. Prepare photocopies for the entire class. Ask students to note the high caloric value of many of these foods. Ask students to calculate the percentage of Calories derived from fat and carbohydrates. For fats, multiply the grams of fat per serving by 9 and divide this number by total Calories per serving to get the percentage of Calories from fats for one serving. For carbohydrates, multiply the grams of carbohydrates per serving by 4 and divide this number by total Calories per serving to get the percentage of Calories from carbohydrates for one serving. Add the two percentages and see how close to 100% the sum is.

MEETING INDIVIDUAL NEEDS

Ask students working at or below grade level to examine the labels of some "junk" foods. You may wish to supply photocopies of labels from non-diet soda pop, cheese curls, and cookies. Have them record the nutrients in one of the foods. Ask them to assume that their entire food intake for the day would consist of ten portions of the same junk food. Have them describe what nutrients would be in short supply for that one day and why the term *junk food* is appropriate. LEP

Different Viewpoints in Biology

Junk Foods

The label "junk food" is subjective. It tends to be applied to foods that contain a lot of sugar and/or fat, particularly those that seem to tempt people to eat them in unusually large quantities or that provide a large portion of daily Calorie requirements without also providing a corresponding range of nutrients. Still, barring the presence of harmful ingredients, is there any food that is inherently junk food? There may be nothing wrong with eating a candy bar or a bag of chips as long as it is in the context of a balanced daily diet. Conversely, even broccoli could be considered junk food if people had an inordinate craving to eat it in excess. Ask students to list what they consider to be junk foods and then consider the points made above. Have them formulate their own definitions of junk food.

Activity

Have students prepare the following chart. Label two columns "Aid in Physical Changes" and "Aid in Chemical Changes." Ask students to enter the following under the proper headings: mouth, teeth, enzymes, salivary glands, mucus, saliva. Advise students that some of the terms may be correctly recorded under both columns. Have them add other terms to the chart as they complete the section. **LEP**

The Beginning of Digestion

Digestion begins when you put food in your mouth. In the mouth, both physical and chemical processes begin to break down the food. Teeth physically grind and tear the food into smaller pieces. This process makes the food particles small enough to swallow and increases their surface area. When food is chewed well, the enzymes are better able to begin the chemical process of digestion. Another important function of the mouth is to evaluate the quality of food by sensing taste and texture. This evaluation allows us to spit out food that may be spoiled, contain disagreeable substances, or contain foreign matter that could be harmful.

Salivary Glands Several structures along the length of the digestive tract aid in digestion. In and near the mouth are three pairs of **salivary glands,** which secrete saliva into the mouth. The taste, smell, or sometimes even the thought of food causes nerves to stimulate the glands and increase their secretion of saliva. Like other structures that secrete fluids important in digestion, the salivary glands secrete saliva into the mouth through small tubes called ducts.

Saliva contains mucus, which moistens and lubricates food, thus making it easier to swallow. Saliva also contains an enzyme that begins the breakdown of starch into molecules of maltose, a disaccharide. Chemical digestion of fats and proteins does not take place in the mouth.

GLOBAL CONNECTION

Salt of the Earth

"Here it comes!" shouted a merchant in the ancient city of Timbuktu. Squinting against the desert sun, she spotted the huge caravan, with its 2000 camels and hundreds of guards, weaving slowly across the Sahara. The bulky, 300-pound load on each camel's back represented wealth to finance schools, libraries, and other public services in this affluent west African city. The caravan's cargo was not gold or glittering jewels; it was sodium chloride—everyday salt.

In ancient times, salt was in great demand because it is an essential nutrient, a seasoning, and a food preservative. The problem was that salt was available in large quantities only at a few sites. Also, in those times, shipping salt over great distances was expensive, risky, and often took many months. All across Africa, Europe, and Asia, ancient salt routes were established to trade the precious commodity. The city of London, among other cities, began as a stop along a trade route for salt. In some places, salt was even used as money. Roman soldiers received part of their pay in salt, a practice that was the origin of the English word "salary."

Salt also played an important part in religious life. In many early societies along the Mediterranean,

offerings of salt were made to the gods. On the North American continent, the Aztecs honored a salt goddess, the Navajos prayed to Salt Woman, and the Hopis' war god was Salt Man.

Because salt was widely used as a food preservative, it came to symbolize permanence in many societies. An Arab saying, "There is salt between us," implies a lasting trust. The Hebrew expression, "To eat the salt of the palace," means to think highly of someone. When English-speakers call a person "the salt of the earth," they mean that he or she possesses admirable basic qualities.

In contrast, salt has often been a cause of dissension. During the first century A.D., a spear battle between

560 ❧ NUTRITION AND DIGESTION

PORTFOLIO

Have students prepare a chart that is to be completed as the remainder of this section is covered. The chart should be titled "Organs That Affect Digestion." The chart is to be divided into three columns marked "Fat," "Protein," and "Carbohydrate." Label the side rows "Mouth," "Stomach," "Liver/Gallbladder," "Pancreas," "Small Intestine," and "Large Intestine." Students should enter a description of what, if any-

thing, happens to each food type as a result of the activity of the listed organ. Students may include the completed charts in their portfolios. **L1**

The Esophagus Next, chewed, moistened, slightly digested food is swallowed through the pharynx and pushed into the long, slender esophagus. Digestive fluids are not added to the food while it is in the esophagus. Food is moved down the esophagus and through the rest of the digestive tract by **peristalsis,** the alternating contraction and relaxation of muscles along the digestive tract. First, one area of the esophagus contracts, squeezing the food from above and pushing it down. Then the muscle in that first area relaxes, and the next area contracts, again squeezing the food from above and moving it farther along. Alternating contractions and relaxations continue to push the food into the stomach. Similar contractions move food through the remainder of the digestive tract.

The Stomach

The **stomach** is a large, hollow organ in the digestive tract. The stomach performs three main functions. (1) The stomach's muscular walls provide a churning action that continues the physical breakup of food particles. (2) The stomach secretes acid and certain enzymes that begin breaking up protein. (3) The stomach acts as a storage area for food, which allows food to be released slowly into the intestine.

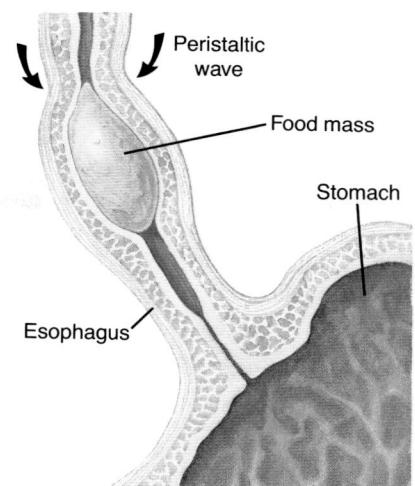

Figure 20-15 When you swallow food, waves of muscular contraction, called peristalsis, push the food through your esophagus and into the stomach.

two German groups left thousands of dead warriors beside the contested prize, a salty stream. In France, the peasants' revolt against a heavy tax on salt contributed to the French Revolution that began in 1789. Similarly, Mahatma Gandhi of India led a "Salt March" in 1930 to protest the tax on salt that the English imposed on his country.

Victory and defeat in wartime has also been influenced by salt. The army of the French general Napoleon lost contact with its supply wagons during the 1812 invasion of Russia. Deprived of salt, the soldiers became sick and their wounds would not heal. During the American Civil War, the South ran low on salt, and the price of a

pound of salt shot from one-quarter cent to five dollars. In more modern times, World War II fighter pilots flying over China carried salt in their emergency kits. If they were shot down in rural areas, the pilots could use the salt in exchange for help from local people.

Salt has even been a sign of social rank. At royal banquets in past centuries, guests eagerly surveyed where their assigned seats were in relation to the salt on the table. Those seated "below the salt" realized that they were unlikely to win favors from the king or queen.

Because salt is so vital to human health, it is fortunate that today the mineral is plentiful and cheap in most parts of the world.

1. **Connection to Literature:** From what you've learned about salt, tell what you think are the meanings of these sayings.
   (a) That worker isn't worth his salt.
   (b) I've salted away my allowance instead of spending it.
   (c) Wit is the salt of conversation, not the food.
   —William Hazlitt
2. **Solve It:** When humans lived a hunting, gathering, and herding way of life, their diet contained a lot of milk and roasted meat. When societies turned to farming, they began to need salt for good health. How can you explain this observation?

MEETING INDIVIDUAL NEEDS

Visually Impaired: Obtain a model (preferably dissectable) of the human head and torso. Provide each team with a list of organs and ducts of the digestive system to locate, starting with salivary glands. Make sure students see the entry of salivary ducts into the mouth. Ask students to estimate the length of the esophagus. Have them explain the reason food might enter the nasal chamber when a person throws up. Ask them why food passes into the esophagus rather than into the trachea when swallowed. [LEP]

GLOBAL CONNECTION

Purpose
Students will gain insight into the role that salt has played in historical events.

Teaching Strategies
Ask students to describe how salt can serve as a preservative. Then ask them for examples of foods that are preserved even today with salt. Have students determine the role of sodium and chloride ions in the body. Have students find the reason for adding iodine to salt. Ask them to suggest a reason for adding iodine to salt rather than adding it to some other food or condiment.

Possible Answers
1. (a) It refers to the time when workers were paid in salt. The worker is not earning his salary.
   (b) The person is "preserving" the money just as people preserved food by salting.
   (c) It means that wit flavors conversation just as salt improves the taste of bland food.
2. Plants typically contain very little salt. A diet that consists mainly of plant material must be supplemented with salt.

Going Further
Have students use the nutritional information on a bag of potato chips to calculate the percentage of salt in a serving of chips. The information is usually given as "milligrams of sodium." Sodium is roughly 40% of the mass of salt. Therefore, multiply the mass of sodium by 2.5 to obtain the mass of salt. Students will have to determine the mass of chips in one serving. L1

The pH Scale: Acids are defined as substances that ionize in water to form hydrogen ions (H^+). Each step downward on the pH scale represents a 10-fold increase in the concentration of hydrogen ions. Therefore, stomach acid at pH 2 represents an increase of 10^5 (100 000) times the concentration of hydrogen ions in pure water at pH 7.

Using Science Terms

Ask students to list several terms that are derived from or related to the word *gastric*. Have them define these terms. For example: gastrovascular cavity, gastroenterologist, gastric juice. L2

Demonstration

Obtain biuret reagent from a supply house. Biuret reagent is normally blue but will turn violet in color when in contact with protein. **CAUTION:** *Biuret reagent is caustic and can burn the skin. Wear goggles and an apron.* Wash away any spills immediately. Test a variety of foods such as canned pet foods, baby foods, eggs, and milk. Ask students to predict which foods will give a positive test for protein.

Digestion in the Stomach   Food enters the stomach through a ring of muscle that is normally closed tight. This muscle prevents food from moving back up into the esophagus. As the food moves into the stomach, it is moistened further by mucus that coats the inner lining of the stomach. The presence of proteins in the food stimulates nerves that signal the gastric glands lining the stomach wall to release gastric juice. Gastric juice contains hydrochloric acid and an enzyme that is in an inactive form until it comes into contact with the acid in the stomach. The hydrochloric acid gives the stomach fluid an acidic pH of about 2. The enzyme begins protein digestion by breaking some of the bonds between amino acids. However, because the enzyme can't break the bonds between all amino acids, it cannot complete protein digestion. Instead, the proteins are broken down into smaller polypeptide molecules.

As polypeptides are formed, their presence stimulates cells in the stomach lining to release a hormone into the bloodstream. Although the hormone travels throughout the body, it affects only the gastric glands, signaling them to release more gastric juice. As a result, large amounts of gastric juice are secreted only when protein is present in the stomach.

Digestion is also aided by a churning motion that constantly mixes the food in the stomach. This action continues to break up food and helps bring the surfaces of all food particles into contact with the enzymes.

When this stage of digestion is complete, the food is in the form of an acidic liquid mixture known as chyme.

The stomach plays yet another important role. Like the crop of an earthworm, it stores food. Adaptations for food storage are important because they enable an animal to eat periodically, rather than having to eat almost continuously.

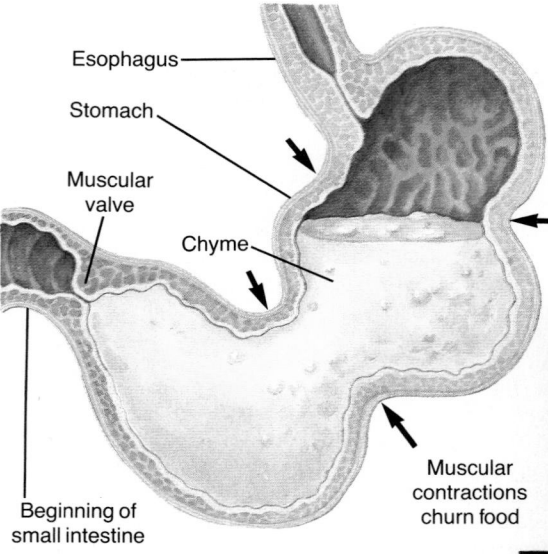

Esophagus

Stomach

Muscular valve

Chyme

Beginning of small intestine

Muscular contractions churn food

Figure 20-16   **After food enters the stomach, acid is secreted along with enzymes that begin protein digestion, and muscular contractions churn the food. The stomach also acts as a storage container, releasing food into the intestine at a slow rate for maximum efficiency in digestion and absorption.**

562 🍂 NUTRITION AND DIGESTION

Visually Impaired: Obtain a plastic "baggie" that measures about 30 by 15 cm in size. Allow students who are visually impaired to feel the empty bag. This bag is close to the size of the stomach when empty. Then fill the bag to capacity with water and allow students to again feel its capacity. Explain that the stomach, much like the bag, can expand to a capacity of 2 to 3 liters if necessary.

Teacher Classroom Resources
Study Guide, pp. 118-120 L1
Concept Mapping, p. 20 L1 LEP
Color Transparency #38, 52 L1 LEP
Probing Levels of Life, Lab 50, p. 129 L2
Investigating Living Systems, Labs 53-55, pp. 201-205 L2

The Small Intestine

Another muscular ring regulates the passage of chyme from the stomach into the longest part of the digestive tract, the small intestine. It is in the **small intestine** that the chemical digestion of food is completed and that most of the nutrient molecules are absorbed. The small intestine in an adult human is about seven meters long. The length of the small intestine helps ensure that the food stays in the organ long enough to be completely digested and absorbed.

The Gallbladder   Two organs that are not part of the digestive tract secrete important digestive fluids into the small intestine. The first of these organs is the **gallbladder.** The liver produces **bile,** which is stored in the small, saclike gallbladder. As soon as proteins or fats are detected in the intestine, certain cells of the intestine release a hormone that stimulates the gallbladder to empty the stored bile into the small intestine. Bile moves from the gallbladder into the small intestine via the common bile duct as shown in Figure 20-17.

Bile is made up of several substances, but only bile salts are important in digestion. Bile salts are a mixture of soaplike substances that the liver makes from cholesterol. These bile salts break up fats into small globules. This process is called emulsification and is similar to what takes place when you use detergent to wash fats and oils from dirty dishes. In the intestine, emulsification increases the surface area upon which fat-digesting enzymes can operate. The bile salts also aid in the absorption of digested fats.

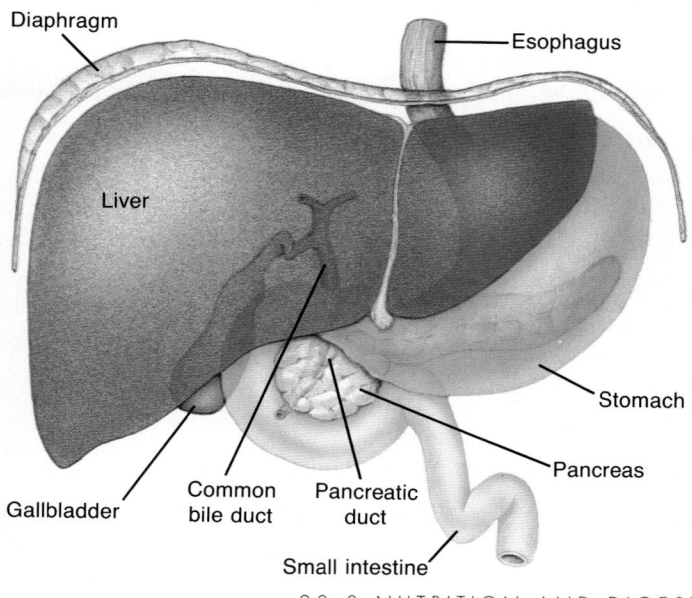

Figure 20-17   When food passes into the small intestine, digestion is continued by enzymes from the pancreas. Bile, which is produced by the liver and stored in the gallbladder, is released. Bile salts break up fat globules so that they can be attacked more efficiently by enzymes. Further along, enzymes secreted by the small intestine itself complete digestion. Sometimes people must undergo surgery to remove most of the small intestine because of disease or injury. What kinds of foods would these people have to eat after such surgery?

20.3 NUTRITION AND DIGESTION IN HUMANS **563**

MEETING INDIVIDUAL NEEDS

Ask students working at or below grade level to prepare a concept map that summarizes the important information found in the two paragraphs below the heading marked "The Gallbladder." Completed maps may become part of the students' portfolios. LEP

Concept Development
The gallbladder is not part of the digestive tract. Ask students what the term *tract* means and what organs associated with the digestive system are not part of the digestive tract (salivary glands, gallbladder, liver, and pancreas). LEP

Enrichment
The hormone responsible for gallbladder contraction is called cholecystokinin. Ask students to use a dictionary to determine the derivation for the name of this hormone. Point out that a hormone signals the gallbladder to release bile when fats are present in the intestine. Have students explain why digestion is more efficient with this system rather than one in which bile is released continuously.

Using the Diagram
Have students refer to Figure 20-17. Ask them to describe the location of the gallbladder, the location of both muscular rings of the stomach, and how far along the small intestine the common bile duct enters. LEP

Brainstorming
- Have students explain how it is possible for a person to live without a gallbladder; why a person with no gallbladder can still form bile; and why a person with no gallbladder can still digest fats but less efficiently. COOP LEARN
- Ask students to recap the many different roles of the pancreas that are related directly to digestion. Then ask them if they believe that a person can survive without a pancreas as was the case with no gallbladder. Have them justify their answers. COOP LEARN

Figure Caption Question
What kinds of foods would these people have to eat after such surgery? They would have to eat foods that are rich in nutrients that require little digestion. Often, artificial supplements are needed.

Minilab 2

Purpose
To observe evidence of protein digestion by an enzyme.

Skills
observe and infer, classify

Teaching Strategies
- Supply students with test tubes or small plastic cups, markers, beaker, mashed fruit samples, and warm gelatin solution.
- Use unflavored gelatin and prepare it according to directions on the package. Timing is important because gelatin must be warm and liquid but not hot enough to destroy enzymes in fruit.

Expected Results
Kiwi and pineapple contain enzymes that digest protein enough to keep gelatin from jelling. The gelatin in contact with these fruits will remain liquid while that with other fruits will jell.

Answers
Kiwi and pineapple contain proteolytic enzymes. The gelatin in contact with these fruits did not jell. Similar enzymes would be produced by the pancreas and cells lining the stomach and small intestine.

✔ Assessment
Portfolio: Have students summarize protein digestion in humans by creating a chart using information on pages 562-565 and in Table 20.3. Students should include the chart in their portfolios.

Minilab 2

Which fruits keep gelatin from jelling?

Gelatin that you use to make desserts is partially composed of protein. Certain raw fruits contain an enzyme that digests protein. When these fruits are added to gelatin, it will no longer jell when cooled. Fill five test tubes with a warm (not hot) solution of gelatin. Label them 1 through 5. Add the following: 1 = nothing, 2 = fresh mashed pineapple, 3 = fresh mashed apple, 4 = fresh mashed kiwi fruit, 5 = fresh mashed orange. Allow all tubes to cool overnight. Observe whether each tube did or did not jell.

Analysis *Which fruits contained a protein-digesting enzyme? How were you able to tell? If this same enzyme were present in your body, what organs might produce it?*

The Pancreas The second organ that secretes digestive fluid into the small intestine is the **pancreas,** which lies behind and partly below the stomach. It secretes enzyme-containing pancreatic juices into a duct that merges with the common bile duct. The pancreas releases its juices in response to the same hormonal signal that causes the release of bile from the gallbladder.

Presence of the acidic chyme in the small intestine causes the secretion of yet another hormone from cells of the intestine. This hormone causes the pancreas to release sodium hydrogen carbonate along with its enzymes. Sodium hydrogen carbonate is the same substance as baking soda and helps neutralize the acidic chyme. Bile also contains basic substances and, together with sodium hydrogen carbonate, raises the pH of the chyme to about 8. The pancreatic enzymes work most effectively in this slightly basic environment. Over-the-counter remedies used to relieve acid indigestion and heartburn contain either sodium hydrogen carbonate or other basic substances such as magnesium hydroxide. Heartburn is a painful condition that occurs when acidic gastric juice from the stomach enters and irritates the esophagus. The basic substances in the medicine neutralize stomach acid, thus relieving the symptoms of heartburn.

One of the pancreatic enzymes is similar to the salivary enzyme that converts starch to maltose. A second pancreatic enzyme helps convert fats to fatty acids and glycerol. A third group of enzymes acts on the polypeptides that were produced in the stomach, breaking them down into smaller polypeptides. Several enzymes of this third type are needed because each one serves to break only the bonds between certain amino acids. A fourth type of pancreatic enzyme converts nucleic acids to nucleotides.

Thinking Lab
DRAW A CONCLUSION

Why are Michael's data different?

Background
Salivary glands form an enzyme that digests starch into disaccharides. The amount of enzyme present in saliva varies from person to person. A deep blue color appears when iodine is added to starch. The color becomes progressively lighter as the amount of starch decreases. A number system from 10-0 can be used to judge color intensity and starch amounts. Let 10 = deep blue and 0 = no blue color.

You Try It
Each of six students received a tube containing 10 mL of a starch suspension. They then added 5 drops of their saliva and stirred the mixture thoroughly. After 10 minutes, each student added a drop of iodine to the tube and mixed thoroughly. The students' results are shown in Table A.

Draw a conclusion to explain Michael's results. Michael correctly repeated the experiment five more times and recorded the same results each time. Draw another conclusion for his five similar results.

Table A

Student	Color Intensity
Shawana	3
Talyn	1
Jay	8
Maria	2
Larry	1
Michael	10
Control	10

Thinking Lab
DRAW A CONCLUSION

Purpose
Students learn that enzyme levels can vary among people, possibly for genetic reasons.

Skills
interpret data, observe and infer

Teaching Strategies
- Have students first think about and explain the results based only on the data given. Then have them reconsider their conclusions, assuming that repetitions of the experiment gave similar results.

Answers
Explanations for one trial might include the idea that Michael made a mistake or did not wish to provide a saliva sample. To account for multiple trials giving similar results, students should conclude that Michael's saliva has very little amylase, at least on this day.

✔ Assessment
Knowledge: Ask students to speculate on the reasons that enzyme levels might vary greatly from person to person. They should discuss genetic variation in their responses.

Final Steps in Digestion   At this point, the food in the small intestine is being acted upon by bile and pancreatic enzymes. The intestine now contains both simple nutrients—vitamins, mineral ions, and water—and complex nutrients. Of the complex nutrients, only the fats have been fully digested. They have been broken down into fatty acid and glycerol molecules. Proteins and carbohydrates have been only partially digested. So far, proteins have been broken down into small polypeptides, nucleic acids have been broken down into nucleotides, and carbohydrates exist in the form of the disaccharides maltose, sucrose, and lactose.

Protein and nucleic acid digestion is completed by enzymes secreted in the intestinal walls. A group of these enzymes converts nucleotides into their component sugars, bases, and phosphates. Other enzymes break down polypeptides into dipeptides and then into amino acids.

Carbohydrate digestion is completed by enzymes that convert disaccharides to monosaccharides. These enzymes are located in the membranes of cells lining the intestine. By the time digestion in the small intestine is complete, all complex food molecules have been converted to smaller molecules that can pass across cell membranes. A summary of the process of human digestion is shown in Table 20.3. The right column in the table shows the overall enzyme reactions that occur in digestion. The names of the enzymes involved are printed over the arrows.

Table 20.3   Summary of Digestion in Humans

Digestive Organ	Major Physical Actions	Major Chemical Actions
Mouth	Chewing Grinding Moistening	starch $\xrightarrow{\text{salivary amylase}}$ maltose
Esophagus	Moistening, Peristalsis	
Stomach	Moistening Churning Peristalsis Some water absorption	proteins $\xrightarrow{\text{pepsin}}$ polypeptides
Small intestine	Peristalsis Fat emulsification Most nutrient absorption Some water absorption	starch $\xrightarrow{\text{pancreatic amylase}}$ disaccharides proteins $\xrightarrow{\text{proteases}}$ polypeptides polypeptides $\xrightarrow{\text{peptidases}}$ amino acids fats $\xrightarrow{\text{lipases}}$ fatty acids and glycerol disaccharides $\xrightarrow{\text{maltase, lactase, sucrase}}$ monosaccharides
Large intestine	Most water absorption Peristalsis Waste elimination	some vitamins synthesized

SECTION 20.3

Concept Development

- The small intestine receives simple nutrients such as vitamins and mineral ions as well as complex nutrients from the stomach. Have students explain the meaning of "simple" and "complex" nutrients.
- Have students review the processes of extracellular and intracellular digestion. Then have them explain which process the human digestive system relies on. Ask them to explain their answers.

Using the Table

Have students study Table 20.3. Then ask them to answer the following questions. (a) Why is water absorption a physical rather than chemical action? (b) Which organs contribute to pushing food through the digestive tract by peristalsis? (c) Which organs are involved with carbohydrate digestion? (d) Which organs are involved with fat digestion? (e) Which organs are involved with protein digestion? (f) How can a person without a stomach still manage to digest food? (g) Why may the small intestine be the most important organ of the digestive system? (h) What specific changes and enzymes are needed to convert starch to glucose? (i) What specific changes and enzymes are needed to convert fat to fatty acids and glycerol? (j) What specific changes and enzymes are needed to convert protein to amino acids?

MULTICULTURAL CONNECTION

Digestion of Lactose: The enzyme lactase is needed to properly digest lactose, the sugar in milk. However, not everyone has this enzyme as part of his or her digestive system. Without it, drinking milk or eating some milk products can result in indigestion, cramps, bloating, gas, and diarrhea because the lactose is broken down by bacterial fermentation. African groups such as the Ibo and Yoruba have no lactase as adults and therefore use very little milk in their diet. Understandably, they do not herd dairy animals. Some other ethnic groups around the world have high percentages of adult members who cannot digest lactose.

Using the Photograph

Ask students to examine Figure 20-18. Remind them that the photo on the right is a cross-section view. Have them explain what the large, shadowy circle in the center represents, and what the outer ring surrounding the villi might represent and what its function might be. **LEP**

Using Science Terms

Ask students to determine the meaning of the terms *villus* (hair) and *microvilli* in Latin. Have them explain how this meaning justifies the appearance of these structures. **L1**

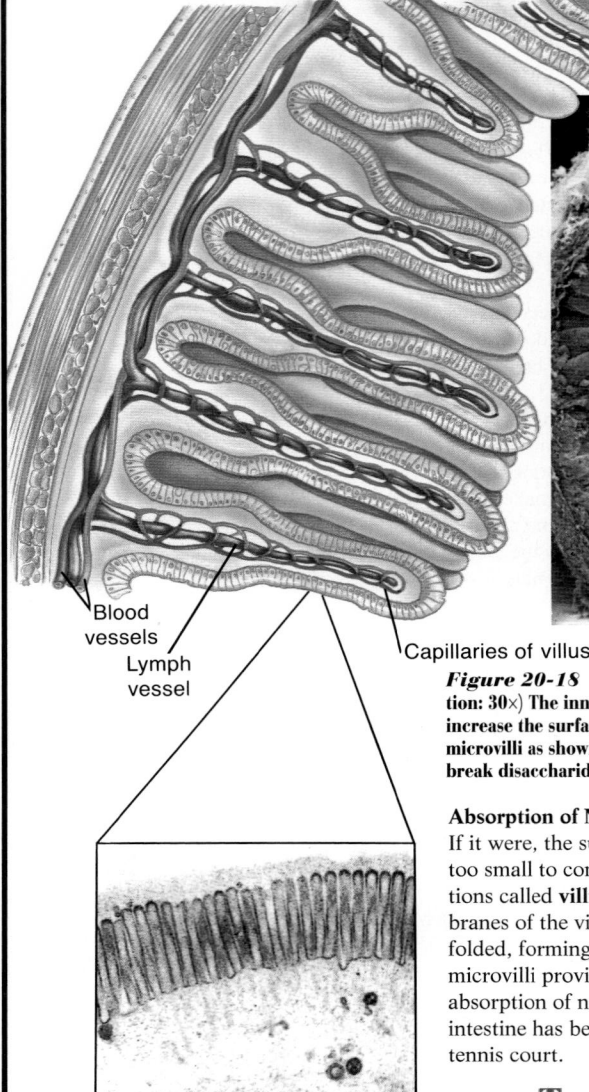

Villus

Blood vessels
Lymph vessel

Capillaries of villus

Figure 20-18 The photo above is a cross section of a rat intestine. (Magnification: 30×) The inner lining of the intestine is divided into many villi, which greatly increase the surface area for absorption. In addition, each cell has projections called microvilli as shown in the photo below left. (Magnification: 6000×) Enzymes that break disaccharides into monosaccharides are located in the microvilli.

Absorption of Nutrients The lining of the small intestine is not smooth. If it were, the surface area available for absorbing digested food would be too small to complete the job. The lining is folded, and fingerlike projections called **villi** extend inward from each of the many folds. The membranes of the villi cells that face the intestine's interior are also highly folded, forming microvilli, as shown in Figure 20-18. The villi and microvilli provide a very large surface area inside the intestine where absorption of nutrients can take place. The surface area inside the human intestine has been estimated as 300 m², which is roughly the area of a tennis court.

Transport of Nutrients

Before nutrients can reach all body cells, they must first enter villi cells. Then they are absorbed by the blood and transported through the body. Passage into villi cells and from there into the blood involves both diffusion and active transport. Within the villi are many tiny blood vessels called capillaries. Monosaccharides, dipeptides, amino acids, products of nucleotide digestion, minerals, small fatty acids, and vitamins enter the blood flowing through the capillaries. The blood, laden with nutrients, then moves on to the vein that carries blood to the liver.

566 🐾 NUTRITION AND DIGESTION

Glucose and Amino Acids The liver has the important task of monitoring some nutrients as they leave the small intestine. Under the direction of hormones, the liver controls the levels of these nutrients in the body. For example, it is important that the level of glucose in the blood be kept fairly constant. If all the glucose produced during digestion of a meal remained in the bloodstream, the level of glucose in the blood would increase dramatically. To prevent this, the liver converts excess glucose to the polysaccharide glycogen, which is stored for later use. Thus, the blood that leaves the liver and transports nutrients to the rest of the cells in the body has the correct glucose level. As time passes between meals, the level of glucose in the blood gradually falls. To keep the level constant, the liver gradually converts the stored glycogen back into glucose and releases it into the bloodstream as needed.

The liver also regulates the levels of amino acids in blood that passes through it. Excess amino acids, unlike excess glucose, can be stored only for a short time. As a result, most are converted to other organic molecules such as carbohydrates or fats. The body's inability to store amino acids is the primary reason why it is important to eat a diet that provides a constant intake of proteins containing all the essential amino acids.

Fatty Acids and Glycerol Large fatty acid molecules and glycerol do not enter the blood directly. After they pass from the intestine into villi cells, they are recombined to form molecules of fat, which are then coated with proteins. These particles are absorbed into small vessels in the villi that are part of the lymphatic system, which will be described in more detail in Chapter 22.

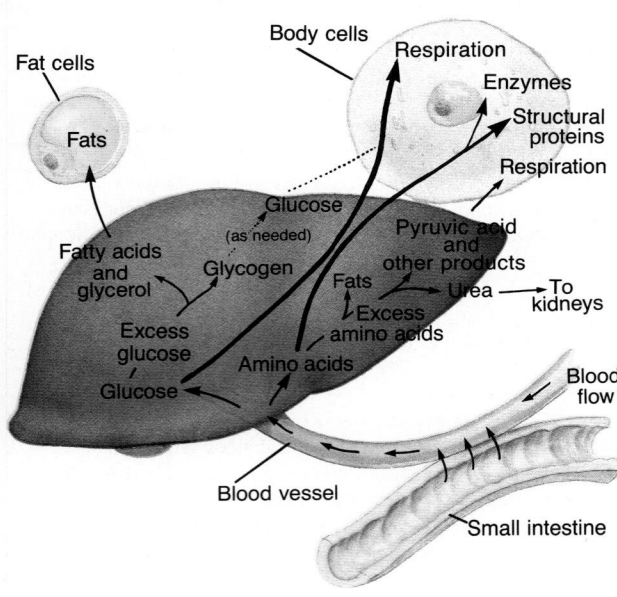

Figure 20-19 This diagram shows how the liver handles the products of carbohydrate and protein digestion. Notice that excess glucose from carbohydrate digestion is stored as glycogen. Any excess beyond what can be stored as glycogen is converted to fats and stored in fat cells. Amino acids, on the other hand, cannot be stored in reserve. Excess amino acids are converted either to products that can enter respiration or to fats. In either case, urea is formed as a waste product and must be eliminated by the kidneys.

20.3 NUTRITION AND DIGESTION IN HUMANS **567**

Teacher FYI
The concentration of glucose in the blood is normally maintained at between 75-110 milligrams per deciliter. This concentration could be illustrated by dissolving 0.1 g of sugar in 100 mL of water.

Bioethics

A Question of Feeding: Should a patient who is not likely to ever regain consciousness be fed through a tube inserted into his or her stomach? Those who say "yes" believe that: (a) it is never morally right to starve a human being, (b) euthanasia is not morally justified, and (c) it is never right to withhold food and fluids from persons who are unconscious or seriously debilitated. There are those who disagree. They believe that: (a) the procedure needed to introduce the feeding tube can be risky for the patient, (b) the food and liquids that are received are of no benefit to the patient, and (c) the cost and burdens of receiving the treatment may outweigh the benefit. Have students hold a debate on this question.

MEETING INDIVIDUAL NEEDS

Visually Impaired: Illustrate the total surface area of the human intestines having students walk (with help if necessary) a length of 7 meters. This corresponds to the length of the small intestines. Then, have them walk along the perimeter of a tennis court (or similar area) to represent the area of the intestines with villi (300 m²). | LEP |

STUDENT JOURNAL

Have students track the path of a molecule of glucose that has just arrived in the small intestine. Ask them to describe the trip from small intestine to liver. From this point, students should track the fate of the molecule as if it remained mobile and as if it were "excess." | L2 |

Brainstorming

Many people believe that cholesterol is a chemical that is always harmful. Have students cite two specific facts that can dispel this misconception.

COOP LEARN

NUTRITION CONNECTION

Limiting Cholesterol:

Provide students with the following data on cholesterol levels in certain foods. All values are in milligrams per serving.

Food	Serving	Choles-terol (mg)
Bacon	4 strips	30
Hot dog	1	30
Sirloin	3.5 oz.	90
Ribs, pork	3.5 oz.	120
Liver	3.5 oz.	390
Chicken (no skin)	3.5 oz.	90
Duck (no skin)	3.5 oz.	90
Catfish	3.5 oz.	30
Snapper	3.5 oz.	50
Herring	3.5 oz.	80
Crab	3.5 oz.	100
Oysters	3.5 oz.	110
Egg white	1	0
Feta cheese	1 oz.	25
Cream cheese	1 oz.	30
Egg, whole	1	220
Spaghetti	1 cup	0

The recommended daily intake of cholesterol should not exceed 300 milligrams. Have students consider portion size, and then compile a list of foods to avoid. **L1**

Figure Caption Question

Page 570: *Which part do you think goes with each term? Why?* The terms reflect the direction of movement of material. Ascending is on the right side of the abdomen and descending is on the left. Transverse crosses between the ascending and descending.

Cholesterol molecules are coated with protein to form molecules known as LDL complexes. These complexes also enter the lymphatic vessels. These and other substances that travel through lymph vessels are eventually emptied into the bloodstream. Fat and cholesterol molecules must be coated with proteins because they are not soluble in water. Insoluble particles cannot be transported in the watery liquid part of the blood. In the blood, the protein-coated fats are slowly broken apart and delivered to cells for use as a source of energy. If they are not needed for energy, the fats are stored in fat cells. The LDL complexes remain intact. The liver absorbs the LDLs and regulates blood cholesterol by storing or releasing it.

Absorption of Nutrients by Cells When digested nutrients reach the bloodstream, they are in a form that can enter your cells. Some nutrients, such as fatty acids and glycerol, diffuse directly through cell membranes. Others, such as glucose, amino acids, and mineral ions, enter cells by means of facilitated diffusion. LDL complexes are brought into cells by receptor-aided endocytosis. Glucose and some fats are used in cellular respiration, which releases energy for the cell's many functions. Other nutrients are used for growth. For example, amino acids that were linked to form proteins in the beef, chicken, fish, or beans you ate for dinner can now be joined in different sequences to form human proteins. Fats and cholesterol are used to build new membranes, and certain cells convert cholesterol to hormones.

HISTORY CONNECTION

Lillie Rosa Minoka-Hill

A squawking chicken, a bushel of newly dug potatoes, or a bucket of foamy and still-warm milk—that was the kind of payment doctors in rural America often received in the early 1900s. Dr. Minoka-Hill, a physician in the small town of Oneida, Wisconsin, accepted these offerings graciously. She understood her patients' financial situations and explained, "If I charged too much, I wouldn't have a very good chance of going to heaven."

Dr. Minoka-Hill (1876-1952) was a Native American born on a Mohawk reservation in New York state. After her mother's death, she stayed on the reservation with her maternal relatives until she was old enough to go to school. Then her Quaker father, a doctor, brought her to Philadelphia, where he taught her about her Mohawk heritage and sent her to a Quaker boarding school.

She continued her education at the Woman's Medical College in Philadelphia. After graduation, she helped penniless immigrant women at a clinic associated with the medical school.

When she married Charles Hill, a member of the Oneida tribe, and moved to Wisconsin, Dr. Minoka-Hill thought that her days of practicing medicine were over. There were too many other chores on the land she and her husband farmed. However, she found time to visit the nearby Oneida reservation and talk with the people living there. They taught her about traditional herbal remedies for illness and injuries. Soon, neighbors began to come to Dr. Minoka-Hill for her combination of traditional and modern medical knowledge.

Charles Hill died in 1916, leaving his wife with only a debt-ridden farm and a few farm animals to support six young children. Dr. Minoka-Hill ignored the advice of friends who urged her to move

568 ☙ NUTRITION AND DIGESTION

STUDENT JOURNAL

Have students assume they have just eaten a roast beef sandwich with cheese. Have them explain what molecules will result from digestion of the sandwich. Review the fact that (other than water) bread is mostly carbohydrates, beef is mostly protein, and cheese contains fat. Then have students describe where they might find the molecules in their bodies 24 hours after eating the sandwich, and ask them to explain why they are in those locations. **L1**

The Large Intestine

After the small intestine has absorbed most of the nutrients from digested food, undigestible solids and some water remain. These materials pass from the small intestine into the **large intestine** or **colon.** This organ is composed of three sections that loop around and over the coiled small intestine. Slightly below the point at which the small and large intestines join is the appendix, a vestigial structure.

Absorption of Water   During digestion, a lot of water has been added to the food by secretions from the mouth, stomach, and small intestine. A major function of the colon is to reclaim that water by absorption. In this process, water and dissolved minerals pass from the hollow interior of the colon into the bloodstream of the colon walls. Absorption of water causes the remaining material to become a mass of damp solids, called feces. These solids are stored in the rectum and pass out of the body through the anus. Some excess minerals, such as iron and calcium, may pass from the bloodstream into the colon to be eliminated along with feces.

The interior of the human colon provides an ideal habitat for many species of bacteria. These bacteria have a mutualistic relationship with humans. The wastes of digestion provide the bacteria with food, and the bacteria make the vitamins B-12 and K along with some amino acids. These bacteria also inhibit the growth of disease-causing bacteria.

back to New York. She said, "While in college, I resolved to spend some time and effort to help needy Indians. In Wisconsin I found my work."

From seven in the morning until ten at night, Dr. Minoka-Hill welcomed patients to what she called her "kitchen-clinic." She traveled long distances to treat patients or deliver babies, sometimes taking her younger children along. She also spent much of her time teaching the Oneida people about nutrition and good eating habits in an effort to relieve their constant problem of malnutrition. Because of her dedication, the Oneida adopted the doctor into their tribe and gave her

an Oneida name, You-da-gent, which means "she who serves."

Dr. Minoka-Hill died in 1952. A memorial erected by her friends has this simple inscription: "I was sick and you visited me."

1. **Explore Further:** What "home remedies" are used by people in your family or community?

2. **Connection to Health:** Why do you think today's recent immigrants to the United States might find it difficult to get health care?

HISTORY CONNECTION

Purpose
Students learn that combinations of traditional and modern medicine can prove effective.

Teaching Strategies
• Have students work in cooperative groups in order to: (1) define the terms *herbal remedies* and *malnutrition,* (2) determine through references what constitutes malnutrition, (3) answer the questions at the conclusion of this feature, and (4) determine, through ethnobotany references, examples of herbal remedies.

COOP LEARN

Possible Answers
1. Answers will vary, but may include drinking herbal teas, gargling with salt water to ease a sore throat, applying camphor or menthol salve around neck to ease congestion, and eating chicken soup to cure a cold.
2. Many immigrants do not have jobs that provide health care benefits and may not be eligible for programs available to citizens.

Going Further
Have students determine through references how long the human body can survive without food or water. Ask them to describe the events within the body that occur as starvation progresses. L2

MEETING INDIVIDUAL NEEDS

• Ask students working at or below grade level to list at least five facts regarding the large intestine. Have students also describe how each fact differentiates the large from the small intestine. Point out that there are no villi in the large intestine. LEP

• **Visually Impaired:** Provide students who are visually impaired with 1.5 m of tubing. Allow students to run their hands along its entire length. Advise them that the tubing corresponds in length to that of the large intestine. For comparison, a length of tubing 7 meters long would be needed for the small intestine.

3 Assess

Check for Understanding
Ask students to explain the role or roles of (a) a balanced diet in keeping healthy, (b) saliva and the mouth in digestion, (c) the stomach and its enzymes, (d) the gallbladder and its contents, (e) the pancreas and its enzymes, and (f) the small intestine and its enzymes. L1

Reteach

Have students work in cooperative groups in order to respond to each of the six items listed in the "Check for Understanding" section.

Extension

Ask students how they would redesign the small intestine to (a) decrease the amount of food absorbed into the bloodstream, or (b) increase the amount of food absorbed into the bloodstream.

✔ Assessment

Skill: Have students sequence the following events associated with digestion: (a) absorption of excess water into bloodstream, (b) release of bile into small intestine, (c) release of saliva into mouth, (d) release of pepsin by stomach, (e) passage of food through esophagus, (f) final digestion of all nutrients, (g) elimination of feces, and (h) movement of chyme into small intestine.

4 Close

Activity

Have students prepare a line segment that measures 38.4 cm. Advise them that this line represents the human digestive tract. Each 4 cm on the line represents one meter of actual tract. Have students mark off and label the lengths of the following organs: mouth = 0.1 meter, esophagus = 0.25 meters, stomach = 0.25 meters, small intestine = 7.5 meters, large intestine = 1.5 meters. Have them include the label "Human Digestive Tract" and include the diagram in their portfolios.

Figure 20-20   Shown here are the major organs of the digestive system. Notice how the shape of the large intestine adapts it to collect undigested waste, absorb water from the waste, and compact the waste. In this diagram, the front of the liver is raised slightly so that you can see the gallbladder underneath. The large intestine is usually described as having three parts—ascending, descending, and transverse. Which part do you think goes with each term? Why?

LOOKING AHEAD

Y OU HAVE LEARNED in this chapter that autotrophs take in simple inorganic materials that they can use in photosynthesis to produce food molecules. Heterotrophs digest complex molecules in their food into simpler molecules. The simple inorganic nutrients and the products of photosynthesis of autotrophs must be distributed to all of the organism's cells. The products of digestion in heterotrophs also must be distributed. This distribution depends upon some type of transport mechanism. In the next chapter, you will study the function of transport, not only of nutrients, but also of other substances important to life. You will also learn about how part of the transport system of animals functions in other vital ways. ❧

Section Review

Understanding Concepts

1. Suppose a person always ate a breakfast that included buttered toast, two eggs, and bacon. How would eating only those foods be likely to affect the person's health? How could this person improve his or her diet?

2. How can the human digestive tract be compared with an assembly line?

3. How do physical and chemical processes of digestion work together in your mouth, your stomach, and your small intestine?

4. **Skill Review—Classifying:** Think about what you have eaten in the last two days. Use the information provided in Figure 20-12 to arrange the various foods by food groups. Is your diet of the last two days a balanced one? For more help, refer to Organizing Information in the **Skill Handbook**.

5. **Thinking Critically:** What is the advantage of having the same starch-digesting enzyme in both the mouth and the small intestine?

Answers to Section Review

1. That diet is rich in fats and cholesterol and could promote obesity and plaque buildup, and possibly increase the risk of a heart attack or stroke. The person could include more cereals, fruits, vegetables, and lean meat.

2. Each specialized region of the digestive tract performs a function that prepares the food for the next region.

3. In the mouth, food is broken into smaller chunks, thus increasing the surface area. An enzyme in saliva converts starch to maltose. The churning action of the stomach exposes food to pepsin, which begins protein digestion. As food is moved through the small intestine by peristalsis, the final breakdown of organic molecules occurs, producing amino acids, fatty acids and glycerol, and monosaccharides.

4. **Skill Review—Classifying:** Answers should reveal that students know the major food groups and examples of foods within each of those groups.

5. **Thinking Critically:** Starch is an important energy source for the body. Having similar enzymes in two locations ensures that starch receives maximum digestion.

BIOLOGY, TECHNOLOGY, AND SOCIETY

Health Connection

Does cholesterol count?

Suppose that in the grocery store, you see two one-pound jars of peanut butter, Dippy's brand and Duffy's brand. The price tags are identical, and about the only difference you can spot is the claim printed in bright yellow letters on the Dippy's jar: *Now! Cholesterol-Free!* Which jar will you put into your shopping cart?

If you choose Dippy's because of the label, the manufacturer's strategy has worked. Of course, Dippy's Peanut Butter contains no cholesterol. But, neither does Duffy's or any other brand of peanut butter. Only foods containing animal products are likely to contain this fat-like, soft, waxy substance. Peanut butter contains no animal products.

Advertisers' claims may have persuaded you that cholesterol is always a villain, but that idea is misleading, too. As you learned in Chapter 4, cholesterol is an important part of the membranes of cells. In your body, cholesterol is used to make several types of hormones, the chemical messengers of the body. Problems occur when your body has too much cholesterol.

Cholesterol is transported in two forms, low-density lipoproteins (LDLs) and high-density lipoproteins (HDLs). Although it's not entirely accurate, the label of "good" has been attached to HDLs

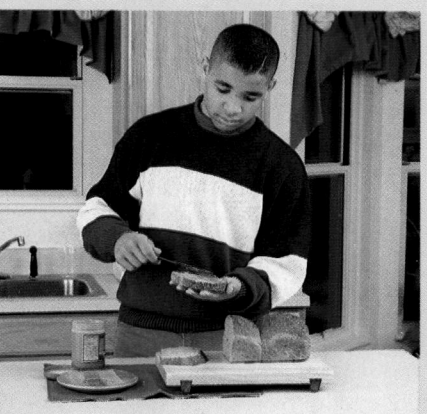

because they seem to act something like a vacuum cleaner, taking cholesterol from cells and delivering it to the liver. In contrast, LDLs tend to deposit cholesterol on the inside lining of arteries. These deposits are referred to as *plaque.* As layers of this plaque thicken, they can block the flow of blood in much the same way that mineral deposits inside water pipes can restrict water flow.

When blood flow is blocked, a heart attack or stroke can result.

Eating saturated fats tends to increase a person's cholesterol. As a result, the National Heart, Lung, and Blood Institute recommended in 1990 that everyone eat a diet with only 10% of daily Calories coming from saturated fats. Instead, people are advised to replace saturated fats in the diet with unsaturated fats. Vegetable oils such as corn oil, olive oil, and peanut oil are typically low in saturated fats.

However, "vegetable oil" printed on a label is no guarantee that the food contains no saturated fats. The so-called tropical oils such as palm oil and coconut oil can properly be called vegetable oils. However, these tropical oils usually contain saturated fatty acids and should only be used in moderation, just as with animal fats.

Most of the earliest findings about cholesterol were based on a study of 362 000 middle-aged men. Some scientists have criticized the application of these results to women and people of other ages. Currently, research is taking place

Going Further
Have students contact local physicians or hospitals. Ask them to find out what the normal or acceptable levels in the blood are for cholesterol, both HDL and LDL. Are these levels always the same or do they differ by age groups or other factors? **L1**

BIOLOGY, TECHNOLOGY, AND SOCIETY

Health Connection

Purpose
Students learn that fat is not necessarily bad or good. Much depends on the type of fat consumed.

Background
Saturated fats contain fatty acid chains in which all carbons are linked by single bonds. Unsaturated fats contain fatty acid chains in which one or more double bonds between carbons exist.

Teaching Strategies
- Have students review the structure of fats and the meaning of *saturated* and *unsaturated* in Chapter 3.
- Have students compare structural formulas of saturated and unsaturated fatty acids on the chalkboard so that the chemical difference is clearly illustrated.
- Have students work in cooperative groups as they read this feature, outline it, and answer the questions. The outline and answers may be added to the students' portfolios. **COOP LEARN**
- Provide food label photocopies that list the mass of saturated and unsaturated fats separately. Ask students to compare labels and make judgments about which foods people should eat if they are attempting to lower cholesterol levels. **COOP LEARN**

Possible Answers
1. Diet is the critical factor. Wealthy countries tend to have more fat in their diet from animal sources. Less affluent nations rely more on diets of plants, grains, and beans, which are low in cholesterol.
2. Advantages include lowering of cholesterol and fat intake, loss or control of weight, and reduction of plaque formation. Disadvantages include the fact that the human body needs some fat for energy and construction of plasma membranes and organelles.

Issues

Purpose

Students are introduced to the advantages and problems associated with the use of liquid diets to lose weight.

Teaching Strategies

- Have students look up the meaning or significance of the following terms: *obese, diabetes, stroke, high blood pressure, electrolyte level, Calorie, thyroid, sympathetic nervous system.*

- Make photocopies of warning labels that appear on liquid diets. Allow students to examine these copies. Ask them to explain why a liquid diet could have serious medical consequences relating to the heart.

- Have students use references to determine what standards are used to determine if a person is or is not obese. Males should have a body fat reading of between 12% and 23% and females between 16% and 28%. Values much above these indicate a trend toward obesity.

- Discuss Calories with your students. Review the Calorie content of certain foods by examining food labels or transparencies of labels. Have students find out the number of excess Calories needed to add one pound of body mass (3500 Calories). Discuss the difference in Calorie content of fats (9 per gram) compared to carbohydrates and protein (4 per gram).

- Have students read the articles listed at the bottom of page 573 and write a report on their findings. This report could be placed in their portfolios or be given as an oral report to the class.

---

to determine the relationship between cholesterol and arterial disease in diverse groups of people.

1. **Connection to Economics:** People living in wealthy countries tend to have more cholesterol in their blood than people in less affluent nations. What might account for the difference?

2. **Connection to Chemistry:** Chemists are synthesizing and testing fake fats, substances that can be used in food preparation because their physical properties closely resemble real fats. However, fake fats pass through the digestive system without being absorbed. What advantages and disadvantages could result from using fake fat in your diet?

Issues

Are liquid diets a losing proposition?

How much are Americans willing to spend to become thin? Apparently, quite a lot, because the U.S. diet industry takes in more than $30 billion a year. Displaying the typical American trait of trying to accomplish things quickly, the fastest-growing group of dieters are

those on liquid diets that substitute high-protein "milkshakes" for regular meals.

Winning with Liquid Diets

Liquid diets have been around since the late 1970s. At that time, some

were considered dangerous and were linked to more than 50 deaths, mostly from heart problems. Since 1984, the U.S. Food and Drug Administration has required all very-low-calorie protein diets to carry a warning that they may cause serious illness and should be medically supervised. Today's liquid-protein mixes contain more and better quality protein than those of the 1970s. In addition, carbohydrates, vitamins, and minerals are now included.

For those patients who are truly obese, medically monitored liquid-protein weight-loss diets can be life-saving. Most programs run by hospitals or through doctors' offices accept only adult patients who are 20 to 50 percent over their ideal weights. These people are at risk for serious heart problems, stroke, high blood pressure, gallbladder disease, diabetes, and other life-threatening medical problems if they don't lose weight.

The psychological benefits of quick weight loss for people with many pounds to lose must also be considered. Ordinary, slow-paced diets, with their losses of only a pound or two a week, may be too discouraging for very obese people.

The most regimented liquid-protein diet plan replaces food entirely for weeks at a time. In the first stage of the program, dieters consume protein shakes that provide 400 to 800 Calories a day. Weight loss averages three to ten pounds a week. Dieters must have weekly checks of blood pressure, heart function, urine content, and electrolyte levels.

Following the initial stage, the "refeeding" portion of the diet begins. The protein shakes are gradually replaced with sensible meals that are low in fat.

When patients reach their ideal weight, the third phase of the program, maintenance, begins. During this phase, patients practice eating a moderate, balanced diet on their own to keep the lost pounds from returning.

Dieters who decide to use liquid diets have several plans from which to choose. Some programs involve the supervision of only a doctor, while others promote a team approach that includes a doctor, dietitian, exercise physiologist, and psychologist.

Losing with Liquid Diets It's hard to pick up a magazine without finding articles with titles such as "One-Day Quick-Fix Diet" or "Holiday Weight-Watching." The magazines' publishers know their audience well, because about one-third of American women and one-fourth of American men are trying to lose weight.

Television, too, makes people aware of weight-loss programs. Fans of a popular TV talk show cheered when the formerly plump hostess of the program modeled her size-10 jeans in front of 20 million viewers and touted the wonders of a liquid-protein diet. Unfortunately, in the following months, she regained many of her banished 67 pounds.

Why do liquid diets often fail? In most cases, it is because the people who have lost weight on these diets have not changed their lifestyles. When they return to eating regular meals, they often cannot eat sensibly and maintain an exercise program. They discover the harsh truth that there is no magic in a liquid-protein diet itself and that losing weight means limiting caloric intake, no matter what the source of those Calories is.

The big selling point for liquid-protein diets is how quickly they

work. However, this type of rapid weight loss can have bad effects on the body's chemistry. When fueled with few Calories, the body is fooled into thinking it is in a state of starvation. Then, to save energy, the thyroid and sympathetic nervous systems slow down the body's metabolic rate. Because the body has to decide where to spend its limited energy, people on rapid weight-loss diets often complain about dry skin, bad breath, and hair loss and of being cold, tired, or dizzy.

Scientists think that after repeated diet cycles, the body stays in this semi-starvation mode. As a result, the repeat dieter's metabolism slows with each diet cycle, and it becomes harder to lose weight or to maintain a weight loss. This effect is sometimes dubbed the "yo-yo syndrome."

Are liquid-protein diets the miracle weight-loss method of the future? Probably not. Although the diets help with initial weight loss, most dieters fail to maintain that loss. In fact, 90 percent of dieters who lose weight regain it within three years, and half gain even more.

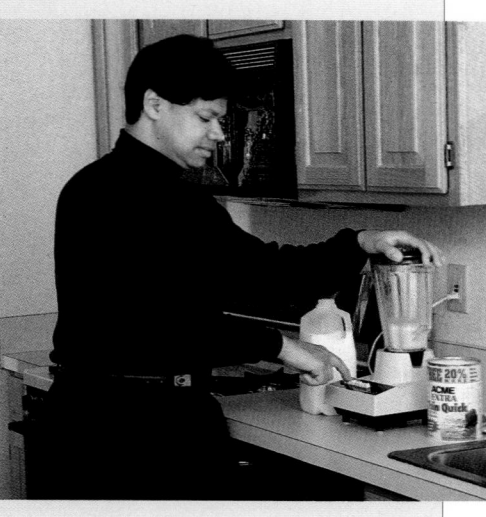

Understanding the Issue

1. Many liquid diets are sold in drug stores and grocery stores. What steps would you recommend that a person take before starting one of these programs? What criteria do you think should be used in choosing a program?

2. How would you advise someone who is ten pounds overweight and is considering a liquid weight-loss program?

3. The medically supervised team approach to dieting seems to be more successful for maintaining weight loss than are personal diet plans. How can you account for this difference?

4. Many teenagers have an inaccurate view of their bodies and consider themselves fat even when they are not. How do you think they could get a more realistic picture of themselves?

5. While on a liquid-protein diet, people can just mix a packet of powder with water at mealtime. Why do you think this approach appeals to many dieters?

Readings

- "The Losing Formula." *Newsweek,* April 30, 1990, p. 52.
- "Inside America's Hottest Diet Programs: Losing BIG with Optifast." *Prevention,* January 1990, p. 52.

Possible Answers

1. Consult with a nutritionist or physician before starting a liquid diet. Criteria may include the amount of weight loss to be obtained, the rate of weight loss desired, and the health of the person with special attention to current illnesses.
2. Weight loss may be achieved more safely by exercising and reducing Calorie input from regular meals. In addition, the results are more likely to be long lasting.
3. A team approach addresses all aspects of a person's problem. Medical personnel can monitor any physiological changes or side effects. Psychologists can help with mental and emotional problems related to obesity and weight loss. Nutritionists can help with planning nutritious and proper meals.
4. Students' answers will vary and could be used to spark a debate. Students may suggest consulting with friends, medical personnel, counselors, and family members.
5. It requires no preplanning, takes little time, is very convenient, and requires no calculating of Calories and portions.

Going Further

Obtain skin calipers from a supply house, another department in your school, a hospital, a weight-loss clinic, or an athletic department. Use these calipers to allow students to measure their body fat. Directions on use and interpretation of data usually accompany the calipers. **L1**

CAREER CONNECTION

For more information, have interested students contact a hospital or college/university food service. These institutions may be able to suggest a source for classroom speakers.

CHAPTER 20

CHAPTER REVIEW

Summary

The summary can be used by students to review the major concepts of the chapter.

Language of Biology

Answers should go beyond defining the terms. Accept any answer that uses the term correctly and in the proper context.

Understanding Concepts

1. It does not contain food. Plant food contains minerals needed for plant growth and development—typically nitrogen, phosphorus, and potassium.
2. It could be either. For example, a baleen whale still has extracellular digestion like other mammals, whereas sponges employ mainly intracellular digestion.
3. Intracellular digestion in protozoa occurs within vacuoles, which are analogous to hollow digestive organs characteristic of animals with extracellular digestion.
4. It must obtain vitamins, carbohydrates, proteins, and lipids, substances manufactured from simple substances by an oak tree.
5. Digestion is more efficient in the segmented worm because that animal has two body openings and one-way digestive traffic. The digestive tract consists of regions specialized for specific functions.
6. The animal probably filter feeds on microscopic organisms.
7. Excess amounts of starch, fats, and cholesterol could lead to obesity and deposits of plaque. The person would be susceptible to a heart attack or stroke. The point of this question, however, is that anything eaten in excess can be harmful to health.
8. (a) small, moistened chunks; small amount of starch converted to maltose; (b) a semi-liquid known as chyme in which proteins have been broken into smaller polypeptides; (c) the food is liquefied and

the nutrients present are water, ions, vitamins, amino acids, fatty acids and glycerol, monosaccharides, cholesterol, and nitrogen bases that are the products of nucleic acid digestion; (d) undigestible parts of food from which most water has been absorbed.
9. Although amino acids are removed from the blood by the liver, the excess cannot be stored until all necessary amino acids are present. To have all amino acids available at one time, vegetarians eat combinations of grains and vegetables at the same meal.

574

Summary

Organisms must take in either complex molecules or the simple materials to make them. Autotrophs make complex organic molecules by using the products of photosynthesis, plus other nutrients absorbed from the surroundings. However, heterotrophs must get complex molecules that are already made.

Digestion, which may be intracellular or extracellular, breaks up complex organic molecules into smaller ones that can pass through cell membranes.

Animals may be either filter feeders or chunk feeders, and the digestive system of either type may be simple or complex. Digestion is more efficient in animals having two body openings than in animals in which food and wastes must pass through the same opening.

Humans should eat a balanced diet that includes sufficient amounts of food from all five food groups. Digestion in humans and many other animals is a complex, step-by-step process involving both physical breakdown of food chunks and chemical breakdown of complex molecules. Nutrients are absorbed by the capillaries or lymphatic vessels in villi and transported to all body cells.

Language of Biology

Write a sentence that shows your understanding of each of the following terms.

anus	intracellular digestion
bile	large intestine
colon	nutrient
crop	pancreas
digestion	peristalsis
esophagus	pharynx
extracellular digestion	salivary gland
gallbladder	small intestine
gastrovascular cavity	stomach
gizzard	villi

Understanding Concepts

1. Plant food can be purchased at garden shops. Does this product really contain food? What does it contain?
2. Would you expect digestion in filter feeders to be mainly intracellular or extracellular? Explain.
3. Digestion in protozoans is intracellular. In what way, however, does it resemble extracellular digestion?
4. What nutrients would a chimpanzee require that an oak tree would not?
5. In which animal, a flatworm or a segmented worm, would digestion be more efficient? Why?
6. A certain aquatic animal is slow moving, is enclosed by shells, and has gills. What is the probable diet of this animal and how does it obtain its food?
7. A cheeseburger on a bun consists of many substances including starch, fats, cholesterol, protein, minerals, and vitamins. Which of these, if eaten in excess, could lead to health problems and what are those problems?
8. A person has just begun a meal of foods containing starches, fats, and proteins. Describe the state of that food, physically and chemically, by the time it (a) leaves the mouth; (b) leaves the stomach; (c) has been digested in the interior of the small intestine; and (d) has moved through the colon.

Applying Concepts

10. Because the stomach is smaller, the person would have to eat smaller portions and do so more frequently to compensate for the loss of food-storing ability.
11. Protein-digesting enzymes in the small intestine will perform the same functions as the enzymes in the stomach.
12. Without a gallbladder, bile cannot be stored. Instead, it passes continuously into the small intestine. Therefore, fats can be emulsified only a little at a time.

574

9. In terms of events in the liver, explain why vegetarians should eat vegetables and grains that contain a variety of proteins.

Applying Concepts

10. Some people develop stomach ulcers, which are sores in the stomach wall. In severe cases, the ulcer does not respond to medication or diet and the part of the stomach containing the ulcer is removed surgically. How do you think a person's eating habits might change after such surgery?

11. Even if a person's entire stomach is removed, protein digestion can occur normally. Can you suggest a reason for this fact?

12. After removal of the gallbladder, a patient is told to stick to a low-fat diet. Why?

13. The inner surface of a shark's intestine is coiled like a carpenter's drill, and the food must move through the intestine in a spiral fashion. What is the adaptive advantage of such a structure?

14. Normally, materials pass through the colon at a relatively slow rate. What condition results from too rapid a passage? How might that condition, if prolonged, become dangerous?

15. How would the relative lengths of the small intestine of a lion (a meat eater) and a zebra (a plant eater) compare? How do you suppose the relative length of a human's small intestine compares to the intestines of these two animals?

16. It is thought that the evolution of a digestive system that allowed animals to consume a large meal and then digest it gradually was a major factor that allowed animals to become highly mobile. Explain how this could be true.

17. Hospitalized people must sometimes be fed by means of solutions that flow directly into the bloodstream. What might these solutions contain? Why is it difficult to maintain nutrition over time by this means?

18. **Global Connection:** Why do you think salt is cheap and plentiful today instead of expensive and scarce as it was in ancient times?

19. **Health Connection:** Suppose you saw a muffin mix that advertised, "Contains no cholesterol or animal fats!" Do you think such a product would be safe for a person who needs to reduce blood cholesterol? Explain your answer.

Lab Interpretation

20. **Investigation:** Suppose you conducted this investigation by placing the starch suspension and enzyme in an open container and filling the dialysis tubing with plain water. Would the results be different? Explain what you would observe.

21. **Thinking Lab:** Explain how it is possible for a person to survive if the person forms no salivary amylase enzyme.

22. **Minilab 2:** A student conducts Minilab 2 to compare the effects of cooked, fresh, and frozen fruits on gelatin. Write a conclusion based on the data shown in the following table.

Condition after cooling

Fruit	Fresh	Frozen	Cooked
Pineapple	Not Jelled	Not Jelled	Jelled
Orange	Jelled	Jelled	Jelled

Connecting Ideas

23. A protein deficiency can be especially harmful early in life. Why?

24. Explain how an increase of blood-glucose level above normal would result in osmotic imbalance between the blood and body cells. What would result from such an imbalance?

Connecting Ideas

23. **Patterns of Change:** Growth and development are characteristics of early stages of life. Large amounts of protein synthesis are essential for that growth and development to occur properly.

24. **Systems and Interactions:** As the concentration of glucose in blood increases, the blood comes to have a lower concentration of water than the interior of cells. Thus, water moves by osmosis from the cells and into the blood. This loss of water from cells leads to dehydration.

PROGRAM RESOURCES

Teacher Classroom Resources
Chapter Assessment, pp. 77-80 L1
Performance Assessment in Biology, p. 40 L2
Alternate Assessment in the Science Classroom
Computer Test Bank L1

13. The coiled inner surface increases the surface area available for absorption of digested food.

14. Diarrhea results and may lead to severe dehydration and mineral imbalance. This condition occurs because material does not remain in the large intestine long enough for water and dissolved minerals to be absorbed.

15. Plant materials are harder to digest and contain a lower concentration of nutrients. Thus, the zebra has a relatively longer small intestine. Because humans eat both meat and plant material, nutrients are more concentrated. Therefore, the relative length of the small intestine would be between that of the zebra and lion.

16. Animals with such a system can move in search of a new food supply. They do not have to remain in one area where food is in constant supply.

17. Those solutions contain a complete set of nutrients including monosaccharides, amino acids, vitamins, and so on. Because these nutrients must be given in low concentrations compatible with blood, patients can be fed only at a very slow rate.

18. Technology has improved the means of obtaining and transporting salt. For example, deep mines into salt deposits produce huge amounts of cheap salt.

19. The person should read the instructions. The mix may contain no animal fats, but perhaps you have to add milk and/or eggs.

Lab Interpretation

20. The results should be no different as long as the water inside the tube is tested in place of the water in the beaker in the original experiment.

21. The pancreas produces pancreatic amylase, which performs the same function as salivary amylase.

22. The student should conclude that freezing does not destroy the enzyme, but heating it to high temperatures does. No enzyme was present in the orange.

SECTION	OBJECTIVES	TEXT LABS/FEATURES
21.1 Nutrient Transport in Plants (2 days)	**Determine** why simple organisms do not have a transport system. **Compare** the transport of water and minerals with transport of organic molecules in a vascular plant.	**Art Connection:** Is a root more than a root? p. 584
21.2 Transport in Animals (3 days)	**Distinguish** between open and closed circulatory systems. **Sequence** the flow of blood in the circulation of birds and mammals. **Discuss** the various means by which materials are exchanged between the blood and the body cells.	**Minilab 1:** What affects pulse rate? p. 592 **Investigation:** The Effect of Stress on Blood Pressure, p. 596 **Minilab 2:** How do you interpret an EKG? p. 598 **History Connection:** A Pioneer in Medicine, p. 599
21.3 The Blood (2 days)	**Compare** the structure and function of components of the blood. **Define** the roles of white blood cells and platelets. **Predict** the outcomes of mixing the four blood types of humans.	**Thinking Lab:** What are the effects of iron deficiency? p. 602
BIOLOGY, TECHNOLOGY, AND SOCIETY		**Biotechnology:** Looking Inside Your Body, p. 606 **Career Connection:** Medical technologist, p. 606 **Health Connection:** Protect Your Heart, p. 607

LAB MATERIALS

INVESTIGATION	MINILAB	ALTERNATE LAB
page 596 cotton balls rubbing alcohol sphygmomanometer stethoscope	**page 592** backpack or bookbag books watch with second hand **page 598** EKGs, normal and abnormal	**page 598** labels microscope nickel prepared slide of human blood scissors

TEACHER CLASSROOM RESOURCES	OTHER RESOURCES
Study Guide, pp. 121-122 ***PLL:** *Root Anatomy,* p. 133 ***PLL:** *Stem Anatomy,* p. 135 ***PLL:** *Leaf Structure and Function,* p. 137 ***PLL:** *Transpiration in Plants,* p. 140 ****ILS:** *Roots and Stems,* p. 211 ****ILS:** *Leaf Anatomy,* p. 217	***STVS:** *Sound of Thirsty Plants,* Plants and Simple Organisms (Disc 4, Side 2) **Color Transparency 22:** *A Plant's Vascular System* **Color Transparency 23:** *Leaf Structure*
Study Guide, pp. 123-124 **Concept Mapping,** p. 21 **Critical Thinking/Problem Solving:** *The Path of Circulation in* *Mammals,* p. 21 ***PLL:** *Capillary Circulation,* p. 143 ***PLL:** *Effects of Exercise on the Heartbeat Rate,* p. 145 ****ILS:** *The Human Heart,* p. 221	***STVS:** *Measuring Blood Pressure,* Human Biology (Disc 7, Side 1) ***STVS:** *Modeling Blood Flow,* Human Biology (Disc 7, Side 1) **Color Transparency 28:** *Earthworm Body Systems* **Color Transparency 39:** *The Human Heart* **Color Transparency 52:** *Human Body Systems*
Study Guide, pp. 125-126 ****ILS:** *Blood,* p. 227	**Color Transparency 42:** *The Lymphatic System*
Assessment Materials **Chapter Assessment,** pp. 81-84 **Performance Assessment in Biology,** p. 42 **Alternate Assessment in the Science Classroom** **Computer Test Bank**	**Spanish Resources** **Cooperative Learning Resource Guide** **Videodisc Correlations** (to Optical Data's and Videodiscovery's videodiscs)

* Probing Levels of Life
** Investigating Living Systems

* Science Technology Videodisc Series

ADDITIONAL RESOURCES

Infinite Voyage *Unseen Worlds*
New tools enable biologists and other scientists to study previously unseen organs such as the heart and brain.

Audiovisual
Circulation, video, Insight Media.
Plant Movement and Transport, video, Insight Media.

Software
The Heart Simulator, Apple 48K, Focus.
Transport, Apple II/TRS-80/Model III, J and S.

CHAPTER

21

TRANSPORT

Chapter Overview

Students begin the chapter exploring the idea that a means of transport is needed to move materials between cells and the external environment. They will come to realize that complex organisms, in which most cells are distant from that environment, require a system for transport, and that materials are carried to and away from cells by a fluid, which makes up the internal environment.

First, students will apply these fundamental ideas to the study of transport in vascular plants. They will examine anatomy of the root, stem, and leaf and relate that anatomy to the functions of uptake and transport of water and ions and to the transport of organic nutrients. In so doing, students will gain an appreciation of the relationship between structure and function.

Students will then analyze the idea of circulation in animals, and they will compare and contrast closed and open systems. They will then examine circulation among vertebrate groups and analyze the relative efficiency of two-, three-, and four-chambered hearts. Finally, students will study aspects of human circulation—heartbeat, role of the lymphatic system, and the structure and functions of blood.

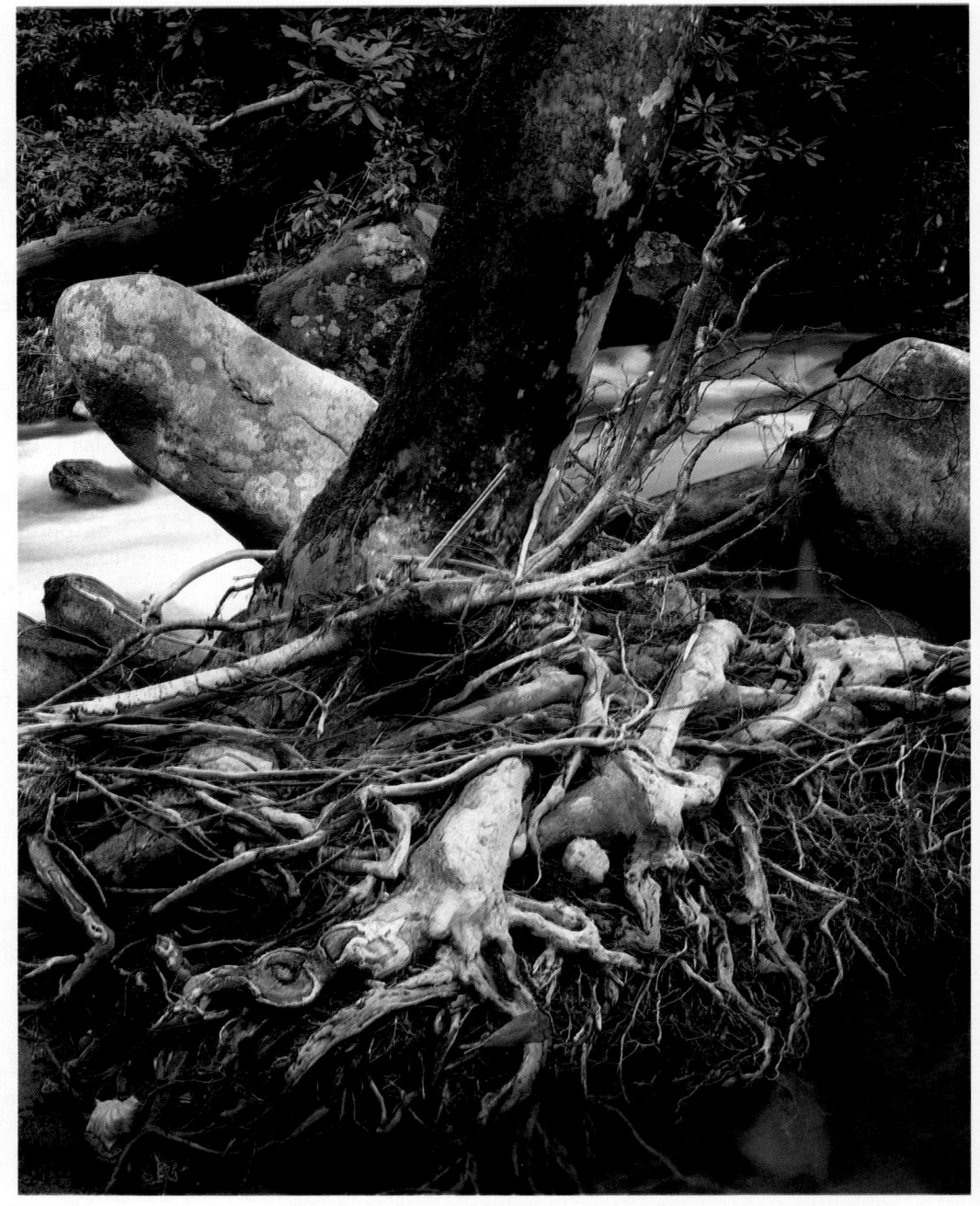

576

KEY TERMS

antibody	phloem	ventricle
antigen	platelet	vessel
aorta	red blood cell	white blood cell
artery	root hair	xylem
atrioventricular (A-V) node	sieve tube	
atrium	sinoatrial (S-A) node	
capillary	stoma	
guard cell	transpiration	
lymph node	vein	

21

TRANSPORT

"OH, WHAT big roots you have!"

"The better to nourish myself with, my dear."

This revision of some dialogue from "Little Red Riding Hood" illustrates a point—people don't realize how much of a plant is underground until they see the exposed roots of a fallen tree or of a tree on a riverbank as shown here. The exposed roots of this tree mean that the tree will soon die. Its fragile root system has been extensively damaged. Fragile? Yes. Even though many of the tree's roots are as big around as your arm, about 90 percent of all absorption of water and minerals from the soil is done by tiny root hairs.

Root hairs grow near the root tips and are composed of just one cell. They worm their way between soil particles and help to absorb water and nutrients for the plant. From within the roots, the water and minerals spire upward through columns of tubes to every part of the plant. Another set of tubes transports sugars and other nutrients from the leaves, around the plant, and back to the roots for growth. This tree's roots have been exposed by water erosion, but much of the root system still remains hidden. Such extensive damage to a plant's transport system greatly reduces its capacity for absorption and often results in death.

Root systems may be huge. A single rye grass plant has been found to have almost 14 million roots after only four months of growth. The total surface area of the root hairs was more than half the size of a basketball court.

Animals, too, can have a system of tubes in which water, nutrients, and other substances move throughout their bodies. Unlike plants, though, the nutrients in animals are circulated all together throughout their bodies. In this chapter, you will read about how the transport systems in plants and animals are vital to survival of these organisms.

How are these plant cells, which connect roots to leaves and are stacked end to end to form long tubes, like drinking straws? (Magnification: 300×)

Chapter Preview

Contents

ASSESSMENT PLANNER

Choose assessment strategies from the following pages to evaluate the progress of your students.

Assess, pp. 587-588, 600, 604-605
Portfolio, pp. 579, 584, 588, 595, 599, 604, 605
Alternate Lab, pp. 598-599
Thinking Lab, p. 602

Minilab 1, p. 592
Minilab 2, p. 598
Investigation, pp. 596-597
Chapter Review, pp. 608-609

Introducing the Chapter

Call students' attention to the photograph on page 576. Conduct a quick review of photosynthesis and plant nutrition, concentrating first on the raw materials. Use this review as a lead-in to a discussion of the sources of plant nutrients—water and mineral ions from the soil, carbon dioxide from air. Where must the water and ions go? What path must they follow? Is a system of transport needed to get them there? Now turn attention to the products of photosynthesis. Where must some of the sugars and other organic molecules produced go? What path(s) do they follow? Next, discuss the photograph on page 577. Use it to introduce the idea of transport "pipelines."

Theme Development

Students should recognize the theme of unity within diversity throughout the chapter. Unity is seen in the fact that very different complex organisms share a common need for a transport system that serves as a link between their cells and the external environment. Students will see that the transport systems and the fluids within them are quite different in plants and animals. They will also recognize the diversity of systems of circulation among animals. Also evident in this chapter is the theme of systems and interactions as students study the tissues and organs of which transport systems are comprised.

Tying to Previous Knowledge

Students can apply their knowledge of evolution to many of the concepts presented in this chapter; for example, how heart and circulatory systems of different classes of vertebrates have evolved. Having just completed a study of obtaining and processing nutrients, students can now more fully understand the means by which those nutrients are transported.

Prepare

Key Concepts

Students will discover the need for transport systems in multicellular organisms. They will be able to correlate the functions of diffusion, osmosis, active transport, and transpiration with plant structures.

Key Terms

xylem, vessel, phloem, sieve tube, root hair, stoma, transpiration, guard cell

Materials

1 Focus

Objectives

The objectives are listed on the student page. Remind students to preview these objectives as a guide to this numbered section.

Demonstration

Show students a cork, length of twine, piece of cotton fabric, and a block of wood. Ask them where all of these materials come from. *plants* Then ask what part of the plant is represented by each item. *cork—bark, twine—stem fibers, fabric—seeds, wood—stem* Ask which item most likely was associated with transport of materials through the plant. Most will guess the twine. Point out that only the block of wood is made of transport vessels. Twine is typically supportive lignified fibers, while wood is mainly conducting xylem vessels. **LEP**

2 Teach

Microscope Activity

Expose *Elodea* to bright light for at least four hours. Have students prepare wet mounts of leaf cells of *Elodea*. Under high power, students will be able to observe cytoplasmic streaming. Streaming will be most obvious when chloroplasts are pulled along by the cytoplasm. **L1**

Objectives

Determine why simple organisms do not have a transport system.

Compare the transport of water and minerals with transport of organic molecules in a vascular plant.

21.1 Nutrient Transport in Plants

Imagine a busy factory. New supplies continually arrive at the factory and are unloaded. These supplies—raw materials used in making products or fuel to provide the energy to make them—then must be transported to the areas within the factory where they are needed. Once made, the products are sent to different areas of the factory for packaging and storage. Eventually, they are shipped out. As the raw materials and fuel are used, wastes are produced. These wastes somehow must be removed from the factory. Like factories, organisms must take in raw materials from the outside world, and those materials must be transported to cells to supply life's processes. Products and wastes made by cells then must be transported away and removed from the organism.

Nutrient Supplies for All Cells

Every cell is surrounded by a liquid environment from which needed materials enter the cell and into which wastes are dumped. The liquid surrounding unicellular organisms is the external environment in which they live. These organisms take in needed materials such as gases, ions, and food directly from their external environment and pour their wastes back out. Distribution of materials within the cells often occurs by diffusion. However, diffusion within a cell is effective only over short distances. Movement of substances within cells is aided in many cells by the streaming of cytoplasm. There is a gentle but steady flow of cytoplasm within the cell. Streaming also helps in the distribution of larger substances, as shown in the amoeba in Figure 21-1.

Figure 21-1 The internal environment of this hydra (left) is in direct contact with the watery external environment. The cells of this simple multicellular organism and unicellular organisms such as the amoeba (right) obtain their nutrients directly from the surrounding water.

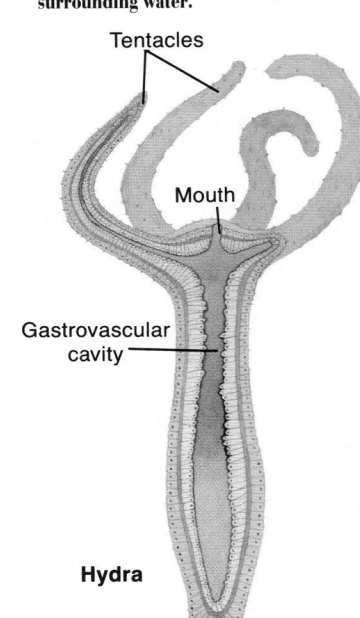

Tentacles

Mouth

Gastrovascular cavity

Hydra

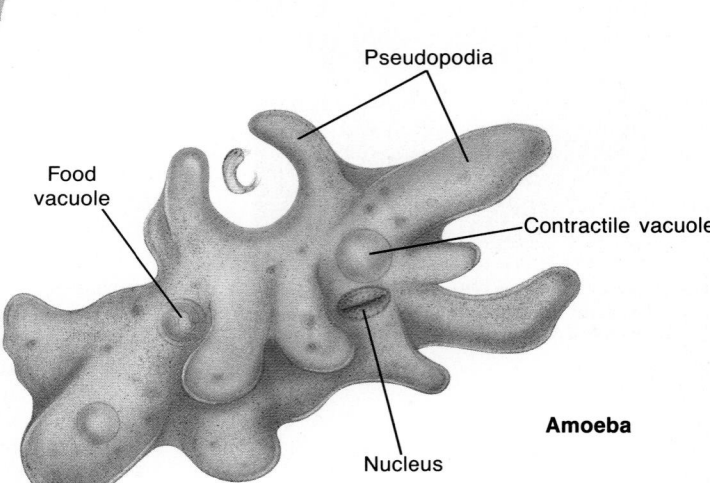

Pseudopodia

Food vacuole

Contractile vacuole

Nucleus

Amoeba

MEETING INDIVIDUAL NEEDS

Have students prepare a three-column table that lists all the animal phyla in the first column. Encourage students to use Appendix A. Ask them to complete the second column by indicating if the majority of animals present in the phylum are land or water dwellers. The third column should indicate if the animals do or do not have a transport (circulatory) system. **LEP**

STUDENT JOURNAL

Ask students to write a paragraph explaining why a chemical such as carbon dioxide that is produced by a one-celled organism as a waste chemical will diffuse out of the cell. Have them include in their paragraph the nature of the cell membrane in order to allow for CO_2 diffusion, the concentration of CO_2 inside and outside the cell, and if the process requires energy. **L1**

The cells of multicellular organisms such as most algae, fungi, nonvascular plants, sponges, cnidarians, and flatworms also interact directly with their external environment. Some of these organisms, such as kelp seaweed, may be large in terms of length, but they all are relatively thin, consisting of just a few layers of cells. Thus, each cell is in direct contact with or very close to the external environment. Gases, water, ions, and wastes can be exchanged between each cell and the environment. Most cells of organisms with little tissue differentiation act independently of one another in exchanging materials with their environment or can easily get materials by diffusion from other cells. There is no organized transport system in these organisms.

On the other hand, in plants and animals that have more complex tissue organization, most cells are too far away from the external environment for direct exchange of materials. Diffusion within an organism is ineffective over several thicknesses of cells. In these complex organisms, materials enter and leave only at certain points and then are carried between the cells and these points by some kind of fluid. The fluid is part of the organism's transport system, a link between the organism's cells and the external environment. Because exchange of materials occurs between cells and the transport fluid, the fluid can be called the internal environment of the organism. Evolution of an internal environment in complex organisms provided each of their cells access to an environment much like the external environment of their unicellular or simpler multicellular ancestors.

Figure 21-2 **The cells of many multicellular protists, such as seaweed (left), are in direct contact with water that contains their required nutrients. A giraffe is an unusual and very complex organism. How can all the cells of a giraffe obtain the nutrients they need to survive?**

Microscope Activity

Have students prepare a wet mount of *Ulva*—a marine, green seaweed. When examined under low and high power, students will be able to appreciate the transparent nature of this organism. **L1**

Chalkboard Example

Diagram a square on the chalkboard measuring 30×30 cm. This square will represent a cell. Use colored chalk to make ten dots inside the cell to represent Na^+ and Cl^- ions. Draw 20 molecules outside the square. Ask students to predict direction of movement of ions via osmosis. Redraw the square with 20 ions inside and ten ions outside. Ask students to predict direction of movement of ions. Explain that the square boundary represents a cell membrane that is permeable to salt ions. In both examples, have students explain their answers using such terms as *low/high concentration of salt ions.* **LEP**

Using the Photograph

Ask students to name some of the molecules that may be exchanged between the seaweed in Figure 21-2 and its surrounding water. Have them do the same for the giraffe and the fluid of its internal environment. **LEP**

Figure Caption Question

How can all the cells of a giraffe obtain the nutrients they need to survive? Nutrients are supplied to cells in a multicellular organism by means of a transport system.

PROGRAM RESOURCES

Teacher Classroom Resources
Study Guide, pp. 121-122 **L1**
Probing Levels of Life, Labs 51, 52, 53, 54, pp. 133, 135, 137, 140 **L2**

PORTFOLIO

Ask students to diagram the direction of chemical movements in or out of the cell for each of the following scenarios. (a) Carbon dioxide concentration inside the cell is lower than outside the cell; (b) Carbon dioxide concentration inside the cell is higher than outside the cell; (c) Water concentration inside the cell is lower than outside the cell. **L1**

SECTION 21.1

Using Science Terms

Have students discuss and then decide on the technical term used to describe the system of blood vessels in animals. Have them relate the term *vascular* in connection with blood transport. Correlate the function of the human vascular system with that of a plant vascular system. **L1** **LEP**

Building a Model

- Supply students with two 8-cm lengths of straws, tape, and a sheet of blank paper. Ask them to build a model illustrating xylem tissue. Have them label xylem cells and xylem vessel. Make sure that the ends of the straws are open. **L1** **LEP**

- Supply students with four 8-cm lengths of straw, tape, dissecting needle, scissors, and a sheet of blank paper. Ask them to build a model illustrating phloem tissue. Have them label phloem cell, companion cell, phloem tissue, sieve tube. Make sure that the straw ends are folded inward and perforated with the needle to simulate the sieve ends. **L1** **LEP**

Microscope Activity

Have students prepare wet mounts of wood shavings from a pencil sharpener. This will allow them to see xylem cells. As an alternative, strip out the "veins" from a celery leaf petiole (usually referred to as the celery stalk). Place on a glass slide. Add water and a second glass slide over the tissue. Press down to squash the celery tissue. Remove the top glass slide and replace with a coverslip. **L1**

Figure Caption Question

How does the arrangement of xylem tissue change as it moves up into the stem? In the roots of a plant, xylem tissue is located in the center. As it moves up into the stem, xylem tissue becomes organized into discrete bundles arranged closer to the outside. In woody plants, the xylem tissue forms a cylinder within the stem.

580

Transport Tissues in Vascular Plants

One group of organisms that uses a transport system is the vascular plants, so named because they contain vascular tissues that transport water, minerals, and food in the form of sugars. These vascular tissues are of two types: xylem tissue and phloem tissue.

Xylem and Phloem   Water and dissolved mineral ions are transported upward from roots to leaves within a series of tubular cells that make up **xylem** tissue. In the roots of a young plant, xylem cells are at first short and narrow, but as the plants mature the xylem cells elongate, the end walls break down, die, and the cells then form hollow tubes consisting only of the cell walls. The cells are linked end to end, forming long pipelines called **vessels.** Xylem vessels extend from near the tips of the roots up into the rest of the plant. The water transported in xylem vessels helps to keep the plant from wilting and is important in the process of photosynthesis in the leaves. Some of the sugars produced during photosynthesis are transported within the plant by cells of **phloem** tissue. Phloem is another part of the vascular plant's transport system. As in xylem, phloem is composed of cylindrical cells joined end to end to form pipelines. Unlike xylem, however, phloem cells are not dead. They have cytoplasm but lose their nuclei as they age. Their life processes are controlled by smaller companion cells that retain their nuclei. The end wall of each phloem cell is perforated, like a sieve. Therefore, a pipeline of sieve cells is called a **sieve tube.** The tissues of xylem and phloem form vascular bundles throughout the vascular plant.

Figure 21-3   The strands of vascular tissue in a plant supply all the different organs with required nutrients. How does the arrangement of xylem tissue change as it moves up into the stem?

Cross Section of a Leaf

Transport in a Plant

Cross Section of a Root

Cross Section of a Stem

580 TRANSPORT

MEETING INDIVIDUAL NEEDS

Have students prepare the following table. Headings across the top should be as follows: "What is Transported"; "Shape of Cells"; "Living or Dead in Mature Plants." Headings down the side should be: "Xylem"; "Phloem." Ask students to complete the table. **LEP**

PROGRAM RESOURCES

Teacher Classroom Resources
Color Transparency #22, 23 **L1** **LEP**
Investigating Living Systems, Labs 56, 57, pp. 211, 217 **L2**

580

Transport into a Root

Cortex
Root hair
Endodermis
Pathway A
Phloem
Xylem
Epidermis
Waxy strip
Pathway B
Water and ions
Endodermal Cells

Root Tissues Water and minerals enter a plant via the roots, which are also important in anchoring the plant and in storage of food in the form of starch. Figure 21-4 shows a cross section of a typical root of a flowering plant such as a sunflower. Notice that the tissues are arranged somewhat in circular layers. Notice also the numerous **root hairs,** which are outgrowths of the outer layer of cells, or epidermis, of the root. The hundreds of tiny root hairs together provide a very large surface area for absorbing water and dissolved ions from the film of moisture around soil particles. Entrance of water into the epidermal cells by osmosis results in a greater concentration of water molecules there than in the layer of loosely packed cells that form the next inner tissue layer. Thus, water moves by osmosis into this inner tissue, called the cortex. In addition to being involved in transport, cells of the cortex are food storage areas. For example, when you eat carrot sticks you are eating the cortex with stored carbohydrates of a carrot root.

Endodermis: The Plant's Gatekeeper Some water and dissolved ions pass from the soil all the way through the root cortex without actually entering the cells. Instead, they pass *between* the cells of the cortex. This uncontrolled flow is stopped short by the ring of endodermis. The endodermis is a layer of cells one cell thick that completely surrounds the central core of the root. The radial and end walls of endodermal cells are surrounded by a strip of wax. These strips form a waterproof seal between the outer and inner layers of the root. Water and ions can no longer pass between cells. Instead, they are forced to enter the endodermal cells.

Although water readily diffuses across the cell membranes, ions in the water cannot cross these membranes by simple diffusion. Rather, ions pass into the cells of the endodermis by facilitated diffusion or by active transport. From the cortex, water and ions pass through the endodermis

Figure 21-4 The cross section of a root (right) shows that the xylem tissue forms a central core surrounded by a single layer of cells called the endodermis. Follow the pathways A and B of water molecules into a root. What happens when they reach the waterproofed cells that make up the endodermis?

21.1 NUTRIENT TRANSPORT IN PLANTS **581**

SECTION 21.1

Brainstorming
Ask students to list examples of structures that provide large surface areas for gas exchange and nutrient absorption. Examples may include frog skin for absorption of water/oxygen, fish gills for oxygen/carbon dioxide exchange, earthworm skin for oxygen/carbon dioxide exchange, and human lungs for oxygen/carbon dioxide exchange. COOP LEARN

Microscope Activity
Provide prepared slides of cross sections of sunflower (*Helianthus*) roots and stems for your students to observe the various tissues being described. As an alternative, project a 35-mm slide onto a screen. Ask students to name the different tissue layers. L1

Demonstration
Soak radish or mustard seeds overnight. Place onto moist, black construction paper squares and slide into a sealable plastic bag. Have students observe the extensive root hair growth that is visible within 48 to 72 hours. As an added enrichment, have students prepare wet mounts of hairs to confirm that they are indeed only one cell. L1

Using Science Terms
Have students compare the prefixes *endo* and *epi.* Have them then add these prefixes to the root word *dermis.* Ask them to explain the meaning of *endodermis* after they have reviewed the meaning of *epidermis.* L1 LEP

Figure Caption Question
What happens when water molecules reach the waterproofed cells that make up the endodermis? They are forced to pass into the endodermal cells before they can enter the xylem tissue.

SECTION 21.1

Demonstration

- Obtain 35-mm slides of typical monocotyledonous and dicotyledonous stem cross sections. Project these onto a screen. Have students distinguish between the two arrangements of vascular tissues. Ask students to identify various tissues by name. For examples of monocotyledonous and dicotyledonous plants, see Appendix A. The pattern of vascular tissue scattered throughout the stem is typical of monocotyledons such as grasses, daffodils, palms, and lilies. **L1**

- Place a celery stalk into a beaker of water with added food coloring. After 24 hours, allow students to examine cross-sectional slices. Students will note that the uptake of colored water is confined to the strings (vascular bundles) that run the length of the stalk. **LEP**

Using Science Terms

Review the meaning of the term *meristematic.* Have students explain why vascular cambium fits the definition. **L1**

Enrichment

Discuss and illustrate the formation of annual rings within the xylem tissue of a woody dicotyledon. Annual rings result from uneven growth of xylem tissue as a consequence of varying climatic conditions. Rapid growth during the spring results in a wider band of larger xylem cells than produced by slower growth of the summer and fall. As a consequence, alternating rings of more open and more dense xylem tissues are formed. Rings of xylem usually correspond to the age of a woody plant because one annual ring is formed each year. Point out that tropical trees do not have annual rings because environmental conditions are constant year round.

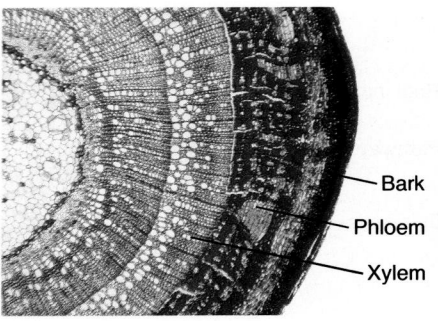

Figure 21-5 **In the stems of many flowering plants such as this Queen Anne's lace (left), the vascular tissues are arranged in a circle of discrete bundles. In stems of plants such as lilies, palms, or grasses, the vascular bundles are scattered throughout the stem. In woody stems (right), new layers of xylem and phloem form complete cylinders of woody tissue surrounded by a protective bark.**

and into the xylem in the central core of vascular tissues. Only substances that can cross the cells' plasma membranes can get into the inner column of vascular tissue and up into the plant. At the same time, the endodermis prevents a backflow of ions. Thus, the membranes of the endodermal cells regulate the passage of ions by active transport into the xylem. The higher ion concentration in the central core of vascular tissue is a major driving force of water flow up a plant. In other words, the endodermis acts as a checkpoint or gatekeeper to control substances entering the plant. Once in the xylem, the water and some of the ions move up the stem of the plant to the leaves for use in photosynthesis and other cell processes. Other ions remain in the root cells and are used for their cell processes.

Stem and Leaf Tissues From the roots, the water and ions move up the xylem vessels and into the stem. Figure 21-5 shows a cross section of a herbaceous plant stem. Note the position of xylem and phloem in the vascular bundles. These bundles are continuous with the core of vascular tissues in the roots. Water and ions that have entered the xylem of roots now pass up the xylem of stems and into the vascular bundles of the leaves. In many plants, xylem and phloem cells develop on either side of a ring of meristematic tissue called vascular cambium. This vascular cambium is an active region of cell division. In plants that live longer than one year, the cells that are produced in the vascular cambium each year develop either into new xylem or new phloem cells; xylem cells form toward the inside of the stem, and phloem cells form toward the outside. The vascular cambium links each bundle of xylem and phloem to form a cylinder of vascular tissue. Addition of new xylem and phloem thickens the stem. A woody stem is usually formed by the buildup of xylem tissue and by the formation of bark, a thinner outer layer of corklike cells that includes and protects the phloem (Figure 21-5).

STUDENT JOURNAL

Tell students that they are a molecule of water sitting in the soil just outside of a root hair. Ask them to write a paragraph that describes the process responsible and the pathway they follow as they move from soil up into a leaf of the plant. They are to name all the tissues that they pass through on their journey. **L2**

MEETING INDIVIDUAL NEEDS

Visually Impaired: Provide students who are visually impaired with the following materials: small plastic cup, plastic film container with bottom removed (use a pair of scissors to snip out bottom), several drinking straw sections each about 8 cm long. Ask students to construct a model of a root. Ask them to name the various tissue layers. **L1** **LEP** **COOP LEARN**

From the stem, the water and ions enter the xylem of the leaves. Located throughout a leaf are vascular bundles, which cause the appearance of veins on the leaf's surface. Veins in a leaf are continuous with the vascular bundles of the stem. As water enters a leaf, it moves from the xylem in the veins into layers of leaf cells that make up the palisade tissue and spongy tissue. Cells in the palisade layer are long and narrow, packed closely together, and contain chloroplasts. They are lined up side by side like notes on a keyboard (Figure 21-6). Cells in the spongy layer also contain chloroplasts. The spongy cells are round and loosely packed and have many air spaces between them, like a sponge. It is in these two layers that most of a plant's photosynthesis occurs. The epidermis is the outer layer of cells of a plant. The epidermis of the leaf protects the cells inside and is coated by a cuticle, a layer of waxy secretion from the epidermal cells that prevents evaporation.

You know that carbon dioxide is needed for photosynthesis. It enters through structures with openings, called **stomata** (*sing.,* stoma), in the epidermis and passes to the air spaces between the palisade and spongy cells. It then dissolves in the watery film around those cells and diffuses into them and on into the chloroplasts. Oxygen produced during photosynthesis passes out of the leaf through the pores in the stomata. Oxygen also enters the leaf for use in respiration by the plant. In this process, carbon dioxide is released by the plant via the stomata.

Figure 21-6 The veins of a leaf are clearly visible (left). However, a cross section of a leaf (right) will provide a better understanding of the function of this complex plant organ. Notice the stomata in the epidermis where gases are exchanged and the compact palisade layer where the energy of sunlight is captured.

Palisade layer   Vein

Spongy layer   Stoma

SECTION 21.1

Microscope Activity

Veins of a leaf can be seen easily in lettuce. Have students use the thinnest portion of a lettuce leaf to prepare a wet mount. Have students observe the vascular tissue under low power. L1

Using an Analogy

Remind students of the technical term for their skin. *epidermis* Ask them to describe its function. Draw attention to oils formed by skin cells. Then, make a comparison between the leaf epidermis and its cuticle and human epidermis with its oil. LEP

Demonstration

Do the following to illustrate the role of a leaf's cuticle. Bring samples of leaves to class. Use a spray bottle to squirt water onto the upper surface of a leaf, and have students note the beading of water on this waxy layer. Then repeat the process of spraying water onto a sheet of wax paper, and again note the beading of water on this surface. LEP

Chalkboard Example

Use a rectangular outline on the board to represent a sectional side view of a leaf. Have students volunteer to come up to the board and: (a) draw and label the different tissues that form the leaf; (b) indicate by shading with chalk those tissues that are photosynthetic; (c) use arrows to indicate direction of oxygen and carbon dioxide as it enters and exits the leaf during the day; (d) indicate above the arrows if the gas is being used or given off during photosynthesis or respiration.

STUDENT JOURNAL

Tell students that they are a molecule of carbon dioxide gas. They are to write a paragraph that traces the pathway that they might follow from air to a chloroplast located in a spongy cell of a leaf. Students are to describe what they pass through, the processes that are involved in their passage, and their eventual fate once inside the chloroplast. L2

MEETING INDIVIDUAL NEEDS

Provide students with a diagram of a simple cross section of a leaf. Have them perform the following tasks: (a) Identify and label epidermis, guard cells, stoma, spongy and palisade layers, vein; (b) Briefly describe the function of each tissue or structure just labeled; (c) Color in green those tissues or cells that are photosynthetic. L1

Cohesion of Polar Molecules:
Each molecule of water attracts four additional water molecules, resulting in cohesion. A single water molecule consists of a single oxygen atom with two hydrogen atoms attached toward the same end. The oxygen "end" attracts the hydrogen "end" of two other water molecules. Each "hydrogen end" attracts the "oxygen end" of two different water molecules.

Different Viewpoints in Biology

Climbing Water
Movement of water through a vascular plant depends on several physical factors working in concert. One factor is root pressure. As water moves into roots via osmosis, pressure builds up within roots. This pressure forces water into the xylem tissue. Plant physiologists, however, have found that root pressure alone cannot account for the rise of water within xylem. It can account for part of the rise in short plants but does not exert enough force to move water to heights of 350 meters. Might capillary action enable water to rise to the heights of the tallest trees? Apparently not. When measuring capillary action alone, the ability of water to rise is limited to only 1 meter in glass tubes the diameter of a xylem cell. The movement of water out of a plant by transpiration may be an added force behind movement of water through a plant.

Water Movement in a Vascular Plant

To get to the leaves, water from the roots sometimes must travel 100 meters or more. How can this be done? Plants do not contain a pump to push the water upward.

Properties of Water In fact, the water is not pushed from below, but rather is pulled from above. For such a pull to occur, water must form unbroken columns from roots to leaves, as the lead in a pencil extends from point to eraser. Two properties of water combine to produce such continuous columns. Because of the polarity of water molecules (Chapter 3), they tend to cling to one another like magnets; the positive end of one molecule attracts the negative end of another. This attraction among the same kind of molecules is known as cohesion. You can see cohesion of water molecules when you turn on a faucet. The water flows out in a solid, steady stream, rather than sprinkling out like separate grains of sand. Water molecules also are attracted to the inner walls of xylem vessels, a property known as adhesion. You can see adhesion of water molecules when you step out of a shower—water droplets cling to your skin. Remember that xylem cells are microscopic. In the very narrow pipelines that xylem cells form, the combination of cohesion and adhesion gives a column of water properties more like those of a solid than of a liquid. The

A R T   C O N N E C T I O N

Is a root more than a root?

Diego Rivera returned to Mexico in 1921, after the revolution of 1910-1917 had brought about land reform and a more democratic constitution. He had been in Europe since 1907 painting and studying, but once back in Mexico, art became a way for him to communicate the history of Mexico's political struggles against foreign powers and the ruling classes. Rivera is best known for the murals he painted both in Mexico and the United States illustrating the social conditions and the heritage of the

584 TRANSPORT

PORTFOLIO

Have students prepare a concept map that describes both cohesion and adhesion. They should include the derivation of these two words and at least one other related word with the same root word parts and its definition. *adhere, adhesive, cohesive; stick, sticky, together* L1 column of water remains continuous, in complete contact with the walls of the xylem vessels, and could be pictured as a long but very fine thread, extending from roots to leaves.

Cohesion of water molecules

H_2O Transpiration

H_2O

Xylem pathways

Adhesion to xylem vessel wall

H_2O

Absorption

Figure 21-7 When water moves up the xylem vessels in a plant, the molecules stick together by cohesion and to the walls of xylem vessels by adhesion.

Mexican people. Rivera and his fellow muralists helped to give Mexico contemporary art based on native tradition.

Roots The geography of Mexico is part of that native heritage, and many of Rivera's paintings and murals show the tie between the people and the land. "Roots," painted in 1937, is one of six watercolors Rivera did of Mexican plants. The "roots" of this ancient-looking plant appear to be more like rhizomes, which are underground storage organs modified from stems. In Rivera's painting, the eye is immediately drawn to the rhizomatous "root" system that seems to be pushing its way up through massive rocks. There appears to be little or no soil or water anywhere. The rhizomes look old and gnarled, as if their push to the surface has been long and difficult. At the tips of the giant rhizomes, thin, flowerlike shoots of yellow and green burst out, almost like firecrackers. They alone seem to be young and healthy.

The Struggle for Survival
Knowing Rivera's use of art to tell a story, one wonders whether the rocks perhaps represent the government and the ruling class of Mexico, and the "roots" the long struggle of the Mexican people to overthrow them. In some of Rivera's other paintings, trees and plants take on clearly animal or human shapes. Some of the "roots" in this picture look dead, perhaps representing the people who died in the struggle. The flowerlike shoots seem to symbolize the people who have finally won the struggle and are just beginning to claim their own land. What at first looks like a bleak, gray scene becomes a sign of hope for the future.

1. **Connection to the Environment:** How might this picture tell a story about the environment?
2. **Writing About Biology:** Describe how desert plants might be adapted for survival.
3. **Explore Further:** Compare the tissues of roots and rhizomes.

21.1 NUTRIENT TRANSPORT IN PLANTS **585**

Demonstration

Fill a small beaker with water. Cover it with tin foil and seal the edges of the foil with rubber bands. Cut a small hole in the center of the foil. Insert the stem end of a small plant such as a cutting of a geranium through the opening. Make sure the cut end is immersed in the water. Seal the opening around the stem with clay to make the beaker airtight. Completely cover the beaker and plant with a plastic bag. Close the bag with a metal tie. Have students account for the moisture that accumulates on the inside of the bag after 24 hours.

Using Science Terms

In Greek, *stoma* means mouth, and the term is often used with reference to the stomatal pore only. However, in many plant anatomy texts, the term *stoma* includes both the guard cells and the pore that they surround.

MATH CONNECTION

Numbers of Stomata:
Provide each student with a lettuce leaf. Have them determine the area of the leaf. Ask them to prepare a wet mount of a small piece of the leaf, and have them count the number of stomata observed under one high-power field. Have them determine the area of their high-power field. Typically, the diameter of the field will be close to 0.35 mm. Once the area of the scope field is determined, have them calculate the total number of scope areas for the entire leaf area. This number multiplied by the number of stomata per high-power field will tell them the total number of stomata on the leaf. **L2**

Figure 21-8 A common sight over a forest on an early summer morning is the rising of a cloud of water vapor. This is one sign that the forest is alive. Most of the water taken up by plants is given off by transpiration from stomata in the leaves.

Transpiration What causes the pull? Water is lost constantly through the pores in stomata in a process called **transpiration.** As water molecules exit the leaf tissues through stomata, they are replaced by water molecules from the xylem vessels in the veins of the leaf. Because of cohesion, this movement of water molecules creates a tension, or pull, on the rest of the water column up the stem. This pull can be thought of as a stretching effect that extends all the way to the roots. As the water in the root xylem is pulled up, more water moves into the xylem from the surrounding root cells and ultimately from the soil. It's like a magician pulling an unending string of scarves from a sleeve. According to this model, known as the transpiration-cohesion theory, it is important that no air bubbles form in a xylem vessel. Such bubbles would break the continuous column of water. Obviously, movement of water columns from roots to leaves is work. What is the source of energy for this work?

Stomata: The Pores of a Plant

Transpiration is important in the upward transport of water and dissolved ions. However, excess water loss from the leaves could cause a plant to dehydrate and die. Each stoma in a leaf is a pore surrounded by **guard cells** that regulate the pore's size. Guard cells prevent a plant from drying out. During the day, the pores of the stomata are wide open, allowing an ample supply of carbon dioxide to enter the leaf for photosynthesis. But much water escapes from these stomata also during the day. At night, however, the light reactions of photosynthesis do not occur, and large supplies of carbon dioxide are not needed. At that time stomata are partially closed, decreasing the amount of transpiration and conserving water. Stomata do not close up completely because respiration continues both day and night. The stomata still allow the exchange of oxygen and carbon dioxide for this essential life process.

PROJECT

Comparing Stomata: Ask students to observe a number of leaf samples under the microscope. Their project is to compile a table of the number of stomata observed per high-power field for each sample. Suggested plant leaf material might include green onions, lettuce, spinach, brussels sprouts, bok choy, parsley, and cabbage. **L1**

MEETING INDIVIDUAL NEEDS

Ask students to wet a piece of paper toweling and note how long it takes to dry out. Compare this time with how long it takes for a wet towel covered with a sheet of wax paper in which a series of pinholes have been pricked to dry out. Make sure that students realize the connection between wax paper and the plant's cuticle, pinholes and stomata, and wet towel and a leaf **LEP**

How do guard cells control opening and closing of stomata? When guard cells take in water by osmosis, they swell. The cell walls of guard cells have rings of cellulose microfibrils (Figure 21-9) similar to the belts in radial tires. When water enters the guard cells, the rings of microfibrils prevent the cells from swelling in width. They can only swell in length and thickness. Because the guard cells are joined at each end, they bow apart when they swell. They take on a balloonlike crescent shape. Thus, the size of the stoma between them increases. At night, or when there is a water shortage, water moves by osmosis from the guard cells into neighboring epidermal cells. The guard cells collapse and lose their crescent shape, and the size of the stoma decreases.

What determines when guard cells swell or collapse? As day breaks, light stimulates photosynthesis in the guard cell chloroplasts, which makes ATP available for the active transport of potassium ions from neighboring cells. This uptake of ions causes water to enter by osmosis and the guard cells swell. At night, when potassium ions leave the guard cells, water is lost by osmosis and the stoma closes.

Transport in Phloem Tissue

From the leaf, the sugars made during photosynthesis are converted to sucrose, a more soluble form of sugar, which then meanders through the phloem to all parts of the plant. You know that the sieve cells of phloem pipelines, which transport sugars, are not dead and that they contain cytoplasm. The sieve tubes, therefore, are not comprised of continuous hollow pipelines as in the xylem. The side walls of phloem sieve cells have small holes, and strands of cytoplasm pass horizontally between them and their companion cells. Ions and amino acids are known to pass into sieve tubes via these strands of cytoplasm. Phloem tissue is a living tissue.

Figure 21-9 The stomata in a leaf, as seen in this electron micrograph (magnification: 257×), are the doorways between a plant's internal and external environments (right). When light stimulates the movement of potassium ions (K^+) into the guard cells (left) the cells take up water and swell, and the stoma opens. The stoma closes later when daylight fades and the movement of potassium ions is reduced.

Stoma Opening
Water moves into guard cells

Stoma Closing
Water moves out of guard cells

Microfibrils · H_2O · H_2O · H_2O · Stoma · K^+ · H_2O · Guard cell · Epidermal cells · K^+ · H_2O · H_2O · K^+ · H_2O

Light

CO_2 · O_2 · H_2O · Vein · Stoma

21.1 NUTRIENT TRANSPORT IN PLANTS **587**

SECTION 21.1

Reteach

Divide the class into nine groups. Assign a pair of phrases from the Check for Understanding. Have them present a brief explanation of their phrases.

Extension

Have students determine if all leaves have more, less, or equal numbers of stomata on the upper surface or lower leaf surface. Provide them with a variety of leaf samples for their study. Ask them to explain their findings.
L2

✔ Assessment

Portfolio: There are a number of situations in which the processes of diffusion, osmosis, active transport, and evaporation are used within roots, stems, and leaves. Ask students to provide an example where each process is used, and explain its role in the normal functioning of the plant. Have students place these examples in their portfolios. **L1**

4 Close

Discussion

Ask students to reread the opening paragraphs on page 577. Then ask them to: (a) Explain why trees that are being transplanted always have a huge ball of dirt connected to the roots; (b) Tell why a plant usually dies when "pulled" from the ground or a pot even if transplanted immediately into a new area or pot.

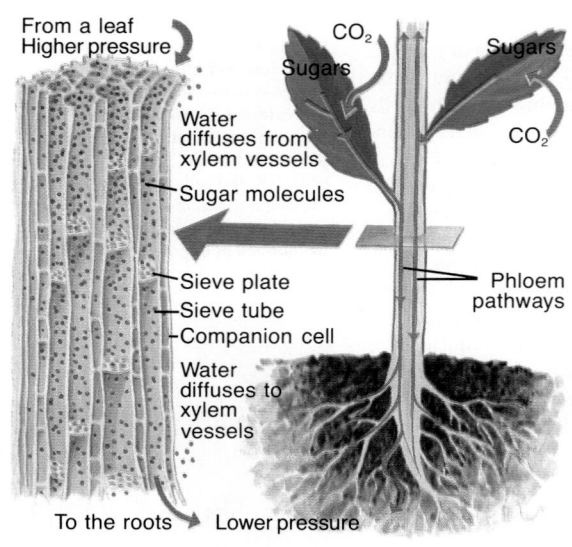

Figure 21-10 **The pressure flow (from the phloem in the leaves down sieve tubes in the stem to the roots) is due to a higher concentration of sugar in the leaves. Sugar molecules enter companion cells by active transport. The sugar then passes into the sieve tubes across the interconnecting strands of cytoplasm and on down to the roots, where it is stored as starch or used for growth and metabolism.**

The dissolved sucrose and other nutrients made in the cells pass from the palisade and spongy tissues of the leaf into the sieve tubes in the leaf's veins. This increase in concentration of solutes in the sieve cells causes water to enter by osmosis. The sucrose and nutrients are carried by this water downward to the roots to be used in cell processes as an energy source or converted to starch for storage. Sucrose also can be transported upward, where it could be stored in fruits or used as an energy source for the development of new leaf or flower buds.

How does phloem transport work? One model suggests that transport in phloem is a result of pressure. The entrance of water from the surrounding cells into the sieve cells increases the pressure inside the cells at the top of the sieve tubes. Because of this pressure, the sucrose, nutrients, and water are forced out through the sieve end and into the next lower sieve cell, where pressure is lower. The pressure differences in sieve cells from leaves to roots may account for this downward movement. As the solution works its way down to the roots, some of the sucrose, nutrients, and water leaves the sieve cells to nourish the developing tissues of the roots or to be held for storage. Thus, pressure remains lower in the roots. This model of movement in phloem tissue is called the pressure-flow hypothesis.

The pressure-flow hypothesis also explains the upward movement of organic molecules. For example, in spring, starch stored in the roots is converted to sucrose, which then enters sieve cells. Water enters the sieve cells from other root cells by osmosis, increasing the pressure within them. In this case, the higher pressure is in the sieve cells at the bottom of the phloem pipeline. As a result, the sucrose is forced upward.

Section Review

Understanding Concepts

1. Explain why humans must have a transport system, whereas a planarian can exist without one.
2. How are the structures of xylem and phloem cells adapted to their functions?
3. Explain how the various parts of a leaf contribute to its ability to carry out photosynthesis.
4. **Skill Review—Recognizing Cause and Effect:** Sieve tubes form a circle of tissue within the bark of a woody stem. What would be the result of removing a strip of bark all the way around such a stem? For more help, see Thinking Critically in the Skill Handbook.
5. **Thinking Critically:** How can it be explained that organic molecules can be moving both upward and downward in the same kind of vascular tissue at the same time?

Answers to Section Review

1. A transport system is necessary in organisms in which most cells are too far from the external environment to exchange materials directly. That is the case in humans, but not planarians.
2. Both types of cells are cylindrical and form tubes suitable for transport.
3. Xylem brings the water needed for photosynthesis, and carbon dioxide enters via stomata. The palisade cells, in which most photosynthesis occurs, are near the top surface where light is most readily available. Phloem delivers organic molecules, products of photosynthesis, to nonphotosynthetic parts of the plant.
4. **Skill Review—Recognizing Cause and Effect:** The plant would die due to damage to an entire circle of phloem tissue. Sugars and other photosynthetic products could not be transported to tissues beyond the point from which the bark was stripped. Food supply to the roots would be cut off.
5. **Thinking Critically:** Some phloem may be carrying sucrose downward from the leaves while other phloem pipelines may be transporting organic molecules, such as amino acids, upward from the roots.

21.2 Transport in Animals

Vascular plants, as you have read, obtain their nutrients by a system of two kinds of tissues that make up an internal transport system. Most animals, too, have a transport system to move materials to and from body cells. As in plants, each cell requires a supply of oxygen and food molecules, and each cell must get rid of waste products. In all animals that have a transport system, two parts are essential: (1) circulating fluid, and (2) one or more hearts to pump the blood. All of the materials moved by a transport system travel together in the same fluid, which circulates over and over again from the cells, sometimes through vessels, in and out of the heart, and back to the cells. Thus, the transport system of animals is a *circulatory* system.

Closed Circulatory System—The Earthworm

Segmented worms are the least complex animals to have a true circulatory system. The system is closed; that is, the blood is carried within blood vessels. It does not slosh around freely in the worm's body cavity. This kind of animal transport system, in which the blood is enclosed at all times within vessels, is called a closed circulatory system.

Although simple in structure, the worm's circulatory system permits rapid and efficient exchange of materials. In an earthworm, the blood flows through two major blood vessels—the dorsal blood vessel and ventral blood vessel, shown in Figure 21-11. These two vessels are connected near the anterior end of the worm by a series of five pairs of pumps. These tubelike pumps, known as aortic arches, function as hearts. The hearts, like all hearts, contract rhythmically and pump the blood along. The elastic dorsal vessel also helps squeeze the blood. Under these pressures, the blood flows away from the hearts through the ventral vessel. It returns to the hearts from the body tissues and through the dorsal vessel. Valves in the hearts and in the dorsal vessel, like one-way doors, keep the blood flowing in the right direction.

Objectives

Distinguish between open and closed circulatory systems.

Sequence the flow of blood in the circulation of birds and mammals.

Discuss the various means by which materials are exchanged between the blood and the body cells.

Figure 21-11   Notice how the dorsal (back) and ventral (belly) blood vessels of an earthworm are connected by the five pairs of hearts at the anterior or head end. How do nutrients enter the blood of an earthworm?

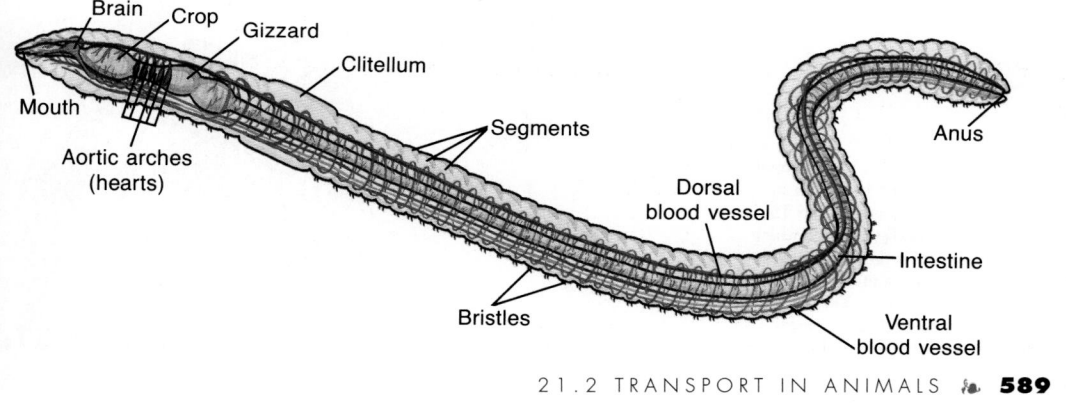

21.2 TRANSPORT IN ANIMALS **589**

SECTION 21.2
Prepare

Key Concepts
Closed circulatory systems consist of blood vessels and a pumping organ. In an open system, blood does not follow a pathway but is free to slosh within the animal's body. Vertebrates have evolved either two-, three-, or four-chambered hearts to meet increasingly complex lifestyles. The human heart is a dual system. The heart's right side pumps blood to the lungs. The heart's left side pumps blood to the body.

Key Terms
capillary, aorta, atrium, ventricle, artery, vein, sinoatrial node (S-A node), atrioventricular node (A-V node), lymph node

Materials
- Obtain a scale to mass the books needed in Minilab 1. Remind students to bring backpacks and textbooks on the day of this lab.
- Obtain a stethoscope and a sphygmomanometer for the Investigation.
- Secure EKG tracings from your local hospital.

1 Focus

Objectives
The objectives are listed on the student page. Remind students to preview these objectives as a guide to this numbered section.

Activity
Have students determine the average class pulse as well as the extreme low and high rate per minute for the class. **L1**

2 Teach

Figure Caption Question
How do nutrients enter the blood of an earthworm? Nutrients pass from the digestive tract of the earthworm into the blood by diffusion.

PROGRAM RESOURCES

Teacher Classroom Resources
Study Guide, pp. 123-124 **L1**
Concept Mapping, p. 21 **L1** **LEP**
Probing Levels of Life, Labs 55, 56, pp. 143, 145 **L2**

Critical Thinking/Problem Solving, p. 21 **L2**
Color Transparency #28, 39, 52 **L1** **LEP**
Investigating Living Systems, Lab 58, p. 221 **L2**

The blood flows from the ventral blood vessel through smaller and smaller branches of the vessel to the worm's tissues. Exchange of materials between blood and cells takes place through the smallest blood vessels, called **capillaries.** Capillaries have walls only one cell thick, so materials can pass easily in and out of them. The blood picks up digested food molecules from within capillaries in the intestine and picks up oxygen from within capillaries in the skin. As the blood in the capillaries passes by cells, food and oxygen molecules in the blood pass through the capillary wall to the cells. Wastes pass from the cells, through the capillary wall, to the blood. The capillaries then converge into larger and larger branches of blood vessel until they eventually empty into the dorsal blood vessel. From there, the blood flows back to the hearts, and the circuit continues. Capillaries are so numerous that no cell is far from the blood. Thus, each cell is linked by means of blood, the animal's internal environment, to the external environment.

Open Circulatory System—The Grasshopper

A different kind of circulation later evolved among arthropods. For example, in a grasshopper, blood is pumped toward the head by a dorsal, segmented heart, into the **aorta,** the only blood vessel in its body, Figure 21-12. From the aorta, the blood empties into the insect's body cavity, where it moves into spaces surrounding the internal organs. While in these spaces, the blood bathes the cells directly and exchange of materials occurs. Muscular movements of the grasshopper circulate the blood within the spaces. Eventually, the blood collects in the space surrounding the heart and passes into the heart through tiny openings. This system, in which blood does not always move within vessels, is known as an open circulatory system.

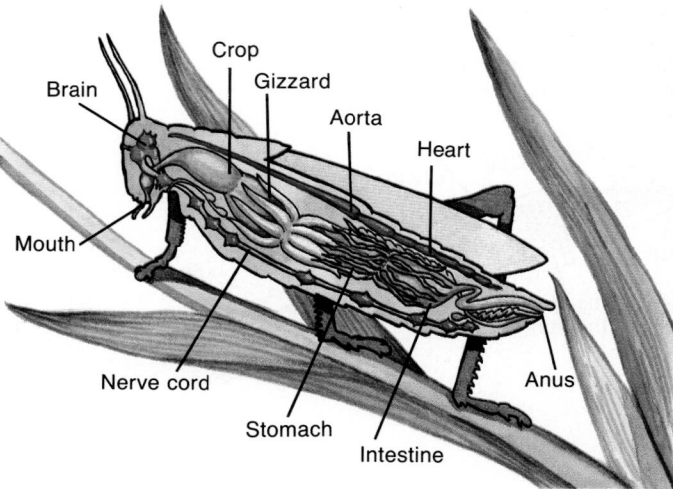

Figure 21-12 The dorsal blood vessel is the only blood vessel in an insect such as this grasshopper. The tubular heart has slits through which blood enters and is then pumped forward along the aorta to the head and out into the body cavity. The direction of blood flow around the organs is controlled by partitions of tissues.

590 TRANSPORT

An open circulatory system may seem less efficient than a closed system because movement of blood around the body is less rapid and under less pressure. Insects are active animals with high energy demands. How can the open system of an insect provide a sufficient supply of oxygen for cellular respiration? The answer is that it doesn't. Oxygen is not transported by the blood at all. It is transported very quickly to the cells by a separate system of tubes, as you will learn in the next chapter. Food and wastes, though, are carried efficiently by the blood.

Other arthropods, such as spiders and crayfish, have open circulatory systems in which the blood does indeed carry oxygen and carbon dioxide. In crayfish, the gills have a rich supply of blood. Within the gills, oxygen from the water diffuses into the blood, and carbon dioxide in the blood is expelled into the water.

Circulation in Vertebrates

Vertebrates have a closed circulatory system made up of a single heart and three types of blood vessels. The heart has two kinds of chambers. An **atrium** is a thin-walled chamber—a kind of receiving room in which incoming blood from the body is collected. A **ventricle** is a larger, more muscular, thicker-walled chamber. It pumps blood to the body. The three types of blood vessels differ in structure and function, as seen in Figure 21-13. Arteries and veins are thick-walled, large-diameter vessels composed of three layers of cells. **Arteries** transport blood away from the heart, and **veins** transport blood back to the heart. Veins contain one-way valves that aid in the return flow of blood to the heart. Capillaries, as you have already read, consist of just one layer of cells. The function of these very narrow vessels is exchange of materials.

Figure 21-13 Arteries (left, 440×) carry blood away from the heart to supply the body's tissues with a network of thin-walled capillaries (center, 28 000×). Veins (right, 16×) carry blood back to the heart. One-way valves (lower right) keep blood from flowing back.

Artery

Vein

Blood flow

Valves open

Valves close

Capillaries

21.2 TRANSPORT IN ANIMALS **591**

SECTION 21.2

Brainstorming

Ask students to predict if gills in crayfishes may have large or small surface areas with the outside environment. Have students explain their predictions. **COOP LEARN**

Demonstration

A live or preserved crayfish (available from local bait shops) will allow students to observe the extensive gill system present in these animals. Lift the carapace or skeleton up along the sides of the animal's body near its walking legs. The feathery structures attached near the top of its legs are the gills.

Using an Analogy

Water systems in cities consist of a pumping station, water mains carrying water to homes and apartments, and sewage pipes carrying waste water away from homes and apartments. Individual faucets link the clean water to sewage lines. Have students correlate these parts of a water system with the heart, arteries, veins, and capillaries. **LEP**

Using Science Terms

Ask students to provide examples other than in the circulatory system that use the term *atrium* in a manner similar to how it is used as a structure of the heart. Point out that one way to remember that the direction of blood flow in arteries is away from the heart or away from the lungs is to note that both words begin with the letter *a*. **LEP**

Minilab 1

Purpose
To compare pulse rate at rest with pulse rate after exercise.

Skills
sequence, observe and infer, compare and contrast, recognize cause and effect, calculate

Teaching Strategies
- **Safety Precautions:** Students who have knee problems should not do deep knee bends. Exercise immediately after a meal may cause stomach discomfort. Ascertain, before this activity, if any of your students should not participate for health reasons.
- If students have come from physical education class, have them rest for at least ten minutes before calculating resting pulses.
- Tell students to bring a book bag or backpack with extra books to class for this activity.
- Make sure students take their pulse in the order prescribed. The pulse should be taken with the index and middle fingers, not the thumb.

Expected Results
Answers will vary depending on a student's state of health and whether the student is under stress. Illness or poor health may cause a pulse to be higher. Trained athletes will have lower pulse rates.

Answers
Pulse rate will be higher because the heart must work harder to carry more food and oxygen to muscle cells. Pulse rate will be even higher with added weight because the heart must work even harder.

✔ Assessment
Knowledge: Ask students to write in their journals how what they have just learned will be important in their futures.

Minilab 1

What affects pulse rate?

Take your resting pulse rate by counting the pulse on your wrist for 20 seconds. Multiply by three to find your pulse rate for one minute. Repeat this procedure for four trials. Find the average. To find your after-exercise pulse rate, do 20 deep-knee bends in 40 seconds. Immediately take your pulse and find the average rate as before. To find the effect of increased weight on pulse rate, first wait about 10 minutes to be sure your pulse has returned to normal. Put 10 lbs. (4.5 kg) of books in a backpack on your back. Do knee bends as before, then find your new average pulse rate.
Analysis *What is the effect of exercise on pulse rate? Explain. What is the effect of increased weight on your pulse rate? Explain.*

A Heart with Two Chambers   As vertebrates evolved, they developed a greater body complexity and a more active lifestyle from life in the water to life on land. These changes made necessary a more efficient gas exchange with the environment, and a high-pressure circulatory system that supplies all the cells of the animals with necessary nutrients and removes the waste products.

The vertebrate heart is one organ that shows a range of adaptations to different vertebrate lifestyles. For example, fish have a heart with two chambers, an atrium and a ventricle. The atrium receives blood, and the ventricle forces blood out to the gills. The blood flow back from the gills is much slower than to the gills. Due to friction, the pressure of the blood is reduced as it passes through narrower and narrower vessels. Blood pressure in a fish drops as blood passes through the gill capillaries. The blood moves sluggishly from the gills to other parts of the body, and cells do not receive oxygen quickly. The low pressure of fish circulation is adapted to the lower energy demands of these ectotherms, animals whose body temperature changes with the temperature of the environment.

The Three-chambered Heart   Amphibians have three heart chambers—two atria and one ventricle. One atrium receives blood directly from the lungs and skin; another receives blood from the body tissues. Blood from both atria is then pumped into the ventricle. The oxygen-rich blood from the lungs and skin is then pumped to the body systems, and the oxygen-poor blood is pumped back to the lungs and skin where gas exchange takes place. Although the blood pressure falls as it passes through lung and skin capillaries, the blood returns to the heart before being pumped to the rest of the body. Therefore, the circulation is repressurized for its journey to body tissues. Amphibians are also ectotherms, and their circulatory system is an adaptation to their lifestyle. There is some mixing of oxygen-rich and oxygen-poor blood in the heart, although the internal structure of the ventricle keeps this to a minimum.

The Four-chambered Heart   In reptiles, some animals have a three-chambered system and others, such as alligators, have four chambers, just as in birds and mammals. The evolution of this high-pressure, double circulation—once through the lungs and once through the body tissues—is an adaptation to the active lifestyles of complex vertebrates. A wall of muscle divides the ventricle keeping oxygen-rich and oxygen-poor blood separate. As a result, body cells receive a steady supply of oxygen. Compare the circulatory systems of vertebrates in Figure 21-14.

Circulation in Mammals

Mammals are endotherms, animals that maintain a constant body temperature and have high energy demands. It is essential that their cells receive as much oxygen as possible and as quickly as possible. The evolution of a four-chambered heart consisting of two atria and two ventricles has made this possible. As an example of circulation in mammals, we will study human circulation. Follow Figure 21-15 as you read the description that follows.

PROJECT

Heart Models: A series of heart models can be constructed from simple materials such as paper cups, straws, labels, and tape or glue. Paper cups are available in a variety of different sizes. Have students work in cooperative groups and ask them to construct models of a two-, three-, and four-chambered heart. Small cups can represent atria and large cups can represent ventricles. Straws can be used to represent blood vessels. Labels can be used to name the blood vessels and/or to indicate the condition of blood within them. To conserve on time and materials, you may wish to assign a specific model to each student group. **L1**
COOP LEARN

Largemouth Bass

Two-chambered Heart

Leopard Frog

Three-chambered Heart

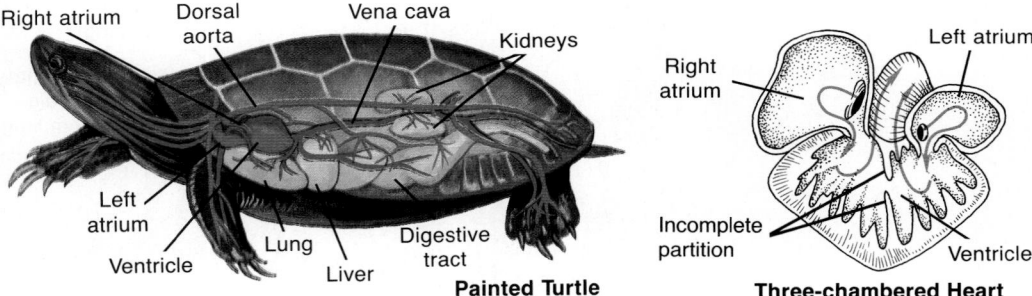

Painted Turtle

Three-chambered Heart

Figure 21-14 The circulatory systems of vertebrates show a trend from the two-chambered heart of a fish (top) to the three-chambered heart of amphibians (center) and reptiles (bottom).

SECTION 21.2

Concept Development

A four-chambered human heart prevents mixing of oxygen-rich and oxygen-poor blood. This is not the case with fish, amphibians, and some reptiles. Have students predict the condition of blood in the atrium and ventricle of a fish heart. Have students predict the condition of blood in the atria and ventricle of an amphibian.

Bioethics

Baboon Hearts for Humans: "Baby Fae," a 14-day-old infant, received an implant of a baboon heart. She was born with a defective heart and was not expected to live longer than a few days. Baby Fae was the first newborn to receive a cross-species transplant. She survived for just three weeks. Those who support this type of implant do so for several reasons. One, there is an acute shortage of available human organs for transplant. Being able to use organs from closely related species relieves this shortage. Two, animals are killed for food and as recreation. Is the killing of animals for their organs any different? Three, transplants are typically done as last-resort measures to prolong human life. Is a human life more important than that of any other animal? Those opposed to cross-species organ transplants claim that "Baby Fae" was unable to consent herself for the procedure. Second, research on this practice has not yet proved to be successful on adults. Therefore, this type of procedure should not be carried out on infants. When the pain and short-term nature of survival after transplant are considered, is it worth the physical, emotional, or financial investment required?

MEETING INDIVIDUAL NEEDS

Ask students to make simple concept maps to illustrate the cyclic movement of blood around the bodies of a fish, an amphibian, and a reptile. Have them complete the fish diagram by using the following labels: ventricle, gills, atrium, body. Have them complete the amphibian diagram by using the following labels: body, atrium, ventricle lungs and skin, atrium. Have them complete the reptile diagram by using the following labels: body, lungs, left heart, right heart. **L1** **LEP**

William Harvey: Prior to the early 1600s, the human circulatory system was poorly understood. William Harvey, a court physician for King James I and Charles I, was responsible for correctly describing the anatomy and physiology of the human circulatory system. Some of the main contributions he made are as follows: Contractions of heart chambers are not simultaneous; atria contract first and then the ventricles. As chambers contract, blood is pumped out of the heart. Previously, it was thought that blood was sucked into the heart as it expanded during relaxation. Blood does not pass from right to left ventricle across the septum. Instead, it passes from right ventricle to lungs and then returns to the heart's left side.

Using the Illustration

Have students examine Figure 21-15. Ask them to explain why not all veins carry blood low in oxygen, which vein carries blood high in oxygen, which arteries carry blood high in oxygen, and which artery carries blood high in oxygen. LEP

Using an Analogy

A medicine dropper can be used to represent the action of the heart as it contracts and relaxes. Expel the air within the dropper. Then, while holding the bulb compressed, stick it into a beaker of water and release the bulb. Ask students what this event compares to in the heart. Depress the bulb. Ask students what this event compares to in the heart. LEP

Human Circulatory System Blood low in oxygen and high in carbon dioxide enters the right atrium through the superior and inferior vena cavae, large veins leading into the heart from above and below. Contraction of the right atrium forces blood into the right ventricle. The right ventricle contracts, forcing blood into the pulmonary artery. Branches of this artery lead to capillaries in each lung where blood picks up oxygen and carbon dioxide is given off.

Oxygen-rich blood from the lungs courses to the left atrium along four pulmonary veins. As the left atrium contracts, blood is forced into the left ventricle. A powerful contraction of the left ventricle forces blood into the aorta, the largest blood vessel in the body. The aorta forms an arch, like the handle of a cane, that bends down behind the heart. Smaller arteries branching from the aorta direct blood to all parts of the body. The arteries branch and rebranch to form capillaries in which the blood gives up

Figure 21-15 **Some activities require large supplies of oxygen to the muscles. Olympic athletes learn to understand efficient use of their body's circulatory system as they strive to reach their greatest physical potential.**

594 TRANSPORT

Heart Diseases: Cardiovascular diseases (CVD) include many different diseases. Some people are more likely than other people to develop certain diseases. Interesting studies have been compiled on the occurrence of CVD in people of different ethnic backgrounds. Heart attacks are rarer in East Asian countries such as Japan, China, and India than in the United States and Europe. Studies have shown that heart attacks may be two times more common in African Americans than in Caucasians. Some studies have shown that, unfortunately, CVD is the main cause of death among African Americans. However, strokes are more common in Caucasians than in African Americans.

oxygen to body cells and receives carbon dioxide from these cells. In turn, these capillaries merge to form larger and larger veins that eventually form the superior and inferior vena cavae that return blood to the right atrium.

One-way valves between the atria and ventricles and at the base of the arteries leading from the ventricles allow blood to flow in only one direction. In the heart, valves are found between the right atrium and right ventricle, and between the left atrium and left ventricle. Valves also are located at the entrances of the pulmonary artery and the aorta. Find these structures in the heart in Figure 21-14. Why do you think that blood must flow in only one direction?

All blood travels through the heart twice during each circulation of the body. Oxygen-poor blood travels through the right side of the heart and to the lungs, where it picks up oxygen. The oxygen-rich blood travels through the left side of the heart, where it is forced out under great pressure to the body. Presence of two distinct ventricles ensures no mixing of oxygen-rich and oxygen-poor blood.

Blood Pressure As blood is pumped, it exerts a pressure on the walls of blood vessels. In arteries, the pressure causes the walls to bulge outward and then bounce back. You can feel this as a pulse in arteries near the surface of your skin. The surface area of blood is reduced on its journey along this passageway of narrowing vessels. The greatest loss of pressure occurs as blood travels through capillaries. Thus, when blood enters veins on its way back to the heart, the pressure is quite low. How does it get back to the heart, especially from the lower parts of the body? The one-way valves in the veins are important in this return flow of blood. Contraction of skeletal muscles squeezes the veins, forcing blood to move through the valves, which open only toward the heart. When muscles relax, the valves snap shut, preventing blood from flowing down and away from the heart. By the time blood enters the inferior vena cava, the pressure is very low. Breathing creates a vacuum effect in the chest cavity that helps draw the blood from the veins to the heart.

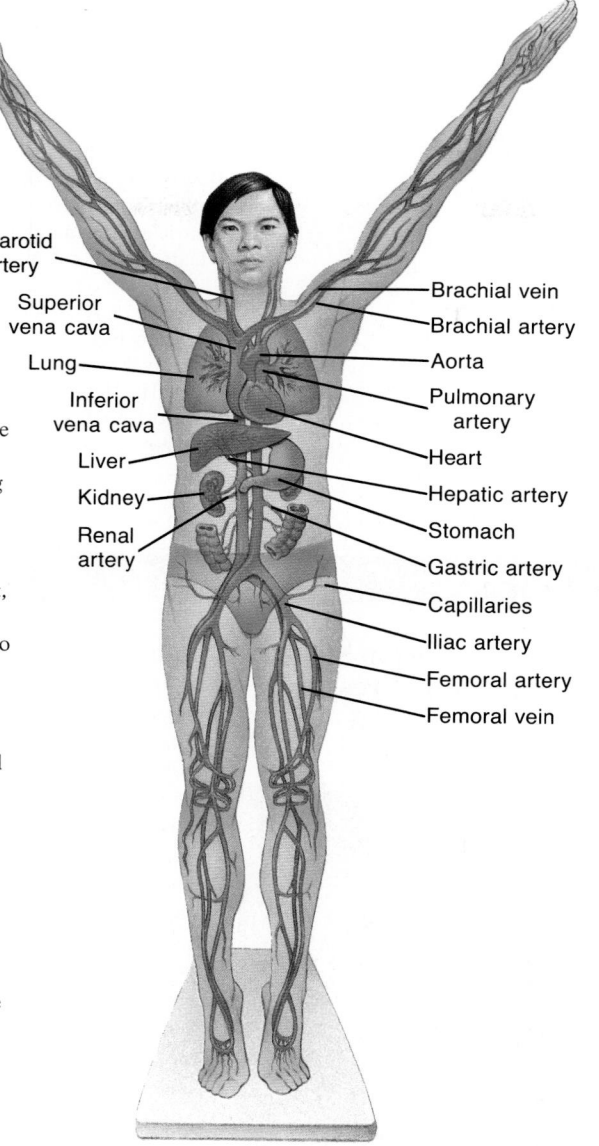

Carotid artery
Superior vena cava
Lung
Inferior vena cava
Liver
Kidney
Renal artery

Brachial vein
Brachial artery
Aorta
Pulmonary artery
Heart
Hepatic artery
Stomach
Gastric artery
Capillaries
Iliac artery
Femoral artery
Femoral vein

Figure 21-16 **The human circulatory system comprises blood circulation to and from the lungs, and circulation of blood to and from all the other organs, tissues, and cells of the body. The thousands of arteries and veins are linked by capillaries within the tissues and form a closed circulatory system.**

21.2 TRANSPORT IN ANIMALS **595**

Misconception

A student hears the thumping of his or her heart. The student believes that the thumping results from the contraction and relaxation of heart muscle. The sounds are actually caused by closure of the valves. Illustrate this fact first by asking if muscles make sound as they contract or relax. Ask students if they have ever heard their leg muscles contract or relax. Compare the heart valves to the closing of a door. Slam the classroom door. Do students hear it close? Now open the classroom door. Do students hear it open?

Demonstration

- Prove that the pulse and heartbeat are identical. Have students take their pulse for five trials of 30 seconds each trial. Ask them to calculate an average. Then have them repeat the five trials with their hand over their chest so as to detect their heartbeat. Both pulse and heartbeat rates should be almost identical. Collect their data on the chalkboard. Discuss why there could be a minor discrepancy between the two values. **L1**

- The effect of warm and cold temperatures on heartbeat rate can be illustrated by using earthworms. **CAUTION:** *Handle animals with care and consideration for their later release.* The dorsal blood vessel of the earthworm contracts in a wavelike pattern and can be seen through the animal's skin. Have students establish a "control" heartbeat for their worm while placed in a petri dish containing moist paper. Then, add cool water to the dish and record the earthworm's new heartbeat. Repeat this procedure using warm (not hot) water. Data collected may be averaged for the class, graphed, and placed as a report in the students' portfolios. **L1**

INVESTIGATION

The Effect of Stress on Blood Pressure

Time Allotment
1-1/2 class periods

Objectives
Upon completing this investigation, students will be able to:
- Evaluate the effects of stress on blood pressure.
- Demonstrate an understanding of how blood pressure is measured.

Skills
work cooperatively in groups, recognize cause and effect, interpret data, separate and control variables, use a stethoscope and sphygmomanometer

Materials
sphygmomanometer, stethoscope, cotton balls, rubbing alcohol, other materials supplied by students as necessary for producing stress

Preparation
1. Use alcohol to clean the parts of the stethoscope that fit in the ear.
2. Contact the school nurse or other qualified person for information on how to take blood pressure.

The Heartbeat

The source of each heartbeat is from within the heart itself. Each beat of the heart originates in a small bundle of tissue in the right atrium. This bundle of tissue is called the **sinoatrial node,** or **S-A node,** and also is known as the pacemaker. The S-A node acts like a kind of spark plug. A flow of ions acts as the electrical impulse that causes the muscle fibers of both atria to contract. The contraction forces blood from the atria into the ventricles. The impulse then reaches another small bundle, the **atrioventricular node,** or **A-V node,** located between the atria and the ventricles.

The A-V node causes an impulse that sweeps outward and downward along the muscle walls of the ventricles, which makes them contract. The squeezing increases the pressure of the blood. This pressure closes the heart's valves and opens the valves of the arteries that lead away from the heart. The "lub-dup" of a heartbeat is the sound of these valves opening and closing. The heart of an adult human at rest beats on average about 70 times per minute.

INVESTIGATION

The Effect of Stress on Blood Pressure

Your teacher hands out the big test. Your hands feel cold and clammy. Your mouth is dry, and the back of your neck is tight and stiff. You are experiencing stress. Stress has many physiological effects on the body, with wide variations from one person to another. Anxiety, which is stress over a long period of time, can cause a rise in blood pressure. This higher blood pressure might place a person at greater risk for stroke or heart attack.

The average normal blood pressure is around 120 over 80. Each heartbeat consists of two phases. The forceful, muscular contraction of the ventricles is called the systole. The top or first number in a blood pressure reading is the systolic pressure. Systole is followed by a short period called diastole, during which time the ventricles fill back up with blood. The second or bottom reading is the diastolic pressure. In this lab, you will test your blood pressure before and after a stressful event.

Problem
What effect does stress have on blood pressure?

Safety Precautions
Do not pump the blood pressure cuff beyond 180. Do not leave the cuff inflated any longer than necessary.

Hypothesis
Make a hypothesis about how your blood pressure will change following a stressful experience. Explain your reasons for making this hypothesis.

596 ⬥ TRANSPORT

Possible Hypotheses
My blood pressure will go up when I am asked personal questions by my group or when someone bursts a balloon when I am not expecting it.

Possible Procedures
- After taking a student's blood pressure, ask him or her to stand in front of a large group of students. Ask personal questions about grades, social relationships, and habits. The student may refuse to answer specific questions. Take blood pressure immediately after the questions are asked.
- Take blood pressure. Later, pop a balloon behind the student when it would be unexpected. Take blood pressure.

Teaching Strategies
- **Safety Precautions:** Before commencing with this investigation, ascertain if any of your students have a heart condition. These students should not participate in stressful activities.

Control of the heartbeat is an example of homeostasis, which, as you learned in Chapter 1, is the maintenance of a constant internal environment despite external change. Blood is part of the internal environment of humans. The blood must deliver and remove materials from body cells under varying conditions. At rest, a heartbeat rate of 70 beats per minute is adequate, but during heavy exercise, cells require more oxygen and glucose and produce more wastes. The heartbeat rate must increase so that the exchanges between blood and cells occur more quickly. Once exercise stops, the heartbeat rate gradually slows and soon returns to the resting rate. Heartbeat rate is under the control of part of the nervous system, which will be discussed in Chapter 25.

Exchange of Materials

Capillaries are the sites of exchange. However, there are several methods by which different materials are exchanged between the body cells and the blood in the capillaries. One method is diffusion, the means by which

Concept Development

The heartbeat sounds are identified as "lub-dup." Ask students to correspond the "lub" sound to an event. What does the "dup" sound correspond to? Ask students which heart chambers contract first. Explain that the valves between atria and ventricles do not close at this time. Ask which valves are therefore responsible for the first heart sound. Ask students which chambers contract next. Point out that blood does not flow backward into atria during this event. Ask, therefore, which valves must close, resulting in the second heart sound.

- To develop interest and focus, ask what causes stress in your life and what are the effects of stress on the body?
- Demonstrate the proper use of the sphygmomanometer.
- Advise students not to insult, degrade, or abuse other students.
- Make certain that blood pressure is taken immediately after the stressful situation.

Data and Observations

Evaluate each group's graphs and interpretations of data. Systolic pressure will be between 110 and 140. Diastolic pressures will be between 70 and 80 before stress. After stress, some pressures will not change a great deal. Most diastolic pressures will not go above 95; most systolic pressures will not go above 180.

Data Analysis

1. Numbers will vary. Systolic pressure is the pressure created by the muscular contraction of the ventricles.

Experimental Plan

1. In your group, make a list of possible ways you might test your hypothesis.
2. Agree on one idea from your group's list that could be investigated in the classroom. Be sure that your subjects will be treated humanely.
3. Design an experiment that will test one variable at a time. Plan to collect quantitative data.
4. Following the style of a recipe, write a numbered list of directions that anyone could follow.
5. Make a list of materials and the quantities you will need.

Checking the Plan

Discuss the following points with other group members to decide the final procedures for your experiment.
1. What variables will need to be controlled?

2. What is your control?
3. What procedures or props will you use to cause stress?
4. What will you measure or count?
5. How long will you apply stress?
6. How many trials will you run?
7. Have you designed and made a table for collecting data?

Make sure your teacher has approved your experimental plan before you proceed further.

Data and Observations

Carry out your experiment, make your measurements, and complete your data table. Make a graph of your results.

Analysis and Conclusions

1. What is your measured systolic pressure before stress? What does this number represent?

2. What is your measured diastolic pressure before stress? What does this number represent?
3. How did stress alter your blood pressure?
4. How is this change beneficial?
5. If the source of stress did not alter your blood pressure, why do you think it didn't?
6. If you were subjected to a continual high level of stress, how might this stress level affect your health?
7. What could you do to alleviate some stress in your life?

Going Further

Based on this lab experience, design another experiment that would help explain the effects of different kinds of stress in everyday life. Assume that you will have unlimited resources and will not be conducting this lab in class.

---

2. Numbers will vary. Diastolic pressure is created when the heart is at "rest" and the atria and ventricles are filling with blood.
3. Answers will vary.
4. A rise in blood pressure might indicate that the heart is working harder, perhaps getting ready for possible "danger."
5. Individual students will have different levels of tolerance.
6. There will be an increased risk over the long term for heart attack.
7. Answers could include: exercise, meditation, counseling or modifying the lifestyle.

✔ Assessment

Oral: Both systolic and diastolic blood pressures of teenagers in one of two big city schools were higher than in the other. Propose and justify a hypothesis that would explain these results.

Extensions

Lead students with questions about other experiments they could conduct. For example, which situations would produce the most stress as reflected by changes in blood pressure? Or, are there gender differences?

Minilab 2

Purpose
To compare a normal EKG with actual EKGs that may be abnormal.

Teaching Strategies
- EKGs may be obtained from local hospitals or doctors' offices. Ask for some that are normal and some that are abnormal. Make copies to supply all students. Explain that common abnormalities might result from abnormal valve structure, abnormal structure or size of the heart muscle, or abnormal transmission or reception of the electrical impulse. Point out the effect of each abnormality on an EKG.

Expected Results
Results can be obtained by counting the vertical lines representing 0.1 seconds on the normal EKG. Time at rest is 0.3 seconds; for atrial contraction, 0.2 seconds; for ventricle contraction, 0.4 seconds.

Answers
Answers will vary.

✔ Assessment
Knowledge: Ask students to explain in their journals why it would be important to have an EKG made when you are in good health. *If you have a problem later, there will be a basis for comparison.*

Minilab 2

How do you interpret an EKG?
Examine the graph below of a normal human heartbeat. This is called an electrocardiogram or EKG. By placing electrodes on the body, the pattern of electrical messages stimulating the heart muscle can be recorded. Segment T-P in the graph represents the heart at rest; P-Q represents atrial contraction; Q-T represents ventricles contracted. Study the samples of actual EKGs provided by your teacher. Label them with the appropriate letters.

Analysis *Examine the normal EKG. Compare the times spent by the heart in each segment—at rest, atrial contraction, and ventricle contraction. Were the sample EKGs normal or abnormal? Explain.*

carbon dioxide and oxygen can pass between the blood and the body cells. For example, oxygen diffuses from blood in capillaries to muscle cells. Together, the great number of capillaries provide an enormous surface area for exchange. Because these tiny vessels branch and rebranch many times, no cell is far from a capillary. These two features promote ready exchange of materials between cells and blood. In a second method, dissolved materials are transported across the cells that make up the capillary wall in small vesicles. The vesicles form on one side of a capillary cell by endocytosis, and the material is deposited on the other side by exocytosis.

Tissue Fluid A third method for exchange involves seepage of fluid through the spaces between capillary cells. As blood passes through the capillaries, pressure is exerted on the capillary walls. The pressure is greatest at the arterial end of the capillary. This pressure forces some water and small dissolved particles out of the capillaries and into the tissues. The water and particles are called tissue fluid. Large molecules such as proteins, as well as blood cells, remain in the capillaries. At the venous end of the capillary, blood pressure is lower. Some tissue fluid re-enters that end of the capillary by osmosis. Osmosis occurs in this direction because there is a larger concentration of protein and a smaller concentration of water inside the capillaries than in the surrounding tissue fluid. The tendency of fluid to move into the capillary by osmosis at the venous end of the capillary is greater than the tendency of fluid to move out due to blood pressure.

Tissue fluid is important in the exchange of materials to and from cells. Materials such as fatty acids and sodium ions enter cells from tissue fluid. Also, wastes, such as urea, and products produced by cells, such as hormones, enter the tissue fluid. Thus, tissue fluid is part of the internal environment. When you scrape your knuckle, the sticky fluid (not the red blood) that collects is tissue fluid.

Figure 21-17 The pacemaker is a mass of muscle tissue that controls the rhythm of the heartbeat (a). This activity can be recorded as an electrocardiogram (EKG) (b).

ALTERNATE LAB: Observing Blood Components

Purpose
Students will observe and compare prepared slides of human blood smears.

Materials
microscope, scissors, a nickle, self-adhesive label, prepared slide of human blood

Procedure
Give the following directions to students.
1. Make a data table with three columns labeled Blood component type, Number per field of view, and Average number. Make three rows labeled *white blood cells, platelets,* and *red blood cells.*
2. Locate blood cells under your microscope using low- and then high-power magnification.
3. Count and record the number of white blood cells seen in a high-power field of view. White cells are stained blue and are the largest cells in the blood.
4. Repeat step 2 for two more different fields of view.
5. Repeat steps 2 and 3. This time count and record the number of platelets in each field of view. Platelets will appear as dot-like purple spots.
6. Draw a circle on a self-adhesive label using a nickel as the outline. Cut out a pie section 1/16 the total area of the circle and discard this section.

The Lymph Network Not all tissue fluid that leaves a capillary returns to it by osmosis. Some of the fluid enters a network of small vessels, called lymph vessels, that are closed at one end. The fluid that collects in lymph vessels is then called lymph fluid. There is no pump for lymph circulation, but random body movements force the lymph toward a major collecting duct located near the heart. This duct empties into a large vein. In this way, the liquid portion of blood lost from within the capillaries is restored to the blood.

Scattered throughout the lymphatic system are **lymph nodes,** small, spongy capsules—more than 100 of them—that appear as bumps along the lymph vessels.

Figure 21-18 Exchange of carbon dioxide and oxygen between the red blood cells and body cells occurs in the thin-walled capillaries.

HISTORY CONNECTION

A Pioneer in Medicine

Today, surgeons can replace diseased heart valves, clear blocked arteries or put in a new artery to bypass the blocked one, implant a pacemaker to make the heart beat regularly, and even transplant a heart from one person to another. Until the middle of this century, however, such heart operations were unheard of.

Dr. Myra Logan was one of the pioneers of heart surgery. Not only was she one of the first surgeons to operate on the heart, she was the first woman ever to do so. In 1951, she became the first African American woman to be elected to the American College of Surgeons, a prominent medical honor society. When Dr. Logan graduated from medical school in 1929, however, a surgeon did all kinds of operations.

During her internship and residency at Harlem Hospital, she did everything from delivering babies to closing stab wounds to the heart. Today, heart surgery is performed by specialists called cardiovascular surgeons.

In addition to performing heart surgery, Dr. Logan continued to perform many other kinds of operations, especially on children. She was one of the first doctors to practice group health maintenance, in which several doctors with different specialties work together. In the 1960s, she conducted an important study on breast tumors and improved the use of X rays to detect breast cancer in women. Dr. Logan was a pioneer not only as a successful female African American, but also as an outstanding medical researcher and a surgeon who served the Harlem community for more than 35 years.

1. **Explore Further:** Breast cancer is the third leading cause of death from cancer. How can a breast X ray, called a mammogram, help prevent breast cancer?
2. **Writing About Biology:** Explain why heart transplant operations are not always successful.

7. Place the label onto the eyepiece of your microscope. Count the number of red cells seen through the section using high power.
8. Multiply your count by 16 before recording it. Repeat your count for two more fields of view.
9. Calculate and record an average number for each cell type.

Analysis
Ask students the following questions.
1. Sequence the cell types observed from least to most common. *white— platelet—red*
2. Compute the ratio of white cells to platelets to red cells. *Answers will vary, example 1: 27 : 1270*
3. The actual ratio of white cells to platelets to red cells is 1 : 40 : 500.

Offer a possible explanation for why your calculated ratios and the actual ratios do not match. *The sample size should be larger to reduce errors in counting or errors in calculating.*

✔ Assessment
Portfolio: Make labeled diagrams of the three blood cell types. Add them to your portfolio. **L1**

3 Assess

Check for Understanding

Have students list the term or statement that is the pair of the one provided. **L1**
(a) open circulatory system
(b) artery
(c) atrium

Reteach

Ask students to explain their answers provided for the "Check for Understanding" above.

Extension

During early human development, blood bypasses the lungs and moves from right to left atrium through an opening. Ask students to explain why this opening is harmful if it persists in the newborn. **L3**

✔ Assessment

Skill: Provide students with a diagram similar to Figure 21-15. Have students label all heart chambers and major blood vessels, provide arrows that trace the pathway of blood, and shade in all blood vessels with oxygen-poor blood. **L1**

4 Close

Demonstration

Obtain a whole preserved sheep heart from a biological supply house. Slice the heart open to view the internal structure. Ask students to identify chambers, valves, and major blood vessel points of entry and exit.

Figure 21-19 Fluid lost from the capillaries to the lymphatic system is later returned to the blood via a duct near the heart.

Destruction of bacteria occurs mainly within the lymph nodes. You will read more about the lymphatic system and its role in immunity in Chapter 23. Your tonsils and adenoids act in much the same way as your lymph nodes. Have you ever experienced swelling in the lymph nodes in your neck? What does such swelling indicate?

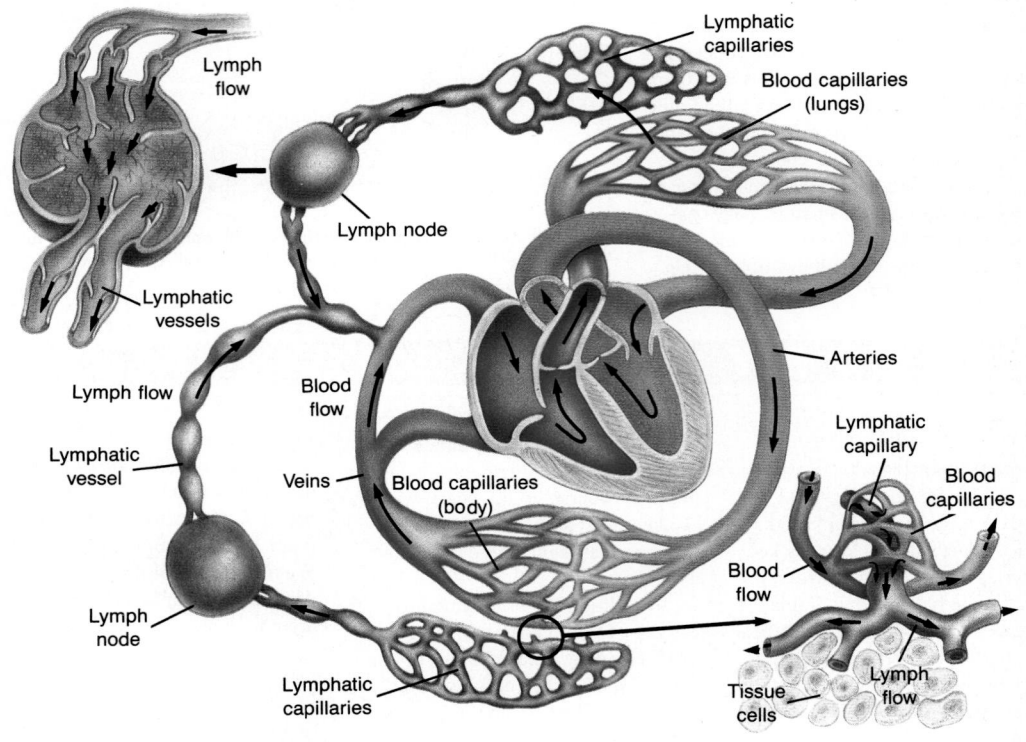

Section Review

Understanding Concepts
1. Why is circulation more efficient in an animal with a closed circulatory system than in an animal with an open circulatory system?
2. For each pair of fish circulatory structures, indicate where the amount of oxygen is higher: ventral aorta— dorsal aorta; ventral aorta—gill capillaries; dorsal aorta—atrium; atrium—ventricle.
3. How is circulation in an amphibian more efficient than in a fish?
4. **Skill Review—Sequencing:** Sequence all the structures through which blood passes as it circulates from your heart to your left foot and back again. For more help, see Organizing Information in the **Skill Handbook.**
5. **Thinking Critically:** Blood flows most slowly in capillaries. How is that rate of flow adaptive?

Answers to Section Review

1. Blood in a closed circulatory system is continually within vessels, follows a fixed path, and is pushed along continually by the beating of the heart(s). Blood in an open system follows no fixed path, its movement is dependent on the movement of the animal, its circulation is less rapid, and it moves under less pressure.

2. dorsal aorta; gill capillaries; dorsal aorta; no difference
3. Because there are two atria in an amphibian heart, blood going out to body tissues is oxygen rich and under high pressure. In a fish, the blood is under less pressure.
4. **Skill Review—Sequencing:** inferior vena cava→ right atrium→ valve→ right ventricle→ valve→ pulmonary

artery→ lung capillaries (blood picks up oxygen)→ pulmonary veins→ left atrium→ valve→ left ventricle→ valve→ aorta→ smaller arteries→ capillaries in left foot (blood gives up oxygen)→ veins→ inferior vena cava
5. **Thinking Critically:** A slow rate of flow permits more time for gas and nutrient exchange between capillaries and tissues.

21.3 The Blood

As your internal environment, your blood has many functions. It transports nutrients such as glucose, fats, amino acids, ions, and vitamins to your body cells. It delivers oxygen, removes carbon dioxide, and carries hormones from the glands where they are formed to the tissues or organs they regulate. Blood passing through your liver picks up a nitrogenous waste called urea, which is carried via the bloodstream to the kidneys, where it is removed from the body. Blood also has a major role in protecting the body from infection.

Gas Transport

A microscope reveals that a drop of human blood is a pale yellow fluid, called plasma, that contains a variety of cell-like structures as shown in Table 21.1 below. These structures differ from most other body cells and include red blood cells, white blood cells, and platelets, which are cell fragments. All are produced from central bone tissue called marrow—a mesh of delicate connective tissue and blood vessels. Blood cells are formed in the marrow of long bones, such as the thighbone, and flat bones, such as ribs and the breastbone. The characteristics of blood components are outlined in Table 21.1.

Objectives

Compare the structure and function of components of the blood.

Define the roles of white blood cells and platelets.

Predict the outcomes of mixing the four blood types of humans.

Table 21.1 Blood Components

Component	Characteristics
Red blood cells	biconcave, disk-shaped cells with no nuclei; contain hemoglobin, transport oxygen and some carbon dioxide
White blood cells	five types; shape is round with a nucleus; some fight infection; some control immunity
Platelets	cell fragments that liberate substances necessary for clotting blood
Proteins	some are involved with clotting activities; some are antibodies
Hormones	chemicals secreted by glands; control and coordinate the activities of the body
Urea	waste product formed by liver; transported to kidneys, where it is filtered out of the body
Glucose, amino acids, fats, vitamins, minerals, lipids	nutrients transported to all cells and tissues; necessary for metabolism

White blood cells

Platelets

Red blood cells

MEETING INDIVIDUAL NEEDS

Visually Impaired: Students who are visually impaired may be able to experience the shape and relative size of red cells, white cells, and platelets by feeling different kinds of candy: candy with concave surfaces for red cells, candy with a soft center for white cells, and tiny candy for platelets.
LEP

Key Terms
red blood cell, platelet, white blood cell, antigen, antibody

Materials
none

1 Focus

Objectives
The objectives are listed on the student page. Remind students to preview these objectives as a guide to this numbered section.

Demonstration
Fill five 1000-mL graduated cylinders with water to which red food coloring has been added. Ask students to predict the volume of blood present in an adult human. Show them their choices of one to five liters. Few will guess that it is five liters.

2 Teach

Using the Table
Ask students to use the table to determine the chemicals present in plasma. L1

Microscope Activity
Provide students with prepared slides of human blood smears. These slides are available from biological supply houses. Have them identify red cells. Ask the students to estimate the diameter of a typical red cell. Advise them that the diameter of their high-power field is about 0.35 millimeters across. L1

Red Blood Cells: Tell students that 1 cubic millimeter = 1 milliliter; blood volume of an adult human = 5 liters. Knowing from the text that there are 5 million red blood cells in a cubic millimeter of blood, have them calculate the number of red blood cells in the human body. **L1**

Science, Technology, and Society

Modified Hemoglobin: Blood banks can only store donated blood for 42 days, and the transfused blood must match the recipient's rather closely. Artificial blood would overcome these problems. The answer to finding such a solution may be found among recombinant DNA techniques. A company in Boulder, Colorado, has placed the genes responsible for forming human hemoglobin into the bacterium *Escherichia coli*. The human hemoglobin is slightly modified. It has two amino acids different from those found in normal hemoglobin. The bacterial cells open to release the modified hemoglobin. Initial trials show it to be most promising.

The Work of Red Blood Cells   The most numerous of all kinds of blood cells are the **red blood cells.** About 5 million red blood cells are present in a cubic millimeter of blood. Disk-shaped and concave on each side, these blood elements lose their nuclei as they age. Red blood cells carry an iron-containing protein molecule—hemoglobin—that functions in the transport of oxygen. In the lungs, oxygen combines with hemoglobin to form the compound oxyhemoglobin, which makes the blood bright red. Oxyhemoglobin is then transported to the heart and the body cells.

In the capillaries, oxyhemoglobin breaks down into hemoglobin and oxygen. The liberated oxygen then diffuses from the red blood cells to the body cells. As oxygen leaves the blood, the blood turns a dark red, or maroon. At the same time, carbon dioxide diffuses from body cells into the capillaries. Some of the carbon dioxide forms ions in the plasma. Some combines with hemoglobin. The remaining carbon dioxide dissolves in the liquid within the red blood cells. The blood then returns to the lungs, where the carbon dioxide is released and oxygen is picked up.

Thinking Lab

INTERPRET THE DATA

What are the effects of iron deficiency?

Background
Have you ever heard the expression "tired blood"? This expression refers to iron deficiency in blood. Iron is an important element of the hemoglobin molecule. Without enough iron, the body cannot make adequate amounts of hemoglobin, which is the molecule that carries oxygen to body cells. Iron deficiency also interferes with the exchange of oxygen and carbon dioxide in muscle cells.

The Harvard step test is designed to test physical ability. The subject steps up and down from a platform for a specified time, after which the pulse is measured. This pulse rate after exercise can be correlated to the body's ability to do physical work.

You Try It
Examine Graph A below, which demonstrates the results of the Harvard step test on a small population of people. **Interpret** the results. Look at Graph B, which compares available iron content of different foods, and describe a meal that might help someone with an iron deficiency.

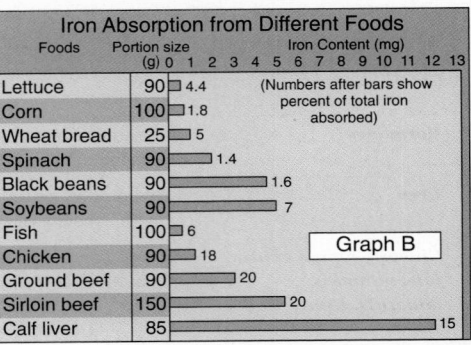

Thinking Lab

INTERPRET THE DATA

Purpose
Students will find the relationship between hemoglobin and work performance.

Teaching Strategies
Review graph interpretation with students if necessary.

Further Background
Anemia is the result of iron deficiency. This deficiency has symptoms that often go undetected: pallor, listlessness, and fatigue. Anemia can affect learning ability and immune processes as well as oxygen transport.

Answers
Graph A: As amounts of hemoglobin increase, work performance increases because more hemoglobin is available to carry more oxygen to muscle cells.

Graph B: Corn flour tortilla with soybean and chopped sirloin steak filling, iceberg lettuce salad.

✔ Assessment
Knowledge: Ask students to make a brief entry in their journals about how what they learned might be important to them. **L1**

in the donor's plasma will not affect your blood cells as much because they will be greatly diluted by your own plasma. This is the reason why type O blood, which has no antigens but has both anti-A and anti-B antibodies, can be transfused into all persons no matter what their blood type. People with type A blood have type anti-B antibodies. If type B blood is mistakenly transfused into a person with type A blood, clumping in the recipient's blood will occur. Such clumping may plug up blood vessels, causing the recipient's death. The reverse is also true; that is, type B blood has type anti-A antibodies. Clumping of the recipient's blood will occur if type A blood is given to a person with type B blood. People with type AB blood have neither type of antibody. Transfusion possibilities are summarized in Table 21.2.

Because people with type AB blood have no antibodies, they can, therefore, receive any blood type. Such people are known as universal recipients. People with type O blood are known as universal donors because their red blood cells have no antigens. If no foreign antigens are present, clumping will not occur. Thus, when transfusions are performed, it is important that no foreign antigens be introduced.

LOOKING AHEAD

As you have read, transport within organisms is accomplished in a variety of ways. Cells must take in nutrients and oxygen for life processes, and waste by-products from these processes must be removed. What prevents so much material from entering the cells that they burst? What prevents so much material from leaving the cells that they collapse? And once the wastes leave a cell, how are they removed from the organism? In the next chapter, you will explore how osmotic balance is maintained, how gases are exchanged, and how cell wastes are removed from the body.

Section Review

Understanding Concepts

1. Why do you think the number of red blood cells is so much greater than the number of other blood components?

2. Sometimes a blood clot forms on the inner wall of a blood vessel and then breaks free. How might that event be dangerous?

3. Explain what will happen if a person with type O blood receives a transfusion of type B blood.

4. **Skill Review—Making Tables:** Make a table comparing the components of blood in terms of their structure, number, and function. For more help, see Organizing Information in the **Skill Handbook**.

5. **Thinking Critically:** Why are people with certain immune system problems sometimes given a bone marrow transplant?

Extension

Blood is a transporter of both oxygen and carbon dioxide. Ask students to describe the variety of ways in which carbon dioxide is transported by blood. Describe the one way in which oxygen is transported by blood. **L2**

✔ **Assessment**

Portfolio: Have students make a diagram of components in a drop of blood. Their diagrams should include plasma. Students should label the component parts and add a brief description of the function of each component. Diagrams are to be placed in students' portfolios. **L1**

4 Close

Discussion

Prepare a model of a test tube of blood. Half fill a test tube with water containing a few drops of red food coloring. Fill the test tube by adding cooking oil. Ask students to explain what the oil layer represents and approximately what percentage of blood is composed of this component. *plasma, 50 percent* Have students assume the model represents either type A, B, AB, or O blood. Which blood type's plasma could be used as a suitable transfusion liquid into any other person and why? *AB, because it lacks antibodies* **LEP**

Answers to Section Review

1. Transport of oxygen is a vital function. The greater number of red blood cells maximizes the amount of oxygen that can be carried to body cells.

2. The clot could later lodge in a capillary with a smaller diameter, blocking blood flow to tissues in that area. Clots causing blockages can lead to heart attacks and strokes.

3. The transfusion will not be successful. A person with type O blood has anti-A and anti-B antibodies. The latter will cause clumping as they encounter the B antigens of the type B blood.

4. **Skill Review—Making Tables:**

Blood component	Number per mL^3	Function
red	5 million	transport O_2 and some CO_2
white	10 000	fight infection
platelets	400 000	help clot blood

5. **Thinking Critically:** The transplanted marrow produces white blood cells that the patient cannot make.

Biotechnology

Purpose
Students will be introduced to modern, non-invasive techniques for the diagnosis and treatment of problems concerning the circulatory system.

Teaching Strategies
- Make sure that students understand the meaning of the following terms: *catheter, laser, radiant energy, coagulate, angioplasty.*
- Ask students to work in cooperative groups to answer questions at the end of this feature.

  COOP LEARN
- A video of an angiogram is viewed by the cardiologist after the procedure. Check with your local cardiologist to determine if a tape from a patient could be used for viewing in the classroom.

Possible Answers
1. Laser angioplasty is a temporary measure. The removal of blockage of a blood vessel via angioplasty does not guarantee a permanent cure from reforming plaque. Also, plaque formation may be so extensive that laser angioplasty cannot reach all the affected blood vessels.
2. Student descriptions may cover X ray, sonogram or ultrasound, MRI or magnetic resonance imaging, or CAT scan or computerized axial tomography technologies.

Going Further
Ask students why a cardiologist may wish to know the pH of a patient's blood. What factors affect blood pH? Your physics department may have a demonstration laser. Ask a physics teacher to demonstrate and explain its use to your students.

BIOLOGY,
TECHNOLOGY, AND
SOCIETY

Biotechnology
Looking Inside Your Body

A new way of operating without making large cuts into your body is no longer science fiction. Already, doctors can look inside organs such as your heart by making a tiny cut and threading optical fibers through your blood vessels.

Viewing with a Fiberscope   The first fiberscope was tested in 1957. A fiberscope has two bundles of optical fibers made of very pure glass called silica. One bundle transmits light to the body tissue being examined. The other bundle sends back an image to an eyepiece, camera, or TV screen. Each bundle contains about 10 000 optical fibers and measures less than 1 mm in diameter. The two bundles are wrapped in a flexible catheter thin enough to fit into the blood vessels.

A fiberscope lets doctors observe your body at work. They can watch your heart valves open and close and spot cholesterol in your arteries. A light reflected from the tip of the catheter can tell them how much oxygen is in your blood and how fast the blood is flowing. By adding special sensors called optrodes, doctors can measure the pressure in your arteries and the pH of your blood. They can also peer into your lungs, your stomach and intestines, and other organs.

Operating with an Endoscope   A fiberscope is often part of a larger instrument called an endoscope. Endoscopes contain other fibers through which doctors can withdraw fluids or perform surgery. An entire endoscope can measure as little as 2.5 mm in diameter—about a third of the diameter of a pencil.

Endoscopes are used in laser surgery. Laser light is a form of radiant energy. Low-power lasers cause blood to coagulate by gentle heating, while high-power lasers boil tissue away. During laser surgery, high concentrations of laser energy are beamed through optical fibers made of quartz or crystals onto the tissue to be treated.

Cleaning the Arteries   Laser surgery offers a new way to treat heart disease. Blood clots and plaque in the arteries reduce blood circulation to the heart and brain. If circulation is cut off completely, a heart attack or stroke occurs. Until recently, open heart surgery was the only way to open clogged arteries. Now doctors are testing a procedure called laser angioplasty. A laser beam is transmitted through an optical fiber to a metal tip, which heats up and melts the plaque or blood clot.

1. **Issue:** Why is laser angioplasty not the perfect solution to atherosclerosis?
2. **Writing About Biology:** Describe other technologies that doctors use to view what is going on in your body.

CAREER CONNECTION

Medical technologists at a blood bank are responsible for making sure that blood is safe for transfusion. After they draw a unit of blood from the donor, they determine its type. They screen the blood to be sure there are no traces of viruses, and then they seal and label the blood for storage. Medical technologists work for the Red Cross, for local blood banks, and for hospitals.

CAREER CONNECTION

For more information, contact your local hospital. Most medical technologists are trained by attending a licensed program usually associated with a hospital or nursing school.

Health Connection

Protect Your Heart

More than twice as many Americans die from diseases of the heart and blood vessels than from any other cause. The risk of heart disease rises as you get older, but the early stages can start in your teens. The culprit is atherosclerosis, a buildup of fat deposits on the artery walls.

Clogged Arteries Your liver removes fats called cholesterol from your blood, but if there is too much cholesterol for your liver to handle, the excess stays in your blood. Some of it seeps into the lining of your arteries. White blood cells come along, gobble up the cholesterol, and then swell and get trapped in the artery wall. A small mass of these bloated white cells causes a fatty streak.

As more and more bloated white blood cells clump together, they create a bulge on the inside of the artery and damage the lining of the artery wall. Other cells move in to repair the damage, but they end up turning the bulge into a buildup of fats and dead cells, called plaque. The artery wall becomes hard. Less blood can flow through the artery, so your heart doesn't get as much oxygen. You are now at risk for a heart attack or stroke.

Hypertension Some people are more prone to atherosclerosis, but there are things you can do now to help reduce your risks. High blood pressure, called hypertension, is thought to be the biggest risk factor in heart disease. An average normal blood pressure is around 120 over 80. Diastolic blood pressure (the bottom number) higher than 90 signals hypertension. High blood pressure causes the walls of the arteries to become thick and hard, although exactly how is not fully known. You can greatly reduce your risks of developing hypertension by keeping your weight down, eating a low-salt diet, and getting regular exercise.

High Cholesterol Research studies show that high cholesterol is directly linked to heart disease. High cholesterol leads to a buildup of plaque in your arteries. The best way to keep your cholesterol low is to eat low-fat foods. That means cutting down on hamburgers, milk shakes, potato and corn chips, fried foods, ice cream, and cheese.

Smoking Smoking is another major risk factor in heart disease. More than 170 000 people die each year from the damage cigarette smoke causes to their arteries. Smokers are two to four times more likely to have heart attacks than nonsmokers, and their heart attacks are more likely to end in death. Researchers have found that cigarette smoke increases the buildup of plaque in your arteries. Ten to 15 years after you stop smoking, your risk of dying from a heart attack approaches the same level as that of a nonsmoker.

Control of Risk Factors If you don't smoke and don't have high blood pressure or high cholesterol now, are you home free? Not totally. Several other factors play an indirect role in atherosclerosis.

Obesity is one. Extra pounds strain your heart muscles and often cause your blood pressure and cholesterol to go up. Obesity can also cause the breakdown of pancreatic tissues resulting in adult diabetes. Diabetes raises cholesterol levels. Lack of exercise is another risk factor. Exercise lowers blood pressure and cholesterol and strengthens your heart muscles.

You can't absolutely prevent heart disease, but exercising, eating a low-fat, low-salt diet, and not smoking can greatly reduce your risks. You'll feel better and look better, too.

1. **Writing About Biology:** Describe some of the risk factors of heart disease that you can't control.
2. **Explore Further:** Why is taking aspirin thought to help prevent atherosclerosis?

involving more than 20 000 physicians, those who took an aspirin every other day had 44 percent fewer heart attacks over a five-year period than those who didn't.

Going Further

Obtain a model of a heart. Have students locate the coronary blood vessels. Ask them to trace a drop of blood through this system. Make sure that they can visualize where the coronary arteries connect to major vessels (aorta) and where coronary veins return (vena cava). Have them explain what a heart attack actually is and how it relates to the coronary system. L1

CHAPTER 21

Health Connection

Purpose
Students are exposed to some of the problems that can affect the circulatory system. They are made aware of the importance of changing certain habits while young in order to prevent heart problems later in life.

Background
The coronary circulation vessels, blood vessels that supply heart muscle with its needed nutrients and oxygen, are the vessels most prone to atherosclerosis. This may be because of the fact that these vessels are initially rather narrow. Thus, any further narrowing from plaque buildup makes them easy candidates for causing heart damage.

Teaching Strategies
- Have students work in cooperative groups to research the role and anatomy of the heart's coronary circulation. COOP LEARN
- Ask students to prepare lists of foods that are high and low in cholesterol. Have them plan a meal that is low in cholesterol.
- Have students list some of the foods that they have eaten in the past few days. Provide them with a food chart so they can calculate the cholesterol value for these foods.

Possible Answers
1. Some people inherit a tendency for heart disease. However, members of the same ethnic origin living in different countries, such as Japanese living in Japan and Japanese living in the United States, show very different rates of heart disease, suggesting the influence of diet and lifestyle. Men are more likely to develop heart disease than women; however, a woman's risk of heart disease goes up after menopause. Age is a factor for everyone; the older you are, the more likely you are to develop heart disease.
2. Aspirin keeps platelets from sticking together and forming blood clots. Blood clots cause about 70 percent of heart attacks. In a study

CHAPTER REVIEW

Summary

Summary statements can be used by students to review the major concepts of the chapter.

Language of Biology

Answers should go beyond defining the terms. Accept any reasonable answer that uses the term correctly and in the proper context.

Understanding Concepts

1. Water enters root hairs and passes across the cortex and endodermis by osmosis, and then moves into the xylem. The water moves upward in xylem through the stem and into the leaves. Upward transport of water results from the pull due to transpiration. Cohesion of water molecules and their adhesion to the inner walls of xylem vessels help this movement.

2. The glucose would be converted to sucrose, which would move into sieve tubes within the veins of the leaf. Water moves into the sieve tubes by osmosis, resulting in greater pressure in the leaf sieve cells than in sieve cells higher up. The difference in pressure forces the sucrose upward to the bud.

3. In an animal, the single transport fluid carries many different substances, and the fluid circulates from heart to tissues and back. In a plant, there are separate pipelines containing different fluids that do not circulate.

4. Xylem cells have thicker cell walls and appear hollow. Phloem cells are filled with cytoplasm.

5. Because there are two distinct and fully separated ventricles, oxygen-rich blood leaving the heart to go to the body does not mix with oxygen-poor blood in the right ventricle, which is destined for the lungs. Although blood pressure decreases as blood moves through lung capillaries, blood is repressurized by contraction of the left ventricle.

Summary

Cells take needed materials from and release wastes into their external environment. Unicellular organisms and cells of many simple multicellular organisms can directly exchange materials with their external environment. However, more complex organisms cannot do so. They have transport systems in which internal fluids carry materials to and from their cells, and which link them to the external environment.

In vascular plants, water and dissolved minerals are pulled upward in xylem vessels as a result of transpiration. Due to pressure differences, organic molecules made by these plants move either up or down within phloem sieve cells.

In animals that have a transport system, blood circulates around the body, returning to the heart, which has a pumping action that keeps the blood moving. Circulatory systems may be open or closed.

Humans have a four-chambered heart that rapidly moves fully oxygenated blood to body cells. Besides gas transport, the blood cells also function in clotting and defense against infectious disease. Different blood types are due to presence or absence of antigens on red blood cell membranes.

Language of Biology

Write a sentence that shows your understanding of each of the following terms.

antibody	red blood cell
antigen	root hair
aorta	sieve tube
artery	sinoatrial (S-A) node
atrioventricular (A-V) node	stoma
atrium	transpiration
capillary	vein
guard cell	ventricle
lymph node	vessel
phloem	white blood cell
platelet	xylem

Understanding Concepts

1. Trace the path of water from soil to the leaves of a vascular plant. Explain how that water moves into and up through the plant.
2. Trace the movement of glucose produced in a leaf to a bud on a higher branch and explain how the sugar is transported.
3. In general, how is the transport system of an animal different from that of a vascular plant?
4. Suppose you were viewing a cross section of vascular tissue from a root, stem, or leaf. How would you distinguish between xylem and phloem?

608 CHAPTER 21 TRANSPORT

---

6. Atria send blood only to the ventricles. Ventricles must send blood to the lungs or the body.

7. Blood pressure forces some of the liquid part of blood from capillaries. The tissue fluid serves as an exchange medium with them.

8. Both platelets and injured tissue release chemicals that cause production of an insoluble protein, fibrin, which forms a clot.

Applying Concepts

9. If there were a hole between the atria or ventricles, some blood that should be sent to the lungs would instead be sent to the body. That blood would not contain a quantity of oxygen sufficient to meet the body's energy demands.

10. Type O blood, because the red cells contain no antigens.

11. On a dry day, water passes more quickly to the dry air outside. The size of the stoma would be reduced to conserve water. Less water would be lost on a humid day, so the stomatal aperture would be larger.

5. Identify the two adaptations in the circulatory system of humans that enable fully oxygenated blood to be quickly delivered to body cells.
6. Why are the walls of atria much thinner than those of ventricles?
7. Explain the origin and importance of tissue fluid.
8. How is your blood adapted to preventing blood loss and infection after the vessels are damaged?

Applying Concepts

9. Describe and explain the effects of a birth defect in which the infant had a hole between either the left and right atria or the left and right ventricles.
10. What blood type could be given safely to a person in an emergency? Explain.
11. Compare and explain the size of a stoma on a humid day and a dry day.
12. Can you suggest a reason why a soldier standing at attention for a long period of time might faint?
13. A roundworm, *Filaria*, is a parasite that lives in lymph vessels. Suppose many of these worms were in the lymph vessels of a person's leg. Describe and explain how the leg would be affected.
14. Oxyhemoglobin releases more oxygen at higher temperatures than at lower ones. How is that property important to muscle tissue?
15. Describe and explain the probable location of stomata on a floating lily pad.
16. An artificial blood that carries oxygen has been developed. Explain why this could not replace normal blood.
17. **Biotechnology:** How can a laser be used to view tissues and also to cut tissues?
18. **Health Connection:** How is plaque in an artery different from plaque on your teeth?

Lab Interpretation

19. **Investigation:** You go for a checkup by your doctor, who tells you that your blood pressure has gone up. What are some possible causes of this increase?

20. **Thinking Lab:** The following are Harvard step test measurements of adults from various countries. Which countries might have adults with a diet low in red meat? Explain.

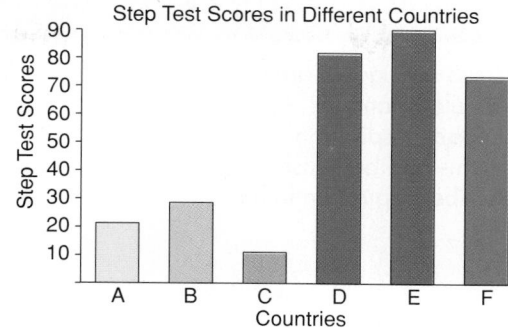

Step Test Scores in Different Countries

21. **Minilab 2:** Examine the abnormal EKG shown here. What part of the heart might be affected? Explain.

Connecting Ideas

22. In a human fetus, most blood passes directly from the right atrium to the left atrium, and some blood passes through a duct from the pulmonary artery to the aorta. As a result, only a small amount of blood passes to the lungs. Explain the reason for this circulatory pattern.
23. Trace the pathway of blood in a human from the heart to the small intestine and back again. What materials are exchanged along the way and where does the exchange occur?

lungs is already oxygenated and is adequate to serve the needs of the lungs during development.
23. **Systems and Interactions:** Left ventricle—aorta—intestine—villi. Nutrients pass into the capillaries, which merge to form veins that lead to the liver. Excess glucose and amino acids are removed at the liver. The blood returns to the heart via the inferior vena cava and is pumped throughout the body, where nutrients enter body cells.

PROGRAM RESOURCES

Teacher Classroom Resources
Chapter Assessment, pp. 81-84 L1
Performance Assessment in Biology, p. 42 L2
Alternate Assessment in the Science Classroom
Computer Test Bank L1

12. Lack of movement hinders return of blood upward to the heart. As blood collects in the legs, less blood is available to be sent to the brain. Thus, less oxygen is delivered to the brain and fainting might result.
13. Lymph vessels return tissue fluid to the bloodstream. Blockage of the lymph vessels would prevent that return, and tissue fluid would accumulate in the affected area, resulting in swelling.
14. Actively working muscles generate heat. The heat would facilitate passage of oxygen, needed for cellular respiration.
15. The stomata would be located in the upper epidermis layer to allow movement of gases to the air outside.
16. Oxygen transport is not the only function of blood.
17. At low intensity, lasers provide light to view tissues. At higher power, lasers have enough energy to be used as a "radiant scalpel."
18. Plaque in an artery is an accumulation of fats within artery walls. Plaque on teeth is the buildup of dead bacteria following their breakdown of sugars on the surface enamel.

Lab Interpretation

19. Increased stress in relationships, a high salt diet, disease, or a lack of exercise
20. Countries A, B, and C. Step results are poor when hemoglobin in the blood is low. Diets without red meat might be low in iron unless effort is made to include other foods high in iron.
21. P-Q, representing the atria, is abnormal.

Connecting Ideas

22. **Patterns of Change:** A fetus receives its oxygen from the mother via the placenta. Passage of fetal blood from right atrium to right ventricle and from pulmonary artery to aorta bypasses the lungs, which are not functioning in gas exchange in the fetus. The blood that does reach the

SECTION	OBJECTIVES	TEXT LABS/FEATURES
22.1 Gas Exchange (2 days)	**Discuss** how gases are exchanged in vascular plants. **Compare** respiration in segmented worms and bony fish. **Describe** respiration in humans.	**Minilab 1:** Will water temperature influence the breathing rate of a goldfish? p. 615 **Investigation:** Carbon Dioxide Levels, p. 616 **Leisure Connection:** Scuba Diving: Exploring Below the Surface, p. 619 **Global Connection:** How high can we live? p. 621 **Minilab 2:** How much air do you inhale in one minute? p. 622
22.2 Excretion and Maintenance of Osmotic Balance (3 days)	**Discuss** why many organisms must have adaptations for maintaining osmotic balance. **Describe** maintenance of osmotic balance and the process of excretion in simple freshwater organisms. **Discuss** the function of excretion and maintenance of osmotic balance in animals having circulatory systems.	**Thinking Lab:** What may cause "fish kills" in the summer? p. 624
BIOLOGY, TECHNOLOGY, AND SOCIETY		**Health Connection:** Let's Clear the Air, p. 633 **Career Connection:** Respiratory therapist, p. 633 **Biotechnology:** A Treatment for Respiratory Distress Syndrome, p. 634 **Issues:** Asbestos Hazard, p. 635

LAB MATERIALS

INVESTIGATION	MINILAB	ALTERNATE LAB
page 616 bromthymol solution flasks, 250-mL or 500-mL glass tubing, bent (or plastic straws) graduated cylinder hole stoppers paper, white	**page 615** beaker, 250-mL or 500-mL fish net goldfish ice plastic cups thermometer watch or clock **page 622** watch or timer calculator	**page 620** basin marking pen measuring cup soda bottle, 2-L straw, flexible

TEACHER CLASSROOM RESOURCES	OTHER RESOURCES
Study Guide, pp. 127-129 **Concept Mapping,** p. 22 ***PLL:** *Effect of Temperature Changes on Breathing Rate of Fish,* p. 149 ***PLL:** *Effect of Exercise on Carbon Dioxide Release in the Human Body,* p. 151 ****ILS:** *Gas Exchange in Microorganisms,* p. 229 ****ILS:** *Comparing Dormant and Germinating Seeds,* p. 233 ****ILS:** *Lung Capacity,* p. 237	***STVS:** *Children and Smog,* Human Biology (Disc 7, Side 2) **Color Transparency 40:** *The Respiratory System* **Color Transparency 47:** *Crustacean Body Systems* **Color Transparency 49:** *Fish Body Systems* **Color Transparency 50:** *Frog Body Systems* **Color Transparency 52:** *Human Body Systems*
Study Guide, pp. 130-132 **Critical Thinking/Problem Solving:** *Human Excretion,* p. 22 ****ILS:** *Urinalysis,* p. 241 **Exploring Environmental Issues:** *The Air We Breathe,* p. 5	**Color Transparency 41:** *The Urinary System* **Color Transparency 47:** *Crustacean Body Systems* **Color Transparency 49:** *Fish Body Systems* **Color Transparency 50:** *Frog Body Systems* **Color Transparency 52:** *Human Body Systems*
Assessment Materials **Chapter Assessment,** pp. 85-88 **Performance Assessment in Biology,** p. 44 **Alternate Assessment in the Science Classroom** **Computer Test Bank**	**Spanish Resources** **Cooperative Learning Resource Guide** **Videodisc Correlations** (to Optical Data's and Videodiscovery's videodiscs)

* **Probing Levels of Life**
** **Investigating Living Systems**

* **Science Technology Videodisc Series**

Key to Teaching Strategies

The following designations will help you decide which activities in the teacher margin are appropriate for your students.

L1 Level 1 activities should be within the ability range of all students.

L2 Level 2 activities should be within the ability range of the average to above-average student.

L3 Level 3 activities are designed for the ability range of above-average students.

LEP LEP activities are appropriate for Limited English Proficiency students.

COOP LEARN Cooperative Learning activities are designed for small group work.

ADDITIONAL RESOURCES

Infinite Voyage *Crisis in the Atmosphere*
The atmosphere protects Earth from harmful sunlight and traps energy to keep us warm, but air pollution is destroying it. Students will learn what air pollution is and how to stop it.

Software
Excretion, Apple II/TRS-80/Model III, J and S.
Respiration, Apple II, Learning Arts.

22

GAS EXCHANGE AND EXCRETION

Chapter Overview

Students begin the chapter by comparing the basic ideas of gas exchange in simple and complex organisms and by examining the special problems the latter organisms face. They learn that while gas exchange occurs at many points in plants and no transport of those gases is needed, most complex animals have localized exchange areas, and gases must be transported between those areas and body cells. Students compare respiratory systems of segmented worms, bony fish, insects, and humans and learn the different ways that each of those animals is adapted to solve the problems of gas exchange.

Next, students come to understand the source of nitrogenous wastes, why those wastes must be excreted, and how osmotic balance is maintained. As they compare these functions in a paramecium and a variety of animals, they realize that the means of carrying out the functions is related to the environment in which these organisms live. They also come to appreciate why excretion and maintenance of osmotic balance are carried out together in animals having circulatory systems.

GAS EXCHANGE AND EXCRETION

ARE THESE FISH puzzled by the odd equipment this diver is wearing? It's not likely, because they have probably never seen a human without it. What is the purpose of all that equipment? If the diver could talk with that thing in his mouth, he would explain that the mouthpiece is the part of the scuba equipment that controls the volume of air leaving the air tanks and entering the lungs. The deeper the diver goes, the greater the water pressure will be and the more air the lungs will require. Increased air pressure in the lungs helps equalize the pressure inside and outside the body.

Why don't fish release bubbles under water the way a human diver does? Don't they both have to breathe? Of course they do. But the fish is adapted to take oxygen from the water and return carbon dioxide to the water. Humans are adapted to take oxygen from the air and return carbon dioxide to the air. A human diver, therefore, has to carry air along in tanks in order to breathe under water, and the water bubbles as the diver exhales carbon dioxide from his lungs. The only way a fish could survive away from its underwater home would be to take along a water tank—one that is built in, not one that it carries on its back. Before you finish this chapter, you will understand why fish and people breathe differently. You will also see how organisms are adapted to getting rid of bodily wastes and maintaining osmotic balance in different environments.

610

KEY TERMS

alveolus	nephridium
Bowman's capsule	nephron
	respiration
bronchus	trachea
diaphragm	tracheole
excretion	ureter
gill	urethra
glomerulus	urinary bladder
kidney	
lung	urine
Malpighian tubule	vasopressin

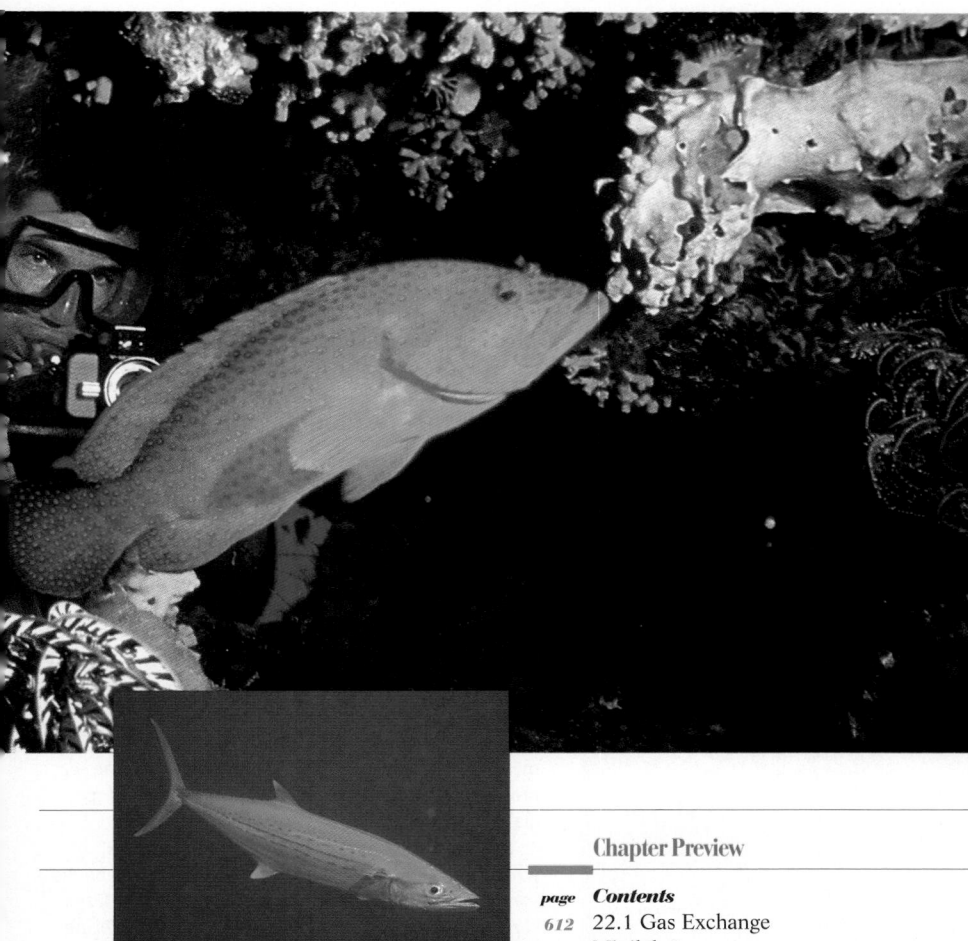

Mackerel live in the Atlantic Ocean. They swim with their mouths open. This forces water to flow into their mouths and out the gills. What would happen if the mackerel in the photo were placed in an aquarium with limited space? Why?

Chapter Preview

611

Introducing the Chapter

The photographs on pages 610 and 611 can be used to introduce the idea that an animal's respiratory system is related to the environment in which it lives. Lead students to understand that oxygen is either dissolved in water or is part of the mixture they know as air. Both the human and the fish must draw the source of oxygen (air or water) into its body and then transport the oxygen to all body cells. Ask students whether all animals face the same task. When they agree that they do, ask them to name examples of other animals that have a respiratory system similar to that of the fish and of the human. Can they name some animals that do not respire by either of those methods? What about simple organisms such as bacteria or protozoa? Finally, turn their attention to plants. Do plants take in oxygen and give off carbon dioxide? If so, where do those gases enter and leave the plant? Do plants also take in carbon dioxide and expel oxygen?

Theme Development

Systems and interactions is an obvious theme in the study of both gas exchange and excretion. Students will see the interdependence of the many parts of both systems as well as how both systems may interact with others. The theme of unity and diversity will be recognized as students come to understand that organisms must solve common problems of gas exchange and excretion but do so in a variety of ways.

Tying to Previous Knowledge

Students will make use of their recently gained knowledge of transport systems as they learn about the role of those systems in carrying gases and wastes in many animals. They will also make use of and strengthen their understanding of concepts such as diffusion, osmosis, and active transport as they learn about gas exchange, excretion, and maintenance of osmotic balance.

ASSESSMENT PLANNER

Choose assessment strategies from the following pages to evaluate the progress of your students.

Assess, pp. 622, 631-632
Portfolio, pp. 613, 617, 621, 622, 624, 625, 632
Alternate Lab, pp. 620-621
Thinking Lab, p. 624

Minilab 1, p. 615
Minilab 2, p. 621
Investigation, pp. 616-617
Chapter Review, pp. 636-637

Prepare

Key Concepts

Students will learn similarities and differences in the gas exchange processes of plants, earthworms, insects, fish, and humans.

Key Terms

respiration, gill, trachea, tracheole, lung, bronchus, alveolus, diaphragm

Materials

- Gather beakers, water, goldfish, and thermometers for the Minilab.
- Gather lab equipment and bromothymol blue solution for the Investigation.
- Gather basins, soda bottles, measuring cups, soda straws, and water for the Alternate Lab.
- Gather plant stems and leaves, and prepared slides of leaves and mammalian lung tissue for microscope activities.
- Gather pond weed, bean seeds, salamander, and aquarium for demonstrations and display.

1 Focus

Objectives

The objectives are listed on the student page. Remind students to preview these objectives as a guide to this numbered section.

Discussion

Review the chemical reactions that enable living organisms to obtain energy from the environment. Write on the chalkboard the reactions for photosynthesis ($CO_2 + H_2O$ + light = glucose + O_2) and cellular respiration (glucose + O_2 = $CO_2 + H_2O$ + energy). Highlight the gases O_2 and CO_2 by underlining or using colored chalk.

Objectives

Discuss how gases are exchanged in vascular plants.

Compare respiration in segmented worms and bony fish.

Describe respiration in humans.

22.1 Gas Exchange

Almost every organism on Earth lives in close relationship with two gases—carbon dioxide and oxygen. Most autotrophs take carbon dioxide from their environment and use it as one of the raw materials for photosynthesis. They release oxygen as a by-product of photosynthesis. In addition, nearly all autotrophs and all heterotrophs require oxygen for cellular respiration. As they carry out the respiration process, organisms take in oxygen from their physical surroundings and return carbon dioxide in a continuous process. This general back-and-forth movement of carbon dioxide and oxygen between organisms and their environment is known as gas exchange. All organisms, from the simplest to the most complex, meet certain requirements in order to accommodate gas exchange.

Simple Organisms vs. Complex Organisms

In order for a gas to pass into or out of a cell, it must be dissolved in a liquid. Think for a moment about where unicellular and simpler multicellular organisms are found. They live either in water, in damp areas on land, or within the moist environment of a host. Every cell among these organisms lives in direct or close contact with a damp environment. Each cell exchanges gases directly with the liquid that surrounds it.

Among larger organisms, gas exchange cannot occur as readily as among simple life forms. Many do not live in watery environments. And even if they do, most organisms' bodies are too thick for each cell to exchange gases directly with the external environment. To accommodate gas exchange among the more complex forms of life, certain body areas specialized in gas exchange have evolved.

Body tissues in gas exchange areas are moist, which takes care of the requirement that gases be dissolved in liquid. Gas exchange areas also have large surfaces to ensure that the volume of gases entering and leaving the organism is sufficient to meet its

Figure 22-1 **Among organisms, there is a wide variety of structures designed for gas exchange. Most land organisms such as humans have protected internal respiratory structures. Small aquatic organisms exchange gases directly with their environment.**

612 🔷 GAS EXCHANGE AND EXCRETION

MEETING INDIVIDUAL NEEDS

Help students visualize how O_2 and CO_2 move in and out of plants with a simple chalkboard diagram. Draw a shape labeled "plant." Using chemical symbols and arrows, show CO_2 entering and O_2 exiting the plant. Label these arrows "photosynthesis." Show O_2 entering and CO_2 exiting the plant, and label these arrows

"respiration." Point out that photosynthesis takes place only when light is available, while respiration takes place all the time.

LEP

needs. Tissue membranes that make up the gas exchange surfaces are usually thin, so that gases can easily cross over. Because these tissues are so delicate, the bodies of most large, complex animals have evolved structures that shield the gas exchange area from possible injury. Finally, many complex organisms have further specialized structures that work together as a transport system. The job of the transport system is to carry the gases back and forth between the exchange area and other body cells.

Gas Exchange in Plants

Most plants could be considered large organisms, especially some vascular plants like trees. Yet plants do not have a specialized gas transport system. There is no need for one. Gas exchange occurs at many different places within plant structures.

Photosynthesis may be the first process in which gas exchange occurs that you think about when it comes to plants. Leaves of plants do take in carbon dioxide and give off oxygen during photosynthesis. But leaves, and other parts of plants, also do the reverse. They take in oxygen and give off carbon dioxide during cellular respiration. As in all organisms, cellular respiration occurs in plants at all times, in sunlight and in darkness. Photosynthesis, on the other hand, occurs only in sunlight.

Gas Exchange in Roots   Plant roots extract some mineral nutrients from water by active transport. Roots get the energy they need for active transport and for other processes from cellular respiration. The oxygen needed for cellular respiration is in the air spaces between soil particles. This oxygen dissolves in the moisture of the soil and then diffuses into the root hairs. Further diffusion distributes the oxygen to other root cells, such as the cortex. As cellular respiration occurs within the root cells, carbon dioxide is produced. The carbon dioxide diffuses from the root cells to the root hairs and then to the soil.

Figure 22-2   Plants obtain oxygen from water they absorb through their roots. Root hairs increase the surface area of the root system, facilitating gas exchange.

22.1 GAS EXCHANGE **613**

SECTION 22.1

2 Teach

Demonstration

Demonstrate how a gas can be dissolved in a liquid by pouring water back and forth several times between two beakers. Viewing the beaker against a bright background, students can easily observe the tiny bubbles of air that have been incorporated into the water. The bubbles are evidence that the gases dissolved in the water are coming out. Point out that there is more air dissolved in water that has just spilled over a waterfall than in the still water of a stagnant pool.
LEP

Reinforcement

Prove that soil contains air. Let a beaker of water stand undisturbed until bubbles of air can no longer be seen in it. Gently place a scoop of soil in the bottom of the beaker. Students will observe air bubbling out of the soil. **LEP**

PHYSICS CONNECTION

Behavior of Gases: Gases move into any available space, even the tiny openings of lenticels or stomata. This behavior is explained in part by the Kinetic Theory of Gases, which states that the molecules of a gas are in constant, random motion. Molecules of solids and liquids do not have the same freedom of motion.

PORTFOLIO

Have students draw and describe each classroom demonstration, microscope activity, and lab activity they perform during study of this section of the text for their use in reviewing the information. Let students select their best work for inclusion in their portfolios. **L1**

PROGRAM RESOURCES

Teacher Classroom Resources
Study Guide, pp. 127-129 **L1**
Concept Mapping, p. 22 **L1** **LEP**

Demonstration

- Sprout bean or sunflower seeds in a clear glass beaker stuffed with damp paper toweling. Place seeds between the toweling and the glass so students can observe the roots as they grow. When fine root hairs are well developed, remove the sprouts and have students examine them under low-power magnification. **L1**

- To demonstrate the release of oxygen during photosynthesis, place some pond weed or an aquarium plant in a basin of water. Fill a clear, widemouth jar with water and invert it over the plant in the basin. To make sure there are no pockets of air in the jar, assemble the materials in a sink, under water. Place the assembly in a sunny window. Oxygen bubbles will rise from the leaves to the top of the water in the inverted jar, gradually creating a pocket of gas. **LEP**

Microscope Activity

- Have students use low-power magnification to locate and examine lenticels on a variety of woody plant stems. Lenticels may appear as elongated, circular, or raised areas on the stem. Students can also observe stomata in leaves viewed at low power against a bright background. The stomata will appear as tiny bright spots covering the leaf surface. **L1**

- Have students examine prepared slides of leaf cross sections under the microscope. Ask students to draw and label each cell layer and indicate the movement of oxygen and carbon dioxide through them, making sure they differentiate between photosynthesis and respiration. **L1**

Figure Caption Question

How do you think the worm benefits from having these specialized structures for gas exchange? These structures provide an increased surface area for more efficient gas exchange.

Gas Exchange in Stems Most of a tree's stem, which we usually call the trunk, consists of dead xylem cells. That's what wood is. But some cells, namely those in the bark region, are alive and so need oxygen for respiration. Although a tough barricade made up of dead cells and a waxy substance surrounds the stem to protect it and prevent evaporation, oxygen can still get in through tiny openings called lenticels. After entering the stem via these lenticels, oxygen travels by diffusion through tiny air spaces and then diffuses across the moist membranes of nearby cells. Carbon dioxide travels and finally exits in the opposite direction.

Gas Exchange in Leaves In the discussion of photosynthesis in Chapter 21, you read how carbon dioxide and oxygen enter and exit a leaf through stomata. The actual exchange of gases takes place in the cells of the palisade and spongy layers, headquarters for photosynthesis. A thin film of moisture surrounding the palisade and mesophyll cells dissolves the gases so they can pass in and out of the cell.

Palisade and spongy cell layers are also responsible for a lot of the leaf's cellular respiration, which occurs at the same time that photosynthesis occurs. The cells can use oxygen produced by photosynthesis for cellular respiration, and carbon dioxide released during cellular respiration for photosynthesis. Some of the oxygen produced by photosynthesis is used in cell respiration. Additional oxygen enters the leaf through stomata; carbon dioxide departs through the same openings.

Figure 22-3 Gases can be exchanged in a plant stem through tiny openings called lenticels. Plants also exchange gases through the cells of the palisade layer and spongy layer of the leaf. The stomata also allow gases to be exchanged in a leaf.

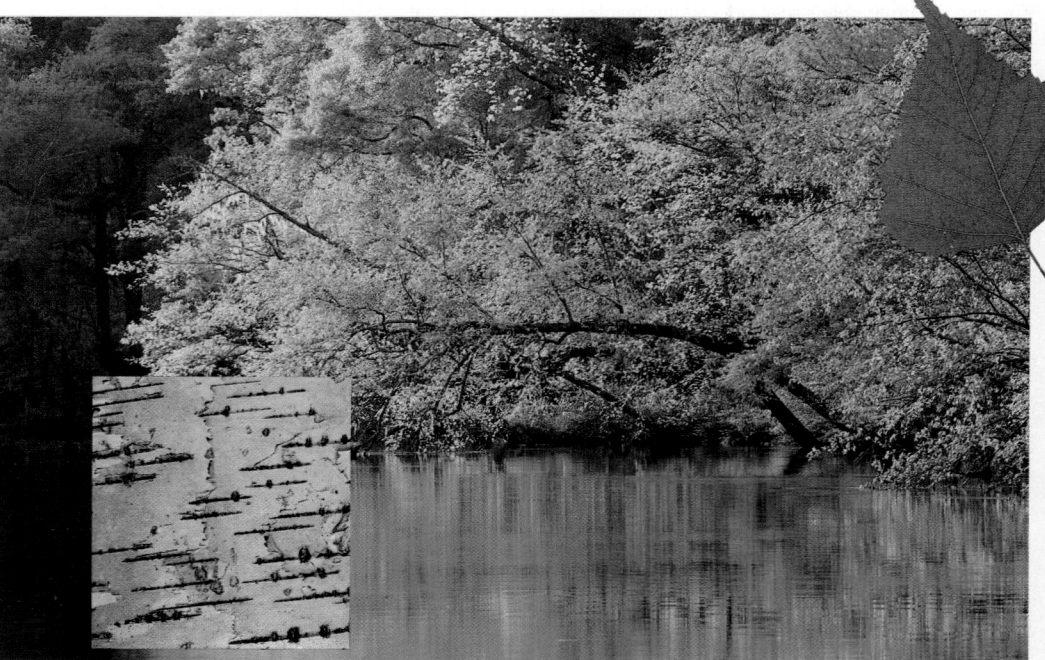

614 ♠ GAS EXCHANGE AND EXCRETION

PROJECT

Animal Respiratory Systems: Have students, individually or in pairs, research the respiratory system of a specific animal. Ask them to create a written report or poster display, with illustrations, that describes how the animal obtains oxygen from the environment, how oxygen reaches the body cells, and how carbon dioxide is released. Ask students to speculate about how the animal's respiratory system is adapted for its environment and behavior. **L1** **COOP LEARN**

Animal Respiratory Systems

Cellular respiration is vital for animals just as it is for plants. In contrast to plants, however, complex animals require a transport system to move around the gases involved in cellular respiration. Complex animals have evolved complete respiratory systems with the sole purpose of acquiring oxygen from the external environment, distributing it throughout the body, and discharging carbon dioxide. The work of animal respiratory systems is simply referred to as **respiration.**

A gas exchange area, where specialized cells exchange gases with the external environment, is part of an animal's total respiratory system. Commonly, but not always, blood is the transport vehicle. Certain blood cells, traveling the routes of the blood vessels, carry oxygen to all body cells. Oxygen diffuses into the cells; carbon dioxide diffuses out of the cells. The carbon dioxide is carried back to the exchange area and then is released into the external environment. Because of the requirement that the exchange area be moist, the type of respiratory system an animal has is related to the environment in which it lives. Animals that live in watery environments are adapted to obtain oxygen from water. Those that live in dry air environments are adapted to obtain oxygen from the atmosphere.

Respiration in Segmented Worms

The earthworm lives in moist soil. In this damp environment, it might seem appropriate that the earthworm's gas exchange area be located somewhere close to its outer surfaces. And such is the case. The entire skin area of the earthworm, in fact, is its gas exchange area. Thus, the earthworm's respiratory solution meets the requirement that the exchange area be large as well as moist.

Mucus secreted by the worm, as well as water in the soil, maintains a film of moisture all over the earthworm's skin. Oxygen from water in the soil dissolves in the film, diffuses across the thin skin, and enters capillaries. The blood transports the oxygen to all body cells, exchanges it for carbon dioxide, and transports the carbon dioxide to the skin. From the skin, the carbon dioxide diffuses into the soil.

Figure 22-4   Some species of segmented worms, such as this marine fireworm, have parapodia—thin, paddle-like, bristled extensions of the body where gas exchange occurs. How do you think the worm benefits from having these specialized structures for gas exchange?

22.1 GAS EXCHANGE **615**

Minilab 1

Will water temperature influence the breathing rate of a goldfish?

Add 250 mL of water to a beaker. Add either warm or cold water until a temperature of 20°C is reached. Place a goldfish in the water. **CAUTION:** *Use care when handling live animals.* Wait five minutes, then count the number of times in one minute that the fish opens its gill covers. Repeat for four more trials. Adjust the water temperature to 15°C. Repeat steps above. Adjust the water temperature to 10°C. Repeat steps again. For each trial, calculate the average number of gill cover openings per minute. Plot your data on a graph.

Analysis   *Offer a possible explanation for your observations. See the Thinking Lab in this chapter if you need help.*

Minilab 1

Purpose

Students will correlate water temperature with respiration rate in goldfish. They will experimentally determine that fish-breathing rate will decrease with a decrease in water temperature.

Skills

observe and infer, interpret data, recognize cause and effect

Teaching Strategies

- Students will need the following materials: glass or plastic beaker—250- or 500-mL capacity, goldfish, thermometer, watch or room wall clock, ice cubes or cold water, warm water, small plastic cups for warm water and ice cubes, fishnet.
- You may wish to have students count mouth openings rather than gill openings as a measure of respiration rate. Mouth and gill opening are directly related.
- It is important that students take five trials at each temperature and average each temperatures' trials.
- **Safety Precautions:** Advise students against "shaking down" of thermometers.
- Remind students to handle the goldfish with care.

Expected Results

Sample data:

Water Temperature °C	Average Gill Openings
20°	67
15°	60
10°	48

Answers

- The amount of available oxygen in water increases as water temperature decreases. Thus, the fish may have to breathe less often in colder water because they are getting more oxygen into their blood than they would in warmer water.

✔ Assessment

Knowledge: Students are to enter their data into their journals along with their graphs. Check to see that student graph axes are correctly marked and that suitable intervals are used on the graph.

INVESTIGATION

Carbon Dioxide Levels

Time Allotment
1 class period

Objectives
Upon completing this investigation, students will be able to:
- Design their own investigation.
- Use the scientific method to test their hypothesis.
- Determine the chemical difference for carbon dioxide between inhaled and exhaled air.

Skills
form a hypothesis, design an experiment, separate and control variables, interpret data

Materials
flasks—250 or 500 mL, four per group (or substitute jars), two-hole stoppers to fit flasks (3), bent glass tubing as shown in diagram (or substitute plastic tubing or straws), bromothymol blue solution—1000 mL per group, graduated cylinder, white paper sheets

Preparation
See page 27T to prepare bromothymol blue solution. Assemble all glass tubing and stoppers in advance. Use of straws rather than glass tubing will eliminate much of the safety hazard associated with glass tubing.

Possible Hypotheses
- If exhaled air and inhaled air contain the same amount of carbon dioxide, then exhaling and inhaling into the blue liquid should show the same color after completion of the experiment.
- If inhaled air contains less carbon dioxide than exhaled air, then the color of the liquid in inhaled air should show less of a change than liquid in the exhaled air.

Possible Procedures
Students' approaches may vary. However, the following is the most probable approach by student groups.
- Exhaled air: students should add 150 mL of bromothymol blue solution (BTB) to two flasks.

Respiration in Bony Fish

Like earthworms, aquatic animals such as mollusks, certain aquatic arthropods, echinoderms, and fish spend their lives surrounded by liquid. Aquatic animals, too, have gas exchange areas located near body surfaces. Their exchange areas, however, are not spread over their entire outer body surfaces. Instead, their exchange areas are concentrated in organs called **gills.** Gills vary in appearance among different aquatic animals, but most often they have a delicate, feathery structure.

INVESTIGATION

Carbon Dioxide Levels

Is there a difference in the chemical makeup of air inhaled versus air exhaled? A more specific question might be, does inhaled air contain more, the same, or less carbon dioxide than air exhaled? To help answer this question, a chemical called bromothymol blue can be used to detect carbon dioxide. This chemical, as its name suggests, is normally blue. However, if carbon dioxide gas is added, bromothymol blue changes color progressively from blue to aqua to green to yellow as the amount of carbon dioxide increases.

The two pieces of equipment supplied by your teacher allow you to pass either your inhaled or exhaled air through the bromothymol blue solution. Any differences in the concentration of carbon dioxide gas in inhaled versus exhaled air can be observed.

Working in groups of two, form a hypothesis that could be tested.

Problem
Is there a difference in carbon dioxide concentration between inhaled and exhaled air?

Hypothesis
What is your group's hypothesis?

Safety Precautions
The chemical bromothymol blue may stain clothing.

Experimental Plan
1. Decide on a way to test your group's hypothesis. Keep the available materials provided by your teacher in mind as you plan your procedures.
2. Remember to test only one variable at a time and use suitable controls.
3. Record your procedure and list materials that you will need.

Checking the Plan
1. What controls will be used and what variables will have to be controlled?
2. What data will you collect and how will it be recorded?
3. How will you determine if there is a difference in carbon dioxide amounts between inhaled and exhaled air?

616 GAS EXCHANGE AND EXCRETION

- While a partner either counts numbers of exhalations or watches the time agreed upon, one student should continue to exhale through the long tube.
- After exhaling, students will compare flask color to that of the flask not used (control flask). Exhaled air has passed directly through the BTB solution.
- Inhaled air: prepare two flasks as shown in the introduction. The second flask is to prevent students from inhaling any of the liquid from the first flask. Fill the first flask with 150 mL of BTB.

- Fill a third flask with the same volume of BTB liquid to be used as a control.
- The same student who participated in the exhaling should now inhale for the same amount of time or same number of inhalations as in the exhaling part of the experiment. Note: Inhaling through the mouth with the tube in the mouth draws outside air into the flask and through the BTB solution.
- Compare color of this flask with control flask.

In bony fish, oxygen-rich water enters through the mouth and passes back to the throat or pharynx. From the pharynx, the water travels to the gills. As water is taken into the mouth, the bony gill cover closes. Contraction of the pharynx forces water over the gills, the gill cover opens, and water is expelled. You have probably seen the gill cover opening and closing if you have observed a bony fish in an aquarium.

Each arch of the gill has rows of feathery gill filaments. The surface area of these filaments is further increased by tiny extensions called lamellae that protrude from the filaments. The gill filaments and lamellae house

- The same amount of liquid must be used in both flasks.
- The same amount of time inhaling and exhaling or the same number of inhalations and exhalations must be maintained.
- The same student should do both parts of the experiment.
- BTB is actually a pH indicator and does not detect carbon dioxide directly. It is detecting a change in pH from neutral to acid as carbon dioxide gas is added to water. This creates a weak acid condition due to the formation of carbonic acid (carbon dioxide + water = carbonic acid). Student data will vary depending on: amount of BTB used in each flask, amount of time exhaled or inhaled into tubes, and number of inhalations or exhalations decided upon.
- Too few exhalations into the BTB or too much BTB used per flask may yield no color change in the experimental flask.

4. How many trials will your experiment need?
5. Assign roles for this investigation.

Make sure your teacher has approved your experimental plan before you proceed further.

Data and Observations
Carry out your experiment. Prepare a data chart to record your findings.

Analysis and Conclusions
1. What is the role of bromothymol blue in this experiment?
2. What type of control was used?
3. What are the variables?

4. Two terms are used to describe data, *quantitative* and *qualitative*. Quantitative refers to data presented with numbers (quantities). Qualitative data usually is presented with a general description that uses words. An example might be: thick, moderate, or thin (quality).
(a) Was your experiment qualitative or quantitative? Explain why.
(b) Suggest a way that the experiment might be changed to make the data the opposite of (a).

5. Explain how your experimental findings tend to confirm what you already know about the processes of cellular respiration and external respiration.
6. Write a conclusion to this investigation.

Going Further
Based on this lab experience, design an experiment that would help to answer another question that arose from your work. Assume that you will have limited resources and will be conducting the lab in class. Include this in your conclusion.

Data and Observations
Students should find that exhaling produces a color change from green to blue. Inhaling produces no color change.

Data Analysis
Student answers will vary.
1. BTB is a liquid that detects the presence of carbon dioxide gas.
2. The flask receiving no inhaled or exhaled air was the control.
3. Same amount of time for exhaling and inhaling, same volume of liquid in control and experimental flasks, same student performing both inhaling and exhaling.
4. (a) qualitative. No numbers were used to describe color change. Colors (words) were used.
   (b) Devise some way to measure the color change with an instrument that gives a numerical reading to the colors in each flask (or use a titration technique to return flask color back to original color).
5. Internal respiration adds carbon dioxide gas to blood. This addition is reflected in the increased

Exhaled air

Inhaled air

a

b

amount of this gas being released to the lungs and then exhaled.
6. Exhaled air contains more carbon dioxide than inhaled air. Inhaled air failed to show any color change associated with the presence of carbon dioxide gas when passed through BTB. Exhaled air did show the presence of carbon dioxide gas when passed through BTB.

✔ Assessment
Portfolio: Have students write an evaluation of the Investigation in their portfolios. They

should include all data and conclusions. They should also include notes on changes in experimental design that would have improved the Investigation.

Extensions
What is the minimum number of exhalations needed to show a color change in the experimental flask? How would different volumes of BTB influence the results? Is there a chemical that could detect and measure the amount of oxygen gas in exhaled versus inhaled air?

How do you think CO$_2$ is eliminated from the blood? CO$_2$ diffuses into the water where the concentration of CO$_2$ is less.

Different Viewpoints in Biology

Amphibian Ancestors

Lungfish have both lungs and gills. They can survive periods of drought by lying buried in mud burrows and breathing air through openings to the surface. According to the fossil record, lungfish first appeared on Earth about 80 to 100 million years before the dinosaurs. Biologists once thought lungfish were direct ancestors of amphibians. Today, most biologists think amphibians and lungfishes are two separate evolutionary lines descended from crossopterygian fishes.

Teacher FYI

It is more difficult to obtain oxygen from water than from air. Air contains about 210 mL of oxygen per liter. Water contains 3 to 9 mL of oxygen per liter, so more water must move across a gas exchange surface to extract a given amount of oxygen. Water is about 800 times more dense than air, so it also takes more energy to move water across gas exchange surfaces.

a broad network of capillaries, which provides a very large surface area for gas exchange. The gills lie very close to the heart of the fish. Blood low in oxygen leaves the heart and travels to the gill capillaries. As water passes over the gills, oxygen dissolved in the water diffuses into blood in the capillaries, and carbon dioxide diffuses from blood to the water. Oxygen-rich blood is transported from the gills to all parts of the body, where exchange of oxygen and carbon dioxide takes place.

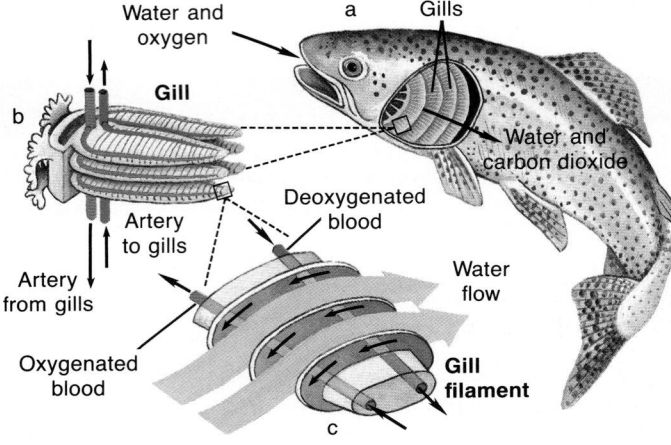

Figure 22-5 In bony fish, the gills are covered by a bony flap called an operculum. The operculum of this fish (a) is raised, exposing the gills. As water passes over the gill filaments, oxygen enters the blood in the capillaries and is circulated to the body of the fish (b,c). How do you think CO$_2$ is eliminated from the blood?

Respiration in Insects

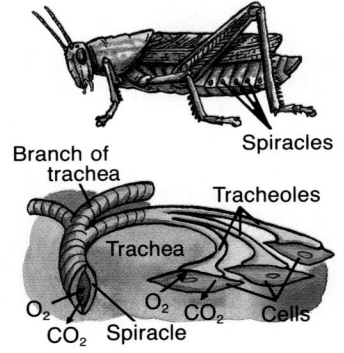

Figure 22-6 A grasshopper has a specialized respiratory system composed of spiracles and tracheae. The tracheae branch and rebranch until they end in tiny air sacs called tracheoles.

Most land animals live in an environment that exposes them to dry air. They cannot undergo gas exchange on their body surfaces because there is not enough moisture to dissolve the needed gases. Instead, dry air is drawn into moistened areas inside their bodies.

In some land arthropods (insects and their relatives), air enters the animals through small openings located along the sides of the body called **spiracles**. These external openings lead into tubes called **tracheae**. Tracheae branch and rebranch inside an animal. The smallest branches end in tiny air sacs, called **tracheoles**, that contain moisture (Figure 22-6). External openings, tracheae, and tracheoles make up the tracheal respiratory system.

In an animal with a tracheal system, oxygen in the air dissolves inside the moist tracheoles and passes directly to the cells by diffusion. Carbon dioxide from the cells diffuses to the tracheoles and is expelled through the external side openings. The system works because no cell is very far from a tracheole. The large number of tracheoles provides a large surface area for gas exchange.

Blood does not transport gases in a tracheal system. Gases travel via simple diffusion or, in large insects, via muscular contraction. The blood's main function is limited to the transport of nutrients and wastes.

STUDENT JOURNAL

Ask students to imagine being an oxygen molecule entering the body of an organism of their choice. Ask them to write a story, from the point of view of the oxygen molecule, that describes the journey. Ask them to describe the journey in three stages: how the molecule gets from the environment into the organism, what happens to the molecule inside the organism, and how the molecule is released back into the environment. **L1**

Respiration in Humans

As a human, you live on the land in a dry air environment. Does this mean that you have a tracheal respiratory system, like an insect's? No, but you do have a tube called a trachea, which conducts air from the outside into an internal gas exchange area. That gas exchange area is composed of two organs called **lungs.** Your lungs have many tiny, moist air sacs similar to those in a tracheal system. But unlike the insect's, your respiratory system relies on circulating blood to transport gases between body cells and the gas exchange area. All other mammals, as well as reptiles, birds, and most adult amphibians, have respiratory systems that have lungs and use blood to transport gases.

From Atmosphere to Air Sac   You know your body well enough to sense that your lungs are located deep inside your body structure. This is a safe place for them, considering that gas exchange surfaces are always thin and delicate. But how does oxygen reach the lungs?

LEISURE CONNECTION

Scuba Diving: Exploring Below the Surface

People have always wanted to explore places that are beyond the physical abilities of their bodies to reach. For example, the ancient Greeks seemed eager to explore both the heavens and the oceans. One myth tells of Icarus and Daedalus flying with wings of wax. The ancient philosopher Aristotle is credited with describing a crude diving bell that allowed a diver to work under water. It wasn't until this century, however, that people have been able to explore both places. Just as the Wright brothers opened up the sky with their invention of the airplane, Jacques Cousteau and Emile Gagnan opened up the oceans to exploration with their invention of scuba,

or *Self-Contained Underwater Breathing Apparatus.*

Several factors inhibit a person's ability to work under water. The most obvious is that while fish have gills to remove oxygen from water, your lungs function only on land. The second factor involves the amount of pressure exerted on your body. Your body is adapted to function at sea level. At sea level, the mass of air in the atmosphere presses on your body at a force of 14.7 psi (pounds per square inch), or 1 atmosphere. You inhale and exhale at a normal rate and without much effort. As you descend into the ocean, the mass of the water increases the pressure on your body. The pressure doubles to 2 atmospheres at a depth of 10 meters and is 3 atmospheres at a depth of 20 meters. On land, an increase in pressure like this would make it impossible for you to inhale

and inflate your lungs. Scuba equipment provides a way for you to breathe under the increased pressure. A tank of compressed air and a demand regulator make up the scuba equipment. With this equipment, air is supplied from the tank to your lungs, at the same pressure as the surrounding water, when you inhale. As you exhale, air is released through the regulator into the water. You can breathe easily as you explore the wondrous habitat of the ocean organisms.

1. **Find Out:** Why do divers have to take time to "decompress" when they go back up to the surface after a deep dive?
2. **Connection to History:** How can scuba gear be used to find out about how Spanish explorers lived in the newly discovered lands of North and South America?

SECTION 22.1

LEISURE CONNECTION

Purpose
Students learn how gas volume correlates with pressure and how an increase in air pressure affects the body.

Teaching Strategies
Point out that just as pockets of air in the body (inner ear, sinuses, digestive system) are affected by changes in air pressure, so are the gases dissolved in blood or tissue.

Possible Answers
1. When scuba divers breathe under pressure, their blood and tissues absorb gases at that pressure. When the diver surfaces, the pressure is released and the gases increase in volume. If pressure is released too quickly, bubbles may form and cause decompression sickness.
2. Underwater archaeologists can investigate Spanish shipwrecks.

Going Further
Have students devise and carry out an experiment demonstrating how the volume of a gas decreases with an increase in pressure. **L3**

Science, Technology, and Society

Developments in Treating Respiratory Illnesses:
Have groups of students research the causes, symptoms, and possible cures or preventive measures for serious respiratory diseases of concern today. Cystic fibrosis is a hereditary disease for which gene therapy looks promising. Tuberculosis is again becoming prevalent. Lung cancer continues to be linked to air pollutants like tobacco smoke and asbestos. **L2**   **COOP LEARN**

Purpose
Students will deepen their understanding of the relationship between gas pressure and volume and learn how reduced air pressure can affect the body.

Teaching Strategies
Draw two sets of lungs—one belonging to a surfer at sea level, the other to a mountain climber at 3000 meters. Using dots to represent oxygen molecules, show how the surfer takes in more oxygen per lungful of air than the climber. Use the diagrams to help students visualize that more high-altitude air has to pass over the alveoli to supply the same amount of oxygen to the blood as sea-level air. **LEP**

Possible Answers
1. Acclimate to high altitudes by climbing in increments of 500 to 1000 feet a day; rest during the first day or two at a higher altitude; drink plenty of water.
2. The air in aircraft cabins is pressurized to simulate much lower altitudes.

Going Further
Ask students why it is dangerous for vacationing scuba divers to go on a deep dive in the morning and take an airplane flight home that same afternoon. **L1**

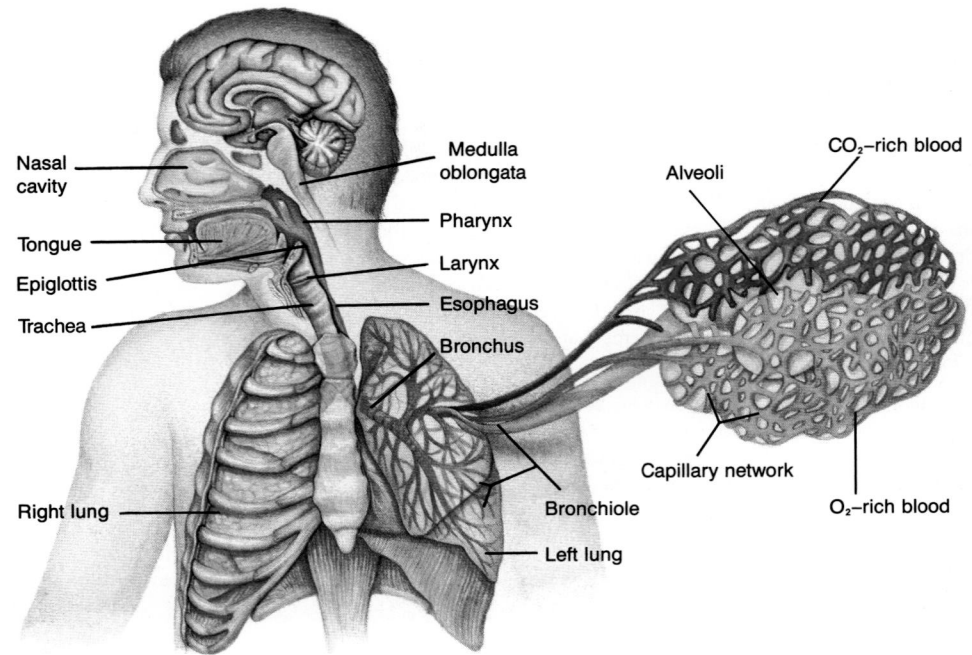

Figure 22-7 The human respiratory system consists of air passageways and the lungs. The bronchioles end in clustered air sacs called alveoli. Diffusion of oxygen and carbon dioxide into and out of the lungs occurs at the alveoli.

When you inhale, oxygen (as part of the air) enters the nose or mouth, passes to the pharynx, and then moves downward into the trachea, also called the windpipe. The opening of the trachea is protected by a structure called the epiglottis. During breathing, the trachea is open. When a person swallows food, the epiglottis closes over the top of the trachea so food goes down only the esophagus. Have you ever choked from talking while eating? Choking occurs when the epiglottis fails to close properly and food starts into the trachea.

Branching from the trachea are two large tubes called **bronchi.** The bronchi branch and rebranch into many smaller bronchial tubes that end as numerous small, moist sacs called **alveoli.** Gas exchange occurs in the alveoli. Like the tracheoles in insects and gill filaments in fish, groups of alveoli greatly increase the surface area of the lungs for gas exchange. Thus, the human body is assured an adequate supply of oxygen.

Blood as Transporter of Gases Oxygen in the bloodstream travels exclusively in the red blood cells. Red blood cells, you may remember from Chapter 21, contain hemoglobin—an iron-rich protein that can combine with and carry oxygen. Carbon dioxide, on the other hand, is not so limited in its travel arrangements. It combines with hemoglobin, with liquid in the red blood cells, and with the watery portion of blood.

Blood rich in carbon dioxide reaches the alveoli via capillaries that branch from the pulmonary arteries. In the alveoli, the level of carbon dioxide is low and the level of oxygen is high. Under these conditions, the

620 🐾 GAS EXCHANGE AND EXCRETION

ALTERNATE LAB: Lung Capacity

Purpose
Students measure their own lung capacity and calculate the class average.

Materials
basin, 2-L soda bottle, flexible straw, measuring cup, marking pen, water

Procedure
Give the following directions to students.
1. Pour 500 mL of water into the soda bottle. Mark this level "500 mL" on the bottle with the marking pen. Add water in 500-mL increments and mark the levels until the bottle contains 2 L.
2. Fill the soda bottle all the way to the top. Fill the basin 1/4 full of water. Make sure it can hold another 2 L.
3. With one hand placed tightly over the top of the soda bottle, submerge it upside down in the basin.
4. While your partner holds the bottle steady, insert the flexible end of the straw into the neck of the bottle. Inhale normally, then exhale through the straw while holding your nose.
5. Record the volume of water displaced by your exhalation. Measure three normal exhalations.

Analysis
Ask students to answer the following questions.
1. Calculate their "resting" lung capacity by averaging their three measurements.

carbon dioxide diffuses from the blood into the alveoli and is exhaled. At the same time, oxygen diffuses from the alveoli into the blood and there combines with hemoglobin to form oxyhemoglobin. The oxygen-rich blood returns via the pulmonary vein to the left side of the heart. From there, it is pumped throughout the body.

At the body tissues, cells are rich in carbon dioxide and poor in oxygen. Under these conditions, oxyhemoglobin readily breaks down into hemoglobin and oxygen, and the oxygen diffuses from the blood to the tissues. Carbon dioxide diffuses from the tissues to the blood and is carried back toward the heart and lungs.

Control of Breathing

What happens when you inhale? Air is drawn from the environment into your lungs. When you exhale, air is pushed out of your body into the environment. This movement of air is called breathing.

Breathing requires action inside the body. Taking in air (inhalation), requires the action of the rib muscles and a large flat muscle called the

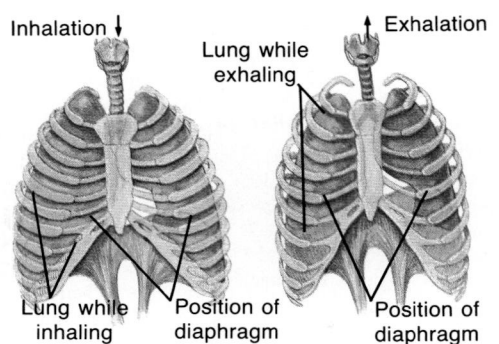

Figure 22-8 During inhalation, rib muscles contract, lifting the ribs apart, and the diaphragm flattens. This increases the size of the chest cavity, allowing air to enter the lungs. During exhalation, the rib muscles relax, the diaphragm moves up, and the size of the chest cavity decreases.

GLOBAL CONNECTION

How high can we live?

Imagine a hot summer morning in the California desert. To escape the oppressive heat, you ride the aerial tramway to the top of Mt. San Jacinto. On the way up, you watch the rugged desert landscape fall far below. At the station on top of the mountain, you see squirrels and chipmunks scampering among pine trees. The air is refreshing and you look forward to a day of hiking. However, a few hours later you begin to feel a little dizzy. You're breathing faster and you can't walk very quickly. Your symptoms are caused by the high altitude of Mt. San Jacinto, which has a summit more than 2000 meters above sea level.

High altitude sickness, or hypoxia, often strikes skiers, hot air balloonists, mountain climbers, and people who visit places like Mexico City, the Himalayas, and the Andes. Hypoxia is caused by a reduction in the amount of oxygen that enters a person's body. While the atmosphere has the same percentage of oxygen at all altitudes, the air is less dense and the air pressure is lower at higher altitudes; thus, less oxygen can move into the lungs, the blood, and the individual body cells. A person suffering from hypoxia will try to compensate for the oxygen deficiency by hyperventilating, or breathing more quickly and more deeply than normal.

People who live at high altitudes are adapted to the lower air pressure. For example, the native

Aymara and Quechua Indians that live in the Andes mountains have barrel-shaped chests, strong diaphragms, and large lungs that have a greater capacity than the lungs of people who live at lower altitudes. The Aymara and Quechua also have more capillaries around their alveoli, larger hearts, and more red blood cells. All of these adaptations help deliver oxygen to their body cells and tissues.

1. **Find Out:** How can the effects of high altitude sickness be reduced or avoided?
2. **Explore Further:** Modern jets fly at altitudes of 10 000 to 13 000 meters. Why don't passengers have difficulty breathing?

SECTION 22.1

Minilab 2

Purpose
Students will measure their breathing rate for one minute. This data will then be used to calculate the actual volume of air reaching their lungs in one minute.

Skills
observe and infer, measure in SI

Teaching Strategies
• Remind students that they are to count only the "ins" or the "outs," but not both, that take place within a minute.

Expected Results
Breathing rate for one minute = 15
Volume of air inhaled in one minute = 15 × 500 mL = 7500 mL
Volume of air in contact with alveoli for one minute = 15 × 350 mL = 5250 mL

Answers
More oxygen is present in inhaled air than in exhaled air; less carbon dioxide is present in inhaled air than in exhaled air. The concentration of oxygen and carbon dioxide will not vary with the 150 mL of air as part of the dead air space. This air does not come in contact with alveolar lung tissue and therefore does not carry on gas exchange.

✔ Assessment
Performance: Ask students to record their data in their portfolios. Provide them with some sample data and ask them to calculate volume of air inhaled per minute and volume of air reaching alveoli.

2. Compare your findings with the findings of other students. Speculate why lung capacities are similar or different. *Body size, fitness, and respiratory problems affect lung capacity.*
3. Calculate average lung capacity for the entire class. At rest, the average adult takes in about 1/2 L of air with each breath. During strenuous activity, the lungs can expand to hold more than 6 L.

4. Have students repeat the lab to measure lung capacity following exercise. Replace the 2-L bottle with a 6- to 7-L (or 2-gallon) plastic container marked off in liters or half liters. Instead of the basin, conduct the experiment in a sink partially filled with water.

✔ Assessment
Portfolio: Have students make a data sheet to record their findings to include in their portfolios. Ask them to identify the factors that could explain individual differences in lung capacity and the difference in their own lung capacity at rest and following exercise. **L1**

3 Assess

Check for Understanding

List the organisms studied in this section of the text and list structures involved in gas exchange. Have students match each organism with its gas exchange structures. **L1**

Reteach

Have pairs of students formulate one or more questions on points about gas exchange they are having trouble understanding and would like to have clarified. Have pairs join into groups of four or six students to answer each other's questions. Allow students to use the text and other classroom materials to aid them in their explanations. **LEP** **COOP LEARN**

Extension

Give pairs of students a description of the gas exchange system of an unidentified organism. Give each pair a different description and ask them to identify the type(s) of organism(s) that match it. **L2** **COOP LEARN**

✔ Assessment

Portfolio: Have students draw a diagram and write a paragraph describing how gas exchange takes place in each type of organism studied in this section of the text. Have them color code their diagrams. **L1**

4 Close

Activity

Have pairs of students play a version of "hangman" using terms from this section of the text. **COOP LEARN**

Minilab 2

How much air do you inhale in one minute?

An average adult breathes in 500 mL of air each time he or she inhales but only 350 mL reach the alveoli. The remaining 150 mL is called dead air. It fills your nasal chamber, trachea, and bronchial tree. Determine the number of times in one minute that you inhale. Calculate the total volume of air in one minute: (a) that you breathe in, and (b) that comes in contact with your alveoli.
Analysis How might the concentration of oxygen and carbon dioxide gas vary with: (a) The 350 mL of air inhaled compared to air exhaled? Why? (b) The 150 mL of dead air inhaled compared to dead air exhaled? Why?

diaphragm, which stretches across the base of the rib cage. The diaphragm and the rib muscles contract at the same time. As a result, the diaphragm muscle pulls downward and the ribs move upward and outward. At this point, the size and volume of the chest cavity have expanded. Air pressure inside the cavity is less than air pressure in the atmosphere. Air rushes into the trachea and the lungs to correct the imbalance. About 500 mL of air are brought into the lungs at a time. Now the muscles relax. The diaphragm pushes upward and rib muscles allow the rib cage to relax, thus decreasing the size of the chest cavity. Inside air pressure becomes greater than air pressure in the atmosphere, so the air rushes out. This is called exhalation.

When you think about it, you can control the action of the diaphragm and rib muscles. But you don't have to worry about remembering to breathe. Specialized nerve cells, which are scattered throughout certain arteries and concentrated in the medulla, control your breathing for you. The medulla is the part of the brain that contains the breathing control center. The nerve cells along the arteries send impulses to the medulla, keeping it informed about the levels of carbon dioxide in the blood. If the level of carbon dioxide gets too high, the medulla sends impulses of its own along nerves leading to the diaphragm and rib muscles. These nerves stimulate the muscles to contract more frequently and so increase the breathing rate. The faster a person breathes, of course, the greater the amount of carbon dioxide leaving the blood and the greater the amount of oxygen entering the blood. Too much carbon dioxide can build up acidity in the bloodstream and cause illness, even death in extreme cases. Too little oxygen inhibits the work of the cells.

When you exercise, you are asking the cells to work harder to give you the energy you need. Thus, you raise the level of carbon dioxide and lower the level of oxygen in the blood. Your breathing rate increases to adjust the rate of gas exchange to the needs of the cells. Smoking or breathing heavily polluted air can raise levels of carbon dioxide in the blood. The respiratory system may not be able to adjust to these conditions, and illnesses such as chronic coughing, persistent respiratory infections, and eventually emphysema and cancer could result.

Section Review

Understanding Concepts
1. Explain why gases need not be carried by a specialized transport system in plants.
2. How are the respiratory systems of an earthworm and a bony fish similar? Why?
3. Explain how the respiratory system of a grasshopper is adapted with respect to each of the following: maintaining a moist gas exchange area; having a gas exchange area with a large surface; protecting the gas exchange area; and transporting gases between body cells and the gas exchange area.
4. **Skill Review—Sequencing:** Trace the path of oxygen in a human from the point of air intake to body cells. For more help, refer to Organizing Information in the **Skill Handbook.**
5. **Thinking Critically:** Why is it not possible for you to hold your breath for very long?

622 ♠ GAS EXCHANGE AND EXCRETION

Answers to Section Review

1. Gases are exchanged at many points in plants—leaves, stems, and roots. Gases simply diffuse to and from individual cells in these organs.
2. Both have respiratory surfaces located on their outer body surface. Blood is needed for transport because most body cells are too far from the exchange area for diffusion to be effective.
3. Exchange area—tracheoles deep in body. Large surface area—great number of tracheoles. Protection—by exoskeleton and surrounding tissues. Transport—by diffusion, no cell is far from a tracheole.
4. **Skill Review—Sequencing:** Air enters via the nose or mouth. It passes through the pharynx and into the trachea. The air passes through the bronchi and bronchioles to the alveoli. Oxygen diffuses from alveoli into capillaries, where it combines with hemoglobin. As the blood passes, the oxygen diffuses into body cells.
5. **Thinking Critically:** Carbon dioxide level in blood becomes so high that the breathing center is stimulated to send messages to the rib muscles and diaphragm, causing them to contract.

22.2 Excretion and Maintenance of Osmotic Balance

If you light a fire using several wood logs in a fireplace, you will have ashes to clear away after the fire has died. The ashes are wastes left after the wood has burned. Your body cells also produce wastes as they metabolize nutrients. So do the body cells of all animals and protozoans. Some of these wastes are potentially toxic and must be removed. Humans and many other animals have specialized systems that clear away the unwanted wastes.

Adaptations that dispose of cellular wastes often serve double duty. That is, they may also be responsible for maintaining osmotic balance. A cell is bathed in liquids, both internally and externally. The liquids hold dissolved particles. If the liquids inside and outside a cell do not contain about the same concentration of dissolved particles, the cell is not in osmotic balance. The kinds of adaptations animals may or may not have for disposing of wastes and maintaining osmotic balance are closely related to the environments in which they live.

Aquatic Environments

The watery environment of simple organisms influences the way they remove cellular wastes as much as it affects the way they exchange carbon dioxide and oxygen in respiration. It also determines the way they maintain osmotic balance.

Excretion Metabolism of nutrients in animals and protozoans produces waste products. These waste products include carbon dioxide gas, excess water, and nitrogen wastes. Nitrogenous chemicals are released during the cellular breakdown of proteins to produce energy or to make carbohydrates or fats. The nitrogen-containing waste product is ammonia. Ammonia is a highly toxic molecule and must be either excreted directly or converted to a less toxic waste such as urea or uric acid. Figure 22-9 shows the molecules of ammonia, urea, and uric acid. The production of uric acid and urea are two important adaptations of land animals that enable them to excrete nitrogenous wastes with a minimum of water loss.

A liquid environment facilitates the removal of ammonia. Since ammonia dissolves readily, it simply diffuses from the organism into the external environment. Land animals and complex aquatic animals cannot rely on such direct methods for removal of wastes. But whatever the methods or steps required, removal of toxic nitrogenous wastes is called **excretion.**

Objectives

Discuss why many organisms must have adaptations for maintaining osmotic balance.

Describe maintenance of osmotic balance and the process of excretion in simple freshwater organisms.

Discuss the function of excretion and maintenance of osmotic balance in animals having circulatory systems.

Figure 22-9 Birds excrete uric acid as a pastelike substance that contains almost no water. How is the excretion of uric acid a beneficial adaptation to animals that live in dry environments?

22.2 EXCRETION AND MAINTENANCE OF OSMOTIC BALANCE 🐾 **623**

SECTION 22.2

Prepare

Key Concepts

Students will distinguish between the excretion of nitrogenous wastes and the maintenance of osmotic balance and learn how aquatic animals, land animals, and humans perform these functions.

Key Terms

excretion, nephridia, Malpighian tubule, nephron, Bowman's capsule, glomerulus, urine, ureter, urinary bladder, urethra, vasopressin

Materials

- Gather live protozoan cultures and prepared slides of mammalian kidney tissue for microscope activities.
- Gather copies of *The Human Anatomy Coloring Book* and *The Zoology Coloring Book* for reinforcement activities.
- Gather earthworm and grasshopper specimens for dissection.
- Provide a model of the human kidney or urinary system for classroom display.

1 Focus

Objectives

The objectives are listed on the student page. Remind students to preview these objectives as a guide to this numbered section.

Figure Caption Question

How is the excretion of uric acid a beneficial adaptation to animals that live in dry environments? Uric acid contains little or no water; therefore water is conserved.

STUDENT JOURNAL

Ask students to imagine being a nitrogen molecule in a single-celled organism captured and engulfed by an amoeba. Tell them that this molecule becomes part of an NH_2 amino group produced during the breakdown of the prey's proteins in the cell of the amoeba. Have students write a story or "travelogue" describing what happens to this molecule during and after cellular digestion of the prey. Have students write another story from the viewpoint of a nitrogen molecule consumed by an earthworm or grasshopper. Ask them to write a third story from the viewpoint of a nitrogen molecule consumed by a human. After all three journeys have been written, have students compare and contrast the events that took place inside each organism. Have students include one or more of their stories in their portfolios.

Using an Analogy

Ask students to recall the definition of *cellular metabolism.* Point out that the oxidation of chemicals within a cell is like a very slow-burning, low-temperature fire. The ash, or waste products, must be eliminated. Remind students that proteins are made up of amino acids, which include nitrogen and hydrogen atoms, and that protein breakdown within the cell produces nitrogen-containing wastes. LEP

2 Teach

Misconception

Students may not have a clear understanding of the difference between excretion of metabolic wastes and elimination of digestive wastes. Metabolic wastes are produced within the cell and often pass out of the organism's body in liquid form. Digestive wastes are indigestible food particles that never enter cells and are eliminated directly from the digestive system.

Figure 22-10 Many marine organisms, such as this scarlet reef lobster, are able to maintain osmotic balance without much trouble. To excrete nitrogenous wastes, most often in the form of ammonia, they have simple excretory organs located in the head.

Osmotic Balance and Sea Water Among simple organisms, excretion and osmotic balance are independent of each other. Life is thought to have first evolved in the sea, a saltwater environment. Both the cytoplasm of those first cells and the surrounding sea water doubtless had similar concentrations of dissolved particles, such as salts. Thus, the first organisms would have been in osmotic balance with their environment. Descendants of these early forms of life that remained in the sea continued to maintain that balance. Organisms such as today's seaweeds, sponges, and jellyfish have cells directly bathed by ocean water; their cells are in osmotic balance with that water. More complex organisms, such as lobsters or clams, have internal tissue fluids and blood that bathe their cells. The concentration of dissolved particles in the tissue fluid and blood is close to the concentration of dissolved salts in ocean water. Thus, these animals, too, are able to maintain osmotic balance without any special adaptation.

Osmotic Balance in Fresh Water During the course of evolution, many organisms moved to environments other than sea water. Consider for a moment a single-cell organism bathed by fresh water. The surrounding water has a much higher concentration of water and a much lower concentration of salts than the cytoplasm of the cell. As a result, there is a net movement of water into the cell. If there were no way to counteract this inward flow of water, the cell would eventually burst. Multicellular organisms in fresh water face this situation many times over. They can survive in such an environment only if they have adaptations that allow them to maintain osmotic balance between their cells and the surrounding fluid.

Thinking Lab
INTERPRET THE DATA

What may cause "fish kills" in the summer?

Background
In late summer, fish may die off in small lakes as water temperatures rise. Are the fish boiling? This is not likely, as the water doesn't get that hot. What else could be affecting them?

You Try It
Examine the data in the table. It shows the amount of dissolved oxygen available at different water temperatures. The amount of oxygen available to fish is in units marked ppm or "parts per million." A reading of 8 ppm means 8 parts oxygen for 1 million parts of water. The higher the ppm reading, the more oxygen there is. Prepare a graph and then **interpret the data.**

Water temperature	Amount of dissolved oxygen
30°C	7.8 ppm
20°C	9.0 ppm
10°C	10.5 ppm
0°C	14.1 ppm

Why do fish require oxygen? What happens to dissolved oxygen as water temperatures rise? When they fall? Explain why fish may die off when water temperatures rise.

624 🦐 GAS EXCHANGE AND EXCRETION

Thinking Lab
INTERPRET THE DATA

Purpose
Students will interpret the data to show that as water temperature increases, dissolved oxygen amounts decrease.

Skills
interpret data, recognize cause and effect

Teaching Strategies
• Ask students to make observations of a pot of water as it is heated. Tell them that the bubbles are actually air that is expanding and leaving the water as temperature increases.

Answers
Oxygen is required for respiration. Dissolved oxygen amounts decrease with increasing temperature and increase with decreasing temperature. Fish may die off due to the decreasing amount of dissolved oxygen available to them as water temperatures rise.

✔ **Assessment**
Portfolio: Ask students to write a conclusion and/or evaluation of this lab in their portfolios. Have them include their graphs.

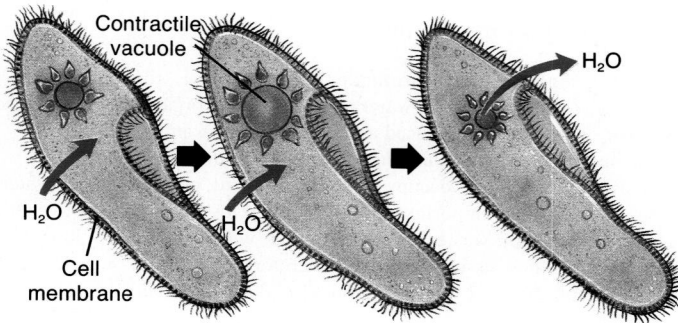

Contractile vacuole

H₂O

H₂O

Cell membrane

H₂O

Figure 22-11 **Paramecium maintain osmotic balance by means of contractile vacuoles. Water moves into these vacuoles, which expel the excess through the cell membrane into the environment. What would happen to this organism if the contractile vacuoles failed to function?**

A single-cell *Paramecium* is adapted to maintain osmotic balance in fresh water. This protozoan has contractile vacuoles (Chapter 5) that remove excess water. The net movement of water into the cell fills the canals that surround these vacuoles. When a vacuole is full, its membrane contracts, forcing the water from the vacuole and out through the cell membrane. ATP energy is needed for the contraction of the vacuole.

A planarian is a freshwater animal that has a special system to maintain osmotic balance. A planarian has no circulatory system to transport wastes and excess water to a collecting site. Instead, a system of excretory canals and flame cells is found throughout the animal. Each flame cell has several flagella, the movement of which reminded scientists of candle flames—thus the name *flame cells*. Excess water and some wastes are drawn into the flame cells, where movement of the flagella sets up a current. This current moves the water into and along the excretory canals. At certain places, the canals branch into excretory ducts that open as pores on the surface of the planarian. Water is given off through these pores.

Most of the nitrogenous wastes of a planarian do not enter the excretory canals. They pass from cells to the digestive system and are excreted through the mouth. Some wastes may diffuse directly from cells to the water.

Because their chemical reactions differ from those of protozoans and animals, plants do not build up dangerous nitrogenous wastes. Thus, they have no mechanisms for excretion. However, the fluid that bathes their cells is fresh water, and they must have a means of maintaining osmotic balance. You learned how they do this in Chapter 4. Some water enters plant cells by osmosis, but the cell wall prevents much swelling from occurring. The presence of the cell wall prevents the bursting of cells that would otherwise occur.

Figure 22-12 **Flagella in the flame cells of *Planaria* draw excess water from the body. The water collects in ducts and moves out of the body through pores.**

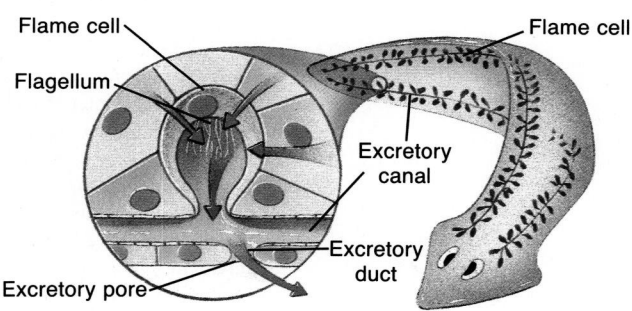

Flame cell

Flame cell

Flagellum

Excretory canal

Excretory duct

Excretory pore

Microscope Activity

Have students observe live protozoans such as Amoeba or Paramecium under a microscope. Instruct students to look for contractile vacuoles (clear regions that contract, disappear, and reappear) and the canals surrounding them. Students may also be able to locate openings where digestive wastes are ejected from the cell. Have students make labeled drawings and explain the function of the structures they observe. **L1**

Reinforcement

Have students color the plates illustrating Paramecium and Amoeba in *The Zoology Coloring Book.* **LEP**

Figure Caption Question

What would happen to this organism if the contractile vacuoles failed to function? The organism would explode.

PORTFOLIO

Invite students to include in their portfolios any or all of their drawings of the excretory structures of protozoan, earthworm, grasshopper, or human. Ask students to make sure all important structures are labeled and to use arrows to show the direction of movement of waste materials and blood, if applicable.

PROGRAM RESOURCES

Teacher Classroom Resources
Study Guide, pp. 130-132 **L1**
Critical Thinking/Problem Solving, p. 22 **L2**
Investigating Living Systems, Lab 63, p. 241 **L2**
Color Transparency #41, 47, 49, 50, 52 **L1** **LEP**
Exploring Environmental Issues, p. 5 **L3**

Chalkboard Example

Diagram the chemical structures of ammonia, urea, and uric acid on the chalkboard. Circle the amino groups (NH$_2$) in each molecule. Point out that ammonia is a gas that can be dissolved in water, urea is a liquid that can be diluted with water, and uric acid is an almost insoluble crystal (solid).

Ammonia NH$_3$

$$H—N—H$$
$$|$$
$$H$$

Urea CO(NH$_2$)$_2$

$$NH_2—C—NH_2$$
$$\|$$
$$O$$

Uric acid C$_5$H$_4$N$_4$O$_3$

Land Environments

Animals living on land are surrounded by dry air. Thus, they cannot diffuse dissolved ammonia into water as some aquatic organisms do. In these animals, the ammonia produced must be changed to another form—a substance that can safely build up in body fluids until it is excreted.

Because land animals occupy a dry environment, conservation of water is crucial. Thus, it is important that they do not lose a great deal of water as they excrete their wastes. In these animals, wastes are picked up and carried by blood or tissue fluid. Their excretory systems not only rid the animals of nitrogenous wastes, but are also a factor in maintaining osmotic balance.

The Earthworm Fluid in the body cavity of the earthworm contains both useful substances and wastes. The wastes take two forms: ammonia and another much less toxic compound called urea. Because the earthworm lives in the land rather than on it, its environment contains soil moisture. Thus, the earthworm diffuses ammonia wastes into the soil. But the urea is excreted through its excretory system.

Figure 22-13 shows the excretory system of an earthworm. Pairs of excretory organs, **nephridia,** are found in almost every segment. Body fluid is drawn into the funnel-shaped entrance of a nephridium by the action of cilia and muscles. As the body fluid flows through the long, narrow tubule of the nephridium, the useful materials such as water, food molecules, and ions are taken in by certain cells of the tubule. These materials then pass to surrounding capillaries and can be recirculated. The nitrogen wastes and a small amount of water remain in the nephridium and are eventually excreted to the outside.

Nephridia in the earthworm act as filters, removing wastes and returning usable substances to the circulatory system. Excretory systems, likewise based on filtration and the return of usable substances to the circulatory system, are found in most complex animals.

The Grasshopper True land animals, such as insects, cannot excrete ammonia and also must conserve water in their body fluids. The ammonia their cells produce is converted to a less toxic compound called uric acid.

Uric acid takes the form of insoluble crystals. The insolubility of uric acid is important for two reasons. First, because it does not dissolve in water, it does not enter into chemical reactions within fluids and so can be concentrated in the body without interfering with cellular metabolism. Second, it does not require excretion of water, so water is conserved. Uric acid's insolubility is important not only in the adult stage of life, but also for the embryo. Insects develop in a shelled egg. That means their wastes must be stored safely until they hatch out of the egg. Uric acid meets that requirement. Other embryos that develop in shelled eggs—reptiles, birds, and some land snails—also produce uric acid.

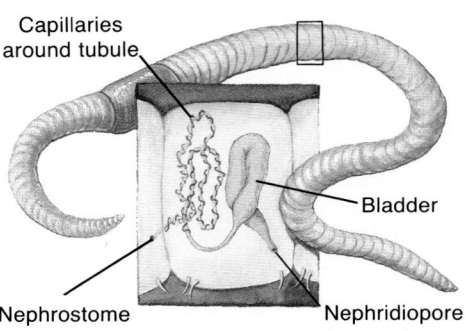

Capillaries around tubule

Bladder

Nephrostome

Nephridiopore

Figure 22-13 In an earthworm, wastes are separated in the nephridia and excreted through nephridiopores. Certain materials are reabsorbed by tubules and passed to capillaries for recirculation.

Make construction paper cutouts of the parts of the excretory systems of earthworms and of humans. Help students visualize how the parts fit together by having them identify, label, and assemble them.

Attached to the intestine of a grasshopper, as seen in Figure 22-14, is a group of stringlike excretory structures. The free ends of these structures, known as **Malpighian tubules,** lie among the cavities of the body. Blood enters and passes through these tubules. As it does so, needed materials and most of the water are resorbed, meaning taken back, into the body, usually through osmosis and active transport. The uric acid and remaining water enter the intestine, where the rest of the water is resorbed. The solid uric acid crystals are excreted from the anus as undigested food is expelled.

Filtration and Excretion in Humans

Like other animals, humans have an excretory system that filters out nitrogen wastes and helps maintain osmotic balance. The main excretory organs are two **kidneys,** fist-sized, bean-shaped structures that lie near the dorsal abdominal wall. Each kidney consists of an outer part, an inner layer, and a center hollow cavity, as seen in Figure 22-15.

Nephron Filtration Centers   Inside each kidney are about a million tiny units called **nephrons.** Nephrons are similar in function to the nephridia of an earthworm. Each nephron is made up of a cup-shaped **Bowman's capsule,** which narrows into a long, coiled tubule. In the center of each Bowman's capsule is a mass of capillaries called the **glomerulus.**

A glomerulus forms from a small artery that branches from one of the two renal arteries. The renal arteries direct blood from the aorta into the kidneys. Another small artery loops away from the glomerulus, outside the wide entrance to the Bowman's capsule. This artery, too, divides into a set of capillaries, which extend to surround the outside of the tubule. The capillaries merge to form small veins. These veins merge to form one of the two renal veins, which return purified blood to general circulation.

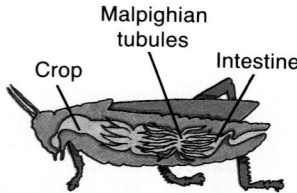

Figure 22-14   In a grasshopper, Malpighian tubules absorb uric acid and water from blood. Water is reabsorbed, but uric acid is passed to the intestines and excreted through the anus.

Figure 22-15   A human kidney consists of three distinct areas. The outer layer or cortex, the inner layer or medulla, and the inner collecting area, the pelvis. A detailed diagram of an individual nephron is shown on the right.

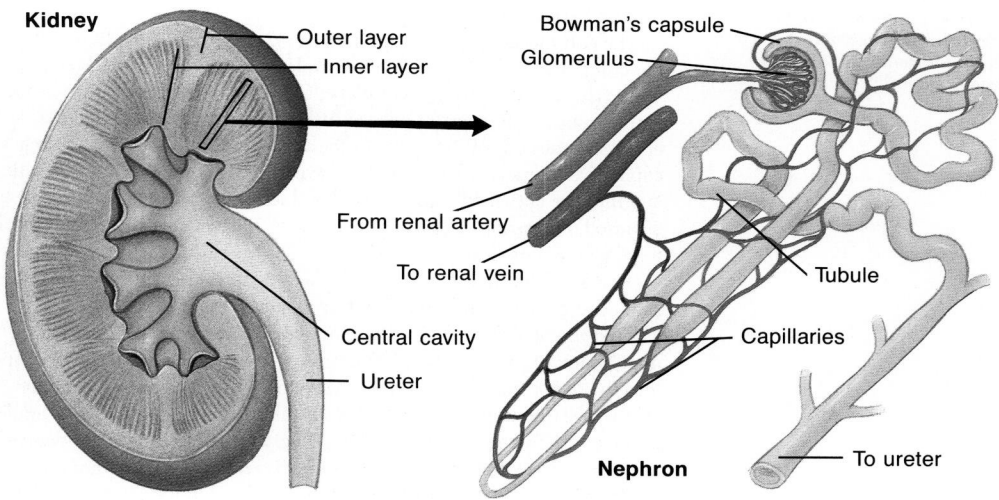

22.2 EXCRETION AND MAINTENANCE OF OSMOTIC BALANCE ❧ **627**

SECTION 22.2

Activity
Have students dissect, or dissect for their observation, an earthworm and a grasshopper. Ask students to locate and identify nephridia and Malpighian tubules. Point out that in the earthworm urea is released to the outside of the animal through the nephridial openings. In the grasshopper, metabolic waste takes the form of uric acid which is released, not directly to the outside, but into the intestine for excretion along with digestive wastes. **L1**

Reinforcement
Have students color the plates illustrating the earthworm and the grasshopper in *The Zoology Coloring Book.* **LEP**

Concept Development

Although earthworm nephridia and human nephrons are similar in both structure and function, they developed independently. They are examples of convergent evolution—the independent development of structures with similar functions.

Display

Set up a plastic or paper model of the human kidney in the classroom. Or display a model of the human body that can be taken apart and put back together, and let each student have an opportunity to assemble the parts of the urinary system. **L1** **LEP**

Reinforcement

Have students color the plates from *The Anatomy Coloring Book* that illustrate the urinary tract, the urinary system in the abdominal cavity, and the kidney. **LEP**

Artery:
Blood cells, water, salts, nutrients, urea

Urea Water

Collecting duct to ureter

Nutrients

Salts

Bowman's capsule

Capillaries

Water

Vein:
Blood cells, water, salts, nutrients

Salts

Urine, excess water and salts

Nutrients

Tubule

Figure 22-16   This single nephron is one of approximately one million functional units of a kidney. The arrows show the movement of materials through the nephron. Water, nutrients, and salts are returned to circulation. Excess water and salts, as well as urea, form urine and are excreted. The glomerulus of one nephron is shown at the left. Magnification: 300×

The Filtering Process   Blood entering a kidney contains needed materials being transported to body cells, plus urea and excess salts. The blood acquires urea when it passes through the liver, which converts ammonia to urea. Urea is less toxic than ammonia and also conserves water because it requires less water for excretion.

From a renal artery, blood is channeled into smaller arteries that lead to each nephron and its glomerulus. The first step in the filtering process takes place as blood pressure forces most of the water and dissolved particles out of the glomerulus and into the cup portion of the Bowman's capsule. Large proteins and the formed elements of blood (red and white blood cells, platelets) do not normally enter the capsule. They remain in the capillaries of the glomerulus.

The continuous flow of blood into the kidneys forces the liquid out of the cup portion of the Bowman's capsule and into the tubule. Here is where the actual filtering takes place. Certain cells lining the tubule use active transport to transfer needed materials such as food molecules, ions, and hormones out of the liquid in the tubule and into the surrounding capillaries. Some of the water also travels, by osmosis, out of the tubule and into the entwined capillaries. The blood, now reassembled and cleansed, makes its way out of the kidneys through a renal vein and back to general circulation.

The liquid left to move into the collecting duct contains urea, excess salts, and a great deal of the water originally present in the blood that entered the nephron. As this liquid moves down through the collecting duct, much of the remaining water moves by osmosis out of the duct and into the tissue fluid of the kidney. Movement of water in this direction occurs because the surrounding tissue fluid is less watery than the liquid in the duct. This resorption of water is very efficient. In fact, 99 percent of the water passing through the kidneys is resorbed! The amount of water lost through excretion is replaced by water in food and beverages.

628 🐌 GAS EXCHANGE AND EXCRETION

Excretion of Urine   What remains in the collecting duct—urea, salts, and a small amount of water—is called **urine.** Slowly but constantly, urine passes from the collecting ducts in the outer layers of a kidney to the center cavity. Leading from the center of each kidney is a tube called the **ureter,** which conveys the urine to a muscular storage sac, the **urinary bladder.** When the bladder becomes filled, a muscular valve relaxes, and urine is excreted through the **urethra** (Chapter 18). Table 22.1 compares the contents of urine with the contents of blood.

Kidney Failure   When a person's kidneys fail to function, the body has a big problem. The kidneys may fail to work properly for a number of reasons. Bacteria may attack the kidneys and do damage. Kidneys may also be damaged by environmental toxins such as mercury and lead. When enough of a person's nephrons are affected, the kidneys fail to filter the blood effectively. Persons whose kidneys have failed must have their blood filtered by an artificial kidney machine in a process called dialysis. During dialysis, blood is pumped from the person's artery through tubing that is bathed in a salt solution similar to plasma. Waste materials diffuse from the tube containing blood and are washed away by the salt solution. The cleaned blood left behind is returned to a vein. Dialysis sessions may last from five to ten hours every two to three days.

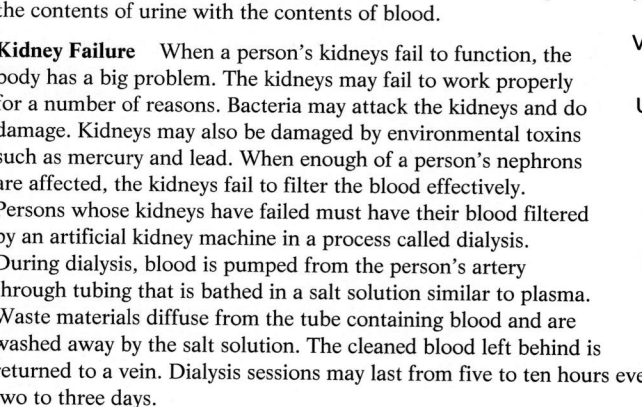

Figure 22-17   **The human urinary system is made up of a pair of kidneys, ureters, a urinary bladder, and a urethra.**

Table 22.1   **Composition of Urine and Blood**

Substance	In Blood	In Urine
Urea	small amount	large amount
Water	large amount	small amount
Salts	small traces	moderate traces
Glucose	present	usually absent
Amino Acids	present	usually absent
Proteins	present	usually absent
Blood Cells	present	usually absent

Control of Osmotic Balance

The removal of excess water and salts by the kidneys is as crucial as the removal of urea. The amount of water and salts removed—or not removed—affects the composition of blood and tissue fluid. These liquids must contain appropriate amounts of salts and water in order to help maintain osmotic balance between internal fluids and body cells.

HEALTH CONNECTION

Need for Water: The average human body uses 2.5 to 3 quarts of water each day. Some is replenished from the water in food, but most people need to drink six to eight glasses of water every day to make up the difference.

Teacher FYI

Urinalysis is a routine, easily performed test used to screen people for a variety of disease symptoms. Excess glucose in the urine is a sign of diabetes. Bacteria or large numbers of white blood cells may signify an infection of the urinary tract. The presence of protein or blood cells indicates possible kidney malfunction.

Microscope Activity

Have students examine prepared slides of mammalian kidneys. Students should be given slides showing nephrons. They should make drawings of what they see and label apparent structures. Magnification should be recorded. These drawings can be placed in their portfolios.

STUDENT JOURNAL

Have students find out more information about kidney dialysis and the effect it has on the daily lives of the people who require it. Have them write a reaction in their journals to their findings. **L1**

Bioethics

Drug Testing and Human Rights: Increasing numbers of employers—including government agencies, private companies, and even sports associations—are requiring that their members or employees submit to urine tests designed to determine whether they abuse drugs or use illegal substances. Some people feel that drug testing is needed to make sure that airplane pilots, bus drivers, firefighters, and others who are responsible for other people's safety are not impaired by drug use. Others feel that drug testing is an invasion of privacy and a violation of constitutional rights. Some experts have acknowledged that the drug tests are not foolproof, and cases of false positive results have occurred. Have students research this issue and hold a class debate. **COOP LEARN**

a **Low fluid intake**

Hypothalamus

ADH

Blood low in water is detected by the brain.

Result: Amount of ADH increases

Kidney returns more water to blood.

Result: Decreased urine output

b **High fluid intake**

Hypothalamus

Blood with much water is detected by the brain.

Result: Amount of ADH drops

Kidney returns less water to blood.

Result: Increased urine output

Figure 22-18 The amount of urine produced by the kidneys is a result of an interaction between body fluid levels and ADH.

You have learned that almost all the water that enters the kidneys is conserved. Exactly how much water is conserved or excreted in urine can vary, however. For example, a person may need to conserve even more water than usual if much has been lost because of heavy perspiration or illness. On the other hand, removal of more water than usual may be necessary for a person who has consumed a large volume of liquid.

The kidneys respond to a variety of regulatory substances called hormones, secreted by various parts of the body, to monitor the amount of water and salts excreted. The amount of water excreted in urine is controlled by the hormone **vasopressin**. Vasopressin causes the collecting ducts of the kidneys to resorb more water. Thus, a higher level of vasopressin will result in more water resorption and a more concentrated (less watery) urine. When too much water is present in the blood, the opposite occurs. The level of vasopressin is reduced, a lesser amount of water is resorbed in the collecting ducts, and a more dilute (watery) urine is produced.

Other hormones play a role in determining the amount of certain salts excreted in urine. Control over the amount of water and salts in the body is an important means of homeostasis. Homeostasis refers to the ability of an organism to maintain a steady state of internal operation regardless of changes in the external environment. By regulating the salt and water content in the blood and tissue fluids, the kidneys help maintain a constant internal environment for cells regardless of changes in diet, activity, or other factors that affect the body.

630 GAS EXCHANGE AND EXCRETION

MULTICULTURAL CONNECTION

Government Appointment: In 1990, the first woman and first Hispanic surgeon general of the United States, Dr. Antonia Novello, was appointed by President Bush. Dr. Novello was born in Puerto Rico. She received her M.D. from the University of Puerto Rico in 1970, and has specialized in pediatrics with an emphasis on nephrology. Dr. Novello has been on the staff of several large hospitals in the United States and has directed research projects dealing with kidney disease in children. As surgeon general, Dr. Novello has spoken out against advertising that entices children to smoke. She is also interested in pursuing other health risks that affect children, such as underage drinking and AIDS among adolescents, as well as the health problems of all Americans.

Kidneys in Other Vertebrates

Over the course of evolution, freshwater fish were the first vertebrates with kidneys. The structure and function of the kidneys were modified, however, as later vertebrates began occupying different environments. Bony fish, for example, all have kidneys, but the role of the kidneys in both excretion and maintaining osmotic balance is more vital for freshwater fish than for saltwater fish.

Bony Fish   Body fluids of bony fish are not in osmotic balance with the water in which they live. Most of the surface of a fish is covered with scales, which water and salts cannot cross. Water and salts may enter or leave the fish at the gills, however, causing an imbalance between internal fluids and the cells.

Body fluids of freshwater bony fish are more concentrated than the surrounding water. Thus, these fish tend to gain water and lose salts through the gill membranes. Three factors compensate for these conditions. First, the kidneys of freshwater fish resorb most salts but very little water. As a result, the urine produced is dilute, and large amounts of urine are excreted. Second, a freshwater fish drinks very little water, so no additional water builds up in its fluids. Finally, salts are actively transported from water into the gills. Together, these adaptations enable the animal to conserve salts, rid itself of excess water, and excrete wastes.

You might expect the internal fluids of marine bony fish to be in osmotic balance with sea water. But marine fish descended from freshwater fish, not saltwater organisms. Thus, the salt content of their body fluids is less concentrated than that of the water in which they live.

Figure 22-19   Freshwater and marine bony fish have evolved different adaptations for maintaining osmotic balance.

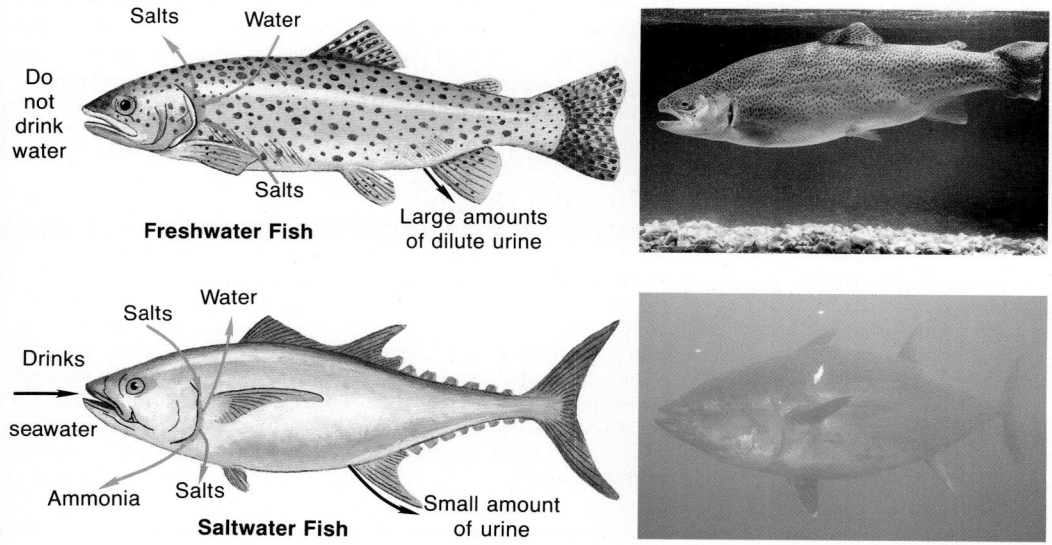

Salts   Water
Do not drink water
Salts
Freshwater Fish
Large amounts of dilute urine

Salts   Water
Drinks seawater
Ammonia   Salts
Saltwater Fish
Small amount of urine

Guest Speaker

Invite a nurse or dialysis technician from a local hospital or dialysis center to talk to the class about the duties and responsibilities of assisting dialysis patients and the training necessary to prepare someone for this type of job.

MATH CONNECTION

Size of Kidneys: Adult kidneys weigh only about five ounces each. The kidneys of an average adult process about 425 gallons of liquid a day, most of which is recycled. Have students calculate how many gallons an adult's kidneys process in a year, in a decade, and in 75 years.   **L1**

3 Assess

Check for Understanding

List on the chalkboard the organisms studied in this section of the text and the structures involved in excretion and osmotic balance. Have students match the structures with the organisms, then identify whether each match refers to excretion, osmotic balance, or both.   **L1**

Reteach

Divide students into pairs to play a version of "hangman" with terms studied in this section. One student chooses a term, and the other student not only has to determine what the word is, but also give the correct definition before being "hung." **COOP LEARN**

Extension

Provide students with colored modeling clay to use in building models of earthworm nephridia or human nephrons. **L2**

✔ Assessment

Portfolio: Ask students to imagine that humans have established contact with intelligent life forms in a nearby galaxy. Their job is to write a letter explaining to these new, nonhuman friends how the human excretory system works. **L1**

4 Close

Discussion

Have students determine the effect on the amount and concentration of urine during each of the following: (a) meal rich in proteins, (b) drinking large quantities of water, (c) hot, dry day, (d) high blood pressure, (e) disease or destruction of the hypothalamus. **COOP LEARN**

Figure 22-20 The kangaroo rat, a desert animal, excretes highly concentrated urine and, thus, conserves water. This animal obtains enough water from food and its metabolic reactions to survive without drinking water.

The gills play a major role in the adaptation of marine bony fish to their saltwater environment. Some of the water lost from their body fluids is restored by drinking large amounts of sea water. However, this water contains salts, so even more salts build up in the fluids. This excess salt is removed by active transport across the gill tissue to the water. Also, most nitrogenous wastes in these fish are excreted from the gills in the form of ammonia. Because very little water enters the kidneys, even more water is conserved. The end result is that the kidneys play only a minor role in both excretion and osmotic balance.

Land Animals Vertebrates living on land also exhibit variety in the structure, function, and efficiency of their kidneys. Amphibians and mammals, for instance, need to drink a certain amount of water to make up for water loss through their kidneys. Birds and reptiles conserve water by excreting uric acid and so resorb almost all the water passing through their kidneys. The tiny kangaroo rat, a desert dweller, can survive without drinking any water at all. Its kidney tubules resorb most of the water that passes through them. So efficient are its kidneys that a kangaroo rat can survive without drinking water. Kangaroo rats obtain enough water from the food they eat and as a by-product of metabolism.

LOOKING AHEAD

YOU HAVE OBSERVED that organisms are closely involved with the external environment for many vital functions including gas exchange, excretion, and maintaining osmotic balance. While the environment is a source of air, water, and food, it is also a potential source of danger. Any number of viruses and microorganisms can contaminate life-sustaining materials in the environment. In the next chapter, you will learn about some of the diseases these tiny organisms can spread. You will also study the means by which the body defends itself against the agents of disease.

Section Review

Understanding Concepts

1. In terms of osmotic balance, what common problem is faced by a tomato plant and an amoeba?
2. In general, how are the excretory systems of an earthworm and a grasshopper similar?
3. Could a marine bony fish survive in fresh water? Explain.

4. **Skill Review—Sequencing:** Trace the path of blood from a renal artery to a renal vein, indicating how the various structures through which blood passes function in excretion and maintenance of osmotic balance. For more help, refer to Organizing Information in the **Skill Handbook.**

5. **Thinking Critically:** A urinalysis is a common test from which much can be learned about a patient's health. A urinalysis reveals the presence of proteins in the urine. Is the patient healthy? Explain. What part of the excretory system is not functioning properly?

Answers to Section Review

1. The tomato plant cells and the amoeba are surrounded by fresh water. In both, water moves in by osmosis.
2. Both systems operate by separating needed materials from wastes. The needed materials are returned to the blood, and the wastes are excreted.
3. The marine fish could not survive in fresh water. Given its mechanisms of maintaining osmotic balance—drinking large amounts of water, and excreting little, and actively removing salts—the fish would gain water.
4. **Skill Review—Sequencing:** Blood passes through the glomerulus, where blood pressure forces most of the liquid part of the blood and dissolved materials into the Bowman's capsule. The liquid passes along the tubule where materials such as nutrients and some ions are actively transported back to surrounding capillaries. Material remaining in the tubule consists of excess salts, water, and urea. Most water is resorbed in the collecting duct.
5. **Thinking Critically:** The glomerulus is allowing proteins to pass into the Bowman's capsule, which should not happen.

Health Connection
••••••••••••••••••••••••••••

Let's Clear the Air

By now, most people know the serious damage smoking does to a person's health. A smoker is twice as likely to die from heart disease, ten times more likely to have mouth or throat cancer, and 25 times more likely to develop lung cancer than a non-smoker. Bronchitis, an inflammation of the air tubes leading to the lungs, is more common and harder to cure in smokers. Many long-term, heavy smokers contract emphysema, a disease that causes the flexible air sacs of healthy lungs to break down, reducing the amount of oxygen the body can absorb. This makes breathing extremely difficult, and eventually restricts a patient's activities to the bare minimum.

All of this information has little relevance for the average young person who lights up a cigarette. The dire consequences of smoking lie not in the present but in the dim future. The cold statistics don't translate into a meaningful, real-life situation. Maybe it would help to think about the risks of smoking in other ways. Suppose you attended a

large high school of 1000 students. All of the students smoked. Cold statistics show that on average, one of the 1000 will be murdered, six will die in traffic accidents, and 250

(or one out of four) of your fellow classmates will die because of a smoking-related disease before reaching the age of 65.

CAREER CONNECTION

A **respiratory therapist** assists patients who have cardiorespiratory problems arising from illnesses, heart attacks, or strokes. Respiratory therapists operate and monitor equipment that patients may need to support their breathing. They also teach breathing exercises.

While this statistic may be more meaningful, it doesn't show how smoking might influence your immediate life. Perhaps the following situation will show how smoking can make an unattractive impression on someone you might want to meet.

What a week! Three tests, an essay, and a science project due at the same time. By Friday, you're looking forward to a movie with some friends. As you enter the theater, your eyes settle on a stranger buying a soft drink at the concession stand. Wow! Even from a distance you know that you really want to meet this person. Taking a deep breath, you boldly step up, tap the shoulder, and wait as the stranger slowly turns around. Suddenly, anticipation turns to disappointment. The stale odor of cigarette smoke drifts from the stranger's hair and clothes to your nose. Red-rimmed eyes peer at you. Yellowed teeth and the unmistakable odor of smoker's breath flash your way as the stranger searches for a breath mint and brushes away some ashes that have just burned a

Health Connection

Purpose
Students will have an opportunity to think about and discuss the health and social consequences of smoking.

Teaching Strategies
• Have students work in groups to investigate sources of air pollution in and around their school and neighborhoods and to come up with ideas about improving air quality in these areas.

Possible Answers
1. Some students may feel that employers would be violating a smoker's constitutional rights of privacy by refusing to hire a smoker who does not smoke at work. Others may feel that, since the employer loses money when a smoker is ill and misses work, refusal to hire smokers is justifiable.
2. Skin cells, like all cells, must be well supplied with oxygenated blood to stay healthy. Smoking reduces the lungs' ability to oxygenate the blood and replaces some oxygen with carbon monoxide.

Going Further
Have students investigate the difficulties of quitting smoking by interviewing a smoker they know who is trying to quit or attending a meeting of a quit-smoking group. L1

CAREER CONNECTION

Have students contact a local hospital, university, or health clinic and ask for information on careers in respiratory therapy.

Biotechnology

Purpose
Students learn how premature birth can affect a baby's respiratory system.

Teaching Strategies
Simulate the oily liquids on the surface of lung tissue with a thin film of oil poured over water in a beaker. Add a few drops of a soap or detergent solution to show students how a surfactant can break up surface tension. `LEP`

Possible Answers
1. Good prenatal care ensures that an expectant mother receives proper nutrition and provides early detection of health problems that could result in premature birth.
2. Almost any cleaning agent is a surfactant. Soaps and detergents not only break up grease films but also help water penetrate clothing fibers during washing.

Going Further
Have students visit a neonatal nursery or intensive care unit, or have a neonatal intensive care nurse speak to the class. `L1`

---

hole in what looks like a new sweater. Unable to hide a look of disappointment, you mumble an apology of mistaken identity and walk away.

1. **Issue:** Smokers usually have more health problems than non-smokers. They often suffer from frequent respiratory infections such as colds, bronchitis, and pneumonia. These illnesses cause many days of missed work. Because of the rising cost of health insurance, some companies are refusing to hire smokers, and are even firing some present employees who smoke only in their own homes. How much right does a company have to regulate what a person does within his or her home?
2. **Writing About Biology:** Explain how smoking can make your skin look older than your actual age.

Biotechnology

A Treatment for Respiratory Distress Syndrome

The birth of a baby is often a time of great joy. However, sometimes the joy is erased by fear and apprehension when the newborn arrives prematurely. Premature babies may be affected by a disorder called respiratory distress syndrome, or RDS. The lungs of babies with RDS are not flexible and elastic enough to stay inflated. Until recently, babies with this disorder died when the air sacs of their lungs collapsed.

Doctors know that fully developed lungs secrete a natural mucus-like substance that is a combination of fats and proteins. The substance is called a surface-active agent or surfactant. Surfactants lower the surface tension of liquids. They act as lubricants to prevent tissues from sticking together. The natural surfactant produced in healthy lungs lowers the surface tension of fluids found in the air sacs and enables the lungs to remain inflated. Most babies do not produce enough surfactant to prevent the lungs from collapsing until they are at least 32 weeks gestational age. Without this substance, babies born prematurely are unable to breathe independently.

Thus, the most effective way of preventing RDS is to prevent premature births.

While prevention is the best method, doctors now have an additional method of treating the disorder. Since the 1980s, surfactant-replacement therapy has saved the lives and reduced the suffering of babies with RDS. Synthetic surfactant is mixed with sterile water and administered directly into the windpipe of an infant suffering from RDS. Almost half of the infants improve within hours. After a short time, an affected baby's lungs will begin manufacturing surfactant by themselves. Based on the results of clinical trials, the Food and Drug Administration has now approved for use a surfactant that is produced from calf lung tissues and a synthetically produced surfactant. Continued research on the disorder should provide for even better treatment in the future.

1. **Connection to Health:** What measures can be taken to reduce the number of premature births in the United States?
2. **Find Out:** What common household products are surfactants?

634 CHAPTER 22 GAS EXCHANGE AND EXCRETION

Issues

Asbestos Hazard

The scene looks like something out of a science fiction movie. Workers wearing gloves, special hooded suits, and face masks enter the furnace room of an old basement. The area around the furnace has been sealed off so that air can't escape and contaminate the outside. What's the danger? It isn't a new form of virus or a radiation leak. These workers are about to remove a furnace that had been insulated with asbestos.

Asbestos has been used for thousands of years. Romans used it for wicks in oil-burning lamps, and Egyptians clothed their mummies in garments made with asbestos fibers. More recently, asbestos has been mixed with paint, cement, plastic, rubber, and asphalt to produce a variety of products used by industries and in construction. Asbestos adds texture to paint. When mixed with cement or wall and ceiling materials, it insulates pipes and buildings. It even helps soundproof rooms. The brake linings of new cars are still made from asbestos materials, and firefighters wear asbestos suits so they can work in burning buildings without fear of being burned.

To understand the dangers of asbestos, you must know about the properties of this material. Asbestos is a fibrous, or flexible mineral found in serpentine and amphibole rocks. Asbestos fibers from amphibole rocks are blue or brown in color, brittle, straight, and needle-like. When people inhale the fibers of blue and brown asbestos, these fibers become lodged in the lungs.

Over time, the lungs become scarred, breathing becomes difficult, and a disease called asbestosis develops. In some cases, the lodged fibers cause lung cancer to develop. Asbestos fibers have even contaminated the water supply of older homes. This happens when fibers from insulating materials around the water tank or pipes crumble and fall into the tank. The fibers may then become lodged in the stomach or intestines of people who drink the water. Doctors suspect that some cancers of the gastrointestinal system have been caused by the fibers. Some cancers of the larynx, pancreas, kidneys, ovaries, and lymph glands may also be traced to asbestos. Because of these health problems, the use of blue and brown asbestos has been banned. Possibly because of its spiral shape, the fibers of white asbestos are not as dangerous as blue and brown asbestos. Although these fibers may also be inhaled or ingested, they don't remain lodged in the tissues. The use of white asbestos is greatly restricted, and safer alternatives are used whenever possible.

An immediate danger now involves removing asbestos materials installed in schools, homes, and office buildings before the dangers of the mineral were identified. As these materials get older, they deteriorate and crumble apart, releasing the fibers into the air and water. Only qualified workers using spe-

cial equipment and following carefully developed precautions should remove asbestos. These activities may remind you of a movie scene, but the results help provide a greater chance of good health for those people living and working in the building.

Understanding the Issue
1. Should old asbestos insulation be removed even though it hasn't begun to break apart or crumble?
2. What new products are being used to replace asbestos?

Readings
- Mathews, J. "To Yank or Not to Yank?" *Newsweek,* April 13, 1992, p. 59.
- Stone, R. "No Meeting of the Minds on Asbestos." *Science,* Nov. 15, 1991, pp. 928-931.

Issues

Purpose
Students learn about how asbestos fibers can endanger the respiratory system.

Teaching Strategies
- Point out to students that it is dangerous for nonexperts to try to remove asbestos, since asbestos fibers can pass through the filters of ordinary household vacuum cleaners or dust masks available in hardware stores.
- Show students samples of asbestos minerals such as serpentines or amphiboles. Make sure these samples are enclosed to prevent students from coming into contact with asbestos.

Possible Answers
1. Experts feel that as long as the material is intact, its removal is not necessary.
2. Fiberglass, Styrofoam, calcium silicate, and a wide variety of other heat-resistant fibrous materials that do not pose a danger to the respiratory system

Going Further
Visit an asbestos removal site or have a contractor talk to the class about the steps required for safe removal. **L1**

CHAPTER REVIEW

Summary

The summary can be used by students to review the major concepts of the chapter.

Language of Biology

Answers should go beyond defining the terms. Accept any reasonable answer that uses the term correctly and in the proper context.

Understanding Concepts

1. Gas exchange is applicable whether discussing photosynthesis or respiration. Both processes involve movement of oxygen and carbon dioxide, but in different directions.
2. In both cases, oxygen is taken in and carbon dioxide is expelled.
3. Large surface: many alveoli. Protection: lungs surrounded by ribs and muscles. Moist surface: alveoli located deep within the body where moisture can be retained. Transport of gases: by blood.
4. Large surface: many gill filaments. Protection: gill cover. Moist surface: gills in contact with watery environment. Transport of gases: by blood.
5. During inhalation, the ribs move up and out and the diaphragm moves down, decreasing pressure in the chest cavity. Air rushes into the lungs, and oxygen moves from the alveoli into the blood of surrounding capillaries. When the ribs move down and in and the diaphragm moves up, air pressure in the chest cavity increases, forcing air, and the carbon dioxide it contains, out of the lungs.
6. Such organisms evolved in that environment and are in osmotic balance with it.
7. Removal of wastes from blood affects the concentration of dissolved substances in blood. Change in concentration of dissolved particles affects osmotic balance.

Summary

Simple organisms have no specialized structures for gas exchange; each of their cells carries out that function independently. Gas exchange areas in plants are located in stems, leaves, and roots, and there is no transport of gases from one part of the plant to another.

Location of respiratory exchange surfaces of animals is related to the environment in which they live. In aquatic animals, the exchange area is near or projecting from the surface, where it is kept moist by the surrounding water. In land animals, the exchange surface must be deep within the body where the delicate tissues can be surrounded by moisture. Humans exchange gases at the lungs, and gases are transported between lungs and body cells by blood.

Terrestrial and freshwater organisms as well as some marine forms must have a means of maintaining an osmotic balance between their cells and the fluid that bathes those cells. Protozoans and animals excrete various forms of nitrogenous wastes. In animals with a circulatory system, the excretory system also functions in maintaining osmotic balance. Kidneys are the excretory organs of humans and other vertebrates.

Language of Biology

Write a sentence that shows your understanding of each of the following terms.

alveolus	nephridium
Bowman's capsule	nephron
bronchus	respiration
diaphragm	trachea
excretion	tracheole
gill	ureter
glomerulus	urethra
kidney	urinary bladder
lung	urine
Malpighian tubule	vasopressin

Understanding Concepts

1. Why is the phrase *gas exchange* suitable when talking about gases moving into and out of all kinds of organisms?
2. What do the terms *respiration* and *cellular respiration* have in common?
3. How is the human respiratory system adapted for each of the following: a large gas exchange surface; protection of the exchange surface; a moist environment for the exchange surface; transport of gases between body cells and the exchange surface?
4. How is a bony fish adapted for each of the features or functions listed in question 3?
5. Describe inhalation, gas exchange, and exhalation in a human. List all the structures of the respiratory system and their functions, in order, for each process.
6. Why have most marine organisms not evolved a means of regulating their body fluids?
7. Why are excretion and maintenance of osmotic balance linked together in animals having a circulatory system?
8. Many people add plants to their freshwater aquaria. How can the plants maintain osmotic balance in that environment?
9. Could a seaweed survive in a freshwater aquarium? Explain.

636 CHAPTER 22 GAS EXCHANGE AND EXCRETION

---

8. The plants take in some water by osmosis, but the presence of the cell wall prevents too much water from entering.
9. A seaweed could not survive in fresh water because it would tend to lose too much water by osmosis and it has no adaptations to prevent that water loss.
10. Varying amounts of water and salts must be excreted in order to maintain osmotic balance under varying conditions. The amounts excreted are controlled by hormones.

PROGRAM RESOURCES

Teacher Classroom Resources
Chapter Assessment, pp. 85-88 L1
Performance Assessment in Biology, p. 44 L2
Alternate Assessment in the Science Classroom
Computer Test Bank L1

10. Explain why the amount of water and salts excreted by a human is not always the same. How are the amounts that are excreted controlled?

Applying Concepts

11. Shore crabs can exist in sea water, but can also live in brackish water, water that contains a mixture of salt water and fresh water. In which environment are their internal fluids in osmotic balance with the water? In general, what adaptation must they have to be able to live also in the other environment?

12. Why must the space shuttle contain equipment that removes carbon dioxide from the cabin?

13. A person is caught in an avalanche of snow. The snow is tightly packed around the person up to the neck. Help is three days away. Will the person be able to survive that long? Explain.

14. A person is adrift on a raft in the ocean and is very thirsty. Will drinking sea water help? Explain.

15. On a relative basis, do you think that the tubule and collecting duct of a kangaroo rat nephron are longer or shorter than those of a human nephron? Why?

16. You are observing a paramecium under high power of a microscope and measuring the rate at which its contractile vacuole is contracting. How will that rate change if you slowly add more and more salt to the water? Explain.

17. Why do marine birds have special glands that excrete salt?

18. **Health Connection:** Cigarette smoking is hazardous to a person's health, but becomes much more hazardous when the individual is exposed to other air pollutants as well. The two pollutants may work together to create an even more toxic situation. What other pollutants might a smoker encounter daily that may cause more lung damage than the smoke alone?

19. **Leisure Connection:** High altitudes and low air pressure create problems for mountain climbers. Would scuba equipment be beneficial for these people? How might it be adapted?

Lab Interpretation

20. **Investigation:** A student group ended up with the following data: inhaled air flask = bright blue, exhaled air flask = bright blue. Suggest a possible reason for their results.

21. **Minilab 2:** You are provided with the following data: breathing rate = 10 times per minute, volume of air inhaled = 400 mL, dead air space = 100 mL, inhaled air is 20% oxygen.
    (a) Calculate the volume of air reaching the alveoli in one hour.
    (b) Calculate the volume of oxygen reaching the alveoli in one minute.

22. **Thinking Lab:** Water gets its dissolved oxygen from the air that mixes into it. How might it be possible for fish to survive in bodies of water that are covered during the winter by a layer of ice?

Connecting Ideas

23. Based on what you learned about digestion in humans, how does the liver play a role in maintaining osmotic balance? The colon?

24. Compare the amounts of urea and oxygen present in blood in the right atrium with the amounts present in the left ventricle.

CHAPTER 22

Applying Concepts

11. The internal fluids are in balance with the seawater. The crabs must have adaptations that compensate for the amount of water taken in and salt lost in brackish waters.

12. Buildup of carbon dioxide would cause an increase in breathing rate.

13. The person will probably not survive because the tightly packed snow will not allow breathing to occur.

14. Drinking seawater will only exacerbate the problem. The salty water will cause water to move from body cells to the blood. In addition, more water will be needed to excrete the salts. The person will become even more dehydrated.

15. The kangaroo rat has a relatively longer tubule and collecting duct. More water can be resorbed in a longer duct.

16. The rate of contraction would decrease as salt was added to the water.

17. Marine birds drink salt water and eat foods rich in salt. The glands are adaptations for ridding their bodies of that salt.

18. Air pollutants could be added to cigarette smoke as a possible source of lung damage.

19. Scuba equipment could be used to provide air, but could also be modified to deliver the air under higher pressure. Thus, the air would move more easily into the lungs. Smaller, lighter tanks would need to be designed because the air does not support the tanks as well as water does.

Lab Interpretation

20. Some possible reasons are: they did not exhale enough times into the solution; they may not have exhaled directly into the tube; equipment was faulty, allowing air to escape from flask before passing through the solution of BTB.

21. (a) 10×300 mL = 3000 mL per minute $\times 60$ = 180 000 mL (Note: 400 mL inhaled air— 100 mL dead air = 300 mL reaching alveoli)

    (b) 10×60 mL = 600 mL per minute (Note: 20% of 300 mL = 60 mL)

22. Water temperature of lakes and ponds is very cold (but never below 0°C) during the winter. Therefore, the amount of dissolved oxygen present must be at its maximum levels providing enough oxygen for fish.

Connecting Ideas

23. **Systems and Interactions:** The liver removes excess glucose and amino acids coming from the small intestine. The colon absorbs water from undigested food and also excretes excess iron and calcium.

24. **Systems and Interactions:** The amount of urea would be the same in both chambers because the blood contains urea picked up from the liver and that has not yet been sent to the kidneys. The amount of oxygen is greater in the left ventricle because that blood has just returned to the heart from the lungs.

ORGANIZER

CHAPTER 23

SECTION	OBJECTIVES	TEXT LABS/FEATURES
23.1 Bacterial and Viral Agents of Disease (2 days)	**Describe** various ways in which pathogens are transmitted. **Compare** how bacteria and viruses may cause disease.	**Minilab 1:** How is disease spread? p. 642
23.2 Defending Against Pathogens (2 days)	**Discuss** nonspecific lines of defense against pathogens. **Describe** how the immune system defends against pathogens present in blood and tissue fluid. **Demonstrate** how the immune system functions in destruction of infected, abnormal, or foreign cells.	**Minilab 2:** Do mouthwashes kill bacteria? p. 646 **Thinking Lab:** How do helper T cells act? p. 651
23.3 Immunity and Prevention of Disease (2 days)	**Distinguish** between active and passive immunity. **Discuss** the use of drugs in treating bacterial and viral diseases. **Relate** the life cycle of HIV to the symptoms of AIDS.	**Investigation:** Antibiotic Properties of Plants and Other Substances, p. 658 **Psychology Connection:** How Attitudes Affect Health, p. 662
BIOLOGY, TECHNOLOGY, AND SOCIETY		**Biotechnology:** Defending Against Thousands of Antigens, p. 664 **Career Connection:** Epidemiologist, p. 664 **Issues:** Organ Transplants—Who Decides? p. 665

LAB MATERIALS

INVESTIGATION	MINILAB	ALTERNATE LAB
page 658 beaker, 250-mL Bunsen burner *E. coli* culture forceps hot plate marking pencil masking tape metric ruler paper punch petri dish plant material toothpicks	**page 642** beakers or cups label NaOH solution phenolphthalein **page 646** agar masking tape mouthwash toothpicks	**page 646** library sources on blood cells microscope prepared slide of human blood

TEACHER CLASSROOM RESOURCES	OTHER RESOURCES
Study Guide, p. 133 ***PLL:** *Assay of Bacteriophage,* p. 153 ***PLL:** *The Regional Spread of a Disease-Causing Protozoa,* p. 158 ****ILS:** *Control of Disease-Causing Bacteria,* p. 245	
Study Guide, pp. 134-135 ***PLL:** *Controlling Microbial Growth,* p. 156	***STVS:** *Combined Immune Deficiency,* Human Biology (Disc 7, Side 1) **Color Transparency 42:** *The Lymphatic System*
Study Guide, pp. 136-138 **Concept Mapping,** p. 23 **Critical Thinking/Problem Solving:** *Constructing a Vaccine for AIDS,* p. 23 ****ILS:** *Using Antibiotics to Stop Bacterial Growth,* p. 247	***STVS:** *Anticavity Vaccine,* Plants and Simple Organisms (Disc 4, Side 1)
Assessment Materials **Chapter Assessment,** pp. 89-92 **Performance Assessment in Biology,** p. 46 **Alternate Assessment in the Science Classroom** **Computer Test Bank**	**Spanish Resources** **Cooperative Learning Resource Guide** **Videodisc Correlations** (to Optical Data's and Videodiscovery's videodiscs)

* **Probing Levels of Life**
** **Investigating Living Systems**

* **Science Technology Videodisc Series**

Key to Teaching Strategies

The following designations will help you decide which activities in the teacher margin are appropriate for your students.

L1 Level 1 activities should be within the ability range of all students.

L2 Level 2 activities should be within the ability range of the average to above-average student.

L3 Level 3 activities are designed for the ability range of above-average students.

LEP LEP activities are appropriate for Limited English Proficiency students.

COOP LEARN Cooperative Learning activities are designed for small group work.

ADDITIONAL RESOURCES

Infinite Voyage *The Champion Within*
Why do some people stay fit as they age whereas others don't? Students will learn about the human body and its capabilities in this video.

Audiovisual
Cell Wars, video, Films for the Humanities and Sciences.
Don't Get It! Teenagers and AIDS, video, Sunburst.

Software
Pathology: Disease and Defense, IBM, Gemstar.
Understanding AIDS, Apple II 64K/IBM 128K, Carolina.

Chapter Overview

Before examining the means by which the body wards off or defends against pathogens, students first learn about diseases caused by bacteria and viruses, how they are transmitted, and how they exert their effects on their hosts. They also come to see that many human pathogens may be descendants of pathogens that infect other hosts.

Then students learn of nonspecific mechanisms of defense against pathogens—skin and membranes and the inflammatory response. They learn that the key to the specificity of the immune response is the recognition of antigens by antibodies. They examine the means by which the immune system recognizes and defends against pathogens present in blood or tissue fluid and compare that to the manner in which the system destroys infected, foreign, or cancerous cells. Principles of immunity are then related to the topics of allergies, rejection of transplants, and autoimmune diseases.

Students' understanding of the immune system is then applied to the concepts of active and passive immunity and the prevention and treatment of infectious diseases. Finally, they relate the cause of AIDS and its consequences to destruction of the immune system.

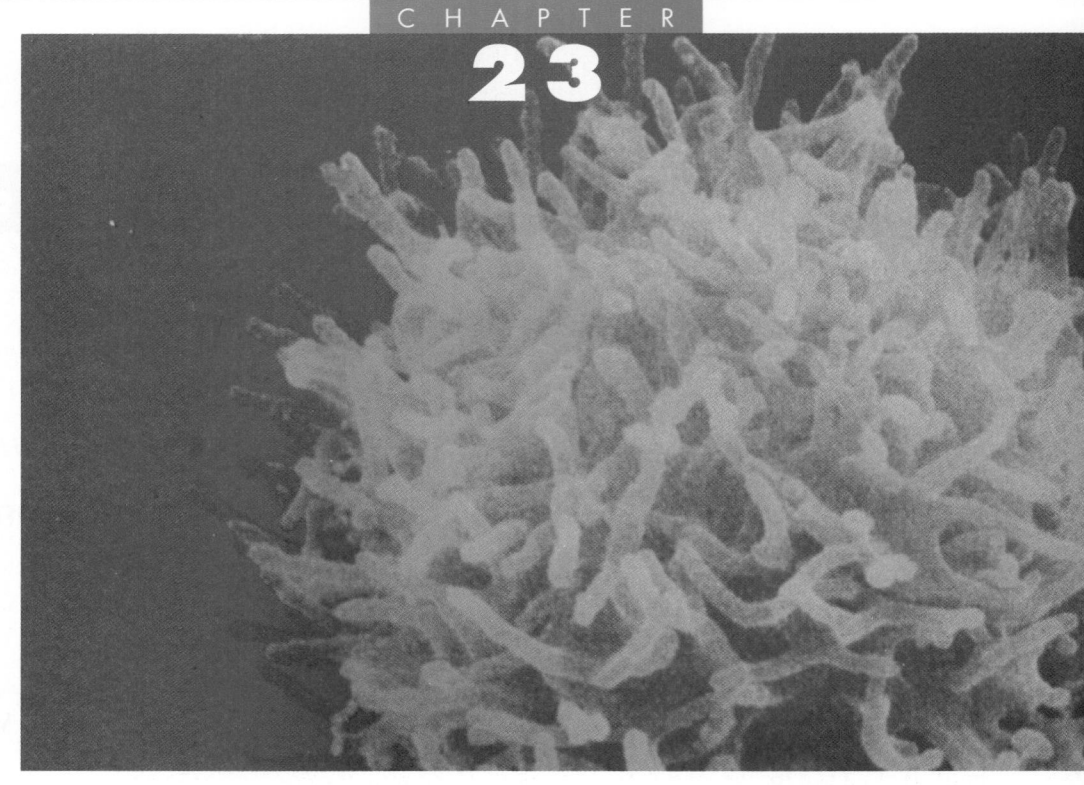

CHAPTER

23

IMMUNE SYSTEM

YOU MAY NOT realize it, but at this very moment, a battle might be raging inside your body. Are you sniffling? Do you have a scratchy throat? These symptoms may mean you are fighting off an infection. Within your body, white blood cells like the one shown in the photograph are busy consuming the bacteria or viruses that are causing the disease. At first, the invaders reproduce rapidly and seem likely to overwhelm your defenses. But then your body rallies. Thousands of white blood cells go on the counterattack. The battle rages on. At times, the outcome may appear to be in doubt. But if you recover, you can be sure your body has won the war.

The response of the body to attack by outside agents is a remarkable process to experience, whether it is going on inside you or you are viewing it under a microscope. It involves thousands of troops as well as time and energy. Because of it, some infections—such as colds—are of no permanent concern. Others—such as pneumonia—are more serious but still likely to be conquered by most people. Our knowledge of the body's ability to fight disease has helped us prevent diseases such as polio and eliminate smallpox. Perhaps someday that knowledge will extend to a cure for the disease called AIDS.

638

KEY TERMS

active immunity
antiserum
autoimmune disease
B cell
cytotoxic T cell
endotoxin
exotoxin
helper T cell
interferon

lymphocyte
macrophage
memory cell
monoclonal antibody
passive immunity
pathogen
plasma cell
receptor
suppressor T cell

T cell
thymus gland
vaccine

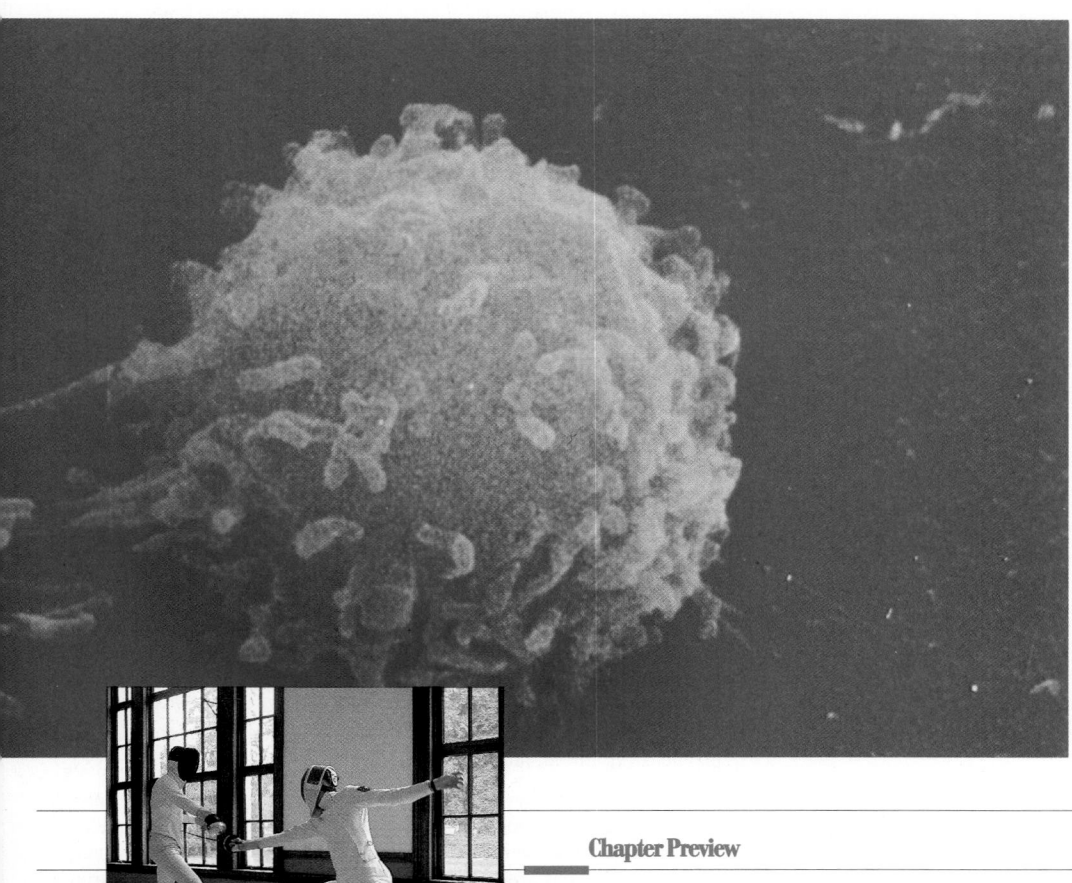

Introducing the Chapter

Call your students' attention to the photograph on pages 638 and 639. The white cells pictured here are part of an army of cells and tissues that are constantly on the lookout for and ready to defend against foreign invaders. Ask students to identify examples of infections they have had. Which ones did they fight off without the aid of medicines? For which did they take medicines? Ask them if they know the kind of pathogen in each case. Now ask them to explain how they have been prevented from contracting many infectious diseases. This discussion should generate many ideas to be explored and questions to be answered in this chapter.

Theme Development

As students begin to understand the interplay between the many cells and tissues of the immune system, they will recognize the theme of systems and interactions. The theme of patterns of change will also be reinforced as students study the sequence of events in the body's response to the onset of infection, appearance of disease symptoms, and return to normalcy.

Tying to Previous Knowledge

Students have previously studied bacteria and viruses and their means of reproduction. In this chapter, they will relate some of that information to infectious diseases. For example, students will learn more clearly how reproduction of viruses within specific host cells is tied to diseases affecting particular tissues of the body, e.g., in polio, the common cold, or AIDS. Students will also put to use their knowledge of methods of science as they examine the promise of new techniques such as production of synthetic vaccines and monoclonal antibodies and the possible applications of those advances.

These fencers are fighting a mock battle in which no one will be hurt. Does this type of battle go on inside your body?

Chapter Preview

639

ASSESSMENT PLANNER

Choose assessment strategies from the following pages to evaluate the progress of your students.

Assess, pp. 643, 655-656, 663
Portfolio, pp. 642, 643, 648, 650, 653, 661, 663
Alternate Lab, pp. 646-647
Thinking Lab, p. 651

Minilab 1, p. 642
Minilab 2, p. 646
Investigation, pp. 658-659
Chapter Review, pp. 666-667

Prepare

Key Concepts

Students will study how bacteria and viruses are transmitted and how they cause disease. The evolution of disease will also be addressed.

Key Terms

pathogen, exotoxin, endotoxin

Materials

- Gather small beakers or cups, phenolphthalein indicator, droppers, and goggles, and goggles, and prepare 0.01*M* NaOH for the Minilab.

1 Focus

Objectives

The objectives are listed on the student page. Remind students to preview these objectives as a guide to this numbered section.

Demonstration

Ask students if they think insects transmit disease. Ask them how they could tell if a housefly were carrying microbes. Attempt to answer this by allowing a cockroach, a housefly, or a cricket to walk across the surface of a plate of sterile nutrient agar. Close and seal the dish with masking tape, and incubate in a dark place at room temperature for three to four days or in an incubator for two days. Ask students to observe bacterial colonies growing on the agar. **LEP**

Objectives

Describe various ways in which pathogens are transmitted.

Compare how bacteria and viruses may cause disease.

23.1 Bacterial and Viral Agents of Disease

When is the last time you had a cold? Not only were you sneezing and coughing, but you also probably had a sore throat and a fever. Did you ever suffer from an intestinal flu? Have you ever had strep throat? Do you know why you were vaccinated against measles, mumps, and polio? All these illnesses are caused by either bacteria or viruses, unseen enemies that can enter human tissues. There, they may cause discomfort, disease, and sometimes even death. Not all microorganisms cause disease. In fact, many are important in nature or useful to humans.

Microorganisms that do cause disease are called **pathogens.** Besides bacteria and viruses, simple organisms such as fungi and protozoa may also be pathogens. Many diseases caused by pathogens—including the common cold, the flu, and strep throat—are spread from one person to another and are known as infectious diseases.

Bacteria and Disease

The relationship between bacteria and certain diseases was not well understood until the middle of the 19th century. At that time, Louis Pasteur proposed the idea that bacteria can cause disease. About the same time Pasteur developed this germ theory of disease, a standard method of identifying bacterial pathogens was devised. Since then, many bacteria have been found to be responsible for infectious diseases in animals. Among humans, bacterial diseases include bacterial pneumonia, bubonic plague, strep throat, and meningitis.

Transmission of Bacterial Diseases Bacteria are adapted to be transmitted from one host to another in a variety of ways. Often, their mode of transmission is related to the symptoms they cause. For example, some bacterial pathogens are airborne. That is, the bacteria are carried through the air on small liquid droplets produced when the infected person coughs or sneezes. The bacteria responsible for strep throat are transmitted in this way.

Figure 23-1 **Bacteria that cause diseases include various species of *Streptococcus*, left; *Vibrio cholerae*, the organism that causes cholera, center; and *Yersinia pestis*, right, the bacteria that cause bubonic plague. Magnifications: 40 000× (left), 6500× (center), 1200× (right)**

640 IMMUNE SYSTEM

Figure 23-2 When you sneeze, bacteria carried on tiny water droplets spread out in all directions. Does sneezing spread pathogens?

Other bacterial pathogens are carried in water that has not been treated, or purified. Waterborne bacteria are spread when a person drinks water or eats food that once lived in water contaminated by human wastes. The bacteria responsible for cholera are transmitted in this way. When a person contracts cholera, the bacteria cause the intestine to secrete excessive amounts of fluids. This constant secretion results in diarrhea. The diarrhea, if untreated, can quickly lead to dehydration, decreased blood pressure, kidney failure, and then death. Bacteria may reproduce within a host, but if the host dies before the bacteria find another host, the bacteria will die too. However, even if a person dies of cholera, the bacteria responsible for the disease can be spread because they are present in the fluids lost by the dying host. If those fluids enter water supplies from which people drink or obtain food, the bacteria may be transmitted to others. An outbreak of cholera that began in Peru in early 1991 spread along the entire Pacific coast of South America and east to Brazil by 1992, infecting more than 300 000 people.

Still other bacterial pathogens are transmitted by direct contact. The bacteria are spread when one person touches an object or a living thing on which the bacteria are located. Sexually transmitted diseases caused by bacteria—syphilis and gonorrhea—are spread by sexual contact. Some other bacterial diseases are transmitted by arthropods. For example, bubonic plague is spread by fleas, epidemic typhus fever is transmitted by lice, and Lyme disease is carried by ticks. The bacteria may enter the body when the arthropod bites or pierces the skin.

Causes of Bacterial Diseases When bacteria enter the body, they can cause disease in several ways. One way many bacteria cause disease is by producing poisonous chemicals called toxins.

Exotoxins are released by living bacteria. They travel through the bloodstream and affect particular tissues or act locally. For example, one species of bacterium secretes a toxin that stimulates certain nerves, causing some muscles to remain contracted. The result is tetanus, a condition that can be very painful and may even result in death. The bacterium that causes diphtheria secretes a toxin that may damage the heart, kidneys, and nerves.

Figure 23-3 Syphilis is a sexually transmitted disease caused by the bacterium *Treponema pallidum.* Magnification: 10 000×

23.1 BACTERIAL AND VIRAL AGENTS OF DISEASE **641**

PROGRAM RESOURCES

Teacher Classroom Resources
Study Guide, p. 133 L1
Probing Levels of Life, Labs 59, 61, pp. 153, 158 L2
Investigating Living Systems, Lab 64, p. 245 L2

PROJECT

Statistics on Infectious Diseases: Ask a group of students to research the historical incidence statistics for a variety of infectious diseases. Ask them to make line graphs of the data that would demonstrate the trends over the course of many years. Ask them to speculate about reasons for the curves in their graphs. L3 COOP LEARN

---

2 Teach

Figure Caption Question
Does sneezing spread pathogens?
Yes, the pathogens are carried on tiny water droplets through the air.

Different Viewpoints in Biology

Protection Against Lyme Disease?

An experimental vaccine made from genetically engineered bacterial proteins provides mice with complete protection against Lyme disease. The incidence of Lyme disease, with its associated nerve, joint, and heart problems, has increased dramatically in the last few years. The bacterium, *Borrelia burgdorferi,* can deceive the body's defenses. There also have been no animal models to test vaccines for this disease. Both of these factors have slowed the search for a human vaccine. Current research uses a strain of mice that show some of the same symptoms as humans after being infected by the bacterium. Scientists, using recombinant DNA methods, produced a protein called OspA, a surface protein of *B. burgdorferi.* After vaccinating the mice with this protein and injecting them with the bacteria, they found that the vaccinated mice showed no sign of infection. Another group of researchers claim that this evidence is not as substantial as first indicated because the bacteria are transmitted to the mice by injection rather than by live ticks. They say that lab strains of the bacteria growing on culture dishes may not be as virulent as the wild strains, and that tick saliva may enhance this virulence. Scientists are testing the mice to see how long the immunity lasts.

Minilab 1

Purpose

Students will be able to explain how diseases, such as AIDS, are spread by exponential growth.

Skills

sequence, observe and infer, form a hypothesis

Teaching Strategies

- Make sure that each student has two beakers or cups.
- Give 10 percent of your students $0.01M$ NaOH in their cups. Refer to p. 27T for solution preparation directions. Give the rest of your students water in one of their cups. Explain to students that 10 percent of them will have a virus in their liquid. Explain that the exchange of liquids represents contact that can transmit disease. Make sure students do not exchange liquids with the same person twice.
- Phenolphthalein is an indicator that can be purchased from a biological suppy company.

Expected Results

In a class of 20, two students (10 percent) had the disease. They spread it to four others who spread it to eight others who spread it to 16 others. These numbers represent a maximum because some may exchange with others who have already been "infected."

Answers

Answers will vary, but will most likely be between 50 percent and 80 percent. It is spread by exponential growth.

✔ Assessment

Portfolio: Ask students to explain in their portfolios what they have learned from this lab. If you have asked students to keep track of their exchanges and write their results on the board, you might also ask them to try to trace the infection to its origin.

Minilab 1

How is disease spread?

Your teacher will give you 2/3 of a cup of clear liquid. Ten percent of the class will have "diseased" liquid and 90 percent will have water. Pour 1/4 of your liquid into your empty cup and mark it "control." Exchange your original liquid with another student by pouring half of your remaining liquid into his or her liquid, then taking half back. Do this two more times with a different student each time. Add 1 to 2 drops of phenolphthalein to both of your cups. **CAUTION:** *Be careful using phenolphthalein. It can stain clothing.* The dark pink liquid indicates which cups have the "disease."

Analysis *What is the percentage of students who had the "disease" at the end of this lab? How does this lab simulate the spread of an infectious agent?*

Endotoxins are released by dead bacteria. These toxins are associated with bacterial membranes until the bacteria die and break open. Endotoxins are released when the bacterial cells rupture. Endotoxins are the cause of tuberculosis and bubonic plague.

How do toxins produce their effects? The answer is not always known. But in the case of cholera, the bacterium exerts its deadly effects by means of a toxin whose action *is* understood. The toxin alters a protein in the membrane of intestinal cells, causing negatively charged chloride ions to continually leave the cells. Positively charged sodium ions, attracted to the chloride ions, follow them out. As a result of the loss of these ions, the cells lose water by osmosis. The effect is like opening a gate in a dam, and the constant loss of water results in the symptom of diarrhea.

Disease symptoms do not always result from the action of toxins. In some cases, symptoms result from the host's reaction to the invasion of the bacteria. Bacterial pneumonia is an example. The presence of the bacteria results in the loss of a great deal of fluid from cells. This fluid accumulates in the lungs, interfering with breathing.

Viruses and Disease

Since viruses were first isolated in 1935, a large number have been discovered and studied. Many viruses cause diseases and are transmitted in the same ways as bacterial pathogens. Human diseases caused by viruses include the common cold, polio, the flu, measles, mumps, rabies, and AIDS. One form of a herpes virus causes a sexually transmitted disease. Other herpes viruses cause infectious mononucleosis and cold sores.

Some viruses that infect humans also attack other animals. For example, the virus that causes encephalitis, an inflammation of the brain, invades horses as well as humans. In addition, viruses that cause disease in both humans and other animals can be spread among the different host species. Rabies is such a disease. It can be spread among animals such as raccoons, dogs, and humans when a rabid animal bites another animal.

The symptoms of viral diseases vary with the virus and the tissues under attack. Recall that as viruses reproduce, they often destroy their host cells. For example, polio viruses attack and damage or destroy nerves in the brain and spinal cord, causing paralysis or even death.

Figure 23-4 **Viruses contain either DNA or RNA, but not both. The RNA viruses shown here cause poliomyelitis (left) and influenza (center). The smallpox virus (right) contains DNA. Magnifications: 4000× (left), 300 000× (center), 65 000× (right)**

642 ● IMMUNE SYSTEM

PORTFOLIO

Have students do research on polio and write an essay describing life in an iron lung. You could have a small group of students interview a polio survivor and report to the class. Essays may be added to the students' portfolios.

The Evolution of Disease

How did the pathogens that infect humans come to do so? Many human pathogens may be descendants of pathogens that invade other animal hosts. Most bacteria and viruses that pass from other animals to humans cannot survive and cause disease in humans. However, some of these pathogens may have evolved over time, increasing their chances of survival. For example, the virus that causes smallpox in humans is thought to have evolved from a virus that causes a disease in cattle called cowpox. Scientists hypothesize that the virus responsible for AIDS may have descended from a usually harmless virus present in the African green monkey. In addition to infecting new hosts, some pathogens also evolved different ways of being transmitted from one host to another.

Figure 23-5 Pathogens that affect humans may have evolved from bacteria and viruses that are found in animals like the African green monkey, cow, and red fox.

Section Review

Understanding Concepts

1. Malaria is caused by a protozoan and is transmitted by a particular species of mosquito. How is this protozoan transmitted? Explain why malaria is considered an infectious disease.

2. A person is infected with the bacterium that causes cholera. How does the transmission of the bacterium relate to how it causes the disease?

3. Given the symptoms of a common cold, in what kinds of cells must cold viruses reproduce?

4. **Skill Review—Designing an Experiment:** How would you set up an experiment to test the hypothesis that a certain bacterium causes a disease? For more help, see Practicing Scientific Methods in the **Skill Handbook.**

5. **Thinking Critically:** What would be a logical plan of attack for preventing the spread of waterborne diseases? Of those spread by insects?

23.1 BACTERIAL AND VIRAL AGENTS OF DISEASE **643**

SECTION 23.1

3 Assess

Check for Understanding
Have students work in groups to draw an infection cycle involving a vector. Ask them to describe ways of disrupting and preventing this type of infection cycle. COOP LEARN

Reteach
Create a "web" on the chalkboard of possible transmission pathways of a cold virus from student to student. LEP

Extension
Ask a group of students to read about some major epidemics, such as the bubonic plague, and write newspaper articles set in that time describing the current status of the epidemic. L2

✔ Assessment
Portfolio: Ask students to imagine that they are restaurant managers preparing a memo for new employees about precautions to take to avoid the transmission of disease. They should be as detailed as possible and include their memos in their portfolios. L1

4 Close

Discussion
Ask a hotel or motel manager to speak to the class about practices that must be followed in their facilities in the areas of food service, room cleaning, and maintenance of air conditioning and swimming pools to prevent transmission of disease.

Answers to Section Review

1. Malaria is a disease spread by direct contact. It is infectious because it is spread from one person to another, in this case by an arthropod.

2. The bacterium results in the symptom of diarrhea, and it is spread in the fluid lost from the disease victim.

3. The cold virus attacks tissues in the nose and throat.

4. **Skill Review—Designing an Experiment:** Two groups of mice could be given injections. The fluid injected into the mice in the experimental group would contain the bacteria; the fluid injected into the control group of mice would not. All other factors would be identical.

5. **Thinking Critically:** Sanitation is a means of preventing spread of waterborne diseases. Elimination of the insect can eliminate the disease caused by the pathogen it carries.

Prepare

Key Concepts

Students will study defense mechanisms against disease including the skin and membranes, inflammatory response, lymphocytes, macrophages, B cells, antibodies, and T cells. They will also learn about defense against cancer, allergies, autoimmune disease, and about monoclonal antibodies.

Key Terms

macrophage, lymphocyte, B cell, thymus gland, T cell, plasma cell, helper T cell, receptor, suppressor T cell, cytotoxic T cell, autoimmune disease, monoclonal antibody

Materials

- For the Minilab, prepare petri dishes with nutrient agar, and sterilize toothpicks. Gather mouthwashes, masking tape, and magnifying lenses.

1 Focus

Objectives

The objectives are listed on the student page. Remind students to preview these objectives as a guide to this numbered section.

Analogy

The armed forces of a nation might go into battle in the same way that the immune system does in the body. Compare the following lines of defense in the armed forces to the immune system lines of defense: marines = skin and membranes; infantry = inflammatory response; armored division = macrophages; communications = lymphocytes. Ask students to expand on this analogy as you proceed through the chapter. They should include B cells, T cells, lymph, antibodies, plasma cells, and receptors. An example might be: internal security patrol = cytotoxic T cell. LEP

Objectives

Discuss nonspecific lines of defense against pathogens.

Describe how the immune system defends against pathogens present in blood and tissue fluid.

Demonstrate how the immune system functions in destruction of infected, abnormal, or foreign cells.

23.2 Defending Against Pathogens

The environment that you and other humans inhabit includes a great number and a great diversity of potential pathogens. Those pathogens, however, can cause disease only if they gain entry into your body. If they do, an army of specialized cells and tissues is present and ready to respond to the invasion. Working together, these cells and tissues become mobilized to identify, seek out, and destroy the pathogens. While the battle is raging, you feel sick. The symptoms you feel are the result not only of the effect of the pathogens, but also of your body's defense against the pathogens.

Your body possesses several lines of defense against diseases. Some are nonspecific in their response; that is, they attempt to take on all potential invaders. Others target specific pathogens.

Nonspecific Defense Mechanisms

The first line of defenders to meet invading pathogens are nonspecific. They stand guard at or near the entryways to your body.

Skin and Membranes Your first line of defense against pathogens is your skin and the membranes of body openings. Your outer layer of skin is made up of dead cells that microorganisms cannot penetrate. Only if your skin is broken, as when a cut occurs, can microscopic pathogens enter.

Membranes that line openings in your body, such as your nostrils and mouth, are more vulnerable to entry of pathogens. Microorganisms can easily enter through your nose, for example. However, several adaptations prevent pathogens from gaining an upper hand. For example, hairs in your nose filter the air, while mucus in the lining of your nose traps and destroys microorganisms. Saliva in your mouth and tears in your eyes both contain substances that kill microorganisms. An enzyme in tears breaks down the cell walls of bacteria that enter the tear ducts of your eyes. The lining of your trachea and bronchi consists of cells that bear many of the tiny hairlike structures called cilia. These cilia wave as they move mucus from your lungs to your mouth. As air moves toward your lungs, potential pathogens are trapped in the mucus. Action of the cilia and mucus together prevents respiratory infection.

You have still other defense mechanisms against infectious diseases. Acids and enzymes in your body can kill many pathogens that enter body openings. Your stomach and other digestive organs produce a variety of chemicals that destroy pathogens. Bacteria present in your lower intestine also attack pathogens.

Figure 23-6 **Cilia lining your windpipe trap foreign particles to prevent them from entering your lungs. Magnification: 3570×**

644 ᴵᴹᴹᵁᴺᴱ ˢʸˢᵀᴱᴹ

PROJECT

The Grim Reaper: Tell students that Thomas Malthus proposed that three "grim reapers" would keep the human population from expanding beyond limits that the environment could sustain. One of these "grim reapers" he described as pestilence or disease. Ask students to use library resources such as almanacs to determine how effective disease is as a population limiting factor in developed countries versus lesser-developed countries. Ask them to write an essay defending or opposing his view. Students should also find out what the other two grim reapers are, according to Malthus.

The Inflammatory Response   If pathogens get by the first line of defense, a second line begins to function. Suppose you cut your finger, and pathogens enter your body. Within a short time, you notice that the cut area has become swollen, hot, painful, and red. Specialized white blood cells in the area have released a chemical called histamine. Histamine increases the flow of blood to the wound. It also increases the permeability of capillaries, allowing fluid and a variety of other white blood cells to escape into the surrounding tissue. Some of the white blood cells, called **macrophages,** are scavengers. Like amoebas, they engulf and digest pathogens that entered the cut area. The increased blood flow and accumulation of fluid are the reasons that the cut area becomes inflamed.

The temperature in the cut area often rises. This response is still another adaptation, one that interferes with the reproduction of the pathogens. Together, these various events are known as the inflammatory response.

Besides these localized events, inflammation can also cause responses throughout your body. Some injuries result in production of large numbers of white blood cells. Physicians use the relative numbers of white blood cells in a sample of your blood to help them make a diagnosis of illness. Another such response is fever. A fever is caused by a protein released by white blood cells during an inflammatory response.

Over time, these nonspecific defense mechanisms destroy most pathogens, and the infected tissue returns to normal. If a cut results in a particularly bad infection, pus may form. Pus is tissue fluid containing macrophages, other white blood cells, and dead pathogens.

Figure 23-7   When your skin is cut, the inflammatory response rids the injured area of pathogens. Sometimes a bad infection results in the formation of pus, a combination of tissue fluid, white blood cells, and dead pathogens.

Injured area

Tissue fluid and macrophages move into injured area

Release of histamine causes blood vessels to dilate

Macrophage

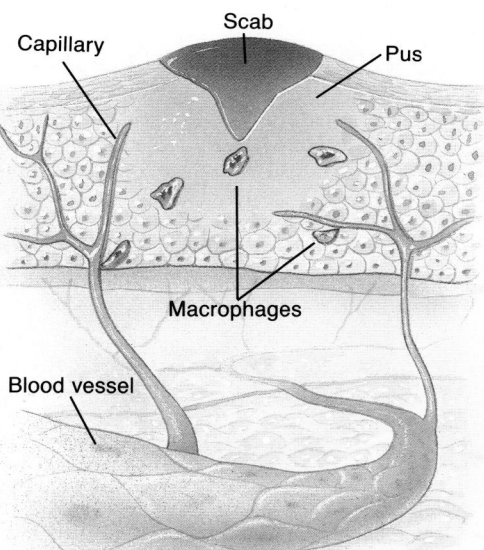

Capillary

Scab

Pus

Macrophages

Blood vessel

2 Teach

Display
Ask students to make a large poster of everything that happens during the inflammatory response. They should indicate what is happening both at the site of the infection or injury and in other parts of the body away from the site. They should make their diagrams colorful and mark them with all the appropriate labels. **L1** **LEP**

Brainstorming
Ask students to brainstorm a list of different diseases, their causes, how they are transmitted and prevented, and the body's defense against each. Explain to them that you do not expect that they will know all this information, but that you are looking for their present level of knowledge. **L1** **COOP LEARN**

Enrichment
Ask students to prepare a skit about the inflammatory response. The following characters should be included: pathogens (several students), histamine, white blood cells that are releasing histamine, blood fluids (several students), macrophage, protein that causes fever, narrator (person explaining response), and pus. **L1** **LEP**

STUDENT JOURNAL

Tell students that they are the body's immune system personnel department and they are going to "hire" new macrophages and other white blood cells that release various proteins during the inflammatory response. Each group should be "in a meeting" to decide what questions to ask potential candidates for the position. Ask them to write at least ten questions for each candidate to fill the positions of macrophage, white blood cells, and proteins involved in inflammation. The questions should reflect the kinds of jobs they will have to perform. **L1**

Minilab 2

Purpose
Students will test the effectiveness of mouthwashes in killing mouth bacteria.

Skills
observe and infer, compare and contrast, recognize cause and effect

Teaching Strategies
- Sterile petri dishes with nutrient agar are available from biological supply houses, or you may make your own.
- Explain sterile technique: Touch only one end of the toothpick. Do not touch the inside of the petri dish or cover during inoculation. Do not open dish during or after incubation.
- Make sure used toothpicks are disposed of in trash containers.

Expected Results
Bacteria colonies will be small, round spots on the agar. Sizes will vary from pinpoint to dime size. Some will be raised; colors will vary from white to tan or yellow. Both sections of the dish will have equal numbers of bacteria colonies.

Answers
Both sections had about the same numbers of colonies. Mouthwashes do not kill bacteria.

✔ Assessment
Knowledge: Design an experiment in which you could test the effects of using salt water as a mouthwash to kill bacteria.

Minilab 2

Do mouthwashes kill bacteria?

On the bottom of a petri dish prepared with sterile nutrient agar, draw a line that divides the dish in half. With a sterile toothpick, gently scrape the side of a back tooth. **CAUTION:** *Do not scrape hard enough to cause the gum to bleed.* Being careful not to cut into the surface of the agar, gently run the toothpick in an *S* shape on the surface of 1/2 of the agar. Mark C for control on the bottom of that half of the dish. Rinse your mouth with your favorite mouthwash or that supplied by your teacher. Follow the same procedure as above with another sterile toothpick. Mark an M for mouthwash on that side of the bottom of your dish. Put on the lid and seal your dish all the way around with masking tape. Incubate in a warm place for three to four days. Without opening the dish, count the bacterial colonies on each side of the dish. **CAUTION:** *Handle petri dishes with care. Be sure to wash your hands after handling petri dishes.* Put your results on the board. Make a graph of class results.
Analysis *According to class results, which section of the dish had the most bacteria colonies? According to class results, does mouthwash kill bacteria? Explain.*

Specific Defense Mechanisms

Of course, you're well aware that the adaptations you just read about are not foolproof. Pathogens can sometimes escape the first and second lines of defense. Your last cold or strep throat infection will remind you of this fact. You know, too, that you survived that cold or throat infection. You regained your health as a result of a third line of defense, called the immune response. The immune response is a highly specific means of defense. The response involves recognition and destruction of a particular pathogen. In the case of your cold or strep throat, for example, it involves recognizing and destroying the virus that causes the cold or the bacterium that causes strep throat.

The Immune Response   The ability to recognize a particular pathogen occurs early in development, as an embryo learns to detect the difference between self and non-self. That is, it becomes able to distinguish between its own chemicals and those foreign to it. In general, any foreign chemical is called an antigen. An antigen may be a protein in the membrane of a bacterium or coat of a virus. It may also be a chemical secreted by a pathogen, such as a toxin. Strep throat bacteria are distinguished from all other bacteria because of their unique antigens. Similarly, cold viruses have antigens different from antigens of other viruses. A single bacterial cell's surface may have a number of different antigens. Antigens are chemical identification markers.

Lymphocytes   How does your body use antigens to defend itself against infection? The immune response is carried out by the interaction of different white blood cells. Among them are cells known as **lymphocytes,** which recognize antigens and then begin to destroy specific pathogens. Lymphocytes are produced by bone marrow, the tissue in the hollow parts of some bones. Some lymphocytes mature within the bone marrow itself and are called **B cells.** Other lymphocytes pass from the bone marrow and mature in the **thymus gland,** which is located beneath the breastbone above the heart. Such lymphocytes are called **T cells** because they are processed in the thymus.

Figure 23-8   **Lymphocytes are one type of white blood cell. They may be B cells or T cells. Magnification: 10 000×**

ALTERNATE LAB: Identifying White Blood Cells

Purpose
Students will identify different kinds of white blood cells and determine the percentage of each in human blood.

Materials
prepared slide of human blood, microscope, library sources on blood cells

Procedure
Give the following directions to students.
1. Make a data table for the following data: number counted and percent of total, and space for diagrams of these cells: neutrophil, lymphocyte, monocyte.
2. Mount the slide on the microscope and focus on low power, then turn the slide to high power.
3. Locate a neutrophil, a cell with a nucleus and several lobes. Diagram it.
4. Locate a lymphocyte. Lymphocytes have nuclei that nearly fill the cell. Diagram a lymphocyte.
5. Locate a monocyte, the largest cell. A monocyte contains a round nucleus that fills about half the cell. Monocytes are called macrophages when they leave the bloodstream. Diagram a monocyte.
6. Develop a hypothesis as to the percentage of each type of white blood cell you will find.
7. Count a total of 50 white blood cells and keep track in your table of how many of each type you see.

Macrophages Macrophages, which are involved in nonspecific defense, are also involved in specific immune responses. Once mature, some of these cells take up residence in a variety of structures around your body—the lymph vessels and lymph nodes, the spleen, and the tonsils. These structures, along with the bone marrow and thymus, form the human immune system, which you can see in Figure 23-10.

Lymph You learned in Chapter 21 that lymph vessels carry fluid from the microscopic spaces around cells in body tissue back to your bloodstream. This tissue fluid contains lymphocytes and macrophages. Microorganisms, as well as foreign particles, are also present in tissue fluid. Located among the lymph vessels are lymph nodes through which the fluid—at this point called lymph—passes. Lymph nodes are scattered throughout your body, but they are most prominent in your neck, groin, and armpits. The lymph nodes act as filters, as macrophages within them trap and destroy some pathogens as well as debris present in the lymph fluid. B cells in the lymph nodes recognize particular pathogens and begin to kill them.

Not all pathogens, though, are present in lymph. Some are in the blood. These pathogens are detected, and some are destroyed as the blood passes through the spleen. Other pathogens are present in the air as it enters your body through your nose or mouth. These pathogens may be trapped by your tonsils.

Figure 23-9 Macrophages are white blood cells that engulf and digest pathogens. Magnification: 9000×

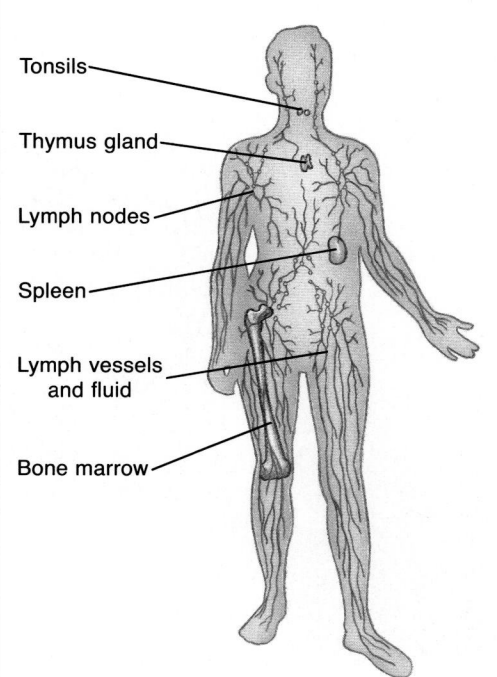

Tonsils

Thymus gland

Lymph nodes

Spleen

Lymph vessels and fluid

Bone marrow

Figure 23-10 The human immune system includes the tonsils, thymus gland, spleen, lymph vessels and fluid, lymph nodes, and bone marrow.

23.2 DEFENDING AGAINST PATHOGENS **647**

SECTION 23.2

Microscope Activity

Obtain slides of bone marrow, and ask students to make diagrams of macrophages as they see them under the microscope. Provide library resources and have them look at the photos in the text.

Discussion

Ask students what effect high-level exposure to radiation would have on macrophages and lymph. It decreases the amounts of both.

HISTORY CONNECTION

A Cure for Smallpox: In 1796 Edward Jenner, a country doctor in England, did an experiment that began the study of immunology. He had observed that milkmaids who had contracted cowpox, a milder form of smallpox, never contracted smallpox. He decided to test the idea that cowpox provided protection against smallpox by inoculating people with material that induced cowpox. These patients contracted cowpox but never got smallpox, even though they were exposed to that disease. Jenner's vision altered the world forever, beginning the work that eventually wiped out a deadly disease and also opened a new medical field—immunology.

---

8. To calculate the percent of each type of white blood cell, multiply the number of each cell type by two. Record the percent of each type in your data table.

Analysis

Ask students to answer the following questions.

1. Which type of blood cell was most common? Second most common? *neutrophil, lymphocyte*

2. What major difference did you notice between red and white blood cells? *Red blood cells don't have nuclei, while the white blood cells have large nuclei.*

3. Why would you expect the white blood cell count to go up during an infection? *White blood cells increase in number and move to the infection site to destroy invading pathogens.*

4. What are the percentages of different kinds of white blood cells? *Common*

percentages of white blood cells are: neutrophils, 60-70 percent; lymphocytes, 20-25 percent; monocytes, 3-8 percent.

✔ **Assessment**

Knowledge: Tell students that they are analyzing blood samples. One sample contains twice as many lymphocytes as they would expect. Give an explanation of what could be happening to the body. **L1**

Enrichment

Divide the class into groups of four. Each group should be assigned to one specific antibody. Using library resources, have students find out how their antibodies are unique and how they function. Then, one student should act as a talk show host interviewing the antibodies about their functions. Encourage students to use costumes and props that are creative and instructional. **L1** **COOP LEARN**

Using an Analogy

Ask students to think of ten analogies about antigen/antibody specificity. They should think of everyday life examples that would compare to the antigen/antibody complex in function and in appearance. Examples might be a lock and key or shoes and feet. **LEP**

Building a Model

Ask students to make salt dough models of antigens and antibodies and explain and demonstrate how they work to the rest of the class. Prepare salt dough in proportions of one part salt to one part flour and add water while mixing to form a bread dough-like consistency that does not stick to the hands when touched. If it remains sticky, add more flour. **L1** **LEP**

B Cells and Antibody Formation

The lymphocytes called B cells help defend against bacteria, viruses, and foreign chemicals that may be present in blood or tissue fluid. There are easily millions of possible antigens that may be detected. How can B cells recognize all of them?

Antibodies   B cells have protein molecules called antibodies embedded in their outer membranes. An antibody molecule is Y-shaped, composed of two smaller (sometimes called light) polypeptide chains bound to two larger (sometimes called heavy) polypeptide chains. Each kind of B cell bears a slightly different kind of antibody on its surface. Recognition occurs when the shape of an antibody molecule on a B cell matches the shape of part of an antigen molecule on a pathogen.

How can there be so many differently shaped antibody molecules? Look at Figure 23-11. You can see that certain areas of both the light and heavy regions are constant. That is, they have the same sequence of amino acids. But other regions of the light and heavy regions that form the two branches of the Y vary from one antibody molecule to another. In other words, they have different sequences of amino acids. The variations in amino acid sequence determine the shape of these variable regions. Each kind of antibody molecule has variable regions with a distinctive shape. In addition, each shape matches part of a specific antigen molecule in much the same way that the active site of an enzyme matches a portion of its substrate (Chapter 3). Because the two branches of the Y are the same as one another, one antibody molecule can bind to two antigen molecules.

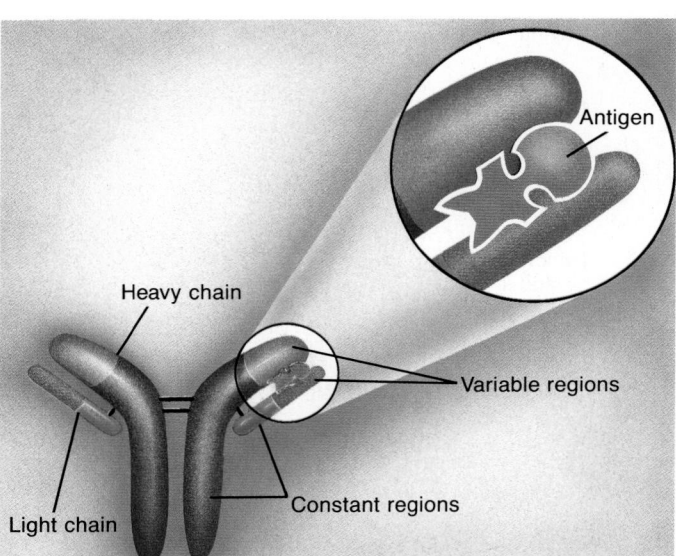

Figure 23-11   A Y-shaped antibody consists of light and heavy polypeptide chains. The tips of the Y are variable regions. The variable regions are so specific that each antibody can bind with just one type of antigen.

648 IMMUNE SYSTEM

PROGRAM RESOURCES

Teacher Classroom Resources
Study Guide, pp. 134-135 **L1**
Probing Levels of Life, Lab 60, p. 156, **L2**
Color Transparency #42 **L1** **LEP**

B Cells in Action Look at an example of how B cells work. Suppose a person with strep throat coughs, and you inhale some of the bacteria that cause this illness. The bacteria escape your first and second lines of defense and begin to reproduce within your throat tissues. Some of the bacteria enter lymph fluid, traveling with it to lymph nodes in your neck. In the nodes are B cells whose antibodies match the antigens on the bacteria. Because they match, the antibodies and antigens become linked.

Once the antibodies of a B cell are linked to antigens, the B cell becomes activated. It begins to enlarge. The large B cell divides many times to form two types of cells—plasma cells and memory cells. You will learn about memory cells later in this chapter. **Plasma cells** produce thousands of antibody molecules per second. These antibodies, identical to the ones in the membrane of the original B cell, are released into the bloodstream and lymphatic system. There they move to the site of the invasion. When the free antibodies locate their matching antigens, they bind to them. Because each antibody joins to two antigens, one antibody molecule may bind to antigens located on two different bacteria. You can see this clumping together of antibodies and bacteria in Figure 23-12. Recall from Chapter 21 that a similar clumping occurs when an improper blood transfusion is given.

Once B cell antibodies and antigens have matched and clumping has occurred, the bacteria may be destroyed. Macrophages may engulf the bacteria by phagocytosis and digest them. This process occurs within the lymph nodes, which become swollen and tender during an infection such as strep throat. In other cases, a set of blood proteins becomes activated, forming a protein that creates an opening in the bacterium. Water enters the opening by osmosis, causing the bacterium to burst.

MATH CONNECTION

Multiplying Bacteria:
Make a table showing how quickly bacteria multiply if they divide every 20 minutes. The table should illustrate an eight-hour period of time. Explain what you have found and how the immune system would have to function based on the results you see in your table. The immune response must happen quickly to attack rapidly multiplying bacteria.

Demonstration
Prepare nutrient agar plates. Spread a drop of pure bacterial culture such as *E. coli* over the agar. Place an antibiotic disc on the agar. Incubate for 24 hours. Use this to demonstrate the zone of inhibition that develops around the disc. Try several types of antibiotic discs. You can also dip circles of filter paper into antiseptics or cleaning products to see if a zone of inhibition will develop.

Bacteria with antigens enter lymph nodes

Antibodies on B cells in lymph nodes link to antigens

B cell enlarges and divides many times

Antigens

Bacterium

Antibodies

Figure 23-12 Inhaled bacteria may end up in the lymph nodes, where B cells with the correct antibodies bind with the bacteria's antigens. This begins a process that results in destruction of the invading bacteria.

Antibodies bind to antigens on bacteria

Memory cells

Plasma cells produce antibodies

Antibodies released into bloodstream

23.2 DEFENDING AGAINST PATHOGENS **649**

STUDENT JOURNAL

- Ask students to draw single-frame cartoons of B cells in action. Show them Gary Larson cartoons that have a biological emphasis as examples. Have them put their cartoons in their journals. **L1**

- Tell students to brainstorm a list of ideas for a completely different mechanism for immunity in the body. They must assume that the immune system is not a part of the blood. They must use their imaginations, but still keep within the limits imposed by what the function of the immune system actually is.

Using an Analogy

Tell students to use and add to the following analogy to describe B cells, plasma cells, and T cells. Tell them that their bodies are defended in a manner similar to the way knights defended medieval cities. Walls and moats surround the city and make entry inconvenient. Soldiers patrol the city and attack strangers. Lookouts demand identification for anyone loitering about and summon the patrol if a person does not have proper identification. **LEP**

Display

Ask students to draw a detailed series of diagrams in color on a large sheet of butcher paper or poster board about the actions of B and T cells from the time that the pathogen enters the body through the first line of defense. Have students put up their diagrams around the room for display. **LEP**

CHEMISTRY CONNECTION

Immunity and Chemistry:
Students can make the analogy that B cells and their antibodies recognize antigens in a manner similar to enzymes matching their substrates. Ask them to make another analogy to match the role of Helper T cells to the role of a catalyst in a chemical reaction. *A catalyst must be present for the reaction to occur, but at the end it is unchanged; helper T cells must link with B cells to be activated and thus activate B cells to produce antibodies, yet helper T cells are unchanged.*

Figure 23-13 Helper T cells have receptors that recognize self proteins on B cells. When the self proteins have antigen fragments, helper T cells bind with them and become activated.

Regulation of B Cells by T Cells Can you see how the formation of antibodies depends on the activation of B cells? In turn, the growth and division of activated B cells depend on their binding with certain T cells. These special cells are called **helper T cells.** In order to bind with a B cell—or, for that matter, to affect any cell—a T cell must first recognize the other cell. How does a T cell recognize a B cell?

Embedded in the membrane of all T cells are **receptors,** proteins similar to the antibodies of B cells. Receptors recognize certain self proteins that are present in the membranes of other cells in the body. However, they will bind to a self protein only if that protein is linked to an antigen. If any T cell encounters another cell displaying a self protein and an antigen that matches its receptor, the receptor will bind to the self protein and antigen, and the T cell will become activated.

For a helper T cell to bind with a B cell, therefore, the B cell must first be joined with an antigen. After a B cell's antibodies have linked with their matching antigens, some of those antigens are brought into the B cell by endocytosis. There, the antigens are broken up. A fragment of the original antigen is linked to a self protein inside the B cell. Once linked, the fragment and self protein are shuttled back to the B cell's membrane. The helper T cell's receptor recognizes the self protein and binds to it and the antigen fragment on the B cell, and the T cell becomes activated.

Helper T cells can also be activated by binding to macrophages. Macrophages break up antigens they have engulfed and, like B cells, send fragments linked with self proteins back to the membrane. Once activated, the helper T cell releases chemicals that stimulate the B cell to divide and form plasma cells. These events are summarized in Figure 23-13.

PORTFOLIO

Tell students to design a 30-minute educational presentation for seventh grade students that would teach them about B and T cell interactions. Have them record their plans in their portfolios. Tell them to be creative with illustrations, models, analogies, and hands-on manipulatives. If there is an opportunity to do the presentation, allow a group that has especially good ideas to do their presentation to a seventh grade class and then report on what they thought was effective and what could have been improved. **L3**

The chemicals released by activated helper T cells also attract macrophages and activate other kinds of T cells. **Suppressor T cells** counteract the effect of helper T cells by releasing chemicals that inhibit activity of B cells and macrophages. The number of helper T cells decreases and the number of suppressor T cells increases as an infection is brought under control.

Allergies Do you suffer from hay fever or know someone who does? Hay fever is an immune response to an antigen that does not cause a reaction in most people. As such, it is an allergy. In hay fever, pollen acts as an antigen against which plasma cells begin producing antibodies. Some of the antibodies cause release of histamine. The continued high level of histamine accounts for the sneezing and runny noses of hay fever victims. Allergies are thought to result when suppressor T cells fail to balance the effects of the plasma cells, antibodies, and histamine. Other allergies can be caused by certain foods. Hives, reddened swellings on skin similar to a rash, are a common indication of such allergies.

Thinking Lab
DRAW A CONCLUSION

How do helper T cells act?

Background
How do you fight off a cold, "strep" throat, or cancer? Your immune system protects you from harmful microorganisms. Recently, scientists have learned how different white blood cells function as part of your immune system. B cells, white blood cells made in the bone marrow, make receptors called antibodies that can deactivate toxins produced by bacteria. Helper T cells,

made in the thymus gland, get information from another white blood cell, a macrophage, about the type of toxin present in the body. The helper T cell, activated by the macrophage, gives off a substance which stimulates B cells.

You Try It
Study the summary diagram of recent discoveries of interactions of B cells, helper T cells, and macrophages.

Draw conclusions about the diagram by answering the following questions.
1. How do macrophages get information about bacterial toxins?
2. What do B cells do in the presence of interleukin?
3. Where does interleukin come from?
4. What happens to the antibodies produced by B cells?

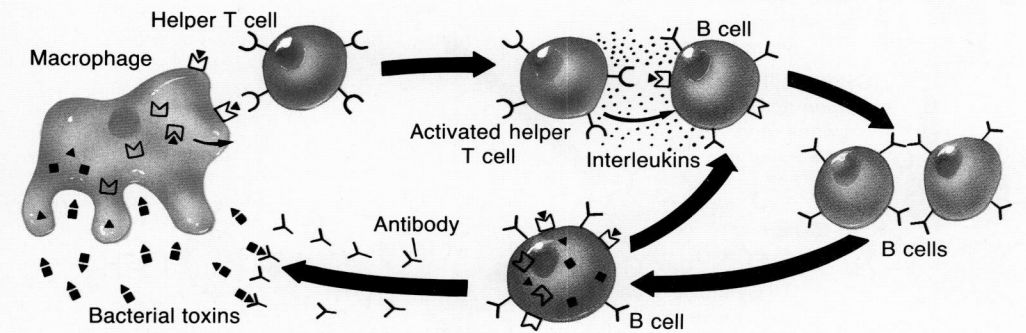

23.2 DEFENDING AGAINST PATHOGENS 🔊 **651**

Thinking Lab
DRAW A CONCLUSION

Purpose
Students will gain an understanding of the complexity of the immune system.

Skills
interpret scientific illustrations, recognize cause and effect

Teaching Strategies
• Ask students why they haven't gotten chicken pox more than once.

Further Background
Cytotoxic T cells, also made in the thymus, get information about abnormal cells and the antigens they display. After obtaining this information, they multiply and secrete destructive enzymes, which kill the abnormal cells.

Answers
1. They engulf the toxins.

2. They divide and produce more B cells with antibodies for the toxin.
3. activated helper T cells
4. They are given off by the B cell and deactivate bacterial toxins.

✔ Assessment

Knowledge: In their journals, have students describe the most impressive things they learned from this lab.

Concept Development

Ask students to make a chart comparing and contrasting the similarities and differences of B cells, helper T cells, suppressor T cells, and cytotoxic T cells. **L2**

Display

Have students make mobiles of the cells involved in the immune response. They can use construction paper, string, and coat hangers. The length of the string should correlate to the sequence of the events in the immune response, with the events happening first at the highest levels with shortest strings and the longest strings indicating the events that take place later in the sequence. The mobiles should have labels of the immune cells and tissues. They should try to make their mobiles self-explanatory by using arrows and diagrams that will help in understanding the sequence of events in the immune response. **L1** **LEP**

Misconception

Some people think they are allergic to the feathers in feather pillows. New evidence shows that people are not allergic to the feathers, but instead are allergic to the mites that live on the feathers. These microscopic animals live on the scales of dead human skin, which are shed on pillows and mattresses. The feces of the mites lead to allergic reactions in the form of skin rashes or respiratory problems.

Text Question

How is a cytotoxic T cell similar to a helper T cell? Both recognize self proteins linked with antigen fragments and bind to them.

T Cells and Cellular Immunity

You've just read how B cell stimulation leads to the production of antibodies that detect and destroy pathogens present in blood and tissue fluid. You've also seen how different T cells are involved in that process. Yet T cells function in ways other than regulating the activity of B cells and macrophages. They also interact directly with cells infected by viruses and with foreign cells.

One kind of T cell defends against body cells in which viruses are reproducing. This cell, called a **cytotoxic T cell,** acts to destroy the infected cell. But like any other T cell, to be activated it must first bind with a self protein linked to a foreign antigen. The viral mRNA within the infected cell directs the production of proteins needed to make new virus coats. Those proteins are foreign to the person's body and therefore serve as antigens. Some of those antigens move to the infected cell's membrane attached to a self protein. At this point, a receptor on a cytotoxic T cell recognizes the antigen linked to the self protein on the infected cell's membrane and binds with it. After binding to the infected cell, the cytotoxic T cell becomes activated. It then forms a clone of cells that destroy the infected cells. It also releases chemicals that attract macrophages. Some cytotoxic T cells secrete powerful chemicals that kill the infected cells. Helper and suppressor T cells help regulate the activity of cytotoxic T cells. How is a cytotoxic T cell similar to a helper T cell?

Figure 23-14 Cytotoxic T cells kill infected body cells indirectly by attracting macrophages. Cytotoxic T cells also kill infected cells directly by releasing proteins that disrupt the cells' plasma membranes.

Body cell infected by viruses

Virus fragments presented by self protein

Cytotoxic T cell recognizes and binds with self protein and virus fragment

Cytotoxic T cell becomes activated, divides, and forms a clone

Clone of T cells

Cytotoxic T cells move to site of infection

Cytotoxic T cells release chemical to attract macrophage

Macrophage destroys infected cell by phagocytosis

Cytotoxic T cell binds with infected cell and kills it

652 IMMUNE SYSTEM

Molecular Biology: Cesar Milstein is an Argentinean molecular biologist who has done research on genetics, biosynthesis, and chemistry of immunoglobins (antibodies). He has developed a strategy for making chemically pure antibodies. Milstein and his colleagues were one of the first teams of scientists to determine the complete nucleotide sequence of the immunoglobin molecule. To prepare chemically pure monoclonal antibodies, he fused myeloma cells with spleen cells to make hybrid cells that can be cultured to produce antibodies against a wide range of antigens. The permanent cultures that come from the clones can be propagated indefinitely and can produce an unlimited supply of immunoglobin.

Why You Feel Sick

Some of the chemicals that act to signal and regulate various parts of the immune system are also responsible for making a person feel sick. You've already learned about histamine and its effects. When you are fighting an infection, macrophages release another chemical that resets your body's thermostat to a higher setting, resulting first in chills and then in fever. Though fever may make you feel uncomfortable, it is an adaptation. A slightly higher-than-normal body temperature interferes with the ability of viruses and bacteria to reproduce. It also increases the production of antibodies and replication of T cells. The same chemical that increases your body temperature also causes an increase in the production of certain hormones that are secreted during periods of stress. High levels of these hormones inhibit reactions that store fat or convert glucose to glycogen. Instead, fats and sugars are promptly delivered to your body tissues, where they provide the energy needed to fuel the immune response. In addition, the hormones tend to decrease your appetite and cause sleepiness. They also make a sick person more susceptible to pain, which explains why many illnesses are accompanied by headaches and sore joints. Aspirin is effective in combating fever and pain associated with many illnesses because it interferes with chemical changes that lead to those symptoms.

Defense Against Cancer

Cytotoxic T cells defend not only against infectious diseases but also against cancer. Recall from Chapter 10 that cancers are diseases in which cells grow and reproduce uncontrollably. In addition, the cells are abnormal, resembling embryonic cells rather than differentiated cells. They also differ in shape from normal cells, have unique antigens on their surfaces, and have self antigens. Cytotoxic T cells can bind to these cancer cells and destroy them. It is likely that many cells become cancerous during a person's life, but they are destroyed by the immune system before they can multiply and cause damage. A person may develop cancer when his or her immune system fails to perform its normal function of detecting and destroying cancer cells.

Figure 23-15 **Cancer cells like these are usually killed by cytotoxic T cells. What happens if cancer cells are not destroyed? Magnification: 2000×**

Teacher FYI

In mice, exposure to tobacco smoke increases the chances of the female contracting cervical cancer. Cervical cancer kills about 4500 women in the U.S. each year. Cigarette smoking alone doesn't increase the risk, but if a woman is infected with HPV, the human papillomavirus, her chances of developing cancer increase. HPV is a common sexually transmitted disease. Scientists suspect that a two-step process is at work. HPV causes the epithelial cells of the cervix to divide rapidly. If these cells are exposed to carcinogens from tobacco smoke, they become malignant. Now that mouse studies are complete, scientists are working on similar experiments with human cervical cells in laboratory cultures.

Brainstorming

Ask students to brainstorm a list of at least 10 infectious diseases they have had. They should decide which five diseases they want to discuss. For each disease, they should make a list of symptoms and the immune response that caused these symptoms to develop. They should explain the treatment they received and describe how it helped. Have them hypothesize why some symptoms lasted longer than others. **L1** **COOP LEARN**

Display

Ask students to find and cut out from their favorite magazines advertisements for products that make health claims or claim to help fight disease. Substances such as mouthwashes, vitamins, and sport drinks are examples. Ask students to make a bulletin board collage of their advertisements and speculate about which claims might not be true. **L2** **COOP LEARN**

Figure Caption Question

What happens if cancer cells are not destroyed? A person may get cancer.

Concept Development

Autoimmune disorders are not understood very well and may involve several biochemical and immune pathways. In some, antibodies or effector T cells may react with the patient's own tissues. An example of that can be found when the strep bacteria that cause rheumatic fever induce antibodies that attack the heart muscle. In other cases, viruses, drugs, or genetic mutations may cause differences in the cell components so that they are identified as foreign particles by the immune system. Patients with lupus erythematosus have immune reactions against the genetic machinery of their own cells. Symptoms include inflammation of joints and damage to the kidneys. Rheumatoid arthritis causes joints to stiffen, swell, and become painful. The area in the joint where two bones meet is enclosed in a capsule that contains fluid. The capsule has an inner lining called the synovial membrane. Inflammation starts here, swelling the membrane and spreading to other parts of the joint. Outgrowths of inflamed tissue invade the cartilage surrounding the bone ends, eventually eating it away. Finally, scar tissue can form between the bone ends and sometimes change to bone so that the joint becomes fused and immovable. Treatment programs are designed to relieve pain, reduce inflammation, prevent damage to joints, prevent deformities, and keep joints movable and functioning properly.

Figure Caption Question

What other organs are routinely transplanted? Students may know that kidneys, lungs, corneas, and livers may be transplanted.

Figure 23-16 **Heart transplants are no longer rare in the United States. What other organs are routinely transplanted?**

Figure 23-17 **In the autoimmune disease called rheumatoid arthritis, the membranes around joints are attacked by the immune system. Rheumatoid arthritis is extremely painful and often leads to crippling like this.**

654 ❧ IMMUNE SYSTEM

Rejection of Transplants

Organ transplants are considered by many to be a miracle of modern medicine. Replacement of a failed heart or liver offers a person a promise of survival when no other medical technology can do so. However, the person's immune system treats the transplanted organ as it has evolved to do—as foreign matter to be destroyed. The foreign tissue will have some self proteins in common with the person into which it has been transplanted. However, it will also have self proteins of its own, which are foreign to the transplant recipient. Cytotoxic T cell receptors will bind to both proteins, and ultimately the T cells will destroy the tissue. Because the T cell receptors can bind only to both a self protein and an antigen, the closer the match between donor and recipient tissues, the less the chance for rejection. In other words, if the transplanted tissue has many proteins like the self proteins of the recipient, fewer T cells will be able to attack.

To combat the rejection of transplanted tissue, patients are usually given drugs that dampen the immune response. The problem with many of these drugs, though, is that the patient then becomes susceptible to other diseases. Transplant recipients, for example, have an increased risk of cancer. However, a drug called cyclosporin affects only the T cells that fight the transplant. Thus, the other cells of the immune system are left to defend against other antigens.

Autoimmune Diseases

Recall that an embryo becomes able to distinguish self from non-self early in its development. This distinction is usually retained throughout life. However, for reasons we still don't know, some people's immune systems turn against them. For these people, certain of their own tissues are attacked by antibodies or by cytotoxic T cells as if they were transplanted tissues. This abnormal response of the immune system to part of a person's own body may cause a variety of **autoimmune diseases.**

Examples of autoimmune diseases include myasthenia gravis and multiple sclerosis, diseases affecting the nervous system. In myasthenia gravis, antibodies attack the connections between nerves and muscles. In multiple sclerosis, T cells attack the outer covering around certain nerve cells. Rheumatic fever is another autoimmune disease in which antibodies against certain bacteria react with heart and skeletal muscles. Juvenile onset diabetes mellitus is caused by T cells that attack certain pancreas cells. In this case, the body cells may be infected with a virus.

Treating Autoimmune Diseases Scientists are working to find ways of helping people with autoimmune diseases. However, their work is hampered by the fact that they do not fully understand what makes the immune system turn against the body of which it is a part.

One possible method of treatment is to introduce toxic chemicals that bind to and kill the T cells that cause the disease. This cure might be effected by producing an antibody that matches the T cell's receptor and then linking the toxic chemical to that antibody. The antibodies, attached to the toxic chemicals, would be injected into the body. Because the antibody would match only with receptors of a particular T cell, only that kind of T cell would be destroyed by the toxic chemical. It may also be possible to inject substances that would bind to the self proteins of the body cells under attack. The substances, once attached to the self proteins, would prevent the T cell receptors from binding with them.

Monoclonal Antibodies   You've just read how particular antibodies might be made and used to treat autoimmune diseases. A means of producing pure antibodies has been available since the 1970s. These antibodies are not produced in a test tube. Rather, they are produced by mice.

To produce a specific antibody, a mouse is injected with the proper antigen. Lymphocytes in the mouse's spleen respond by making antibodies against the antigen in the injection. Each lymphocyte makes a specific antibody. The lymphocytes are then removed from the spleen and fused with certain cancer cells, which divide repeatedly in a culture medium in the laboratory. Each fused cell is cultured and forms a pure clone. The clone consists of cells that make only one kind of antibody, so the antibodies produced are called **monoclonal antibodies.**

After the antibody produced by each clone is identified, the clones are grown in culture. Even greater quantities of pure antibody can be obtained by injecting a mouse with the fused cells. The cells form a tumor that produces a large amount of the antibody. The antibody is later filtered from the body fluids of the mouse. These techniques are pictured in Figure 23-18.

Figure 23-18   Monoclonal antibodies can be produced in the laboratory and might be used to fight autoimmune diseases.

Antigens

Bacteria

Activated B cells make antibodies

B cells fused with cancer cells

Fused cells cultured

B cells   Cancer cells

Clones of fused cells

Monoclonal antibodies

Enrichment
Ask students to interview a physician to find out how the following autoimmune diseases are treated: multiple sclerosis, arthritis, rheumatic fever, juvenile diabetes mellitus, and myasthenia gravis. They should also ask about the symptoms, what population is most affected, genetic and environmental factors, and any late-breaking research regarding the disease. L2

3 Assess

Check for Understanding
Ask students to select an infectious disease that they are familiar with. Ask them to list the symptoms, causes of the symptoms, and the immune response that occurred. L1

Reteach
Make a list of the components of the immune system on the board. Ask students to describe the function of each component.

STUDENT JOURNAL

Tell students that they work for a biological research company that has just perfected and patented a new monoclonal antibody system that is better than what is currently available. Ask them to make an advertisement for a page in a physicians' magazine that will sell their product. Ask students to design, for a page in their journals, an advertising campaign for doctors about the new product. L1

Extension

Ask students to do library research and report on the effect of tobacco use on the immune system. Ask them to find out how other stresses on the body affect the immune system. Examples of stress might be heat, cold, hunger, emotional stress, anger, lack of sleep, and others students may wish to research. **L2**

✔ Assessment

Performance: Have students write the script for a play about a person who inhales pathogens and the various responses made by the immune system. Have one student be the casting director, another the props and costume manager, etc. Create simple costumes and have students put on the play. Afterwards, have several students critique the play. **COOP LEARN**

4 Close

Activity

Ask the school building engineer and the school cafeteria manager to explain to the class what they do as part of their jobs to prevent the spread of pathogens in the school.

Figure 23-19 Cancer cells in humans vary in size and shape. The photograph on the right shows cancer cells from a brain tumor. In the photograph on the left, a cytotoxic T cell is attacking a cancer cell. Magnification: 500× (right); 2500× (left)

Monoclonal antibodies have taught us a great deal about how the immune system operates. They are also used in home pregnancy tests. In such tests, antibodies react with a chemical present only in the urine of a pregnant woman. Combining the antibodies with the chemical in the urine results in a visible change that the woman can easily see.

In the future, monoclonal antibodies might also be used to detect and treat cancer. The antibodies would be designed to recognize abnormal antigens present on cancer cells. Attaching a poison to the antibodies would lead to the destruction of the cancer cells. After the antibodies bind to the antigens on the cancer cells, the poison would enter and kill the cells. This technique has already proved successful in killing certain cancer cells grown in culture.

Section Review

Understanding Concepts

1. You get a splinter in your foot while walking barefoot. The next day, the area around the splinter is swollen, sore, and red. Explain why.
2. How do two antibodies that recognize two different antigens differ from one another? How are they the same?
3. Explain why skin grafts might be rejected.
4. **Skill Review—Sequencing:** Sequence the steps by which the immune system would identify and destroy a bacterium present in your tissue fluid. For more help, see Organizing Information in the **Skill Handbook.**
5. **Thinking Critically:** Explain why burn victims are susceptible to infection.

656 🔬 IMMUNE SYSTEM

Answers to Section Review

1. The inflammatory response results in swelling and redness due to release of histamine.
2. Each kind of antibody molecule has unique variable regions at the tips of its Y shape. The rest of each antibody has basically the same structure.
3. Skin grafts are foreign tissue. Cells of the graft have some self antigens in common with the recipient, but they also bear foreign antigens. Cytotoxic T cells bind to the combination of self and foreign antigens and destroy the graft.
4. **Skill Review—Sequencing:** Some B cells have antibodies on their membranes that match the antigens on the bacterium. After the antibodies are linked to the antigens, the B cell forms a clone of plasma cells that release antibodies into the blood and lead to clumping of the bacteria. The bacteria may be destroyed by macrophages or by cytotoxic T cells.
5. **Thinking Critically:** Burned skin becomes vulnerable to entrance of pathogens.

23.3 Immunity and Prevention of Disease

Did you have chicken pox as a child? If you did, you might recall having a fever and certainly will remember the rash that appeared all over your body. You also know that you will probably not get chicken pox again. Why are you protected from a second bout of this disease? Why do you get some other infections over and over again? How can many diseases be prevented from occurring in the first place? Why can medicines be used to treat some diseases but not others? The answers to all those questions concern whether and how your body develops immunity to diseases.

Active Immunity

The first time you are exposed to a particular antigen, your immune system springs into action, producing clones of plasma cells or cytotoxic T cells that help stop the infection. However, it takes several days for your immune system to mobilize its forces against the pathogens. During that time, you feel sick. Gradually your symptoms disappear, and your immune system wipes out the enemy. In many cases, the next time you are exposed to the same antigen, your immune system responds much more quickly and you don't become sick at all. Why?

During your first exposure to an antigen, when clones of plasma cells or cytotoxic T cells are being produced, clones of **memory cells** are also produced. Those memory cells remain in your body long after an infection is over. Some live for months or years; others last your lifetime. Thus, if a pathogen reappears, your body can react very quickly, bypassing the early steps of the immune response. The antigens of the pathogen are recognized very quickly by either antibodies or cytotoxic T cells and destroyed before the pathogen can cause symptoms. In such a case, you have become immune to the pathogen. When memory cells enable you to resist a disease, you have what is known as **active immunity.**

Objectives

Distinguish between active and passive immunity.

Discuss the use of drugs in treating bacterial and viral diseases.

Relate the life cycle of HIV to the symptoms of AIDS.

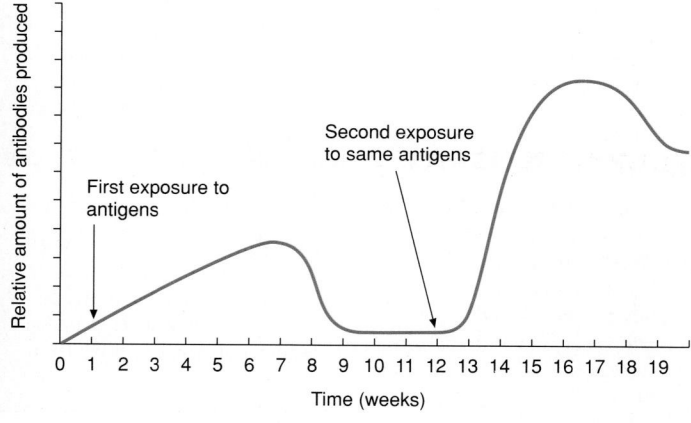

Figure 23-20 Memory B cells have antibodies for antigens that have attacked your body in the past. Memory cytotoxic T cells have receptors. Both types of memory cells allow the immune system to respond quickly to new infections of the same antigen.

SECTION 23.3

Prepare

Key Concepts
Students will study active and passive immunity, vaccines, treatment of disease, interferon, and AIDS.

Key Terms
memory cell, active immunity, vaccine, antiserum, passive immunity, interferon

Materials
- Gather the following materials for the Investigation: petri dish cultures of *E. coli,* permanent marking pencil, masking tape, sterile toothpicks, sterile paper punches, metric ruler, plant material and other substances to be tested depending on students' requests, 250-mL beakers, forceps, Bunsen burner, hot plates.

1 Focus

Objectives
The objectives are listed on the student page. Remind students to preview these objectives as a guide to this numbered section.

Activity
Ask students to make a table of all the communicable diseases they have had. Next to each disease, they should write the treatment they received. In the third column, they should indicate whether they got the disease more than once. Ask them to make another list of diseases they have never had and why they haven't contracted them. **L1**

2 Teach

Enrichment
Have students visit a local swimming pool and ask what kinds of practices are followed to prevent disease transmission, then report to the class.

INVESTIGATION

Antibiotic Properties of Plants and Other Substances

Time Allotment
1 1/2 class periods spread over several days

Objectives
Upon completing this investigation, students will be able to:
- Compare the antibiotic properties of plants and other substances.
- Interpret zones of inhibition in bacteria cultures.

Skills
observe and infer, design an experiment, interpret data

Materials
petri dish cultures of *E. coli,* permanent marking pencil, masking tape, sterile toothpicks, sterile paper punches, metric ruler, plant material and other substances for testing, 250-mL beaker, forceps, Bunsen burner, hot plates

Preparation
- Obtain petri dishes with agar and *E. coli* cultures, or prepare your own.
- Sterilize toothpicks and paper punches by wrapping separately in aluminum foil and autoclaving or use a home pressure cooker.
- About one week prior to the lab, prepare one of the above petri dishes for your introductory demonstration. Place four different antibiotic discs on a culture of *E. coli* that is marked into quadrants on the bottom. Discs are available from biological supply houses, or your local hospital lab may be willing to provide outdated ones. Most will still work well enough for your purposes. Seal the dish with masking tape around the outside.

Possible Hypotheses
1. Onion and garlic have antibiotic properties, but dandelion does not.
2. Regular tea has antibiotic properties, but mint tea does not.

Use of Vaccines   The principle of active immunity may be used to prevent certain diseases from occurring. Solutions prepared from weakened or dead microorganisms, viruses, or toxins are called **vaccines.** Vaccines injected into a healthy person do not normally cause the disease, but they do cause antibodies or cytotoxic T cells to form. When you are vaccinated, you may suffer mild discomfort, but the antibodies or cytotoxic T cells will protect you from the more potent disease organisms or toxins if you are later exposed to them.

Vaccines have been developed for such diseases as polio, measles, mumps, some forms of influenza, tetanus, diphtheria, and bacterial pneumonia. Why is there no vaccination for the common cold? Why, for that matter, do you keep getting colds over and over again?

The reason is that there is no single cold virus. In fact, there are 100 different forms of one kind of cold virus alone. Moreover, these viruses mutate. Mutations result in different alleles, which result, in turn, in different protein antigens. Therefore, one generation of cold virus may have different antigens from its ancestors. Yet one region of the virus's protein coat must remain the same. It is the part of the coat that matches with a receptor on the membrane of cells in the nasal lining. Though different, at least half of all cold viruses attach to the same receptor on nose cell

INVESTIGATION

Antibiotic Properties of Plants and Other Substances

Medicine men and women of the past used a variety of plants for healing. Scientists have studied the medicinal effects of a variety of these plants and find that in some cases there is a medicinal effect. However, some folklore remedies have no merit; in fact, some can be harmful. In this lab, you will test the antibiotic properties of plants and other substances you may have heard have healing effects.

Problem
Do plants and other substances have antibiotic properties?

Safety Precautions
Take appropriate precautions when using a Bunsen burner. Wear goggles. Wash hands at the end of this lab. Do not use poisonous plants or substances. Even though *E. coli* is not pathogenic under normal circumstances, it is wise to treat your cultures with caution.

Hypothesis
Make a hypothesis about what plants or other substances might have antibiotic properties. Explain your reasons for making this hypothesis.

Experimental Plan
1. As a group, make a list of possible ways you might test your hypothesis using the materials your teacher has made available or materials you can bring from home.

658 IMMUNE SYSTEM

Possible Procedures
- Heat paper punches in three different kinds of tea and one in water. Place the paper punches on four quadrants of the petri dish bacteria culture. Measure zones of inhibition.
- Place yogurt, ginger, and a small piece of adhesive tape on three quadrants of a petri dish bacteria culture. Leave the other 1/4 of the dish free. Measure zones of inhibition.

membranes. Based on that knowledge, scientists are attempting to produce antibodies that would link to the receptors, preventing the viruses from attaching. The antibodies might be given in the form of drops or a spray. The drug would not cure a cold, but it would prevent one. Vaccinations in the future may be sprayed into your nose!

Synthetic Vaccines Vaccines made from weakened bacteria, viruses, or toxins often take a long time to produce and are usually expensive to develop. They also may cause side effects. Recent advances have made possible the production of synthetic viral vaccines. The idea behind these vaccines is that an entire virus is not necessary. Only a specific antigen, a part of a protein in the virus's coat, is recognized by the host. Synthetic vaccines contain only these recognizable antigens. Another advantage of synthetic vaccines is the possibility of producing a single vaccine that would provide immunity against several viral diseases.

Figure 23-21 Vaccination programs protected children against poliomyelitis in the 1950s.

2. Agree on one idea from your group's list that could be investigated in the classroom.
3. Design an experiment that will test one variable at a time. Plan to collect quantitative data.
4. Following the style of a recipe, write a numbered list of directions that anyone could follow.
5. Make a list of materials and the quantities you will need.

Checking the Plan

Discuss the following points with other group members to decide the final procedures for your experiment.
1. What variables will need to be controlled?
2. What is your control?
3. What will you measure or count?
4. How will you make your counts?

5. Have you designed and made a table for collecting data?

Make sure your teacher has approved your experimental plan before you proceed further.

Data and Observations

Carry out your experiment; make your measurements; and complete your data table. Make a graph of your results.

Analysis and Conclusions

1. According to your results, which of the plants or substances that you tested have antibiotic properties? Explain.
2. Were your results supported by your hypothesis? Explain.
3. If your hypothesis was not supported, what types of experimental error could be responsible?

4. Consult with another group that tested the same plants or substances. Were their results the same as yours? Explain.
5. Of the plants or substances you tested, which ones had the most antibiotic effect? How could you tell?
6. Why is it important that new antibiotics be developed?

Going Further

Based on this lab experience, design an experiment that would help to answer another question that arose from your work. Assume that you will have unlimited resources and will not be conducting this lab in class.

23.3 IMMUNITY AND PREVENTION OF DISEASE **659**

Extensions

Lead students with questions about other plants and substances they might test. Ask them to think about how they could vary the environmental conditions for growth to determine if zones of inhibition might change size under varying conditions.

Teaching Suggestions

- Introduce the lab by explaining how you prepared the petri dish. Explain what antibiotic discs are and ask students what the zones of inhibition might represent. Pass the dish around and ask them not to open it, but to hold it up to the light to see the zones of inhibition more easily.
- Demonstrate how to prepare a petri dish using sterile technique. Ask a student to come to the front and direct him or her to prepare a plate similar to the one you made using sterile technique.
- Ask students if they have heard about any plants or substances other than medications that have antibiotic properties. They may suggest plants such as garlic, onion, ginger, sugar, tea, vitamin C, yogurt, aloe, and adhesive tape.
- Explain to students that *E. coli* is a common nonpathogenic (under ordinary circumstances) bacterium that inhabits the human body. They should still use care with a bacteria culture and not open the seal after inoculation. Make sure they wash their hands at the end of each lab.
- Cultures should be incubated in a warm place for two to three days or at room temperature for three to four days.
- Be sure students can identify poisonous plants of the area.

Data and Observations

Examine each group's graphs and evaluate the group's interpretation of the data.

Data Analysis

1-5. Answers will vary according to the plants and other substances chosen for testing.
6. Resistance to antibiotics has developed in a number of different bacteria that cause human disease.

✔ **Assessment**

Oral: Have each student group choose a spokesperson to give an oral report on the results of their experiment.

Figure Caption Question

What kind of immunity is passed from the mother to a nursing baby?
passive immunity

Different Viewpoints in Biology

Antibodies or Proteins in Mother's Milk?

Doctors have always assumed that breast-fed infants have fewer diseases because breast milk contains the mother's antibodies for various diseases. However, new studies show that perhaps infants' resistance to infection by viruses that cause severe diarrhea is controlled equally by a slimy protein called mucin in the milk. Scientists removed antibodies from the milk and found that growth of viruses was inhibited as long as mucin was still present. If mucin protein can be synthesized in the lab, it could be added to infant formulas. The scientists hypothesize that adults develop natural mucins in their intestines, while newborns do not have intestinal mucins. They speculate that as babies develop, they generate their own mucins. Cow's milk contains some mucin, but because most of the protein is filtered out of cow's milk formulas during preparation, it is not a good source of mucin.

Figure 23-22 What kind of immunity is passed from the mother to a nursing baby?

Passive Immunity

When a person becomes infected, the body often cannot produce antibodies quickly enough to fight the disease. In the case of some diseases—for example, tetanus—this slow response could be fatal. However, a person might survive the disease by receiving antibodies against the disease made by another animal. The antibodies are extracted from the animal's blood. A solution of antibodies and blood serum is called an **antiserum.** Injection of an antiserum provides borrowed antibodies to fight the disease. Protection in this case results in what is called **passive immunity** because the antibodies are not being made by the person exposed to the pathogen.

Passive immunity works more quickly than active immunity, but its effects last for a shorter time. Human infants have passive immunity at birth because they have some antibodies that passed across the placenta from the mother. Borrowed antibodies may later be passed to an infant in the mother's milk. Passive immunity protects an infant during its early life when its own immune system is just developing and when it is exposed to a variety of pathogens for the first time.

Treatment of Disease

You know that a person is sick while his or her immune system is building its response to a pathogen. If the infection is bacterial, the bacteria are reproducing rapidly during this time. The length of an illness caused by some bacterial pathogens can be decreased by antibiotic medicines, which reduce the rate of bacterial reproduction. Antibiotics are produced by many kinds of simple organisms and destroy bacteria in a variety of ways. Penicillin, for example, interferes with the production of the cell walls of some bacteria.

Viral Disease Treatment Antibiotics cannot be used against viruses because viruses are not living organisms. Viral diseases must be treated differently from bacterial diseases. Drugs that disrupt the life cycle of a virus cannot be used if they also destroy the infected host cell. Some drugs used to treat viral diseases prevent the viral nucleic acid from replicating. Others interfere with transcription or translation. Still others might work by preventing viruses from entering host cells, as with the possible cold virus drug discussed earlier.

Interferon Protection from a first attack by viruses is not the result of the immune system. Instead, a protein is released by the infected host cell. The protein, called **interferon,** travels to and enters a healthy cell, where it prevents viral reproduction. Several kinds of interferons have been discovered. Some work by activating an enzyme that breaks down viral mRNA. Others prevent translation of viral mRNA or stop the packaging and release of new viruses.

660 IMMUNE SYSTEM

When interferon was discovered, it was believed that it might be used in antiviral drugs. Using recombinant DNA techniques, researchers have produced large quantities of interferon. Tests have been conducted to determine whether interferon can be used to prevent or to treat a variety of viral diseases or certain forms of cancer. Although the results of many tests have not been promising, interferon has been shown to be effective against the virus that causes hepatitis B, a disease that can lead to liver cancer and other liver problems. A recent study showed that injections of interferon prevented the virus from destroying the liver in about half the patients tested; it cured about one in ten. Considering that 300 million people worldwide suffer from hepatitis B, this study is particularly encouraging.

AIDS

With autoimmune diseases, the body turns against itself; the immune system responds to body tissues as if they were foreign. When a person has AIDS (acquired immune deficiency syndrome), his or her immune system is slowly destroyed. As this destruction occurs, the person suffering from AIDS is not able to fight off pathogens or abnormal cells that would normally be attacked by the immune system of a healthy person. The destruction of the immune system is so overwhelming that AIDS is always a fatal disease.

Transmission   AIDS is caused by a retrovirus (Chapter 15) named human immunodeficiency virus, or HIV. In infected persons, HIV is present in body fluids such as blood and semen. Infection occurs when the virus enters the bloodstream through a cut or tear in the tissues.

HIV can be transmitted in four known ways, all of which involve the exchange of body fluids: (1) Transmission can occur during sexual intercourse in semen or vaginal secretions. (2) Sharing needles during intravenous drug use is another mode of transmission. A small amount of blood can remain on a needle used by a person infected with HIV. If this needle is used by a second person, the virus present in the blood can be injected into the second person's blood. (3) Many cases of infection with the virus have resulted from transfusions of blood or blood products that contained HIV. However, since 1985, this means of transmission has declined as a result of a test that screens blood for the presence of HIV antibodies. Currently, an extremely small chance exists that HIV can be spread through transfusions. (4) Finally, the virus can be transmitted from the blood of an infected female to a fetus during pregnancy. The virus passes to the fetus through the placenta.

Figure 23-23   The AIDS virus consists of an outer covering taken from the cells it infects and an inner protein capsule that contains RNA and an enzyme. In this photograph, the AIDS virus is the small red sphere near the top. Magnification: 32 400×

Display
Ask students to cut out articles from the newspaper on current AIDS-related issues and mount them on the bulletin board. You might want to have a corner of the board deal with misconceptions about AIDS and methods of transmission. L1 LEP

PORTFOLIO

Have students imagine their best friends have just found out they are HIV positive. Ask them to write entries in imaginary diaries that describe how they feel about their friends and include these in their portfolios.

MEETING INDIVIDUAL NEEDS

Ask a group of students who are gifted to assume that they are doctors who have just learned that a patient has AIDS. Have students devise a way to tell the patient he or she has AIDS and what kinds of precautions the patient should take to be sure he or she doesn't spread the disease. Students should design a profile of the patient first. L3

Purpose

Students will learn about a study underway to determine the effects of stress on the immune system.

Background

A number of diseases—including heart disease, high blood pressure, asthma, ulcers, colitis, and migraine headaches—are thought to be related in some way to stress. In some cases, stress seems to be a contributing factor. There is increasing evidence that emotions cause physical reactions which, over time, may be damaging to the body.

Teaching Strategies

- Have a discussion about the causes of stress in students' lives. Ask them to brainstorm, in their groups, a list of factors that create stress, and then prioritize them as to which causes the most stress. Discuss what kinds of strategies they can use to combat stress. Emphasize rest, proper nutrition, planning time for relaxing, using imagery, exercise, and counseling. **COOP LEARN**

Possible Answers

1. Vitamins A and C help to maintain epithelial membranes, which may be more susceptible to infection during stress. Vitamin E prevents the breakdown of Vitamin A.
2. They tested a control group of similar age who were not caregivers.

Going Further

Ask students to make a diagram of how stress affects the body. They should include in their diagrams and label the hypothalamus, pituitary gland, adrenal gland, adrenaline, breathing passages, oxygen, and muscles. **L1**

Infection and Onset of Symptoms   After entering the blood, HIV attacks and destroys helper T cells. HIV can recognize those cells because the proteins projecting from the virus match with receptors on the cells' membranes. Eventually, the viruses destroy the helper T cells as they leave them and move on to infect other helper T cells.

Because helper T cells trigger the production of antibodies by B cells and also stimulate cytotoxic T cells, their destruction causes the immune system to begin to break down. In addition, the activities of macrophages and suppressor T cells are affected. As HIV reproduction begins, so, too, do early symptoms of AIDS. Weight loss, fatigue, and swollen lymph nodes are common. Although antibodies against HIV are produced, they are not made quickly enough, and the immune system gradually becomes overwhelmed. The infected person is then prone to a variety of diseases that normally would be fought off by the immune system.

Three major diseases associated with AIDS are a rare type of pneumonia, a rare form of cancer that appears as spots on the skin or in the mouth, and tuberculosis. In the later stages of AIDS, there may also be a loss of normal mental functions as HIV invades and destroys nerve cells. Eventually, the patient dies from one of these diseases or from heart failure. At this time, it seems that anyone infected with HIV will eventually die from AIDS. The time from infection to onset of symptoms may be as long as ten years, but most cases develop more rapidly.

PSYCHOLOGY CONNECTION

How Attitudes Affect Health

Do people who are depressed get sick more often? That is the question that researchers at The Ohio State University have been studying. What is the effect of the constant stress of caring for people with Alzheimer's disease on the caregivers? Earlier studies indicate that elderly caregivers were more depressed and had twice as many colds and bouts with the flu as a control group of similar age who weren't caregivers.

It has long been established that stress and anxiety promote heart disease and other maladies, but this study seeks to establish a connection to a specific response by the immune system. One hypothesis to be tested is that stress affects immunity because it causes the release of hormones. Scientists hypothesize that these hormones either suppress or interfere with the immune system.

The study of elderly caregivers and a control group of similar age who are not caregivers involves inoculation with an influenza vaccine. After inoculation, the response of the immune systems of the test subjects will be monitored. The data should yield valuable information on how stress affects parts of the immune system and lead to further discoveries about how to lead a healthy life.

1. **Connection to Nutrition:** Many people under stress have been advised to adopt an ACE diet. This diet is named after three vitamins featured in the cuisine—A, C, and E. Find out why these particular vitamins are recommended and what their effects are.

2. **Solve the Problem:** One problem with the study in the story is that the study population (caregivers) is more isolated than the control group. That is, they tend to remain at home with their ill loved one and do not get out for other activities. Thus, they would be less likely to be exposed to disease than the controls. How have the researchers compensated for this difference?

662 IMMUNE SYSTEM

STUDENT JOURNAL

Provide students with library resources on the latest findings about AIDS. Ask them to write a report in their journals about the latest research on a vaccine, a cure, prolonging life, new strains, how quickly it is spreading, how many people have it, and what groups are most affected by AIDS. **L2**

PROJECT

School Attendance and AIDS:
Ask students to find out what the local school district policy is regarding children who have AIDS and school attendance. Have them compare their school district with other districts. Ask them to report back to class about the policies they discover. **L2**

Prevention and Treatment   Clearly, AIDS is a major health problem. To stop the spread of infection by HIV, high-risk behavior associated with transmission of the virus must be avoided. Needles used to inject drugs must not be shared. People must exercise good judgment about their sexual activities and choice of partners. A person infected with HIV may have no symptoms and can unknowingly infect others. Remember that once infected, a person will die from AIDS.

Ideally, AIDS could be prevented if a vaccine against HIV could be produced. A major problem in developing such a vaccine is the fact that the structure of some of the HIV proteins varies greatly, and the proteins are subject to constant mutation. There can be no single vaccine to prevent AIDS. In addition, there have been no animal models in which to study AIDS and test vaccines as they are developed.

Another direction of research is the development of drugs to relieve symptoms or destroy the virus. To date, only two drugs have been approved for use in all patients, AZT and DDI. Although the drugs have been effective in slowing the progress of AIDS symptoms, they do have toxic side effects. New therapies using these drugs have been encouraging.

LOOKING AHEAD

THIS CHAPTER concludes the unit in which you have studied several systems—reproduction, development, digestion, excretion, transport, immunity—that carry out functions. Systems must have controls so that the various tissues and organs operate smoothly under a variety of conditions. One means of control is chemical, which you will study in the next chapter. You will learn about the responses caused by a variety of chemicals and how levels of chemicals change according to the needs of the organism.

Section Review

Understanding Concepts

1. Explain why you would most likely not get measles a second time.
2. How does reproduction of HIV lead to the symptoms of AIDS?
3. Many antibiotics can be used to kill a broad range of bacteria. Why do you think discovery of interferon caused biologists to hope that it could be used against a broad range of viruses?

4. **Skill Review—Comparing and Contrasting:** One person has been vaccinated against tetanus. Another person has received an antiserum to treat tetanus. Compare the degree and type of immunity to tetanus in the two people three years later. Explain. For more help, see Thinking Critically in the **Skill Handbook**.

5. **Thinking Critically:** Suppose a drug were developed that interfered with synthesis of proteins needed for reproduction of a virus causing a particular disease. Why might such a drug not be able to be used safely?

23.3 IMMUNITY AND PREVENTION OF DISEASE   **663**

SECTION 23.3

3 Assess

Check for Understanding
Ask students to make a table comparing active and passive immunity. L1

Reteach
Divide the class into two teams, A and B. Make a list of words, related to this section, on cards. One person from group A will be the clue giver. The clue givers change with each turn. The clue giver draws one card and describes to the rest of the team the guess word. Teammates guess while the clue giver continues to give oral clues. Team A has one minute to get through as many cards as possible. After one minute, add up how many cards were guessed correctly. Then it is team B's turn.
COOP LEARN

Extension
Ask students to make a list of steps in the replication sequence of the AIDS virus and indicate where in the sequence drugs might be used to intervene. L2

✔ Assessment
Portfolio: Ask students to design a billboard poster that would caution people about how to avoid AIDS and about current myths regarding AIDS. L1

4 Close

Activity
Show a recent film containing updated information about AIDS.

Answers to Section Review

1. A clone of memory cells was produced as a response to the original infection. These cells remain in the body, quickly destroying the measles virus if it reappears.
2. The host cells of HIV are helper T cells, which play an important role in regulating B cells and other T cells. As HIV reproduces, it destroys T cells. As a result, immune functions are depressed and the body is unable to defend against other infections. The person with AIDS most often dies from a rare form of pneumonia or cancer.
3. Interferon is a naturally produced substance that protects a variety of host cells from infection by viruses. It was thought that a drug containing interferon would have the same effect.

4. **Skill Review—Comparing and Contrasting:** The vaccinated person has active immunity, which is long-lasting. The person who received the antiserum has passive immunity, which lasts for a shorter period of time.
5. **Thinking Critically:** That drug might also interfere with protein synthesis in the host cells in which the virus reproduces.

Biotechnology

Purpose
Students will study how Susumu Tonegawa discovered how sequences of genes combine and recombine to allow the body to fight off thousands of different antigens.

Teaching Strategies
- Before students read the selection, ask them how many different antibodies they would speculate the human body has. Ask them to give reasons for their speculations. After the reading, ask them to suggest some ways that Tonegawa's discovery will help in the fight against disease.

Possible Answers
1. Opposition might say that if money were delegated to AIDS research, there might be a cure; that there are starving children dying in the U.S. every day; that Tonegawa's mind should be put to better use on more important projects; that this research will not cure the ills of this country—problems such as crack babies, AIDS, alcoholism, and heart disease. The defense might say that without this biological basis for understanding of physiology at the molecular level, there can be no cure for anything; that scientists should be able to choose the projects that most interest them; and that this is not a scientific problem, but a cultural one.
2. $400 \times 12 \times 4 = 19\ 200$.

Going Further
Ask a group of students to look up the articles about Tonegawa's work and make a diagram that would illustrate the concept presented in the papers. **L3**

BIOLOGY,
TECHNOLOGY, AND
SOCIETY

Biotechnology

Defending Against Thousands of Antigens

There are thousands of different disease-causing antigens that could make a person sick. They attack your body every day. But very few cause illness even after they penetrate your defenses. How can this be? How can the body create specific antibodies to fight off thousands of different antigens?

Structure of Antibodies Antibodies consist of two long polypeptide chains and two short ones. Each of these chains has a portion that carries the "self" identifier. This identifier allows the antibody to do its work without being mistaken for an antigen and inviting attack by other lymphocytes. But the other portion of the antibody can respond to thousands of different antigens. How does this happen?

Tonegawa's Discovery Japanese scientist Susumu Tonegawa discovered that the DNA for the parts of the chains that vary consists of more than 400 *variable* gene sequences, about 12 different *diversity* sequences, and four *joining* sequences. Different combinations of these sequences can produce thousands of different antibodies. Here's how.

If *variable* sequence number one (V_1) is combined with *diversity* sequence number one (D_1) and

joining sequence number one (J_1), you get a specific antibody $(V_1D_1J_1)$. However, if you substitute *variable* sequence number two (V_2), you get an entirely different antibody $(V_2D_1J_1)$.

The immune system has adapted to the variability of antigens by combining and recombining a small number of gene sequences into a large number of possible responses. The number of possible combinations of gene sequences that code for antibody formation has been estimated at more than 18 billion. Knowledge of how combinations code for millions of antibodies not only helps scientists understand how the cells of the immune system do their work but also opens up new areas of research on how genes might be manipulated to assist the body in fighting disease.

1. **Issue:** Tonegawa's studies were pure research—they uncovered new knowledge but had little immediate practical application. Some people argue that in today's world, where war, famine, and disease are rampant, we should not be spending our resources on efforts that do not directly help to solve these problems. Write an essay defending or opposing pure research in science.

2. **Mathematics Connection:** If there are at least 400 *variable*, 12 *diversity*, and 4 *joining* sequences, how many different antibodies can be made?

CAREER CONNECTION

Epidemiologists study diseases that spread rapidly through populations. Most modern epidemiologists are doctors (MD) and are experts at gathering and interpreting disease statistics. Almost all practitioners work for governmental agencies or universities.

CAREER CONNECTION

For more information about a career as an epidemiologist, have students contact a local college or university.

Organ Transplants—Who Decides?

For many years, only organs from an identical twin or close relative could be used for transplant. But now anti-rejection drugs that either fool the immune system or block its action have been developed. Further development of these drugs may lead to the day when transplanted organs are not rejected, even if the donor is not a close relative. However, there are more people needing transplants than there are organ donors.

Sources of Organs Most organs used for transplantation today are from accident victims. These organs come from individuals who are brain dead, but whose organs continue to function. Some potential donors have been kept "alive" by machines. When their families have agreed to donate their organs for transplantation, the machines are turned off, and their organs are saved and implanted in recipients who need them. In order to make this process as efficient and fair as possible, a computerized network called the United Network for Organ Sharing (UNOS) has been set up by the more than 140 organ transplant centers in the United States. Each network member maintains information on patients who need organs and where they are located. The transplant centers also maintain records of the donor's major histocompatibility complex (MHC), blood type, and other data. MHC is a measurement of the kinds of antigens produced by the organ and includes four important antigens. For a transplant to occur, there has to be at least one matching antigen between donor and recipient. A perfect match of four antigens would reduce the chances of rejection to a minimum.

Choosing a Recipient Because there are so many more potential recipients than donors, transplant centers maintain waiting lists. When an organ becomes available, the recipient with the best match of antigens usually gets it. Sometimes, however, the organ will go to a recipient who is not as close a match, but desperately ill, especially if the best match has a good chance of surviving the wait for another organ. Other factors also influence the choice of recipient. Doctors try to match the weight of donor to recipient, for example.

Who Makes the Decision? Today, the decision as to who receives particular donated organs is made by doctors, usually part of a committee at a hospital that does transplants. But some people feel that this should not be just a medical decision. What happens when one organ is available that matches two needy patients? How do doctors choose between two heart patients—say a young boy and a young woman who has just had her first baby? Obviously, these are tough, if not impossible, decisions to make.

Would these decisions be easier if more organs were available for donation? The answer is probably yes, but it is not easy to increase the supply. People who have just lost a loved one in an accident are not thinking about organ donation. By the time they do, it may be too late to remove healthy organs.

Understanding the Issue

1. Outline the issues surrounding organ transplants. List opposing viewpoints on each of the major issues, adding your own facts and opinions. Use the outline to make a balanced presentation on the subject to your class or other group.

2. One major problem with organ transplants is the cost. Not only does an operation cost hundreds of thousands of dollars, but drugs to prevent rejection must be taken for the rest of the recipient's life. Find out how much an organ transplant operation costs and how these operations are usually paid for, and give a report to your class.

Readings

- Pekkanen, John. *Donor.* Boston, MA: Little Brown, 1986.
- Chandra, Prakash. "Kidneys for Sale," *World Press Review,* February 1991, p. 53.

Going Further

Ask students to put on a skit in which there has been a death and two group members represent the family of the donor; another, the family of the recipient; another, the doctor. **L2**

Issues

Purpose

Students will learn who can be an organ donor and how the decision is made to give the organ to a specific patient.

Background

In 1982, Jamie Fiske received a liver transplant. She received the transplant after her father, a hospital administrator, telegraphed 500 pediatricians, wrote an appeal in a newsletter, spoke to a senator and the speaker of the House, notified television news anchors who broadcasted the dilemma nationwide, and spoke of his daughter's need at the American Academy of Pediatrics meeting. Although Jamie was in dire need of a liver, she got it due to the immense publicity.

Teaching Strategies

- Have students decide who should get a heart transplant, a male teenage athlete or a 40-year-old female doctor.

Possible Answers

1. Issues concern getting families to allow their brain dead relatives to donate organs: It is not polite to ask families that are grieving; another family could be saved this grieving if an organ were donated. Who should get the organ: the person who is most compatible with the tissue because he or she will be more likely to live, the person in greatest need because he or she will die sooner, or the youngest because that person's whole life lies ahead? Issues concerning who makes the decision: doctors should because they are most knowledgeable, or they should take into consideration the circumstances of the recipients.

2. Drugs to prevent rejection: cyclosporin A = $4000 to $6000 per year. Transplant operations:
Cornea: $2500 to $5000
Bone Marrow: $60 000 to $150 000
Lung: $50 000 to $150 000
Heart-Lung: $78 000 to $92 000
Heart: $57 000 to $110 000
Liver: $54 000 to $238 000
Pancreas: $18 000 to $50 000
Kidney: $25 000 to $35 000

CHAPTER 23

CHAPTER REVIEW

Summary

Summary statements can be used by students to review the major concepts of the chapter.

Language of Biology

Answers should go beyond defining the terms. Accept any reasonable answer that uses the term correctly and in the proper context.

Understanding Concepts

1. The cold virus invades cells of the nasal lining. Some proteins of the new viral coats being made become linked to a self protein, which appears on the infected cell's membrane. Cytotoxic T cells bearing receptors that match the self and foreign antigen bind to them. The cytotoxic T cell becomes activated, forming a clone of cells that destroy the infected cell. Helper and suppressor T cells regulate the activities of cytotoxic T cells.

2. The transplanted kidney has the same DNA and thus the same self proteins as the recipient's tissues.

3. The mouse has not yet learned to detect self from nonself, i.e., foreign tissue.

4. The transplant would not be rejected because the mouse would not recognize it as being foreign.

5. Aspirin relieves symptoms but does not cure the infection. Aspirin is an anti-inflammatory drug, so it reduces inflammation of tissues and reduces associated pain.

6. Penicillin and other antibiotics are effective only against bacteria. Flu is caused by viruses.

7. These people have an allergic reaction to the dust. Their immune systems are responding to the antigens present on the dust particles.

8. An antiserum containing antibodies against the toxin could be administered.

9. People may have no symptoms of AIDS but may be infected with HIV. A person who has had many sexual partners may have contracted HIV from one of them.

10. In both cases, the first line of defense is not protecting the person.

Summary

Pathogens are adapted so that they can be spread from one host to another. Many bacteria and viruses are pathogens spread through air, water, or direct contact. Bacteria often cause disease by producing toxins. Viral diseases occur as viruses reproduce within and destroy their host cells.

Your skin, membranes, and certain body chemicals form a first line of defense against pathogens. The inflammatory response is a second line of defense. Both these lines of defense are nonspecific.

The immune response is a specific defense that destroys pathogens in the blood or tissue fluid and rids the body of infected, abnormal, or foreign cells. Allergies and autoimmune diseases are conditions in which the immune system either overreacts to antigens or destroys the body's own tissues.

Active immunity may result from exposure to a disease or from a vaccination. Passive immunity makes use of antibodies produced by another organism. Antibiotics can be used to treat many bacterial diseases, but few antiviral drugs have been developed.

AIDS, caused by HIV, gradually destroys the immune system, leading eventually to death.

Language of Biology

Write a sentence that shows your understanding of each of the following terms.

active immunity	memory cell
antiserum	monoclonal antibody
autoimmune disease	passive immunity
B cell	pathogen
cytotoxic T cell	plasma cell
endotoxin	receptor
exotoxin	suppressor T cell
helper T cell	T cell
interferon	thymus gland
lymphocyte	vaccine
macrophage	

Understanding Concepts

1. Outline the events of a cold and the immune system's response to it from the onset of infection until the infection is over.

2. The first organ transplants ever done were kidney transplants. A kidney of a healthy person was removed and donated to an identical twin, whose two kidneys were failing. Why would a transplant between identical twins not result in rejection?

3. Tissue from one mouse is transplanted to a mouse fetus very early in its development. Why is the tissue not rejected by the fetus?

4. Would the fetus in question 3 reject a transplant from the same donor mouse after it is born? Explain.

5. Does aspirin cure you of the flu? Explain. Why do you take aspirin when you have the flu?

6. Should you take penicillin when you have the flu? Explain.

7. Some people, when exposed to dust, begin to have itchy eyes and sneeze repeatedly. Why?

8. Botulism is a disease that may result from eating improperly canned or preserved food. It is caused by a powerful toxin produced by bacteria in the food and may quickly lead to paralysis and death. How might a person who begins to have symptoms of botulism be treated?

9. In terms of AIDS, why is sexual contact between two people who do not know each other's sexual history a risky behavior?

10. What line of defense is not protecting a person when HIV is transmitted by sexual intercourse? By sharing needles?

666 🐾 CHAPTER 23 IMMUNE SYSTEM

Applying Concepts

11. If cilia are inactivated, mucus cannot be swept up from the lungs. Mucus is important for trapping pathogens that enter the respiratory tract.

12. The booster shots increase the number of memory cells, thereby offering greater protection against the pathogen.

13. Swollen lymph nodes may be a sign of infection.

Applying Concepts

11. Smoking can inactivate the cilia lining the trachea. Why are long-time heavy smokers susceptible to respiratory infections?
12. Many vaccinations require booster shots a few years later. Why do you think they are necessary?
13. Why does a physician usually examine the lymph nodes during a checkup?
14. What do you think might be an effective treatment to prevent death from cholera? Why?
15. Explain why preventing a cold might be a more realistic goal than developing a cure for the cold.
16. Can you suggest a reason that some people are advised to have a flu vaccination each year even though they have had the flu and other vaccinations before?
17. Why are bone marrow transplants sometimes suggested for patients with certain immune system deficiencies?
18. Could monoclonal antibodies be useful in terms of passive immunity? Explain.
19. **Psychology Connection:** Find out some of the symptoms of Alzheimer's disease, then answer the following question. Why would caring for a person who had Alzheimer's disease cause stress to the caregiver?
20. **Issues:** Research on transplantation of organs is often done on animals before attempted with human subjects. Do you think this practice should continue? Defend your answer.

Lab Interpretation

21. **Investigation:** Study the following zones of inhibition produced by a variety of plants in a petri dish culture of a specific bacterium.

    | Plant A | 1 mm |
    | Plant B | 4 mm |
    | Plant C | 1 cm |
    | Plant D | 3 mm |

    Which plant would you continue to investigate as a possibility for producing a new antibiotic? Why?
22. **Thinking Lab:** What would happen if the antibodies made by B cells were not given off into the blood stream, but remained attached to the B cell? Be specific in your answer.
23. **Minilab 2:** The following graph shows the results of an experiment to test how effective brushing teeth with toothpaste is in combating mouth bacteria. Explain these results.

Connecting Ideas

24. Explain how many bacteria become resistant to certain antibiotics over time.
25. Would you expect that a woman's immune system is somehow different when she is pregnant? Explain.

CHAPTER 23

14. Replacement of body fluids is crucial because death is ultimately associated with fluids lost in diarrhea.
15. It is difficult to develop drugs that can destroy viruses without also destroying host cells. In addition, colds are caused by more than 100 different viruses.
16. Flu viruses mutate frequently. New vaccines are developed for the new strains of viruses that appear.
17. Certain immune system deficiencies result from low numbers of white blood cells. The transplanted tissue may produce the white cells that the patient's own bone marrow cannot.
18. Monoclonal antibodies could be used in much the same way as antisera are. Administration of such antibodies could offer immediate protection against certain pathogens or toxins.
19. Students may cite such symptoms as memory loss and confusion as factors causing stress in caregivers over an extended period of time.
20. Some students will defend the use of animal experimentation, feeling that saving human lives is more important than the lives of the animals. Others may argue that lives of animals are just as important and that research might be able to be conducted using other techniques, such as computer modeling.

Lab Interpretation

21. Plant C. It has the largest zone of inhibition and thus may have the strongest antibiotic effect.
22. Only toxins that came in contact with the B cell could be deactivated. Toxins would remain in the blood and the person would not get well as quickly, or perhaps not at all.
23. Toothpaste is effective in killing some mouth bacteria, but not all.

Connecting Ideas

24. **Evolution:** Bacteria reproduce asexually and very quickly. Any bacterium that has a variation for resistance to a given antibiotic

---

will be naturally selected, passing on its variation to the two new cells produced by binary fission. A new strain of bacteria will evolve very rapidly.

25. **Systems and Interactions:** A developing fetus is foreign tissue to the pregnant woman, yet the fetus is not rejected. Thus, it is reasonable to assume that the woman's immune response, at least with respect to the fetus, is somehow depressed during pregnancy.

Controlling Living Systems

Unit Overview

Unit 6 consists of chapters covering chemical and nervous control and a chapter on movement. Chemical and nervous control mechanisms are related back to life functions previously studied and tied logically to the discussion of movement. Chapter 24 introduces students to the roles of various plant and animal hormones and the means by which those hormones exert their effects. In Chapter 25, students learn about neuron structure and the nature of the nerve impulse and compare animal nervous systems. Chapter 26 focuses on the interaction of skeletal and muscular systems in effecting responses to stimuli.

Theme Development

In this unit, the theme of energy as it applies to conduction of nerve impulses and contraction of muscle is apparent. Students will perceive the theme of systems and interactions as they study concepts such as how different hormones together regulate many responses and themselves are often controlled by negative feedback, the second-messenger hypothesis, types of vertebrate joints, flexors and extensors, and the interdependence between hormones or nerves and the effectors that respond to them. The themes of unity within diversity and evolution become clear in the comparison of exoskeletons and endoskeletons.

Advance Planning

Chapter 24
- Prepare gibberellin solution for the Investigation.
- Order prepared slides of pancreas tissue for Minilab 2.

UNIT SIX

Controlling Living Systems

Sometimes people who have lost an arm or a leg still feel pain in the lost limb. How can that happen? Even though there is no muscle to be stimulated, nerve impulses are still being sent to the brain. Nerve pathways that existed before the limb was lost still exist.

Octopuses change color depending on their state of arousal. At rest, an octopus matches its surroundings and is a mottled gray-brown color. To signal alarm, an octopus can suddenly exhibit strong contrasting light and dark bars or spots. When engaged in a visual battle with another octopus, it changes colors so rapidly that waves of color appear to wash over it.

668

- Order prepared slides of mammalian adrenal gland, thyroid gland, testes, and ovaries for the Alternate Lab.

Chapter 25
- Order *Daphnia* culture for the Investigation.
- Order *Daphnia* culture, *Planaria* culture, and vinegar eels for the Alternate Lab.

Chapter 26
- Procure crab or lobster exoskeletons for the Investigation.

- Procure arthropod and turtle skeleton, snake skins, sea urchin spines, sand dollars, shells, and puffballs for Minilab 1. Order prepared slides of diatoms.
- Order live crayfish for the Alternate Lab.

What color is the common octopus, *Octopus vulgaris?* If you answered white, brown, gray, black, red, yellow, or orange-red, you would be correct. Octopuses and their relatives, the squid and cuttlefish, are members of a group of invertebrate animals that have complex brains and highly developed central nervous systems. Octopuses can completely change color in less than half a second. Color change in an octopus is controlled by nerve impulses from the brain to pigment cells in the animal's skin.

What does an octopus have in common with a person who has lost an arm or a leg? People who have lost a limb are often fitted with an artificial arm or leg called a prosthesis. Muscle contractions in the remaining portions of a person's arm or leg generate an electric current that activates electrodes implanted in the prosthesis. Color change in an octopus and operation of an artificial arm are both a result of nervous control. The nervous system is one of the living systems you will be studying in this unit.

Using the Photos
The photographs illustrate the point that stimuli lead to responses. Some responses, such as the octopus's changing color, occur quite rapidly and are under nervous control. Other responses occur over longer periods of time, such as the growth of a plant stem toward light, or the maturation of an egg and preparation of the uterus for pregnancy. Those responses are chemically controlled. Many, but not all, responses to stimuli result in movement of part of an organism or in its locomotion. Most often, movement or locomotion is associated with nervous control.

Previewing the Chapters
Chapter 24 examines the discovery of auxins and explores some of the functions of those plant hormones as well as the gibberellins. As students study both plant and human hormones, they come to see that hormones interact to regulate a broad spectrum of functions. A primary example of such interaction is the discussion of hormonal control of the menstrual cycle, which also illustrates the concept of negative feedback control. The chapter also presents information about how hormones actually exert their effects on target tissues.

In Chapter 25, students contrast nervous control with chemical control, but come to understand that the two means of control are closely related. They study neuron structure and physiology and the means by which synapses are crossed. The chapter then turns to a discussion of nervous systems, and tne roles of the sensory somatic and autonomic nervous systems are examined. Examples are provided of how the nervous system controls functions that students have previously studied.

Chapter 26 begins as students compare and contrast exoskeletons and endoskeletons. They examine the advantages of the latter and study development and structure of bone and types of vertebrate joints. Next, students discover how animals that

lack a skeleton can move. Students also come to realize the adaptive advantages of movement resulting from interaction of muscles and skeleton. They compare the structure and functions of vertebrate muscle types and analyze the sliding filament hypothesis. In so doing, students see the relationship between nervous control and movement. Students complete the chapter by studying how energy is made available for muscle contraction and by learning of the similarities between contraction of muscle and ciliary and flagellar motion.

ORGANIZER
C H A P T E R
24

SECTION	OBJECTIVES	TEXT LABS/FEATURES
24.1 Chemical Control in Plants (2 days)	**Summarize** the experiments that led to the discovery of auxins. **Discuss** the roles of auxins in the growth and development of plants. **Describe** the effects of other plant hormones and how they interact in control of plant growth and development.	**Investigation:** Where to Apply Gibberellin, p. 676 **Minilab 1:** Is light a factor in geotropism? p. 678
24.2 Chemical Control in Animals (3 days)	**Explain** the role of insulin in regulation of blood sugar level. **Describe** the operation of feedback mechanisms that control levels of some hormones. **Discuss** the interaction of hormones in control of the menstrual cycle. **Explain** how hormones cause responses in their target tissues.	**Minilab 2:** What does pancreas tissue look like? p. 683 **Health Connection:** Choh Hao Li, p. 687 **Thinking Lab:** Which hormones control egg release or uterine thickening? p. 690
BIOLOGY, TECHNOLOGY, AND SOCIETY		**Considering the Environment:** The Pesticide Tree, p. 693 **Career Connection:** Entomologist, p. 693 **Biotechnology:** Insulin Without the Sting, p. 694 **Issues:** Steroids and Athletes, p. 695

LAB MATERIALS

INVESTIGATION	MINILAB	ALTERNATE LAB
page 676 bean plants cotton swabs foil gibberellin solution graduated cylinder labels petroleum jelly plastic cups ruler scissors toothpicks	**page 678** clay foil paper towels petri dishes radish seeds scissors tape **page 683** microscope prepared slide of pancreas tissue	**page 688** microscope prepared slides of: mammalian adrenal gland thyroid gland testes ovaries

TEACHER CLASSROOM RESOURCES	OTHER RESOURCES
Study Guide, pp. 139-140 ***PLL:** *Tropisms in Plants,* p. 161 ****ILS:** *Influence of Hormones on Plant Growth,* p. 251	***STVS:** *Growing Plants in Space,* Plants and Simple Organisms (Disc 4, Side 2)
Study Guide, pp. 141-144 **Concept Mapping,** p. 24 **Critical Thinking/Problem Solving:** *The Menstrual Cycle,* p. 24 ***PLL:** *Effects of Iodine Compounds on Tadpole Metamorphosis,* p. 163 ***PLL:** *Effects of Adrenaline on Daphnia Heartbeat,* p. 165 ***PLL:** *The Human Menstrual Cycle,* p. 167 ****ILS:** *The Menstrual Cycle,* p. 257 ****ILS:** *Thyroid Gland,* p. 263	***STVS:** *Insulin Pills,* Human Biology (Disc 7, Side 2) **Color Transparency 43:** *The Menstrual Cycle*
Assessment Materials **Chapter Assessment,** pp. 93-96 **Performance Assessment in Biology,** p. 48 **Alternate Assessment in the Science Classroom** **Computer Test Bank**	**Spanish Resources** **Cooperative Learning Resource Guide** **Videodisc Correlations** (to Optical Data's and Videodiscovery's videodiscs)

* **Probing Levels of Life**
** **Investigating Living Systems**

* **Science Technology Videodisc Series**

Key to Teaching Strategies

The following designations will help you decide which activities in the teacher margin are appropriate for your students.

L1 Level 1 activities should be within the ability range of all students.

L2 Level 2 activities should be within the ability range of the average to above-average student.

L3 Level 3 activities are designed for the ability range of above-average students.

LEP LEP activities are appropriate for Limited English Proficiency students.

COOP LEARN Cooperative Learning activities are designed for small group work.

ADDITIONAL RESOURCES

Infinite Voyage *Prisoners of the Brain*
Scientific research shows an increasing awareness of the linkage between disorders and the chemistry of the brain.

Audiovisual
Hormonal Control, video, Films for the Humanities and Sciences.
Messengers, video, Films for the Humanities and Sciences.

Software
The Endocrine System, Apple II/TRS-80/Model III, J and S.

CHAPTER

24

CHEMICAL CONTROL

Chapter Overview

Students begin their study of chemical control by learning how the role of auxin in positive phototropism of stems was discovered. They learn that auxins, like all hormones, exert an effect by either triggering chemical reactions directly or activating a gene that indirectly leads to chemical change within a target tissue. They conclude their study of plant hormones with a look at the functions of gibberellins, cytokinins, and ethylene.

Students next study chemical control in animals. They learn that the target tissue determines the response to a hormone. Then, they study the control of blood glucose as an example of hormonal control. They examine the idea of negative feedback and the interaction of the hypothalamus and pituitary gland. Students compare the means by which proteinaceous and steroid hormones exert their effects on target tissues. Finally, their knowledge of the mechanisms of human hormones is brought together as students consider hormonal control of the menstrual cycle.

670

KEY TERMS

abscission
apical
  dominance
auxin
corpus luteum
corpus luteum
  stage
endocrine
  gland
follicle stage
gibberellin
hypothalamus
negative
  feedback
pituitary
  gland
second
  messenger
  hypothesis
stimulus
tropism

CHEMICAL CONTROL

PICTURE YOURSELF in a beautiful green garden on a warm summer day. The sounds of insects fill the air with peaceful background buzz, flowers are in full bloom, and the graceful leaves of small plants and trees seem to stretch outward, as if to grab every ray of sunlight. Farther along, you notice young fruits and berries starting to appear on small branches, and slender vines twining around poles and fences. Have you ever wondered why some vines wind around poles or why leaves seem to turn to face the sun? If you're a sharp observer, you'll probably wonder whether plants also sense the world around them. Do plants, like animals, respond to the environment?

Unlike animals, plants do not possess nervous systems that allow them to respond quickly to a stimulus. But plants, like all other living organisms, react to changes in their environments. The adjustments plants make are usually slow, and it often takes an entire summer to witness these dramatic changes. In this chapter, you'll learn how plants respond slowly to stimuli through chemical, rather than nervous, control. Animals have the ability to respond to changes both slowly and quickly, and in this chapter, you'll also find out how a plant's chemical control system compares to your own.

Growth patterns in both plants and humans are under chemical control, but the chemicals differ greatly.

Chapter Preview

ASSESSMENT PLANNER

Choose assessment strategies from the following pages to evaluate the progress of your students.
Assess, pp. 678-679, 691-692
Portfolio, pp. 674, 678, 682, 683
Alternate Lab, pp. 688-689
Thinking Lab, p. 690
Minilab 1, p. 678

Minilab 2, p. 683
Investigation, pp. 676-677
Chapter Review, pp. 696-697

Introducing the Chapter

Begin the chapter by calling students' attention to the photograph on page 670. Point out that organisms are constantly bombarded by stimuli, both from without and within, and must respond appropriately to those stimuli. The climbing vine responds to the stimuli of light, gravity, and touch as it winds its way along. Growth toward the light promotes photosynthesis. Ask students to suggest the type of signal that might guide the growth response. They should conclude that it must be chemical because they know that plants lack nerves. Ask them whether they can identify other examples such as development of fruit or falling of leaves.

Theme Development

The theme of systems and interactions is evident throughout the chapter. Students should perceive it as they learn that hormones secreted by one part of an organism exert their effects in another part; as they examine the interaction among hypothalamus, pituitary, and other endocrine glands; and as they determine the manner in which hormones actually cause a response in target tissues. Students should also recognize the theme of unity within diversity as they come to realize that chemical control is characteristic of a wide variety of organisms.

Tying to Previous Knowledge

In Unit Five, students studied a variety of basic life functions. Now, they will see how those functions are carried out and controlled as they learn the roles of various hormones. They will now see, for example, how the conversion of excess glucose to glycogen is controlled, how hormones coordinate the events of the menstrual cycle, and how hormones guide plant development.

Prepare

Key Concepts

Students analyze the role of hormones in the control of plant growth.

Key Terms

stimulus, tropism, auxin, apical dominance, abscission, gibberellin

Materials

- Obtain radish seeds for Minilab 1.
- Start bean seedlings. They should be at least at the two-leaf stage for the Investigation.
- Locate prepared slides of the pancreas and other glands for Minilab 2 and the Alternate Lab.

1 Focus

Discussion

Point to the lateral and terminal buds on a plant or tree branch. Explain that plant growth occurs with cell division at the tips of branches and side shoots, and the further division and elongation of these cells as they trail behind the growing tips. Exhibit two identical plants having definite growing tips (e.g. *Coleus* or marigold seedlings). Pinch off the tip of one plant and have students compare the plants' growth for several days.

Objectives

Summarize the experiments that led to the discovery of auxins.

Discuss the role of auxins in the growth and development of plants.

Describe the effects of other plant hormones and how they interact in control of plant growth and development.

24.1 Chemical Control in Plants

Picture a tree near your home or school. Each year that tree gets taller and the size of its trunk increases. In spring, new branches appear and leaves develop on them. Flowers begin to form, pollination occurs, and new seeds are produced. Eventually, leaves are shed, either constantly or once each year. Beneath the surface of the soil, there are similar changes. New roots develop, enabling the tree to absorb necessary nutrients. What controls these changes? In this section, you'll learn that all of these changes in a plant are under control of chemicals that interact to guide growth and development.

Phototropism and the Discovery of Auxins

Although changes such as flowering and leaf development are usually not observable in short periods of time, you know from experience that plants are not inactive. In fact, like yourself and other organisms, plants respond to changes in the environment. They respond to factors such as light, water, and the force of gravity. Such factors, which lead to a reaction or change in an organism, are called **stimuli.** Like other living organisms, you respond to stimuli constantly. In school, when a bell rings, what do you do? You move to another class, right? In this case, the ringing bell is a stimulus; it makes you react.

Phototropism   Biologists have studied for many years how plants respond to stimuli. One example of such a response is probably familiar to you. Have you ever noticed that a houseplant on a windowsill grows toward the light? In this case, light from one side is a stimulus, and the plant's response is to grow toward the light.

Figure 24-1   **Plants seem to grow naturally toward light. This tendency is called phototropism and is caused by substances produced within the plant.**

672 CHEMICAL CONTROL

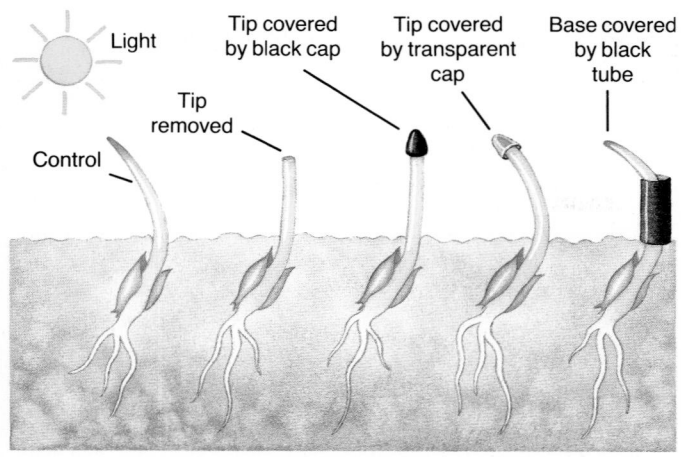

Light

Control

Tip removed

Tip covered by black cap

Tip covered by transparent cap

Base covered by black tube

Figure 24-2 The Darwins' experiment showed that grass seedlings curved toward light, but only when light reached the growing tip. When the tip was cut off or covered by an opaque material, the seedlings did not curve.

Why do plants grow toward light? It happens because there is unequal growth stimulation on opposite sides of the plant stem. Any plant response caused by unequal stimulation is called a **tropism.** Growth of a plant part toward a stimulus is called positive tropism, and growth away from the stimulus is called negative tropism. A growth response to light is called phototropism. The stem of a plant is said to show positive phototropism because it bends toward the light. Positive phototropism is adaptive for plants because it causes them to grow toward regions where light is more abundant.

Charles Darwin and his son Francis began investigating the causes of positive phototropism in stems more than 100 years ago. They worked with very young seedlings of grass plants, conducting several experiments in which the seedlings were exposed to light from one side. In one experiment, they covered the tips of one group of seedlings with black caps. The seedlings did not curve, but instead grew straight upward. Then, the scientists covered the tips of another group of seedlings with transparent caps. Still another group was left uncovered as a control. Both the plants with transparent caps and the uncovered controls curved toward the light as usual.

The Darwins also showed that enclosing the base of the young stem with a black tube did not prevent the plant from curving toward light. However, when the tip of a stem was removed, the stem failed to grow toward the light. Results of the various experiments, shown in Figure 24-2, all led to the same conclusion. The tip of the stem somehow detects the presence of light and controls the growth of the stem below. How does this control occur?

The Discovery of Auxins   Over the years, through much experimentation with young plants, understanding of this plant growth response increased. Many scientists thought that a chemical secreted by the tip of the stem causes plants to grow toward light. In 1926, a Dutch scientist,

2 Teach

Demonstration

Using grass or onion seedlings, replicate some of the Darwins' phototropism experiments in the classroom, or expose seedlings to a bright window or other directional source of light to demonstrate phototropism. Once the plants have curved toward the light, ask students which side of the stem has the highest concentration of auxin. *the side opposite the light*

MEETING INDIVIDUAL NEEDS

Help students who speak English as a second language to develop vocabulary and speaking skills by pairing them with native English speakers. Have the students work together to learn the meaning of terms introduced in this section and to study how auxins affect plant growth. Have students practice their oral skills by explaining the terms and concepts to their partners. LEP   COOP LEARN

Figure 24-3 Went used agar to absorb chemicals from the tips of seedlings. He found that a chemical in the agar blocks would cause growth in seedlings whose tips had been removed. When the block was placed off center, the stem curved toward the side opposite the side on which the agar block had been placed. What do you think Went did to prove that the effects were not due to the agar itself?

Frits Went, carried out a famous experiment. He removed tips from many young stems and placed them on agar, a gelatin-like substance that permits chemicals to diffuse through it.

Went thought that if growth-control chemicals were produced in the tips, then those chemicals would diffuse into the agar. After the tips had rested on the agar for about an hour, he cut the agar into small squares. Next, he placed the squares on the cut ends of the stems from which the tips had been removed. He found that the stems continued to grow, even in darkness. In fact, Went found that the direction in which a stem grew depended on the position of the agar square. When he placed the agar square on the center of the cut end of the stem, the stem grew straight upward. When the agar square was placed only on one side of the cut end, the stem grew in the direction of the opposite side, as you can see in Figure 24-3. As a control, Went used squares of agar on which no tips had been placed. When these agar squares were placed on cut stems, the stems did not grow, regardless of where the squares were placed. From these results, Went concluded that a chemical produced in the tips of stems controls plant growth. Went named the chemical an **auxin,** from the Greek word *auxein* meaning "to grow."

How Auxins Work   Today, we can partially explain how auxins cause stems to grow toward light. A major effect of auxins in some tissues of plants is to cause cells to elongate rapidly. Light coming from one side causes auxin molecules in the tip to move toward the darker side. Thus, auxin becomes more concentrated on the shaded side. By active transport, the auxin moves downward, causing cells on the shaded side to elongate more quickly than cells on the lighted side. Because of this unequal growth in cells, the stem seems to bend toward the light. In stems exposed equally to light from all sides, auxin concentration is the same in cells throughout the stem. In this case, the stem simply grows upward and does not curve. Figure 24-4 summarizes these findings. It's interesting to note that after more than 100 years of research, scientists still do not completely understand how auxins act.

Auxins, as well as other chemical regulators in plants, are examples of hormones. A hormone is a chemical that is produced in one tissue of an organism and then is transported to another tissue where it causes a response. The tissue in which the hormone causes a response is often called a target tissue. How does a hormone cause a response in the cells of a target tissue? It does so in one of two ways. One way is to trigger certain chemical reactions within the cell. The other way is to activate a gene, causing the cell to synthesize a certain protein. In the case of auxin, scientists have found that it lowers the pH in stem cell walls, making them more acidic. This action causes an enzyme in the cell walls to separate cellulose molecules from one another allowing cell elongation to occur more easily.

Other Effects of Auxins

Plant stems grow toward light but grow away from the force of gravity. A growth response to the force of gravity is called geotropism. The stem of a plant placed on its side will respond by growing upward, even in the dark. Because the growth response of a stem is opposite to the direction of the force of gravity, it is called negative geotropism.

Negative geotropism of stems also occurs because of auxins. When a stem is placed on its side, more auxin collects in cells on the stem's lower side. As a result, the cells on the lower side elongate more rapidly than those of the upper side, and the stem grows upward. In contrast to stems, roots grow in the direction of gravitational force—in other words, downward. This response is an example of positive geotropism, and auxin also may play a major part in this process. Increases in auxin concentration inhibit root growth. If a root is placed sideways, auxin collects along its lower side.

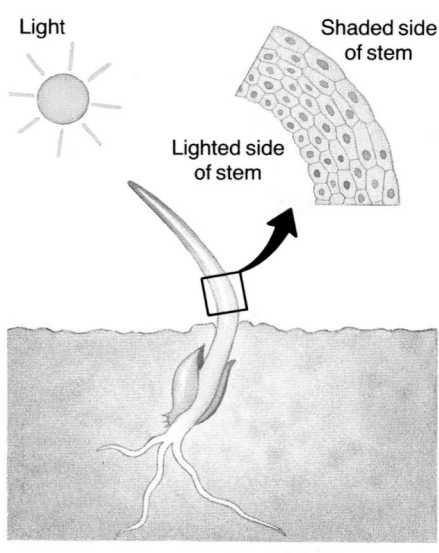

Figure 24-4 Stems grow toward light because auxin collects in the cells on the shaded side of the stem, stimulating elongation of these shaded cells. As a result, the stem curves toward the light.

Figure 24-5 Plant roots grow downward in the direction of the force of gravity. This phenomenon is an example of positive geotropism. On the other hand, stems exhibit negative geotropism because they grow away from the force of gravity. The corn grains you see here were germinated with the dish standing vertically. The arrow points in the direction of gravitational force.

Reinforcement

Point out that auxins have different effects on root, stem, and bud tissue. Chart these differences on the chalkboard. In a column labeled "promotes," list "elongation of cells on the darker side of the stem" and "elongation of cells on the lower side of stems." In a column labeled "inhibits," list "growth on lower sides of roots" and "bud growth on the sides of stems." **L1** **LEP**

Misconception

Students may not realize that the terms *auxin* and *gibberellin* each refer to a type of hormone, not a single chemical. There are many different auxins and gibberellins in the plant kingdom.

Teacher FYI

Auxins are associated with cell elongation. Cytokinins are plant hormones associated with cell division. They interact with auxins to stimulate growth. Cells exposed to an auxin alone will elongate or enlarge without dividing. Cells exposed to both a cytokinin and an auxin will divide as well as elongate.

STUDENT JOURNAL

Have students write a journal entry describing one of the Darwins' experiments on phototropism or Went's experiments with auxins. Ask students to write the entry as if it were a laboratory report that the Darwins or Went entered in a laboratory notebook. Students should include the experimenter's hypothesis, procedure, some plausible data, data analysis, and conclusions.

INVESTIGATION

Where to Apply Gibberellin

Time Allotment
1 class period to set up; a few minutes each day for about 2 weeks to make observations

Objectives
Upon completing this investigation, students will be able to:
- Describe an effect of gibberellin on plant growth.
- State two effective ways of treating plants with gibberellin.

Skills
separate and control variables, interpret data, measure in SI

Materials
bean plants that are at the two-leaf stage (8 per group), gibberellin solution and paste, cotton swabs, toothpicks, plastic cups or tubes for growing beans in water, labels, ruler, graduated cylinder, foil, scissors, lanolin or petroleum jelly for control

Preparation
Gibberellin paste (500 ppm in lanolin) and gibberellin powder are available from supply houses and some garden stores. Prepare 500-ppm solution by dissolving 1 g gibberellin in 2 L of water. Germinate beans in containers filled with sand or artificial soil mix. You can use milk or egg cartons and plastic cups. For convenience, purchase 72-hole seed-starter flats from a garden store.

Possible Hypotheses
Students may suggest that root application will be ineffective or that location will make no difference.

Possible Procedures
- Lanolin paste should be applied at the point where new leaves are just emerging from the stem.
- To prepare plants for growing in water, students should lift the plant along with its soil. Hold the plant only by one leaf, not by the stem or tip. Dip the roots up and down in a large container of room-temperature water until all soil

Cell growth is inhibited on that side while the cells along the upper side continue to elongate. As a result, the root turns downward. Scientists still cannot fully explain the details of positive geotropism in roots.

How Auxin Affects the Shape of a Plant Auxins are also responsible for actions other than phototropism and geotropism. As an example, let's look at the overall growth pattern of trees. You have probably noticed that many trees grow into cone shapes. This appearance results from the fact that branches near the bottom of the trunk are much longer than those near the top. The actively growing bud at the tip (apex) of a stem is known as the apical meristem. This growing tissue produces auxin, which travels downward through the stem. The presence of auxin in the stem inhibits the growth of buds, including the tips of branches, along the sides of the stem.

Buds along the stem of a plant are known as lateral buds. In the case of a tree, the stem is the tree's trunk. Buds and branches nearest the top of the stem are inhibited the most, because the concentration of auxin is greater there. Those farther down the stem are inhibited less because they are farther from the apical meristem, and thus the concentration of auxin

I N V E S T I G A T I O N

Where to Apply Gibberellin

Gibberellin is a plant hormone that stimulates cell elongation. The result is that some plants tend to grow very tall when this hormone is present in the plant. If you could apply gibberellin to an experimental plant, where do you suppose would be the best place to apply it?

Your task is to determine if the site where the gibberellin is applied causes any difference in growth stimulation. Two different stimulation sites will be tested. One site is the roots. To test the effectiveness of this site, you will add the chemical to the water in which a bean plant is growing. The second site is the growing tips of stems, which you will test by applying gibberellin paste directly to them. Both the paste and liquid have identical strengths of 500 ppm (parts per million). This means that 500 parts gibberellin are present for every 1 million parts of mixture.

Problems
Will gibberellin taken in through a bean's roots influence growth the same as when it is applied to the bean stem's growing tips?

Hypothesis
Form a hypothesis that could be tested using gibberellin on bean plants. Record your group's hypothesis.

Safety Precautions
Wear aprons and goggles to protect your eyes and clothing.

Experimental Plan
1. Decide on a way to test your group's hypothesis. Keep the

falls free. Then, place plant into container with gibberellin solution or plain water. The quantity of solution should be determined by the volume of the container. Support the plant and limit evaporation by covering the container with foil having a slit for the plant's stem. An alternative is to stuff cotton around the stem and the top of the container. Plants in soil may be grown in their original containers.
- Students will have to devise a method so that heights are always measured from the same reference point. This could be a mark

near the top of each container. Try to find points so that the soil-grown and water-grown plants have similar starting heights. This method will be less confusing to students. Have students measure heights each day for two weeks.

Teaching Strategies
- Each group should run experiments on two treated and two untreated plants in soil along with two plants in gibberellin solution and two plants in plain water.
- Make certain students label plants for clear identification and that they have prepared a

is lower. This inhibition of lateral bud development by auxins is called **apical dominance.**

Gardeners put this knowledge about apical dominance to practical use. Many gardeners produce bushy plants by cutting off the apical buds. If the apical bud is removed, auxin production ceases. The lateral buds then develop into many longer branches because they are no longer inhibited by high concentrations of auxin. As a result, the plant becomes bushier instead of growing taller. Contrast the two photos in Figure 24-6.

Figure 24-6 The cone-shaped tree on the left shows apical dominance. Flower growers pinch the tips of plants to prevent apical dominance.

data table that correlates to their labeling with spaces for all relevant information.
- Help students apply the paste to the correct location by drawing a diagram on the chalkboard.
- One application of lanolin paste is sufficient. However, students will need to replenish water or gibberellin solution from time to time. Use a long-stem plastic dropper to avoid displacing plants.
- If stems curl, bend, or fall over as they grow, the plants should be straightened out long enough for measuring.

Data and Observations
Students should discover that both sets of treated plants grow taller than the untreated plants. Students should begin to see significant differences in growth at about days 4 to 6. By days 8 or 9, differences should be very apparent (8 or 9 cm versus about 6 cm). In trials of this experiment, treated plants achieved heights of 16 to 20 cm after 14 days, whereas untreated plants achieved heights of 8 to 10 cm. Plants in liquid may be set back somewhat if they are improperly handled. Emphasize gentleness when washing roots and making the transfer.

Data Analysis
1. See Data and Observations.
2. See Data and Observations.
3. If all plants were handled carefully, growth should be nearly the same.
4. Answers will depend on student hypotheses. Students should observe that gibberellin causes increased growth.
5. Answers will depend on student hypotheses. Students' explanations should be based entirely on measured data.
6. It must be taken up through the plant roots. Gibberellin absorbed by the roots was able to move rapidly through the entire plant. Applied as a paste, gibberellin was first absorbed only by the growing tip, although it may have spread with time.

available materials provided by your teacher in mind as you plan your procedure.
2. Remember to test only one variable at a time and use suitable controls. A paste like the one with gibberellin is also available with no gibberellin added.
3. Record your procedure and list the materials and amounts that you will need.

Checking the Plan
1. What controls will be used and what factors will have to be controlled?
2. How long will your experiment run and how many plants will you use?
3. What data will you collect and how will it be recorded? Prepare a data table to record your findings.
4. Assign roles for this investigation.

Make sure your teacher has approved your experimental plan before you proceed further.

Data and Observations
Carry out your experiment. Record your findings in your data table. Show your results by plotting graphs of your data.

Analysis and Conclusions
1. Make a statement comparing the plants treated with gibberellin paste to those treated with paste containing no gibberellin.
2. Make a statement comparing the plants treated with gibberellin solution to those treated with plain water.
3. Make a statement comparing the paste-treated plants to the liquid-treated plants.
4. Do your experimental and control data support your hypothesis?

5. Do your experimental paste and experimental liquid data support your hypothesis? Explain your answer.
6. How does the gibberellin added to water enter a bean plant? How might this affect distribution of gibberellin compared to the distribution of gibberellin applied as a paste?
7. Write a conclusion to the experiment. Make sure your conclusion is based entirely on the results you observed.

Going Further
Based on this lab experience, design an experiment that would help answer another question that arose from your work. Assume that you will have limited resources and will be conducting the lab in class.

24.1 CHEMICAL CONTROL IN PLANTS **677**

7. Conclusions should mirror actual observations. Students should conclude that it makes little difference whether gibberellin is applied to growing tips or to roots and that gibberellin increases length in both cases.

✔ Assessment
Skill: Set up exhibits of typical sets of experimental and control plants. Include a metric ruler. Ask each student to measure the experimental and control plants and to record the values he or she obtains. Ask students which

plants have probably received gibberellin and to describe how they know.

Extensions
Students could carry out experiments to determine whether gibberellin has similar effects on other plants. Students could obtain growing plants from garden stores to test. The effects of gibberellin on dwarf and rosette plants can be particularly dramatic. They may find little effect on vining plants and others that typically grow long and thin.

Minilab 1

Purpose
Students will observe geotropism and determine whether or not it is influenced by light.

Skills
observe and infer, recognize cause and effect

Teaching Strategies
- An alternative method is to stand dishes up for germination and then keep vertical but rotate 90° for the light test. Seeds will have to be tight against lid if this method is used.

Expected Results
Upon germination, stems grow upward and roots downward, demonstrating geotropism. In both exposed and covered dishes, stems turn to grow upward and roots will grow downward. Any directional effect of light is independent of the effect of gravitational force.

Answers
See Expected Results above. Effects due to gravity were evident in both covered and uncovered plants. Plants may have responded to light direction also.

✔ Assessment
Portfolio: Have students draw and label their dishes at each stage in the activity, starting with the initial setup. Before each pair of drawings, students should summarize the experimental conditions up to that point. After each pair of drawings, they should summarize their observations and state what they can conclude at that point.

3 Assess

Check for Understanding
Ask students to describe, at a cellular level, what causes a stem to grow toward light and a root to grow downward. Have them explain how auxins influence plant shape and how they affect the falling of leaves and fruit. L1

678

Minilab 1

Is light a factor in geotropism?

Line the bottoms of two petri dishes with four layers of paper toweling cut to fit the round shape. Wet the toweling. Add ten radish seeds to each dish and spread them out evenly. Sketch their appearance. Keep dishes moist and flat for four days. On day five, record the position of all young stems. Stand both dishes up on their edges. Next, label the dishes A and B. Tape the covers on. Cover dish A with foil. After 24 hours, record the position of stems. **Analysis** *How does direction of stem growth compare for plants in the light versus those in the dark? Were the plants responding to light, gravity, or both? How do you know?*

Effects of Auxin on Fruit and Leaves   Development of fruit also depends on auxins. You learned in Chapter 18 that a fruit develops from the ovary of a flower. When pollination occurs, pollen grains produce an auxin that causes the ovary to begin growing. As seeds develop in the fruit, the seeds release auxin, which continues to stimulate the formation of the fruit. The high level of auxin that leads to development of fruit also prevents the dropping of fruit from the plant. The dropping of fruit or leaves from a plant is called **abscission.** However, the level of auxin declines as the fruit matures and a layer of cells, the abscission layer, forms across the stalk that holds the fruit. Because the cells of the abscission layer are weak, the stalk breaks and the fruit falls from the plant.

High concentration of auxin also inhibits leaf abscission. Deciduous plants are plants that lose their leaves at the end of the growing season. In these plants, auxin concentration declines in autumn. As in fruits, an abscission layer forms across the stalk of the leaf. Eventually the leaf falls, usually because of wind or rain.

Auxin also stimulates cell reproduction within some plant tissues. For example, in spring, auxin produced by buds causes the development of new xylem and phloem tissue. It is also known that application of auxins to stem cuttings can cause the formation of roots from those cuttings.

Gibberellins

A second type of hormone was discovered in Japan, where rice farmers had long noticed that many of their plants grew unusually tall. Because these tall plants usually fell over and did not live to maturity, they were long ignored. But in 1926, scientists found that the tall plants were being

Figure 24-7   **Application of gibberellin to some plants causes them to grow much taller than normal. Compare the gibberellin-treated mustard plants on the right of the photo with the normal plants on the left.**

678 CHEMICAL CONTROL

affected by a parasitic fungus of the genus *Gibberella*. It was later found that the fungus produces a hormone, named **gibberellin,** that is responsible for the unusual growth of the rice plants. Many different gibberellins have since been discovered, both in fungi and in plants.

Action of Gibberellins Gibberellins, like auxins, help to control cell growth but they do so in a way unlike auxins. Often, gibberellins and auxins contribute to the same response, as in the case of cell elongation. In other cases, gibberellins and auxins counter the effects of one another, as in control of leaf abscission. Gibberellins also increase the rate of germination of many seeds and the development of buds. They may also induce flowering and fruit formation in some species.

You might think that application of gibberellins could produce bigger food plants. However, gibberellins applied artificially often cause abnormalities. They have been successfully used, though, to produce larger seedless grapes and more tender stalks of celery.

Both auxins and gibberellins are hormones that promote growth and development of plants. Their effects are also balanced by a group of plant hormones called inhibitors. Many inhibitors promote dormancy in seeds and buds. Dormancy is important because it prevents development during unfavorable conditions, such as when not enough water is available for seeds to germinate or when cold weather would damage new leaves or flowers. Concentration of inhibitors eventually declines as they are washed away by water, destroyed by cold, or as they simply break down with time. When that happens, hormones such as gibberellins, which promote development, exert their effects. Other hormones work along with auxins, gibberellins, and inhibitors to regulate plant growth. Cytokinins, for example, stimulate lateral bud development, whereas auxin inhibits it. Ethylene, a gas, promotes the formation of an abscission layer and causes some fruit to ripen.

Figure 24-8 **Seedless grapes treated with gibberellin develop into larger, juicier fruit than untreated grapes.**

Section Review

Understanding Concepts

1. At the time of Went's experiments, it was thought that the tip of a stem "informs" the rest of the stem by some electrical means. How did Went's work show that it is a chemical that passes from the tip to the rest of the stem and not an electric current?

2. Using information from this section, explain why many orchard keepers spray developing fruits with auxin.

3. Give two examples of how different plant hormones interact to control growth and development.

4. ***Skill Review—Designing an Experiment:*** How would you conduct an experiment to test the idea that auxin prevents abscission of leaves? For more help, see Practicing Scientific Methods in the **Skill Handbook.**

5. ***Thinking Critically:*** Review how auxin affects the shape of a plant. How is cone-shaped growth in a plant an adaptive advantage? Hint: Think about photosynthesis.

Answers to Section Review

1. Blocks of agar upon which tips of young stems had been placed were found to promote growth. They must have absorbed chemicals from the tips.
2. Such spraying promotes growth of fruits and also prevents their abscission.
3. Cytokinins stimulate development of lateral buds, while auxin inhibits it. Ethylene causes abscission layers to form; auxin inhibits their formation.

4. **Skill Review—Designing an Experiment:** The blades of leaves could be removed from their petioles. Auxin could be applied to the cut ends of some petioles. Others would be left untreated as controls. Petioles to which no auxin was applied should fall off first. Other answers are possible.
5. **Thinking Critically:** Such a shape exposes more leaves to sunlight.

Prepare

Key Concepts

Students learn how endocrine hormones influence physiological processes, particularly in humans.

Key Terms

endocrine gland, negative feedback, pituitary gland, hypothalamus, second messenger hypothesis, follicle stage, corpus luteum, corpus luteum stage

Materials

- Gather prepared slides of several mammalian endocrine tissues for the Alternate Lab.
- Gather prepared slides of pancreas tissue for Minilab 2.

1 Focus

Using an Analogy

Point out to students that nervous responses, such as catching a ball or tasting food, are relatively rapid, short-term events elicited by external stimuli. Chemical, or hormonal, responses are relatively slow and long lasting; may be associated with either external or internal stimuli; and are involved with growth and development, reproduction, metabolism, and digestion. Compare nervous responses to turning the key in the ignition of a car on a cold day, starting the engine quickly. Hormonal responses might be compared to obtaining heat from the heater, which takes a while because coolant must first be warmed by heat output from the engine. **L1** **LEP**

Objectives

Explain the role of insulin in regulation of blood sugar level.

Describe the operation of feedback mechanisms that control levels of some hormones.

Discuss the interaction of hormones in control of the menstrual cycle.

Explain how hormones cause responses in their target tissues.

Figure 24-9 **Chemical control isn't limited to plants and humans. Chemical substances play important roles in controlling the development of a polyphemus moth from egg to larva to pupa to adult.**

24.2 Chemical Control in Animals

Like plants, animals also respond to stimuli. The stimuli come from outside or inside the body—a sudden drop in temperature, a baseball speeding toward you, hunger pangs, or a rise in the level of carbon dioxide in the blood. In plants, hormones regulate growth and development. There are some hormones that control these functions in animals. However, many other hormones regulate responses to stimuli inside and outside the body in order to maintain homeostasis. In this section, we will focus mostly on the hormones that maintain this condition.

Endocrine Control

In the next chapter, you will learn how the nervous system in animals quickly responds to stimuli by sending electrical "messages" along nerves to various parts of the body. The chemical control system in animals, on the other hand, is usually a much slower system because most hormones must travel through the bloodstream to reach their target tissues. Like plant hormones, though, their effects on the organism may last hours, days, weeks, or even years.

Glands In animals, chemical control is regulated by several glands located throughout the body. Glands are organs that are specialized for secreting substances needed by the organism. Some glands, such as those in the digestive system, produce substances that are needed quickly. These glands secrete products through small ducts and are known as exocrine glands. Other exocrine glands include sweat glands and milk glands. The glands you will study in this section secrete hormones directly into the bloodstream without the use of ducts. Such glands are the **endocrine glands,** which are sometimes called ductless glands.

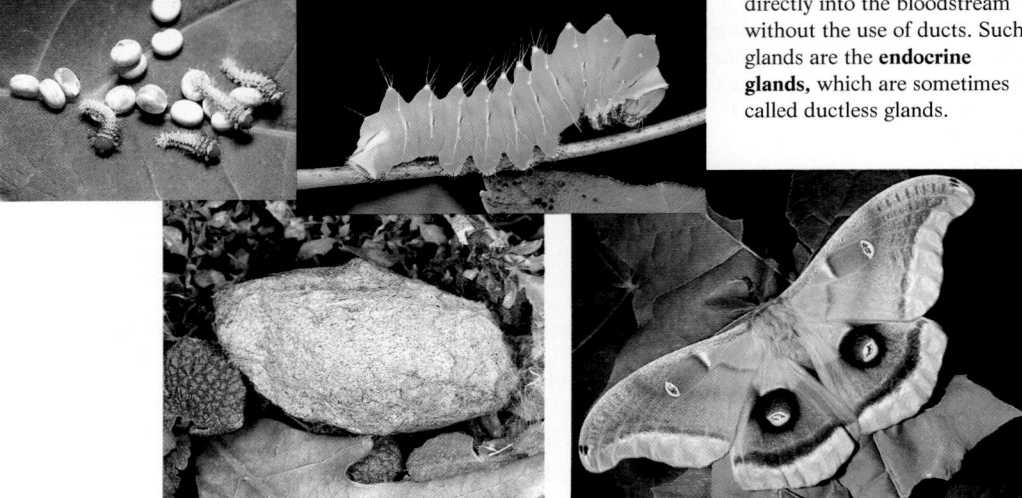

680 🦋 CHEMICAL CONTROL

PROGRAM RESOURCES

Teacher Classroom Resources

Study Guide, pp. 141-144 **L1**
Concept Mapping, p. 24 **L1** **LEP**
Critical Thinking/Problem Solving, p. 24 **L2**

Probing Levels of Life, Labs 63, 64, 65, pp. 163, 165, 167 **L2**
Investigating Living Systems, Labs 67, 68, pp. 257, 263 **L2**
Color Transparency #43 **L1** **LEP**

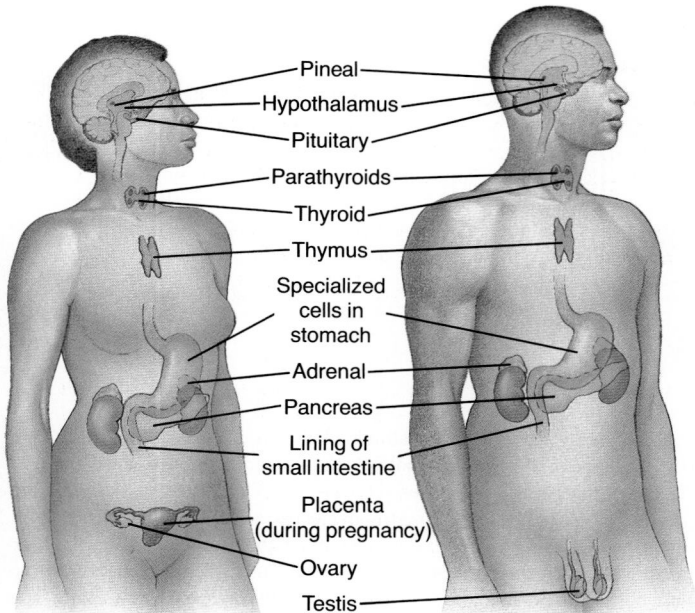

Pineal
Hypothalamus
Pituitary
Parathyroids
Thyroid
Thymus
Specialized
cells in
stomach
Adrenal
Pancreas
Lining of
small intestine
Placenta
(during pregnancy)
Ovary
Testis

Figure 24-10 This illustration shows the locations of the major endocrine glands. The small intestine and stomach are listed because certain of their cells produce hormones that affect digestion.

Endocrine glands are found in the brain, chest, abdomen, and pelvis in vertebrate animals. Figure 24-10 shows the names and locations of the major endocrine glands in humans.

Animal Hormones   Animal hormones, like auxins, are recognized only by specific target tissues. In general, hormones either stimulate a target tissue and increase its activities, or inhibit a target tissue and decrease its activities. It's important to note that the target tissue determines the response to a hormone, not the hormone itself. Like auxins, animal hormones also affect the target tissues by affecting chemical reactions. In animals, hormones regulate growth, development, and reproduction as well as maintain homeostasis.

In terms of chemical structure, there are two major types of hormones. Some hormones, such as insulin, are composed of chains of amino acids and are known as protein-type hormones. Others, such as testosterone and estrogen, are called steroid hormones. The chemical structures of the steroid hormones are closely related to cholesterol.

Negative Feedback   How do hormones work? In general, endocrine glands don't secrete hormones into the bloodstream at a constant rate. Rather, the rate of hormone secretion is determined by the needs of the animal at the particular time. Often, the message that causes a gland to speed up or slow down comes from the nervous system responding to some stimulus. In most cases, however, messages come in the form of other hormones.

24.2 CHEMICAL CONTROL IN ANIMALS   **681**

2 Teach

Brainstorming

Ask students to name some familiar biological processes that are controlled by animal hormones. Examples include molting in crustaceans, metamorphosis in insects, development of frogs from tadpoles, differentiation of tissues in developing embryos, development of breeding plumage in birds, and growth and maturation in all vertebrates. COOP LEARN

Bioethics

Research on Animals: Animal rights activists feel that scientists should not conduct any experiments on animals. Medical scientists point out that animal research has made possible many important discoveries that otherwise might not have been achieved. For example, without animal research, insulin may not have been isolated and many diabetics would not be alive today. Have students analyze this issue by interviewing or reading materials published by animal rights groups and those who oppose them. Be sure that students separate product safety tests from scientific research when considering this issue. L1

MEETING INDIVIDUAL NEEDS

Visually Impaired: Make an enlarged version of Figure 24-10 on butcher paper or poster board, or make a transparency of the diagram and project it using an overhead projector. Refer to the enlargement while discussing each gland, its hormones, and its corresponding target tissues. Hormone pathways through the body can be traced with a marking pen or a pointer.

Figure Caption Question

Why would feedback responses in humans be slower than with a thermostat and furnace? The thermostat involves an electrical switch that can turn on and off instantaneously. Hormones must be transported by the bloodstream and control biochemical processes that sometimes require several steps.

Chalkboard Example

Draw a feedback loop on the chalkboard. Show students how information from the output of a system is fed back as input to the system. Point out that input to the system can be any kind of information, whether it's the temperature of a room or the level of a hormone in the bloodstream. `L1` `LEP`

Using Science Terms

The term *endocrine* is derived from the Greek *endo-* (within) and *krinein* (to separate). *Insulin* is from the Latin word *insula,* meaning "island." *Diabetes* is from the Greek *bainein* (to walk or stand) and *dia* (across, apart). Although there is some uncertainty, it is assumed that the word refers to the act of urinating as a result of the large volumes of urine associated with the disease. *Hypothalamus* is from the Greek *hypo-* (under) and *thalamos* (inner room) and means literally "under the thalamus." *Hormone* is from the Greek word *horman,* meaning "to excite" or "to urge on." `LEP`

Display

Set up a plastic model of the human body in the classroom. Give each student an opportunity to locate, remove, and replace the components of the human endocrine system. `L1` `LEP`

Mercury switch in the "On" position

Thermostat shuts off current

Temperature setpoint

Temperature

Time →

Thermostat turns on current

Figure 24-11 **A furnace thermostat is a device that operates on the principle of negative feedback. It responds to temperature and switches heat on and off to keep the temperature within a degree or two of the set point. Negative feedback in humans is similar except that changes aren't as quick as with an on-off switch in a thermostat. Why would feedback responses in humans be slower than with a thermostat and furnace?**

Many body processes are maintained at an appropriate level through the mechanism of **negative feedback.** A familiar example of a negative feedback mechanism is an oven thermostat, which is used to maintain an oven at a constant temperature. In an electric oven, when the electric element raises the oven temperature just above the set temperature, the thermostat shuts off the current to the element. Then, the oven cools down to just below the setting, and the thermostat turns on the current again. You know also that you can set a thermostat to a higher or lower setting as needed. Likewise, negative feedback by the endocrine system maintains body processes at the levels required by the body. Those levels can vary according to the conditions of the body. Those conditions might include sleeping, working, fleeing danger, growing, fighting off an infection, and pregnancy.

In the body, negative feedback works like this. Suppose the concentration of a particular substance, such as thyroid hormone in the blood, increases above the level required by the body. Then, negative feedback acts to decrease it. On the other hand, if the concentration becomes too low, negative feedback will act to increase the level. Now let's look at some specific examples of hormonal control in humans.

Control of Blood Glucose Level

When you digest a meal, carbohydrates are broken down into glucose. As a result, a high concentration of glucose begins to build in the small intestine. In Chapter 20, you learned that after glucose enters the bloodstream, it is transported to the liver, where some of it is stored as glycogen. When glucose is needed by the body, some of the stored glycogen is broken down and the resulting glucose is released back into the bloodstream. This storage and release of glucose from the liver helps maintain the concentration of blood sugar at a level appropriate to the body's activities. Glucose is also stored as glycogen in skeletal muscle, the muscle attached to bones. Excess glucose is also transported into fat cells, where it is converted to fats.

682 🐾 CHEMICAL CONTROL

PORTFOLIO

Inside an outline of the human form, have students draw and label each endocrine gland, the hormone(s) each gland produces, and each hormone's target tissues. Have students select one hormone and create a series of "textbook illustrations" that show how the body senses the need for the hormone, where the hormone is synthesized, how the hormone gets to the target tissue, and how it affects the target tissue. Students may need to use reference books for additional information on the hormones to be discussed. Suggest to students that they look through a variety of books for ideas on presenting information in visual form. You may want to challenge more able students by assigning them hormones that are not discussed in detail in the textbook. `L1`

Action of Insulin   The uptake of glucose by the liver, skeletal muscle, and fat cells is under control of the hormone insulin. Insulin is produced by a group of cells located in the pancreas. After a carbohydrate-rich meal, the increased level of glucose in the blood is detected and these pancreatic cells respond by increasing their output of insulin. The net effect is the storage of blood glucose as described previously. The cells in the pancreas detect the reduced glucose level. As a result, the pancreas decreases its output of insulin, thus ensuring that some glucose remains in the blood rather than in storage.

Diabetes Mellitus   If the level of blood sugar is not regulated properly, such that a person has too much glucose in the blood, a variety of problems will arise. Such a person suffers from the disease diabetes mellitus, or sugar diabetes. In Chapter 22, you learned that one function of the kidneys is to conserve important substances including glucose by resorbing them into the blood. However, in diabetes, so much glucose is in the blood that not all of it can be resorbed, and glucose passes into the urine. Also, because there is an increased concentration of glucose in the blood, water and salts move from body cells into the blood because of osmosis and diffusion. This condition also forces the kidneys to work harder as they act to remove the excess water and salts in the bloodstream. As a result, thirst and frequent urination are common symptoms of untreated diabetes mellitus. A series of complications resulting from untreated diabetes can depress brain function, leading to a condition called diabetic coma.

What is the cause of this disease? You have learned that insulin enables glucose to enter body cells from the blood. In one form of diabetes, lack of insulin prevents glucose from entering cells. Thus, glucose levels in the blood remain high. It's as if the shelves are full of groceries, but there is no way to get at all the food. Thus, even though a person with

Minilab 2

What does pancreas tissue look like?

Observe a prepared slide of pancreas tissue under low power. You should see two different tissues. One appears as scattered, round, light-colored patches of cells with dark nuclei. They are surrounded by slightly darker tissue that makes up the bulk of the pancreas. The round patches are endocrine tissue that secretes hormones. The surrounding tissue forms digestive enzymes. Draw what you see in the microscope field, and label the two types of tissue seen. Name the two hormones made by the endocrine tissue and describe their functions. The endocrine patches are called islet cells.

Analysis   *Why do you think this name is appropriate? How are hormones made in islet cells carried from the pancreas to the rest of the body?*

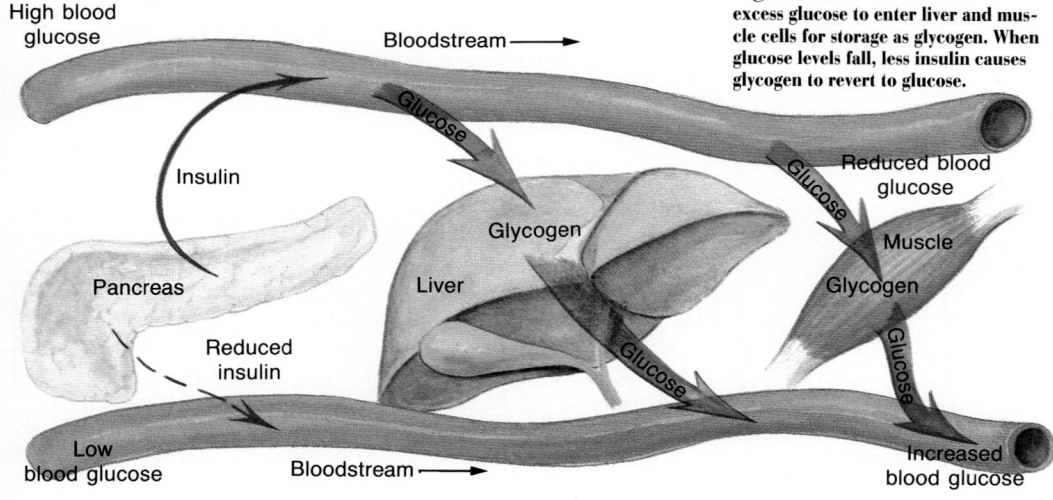

Figure 24-12   **Insulin causes excess glucose to enter liver and muscle cells for storage as glycogen. When glucose levels fall, less insulin causes glycogen to revert to glucose.**

High blood glucose

Bloodstream →

Glucose

Insulin

Pancreas

Glycogen

Liver

Reduced insulin

Low blood glucose

Bloodstream →

Glucose

Reduced blood glucose

Glucose

Muscle

Glycogen

Glucose

Increased blood glucose

Minilab 2

Purpose
Students are able to observe the different secretory tissues present within the pancreas.

Skills
observe, compare and contrast

Teaching Strategies
- Remind students about the proper handling of microscopes and slides.
- Prepared slides are available from supply houses or perhaps from the pathology department of a hospital.
- Provide students with photographs of similar tissue from reference books so they will know what to look for. Students should start by scanning the specimen under low power.

Expected Results
Students should see patches of islet cells within surrounding tissue. Students are not likely to be able to differentiate between alpha and beta islet cells.

Answers
The cells are part of small bits of different tissue that are surrounded by tissue that secretes digestive enzymes. The hormones from islet cells enter the bloodstream.

✔ Assessment
Portfolio: Have students make carefully labeled drawings of the fields they observe and place them in their portfolios. You may want students to combine them with similar drawings from the Alternate Lab on pages 690 and 691.

Misconception

Help clarify student understanding of the difference between endocrine glands and other (exocrine) glands. The prefix *exo-* means "outside" or "out of," and exocrine glands have ducts that transport materials such as sweat, milk, and sebum to the outside of the gland. The prefix *endo-* means "within" or "inside," and endocrine glands secrete hormones into the bloodstream as it passes through the gland.

Reinforcement

Have students color the plates illustrating the human endocrine system in The Anatomy Coloring Book. **LEP**

HISTORY CONNECTION

Diabetes: The earliest evidence that diabetes was recognized as a disease dates from around 1500 B.C. It was at first thought to be a kidney malady because of the primary symptom, the excretion of copious amounts of urine. In the 1800s, the German scientist Paul Langerhans observed clusters of cells in the pancreas, and others found that diabetes resulted when the pancreas of an animal was removed. It wasn't until 1921 that scientists learned that insulin is produced in tissue called the "islets of Langerhans" embedded in the pancreas. The discovery of insulin has saved the lives of millions of people with diabetes, but there is still no cure for the disease.

Figure Caption Question

How would the number of transport proteins in the plasma membrane affect the rate at which glucose enters a cell? More transport proteins provide more locations at which glucose can pass through a cell membrane.

untreated diabetes may have recently eaten a meal, he or she may feel fatigued and hungry. Long-term complications of untreated diabetes include strokes, blindness, kidney failure, and serious circulatory problems.

There are two types of diabetes. In one type, glucose cannot enter cells because cells in the pancreas do not produce enough insulin. This form of diabetes usually develops in people under 20 years of age and is known as type I diabetes. Type I diabetes is usually controlled by injections of insulin to maintain needed levels.

Type II diabetes occurs because muscle and fat cells that normally take up glucose after a meal do not carry out that function adequately. It is much more common and occurs most frequently in overweight people over 40 years old. Diet and exercise have been shown to help reduce blood glucose in these cases. However, as the disease progresses, many people must rely on insulin injections.

Insulin and Uptake of Glucose If the blood of people with untreated diabetes is so rich in glucose, why can't glucose pass from blood to body cells? Recent research has revealed a great deal about how glucose is transported across cell membranes. The transport relies on proteins called transporters in cell membranes. It is thought that transporters act to form pores that extend through the cell membrane. Figure 24-13 shows the series of steps by which glucose is thought to pass through the transporter and into a cell's interior. Once a glucose molecule enters a pore, the pore changes shape, closing behind the glucose molecule. When the molecule is in the cell, the pore takes its original shape. Scientists have found that the rate at which this transport can occur is greatly influenced by presence of insulin in the bloodstream.

Scientists have worked out a partial explanation of how insulin influences absorption of glucose into cells. In experiments with fat and muscle cells, scientists have found that some transporters are in the plasma membrane, but many more are on the surface of vesicles inside the cell. Evidence indicates that insulin links with a receptor present in the membrane. This linking sets off a chain of events that causes vesicles that have transporters to be brought from inside the cell and to fuse with the

Figure 24-13 Glucose enters cells through the action of transport proteins in the cell membrane. How would the number of transport proteins in the plasma membrane affect the rate at which glucose enters a cell?

684 CHEMICAL CONTROL

Plasma membrane

Vesicle fuses with plasma membrane

Glucose transporter

Glucose enters cell

Insulin

Glucose transporters

Insulin receptor

Vesicle with transporters

plasma membrane. The cell can then take up glucose more quickly because of the increased number of transporters. Research continues to lead to more information about this process.

Interaction of Hormones In the first section of this chapter, you learned that some plant hormones interact to control growth. Hormone interaction occurs in animals as well. For example, glucagon is another hormone secreted by cells in the pancreas. Instead of promoting the uptake of glucose by cells, it has nearly the opposite effect. Glucagon increases blood sugar by causing glycogen in the liver to break down and release glucose into the bloodstream. In fact, there are at least five other hormones that interact to maintain blood glucose at a proper level. You will see several examples of hormone interaction in the remainder of the chapter.

The Pituitary Gland

In order to maintain homeostasis, levels of hormones must change in response to different stimuli. Secretion of hormones from many endocrine glands is under control of the **pituitary gland.** The pituitary gland is a three-lobed structure located at the base of the brain. The two major lobes are known as the anterior pituitary and posterior pituitary. Working with a nearby brain structure, the **hypothalamus,** the pituitary releases hormones of its own. The targets of many of these hormones are other endocrine glands around the body, and they cause the glands to either increase or decrease activity.

Figure 24-14 Scientists believe that insulin helps glucose enter cells by a process that brings more transport proteins to the plasma membrane from inside the cell. When insulin binds to a receptor, a chain of events causes vesicles containing transport proteins to fuse with the cell's plasma membrane, providing more transporters to bring glucose into the cell.

24.2 CHEMICAL CONTROL IN ANIMALS **685**

Different Viewpoints in Biology

New Ways to Take Insulin
People with type II diabetes are often treated with oral drugs that stimulate the pancreas to produce more insulin. Because people with type I diabetes produce very little if any insulin, they cannot use these drugs. Research on the long-term effect of these drugs has suggested a connection with cardiovascular disease. Although results are not yet certain, many doctors prefer to treat patients with diet and exercise and add insulin if necessary. They reserve oral drugs for those who cannot take insulin for some reason.

One of the major problems with the administration of insulin is in trying to maintain normal levels by means of injection. The natural fluctuation of insulin levels in response to various stimuli cannot be duplicated with insulin injections. Mechanical insulin pumps that deliver a more steady supply are now available. Patients can also give themselves extra quantities when needed, such as at mealtime. The drawback to this device is that continual medical supervision is needed to deal with the needle that remains inserted below the skin on the abdomen.

STUDENT JOURNAL

Have students write a report on what happens to a glucose molecule as it moves out of the digestive system into the bloodstream. Have them follow the glucose molecule's path into a cell of a healthy individual, and compare that with the pathway of a glucose molecule in the bloodstream of a person with untreated diabetes. L2

Lifetime of Insulin: Insulin, a simple protein molecule, is made up of 51 amino acids arranged in two chains linked by three pairs of sulfur atoms. Because the sulfur links are easily broken, half of the insulin molecules present at a given time are gone ten to 30 minutes later. Cells in the islets of Langerhans of a healthy pancreas store insulin as unlinked amino acid chains. These cells detect blood glucose level and, when the level rises, the amino acid chains are linked. Thus, the proper amount of insulin is released into the bloodstream within one and a half minutes.

Concept Development

Emphasize to students that insulin is required by nearly every type of cell in the body because every cell needs to take in glucose. Point out that, by releasing hormones directly into the bloodstream, endocrine glands efficiently distribute hormones to all body cells.

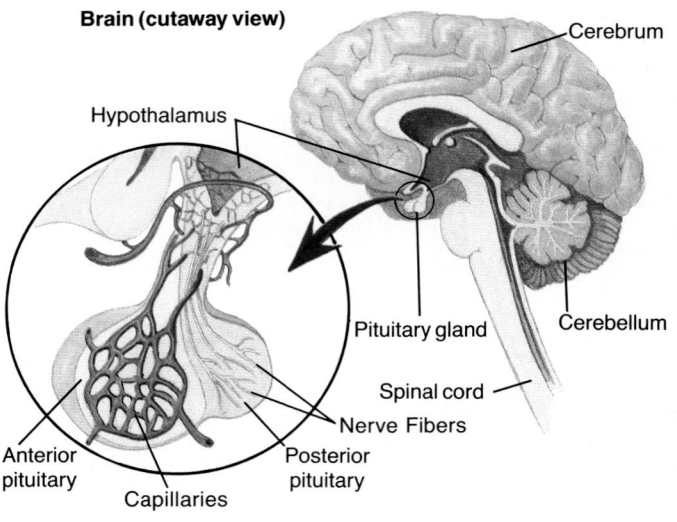

Figure 24-15 The pituitary gland is embedded in bone below the hypothalamus of the brain. The hypothalamus senses the levels of various substances in the blood. As a result, it secretes (or stops secreting) releasing factors. These factors enter the bloodstream and cause the anterior pituitary to release its own hormones.

Figure 24-16 This diagram shows how negative feedback by hormones keeps the amount of thyroxine at a level suitable to the body's needs.

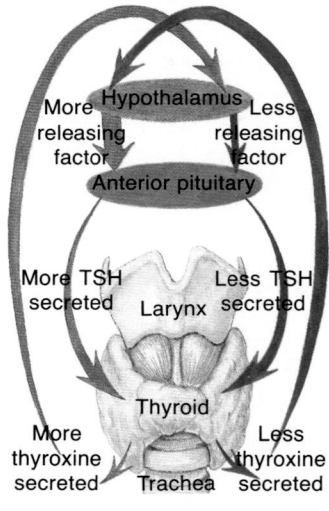

Anterior Pituitary   As an example of negative feedback, consider control of the level of thyroxine, a hormone produced by the thyroid gland. Thyroxine increases the rate of metabolism in cells, and the level of thyroxine in the blood must be maintained at a level that meets the needs of the body. Output of thyroxine by the thyroid is controlled by a hormone from the anterior pituitary called thyroid stimulating hormone, usually referred to as TSH. An increase in level of TSH stimulates the thyroid to release more thyroxine and vice versa. How do the two interact and what signals the pituitary to release more or less TSH?

As the level of thyroxine in the blood falls below the proper point, that lower level is detected by the hypothalamus as blood passes through it. The hypothalamus secretes a hormone of its own, called TSH releasing factor, which enters the bloodstream. As the releasing factor reaches the anterior pituitary, the anterior pituitary responds to the stimulus by secreting more TSH. TSH enters the bloodstream and, upon reaching the thyroid, stimulates it to secrete more thyroxine. With time, the thyroxine level rises above the "set point," and this level is also detected by the hypothalamus, which stops secreting TSH releasing factor. The anterior pituitary then decreases TSH output, and the level of thyroxine in the blood begins to fall.

This interaction of hypothalamus, anterior pituitary, and thyroid is another example of negative feedback. Information—in this case high thyroxine level in blood—is fed back as a drop in releasing factor to the structure responsible for controlling that level. The structure, the anterior pituitary, responds accordingly by shutting off production of the stimulating hormone. The fact that the hypothalamus, a part of the nervous system, plays a role in chemical control shows a close link between nervous and endocrine systems.

686 ⚬ CHEMICAL CONTROL

Percy Julian: The chemist Percy Julian developed methods for synthesizing cortisone, testosterone, and progesterone. Instead of extracting these hormones from animal tissues, he used sterol molecules from soybeans as raw materials for the manufacture of these human hormones. Cortisone can relieve the pain of inflammatory diseases such as arthritis. Dr. Julian's discoveries made it possible to manufacture cortisone inexpensively. Born in Montgomery, Alabama, in 1899, he grew up at a time when it was extremely difficult for an African American to obtain a college education. Through hard work, Dr. Julian obtained a master's degree in chemistry from Harvard University and a Ph.D. from the University of Vienna in Austria. Included among his many achievements is the development of a foam used in fire extinguishers.

The Posterior Pituitary   The posterior pituitary secretes two hormones, which are actually made in the hypothalamus. Neither of these hormones controls other endocrine glands. One of them, oxytocin, stimulates contraction of muscles of the uterus, leading to labor and childbirth. The other is vasopressin, which helps maintain the body's water balance by regulating the amount of water lost in urine. Unlike secretions by the anterior pituitary, secretion of hormones from the posterior pituitary is not controlled by other hormones, but by nervous stimulation from the hypothalamus. Still, the control is by feedback.

Hormone Action

How do hormones work to cause a response by a target tissue? In Section 24.1, you learned that hormones can work in one of two ways. In one way, hormones cause a response by triggering chemical reactions within cells of target tissue. In general, protein-type hormones work this way. Steroid hormones work in another way. They activate genes within cells of target tissue. In either case, the hormone must first recognize its target tissue before a response can occur.

HEALTH CONNECTION

Choh Hao Li

Choh Hao Li dedicated his scientific career to the study of the hormones of the pituitary gland. He and his research teammates were either the first or among the first to isolate and identify the eight hormones produced by the anterior pituitary.

Born in China in 1913, Li studied and then taught chemistry at Nanking University. He earned a Ph.D. in the United States at the University of California at Berkeley, and stayed on afterwards as a faculty member. In 1950, he became director of the university's Hormone Research Laboratories. Five years later, he was granted U.S. citizenship.

Among Dr. Li's most famous discoveries is adrenocorticotropic hormone (ACTH), a protein hormone from the anterior pituitary. ACTH stimulates the outer layer of the adrenal gland, called the adrenal cortex, to produce corticoids, also known as corticosteroids. Corticoids are hormones the body needs in order to use nutrients properly and maintain the right balance of salts and water in body fluids. They also affect inflammation and immune response. Li worked out the structure of ACTH and showed that only portions of the hormone's molecule were necessary for it to be effective in the body.

It was also Dr. Li who isolated and discovered the structure of human growth hormone (HGH), also called somatotropin. His work with pituitary growth hormones proved that the hormones work only for the species that produces them. A dog's growth hormone, for example, will help a dog grow, but it will do nothing for a cat or any other non-canine animal.

In 1970, he succeeded in synthesizing HGH. With its 256 amino acid chains, it was the largest protein molecule ever synthesized up to that time. Li's work paved the way for research showing that doctors can use HGH to help children lacking the hormone to grow normally.

1. **Solve the Problem:** Many scientists are concerned about the possible misuse of HGH. In what ways do you think this hormone might be misused?
2. **Explore Further:** ACTH is a protein-type hormone. How do you think it exerts its effect on the cells of the adrenal cortex?

HEALTH CONNECTION

Purpose
Students see how discoveries made in one scientific discipline, such as chemistry, can have a significant effect on progress in other disciplines, such as medicine.

Teaching Strategies
- Draw a silhouette of the human body on the chalkboard showing the location of the pituitary and adrenal glands. Point out that ACTH moves, via the bloodstream, to the adrenal cortex and that corticosteroids then move from the adrenal cortex, again via the bloodstream, throughout the body. **LEP**

Possible Answers
1. Young athletes might want to use HGH to become taller than they would normally grow. Parents might want to make a short child taller by giving him or her HGH. However, serious side effects can result. For example, although HGH will speed the growth of bones, it will also cause the bones to mature before they have reached full growth. As a result, a child could actually end up being shorter than average.
2. It attaches to receptors in the membrane of adrenal cortex cells, stimulating the production of corticosteroid molecules within the cell.

Going Further
Have students look up information on scientists who have discovered or synthesized endocrine hormones. F.G. Banting and C.H. Best discovered insulin, E.C. Kendall isolated thyroxine and cortisone, P.S. Hench discovered that cortisone had a beneficial effect on inflamed tissues, and Starling and Bayliss discovered secretin. **L2**

Protein-type Hormones   Protein-type hormones locate their target tissue by matching with receptor proteins in the plasma membranes of the cells of their target tissues. Because each hormone can link with only a certain receptor, the target tissue is easily recognized. As a specific example, adrenaline molecules can dock with adrenaline receptors located on certain liver cells and on cells of skeletal muscle. One action of adrenaline is to cause conversion of glycogen to glucose in those target cells.

However, adrenaline does not cause a response directly. After an adrenaline molecule links to its receptor, the receptor activates an enzyme in the cell membrane. This enzyme converts one substance to another substance called a second messenger, which causes a series of reactions. These reactions activate an enzyme that converts glycogen to glucose. In just a few seconds, one adrenaline molecule can lead to production of 10 billion molecules of glucose. This model has become known as the **second messenger hypothesis**. In this case, adrenaline is the first messenger, but it never enters the target cell. It is the second messenger that actually causes the response.

Steroid Hormones   Steroid hormones actually pass through the membranes of target cells. Once inside the cell, the hormones combine with receptors in the cytoplasm. No second messengers are involved. Instead, the steroid-receptor complex moves into the nucleus, where it activates a gene. When the gene becomes active, it is transcribed and translated. The protein formed then changes the cell's chemistry, leading to a response.

So far, you've looked at some human hormones, how they function, and a relatively simple example of negative feedback. Now, let's look at how hormones interact to regulate a more complex body process.

Figure 24-17   **The diagram on the left illustrates the action of adrenaline, a typical protein-type hormone. When adrenaline binds to its receptor, a second messenger is produced. This second messenger initiates a series of reactions that finally activates an enzyme that converts stored glycogen to glucose. In contrast, the right diagram illustrates the action of a steroid hormone, which enters the target cell and binds with a receptor. Together they enter the nucleus and cause a gene to be transcribed. Translation of the resulting mRNA produces the needed protein.**

Action of Protein-type Hormone

Action of Steroid Hormone

ALTERNATE LAB: Comparing Endocrine Tissue

Purpose
Students examine glandular tissue under the microscope and relate their observations to the tissues' functions.

Materials
prepared slides of mammalian adrenal gland, thyroid gland, testes, and ovaries showing the corpus luteum

Procedure
Give the following directions to students.

1. Examine each slide under the microscope.
2. The adrenal gland is made up of the adrenal medulla and the surrounding cortex. The medulla contains nerve cells and secretory cells that release epinephrine (adrenaline). Look for three layers of cells in the adrenal cortex. These cells secrete aldosterone, cortisol, and other steroid hormones.

3. Look for thyroxine-filled follicles embedded in the thyroid tissue. In humans, the thyroid gland is the largest of the endocrine glands.
4. Look for developing sperm cells lining the seminiferous tubules coiled within the testes. Interstitial ("in between") cells, distributed throughout the seminiferous tubules, include the "cells of Leydig," which secrete testosterone.

Table 24.1 Some Human Hormones and Their Main Functions

Hormone	Sources	Location of Source	Functions
Thyroxine	Thyroid gland	Neck	Regulates metabolic rate of body cells
Insulin	Islets of Langerhans (beta cells)	Pancreas	Decreases level of sugar in blood
Glucagon	Islets of Langerhans (alpha cells)	Pancreas	Increases level of sugar in blood
Adrenaline	Adrenal medulla	On kidneys	Prepares body to cope with stress; converts glycogen to glucose
Cortisone	Adrenal cortex	On kidneys	Prevents inflammation Increases level of sugar in blood
Testosterone	Testes	In scrotum	Causes secondary sexual characteristics in males; stimulates sperm production
Estrogen	Ovaries	In abdomen	Causes development of secondary sexual characteristics in females Prepares uterus for pregnancy
Progesterone	Corpus luteum	In abdomen	Maintains uterus during pregnancy
FSH	Anterior pituitary	Base of brain	Causes maturation of egg in females Stimulates sperm production in males
LH	Anterior pituitary	Base of brain	Causes ovulation in females Causes release of testosterone in males
TSH	Anterior pituitary	Base of brain	Stimulates thyroxine production
HGH	Anterior pituitary	Base of brain	Regulates growth of body
ACTH	Anterior pituitary	Base of brain	Stimulates release of adrenal cortex hormones
Oxytocin	Posterior pituitary	Base of brain	Stimulates contraction of uterine muscles
Vasopressin	Posterior pituitary	Base of brain	Regulates water balance by kidneys
Gastrin	Stomach cells	Stomach	Stimulates release of gastric juice
Secretin	Intestinal cells	Intestine	Stimulates release of sodium hydrogen carbonate from pancreas and bile from gallbladder
Cholecystokinin	Intestinal cells	Intestine	Stimulates release of pancreatic enzymes and bile

SECTION 24.2

Using the Table

Explain to students that hormones produced by the adrenal cortex and the gonads are steroids, and hormones produced by the hypothalamus, pituitary, gut, and thyroid are proteins. Point out that protein hormones are stored in gland cells and can be secreted into the bloodstream very quickly, usually within minutes. Steroid hormones cannot be stored and so must be synthesized as needed. As a result, responses to steroid hormones take place in a matter of hours rather than minutes. **LEP**

CHEMISTRY CONNECTION

Steroid Structure: All steroid hormones are based on the same four-ring carbon skeleton of cholesterol. When a steroid hormone is needed, the endocrine gland removes cholesterol molecules from the blood, converts them to hormone molecules, then returns them to the bloodstream.

---

5. Look for oocytes, or undeveloped eggs, located near the edge of the ovary. As each egg matures, it grows larger and is surrounded by an increasing number of follicle cells. After a follicle ruptures and releases the mature egg, the follicle cells accumulate large amounts of fat and become the large, yellowish corpus luteum.

Analysis
Have students draw each type of tissue observed and label each type of cell they are able to identify, including those cells that secrete hormones. If possible, furnish visual references from college textbooks or other sources. Cells of the adrenal gland secrete a variety of steroid hormones, thyroid follicles secrete thyroxine, cells of Leydig secrete testosterone, a developing ovarian follicle secretes estrogen, and the corpus luteum secretes estrogen and progesterone.

✔ Assessment
Knowledge: Have students identify one or more hormones associated with each gland and describe how each hormone affects the body.

Using Science Terms

Follicle, a general term for a small anatomical cavity, is from the Latin word *folliculus,* meaning "small bag." *Corpus* is Latin for "body" and *luteum* means "yellow."

Concept Development

As the hormonal changes that take place during the menstrual cycle are discussed, point out that some contraceptive drugs disrupt the menstrual cycle by suppressing ovulation. Many of these drugs contain a combination of estrogen and progesterone, though some contain only progesterone. Taken during the first 21 days of the cycle, the hormones suppress secretion of FSH and LH, so ovulation is never triggered.

Control of the Menstrual Cycle

Control of the menstrual cycle involves several different hormones and illustrates the principle of negative feedback very well. You learned in Chapter 18 that the menstrual cycle lasts an average of 28 days. During that time, an egg matures within the follicle of an ovary, and the uterine tissue becomes spongier and enriched with blood. Because the menstrual cycle is a cycle, we could begin studying it at any point. For convenience, let's begin with menstruation, which is marked by loss of blood and some uterine tissue through the vagina and lasts three to five days.

The Follicle Stage   As menstruation is proceeding, a new egg is already beginning to mature within a follicle of the ovary. This event marks the beginning of the **follicle stage,** which lasts for about ten days. Maturity of an egg is controlled by the anterior pituitary gland, which releases follicle-stimulating hormone, or FSH. Secretion of luteinizing hormone, LH, from the anterior pituitary is also increased. As the follicle develops, it also secretes a hormone, estrogen, which stimulates the tissues of the uterus to thicken and the blood supply to increase. This action begins to prepare the uterus for possible pregnancy.

The Corpus Luteum   As the level of estrogen in the blood increases, it is detected by the hypothalamus. In a feedback process, the hypothalamus responds by causing the pituitary to decrease FSH production and increase output of LH. The increased concentration of LH in the blood leads to ovulation, the bursting of a follicle and release of an egg into the oviduct.

Thinking Lab

DRAW A CONCLUSION

Which hormones control egg release or uterine thickening?

Background
The menstrual cycle consists of a number of events that follow a recurring pattern. This pattern repeats because of the interaction of hormones. Two events of this cyclic pattern are (1) release of an egg from an ovary and (2) the buildup of the uterine lining.

You Try It
Use the table to predict which hormone(s) would be associated with the two events described above. Assume that the cycle is one of average length (28 days) and the egg is not fertilized.

Day of Menstrual Cycle	Concentration of Hormones		
	A	B	C
1	12	5	10
5	14	5	14
9	14	5	13
13	70	10	20
17	12	60	9
21	12	150	8
25	8	100	8
1	12	5	10

Draw a conclusion by answering the following questions. Which hormone(s) may be involved with the: (a) thickening of the uterine lining and (b) release of an egg from the ovary? Explain your answers.

690 CHEMICAL CONTROL

Thinking Lab

DRAW A CONCLUSION

Purpose
Students will correlate hormone levels with events of the menstrual cycle.

Skills
interpret data, sequence

Teaching Strategies
• Students may need to refer to Figure 24-19 for help. However, caution them that patterns of hormone levels may vary among women.
• You may find this Thinking Lab a useful teaching tool to motivate students to read and study pages 690-692.

Answers
Hormone B (progesterone) must be involved with thickening the uterine lining because B begins to increase just before the middle of the cycle and rises to a high level at about the beginning of the fourth week. Hormones A and C (LH and FSH) are associated with ovulation because their levels become high at the middle of the cycle.

✔ **Assessment**
Oral: Copy the data chart on the chalkboard and have students point out trends while telling how they arrive at their conclusions.

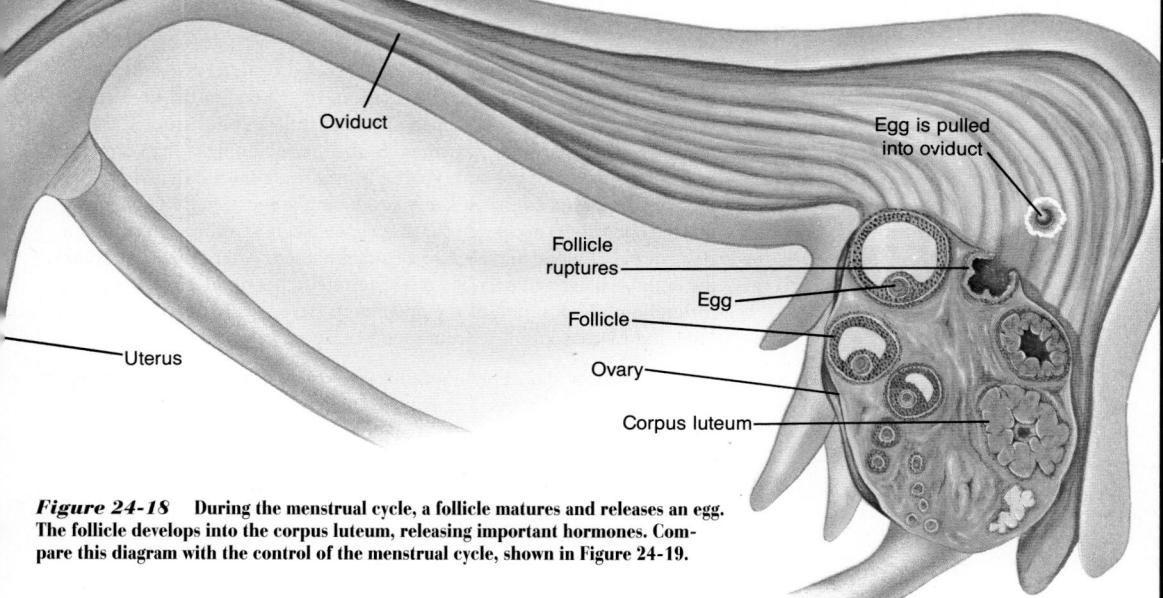

Oviduct

Egg is pulled
into oviduct

Follicle
ruptures

Egg

Follicle

Ovary

Uterus

Corpus luteum

Figure 24-18 During the menstrual cycle, a follicle matures and releases an egg. The follicle develops into the corpus luteum, releasing important hormones. Compare this diagram with the control of the menstrual cycle, shown in Figure 24-19.

This release is called ovulation, which usually occurs about midway through the cycle.

LH also causes the ruptured follicle to be converted to a yellowish body, the **corpus luteum.** Under the influence of LH, the corpus luteum secretes some estrogen and the hormone progesterone. Progesterone further prepares the uterus for pregnancy. The high concentration of progesterone in the blood is again detected, and the pituitary reduces output of FSH and LH. This stage of the cycle, which lasts about two weeks, is called the **corpus luteum stage.**

Figure 24-19 This diagram of the menstrual cycle shows the relationship among the levels of pituitary hormones, levels of ovarian hormones, events in the ovary, and the condition of the uterine lining.

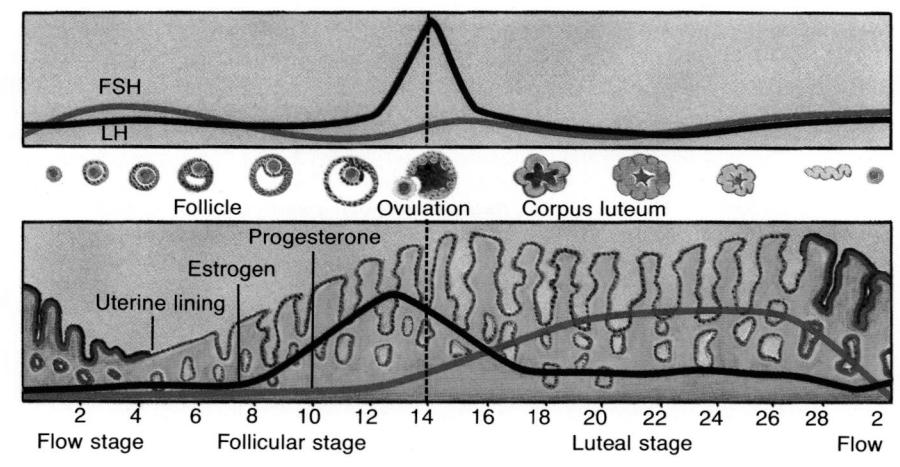

Levels of pituitary hormones

FSH

LH

Events in the ovary

Follicle   Ovulation   Corpus luteum

Thickness of uterine lining and levels of ovarian hormones

Progesterone

Estrogen

Uterine lining

Time (days)

2   4   6   8   10   12   14   16   18   20   22   24   26   28   2

Flow stage   Follicular stage   Luteal stage   Flow

24.2 CHEMICAL CONTROL IN ANIMALS   **691**

✔ **Assessment**

Oral: Divide the class into four or five groups. Have each group member select a different endocrine gland and describe to the rest of the group its function and the sequence of events involved in a hormonal response associated with that gland. Students should be invited to use visuals to enhance their presentations. `L1` `COOP LEARN`

4 Close

Activity

Provide pairs of students with a set of cards or slips of paper, each of which describes an event involved in a specific hormonal response. Have the students arrange the cards in the proper sequence. After completing the first puzzle, have students shuffle and exchange cards with another group. A logical progression would be from insulin to thyroxine to the menstrual cycle. Students could also sequence events to compare the action of protein-type hormones with that of steroid hormones. `L1`

When Fertilization Occurs   When an egg has been fertilized in the oviduct, it begins to undergo cell division. By the end of the first week of growth, the zygote has developed into a blastula and has entered the uterus. Here, it becomes implanted in the uterine lining. When implantation occurs, some of the embryo's cells produce a hormone that maintains the corpus luteum so that it keeps producing progesterone. Thus, the uterine conditions necessary for pregnancy, such as a thick lining and a rich supply of blood vessels, are also maintained. After about five weeks, the embryo itself will produce progesterone to maintain the uterus throughout the duration of the pregnancy. Because progesterone inhibits FSH and LH output, menstrual cycles cease during pregnancy.

Menstrual Flow   If implantation of an embryo does not occur during the corpus luteum stage, the corpus luteum begins to break down. As it does so, progesterone level declines and the uterine lining cannot be maintained. The uterine lining begins to break down, and menstruation occurs once more. In addition, production of FSH and LH is no longer inhibited, and output of those two hormones increases. The net result is the development of a new follicle and, consequently, a new cycle.

LOOKING AHEAD

Organisms respond to stimuli by means of chemical control—hormones. Chemical response to stimuli is slow, but in Chapter 25 you will examine a faster means of response—nervous control. You will learn how stimuli are detected and how those stimuli set off impulses that are transmitted from one cell to another and to the structures that respond to the stimuli.

Section Review

Understanding Concepts

1. Explain why the blood glucose level is often high in people with untreated diabetes.
2. Ecdysone, a steroid, stimulates metamorphosis in insects. Describe how this hormone causes a response in target tissue.
3. How does the follicle stage of the menstrual cycle illustrate the idea that some hormones work together to cause a response? Give examples of negative feedback at work in control of the menstrual cycle.
4. **Skill Review—Sequencing:** Output of cortisone from the adrenal gland is under control of ACTH, an anterior pituitary hormone. Sequence the series of events that would lead to a decrease in output of cortisone. For more help, see Organizing Information in the **Skill Handbook**.
5. **Thinking Critically:** People who do not produce enough of the hormone vasopressin suffer from the disease diabetes insipidus. Consider what their symptoms might be and why the term *diabetes* applies to their illness, as well as to people with diabetes mellitus.

692 ❧ CHEMICAL CONTROL

Answers to Section Review

1. Lack of insulin results in lack of glucose transporters at cell surfaces. Therefore, glucose builds up in blood.
2. Ecdysone combines with a receptor in the cytoplasm. The complex moves into the nucleus, where it activates a gene, producing a protein that leads to a chemical change.
3. High estrogen at the end of the follicle stage is detected by the hypothalamus, which decreases FSH output and increases LH output from the pituitary. Ovulation follows. In the corpus luteum stage, the high level of progesterone inhibits FSH and LH output.
4. **Skill Review—Sequencing:** Cortisone increases and is detected by the hypothalamus, which stops secreting ACTH releasing factor, and the anterior pituitary decreases output of ACTH. Reduced ACTH leads to decreased cortisone from the adrenal gland.
5. **Thinking Critically:** The kidneys retain less water and the person suffers from thirst and frequent urination, both of which are also symptoms of diabetes mellitus.

BIOLOGY, TECHNOLOGY, AND SOCIETY

Considering the Environment

The Pesticide Tree

Since the dawn of agriculture, farmers have been at war with insects seeking to steal crops for their own food. For the past several decades, humans have been winning the war on insect pests, thanks in great part to chemical insecticides. But there's been growing concern about the environmental damage that some of these insecticides may cause. As a result, there's been an increasing demand for safer ways to control insect pests.

Recently, a lot of scientific interest has been focused on the neem tree, a plant long known in India for its insect-fighting properties. Of particular interest is the oil from neem seeds. Neem oil shows insecticidal properties that are effective against a wide range of insect pests. One component of neem oil is a compound called azadirachtin, which fatally disrupts insect growth.

How Neem Oil Acts   One reason azadirachtin is so effective is that it has a molecular structure very similar to ecdysone. In some insects, it bonds to ecdysone receptors, blocking the insect's natural hormone and preventing it from acting. Molting stops and the larva dies.

Safety of Neem Oil   Despite its toxicity to many insect pests, azadirachtin has so far shown no ill effects on most other animals. Laboratory tests indicate it to be safe for birds and rats, although it might pose a threat to some fish. It seems to offer no danger to humans or pets.

Many beneficial insects, such as those that prey on pests, have also survived well among azadirachtin-treated test plants. The reason seems to be that plants absorb the compound. Those insects that feed on the plant die, while those that don't remain safe.

Another advantage of neem-based insecticides is that they rapidly degrade, losing all toxicity. That may mean extra work for

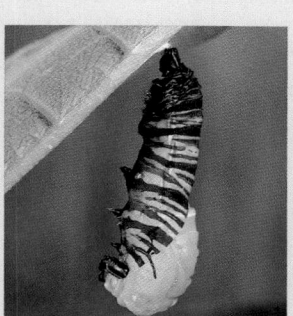

farmers since they might have to treat crops several times each growing season. However, it greatly reduces any risk of buildup in the soil or groundwater.

1. **Explore Further:** Do library research to find out about other insecticides that have been derived from plants. Against what insects are they effective?
2. **Connection to Economics:** Many substances that are useful to humans can be found in plants and other organisms. Assume that a substance from plants found only in a desert environment is discovered to be very active in treating heart disease in humans. It is complex and cannot be manufactured. What do you think would be the consequences of such a discovery, both economic and ecological?

CAREER CONNECTION

Entomologists study insects. They work to better understand insect anatomy, behavior, classification, development, and roles in their ecosystems. Some entomologists are interested purely in expanding our knowledge of insects. Other entomologists work to protect crops, animals, and people from insect pests or to safeguard and increase the population of beneficial insect species. Entomologists commonly work for agricultural and health organizations, pesticide manufacturers, museums, and universities.

CAREER CONNECTION

Have students contact a local agricultural extension office, university biology department, or companies that manufacture insecticides to learn more about careers in entomology.

Considering the Environment

Purpose
Students explore the use of a substance derived from a natural source to control pests.

Background
The neem tree is also known as the bead tree or Indian lilac tree. Its botanical name is *Azadirachta indica*.

Teaching Strategies
* Show students a photograph or drawing of a neem tree, or bring a neem oil product to class. Many people of south Asia use neem-derived products in a variety of body care products, including soap and toothpaste.

Possible Answers
1. Pyrethrum, made from a flower of the chrysanthemum family, controls aphids, beetles, caterpillars, moths, and many other insects. Rotenone, derived from several tropical plants, kills insects, including fleas and ticks, but is toxic to fish. Other botanical pesticides include sabadilla seeds, quassia wood chips, and tobacco.
2. A possibility is that deserts would become more important, causing a rise in the value of desert land that can grow the plants commercially. On the other hand, poachers might destroy the desert ecosystem while trying to obtain the plants. Other answers are possible.

Going Further
Have students interview local gardeners or farmers to find out whether they use botanical insecticides and to learn about non-chemical means of controlling pests. **L2**

CHAPTER 24

Biotechnology

Purpose
Students learn a new approach to the treatment of diabetes with insulin.

Teaching Strategies
- Explain that persons with type I diabetes must rotate injection sites on the body to avoid development of abscesses or infection, and that usually one or two injections are given daily.

Possible Answers
1. People with type I diabetes would no longer have to purchase syringes, needles, and disinfectants needed for injections. The ability to take insulin by mouth could increase the control people have over blood sugar levels because they could take smaller, more frequent doses.
2. A positive ion has lost an electron. A negative ion has an extra electron.

Going Further
Have students talk to a pharmacist or physician about other drug delivery methods, such as patches for delivering nicotine to the bloodstream of a person who is trying to quit smoking or suppositories for giving medicines to infants or patients who are nauseated and cannot swallow drugs. **L1**
LEP

Biotechnology
Insulin Without the Sting

Nobody enjoys taking shots, but people who suffer from juvenile diabetes mellitus have learned to live with them, because the alternative may be not living at all. The name "juvenile diabetes" does not mean that everyone who has it is a child. Rather, it's called "juvenile" because its onset is usually during childhood.

Causes of Diabetes   People who have diabetes mellitus either don't produce enough insulin in their bodies or can't efficiently use the insulin they do produce. The form of diabetes mellitus known as adult diabetes can often be controlled with careful diet and exercise. The form called juvenile diabetes, however, usually cannot. Those with juvenile diabetes need to take regular doses of insulin to keep their blood sugar under control.

Unfortunately, insulin can't be taken by mouth. It's a simple protein—exactly the sort of material your stomach easily digests. Insulin would be quickly broken

down by digestive enzymes and would never make it into the bloodstream. Diabetics in need of insulin have to take it by frequent injections.

A New Way to Take Insulin   The good news is that the need for injections may soon disappear. New coatings are being developed that go beyond allowing insulin in tablet form to survive the digestive system. These coatings actually use the digestive process to release the insulin at the right time and place.

The new coatings are made of substances called proteinoids, combinations of amino acids that aren't quite normal proteins and so resist digestion. The unusual thing about proteinoids is that they shape themselves into tiny bubble-like spheres when placed in water. Put insulin, or any other organic material, in the water with them and some will be caught up inside the spheres. Since the spheres are so small that millions would fit in a single tablet, they're referred to as microspheres.

The molecules in proteinoids can be treated so that they have electrical charges. Some become positively charged and others negatively charged. By selecting ingredients carefully, it's possible to make microspheres with an abundance of either positively or negatively charged molecules on the outside.

How Microspheres Avoid Digestion   To carry insulin, it's best to have microspheres with a shell of positive charges. Because the stomach contains acid, there is a high concentration of positive

hydrogen ions. Because like charges repel each other, the positive charge on the outside of the microsphere would deflect attacks by digestive acid. The microspheres would then carry their cargo of insulin safely into the small intestine where they are absorbed without having been broken down.

In the bloodstream, the microspheres are in a very different chemical environment. Because opposite charges attract, the negative ions would attract the microspheres and begin breaking them down. Soon, the microspheres would rupture, releasing insulin directly into the bloodstream.

Other Roles for Microspheres
Proteinoid microspheres aren't limited to carrying insulin. They could transport just about any type of medication into the bloodstream—including vaccines. By carefully selecting the proteinoids to be used, pharmaceutical companies can engineer microspheres to release each medicine at its most beneficial point.

1. **Issue:** When encapsulated insulin finally becomes available, it is likely to be expensive. What factors might offset this expense for people who must take frequent insulin injections? Can you think of any health advantages that encapsulated insulin might have over injected insulin?
2. **Connection to Chemistry:** What causes an ion to have a positive or a negative electrical charge?

Issues

Steroids and Athletes

There's an old doctor's joke about the hospitalized patient whose condition kept improving day by day until he died. He died of too much improvement. That joke has become a tragic reality for some athletes and for some who merely want to look like athletes. The people are those who have "improved" their muscle size and strength using drugs called anabolic steroids.

The Action of Anabolic Steroids
Anabolic steroids are synthetic chemicals similar to testosterone, which is normally produced in the testes of the male. Although both males and females have testosterone, males have greater amounts.

Because anabolic steroids mimic testosterone, some obvious side effects occur in female users. These effects include deeper voices, beard growth, and male pattern baldness.

Males, on the other hand, do not grow increasingly "masculine" in appearance except for larger muscles and an increase in facial and body hair. The testosterone-like action of the steroids tends to shut down natural testosterone production. As a result, male users' testicles may permanently shrink and their breasts may enlarge.

Side Effects of Anabolic Steroids
Anabolic steroids can greatly reduce the body's level of HDLs, substances necessary for a healthy heart. As a result, many young users have died from sudden heart attacks. Long-term use of the drugs has been linked to liver damage, kidney disease, strokes, immune system disorders, and cancer.

Teenage users face even more dangers. Teenage bodies are not yet fully formed, and some parts, such as the skeletal and reproductive systems, are still developing. Anabolic steroid use can bring that development to a premature and permanent halt.

Can They Be Used Safely? Still, many who bulk up their muscles with anabolic steroids are convinced that the drugs are safe if used wisely and carefully. A number of doctors say that this might be true, although they stress that it's by no means certain. Furthermore, medical experts insist that wise and careful use requires a high level of medical supervision. Very few users have such guidance, and the temptation to overuse is very great.

Nor are many likely to get the medical help required because the use of anabolic steroids without a doctor's prescription is illegal. In addition, all anabolic steroid use is against the rules of most professional and amateur sports. It's considered cheating.

Psychological Effects Anabolic steroids affect the brain as well as the body. The drugs tend to give users feelings of extreme self-confidence while making them more aggressive.

These psychological effects can be drastic. Many users have undergone major personality changes. Steroid use has been linked with cases of violent behavior, and one psychiatric study showed that 14 out of 41 anabolic steroid users displayed signs of mental illness.

1. **Understanding the Issue:** In some countries, sports organizations and schools require athletes to take random tests for steroid use. Do you think random testing of athletes for steroid use should be carried out? Do you believe it's an invasion of privacy? Explain your position.

2. **Explore Further:** Some athletes feel that anything they can do to improve their performance should be legal and that steroid use is as fair as having a proper diet. Others think that strength from steroids is an artificial boost and should be illegal. Do you think a steroid advantage is fair or unfair? Why?

Readings
- "Pumped Up." *U.S. News and World Report,* June 1, 1992, pp. 54-63.
- "Roid Rage." *American Health,* May, 1991, pp. 60-65.

CHAPTER 24 CHEMICAL CONTROL 🏃 **695**

Issues

Purpose
Students learn of the dangers involved in abusing a hormone.

Teaching Strategies
- Ask students to discuss whether taking steroids to improve their own athletic performance would be worth the risk of serious side effects, perhaps even a shortened life span. Ask students to discuss athletes they may have known or read about who have taken steroids.

Possible Answers
1. Since most sports organizations consider taking steroids a form of cheating, students may believe that drug testing of athletes is fair. Others may think that testing is an invasion of privacy but that taking steroids is still wrong.
2. Opinions will vary. An argument could be made that some individuals naturally produce less hormone than others, and so should be allowed to take hormone supplements. Students may want to consider how a person who must take steroids for medical reasons might be viewed by athletic organizations.

Going Further
Have students interview sports medicine specialists to find out more about the potential benefits and adverse effects of taking anabolic steroids. **L1**

CHAPTER 24

CHAPTER REVIEW

Summary

The summary can be used by students to review the major concepts of the chapter.

Language of Biology

Answers should go beyond defining the terms. Accept any answer that uses the term correctly and in the proper context.

Understanding Concepts

1. The stem covered with the black tube showed that the substance that influenced curvature was produced only by the stem tip.
2. The stem exhibits negative geotropism. As auxin accumulates on the lower side of the stem, it causes elongation of cells on that side, and the stem grows upward. Accumulation of auxin on the lower side of the roots seems to inhibit elongation. Thus, the root grows downward.
3. A high concentration of auxin stimulates growth of stems but inhibits lateral bud development. Also, it stimulates elongation of stem cells but inhibits elongation of root cells.
4. Such chemicals, in high concentrations, speed growth in an uncoordinated way, leading to death of the weeds. Therefore, plants must be growing to be killed. When plants are dormant, they cannot be killed by these herbicides.
5. vasopressin
6. Insulin's effect is to cause the movement of glucose transporters to the outer plasma membranes of target cells. Low levels of insulin result in cells having fewer membrane transporters, so less glucose can be absorbed.
7. The high concentration of progesterone inhibits secretion of FSH and LH.
8. Adrenaline combines with receptors in the membranes of target tissues, activating an enzyme that sets off a series of enzyme reac-

REVIEW
CHAPTER
24

Summary

Plants respond to stimuli by means of hormones that interact to control growth and development. Hormones control such activities as tropisms, seed germination, cell division, fruit formation, and abscission of fruit and leaves. A plant's overall pattern of growth and development depends upon a balance among those hormones that promote these activities and those that inhibit them.

Hormones are one means of controlling responses in animals. Some animal hormones control growth and development. Others play a role in maintaining homeostasis—for example, the hormones that regulate blood sugar level. As in plants, hormones may work together to cause a response or in opposition to one another. Levels of many hormones in the blood are regulated by negative feedback mechanisms such as those that occur during the menstrual cycle.

As in plants, hormones in animals cause a response in one of two ways, each of which results in a chemical change within target tissues. A hormone may cause such a change by directly activating an enzyme within a target cell or by indirectly activating a gene.

Language of Biology

Write a sentence that shows your understanding of each of the following terms.

abscission	hypothalamus
apical dominance	negative feedback
auxin	pituitary gland
corpus luteum	second messenger
corpus luteum stage	hypothesis
endocrine gland	stimulus
follicle stage	tropism
gibberellin	

Understanding Concepts

1. In the Darwins' experiment, what was the purpose of the stem with the black tube?
2. A plant is placed on its side in the dark. Explain the growth of the plant's stem and roots in terms of stimuli and the action of hormones.
3. In terms of plant growth and development, discuss an example that shows that it is the target tissue, not the hormone, that determines a response.
4. Some weed killers are chemicals with powerful auxin-like activity. Suggest a way that these chemicals kill a plant. Why do you think that auxin-like weed killers would not kill plants during cold or very dry weather?
5. Drugs called diuretics cause the body to eliminate more water. Which hormone in Table 24.1 would be most affected by diuretics?

6. Explain the high blood sugar level of a person with type I diabetes in terms of insulin's effect on body cells.
7. Explain why a female does not usually ovulate during the corpus luteum stage.
8. You have probably heard of the idea that adrenaline can result in a burst of energy. Explain why this is true in terms of how adrenaline causes a response in liver and skeletal muscle cells.
9. Glucagon, a protein-type hormone, causes the same response in liver cells as adrenaline. How can it be explained that two different hormones can cause the same response in the same target cell? Can you suggest a reason why adrenaline, but not glucagon, can cause that response in skeletal muscle cells?

696 🐾 CHAPTER 24 CHEMICAL CONTROL

tions. The final reaction converts glycogen to glucose, the energy source.

9. Whether a protein-type hormone has an effect on cells depends on whether or not those cells have receptors for the hormone. Both glucagon and adrenaline receptors are present in the membrane of the liver cell, and both lead to the same series of reactions. Skeletal muscle cells have no glucagon receptors.
10. Combination of insulin with receptors in liver cell membranes leads to production of a different second messenger that causes a

different series of reactions.

Applying Concepts

11. Apical buds could be removed from several plants. Auxin could be applied to the cut ends of some plants. Other plants would have no auxin applied. The plants to which auxin was applied should exhibit apical dominance as if the bud were present; the others should not.
12. Though chemically similar, the two hormones are recognized by different receptors

REVIEW

10. Insulin causes a response in liver cells opposite to that caused by adrenaline and glucagon. It exerts its effect by a second messenger. How can these opposite responses be explained if all three hormones involve a second messenger?

Applying Concepts

11. How would you design an experiment to show that it is auxin secreted from an apical bud that controls apical dominance?
12. Oxytocin and vasopressin are protein-type hormones composed of eight amino acids, only two of which differ. How can the different responses to these two hormones be explained?
13. Explain why unfertilized flowers fall from a plant much more quickly than fertilized flowers.
14. Explain why auxins are used to cause seedless varieties of some plants to develop fruit.
15. Suggest an explanation for the fact that a given protein-type hormone can cause two different responses in the same target cell.
16. Using Table 24.1 as a guide, identify the hormone(s) that would be associated with each of the following: (a) increased heartbeat rate and blood pressure; (b) loss of weight; (c) infertility in males; (d) infertility in females; (e) failure to maintain a balance of osmotic pressure between cells and surrounding fluid or blood.
17. In the menstrual cycle, when the corpus luteum breaks down, the uterine lining begins to break down also. Why does the corpus luteum break down if fertilization does not occur?
18. People with insulin-treated diabetes run some risk of a condition called insulin shock, which usually results from taking too much insulin. Why would this condition affect the body adversely? Why do some diabetics carry candy to eat in case insulin shock sets in?
19. **Health Connection:** Why do you think it's difficult to synthesize human growth hormone and similar substances in the laboratory?
20. **Biotechnology:** There are medicine capsules available that will pass through the stomach without being digested. Why not just fill these capsules with insulin?

Lab Interpretation

21. **Investigation:** You have tested the effect of various concentrations of gibberellin applied as a solution to the roots of bean plants. The data you obtained are shown in the following graph. Write a conclusion to the experiment.

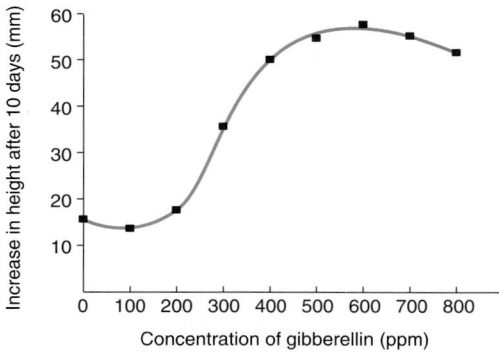

22. **Minilab 1:** After the activity is finished, what steps would be needed to return the plant stems back to their original vertical position? Explain why your idea would work.
23. **Minilab 2:** Which tissue found in the pancreas should have ducts leading from it? Which should not have ducts leading from them? Explain your answers.
24. **Thinking Lab:** Using what you learned in the text, identify hormones A, B, and C.

Connecting Ideas

25. Explain the following events in plant development in terms of chemical control: (a) dormancy of the seed after the embryo begins its development; (b) breaking of dormancy and onset of germination; (c) lengthening of cells in the zone of elongation of the root; (d) growth of the root downwards even if the seed begins germinating with the radicle growing horizontally; (e) the different lengths of branches.
26. Why must insulin be taken by injection rather than orally?

CHAPTER 24

on different target tissues. Thus, different responses result.
13. Unfertilized flowers produce no seeds. Seeds produce auxin, which inhibits the formation of an abscission layer.
14. Auxins stimulate fruit formation. Normally, auxin is secreted by developing seeds. In the absence of seeds, applying auxin will cause fruit to develop.
15. It is possible that the same second messenger can cause one set of reactions while inhibiting another.
16. (a) adrenaline, and/or thyroxine (b) thyroxine; (c) FSH and/or LH; (d) FSH and/or LH; (e) vasopressin
17. because there is no embryo to produce the hormone that maintains the corpus luteum
18. Too much insulin drastically reduces blood sugar level and brain cells cannot get enough glucose. Candy is rich in glucose, which enters the bloodstream rapidly.
19. Such protein-type hormones are very complex, consisting of many amino acids, which must be linked in the correct sequence.
20. When the capsules finally dissolve in the small intestine, the insulin would be broken down by the proteolytic enzymes present there.

Lab Interpretation

21. An increase in height was evident at a concentration of 300 ppm of gibberellin. Concentrations beyond 500 ppm produced little additional effect. Gibberellin applied to the roots of bean plants increased growth when present in sufficient concentration, but increasing its concentration beyond an optimum point did not enhance its effect.
22. To restore the original direction, just turn dishes to their original positions. Geotropism caused by auxin will cause the plant to turn back to its original direction of growth.
23. The islet cells will have no ducts because they make up endocrine tissue. The remaining tissue should have ducts because it secretes digestive enzymes.

---

24. Hormone A is luteinizing hormone; hormone B is progesterone; hormone C is follicle-stimulating hormone.

Connecting Ideas

25. **Systems and Interactions:** (a) Dormancy is induced by inhibitors. (b) Breaking of dormancy requires gibberellins. (c) Cell elongation is stimulated by an auxin. (d) Negative geotropism is influenced by an auxin. (e) Length is controlled by an auxin.
26. **Systems and Interactions:** Insulin is a protein easily digested in the stomach.

PROGRAM RESOURCES

Teacher Classroom Resources
Chapter Assessment, pp. 93-96 L1
Performance Assessment in Biology, p. 48 L2
Alternate Assessment in the Science Classroom
Computer Test Bank L1

SECTION	OBJECTIVES	TEXT LABS/FEATURES
25.1 Conduction of Impulses (3 days)	**Diagram** the transmission of an impulse along a neuron. **Explain** why an impulse is an all-or-none response. **Sequence** the events in the transmission of an impulse from one neuron to another, and describe how each neuron may respond.	**History Connection:** Dr. Humberto Fernandez-Moran, p. 702 **Minilab 1:** How sensitive is skin to the sense of touch? p. 706
25.2 Nervous Systems (3 days)	**Compare** the nervous systems of invertebrates and vertebrates. **Explain** the functions of the parts of the central nervous system of humans. **Describe** examples of reflexes and how those responses are carried out by the nervous system in humans. **Explain** the functioning of the human ear and eye.	**Thinking Lab:** Can brain cells regenerate? p. 714 **Investigation:** The Effect of Stimulants on *Daphnia*, p. 716 **Minilab 2:** How do distractions affect your reaction time? p. 719
BIOLOGY, TECHNOLOGY, AND SOCIETY		**Biotechnology:** Fighting Noise Pollution, p. 724 **Career Connection:** Audiologist, p. 724 **Issues:** Alzheimer's: The Disease that Takes Everything, p. 725

LAB MATERIALS

INVESTIGATION	MINILAB	ALTERNATE LAB
page 716 caffeine solution *Daphnia* dropper microscope petri dish	**page 706** masking tape toothpicks **page 719** meterstick	**page 704** construction paper, black *Daphnia* droppers duct tape flashlight hand lens marking pencil, wax *Planaria* ruler test-tube rack thermometer tubes with caps, plastic vinegar eels (*Turbatrix aceti*)

| --- | --- |
Study Guide, pp. 145-146 **Exploring Environmental Issues,** *Toxic Waste—Where Does It Go?* p. 11	
Study Guide, pp. 147-150 **Concept Mapping,** p. 25 **Critical Thinking/Problem Solving:** *Analyzing Sensory-Somatic Responses,* p. 25 ***PLL:** *Response of Protists to Chemical and Physical Stimuli,* p. 169 ***PLL:** *Response of Multicellular Animals to Light,* p. 173 ***PLL:** *Taste Perception in Humans,* p. 177 ****ILS:** *The Eye,* p. 267 ****ILS:** *Reflex Arc,* p. 271 ****ILS:** *Reliability of Your Visual Sense,* p. 275	***STVS:** *PET Scanner,* Human Biology (Disc 7, Side 1) ***STVS:** *Vision Diagnosis,* Human Biology (Disc 7, Side 1) **Color Transparency 27:** *Mollusk Body Systems* **Color Transparency 28:** *Earthworm Body Systems* **Color Transparency 44:** *The Central Nervous System* **Color Transparency 45:** *Structure and Function of Sensory Organs*
Assessment Materials **Chapter Assessment,** pp. 97-100 **Performance Assessment in Biology,** p. 50 **Alternate Assessment in the Science Classroom** **Computer Test Bank**	**Spanish Resources** **Cooperative Learning Resource Guide** **Videodisc Correlations** (to Optical Data's and Videodiscovery's videodiscs)

* **Probing Levels of Life**
** **Investigating Living Systems**

* **Science Technology Videodisc Series**

Key to Teaching Strategies

The following designations will help you decide which activities in the teacher margin are appropriate for your students.

L1 Level 1 activities should be within the ability range of all students.

L2 Level 2 activities should be within the ability range of the average to above-average student.

L3 Level 3 activities are designed for the ability range of above-average students.

LEP LEP activities are appropriate for Limited English Proficiency students.

COOP LEARN Cooperative Learning activities are designed for small group work.

ADDITIONAL RESOURCES

Infinite Voyage *Prisoners of the Brain*
Students will see how drugs can affect the chemistry of the brain for good or ill, and will learn ways to maintain good mental health.

Audiovisual
Inside Information, video, Films for the Humanities and Sciences.
The Nature of the Nerve Impulse, video, Films for the Humanities and Sciences.

Software
Human Eye, Apple 64K, Queue.
Nervous System, Apple II/TRS-80/Model III, J and S.

25

NERVOUS CONTROL

Chapter Overview

After studying the general requirements necessary for a nervous response and the types and structure of neurons, students learn how the resting potential of a neuron is converted to an action potential in the transmission of a nerve impulse. They then come to understand that an impulse is an all-or-none response. Next, transmission across synapses is studied, and students find out that neurotransmitters may either excite or inhibit postsynaptic cells and that many drugs exert their effects at synapses.

Next, students explore nervous responses in unicellular organisms and trace the evolution of nervous systems among invertebrates and vertebrates. They then distinguish between the central and peripheral nervous systems of humans, and between the two divisions of the latter—sensory-somatic and autonomic. Finally, they study the structure and function of two sense organs, the ear and the eye.

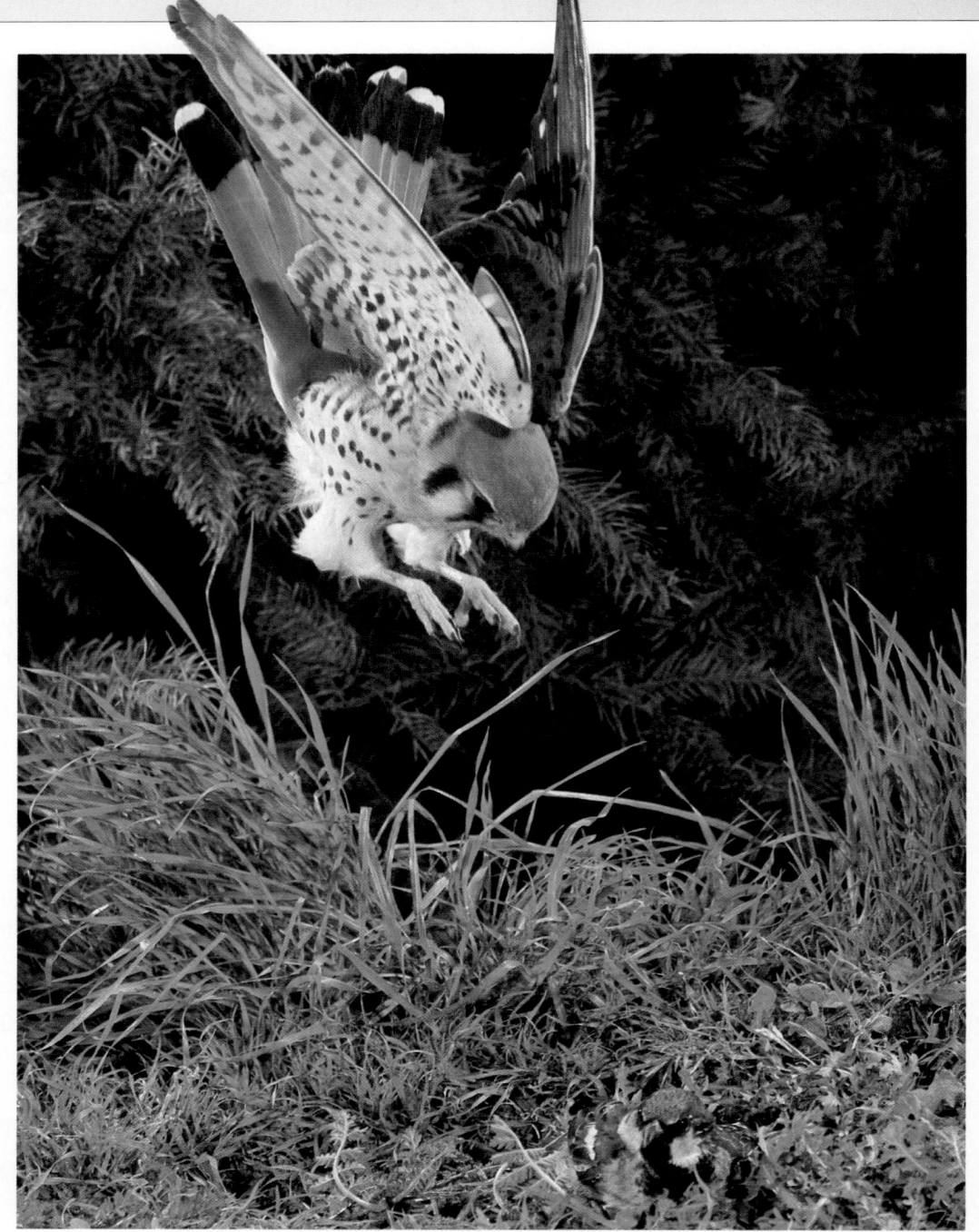

698

KEY TERMS

action potential	lens	retina
autonomic system	medulla oblongata	rod cells
axon	motor neuron	sensory neuron
central nervous system	nerve	sensory-somatic system
cerebellum	neuron	synapse
cerebrum	neurotransmitter	
cone cells	peripheral nervous system	
cornea	reflex	
dendrite	reflex arc	
interneuron	resting potential	

CHAPTER
25

NERVOUS
CONTROL

A HAWK SOARS majestically through the air, its sharp eyes surveying a meadow hundreds of feet below. On the ground, small animals carry on with their activities, oblivious to the hawk above. The instant the hawk catches sight of its prey it swoops down in a steep dive and snatches the unsuspecting animal in its talons. Hawks and other birds of prey have such a keen sense of sight that they can hunt from a distance and take their quarry by surprise.

When a hawk is hunting, light rays entering its eyes are transformed into electrical impulses that travel to its brain. The brain processes the information and transmits impulses to the bird's muscles that send it into a dive. How do light rays become electrical impulses? How do these impulses cause muscle action? How does this happen quickly enough for a hawk to catch its prey? In this chapter, you will learn how animals and other organisms sense their environment, and how those sensations are transformed into responses. You will discover that nerves enable organisms to respond to stimuli very quickly. And you will learn how the most highly developed nervous system in the animal kingdom—the human nervous system—operates.

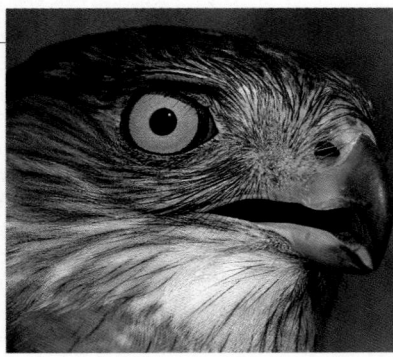

A hawk's eyes are able to focus on two objects at the same time. What advantage is this to the hawk?

Chapter Preview

Introducing the Chapter

Have students consider the photographs on pages 698 and 699. A discussion of the events from the hawk's sighting of its prey to the time it snares it should provide the general idea of the elements needed for a nervous response to occur. Students should be able, in general terms, to come up with the idea that nerves pick up the sensory information and somehow transmit it to the brain, where it is sorted out. They can then reason out that other nerves must carry messages to the muscles, whose movement is necessary for the hawk's response to the prey. Ask students to name other kinds of organisms that respond to stimuli in similar ways. It will become apparent that it is mainly animals that are capable of doing so.

Theme Development

Systems and interactions is a theme that can be applied at many levels in this chapter. For example, the various kinds of neurons—sensory, interneurons, and motor—interact in detecting stimuli and affecting responses. Responses, in turn, involve interaction of the nervous and muscular systems. The theme of evolution is exemplified in the discussion of the changes in complexity of nervous systems among various animal groups.

Tying to Previous Knowledge

Having just completed a study of hormones, students will expand their understanding of the close relationship between endocrine and nervous systems as they study this chapter. Their knowledge of such topics as ATP and active transport, membrane proteins, diffusion, and ions will be put to use as they study transmission of impulses along neurons and across synapses.

ASSESSMENT PLANNER

Choose assessment strategies from the following pages to evaluate the progress of your students.

Prepare

Key Concepts

Students will study the nervous response related to the structure and function of neurons. Transmission, inhibition, and suppression of impulses also will be presented.

Key Terms

neuron, sensory neuron, motor neuron, interneuron, nerve, axon, dendrite, resting potential, action potential, synapse, neurotransmitter

Materials

- For the Minilab, gather masking tape, 12 toothpicks per team, and metric rulers.

1 Focus

Objectives

The objectives are listed on the student page. Remind students to preview these objectives as a guide to this numbered section.

Activity

Ask your students to hold a small bean in the palm of one hand. Then have them cross the middle finger over the index finger of the other hand and roll the bean with their crossed fingers. Ask them what they feel with their crossed fingers. Do not tell them that they will feel as if they are holding and touching two beans. Ask them to speculate about how this could happen. **L1**

Objectives

Diagram the transmission of an impulse along a neuron.

Explain why an impulse is an all-or-none response.

Sequence the events in the transmission of an impulse from one neuron to another, and describe the different ways the neuron may respond.

Figure 25-1 This electron micrograph shows one of the body's billions of neurons.

25.1 Conduction of Impulses

You learned in the last chapter that many of an organism's responses to stimuli are controlled chemically by hormones. Hormonal control is usually involved in responses that occur slowly, such as positive phototropism in plants, metamorphosis in insects, or growth in humans. But what about responses that must take place within a fraction of a second, like jerking your hand away from a hot stove or dodging out of the path of a speeding car? Rapid responses such as these are controlled by the nervous system. The nervous system is responsible for receiving information from internal and external stimuli and responding to that information. While bacteria, protists, and some plants are capable of nervous response, animals are the only organisms that possess true nervous systems.

Nervous Response

What kinds of cells, tissues, and organs are involved in your response to a hot stove or a speeding car? Four requirements must be met for a nervous response to occur. First, there must be a means of detecting a stimulus. In most animals, stimuli are detected by sensory receptors, which may be either individual nerve cells, such as touch-sensitive cells in your skin, or nerve cells that form part of a sense organ, such as the eye or ear. These cells transform sensory input into electrical impulses.

Second, there must be a way for the impulses to be transmitted to other parts of the body. Impulses are transmitted along a network of **neurons**—cells that are specialized for conducting nerve impulses. Third, the impulses must be interpreted and analyzed. This process takes place in a coordination center, such as the brain or spinal cord of vertebrates.

Fourth, an appropriate response must be carried out by an effector. An effector is usually a muscle or gland. For example, the muscles of your arm are the effectors that pull your hand away from the stove. Your adrenal glands are effectors that participate in your response to a speeding car by secreting adrenalin, which increases your metabolic rate and helps you respond more quickly to the emergency.

Nerve Tissue

Nerve tissue is composed of specialized cells that transmit nerve impulses through the body. Vertebrates and the more complex invertebrates, such as mollusks, annelids, and arthropods, have nerve tissue that is made up of different types of neurons. Each type differs in its structure and in the direction in which it carries impulses.

Sensory Neurons   In most animals, **sensory neurons** transmit incoming impulses from receptors in sense organs to a coordination center, where the impulses are interpreted. For example, a sensory neuron picks up impulses from touch-sensitive receptors in your fingertips and transmits those impulses to your brain or spinal cord for interpretation and processing.

700 🔹 NERVOUS CONTROL

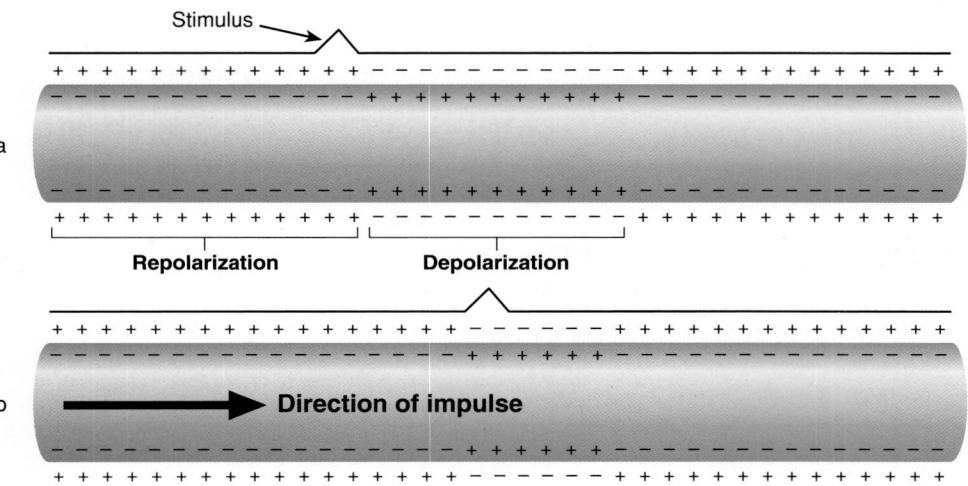

a

Repolarization   Depolarization

b   **Direction of impulse**

consists of electrons flowing smoothly along a wire. A current in a nerve impulse is caused by the flow of ions across the cell membrane. Thus, a nerve impulse is an electrochemical reaction that behaves somewhat like a fuse. Ignited at one end, a fuse will burn continually and very rapidly. Like a nerve impulse, this action can move in only one direction. Unlike the fuse, the nerve impulse can restore itself.

Restoring Resting Potential   After an action potential has swept along a neuron, some of the sodium ions that were originally outside the cell membrane are now inside it. Similarly, some potassium ions have moved from inside the cell into the fluids surrounding it. However, because the number of sodium ions that were originally outside the cell is very large, there are still more sodium ions outside the cell than inside it. Similarly, there are still more potassium ions inside the cell than outside it.

But as action potentials continue moving along the neuron, a point is reached when the balance of sodium and potassium ions inside and outside the cell becomes equalized. It is at this point that the sodium-potassium pump operates to once again create a resting potential across the cell membrane. Sodium ions once again move into the cell and potassium ions move out in a ratio of approximately three to two. Each pump can move several hundred ions per second, and a single neuron has about 1 million pumps. So, even though the neuron cannot carry a nerve impulse while the sodium-potassium pumps are restoring the resting potential, there is little effect on the nervous system. Resting potential can be restored in about 1.0 to 1.5 milliseconds.

Figure 25-8   Repolarization occurs as K⁺ flows out of the cell, restoring resting potential (a). Transmission of an impulse occurs as the action potential (polarity change) moves along an axon (b).

Figure 25-9   The burning of this fuse resembles the way an impulse travels down an axon. Unlike the fuse, however, the nerve impulse can be restored.

Concept Development

- In an unmyelinated fiber, each part of the nerve fiber becomes depolarized in a sequence along the fiber. The message moves faster on a myelinated fiber as the wave of depolarization jumps electrically from node to node without depolarizing the insulated axon membrane between the nodes. This is called saltatory conduction.

- The velocity of conduction along a nerve fiber is determined by whether or not the fiber is myelinated and the diameter of the fiber: The larger the fiber, the higher the velocity of conduction. An unmyelinated nerve with a diameter of 10 microns would conduct messages at about 0.5 meters per second. If this fiber is myelinated, conduction velocity would increase to about 50 meters per second.

- When the membrane returns to resting potential, two factors are at work. Na⁺ channels close spontaneously while the membrane is still depolarized. The same depolarization opens K⁺ channels, thereby increasing the permeability of K⁺. This results in rapid repolarization of the membrane. Once they have been inactivated, the Na⁺ channels need time to recover. During this time, a new action potential cannot be generated. This time period is called the absolute refractory period.

---

black paper and flashlight after five minutes, and count the planarians in the lighted third of the tube and the number in the dark third.
5. Repeat these steps with *Daphnia* and vinegar eels.

Analysis

1. Which species exhibited positive responses to light? Gravity?
2. Which species exhibited negative responses to light? Gravity? *Negative*

to light: Planaria, Daphnia; *Negative to gravity:* Daphnia, *vinegar eels*
3. Which species exhibited the most diverse response to gravity? Light? *Gravity:* Planaria, *Light: vinegar eels*
4. Is diversity of response among individuals of a species a sign of a greater or less complex nervous system? Explain. *Diversity of response is a sign of greater complexity of the nervous system. These organisms respond to more stim-*

uli and so are less predictably stimulated by any one stimulus.

✔ Assessment

Portfolio: Ask students to write in their portfolios a design for an experiment that would show whether invertebrates can learn. Tell students that they should plan to gather quantitative data and use information that they have gained in this lab to plan their study. L1

Minilab 1

Purpose
Students will test various body locations to determine which are most sensitive to touch.

Skills
recognize cause and effect, interpret data

Teaching Strategies
- Tell students to test parts of the skin that do not have calluses. Instead of toothpicks, students might use paper clips that have been bent into U shapes and are held the specified distance apart with clear tape.

Expected Results
In general, the tips of the fingers are the most sensitive and the back of the neck or forearm is least sensitive.

Answers
1. Fingertips will be most sensitive in general, but results may vary. The back of the neck or forearm will probably be least sensitive. Sensitive areas have receptors that are closer together and can detect stimulation by two points that are closer together than areas that are less sensitive.
2. Fingertips must have more receptors for touch because they investigate and explore objects and are important for any work done with the hands.

✔ Assessment
Performance: Test area of the foot and leg below the knee to determine which areas are most sensitive. Speculate why. *Generally, the soles of the feet are most sensitive, perhaps because it was important for early hominids to know if the surface being walked on would injure the feet.*

Minilab 1

How sensitive is skin to the sense of touch?

Tape two toothpicks to six separate pieces of masking tape the following distances apart: 2, 4, 6, 8, 10, 12 mm. Allow a small amount of the toothpick to extend beyond the edge of the tapes. Working with a partner, test the fingertip, palm, back of hand, inside forearm, and back of neck.

Be sure to apply the same pressure each time. **CAUTION:** *Be sure not to press too hard with the toothpicks.* The subject should let the tester know when two points are felt and when one point is felt. Conduct four trials in each location. Make a graph of the average for each location.
Analysis *Which location was most sensitive to touch? How could you tell? Which location was least sensitive to touch? How could you tell? How might the distribution of receptors for touch be a reflection of the functions of those body parts?*

All-or-none Response

Not all stimuli cause action potentials (impulses). A weak stimulus might generate some changes in the dendrites and cell body neuron, but unless the depolarization is of sufficient strength when it reaches the axon, there will be no nerve impulse. A stimulus must have a certain intensity to change polarity in the beginning of the axon and start an impulse. This level of intensity is called the threshold.

A stimulus stronger than threshold level will produce the same depolarization of the axon and thus the same impulse as a stimulus just at the threshold level. No matter how strong the stimulus is, as long as it is at or above the threshold level, the nerve impulse it causes will travel at the same speed and in the same way. Thus, a nerve impulse is an all-or-none response, meaning the impulse is either sent or not sent. If impulses are the same whether the stimulus is at or above threshold, how do you detect different strengths of stimuli? This detection depends on the number of impulses carried along a neuron in a given period of time and the number of neurons carrying the impulse. For example, you can tell whether the metal handle of a frying pan is warm or burning hot because the stimulus of a hot handle will excite more neurons, and cause those neurons to send impulses more frequently, than the stimulus of a warm handle.

All nerve impulses are essentially the same. If this is so, how do you interpret *what* the stimulus is? How do you know whether you are sensing light or sound or touch? The answer is that your interpretation and response to a stimulus depend on the pathway of the nerve impulse. For example, when a touch-sensitive receptor in your skin is stimulated, the nerve impulse travels to a specific area of your brain or spinal cord that interprets nerve impulses coming from touch receptors. Impulses transmitted by receptors in your eyes or ears travel to areas of your brain that determine your response to light or sound. Impulses traveling along a particular nerve pathway will always go to the same area of the brain or spinal cord.

Figure 25-10 A "strong enough" push is needed to begin these dominos falling. The same is true for a nerve impulse. A stimulus must be of a certain intensity to begin an impulse. This level of intensity is called the **threshold.**

706 NERVOUS CONTROL

Transmitting Impulses from Neuron to Neuron

So far, you have learned how an action potential, or nerve impulse, moves along the axon of a single neuron. Virtually all nerve impulses must travel through many neurons before reaching their target. But there is a very small, fluid-filled space, or **synapse,** between each neuron along a nerve pathway. How does a neuron transmit across a synapse?

Remember, an action potential can travel through a neuron in one direction only—through the dendrites, into the cell body, and then along the axon. It follows that the impulse travels across a synapse in one direction only—from the axon of one neuron, across the synapse, to the dendrites of the next neuron. Since the end of the axon is so highly branched, a single neuron can send impulses across the synapse to the dendrites of many neurons.

Neurotransmitters   Located in the cell membrane of the end brush of the axon are membrane proteins that act as calcium ion gates. When the neuron is at rest, the concentration of calcium ions outside the membrane is much greater than inside it. As an action potential sweeps toward the end brushes of the axon, the calcium gates open, permitting an inward rush of calcium ions. Once inside the end brushes of the axon, the calcium ions stimulate vesicles in the cytoplasm to move toward the membrane. These vesicles contain **neurotransmitters,** which are chemicals that transmit the nerve impulse across the synapse. The vesicles fuse with the

Figure 25-11   At a synapse, neurotransmitters pour into specific sites on nearby dendrites. Compare the diagram and the electron micrograph. Find the synaptic vesicles in the micrograph.

25.1 CONDUCTION OF IMPULSES 🐾 **707**

Figure Caption Question
Find the synaptic vessicles in the micrograph. Students should be able to find synaptic vessicles at the edge of the cell in the electron micrograph.

Different Viewpoints in Biology

Causes and Treatment of Phantom Pain
People who have lost a limb often feel as though the arm or leg is still there. They may also feel excruciating pain in parts of the missing limb. Researchers disagree on the cause of this phantom pain as well as on the best method of treatment. Electrical currents, acupuncture, hypnosis, and drugs used to treat epilepsy, depression, or drug addiction are treatments that meet with limited success. Neurosurgeons have recently developed a procedure in which the spinal cells receiving the messages from the nerves of the stump are eliminated surgically. Long-term results cannot be predicted for this procedure. Other scientists think that the limbic system is involved even though limbic structures are not actively affected by injurious stimuli. The phenomenon of phantom pain challenges the idea that sensations are produced only by stimuli and that perceptions without stimuli are abnormal. Phantom pain indicates that the brain does not just detect and analyze information coming in on sensory nerves. It may also generate an experience of the body. People born without limbs also experience phantoms. Even without ever having sensory input from a limb, neurons generate messages about the missing parts. These phenomena indicate that perhaps the neural networks for perceiving the parts of the body are built into the brain.

Concept Development

- About 60 years ago, the first neurotransmitter, acetylcholine (ACh), was discovered. It is released by neurons with connections to skeletal muscles and the heart muscle, causing them to contract. ACh is made in the axon terminals and is released into the synapse when an action potential arrives and releases calcium into the axon. In the synapse, it attaches to ACh receptors in skeletal muscles. In the muscle, this causes sodium ion channels to open and skeletal muscle contraction. Interference with ACh activity in skeletal muscles produces a disease called myasthenia gravis in which the patient is easily fatigued and has weak muscles. In the brain, ACh is thought to be important for normal intellectual activity. Patients with Alzheimer's disease have a low amount of ACh in their brains.
- Norepinephrine is secreted by the adrenal gland when a person is under stress. Ability to learn and memory are affected when this neurotransmitter is low.

Figure Caption Question

What other food products contain caffeine? Caffeine is contained in chocolate and cola as well as coffee.

3 Assess

Check for Understanding

Prepare a quiz of ten questions about the structure of neurons and transmission of nerve impulses. Give one quiz paper to each student. Have each individual write, independently, the answer to the first question, then pass the paper to the left. This student should answer the next question, then pass on the papers. The process continues until all students have answered all of the questions. Collect one paper at random from each group to grade. **COOP LEARN**

axon membrane, and the neurotransmitters are released into the synapse by exocytosis. The neurotransmitters diffuse across the fluid-filled synapse and combine with receptor molecules embedded in the membrane of the dendrites of neighboring neurons.

Excitation   There are many types of neurotransmitters and many types of receptor molecules. Some neurotransmitters, when combined with certain receptor molecules on the dendrites, will cause the dendrite membrane to become more permeable to sodium. When this happens, sodium ions rush into the neuron and an action potential is started. In this case, the neurotransmitter is said to excite the neuron.

Inhibition   Other combinations of neurotransmitters and receptor molecules may have the opposite effect. In this case, the combination may cause the dendrite membrane to become more permeable to negatively charged chloride ions, which enter the cell and reinforce its resting potential. The polarization of the cell increases (the interior becomes even less positive than the exterior), which prevents an action potential from starting. Some neurotransmitters produce the same inhibitory effect by inducing the dendrite membrane to release positively charged potassium ions.

Determining the Effect of a Neurotransmitter   Recall that a single axon may pass impulses to the dendrites of many neurons. In addition, the dendrites of a single neuron may receive neurotransmitters from many axons. Some neurotransmitters will excite the target neuron, while others will inhibit it. The net effect of these excitatory and inhibitory neurotransmitters determines whether or not the target neuron will carry an action potential.

The effect of a particular transmitter on a neuron depends on the receptors and membrane proteins in the dendrites of the target neuron. For example, the transmitter acetylcholine excites the neurons that activate skeletal muscle and muscles of the digestive tract, but inhibits neurons that activate heart muscle. Noradrenaline, another neurotransmitter, excites heart muscle, inhibits muscles of the digestive tract, and has no effect at all on skeletal muscle. It is the target, not the transmitter, that determines the response. Do you see that nerves ultimately cause a response by means of chemicals? Many of those chemicals, such as noradrenaline, are very similar to hormones. Not only that, but some transmitters within the brain, are, in fact, hormones such as vasopressin, oxytocin, and ACTH. As transmitters, they have evolved different functions. It is clear that endocrine and nervous control systems are closely related. Nerves can be thought of as structures specialized for delivering chemicals quickly to target organs of animals, thus ensuring the rapid responses animals need to survive.

The hormones of the endocrine system for the most part control slow, long-lasting processes such as growth and development. The nervous system is specialized for much faster movement of chemicals through the body. A nervous system of this type is needed to enable animals to make rapid responses necessary for survival, such as fleeing from danger or capturing prey.

Figure 25-12   **The dendrites of a single neuron may receive neurotransmitters from many axons.**

Suppression of Neurotransmitter Soon after a neurotransmitter is released from the axon, it is suppressed so that the target neuron does not continue to respond. For example, after acetylcholine has combined with the receptor proteins of a dendrite membrane, it is broken down by an enzyme into two smaller molecules. Neither of these smaller molecules can excite or inhibit the neuron. Noradrenaline is not chemically changed by the target neuron. Instead, it is recaptured by the axon that released it.

Effects of Drugs Many drugs, both legal and illegal, exert their effects at the synapse. Depressants such as hypnotics and anesthetics are drugs that reduce nerve transmission. This reduction in transmission can result in impaired coordination, shortened reaction time, and impaired judgment. Some depressants have molecular structures that are very similar to those of neurotransmitters that occur naturally in the body. These depressants combine with receptors in the cell membranes of dendrites, blocking the natural neurotransmitters and reducing the number of impulses transmitted along the neuron. Other depressants may prevent the production of neurotransmitters or prevent their release from the vesicles of the axon.

Stimulants such as caffeine increase the activity of the nervous system. This causes heartbeat rate to increase, an increase in blood pressure, and an increase in mental alertness. Some stimulants combine with receptors in the dendrite and excite the neuron by causing action potentials. This occurs in the same way as the transmitters that normally link with the receptors. Other stimulants prevent the recapture or destruction of neurotransmitters or cause the excessive release of neurotransmitters.

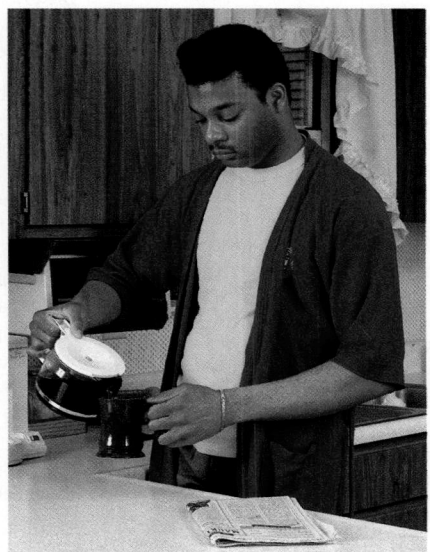

Figure 25-13 **Many people use the caffeine in coffee as a stimulant in the morning. What other food products contain caffeine?**

Section Review

Understanding Concepts

1. Suppose you accidentally stick your finger with a pin. Explain how a neuron in your finger responds by conducting an impulse.

2. In a lab, an axon is exposed to 1 volt of electricity, then 3 volts, and then 5 volts. The axon does not carry an impulse until stimulated by 5 volts. Why not? How will stimulating the axon with 10 volts affect the axon? Explain.

3. An interneuron in the brain synapses with hundreds of sensory neurons. What factor determines whether or not that interneuron will carry an action potential at any given time?

4. ***Skill Review—Recognizing Cause and Effect:*** Novocaine interferes with operation of the sodium-potassium pump. Explain why Novocaine causes numbness. For more help, see Thinking Critically in the **Skill Handbook.**

5. ***Thinking Critically:*** Suppose your nervous system were rewired so that the nerve from your eye led to the area of your brain to which the nerve from the ear is supposed to lead and vice versa. How would you respond to light and sound? Explain.

SECTION 25.1

Reteach

Ask students to write a letter to a friend beginning with: "What I understand about transmission of nerve impulses is...," followed by: "But what I still don't understand is.... Please help me understand this idea better." Ask students to exchange notes with someone who is not having the same trouble, and the partner should respond in writing with another note including an explanation. **COOP LEARN**

Extension

Ask students to report about drugs that affect transmission of the action potential and chemical transmission at the synapse. **L2**

✔ **Assessment**

Portfolio: Ask students to write an analogy of transmission of the action potential in their portfolios. They should begin by brainstorming as a group a list of ideas that could be used. They should think of some other process or sequential event in everyday life that can be compared to the sequence of nerve impulse transmission. Students should use appropriate neurological terms. **L1**

4 Close

Audiovisual

Show a film or filmstrip about neurons and conduction of impulses along a nerve fiber.

709

Prepare

Key Concepts

Students will compare and contrast the nervous systems and brains of a variety of invertebrates and vertebrates and then analyze the details of structure and function of the human central and peripheral nervous system with its associated senses.

Key Terms

central nervous system, peripheral nervous system, cerebrum, cerebellum, medulla oblongata, sensory-somatic system, reflex, reflex arc, autonomic system, cornea, lens, retina, rod cells, cone cells

Materials

- For the Minilab, provide meter-sticks.
- For the Investigation, gather petri dishes, droppers, *Daphnia,* and microscopes. Order or collect *Daphnia.*

1 Focus

Discussion

Divide the class into groups to discuss and come to consensus about whether death occurs when the heart stops beating or when the brain stops functioning. Ask each group to prepare justification that they share with the rest of the class. L1

COOP LEARN

Objectives

Compare the nervous systems of invertebrates and vertebrates.

Explain the functions of the parts of the central nervous system of humans.

Describe examples of reflexes and how those responses are carried out by the nervous system in humans.

Explain the functioning of the human ear and eye.

25.2 Nervous Systems

Although animals (except sponges) are the only living organisms that have nervous systems, all cells possess the basic elements of nervous control. Even unicellular organisms are capable of detecting stimuli. They can transmit signals from one part of the cell to another, analyze those signals, and respond accordingly. As animals evolved, certain cells became specialized for the functions involved in the rapid responses that are crucial to survival. Those specialized cells gradually evolved into the nervous systems of animals. As more complex animals evolved, their nervous systems also became more complex. Today, the nervous systems of complex organisms, such as humans and other vertebrates, exert a great deal of control over behavior and permit a large variety of responses to a given stimulus.

Unicellular Organisms

Many bacteria can sense the presence of chemicals in their environment. They move toward useful substances and away from harmful ones. The movement of an organism toward or away from a stimulus is called a taxis. It is thought that the bacteria detect stimuli by means of receptor proteins in their cell membranes and cell walls. Stimulation of these receptors leads to production of chemicals within the cell. After these chemicals are "analyzed" by the cell, an electrical signal travels through the cytoplasm to effectors, such as the flagella. The flagella respond to the signal by beating in a direction that propels the cell toward or away from the stimulus.

Some simple eukaryotes have cell parts that are specialized for responding to the environment. For example, *Euglena* has a light-sensitive structure under the eye-spot or "stigma." The pigment in the stigma

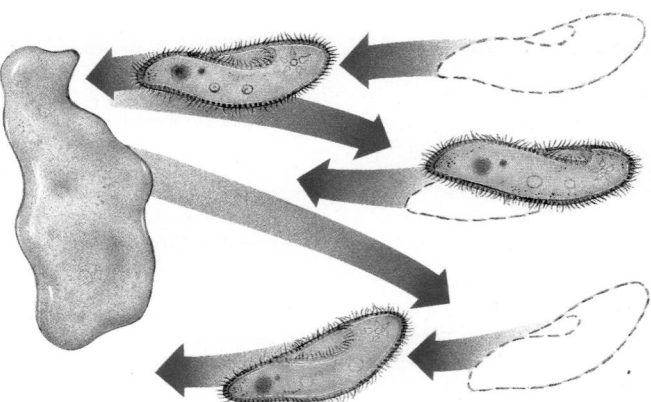

Figure 25-14 Paramecium responds to obstacles in its path by turning and moving forward again. The organism continues responding this way until it has cleared the obstacle.

MEETING INDIVIDUAL NEEDS

Visually Impaired: For students who are working below grade level and for those who are visually impaired, make large diagrams of the brain with bright colors distinguishing the different parts. It will help students to associate the names of the parts of the brain with different colors. Make another diagram of the brain that has different grades of sandpaper glued to the different lobes. It will help students working below grade level and those with visual impairments to use their kinesthetic sense to associate tactile features of the brain lobes with names.

allows this protozoan to detect the direction of the light source. This allows *Euglena,* a photosynthetic protist, to swim in the direction of light.

Paramecium can respond to obstacles in its path. If *Paramecium* comes into contact with an object, it will reverse the beating of its cilia and back away. Then it turns at an angle of about 30° and moves forward again. The organism continues to respond in this way until it passes the object (Figure 25-14). Responses in *Paramecium* seem mainly to be under electrical control.

Invertebrates

The cnidarians are the simplest phylum of animals that possess a nervous system. Recall that cnidarians are radially symmetrical. They have no front or back, and no left or right sides. Those that can move do not travel in a definite direction. There is no center of nervous control in these animals. Instead, many short neurons are scattered throughout the animal, forming what is called a nerve net. Figure 25-15 shows the nerve net of *Hydra.* All its neurons are short and similar in structure, and there are no definite nerve pathways. Because the neurons are short, an impulse must cross many synapses, and the impulse often dies out before being transmitted very far. As a result, most responses are localized, involving only one part of the body such as a single tentacle. Strong stimuli, though, may lead to a response of the entire organism. For example, *Hydra* may respond to a strong disturbance by contracting into a ball. Unlike the synapses described earlier, those of cnidarians send messages in both directions. A light touch to one tentacle of a *Hydra* causes the tentacles on either side to respond at the same time.

Flatworms   Flatworms, unlike cnidarians, have bilateral symmetry. Like most animals, they have anterior and posterior ends and a definite head-first direction of movement. Animals with these characteristics have evolved a nervous system that is especially suited for movement in one direction. Animals with bilateral symmetry have nervous systems with a control center, or centers, and specific nerve pathways.

A planarian is a flatworm whose nervous system shows the early evolution of such systems. At its anterior end are two bundles of neuron cell bodies called ganglia, which are like the brains of more complex animals. Extending from the ganglia are two ventral nerve cords that run the length of the body. The cords consist of the axons of the neurons. Connecting nerves join the two main cords. Smaller neurons branch from the cords and act much like a nerve net. The planarian's primitive brain does not exert much control.

Other Invertebrates   Segmented worms, such as the earthworm, have two ventral nerve cords, like planarians. However, in each segment of the worm there is a pair of ganglia along the nerve cord. These ganglia act as control centers. The brain, which is located on the dorsal side of the head, is really just a slightly larger ganglion. It exerts a bit more control than do the other ganglia. Arthropods are segmented, too, but they have fewer

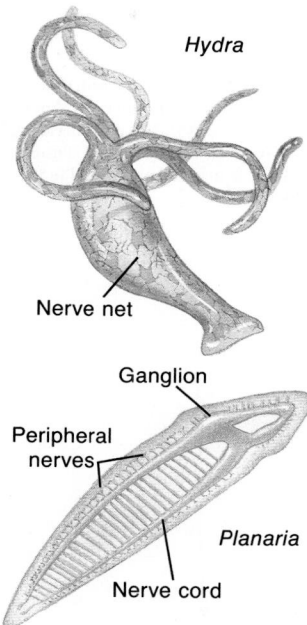

Figure 25-15 *Hydra* (a) has a nerve net nervous system. *Planaria* (b) has a ladder-type nervous system with the beginnings of central control in the ganglia of the head region.

2 Teach

Demonstration
Set up a demonstration in which students can observe how paramecia adjust their paths of movement when they bump into an object (algae or pieces of cotton) in their path. **LEP**

Activity
Tell students to design and carry out a controlled experiment in which they gather quantitative data to determine how *Hydra,* planarians, crickets, other available insects, and earthworms respond to light. Make sure they plan to use simple equipment that is available in your lab, and check the design of their experiments before they begin. **L1**   **COOP LEARN**

Activity

Make available to students a variety of preserved brain specimens of invertebrates and vertebrates. Ask them to compare and contrast the brains for numbers of lobes and complexity. Ask them to speculate how the differences in the brains reflect differences in the capabilities of the animals. `L1`

Demonstration

Using a model of a human skeleton, point out the locations of the central and peripheral nervous systems. If a preserved brain or plastic model is available, point out the forebrain, midbrain, and hindbrain. `LEP`

Guest Speaker

Invite a neurologist to speak to the class about the nervous system. Ask him or her to bring in a sample electroencephalogram (EEG) tracing to share with the class.

ganglia and a somewhat more prominent brain that exerts a greater degree of control than the earthworm's brain. Like other bilateral invertebrates, arthropods have a dorsal brain and ventral nerve cords.

Definite evolutionary trends can be seen when you examine the nervous systems of bilaterally symmetrical animals. As more complex animal phyla evolved, the brain began to exert more control, and the nerve cords gradually lost many of their control functions. Location of the major control center, the brain, at the animal's anterior end allowed organisms to adapt more easily to the environment. As an animal moves, its anterior end is the first part to encounter stimuli from the environment. As sense organs—such as eyes, antennae, and hearing structures—evolved, they became more concentrated at the anterior end. It makes sense that sensory organs, which gather information, and the brain, which analyzes the information, should be located near each other.

Vertebrates

Evolutionary trends observed among invertebrates continued as the vertebrate nervous system evolved. The nervous systems of bilaterally symmetrical animals are divided into two main parts. The **central nervous system,** or CNS, consists of a brain and one or more nerve cords, which serve as control centers. The **peripheral nervous system** consists of sensory and motor neurons connected to the CNS. Information about the animal's environment is gathered by receptors and brought to the CNS by sensory neurons. That information is analyzed by means of interneurons in the CNS, and impulses are then carried to appropriate effectors by motor neurons of the peripheral nervous system. Vertebrates have an anterior brain, which serves as the major center for coordinating nervous response, and much of the sensory equipment is located in the head. Although ganglia are located along the length of the single, dorsal spinal cord, they do not control complex responses. The spinal cord is an extension of the vertebrate brain; together, the brain and spinal cord make up the CNS.

The peripheral nervous system consists of nerves leading to and from the brain and spinal cord. In humans, the peripheral nervous system is composed of 12 pairs of cranial nerves attached to the brain, and 31 pairs of spinal nerves attached to the spinal cord.

Vertebrate brains are made up of three general areas—forebrain, midbrain, and hindbrain. The structure of each area and the functions it performs differ from one kind of vertebrate to another. We'll study the human nervous system as a model of the vertebrate nervous system as it exists in the most complex vertebrate.

Figure 25-16 The brain and spinal cord make up the central nervous system (CNS). The peripheral nervous system (PNS) is made of sensory and motor neurons connected to the CNS.

Brain
Spinal cord
Central Nervous System
Spinal nerves
Peripheral Nervous System

712 NERVOUS CONTROL

Skull
Meninges
Cerebrum
Thalamus
Hypothalamus
Pituitary gland
Midbrain
Pons
Medulla oblongata
Cerebellum
Spinal cord

Figure 25-17 The human brain is composed of three major regions—the forebrain, or cerebrum; the midbrain; and the hindbrain, made up of the medulla oblongata and the cerebellum.

Central Nervous System of Humans

The human brain is the most complex structure known to humans. It is a soft, wrinkled mass composed of billions of neurons. A human brain is protected by the skull and three layers of membranes called the meninges. These membranes protect and nourish both the spinal cord and brain. The space between the inner two meninges is filled with cerebrospinal fluid. Cerebrospinal fluid also fills the ventricles (cavities) of the brain. Capillaries in the walls of the ventricles exchange nutrients and waste materials between the blood and the cerebrospinal fluid. The fluid, in turn, exchanges these materials with the brain cells. This clear fluid cushions the brain against mild shock, though a severe shock, such as a blow to the head, can sometimes damage the brain. For example, a concussion, a brain injury resulting from a severe blow to the head, temporarily affects the brain's ability to function and can cause dizziness or unconsciousness.

The Forebrain The largest part of the forebrain is the **cerebrum,** which consists of two hemispheres. Each hemisphere is made up of four lobes, Figure 25-18. The surface of the cerebrum is called the cerebral cortex and is composed of neuron cell bodies that are collectively known as gray matter. These cells are gray in color because they are not covered with a myelin sheath. The interior of the cerebrum is made up of white, myelin-sheathed axons.

The cerebral cortex is highly folded. These folds provide more surface area, and therefore more space for neuron cell bodies, than a smooth surface would. The large number of neuron cell bodies in the human brain is

Figure 25-18 The cerebrum is divided into two hemispheres, each consisting of four lobes. These lobes are named after the bones of the skull that protect them.

Frontal lobe
Parietal lobe
Occipital lobe
Temporal lobe

25.2 NERVOUS SYSTEMS **713**

PROJECT

Concussions: Ask a group of students to do research and report to the rest of the class on concussions. They should find out how they occur, what happens to the brain, symptoms, and treatment. Preventive measures, such as wearing seat belts, should also be brought out.

SECTION 25.2

MUSIC CONNECTION

Music and the Brain: Maurice Ravel, a French composer of the first part of this century, developed a progressive brain disease that caused him to lose his ability to write music and perform many basic motor skills. He continued to enjoy listening to music until his death in 1937, but could not play music or compose. Neuroscientists have recently discovered the parts of the brain that become active during a musical performance, and now have more ideas about what parts of Ravel's brain may have been affected. In a study of classical pianists, scientists injected a radioactive labeled compound into subjects who were either reading music or performing it on a simple keyboard while sight-reading the music. A positron emission tomography (PET) scanner was used to measure the gamma rays from the decaying radioactive marker in the brain. Magnetic Resonance Imaging (MRI) was also administered to determine the areas of the brain with most blood flow.

Results show that sight-reading and piano performance activate the outer layer of the brain, the cerebral cortex, and the cerebellum at the base of the cortex. Sight-reading and playing the piano are only a small part of the whole range of musical experience, which would include the pleasure and emotions stimulated by music. This research is only the beginning glimpse into how the brain helps compose, play, and enjoy music.

Audiovisual

- Show the filmstrip *The Brain: Its Wonders and Its Mysteries,* National Geographic Educational Services.
- Eight videocassettes are available from the PBS series "The Brain." These videocassettes are available from WNET Education, 356 West 58th Street, New York, NY 10019.

Teacher FYI

The hypothalamus regulates food intake through two centers. The feeding center is stimulated by an empty stomach. The satiety center is stimulated by a full stomach and sends out impulses to inhibit the feeding center.

Figure 25-19 The medulla oblongata and the pons make up the brainstem. The brainstem connects the brain and the spinal cord.

important to our capacity for complex behavior and intelligence. Many human abilities are related to our very large cerebrum; for example, speech, reasoning, emotions, and personality are all functions controlled by this area of the brain. The cerebrum is also where sensory inputs are interpreted and motor impulses are started.

Located under the cerebrum are the thalamus and hypothalamus. The thalamus aids in sorting sensory information. The hypothalamus, which is a small structure just under the thalamus, controls hunger, body temperature, aggression, and other aspects of metabolism and behavior. It also plays an important role in endocrine control.

Midbrain The midbrain is an important and prominent structure in fish and amphibians. But in humans and other mammals, it mainly functions as a station for message exchange between the forebrain and hindbrain. The midbrain also is involved in some sight, hearing, and orientation responses.

Hindbrain: The Cerebellum The **cerebellum,** a motor area of the brain, lies at the back of the head, below the cerebrum. Like the cerebrum, the cerebellum is highly folded; its outer surface is made up of gray matter, and its interior is made up of white matter. The cerebellum coordinates

Thinking Lab

DRAW A CONCLUSION

Can brain cells regenerate?

Background
Human brains do not have the ability to replace nerve cells that have been damaged through disease or injury. A team of scientists recently decided to try to grow brain cells in a laboratory. They obtained brain tissue from an infant with a rare brain disease. One side of this infant's brain was growing at an extremely rapid rate. The researchers began growing these cells from the cerebral cortex of the child. Growing human cells in laboratory dishes is very difficult. They must be given precisely the same amounts and kinds of nutrients and growth hormones that they have in the body. Surprisingly, some of the brain cells in the lab dishes began to grow. The scientists had to decide if they were neuron or other types of neuron tissue called glial

cells—cells that provide support to the brain. Neurons have a pyramid-shaped cell body and long, thin tendrils that stretch out from the cell body. The support glial cells are flat and many-sided with no tendrils, and these cells have the ability to divide.

A   B

You Try It
Draw conclusions by examining the microscopic views of the brain cells in this study. Figure A shows brain cells before treatment with nutrients and hormones. Figure B shows brain cells after treatment. (1) If you were a scientist

working on this study, what hypothesis would you make after observing these cells? (2) Did the brain cells reproduce forming new nerve cells? How could you tell? (3) Remember that the cells were originally taken from the brain of a child with a brain disease. How would this fact affect your conclusion?

Thinking Lab

DRAW A CONCLUSION

Purpose
Students will analyze and interpret data about brain cell growth in a laboratory.

Skills
interpret data, observe and infer, interpret scientific illustrations

Teaching Strategies
- Ask students what kinds of body cells can reproduce. Bring out the idea that

up until this time, neural brain cells have not been known to reproduce.

Answers
1. Brain nerve cells were reproduced in lab dishes. Prior to treatment with nutrients and hormones, they did not look like brain cells, but after treatment they took on characteristics of brain nerve cells.
2. Yes. The cells had pyramid-shaped cell

bodies with long tendrils.
3. Perhaps all young children's brain cells would reproduce, or perhaps the diseased tissue had unique properties allowing it to reproduce.

✔ **Assessment**
Portfolio: Ask students to record a short statement proposing what direction the current research should take and why.

impulses sent out from the cerebrum. It constantly receives sensory impulses from certain receptors in muscles, tendons, and joints. If the sensory information and cerebral impulses do not agree, the cerebellum sends messages to the cerebrum and the cerebral impulses change. The cerebellum also controls posture and balance and maintains muscle tone. Extending down from the center portion of the brain is the **medulla oblongata,** which controls many responses of internal organs, such as breathing rate, heartbeat rate, peristalsis, and some gland secretions. The medulla oblongata and the pons make up the brainstem. The pons links the spinal cord, medulla, and the midbrain. It is composed of a bundle of fibers that transmit impulses from one side of the cerebellum to the other. The pons, together with the respiratory center in the medulla, helps to control respiration.

Spinal Cord　Extending down from the medulla oblongata is the long spinal cord, which has a fluid-filled central canal. The spinal cord is surrounded and protected by an extension of the three-layered meninges that cover the brain and by a series of bony vertebrae. The outer surface of the spinal cord is composed of white matter (myelin-sheathed axons), and its interior is made up of gray matter (unsheathed cell bodies), an arrangement opposite of that in the brain (Figure 25-20).

　In humans, the spinal cord connects the brain with the peripheral nervous system. The spinal nerves, which are part of the peripheral system, serve as the communication link between the spinal cord and the rest of the body. Spinal nerves contain both sensory and motor neurons, which enter and leave the spinal cord through nerve roots. Impulses reach the spinal cord from receptors via sensory neurons and then travel to interneurons in the spinal cord. The impulses may be transferred to the brain for interpretation or may be passed directly to motor neurons in the spinal cord. Impulses travel to effectors by motor neurons of the peripheral nervous system.

The Sensory-Somatic System of Humans

The sensory and motor neurons of the spinal and cranial nerves are part of the human's peripheral nervous system. Some sensory neurons carry impulses from receptors to the CNS and are linked to motor neurons that carry impulses to skeletal muscles. They are part of the peripheral nervous system known as the **sensory-somatic system.** Responses that are under conscious control—voluntary responses—are part of this system. The sensory-somatic system is also responsible for controlling certain responses not under conscious control—involuntary or automatic responses to stimuli. Such responses are called **reflexes.** Reflexes involve the CNS but require no conscious control or decision making because they are determined by fixed pathways of the nervous system. We are aware of reflexes controlled by the sensory-somatic system.

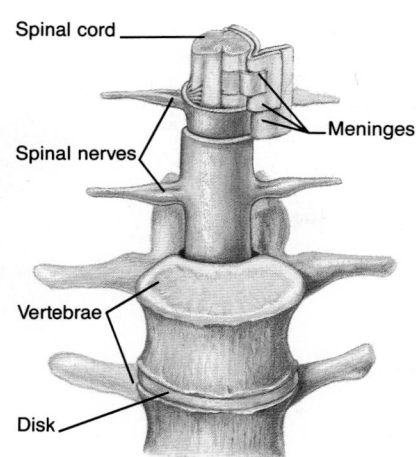

Figure 25-20　The spinal cord is protected by vertebrae and discs made of cartilage. Even with this protection, many thousands of people incur spinal injuries every year. Many happen during sports activities such as diving and skiing.

25.2 NERVOUS SYSTEMS ❧ **715**

Science, Technology, and Society

Fat Protein: In the past, cravings for fatty foods such as potato chips, fried chicken, and ice cream were thought to be related to a person's emotional state and under voluntary control. People who ate large amounts of fatty foods and gained weight were thought to lack self control and willpower. The inability to control the amount of fatty food intake has been recently associated with a brain protein called galanin. This protein in rats dictates their craving for fatty foods. In addition, a drug that blocks galanin's activity can reduce an animal's appetite for fat.

PROJECT

Inborn Reflexes: Ask a group of students to research the motor reflexes a child is born with. As part of their research, they should interview a pediatrician.

Effects of Caffeine on *Daphnia*

Time Allotment
1 class period

Objectives
Upon completing this Investigation, students will be able to:
• Compare *Daphnia* with and without the effects of caffeine.
• Demonstrate understanding of the effect of caffeine on animals.

Skills
observe, form a hypothesis, design an experiment, separate and control variables, interpret data

Materials
petri dish, 1 per group; dropper; caffeine solution; *Daphnia;* microscope

Preparation
Purchase *Daphnia* from a biological supply house. Other aquatic invertebrates may be substituted for *Daphnia.* Keep *Daphnia* in dechlorinated water. Prepare a solution of caffeine from caffeine tablets purchased at a pharmacy. Prepare it in a cup of hot water as if you were making coffee. One tablet is generally equivalent to the caffeine in one cup of coffee. Make serial dilutions for 1/2 strength and 1/4 strength of the original. Allow to cool to room temperature prior to lab. Prepare dechlorinated water by keeping tap water in an open container in the room for two days.

Possible Hypotheses
1. *Daphnia* will have an increase in heartbeat rate when full-strength caffeine is added.
2. *Daphnia* will demonstrate increasing activity as caffeine increases in concentration.

Possible Procedures
• Count heartbeat rate before and after exposure to most highly concentrated caffeine solution.
• Count number of times *Daphnia* move across the midline of a petri dish as caffeine concentration is increased.

Figure 25-21 The response to stepping on a sharp object takes nearly 100 muscles. Not only do you jerk your foot away but you extend your arms to balance yourself on one foot, too.

INVESTIGATION

The Effect of Stimulants on *Daphnia*

How many people do you know who start each morning with a cup of coffee? What do you do when you're feeling sleepy in mid-afternoon? You might drink a cola beverage with caffeine. Caffeine is a drug. It is a stimulant that is addictive and can produce withdrawal symptoms such as headaches when limited or eliminated from a person's diet. Caffeine is contained in many carbonated soft drinks, coffee, tea, chocolate, and many over-the-counter medications. It can produce such physical symptoms as ulcers, heart irregularities, and irritability. Recently, it has become a suspect in the cause of fetal development problems. In this lab, you will determine the effect of caffeine on the crustacean *Daphnia.*

Problem
What is the effect of a stimulant on *Daphnia?*

Safety Precautions
Do not drink any of the beverages used during this lab. Treat invertebrates used in a humane fashion at all times.

Hypothesis
Make a hypothesis about how caffeine will affect *Daphnia.* Explain your reasons for making this hypothesis.

Experimental Plan
1. As a group, make a list of possible ways you might test your hypothesis using the materials your teacher has made available.

Reflex—Initial Response In some reflex actions such as blinking, the fixed pathway runs through the brain. For other reflexes, the fixed pathway runs through the spinal cord. For example, consider your response to stepping on a sharp rock while walking barefoot. Before you are aware of what is happening, certain muscles in your leg have contracted, lifting your foot from the ground. What is the nerve pathway of this response?

Receptors in the skin of your foot are activated by the pressure of the rock and the pain it causes. Each receptor stimulates a sensory neuron and causes an impulse to travel to the spinal cord via one of the spinal nerves. Each impulse crosses a synapse to an interneuron.

The impulse travels along the interneuron and across another synapse to a motor neuron, which leaves the spinal cord. As the impulse passes out of the end branches of the motor neuron, it crosses several synapses and activates several muscle cell effectors. Acetylcholine is the neurotransmitter that carries the impulses across these synapses and causes the muscles to contract. Once the reflex action has taken place, the motor neuron stops carrying impulses, acetylcholine is no longer released, the muscles relax, and your foot returns to the ground.

2. Agree on one idea from your group's list that could be investigated in the classroom.
3. Design an experiment that will test one variable at a time. Plan to collect quantitative data.
4. Following the style of a recipe, write a numbered list of directions that anyone could follow.
5. Make a list of materials and the quantities you will need.

Checking the Plan

Discuss the following points with other group members to decide the final procedures for your experiment.
1. What variables will need to be controlled?
2. What is your control?
3. What will you measure or count?
4. How many *Daphnia* will you examine?
5. How many trials will you run?

6. Have you designed and made a table for collecting data?

Make sure your teacher has approved your experimental plan before you proceed further.

Data and Observations

Carry out your experiment; collect your data and complete your data table. Make a graph of your results.

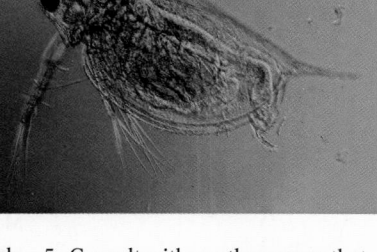

Analysis and Conclusions

1. According to your results, how does caffeine affect *Daphnia*?
2. What is your experimental evidence for your conclusion in question 1?
3. Was your hypothesis supported by your data? Explain.
4. If your hypothesis was not supported, what type of experimental error could be responsible?

5. Consult with another group that used a different procedure to examine this problem. Were their conclusions the same as yours? Why or why not?

Going Further

Based on this lab experience, design an experiment that would help to answer another question that arose from your work. Assume that you will have unlimited resources and will not be conducting this lab in class.

Teaching Strategies
- Tell students that they should not add more than 10 drops of the most concentrated caffeine solution to the water in their petri dish as it will kill the *Daphnia*.
- Tell students to dispose of their *Daphnia* in a container of fresh water you provide. They should not be reused in other classes.
- To introduce the lab, ask students to observe *Daphnia* behavior and internal structure using a dissecting microscope. You might ask them to determine the heartbeat rate by observing the number of beats in a minute. Discuss with students their use of beverages with caffeine. Ask how many soft drinks with caffeine or how much coffee and tea they drink each day. Ask them what the side effects of caffeine use might be.
- Be sure that all water temperature is kept the same.

Data and Observations

Examine each group's graphs and evaluate the group's interpretation of the data. In general, students' data should show an increase in heartbeat rate and activity of *Daphnia*. Graphs should be labeled correctly and have a title.

Data Analysis

1-5. Answers will vary. In general, the heartbeat rate and activity of *Daphnia* increase with increasing concentrations of caffeine.

✔ **Assessment**

Oral: Have students analyze the process and results of their experiments with you. They should concentrate on their experimental procedure and changes they would make if doing the experiment again.

Extension

Ask students what other invertebrates they might test and what other stimulant or depressant drugs they might test. *Alcohol and nicotine are possibilities.*

Activity

Have students observe the following reflexes with a partner:

1. Tell students to have one partner hold a 30 cm × 30 cm piece of plexiglass in front of his or her face. The other partner should throw a paper wad at his or her partner's face. The subject should be encouraged not to blink. Ask them if they can keep from blinking, then trade partners.

2. Tell one partner to sit on the edge of a table with legs dangling but not touching the floor. The other partner should tap, with the side of the hand, just below the knee. They should explain what happens and then trade partners.

Figure 25-22 Reflexes operate with such speed that you can move away from a potentially dangerous situation quickly—hopefully without much injury.

The path a nerve impulse takes during a reflex action is called a **reflex arc.** A reflex arc often includes five parts—receptor, sensory neuron, interneuron, motor neuron, and effector.

Reflex—Secondary Response A reflex action takes place within a fraction of a second. Since your response to a sharp rock underfoot does not involve your brain, how do you become aware of what is going on? Some of the spinal cord interneurons that receive sensory impulses connect with other neuron pathways leading to the brain. The brain becomes aware of what has happened. At this point, secondary responses occur. A loud "ouch" is a common secondary response to stepping on a sharp rock.

The Autonomic System of Humans

Many reflexes involve effectors other than skeletal muscle, including glands and muscles of the heart and digestive tract. You usually remain unaware of these reflexes, which are often responses to internal stimuli. These responses—such as the beating of your heart, or the peristaltic motions of your intestines—are under the control of the **autonomic system.** The autonomic system is made up of two groups of nerves that serve to check and balance each other. These two groups are called the sympathetic and parasympathetic nerves.

Sympathetic Nerves Imagine you're out riding your bicycle on a pleasant Saturday afternoon. As you pedal up a long, steep hill, your breathing gets faster and deeper, and you can tell by the pounding in your temples how fast your heart is pumping. You are sure it's going to take all your strength to get up this hill without stopping. Suddenly, a car comes speeding out of a parking lot right in front of you. You see it just in time to put on an extra burst of speed and swerve out of its path.

Sympathetic nerves speed up the activity of the heart and lungs during emergencies or strenuous exercise. A high rate of cellular respiration increases the level of carbon dioxide in your blood. Receptors in your aorta and other major arteries detect the higher carbon dioxide level and send impulses to the part of your medulla oblongata that controls heartbeat rate. This region of your brain is also receiving signals from the right atrium of your heart that indicate this chamber is receiving an increased volume of blood. In response to these signals, your brain sends impulses along the spinal cord and spinal nerves that release the neurotransmitter noradrenaline, which stimulates heart muscle contractions and increases your heartbeat rate.

The fear that you feel when you see the speeding car in your path also stimulates the acceleration center of your medulla oblongata. As a result of all this sympathetic nerve activity, you get an unusual burst of energy that enables you to not only pedal up the hill, but also to get out of the way of that car.

Parasympathetic Nerves   Once you've escaped a potential collision and reached the top of the hill, your heart no longer needs to work so hard. In fact, a too-rapid heartbeat can damage blood vessels. Your sympathetic nerves are capable only of speeding up your heartbeat rate. Slowing it back down to normal is the job of the parasympathetic nerves.

When your heartbeat rate increases, so does your blood pressure because the blood vessels have constricted. The increase in blood pressure is detected by receptors located in the same blood vessels that have receptors to detect high carbon dioxide levels. The blood pressure receptors send impulses to the inhibition center of the medulla oblongata, which sends impulses that cause the release of acetylcholine, a neurotransmitter that inhibits heart muscle contractions.

The responses of most of your internal organs are regulated by the two parts of the autonomic nervous system. For example, sympathetic nerves cause the pupils of your eyes to become larger in response to low light levels, and parasympathetic nerves reduce the size of the pupils when light levels are high. In other words, the sympathetic system copes with stress or emergencies and the parasympathetic system does the opposite.

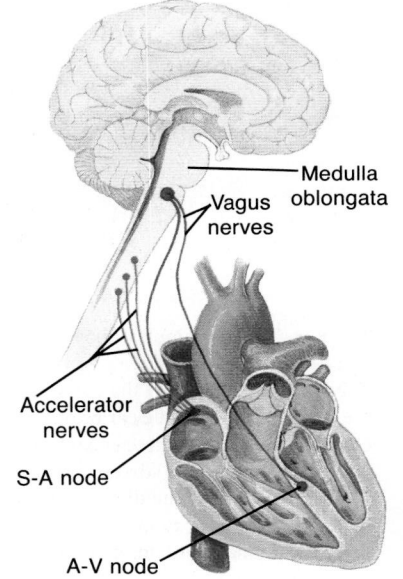

Medulla oblongata
Vagus nerves
Accelerator nerves
S-A node
A-V node

Figure 25-23   **Heartbeat rate is controlled by nerves and the medulla oblongata. The medulla sends messages by way of nerves to the heart to accelerate it or to slow it down.**

Minilab 2

How do distractions affect your reaction time?

Place your arm on your desk so that your hand is just over the edge. Hold your thumb and index finger about 2 cm apart. Your partner will hold a meter stick vertically with the zero end between your fingers. Your partner will drop the stick without warning you. Catch the stick as soon as it begins to fall. Record the number of centimeters the stick fell before you caught it. Repeat for 10 trials. Record and average the distance the meter stick falls before it is caught. Trade partners and conduct the same test. To determine the effects of a distraction on reaction time, choose something such as spelling words or chatting with a friend while repeating the test.

Analysis   *Did you improve your reaction time as you completed more trials? Why or why not? How did the distraction affect your reaction time?*

Minilab 2

Purpose
Students will compare their reaction time with and without distractions.

Skills
observe and infer, recognize cause and effect

Teaching Strategies
- Ask the student being tested to sit and the other to stand. Tell them to be sure that the meterstick is perpendicular to the floor.

Expected Results
Results will vary. Averages will vary between 10 cm and 20 cm without distraction. With distraction, the distance will increase, perhaps by more than 10 cm.

Answers
1. Answers will vary. Many students will improve their time. Learning occurs and students begin to anticipate the drop.
2. Reaction time is increased by distractions.

✔ **Assessment**
Portfolio: Ask students to write in their portfolios a list of activities that require quick reaction time. Ask them to make another list of factors that may reduce reaction time.

Misconception
Students often confuse the term *autonomic* with the term *automatic*. Make sure they understand that autonomic is used to designate nerves not under voluntary control and *somatic* is used to designate nerves under voluntary control.

PROJECT

MRI and PET: Ask a group of students to visit a clinic where MRIs and PET scanning are done. They should take photos and prepare a slide presentation or photo essay of their findings. They should also bring back examples of images of the brain made by the two different techniques.

Activity

Obtain tuning forks for the following activity. If tuning forks are not available, an all-metal kitchen fork will be an acceptable substitute. Tell students to strike the tines on a metal surface, then hold the fork next to the ear until the sound is almost gone. Next, they should place the fork (the handle, not the tines) on their foreheads. Ask them what that demonstrates about the transmission of sound. Ask them to repeat the same experiment using other parts of their body. Ask them what they conclude.

L1 **LEP**

Concept Development

The process of hearing begins with sound waves coming into the ear canal. The sound travels like ripples on a pond by the successive vibrations of molecules. When the waves hit the eardrum, it moves back and forth slightly. The malleus takes this pressure from the inner surface of the eardrum and passes it to the incus, which in turn passes it to the stapes so that the pressure is multiplied about 20 times as it moves across these bones in succession. The stapes strikes the oval window, which causes the pressure to be passed to the fluid of the inner ear. As a result of cochlear fluid movement, the basilar membrane (the organ of Corti) moves up and down and the attached cilia of the hair cells, when bent, initiate nerve impulses that pass by way of the cochlear nerve to the temporal lobe of the brain where the impulse can be interpreted as sound.

The Senses

Animals are constantly bombarded by stimuli from their environment. Detecting and reacting to stimuli are important for an animal's survival. Humans have adaptations to sense a variety of stimuli. Whether stimuli are detected by a simple nerve ending or special cells of the ear, eye, or other complex organs, sensory information causes action potentials in neurons. Each receptor or sense organ sends impulses to particular parts of the brain where they are interpreted. We have the ability to then act on the information that has been provided.

There are five major human senses—vision, hearing, smell, taste, and touch. Touch is a general term that includes several related senses such as pain, pressure, heat, and cold. Each of these "touch" senses is detected by separate skin receptors. Each kind of receptor detects only one sense. The number and location of touch receptors around the body varies. For example, there are more cold receptors than heat receptors, and there are more touch receptors in the fingertips than in the legs.

The senses of taste and smell are not essential to the survival of humans, but for many, many animals, they are the most important senses. For nocturnal animals and very small mammals, the sense of smell provides the most information about what is happening in their environments. Can you think of a reason smell is not more highly evolved in humans?

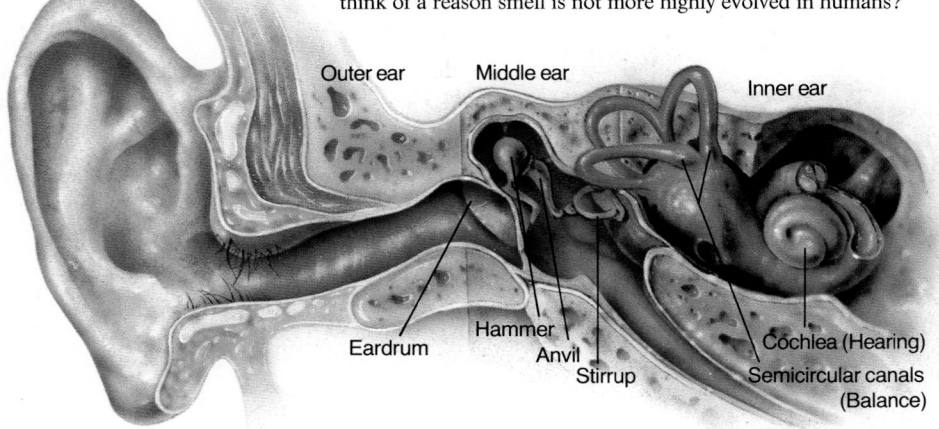

Figure 25-24 **The human ear is a complex sense organ that converts sound waves into vibrations. These vibrations ultimately trigger action potentials in the neurons of the auditory nerve, which ultimately connect with neurons in the auditory center of the brain.**

The Ear As an example of how a sense organ works, consider the ear. The ear is made up of three areas—outer ear, middle ear, and inner ear. The outer ear consists of the outer flap, the auditory (hearing) canal, and the eardrum. The middle ear begins on the inner side of the eardrum and consists of a chain of three small bones commonly called the hammer, anvil, and stirrup. The stirrup contacts a second membrane called the oval window. Also in the middle ear is the eustachian tube, a canal that connects the middle ear to the nasal passages and throat. The eustachian tube contains air and maintains equal air pressure between the middle and outer ear. This is unfortunately a prime breeding ground for infectious

STUDENT JOURNAL

Ask students to cut advertisements in the help wanted section of the newspaper about jobs that require keenness of certain senses such as hearing, vision, balance and coordination, or smell. They should put these ads, along with brief descriptions of how and why specific senses would be involved, in their journals.

microorganisms that enter the body through the mouth or nose. The inner ear contains two sets of fluid-filled canals. One set, the semicircular canals, controls the sense of motion and is not involved in hearing. The other fluid-filled canal is a coiled structure called the cochlea, which is involved in hearing. Part of the cochlea is in contact with the oval window. The cochlea contains sensitive hair cells that are connected to fibers of the auditory nerve.

Detecting Sound   How does hearing occur? Sound waves enter the outer ear, pass through the auditory canal, and cause the eardrum to begin vibrating. The vibrations are picked up by the middle ear bones, which amplify the vibrations and transfer them to the oval window. The oval window then vibrates, causing the fluid in the cochlea to move. Movement of the fluid within the cochlea causes the sensitive hairs to bend, and to cause an action potential along axons of the auditory nerve.

Transmitting and Interpreting Sound Impulses   There are thousands of sensitive hairs inside the fluid-filled cochlea. When each hair bends, even slightly, in response to a vibration, it creates an action potential in the auditory nerve fiber to which it is attached. These impulses travel to the auditory cortex located on each side of the cerebrum.

How does the brain interpret these impulses? How can you tell the difference between a bass guitar and a bird's song? The hairs in different regions of the cochlea respond to different sound frequencies. Each hair is connected via a neuron pathway to a specific location in the auditory cortex. The frequency of a sound vibration determines which of the hair cells will be stimulated. The loudness of the sound determines how many times the hair cell will be stimulated. What you hear depends on the pattern of hair cells stimulated into movement by the sound. You respond, perhaps by turning down the volume of a too-loud stereo or jumping up to dance to a favorite tune.

Figure 25-25   **The eardrum or tympanic membrane (a) begins sending vibrations through the rest of the ear structures. The hammer, anvil, and stirrup are located in the middle ear (b). The semicircular canals are located in the inner ear (c).**

a

b

c

Concept Development

There are two main kinds of deafness: conduction deafness and nerve deafness. Conduction deafness occurs when the sound waves cannot be conducted properly through the ear. It can be due to a congenital defect such as those that result when a pregnant mother contracts German measles. Conduction deafness can also be due to repeated infections of the middle ear. Many children suffer from these infections. If infections are repeated, physicians sometimes insert tiny plastic tubes into the tympanic membrane to keep the middle ear dry. Conduction deafness may also occur when the ossicles fuse together, limiting their ability to transmit sound waves.

Nerve deafness occurs when cilia on the sense receptor in the cochlea wear away. This may happen to some extent with normal aging, but also occurs in young people who listen to loud music amplified to 130 decibels. Hearing aids cannot correct nerve deafness. For this reason, it is important to protect the ears against any continuous loud noise. Cochlear nerve implants have been done, but it is extremely costly and patients say that the speech they hear sounds like a robot.

Activity

Have students find their blind spot using the following method. On a piece of paper, draw two circles (2 mm diameter) 10 cm apart. Have students hold the paper about 20 cm away from their eyes, directly in front of their eyes. Students should close their right eye, and with their left eye focus on the right circle. Have each student slowly move the paper away from his or her face and notice that the left circle seems to disappear. Repeat with the left eye closed. When the circle disappears, the image has reached the blind spot on the retina. This is an area where there are no light receptor cells. **L1** **LEP**

Demonstration

- Obtain test patterns for color blindness and astigmatism from your school nurse or local medical center. Ask students to test themselves and look up explanations for color blindness and astigmatism.

- Dissect a cow or sheep eye so that students can see the parts. Cow and sheep eyes have a layer of the inner choroid coat that is not present in humans. This iridescent layer, called the tapetum lucidum, causes the eyes of animals to reflect light at night and appears to enhance night vision by reflecting some light back into the retina. **LEP**

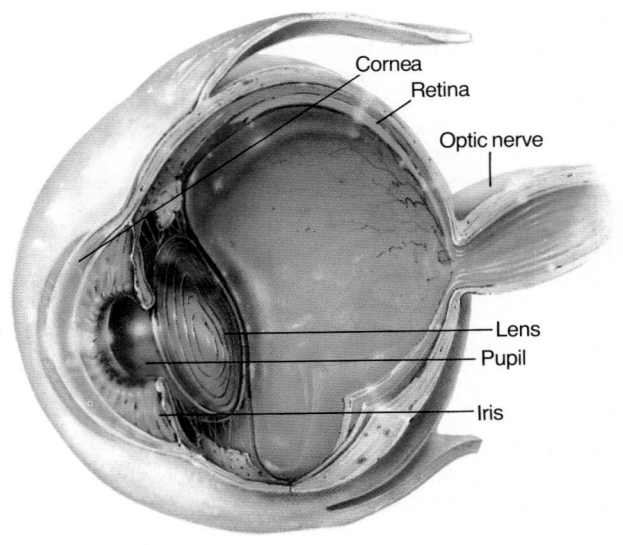

Figure 25-26 The eye is a sensory structure composed of three layers of tissue that enclose a fluid-filled space. The innermost layer, the retina, contains rods and cones, the photoreceptor cells. These cells transmit impulses to the brain, where they are interpreted.

The Eye Ability to detect light, an important source of information about the environment, has evolved among a wide variety of organisms. *Euglena*, a unicellular protist, and planarians, flatworms, both have structures that enable them to distinguish between light and dark. Light detection pigments are also present in plants to aid in phototropism and flowering. Only in certain animals, however, have structures evolved that enable the organism to form an image. Image-forming structures, eyes, are characteristic of arthropods, some mollusks, and vertebrates.

Humans (and other vertebrates) have what is known as a camera eye, so named because it works much like a camera. Rays of light reflected from an object enter the front of the eye, pass through a lens, and are focused on the back of the eye much as light passing through a camera lens is focused on film at the rear of the camera.

Figure 25-26 shows the structure of the human eye. Notice that only the front of the eye is exposed. The rest of the eye is protected by the skull. Surrounding most of the human eye is a tough layer of connective tissue, the sclera, which you know as the white of the eye. At the front of the eye, the transparent sclera bulges outward and is known as the **cornea.** The cornea admits light into the eye. Beneath the sclera is a dark layer, the choroid, which contains many blood vessels that nourish the eye. The dark color of the choroid reduces reflection within the eye. Toward the front of the eye, the choroid extends upward, forming a ring of cells known as the iris. The iris contains pigments, which give the eye its color. The iris contains sets of muscles that control the size of the opening in its center, the pupil. When one set of iris muscles is contracted, the pupil is dilated, admitting more light. When the other set of muscles is contracted, the size of the pupil is reduced and less light can enter.

722 🐾 NERVOUS CONTROL

Light passing through the cornea travels through a watery fluid, the aqueous humor, and then through the pupil. From there, the light rays pass through the transparent **lens** of the eye. The lens is an elastic ball that bends rays of light. The shape of the lens is changed by the action of very small muscles. Such changes in shape focus the rays of light.

Light focused by the lens strikes the innermost layer of the eye. That layer, the "film" of the camera eye, is called the **retina.** The retina contains two types of photoreceptor cells that are stimulated by the rays of light striking them. **Rod cells** are most sensitive and permit vision even in dim light. However, they do not function in color vision. Distinguishing colors is the function of the **cone cells,** most of which are located near the center of the retina. Cone cells also contribute to sharper images.

Light rays falling on rods and cones cause changes in pigment molecules present in those cells. Those changes lead to action potentials in the rods and cones. Impulses cross synapses to other retinal nerve cells, and eventually are carried along axons that form the optic nerve, which leads to vision centers in the cerebrum of the brain. Because of the way that light rays behave as they pass through a structure such as the lens of the eye, the image formed on the retina is upside down. Our brain, however, interprets images as being right side up, and that is the way we see them.

Figure 25-27 **This electron micrograph shows the rods and cones of the human eye. Magnification: 10 000×**

LOOKING AHEAD

I N THIS CHAPTER, you have studied neuron structure and function and the nervous pathways involved in reflex responses, some of which depend upon skeletal muscle. In the next chapter, you will learn how the skeleton and muscles interact to provide support and locomotion, and will study the mechanism by which skeletal muscle causes movement. You will also examine various ways in which energy is made available for the activities of skeletal muscle.

Section Review

Understanding Concepts
1. Compare and contrast the nervous systems of invertebrates and vertebrates. Concentrate on major differences.
2. Suppose a person suffered brain damage as a result of an accident. What part of the brain was injured if the symptoms of the injury were (a) loss of speech, (b) emotional problems; (c) loss of control of internal organs; or (d) loss of balance and coordination?
3. What is the difference between a reflex arc and a reflex act? Name the components of a typical reflex arc.
4. ***Skill Review—Sequencing:*** Sequence the nervous pathway structures involved in the response made to touching a hot stove. For more help, see Organizing Information in the **Skill Handbook.**
5. ***Thinking Critically:*** Why do the ears of a person going up or coming down in an airplane often feel stuffed up?

Answers to Section Review

1. In invertebrates with bilateral symmetry, the brain does not exert as much control, the nerve cords are ventrally located, and ganglia located throughout the body exert much of the control. Vertebrate brains exert more control. There is a single dorsal nerve cord, and ganglia exert less control than in invertebrates.
2. (a) cerebrum; (b) cerebrum; (c) medulla oblongata; (d) cerebellum
3. A reflex arc is the pathway impulses follow in a reflex, which is an automatic response to a stimulus. A typical reflex arc consists of receptor, sensory neuron, interneuron, motor neuron, and effector.
4. **Skill Review—Sequencing:** Pain receptor in hand → sensory neuron → interneuron in spinal cord → motor neuron → muscles in arm
5. **Thinking Critically:** As the plane ascends or descends, air pressure in the outer ear varies and is not equal to the pressure of the air within the eustachian tube. This difference causes the ears to feel stuffed up.

Biotechnology

Purpose
Students will study what generates noise pollution, its effect on the body, and efforts being made to control it.

Background
Sixteen million people in the United States suffer some hearing loss because of exposure to noise. In a recent study, degrees of sensory deafness, an incurable hearing loss caused by excessive noise over a long period of time, were detected in 60% of college freshmen. Sensory deafness is caused when the special sensory hair cells in the inner ear are damaged. The hairs spring back if the sounds are not too loud. After years of exposure to damaging sound levels, the hair cells do not spring back any more. They stay flattened out and eventually die.

Teaching Strategies
* Borrow a sound-level meter from the physics department. Measure the sound level as students enter the room, and record the decibels on a chalkboard or transparency.
* Before class, set up a variety of items that create sound—radio, musical instruments, kitchen appliances, computer printer, and others. With student help, measure the sound levels of each. Note that 130 decibels is uncomfortably loud; 100 very loud; 80 moderately loud; 50 quiet; 30 very quiet; 20 just audible.
* Tell students that sound above 70 dB can eventually damage hearing. This would be the loudness of an ordinary vacuum cleaner.

Possible Answers
1. When two sound waves with different amplitudes move toward each other from opposite directions, the meeting of the two waves produces a larger amplitude than the two waves added together. When this meeting of waves

continues at specific intervals of time, a musical beat is heard.
2. Yes, any sound that is continuous and becomes annoying is having a physiological effect on your body and can be called noise pollution.

Going Further
Find out what regulations OSHA, the government agency responsible for safety in the workplace, has for noise and noise pollution in the workplace.

Biotechnology

Fighting Noise Pollution

When you think of pollution, usually water and air pollution quickly come to mind. Generally, people don't think of sound as a polluting agent. Yet sound can cause people to become nervous, irritable, or tired. It can make people nauseous and damage their hearing. Loud

sounds such as fireworks and the roar of jet engines would seem the obvious cause of these health problems, yet scientists and doctors know that the sound doesn't have to be loud to cause problems. It only has to be constant or prolonged. Scientists who work to control sound or noise pollution are in the field called environmental acoustics.

Acoustical engineers know that noise pollution can be controlled in several ways. For example, people who work around loud sounds, such as the operators of printing presses and rock musicians, should wear earplugs or muffs to deaden the constant loud noise. Architects and acoustical engineers can design buildings with rooms that absorb the sounds of appliances and office machinery. Special acoustic tiles that trap sound are placed on walls and ceilings. Carpets cover the floor. Draperies are used as window treatments. Even fabric is used on office walls to absorb sounds.

Recently, technology has provided an additional means to control noise pollution. Scientists know that if an identical tone is produced by two different sources, the sound waves may cancel out each other.

CAREER CONNECTION

Audiologists work with both children and adults who have hearing disorders. They identify and evaluate the severity of the hearing disorder as well as provide a therapy program to treat the problem. Most states require audiologists to have a master's degree in audiology and to meet special licensing requirements.

No sound is heard. This phenomenon is called *interference.* They have used this knowledge to build active noise control (ANC) devices. Sounds produced by active noise control devices match the frequency and amplitude of the polluting sound; however, the two sounds vibrate in opposite directions. This results in interference, and as a result, neither sound is heard. Think of the improvement that ANC devices can make on annoying machines such as air conditioners and heaters. Such devices can even make a whole office a quieter place to work.

1. **Find Out:** Two sound waves that cancel each other out are an example of destructive interference. Find out how destructive interference is related to constructive interference and the production of musical beats.
2. **Issue:** Suppose you work after school in an office. The copying machine is located next to your desk. The machine doesn't make a loud sound, but after sitting next to it for an hour, you find yourself becoming annoyed by its sound. Is the sound produced by the machine an example of noise pollution? Explain.

CAREER CONNECTION

For more information, have students contact a local audiology clinic or hospital to find out more about a career as an audiologist.

Issues

Alzheimer's: The Disease that Takes Everything

Jackson walked up the front steps of his grandmother's house. It had been months since he was last there and he was eager to see her. His excitement turned to dismay as he looked around the familiar house. His grandmother had always been a meticulous housekeeper. She took pride in keeping herself well-groomed as well. But as Jackson looked around the living room, he saw that the once-tidy room was now cluttered and unkept. In fact, Grandma Sweetwell herself looked unkept. Even more disturbing, his grand-mother did not seem to recognize him. What had happened? Something was quite wrong. Jackson's grandmother was the victim of a progressive, degenerative, terminal disease that attacks the brains of approximately 5 percent of people over the age of 65. This disease, called Alzheimer's disease, impairs the memory, thinking ability, and behavior of its victims. In the final stages, its victims are bedridden and completely helpless. Today, Alzheimer's is the fourth leading cause of death in the elderly population following heart disease, cancer, and strokes. As Jackson was to find out, coping with the mental and physical degeneration of the victim is only part of the problems facing Alzheimer's patients and their families. The other part deals with the financial burdens incurred.

At first, Jackson's parents were able to care for Grandma Sweetwell. They had her move into their house. As the disease pro-

gressed, they took turns dressing her and caring for her needs. They watched to be sure she didn't wander out of the house, hurt herself, or damage the house. But as the disease progressed, she needed more care. Doctors suggested a nursing home; however, the cost of one month in a home was more than $2000. Jackson's parents couldn't afford that. Grandma Sweetwell's health insurance paid for hospital and doctor bills, but it didn't pay for long-term care in a nursing home. The federal program, Medicare, paid for "skilled care" in a nursing home; but Jackson's grandmother didn't need that. She needed custodial care. The program Medicaid would cover custodial care but she had a savings account, a small monthly pension, and owned her own house. She had too many assets to qualify for Medicaid.

Jackson's parents were forced to go to the courts to get authority to

sell Grandma Sweetwell's house and its contents. They used the money from the sale and her savings to pay for the nursing home. Once all of these assets were gone, she qualified for government assistance. Jackson's grand-mother died nine months after getting government assistance. Alzheimer's had stripped away her mental and physical abilities, her dignity, and just about everything else that she owned.

Understanding the Issue

1. How do you think Jackson's parents felt about having to sell all of Grandma Sweetwell's possessions and using all of her savings before she could qualify for government assistance?

2. The cost of health care is a crisis in the United States. The number of senior citizens is increasing. How will this increased population impact the cost of health care? What suggestions might you make to provide the necessary care for this segment of the population, yet still keep down the costs?

Readings

- Sandstrom, B. "Difficult decisions: A family deals with Alzheimer's disease." *Aging*, no. 363-364: 22-3, 1992.
- Stoneman, D. "The other side of Alzheimer's." *Health*, May/June 1992.

Purpose

Students will read a case study of an Alzheimer's patient and her family and learn about the day-to-day problems faced by the patient and her family.

Background

Alzheimer's disease causes people to gradually lose their memory and powers of judgment. Speech and body coordination may also be affected. The disease seems to affect people who are over 40 years old, and gets progressively worse as patients get older. The disease attacks and destroys brain cells. At present, science does not know the cause of the disease or how it operates. It may have viral and hereditary factors involved in its onset.

Teaching Strategies

- Ask students to share experiences or reports from the media about individuals with Alzheimer's disease.

Possible Answers

1. The family would feel guilty and devastated about having to sell the grandmother's possessions.
2. The cost of health care will rise. Some people advocate a national health care insurance plan that would make health care affordable to all.

Going Further

Ask a group of students to contact the nearest Alzheimer's Society and ask what kinds of services they supply to patients and families, and what types of educational and research programs they sponsor.

CHAPTER 25

CHAPTER REVIEW

Summary

Summary statements can be used by students to review the major concepts of the chapter.

Language of Biology

Answers should go beyond defining the terms. Accept any reasonable answer that uses the term correctly and in the proper context.

Understanding Concepts

1. The anatomy of the nervous system is such that impulses begin in the dendrites, located at the ends of neurons. They travel in only one direction from that point.
2. Skeletal muscle has no receptors for noradrenaline.
3. After transmission of many impulses, most sodium ions are trapped on the inside of the neuron and most potassium ions have moved to the outside. The original distribution and concentration of ions must be restored by the sodium-potassium pump, which pushes out more sodium ions than potassium ions pulled in.
4. Neurons release chemicals, neurotransmitters, some of which are very similar to hormones. Some hormones act as neurotransmitters in the brain.
5. The skeletal muscle would continue to be stimulated; thus, it would remain contracted.
6. Drugs that are depressants reduce nerve impulse transmission. This can result in impaired coordination, shortened reaction time, and impaired judgment. Stimulants increase nervous system activity. Heartbeat rate increases as well as blood pressure.
7. Peristalsis is regulated by the autonomic nervous system. It is inhibited by sympathetic nerves and stimulated by parasympathetic nerves. Inhibition is adaptive during emergencies, when other activities are more important than digesting food.

Summary

With the exception of sponges, animals have nervous systems that control responses to many stimuli. Nervous control requires detection of stimuli, transmission of impulses, analysis of impulses, and an appropriate response to the stimuli.

Transmission of impulses in animals depends upon reversals of polarity along neurons. Those reversals result from changes in membrane permeability to different ions, which cause action potentials, or impulses. Impulses cross synapses by means of chemical transmitters, which may either excite or inhibit the target cell. Analysis of impulses is made on the basis of the number of excitatory and inhibitory effects of transmitters at any given time.

Nervous systems in animals became more complex as more complex animals evolved. Most animals have a central nervous system that analyzes information from sensory neurons, and in response sends impulses along motor neurons to effectors. In humans, many responses are voluntary, but others are involuntary reflexes. The sense perceived depends on the region of the brain receiving the sensory message. The strength of the sensation is reflected in the frequency of nerve impulse in the sensory nerves.

Language of Biology

Write a sentence that shows your understanding of each of the following terms.

action potential	nerve
autonomic system	neuron
axon	neurotransmitter
central nervous system	peripheral nervous
cerebellum	system
cerebrum	reflex
cone cells	reflex arc
cornea	resting potential
dendrite	retina
interneuron	rod cells
lens	sensory neuron
medulla oblongata	sensory-somatic system
motor neuron	synapse

Understanding Concepts

1. A neuron stimulated in a laboratory will carry an impulse in either direction away from the point of stimulation. Why don't impulses travel in two directions along your neurons?
2. Can you suggest a reason why noradrenaline has no effect on skeletal muscle?
3. When does the sodium-potassium pump go into action? Why must it do so?
4. Cite two examples from this chapter that illustrate the close relationship between the endocrine and nervous systems.
5. What would be the effect on skeletal muscle if the enzyme that breaks down acetylcholine were not present?
6. Explain several ways in which drugs affect the nervous system.
7. Muscles controlling peristalsis are inhibited during an emergency or stress situation. Afterwards, peristalsis again occurs normally. How is regulation of peristalsis controlled? How is such regulation adaptive?
8. How are the nervous systems of a hydra and a planarian related to the body plans of those animals?
9. Relate the concepts of action potentials and crossing of synapses to a reflex arc of your choosing.
10. During an outer ear infection, the auditory canal may become inflamed and swollen. Explain why hearing is impaired during such an infection.

8. The nerve net of a hydra enables it to sense and respond to stimuli coming from all directions around its radially symmetrical body. The planarian has sense organs and a primitive brain located at the front of its bilaterally symmetrical body, the part that encounters stimuli first.
9. An action potential occurs in a receptor when a stimulus at or above threshold level alters permeability in the membrane of neurons. The action potential sweeps along, causing release of neurotransmitters across a synapse to a sensory neuron. Combining neurotransmitters with receptors in the membrane of the sensory neuron sets off an action potential in the sensory neuron. This pattern of action potentials and release of transmitters across synapses continues from sensory neuron to interneuron to motor neuron to effector.
10. The swelling due to infection interferes with transmission of sound waves toward the eardrum.

Applying Concepts

11. Nicotine mimics the effect of acetylcholine. Is nicotine a stimulant or depressant? Explain.
12. Other than arthropods, can you think of invertebrates in which the brain is complex and exerts much of the control over behavior? Explain.
13. How would a drug that occupies sodium-potassium pumps affect transmission of impulses? Explain.
14. In the cerebrum, the areas that receive impulses from sensory neurons vary in size. For example, the area receiving impulses that originate in the fingers is larger than the area receiving impulses that originate in the upper arm. Explain the reason for the differences.
15. Brains that exert greater control over responses have relatively more interneurons than brains that do not exert so much control. Can you explain that fact?
16. Muscle cells, like neurons, have resting potentials and action potentials. They contract in response to an action potential. Explain how transmitters released from sympathetic and parasympathetic motor neurons can have opposite effects on the same muscle tissue.
17. Based on your own experience, what kinds of responses, in general, are reflexes? How is it adaptive that such responses occur automatically rather than as a result of conscious effort?
18. **Biotechnology:** Explain how sounds can damage your ears and cause hearing loss.
19. **Issues:** What part of the brain does Alzheimer's affect? Explain.

Lab Interpretation

20. **Thinking Lab:** Oncogenes are genes that produce cancerous cells—cells that multiply very rapidly. Adult brain neurons ordinarily do not reproduce once they have been destroyed by accident or disease. Can you think of a way oncogenes might be used to solve the problem of lack of brain cell division?

Effects of nicotine on *Daphnia*

Heart rate (beats/min.) vs. Drops nicotine solution added to H_2O

21. **Investigate:** A student conducts an experiment to determine the effect of nicotine on *Daphnia*. Examine the results in the graph and tell how nicotine affects *Daphnia*.
22. **Minilab 2:** Reaction time may be affected by a variety of circumstances. Make a hypothesis about how reaction time would be affected by the following: alcohol, lack of sleep, after a meal, after eating a chocolate bar.

Connecting Ideas

23. Review the means by which breathing rate is controlled. Is that control by the sensory-somatic or autonomic system? Explain.
24. How do hearing and sight illustrate the principle of energy transformation?

Applying Concepts

11. Nicotine is a stimulant. Like acetylcholine, it causes contraction of skeletal muscles.
12. Active mollusks, such as squid and octopuses, have a complex brain. They have good vision and are efficient predators.
13. Such a drug would prevent transmission of impulses because the resting potential of the neuron could not be established.
14. The size of the area of the brain is correlated with the importance of the areas from which the sensory neurons originate. Fingers, for example, detect many more stimuli than do the upper arms.
15. A greater number of interneurons makes possible a greater number of synapses. More information can be received and analyzed.
16. Some transmitters increase permeability of muscle cell membranes to sodium, thereby setting off an action potential. Other transmitters prevent action potentials by making the muscle cell membranes even more polarized.
17. Responses to emergency situations are reflexes. Such responses can be made quickly without the need to take the time to make a decision.
18. Very loud noises could possibly break the eardrum. Such breakage could not only interfere with transmission of vibrations, but also lead to infections that could damage other parts of the ear.
19. Given such symptoms as memory loss and changes in behavior, Alzheimer's disease must affect the cerebrum.

Lab Interpretation

20. Perhaps oncogenes could be genetically engineered to be inserted into brain cells to encourage cell division.
21. Nicotine speeds up heartbeat rate.
22. Alcohol and lack of sleep cause a decrease in reaction time.

PROGRAM RESOURCES

Teacher Classroom Resources
Chapter Assessment, pp. 97-100 [L1]
Performance Assessment in Biology, p. 50 [L2]
Alternate Assessment in the Science Classroom
Computer Test Bank [L1]

Connecting Ideas

23. **Systems and Interactions:** Breathing rate is under the control of the sensory-somatic system. Contraction and relaxation of rib muscles and the diaphragm are under control of just one nerve. Also, this activity can be voluntarily controlled, up to a point.
24. **Energy:** The eye transforms light energy to electrical energy, while the ear transforms mechanical energy (vibrations) to electrical energy.

ORGANIZER

CHAPTER 26

SECTION	OBJECTIVES	TEXT LABS/FEATURES
26.1 Skeletal Systems (2 days)	**Compare** the structures and functions of exoskeletons and endoskeletons. **Discuss** the development of bone and its structure. **Demonstrate** various ways in which different bones form joints.	**Minilab 1:** How do exoskeletons and endoskeletons compare? p. 732
26.2 Effectors and Their Actions (3 days)	**Describe** examples of movement in animals lacking skeletons. **Distinguish** among the three types of vertebrate muscles and their characteristics. **Relate** the events of muscle contraction to the ways in which energy is made available for that contraction.	**Math Connection:** How fast do animals move? p. 740 **Investigation:** Bone and Muscle Density, p. 742 **Thinking Lab:** What kind of muscle is being used? p. 745 **Minilab 2:** How quickly do our muscles fatigue? p. 747 **Leisure Connection:** Exercise for Muscle Fitness, p. 748
BIOLOGY, TECHNOLOGY, AND SOCIETY		**Biotechnology:** Bionics and Artificial Limbs, p. 751 **Issues:** A Day in the Life of a Physically Challenged Person, p. 752 **Career Connection:** Physical therapist, p. 752

LAB MATERIALS

INVESTIGATION	MINILAB	ALTERNATE LAB
page 742 balance beef bones bird bones cartilage exoskeletons (crab or lobster) graduated cylinder meat chunks paper towels pennies tape	**page 732** bones cards, numbered 1-20 exoskeletons (shed) of arthropods microscope prepared slide of diatoms puffball sand dollar sea urchin spine shells snake skin turtle skeleton **page 747** book, heavy watch or clock with second hand	**page 730** crayfish distilled water shoeboxes, plastic

TEACHER CLASSROOM RESOURCES	OTHER RESOURCES
Study Guide, pp. 151-152 **Critical Thinking/Problem Solving:** *Joints in Action,* p. 26 ***PLL:** *Muscle and Bone Tissue,* p. 179	***STVS:** *Measuring Calcium Deficiency,* Human Biology (Disc 7, Side 2) **Color Transparency 46:** *The Skeletal System* **Color Transparency 50:** *Frog Body Systems* **Color Transparency 51:** *Bird Body Systems* **Color Transparency 52:** *Human Body Systems*
Study Guide, pp. 153-156 **Concept Mapping,** p. 26 ***PLL:** *Muscle and Bone Tissue,* p. 179 ***PLL:** *Locomotion in Earthworms,* p. 181 ***PLL:** *Locomotion in Protists,* p. 183 ***PLL:** *Earthworm Anatomy,* p. 187 ***PLL:** *Frog Anatomy,* p. 190 ****ILS:** *Skeletal Muscles,* p. 279 ****ILS:** *Measuring Differences in Muscular Activity,* p. 285	***STVS:** *Sea Turtle Mystery,* Animals (Disc 5, Side 2) **Color Transparency 27:** *Mollusk Body Systems* **Color Transparency 48:** *Starfish Body Systems*
Assessment Materials **Chapter Assessment,** pp. 101-104 **Performance Assessment in Biology,** p. 52 **Alternate Assessment in the Science Classroom** **Computer Test Bank**	**Spanish Resources** **Cooperative Learning Resource Guide** **Videodisc Correlations** (to Optical Data's and Videodiscovery's videodiscs)

* Probing Levels of Life
** Investigating Living Systems

* Science Technology Videodisc Series

Key to Teaching Strategies

The following designations will help you decide which activities in the teacher margin are appropriate for your students.

L1 Level 1 activities should be within the ability range of all students.

L2 Level 2 activities should be within the ability range of the average to above-average student.

L3 Level 3 activities are designed for the ability range of above-average students.

LEP LEP activities are appropriate for Limited English Proficiency students.

COOP LEARN Cooperative Learning activities are designed for small group work.

ADDITIONAL RESOURCES

Infinite Voyage *The Champion Within*
Students will learn all about the human body and its potential in this video about exercise and health.

Audiovisual
Locomotion and Skeletons, video, Frey Scientific.
Muscle Power, video, Films for the Humanities and Sciences.

Software
Locomotion, Apple II/TRS-80/Model III, J and S.

MOVEMENT

Chapter Overview

Students are introduced to the functions of skeletal systems. They compare the exoskeletons of arthropods and the endoskeletons of vertebrates. As they do so, they learn how the latter overcome certain limitations imposed by the former. Students study the development, structure, and functions of bones as well as the various types of joints they form.

Students then study means of movement in animals having muscles but no skeletons. They compare such movement in cnidarians, earthworms, clams, and starfish. Students then focus upon movement and locomotion in arthropods and vertebrates, learning how coordination of both muscles and skeleton contributes to greater efficiency. They explore the antagonistic roles of flexors and extensors and then compare and contrast the structure and functions of vertebrate muscle types. After studying the sliding filament hypothesis, students learn of the various means by which ATP is made available for contraction. Finally, they find out that cilia and flagella function in a manner analogous to muscle.

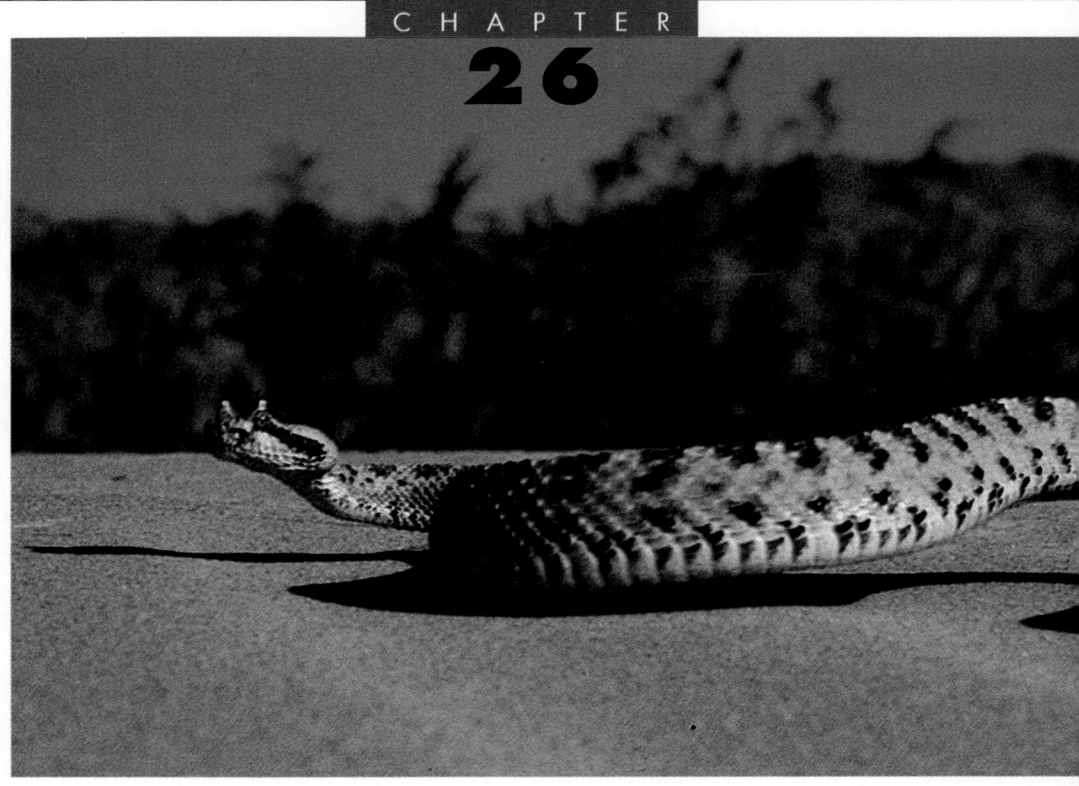

MOVEMENT

LIKE HUNDREDS of tiny oars, the many cilia of *Paramecium* propel it through the water. Powered by contraction of muscles in its hind legs, a frog leaps into the air. Muscles also control the burrowing of an earthworm, the graceful flight of a butterfly, the sidewinding movement of a snake, the creeping of a snail, and the jumping and tumbling of a cheerleader. Cilia and muscles are examples of effectors. After stimulation by a motor nerve, effectors such as muscles respond.

Muscle contraction may contribute to locomotion, the movement of an entire organism, as in the examples above. Effectors also may contribute to the movement of individual parts of an organism, like the tentacle of a hydra, the mouthparts of a grasshopper, or the fingers of a violin player. Movement, whether of the organism or one or more of its parts, is a characteristic of animals and animal-like organisms. It is related to their heterotrophic way of life, in which they must secure food and avoid becoming food for some other organisms.

KEY TERMS

cardiac muscle	oxygen debt
cartilage	sarcomere
extensor	sliding filament hypothesis
fiber	
fibril	smooth muscle
flexor	striated muscle
Haversian canal	tendon
joint	water-vascular system
ligament	
ossification	
osteocyte	

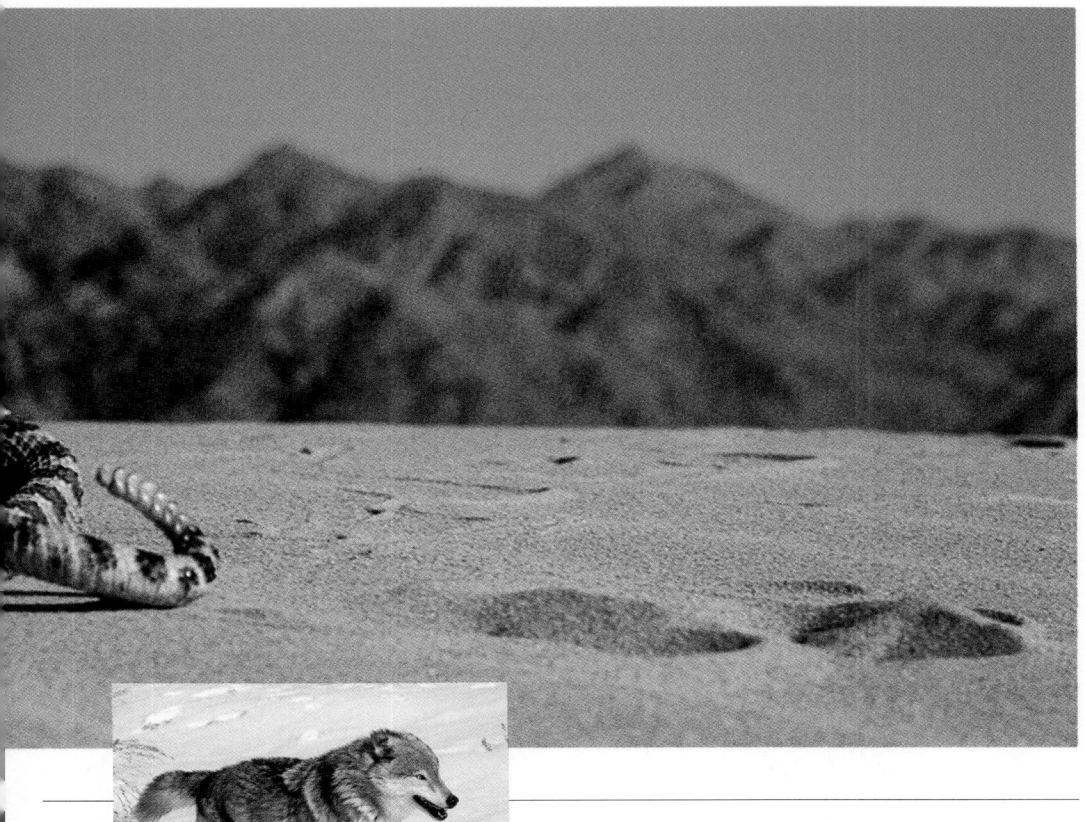

Predators like the wolf are adapted to capturing prey on the run. How are the wolf and the snake alike? What features enable both organisms to capture their food?

Chapter Preview

Introducing the Chapter

Discussion of the sidewinding movement of the snake pictured on pages 728 and 729 will motivate students to think about various modes of movement and locomotion. Have them distinguish between the two and then ask them to give examples of both, for example, flying, walking, hopping, and swimming for locomotion. Ask them to provide specific examples of organisms for each category they have identified. At the end of this exercise, ask them what kinds of organisms are missing from their list of examples (plants and fungi, most probably). Following up on the organisms that exhibit neither movement nor locomotion, guide students to recognize the roles of nerves, muscles, and skeletons in most types of movement.

Theme Development

Systems and interactions is an important theme throughout the chapter. The interplay between flexors and extensors, muscles and bones, nerves and muscles, and, on the molecular level, between thin and thick filaments illustrates the theme of systems and interactions. The theme of energy is also important as students examine the need for ATP energy in muscle contraction and in movement of cilia and flagella.

Tying to Previous Knowledge

Students have previously learned that arthropods have exoskeletons and vertebrates have endoskeletons. They will compare and contrast these two types of skeletal systems in this chapter. The knowledge of muscle structure and function they will gain in this chapter relates to nerve impulses and synapses, topics just studied in Chapter 25; the two chapters can be tied together. Students will also apply their understanding of aerobic respiration, fermentation, and ATP function as they learn about the sliding filament hypothesis.

ASSESSMENT PLANNER

Choose assessment strategies from the following pages to evaluate the progress of your students.

Assess, pp. 736-737, 749-750
Portfolio, pp. 732, 735, 744, 749, 750
Alternate Lab, pp. 730-731
Thinking Lab, p. 745

Minilab 1, p. 732
Minilab 2, p. 747
Investigation, pp. 742-743
Chapter Review, pp. 754-755

Prepare

Key Concepts

Students will compare and contrast exoskeletons and endoskeletons of a variety of animals. They will study the development and structure of bones and joints.

Key Terms

joint, cartilage, ossification, Haversian canal, osteocyte, ligament

Materials

- Gather a variety of exoskeletons, endoskeletons, and other materials for the Minilab.

1 Focus

Objectives

The objectives are listed on the student page. Remind students to preview these objectives as a guide to this numbered section.

Activity

Assign students to one of several groups. Give each group of students three containers and an earthworm, a crayfish, and a frog. Have students place one animal in each container. Ask them to observe and describe how these animals move. They should explain the ways in which the movements are alike and how they are different. Ask them to explain why the earthworm cannot jump and why the frog cannot crawl. **L1** **LEP**

COOP LEARN

Objectives

Compare the structures and functions of exoskeletons and endoskeletons.

Discuss the development of bone and its structure.

Demonstrate various ways in which different bones form joints.

Figure 26-1 Arthropods, left, and vertebrates, right, have skeletons and muscles that work together to create movement. What types of organisms have no skeletons?

26.1 Skeletal Systems

Most animals have the ability to move at some stage of their lives. Even if an animal does not move, it requires some kind of support. Without support, an animal would collapse from its own body weight. Many aquatic invertebrates such as jellyfish are supported by the water in which they live. Movements of these animals, though, are most often slow and sluggish.

The Exoskeleton

Think about the most active animals you know. You probably thought of animals belonging to two groups—arthropods and vertebrates. These animals, whether living in water or on land, have muscles that function in both movement and support. They also have an additional means of support—a skeleton. The muscles and skeleton work together, providing an efficient means of locomotion and movement of individual body parts. The skeletons of arthropods and vertebrates also protect the organism and serve as holding areas for needed minerals. Invertebrates such as sponges, sea stars (starfish), and clams do not have skeletons, although they do have mineral deposits in their tissues. These deposits contribute to support and protection of the organism, but not to movement.

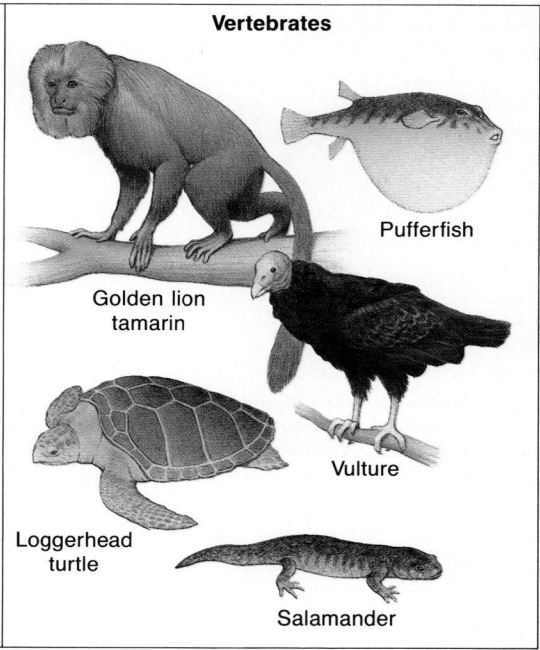

Arthropods

Flea

Dragonfly

Walking stick

Centipede

Lobster

Horseshoe crab

Scorpion

Vertebrates

Pufferfish

Golden lion tamarin

Vulture

Loggerhead turtle

Salamander

730 🐚 MOVEMENT

ALTERNATE LAB: How do crayfish move?

Purpose

Students will determine how crayfish move under a variety of conditions.

Materials

1 crayfish, 2 plastic shoeboxes or similar containers, distilled water

Procedure

Give the following directions to students.

1. Pick up your crayfish and put it in a dry, plastic shoebox. Grasp the animal with thumb and forefinger on either side of the cephalothorax above the walking legs. Describe how your crayfish walks in the dry, plastic container.

2. Place distilled water in the other container to a depth of about 6 cm. Now pick up the crayfish and put it into the water. Describe how your crayfish swims in the container with water.

3. Make a data table for the speed of your crayfish walking and swimming.

4. Mark a space of a known distance on the side of the shoebox. Time how long it takes for your crayfish to traverse this space. To determine the speed of the crayfish, divide the distance by the time. This will give you a speed in cm/sec. Record your results in the table.

Analysis

Ask students to answer the following questions.

Composition of Exoskeletons   Recall from Chapter 17 that the skeleton of arthropods is external and called an exoskeleton. Exoskeletons are composed of proteins and a specialized carbohydrate material called chitin. The outer surface of many arthropods is waxy. The waxy layer protects against water loss in terrestrial arthropods. Parts of the exoskeleton may also extend inwards. In arthropods, such as insects, the muscles are attached to these inward sections of the exoskeleton. The exoskeleton of insects also forms the lining of the tubes through which air enters the body, the tracheae, thus supporting them and keeping them open.

An exoskeleton is a tough, rigid structure that is produced by the epidermal cells. The exoskeleton is divided into segments connected by soft, flexible **joints.** Joints are located between body segments, at the base of appendages, and between segments of appendages. Without joints, movement of body parts and of the entire animal would be impossible. Though protected, an arthropod would be a prisoner in its own armor.

Disadvantages of Exoskeletons   An exoskeleton has certain disadvantages. It limits the size and movement of an arthropod. Because the heavy exoskeleton needed to support a large arthropod would seriously limit movement on land, most adult terrestrial arthropods are small. However, some arthropods that live in water are able to grow much larger than those on land. A giant crab that lives in the ocean near Japan can be as large as 3.6 m across!

Growth is also limited in arthropods. Once the exoskeleton is made and it hardens, its size cannot be changed. Growth only takes place because molting, the shedding of the exoskeleton, occurs. When an arthropod sheds its exoskeleton, the new exoskeleton underneath is stretched by increased blood pressure, and by the intake of air or water by the organism. This increases the size of the animal before the new exoskeleton hardens. Molting may occur many times before an arthropod reaches its final adult size. Some spiders molt 10 times before they reach sexual maturity and molting stops. After each molt, the new skeleton is soft, making an arthropod easy prey for predators. For example, soft-shell crabs are merely crabs that have been caught after a molt but before the exoskeleton has hardened. The animal has neither its armorlike protection nor the ability to move rapidly. Land arthropods lose water when molting. Would you expect to find terrestrial arthropods hiding under rocks just after they have molted? Why?

Figure 26-2   **In this photograph of a praying mantis, you can see why insects are arthropods. The word *arthropod* means *jointed leg.***

Figure 26-3   **Arthropods must shed their exoskeletons in order to increase in size.**

26.1 SKELETAL SYSTEMS **731**

S E C T I O N   26.1

2 Teach

Using an Analogy

Make an analogy between a full suit of armor and an arthropod's exoskeleton. Have students identify limitations that might be imposed on life activities by the exoskeleton of an arthropod. **L1**   **COOP LEARN**

Figure Caption Question

What types of organisms have no skeletons? Invertebrates, excluding arthropods

Activity

Ask students to bring in pill bugs and sow bugs. They are isopods that can be found under moist, fallen logs and in other moist, dark places. Pill bugs curl into a ball when threatened, and sow bugs try to escape by moving away. Have them examine the exoskeletons of pill bugs and sow bugs. Have them describe the exoskeletons. Have them answer the following questions: How are the exoskeletons alike? How are they different? **L1**   **LEP**

Using the Photo

In Figure 26-3, the students may be unable to determine which is the organism and which the shed exoskeleton. The exoskeleton is on the left side of the photograph.

Text Question

Would you expect to find terrestrial arthropods hiding under rocks just after they have molted? Why? Yes, because newly molted organisms are not protected by a hard exoskeleton; they hide until the new exoskeleton has hardened.

---

1. What are crayfish adaptations to walking? *Walking legs*
2. What are crayfish adaptations to swimming? *Abdomen and tail*
3. How does the crayfish's exoskeleton help it survive? *It protects it from predators and other harmful factors.*
4. How is the exoskeleton constructed to allow for movement? *It has flexible joints.*

5. Compare how a crayfish walks with how it swims. *The crayfish walks with four pairs of legs. It swims awkwardly by making a series of rapid downward movements of the abdomen, which moves it backward in a jerky manner.*

✔ Assessment

Performance: Have students choose an invertebrate from a list you prepare. Each student must then pretend to move as that animal would in front of the class. Have other students guess what the organism is. **L1**   **COOP LEARN**

Minilab 1

Purpose
Students will be able to compare exoskeletons and endoskeletons and discover that endoskeletons are articulated.

Skills
observe and infer, compare and contrast, interpret data

Teaching Strategies
- On a table at the side of the room, set up 10 to 20 objects with a numbered card next to each one. Include various bones, a turtle skeleton, spines from a sea urchin, a sand dollar, one or two shells, shed exoskeletons of arthropods, a puffball, and a microscope with a slide of diatoms on the stage.
- Have students walk past the table and record their impressions. Then, collect their papers and record their answers on the chalkboard before you tell them what each item is.
- You may want to include the shed skin of a snake in your display as well.

Expected Results
Students should be able to identify bones or skeletons as endoskeletons and shed exoskeletons. They may have trouble with sand dollars, sea urchin spines, shells, or the shed skin of a snake. Students should be able to state that skeletons permit or aid movement, whereas shells, spines, and skin do not.

Answers
Student answers should include all bones as endoskeletons and all shed exoskeletons as exoskeletons. They should be able to state that shells do not aid in movement and thus are not skeletons.

✔ Assessment
Skill: Have students write an essay describing the differences between endoskeletons and exoskeletons, and how they know that a clam shell is neither an endoskeleton nor an exoskeleton.

Minilab 1

How do exoskeletons and endoskeletons compare?

Your teacher has placed a variety of objects on display. Some are exoskeletons, some are endoskeletons, and some are neither exoskeletons nor endoskeletons. On a piece of paper, write the numbers corresponding to each object, then write beside each number the word *endo*, *exo*, or *neither*.

Analysis *Which objects did you label as exoskeletons? As endoskeletons? As neither? How do you know which are which? Explain your answers.*

Advantages of Exoskeletons Despite the limitations on size and growth, the exoskeleton has certain advantages. An exoskeleton protects animals from predators and from physical harm. In terrestrial arthropods, the exoskeleton guards against water loss. The exoskeleton also allows movement and supports the animal. Many scientists credit the evolution of the exoskeleton as the reason for the amazing versatility of the arthropods. There are more species of arthropods known than are found in all other animal phyla combined. This great diversity of arthropods is due in part to the exoskeleton. In fact, the presence of an exoskeleton may have been critical to the success of arthropods on land.

The Endoskeleton

In vertebrates, the skeleton lies within the soft tissues of the body rather than outside the body. Recall that such an internal skeleton is called an endoskeleton. Although an endoskeleton and an exoskeleton function similarly, they differ in development and structure and are not homologous. Vertebrates and arthropods (which are invertebrates) evolved from different ancestors.

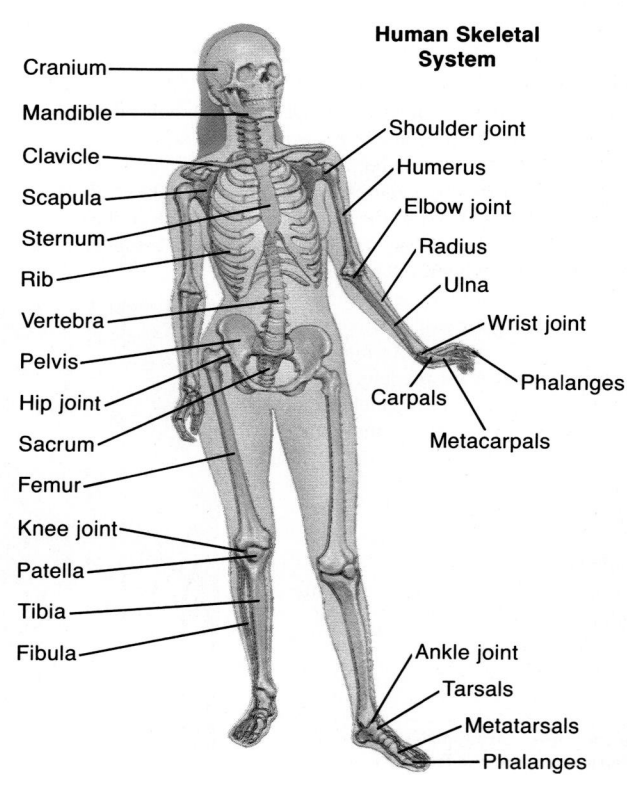

Human Skeletal System

Cranium — Mandible — Clavicle — Scapula — Sternum — Rib — Vertebra — Pelvis — Hip joint — Sacrum — Femur — Knee joint — Patella — Tibia — Fibula

Shoulder joint — Humerus — Elbow joint — Radius — Ulna — Wrist joint — Phalanges — Carpals — Metacarpals — Ankle joint — Tarsals — Metatarsals — Phalanges

Figure 26-4 The human skeletal system includes 206 bones. Why do you think an endoskeleton has so many parts?

Functions of Endoskeletons Unlike an exoskeleton, which covers the entire animal in one continuous unit, an endoskeleton is subdivided into many distinct parts. These individual parts, called bones, are specialized for certain functions and types of movements.

Some bones function in protection. Skull bones, ribs, and the breastbone protect the brain, lungs, and heart. The column of vertebrae called a backbone forms a hollow tube to protect the spinal cord.

In humans, the vertebrae also function in another way. The shape of the human vertebral column is unique. Humans have upright posture and locomotion. The "s" curve of the vertebral column aids in distributing and supporting body weight, thus making upright locomotion possible.

Bones also function in support. The long, dense thighbones support the weight of the body and aid the speed and strength of movement. Some bones, such as the delicate finger bones, are adapted for precise, small movements. Many bones function in several ways. For example, the ribs not only provide protection, but also aid breathing.

Advantages of Endoskeletons Internal skeletons protect the internal organs of the body but give little external protection, except the skull, which protects the brain. Some animals with endoskeletons also have skeletal adaptations that give more external protection. For example, turtles are covered by a shell made of bony plates. The plates are made of bone covered by scales. The plates are fused with the ribs of the endoskeleton but do not originate from the ribs in their development.

Limited size and growth are the main disadvantages of an exoskeleton, but size and growth are not as limited in animals with endoskeletons. Because bones are alive and can grow, there is no loss of protection or support as the animal grows. Animals with endoskeletons do have an upper size limit, but as bones are stronger than exoskeletons, they can support greater mass. Muscles of animals with endoskeletons are larger, too, thus providing additional support.

Figure 26-5 **Like the exoskeleton of a crab, a turtle's shell protects it from predators. Is a turtle's shell homologous to the shell of a crab?**

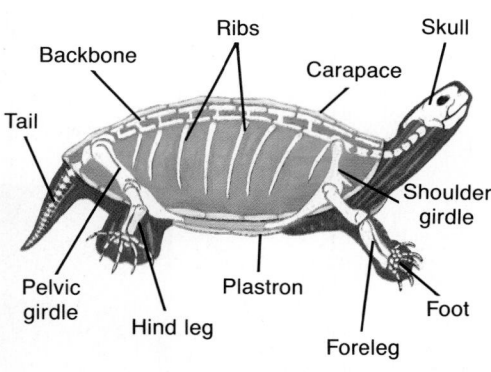

Turtle Skeleton

26.1 SKELETAL SYSTEMS ❧ **733**

Brainstorming
Give students the following list of types of movement and ask them to think of as many animals as they can that use that type of locomotion as their primary means of movement: walking, running, crawling, leaping, flying, swimming, climbing, and gliding. Ask them to decide how endoskeletons of the above groups are adapted to that particular type of locomotion. **L1** **COOP LEARN**

Misconception
Many students think that bone is dead tissue. Explain to them that it consists of living cells and completely renews itself every two years.

Demonstration
Use a model of the human skeleton to demonstrate how the skull and ribs function in protection; how the strong thighbones function in support; and how the delicate finger bones are adapted for precise, small movements. Point out a variety of other bones and ask students how they are adapted for specific functions.

Figure Caption Question
Is a turtle's shell homologous to the shell of a crab? No, the crab's shell is an exoskeleton, whereas the turtle's shell is formed from bone.

Activity
Provide students with animal skeletons purchased from a biological supply house, or prepare chicken skeletons by boiling chickens and removing the meat. Take the skeletons apart before class. Ask students to lay the bones out in correct order on large sheets of paper. **L1** **LEP** **COOP LEARN**

MEETING INDIVIDUAL NEEDS

Visually Impaired: Make photocopies of the diagrams in the chapter. Ask a group of students to cut out sandpaper outlines of features of the diagrams and glue these onto the diagrams for use by students who are visually impaired.

PROJECT

Types of Fractures: Ask a group of students to report on various types of fractures in bones and the treatment required for each type of fracture. **L2** **COOP LEARN**

733

SECTION 26.1

Different Viewpoints in Biology

Treating Osteoporosis
Osteoporosis is a disease in which bones lose calcium and become brittle and easily broken. It is a disorder that is common in women after menopause. Lack of estrogen is thought to cause progressive symptoms, and hormone therapy is often standard treatment. In an experimental therapy, a drug that suppresses osteoclasts is given for two weeks, then alternated with two weeks of calcium treatments in order to allow the osteoblasts to build bone. After two years of treatment, women being treated for osteoporosis with this therapy showed a 4 to 5 percent increase in spinal bone density. Researchers are studying these patients to determine if bone building continues over a long period of time.

Text Question

Where in the human body is cartilage found? How is that cartilage important? Cartilage is found in the ears, nose, ends of bones, joints, and wherever flexibility is needed.

Development of Bone

Because bone is made up of minerals and is hard, many people think that it is not living material. But a bone in a living animal is a living tissue.

Ossification In a vertebrate fetus, most of the skeleton is made up of **cartilage,** a tough, flexible tissue that has no minerals. As the fetus grows, living cells called osteoblasts slowly replace cartilage cells and ossification begins. **Ossification** is the replacement of cartilage with bone by the activity of osteoblasts and addition of minerals such as calcium compounds. By the time an animal is born, many of the bones have been at least partly ossified. Some bones are not formed by ossification of cartilage. Bones of the face and skull, for example, are formed as osteoblasts fill in membranes. In humans, ossification is not completed until about age 25. During this period, the stresses of physical activity result in the strengthening of bone tissue. This process continues until about age 40, when the activity of osteoblasts slows and bones become more brittle.

Materials Used in Ossification Calcium compounds must be present for ossification to take place. Osteoblasts do not make these minerals, but must take them from the blood and deposit them in the bone. Because this process begins in the fetus, the minerals are first obtained from the mother's blood through the placenta. Thus, it is important that the mother eat a well-balanced diet, taking in the proper amounts of minerals and other nutrients.

Because bones grow after the birth of an animal, ossification continues and calcium compounds are still needed. Foods rich in calcium include milk, cheese, meats, vegetables, and whole grain cereals. Vitamin D is needed for proper bone development because it is necessary for calcium absorption from blood. Vitamin D is present not only in milk, but also in egg yolk, fish oils, and liver. It is also made in the skin in the presence of sunlight. Rickets, a disease that results in severe bone deformities, is caused by inadequate amounts of vitamin D.

Not all cartilage is replaced by bone. Some cartilage remains at the ends of bones to provide smooth joint surfaces. In some vertebrates, such as sharks, the whole skeleton remains cartilage throughout the life of the animal. However, in most vertebrates, only a few parts remain as cartilage. Where in the human body is cartilage found? How is that cartilage important?

Figure 26-6 **A child with rickets, left, is unable to form bone properly due to a lack of vitamin D. Sharks, right, are fish that do not undergo complete ossification.**

734

Cartilage
Spongy bone
Osteocyte
Compact bone
Marrow cavity
Blood vessel
Periosteum
Haversian canals

Structure of Bone

Have you ever broken a bone? Did your bone bleed? Bleeding is not surprising when you have broken a bone because bones are living tissue.

Types of Bone Tissue   All bones are enclosed by an outer membrane called the periosteum. The periosteum supplies blood vessels and nerves to the bone, and contains cells needed by the bone for growth and repair. Most bones are made up of two types of bone tissue: compact bone and spongy bone. The shafts of long bones, such as the femur, are composed of hard, compact bone. The ends of these bones are composed of spongy bone underneath a layer of compact bone. Compact bone is made of alternating layers of a protein called collagen and minerals, and contains many tiny channels called **Haversian canals.** Haversian canals carry blood vessels and nerves that supply osteocytes in the bone tissue. **Osteocytes** are mature osteoblasts found in most formed bone tissue. Spongy bone is composed of a system of cavities and intersecting plates. Spongy bone contains blood vessels and marrow, a tissue that produces blood cells and stores fat.

Bone Marrow   Marrow is found in the central hollows of the sternum, ribs, pelvis, vertebrae, skull, and the long bones of the arms and legs. Red marrow produces red blood cells, some white blood cells, and platelets. Yellow marrow stores excess fat. Marrow also functions in formation of bone cells. Bones without marrow—such as the small bones of the wrist and ankle—are spongy bone.

Figure 26-7   **There are three types of bone cells—osteoblasts, osteoclasts, and osteocytes. Osteoblasts form new bone, whereas osteoclasts break down bone. Osteocytes, as seen in the diagram, are found in most formed bone tissue. What kind of bone cells would you expect to see at the site of a broken bone? Magnification: 400×**

Science, Technology, and Society

Making Bones from Muscles: Recently, biologists have made a leg bone and jaw bone for a rat from muscle. Into tiny bone-shaped molds they placed a piece of rat thigh muscle treated with osteogenin, a bone protein that promotes bone growth in the fetus, and pulverized bone. After 10 days of incubation in a surgically produced abdominal pouch, the muscle changed to bone. Biologists hope that one day similar human natural bone might be used to replace broken, diseased, and worn out human bones.

Activity

- Obtain bones from the meat department of a grocery store or butcher shop. Ask the meat cutter to cut some bones crosswise and others lengthwise. Keep the bones frozen until you plan to use them in class. Ask students to identify the compact bone, spongy bone, and marrow, and discuss the differences in structure and function of these tissues. [L1] [LEP]

- Ask a local physician or hospital for old or imperfect X rays showing different bones, joints, fractures, and repairs using metal parts. Ask students to use the overhead projector to compare them to a model skeleton or diagram to determine what part of the skeleton is represented in the X ray. Ask them if they can tell the difference between males and females and between adults and children. [L1] [LEP]

26.1 SKELETAL SYSTEMS   **735**

PORTFOLIO

Ask students to design, in their portfolios, a model of an arm based on their observations of a model skeleton. They should use the tubes from paper towel rolls for bones, unbent paper clips for fasteners, and slightly inflated long balloons for muscles. After their diagrams are complete, they should try to build their models. [LEP]

Teacher FYI

Bone marrow in an adult produces more than 200 billion red blood cells each day.

Building a Model

Collect old tennis balls, plastic cups, rulers, and adhesive tape to use in making models of hip joints. Tell students to make two cuts on opposite sides of a tennis ball. The cuts should be about 3 cm down from the same point on opposite sides of the ball and about 5 cm wide. Students should push a wood or plastic ruler through the cuts. This model represents the femur and ball. Next, have them place a plastic cup over the ball so that it fits just inside the rim of the cup. This represents the acetabulum. Next, they should attach adhesive tape loosely around the bottom of the cup and tape the ends to each side of the ruler. Ask them how much movement the "hip" can undergo before it comes out of the cup. Students will have varying amounts of movement in their "hips." Ask them what the tape represents. *Ligaments* Ask them if the variations in "flexibility" of their "hips" reflect similar flexibility in humans. L1 LEP

Text Question

Are there other ball-and-socket joints in the human body? If so, where? Yes, where the humerus enters the shoulder

Figure Caption Question

What kind of joint is found in your ankle? Gliding joint

3 Assess

Check for Understanding

Give students an exoskeleton from a mealworm and a bone from any vertebrate. Ask them to make a list of the advantages and disadvantages of the type of skeleton each item represents. Also ask them to explain the development and structure of the bone you have provided. L1

Joints in Vertebrates

Every time you open a door, you are using a type of joint. The door is joined to the door frame with a joint called a hinge. In vertebrates, joints are the points where bones connect with one another. Most joints are movable and are held together by muscles and by connective tissue called **ligaments.** Ligaments are made of collagen and some elastic fibers. The ends of bones are covered by a layer of cartilage. Between cartilage and the ends of the bones are fluid-filled bags called bursas. Bursas cushion the ends of the bones and prevent them from rubbing against each other.

Types of Joints   There are four main types of joints in vertebrates: ball-and-socket joints, hinge joints, pivot joints, and gliding joints. You can see the types of joints in Figure 26-8.

The most flexible of all joints is the ball-and-socket joint. In humans, this type of joint is found where the upper end of the femur (thighbone) joins the pelvis (hipbone). The end of the femur is rounded into a knob that fits into a depression in the pelvis. The femur can rotate, as well as move from front to back or side to side. Are there other ball-and-socket joints in the human body? If so, where?

Hinge joints exist in many places within the human body, such as the fingers. Like a hinge on a door, hinge joints can move in only one direction. A door can only be opened or closed; your fingers can only be bent toward your palm or straightened. They cannot be bent in another direction. Hinge joints are also found in the elbows, knees, and toes.

Shoulder
Ball-and-Socket Joint

Neck Vertebrae
Pivot Joint

Elbow
Hinge Joint

Wrist
Gliding Joint

Figure 26-8   The four main types of joints in vertebrates are the ball-and-socket, pivot, hinge, and gliding joints. What kind of joint is found in your ankle?

PROJECT

Testing for Flexibility: Have students conduct tests for flexibility at home. Here are a few suggestions students may use.
(a) Take your shoes off and point your toes. How close to a straight line is it between your shin and the tips of your toes?
(b) With shoes off, how far can you bend your knees without lifting your heels off the floor? Keep your back straight.
(c) Lay on your back and pull one leg toward your head. How far can you go?
(d) Lay on your stomach; push up with your hands at the same time you bend your knees to try to touch your head with your toes.
Have students keep results of their tests and record them in their journals. L1

Femur
Ligaments
Cartilage
Cartilage
Ligament
Ligament
Ligament (cut)
Fibula
Tibia

Figure 26-9 This diagram of the right knee with the knee cap removed shows how the femur is attached to the lower leg bones by ligaments. Most knee injuries are the result of torn ligaments. Can you see why ligaments would be torn if a hinge joint like the knee was hit from the side?

Rotation can occur in a pivot joint. One example of a pivot joint is where the bones of the lower arm connect near the elbow. This joint allows the radius to rotate over the ulna when the hand is turned over. The cranium, or skull, is connected to the spine by a pivot joint. With this joint, the head can turn, as well as move up and down.

Vertebrae are linked by gliding joints. In gliding joints, the bones move easily over one another in a back-and-forth manner. Gliding joints aid the flexibility of the backbone and are found in wrists and ankles.

Fixed Joints   Some joints in vertebrates do not move. In adult humans, the individual bones of the skull are held together by fixed joints. In fixed joints, the bones are fused; these joints are not connected by ligaments. In babies and children, the skull bones are not fused together, but rather have soft spots between them. Why do you think this is so?

Figure 26-10 The bones of the skull meet in fixed joints. Where are the fixed joints on this human skull?

Section Review

Understanding Concepts
1. Think about an arthropod, such as an ant, and a vertebrate, such as a lizard. What functions do the skeletons of these animals have in common? Do they have a common structure? Explain.
2. Why do you think spongy bone has an outer layer of compact bone?

3. Think about the possible movements of your lower arm and lower leg. How do the movements differ and why?
4. **Skill Review—Comparing and Contrasting:** Compare and contrast exoskeletons and endoskeletons in terms of how they determine growth and size of the animals that

have them. For more help, see Thinking Critically in the **Skill Handbook.**
5. **Thinking Critically:** Why are the largest arthropods, such as lobsters, found living in water?

SECTION 26.1

Reteach
Make photocopies of the figures in the chapter. Make them into flash cards with the diagram on one side and the caption on the other. Ask students to work together in small groups to check one another's understanding of this section.

Extension
Ask students to investigate common joint injuries such as sprains, cartilage injuries, and dislocations and find out what part of the joint is affected in each. They should also research common inflammatory conditions such as arthritis, bursitis, and tendonitis. **L2**

✔ Assessment
Knowledge: Set up a practical exam in which you place specimens and diagrams of exoskeletons and endoskeletons on a display table. Mark each item with pins or tape labels and questions about animal movement, bone structure, and development. Give students about one minute at each station in the display before they move on. **L1**

4   Close

Activity
Invite a forensic pathologist to speak to the class about the kinds of information that can be learned from skeletal remains about the health and medical history of the victim.

Prepare

Key Concepts

Students will compare and contrast movement in animals that have skeletons and animals that do not. They will study the types of vertebrate muscles and learn about their structures and functions.

Key Terms

water-vascular system, tendon, flexor, extensor, striated muscle, fiber, smooth muscle, cardiac muscle, fibril, sarcomere, sliding filament hypothesis, oxygen debt

Materials

- Gather various types of bones, cartilage, and muscle for the Investigation.
- Gather stopwatches for the Minilab.

1 Focus

Objectives

The objectives are listed on the student page. Remind students to preview these objectives as a guide to this numbered section.

Activity

Provide students with a hydra, a snail, and a mouse. Ask them to describe the movements of these animals. Ask them to speculate how the muscles of each of the animals are different. Ask them how the muscles are adapted to the lifestyle of the animal. L1

Objectives

Describe examples of movement in animals lacking skeletons.

Distinguish among the three types of vertebrate muscles and their characteristics.

Relate the events of muscle contraction to the ways in which energy is made available for that contraction.

26.2 Effectors and Their Actions

Locomotion and movement of body parts are important in many ways: obtaining food, avoiding predators, reproducing, and reacting to a variety of environmental factors such as light, heat, and chemicals. How do the effectors that contribute to movement work? How do muscles of arthropods and vertebrates attach to the skeleton, and how do the two work together to cause movement? How do animals lacking skeletons move by muscles alone? How do unicellular organisms lacking both muscles and skeletons move?

Movement Without a Skeleton

Movement in animals without a skeleton is limited. How do invertebrates move? Recall from Chapter 17 that cnidarians exist in two forms, polyp and medusa. Let's see how some cnidarians move.

Hydra is most often a sessile polyp, but it can move by somersaulting, as seen in Figure 26-11. Other cnidarians spend most of their life cycles as medusas, such as jellyfish. Jellyfish float freely in the water or move by contracting their muscle cells, forcing water from under the bell-shaped medusa to create a jet propulsion effect. The jellyfish moves in the direction opposite to that of the expelled water.

Earthworms are adapted for locomotion in soil. Their movement is controlled by two sets of muscles. As one set of muscles contracts to shorten the body, the other set then contracts, resulting in a lengthening of the body. Interaction of these two sets of muscles causes movement. In addition, bristles called setae extend backward from each segment of an earthworm. With setae, a worm "grasps" the soil, resulting in smoother movement.

Other means of locomotion occur in mollusks and echinoderms. Clams have a muscular foot that can be extended between the shells. To move, a clam extends the foot and anchors it in the sand. The muscles of the foot contract at the rear, lifting and coming down again. The rest of the foot moves forward from the rear in a wavelike series of movements.

Figure 26-11 Invertebrates have evolved unique ways to move. *Hydra*, left, somersaults from place to place. The setae of earthworms, right, grip the soil so that muscles can contract and move the earthworm forward.

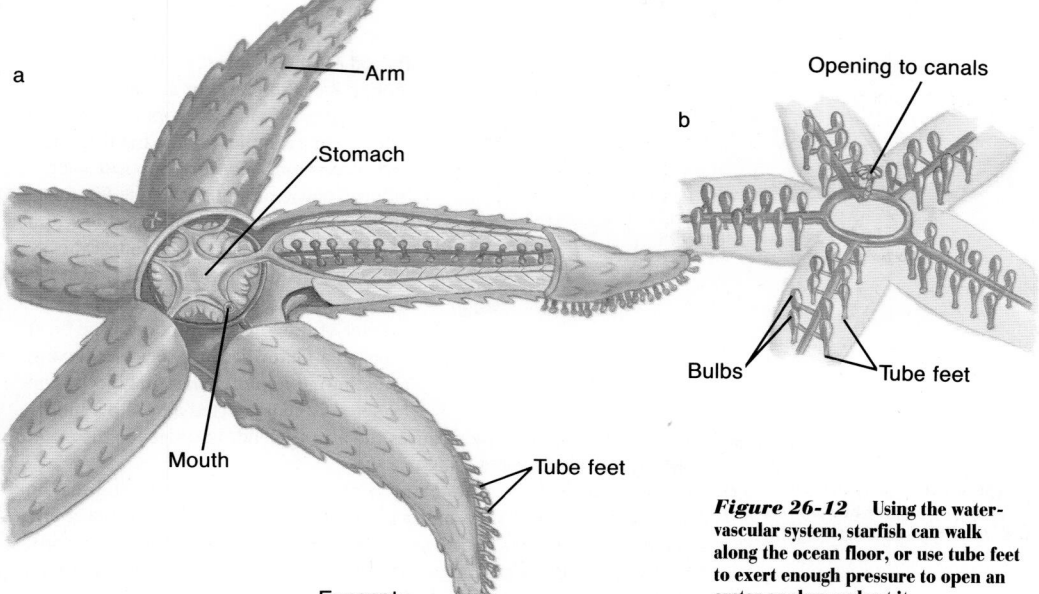

a

Arm

Stomach

Mouth

Tube feet

Eyespot

b

Opening to canals

Bulbs

Tube feet

Figure 26-12 Using the water-vascular system, starfish can walk along the ocean floor, or use tube feet to exert enough pressure to open an oyster or clam and eat it.

In starfish, movement is controlled by a unique **water-vascular system,** pictured in Figure 26-12. Water is drawn into the animal through a small opening in the central disc and is passed to canals running along each "arm." Along each canal are hollow, muscular tube feet that are found on the underside of the starfish. The bottom part of each tube foot flattens out like a sucker. The upper part of the tube foot is a bulb-like structure. The bulb contains water that comes from the canal. When the bulbs contract, water is forced into the tube feet and they lengthen. If pressed against a surface, the tube feet stick on like small suction cups. When muscles of the bulbs relax, water pushes back up through the canals and the tube feet shorten, releasing the suction. Each tube foot works independently of the others. A starfish can creep along rocks by alternately pushing out and pulling in its tube feet.

Movement: Vertebrates and Arthropods

Because they have both muscles and a skeleton, vertebrates are capable of a great variety of movement. Muscles are attached to the skeleton. As muscles contract, they pull on the skeletal system. The pull results in movement. In vertebrates, most muscles are attached to bones by tough connective tissues called **tendons.** Muscles are attached to bones at two different sites. During contraction, one end of the muscle and the bone to which it is attached do not move. This attachment site is called the point of origin. The other end of the muscle and the bone to which it is attached move when the muscle contracts. This attachment site is called the point of insertion. Attachment of a muscle to two sites is necessary for movement.

26.2 EFFECTORS AND THEIR ACTIONS **739**

LEISURE CONNECTION

Choosing Athletic Shoes: What should students look for in an athletic shoe? The shoe serves two functions for a runner: it must create friction with the running surface to keep the runner from slipping, and it must act as an extension of the Achilles tendon. When running, the front foot lands with a force triple that of the body weight. The Achilles tendon compresses like a spring storing energy. When the runner rolls forward onto the ball of the foot, the tendon springs forward, pushing the runner ahead. Because a sprinter spends more time on the balls of the feet, the shoes should have more cushioning in the front. A middle-distance runner needs more cushioning in the middle of the foot and heel. A marathoner needs most cushioning in the heel. If the shoes are worn for five to ten hours per week during exercise, they should probably be replaced in six months in order to maintain good cushioning.

STUDENT JOURNAL

Give students a diagram of the main muscles of the human body. Ask them to look up their names and functions and be able to demonstrate the functions with their partners. They should put this information into their journals.
L1

PROGRAM RESOURCES

Teacher Classroom Resources
Study Guide, pp. 153-156 L1
Concept Mapping, p. 26 L1 LEP
Color Transparency #27, 48 L1 LEP
Probing Levels of Life, Labs 69-73,
  pp. 179-190 L2
Investigating Living Systems, Labs 72, 73,
  pp. 279, 285 L2

MATH CONNECTION

Purpose
Students will study a variety of ways animals move and compare relative speeds of animals.

Background
A hummingbird's wings look like the wings of other birds, but the joints in the "hand" bones are rigid and the shoulder joint is more flexible, allowing the wing to move freely in almost any direction. This flexibility does not allow the hummingbird to soar or glide. It must flap its wings continuously.

Teaching Strategies
- On the chalkboard, list the organisms shown in the table. Ask students to list the organisms in order of their speed, from fastest to slowest. Ask students to give reasons for their selections.

Possible Answers
1. To travel one meter, it takes an ant 1/.03 = 33.3 seconds. In 33.3 seconds, a squirrel travels 33.3 × 2 = 66.6 meters.
2. Examples of speed records for running 100 m: men, 9.86 seconds; women, 10.49 seconds. Examples of speed records for swimming 100 m: men, 48.42 seconds; women, 54.73 seconds. People can run faster than they can swim because arm muscles are not as strong as leg muscles and because water provides more resistance than air.

Going Further
Ask students to get a copy of the National Wildlife Federation's book titled *Amazing Animals* by Thomas B. Allen, Karen Jensen, and Philip Kopper. Ask them to read and report on the first section, titled "Wonders in Motion." L2

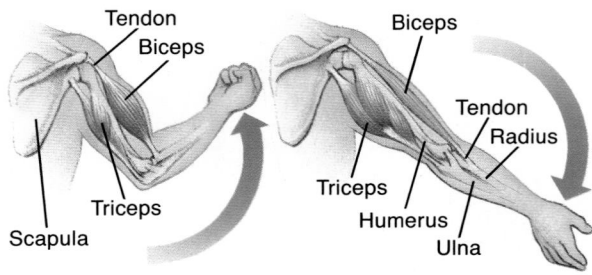

Figure 26-13 To bend your arm, the biceps muscle contracts while the triceps muscle relaxes (left). Your arm straightens when the biceps relaxes and the triceps contracts (right).

Paired Muscles Muscles that cause locomotion work in pairs (or at least in two opposing groups) in arthropods and vertebrates. For example, in humans the biceps and triceps muscles work opposite each other to cause motion. Examine Figure 26-13. The biceps originates on the scapula (shoulder blade). The other end of the biceps is attached to the radius (lower arm), the point of insertion. The radius is the smaller of the lower arm bones. The biceps is called a **flexor** because it causes flexing (bending) at a joint. When the biceps contracts, a force is exerted across the hinge joint of the elbow, which causes the arm to bend. In order for the arm to bend, the triceps must relax.

To straighten the arm, the process is reversed. The triceps muscle links the back of the humerus and scapula with the ulna, the other lower arm bone. As the triceps contracts, the ulna is pulled downward, the biceps relaxes, and the arm straightens. The triceps is called an **extensor** because

---

M A T H C O N N E C T I O N

How fast do animals move?

In the United States, most humans don't often need to think about how fast they can move on foot. If they're in a hurry, they ride bicycles, drive cars, catch buses, or even take jet planes. Some animals, though, would break the speed laws if they ran on the road at top speed. For example, a cheetah can sprint at 113 kilometers (70 miles) per hour!

Locomotion Speed in Animals
Without transportation, how do humans compare in speed of locomotion to other animals? Which animals can move faster than the fastest humans? Of the animals that are faster than humans, some swim, some fly, and others run. For example, cheetahs, horses, blue whales, and vultures all travel faster than humans do.

Some animals can travel only through water. Many are amphibious and can swim or travel on land. Birds are the most versatile travelers. Many of them can swim, fly, and walk.

Locomotion Systems Locomotion systems in vertebrates use movable bones that interact with attached muscles. Most vertebrates use legs, arms, wings, tails, or fins to propel themselves, but snakes move even without limbs.

Invertebrates use a variety of specialized structures, systems, and interactions to move. They may use waving hairs or spines, for example.

Some, like vertebrates, use legs, wings, fins, or tails.

The speeds listed in the following table are the fastest speeds ever recorded for given animals. An animal can move only a short distance at its top speed. The average speed for an animal is lower than its top speed.

The animals that can move body parts fastest are not necessarily the ones that cover the greatest distance in the shortest time. For example, a hummingbird's wings move much faster than a duck hawk's do, but a duck hawk soars through the air more than twice as fast as a hummingbird. An ant's legs move rapidly, but you can see from the chart that a turtle can travel a given distance in less time.

740 🦎 MOVEMENT

MULTICULTURAL CONNECTION

Uses of Steroids: In the 1930s, Julian Percy, an African American scientist, was trying to synthesize steroids in the laboratory. Steroids are commonly thought of as dangerous drugs taken by athletes to build muscle, but steroids include some important medicinal drugs. One of the best known is cortisone, which can help to soothe and heal skin rashes, reduce inflammation of injured muscle tissue, and treat inflammatory diseases such as arthritis. When Percy began his work, steroids were very expensive and had to be extracted from cows. He used inexpensive soy bean oil from which he isolated stigmasterol, a key building block needed to make steroids.

it causes the extension (straightening) of a joint. What are the points of origin and insertion of the triceps?

Note that the bending of a joint is always due to contraction of one of the muscles of the pair. In other words, both flexing and extending are due to contraction. In order for one muscle of a pair to contract, the other must relax.

Besides bending or straightening a joint, paired muscles are important in another way. No muscle is ever completely relaxed; both muscles of a pair are always slightly contracted whether or not a movement is taking place. This condition provides enough contraction of the muscles to help support the body. Called muscle tone, this condition also keeps the muscles ready for quick contractions.

Arthropod Movement In arthropods, muscles are attached to the inside surface of the exoskeleton. Contraction of one muscle exerts a pull on the exoskeleton that results in the bending of a joint and a movement. When this muscle relaxes and the opposing muscle contracts, an opposite movement occurs.

Note that the paired muscles of arthropods function as flexors and extensors. Although arthropods and vertebrates are not closely related, they have evolved a similar type of muscular control of skeletal movements.

In general, large animals move faster than smaller ones, but many exceptions exist. For example, cheetahs are smaller than horses or elephants, but much faster. The cheetah has an unusually long stride for its size because of a flexible spine that lets its hind legs reach ahead of its front legs as it runs. Its structure and the interaction of its parts enable it to accelerate from standing still faster than most automobiles.

1. **Solve the Problem:** At the speeds provided in the chart, how many meters could a squirrel travel while an ant was traveling one meter?

2. **Explore Further:** Examine speed records for running and swimming. Why can people run faster than they can swim?

Speeds of Animals

Mammals		Reptiles	
cheetah	26.7 m/s	lizard	6.7 m/s
racehorse	19.1 m/s	turtle	2.0 m/s
blue whale	18.0 m/s	**Amphibians**	
dog	16.0 m/s	frog	1.5 m/s
human	11.0 m/s	**Fish**	
cat	10.0 m/s	tuna	20.0 m/s
rabbit	8.0 m/s	flying fish	10.0 m/s
squirrel	2.0 m/s	salmon	3.0 m/s
Birds		**Invertebrates**	
vulture	17.0 m/s	locust	4.5 m/s
ostrich (running)	9.5 m/s	dragonfly	3.0 m/s
penguin (swimming)	3.5 m/s	ant	0.03 m/s
duck (swimming)	0.7 m/s	snail	0.0025 m/s

26.2 EFFECTORS AND THEIR ACTIONS ❧ **741**

PROJECT

Laws of Physics: Ask students to find out the laws of physics involved in the following swimming motions: the push forward with the hand and arm in the water makes the water push back equally hard. *Newton's third law of motion*

The snaking S-shaped movement of hands moving through the water, while keeping them at an angle instead of pushing straight back, is more effective than pushing straight through the water. *Bernoulli's principle* L2

INVESTIGATION

Bone and Muscle Density

Time Allotment
1 class period

Objectives
Upon completing this Investigation, students will be able to:
- Understand the technique used to measure density.
- Compare density of bone from different animals.
- Compare density of bone, cartilage, and muscle.

Skills
observe and infer, compare and contrast, measure in SI

Materials
bird bones, beef bones, cartilage (removed from ends of bones), crab or lobster exoskeletons, small chunks of meat (muscle), tape, pennies, balance, large graduated cylinder, water, paper towels

Preparation
Gather all the materials listed above for each group of students. Students may bring bones from home.

Possible Hypotheses
- If the compactness of chicken bone and that of beef bone are the same, then their densities will be similar.
- If the compactness of bone is greater than that of cartilage, then the density of bone will be higher than that of cartilage.
- If the compactness of bone is greater than that of muscle, then the density of bone will be higher than that of muscle.
- If the compactness of exoskeleton is greater than that of endoskeleton, then the density of exoskeleton will be higher than that of endoskeleton.

Possible Procedures
- Most students will determine the mass of samples and then determine volume through water displacement.
- If cartilage or muscle samples float in the graduated cylinder, they can

be held just below the water surface with a pencil to keep them submerged.

Teaching Strategies
- One sample is needed per group of beef bone, chicken bone, cartilage, muscle (beef or chicken), and exoskeleton from crab or lobster. If materials are in short supply, have groups share samples with other groups.
- Students must be advised to dry bones, muscle, or cartilage before using the balance for estimating mass of samples.
- Bone size must be small enough to fit inside the graduated cylinders that are available.

- Data on pennies should be similar to the following: mass = 28.2 g, volume = 4 mL, density = 7.05 g/mL.

Types of Vertebrate Muscles

Have you ever felt nervous before riding a roller coaster at an amusement park? Perhaps you took a deep breath to try to control all the butterflies fluttering in your stomach. Did it work? In vertebrates, there are some muscles that the animal cannot control, like the muscles of your stomach or heart. Other muscles can be controlled by your actions. Why is there a need for different kinds of muscles?

Striated Muscle Three types of muscle tissue are present in vertebrates. Of these, the most important in terms of locomotion is **striated muscle** (also known as skeletal muscle). Striated muscles are so named because of their striped appearance when viewed with a microscope. Striated muscle

INVESTIGATION

Bone and Muscle Density

The term *density* refers to compactness. It is an indication of how much mass is packed into a specific space. For example, the density of a pillowcase filled with feathers is very low, whereas the density of the same pillowcase filled with sand would be much higher. One can express density in a mathematical formula as follows:

$$\text{Density} = \frac{\text{Mass}}{\text{Volume}}$$

How might one go about measuring density of an object? Try these steps to find the density of a stack of ten pennies:

1. Use a balance to find and record their mass in grams.
2. Find the volume in mL of the stack using water displacement.
3. Divide volume into mass. This gives you density in g/mL.

Repeat the entire procedure for a stack of five pennies. How do the densities compare for five or ten pennies? How should they compare if you were finding the density of the same coin type in both trials?

Now that you know how to find density, this technique will be used to solve several problems. How might the densities of muscle and bone compare? How might densities of bone and cartilage compare? How might densities of bones of different animals compare? Work with a group assigned by your teacher. Form hypotheses that could be tested using bone, cartilage, and muscle.

Problems
(1) How does density of bird bone compare to beef bone? (2) How does density of bone compare to cartilage? (3) How does density of bone compare to muscle? (4) How does density of an exoskeleton compare to that of an endoskeleton?

742 MOVEMENT

consists of long cells, each called a **fiber,** that have many nuclei. Fibers have many nuclei because they are formed by the fusion of many embryonic cells during the development of a fetus. Each fiber is surrounded by connective tissue, and the fibers and connective tissue together make up a muscle. Striated muscles are attached to the bones. They are voluntary muscles because they can be controlled at will.

Each skeletal muscle fiber is stimulated by just one nerve. Your brain sends impulses to motor neurons in your right arm. The motor neurons in turn stimulate several muscle fibers in your right arm muscle. These nerve impulses cause the muscle fibers to respond (contract). Muscle contraction causes your arm to bend at the elbow joint. When the impulses stop, the muscle fibers relax and your arm can straighten. Remember that your arm straightens because it is pulled by the contraction of the opposing muscle.

Hypothesis

What are your group's four hypotheses?

Experimental Plan

1. Decide on a way to test your group's four hypotheses. Keep the available materials provided by your teacher in mind as you plan your procedure.
2. Record your procedure and list materials and amounts that you will need.

Checking the Plan

Discuss the following points with other group members to decide the final procedure for your experiment.

1. What data will you collect and how will it be recorded?
2. What variables will have to be controlled?
3. Assign roles for this investigation.

Make sure your teacher has approved your experimental plan before you proceed further.

Data and Observations

Carry out your experiment. Prepare a data chart to record your findings.

Analysis and Conclusions

1. State each hypothesis separately. Explain how your data either support or reject each hypothesis.
2. (a) What advantage to birds is having a bone density that is different than that of a cow?
   (b) What advantage to a cow is having a bone density that is different than that of a bird?
   (c) What advantage to animals is having an exoskeleton density that is different than that of animals having an endoskeleton?
3. Offer an explanation as to why the densities of bone differ from cartilage.
4. What advantage to animals is having bone density that differs from muscle?
5. The student group working next to you had bone samples that were much larger than yours. Yet, your data and theirs were almost identical. Explain how

this is possible. Offer several reasons why your data may have differed slightly.

Going Further

Based on this lab experience, design another experiment that would help to answer questions that arose from your work. Assume that you will have limited resources and will be conducting this lab in class. Include this as part of your report.

26.2 EFFECTORS AND THEIR ACTIONS 🐚 **743**

Data and Observations

Student data and their methods of reporting will vary. The following is an example of the type of data and a sample chart that might be used.

Sample	Mass	Volume	Density
Chicken bone	34.0 g	30 mL	1.1 g/mL
Beef bone	38.0 g	23 mL	1.6 g/mL
Cartilage	4.8 g	6 mL	0.8 g/mL
Muscle	42.8 g	40 mL	1.07 g/mL
Crab	22.8 g	10 mL	2.28 g/mL

Data Analysis

1. (a) If the compactness of chicken bone and that of beef bone are the same, then their densities will be similar. Data do not support the hypothesis—chicken bone density = 1.1 g/mL while beef bone density = 1.6 g/mL.
   (b) If the compactness of bone is greater than that of cartilage, then the density of bone will be higher than that of cartilage. Data support the hypothesis—beef density = 1.6 g/mL while beef cartilage = 0.8 g/mL.
   (c) If the compactness of bone is greater than that of muscle, then the density of bone will be higher than that of muscle. Data support the hypothesis—muscle density = 1.07 g/mL while beef bone density = 1.6 g/mL.
   (d) If the compactness of exoskeleton is greater than that of endoskeleton, then the density of exoskeleton will be higher than that of endoskeleton. Data support the hypothesis—exoskeleton density = 2.28 g/mL while endoskeleton density = 1.6 g/mL for cow and 1.1 g/mL for chicken.
2. (a) The lighter bone density of birds reduces body mass and therefore may help with flight.
   (b) The higher bone density of cows provides greater strength for support of a heavy body.
   (c) For crab and lobsters, the compact exoskeleton provides a strong protective covering. Insects also show a less dense exoskeleton, which reduces body mass and therefore helps them with flight.

---

3. Cartilage is free of calcium deposits, thus making it less dense than bone.
4. A high muscle density may add too much mass to the animal body or may prevent muscle ease in contraction and relaxation.
5. Density is a property that does not vary as long as the same sample is being compared.

✔ Assessment

Knowledge: Have students write a summary of their conclusions about density and include it in their portfolios.

Going Further

Students may wish to compare the densities of: shrimp versus lobster exoskeletons, clam shell density versus oyster or snail shell density (shells are available from local restaurants), muscle tissue density of shrimp versus beef, or density of dark chicken muscle versus light chicken muscle.

Spacelab J: In 1992, Spacelab J was launched into space for eight days. Twenty-nine white rats were tested for adaptations of the "antigravity" muscles that support the body and maintain posture in Earth's gravity. Results were unexpected. In Earth's gravity, muscle cells use both fatty acids and carbohydrates for energy production. In space, muscles seem to lose the ability to use fatty acids and rely instead on carbohydrates. Further studies may indicate that astronauts in space may need special diets. In a related project, rats lost up to 25 percent of the mass in their antigravity muscles, but muscles used in locomotion did not atrophy as much. After returning to Earth, it took the rats twice as much time to regain the muscle mass lost as it took to lose it originally. These studies may demonstrate that astronauts will need to add new exercises to their routines in space.

Smooth Muscle   As well as muscles for locomotion, vertebrates have muscles for other functions. Nonstriated or **smooth muscle** moves many of the internal parts of the body. Smooth muscle is made up of sheets of distinct, tapered cells, each with a nucleus. Smooth muscles are called involuntary muscles because an animal cannot control the activities of these muscles at will. Smooth muscles make up the walls of the hollow organs of the body, such as those of the digestive tract. Blood vessels also have a layer of smooth muscle. Contraction and relaxation of these muscles can regulate the activity of the organs or the diameter of vessels. Peristalsis is caused by smooth muscle contractions.

Structures of which smooth muscles are a part are controlled by a pair of nerves. These nerves belong to the autonomic nervous system. One nerve causes contraction; the other inhibits it. Smooth muscles contract less forcefully and somewhat more slowly than skeletal muscles and are not involved in locomotion.

Cardiac Muscle   The heart is composed of individual muscle cells. The cells are branched and form networks which wrap around the chambers of the heart. Heart muscle is similar to smooth muscle in that it is an involuntary muscle and it is controlled by two nerves. Heart muscle looks much like striated muscle in that both show striations, but heart muscle is different from striated muscle because it contracts rhythmically. The contraction of heart muscle cells forces blood out of the heart chambers and into arteries. Heart muscle is known as **cardiac muscle**. All three types of vertebrate muscle are shown in Figure 26-14.

Figure 26-14   **Three types of muscle in vertebrates include striated, smooth, and cardiac muscles. Striated muscles, left, are muscles that attach to bones. (Magnification: 250×) Smooth muscles line internal organs and blood vessels. (Magnification: 100×) Cardiac muscles, right, are found only in the heart. (Magnification: 140×)**

TYPES OF MUSCLE

Striated Muscle — Rectus femoris

Smooth Muscle — Small Intestine

Cardiac Muscle — Heart

PORTFOLIO

Obtain a cow or lamb heart from the meat department of a local grocery store or butcher shop. Ask students to examine the thickness of the muscles in the four chambers and the muscles controlling the valves. Ask them how the thickness of the muscle reflects the function of each chamber. Cut the heart in half lengthwise so that students can see the valves, chambers, main arteries, and veins. Ask them to make, in their portfolios, a diagram of the heart that reflects the nature of the muscle. **L2**

Contraction of Vertebrate Skeletal Muscle

The fibers of a skeletal muscle are closely packed together. Each cylindrical fiber is made up of smaller units called **fibrils**. Fibrils consist of many microfilaments. You learned in Chapter 5 that microfilaments are composed of the proteins actin and myosin. In vertebrate muscle cells, microfilaments are more simply called filaments. The arrangement of filaments gives striated muscle its striped appearance. There are two kinds of filaments, thick and thin. The thick filaments are made of the protein myosin, and the thin ones are made mainly of the protein actin. At each end of the thick filaments are knoblike structures that may bridge (link) the two kinds of filaments together. The thin filaments are anchored to vertical bands called Z lines. The part of a fibril from one Z line to the next is called a **sarcomere**.

Figure 26-15 Muscles consist of bundles of fibers that are made up of smaller fibrils. Fibrils consist of filaments of the proteins actin and myosin.

Thinking Lab

DRAW A CONCLUSION

What kind of muscle is being used?

Background
The three muscle types each have their own characteristics. For example, smooth and cardiac muscle are involuntary, while skeletal muscle is voluntary. Smooth muscle does not fatigue easily, but skeletal muscle does. Cardiac muscle is only found in the heart.

You Try It
Chewing food with jaw muscles must be voluntary. Therefore, jaw muscles must be skeletal. Swallowing and the passage of food down your esophagus also depend on muscles. Using your own experience with swallowing and what happens after you swallow, **draw** **a conclusion** and offer support for your answer for: (a) the type of muscle found toward the back of your mouth; and (b) the type of muscle found in your esophagus.

Science, Technology, and Society

Open-heart Surgery:
During open-heart surgery, the heart must be chilled and bathed in specific chemicals in order to prevent inflammation of the heart muscle, a condition in which the heart becomes rigid and restoration of blood flow is impossible. Research is underway to prevent inflammation of the heart muscle. Scientists are using genetically engineered proteins found in the body that naturally suppress inflammation. Applications of these proteins may be useful in treating other inflammatory diseases such as rheumatoid arthritis.

Activity
Have students rest their elbows on the table and open and close their preferred hand rapidly and forcefully as many times as they can in 20 seconds. Ask them what produces muscle fatigue. L1

Thinking Lab

DRAW A CONCLUSION

Purpose
Students will determine that swallowing is dependent on both skeletal muscles and smooth muscles.

Skills
form a hypothesis, observe, interpret data

Teaching Strategies
• A model of the upper torso will show the pharynx and the esophagus.

Further Background
The back of the mouth or pharynx is composed of skeletal muscle. The esophagus is composed of smooth muscle. You can control swallowing, but you have no control once food passes into the esophagus.

Answers
(a) You can control swallowing. Therefore, the back part of your mouth is made up of skeletal muscle.
(b) You cannot control food once it enters your esophagus. Therefore, this tube is composed of smooth muscle.

✔ **Assessment**
Knowledge: Ask students to make a diagram of the mouth, pharynx, esophagus, and stomach. Have them label these areas.

Teacher FYI

Each striated muscle fiber contains myofibrils that are covered by the sarcoplasmic reticulum. The sarcoplasmic reticulum is derived from the endoplasmic reticulum. During contraction, it is the sarcoplasmic reticulum that releases calcium ions into the myofibrils.

Text Question

Why is constant readiness of a muscle for contraction important? It enables an organism to respond quickly to stimuli.

Bioethics

Overtraining of Athletes:

In competition, athletes continually push themselves to make better times and improve their records in other ways. When muscles are pushed to these limits, the high oxygen consumption causes the muscles to be exposed to high levels of damaging oxygen-derived free radicals. Damage to muscle membranes produces a variety of symptoms sometimes referred to as "overtraining," a condition that inhibits the level of athletic performance. Recent research shows that treatment with vitamin E and vitamin C for three months prior to and during training reduces tissue oxidation by 25 percent. Antioxidant supplementation may not improve athletic performance but may reduce the damage done by oxidants released during strenuous athletics. Students may be asked how they feel about athletes pushing themselves beyond their natural limits and needing vitamin supplements in order to avoid the overtraining syndrome.

Figure 26-16 The sliding filament hypothesis suggests that actin and myosin filaments slide over one another to shorten the fibrils during muscle contraction.

Sliding Filament Hypothesis Electron microscope studies show that Z lines of each sarcomere are closer together when a muscle is contracted than when a muscle is relaxed. Such observations as well as experiments on striated muscle have led to the **sliding filament hypothesis,** a model that explains contraction.

Motor nerves leading to a skeletal muscle branch many times so that a number of individual muscle fibers are stimulated. Acetylcholine is released by the motor neuron and diffuses across the synapse to the muscle fiber. The membranes of muscle fibers, like neurons, are polarized. The acetylcholine causes depolarization of the membranes of the fibers. This action potential causes a release of calcium ions stored in special membranes inside the fiber. Calcium ions are needed to allow the ends of the myosin molecules of the thick filaments to form bridges with the actin molecules of the thin filaments. Bridges form as the ends of the myosin molecules "hook" into grooves along the actin molecules. Using energy of ATP, the bridges bend, causing thin filaments to slide past thick filaments. Myosin detaches from actin and combines with another site to repeat the process. As a result of this repeated pattern, the thin filaments slide toward and over one another. The chemical energy of ATP is thus transformed to the mechanical energy of sliding filaments. Note that the filaments themselves do not shorten, but the filaments' sliding over each other causes the muscle fiber to shorten. After the nerve impulse is over, the calcium ions are once again stored. Bridges cannot form and the muscle relaxes. These events are diagrammed in Figure 26-16.

PROJECT

Sliding Filament Model: Ask students to make, with simple household materials, a working model of the concept of the sliding filament hypothesis. Paper clips, pipe cleaners, wire, string, yarn, and other materials might be used. `L1` `LEP` `COOP LEARN`

All-or-none Response Once an impulse reaches a muscle fiber, there is an all-or-none response. That is, either the muscle fiber contracts fully or it does not contract at all; there is no partial contraction for a given fiber. Also, all contractions are of the same intensity. How, then, can a muscle contract to a greater or lesser degree? The number of fibers that contract at one time determines the strength of the contraction of the whole muscle. The greater the number of fibers that contract, the greater the contraction of the muscle as a whole.

The all-or-none response can also explain muscle tone. The nervous system constantly sends out messages that you are not aware of. These messages keep some fibers in each muscle relaxed and some fibers contracted. A muscle fiber must undergo a short recovery period after it contracts before it can contract again. The nerves constantly cause different fibers to contract so that while some fibers are contracting, others are recovering. Thus, some fibers will always be able to contract, and the muscle as a whole is always prepared for a complete contraction. Why is constant readiness of a muscle for contraction important?

Energy for Skeletal Muscle Contraction

Contraction of muscles is biological work requiring ATP energy. The energy needed for muscle contraction is made available in several ways, depending on muscle activity.

Aerobic Respiration Provides ATP During rest or very light activity, ATP is produced in muscle cells by aerobic respiration. Some of the ATP produced this way is immediately used for muscle contraction. The remaining ATP is stored in the muscle cells either as ATP itself or as another compound, creatine phosphate (CP), that can be converted quickly to ATP. The CP is formed when molecules of ATP donate phosphate groups to molecules of a compound called creatine. As muscles become more active, the energy stored in CP can be used. CP is changed to creatine, and the phosphate released combines with ADP to form ATP. The energy in the ATP can then be used for muscle contraction.

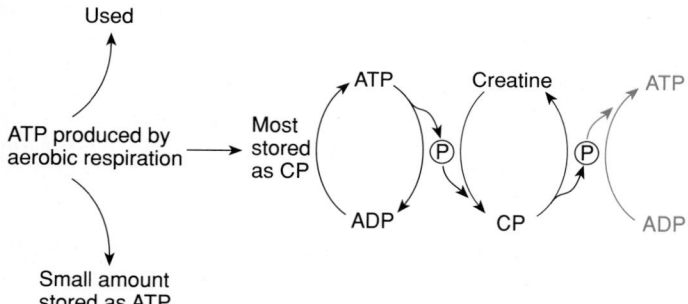

Figure 26-17 The source of energy for muscle contraction is ATP.

Minilab 2

How quickly do our muscles fatigue?

Skeletal muscles fatigue as oxygen is used up and a waste chemical called lactic acid forms. Fatigue can be shown by doing the following. Have a classmate hold a rather heavy textbook in the palm of his or her hand with the arm extended straight out and parallel to the floor. Time and record how long your classmate can hold the book in this position before he or she tires from muscle fatigue. Give your classmate 15 seconds to rest and have him or her repeat the process while you again record the time. Repeat again for as many trials as possible.

Analysis *What happens to the length of each trial? Why?*

Minilab 2

Purpose
Students will be able to feel the effects of muscle fatigue and will also note that the onset of fatigue is quicker when a set of already used and previously fatigued muscles are continuously being reworked.

Skills
observe and infer, compare and contrast, recognize cause and effect

Teaching Strategies
• Have students work in pairs for this activity.
• Alter the weight of the books being used to compensate for student size and possible endurance.
• It is critical that the student doing the recording keep accurate data as to the trial and length of time that the book is held for each successive trial.
• If students show no decrease in endurance in that they are capable of holding the book for successive trials, reduce the waiting time from 15 to 5 seconds.

Expected Results
The length of time that each successive trial will take becomes shorter and shorter.

Answers
The length of time that each trial took became shorter and shorter. More rapid onset of fatigue with each trial may be caused by the inability of muscle tissue to receive enough oxygen or to get rid of the lactic acid buildup.

✔ **Assessment**
Knowledge: Have students record the experimental data in their journals. A conclusion should also be included. Ask students to design an experiment that would determine the length of time needed to rest between trials so that each successive trial will not change in terms of time before the onset of fatigue.

Purpose
Students will study the benefits of exercise, both for health of the body and for mental health.

Background
Most sports require a combination of cardiovascular endurance, muscular endurance, strength, flexibility, skill, and psychological factors that give the athlete a positive mental attitude for a good performance. Warming up is important in any vigorous sporting activity because it prevents injuries.

Teaching Strategies
Ask students to tell whether the following statements are true or false.
1. Spot reduction, for example getting rid of a "spare tire," can be done with specific exercises such as sit-ups. *False*
2. Wearing a sweatsuit will cause more calories to be burned and therefore more weight loss. *False*
3. If some exercise is good, even more will be better. *False*

Possible Answers
1. Cross-country skiing, uphill hiking, ice hockey, jogging, jumping rope, rowing, running in place, stationary cycling
2. Anaerobic exercise centered on specific groups of muscles will build muscle mass and strength. Weight training is most effective.

Going Further
Ask students to plan an exercise program for themselves that fits in with the time they have available. **L1**

Need for Lactic Acid Fermentation   During prolonged or heavy exercise, the supplies of stored energy (both ATP and CP) are quickly used. Even though the heartbeat and breathing rates are increased during heavy exercise, not enough oxygen is delivered to muscle cells for aerobic respiration to continue. Under these conditions, the muscle cells switch to lactic acid fermentation. During lactic acid fermentation, glycogen stored in muscles is converted to lactic acid, and ATP is produced in the process. The ATP provides energy for muscle contraction. During this process, the muscles are said to acquire an oxygen debt. **Oxygen debt** occurs when the cell is obtaining ATP energy without going through normal, aerobic respiration. The cell is "borrowing" against future oxygen intake.

After strenuous activity, rapid breathing occurs, increasing the supply of oxygen to cells. With an increase in oxygen, aerobic respiration is again possible. Blood circulation removes the lactic acid from your muscles and transports it to the liver. Using ATP produced by the oxidation of some lactic acid, the liver converts the remaining lactic acid to glycogen. The oxygen debt is "paid" when all the lactic acid is removed.

LEISURE CONNECTION

Exercise for Muscle Fitness

How many hours of television do you watch in a week? How much of your leisure time is spent sitting around? Outside school, exercise for some young people consists of getting up for a snack. They don't even need to get up to change the channel on the television set. As a result, many young people are overweight and out of shape.

In a 1985 National Adolescent Health Survey, of the students polled in grades eight and nine, 41 percent exercised 20 minutes or more five times per week. Almost 16 percent didn't exercise, or did so only once per week.

Why You Need to Exercise Your muscles need exercise to stay strong and flexible. Muscles that are toned resist injury from strenuous or unexpected activity.

Exercise has other benefits as well. Like other muscles, the muscles in the heart need regular exercise to stay strong. A strong heart muscle will pump more blood per heartbeat to your body's cells. The more blood pumped with each heartbeat, the greater the amount of oxygen provided to body cells.

The most healthful exercises are aerobic, the kind that keep your heart beating faster and your lungs drawing more air for an extended period of time. Aerobic exercise will strengthen your heart and lungs, open your arteries, and keep these systems working and interacting efficiently. Thirty minutes of continuous aerobic activity every other day is recommended.

Exercise can have many benefits. It helps reduce blood cholesterol levels and weight. The bones of people who exercise are stronger. In fact, as people age, they tend to lose calcium from their bones from lack of exercise.

Exercise for Mental Health   In addition to physical health, exercise enhances mental and emotional health. It also boosts energy and releases tension, anger, and

748 MOVEMENT

Muscular Diseases: Ask students to report on two diseases of the muscular system: myasthenia gravis and muscular dystrophy. They might contact the local muscular dystrophy association to determine how it assists patients and their families. **L2**

Ciliary and Flagellar Motion

Some organisms or specialized cells can move even though they lack both muscles and skeletons. Many unicellular eukaryotes have cilia or flagella composed of microtubules. These effectors may be used not only to propel cells, but also to move particles past cells. In a paramecium, the cilia do both, moving the protozoan through the water and setting up a current that draws food into its oral groove.

Microtubules in cilia and flagella of eukaryotes are arranged in nine pairs with a pair in the middle. Figure 26-18 shows the arrangement of the microtubules, although it is not detailed enough to show that the outer pairs of microtubules are connected to one another. The connections are projections, or arms, made of a protein. Each outer pair is also connected to the pair in the center by structures resembling the spokes of a wheel.

Paired microtubules

Cilium

Figure 26-18 **The cilia and flagella bend when one tubule of each pair slides past the other, similar to the sliding found in muscle filaments.**

stress. Studies have shown that exercise is helpful in fighting depression. Regular aerobic exercise can result in elevated self-confidence, personal responsibility, and a sense of well-being. By contrast, inactivity tends to make your mind and body sluggish.

If you develop the habit of exercising regularly now, you are more likely to incorporate exercise into your life as an adult. Exercise needn't be a chore if you choose an activity you enjoy. Skiing, soccer, rowing, hiking, swimming, bicycling, basketball, dancing, and many competitive sports are all excellent forms of exercise. For some people, such activities are the best part of a weekend. Many are social activities that help them make new friends and enjoy the ones they have. What television program or video game could provide so many benefits and so much fun?

1. **Explore Further:** Examine some studies comparing various types of exercise. Which are best for weight control?

2. **Explore Further:** Which types of exercises are most effective for building muscle mass and strength?

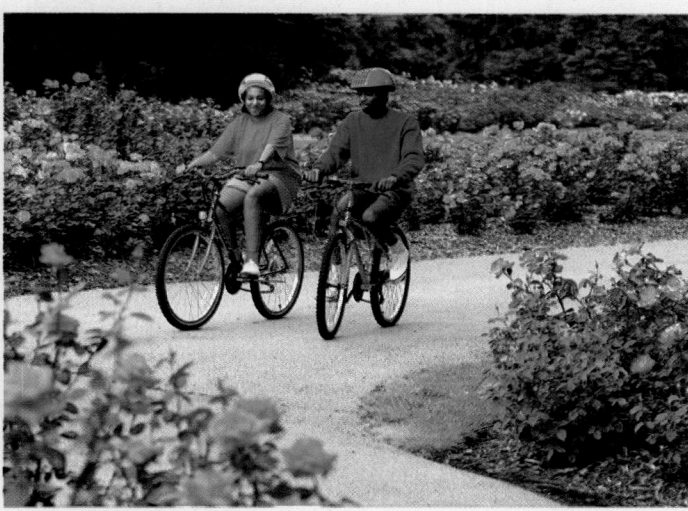

26.2 EFFECTORS AND THEIR ACTIONS **749**

SECTION 26.2

Demonstration

Ask people who work in the sports or exercise fields to speak to the class about the importance of warming up and cooling down in a sports or exercise program. Examples of people who could speak are physical therapists, trainers, dancers, and aerobic instructors. They should describe the type of training they have had and what a day on the job is like. **L1**

3 Assess

Check for Understanding

Ask students to go to the chalkboard and make sketches of microscopic views of muscle types and diagrams explaining muscle movement in terms of the sliding filament hypothesis. **L1**

Reteach

Have students play a word game. Make sets of cards with words from the chapter, one set for each team of six students. At your signal, one person from each team picks up a card, looks at it, and passes it to one person on another team. The students who have seen the card draw hints on paper for their teams to guess the word. The person drawing may not speak or write words, letters, or numbers. The first team to guess the word gets a point. You should allot about one minute per word. **LEP**

COOP LEARN

Extension
Ask a group of students to report on the details of the research evidence for the sliding filament theory of muscle contraction. They should make detailed diagrams to make their explanations clear. **L3**

✔ **Assessment**
Portfolio: Ask students to use an exercise video and make their own narration about movement, muscles, types of muscles, muscle contraction, and energy use by muscles. They should freeze appropriate frames of the video as they do their narration. Ask them to include their narration in their portfolios. **L1**

4 Close

Demonstration
Arrange for a body builder from a local health club to visit the class. Describe the origins, insertions, and functions of some of the major muscles as they are flexed.

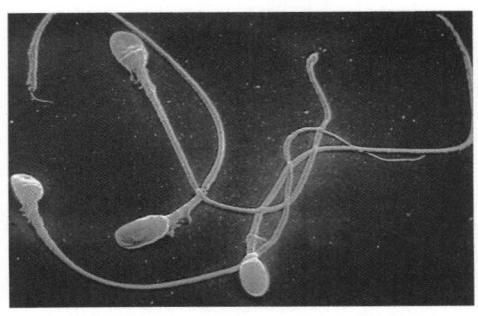

Figure 26-19 Each human sperm moves by means of a flagellum. Magnification: 5000×

It is thought that the outer pairs of microtubules slide past one another in much the same way as the filaments of a muscle fiber do. According to this model, the arms that connect the outer pairs of microtubules act in much the same way as the bridges that connect thick and thin muscle filaments. The energy of ATP is necessary for the arms to form these connections between microtubule pairs and to cause them to move. As the pairs of outer microtubules slide over one another, the cilium or flagellum bends, because all the microtubules are interconnected. Sliding of different pairs of microtubules results in movement such as that which occurs as an oar moves through the water.

Locomotion of unicellular eukaryotes thus has similarities to locomotion of vertebrates. However, the two systems of locomotion—bending of cilia and the mechanics of muscle contraction—evolved independently, another good example of convergent evolution.

LOOKING AHEAD

THIS CHAPTER completes a unit in which you have studied how chemical control, nervous control, and effectors enable organisms to respond to stimuli. Many of those stimuli are present in the external environment. In the next chapter, you will begin to explore the relationship between organisms and their environment from another point of view. You will study how various factors limit the growth of populations of organisms. Those factors include other organisms as well as physical factors of the environment.

Section Review

Understanding Concepts
1. As an earthworm moves, part of its body seems to get shorter, and then the body gets longer again. How are these changes in body length explained?
2. You are observing a section of muscle tissue with a microscope. You have difficulty distinguishing separate cells but notice that the muscle has a branched appearance. Is the muscle tissue you are observing voluntary or involuntary? Explain.
3. You are sitting watching TV, but some of your skeletal muscles are moving. By what process is energy made available for that movement? How, specifically, does the ATP contribute to contraction of your muscles?
4. **Skill Review—Designing an Experiment:** Assuming you had the necessary equipment, how would you test the idea that a muscle contraction is an all-or-none response? For more help, see Practicing Scientific Methods in the **Skill Handbook**.
5. **Thinking Critically:** What effect would a chemical that interferes with ATP production have on cilia and flagella? Discuss the role of ATP in explaining your answer.

Answers to Section Review

1. Contraction of one set of muscles shortens the body while another set lengthens it.
2. The tissue is cardiac muscle, which is involuntary.
3. ATP is made available by means of aerobic respiration under these conditions. The ATP is needed for the bridges binding thick filaments to thin filaments to swivel, causing contraction.
4. **Skill Review—Designing an Experiment:** A muscle could be stimulated by electricity. Different voltages could be used. If the all-or-none response is true, once contraction is made to occur, higher voltages will not cause the muscle to contract any more forcefully.
5. **Thinking Critically:** The cilia and flagella would not be able to bend because ATP is needed to connect the arms of the outer pairs of microtubules. Without those connections, the microtubules cannot slide past one another.

Biotechnology

Bionics and Artificial Limbs

Most people take locomotion for granted. A person with full use of all body parts can scarcely imagine the impact of paralysis or the loss of a limb. In fact, to most wild animals, the loss of a limb is so disabling that the animal is unable to survive.

The First Substitute Limbs
The development of human societies has enabled humans to survive the loss of limbs. According to archaeologists, humans were caring for the physically challenged among them as early as 250 000 years ago. More than 2000 years ago, humans began using substitutes for lost legs, arms, and hands. The earliest known artificial leg, made of metal plates around a wooden core, dates from 300 B.C. By 1990, human technology had evolved to the point where some quadriplegics could thread needles, and individuals with artificial legs could walk up and down stairs, jump, ski, and run marathons.

Artificial Limb Replacement
Modern surgeons can amputate limbs, leaving enough muscle structure in place to control an artificial replacement. If enough stump and muscle remain after amputation of a hand or an arm, replacements are

usually operated by voluntary muscle control. An artificial hand, for example, may be held closed with a built-in spring. Straps connected to the opposite shoulder pull the fingers and thumb apart.

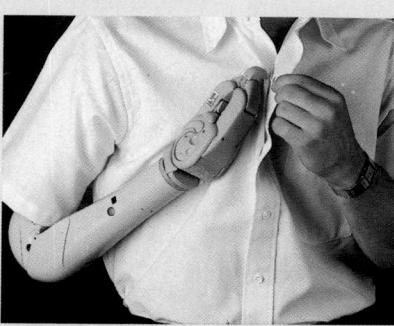

Designing an Artificial Limb To design an artificial limb, a prosthetist needs to examine the function of the natural limb and how it contributes to locomotion. For example, a living foot extends and flexes, bends at the ball for walking or running, and acts as a shock absorber, bearing the entire weight of the body. Some modern artificial feet are designed to flex at the ball like natural feet. They contain springs to simulate the action of the sole of the foot in walking.

Stimulating Muscles by Electrodes
Locomotion requires more than the

presence of the necessary limbs, muscles, and joints. The muscles must receive stimulation from the nerves. Injuries to the nerves or spinal column can leave victims unable to control the muscles that move their limbs. However, researchers learned to use electrodes to stimulate the muscles in paralyzed limbs. Muscles can be made to contract or relax to control the limbs. Using these electrodes, patients have learned to walk with paralyzed legs. Some people with paralyzed arms can even write.

Nothing can fully replace a functioning limb. However, modern researchers constantly seek ways of improving survival and quality of life for those who have lost use of limbs.

1. **Writing About Biology:**
   Experiment with your leg, knee, ankle, or hand. Observe the body part while performing several everyday functions. In order to replace that part fully, what would an artificial body part need to do?
2. **Explore Further:** Research the latest developments in one of these areas: electrical stimulation of paralyzed limbs, artificial hands, artificial feet.

fingers, make a fist, thumb must be able to touch all fingers.
2. Using a battery-powered computer pack worn at the waist, paraplegic muscles are stimulated to move the legs, stabilized in braces, in walking motions. The newest programs allow the patient to go up and down stairs and walk forward and backward. Crutches or walkers are needed to assist, and the wiring is built into "hot pants" that can be worn easily under clothes.

Going Further
Ask students to research regeneration in animals such as salamanders, lizards, and earthworms. Ask them to find out why humans cannot regenerate lost limbs. L2

Biotechnology

Purpose
Students will trace the development of artificial limbs from the time they first were used until today. They will learn how a variety of artificial limbs function.

Background
Artificial hips, knees, and teeth are becoming more common. An artificial hip or knee is often used to replace one that has been destroyed by accident or disease. An artificial hip joint consists of a ten-inch metal spike inserted into the femur. The spike has a sphere on the top that fits into a cup of polyethylene. These parts are custom made by computer design to fit precisely, and the stainless steel or titanium from which they are made must have mirror finishes to fit smoothly. Artificial knees are used only as a last resort for young people, as they must be replaced every ten years.

False teeth do not work as well and are not as comfortable as teeth anchored in the jaw. Permanent tooth replacements are fixtures that look like screws, made of titanium, that are implanted into the jawbone and then covered with artificial teeth. The technique works well for a single tooth or an entire mouth.

Teaching Strategies
• Bring in several borrowed prostheses that students can manipulate as you explain how they work. They may be available from a physical therapist or orthopedic clinic.

Possible Answers
1. Leg—must be able to support weight, bend and straighten at the knee, rotate and lift at the hip, and provide stability; knee—bend, support weight, provide stability; Ankle—rotate the foot, support weight, provide stability; hand— rotate the wrist, flex and extend

CHAPTER 26

Issues

Purpose

Students will follow a physically challenged policeman through a typical day and see the obstacles faced by a person in a wheelchair.

Background

In this country, there are millions of people who have difficulty hearing, seeing, moving, learning, controlling their emotions, or talking. There are four main barriers to people who are physically challenged: architectural barriers (limitations imposed by the construction of buildings and transportation systems); attitudinal barriers (studies show that even though they may feel positive about people who are physically challenged, others still have higher anxiety in the company of people who are physically challenged); educational barriers (up to half are not getting appropriate education); occupational barriers (less than half are employed); and personal barriers (adjusting to the new demands of daily living and societal perceptions of their abilities).

Teaching Strategies

- Ask students to speculate about what kinds of changes could be made to accommodate wheelchairs in buildings, in public transportation, and in schools.

A Day in the Life of a Physically Challenged Person

"One of the biggest differences is that everything takes a lot longer," said former police officer Chris Barrett, describing changes in his life since a bullet paralyzed him from the waist down. It took just a fraction of a second for the bullet to damage his spine and destroy the systems he used for locomotion and everyday activity. However, the pace of recovery was laborious and slow as he trained his body parts to interact in new ways. For example, since his injury it takes him six times as long to get up and prepare for work.

Getting Out of Bed   First, he needs to get out of bed. With his back to the wheelchair beside the bed, he uses his arms to push himself to a sitting position. Then he uses his arms to pull his torso onto the seat. Next he uses his arms to lift his legs onto the footrest of his wheelchair. When the legs and stomach muscles can't interact with the arms, head, and torso, all these maneuvers require abundant energy and tremendous strength in the arms. Fortunately, Barrett was an athlete before his injury. Injured people in poor shape have much more trouble developing the necessary strength.

Upon arising, Barrett navigates the doorways and hallways to the kitchen. In the kitchen, most cabinets are too high or too low for him to reach from a wheelchair. He uses a set of tongs to grab the food and dishes he needs. The sink is too high, but by placing his wheelchair beside it, he is able to reach up and to the side to use it. "Some disabled people who live alone have special cabinets and counter tops that can be raised or lowered at the touch of a button. Even the sink moves up and down," says Barrett.

How to Use the Bathroom

Wheeling to the bathroom, Barrett is grateful that the family rebuilt their home, widening doorways and hallways. After Barrett's injury, he had to maneuver his wheelchair through narrow doorways and hallways, and cross raised thresholds when going from one room to another.

The bathroom presented problems, too. When Barrett was injured, his bathroom was small and the door opened inward.

Imagine trying to wheel a chair into a small bathroom and close the door behind you, especially if the door opens inward.

Unfortunately, as Barrett points out, many physically challenged people are renters and can't remodel their homes. Those who don't have much money must choose housing they can afford and can't shop around for homes where they can easily navigate. They must wrestle with thresholds, narrow doors and hallways, and cramped bathrooms without space to maneuver.

Obstacles in Public   Even if physically challenged people can afford to design their homes to accommodate their challenges, they have no control over public streets and buildings, friends' homes, or the work place.

Because the front of a wheelchair extends about two feet in front of the torso, it can't be pulled close to tables and desks. As a result, there are many restaurants that Barrett can't use. Transferring to a chair or booth doesn't work well for him. Unless he supports himself with his

---

CAREER CONNECTION

Sometimes, due to illness or injury, a person's mobility becomes limited. **Physical therapists** help restore and maintain muscle strength, range of motion, and coordination. They may do this by manipulation to provide passive exercise for the muscle, or by supervising active exercise. Physical therapists may work for hospitals, rehabilitation centers, sports medicine clinics, or school districts.

CAREER CONNECTION

To find out more about the career of a physical therapist, contact a local physical therapy or sports medicine clinic.

hands, he tends to fall over if he leans too far forward or to the side.

Challenges at the Work Place Barrett faces additional challenges at work. For example, he must go through heavy, self-closing doors. Fortunately, the doors open with levers. Barrett works up some speed with his wheelchair and runs into the door. If he depresses the lever fast enough, the momentum opens the door. Then he holds it open with his footrest while he struggles to wheel the chair through.

Turning a knob, pushing a heavy door open, and holding it open while wheeling a chair through is more than many physically challenged people can manage. "Levers are a big improvement," says Barrett. "Some quadriplegics are accompanied by dogs, and the dogs can trip the levers to open these doors." Quadriplegics have injuries high on the spinal cord and can't control their arms and legs.

The two-story building where Barrett works doesn't have elevators, and Barrett has duties on both floors. Fortunately, the building has a two-story garage with entrances on both levels. "It takes a lot of planning," says Barrett. First, he completes all his duties on the top floor. Then he goes outside, gets into his car, and drives to the ground floor.

Barrett doesn't want to make the drive more often than necessary. Getting in and out of the car and collapsing or opening his wheelchair takes time, energy, effort, and careful maneuvering. In Barrett's car, all controls are operated by

hand. "There's a quadriplegic in town who drives his car with his mouth," says Barrett. "Plenty of people have it harder than I do."

Laws Help the Physically Challenged Laws now require public buildings to provide automatic doors, and ramps for people who can't use stairs. Hallways, aisles, and doorways must be wide enough so that people with wheelchairs can use them. Rest rooms must be constructed so that people in wheelchairs can get in and out of them. Handrails are provided beside toilets and in some showers and bathtubs.

For the sake of people who find locomotion difficult, handicapped parking spaces are required in public parking lots. Such spaces are located near the entrances and have safety areas where people can get in and out of wheelchairs. In many cities, physically challenged citizens may have blue-curbed handicapped parking spaces designated outside their homes.

In addition to wheelchair-friendly construction, Barrett reports that he has found workers in public and commercial buildings very helpful. For example, in restaurants with steps but no eleva-

tors, staff members willingly take him through the kitchen or carry him up steps. However, like most physically challenged people, Barrett wants to be as independent as possible. What he appreciates most are the facilities that allow him to be independent in public places.

Fortunately, technology is constantly creating new devices to enable the physically challenged to be more independent. Many devices, for example, can be activated by voice, breath, or head movements. Researchers continuously seek to improve not only locomotion, but the quality of life and the range of possible activity for the physically challenged.

1. **Writing About Biology:** Examine the doors to your school and classroom. Describe what a person in a wheelchair would need to do to enter the school, travel to the classroom, enter the room, and reach your desk.
2. **Explore Further:** Examine ten public or commercial buildings in your community. How many are designed to accommodate the physically challenged? What challenges would the other buildings present for someone in a wheelchair or walker?

Readings
- Hertz, Sue. "The User-Friendly Home." *House Beautiful,* Nov. 1992, p. 90.
- Kridler, Charles and R.K. Stewart. "Access for the Disabled." *Progressive Architecture,* Sept. 1992, p. 45.

Possible Answers
1. If the school has not been constructed with people who are physically challenged in mind, it may have outside steps, doors that are difficult to open and hold open while getting a wheelchair through, stairs between floors, recessed classroom doorways with limited space and outward opening doors in the recesses, making entry to the classroom impossible. Once in the classroom, the chairs and lab benches may be bolted to the floor with aisles too narrow to make access by wheelchair possible.
2. Steps to entrance, steps inside, small hallways, elevator buttons too high, lack of restroom facilities that would accommodate a wheelchair, door handles and knobs difficult to reach and opening in inconvenient ways, high step between room and hall, floor covering on which a wheelchair does not roll easily, office space set up with lack of regard for wheelchair access to desks and files, files too high or low, shelves too high or low, cafeteria that will not accommodate a wheelchair

Going Further
Ask students to do research about how society could make accommodations for other people who are challenged with hearing loss, vision loss, and other types of challenges.
L1

CHAPTER REVIEW

Summary

Summary statements can be used by students to review the major concepts of the chapter.

Language of Biology

Answers should go beyond defining the terms. Accept any reasonable answer that uses the term correctly and in the proper context.

Understanding Concepts

1. A cartilaginous skeleton would not provide enough support for a terrestrial vertebrate.
2. The water contributes to the support of these large animals.
3. The knee is a hinge joint, adapted for movement in only one plane. Many injuries occur as the knee is twisted during athletic activities.
4. The heart muscle has a branching pattern.
5. Operation of the water-vascular system occurs slowly, and the many tube feet function independently. The earthworm has two sets of muscles that control movement of the entire body.
6. A torn ligament would impede movement because ligaments attach bones across moveable joints.
7. Such an injury would preclude movement because tendons attach muscles to bones.
8. Acetylcholine is released across a synapse and diffuses to muscle fiber, where it causes depolarization and the onset of an action potential. Release of calcium ions from within the fiber allows formation of bridges between thick and thin filaments. ATP energy causes the bridges to bend, sliding the thin filaments toward one another. Continued sliding of the filaments results in contraction of the flexor.
9. Additional energy could be provided by means of fermentation.
10. Like muscle, cilia and flagella require ATP energy. ATP results

---

Summary

Effectors such as cilia or muscles are structures by which organisms respond to stimuli. Muscles not only aid in movement, but also provide support. Animals having skeletons, arthropods and vertebrates, are capable of the most efficient movement, and their skeletons also provide support and protection.

Arthropods have a nonliving exoskeleton that limits their size and growth patterns. Vertebrates, having an endoskeleton, are not so severely limited. Most vertebrates have a skeleton composed of bone, which replaces cartilage during development. The individual bones are joined in different ways, providing a great variety of movements.

Much movement in arthropods and vertebrates depends upon interaction of muscles and skeleton. Flexors and extensors work together to move parts of the body. Smooth muscle and cardiac muscle also cause movement, but do not interact with the skeleton. Energy for muscular movement is provided by ATP, which also fuels the movement of cilia and flagella.

Language of Biology

Write a sentence that shows your understanding of each of the following terms.

cardiac muscle	ossification
cartilage	osteocyte
extensor	oxygen debt
fiber	sarcomere
fibril	sliding filament hypothesis
flexor	smooth muscle
Haversian canal	striated muscle
joint	tendon
ligament	water-vascular system

Understanding Concepts

1. Sharks have an endoskeleton composed entirely of cartilage. Why are there no terrestrial vertebrates with such a skeleton?
2. Do you think that it is a coincidence that the largest vertebrates, whales, and the largest arthropods, such as lobsters, both inhabit water? Explain.
3. Can you offer an explanation of why there are so many knee injuries in athletics?
4. How can you tell if a striated muscle is skeletal muscle or heart muscle when viewed under a microscope?
5. Why can't a starfish move as rapidly and smoothly as an earthworm?
6. Have you heard of someone suffering from a torn ligament? How would such an injury affect a person?
7. What effect would a cut or injured tendon have?
8. Explain the series of events beginning with an impulse from a motor neuron and ending with contraction of a flexor in your lower leg.
9. Suppose you were running a race. Toward the end of the race, you are gasping for breath. How do you manage to keep running a little bit more?
10. How is the movement of cilia and flagella similar to the contraction of muscle?

in sliding of filaments in muscle and sliding of microtubules in cilia and flagella.

Applying Concepts

11. A graph of arthropod growth would indicate periods of growth followed by periods of no growth in a stairstep pattern. That pattern is explained by the molting of the arthropod.
12. The femurs (thighbones) support most of the body's mass.
13. Energy would be provided by fermentation because not enough ATP could be made available by aerobic respiration or from creatine phosphate.

Applying Concepts

11. The graph below indicates growth of a vertebrate over time. How would you graph the growth of an arthropod? Explain.

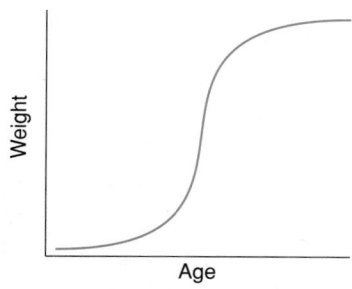

12. Which bone(s) of the human body would you expect to be the strongest? Explain.
13. How would ATP be provided when a person is lifting a heavy object for a very long time? Explain.
14. How is the slow contraction of smooth muscle adaptive?
15. Why can skeletal muscles be controlled by just one nerve rather than two, like smooth or cardiac muscle?
16. Parathyroid hormone acts to stimulate release of calcium from bones to blood. Calcitonin has an opposite effect. What symptoms might arise if the levels of these hormones were not in normal balance?
17. **Biotechnology:** Why would the loss of a leg be disabling to an animal such as a rabbit?
18. **Issues:** Walk around your home and make an inventory of areas that you think would be difficult to maneuver in if you were in a wheelchair. Look carefully at both the kitchen and the bathroom. How could you remodel these areas if you had no money for major changes?

Lab Interpretation

19. **Investigation:** The following data are provided for your use. Determine which sample is bone and which is cartilage. Explain your answers.

Sample	Mass	Volume
A	6.2 g	8 mL
B	88.4 g	52 mL

20. **Thinking Lab:** Explain why you cannot stop vomiting once the process begins.
21. **Minilab 2:** Suggest two ways in which you could delay the onset of fatigue with each succeeding trial if doing an experiment similar to the one you did with the book.

Connecting Ideas

22. How is it possible for mollusks such as squid and octopuses to move much more rapidly than most other mollusks? How is that movement related to their food-getting abilities?
23. Explain why skeletal muscles and cilia and flagella illustrate convergence rather than homology.

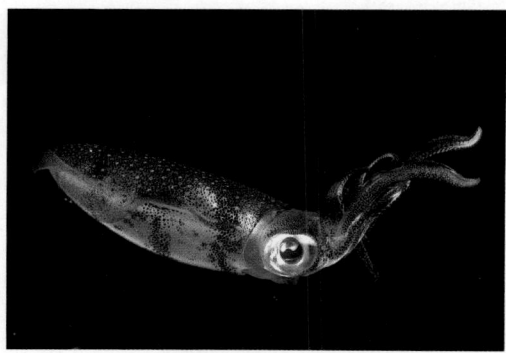

CHAPTER 26

14. Slower contraction is less forceful and more appropriate for such movement as peristalsis or constriction of blood vessels.
15. Skeletal muscles work in pairs, and each member of a pair is controlled by a nerve. Smooth and cardiac muscle do not work in pairs. Thus, one nerve stimulates the muscle and another inhibits it.
16. An imbalance in these hormones could cause loss of too much calcium from bones, causing them to become weak. (Too much calcium in the blood could also result in a loss of osmotic balance between blood and cells.)
17. The rabbit often depends upon a hopping mode of locomotion.
18. Answers should reveal careful thought about the special needs of a person confined to a wheelchair.

Lab Interpretation

19. Sample A is cartilage, B is bone. Density calculations for each sample will disclose that A (0.77 g/mL) is much less compact than B (1.7 g/mL). This is typical of cartilage density compared to bone density.
20. This event results from the contraction of muscles in the stomach and esophagus. These muscles are smooth muscles and thus cannot be controlled voluntarily.
21. Answers will vary. These could include reducing the mass of the book being held, resting between trials for a longer time, strengthening muscles through training periods prior to trying the experiment, and bending the arm at an angle rather than keeping it straight out.

Connecting Ideas

22. **Evolution:** These mollusks, unlike most others, have no confining outer shells. Thus, they can be much more mobile and more efficient predators.
23. **Evolution:** Skeletal muscles and cilia and flagella function in the same way. However, their structures are far different and therefore not homologous.

Interactions in the Environment

Unit Overview

This concluding unit focuses upon the highest levels of biological organization, from populations to the biosphere. Chapter 27 examines populations, their growth, and the factors that limit their size. The chapter also includes an in-depth study of the human population explosion. In Chapter 28, students learn about ecosystems, the biotic relationships that exist in an ecosystem, and the influence of abiotic factors on organisms. Chapter 29 covers the development of communities through ecological succession, and also explores the characteristics of the world's major biomes and the physical factors that cause different biomes to exist. Chapter 30 takes a look at some of the ways in which humans have exploited their environment, and examines possible solutions to correct mistakes, past and present.

Theme Development

The theme of patterns of change pervades all the chapters in this unit and is evident in the discussion of such concepts as population growth, succession, and pollution. Energy is a theme stressed from one point of view in the study of ecosystems and from another in the study of conservation of resources. The theme of systems and interactions is made clear in the study of the importance of both biotic and abiotic factors of the environment.

Advance Planning

Chapter 27
- Order duckweed and nitric acid and prepare fertilizer solution and salt solution for the Investigation.
- Procure photos taken by remote-sensing satellites for Minilab 1.

Interactions in the Environment

How is a city like any other environment? Organisms that live in a city interact with other living and nonliving things. Dandelions sprout in sidewalk cracks, and robins pull worms out of the soil in vacant lots. A city, like other environmental systems, has a life of its own.

Grasslands, such as this one in Africa, are characterized by the lack of trees and the presence of various types of grasses. Large herds of grass-eating mammals are generally found on grasslands, but the species vary depending upon where the grassland is located. Wind, rainfall, and temperature also influence the formation of grasslands, as does soil type. Living and nonliving things interacting help to define a grassland.

756

Chapter 28
- Prepare bromthymol blue solution for Minilab 1.
- Order litmus paper for the Alternate Lab.

Chapter 29
- Prepare charate for the Investigation. Two months prior to doing the Investigation, refrigerate a portion of the grass seeds.
- Procure Potential Natural Vegetation Maps for Minilab 2.

Chaper 30
- Order pH paper for Minilab 2.
- Order *Daphnia* culture for the Alternate Lab.

What organisms can you see in a grassland? Shrubs, grasses, giraffes, zebras, and wildebeests are residents of this African grassland. Waterholes harbor protists and algae, and even fingerling fish. Nonliving factors also influence what goes on in the grassland. The amount of sunlight, rainfall, and wind intensity are all important to the life of the grassland.

What do you see when you look at a photograph of a city? You see buildings, vehicles, and people; but, a city also has a natural environment just like a grassland.

Pigeons are found in many cities, but so are peregrine falcons that nest on tall skyscrapers. Cities near the ocean have gulls that wheel overhead. Look closely at the trees in a city park, and you will see rows of holes made by woodpeckers looking for an insect meal. The next time you visit a city, look for signs of living things. There are complex relationships among the organisms in a city, just like there are in a grassland. Interactions among living and nonliving things are the focus of this final unit.

Introducing the Unit

Using the Photos
The activities of organisms in a city reflect the same kinds of interactions that mark the lives of organisms in natural communities. Organisms depend upon one another for food, shelter, and reproduction. They are not only influenced by other life forms, but also by physical factors of their environment. Organisms, in turn, exert an effect upon their physical environment. Humans play a unique role in cities, and their activities uniquely affect natural environments as well, often in ways that threaten themselves and other living systems.

Previewing the Chapters
In Chapter 27, students learn that limiting factors check the growth of populations. Some of those factors are density dependent, others density independent. Students compare those factors and distinguish between the kind of population growth governed by each. They come to understand that growth of the human population has been unique because of the lack of limiting factors acting upon it.

Chapter 28 centers on ecosystems. Students are introduced to the concept of trophic levels; the pyramids of energy, numbers, and biomass; and the reasons for those patterns. They compare other biotic relationships—mutualism, commensalism, and parasitism—and then study how organisms are influenced by, and influence, in turn, physical factors of the environment.

Chapter 29 begins with a comparison of primary and secondary ecological succession, factors leading to each type, and trends common to both. After learning how temperature, rainfall patterns, and topography contribute to different climates, students compare major world biomes and come to understand that all communities in the biosphere interact with one another.

Chapter 30 presents a variety of contemporary ecological issues and problems related to human activities—pesticide use, pollution of air and water, depletion of the ozone layer, the possibility of global warming, and conservation of natural resources. The consequences of these problems, both for humans and other organisms, are discussed, as are the factors that make finding solutions so complex.

SECTION	OBJECTIVES	TEXT LABS/FEATURES
27.1 Growth of Populations (3 days)	**Examine** the potential of organisms to reproduce in great numbers. **Compare** the growth of populations when limited by density-dependent or by density-independent factors.	**Minilab 1:** What are land use trends in your area? p. 763 **Investigation:** Limiting Factors for Duckweed Growth, p. 764
27.2 Regulation of Population Size (3 days)	**Predict** how predation and food supply may interact to limit two populations. **Discuss** the roles of parasitism and disease as density-dependent limiting factors. **Distinguish** between interspecific and intraspecific competition, and identify ways in which both may be reduced. **Analyze** the growth of the human population.	**Thinking Lab:** Why do newts survive their parasites? p. 769 **Minilab 2:** How does crowding affect plant growth? p. 774 **Literature Connection:** Rafael Jesús González, p. 776
BIOLOGY, TECHNOLOGY, AND SOCIETY		**Issues:** Old Versus Young in America? p. 780 **Career Connection:** Demographer, p. 781 **Considering the Environment:** Pile It On! p. 781

LAB MATERIALS

INVESTIGATION	MINILAB	ALTERNATE LAB
page 764 aluminum foil aquarium with pump beakers binocular microscope droppers duckweed fertilizer solution light source nitric acid solution ruler salt solution thermometer	**page 763** photos taken by remote-sensing satellites ruler **page 774** cups light source potting soil radish seeds ruler	**page 762** beans, navy and pinto beaker, 1-L

TEACHER CLASSROOM RESOURCES	OTHER RESOURCES
Study Guide, pp. 157-158 ***PLL:** *Dandelion and Plantain Populations,* p. 195 ***PLL:** *Microarthropod Populations in Leaf Litter,* p. 199 ****ILS:** *A Yeast Population Study,* p. 289 **Exploring Environmental Issues:** *How Many Is a Crowd?* p. 23	***STVS:** *Fish Survey,* Ecology (Disc 6, Side 1)
Study Guide, pp. 159-162 **Concept Mapping,** p. 27 **Critical Thinking/Problem Solving:** *Limiting Populations,* p. 27 ***PLL:** *Predation—A Limiting Factor in Population Growth,* p. 202 ***PLL:** *Growth of the Human Population in the United States,* p. 205 ****ILS:** *Changes in the Survival Rate of U.S. Population,* p. 293	***STVS:** *Sheep Parasite,* Animals (Disc 5, Side 1)
Assessment Materials **Chapter Assessment,** pp. 105-108 **Performance Assessment in Biology,** p. 54 **Alternate Assessment in the Science Classroom** **Computer Test Bank**	**Spanish Resources** **Cooperative Learning Resource Guide** **Videodisc Correlations** (to Optical Data's and Videodiscovery's videodiscs)

* Probing Levels of Life
** Investigating Living Systems

* Science Technology Videodisc Series

Key to Teaching Strategies

The following designations will help you decide which activities in the teacher margin are appropriate for your students.

L1 Level 1 activities should be within the ability range of all students.

L2 Level 2 activities should be within the ability range of the average to above-average student.

L3 Level 3 activities are designed for the ability range of above-average students.

LEP LEP activities are appropriate for Limited English Proficiency students.

COOP LEARN Cooperative Learning activities are designed for small group work.

ADDITIONAL RESOURCES

Infinite Voyage *The Keepers of Eden*
Students will see how scientists study populations of endangered species, and how human intervention may help to prevent the extinction of some species.

Audiovisual
Population Ecology Set, 35mm slide set, video, or filmstrip, Carolina.
Survival of the Fittest, video, Films for the Humanities and Sciences.

Software
Community Dynamics, Apple 128K, EME.
Coexist, Apple II, Conduit.

27

POPULATION BIOLOGY

Chapter Overview

Students begin their study of population biology as they learn about the growth of populations under ideal conditions. They find that growth of populations is checked by limiting factors, however, and then they compare the patterns of population growth influenced by density-dependent and density-independent factors, and analyze the reasons for the differences.

Next, students examine a variety of density-dependent limiting factors—predation and food, parasitism, disease, and competition, both interspecific and intraspecific. Finally, they study the growth of the human population and come to see that, at present, it is not affected by limiting factors to the same extent as are other populations. They learn why the human population will continue to grow worldwide and examine possible consequences of and solutions to the human population explosion.

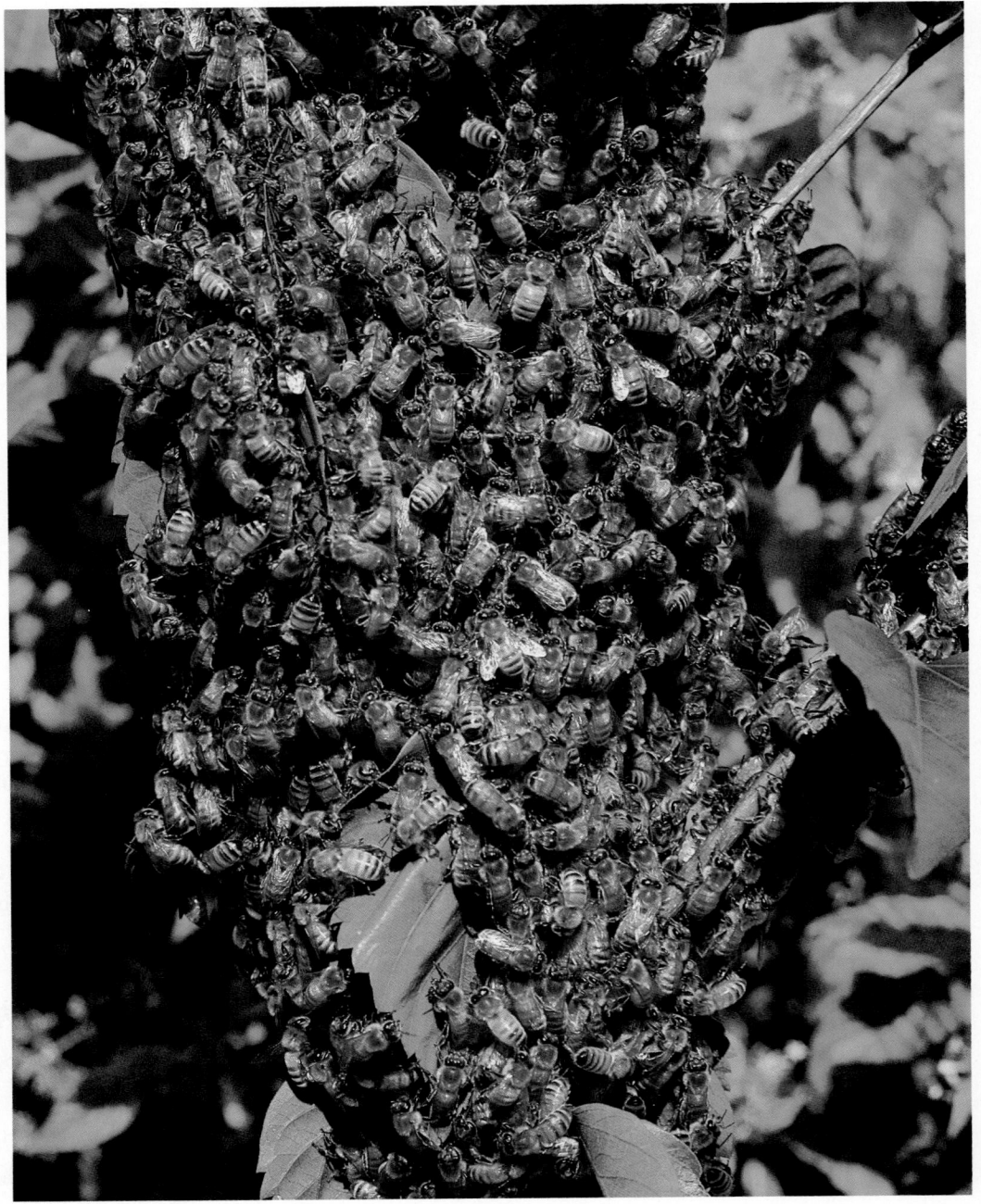

758

KEY TERMS	
biotic potential	population growth curve
birthrate	population growth rate curve
carrying capacity	population size
death rate	predation
interspecific competition	social hierarchy
intraspecific competition	territoriality
limiting factor	zero population growth
parasitism	
population density	
population growth	

POPULATION BIOLOGY

THERE'S A PLACE for everything—food, nursery, work places—and everything is in its place inside a beehive. Each individual has a role, which it performs faithfully. All the work gets done inside and outside the hive. Everybody eats and nobody fights. Sounds like the perfect success story, doesn't it? And it is, until success fills the hive with too many bees. But not to worry; the bees have an adaptive mechanism for handling the situation.

It's time to move—for the bees, as well as for anyone who might be in the path of a swarm such as the one shown here. If a hive becomes too crowded, a new queen bee is produced. The old queen gathers together a group of bees, and they move away to start a new hive. Does it matter how far away the bees move from their old home? Will other species of organisms living in the area of the new home site compete with the bees for food? In this chapter, you will think about questions such as these. You will also see how whole populations of organisms can reproduce successfully without overcrowding the planet.

How many family members would it take to create a crowd in your home? For bees in this hive, the number is in the tens of thousands. But even bees have their limits.

Chapter Preview

Contents

ASSESSMENT PLANNER

Choose assessment strategies from the following pages to evaluate the progress of your students.

Assess, pp. 766, 778-779
Portfolio, pp. 761, 768, 778
Alternate Lab, pp. 762-763
Thinking Lab, p. 769
Minilab 1, p. 763

Minilab 2, p. 774
Investigation, pp. 764-765
Chapter Review, pp. 782-783

Introducing the Chapter

The photographs on pages 758 and 759 will make very real the idea of population size and population density. Have students identify some factors that limit population size and lead them to distinguish between those factors related to density and those independent of density. Then, have students consider the human population, how its growth compares to that of other populations, and the reasons for the differences.

Theme Development

Students will recognize the theme of patterns of change as they examine population growth and the changing rates of birth and death over time. The theme is also evident as they study fluctuations in predator/prey relationships and examples of adaptations that serve to reduce competition. Systems and interactions is a major theme as well, as students explore relationships between predators and prey, parasites and hosts, pathogens and hosts, and competition among members of the same and different species.

Tying to Previous Knowledge

This chapter ties, in several ways, to evolution. Students have learned that it is the population that evolves, and that competition is often an important factor determining evolutionary change. Here they will examine the role of competition within and between species in greater detail. They can be reminded that Darwin recognized that although organisms tend to reproduce in great numbers, their population size tends to remain constant. Students will examine the reasons why this is so. The concept of cultural evolution comes into play once again as students learn why growth of the human population is unlike that of any other.

Key Concepts

This section outlines the concept of a population in terms of potential for growth. Patterns of population growth are compared. Limiting factors that keep population growth potentials from being reached are described.

Key Terms

population size, population growth, biotic potential, limiting factor, population growth curve, population growth rate curve, carrying capacity, birthrate, death rate, population density

Materials

- Order Landsat photos for Minilab 1.
- Acquire duckweed and fertilizer, and assemble aquariums for the Investigation.
- Purchase beans for the Alternate Lab.

1 Focus

Objectives

The objectives are listed on the student page. Remind students to preview these objectives as a guide to this numbered section.

Objectives

Examine the potential of organisms to reproduce in great numbers.

Compare the growth of populations when limited by density-dependent or by density-independent factors.

Figure 27-1 Dandelions seem to sprout up everywhere in the springtime. They produce huge numbers of seeds that are carried by air currents (right).

27.1 Growth of Populations

People who live in climate zones with four seasons expect new populations of living things to arrive every spring. Perhaps you, too, have watched dandelions sprout up in lawns or vacant lots in springtime. At first, there are just a few here and there. After a week or so, there may be more than you can easily count. As the summer months progress, you may see numerous grasshoppers and houseflies, or feel the sting of mosquitoes. At the same time you are observing—or experiencing—the dandelions and insects, you know that their days are limited. Their populations may grow rapidly for a while, but they will not continue to grow endlessly. They will, in fact, all disappear with a new change of season. Scientists of Charles Darwin's day took careful note of the fact that no population continues to grow unchecked. This realization helped Darwin form his ideas about natural selection.

Biotic Potential

How big is a population? The answer depends partly on where the organisms live. Suppose you discover a pond where 40 frogs are living. The frog population of the pond at this time is 40. Suppose you can count 75 cattails growing along the edges of the pond. The cattail population of the pond is 75. The frogs make up one population at the pond; the cattails make up another. There probably are populations of other kinds of organisms at the pond as well. A population is a group of organisms belonging to the same species and living within a certain area, such as the pond. The number of organisms in each group is the **population size.** As the organisms reproduce, the population size increases.

Look at the growth curve, shaped like the letter J, in Figure 27-2. It shows that under ideal conditions—unlimited food, absence of disease, lack of predators, favorable temperatures, and so on—the size of a population would increase indefinitely. Increase in the size of a population with time is called **population growth.**

760 POPULATION BIOLOGY

Under ideal conditions, many species of bacteria reproduce by binary fission and double their population size every 20 minutes. If no environmental factors limited their survival, in 36 hours one bacterium could give rise to enough descendants to cover Earth with a layer of bacteria 30 cm deep! Even organisms that reproduce more slowly could produce many offspring under ideal conditions. Darwin estimated that, starting with one pair of elephants, there would be more than 19 million elephants in only 750 years. This highest rate of reproduction under ideal conditions is called a population's **biotic potential.**

Do most organisms reach their biotic potential? Obviously, they do not. If they did, Earth would be overrun with elephants, bacteria, cattails, grasshoppers, and other organisms. **Limiting factors,** which are circumstances that keep organisms from reaching their biotic potential, prevent such chaos. For many organisms, such as grasshoppers and mosquitoes, unfavorable temperatures that come with seasonal changes are limiting factors. Disease, predators, and lack of food or space are other common limiting factors.

Population Growth Curves

How do we know how populations grow and respond to their environment? Growth of populations can best be studied in the laboratory because conditions can be controlled. To study the population growth of yeast cells, a culture medium can be inoculated with a few yeast cells. Counting the yeast cells at regular time intervals would give data much like those shown in Table 27.1. Note that the size of the population increases slowly at first. This period of slow growth in population size is followed by a period of rapid

Figure 27-2 Under ideal conditions, a population's size would continue to increase indefinitely. This increase can be shown graphically and resembles the letter *J.*

Table 27.1 Growth of a Yeast Population

Population Age (hours)	Number of Cells/mL	Increase in Cell Number/mL
0	10	
2	29	19
4	71	42
6	175	104
8	351	176
10	513	162
12	595	82
14	641	46
16	656	15
18	662	6

Demonstration

Obtain a set of 5-cm wooden cubes that have been painted blue, brown, and green. You can obtain the wooden cubes from a lumber yard and paint them yourself. Explain to students that the blue cubes represent oceans, brown cubes represent land masses, and green cubes represent a population of animals. Place seven blue cubes and three brown cubes in a group on the table. Tell students that this group of cubes represents Earth. Begin with one green cube and stack it on one of the brown cubes. Add a second green cube on top of the brown and green cubes after one minute, explaining that the population has doubled. After another minute, add two more green cubes to the stack. Continue doubling the population size each minute. When the stack falls, begin a new stack on another brown cube. Continue the process until all of the stacks have fallen and there are no more brown cubes to begin another stack. Ask students to comment on what they have learned. Point out that this chapter explains many of the concepts illustrated by the demonstration. **L1** **LEP**

2 Teach

Using the Illustration

Point out to students that the J-shaped growth curve in Figure 27-2 is theoretical for most populations. Explain that populations never continue such growth indefinitely because conditions never remain ideal.

Demonstration

Set up a series of culture dishes with equal amounts of pond water that have been adjusted to various pH levels, pH 4 to pH 9. Inoculate each culture dish with five planarians and feed them a bit of raw liver every two days. Observe the dishes for a week. Have students explain how pH level of water is a limiting factor for planarians. **L1**

PORTFOLIO

Have students write a short story for their portfolios explaining the plight of a density-dependent factor, such as a disease organism, from the point of view of the density-dependent factor. Use this teaching strategy with material on page 764 of the text. **L1**

STUDENT JOURNAL

Have students make an entry in their journals that lists all of the density-independent limiting factors they are aware of for one day. The factors may limit populations of humans or any other organism they see. Use this teaching strategy with material on page 765 of the text. **L1**

SECTION 27.1

Concept Development

Explain that J-shaped curves represent population growth under ideal conditions and that S-shaped curves occur when limiting factors come into play. A population may begin growth similar to a J-shaped curve but then decline. Point out that the population growth curve may be altered as environmental conditions change.

Is Coexistence Possible?

Obtain a copy of the painting *The Peaceable Kingdom* by Edward Hicks. Ask students to identify the animals included in the painting and suggest reasons why it would be impossible for populations of these animals to exist as portrayed. There is a wide variety of domestic and wild animal species in the painting, native to different continents. Explain that, in real life, the predators would reduce the domesticated animals to extinction. **L1**

COOP LEARN

Using the Illustration

In mathematics, the rate of change of a straight line graph is determined by dividing the vertical rise of the curve by the length of the run. This same principle holds true in determining the rate of change of population growth when graphed, as shown in Figure 27-4.

Figure 27-3 A yeast population can be grown under controlled laboratory conditions. When the growth is graphed, an S-shaped population growth curve results. Growth levels off at the carrying capacity of the environment. The liquid medium in which the yeast are grown becomes cloudier as the number of yeast cells increases. Each tube corresponds to a population at the portion of the growth curve shown above it. Data for this graph are shown in Table 27.1.

growth, followed by another period of slow growth. Eventually, the population stops increasing altogether. The population size remains stable after that point. Limiting factors such as available food supply or the buildup of wastes have determined that the yeast population will grow no larger.

If you were to graph the changes in the size of the yeast population, you would get an S-shaped curve, as in Figure 27-3. An S-shaped curve is also known as a **population growth curve.** The low end of the curve, on the left, indicates the early slow growth. The steep rise in the curve illustrates the period of rapid growth over a comparatively short span of time. The high end, on the right, indicates the final, stable population size. At this point, the population has stopped increasing in size.

The growth of animal populations shows a similar pattern. Imagine several families of raccoons newly relocated to a woodland where there were no raccoons before. If you could keep count of the raccoons over several years, you would find that the size of the raccoon population grows in much the same way as that of the yeast population. Eventually, the population would stop increasing in size and then would remain stable. Limiting factors such as available food supply, space, or predators have determined that the raccoon population will grow no larger.

762 POPULATION BIOLOGY

ALTERNATE LAB: Estimating Population Size

Purpose
Students will model a method for estimating the size of a population of organisms.

Materials
1-L beaker, 500-mL volume each of pinto beans and white navy beans

Procedure
Give the following directions to students.
1. Consider 500 mL of pinto beans in the beaker to be a deer population. Capture a sample of deer by removing a handful of pinto beans.
2. Count the number of "deer" captured and record the number in a data table that you have made.
3. In a real investigation, the deer would be marked and released into the population. Model the capture-and-release technique by counting out an equal number of white navy beans to put in the beaker. The white beans represent the captured and released deer. Put the pinto beans you removed to the side.
4. Biologists studying a real deer population would allow the deer to become distributed again. Model this by stirring the beans so that the captured "deer" are evenly distributed in the beaker.
5. Now, capture a second sample of "deer" from the population. Count and record the total number captured and the number that were previously

If you were to make similar studies of deer, mice, snakes, different species of trees, shrubs, or other complex organisms in the woodland, your population growth curves would also follow an S-shaped pattern. The limiting factors might vary from population to population, but eventually they would check each population's growth.

Population Growth Rate Curve   You could also use graphs to show how fast the yeast population and other populations grow. Such a graph, as seen in Figure 27-4, is called a **population growth rate curve**. It demonstrates that, up to a point, the size of a population increases more and more rapidly. Then the rate of increase slows down. The *number* of organisms still increases, but the *rate* at which new organisms are added to the population decreases. When the population growth levels off, the population growth rate approaches zero. To picture this another way, think about the acceleration of a car. As the car pulls away from a stop sign, it moves slowly at first. Then the speed rapidly increases, and more distance is covered in less and less time. As the car approaches the speed limit, its speed continues to increase, but not as quickly as before. The car continues to move; eventually, its speed no longer increases. Instead, it remains steady at the speed limit.

Carrying Capacity   When a population arrives at the point where its size is no longer increasing, it has reached the carrying capacity of the environment. The **carrying capacity** is the greatest number of individuals in a certain population that a given environment—such as a pond or a woodland—is capable of supporting under a specific set of conditions. The carrying capacity of an environment can vary with the time of year as conditions change. For example, as the weather becomes colder in winter, food supply may diminish and the environment will not be able to support as many organisms. For plant populations, the carrying capacity may decrease in summer as water supply or access to sunlight becomes limited. At the carrying capacity, the number of organisms born or produced in a given period of time, the **birthrate,** balances the number of organisms that die during that time, the **death rate.** At this point, the size of the population remains fairly stable.

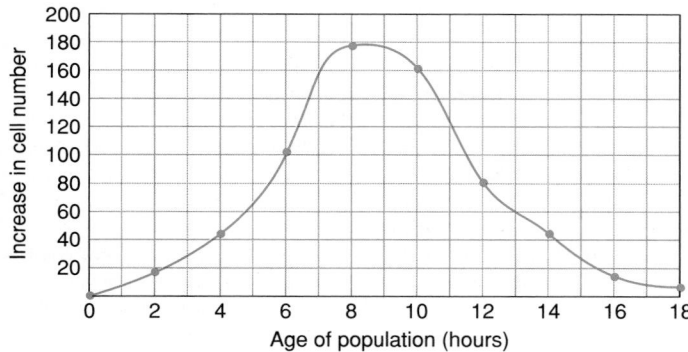

Figure 27-4   **The growth rate of a population can be graphed. This growth rate curve is for the same yeast population whose growth is graphed in Figure 27-3. The growth rate data are shown in the right-hand column of Table 27.1.**

Minilab 1

What are land use trends in your area?

What is happening to land in your area? Are marshes or forests disappearing? Is your city getting larger? Is cropland increasing or decreasing? To learn the answers to these questions, a remote-sensing satellite program with its satellite, Landsat, has been in operation since 1986. This system does environmental monitoring and land use analyses by using photographic studies called remote sensing. Use the before and after remote-sensing photos provided by your teacher to determine what is happening to the land. Take measurements and calculate percentages of land undergoing changes.

Analysis   *What kind of change is the land in your photograph undergoing? Why? What percentage of the land changed from the before photo to the after photo?*

Minilab 1

Purpose
Students will examine remote-sensing satellite photos to determine changes in land use.

Skills
observe, compare and contrast, measure in SI

Teaching Strategies
- Obtain satellite remote-sensing photos from: EOSAT, Landsat Data Users Notes, 4300 Forbes Blvd., Lanham, MD 20706; 800-344-9933. If photos are not available for your area, request photos of areas that have disappearing cropland, land cover changes in major cities, wetlands drainage, or other land use analyses.
- Give students rulers to measure areas where change has occurred.
- Review how to calculate percentages.

Expected Results
Answers will vary depending on photos.

Answers
Answers will vary depending on photos.

✔ Assessment
Knowledge: Have students summarize their findings in their journals. If their findings indicate that a land problem is developing, ask them to make suggestions as to what could be done to alleviate the problem.

---

marked and recaptured.
6. After you finish, count all the beans in the beaker. This is the actual size of the population. The estimated number of "deer" in the population is given by the formula $T = (O \times S)/M$ where T = the estimated population size, O = the number captured and marked in the first sample, S = the number captured in the second sample, and M = the number of marked individuals in the

second sample.
Analysis
Ask students to answer the following.
1. What are important factors in the capture? *size of the animal, where it lives*
2. What data were obtained? *Answers should include data needed to obtain the theoretical population size.*
3. Find the percent error by subtracting the estimated size from the actual size, dividing by the actual size, then multi-

plying by 100. What was your percent error? *Answers should range between 5% and 50%.*

✔ Assessment
Performance: Have students design a model to investigate the size of a population of pigeons in a city park. Students should list their methods of marking and recapturing, and include illustrations of their design. **L1**

Microscope Activity

Set up a hay infusion by adding a couple of wheat seeds and a pinch of hay to a 1-liter jar half full of water. Inoculate the infusion with a few paramecia. Have students monitor the population explosion of paramecia by observing one drop of water each day for two weeks. `L1` `LEP`

Audiovisual

Show the filmstrip *Population Ecology,* available from Carolina Biological Supply Company.

Software

Populous: Simulations of Population Biology is an inexpensive program available from Don Alstat at the University of Minnesota, Minneapolis, MN 55455-0302.

INVESTIGATION

Limiting Factors for Duckweed Growth

Time Allotment

1 class period, then 10 minutes every other day for 2 to 3 weeks

Objectives

Upon completing this Investigation, students will be able to:
- Describe limiting factors for growth and reproduction of duckweed.
- Interpret data in terms of limiting factors.

Skills

observe and infer, form a hypothesis, design an experiment, interpret data

Materials

duckweed, beakers, aquariums and pumps, light source, aluminum foil for making dark environments, thermometer, ruler, serial dilutions of 5-10-5 fertilizer (1%, 0.1%, 0.01%), dilute nitric acid (pH 5), droppers, serial dilutions of salt solution (1%, 0.1%, 0.01%), binocular microscope

---

Density-dependent Limiting Factors

Suppose you wanted to predict population growth among a group of organisms, perhaps among the frogs in a pond. You would need to know as much as possible about the limiting factors of the frogs' environment. Limiting factors for organisms whose growth pattern takes an S-shaped curve, as is the case with frogs, are almost always density dependent. This means that the influence of any limiting factor varies with the population density. **Population density** refers to the size of a population that occupies a given area at any given point in time. A small population of frogs living in a given pond has a low population density. A large population living in the same pond has a high population density.

The growth of many populations decreases as density increases. Thus, whatever limiting factor is acting on the population—possibly a shortage in the food supply—is tied to population density. The greater the density becomes, the more vigorously the limiting factor slows down population

---

INVESTIGATION

Limiting Factors for Duckweed Growth

Duckweed

During the summer, you may have noticed green mats of plants on the surface of ponds or in areas of slowly moving streams. Some of this green material was probably algae, but some may have been duckweed—the smallest flowering plant in the world. Its tiny, round "leaves" are actually the stems of the plant. They can be as small as 1 mm in diameter. Duckweed reproduces asexually with the daughter plants clinging to the parent plant. As growth progresses, the plant bodies separate, producing new individuals.

Conditions for growth must be optimal if plants are to grow well. For example, water temperature and pH must be in a narrow range that the plants can tolerate, light must be available, and the water must contain sufficient minerals. If any of these factors are limiting, plants will not grow well.

Problem

What are the limiting factors for duckweed growth?

Safety Precautions

Be sure to wash your hands at the end of each lab session in which you count or handle duckweed.

Hypothesis

Make a hypothesis about what might be a limiting factor for duckweed growth. Explain your reasons for making this hypothesis.

Experimental Plan

1. As a group, make a list of possible ways you might test your hypothesis using the materials your teacher has made available.

764 POPULATION BIOLOGY

(See page 27T for instructions for making serial dilutions of fertilizer and salt solution.)

Preparation

Collect duckweed from local ponds or still places in streams, or order it from a biological supply company.

Possible Hypotheses

1. Low pH will inhibit growth and reproduction of duckweed.
2. Oxygenated water will cause an increase in growth and reproduction of duckweed.

Possible Procedures

- A possible procedure might be to place 25 duckweeds in each of four equal-size beakers of pond water containing serial dilutions of fertilizer. Set up two controls, one of plain pond water and one of distilled water. Count plant bodies every other day for three weeks.

growth. Gradually, the population density approaches the carrying capacity of the environment. After the density reaches the carrying capacity, birthrate and death rate become about equal; population growth levels off.

Density-independent Limiting Factors

Organisms such as the ladybugs shown in Figure 27-5 show a different pattern of population growth. The size of the population does not level off in a smooth S shape. Rather, the curve showing the growth of these organisms begins in a way that resembles the J-shaped curve in Figure 27-2. First there is a rapid increase in population size, also similar to the early stages of S-shaped growth but occurring at a higher rate. But then the population crashes, which means that it rapidly declines rather than levels off, and the population size never reaches the carrying capacity of the environment. The factor limiting the growth of the ladybug

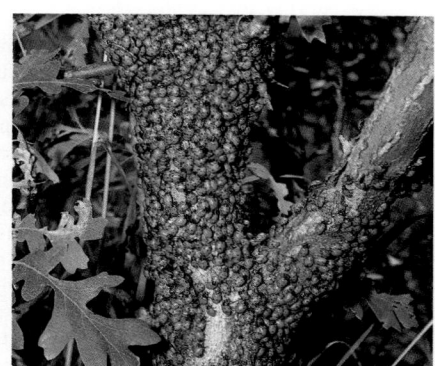

Figure 27-5 This dense population of ladybugs probably will never reach the carrying capacity of the environment. Why might this be so?

EARTH SCIENCE
CONNECTION

Population Studies: Newly formed volcanic islands provide scientists with a natural laboratory in which the population growth rates of plants and animals can be observed. Islands off the coast of Iceland have been the scene of carrying capacity studies for 30 years or more.

Figure Caption Question
Why might a ladybug population never reach the carrying capacity of the environment? Cold weather will limit the population and it will rapidly decline.

---

2. Agree on one idea from your group's list that could be investigated in the classroom.
3. Design an experiment that will test one variable at a time. Plan to collect quantitative data.
4. Following the style of a recipe, write a numbered list of directions that anyone could follow.
5. Make a list of materials and the quantities you will need.

Checking the Plan

Discuss the following points with other group members to decide on the final procedures for your experiment.
1. What variables will need to be controlled?
2. What is your control?
3. What will you measure or count?
4. How many setups will you make?
5. How many groups of duckweed plants will you start with? How many plants will be in a group?

6. How will you raise the plants? What kinds of containers will you keep them in? Will you supply any nutrients?
7. How long will your experiment run?
8. Have you designed and made a table for collecting data?

Make sure your teacher has approved your experimental plan before you proceed further.

Data and Observations

Carry out your experiment, make your measurements, and complete your data table. Make a graph of your results.

Analysis and Conclusions

1. Under what conditions did your duckweed reproduce faster?
2. What was your experimental evidence for this conclusion?
3. Was your hypothesis supported by your data?

4. If your hypothesis was not supported, what types of experimental error could be responsible?
5. Consult with another group that used a different procedure to examine this problem. What are its conclusions?
6. What does your experimental evidence tell you about limiting factors for duckweed growth?
7. What other limiting factors might affect duckweed growth?

Going Further

Based on this lab experience, design an experiment that would help to answer a question that arose from your work. Assume that you will have unlimited resources and will not be conducting this lab in class.

Teaching Strategies
- If two groups decide to do the same experiment, encourage one group to choose a different limiting factor. You will have a more interesting discussion if groups have investigated a variety of variables.
- Remind students to wash their hands each time they work with the duckweed.
- To introduce the lab, ask students to observe duckweed plants under the microscope. Point out that each "leaf" has one root with no root hairs.
- Review vegetative reproduction.
- Make sure students know that when the plants begin to reproduce, each lobe is a separate plant.
- Make sure students keep their duckweed containers supplied with an adequate amount of pond water.

Data and Observations
Examine each group's graphs and evaluate the group's interpretation of data.

Data Analysis
1-7. Answers will vary depending on variables selected. Light, fertilizer, pH, and water temperature are all limiting factors in duckweed growth.

✔ **Assessment**
Knowledge: Have students summarize the class results by compiling a list of all factors that were found to be limiting to duckweed growth. They should subdivide the list into density-dependent and density-independent factors. | COOP LEARN |

Extensions
Students might test other plants, such as *Elodea,* and compare growth with duckweed growth under the same experimental conditions.

3 Assess

Check for Understanding

Have students invent and play a board game that illustrates the concepts of this chapter. Game elements should include additional points for strategies that maximize sustainable populations and negatives for strategies that encourage overpopulation. `L1` `COOP LEARN`

Reteach

Have student teams imagine that they are a population of wild mustangs. Have students discuss the limits on their population growth that are density dependent and those that are density independent. Teams should prepare and give oral reports on their discussion. `COOP LEARN`

Extension

Have students design a bulletin board display that illustrates factors that limit population growth of organisms. Students can use photos from magazines and newspapers. `L1` `LEP`

✔ Assessment

Oral: Assign students to make up three questions about limiting factors for their classmates to answer. Have students pair up, and have them ask each other their questions. Monitor the groups to be sure that students are on task and understand the concepts presented. `L1` `COOP LEARN`

4 Close

Discussion

Present the following scenario to students. Populations of a certain insect pest and one of its predators have been detected in a field. Have students make statements about the pest insect's biotic potential, population growth rate, and limiting factors. Then, have students determine if they would spray the field with insecticide, based on what they have decided about the pest insect population. Ask students to defend their answers.

Figure 27-6 An insect population in a temperate climate, such as the ladybugs shown on the previous page, increases each spring and summer and dies rapidly with the freezing weather of late fall. Temperature is therefore a density-independent limiting factor.

population is, thus, not related to population density and is said to be density independent. Density-independent factors, such as temperature and oxygen supply, are often related to physical aspects of the environment.

Temperature is a physical factor that frequently limits the size of insect populations. In temperate zones, the population size begins to grow slowly in late spring and then more rapidly through the summer. Then, when cold weather begins in late autumn, population size declines rapidly as adults die. The environment could support further population growth, but the population declines before that point is reached. However, the population is not destroyed by the weather. Before they die, the insects deposit their fertilized eggs in a weather-resistant area. The following spring, the young insects emerge and begin another population explosion.

Oxygen can be a physical limiting factor in aquatic communities. Oxygen is needed for cellular respiration by almost all organisms. If the oxygen level drops too low, many animals that have a high demand for oxygen cannot survive. Decline in oxygen content of water can be caused by the decomposition of polluting organic wastes or by an increase in water temperature. More oxygen can dissolve in cold water than in warm water. Sometimes, hot water is released into lakes or rivers from factories or power plants. The hot water raises the temperature of the water to which it is added, causing the oxygen content to be lowered. Lack of oxygen becomes a limiting factor. As fish and other organisms die, their overall populations decline.

Section Review

Understanding Concepts

1. Suppose you were to observe the growth of a population of amoebas in a very large container. You provide unlimited numbers of smaller microorganisms for food, the water contains plenty of dissolved oxygen, and all other conditions are favorable for growth. Describe the growth of such a population.
2. Now suppose you repeat the experiment in question 1, but this time you limit the amount of food organisms. Assuming all other factors are the same as in the first experiment, describe the growth of this population of amoebas.
3. Suppose you were conducting the experiment as in question 1, but after several weeks you add a chemical that the amoebas cannot

tolerate. Describe the growth of the population up to and after the addition of the chemical.
4. **Skill Review—Making and Using Graphs:** The following table shows the growth of a population of unicellular organisms.

Time (hours)	Number of Organisms/mL
0	17
4	41
8	89
12	202
16	418
20	510
24	530
28	537
32	542
36	544

Prepare a graph of these data. What kind of factor is limiting the population's growth? Explain. For more help, refer to Organizing Information in the **Skill Handbook.**
5. **Thinking Critically:** Which kinds of populations, those limited by density-dependent or by density-independent factors, are more likely to be made up of individuals that reproduce quickly and produce many offspring? Why?

766 POPULATION BIOLOGY

Answers to Section Review

1. The growth would illustrate the idea of biotic potential, and data would generate a J-shaped curve.
2. Data would generate an S-shaped curve.
3. Addition of the chemical would be a density-independent limiting factor. The population's growth would be very rapid before addition of the chemical, but, once added, the chemical would result in the sudden death of the organisms.

4. **Skill Review—Making and Using Graphs:** The data produce an S-shaped graph. Thus, the limiting factor was density dependent.
5. **Thinking Critically:** Populations influenced by density-independent factors reproduce this way. Such populations will not be influenced by the carrying capacity of the environment, so the number of organisms produced is not significant.

27.2 Regulation of Population Size

You have learned that density-independent limiting factors, such as climate and seasonal temperature change, have the same effect on a population regardless of its size. A large population of houseflies will die in the autumn cold just as surely as a small one will. In contrast, the effect of density-dependent limiting factors varies with the size of the population. The larger the population size, the more intense a density-dependent factor will be.

While density-independent limiting factors tend to be rooted in the physical environment, density-dependent factors most often involve interactions among organisms, and so they are biological. A population may be limited by availability of food, or by other organisms that feed or prey upon it or cause disease. Members of a population may compete with one another for some important resource in the environment. Organisms belonging to different populations may also compete. In any case, populations responding to density-dependent factors can attain a maximum population size that matches the carrying capacity of the environment.

Predation and Food

Almost all organisms are food for other organisms. **Predation,** the feeding of one organism on another, can be a factor limiting the size of a population. Often it is hard to tell, however, if predation is a limiting factor. For example, the Canadian lynx preys on the snowshoe hare. At about ten-year intervals, the sizes of both populations rise and fall almost simultaneously. Does this mean that the lynx regularly overkill their prey? It has been observed that snowshoe hare populations on islands where the lynx does not live show similar cycles. Perhaps the hare's food supply or another limiting factor periodically increases and decreases. If so, both lynx and hare populations would increase and decrease with it. Or, perhaps the lynx

Objectives

Predict how predation and food supply may interact to limit two populations.

Discuss the roles of parasitism and disease as density-dependent limiting factors.

Distinguish between interspecific and intraspecific competition, and identify ways in which both may be reduced.

Analyze the growth of the human population.

Figure 27-7 As the prey population rises and falls in number, so does the predator population, but with a slight lag. These data come from records of hare and lynx pelts sold by trappers to the Hudson Bay Company in northern Canada.

Number of organisms (in thousands)

Time (in years)

27.2 REGULATION OF POPULATION SIZE ❧ **767**

SECTION 27.2
Prepare

Key Concepts
The roles of symbiotic and predator-prey relationships and competition as limiting factors of population growth are outlined. Human population growth is compared with that of other populations for similarities and differences.

Key Terms
predation, parasitism, interspecific competition, intraspecific competition, social hierarchy, territoriality, zero population growth

Materials
• Obtain potting soil, cups, and radish seeds for Minilab 2.

1 Focus

Objectives
The objectives are listed on the student page. Remind students to preview these objectives as a guide to this numbered section.

Demonstration
Feed an earthworm to an African clawed frog, *Xenopus laevis,* or a cricket to a spider. Ask students to describe the relationship between the two organisms. (They should say that one eats the other or one is harmed while the other benefits.) Explain that this is essentially what the term *predation* means in real life.

PROGRAM RESOURCES

Teacher Classroom Resources
Study Guide, pp. 157-158 L1
Concept Mapping, p. 27 L1 LEP
Critical Thinking/Problem Solving, p. 27 L2
Probing Levels of Life, Labs 76, 77, pp. 202, 205 L2
Investigating Living Systems, Lab 75, p. 293 L2

2 Teach

Bioethics

Predators: Because of losses in their sheep and cattle herds, many ranchers are of the view that all populations of predators such as eagles, wolves, and coyotes should be eliminated. Many environmentalists contend that predator populations serve a valuable role in reducing the populations of rodents and other pest species. Ask students if they think predator species should be eliminated to protect domesticated animals. Ask students to consider whether losses caused by predators are density dependent or density independent. *Because the number of losses is dependent upon the density of the herd and the density of the predators, the relationship is density dependent.*

Chalkboard Example

Have students relate as many predator-prey relationships as they can. Write all contributions on the board. Ask students if some of the prey have more than one predator. *The answer is yes.* **L1**

Enrichment

Point out that predators generally weed out the weakest individuals. Any unusual behavior on the part of the prey almost instantly catches the attention of the predator.

Figure Caption Question

What would you expect to happen to a fish population in this river if the eagle population declined? Because fewer fish would be eaten by eagles, the fish population would increase.

Figure 27-8 Eagles are predators of fish. What would you expect to happen to a fish population in this river if the eagle population declined?

undergoes a regular cycle, independent of the hares but affecting them. The situation is complex, yet it is clear that the size of most populations is at least partly checked by predators.

Predation as a Density-dependent Factor How may predation be density dependent? Consider a prey population such as rabbits. The greater the number of rabbits in a given area, the more likely it is that a predator, perhaps a coyote, will find and kill one. As the density of the prey population begins to fall as a result of predation, fewer prey are killed.

Most often, a balance is reached in a predator-prey relationship. The size of one population affects the size of the other. An increase in size of the prey population leads to an increase in size of the predator population because more food is available for the predators. Later, the size of the prey population begins to fall. Soon, because less food is available, fewer predators survive, and the size of the predator population falls. Thus, with fewer predators in its environment, the prey population will rise again.

The predator-prey interaction creates a cycle of population increase and decrease in both populations. Notice in Figure 27-7 on the previous page that changes in the size of the predator population follow those in the prey population. In a typical predator-prey relationship, predation is the limiting factor for the prey population, and the availability of food is the limiting factor for the predator population.

Predation as Beneficial Predation is healthy for a prey population. Very often, the prey caught and killed are those that are very young, very old, or less capable of coping with the environment. Thus, the healthiest, best-adapted individuals are most likely to survive, reproduce, and pass their genes on to the next generation. In this sense, predation is a form of natural selection that benefits the population as a whole.

Predation may also maintain prey population size very near the carrying capacity while other factors would not. Suppose, for example, predators were removed from the environment. At first, in the absence of predators, the size of the prey population would probably increase, exceeding the carrying capacity. However, food might then become a limiting factor. The unusually large number of prey organisms might overbrowse, eating plants more quickly than the plants could reproduce. Eventually, almost all of the animals would starve to death, and the population size would decline to a point well below the carrying capacity.

Such a case happened in a moose population on an island in Lake Superior. Before wolves lived on the island, many moose starved. In the absence of predators, the size of the moose population increased unchecked. Food then became a limiting factor, and the majority of the moose starved. Later, wolves walked across the frozen lake to the island and began to prey on the moose. Since that time, the size of the moose population has remained stable at a point closer to the carrying capacity.

PORTFOLIO

Ask students to use the library to research the introduction of Russian thistle, starlings, English sparrows, gypsy moths, or kudzu into the United States; or have students read and report on the work of John Garcia, who studies the interactions of animals and their environments in California. Students should add their reports to their portfolios. **L2**

Parasitism

When you think of a predator stalking prey, you probably think of a larger or stronger animal, such as a lion, attacking a smaller or gentler animal, such as a zebra. There are many instances, however, in which smaller—much smaller—organisms attack organisms much larger than they are. These kinds of harmful organisms are called parasites. Parasites include such organisms as fleas and leeches, which live on another organism called the host. Parasites also include many organisms, such as tapeworms and flukes, that live inside host organisms.

Parasitism can be a limiting factor for population size. Almost all organisms have some parasites. Parasites usually harm the host but typically do not kill it, because the death of the host would result in the death of the parasites. However, if a host has too many parasites, the host might die. Dogs, for example, may die from the effects of harboring large numbers of heartworms.

Parasitism is a density-dependent factor. The possibility that different kinds of parasites will be passed from one organism to the next is greater in a dense host population. As the rate of transfer increases, the number and kinds of parasites in each host also increase. Too many parasites on one host may cause death by interfering with the host's nutrition or immune responses. The parasites may also reduce fertility of the host. As a result, the size and density of the host population decreases. Host organisms are then more widely spaced, and transfer of parasites is less frequent. Because hosts have fewer parasites, the host population can survive and increase in number again. Thus, the cycle continues.

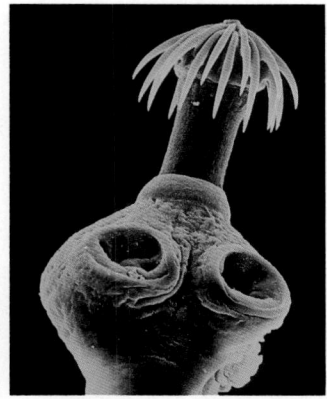

Figure 27-9 The head of a tapeworm is adapted with hooks and suckers for grasping the inner lining of the host's intestine. Magnification: 80×

Thinking Lab
DRAW A CONCLUSION

Why do newts survive their parasites?

Background
Why is it that parasites haven't killed everything on the planet? This question can be answered in part by examining the way in which parasites are transmitted from one host to another. If a parasite kills its host, it must have a method of transportation for moving to a new host. A biting fly or mosquito would serve this purpose. If a parasite has no way to get to another host except by contact with that host, then the parasite must not kill the first host. The host must

be permitted to live and associate with other, potential host organisms.

Red-spotted newts often are infected with a parasite that is transmitted by the bite of a leech. Therefore, infection can be transmitted only in ponds, the leech's habitat. At the end of their first summer, young newts leave the pond and spend about six years maturing before they return to the pond to reproduce. When the newts are analyzed for parasites, it is found that they do not suffer from any adverse effects—even

when their blood contains a million parasites per milliliter of blood. This number is about the same as the number of red blood cells in the blood of a newt!

You Try It
In general, parasites that kill their hosts have intermediate hosts such as insects or leeches. Why are the newts, with a leech as intermediate host, not killed by their parasites? Analyze the information and **draw a conclusion.** Hint: Think about the newt's life cycle.

Thinking Lab
DRAW A CONCLUSION

Purpose
Students will interpret the pattern of parasitism in red-spotted newts.

Skills
recognize cause and effect, interpret data

Teaching Strategies
• Ask students what would happen to the newts in the forest if the parasite were very harmful. What would happen to the

newts if they became ill in the forest and did not return to the pond to reproduce? What would happen to the parasite?
• Make sure that students are aware of the close relationship between the evolution of the parasite and that of the host.

Answers
The six years that newts spend in the forest prevent harmful parasites from surviving.

Only those that do not harm the newt survive, reproduce, and infect new hosts when the newt returns to the pond. Newts with harmful parasites will die before they return to the pond. Therefore, harmful parasites cannot infect new hosts.

✔ **Assessment**
Knowledge: Have students describe their reasoning process as they draw a conclusion.

SECTION 27.2

Concept Development
The human population is estimated to be greater than 5 billion. It is also estimated that there are 10 billion parasitic infections in humans. Ask students to explain how this can be. *Studies by parasitologists indicate that, on average, most humans carry more than one species of parasite at any one time.*

Microscope Activity
Have students observe prepared slides of tapeworms, pinworms, trichinella, or similar human parasites. **L1**

Enrichment
Allow students to research various human parasites. If you have students who plan to become veterinarians, you might suggest that they research parasites of some animal they are interested in. **L2**

Reinforcement
Emphasize the fact that most parasites do not kill their hosts. Human autopsies sometimes reveal large numbers of intestinal parasites in otherwise healthy individuals who have been killed in automobile accidents.

SECTION 27.2

Misconception

Students often have a limited understanding of disease organisms and the disease process. This section provides an excellent opportunity to explain the similarities between the disease organism-host relationship and the predator-prey relationship.

Reinforcement

Explain that most disease organisms are transferred by other organisms called vectors. Vectors that students may be aware of include rats, roaches, mosquitoes, and similar organisms. Other diseases, like the common cold virus, are spread by contact and aerosols.

Concept Development

Have students relate the rabbit population problem in Australia to a population growth curve. Before the introduction of the virus, the population growth curve resembled the J-shaped curve. After the introduction of the virus, the curve turned rapidly downward. The population now oscillates around the carrying capacity of the range.

Disease and Populations

Population density is closely related to the spread of certain diseases. For example, malaria is a disease caused by the sporozoan protist *Plasmodium*, which is carried by female *Anopheles* mosquitoes and transferred to humans by the bites of these mosquitoes. Malaria is a density-dependent factor because the denser the human population, the greater the chance of the disease being passed to others. The spread of malaria is also dependent on the density of the mosquito population. Without these mosquitoes, malaria could not be transmitted, even if people stood cheek-to-cheek.

Disease can control the size of animal populations. In a dense population, disease can spread rapidly and kill many organisms in a matter of days. Sometimes people use this fact as a way to control oversized animal populations. For example, rabbits are not native to Australia; they were brought there from Europe by humans. The result was a disaster. Because there were no effective native predators or competitors at the time, the size of the rabbit population increased rapidly. Soon rabbits began competing with sheep for food. In order to reduce the rabbit population and preserve the sheep population, biologists injected some of the rabbits with a virus from South America. The virus was transferred directly from rabbit to rabbit, and rapidly killed large numbers of the animals because most had no immunity to the disease. As the number and density of rabbits decreased, the rate of disease transfer also decreased. A few rabbits were resistant enough to the virus to survive the disease. Because resistance is an inherited trait, the rabbit population became more resistant through natural selection. At the same time, there was selection for less virulent viruses, which had greater success at being transmitted by hosts that survived. Today, Australia's rabbit population is stable.

Killing pests by using disease-causing organisms must be carefully controlled. Care must be taken that only the pest population is affected. If other organisms are killed, the balance of nature could be upset, causing even more harm.

Figure 27-10 **Large populations of caterpillars, such as these tent caterpillars, can be controlled by spraying them with bacteria that cause the caterpillars to become sick and die. Other types of organisms, such as birds and humans, are not affected by these bacteria.**

770 POPULATION BIOLOGY

STUDENT JOURNAL

Ask students to research ways that human diseases are spread and examples of diseases that are spread in each way. Students should be able to list food (trichinella), water (cholera), air (common cold), sex (any STD), and insects (malaria), among others. Reports can be written in student journals. **L2**

Interspecific Competition

As you have perhaps observed, a number of different species usually occupy the same area at the same time. How many species of birds, for instance, or rodents such as squirrels or field mice, can you spot in your locality? Now suppose a food source shared by several populations in a given area becomes limited. What happens? The populations of different organisms compete for it, and the competition itself may become a limiting factor. Competition among populations of different species is called **interspecific competition.** As a limiting factor, it is density dependent.

Extinction When two or more species living in the same environment compete for the same resources, one of several different events may occur. One possibility is that one of the species will die out and become extinct in that environment. This event was demonstrated in a classic lab experiment using two species of paramecia. First, *Paramecium caudatum* and *Paramecium aurelia* were grown in two separate culture dishes. Food was kept at a constant level in both cultures by adding a species of bacterium that both paramecium species use for food. Wastes were removed regularly so they did not accumulate. The growth of each *Paramecium* population was measured and recorded, Figure 27-11 a and b. Then the two species of paramecia were placed in the same culture dish with a constant limiting supply of the same kind of bacteria as the food source. Wastes were removed by washing the cultures. This was done to ensure that competition for the fixed amount of food was the limiting factor. In the competition that followed, *Paramecium aurelia* proved better adapted to rapid growth and so trapped a larger share of the limited food supply. In the end, *Paramecium aurelia* survived, but *Paramecium caudatum* died.

Figure 27-11 **Population growth curves show that *Paramecium aurelia* (a) grows to a higher density than *Paramecium caudatum* (b) before leveling off. In this experiment, when the two species are grown together, interspecific competition occurs (c). *P. aurelia* survives while *P. caudatum* dies.**

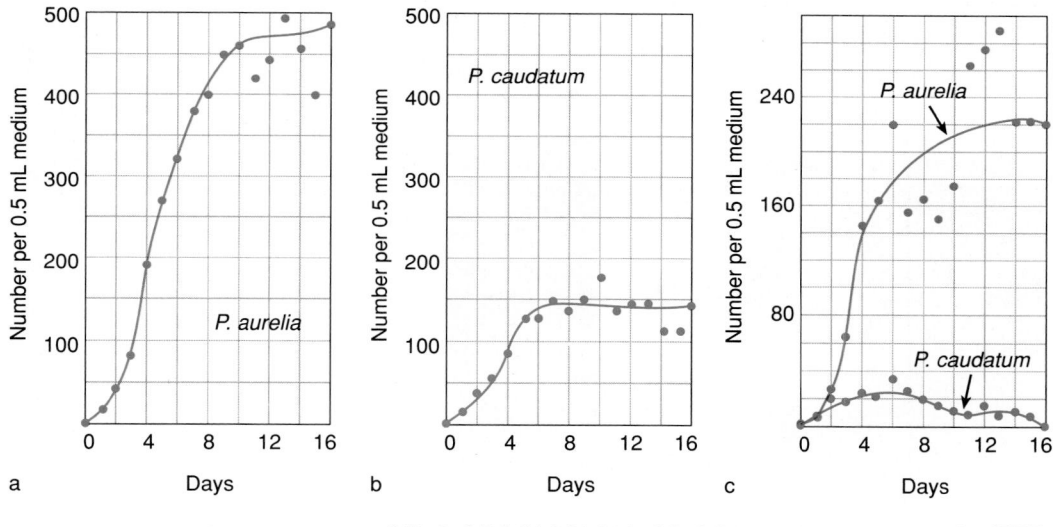

a Days   b Days   c Days

27.2 REGULATION OF POPULATION SIZE **771**

SECTION 27.2

Concept Development

Allow students to create cartoons that illustrate the concept of interspecific or intraspecific competition. L1

Reinforcement

Ask students to describe reasons why intraspecific competition might be beneficial. Answers should include that only the most fit males or females survive and pass on their genes, that the population is limited to the carrying capacity, and that most overt damaging conflict is eliminated or reduced. L1

CHEMISTRY CONNECTION

That's My Turf! One interesting example of intraspecific competition involves polyps of sea anemones. Although the anemones appear to be stationary to the unaided eye, time-lapse video shows that these organisms release a chemical that warns other members of the species to keep away. Thus, the sea anemones avoid competition for space.

Figure Caption Question

Can you think of an adaptation that would help the seed cling to the animal's fur? Adaptations might include hooks, burrs, or stickers that would cling to the fur.

Figure 27-12 Several species of warblers are able to feed and nest in the same kind of spruce tree without competing because they live in different parts of the tree.

Figure 27-13 Animals disperse seeds to distant locations, where the new plants will not compete with the parent plant. Can you think of an adaptation that would help the seed cling to the animal's fur?

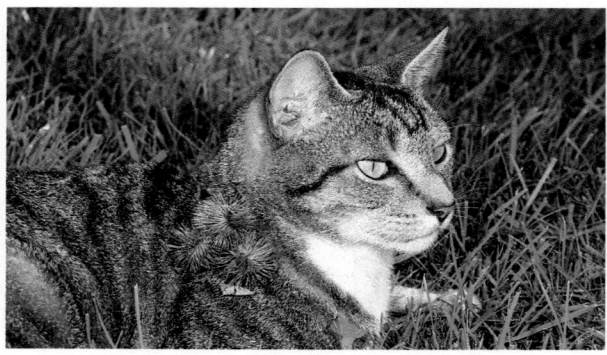

Movement A second possible outcome of interspecific competition is that one species will move into another, usually close-by, environment. Several species of Maine warblers, for instance, feed and nest in the same kind of spruce tree at the same time each year. But no interspecific competition takes place. Instead, each species of warbler spends most of its time in a certain zone in the tree—the crown, lower branches, outer branches, or other specified area—and eats insects only in that zone.

Adaptation Third, interspecific competition may spur rapid evolution in which species acquire different traits. As a result, the populations no longer compete with each other. You may recall that several of Darwin's finches live on the ground and eat seeds. But the size and shape of the different birds' beaks provide each species with an adaptation that allows its members to feed on seeds of different sizes and shapes. The insect-eating finches also have different kinds of beaks—ones that allow the birds to pick out insects from different kinds of places. Hence, interspecific competition loses its limiting effect.

Intraspecific Competition

Often, competition occurs between members of the same species. This competition is called **intraspecific competition.** It is more severe than interspecific competition because all members of the species have the same requirements. Intraspecific competition also is density dependent. The greater the population density, the greater the chance for competition because there are more contacts among individual organisms. Some degree of competition is desirable for a species because, through natural selection, the best adapted individuals survive to reproduce. However, too much competition is not desirable because it could lead to a drastic decline in population size.

Life Cycles and Life Spans Excess intraspecific competition is avoided in many ways. Life cycles may be such that competition is avoided within a species. For example, adult frogs do not compete with tadpoles because the habitats and foods of frogs and tadpoles are different. Life spans also may reduce competition. In many animal species, such as insects, adults die shortly after the young are produced. Thus, old and young do not compete for food, space, or other factors. In animal species in which the parent does not die after the young are produced, parental care is common. This avoids competition because the offspring depend on the parents. In plants and fungi, dispersal of seeds or spores to distant locations by wind and animals also prevents competition among members of the same species.

772 POPULATION BIOLOGY

MEETING INDIVIDUAL NEEDS

Bilingual or multicultural students may have difficulty recognizing the animal and plant populations mentioned and pictured in the text. Whenever possible, encourage these students to share information about organisms in their native countries. Relate these living things to those illustrated in the text; for example, Japanese students might know of a predator-prey example that is found only in Japan. The assistance of a bilingual student or parent may be effective. LEP

772

Dominance and Social Hierarchy Social behavior can reduce intraspecific conflicts. Consider, for example, how levels of authority reduce conflicts and preserve order in certain human groups, such as the military or a business. A designated chain of command, based on dominance, eliminates confusion and promotes group efficiency. Behavior patterns based on dominance and chains of command are characteristic of some animal populations. Such a pattern is known as a pecking order or **social hierarchy.**

The term *pecking order* grew out of studies of dominance relationships among chickens. A society of chickens forms a hierarchy by pecking at each other. Two chickens approach each other and may fight, or one may peacefully give way to the other, Figure 27-14. In either case, a dominance relationship results between these two chickens.

Dominance leads to a system of authority relationships spread throughout a society. Contacts similar to the one between the two chickens just described occur throughout a flock, and a total hierarchy emerges. One chicken becomes dominant to all the others. Another chicken may be dominant to all but the first one, and so on. Once the order is decided, it remains constant unless new chickens join the flock. Then the entire pecking order must be reestablished. Sometimes a chicken with lower status challenges a more dominant one, but such encounters rarely change the pecking order. This type of social hierarchy occurs in many groups of animals such as birds, some reptiles, and mammals, particularly wolves, dogs, and a variety of primates.

A hierarchy promotes survival in several ways. The overall result of dominance is increased order and reduced aggression throughout the society. After the first pecking is over, the less dominant individual accepts its status, and there is less fighting over food and mates. If conditions are such that not every individual can eat and mate, then at least the more dominant ones will be able to do so. These members are usually the better

Figure 27-14 **Chickens form a pecking order, a social hierarchy in which more dominant individuals peck at less dominant individuals.**

Figure 27-15 **Some animals engage in aggressive behaviors in order to establish a social hierarchy. Once established, the hierarchy reduces conflict.**

27.2 REGULATION OF POPULATION SIZE 🐦 **773**

SECTION 27.2

Using the Illustration
Point out that many organisms exhibit social hierarchy. Most of these behaviors are concerned with reducing energy expended by the top organisms in search of food or mates. LEP

HISTORY CONNECTION

Human Hierarchies: Ask students how social hierarchy among humans has been demonstrated in the past in such countries as England and India. (England has a monarchy and India has the caste system.)

Concept Development
Ask students to discuss dominance relationships they have observed. Find out if they have made the observation that even very young children show similar aggressive types of behavior and a subtle or not-so-subtle pecking order similar to that discussed in chickens.

Using Science Terms
The word *hierarchy* comes from two words in Greek that mean "sacred" and "leader." Ask students to explain how the two Greek root words are useful in describing the relationship that we call hierarchy. LEP

PROJECT

Name That Competition: Have students make a game—Name That Competition—in which they name the relationship that exists between two organisms. Have each student group write a description of a relationship on a 3 x 5 card, then exchange the card with another group, who will identify the relationship. Examples might include black vultures at a carcass (intraspecific competition), Egyptian vultures and Griffin vultures at a carcass (interspecific competition), two robins and one worm (intraspecific competition), or mosses and liverworts on a shady stream bank (interspecific competition). **L2** **COOP LEARN**

Minilab 2

Purpose
Students will grow radish seeds and observe the effects of crowding on the growth of these seeds.

Skills
observe and infer, compare and contrast, measure in SI, interpret data

Teaching Strategies
- Have students measure the height of the plants with a ruler to determine amount of growth.
- Provide a well-lighted place after the seeds germinate.
- You might ask your class to pool their results on the board and take averages. Ask them to make graphs of their results.

Expected Results
Radish plants that are crowded will be shorter. If the crowded plants were pulled out of the soil, students would see that the edible root is smaller.

Answers
Crowded plants do not grow as tall as uncrowded plants. Roots of crowded plants are not able to get enough minerals and water, as they are competing for the same resources. The roots of crowded plants may secrete growth inhibitors that prevent roots from growing. Without sufficient surface area for absorption, the plant will not get enough water and minerals for growth.

✔ Assessment
Performance: Have students conduct this same experiment with other plant seeds and summarize their results in their journals.

Using Science Terms
Emigration is derived from two Latin words. The prefix *e* means "away," and the suffix *migrate* means "to move." LEP

Minilab 2

How does crowding affect plant growth?

Radishes are your favorite garden vegetable. You want to plant enough so that you will have radishes for many months of salads, but you have only a small garden patch. If you plant the radish seeds very close together, will you get as many good-quality radishes as you will if you follow package directions? In one cup of potting soil, plant five radish seeds according to package directions. In another cup with the same amount and type of soil, plant 30 seeds. Keep the soil moist and place the cups in a well-lighted area. Measure growth at the end of one week and at the end of two weeks.

Analysis *What is the effect of crowding on the growth of radish seeds? Speculate about why crowding is a limiting factor for plant growth.*

---

adapted. Thus, a social hierarchy is good insurance that the most adaptive genes are the ones passed on. A social hierarchy also prevents overbreeding because the most dominant individuals may prevent the lower individuals from mating. In any event, the pecking order reduces competition among the members of a population. Therefore, it is adaptive to the total group of animals and promotes group survival.

Role Separation Competition is also reduced in societies in which members have definite roles. In insect societies such as those of bees, ants, and termites, roles are both genetically and physiologically determined. Usually, there is one queen that produces all new members of the society. Other members may have roles as workers, soldiers, or foragers. Among termites, the relative densities of workers, soldiers, and foragers seem to determine what role an individual will play. Spreading out the work reduces conflict and competition among the members of the society.

Behavioral and Physiological Changes Overcrowding can lead to behavioral and physiological changes among members of the same species. If rats are overcrowded and cannot escape, they may become increasingly aggressive to the point where more deaths than usual occur. They may build poorly constructed nests or none at all. Hormonal changes resulting from stress may reduce litter size. In some cases, no young are produced. In other cases, the young are abandoned or eaten by their parents.

As a result of these behavioral and physiological changes, birthrate decreases and death rate increases. The outcome is a reduction in the size of the population to a number that the environment can support.

Emigration Another solution to overcrowding in some populations is emigration, the moving out of an area. You read in the chapter opener that bees swarm to new areas when the hive becomes overcrowded. Not all the bees in the hive emigrate, however. Some remain in their original environment with a new queen and are able to survive under conditions of reduced population size and density.

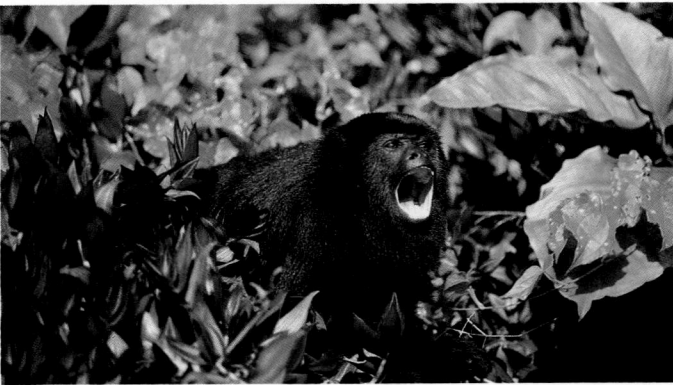

Figure 27-16 Howler monkeys establish and protect their territory by howling loudly when an intruder approaches. This practice ensures that each group of monkeys will have sufficient living space.

PROJECT

Pheromones: Many animals produce chemicals, called pheromones, for marking territories and locating mates. Pheromones can be illustrated using two different species of snails. Have students divide a rectangular pan in half with a wax pencil line and add a thin film of water. Have them place a piece of cardboard on the pencil line as a barrier, then place one species of snail on one side of the pan and the other species on the other side. Cover with aluminum foil and allow them to move for about an hour. Then have students remove the barrier and place all the snails on the line, alternating species. Cover the pan again for an hour. Students will find that the snails will move to the side of the pan where they were previously, following the pheromone in the mucous slime. L3

Territoriality Intraspecific competition among some animals may be held in check as animals occupy and defend specific territories. This behavior, known as **territoriality,** was first observed in birds. Among many bird species, the song of the male announces that he has established his territory. The song tells other males to stay away and informs females of the species that a male has staked out his territory. Howler monkeys, another territorial species, travel in clans. They establish and then defend their territory against rival howler clans by howling and bluffing attacks against the rivals. Rarely is anything more serious needed to preserve a clan's territory.

Like a social hierarchy, possession of territories reduces conflicts within a species. It spreads the members of a population over a large area, thus ensuring a better food supply for all members. In addition, it is usually the strongest, largest, most aggressive, and otherwise best-adapted members of the species that win a territory and mate. Thus, their genes are the ones most likely to be passed on.

The Human Population—Without Limits?

If you examine Figure 27-18, you will see that the human population grew very slowly at first. Even after the year A.D. 1, it took 1600 years for the number of humans to double. After the year 1650, however, the rate of doubling rapidly increased. About this time, the rapid development of science, technology, and industrialization led to an explosion of the population. The population doubled between the years 1650 and 1850, then doubled again by 1930. By 1990, the world's population was estimated at 5.3 billion. Projections suggest that it will be 6.3 billion by the end of this century and 10.8 billion by the year 2050. Thus, the current population will double in roughly 50 years. The graph of human population growth closely resembles the graph of population growth under ideal conditions—the J-shaped curve you saw in Figure 27-2. Such a pattern, remember, occurs in the absence of limiting factors.

Figure 27-17 Much of the world's human population is crowded together in cities.

Figure 27-18 Worldwide, human population growth has risen dramatically since the middle of the nineteenth century. The dotted portion of the curve represents projected future growth. Note the dip in the curve, due to the death of 75 million Europeans by bubonic plague between 1347 and 1351.

Bioethics

Limiting Populations: China has instituted a governmental policy encouraging families to have no more than one child. Families are urged by social pressure, incentives, and disincentives not to exceed the limit dictated by the national birth control programs. Newlyweds are asked to pledge to have no more than one child. Ask students if they consider such a government position to be ethical or beneficial. Encourage students to discuss the pros and cons of such a population policy.

Debate

Ask students to debate the relevance of role separation in humans as a mechanism for reducing competition.

COOP LEARN

Demonstration

Before discussing the concept of territoriality, ask for two student volunteers to stand and face each other on opposite sides of the room. Every 30 seconds, have them take one step toward each other without talking. Continue this until it becomes evident that they have mapped out their spatial territories. Ask them to explain what happened as they got closer and closer to each other.

Concept Development

Explain that most species, including humans, have some territorial instinct. Territories may be very small for species such as nesting seabirds or very large, as for Alaskan brown bears.

Misconception

Many students will think that the human population is immune to the concepts of population growth presented in this chapter. Point out that human populations may grow above the carrying capacity but, if that happens, they will eventually suffer the same consequences as any other population that does so.

MULTICULTURAL CONNECTION

Birthrates: There are cultural differences between developing and industrialized countries that contribute to their population growth rates. The countries in the world with the highest birthrates of greater than 50 per 1000 are all in Africa. In order from highest, they are Uganda, Ivory Coast, Rwanda, Zambia, and Tanzania. The countries in the world with the lowest birthrates of less than 13 per 1000 are all in Europe. In order from lowest, they are Italy, Germany, Austria, Denmark, and Hungary.

775

LITERATURE CONNECTION

Purpose

This feature and poem presents the view one person has of the elderly in society. However, the view is representative of the author's entire culture. The expressed view contrasts sharply with that held by many people in the United States today.

Teaching Strategies

- Ask students if they feel differently about small children than they do about adults or teenagers. Allow them to discuss their feelings. Then ask the students if they feel differently about teenagers and old people. Again allow them to discuss their feelings. Point out that the poem in this feature represents the view of one person from one culture. Then, have students read the poem and answer the questions. **COOP LEARN**

Possible Answers

1. Some activities such as the contact sports of football and basketball have traditionally been restricted to males. Attending certain movies, drinking alcohol, and smoking have been restricted by age. Such restrictions may have had their roots in protection or in reducing intraspecific competition.
2. Results will vary, but most adults surveyed will likely disclose a higher age for *old* than students will. Many students will consider 40 to be old, while many adults do not consider 60 to be old.

Going Further

Have students write a poem that expresses how they feel about the elderly in society.

Declining Growth Rate Percentages are often used to illustrate the population growth rate pattern. To arrive at such percentages, think of the birthrate as the number of births each year for every 1000 persons. The death rate is the number of deaths each year for every 1000 persons. To obtain a growth rate, figure the difference between the two numbers and express it as a percentage of 1000. For example, think of a population where the birthrate is 30. The death rate is 10. The difference between the two figures is 20. The population growth rate, then, is 2 percent because 20 is 2 percent of 1000. A growth rate of 2 percent is high. At that rate, a population would double its size about every 35 years.

Given the predictions for human population growth in the next 50 years, you might conclude that the rate of growth will continue to increase. That is not the case, however. Since the 1970s, the worldwide growth rate has actually been decreasing. In 1989, the rate of growth was 1.8 percent, and it is expected to fall to 1.3 percent by 2025. Despite lowered growth rates, the human population will continue to increase in size. It will just grow more slowly than in recent centuries.

Uneven Growth Rates Worldwide Declines in population growth rates are expected to occur in almost all countries of the world. But the rates will vary. The steepest declines are expected among developed countries—those that are highly industrialized and able to provide healthful, comfortable living conditions for their people. Such countries can expect their growth rates to drop from a present rate of about 0.5 percent to about 0.3 percent. Some industrialized countries, such as Germany and

---

LITERATURE CONNECTION

Rafael Jesús González

Needing to borrow the sharp eyes of youth to help her make her embroidered flowers and birds come to colorful life, the old woman always sought out Rafael. The young man, a pre-med college student, worked in a five-and-dime store on the Mexico-Texas border. The pair's frequent consultation over the rainbow-hued display of thread drew them into a special friendship. Then, one day the old woman stopped coming to the store. Missing her visits, Rafael wrote this poem, *To an Old Woman*, to honor his older friend.

To an Old Woman

Come mother—
    your rebozo trails a black web
and your hem catches on your
    heels;
you lean the burden of your years
on shaky cane and palsied hand
pushes
    sweat-grimed pennies on the
    counter.
Can you still see, old woman,
the darting color-trailed needle of
your trade?

The flowers you embroider
    with three-for-a-dime threads
cannot fade as quickly as the leaves
of time.
    What things do you remember?
Your mouth seems to be forever
tasting
the residue of nectar-hearted years.
    Where are the sons you bore?
Do they speak only English now
and say they're Spanish?
    One day I know you will not
come
and ask for me to pick
    the colors you can no longer see.
I know I'll wait in vain
    for your toothless benediction.

776 POPULATION BIOLOGY

PROJECT

Comparing Population Growth: Have teams of students research the population sizes, population growth rates, or energy consumption of various countries of the world. Each team should create a map that details the results of their research. Maps may be two dimensional, but three-dimensional maps of plaster of paris or papier mâché should be encouraged. Provide time for the groups to present their findings and compare their maps. **LEP** **COOP LEARN**

Figure 27-19 Many people in developing countries struggle to grow enough food to feed their families. In developed countries, however, surplus food is grown by modern agricultural practices.

Denmark, have already begun to experience declines in not only growth rate, but also population size. The rest of Europe and Japan will probably see the same kinds of decreases over the next 50 years.

The outlook is much different in the world's developing countries. Developing countries are those in which industrialization is only in its early stages. Many of their people, a large portion of whom try to grow their own food on small farms, have trouble meeting their needs. In these countries, the present growth rate of about 1.9 percent is expected to

I'll look into the dusty street
made cool by pigeons' wings
until a dirty child will nudge me
and say:
    "Señor, how much ees thees?"

As he grew up on the Mexico-Texas border, Rafael Jesús González (1935-   ) was surrounded by older family members who were highly valued and respected. Moving further into the United States, he was saddened to find such a division between age groups. He expressed this contrast in his poem. The last line of the poem completes the contrast of the values of the old woman and the more materialistic values of the young.

Today, Rafael wears a denim jacket with a beautiful embroidered flower, heart, and yin-yang symbol. It's a piece of art that he created. He says that he certainly couldn't have taken up an embroidery needle when he was young because friends his age would have teased him for doing what they considered women's work. "Hopefully, when we get older, we can see through nonsense and can understand that some strictures make no sense," he explains. "I would also

hope that old age brings increased patience, a more life-accepting set of values, and the ability to love more wisely and fully."

1. **Issue:** What activities in American culture seem to be restricted by gender or age? Why do you think this has happened?
2. **Explore Further:** Conduct an informal opinion survey in your class, school, or neighborhood. Ask how people define *old*.

27.2 REGULATION OF POPULATION SIZE 🐌 **777**

Science, Technology, and Society

High-tech Agriculture: One of the reasons the United States has been able to maintain its population growth while reducing the amount of farmland and the number of farmers is the development of high-tech agricultural equipment and practices that enable farmers to produce more grain with higher protein value in less space.

Debate

Assign pairs of students a debate topic. Depending on time available, students should be able to research and prepare their debate in one to four weeks. Possible topics include the following. Are there limits to human population growth? Do environmental problems demand a change in values? Should the government limit human births? An article by Stephen Zipko in the March, 1991 *American Biology Teacher* gives additional topics and strategies. **COOP LEARN**

ART CONNECTION

Lifestyle Differences: Obtain copies of *A Sunday Afternoon on the Island of La Grande Jatte* by Georges Seurat and *The Beanery* by Edward Kienholz, or similar artworks that show extremes of lifestyles that reflect different population densities. Ask students to compare the styles of the artists, as well as the differences in lifestyles the people had in different population densities. Have students list indications in the paintings that suggest the population densities of the people illustrated.

What Does the Future Hold?

Most biologists share the views of Garrett Hardin and Paul Ehrlich that the human population growth rate will eventually cause widespread famine when the population size exceeds the carrying capacity of Earth. For more than two decades, these biologists have supported measures to limit the population growth rate by political means. A few biologists point out that the disastrous results predicted by Hardin and Ehrlich have not occurred, and they maintain that increased use of technology will continue to protect our species from destroying itself by overpopulation.

Audiovisual

Show the 6.5-minute film *World Population,* available from ZPG, 1400 16th Street NW, Washington, DC 20036.

3 Assess

Check for Understanding

Present students with population data for any population whose growth shows an S-shaped curve. Have students graph the data. Ask them to describe when the population is growing fastest, when it reaches the carrying capacity, and why the population begins to grow slowly at that point. Then ask students to compare the graphed data with the human population. **L1**

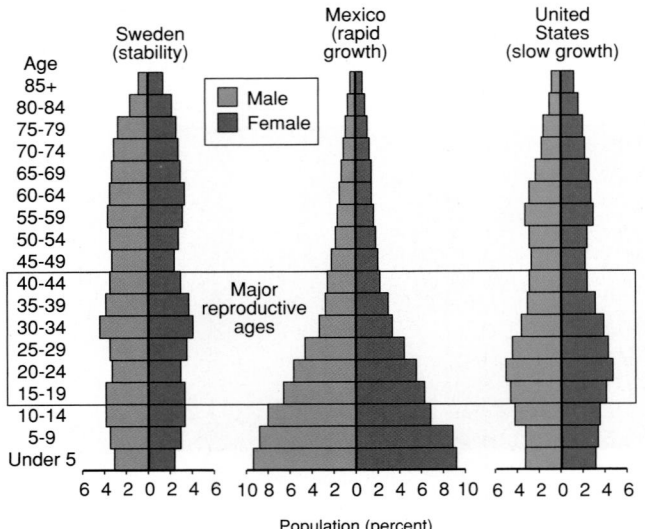

Figure 27-20 **The proportion of females of reproductive age in a population has a significant impact on the future growth of that population.**

drop to about 1.5 percent. Even 1.5 percent is still a substantial rate of growth. Two factors account for it. First, birthrates in developing countries are high, as much as four times higher than in developed countries. Second, a very large segment of the total population in developing countries is of reproductive age, Figure 27-20. Worldwide, the increases in population sizes of developing countries will more than make up for the decreases in developed countries. The total world population, therefore, will continue to grow.

Another way to study population growth is to look at the number of births among women of reproductive age. For example, the birthrate in the United States has dropped from a peak of nearly 3.8 births per woman in the late 1950s to 1.84 by the late 1980s. However, the size of the population still increased. A rate of 2.1 births per woman for many generations is necessary to attain **zero population growth,** a condition in which the birthrate equals the death rate and the rate of population growth equals zero. Because a large proportion of the United States population is now of reproductive age, even a birthrate of 1.84 births per woman—well below 2.1—would continue to cause significant increases in population size in the years ahead. According to U.S. Census figures, the United States population was 248.7 million in 1990. It is projected to grow to 268.1 million by the year 2000 and to 312.7 million by 2025. At this rate, the population in the United States will double in fewer than 100 years.

Future of the Population Explosion

What has caused the human population explosion—especially in the last several hundred years? It has not happened because the birthrate steadily increased. You learned in Chapter 13 that agriculture and technology are unique attributes of the human population. You also saw that recent human progress stems not from biological evolution, but from cultural evolution. Cultural advances have greatly improved the quality of life among many individuals. They have also greatly impacted the growth of the human population, mainly by reducing the death rate. Consider the importance of sanitation, for instance. Bubonic plague is a bacterial disease carried by fleas that hitchhike on rats. In the 14th century, one-fourth of the population of Europe died of that disease. Later, improved sanitation eliminated most rats, which reduced people's contact with fleas and, therefore, the incidence of the plague.

So far, cultural evolution has placed the human population beyond the environmental factors that limit all other populations. But the human population cannot continue to expand indefinitely. It, too, is subject to a point at which the environment cannot support additional growth. There is also the chance that a density-independent factor could take effect. Based upon what you've learned, what might happen if the human population reaches carrying capacity? What could happen if a density-independent factor, such as an earthquake or volcanic eruption, intervenes?

Most natural checks of population growth cause an increase in the death rate. One alternative for controlling population growth of humans would be to decrease the birthrate. This can be accomplished as part of family planning methods. Biologists and physicians have developed several artificial ways of preventing pregnancy based on the biological aspects of reproduction. Natural methods that prevent pregnancy have also been studied.

Many countries around the world educate their citizens about family planning. Which, if any, family planning method is used depends on physical, emotional, religious, and moral factors. The results of this education may be a factor in the recently declining growth rates in some countries.

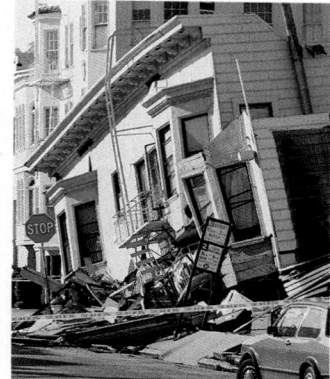

Figure 27-21 Human populations are affected by density-independent factors such as earthquakes.

LOOKING AHEAD

THE GROWTH OF populations is affected by environmental factors, both living and nonliving. In the next chapter, you will look at the bigger picture as you explore factors that influence the functioning of entire communities. You will study ways in which different populations interact with one another, how populations respond to the availability of energy, and how materials are continually made available to organisms.

Section Review

Understanding Concepts

1. A population of insects is fed upon by spiders. What change in the insect population will cause a decline in the size of the spider population? Why? What will then happen to the size of the insect population? Why? What is the limiting factor for each population?

2. Explain why clearing land and planting a large area with a single crop makes that crop subject to destruction by parasites.

3. Why did the human population size not begin to increase rapidly until after 1650?

4. **Skill Review—Comparing and Contrasting:** Caterpillars of two different species of insects both feed on leaves. Members of a population of birds compete for the same nesting sites. Compare the two types of competition and mechanisms for avoiding each type of competition. For more help, refer to Thinking Critically in the **Skill Handbook.**

5. **Thinking Critically:** What method might prove most effective in preventing the spread of malaria?

SECTION 27.2

Reteach

If students fail to understand the concepts of population growth and the predicament of the human population, conduct a discussion of factors that might influence the growth of a population of pigeons in a city. Then have students describe the similarities and differences between factors affecting pigeon population growth and those affecting human population growth.

Extension

Have students read Garrett Hardin's essay, *Tragedy of the Commons.* Have students discuss whether they agree or disagree with Hardin's assessment of human population growth in the essay. L3

✔ Assessment

Skill: Have students create a headline for a news story about a problem that is meaningful to them and has a root cause in overpopulation. Then have students write a story that fairly portrays both sides of the problem. L1

4 Close

Discussion

End your study of this chapter with a discussion of the importance of the individual in solving problems that have social and political overtones. Point out that the problems discussed in this chapter will be dealt with by them. COOP LEARN

Answers to Section Review

1. A reduction in the size of the insect population will lead to a reduction in the size of the spider population because the spiders will be limited by food supply. With fewer spiders, the insect population will rise. The insect population is limited by predation by the spiders. The spider population is limited by the food supply.

2. This practice results in a very great population density, making transmission of parasites from one host to another more certain.

3. Cultural evolution, especially advances in sanitation, medicine, and technology, contributed to population growth after 1650.

4. **Skill Review—Comparing and Contrasting:** The caterpillars are limited by interspecific competition, the birds by intraspecific competition. The former is reduced by extinction of one species, movement of one species to a different habitat, or rapid evolution leading to novel adaptations in each species. The latter may be avoided by any of the mechanisms discussed on pages 772-775.

5. **Thinking Critically:** Reducing the size of the *Anopheles* mosquito population would reduce the chances of *Plasmodium* spreading to humans.

779

Issues

Purpose

Students will learn about some of the properties of an age class in a population, and the problems associated with an aging population in our society.

Teaching Strategies

• Ask students if they have ever played the baby boomer edition of the board game *Trivial Pursuit.* Ask why there might be a special edition for this group. *Not only is this age class one that is interested in playing such games, but it is one of the largest age classes and is old enough to be able to easily afford the game.* Have them hypothesize why this group may be so large.

Possible Answers

1. Older people usually have more money and more time to do the things they may not have done while they were engaged in a career. However, the disadvantages are a decline in health, strength, and stamina.

2. Most United States presidents are or were in their older years as far as students are concerned. Older scientists include James Watson, who headed the Human Genome Project until 1992 and won a Nobel Prize for co-discovering the structure of DNA, and Barbara McClintock, who continued her Nobel Prize-winning research in corn genetics until her death at age 90.

Going Further

Ask students to write a position paper on aging that supports or rejects additional taxes on younger workers to pay for Social Security benefits of older Americans.

BIOLOGY, TECHNOLOGY, AND SOCIETY

Issues

Old Versus Young in America?

Take a look at your parents. They don't look much like babies, do they? But to demographers, scientists who study population trends, your parents will always be "baby boomers." That's the name tag that has been pinned on all people born in the United States between 1947 and 1961. In those years, the number of babies born seemed to explode with a resounding boom.

An Aging Population The baby boomers make a "bulge" in the population of the United States. When they started school, they crowded the classrooms. Entering the work force, they composed a group to which marketers eagerly geared their products. And, of course, baby boomers will grow old together. The number of Americans age 65 and over is expected to leap beginning in the year 2010.

Better health care and nutrition account for some of the growth in the over-65 category. In 1900, the average American could expect to live to 47. Today, the average American will quite likely have a 75th birthday party. By the time the baby boomers reach old age, they may have an even longer life span.

With their professional responsibilities accomplished and their children grown, older Americans have more leisure time to develop their minds and their imaginations. Although modern technology has caused enormous changes in lifestyles, most older Americans have been able to keep up through education, both formal and informal. The number of people over 65 who take classes in everything from computer science to painting has never been higher.

Many older Americans disregard the traditional retirement age of 65 and continue to work. They may continue their careers or even enter entirely new job areas.

Many older Americans are the backbone of volunteer organizations. These people are generous in giving their time to run soup kitchens, help people learn to read, provide child care and hospital services, and so much more.

Problems of an Aging Population An aging population could bring some difficult problems for the United States. Although today's older Americans are the healthiest in history, they do inevitably require more health care. Can America afford health care for both ends of the age spectrum?

Another area of concern is the Social Security system. Older Americans paid into the system during their working years and deserve to draw the benefits after they retire. However, that system depends on a balance between working people and retired people. In 1985, that ratio was 3.4 to 1; by 2030, it is projected to decline to 2 to 1. That means there will be fewer people in the work force supporting more people outside it.

Even in everyday life, an aging population may require some accommodation. For example, traffic signals might have to stay green longer for older pedestrians, and the soundtracks of movies may need to be turned up.

Clearly, changes will have to be made to accommodate our aging population. Older Americans are too valuable a resource to be ignored.

780 CHAPTER 27 POPULATION BIOLOGY

CAREER CONNECTION

Demographers are responsible for demographic and human ecology studies. Demographics include birth and death rates and migration patterns, in addition to those listed on the student page. Human ecology deals with the structure of urban environments and patterns of settlement and growth. Students may write to the American Sociological Association, 1722 N Street NW, Washington, DC 20036.

Understanding the Issue

1. What do you see as advantages and disadvantages of old age?
2. Find out about Americans who have made important contributions in their older years.

Readings

- Ames, K. "Cheaper by the Dozen." *Newsweek*, Sept. 14, 1992, pp. 52-53.
- Baltes, Paul B. "Wise, and Otherwise." *Natural History*, Feb. 1992, pp. 50-51.

Considering the Environment

Pile It On!

The Great Wall of China snakes across 2400 kilometers of hilly terrain. It averages about 8 meters in height and 4 meters in width. The Wall has been for centuries the largest human construction on Earth. However, it may lose that distinction in the next few years. Every day in New York, another structure grows a little larger. It's not a wall or a beautiful building—it's a garbage dump! The 3000-acre Fresh Kills landfill will soon rise to a height of almost 170 meters, making it the tallest "mountain" on the east coast of the United States.

The Fresh Kills landfill is only one of 7300 dumps in the United States, about half of which are nearing capacity. As the human population continues to grow, city officials are asking where they are going to put all the trash.

Mulch   There is a large component of landfills that many people can reuse directly. That's the material that consists of yard wastes—leaves, twigs, and lawn clippings. When people take care of their yards, they often throw these materials into the garbage can. Then they spend money on mulch to control weeds and retain soil moisture. And what is mulch made of? Leaves, twigs, and lawn clippings—the same

materials they just discarded! Some people have added chippers and shredders to their yard-care equipment to make their own mulch.

Compost   Another resource that you can save from landfills and turn into garden "gold," or compost, is organic kitchen scraps. You don't want all of it; meat, bones, or anything oily won't do. Fruit and vegetable peelings, coffee grounds, teabags, and eggshells are good materials for compost. So are small materials from your yard, such as leaves and grass clippings.

You can buy or make a container for your compost pile, or you can just start a pile in an out-of-the-way spot. To begin, make a pile of kitchen and garden leftovers. When the pile is about one meter high and equally wide, buy some nitrogen fertilizer, which will speed the

breakdown of your compost. Add a handful or two of fertilizer, sprinkle the compost pile with water, and cover it with black plastic anchored with rocks.

Wait about a week. Then remove the cover and stir up the pile. You'll probably find that the middle is warm. That's because the materials are decomposing. Add a little more water, just enough so that the material is as damp as a squeezed-out sponge. Put the cover back on, and repeat the process every week. In a month or two, the compost will look dark and crumbly. Then you can dig it into your garden plot. You will have done two good deeds at once—improved the soil and saved space in a landfill.

1. **Explore Further:** Where does your garbage go? Call a city official and find out. Try to learn how much trash is dumped in your local landfill.
2. **Solve the Problem:** Scientists have discovered 20-year-old newspapers that are still readable and five-year-old hotdogs that are recognizable although certainly not appetizing. Why do you think these items haven't decomposed the way material in a compost pile does?

Considering the Environment

Purpose
This feature contrasts human population growth with the problem of increasing refuse production.

Teaching Strategies
- Ask students to give reasons why they should be concerned about the trash and yard wastes they create. Allow students to discuss the importance of waste management.

Possible Answers
1. Most garbage in the United States goes to landfills. However, there is a growing trend to remove some types of garbage for recycling.
2. Landfills are anaerobic environments, and air is needed for decomposition. Some communities are beginning to aerate the landfill by picking up the garbage in huge machines and turning it over. By oxygenating the garbage, it is hoped that biological degradation will occur.

Going Further
If possible, visit the local landfill on a field trip, or have the person responsible for the landfill nearest you come to visit the class.

CHAPTER 27

CHAPTER REVIEW

Summary

Summary statements can be used by students to review the major concepts of the chapter.

Language of Biology

Answers should go beyond defining the terms. Accept any reasonable answer that uses the term correctly and in the proper context.

Understanding Concepts

1. Both curves show that the size of the population increases slowly at the outset, then increases more and more rapidly, then increases less rapidly, and then finally stops increasing and levels off.
2. The greater the density, the greater the effect of the factor limiting population growth. The effect of that factor increases as the size of the population approaches the carrying capacity.
3. In both cases, as more and more organisms are produced, they, in turn, can reproduce. An increase in the number of organisms means more offspring can be produced per unit of time.
4. Students in classrooms represent a high population density. Spread of the measles virus was facilitated by that high density.
5. Legalized hunting can be beneficial by preventing the hunted animals' population from exceeding the carrying capacity.
6. Crops are populations having extremely high density. In planting crops, farmers make the spread of parasites and disease-causing organisms that much easier and increase the food supply of many animal species. Without the use of pesticides, the crops would be partly or even totally destroyed.
7. Two species cannot successfully compete for the same resources, so one species will die out.
8. Motile larvae are a means of dispersal, reducing competition between young and their parents.

REVIEW
CHAPTER
27

Summary

Under ideal conditions, a population would continue to expand indefinitely. However, environmental factors limit the growth of populations. Some of these factors may be related to the density of a population. The size of the population levels off at the carrying capacity of the environment. The size of populations limited by density-independent factors, often involving a sudden environmental change, never reaches the carrying capacity.

Density-dependent factors include availability of food, predation, disease and parasitism, and competition within or between species. Each of these factors becomes more severe as the number of organisms in the population increases.

Growth of the human population is unlike that of any other population. Advances due to cultural evolution have allowed humans to escape the effect of limiting factors, resulting in a decrease in the death rate and contributing to a population explosion. Even though the growth rate of the human population has recently begun a slight decline, the population size will continue to increase in the future because there are so many people of reproductive age. Decreasing the birthrate seems to be the most logical and least drastic means of reversing this trend.

Language of Biology

Write a sentence that shows your understanding of each of the following terms.

biotic potential	population growth
birthrate	population growth curve
carrying capacity	population growth rate
death rate	curve
interspecific competition	population size
intraspecific competition	predation
limiting factor	social hierarchy
parasitism	territoriality
population density	zero population growth

Understanding Concepts

1. Explain how an S-shaped curve and a population growth rate curve illustrate the same ideas in different ways.
2. Explain why, in terms of population density, population growth slows more and more as population size approaches the carrying capacity.
3. Why is there a similarity between the early stages of population growth that is limited by density-dependent factors and by density-independent factors?
4. Prior to development of the measles vaccine, that disease spread rapidly among young schoolchildren. Why?
5. Can legalized hunting be "good" for a population of animals? Explain.

6. Why do farmers find it necessary to spray their crops with pesticides? What might happen if they didn't? Why?
7. Will two species of amoebas with identical growth requirements both survive if they are placed in the same container in a lab? Explain.
8. Although some adult animals are sessile, their larvae are motile. How are motile larvae important with respect to competition?
9. Life expectancy in developed countries is far greater than in developing countries. Why is population growth greater in developing countries if people do not live as long?

782 CHAPTER 27 POPULATION BIOLOGY

9. The birthrate is much higher in developing countries than in developed ones, and there are many more individuals of reproductive age and those who have yet to reach that age.
10. Reduction in infant mortality is one significant factor contributing to the increase in size of the human population.

Applying Concepts

11. One species will die out due to interspecific competition.
12. The glass tubing provides a different habitat for one species. Thus, the two species are not competing for exactly the same resources.
13. The human female could produce 30 offspring. If half of them were females, they could produce a total of 450 offspring during their reproductive life span. This calculation shows that the biotic potential of

10. Reduction in death rate among humans has been especially important with respect to infant mortality. Many more infants survive today, at least in developed countries, than in the past. How has reduction of infant mortality played a role in population growth?

Applying Concepts

11. Two species of flour beetles are introduced into a single jar of flour. What will happen? Why?

12. Two species of flour beetles are placed in a single container of flour to which some glass tubing has been added. One species is found to occupy the glass tubing and both species survive. What idea do these results show?

13. Assuming that a human female has a reproductive life span of 30 years, how many offspring could a couple hypothetically produce during that time? Assume one birth per year, with no multiple births. If half of all the offspring were females, how many children could be produced in the next generation? What do your answers indicate about the biotic potential of humans?

14. Choose a particular example of technology and explain how it has contributed to growth of the human population.

15. Suppose a few mice had invaded a new habitat and their population size had begun to grow. A flood then swept over the habitat of the mice. What kind of limiting factor is the flood? Why?

16. What kind of factor might act to limit the growth of a population of dandelions in a lawn? Explain.

17. What factor probably explains why desert plants of the same species are widely spaced? Explain.

18. Look again at the S-shaped curve in Figure 27-3. Suppose the graph represented a population of fish regularly caught by humans and that at a given point in time, the population was at the carrying capacity. How far should the fish population be allowed to fall in order to ensure that the population will once again grow to maximum size as quickly as possible? Explain.

19. In India, the number of people between 15 and 40 is more than twice the number of people of those ages in Sweden. Predict the future growth of the population of each of those countries.

20. **Issues:** What do you think caused the boom in the number of babies born beginning in 1947?

21. **Considering the Environment:** What makes compost such good fertilizer?

Lab Interpretation

22. **Investigation:** Growth of a bacterial species under different pH conditions is shown below. Examine the graph and determine if pH is a limiting factor for growth of this bacterium. Explain.

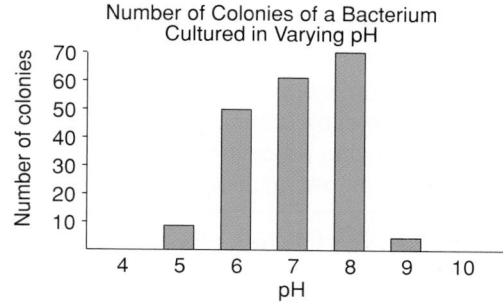

Number of Colonies of a Bacterium Cultured in Varying pH

23. **Minilab 1:** You examine remote sensing photos of the same farmland today and 10 years ago. In the most current photos, the crop fields are larger and contain only one type of crop. Ten years ago, the fields were smaller and had a variety of crops. Discuss the pros and cons of the conversion to larger fields and one type of crop.

24. **Minilab 2:** Might the results of this experiment have been different if two species of plant seeds had been planted together? Explain your answer.

Connecting Ideas

25. Explain how natural selection might lead to evolution of different traits among members of two similar species living in the same environment.

26. How can you explain the fact that many different mammals limited by density-dependent factors share the following characteristics: They usually live in stable environments, they reproduce only a few offspring at a time and do so slowly, and their offspring mature slowly and live a long time?

way would be naturally selected because competition would be reduced.

26. **Unity Within Diversity:** The stable environments in which they live indicate they will not normally be influenced by density-independent factors. Thus, it is important they not exceed the carrying capacity of their environments. Their production of few offspring that mature slowly and have long life spans are adaptations that prevent them from doing so.

humans, like that of all other organisms, is high.

14. Students may choose such examples as better nutrition and health care or a variety of technological innovations.

15. The flood would be a density-independent limiting factor. The mice were not limited as a result of their population's density.

16. Dandelions might be limited by competition with the grass for water, minerals, and space.

17. Wide spacing would reduce competition for water.

18. The population should be reduced to the density that represents the point at which the rate of increase is greatest. Doing so would leave the number of fish needed to bring the population rapidly back to maximum size.

19. The size of the population in India will continue to grow much more quickly than that of Sweden because India contains so many more people of reproductive age.

20. The increase can be attributed to the return of servicemen from World War II.

21. Compost is rich in a variety of inorganic and organic nutrients.

Lab Interpretation

22. pH is a limiting factor. Growth is inhibited above pH 8 and below pH 6.

23. Pros: It takes less time to care for and harvest large fields. Cons: If a pest of the single crop gets out of hand, the entire crop can be lost, whereas if a variety of crops is planted, some types of crops may survive. The soil will be in better condition if a variety of crops is planted in rotation because different plants deplete the soil of different minerals.

24. Two species might have different needs or might germinate at different times.

Connecting Ideas

25. **Evolution:** Any variations that enabled the two species to exploit their environments in a different

SECTION ·	OBJECTIVES	TEXT LABS/FEATURES
28.1 Interactions Among Organisms (3 days)	**Trace** the passage of energy from producers to consumers in an ecosystem. **Relate** the flow of energy through an ecosystem to the pyramid of energy. **Analyze** the importance of recycling of materials in an ecosystem and **describe** how such recycling occurs. **Distinguish** among parasitism, commensalism, and mutualism.	**Thinking Lab:** How do root nodule bacteria benefit clover plants? p. 793
28.2 Abiotic Factors of the Environment (3 days)	**Analyze** the ways in which abiotic factors of an environment may influence the activities and distribution of organisms. **Predict** the effects of changes on the balance of an ecosystem.	**Art Connection:** *Abuelitos Piscando Napolitos*, p. 796 **Investigation:** Do soil samples differ in amount of humus present? p. 798 **Minilab 1:** Do plant roots help with soil formation? p. 800 **Minilab 2:** Can composting be observed? p. 804
BIOLOGY, TECHNOLOGY, AND SOCIETY		**Considering the Environment:** Is the lowly lichen smarter than we are? p. 806 **Issues:** Can agriculture be climate free? p. 808 **Career Connection:** Hydrologist, p. 809

LAB MATERIALS

INVESTIGATION	MINILAB	ALTERNATE LAB
page 798 glass tube goggles graduated cylinder, 100-mL graduated cylinder, small 1-hole stopper hydrogen peroxide peat moss rubber tubing or plastic tygon shallow pan test tube, large test-tube rack	**page 800** bean plant bromthymol blue solution clay labels test tube **page 804** labels lens paper metric ruler plastic cups scissors soil tweezers	**page 800** field guides light meter litmus paper thermometer twine wood stakes

TEACHER CLASSROOM RESOURCES	OTHER RESOURCES
Study Guide, pp. 163-165 **Concept Mapping,** p. 28 ***PLL:** *Interspecific Relationships Between Populations,* p. 208 ****ILS:** *Earthworm Behavior,* p. 297 **Exploring Environmental Issues:** *Is It Getting Hot in Here?* p. 7; *Balancing Act,* p. 43	***STVS:** *Shorebird Preserves,* Ecology (Disc 6, Side 1) **Color Transparency 53:** *A Food Web*
Study Guide, pp. 166-168 **Critical Thinking/Problem Solving:** *How Does the Environment* *Affect Life?* p. 28 ***PLL:** *Physical Factors of Soil,* p. 213 ***PLL:** *Field Studies of a Freshwater Ecosystem,* p. 217 ***PLL:** *Effect of Temperature on Seed Germination,* p. 215 ***PLL:** *Field Study of a Terrestrial Community,* p. 223 ****ILS:** *Testing Water Quality,* p. 301 ****ILS:** *Soil Chemistry,* p. 305	***STVS:** *Cloud Chemistry,* Ecology (Disc 6, Side 2) **Color Transparency 54:** *The Carbon Cycle* **Color Transparency 55:** *The Nitrogen Cycle* **Color Transparency 56:** *The Phosphorus Cycle* **Color Transparency 57:** *The Water Cycle*
Assessment Materials **Chapter Assessment,** pp. 109-112 **Performance Assessment in Biology,** p. 56 **Alternate Assessment in the Science Classroom** **Computer Test Bank**	**Spanish Resources** **Cooperative Learning Resource Guide** **Videodisc Correlations** (to Optical Data's and Videodiscovery's videodiscs)

* **Probing Levels of Life**
** **Investigating Living Systems**

* **Science Technology Videodisc Series**

Key to Teaching Strategies

The following designations will help you decide which activities in the teacher margin are appropriate for your students.

L1 Level 1 activities should be within the ability range of all students.

L2 Level 2 activities should be within the ability range of the average to above-average student.

L3 Level 3 activities are designed for the ability range of above-average students.

LEP LEP activities are appropriate for Limited English Proficiency students.

COOP LEARN Cooperative Learning activities are designed for small group work.

ADDITIONAL RESOURCES

Infinite Voyage *Living with Disaster*
Nature is unpredictable, yet living things manage to survive. Students will see that living things always interact with the forces of nature.

Audiovisual
Living Together, video, Frey Scientific.
The Balance of Nature, video, Films for the Humanities and Sciences.

Software
The Environment I: Habitats and Ecosystems and *The Environment II: Cycles and Interactions,* IBM, IBM.

28

ECOSYSTEMS

Chapter Overview

Students begin their study of ecosystems as they explore feeding relationships within them. They distinguish between food chains and food webs and come to understand their importance in distribution of energy. They discover the several reasons why less and less energy is available to each succeeding trophic level and the pyramid of energy that results from such energy loss. They then relate the pyramid of energy to pyramids of numbers and biomass. This knowledge leads them to appreciate the fact that energy is not recycled and that each ecosystem needs a continual input of energy in order to survive.

Next, students study the pathways of materials in an ecosystem and learn that those materials are not in endless supply. They explore the role of all organisms, including decomposers, in the cycling of materials. In doing so, they realize another important way in which organisms in an ecosystem interact. They then study other biotic relationships—commensalism, mutualism, and parasitism.

Students complete their study of ecosystems by examining abiotic factors—water, soil, light, and temperature.

ECOSYSTEMS

HAVE YOU EVER wondered what those colorful, fuzzy patches of blue, red, brown, or green growing on damp trees and rocks are? What about the small, gray, shrublike organisms that sprout from the soil in all types of weather? Such organisms are called lichens, and they certainly rank among the most unusual of all living things. Lichens defy insertion into any general classification because they are actually dual organisms, an alga and a fungus. The typical lichen consists of a sac fungus and either a photosynthetic bacterium or a green alga, and their relationship represents one of the more classic examples of mutualism in nature. In this relationship, fungi provide crucial protection from the elements, while the photosynthetic bacteria or algae manufacture food that is used by both organisms. Together, the two components form a compact and highly efficient unit that may occupy even the most inhospitable habitats.

In nature, living organisms interact in a variety of ways. Sometimes, these relationships are surprising, as in the case of lichens. But more often, interactions between organisms are much simpler. In this chapter, you'll learn how groups of organisms interact and depend on each other for survival. You'll also consider how organisms are affected by physical factors in the environment.

784

KEY TERMS

abiotic factor	food web	third-order consumer
algal bloom	herbivore	trophic level
biomass	humus	
biotic factor	niche	
carnivore	omnivore	
commensalism	pyramid of biomass	
ecosystem	pyramid of energy	
estivation	pyramid of numbers	
first-order consumer	second-order consumer	

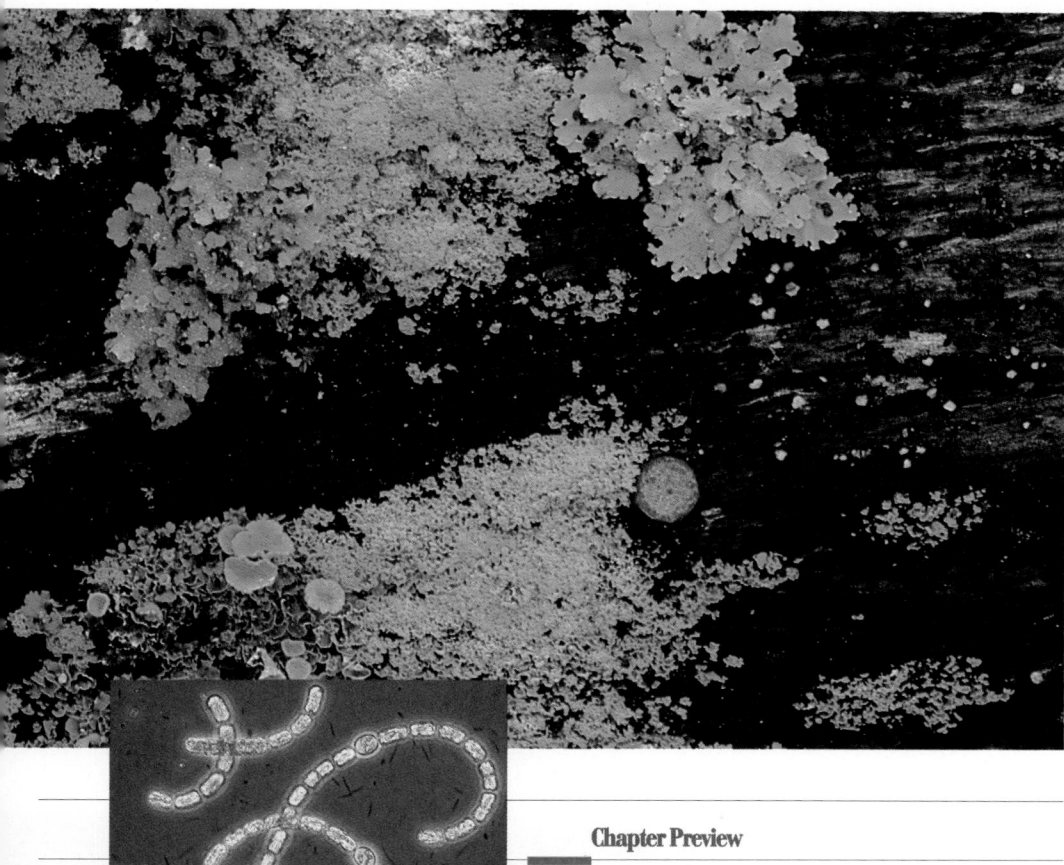

In communities, organisms depend on and interact with each other in ways similar to the way this alga depends on and interacts with the fungus. In what ways do the members of the community you live in interact like organisms in these environments?

Chapter Preview

785

Introducing the Chapter

Use the photograph on page 784 to introduce the idea of interactions within ecosystems. After reviewing how the organisms that make up a lichen interact, ask students to identify other ways in which organisms interact with one another. Urge them to consider relationships other than those related to feeding. Perhaps they will think of examples such as pollination of flowering plants by animals or birds nesting in trees. Having established the importance of the interaction among organisms, turn the attention of the class to ways in which organisms interact with the physical aspects of their environment. Ask them what kinds of physical factors can affect populations of organisms. They may identify factors such as temperature, light, topography, and amount of oxygen.

Theme Development

The theme of energy is apparent early in the chapter as students explore the flow of energy through an ecosystem. The theme of systems and interactions is emphasized throughout the chapter, e.g., in the discussions of food chains and webs, recycling of materials, symbiotic relationships, and the interplay between organisms and the physical aspects of their environment.

Tying to Previous Knowledge

This chapter will expand students' understanding of ecological relationships first studied in Chapter 1 and will add to their appreciation of the importance of and relationship between the processes of photosynthesis and cellular respiration. They will make use of their knowledge of chemistry as they study cycling of materials. They will also come to apply their knowledge of population biology as they realize that an ecosystem consists of many interacting populations.

ASSESSMENT PLANNER

Choose assessment strategies from the following pages to evaluate the progress of your students.

Assess, pp. 793-794, 805
Portfolio, pp. 790, 803
Alternate Lab, pp. 800-801
Thinking Lab, p. 793
Minilab 1, p. 800

Minilab 2, p. 804
Investigation, pp. 798-799
Chapter Review, pp. 810-811

Prepare

Key Concepts

Students trace the path of energy through an ecosystem. They will learn about the interactions of biotic and abiotic factors in an ecosystem. Students will also learn more about the interdependence of organisms and their environment.

Key Terms

biotic factor, ecosystem, trophic level, niche, first-order consumer, herbivore, carnivore, second-order consumer, third-order consumer, omnivore, food web, pyramid of energy, pyramid of numbers, biomass, pyramid of biomass, commensalism

Materials

- Gather hand lenses and field guides for the outdoor activity.

1 Focus

Objectives

The objectives are listed on the student page. Remind students to preview these objectives as a guide to this numbered section.

Discussion

Use students' relationships with other living things as an example of an ecosystem. Ask students to identify organisms in their community with which they interact, including plants, insects, birds, mammals, and other humans. Ask students to describe their relationship with each organism. Use these descriptions to introduce the terms *ecosystem, community,* and *niche.*

Objectives

Trace the passage of energy from producers to consumers in an ecosystem.

Relate the flow of energy through an ecosystem to the pyramid of energy.

Analyze the importance of recycling of materials in an ecosystem and **describe** how such recycling occurs.

Distinguish among parasitism, commensalism, and mutualism.

28.1 Interactions Among Organisms

Can you picture a lake and think about the many living things that inhabit such a community? Around the edge live a variety of plants—grasses, cattails, and ferns, perhaps. The water itself is home to a great diversity of invertebrates such as worms, snails, hydras, and insect larvae. Vertebrates include a variety of fish, tadpoles and adult frogs, snakes, turtles, and maybe ducks or coots. Unseen are the many microscopic organisms present: bacteria and fungi, algae, and tiny crustaceans. In what ways do these many organisms interact with one another? How does each organism obtain the materials and energy it needs to remain alive? Do the organisms depend upon one another in ways other than as food sources? Could the community continue to exist if the diversity of life forms were altered in some way? Knowing answers to questions such as these will be important to you when you must make informed decisions concerning the environment.

Trophic Levels

Just as the homes, schools, and businesses in your town make up a community, populations of organisms living together in the same area make up a community. Within any community, the organisms interact with members of their own species and with those of other species. Such relationships between or among different organisms are known as **biotic factors** of the environment. These organisms interact with their physical environment as well. Interaction of a community with its environment is an ecological system or **ecosystem.**

Figure 28-1 **This pond is an example of an ecological system or ecosystem. The microscopic plants and animals (left), pintail duck (top right), and sunfish (bottom right) all contribute to the balance of the pond ecosystem.**

786 ECOSYSTEMS

MEETING INDIVIDUAL NEEDS

Help ESL students develop vocabulary and speaking skills by pairing them with native English speakers. Ask students to name foods eaten at a recent meal. Using labeled drawings or magazine cutouts, have students trace the passage of energy from sunlight to each food item. For example, the meat in a hamburger is traced back from a cow, through grass and grain, to sunlight. Have students place the drawings on a trophic level chart, with producers at the bottom, herbivores on the next level, and so on. Ask students to orally describe the passage of energy from sunlight to each food item, naming each trophic level. Use these charts when introducing the pyramid of energy concept. LEP

The interactions between a community of organisms and the environment are give-and-take relationships. Organisms take from their environment materials and energy needed for life, and, as they are used, they are transferred back to the environment. Because there is a tight relationship between a community of organisms and the environment, there is a delicate balance among the many forms of life in a healthy ecosystem.

How do organisms interact with each other? Perhaps the most obvious way in which different populations of organisms interact is by feeding upon one another. Because food is a source of energy, availability of food is a limiting factor for many animal populations. You are well aware by now that all organisms require energy in order to carry out their many functions. In almost all ecosystems, the original source of that energy is sunlight. The light can be used directly only by autotrophs such as grasses, trees, or algae. In photosynthesis, autotrophic organisms trap light energy and change it to chemical energy stored in the form of sugars and other organic compounds.

Because only photosynthetic autotrophs can trap and change light energy to chemical energy, all other organisms depend on them for their energy sources. Energy stored in energy-rich organic molecules is transferred from one organism to another as organisms feed upon each other within an ecosystem. In this way, each organism represents a feeding step, or **trophic level,** in the passage of energy and materials.

All organisms within an ecosystem have functions in that ecosystem. An organism's **niche** describes how an organism fits into an ecosystem. Where an organism lives, what it eats and what eats it, and how it interacts with all the biotic and abiotic parts of the ecosystem describe its niche. Since each organism plays a unique role, no two organisms can occupy the same niche in an ecosystem.

28.1 INTERACTIONS AMONG ORGANISMS **787**

2 Teach

Using the Illustration

On the chalkboard, create a chart with the headings *Organism, Home, Food, Predators, Interactions.* Ask students to define the niches of each organism illustrated in the pond community by filling in the chart. Extend the discussion to other biotic communities the students are familiar with, such as lawn, flower bed, woodland, rotting log, beach, vegetable garden, or vacant lot. LEP

PROGRAM RESOURCES

Teacher Classroom Resources

Study Guide, pp. 163-165 L1

Concept Mapping, p. 28 L1 LEP

Probing Levels of Life, Lab 78, p. 208 L2

Investigating Living Systems, Lab 76, p. 297 L2

Exploring Environmental Issues, pp. 7, 43 L3

Color Transparency #53 L1 LEP

Misconception

Students may not clearly understand the difference between a biotic community and an ecosystem and the difference between a niche and a habitat. A community is made up of organisms that live on or near each other and interact in ways that sustain and regulate their relationships. An ecosystem is a stable system made up of a community of living organisms plus the nonliving, or abiotic, factors that characterize that environment. A niche is an organism's responses and behaviors, while a habitat is the physical place that is its home.

Brainstorming

Ask students to name familiar organisms from each trophic level. Point out that a single species may feed on more than one level, depending on the availability of different food items. For example, while mice usually eat seeds and grain, they can also catch and eat insects. Producers include algae, phytoplankton, and plants. Herbivores include rabbits, mice, humans, bear, deer, elephants, seed-eating birds, and zooplankton. Second-order consumers include humans, baleen whales, and birds that eat insects, worms, or mice (robins, flycatchers, hawks). Third-order consumers include lions, tigers, sharks, killer whales, and birds that prey on birds (hawks, gulls).

COOP LEARN

Trophic Levels   In order for a community to function, people depend on other people. How do you depend on work done by police? Mail carriers? The same is true for organisms within an ecosystem. In order for an ecosystem to function, organisms also depend upon each other. For an ecosystem to be successful, energy must first pass from producers to consumers. A consumer that feeds directly on a producer is called a **first-order consumer.** First-order consumers are also called **herbivores,** or plant eaters. A cow grazing on grass, a deer browsing on foliage, and a tadpole eating algae are examples of herbivores. Herbivores make up the second trophic level in ecosystems.

Consumers that feed on other consumers are called **carnivores,** or meat eaters. A mouse is preyed upon by snakes. Therefore, a snake is a carnivore and a **second-order consumer.** An owl that eats the snake is a **third-order consumer.** Second-order and third-order consumers make up higher trophic levels.

Decomposers are consumers as well. Protists and fungi are common types of decomposers. Scavengers such as vultures may prey on decomposers as well as feeding on dead animals. Decomposers break down and consume dead organisms and wastes at every trophic level. In the process, they recycle a large part of the broken-down substances back to the producers.

Food Chains   The transfer of materials and potential energy from organism to organism (trophic level to trophic level) forms a series called a food chain. A food chain is represented using arrows that indicate the direction in which materials and energy are transferred from one organism to another. Decomposers can function at any point in a food chain.

plant   →   mouse   →   snake   →   owl   →   decomposer
(producer)   (first-order   (second-order   (third-order
             consumer)   consumer)   consumer)

A food chain represents *one* possible route for the transfer of materials and energy through an ecosystem. Many other routes exist. In an ecosystem, many species are found at each trophic level, and one species does not always feed on the same food source. A snake may also eat a lizard or a toad; an owl may feed directly on a mouse. Can you think of any other possible food chains? In addition, some animals are **omnivores,** organisms that eat both plants and animals. Humans are omnivores. All the possible feeding relationships that exist in an ecosystem make up a **food web,** pictured in Figure 28-2.

PROJECT

Earth's Ecosystems: Have small groups of students research and report on one of the major ecosystems on Earth, such as tundra, taiga forest, tropical forest, grassland, open ocean, rocky ocean shore, desert. Individual students could be assigned aspects of the ecosystem to report on, such as the abiotic factors in the environment, the producers, the herbivores, the second- and third-order consumers, or the culture of the people living in the area. Or students could be assigned separate geographic areas. For example, one student from the grassland group might report on the prairies of North America and another on the savannahs of Africa.

L1   **COOP LEARN**

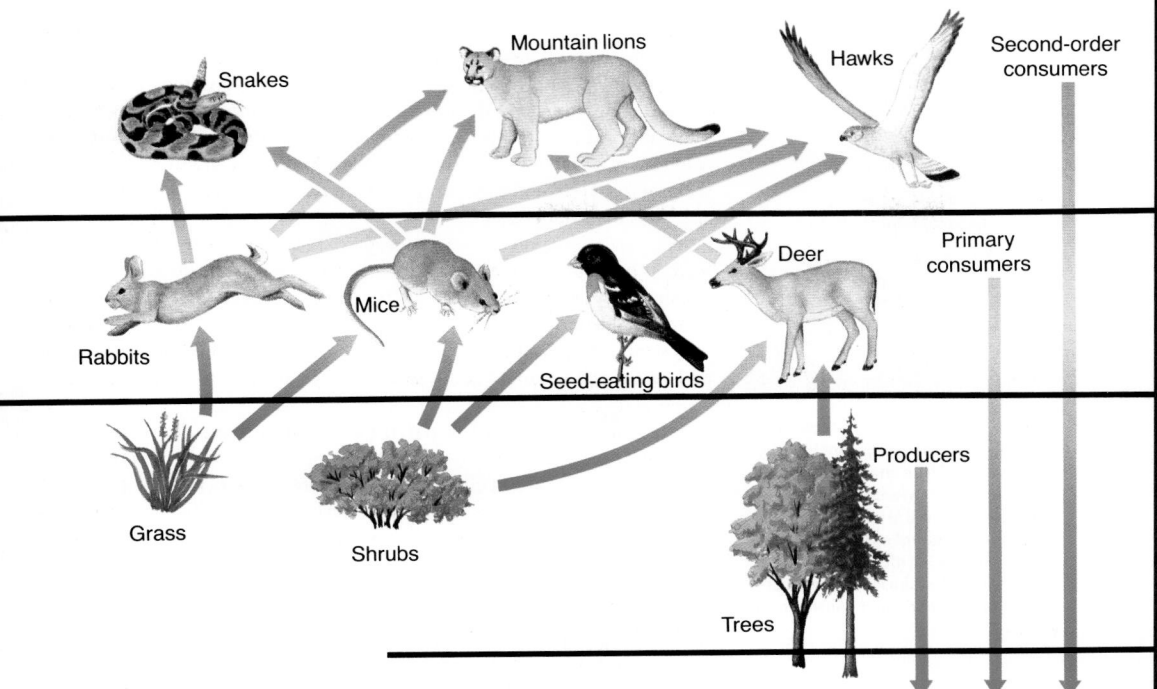

Mountain lions

Snakes

Hawks

Second-order consumers

Rabbits

Mice

Deer

Primary consumers

Seed-eating birds

Grass

Shrubs

Producers

Trees

Decomposers

Figure 28-2   The food web pictured here describes some of the feeding relationships within an ecosystem. The arrows show the direction of energy flow. In a real ecosystem, many more plants and animals would be involved in the food web.

Pyramid of Energy

Food chains enable all organisms to obtain a part of the energy entering the ecosystem. However, some energy is always lost between each link in a food chain. The amount of energy actually transferred at each level depends on the ecosystem. Accurate data are difficult to obtain because of variables such as season, age and size of organisms, and amount of sunlight. A study of a river ecosystem in Silver Springs, Florida, was made by Howard Odum. It showed that only 16 percent of the potential energy in producers was transferred to herbivores. Second-order consumers obtained only 11 percent of the potential energy in herbivores. Only about 5 percent of the energy in second-order consumers was transferred to third-order consumers. The third-order consumers received only about 0.1 percent of the potential energy originally available in the producers. A graph of data such as these has the pyramid shape shown in Figure 28-3. Thus, ecologists refer to the transfer of energy as a **pyramid of energy.**

What happens to the energy originally produced? According to the law of conservation of energy, the energy is not lost—it still exists—but it is in a form that cannot be used again. Remember, some stored energy is used by the producers themselves for their life processes. Some energy is bound up in molecules the consumer cannot digest. More than half of the potential energy present in each food molecule is lost as heat energy during cellular respiration.

28.1 INTERACTIONS AMONG ORGANISMS ❧ **789**

SECTION 28.1

Chalkboard Example

Help students visualize the magnitude of the reduction in available energy at higher trophic levels. On the chalkboard, diagram the river ecosystem food chain described in the student text. For each link in the chain, draw a pie diagram to illustrate the amount of energy available:

Producer
100%

Herbivore
17%

2nd-Order Consumer
0.86%

3rd-Order Consumer
0.1%

Figure Caption Question

What types of organisms are found at the top of the energy pyramid? Which trophic level contains the most energy? Why is eating low on the food chain most energy efficient?
Large predators are found at the top of the pyramid. The most energy is found at the level of the producers. Feeding is most efficient at the producer level because no energy has been lost to the next level.

Concept Development

Ask students to describe how carbon is incorporated into the tissues of an apple or other fruit tree as it grows to maturity from a seed. Remind students that carbon dioxide gas from the air is used as a component of the sugars made during photosynthesis. Ask which tissues of the tree contain carbon. *all* Then ask for ways in which that carbon is distributed to other organisms or back into the atmosphere. For example, the carbon in pollen is collected by bees and used to make honey; carbon in bark and leaves is eaten by insects and is in turn eaten by birds. The fruit is eaten by birds, squirrels, deer, and humans. Carbon is released into the atmosphere when branches are burned at pruning time.

790

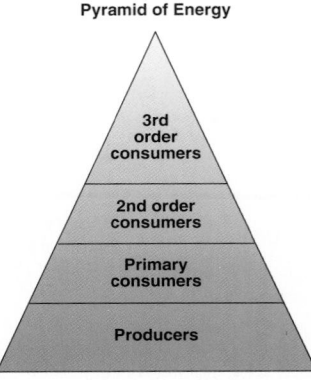

Pyramid of Energy

3rd order consumers

2nd order consumers

Primary consumers

Producers

Figure 28-3 **A pyramid can be drawn to show the energy levels within an ecosystem. Little energy is available at the top of the pyramid because some is lost at each level. What types of organisms are found at the top of the energy pyramid? Which trophic level contains the most energy? Why is eating low on the food chain most energy efficient?**

There are other reasons why the amount of energy available to each level decreases. Some organisms die and are acted on by decomposers. Also, members of higher trophic levels often don't consume every part of an organism. For example, only a small fraction of the organic material in a tree is consumed by herbivores. In addition, not all parts of the material eaten by an organism, such as bones or cellulose, are digested. For all these reasons, each link in the food chain has less potential energy available to it than the previous link.

The pyramid of energy also offers an explanation as to why organisms feed on particular organisms and not others. Lions prey on large animals because they can get more energy from a large animal than from a small animal. In fact, lions might use more energy trying to catch a rodent than they would get by eating the rodent. Therefore, lions hunt and eat zebras, and a single chase might result in an energy "profit" for the lion.

Pyramids of Numbers and Biomass

Loss of energy in a food chain explains several ecological principles. A food chain rarely includes more than four links. So much energy is lost at each trophic level that enough energy seldom remains to support fourth- and fifth-order consumers. The loss of energy also explains why there are usually fewer organisms in each higher trophic level than in the previous level. For example, there are more mice than there are weasels that feed on those mice. This relationship is known as the **pyramid of numbers.** Each trophic level has fewer organisms than the previous level. A pyramid of numbers shows the same general pattern as a pyramid of energy.

The pyramid of numbers does not apply to all food chains, especially where a large organism is fed upon by smaller ones. For example, a single tree might be food for thousands of caterpillars, and a dog might be infested with many parasites.

Decrease in energy along food chains suggests that the total amount of organic matter present at each trophic level should also decrease because energy is required to build organic matter. Research has shown that this

Table 28.1 **Biomass in an Ecosystem**

Trophic Level	Biomass (g/m²)	Percent of Biomass Compared to Previous Level
Producers	809	—
Herbivores	37	4.5
Second-order consumers	11	29.7
Third-order consumers	1.5	7.3

PORTFOLIO

Have students diagram a food web for a biotic community of their choice. Rather than choosing large communities or ecosystems, encourage students to select smaller, perhaps even local, communities. Good choices might include oak woodland, redwood forest, kelp forest, sandy beach, salt marsh, rotting log, or beech-maple forest. Ask students to write a brief description of the feeding or growth habits and other niche characteristics of major organisms in the community. Ask students to describe, in addition to predator-prey relationships, any commensal, mutualistic, or parasitic relationships that exist within the community. **L1**

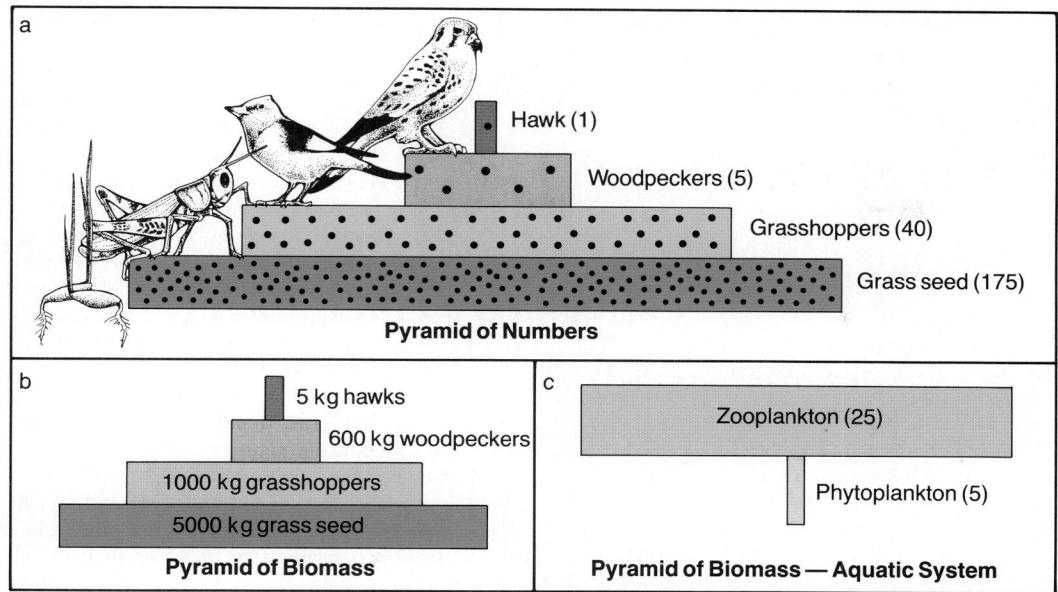

a

Hawk (1)

Woodpeckers (5)

Grasshoppers (40)

Grass seed (175)

Pyramid of Numbers

b

5 kg hawks

600 kg woodpeckers

1000 kg grasshoppers

5000 kg grass seed

Pyramid of Biomass

c

Zooplankton (25)

Phytoplankton (5)

Pyramid of Biomass — Aquatic System

prediction is true in some cases. Examine Table 28.1, which lists biomass data from the Silver Springs ecosystem. These data represent the total amount of dried weight of organic matter, called **biomass,** at different trophic levels. Do you see that there is indeed a decrease in total biomass? If data such as these are graphed, the familiar pyramid shape results, showing a **pyramid of biomass** for most ecosystems on land. The reverse is true, though, for aquatic ecosystems, because the producers are mainly microscopic algae, not large plants or trees. Though the total number of algae is great, their total biomass is quite small at any given time.

Figure 28-4 **Pyramids of numbers (a) show how many individuals an ecosystem can support. Pyramids of biomass (b) show how much living matter an ecosystem can support. The inverted pyramid (c) shows that a relatively small biomass can support a larger biomass, such as a whale being supported by microscopic plants and animals.**

Cycling of Materials

Although energy is not cycled in an ecosystem, the energy lost is constantly replaced by energy of sunlight. As a result, an ecosystem always has a new supply of energy. However, if loss of materials occurred, an ecosystem could not continue to survive, because the amount of matter is limited. No new matter is being made. Thus, matter must be recycled—the same materials used over and over again—if an ecosystem is to continue to function.

Look at Figure 28-5, which illustrates the carbon cycle. Almost every member of an ecosystem contributes to the cycling of carbon. Producers do so as they carry out both photosynthesis and aerobic respiration. Consumers do so as they undergo aerobic respiration. The products of aerobic respiration, carbon dioxide and water, are cycled to producers, which use those products to make sugars and other organic compounds in

Figure 28-5 **The processes of photosynthesis and respiration cause carbon to cycle through the environment. As the diagram shows, some carbon can accumulate for years in the wood of trees and in the soil. How is this carbon eventually returned to the atmosphere?**

photosynthesis. Most producers and consumers use those organic compounds, along with oxygen produced during photosynthesis, in aerobic respiration. Thus, carbon is continually cycled from inorganic form, carbon dioxide, to organic form, such as sugars. Note, too, that hydrogen and oxygen atoms are cycled as well.

As organisms live, they produce a variety of wastes. Eventually, all organisms die. Both wastes and dead organisms contain materials. Some are organic, such as carbohydrates, fats, and proteins. Others are inorganic, such as a variety of minerals. These materials are cycled, too. If they weren't, all available matter would one day be locked up in wastes or dead bodies. How are they cycled?

Wastes and dead organisms are the food of a variety of organisms in an ecosystem. Decomposers, such as many bacteria and fungi, use this food in cellular respiration, just as other consumers do. Therefore, they, too, release carbon dioxide and water back into the environment, making them available to producers. Various animals also cycle carbon as they feed upon dead organisms and wastes. Among them are insects, buzzards, lobsters, crabs, and jackals. Such animals are often called scavengers.

Carbon is also recycled in other ways. For example, the burning of fossil fuels such as oil, gasoline, and coal by humans releases large amounts of carbon dioxide into the environment. Carbon dioxide is also released during volcanic eruptions, and when carbonate ions present in rock are slowly changed in chemical reactions.

Many decomposers recycle materials other than carbon as well. Some break down nitrogen-containing organic molecules such as nucleic acids, proteins, and urea, converting them to inorganic ions. Others then convert those ions to other forms, such as nitrates, which are absorbed by producers. Producers use nitrates to manufacture the organic nitrogen-containing molecules mentioned above, which can then be passed along food chains. In addition to nitrogen, decomposers play a role in recycling of other materials, such as phosphorus and sulfur. Availability of these inorganic materials is crucial, and the supply of them may act to limit distribution of organisms and the size of their populations.

Other Biotic Relationships

Many relationships and interactions exist among organisms of different species. Some of these relationships are necessary to the survival of both organisms. Other relationships are of no consequence to either organism. In ecosystems, the most obvious biotic relationships involve feeding, but organisms also interact in other ways.

Commensalism In some relationships, one organism benefits from a host without aiding or harming the host. Such a relationship is called **commensalism,** and an organism that benefits is called a commensal. For example, in dense tropical rain forests, the tree branches are so thick that the forest floor is dark. As a result, small plants cannot grow on the forest floor. Some small plants, such as orchids, live in the branches of trees and, thus, get enough light. Because of the high humidity in a rain forest, their roots absorb water from the air. Orchids benefit greatly in this relationship because they can receive ample sunlight. Large trees receive no benefit from this relationship, but they also are not harmed in any way.

The bromeliad, a member of the pineapple family, also lives in the branches of rain forest trees. Not only is a bromeliad a commensal, it is also a small ecosystem. The leaves of a bromeliad overlap to form a hollow in which water collects. Many arthropods and even tree frogs reproduce in the water. Some of these frogs live entirely in the treetops.

Animals exhibit commensalism also. A remora is a small fish that attaches itself to the belly of a larger animal, such as a shark. The shark provides a "free ride" for the remora, which feeds from the leftovers of the shark's meals. Are sharks harmed in any way from this relationship?

Mutualism Often, both organisms in a relationship benefit in some way. As you know, this relationship is called mutualism. For example, bees pollinate plants and at the same time receive food in the form of nectar and pollen. Termites show another classic example of mutualism. Termites are able to obtain energy from wood because their intestines are home to protozoans that digest the cellulose of which the wood is composed. How do

Figure 28-6 This orchid depends on a tree for a place to live. The tree neither benefits nor is harmed by this relationship.

Thinking Lab
ANALYZE THE PROCEDURE

How do root nodule bacteria benefit clover plants?

Background
Scientists have known for years that clover roots contain nodules filled with bacteria. They thought that the bacteria were parasites and caused harm to clover. Then, when checking on this "parasite," they found that clover with bacteria grew better than when no bacteria were present.

You Try It
Analyze each experiment listed below. Explain why you think it would or would not be helpful in explaining why or how these bacteria improve clover growth. Explain what information, if

any, each experiment would give you. Describe the errors in experimental method you find. (1) Clover with bacterial nodules was grown in soils having different nutrients available. Clover was observed for differences in growth. (2) Clover was grown with and without nodules in beakers of water. Kinds of chemicals present in the water before and after several weeks were analyzed and compared. (3) Clover nodule bacteria were grown in culture medium at different temperatures. The optimum temperature for their growth was determined.

Thinking Lab
ANALYZE THE PROCEDURE

Purpose
Analyze experimental procedures to determine if they are meaningful.

Skills
separate and control variables, interpret data

Teaching Strategies
• Review the concepts of parasitism, mutualism, and commensalism with

your students. Which relationship exists between bacteria and clover roots?

Answers
1. No control was provided in the procedure.
2. A control is being used. The difference in chemical makeup of the water before and after may provide valuable data as to the role of the bacteria.

3. Temperature may be a factor in speeding up or slowing growth of bacteria.

✔ **Assessment**
Knowledge: Ask students to design other experiments that may be helpful in answering the questions asked about improved clover growth. Experiments may focus on the growth of the bacterium itself outside of the clover nodules.

Display
Have students do research to find several relationships between organisms. Have them determine if the relationship is mutualistic, commensal, or parasitic. They should then display pictures of these relationships with a short explanation of each.

Misconception
Students may think that parasites kill their hosts. Parasites generally do not kill their host because they would then lose their home and food supply.

3 Assess

Check for Understanding
Ask each student to formulate one or more questions about material studied in this section and write each question on a 3×5 note card. Collect the cards, shuffle them, and have each student draw one without looking. Divide the class into small groups, and have each student answer his or her question orally for the group. Encourage students to explain answers to each other when help is needed. **L1** **COOP LEARN**

Reteach
Choose an ecosystem, and have each student represent an organism's niche. Make sure all trophic levels are represented. Give a "producer" a spool of twine. Ask students to use the twine to represent the pathway of energy moving through the ecosystem. As each organism consumes a food item, it wraps the twine around one hand.

Extension

Have students investigate how the food webs of two neighboring communities might overlap. Ask them to diagram an example of overlap, such as an owl living in a forest that travels to a meadow at dusk to hunt for mice. **L2**

✔ Assessment

Performance: Using a 3 × 5 card for each unnamed organism belonging to a "mystery" ecosystem, provide students with data such as the organism's population size, feeding habits, and relationships with other organisms. For example, "organism A" might belong to a population of thousands of individuals, obtain its food without eating, and provide a home for several herbivore species and one second-order consumer. Have students organize the cards into a reasonable food web and identify the type(s) of ecosystem(s) the web might represent. **L1**

4 Close

Discussion

Using food webs constructed during study of this section, ask students to speculate about what might happen if one or more species were removed from a community.

Figure 28-7 Bur marigold seeds, commonly called sticktights, cling to fur, feathers, or even clothing. This plant depends on other members of the ecosystem to disperse its seeds.

termites and protozoans benefit from this relationship? Another example of mutualism is that of the yucca plant and yucca moth. Female yucca moths transfer pollen from one yucca flower to another. These moths also deposit eggs in the developing seedpods of yucca plants. In this relationship, moths benefit because the eggs have a source of food when they hatch, and yucca plants benefit because pollination and reproduction of yucca plants is assured.

Cycling of nitrogen depends in part on a mutualistic relationship. The atmosphere consists of about 78 percent nitrogen gas by volume, but most organisms cannot use nitrogen in that form. Many forms of bacteria, though, can convert nitrogen gas to a usable form, a process known as nitrogen fixation. Many of those bacteria live in the roots of certain plants, especially legumes such as peas, clover, and alfalfa, where they break down dead plant material for food. These bacteria reside in the cortex cells of the roots and cause them to become swollen areas called nodules. Within the root cells, the bacteria convert nitrogen gas to ammonia. The plant uses the ammonia to make proteins and other nitrogen compounds. The bacteria benefit by having a place to live and a constant food supply.

Parasitism Parasitism is another relationship between organisms. In parasitism, one organism, the parasite, is completely dependent at some point in its life cycle upon a host. Unlike mutualism and commensalism, the host is usually harmed in some way.

Besides these specific biotic relationships, many more relationships exist among organisms. Each ecological niche involves many obvious and not-so-obvious relationships among living or once-living organisms. For example, many species of birds build nests in trees. Rotten logs provide a place for some types of insect larvae. And some plants such as the bur marigold and tick trefoil depend on animals for seed dispersal. Think of some of the ways humans depend on other organisms.

Section Review

Understanding Concepts

1. A certain fish feeds upon tiny crustaceans in the ocean. The crustaceans feed upon algae. How do these feeding relationships provide energy to the organisms involved?
2. In a certain ecosystem, owls feed on field mice. Explain two reasons why the total energy present in field mice is not available to the owls.
3. Suppose a polluting chemical entered a lake and that it killed most bacteria but not other life forms. What effect would that chemical have on the lake ecosystem? Why?
4. **Skill Review—Making Tables:** Make a table that compares the effect on both organisms in each of the following relationships: mutualism, parasitism, commensalism. Use a "+" to indicate benefit, a "–" to indicate harm, and a "0" to indicate no effect. For more help, see Organizing Information in the **Skill Handbook**.
5. **Thinking Critically:** Consider a New England forest ecosystem in summer and winter. How would the number of organisms at each trophic level differ during those two seasons? Explain.

Answers to Section Review

1. Algae trap light energy and use it to manufacture sugars and other organic compounds, the food of animals in the ecosystem. The crustaceans obtain energy as they use the organic molecules of the algae in cellular respiration. Similarly, the fish obtain energy from the organic molecules in the crustaceans.
2. Energy is lost as the field mice carry out their functions, during cellular respiration, because not all parts of the mice are eaten, because not all parts eaten can be digested, and because some mice die and are acted upon by decomposers.
3. Death of most bacteria would lead to a decreased rate of decomposition. Necessary materials would accumulate at the bottom of the lake instead of being recycled. As a result, other organisms might also die, compounding the problem.
4. **Skill Review—Making Tables:** Mutualism: +/+; parasitism: parasite +; host –; commensalism: commensal +; host 0.
5. **Thinking Critically:** The numbers would decrease during winter because of the decrease in food production.

28.2 Abiotic Factors of the Environment

In the previous section, we focused on ways in which organisms interact. But organisms are affected not only by other organisms, but also by physical factors of the environment. Let's think again about a lake ecosystem. Why are plants such as grasses and cattails found only around the edges of the ecosystem? Why are the algae located only near the surface? Does the temperature of the water affect the kinds of animals that live there or the activity of those animals? How much oxygen is dissolved in the water, and how does that oxygen supply influence the organisms? Do different animals live at different depths? If so, why? Such questions can be answered by analyzing physical factors of an environment and their effects.

Water

Physical aspects of the environment are important in many ways. They can influence the distribution and range of organisms, as well as their reproduction, feeding, growth, and metabolism. Physical aspects of the environment, known as **abiotic factors,** can also limit the size of a population, as you learned in Chapter 27. Therefore, an entire ecosystem, composed of many different populations, can be affected by abiotic factors. Pinpointing the role of a particular abiotic factor is often difficult because many of those factors interact to affect the makeup and functions of the ecosystem. We'll take a look at a few of these factors separately, but keep in mind that they operate together.

All organisms need water. Water is important as a medium in which many organisms live. The organisms living in a pond or lake ecosystem, or in a river, stream, or ocean, are adapted for living in water and could not live in the dry medium of air. If you consider functions such as gas exchange, excretion, and locomotion, you'll understand why aquatic organisms could not carry out those functions on land.

Water is crucial for organisms in other ways. It is a major component of cytoplasm and of the fluids that bathe cells. It is also the substance in which numerous metabolic reactions take place.

Because water is so important for living organisms, availability of water can affect the distribution of land plants. Why? Plants require water for photosynthesis, and plants such as mosses and ferns

Objectives

Analyze the ways in which abiotic factors of an environment may influence the activities and distribution of organisms.

Predict the effects of changes on the balance of an ecosystem.

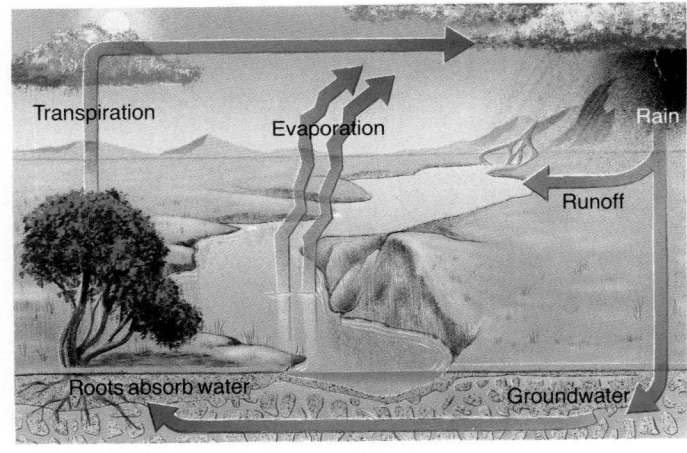

Figure 28-8 **Water moves in a cycle between organisms on land, the land itself, and the atmosphere. From where do you think the largest amount of evaporation of water occurs?**

28.2 ABIOTIC FACTORS OF THE ENVIRONMENT **795**

PROGRAM RESOURCES

Teacher Classroom Resources
Study Guide, pp. 166-168 [L1]
Critical Thinking/Problem Solving, p. 28 [L2]
Probing Levels of Life, Labs 79-82, pp. 213-223 [L2]

Investigating Living Systems, Labs 77, 78, pp. 301, 305 [L2]
Color Transparency #54, 55, 56 [L2] [LEP]
Color Transparency #57 [L1] [LEP]

Prepare

Key Concepts
Students analyze the roles that non-living environmental factors play in maintaining the balance of an ecosystem.

Key Terms
abiotic factor, humus, estivation, algal bloom

Materials
- Gather empty aquarium or large glass jar, potting soil, sand or gravel, rocks, plants, fish, reptiles, insects, and other organisms for terrarium model of a community.
- Gather live cactus, prickly pear fruit, beakers, and thermometers for the demonstrations.
- Gather sturdy twine, wooden stakes, measuring tape, hand lenses, pH paper, thermometers, and field guides for the Alternate Lab.

1 Focus

Objectives
The objectives are listed on the student page. Remind students to preview these objectives as a guide to this numbered section.

Model
Set up a terrarium in class that models a woodland, grassland, pond, or desert community. Have students monitor and record moisture, light, temperature, and soil conditions to determine the conditions most favorable for that community. If possible, set up more than one model so students can make comparisons of the optimal conditions in different communities. [LEP]

Figure Caption Question
From where do you think the largest amount of evaporation of water occurs? From the oceans

Purpose
Students deepen their understanding of how local ecology influences human culture.

Teaching Strategies
Bring to the classroom a living cactus plant students can examine during discussion of the adaptations that enable cacti to survive with little water. Obtain prickly pear fruit, preserves, or candy for students to taste.

Possible Answers
1. The prickly pear cactus is important to semiarid regions like the southwest, northern Mexico, and North Africa as food for range cattle during periods of drought. It is planted to create a windbreak and help prevent soil erosion during the dry, windy season, as well as to serve as a fence. The pads are broken down into a sticky substance that is used in making bricks.
2. Answers will vary but should include effects of weather patterns, water supply, native plants and animals, and important landforms on agriculture, diet, housing, clothing, transportation, customs, and recreation.

Going Further
Have students bring food, dress in costumes, or play a game from another culture. L1

Figure 28-9 Grasslands cover about 25 percent of Earth's land surface and are North America's largest biome. Grasslands typically receive between 25 and 75 cm of rainfall each year.

also need at least a thin film of water in which sperm cells can swim to eggs. The amount of water on land is controlled by rainfall. The amount of rainfall, in combination with temperature, determines the type of plant that will be dominant in a given area. For example, forests are common in areas receiving 75 cm or more of rain per year. However, in regions where rainfall is between 25 and 75 cm per year, grasslands are common. Water is scarce in desert regions, and the plants living in such ecosystems are those adapted to obtain and conserve the small amount of water that is available. Thus, water availability is a limiting factor. The types of plants in an area determine, in turn, the animal life in that area. For example, monkeys can live in a tropical forest, but not in a grassland.

You know that water is constantly cycled as organisms carry out cellular respiration. However, that process is just one aspect of water cycling. Examine Figure 28-8 on the previous page. It shows how physical events—evaporation, condensation, and transpiration (water loss from leaves)—are all important components of the water cycle.

ART CONNECTION

Abuelitos Piscando Napolitos

The painting *Abuelitos Piscando Napolitos* shows the harvest of prickly pear cactus fruits in the southwest. The artist, Carmen Lomas Garza, grew up in Kingsville, Texas, where her mother's family had lived for many generations, working as ranch hands and on the railroads. She inherited her artistic talent from her grandmother, a skilled needle-worker, and from her mother, a self-taught artist. In choosing a career as a professional artist, however, Garza has challenged the traditional roles that many Latin women have followed.

Abuelitos Piscando Napolitos is one of several works in which Garza shows her response to the Latino movement. In painting these pictures, Garza has said that she wanted to portray events that are meaningful to all Mexican-American culture.

The prickly pear cactus has long played an important part in the life of Mexico and the southwest. Fossil evidence indicates that the fruit of the prickly pear cactus was part of the diet of the native Indians of this region as long as 9000 years ago. The Aztecs prized the prickly pear cactus for the red dye that was extracted from the bodies of an insect that lived on the plant. After Cortes invaded the Aztec empire, there was a great demand for the dye in Europe, and prickly pear cac-

tus plants were exported to Spain and the Canary Islands. Today, the fruit of the prickly pear cactus is eaten raw or cooked and made into preserves, pickles, a sweet drink called "miel de tuna," and even a taffylike candy called "queso." The pads can be used as an ingredient in soup.

While most plants cannot survive in a very dry climate, the prickly pear cactus is well adapted to its desert environment and plays an important part in the local ecology. The fleshy pads of the prickly pear and other cacti are actually stems whose spongy tissues retain moisture. During the short rainy season, these stems expand quickly to hold the water absorbed by the plant's shallow but extensive roots. The vascular tissue of the cactus is

796 ECOSYSTEMS

Visually Impaired: Pair visually impaired students with sighted students during outdoor activities. Ask the sighted student to describe the study area and help the visually impaired student touch or smell leaves, twigs, flowers, bark, and other organisms from the study area.

Soil

Soil is important in many ways to land organisms. Most plants are anchored in soil, which is also the source of water and minerals the plants require. Soil is the surface upon which many animals move and the home for countless microorganisms and decomposers. Activities of these soil-inhabiting organisms not only help to enrich and aerate the soil, but also play an important role in cycling materials to other organisms in the ecosystem.

Soil Formation Organisms do more than enrich existing soil. They also play a major role in early steps of soil formation. Soil formation begins with a mechanical process in which weathering (freezing, thawing, and erosion) breaks rock into small mineral particles. Lichens erode away rock surfaces by secreting carbonic acid. Activities of organisms that inhabit soil further modify it. Leaching continues the breakdown of the rock. Leaching is the dissolving of minerals out of the rock or soil by water. Eventually, fine particles such as sand or clay are formed.

continuous from roots into the stem, so that water is easily distributed throughout the plant. The cacti also grow special rain roots within a few hours to a few days after rainfall, which helps them absorb water more rapidly. Most of the water is stored in the cortex and the pith of the stem. The stomata of cacti open mostly at night, when temperatures are lower, so that less water is lost by transpiration. Thus, the cactus retains a large internal store of water—enough to carry it through the long dry season.

Spines on the cactus take the place of leaves and help to discourage predators. Small desert animals, such as the cactus wren, use the stems to protect the entrance to their burrows. Larger animals, however, find the stems very unpleasant because they break off easily. A number of desert animals, including the pack rat, use the prickly pear cactus as a source of food and water.

In these ways, the prickly pear and other cacti have both adapted to their dry environment and become highly useful to the people and animals sharing their habitat.

By painting Mexican-Americans picking the fruit of the prickly pear cactus, Carmen Garza is portraying something that her culture finds important and beautiful.

1. **Explore Further:** In what other ways does the prickly pear cactus play an important role in the ecology of the desert?
2. **Writing About Biology:** Choose another ecological area, such as the coast, tundra, rain forest, tropics, savannah, or high mountains, and research the ways in which the ecology of the area influences the culture of the people who live there.

ART CONNECTION

Biological Illustration: Have students try their hands at biological illustration. Outdoors or in the classroom, have students select a live organism as a model. Have them use pencil, charcoal, or ink to draw as life-like a portrayal of the organism as possible. If there are students in class who are uncomfortable with drawing, have them look up information on some of the techniques used in biological and medical illustration, such as stippling or the use of a camera lucida. Let students experiment with these techniques rather than drawing from life. LEP

STUDENT JOURNAL

Have each student write a description of the niche of an organism that can live under extreme environmental conditions. Ask students to include in their descriptions some of the adaptations that enable the organism to survive. Biotic communities characterized by extreme temperatures or lack of sunlight include Arctic waters, the Antarctic, the deep sea, ice-covered lakes, the highest elevations of the Himalayan range and other very tall mountains, hot springs, or extremely dry desert regions such as parts of the Sahara. L2

SECTION 28.2

INVESTIGATION

Do soil samples differ in amount of humus present?

Time Allotment
2 class periods

Objectives
Upon completing this Investigation, students will be able to:
- Understand what humus is, why the amount of humus may differ from soil type to soil type, and why it may vary depending on soil depth.
- Learn a technique that can be used to measure and compare in a qualitative way the amount of humus present in a soil sample.

Skills
observe, form a hypothesis, design an experiment, separate and control variables, interpret data

Materials
Each group will need the following: graduated cylinder with minimum capacity of 100 mL, large test tube, one-hole stopper to fit tube, small graduated cylinder for measuring hydrogen peroxide, plastic tygon or rubber tubing, short glass tube to fit stopper, test-tube rack or support, shallow pan, water, 200 mL fresh 3 percent hydrogen peroxide (available from local drugstore—already at 3 percent), peat moss. Note: Teacher pre-assembly of glass tube and stopper is advised.

Safety Precautions: Safety goggles must be worn during the experiment and while all solutions are poured. Students should take care when handling equipment and pouring solutions.

Preparation
Gather soil samples from different local areas—include a sample with as much decaying organic matter as possible, clay soil samples, sand samples, playground or football field samples, and soil samples taken at two different depths with one sample at surface and another 30 cm below the surface.

After the breakdown of rock into soil begins, organic material is added as organisms die. More plants begin to take root in the soil, and then the diversity of animal life both in and on the soil increases. As these plants and animals die, they build up on the surface of the soil and are gradually decomposed. The decayed remains of organisms are called **humus.** Humus is an important part of soil because it contains organic material that enriches the soil. Thus, the remains of once-living organisms provide the materials that living organisms will later use. Humus also increases the soil's capacity for holding the water and air necessary for plant growth. Humus is found in the dark upper layers of soil called topsoil. Removal of topsoil by erosion is a serious agricultural problem.

INVESTIGATION

Do soil samples differ in amount of humus present?

Humus is the decomposed organic matter in soil. This means that anything that was once alive (organic matter such as leaves, insects, roots, and dead birds or mammals) that is now in the soil is part of humus. Decomposition takes place as soil bacteria use this organic matter for food and slowly break it down into mineral nutrients.

Do all soils contain the same amount of humus? It might depend on the amount of organic matter originally present in the soil. Which types of soils would have the most or least humus? Would depth of a soil sample make any difference as to amount of humus present? How can you find out?

The following experimental setup can be used to indirectly measure the amount of humus in a sample of soil. Look it over carefully. The amount of gas collected in the graduated cylinder after waiting 10 minutes is an indication of the amount of humus in the soil sample.

Now that you know how to measure soil humus, use the technique to solve several problems. How might soil humus differ if samples are taken from the surface and 30 cm below the surface? Will humus vary in soil samples taken from different areas? Work with a group assigned by your teacher. Form hypotheses that could be tested using soil samples.

Problem
Does humus vary in different soil samples? Does humus vary in the same samples of soil taken from different depths?

Safety Precautions
Be sure to wash your hands carefully after handling soil.

Hypotheses
What are your group's hypotheses?

Experimental Plan
1. Decide on a way to test your group's two hypotheses. Keep the available materials provided by your teacher in mind as you plan your procedure. If possible, you may wish to collect your own soil samples for testing.
2. Record your procedure and list materials and amounts that you will need.

Note: You may wish to have students collect their own samples and bring them to class on the day of the experiment.

Possible Hypotheses
- If each soil sample differs in amount of humus, then the amount of gas released from each sample will differ.
- If soil samples differ in the amount of humus present, then the sample with the most humus will generate the most gas.
- If the amount of humus increases with soil depth, then the amount of gas released will

increase with the depth of the soil sample tested.

Possible Procedures
- Students will follow the procedure outlined in the introduction to the experiment. There is no opportunity for variation in the procedure. The only variation will be in the sample tested and amount of gas generated with each sample.
- Controls for the experiment will usually consist of a tube of hydrogen peroxide with no soil sample added. No gas release will occur.

Types of Soil The relative amounts of minerals present in soil influence the kinds of plant life that can exist. Consider, for example, a sandy soil. There are many air spaces in such soil, but the minerals do not attract water. Water drains rapidly through the soil. Since little water is held in the soil, water is not available for plant life. These facts explain why you see no life on a beach or a scarcity of life in the middle of a desert. While there is no "best" type of soil, some soils support more plant life than others. Clay particles are minerals in soil that retain water. A soil that contains a higher proportion of clay will, therefore, be able to sustain more plant life. Too much clay, however, prevents drainage of water and the air spaces become filled.

Checking the Plan

Discuss the following points with other group members to decide the final procedure for your experiment.

1. What data will you collect and how will it be recorded?
2. What variables will have to be controlled?
3. What control will be used?
4. Assign roles for this investigation.

Make sure your teacher has approved your experimental plan before you proceed further.

Data and Conclusions

Carry out your experiment. Prepare a data chart to record your findings.

Analysis and Conclusions

1. State your hypothesis regarding the amount of humus present in the soil samples taken from different depths. Explain whether your hypothesis supports or rejects the information you now have from the answer to question 1. Use specific experimental data to confirm or reject your hypothesis.

2. State your hypothesis regarding the amount of humus present in different soil samples. Explain whether your hypothesis supports or rejects the information you now have from the answer to question 1. Use specific experimental data to confirm or reject your hypothesis.

3. Explain what you believe may have been the role of adding hydrogen peroxide (H_2O_2) to each soil sample.

4. Describe some of the variables that had to be controlled in this experiment. How were they controlled?

5. Describe the control that was used and how it enabled you to conclude that the gas being released did come from the soil. Did your experi-ment actually show that the gas given off did come directly from the humus alone? Explain how you might have altered your experimental procedure to prove this.

Going Further

Based on this lab experience, design another experiment that would help to answer questions that arose from your work. Assume that you will have limited resources and will be conducting this lab in class. Include this as part of your report.

Glass tube — Plastic tube — Hydrogen peroxide — Water — Soil — Pan

means for judging the amount of humus present in a soil sample.

4. Some variables include the following. Volume of soil used for each trial should be the same. Volume of hydrogen peroxide used should always be the same. Use a graduated cylinder to measure the volume of soil and hydrogen peroxide being used.

5. The control was a tube of hydrogen peroxide with no soil sample. No gas was released. This proved that gas collected with the soil sample came from a reaction of hydrogen peroxide and soil.

✔ Assessment

Performance: Have students write an evaluation of this lab for their portfolios. Have students show how they used their lab setup in a demonstration to you. They should be able to explain how the apparatus works.

Extensions

Students may wish to determine the amount of humus in pure leaf litter or pure dead plant material. Compare the amount of humus in a compost heap to that of soil. Compare the amount of humus in a soil sample at different times of the year.

Teaching Strategies

- Fresh H_2O_2 must be used with each new trial.
- Students must control the following: use same volume of soil for each sample tested, use same volume of hydrogen peroxide for each sample tested, wait same length of time for gas generation.
- Allow students to set up equipment and perform a pretrial using hydrogen peroxide and a sample of peat moss.
- Demonstrate the procedure for filling and inverting the cylinder into the water-filled pan. Students can use the palm of their hand to prevent water from escaping while inverting the cylinder. If any air enters the cylinder while inverting into the pan, remind students to subtract this volume from the volume of gas generated by the soil sample.
- A review of the chemical reaction occurring may be helpful. The carbon present in humus reacts with H_2O_2 to release oxygen gas. The greater the amount of carbon available, the more oxygen gas released.

Data and Observations
Sample data

Soil sample	Volume of gas collected
Control	0 mL
Sand	3 mL
Football field	8 mL
Forest	32 mL
Empty lot	22 mL
Garden at surface	28 mL
Garden 30 cm below surface	12 mL

Data Analysis
Student answers may vary.

1. Accept all reasonable hypotheses. Make sure students use experimental data to accept or reject their hypothesis.
2. Accept all reasonable hypotheses.
3. The hydrogen peroxide reacts chemically with the humus (carbon) to release a gas. The amount of gas released will vary with the amount of humus present. Therefore, the gas serves as a

Minilab 1

Purpose

Students will determine that plant roots do release carbon dioxide. They should then be able to state that this gas production can aid in the formation of soil.

Skills

design an experiment, observe, infer

Teaching Strategies

- Begin growing bean plants about 2 weeks in advance of this Minilab. As an alternative, use small store-bought plants such as ivy, coleus, or potted herbs. Have students rinse soil from the roots. Soil itself contains microbes, which also carry out respiration.
- Other materials needed will include BTB solution, test tubes for holding the plants overnight, clay, and labels.
- See page 27T for solution preparation.

Expected Results

Test tubes with plant roots inside will turn green or yellow overnight. Control tubes with no plants will remain blue overnight.

Answers

Plant roots do give off carbon dioxide. Respiration is the process responsible.

✔ Assessment

Knowledge: Have students record their findings in their journals. Ask them to predict the color that would appear in test tubes if the following were used instead of the one bean plant and explain why: three bean plants, dead bean plants.

Minilab 1

Do plant roots help with soil formation?

Plant roots may chemically aid in soil formation if they give off CO_2 gas into soil water. CO_2 plus water forms carbonic acid, which hastens the change of rock minerals into soil. Do plant roots give off CO_2? Put the root portion of a bean plant into a test tube of bromothymol blue (BTB) solution. **CAUTION:** *Be careful handling BTB solution. It will stain clothing.* Be sure all soil is rinsed from the roots. The change in color of BTB indicates the presence of CO_2. Seal the stem from outside air with a clay plug. Prepare a suitable control for this experiment. Note the color of the BTB 24 hours later. A color change means CO_2 has been given off. **Analysis** *Explain the results of your experiment. Do plant roots give off CO_2? Why is CO_2 given off?*

Figure 28-10 In a mature forest, only a limited amount of vegetation is able to survive on the forest floor due to the unavailability of enough sunlight. In deciduous forests, many plants begin to grow before the leaves appear on the trees in order to utilize the sunlight available.

Plants have adapted to grow in many different types of soil. Cacti, for example, have adaptations to grow in extremely dry, sandy soils. Water lilies are adapted to a different type of soil. They grow in fresh water, sometimes up to 15 feet deep.

In addition to organic and mineral content, soil fertility is also determined by pH. Some plants such as azaleas, cranberries, and rhododendrons can grow well in acidic soils, but most cannot. Most grow best in neutral or basic soils. Lime, a basic material, is often added to acidic soils to make them neutral. Acid rain, which you will study in Chapter 30, alters the pH of soil and therefore affects plant life.

Studying soil is an excellent way to learn how organisms are affected by the physical environment and how they, in turn, affect that environment. The nature of soil determines the diversity of plants and all other organisms in an ecosystem on land. At the same time, the presence of organisms is crucial to the formation and enrichment of the soil.

Light

As you've learned, light, or radiant energy, is the source of energy for almost all ecosystems. By photosynthesis, light energy is changed to the chemical energy needed by every living system.

As you may have guessed, plant and protist distribution is also affected by the amount of light. Because light cannot penetrate deep into water, most algae live near the surface of aquatic ecosystems. In a forest, trees are exposed to the greatest amount of light through leaf arrangements that are adaptations for maximum light exposure. In temperate forests, other plants are adapted to grow in the dim light of the forest floor. Some of these other plants begin to grow before leaves appear on the trees. In tropical rain forests, many plants, like bromeliads, receive enough light by growing among tree branches.

ALTERNATE LAB: Transect Survey

Purpose

Students are introduced to the concept of species diversity and learn how a transect survey is used in ecological studies.

Materials

strong twine, wooden stakes, thermometers, field guides, litmus or Hydrion paper, light meter (optional)

Procedure

Give the following directions to students.

1. Go to a park, vacant lot, or other area with a variety of plant populations, such as lawn, trees or bushes, clumps of weeds or flowers, a stream or pond.
2. Using two stakes and twine, string a transect line across your assigned portion of the area. Have students work in groups. Preview the area to decide how long transects should be. Each transect should survey one community.
3. Observe and record the number of different types of organisms present at predetermined intervals along the transect. If the community is very uniform, include several feet on both sides of the transect line in the survey. If the community is diverse, limit the survey to an area closer to the line.
4. At each interval, note temperature, soil pH, light intensity (if light meters are used), and whether the area has standing water or is moist or dry.

Light is also important to organisms in other ways. Light is required for vision. Some animals see well in dim light, but no animal can see in the complete absence of light. Light is also a factor in the migration of birds and the flowering of certain plants. Light energy is needed to make vitamin D in humans. Can you think of other examples of the importance of light?

Only about two percent of the light striking Earth is used for photosynthesis. Much of it is absorbed by the atmosphere, land, and seas and is converted to heat or thermal energy. Light absorbed by the surfaces on Earth and trapped by atmospheric gases helps maintain its temperature.

The heat produced by this absorption of light also plays a role in maintaining life. For example, heat is needed for the transpiration of water from plants. Heat also causes the evaporation of water from oceans and rivers. Without heat, water could not be cycled. As you'll learn, temperature also plays a more direct role in the survival of organisms.

Temperature

Temperature, along with factors such as wind and amount of rainfall, plays an important role in the distribution of organisms. In general, temperature changes with altitude and latitude; that is, temperature decreases from Earth's surface upward, and from the equator north and south to the poles. Thus, the types of organisms found in Alaska or high on a mountain are different from those living in Florida or in a valley. Would you expect to find polar bears in Florida or orange groves in Alaska? Organisms are adapted to survive within particular average temperature ranges.

Figure 28-11 Temperature plays an important role in the distribution of organisms. Organisms are adapted to survive within certain temperature ranges: Adelie penguins, Antarctica (top left); bananas, Madagascar (bottom left); saxifrage, New York State (center); Eastern Rosella parrot, Australia (right).

SECTION 28.2

Teacher FYI

Keystone species are so important to ecological balance that their population size can serve as an indicator of the health of a community. The sea otter is a keystone species in kelp forest communities. Kelps are seaweeds that grow 100 to 200 feet long in the coastal waters of the Pacific Ocean. During the 19th and early 20th centuries, sea otters were almost completely wiped out by fur hunters. One of the otters' primary foods is the spiny sea urchin, an echinoderm that feeds on kelp. Without otters to control the urchin population, large stands of kelp disappeared, resulting in a reduction in the populations of fish and other organisms that depend on kelp for food or shelter.

Concept Development

Ask students to think about the biological activities that occur during the fall and winter. Ask them to speculate about how light could affect the timing of bird migrations, the breeding season of mammals like ferrets and foxes, or the growth of plants (bulb formation in onions, for example). Point out that these biological activities are influenced by day length—the number of hours of daylight in a 24-hour period.

5. Use field guides or consult a local expert, such as a park gardener, to identify plants, insects, and other organisms. Draw or describe in writing any that cannot be identified or, with permission, take samples back to class.

Analysis

1. Count the number of species present along each transect.
2. Note changes in types or numbers of species present, or in abiotic factors measured, at different points.

✔ Assessment

Oral: Have students write a description of their transects in their journals. Have groups enter their data on a class chart. Ask them to compare the number of species, or species diversity, of each area. Have them answer the following questions: Were any species found along more than one transect? Which area has the highest species diversity? Which has the lowest? How do abiotic factors correlate with these observations? Do you think the transect method enabled you to observe and identify the most important organisms in an area? Have students include their journal entries and any other information they obtained from the discussion in their portfolios. **L1**

CHEMISTRY CONNECTION

Antifreeze in Animals:
The freezing point of a liquid is the temperature at which it begins turning to a solid; the boiling point is the temperature at which it begins evaporating into a gas. People add antifreeze to their cars to lower the freezing point and raise the boiling point of water in the cooling system. Ocean water remains liquid at temperatures below freezing because the salts in it reduce the freezing point. Some species of fish in the suborder notothenioidei produce biological antifreezes that keep their body fluids from freezing. These fish live in below-freezing Antarctic waters.

Temperature varies with time as well as with location. Temperatures differ from day to night and from season to season. Temperature differences also exist between times of sunshine and times of cloudiness. Such changes affect land organisms more than water organisms because air temperatures change more rapidly and to a greater degree than water temperatures. Air temperatures can change as much as 40°C between day and night. In the same time period, the temperature of the surface (top ten meters) of the ocean changes no more than 4°C. Below ten meters, there is little change in ocean temperature. How do you think the differences in temperature at different depths affect the diversity of organisms that live there? In terms of temperature, water is a more stable environment than land, but temperature on land is also an important ecological factor. Bacteria can live within the greatest temperature range. Some bacteria form endospores and can withstand temperatures above the boiling point and far below the freezing point of water (Chapter 15). For this reason, bacteria are found almost everywhere. The spores of fungi and seeds from some plants are adapted to survive temperatures that would kill mature fungi and plants. In this way, many species are able to survive extreme temperatures.

Temperature often starts biological processes. That is, temperature changes act as stimuli that activate chemical control systems of some organisms. For example, peach trees bloom when it is warm, but they must first be exposed to chilling during winter. The trees will not bloom without the chilling. Gypsy moth pupae will not develop into adults unless a freezing temperature has occurred. An adult, though, would die in freezing temperatures. Temperature requirement is a limiting factor that affects distribution of organisms. Do you think peach trees and gypsy moths could reproduce in the tropics?

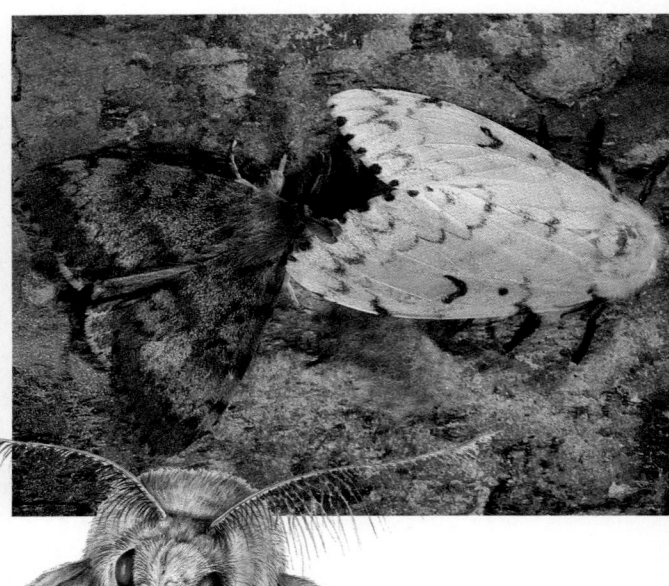

Figure 28-12 Gypsy moth pupae need freezing temperatures in order to develop into adults.

Temperature and day length can also affect the movement of organisms from place to place. You know that many birds and some mammals migrate in the winter. Animals such as bighorn sheep, caribou, and many birds migrate annually because temperature, length of day, and weather changes in winter create food shortages for these organisms.

Metabolic rate in some animals varies with temperature as well. Examine Figure 28-13. As you see in the graph, up to about 45°C, metabolic rate increases two or three times for every 10° the temperature rises. Remember that metabolism is related to the activity of enzymes. At high temperatures, metabolic reactions cannot occur; thus, most forms of life cannot survive when their body temperatures are above 50°C as enzymes are destroyed above this temperature.

Many animals have behavioral and physiological adaptations that prevent severe changes in body temperature and metabolism as the temperature of the environment changes. Desert lizards, for example, are active only in the early morning when it is cool. They spend the hottest part of the day under rocks where it is cooler. Also, certain species of frog go through dormant periods during the summer. This period of summer dormancy is called **estivation.**

Animals such as birds and mammals maintain constant body temperatures. A human has a body temperature of about 37°C, and a polar bear's body temperature is about 38°C. Why are these temperatures so similar? Look again at Figure 28-13. This temperature range is one at which metabolic reactions operate most efficiently. During severely cold weather, though, this body temperature is difficult to maintain because food is scarce. That's why many small mammals, such as chipmunks and bats, hibernate during the winter. During hibernation, metabolic rate decreases as body temperature decreases. In this way, food is conserved.

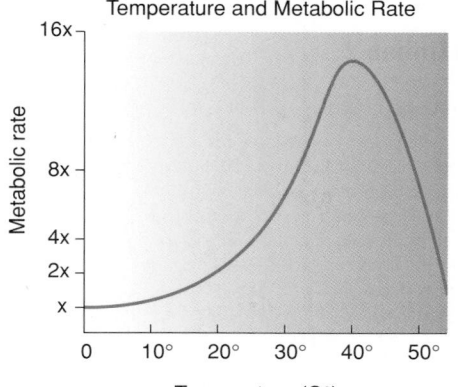

Temperature and Metabolic Rate

Figure 28-13 As this graph shows, metabolic rate is highest at approximately 40°C.

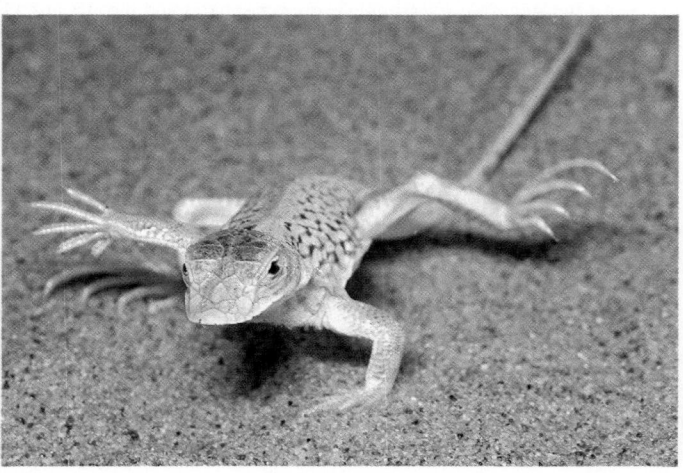

Figure 28-14 Many organisms have behavioral adaptations that allow them to maintain constant body temperatures. This sand-diving lizard cools itself by lifting its feet off the hot sand.

28.2 ABIOTIC FACTORS OF THE ENVIRONMENT **803**

Minilab 2

Purpose
Students will be able to observe the decomposition of cellulose during composting.

Skills
design an experiment, recognize cause and effect

Teaching Strategies
- Materials needed include: lens paper, metric ruler, scissors, water, soil, labels, tweezers (optional), and two small plastic cups or containers for soil and water.
- Students will fill one cup with provided soil. The other cup will be filled with water. Cups should be labeled with student names and the date.
- You may want to suggest that the lens paper strip buried in soil have a small corner remaining out of the soil to facilitate retrieval at the end of the week.

Expected Results
The following data table may be typical of students' reported data.

Composting Data

Lens paper	Date 5/6	Date 5/13
Lens paper in water	clean, intact piece of paper	clean, intact piece of paper
Lens paper in soil	clean, intact piece of paper	shreds of rotting paper

Answers
Changes were due to what was in the soil. The control piece of paper in water showed no change or decomposition. Fungi and/or bacteria in the soil caused the changes in decomposition of the paper.

✔ Assessment
Knowledge: Have students record their data and answers to questions in their journals. Ask them to predict the changes that might occur to the lens paper if the experiment were to be continued for another week or month.

Minilab 2

Can composting be observed?

Cut two pieces of cellulose lens paper into strips 2 cm by 10 cm. Draw a diagram of each strip to scale. Place one strip into a water-filled plastic cup. Place the other strip in a soil-filled cup. The strip should be just below the surface but completely covered with soil. Moisten the soil with water and keep it moist for the next week. After one week, carefully remove both strips and examine them. Record your observations and diagram each strip to scale.

Analysis *What caused the observed changes? Were they due only to the effect of water or what was in the soil? Explain. What microbe types in soil may have caused the changes? How does this Minilab demonstrate composting?*

You may be familiar with some of your own adaptations to temperature. For example, humans often perspire when hot. As perspiration occurs, the skin is cooled. When you're hot, arteries in your skin also expand to increase heat loss. Humans also tend to be less active when hot, so less heat is generated by the muscles. When you are cold, you may become more active and even shiver. When this occurs, arteries in the skin contract, conserving heat.

Disrupting the Balance

An ecosystem's balance can be altered temporarily by natural biotic and abiotic factors. Both biotic and abiotic factors play a role in limiting population sizes in such a way that the resources of the environment are not overused. Energy is captured in photosynthesis by green plants and made available to all organisms by means of food webs. Materials are cycled and can be used over and over again. Organisms are adapted to both living and physical factors of the environment and are capable of responding to some changes, such as different seasons or a temporary shortage of water. However, drastic or prolonged changes can affect the delicate balance of an ecosystem.

Natural occurrences such as a flood, earthquake, or volcanic eruption may certainly upset the balance of an ecosystem. Such events cannot be prevented. Other events, though—ones that might not be predicted to cause disturbances—may, in fact, lead to major problems in an ecosystem. Often, those events are a consequence of human activities. The real threat to ecosystems is the frequency, intensity, and uniqueness of human activity.

As an example of how human activities can upset the balance in an ecosystem, let's return once more to our lake community. Phosphates are chemicals present in detergents. Phosphates may enter a lake from sewage treatment plants. Phosphates, as well as nitrates present in fertilizers, may also enter the lake from soil runoff. These phosphates and nitrates are important nutrients for algae. Low levels of these chemicals limit the growth of algal populations. However, with large amounts of these chemicals and in the presence of warm temperatures, the algal populations thrive and grow rapidly in what is called an **algal bloom.** You might think that an increase in the algal population would be a benefit because more food would be available for first-order consumers.

Figure 28-15 An extreme increase in the population of one organism in an ecosystem can disrupt the balance of the entire ecosystem. In this case, an algal bloom caused this pond to become stagnant.

At best, though, the benefit is temporary. The algal population may become so large that the algae finally use up all available nutrients and begin to die. The dead algae settle to the bottom where they are decomposed. Large amounts of oxygen are used up as decomposition occurs. As a result, less oxygen is available for cellular respiration, and other organisms begin to die. Death of a large number of organisms disrupts the food web, and continued decomposition uses even more oxygen. Consumers such as oxygen-sensitive insect larvae, mayflies, and fish may die, while other organisms such as bacteria and mosquitoes may thrive. The entire lake may become stagnant as the ecological balance is drastically altered to the new factors.

Analysis of an algal bloom shows how a change in just a single physical factor, amount of a particular chemical, can have serious consequences for an ecosystem. Changes in other factors, both abiotic and biotic, can also affect and disrupt the balance of ecosystems. In Chapter 30, you'll study examples of how human actions contribute to the disruption of ecosystems.

LOOKING AHEAD

ORGANISMS IN an ecosystem interact with each other and are affected by them as well as by physical factors in the environment. In this chapter, you've considered how disruptions caused by biotic and abiotic factors can alter the delicate balance of ecosystems. In the next chapter, you'll discover how ecosystems develop over time and how ecosystems are replaced after being destroyed. You'll also learn how physical factors operate together to determine the various kinds of ecosystems found throughout the world.

Section Review

Understanding Concepts

1. Grasslands are common in Iowa and beech-maple forests are natural ecosystems in New England. Why are the ecosystems different in these two areas?
2. Food chains exist within soil, yet no food is produced there. How can this be explained?
3. In northernmost regions, the ground is permanently frozen except for the very top layer, which thaws in spring and summer. What effect does this physical factor have on plant and animal life in such regions? Explain.
4. **Skill Review—Recognizing Cause and Effect:** In an abandoned field, grasses and shrubs begin to grow. Later, the number of these smaller plants decreases as trees sprout up. How does the presence of trees result in a decrease in the numbers of grasses and shrubs?

For more help, see Thinking Critically in the **Skill Handbook.**

5. **Thinking Critically:** Suppose a pesticide were applied to rid a forest of insect larvae that were hungrily consuming leaves of the trees. Suppose, too, that the pesticide killed natural predators of the insect larvae. The natural predators are food for other animals. Describe some possible consequences of applying the insecticide to this forest ecosystem.

3 Assess

Check for Understanding

Have students choose an ecosystem and list biotic and abiotic factors that are part of the ecosystem. Have them form a realistic food web for that ecosystem. **L1**

Reteach

Have students work in pairs to review and correct their Check for Understanding assignments.

Extension

Provide each student with temperature, light, and soil conditions for a real or imaginary ecosystem. Have students describe the niche of a hypothetical organism that could survive under those conditions. **L2**

✔ Assessment

Knowledge: Ask students to identify biotic and abiotic factors that influence a particular ecosystem. **L1**

4 Close

Discussion

Give half the students 3 × 5 cards containing terms introduced in this chapter. Give the other students cards with the definitions. One by one, have students holding terms answer questions from the group of students holding definitions, without using the term itself in questions or answers. Definition-holders try to identify their matching term.

Answers to Section Review

1. The major reason for the difference is amount of annual rainfall.
2. The food is in the form of dead organisms (or parts of dead organisms) and wastes.
3. Presence of frozen soil prevents growth of trees. Shrubs and wildflowers can complete their life cycles quickly when the soil thaws. Because of the low number of producers, animal life is limited.

4. **Skill Review—Recognizing Cause and Effect:** Presence of trees reduces the amount of light available to grasses and shrubs.
5. **Thinking Critically:** Death of the predators would remove a natural factor that controls the insect population. The insects that survive the pesticide may undergo a population explosion, causing a more severe problem than

before the pesticide was applied. Death of the insect predators would also affect the populations that feed on those predators. Those populations would have to find alternate food sources or emigrate or they would die out.

Considering the Environment

Purpose

Students learn that some organisms can be used as indicators of the environmental health of an area.

Teaching Strategies

- Locate Chernobyl on a world map and describe the movement of radioactive fallout into Scandinavia.
- Have students research the Lapps or Sami. Have them find out about the lifestyle of these people and all the ways their lives were affected by the Chernobyl accident.
- Have students debate the use of nuclear power. They should first do research to back up their arguments.

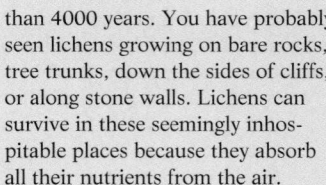

BIOLOGY, TECHNOLOGY, AND SOCIETY

Considering the Environment

Is the lowly lichen smarter than we are?

What plant-like organism can live in both arctic regions and deserts, doesn't need soil to supply its food, and can tell you how bad the air is? Answer: the lichen, a rootless organism that is actually a combination of a fungus and a green alga or

photosynthetic bacterium. Lichens are perhaps the hardiest organisms on Earth. They are largely unaffected by extremes of temperature, and they can lie dormant through long periods of drought. Some lichens are known to live for more

than 4000 years. You have probably seen lichens growing on bare rocks, tree trunks, down the sides of cliffs, or along stone walls. Lichens can survive in these seemingly inhospitable places because they absorb all their nutrients from the air.

Just as most plants are vulnerable to pollutants in the soil and water, lichens are vulnerable to pollutants in the air. They absorb anything the air brings their way, including sulfur dioxide from industrial and urban emissions, heavy metals, and radiation. This makes them good early indicators of air quality. Scientists noted more than a century ago that most lichens don't survive in cities and industrial areas because of the poor air quality. Today, by chemically analyzing lichens or charting their presence or absence in an area, scientists can determine the amount and kind of pollution present in the air.

There are more than 18 000 varieties of lichens, and different varieties are more sensitive to some pollutants than to others. Sulfur dioxide, for example, kills some lichens, causes others merely to sicken, and doesn't affect several types at all. By studying different lichens, scientists have been able to categorize them according to which pollutants they are sensitive to. The presence or absence of these particular varieties in an area then alerts the scientists to the presence of pollutants in the air long before other kinds of plants start to die or people become affected. Sometimes lichens tell a story of air pollution in remote rural areas long before any hint of haze can be detected in the air.

One variety of lichen, *Cladina*, is commonly known as reindeer moss. It grows like a thick, green carpet in arctic regions and is the main source of food for caribou and reindeer in North America and Eurasia. The animals dig through the snow with their hooves to eat the lichen during the long winters. For the Lapps, or Sami as they prefer to be called, semi-nomadic herders who live on the tundra of Scandinavia, the reindeer are the basis of their economy. Each Sami eats an average of eight to ten reindeer a year. They also make their coats, shoes, and tents from reindeer hides, use the antlers to make knife handles and glue, and sell reindeer meat to markets in the southern cities. Following the migration of reindeer herds has been their way of life for more than 10 000 years.

In the fall of 1986, that way of life was suddenly interrupted because of the lichen's ability to soak up pollution from the air. On April 26, 1986, a huge reactor at the Soviet nuclear power plant in Chernobyl burned, releasing a cloud of radioactive particles. The cloud blew northwest, arriving over Norway and Sweden within two days. Rain in parts of these countries brought radioactive particles, especially cesium-137, to Earth. The *Cladina* absorbed the cesium-137 along with its usual nutrients, and when the reindeer began to feed on the moss in the early fall, they, in turn, absorbed cesium-137. Passed through the food chain to humans, cesium-137 can cause cancer. Fortunately, the Swedish government detected the

radioactive material in the reindeer meat and acted to prevent its sale. However, about 50 000 reindeer had to be destroyed. The government provided commercial feed for some reindeer herds and moved others to Norway, which received less radioactive fallout. This disrupted the traditional Sami economy and way of life and cost the Swedish government millions of dollars. The price of uncontaminated reindeer meat rose, and consumer demand fell as people worried about its safety or could not afford the higher price. Cesium-137 decays slowly, and it may be more than 30 years before the lichen is safe again for grazing.

Lichen such as the reindeer moss on the arctic tundra act as a kind of advance warning system, telling us that we are polluting our world without even knowing it. New technologies now allow scientists to test lichen to detect the presence of

many chemicals that are dangerous to humans, including lead, nitrates, fluorides, and ammonium. The lowly lichens may prove to be one of our best friends.

1. **Explore Further:** The 1986 accident at the Chernobyl nuclear power plant led to the largest release of radioactive material ever from one accident. What were some of the other effects of this disaster?
2. **Writing About Biology:** Find out more about the Sami. Locate where they live on a map. Write a paragraph about the niche these people fill in the ecosystem.

Readings

- Bruemmer, Fred. "In Praise of Lowly Lichen." *International Wildlife,* Vol. 21, No. 6, Nov./Dec. 1991, pp. 30-33.
- Kiester, Edwin, Jr. "Prophets of Gloom." *Discover,* Nov. 1991, pp. 53-56.
- Lofstedt, Ragnar, and Allen White. "Chernobyl: Four Years Later." *Environment,* Vol. 32, No. 3, April 1990, pp. 1-8.

Possible Answers

1. Food, especially meat, milk, and produce, was contaminated throughout Europe and the former Soviet Union and had to be destroyed. However, some contaminated food, such as powdered milk from Germany, was shipped to third-world countries. Contaminated food is the main path of radiation exposure to humans, and it is thought to account for about 90% of the radiation exposure from Chernobyl. People living in the Chernobyl area were not evacuated for more than two days after the incident and were exposed to radioactivity through air and water as well as food. The overall consequences of the incident will not be known for many years.
2. Student answers may vary. One possibility is that the Sami control reindeer populations, not letting them get too large or small. This also keeps the food supply in balance for both the reindeer and the people.

Going Further

Have students look up news reports on the Chernobyl incident and its aftermath. Have students find out how lichens grow and reproduce and investigate their uses. *animal food, perfumes, dyes* L2

CHAPTER 28

Issues

Purpose
Students learn there can be long-lasting consequences to the use of modern technologies.

Teaching Strategies
• Create a model of an underground aquifer and well with a tall narrow jar, a wooden skewer, a soda straw, and a pipette bulb. Partly fill the jar with aquarium gravel, topped with about an inch of sand or soil. Use the skewer as a "drill" to dig a hole through the soil and most of the way through the gravel. Do this at the edge of the jar so the "well" can be seen. With a straight pin, poke a few holes in the bottom of the soda straw. Use the straw to simulate a well casing, pushing it down over the skewer into the jar. Then remove the skewer. Use the pipette bulb to "pump" the water from the well. Show students how the aquifer can be rapidly depleted if water is removed faster than it is replenished.

Issues

Can agriculture be climate free?

The Southwest is the driest region of the United States. Average annual rainfall is less than 20 inches. Summers are hot and dry, winters cold and windy, and drought years are frequent. Yet if you drive through the Texas Panhandle, you will see fields of cotton, wheat, grain sorghum, and corn, as well as sugar beets, potatoes, and hay. In all, more than 5 million acres, or one-fourth of the land in northwest Texas, have been turned into productive cropland.

Farming in the Texas High Plains began to boom in the 1950s with introduction of the central-pivot irrigation, or watering, system. This strange looking structure is made of a vertical pipe, or tower, connected to a horizontal pipe. Both are on wheels so they can rotate. The horizontal pipe, sometimes as long as 1000 feet, circles slowly around the field, about eight feet above ground, spraying water from holes along its length. The tower, usually the height of a house, is connected to a well that pumps water from underground. A thousand gallons of water spew each minute from the biggest of these center-pivot irrigation systems. The force of the water moves the pipe slowly around in a circle, usually taking about 12 hours to complete a full turn around a quarter-square-mile area.

Beneath the Texas High Plains lies the southern part of the Ogallala aquifer. An aquifer is an underground formation of sand, gravel, and clay saturated with water. The top of the aquifer is called the water table. The Ogallala stretches under six states: Texas, New Mexico, Colorado, Oklahoma, Kansas, and Nebraska. In Texas alone, the Ogallala covers 35 000 square miles and holds an estimated 400 million acre-feet, or more than 1.3 quadrillion gallons of water.

Farmers in Texas started tapping the Ogallala with small wells in the late 1800s. Agriculture expanded in the area during the first half of the 20th century, but the drought in the 1930s wiped out much of the area. It was the invention of better irrigation systems in the 1950s that opened the way for large-scale farming in this semiarid region. Crop production per acre more than doubled, the economy boomed, and more farmers moved into the Southwest. Technology, it seemed, could change the course of nature. Climate-free agriculture it was called.

But now we are realizing that the technology that turned the Texas High Plains into an agricultural gold mine may be leading to its ultimate ruin. Today, more than 150 000 wells dot the Ogallala, most of them driving center-pivot irrigation towers. Together, they are capable of pumping more than 50 billion gallons of water from the aquifer in one 12-hour period. How does all that water get replaced?

The Ogallala was once called the "land of underground rain" or the "sixth" Great Lake. Everyone assumed that its supply of water was endless. But we now know that the Ogallala is slowly drying up. At its northern end, there is enough rainfall to nearly recharge the Ogallala each year. In the dry High Plains, however, there is very little rainfall. In some places, only a teacupful of water is put back for every gallon that is pumped out. Each year, almost 5 trillion gallons of water are taken from the Ogallala without being replaced. That's almost as much water as flows through the entire Colorado River. And only 60 to 70 percent of that water gets into the soil; the rest is lost to evaporation and runoff. The Ogallala took about 10 million years to fill. At the present rate of water use, it may be emptied in fewer than 100 years.

The first effects are already being felt. As the aquifer is depleted, the water table sinks lower and lower.

It becomes more expensive to pump water to the surface, which in turn makes crops less profitable to grow. Some farmers already have to redrill their wells every year, or connect smaller wells to the central well in order to have enough water power to drive their irrigation systems. Eventually, fields may be left unplanted, and then wind will erode the soil, just as it did during the Dust Bowl of the 1930s.

In parts of the Texas High Plains, more than water is disappearing. When the water table drops, the soil above it compacts. If it compacts enough, the ground will sink and form cracks. This process is called land subsidence. Eventually, these cracks widen and deepen into huge ditches called fissures. Fissures have opened up all across the plains, damaging wells, water pipes, and roads; trapping cattle; and making fields impossible to irrigate.

Thus, the High Plains face a dilemma. While irrigation has turned this and other dry regions of

the southwest, such as California's Imperial Valley, into an agricultural gold mine supplying food to millions of people and livestock, it has also depleted sources of underground water that can never be replaced. Eventually, the Ogallala may run dry. That is a price we may have to pay for climate-free agriculture.

Understanding the Issues
1. What might be some ways to conserve water on the High Plains without giving up agriculture?
2. Do you think it is more important to conserve our groundwater supplies or grow as much food as possible? Why?

Readings
- Barnes-Svarney, Patricia. "Ground Water in Peril." *Earth Science*, Vol. 42, No. 4, Winter 1989, pp. 14-16.
- Glantz, Michael. "An Analog for the Texas High Plains." *Environment*, Vol. 33, No. 5, June 1991, pp. 30-31.

CAREER CONNECTION

Hydrologists study Earth's water system including precipitation, storm patterns, the causes and effects of droughts and floods, the water supply in aquifers, and the exchange of water between the oceans and the atmosphere. They plan soil and water conservation programs, flood control systems, and irrigation and drainage projects for agriculture. They work for the government and in private industry.

Possible Answers
1. Plant crops like milo, wheat, sunflowers, and sorghum that require less water. Water crops by using drip irrigation rather than overhead watering. Use reclaimed wastewater instead of ground water. Retire eroding fields for a few years and plant a drought-tolerant ground cover to prevent the soil from blowing away.
2. Answers will vary. Some may say we need to save resources for future generations, keep groundwater from becoming polluted, and prevent dust bowl conditions from developing. Others may argue that we can't let people starve or lose their way of making a living just because we might run out of water someday, and that we might find other ways to get water, such as melting polar ice caps or inventing machines to make water from oxygen and hydrogen.

Going Further
Have students investigate the water resources in their county or state, and find out where irrigation water comes from and what irrigation methods are used. L1

CAREER CONNECTION

Have students interview hydrologists or hydrogeologists working with the county agency that deals with flood control or water well safety, the local office of the U.S. Geological Survey, or the state water agency.

CHAPTER 28

CHAPTER REVIEW

Summary

The summary can be used by students to review the major concepts of the chapter.

Language of Biology

Answers should go beyond defining the terms. Accept any answer that uses the term correctly and in the proper context.

Understanding Concepts

1. Students may need help getting started. Have them think about a natural area with which they are familiar. You may wish to remind them not to use a decomposer as the fourth trophic level.
2. Answers will depend upon the particular food chain used.
3. There is more energy present in the herbivores than in the animals in the next trophic level. The herbivores use some of their energy in carrying out their life functions, and some is transformed to heat during cellular respiration. Not all parts of the herbivores are eaten and digested.
4. There would be a pyramid of biomass. Less biomass can exist at each trophic level because there is less energy available to support it.
5. Most food chains show a pyramid of numbers. However, there are exceptions, as when a single tree is being fed upon by thousands of insect larvae.
6. The producers take up carbon dioxide and use it in photosynthesis. All members of the food chain release carbon dioxide as they carry out cellular respiration. Decomposers do the same as they act on the wastes of the animals and on dead organisms.
7. Nitrates are the source of nitrogen for most plants. Planting of legumes reduces the need for fertilizers because bacteria in the roots of legumes can fix nitrogen.
8. This relationship is an example of mutualism. Both the fungi and the conifers benefit.

810

REVIEW
CHAPTER
28

Summary

Producers are the breadwinners of an ecosystem. In almost all ecosystems, producers trap the energy of sunlight, changing it to chemical form. All other members of the ecosystem depend directly or indirectly on producers as a source of energy, which they obtain via food webs.

Less and less energy is available to each trophic level in an ecosystem, and, because energy is lost and cannot be recycled, each ecosystem must have a continual input of energy in order to survive. However, materials are constantly recycled and can thus be used over and over again.

In addition to their need for food, organisms depend upon one another in other ways. Specialized relationships include mutualism, commensalism, and parasitism.

Organisms are influenced not only by other organisms, but also by abiotic factors of their environment. Factors such as water, soil, light, and temperature may affect the distribution and activities of organisms and may act to limit population sizes. A stable ecosystem is a delicate balance of biotic and abiotic interactions. Changes in even one of these factors may disrupt that delicate balance.

Language of Biology

Write a sentence that shows your understanding of each of the following terms.

abiotic factor	herbivore
algal bloom	humus
biomass	niche
biotic factor	omnivore
carnivore	pyramid of biomass
commensalism	pyramid of energy
ecosystem	pyramid of numbers
estivation	second-order consumer
first-order consumer	third-order consumer
food web	trophic level

Understanding Concepts

1. Identify a particular food chain of four links in an ecosystem of your choosing. You will use your food chain to answer questions 2-6.
2. Identify the producer and second-order consumer in your food chain. Are there any omnivores? If so, identify them.
3. Compare the total amount of energy present in the herbivores in your food chain with the amount available to the organisms in the next trophic level. Explain several reasons why the amounts are not the same.
4. If you could determine the amount of biomass present in each trophic level, what pattern would you see? Explain the reason for that pattern.
5. Does your food chain show a pyramid of numbers? If so, explain why. If not, explain why.
6. How does each member of your food chain contribute to the cycling of carbon? Where do decomposers "fit" in your food chain? How do they contribute to the cycling of carbon?
7. Why do fertilizers contain nitrates? Could planting of legumes reduce the need for fertilizers? Explain.
8. Certain fungi grow on the roots of conifers. The fungi absorb nutrient-rich fluids from the roots and help draw water and mineral ions from the soil into the roots. Of what type of relationship is this an example?

9. Absence of leaves reduces surface area, thus reducing water loss due to transpiration.
10. Moss plants require water for sexual reproduction. Moisture would be available at the shaded base of a tree, but not in an open spot where evaporation rate is very high.
11. A change in temperature, such as in a temperate forest during winter, reduces food production by the major producers, the trees, as well as by most other plants.
12. An increase in body temperature speeds the metabolism of the snake.
13. Removal of too many fish might disrupt the balance of the lake ecosystem.

Applying Concepts

14. Smaller endotherms have a higher metabolic rate.
15. Smaller extremities have less surface area, thus reducing heat loss. The opposite is true for larger extremities.
16. Most photosynthesis occurs in algae in the oceans.

9. In cacti, the stem is the organ of photosynthesis rather than leaves. Explain this fact in terms of an abiotic factor.

10. Why would you expect to find moss plants growing on or near the base of a tree rather than in an open spot in a forest?

11. How can temperature cause food to become a limiting factor for some animals?

12. Why does a desert snake sun itself on a rock early in the day?

13. How might a lake ecosystem be affected if there were no limits on the number of a certain fish that humans are allowed to catch?

Applying Concepts

14. Even though mammals are endotherms, heat is lost from the surfaces of their bodies. Smaller endotherms lose relatively more heat than do larger ones. How would you expect the relative metabolic rates of small and large endotherms to compare? Why?

15. Allen's rule states that the size of extremities (ears, for example) of animals decreases as temperature decreases. Why are extremities smaller in cold temperatures and larger in warm temperatures?

16. In what ecosystem do you suppose the greatest amount of photosynthesis occurs? Why?

17. A home aquarium can be considered a miniature balanced ecosystem. Explain how balance is maintained in this tiny ecosystem.

18. Explain why more people could be fed if food chains were shortened.

19. How may clearing land for agriculture affect a natural ecosystem?

20. How does destruction of large portions of tropical rain forests affect the carbon cycle?

21. **Issues:** Using more water from an aquifer than is replaced is called overdrafting. Overdrafting is one threat to our groundwater. What are other possible threats?

22. **Considering the Environment:** Why do you think that lichens are particularly sensitive to air pollutants?

Lab Interpretation

23. **Investigation:** The following bar graph depicts the data that a student group presented of their results when measuring gas release from soil treated with hydrogen peroxide. Which bar letter best represents:
    (a) Their control? Explain why.
    (b) A tube in which sand was tested? Explain why.
    (c) A soil sample in which they forgot to add hydrogen peroxide? Explain why.
    (d) The soil sample with the most humus? Explain why.

Measure of Gas Release from Soil

24. **Minilab 1:** Predict the experimental outcome of this same experiment if the bean plant placed in BTB solution had been supplied with light overnight and explain your answer.

25. **Minilab 2:** Predict and explain your observation on lens paper after one week if it had been placed in sterile soil. Note: All life forms in sterile soil have been killed.

Connecting Ideas

26. Cite and explain several structural adaptations that permit endotherms to withstand extreme cold.

27. In what way is a mutualistic relationship between two organisms in an ecosystem similar to the relationship that is thought to have existed between the first mitochondria and chloroplasts and their host cells?

17. The plants are the producers of the aquarium's food chain. Materials are recycled by the plants, snails, fish, and decomposers.

18. Less energy would be lost if some trophic levels were eliminated.

19. Clearing land for agriculture necessarily disrupts a natural ecosystem. The producers are eliminated, and the consumers must find new food sources or they will die out.

20. The trees and other plants of the rain forest would normally take in large volumes of carbon dioxide for photosynthesis. In their absence, carbon dioxide would accumulate in the atmosphere.

21. Groundwater is also threatened by pollution resulting from improper storage of hazardous chemicals.

22. All of the lichen's nutrients are absorbed from the air.

Lab Interpretation

23. **Investigation:**
    (a) B, very little gas was collected
    (b) C, little gas was collected—sand contains little humus
    (c) A, much gas was collected—vacant lots tend to have much humus
    (d) B, no gas will be released without hydrogen peroxide
    (e) A, the most humus present corresponds to the most gas released

24. **Minilab 1:** Light would have no effect on the outcome. The BTB will change to a green or yellow color. Respiration is light independent. Therefore, roots carry out only respiration and do not carry on photosynthesis.

25. **Minilab 2:** No change in the lens paper would be observed. Without soil microbes, decomposition will not occur.

Connecting Ideas

26. **Evolution:** Endotherms are protected from cold by such adaptations as fur, feathers, and layers of fat.

27. **Evolution:** Mitochondria and chloroplasts are thought to be descendants of free-living

prokaryotes. Both the organelles and their host cells would benefit. For example, the primitive mitochondrion would enable the host to undergo aerobic respiration, and the host would provide the food for both. The chloroplast would enable what was a heterotrophic cell to trap light and make its own food, and the chloroplast might have been afforded protection by the host.

ORGANIZER
CHAPTER 29

SECTION	OBJECTIVES	TEXT LABS/FEATURES
29.1 Ecological Succession (3 days)	**Relate** the events of a particular ecological succession to the factors that cause succession. **Compare and contrast** primary succession and secondary succession. **Apply** the ideas of the general trends seen in succession to a particular example of succession.	**Minilab 1:** How do different soils compare? p. 815 **Investigation:** Factors Involved in Grass Seed Germination, p. 818
29.2 Biomes (3 days)	**Explain** how physical factors interact to determine the life forms found in different biomes. **Compare** the climates and common life forms of the world's major land biomes. **Differentiate** among the various zones of which the oceans are composed.	**Literature Connection:** *Winter Poem* by Nikki Giovanni, p. 822 **Thinking Lab:** How are tropical rain forests studied? p. 828 **Minilab 2:** Which biomes are in the United States? p. 830
BIOLOGY, TECHNOLOGY, AND SOCIETY		**Considering the Environment:** Wetlands, p. 837 **Career Connection:** Agronomist, p. 838 **Issues:** Friendly Fires, p. 839

LAB MATERIALS

INVESTIGATION	MINILAB	ALTERNATE LAB
page 818 aluminum foil charate fertilizer or plant food grass seed light source masking tape paper towels petri dish scissors	**page 815** filter paper lab burner soil samples thermal gloves **page 830** atlas of U.S. Potential Natural Vegetation Map	**page 816** beaker, 1-L coverslips droppers glass slides hay leaves microscope soil

812A

TEACHER CLASSROOM RESOURCES	OTHER RESOURCES
Study Guide, pp. 169-170 ***PLL:** *Ecological Succession in a Microenvironment,* p. 232 ****ILS:** *A Soil Community,* p. 309 ****ILS:** *Microcommunities,* p. 313	***STVS:** *Managing a Forest,* Plants and Simple Organisms (Disc 4, Side 2)
Study Guide, pp. 171-174 **Concept Mapping,** p. 29 **Critical Thinking/Problem Solving:** *Where Am I?* p. 29 **Exploring Environmental Issues:** *Be an Earthwise Consumer,* p. 47	***STVS:** *Simple Forms of Life in the Antarctic,* Plants and Simple Organisms (Disc 4, Side 1) **Color Transparency 58:** *Terrestrial Biomes*
Assessment Materials **Chapter Assessment,** pp. 113-116 **Performance Assessment in Biology,** p. 58 **Alternate Assessment in the Science Classroom** **Computer Test Bank**	**Spanish Resources** **Cooperative Learning Resource Guide** **Videodisc Correlations** (to Optical Data's and Videodiscovery's videodiscs)

* Probing Levels of Life
** Investigating Living Systems

* Science Technology Videodisc Series

Key to Teaching Strategies

The following designations will help you decide which activities in the teacher margin are appropriate for your students.

L1 Level 1 activities should be within the ability range of all students.

L2 Level 2 activities should be within the ability range of the average to above-average student.

L3 Level 3 activities are designed for the ability range of above-average students.

LEP LEP activities are appropriate for Limited English Proficiency students.

COOP LEARN Cooperative Learning activities are designed for small group work.

ADDITIONAL RESOURCES

Infinite Voyage *To the Edge of the Earth*
Students will learn in this video that organisms have adapted to difficult environments, from underwater caves to wind-swept Tibetan plateaus.

Audiovisual
Primary Ecological Succession, video, Insight Media.
Splendors of the Sea, video, Frey Scientific.

Software
Biomes, Apple II, Queue.

CHAPTER

29

ORIGIN AND DISTRIBUTION OF COMMUNITIES

Chapter Overview

Students begin the chapter by considering familiar examples that illustrate the point that communities change over time. They are then introduced to the concept of ecological succession, and they learn that the major factor in succession is the alteration of the physical environment by the organisms present at each stage. They then distinguish between and study examples of primary and secondary succession, coming to understand that certain trends are common to both types.

Students next examine how climate is a function of temperature and rainfall and the factors that determine those parameters. They learn that similar climatic conditions are found in many land areas on Earth, producing similar biomes. As students study examples of major land biomes (as well as ocean zones) and the organisms common to them, they come to realize that no biome is isolated and that they all interact to form the biosphere.

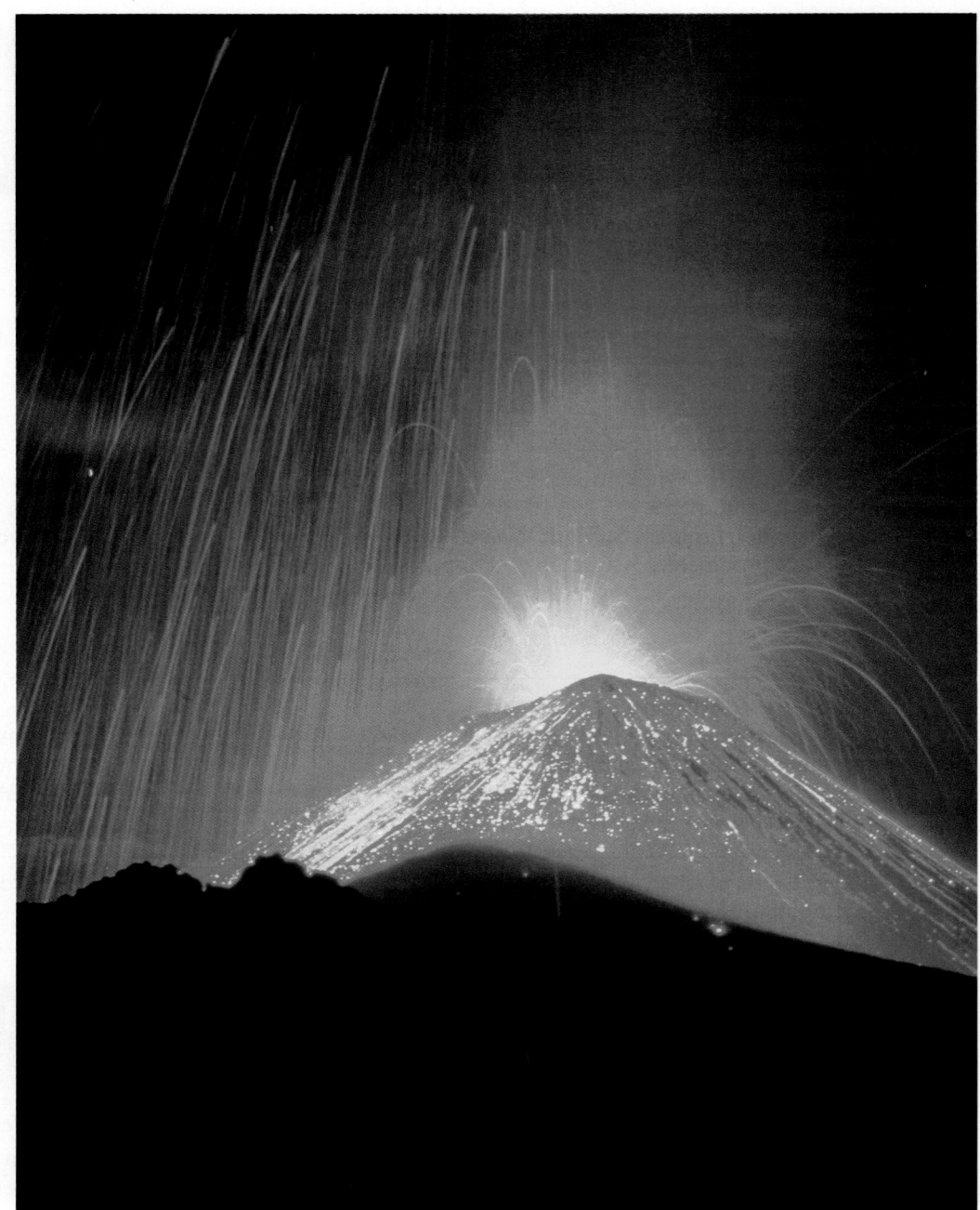

812

KEY TERMS

benthos	microenvironment	taiga
biome	nekton	temperate forest
biosphere	neritic zone	tropical rain forest
climax community	oceanic zone	tundra
desert	permafrost	
ecological succession	pioneer stage	
geothermal energy	plankton	
grassland	primary succession	
littoral zone	secondary succession	

29

ORIGIN AND DISTRIBUTION OF COMMUNITIES

ON AUGUST 27, 1883, what may have been the loudest sound in recorded history was heard when the volcano on the island of Krakatau blew apart. It was heard 4800 km away. The island, which is near Indonesia and was about the size of Manhattan before the blast, was now only one-quarter that size.

When it was all over, the first landing party on what was left of the island found not a tree, shrub, or blade of grass growing. All vegetation was buried under ash and cinders and hardened lava. Within a year, however, grasses and other pioneer plants began to appear in the ashes. As these plants died and decayed, they formed a fertile soil; less hardy plants could then grow there. Airborne spores and seaborne seeds could germinate and begin to grow. Within 50 years, the island was well on its way to renewing itself; it was covered with a thick, young forest.

Like human pioneers, plant pioneers must withstand the harshest conditions—among them, intense sunlight and scarce or infertile soil. The growing conditions are not suitable for most other species, so pioneer plants have the area pretty much to themselves. Few competitors will challenge their existence until the pioneers have done the homesteading—that is, until the pioneers have changed the site enough for others to survive.

As you read this chapter, you will see how pioneer organisms modify their environment. You will follow the sequence of events that occurs as an area changes over time from a barren wasteland to a stable, flourishing community of living things. You will also examine the major kinds of ecosystems that exist on Earth.

Like Davy Crockett and Johnny Appleseed, this plant is a pioneer. It won't tussle with bears or sow apple trees, but it will change its environment so other seeds that land there can sprout and survive.

Chapter Preview

813

ASSESSMENT PLANNER

Choose assessment strategies from the following pages to evaluate the progress of your students.

Introducing the Chapter

Begin by having students identify different types of communities. Then refer to the photograph on page 812. Point out that a community is always subject to change, be it natural or as a consequence of human intervention. Have students cite examples of changes that may alter communities. Return again to the discussion of Krakatau and the renewal of life after the eruption. Referring to the photo on page 813, introduce the concept of pioneer organisms and their alteration of the physical environment. This discussion should lead students to the general conclusion that communities change over time. Complete the introduction by asking students whether similar types of communities are found in different parts of the world, and why.

Theme Development

The theme of patterns of change pervades the discussion of ecological succession. Students will recognize this theme as they study stages of succession and the causes and consequences of the different stages. Study of successional stages also illustrates the theme of systems and interactions. Students will perceive this theme as they come to understand how organisms modify the physical environment and how succession produces more stable communities characterized by more complex interactions.

Tying to Previous Knowledge

Students have recently completed studies of population biology and ecosystems. In this chapter, they will come to see those topics from a different viewpoint as they realize that populations, patterns of energy flow, biotic interactions, and physical factors of the environment change during ecological succession. They will also come to realize that similar ecosystems exist in different parts of the world and that all ecosystems interact within the biosphere.

Prepare

Key Concepts

The events of succession, causes of primary and secondary succession, and applications are presented in this section.

Key Terms

ecological succession, primary succession, pioneer stage, microenvironment, climax community, secondary succession

Materials

- Gather lab burners and balances for Minilab 1.
- Collect soil, leaves, and hay for the Alternate Lab.
- Buy grass seed, fertilizer, and radish seeds, and prepare charate for the Investigation. The grass seed must be purchased two months in advance.

1 Focus

Objectives

The objectives are listed on the student page. Remind students to preview these objectives as a guide to this numbered section.

Discussion

Ask students what would happen if people stopped mowing their lawns. Allow the student answers to this question to develop into a definition of succession. After students have defined the changes they would expect, point out that similar kinds of changes naturally occur in communities over time.

2 Teach

Misconception

Students have a tendency to think that ecosystems are static. Explain that forests, deserts, grasslands, and other communities are in a state of slow but measurable change.

Objectives

Relate the events of a particular ecological succession to the factors that cause succession.

Compare and contrast primary succession and secondary succession.

Apply the ideas of the general trends seen in succession to a particular example of succession.

29.1 Ecological Succession

Have you ever walked along an abandoned railroad track and seen young shrubs sprouting up beside and between the tracks? Have you ever noticed moss growing in cracks in the sidewalk or along a curb—or the grasses growing around a house or building where the land has not been tended? Although you probably haven't thought about it, the shrubs or moss or grasses could be the beginnings of new, natural communities. If these areas were not altered by human activities, each would undergo a series of changes in which different species of organisms would appear, only to be replaced later by others. Given enough time, each area would become a complex and stable community.

Succession and Its Causes

Picture several types of communities—lake, forest, desert. Each of these communities has a history. The diversity of organisms living in each community today is not the same as it was in the past. Biotic and abiotic factors have changed over time. Some communities today may be stable, having undergone many changes over a long period of time. Others may not be quite so stable and will undergo still further change. The series of changes in a community is called **ecological succession.** Succession may occur in areas where no life has previously existed, or it may occur where an established community has been affected by a disaster such as a fire or volcanic eruption, or by human activities such as the clearing of a forest. In either case, succession is marked by differences in organisms and physical factors over time.

What causes ecological succession? A major factor is the effect a particular set of organisms has on the physical environment. Think back, for example, to the effect of organisms on the formation and characteristics of soil. During succession, organisms alter their physical surroundings in a way that makes those surroundings more suitable for other kinds of organisms and less suitable for themselves. As a result, new organisms invade a habitat, and the organisms previously living there cannot compete with them. Thus, many of the earlier organisms gradually disappear.

Physical changes in the environment during succession may result from factors other than the action of organisms. For example, soil from surrounding land may run off into a pond, causing the pond to become shallower and eventually fill in entirely.

Figure 29-1 **When a forest is cleared, either by natural causes or by human intervention, the process of succession soon will follow.**

Climax Community

Beeches and maples are the dominant species in the mature New England forest. The beech-maple forest is the final, stable stage in the development of the community and is known as the **climax community**. The type of climax community that emerges in a given area depends on the interaction of all factors of the environment, both abiotic and biotic. In the southeastern United States, the climax community might be an oak-hickory forest. In the climax community of a North American desert, the creosote bush may be the dominant species.

Because it is stable and complex, a climax community tends to remain the same over a long period of time without further succession. But factors such as changes in climate, disease, a natural disaster, or human interference could be so severe that succession might start over again later, though not necessarily from the pioneer stage.

From Pond to Forest

A pond is a small body of water surrounded by land. It is an ecosystem in which blue-green bacteria and green algae are the main producers. Toward the shore, plants such as cattails and reeds also trap energy from the sun. Consumers consist of ciliates and other protists, insect larvae, worms, crayfish, and fish.

A pond is organized, but it is not a climax community. A pond is not a permanent ecosystem; it undergoes succession. The life span of a pond depends on its size and the conditions of the environment. Consider a pond surrounded by a forest. As the pond ages, sediments collect at its bottom, in much the same way as dust collects under your bed. The shallow portions around the shoreline fill in first. In this marshy soil, simple plants such as sphagnum moss, insectivorous plants, and shrubs take root and help bind the soil. Sediments continue to collect on the bottom of the pond, decreasing its depth. As land takes the place of water, simple plants continue to grow. Meanwhile, the areas around the old shore undergo further succession. Shrubs are replaced by trees, and finally trees become dominant. This pattern of simple plants to shrubs to trees continues until no more water remains, as seen in Figure 29-5. A forest—the climax community—gradually replaces the pond.

Secondary Succession

Succession often begins as a result of natural destruction, such as a fire started by lightning. It also may result from interference by humans, such as logging. In either case, new succession begins when the dominant plants of a plant community are removed. If the land is later left untended, **secondary succession** will occur. Secondary succession occurs more rapidly than primary succession, especially in its early stages, because soil is already formed and a few life forms such as seeds may be present. Thus, the area does not have to "start from scratch."

Figure 29-5 **A pond is not a climax community. Over a period of time, a pond becomes filled in with soil and plant material, and eventually is replaced by the surrounding climax community—the forest.**

LITERATURE CONNECTION

Birches: Read Robert Frost's poem, *Birches*. Ask students to identify physical reasons for succession in birch forests.

Software

WAQUAL, Pond Study, and *Lake Study* is a series of simulations available from Project Seraphim, Department of Chemistry, University of Wisconsin-Madison, 1101 University Avenue, Madison, WI 53706. These simulations are interesting ways to relate the problems in aquatic communities with the scientific methods available for studying the problems. **L1**

Different Viewpoints in Biology

How important are climax communities?
Climax communities are viewed by most ecologists and environmentalists as essential for aesthetic beauty, maintenance of biodiversity, and a healthy environment. However, the view of logging interests and ranchers is often that subclimax communities and forest monocultures are more important for their economic productive capacity.

29.1 ECOLOGICAL SUCCESSION **817**

Analysis

Ask students to answer the following questions.
1. Draw and label each species of organism you were able to identify. *Student drawings will vary with the types of organisms they observe.*
2. Which organisms were most numerous? *Species of ciliates usually are the most numerous, but students may observe a different group of organisms.*
3. Which organisms appeared first in the community? Which appeared last? *Typically, paramecia or other ciliates appear first and are eventually followed by high numbers of rotifers.*
4. What changes did you notice in the community? *Populations appear and are replaced by other populations. The ecosystem is changed by the organisms.*

✔ Assessment

Skill: Have students prepare a graph of the rise and fall of the various populations over time. Ask them to explain how these population changes represent succession. *One population displaces another population and changes the physical parameters of the ecosystem.* **L1**

INVESTIGATION

Factors Involved in Grass Seed Germination

Time Allotment

1 class period, then 10-minute observations every other day for 2 to 3 weeks

Objectives

On completing this Investigation, students will be able to:

- Analyze the conditions necessary for fastest germination of grass seed.
- Relate the germination conditions to stages of succession.

Skills

make a hypothesis, design an experiment, interpret data, observe and infer

Materials

grass seed, petri dishes, masking tape, light source, aluminum foil for making dish dark, charate, commercial fertilizer or houseplant "food," paper towels, scissors

Preparation

- Obtain a type of grass seed adapted for germination and growth in the sun that also grows quickly in your part of the country.
- Prepare charate by charring birch or balsa wood dowels. Do not burn them to ash. Then grind the charred dowels to a fine powder. If there is no mill for grinding, soak the charred dowels in water for two days and use this water for wetting paper toweling. Activated charcoal will not work as a substitute.
- Refrigerate a portion of the seeds for two months prior to the lab. Heat a second portion of the seeds for five minutes at 120°C. Soak a third portion of the seeds for 24 hours in 0.1N HCl (1N HCl diluted 1 to 10) (mimics passage through an animal's digestive system).
- Five days prior to the lab, set up 20 radish seeds in a petri dish on top of two wet circles of paper

During the early history of the United States, much of the forest land of New England was cleared and used for farming. As people moved westward, many of these farms were abandoned. Secondary succession then began in the abandoned fields. This type of succession is still occurring today in New England (and in other parts of the world). At first, hardy pioneer grasses and weeds appear in the fields. Later, shrubs grow, followed by junipers, poplars, and white pines. Eventually, beeches and maples begin to sprout in the shadow of the other trees. What was once an open field becomes a beech-maple forest.

In this example, the sequence of stages of community development is different from that beginning with bare rock, but the climax community is the same. However, succession in a given area does not necessarily lead to the same climax community each time. The characteristics of a climax community probably result from many chance occurrences including biotic and abiotic environmental factors over long periods of time. In general, though, each climax community is more stable and productive than previous stages of the succession that produced it.

INVESTIGATION

Factors Involved in Grass Seed Germination

Did you ever have a garden or grow seeds in a paper cup? What caused your seeds to grow? Some seeds require a period of cold before they will germinate. Others need to have their seed coats burned by a fire or exposed to charate, which is the remains of burned plants. Some seeds must pass through the digestive system of an animal before they will germinate. Others must be in the light, while still others must have darkness for germination.

Ranchers and farmers use a variety of methods to stimulate growth of the fields of grasses they make into hay. Some fertilize their fields either with organic manure or synthetic fertilizer; some burn their fields before the growing season begins; some irrigate heavily, ensuring adequate water supply.

During various stages of succession, conditions for growth change. In a recently burned meadow, seeds requiring charate, heat, and sunlight may germinate best. Later, as plants grow in this meadow, shade creates different conditions more suited for germination of other kinds of seeds.

Problem

Under what conditions does grass seed germinate fastest?

Safety Precautions

Wash your hands after setting up this lab and after making measurements.

Hypothesis

Make a hypothesis about the conditions under which you think grass seed will germinate fastest. Explain your reasons for making this hypothesis.

towels cut to fit the bottom of the dish. Seal the edges of the dish with masking tape to keep the seeds from drying out.

Possible Hypotheses

1. Charate promotes faster germination of grass seed.
2. HCl treatment promotes faster germination of grass seed.

Possible Procedures

- Place 20 grass seeds treated for 24 hours with HCl on moistened paper toweling in a sealed petri dish. Do the same with 20 untreated seeds.
- Place 30 grass seeds treated with cold temperature for two months on moistened paper toweling in a sealed petri dish. Do the same with an untreated group.

Desert communities may not always follow the same sequence. In climates more favorable for plant growth, the plants compete for space; the result is dominance by some plants and elimination of others. In the desert, however, the primary struggle of the plants is for water. Also, there is little plant debris on the ground to help form fertile soil for successional changes. When a forest is destroyed by cutting or burning, new light-loving species spring up, and it may take decades for the forest to regain its original appearance. When a desert community is destroyed, the first plants that spring up are almost always the very same species that were destroyed.

Trends in Succession

Whether primary or secondary, every succession on land has common characteristics. As succession occurs, small plants with short life cycles are replaced by larger plants with longer life cycles. With more producers, the amount of energy trapped during photosynthesis increases. In the

Experimental Plan

1. As a group, make a list of possible ways you might test your hypothesis using the materials your teacher has made available.
2. Agree on one idea that could be investigated in the classroom.
3. Design an experiment that will test one variable at a time. Plan to collect quantitative data.
4. Following the style of a recipe, write a numbered list of directions that anyone could follow.
5. Make a list of materials and the quantities you will need.

Checking the Plan

Discuss the following points with other group members to decide the final procedures for your experiment.

1. What variables will need to be controlled?
2. What is your control?
3. What will you measure or count?

4. How many groups of seeds will you count, measure, or examine? How many seeds will you have in each group?
5. What treatment will each group of seeds receive?
6. Have you designed and made a table for collecting data?

Make sure your teacher has approved your experimental plan before you proceed further.

Data and Observations

Carry out your experiment, make your measurements, and complete your data table. Make a graph of your results.

Analysis and Conclusions

1. According to your results, what conditions promote faster grass seed germination?
2. What was your experimental evidence for your conclusion?

3. Was your hypothesis supported by your data? Explain.
4. If your hypothesis was not supported, what types of experimental error might be responsible?
5. Consult with another group that used a different procedure to examine this problem. What was its conclusion?
6. In what way might farmers or ranchers benefit from the results of your experiment?
7. During what stage of succession after a forest fire would grass grow fastest?
8. Write a brief conclusion to your experiment.

Going Further

Based on this lab experience, design an experiment that would help answer a question that arose from your work. Assume that you will have unlimited resources and will not be conducting this lab in class.

29.1 ECOLOGICAL SUCCESSION **819**

SECTION 29.1

Teaching Strategies

- To introduce the lab, show students the petri dish you have prepared with wet paper towels and radish seeds. Some seeds should have germinated. Ask students what conditions seeds need for germination. Ask them what kinds of seeds begin to grow first after a forest fire. Bring out the idea that as succession progresses, conditions become different, promoting growth of different plant species.
- Advise students to wash their hands after setting up the lab and after making their observations.
- You may want to substitute the seed of local plants.
- Make sure students keep their seeds moist.
- You may want to ask students to put data on the board for all the class to compare results.

Data and Observations

Examine each group's graphs and evaluate the group's interpretation of the data.

Data Analysis

1-5. Answers will vary depending on which variables students choose.
6. If germination could be speeded up, farmers or ranchers might be able to grow a crop where it otherwise might not grow.
7. Grass would grow fastest immediately after a fire if charate speeded up germination.
8. Answers will vary depending on the variables tested.

✔ Assessment

Oral: Ask students how they could test which seeds would germinate faster in the later stages of succession of a forest. L1

Extensions

Lead students with questions about what other plants and other conditions they might test.

3 Assess

Check for Understanding

Make a list of terms and concepts associated with primary and secondary succession. Have students create a concept map showing the relationships between the terms and concepts on the list. **L1**

Reteach

If students have difficulty with the Check for Understanding activity, allow them to work in groups. Assign each group to review the succession of a particular community. Then have each group present its findings to the class. **COOP LEARN**

Extension

Have students study the temperature of a microclimate created near the entrance to a mall, in the parking lot, and in an associated area that contains plants. Students should graph the results at the end of their study for comparison of the microclimatic conditions in the three areas. **L2**

✔ Assessment

Performance: Have students write a poem that describes the events in the succession of a particular community.

4 Close

Discussion

Lead a class discussion of how microclimates created by organisms in a community can cause succession. Have students explain how humans cause succession by their activities.

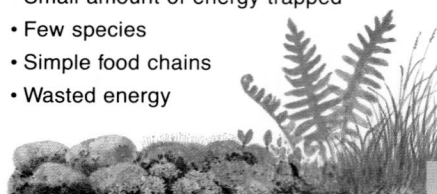

Figure 29-6 Every succession has common characteristics, which are summarized here.

- Small plants with short life cycles
- Small amount of energy trapped
- Few species
- Simple food chains
- Wasted energy

- Larger plants with longer life cycles
- Larger amount of energy trapped
- Many species
- Complex food webs
- Efficient energy use

Early stage → **Climax community**

early stages of succession, few species are involved, but as time goes on, the diversity of species increases. Food chains are simple at first, consisting mainly of producers, first-order consumers, and decomposers. Later, as the diversity of species increases, more complex food webs develop that include higher trophic levels and a greater variety of decomposers. More complex food webs result in greater use of the energy that enters the community, as less energy is wasted. Recycling of materials also becomes more efficient. Population sizes are kept steady by both biotic and abiotic factors.

All of these trends contribute to production of the climax community, which is complex and stable. At this point, the activities of the organisms are not likely to alter the physical environment in ways that would lead to further change. Thus, the community will remain basically the same unless disturbed by outside influences of nature or the activities of humans.

Section Review

Understanding Concepts

1. Use two examples from this section to explain how organisms alter the physical environment in such a way as to lead to their own elimination.
2. Suppose a meadow community were destroyed by fire. Will succession in that community occur more rapidly than the succession that originally produced the community? Explain.
3. Using the primary succession of a forest community from bare rock as

an example, explain how changes during succession illustrate each of the following trends in succession: (1) increase in species diversity; (2) change in size of dominant plant forms; (3) greater complexity of food webs; and (4) increase in amount of light energy trapped.

4. **Skill Review—Sequencing:** Sequence the steps you might expect to occur in a succession that begins on rock that has formed from lava after a volcanic eruption.

Assume the volcano erupted in a tropical climate. For more help, refer to Organizing Information in the **Skill Handbook**.

5. **Thinking Critically:** You know that a pond will undergo further succession eventually. How do you think the pond community developed in the first place?

Answers to Section Review

1. Examples may include how pioneer organisms enrich the soil making it more suitable for other forms of plant life, or how large plants cast shade that prevents growth of smaller plants.
2. The secondary succession will occur more rapidly because conditions that support life are already present.
3. Lichens and then mosses are replaced by ferns, grasses, and shrubs, then by

pines, and finally by beeches and maples. Changes in plant life increase the diversity of animal life, both within the soil and above it. The shift from low plants to trees illustrates the trend toward larger size of plants. With greater diversity, more feeding relationships are possible. Increase in number of complex plants results in more photosynthesis.

4. **Skill Review—Sequencing:** The sequence should start with pioneer organisms and their role in soil formation. Answers should reflect an understanding of the trends common to successions. The climax community would be a tropical rain forest.
5. **Thinking Critically:** The pond developed by primary succession. The bottom of the pond was once bare rock.

29.2 Biomes

Within the United States are several types of communities. In much of the eastern part of the country, forests predominate. In the Midwest, grasslands are common. Deserts are found in the Southwest. These types of communities are not limited to the United States. They are found elsewhere in the world, too—forests in Scandinavia, grasslands in Argentina, and deserts in Northern Africa. Why are certain kinds of communities found only in certain parts of the world? What do those parts of the world have in common? Basically, they share similar climates.

Climate

Climates are a function of many factors. Among them are amount and pattern of rainfall, humidity, and temperature ranges. Such factors are determined by altitude, latitude, wind patterns, and topography (surface characteristics).

Temperature   The sun is important to organisms not only because it provides the light energy for photosynthesis but also because it heats Earth, providing temperatures at which organisms can live. Not all parts of Earth, however, receive the same amount of sunlight. Because of Earth's curvature, sunlight hitting areas at higher latitudes is spread over a wider area than is the sunlight striking near the equator, Figure 29-7a. Put another way, the area of Earth near the equator receives more light energy per unit area than areas north and south of the equator. Because they receive different amounts of light energy, different areas have different temperatures. These temperature differences are a major factor influencing distribution of organisms.

The tilt of Earth and its orbit around the sun influence the angle at which sunlight is received and, thus, the temperature, as seen in Figure 29-7b. For example, during the summer the United States is tilted

Objectives

Explain how physical factors interact to determine the life forms found in different biomes.

Compare the climates and common life forms of the world's major land biomes.

Differentiate among the various zones of which the oceans are composed.

Figure 29-7   **Sunlight is five times stronger at the equator than at the poles because the surface of Earth is curved (a) and because Earth's axis is tilted (b). Seasons occur because of Earth's tilted axis and its orbit around the sun. December is winter in the Northern Hemisphere because the North Pole is tilted away from the sun. Why is June warm in the Northern Hemisphere?**

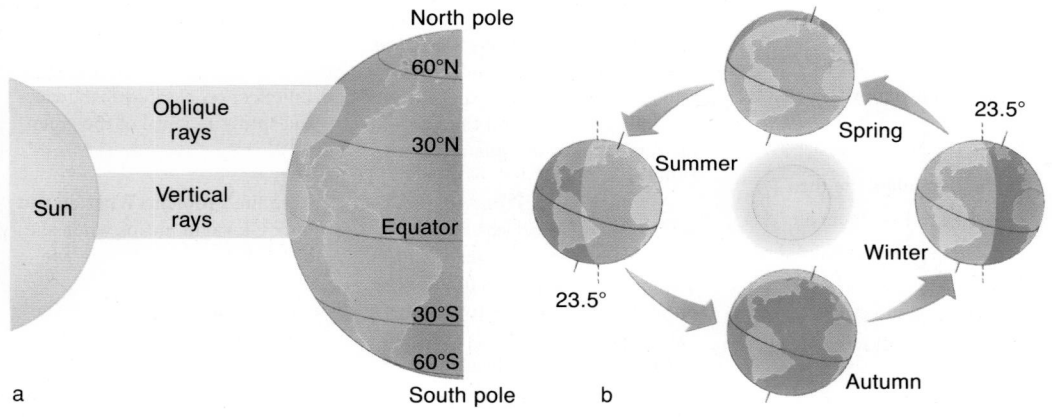

a

b

29.2 BIOMES ❧ **821**

Prepare

Key Concepts

This section explains how physical factors interact to determine climate and the life forms found in the world's land biomes. It also discusses the life zones of the oceans.

Key Terms

biome, tundra, permafrost, taiga, temperate forest, tropical rain forest, grassland, desert, plankton, nekton, benthos, neritic zone, oceanic zone, littoral zone, geothermal energy, biosphere

Materials

- Order Potential Natural Vegetation Maps for Minilab 2.

1 Focus

Objectives

The objectives are listed on the student page. Remind students to preview these objectives as a guide to this numbered section.

Activity

Pass out photographs of plants or animals from magazines such as *National Geographic* and *Natural History.* Ask students to guess where the organism lives. In giving their answers, students should give their reasoning. This will give you some insight into what students already know and don't know about biomes. `L1` `LEP`

2 Teach

Figure Caption Question

Why is June warm in the Northern Hemisphere? In June, the Northern Hemisphere is tilted toward the sun and receives direct rays of the sun.

SECTION 29.2

Purpose
Students will encounter one poet's view of the cyclic nature of the seasons, the cycle of water, and the cycle of the human spirit in one short poem.

Teaching Strategies
• Ask students to describe how they feel when summer gives way to autumn, or when winter loses its grip to spring. Then, ask them to make a statement about their feelings using a living thing or event that they associate with a particular season. Have students read the poem and information about the author before answering the questions at the end.

Possible Answers
1. Students will express various meanings, and the statement is open to some interpretation. One of Giovanni's probable meanings is that when people understand the reason for their existence, they will begin to take better care of Earth.
2. Temperature and other changes in the cycle of seasons govern the life cycle of plants.

Going Further
Suggest that students study other poems by Nikki Giovanni and perhaps other authors, such as Frost and Longfellow, who express a similar understanding and wonderment of nature.

Concept Development
The water cycle is influenced by weather and land surface. Rainfall is influenced by the location of mountain ranges and wind action. Have students notice that the larger the area, the smaller the annual average precipitation for the area.

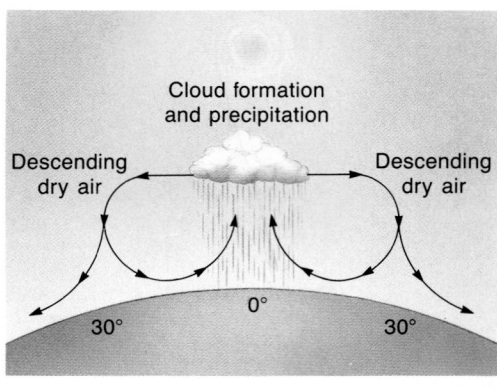

Figure 29-8 Deserts are common at latitudes 30° north and south because the descending air is so dry.

closer to the sun than in the winter, so it receives sun more directly in the summer. Less energy is lost as sunlight travels toward the United States in summer. In addition, the United States receives more hours of sunlight. As a result, temperatures are higher in summer than in winter. Seasonal temperature differences are greater at latitudes farther from the equator. You know this by comparing the seasonal differences in temperature in Maine or Michigan with those in southern Florida. Tropical areas, at or close to the equator, receive about the same large amounts of solar energy year round, resulting in a steady, warm temperature and no changing seasons.

Precipitation   Differences in temperature contribute to precipitation patterns. Warm temperature causes air to rise because warm air is less dense than cooler air. Near the equator, where air is warmest, the rising warm air takes with it a great deal of moisture from the oceans, Figure 29-8. As the warm air rises, it begins to cool. Because cooler air cannot hold as much moisture as warmer air, the moisture condenses as rain. Tropical areas receive large amounts of rainfall all year long. The cooled air that rises from the tropics and loses its moisture then spreads to latitudes 30° north and south before descending.

LITERATURE CONNECTION

Winter Poem
by Nikki Giovanni

once a snowflake fell
on my brow and i loved
it so much and i kissed
it and it was happy and called its
cousins
and brothers and a web
of snow engulfed me then
i reached to love them all
and i squeezed them and they
became
spring rain and i stood perfectly
still and was a flower

Nikki Giovanni (1943-   ) is an African American poet, writer, and lecturer at Queen's College of the City University of New York. She says of poetry and life in general, "I just think things should mean something and i get confused when no meaning is found. We waste too much, we humans, because we refuse to recognize that there is a possibility of order and things making sense and us as a planet doing better."

As you can see, *Winter Poem* evokes not only the season of winter, but the quiet passage of winter into spring. Giovanni is fond of the order expressed in the quotation, "To everything, there is a season and a purpose under heaven."

Winter Poem suggests the flowering of the human spirit in the growth of a new season. It also describes the acceptance and joyful challenge of difficult times as in winter. On another level, the poem describes not only the cycle of seasons, but the cycle of phase change in water from solid to liquid. This, in turn, has an effect on plant growth, causing the spring renewal of the green Earth.

---

1. **Solve the Problem:** What do you think Giovanni means when she says, "We waste too much, we humans . . ."?
2. **Explore Further:** How does the cycle of seasons affect the life cycle of plants?

MEETING INDIVIDUAL NEEDS

For students who are working below grade level, provide a globe and penlight to illustrate how sunlight strikes Earth at different latitudes and how the tilt of Earth's axis influences the angle at which sunlight is received. This demonstration is more effective in a darkened room. **LEP**

When it does descend, it is very dry. This dry air is a factor in the formation of deserts common at these latitudes, such as the Sahara Desert of northern Africa and the vast deserts that cover much of Australia. Changes in the temperature and moisture content of air occur at other latitudes as well. Depending on differences in temperature at those latitudes, different patterns of precipitation and climate result. In general, air moves from the equator north and south toward the poles. As Earth spins on its axis, that spin causes wind patterns in the air moving toward the poles.

Topography Mountain ranges illustrate the importance of topography in determining climate. Mountains can contribute to rainfall patterns. When wind pushes air toward mountains, the air is forced upward along the mountain slopes. As the air rises, it cools, and the moisture it holds condenses. Rain falls, like water being wrung from a wet sponge, on the side from which the wind is blowing (the windward side). The ample rainfall may be sufficient to support a forest community. By the time the cool air descends on the other side of the mountains (the leeward side), it has been wrung dry. Little precipitation falls on this side of the mountains, giving rise to a desert community.

Wind, temperature, altitude, and latitude interact to produce similar climates in large land areas around the world. These large geographic regions are known as **biomes.** Each type of biome is characterized by similar forms of dominant plant life such as grasses, conifers, or cacti.

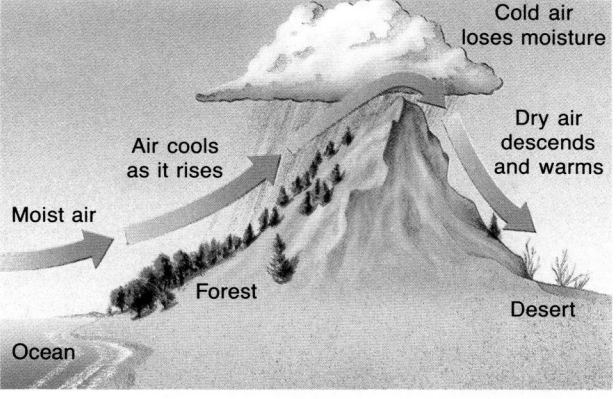

Figure 29-9 Warm, moist air moving up the mountains cools and forms rain. Deserts form on the leeward side of the mountains as dry air descends to the surface and warms. These conditions exist on either side of the Sierra Nevada range in California.

Figure 29-10 The distribution of the world's biomes is shown on this map. Notice how areas with similar climates have the same biomes.

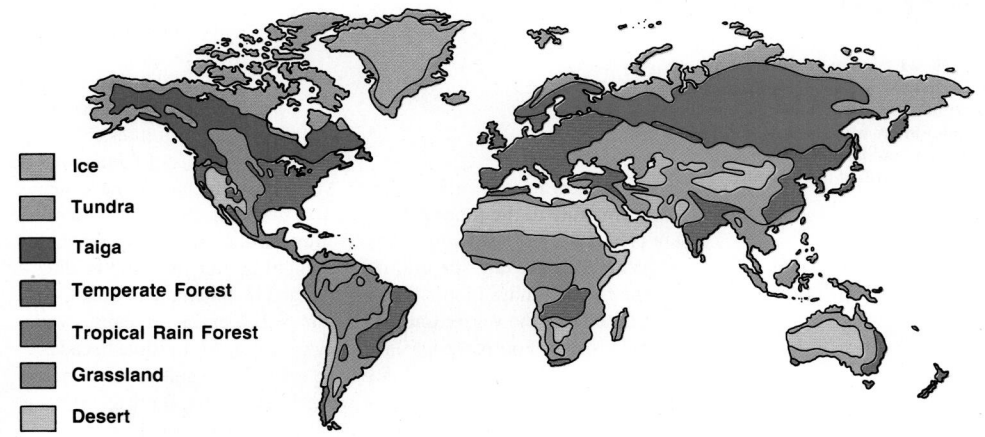

Ice
Tundra
Taiga
Temperate Forest
Tropical Rain Forest
Grassland
Desert

29.2 BIOMES **823**

Display

Obtain a large world map from *National Geographic* and prepare a bulletin board display that shows each of the biomes mentioned in this section. Ask students to compare what they know about climate zones and biomes. `LEP`

Using Science Terms

Tundra is a Russian word that means "treeless plain."

Discussion

Ask students to discuss why there is no tundra biome in the southern latitudes. (There is no land at these latitudes.)

Concept Development

Point out that the average annual precipitation of the tundra biome is less than that of the desert biome. Many scientists contend that tundras should be called cold deserts to differentiate them from the warm deserts.

Audiovisual

Show *Scientists and the Alaska Oil Spill,* available free from Exxon Corporation. Ask students to analyze the film for any inaccuracies. `L1`
`LEP`

Tundra

Circling the globe at the northernmost latitudes is a biome having low average temperatures and little annual precipitation. The precipitation that does fall is mostly in the form of snow, in an amount equivalent to about 12 cm of rain per year. This biome, called the **tundra,** includes areas where the water in the soil is frozen during winter. The winter is long in the tundra. There are many months of twilight and darkness, when the sun is below the horizon the entire day. The result is a growing season that is very short. Although the top layer of soil thaws during the short summer season, the lower layer remains permanently frozen. This permanently frozen soil layer is known as **permafrost.** Low temperatures, poor soil, and limited water are the critical factors that determine which plants grow in this biome. Permafrost and the low precipitation level prevent the rooting and growth of forests in the tundra. There may be a few small trees, but they are widely scattered. Thus, the tundra resembles a plain. Lakes and ponds are plentiful.

Producers of the tundra include lichens known as reindeer moss, true mosses, grasses, sedges, and some low, stunted shrubs. During the brief summer season, which is quite cool, a variety of small perennial plants sprout and quickly flower.

Common consumers of a tundra include rodents such as mice, voles, and lemmings. Snowshoe hares, reindeer and caribou, wolves, and foxes live there, as do polar bears in areas near the ocean. Biting flies and mosquitoes are numerous; great swarms of them make life almost unbearable for other animals. Many birds, including ducks and geese, migrate to the tundra in summer to nest. Insects, seeds, and berries are plentiful. For the few months of summer, when the sun is above the horizon the entire day, the unbroken daylight permits nonstop feeding.

The fragile tundra biome is being changed by human activities. Disturbance of the vegetation that insulates the permafrost causes widespread erosion. Footpaths used for one season are still visible decades later. Vehicles have left tracks that have eroded into gullies three meters deep. The search for oil also poses grave threats to the tundra, reducing grazing ranges and disturbing the migratory patterns of animals.

Figure 29-11 Animals of the tundra are adapted to life in the cold. Musk oxen, caribou, and snowy owls (from top to bottom) are found here. Harsh winters with strong winds, permafrost, short summers, and lack of available water prevent growth of large plants.

PROJECT

Biome Boxes: If you have contacts with schools located in biomes different from your own, have groups of students exchange "biome boxes" with groups of students from those schools. Each biome box should contain a sample of soil, small rock, pressed common plants, and photographs of common animals. In addition to the physical samples, each group should include a paper that summarizes the biome in which they live. When students receive their biome boxes from their complementary school, they should share the contents with the class. `L1`
`COOP LEARN`

Taiga

South of the tundra are the great coniferous forests that cover large portions of Canada, Alaska, and Eurasia. This biome, called **taiga,** is probably the largest of the world's biomes. The more southern areas of the taiga have a rainfall of about 35 to 40 cm per year. The taiga also has frequent fog and a low evaporation rate that results in very wet conditions. The soil is saturated with water and is acidic. There is no permafrost because the temperature is higher than that in the tundra.

Trees can grow in taiga soil. Once spruce and firs take hold, they further change an area by creating microenvironments. Trees of the taiga provide shade, protection, and homes for many organisms. Trees also cause changes in the soil. Although conifers are prominent, other trees grow there too.

Animal life common in the taiga includes moose, caribou, black bears, wolves, porcupines, weasels, and mink. Crossbills are birds well adapted to the taiga. Because their upper and lower bills overlap like a pair of scissors, Figure 29-12 (right), crossbills are able to break apart pine and spruce cones and feed on the seeds.

Temperate Forest

South of the taiga, where rainfall is greater and summers are longer and warmer, a different kind of forest biome is found. These regions, with a rainfall totaling about 100 cm per year, make up the **temperate forest** biome. As the name suggests, this biome is found in temperate regions of North America, South America, Europe, and Asia. Temperate forests are usually characterized by definite seasons. The growing season lasts at least six months.

Figure 29-12   The taiga, land characterized by coniferous forests, is the largest of the world's biomes. Taiga animals include moose (left), porcupines (center), and crossbills (right).

29.2 BIOMES 🐾 **825**

Using Science Terms
Taiga is derived from the Russian word *tajga,* which means "swampy forest."

Misconception
Unlike the ferocious monster plants highlighted by commercial horror movies, the insectivorous plants of bogs in the taiga are generally small. Sundews, for instance, may have a diameter about the size of a quarter.

Discussion
Have students discuss whether or not they think the taiga is an inviting biome for humans. Ask students to defend their answers by citing environmental or biological factors that justify their decision.

Audiovisual
Show *Spruce Bog—an Essay in Ecology,* available from the National Film Board of Canada. L1 LEP

Enrichment
Give each student a copy of a world map with the biomes drawn on it. Have students use their own methods to calculate and compare the area of each biome. Ask them to explain how much larger the taiga is than the other biomes. L2

MULTICULTURAL CONNECTION

Biome Dependencies: Explain to students how different cultures are dependent upon the biomes in which they live. For example, Laplanders depend on the reindeer that are the dominant large animal where they live in the taiga. Similarly, people who live in grasslands tend to depend upon grains that grow in that biome. Have students explore the ways other cultures depend upon the biomes in which they live. Students should examine diet, clothing, housing, and other aspects of the culture they explore.

SECTION 29.2

Concept Development

Most students in the United States live in or fairly near the temperate forest biome, the largest biome of the U.S. However, if your students live in the inner city, they may be unaware of the forest biome. It will be important to relate factors outside the city that are examples of the biome to students.

Activity

Have students describe food chains that exist within the temperate forest biome. Be sure that students always begin their food chain with a plant. **L1**

Audiovisual

Show *Forests,* an extraordinary film from Churchill Films that teaches the principles of forest growth and the variety of forest types in the United States. **L1** **LEP**

Reinforcement

Compare maps that show the amount of forested area of the United States 100 years ago with current maps. Have students research the reasons for the disappearance of the forests during this time period. (Most of the changes are human induced and result from building and farming activities.)

Figure Caption Question

Why might a plant such as a vine be able to grow in the canopy but not in the shrub layer or on the forest floor? There may not be enough light in the shrub layer or forest floor.

Layers of Vegetation   Temperate (and other) forests form a series of layers of vegetation from top to bottom. The top layer is the canopy (branches) of the trees. The canopy shades the ground below, much as an awning shades a window. It provides homes for animals such as insects, squirrels, and birds. Most of the food for these animals is produced in the canopy. Next is the shrub layer, consisting of shorter, shade-tolerant bushes. Under this is the forest floor. Light is scarce on the floor, so only plants that can grow well in dim light are present. Insects, other arthropods, and snakes are common on the forest floor. A fallen, rotting log may contain a microcommunity of life. Beneath the ground, in the soil, is the lowest level with many small arthropods, worms, and decomposers.

Each level of the forest has its own set of environmental conditions. Each is a separate microenvironment. Although an organism usually lives in only one level, the organization of the community depends on the interaction of all organisms.

Temperate Deciduous Forest   Most temperate forests in North America and Europe are composed of trees that lose their leaves each autumn. During the winter season, the trees are bare. Such trees are called deciduous, and the biome is known as a temperate deciduous forest. Most of the region east of the Mississippi River is the temperate deciduous forest biome of the United States, and is shown in Figure 29-2 (left) on page 815.

A temperate deciduous forest changes with the seasons. The falling of leaves in the autumn affects the community in many ways. Most important is that the food supply is reduced because food sources such as leaves, seeds, and fruits are less abundant. Also, without leaves, the effects of cold temperatures and wind are more severe. The net effect of these changes is a dormant period during the winter months. The forest floor is covered with dead leaves. Animal life is scarce as hibernation and long winter sleeps are common among the animals. The spring brings a rapid burst of growth as plants on the forest floor bloom and leaves on the trees unfurl.

Some of the major animals of the temperate deciduous forest in the United States are white-tailed deer, black bears, opossums, salamanders, and squirrels. Birds and insects are abundant.

Tropical Rain Forest

A different kind of forest occupies the equatorial regions around the world. These regions comprise the **tropical rain forest** biome. Tropical rain forests are found in Central and South America, central Asia, parts of Australia, and Africa. In a tropical rain forest, the temperature is almost

Canopy

Shrub layer
Forest floor
Soil

Figure 29-13   **Forests form layers of vegetation in which life forms vary. Why might a plant such as a vine be able to grow in the canopy but not in the shrub layer or on the forest floor?**

constant at 25°C, and rainfall is heavy. A total of 200 cm or more of rain falls per year. Heavy rainfall and high temperatures produce a humid environment much like a florist's greenhouse, and growth occurs constantly. The tropical rain forest has the most abundant growth and the greatest species diversity of any biome.

Plants   Most prominent of the plants in the tropical rain forest are large trees reaching 30 to 40 meters in height. Unlike coniferous and deciduous forests, a tropical rain forest has no dominant species of tree. In fact, hundreds of species may inhabit the same forest, and the few individuals of each species are widely scattered. As in a temperate forest, the branches of the trees form a large canopy, which is a major layer of the forest. Some taller trees may poke out above the canopy. The canopy is so thick that the forest floor may be dark even at noon. Because the forest floor is so dim, plant life there is scarce. A few shrublike plants may survive, but often the soil is bare.

Common in this biome are woody, vinelike plants called lianas. Lianas are rooted in the ground, but their leaves are up in the canopy where they receive sunlight. Also in the canopy are commensals such as orchids and bromeliads. The bromeliads trap and store water in the hollow, cuplike areas where their rosettes of leaves are joined. This water is used by the plant and by the animals that live in the canopy.

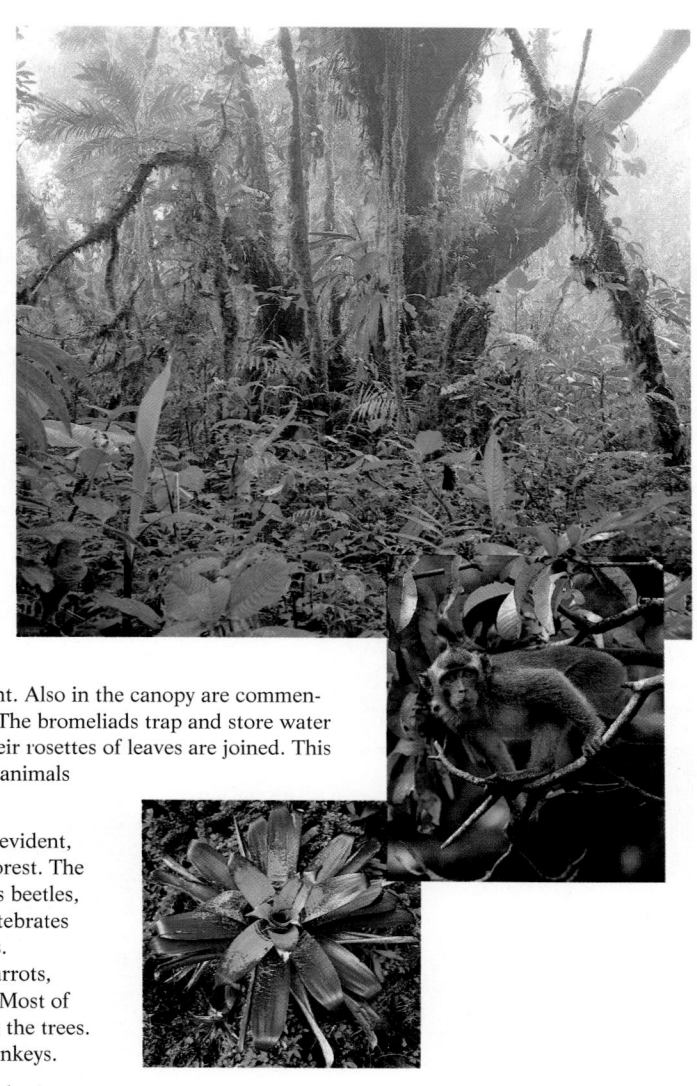

Figure 29-14   Monkeys (center) and bromeliads (bottom) are among the enormous number of species that live in the hot, humid tropical rain forest.

Animals   Although plants are more evident, animals abound in the tropical rain forest. The forest is alive with arthropods such as beetles, butterflies, and grasshoppers and vertebrates such as snakes, lizards, and tree frogs. Beautifully colored birds including parrots, parakeets, and toucans are common. Most of the mammals in the rain forest live in the trees. Among them are bats, sloths, and monkeys.

Effects of Destruction   Many tropical rain forests exist in developing countries of the world. For economic reasons, huge tracts of these forests are being destroyed. Trees are sometimes

29.2 BIOMES **827**

Brainstorming
Have students brainstorm possible scenarios about what the rain forest will be like in 20, 50, 100, and 500 years if biodiversity continues to decline. Write all student ideas on the board. **COOP LEARN**

Science, Technology, and Society

Rain Forest Resources: Earth scientists have found tremendous amounts of resources—gold, oil, precious stones—in the rain forests of South America. The native people of the rain forests have lived there for thousands of years and are uniquely adapted to living in that environment. Technology now exists that can quickly eliminate the forests to harvest these resources. Ask students to discuss the issues from the point of view of the native people, the South American governments, and people in the United States who supply the technology.

PROJECT

Rain Forest Destruction: Have students make a bulletin board that illustrates how humans are destroying rain forests. The display should show controlled fires, farming, logging, and buildings. After students have had a chance to study the display, ask them to describe which activities of humans they think are positive and which are negative. **L1** **LEP**

STUDENT JOURNAL

Have students write a short story detailing a scenario of what a rain forest will be like in the future. They may get some ideas as a result of the Brainstorming activity on this page. Suggest that the story be about a typical day in the life of a rain forest organism (up to 500 years in the future). **L1**

Chalkboard Example

Draw a cross section of a tropical rain forest on the chalkboard. Use different colors of chalk to show the layers of the rain forest, a thin soil, and a stream. Have students use the cross section to describe how the water normally flows through the ecosystem. Erase the trees as would happen in slash-and-burn agriculture and mining. Then have the students describe how water leaches the soil.

LEP

Enrichment

Insects are particularly plentiful in tropical rain forests. Until recently, there was no way to determine insect numbers in the rain forest. One enterprising entomologist decided to place large sheets of cloth beneath a tree and then fog the tree with a quickly degradable insecticide. Entomologists have since found more than a thousand species of insects in a single tree. Taxonomists suggest that insects may make up as many as 90% of all known species on Earth.

---

slashed, dried, and then burned, and crops are planted right in the ashes. Some cleared areas have been planted with grass to feed cattle. However, these cleared areas can be used in this way for only a few years. Because high temperature and humidity cause rapid decay of organisms, little humus accumulates in the thin tropical rain forest soil. Heavy rainfall leaches minerals from the soil. Thus, the soil is poor in nutrients to begin with, and those that are present are quickly used up by the new plants. The land is then abandoned as useless.

Tropical rain forests also have been cleared to provide a source of wood and to make space for new roads and mines. In the process, a great many species have been destroyed. Because the biodiversity in the tropical

Thinking Lab

ANALYZE THE PROCEDURE

How are tropical rain forests studied?

Background

Fifteen places in the world, totaling about half the size of Mexico, grow one-third to one-half of all the world's species of plants. These areas are parts of tropical rain forests that have been declining in area from more than 3.5 billion total acres in the early 1980s to fewer than 2 billion acres today. This map illustrates the 15 "hot spots," the most diverse parts of tropical forests.

Deforestation of 42 million acres per year results in losses of hundreds of species annually as roads are built and logging, ranching, farming, and con-

struction of settlements continue. Scientists agree that something must be done, but they disagree on which of two different research procedures should be used to study the problems of tropical rain forests. One procedure uses lengthy studies of entire forests and examines changes as they occur over long periods of time. Scientists from different parts of the world collect data from the rain forests, then take their data home, analyze it, and submit reports and recommendations for protection and management to the countries involved. In a contrasting proce-

dure, the focus of study is limited to gathering data over a short time in a few selected "hot spots" of biodiversity. Scientists then share their findings, which are used immediately in land-use planning and conservation efforts. Some researchers say that short-term studies cannot give accurate information about long-term ecological effects. These scientists also say that complex ecosystems cannot be studied for a brief period and yield useful data needed for long-term management. Advocates of short-term study say that their findings could be applied immediately and thereby give immediate protection to critical habitats.

You Try It

You are the scientist in charge of making a grant proposal for a research project that will provide data for developing conservation methods in South American tropical rain forests. **Analyze the procedures** that could be used in your research project. Write a short proposal that advocates one of the two procedures described above. Remember that what you write will determine how much money you get for your project.

828   ORIGIN AND DISTRIBUTION OF COMMUNITIES

Thinking Lab

ANALYZE THE PROCEDURE

Purpose

Students will analyze two procedures used to study tropical rain forests and decide which to use for a proposed study.

Skills

compare and contrast, interpret scientific illustrations

Teaching Strategies

• Introduce the lab by asking students to

list foods, medicines, and other products that have origins in tropical rain forest organisms. Ask why tropical rain forests are being destroyed, and why they should be saved.

• Provide library resources for students to read about deforestation in rain forests.

Answers

Answers will vary. Be sure that they are

based on one of the two methods given or on a combination of strategies given.

✔ Assessment

Portfolio: Ask students to write about the specific problems facing one rain forest on the map. They should include ideas for resolution of the problems, including methods by which the forest could be studied.

rain forest is the greatest in the world, biologists are concerned that potentially useful organisms (and chemicals produced by those organisms) are being eliminated before they can be discovered. It is also possible that removal of the forests may affect concentrations of both oxygen and carbon dioxide in the atmosphere and contribute to an increase in temperature worldwide. We will explore this idea in Chapter 30. It is clear that succession will not lead to restoration of a climax community like the original. Once destroyed, a tropical rain forest cannot be replaced. Recent efforts by scientists, governments, and environmental groups offer hope that the rate of destruction will be greatly reduced in the years ahead.

Grassland

Some areas in both temperate and tropical regions receive between 25 and 75 cm of unevenly distributed rainfall per year. Grasses are the major species of the climax community in these areas. Grasses also will grow where there is more than 75 cm of rain per year, but they are often crowded out in the shade of trees. Biomes in which grass is predominant have different names in different regions of the world. These names include steppe, prairie, plain, pampa, savannah, and veldt. In some regions where grasses predominate, there are also scattered trees. However, in general, these biomes are all **grasslands.**

Plants and Animals   In the United States, grassland is found west of the Mississippi River to the foothills of the Rocky Mountains. Grasses are the natural climax species of this biome. The height of the grasses increases from west to east as average rainfall increases. At one time, grasses close to two meters tall were common.

Wildlife of the grasslands in the United States once included grizzly bears, bighorn sheep, and bison. Today, the wildlife includes antelopes, jackrabbits, gophers, ground squirrels, and meadowlarks. Hunting of ground-nesting birds, such as the prairie chicken, is restricted to prevent their extinction.

Effects of Humans   Grasslands are important to humans because of their use in agriculture. To take advantage of the high fertility of grassland soils, humans have changed this biome. They have replaced the natural grasses with cereal grains such as wheat and corn. Humans have been

Figure 29-15   **Herds of bison (bottom) and colonies of prairie dogs (top) are native to the North American grasslands.**

29.2 BIOMES **829**

Concept Development

- Explain that at one time, half of the land on Earth was grassland. Today, that land is used by humans to grow crops, raise animals, or for housing.
- When grasslands are overgrazed, they can be irreparably damaged. The perennial grasses are replaced by annuals for a few years. Then the annuals are replaced by other plants that are not used by grazers. Ask students to give the term that describes this set of events. *Succession*

Enrichment

Have students compare the animals of the African grasslands with those in North America. Ask what type of evolution appears to be at work in shaping these examples. (Convergent evolution shapes organisms in widely separated biomes to resemble each other in appearance and function.)

L2

MULTICULTURAL CONNECTION

Grassland Dwellers: There are often parallels between cultures that share the same type of environment even though the cultures are continents apart. Ask students to compare and contrast the cultures inhabiting the grasslands of North America (farmers), South America (gauchos), and Africa (Masai herders of Kenya).

Minilab 2

Purpose
Students will gain an understanding of how vegetation types have changed due to human interference and develop an understanding of what biomes make up the United States.

Skills
sequence, classify, interpret scientific illustrations

Teaching Strategies
- Obtain "Potential Natural Vegetation Maps" of the United States from the U.S. Geological Survey, Reston, VA 22092 or from your local USGS office. Other vegetation-type maps of the United States may be substituted.
- Supply an atlas of the United States so students can decide on travel routes. Vegetation maps do not have cities identified.

Expected Results
Answers will vary depending on the routes students choose.

Answers
Answers will vary. If students travel in a straight line, they will probably pass through at least two biomes.

✔ Assessment
Knowledge: Have students predict in their journals what might happen if no conservation measures were in effect for 50 years in the spots they stopped to see during their trips. What kinds of conservation measures could be put in place to keep things in a better balance than they are in today at those sites?

Concept Development
Ask students why desert communities are favored by many biologists who study energy relationships among organisms. (Desert food chains tend to be shorter than those in most other biomes, and there are fewer organisms with which to contend.)

Minilab 2

Which biomes are found in the United States?

The Potential Vegetation Map provided by your teacher is a map of the natural vegetation that could grow if humans had not interfered with the natural course of events. Using this map, plot a trip of 2000 miles between two major cities in the United States. Plan stops every 400 miles. Assume that the potential vegetation is growing. Describe what you would see at the beginning and end of your trip and at each of the 400-mile stopping points.

Analysis *What biomes were you in at the beginning and end of your trip and at each 400-mile stopping point? How have human activities changed the environments where you stopped?*

careless with this biome. Overgrazing and trampling by herds of domestic animals have killed much of the grass. Much of the rich topsoil has been lost as a result of wind and water erosion of plowed soil. Constant plowing and lack of rain change the rich soil into loose dust. In the 1930s, winds picked up the dry soil and carried it for great distances. The south central part of the United States became known as the Dust Bowl, and many farms had to be abandoned. The tragedy of the Dust Bowl was a major factor in starting conservation practices.

Desert

Where rainfall is less than 25 cm per year and evaporation is rapid, there is little plant and animal life. Such areas are desert biomes. **Deserts** are found in the western United States, Africa, India, Asia, South America, and Australia. Depending on the amount of rainfall relative to the average temperature, deserts can be hot, cold, or temperate. The Mojave Desert of southern California is an example of a hot desert. The Northern Great Basin Desert in parts of Nevada, Utah, and California is a cold desert.

Deserts have little plant cover; bare ground is a common sight. However, the endless stretches of barren sand dunes that you probably picture in your mind are not typical of most deserts. The plants that are present are widely spaced due to the scarcity of water, Figure 29-16.

Not only is water scarce, but there is no regular pattern of rainfall. Long periods of drought are not uncommon and may last for many years. When it does rain, much of the water quickly runs off and is not available for use by the plants.

Adaptations of Plants   Organisms in desert biomes have many adaptations to dryness and temperature extremes. In plants, these include reduction of the surface area of leaves, waxy coatings on the leaves and stems, storage of water in fleshy parts, and large, shallow root systems for

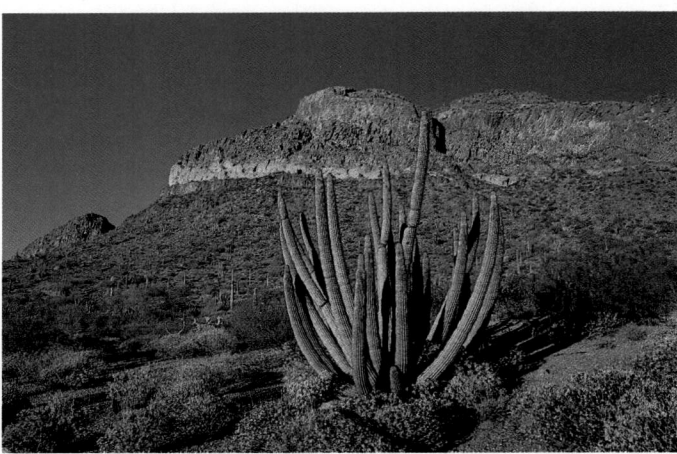

Figure 29-16   **Poor soil and lack of water cause desert plants to be widely spaced.**

STUDENT JOURNAL

Have students write a short story about one day in the life of a particular animal or plant that lives in a different biome from that in which they live. The short story should be written from the perspective of the inhabitant of the biome and include physical factors that determine the biome and other animals and plants found in the biome. **L1**

Figure 29-17 Desert organisms, such as lizards and cacti, are adapted to hot, dry conditions.

absorbing water quickly. Cactus leaves have become modified into spines, and the stem of the plant carries out photosynthesis. Some plants mature quickly and produce seeds in the few days when water is available. During droughts, some parts of plants may die, but the remaining parts can produce new growth when water again becomes available. Seeds of some desert plants can remain dormant for 50 years or more, so a species can survive even under the most adverse conditions. Other seeds contain inhibitors that prevent germination until the inhibitor is dissolved by water. Because a large amount of water is needed to dissolve the inhibitor, the plant starts to grow only when water is plentiful.

Adaptations of Animals   Animals, too, are adapted to desert life. Conservation of water is important to their survival. Some desert animals obtain water from their metabolism. Water produced as a by-product of the breakdown of foods can be used for other purposes. Also, animals such as kangaroo rats excrete concentrated urine to conserve water.

Due to the sparse vegetation, temperature extremes are common in deserts, and many animals have evolved behavioral adaptations for protection. Small, burrowing rodents are active only in evening or during early morning or late afternoon. By staying in their burrows, they avoid the heat of the day and the cold of the night. Others stay in shady places during the hottest part of the day. Some burrowing animals undergo a period of estivation. As in hibernation, metabolism is slowed down. In this way, an animal survives adverse conditions.

Many desert animals, such as jackrabbits and kangaroo rats, move by jumping, allowing them to move quickly from place to place. Large animals do not usually live in a desert. They would be unable to find enough food, and they are not adapted to drought and temperature extremes.

29.2 BIOMES 🌿 **831**

Audiovisual

- Show *Land of Lost Borders: Chihuahuan Desert Trilogy,* available from the Chihuahuan Desert Research Institute. The film reveals the factors involved in the creation of the desert and illustrates the ecology of this large desert that extends from New Mexico and Texas into Mexico. L1 LEP

- *A Desert Place,* produced by Time Life Films, shows the extraordinary plant and animal life of the Sonoran Desert, where environmental extremes create an extravagant variety of forms. L1 LEP

Demonstration

Obtain various species of cacti and other desert plants. Ask students to describe the adaptations the plants have for the conditions found in a desert biome. (Cacti have spines, thick cuticles, fleshy pads, and few stomata as adaptations to high temperatures and light intensity in this unique biome.) LEP

Activity

Have students use the library to find out about the adaptations of a desert animal. After students have done their research, they should give oral reports to the class. L2

Reinforcement

Remind students that all organisms are adapted to their habitats. Ask students to define the term *adaptation.* (Adaptations are inherited characteristics that provide survival value in nature.)

Using an Analogy

Point out to students that jackrabbits do not hear any better than most other mammals do. Ask why their ears are so large. An analogy for the adaptation of the ears of a jackrabbit is a radiator. The large surface areas of the ear and the radiator allow heat to leave. LEP

PORTFOLIO

Have students select two biomes. Then have them write a poem that compares the two biomes. The poems should contain references to climatic, geographical, and precipitation factors, as well as examples of plants and animals of each biome. L1

831

Reinforcement

Have students refer back to Chapter 28 for a discussion of biotic and abiotic factors.

Concept Development

More than 70% of Earth's surface is covered by oceans. The plankton of the oceans provide most of the oxygen available for animals. Oceans also act as a carbon dioxide sink, and without this sink the greenhouse effect would be magnified significantly.

Different Viewpoints in Biology

What is the role of the oceans?

Some people support the use of the ocean as a place to dump large amounts of waste generated by humans. These people say that the ocean volume is so large that the amount of waste being dumped is insignificant. Other people suggest that the ocean should be considered a support system for life on Earth rather than a dumping ground. Ask students to defend their viewpoints.

Using Science Terms

Plankton is derived from the Greek word *planktos,* meaning to drift or wander. Ask students how this name is appropriate. (Ocean plankton drift on the wandering ocean currents.)

LEP

Ocean

You are familiar with life on land. However, if you examine a globe, you will see that the surface of Earth is more than two-thirds water, mostly in the form of oceans. The kinds and number of organisms living in the oceans far exceed those on land.

Abiotic Factors Distribution of organisms in the oceans depends mostly on abiotic factors. The most important of these is light. Light intensity decreases with depth because light is both reflected and absorbed by the water. The penetration of light varies with the contents of the water and with latitude, but it generally does not reach a depth greater than 200 meters. The oceans have an average depth of about 4000 meters, so the zone of water in which light is present is relatively small. Producers, which affect the makeup of any ecosystem, live only where light is sufficient for photosynthesis to occur. Thus, light is an important factor in limiting distribution of life in the ocean.

Temperature is also important to life in water. However, temperature does not vary as much in the ocean as on land because bodies of water absorb heat during the warm seasons and hold it during cold seasons. Thus, the sea is a more stable environment than the land. In the middle North Atlantic, for example, water temperature varies only about 10 C° from surface to ocean floor.

Organisms Ecologists classify aquatic organisms into three major groups. Organisms that float in the water and are carried by ocean currents are called **plankton.** These include many types of unicellular algae, heterotrophic protists, and small multicellular animals. Copepods, which are microscopic crustaceans, are a major form of animal plankton. Jellyfish and their relatives and the larval forms of some other animals are also plankton.

Figure 29-18 Jellyfish (right) are plankton because they are carried by ocean currents. Fish (left) can swim, and thus are examples of nekton.

832 ORIGIN AND DISTRIBUTION OF COMMUNITIES

PORTFOLIO

Have students choose one zone of the ocean and make a poster showing the organisms found in that zone and the food webs that exist there. Posters should be added to student portfolios.

L1   LEP

A variety of animals can move freely through the water under their own power. These animals are called **nekton.** Nektonic animals include fish, whales, shrimp, and squid. Other animals live attached to or crawl on the ocean floor. They are called **benthos.** Included in this group are organisms such as barnacles, starfish, sponges, and clams. Benthic organisms are mostly found close to shore or in shallow water.

Zones Different parts of an ocean differ from one another in terms of both physical factors and the organisms present. Rather than referring to these different parts of the ocean as biomes, ecologists usually identify them as zones. Two zones are classified on the basis of presence or absence of light. Other zones are based on depth and the kinds of life present at different depths. These zones overlap one another. For example, the lighted zone is part of the top 200 meters of the entire ocean, regardless of total depth at any point. The different zones of the ocean interact with one another to a greater extent than do distinct biomes on land.

Ecologists often classify two main ocean regions with respect to depth. The area above the continental shelf is known as the **neritic zone.** The region of the deeper waters of the ocean basin is called the **oceanic zone.**

The portion of the neritic zone closest to the shore is the region most subject to change. Organisms in this area, called the **littoral zone,** are influenced by the action of tides, exposure to both water and air, temperature changes, and changes in amount of light and salinity of the water. Algae, both nekton and forms that are attached, are the producers of this zone. Animal life is diverse and includes clams, crabs, and barnacles—animals adapted to the changing conditions.

The littoral zone extends out to a point at which conditions become more stable. Life in this portion of the neritic zone is different. All organisms living there are strictly aquatic. Plankton and nekton populate the surface waters, and benthic animals are plentiful.

Figure 29-19 Barnacles are examples of benthic animals that live attached to surfaces.

Figure 29-20 The ocean is divided into zones based on depth and amount of sunlight penetration.

Neritic zone
Littoral zone
Sea level
200 m
Continental shelf
Lighted zone
Oceanic zone
Unlighted zone
1800 m
5000 m

29.2 BIOMES **833**

Audiovisual

Show *Oceanography: Role of People in Ocean Sciences,* available from BFA Educational Media. L1 LEP

Enrichment

The "lure" of the angler fish is actually a modified ray of the dorsal fin. Stephen Jay Gould has written several essays about the evolution of this and similar structures in *Natural History* magazine and several books. L3

Demonstration

You can show that warm water circulates faster than cold water. Put a crystal or two of potassium permanganate into each of two beakers, one filled with warm water and one with cold water. Watch the diffusion and circulation rates in the two beakers. LEP

Concept Development

In 1979, the Galapagos expeditions brought up specimens of tube worms, *Riftia pachyptila,* the thick-plumed rift worm. The giant worms were named for the red tip that looked superficially like a feather, but functioned as a strainer for collecting the hydrogen sulfide that gave the worm an obnoxious odor. More importantly, the worms lacked a mouth, a gut, and an anus, but contained red blood. Ask students how they think the tube worms get energy if they cannot ingest food.

Figure 29-21 The "headlight" of the angler fish attracts prey.

In the deepest part of the ocean, the oceanic zone, life in the surface waters is similar to that of the neritic zone. In deeper waters, though, conditions and life forms are quite different. There light is absent, so no photosynthesis occurs. Some nektonic animals, mostly fish, live there. They feed on other fish and on dead organisms that sprinkle down from above. Some organisms that live in deep waters emit light. The light given off by the "lure" of one type of angler fish attracts prey.

Bacteria decompose organic materials that settle onto the ocean floor when organisms die. The organic materials are broken down into simpler molecules such as carbon dioxide, nitrates, and phosphates. These simple molecules must be made available to producers in the ocean. If materials continue to build up on the ocean bottom, a point would be reached where life could no longer continue. An ecosystem can survive only if materials are recycled.

Circulation of Water　Return of materials to the surface of the oceans is affected mostly by water temperature and wind. In cold climates, surface water becomes colder than water below the surface. Because cold water is more dense than warm water, cold surface water sinks and warm bottom water rises, setting up a vertical current. Also, the wind causes horizontal currents that move the surface water. Water below the surface rises to replace the water displaced by the wind. Thus, the ocean water is stirred as if in a huge mixing bowl. Although both of these processes return decomposed materials to the surface, water temperature differences account for most of the return.

Unique Ocean Communities

Most of the ocean floor is like a cold, barren desert. Light does not reach the ocean floor so there can be no photosynthesis. Because of this, it was long thought that few, if any, life forms could exist in this area. However, in recent years, scientists have discovered unique communities of animals living on the ocean floor at depths as great as 3000 meters.

Deep-sea Vents　Many of these unusual communities exist in the Pacific Ocean. The first community was found in 1977 off the Galapagos Islands, and others were later discovered off the coasts of Mexico and Peru. Although the water temperature on most of the ocean's floor is near freezing, each of these Pacific communities is in an area of warm water. The communities are located over areas of molten rock where new ocean floor is forming. Cold seawater seeps into cracks in the new crust of the ocean floor, comes into contact with the molten rock below, and becomes heated. The hot water, which may be as hot as 350°C, gushes up through deep-sea vents—openings that look like small volcanoes. The newly discovered communities thrive in the warm water around the vents.

Animal life never before seen inhabits these communities. Brown mussels and white clams that average 30 cm long live among pillows of cooling lava. Clusters of orange and white crabs, starfish, octopuses, and unusual fish move around the vents. Strangest of all are colonies of giant tube worms, Figure 29-22, some of them as long as three meters, that live around the vents. Many other life forms collected from the sites differ so much from known animals that they have not yet been classified.

Deep-sea Energy Relationships   Every community must have an outside energy source and producers that trap the energy to make food. In most communities, light is the energy source, plants or algae are the producers, and carbohydrates are made by photosynthesis. But, there is no light energy in these ocean floor communities. Instead, there is geothermal energy. **Geothermal energy** is heat energy from the interior of Earth. This energy, present in the molten rock, increases the temperature of the water. The very hot water is important because it reacts with minerals in the rocks and the seawater to produce an energy-rich compound—hydrogen sulfide. Chemosynthetic bacteria are the producers of these unique communities. Like other producers, chemosynthetic bacteria make organic molecules. However, these bacteria make carbohydrates by using the energy in hydrogen sulfide. Thus, these bacteria are the basis of the community's food web. Animals such as mussels and fish feed on the bacteria and are, in turn, preyed on by other animals.

Tube worms and clams depend on the bacteria as well, but in a unique way. Instead of feeding on the bacteria, these animals live with them in a mutualistic relationship. The bacteria live in different parts of the tube worm's body. In clams, the bacteria live in the gills. Both animals extract hydrogen sulfide from the water and transport it in their blood to the bacteria. In turn, the bacteria use the chemical energy in hydrogen sulfide to provide food for the animals through chemosynthesis.

In 1986, deep-sea vents were discovered in the Atlantic Ocean. This discovery suggests that hot-spring ocean communities may occur wherever new ocean floor is forming. It also may mean that these vents have a marked effect on both the temperature and mineral content of the oceans. More recently, a freshwater vent was discovered in a lake in Siberia. The water there is not nearly as hot as that around ocean vents, and the community around the vent has fewer animals. It is thought that the community is quite young, and study of it should shed light on how new species colonize the area.

Figure 29-22   Sulfide-blackened hot water pours from a deep-sea thermal vent (left). Water from the vents contains minerals that nourish a unique community of organisms, such as the tube worms shown here (right).

CHEMISTRY CONNECTION

Hydrogen Sulfide:
Hydrogen sulfide is formed in the laboratory by burning sulfur in hydrogen gas or by displacement reactions. The odor of rotten eggs is due chiefly to the presence of hydrogen sulfide.

Enrichment
Discuss the energy flow in each of the biomes discussed in this section. Relate biodiversity to energy conversion. **L2**

3 Assess

Check for Understanding
On the chalkboard, make a blank table with six rows and six columns. Heads for the columns should be: Biomes, Precipitation, Temperature, Plants, Animals, Description. Each row should be a biome. Randomly ask students to fill in different blocks of the table. Allow the students to choose the block they would like to complete. **L1**

Reteach
Use an overhead projector to show a map of the world. Put numbers in different areas. Randomly ask students to describe the biome of the area and give an example of a common plant or animal of the biome. Have the student who answers choose another student to describe the climate of the biome.

STUDENT JOURNAL
Have interested students research the use of geothermal energy as an alternate energy source and write a short report in their journals. Students should consider whether the energy from deep-sea thermal vents can be captured for use by humans. **L3**

Extension

Have students prepare a question-naire that pertains to the awareness and attitudes of different people about the impact of long- and short-term solutions to environmental problems dealing with entire biomes. As an example, one set of questions might relate to increasing desertification and ways to reverse the trend. Provocative questions can give real insight into the true awareness of people to environmental problems and attitudes about possible solutions. **L2**

✔ Assessment

Portfolio: Have students describe the root problems and possible solutions to the decline of rain forest, temperate forest, or grassland biomes. **L1**

4 Close

Activity

Allow student groups to coopera-tively create skits and role play differ-ent parts of a biome. Each group should have roles that include a plant, animal, and the climate of the biome. **COOP LEARN**

The Biosphere   Just as the many zones of an ocean interact with one another, so, too, do the various biomes on land. There are no sharp divisions between biomes. Rather, one type of biome gradually gives way to another, much as wet strokes of watercolors blend into each other along their edges. All the world's land biomes, as well as ocean and freshwater ecosystems, interact with one another. Together, they make up the highest level of biological organization, the **biosphere.** No one part of the biosphere is isolated from another. Therefore, what happens in one region may affect other regions as well. Understanding of this rela-tionship among the world of life and making sound deci-sions based on such understanding is crucial to the future of humans and all other life forms.

Figure 29-23   **The biosphere is the thin layer of Earth's surface where life exists.**

LOOKING AHEAD

COMMUNITIES DEVELOP over time as they undergo ecological succes-sion. Biotic and abiotic factors interact to influence the distribution of communities on Earth. What role have humans played in ecological suc-cession? How can we lessen the harm we do to the environment? In the next chapter, you will study ways in which human activities have adversely affected individual organisms, communities, and entire ecosys-tems, and how many of those activities pose a threat to humans them-selves. You will also examine possible remedies for correcting past mistakes and plans for avoiding future ones.

Section Review

Understanding Concepts

1. How can the cold, dry conditions of the tundra biome be explained?
2. Why do you think the taiga receives more precipitation than the tundra?
3. Describe the changes in benthos you would note if you could walk along the ocean bottom from the shoreline to the greatest depths.

4. ***Skill Review—Making Tables:*** Construct a table compar-ing the following characteristics in the tundra, taiga, temperate decidu-ous forest, desert, grassland, and tropical rain forest biomes: average precipitation; temperature range; dominant plant species; and com-mon forms of animal life. For more

help, refer to Organizing Information in the **Skill Handbook.**

5. ***Thinking Critically:*** Consider the layers of vegetation in a tropical rain forest. Most organisms in that forest inhabit mainly one layer, such as monkeys in the canopy. How is the survival of the monkeys linked to organisms living in different layers?

836 ORIGIN AND DISTRIBUTION OF COMMUNITIES

Answers to Section Review

1. The cold is a function of the amount of light energy received per unit area. At higher latitudes, there is less warm air to rise; thus, less moisture enters the air.
2. The taiga exists at lower latitudes. Thus, temperature is slightly warmer and the air holds more moisture. When that air rises and cools, rain is formed.
3. The diversity of benthos close to the shoreline would be great because in

shallow waters, light is available to support a diversity of food chains. Farther out, the ocean bottom is far removed from light; thus, fewer and fewer benthic organisms exist.

4. **Skill Review—Making Tables:** Precipitation: tundra—12 cm; taiga—35-40 cm; temperate forest—100 cm; desert—less than 25 cm; grassland—25-75 cm; tropical rain forest—200

cm. Temperature: tundra—low; taiga—slightly higher than tundra; temperate forest—warmer with definite seasons; desert—hot, cold, or temperate; grass-land—temperate or tropical; tropical rain forest—25°C. Plant and animal species are cited on pages 824 to 831.

5. **Thinking Critically:** Decomposers in the soil recycle nutrients needed by the trees in which the monkeys live.

Considering the Environment
Wetlands

Swamps, bogs, potholes, muskegs, marshes—the names vary by region and location, but they are all lands that are wet for at least part of the year. Historically, wetlands have been places of legends and loathing. These myths, combined with a proven relationship between wetlands and certain mosquito-borne diseases such as malaria and yellow fever, have shaped our attitudes about wetlands.

Two thousand years ago, one of the first large-scale public works programs was the draining of the Pontine Marshes in Italy. This project was started by the Roman emperors as a solution to a problem with malaria and to create prime farmland. In the early history of the United States, the federal government encouraged the draining of swamps by giving 64 million acres of wetlands to those states that would drain them.

But a lot has been learned since then. We have found more effective ways to control disease and have discovered that wetlands are essential to a healthy ecosystem. After centuries of neglect, why are we so concerned about the preservation of wetlands?

Coastal Wetlands   Consider just one type of wetland—the type that borders our coasts. These coastal marshes, swamps, and bogs are the homes of many unique plants and animals. Besides providing humans with food such as cranberries, ducks, geese, and turtles, coastal wetlands filter water before it enters underground reservoirs. These reservoirs are the source of much of the water we use for drinking and washing. Another benefit of coastal wetlands is that they absorb many pollutants in the rivers and streams that feed them, preventing contaminants from entering the ocean. Coastal wetlands also have a direct effect on jobs. Most of the fish harvested by the United States fishing industry live part of their life cycle in coastal marshes. In addition to providing a livelihood for people along the coast, wetlands also provide a protective buffer against the seasonal storms and flooding that threaten coastal communities every year.

Potholes   Other wetlands, such as the potholes in the northern prairies, have a direct effect on wildlife. The potholes serve as the breeding ground for about half the wild ducks in North America. For decades, farmers were encouraged to drain and fill these small ponds and marshes, turning them into farmland. However, when the duck population started to decline, it was realized that the potholes were a valuable resource. Efforts are now underway to preserve them.

Bogs   A fascinating type of wetland with many unique inhabitants is the bog. In the northern part of North America, these diverse communities are called muskegs. Floating on the acidic water of these bogs is a mat of sphagnum moss thick enough to support a person's weight. You may have seen sphagnum moss at garden centers, where it is sold as a soil conditioner. Because it absorbs large amounts of water and has antibiotic properties, it was used as a diaper by Native Americans and as a surgical dressing in World War I.

Bog Life   Bogs support a unique and diverse community of plants

Considering the Environment

Purpose
This feature explains how environments are important in the lives of humans and inhabitants of the environment. The feature explores the importance of human disruptions in wetland ecosystems.

Background
Wetlands occur in many different biomes. They are considered by many environmentalists to be as important to maintaining biological diversity as are tropical rain forests.

Teaching Strategies
- Tell students to imagine that they are farmers. The margin of one of their fields is damp, marshy, and covered with water for part of the year. They must plow around the area, so it does not produce any crops for them to harvest. Ask if they should be encouraged or allowed to fill in the area so that it will be able to produce crops. Allow students to discuss the pros and cons of both sides of the issue.

CHAPTER 29

and animals. Because the water is acidic and nutrient-poor, most species of plants cannot grow there. However, the ones that do survive among the sphagnum are adapted in unusual ways. A major requirement for plant growth is nitrogen, and bogs have notoriously low levels of nitrogen. But plants such as the Venus's flytrap, pitcher plant, and sundew solve this problem in a distinctive way—they trap and digest insects. Pitcher plants are shaped like a funnel. Along the sides are attractive spots of color and drops of nectar. When the insect enters the funnel, it follows the nectar deep into the plant. However, when the insect tries to leave, it finds that its path is blocked by inward-bending hairs. Exhausted by the struggle to get out, it eventually falls to the water-filled base of the plant and is digested. An even more active bog-based insect hunter is the Venus's flytrap from North and South Carolina. These plants have V-shaped leaves that are fringed with long spines. When an insect lands on the leaf, attracted by the color and nectar on the surface, it brushes against one or more trigger hairs in the center of the leaf; the leaf then closes. In a short time, the insect is digested and the leaf opens again, ready for the next victim.

CAREER CONNECTION

Agronomists are agricultural scientists who study soil management and growth of field crops such as corn, wheat, and cotton in various soils. They study ways to improve the quality and yield of crops by improving soil conditions and developing new growth methods.

Because bogs are acidic and lack oxygen, plants do not decay rapidly when they die. Thus, bogs build up thick layers of plant material called peat. Peat, after drying, is used as fuel in many parts of the world. Ireland, for example, uses peat as a major source of energy and, because of overharvesting, has destroyed the majority of its bogs. Fortunately, most North American bogs are untouched, so we have the opportunity to preserve these unique and productive ecosystems.

The Everglades The Everglades, a huge swamp in Florida, is a study of what can happen if humans aren't careful when they manage wetlands. For 5000 years, a huge wet prairie of plants growing in constantly wet muck prospered on the southern tip of Florida. Fresh water from Lake Okeechobee and the Big Cypress Swamp combined to form a river 50 miles wide, but only inches deep, flowing south. The constantly saturated muck underlying this river supported a lush and varied freshwater ecosystem that was unique in all the world. An added benefit in low-lying Florida was that this constant flow of fresh water replenished the water table and kept salt water from the ocean from migrating inland.

But the winter climate in this area is very comfortable, and increasing numbers of people have moved to Florida to live. In addition, it is a prime area for agriculture. So some of the land was drained and the natural system was replaced with a series of artificial canals and levees. These allow engineers to adjust the water levels and prevent flooding during hurricanes. However, there isn't enough reserve water to keep the Everglades wet during a drought and it dries out. Under these conditions, massive fires have erupted. Because the soil is almost pure organic matter, it can smolder and burn for months, destroying the soil and seeds of the future generations. At the same time, the lack of fresh water allows salt water from the surrounding ocean to infiltrate the water table, making it unsuitable for human or plant consumption.

Now that these relationships are better understood, efforts have been proposed to prevent drying and to preserve the wildlife in the Everglades. These will require billions of dollars and years of time to accomplish. Perhaps the best lesson to be learned is that humans must proceed very carefully when changing what millions of years of natural processes have built.

1. **Connection to Chemistry:** Research the composition and chemistry of swamp gas. Propose ways in which it could be used by humans.

2. **Connection to History:** George Washington was one of the surveyors who laid out the plan to drain the Dismal Swamp. Where is the Dismal Swamp? Find out if the plan was carried out.

CAREER CONNECTION

Agronomists work in agricultural experimental stations, universities, and as teachers. Students can get additional information about this career from the U.S. Department of Agriculture, 14th Street and Independence Avenue SW, Washington, DC 20001.

Friendly Fires

Fire can be deadly, and it may come as a surprise to you that wildlife biologists sometimes start fires deliberately. Are these biologists literally playing with fire?

Most forest fires that reach the evening news are terrifying. Some, such as the huge lightning-triggered 1988 conflagration in Yellowstone National Park, create fire storms measuring more than 1000°C with tornado-like winds that incinerate everything in their path. Why would anyone deliberately start something that had such a devastating potential?

One reason is that controlled fires can actually be beneficial to a wild community, which needs periodic fires to maintain a healthy environment. If a wild area is protected from fire, the underbrush grows thick, and dead branches build up on the forest floor. This inhibits healthy new growth, and when a fire does occur, it is much larger and hotter than normal. However, if burning is controlled, the size and temperature can be held to levels that encourage recovery.

A fire triggers germination of many seeds, which starts the rebuilding process. For example, the lodgepole pine produces two kinds of cones. One type is like other pine cones and opens in the fall, releasing seeds. However, the other type opens only when it is heated. This ensures that the species will survive a fire. Other species survive by producing tough-coated seeds that can resist fire and germinate only when wet.

Why Not Set Friendly Fires?
Opponents of controlled burns point out that these fires sometimes grow uncontrollably and exceed the ability of humans to manage them. If the wind shifts or something unforeseen happens, there is little that humans can do to reestablish control. In the past, homes and businesses have been lost to controlled fires that got out of control. Opponents ask, Why burn trees that can provide jobs and lumber, when loggers could accomplish the same results? Opponents feel that humans have been given a responsibility to manage these resources, and anything less than our maximum effort to preserve and use them wisely is a breach of trust.

Prairie Fires Another area where fire is in the natural scheme of life is the prairie. If not burned regularly, woody plants and other invaders start to take over these fertile grasslands. Before it was settled by humans, the prairie was regularly ignited by lightning and other natural causes. Prairie grasses are protected from fire by their deep roots. When fires race across the flat grasslands, the tops of the grasses are burned along with everything else. However, deep in the rich turf, the roots survive—ready to burst forth in growth after the first rain. Other seed plants are not so well adapted. The fire destroys the mature plants and seeds alike, and it may take several decades before a tree can grow again. By that time, other fires may have destroyed any succeeding seed

plants that have begun to grow. Thus, the vast sea of grass that covered the Midwest prospered, in part, because of fire.

Understanding the Issue

1. Recently, the United States Park Service adopted plans that give managers great latitude in deciding whether to actively fight fires ignited by natural causes such as lightning. Unless they threaten human lives or property, many fires have been allowed to burn themselves out as part of a natural process. Discuss the advantages and disadvantages of this policy.

2. Do you agree with opponents of controlled fires when they say that loggers could accomplish the same results as a fire? Why or why not?

Readings

- Farney, Dennis. "The Tallgrass Prairie: Can It Be Saved?" *National Geographic,* January, 1980, pp. 37-61.
- Jeffery, David. "Yellowstone, The Great Fires of 1988." *National Geographic,* February, 1989, pp. 255-273.

Issues

Purpose
Students will learn that fire is one density-independent factor that affects ecosystems and speed of succession. The feature also points out that issues may be seen quite differently by different groups.

Background
Point out that the Yellowstone event was not a single fire, but a series of fires. The patchy occurrence of the fires is evident from satellite views of the park, as shown in the 1989 *National Geographic* article referenced on the student page. Students should not be given the impression that concern about fires was raised only with the Yellowstone fires of 1988. Management issues with regard to wildfires and human-caused fires have been raised for at least 50 years within the National Parks system.

Teaching Strategies
- Ask students if they have ever visited Yellowstone. Allow students to describe their visits. Ask other students if they think that Yellowstone National Park and other national parks should be managed for human use, wild habitat preservation, or some combination of the two.

Possible Answers
1. The advantages of the new plans are that natural habitats will be preserved and processes will be uninterrupted by humans. However, one disadvantage is that the parks may be unsightly just after a fire, and signs of fires may be apparent for years.
2. Some students will agree with logging interests, saying that humans know how to control the environment appropriately. Most students will disagree with the statement, saying that nature is the best manager of ecosystems.

Going Further
Have students research the effects of the Yellowstone fires since 1988. This event will be the subject of research for years to come as the area recovers from the effects of the fires. **L2**

CHAPTER 29

CHAPTER REVIEW

Summary

Summary statements can be used by students to review the major concepts of the chapter.

Language of Biology

Answers should go beyond defining the terms. Accept any reasonable answer that uses the term correctly and in the proper context.

Understanding Concepts

1. The meadow is undergoing succession and will probably become a temperate deciduous forest. The existing forest was probably once a meadow.
2. The soil will gradually fill in the lake, which will undergo succession to the type of climax community common in that area.
3. The diversity of both plant and animal species will increase with time; however, the diversity of plant species will increase more rapidly.
4. The climax community is complex and stable, characterized by efficient trapping and use of energy and recycling of nutrients.
5. Such an arrangement allows for maximum exposure to sunlight in the dense forest.
6. Early stages contribute to the formation of the soil layer. Life begins to abound on the surface of the soil, forming what will be the forest floor. Plants that are shade tolerant will compose the shrub layer, which will survive beneath the trees, the branches of which form the canopy layer.
7. As new layers form, microenvironments are created, resulting in differences in such factors as available light, temperature, and humidity.
8. Areas of greater moisture would allow mosses and ferns to flourish. Presence of shade would allow shade-tolerant plants to supplant species requiring more light. Fallen branches and leaves would make possible the invasion of worms, insects, and fungi.

840

Summary

During ecological succession, communities change over time. Succession may begin where no community has existed before or may follow destruction or alteration of a previously existing community.

In each stage of succession, the organisms alter the physical environment, making it more suitable for other organisms and less suitable for themselves. Succession ends with the development of a climax community characterized by stable population ·sizes, complex food webs, and efficient use of energy and materials.

Physical factors including temperature, rainfall, altitude, latitude, and topography interact to produce major regions of climate called biomes. Each type of biome is home to a similar group of communities.

Major world biomes include tundra, taiga, temperate forests, tropical rain forests, grasslands, and deserts. The ocean consists of several zones that are similar to but more closely interdependent than biomes. All the world's biomes and aquatic ecosystems interact. Together they form the total world of life—the biosphere.

Language of Biology

Write a sentence that shows your understanding of each of the following terms.

benthos	neritic zone
biome	oceanic zone
biosphere	permafrost
climax community	pioneer stage
desert	plankton
ecological succession	primary succession
geothermal energy	secondary succession
grassland	taiga
littoral zone	temperate forest
microenvironment	tropical rain forest
nekton	tundra

Understanding Concepts

1. A meadow exists next to a temperate deciduous forest. Is the meadow undergoing succession? Explain.
2. The banks around a small lake are sloped, and soil slowly but constantly runs off into the lake. What effect will such runoff have on the lake? Explain.
3. Construct a graph in which the x-axis represents time and the y-axis represents number of species. Use a dotted line to represent plant species and a solid line to represent animal species present during the course of a succession.
4. Why is a climax community not likely to alter the physical environment in such a way as to lead to further succession?
5. Branches of tropical rain forest trees are arranged in a crown near their very tops. Why?
6. Explain how stages of succession would result in the formation of layers of vegetation in a temperate deciduous forest.
7. In what ways does a pattern of layers of vegetation, as it is established, modify the environment?
8. Predict how modification due to the formation of layers of vegetation may influence the kinds of organisms that appear later in the succession.
9. What factor limits life on the floor of a tropical rain forest and in deep ocean waters? How is life in those two places similar? Why?
10. Cite an example that shows how different ocean zones are interdependent.

840 CHAPTER 29 ORIGIN AND DISTRIBUTION OF COMMUNITIES

---

9. Both forest floor and deep ocean waters are limited by availability of light. Both places are characterized by a much lesser diversity of life than is found in layers closer to light.
10. Availability of nutrients in the neritic zone depends upon activity of decomposers on the ocean bottom.

Applying Concepts

11. The rotting railroad ties enrich the soil.
12. A variety of grasses and shrubs could begin to take root in the soil, and animals such as worms and arthropods could live within it.
13. The ocean could be considered to be composed of layers, much like a forest. There is a lighted zone and an unlighted zone. There is also the neritic zone and the oceanic zone.

Applying Concepts

11. How would the rotting of railroad ties on abandoned tracks modify the environment?
12. What might be the results of the modification of the environment caused by the rotting of the railroad ties?
13. Would you say that there is a pattern of layers in an ocean? Explain.
14. Think about the general pattern of biome types that exists from the equator to the poles. Do you think that you would see a similar pattern if you were to climb from the base to the top of a very high mountain? Explain.
15. If you were in the commercial fishing business, would you fish in coastal regions or far out in an ocean? Why?
16. Suppose you are analyzing two soil samples, one from a temperate deciduous forest and one from a tropical rain forest. Which sample would you expect to have a greater concentration of organic material? Why?
17. Compare the length of plant life cycles in a tundra or desert and in a tropical rain forest. How is the difference related to climate?
18. How would you expect differences in plant species to affect differences in bird species during a succession?
19. **Considering the Environment:** Why is sphagnum moss sold in garden supply stores as a soil conditioner?
20. **Issues:** What would most likely be the climax community of a prairie if fires did not occur regularly? Explain your reasoning.

Lab Interpretation

21. **Investigation:** Examine the graph at the top of the next column. What conditions are needed for radish seed germination?

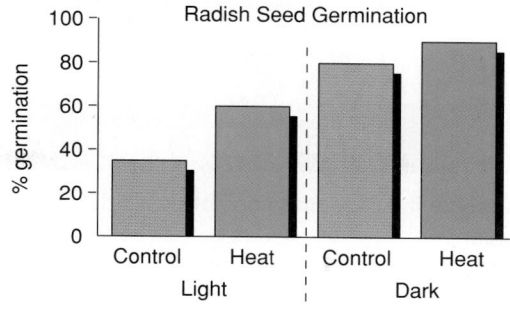

22. **Minilab 1:** The following graph represents percentages of organic matter in four soil samples. Which sample would be best for plant growth? Explain why.

23. **Minilab 2:** Assume that you are a scientist studying the effects of acid rain in the United States. You want to determine its effects on temperate deciduous forests. To what part of the country would you travel to study these forests?

Connecting Ideas

24. Could a succession involve evolution of new species? Hint: Think about the Galapagos Islands. Was succession on the Galapagos Islands primary or secondary?
25. In what ways are the organelles in a cell or the organs in a system like the biomes of the biosphere? Explain.

14. A similar pattern would exist as a result of changes in temperature and rainfall associated with differences in altitude.
15. Many more fish would be found in coastal waters. Closer to shore, the diversity of life is much greater, supporting more complex food webs. More food for fish means more fish.
16. There would be more organic matter in the soil of the temperate deciduous forest. The constant growth and great diversity of life in the tropical rain forest does not allow for much accumulation of nutrients in the soil.
17. Plant life cycles in the tundra or desert must be completed much more rapidly than in a tropical rain forest. Desert plants must take advantage of water when it is available, and many tundra plants can only survive when permafrost thaws.
18. Birds depend upon plants for food as well as for nesting sites. As the diversity of plant species increases, so does that of bird species.
19. Sphagnum moss absorbs and holds water. It is especially useful for conditioning sandy soils.
20. Woody plants would readily invade the prairie. If rainfall were sufficient, a grassland might be replaced by a forest.

Lab Interpretation

21. Heat and darkness are needed.
22. Sample B. The organic matter would hold moisture in the soil where it would be available to growing plants.
23. Eastern states and Oregon, Washington, and California

Connecting Ideas

24. **Evolution:** Speciation could occur as succession proceeds. The Galapagos Islands are volcanic in origin; thus, succession was primary. Many forms of life reaching the islands gave rise to new species, such as Darwin's finches.

25. **Systems and Interactions:** Organelles in a cell interact to maintain the life of the cell, and organs interact to carry out the functions of the system of which they are a part. The many biomes of the biosphere also interact as the events in one biome affect events in another.

ORGANIZER
CHAPTER 30

SECTION	OBJECTIVES	TEXT LABS/FEATURES
30.1 The Pesticide Dilemma (2 days)	**Analyze** the pros and cons of pesticide use. **Discuss** methods that can be used to control pests while also safeguarding the environment.	
30.2 Pollution of Air and Water (2 days)	**Discuss** the effects of various pollutants that contaminate the air. **Analyze** the cause and consequences of destruction of the ozone layer. **Explain** the difficulties involved in determining the extent of the greenhouse effect and finding solutions to the problem of global warming. **Describe** the sources and effects of pollutants entering ground and surface waters.	**Minilab 1:** Why are oil spills lethal to birds? p. 855 **Investigation:** Effects of Pollutants on Seed Germination and Plant Growth, p. 856 **Global Connection:** Michiko Ishimure, p. 861 **Minilab 2:** How acid is rain? p. 862
30.3 Conservation of Resources (2 days)	**Relate** availability of food resources to the resource of soil. **Analyze** the need for developing non-fossil fuels. **Discuss** the importance of preserving forests and wildlife.	**Thinking Lab:** How much and what do we throw away each day? p. 868
BIOLOGY, TECHNOLOGY, AND SOCIETY		**Considering the Environment:** New Uses for Waste Material, p. 870 **Career Connection:** Chemical engineer, p. 870

LAB MATERIALS

INVESTIGATION	MINILAB	ALTERNATE LAB
page 856 bean plants ruler clay sand labels test tubes light bank test-tube rack milk carton vermiculite paper towels chemicals: peat pots insecticides plastic cups oil plastic bags, laundry detergent self-sealing fertilizer	**page 855** balance dish, shallow feathers motor oil (or vegetable oil) paper towels **page 862** bottles distilled water funnel labels pH paper color chart pH paper strips rain (or snow) samples	**page 848** beakers, 100-mL *Daphnia* droppers goggles magnifiers pesticides (rotene, pyrethrum) plastic gloves

TEACHER CLASSROOM RESOURCES	OTHER RESOURCES
Study Guide, pp. 175-176 ***PLL:** *Effects of a Pollutant on Protozoa Populations,* p. 235	***STVS:** *Soldier Bug,* Ecology (Disc 6, Side 1)
Study Guide, pp. 177-178 **Concept Mapping,** p. 30 ****ILS:** *Thermal Pollution,* p. 317 ****ILS:** *Acid Rain,* p. 321	***STVS:** *Modeling Pollutants,* Ecology (Disc 6, Side 2) **Color Transparency 59:** *Acid Precipitation*
Study Guide, pp. 179-180 **Critical Thinking/Problem Solving:** *Science and Language Arts: A Wildlife Preserve,* p. 30 **Exploring Environmental Issues:** *Using Land Wisely,* p. 25; *Sort It Out with Recycling,* p. 27	
Assessment Materials **Chapter Assessment,** pp. 117-120 **Performance Assessment in Biology,** p. 60 **Alternate Assessment in the Science Classroom** **Computer Test Bank**	**Spanish Resources** **Cooperative Learning Resource Guide** **Videodisc Correlations** (to Optical Data's and Videodiscovery's videodiscs)

* Probing Levels of Life
** Investigating Living Systems

* Science Technology Videodisc Series

Key to Teaching Strategies

The following designations will help you decide which activities in the teacher margin are appropriate for your students.

L1 Level 1 activities should be within the ability range of all students.

L2 Level 2 activities should be within the ability range of the average to above-average student.

L3 Level 3 activities are designed for the ability range of above-average students.

LEP LEP activities are appropriate for Limited English Proficiency students.

COOP LEARN Cooperative Learning activities are designed for small group work.

ADDITIONAL RESOURCES

Infinite Voyage *Secrets from a Frozen World*
Antarctica can be seen as an early warning system of global change and as a living laboratory to test the impact of a changing environment. Nature, in this video, is a study of conflict and contrast.

Audiovisual
Putting Aside Pesticides, video, Films for the Humanities and Sciences.
The Endangered Earth, video, Films for the Humanities and Sciences.

Software
Air Pollution, Apple II/IBM, EME.
Hothouse Planet, Apple II/IBM, EME.

HUMANS AND THE ENVIRONMENT

Chapter Overview

Students begin the chapter by learning that pollution is a function of modern agricultural and technological techniques. They examine the need for and use of pesticides and the harmful consequences of such use, and come to appreciate the dilemma between economic realities and the need to protect the environment. They learn how integrated pest management may be the best means of dealing with that dilemma.

Students next study causes and consequences of and possible solutions to problems associated with air pollution, including destruction of the ozone layer and the many effects of acid precipitation. As they examine the question of global warming, students appreciate the idea that science cannot answer all questions, and that scientists may interpret data in different ways. Students also compare pollution problems in surface waters, the oceans, and groundwater.

Students complete the chapter with a study of resources and the need to conserve them—food, soil, fuels, wildlife, and forests. They come to understand that rectifying past mistakes and preventing new problems are possible if humans use good judgment in weighing economic realities against the possible adverse effects of their activities on the environment.

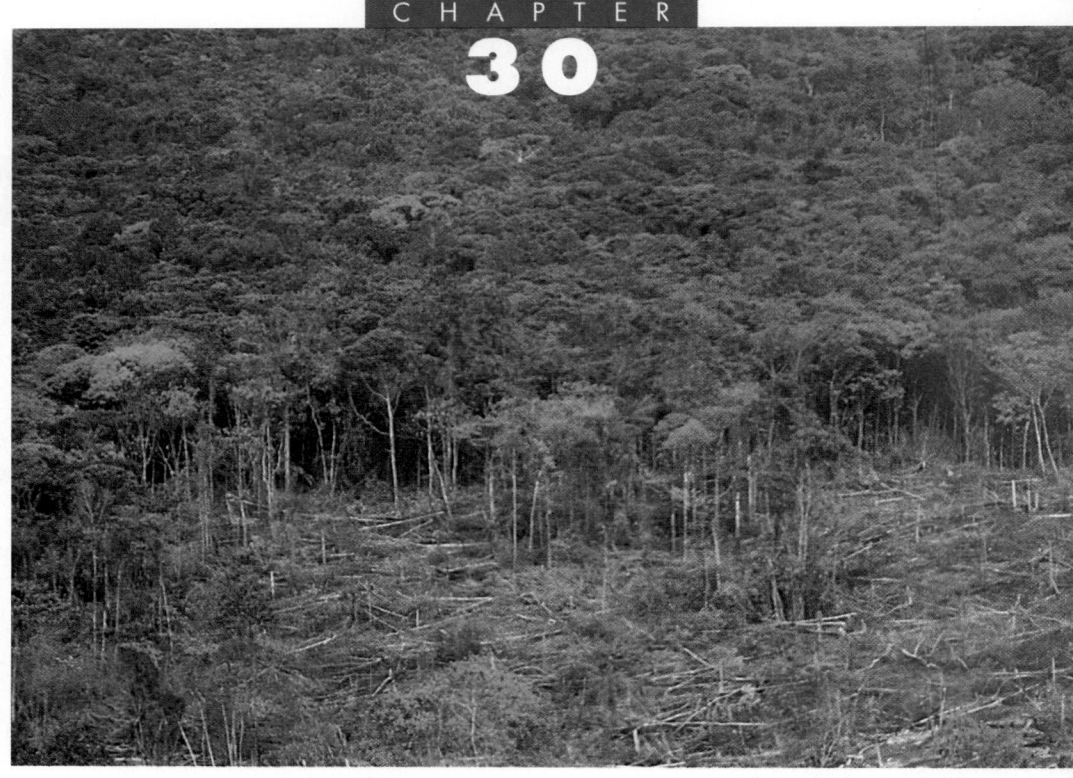

HUMANS AND THE ENVIRONMENT

RAIN FALLS in this tropical forest almost every day. The tallest trees and vines grow hundreds of feet above the ground and are the first to catch the rain. They bend and sway under the powerful force of torrential downpours. Water runs off one leaf onto another, then another, then along a mossy tree branch. Now flowing gently, the rainwater continues its downward course, dripping softly onto ferns and other delicate undergrowth. Finally, the water soaks into the soil of the forest floor.

What would happen if those torrential rains fell, not on the lush growth of a forest, but on bare ground? When forest, grassland, or other plant cover is destroyed, the soil is left exposed to the ravages of rain and wind. Precious topsoil can be washed or blown away, making it difficult for plants to take root. The forces of erosion can gouge out barren gullies where healthy plant life once thrived. In this chapter, you will learn how the activities of humans can change the environment. You will find out how pesticides have been both helpful and harmful. You will learn the causes of several environmental problems humans face today, including acid rain, global warming, and ozone depletion. And you will discover how conservation of Earth's forests and other natural resources can help us overcome these problems.

842

KEY TERMS

acid precipitation
autocidal control
biological control
biological magnification
chloroflurocarbon (CFC)
crop rotation

cultural control
erosion
greenhouse effect
integrated pest management
nonbiodegradable
nonrenewable resource

pesticide
pollution
renewable resource
soil depletion

What do you think are the biggest environmental problems facing the human population today? What kinds of actions can you and your classmates take to help reduce pollution in your community?

Chapter Preview

843

ASSESSMENT PLANNER

Introducing the Chapter

Refer students to the photograph on page 842. A functioning ecosystem, such as a tropical rain forest, supports a great diversity of life and is characterized by complex interactions among those many life forms. While natural disasters or long-term changes can have an effect on an ecosystem, human activities can result in far more severe consequences and do so much more quickly. Point out that not all human activities result in complete removal of ecosystems, but that many are nevertheless harmful to the environment. Ask students to provide examples. They should be able to think of various pollutants as well as ways in which humans have overexploited resources.

Theme Development

The theme of systems and interactions is evident throughout the chapter as students learn of the kinds of "chain reactions" that can result from human activities. They see, for example, how pesticides can affect many different organisms in an ecosystem through the process of biological magnification and how acid precipitation can have a rippling effect on the organisms. The theme of patterns of change is also exemplified in many ways, such as the long-term changes in composition of ecosystems related to the events mentioned above and in the discussion of the possible effects of global warming.

Tying to Previous Knowledge

As you teach this chapter, relate examples of humans' effects on the environment to each of these topics, pointing out that humans have the ability to affect populations, communities, ecosystems, biomes and the entire biosphere in an adverse way. Humans also have the ability to solve problems they have caused and to prevent future ones from developing.

Prepare

Key Concepts

Students will study the dilemma of pesticide use in homes and in agriculture. Benefits and problems will be presented as well as alternatives to pesticide use.

Key Terms

pollution, pesticide, nonbiodegradable, biological magnification, cultural control, biological control, autocidal control, integrated pest management

Materials

1 Focus

Objectives

The objectives are listed on the student page. Remind students to preview these objectives as a guide to this numbered section.

Discussion

Display two of each of the following fresh fruits or vegetables or other local fruits and vegetables: tomato, orange, melon, green beans, spinach, turnips, and apples. One of each fruit should not be a perfect specimen but should show signs of insect damage. Ask students to pick which of the two fruits or vegetables they would buy. Ask them why. Bring out the idea that when consumers demand perfect fruits and vegetables, farmers might use more chemical pesticides. In fact, the less-perfect fruit may be better to consume because it may have had less pesticide contact. **LEP**

Objectives

Analyze the pros and cons of pesticide use.

Discuss methods that can be used to control pests while also safeguarding the environment.

30.1 The Pesticide Dilemma

Imagine taking a long car trip. Perhaps you're traveling from New York to Los Angeles, or from Chicago to Dallas. Your journey begins downtown, where streets and freeways are crowded with cars, trucks, and buses, and high-rise office buildings tower overhead. As you reach the outskirts of the city, you pass warehouses, factories, railroad yards, and finally, the airport. Next, you travel past row after row of suburban houses and lawns. Then you begin to see herds of dairy and beef cattle. Fields of wheat or corn, and rows of tomatoes, squash, and melons stretch out into the distance. Farther on, you see streams, meadows, a lake, and perhaps some distant mountain peaks.

Sources of Pollution

Without modern advances in technology, this trip wouldn't be possible. The car itself, the gasoline that fuels it, and the highways it travels on are all products of technology. So are factories, power plants, trains, and planes. Today's food crops are grown by agricultural techniques—including the use of pesticides, fertilizers, and farm machinery—that help with almost every task from plowing the ground and planting the seed to harvesting the crop. Technology also provides us with television, artificial lighting, computers, telephones, and many other items we consider indispensable. But are we paying an unexpectedly high price for our modern conveniences?

Figure 30-1 **Technology has provided us with many modern conveniences. Most of them come with a high environmental cost.**

While advances in agriculture and industry have been responsible for enriching and prolonging the lives of humans, they have also created undesirable by-products. The exhaust from your car or the smoke from a city factory may have an effect on the lake you've traveled hundreds of miles to see. The pesticides that protect a corn crop from insect damage also affect the health of birds, fish, and humans that consume the corn. Automobile exhaust, factory emissions, and pesticides are examples of materials that can cause **pollution,** which is the contamination of air, water, or soil by materials released into the environment by the ever-increasing numbers of humans and their activities.

844 HUMANS AND THE ENVIRONMENT

MEETING INDIVIDUAL NEEDS

Ask gifted students to accompany, for a day, a commercial pesticide applicator who is applying pesticides in residential homes. It would be wise to select a national chain that is required to follow stringent regulations for applicator safety. Make sure you arrange with the company for students to wear protective garments and respirators if necessary. Ask them to take photos of their experience and present them in the form of slides or a photo essay for the rest of the class. **L3**

Pest Control and Pollution

Have you ever put a flea collar on a cat or dog, put out poisoned bait for ants or cockroaches, or watched a gardener spray weed killer on a patch of crabgrass? These are examples of pesticide use. A **pesticide** is a chemical poison that is used to kill an unwanted organism. There are many organisms that humans consider pests, including termites that destroy wood, moths that eat woolen fabrics, and aphids that can kill houseplants.

Agricultural Pests   In addition to pests that directly affect humans in and around the home, there are many pests that cause severe damage to agricultural crops, livestock, and forests. For example, weeds compete with and crowd out cultivated plants, causing nearly ten percent of each year's crop losses. Types of fungi known as "rusts" reduce the yield of wheat and other grain crops by millions of bushels each year.

Many agricultural pests were brought to North America from other parts of the world. Among these are the European corn borer, a moth larva that attacks ears of corn and limits the corn growing season in some parts of the country. Another example is the Mediterranean fruit fly, sometimes called the medfly. The larvae of this tiny fly can so severely damage citrus, apple, and other fruit crops that infested fruit cannot be shipped to market for fear the pest will be carried to other regions.

Altering Natural Ecosystems   A field of corn can tolerate a few corn borers without suffering much damage. And a few medflies probably wouldn't destroy all the apples in an orchard. These organisms become pests when their populations grow so large that they cause severe damage and significantly reduce crop yields.

Humans have actually contributed to pest problems by altering natural ecosystems. For example, in nature, several plant species usually grow together. One plant may serve as host to an organism that preys on the pest of a neighboring plant. By planting large areas of land with a single food crop, humans reduce this natural diversity and disturb the relationships among predators and prey, beneficial and pest organisms. As a result, single-crop planting can give pests an opportunity to thrive because fewer of their natural enemies are present.

Humans have also contributed to changes in natural ecosystems by transporting organisms from one part of the world to another. For example, medflies were probably originally introduced into the continental U.S. in fruit smuggled from Hawaii. Since medflies had no natural predators here, their numbers grew unchecked, their population density increased, and they became a pest. Many other pests, including the Japanese beetle and the gypsy moth, have been introduced into the U.S. from other parts of the world.

Figure 30-2   Medfly larvae can damage crops of fruit severely. The pesticide malathion was used widely in California to control the medfly.

30.1 THE PESTICIDE DILEMMA ❧ **845**

HISTORY CONNECTION

History of Pesticide Use: Pesticides have been used over the course of centuries. In the 15th century, inorganic compounds made from toxic metals were used on crop plants as pesticides. In use were arsenic, lead, and mercury. These chemicals were used until the late 1920s when poisonings and fatalities reached high enough numbers to prompt a search for less toxic materials.

In the mid 1800s, two natural pesticides were discovered: rotenone and pyrethrum. Rotenone was extracted from the root of the derris plant and other tropical legumes. Pyrethrum was a powder that resulted from grinding the heads of chrysanthemum flowers. Other natural insecticides that were popular were red pepper for ant control, and garlic oil and lemon oil for fleas, mosquito larvae, houseflies, and other insects.

After 1945, chemists developed many synthetic organic chemicals for use as pesticides. In the United States today, there are about 55 000 pesticide products made from about 600 biologically active ingredients. Of the pesticides in use currently, 80 percent are used by agriculture and 20 percent are applied to lawns, gardens, parks, golf courses, and cemeteries. Of the pesticides used by farmers, about 70 percent are herbicides, 20 percent insecticides, and about 10 percent fungicides. In the United States, the average homeowner uses about five times more pesticide per unit of land than do farmers. Overall, the amount of pesticides used in this country has tripled since 1964 and comes to about 2 kg per person per year.

STUDENT JOURNAL

Ask students to investigate the crops grown nearby and the kinds of pest control used on these crops. Ask them to make a table in their journals indicating the crop, the type of pest control commonly used, and improvements that might be undertaken. **L1**

PROGRAM RESOURCES

Teacher Classroom Resources
Study Guide, pp. 175-176   **L1**
Probing Levels of Life, Lab 84, p. 235   **L2**

SECTION 30.1

Bioethics

Herbicide-resistant Crops:
The world's largest chemical companies are producing genetically engineered crop plants that are herbicide resistant. Some scientists think that herbicides can be liberally applied to cause harvests to be bigger. This will mean that there will be more food for more people, more fiber from cotton plants, and more cattle feed. Others say that in developing countries, there could be serious problems with herbicide-tolerant crops because wild forms of rice, wheat, soybeans, and potatoes grow adjacent to crop fields. Scientists think that herbicide-tolerant crops might cross-pollinate with their wild cousins that are really weeds. Herbicide tolerance would then be passed to weeds, an intolerable thought for farmers.

Others are opposed to herbicide-resistant crops because they say it will encourage farmers to continue to use chemical herbicides rather than switching to less environmentally threatening means of control. Producing these types of resistant crops benefits the chemical companies because these crops will encourage farmers to keep buying their herbicides.

Figure 30-3 Although pesticides are useful in eliminating pests from crops and allowing us to purchase mold-free and worm-free fruit, they do not come without problems. In some instances, pesticides destroy not only the target pest but another whole population. Dragonflies are natural predators of aphids. Spraying an area with a pesticide to kill aphids may kill all dragonflies, while some aphids may survive. Without the natural predator, the aphid population would grow even larger than it was originally.

The Benefits of Pesticides Chemical pesticides have made it possible for humans to successfully replace natural ecosystems with farmland, lawns, golf courses, and gardens. Pesticides have enabled farmers to produce larger quantities of food and have helped reduce the incidence of insect-borne diseases such as malaria, yellow fever, and typhus by reducing the populations of the disease-carrying insects. Because pesticides are effective, easily obtainable, and relatively inexpensive, they have become convenient weapons for farmers, homeowners, and public health workers all over the world. Today, about 2.3 million metric tons of synthetic pesticides are used worldwide each year.

Problems with Pesticides

If pesticides killed only the pests for which they were intended, there would be few problems with their use. Unfortunately, that is rarely the case. When a pesticide is sprayed on a crop, it is estimated that only ten percent, or even less, of the chemical spray actually comes into contact with the insect pests that are being targeted. The remaining 90 percent is taken up by other, often harmless, organisms, as well as soil and water.

Pesticides often destroy not only pest organisms, but also their natural predators. Predators are fewer in number than their prey, and it is possible for a pesticide to completely destroy the predator population. If any pests survive and reproduce, or if they are reintroduced from another area, there may no longer be any natural predators to keep their numbers in check. As a result, the pest problem can become worse than it was originally. Other beneficial organisms, such as honeybees and other insects that help pollinate flowering plants, may also be destroyed by pesticide applications. Entire ecosystems are affected by pesticide use. Sometimes these effects can spread over great distances and last for many years.

DDT In 1939, a chemical called DDT was found to be extremely effective in controlling insect pests. It quickly gained popularity and was used all over the world to control many kinds of insects from malaria mosquitoes and corn borers to fleas and houseflies. However, DDT has some very serious side effects that were not immediately evident. By 1972, the severity of these side effects had become so alarming that the use of DDT was banned in the U.S. Even though DDT is banned in the U.S., it is still used in large quantities around the world. It is very inexpensive to manufacture, and more DDT than ever before is being sold—mostly to developing countries.

Biological Resistance During the 1940s, DDT was widely used to kill houseflies. However, some flies were genetically resistant to the chemical. These resistant flies survived and reproduced, passing their DDT-resistant genes on to their offspring. As a result of natural selection, a resistant strain of houseflies rapidly evolved.

DDT is not the only pesticide to which insect pests have developed resistance. There are several species of mosquitoes that transmit malaria; most of these have become resistant to a number of pesticides, including

846 HUMANS AND THE ENVIRONMENT

PROJECT

Role Play: Ask students to role play members of a community town meeting deciding on whether to spray the nearby marsh for mosquitoes in the summer. Prepare role cards and statements for a: farmer, homeowner near marsh, mother with children, mayor, biologist, pest control company representative, owner of a motel near marsh, and biology student. **L1** **COOP LEARN**

PORTFOLIO

Ask students to write in their portfolios a public service announcement that explains to the community why the town voted in favor of or against spraying for mosquitoes. **L1**

DDT. This resistance was responsible for a great increase in the number of cases of malaria during the 1970s and 1980s. It is estimated that a total of 500 insect species around the world have become resistant to some of the pesticides that are currently in use. Twenty insect species are thought to be resistant to all currently used pesticides.

This trend toward development of pesticide resistance also has been observed among non-insect pests including rodents, fungi, and weeds. As organisms develop resistance to pesticide chemicals, it becomes necessary to apply the chemicals in stronger concentrations or spend time and money developing more effective, and sometimes more poisonous, compounds.

Figure 30-4 One of the most effective and toxic pesticides ever used to kill insects was DDT. It was developed in the 1940s and used extensively to kill disease-carrying mosquitoes, as well as household pests and insects that destroyed crops. DDT was even used on mattresses in Army barracks to fight bed bugs. Unfortunately, DDT affected many organisms besides pests, disrupting entire ecosystems.

Biological Magnification   Another problem with DDT is that it remains toxic long after it has been released into the environment. A chemical or other substance that cannot be broken down or degraded into harmless, inactive compounds by the metabolism of living organisms is **nonbiodegradable.** A number of nonbiodegradable pesticides that are chemically related to DDT have been developed, including DDD, DDE, dieldrin, and chlordane. DDT breaks down into DDD or DDE in the environment. DDT and its chemical relatives are insoluble in water but can be dissolved in fats and oils. Molecules of these substances remain on plants or in the soil for long periods because they are not easily washed away. Organisms that absorb molecules of DDT, or consume plants or soil contaminated with it, cannot break down the chemical in their bodies. Instead, it is stored in their fatty tissue.

Concept Development

The opposition to pesticide use cites many examples of problems created by use of pesticides. Estimates show that about 3 million people are poisoned by pesticides each year, and about 5000 to 20 000 die. Most are farmers in developing countries where educational levels are low, and regulations, warnings, and controls are lax or do not exist at all. In the United States, 45 000 cases of pesticide poisoning occur each year, mostly due to unsafe storage and use of chemicals. About 10 000 Americans including pesticide applicators, manufacturing plant workers, crop pickers, and home gardeners get cancer from handling pesticides. The Food and Drug Administration reports that 3 percent of supermarket food has levels above the legal limit for pesticides. Community spraying programs are used to control mosquitoes or other pests, and pesticide-sprayed lawns, parks, golf courses, forests, and roadsides have been shown to expose people to even higher levels of pesticides than that in foods.

30.1 THE PESTICIDE DILEMMA **847**

SECTION 30.1

Activity

Divide the class into groups. Make a set of cards for each group with the following information on each card.

A. In the summer of 1940, a dairy farmer notices that the barn is full of flies. Pesticide applicators are hired to spray DDT. The applicators notice that after they spray, 1000 flies die and 10 remain. What percentage of the flies were killed? Explain why most flies die and a few live.

B. The applicators come back a month later and notice that there are fewer flies than before. They spray again and find 500 flies dead and 20 remaining. What percentage of the flies were killed? Explain why more flies are surviving.

C. The applicators come back a month later and find that there seem to be even more flies than before the spraying. They spray again. Predict what might happen and justify your prediction.

Have the cards in piles A, B, and C on your desk. Ask one person in each group to come up and get card A. The group should read it and answer the questions. When they return it to you, they may pick up card B, read it, and answer the questions. They should do the same with all the cards in sequence. In this way, they cannot look ahead to figure out what might be happening next. **L1** **LEP** **COOP LEARN**

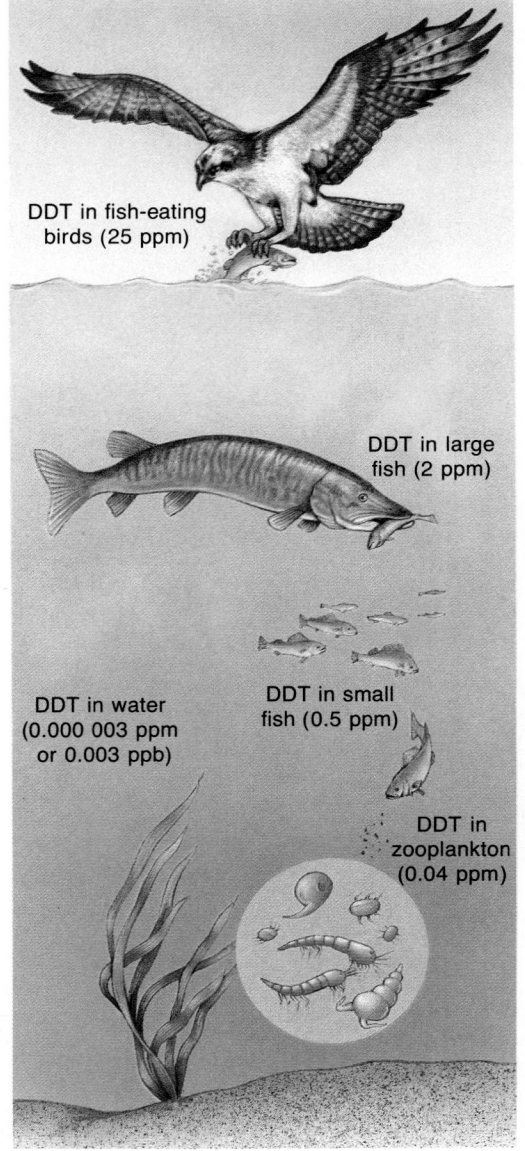

DDT in fish-eating birds (25 ppm)

DDT in large fish (2 ppm)

DDT in water (0.000 003 ppm or 0.003 ppb)

DDT in small fish (0.5 ppm)

DDT in zooplankton (0.04 ppm)

Figure 30-5 As top-level carnivores, ospreys can accumulate large concentrations of DDT in their fatty tissues. DDT concentration is measured in parts per million (ppm) or parts per billion (ppb).

Since DDT isn't metabolized, it is passed along the food chain from one animal to another. Imagine a stream that runs through acre after acre of farmland or forest. DDT is sprayed to control insect pests that are reducing farm yields or damaging valuable timber. Some of the DDT molecules are ingested by the pests, and these insects die. But the DDT in their dead bodies remains toxic. The remainder of the DDT may kill beneficial insects or adhere to leaves or particles of soil. As the dead insects decay, the DDT contained in their bodies is also added to the soil.

With each rainfall, some of these soil particles are washed into the stream. Small amounts of DDT are absorbed or ingested by the organisms that serve as food for fish living in the stream. As time goes by, DDT builds up in the fatty tissues of the fish. Now imagine an osprey or other fish-eating predator that gets most of its food from this stream. It will consume many DDT-contaminated fish over time. This organism will build up a higher and higher concentration of DDT in its fatty tissues. You can see how the concentration of DDT increases as it passes higher up the food chain—the osprey has a much greater concentration of DDT in its fatty tissues than any single fish. This increasing concentration of nonbiodegradable chemicals along a food chain is called **biological magnification.**

In small doses, DDT is not lethal to birds and other animals. But its gradual buildup in the fatty tissues of an animal eventually affects the animal's health. One of the effects of biological magnification of DDT, and one of the discoveries that led to its ban in the U.S., was the thinning of eggshells in birds. Top carnivores—including ospreys, falcons, eagles, and pelicans—with high levels of DDT in their bodies often could not reproduce successfully. Many of these birds produced eggs with shells so thin that they broke long before the embryo had a chance to develop into a hatchling. The populations of these birds decreased so sharply that many biologists feared they would become extinct.

In a study done in 1984, 12 years after DDT had been replaced in this country with other types of pesticides, DDT was still the most common pesticide residue found on fruits and vegetables. Even though it has been banned in the U.S. for more than 20 years, DDT is still being used for pest control in countries that supply the United States with produce.

848 HUMANS AND THE ENVIRONMENT

ALTERNATE LAB: Toxicology Testing of *Daphnia*

Purpose

Students will compare the effects of different dilutions of pesticides on *Daphnia*.

Materials

1%, 5%, 10%, 20% solutions of 2 pesticides such as rotenone or pyrethrum, plastic gloves, 100 mL beakers (10), *Daphnia*, droppers, magnifiers (optional), safety goggles
For solution preparation, refer to p. 27T.

Procedure

Give the following directions to students.
1. Mark five beakers with percent of dilution and control for each pesticide.
2. **Safety Precaution:** Be sure to wear gloves and safety goggles when handling pesticide solutions.
3. Make a hypothesis about what will happen to *Daphnia* in the solutions.
4. With a dropper, add one *Daphnia* to each beaker. Be careful not to touch the

pesticide solutions with the dropper.
5. Begin timing as soon as you have added the *Daphnia* to the solution. Note in a table how long it takes for the *Daphnia* to stop moving.
6. Note of other behaviors you observe.
7. After 15 minutes, dispose of your *Daphnia* in solution as your teacher directs. Wash your beakers well with soapy water, and rinse.
8. Make a bar graph of your data.

Biodegradable Pesticides Another group of pesticides that, unlike DDT, are water soluble and break down quickly, have also been developed. These pesticides—which include parathion, malathion, and phosdrin—have taken the place of DDT and other fat-soluble pesticides and are presently in use. Since they are biodegradable, they do not spread from one animal to another through the food chain. Although these pesticides do not persist in the environment like DDT, their use still poses pollution problems. For example, since they are water soluble, they more easily contaminate water supplies. Also, these pesticides are actually more toxic than DDT, and are highly poisonous not only to insects but also to vertebrates, including humans. And, like DDT, they kill both pests and their predators, and so disturb natural controls of pest populations. Because they break down so quickly, they are applied frequently. As a result, they are almost always present and, in that sense, are similar to DDT and other pesticides that break down slowly.

Alternatives to Pesticides

Pesticides are not the only answer to pest control problems. Since natural population controls already exist in nature, it makes sense to try to take advantage of them. Some alternative solutions to pest problems involve using natural predators or a pest's own biochemical characteristics to control its population. Other alternatives called **cultural controls** involve devising growing methods that discourage pest growth, or breeding plants that are resistant to pests.

These alternatives are not foolproof—they don't always work quickly enough to keep a pest population from severely damaging a crop. Sometimes pesticides are needed. But if alternative pest control methods are implemented before a pest population gets completely out of hand, they can help reduce the need for pesticides.

Biological Control Natural predators of agricultural pests include insects, spiders, frogs, and birds. Preserving the natural predators living in an infested area, or introducing predators from another area to help keep a pest population in check, is called **biological control.** The first use of this type of pest control took place in 1888. An insect called the cottony cushion scale had become a severe pest in the citrus groves of California. Scale insects exude a sticky, sweet, honeydew material that encourages mold growth, which destroys the fruit. The Australian ladybird beetle, a predator of scale insects, was introduced to control the pest. The beetle saved the citrus industry.

Introducing predators from other parts of the world has proven to be a useful method of pest control. Can you think of some precautions that should be taken before a "foreign" insect is introduced into an ecosystem?

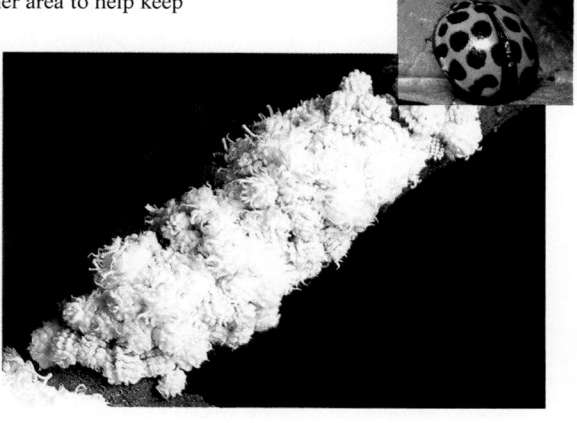

Figure 30-6 The Australian ladybird beetle was introduced to control the cottony cushion scale that was causing great damage to the citrus groves of California.

30.1 THE PESTICIDE DILEMMA 🐞 **849**

SECTION 30.1

Teacher FYI

Another example of biological control involves parasitic wasps that prey on gypsy moth caterpillars. Serious infestations of the leaf-devouring larvae of the gypsy moth are responsible for destroying millions of acres of valuable timber and forest trees in the U.S. every year. Two species of parasitic wasps have been imported from India to help control this pest. The adult wasp lays its eggs in the body of the caterpillar. Within two to three weeks, the eggs hatch and the wasp larvae consume their caterpillar host.

Figure Caption Question

Page 850: *What other factors must be taken into consideration for this type of control to be successful?* The size of the area, the number of fertile mates that may be in the area, the size of the insect population

3 Assess

Check for Understanding

Tell students that they are the new managers of a large farm in Iowa. The farm has always produced large amounts of corn as the primary crop. Tell them that the county government is requiring that all farms submit for approval an integrated pest management program. Ask students to prepare the basics of a report for submission to the county. **L1** **COOP LEARN**

Analysis
Ask students to answer the following questions.
1. In which cups do the *Daphnia* move for the longest time? Explain. *1 percent solutions, less toxic to* Daphnia
2. In which cups do *Daphnia* move for the least time? Explain. *20 percent solutions, more toxic to* Daphnia
3. Is there a difference between the two pesticides and their effects on *Daphnia*? Speculate about the reasons for the difference or lack of difference. *They are about the same. Both pesticides have the same toxicity.*
4. How do the control *Daphnia* behave differently from the experimental group? Speculate about why this happens. *The control stays nearer to the top of the beaker and moves with faster swimming motions, while the experimental* Daphnia *move to the bottom of* the water and do not display as active swimming motions.
5. Did your results support your hypothesis? *Answers will vary.*

✔ **Assessment**
Knowledge: Design an experiment in which you test the toxicity of a new pesticide. Make sure you plan to gather quantitative data and use a control. **L2**

SECTION 30.1

Reteach

Tell students to assume that DDT is still legal. Ask them to write a petition to the state government to change the laws. They should explain the evidence that shows that DDT should not be used and what alternatives should be promoted.

Extension

Ask students to do library research on the studies of declines in fish-eating birds such as ospreys, cormorants, eastern and California brown pelicans, and bald eagles. **L2**

✔ Assessment

Portfolio: Ask students to design the ideal pesticide. They do not need to pick specific chemicals, but assume that there are combinations of chemicals that would have specific effects and not have other effects. Tell students that they should be creative but use good science. Have them include their descriptions in their portfolios. **L3**

4 Close

Discussion

Ask students to bring in a list of the pesticides they have in their homes. Ask them to make three columns on the chalkboard: one listing the pesticides, another listing the use of the pesticide, and the third column listing an alternative.

Figure 30-7 The release of sterile males into an area can help control the numbers of a pest population. When a sterile male mates with a female, no offspring will be produced. What other factors must be taken into consideration for this type of control to be successful?

Autocidal Control In another type of alternative pest control, called **autocidal control,** the insect actually contributes to its own population control. One type of autocidal control involves sterilizing males of a pest species and introducing them into the infested area. Males of the pest species are raised in the laboratory, where they are exposed to radiation that renders them incapable of producing viable sperm. When the sterilized males are released into the infested area, they mate with the females but the eggs are not fertilized and no offspring are produced.

This type of control can work only if a huge number of sterilized males is introduced into the area to make certain that very few of the normal, unsterilized males are able to find females that have not already mated. Research indicates that if there are ten times more sterile males than fertile ones in a population, the entire population can be destroyed within four generations. In California, application of the conventional pesticide malathion, followed by the introduction of sterile males to mate with surviving females, has proved useful in controlling the spread of the medfly.

Integrated Pest Management As we learn more about relationships among organisms, it becomes clear that the problems of pest control are complex, and solutions must be carefully thought out. The most successful, least toxic solution to a problem takes advantage of all available methods of pest control. Several control methods used simultaneously can be much more effective than a single control method used alone. **Integrated pest management** is a system that uses biological, autocidal, and cultural controls along with chemical pesticides to manage the size of pest populations. An integrated pest management system designed to check population growth of the medfly, for example, might include an initial pesticide application followed by trapping with chemical lures and the periodic release of large numbers of sterilized males. The goal of any integrated pest management program is to reduce the numbers of pest organisms to tolerable levels to maximize crop yields at a minimal cost.

Section Review

Understanding Concepts
1. A new insecticide is developed. When first applied to a population of disease-carrying insects, it successfully eliminates most of them. Within several years, however, the insecticide is no longer effective against these insects. How does this case illustrate the benefits and drawbacks of pesticide use?
2. Suppose an insecticide with properties similar to those of DDT accumulates over the years in a lake as a result of runoff from land. What animals are likely to be most severely affected by the insecticide? How might other animals also be affected as a result?
3. Crops are being destroyed mainly by one type of insect. Another kind of insect does not cause much damage because of its small numbers. An insecticide is applied to the crops and kills the natural predators of both insects. What may be the consequences?
4. **Skill Review—Making Tables:** Construct a table that compares the pros and cons of pesticide use. For more help, see Organizing Information in the **Skill Handbook.**
5. **Thinking Critically:** Explain several ways that biological and autocidal control methods may overcome the disadvantages of using chemical pesticides.

850 🐦 HUMANS AND THE ENVIRONMENT

Answers to Section Review

1. Although an insecticide may be effective at first, insects may develop a resistance to it over time. Either greater doses of the insecticide must then be applied or new insecticides used.
2. Top predators in the lake may be affected as biological magnification occurs. A decrease in the population size of the top predators could lead to an increase in numbers of other animals upon which those predators normally feed. Normal feeding relationships in the lake could be disrupted.
3. The insecticide may completely eliminate the predator population. Both types of insects would undergo a population explosion, resulting in more damage to crops than occurred before application.
4. **Skill Review—Making Tables:**

Pros: prevention of spread of disease, reduced damage to food crops, protection of gardens or lawns. Cons: death of non-pest organisms, and of natural predators, effects of biological magnification, and disruption of food webs.
5. **Thinking Critically:** Biological and autocidal control methods do not introduce potentially toxic and nonbiodegradable pollutants into ecosystems.

30.2 Pollution of Air and Water

Pesticide pollution is associated primarily with agriculture. You've learned that pesticides can affect the health of virtually all members of an ecosystem including birds, insects, fish, and humans. Pollutants associated with industry, transportation, and other aspects of technology also affect Earth and its inhabitants. Remember the imaginary car trip you took at the beginning of this chapter? Your journey started in the center of a big city, where the air is full of exhaust fumes from automobiles, factory smokestacks, and jet airplane engines. Most pollutants associated with technology are waste materials produced during the manufacture of goods and the burning of fuels.

Air Pollution

Take a moment to think about some of the reasons why humans burn fossil fuels such as oil, coal, natural gas, and gasoline. We burn fuel to heat homes and businesses; to cook food; to run plane, car, train, and bus engines; to produce electricity in power plants; and to drive manufacturing and industrial processes of all kinds. Most of today's air pollution problems result from the burning of fossil fuels. The smoke produced from burning these fuels releases materials into the atmosphere that can either harm living organisms directly or change the environment in ways that are harmful to life. One of the chief causes of air pollution is the burning of gasoline in automobiles. By-products of the combustion of fossil fuels include carbon monoxide, carbon dioxide, sulfur dioxide, nitrogen oxides, lead compounds, and hydrocarbons. All of these by-products are considered pollutants.

Objectives

Discuss the effects of various pollutants that contaminate the air.

Analyze the cause and consequences of destruction of the ozone layer.

Explain the difficulties involved in determining the extent of the greenhouse effect and finding solutions to the problem of global warming.

Describe the sources and effects of pollutants entering ground and surface waters.

Figure 30-8 The burning of fossil fuels is the cause of most of today's air pollution problems. How many of our modern conveniences are available due to the burning of fossil fuels?

STUDENT JOURNAL

Ask students to examine a square of nylon stocking under a binocular microscope. They should make diagrams in their journals of the nature of the fibers. Have them put masking tape around the edges of the fabric samples to keep them open to the air. Have them hang the experimental squares in areas where there may be air pollution, and a control in their home or an area where there will not be pollution. After two weeks, they should collect their samples and examine them microscopically again. Then, they should make diagrams of the fabric. Air pollution damages nylon fabric. **L1** **LEP**

Prepare

Key Concepts
Students will study the problems and possible solutions for air pollution, ozone depletion, acid rain, global warming, surface and ground water pollution, and biological and technological wastes.

Key Terms
chlorofluorocarbons (CFCs), acid precipitation, greenhouse effect

Materials
- Gather feathers, motor oil, and paper towels for Minilab 1.
- Gather pH paper, rain samples, funnels, and distilled water for Minilab 2.
- Gather two-week-old bean seedlings; test tubes; test-tube racks; clay or cotton; plastic bags; radish, mustard or bean seeds; and chemicals for testing.

1 Focus

Objectives
The objectives are listed on the student page. Remind students to preview these objectives as a guide to this numbered section.

Discussion
Ask students what they would do under the following circumstances:
1. After a picnic, your friends start tossing the aluminum drink cans into the trash container even though there is a recycling container nearby. When you point out the recycle box, they laugh and call you an eco-freak.
2. Your favorite music group has just come out with a new compact disc. When you go to buy it, you notice that it is wrapped in a lot of extra packaging material.
3. In your school, the temperature is maintained at 72 degrees and the lights are left on in all rooms all day regardless of whether or not they are occupied. **L1**

COOP LEARN

2 Teach

Concept Development

- Some fossil fuels, particularly fuel oil and coal, contain sulfur. Burning these fuels produces sulfur dioxide gas. This gas damages an organism's respiratory tract and lungs by weakening the ciliated cells lining the air passages. These cells, when healthy, help to move foreign particles out of the respiratory system. Exposure to sulfur dioxide makes the respiratory system vulnerable to injury by dust and other pollutants.

- In addition to fossil fuels as a source of air pollution, many pollutants are released into the air by industrial processes. For example, asbestos fibers—used in insulation, brake linings and pads, plaster, cement, and many other products—can become trapped in lung tissue where they can cause lung cancer and other respiratory illnesses. These fibers are easily dislodged, and even short exposures can lead to illness. The use of asbestos for insulation, fireproofing, and other purposes was banned in the U.S. in 1978. In 1979, the EPA began helping to identify and remove hazardous asbestos from public areas.

Carbon Monoxide Hemoglobin is the component of blood that carries oxygen from the lungs to the rest of the body. When carbon monoxide (CO) is breathed into the lungs, it enters the bloodstream and bonds with hemoglobin at sites usually reserved for oxygen molecules. If hemoglobin's oxygen-carrying sites are taken up with CO, tissues are deprived of the oxygen needed for metabolism. Unfortunately, the bond between CO and hemoglobin is more stable than the bond between oxygen and hemoglobin, so oxygen deprivation occurs even when the concentration of CO in the air is very low.

Nitrogen Oxides When fossil fuels are burned at high temperatures, nitrogen from the fuel and oxygen from the air combine to form compounds called nitrogen oxides. Nitric oxide (NO) is made up of one nitrogen and one oxygen atom. It can interact with oxygen in the air to form nitrogen dioxide (NO_2), which has two oxygen atoms. Nitrogen dioxide is a brownish-colored gas that can kill lung cells and cause fluid to build up in the lungs.

In the presence of sunlight, NO and NO_2 combine with hydrocarbons (also produced by combustion) to form carbon compounds that irritate the eyes and stimulate the production of tears. Nitrogen dioxide also contributes to the formation of ozone. The oxygen molecules we breathe are made up of two atoms of oxygen; ozone is composed of three atoms of oxygen bound together. Ozone and eye-irritating carbon compounds contribute to photochemical smog—that is, smog produced by the interaction of sunlight and air pollutants. This type of smog, which often surrounds large cities such as Los Angeles, Denver, and Washington, DC, is damaging to lung tissue and can be extremely dangerous to people who already suffer from respiratory illnesses like asthma or emphysema.

One of the major difficulties in analyzing and solving air pollution problems stems from the tendency of many pollutants to interact with one another and form compounds that may be even more dangerous than the original substances. Examples of this phenomenon include the interaction of nitrogen oxides with hydrocarbons and sunlight to form components of photochemical smog.

Figure 30-9 **Photochemical smog, the smog that surrounds cities, is produced by the interaction of chemicals released from the burning of fossil fuels and sunlight.**

852

Figure 30-10 Ozone, a layer of gas located in the stratosphere, absorbs almost all the UV radiation that reaches Earth from the sun. Many scientists think that the ozone layer is thinning due to the release of CFCs into the atmosphere.

The Ozone Hole

The atmosphere extends several miles above Earth's surface and is made up of four layers, as shown in Figure 30-10. The layer closest to the surface, the troposphere, is about seven miles thick and contains the air we breathe. Most weather events take place in the troposphere, and most air pollution is confined to this layer. The next layer is the stratosphere, which extends to about 30 miles from Earth's surface.

The Ozone Layer At the top of the stratosphere, just before the mesosphere begins, is a layer of ozone gas. While ozone in the troposphere can be dangerous and is considered an air pollutant, the ozone layer in the stratosphere is important to the health of all organisms living on Earth. This ozone layer absorbs almost all of the ultraviolet (UV) radiation that reaches Earth from the sun. UV radiation can be extremely damaging. The small amount that does penetrate the ozone layer is responsible for sunburn, can cause skin cancer, and can cause mutations in the genetic material of cells exposed to it. It can reduce crop yields and even kill small organisms such as plankton. If the ozone layer did not exist, it is doubtful that life could survive on the surface of Earth.

During the 1980s, it became evident that protective ozone is being lost from the stratosphere. The ozone layer above Antarctica becomes thinner during every Antarctic spring. This thinning has become known as the "ozone hole." In some years, ozone in this region has decreased by as much as 50 percent. The apparent loss of ozone is not limited to the Antarctic; it is just most severe there. Decreases as great as 10 percent have been detected over parts of Europe and North America.

30.2 POLLUTION OF AIR AND WATER **853**

Different Viewpoints in Biology

Haze: Benefits and Problems

Haze is a suspension of sulfates and other pollutants in the lower atmosphere produced by combustion. It interferes with daytime visibility and is associated with all the other problems generated by air pollution. However, a new study shows that it also filters out harmful ultraviolet rays. Studies show that the amount filtered is equal to or greater than the amount coming through the ozone layer in areas where it is broken and thinning. Scientists think that the benefits of haze pollution will not last as industrial regulations get stricter and stratospheric ozone continues to diminish. Some scientists think that since the advent of the industrial age, UV levels have been cut by 20 to 30 percent because of air pollution. When air pollution diminishes and the ozone hole increases, UV light coming into our atmosphere may be greater than originally anticipated.

Activity

Ask students to examine recent maps published in science magazines and journals of the arctic and antarctic ozone holes at various times of the year. Supply them with four maps of the world labeled spring, summer, fall, and winter, and ask them to shade in the part of the world that would be at risk from increased UV light during specific times of the year. Tell students to remember that the seasons are reversed in the southern hemisphere. **L1** **LEP**

PORTFOLIO

Ask students to prepare, an argument that takes a stand, on the following question: Are current environmental problems a reflection of a fundamental change in human values over the past 50 years? To defend their opinions, they should conduct a survey of different age groups of people and use library resources for specific examples of the points they wish to make.

Figure Caption Question

How are CFCs in these appliances lost to the atmosphere? They leak from broken parts and from when old appliances are disposed of improperly without recovering the CFCs.

Activity

Ask half of your students to do a survey of labels of aerosol products on the shelves of the cosmetic/health section of a nearby market or pharmacy. They should make a list of products that have CFCs on the ingredients label. The other half of your students should examine the grocery store shelves to determine which aerosol cleaning products are made with CFCs as propellants. In class, they should write letters to companies that produce these products and encourage them to switch to non-aerosol containers or use propellants that will not damage the atmosphere. L1

Concept Development

Acid rain falling on ancient stone cathedrals and statues in Europe or on brick or stone buildings and monuments is causing their surfaces to dissolve. Some of the most famous monuments ever built such as the Sphinx and the Great Pyramids of Giza in Egypt now are suffering damage from acid rain.

Figure 30-11 CFCs work as coolants in appliances such as refrigerators and air conditioners. How are the CFCs in these appliances lost to the atmosphere?

CFCs What is causing the thinning of the ozone layer? Most of the blame has been placed on air pollutants called **chlorofluorocarbons,** which are also known as **CFCs.** These chemicals are used as coolants in refrigerators and air conditioners, as foaming agents in the manufacture of Styrofoam, and as propellants in spray cans. CFCs contain chlorine. Scientists have found that as amounts of chlorine in the atmosphere increase, the amount of ozone decreases. In the stratosphere, CFCs destroy ozone by reacting with it to form chlorine gas and oxygen.

What can humans do to stop this loss of ozone? In 1987, governments of the world's industrial nations became concerned enough to sign an agreement to reduce the production of CFCs. In 1990, the agreement was revised. This time, it called for complete elimination of CFCs, worldwide, by the year 2000. What about the CFCs already present in refrigerators and air conditioners? Removing the coolants from discarded appliances and recycling them instead of just releasing them into the atmosphere can help. The efforts of government and industry will probably not be able to prevent CFC levels from continuing to increase, perhaps by as much as 20 percent, by the end of the 20th century. The effect of this increase on the ozone layer remains to be seen.

CFCs can remain unchanged in the troposphere for as long as 70 to 150 years, rising into the stratosphere very slowly. It is believed that CFCs already released at ground level will continue to rise into the stratosphere for many more years. As a result, ozone depletion would likely continue to worsen even if we stopped all CFC use immediately.

Acid Precipitation

Water, in the form of water vapor, enters the atmosphere by the processes of evaporation, transpiration, and respiration. Water returns to Earth's surface in the form of rain, snow, and other types of precipitation. While in the atmosphere, water molecules may come into contact with air pollutants. Analysis of rain and snow falling over many parts of Earth today illustrates how pollutants can react with other compounds to cause unforeseen problems.

In the atmosphere, carbon dioxide gas dissolves into droplets of water to form weak carbonic acid. As a result, rain is normally acidic, with a pH of about 5.6 to 5.7. Release of sulfur dioxide and nitrogen oxides into the atmosphere can further reduce the pH of rain and snow. In the presence of sunlight, these pollutants react with water and/or oxygen in the air to form sulfuric acid and nitric acid. In some urban and heavily industrialized areas, the amount of these pollutants released into the air is so great that the pH of rain or snow may be as low as 3.0, which is about the same as the pH of vinegar. Precipitation with a pH below 5.6 is called **acid precipitation.** Dew, fog, and even airborne dust can also become acidic as a result of air pollution.

The region of the United States that has suffered the most damage from acid precipitation is the northeast, where the average pH of rain and snow is between 4.0 and 4.5. However, most of the sulfur dioxide pollution

854 ☙ HUMANS AND THE ENVIRONMENT

Auto Necessity? Ask students to write essays about the pros and cons of the automobile in our lives. They should bring out ideas about transportation and jobs provided, as well as the dangers of accidents and air pollution they cause. They should discuss in detail each of the air pollutants produced by cars and explain the effect on the environment of each pollutant. In addition, they should provide information about research projects underway on cars of the future such as electric and solar cars and cars that use other alternative fuels. L2 that causes this acid precipitation does not originate in the northeastern part of the country. It comes from coal-burning power plants located as far west as Illinois, hundreds of miles away. Prevailing winds move the acids toward the east. Emissions from factories and automobiles in the northeast compound the problem. As you can see, air pollution events in one part of the biosphere can affect other regions.

Effects of Acid Rain Precipitation that is only slightly more acidic than normal may actually increase the yield of some crops, especially those grown in fields that receive little or no fertilizer. Depending on the nutrient balance of the soil, tomatoes, green peppers, and strawberry plants may benefit from the nitrogen and sulfur added to the soil by acid rain. However, as acidity increases (and pH decreases), nutrients that are easily dissolved in acid, such as calcium and potassium, are washed out of the soil. As these nutrients are washed away, the soil becomes less fertile and soil microorganisms become less numerous. Decomposition and the cycling of essential nutrients slows down so that fewer nutrients are available to plants. This loss of nutrients can lead to the death of trees, especially conifers.

Acid rain and snow can damage or destroy leaves and other plant tissues, reduce photosynthesis and nitrogen fixation, and limit the types of plants that can grow in the affected area. Acid precipitation can also have severe effects on lake ecosystems. Acid precipitation falling into a lake, or entering it as runoff from streams or neighboring slopes, causes the pH of the lake water to fall below normal. This acidity may be great enough to cause the death of plankton; destroy the eggs of fish, salamanders, and frogs; and even kill adult fish. Lake food chains can be destroyed because

Figure 30-12 **Many trees in the mountains of New England are dying at a high rate due to acid rain. Acid rain may damage plant tissues and interfere with photosynthesis and nitrogen fixation.**

Minilab 1

Why are oil spills lethal to birds?

Obtain five feathers from your teacher. Tag one feather and make a drawing of it to actual size. Label this drawing "Before oil." Find the mass of the five feathers using a balance. Record your data. Place all feathers in a dish of motor oil. Remove them from the oil and place on paper towels to remove as much oil as possible. Remass the feathers and record your data. Make an outline diagram of the original tagged feather. Keep it from touching your paper as the outline is made. Label it "After oil."

Analysis *Explain how your "before-and-after" data and diagrams may explain why birds are killed when they come in contact with oil spills.*

Minilab 1

Purpose
Students will be made aware of why oil spills are so harmful to birds.

Teaching Strategies
- Materials needed: shallow dish, paper towels, 5 feathers, balance, motor oil (approximately 50 mL). Most hobby and craft stores carry packaged feathers.
- Vegetable oil may be substituted for motor oil.
- **Safety Precautions:** Have students wear aprons and have them wash their hands thoroughly after handling motor oil.

Expected Results
Student data tables and actual data may vary.

	Mass	*Shape*
Before (dry feathers)	1.2 g	wide, fluffy light
After (oil-soaked feathers)	2.3 g	narrow, compressed, heavy

Answers
Student answers may vary. The mass of feathers with oil is almost double dry mass. Feather shape becomes distorted when soaked in oil. The extra mass makes it difficult for birds to fly. The distorted feather shape makes it difficult to fly and to trap air below that normally serves an insulatory function.

✔ Assessment
Performance: Have students record their answers and data in their journals. Have them determine through experimentation if the rinsing of oil-soaked feathers in water or in detergent added to water is an effective means for reducing mass and returning shape back to normal. Ask why this type of effort on the part of humans has only limited success.

INVESTIGATION

Effects of Pollutants on Seed Germination and Plant Growth

Time Allotment

1 class period initially and then 5 to 10 minutes each day for a week

Objectives

Upon completing this investigation, students will be able to:

- Use the scientific method to test their hypotheses.
- Better understand the influence of pollutants on plant growth and seed germination.

Skills

form a hypothesis, design an experiment, separate and control variables, interpret data

Materials

Materials needed per group include: young bean plants, test tubes, ruler, labels, test-tube rack, clay or cotton, light bank (optional), paper towels, radish or mustard or bean seeds, self-sealing or regular plastic lunch bags, chemicals to be tested such as oil, insecticides, laundry detergents, fertilizer.

Preparation

- Grow young plants such as beans from seed at least 2 weeks prior to doing this activity. Store-bought plants such as coleus or other decorative plants may be used.
- Small plastic cups, milk cartons, or peat pots may be used for growing beans.
- Purchase seeds from your local grocery store. Use kidney or pinto but avoid lima beans.
- Using sand or vermiculite as the growing medium will aid in removing them from the soil.

Possible Hypotheses

- If chemical pollutants affect seed germination, then a lower percentage of seeds will germinate among those exposed to the pollutants.
- If only certain chemical pollutants affect seed germination, then the number of seeds germinating will

---

many organisms disappear as a direct result of acid rain or because their food supply is gone. Low pH can reduce the availability of nutrients the same way nutrient availability is reduced in soils—microorganisms become less numerous, slowing decomposition and the recycling of nutrients.

Low pH also increases the solubility of dangerous metals such as mercury, aluminum, and lead. Under normal circumstances, molecules of these metals cannot dissolve in water. They remain buried in the sediments at the bottom of the lake and pose little hazard to life. But once they become dissolved in lake water, they can be taken up by plants, fish, and other organisms.

Acid rain also has a direct effect on human health. It can reduce the pH of dust particles in the air. A buildup of these particles in the lungs could become a factor in the onset of diseases such as bronchitis, asthma, and emphysema.

INVESTIGATION

Effects of Pollutants on Seed Germination and Plant Growth

Pollution of land and water by everyday common chemicals is a concern of everyone. Barely a day goes by without the news of some chemical that has leaked from a truck, train, or storage site into the ground or water supply. How much damage is being done to life from these kinds of chemical spills? It may be difficult for you to evaluate the damage on animals directly. However, you could experiment with seeds to determine if these chemicals do have a harmful effect on their germination and growth.

What might be the effect on germination if seeds were exposed to such chemicals as oil, cleaning detergents, insecticides, and excess fertilizers? You may wish to use chemicals other than those suggested as you plan your investigation. What might be the effect on growth if young plants were exposed through their roots to such chemicals as those listed above? You may wish to use chemicals other than those suggested as you plan your investigation.

Work with a group assigned by your teacher. Form hypotheses that could be tested using the chemicals suggested or those of your choice.

Problem

(1) How might seed germination be affected by soaking seeds in oil, cleaning detergent, insecticides, and excess fertilizers? (2) How might growth of young plants be affected by having their roots exposed to oil, cleaning detergent, insecticides, and excess fertilizers?

Hypotheses

What are your group's two hypotheses?

Safety Precautions

Be careful when handling oil, insecticides, and fertilizer.

---

be lower than in other chemicals and the control.

- If only certain chemical pollutants affect plant growth, then changes in the appearance and continued growth of these plants will differ from those in other pollutants and the control plants.

Possible Procedures

- Students should check seed germination each day for at least one week. The same species of seed should be used throughout their study.

- Young bean plants may have their root systems placed directly into the chemical pollutant being tested. Make sure that the same plant type is used by the same group for all their growth studies.
- Concentration of insecticide, detergent, or fertilizer may vary from group to group. Remind students to record the concentrations used of each of these pollutants.
- Controls will usually consist of a plant placed into a test tube filled with water.
- For seed germination, data collection may take the format of students observing,

Possible Solutions   Acid rain, along with ozone depletion, is yet another pollution problem resulting from the burning of fossil fuels. The burning of coal is an especially important source of acid precipitation because most coal contains fairly large amounts of sulfur. Much of the electricity we use is produced by coal-burning power plants. In 1992, 17 million tons of sulfur dioxide were released by coal-fired power plants. Reducing these sulfur dioxide emissions could help reduce the acid rain problem. Regulations that are part of the Clean Air Act of 1990 are intended to do just that. According to these regulations, by the year 2010 most power plants will have to reduce sulfur dioxide emissions by half. How can this goal be accomplished? Emissions can be reduced by burning low-sulfur coal, producing less electricity, by installing scrubbers in coal-burning power plants to filter pollutants from emissions, and by using alternative fuels such as solar or hydroelectric power.

Experimental Plan

1. Decide on a way to test your group's two hypotheses. Keep the available materials provided by your teacher in mind as you plan your procedure.
2. Record your procedures and list materials and amounts that you will need.

Checking the Plan

Discuss the following with other group members to decide the final procedure for your experiment.
1. What data will you collect and how will it be recorded?
2. What will be your controls and what variables will have to be controlled?
3. Assign individual roles for this investigation.

Make sure your teacher has approved your experimental plan before you proceed further.

Data and Observations

Carry out your experiment. Prepare a data chart to record your findings.

Analysis and Conclusions

1. State your hypothesis that relates to the effect of chemicals on seed germination. Use specific data from your experiment to support or reject your hypothesis.
2. Might you be able to conclude from your data that:
   (a) different chemical pollutants will have the same effect on the type of seeds used in your investigation? Explain.
   (b) those chemical pollutants used in your investigation will have the same effect on different seed types? Explain.
3. State your hypothesis that relates to the effect of chemicals on plant growth. Use specific data from your experiment to support or reject your hypothesis.
4. Might you be able to conclude from your data that:
   (a) different chemical pollutants will have the same effect on the type of plants used in your investigation? Explain.
   (b) those chemical pollutants used in your investigation will have the same effect on different plant types? Explain.
5. Explain the advantage of using plants rather than animals in this investigation. Might you be able to conclude from your data that those chemicals used in your investigation will have the same effects on animals as they did on plants? Explain.
6. Design and describe an experimental procedure that you could use to test the effects of chemicals such as lead or mercury on:
   (a) seed germination and (b) young plant growth.

Going Further

Based on this lab experience, design another experiment that would help to answer questions that arose from your work. Assume that you will have limited resources and will be conducting this lab in class. Include this as part of your report.

---

counting, and recording the number of seeds germinating each day. For young plant reaction, data collection may take the format of student diagrams being made each day of general plant appearance including such things as height, leaf color...

Teaching Strategies
- Soak seeds overnight in the liquids to be tested.
- Oil may be motor or vegetable cooking oils, laundry detergents may be either liquid or powder, fertilizer and insecticides would be more manageable if in liquid form. Let students decide on the concentration of fertilizer to be used. The concentration chosen should be higher than what is recommended on the container.
- Review the procedure for the preparation of a certain solution percentage:
  (a) Percentage by weight—mass the amount of chemical to be used, add to a graduated cylinder, and add water to the 100-mL mark. Example: 20% fertilizer solution = 20 g of fertilizer placed into a graduated cylinder and add water until the 100-mL mark is reached.
  (b) Percentage by volume—measure the volume of chemical to be used equal to the percentage needed for the new solution. (You may have to assume that insecticides and detergents are at 100%.) Add water to the 100-mL mark.

Data and Observations
Student data and the reporting format will vary. Students should set up data tables to record data daily. Make sure tables have an appropriate title.

Data Analysis
Student answers may vary.
1. Students' answers will vary depending on their hypotheses. Accept all logically constructed answers.
2. For each a and b, the answer is no. Each different pollutant and seed type would have to be experimentally tried.
3. Students' answers will vary depending on hypotheses and experimental data.

---

4. For each a and b, the answer is no. General conclusions cannot be drawn. Each chemical and seed needs to be tested.
5. Animals would possibly have to be sacrificed if repeating the same experiment. Since animal and plant physiology is so different, generalizations should not be made.
6. (a) Soak seeds in solutions that contain lead or mercury. Compare germination rates with controls.
   (b) Place young plants in solutions that contain lead or mercury. Compare their growth with controls.

✔ **Assessment**
Knowledge: Write an analysis of this experiment for your portfolio. Design another experiment to test the maximum concentration of a pollutant a plant can tolerate before its growth is disrupted. Include a full description of the experiment in your portfolio.

Extensions
Students may wish to test the effect of pollutants applied to plants via their leaves and stems rather than through their roots. Other pollutants or household chemicals/products may be tested.

Debate

Divide the class in half and give one half copies of articles to read that explain that global warming is inevitable and that we should be taking action now to control it by cutting carbon dioxide production by 20% and phasing out CFCs. This group would be in favor of research on and switching to alternative energy, a tax on gasoline, cars that get better gas mileage, increased availability of public transportation, and prevention of any more burning of tropical rain forests. Give the other half of the class articles that say that more research needs to be done before any action can be taken. This group will say that different computer models predict different results for the changes currently going on in Earth's atmosphere. People in developing countries that are just becoming industrialized and getting cars would be under great hardship. In the U.S., it would cost billions to cut CO_2 production. Small industries would go out of business if they had to pay the expenses of using alternative fuels. After the debate, ask students to write a paragraph that is a compromise between the two opposing views. **L1** **COOP LEARN**

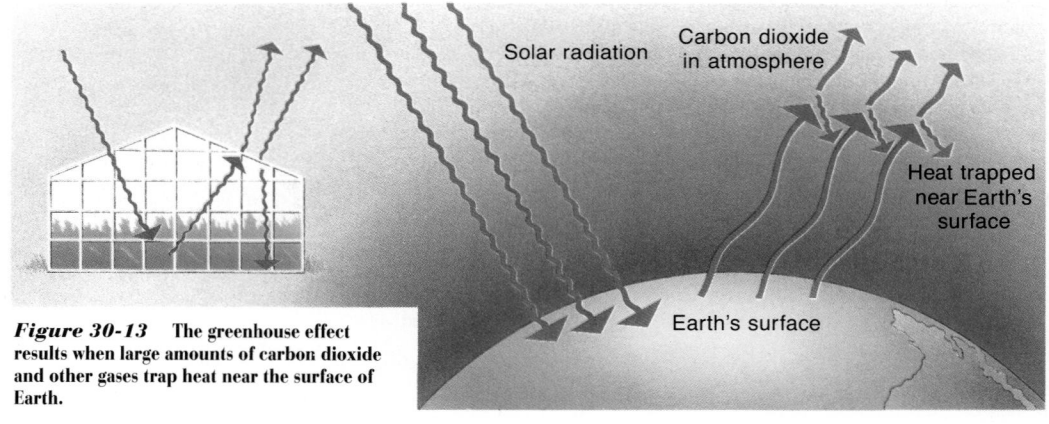

Figure 30-13 The greenhouse effect results when large amounts of carbon dioxide and other gases trap heat near the surface of Earth.

Global Warming—Is There a Problem?

You may have heard a great deal of talk in recent years about possible changes in Earth's climate. Many scientists are concerned that average temperatures are slowly getting warmer, a change often referred to as global warming. This problem, too, is related to the burning of fossil fuels, which releases large amounts of carbon dioxide into the atmosphere. Over the past 125 years, as humans have burned more and more fossil fuels for heat, transportation, and industry, the amount of carbon dioxide in the atmosphere has increased by at least 11 percent.

Carbon dioxide levels are also affected by the amount of forest land on Earth's surface. Do you remember the chemical reaction that takes place during photosynthesis? Because trees and other green plants use carbon dioxide, water, and sunlight to manufacture sugars, they help remove carbon dioxide from the atmosphere. But as the global human population has increased, so has the pressure for people to clear forest land for agriculture. In some areas, particularly the tropical countries of South America, millions of acres of forest are burned each year to make way for food crops and livestock pasture. Not only are the forests disappearing, they are being burned away, which adds even more carbon dioxide to the atmosphere.

Greenhouse Effect What does atmospheric carbon dioxide have to do with temperature? Sunlight passes through the atmosphere to Earth's surface. Part of the heat from sunlight is absorbed by objects and organisms, but much of it is radiated back into the atmosphere. Some of this reradiated heat passes all the way through the atmosphere and escapes into space. The rest bounces off certain atmospheric gases, such as carbon dioxide and water vapor, and returns to Earth's surface. As the amount of carbon dioxide in the atmosphere grows larger, the amount of heat reflected back to Earth instead of escaping into space may also increase.

Carbon dioxide traps heat near Earth's surface in the same way that glass traps heat inside a greenhouse. The increase in temperatures that could result from a buildup of heat-reflecting atmospheric gases is known as the **greenhouse effect.** The heat-reflecting gases that contribute to global warming are called greenhouse gases. They include carbon dioxide, methane (natural gas), nitrogen oxides, and CFCs.

Possible Effects Several groups of scientists have used computer modeling to try to predict future temperatures. Some models suggest that global temperatures will increase only one degree Celsius by the year 2050. Others suggest an increase of up to five degrees Celsius. That may not sound like much, but even a small change in temperature can have a serious effect on the global climate. For example, during the last Ice Age, when glaciers covered most of North America, the average temperature was only five degrees Celsius colder than it is today.

What might happen if the temperature were to rise five degrees during the next half century? The polar ice caps might begin to melt, causing sea levels to rise and possibly submerging some populated coastal areas. The temperate zone could become subtropical, and more northerly regions could become temperate. Such changes would alter the distribution of plants and other life forms, creating major changes in ecosystems around the world. For example, crops like wheat and corn, which are presently grown in abundance in the United States, would no longer thrive here. You might think they could be grown in areas that were formerly cooler, such as Canada, but that is not the case. Even though the weather might be favorable, soil conditions in Canada are not suitable for these crops.

Rising temperatures might change wind and weather patterns, converting grasslands to desert or tundra to taiga. Warmer weather could lead to the spread of diseases now limited to the tropics and might favor the reproduction of crop-destroying insects.

Figure 30-14 **Global warming may result in a decrease in the amount of rainfall different regions of the world receive. The map shows the possible percent decrease in the amounts of rainfall in areas of the United States by 2075 if atmospheric levels of carbon dioxide continue to rise at present rates. Another possible effect of global warming is rising ocean levels due to the melting of polar ice caps. This could result in serious consequences for coastal cities.**

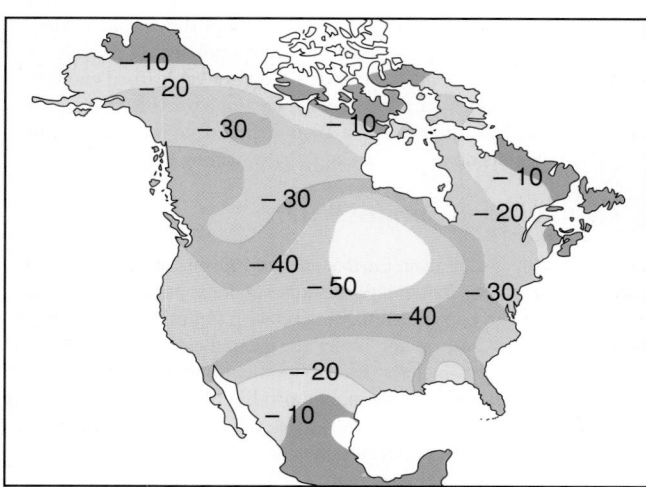

SECTION 30.2

Concept Development

Most scientists conclude that temperatures will rise as the levels of carbon dioxide and other greenhouse gases rise. But how much will temperatures increase, and what effects will this increase have on life on our planet? There is no doubt that atmospheric levels of carbon dioxide have risen. In 1880, the atmosphere contained 290 parts per million, and in 1990 the level was 352 parts per million. Many experts have predicted that the level of carbon dioxide will reach 540 parts per million by the middle of the next century. What we don't know is how this increase will affect temperatures.

Bulletin Board Display

Ask students to collect and bring in articles about global warming from the local newspaper and from magazines. Ask them to make a bulletin board display from these articles.
 LEP

Humor in Biology

A recent study shows that cows, worldwide, may contribute to global warming by releasing 60 million tons of methane gas into the air due to flatulence each year. Methane is an important greenhouse gas that contributes to global warming. A group of scientists is at work developing a method of changing the cow's stomach chemistry so not as much methane will be produced. Others have calculated that one cow, releasing methane, warms the world no more than a 75-watt bulb shining for a year. This amount, they say, is not much.

PORTFOLIO

Ask students to collect articles about global warming from newspapers and magazines. In their portfolios, they should summarize each article and write an essay that compares and contrasts the coverage of this issue in the various articles. They will find that scientists are undecided about the extent of the effects of future global warming and when this warming will take place. Ask them to conclude with an analysis about why laws are not being passed that would prevent escalation of global warming. L2

Poisonous Paints: In the mid-1800s, cadmium sulfide pigments were introduced to artists and produced brilliant yellow color never found before. Cadmium yellows have been used by painters and appreciated in paintings by people worldwide ever since. Cadmium, however, is a heavy metal that can cause kidney damage and may trigger various cancers. Cadmium wastes now enter streams as a result of industrial production of plastic bottles and chemicals, textiles, batteries, and a variety of other products including artists' paint. As environmentalists try to get legislation passed that will protect the public from cadmium wastes, artists fear that their zeal will also include cadmium-based paint. Without cadmium colors, artists claim that they will not be able to convey the sensory beauty of a sunset and other natural settings requiring yellows, golds, orange, and red. To give an example, artists point to Van Gough's *Sunflowers*, which they say he could not have painted without cadmium paints.

Figure 30-15 One way to reduce the burning of fossil fuels is to find alternate methods of transportation.

Possible Solutions   These are frightening possibilities. Could they really happen? Many ideas for reducing the potential for global warming have been proposed. For example, we could make more use of alternative energy sources, such as solar and wind energy, which do not require the burning of fuels. Reducing the use of fossil fuels would, of course, also reduce the output of many pollutants. We could stop removing vegetation, such as tropical rain forests, and start growing new forests. In addition, we could make use of our knowledge of genetics to develop crops capable of tolerating warmer temperatures and a variety of insect pests.

   The cost of making these changes would be great, and people would have to endure many alterations in lifestyle. Energy costs would rise. We might have to dramatically reduce the number of car trips we take and severely curtail our use of electricity. As you can see, dealing with environmental problems involves politics and economics as well as science. The issue of global warming may be the most difficult ecological dilemma of our time, yet we are still uncertain of the extent of the problem. This uncertainty is a prime example of how science cannot always provide an immediate solution to a problem. Scientists have not yet learned enough to predict how severe global warming may be, let alone provide safeguards against it. Furthermore, there is still a great deal of disagreement on this issue—some scientists do not foresee a global warming problem at all.

Pollution of Surface Waters

Water is constantly cycled from Earth's surface into the atmosphere and back again. Water vapor that enters the atmosphere is pure, but once in the atmosphere, it can become contaminated with pollutants as in the formation of acid rain. Water on and under the ground can also become contaminated. Contaminants include not only pesticides, oils, detergents, and other substances released by humans, but also biological materials such as decaying plants and animals or animal wastes. These pollutants can enter the water directly from sewers, drainpipes, or runoff from land, or indirectly, picked up as the water flows through polluted soil.

Ask students to select a body of water nearby. It could be a pond, stream, river, or lake. Provide them with materials to test the water. Ask them to find out how the quality of the water could be improved and design a community campaign to improve the quality of the water. Help for such a project can be provided through the U.S. Environmental Protection Agency. Local community leaders or environmental groups could be asked to provide advice and assistance. Ask students to keep records of their progress in their journals.

Most of the water on Earth is salt water; less than 0.1 percent is fresh. Organisms that dwell on land need a constant supply of fresh water, as do the organisms that live in lakes, ponds, and streams. Pollution of this tiny percentage of Earth's water can present a serious threat to life. Pollution of fresh water can also affect marine organisms because almost all fresh water eventually finds its way to the ocean. This is another example of how ecosystems interact with one another. Let's take a closer look at some of the ways in which fresh water can become contaminated.

Biological Wastes In most communities, sewage treatment plants ensure that human wastes, pathogens, and other contaminants are removed from water before it is released into local waterways. But in areas where there is no treatment of sewage, or where treatment systems fail, these wastes find their way into bodies of water, where they are broken down by bacteria and other organisms. If the accumulation of waste materials is large, the decay process may use up all of the oxygen dissolved in the water. Fish and other water dwellers cannot survive without oxygen, and the water may become stagnant and lifeless.

G L O B A L   C O N N E C T I O N

Michiko Ishimure

Michiko Ishimure became familiar with one of the worst effects of water pollution long before anyone knew its cause. In her Japanese fishing village, it was known as the "cat's dance disease." Cats inflicted with the malady would go mad and drown themselves. After a while, the problem started showing up in humans, who would become crippled and die.

Ishimure became involved when university studies showed that the disease was a neurological disorder caused by mercury poisoning. The source was a chemical plant that had been dumping mercury-carrying waste into the bay. For years, mercury had been thought to be harmless in seawater because it didn't dissolve. It wasn't known that chemical reactions between

mercury and seawater would allow the poisonous metal to enter the food chain.

Ishimure helped expose the toxic waste problem to the world by writing books about the people who suffered from the poisoning. She took a leading role in efforts to limit the wastes that industry was allowed to dump.

Yet, while she was defending her village from the immediate threat of the poisons being dumped into its waters, her fellow villagers wouldn't support her. Instead, they made her an outcast. Too many of the villagers depended upon the chemical plants for jobs. To them, an attack on the plant was a threat to their livelihood.

Yet, her books helped make the Japanese government aware of the toxic waste program. They greatly contributed to the passing of pollution control legislation in Japan and around the world.

1. **Explore Further:** Research the famous Love Canal toxic dump site. What happened there? Who were the key people in uncovering the problem?

2. **Writing About Biology:** Write several paragraphs describing human responsibility to control toxic waste worldwide.

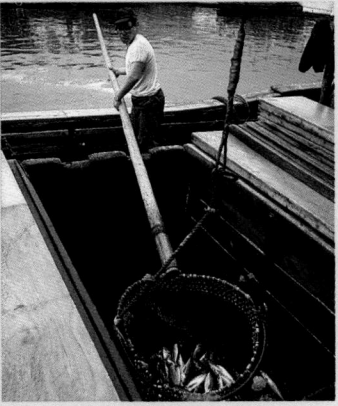

GLOBAL CONNECTION

Purpose
Students will study the work of Michiko Ishimure in exposing the effects of mercury poisoning on the citizens of a Japanese fishing village.

Teaching Strategies
Explain to students that, like DDT, soluble mercury is biologically magnified as it moves from one trophic level to another.

Possible Answers
1. The Love Canal in New York was used as a dump by a major chemical company in the 1940s and 1950s. It was covered with clay and developed as a residential site. Residents of the area began to notice bad-smelling sludges leaking into their basements, and local health officials noticed a large number of birth defects, miscarriages, liver disease cases, and cancer cases. Love Canal was declared a disaster area due to the efforts of Lois Marie Gibbs, a housewife living near the canal. She organized a group of "amateurs" who brought hazardous wastes to national attention.

2. Students should discuss the responsibility of limiting as much as possible the initial production of toxic waste. The toxic waste that is generated should be dealt with in a way that will not be just a quick fix, but be a lasting solution that will not need fixing again by future generations.

Going Further
Ask students to find out about federal and state legislation that protects the local area from toxic waste. **L2**

PROJECT

Sewage Treatment: Ask a group of students to visit a sewage treatment plant. They should ask for a tour that will show them all the levels of treatment and how the treatment and testing is done. If the sewage sludge is not being processed and recycled, ask them to find out if there are plans to do this. They should take photos of their tour and present them to the class in the form of a photo essay or a slide presentation. If the sewage treatment plant could be improved, ask them to present ideas for improvements that could be undertaken. **L3** **COOP LEARN**

Minilab 2

Purpose

Students will learn how to use pH paper as a tool for judging if rain and water samples are acid, base, or neutral. They will determine if rain samples in their area are acidic.

Teaching Strategies

- Collect three different rain (or melted snow) samples in bottles marked with the date of collection.
- If rain samples are not available close to the day when you wish to run the experiment, provide students with water samples that have been prepared with weak acid to achieve a variety of pHs.
- Materials needed include pH paper strips, pH paper color chart, rain samples, funnels, tap water, and distilled water.
- Have students review the pH scale in Chapter 3.

Expected Results

Students will most likely find pHs ranging from 4 to 7. Tap water will most likely measure 6 and distilled water 7. Rain samples will vary. Normal rain has an average pH of 5.6.

Answers

Student answers may vary. Acid numbers are from 1 to 6. Rain is acid due to the normal presence of carbon dioxide plus the presence of gas pollutants such as sulfur dioxide and nitrogen oxide, which react with water to form acid.

✔ Assessment

Knowledge: Have students record their data and answers in their journals. Provide students with a "practical" quiz. Ask them to determine the pH of several samples of liquid. Grade them on their understanding of the proper technique for using pH paper as well as their accuracy for determining pH.

Minilab 2

How acid is rain?

Use funnels and bottles to collect three samples of rain on three different days. Mark the date on each sample collected. Measure the pH of each sample using pH paper. Use a new piece for each sample. Dip the pH paper into a sample. Compare the color that appears on the paper to the color scale provided in class. Record the pH number that corresponds to the matching color in a data table. Measure and record the pH of tap and distilled water.

Analysis What numbers on the pH scale indicate acid? Which samples had the lowest pH numbers? The strongest acid values? Why might rain be acid?

Technological Wastes In technological societies like ours, most water pollutants are by-products of industrial and agricultural activities. These pollutants range from poisonous substances such as pesticides and potentially toxic metals, to biodegradable or inert materials like glass, paper, and chunks of concrete.

PCBs (polychlorinated biphenyls) are a type of industrial pollutant once found in chemical plant wastes and in large electrical transformers, such as those located at the top of power line poles. Their use was banned in 1979. Because they are nonbiodegradable, PCBs remain in the environment. They also pose a health threat to humans. PCBs affect the nervous and muscular systems, and experiments suggest that they may cause cancer and birth defects in animals. Humans come into contact with PCBs through contaminated water, through contact with contaminated soil, or by ingesting PCB-contaminated fish. Most of this contact comes from the improper disposal of waste containing PCBs.

Ocean Pollution The water in a small stream flows into a larger stream, then into a river, which empties into the ocean. Any pollutants carried in this water will affect the waterways along the coast. These areas of the ocean support the greatest diversity of marine life. They serve as nursery grounds for many species of fish and for marine mammals such as seals and sea lions. Many water birds feed and raise their young there. In regions where a number of rivers and streams flow into the same bay or coastal area, pollutants can become highly concentrated, with severe consequences to marine life.

You have probably heard about oil spills that occur in ocean waters. Sometimes huge quantities of oil are lost from giant tankers as a result of accidents at sea. Smaller quantities leak from offshore oil-drilling rigs or from boat motors. It is estimated that about 0.1 percent of the oil produced each year finds its way into the world's oceans. Some of this oil evaporates and some is broken down by bacteria, but these are very slow processes. Before it breaks down, the oil can be lethal to plankton, fish larvae, crustaceans, birds, and many marine mammals.

Figure 30-16 Oil spills are very costly to marine and coastal ecosystems. After a major oil spill, it can take up to ten years for organisms to recover.

862 🐟 HUMANS AND THE ENVIRONMENT

Pollution of Groundwater

Fresh water is present not only in surface waters but also underground in reservoirs called aquifers. Underground water supplies can become contaminated by pollutants washed down through layers of soil. Some pollutants leach into groundwater from landfills where hazardous wastes have been stored. Pollutants also enter groundwater from buried gasoline tanks, septic systems, municipal and industrial landfills, agriculture, and from illegally dumped materials.

Some of the pollutants that have entered groundwater supplies include PCBs, pesticides, and a variety of other organic chemicals. These contaminants most often reach groundwater due to improper disposal. A chemical called TCDD, a dioxin, a by-product of the manufacture of some herbicides, has contaminated groundwater supplies. TCDD is toxic to some animals, but its long-term effects on humans are not yet known. Radioactive wastes, which come from spent nuclear power plant fuel, the manufacture of atomic devices, and from medical waste materials, also pose a threat to groundwater. These materials are usually stored in containers, but leakage sometimes occurs. Radiation from some of these isotopes can be lethal, even in very small amounts.

Pollution of an underground aquifer poses a grave threat to people who depend on it as their primary water supply. It is difficult and expensive to clean large quantities of contaminated groundwater. In many parts of the United States, wells have been shut down and people have been forced to use bottled water. Efforts are being made to clean up existing hazardous waste dumps and to develop safer methods of storage and containment of hazardous wastes to prevent further groundwater contamination.

In examining the effects of pesticides, air and water pollution, acid rain, ozone depletion, and global warming, you have come to see how modern technology contributes to environmental problems. Finding solutions will require contributions from individuals, industries, governments, and scientists. Cooperation is crucial as we explore ways to reverse damage already done to our environment and to prevent future damage.

Figure 30-17 **Aquifers become polluted by the improper disposal of hazardous wastes. Contaminants leak into the ground and ultimately into the groundwater from improper storage containers, buried gasoline tanks, and from illegally dumped materials.**

Section Review

Understanding Concepts

1. How is the production of the electricity used by many people related to acid precipitation?
2. Landfills may contain old Styrofoam containers, refrigerators, and spray cans. In what way are these materials dangerous to the environment?
3. How does dealing with the issue of global warming illustrate the roles of science, government, and economics in solving environmental problems?
4. ***Skill Review—Designing an Experiment:*** How would you conduct an experiment, using a terrarium, to test the adverse effects of acid precipitation? For more help, see Practicing Scientific Methods in the **Skill Handbook.**
5. ***Thinking Critically:*** Explain how old motor oil dumped in a vacant lot could affect life in the ocean.

Check for Understanding

Ask students to make a list of environmental concerns in your area and in the state. They should make a recommendation about what might be done about each problem. **L1**

Reteach

Ask students to make a list of the lifestyle changes they could make in their lives to reduce environmental pollution. **L2**

Extension

Ask students to visit a nearby major industry and ask officials there what they are doing to protect the environment from damage from their industrial processes.

✔ Assessment

Portfolio: Ask students to write a letter to a local official about problems in the local environment. Tell students that they should put this letter into their portfolios. They should describe the problem and the history of the problem fully, and then make recommendations for how to deal with this problem. Then they should justify their recommendations. **L1**

4 Close

Portfolio

Ask a member of the local government to do a presentation about local environmental issues to the class. Students should place written summaries of the presentation into their portfolios.

Answers to Section Review

1. Burning of coal to generate electricity releases sulfur dioxide into the air. Sulfur dioxide may combine with water, forming sulfuric acid, which reduces the pH of precipitation.
2. All of these substances are sources of CFCs. The chlorine they contain reacts with ozone, thus leading to a thinning of the ozone layer.
3. Predicting the extent to which global warming may occur and devising possible solutions to deal with these unknown factors requires consideration of scientific data, governmental policies, and the costs involved.
4. **Skill Review—Designing an Experiment:** Two uncovered terraria could be set up and established. The plant life would be identical in each, as would all other factors. Each terrarium would initially receive equal amounts of water with a pH greater than that of acid rain. Then, one terrarium could be given water with a pH below 5.6. The effects of that water on the life in the terrarium could then be monitored.
5. **Thinking Critically:** The motor oil could eventually find its way into a stream, which feeds into a river, and finally the ocean.

Prepare

Key Concepts

In a consideration of conservation of natural resources, students will study availability and new sources of food, prevention of soil depletion, energy, and wildlife and forests.

Key Terms

renewable resource, nonrenewable resource, soil depletion, crop rotation, erosion

Materials

1 Focus

Objectives

The objectives are listed on the student page. Remind students to preview these objectives as a guide to this numbered section.

Discussion

Guide students in a discussion about a local or state conservation issue such as cleaning up an area, dealing with a landfill, organic farming, recycling projects, erosion control, disposal of city wastes, logging practices, or endangered species of the area.

Figure Caption Question

How is this technology beneficial to the environment as well as to famine-stricken countries? With larger production in a smaller area, less fuel will be used in harvesting. With larger crop yields, more food will be available for famine-stricken countries.

Objectives

Relate availability of food resources to the resource of soil.

Analyze the need for developing non-fossil fuels.

Discuss the importance of preserving forests and wildlife.

30.3 Conservation of Resources

For humans—and all other organisms—the environment is the only source for all materials needed for survival. Humans depend on other organisms as sources of food, clothing, tools, shelter, medicines, and fuel. Humans mine minerals from Earth and the oceans. The development of modern agriculture and technology has enabled humans to extract more and more resources from the environment. How long can we continue to depend on these natural resources? At some point, will we begin to run out of some of the materials we need? How does our use of these resources affect other organisms, and our own future?

Food

In a broad sense, resources are either renewable or nonrenewable. **Renewable resources** can be replaced; **nonrenewable resources** such as minerals and fossil fuels cannot. One of the most important of all resources is food. Food provides the energy needed for life. Because crops can be replanted and livestock can be bred, food is a renewable resource. However, availability of food varies in different parts of the world. Food shortages exist. The problem is most severe in developing countries, where the combination of dense populations, nonproductive farming methods, and poverty results in poor food supplies. Fuel for harvesting crops is expensive and difficult to obtain, limiting food production even more. Prolonged drought in some areas has led to widespread famine. How can food shortages, famine, and starvation be prevented?

Figure 30-18 Selective breeding practices have resulted in strains of wheat that produce more grain per plant than other varieties. How is this technology beneficial to the environment as well as to famine stricken countries?

Genetic Engineering Using selective breeding, geneticists have produced new strains of plants, such as rice and wheat, that produce more grain per plant than other varieties. The new strains also respond well to chemical fertilizers. An acre of land planted with these new strains can produce food for more people than the same acre planted with other varieties.

Geneticists have also begun developing a strain of corn that is richer in protein than other types of corn. This protein-rich strain is not yet ready for use because it has several undesirable traits that must be bred out of it, including soft kernels and lack of resistance to pests.

Concentrated Protein One of the major health problems people experience during food shortages is protein deficiency. Protein is very important for normal growth and development. Growing children who don't get enough protein experience severe weight loss, anemia, and liver damage. A possible solution to protein shortage is to make the best possible use of known protein-rich plant foods and to find new sources of protein.

864 HUMANS AND THE ENVIRONMENT

The seeds of many types of plants, especially beans, are good sources of protein. Soybean plants resist drought, thrive in a variety of soils, and can be grown for use as a source of protein in many areas of the world. The fresh seeds can be cooked and eaten, or they can be dried and stored for later use. They can also be ground to make flour or meal. The oil extracted from soybeans can be used to make a concentrated protein to be eaten as a meat replacement, or added to meat for a protein-rich meal.

Soil

Growing food crops on land requires fertile soil. In uncultivated areas, the organic nutrients plants remove from the soil are returned with the decay of the plants or the animals that ate the plants. When humans grow food crops, the plants are taken away from the area. If the soil nutrients are not replaced, the fertility of the soil is reduced and its ability to support crop growth diminishes. This process is called **soil depletion**. Fertilizers, both organic and synthetic, are used in an effort to replace the nutrients that are removed.

Crop Rotation Another method of reducing soil depletion involves alternating the crops grown on a plot of land. In this process, known as **crop rotation**, a soil-enriching plant such as a legume is grown one year; the next year, a soil-depleting crop such as corn or wheat is grown. The legumes return nitrogen and other nutrients to the soil, making it more fertile. As you already know, crop rotation also helps reduce pest problems by removing a pest's host plant.

Erosion Soil is usually considered a renewable resource because it is constantly being formed, primarily by the decay of organisms living on and in it. However, soil resources can be lost as a result of **erosion**, a natural process in which soil is removed by the action of rain and wind. Under the cover of plants, soil is held in place. However, careless farming methods can increase the erosion rate, as happened in the dust bowl, described in Chapter 29. Harvesting and plowing expose topsoil by removing the plant cover. Without rooted plants holding the soil in place, it is easier for wind and water to carry the soil away.

There are several farming methods that can be used to reduce erosion. Many of these involve plowing techniques that reduce erosion caused by the flow of rainwater. They include contour plowing, in which plowed furrows follow the shape of the land, and terracing, which involves creating level banks of land on a slope to slow the downhill flow of water.

Figure 30-19 **Rows of taller plants, such as corn planted in strips between rows of small grain plants, can protect the smaller plants from the effects of the wind. Strip-cropping is used to conserve soil in fields that are subject to erosion by wind or water.**

30.3 CONSERVATION OF RESOURCES ❧ **865**

2 Teach

Concept Development

- Experiments are underway to develop agricultural methods for growing other types of grain plants called amaranths, which were once a staple diet of the Aztecs. Amaranths contain more protein than the grains most often used for food today.

- The oceans can provide new sources of protein. For example, many species of fish are too small or too oily to make pleasant eating, so humans don't usually use them as food. However, modern food-processing methods could make it possible to create a nutritious protein concentrate or meat substitute from these fish.

- Recent experiments also suggest that genetic and biochemical techniques could be used to make synthetic foods for use in the future. These foods would be very similar to foods obtained from plants and animals, but they would come from a different source. For example, bacteria and yeasts can be genetically engineered to produce the same proteins that are found in meats, fish, and other foods. These proteins could be made into a powder that can be mixed with other food to increase the amount of protein in the diet.

- Using recombinant DNA techniques, bacteria have been engineered that produce one of the enzymes present in the stomachs of calves. This particular enzyme is used in the production of puddings and cheeses. With availability of synthetic versions of the enzyme, more of these foods could be produced at a lower cost.

MULTICULTURAL CONNECTION

Women in Science: Wangari Maathai was the first Kenyan woman to earn a Ph.D. in science. She became head of the department of veterinary medicine at the University of Nairobi and also organized the internationally recognized Green Belt Movement in 1977. The goal of this women's community action group was to plant a tree for each of Kenya's 25 million people. Her organization numbered 50 000 members who planted more than 10 million trees. Her project was the beginning of many other such movements in Africa and around the world.

Activity

- Take students on a walk through the school and have them keep track of all the places and ways in which materials and energy could be saved. Have them suggest alternate ways of doing things that would protect the environment. **L1**

- Have students determine what materials are best for absorbing sunlight and converting it to heat. They should place different types and colors of materials on the ground in sunlight. Then, cover and tape the bulb of a thermometer to the sample. After 5 minutes, ask students to record the temperatures. **L1** **LEP**

Figure Caption Question

What are some major limitations to the use of solar energy? It is not practical in areas with limited hours of sunlight and many cloudy days.

Minimum tillage is another method in which fields are not plowed after a crop is harvested. The stalks are kept in place. This can decrease erosion by as much as 90 percent for some crop fields. Wind erosion can also be reduced by planting trees as windbreaks and by plowing at right angles to prevailing winds.

Fuels

The fossil fuels and other petroleum products we rely on today took millions of years to form. Estimates are that humans may use up known petroleum deposits in as little as 645 years at current rates of consumption. New sources of oil and natural gas are constantly being sought. Offshore drilling may provide new supplies, and some shale formations may provide a new source of oil. But petroleum is not a renewable resource. Eventually, the demand is likely to exceed the supply. Humans can help preserve this resource by replacing fossil fuels with other sources of energy.

Figure 30-20   Solar heating systems are available to heat and cool homes. Active solar systems have tracking systems that actually allow solar collecting panels to track the sun across the sky. What are some major limitations to the use of solar energy?

Nuclear Power   The United States and other countries are already making use of nuclear power as a source of energy. There are several types of nuclear power plants. In one type, the nuclear reactor contains radioactive isotopes of uranium. These isotopes are split apart in a reaction called nuclear fission. The energy released by nuclear fission is used to generate electricity.

Only a small part of the electricity generated in the United States is produced by nuclear power. While this type of power plant conserves fossil fuels, the radioactive isotopes of uranium used as fuel are also a nonrenewable resource. Radioactive wastes produced by nuclear reactors pose a difficult disposal problem. And the water used to cool the reactors may cause thermal pollution of rivers and lakes. In a properly functioning reactor, radiation does not escape into the environment during fission. However, in the event of a large accident, some radiation could be released.

Solar Energy   The energy contained in sunlight is a plentiful, renewable resource. Our use of solar energy is slowly increasing. Solar-heated houses and other buildings are built of heat-absorbing materials and are oriented to catch sunlight during the winter months. You may have seen solar panels installed on the roofs of homes in some parts of the country. These panels collect solar energy for use in heating water. Solar cells have been developed to operate small devices such as calculators and watches. Larger solar cells are being used to power a factory in Saudi Arabia that makes fresh water from salt water, to power satellites, and to power portable field telephones for the military. As the cost of solar cells decreases, more uses for them will undoubtedly be found.

866 🔖 HUMANS AND THE ENVIRONMENT

PORTFOLIO

Ask student groups to prepare in their portfolios a presentation of the merits and drawbacks of one of the following types of energy: oil, coal, natural gas, hydropower, solar power, nuclear power, and other alternatives. They should illustrate with posters and transparencies, and should create a hands-on demonstration emphasizing a point.

PROJECT

Nuclear Winter: Ask a group of students to look up information about "nuclear winter." Ask them to compare views of experts on the subject and draw conclusions about whether they think nuclear winter is a possibility.

Other Energy Sources Still other sources of energy are being investigated for use in the future. Possible sources of untapped energy include hydrogen gas, wind, geothermal energy, and tidal power. These energy sources have two advantages—they are renewable, and they produce little or no pollution.

Wildlife and Forests

There have been many cases of human interference causing the extinction of plant and animal species. The dodo bird—a flightless, turkey-sized bird that nested on the ground—was wiped out when explorers brought dogs and pigs to its native island. The bird could not protect its eggs and young from being trampled or eaten by these new predators. Hunters were responsible for the extinction of the passenger pigeon and have almost wiped out other species, such as the tiger. When an organism becomes extinct, the natural balance of the ecosystem is irreversibly altered. It is important to realize that an extinct species will never again live on Earth—once it is gone, it is gone forever. Today, the major cause of extinction is the destruction of natural habitats. It is estimated that humans are causing the extinction of about one species each day.

Wildlife Conservation Efforts to conserve wildlife have included setting up wildlife preserves and imposing limits on hunting and fishing of some species. Wildlife preserves provide a means of making sure the habitat an endangered species needs for survival is not destroyed. Populations of many nearly extinct animals have been increasing as a result of wildlife conservation efforts in the United States. Whooping cranes, bison, sea otters, wild turkeys, and white-tailed deer have all benefited from these efforts. However, animals such as the California condor and the black-footed ferret are still in danger of disappearing.

Forest Conservation Scientists have estimated that approximately 30 to 50 percent of the world's forests have been destroyed for agriculture, fuel, and commercial use. Before Europeans arrived in North America, forests covered most of the eastern and western regions of the continent. Settlers cleared these forests for farmland, and the timber was burned for fuel or used for building. By the early 1900s, when it was becoming evident that too much of this natural resource was being destroyed, forest conservation efforts began.

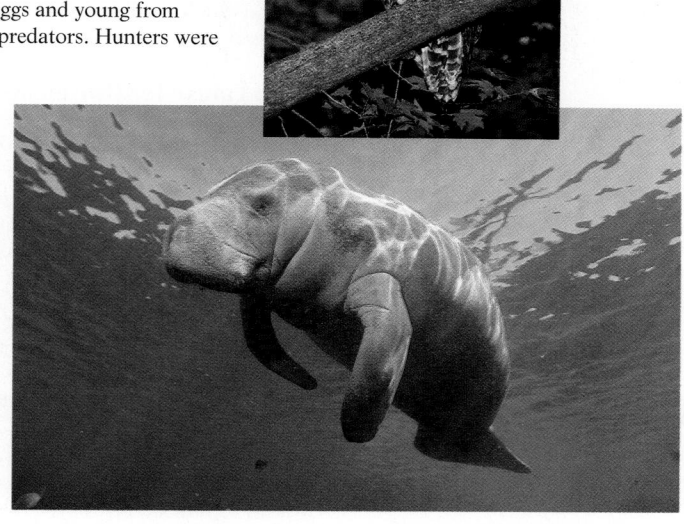

Figure 30-21 Manatees and the spotted owl are two animals that are facing extinction due to human interference. For these animals, the major threat is habitat destruction.

Activity
Ask students to select a spot on school grounds or a nearby vacant lot that could be improved for wildlife. Even city sites can be improved for city wildlife such as squirrels and birds. Ask students to make a map to scale of this area prior to making suggestions for improvements. Then, ask them to make another map with all the improvements that could be made for wildlife. Tell them that they will have unlimited budgets and that creativity is important. **L1**

MULTICULTURAL CONNECTION

Conservation of Trees: The Chipko Movement began in India in 1730 when the Maharajah of Jodphur sent his woodcutters to cut down the few trees left in the area. The Bishnois, a religious sect for whom the protection of trees and wildlife was a sacred duty, prevented this action. Bishnois women rushed in and put their arms around the trees to protect them. In 1973, a sports company was to come in to an area of Himalayan forest to cut trees for making racquet sports equipment. A community leader urged the people of the area to "chipko" or hold fast to the trees in their forest. When the tree cutters arrived, women of the village rushed in and threw their arms around the trees. Their successful action inspired other such movements around the country and the world.

SECTION 30.3

LITERATURE CONNECTION

The Lorax: Read the story *The Lorax* by Dr. Seuss to your class. This is a short essay about environmental problems. Tell students, in groups of three, that they are to assume the roles of the characters in the book: The Lorax, a Bar-ba-loot, and a Swomee-Swan. They should select a real environmental problem related to wildlife and forests and debate this issue from the points of view their story characters would have had. They should assume that they are serving on a committee that will decide what to do about the problem selected. They should represent and defend the point of view of the character assigned, even if they think it is not right. **L1**

COOP LEARN

Many of today's forest conservation efforts involve harvesting techniques used by the timber industry. To satisfy the demand for lumber, many timber harvesting companies are "farming" forest land by planting trees, both to replace those that are cut and to produce timber for future harvests. They are also planting private tree farms rather than depending on harvesting and replanting public forest lands. Clear cutting—a process of cutting all the trees in an area at one time—is now being replaced with other methods. For example, blocks of trees are sometimes left to reseed nearby cut areas and to maintain part of the complex forest community. Selective cutting and improvement cutting are also being used. In selective cutting, only mature trees are harvested, while young trees are left to mature. In improvement cutting, old, crooked, or diseased trees that will never be useful for timber are removed to make room for more valuable trees to grow.

Cause for Optimism

Pollution of the environment, overconsumption of natural resources, and an expanding human population are real and important problems facing humans today. For too many years, people ignored or failed to recognize the consequences of their actions with respect to the environment. As we improve our understanding of the consequences of our actions, we can make better, more informed choices.

Thinking Lab

DRAW A CONCLUSION

How much and what do we throw away each day?

Background
The graph shows the approximate mass percent of solid waste thrown away each day by each person in the U.S.

You Try It
Draw the following conclusions.
Calculate the mass of solid waste generated in the U.S. each day. If starting a recycling program to reduce solid waste being buried in landfills: (a) What material should be recycled first? Why? (b) What should be recycled last? Why? Does your community recycling program tend to agree with your last answers? Why are they good environmental choices? Explain why it may be a poor choice to begin a recycling program for leather and rubber.

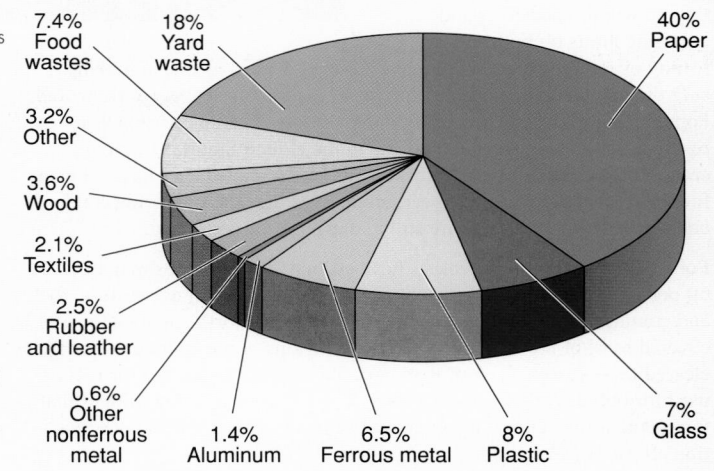

7.4% Food wastes
18% Yard waste
40% Paper
3.2% Other
3.6% Wood
2.1% Textiles
2.5% Rubber and leather
0.6% Other nonferrous metal
1.4% Aluminum
6.5% Ferrous metal
8% Plastic
7% Glass

868 HUMANS AND THE ENVIRONMENT

Thinking Lab

DRAW A CONCLUSION

Purpose
Students will use a pie graph to draw conclusions regarding the mass of solid waste disposed of each day by every American.

Skills
interpret scientific illustrations, interpret data

Teaching Strategies
Tell students the population of the U.S.

(approximately 250 million). Use a single-pan laboratory balance to illustrate and demonstrate what a mass of 1.8 kilograms looks like.

Answers
Mass of waste generated each day = 1.8 × 250 000 000 = 450 000 000 kg. Paper, being the highest contributor to solid waste, should be first to be recycled.

✔ **Assessment**
Knowledge: Have students record their answers in their journals. Ask them to give an opinion as to the success of and value of recycling programs in their community. Ask students to calculate the mass of solid waste generated each day/week/year in their city or community.

With careful planning and cooperation, we can reverse many existing problems and avoid creating new ones. Using human reason and intelligence, by balancing scientific facts against sound economic realities, we can take steps to maintain the health of the environment that supports all life on Earth.

LOOKING AHEAD

YOU HAVE NOW completed your course in biology. There are no more chapters to read. You've learned a great deal about life at all levels, from cell to biosphere. You know that all organisms use energy to carry out similar functions and that the instructions for being alive are coded in molecules of DNA. You know now that DNA is copied and transmitted to offspring, and you understand why organisms have the traits they do. You've learned that organisms evolve over time, adapting to environmental changes, and that evolution explains both the similarities and differences among living things. You understand that organisms live together in complex communities, and that they interact with one another and with the physical aspects of their environment. In this chapter, you learned how human activities have caused harm to the environment and some steps that need to be taken to correct and prevent environmental problems. You probably won't remember all of the details you've learned this year. We hope, though, that you will remember and make use of the major ideas. The knowledge you've gained of biology will enable you to make sound decisions concerning your personal life, the lives of fellow humans, and all other living systems. 🐾

Section Review

Understanding Concepts

1. A farmer has many acres of land. Each year, he sets several acres aside, planting no crops on that land. He varies the unplanted acres each year. Why?

2. The impact of humans on the environment can be described by the following equation: Impact = Population × Affluence × Techology. Explain how this equation describes the pollution problems in the U.S. and in a developing country. (Hint: You may wish to review Chapter 27.)

3. Some people argue, "What is so important about saving an endangered species?" What would you tell them?

4. **Skill Review—Making Models:** Use mounds of soil to demonstrate the principles of contour plowing and terracing. How can you demonstrate that these practices reduce erosion? For more help, see Representing and Applying Data in the **Skill Handbook.**

5. **Thinking Critically:** Irrigation can make dry land suitable for growing crops. In most irrigation methods, water is "sprayed" over the land. As this occurs, salt accumulates in the soil. The salt may have been present in the water added or it may have come from below as the salty water table rose. What would be the long-range effect of this irrigation procedure?

3 Assess

Check for Understanding
Have students make a list of the things each of them can do to help conserve and preserve our vital resources. They should include soils, energy, wildlife, and forests.

Reteach
Have students who have mastered this section tutor those who are still having trouble.

Extension
Ask students to do research on the endangered species. They should report about how they became endangered, and what is being done to improve their situations. **L2**

✔ Assessment
Portfolio: Ask students to assume that they are members of a committee from an environmental research company. They must develop a proposal for funding for a project to learn more about a specific environmental problem related to soils, energy, wildlife, or forests. They should explain the problem fully and propose what they hope to discover, how they intend to proceed, and why their ideas are so important. **L1**

4 Close

Guest Speaker
Ask a member of a local environmental group or agency to address your class on local environmental issues.

Answers to Section Review

1. Leaving some land unplanted each year slows removal of nutrients from the soil. By varying the unplanted areas, the farmer maximizes the fertility of his or her farmland.

2. Although the population size in the U.S. is not as great as in some developing countries, "values" for affluence and technology are high. Thus, the impact is great. In developing countries, affluence and technology have lower values, so the impact on the environment may be less even though the population size is great.

3. Some students may argue that human needs are more important than saving a species. Others may counter that it is our responsibility to save endangered species and that extinction could lead to disruption of ecosystems.

4. **Skill Review—Making Models:** Students can use the description of these practices in the text to construct their mounds of soil. They can test the effectiveness of each technique by noting the effects of water runoff as compared to a control mound of soil.

5. **Thinking Critically:** Over time, the soil would become so salty that it would become unsuitable for plant life.

CHAPTER 30

BIOLOGY, TECHNOLOGY, AND SOCIETY

Considering the Environment

Purpose
Students will study the benefits and problems associated with recycling paper, plastic, and tires.

Background
Today, only ten states have returnable bottles. Refillable bottles, collected and filled at nearby bottling plants, would reduce transportation and energy costs. In Ecuador, the beverage container deposit fee is 50 percent higher than the cost of the drink. This method of encouraging recycling has been very successful, and some bottles that are still in circulation are ten years old. Only two sizes of bottles are allowed so that sorting is not a problem. In Finland, 95 percent of beverage containers are refillable, and in Germany 75 percent.

Teaching Strategies
Display a variety of items and tell students that they may or may not be recyclable: newspaper, carrot, plastic soda bottle, plastic bleach bottle, piece of carpet, T-shirt, glass bottle, rechargeable battery, tire, motor oil, and aluminum can. Ask them if they know which products can be recycled.

BIOLOGY, TECHNOLOGY, AND SOCIETY

Considering the Environment
New Uses for Waste Material

Every year, the average American creates approximately 2000 pounds of trash. We're running out of places to put it. So much garbage has already been dumped

into New York's Fresh Kills landfill on Staten Island that it has become the largest human-made object in the world, surpassing the Great Wall of China.

Across the country, existing landfills are filling up but few new ones are opening. Inexpensive land suitable for landfills is becoming rare and few communities are willing to have a landfill nearby.

Approximately 40 percent, by weight, of the trash in landfills is paper. It's paper's role in the landfill crunch that has been behind the growing demand for paper recycling.

During the past decade, paper recycling technology has improved to the point that the only thing holding it back is customer demand. As of 1992, far more paper has been turned in for recycling than the paper companies could accept. They could make only so much recycled paper because they couldn't sell any more. As increasing numbers of people use recycled paper, less and less paper will end up in landfills.

In contrast to paper, plastic accounts for only 8 percent of landfill trash by weight. Although this is true, it makes up approximately 20 percent by volume. That makes plastic a major part of the landfill problem, because volume determines when a landfill is full.

Unlike paper, plastic has been notoriously hard to recycle. One major problem is that there are hundreds of different types of plastic and they usually cannot be mixed. You can melt down soda bottles for reuse easily enough. But, if a single bleach bottle made of a

different type of plastic were accidentally melted down with them, all the plastic would be ruined.

To keep the many types of plastic apart, all plastic has to be hand sorted. The type of plastic is indicated on each container by a number. The type of plastic can be determined easily enough, but hand sorting is an expensive process.

Furthermore, plastic is so inexpensive to manufacture from scratch that recycling has always been more costly. Until the landfill crunch created a demand, few plastic buyers were willing to pay extra for recycled supplies.

Fortunately, new techniques and new products have combined with the growing demand for recycled products to make plastic recycling practical. Among the techniques

CAREER CONNECTION

Chemical engineers develop the manufacturing processes, equipment, and plants that convert raw materials into commercial products. To do their job, they must be skilled in mathematics, chemistry, and physics. A variety of industries require chemical engineers, including plastics, cosmetics, pharmaceuticals, soap, fuels, explosives, and food products.

870 CHAPTER 30 HUMANS AND THE ENVIRONMENT

CAREER CONNECTION

For more information, have students contact a nearby college or university to ask about careers in chemical engineering.

870

being pioneered are several processes that completely disassemble plastics to their original chemical components. The components can then be remixed to make fresh plastics or be used for other purposes. For example, since plastics are petroleum-based, scrap plastic can be a source of fuel and fuel additives.

Recycling plastic into fuel may keep it out of the landfills, but it isn't likely to win the hearts of many environmentalists. One use and the fuel is gone in a burst of exhaust fumes. Maybe that's one reason recycled plastic has generated a lot of interest as a construction material.

Plastic lumber has earned itself a place in the construction world. It has proven particularly good for park benches, decks, and other outdoor uses. Plastic makes good lumber for the same reason it makes bad landfill material—it doesn't degrade easily. Plastic is waterproof and rot proof. Insects don't eat it. And it requires no preservatives, as wood does.

Unfortunately, plastic lumber looks like plastic, not like lumber. But another new building material combines recycled plastic with recycled wood to give a more natural appearance. Fibers from scrap wood are encapsulated in the plastic and molded into the desired shape. One of the first uses of this material is in exterior doorways. The material is used at the bottom of the door jamb because it seals well against the weather and resists rot due to moisture.

Recycled plastic is showing up in other parts of new homes and commercial buildings. Plastic foam is being processed into insulation board, while discarded plastic computer housings have been reincarnated as roofing panels.

Discarded tires have created a problem very similar to that caused by plastic. About 242 million tires are tossed away in the United States every year, most of them ending up in landfills, illegal dumping sites, or near-useless stockpiles. One recent Environmental Protection Agency estimate is that the U.S. has a stockpile of more than 2 billion old tires. These old tires are also finding new uses.

The development of rubberized asphalt is putting old tires back on the road. This form of asphalt, made with rubber from discarded tires, has made a name for itself as road repair material. While it costs twice as much as normal asphalt, it also lasts twice as long. What's more, it's less expensive to use and maintain.

One experimental technique that holds much promise involves grinding old tires into small particles and

bonding them with other substances to produce new composite materials. The new materials may be used for such things as shoe soles, hoses, and conveyer belts.

Still another technique mixes granules of recycled tire rubber with resins to produce an outdoor flooring material. It's particularly good for coating concrete. It has been used on swimming pool decks at the Disneyland Hotel and the University of California at Los Angeles and to coat the eroding top of a hydroelectric dam.

Another aquatic use for old tires is under water. They've been used to help construct artificial reefs. It takes only days before barnacles and other reef-building organisms start growing on the tires and connecting material. Eventually, reefs they produce become havens for fish and scuba divers.

None of the innovations we've discussed here come close to solving the enormity of the United States' landfill problem. However, they show what's possible when the will to recycle is combined with effort and ingenuity.

1. **Find Out:** Plastic lumber and rubberized asphalt have been used in many city and county government projects. Has your community used these or any similar materials? How?
2. **Issue:** Should city governments require citizens to separate and recycle their trash? Defend your answer.

Possible Answers
1. Answers will vary. Some students will find that their community uses rubberized asphalt and park and playground equipment and lumber made of recycled plastic or tires. Other communities will not use such materials.
2. Most students would be in favor of recycling. Some will say that the city should do the separation of trash as it creates, for the homeowner, a problem of storage of all the different kinds of trash, and it takes time to do the work required to clean and separate trash. Others will say that the process of recycling is a waste of time and energy and will think we should make all our products from new materials. Others might be in favor of recycling, but not in favor of laws that require it. They might say that citizens should be free to make their own choices about whether or not to recycle.

Going Further
Tell students that they are directors of a project to get rid of old tires that have been piled up in a community dumping spot for 50 years. They must think of a new product to make from the tires and develop a community service announcement encouraging residents to buy this product. **L1**

CHAPTER REVIEW

Summary

The summary can be used by students to review the major concepts of the chapter.

Language of Biology

Answers should go beyond defining the terms. Accept any reasonable answer that uses the term correctly and in the proper context.

Understanding Concepts

1. The question emphasizes the economic considerations and benefits of pesticide use. Availability of an abundance of "undamaged" fruits and vegetables is crucial to the grocer's livelihood.
2. It would be best, if possible, to use integrated pest management methods in order to reduce potential harm to organisms other than the insect larvae.
3. Student opinions will doubtless vary, some supporting each side of the issue. The fact that people view such matters in different ways illustrates the complexity of environmental problems.
4. Limiting sunbathing is wise, especially in view of ozone layer depletion, which allows even more ultraviolet radiation to reach Earth's surface. Such radiation is known to cause skin cancer.
5. Students might choose examples such as use of pesticides or burning of fossil fuels. They should explain the economic consequences of reducing amounts of the pollutants they choose. Costs borne by industries are usually passed along to consumers and that consumers often act unfavorably to such cost increases.
6. An asthma sufferer would doubtless be pleased by such regulations and would gladly pay a bit more to ensure better health.
7. Some of the heat entering and then reflected from the room on the sunny side of the building is reflected back into the room by the windows.

872

REVIEW
CHAPTER
30

Summary

Modern technology and agricultural practices have led to pollution of the environment.

Pesticides are an example of chemicals that have positive value but that also have adverse effects including destruction of natural predators of pests and harm to non-pest organisms as well. Use of less toxic, quickly biodegradable pesticides coupled with biological, autocidal, and cultural means of pest control is a reasonable solution to the problem.

By-products of technology often become pollutants of air and water. Individually, many of these pollutants threaten the health and well-being of humans, other organisms, and entire ecosystems. Many of them interact with each other or other chemicals, giving rise to additional problems such as smog, acid precipitation, and destruction of the ozone layer.

Reducing pollution and preventing further harm to the environment involves a cooperative effort among scientists, governments, and individuals.

Not only have humans added pollutants to the environment, they have also depleted it of many resources. Development of new food and fuel sources and conservation of soil, forests, and wildlife are crucial goals if our planet is to continue to support the lives of humans and all other organisms.

Language of Biology

Write a sentence that shows your understanding of each of the following terms.

acid precipitation
autocidal control
biological control
biological magnification
chlorofluorocarbon (CFC)
crop rotation
cultural control
erosion
greenhouse effect

integrated pest
 management
nonbiodegradable
nonrenewable
 resource
pesticide
pollution
renewable resource
soil depletion

Understanding Concepts

1. You are a grocer whose income depends partly on the sale of fresh fruits and vegetables. Are you for or against the use of pesticides? Why?
2. Suppose you are a member of your local town council. Larvae of a certain insect are devouring the leaves on the trees along Main Street. What method(s) would you suggest to your fellow council members to preserve the trees? How would you convince them?
3. More than ten years ago, residents of Times Beach, Missouri, were ordered to evacuate the town permanently. This order was to protect residents against the dangers of dioxin that contaminated roadways in the area. Did scientists act hastily? Did they overestimate the risks of exposure to dioxin? Should they have waited to evacuate the area until further analysis and testing of the hazards of dioxin? How does this story affect your thinking about how we should respond to pollutants and environmental problems in general? Is it better to be safe than sorry, or do you favor a "wait-and-see" approach?
4. Why would it be wise for you to limit your sunbathing?

Applying Concepts

8. The danger of oil entering the ocean waters is always present. Oil is lethal to a variety of marine life—plankton, fish larvae, crustaceans, birds, and mammals.
9. Students may think of countless ways in which a technological society depends upon energy—for transportation, in manufacture of goods, and for production of electricity.
10. No area is completely isolated from any other. Students may cite examples such as acid rain to support the idea that the area is not safe from pollution.
11. Runoff of soil and remains of dead organisms from the field bring pesticides to the lake. There, the pesticides, if nonbiodegradable, can enter food chains and be subject to biological magnification. Large fish accumulate the greatest amount of pesticides and may die.

5. Choose two examples of pollutants discussed in this chapter and explain how solutions to the problems of decreasing those pollutants involve economic factors. If you were the president of a company, how would you feel if regulations forced you to spend more money to counteract pollution? How would you make up your losses? How might your customers react?

6. If you suffered from asthma, how would you feel about regulations like the ones that call for reduced output of sulfur dioxide emissions? Would you be willing to pay a higher electric bill?

7. It's a bright, sunny, though cold day in winter and the heat is on. Why are the rooms on the sunny side of the school warmer than those on the other side?

Applying Concepts

8. Why must offshore oil-drilling procedures be well controlled?

9. Outline some ways in which an energy shortage would affect a technological society.

10. Suppose today a particular area of the United States is not heavily industrialized and is relatively free of pollution. Suppose, too, that the area remains industry-free. Is it safe from pollution in the future? Explain.

11. How can application of pesticides to a field have an effect on large fish in a lake?

12. Which animals, insects or birds, are likely to develop a resistance to a pesticide more quickly? Why?

13. **Considering the Environment:** Explain how recycling reduces pollution problems and helps preserve resources.

14. **Global Connection:** Why is our knowledge of the effects of toxic chemicals on humans so limited?

Lab Interpretation

15. **Thinking Lab:** A recycling program for waste wood is being considered by your community. How would you advise them? Explain why.

16. **Investigate:** The following data were gathered by a student using different detergent concentrations on bean seed germination.

Concentration of detergent	Number of seeds used	# germinated after 5 days
0	100	98
1	100	97
2.5	100	90
5	100	63
10	100	14
20	100	0

(a) At what range may the maximum concentration of detergent be found for a 50% germination rate?

(b) Explain how this data may be used to predict germination of radish seeds in different concentrations of insecticide.

17. **Minilab 2:** The following data gives the pH values for samples of rainwater:

Sample	pH
A	4
B	3
C	5
D	6

(a) Which sample(s) are acid?

(b) Which sample is the strongest acid?

(c) Which sample may contain the fewest air pollutants?

(d) Which sample may contain the most air pollutants?

Connecting Ideas

18. Suppose global warming occurs to an extent such that temperatures in the midwest become more like those of subtropical areas, and farmlands are abandoned. What would happen to those abandoned lands if left undisturbed?

19. Review the graph of human population growth in Chapter 27. Do you see a correlation between that growth and the onset of major environmental problems? What does that suggest to you about another important factor in reducing environmental concerns?

12. Insects will likely develop a resistance first. They produce more offspring and do so much more quickly than birds. Thus, there is a greater chance of some individuals having the variation of resistance, which they can pass on to their descendants.

13. Recycling not only lengthens the life of landfills, but it also conserves resources by using the same materials over and over again.

14. Knowledge is limited because it is often difficult to establish a link between a toxic chemical and symptoms that may appear among humans.

Lab Interpretation

15. Student answers may vary. Wood accounts for only 3 percent of the total mass of solid waste thrown away each day. It is not responsible for the bulk of waste material. Therefore, it may not be efficient or effective to attempt to recycle such a small amount of waste.

16. (a) between 5 and 10 percent concentration; (b) A different seed type and pollutant is being used than what is given in the experimental data. Therefore, no conclusions can be drawn from this data.

17. (a) A-D; (b) A; (c) D; (d) B

Connecting Ideas

18. **Patterns of Change:** The abandoned lands would undergo secondary succession. However, considering the changes in climate, they would probably develop into a community more like a tropical rain forest.

19. **Patterns of Change:** The significant increase in human population size can be correlated with technological advances. Technology, in turn, has been a source of pollution and other environmental concerns such as depletion of resources. The more people, the more technology. More technology brings with it more pollution and depletion of resources. Decreasing

PROGRAM RESOURCES

Teacher Classroom Resources
Chapter Assessment, pp. 117-120 **L1**
Performance Assessment in Biology, p. 60 **L2**
Alternate Assessment in the Science Classroom
Computer Test Bank **L1**

the rate at which the human population size is increasing will be an important factor in reducing pollution and other environmental problems.

Skill Handbook

Organizing Information

Thinking Critically

Practicing Scientific Methods

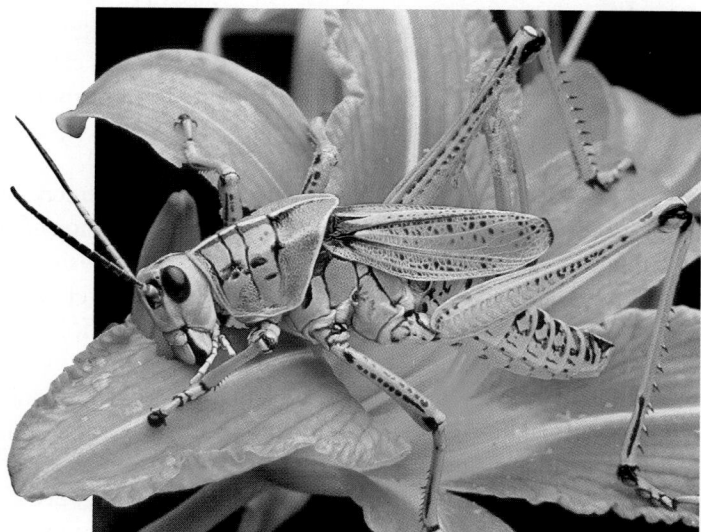

Organizing Information

Classifying

You may not realize it, but you impose order on the world around you. If your shirts hang in the closet together, your socks take up a corner of a dresser drawer, or your favorite CDs are stacked in groups according to recording artist, you have used the skill of classifying.

Classifying is grouping objects or events into groups based on common features. When classifying, you first make careful observations of the group of items to be classified. Select one feature that is shared

by some items in the group but not others. Place the items that share this feature in a subgroup. Place the remaining items in a second subgroup. Ideally, the items in the second subgroup will have some feature in common with one another. After you decide on the first feature that divides the items into subgroups, examine the items for other features and further divide each subgroup into smaller and smaller groups until the items have no features in common.

How would you classify a collection of CDs? Classify the CDs based on observable features. You

might classify CDs you like to dance to in one subgroup and CDs you like to listen to in another. The CDs you like to dance to could be subdivided into a rap subgroup and a rock subgroup. Note that for each feature selected, each CD only fits into one subgroup. For example, you wouldn't place a CD into both rap and rock categories. Keep selecting features until all the CDs are classified. The chart shows one method of classification.

Remember, when you classify, you are grouping objects or events for a purpose.

Sequencing

A sequence is an arrangement of things or events in a particular order. A common sequence with which you are familiar is students sitting in alphabetical order. Think also about baking chocolate chip cookies. Certain steps have to be followed in order for the cookies to taste good.

When you are asked to sequence things or events, you must first identify what comes first. You then decide what should come second. Continue to choose things or events until they are all in order. Then, go back over the sequence to make sure each thing or event logically leads to the next.

Suppose you wanted to watch a movie that just came out on videotape. What sequence of events would you have to follow to watch the movie? You would first turn the television set to Channel 3 or 4. You would then turn the videotape player on and insert the tape. Once the tape has started playing, you would adjust the sound and picture. Then, when the movie is over, you would rewind the tape and return it to the store. What would happen if you did things out of sequence, such as adjusting the sound before putting in the tape?

Concept Mapping

If you were taking an automobile trip, you would probably take along a road map. The road map shows your location, your destination, and other places along the way. By examining the map, you can understand where you are in relation to other locations on the map.

A concept map is similar to a road map. But, a concept map shows the relationship among ideas (or concepts) rather than places. A concept map is a diagram that visually shows how concepts are related. Because the concept map shows the relationships among ideas, it can clarify the meaning of ideas and terms and help you to understand better what you are studying.

Look at the construction of a concept map called a **network tree.** Notice how some words are circled while others are written on connecting lines. The circled words are science concepts. The lines in the map show related concepts, and the words written on the lines describe relationships between the concepts. A network tree can also show more complex relationships between the concepts. For example, a line labeled "affected by" could be drawn from plants and animals to chemistry, because chemical processes occur in plants and animals.

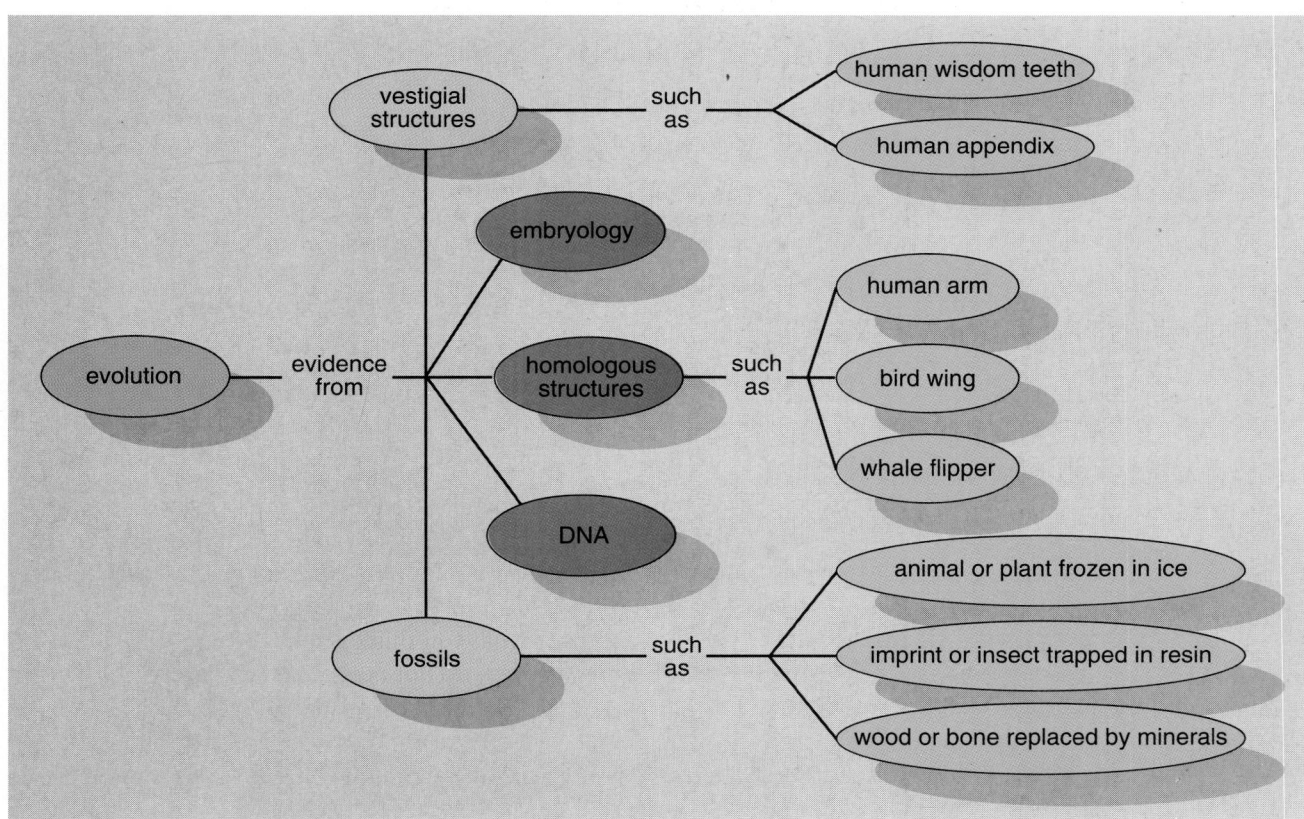

When you are asked to construct a network tree, state the topic and select the major concepts. Find related concepts and put them in order from general to specific. Branch the related concepts from the major concept and describe the relationships on the lines. Continue to write the more specific concepts. Write the relationships between the concepts on the lines until all concepts are mapped. Examine the concept map for relationships that cross branches, and add them to the concept map.

An **events chain** is another type of concept map. An events chain map is used to describe ideas in order. In science, an events chain can be used to describe a sequence of events, the steps in a procedure, or the stages of a process.

dinner dishes. An events chain map might look like the one in the left column. Notice that connecting words may not be necessary.

A **cycle concept map** is a special type of events chain map. In a cycle concept map, the series of events do not produce a final outcome. The last event in the chain relates back to the initiating event.

As in the events chain map, you first decide on an initiating event and then list each important event in order. Since there is no outcome and the last event relates back to the initiating event, the cycle repeats itself. Look at the cycle map of insect metamorphosis.

Complete Insect Metamorphosis

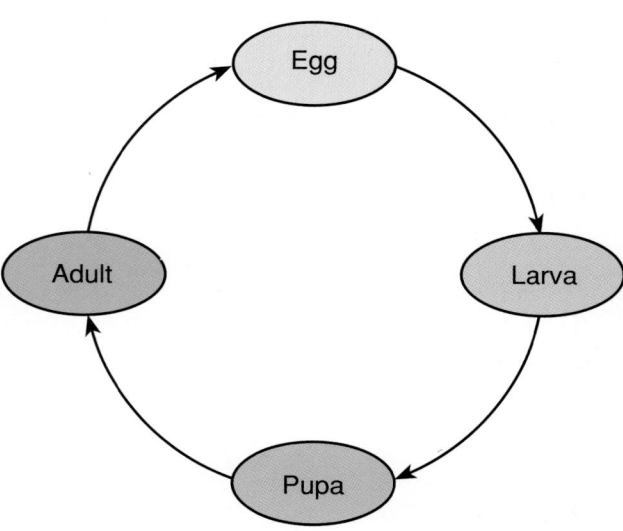

When making an events chain, you first must find the one event that starts the chain. This event is called the initiating event. You then find the next event in the chain and continue until you reach an outcome. Suppose your mother asked you to wash the

There is usually not one correct way to create a concept map. As you are constructing a map, you may discover other ways to construct the map that show the relationships between concepts better. If you do discover what you think is a better way to create a concept map, do not hesitate to change it.

Concept maps are useful in understanding the ideas you have read about. As you construct a map, you are constructing knowledge and learning. Once concept maps are constructed, you can use them again to review and study and to test your knowledge.

Making and Using Tables

Browse through your textbook, and you will notice many tables both in the text and in the labs. The tables in the text arrange information in such a way that it is easier for you to understand. Also, many labs in your text have tables to complete as you do the lab. Lab tables will help you organize the data you collect during the lab so that it can be interpreted more easily.

Most tables have a title telling you what is being presented. The table itself is divided into columns and rows. The column titles list items to be compared. The row headings list the specific characteristics being compared among those items. Within the grid of the table, the collected data are recorded. Look at the following table and then study the questions that follow it.

Effect of Exercise on Heartbeat Rate

| Pulse taken | Heartbeat rate | |
	individual	class average
at rest	73	72
after exercise	110	112
1 minute after exercise	94	90
5 minutes after exercise	76	75

What is the title of this table? The title is "Effect of Exercise on Heartbeat Rate." What items are being compared? The heartbeat rate for an individual and the class average are being compared at rest and for several durations after exercise.

What is the average heartbeat rate of the class 1 minute after exercise? To find the answer, you must locate the column labeled "class average" and the row "1 minute after exercise." The data contained in the box where the column and row intersect is the answer. Whose heartbeat rate was 110 after exercise? If you answered the individual's, you have an understanding of how to use a table.

Making and Using Graphs

After scientists organize data in tables, they often display the data in graphs. A graph is a diagram that shows a comparison between variables. Since graphs show a picture of collected data, they make interpretation and analysis of the data easier. The three basic types of graphs used in science are the line graph, bar graph, and pie graph.

A line graph is used to show the relationship between two variables. The variables being compared go on two axes of the graph. The independent variable always goes on the horizontal axis, called the x-axis. The independent variable is the condition that is manipulated. The dependent variable always goes on the vertical axis or y-axis. The dependent variable is any change that results from manipulating the independent variable.

Suppose a school started a peer study program with a class of students to see how it affected their science grades.

Average Grades of Students in Study Program

Grading Period	Average Science Grade
first	81
second	85
third	86
fourth	89

You could make a graph of the grades of students in the program over a period of time. The grading period is the independent variable and should be placed on the *x*-axis of your graph. Instead of four grading periods, we could look at average grades for the week or month or year. In this way, we would be manipulating the independent variable. The average grade of the students in the program is the dependent variable and would go on the *y*-axis.

After drawing your axes, you would label each axis with a scale. The *x*-axis simply lists the grading periods. To make a scale of grades on the *y*-axis, you must look at the data values. Since the lowest grade was 81 and the highest was 89, you know that you will have to start numbering at least at 81 and go through 89. You decide to start numbering at 80 and number by twos through 90.

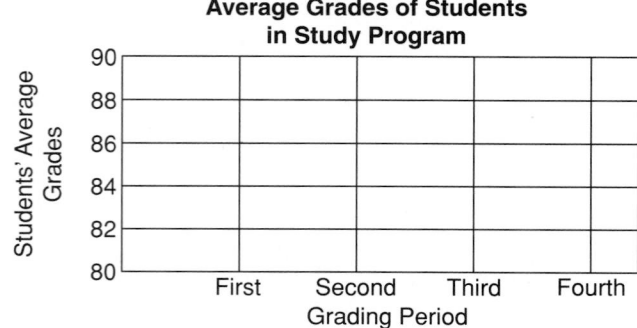

You next must plot the data points. The first pair of data you want to plot is the first grading period and 81. Locate "First" on the *x*-axis and 81 on the *y*-axis. Where an imaginary vertical line from the *x*-axis and an imaginary horizontal line from the *y*-axis would meet, place the first data point. Place the other data points the same way. After all the points are plotted, connect them with a smooth line.

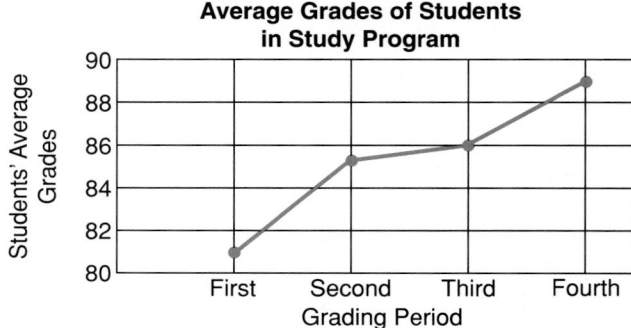

What if you wanted to compare the average grades of the class in the study group with the grades of another class? The data of the other class can be plotted on the same graph to make the comparison. You must include a key with two different lines, each indicating a different set of data.

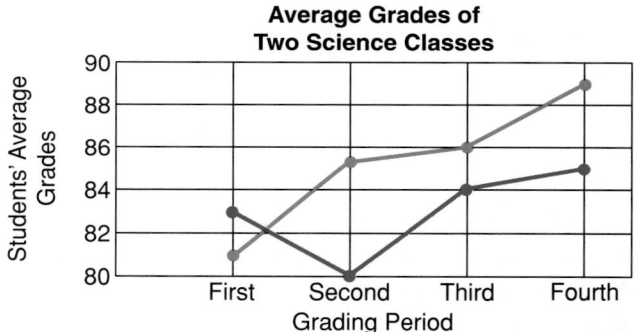

Bar graphs are similar to line graphs, except they are used to show comparisons between data or to display data that does not continuously change. In a bar graph, thick bars show the relationships between data rather than data points.

To make a bar graph, set up the *x*-axis and *y*-axis as you did for the line graph. The data is plotted by drawing thick bars from the *x*-axis up to an imaginary point where the *y*-axis would intersect the bar if it were extended.

Look at the bar graph comparing the wing vibration rates for different insects. The independent variable is the type of insect, and the dependent variable is the number of wing vibrations per second. The number of wing vibrations for different insects is being compared.

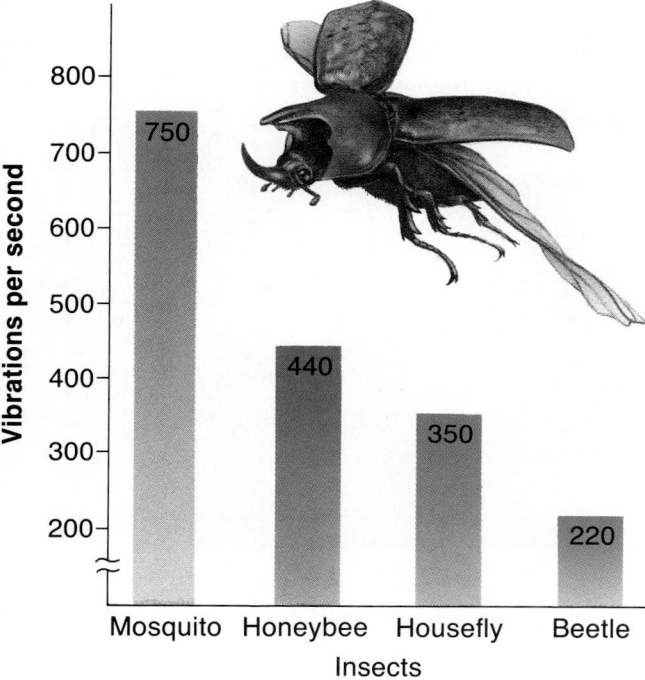

A pie graph uses a circle divided into sections to display data. Each section represents part of the whole. When all the sections are placed together, they equal 100 percent of the whole.

Suppose you wanted to make a pie graph to show the number of seeds that germinated in a package. You would have to determine the total number of seeds and the number of seeds that germinated out of the total. You count the seeds and find that there are 143 seeds in the package. Therefore, the whole pie will represent this amount.

You plant the seeds and determine that 129 seeds germinate. The group of seeds that germinated will make up one section of the pie graph, and the group of seeds that did not germinate will make up another section.

To find out how much of the pie each section should take, you must divide the number of seeds in each section by the total number of seeds. You then multiply your answer by 360, the number of degrees in a circle. Round your answer to the nearest whole number. The number of seeds that germinated would be determined as follows:

$$\frac{143}{129} \times 360 = 324.75 \text{ or } 325 \text{ degrees}$$

To plot this data on the pie graph, you need a compass and a protractor. Use the compass to draw a circle. Then, draw a straight line from the center to the edge of the circle. Place your protractor on this line and use it to mark a point on the edge of the circle at 325 degrees. Connect this point with a straight line to the center of the circle. This is the section for the group of seeds that germinated. The other section represents the group of seeds that did not germinate. Complete the graph by labeling the sections of your graph and giving the graph a title.

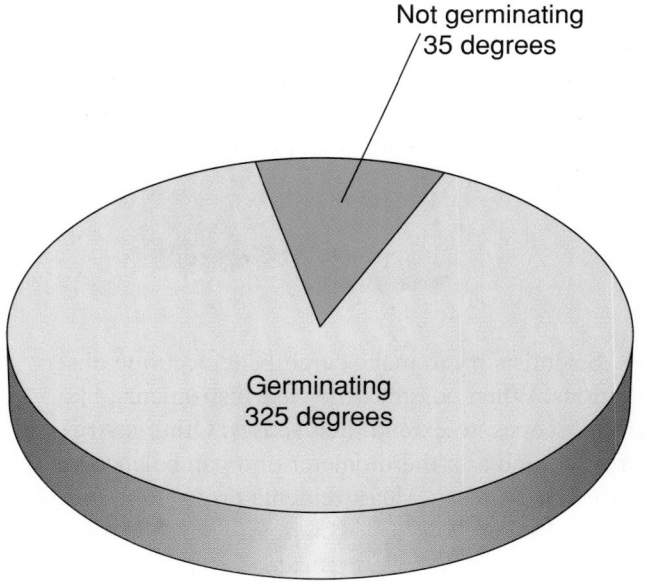

Thinking Critically

Observing and Inferring

Imagine that you have just finished a volleyball game with your friends. At home, you open the refrigerator and see a jug of orange juice at the back of the top shelf. The jug feels cold as you grasp it. "Ah, just what I need," you think. When you drink the juice, you smell the oranges and enjoy the tart taste in your mouth.

As you imagined yourself in the story, you used your senses to make observations. You used your sense of sight to find the jug in the refrigerator, your sense of touch to feel the coldness of the jug, your sense of hearing to listen as the liquid filled the glass, and your sense of smell and taste to enjoy the odor and tartness of the juice. The basis of all scientific investigation is observation.

Scientists try to make careful and accurate observations. When possible, they use instruments, like microscopes, to extend their senses. Other instruments, such as a thermometer or a pan balance, measure observations. Measurements provide numerical data, a concrete means of comparing collected data that can be checked and repeated.

When you make observations in science, you may find it helpful first to examine the entire object or situation. Then, look carefully for details using your sense of sight. Write down everything you see before using another sense to make additional observations.

Scientists often use their observations to make inferences. An inference is an attempt to explain or interpret observations or to determine what caused what you observed. For example, if you observed a CLOSED sign in a store window around noon, you might infer that the owner is taking a lunch break. But, perhaps the owner has a doctor's appointment or has a business meeting in another town. The only way to be sure your inference is correct is to investigate further.

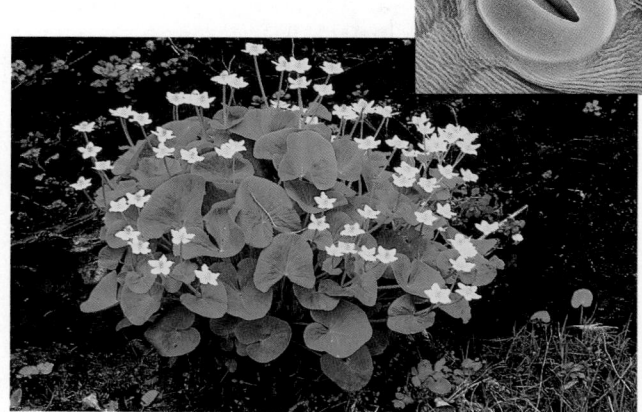

When making an inference, be certain to make accurate observations and to record them carefully. Collect all the information you can. Then, based on everything you know, try to explain or interpret what you observed. If possible, investigate further to determine if your inference is correct.

Comparing and Contrasting

Observations can be analyzed and then organized by noting the similarities and differences between two or more objects or situations. When you examine objects or situations to determine similarities, you are comparing. Contrasting is looking at similar objects or situations for differences.

Suppose you were asked to compare and contrast a grasshopper and a dragonfly. You would start by making your observations. You then divide a piece of paper into two columns. List ways the insects are similar in one column and ways they are different in the other. After completing your lists, you report your findings in a table or in a graph.

Similarities you might point out are that both have three body parts, two pairs of wings, and chewing mouthparts. Differences might include large hind legs on the grasshopper, small legs on the dragonfly; wings held close to the body in the grasshopper, wings held outspread in the dragonfly.

Recognizing Cause and Effect

Have you ever observed something happen and then tried to figure out why or how it came about? If so, you have observed an event and inferred a reason for the event. The event or result of action is an effect, and the reason for the event is the cause.

Suppose that every time your teacher fed fish in a classroom aquarium, she tapped the food container on the edge. Then, one day she tapped the edge of the aquarium to make a point about an ecology lesson. You observe the fish swim to the surface of the aquarium to feed.

What is the effect and what would you infer would be the cause? The effect is the fish swimming to the surface of the aquarium. You might infer the cause to be the teacher tapping on the edge of the aquarium. In determining cause and effect, you have made a logical inference based on careful observations.

Perhaps the fish swam to the surface because they reacted to the teacher's waving hand or for some other reason. When scientists are unsure of the cause for a certain event, they often design controlled experiments to determine what caused their observations. Although you have made a sound judgment, you would have to perform an experiment to be certain that it was the tapping that caused the effect you observed.

Measuring in SI

You are probably familiar with the metric system of measurement. The metric system is a uniform system of measurement developed in 1795 by a group of scientists. The development of the metric system helped scientists avoid problems with different units of measurement by providing an international standard of comparison for measurements. A modern form of the metric system called the International System, or SI, was adopted for worldwide use in 1960.

SKILL HANDBOOK

You will find that your text uses metric units in all its measurements. In the labs you will be doing, you will use the metric system of measurement.

The metric system is easy to use because it has a systematic naming of units and a decimal base. For example, meter is the base unit for measuring length, gram for measuring mass, and liter for measuring volume. Unit sizes vary by multiples of ten. When changing from smaller units to larger, you divide by a multiple of ten. When changing from larger units to smaller, you multiply by a multiple of ten. Prefixes are used to name larger and smaller units. Look at the following table for some common metric prefixes and their meanings.

Metric Prefixes

Prefix	Symbol	Meaning
kilo-	k	1000 thousand
hecto-	h	100 hundred
deka-	da	10 ten
deci-	d	0.1 tenth
centi-	c	0.01 hundredth
milli-	m	0.001 thousandth

Do you see how the prefix *kilo-* attached to the unit *gram* is *kilogram* or 1000 grams, or the prefix *deci-* attached to the unit *meter* is *decimeter* or one tenth (0.1) of a meter?

You have probably measured distance many times. The meter is the SI unit used to measure distance. To visualize the length of a meter, think of a baseball bat, which is about one meter long. When measuring smaller distances, the meter is divided into smaller units called centimeters and millimeters. A centimeter is one hundredth (0.01) of a meter, which is about the width of the fingernail on your index finger. A millimeter is one thousandth of a meter (0.001), about the thickness of a dime. The photograph at the top of the page shows this comparison.

Most metric rulers have lines indicating centimeters and millimeters. The centimeter lines are the longer numbered lines, and the shorter lines between the centimeter lines are millimeter lines.

When using a metric ruler, you must first decide on a unit of measurement. You then line up the 0 centimeter mark with the end of the object being measured, and read the number of the unit where the object ends.

Units of length are also used to measure surface area. The standard unit of area is the square meter (m^2), or a square one meter long on each side. Similarly, a square centimeter (cm^2) is a square one centimeter long on each side. Surface area is determined by multiplying the number of units in length times the number of units in width.

884 ❧ SKILL HANDBOOK

The volume of rectangular solids is also calculated using units of length. The cubic meter (m^3) is the standard SI unit of volume. A cubic meter is a cube one meter on a side. You can determine the volume of rectangular solids by multiplying length times width times height.

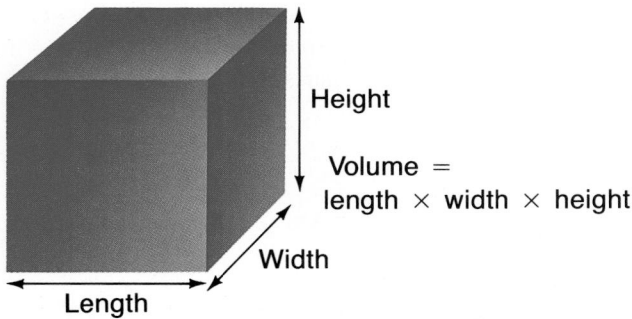

Height

Volume =
length × width × height

Width

Length

Liquid volume is measured using a unit called a liter. A liter has the volume of 1000 cubic centimeters. Because the prefix *milli-* means thousandth (0.001), a milliliter equals one cubic centimeter. One milliliter of liquid would completely fill a cube measuring one centimeter on each side.

During biology labs, you will measure liquids using beakers and graduated cylinders marked in milliliters. A graduated cylinder is a tall cylindrical container marked with lines from bottom to top. Each graduation represents one milliliter. You will likely use a beam balance when you want to find the masses of

objects. Often you will measure mass in grams. On one side of the beam balance is a pan and on the other side is a set of beams. Each beam has an object of a known mass called a rider that slides on the beam.

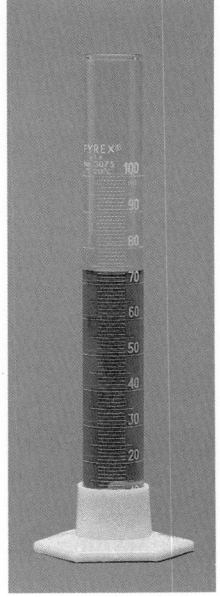

Before you find the mass of an object, you must set the balance to zero by sliding all the riders back to the zero point. Check the pointer to make sure it swings an equal distance above and below the zero point on the scale. If the swing is unequal, find and turn the adjusting screw until you have an equal swing.

You are now ready to use the balance to find the mass of the object. Place the object on the pan. Slide the rider with the largest mass along the beams until the pointer drops below the zero point. Then move it back one notch. Repeat the process on each beam until the pointer swings an equal distance above and below the zero point. Read the masses indicated on the beams. The sum of the masses is the mass of the object.

Never place a hot object or pour chemicals directly on the pan. Instead, find the mass of a clean container, such as a beaker or a glass jar. Place the dry or liquid chemicals you want to measure into the container. Next, find the combined mass of the container and the chemicals. Calculate the mass of the chemicals by subtracting the mass of the empty container from the combined mass.

Interpreting Scientific Illustrations

Illustrations are included in your science textbook to help you understand, interpret, and remember what you read. Whenever you encounter an illustration, examine it carefully and read the caption. The caption is a brief comment that explains or identifies the illustrations.

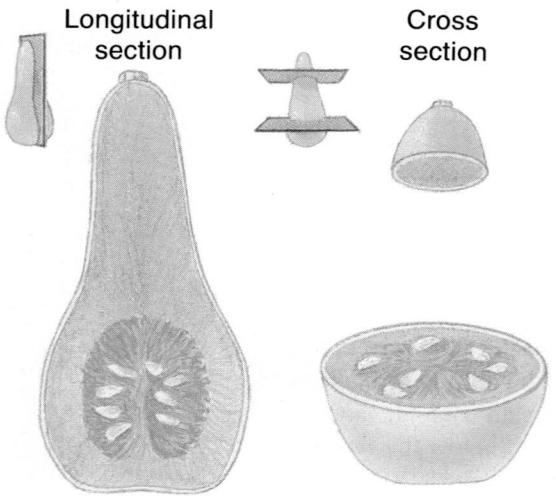

Longitudinal section

Cross section

Other organisms and objects have radial symmetry. Radial symmetry is the arrangement of similar parts around a central point. The anemone in the figure below has radial symmetry. See how it can be divided anywhere through the center into similar parts.

Some organisms and objects cannot be divided into two similar parts. If an organism or object cannot be divided, it is asymmetrical. Study the sponge. Regardless of how you try to divide a sponge, you cannot divide it into two parts that look alike.

Some illustrations are designed to show you how the internal parts of a structure are arranged. Look at the illustrations of a squash. The squash has been cut lengthwise so that it shows a section that runs along the length of the squash. This type of illustration is called a longitudinal section. Cutting the squash crosswise at right angles to the length produces a cross section.

Symmetry refers to a similarity or likeness of parts. Many organisms and objects have symmetry. When something can be divided into two similar parts lengthwise, it has bilateral symmetry. Look at the illustration of the butterfly. The right side of the butterfly looks very similar to the left side. It has bilateral symmetry.

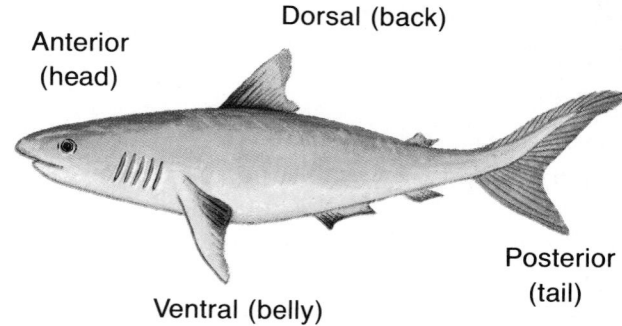

Dorsal (back)

Anterior (head)

Ventral (belly)

Posterior (tail)

In your reading and examination of the illustrations, you will sometimes see terms that refer to the orientation of an organism. The word *dorsal* refers to the upper side or back of an animal. *Ventral* refers to the lower side or belly of the animal. The illustration of the shark has both dorsal and ventral sides.

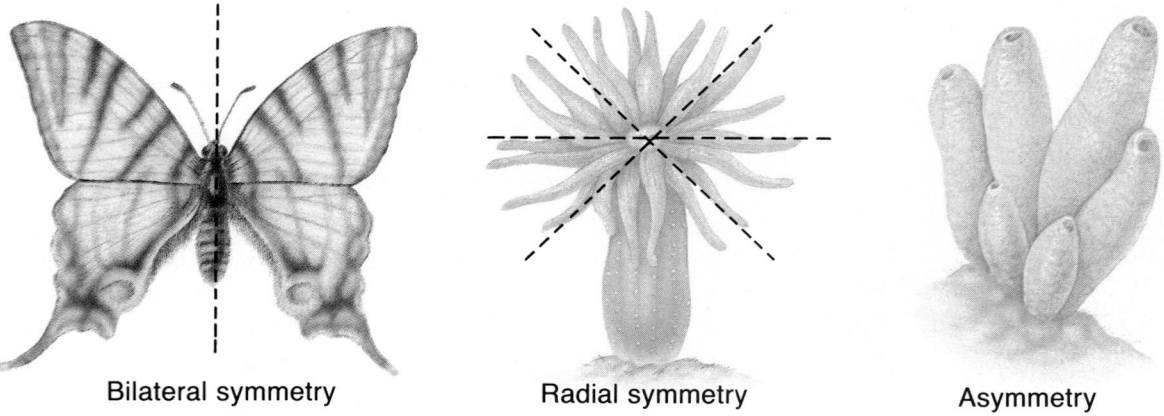

Bilateral symmetry　　　　Radial symmetry　　　　Asymmetry

Practicing Scientific Methods

You might say that the work of a scientist is to solve problems. But when you decide how to dress on a particular day, you are doing problem solving, too. You may observe what the weather looks like through a window. You may go outside and see if what you are wearing is warm or cool enough.

Scientists generally use experiments to solve problems and answer questions. An experiment is a method of solving a problem in which scientists use an organized process to attempt to answer a question.

Experimentation involves defining a problem and formulating and testing hypotheses, or proposed solutions, to the problem. Each proposed solution is tested during an experiment, which includes making careful observations and collecting data. After analysis of the collected data, a conclusion is formed and compared to the hypothesis.

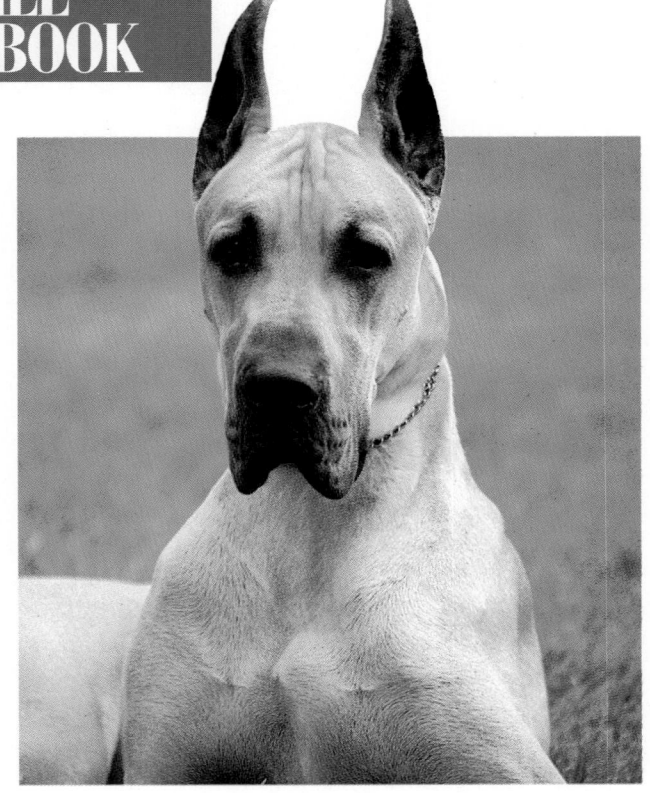

Observing

You observe all the time. Anytime you smell wood burning, touch a pet, see lightning, taste food, or hear your favorite music, you are observing. Observation gives you information about events or things. Scientists must try to observe as much as possible about the things and events they study.

Some observations describe something using only words. These observations are called qualitative observations. If you were making qualitative observations of a dog, you might use words such as furry, brown, short-haired, or short-eared.

Other observations describe how much of something there is. These are quantitative observations and use numbers as well as words in the description. Tools or equipment are used to measure the characteristic being described. Quantitative observations of a dog might include a mass of 45 kg, a height of 76 cm, ear length of 11 cm, and an age of 412 days.

Forming a Hypothesis

Suppose you wanted to earn a perfect score on a spelling test. You think of several ways to accomplish a perfect score. You base these possibilities on past observations. All of the following are hypotheses you might consider to explain how you could score 100% on your test:

If the test is easy, then I will get a good grade.
If I am intelligent, then I will get a good grade.
If I study hard, then I will get a good grade.

Scientists use hypotheses that they can test to explain the observations they have made. Perhaps a scientist has observed that fish activity increases in the summer and decreases in the winter. A scientist may form a hypothesis that says: If fish are exposed to warmer water, their activity will increase.

Designing an Experiment to Test a Hypothesis

Once you have stated a hypothesis, you probably want to find out whether or not it explains an event or an observation. This requires a test. To be valid, a hypothesis must be testable by experimentation. Let's figure out how you would conduct an experiment to test the hypothesis about the effects of water temperature on fish.

First, obtain several identical clear glass containers, and fill them with the same amount of water. Let the containers set. On the day of your experiment, you fill a container with an amount of aquarium water equal to that in the test containers. After measuring and recording the water temperature, you heat and cool the other containers, adjusting the water temperatures in the test containers so that two have higher temperatures and two have lower temperatures than the aquarium water temperature.

You place a guppy in each container. You count the number of horizontal and vertical movements each guppy makes during five minutes and record your data in a table. Your data table might look like this:

Number of Guppy Movements

Container	Temperature (°C)	Number of movements
aquarium water	38	56
A	40	61
B	42	70
C	36	46
D	34	42

From the data you recorded, you will draw a conclusion and make a statement about your results. If your conclusion supports your hypothesis, then you can say that your hypothesis is reliable. If it did not support your hypothesis, then you would have to make new observations and state a new hypothesis, one that you could also test. Do the data above support the hypothesis that warmer water increases fish activity?

Separating and Controlling Variables

When scientists perform experiments, they must be careful to manipulate or change only one condition and keep all other conditions in the experiment the

Appendices

Classification of Organisms

Kingdom Monera

Archaebacteria (Ancient Bacteria)

Phylum Aphragmabacteria (thermoacidophiles)
Shape irregular or bloblike due to lack of cell wall; found in hot springs of Yellowstone National Park at temperatures of 60°C and having a pH of 1 to 2, and in humans and domesticated animals where they cause certain types of pneumonia. **Examples:** *Mycoplasma pneumoniae, Thermoplasma acidophilum*

Phylum Halobacteria (halophiles)   Rod- or cocci-shaped; move by flagella; tolerate and live only in areas of high salt (sodium chloride) concentrations, such as in brine or salt flats. **Examples:** *Halobacterium halobium, Halobacterium salinarium*

Phylum Methanocreatrices (methanogens)   Rod, spiral, or coccus in shape; may move via flagella or are immobile; found worldwide in sewage, marine and freshwater sediments, swamps, and even cows' stomachs; responsible for producing marsh gas or methane. **Examples:** *Methanobacillus omelianski*

Eubacteria (True Bacteria)

Phylum Actinobacteria   Composed of rods, long complex filaments, or short multicellular filaments; filaments resemble hyphae of fungi; some cause diseases such as tuberculosis, leprosy, or skin lesions; others produce the antibiotic streptomycin; others found living in plant root nodules remove or fix nitrogen from the air. **Examples:** *Mycobacterium tuberculosis (tuberculosis), Mycobacterium leprae* (leprosy), *Streptomyces griseus*

Phylum Omnibacteria   A mixed group of bacteria having rod or comma-like shapes; can live with or without oxygen; many cause plant, human, and other animal diseases such as food poisoning, gonorrhea, meningitis; *Escherichia coli,* the most studied bacterium in the world, belongs to this phylum. **Examples:** *Salmonella typhi, Neisseria gonorrhoeae*

Phylum Spirochaetae (Spirochaetes)   Look like coiled springs, as suggested by the beginning of the phylum name (spiro); found in sewage, marine, and fresh water as well as in tooth plaque and the intestines of different animals; help to digest wood in the gut of termites; cause diseases in humans. **Examples:** *Treponema pallidum* (syphilis), *Leptospira icterohaemorrhagiae* (infectious jaundice)

Kingdom Monera

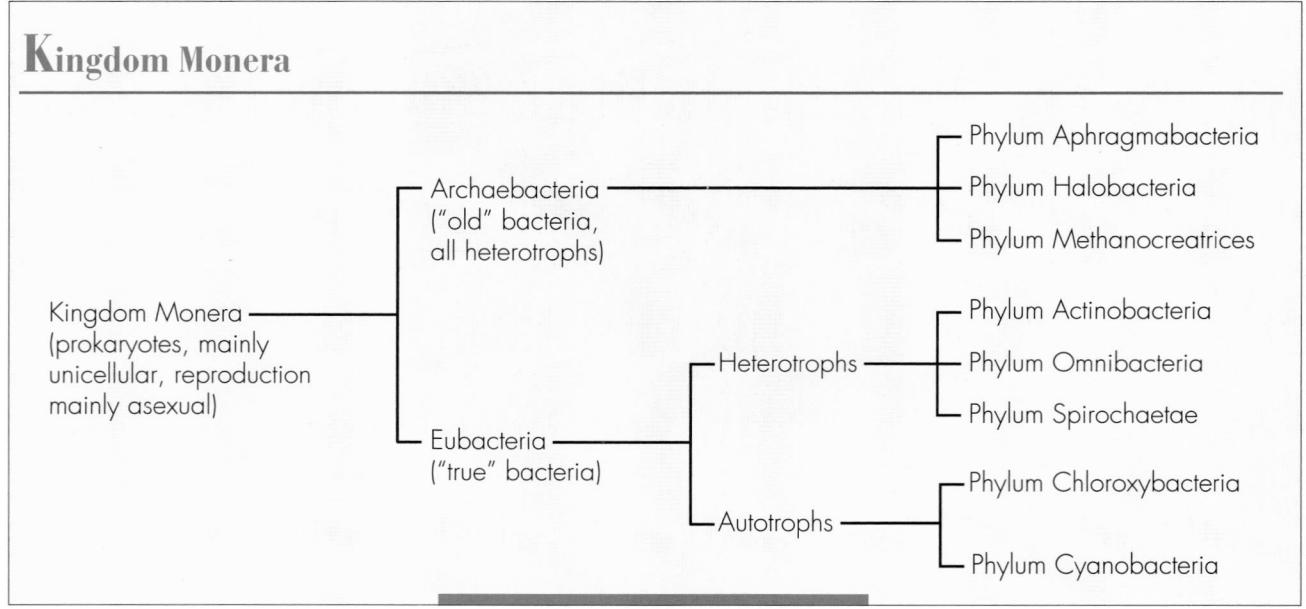

Phylum Chloroxybacteria (Grass-green Bacteria)
All spherical in shape and contain chlorophyll, thus
making them autotrophic; found living on or in the
body of marine organisms called tunicates, also
known as sea squirts; structure strongly resembles
chloroplasts, the photosynthetic organelles found in
plants. **Examples:** *Prochloron sp., Prochlorothrix sp.*

Phylum Cyanobacteria (Blue-green Algae)
Autotrophic due to the presence of chlorophyll; have
a bluish tinge due to blue-colored pigments; some
cyanobacteria found as fossils dating as far back as 3
billion years ago (stromatolites); some found floating
on or just below the surfaces of lakes and ponds,
some fix nitrogen from the air. **Examples:** *Nostoc
parmeloides, Anabaena subcylindrica*

Kingdom Protista

Animal-like Protists

Phylum Rhizopoda (Amoebas)   Found in soil, fresh
and marine waters; unicellular; move about by flowing cytoplasmic extensions called pseudopodia; many
are parasitic. **Examples:** *Amoeba proteus, Entamoeba
histolytica* (amoebic dysentery)

Phylum Ciliophora (Ciliates)   Hairs called cilia that
are used for locomotion; may reproduce asexually or
sexually; two types of nuclei–a, small micronucleus
used in sexual reproduction and a larger macronucleus used for growth and asexual reproduction.
Examples: *Paramecium caudatum, Stentor coeruleus*

Kingdom Protista

Kingdom Protista (eukaryotic cells, may be autotrophs or heterotrophs)

- Animal-like (heterotrophic, unicellular)
  - Move by pseudopodia —————— Phylum Rhizopoda
  - Move by cilia —————— Phylum Ciliophora
  - Nonmotile —————— Phylum Sporozoa
  - Move by flagella —————— Phylum Zoomastigina
- Plantlike (autotrophic)
  - Unicellular
    - No flagella —————— Phylum Bacillariophyta
    - Two flagella of unequal lengths
      - Phylum Euglenophyta
      - Flagella at right angles — Phylum Dinoflagellata
  - Multicellular
    - Red and green pigments —————— Phylum Rhodophyta
    - Brown and green pigments —————— Phylum Phaeophyta
  - Unicellular or multicellular
    - Green and orange pigments —————— Phylum Chlorophyta
- Funguslike (heterotrophic)
  - No cellulose in cell walls
    - Unicellular —————— Phylum Acrasiomycota
    - Multicellular —————— Phylum Myxomycota
  - Cellulose in cell walls —————— Phylum Oomycota

Phylum Sporozoa (Sporozoans) Protists with no means for locomotion; form spores, as their name suggests, that aid in their dispersal from host to host; many are bloodstream parasites. **Examples:** *Plasmodium malariae* (malaria), *Monocystis agilis*

Phylum Zoomastigina (Flagellates) One or many whiplike hairs called flagella that are used for locomotion; include human parasites; others are found in the gut of wood-eating termites and aid the digestion of cellulose. **Examples:** *Trichomonas muris, Trypanosoma gambiense* (sleeping sickness)

Plantlike Protists

Phylum Euglenophyta (Euglenoids) Lack cellulose cell walls; easily change shape; most live in fresh or stagnant waters; photosynthetic, but can become heterotrophic organisms. **Examples:** *Euglena gracilis, Euglena spirogyra*

Phylum Bacillariophyta (Diatoms) Appear in the fossil record as far back as the Cretaceous period; cells like the two parts that make up a pillbox; beautiful silica-impregnated shells; important food source for marine and freshwater organisms. **Examples:** *Navicula lyra, Frustulia rhomboides*

Phylum Dinoflagellata (Dinoflagellates) Found in warm marine waters; some are bioluminescent; others form toxic poisons dispersed in blooms, such as red tides; many form symbiotic relationships with corals and sea anemones; all have two flagella located at right angles to one another. **Examples:** *Gonyaulax tamarensis, Gymnodinium microadriaticum*

Phylum Rhodophyta (Red Algae) Usually complex marine algae; red color due to the presence of photosynthetic pigments; some forms are edible; others provide a chemical substance called agar, used in bacteria cultures. **Examples:** *Polysiphonia harveyi, Chondrus crispus*

Phylum Phaeophyta (Brown Algae) Large kelps found along ocean coastlines forming underwater forests of seaweed beds; some are used as food or fertilizers; algin, a chemical formed by these algae, is used as a gel in soft ice creams. **Examples:** *Macrocystis pyrifera* (kelp), *Fucus vesiculosus*

Phylum Chlorophyta (Green Algae) Many green algae are unicellular, but colonies and large multicellular forms exist; considered to be the ancestors of higher land plants; are important oxygen-formers and provide food for many

marine and freshwater heterotrophs. **Examples:** *Ulva lactuca* (sea lettuce), *Volvox aureus*

Funguslike Protists

Phylum Acrasiomycota (Cellular Slime Molds) They share features of the plant, animal, and fungi kingdoms; grow in or on fresh water, damp soil, or rotting vegetation, such as decaying logs; slime molds help break down dead organic matter. **Examples:** *Dictyostelium discoideum, Acrasia sp.*

Phylum Myxomycota (Plasmodial Slime Molds) Found as slimy wet scum on fallen logs and bark; a favorite for laboratory study because they show streaming and back-and-forth pulsating of their protoplasm; advanced protists showing alternation of generations in their life cycle. **Examples:** *Physarum polycephalum, Stemonitis splendens*

Phylum Oomycota (Water Molds, Mildews, Rusts) Includes water mold that caused the infamous 19th-century blight that destroyed potato crops in Ireland and Germany; another parasitic form called "ich" is a common, often fatal pest of aquarium fish, seen as a white fuzz on their fins; many cause diseases of garden and crop plants. **Examples:** *Saprolegnia parasitica, Phytophthora infestans* (potato blight)

Kingdom Fungi

Phylum Zygomycota (Sporangium Fungi) These fungi grow by feeding on any decaying vegetation or animal; they may reproduce by forming spores inside a round sporangium that is borne aloft by a long, thin hypha. **Examples:** *Rhizopus stolonifer* (black bread mold), *Mucor hiemalis*

Phylum Ascomycota (Cup Fungi and Yeasts) Includes yeasts, morels, and truffles; causes athlete's foot and ringworm of the scalp; may reproduce by forming spores that are enclosed inside an ascus; important as decomposers; yeasts are essential for making wine and beer, and as an aid in baking. **Examples:** *Saccharomyces cerevisiae* (bread yeast), *Neurospora sitophila*

Phylum Basidiomycota (Club Fungi) Includes smuts, rusts, and puffballs; reproduce with a microscopic clublike part, called a basidium, that contains spores; fatal, hallucinogenic, and edible mushrooms all belong to this phylum. **Examples:** *Amanita phalloides* (death cap), *Agaricus brunnescens* (edible mushroom)

Phylum Deuteromycota (Imperfect Fungi) Only asexual reproduction has been observed; the antibiotic penicillin is produced by a fungus in this phylum. One member of this phylum causes moniliasis, a vaginal infection of humans; other members cause root rot of many cultivated plants. **Examples:** *Penicillium chrysogenum* (penicillin antibiotic), *Candida albicans* (moniliasis)

Phylum Mycophycota (Lichens) This phylum is made up of organisms formed through a symbiotic union of a fungus and a unicellular chlorophyte algae or cyanobacterium; are the first organisms that grow on volcanic areas or bare rock; ecologically important because they dissolve rocks, thus providing conditions suitable for the growth of rooted plants; are an important food for tundra reindeer. **Examples:** *Cladonia cristatella, Peltigera rufescens*

Kingdom Fungi

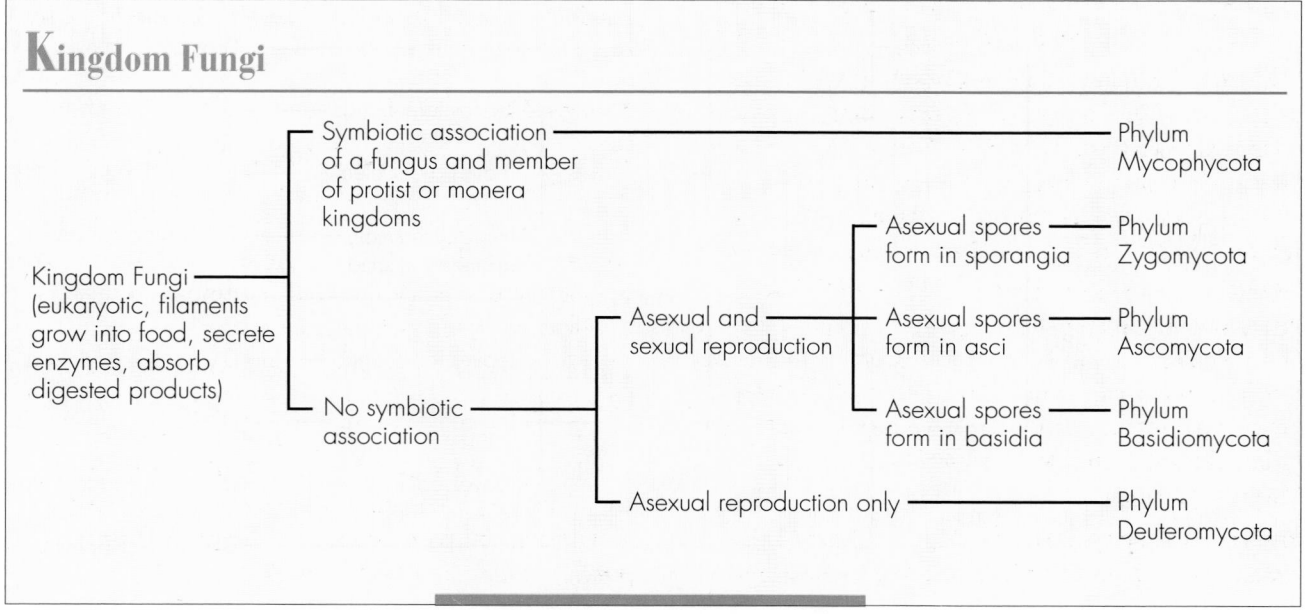

Kingdom Plantae

Spore Plants

Division Bryophyta (Mosses and Liverworts)   This division includes the mosses and liverworts, which grow in moist habitats; have no vascular tissue; the most conspicuous stage in the life cycle is a leaflike, green gametophyte generation; spores are formed in capsules; sporophyte dependent on gametophyte for water and nutrients.

Class Mucopsida (Mosses)   More than 14 000 species; Gametophyte generations are creeping along ground or upright; multicellular rhizoids; ecologically important as soil contributors, increasing water retention in soil; peat moss can be burned as a fuel. **Examples:** *Polytrichum juniperinum, Sphagnum squarrosum*

Class Hepaticopsida (Liverworts)   So-called because of the liverlike, flat shape of the gametophyte generation; about 9000 species of liverworts; most found in the tropics; obtain water from long, single-celled rhizoids. **Examples:** *Marchantia polymorpha, Pellia epiphylla*

Division Psilophyta (Whisk Ferns)   The conspicuous generation is a green sporophyte; sporophyte is a thin, leafless stem (about 30 cm); stem has small, leaflike scales along its length; no roots; found in tropical and subtropical regions of the world. **Examples:** *Psilotum nudum, Rhynia gwynnevaughanii* (*Rhynia* is an extinct plant.)

Division Lycophyta (Club Mosses)   The conspicuous generation is the sporophyte; most species extinct; fossil club mosses are giant treelike plants that lived more than 280 million years ago and helped form present-day coal beds; present-day species are very small and have often been used as holiday decorations—the main reason for their threatened condition. **Examples:** *Lycopodium obscurum, Selaginella lepidophylla*

Kingdom Plantae

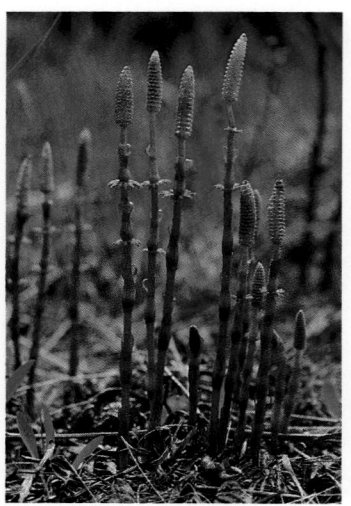

Division Sphenophyta (Horsetails) Stems jointed and have a rough, ribbed feel; stem looks like a pipe with small, scalelike leaves arranged in whorls at each node; commonly called "scouring rushes"; only one living genus with about five species; all present-day horsetails are short, whereas their fossil relatives were treelike; contributed to the formation of coal beds. **Examples:** *Equisetum arvense, Calamites carinatus* (*Calamites* is an extinct plant group.)

Division Pterophyta (Ferns) Most complex of all spore-forming plants; usually have lacy leaves called fronds; size of fronds varies from 1 cm to 500 cm long; two-thirds of the 12 000 present-day species are found in the tropics; many are cultivated for use as houseplants. **Examples:** *Polypodium virginianum, Osmunda cinnamonea*

Seed Plants

Division Ginkgophyta (Ginkgos) Only one living species of this division, which explains why it is called a living fossil; native to China; leaves deciduous and fan-shaped; trees are either male or female; very hardy and resistant to pollution and insects; popular choice for street plantings in many cities. **Examples:** *Ginkgo biloba* (maidenhair tree), *Ginkgoites digitata.* (*Ginkgoites* is an extinct plant group.)

Division Cycadophyta (Cycads) Some are small plants that look like pineapple fruits; others look like palm trees; stems are typically unbranched and covered with the woody bases of shed leaves; bear male and female reproductive organs in cones; grow only in tropical or subtropical climates; about 100 species. **Examples:** *Zamia floridana, Cycas revoluta*

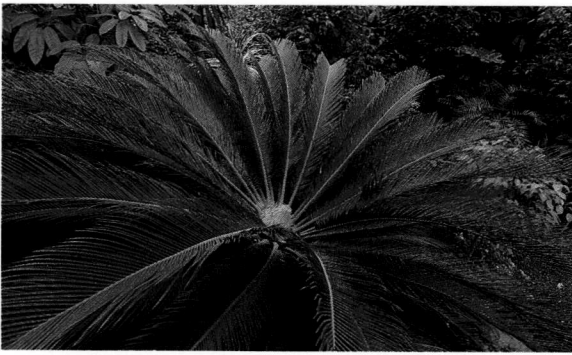

Division Coniferophyta (Conifers) Reproduce by forming cones; commonly known as evergreen or conifer trees; includes the largest living plant, the giant Sequoia of California; leaves are usually needle-shaped and not deciduous; a major source of lumber, paper, turpentine, pitch, tar, amber, and resin; about 400 species. **Examples:** *Pinus virginiana* (Virginia pine), *Sequoiadendron gigantea* (giant redwood)

Division Gnetophyta Most are either desert-dwellers or found on mountainsides in Asia, Africa, and Central and South America; some are scrubby, cone-bearing, and pinelike; others are flat plants consisting of

two long, very large, thick leaves that lie on the ground; only 70 species are known; a drug called ephedrine comes from one of these plants and is used to treat asthma, emphysema, and hay fever. **Examples:** *Welwitschia mirabilis, Gnetum gnenom*

Division Anthophyta (Flowering Plants) Reproduction occurs in flowers; seeds are protected within an ovary in the flower; the most diverse and largest group of modern plants with over 230 000 species and 300 families; gametophyte generation is microscopic; sporophyte generation may reach tree size; plants grown commercially for food and decorations belong to this division.

Class Dicotyledones (Dicots)   Flowering plants with two (di) cotyledons, or seed leaves, in their seeds; flower parts are in fours or fives.

Family Magnoliaceae (Magnolias)   Found mainly in tropic or subtropic regions but a few species are found in temperate zones; about 100 species, most of which are magnolias; 2 species of tulip trees. **Examples:** *Magnolia virginiana, Liriodendron tulipifera*

Family Fagaceae (Beeches)   Familiar members of this group are the oaks and beeches; used primarily for wood in building furniture, floors, and interior moldings; used almost exclusively by early shipbuilders; about 350 species. **Examples:** *Fagus grandifolia, Quercus alba*

Family Cactaceae (Cacti)   Strictly desert dwellers, native to the new world; familiar succulents and spiny cacti that range in height from very small to treelike; flowers with numerous petals, many stamens often joined to the petals; fruit a many-seeded berry; about 2000 species. **Examples:** *Opuntia fragilis, Carnegiea gigantea*

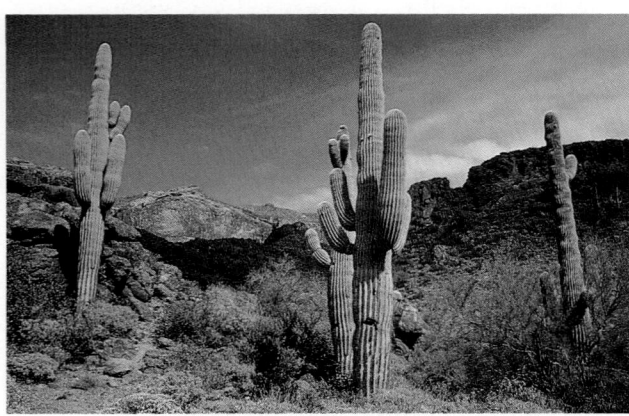

Family Malvaceae (Mallows)   Most important member commercially is the cotton plant; hollyhocks and hibiscus are common cultivated garden plants. Five separate petals; stalks of many stamens all fused and surrounding a long style; fruit a capsule; about

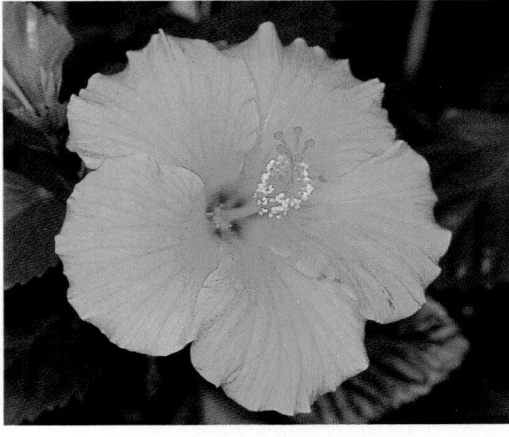

1500 species. **Examples:** *Gossypium hirsutum* (cotton), *Hibiscus tiliaceus*

Family Brassicaceae (Mustard)   Commonly called the mustard group; most familiar as foods that are eaten throughout the world; includes cabbage, turnips, radish, Brussels sprouts, cauliflower, and broccoli; about 2000 species. **Examples:** *Brassica oleracea, Raphanus sativus*

Family Rosaceae (Rose)   Worldwide in distribution; includes common garden rose, raspberries, strawberries; about 1200 species, 300 of which are found in the U.S. **Examples:** *Rosa alba, Rubus idaeus*

Family Fabaceae (Pea)   Second largest family of plants; includes large trees, shrubs, vines, and perennial and annual herbs; includes clover, alfalfa, peas, beans, soybean, and peanuts; over 12 000 species. **Examples:** *Medicago sativa, Arachis hypogaea*

Family Aceracea (Maple) Includes maples and boxelders; most abundant in the eastern half of U.S.; noted for their use in fine furniture, musical instruments, and as a source for sugar maple; about 100 species. **Examples:** *Acer saccharum, Acer negundo*

Family Lamiaceae (Mint) Best known for their fragrance and oils that are used as flavorings and in some medicines; includes plants such as peppermint, catnip, thyme, and sage; about 3000 species. **Examples:** *Mentha piperita, Thymus vulgaris*

Family Asteraceae (Daisies) The largest family; found growing worldwide and in almost every ecological condition; includes sunflower, goldenrod, lettuce, dandelion, ragweed, and chrysanthemum; more than 15 000 species. **Examples:** *Helianthus annuus, Lactuca sativa*

Class Monocotyledones (Monocots) Flowering plants with one (mono) cotyledon, or seed leaf, in their seeds; flower parts are in threes or multiples of three.

Family Poaceae (Grasses) Includes important herbaceous plants such as corn, rice, oats, wheat, sugarcane, and Kentucky bluegrass; flowers often inconspicuous; enclosed in two scalelike bracts; fruit a caryopsis; about 10 000 species. **Examples:** *Triticum aestivum* (wheat), *Zea mays* (corn)

Family Palmae (Palms) Tropical and semitropical trees and shrubs; includes date palms, coconut palms, and palmettos; about 1200 species. **Examples:** *Phoenix dactylifera, Cocos nucifera*

Family Liliaceae (Lilies) Many ornamental perennial plants such as lilies, tulips, and hyacinths that grow from bulbs or corms; also includes food plants such as onion and asparagus; leaves linear; flowers with three sepals, three petals, and six stamens; fruit a capsule or berry; about 6500 species. **Examples:** *Lilium philadelphicum, Asparagus officinalis*

Family Orchidaceae (Orchids) Largest family of monocotyledons; flower complexity surpasses everything in the plant kingdom; best known examples are orchids and ladyslippers; 15 000 species. **Examples:** *Cypripedium hirsutum, Spiranthes cernua*

APPENDIX A

Kingdom Animalia

Invertebrates

Phylum Porifera (Sponges)   Body tissues organized into pores and canals; found in either fresh or marine water; lack organs and symmetry; shapes may be like cups, fans, crusts, or tubes; sponge body is riddled with pores (porifera) and contain skeletal needles called spicules; larval stage free-swimming; adults are sessile; most are both male and female; feed by circulating water through pores and canals; about 10 000 species. **Examples:** *Spongilla lacustris, Tethya auvantitium* (sea orange)

Phylum Cnidaria (Corals, Jellyfish, Hydras)   First animal group with organ level of organization; saclike bodies include mouth surrounded by tentacles that sting and paralyze prey; have radial symmetry; almost all marine; certain species show alternation of generations between a polyp and medusa stage; others may spend lives as either medusas or polyps; about 10 000 species.

Class Hydrozoa (Hydroids)   About 3100 species known, including hydroid types and Portuguese man-of-war; tentacles give off a poison; paralyzed prey carried by tentacles to the mouth. **Examples:** *Hydra littoralis, Physalia physalis* (Portuguese man-of-war)

Class Scyphozoa (Jellyfish)   Marine species; often called medusae because this shape is dominant; 95-98 percent of body weight consists of water; about 200 species exist. **Examples:** *Aurelia aurita, Cyanea arctica*

Kingdom Animalia

Class Anthozoa (Sea Anemones, Corals)
Includes sea pens, sea fans, coral, and sea anemones; about 6200 species; polyp stage is dominant; coral reefs are home to thousands of different marine vertebrate and invertebrate species. **Examples:** *Corallium rubrum, Adamsia palliata* (sea anemone always found living with a species of hermit crab)

Phylum Platyhelminthes (Flatworms)   Includes all flat (platy), ribbon-shaped worms; about 15 000 species; all bilaterally symmetrical; have soft body and mouths but no anuses; organs forming simple systems are present; can regenerate and reproduce sexually; most species both male and female; some forms free-living; others parasitic.

Class Turbellaria (Free-living Flatworms)
Flatworms that are free-living; found on land in damp soil, and in fresh or marine waters; body shows a head region with eyespots; familiar example is *Planaria,* often used in regeneration experiments. **Examples:** *Dugesia tigrina, Bipalium kewense* (tropical land planarian)

Class Trematoda (Flukes)   All are parasitic; most live inside vertebrates, including humans; commonly called flukes; have a head region with suckers that attach to a host; can be found in host's liver, lungs, intestines, and blood; some cause diseases in hosts. **Examples:** *Fasciola hepatica* (liver fluke of cattle), *Clonorchis sinensis* (Oriental liver fluke)

Class Cestoda (Tapeworms)   Includes tapeworms; bodies very long, flat, and formed of many short sections; some longer than 7 meters; all parasitic; found in intestines of dogs, cats, fish, cattle, pigs, and humans; lack digestive system and mouth, but have suckers for attaching to host. **Examples:** *Taenia solium, Diphyllobothrium latum* (broad tapeworm)

Phylum Nematoda (Roundworms)   Made up of worms that are bilaterally symmetrical; have round bodies; have complete digestive systems with mouths and separate anuses; about 80 000 species; both free-living and parasitic species exist; pork worm (responsible for trichinosis) and hookworm are parasitic species of phylum; majority nonparasitic soil dwellers. **Examples:** *Trichinella spiralis* (roundworm that causes trichinosis), *Necator americanus*

Phylum Mollusca (Mollusks)   Includes soft-bodied animals such as clams, snails, octopuses, and squid; about 110 000 species; have bilateral symmetry; have either external shell, internal shell, or no shell; all have a mantle; locomotion achieved through muscular foot; many species used as human food; at least 110 000 species.

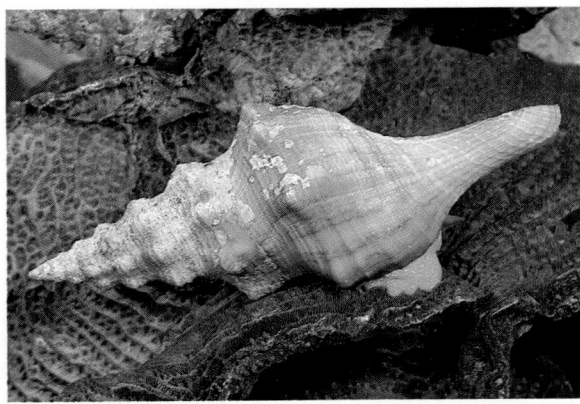

Class Gastropoda (Snails and Slugs) Includes snails, slugs, whelks, and conches; most members have a spiral shell and a head; called "univalves" because of one shell; land slugs and nudibranchs have no shell. **Examples:** *Helix aspersa* (European edible snail), *Achatina achatina* (African land snail)

Class Bivalvia (Bivalves) All have rigid shell of two (bi) parts; includes clams, oysters, and mussels; lack head; have wedge-shaped muscular foot for locomotion or protection; most species marine, but a few live in fresh water. **Examples:** *Arca zebra* (zebra mussel), *Ostvea edulis* (European flat oyster)

Class Cephalopoda (Octopuses, Squid) Most highly developed mollusks with large eyes, arms, and tentacles surrounding the mouth; shell may be external, internal, or lacking; includes squid, octopuses, and chambered nautilus; can move forward or backward with great speed by expelling water through a siphon. **Examples:** *Nautilus macromphalus* (nautilus), *Octopus vulgaria* (common odepus)

Phylum Annelida (Annelids) Segmented worms; have bilateral symmetry, closed circulatory system, and complete digestive system; almost 9000 species live on land or in marine or freshwater bodies; earthworm is an annelid; about 12 000 species.

Class Polychaeta (Polychaetes) Mainly marine; have distinct head with sensory appendages and eyes; each body segment has many setae (bristles) extending from it; most are either male or female; includes clam worms, tube worms, and sandworms. **Examples:** *Nereis virens, Pectinaria gouldii*

Class Oligochaete (Earthworms) Found mainly in soil or fresh water; no distinct head region; setae are short and few per segment; worms are both male and female; includes the common earthworm. **Examples:** *Lumbricus terrestris* (earthworm), *Allolobophora caliginosa*

Class Hirudinea (Leeches) Both male and female; usually predators or parasitic; have a large sucker at the front end, enabling them to attach to their hosts; includes leeches; feed off the blood of hosts; one meal can last worms several months. **Examples:** *Hirudo medicinalis* (European medicinal leech), *Macrobdella decora*

Phylum Arthropoda (Arthropods)   Largest phylum in Animal Kingdom; bilaterally symmetrical; have appendages that are jointed; have tough exoskeletons of chitin; sense organs are well developed; open circulatory systems; includes insects, crayfish, crabs, millipedes, centipedes, and spiders; group is important as pollinators of flowers, carriers of disease, and as food; about 1 million species known at present.

Class Arachnida (Spiders, Mites, Scorpions)
Two body regions; have four pairs of walking legs, a pair of chelicerae (fangs), and a pair of pedipalps used to squeeze and chew food; carnivorous; no antennae; respire through book lungs or tracheae; includes spiders, scorpions, ticks, and mites; about 57 000 species. **Examples:** *Latrodectus mactans* (black widow spider), *Mastigo proctus giganteus* (American whip scorpion), *Dermacentor variabilis* (wood tick)

Class Merostomata (Horseshoe Crabs)   Two body regions; have five pairs of walking legs; have chelicerae like Arachnida; marine organisms; appendages all found on bottom of abdomen; have book gills for respiration; have compound eyes; front body region covered by a large horseshoe-shaped carapace, thus common name horseshoe crabs; only four species exist. **Examples:** *Limulus polyphemus* (horseshoe crab), *Eurypterus fischeri* (Eurypterus is extinct)

Class Crustacea (Lobsters, Crayfish, Crabs)
Two body regions; appendages two-branched and found on each segment; five pairs of walking legs and three pairs of mandibles (jaws) for chewing; two pairs of antennae; respire through gills; mainly aquatic; many have compound eyes; examples are crabs, lobster, shrimp, crayfish, barnacles, and land sowbugs or pillbugs; about 35 000 species. **Examples:** *Macrocheira kaempferi* (Japanese giant spider crab), *Homarus americanus* (American lobster)

Class Chilopoda (Centipedes)   Two body regions; have head with pair of long antennae and a pair of mandibles; two pair of maxillae (which hold their captured food); carnivorous; head followed by 15 to 177 body segments; first body segment has pair of poisonous claws; all other segments have one pair of jointed legs; tracheae used for respiration; class of centipedes; do not have 100 legs (as their common name suggests). **Examples:** *Lithobius forficatus, Scutigerella immaculata*

Class Diplopoda (Millipedes)   Three body regions; head followed by 20 to 200 segments; one pair of antennae; pair of mandibles and one pair of maxillae; two pairs of jointed legs on each segment; tracheae used for respiration; mostly herbivorous; class of millipedes; do not have 1000 legs (as the common name suggests). **Examples:** *Julus terrestris* (garden millipede), *Oxidus gracilis* (greenhouse millipede)

Class Insecta (Insects) Three body regions (head, thorax, and abdomen); one pair of antennae on head; have complex mouth parts with one pair of maxillae and mandibles; three pairs of walking legs located on thorax; only group of invertebrates capable of flight; have one or two

pairs of wings on thorax (when wings are present); tracheae used for respiration; have compound eyes; includes bees, flies, grasshoppers, lice, butterflies, moths, and beetles; single largest class of organisms with 750 000 known species; most insects are 2 to 40 mm in length, but some can reach lengths of 250 mm or have wingspans of 280 mm; most live on land; many have complete metamorphosis. **Examples:** *Bombus americanorum* (bumblebee), *Vanessa virginiensis* (American painted lady)

Phylum Echinodermata (Echinoderms) Marine invertebrates; includes sea stars, brittle stars, sea urchins, sea cucumbers, and sand dollars; usually have radial symmetry in the adult stage; skin covered with spines; only phylum having a water-vascular system that uses tube feet for locomotion; about 6000 species, all marine; many can regenerate lost parts.

Class Crinoidea (Sea Lilies, Feather Stars) Filter-feeders with mouth and anus in a disc on upper surface; includes sea lilies and feather stars; have a flowerlike appearance; marine, living below low tide line to depths of over 3000 meters; most have a long stalk with five to 200 arms around disc that forks into narrow, feather

like appendages; 2100 species of class are extinct; about 600 living species. **Examples:** *Ptilocrinus pinnatus, Antedon spinifera* (sea lily)

Class Asteroidea (Sea Stars) Star-shaped sea stars, commonly called starfish, make up this class; have five to 50 arms surrounding a central disc; mouth and anus on lower surface; have endoskeleton formed from flexible calcareous plates; have ability to bend and turn with ease; move by means of tube feet; about 1500 species. **Examples:** *Asterias forbesi, Acanthaster planci* (crown of thorns starfish)

Class Ophiuroidea (Brittle Stars) Also star-shaped; includes basket stars and brittle stars; arms very long, slender, jointed, and fragile; found in shallow to deep ocean waters; usually hide beneath stones or seaweed or bury themselves in sand; most active at night; about 2000 species. **Examples:** *Ophiura sarsi, Amphipholis squamata*

Class Echinoidea (Sea Urchins and Sand Dollars)
No distinct arms; have rigid external covering; includes sea urchins, sand dollars, and sea biscuits; bodies rounded and covered with many long, flexible spines (*Echinoidea* means "like a hedgehog"); most live on rocks and mud of seashore or buried in sand; move by tube feet or jointed spines; about 950 species. **Examples:** *Arbacia punctulata* (common sea urchin), *Heterocentrotus mammillatus* (slate-pencil sea urchin)

Class Holothuroidea (Sea Cucumbers) Soft, slug-like echinoderms that lie on their sides; includes sea cucumbers; almost leathery body has an elongated cucumber shape; no arms or spines present; some species have small tentacles surrounding mouth; sluggish animals that burrow into ocean sand; when disturbed, sea cucumbers shoot out long, sticky tubules from anuses that entangle and often kill enemies; others completely throw up digestive and respiratory tracts (these systems regenerate); about 1500 species. **Examples:** *Thyone briaereus, Cucumaria frondosa* (sea cucumber)

Vertebrates

Phylum Chordata (Chordates) Best known of all animal phyla, numbering some 45 000 species; all chordates have bilateral symmetry; four chordate characteristics that appear at some stage of development include (1) a single, dorsal nerve cord, (2) a cartilaginous, dorsal rod called a notochord, (3) gill slits, and (4) a tail; includes tunicates, lancelets, fish, amphibians, reptiles, birds, and mammals; includes three subphyla.

Subphylum Urochordata (Tunicates) Free-swimming larvae have notochord and nerve cord, structures absent in sessile adults; includes tunicates (sea squirts); bodies covered by saclike coverings called "tunics" (thus, tunicates); look like soft potatoes; marine organisms that obtain food using cilia; gill slits also remain in adults; about 1250 species. **Examples:** *Polycarpa pomaria, Ecteinascidia turbinata*

Subphylum Cephalochordata (Lancelets) Marine, fishlike chordates with permanent notochord; no internal skeleton; includes small animals called lancelets or amphioxus; have bladelike shape; gill slits and nerve cord remain in adult; filter feeders that draw in food with cilia; about 23 species. **Examples:** *Branchiostoma virginiae, Branchiostoma californiense*

Subphylum Vertebrata (Vertebrates) Found on land and in fresh and marine waters; notochord replaced by cartilage or bone, forming segmented vertebral column (the backbone); have distinct head and brain inside a skull; gill slits may remain or be modified into other structures during development; hollow dorsal nerve cord remains, protected by backbone; *vertebrata* refers to the vertebrae (segments of backbone) surrounding dorsal nerve cord; about 43 700 species.

Class Agnatha (Lampreys and Hagfish) Aquatic organisms with smooth skin; includes eel-like animals called lampreys and hagfish; all lack jaws; have slender bodies; are parasitic or scavengers; have no scales; skeleton made of cartilage; notochord present throughout life. **Examples:** *Petromyzon marinus* (sea lamprey), *Polistotrema stouti*

Class Chondrichthyes (Sharks, Skates, Rays) Cartilagenous fish that are mostly marine; includes sharks, skates, and rays; skin covered with small, toothlike scales; have paired fins; skeleton remains cartilagenous even in adults; notochord remains in adults; dorsal nerve cord protected by individual vertebrae; all are predators; do not have air bladders. **Examples:** *Squalus acanthias, Raja undulata* (skate)

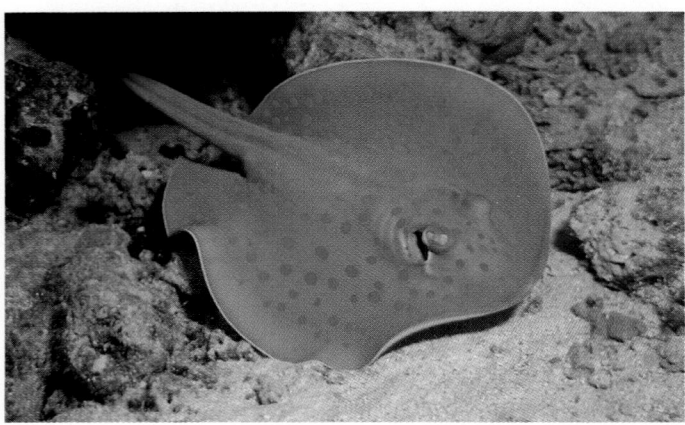

Class Osteichthyes (Bony Fish) Bony fish (except sturgeons) that have skeletons made from bone (ostei); abundant in marine and fresh waters; includes sea horses, goldfish, eels, catfish, trout, gar, salmon; skin covered with scales; have paired fins; notochord usually has disappeared; gills covered by flap (operculum); have air bladders to regulate their densities in water; about 18 000 species. **Examples:** *Perca flavescens* (yellow perch), *Hippocampas erectus* (sea horse)

Subclass Crossopterygii (Lobe-finned Fish) Called lobe-finned fish because of the lobelike nature of their fins; only one living species—the rest are extinct; a species thought to be extinct was caught off the coast of Africa in 1938. **Examples:** *Macropoma sp.* (extinct), *Latimeria chalumnae*

Subclass Dipneusti (Lungfish) Fish with a modified air bladder that enables them to breathe air; found living in Australia, Africa, and South America; six species. **Examples:** *Neoceratodus forsteri, Proptoperus annectens*

Subclass Actinopterygii (Ray-finned Fish) So called because the fins themselves are supported on fin rays, which appear like thin bones but really are extensions of the skin; the largest group of bony fish; over 20 000 species. **Examples:** *Acipenser sturio, Ameiurus melas*

Class Amphibia (Amphibians) Includes salamanders, toads, and frogs; were first vertebrates to live on land; most species spend part of life cycle in fresh water and part on land; larvae use gills and adults use lungs for respiration; skin is smooth with no scales; have two pairs of limbs (except for a few species; have three-chambered hearts; skeleton is bone; no trace of notochord found in adults; lay eggs; are cold-blooded (ectothermic); about 2800 species. **Examples:** *Rana pipiens, Agalychnis spurrelli* (Costa Rican flying tree frog)

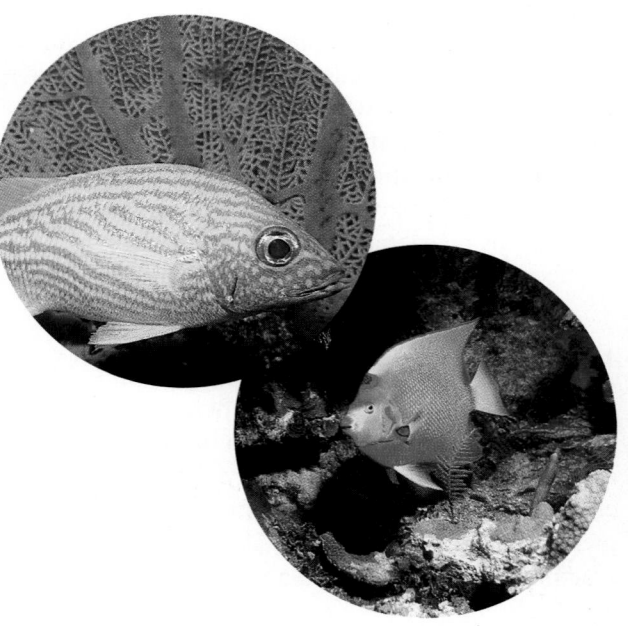

Order Gymnophiona (Caecilians) Slender, wormlike bodies with no limbs; order name means "naked of a snake"; burrow in moist ground; live mainly in the tropics; about 160 known species. **Examples:** *Ichthyophis glutinosus, Gymnopis sp.*

Order Urodela (Salamanders, Newts) Includes mud puppies, salamanders and newts; distinct head, trunk and tail regions; limbs about equal in size; about 300 species. **Examples:** *Triturus viridescens, Necturus punctatus*

Order Salientia (Frogs, Toads) Order name means "leaping"; front legs are usually short, while the rear legs are larger and aid in leaping; no tail; about 2000 species. **Examples:** *Hyla arenicolor, Bufo boreas*

Class Reptilia (Reptiles) Includes lizards, alligators, turtles, snakes, and extinct dinosaurs; skin is dry with scales that protect skin from drying out; most are land dwellers, though a few are aquatic; have imperfect, four-chambered hearts; use lungs for respiration; lay amniotic eggs; are ectothermic; legs absent in snakes and a few lizards; many are poisonous; about 6000 species. **Examples:** *Anolis carolinensis* (green anole), *Chelonia mydas* (green turtle)

Order Testudines (Turtles) Turtles, tortoises, and terrapins; bodies enclosed in a rigid shell of plates; lack teeth; marine, fresh water, or terrestrial; about 330 species. **Examples:** *Chelydra serpentina, Trionyx ferox*

Order Squamata (Snakes, Lizards) Horny skin with scales; lizards typically have four limbs, as seen in newts, skinks, iguanas, and chameleons; snakes do not have legs but show vestiges (remains) of hind

leg bones; about 2700 species of snakes, and 3000 species of lizards. **Examples:** *Chamaeleo chamaeleon, Crotalus viridis*

Order Crocodilia (Crocodiles, Alligators) Front legs with five toes, rear legs with four; crocodiles have a narrower snout than alligators and are considered more dangerous; about 25 species. **Examples:** *Crocodylus americanus, Alligator mississippiensis*

Class Aves (Birds) Includes all birds; first group of Chordates to be warm-blooded (endothermic); have complete four-chambered hearts; respire with lungs; bodies covered with feathers; forelimbs modified into wings; most are capable of flight; mainly land dwellers; fertilization is internal; amniotic eggs are deposited externally for incubation by a parent; have complete double circulation; ostrich is largest bird (over 200 cm tall with mass of 140 kg) while hummingbirds are smallest (6 cm long with mass of 35 g); about 9000 species. **Examples:** *Casuarius casuarius* (Australian cassowary), *Mellisuga helenae* (bee hummingbird)

Order Anseriformes (Ducks, Geese, Swans) Broad bill covered with a soft skin; legs and tails tend to be short with webbing between toes; more than 200 species. **Examples:** *Olor columbianus, Chen hyperboreus*

Order Falconiformes (Hawks, Eagles)
Vultures, kites, hawks, condors, falcons, and eagles; all are predators with keen vision and sharp, curved claws for capturing food; all are daytime hunters and fliers; more than 250 species. **Examples:** *Falco peregrinus, Haliaeetus leucocephalus*

Order Galliformes (Ground Birds) Pheasants, grouse, partridges, and quails; worldwide in distribution; often desirable game birds; chicken-like vegetarians with strong, short beaks and feet well adapted for running and scratching; about 275 species. **Examples:** *Perdix perdix, Bonasa umbellus*

Order Charadriiformes (Shore Birds) Shore birds or waders; includes gulls, terns, puffins, auks, plovers, sandpipers, woodcocks, and snipe; usually live in colonies and are strong fliers; found worldwide; over 300 species. **Examples:** *Oxyechus vociferus, Philohela minor*

Order Passeriformes (Perching Birds, Including Songbirds) Largest of all bird groups; contains over 60 percent of all bird species; larks, swallows, crows, jays, nuthatches, creepers, wrens, robins, bluebirds, vireos, orioles, meadowlarks, and sparrows; perching birds with three toes in front and one in back; more than 5000 species. **Examples:** *Spizella passerina, Turdus migratorius*

Class Mammalia (Mammals) Endothermic organisms; have hair at some stage of development; provide milk to young through mammary glands; have muscular diaphragm; have four-chambered heart; respire with lungs; forelimbs sometimes modified into flippers in aquatic animals or wings (in bats); give birth to live young (except monotremes); about 4500 species in 22 orders.

Order Monotremata (Monotremes) Egg-laying mammals; includes duck-billed platypus and species of echidna; the spiny anteaters; native to Australia, New Guinea, and Tasmania only; platypuses mostly aquatic, having duck-like bill, flattened tail, and webbed feet; echidnas mostly found on land; eggs similar to eggs of reptiles; have some other reptilian features; are toothless as adults. **Examples:** *Ornithorhynchus anatinus* (duck-billed platypus), *Zaglossus bruijnii* (long-nosed echidna)

Order Marsupialia (Marsupials) Pouch for-rearing their young; only one species found in the U.S.—the opossum; all other species found in Australia, where they comprise the dominant mammal order; order includes kangaroos, opossum, koala, wombats, and bandicoots; about 250 species. **Examples:** *Didelphis marsupialus, Phascolarctos cinereus*

Order Insectivora (Insect Eaters) Small with a long, tapered snout; feed on insects; includes the shrews, moles, and hedgehogs; typically five clawed toes for burrowing; about 400 species. **Examples:** *Scapanus latimanus, Suncus etruscus*

Order Chiroptera (Bats) Includes bats, the only mammals capable of sustained flight; most are nocturnal; most feed on insects; a few eat fruit, pollen, and nectar; true vampire bats feed on blood of large birds and mammals such as livestock; use echoes to orient themselves (echolocation); smallest bat (Philippine bamboo bat) only 1.5 g and has wingspan of 15 cm; largest bat (flying fox) 1 kg with wingspan of 1.5 m; about 900 species. **Examples:** *Desmodus rotundus* (vampire bat), *Noctilio leporinus* (fishing bat)

Order Carnivora (Carnivores) Includes flesh eaters (carnivores) such as bears, dogs, walruses, seals, skunks, otters, wolves, raccoons, and cats; canine teeth usually large and designed to tear flesh; some eat plants primarily (bears and raccoons); includes domestic cats and dogs

kept as pets; most live on land; lower jaws can only move vertically, but are very strong; have large brains; have simple stomachs; about 274 species. **Examples:** *Ursus arctos* (grizzly bear), *Castor canadensis* (beaver)

Order Rodentia (Rodents) Squirrels, beavers, rats, mice, porcupines, rabbits, and woodchucks; gnawing mammals with long, chisel-like incisors; typical rodent pets include guinea pigs, hamsters, and gerbils; about 1700 species. **Examples:** *Cavia porcellus, Lepus californicus*

Order Cetacea (Whales, Dolphins) Aquatic mammals; toothed whales, baleen whales, and dolphins; three distinct groups; streamlined bodies; tails (flukes) and dorsal fins lacking bones; breathe through blowholes on top of head; use echolocation; sperm whale reaches lengths of 20 meters and has a mass equal to that of 10 elephants; baleen whales reach lengths of 30 meters; blue whale is largest animal on Earth; about 80 species. **Examples:** *Delphinus delphis* (common dolphin), *Orcinus orca* (killer whale)

Order Primates (Primates) Includes lemurs, baboons, gorillas, monkeys, and humans; large brain with complex cortex; binocular vision; varied teeth; ability to hold body upright; prehensile (grasping) hands with opposable thumbs; most primates live in trees; finger- and toenails; about 197 species. **Examples:** *Gorilla gorilla* (gorilla), *Homo sapiens* (human)

Plant Life Cycles

In their life cycles, plants exhibit alternation of a sporophyte generation with a gametophyte generation. Ferns, mosses, gymnosperms, and angiosperms all go through alternation of generations. In Chapter 18, you studied the life cycle of a representative angiosperm. Life cycles of ferns, mosses, and gymnosperms are presented here in Appendix B. As you study these life cycles, note the similarities and dif-

ferences. Similarities include alternation of diploid (2*n*) and haploid (*n*) generations; presence of sporophyte and gametophyte at some point during the life cycle; production of spore in some form during the life cycle; production of gametes during the life cycle. The most notable difference is the relative size and duration of the gametophyte generation as compared to the sporophyte generation.

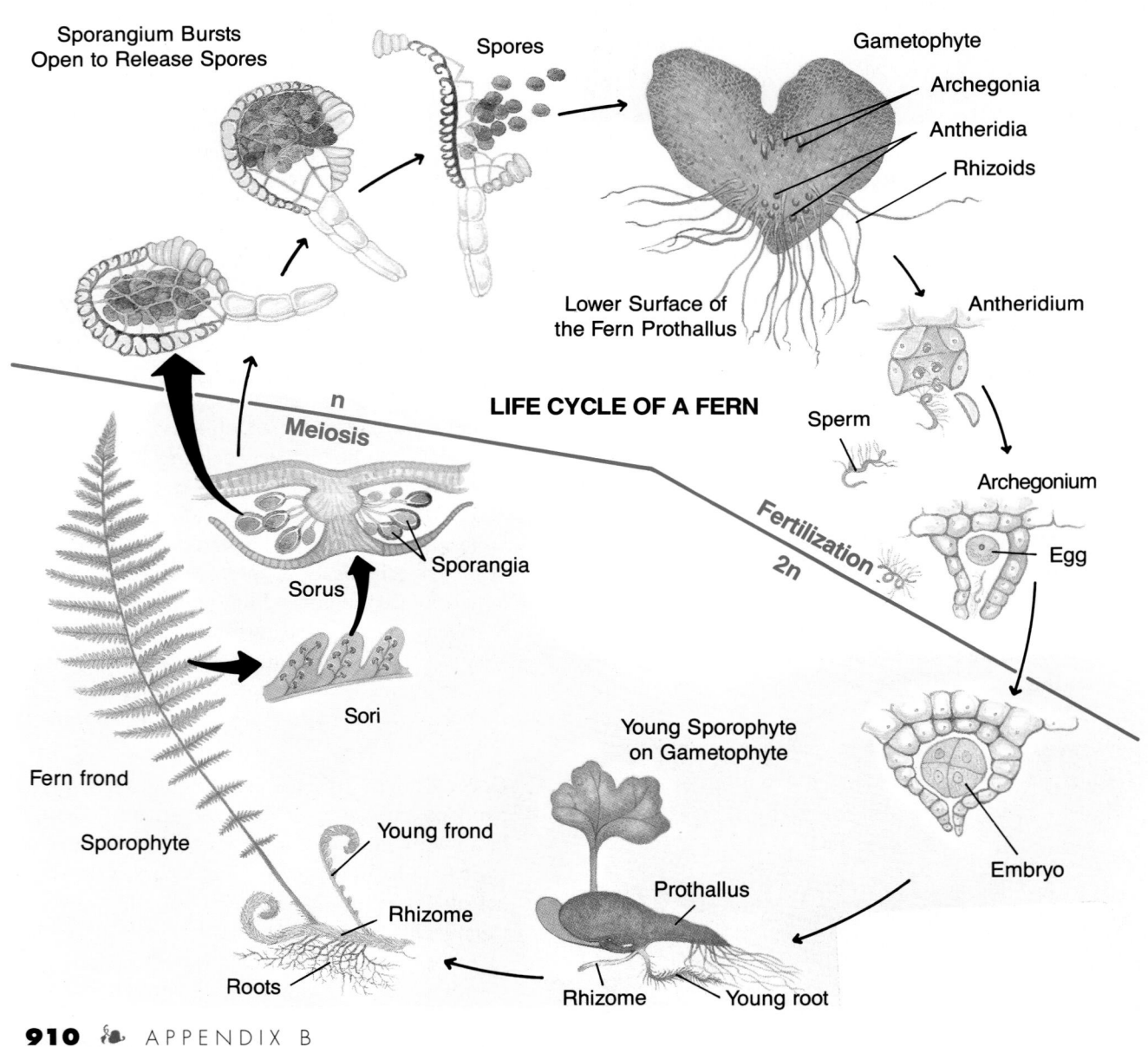

LIFE CYCLE OF A FERN

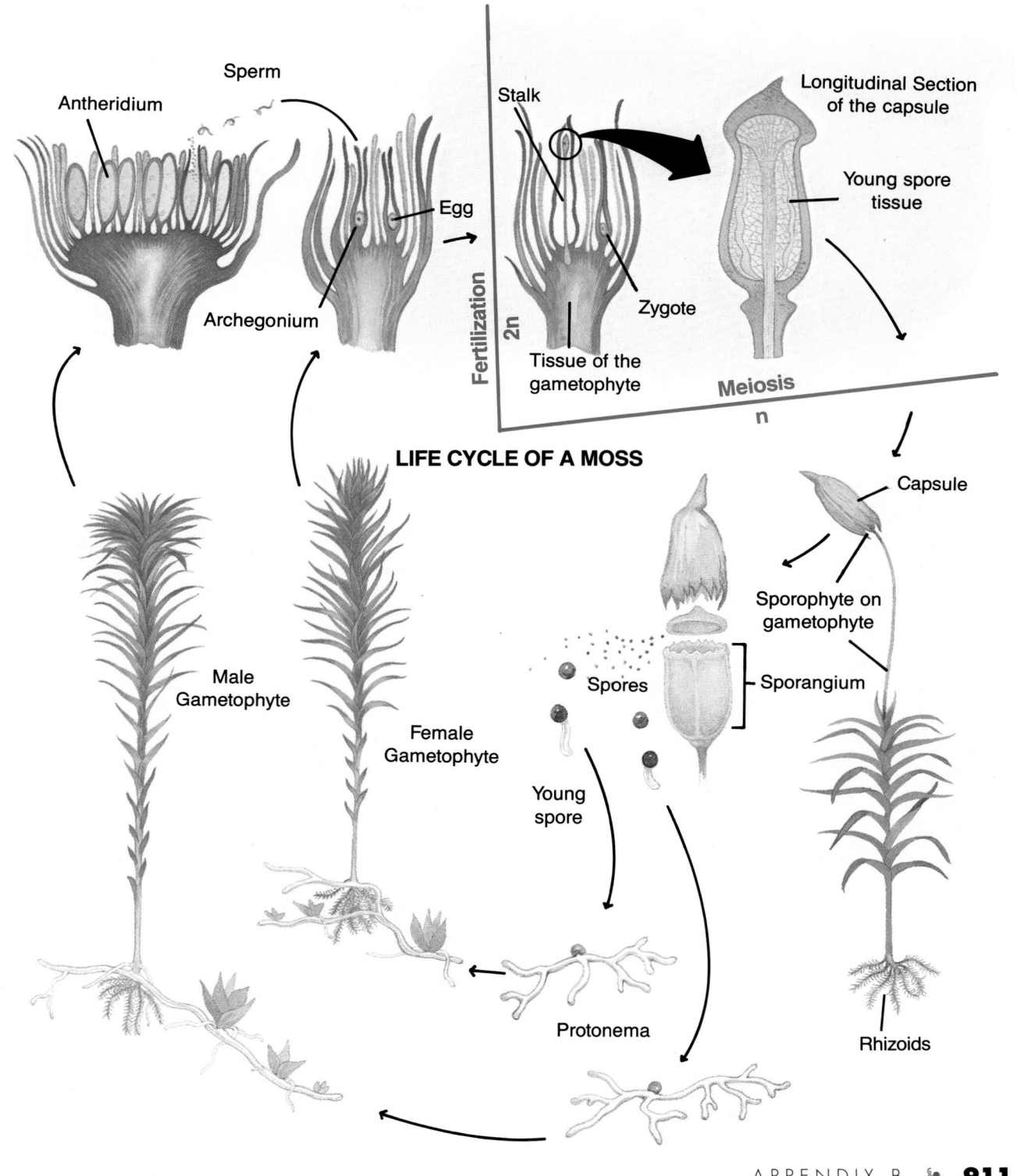

Sperm

Antheridium

Archegonium

Egg

Stalk

Fertilization
2n

Zygote

Tissue of the
gametophyte

Meiosis
n

Longitudinal Section
of the capsule

Young spore
tissue

LIFE CYCLE OF A MOSS

Male
Gametophyte

Female
Gametophyte

Capsule

Sporophyte on
gametophyte

Sporangium

Spores

Young
spore

Protonema

Rhizoids

LIFE CYCLE OF A GYMNOSPERM

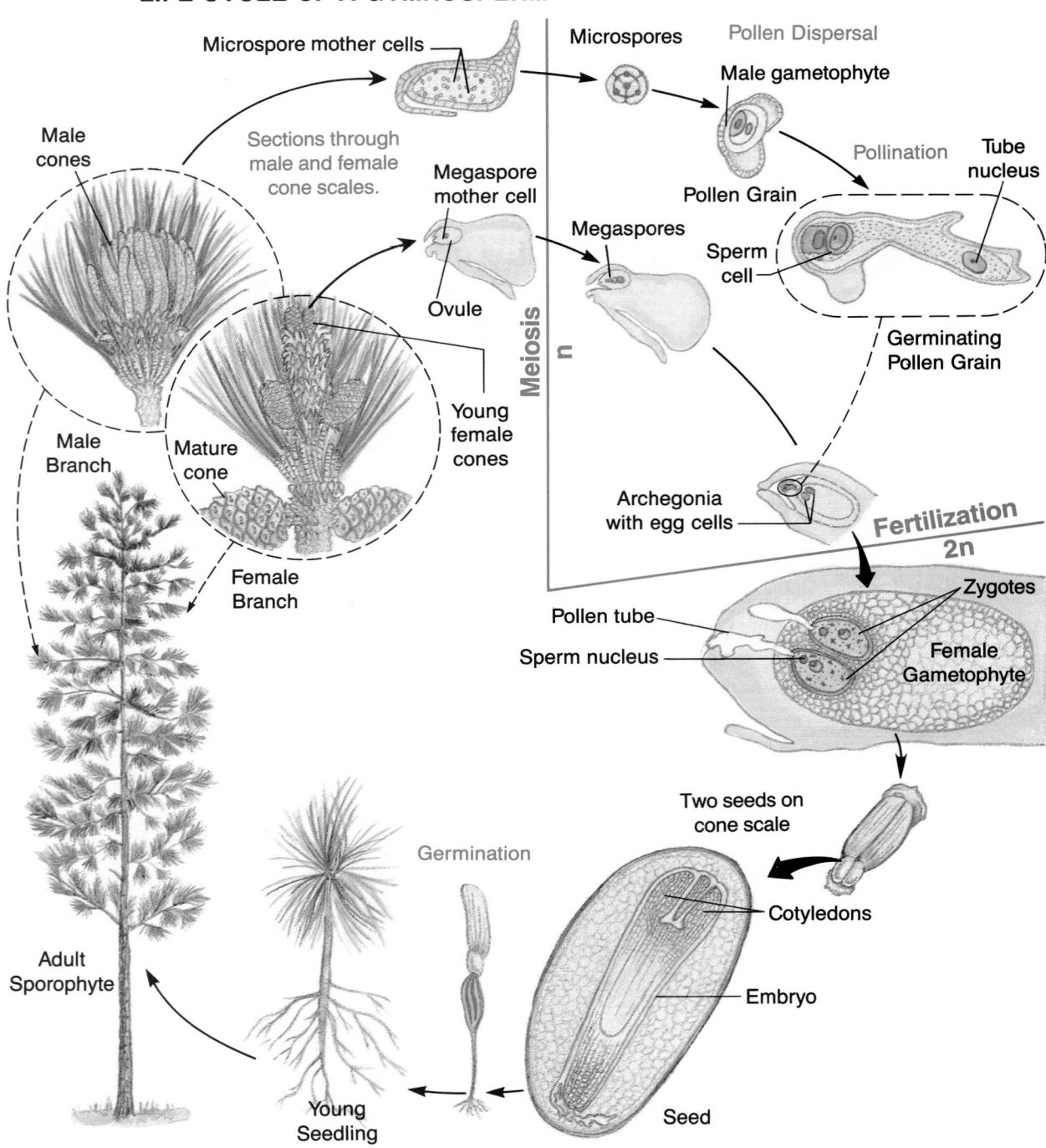

Microspore mother cells

Microspores

Pollen Dispersal

Male gametophyte

Male cones

Sections through male and female cone scales.

Pollen Grain

Pollination

Tube nucleus

Megaspore mother cell

Megaspores

Sperm cell

Ovule

Germinating Pollen Grain

Meiosis

n

Young female cones

Male Branch

Mature cone

Female Branch

Archegonia with egg cells

Fertilization 2n

Pollen tube

Zygotes

Sperm nucleus

Female Gametophyte

Two seeds on cone scale

Germination

Cotyledons

Adult Sporophyte

Embryo

Young Seedling

Seed

APPENDIX C

Cell Chemistry

Cellular Respiration

During aerobic respiration, the energy in the bonds of glucose (or other energy-rich compounds) is transferred to the bonds of ATP. How does this transfer of energy occur? Remember that the process involves many separate chemical reactions. Those reactions can be grouped into four major stages: glycolysis, pyruvic acid oxidation, citric acid cycle, electron transport chain. As you study them, focus on the main point: that energy is transferred from bonds of glucose to bonds of ATP.

Glycolysis

The first stage of aerobic respiration occurs in the cytoplasm. Because the glucose molecule is split apart, this stage is known as **glycolysis.** As a result of many enzyme-controlled reactions, one molecule of glucose, a six-carbon (C_6) compound is changed to two molecules of pyruvic acid, a C_3 compound. Two molecules of ATP are used early in glycolysis, because some of the first steps are endergonic. However, as the reactions occur, chemical bonds are broken and energy is released. In one important energy-releasing step, four hydrogen atoms are removed and join two each with a coenzyme, NAD, forming 2NADH + 2H+. Part of the energy released is used to make the NADH molecules and H+ ions, whose importance

will be discussed later. Most of the other energy released is used to form two molecules of ATP from 2ADP + 2P$_i$. The last step, which forms pyruvic acid, releases more energy, which is used to form two more ATP. Thus, there is a net "profit" of 2ATP. Some of the energy released is not trapped and escapes as heat. Note that glycolysis is not an aerobic process even though it is the first step in aerobic respiration.

Pyruvic Acid Oxidation

The next stage of aerobic respiration occurs in mitochondria. You have learned that a mitochondrion has an outer membrane and an inner, folded membrane. The folds of the inner membrane are called cristae. The space between the outer and inner membranes is known as the outer compartment. The rest of a mitochondrion, bordered all around by the inner membrane, is called the inner compartment. The two pyruvic acid molecules formed during glycolysis move into the inner compartment, where, in several steps, each is converted to acetic acid, a C_2 molecule. The carbon atoms and two oxygen atoms removed from each pyruvic acid molecule form CO_2, which you know is released during respiration. Each acetic acid molecule combines with a molecule of coenzyme A (CoA) forming acetyl-CoA. As this step occurs, two more hydrogen atoms are removed from each acetic acid, forming two more NADH + 2H+. Because removal of hydrogen with its electron is a type of oxidation reaction, this stage is known as pyruvic acid oxidation. Let's

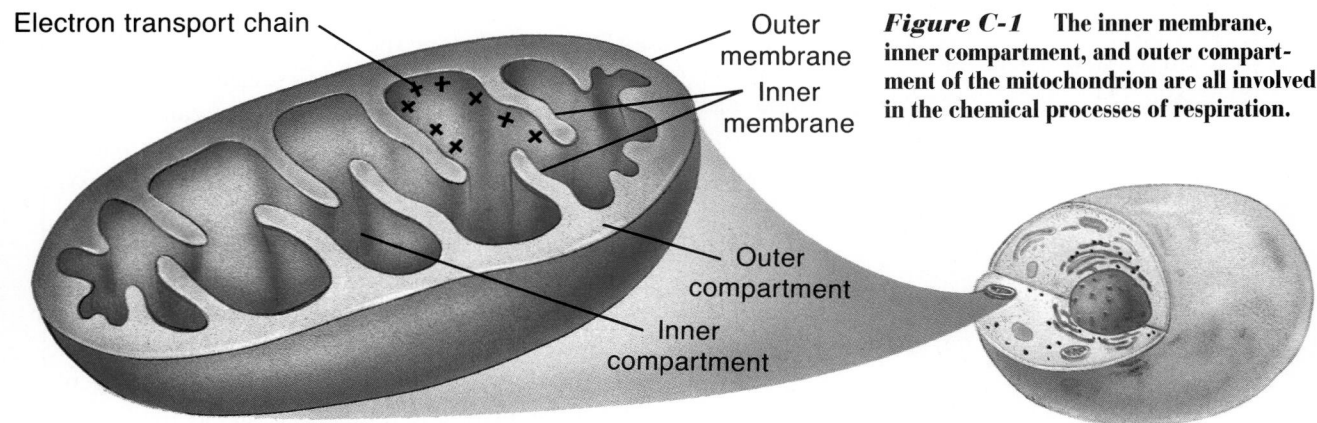

Electron transport chain
Outer membrane
Inner membrane
Outer compartment
Inner compartment

Figure C-1 The inner membrane, inner compartment, and outer compartment of the mitochondrion are all involved in the chemical processes of respiration.

stop for a moment and take account. So far, a glucose molecule has been converted to two acetyl-CoA molecules and two molecules of CO_2. Also produced were 2ATP (net) and four units of NADPH + H$^+$.

Citric Acid Cycle

In the inner compartment, each C_2 molecule of acetyl-CoA combines with a C_4 compound, oxaloacetic acid, yielding a molecule of citric acid, a C_6 compound. The next series of reactions is known as the citric acid cycle. It is also called the Krebs cycle in honor of Hans Krebs, the biochemist who worked out many of its details. At the beginning of the cycle, each citric acid is broken down to a C_5 molecule and then finally to the original C_4 molecule, giving off $2CO_2$ in the process. Since two acetyl-CoA molecules enter the cycle for each original molecule of glucose, a total of $4CO_2$ molecules are given off. These four CO_2 plus the two CO_2 from the previous stage make a total of $6CO_2$, which accounts for all of the carbon atoms in the original glucose. For each acetyl-CoA that enters the citric acid cycle, $3H_2O$ are used and 8 hydrogens are removed. Because 2 acetyl-CoA enter for each glucose molecule being broken down, $6H_2O$ are used and 16 hydrogens are removed in the Krebs cycle. Twelve hydrogens combine with 6NAD to form 6NADH + 6H$^+$, and 4 hydrogens

Figure C-2 **Fats and proteins can be converted to simpler compounds that may enter the respiration pathway at several points and release energy for ATP formation.**

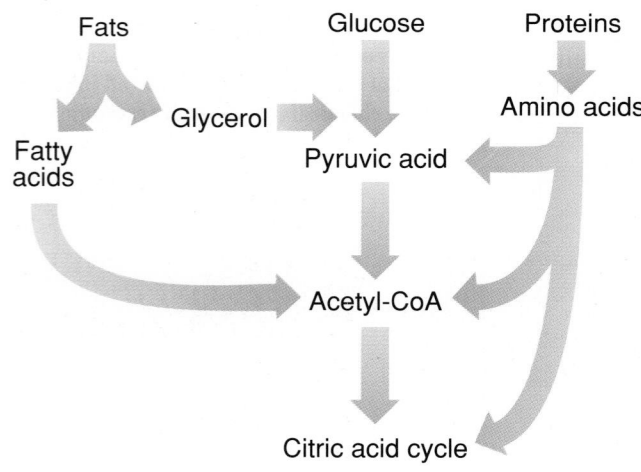

combine with two molecules of another coenzyme, FAD, forming 2FADH$_2$. Much energy is released during the Krebs cycle. Most has been used to make molecules of NADH and FADH$_2$. A small amount is used to produce 2ATP from 2ADP + 2P$_i$. The entire process so far has produced $6CO_2$, 4ATP, 10NADPH + 10H$^+$, and 2FADH$_2$. Six water molecules have been used.

Four ATP do not seem like a very impressive energy payoff for this complex process. Keep in mind, though, that a great deal of the energy released from the breakdown of glucose has been used to make NADPH + H$^+$ and FADH$_2$. As you will see, it is in the final stage of aerobic respiration that the major energy payoff occurs.

Electron Transport Chain

Molecules of NADPH and FADH$_2$ produced during respiration contain electrons at high energy levels. However, the energy of these electrons cannot be released all at once because the amount would be too large for normal biological processes. Instead, the energy of the electrons is released in a stepwise fashion as the electrons are passed down through a series of electron acceptors. Each successive acceptor takes in electrons at a lower energy level. The energy released by the electrons as they pass through these acceptors is used to form several molecules of ATP from ADP + P$_i$. This series of electron acceptor molecules is located in the cristae and is known as the **electron transport chain** or **respiratory chain.** For each glucose molecule broken down, a total of 12 pairs of electrons, 10 pairs from NADH and 2 pairs from FADH$_2$, travel along the chain. Some of the electrons do not enter the chain at the first electron acceptor, but at a later one. The energy released can convert a maximum of 32ADP + 32P$_i$ to 32ATP. Each pair of electrons, at the end of the chain, combines an oxygen atom, which combines with two hydrogen ions to form water. A total of 12 water molecules are thus formed. Because six water molecules were used in the citric acid cycle, there is a net production of six water molecules in aerobic respiration of one glucose molecule. You can now understand the need for oxygen for aerobic respiration. It is necessary as the final electron acceptor in the electron transport chain.

	REACTANTS	PRODUCTS
	$C_6H_{12}O_6$ 2 ATP 4 ADP 4 P_i 2 NAD	2 ADP + 2 P_i 4 ATP 2 Pyruvic Acid 2 NADH + 2H^+
	2 Pyruvic Acid 2 NAD$^+$ 2 CoA	2 Acetyl-CoA 2 CO_2 2 NADH + 2H^+
	2 Acetyl-CoA 6 NAD$^+$ 2 FAD	6 NADH + 6H^+ 2 FADH$_2$
	6 H_2O 2 ADP 2 P_i	4 CO_2 2 ATP
	10 NADH$^+$ 10 H^+ 2 FADH$_2$	10 NAD 2 FAD
	6 O_2 32 ADP 32 P_i	12 H_2O 32 ATP

GLYCOLYSIS — anaerobic — in cytoplasm

$C_6H_{12}O_6$
1 Glucose (6C)

2 ATP → 2 ADP + 2 P_i
4 ADP + 4 P_i → 4 ATP } → Net 2 ATP

4 H — 2 NADH + 2H^+

2 NAD$^+$

2 Pyruvic Acid (3C)

FORMING AC-COA

→ 2 CO_2

2 Acetic Acid (2C)

2 CoA →

4 H — 2 NADH + 2H^+

2 NAD$^+$

2 Acetyl-CoA (2C)

CITRIC ACID CYCLE — aerobic — in mitochondrion

→ 2 CoA

2 (4C) molecules

2 Citric Acid (6C)

6 H_2O
2 ADP + 2 P_i

16 H — 6 NADH + 6H^+
2 FADH$_2$

2 CO_2

2 ATP

2 (5C) molecules

2 CO_2

6 NAD$^+$
2 FAD

ELECTRON TRANSPORT CHAIN

Electron Potential Energy — High / Low

24 H

10 NAD$^+$
2 FAD

12 pair e^- ← → 12 pair H^+

Electron transport chain

ENERGY

32ADP + 32P_i → 32ATP

24 e^- → 12 H_2

6 O_2
(from air)

12 H_2O

Net 6 H_2O

32 ATP

Net: 36ADP + 36P_i + $C_6H_{12}O_6$ + 6O_2 ⟶ 6CO_2 + 6H_2O + 36ATP

Figure C-3   In aerobic respiration, energy in the bonds of glucose is released and used to produce ATP. The process consists of four interrelated stages.

APPENDIX C

Production of ATP During Respiration

How is the movement of pairs of electrons along the electron transport chain related to production of ATP? As the electrons pass from one acceptor molecule to another, the energy released is used to pump hydrogen ions from the inner compartment of the mitochondrion to the outer compartment. The result of this movement of hydrogen ions is a difference in both concentration and charge on either side of the inner membrane. There are more hydrogen ions in the outer compartment than in the inner compartment. There is also a difference in charge because the outer compartment becomes more positively charged and the inner compartment becomes more negatively charged. Located in the inner membrane are complex membrane proteins through which hydrogen ions can pass. Because of the difference in both concentration and charge, hydrogen ions pass through the membrane protein from the outer compartment to the inner compartment, much as electrons flow in a battery. The passage of the ions releases energy, and that energy is used to convert ADP and P_i to ATP.

Other Energy Sources

Besides carbohydrates, fats and proteins can be used as energy sources. Fats are broken down into fatty acids and glycerol. Proteins are converted to amino acids. These simpler molecules are changed to others that enter the respiration pathway at various points, indicated in Figure C-2. As with glucose, energy in the bonds of these substances produced from fats and proteins is released and used to produce ATP.

Fermentation

You know that the process of fermentation results in a much smaller number of ATP molecules produced than in aerobic respiration. What is the reason for the lesser energy harvest of fermentation?

Glycolysis is the first stage of fermentation, as it is in aerobic respiration, and produces two pyruvic acid molecules. The same steps occur, releasing energy used to produce a total of 2NADH + 2H+ and a net of 2ATP. When oxygen is available, the NADH, as you have just learned, will pass electrons to the electron transport chain, and those electrons are eventually

accepted by oxygen. However, when oxygen is not available, fermentation occurs.

Because there is no oxygen to accept them, electrons from NADH cannot be passed to the electron transport chain. Instead, they are donated to the molecules of pyruvic acid. In plant cells and yeasts, the addition of electrons to pyruvic acid molecules results in production of ethyl alcohol and CO_2. In some bacteria and in your skeletal muscle cells, the reactions produce two molecules of lactic acid from the two molecules of pyruvic acid. Much of the energy originally present in the bonds of glucose remains "locked" in molecules such as ethyl alcohol and lactic acid. The difference in energy yield between aerobic respiration and fermentation is like the difference in energy released when a ball bounces down an entire flight of stairs and when it bounces down just a few. More energy is released if the ball is allowed to bounce all the way down (as in aerobic respiration), than if the ball stops after bouncing down just a few steps (fermentation). Aerobic respiration is a far more efficient process of releasing energy.

Photosynthesis

Photosynthesis is a process by which light energy is trapped as chemical energy and used in the production of simple sugars. In many ways, photosynthesis is

Figure C-4 **Anaerobic respiration may result in the production of ethyl alcohol or lactic acid.**

Thylakoid membrane, site of photosystems I and II

Figure C-5 **Thylakoid membranes within the chloroplast are the site of photosynthesis.**

a process opposite to aerobic respiration. Respiration starts with simple sugars and produces CO_2, H_2O, and energy from them. Photosynthesis starts with CO_2, H_2O, and energy and produces simple sugars. Whereas aerobic respiration is exergonic, photosynthesis is endergonic. Like aerobic respiration, photosynthesis is a process involving many steps, which can be divided into two related series of events, the light reactions and the Calvin cycle.

The Light Reactions

How does light interact with chlorophyll, and how is light energy transformed to chemical energy? The reactions in which these events occur are the light reactions. In eukaryotes, they occur in membranes, called *thylakoids,* within chloroplasts. Recall that these membranes may be separate in the stroma or stacked together to form grana.

Embedded in the thylakoid membranes are groups of chlorophyll and carotenoid molecules. These groups are of two types, called **photosystem I** and **photosystem II.** Chlorophyll and carotenoid pigments absorb specific wavelengths of light energy and pass that energy along to a particular molecule of chlorophyll known as the *reaction center.* The energy moves certain electrons of the reaction center molecule to a higher energy level. Such electrons, having gained energy, are said to be excited electrons.

In photosystem I, excited electrons are passed along a chain of acceptor molecules similar to those in the electron transport chain of a mitochondrion. In

some organisms, the following events occur. The electrons return finally to the chlorophyll molecule in their original energy level or ground state. As the energy-rich electrons travel along the acceptor molecules, their energy is released and used to form ATP from ADP and P_i. Because the electrons return to the chlorophyll molecule of which they were originally a part, this passage of electrons is known as the *cyclic pathway.* The cyclic pathway is the only form of photosynthesis in some bacteria (though they have no chloroplasts), and it does not use water or release oxygen. The cyclic pathway can be studied by following the red arrows in Figure C-6.

In other organisms, such as algae and plants, excited electrons most often follow a *noncyclic pathway* in which water is a reactant and oxygen is produced. Follow the blue arrows in Figure C-6 to study this pathway.

Both photosystems I and II play a role in the noncyclic pathway. Light strikes photosystem II, exciting electrons of the reaction center molecule. These electrons are transferred along a different path of acceptor molecules. As the electrons move from one acceptor to the next, they release energy that is used to make ATP. In the noncyclic pathway, electrons from photosystem II do not return to their original chlorophyll molecule. Instead they are transferred to the reaction center chlorophyll molecule of photosystem I to replace electrons that have left there after being excited by light. This process leaves the reaction center molecule of photosystem I with electron vacancies. These vacancies must be filled if photosynthesis is to continue. From where do the needed electrons come? The answer reveals the importance of water in photosynthesis. To provide electrons, water molecules are split into two H^+ ions, an oxygen atom, as well

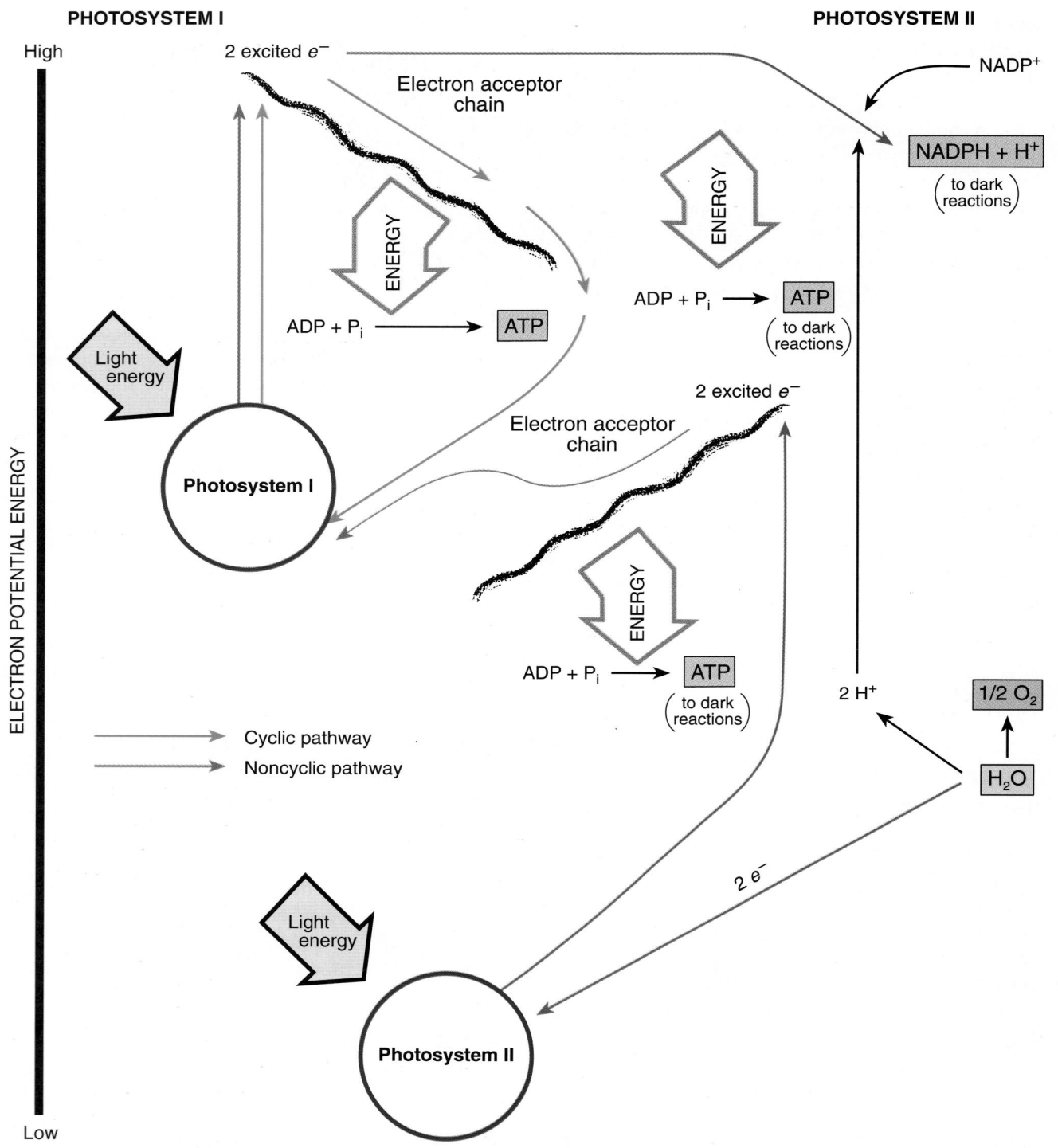

PHOTOSYSTEM I

PHOTOSYSTEM II

High

Low

ELECTRON POTENTIAL ENERGY

2 excited e^-

Electron acceptor chain

$NADP^+$

$NADPH + H^+$
(to dark reactions)

ENERGY

$ADP + P_i \longrightarrow$ ATP

ENERGY

$ADP + P_i \longrightarrow$ ATP
(to dark reactions)

Light energy

Photosystem I

2 excited e^-

Electron acceptor chain

ENERGY

$ADP + P_i \longrightarrow$ ATP
(to dark reactions)

$2 H^+$

$1/2 O_2$

H_2O

Cyclic pathway

Noncyclic pathway

$2 e^-$

Light energy

Photosystem II

Figure C-6   **In the light reactions of photosynthesis, light energy excites electrons. In the returning of these electrons to their ground state, energy is given off as ATP.**

as electrons. The oxygen atoms form O_2 molecules, which are released during photosynthesis. Each water molecule provides two electrons, which are carried to the waiting chlorophyll molecule in photosystem II. Meanwhile, in photosystem I, light excites electrons, which enter another chain of acceptor molecules. Pairs of these high-energy electrons plus pairs of H^+ ions from the water are picked up by the coenzyme NADP, forming NADPH + H^+. The NADPH + H^+ and the ATP formed during the passage of electrons in the noncyclic pathway will be used in the Calvin cycle.

Production of ATP During Photosynthesis

Note that ATP production in the light reactions involves movement of excited electrons along electron acceptor molecules. These same events occur in aerobic respiration as electrons travel the electron transport chain. Synthesis of ATP occurs in the light reactions in much the same way it does during the last stage of aerobic respiration. In the light reactions, the energy released by excited electrons is used to pump hydrogen ions from the stroma to the inside of the thylakoid. This pumping sets up the same kind of concentration and charge differences that occur across the inner membrane of a mitochondrion. As the hydrogen ions pass back across the thylakoid membrane into the stroma, they release energy, which is used to convert ADP and P_i to ATP.

The Calvin Cycle

In the noncyclic pathway of the light reactions, light energy is transformed to chemical energy in molecules of ATP and NADPH + H^+. These two kinds of molecules are essential for building sugars. Manufacture of sugars from carbon dioxide, an endergonic process, occurs within the stroma of a chloroplast.

In a series of reactions known as the **Calvin cycle,** each CO_2 molecule combines with a C_5 molecule, ribulose bisphosphate, which is usually abbreviated RuBP, to form an unstable C_6 molecule that quickly breaks down to form two C_3 molecules. These molecules enter other reactions in which ATP and NADPH + H^+ from the light reactions provide the necessary energy and hydrogen atoms. The products of these

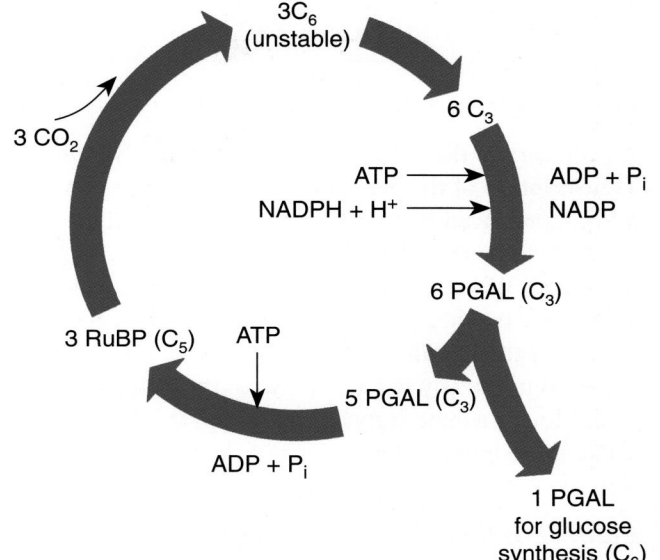

Figure C-7 In the Calvin cycle, CO_2 is converted to PGAL. Two "spins" of the cycle are needed to produce two PGALs for glucose synthesis.

reactions are two molecules of phosphoglyceraldehyde (PGAL), which are simple C_3 sugars that can be considered the end products of photosynthesis. Two PGAL molecules may be combined to make glucose. The other PGAL molecules, using energy from ATP, are converted back to RuBP, thus continuing the cycle. Note that Figure C-7 shows three CO_2 molecules entering the cycle at a time. In all, six CO_2 molecules must enter for each molecule of glucose produced.

Although glucose is a molecule that may be made from PGAL, it is not the only one. Of the glucose that is made, most is quickly changed to other forms. Some is used to make sucrose, the form in which sugars are transported away from the site of photosynthesis. Glucose is also used to make starch, which can be stored as an energy reserve, or to manufacture cellulose necessary for cell wall production.

Much of the PGAL produced in the Calvin cycle is not used to make glucose at all. It can be used directly as an energy source in aerobic respiration. It is also used in making many other organic molecules including lipids, amino acids, and nucleic acids.

Expression of Genotype

Control of Gene Expression

A gene carries the code for synthesis of a polypeptide. Transcription of the gene and then translation of the mRNA produced by transcription are necessary for the code to be deciphered and the polypeptide to be produced. When a polypeptide has been made and a phenotype results, the gene is said to be expressed. Processes that result in expression of a gene do not occur continuously in cells. Instead, the polypeptide coded for by a gene is made only when it is needed. Thus, there must be factors that regulate the expression of genes.

Control of Gene Expression in Prokaryotes

Bacteria called *E. coli* thrive on a culture medium containing glucose, which is their normal energy source. Lactose, a disaccharide, is not normally used by these bacteria as an energy source. Therefore, *E. coli* usually do not produce the enzyme lactase, which breaks down lactose. However, if *E. coli* are grown on a culture medium containing lactose instead of glucose, they will begin to produce lactase. Lactase enables the bacteria to convert lactose to monosaccharides that can be used as energy sources. Thus, the expression of the gene that codes for lactase depends on the presence or absence of lactose. This means of controlling gene expression, in which a substance causes (induces) a gene to be "switched on," is called an **inducible system.** The substance that causes the activation of the genes is known as an inducer. In this case, lactose is the **inducer.** If lactose is not present, the gene for lactase is inactivated or "switched off."

An inducible system consists of several adjacent regions of DNA along a bacterial chromosome. The DNA region that codes for lactase is known as a **structural gene.** Associated with it are two other structural genes that produce other enzymes also

Figure D-1 When no inducer is present (top), a repressor molecule binds to the operator and prevents the synthesis of the enzyme. When an inducer is present (bottom), the inducer binds with the repressor molecule. Thus, the operator is no longer blocked, the structural genes are functional, and enzyme synthesis occurs.

needed for the cells to utilize lactose. All three structural genes are either activated or inactivated as a unit. Other DNA regions play a role in the regulation of the structural genes. A **regulator gene** codes for proteins called **repressors.** Next to the regulator gene is the promoter region, the area of DNA to which the enzyme RNA polymerase may bind, beginning the transcription process. The promoter consists of two separated DNA regions. Between them lies the **operator** region. The operator and its related structural genes are known as an **operon.** Locate these areas of DNA in Figure D-1.

In the absence of lactose, the regulator gene is transcribed and translated, producing repressor molecules. These repressors bind to the operator region. As a result of this binding of repressors and operator, RNA polymerase is blocked from binding to the promoter. Thus, transcription of the structural genes cannot occur, and lactase and the other enzymes are not produced. The structural genes are not expressed. They are "switched off."

When lactose, the inducer, is present, it enters the cells and combines with the repressor molecules. When that happens, the operator is no longer blocked, RNA polymerase can bind to the promoter, and transcription can occur. The mRNA produced from the structural genes is translated, and lactase and the other related enzymes are synthesized. The structural genes have been expressed.

There are several other means by which gene expression is controlled in bacteria. All of them confer an advantage. They insure that enzymes are produced only when they are necessary. Thus, the cell conserves both energy and materials by not producing unnecessary enzymes.

Control of Gene Expression in Eukaryotes

Gene control in eukaryotes is much more complex than in prokaryotes. Unlike bacterial DNA, you know that the DNA of eukaryotes is associated with proteins on the chromosomes. The DNA is wound like thread around spools of these proteins, called histones, and is highly coiled. Before transcription can begin, the DNA must somehow be uncoiled and unwound from the histones. Another type of chromosomal protein, the nonhistones, may function in gene regulation by causing DNA to unwind from the histone spools. This unwinding would be a necessary step leading to transcription.

Although more complicated, control of gene expression by regulating transcription is known to occur in eukaryotic cells. As in bacteria, such control depends upon chemical signals. These chemical signals may take several forms. Steroid hormones, for example, enter a cell, move into its nucleus, and activate a gene. Methylation, the addition of groups of atoms called methyl groups ($-CH_3$), is known to deactivate certain genes. Most important, though, are proteins that regulate transcription. However, these proteins do not function in the simple manner of the repressors (also proteins) of bacteria. In eukaryotes, two different proteins must be zippered together in order to regulate some genes. To further complicate matters, some DNA control regions, called enhancers and silencers, may lie hundreds or thousands of base pairs away from the genes whose activity they help regulate. Much research lies ahead before the picture of control of transcription in eukaryotes becomes clear.

Regulating transcription is only one means of controlling gene expression in eukaryotes. For example, some mRNA molecules can be processed in different ways, depending upon which nucleotides are removed and how the rest are spliced together. Each way of processing results in a different, final mRNA, and, thus, a different polypeptide and a different phenotype.

Expression of a gene may also depend upon changes in a polypeptide after translation has occurred. Consider these examples. Many proteins do not become functional until moved to a certain area within or outside the cell. Some hormones and enzymes cannot function until certain of their amino acids have been removed. The shape of proteins, and thus their functions, is influenced by physical factors such as temperature and pH. Thus, a protein exposed to a pH or temperature that changes its shape cannot function, and the gene coding for that protein will not be expressed.

APPENDIX E

Origin of Science Words

This list of Greek and Latin roots will help you interpret the meaning of biological terms. The column headed *Root* gives many of the actual Greek (GK) or Latin (L) root words used in science. If more than one word is given, the first is the full word in Greek or Latin. The letter groups that follow are forms in which the root word is most often found combined in science words. In the second column is the meaning of the root as it is used in science. The third column shows a typical science word containing the root from the first column. Most of these words can be found in your textbook.

Root	Meaning	Example	Root	Meaning	Example
a, an (GK)	not, without	anaerobic	bursa (L)	purse, bag	bursa
abilis (L)	able to	biodegradable			
ad (L)	to, attached to	appendix	caedere, cide (L)	kill	insecticide
aequus (L)	equal	equilibrium	capillus (L)	hair	capillary
aeros (GK)	air	anaerobic	carn (L)	flesh	carnivore
agon (GK)	assembly	glucagon	carno (L)	flesh	carnivore
aktis (GK)	ray	actin	cella, cellula (L)	small room	protocells
allas (GK)	sausage	allantois	cervix (L)	neck	cervix
allelon (GK)	of each other	allele	cetus (L)	whale	cetacean
allucinari (L)	to dream	hallucinate	chaite, chaet (GK)	bristle	oligochaeta
alveolus (L)	small pit	alveolus	cheir (GK)	hand	chiropteran
amnos (GK)	lamb	amnion	chele (GK)	claw	chelicerae
amoibe (GK)	change	amoebocyte	chloros (GK)	pale green	chlorophyll
amphi (GK)	both, about, around	amphibian	chondros (GK)	cartilage	Chondrichthyes
amylum (L)	starch	amylase	chondros (GK)	grain	mitochondrion
ana (L)	away, onward	anaphase	chorda (L)	cord	urochordata
andro (GK)	male	androgens	chorion (GK)	skin	chorion
anggeion, angio (GK)	vessel, container	angiosperm	chroma, chrom (GK)	colored	chromosome
anthos (GK)	flower	anthophyte	chronos (GK)	time	chronometer
anti (GK)	against, away, opposite	antibody	circa (L)	about	circadian
			cirrus (L)	curl	cirri
aqua (L)	water	aquatic	codex (L)	tablet for writing	codon
archaios, archeo (GK)	ancient, primitive	archaebacteria	corpus (L)	body	corpus luteum
			cum, col, com, con (L)	with, together	convergent
arthron (GK)	joint, jointed	arthropod	cuticula (L)	thin skin	cuticle
artios (GK)	even	artiodactyl			
askos (GK)	bag	ascospore	daktylos (GK)	finger	perissodactyl
aster (GK)	star	Asteroidea	de (L)	away, from	decompose
autos (GK)	self	autoimmune	decidere (L)	to fall down	deciduous
			degradare (L)	to reduce in rank	biodegradable
bakterion (GK)	small rod	bacterium	dendron (GK)	tree	dendrite
bi, bis (L)	two, twice	bipedal	dens (L)	tooth	edentate
binarius (L)	pair	binary fission	derma (GK)	skin	epidermis
bios (GK)	life	biology	deterere (L)	loose material	detritus
blastos (GK)	bud	blastula	dia, di (GK)	through, apart	diastolic
bryon (GK)	moss	bryophyte	dies (L)	day	circadian

Root	Meaning	Example	Root	Meaning	Example
diploos (GK)	twofold, double	diploid	gyne (GK)	female, woman	gynoecium
dis, di (GK)	twice, two	disaccharide			
dis, di (L)	apart, away	disruptive	haima, emia (GK)	blood	hemoglobin
dormire (L)	to sleep	dormancy	halo (GK)	salt	halophile
drom, drome (GK)	running, racing	dromedary	haploos (GK)	simple	haploid
ducere (L)	to lead	oviduct	haurire (L)	to drink	haustorium
			helix (L)	spiral	helix
echinos (GK)	spine	echinoderm	hemi (GK)	half	hemisphere
eidos, oid (GK)	form, appearance	rhizoid	herba (L)	grass	herbivore
ella (GK)	small	organelle	hermaphroditos (GK)	combining both sexes	hermaphrodite
endon, en, endo (GK)	within	endosperm	heteros (GK)	other	heterotrophic
engchyma (GK)	infusion	parenchyma	hierarches (GK)	rank	hierarchy
enteron (GK)	intestine, gut	enterocolitis	hippos (GK)	horse	hippopotamus
entomon (GK)	insect	entomology	histos (GK)	tissue	histology
epi (GK)	upon, above	epidermis	holos (GK)	whole	Holothuroidea
equus (L)	horse	Equisetum	homo (L)	man	hominid
erythros (GK)	red	erythrocyte	homos (GK)	same, alike	homologous
eu (GK)	well, true, good	eukaryote	hormaein (GK)	to excite	hormone
evolutus (L)	rolled out	evolution	hydor, hydro (GK)	water	hydrolysis
ex, e (L)	out	extinction	hyper (GK)	over, above	hyperventilation
exo (GK)	out, outside	exoskeleton	hyphe (GK)	web	hypha
extra (L)	outside, beyond	extracellular	hypo (GK)	under, below	hypotonic
ferre (L)	to bear	porifera	ichthys (GK)	fish	Osteichthyes
fibrilla (L)	small fiber	myofibril	instinctus (L)	impulse	instinct
fissus (L)	a split	binary fission	insula (L)	island	insulin
flagellum (L)	whip	flagellum	inter (L)	between	internode
follis (L)	bag	follicle	intra (L)	within, inside	intracellular
fossilis (L)	dug up	microfossils	isos (GK)	equal	isotonic
fungus (L)	mushroom	fungus	itis (GK)	inflammation, disease	arthritis
gamo, gam (GK)	marriage	gamete	jugare (L)	join together	conjugate
gaster (GK)	stomach	gastropoda			
ge, geo (GK)	earth	geology	kardia, cardia (GK)	heart	cardiac
gemmula (L)	little bud	gemmule	karyon (GK)	nut	prokaryote
genesis (L)	origin, birth	parthenogenesis	kata, cata (GK)	break down	catabolism
genos, gen, geny (GK)	race	genotype	kephale, ceph (GK)	head	cephalopoda
gestare (L)	to bear	progesterone	keras (GK)	horn	chelicerae
glene (GK)	eyeball	euglenoid	kinein (GK)	to move	kinetic
globus (L)	sphere	hemoglobin	koilos, coel (GK)	hollow cavity, belly	coelom
glotta (GK)	tongue	epiglottis	kokkus (GK)	berry	streptococcus
glykys, glu (GK)	sweet	glycolysis	kolla (GK)	glue	colloid
gnathos (GK)	jaw	Agnatha	kotyl, cotyl (GK)	cup	cotylosaur
gonos, gon (GK)	reproductive, sexual	gonorrhea	kreas (GK)	flesh	pancreas
gradus (L)	a step	gradualism	krinoeides (GK)	lilylike	Crinoidea
graphos (GK)	written	chromatograph	kyanos, cyano (GK)	blue	cyanobacterium
gravis (L)	heavy	gravitropism	kystis, cyst (GK)	bladder, sac	cystitis
gymnos (GK)	naked, bare	gymnosperm	kytos, cyt (GK)	hollow, cell	lymphocyte

Root	Meaning	Example	Root	Meaning	Example
lagos (GK)	hare	lagomorph	organon (GK)	tool, implement	organelle
leukos (GK)	white	leukocyte	ornis (GK)	bird	ornithology
libra (L)	balance	equilibrium	orthos (GK)	straight	orthodontist
logos, logy (GK)	study, word	biology	osculum (L)	small mouth	osculum
luminescere (L)	to grow light	bioluminescence	osteon (GK)	bone	osteocyte
luteus (L)	orange-yellow	corpus luteum	ostrakon (GK)	shell	ostracoderm
lyein, lysis (GK)	to split, loosen	lysosome	oura, ura (GK)	tail	anura
lympha (L)	water	lymphocyte	ous, oto (GK)	ear	otology
			ovum (L)	egg	oviduct
makros (GK)	large	macrophage			
marsupium (L)	pouch	marsupial	palaios, paleo (GK)	ancient	paleontology
meare (L)	to glide	permeable	pan (GK)	all	pancreas
megas (GK)	large	megaspore	para (GK)	beside	parenchyma
melas (GK)	black, dark	melanin	parthenos (GK)	virgin	parthenogenesis
meristos (GK)	divided	meristem	pathos (GK)	disease, suffering	pathogenic
meros (GK)	part	polymer	pausere (L)	to rest	decompose
mesos (GK)	middle	mesophyll	pendere (L)	to hang	appendix
meta (GK)	after, following	metaphase	per (L)	through	permeable
metabole (GK)	change	metabolism	peri (GK)	around	peristalsis
meter (GK)	a measurement	diameter	periodos (GK)	a cycle	photoperiodism
mikros, micro (GK)	small	microscope	pes, pedis (L)	foot	bipedal
mimos (GK)	a mime	mimicry	phagein (GK)	to eat	phagocyte
mitos (GK)	thread	mitochondrion	phainein (GK)	to show	phenotype
molluscus (L)	soft	mollusk	phaios (GK)	dusky	phaeophyta
monos (GK)	single	monotreme	phase (GK)	stage, appearance	metaphase
morphe (GK)	form	lagomorph	pherein, phor (GK)	to carry	pheromone
mors, mort (L)	death	mortality	phloios (GK)	inner bark	phloem
mucus (L)	mucus, slime	mucosa	phos, photos (GK)	light	phototropism
multus (L)	many	multicellular	phyllon (GK)	leaf	chlorophyll
mutare (L)	to change	mutation	phylon (GK)	related group	phylogeny
mykes, myc (GK)	fungus	mycorrhiza	phyton (GK)	plant	epiphyte
mys (GK)	muscle	myosin	pinax (GK)	tablet	pinacocytes
			pinein (GK)	to drink	pinocytosis
nema (GK)	thread	nematology	pinna (L)	feather	pinniped
nemato (GK)	thread, threadlike	nematode	plasma (GK)	mold, form	plasmodium
neos (GK)	new	Neolithic	plastos (GK)	formed object	chloroplast
nephros (GK)	kidney	nephron	platys (GK)	flat	platyhelminthes
neuro (GK)	nerve	neurology	plax (GK)	plate	placoderm
nodus (L)	knot, knob	internode	pleuron (GK)	side	dipleurula
nomos, nomy (GK)	ordered knowledge	taxonomy	plicare (L)	to fold	replication
noton (GK)	back	notochord	polys, poly (GK)	many	polymer
			poros (GK)	channel	porifera
oikos, eco (GK)	household	ecosystem	post (L)	after	posterior
oisein, eso (GK)	to carry	esophagus	pous, pod (GK)	foot	gastropoda
oligos (GK)	few, little	oligochaeta	prae, pre (L)	before	Precambrian
omnis (L)	all	omnivore	primus (L)	first	primary
ophis (GK)	serpent	Ophiuroidea	pro (GK and L)	before, for	prokaryote
ophthalmos (GK)	referring to the eye	ophthalmologist	proboskis (GK)	trunk	proboscidean

Root	Meaning	Example	Root	Meaning	Example
producere (L)	to bring forth	reproduction	taxis, taxo (GK)	to arrange	taxonomy
protos (GK)	first	protocells	telos (GK)	end	telophase
pseudes (GK)	false	pseudopod	terra (L)	land, Earth	terrestrial
pteron (GK)	wing	chiropteran	thele (GK)	cover a surface	epithelium
punctus (L)	a point	punctuated	therme (GK)	heat	endotherm
pupa (L)	doll	pupa	thrix, trich (GK)	hair	trichocyst
radius (L)	ray	radial	tome (GK)	cutting	anatomy
re (L)	again	reproduction	trachia (GK)	windpipe	tracheid
reflectere (L)	to turn back	reflex	trans (L)	across	transpiration
rhiza (GK)	root	mycorrhiza	trematodes (GK)	having holes	monotreme
rhodon (GK)	rose	rhodophyte	trope (GK)	turn	gravitropism
rota (L)	wheel	rotifer	trophe (GK)	nourishment	heterotrophic
rumpere (L)	to break	disruptive	turbo (L)	whirl	turbellaria
			tympanon (GK)	drum	tympanum
saeta (L)	bristle	Equisetum	typos (GK)	model	genotype
sapros (GK)	rotten	saprobe			
sarx (GK)	flesh	sarcomere	uni (L)	one	unicellular
sauros (GK)	lizard	cotylosaur	uterus (L)	womb	uterus
scire (L)	to know	science			
scribere, script (L)	to write	transcription	vacca (L)	cow	vaccine
sedere, ses (L)	to sit	sessile	vagina (L)	sheath	vagina
semi (L)	half	semicircle	valvae (L)	folding doors	bivalvia
skopein, scop (GK)	to look	microscope	vasculum (L)	small vessel	vascular
soma (GK)	body	lysosome	venter (L)	belly	ventricle
sperma (GK)	seed	angiosperm	ventus (L)	a wind	hyperventila-tion
spirare (L)	to breathe	spiracle			
sporos (GK)	seed	microspore	vergere (L)	to slant, incline	convergent
staphylo (GK)	bunch of grapes	staphylococcus	villus (L)	shaggy hair	villus
stasis (GK)	standing, staying	homeostasis	virus (L)	poisonous liquid	virus
stellein, stol (GK)	to draw in	peristalsis	vorare (L)	to devour	carnivore
sternon (GK)	chest	sternum			
stinguere (L)	to quench	extinction	xeros (GK)	dry	xerophyte
stolo (L)	shoot	stolon	xylon (GK)	wood	xylem
stoma (GK)	mouth	stoma			
streptos (GK)	twisted chain	streptococcus	zoon, zo (GK)	animal	zoology
syn (GK)	together	systolic	zygotos (GK)	joined together	zygote
synapsis (GK)	union	synapse			
systema (GK)	composite whole	ecosystem			

Periodic Table

1 — Atomic number
1 — Symbol
H — Element name
Hydrogen — Atomic mass
1.00794

Metallic Properties

Transition Elements

Lanthanoid Series

Actinoid Series

Metallic Properties

*Mass of isotope with longest half-life, that is, the most stable isotope of the element

Noble Gases

18					
					2 **He** Helium 4.002602

13	14	15	16	17	
5 **B** Boron 10.811	6 **C** Carbon 12.011	7 **N** Nitrogen 14.0067	8 **O** Oxygen 15.9994	9 **F** Fluorine 18.998403	10 **Ne** Neon 20.179
13 **Al** Aluminum 26.98154	14 **Si** Silicon 28.0855	15 **P** Phosphorus 30.97376	16 **S** Sulfur 32.06	17 **Cl** Chlorine 35.453	18 **Ar** Argon 39.948

10	11	12						
28 **Ni** Nickel 58.69	29 **Cu** Copper 63.546	30 **Zn** Zinc 65.39	31 **Ga** Gallium 69.723	32 **Ge** Germanium 72.59	33 **As** Arsenic 74.9216	34 **Se** Selenium 78.96	35 **Br** Bromine 79.904	36 **Kr** Krypton 83.80
46 **Pd** Palladium 106.42	47 **Ag** Silver 107.8682	48 **Cd** Cadmium 112.41	49 **In** Indium 114.82	50 **Sn** Tin 118.710	51 **Sb** Antimony 121.75	52 **Te** Tellurium 127.60	53 **I** Iodine 126.9045	54 **Xe** Xenon 131.29
78 **Pt** Platinum 195.08	79 **Au** Gold 196.9665	80 **Hg** Mercury 200.59	81 **Tl** Thallium 204.383	82 **Pb** Lead 207.2	83 **Bi** Bismuth 208.9804	84 **Po** Polonium 208.9824*	85 **At** Astatine 209.98712*	86 **Rn** Radon 222.017*

Nonmetallic Properties

■ Metallic Properties   ■ Metalloids   State at Room Temperature:
■ Nonmetallic Properties   □ Synthetic Elements   ■ and □ Solid   ■ Liquid   ■ Gas

63 **Eu** Europium 151.96	64 **Gd** Gadolinium 157.25	65 **Tb** Terbium 158.9254	66 **Dy** Dysprosium 162.50	67 **Ho** Holmium 164.9304	68 **Er** Erbium 167.26	69 **Tm** Thulium 168.9342	70 **Yb** Ytterbium 173.04
95 **Am** Americium 243.0614*	96 **Cm** Curium 247.0703*	97 **Bk** Berkelium 247.0703*	98 **Cf** Californium 251.0796*	99 **Es** Einsteinium 252.0828*	100 **Fm** Fermium 257.0951*	101 **Md** Mendelevium 258.986*	102 **No** Nobelium 259.1009*

APPENDIX G

SI Measurement

The International System (SI) of Measurement is accepted as the standard for measurement throughout most of the world. Four of the base units in SI are the meter, liter, kilogram, and second. The size of a unit can be determined from the prefix used with the base unit name. For example: *kilo* means one thousand; *milli* means one thousandth; *micro* means one millionth; and *centi* means one hundredth. The tables below give the standard symbols for these SI units and some of their equivalents.

Larger and smaller units of measurement in SI are obtained by multiplying or dividing the base unit by some multiple of ten. Multiply to change from larger units to smaller units. Divide to change from smaller units to larger units. For example, to change 1 km to m, you would multiply 1 km by 1000 to obtain 1000 m. To change 10 g to kg, you would divide 10 g by 1000 to obtain 0.01 kg.

Table G-1 Common SI Units

Measurement	Unit	Symbol	Equivalents
Length	1 millimeter	mm	1000 micrometers (μm)
	1 centimeter	cm	10 millimeters (mm)
	1 meter	m	100 centimeters (cm)
	1 kilometer	km	1000 meters (m)
Volume	1 milliliter	mL	1 cubic centimeter (cm^3 or cc)
	1 liter	L	1000 milliliters (mL)
Mass	1 gram	g	1000 milligrams (mg)
	1 kilogram	kg	1000 grams (g)
	1 tonne	t	1000 kilograms (kg) = 1 metric ton
Time	1 second	s	
Area	1 square meter	m^2	10 000 square centimeters (cm^2)
	1 square kilometer	km^2	1 000 000 square meters (m^2)
	1 hectare	ha	10 000 square meters (m^2)
Temperature	1 Kelvin	K	1 degree Celsius (°C)

APPENDIX H

Care and Use of a Microscope

Care of a Microscope

1. Always carry the microscope holding the arm with one hand and supporting the base with the other hand.
2. Don't touch the lenses with your finger.
3. Never lower the coarse adjustment knob when looking through the eyepiece lens.
4. Always focus first with the low-power objective.
5. Don't use the coarse adjustment knob when the high-power objective is in place.
6. Store the microscope covered.

Using a Microscope

1. Place the microscope on a flat surface that is clear of objects. The arm should be toward you.
2. Look through the eyepiece. Adjust the diaphragm so that light comes through the opening in the stage.

3. Place a slide on the stage so that the specimen is in the field of view. Hold it firmly in place by using the stage clips.
4. Always focus first with the coarse adjustment and the low-power objective lens. Once the object is in focus on low power, turn the nosepiece until the high-power objective is in place. Use ONLY the fine adjustment to focus with this lens.

Making a Wet Mount Slide

1. Carefully place the item you want to look at in the center of a clean glass slide. Make sure the sample is thin enough for light to pass through.
2. Use a dropper to place one or two drops of water on the sample.
3. Hold a clean coverslip by the edges and place it at one edge of the drop of water. Slowly lower the coverslip onto the drop of water until it lies flat.
4. If you have too much water or a lot of air bubbles, touch the edge of a paper towel to the edge of the coverslip to draw off extra water and force air out.

Coarse adjustment
Focuses the image under low power

Fine adjustment
Sharpens the image under high and low magnification

Arm
Supports the body tube

Low-power objective
Contains the lens with low-power magnification

Stage clips
Hold the microscope slide in place

Base
Provides support for the microscope

Eyepiece
Contains a magnifying lens you look through

Body tube
Connects the eyepiece to the revolving nosepiece

Revolving nosepiece
Holds and turns the objectives into viewing position

High-power objective
Contains the lens with the most magnification

Stage
Platform used to support the microscope slide

Diaphragm
Regulates the amount of light entering the body tube

Light source
Allows light to reflect upward through the diaphragm, the specimen, and the lenses

APPENDIX I

Safety in the Laboratory

The biology laboratory is a safe place to work if you are aware of important safety rules and if you are careful. You must be responsible for your own safety and for the safety of others. The safety rules given here will protect you and others from harm in the lab. While carrying out procedures in any of the **Biolabs,** notice the safety symbols and caution statements. The safety symbols are explained in the chart on the next page.

1. Always obtain your teacher's permission to begin a lab.
2. Study the procedure. If you have questions, ask your teacher. Be sure you understand all safety symbols shown.
3. Use the safety equipment provided for you. Goggles and a safety apron should be worn when any lab calls for using chemicals.
4. When you are heating a test tube, always slant it so the mouth points away from you and others.
5. Never eat or drink in the lab. Never inhale chemicals. Do not taste any substance or draw any material into your mouth.
6. If you spill any chemical, wash it off immediately with water. Report the spill immediately to your teacher.
7. Know the location and proper use of the fire extinguisher, safety shower, fire blanket, first aid kit, and fire alarm.
8. Keep all materials away from open flames. Tie back long hair.
9. If a fire should break out in the classroom, or if your clothing should catch fire, smother it with the fire blanket or a coat, or get under a safety shower. **NEVER RUN.**
10. Report any accident or injury, no matter how small, to your teacher.

Follow these procedures as you clean up your work area.

1. Turn off the water and gas. Disconnect electrical devices.
2. Return materials to their places.
3. Dispose of chemicals and other materials as directed by your teacher. Place broken glass and solid substances in the proper containers. Never discard materials in the sink.
4. Clean your work area.
5. Wash your hands thoroughly after working in the laboratory.

Table I.1 First Aid in the Laboratory

Injury	Safe Response
Burns	Apply cold water. Call your teacher immediately.
Cuts and bruises	Stop any bleeding by applying direct pressure. Cover cuts with a clean dressing. Apply cold compresses to bruises. Call your teacher immediately.
Fainting	Leave the person lying down. Loosen any tight clothing and keep crowds away. Call your teacher immediately.
Foreign matter in eye	Flush with plently of water. Use eyewash bottle or fountain.
Poisoning	Note the suspected poisoning agent and call your teacher immediately.
Any spills on skin	Flush with large amounts of water or use safety shower. Call your teacher immediately.

APPENDIX I

Safety Symbols

DISPOSAL ALERT
This symbol appears when care must be taken to dispose of materials properly.

ANIMAL SAFETY
This symbol appears whenever live animals are studied and the safety of the animals and the students must be ensured.

BIOLOGICAL HAZARD
This symbol appears when there is danger involving bacteria, fungi, or protists.

RADIOACTIVE SAFETY
This symbol appears when radioactive materials are used.

OPEN FLAME ALERT
This symbol appears when use of an open flame could cause a fire or an explosion.

CLOTHING PROTECTION SAFETY
This symbol appears when substances used could stain or burn clothing.

THERMAL SAFETY
This symbol appears as a reminder to use caution when handling hot objects.

FIRE SAFETY
This symbol appears when care should be taken around open flames.

SHARP OBJECT SAFETY
This symbol appears when a danger of cuts or punctures caused by the use of sharp objects exists.

EXPLOSION SAFETY
This symbol appears when the misuse of chemicals could cause an explosion.

FUME SAFETY
This symbol appears when chemicals or chemical reactions could cause dangerous fumes

EYE SAFETY
This symbol appears when a danger to the eyes exists. Safety goggles should be worn when this symbol appears.

ELECTRICAL SAFETY
This symbol appears when care should be taken when using electrical equipment.

POISON SAFETY
This symbol appears when poisonous substances are used.

PLANT SAFETY
This symbol appears when poisonous plants or plants with thorns are handled.

CHEMICAL SAFETY
This symbol appears when chemicals used can cause burns or are poisonous if absorbed through the skin.

GLOSSARY

A

abiotic factor: physical environmental factor, such as water, temperature, soil, and light, that influences the composition and growth of an ecosystem. (Ch. 28, p. 795)

abscission: dropping of leaves or mature fruit from a plant that results from a lowered level of auxin. (Ch. 24, p. 678)

absorption spectrum: characteristic pattern of wavelengths, or colors, of light absorbed by a particular pigment. (Ch. 6, p. 154)

acid: solution with a higher concentration of hydrogen ions than hydroxide ions; solutions with a pH below 7 are acids. (Ch. 3, p. 68)

acid precipitation: precipitation with a pH under 5.6; can damage leaves and plant tissues, kill plankton, and contribute to human diseases such as asthma and emphysema. (Ch. 30, p. 854)

action potential: temporary change in a neuron's polarity, which creates an electrical current that moves through the dendrites, into the cell body, and along the axon. (Ch. 25, p. 704)

activation energy: minimum amount of energy needed to initiate a chemical reaction. (Ch. 3, p. 80)

active immunity: disease resistance as a result of memory cells recognizing antigens to which they have been previously exposed. (Ch. 23, p. 657)

active transport: energy-requiring process in which particles move from an area of lower concentration to an area of higher concentration. (Ch. 4, p. 105)

adaptation: physical trait of a living organism that helps it survive in its environment; for example, deer are adapted to browse on leaves. (Ch. 1, p. 20)

adaptive radiation: divergent evolution and adaptation of a species over time in response to a new environment. (Ch. 13, p. 348)

adenine: one of four nitrogen bases of DNA; the others are guanine, thymine, and cytosine. (Ch. 9, p. 228)

aerobic respiration: cellular respiration that uses oxygen, sequentially releasing energy and storing it in ATP. (Ch. 6, p. 147)

alcoholic fermentation: anaerobic process whereby enzymes break down glucose into ethanol and CO_2 and transfer energy to ATP. (Ch. 6, p. 151)

algal bloom: explosive population increase in algae that occurs when large amounts of phosphates and/or nitrates enter a body of water in the presence of warm temperatures; can cause stagnation. (Ch. 28, p. 804)

allantois: membrane sac that collects wastes from an embryo. (Ch. 19, p. 528)

allele: either of two alternative forms of a gene for a particular trait such as flower color. (Ch. 8, p. 203)

alternation of generations: reproductive cycle of all plants involving the gametophyte (haploid) and sporophyte (diploid) generations. (Ch. 16, p. 429)

alveoli: within the lungs, numerous, small, moist air sacs where diffusion of oxygen and carbon dioxide into and out of the lungs occurs. (Ch. 22, p. 620)

amino acid: simple compound that is the building block of proteins. (Ch. 3, p. 75)

amniocentesis: withdrawal of amniotic fluid to evaluate the fetal cells for a genetic disorder (for example, Down syndrome) prior to birth. (Ch. 11, p. 291)

amnion: fluid-filled sac developed from the innermost membrane surrounding the embryo; amniotic fluid provides moisture and protection. (Ch. 19, p. 528)

anaerobic: processes that occur in the absence of oxygen (for example, lactic acid fermentation and alcoholic fermentation). (Ch. 6, p. 149)

anaphase: third stage of mitosis during which the two sister chromatids separate and are pulled to opposite poles and only one set of single-stranded chromosomes is seen at each end of the cell. (Ch. 7, p. 176)

angiosperm: flowering plant (for example, wild and cultivated flowers, oats, strawberries, broccoli) whose seeds are contained in a fruit. (Ch. 16, p. 439)

anterior: front end of animals with bilateral symmetry (for example, mollusks); generally contains a head. (Ch. 17, p. 454)

anther: the pollen-bearing part of the stamen in flowering plants. (Ch. 16, p. 441)

antibody: protein contained in plasma that can unite with a specific antigen. (Ch. 21, p. 604)

anticodon: in a tRNA molecule, the set of three bases specific to the kind of amino acid carried by the tRNA; complementary to the mRNA codon. (Ch. 10, p. 254)

antigen: foreign substance that stimulates an immune response in the blood. (Ch. 21, p. 604)

antiserum: solution containing blood serum and antibodies extracted from an animal and injected into another animal in order to fight disease. (Ch. 23, p. 660)

anus: body opening through which undigested materials are eliminated. (Ch. 20, p. 551)

aorta: in arthropods, the only blood vessel; empties blood into the organism's body cavity; in vertebrates, the largest blood vessel in the body; directs blood into arteries and to all body parts. (Ch. 21, p. 590)

apical dominance: hormone-mediated inhibition of lateral bud development; can be used by gardeners to produce bushier plants. (Ch. 24, p. 677)

appendage: in arthropods, pairs of jointed structures, such as a leg, that extend from the body and enable complex movement. (Ch. 17, p. 459)

artery: thick-walled vessel composed of three layers of cells; carries blood away from the heart. (Ch. 21, p. 591)

ascus: saclike structure that produces sexual spores by meiosis; found in the sac fungi (for example, yeasts). (Ch. 15, p. 413)

GLOSSARY

asexual reproduction: involves only one parent—produces a new organism genetically identical to the parent. (Ch. 15, p. 396)

ATP: adenosine triphosphate; energy-carrying molecule, which, when hydrolyzed to ADP and inorganic phosphate, releases free energy. (Ch. 6, p. 145)

atrioventricular (A-V) node: small bundle of tissue in the vertebrate heart through which impulses are passed from the S-A node to the ventricles. (Ch. 21, p. 596)

atrium: thin-walled chamber in the heart that receives the body's incoming blood and passes it to the ventricle. (Ch. 21, p. 591)

autocidal control: release of sterile males into an area to help control a pest population. (Ch. 30, p. 850)

autoimmune disease: disease, such as rheumatoid arthritis, caused by the abnormal response of the immune system against the individual's own body. (Ch. 23, p. 654)

autonomic system: in humans, two groups of nerves—the sympathetic and parasympathetic—that control such reflexes as heartbeat and peristalsis. (Ch. 25, p. 718)

autosomes: chromosomes other than sex chromosomes. (Ch. 8, p. 213)

autotroph: organism that makes its own food through chemosynthesis or photosynthesis; blue-green bacteria are autotrophs. (Ch. 12, p. 327)

auxin: plant hormone with growth-regulating effects, including the growth of stems toward light. (Ch. 24, p. 674)

axon: portion of a neuron that conducts impulses away from the cell body. (Ch. 25, p. 701)

B

B cell: lymphocyte that matures in the bone marrow; can form two types of cells: plasma cells and memory cells. (Ch. 23, p. 646)

bacteriophage: a virus that attacks bacteria. (Ch. 9, p. 228)

base: solution with a higher concentration of hydroxide ions than hydrogen ions; solutions with a pH above 7 are bases. (Ch. 3, p. 68)

basidium: in club fungi, the clublike structure in which sexual spores are formed. (Ch. 15, p. 411)

behavioral adaptation: results from the response of an organism to its external environment (for example, bird migration). (Ch. 13, p. 340)

benthos: aquatic organisms that live attached to the ocean floor or crawl over it; some benthic animals are starfish, barnacles, and clams. (Ch. 29, p. 833)

bilateral symmetry: body plan of organisms, such as flatworms, in which there is only one plane that will divide the organism's body into nearly identical (mirror symmetry) parts. (Ch. 17, p. 454)

bile: digestive fluid produced by the liver, stored in the gallbladder, and released into the small intestine, where it breaks up fat globules. (Ch. 20, p. 563)

binary fission: method by which prokaryotes reproduce whereby their DNA is replicated and distributed equally to daughter cells. (Ch. 7, p. 181)

binomial nomenclature: two-part system of biological classification for naming organisms in which the first part of the name is the genus and the second part is the specific name (species name). (Ch. 14, p. 368)

biological control: preservation or introduction of predators to limit a pest population. (Ch. 30, p. 849)

biological magnification: increasing concentration of non-biodegradable chemicals (for example, the pesticide DDT) from one step in the food chain to the next. (Ch. 30, p. 848)

biology: branch of science that deals with living organisms and processes vital to life. (Ch. 1, p. 11)

biomass: total dried weight of all organic matter at different trophic levels. (Ch. 28, p. 791)

biome: one of the distinctive geographic regions of the world characterized by dominant plant and animal life forms and maintained by similar climates. (Ch. 29, p. 823)

biosphere: thin layer of Earth's surface, composed of the world's biomes and ocean and freshwater ecosystems, that is occupied by living things; highest level of biological organization. (Ch. 29, p. 836)

biotic factors: interspecies and intraspecies relationships of organisms living within a community. (Ch. 28, p. 786)

biotic potential: highest reproductive capacity of a population to increase indefinitely under ideal conditions; most organisms never reach their biotic potential. (Ch. 27, p. 761)

birthrate: number of organisms born or produced in a given time span. (Ch. 27, p. 763)

blastocoel: hollow cavity in the interior of a blastula. (Ch. 19, p. 513)

blastula: hollow ball of cells formed by cleavage during the early development of an embryo. (Ch. 19, p. 513)

Bowman's capsule: cup-shaped structure of the nephron that narrows into a tubule; involved in filtration. (Ch. 22, p. 627)

bronchus: one of two large tubes branching and rebranching from the trachea into smaller bronchial tubes and ending as alveoli. (Ch. 22, p. 620)

budding: in animals such as *Hydra*, asexual reproduction in which a new organism is produced by means of an outgrowth that breaks off from the parent. (Ch. 18, p. 485)

C

Calvin cycle: set of reactions in photosynthesis in which carbon dioxide is converted into sugars; takes place in the stroma. (Ch. 6, p. 158)

capillary: small, thin-walled blood vessel where exchange of carbon dioxide and oxygen occurs between blood and body cells. (Ch. 21, p. 590)

carbohydrate: organic compound containing carbon, hydrogen, and oxygen; carbohydrates such as sugars and starches provide sources of energy for life processes. (Ch. 3, p. 72)

carcinogen: agent such as cigarette smoke or X rays that is capable of causing cancer. (Ch. 10, p. 267)

cardiac muscle: in vertebrates, involuntary muscle found only in the heart. (Ch. 26, p. 744)

carnivore: meat eater; consumer, such as a snake or owl, that feeds on other consumers. (Ch. 28, p. 788)

carotenoid: pigment molecules—usually yellow, orange, and red—that interact with chlorophylls to absorb light energy needed in photosynthesis. (Ch. 6, p. 154)

carrying capacity: greatest number of individuals in a specific population that a specific environment is capable of supporting under particular conditions; can vary, for example, with time of year or access to food. (Ch. 27, p. 763)

cartilage: in a vertebrate fetus, flexible tissue that makes up most of the skeleton. (Ch. 26, p. 734) also found in the notochord of chordates, and as the primary means of internal support in cartilagenous fish. (Ch. 17, pp. 465, 467)

cell cycle: cycle of cell growth and division involving interphase and mitosis. (Ch. 7, p. 173)

cell plate: in the dividing cells of most plants, gives rise to the plasma membranes of the two new plant cells. (Ch. 7, p. 176)

cell theory: the theory that (1) all living things are composed of one or more cells or cell fragments, (2) the cell is the organism's basic unit of structure and function, and (3) all cells arise from other cells. (Ch. 4, p. 91)

cell wall: structure that lies outside the plasma membrane and provides support and protection. (Ch. 4, p. 109)

cellular respiration: process used by producers and consumers to convert the energy in glucose and other sugars into a usable form of energy. (Ch. 1, p. 15)

central nervous system: in bilaterally symmetrical animals, the brain and one or more nerve cords. (Ch. 25, p. 712)

centriole: found in the cells of animals and some algae and fungi; two pairs of centrioles play an important role in cell reproduction. (Ch. 5, p. 133)

centromere: region of attachment for the two chromatids of a chromosome (sister chromatids) during prophase; also attaches the chromosome to the microtubules of the spindle. (Ch. 7, p. 175)

cerebellum: motor area of the brain; coordinates muscular activity. (Ch. 25, p. 714)

cerebrum: largest portion of the human brain; controls speech, reasoning, emotions, and personality. (Ch. 25, p. 713)

chemical formula: a group of symbols showing the number and kind of each atom in a compound; for example, CO_2 is the chemical formula for carbon dioxide. (Ch. 3, p. 62)

chemosynthesis: process by which energy released from the breakdown of inorganic materials is used to synthesize organic compounds. (Ch. 12, p. 327)

chlorofluorocarbon (CFC): chemical used as a coolant in appliances and in spray-can propellants that causes air pollution and thinning of the ozone layer. (Ch. 30, p. 854)

chlorophyll: green substance in producers that traps light energy from the sun, which is then used to combine carbon dioxide and water into sugars in the process of photosynthesis. (Ch. 1, p. 14)

chloroplast: double-walled organelle found in plants and some algae; functions in photosynthesis to trap light energy. (Ch. 5, p. 131)

chorion: thin membrane lining an eggshell that functions with the allantois in gas exchange. (Ch. 19, p. 529)

chorionic villus biopsy: removal of cells from the chorion to determine whether disease-causing genes are present in the fetus. (Ch. 11, p. 293)

chromatid: each strand of the double-stranded chromosome resulting from replication during prophase. (Ch. 7, p. 175)

chromatin: dense mass of material within the nucleus that is composed of individual chromosomes. (Ch. 5, p. 130)

chromosome: structure that carries the genes; composed of proteins and DNA. (Ch. 5, p. 130)

cilia: flexible projections extending outward from a cell that enable locomotion by whiplike motion; *Paramecium* move by the motion of cilia. (Ch. 5, p. 133)

class: taxonomic grouping of related (similar) orders of living organisms. (Ch. 14, p. 376)

cleavage: process of rapid cell division that splits the zygote into many smaller cells to form a multicellular blastula. (Ch. 19, p. 513)

climax community: in ecological succession, the final community, which is complex, stable, and tends to remain basically the same unless disturbed by nature or humans. (Ch. 29, p. 817)

clones: genetically identical copies derived from a single cell. (Ch. 10, p. 269)

codominance: occurs when one allele is not dominant; both alleles are expressed equally. (Ch. 8, p. 210)

codon: basic unit of the genetic code formed by sets of three adjacent bases representing an amino acid. (Ch. 9, p. 239)

coelom: fluid-filled body cavity formed within the mesoderm in which internal organs are suspended and protected. (Ch. 17, p. 457)

coenzyme: nonprotein, reusable helper molecule that helps enzymes activate chemical reactions. (Ch. 3, p. 83)

colon: organ that reclaims water by absorption during digestion, resulting in the remaining material being formed into feces, which is eliminated through the anus. (Ch. 20, p. 569)

commensalism: relationship in which only one organism benefits and the other organism (the host) is unaffected; both plants and animals can exhibit commensalism. (Ch. 28, p. 793)

community: assortment of life forms (for example, bacteria, fish, and algae) living together in a particular place and interacting with and depending on one another in various ways. (Ch. 1, p. 13)

comparative anatomy: study comparing structures of different living organisms (for example, forelimbs of a bird, horse, and human); provides evidence of evolution. (Ch. 12, p. 309)

comparative biochemistry: study of organisms on a biochemical level; compares amino acid sequences, providing evidence of evolution. (Ch. 12, p. 312)

comparative embryology: study of developing organisms showing relationships not obvious in the organism's adult stage. (Ch. 12, p. 312)

compound: substance with two or more atoms of different elements combined chemically; sucrose and table salt are compounds. (Ch. 3, p. 60)

cone cell: type of photoreceptor cell in the retina; distinguishes colors. (Ch. 25, p. 723)

conifer: gymnosperm whose seeds develop in cones; pine trees, junipers, and giant redwoods are conifers. (Ch. 16, p. 436)

conjugation: sexual process in some simple organisms such as fungi in which genetic material is transferred from one cell to another by cell-to-cell contact. (Ch. 18, p. 488)

consumer: organism in a community that is unable to produce its own food. (Ch. 1, p. 15)

continuous variation: gradations in traits (for example, varied lengths of ears of corn) as a result of the presence of many different phenotypes. (Ch. 8, p. 215)

control group: in a controlled experiment, this is the group in which all the variables remain constant, including the independent variable. (Ch. 2, p. 37)

controlled experiment: one in which all variables are kept constant except the one being tested, so the results observed are due to changes in the variable being manipulated. (Ch. 2, p. 36)

convergent evolution: independent development of similar traits between unrelated species as a result of adaptations to similar environments. (Ch. 13, p. 348)

cornea: front surface of the eye; admits light, which then passes through the aqueous humor to the pupil. (Ch. 25, p. 722)

corpus luteum: yellowish body developed from the ruptured follicle after ovulation. (Ch. 24, p. 691)

corpus luteum stage: stage of the menstrual cycle during which the level of progesterone is high and FSH and LH are inhibited by the pituitary. (Ch. 24, p. 691)

cotyledon: leaflike food-storage organ of the embryo of a flowering plant. (Ch. 19, p. 519)

covalent bond: occurs when atoms combine by sharing electrons. (Ch. 3, p. 59)

crop: stretchable food-storage organ found in animals such as earthworms. (Ch. 20, p. 552)

crop rotation: alternating crop growth in a field in order to replace nutrients such as nitrogen and to control pests. (Ch. 30, p. 865)

cultural control: agricultural alternative to pesticides involving growing methods to discourage pests and breeding pest-resistant plants. (Ch. 30, p. 849)

cuticle: waxy layer in plants such as ferns and conifers that helps protect against water loss. (Ch. 16, p. 425)

cytoplasm: substance contained by living cells that is composed of a complex mixture of enzymes, sugars, and amino acids; these substances are constantly involved in chemical reactions. (Ch. 5, p. 123)

cytosine: a nitrogen-containing base of DNA; the other three are adenine, guanine, and thymine. (Ch. 9, p. 228)

cytotoxic T cell: specialized lymphocyte that can kill infected body cells directly by releasing proteins and indirectly by attracting macrophages. (Ch. 23, p. 652)

D

data: collection of bits of information about the natural world; for example, measuring the height of plants in sunny and shady fields provides data. (Ch. 2, p. 33)

death rate: number of organisms that die during a given time span. (Ch. 27, p. 763)

decomposer: organism that derives nourishment by feeding on dead organisms and waste products of living organisms. (Ch. 1, p. 16)

deletion: type of gene mutation in which a nucleotide is left out; results spontaneously from errors in copying. (Ch. 10, p. 261)

dendrite: portion of a neuron that transmits impulses toward the cell body. (Ch. 25, p. 701)

dependent variable: in an experiment, any change that results from the manipulation of the independent variable. (Ch. 2, p. 37)

desert: biome characterized by less than 25 cm of rainfall yearly, rapid evaporation, poor soil, and little plant or animal life; desert organisms show many adaptations such as large, shallow root systems and estivation. (Ch. 29, p. 831)

development: series of changes an organism undergoes in reaching its final, adult form; one of four functions that distinguishes organisms as living creatures. (Ch. 1, p. 8)

diaphragm: wide, flat band of muscle stretched across the base of the rib cage that flattens during inhalation and pushes upward during exhalation. (Ch. 22, p. 622)

differentiation: developmental process by which generalized cells become specialized in order to form such structures as the brain and spinal cord. (Ch. 19, p. 517)

diffusion: random movement of ions and other particles from an area of higher concentration to an area of lower concentration; through air, water and other liquids, and across membranes. (Ch. 4, p. 98)

digestion: chemical, enzymatic process that breaks down large, complex, organic molecules into simpler, smaller ones capable of passing through plasma membranes. (Ch. 20, p. 545)

diploid: cells having two of each chromosome ($2n$). (Ch. 7, p. 183)

divergent evolution: the evolution of a single species into two or more species with different characteristics. (Ch. 13, p. 345)

dominant: form of a trait that dominates another trait and appears in the F_1 generation. (Ch. 8, p. 200)

dorsal: top or back of animals with bilateral symmetry (for example, segmented worms). (Ch. 17, p. 454)

dynamic equilibrium: in diffusion, the point reached when the numbers of particles entering and leaving a region are equal—movement is continuous but produces no overall change. (Ch. 4, p. 98)

E

ecological succession: gradual process by which communities change over time. (Ch. 29, p. 814)

ecosystem: relationship of a community of organisms interacting with its environment. (Ch. 28, p. 786)

ectoderm: outermost tissue layer of an organism. (Ch. 17, p. 454)

ectotherm: animal whose body temperature can change with the environment; ectotherms such as turtles develop behaviors like sunning to regulate their body temperature. (Ch. 17, p. 471)

electron cloud: space that electrons occupy while moving around the nucleus. (Ch. 3, p. 57)

element: substance composed of only one type of atom; examples include gold, lead, and oxygen. (Ch. 3, p. 58)

embryo: a living organism's early stage of development. (Ch. 12, p. 312)

embryonic induction: occurs when one part of an embryo induces (for example, by hormones) the development of another part. (Ch. 19, p. 524)

endergonic: chemical reaction requiring free energy in addition to enzymes and activation energy. (Ch. 6, p. 144)

endocrine gland: in animals, a ductless gland such as the pituitary that secretes hormones directly into the bloodstream. (Ch. 24, p. 680)

endocytosis: process by which the plasma membrane of a cell surrounds material, engulfs it, and takes in the material from its environment. (Ch. 4, p. 106)

endoderm: innermost tissue layer of an organism. (Ch. 17, p. 454)

endoplasmic reticulum: network of interconnected structures found in all eukaryotes; functions include intracellular transport of proteins and the breakdown of harmful substances. (Ch. 5, p. 126)

endoskeleton: in echinoderms (for example, starfish), calcium carbonate spines that project through the skin; provides support. (Ch. 17, p. 463) any internal framework or support system. (Ch. 26, p. 732)

endosperm: in plants, the 3n tissue that is the product of double fertilization and provides the embryo with food. (Ch. 18, p. 495)

endospore: highly resistant, dormant structure formed from a bacterial cell during unfavorable environmental conditions. (Ch. 15, p. 396)

endotherm: animal that maintains a constant body temperature through internal metabolic activity, regardless of external conditions; birds are endotherms. (Ch. 17, p. 471)

endotoxin: poisonous chemical released by dead bacteria when their cell walls rupture, producing disease such as tuberculosis. (Ch. 23, p. 642)

energy: the ability to do work. (Ch. 1, p. 14)

energy level: any of several different regions in which electrons travel about the nucleus. (Ch. 3, p. 57)

enzyme: reusable protein that lowers the required activation energy and allows reactions to happen at the normal temperatures of cells. (Ch. 3, p. 81)

epicotyl: in plants, a structure that forms a pair of small leaves that will open early in development. (Ch. 19, p. 519)

erosion: process by which soil is worn away by rain and wind. (Ch. 30, p. 865)

esophagus: muscular tube found in animals that pushes food by means of muscular contractions through the digestive system. (Ch. 20, p. 552)

estivation: period of summer dormancy that allows organisms to survive heat or drought. (Ch. 28, p. 803)

estrus: hormone-regulated receptive mating periods in many female mammals. (Ch. 18, p. 500)

eukaryote: cell containing a nuclear membrane and a membrane-bound nucleus; the vast majority of living organisms (for example, plants, animals, protists, and fungi) are eukaryotic. (Ch. 5, p. 125)

evolution: the change in living organisms over time. (Ch. 1, p. 20)

excretion: in animals and protozoans, the removal of toxic nitrogenous wastes from the body that are produced by metabolism. (Ch. 22, p. 623)

exergonic: chemical reaction that releases free energy. (Ch. 6, p. 145)

exocytosis: reverse process of endocytosis in which cell products or wastes are enclosed in vesicles and released to the surroundings. (Ch. 4, p. 108)

exons: sets of nucleotides that code for amino acids; during mRNA processing, exons are spliced together. (Ch. 10, p. 253)

exoskeleton: hard, external body covering that provides support for tissues and organs and protects the organism from predators; found in arthropods. (Ch. 17, p. 459)

exotoxin: poisonous chemical produced by living bacteria that causes disease (for example, tetanus). (Ch. 23, p. 641)

experiment: scientific test of a hypothesis used to determine whether or not the hypothesis (or explanation) is correct. (Ch. 2, p. 35)

experimental group: in a controlled experiment, the group in which the independent variable is manipulated. (Ch. 2, p. 37)

extensor: muscle (for example, the triceps) that causes straightening at a joint by contracting. (Ch. 26, p. 740)

extracellular digestion: in multicellular heterotrophs, complete or partial digestion of large pieces of food outside the cells. (Ch. 20, p. 547)

F

facilitated diffusion: use of transport proteins to help the passage of particles across the plasma membrane; a form of passive transport. (Ch. 4, p. 102)

family: taxonomic group of related (similar) genera of living organisms. (Ch. 14, p. 376)

fertilization: process of fusion of two haploid sex cells (egg and sperm) to form a zygote. (Ch. 7, p. 183)

fetoscopy: diagnostic technique used to directly view the developing fetus and surrounding tissue by means of an endoscopic tube. (Ch. 11, p. 295)

fiber: long, multinucleated type of cell surrounded by connective tissues, which together make up striated muscle. (Ch. 26, p. 743)

fibril: threadlike structure composed of filaments of actin and myosin; fibers are made up of fibrils. (Ch. 26, p. 745)

first-order consumer: consumer that feeds directly on a producer (for example, a cow grazing on grass); also called a herbivore and occupies the second trophic level. (Ch. 28, p. 788)

flagella: long, whiplike strands extending from a cell that enable cell locomotion. (Ch. 5, p. 133)

flexor: muscle (for example, the biceps) that causes bending at a joint by contracting. (Ch. 26, p. 740)

fluid mosaic model: a current model of cell membrane structure in which the membrane is a phospholipid bilayer with proteins embedded in it. (Ch. 4, p. 95)

follicles: the groups of cells within the ovary where eggs develop. (Ch. 18, p. 500)

follicle stage: during menstruation, the stage lasting about ten days when a new egg begins to mature in the follicle. (Ch. 24, p. 690)

food chain: series of steps from producers to consumers to decomposers by which food and energy are transferred through the environment. (Ch. 1, p. 15)

food web: all feeding relationships of organisms in an ecosystem. (Ch. 28, p. 788)

fossil: evidence (for example, bones or casts) of organisms that lived long ago. (Ch. 12, p. 306)

fragmentation: asexual reproduction in which whole, new adults are formed from fragments of the original organism. (Ch. 18, p. 486)

free energy: energy available to do biological work; for example, free energy is needed to synthesize proteins from single amino acids. (Ch. 6, p. 144)

fruit: in angiosperms (for example, corn, strawberries, onions), the vessel that contains the seeds; an enlarged ovary. (Ch. 16, p. 439)

G

gallbladder: small, saclike digestive organ that stores bile from the liver and secretes it into the small intestine. (Ch. 20, p. 563)

gamete: a sex cell—a sperm in the male parent and an egg in the female parent. (Ch. 7, p. 183)

gametophyte generation: gamete-producing haploid (*n*) stage of all plants. (Ch. 16, p. 429)

gastrovascular cavity: fluid-filled digestive cavity with only one body opening. (Ch. 20, p. 551)

gastrula: cup-shaped form of the developing embryo; contains ectoderm, endoderm, and mesoderm. (Ch. 19, p. 515)

gene: factor containing information for every trait; genes can be dominant or recessive. (Ch. 8, p. 201)

gene pool: total collection of genes, including the new alleles that occur and are recombined, within a specific population. (Ch. 12, p. 322)

gene therapy: treatment of genetic disorders through the introduction of normal genes into body cells. (Ch. 11, p. 296)

genetic counseling: gives parents information concerning the chances of having a child with a genetic disorder based on family history, patterns of heredity, and new diagnostic techniques. (Ch. 11, p. 290)

genetic drift: random changes in the gene pool of a population; a driving force in speciation. (Ch. 13, p. 345)

genetic recombination: the formation of new gene combinations during meiosis and sexual reproduction. (Ch. 7, p. 189)

genetics: science of inheritance of traits. (Ch. 8, p. 198)

genotype: combination of alleles for a certain trait. (Ch. 8, p. 203)

genus: taxonomic grouping of related species. (Ch. 14, p. 368)

geographic isolation: geological change that isolates segments of a population. (Ch. 13, p. 344)

geothermal energy: energy of ocean floor communities that is released as heat energy from Earth's interior; the hot water reacts with minerals in the molten rock to produce hydrogen sulfide, which is used by chemosynthetic bacteria to make carbohydrates. (Ch. 29, p. 835)

germination: development of a seed into a new plant; occurs when environmental conditions are favorable. (Ch. 19, p. 519)

gibberellin: plant hormone that promotes growth and development (for example, stimulates the germination rate of seeds). (Ch. 24, p. 679)

gill: in aquatic animals (for example, fish), the respiratory organ in which gas exchange takes place. (Ch. 22, p. 616)

gizzard: muscular, thick-walled chamber found in animals such as earthworms; with the help of coarse particles ingested with food, grinds food into smaller pieces. (Ch. 20, p. 552)

glomerulus: cluster of capillaries in Bowman's capsule; involved in filtration. (Ch. 22, p. 627)

Golgi body: flattened, saclike organelle that functions as a processing, packaging, and delivery system in eukaryotes. (Ch. 5, p. 127)

gradualism: evolutionary change in a species that progresses at a slow and steady rate. (Ch. 13, p. 350)

grana: in chloroplasts, stacked internal membranes (thylakoids) at which the light reactions of photosynthesis take place. (Ch. 6, p. 156)

grassland: biome in which grasses are the major species; also known as steppe, prairie, or savanna, and can include such animals as antelopes, bison, and prairie dogs. (Ch. 29, p. 829)

greenhouse effect: results when carbon dioxide traps heat near Earth's surface; could be producing global warming, which may eventually have a serious effect on climate. (Ch. 30, p. 859)

growth: an increase in the amount of living material in an organism; a function carried out by all organisms. (Ch. 1, p. 8)

guanine: a nitrogen-containing base of DNA; the other three are adenine, thymine, and cytosine. (Ch. 9, p. 228)

guard cells: specialized cells in plants that surround each stoma, regulating its size and preventing the plant from drying out. (Ch. 21, p. 586)

gymnosperms: "naked seeds"; plants in which seeds develop on the woody scales of reproductive structures that form cones (for example, pine and spruce trees). (Ch. 16, p. 436)

H

haploid: cells having only one chromosome (*n*) from each homologous pair. (Ch. 7, p. 183)

Haversian canal: tiny channel in compact bone that carries blood vessels and nerves. (Ch. 26, p. 735)

helper T cell: specialized lymphocyte that binds with B cells and can release chemicals to stimulate B cells to form plasma cells. (Ch. 23, p. 650)

herbivore: plant-eating animal, such as a cow, that occupies the second trophic level in an ecosystem. (Ch. 28, p. 788)

heredity: transmission of traits from parents to offspring. (Ch. 8, p. 198)

hermaphrodite: an organism with both male and female reproductive organs; earthworms are hermaphrodites. (Ch. 18, p. 497)

heterotroph: organism requiring complex organic molecules for energy, and that must feed on matter produced by other organisms. (Ch. 12, p. 327)

heterozygous: organism in which each cell contains two different alleles for a certain trait. (Ch. 8, p. 203)

homeostasis: steady state of the internal operation of a living organism regardless of external changes. (Ch. 1, p. 9)

homologous: similar in structure, in function, or both; the more homologous structures shared by different kinds of organisms, the closer their relationship. (Ch. 12, p. 310)

homologues: in diploid cells, the two members of each pair of chromosomes that carry DNA with information for corresponding traits. (Ch. 7, p. 183)

homozygous: organism in which each cell contains two of the same alleles for a particular trait. (Ch. 8, p. 203)

hormone: chemical secreted by one part of an organism that affects another part of the organism. (Ch. 18, p. 500)

humus: decayed remains of organisms that contain organic material, enrich soil, and increase the capacity of the soil to hold air and water. (Ch. 28, p. 798)

hyphae: multinucleate mass of cytoplasm forming the basic structure of fungi. (Ch. 15, p. 410)

hypocotyl: stalklike part of embryo that will eventually become the upper part of the primary root and the lower part of the stem. (Ch. 19, p. 519)

hypothalamus: brain structure that secretes releasing factors that cause the anterior pituitary to release its own hormones. (Ch. 24, p. 686)

hypothesis: statement formed by analyzing observations and sorting through possible causes of the effect noted. (Ch. 2, p. 34)

I

incomplete dominance: pattern of inheritance in which neither allele is dominant and three totally different phenotypes can occur. (Ch. 8, p. 209)

independent variable: the only variable to be manipulated (or changed) in a controlled experiment. (Ch. 2, p. 37)

insertion: type of mutation in which an extra nucleotide is added during replication; produces very different amino acid sequences from those coded by normal genes. (Ch. 10, p. 261)

integrated pest management: use of biological, autocidal, and cultural controls in addition to chemical pesticides to control pest populations. (Ch. 30, p. 850)

interferon: protein made by a virus-infected host cell that prevents viral reproduction in healthy cells. (Ch. 23, p. 660)

International System of Measurement, (SI): a universal language of measurements and its symbols used by scientists; a decimal system based on tens, multiples of tens, and fractions of tens. (Ch. 2, p. 46)

interneuron: neuron that carries impulses from sensory neurons to motor neurons. (Ch. 25, p. 701)

interphase: cell division stage in which each chromosome and the DNA it contains replicates, producing a second set of chromosomes. (Ch. 7, p. 173)

interspecific competition: interaction that takes place when populations of different species compete for the same resources (for example, food); density-dependent limiting factor. (Ch. 27, p. 771)

intracellular digestion: efficient means of digestion that takes place inside a cell; used by heterotrophs such as amoebas to break down microorganisms and starch molecules. (Ch. 20, p. 547)

intraspecific competition: density-dependent competition between members of the same species for the same resources (for example, water). (Ch. 27, p. 771)

introns: sets of nucleotides that do not code for amino acids; during mRNA processing, introns are cut out. (Ch. 10, p. 253).

invertebrates: animals without backbones—examples are sponges and cnidarians. (Ch. 17, p. 450)

ion: a charged atom (or group of atoms) resulting from an atom's loss or gain of one or more negative charges (electrons). (Ch. 3, p. 61)

ionic bond: force of attraction between ions; for example, because sodium and chloride ions are oppositely charged, they attract one another. (Ch. 3, p. 61)

isomers: organic molecules with the same chemical formula but different structural formula. (Ch. 3, p. 71)

joint: in arthropods, the flexible connector located between segments of appendages and between segments of exoskeleton; in vertebrates, the points where bones connect with one another; makes body movement possible. (Ch. 26, p. 731)

karyotype: appearance of chromosomes in an organism regarding number, size, and shape; used to detect certain chromosomal abnormalities. (Ch. 11, p. 288)

kidney: main excretory organ that filters out nitrogenous wastes and helps maintain osmotic balance. (Ch. 22, p. 627)

kinetic energy: the energy of motion. (Ch. 3, p. 79)

kingdom: broadest taxon in the classification of living organisms; divided into more specific taxa: phylum, class, order, family, genus, and species. (Ch. 14, p. 376)

lactic acid fermentation: anaerobic process whereby enzymes break down glucose into lactic acid and transfer energy to ATP; sauerkraut is produced by lactic acid fermentation. (Ch. 6, p. 150)

large intestine: digestive organ that collects undigested waste, absorbs water from the waste, and compacts the waste. (Ch. 20, p. 569)

larva: immature stage that usually does not resemble the adult form but will eventually change into that form; tadpoles are larvae. (Ch. 19, p. 525)

law: a statement about events that always occur in nature; for example, the law of gravitation. (Ch. 2, p. 42)

lens: eye structure that focuses light on the retina. (Ch. 25, p. 723)

ligament: strong band of tissue composed of collagen and elastic fibers that connects bones. (Ch. 26, p. 736)

light reaction: in photosynthesis, the series of changes that occurs only in the presence of light, converting light energy into chemical energy. (Ch. 6, p. 156)

limiting factor: unfavorable factor such as temperature, disease, or predation that prevents organisms from achieving their biotic potential. (Ch. 27, p. 761)

lipid: organic compound composed of carbon, hydrogen, and oxygen, with the number of hydrogen atoms per molecule being much greater than the number of oxygen atoms; fats, oils, and waxes are lipids. (Ch. 3, p. 73)

littoral zone: in the ocean, the region of the neritic zone that is closest to the shore; organisms adapted to changing environmental conditions abound including algae, clams, and crabs. (Ch. 29, p. 833)

lung: in terrestrial vertebrates, organ used for gas exchange. (Ch. 22, p. 619)

lymph node: small, spongy capsule scattered through the lymphatic system in which destruction of bacteria occurs. (Ch. 21, p. 599)

lymphocyte: white blood cell involved in the immune response; may be either a B cell or T cell. (Ch. 23, p. 646)

lysogenic cycle: occurs when a cell containing a provirus reproduces—the host cell lyses and new viruses are released to become part of the chromosomes of other cells. (Ch. 15, p. 392)

lysosome: organelle containing digestive enzymes that break down food and digest worn out cell parts. (Ch. 5, p. 132)

lytic cycle: reproductive process in which a virus takes over all metabolic activities of a cell, replicates itself many times, and destroys the host cell. (Ch. 15, p. 391)

macrophage: white blood cell that engulfs and digests pathogens; plays an important role in inflammatory and immune responses. (Ch. 23, p. 645)

Malpighian tubules: in a grasshopper, stringlike excretory system that absorbs uric acid and water from blood. (Ch. 22, p. 627)

medulla oblongata: center portion of the brain; controls heartbeat rate and many other internal responses. (Ch. 25, p. 715)

meiosis: cellular process that occurs only in certain cells of reproductive organs by which haploid nuclei are formed from diploid nuclei; ensures genetic continuity between generations and promotes variation. (Ch. 7, p. 183)

memory cell: produced during the first exposure to an antigen; if a pathogen reappears, memory cells recognize its antigens and the immune system responds quickly. (Ch. 23, p. 657)

menstrual cycle: in human females, the series of monthly hormone-regulated changes that results in the maturation of an egg and preparation of the uterus for possible pregnancy. (Ch. 18, p. 502)

menstruation: phase of the menstrual cycle involving the loss of the egg and uterine tissue through the vagina. (Ch. 18, p. 502)

meristems: regions of cell division that in many plants can develop new structures throughout the plant's lifetime. (Ch. 19, p. 519)

mesoderm: in flatworms, the tissue layer between the ectoderm and endoderm containing several primitive organ systems; in animals with coeloms, the tissue layer in which the coelom forms and from which some organs develop. (Ch. 17, p. 455)

messenger RNA (mRNA): carries the genetic information representing a certain order of amino acids from the nucleus to the cytoplasm where translation takes place; RNA is transcribed from DNA. (Ch. 10, p. 252)

metabolism: sum of all chemical reactions that occur in cells; hydrolysis is one such chemical reaction. (Ch. 5, p. 123)

metamorphosis: various patterns of development that involve a series of changes in body structure—for example, some insects have three stages of change: egg, nymph, and adult. (Ch. 19, p. 525)

metaphase: second stage of mitosis during which the chromosomes gather at the equator of the spindle and become aligned. (Ch. 7, p. 176)

microenvironment: during each stage of succession, the slightly different environment created as organisms grow and affect their surroundings, which allows for the growth of other kinds of organisms better adapted to the changed conditions. (Ch. 29, p. 816)

microfilament: structure of the cytoskeleton in eukaryotes; composed of actin and myosin, it provides structural support and assists cell movement (for example, muscle movement). (Ch. 5, p. 133)

microtubule: structure of the cytoskeleton in eukaryotes that helps certain organelles move within the cell. (Ch. 5, p. 133)

middle lamella: in plants, the secondary wall, which lies inside the primary wall; composed of pectin; it strengthens the cell wall and provides support. (Ch. 4, p. 110)

mitochondria: organelles, bound by a double membrane, found in all eukaryotes; mitochondria break down organic molecules to release energy for cell reactions. (Ch. 5, p. 128)

mitosis: process by which chromosomes are duplicated and distributed to daughter nuclei; each daughter nucleus carries the same set of genetic information as the parent nucleus. (Ch. 7, p. 173)

modifier genes: genes interacting with each other to control particular traits, such as eye color. (Ch. 8, p. 217)

molecule: combination of two or more atoms joined by a covalent bond; water is a molecule. (Ch. 3, p. 59)

monoclonal antibody: specific antibody produced in the laboratory from the fusion of cancer cells and lymphocytes. (Ch. 23, p. 655)

morphogenesis: development of the species-specific form or structures of an organism. (Ch. 19, p. 514)

motor neuron: specialized cell that carries impulses from the brain or spinal cord to an effector (typically a muscle or gland). (Ch. 25, p. 701)

multiple alleles: set of three or more different alleles that control a trait—for example, the three alleles in humans that determine blood type are multiple alleles. (Ch. 8, p. 210)

multiple genes: pattern of inheritance (continuous variation) produced by many genes affecting a particular trait (for example, skin color in humans). (Ch. 8, p. 216)

mutagen: external chemical or physical agent such as radiation that causes mutations; some mutagens play a role in cancer development. (Ch. 10, p. 262)

mutation: a change (mistake) in the replication of genetic material; mutations occur in all living organisms as a result of changes to individual genes or the gene arrangement on chromosomes. (Ch. 10, p. 261)

mutualism: mutually beneficial relationship between different kinds of organisms. (Ch. 15, p. 405)

mycelium: mat of filaments composed of a mass of hyphae that form the body of fungi. (Ch. 15, p. 410)

N

natural selection: process resulting in the survival of the best-adapted individuals in a population. (Ch. 12, p. 320)

negative feedback: control mechanism whereby various body processes are kept at levels suitable to the body's changing needs; often involves the release of hormones to speed up or slow down other chemical reactions in the body. (Ch. 24, p. 682)

nekton: aquatic organisms that swim freely through the ocean; whales, fish, shrimp, and squid are nektonic animals. (Ch. 29, p. 833)

nephridium: tubular excretory organ of an earthworm, which acts as a filter, removing wastes and returning usable materials to the circulation system. (Ch. 22, p. 626)

nephron: functional unit of the kidney; the human kidney has about 1 million nephrons. (Ch. 22, p. 627)

neritic zone: shallow, lighted zone of the ocean, above the continental shelf, with diverse and plentiful animal life. (Ch. 29, p. 833)

GLOSSARY

nerve: bundle of neuron axons with accompanying connective tissue. (Ch. 25, p. 701)

neural tube: hollow tube formed by the folding and fusing of the neural plate; develops into the brain and spinal cord in the early vertebrate embryo. (Ch. 19, p. 517)

neuron: specialized nerve cell, consisting of a cell body, dendrites, and an axon, that transmits impulses from one part of the body to another. (Ch. 25, p. 700)

neurotransmitter: chemical agent that conducts nerve impulses across the synapse into specific sites on nearby dendrites. (Ch. 25, p. 707)

niche: in an ecosystem, the unique place occupied by an organism in relationship to all the biotic and abiotic factors. (Ch. 28, p. 787)

nonbiodegradable: chemical or other substance that living organisms cannot break down or degrade into harmless compounds; DDT, a pesticide, is nonbiodegradable. (Ch. 30, p. 848)

nonrenewable resource: resource such as fossil fuels that cannot be replaced. (Ch. 30, p. 864)

nucleic acid: biological compound (for example, DNA and RNA) that forms a code to determine a living thing's appearance and behavior. (Ch. 3, p. 76)

nucleoli: prominent bodies found in the nucleus of eukaryotes; the site of RNA synthesis. (Ch. 5, p. 130)

nucleotide: molecule composed of a phosphate group, a sugar molecule, and one of four nitrogen-containing bases (adenine, guanine, thymine, or cytosine). (Ch. 9, p. 229)

nucleus: control area of eukaryotic cells; contains chromatin and a nucleolus. (Ch. 5, p. 130)

nutrients: complex organic molecules and simpler substances needed by living organisms to carry out such life processes as respiration, protein synthesis, and reproduction. (Ch. 20, p. 544)

nymph: immature developmental stage of some insects (for example, grasshoppers) that closely resembles the adult stage. (Ch. 19, p. 528)

O

oceanic zone: deepest region of the ocean in which there is no light, no photosynthesis; populated by some nektonic animals, mostly fish. (Ch. 29, p. 833)

omnivore: organism that eats both plants and animals; humans are omnivores. (Ch. 28, p. 788)

oncogene: gene that has mutated into a cancer-causing gene; descendant cells will inherit the oncogene, which will disrupt the organism's cell cycle, causing cancer. (Ch. 10, p. 267)

order: taxonomic grouping of related (similar) families of living organisms. (Ch. 14, p. 376)

organ: a group of different tissues that work together to carry out a particular function; the stomach is an example. (Ch. 5, p. 122)

organism: anything capable of carrying on the life processes of reproduction, growth and development, homeostasis, and organization; more than 2 million organisms have been identified. (Ch. 1, p. 12)

organization: orderly, interrelated system of vital life processes or functions performed by a living organism; for example, different kinds of cells group together to make up structures with complex organization. (Ch. 1, p. 9)

osmosis: diffusion of water into and out of cells through a selectively permeable membrane from a region of higher concentration to a region of lower concentration. (Ch. 4, p. 100)

ossification: mineral-requiring process by which bone replaces cartilage as the skeleton develops. (Ch. 26, p. 734)

osteocyte: type of bone cell found in most formed bone tissue; the mature form of an osteoblast. (Ch. 26, p. 735)

ovary: structure in a flower's pistil in which the female gametes are produced. (Ch. 16, p. 441) in sexually reproducing animals, the structure that produces eggs. (Ch. 18, p. 500)

oviduct: tube that transports eggs to the uterus. (Ch. 18, p. 501)

ovulation: release of the immature egg from a follicle. (Ch. 18, p. 501)

ovule: part of a plant ovary that will develop into a seed if fertilization occurs. (Ch. 18, p. 493)

oxygen debt: amount of oxygen needed to metabolize lactic acid after exercise. (Ch. 26, p. 748)

ozone layer: found at the top of the stratosphere, the layer of ozone gas that absorbs almost all the UV radiation that reaches Earth from the sun. (Ch. 12, p. 329)

P

pancreas: digestive organ behind and partly below the stomach that secretes enzyme-containing pancreatic juice to break down polypeptides, convert nucleic acids to nucleotides, etc. (Ch. 20, p. 564)

parasite: organism living on or in another organism (the host) in order to obtain nourishment; parasites always harm the host. (Ch. 15, p. 379)

parasitism: density-dependent (often limiting) factor for population size in which harmful organisms live on or in a host organism, from which they draw nourishment. (Ch. 27, p. 769)

passive immunity: temporary immunity acquired by transfer of antibodies to the recipient. (Ch. 23, p. 660)

passive transport: movement of particles across membranes from an area of greater concentration to an area of lesser concentration as a result of a net random motion; diffusion and osmosis are examples. (Ch. 4, p. 100)

pathogen: disease-causing microorganism (for example, bacteria such as *Treponema pallidum,* which causes syphilis). (Ch. 23, p. 640)

GLOSSARY

peripheral nervous system: the sensory and motor neurons connected to the CNS in bilaterally symmetrical animals. (Ch. 25, p. 712)

peristalsis: alternating waves of muscular contraction and relaxation that push food through the esophagus and into the stomach. (Ch. 20, p. 561)

permafrost: permanently frozen soil layer of the tundra. (Ch. 29, p. 824)

pesticide: chemical agent used to kill pests such as termites, moths, and aphids; pesticides often destroy not only the target pests but also their natural predators. (Ch. 30, p. 845)

petals: a flower's inner row or rows of leaflike structures; often highly perfumed, brightly colored structures that dispense nectar. (Ch. 16, p. 440)

phagocytosis: process by which the cell takes in solid chunks of material; a form of endocytosis. (Ch. 4, p. 107)

pharynx: in animals such as earthworms, the muscular tube that moves food from the mouth to the esophagus by means of muscular contractions. (Ch. 20, p. 552)

phenotype: physical appearance of an organism as determined by a particular genotype. (Ch. 8, p. 203)

phloem: one of two types of vascular tissue in plants; conducts some of the sugars produced during photosynthesis. (Ch. 21, p. 580)

photosynthesis: process by which carbon dioxide and water are combined in the presence of sunlight and water to produce simple sugars and give off oxygen as a by-product. (Ch. 1, p. 14)

phylogeny: evolutionary history of a living organism based on such factors as fossil evidence and biochemical comparisons of enzymes. (Ch. 14, p. 374)

phylum: taxonomic grouping of related (similar) classes of living organisms. (Ch. 14, p. 376)

physiological adaptation: adaptation with a chemical basis that is associated with an organism's function; the spider's web is an example. (Ch. 13, p. 340)

pinocytosis: process by which a cell takes liquid droplets into itself; a form of endocytosis. (Ch. 4, p. 107)

pioneer stage: first stage of primary succession that begins with hardy organisms that can grow and reproduce under adverse conditions. (Ch. 29, p. 815)

pistil: a flower's female reproductive organ; produces female gametes. (Ch. 16, p. 441)

pituitary gland: three-lobed endocrine gland that works with the hypothalamus to release activity-regulating hormones such as vasopressin and oxytocin. (Ch. 24, p. 685)

placenta: tissue formed for exchange of gases, nutrients, and wastes between the mother and embryo. (Ch. 19, p. 530)

plankton: aquatic organisms, such as copepods and jellyfish, that are carried by ocean currents rather than swimming freely. (Ch. 29, p. 832)

plasma cell: antibody-producing cell resulting from division of a B cell. (Ch. 23, p. 649)

plasma membrane: outer boundary of a cell that regulates which particles enter and leave the cell. (Ch. 4, p. 92)

plasmid: structure in the cytoplasm of a bacterium with which foreign DNA is combined in genetic engineering techniques. (Ch. 10, p. 268)

plasmodium: slimy multinucleate mass with an amoeba-like feeding stage that is produced by a slime mold as part of its life cycle; engulfs bacteria and organic matter by phagocytosis. (Ch. 15, p. 407)

platelet: cell fragment involved in blood clotting. (Ch. 21, p. 603)

point mutation: type of gene mutation affecting only one amino acid in the polypeptide. (Ch. 10, p. 262)

pollen: protective structure enclosing the sperm of all seed plants; the pollen grain is often distributed by wind or air currents. (Ch. 16, p. 437)

pollination: sexual reproduction in plants in which pollen is transferred from anther to stigma either by cross-pollination or self-pollination. (Ch. 18, p. 494)

pollution: contamination of the air, water, or soil by such industrial or agricultural by-products as pesticides, automobile exhausts, and factory emissions. (Ch. 30, p. 844)

polypeptide: many amino acids bonded together form a polypeptide. (Ch. 3, p. 75)

polysaccharide: the most complex carbohydrate—such as cellulose, glycogen, or starch—which is formed by long chains of monosaccharides. (Ch. 3, p. 73)

population: all organisms within a breeding group. (Ch. 12, p. 313)

population density: number of one kind of organism in a given area. (Ch. 27, p. 764)

population growth: increase in population size over time; under ideal conditions (without being held in check by limiting factors), growth would increase indefinitely. (Ch. 27, p. 760)

population growth curve: used to graph changes in the size of a population. (Ch. 27, p. 762)

population growth rate curve: graph to show how fast a population grows. (Ch. 27, p. 763)

population size: number of organisms belonging to a population group; increases as organisms reproduce under favorable conditions. (Ch. 27, p. 760)

posterior: back end of animals with bilateral symmetry (for example, roundworms); generally contains a tail. (Ch. 17, p. 454)

potential energy: stored energy or energy of position; an example is the potential chemical energy of unlit wood in a fireplace. (Ch. 3, p. 79)

predation: feeding of one organism on another; the size of most populations is at least partially controlled by predation. (Ch. 27, p. 767)

primary succession: succession that begins in areas in which there is no life, such as barren rock. (Ch. 29, p. 815)

producer: food-producing member of a community; examples include plants and algae. (Ch. 1, p. 14)

prokaryote: cell that lacks a membrane-bound nucleus and membrane-bound organelles; bacteria are prokaryotes. (Ch. 5, p. 125)

prophase: first stage of mitosis in which the nucleoli disintegrate and the chromatin shortens and thickens. (Ch. 7, p. 175)

proteins: organic molecules used to build living material, carry out chemical reactions, fight disease, or transport particles out of cells. (Ch. 3, p. 75)

provirus: occurs when viral nucleic acid becomes part of the host cell's chromosomes; may cause phenotypic changes in the host but does not destroy the host. (Ch. 15, p. 392)

pseudopodia: "false feet," or extensions of the plasma membrane of amoebas that are used for locomotion and to engulf food. (Ch. 15, p. 404)

punctuated equilibrium: rapid evolutionary change in a species as the result of a sudden change in the environment. (Ch. 13, p. 350)

pupa: developmental stage of most insects (for example, butterflies) during which time the tissues are reorganized; the adult form emerges from the pupa. (Ch. 19, p. 527)

pyramid of biomass: diagram that shows how much living matter can be supported by an ecosystem. (Ch. 28, p. 791)

pyramid of energy: diagram of the transfer of energy in a food chain that shows the energy levels within an ecosystem. (Ch. 28, p. 789)

pyramid of numbers: diagram of energy loss in a food chain that shows how many individual organisms an ecosystem can support. (Ch. 28, p. 790)

R

radial symmetry: body plan in which all body parts of an organism are arranged equally around a center point; cnidarians exhibit radial symmetry. (Ch. 17, p. 454)

radicle: first part of the embryo to emerge from the seed; becomes the primary root of the plant. (Ch. 19, p. 519)

receptor: a protein embedded in the membrane of T cells that can recognize self proteins on B cells. (Ch. 23, p. 650)

recessive: the form of a trait that is hidden in the F_1 generation. (Ch. 8, p. 200)

recombinant DNA: DNA of an altered bacterium through insertion of a foreign gene; recombinant DNA techniques can engineer *E. coli* to produce insulin. (Ch. 10, p. 268)

red blood cell: most numerous blood cell; carries hemoglobin, which functions in oxygen transport. (Ch. 21, p. 602)

reflex: involuntary or automatic response to a stimulus—for example, blinking. (Ch. 25, p. 715)

reflex arc: in the nervous system, the path a nerve impulse takes during a reflex action. (Ch. 25, p. 718)

regeneration: replacement or regrowth of tissue in plants and animals. (Ch. 18, p. 486)

renewable resource: resource such as food that can be replaced. (Ch. 30, p. 864)

reproduction: production of offspring; living things reproduce, but nonliving things do not. (Ch. 1, p. 8)

reproductive isolation: results from the inability to exchange genes among species. (Ch. 13, p. 345)

resolving power: ability of a microscope to distinguish two objects as separate things. (Ch. 2, p. 44)

respiration: in complex animals, the intake of oxygen and the discharge of carbon dioxide. (Ch. 22, p. 615)

resting potential: unequal distribution of ions inside and outside the cell membrane (difference in electrical charge) that polarizes a neuron. (Ch. 25, p. 704)

retina: innermost layer of the eye; contains rod cells and cone cells. (Ch. 25, p. 723)

retrovirus: RNA virus that performs transcription from RNA to DNA; the virus that causes AIDS is a retrovirus. (Ch. 15, p. 394)

rhizoid: rootlike organ of zygote fungi; rhizoid enzymes break down food molecules into simpler molecules. (Ch. 15, p. 411)

rhizome: in vascular plants, a thick, underground stem that functions as a food storage organ. (Ch. 16, p. 434)

ribosomal RNA (rRNA): the RNA present in ribosomes; rRNA is transcribed from DNA. (Ch. 10, p. 252)

ribosomes: organelle composed of RNA and protein; site where proteins are made from amino acids. (Ch. 5, p. 126)

rod cell: type of photoreceptor cell in the retina; sensitive to very dim light but does not distinguish colors. (Ch. 25, p. 723)

root hairs: tiny, fine outgrowths of the epidermal cells of plants; provide a large surface area for absorbing water and dissolved ions. (Ch. 21, p. 581)

S

salivary gland: gland of the digestive system that secretes saliva into the mouth through ducts. (Ch. 20, p. 560)

saprophyte: organism that feeds on decaying organic matter; saprophytes such as some heterotrophic bacteria help recycle nutrients and prevent decayed matter from enveloping Earth. (Ch. 15, p. 397)

sarcomere: in a skeletal muscle, the structural subunit from one Z line to the next. (Ch. 26, p. 745)

scanning electron microscope (SEM): produces a three-dimensional image by sweeping a beam of electrons across an object and then bouncing off; used to study cell interaction and cell surfaces. (Ch. 2, p. 45)

science: looking at and learning about the natural world and producing a body of knowledge about nature; a process based on observing, interpreting observations, explaining observations, and testing the explanation. (Ch. 2, p. 33)

GLOSSARY

scrotum: sac of skin outside the male body wall that contains the testes, thereby providing the lower body temperature needed by sperm. (Ch. 18, p. 501)

second messenger hypothesis: model used to describe a cellular response wherein the first messenger never enters the target cell and the second messenger causes the response. (Ch. 24, p. 688)

second-order consumer: carnivorous consumer such as a snake that feeds directly on first-order consumers such as mice. (Ch. 28, p. 788)

secondary succession: new succession beginning when the dominant plants of a plant community are removed and the environment is left untended; can be caused by natural destruction such as fire or activities of humans such as logging. (Ch. 29, p. 817)

seed: embryonic plant consisting of the embryo, a food supply, and a protective coat; seed-bearing plants are the most numerous and diverse plants today. (Ch. 16, p. 435)

selective breeding: directing evolution by selecting only individuals with the most desirable traits and breeding them to pass these traits to the offspring. (Ch. 12, p. 313)

selectively permeable membrane: a membrane that is able to expel or admit particles used by the cell. (Ch. 4, p. 92)

semen: sperm and sperm-carrying fluids. (Ch. 18, p. 501)

sensory neuron: specialized cell that transmits impulses from sensory receptors to the brain or spinal cord for interpretation and processing. (Ch. 25, p. 700)

sensory-somatic system: part of the human peripheral nervous system that controls both conscious and involuntary responses to stimuli. (Ch. 25, p. 715)

sepal: a flower's outer row of leaves whose function is to enclose the bud and protect it. (Ch. 16, p. 440)

sex chromosomes: X and Y chromosomes that are different between the sexes and that are involved in sex determination. (Ch. 8, p. 213)

sex-linked trait: an inherited trait, such as eye color in fruitflies, determined by a gene on the sex chromosome. (Ch. 8, p. 214)

sexual reproduction: reproduction involving production and fusion of egg and sperm to form a diploid zygote, which will develop into a mature multicellular adult. (Ch. 7, p. 183)

sieve tube: series of sieve cells that form a pipeline and conduct sugars in plants. (Ch. 21, p. 580)

sinoatrial (S-A) node: small bundle of tissue (the pacemaker) in the right atrium of the vertebrate heart in which the heartbeat originates. (Ch. 21, p. 596)

sliding filament hypothesis: a model suggesting that muscle filaments slide over each other, shortening the fibrils during contraction of muscles. (Ch. 26, p. 746)

small intestine: longest part of the digestive tract; completes the chemical digestion of food and most of the absorption of nutrients. (Ch. 20, p. 563)

smooth muscle: nonstriated, involuntary muscle of vertebrates that lines the hollow internal organs of the body. (Ch. 26, p. 744)

social hierarchy: system of authority relationships ("pecking order") that is based on dominance and spread throughout a society. (Ch. 27, p. 773)

soil depletion: occurs when soil nutrients are not replaced in soil cultivated for crops. (Ch. 30, p. 865)

solution: a mixture of different substances in which every part of the mixture is the same. (Ch. 3, p. 65)

speciation: process by which new species are formed. (Ch. 13, p. 344)

species: group of organisms that can interbreed and produce fertile offspring; can include a broad range of variations. (Ch. 13, p. 342)

spindle: in newly dividing cells, the football-shaped structure formed from microtubules; functions to move the chromosomes during mitosis. (Ch. 7, p. 175)

spontaneous generation: disproved hypothesis that living organisms can arise from nonliving things. (Ch. 7, p. 170)

sporangium: reproductive structure of plants that produces spores. (Ch. 16, p. 432)

spore: reproductive cell capable of developing into a new haploid organism without first fusing with another cell. (Ch. 7, p. 184)

sporophyte generation: spore-producing diploid ($2n$) stage of all plants. (Ch. 16, p. 429)

stamen: a flower's male reproductive organ; produces male gametes and pollen. (Ch. 16, p. 441)

stigma: in a flower, the rough or sticky structure found at the tip of the style. (Ch. 16, p. 441)

stimulus: any change in the environment (for example, light) that influences an organism's activity. (Ch. 24, p. 672)

stoma: tiny opening in the epidermis of plants through which gases are exchanged. (Ch. 21, p. 583)

stomach: large, hollow organ in the digestive tract that churns food, secretes acid and enzymes to begin breaking up protein, and stores food. (Ch. 20, p. 561)

striated muscle: voluntary muscles with a striped appearance that are attached to bone and are important in vertebrate locomotion. (Ch. 26, p. 742)

stroma: fluid part of the chloroplast containing molecules used to synthesize sugars. (Ch. 6, p. 158)

structural adaptation: internal or external anatomic adaptation by an organism that promotes its fitness in its environment; the long, narrow tongue of woodpeckers, which is helpful in obtaining food, is an example. (Ch. 13, p. 339)

style: the neck of a flower's ovary. (Ch. 16, p. 441)

suppressor T cell: specialized lymphocyte that can release chemicals that reduce the response of macrophages and B cells. (Ch. 23, p. 651)

symbiosis: living together of two dissimilar organisms for their mutual benefit. (Ch. 5, p. 136)

synapse: small, fluid-filled space between neurons across which impulses are chemically transmitted. (Ch. 25, p. 707)

system: group of organs that depend on other organs to complete a biological process such as digestion, respiration, or reproduction. (Ch. 5, p. 122)

T

T cell: lymphocyte that matures in the thymus gland; can defend against body cells in which viruses are reproducing. (Ch. 23, p. 646)

taiga: biome south of the tundra characterized by coniferous forests, frequent fog, and acidic soil; typical animals include moose, caribou, and mink. (Ch. 29, p. 825)

taxa: particular categories in the biological classification system created for all living organisms and used to help organize information about the natural world. (Ch. 14, p. 366)

taxonomy: science of classification of living organisms that creates a hierarchy based on their similarities and differences. (Ch. 14, p. 366)

technology: application of knowledge gained through scientific study to real problems. (Ch. 2, p. 33)

telophase: fourth state of mitosis during which two cells begin to form from one; the nucleoli reappear and a nuclear membrane encloses each set of chromosomes. (Ch. 7, p. 176)

temperate forest: biome south of the taiga characterized by definite seasons (a growing season at least six months long), layers of vegetation, and, commonly, deciduous trees; typical animals include white-tailed deer, opossums, and squirrels. (Ch. 29, p. 826)

tendon: in vertebrates, the tough connective tissue that attaches most muscles to bone. (Ch. 26, p. 739)

territoriality: possession and defense of specific territories; reduces conflict within a species. (Ch. 27, p. 775)

testes: sperm-producing organs of animals. (Ch. 18, p. 497)

thallus: a liverwort's flat, liverlike body, which is only a few cells thick; produces sugars (which move by diffusion) during photosynthesis. (Ch. 16, p. 427)

theory: a major hypothesis that has withstood the test of time; although always subject to revision, theories—which are based on observations—are the closest to a complete explanation that science can offer. (Ch. 2, p. 42)

theory of natural selection: explanation for how evolution occurs, stressing the importance of variations among organisms and that variations can be inherited. (Ch. 12, p. 320)

third-order consumer: carnivorous consumer such as an owl that feeds directly on second-order consumers such as snakes. (Ch. 28, p. 788)

thymine: one of four nitrogen bases of DNA; the others are adenine, guanine, and cytosine. (Ch. 9, p. 228)

thymus gland: organ in which lymphocytes mature into T cells. (Ch. 23, p. 646)

tissue: in multicellular organisms, a specialized group of cells with the same basic structure that perform the same function. (Ch. 5, p. 121)

trachea: in some arthropods, branching and rebranching tube ending in tiny air sacs (tracheoles); in terrestrial vertebrates, the tube that conducts air to the lungs. (Ch. 22, p. 618)

tracheoles: tiny, moisture-containing air sacs of some arthropods that provide a large surface area for gas exchange. (Ch. 22, p. 618)

transcription: process whereby RNA is made from DNA; in prokaryotes, transcription is relatively simple but in eukaryotes is more complex. (Ch. 10, p. 252)

transfer RNA (tRNA): brings amino acids to the ribosomes, which are the site of translation in protein synthesis; acts as an interpreter translating nucleic acid language into protein language. (Ch. 10, p. 254)

translation: process by which genetic information present in a molecule of mRNA directs the synthesis of a polypeptide; depends on the correct joining of mRNA codons and tRNA anticodons. (Ch. 10, p. 253)

transmission electron microscope (TEM): used to view parts of very small, nonliving structures such as thin sections of cells embedded in plastic; forms an image by passing a beam of electrons through the object. (Ch. 2, p. 45)

transpiration: in plants, the loss of water through the pores in stomata. (Ch. 21, p. 586)

transport proteins: membrane proteins that play a role in the passage of particles—such as certain ions, sugars, and amino acids—through the plasma membrane. (Ch. 4, p. 102)

trisomy: having three of one kind of chromosome resulting in inherited defects such as Down syndrome (trisomy 21). (Ch. 11, p. 288)

trophic level: in an ecosystem, an organism's position in a food chain—for example, herbivores make up the second trophic level and carnivores make up higher trophic levels. (Ch. 28, p. 788)

tropical rain forest: biome characterized by heavy rainfall and constantly warm temperatures; has the most abundant plant growth and greatest species diversity of any biome and is populated, for example, by monkeys, parrots, beetles, and snakes. (Ch. 29, p. 827)

tropism: positive or negative response to a specific stimulus (e.g., positive phototropism causes plants to grow toward light). (Ch. 24, p. 673)

tundra: biome characterized by harsh winters, permafrost, short summers, little precipitation; typical life forms include mice, deer, wolves, true mosses, and stunted shrubs. (Ch. 29, p. 824)

U

ultrasonography: diagnostic technique using high-frequency sound waves and a screen image (echogram) to determine, for example, the position and anatomy of a fetus. (Ch. 11, p. 294)

GLOSSARY

umbilical cord: contains large blood vessels that transport blood between the fetus and placenta; connects the fetus to the placenta. (Ch. 19, p. 531)

uracil: the nucleic acid RNA contains uracil as one of its four bases; uracil in RNA takes the place of thymine in DNA. (Ch. 10, p. 250)

ureter: tube carrying urine from each kidney to the urinary bladder. (Ch. 22, p. 629)

urethra: structure through which urine is passed when the bladder fills. (Ch. 22, p. 629)

urinary bladder: muscular urine-storage sac; together with the kidneys and ureters makes up the human urinary system. (Ch. 22, p. 629)

urine: waste filtered by the kidney from the blood; composed of urea, salts, and a small amount of water. (Ch. 22, p. 629)

uterus: thick-walled, muscular organ of female mammals in which embryonic development takes place. (Ch. 18, p. 501)

V

vaccine: preparation created from weakened or killed microorganisms, viruses, or toxins that causes an immune response and prevents specific diseases. (Ch. 23, p. 658)

vacuole: membrane-bound, fluid-filled structure functioning in storage, digestion, and maintenance of osmotic balance. (Ch. 5, p. 132)

vagina: muscular tube that serves as the birth canal, leading to the outside of a female mammal's body, and also allows the passage of sperm to the uterus. (Ch. 18, p. 501)

vascular tissue: tissue that transports food, water, and other nutrients from one part of a plant to another. (Ch. 16, p. 426)

vasopressin: hormone that controls the amount of water excreted in urine—a reduced level results in a more dilute urine being produced. (Ch. 22, p. 630)

vegetative reproduction: asexual reproduction in plants that produces new plants from leaves, roots, or stems. (Ch. 18, p. 485)

vein: thick-walled vessel that carries blood back to the heart; contains one-way valves and is composed of three layers of cells. (Ch. 21, p. 591)

ventral: belly or bottom side of animals with bilateral symmetry (for example, segmented worms). (Ch. 17, p. 454)

ventricle: muscular chamber in the heart that receives blood from the atrium and pumps it to the body. (Ch. 21, p. 591)

vertebrae: bony or cartilaginous segments making up the backbone in vertebrates that provide protection and allow flexibility. (Ch. 17, p. 466)

vertebrates: animals with a backbone; subdivided into two major groups—the fish and the tetrapods. (Ch. 17, p. 450)

vesicle: small substance-containing sac formed from the plasma membrane in the process of endocytosis. (Ch. 4, p. l07)

vessel: tubelike element of the xylem formed from dead cells linked end to end; conducts water. (Ch. 21, p. 580)

vestigial: structure once useful for an organism's lifestyle but now has no function. (Ch. 12, p. 311)

villi: fingerlike projection on the intestinal lining that increases the intestine's absorptive area. (Ch. 20, p. 566)

visible spectrum: range of colors that make up white light. (Ch. 6, p. 152)

W

water-vascular system: series of water-filled canals and muscular tube feet that allows starfish to control movement. (Ch. 26, p. 739)

wavelength: a measure of radiant energy (for example, light, radio waves) calculated by the distance from one wave crest to the next. (Ch. 6, p. 152)

white blood cell: one of five types of colorless blood cells that are formed within lymph nodes and bone marrow and guard against foreign invaders such as viruses. (Ch. 21, p. 603)

X

xylem: one of two types of vascular tissue in plants; conducts water and dissolved minerals from the roots to the leaves. (Ch. 21, p. 580)

Z

zero population growth: condition where the birthrate equals the death rate and the population growth rate equals zero. (Ch. 27, p. 778)

zygote: diploid ($2n$) cell that results from fertilization of an egg by sperm. (Ch. 7, p. 183)

INDEX

INDEX

623, David Frazier;

624, Dr. E. R. Degginger/Color-Pic, Inc.;

628, CNRI/Science Photo Library/Photo Researchers, Inc.;

631, (t) Animals Animals/Holt Studios International, (b) Bill Curtsinger;

632, Alford W. Cooper/Photo Researchers, Inc.;

633, Doug Martin;

634, Hank Morgan/Science Source/Photo Researchers, Inc.;

635, David Brownell, The Image Bank;

637, Johnny Johnson;

638-639, ©Don Fawcett & E. Shelton/Science Source/Photo Researchers, Inc.;

639, Michael Kevin Daly/The Stock Market;

640, (bl) Visuals Unlimited/©David M. Phillips, (bc) London School of Hygiene & Tropical Medicine/Science Photo Library/Photo Researchers, Inc., (br) CNRI/Science Photo Library/Photo Researchers, Inc.;

641, (t) Matt Meadows, (b) Science VU/Visuals Unlimited;

642, (bl) Science VU/Visuals Unlimited, (bc) ©Dr. Dennis Kunkel/Phototake NYC, (br) Visuals Unlimited/©Hans Gelderblom;

643, (l) Tim Davis/AllStock, (c) James N. Westwater, (r) Alvin E. Staffan;

644, Prof. Motta, Correr & Nottola/University "La Sapienza", Rome/Science Photo Library/Photo Researchers, Inc.;

646, Robert Becker/Custom Medical Stock Photo;

647,653, Visuals Unlimited/©David M. Phillips;

654, (t) Dr. C. Lowe, Oregon Health Sciences University/AllStock, (b) Biomedical Communications/Photo Researchers, Inc.;

656, (l) Dr. A. Liepins/Science Photo Library/Photo Researchers, Inc., (r) ©Cecil Fox/Science Source/Photo Researchers, Inc.;

658, David M. Stone, PHOTO/NATS Inc.;

659, UPI/Bettmann;

660, ©1991 Lawrence Migdale;

661, Prof. Luc Montagnier, Institute Pasteur/CNRI/Science Photo Library/Photo Researchers, Inc.;

664, Steve Liss/Time Magazine;

665, ©Hank Morgan/Science Source/Photo Researchers, Inc.;

667, file photo;

668, Richard Himelsen/Medichrome;

668-669, Fred Bavendam/Peter Arnold;

670, Tomomi Saito/Dunq/Photo Researchers, Inc.;

671, Doug Martin;

672,675, Runk/Schoenberger from Grant Heilman;

676, Matt Meadows;

677, (l) Visuals Unlimited/©Link, (r) Aaron Haupt;

678, Runk/Schoenberger from Grant Heilman;

679, BLT Production;

680, (tc,bc) M.H. Sharp/Photo Researchers, Inc., (l) J.H. Robinson/Photo Researchers, Inc., (r) J.L. Lepore/Photo Researchers, Inc.; 682, Matt Meadows;

693, Animals Animals/Ed Degginger;

694, Aaron Haupt;

695, David Woods/Tony Stone Images;

698, Superstock;

699, Jim Zapp/Photo Researchers, Inc.;

700, CNRI/Science Photo Library/Photo Researchers, Inc.;

702, ©Lennart Nilsson, The Incredible Machine/The National Geographic Society;

705, Matt Meadows;

706, Jim Pickerell/FPG International;

707, Don Fawcett/Science Source/Photo Researchers, Inc.;

709, Robert Mullenix;

716, Matt Meadows;

717, Dr. E. R. Degginger/Color-Pic, Inc.;

721, (c) ©Lennart Nilsson, The Incredible Machine/The National Geographic Society, (l,r) ©Lennart Nilsson, Behold Man/Little, Brown and Company;

723, ©Lennart Nilsson, The Incredible Machine/The National Geographic Society;

724, Bill Ross/AllStock;

725, John Welzenbach/The Stock Market;

728-729, Bob McKeever/Tom Stack & Associates;

729, Renee Lynn/Photo Researchers, Inc.;

731, (t) Dr. E. R. Degginger/Color-Pic, Inc., (b) Visuals Unlimited/©William C. Jorgensen;

733, Dr. E. R. Degginger/Color-Pic, Inc.;

734, (l) Biophoto Associates/Science Source/Photo Researchers, Inc., (r) Steinhart Aquarium/Photo Researchers, Inc.;

735, Animals Animals/Breck P. Kent;

737, Visuals Unlimited/©Don W. Fawcett;

738, Dwight R. Kuhn;

742, Matt Meadows;

743, Dr. E. R. Degginger/Color-Pic, Inc.;

744, (l) Visuals Unlimited/©J. Venable & D. Fawcett, (m) Dr. E. R. Degginger/Color-Pic, Inc., (r) Michael Abbey/Photo Researchers, Inc.;

748, Robert Mullenix;

749, Doug Martin;

750, Visuals Unlimited/©David M. Phillips;

751, Richard Hineisen/Medichrome;

752, Ted Rice;

753, Robert Mullenix;

755, Dave B. Fleetham/Tom Stack & Associates;

756-757, Animals Animals/Zig Leszczynski;

756, David Ball/AllStock;

758, Visuals Unlimited/David S. Addison;

759, M.E. Warren/Photo Researchers, Inc.;

760, (l) John Lynch, PHOTO/NATS Inc., (r) Lee Saucier, PHOTO/NATS Inc.;

762, Rich Brommer;

764, Visuals Unlimited/©Joe McDonald;

765, Don & Esther Phillips/Tom Stack & Associates;

768, Tom & Pat Leeson/Photo Researchers, Inc.;

769, Cath Ellis, Dept. of Zoology, University of Hull/Science Photo Library/Photo Researchers, Inc.;

770, Dr. E. R. Degginger/Color-Pic, Inc.;

772, Animals Animals/Patti Murray;

773, Tom Ulrich/AllStock;

774, Alan & Sandy Carey;

775, Ben Simmons/The Stock Market;

777, (l) Nick Gunderson/AllStock, (r) R. Hamilton Smith/AllStock;

779, David Weintraub/Photo Researchers, Inc.;

780, Elaine Shay;

781, Ray Pfortner/Peter Arnold, Inc.;

784-785, Jane Grushow from Grant Heilman Photography;

785, Paul W. Johnson/Biological Photo Service;

786, Dwight R. Kuhn;

786-787, Grant Heilman/Grant Heilman Photography;

787, (tr) Charles W. Melton, (br) Labat Jacana/Photo Researchers, Inc.;

793, (t) Viviane Holbrooke/The Stock Market, (b) Visuals Unlimited/©C.P. Vance;

796, Grant Heilman/Grant Heilman Photography;

797, Carmen Lomas Garza;

798, Robert Mullenix;

800, Earth Scenes/E. R. Degginger;

801, (tl) Animals Animals/G.L. Kooyman, (tr) Animals Animals/E. R. Degginger, (m) Bill Larkin, PHOTO/NATS Inc., (bl) Jack S. Grove/Tom Stack & Associates;

802, Dr. E. R. Degginger/Color-Pic, Inc.;

803, Animals Animals/Michael Fogden;

804, Animals Animals/C.C. Lockwood;

806, Animals Animals/Fran Allan;

807, (t) Sovfoto, (b) Brian & Cherry Alexander;

808, Shattil-Rozinski/Tom Stack & Associates;

809, Alan Pitcairn from Grant Heilman;

812, Earth Scenes/Thomas Long;

813, ©Krafft-Explorer/Photo Researchers, Inc.;

814, Chip & Jill Isenhart/Tom Stack & Associates;

815, (l) Aaron Haupt, (r) Dr. E. R. Degginger/Color-Pic, Inc.;

816, St. Meyers/Okapia/Photo Researchers, Inc.;

818, Steve Allen/Peter Arnold, Inc.;

824, (t) Stephen J. Krasemann/Photo Researchers, Inc., (c) ©1988 Tom Bean/AllStock, (b) Dr. E. R. Degginger/Color-Pic, Inc.;

825, (l) Animals Animals/Dan Suzio, (tr) Visuals Unlimited/©Joe & Carol McDonald, (br) Animals Animals/Michael Leach, Oxford Scientific Films;

827, (t) ©1984 Gregory G. Dimijian, M.D./Photo Researchers, Inc., (c) ©James Martin/AllStock, (b) Visuals Unlimited/©1992 David Matherly;

829, (t) Dr. E. R. Degginger/Color-Pic, Inc.,(b) ©Tim Davis/AllStock;

830, ©1987 Tom Bean/AllStock;

831, Animals Animals/Breck P. Kent;

832, (l) Joey Jacques, (r) Dr. E. R. Degginger/Color-Pic, Inc.;

833, ©Jett Britnell/DRK Photo;

834, ©Norbert Wu/Peter Arnold, Inc.;

835, (l) Science VU - WHOI/©Visuals Unlimited, (r) Visuals Unlimited/D. Foster, Wood's Hole Oceanographic Institution;

836, NASA;

837, William J. Weber;

838, Van Vucher/Photo Researchers, Inc.;

839, ©Jeff Henry/Peter Arnold, Inc.;

842-843, Robert Perron;

843, Richard Laird/FPG International;

844, Will & Deni McIntyre/Photo Researchers, Inc.;

845, (t) Runk/Schoenberger from Grant Heilman, (b) Dr. E. R. Degginger/Color-Pic, Inc.;

847, (l) John Paul Kay/Peter Arnold, Inc., (r) UPI/Bettmann;

849, (t) Animals Animals/Rudie H. Kuiter, (b) Louis Quitt/Photo Researchers, Inc.;

850, Animals Animals/Doug Wechsler;

851, (l) Jacques Jangoux/Peter Arnold, Inc., (r) Joe Towers/The Stock Market;

852, Tom McHugh/Photo Researchers, Inc.;

854, Aaron Haupt;

855, Barth Falkenberg/Stock Boston;

856, Robert Mullenix;

859, Vince Streano/The Stock Market;

860, Robin Pranhe/The Stock Market;

861, Martha Cooper/Peter Arnold, Inc.;

862, Mark Reinstein/FPG International;

863, Gary Milburn/Tom Stack & Associates;

864, Inga Spence/Tom Stack & Associates;

865, Larry LeFever from Grant Heilman;

866, H.P Merten/The Stock Market;

867, (t) C. Allan Morgan/Peter Arnold, Inc., (b) D. Holden Bailey/Tom Stack & Associates;

870, Robert Mullenix;

871, Greg Vaughn/Tom Stack & Associates;

875, Matt Meadows;

876, George Disario/The Stock Market;

879, Rod Joslin;

882, (l) Robert Mullenix, (tr) Dr. Jeremy Burgess/Science Photo Library/Photo Researchers, Inc., (br) James N. Westwater;

883, (tl) John Gerlach/Tony Stone Images, (tr) Roger K. Burnard, (br) Matt Meadows;

884, Robert Mullenix;

885, Matt Meadows;

887, (l) courtesy Ohio Disaster Services Agency, (r) Animals Animals/Margot Conte;

889, (l) Robert Mullenix, (r) Doug Martin;

891, Sharon M. Kurgis;

894, (l) Manfred P. Kage/Peter Arnold, Inc., (tr) Visuals Unlimited/©Daniel Gotshall, (br) Dr. E. R. Degginger/Color-Pic, Inc.;

897, (l) Alvin E. Staffan, (tr) Lefever/Grushow from Grant Heilman, (br) Earth Scenes/Michael Fogden;

898, (l) Jim Rorabaugh, (tr) Visuals Unlimited/©W. Ormerod, (br) Dr. E. R. Degginger/Color-Pic, Inc.;

899, (l) Morgan Photos, (tr) Earth Scenes/Richard Smiell, (br) Earth Scenes/E. R. Degginger;

900, William Curtsinger/Photo Researchers, Inc.;

901, (t) Geri Murphy, (b) Dave B. Fleetham/Tom Stack & Associates;

902, (tl) Dr. E. R. Degginger/Color-pic, Inc., (bl) Geri Murphy, (r) Joey Jacques;

903, (l) David M. Dennis, (tr) Animals Animals/T.A.L. Cooke, (br) David M. Dennis/Tom Stack & Associates;

904, (l) Animals Animals/Patti Murray, (tr) Denise Tackett/Tom Stack & Associates, (br) Dave B. Fleetham/Tom Stack & Associates;

905, (l) Dr. E. R. Degginger/Color-Pic, Inc., (r) Fred Bavendam/Peter Arnold, Inc.;

906, (l) Animals Animals/W. Gregory Brown, (tr) Brian Parker/Tom Stack & Associates, (br) Joey Jacques;

907, (t) Alan & Sandy Carey, (b) Alvin E. Staffan;

908, (tl) Animals Animals/Stan Osolinski, Oxford Scientific Films, (bl) Johnny Johnson, (br) Lynn M. Stone;

909, (tl) Stephen Dalton/Photo Researchers, Inc., (bl) Visuals Unlimited/©Leonard Lee Rue III, (r) Visuals Unlimited/© Barbara Gerlach.